ASHTO

The

MS-DOS®

Encyclopedia

The
MS-DOS®
Encyclopedia

Microsoft Press
Redmond, Washington
1988

Ray Duncan, General Editor
Foreword by Bill Gates

Published by
Microsoft Press
A Division of Microsoft Corporation
16011 NE 36th Way, Box 97017, Redmond, Washington 98073-9717
Copyright © 1988 by Microsoft Press

Library of Congress Cataloging in Publication Data
The MS-DOS encyclopedia : versions 1.0 through 3.2 /
    editor, Ray Duncan.
        p.   cm.
Includes indexes.
ISBN 1-55615-049-0
1. MS-DOS (Computer operating system)   I. Duncan, Ray, 1952-
II. Microsoft Press.
QA76.76.063M74   1988   87-21452
005.4'46--dc19   CIP

Printed and bound in the United States of America.

    3 4 5 6 7 8 9 RMRM 8 9 0 9 8

Distributed to the book trade in the
United States by Harper & Row.

Distributed to the book trade in
Canada by General Publishing Company, Ltd.

Distributed to the book trade outside the
United States and Canada by Penguin Books Ltd.

Penguin Books Ltd., Harmondsworth, Middlesex, England
Penguin Books Australia Ltd., Ringwood, Victoria, Australia
Penguin Books N.Z. Ltd., 182-190 Wairau Road, Auckland 10, New Zealand

British Cataloging in Publication Data available

Microsoft Press gratefully acknowledges permission to reproduce material listed below.
Page 4: Courtesy The Computer Museum.
Pages 5, 11, 42: Intel 4004, 8008, 8080, 8086, and 80286 microprocessor photographs. Courtesy Intel Corporation.
Page 6: Reprinted from *Popular Electronics*, January 1975 Copyright © 1975 Ziff Communications Company.
Page 13: Reprinted with permission of Rod Brock.
Page 16: Reprinted with permission of The Seattle Times Copyright © 1983.
Pages 19, 34, 42: IBM PC advertisements and photographs of the PC, PC/XT, and PC/AT reproduced with
permission of International Business Machines Corporation Copyright © 1981, 1982, 1984. All rights reserved.
Page 21: "Big IBM's Little Computer" Copyright © 1981 by The New York Times Company. Reprinted by
permission.
"IBM Announces New Microcomputer System" Reprinted with permission of InfoWorld Copyright © 1981.
"IBM really gets personal" Reprinted with permission of Personal Computing Copyright © 1981.
"Personal Computer from IBM" Reprinted from DATAMATION Magazine, October 1981 Copyright © by Cahners
Publishing Company.
"IBM's New Line Likely to Shake up the Market for Personal Computers" Reprinted by permission of The Wall
Street Journal Copyright © Dow Jones & Company, Inc. 1981. All Rights Reserved.
Page 36: "Irresistible DOS 3.0" and "The Ascent of DOS" Reprinted from *PC Tech Journal*,
December 1984 and October 1986. Copyright © 1984, 1986 Ziff Communications Company.
"MS-DOS 2.00: A Hands-On Tutorial" Reprinted by permission of PC World from Volume 1, Issue 3, March 1983,
published at 501 Second Street, Suite 600, San Francisco, CA 94107.

Special thanks to Bob O'Rear, Aaron Reynolds, and Kenichi Ikeda.

Encyclopedia Staff

Editor-in-Chief: Susan Lammers

Editorial Director: Patricia Pratt

Senior Editor: Dorothy L. Shattuck

Senior Technical Editor: David L. Rygmyr

Special Projects Editor: Sally A. Brunsman

Editorial Coordinator: Sarah Hersack

Associate Editors and Technical Editors:
Pamela Beason, Ann Becherer, Bob Combs,
Michael Halvorson, Jeff Hinsch, Dean Holmes,
Chris Kinata, Gary Masters, Claudette Moore,
Steve Ross, Roger Shanafelt, Eric Stroo,
Lee Thomas, JoAnne Woodcock

Copy Chief: Brianna Morgan. Proofreaders:
Kathleen Atkins, Julie Carter, Elizabeth
Eisenhood, Matthew Eliot, Patrick Forgette,
Alex Hancock, Richard Isomaki, Shawn Peck,
Alice Copp Smith

Editorial Assistants: Wallis Bolz, Charles Brod,
Stephen Brown, Pat Erickson, Debbie Kem, Susanne
McRhoton, Vihn Nguyen, Cheryl VanGeystel

Index: Shane-Armstrong Information Services

Production: Larry Anderson, Jane Bennett, Rick
Bourgoin, Darcie S. Furlan, Nick Gregoric, Peggy
Herman, Lisa Iversen, Rebecca Johnson, Ruth Pettis,
Russell Steele, Jean Trenary, Joy Ulskey

Marketing and Sales Director: James Brown

Director of Production: Christopher D. Banks

Publisher: Min S. Yee

Contributors

Ray Duncan, General Editor   Duncan received a B.A. in Chemistry from the University of California, Riverside, and an M.D. from the University of California, Los Angeles, and subsequently received specialized training in Pediatrics and Neonatology at the Cedars-Sinai Medical Center in Los Angeles. He has written many articles for personal computing magazines, including *BYTE*, *PC* Magazine, *Dr. Dobb's Journal*, and *Softalk/PC*, and is the author of the Microsoft Press book *Advanced MS-DOS*. He is the founder of Laboratory Microsystems Incorporated, a software house specializing in FORTH interpreters and compilers.

Steve Bostwick   Bostwick holds a B.S. in Physics from the University of California, Los Angeles, and has over 20 years' experience in scientific and commercial data processing. He is president of Query Computing Systems, Inc., a software firm specializing in the creation of systems for applications that interface microcomputers with specialized hardware. He is also an instructor for the UCLA Extension Department of Engineering and Science and helped design their popular Microprocessor Hardware and Software Engineering Certificate Program.

Keith Burgoyne   Born and raised in Orange County, California, Burgoyne began programming in 1974 on IBM 370 mainframes. In 1979, he began developing microcomputer products for Apples, TRS-80s, Ataris, Commodores, and IBM PCs. He is presently Senior Systems Engineer at Local Data of Torrance, California, which is a major producer of IBM 3174/3274 and System 3X protocol conversion products. His previous writing credits include numerous user manuals and tutorials.

Robert A. Byers   Byers is the author of the bestselling *Everyman's Database Primer.* He is presently involved with the Emerald Bay database project with RSPI and Migent, Inc.

Thom Hogan   During 11 years working with personal computers, Hogan has been a software developer, a programmer, a technical writer, a marketing manager, and a lecturer. He has written six books, numerous magazine articles, and four manuals. Hogan is the author of the forthcoming Microsoft Press book *PC Programmer's Sourcebook*.

Jim Kyle   Kyle has 23 years' experience in computing. Since 1967, he has been a systems programmer with strong telecommunications orientation. His interest in microcomputers dates from 1975. He is currently MIS Administrator for BTI Systems, Inc., the OEM Division of BankTec Inc., manufacturers of MICR equipment for the banking industry. He has written 14 books and numerous magazine articles (mostly on ham radio and hobby electronics) and has been primary Forum Administrator for *Computer Language* Magazine's CLMFORUM on CompuServe since early 1985.

Gordon Letwin   Letwin is Chief Architect, Systems Software, Microsoft Corporation. He is the author of *Inside OS/2*, published by Microsoft Press.

Charles Petzold   Petzold holds an M.S. in Mathematics from Stevens Institute of Technology. Before launching his writing career, he worked 10 years in the insurance industry, programming and teaching programming on IBM mainframes and PCs. He is the author of the Microsoft Press book *Programming Windows 2.0*, a contributing editor to *PC* Magazine, and a frequent contributor to the Microsoft *Systems Journal*.

Chip Rabinowitz   Rabinowitz has been a programmer for 11 years. He is presently chief programmer for Productivity Solutions, a microcomputer consulting firm based in Pennsylvania, and has been Forum Administrator for the CompuServe MICROSOFT SIG since 1986.

Jim Tomlin   Tomlin holds a B.S. and an M.S. in Mathematics. He has programmed at Boeing, Microsoft, and Opcon and has taught at Seattle Pacific University. He now heads his own company in Seattle, which specializes in PC systems programming and industrial machine vision applications.

Richard Wilton   Wilton has programmed extensively in PL/1, FORTRAN, FORTH, C, and several assembly languages. He is the author of *Programmer's Guide to PC & PS/2 Video Systems*, published by Microsoft Press.

Van Wolverton   A professional writer since 1963, Wolverton has had bylines as a newspaper reporter, editorial writer, political columnist, and technical writer. He is the author of *Running MS-DOS* and *Supercharging MS-DOS*, both published by Microsoft Press.

William Wong   Wong holds engineering and computer science degrees from Georgia Tech and Rutgers University. He is director of PC Labs and president of Logic Fusion, Inc. His interests include operating systems, computer languages, and artificial intelligence. He has written numerous magazine articles and a book on MS-DOS.

JoAnne Woodcock   Woodcock, a former senior editor at Microsoft Press, has been a writer for *Encyclopaedia Britannica* and a freelance and project editor on marine biological studies at the University of Southern California. She is co-editor (with Michael Halvorson) of *XENIX at Work* and co-author (with Peter Rinearson) of *Microsoft Word Style Sheets*, both published by Microsoft Press.

Special Technical Advisor

Mark Zbikowski

Technical Advisors

Paul Allen	Michael Geary	David Melin	John Pollock
Steve Ballmer	Bob Griffin	Charles Mergentime	Aaron Reynolds
Reuben Borman	Doug Hogarth	Randy Nevin	Darryl Rubin
Rob Bowman	James W. Johnson	Dan Newell	Ralph Ryan
John Butler	Kaamel Kermaani	Tani Newell	Karl Schulmeisters
Chuck Carroll	Adrian King	David Norris	Rajen Shah
Mark Chamberlain	Reed Koch	Mike O'Leary	Barry Shaw
David Chell	James Landowski	Bob O'Rear	Anthony Short
Mike Colee	Chris Larson	Mike Olsson	Ben Slivka
Mike Courtney	Thomas Lennon	Larry Osterman	Jon Smirl
Mike Dryfoos	Dan Lipkie	Ridge Ostling	Betty Stillmaker
Rachel Duncan	Marc McDonald	Sunil Pai	John Stoddard
Kurt Eckhardt	Bruce McKinney	Tim Paterson	Dennis Tillman
Eric Evans	Pascal Martin	Gary Perez	Greg Whitten
Rick Farmer	Estelle Mathers	Chris Peters	Natalie Yount
Bill Gates	Bob Matthews	Charles Petzold	Steve Zeck

Contents

Section III: User Commands 723

Section IV: Programming Utilities 961

Section V: System Calls 1175

Appendixes 1431

Indexes 1531

Foreword

Microsoft's MS-DOS is the most popular piece of software in the world. It runs on more than 10 million personal computers worldwide and is the foundation for at least 20,000 applications—the largest set of applications in any computer environment. As an industry standard for the family of 8086-based microcomputers, MS-DOS has had a central role in the personal computer revolution and is the most significant and enduring factor in furthering Microsoft's original vision—a computer for every desktop and in every home. The challenge of maintaining a single operating system over the entire range of 8086-based microcomputers and applications is incredible, but Microsoft has been committed to meeting this challenge since the release of MS-DOS in 1981. The true measure of our success in this effort is MS-DOS's continued prominence in the microcomputer industry.

Since MS-DOS's creation, more powerful and much-improved computers have entered the marketplace, yet each new version of MS-DOS reestablishes its position as the foundation for new applications as well as for old. To explain this extraordinary prominence, we must look to the origins of the personal computer industry. The three most significant factors in the creation of MS-DOS were the compatibility revolution, the development of Microsoft BASIC and its widespread acceptance by the personal computer industry, and IBM's decision to build a computer that incorporated 16-bit technology.

The compatibility revolution began with the Intel 8080 microprocessor. This technological breakthrough brought unprecedented opportunities in the emerging microcomputer industry, promising continued improvements in power, speed, and cost of desktop computing. In the minicomputer market, every hardware manufacturer had its own special instruction set and operating system, so software developed for a specific machine was incompatible with the machines of other hardware vendors. This specialization also meant tremendous duplication of effort—each hardware vendor had to write language compilers, databases, and other development tools to fit its particular machine. Microcomputers based on the 8080 microprocessor promised to change all this because different manufacturers would buy the same chip with the same instruction set.

From 1975 to 1981 (the 8-bit era of microcomputing), Microsoft convinced virtually every personal computer manufacturer—Radio Shack, Commodore, Apple, and dozens of others—to build Microsoft BASIC into its machines. For the first time, one common language cut across all hardware vendor lines. The success of our BASIC demonstrated the advantages of compatibility: To their great benefit, users were finally able to move applications from one vendor's machine to another.

Most machines produced during this early period did not have a built-in disk drive. Gradually, however, floppy disks, and later fixed disks, became less expensive and more common, and a number of disk-based programs, including WordStar and dBASE, entered the market. A standard disk operating system that could accommodate these developments became extremely important, leading Lifeboat, Microsoft, and Digital Research all to support CP/M-80, Digital Research's 8080 DOS.

The 8-bit era proved the importance of having a multiple-manufacturer standard that permitted the free interchange of programs. It was important that software designed for the new 16-bit machines have this same advantage. No personal computer manufacturer in 1980 could have predicted with any accuracy how quickly a third-party software industry would grow and get behind a strong standard—a standard that would be the software industry's lifeblood. The intricacies of how MS-DOS became the most common 16-bit operating system, in part through the work we did for IBM, is not the key point here. The key point is that it was inevitable for a popular operating system to emerge for the 16-bit machine, just as Microsoft's BASIC had prevailed on the 8-bit systems.

It was overwhelmingly evident that the personal computer had reached broad acceptance in the market when *Time* in 1982 named the personal computer "Man of the Year." MS-DOS was integral to this acceptance and popularity, and we have continued to adapt MS-DOS to support more powerful computers without sacrificing the compatibility that is essential to keeping it an industry standard. The presence of the 80386 microprocessor guarantees that continued investments in Intel-architecture software will be worthwhile.

Our goal with *The MS-DOS Encyclopedia* is to provide the most thorough and accessible resource available anywhere for MS-DOS programmers. The length of this book is many times greater than the source listing of the first version of MS-DOS—evidence of the growing complexity and sophistication of the operating system. The encyclopedia will be especially useful to software developers faced with preserving continuity yet enhancing the portability of their applications.

Our thriving industry is committed to exploiting the advantages offered by the protected mode introduced with the 80286 microprocessor and the virtual mode introduced with the 80386 microprocessor. MS-DOS will continue to play an integral part in this effort. Faster and more powerful machines running Microsoft OS/2 mean an exciting future of multi-tasking systems, networking, improved levels of data protection, better hardware memory management for multiple applications, stunning graphics systems that can display an innovative graphical user interface, and communication subsystems. MS-DOS version 3, which runs in real mode on 80286-based and 80386-based machines, is a vital link in the Family API of OS/2. Users will continue to benefit from our commitment to improved operating-system performance and usability as the future unfolds.

Bill Gates

Preface

In the space of six years, MS-DOS has become the most widely used computer operating system in the world, running on more than 10 million machines. It has grown, matured, and stabilized into a flexible, easily extendable system that can support networking, graphical user interfaces, nearly any peripheral device, and even CD ROMs containing massive amounts of on-line information. MS-DOS will be with us for many years to come as the platform for applications that run on low-cost, 8086/8088-based machines.

Not surprisingly, the success of MS-DOS has drawn many writers and publishers into its orbit. The number of books on MS-DOS and its commands, languages, and applications dwarfs the list of titles for any other operating system. Why, then, yet another book on MS-DOS? And what can we say about the operating system that has not been said already?

First, we have written and edited *The MS-DOS Encyclopedia* with one audience in mind: the community of working programmers. We have therefore been free to bypass elementary subjects such as the number of bits in a byte and the interpretation of hexadecimal numbers. Instead, we have emphasized detailed technical explanations, working code examples that can be adapted and incorporated into new applications, and a systems view of even the most common MS-DOS commands and utilities.

Second, because we were not subject to size restrictions, we have explored topics in depth that other MS-DOS books mention only briefly, such as exception and error handling, interrupt-driven communications, debugging strategies, memory management, and installable device drivers. We have commissioned definitive articles on the relocatable object modules generated by Microsoft language translators, the operation of the Microsoft Object Linker, and terminate-and-stay-resident utilities. We have even interviewed the key developers of MS-DOS and drawn on their files and bulletin boards to offer an entertaining, illustrated account of the origins of Microsoft's standard-setting operating system.

Finally, by combining the viewpoints and experience of non-Microsoft programmers and writers, the expertise and resources of Microsoft software developers, and the publishing know-how of Microsoft Press, we have assembled a unique and comprehensive reference to MS-DOS services, commands, directives, and utilities. In many instances, the manuscripts have been reviewed by the authors of the Microsoft tools described.

We have made every effort during the creation of this book to ensure that its contents are timely and trustworthy. In a work of this size, however, it is inevitable that errors and omissions will occur. If you discover any such errors, please bring them to our attention so that they can be repaired in future printings and thus aid your fellow programmers. To this end, Microsoft Press has established a bulletin board on MCI Mail for posting corrections and comments. Please refer to page *xvi* for more information.

Ray Duncan

Updates to the MS-DOS Encyclopedia

Periodically, the staff of *The MS-DOS Encyclopedia* will publish updates containing clarifications or corrections to the information presented in this current edition. To obtain information about receiving these updates, please check the appropriate box on the business reply card in the back of this book, or send your name and address to: MS-DOS Encyclopedia Update Information, c/o Microsoft Press, 16011 NE 36th Way, Box 97017, Redmond, WA 98073-9717.

Bulletin Board Service

Microsoft Press is sponsoring a bulletin board on MCI Mail for posting and receiving corrections and comments for *The MS-DOS Encyclopedia*. To use this service, log on to MCI Mail and, after receiving the prompt, type

```
VIEW  <Enter>
```

The *Bulletin Board name:* prompt will be displayed. Then type

```
MSPRESS  <Enter>
```

to connect to the Microsoft Press bulletin board. A list of the individual Microsoft Press bulletin boards will be displayed; simply choose *MSPress DOSENCY* to enter the encyclopedia's bulletin board.

Special Companion Disk Offer

Microsoft Press has created a set of valuable, time-saving companion disks to The MS-DOS Encyclopedia. They contain the routines and functional programs that are listed throughout this book — thousands of lines of executable code. Conveniently organized, these disks will save you hours of typing time and allow you to start using the code immediately. The companion disks are only available directly from Microsoft Press. To order, use the special bind-in card in the back of the book or write to: Microsoft Press, THE MS-DOS ENCYCLOPEDIA COMPANION DISK OFFER, 16011 NE 36th Way, Box 97017, Redmond, WA 98073-9717. Send $49.95 for each set of disks, plus $2.50 per set for domestic postage and handling, $5.00 per set for foreign orders. Payment must be in US funds. You may pay by check or money order (payable to Microsoft Press), or by American Express, VISA, or MasterCard; please include your credit card number and expiration date. Allow 4 weeks for delivery. Please specify 5.25" disks or 3.5" disks.

Introduction

The MS-DOS Encyclopedia is the most comprehensive reference work available on Microsoft's industry-standard operating system. Written for experienced microcomputer users and programmers, it contains detailed, version-specific information on all the MS-DOS commands, utilities, and system calls, plus articles by recognized experts in specialized areas of MS-DOS programming. This wealth of material is organized into major topic areas, each with a format suited to its content. Special typographic conventions are also used to clarify the material.

Organization of the Book

The MS-DOS Encyclopedia is organized into five major sections, plus appendixes. Each section has a unique internal organization; explanatory introductions are included where appropriate.

Section I, The Development of MS-DOS, presents the history of Microsoft's standard-setting operating system from its immediate predecessors through version 3.2. Numerous photographs, anecdotes, and quotations are included.

Section II, Programming in the MS-DOS Environment, is divided into five parts: Structure of MS-DOS, Programming for MS-DOS, Customizing MS-DOS, Directions of MS-DOS, and Programming Tools. Each part contains several articles by acknowledged experts on these topics. The articles include numerous figures, tables, and programming examples that provide detail about the subject.

Section III, User Commands, presents all the MS-DOS internal and external commands in alphabetic order, including ANSI.SYS, BATCH, CONFIG.SYS, DRIVER.SYS, EDLIN, RAMDRIVE.SYS, and VDISK.SYS. Each command is presented in a structure that allows the experienced user to quickly review syntax and restrictions on variables; the less-experienced user can refer to the detailed discussion of the command and its uses.

Section IV, Programming Utilities, uses the same format as the User Commands section to present the Microsoft programming aids, including the DEBUG, SYMDEB, and CodeView debuggers. Although some of these utilities are supplied only with Microsoft language products and are not included on the MS-DOS system or supplemental disks, their use is intrinsic to programming for MS-DOS, and they are therefore included to create a comprehensive reference.

Section V, System Calls, documents Interrupts 20H through 27H and Interrupt 2FH. The Interrupt 21H functions are listed in individual entries. This section, like the User Commands and Programming Utilities sections, presents a quick review of usage for the experienced user and also provides extensive notes for the less-experienced programmer.

The 15 appendixes provide quick-reference materials, including a summary of MS-DOS version 3.3, the segmented (new) .EXE file header format, an object file dump utility, and the Intel hexadecimal object file format. Much of this material is organized into tables or bulleted lists for ease of use.

The book includes two indexes — one organized by subject and one organized by command name or system-call number. The subject index provides comprehensive references to the indexed topic; the command index references only the major entry for the command or system call.

Program Listings

The MS-DOS Encyclopedia contains numerous program listings in assembly language, C, and QuickBASIC, all designed to run on the IBM PC family and compatibles. Most of these programs are complete utilities; some are routines that can be incorporated into functioning programs. Vertical ellipses are often used to indicate where additional code would be supplied by the user to create a more functional program. All program listings are heavily commented and are essentially self-documenting.

The programs were tested using the Microsoft Macro Assembler (MASM) version 4.0, the Microsoft C Compiler version 4.0, or the Microsoft QuickBASIC Compiler version 2.0.

The functional programs and larger routines are also available on disk. Instructions for ordering are on the page preceding this introduction and on the mail-in card bound into this volume.

Typography and Terminology

Because *The MS-DOS Encyclopedia* was designed for an advanced audience, the reader generally will be familiar with the notation and typographic conventions used in this volume. However, for ease of use, a few special conventions should be noted.

Typographic conventions

Capital letters are used for MS-DOS internal and external commands in text and syntax lines. Capital letters are also used for filenames in text.

Italic font indicates user-supplied variable names, procedure names in text, parameters whose values are to be supplied by the user, reserved words in the C programming language, messages and return values in text, and, occasionally, emphasis.

A typographic distinction is made between lowercase l and the numeral 1 in both text and program listings.

Cross-references appear in the form SECTION NAME: PART NAME, COMMAND NAME, OR INTERRUPT NUMBER: Article Name or Function Number.

Color indicates user input and program examples.

Terminology

Although not an official IBM name, the term *PC-DOS* in this book means the IBM implementation of MS-DOS. If PC-DOS is referenced and the information differs from that for the related MS-DOS version, the PC-DOS version number is included. To avoid confusion, the term *DOS* is never used without a modifier.

The names of special function keys are spelled as they are shown on the IBM PC keyboard. In particular, the execute key is called Enter, not Return. When *<Enter>* is included in a user-entry line, the user is to press the Enter key at the end of the line.

The common key combinations, such as Ctrl-C and Ctrl-Z, appear in this form when the actual key to be pressed is being discussed but are written as Control-C, Control-Z, and so forth when the resulting code is the true reference. Thus, an article might reference the Control-C handler but state that it is activated when the user presses Ctrl-C.

Unless specifically indicated, hexadecimal numbers are used throughout. These numbers are always followed by the designation *H* (*h* in the code portions of program listings). Ranges of hexadecimal values are indicated with a dash — for example, 07–0AH.

The notation *(more)* appears in italic at the bottom of program listings and tables that are continued on the next page. The complete caption or table title appears on the first page of a continued element and is designated *Continued* on subsequent pages.

Section I
The Development of MS-DOS

The Development of MS-DOS

To many people who use personal computers, MS-DOS is the key that unlocks the power of the machine. It is their most visible connection to the hardware hidden inside the cabinet, and it is through MS-DOS that they can run applications and manage disks and disk files.

In the sense that it opens the door to doing work with a personal computer, MS-DOS is indeed a key, and the lock it fits is the Intel 8086 family of microprocessors. MS-DOS and the chips it works with are, in fact, closely connected — so closely that the story of MS-DOS is really part of a larger history that encompasses not only an operating system but also a microprocessor and, in retrospect, part of the explosive growth of personal computing itself.

Chronologically, the history of MS-DOS can be divided into three parts. First came the formation of Microsoft and the events preceding Microsoft's decision to develop an operating system. Then came the creation of the first version of MS-DOS. Finally, there is the continuing evolution of MS-DOS since its release in 1981.

Much of the story is based on technical developments, but dates and facts alone do not provide an adequate look at the past. Many people have been involved in creating MS-DOS and directing the lines along which it continues to grow. To the extent that personal opinions and memories are appropriate, they are included here to provide a fuller picture of the origin and development of MS-DOS.

Before MS-DOS

The role of International Business Machines Corporation in Microsoft's decision to create MS-DOS has been well publicized. But events, like inventions, always build on prior accomplishments, and in this respect the roots of MS-DOS reach farther back, to four hardware and software developments of the 1970s: Microsoft's disk-based and stand-alone versions of BASIC, Digital Research's CP/M-80 operating system, the emergence of the 8086 chip, and a disk operating system for the 8086 developed by Tim Paterson at a hardware company called Seattle Computer Products.

Microsoft and BASIC

On the surface, BASIC and MS-DOS might seem to have little in common, but in terms of file management, MS-DOS is a direct descendant of a Microsoft version of BASIC called Stand-alone Disk BASIC.

Before Microsoft even became a company, its founders, Paul Allen and Bill Gates, developed a version of BASIC for a revolutionary small computer named the Altair, which was introduced in January 1975 by Micro Instrumentation Telemetry Systems (MITS) of

The Altair. Christened one evening shortly before its appearance on the cover of Popular Electronics *magazine, the computer was named for the night's destination of the starship* Enterprise. *The photograph clearly shows the input switches on the front panel of the cabinet.*

Albuquerque, New Mexico. Though it has long been eclipsed by other, more powerful makes and models, the Altair was the first "personal" computer to appear in an environment dominated by minicomputers and mainframes. It was, simply, a metal box with a panel of switches and lights for input and output, a power supply, a motherboard with 18 slots, and two boards. One board was the central processing unit, with the 8-bit Intel 8080 microprocessor at its heart; the other board provided 256 bytes of random-access memory. This miniature computer had no keyboard, no monitor, and no device for permanent storage, but it did possess one great advantage: a price tag of $397.

Now, given the hindsight of a little more than a decade of microcomputing history, it is easy to see that the Altair's combination of small size and affordability was the thin edge of a wedge that, in just a few years, would move everyday computing power away from impersonal monoliths in climate-controlled rooms and onto the desks of millions of people. In 1975, however, the computing environment was still primarily a matter of data processing for specialists rather than personal computing for everyone. Thus when 4 KB

Intel's 4004, 8008, and 8080 chips. At the top left is the 4-bit 4004, which was named for the approximate number of old-fashioned transistors it replaced. At the bottom left is the 8-bit 8008, which addressed 16 KB of memory; this was the chip used in the Traf-O-Data tape-reader built by Paul Gilbert. At the right is the 8080, a faster 8-bit chip that could address 64 KB of memory. The brain of the MITS Altair, the 8080 was, in many respects, the chip on which the personal computing industry was built. The 4004 and 8008 chips were developed early in the 1970s; the 8080 appeared in 1974.

memory expansion boards became available for the Altair, the software needed most by its users was not a word processor or a spreadsheet, but a programming language — and the language first developed for it was a version of BASIC written by Bill Gates and Paul Allen.

Gates and Allen had become friends in their teens, while attending Lakeside School in Seattle. They shared an intense interest in computers, and by the time Gates was in the tenth grade, they and another friend named Paul Gilbert had formed a company called Traf-O-Data to produce a machine that automated the reading of 16-channel, 4-digit, binary-coded decimal (BCD) tapes generated by traffic-monitoring recorders. This machine, built by Gilbert, was based on the Intel 8008 microprocessor, the predecessor of the 8080 in the Altair.

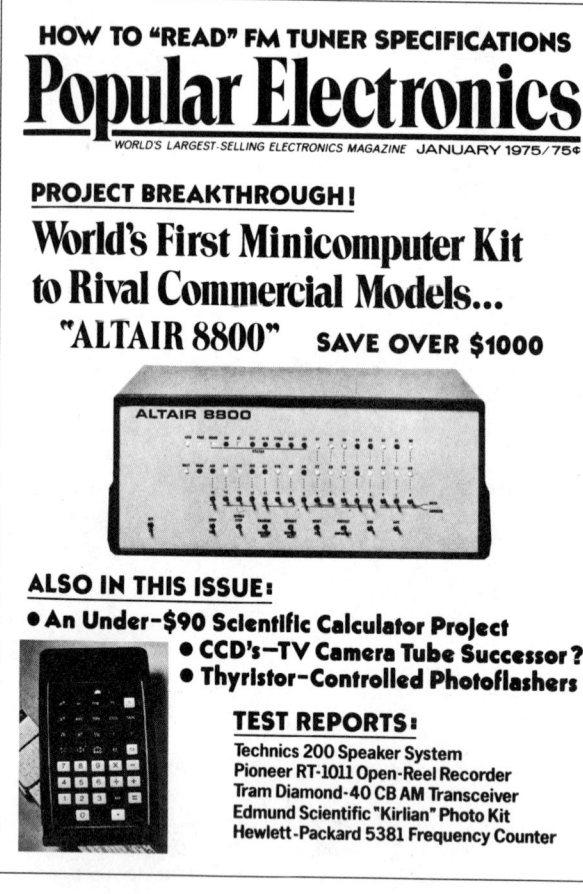

The January 1975 cover of Popular Electronics *magazine, featuring the machine that caught the imaginations of thousands of like-minded electronics enthusiasts — among them, Paul Allen and Bill Gates.*

Although it was too limited to serve as the central processor for a general-purpose computer, the 8008 was undeniably the ancestor of the 8080 as far as its architecture and instruction set were concerned. Thus Traf-O-Data's work with the 8008 gave Gates and Allen a head start when they later developed their version of BASIC for the Altair.

Paul Allen learned of the Altair from the cover story in the January 1975 issue of *Popular Electronics* magazine. Allen, then an employee of Honeywell in Boston, convinced Gates, a student at Harvard University, to develop a BASIC for the new computer. The two wrote their version of BASIC for the 8080 in six weeks, and Allen flew to New Mexico to demonstrate the language for MITS. The developers gave themselves the company name of Microsoft and licensed their BASIC to MITS as Microsoft's first product.

Though not a direct forerunner of MS-DOS, Altair BASIC, like the machine for which it was developed, was a landmark product in the history of personal computing. On another level, Altair BASIC was also the first link in a chain that led, somewhat circuitously, to Tim Paterson and the disk operating system he developed for Seattle Computer Products for the 8086 chip.

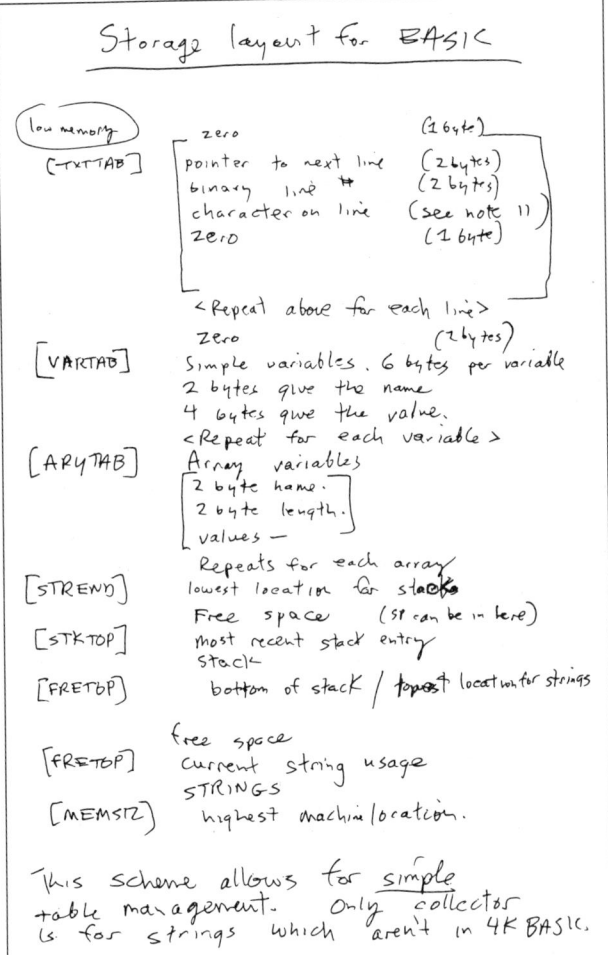

COMPUTER NOTES/JULY, 1975

Loading Software

    Software from MITS will be pro-
vided in a checksummed format.
There will be a bootstrap loader
that you key in manually (less than
25 bytes). This will read a checksum loader (the 'bin' loader) which
will be about 120 bytes.

    For audio cassette loading the
bootstrap and checksum loaders will
be longer. All of this will be explained in detail in a cover package
that will go out with all software.

    For loading non-checksummed
paper tapes here is a short program:

```
STKLOC:  DW GETNEW
             (2 bytes-#1 low byte of
                         GETNEW address
                      #2 high byte of
                         GETNEW address)


START:   LXI H,0
GETNEW:  LXI SP, STKLOC
         IN <flag-input channel>
         RAL  ;get input ready bit
         RNZ  ;ready?
         IN <data-input channel>
CHGLOC:  CPI <043 = INX B>
         RNZ
         INR A
         STA CHGLOC
         RET
                      (22 bytes)
```

    Punch a paper tape with leader,
a 043 start byte, the byte to be
stored at loc 0, the byte to be
stored at 1, - - - etc. Start at
START, making sure the memory the
loader is in is unprotected. Make
sure you don't wipe out the loader
by loading on top of it.

    To run this again change CHGLOC
back to CPI - 376.

On the left, Bill Gates's original handwritten notes describing memory configuration for Altair BASIC. On the right, a short bootstrap program written by Gates for Altair users; published in the July 1975 edition of the MITS user newsletter, Computer Notes.

From paper tape to disk

Gates and Allen's early BASIC for the Altair was loaded from paper tape after the bootstrap to load the tape was entered into memory by flipping switches on the front panel of the computer. In late 1975, however, MITS decided to release a floppy-disk system for the Altair—the first retail floppy-disk system on the market. As a result, in February 1976 Allen, by then Director of Software for MITS, asked Gates to write a disk-based version of Altair BASIC. The Altair had no operating system and hence no method of managing files, so the disk BASIC would have to include some file-management routines. It would, in effect, have to function as a rudimentary operating system.

Microsoft, 1978, Albuquerque, New Mexico. Top row, left to right: Steve Wood, Bob Wallace, Jim Lane. Middle row, left to right: Bob O'Rear, Bob Greenberg, Marc McDonald, Gordon Letwin. Bottom row, left to right: Bill Gates, Andrea Lewis, Marla Wood, Paul Allen.

Gates, still at Harvard University, agreed to write this version of BASIC for MITS. He went to Albuquerque and, as has often been recounted, checked into the Hilton Hotel with a stack of yellow legal pads. Five days later he emerged, yellow pads filled with the code for the new version of BASIC. Arriving at MITS with the code and a request to be left alone, Gates began typing and debugging and, after another five days, had Disk BASIC running on the Altair.

This disk-based BASIC marked Microsoft's entry into the business of languages for personal computers—not only for the MITS Altair, but also for such companies as Data Terminals Corporation and General Electric. Along the way, Microsoft BASIC took on added features, such as enhanced mathematics capabilities, and, more to the point in terms of MS-DOS, evolved into Stand-alone Disk BASIC, produced for NCR in 1977.

Designed and coded by Marc McDonald, Stand-alone Disk BASIC included a file-management scheme called the FAT, or file allocation table that used a linked list for managing disk files. The FAT, born during one of a series of discussions between McDonald and Bill Gates, enabled disk-allocation information to be kept in one location, with "chained" references pointing to the actual storage locations on disk. Fast and flexible, this file-management strategy was later used in a stand-alone version of BASIC for the 8086 chip and eventually, through an operating system named M-DOS, became the basis for the file-handling routines in MS-DOS.

M-DOS

During 1977 and 1978, Microsoft adapted both BASIC and Microsoft FORTRAN for an increasingly popular 8-bit operating system called CP/M. At the end of 1978, Gates and Allen moved Microsoft from Albuquerque to Bellevue, Washington. The company continued to concentrate on programming languages, producing versions of BASIC for the 6502 and the TI9900.

During this same period, Marc McDonald also worked on developing an 8-bit operating system called M-DOS (usually pronounced "Midas" or "My DOS"). Although it never became a real part of the Microsoft product line, M-DOS was a true multitasking operating system modeled after the DEC TOPS-10 operating system. M-DOS provided good performance and, with a more flexible FAT than that built into BASIC, had a better file-handling structure than the up-and-coming CP/M operating system. At about 30 KB, however, M-DOS was unfortunately too big for an 8-bit environment and so ended up being relegated to the back room. As Allen describes it, "Trying to do a large, full-blown operating system on the 8080 was a lot of work, and it took a lot of memory. The 8080 addresses only 64 K, so with the success of CP/M, we finally concluded that it was best not to press on with that."

CP/M

In the volatile microcomputer era of 1976 through 1978, both users and developers of personal computers quickly came to recognize the limitations of running applications on top of Microsoft's Stand-alone Disk BASIC or any other language. MITS, for example, scheduled a July 1976 release date for an independent operating system for its machine that used the code from the Altair's Disk BASIC. In the same year, Digital Research, headed by Gary Kildall, released its Control Program/Monitor, or CP/M.

CP/M was a typical microcomputer software product of the 1970s in that it was written by one person, not a group, in response to a specific need that had not yet been filled. One of the most interesting aspects of CP/M's history is that the software was developed several years before its release date — actually, several years before the hardware on which it would be a standard became commercially available.

In 1973, Kildall, a professor of computer science at the Naval Postgraduate School in Monterey, California, was working with an 8080-based small computer given him by Intel Corporation in return for some programming he had done for the company. Kildall's machine, equipped with a monitor and paper-tape reader, was certainly advanced for the time, but Kildall became convinced that magnetic-disk storage would make the machine even more efficient than it was.

Trading some programming for a disk drive from Shugart, Kildall first attempted to build a drive controller on his own. Lacking the necessary engineering ability, he contacted a friend, John Torode, who agreed to handle the hardware aspects of interfacing the computer and the disk drive while Kildall worked on the software portion — the refinement of an operating system he had written earlier that year. The result was CP/M.

The version of CP/M developed by Kildall in 1973 underwent several refinements. Kildall enhanced the CP/M debugger and assembler, added a BASIC interpreter, and did some work on an editor, eventually developing the product that, from about 1977 until the appearance of the IBM Personal Computer, set the standard for 8-bit microcomputer operating systems.

Digital Research's CP/M included a command interpreter called CCP (Console Command Processor), which acted as the interface between the user and the operating system itself, and an operations handler called BDOS (Basic Disk Operating System), which was responsible for file storage, directory maintenance, and other such housekeeping chores. For actual input and output — disk I/O, screen display, print requests, and so on — CP/M included a BIOS (Basic Input/Output System) tailored to the requirements of the hardware on which the operating system ran.

For file storage, CP/M used a system of eight-sector allocation units. For any given file, the allocation units were listed in a directory entry that included the filename and a table giving the disk locations of 16 allocation units. If a long file required more than 16 allocation units, CP/M created additional directory entries as required. Small files could be accessed rapidly under this system, but large files with more than a single directory entry could require numerous relatively time-consuming disk reads to find needed information.

At the time, however, CP/M was highly regarded and gained the support of a broad base of hardware and software developers alike. Quite powerful for its size (about 4KB), it was, in all respects, the undisputed standard in the 8-bit world, and remained so until, and even after, the appearance of the 8086.

The 16-bit Intel 8086 chip, introduced in 1978. Much faster and far more powerful than its 8-bit predecessor the 8080, the 8086 had the ability to address one megabyte of memory.

The 8086

When Intel released the 8-bit 8080 chip in 1974, the Altair was still a year in the future. The 8080 was designed not to make computing a part of everyday life but to make household appliances and industrial machines more intelligent. By 1978, when Intel introduced the 16-bit 8086, the microcomputer was a reality and the new chip represented a major step ahead in performance and memory capacity. The 8086's full 16-bit buses made it faster than the 8080, and its ability to address one megabyte of random-access memory was a giant step beyond the 8080's 64 KB limit. Although the 8086 was not compatible with the 8080, it was architecturally similar to its predecessor and 8080 source code could be mechanically translated to run on it. This translation capability, in fact, was a major influence on the design of Tim Paterson's operating system for the 8086 and, through Paterson's work, on the first released version of MS-DOS.

When the 8086 arrived on the scene, Microsoft, like other developers, was confronted with two choices: continue working in the familiar 8-bit world or turn to the broader horizons offered by the new 16-bit technology. For a time, Microsoft did both. Acting on Paul Allen's suggestion, the company developed the SoftCard for the popular Apple II, which was based on the 8-bit 6502 microprocessor. The SoftCard included a Z80 microprocessor and a copy of CP/M-80 licensed from Digital Research. With the SoftCard, Apple II users could run any program or language designed to run on a CP/M machine.

It was 16-bit technology, however, that held the most interest for Gates and Allen, who believed that this would soon become the standard for microcomputers. Their optimism was not universal — more than one voice in the trade press warned that industry investment in 8-bit equipment and software was too great to successfully introduce a new standard. Microsoft, however, disregarded these forecasts and entered the 16-bit arena as it had with the Altair: by developing a stand-alone version of BASIC for the 8086.

At the same time and, coincidentally, a few miles south in Tukwila, Washington, a major contribution to MS-DOS was taking place. Tim Paterson, working at Seattle Computer Products, a company that built memory boards, was developing an 8086 CPU card for use in an S-100 bus machine.

86-DOS

Paterson was introduced to the 8086 chip at a seminar held by Intel in June 1978. He had attended the seminar at the suggestion of his employer, Rod Brock of Seattle Computer Products. The new chip sparked his interest because, as he recalls, "all its instructions worked on both 8 and 16 bits, and you didn't have to do everything through the accumulator. It was also real fast—it could do a 16-bit ADD in three clocks."

After the seminar, Paterson—again with Brock's support—began work with the 8086. He finished the design of his first 8086 CPU board in January 1979 and by late spring had developed a working CPU, as well as an assembler and an 8086 monitor. In June, Paterson took his system to Microsoft to try it with Stand-alone BASIC, and soon after, Microsoft BASIC was running on Seattle Computer's new board.

During this period, Paterson also received a call from Digital Research asking whether they could borrow the new board for developing CP/M-86. Though Seattle Computer did not have a board to loan, Paterson asked when CP/M-86 would be ready. Digital's representative said December 1979, which meant, according to Paterson's diary, "we'll have to live with Stand-alone BASIC for a few months after we start shipping the CPU, but then we'll be able to switch to a real operating system."

Early in June, Microsoft and Tim Paterson attended the National Computer Conference in New York. Microsoft had been invited to share Lifeboat Associates' ten-by-ten foot booth, and Paterson had been invited by Paul Allen to show BASIC running on an S-100 8086 system. At that meeting, Paterson was introduced to Microsoft's M-DOS, which he found interesting because it used a system for keeping track of disk files—the FAT developed for Stand-alone BASIC—that was different from anything he had encountered.

After this meeting, Paterson continued working on the 8086 board, and by the end of the year, Seattle Computer Products began shipping the CPU with a BASIC option.

When CP/M-86 had still not become available by April 1980, Seattle Computer Products decided to develop a 16-bit operating system of its own. Originally, three operating systems were planned: a single-user system, a multiuser version, and a small interim product soon informally christened QDOS (for Quick and Dirty Operating System) by Paterson.

Both Paterson (working on QDOS) and Rod Brock knew that a standard operating system for the 8086 was mandatory if users were to be assured of a wide range of application software and languages. CP/M had become the standard for 8-bit machines, so the ability to mechanically translate existing CP/M applications to run on a 16-bit system became one of Paterson's major goals for the new operating system. To achieve this compatibility, the system he developed mimicked CP/M-80's functions and command structure, including its use of file control blocks (FCBs) and its approach to executable files.

An advertisement for the Seattle Computer Products 8086 CPU, with 86-DOS; published in the December 1980 issue of Byte.

At the same time, however, Paterson was dissatisfied with certain elements of CP/M, one of them being its file-allocation system, which he considered inefficient in the use of disk space and too slow in operation. So for fast, efficient file handling, he used a file allocation table, as Microsoft had done with Stand-alone Disk BASIC and M-DOS. He also wrote a translator to translate 8080 code to 8086 code, and he then wrote an assembler in Z80 assembly language and used the translator to translate it.

Four months after beginning work, Paterson had a functioning 6 KB operating system, officially renamed 86-DOS, and in September 1980 he contacted Microsoft again, this time to ask the company to write a version of BASIC to run on his system.

IBM

While Paterson was developing 86-DOS, the third major element leading to the creation of MS-DOS was gaining force at the opposite end of the country. IBM, until then seemingly oblivious to most of the developments in the microcomputer world, had turned its attention to the possibility of developing a low-end workstation for a market it knew well: business and business people.

On August 21, 1980, a study group of IBM representatives from Boca Raton, Florida, visited Microsoft. This group, headed by a man named Jack Sams, told Microsoft of IBM's interest in developing a computer based on a microprocessor. IBM was, however, unsure of microcomputing technology and the microcomputing market. Traditionally, IBM relied on long development cycles — typically four or five years — and was aware that such lengthy design periods did not fit the rapidly evolving microcomputer environment.

One of IBM's solutions — the one outlined by Sams's group — was to base the new machine on products from other manufacturers. All the necessary hardware was available, but the same could not be said of the software. Hence the visit to Microsoft with the question: Given the specifications for an 8-bit computer, could Microsoft write a ROM BASIC for it by the following April?

Microsoft responded positively, but added questions of its own: Why introduce an 8-bit computer? Why not release a 16-bit machine based on Intel's 8086 chip instead? At the end of this meeting — the first of many — Sams and his group returned to Boca Raton with a proposal for the development of a low-end, 16-bit business workstation. The venture was named Project Chess.

One month later, Sams returned to Microsoft asking whether Gates and Allen could, still by April 1981, provide not only BASIC but also FORTRAN, Pascal, and COBOL for the new computer. This time the answer was no because, though Microsoft's BASIC had been designed to run as a stand-alone product, it was unique in that respect — the other languages would need an operating system. Gates suggested CP/M-86, which was then still under development at Digital Research, and in fact made the initial contact for IBM. Digital Research and IBM did not come to any agreement, however.

Microsoft, meanwhile, still wanted to write all the languages for IBM — approximately 400 KB of code. But to do this within the allotted six-month schedule, the company needed some assurances about the operating system IBM was going to use. Further, it needed specific information on the internals of the operating system, because the ROM BASIC would interact intimately with the BIOS.

The turning point

That state of indecision, then, was Microsoft's situation on Sunday, September 28, 1980, when Bill Gates, Paul Allen, and Kay Nishi, a Microsoft vice president and president of ASCII Corporation in Japan, sat in Gates's eighth-floor corner office in the Old National Bank Building in Bellevue, Washington. Gates recalls, "Kay and I were just sitting there at night and Paul was on the couch. Kay said, 'Got to do it, got to do it.' It was only 20 more K of code at most—actually, it turned out to be 12 more K on top of the 400. It wasn't that big a deal, and once Kay said it, it was obvious. We'd always wanted to do a low-end operating system, we had specs for low-end operating systems, and we knew we were going to do one up on 16-bit."

At that point, Gates and Allen began looking again at Microsoft's proposal to IBM. Their estimated 400 KB of code included four languages, an assembler, and a linker. To add an operating system would require only another 20 KB or so, and they already knew of a working model for the 8086: Tim Paterson's 86-DOS. The more Gates, Allen, and Nishi talked that night about developing an operating system for IBM's new computer, the more possible—even preferable—the idea became.

Allen's first step was to contact Rod Brock at Seattle Computer Products to tell him that Microsoft wanted to develop and market SCP's operating system and that the company had an OEM customer for it. Seattle Computer Products, which was not in the business of marketing software, agreed and licensed 86-DOS to Microsoft. Eventually, SCP sold the operating system to Microsoft for $50,000, favorable language licenses, and a license back from Microsoft to use 86-DOS on its own machines.

In October 1980, with 86-DOS in hand, Microsoft submitted another proposal to IBM. This time the plan included both an operating system and the languages for the new computer. Time was short and the boundaries between the languages and the operating system were unclear, so Microsoft explained that it needed to control the development of the operating system in order to guarantee delivery by spring of 1981. In November, IBM signed the contract.

Creating MS-DOS

At Thanksgiving, a prototype of the IBM machine arrived at Microsoft and Bill Gates, Paul Allen, and, primarily, Bob O'Rear began a schedule of long, sometimes hectic days and total immersion in the project. As O'Rear recalls, "If I was awake, I was thinking about the project."

The first task handled by the team was bringing up 86-DOS on the new machine. This was a challenge because the work had to be done in a constantly changing hardware environment while changes were also being made to the specifications of the budding operating system itself.

As part of the process, 86-DOS had to be compiled and integrated with the BIOS, which Microsoft was helping IBM to write, and this task was complicated by the media. Paterson's 86-DOS—not counting utilities such as EDLIN, CHKDSK, and INIT (later named FORMAT)—arrived at Microsoft as one large assembly-language program on an 8-inch floppy disk. The IBM machine, however, used 5¼-inch disks, so Microsoft needed to determine the format of the new disk and then find a way to get the operating system from the old format to the new.

Paul Allen and Bill Gates (1982).

This work, handled by O'Rear, fell into a series of steps. First, he moved a section of code from the 8-inch disk and compiled it. Then, he converted the code to Intel hexadecimal format. Next, he uploaded it to a DEC-2020 and from there downloaded it to a large Intel fixed-disk development system with an In-Circuit Emulator. The DEC-2020 used for this task was also used in developing the BIOS, so there was additional work in downloading the BIOS to the Intel machine, converting it to hexadecimal format, moving it to an IBM development system, and then crossloading it to the IBM prototype.

Defining and implementing the MS-DOS disk format — different from Paterson's 8-inch format — was an added challenge. Paterson's ultimate goal for 86-DOS was logical device independence, but during this first stage of development, the operating system simply had to be converted to handle logical records that were independent of the physical record size.

Paterson, still with Seattle Computer Products, continued to work on 86-DOS and by the end of 1980 had improved its logical device independence by adding functions that streamlined reading and writing multiple sectors and records, as well as records of variable size. In addition to making such refinements of his own, Paterson also worked on dozens of changes requested by Microsoft, from modifications to the operating system's startup messages to changes in EDLIN, the line editor he had written for his own use. Throughout this process, IBM's security restrictions meant that Paterson was never told the name of the OEM and never shown the prototype machines until he left Seattle Computer Products and joined Microsoft in May 1981.

And of course, throughout the process the developers encountered the myriad loose ends, momentary puzzles, bugs, and unforeseen details without which no project is complete. There were, for example, the serial card interrupts that occurred when they should not and, frustratingly, a hardware constraint that the BIOS could not accommodate at first and that resulted in sporadic crashes during early MS-DOS operations.

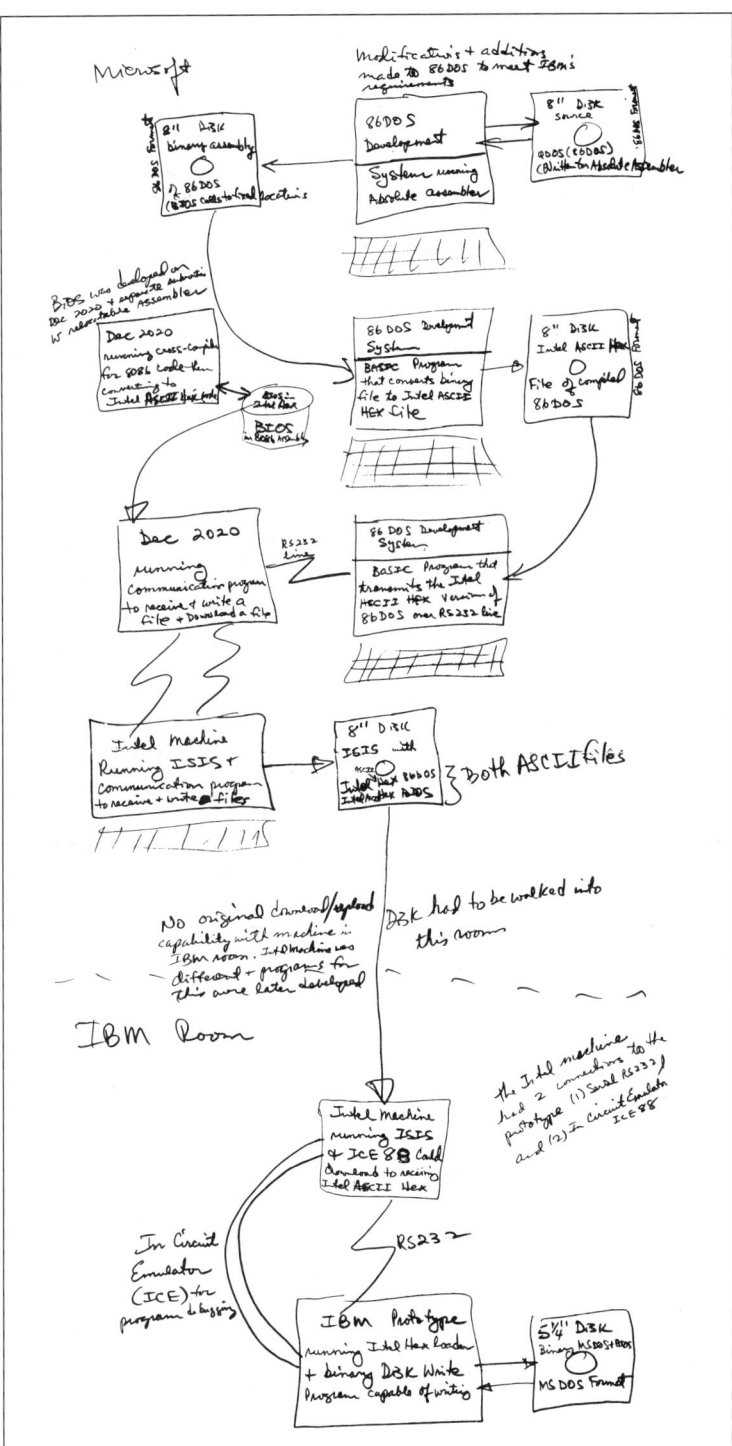

*Bob O'Rear's sketch of
the steps involved in
moving 86-DOS to the
IBM prototype.*

DOS Changes & Fixes

○ 4/20 *Bob* Single drive support, i.e. fix copy to prompt if same diskette

4/20 13. Modify "Format" to do a prompt to allow user to replace disk if formatting a single drive system

4/2 *Bob* Move origin of BIOS to 60:0 and origin of 86 DOS to C0:0. 86 DOS moved to 100:0 due to #21.

4/2 15. Change BOOT program to load the BIOS & DOS into the correct segments and further to locate and identify "if" these routines are on the disk. this is part of the changes necessary to effect data diskettes. BOOT should place an error message indicating no ~~its available if a~~ data ~~diskette~~

○ 4/2 16. ~~~~ of sectors

4/20 17. For diskette see R7.

4/2 18. make sure instruction

4/2 19. Modify the determine m INT ?? acco

4/2 20. Get final str support if a

4/2 21. for speci

○ 4/20 21. Modify CHK b that crosses it to the

4/2

DOS Changes & Fixes

○ 4/2 *DOS* 1. Move 'date' to known location ← 50:2
    50:3

    format   50:2   7 6 5 4 3 2 1 0
                    m m d d d d d
             50:3   y y y y y y y m

    or as a register   [year | month | day]
                       15 14 13 12 11 10 9 8 7 6 5 4 3 2 1 0
                       y y y y y y y m m m m d d d d d

    Requires mods to 86DOS to ~~~~ address date correctly & will take out 86DOS request for date & move to COMMAND

4/2 *Done* 2. Modify COMMAND to search for AUTOEXEC.BAT & if found do a submit on this file. If AUTOEXEC.BAT not found print banner and request date

4/2 *Fixed* 3. Fix DEBUG to do disassembly correctly. Strange problem. This works correctly on the CMC machine.
○

4/2 *Complete* 4. Modify DEBUG to frame its output so that it's readable on both 40X25 & 80X25 screens

4/2 *Done* 5. Modify FORMAT to allocate detected bad tracks to file BADTRK.

4/2 *DOS* 6. Fix problem with ZIBO RUN SPACE where a random read request (function 39) bombs.

4/2 7. Check out RS-232 support in the BIOS

4/2 *DOS* 8. Check out SUBMIT command

4/2 *Done* 9. Check out EDLIN edit of file larger than available memory. depends on #21

○ 4/2 10. Find out why F9 function key does not work correctly in the DOS

4/2 11. Indication from CHKDSK of available directory entries.

Part of Bob O'Rear's "laundry" list of operating-system changes and corrections for early April 1981. Around this time, interim beta copies were shipped to IBM for testing.

In spite of such difficulties, however, the new operating system ran on the prototype for the first time in February 1981. In the six months that followed, the system was continually refined and expanded, and by the time of its debut in August 1981, MS-DOS, like the IBM Personal Computer on which it appeared, had become a functional product for home and office use.

Version 1

The first release of MS-DOS, version 1.0, was not the operating system Microsoft envisioned as a final model for 16-bit computer systems. According to Bill Gates, "Basically, what we wanted to do was one that was more like MS-DOS 2, with the hierarchical file system and everything...the key thing [in developing version 1.0] was my saying, 'Look, we can come out with a subset first and just go upward from that.'"

This first version — Gates's subset of MS-DOS — was actually a good compromise between the present and the future in two important respects: It enabled Microsoft to meet the development schedule for IBM and it maintained program-translation compatibility with CP/M.

Available only for the IBM Personal Computer, MS-DOS 1.0 consisted of 4000 lines of assembly-language source code and ran in 8 KB of memory. In addition to utilities such as DEBUG, EDLIN, and FORMAT, it was organized into three major files. One file, IBMBIO.COM, interfaced with the ROM BIOS for the IBM PC and contained the disk and character input/output system. A second file, IBMDOS.COM, contained the DOS kernel, including the application-program interface and the disk-file and memory managers. The third file, COMMAND.COM, was the external command processor — the part of MS-DOS most visible to the user.

To take advantage of the existing base of languages and such popular applications as WordStar and dBASE II, MS-DOS was designed to allow software developers to mechanically translate source code for the 8080 to run on the 8086. And because of this link, MS-DOS looked and acted like CP/M-80, at that time still the standard among operating systems for microcomputers. Like its 8-bit relative, MS-DOS used eight-character filenames and three-character extensions, and it had the same conventions for identifying disk drives in command prompts. For the most part, MS-DOS also used the same command language, offered the same file services, and had the same general structure as CP/M. The resemblance was even more striking at the programming level, with an almost one-to-one correspondence between CP/M and MS-DOS in the system calls available to application programs.

New Features

MS-DOS was not, however, a CP/M twin, nor had Microsoft designed it to be inextricably bonded to the IBM PC. Hoping to create a product that would be successful over the long term, Microsoft had taken steps to make MS-DOS flexible enough to accommodate changes and new directions in the hardware technology — disks, memory boards, even microprocessors — on which it depended. The first steps toward this independence from

BUSINESS
Digest

Big I.B.M.'s Little Computer

Its Desk-Top
Model Brings
A New Image

Retail Sales
In U.S. Up
1.3% in July

But Analysts
Are Dubious of
General Upturn

IBM's New Line Likely to Shake Up
The Market for Personal Computers

By GEORGE ANDERS
Staff Reporter of THE WALL STREET JOURNAL

NEW YORK — International Business Machines Corp. has made its bold entry into the personal-computer market, and experts believe the computer giant could capture the lead in the youthful industry within two years.

Yesterday the company introduced several versions of a small computer designed for use in homes, schools and offices. Prices ...

... catch-up. The IBM machines operate on an Intel Corp. 8088 microprocessor, a faster and more powerful "chip" than those used in rivals' machines. IBM also has obtained for distribution such popular programs as VisiCalc, a financial forecasting model marketed by Personal Software Inc.

Other programs, or software, for the IBM equipment include the EasyWriter word-processing system, three accounting packages from Peachtree Software Inc. and ...

... far greater, equivalent to more than 1,000 typewritten pages. The new IBM computers don't use all that capacity, but what they do use will enable them to work with longer programs and more data than competing machines and to display images on their video screens in greater detail.

But the added memory comes at a price. IBM acknowledges that a fully stocked computer will cost $6,000 or more. Its basic $1,565 machine comes with 16,000 characters ...

InfoWorld
News For Microcomputer Users

IBM Announces New Microcomputer System

It's Official; One surprise

By Thom Hogan, IW Staff

NEW YORK, NY—Within a month you should be able to order an IBM Personal Computer. Whether or not that will have any effect on the microcomputing industry remains to be seen.

For those of you who have been reading InfoWorld, there were few surprises in the IBM announcement. Although the actual introduction took place a month later than anticipated, the features of the machine are virtually identical to the information we've already published ...

... tion of the unit taking place at the IBM facilities at Boca Raton, Florida, as reported earlier in InfoWorld. ComputerLand, the newly created Sears Business Centers and IBM Product Centers will be selling the Personal Computer. IBM is also setting up a special division of the Data Processing Group to market the machine.

The price begins at $1565, slightly higher than we reported earlier. It includes the keyboard unit, an enhanced Microsoft BASIC, in ...

OUTLOOK

IBM really gets personal.

PERSONAL COMPUTERS

PERSONAL COMPUTER FROM IBM

The mainframer's long-awaited entry into the personal computing market aims for corporate as well as home users.

With uncharacteristic but resounding fanfare, IBM ended the summer's most popular guessing game for the industry by introducing its Personal Computer. Highly comparable to offerings from arch-contenders Apple and Radio Shack, the machine represents several new tacks for the leading computer manufacturer as it attempts to hitch its wagon to one of the fastest growing segments of the industry.

The computer, which is designed to appeal to home users as well as corporate professionals, ranges in price from $1,565 for a bare-bones configuration to $6,300 for the full-blown model. It will be sold through Sears and Computerland computer retail stores as well as directly to large corporate and educational users, IBM says, pointing out that it has set up a special national marketing team to handle such volume orders.

Donald Estridge, the articulate director of IBM's entry systems business who braved strobes and movie lights at the machine's Waldorf-Astoria introduction, declines to say how many personnel have been dedicated to the national marketing effort, but says it will be selling in volumes of 20 machines or more. Several weeks after the unveiling, he said response so far had been "very, very good," with orders being taken but no deliveries to be made before this month.

In addition to the game of Adventure, which Estridge said has been thoroughly exercised by his Boca Raton, Fla., staff, IBM has decked out the machine with an array of packaged applications programs that are expected to make it attractive to the corporate user.

Among these are the popular VisiCalc spreadsheet package from Personal Software, accounting packages from Management Science America's Peachtree Software operation, and Information Unlimited's EasyWriter word processing system. Although IBM wouldn't say, more independently developed packages are certain to be offered for the computer as well as packages ...

... ently unveiled its first offering in the personal computer market—the IBM Personal Computer. The unit, perhaps surprisingly, plays music and includes game software to say nothing of the standard features available.

The machine is impressive. It's starting price is a mere $1565. For that price the buyer gets the 83-key keyboard, the computer itself, based on an 8088 microprocessor, and 16k of main memory. This minimal configuration can use a tape cassette for mass storage and a television set (with an rf ...

... modulator) for a display. (The machine is fully FCC certified for home operation as a class B computing device.)

IBM is cognizant of the fact that this minimally configured machine probably won't last a serious computerist long before he wants to expand. The company offers upgraded versions of the machine, and will sell them in different configurations. For example, the firm lists a more typical configuration for home or school as 64k of main memory, one disk

continued on page 17

12   Personal Computing/October 1981

A sampling of the headlines and newspaper articles that abounded when IBM announced its Personal Computer.

A page from Microsoft's third-quarter report for 1981.

specific hardware configurations appeared in MS-DOS version 1.0 in the form of device-independent input and output, variable record lengths, relocatable program files, and a replaceable command processor.

MS-DOS made input and output device-independent by treating peripheral devices as if they were files. To do this, it assigned a reserved filename to each of the three devices it recognized: CON for the console (keyboard and display), PRN for the printer, and AUX for the auxiliary serial ports. Whenever one of these reserved names appeared in the file control block of a file named in a command, all operations were directed to the device, rather than to a disk file. (A file control block, or FCB, is a 37-byte housekeeping record located in an application's portion of the memory space. It includes, among other things, the filename, the extension, and information about the size and starting location of the file on disk.)

Such device independence benefited both application developers and computer users. On the development side, it meant that applications could use one set of read and write calls, rather than a number of different calls for different devices, and it meant that an application did not have to be modified if new devices were added to the system. From the user's point of view, device independence meant greater flexibility. For example, even if a program had been designed for disk I/O only, the user could still use a file for input or direct output to the printer.

Variable record lengths provided another step toward logical independence. In CP/M, logical and physical record lengths were identical: 128 bytes. Files could be accessed only in units of 128 bytes and file sizes were always maintained in multiples of 128 bytes. With MS-DOS, however, physical sector sizes were of no concern to the user. The operating system maintained file lengths to the exact size in bytes and could be relied on to support logical records of any size desired.

Another new feature in MS-DOS was the relocatable program file. Unlike CP/M, MS-DOS had the ability to load two different types of program files, identified by the extensions .COM and .EXE. Program files ending with .COM mimicked the binary files in CP/M. They were more compact than .EXE files and loaded somewhat faster, but the combined program code, stack, and data could be no larger than 64 KB. A .EXE program, on the other hand, could be much larger because the file could contain multiple segments, each of which could be up to 64KB. Once the segments were in memory, MS-DOS then used part of the file header, the relocation table, to automatically set the correct addresses for each segment reference.

In addition to supporting .EXE files, MS-DOS made the external command processor, COMMAND.COM, more adaptable by making it a separate relocatable file just like any other program. It could therefore be replaced by a custom command processor, as long as the new file was also named COMMAND.COM.

Performance

Everyone familiar with the IBM PC knows that MS-DOS eventually became the dominant operating system on 8086-based microcomputers. There were several reasons for this, not least of which was acceptance of MS-DOS as the operating system for IBM's phenomenally successful line of personal computers. But even though MS-DOS was the only operating system available when the first IBM PCs were shipped, positioning alone would not necessarily have guaranteed its ability to outstrip CP/M-86, which appeared six months later. MS-DOS also offered significant advantages to the user in a number of areas, including the allocation and management of storage space on disk.

Like CP/M, MS-DOS shared out disk space in allocation units. Unlike CP/M, however, MS-DOS mapped the use of these allocation units in a central file allocation table — the FAT — that was always in memory. Both operating systems used a directory entry for recording information about each file, but whereas a CP/M directory entry included an allocation map — a list of sixteen 1 KB allocation units where successive parts of the file were stored — an MS-DOS directory entry pointed only to the first allocation unit in the FAT and each entry in the table then pointed to the next unit associated with the file. Thus, CP/M might require several directory entries (and more than one disk access) to load a file larger than 16 KB, but MS-DOS retained a complete in-memory list of all file components and all available disk space without having to access the disk at all. As a result, MS-DOS's ability to find and load even very long files was extremely rapid compared with CP/M's.

Two other important features — the ability to read and write multiple records with one operating-system call and the transient use of memory by the MS-DOS command processor — provided further efficiency for both users and developers.

The independence of the logical record from the physical sector laid the foundation for the ability to read and write multiple sectors. When reading multiple records in CP/M, an application had to issue a read function call for each sector, one at a time. With MS-DOS, the application could issue one read function call, giving the operating system the beginning record and the number of records to read, and MS-DOS would then load all of the corresponding sectors automatically.

Another innovative feature of MS-DOS version 1.0 was the division of the command processor, COMMAND.COM, into a resident portion and a transient portion. (There is also a third part, an initialization portion, which carries out the commands in an AUTOEXEC batch file at startup. This part of COMMAND.COM is discarded from memory when its work is finished.) The reason for creating resident and transient portions of the command processor had to do with maximizing the efficiency of MS-DOS for the user: On the one hand, the programmers wanted COMMAND.COM to include commonly requested functions, such as DIR and COPY, for speed and ease of use; on the other hand, adding these commands meant increasing the size of the command processor, with a resulting decrease in the memory available to application programs. The solution to this trade-off of speed versus utility was to include the extra functions in a transient portion of COMMAND.COM that could be overwritten by any application requiring more memory. To maintain the integrity of the functions for the user, the resident part of COMMAND.COM was given the job of checking the transient portion for damage when an application terminated. If necessary, this resident portion would then load a new copy of its transient partner into memory.

Ease of Use

In addition to its moves toward hardware independence and efficiency, MS-DOS included several services and utilities designed to make life easier for users and application developers. Among these services were improved error handling, automatic logging of disks, date and time stamping of files, and batch processing.

MS-DOS and the IBM PC were targeted at a nontechnical group of users, and from the beginning IBM had stressed the importance of data integrity. Because data is most likely to be lost when a user responds incorrectly to an error message, an effort was made to include concise yet unambiguous messages in MS-DOS. To further reduce the risks of misinterpretation, Microsoft used these messages consistently across all MS-DOS functions and utilities and encouraged developers to use the same messages, where appropriate, in their applications.

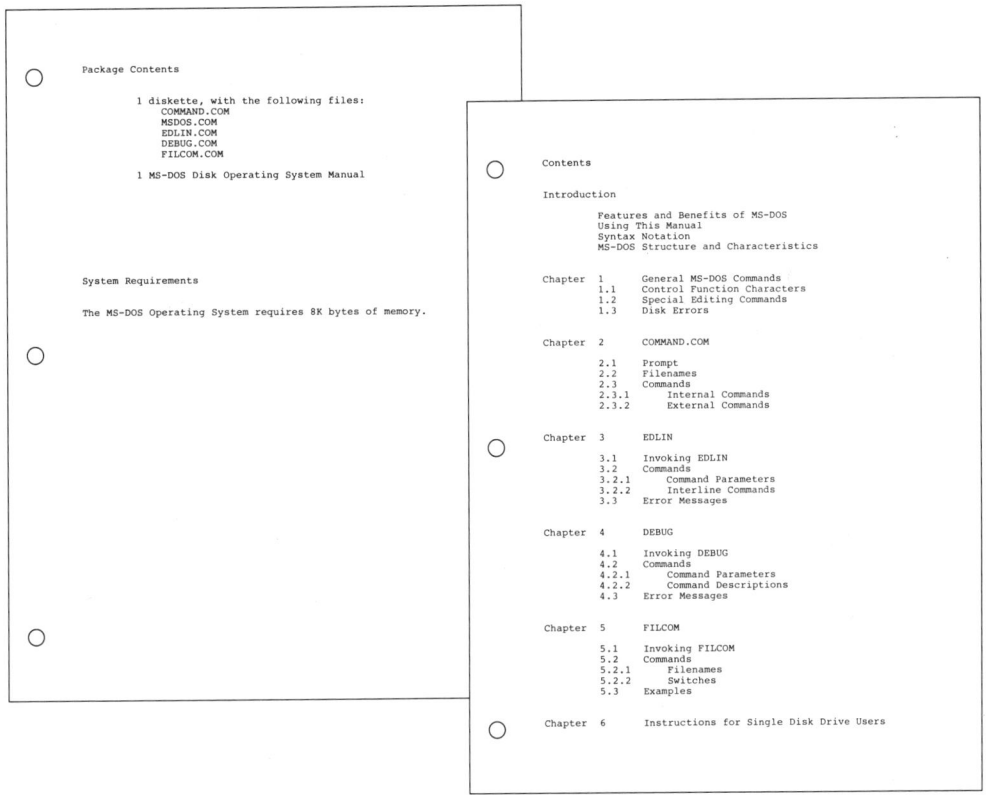

```
        Package Contents

            1 diskette, with the following files:
                COMMAND.COM
                MSDOS.COM
                EDLIN.COM
                DEBUG.COM
                FILCOM.COM

            1 MS-DOS Disk Operating System Manual




        System Requirements

        The MS-DOS Operating System requires 8K bytes of memory.
```

```
        Contents

        Introduction

            Features and Benefits of MS-DOS
            Using This Manual
            Syntax Notation
            MS-DOS Structure and Characteristics

        Chapter 1    General MS-DOS Commands
            1.1      Control Function Characters
            1.2      Special Editing Commands
            1.3      Disk Errors

        Chapter 2    COMMAND.COM

            2.1      Prompt
            2.2      Filenames
            2.3      Commands
            2.3.1        Internal Commands
            2.3.2        External Commands

        Chapter 3    EDLIN

            3.1      Invoking EDLIN
            3.2      Commands
            3.2.1        Command Parameters
            3.2.2        Interline Commands
            3.3      Error Messages

        Chapter 4    DEBUG

            4.1      Invoking DEBUG
            4.2      Commands
            4.2.1        Command Parameters
            4.2.2        Command Descriptions
            4.3      Error Messages

        Chapter 5    FILCOM

            5.1      Invoking FILCOM
            5.2      Commands
            5.2.1        Filenames
            5.2.2        Switches
            5.3      Examples

        Chapter 6    Instructions for Single Disk Drive Users
```

Two pages from Microsoft's MS-DOS version 1.0 manual. On the left, the system's requirements — 8 KB of memory; on the right, the 118-page manual's complete table of contents.

In a further attempt to safeguard data, MS-DOS also trapped hard errors — such as critical hardware errors — that had previously been left to the hardware-dependent logic. Now the hardware logic could simply report the nature of the error and the operating system would handle the problem in a consistent and systematic way. MS-DOS could also trap the Control-C break sequence so that an application could either protect against accidental termination by the user or provide a graceful exit when appropriate.

To reduce errors and simplify use of the system, MS-DOS also automatically updated memory information about the disk when it was changed. In CP/M, users had to log new disks as they changed them — a cumbersome procedure on single-disk systems or when data was stored on multiple disks. In MS-DOS, new disks were automatically logged as long as no file was currently open.

Another new feature — one visible with the DIR command — was date and time stamping of disk files. Even in its earliest forms, MS-DOS tracked the system date and displayed it at every startup, and now, when it turned out that only the first 16 bytes of a directory entry were needed for file-header information, the MS-DOS programmers decided to use some of the remaining 16 bytes to record the date and time of creation or update (and the size of the file) as well.

Batch processing was originally added to MS-DOS to help IBM. IBM wanted to run scripts — sequences of commands or other operations — one after the other to test various functions of the system. To do this, the testers needed an automated method of calling routines sequentially. The result was the batch processor, which later also provided users with the convenience of saving and running MS-DOS commands as batch files.

Finally, MS-DOS increased the options available to a program when it terminated. For example, in less sophisticated operating systems, applications and other programs remained in memory only as long as they were active; when terminated, they were removed from memory. MS-DOS, however, added a terminate-and-stay-resident function that enabled a program to be locked into memory and, in effect, become part of the operating-system environment until the computer system itself was shut down or restarted.

The Marketplace

When IBM announced the Personal Computer, it said that the new machine would run three operating systems: MS-DOS, CP/M-86, and Sof Tech Microsystem's p-System. Of the three, only MS-DOS was available when the IBM PC shipped. Nevertheless, when MS-DOS was released, nine out of ten programs on the *InfoWorld* bestseller list for 1981 ran under CP/M-80, and CP/M-86, which became available about six months later, was the operating system of choice to most writers and reviewers in the trade press.

Understandably, MS-DOS was compared with CP/M-80 and, later, CP/M-86. The main concern was compatibility: To what extent was Microsoft's new operating system compatible with the existing standard? No one could have foreseen that MS-DOS would not only catch up with but supersede CP/M. Even Bill Gates now recalls that "our most optimistic view of the number of machines using MS-DOS wouldn't have matched what really ended up happening."

To begin with, the success of the IBM PC itself surprised many industry watchers. Within a year, IBM was selling 30,000 PCs per month, thanks in large part to a business community that was already comfortable with IBM's name and reputation and, at least in retrospect, was ready for the leap to personal computing. MS-DOS, of course, benefited enormously from the success of the IBM PC — in large part because IBM supplied all its languages and applications in MS-DOS format.

But, at first, writers in the trade press still believed in CP/M and questioned the viability of a new operating system in a world dominated by CP/M-80. Many assumed, incorrectly, that a CP/M-86 machine could run CP/M-80 applications. Even before CP/M-86 was available, *Future Computing* referred to the IBM PC as the "CP/M Record Player" — presumably in anticipation of a vast inventory of CP/M applications for the new computer — and led its readers to assume that the PC was actually a CP/M machine.

Microsoft, meanwhile, held to the belief that the success of IBM's machine or any other 16-bit microcomputer depended ultimately on the emergence of an industry standard for a 16-bit operating system. Software developers could not afford to develop software for even two or three different operating systems, and users could (or would) not pay the prices the developers would have to charge if they did. Furthermore, users would almost certainly rebel against the inconvenience of sharing data stored under different operating-system formats. There had to be one operating system, and Microsoft wanted MS-DOS to be the one.

The company had already taken the first step toward a standard by choosing hardware independent designs wherever possible. Machine independence meant portability, and portability meant that Microsoft could sell one version of MS-DOS to different hardware manufacturers who, in turn, could adapt it to their own equipment. Portability alone, however, was no guarantee of industry-wide acceptance. To make MS-DOS the standard, Microsoft needed to convince software developers to write programs for MS-DOS. And in 1981, these developers were a little confused about IBM's new operating system.

An operating system by any other name...

A tangle of names gave rise to one point of confusion about MS-DOS. Tim Paterson's "Quick and Dirty Operating System" for the 8086 was originally shipped by Seattle Computer Products as 86-DOS. After Microsoft purchased 86-DOS, the name remained for a while, but by the time the PC was ready for release, the new system was known as MS-DOS. Then, after the IBM PC reached the market, IBM began to refer to the operating system as the IBM Personal Computer DOS, which the trade press soon shortened to PC-DOS. IBM's version contained some utilities, such as DISKCOPY and DISKCOMP, that were not included in MS-DOS, the generic version available for license by other manufacturers. By calling attention to these differences, publications added to the confusion about the distinction between the Microsoft and IBM releases of MS-DOS.

Further complications arose when Lifeboat Associates agreed to help promote MS-DOS but decided to call the operating system Software Bus 86. MS-DOS thus became one of a line of trademarked Software Bus products, another of which was a product called SB-80, Lifeboat's version of CP/M-80.

Finally, some of the first hardware companies to license MS-DOS also wanted to use their own names for the operating system. Out of this situation came such additional names as COMPAQ-DOS and Zenith's Z-DOS.

Given this confusing host of names for a product it believed could become the industry standard, Microsoft finally took the lead and, as developer, insisted that the operating system was to be called MS-DOS. Eventually, everyone but IBM complied.

Developers and MS-DOS

Early in its career, MS-DOS represented just a small fraction of Microsoft's business — much larger revenues were generated by BASIC and other languages. In addition, in the first two years after the introduction of the IBM PC, the growth of CP/M-86 and other environments nearly paralleled that of MS-DOS. So Microsoft found itself in the unenviable position of giving its support to MS-DOS while also selling languages to run on CP/M-86, thereby contributing to the growth of software for MS-DOS's biggest competitor.

Given the uncertain outcome of this two-horse race, some other software developers chose to wait and see which way the hardware manufacturers would jump. For their part, the hardware manufacturers were confronting the issue of compatibility between operating systems. Specifically, they needed to be convinced that MS-DOS was not a maverick — that it could perform as well as CP/M-86 as a base for applications that had been ported from the CP/M-80 environment for use on 16-bit computers.

Microsoft approached the problem by emphasizing four related points in its discussions with hardware manufacturers:

- First, one of Microsoft's goals in developing the first version of MS-DOS had always been translation compatibility from CP/M-80 to MS-DOS software.
- Second, translation was possible only for software written in 8080 or Z80 assembly language; thus, neither MS-DOS nor CP/M-86 could run programs written for other 8-bit processors, such as the 6800 or the 6502.
- Third, many applications were written in a high-level language, rather than in assembly language.
- Fourth, most of those high-level languages were Microsoft products and ran on MS-DOS.

Thus, even though some people had originally believed that only CP/M-86 would automatically make the installed base of CP/M-80 software available to the IBM PC and other 16-bit computers, Microsoft convinced the hardware manufacturers that MS-DOS was, in actuality, as flexible as CP/M-86 in its compatibility with existing — and appropriate — CP/M-80 software.

MS-DOS was put at a disadvantage in one area, however, when Digital Research convinced several manufacturers to include both 8080 and 8086 chips in their machines. With 8-bit and 16-bit software used on the same machine, the user could rely on the same disk format for both types of software. Because MS-DOS used a different disk format, CP/M had the edge in these dual-processor machines — although, in fact, it did not seem to have much effect on the survival of CP/M-86 after the first year or so.

Although making MS-DOS the operating system of obvious preference was not as easy as simply convincing hardware manufacturers to offer it, Microsoft's list of MS-DOS customers grew steadily from the time the operating system was introduced. Many manufacturers continued to offer CP/M-86 along with MS-DOS, but by the end of 1983 the technical superiority of MS-DOS (bolstered by the introduction of such products as Lotus 1-2-3) carried the market. For example, when DEC, a longtime holdout, decided to make MS-DOS the primary operating system for its Rainbow computer, the company mentioned the richer set of commands and "dramatically" better disk performance of MS-DOS as reasons for its choice over CP/M-86.

Additional MS-DOS Features and Benefits

- **Written Entirely in 8086 Assembly Language**

  This provides significant speed improvements over operating systems that are largely translated from their 8-bit counterparts.

- **Fast Efficient File Structure**

  The format eliminates the need for "extents," minimizes access to the directory track, and provides for duplicate directory information and verify after write.

- **No Need to Log in Disks**

  As long as no file is currently open, there is no need to log in a new disk by typing Control-C. This greatly improves usability for single disk system users and for people who like to store their data on separate diskettes.

- **No Physical File/Disk Size Limitation**

  Unlike users of operating systems that are limited to 8 megabytes, MS-DOS users would not have to break a 24 megabyte hard disk into three separate drives.

- **No Overhead for Non-128-Byte Physical Sectors**

  One does not have to worry about different physical sector sizes when writing a BIOS.

- **Time/Date Stamps**

  This alleviates, for instance, the need to recompile a file if the time on the relocatable file is more recent than on the source file.

- **Lifeboat Associates**

  The world's largest independent distributor of microcomputer software has chosen to support MS-DOS as its low-end 16-bit operating system. Recognizing the important migration path from the 8-bit level to XENIX OS, Lifeboat will be offering a wide range of software for the MS-DOS environment.

- **100% IBM Compatible**

  IBM is offering software running under MS-DOS. IBM has announced Microsoft BASIC and Microsoft Pascal, along with accounting, financial planning, and word processing software running under MS-DOS.

MS-DOS

Standard Operating System for 8086 Micros

MS-DOS is a disk operating system from Microsoft for 8086/8088 microprocessors. International Business Machines Corp. chose MS-DOS (called IBM Personal Computer DOS) to be its operating system of choice for its Personal Computer. Microsoft's agreements with IBM and several other major computer manufacturers indicate that end-user systems running MS-DOS will be widely available in the near future, making MS-DOS the standard low-end operating system for 8086 micros. Why is MS-DOS becoming popular? MS-DOS is an important advance in microcomputer operating systems.

What Makes MS-DOS Important?

All of Microsoft's languages (BASIC Interpreter, BASIC Compiler, FORTRAN, COBOL, Pascal) are available immediately under MS-DOS. Users of MS-DOS are assured that their operating system will be the first that Microsoft will support when any new products or major releases are announced. In addition, the 8-bit versions of Microsoft's languages are upward compatible with the 16-bit versions. Thus, application programs written in 8-bit Microsoft languages can be run under MS-DOS with little or no modification. Microsoft wants to encourage both the transporting of 8-bit to 16-bit software, and the development of new 16-bit software.

Here are the major features that make MS-DOS the operating system people want to use on 8086 machines:

- **Easy Conversion from 8080 to 8086**

  MS-DOS allows as much transportability of 8-bit machine language software as is possible. MS-DOS emulates system calls to CP/M-80. By simply running assembly language source code through the Intel conversion program, almost all 8080 programs will work without modification. In most cases, a conversion to MS-DOS is easier than conversion to other operating systems.

- **Device Independent I/O**

  MS-DOS simplifies I/O to different devices on the UNIX concept. A single set of I/O calls treats all devices alike from the user's perspective. There is no need to rewrite programs when a new device is added to the system. Simply OPEN the device and READ or WRITE. Also, device independent I/O assures that different control characters (specifically TAB) are handled the same by the different devices.

- **Advanced Error Recovery Procedures**

  MS-DOS doesn't simply fade away when errors occur. If a disk error occurs at any time during any program, MS-DOS will retry the operation three times. If the operation cannot be completed successfully, MS-DOS will return an error message, then wait for the user to enter a response. The user can attempt recovery rather than reboot the operating system.

- **Complete Program Relocatability**

  MS-DOS is a truly relocatable operating system. Not only can the Microsoft relocatable linking loader provide for separate segments, but also the COMMAND program in MS-DOS relocates the modules during loading rather than loading them to preset addresses. Thus, MS-DOS does not have the 64K program space limitation of other operating systems.

- **Powerful, Flexible File Characteristics**

  MS-DOS has no practical limit on file or disk size. MS-DOS uses 4-byte XENIX OS compatible logical pointers for file and disk capacity up to 4 gigabytes.

  Within a single diskette, the user of MS-DOS can have files of different logical record lengths. MS-DOS is designed to block and deblock its own physical sectors. 128 is not a sacred number in MS-DOS.

  MS-DOS remembers the exact end of file marker. Thus, should one open a file with a logical record length other than the physical record length, MS-DOS remembers exactly where the file ends to the byte, rather than rounded to 128 bytes. This alleviates the need for forcing Control-Z's or the like at the end of a file.

MICROSOFT

Microsoft, Inc.
10800 NE Eighth, Suite 819
Bellevue, WA 98004
206-455-8080 Telex 328945

The Future of MS-DOS

Microsoft plans to enhance MS-DOS. The additional addressing space of the 8086 processor makes multi-tasking a particularly attractive enhancement. An upward migration path to the XENIX operating system through XENIX compatible system calls, "pipes," and "forking" is another planned enhancement.

Plans for MS-DOS also include disk buffering, graphics and cursor positioning, kanji support, multi-user and hard disk support, and networking.

A Microsoft original equipment manufacturer (OEM) marketing brochure describing the strengths of MS-DOS.

Version 2

After the release of PC-specific version 1.0 of MS-DOS, Microsoft worked on an update that contained some bug fixes. Version 1.1 was provided to IBM to run on the upgraded PC released in 1982 and enabled MS-DOS to work with double-sided, 320 KB floppy disks. This version, referred to as 1.25 by all but IBM, was the first version of MS-DOS shipped by other OEMs, including COMPAQ and Zenith.

Even before these intermediate releases were available, however, Microsoft began planning for future versions of MS-DOS. In developing the first version, the programmers had had two primary goals: running translated CP/M-80 software and keeping MS-DOS small. They had neither the time nor the room to include more sophisticated features, such as those typical of Microsoft's UNIX-based multiuser, multitasking operating system, XENIX. But when IBM informed Microsoft that the next major edition of the PC would be the Personal Computer XT with a 10-megabyte fixed disk, a larger, more powerful version of MS-DOS — one closer to the operating system Microsoft had envisioned from the start — became feasible.

There were three particular areas that interested Microsoft: a new, hierarchical file system, installable device drivers, and some type of multitasking. Each of these features contributed to version 2.0, and together they represented a major change in MS-DOS while still maintaining compatibility with version 1.0.

The File System

Primary responsibility for version 2.0 fell to Paul Allen, Mark Zbikowski, and Aaron Reynolds, who wrote (and rewrote) most of the version 2.0 code. The major design issue confronting the developers, as well as the most visible example of its difference from versions 1.0, 1.1, and 1.25, was the introduction of a hierarchical file system to handle the file-management needs of the XT's fixed disk.

Version 1.0 had a single directory for all the files on a floppy disk. That system worked well enough on a disk of limited capacity, but on a 10-megabyte fixed disk a single directory could easily become unmanageably large and cumbersome.

CP/M had approached the problem of high-capacity storage media by using a partitioning scheme that divided the fixed disk into 10 user areas equivalent to 10 separate floppy-disk drives. On the other hand, UNIX, which had traditionally dealt with larger systems, used a branching, hierarchical file structure in which the user could create directories and subdirectories to organize files and make them readily accessible. This was the file-management system implemented in XENIX, and it was the MS-DOS team's choice for handling files on the XT's fixed disk.

The MS-DOS version 1.0 manual next to the version 2.0 manual.

Partitioning, IBM's initial choice, had the advantages of familiarity, size, and ease of implementation. Many small-system users — particularly software developers — were already familiar with partitioning, if not overly fond of it, from their experience with CP/M. Development time was also a major concern, and the code needed to develop a partitioning scheme would be minimal compared with the code required to manage a hierarchical file system. Such a scheme would also take less time to implement.

However, partitioning had two inherent disadvantages. First, its functionality would decrease as storage capacity increased, and even in 1982, Microsoft was anticipating substantial growth in the storage capacity of disk-based media. Second, partitioning depended on the physical device. If the size of the disk changed, either the number or the size of the partitions must also be changed in the code for both the operating system and the application programs. For Microsoft, with its commitment to hardware independence, partitioning would have represented a step in the wrong direction.

A hierarchical file structure, on the other hand, could be independent of the physical device. A disk could be partitioned logically, rather than physically. And because these partitions (directories) were controlled by the user, they were open-ended and enabled the individual to determine the best way of organizing a disk.

Ultimately, it was a hierarchical file system that found its way into MS-DOS 2.0 and eventually convinced everyone that it was, indeed, the better and more flexible solution to the problem of supporting a fixed disk. The file system was logically consistent with the XENIX file structure, yet physically consistent with the file access incorporated in versions 1.x, and was based on a root, or main, directory under which the user could create a system of subdirectories and sub-subdirectories to hold files. Each file in the system was identified by the directory path leading to it, and the number of subdirectories was limited only by the length of the pathname, which could not exceed 64 characters.

In this file structure, all the subdirectories and the filename in a path were separated from one another by backslash characters, which represented the only anomaly in the XENIX/MS-DOS system of hierarchical files. XENIX used a forward slash as a separator, but versions 1.x of MS-DOS, borrowing from the tradition of DEC operating systems, already used the forward slash for switches in the command line, so Microsoft, at IBM's request, decided to use the backslash as the separator instead. Although the backslash character created no practical problems, except on keyboards that lacked a backslash, this decision did introduce inconsistency between MS-DOS and existing UNIX-like operating systems. And although Microsoft solved the keyboard problem by enabling the user to change the switch character from a slash to a hyphen, the solution itself created compatibility problems for people who wished to exchange batch files.

Another major change in the file-management system was related to the new directory structure: In order to fully exploit a hierarchical file system, Microsoft had to add a new way of calling file services.

Versions 1.x of MS-DOS used CP/M-like structures called file control blocks, or FCBs, to maintain compatibility with older CP/M-80 programs. The FCBs contained all pertinent information about the size and location of a file but did not allow the user to specify a file in a different directory. Therefore, version 2.0 of MS-DOS needed the added ability to access files by means of handles, or descriptors, that could operate across directory lines.

In this added step toward logical device independence, MS-DOS returned a handle whenever an MS-DOS program opened a file. All further interaction with the file involved only this handle. MS-DOS made all necessary adjustments to an internal structure — different from an FCB — so that the program never had to deal directly with information about the file's location in memory. Furthermore, even if future versions of MS-DOS were to change the structure of the internal control units, program code would not need to be rewritten — the file handle would be the only referent needed, and this would not change.

Putting the internal control units under the supervision of MS-DOS and substituting handles for FCBs also made it possible for MS-DOS to redirect a program's input and output. A system function was provided that enabled MS-DOS to divert the reads or writes directed to one handle to the file or device assigned to another handle. This capability was used by COMMAND.COM to allow output from a file to be redirected to a device, such as a printer, or to be piped to another program. It also allowed system cleanup on program terminations.

Installable Device Drivers

At the time Microsoft began developing version 2.0 of MS-DOS, the company also realized that many third-party peripheral devices were not working well with one another. Each manufacturer had its own way of hooking its hardware into MS-DOS and if two third-party devices were plugged into a computer at the same time, they would often conflict or fail.

One of the hallmarks of IBM's approach to the PC was open architecture, meaning that users could simply slide new cards into the computer whenever new input/output devices, such as fixed disks or printers, were added to the system. Unfortunately, version 1.0 of MS-DOS did not have a corresponding open architecture built into it — the BIOS contained all the code that permitted the operating system to run the hardware. If independent hardware manufacturers wanted to develop equipment for use with a computer manufacturer's operating system, they would have to either completely rewrite the device drivers or write a complicated utility to read the existing drivers, alter them, add the code to support the new device, and produce a working set of drivers. If the user installed more than one device, these patches would often conflict with one another. Furthermore, they would have to be revised each time the computer manufacturer updated its version of MS-DOS.

By the time work began on version 2.0, the MS-DOS team knew that the ability to install any device driver at run time was vital. They implemented installable device drivers by making the drivers more modular. Like the FAT, IO.SYS (IBMBIO.COM in PC-DOS) became, in effect, a linked list — this time, of device drivers — that could be expanded through commands in the CONFIG.SYS file on the system boot disk. Manufacturers could now write a device driver that the user could install at run time by including it in the CONFIG.SYS file. MS-DOS could then add the device driver to the linked list.

By extension, this ability to install device drivers also added the ability to supersede a previously installed driver — for example, the ANSI.SYS console driver that supports the ANSI standard escape codes for cursor positioning and screen control.

Print Spooling

At IBM's request, version 2.0 of MS-DOS also possessed the undocumented ability to perform rudimentary background processing — an interim solution to a growing awareness of the potentials of multitasking.

Background print spooling was sufficient to meet the needs of most people in most situations, so the print spooler, PRINT.COM, was designed to run whenever MS-DOS had nothing else to do. When the parent application became active, PRINT.COM would be interrupted until the next lull. This type of background processing, though both limited and extremely complex, was exploited by a number of applications, such as SideKick.

Loose Ends and a New MS-DOS

Hierarchical files, installable device drivers, and print spooling were the major design decisions in version 2.0. But there were dozens of smaller changes, too.

For example, with the fixed disk it was necessary to modify the code for automatic logging of disks. This modification meant that MS-DOS had to access the disk more often, and file access became much slower as a result. In trying to find a solution to this problem, Chris Peters reasoned that, if MS-DOS had just checked the disk, there was some minimum time

Two members of the IBM line of personal computers for which versions 1 and 2 of MS-DOS were developed. On the left, the original IBM PC (version 1.0 of MS-DOS); on the right, the IBM PC/XT (version 2.0).

a user would need to physically change disks. If that minimum time had not elapsed, the current disk information in RAM — whether for a fixed disk or a floppy — was probably still good.

Peters found that the fastest anyone could physically change disks, even if the disks were damaged in the process, was about two seconds. Reasoning from this observation, he had MS-DOS check to see how much time had gone by since the last disk access. If less than two seconds had elapsed, he had MS-DOS assume that a new disk had not been inserted and that the disk information in RAM was still valid. With this little trick, the speed of file handling in MS-DOS version 2.0 increased considerably.

Version 2.0 was released in March 1983, the product of a surprisingly small team of six developers, including Peters, Mani Ulloa, and Nancy Panners in addition to Allen, Zbikowski, and Reynolds. Despite its complex new features, version 2.0 was only 24 KB of code. Though it maintained its compatibility with versions 1.x, it was in reality a vastly different operating system. Within six months of its release, version 2.0 gained widespread public acceptance. In addition, popular application programs such as Lotus 1-2-3 took advantage of the features of this new version of MS-DOS and thus helped secure its future as the industry standard for 8086 processors.

Versions 2.1 and 2.25

The world into which version 2.0 of MS-DOS emerged was considerably different from the one in which version 1.0 made its debut. When IBM released its original PC, the business market for microcomputers was as yet undefined — if not in scope, at least in terms of who and what would dominate the field. A year and a half later, when the PC/XT came on the scene, the market was much better known. It had, in fact, been heavily influenced by IBM itself. There were still many MS-DOS machines, such as the Tandy 2000 and the Hewlett Packard HP150, that were hardware incompatible with the IBM, but manufacturers of new computers knew that IBM was a force to consider and many chose to compete with the IBM PC by emulating it. Software developers, too, had gained an understanding of business computing and were confident they could position their software accurately in the enormous MS-DOS market.

In such an environment, concerns about the existing base of CP/M software faded as developers focused their attention on the fast-growing business market and MS-DOS quickly secured its position as an industry standard. Now, with the obstacles to MS-DOS diminished, Microsoft found itself with a new concern: maintaining the standard it had created. Henceforth, MS-DOS had to be many things to many people. IBM had requirements; other OEMs had requirements. And sometimes these requirements conflicted.

Hardware Developers

When version 2.0 was released, IBM was already planning to introduce its PCjr. The PCjr would have the ability to run programs from ROM cartridges and, in addition to using half-height 5¼-inch drives, would employ a slightly different disk-controller architecture. Because of these differences from the standard PC line, IBM's immediate concern was for a version 2.1 of MS-DOS modified for the new machine.

For the longer term, IBM was also planning a faster, more powerful PC with a 20-megabyte fixed disk. This prospect meant Microsoft needed to look again at its file-management system, because the larger storage capacity of the 20-megabyte disk stretched the size limitations for the file allocation table as it worked in version 2.0.

However, IBM's primary interest for the next major release of MS-DOS was networking. Microsoft would have preferred to pursue multitasking as the next stage in the development of MS-DOS, but IBM was already developing its IBM PC Network Adapter, a plug-in card with an 80188 chip to handle communications. So as soon as version 2.0 was released, the MS-DOS team, again headed by Zbikowski and Reynolds, began work on a networking version (3.0) of the operating system.

Meanwhile...

The international market for MS-DOS was not significant in the first few years after the release of the IBM PC and version 1.0 of MS-DOS. IBM did not, at first, ship its Personal Computer to Europe, so Microsoft was on its own there in promoting MS-DOS. In 1982, the company gained a significant advantage over CP/M-86 in Europe by concluding an agreement with Victor, a software company that was very successful in Europe and had already licensed CP/M-86. Working closely with Victor, Microsoft provided special development support for its graphics adaptors and eventually convinced the company to offer its products only on MS-DOS. In Japan, the most popular computers were Z80 machines, and given the country's huge installed base of 8-bit machines, 16-bit computers were not taking hold. Mitsubishi, however, offered a 16-bit computer. Although CP/M-86 was Mitsubishi's original choice for an operating system, Microsoft helped get Multiplan and FORTRAN running on the CP/M-86 system, and eventually won the manufacturer's support for MS-DOS.

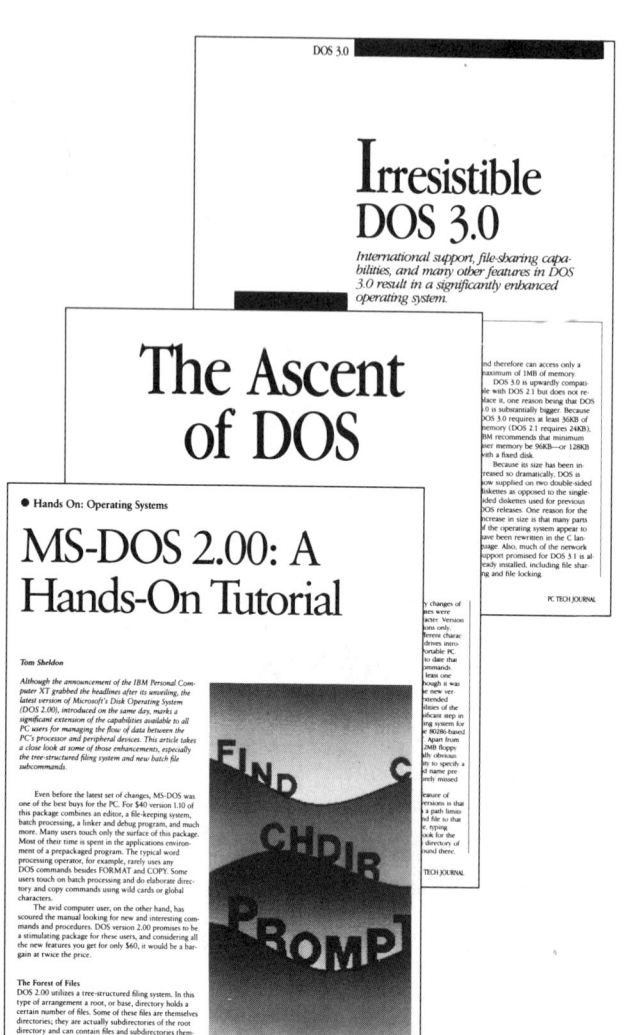

*A sample of the reviews that appeared
with each new version of MS-DOS.*

In the software arena, by the time development was underway on the 2.x releases of MS-DOS, Microsoft's other customers were becoming more vocal about their own needs. Several wanted a networking capability, adding weight to IBM's request, but a more urgent need for many—a need *not* shared by IBM at the time—was support for international products. Specifically, these manufacturers needed a version of MS-DOS that could be sold in other countries—a version of MS-DOS that could display messages in other languages and adapt to country-specific conventions, such as date and time formats.

Microsoft, too, wanted to internationalize MS-DOS, so the MS-DOS team, while modifying the operating system to support the PCjr, also added functions and a COUNTRY command that allowed users to set the date and time formats and other country-dependent variables in the CONFIG.SYS file.

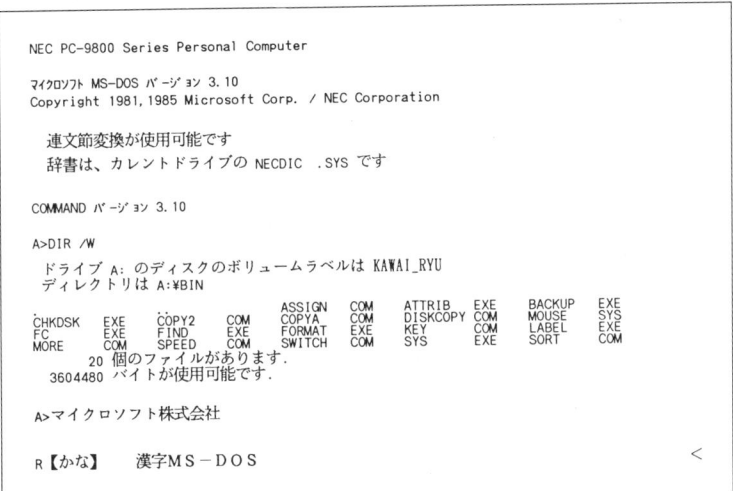

A Kanji screen with the MS-DOS copyright message.

```
NEC PC-9800 Series Personal Computer

マイクロソフト MS-DOS バージョン 3.10
Copyright 1981,1985 Microsoft Corp. / NEC Corporation

   連文節変換が使用可能です
   辞書は、カレントドライブの NECDIC .SYS です

COMMAND バージョン 3.10

A>DIR /W
   ドライブ A: のディスクのボリュームラベルは KAWAI_RYU
   ディレクトリは A:\BIN
                        ASSIGN   COM    ATTRIB   EXE    BACKUP   EXE
CHKDSK   EXE    COPY2    COM    COPYA    COM    DISKCOPY COM    MOUSE    SYS
FC       EXE    FIND     EXE    FORMAT   EXE    KEY      COM    LABEL    EXE
MORE     COM    SPEED    COM    SWITCH   COM    SYS      EXE    SORT     COM
      20 個のファイルがあります.
   3604480 バイトが使用可能です.

A>マイクロソフト株式会社

R【かな】    漢字MS-DOS                                        <
```

At about the same time, another international requirement appeared. The Japanese market for MS-DOS was growing, and the question of supporting 7000 Kanji characters (ideograms) arose. The difficulty with Kanji is that it requires dual-byte characters. For English and most European character sets, one byte corresponds to one character. Japanese characters, however, sometimes use one byte, sometimes two. This variability creates problems in parsing, and as a result MS-DOS had to be modified to parse a string from the beginning, rather than back up one character at a time.

This support for individual country formats and Kanji appeared in version 2.01 of MS-DOS. IBM did not want this version, so support for the PCjr, developed by Zbikowski, Reynolds, Ulloa, and Eric Evans, appeared separately in version 2.1, which went only to IBM and did not include the modifications for international MS-DOS.

Different customers, different versions

As early as version 1.25, Microsoft faced the problem of trying to satisfy those OEM customers that wanted to have the same version of MS-DOS as IBM. Some, such as COMPAQ, were in the business of selling 100-percent compatibility with IBM. For them, any difference between their version of the operating system and IBM's introduced the possibility of incompatibility. Satisfying these requests was difficult, however, and it was not until version 3.1 that Microsoft was able to supply a system that other OEMs agreed was identical with IBM's.

Before then, to satisfy the OEM customers, Microsoft combined versions 2.1 and 2.01 to create version 2.11. Although IBM did not accept this because of the internationalization code, version 2.11 became the standard version for all non-IBM customers running any form of MS-DOS in the 2.x series. Version 2.11 was sold worldwide and translated into about 10 different languages. Two other intermediate versions provided support for Hangeul (the Korean character set) and Chinese Kanji.

Software Concerns

After the release of version 2.0, Microsoft also gained an appreciation of the importance —
and difficulty — of supporting the people who were developing software for MS-DOS.

Software developers worried about downward compatibility. They also worried about
upward compatibility. But despite these concerns, they sometimes used programming
practices that could guarantee neither. When this happened and the resulting programs
were successful, it was up to Microsoft to ensure compatibility.

For example, because the information about the internals of the BIOS and the ROM interface had been published, software developers could, and often did, work directly with the
hardware in order to get more speed. This meant sidestepping the operating system for
some operations. However, by choosing to work at the lower levels, these developers lost
the protection provided by the operating system against hardware changes. Thus, when
low-level changes were made in the hardware, their programs either did not work or did
not run cooperatively with other applications.

Another software problem was the continuing need for compatibility with CP/M. For
example, in CP/M, programmers would call a fixed address in low memory in order to request a function; in MS-DOS, they would request operating-system services by executing a
software interrupt. To support older software, the first version of MS-DOS allowed a program to request functions by either method. One of the CP/M-based programs supported
in this fashion was the very popular WordStar. Since Microsoft could not make changes in
MS-DOS that would make it impossible to run such a widely used program, each new version of MS-DOS had to continue supporting CP/M-style calls.

A more pervasive CP/M-related issue was the use of FCB-style calls for file and record
management. The version 1.x releases of MS-DOS had used FCB-style calls exclusively, as
had CP/M. Version 2.0 introduced the more efficient and flexible handle calls, but Microsoft
could not simply abolish the old FCB-style calls, because so many popular programs used
them. In fact, some of Microsoft's own languages used them. So, MS-DOS had to support
both types of calls in the version 2.x series. To encourage the use of the new handle calls,
however, Microsoft made it easy for MS-DOS users to upgrade to version 2.0. In addition,
the company convinced IBM to require version 2.0 for the PC/XT and also encouraged
software developers to require 2.0 for their applications.

At first, both software developers and OEM customers were reluctant to require 2.0
because they were concerned about problems with the installed user base of 1.0
systems — requiring version 2.0 meant supporting both sets of calls. Applications also
needed to be able to detect which version of the operating system the user was running.
For versions 1.x, the programs would have to use FCB calls; for versions 2.x, they would
use the file handles to exploit the flexibility of MS-DOS more fully.

All told, it was an awkward period of transition, but by the time Microsoft began work on
version 3.0 and the support for IBM's upcoming 20-megabyte fixed disk, it had become
apparent that the change had been in everyone's best interest.

Version 3

The types of issues that began to emerge as Microsoft worked toward version 3.0, MS-DOS for networks, exaggerated the problems of compatibility that had been encountered before.

First, networking, with or without a multitasking capability, requires a level of cooperation and compatibility among programs that had never been an issue in earlier versions of MS-DOS. As described by Mark Zbikowski, one of the principals involved in the project, "there was a very long period of time between 2.1 and 3.0 — almost a year and a half. During that time, we believed we understood all the problems involved in making DOS a networking product. [But] as time progressed, we realized that we didn't fully understand it, either from a compatibility standpoint or from an operating-system standpoint. We knew very well how it [DOS] ran in a single-tasking environment, but we started going to this new environment and found places where it came up short."

In fact, the great variability in programs and programming approaches that MS-DOS supported eventually proved to be one of the biggest obstacles to the development of a sophisticated networking system and, in the longer term, to the addition of true multitasking.

Further, by the time Microsoft began work on version 3.0, the programming style of the MS-DOS team had changed considerably. The team was still small, with a core group of just five people: Zbikowski, Reynolds, Peters, Evans, and Mark Bebic. But the concerns for maintainability that had dominated programming in larger systems had percolated down to the MS-DOS environment. Now, the desire to use tricks to optimize for speed had to be tempered by the need for clarity and maintainability, and the small package of tightly written code that was the early MS-DOS had to be sacrificed for the same reasons.

Version 3.0

All told, the work on version 3.0 of MS-DOS proved to be long and difficult. For a year and a half, Microsoft grappled with problems of software incompatibility, remote file management, and logical device independence at the network level. Even so, when IBM was ready to announce its new Personal Computer AT, the network software for MS-DOS was not quite ready, so in August 1984, Microsoft released version 3.0 to IBM without network software.

Version 3.0 supported the AT's larger fixed disk, its new CMOS clock, and its high-capacity 1.2-megabyte floppy disks. It also provided the same international support included earlier in versions 2.01 and 2.11. These features were made available to Microsoft's other OEM customers as version 3.05.

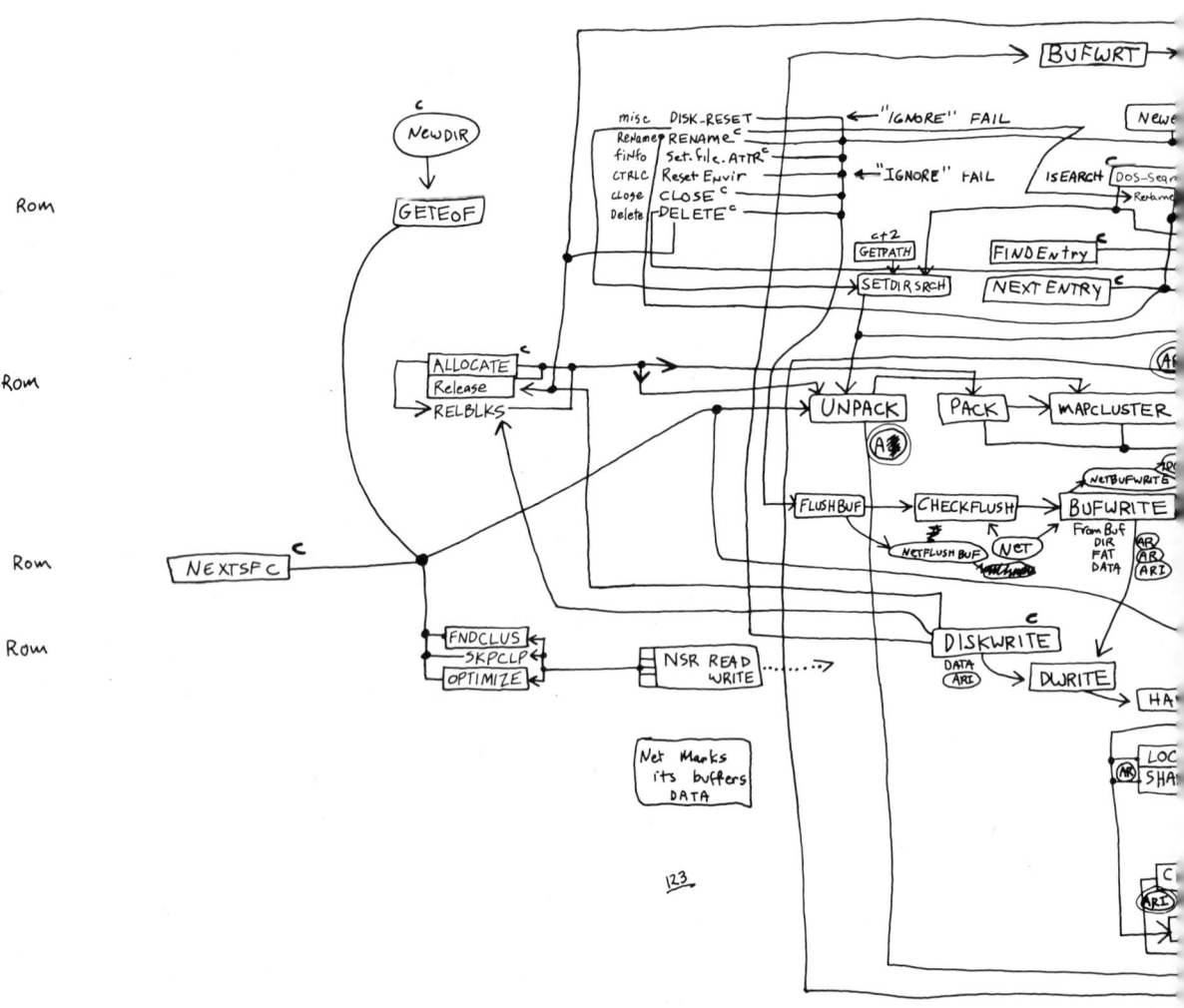

Aaron Reynolds's diagram of version 3.0's network support, sketched out to enable him to add the fail option to Interrupt 24 and find all places where existing parts of MS-DOS were affected. Even after networking had become a reality, Reynolds kept this diagram pinned to his office wall simply because "it was so much work to put together."

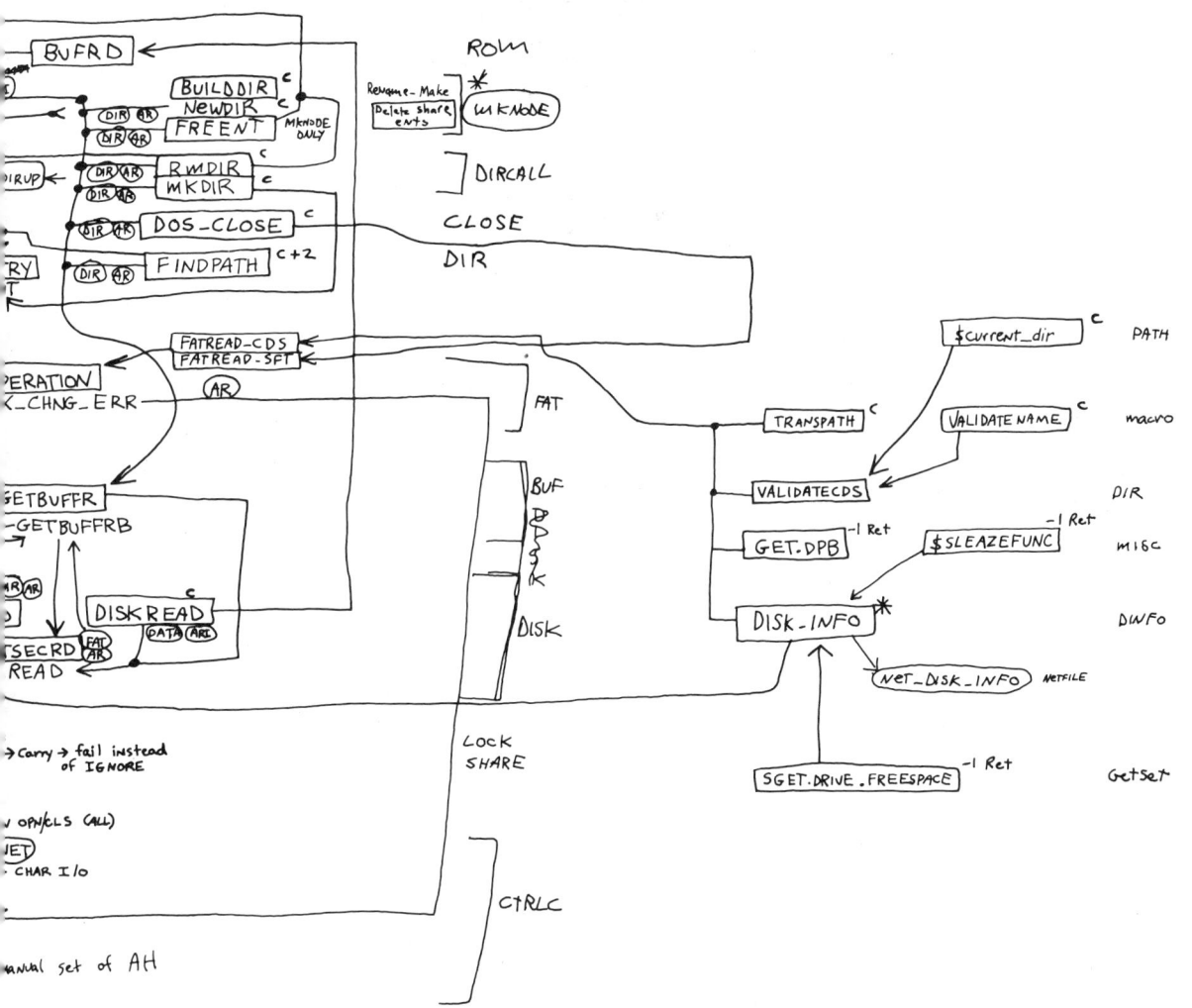

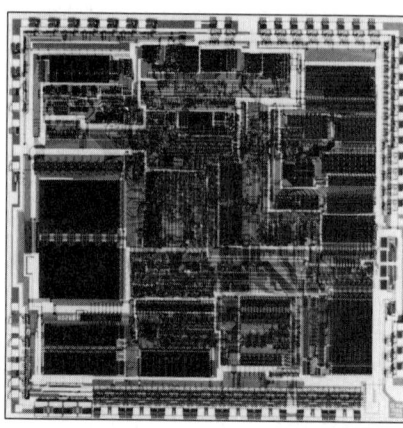

*The Intel 80286 micro-
processor, the chip at
the heart of the IBM
PC/AT, which is shown
beside it. Version 3.0 of
MS-DOS, developed for
this machine, offered
support for networks
and the PC/AT's 1.2-
megabyte floppy disk
drive and built-in
CMOS clock.*

But version 3.0 was not a simple extension of version 2.0. In laying the foundation for networking, the MS-DOS team had completely redesigned and rewritten the DOS kernel.

Different as it was from version 1.0, version 2.0 had been built on top of the same structure.
For example, whereas file requests in MS-DOS 1.0 used FCBs, requests in version 2.0 used
file handles. However, the version 2.0 handle calls would simply parse the pathname and
then use the underlying FCB calls in the same way as version 1.0. The redirected input and
output in version 2.0 further complicated the file-system requests. When a program used
one of the CP/M-compatible calls for character input or output, MS-DOS 2.0 first opened a
handle and then turned it back into an FCB call at a lower level. Version 3.0 eliminated this
redundancy by eliminating the old FCB input/output code of versions 1 and 2, replacing it
with a standard set of I/O calls that could be called directly by both FCB calls and handle
calls. The look-alike calls for CP/M-compatible character I/O were included as part of the
set of handle calls. As a result of this restructuring, these calls were distinctly faster in
version 3.0 than in version 2.0.

More important than the elimination of inefficiencies, however, was the fact that this new
structure made it easier to handle network requests under the ISO Open System Intercon-
nect model Microsoft was using for networking. The ISO model describes a number of
protocol layers, ranging from the application-to-application interface at the top level down
to the physical link — plugging into the network — at the lowest level. In the middle is the
transport layer, which manages the actual transfer of data. The layers above the transport
layer belong to the realm of the operating system; the layers below the transport layer are
traditionally the domain of the network software or hardware.

On the IBM PC network, the transport layer and the server functions were handled by
IBM's Network Adapter card and the task of MS-DOS was to support this hardware. For its
other OEM customers, however, Microsoft needed to supply both the transport and the
server functions as software. Although version 3.0 did not provide this general-purpose
networking software, it did provide the basic support for IBM's networking hardware.

The support for IBM consisted of redirector and sharer software. MS-DOS used an approach to networking in which remote requests were routed by a redirector that was able

to interact with the transport layer of the network. The transport layer was composed of the device drivers that could reliably transfer data from one part of the network to another. Just before a call was sent to the newly designed low-level file I/O code, the operating system determined whether the call was local or remote. A local call would be allowed to fall through to the local file I/O code; a remote call would be passed to the redirector which, working with the operating system, would make the resources on a remote machine appear as if they were local.

Version 3.1

Both the redirector and the sharer interfaces for IBM's Network Adapter card were in place in version 3.0 when it was delivered to IBM, but the redirector itself wasn't ready. Version 3.1, completed by Zbikowski and Reynolds and released three months later, completed this network support and made it available in the form of Microsoft Networks for use on non-IBM network cards.

Microsoft Networks was built on the concept of "services" and "consumers." Services were provided by a file server, which was part of the Networks application and ran on a computer dedicated to the task. Consumers were programs on various network machines. Requests for information were passed at a high level to the file server; it was then the responsibility of the file server to determine where to find the information on the disk. The requesting programs — the consumers — did not need any knowledge of the remote machine, not even what type of file system it had.

This ability to pass a high-level request to a remote server without having to know the details of the server's file structure allowed another level of generalization of the system. In MS-DOS 3.1, different types of file systems could be accessed on the same network. It was possible, for example, to access a XENIX machine across the network from an MS-DOS machine and to read data from XENIX files.

Microsoft Networks was designed to be hardware independent. Yet the variability of the classes of programs that would be using its structures was a major problem in developing a networking system that would be transparent to the user. In evaluating this variability, Microsoft identified three types of programs:

- First were the MS-DOS-compatible programs. These used only the documented software-interrupt method of requesting services from the operating system and would run on any MS-DOS machine without problems.
- Second were the MS-DOS-based programs. These would run on IBM-compatible computers but not necessarily on all MS-DOS machines.
- Third were the programs that used undocumented features of MS-DOS or that addressed the hardware directly. These programs tended to have the best performance but were also the most difficult to support.

Of these, Microsoft officially encouraged the writing of MS-DOS-compatible programs for use on the network.

Network concerns

The file-access module was changed in version 3.0 to simplify file management on the network, but this did not solve all the problems. For instance, MS-DOS still needed to handle FCB requests from programs that used them, but many programs would open an FCB and never close it. One of the functions of the server was to keep track of all open files on the network, and it ran into difficulties when an FCB was opened 50 or 100 times and never closed. To solve this problem, Microsoft introduced an FCB cache in version 3.1 that allowed only four FCBs to be open at any one time. If a fifth FCB was opened, the least recently used one was closed automatically and released. In addition, an FCBS command was added in the CONFIG.SYS file to allow the user or network manager to change the maximum number of FCBs that could be open at any one time and to protect some of the FCBs from automatic closure.

In general, the logical device independence that had been a goal of MS-DOS acquired new meaning — and generated new problems — with networking. One problem concerned printers on the network. Commonly, networks are used to allow several people to share a printer. The network could easily accommodate a program that would open the printer, write to it, and close it again. Some programs, however, would try to use the direct IBM BIOS interface to access the printer. To handle this situation, Microsoft's designers had to develop a way for MS-DOS to intercept these BIOS requests and filter out the ones the server could not handle. Once this was accomplished, version 3.1 was able to handle most types of printer output on the network in a transparent manner.

Version 3.2

In January 1986, Microsoft released another revision of MS-DOS, version 3.2, which supported 3½-inch floppy disks. Version 3.2 also moved the formatting function for a device out of the FORMAT utility routine and into the device driver, eliminating the need for a special hardware-dependent program in addition to the device driver. It included a sample installable-block-device driver and, finally, benefited the users and manufacturers of IBM-compatible computers by including major rewrites of the MS-DOS utilities to increase compatibility with those of IBM.

The Future

Since its appearance in 1981, MS-DOS has taken and held an enviable position in the microcomputer environment. Not only has it "taught" millions of personal computers "how to think," it has taught equal millions of people how to use computers. Many highly sophisticated computer users can trace their first encounter with these machines to the original IBM PC and version 1.0 of MS-DOS. The MS-DOS command interface is the one with which they are comfortable and it is the MS-DOS file structure that, in one way or another, they wander through with familiarity.

Microsoft has stated its commitment to ensuring that, for the foreseeable future, MS-DOS will continue to evolve and grow, changing as it has done in the past to satisfy the needs of its millions of users. In the long term, MS-DOS, the product of a surprisingly small group of gifted people, will undoubtedly remain the industry standard for as long as 8086-based (and to some extent, 80286-based) microcomputers exist in the business world. The story of MS-DOS will, of course, remain even longer. For this operating system has earned its place in microcomputing history.

JoAnne Woodcock

Section II
Programming in the MS-DOS Environment

Part A
Structure of MS-DOS

Article 1
An Introduction to MS-DOS

An operating system is a set of interrelated supervisory programs that manage and control computer processing. In general, an operating system provides

- Storage management
- Processing management
- Security
- Human interface

Existing operating systems for microcomputers fall into three major categories: ROM monitors, traditional operating systems, and operating environments. The general characteristics of the three categories are listed in Table 1-1.

Table 1-1. Characteristics of the Three Major Types of Operating Systems.

	ROM Monitor	Traditional Operating System	Operating Environment
Complexity	Low	Medium	High
Built on	Hardware	BIOS	Operating system
Delivered on	ROM	Disk	Disk
Programs on	ROM	Disk	Disk
Peripheral support	Physical	Logical	Logical
Disk access	Sector	File system	File system
Example	PC ROM BIOS	MS-DOS	Microsoft Windows

A ROM monitor is the simplest type of operating system. It is designed for a particular hardware configuration and provides a program with basic — and often direct — access to peripherals attached to the computer. Programs coupled with a ROM monitor are often used for dedicated applications such as controlling a microwave oven or controlling the engine of a car.

A traditional microcomputer operating system is built on top of a ROM monitor, or BIOS (basic input/output system), and provides additional features such as a file system and logical access to peripherals. (Logical access to peripherals allows applications to run in a hardware-independent manner.) A traditional operating system also stores programs in files on peripheral storage devices and, on request, loads them into memory for execution. MS-DOS is a traditional operating system.

An operating environment is built on top of a traditional operating system. The operating environment provides additional services, such as common menu and forms support, that simplify program operation and make the user interface more consistent. Microsoft Windows is an operating environment.

MS-DOS System Components

The Microsoft Disk Operating System, MS-DOS, is a traditional microcomputer operating system that consists of five major components:

- The operating-system loader
- The MS-DOS BIOS
- The MS-DOS kernel
- The user interface (shell)
- Support programs

Each of these is introduced briefly in the following pages. *See* PROGRAMMING IN THE MS-DOS ENVIRONMENT: STRUCTURE OF MS-DOS: The Components of MS-DOS.

The operating-system loader

The operating-system loader brings the operating system from the startup disk into RAM.

The complete loading process, called bootstrapping, is often complex, and multiple loaders may be involved. (The term *bootstrapping* came about because each level pulls up the next part of the system, like pulling up on a pair of bootstraps.) For example, in most standard MS-DOS-based microcomputer implementations, the ROM loader, which is the first program the microcomputer executes when it is turned on or restarted, reads the disk bootstrap loader from the first (boot) sector of the startup disk and executes it. The disk bootstrap loader, in turn, reads the main portions of MS-DOS — MSDOS.SYS and IO.SYS (IBMDOS.COM and IBMBIO.COM with PC-DOS) — from conventional disk files into memory. The special module SYSINIT within MSDOS.SYS then initializes MS-DOS's tables and buffers and discards itself. *See* PROGRAMMING IN THE MS-DOS ENVIRONMENT: STRUCTURE OF MS-DOS: MS-DOS Storage Devices.

(The term loader is also used to refer to the portion of the operating system that brings application programs into memory for execution. This loader is different from the ROM loader and the operating-system loader.)

The MS-DOS BIOS

The MS-DOS BIOS, loaded from the file IO.SYS during system initialization, is the layer of the operating system that sits between the operating-system kernel and the hardware. An application performs input and output by making requests to the operating-system kernel, which, in turn, calls the MS-DOS BIOS routines that access the hardware directly. *See* SYSTEM CALLS. This division of function allows application programs to be written in a hardware-independent manner.

The MS-DOS BIOS consists of some initialization code and a collection of device drivers. (A device driver is a specialized program that provides support for a specific device such as a display or serial port.) The device drivers are responsible for hardware access and for the interrupt support that allows the associated devices to signal the microprocessor that they need service.

The device drivers contained in the file IO.SYS, which are always loaded during system initialization, are sometimes referred to as the resident drivers. With MS-DOS versions 2.0 and later, additional device drivers, called installable drivers, can optionally be loaded during system initialization as a result of DEVICE directives in the system's configuration file. *See* PROGRAMMING IN THE MS-DOS ENVIRONMENT: CUSTOMIZING MS-DOS: Installable Device Drivers; USER COMMANDS: CONFIG.SYS:DEVICE.

The MS-DOS kernel

The services provided to application programs by the MS-DOS kernel include

- Process control
- Memory management
- Peripheral support
- A file system

The MS-DOS kernel is loaded from the file MSDOS.SYS during system initialization.

Process control

Process, or task, control includes program loading, task execution, task termination, task scheduling, and intertask communication.

Although MS-DOS is not a multitasking operating system, it can have multiple programs residing in memory at the same time. One program can invoke another, which then becomes the active (foreground) task. When the invoked task terminates, the invoking program again becomes the foreground task. Because these tasks never execute simultaneously, this stack-like operation is still considered to be a single-tasking operating system.

MS-DOS does have a few "hooks" that allow certain programs to do some multitasking on their own. For example, terminate-and-stay-resident (TSR) programs such as PRINT use these hooks to perform limited concurrent processing by taking control of system resources while MS-DOS is "idle," and the Microsoft Windows operating environment adds support for nonpreemptive task switching.

The traditional intertask communication methods include semaphores, queues, shared memory, and pipes. Of these, MS-DOS formally supports only pipes. (A pipe is a logical, unidirectional, sequential stream of data that is written by one program and read by another.) The data in a pipe resides in memory or in a disk file, depending on the implementation; MS-DOS uses disk files for intermediate storage of data in pipes because it is a single-tasking operating system.

Memory management

Because the amount of memory a program needs varies from program to program, the traditional operating system ordinarily provides memory-management functions. Memory requirements can also vary during program execution, and memory management is especially necessary when two or more programs are present in memory at the same time.

MS-DOS memory management is based on a pool of variable-size memory blocks. The two basic memory-management actions are to allocate a block from the pool and to return an allocated block to the pool. MS-DOS allocates program space from the pool when the program is loaded; programs themselves can allocate additional memory from the pool. Many programs perform their own memory management by using a local memory pool, or heap — an additional memory block allocated from the operating system that the application program itself divides into blocks for use by its various routines. *See* PROGRAMMING IN THE MS-DOS ENVIRONMENT: Programming for ms-dos: Memory Management.

Peripheral support

The operating system provides peripheral support to programs through a set of operating-system calls that are translated by the operating system into calls to the appropriate device driver.

Peripheral support can be a direct logical-to-physical-device translation or the operating system can interject additional features or translations. Keyboards, displays, and printers usually require only logical-to-physical-device translations; that is, the data is transferred between the application program and the physical device with minimal alterations, if any, by the operating system. The data provided by clock devices, on the other hand, must be transformed to operating-system-dependent time and date formats. Disk devices — and block devices in general — have the greatest number of features added by the operating system. *See* The File System below.

As stated earlier, an application need not be concerned with the details of peripheral devices or with any special features the devices might have. Because the operating system takes care of all the logical-to-physical-device translations, the application program need only make requests of the operating system.

The file system

The file system is one of the largest portions of an operating system. A file system is built on the storage medium of a block device (usually a floppy disk or a fixed disk) by mapping a directory structure and files onto the physical unit of storage. A file system on a disk contains, at a minimum, allocation information, a directory, and space for files. *See* PROGRAMMING IN THE MS-DOS ENVIRONMENT: Structure of ms-dos: MS-DOS Storage Devices.

The file allocation information can take various forms, depending on the operating system, but all forms basically track the space used by files and the space available for new data. The directory contains a list of the files stored on the device, their sizes, and information about where the data for each file is located.

Several different approaches to file allocation and directory entries exist. MS-DOS uses a particular allocation method called a file allocation table (FAT) and a hierarchical directory structure. *See* PROGRAMMING IN THE MS-DOS ENVIRONMENT: Structure of ms-dos: MS-DOS Storage Devices; Programming for ms-dos: Disk Directories and Volume Labels.

The file granularity available through the operating system also varies depending on the implementation. Some systems, such as MS-DOS, have files that are accessible to the byte level; others are restricted to a fixed record size.

File systems are sometimes extended to map character devices as if they were files. These device "files" can be opened, closed, read from, and written to like normal disk files, but all transactions occur directly with the specified character device. Device files provide a useful consistency to the environment for application programs; MS-DOS supports such files by assigning a reserved logical name (such as CON or PRN) to each character device.

The user interface

The user interface for an operating system, also called a shell or command processor, is generally a conventional program that allows the user to interact with the operating system itself. The default MS-DOS user interface is a replaceable shell program called COMMAND.COM.

One of the fundamental tasks of a shell is to load a program into memory on request and pass control of the system to the program so that the program can execute. When the program terminates, control returns to the shell, which prompts the user for another command. In addition, the shell usually includes functions for file and directory maintenance and display. In theory, most of these functions could be provided as programs, but making them resident in the shell allows them to be accessed more quickly. The tradeoff is memory space versus speed and flexibility. Early microcomputer-based operating systems provided a minimal number of resident shell commands because of limited memory space; modern operating systems such as MS-DOS include a wide variety of these functions as internal commands.

Support programs

The MS-DOS software includes support programs that provide access to operating-system facilities not supplied as resident shell commands built into COMMAND.COM. Because these programs are stored as executable files on disk, they are essentially the same as application programs and MS-DOS loads and executes them as it would any other program.

The support programs provided with MS-DOS, often referred to as external commands, include disk utilities such as FORMAT and CHKDSK and more general support programs such as EDLIN (a line-oriented text editor) and PRINT (a TSR utility that allows files to be printed while another program is running). *See* USER COMMANDS.

MS-DOS releases

MS-DOS and PC-DOS have been released in a number of forms, starting in 1981. *See* THE DEVELOPMENT OF MS-DOS. The major MS-DOS and PC-DOS implementations are summarized in the following table.

Version	Date	Special Characteristics
PC-DOS 1.0	1981	First operating system for the IBM PC Record-oriented files
PC-DOS 1.1	1982	Double-sided-disk support
MS-DOS 1.25	1982	First OEM release of MS-DOS
MS-DOS/PC-DOS 2.0	1983	Operating system for the IBM PC/XT UNIX/XENIX-like file system Installable device drivers Byte-oriented files Support for fixed disks
PC-DOS 2.1		Operating system for the IBM PCjr
MS-DOS 2.11		Internationalization support 2.0x bug fixes
MS-DOS/PC-DOS 3.0	1984	Operating system for the IBM PC/AT Support for 1.2 MB floppy disks Support for large fixed disks Support for file and record locking Application control of print spooler
MS-DOS/PC-DOS 3.1	1984	Support for MS Networks
MS-DOS/PC-DOS 3.2	1986	3.5-inch floppy-disk support Disk track formatting support added to device drivers
MS-DOS/PC-DOS 3.3	1987	Support for the IBM PS/2 Enhanced internationalization support Improved file-system performance Partitioning support for disks with capacity above 32 MB

PC-DOS version 1.0 was the first commercial version of MS-DOS. It was developed for the original IBM PC, which was typically shipped with 64 KB of memory or less. MS-DOS and PC-DOS versions 1.x were similar in many ways to CP/M, the popular operating system for 8-bit microcomputers based on the Intel 8080 (the predecessor of the 8086). These versions of MS-DOS used a single-level file system with no subdirectory support and did not support installable device drivers or networks. Programs accessed files using file control blocks (FCBs) similar to those found in CP/M programs. File operations were record oriented, again like CP/M, although record sizes could be varied in MS-DOS.

Although they retained compatibility with versions 1.x, MS-DOS and PC-DOS versions 2.x represented a major change. In addition to providing support for fixed disks, the new versions switched to a hierarchical file system like that found in UNIX/XENIX and to file-handle access instead of FCBs. (A file handle is a 16-bit number used to reference an internal table that MS-DOS uses to keep track of currently open files; an application program has no access to this internal table.) The UNIX/XENIX-style file functions allow files to be treated as a byte stream instead of as a collection of records. Applications can read or write 1 to 65535 bytes in a single operation, starting at any byte offset within the file. Filenames used for opening a file are passed as text strings instead of being parsed into an FCB. Installable device drivers were another major enhancement.

MS-DOS and PC-DOS versions 3.x added a number of valuable features, including support for the added capabilities of the IBM PC/AT, for larger-capacity disks, and for file-locking and record-locking functions. Network support was added by providing hooks for a redirector (an additional operating-system module that has the ability to redirect local system service requests to a remote system by means of a local area network).

With all these changes, MS-DOS remains a traditional single-tasking operating system. It provides a large number of system services in a transparent fashion so that, as long as they use only the MS-DOS-supplied services and refrain from using hardware-specific operations, applications developed for one MS-DOS machine can usually run on another.

Basic MS-DOS Requirements

Foremost among the requirements for MS-DOS is an Intel 8086-compatible microprocessor. *See* Specific Hardware Requirements below.

The next requirement is the ROM bootstrap loader and enough RAM to contain the MS-DOS BIOS, kernel, and shell and an application program. The RAM must start at address 0000:0000H and, to be managed by MS-DOS, must be contiguous. The upper limit for RAM is the limit placed upon the system by the 8086 family—1 MB.

The final requirement for MS-DOS is a set of devices supported by device drivers, including at least one block device, one character device, and a clock device. The block device is usually the boot disk device (the disk device from which MS-DOS is loaded); the character device is usually a keyboard/display combination for interaction with the user; the clock device, required for time-of-day and date support, is a hardware counter driven in a submultiple of one second.

Specific hardware requirements

MS-DOS uses several hardware components and has specific requirements for each. These components include

- An 8086-family microprocessor
- Memory
- Peripheral devices
- A ROM BIOS (PC-DOS only)

The microprocessor

MS-DOS runs on any machine that uses a microprocessor that executes the 8086/8088 instruction set, including the Intel 8086, 80C86, 8088, 80186, 80188, 80286, and 80386 and the NEC V20, V30, and V40.

The 80186 and 80188 are versions of the 8086 and 8088, integrated in a single chip with direct memory access, timer, and interrupt support functions. PC-DOS cannot usually run on the 80186 or 80188 because these chips have internal interrupt and interface register addresses that conflict with addresses used by the PC ROM BIOS. *See* PROGRAMMING IN THE MS-DOS ENVIRONMENT: CUSTOMIZING MS-DOS: Hardware Interrupt Handlers. MS-DOS, however, does not have address requirements that conflict with those interrupt and interface areas.

The 80286 has an extended instruction set and two operating modes: real and protected. Real mode is compatible with the 8086/8088 and runs MS-DOS. Protected mode, used by operating systems like UNIX/XENIX and MS OS/2, is partially compatible with real mode in terms of instructions but provides access to 16 MB of memory versus only 1 MB in real mode (the limit of the 8086/8088).

The 80386 adds further instructions and a third mode called virtual 86 mode. The 80386 instructions operate in either a 16-bit or a 32-bit environment. MS-DOS can run on the 80386 in real or virtual 86 mode, although the latter requires additional support in the form of a virtual machine monitor such as Windows /386.

Memory requirements

At a minimum, MS-DOS versions 1.x require 64 KB of contiguous RAM from the base of memory to do useful work; versions 2.x and 3.x need at least 128 KB. The maximum is 1 MB, although most MS-DOS machines have a 640 KB limit for IBM PC compatibility. MS-DOS can use additional noncontiguous RAM for a RAMdisk if the proper device driver is included. (Other uses for noncontiguous RAM include buffers for video displays, fixed disks, and network adapters.)

PC-DOS has the same minimum memory requirements but has an upper limit of 640 KB on the initial contiguous RAM, which is generally referred to as conventional memory. This limit was imposed by the architecture of the original IBM PC, with the remaining area above 640 KB reserved for video display buffers, fixed disk adapters, and the ROM BIOS. Some of the reserved areas include

Base Address	Size (bytes)	Description
A000:0000H	10000H (64 KB)	EGA video buffer
B000:0000H	1000H (4 KB)	Monochrome video buffer
B800:0000H	4000H (16 KB)	Color/graphics video buffer
C800:0000H	4000H (16 KB)	Fixed-disk ROM
F000:0000H	10000H (64 KB)	PC ROM BIOS and ROM BASIC

The bottom 1024 bytes of system RAM (locations 00000-003FFH) are used by the microprocessor for an interrupt vector table — that is, a list of addresses for interrupt handler routines. MS-DOS uses some of the entries in this table, such as the vectors for interrupts 20H through 2FH, to store addresses of its own tables and routines and to provide linkage to its services for application programs. The IBM PC ROM BIOS and IBM PC BASIC use many additional vectors for the same purposes.

Peripheral devices

MS-DOS can support a wide variety of devices, including floppy disks, fixed disks, CD ROMs, RAMdisks, and digital tape drives. The required peripheral support for MS-DOS is provided by the MS-DOS BIOS or by installable device drivers.

Five logical devices are provided in a basic MS-DOS system:

Device Name	Description
CON	Console input and output
PRN	Printer output
AUX	Auxiliary input and output
CLOCK$	Date and time support
Varies (A–E)	One block device

These five logical devices can be implemented with a BIOS supporting a minimum of three physical devices: a keyboard and display, a timer or clock/calendar chip that can provide a hardware interrupt at regular intervals, and a block storage device. In such a minimum case, the printer and auxiliary device are simply aliases for the console device. However, most MS-DOS systems support several additional logical and physical devices. *See* PROGRAMMING IN THE MS-DOS ENVIRONMENT: PROGRAMMING FOR MS-DOS: Character Device Input and Output.

The MS-DOS kernel provides one additional device: the NUL device. NUL is a "bit bucket"—that is, anything written to NUL is simply discarded. Reading from NUL always returns an end-of-file marker. One common use for the NUL device is as the redirected output device of a command or application that is being run in a batch file; this redirection prevents screen clutter and disruption of the batch file's menus and displays.

The ROM BIOS

MS-DOS requires no ROM support (except that most bootstrap loaders reside in ROM) and does not care whether device-driver support resides in ROM or is part of the MS-DOS IO.SYS file loaded at initialization. PC-DOS, on the other hand, uses a very specific ROM BIOS. The PC ROM BIOS does not provide device drivers; rather, it provides support routines used by the device drivers found in IBMBIO.COM (the PC-DOS version of IO.SYS). The support provided by a PC ROM BIOS includes

- Power-on self test (POST)
- Bootstrap loader
- Keyboard
- Displays (monochrome and color/graphics adapters)
- Serial ports 1 and 2
- Parallel printer ports 1, 2, and 3
- Clock
- Print screen

The PC ROM BIOS loader routine searches the ROM space above the PC-DOS 640 KB limit for additional ROMs. The IBM fixed-disk adapter and enhanced graphics adapter (EGA) contain such ROMs. (The fixed-disk ROM also includes an additional loader routine that allows the system to start from the fixed disk.)

Summary

MS-DOS is a widely accepted traditional operating system. Its consistent and well-defined interface makes it one of the easier operating systems to adapt and program.

MS-DOS is also a growing operating system — each version has added more features yet made the system easier to use for both end-users and programmers. In addition, each version has included more support for different devices, from 5.25-inch floppy disks to high-density 3.5-inch floppy disks. As the hardware continues to evolve and user needs become more sophisticated, MS-DOS too will continue to evolve.

William Wong

Article 2
The Components of MS-DOS

MS-DOS is a modular operating system consisting of multiple components with specialized functions. When MS-DOS is copied into memory during the loading process, many of
its components are moved, adjusted, or discarded. However, when it is running, MS-DOS
is a relatively static entity and its components are predictable and easy to study. Therefore,
this article deals first with MS-DOS in its running state and later with its loading behavior.

The Major Elements

MS-DOS consists of three major modules:

Module	MS-DOS Filename	PC-DOS Filename
MS-DOS BIOS	IO.SYS	IBMBIO.COM
MS-DOS kernel	MSDOS.SYS	IBMDOS.COM
MS-DOS shell	COMMAND.COM	COMMAND.COM

During system initialization, these modules are loaded into memory, in the order given,
just above the interrupt vector table located at the beginning of memory. All three modules
remain in memory until the computer is reset or turned off. (The loader and system initialization modules are omitted from this list because they are discarded as soon as MS-DOS
is running. *See* Loading MS-DOS below.)

The MS-DOS BIOS is supplied by the original equipment manufacturer (OEM) that
distributes MS-DOS, usually for a particular computer. *See* PROGRAMMING IN THE
MS-DOS ENVIRONMENT: Structure of ms-dos: An Introduction to MS-DOS. The kernel
is supplied by Microsoft and is the same across all OEMs for a particular version of
MS-DOS—that is, no modifications are made by the OEM. The shell is a replaceable
module that can be supplied by the OEM or replaced by the user; the default shell,
COMMAND.COM, is supplied by Microsoft.

The MS-DOS BIOS

The file IO.SYS contains the MS-DOS BIOS and the MS-DOS initialization module,
SYSINIT. The MS-DOS BIOS is customized for a particular machine by an OEM. SYSINIT
is supplied by Microsoft and is put into IO.SYS by the OEM when the file is created. *See*
Loading MS-DOS below.

The MS-DOS BIOS consists of a list of resident device drivers and an additional initialization module created by the OEM. The device drivers appear first in IO.SYS because they remain resident after IO.SYS is initialized; the MS-DOS BIOS initialization routine and SYSINIT are usually discarded after initialization.

The minimum set of resident device drivers is CON, PRN, AUX, CLOCK$, and the driver for one block device. The resident character-device drivers appear in the driver list before the resident block-device drivers; installable character-device drivers are placed ahead of the resident device drivers in the list; installable block-device drivers are placed after the resident device drivers in the list. This sequence allows installable character-device drivers to supersede resident drivers. The NUL device driver, which must be the first driver in the chain, is contained in the MS-DOS kernel.

Device driver code can be split between IO.SYS and ROM. For example, most MS-DOS systems and all PC-DOS-compatible systems have a ROM BIOS that contains primitive device support routines. These routines are generally used by resident and installable device drivers to augment routines contained in RAM. (Placing the entire driver in RAM makes the driver dependent on a particular hardware configuration; placing part of the driver in ROM allows the MS-DOS BIOS to be paired with a particular ROM interface that remains constant for many different hardware configurations.)

The IO.SYS file is an absolute program image and does not contain relocation information. The routines in IO.SYS assume that the CS register contains the segment at which the file is loaded. Thus, IO.SYS has the same 64 KB restriction as a .COM file. *See* PROGRAMMING IN THE MS-DOS ENVIRONMENT: PROGRAMMING FOR MS-DOS: Structure of an Application Program. Larger IO.SYS files are possible, but all device driver headers must lie in the first 64 KB and the code must rely on its own segment arithmetic to access routines outside the first 64 KB.

The MS-DOS kernel

The MS-DOS kernel is the heart of MS-DOS and provides the functions found in a traditional operating system. It is contained in a single proprietary file, MSDOS.SYS, supplied by Microsoft Corporation. The kernel provides its support functions (referred to as system functions) to application programs in a hardware-independent manner and, in turn, is isolated from hardware characteristics by relying on the driver routines in the MS-DOS BIOS to perform physical input and output operations.

The MS-DOS kernel provides the following services through the use of device drivers:

- File and directory management
- Character device input and output
- Time and date support

It also provides the following non-device-related functions:

- Memory management
- Task and environment management
- Country-specific configuration

Programs access system functions using software interrupt (INT) instructions. MS-DOS reserves Interrupts 20H through 3FH for this purpose. The MS-DOS interrupts are

Interrupt	Name
20H	Terminate Program
21H	MS-DOS Function Calls
22H	Terminate Routine Address
23H	Control-C Handler Address
24H	Critical Error Handler Address
25H	Absolute Disk Read
26H	Absolute Disk Write
27H	Terminate and Stay Resident
28H–2EH	Reserved
2FH	Multiplex
30H–3FH	Reserved

Interrupt 21H is the main source of MS-DOS services. The Interrupt 21H functions are implemented by placing a function number in the AH register, placing any necessary parameters in other registers, and issuing an INT 21H instruction. (MS-DOS also supports a call instruction interface for CP/M compatibility. The function and parameter registers differ from the interrupt interface. The CP/M interface was provided in MS-DOS version 1.0 solely to assist in movement of CP/M-based applications to MS-DOS. New applications should use Interrupt 21H functions exclusively.)

MS-DOS version 2.0 introduced a mechanism to modify the operation of the MS-DOS BIOS and kernel: the CONFIG.SYS file. CONFIG.SYS is a text file containing command options that modify the size or configuration of internal MS-DOS tables and cause additional device drivers to be loaded. The file is read when MS-DOS is first loaded into memory. *See* USER COMMANDS: CONFIG.SYS.

The MS-DOS shell

The shell, or command interpreter, is the first program started by MS-DOS after the MS-DOS BIOS and kernel have been loaded and initialized. It provides the interface between the kernel and the user. The default MS-DOS shell, COMMAND.COM, is a command-oriented interface; other shells may be menu-driven or screen-oriented.

COMMAND.COM is a replaceable shell. A number of commercial products can be used as COMMAND.COM replacements, or a programmer can develop a customized shell. The new shell program is installed by renaming the program to COMMAND.COM or by using the SHELL command in CONFIG.SYS. The latter method is preferred because it allows initialization parameters to be passed to the shell program.

COMMAND.COM can execute a set of internal (built-in) commands, load and execute programs, or interpret batch files. Most of the internal commands support file and directory operations and manipulate the program environment segment maintained by COMMAND.COM. The programs executed by COMMAND.COM are .COM or .EXE files loaded from a block device. The batch (.BAT) files supported by COMMAND.COM provide a limited programming language and are therefore useful for performing small, frequently used series of MS-DOS commands. In particular, when it is first loaded by MS-DOS, COMMAND.COM searches for the batch file AUTOEXEC.BAT and interprets it, if found, before taking any other action. COMMAND.COM also provides default terminate, Control-C and critical error handlers whose addresses are stored in the vectors for Interrupts 22H, 23H, and 24H. *See* PROGRAMMING IN THE MS-DOS ENVIRONMENT: CUSTOMIZING MS-DOS: Exception Handlers.

COMMAND.COM's split personality

COMMAND.COM is a conventional .COM application with a slight twist. Ordinarily, a .COM program is loaded into a single memory segment. COMMAND.COM starts this way but then copies the nonresident portion of itself into high memory and keeps the resident portion in low memory. The memory above the resident portion is released to MS-DOS.

The effect of this split is not apparent until after an executed program has terminated and the resident portion of COMMAND.COM regains control of the system. The resident portion then computes a checksum on the area in high memory where the nonresident portion should be, to determine whether it has been overwritten. If the checksum matches a stored value, the nonresident portion is assumed to be intact; otherwise, a copy of the nonresident portion is reloaded from disk and COMMAND.COM continues its normal operation.

This "split personality" exists because MS-DOS was originally designed for systems with a limited amount of RAM. The nonresident portion of COMMAND.COM, which contains the built-in commands and batch-file-processing routines that are not essential to regaining control and reloading itself, is much larger than the resident portion, which is responsible for these tasks. Thus, permitting the nonresident portion to be overwritten frees additional RAM and allows larger application programs to be run.

Command execution

COMMAND.COM interprets commands by first checking to see if the specified command matches the name of an internal command. If so, it executes the command; otherwise, it searches for a .COM, .EXE, or .BAT file (in that order) with the specified name. If a .COM or .EXE program is found, COMMAND.COM uses the MS-DOS EXEC function (Interrupt 21H Function 4BH) to load and execute it; COMMAND.COM itself interprets .BAT files. If no file is found, the message *Bad command or file name* is displayed.

Although a command is usually simply a filename without the extension, MS-DOS versions 3.0 and later allow a command name to be preceded by a full pathname. If a path is not explicitly specified, the COMMAND.COM search mechanism uses the contents of the

PATH environment variable, which can contain a list of paths to be searched for commands. The search starts with the current directory and proceeds through the directories specified by PATH until a file is found or the list is exhausted. For example, the PATH specification

```
PATH C:\BIN;D:\BIN;E:\
```

causes COMMAND.COM to search the current directory, then C:\BIN, then D:\BIN, and finally the root directory of drive E. COMMAND.COM searches each directory for a matching .COM, .EXE, or .BAT file, in that order, before moving to the next directory.

MS-DOS environments

Version 2.0 introduced the concept of environments to MS-DOS. An environment is a paragraph-aligned memory segment containing a concatenated set of zero-terminated (ASCIIZ) variable-length strings of the form

variable=value

that provide such information as the current search path used by COMMAND.COM to find executable files, the location of COMMAND.COM itself, and the format of the user prompt. The end of the set of strings is marked by a null string — that is, a single zero byte. A specific environment is associated with each program in memory through a pointer contained at offset 2CH in the 256-byte program segment prefix (PSP). The maximum size of an environment is 32 KB; the default size is 160 bytes.

If a program uses the EXEC function to load and execute another program, the contents of the new program's environment are provided to MS-DOS by the initiating program — one of the parameters passed to the MS-DOS EXEC function is a pointer to the new program's environment. The default environment provided to the new program is a copy of the initiating program's environment.

A program that uses the EXEC function to load and execute another program will not itself have access to the new program's environment, because MS-DOS provides a pointer to this environment only to the new program. Any changes made to the new program's environment during program execution are invisible to the initiating program because a child program's environment is always discarded when the child program terminates.

The system's master environment is normally associated with the shell COMMAND.COM. COMMAND.COM creates this set of environment strings within itself from the contents of the CONFIG.SYS and AUTOEXEC.BAT files, using the SET, PATH, and PROMPT commands. *See* USER COMMANDS: AUTOEXEC.BAT; CONFIG.SYS. In MS-DOS version 3.2, the initial size of COMMAND.COM's environment can be controlled by loading COMMAND.COM with the /E parameter, using the SHELL directive in CONFIG.SYS. For example, placing the line

```
SHELL=COMMAND.COM /E:2048 /P
```

in CONFIG.SYS sets the initial size of COMMAND.COM's environment to 2 KB. (The /P option prevents COMMAND.COM from terminating, thus causing it to remain in memory until the system is turned off or restarted.)

The SET command is used to display or change the COMMAND.COM environment contents. SET with no parameters displays the list of all the environment strings in the environment. A typical listing might show the following settings:

```
COMSPEC=A:\COMMAND.COM
PATH=C:\;A:\;B:\
PROMPT=$p  $d  $t$_$n$g
TMP=C:\TEMP
```

The following is a dump of the environment segment containing the previous environment example:

```
        0  1  2  3  4  5  6  7  8  9  A  B  C  D  E  F
0000   43 4F 4D 53 50 45 43 3D-41 3A 5C 43 4F 4D 4D 41    COMSPEC=A:\COMMA
0010   4E 44 2E 43 4F 4D 00 50-41 54 48 3D 43 3A 5C 3B    ND.COM.PATH=C:\;
0020   41 3A 5C 3B 42 3A 5C 00-50 52 4F 4D 50 54 3D 24    A:\;B:\.PROMPT=$
0030   70 20 20 24 64 20 20 24-74 24 5F 24 6E 24 67 00    p  $d  $t$_$n$g.
0040   54 4D 50 3D 43 3A 5C 54-45 4D 50 00 00 00 00 00    TMP=C:\TEMP.....
```

A SET command that specifies a variable but does not specify a value for it deletes the variable from the environment.

A program can ignore the contents of its environment; however, use of the environment can add a great deal to the flexibility and configurability of batch files and application programs.

Batch files

Batch files are text files with a .BAT extension that contain MS-DOS user and batch commands. Each line in the file is limited to 128 bytes. *See* USER COMMANDS: BATCH. Batch files can be created using most text editors, including EDLIN, and short batch files can even be created using the COPY command:

```
C>COPY CON SAMPLE.BAT  <Enter>
```

The CON device is the system console; text entered from the keyboard is echoed on the screen as it is typed. The copy operation is terminated by pressing Ctrl-Z (or the F6 key on IBM-compatible machines), followed by the Enter key.

Batch files are interpreted by COMMAND.COM one line at a time. In addition to the standard MS-DOS commands, COMMAND.COM's batch-file interpreter supports a number of special batch commands:

Command	Meaning
ECHO*	Display a message.
FOR*	Execute a command for a list of files.

(more)

Command	Meaning
GOTO*	Transfer control to another point.
IF*	Conditionally execute a command.
PAUSE	Wait for any key to be pressed.
REM	Insert comment line.
SHIFT*	Access more than 10 parameters.

* MS-DOS versions 2.0 and later

Execution of a batch file can be terminated before completion by pressing Ctrl-C or Ctrl-Break, causing COMMAND.COM to display the prompt

```
Terminate batch job? (Y/N)
```

I/O redirection

I/O redirection was introduced with MS-DOS version 2.0. The redirection facility is implemented within COMMAND.COM using the Interrupt 21H system functions Duplicate File Handle (45H) and Force Duplicate File Handle (46H). COMMAND.COM uses these functions to provide both redirection at the command level and a UNIX/XENIX-like pipe facility.

Redirection is transparent to application programs, but to take advantage of redirection, an application program must make use of the standard input and output file handles. The input and output of application programs that directly access the screen or keyboard or use ROM BIOS functions cannot be redirected.

Redirection is specified in the command line by prefixing file or device names with the special characters >, >>, and <. Standard output (default = CON) is redirected using > and >> followed by the name of a file or character device. The former character creates a new file (or overwrites an existing file with the same name); the latter appends text to an existing file (or creates the file if it does not exist). Standard input (default = CON) is redirected with the < character followed by the name of a file or character device. *See also* PRO-GRAMMING IN THE MS-DOS ENVIRONMENT: Customizing ms-dos: Writing MS-DOS Filters.

The redirection facility can also be used to pass information from one program to another through a "pipe." A pipe in MS-DOS is a special file created by COMMAND.COM. COMMAND.COM redirects the output of one program into this file and then redirects this file as the input to the next program. The pipe symbol, a vertical bar (¦), separates the program names. Multiple program names can be piped together in the same command line:

```
C>DIR *.* ¦ SORT ¦ MORE  <Enter>
```

This command is equivalent to

```
C>DIR *.* > PIPE0  <Enter>
C>SORT < PIPE0 > PIPE1  <Enter>
C>MORE < PIPE1  <Enter>
```

The concept of pipes came from UNIX/XENIX, but UNIX/XENIX is a multitasking operating system that actually runs the programs simultaneously. UNIX/XENIX uses memory buffers to connect the programs, whereas MS-DOS loads one program at a time and passes information through a disk file.

Loading MS-DOS

Getting MS-DOS up to the standard A> prompt is a complex process with a number of variations. This section discusses the complete process normally associated with MS-DOS versions 2.0 and later. (MS-DOS versions 1.x use the same general steps but lack support for various system tables and installable device drivers.)

MS-DOS is loaded as a result of either a "cold boot" or a "warm boot." On IBM-compatible machines, a cold boot is performed when the computer is first turned on or when a hardware reset occurs. A cold boot usually performs a power-on self test (POST) and determines the amount of memory available, as well as which peripheral adapters are installed. The POST is ordinarily reserved for a cold boot because it takes a noticeable amount of time. For example, an IBM-compatible ROM BIOS tests all conventional and extended RAM (RAM above 1 MB on an 80286-based or 80386-based machine), a procedure that can take tens of seconds. A warm boot, initiated by simultaneously pressing the Ctrl, Alt, and Del keys, bypasses these hardware checks and begins by checking for a bootable disk.

A bootable disk normally contains a small loader program that loads MS-DOS from the same disk. *See* PROGRAMMING IN THE MS-DOS ENVIRONMENT: Structure of ms-dos: MS-DOS Storage Devices. The body of MS-DOS is contained in two files: IO.SYS and MSDOS.SYS (IBMBIO.COM and IBMDOS.COM with PC-DOS). IO.SYS contains the Microsoft system initialization module, SYSINIT, which configures MS-DOS using either default values or the specifications in the CONFIG.SYS file, if one exists, and then starts up the shell program (usually COMMAND.COM, the default). COMMAND.COM checks for an AUTOEXEC.BAT file and interprets the file if found. (Other shells might not support such batch files.) Finally, COMMAND.COM prompts the user for a command. (The standard MS-DOS prompt is A> if the system was booted from a floppy disk and C> if the system was booted from a fixed disk.) Each of these steps is discussed in detail below.

The ROM BIOS, POST, and bootstrapping

All 8086/8088-compatible microprocessors begin execution with the CS:IP set to FFFF:0000H, which typically contains a jump instruction to a destination in the ROM BIOS that contains the initialization code for the machine. (This has nothing to do with MS-DOS; it is a feature of the Intel microprocessors.) On IBM-compatible machines, the ROM BIOS occupies the address space from F000:0000H to this jump instruction. Figure 2-1 shows the location of the ROM BIOS within the 1 MB address space. Supplementary ROM support can be placed before (at lower addresses than) the ROM BIOS.

All interrupts are disabled when the microprocessor starts execution and it is up to the initialization routine to set up the interrupt vectors at the base of memory.

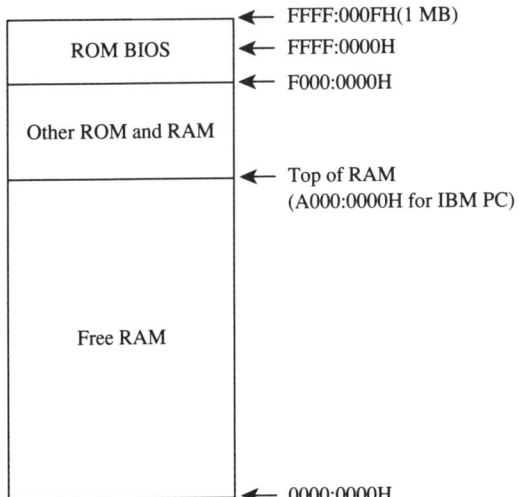

Figure 2-1. Memory layout at startup.

The initialization routine in the ROM BIOS — the POST procedure — typically determines what devices are installed and operational and checks conventional memory (the first 1 MB) and, for 80286-based or 80386-based machines, extended memory (above 1 MB). The devices are tested, where possible, and any problems are reported using a series of beeps and display messages on the screen.

When the machine is found to be operational, the ROM BIOS sets it up for normal operation. First, it initializes the interrupt vector table at the beginning of memory and any interrupt controllers that reference the table. The interrupt vector table area is located from 0000:0000H to 0000:03FFH. On IBM-compatible machines, some of the subsequent memory (starting at address 0000:0400H) is used for table storage by various ROM BIOS routines (Figure 2-2). The beginning load address for the MS-DOS system files is usually in the range 0000:0600H to 0000:0800H.

Next, the ROM BIOS sets up any necessary hardware interfaces, such as direct memory access (DMA) controllers, serial ports, and the like. Some hardware setup may be done before the interrupt vector table area is set up. For example, the IBM PC DMA controller also provides refresh for the dynamic RAM chips and RAM cannot be used until the refresh DMA is running; therefore, the DMA must be set up first.

Some ROM BIOS implementations also check to see if additional ROM BIOSs are installed by scanning the memory from A000:0000H to F000:0000H for a particular sequence of signature bytes. If additional ROM BIOSs are found, their initialization routines are called to initialize the associated devices. Examples of additional ROMs for the IBM PC family are the PC/XT's fixed-disk ROM BIOS and the EGA ROM BIOS.

The ROM BIOS now starts the bootstrap procedure by executing the ROM loader routine. On the IBM PC, this routine checks the first floppy-disk drive to see if there is a bootable

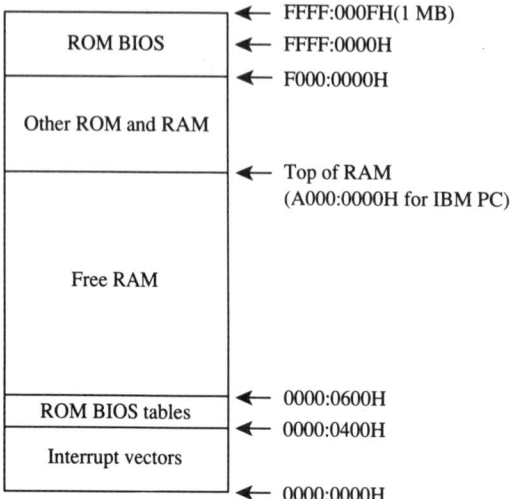

Figure 2-2. The interrupt vector table and the ROM BIOS table.

disk in it. If there is not, the routine then invokes the ROM associated with another boot-able device to see if that device contains a bootable disk. This procedure is repeated until a bootable disk is found or until all bootable devices have been checked without success, in which case ROM BASIC is enabled.

Bootable devices can be detected by a number of proprietary means. The IBM PC ROM BIOS reads the first sector on the disk into RAM (Figure 2-3) and checks for an 8086-family short or long jump at the beginning of the sector and for AA55H in the last word of the sector. This signature indicates that the sector contains the operating-system loader. Data disks — those disks not set up with the MS-DOS system files — usually cause the ROM loader routine to display a message indicating that the disk is not a bootable system disk. The customary recovery procedure is to display a message asking the user to insert another disk (with the operating system files on it) and press a key to try the load opera-tion again. The ROM loader routine is then typically reexecuted from the beginning so that it can repeat its normal search procedure.

When it finds a bootable device, the ROM loader routine loads the operating-system loader and transfers control to it. The operating-system loader then uses the ROM BIOS services through the interrupt table to load the next part of the operating system into low memory.

Before it can proceed, the operating-system loader must know something about the con-figuration of the system boot disk (Figure 2-4). MS-DOS-compatible disks contain a data structure that contains this information. This structure, known as the BIOS parameter block (BPB), is located in the same sector as the operating-system loader. From the con-tents of the BPB, the operating-system loader calculates the location of the root directory

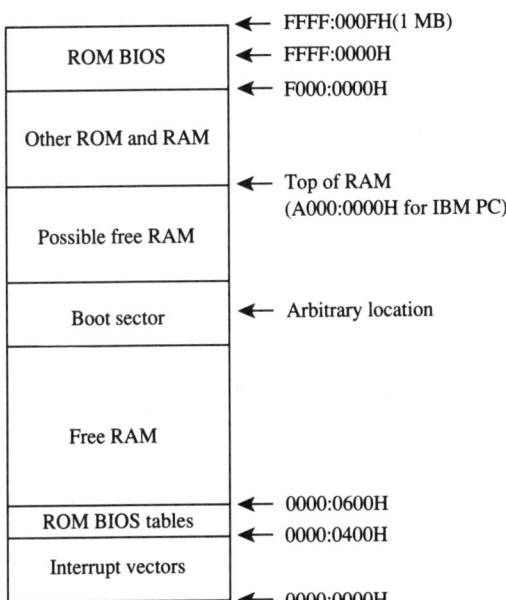

Figure 2-3. A loaded boot sector.

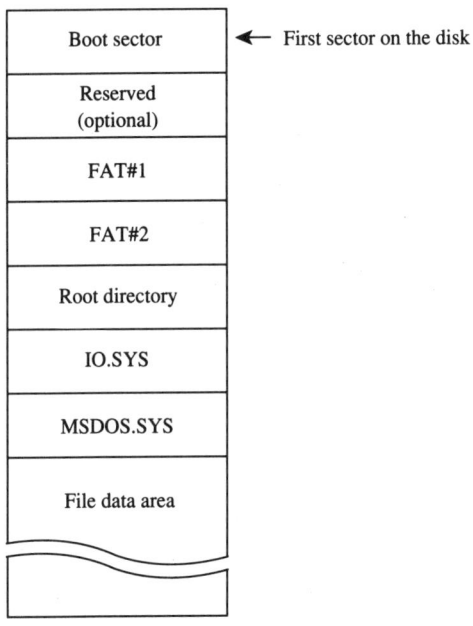

Figure 2-4. Boot-disk configuration.

for the boot disk so that it can verify that the first two entries in the root directory are
IO.SYS and MSDOS.SYS. For versions of MS-DOS through 3.2, these files must also be the
first two files in the file data area, and they must be contiguous. (The operating-system
loader usually does not check the file allocation table [FAT] to see if IO.SYS and
MSDOS.SYS are actually stored in contiguous sectors.) *See* PROGRAMMING IN THE
MS-DOS ENVIRONMENT: STRUCTURE OF MS-DOS: MS-DOS Storage Devices.

Next, the operating-system loader reads the sectors containing IO.SYS and MSDOS.SYS
into contiguous areas of memory just above the ROM BIOS tables (Figure 2-5). (An alternative method is to take advantage of the operating-system loader's final jump to the entry
point in IO.SYS and include routines in IO.SYS that allow it to load MSDOS.SYS.)

Finally, assuming the file was loaded without any errors, the operating-system loader
transfers control to IO.SYS, passing the identity of the boot device. The operating-system
loader is no longer needed and its RAM is made available for other purposes.

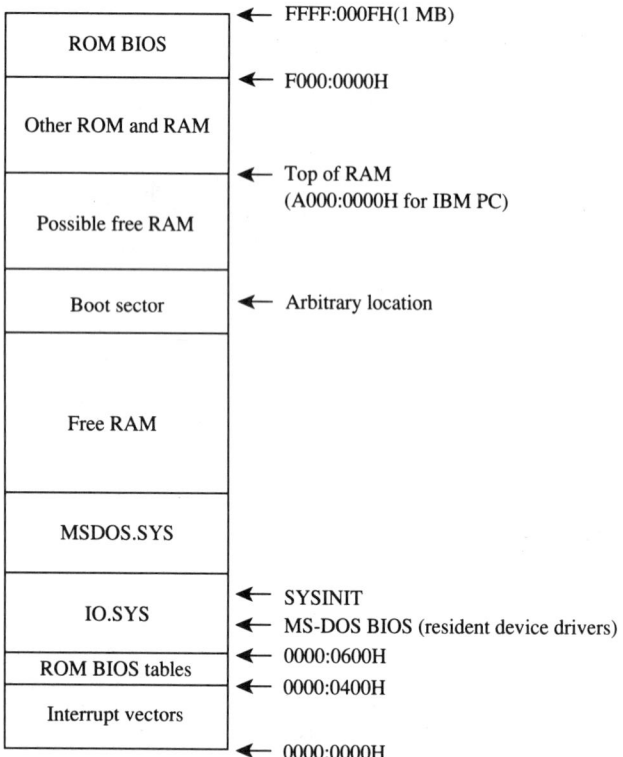

Figure 2-5. IO.SYS and MSDOS.SYS loaded.

MS-DOS system initialization (SYSINIT)

MS-DOS system initialization begins after the operating-system loader has loaded IO.SYS and MSDOS.SYS and transferred control to the beginning of IO.SYS. To this point, there has been no standard loading procedure imposed by MS-DOS, although the IBM PC loading procedure outlined here has become the de facto standard for most MS-DOS machines. When control is transferred to IO.SYS, however, MS-DOS imposes its standards.

The IO.SYS file is divided into three modules:

- The resident device drivers
- The basic MS-DOS BIOS initialization module
- The MS-DOS system initialization module, SYSINIT

The two initialization modules are usually discarded as soon as MS-DOS is completely initialized and the shell program is running; the resident device drivers remain in memory while MS-DOS is running and are therefore placed in the first part of the IO.SYS file, before the initialization modules.

The MS-DOS BIOS initialization module ordinarily displays a sign-on message and the copyright notice for the OEM that created IO.SYS. On IBM-compatible machines, it then examines entries in the interrupt table to determine what devices were found by the ROM BIOS at POST time and adjusts the list of resident device drivers accordingly. This adjustment usually entails removing those drivers that have no corresponding installed hardware. The initialization routine may also modify internal tables within the device drivers. The device driver initialization routines will be called later by SYSINIT, so the MS-DOS BIOS initialization routine is now essentially finished and control is transferred to the SYSINIT module.

SYSINIT locates the top of RAM and copies itself there. It then transfers control to the copy and the copy proceeds with system initialization. The first step is to move MSDOS.SYS, which contains the MS-DOS kernel, to a position immediately following the end of the resident portion of IO.SYS, which contains the resident device drivers. This move overwrites the original copy of SYSINIT and usually all of the MS-DOS BIOS initialization routine, which are no longer needed. The resulting memory layout is shown in Figure 2-6.

SYSINIT then calls the initialization routine in the newly relocated MS-DOS kernel. This routine performs the internal setup for the kernel, including putting the appropriate values into the vectors for Interrupts 20H through 3FH.

The MS-DOS kernel initialization routine then calls the initialization function of each resident device driver to set up vectors for any external hardware interrupts used by the device. Each block-device driver returns a pointer to a BPB for each drive that it supports; these BPBs are inspected by SYSINIT to find the largest sector size used by any of the drivers. *See* PROGRAMMING IN THE MS-DOS ENVIRONMENT: STRUCTURE OF MS-DOS: MS-DOS Storage Devices. The kernel initialization routine then allocates a sector buffer the size of the largest sector found and places the NUL device driver at the head of the device driver list.

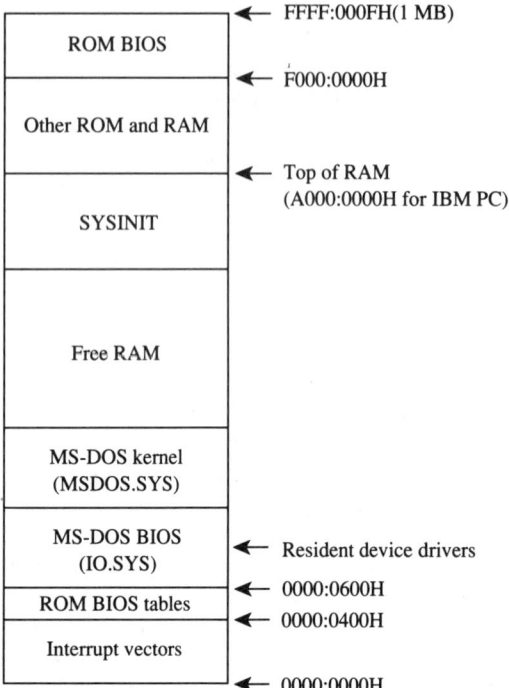

Figure 2-6. *SYSINIT and MSDOS.SYS relocated.*

The kernel initialization routine's final operation before returning to SYSINIT is to display the MS-DOS copyright message. The loading of the system portion of MS-DOS is now complete and SYSINIT can use any MS-DOS function in conjunction with the resident set of device drivers.

SYSINIT next attempts to open the CONFIG.SYS file in the root directory of the boot drive. If the file does not exist, SYSINIT uses the default system parameters; if the file is opened, SYSINIT reads the entire file into high memory and converts all characters to uppercase. The file contents are then processed to determine such settings as the number of disk buffers, the number of entries in the file tables, and the number of entries in the drive translation table (depending on the specific commands in the file), and these structures are allocated following the MS-DOS kernel (Figure 2-7).

Then SYSINIT processes the CONFIG.SYS text sequentially to determine what installable device drivers are to be implemented and loads the installable device driver files into memory after the system disk buffers and the file and drive tables. Installable device driver files can be located in any directory on any drive whose driver has already been loaded. Each installable device driver initialization function is called after the device driver file is loaded into memory. The initialization procedure is the same as for resident device drivers, except that SYSINIT uses an address returned by the device driver itself to determine where the next device driver is to be placed. *See* PROGRAMMING IN THE MS-DOS ENVIRONMENT: CUSTOMIZING MS-DOS: Installable Device Drivers.

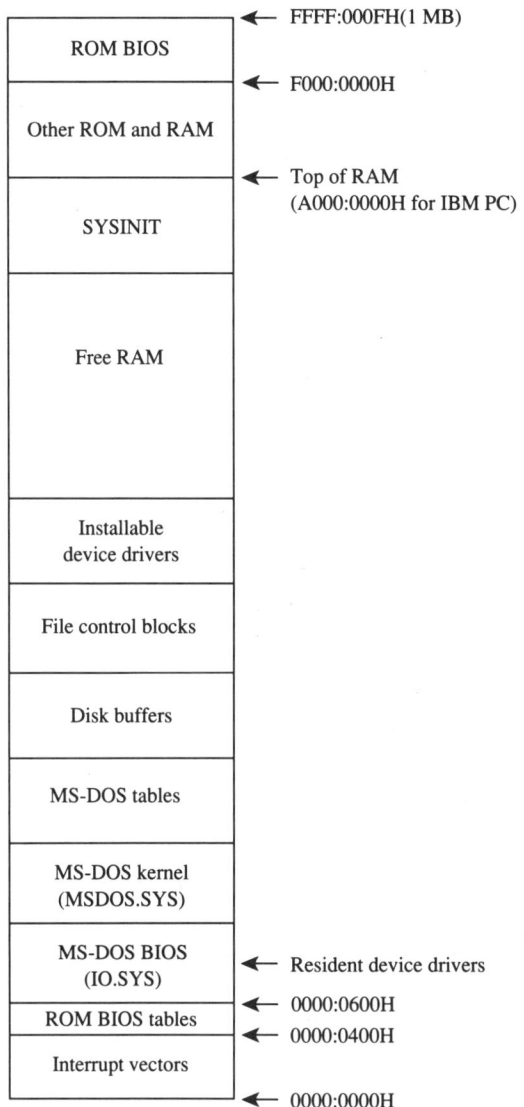

Figure 2-7. *Tables allocated and installable device drivers loaded.*

Like resident device drivers, installable device drivers can be discarded by SYSINIT if the device driver initialization routine determines that a device is inoperative or nonexistent. A discarded device driver is not included in the list of device drivers. Installable character-device drivers supersede resident character-device drivers with the same name; installable block-device drivers cannot supersede resident block-drivers and are assigned drive letters *following* those of the resident block-device drivers.

SYSINIT now closes all open files and then opens the three character devices CON, PRN, and AUX. The console (CON) is used as standard input, standard output, and standard error; the standard printer port is PRN (which defaults to LPT1); the standard auxiliary port is AUX (which defaults to COM1). Installable device drivers with these names will replace any resident versions.

Starting the shell

SYSINIT's last function is to load and execute the shell program by using the MS-DOS EXEC function. *See* PROGRAMMING IN THE MS-DOS ENVIRONMENT: Programming for ms-dos: The MS-DOS EXEC Function. The SHELL statement in CONFIG.SYS specifies both the name of the shell program and its initial parameters; the default MS-DOS shell is COMMAND.COM. The shell program is loaded at the start of free memory after the installable device drivers or after the last internal MS-DOS file control block if there are no installable device drivers (Figure 2-8).

COMMAND.COM

COMMAND.COM consists of three parts:

- A resident portion
- An initialization module
- A transient portion

The resident portion contains support for termination of programs started by COMMAND.COM and presents critical-error messages. It is also responsible for re-loading the transient portion when necessary.

The initialization module is called once by the resident portion. First, it moves the transient portion to high memory. (Compare Figures 2-8 and 2-9.) Then it processes the parameters specified in the SHELL command in the CONFIG.SYS file, if any. *See* USER COMMANDS: command. Next, it processes the AUTOEXEC.BAT file, if one exists, and finally, it transfers control back to the resident portion, which frees the space used by the initialization module and transient portion. The relocated transient portion then displays the MS-DOS user prompt and is ready to accept commands.

The transient portion gets a command from either the console or a batch file and executes it. Commands are divided into three categories:

- Internal commands
- Batch files
- External commands

Internal commands are routines contained within COMMAND.COM and include operations like COPY or ERASE. Execution of an internal command does not overwrite the transient portion. Internal commands consist of a keyword, sometimes followed by a list of command-specific parameters.

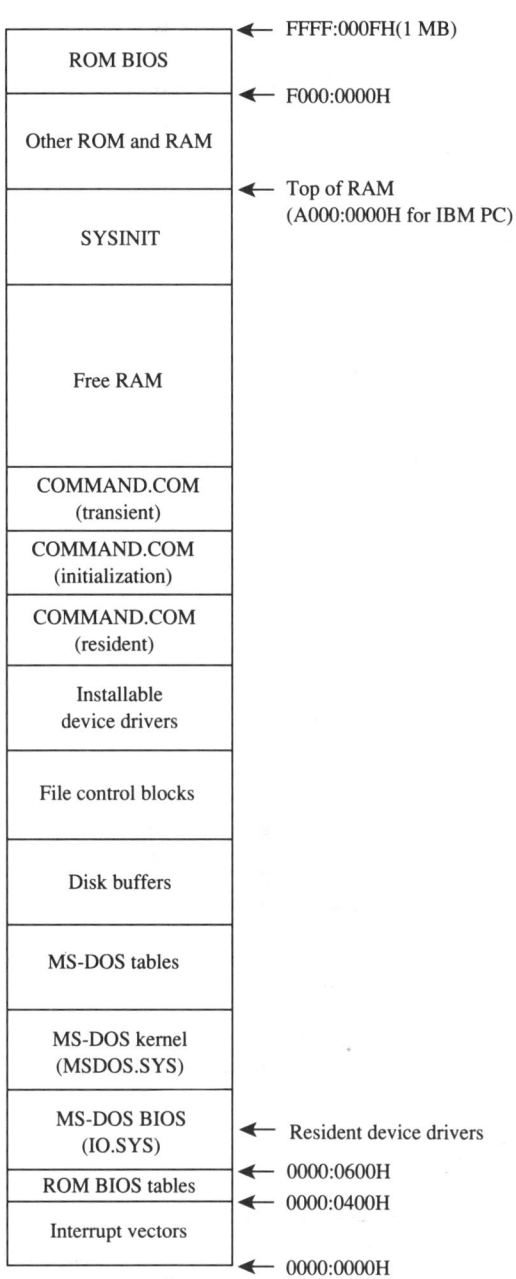

Figure 2-8. COMMAND.COM loaded.

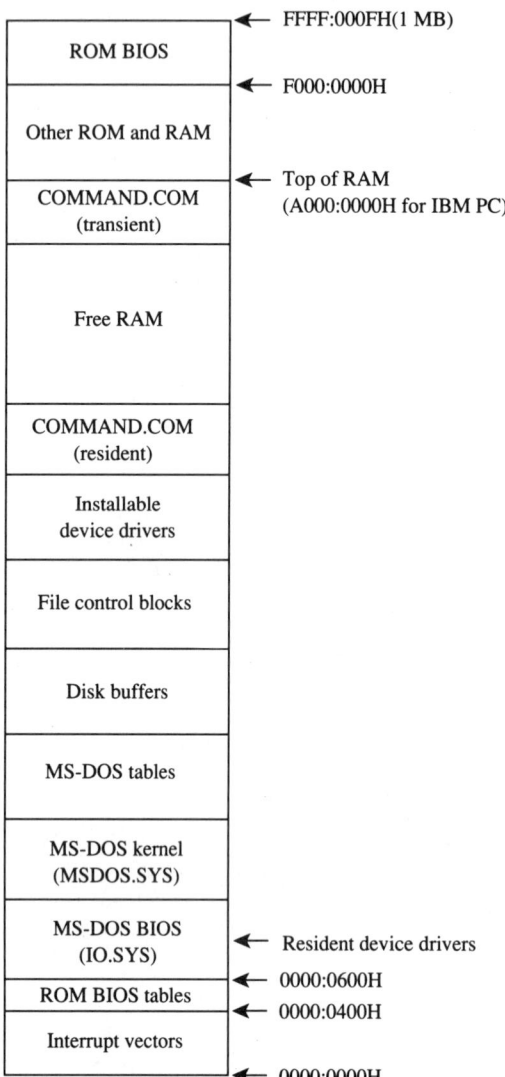

Figure 2-9. COMMAND.COM after relocation.

Batch files are text files that contain internal commands, external commands, batch-file directives, and nonexecutable comments. *See* USER COMMANDS: BATCH.

External commands, which are actually executable programs, are stored in separate files with .COM and .EXE extensions and are included on the MS-DOS distribution disks. *See* PROGRAMMING IN THE MS-DOS ENVIRONMENT: PROGRAMMING FOR MS-DOS: Structure of an Application Program. These programs are invoked with the name of the file without the extension. (MS-DOS versions 3.x allow the complete pathname of the external command to be specified.)

External commands are loaded by COMMAND.COM by means of the MS-DOS EXEC function. The EXEC function loads a program into the free memory area, also called the transient program area (TPA), and then passes it control. Control returns to COMMAND.COM when the new program terminates. Memory used by the program is released unless it is a terminate-and-stay-resident (TSR) program, in which case some of the memory is retained for the resident portion of the program. *See* PROGRAMMING IN THE MS-DOS ENVIRONMENT: Customizing ms-dos: Terminate-and-Stay-Resident Utilities.

After a program terminates, the resident portion of COMMAND.COM checks to see if the transient portion is still valid, because if the program was large, it may have overwritten the transient portion's memory space. The validity check is done by computing a checksum on the transient portion and comparing it with a stored value. If the checksums do not match, the resident portion loads a new copy of the transient portion from the COMMAND.COM file.

Just as COMMAND.COM uses the EXEC function to load and execute a program, programs can load and execute other programs until the system runs out of memory. Figure 2-10 shows a typical memory configuration for multiple applications loaded at the same time. The active task — the last one executed — ordinarily has complete control over the system, with the exception of the hardware interrupt handlers, which gain control whenever a hardware interrupt needs to be serviced.

MS-DOS is not a multitasking operating system, so although several programs can be resident in memory, only one program can be active at a time. The stack-like nature of the system is apparent in Figure 2-10. The top program is the active one; the next program down will continue to run when the top program exits, and so on until control returns to COMMAND.COM. RAM-resident programs that remain in memory after they have terminated are the exception. In this case, a program lower in memory than another program can become the active program, although the one-active-process limit is still in effect.

A custom shell program

The SHELL directive in the CONFIG.SYS file can be used to replace the system's default shell, COMMAND.COM, with a custom shell. Nearly any program can be used as a system shell as long as it supplies default handlers for the Control-C and critical error exceptions. For example, the program in Figure 2-11 can be used to make any application program appear to be a shell program — if the application program terminates, SHELL.COM restarts it, giving the appearance that the application program is the shell program.

SHELL.COM sets up the segment registers for operation as a .COM file and reduces the program segment size to less than 1 KB. It then initializes the segment values in the parameter table for the EXEC function, because .COM files cannot set up segment values within a program. The Control-C and critical error interrupt handler vectors are set to the address of the main program loop, which tries to load the new shell program. SHELL.COM prints a message if the EXEC operation fails. The loop continues forever and SHELL.COM will never return to the now-discarded SYSINIT that started it.

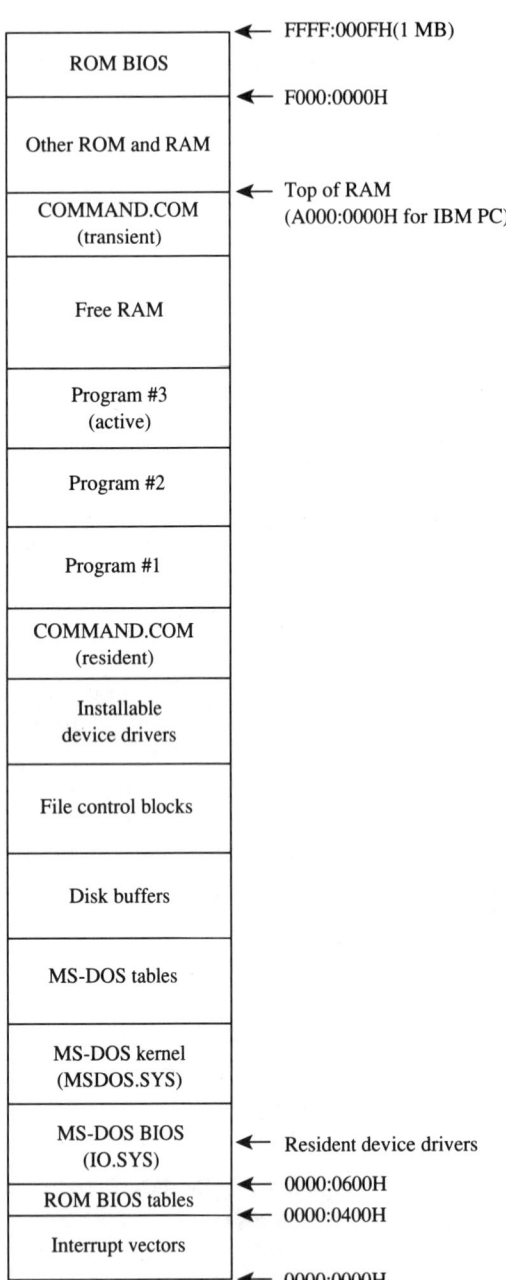

Figure 2-10. Multiple programs loaded.

```
; SHELL.ASM   A simple program to run an application as an
;             MS-DOS shell program. The program name and
;             startup parameters must be adjusted before
;             SHELL is assembled.
;
; Written by William Wong
;
; To create SHELL.COM:
;
;             C>MASM SHELL;
;             C>LINK SHELL;
;             C>EXE2BIN SHELL.EXE SHELL.COM

stderr  equ 2                 ; standard error
cr      equ 0dh               ; ASCII carriage return
lf      equ 0ah               ; ASCII linefeed
cseg    segment para public 'CODE'
;
; --  Set up DS, ES, and SS:SP to run as .COM  --
;
        assume  cs:cseg
start   proc    far
        mov     ax,cs           ; set up segment registers
        add     ax,10h          ; AX = segment after PSP
        mov     ds,ax
        mov     ss,ax           ; set up stack pointer
        mov     sp,offset stk
        mov     ax,offset shell
        push    cs              ; push original CS
        push    ds              ; push segment of shell
        push    ax              ; push offset of shell
        ret                     ; jump to shell
start   endp
;
; --  Main program running as .COM  --
;
; CS, DS, SS = cseg
; Original CS value on top of stack
;
        assume cs:cseg,ds:cseg,ss:cseg
seg_size equ (((offset last) - (offset start)) + 10fh)/16
shell   proc    near
        pop     es              ; ES = segment to shrink
        mov     bx,seg_size     ; BX = new segment size
        mov     ah,4ah          ; AH = modify memory block
        int     21h             ; free excess memory
        mov     cmd_seg,ds      ; setup segments in
        mov     fcb1_seg,ds     ; parameter block for EXEC
        mov     fcb2_seg,ds
        mov     dx,offset main_loop
        mov     ax,2523h        ; AX = set Control-C handler
```

Figure 2-11. A simple program to run an application as an MS-DOS shell.   *(more)*

```
              int     21h               ; set handler to DS:DX
              mov     dx,offset main_loop
              mov     ax,2524h          ; AX = set critical error handler
              int     21h               ; set handler to DS:DX
                                        ; Note: DS is equal to CS
main_loop:
              push    ds                ; save segment registers
              push    es
              mov     cs:stk_seg,ss     ; save stack pointer
              mov     cs:stk_off,sp
              mov     dx,offset pgm_name
              mov     bx,offset par_blk
              mov     ax,4b00h          ; AX = EXEC/run program
              int     21h               ; carry = EXEC failed
              mov     ss,cs:stk_seg     ; restore stack pointer
              mov     sp,cs:stk_off
              pop     es                ; restore segment registers
              pop     ds
              jnc     main_loop         ; loop if program run
              mov     dx,offset load_msg
              mov     cx,load_msg_length
              call    print             ; display error message
              mov     ah,08h            ; AH = read without echo
              int     21h               ; wait for any character
              jmp     main_loop         ; execute forever
shell   endp
;
; -- Print string  --
;
; DS:DX = address of string
; CX    = size
;
print   proc    near
              mov     ah,40h            ; AH = write to file
              mov     bx,stderr         ; BX = file handle
              int     21h               ; print string
              ret
print   endp
;
; -- Message strings  --
;
load_msg db cr,lf
         db 'Cannot load program.',cr,lf
         db 'Press any key to try again.',cr,lf
load_msg_length equ $-load_msg
;
; -- Program data area  --
;
stk_seg   dw    0                       ; stack segment pointer
stk_off   dw    0                       ; save area during EXEC
pgm_name  db       '\NEWSHELL.COM',0 ; any program will do
```

Figure 2-11. Continued.   *(more)*

```
par_blk    dw     0                ; use current environment
           dw     offset cmd_line  ; command-line address
cmd_seg    dw     0                ; fill in at initialization  '
           dw     offset fcb1      ; default FCB #1
fcb1_seg   dw     0                ; fill in at initialization
           dw     offset fcb2      ; default FCB #2
fcb2_seg   dw     0                ; fill in at initialization
cmd_line   db     0,cr             ; actual command line
fcb1       db     0
           db     11 dup (' ')
           db     25 dup ( 0 )
fcb2       db     0
           db     11 dup (' ')
           db     25 dup ( 0 )
           dw     200 dup ( 0 )    ; program stack area
stk        dw     0
last       equ    $                ; last address used
cseg       ends
           end    start
```

Figure 2-11. Continued.

SHELL.COM is very short and not too smart. It needs to be changed and rebuilt if the name of the application program changes. A simple extension to SHELL — call it XSHELL — would be to place the name of the application program and any parameters in the command line. XSHELL would then have to parse the program name and the contents of the two FCBs needed for the EXEC function. The CONFIG.SYS line for starting this shell would be

```
SHELL=XSHELL \SHELL\DEMO.EXE PARAM1 PARAM2 PARAM3
```

SHELL.COM does not set up a new environment but simply uses the one passed to it.

William Wong

Article 3
MS-DOS Storage Devices

Application programs access data on MS-DOS storage devices through the MS-DOS file-system support that is part of the MS-DOS kernel. The MS-DOS kernel accesses these storage devices, also called block devices, through two types of device drivers: resident block-device drivers contained in IO.SYS and installable block-device drivers loaded from individual files when MS-DOS is loaded. *See* PROGRAMMING IN THE MS-DOS ENVIRONMENT: STRUCTURE OF MS-DOS: The Components of MS-DOS; CUSTOMIZING MS-DOS: Installable Device Drivers.

MS-DOS can handle almost any medium, recording method, or other variation for a storage device as long as there is a device driver for it. MS-DOS needs to know only the sector size and the maximum number of sectors for the device; the appropriate translation between logical sector number and physical location is made by the device driver. Information about the number of heads, tracks, and so on is required only for those partitioning programs that allocate logical devices along these boundaries. *See* Layout of a Partition below.

The floppy-disk drive is perhaps the best-known block device, followed by its faster cousin, the fixed-disk drive. Other MS-DOS media include RAMdisks, nonvolatile RAMdisks, removable hard disks, tape drives, and CD ROM drives. With the proper device driver, MS-DOS can place a file system on any of these devices (except read-only media such as CD ROM).

This article discusses the structure of the file system on floppy and fixed disks, starting with the physical layout of a disk and then moving on to the logical layout of the file system. The scheme examined is for the IBM PC fixed disk.

Structure of an MS-DOS Disk

The structure of an MS-DOS disk can be viewed in a number of ways:

- Physical device layout
- Logical device layout
- Logical block layout
- MS-DOS file system

The physical layout of a disk is expressed in terms of sectors, tracks, and heads. The logical device layout, also expressed in terms of sectors, tracks, and heads, indicates how a logical device maps onto a physical device. A partitioned physical device contains multiple logical devices; a physical device that cannot be partitioned contains only one. Each logical device has a logical block layout used by MS-DOS to implement a file system. These various views of an MS-DOS disk are discussed below. *See also* PROGRAMMING IN THE MS-DOS ENVIRONMENT: PROGRAMMING FOR MS-DOS: File and Record Management; Disk Directories and Volume Labels.

Layout of a physical block device

The two major block-device implementations are solid-state RAMdisks and rotating magnetic media such as floppy or fixed disks. Both implementations provide a fixed amount of storage in a fixed number of randomly accessible same-size sectors.

RAMdisks

A RAMdisk is a block device that has sectors mapped sequentially into RAM. Thus, the RAMdisk is viewed as a large set of sequentially numbered sectors whose addresses are computed by simply multiplying the sector number by the sector size and adding the base address of the RAMdisk sector buffer. Access is fast and efficient and the access time to any sector is fixed, making the RAMdisk the fastest block device available. However, there are significant drawbacks to RAMdisks. First, they are volatile; their contents are irretrievably lost when the computer's power is turned off (although a special implementation of the RAMdisk known as a nonvolatile RAMdisk includes a battery backup system that ensures that its contents are not lost when the computer's power is turned off). Second, they are usually not portable.

Physical disks

Floppy-disk and fixed-disk systems, on the other hand, store information on revolving platters coated with a special magnetic material. The disk is rotated in the drive at high speeds — approximately 300 revolutions per minute (rpm) for floppy disks and 3600 rpm for fixed disks. (The term "fixed" refers to the fact that the medium is built permanently into the drive, not to the motion of the medium.) Fixed disks are also referred to as "hard" disks, because the disk itself is usually made from a rigid material such as metal or glass; floppy disks are usually made from a flexible material such as plastic.

A transducer element called the read/write head is used to read and write tiny magnetic regions on the rotating magnetic medium. The regions act like small bar magnets with north and south poles. The magnetic regions of the medium can be logically oriented toward one or the other of these poles — orientation toward one pole is interpreted as a specific binary state (1 or 0) and orientation toward the other pole is interpreted as the opposite binary state. A change in the direction of orientation (and hence a change in the binary value) between two adjacent regions is called a flux reversal, and the density of a particular disk implementation can be measured by the number of regions per inch reliably capable of flux reversal. Higher densities of these regions yield higher-capacity disks. The flux density of a particular system depends on the drive mechanics, the characteristics of the read/write head, and the magnetic properties of the medium.

The read/write head can encode digital information on a disk using a number of recording techniques, including frequency modulation (FM), modified frequency modulation (MFM), run length limited (RLL) encoding, and advanced run length limited (ARLL) encoding. Each technique offers double the data encoding density of the previous one. The associated control logic is more complex for the denser techniques.

Tracks

A read/write head reads data from or writes data to a thin section of the disk called a track, which is laid out in a circular fashion around the disk (Figure 3-1). Standard 5.25-inch floppy disks contain either 40 (0–39) or 80 (0–79) tracks per side. Like-numbered tracks on either side of a double-sided disk are distinguished by the number of the read/write head used to access the track. For example, track 1 on the top of the disk is identified as head 0, track 1; track 1 on the bottom of the disk is identified as head 1, track 1.

Tracks can be either spirals, as on a phonograph record, or concentric rings. Computer media usually use one of two types of concentric rings. The first type keeps the same number of sectors on each track (*see* Sectors below) and is rotated at a constant angular velocity (CAV). The second type maintains the same recording density across the entire surface of the disk, so a track near the center of a disk contains fewer sectors than a track near the perimeter. This latter type of disk is rotated at different speeds to keep the medium under the magnetic head moving at a constant linear velocity (CLV).

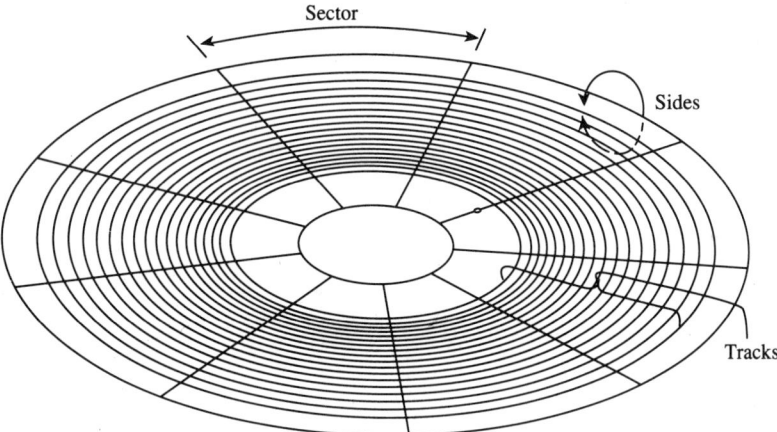

Figure 3-1. The physical layout of a CAV 9-sector, 5.25-inch floppy disk.

Most MS-DOS computers use CAV disks, although a CLV disk can store more sectors using the same type of medium. This difference in storage capacity occurs because the limiting factor is the flux density of the medium and a CAV disk must maintain the same number of magnetic flux regions per sector on the interior of the disk as at the perimeter. Thus, the sectors on or near the perimeter do not use the full capability of the medium and the heads, because the space reserved for each magnetic flux region on the perimeter is larger than that available near the center of the disk. In spite of their greater storage capacity, however, CLV disks (such as CD ROMs) usually have slower access times than CAV disks because of the constant need to fine-tune the motor speed as the head moves from track to track. Thus, CAV disks are preferred for MS-DOS systems.

Heads

Simple disk systems use a single disk, or platter, and use one or two sides of the platter; more complex systems, such as fixed disks, use multiple platters. Disk systems that use both sides of a disk have one read/write head per side; the heads are positioned over the track to be read from or written to by means of a positioning mechanism such as a solenoid or servomotor. The heads are ordinarily moved in unison, using a single head-movement mechanism; thus, heads on opposite sides of a platter in a double-sided disk system typically access the same logical track on their associated sides of the platter. (Performance can be increased by increasing the number of heads to as many as one head per track, eliminating the positioning mechanism. However, because they are quite expensive, such multiple-head systems are generally found only on high-performance minicomputers and mainframes.)

The set of like-numbered tracks on the two sides of a platter (or on all sides of all platters in a multiplatter system) is called a cylinder. Disks are usually partitioned along cylinders. Tracks and cylinders may appear to have the same meaning; however, the term track is used to define a concentric ring containing a specific number of sectors on a single side of a single platter, whereas the term cylinder refers to the number of like-numbered tracks on a device (Figure 3-2).

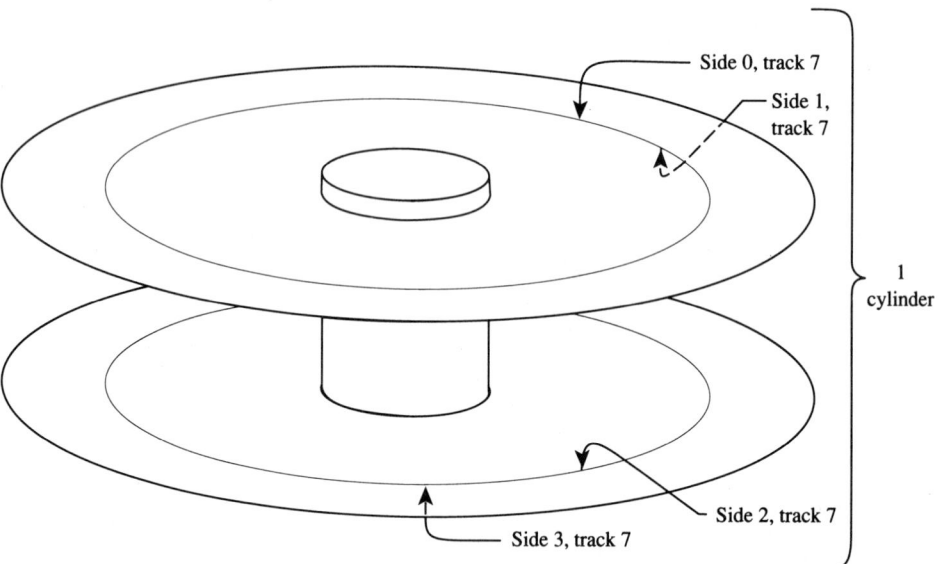

Figure 3-2. Tracks and cylinders on a fixed-disk system.

Sectors

Each track is divided into equal-size portions called sectors. The size of a sector is a power of 2 and is usually greater than 128 bytes — typically, 512 bytes.

Floppy disks are either hard-sectored or soft-sectored, depending on the disk drive and the medium. Hard-sectored disks are implemented using a series of small holes near the center of the disk that indicate the beginning of each sector; these holes are read by a photosensor/LED pair built into the disk drive. Soft-sectored disks are implemented by magnetically marking the beginning of each sector when the disk is formatted. A soft-sectored disk has a single hole near the center of the disk (*see* Figure 3-1) that marks the location of sector 0 for reference when the disk is formatted or when error detection is performed; this hole is also read by a photosensor/LED pair. Fixed disks use a special implementation of soft sectors (*see* below). A hard-sectored floppy disk cannot be used in a disk drive built for use with soft-sectored floppy disks (and vice versa).

In addition to a fixed number of data bytes, both sector types include a certain amount of overhead information, such as error correction and sector identification, in each sector. The structure of each sector is implemented during the formatting process.

Standard fixed disks and 5.25-inch floppy disks generally have from 8 to 17 physical sectors per track. Sectors are numbered beginning at 1. Each sector is uniquely identified by a complete specification of the read/write head, cylinder number, and sector number. To access a particular sector, the disk drive controller hardware moves all heads to the specified cylinder and then activates the appropriate head for the read or write operation.

The read/write heads are mechanically positioned using one of two hardware implementations. The first method, used with floppy disks, employs an "open-loop" servomechanism in which the software computes where the heads should be and the hardware moves them there. (A servomechanism is a device that can move a solenoid or hold it in a fixed position.) An open-loop system employs no feedback mechanism to determine whether the heads were positioned correctly — the hardware simply moves the heads to the requested position and returns an error if the information read there is not what was expected. The positioning mechanism in floppy-disk drives is made with close tolerances because if the positioning of the heads on two drives differs, disks written on one might not be usable on the other.

Most fixed disk systems use the second method — a "closed-loop" servomechanism that reserves one side of one platter for positioning information. This information, which indicates where the tracks and sectors are located, is written on the disk at the factory when the drive is assembled. Positioning the read/write heads in a closed-loop system is actually a two-step process: First, the head assembly is moved to the approximate location of the read or write operation; then the disk controller reads the closed-loop servo information, compares it to the desired location, and fine-tunes the head position accordingly. This fine-tuning approach yields faster access times and also allows for higher-capacity disks because the positioning can be more accurate and the distances between tracks can therefore be smaller. Because the "servo platter" usually has positioning information on one side and data on the other, many systems have an odd number of read/write heads for data.

Interleaving

CAV MS-DOS disks are described in terms of bytes per sector, sectors per track, number of cylinders, and number of read/write heads. Overall access time is based on how fast the disk rotates (rotational latency) and how fast the heads can move from track to track (track-to-track latency).

On most fixed disks, the sectors on the disk are logically or physically numbered so that logically sequential sectors are not physically adjacent (Figure 3-3). The underlying principle is that, because the controller cannot finish processing one sector before the next sequential sector arrives under the read/write head, the logically numbered sectors must be staggered around the track. This staggering of sectors is called skewing or, more commonly, interleaving. A 2-to-1 (2:1) interleave places sequentially accessed sectors so that there is one additional sector between them; a 3:1 interleave places two additional sectors between them. A slower disk controller needs a larger interleave factor. A 3:1 interleave means that three revolutions are required to read all sectors on a track in numeric order.

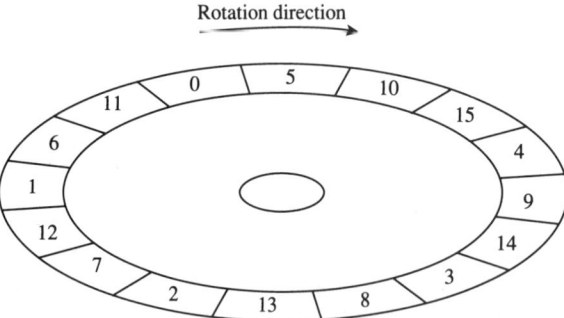

Figure 3-3. A 3:1 interleave.

One approach to improving fixed-disk performance is to decrease the interleave ratio. This generally requires a specialized utility program and also requires that the disk be reformatted to adjust to the new layout. Obviously, a 1:1 interleave is the most efficient, provided the disk controller can process at that speed. The normal interleave for an IBM PC/AT and its standard fixed disk and disk controller is 3:1, but disk controllers are available for the PC/AT that are capable of handling a 1:1 interleave. Floppy disks on MS-DOS-based computers all have a 1:1 interleave ratio.

Layout of a partition

For several reasons, large physical block devices such as fixed disks are often logically partitioned into smaller logical block devices (Figure 3-4). For instance, such partitions allow a device to be shared among different operating systems. Partitions can also be used to keep the size of each logical device within the PC-DOS 32 MB restriction (important for large fixed disks). MS-DOS permits a maximum of four partitions.

A partitioned block device has a partition table located in one sector at the beginning of the disk. This table indicates where the logical block devices are physically located. (Even a partitioned device with only one partition usually has such a table.)

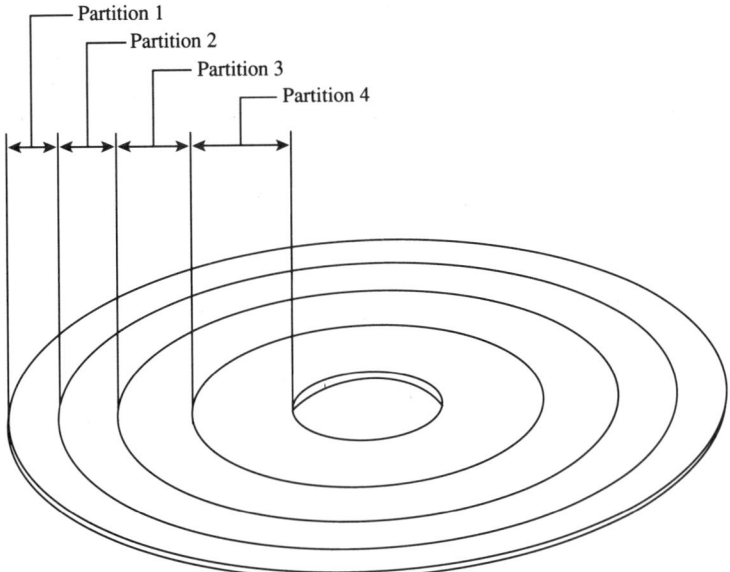

Figure 3-4. A partitioned disk.

Under the MS-DOS partitioning standard, the first physical sector on the fixed disk contains the partition table and a bootstrap program capable of checking the partition table for a bootable partition, loading the bootable partition's boot sector, and transferring control to it. The partition table, located at the end of the first physical sector of the disk, can contain a maximum of four entries:

Offset From Start of Sector	Size (bytes)	Description
01BEH	16	Partition #4
01CEH	16	Partition #3
01DEH	16	Partition #2
01EEH	16	Partition #1
01FEH	2	Signature: AA55H

The partitions are allocated in reverse order. Each 16-byte entry contains the following information:

Offset From Start of Entry	Size (bytes)	Description
00H	1	Boot indicator
01H	1	Beginning head

(more)

Offset From Start of Entry	Size (bytes)	Description
02H	1	Beginning sector
03H	1	Beginning cylinder
04H	1	System indicator
05H	1	Ending head
06H	1	Ending sector
07H	1	Ending cylinder
08H	4	Starting sector (relative to beginning of disk)
0CH	4	Number of sectors in partition

The boot indicator is zero for a nonbootable partition and 80H for a bootable (active) partition. A fixed disk can have only one bootable partition. (When setting a bootable partition, partition programs such as FDISK reset the boot indicators for all other partitions to zero.) *See* USER COMMANDS: FDISK.

The system indicators are

Code	Meaning
00H	Unknown
01H	MS-DOS, 12-bit FAT
04H	MS-DOS, 16-bit FAT

Each partition's boot sector is located at the start of the partition, which is specified in terms of beginning head, beginning sector, and beginning cylinder numbers. This information, stored in the partition table in this order, is loaded into the DX and CX registers by the PC ROM BIOS loader routine when the machine is turned on or restarted. The starting sector of the partition relative to the beginning of the disk is also indicated. The ending head, sector, and cylinder numbers, also included in the partition table, specify the last accessible sector for the partition. The total number of sectors in a partition is the difference between the starting and ending head and cylinder numbers times the number of sectors per cylinder.

MS-DOS versions 2.0 through 3.2 allow only one MS-DOS partition per partitioned device. Various device drivers have been implemented that use a different partition table that allows more than one MS-DOS partition to be installed, but the secondary MS-DOS partitions are usually accessible only by means of an installable device driver that knows about this change. (Even with additional MS-DOS partitions, a fixed disk can have only one bootable partition.)

Layout of a file system

Block devices are accessed on a sector basis. The MS-DOS kernel, through the device driver, sees a block device as a logical fixed-size array of sectors and assumes that the array contains a valid MS-DOS file system. The device driver, in turn, translates the logical sector requests from MS-DOS into physical locations on the block device.

The initial MS-DOS file system is written to the storage medium by the MS-DOS FORMAT program. *See* USER COMMANDS: FORMAT. The general layout for the file system is shown in Figure 3-5.

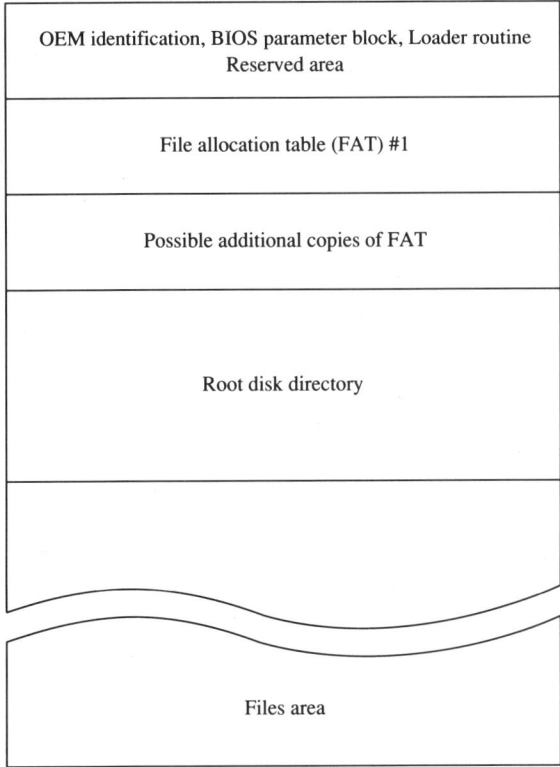

Figure 3-5. The MS-DOS file system.

The boot sector is always at the beginning of a partition. It contains the OEM identification, a loader routine, and a BIOS parameter block (BPB) with information about the device, and it is followed by an optional area of reserved sectors. *See* The Boot Sector below. The reserved area has no specific use, but an OEM might require a more complex loader routine and place it in this area. The file allocation tables (FATs) indicate how the file data area is allocated; the root directory contains a fixed number of directory entries; and the file data area contains data files, subdirectory files, and free data sectors.

All the areas just described—the boot sector, the FAT, the root directory, and the file data area—are of fixed size; that is, they do not change after FORMAT sets up the medium. The size of each of these areas depends on various factors. For instance, the size of the FAT is proportional to the file data area. The root directory size ordinarily depends on the type of device; a single-sided floppy disk can hold 64 entries, a double-sided floppy disk can hold 112, and a fixed disk can hold 256. (RAMdisk drivers such as RAMDRIVE.SYS and some implementations of FORMAT allow the number of directory entries to be specified.)

The file data area is allocated in terms of clusters. A cluster is a fixed number of contiguous sectors. Sector size and cluster size must be a power of 2. The sector size is usually 512 bytes and the cluster size is usually 1, 2, or 4 KB, but larger sector and cluster sizes are possible. Commonly used MS-DOS cluster sizes are

Disk Type	Sectors/Cluster	Bytes/Cluster*
Single-sided floppy disk	1	512
Double-sided floppy disk	2	1024
PC/AT fixed disk	4	2048
PC/XT fixed disk	8	4096
Other fixed disks	16	8192
Other fixed disks	32	16384

* Assumes 512 bytes per sector.

In general, larger cluster sizes are used to support larger fixed disks. Although smaller cluster sizes make allocation more space-efficient, larger clusters are usually more efficient for random and sequential access, especially if the clusters for a single file are not sequentially allocated.

The file allocation table contains one entry per cluster in the file data area. Doubling the sectors per cluster will also halve the number of FAT entries for a given partition. *See* The File Allocation Table below.

The boot sector

The boot sector (Figure 3-6) contains a BIOS parameter block, a loader routine, and some other fields useful to device drivers. The BPB describes a number of physical parameters of the device, as well as the location and size of the other areas on the device. The device driver returns the BPB information to MS-DOS when requested, so that MS-DOS can determine how the disk is configured.

Figure 3-7 is a hexadecimal dump of an actual boot sector. The first 3 bytes of the boot sector shown in Figure 3-7 would be E9H 2CH 00H if a long jump were used instead of a short one (as in early versions of MS-DOS). The last 2 bytes in the sector, 55H and AAH, are a fixed signature used by the loader routine to verify that the sector is a valid boot sector.

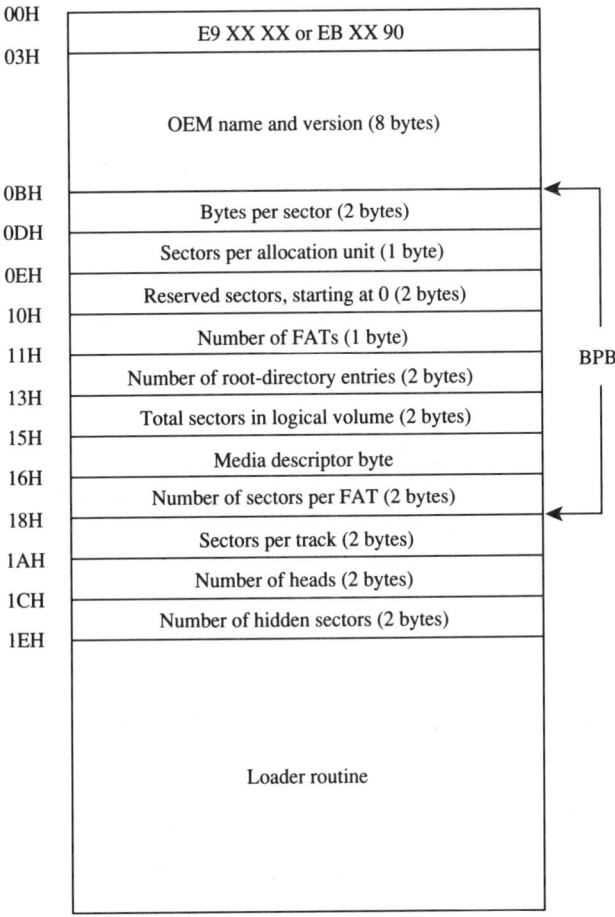

Figure 3-6. Map of the boot sector of an MS-DOS disk. Bytes 0BH through 17H are the BIOS parameter block (BPB).

The BPB information contained in bytes 0BH through 17H indicates that there are

  512 bytes per sector
    2 sectors per cluster
    1 reserved sector (for the boot sector)
    2 FATs
  112 root directory entries
1440 sectors on the disk
 F9H media descriptor
    3 sectors per FAT

```
        0   1   2   3   4   5   6   7   8   9   A   B   C   D   E   F
0000   EB  2D  90  20  20  20  20  20-20  20  20  00  02  02  01  00    k-.        .....
0010   02  70  00  A0  05  F9  03  00-09  00  02  00  00  00  00  00    .p. .y..........
0020   00  0A  00  00  DF  02  25  02-09  2A  FF  50  F6  0A  02  FA    .....—.%..*.Pv..z
0030   B8  C0  07  8E  D8  BC  00  7C-33  C0  8E  D0  8E  C0  FB  FC    8@..X<.¦3@.P.@¦¦
 .
 .
 .
0180   0A  44  69  73  6B  20  42  6F-6F  74  20  46  61  69  6C  75    .Disk Boot Failu
0190   72  65  0D  0A  0D  0A  4E  6F-6E  2D  53  79  73  74  65  6D    re....Non-System
01A0   20  64  69  73  6B  20  6F  72-20  64  69  73  6B  20  65  72     disk or disk er
01B0   72  6F  72  0D  0A  52  65  70-6C  61  63  65  20  61  6E  64    ror..Replace and
01C0   20  70  72  65  73  73  20  61-6E  79  20  6B  65  79  20  77     press any key w
01D0   68  65  6E  20  72  65  61  64-79  0D  0A  00  00  00  00  00    hen ready.......
01E0   00  00  00  00  00  00  00  00-00  00  00  00  00  00  00  00    ................
01F0   00  00  00  00  00  00  00  00-00  00  00  00  00  00  55  AA    ..............*
```

Figure 3-7. Hexadecimal dump of an MS-DOS boot sector. The BPB is highlighted.

Additional information immediately after the BPB indicates that there are 9 sectors per track, 2 read/write heads, and 0 hidden sectors.

The media descriptor, which appears in the BPB and in the first byte of each FAT, is used to indicate the type of medium currently in a drive. IBM-compatible media have the following descriptors:

Descriptor	Media Type	MS-DOS Versions
0F8H	Fixed disk	2, 3
0F9H	3.5-inch, 2-sided, 18 sector	3.2
0F9H	3.5-inch, 2-sided, 9 sector	3.2
0F9H	5.25-inch, 2-sided, 15 sector	3
0FCH	5.25-inch, 1-sided, 9 sector	2, 3
0FDH	5.25-inch, 2-sided, 9 sector	2, 3
0FEH	5.25-inch, 1-sided, 8 sector	1, 2, 3
0FFH	5.25-inch, 2-sided, 8 sector	1 (except 1.0), 2, 3
0FEH	8-inch, 1-sided, single-density	
0FDH	8-inch, 2-sided, single-density	
0FEH	8-inch, 1-sided, double-density	
0FDH	8-inch, 2-sided, double-density	

The file allocation table

The file allocation table provides a map to the storage locations of files on a disk by indicating which clusters are allocated to each file and in what order. To enable MS-DOS to locate a file, the file's directory entry contains its beginning FAT entry number. This FAT entry, in turn, contains the entry number of the next cluster if the file is larger than one cluster or a last-cluster number if there is only one cluster associated with the file. A file whose size implies that it occupies 10 clusters will have 10 FAT entries and 9 FAT links. (The set of links for a particular file is called a chain.)

Additional copies of the FAT are used to provide backup in case of damage to the first, or primary, FAT; the typical floppy disk or fixed disk contains two FATs. The FATs are arranged sequentially after the boot sector, with some possible intervening reserved area. MS-DOS ordinarily uses the primary FAT but updates all FATs when a change occurs. It also compares all FATs when a disk is first accessed, to make sure they match.

MS-DOS supports two types of FAT: One uses 12-bit links; the other, introduced with version 3.0 to accommodate large fixed disks with more than 4087 clusters, uses 16-bit links.

The first two entries of a FAT are always reserved and are filled with a copy of the media descriptor byte and two (for a 12-bit FAT) or three (for a 16-bit FAT) 0FFH bytes, as shown in the following dumps of the first 16 bytes of the FAT:

12-bit FAT:

```
F9 FF FF 03 40 00 FF 6F-00 07 F0 FF 00 00 00 00
```

16-bit FAT:

```
F8 FF FF FF 03 00 04 00-FF FF 06 00 07 00 FF FF
```

The remaining FAT entries have a one-to-one relationship with the clusters in the file data area. Each cluster's use status is indicated by its corresponding FAT value. (FORMAT initially marks the FAT entry for each cluster as free.) The use status is one of the following:

12-bit	16-bit	Meaning
000H	0000H	Free cluster
001H	0001H	Unused code
FF0–FF6H	FFF0–FFF6H	Reserved
FF7H	FFF7H	Bad cluster; cannot be used
FF8–FFFH	FFF8–FFFFH	Last cluster of file
All other values	All other values	Link to next cluster in file

If a FAT entry is nonzero, the corresponding cluster has been allocated. A free cluster is found by scanning the FAT from the beginning to find the first zero value. Bad clusters are ordinarily identified during formatting. Figure 3-8 shows a typical FAT chain.

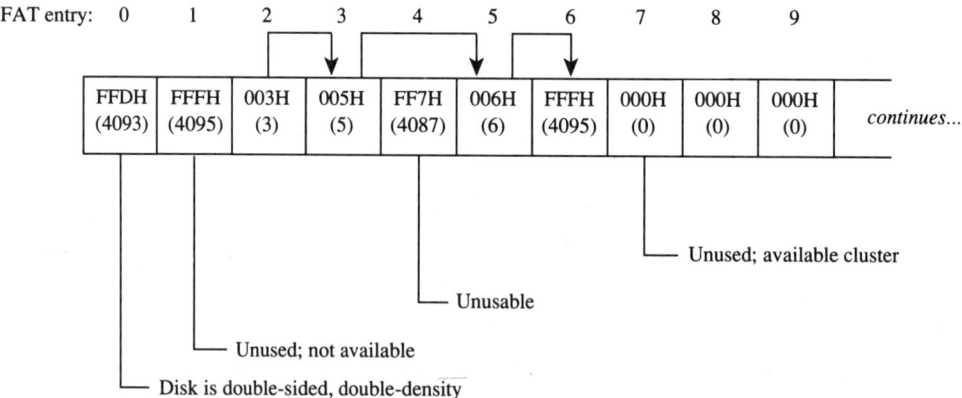

Figure 3-8. Space allocation in the FAT for a typical MS-DOS disk.

Free FAT entries contain a link value of zero; a link value of 1 is never used. Thus, the first allocatable link number, associated with the first available cluster in the file data area, is 2, which is the number assigned to the first *physical* cluster in the file data area. Figure 3-9 shows the relationship of files, FAT entries, and clusters in the file data area.

There is no *logical* difference between the operation of the 12-bit and 16-bit FAT entries; the difference is simply in the storage and access methods. Because the 8086 is specifically designed to manipulate 8- or 16-bit values efficiently, the access procedure for the 12-bit FAT is more complex than that for the 16-bit FAT (*see* Figures 3-10 and 3-11).

Special considerations

The FAT is a highly efficient bookkeeping system, but various tradeoffs and problems can occur. One tradeoff is having a partially filled cluster at the end of a file. This situation leads to an efficiency problem when a large cluster size is used, because an entire cluster is allocated, regardless of the number of bytes it contains. For example, ten 100-byte files on a disk with 16 KB clusters use 160 KB of disk space; the same files on a disk with 1 KB clusters use only 10 KB — a difference of 150 KB, or 15 times less storage used by the smaller cluster size. On the other hand, the 12-bit FAT routine in Figure 3-10 shows the difficulty (and therefore slowness) of moving through a large file that has a long linked list of many small clusters. Therefore, the nature of the data must be considered: Large database applications work best with a larger cluster size; a smaller cluster size allows many small text files to fit on a disk. (The programmer writing the device driver for a disk device ordinarily sets the cluster size.)

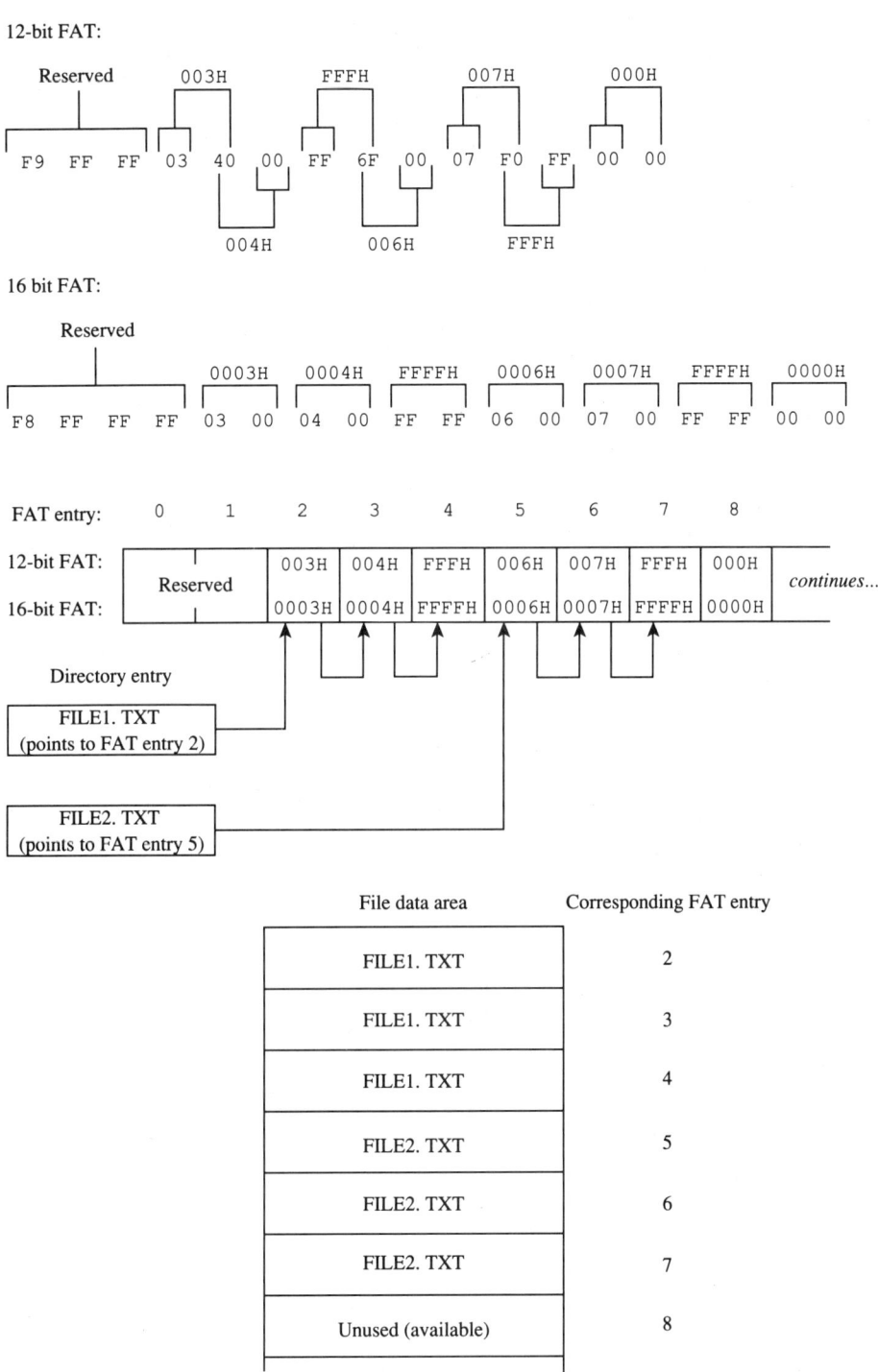

Figure 3-9. Correspondence between the FAT and the file data area.

```
; ---- Obtain the next link number from a 12-bit FAT  -----
;
; Parameters:
;       ax      = current entry number
;       ds:bx   = address of FAT (must be contiguous)
;
; Returns:
;       ax      = next link number
;
; Uses: ax, bx, cx
next12  proc    near
        add     bx,ax           ; ds:bx = partial index
        shr     ax,1            ; ax = offset/2
                                ; carry = no shift needed
        pushf                   ; save carry
        add     bx,ax           ; ds:bx = next cluster number index
        mov     ax,[bx]         ; ax = next cluster number
        popf                    ; carry = no shift needed
        jc      shift           ; skip if using top 12 bits
        and     ax,0fffh        ; ax = lower 12 bits
        ret
shift:  mov     cx,4            ; cx = shift count
        shr     ax,cl           ; ax = top 12 bits in lower 12 bits
        ret
next12  endp
```

Figure 3-10. Assembly-language routine to access a 12-bit FAT.

```
; ---- Obtain the next link number from a 16-bit FAT  -----
;
; Parameters:
;       ax      = current entry number
;       ds:bx   = address of FAT (must be contiguous)
;
; Returns:
;       ax      = next link number
;
; Uses: ax, bx, cx
next16  proc    near
        add     ax,ax           ; ax = word offset
        add     bx,ax           ; ds:bx = next link number index
        mov     ax,[bx]         ; ax = next link number
        ret
next16  endp
```

Figure 3-11. Assembly-language routine to access a 16-bit FAT.

Problems with corrupted directories or FATs, induced by such events as power failures and programs running wild, can lead to greater problems if not corrected. The MS-DOS CHKDSK program can detect and fix some of these problems. *See* USER COMMANDS: CHKDSK. For example, one common problem is dangling allocation lists caused by the absence of a directory entry pointing to the start of the list. This situation often results when the directory entry was not updated because a file was not closed before the computer was turned off or restarted. The effect is relatively benign: The data is inaccessible, but this limitation does not affect other file allocation operations. CHKDSK can fix this problem by making a new directory entry and linking it to the list.

Another difficulty occurs when the file size in a directory entry does not match the file length as computed by traversing the linked list in the FAT. This problem can result in improper operation of a program and in error responses from MS-DOS.

A more complex (and rarer) problem occurs when the directory entry is properly set up but all or some portion of the linked list is also referenced by another directory entry. The problem is grave, because writing or appending to one file changes the contents of the other file. This error usually causes severe data and/or directory corruption or causes the system to crash.

A similar difficulty occurs when a linked list terminates with a free cluster instead of a last-cluster number. If the free cluster is allocated before the error is corrected, the problem eventually reverts to the preceding problem. An associated difficulty occurs if a link value of 1 or a link value that exceeds the size of the FAT is encountered.

In addition to CHKDSK, a number of commercially available utility programs can be used to assist in FAT maintenance. For instance, disk reorganizers can be used to essentially rearrange the FAT and adjust the directory so that all files on a disk are laid out sequentially in the file data area and, of course, in the FAT.

The root directory

Directory entries, which are 32 bytes long, are found in both the root directory and the subdirectories. Each entry includes a filename and extension, the file's size, the starting FAT entry, the time and date the file was created or last revised, and the file's attributes. This structure resembles the format of the CP/M-style file control blocks (FCBs) used by the MS-DOS version 1.x file functions. *See* PROGRAMMING IN THE MS-DOS ENVIRONMENT: PROGRAMMING FOR MS-DOS: Disk Directories and Volume Labels.

The MS-DOS file-naming convention is also derived from CP/M: an eight-character filename followed by a three-character file type, each left aligned and padded with spaces if necessary. Within the limitations of the character set, the name and type are completely arbitrary. The time and date stamps are in the same format used by other MS-DOS functions and reflect the time the file was last written to.

Figure 3-12 shows a dump of a 512-byte directory sector containing 16 directory entries. (Each entry occupies two lines in this example.) The byte at offset 0ABH, containing a 10H, signifies that the entry starting at 0A0H is for a subdirectory. The byte at offset 160H, containing 0E5H, means that the file has been deleted. The byte at offset 8BH, containing the value 08H, indicates that the directory entry beginning at offset 80H is a volume label. Finally the zero byte at offset 1E0H marks the end of the directory, indicating that the subsequent entries in the directory have never been used and therefore need not be searched (versions 2.0 and later).

```
        0  1  2  3  4  5  6  7  8  9  A  B  C  D  E  F
0000   49 4F 20 20 20 20 20 20-53 59 53 27 00 00 00 00    IO      SYS'....
0010   00 00 00 00 00 00 59 53-89 0B 02 00 D1 12 00 00    ......YS....Q...
0020   4F 53 44 4F 53 20 20 20-53 59 53 27 00 00 00 00    MSDOS   SYS'....
0030   00 00 00 00 00 00 41 49-52 0A 07 00 C9 43 00 00    ......AIR...IC..
0040   41 4E 53 49 20 20 20 20-53 59 53 20 00 00 00 00    ANSI    SYS ....
0050   00 00 00 00 00 00 41 49-52 0A 18 00 76 07 00 00    ......AIR...v...
0060   58 54 41 4C 4B 20 20 20 45 58 45 20 00 00 00 00    XTALK   EXE ....
0070   00 00 00 00 00 00 F7 7D-38 09 23 02 84 0B 01 00    ......w}8.#.....
0080   4C 41 42 45 4C 20 20 20-20 20 20 08 00 00 00 00    LABEL      ....
0090   00 00 00 00 00 00 8C 20-2A 09 00 00 00 00 00 00    ....... *.D..R..
00A0   4C 4F 54 55 53 20 20 20-20 20 20 10 00 00 00 00    LOTUS      ....
00B0   00 00 00 00 00 00 E0 0A-E1 06 A6 01 00 00 00 00    ......'.a.&.a...
00C0   4C 54 53 4C 4F 41 44 20-43 4F 4D 20 00 00 00 00    LTSLOAD COM ....
00D0   00 00 00 00 00 00 E0 0A-E1 06 A7 01 A0 27 00 00    ......'.a.'. '..
00E0   4D 43 49 2D 53 46 20 20-58 54 4B 20 00 00 00 00    MCI-SF  XTK ....
00F0   00 00 00 00 00 00 46 19-32 0D B1 01 79 04 00 00    ......F.2.1.y...
0100   58 54 41 4C 4B 20 20 20-48 4C 50 20 00 00 00 00    XTALK   HLP ....
0110   00 00 00 00 00 00 C5 6D-73 07 A3 02 AF 88 00 00    ......Ems.#./...
0120   54 58 20 20 20 20 20 20-20 43 4F 4D 20 00 00 00 00 TX      COM ....
0130   00 00 00 00 00 00 05 61-65 0C 39 01 E8 20 00 00    ......ae.9.h ..
0140   43 4F 4D 4D 41 4E 44 20-43 4F 4D 20 00 00 00 00    COMMAND COM ....
0150   00 00 00 00 00 00 41 49-52 0A 27 00 55 3F 00 00    ......AIR.'.U?..
0160   E5 32 33 20 20 20 20 20-45 58 45 20 00 00 00 00    e23     EXE ....
0170   00 00 00 00 00 00 9C B2-85 0B 42 01 80 5F 01 00    .......2..B.._..
0180   47 44 20 20 20 20 20 20-44 52 56 20 00 00 00 00    GD      DRV ....
0190   00 00 00 00 00 00 E0 0A-E1 06 9A 01 5B 08 00 00    ......'.a...[...
01A0   4B 42 20 20 20 20 20 20-44 52 56 20 00 00 00 00    KB      DRV ....
01B0   00 00 00 00 00 00 E0 0A-E1 06 9D 01 60 01 00 00    ......'.a...'...
01C0   50 52 20 20 20 20 20 20-44 52 56 20 00 00 00 00    PR      DRV ....
01D0   00 00 00 00 00 00 E0 0A-E1 06 9E 01 49 01 00 00    ......'.a...I...
01E0   00 F6 F6 F6 F6 F6 F6 F6-F6 F6 F6 F6 F6 F6 F6 F6    ...............
01F0   F6 F6 F6 F6 F6 F6 F6 F6-F6 F6 F6 F6 F6 F6 F6 F6    ...............
```

Figure 3-12. Hexadecimal dump of a 512-byte directory sector.

The sector shown in Figure 3-12 is actually an example of the first directory sector in the root directory of a bootable disk. Notice that IO.SYS and MSDOS.SYS are the first two files in the directory and that the file attribute byte (offset 0BH in a directory entry) has a binary value of 00100111, indicating that both files have hidden (bit 1 = 1), system (bit 0 = 1), and read-only (bit 2 = 1) attributes. The archive bit (bit 5) is also set, marking the files for possible backup.

The root directory can optionally have a special type of entry called a volume label, identified by an attribute type of 08H, that is used to identify disks by name. A root directory can contain only one volume label. The root directory can also contain entries that point to subdirectories; such entries are identified by an attribute type of 10H and a file size of zero. Programs that manipulate subdirectories must do so by tracing through their chains of clusters in the FAT.

Two other special types of directory entries are found only within subdirectories. These entries have the filenames **.** and **..** and correspond to the current directory and the parent directory of the current directory. These special entries, sometimes called directory aliases, can be used to move quickly through the directory structure.

The maximum pathname length supported by MS-DOS, excluding a drive specifier but including any filename and extension and subdirectory name separators, is 64 characters. The size of the directory structure itself is limited only by the number of root directory entries and the available disk space.

The file area

The file area contains subdirectories, file data, and unallocated clusters. The area is divided into fixed-size clusters and the use for a particular cluster is specified by the corresponding FAT entry.

Other MS-DOS Storage Devices

As mentioned earlier, MS-DOS supports other types of storage devices, such as magnetic-tape drives and CD ROM drives. Tape drives are most often used for archiving and for sequential transaction processing and therefore are not discussed here.

CD ROMs are compact laser discs that hold a massive amount of information—a single side of a CD ROM can hold almost 500 MB of data. However, there are some drawbacks to current CD ROM technology. For instance, data cannot be written to them—the information is placed on the compact disk at the factory when the disk is made and is available on a read-only basis. In addition, the access time for a CD ROM is much slower than for most magnetic-disk systems. Even with these limitations, however, the ability to hold so much information makes CD ROM a good method for storing large amounts of static information.

William Wong

Part B
Programming for MS-DOS

Article 4
Structure of an Application Program

Planning an MS-DOS application program requires serious analysis of the program's size. This analysis can help the programmer determine which of the two program styles supported by MS-DOS best suits the application. The .EXE program structure provides a large program with benefits resulting from the extra 512 bytes (or more) of header that preface all .EXE files. On the other hand, at the cost of losing the extra benefits, the .COM program structure does not burden a small program with the overhead of these extra header bytes.

Because .COM programs start their lives as .EXE programs (before being converted by EXE2BIN) and because several aspects of application programming under MS-DOS remain similar regardless of the program structure used, a solid understanding of .EXE structures is beneficial even to the programmer who plans on writing only .COM programs. Therefore, we'll begin our discussion with the structure and behavior of .EXE programs and then look at differences between .COM programs and .EXE programs, including restrictions on the structure and content of .COM programs.

The .EXE Program

The .EXE program has several advantages over the .COM program for application design. Considerations that could lead to the choice of the .EXE format include

- Extremely large programs
- Multiple segments
- Overlays
- Segment and far address constants
- Long calls
- Possibility of upgrading programs to MS OS/2 protected mode

The principal advantages of the .EXE format are provided by the file header. Most important, the header contains information that permits a program to make direct segment address references — a requirement if the program is to grow beyond 64 KB.

The file header also tells MS-DOS how much memory the program requires. This information keeps memory not required by the program from being allocated to the program — an important consideration if the program is to be upgraded in the future to run efficiently under MS OS/2 protected mode.

Before discussing the .EXE program structure in detail, we'll look at how .EXE programs behave.

Giving control to the .EXE program

Figure 4-1 gives an example of how a .EXE program might appear in memory when MS-DOS first gives the program control. The diagram shows Microsoft's preferred program segment arrangement.

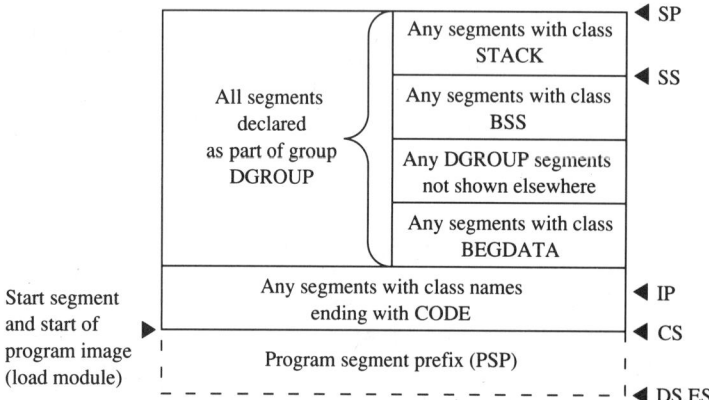

Figure 4-1. The .EXE program: memory map diagram with register pointers.

Before transferring control to the .EXE program, MS-DOS initializes various areas of memory and several of the microprocessor's registers. The following discussion explains what to expect from MS-DOS before it gives the .EXE program control.

The program segment prefix

The program segment prefix (PSP) is not a direct result of any program code. Rather, this special 256-byte (16-paragraph) page of memory is built by MS-DOS in front of all .EXE and .COM programs when they are loaded into memory. Although the PSP does contain several fields of use to newer programs, it exists primarily as a remnant of CP/M— Microsoft adopted the PSP for ease in porting the vast number of programs available under CP/M to the MS-DOS environment. Figure 4-2 shows the fields that make up the PSP.

PSP:0000H (Terminate [old Warm Boot] Vector) The PSP begins with an 8086-family INT 20H instruction, which the program can use to transfer control back to MS-DOS. The PSP includes this instruction at offset 00H because this address was the WBOOT (Warm Boot/Terminate) vector under CP/M and CP/M programs usually terminated by jumping to this vector. This method of termination should not be used in newer programs. *See* Terminating the .EXE Program below.

PSP:0002H (Address of Last Segment Allocated to Program) MS-DOS introduced the word at offset 02H into the PSP. It contains the segment address of the paragraph following the block of memory allocated to the program. This address should be used only to determine the size or the end of the memory block allocated to the program; it must not be considered a pointer to free memory that the program can appropriate. In most cases this address will *not* point to free memory, because any free memory will already have been

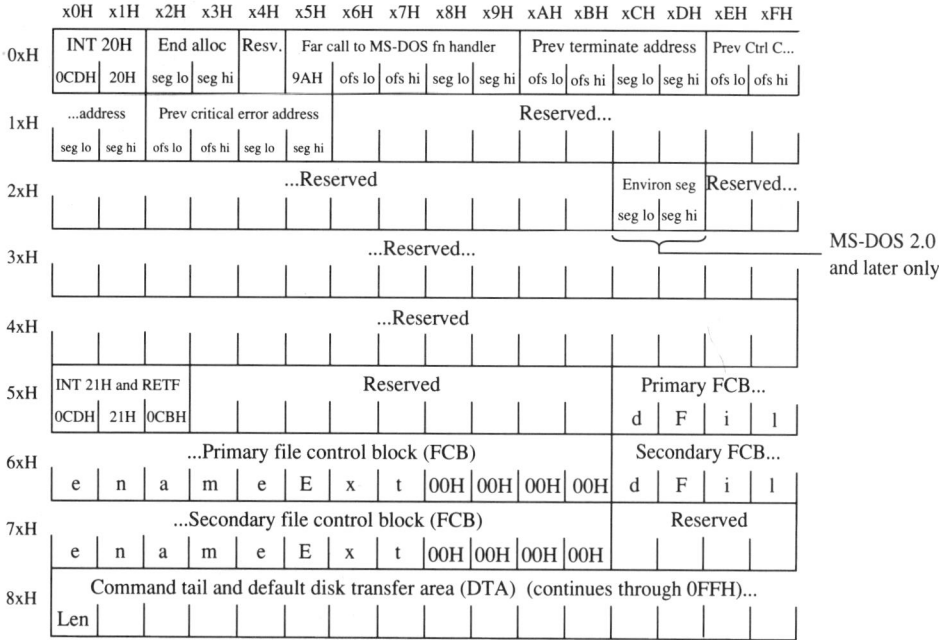

	x0H	x1H	x2H	x3H	x4H	x5H	x6H	x7H	x8H	x9H	xAH	xBH	xCH	xDH	xEH	xFH
0xH	INT 20H		End alloc		Resv.	Far call to MS-DOS fn handler					Prev terminate address				Prev Ctrl C...	
	0CDH	20H	seg lo	seg hi		9AH	ofs lo	ofs hi	seg lo	seg hi	ofs lo	ofs hi	seg lo	seg hi	ofs lo	ofs hi
1xH	...address		Prev critical error address				Reserved...									
	seg lo	seg hi	ofs lo	ofs hi	seg lo	seg hi										
2xH	...Reserved												Environ seg		Reserved...	
													seg lo	seg hi		
3xH	...Reserved...															
4xH	...Reserved															
5xH	INT 21H and RETF			Reserved									Primary FCB...			
	0CDH	21H	0CBH										d	F	i	l
6xH	...Primary file control block (FCB)												Secondary FCB...			
	e	n	a	m	e	E	x	t	00H	00H	00H	00H	d	F	i	l
7xH	...Secondary file control block (FCB)												Reserved			
	e	n	a	m	e	E	x	t	00H	00H	00H	00H				
8xH	Command tail and default disk transfer area (DTA) (continues through 0FFH)...															
	Len															

MS-DOS 2.0 and later only

Figure 4-2. The program segment prefix (PSP).

allocated to the program unless the program was linked using the /CPARMAXALLOC switch. Even when /CPARMAXALLOC is used, MS-DOS may fit the program into a block of memory only as big as the program requires. Well-behaved programs should acquire additional memory only through the MS-DOS function calls provided for that purpose.

PSP:0005H (MS-DOS Function Call [old BDOS] Vector) Offset 05H is also a hand-me-down from CP/M. This location contains an 8086-family far (intersegment) call instruction to MS-DOS's function request handler. (Under CP/M, this address was the Basic Disk Operating System [BDOS] vector, which served a similar purpose.) This vector should not be used to call MS-DOS in newer programs. The System Calls section of this book explains the newer, approved method for calling MS-DOS. MS-DOS provides this vector only to support CP/M-style programs and therefore honors only the CP/M-style functions (00–24H) through it.

PSP:000AH-0015H (Parent's 22H, 23H, and 24H Interrupt Vector Save) MS-DOS uses offsets 0AH through 15H to save the contents of three program-specific interrupt vectors. MS-DOS must save these vectors because it permits any program to execute another program (called a child process) through an MS-DOS function call that returns control to the original program when the called program terminates. Because the original program resumes executing when the child program terminates, MS-DOS must restore these three interrupt vectors for the original program in case the called program changed them. The three vectors involved include the program termination handler vector (Interrupt 22H), the Control-C/Control-Break handler vector (Interrupt 23H), and the critical error handler vector (Interrupt 24H). MS-DOS saves the original preexecution contents of these vectors in the child program's PSP as doubleword fields beginning at offsets 0AH for the program termination handler vector, 0EH for the Control-C/Control-Break handler vector, and 12H for the critical error handler vector.

PSP:002CH (Segment Address of Environment) Under MS-DOS versions 2.0 and later, the word at offset 2CH contains one of the most useful pieces of information a program can find in the PSP — the segment address of the first paragraph of the MS-DOS environment. This pointer enables the program to search through the environment for any configuration or directory search path strings placed there by users with the SET command.

PSP:0050H (New MS-DOS Call Vector) Many programmers disregard the contents of offset 50H. The location consists simply of an INT 21H instruction followed by a RETF. A .EXE program can call this location using a far call as a means of accessing the MS-DOS function handler. Of course, the program can also simply do an INT 21H directly, which is smaller and faster than calling 50H. Unlike calls to offset 05H, calls to offset 50H can request the full range of MS-DOS functions.

PSP:005CH (Default File Control Block 1) and PSP:006CH (Default File Control Block 2) MS-DOS parses the first two parameters the user enters in the command line following the program's name. If the first parameter qualifies as a valid (limited) MS-DOS filename (the name can be preceded by a drive letter but not a directory path), MS-DOS initializes offsets 5CH through 6BH with the first 16 bytes of an unopened file control block (FCB) for the specified file. If the second parameter also qualifies as a valid MS-DOS filename, MS-DOS initializes offsets 6CH through 7BH with the first 16 bytes of an unopened FCB for the second specified file. If the user specifies a directory path as part of either filename, MS-DOS initializes only the drive code in the associated FCB. Many programmers no longer use this feature, because file access using FCBs does not support directory paths and other newer MS-DOS features.

Because FCBs expand to 37 bytes when the file is opened, opening the first FCB at offset 5CH causes it to grow from 16 bytes to 37 bytes and to overwrite the second FCB. Similarly, opening the second FCB at offset 6CH causes it to expand and to overwrite the first part of the command tail and default disk transfer area (DTA). (The command tail and default DTA are described below.) To use the contents of both default FCBs, the program should copy the FCBs to a pair of 37-byte fields located in the program's data area. The program can use the first FCB without moving it only after relocating the second FCB (if necessary) and only by performing sequential reads or writes when using the first FCB. To perform random reads and writes using the first FCB, the programmer must either move the first FCB or change the default DTA address. Otherwise, the first FCB's random record field will overlap the start of the default DTA. *See* PROGRAMMING IN THE MS-DOS ENVIRON-MENT: Programming for ms-dos: File and Record Management.

PSP:0080H (Command Tail and Default DTA) The default DTA resides in the entire second half (128 bytes) of the PSP. MS-DOS uses this area of memory as the default record buffer if the program uses the FCB-style file access functions. Again, MS-DOS inherited this location from CP/M. (MS-DOS provides a function the program can call to change the address MS-DOS will use as the current DTA. *See* SYSTEM CALLS: INTERRUPT 21H: Function 1AH.) Because the default DTA serves no purpose until the program performs some file activity that requires it, MS-DOS places the command tail in this area for the program to examine. The command tail consists of any text the user types following the program name when executing the program. Normally, an ASCII space (20H) is the first character in the command tail, but any character MS-DOS recognizes as a separator can occupy this position. MS-DOS stores the command-tail text starting at offset 81H and always places an ASCII carriage return (0DH) at the end of the text. As an additional aid, it places the length of the command tail at offset 80H. This length includes all characters except the final 0DH. For example, the command line

```
C>DOIT WITH CLASS   <Enter>
```

will result in the program DOIT being executed with PSP:0080H containing

```
0B   20 57 49 54 48 20 43 4C 41 53 53 0D
len sp W  I  T  H  sp C  L  A  S  S  cr
```

The stack

Because .EXE-style programs did not exist under CP/M, MS-DOS expects .EXE programs to operate in strictly MS-DOS fashion. For example, MS-DOS expects the .EXE program to supply its own stack. (Figure 4-1 shows the program's stack as the top box in the diagram.)

Microsoft's high-level-language compilers create a stack themselves, but when writing in assembly language the programmer must specifically declare one or more segments with the STACK *combine* type. If the programmer declares multiple stack segments, possibly in different source modules, the linker combines them into one large segment. *See* Controlling the .EXE Program's Structure below.

Many programmers declare their stack segments as preinitialized with some recognizable repeating string such as *STACK.* This makes it possible to examine the program's stack in memory (using a debugger such as DEBUG) to determine how much stack space the program actually used. On the other hand, if the stack is left as uninitialized memory and linked at the end of the .EXE program, it will not require space within the .EXE file. (The reason for this will become more apparent when we examine the structure of a .EXE file.)

Note: When multiple stack segments have been declared in different .ASM files, the Microsoft Object Linker (LINK) correctly allocates the total amount of stack space specified in all the source modules, but the initialization data from all modules is overlapped module by module at the high end of the combined segment.

An important difference between .COM and .EXE programs is that MS-DOS preinitializes a .COM program's stack with a termination address before transferring control to the program. MS-DOS does not do this for .EXE programs, so a .EXE program *cannot* simply execute an 8086-family RET instruction as a means of terminating.

Note: In the assembly-language files generated for a Microsoft C program or for programs in most other high-level-languages, the compiler's placement of a RET instruction at the end of the *main* function/subroutine/procedure might seem confusing. After all, MS-DOS does not place any return address on the stack. The compiler places the RET at the end of *main* because *main* does not receive control directly from MS-DOS. A library initialization routine receives control from MS-DOS; this routine then calls *main*. When *main* performs the RET, it returns control to a library termination routine, which then terminates back to MS-DOS in an approved manner.

Preallocated memory

While loading a .EXE program, MS-DOS performs several steps to determine the initial amount of memory to be allocated to the program. First, MS-DOS reads the two values the linker places near the start of the .EXE header: The first value, MINALLOC, indicates the minimum amount of extra memory the program requires to start executing; the second value, MAXALLOC, indicates the maximum amount of extra memory the program would like allocated before it starts executing. Next, MS-DOS locates the largest free block of memory available. If the size of the program's image within the .EXE file combined with the value specified for MINALLOC exceeds the memory block it found, MS-DOS returns an error to the process trying to load the program. If that process is COMMAND.COM, COMMAND.COM then displays a *Program too big to fit in memory* error message and terminates the user's execution request. If the block exceeds the program's MINALLOC requirement, MS-DOS then compares the memory block against the program's image combined with the MAXALLOC request. If the free block exceeds the maximum memory requested by the program, MS-DOS allocates only the maximum request; otherwise, it allocates the entire block. MS-DOS then builds a PSP at the start of this block and loads the program's image from the .EXE file into memory following the PSP.

This process ensures that the extra memory allocated to the program will immediately follow the program's image. The same will not necessarily be true for any memory MS-DOS allocates to the program as a result of MS-DOS function calls the program performs during its execution. Only function calls requesting MS-DOS to increase the initial allocation can guarantee additional contiguous memory. (Of course, the granting of such increase requests depends on the availability of free memory following the initial allocation.)

Programmers writing .EXE programs sometimes find the lack of keywords or compiler/ assembler switches that deal with MINALLOC (and possibly MAXALLOC) confusing. The programmer never explicitly specifies a MINALLOC value because LINK sets MINALLOC to the total size of all uninitialized data and/or stack segments linked at the very end of the program. The MINALLOC field allows the compiler to indicate the size of the initialized data fields in the load module without actually including the fields themselves, resulting in a smaller .EXE program file. For LINK to minimize the size of the .EXE file, the program must be coded and linked in such a way as to place all uninitialized data fields at the end of the program. Microsoft high-level-language compilers handle this automatically; assembly-language programmers must give LINK a little help.

Note: Beginning and even advanced assembly-language programmers can easily fall into an argument with the assembler over field addressing when attempting to place data fields after the code in the source file. This argument can be avoided if programmers use the SEGMENT and GROUP assembler directives. *See* Controlling the .EXE Program's Structure below.

No reliable method exists for the linker to determine the correct MAXALLOC value required by the .EXE program. Therefore, LINK uses a "safe" value of FFFFH, which causes MS-DOS to allocate all of the largest block of free memory — which is usually *all* free memory — to the program. Unless a program specifically releases the memory for which it has no use, it denies multitasking supervisor programs, such as IBM's TopView, any memory in which to execute additional programs — hence the rule that a well-behaved program releases unneeded memory during its initialization. Unfortunately, this memory conservation approach provides no help if a multitasking supervisor supports the ability to load several programs into memory without executing them. Therefore, programs that have correctly established MAXALLOC values actually are well-behaved programs.

To this end, newer versions of Microsoft LINK include the /CPARMAXALLOC switch to permit specification of the maximum amount of memory required by the program. The /CPARMAXALLOC switch can also be used to set MAXALLOC to a value that is known to be less than MINALLOC. For example, specifying a MAXALLOC value of 1 (/CP:1) forces MS-DOS to allocate only MINALLOC extra paragraphs to the program. In addition, Microsoft supplies a program called EXEMOD with most of its languages. This program permits modification of the MAXALLOC field in the headers of existing .EXE programs. *See* Modifying the .EXE File Header below.

The registers

Figure 4-1 gives a general indication of how MS-DOS sets the 8086-family registers before transferring control to a .EXE program. MS-DOS determines most of the original register values from information the linker places in the .EXE file header at the start of the .EXE file.

MS-DOS sets the SS register to the segment (paragraph) address of the start of any segments declared with the STACK *combine* type and sets the SP register to the offset from SS of the byte immediately after the combined stack segments. (If no stack segment is declared, MS-DOS sets SS:SP to CS:0000.) Because in the 8086-family architecture a stack grows from high to low memory addresses, this effectively sets SS:SP to point to the base of the stack. Therefore, if the programmer declares stack segments when writing an assembly-language program, the program will not need to initialize the SS and SP registers. Microsoft's high-level-language compilers handle the creation of stack segments automatically. In both cases, the linker determines the initial SS and SP values and places them in the header at the start of the .EXE program file.

Unlike its handling of the SS and SP registers, MS-DOS does *not* initialize the DS and ES registers to any data areas of the .EXE program. Instead, it points DS and ES to the start of the PSP. It does this for two primary reasons: First, MS-DOS uses the DS and ES registers to tell the program the address of the PSP; second, most programs start by examining the command tail within the PSP. Because the program starts without DS pointing to the data segments, the program must initialize DS and (optionally) ES to point to the data segments before it starts trying to access any fields in those segments. Unlike .COM programs, .EXE programs can do this easily because they can make direct references to segments, as follows:

```
MOV     AX,SEG DATA_SEGMENT_OR_GROUP_NAME
MOV     DS,AX
MOV     ES,AX
```

High-level-language programs need not initialize and maintain DS and ES; the compiler and library support routines do this.

In addition to pointing DS and ES to the PSP, MS-DOS also sets AH and AL to reflect the validity of the drive identifiers it placed in the two FCBs contained in the PSP. MS-DOS sets AL to 0FFH if the first FCB at PSP:005CH was initialized with a nonexistent drive identifier; otherwise, it sets AL to zero. Similarly, MS-DOS sets AH to reflect the drive identifier placed in the second FCB at PSP:006CH.

When MS-DOS analyzes the first two command-line parameters following the program name in order to build the first and second FCBs, it treats *any* character followed by a colon as a drive prefix. If the drive prefix consists of a lowercase letter (ASCII *a* through *z*), MS-DOS starts by converting the character to uppercase (ASCII *A* through *Z*). Then it subtracts 40H from the character, regardless of its original value. This converts the drive prefix letters A through Z to the drive codes 01H through 1AH, as required by the two FCBs. Finally, MS-DOS places the drive code in the appropriate FCB.

This process does not actually preclude invalid drive specifications from being placed in the FCBs. For instance, MS-DOS will accept the drive prefix !: and place a drive code of 0E1H in the FCB (! = 21H; 21H−40H = 0E1H). However, MS-DOS will then check the drive code to see if it represents an existing drive attached to the computer and will pass a value of 0FFH to the program in the appropriate register (AL or AH) if it does not.

As a side effect of this process, MS-DOS accepts @: as a valid drive prefix because the subtraction of 40H converts the @ character (40H) to 00H. MS-DOS accepts the 00H value as valid because a 00H drive code represents the current default drive. MS-DOS will leave the FCB's drive code set to 00H rather than translating it to the code for the default drive because the MS-DOS function calls that use FCBs accept the 00H code.

Finally, MS-DOS initializes the CS and IP registers, transferring control to the program's entry point. Programs developed using high-level-language compilers usually receive control at a library initialization routine. A programmer writing an assembly-language program using the Microsoft Macro Assembler (MASM) can declare any label within the program as the entry point by placing the label after the END statement as the last line of the program:

```
END     ENTRY_POINT_LABEL
```

With multiple source files, only one of the files should have a label following the END statement. If more than one source file has such a label, LINK uses the first one it encounters as the entry point.

The other processor registers (BX, CX, DX, BP, SI, and DI) contain unknown values when the program receives control from MS-DOS. Once again, high-level-language programmers can ignore this fact — the compiler and library support routines deal with the situation. However, assembly-language programmers should keep this fact in mind. It may give needed insight sometime in the future when a program functions at certain times and not at others.

In many cases, debuggers such as DEBUG and SYMDEB initialize uninitialized registers to some predictable but undocumented state. For instance, some debuggers may predictably set BP to zero before starting program execution. However, a program must not rely on such debugger actions, because MS-DOS makes no such promises. Situations like this could account for a program that fails when executed directly under MS-DOS but works fine when executed using a debugger.

Terminating the .EXE program

After MS-DOS has given the .EXE program control and it has completed whatever task it set out to perform, the program needs to give control back to MS-DOS. Because of MS-DOS's evolution, five methods of program termination have accumulated — not including the several ways MS-DOS allows programs to terminate but remain resident in memory.

Before using any of the termination methods supported by MS-DOS, the program should always close any files it had open, especially those to which data has been written or whose lengths were changed. Under versions 2.0 and later, MS-DOS closes any files opened using handles. However, good programming practice dictates that the program not rely on the operating system to close the program's files. In addition, programs written to use shared files under MS-DOS versions 3.0 and later should release any file locks before closing the files and terminating.

The Terminate Process with Return Code function

Of the five ways a program can terminate, only the Interrupt 21H Terminate Process with Return Code function (4CH) is recommended for programs running under MS-DOS version 2.0 or later. This method is one of the easiest approaches to terminating *any* program, regardless of its structure or segment register settings. The Terminate Process with Return Code function call simply consists of the following:

```
MOV     AH,4CH              ;load the MS-DOS function code
MOV     AL,RETURN_CODE      ;load the termination code
INT     21H                 ;call MS-DOS to terminate program
```

The example loads the AH register with the Terminate Process with Return Code function code. Then it loads the AL register with a return code. Normally, the return code represents the reason the program terminated or the result of any operation the program performed.

A program that executes another program as a child process can recover and analyze the child program's return code if the child process used this termination method. Likewise, the child process can recover the RETURN_CODE returned by any program it executes as a child process. When a program is terminated using this method and control returns to MS-DOS, a batch (.BAT) file can be used to test the terminated program's return code using the *IF ERRORLEVEL* statement.

Only two general conventions have been adopted for the value of RETURN_CODE: First, a RETURN_CODE value of 00H indicates a normal no-error termination of the program; second, increasing RETURN_CODE values indicate increasing severity of conditions under which the program terminated. For instance, a compiler could use the RETURN_CODE 00H if it found no errors in the source file, 01H if it found only warning errors, or 02H if it found severe errors.

If a program has no need to return any special RETURN_CODE values, then the following instructions will suffice to terminate the program with a RETURN_CODE of 00H:

```
MOV     AX,4C00H
INT     21H
```

Apart from being the approved termination method, Terminate Process with Return Code is easier to use with .EXE programs than any other termination method because all other methods require that the CS register point to the start of the PSP when the program terminates. This restriction causes problems for .EXE programs because they have code segments with segment addresses different from that of the PSP.

The only problem with Terminate Process with Return Code is that it is not available under MS-DOS versions earlier than 2.0, so it cannot be used if a program must be compatible with early MS-DOS versions. However, Figure 4-3 shows how a program can use the approved termination method when available but still remain pre-2.0 compatible. *See* The Warm Boot/Terminate Vector below.

```
TEXT      SEGMENT PARA PUBLIC 'CODE'

          ASSUME  CS:TEXT,DS:NOTHING,ES:NOTHING,SS:NOTHING

TERM_VECTOR     DD      ?

ENTRY_PROC      PROC    FAR

;save pointer to termination vector in PSP

          MOV     WORD PTR CS:TERM_VECTOR+0,0000h ;save offset of Warm Boot vector
          MOV     WORD PTR CS:TERM_VECTOR+2,DS    ;save segment address of PSP
```

Figure 4-3. Terminating properly under any MS-DOS version.   *(more)*

```
;***** Place main task here *****

;determine which MS-DOS version is active, take jump if 2.0 or later

        MOV     AH,30h          ;load Get MS-DOS Version Number function code
        INT     21h             ;call MS-DOS to get version number
        OR      AL,AL           ;see if pre-2.0 MS-DOS
        JNZ     TERM_0200       ;jump if 2.0 or later

;terminate under pre-2.0 MS-DOS

        JMP     CS:TERM_VECTOR  ;jump to Warm Boot vector in PSP

;terminate under MS-DOS 2.0 or later

TERM_0200:
        MOV     AX,4C00h        ;load MS-DOS termination function code
                                ;and return code
        INT     21h             ;call MS-DOS to terminate

ENTRY_PROC      ENDP

TEXT    ENDS

        END     ENTRY_PROC      ;define entry point
```

Figure 4-3. Continued.

The Terminate Program interrupt

Before MS-DOS version 2.0, terminating with an approved method meant executing an INT 20H instruction, the Terminate Program interrupt. The INT 20H instruction was replaced as the approved termination method for two primary reasons: First, it did not provide a means whereby programs could return a termination code; second, CS had to point to the PSP before the INT 20H instruction was executed.

The restriction placed on the value of CS at termination did not pose a problem for .COM programs because they execute with CS pointing to the beginning of the PSP. A .EXE program, on the other hand, executes with CS pointing to various code segments of the program, and the value of CS cannot be changed arbitrarily when the program is ready to terminate. Because of this, few .EXE programs attempt simply to execute a Terminate Program interrupt from directly within their own code segments. Instead, they usually use the termination method discussed next.

The Warm Boot/Terminate vector

The earlier discussion of the structure of the PSP briefly covered one older method a .EXE program can use to terminate: Offset 00H within the PSP contains an INT 20H instruction to which the program can jump in order to terminate. MS-DOS adopted this technique to support the many CP/M programs ported to MS-DOS. Under CP/M, this PSP location was referred to as the Warm Boot vector because the CP/M operating system was always reloaded from disk (rebooted) whenever a program terminated.

Because offset 00H in the PSP contains an INT 20H instruction, jumping to that location terminates a program in the same manner as an INT 20H included directly within the program, but with one important difference: By jumping to PSP:0000H, the program sets the CS register to point to the beginning of the PSP, thereby satisfying the only restriction imposed on executing the Terminate Program interrupt. The discussion of MS-DOS Function 4CH gave an example of how a .EXE program can terminate via PSP:0000H. The example first asks MS-DOS for its version number and then terminates via PSP:0000H only under versions of MS-DOS earlier than 2.0. Programs can also use PSP:0000H under MS-DOS versions 2.0 and later; the example uses Function 4CH simply because it is preferred under the later MS-DOS versions.

The RET instruction

The other popular method used by CP/M programs to terminate involved simply executing a RET instruction. This worked because CP/M pushed the address of the Warm Boot vector onto the stack before giving the program control. MS-DOS provides this support only for .COM-style programs; it does *not* push a termination address onto the stack before giving .EXE programs control.

The programmer who wants to use the RET instruction to return to MS-DOS can use the variation of the Figure 4-3 listing shown in Figure 4-4.

```
TEXT      SEGMENT PARA PUBLIC 'CODE'

          ASSUME  CS:TEXT,DS:NOTHING,ES:NOTHING,SS:NOTHING

ENTRY_PROC      PROC    FAR     ;make proc FAR so RET will be FAR

;Push pointer to termination vector in PSP
          PUSH    DS              ;push PSP's segment address
          XOR     AX,AX           ;ax = 0 = offset of Warm Boot vector in PSP
          PUSH    AX              ;push Warm Boot vector offset

;***** Place main task here *****

;Determine which MS-DOS version is active, take jump if 2.0 or later

          MOV     AH,30h          ;load Get MS-DOS Version Number function code
          INT     21h             ;call MS-DOS to get version number
          OR      AL,AL           ;see if pre-2.0 MS-DOS
          JNZ     TERM_0200       ;jump if 2.0 or later

;Terminate under pre-2.0 MS-DOS (this is a FAR proc, so RET will be FAR)
          RET                     ;pop PSP:00H into CS:IP to terminate
```

Figure 4-4. Using RET to return control to MS-DOS.   *(more)*

```
;Terminate under MS-DOS 2.0 or later
TERM_0200:
        MOV     AX,4C00h        ;AH = MS-DOS Terminate Process with Return Code
                                ;function code, AL = return code of 00H
        INT     21h             ;call MS-DOS to terminate

ENTRY_PROC      ENDP

TEXT    ENDS

        END     ENTRY_PROC      ;declare the program's entry point
```

Figure 4-4. Continued.

The Terminate Process function

The final method for terminating a .EXE program is Interrupt 21H Function 00H (Terminate Process). This method maintains the same restriction as all other older termination methods: CS must point to the PSP. Because of this restriction, .EXE programs typically avoid this method in favor of terminating via PSP:0000H, as discussed above for programs executing under versions of MS-DOS earlier than 2.0.

Terminating and staying resident

A .EXE program can use any of several additional termination methods to return control to MS-DOS but still remain resident within memory to service a special event. *See* PROGRAMMING IN THE MS-DOS ENVIRONMENT: Customizing ms-dos: Terminate-and-Stay-Resident Utilities.

Structure of the .EXE files

So far we've examined how the .EXE program looks in memory, how MS-DOS gives the program control of the computer, and how the program should return control to MS-DOS. Next we'll investigate what the program looks like as a disk file, before MS-DOS loads it into memory. Figure 4-5 shows the general structure of a .EXE file.

The file header

Unlike .COM program files, .EXE program files contain information that permits the .EXE program and MS-DOS to use the full capabilities of the 8086 family of microprocessors. The linker places all this extra information in a header at the start of the .EXE file. Although the .EXE file structure could easily accommodate a header as small as 32 bytes, the linker never creates a header smaller than 512 bytes. (This minimum header size corresponds to the standard record size preferred by MS-DOS.) The .EXE file header contains the following information, which MS-DOS reads into a temporary work area in memory for use while loading the .EXE program:

00–01H (.EXE Signature) MS-DOS does not rely on the extension (.EXE or .COM) to determine whether a file contains a .COM or a .EXE program. Instead, MS-DOS recognizes the file as a .EXE program if the first 2 bytes in the header contain the signature 4DH 5AH

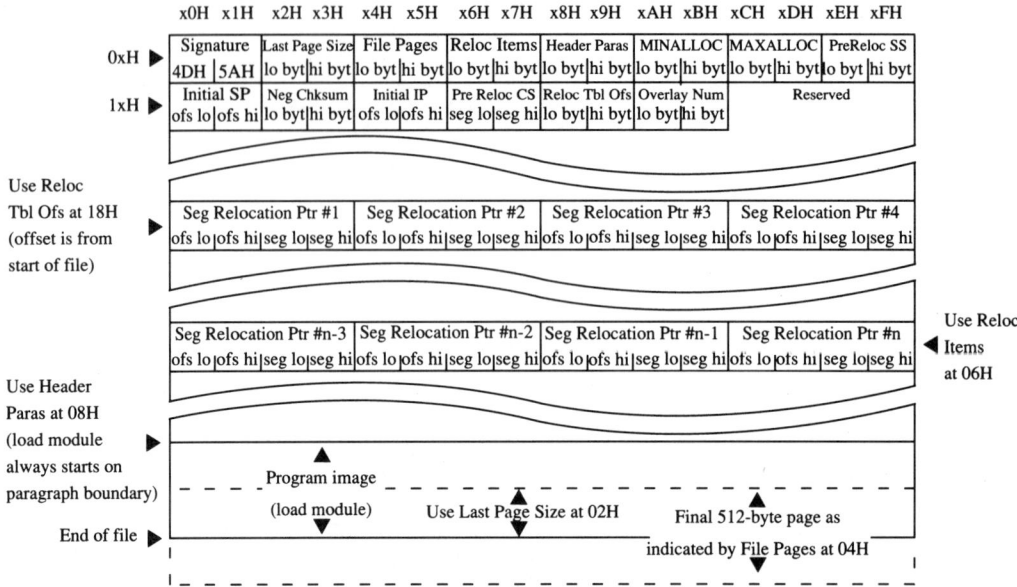

	x0H	x1H	x2H x3H	x4H x5H	x6H x7H	x8H x9H	xAH xBH	xCH xDH	xEH xFH
0xH ▶	Signature	Last Page Size	File Pages	Reloc Items	Header Paras	MINALLOC	MAXALLOC	PreReloc SS	
	4DH 5AH	lo byt hi byt	lo byt hi byt	lo byt hi byt	lo byt hi byt	lo byt hi byt	lo byt hi byt	lo byt hi byt	
1xH ▶	Initial SP	Neg Chksum	Initial IP	Pre Reloc CS	Reloc Tbl Ofs	Overlay Num	Reserved		
	ofs lo ofs hi	lo byt hi byt	ofs lo ofs hi	seg lo seg hi	lo byt hi byt	lo byt hi byt			

Use Reloc
Tbl Ofs at 18H
(offset is from ▶
start of file)

Seg Relocation Ptr #1	Seg Relocation Ptr #2	Seg Relocation Ptr #3	Seg Relocation Ptr #4
ofs lo ofs hi seg lo seg hi	ofs lo ofs hi seg lo seg hi	ofs lo ofs hi seg lo seg hi	ofs lo ofs hi seg lo seg hi

Seg Relocation Ptr #n-3	Seg Relocation Ptr #n-2	Seg Relocation Ptr #n-1	Seg Relocation Ptr #n
ofs lo ofs hi seg lo seg hi	ofs lo ofs hi seg lo seg hi	ofs lo ofs hi seg lo seg hi	ofs lo ofs hi seg lo seg hi

Use Reloc
◀ Items
at 06H

Use Header
Paras at 08H
(load module ▶
always starts on
paragraph boundary)

End of file ▶

▲
Program image
(load module) ▼   Use Last Page Size at 02H ▲ ▼   Final 512-byte page as
indicated by File Pages at 04H ▲ ▼

Figure 4-5. Structure of a .EXE file.

(ASCII characters *M* and *Z*). If either or both of the signature bytes contain other values, MS-DOS assumes the file contains a .COM program, regardless of the extension. The reverse is not necessarily true — that is, MS-DOS does not accept the file as a .EXE program simply because the file begins with a .EXE signature. The file must also pass several other tests.

02–03H (Last Page Size) The word at this location indicates the actual number of bytes in the final 512-byte page of the file. This word combines with the following word to determine the actual size of the file.

04–05H (File Pages) This word contains a count of the total number of 512-byte pages required to hold the file. If the file contains 1024 bytes, this word contains the value 0002H; if the file contains 1025 bytes, this word contains the value 0003H. The previous word (Last Page Size, 02–03H) is used to determine the number of valid bytes in the final 512-byte page. Thus, if the file contains 1024 bytes, the Last Page Size word contains 0000H because no bytes overflow into a final partly used page; if the file contains 1025 bytes, the Last Page Size word contains 0001H because the final page contains only a single valid byte (the 1025th byte).

06–07H (Relocation Items) This word gives the number of entries that exist in the relocation pointer table. *See* Relocation Pointer Table below.

08–09H (Header Paragraphs) This word gives the size of the .EXE file header in 16-byte paragraphs. It indicates the offset of the program's compiled/assembled and linked image (the load module) within the .EXE file. Subtracting this word from the two file-size words starting at 02H and 04H reveals the size of the program's image. The header always spans an even multiple of 16-byte paragraphs. For example, if the file consists of a 512-byte header and a 513-byte program image, then the file's total size is 1025 bytes. As discussed before, the Last Page Size word (02–03H) will contain 0001H and the File Pages word (04–05H) will contain 0003H. Because the header is 512 bytes, the Header Paragraphs word (08–09H) will contain 32 (0020H). (That is, 32 paragraphs times 16 bytes per paragraph totals 512 bytes.) By subtracting the 512 bytes of the header from the 1025-byte total file size, the size of the program's image can be determined — in this case, 513 bytes.

0A–0BH (MINALLOC) This word indicates the minimum number of 16-byte paragraphs the program requires to begin execution *in addition to* the memory required to hold the program's image. MINALLOC normally represents the total size of any uninitialized data and/or stack segments linked at the end of the program. LINK excludes the space reserved by these fields from the end of the .EXE file to avoid wasting disk space. If not enough memory remains to satisfy MINALLOC when loading the program, MS-DOS returns an error to the process trying to load the program. If the process is COMMAND.COM, COMMAND.COM then displays a *Program too big to fit in memory* error message. The EXEMOD utility can alter this field if desired. *See* Modifying the .EXE File Header below.

0C–0DH (MAXALLOC) This word indicates the maximum number of 16-byte paragraphs the program would like allocated to it before it begins execution. MAXALLOC indicates *additional* memory desired beyond that required to hold the program's image. MS-DOS uses this value to allocate MAXALLOC extra paragraphs, if available. If MAXALLOC paragraphs are not available, the program receives the largest memory block available — at least MINALLOC additional paragraphs. The programmer could use the MAXALLOC field to request that MS-DOS allocate space for use as a print buffer or as a program-maintained heap, for example.

Unless otherwise specified with the /CPARMAXALLOC switch at link time, the linker sets MAXALLOC to FFFFH. This causes MS-DOS to allocate all of the largest block of memory it has available to the program. To make the program compatible with multitasking supervisor programs, the programmer should use /CPARMAXALLOC to set the true maximum number of extra paragraphs the program desires. The EXEMOD utility can also be used to alter this field.

Note: If both MINALLOC and MAXALLOC have been set to 0000H, MS-DOS loads the program as high in memory as possible. LINK sets these fields to 0000H if the /HIGH switch was used; the EXEMOD utility can also be used to modify these fields.

0E–0FH (Initial SS Value) This word contains the paragraph address of the stack segment relative to the start of the load module. At load time, MS-DOS relocates this value by adding the program's start segment address to it, and the resulting value is placed in the SS register before giving the program control. (The start segment corresponds to the first segment boundary in memory following the PSP.)

10–11H (Initial SP Value) This word contains the absolute value that MS-DOS loads into the SP register before giving the program control. Because MS-DOS always loads programs starting on a segment address boundary, and because the linker knows the size of the stack segment, the linker is able to determine the correct SP offset at link time; therefore, MS-DOS does not need to adjust this value at load time. The EXEMOD utility can be used to alter this field.

12–13H (Complemented Checksum) This word contains the one's complement of the summation of all words in the .EXE file. Current versions of MS-DOS basically ignore this word when they load a .EXE program; however, future versions might not. When LINK generates a .EXE file, it adds together all the contents of the .EXE file (including the .EXE header) by treating the entire file as a long sequence of 16-bit words. During this addition, LINK gives the Complemented Checksum word (12–13H) a temporary value of 0000H. If the file consists of an odd number of bytes, then the final byte is treated as a word with a high byte of 00H. Once LINK has totaled all words in the .EXE file, it performs a one's complement operation on the total and records the answer in the .EXE file header at offsets 12–13H. The validity of a .EXE file can then be checked by performing the same word-totaling process as LINK performed. The total should be FFFFH, because the total will include LINK's calculated complemented checksum, which is designed to give the file the FFFFH total.

An example 7-byte .EXE file illustrates how .EXE file checksums are calculated. (This is a totally fictitious file, because .EXE headers are never smaller than 512 bytes.) If this fictitious file contained the bytes 8CH C8H 8EH D8H BAH 10H B4H, then the file's total would be calculated using C88CH+D88EH+10BAH+00B4H=1B288H. (Overflow past 16 bits is ignored, so the value is interpreted as B288H.) If this were a valid .EXE file, then the B288H total would have been FFFFH instead.

14–15H (Initial IP Value) This word contains the absolute value that MS-DOS loads into the IP register in order to transfer control to the program. Because MS-DOS always loads programs starting on a segment address boundary, the linker can calculate the correct IP offset from the initial CS register value at link time; therefore, MS-DOS does not need to adjust this value at load time.

16–17H (Pre-Relocated Initial CS Value) This word contains the initial value, relative to the start of the load module, that MS-DOS places in the CS register to give the .EXE program control. MS-DOS adjusts this value in the same manner as the initial SS value before loading it into the CS register.

18–19H (Relocation Table Offset) This word gives the offset from the start of the file to the relocation pointer table. This word must be used to locate the relocation pointer table, because variable-length information pertaining to program overlays can occur before the table, thus causing the position of the table to vary.

1A–1BH (Overlay Number) This word is normally set to 0000H, indicating that the .EXE file consists of the resident, or primary, part of the program. This number changes only in files containing programs that use overlays, which are sections of a program that remain on disk until the program actually requires them. These program sections are loaded into memory by special overlay managing routines included in the run-time libraries supplied with some Microsoft high-level-language compilers.

The preceding section of the header (00–1BH) is known as the formatted area. Optional information used by high-level-language overlay managers can follow this formatted area. Unless the program in the .EXE file incorporates such information, the relocation pointer table immediately follows the formatted header area.

Relocation Pointer Table The relocation pointer table consists of a list of pointers to words within the .EXE program image that MS-DOS must adjust before giving the program control. These words consist of references made by the program to the segments that make up the program. MS-DOS must adjust these segment address references when it loads the program, because it can load the program into memory starting at any segment address boundary.

Each pointer in the table consists of a doubleword. The first word contains an offset from the segment address given in the second word, which in turn indicates a segment address relative to the start of the load module. Together, these two words point to a third word within the load module that must have the start segment address added to it. (The start segment corresponds to the segment address at which MS-DOS started loading the program's

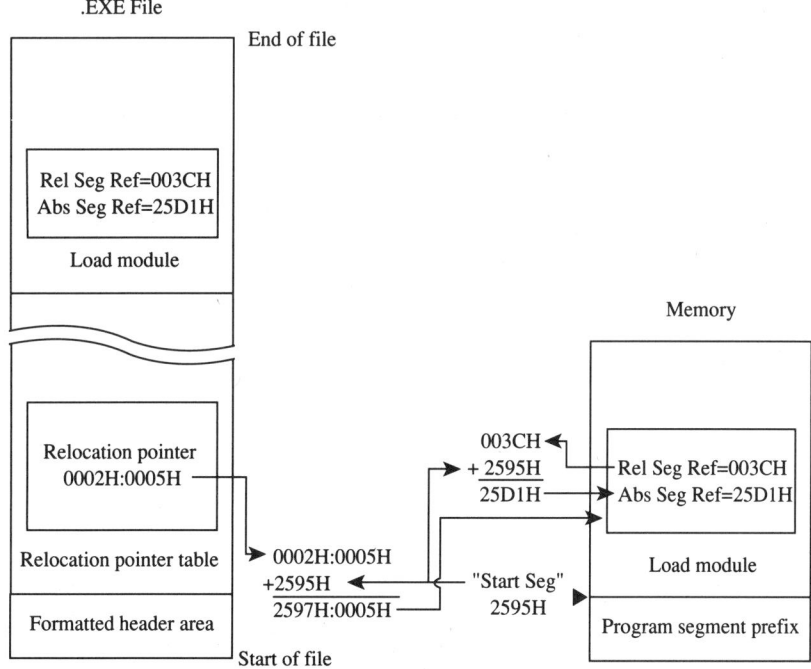

Figure 4-6. The .EXE file relocation procedure.

image, immediately following the PSP.) Figure 4-6 shows the entire procedure MS-DOS performs for each relocation table entry.

The load module

The load module starts where the .EXE header ends and consists of the fully linked image of the program. The load module appears within the .EXE file exactly as it would appear in memory if MS-DOS were to load it at segment address 0000H. The only changes MS-DOS makes to the load module involve relocating any direct segment references.

Although the .EXE file contains distinct segment images within the load module, it provides no information for separating those individual segments from one another. Existing versions of MS-DOS ignore how the program is segmented; they simply copy the load module into memory, relocate any direct segment references, and give the program control.

Loading the .EXE program

So far we've covered all the characteristics of the .EXE program as it resides in memory and on disk. We've also touched on all the steps MS-DOS performs while loading the .EXE program from disk and executing it. The following list recaps the .EXE program loading process in the order in which MS-DOS performs it:

1. MS-DOS reads the formatted area of the header (the first 1BH bytes) from the .EXE file into a work area.
2. MS-DOS determines the size of the largest available block of memory.
3. MS-DOS determines the size of the load module using the Last Page Size (offset 02H), File Pages (offset 04H), and Header Paragraphs (offset 08H) fields from the header. An example of this process is in the discussion of the Header Paragraphs field.
4. MS-DOS adds the MINALLOC field (offset 0AH) in the header to the calculated load-module size and the size of the PSP (100H bytes). If this total exceeds the size of the largest available block, MS-DOS terminates the load process and returns an error to the calling process. If the calling process was COMMAND.COM, COMMAND.COM then displays a *Program too big to fit in memory* error message.
5. MS-DOS adds the MAXALLOC field (offset 0CH) in the header to the calculated load-module size and the size of the PSP. If the memory block found earlier exceeds this calculated total, MS-DOS allocates the calculated memory size to the program from the memory block; if the calculated total exceeds the block's size, MS-DOS allocates the entire block.
6. If the MINALLOC and MAXALLOC fields both contain 0000H, MS-DOS uses the calculated load-module size to determine a start segment. MS-DOS calculates the start segment so that the load module will load into the high end of the allocated block. If either MINALLOC or MAXALLOC contains nonzero values (the normal case), MS-DOS establishes the start segment as the segment following the PSP.
7. MS-DOS loads the load module into memory starting at the start segment.

8. MS-DOS reads the relocation pointers into a work area and relocates the load module's direct segment references, as shown in Figure 4-6.

9. MS-DOS builds a PSP in the first 100H bytes of the allocated memory block. While building the two FCBs within the PSP, MS-DOS determines the initial values for the AL and AH registers.

10. MS-DOS sets the SS and SP registers to the values in the header after the start segment is added to the SS value.

11. MS-DOS sets the DS and ES registers to point to the beginning of the PSP.

12. MS-DOS transfers control to the .EXE program by setting CS and IP to the values in the header after adding the start segment to the CS value.

Controlling the .EXE program's structure

We've now covered almost every aspect of a completed .EXE program. Next, we'll discuss how to control the structure of the final .EXE program from the source level. We'll start by covering the statements provided by MASM that permit the programmer to define the structure of the program when programming in assembly language. Then we'll cover the five standard memory models provided by Microsoft's C and FORTRAN compilers (both version 4.0), which provide predefined structuring over which the programmer has limited control.

The MASM SEGMENT directive

MASM's SEGMENT directive and its associated ENDS directive mark the beginning and end of a program segment. Program segments contain collections of code or data that have offset addresses relative to the same common segment address.

In addition to the required segment name, the SEGMENT directive has three optional parameters:

segname SEGMENT [*align*] [*combine*] ['*class*']

With MASM, the contents of a segment can be defined at one point in the source file and the definition can be resumed as many times as necessary throughout the remainder of the file. When MASM encounters a SEGMENT directive with a *segname* it has previously encountered, it simply resumes the segment definition where it left off. This occurs regardless of the *combine* type specified in the SEGMENT directive — the *combine* type influences only the actions of the linker. *See* The *combine* Type Parameter below.

The *align* type parameter

The optional *align* parameter lets the programmer send the linker an instruction on how to align a segment within memory. In reality, the linker can align the segment only in relation to the start of the program's load module, but the result remains the same because MS-DOS always loads the module aligned on a paragraph (16-byte) boundary. (The PAGE *align* type creates a special exception, as discussed below.)

The following alignment types are permitted:

BYTE This *align* type instructs the linker to start the segment on the byte immediately following the previous segment. BYTE alignment prevents any wasted memory between the previous segment and the BYTE-aligned segment.

A minor disadvantage to BYTE alignment is that the 8086-family segment registers might not be able to directly address the start of the segment in all cases. Because they can address only on paragraph boundaries, the segment registers may have to point as many as 15 bytes behind the start of the segment. This means that the segment size should not be more than 15 bytes short of 64 KB. The linker adjusts offset and segment address references to compensate for differences between the physical segment start and the paragraph addressing boundary.

Another possible concern is execution speed on true 16-bit 8086-family microprocessors. When using non-8088 microprocessors, a program can actually run faster if the instructions and word data fields within segments are aligned on word boundaries. This permits the 16-bit processors to fetch full words in a single memory read, rather than having to perform two single-byte reads. The EVEN directive tells MASM to align instructions and data fields on word boundaries; however, MASM can establish this alignment only in relation to the start of the segment, so the entire segment must start aligned on a word or larger boundary to guarantee alignment of the items within the segment.

WORD This *align* type instructs the linker to start the segment on the next word boundary. Word boundaries occur every 2 bytes and consist of all even addresses (addresses in which the least significant bit contains a zero). WORD alignment permits alignment of data fields and instructions within the segment on word boundaries, as discussed for the BYTE alignment type. However, the linker may have to waste 1 byte of memory between the previous segment and the word-aligned segment in order to position the new segment on a word boundary.

Another minor disadvantage to WORD alignment is that the 8086-family segment registers might not be able to directly address the start of the segment in all cases. Because they can address only on paragraph boundaries, the segment registers may have to point as many as 14 bytes behind the start of the segment. This means that the segment size should not be more than 14 bytes short of 64 KB. The linker adjusts offset and segment address references to compensate for differences between the physical segment start and the paragraph addressing boundary.

PARA This *align* type instructs the linker to start the segment on the next paragraph boundary. The segments default to PARA if no alignment type is specified. Paragraph boundaries occur every 16 bytes and consist of all addresses with hexadecimal values ending in zero (0000H, 0010H, 0020H, and so forth). Paragraph alignment ensures that the segment begins on a segment register addressing boundary, thus making it possible to address a full 64 KB segment. Also, because paragraph addresses are even addresses, PARA alignment has the same advantages as WORD alignment. The only real disadvantage to PARA alignment is that the linker may have to waste as many as 15 bytes of memory between the previous segment and the paragraph-aligned segment.

PAGE This *align* type instructs the linker to start the segment on the next page boundary. Page boundaries occur every 256 bytes and consist of all addresses in which the low address byte equals zero (0000H, 0100H, 0200H, and so forth). PAGE alignment ensures only that the linker positions the segment on a page boundary relative to the start of the load module. Unfortunately, this does not also ensure alignment of the segment on an absolute page within memory, because MS-DOS only guarantees alignment of the entire load module on a paragraph boundary.

When a programmer declares pieces of a segment with the same name in different source modules, the *align* type specified for each segment piece influences the alignment of that specific piece of the segment. For example, assume the following two segment declarations appear in different source modules:

```
_DATA   SEGMENT PARA PUBLIC 'DATA'
        DB      '123'
_DATA   ENDS

_DATA   SEGMENT PARA PUBLIC 'DATA'
        DB      '456'
_DATA   ENDS
```

The linker starts by aligning the first segment piece located in the first object module on a paragraph boundary, as requested. When the linker encounters the second segment piece in the second object module, it aligns that piece on the first paragraph boundary following the first segment piece. This results in a 13-byte gap between the first segment piece and the second. The segment pieces must exist in separate source modules for this to occur. If the segment pieces exist in the same source module, MASM assumes that the second segment declaration is simply a resumption of the first and creates an object module with segment declarations equivalent to the following:

```
_DATA   SEGMENT PARA PUBLIC 'DATA'
        DB      '123'
        DB      '456'
_DATA   ENDS
```

The *combine* type parameter

The optional *combine* parameter allows the programmer to send directions to the linker on how to combine segments with the same *segname* occurring in different object modules. If no *combine* type is specified, the linker treats such segments as if each had a different *segname*. The *combine* type has no effect on the relationship of segments with different *segnames*. MASM and LINK both support the following *combine* types:

PUBLIC This *combine* type instructs the linker to concatenate multiple segments having the same *segname* into a single contiguous segment. The linker adjusts any address references to labels within the concatenated segments to reflect the new position of those labels relative to the start of the combined segment. This *combine* type is useful for accessing code or data in different source modules using a common segment register value.

STACK This *combine* type operates similarly to the PUBLIC *combine* type, except for two additional effects: The STACK type tells the linker that this segment comprises part of the program's stack and initialization data contained within STACK segments is handled differently than in PUBLIC segments. Declaring segments with the STACK *combine* type permits the linker to determine the initial SS and SP register values it places in the .EXE file header. Normally, a programmer would declare only one STACK segment in one of the source modules. If pieces of the stack are declared in different source modules, the linker will concatenate them in the same fashion as PUBLIC segments. However, initialization data declared within any STACK segment is placed at the high end of the combined STACK segments on a module-by-module basis. Thus, each successive module's initialization data overlays the previous module's data. At least one segment must be declared with the STACK *combine* type; otherwise, the linker will issue a warning message because it cannot determine the program's initial SS and SP values. (The warning can be ignored if the program itself initializes SS and SP.)

COMMON This *combine* type instructs the linker to overlap multiple segments having the same *segname*. The length of the resulting segment reflects the length of the longest segment declared. If any code or data is declared in the overlapping segments, the data contained in the final segments linked replaces any data in previously loaded segments. This *combine* type is useful when a data area is to be shared by code in different source modules.

MEMORY Microsoft's LINK treats this *combine* type the same as it treats the PUBLIC type. MASM, however, supports the MEMORY type for compatibility with other linkers that use Intel's definition of a MEMORY *combine* type.

AT address This *combine* type instructs LINK to pretend that the segment will reside at the absolute segment *address*. LINK then adjusts all address references to the segment in accordance with the masquerade. LINK will *not* create an image of the segment in the load module, and it will ignore any data defined within the segment. This behavior is consistent with the fact that MS-DOS does not support the loading of program segments into absolute memory segments. All programs must be able to execute from any segment address at which MS-DOS can find available memory. The SEGMENT AT address *combine* type is useful for creating templates of various areas in memory outside the program. For instance, *SEGMENT AT 0000H* could be used to create a template of the 8086-family interrupt vectors. Because data contained within SEGMENT AT address segments is suppressed by LINK and not by MASM (which places the data in the object module), it is possible to use .OBJ files generated by MASM with another linker that supports ROM or other absolute code generation should the programmer require this specialized capability.

The *class* type parameter

The *class* parameter provides the means to organize different segments into classifications. For instance, here are three source modules, each with its own separate code and data segments:

```
;Module "A"
A_DATA   SEGMENT PARA PUBLIC 'DATA'
;Module "A" data fields
A_DATA   ENDS
A_CODE   SEGMENT PARA PUBLIC 'CODE'
;Module "A" code
A_CODE   ENDS
         END
```

(more)

```
;Module "B"
B_DATA   SEGMENT PARA PUBLIC 'DATA'
;Module "B" data fields
B_DATA   ENDS
B_CODE   SEGMENT PARA PUBLIC 'CODE'
;Module "B" code
B_CODE   ENDS
         END

;Module "C"
C_DATA   SEGMENT PARA PUBLIC 'DATA'
;Module "C" data fields
C_DATA   ENDS
C_CODE   SEGMENT PARA PUBLIC 'CODE'
;Module "C" code
C_CODE   ENDS
         END
```

If the 'CODE' and 'DATA' *class* types are removed from the SEGMENT directives shown above, the linker organizes the segments as it encounters them. If the programmer specifies the modules to the linker in alphabetic order, the linker produces the following segment ordering:

```
         A_DATA
         A_CODE
         B_DATA
         B_CODE
         C_DATA
         C_CODE
```

However, if the programmer specifies the *class* types shown in the sample source modules, the linker organizes the segments by classification as follows:

```
'DATA' class:    A_DATA
                 B_DATA
                 C_DATA

'CODE' class:    A_CODE
                 B_CODE
                 C_CODE
```

Notice that the linker still organizes the classifications in the order in which it encounters the segments belonging to the various classifications. To completely control the order in which the linker organizes the segments, the programmer must use one of three basic approaches. The preferred method involves using the /DOSSEG switch with the linker. This produces the segment ordering shown in Figure 4-1. The second method involves creating a special source module that contains empty SEGMENT–ENDS blocks for all the segments declared in the various other source modules. The programmer creates the list in the order the segments are to be arranged in memory and then specifies the .OBJ file for this module as the first file for the linker to process. This procedure establishes the order of all the segments before LINK begins processing the other program modules, so the programmer can declare segments in these other modules in any convenient order. For instance, the following source module rearranges the result of the previous example so that the linker places the 'CODE' class before the 'DATA' class:

```
A_CODE   SEGMENT PARA PUBLIC 'CODE'
A_CODE   ENDS
B_CODE   SEGMENT PARA PUBLIC 'CODE'
B_CODE   ENDS
C_CODE   SEGMENT PARA PUBLIC 'CODE'
C_CODE   ENDS

A_DATA   SEGMENT PARA PUBLIC 'DATA'
A_DATA   ENDS
B_DATA   SEGMENT PARA PUBLIC 'DATA'
B_DATA   ENDS
C_DATA   SEGMENT PARA PUBLIC 'DATA'
C_DATA   ENDS

         END
```

Rather than creating a new module, the third method places the same segment ordering list shown above at the start of the first module containing actual code or data that the programmer will be specifying for the linker. This duplicates the approach used by Microsoft's newer compilers, such as C version 4.0.

The ordering of segments within the load module has no direct effect on the linker's adjustment of address references to locations within the various segments. Only the GROUP directive and the SEGMENT directive's *combine* parameter affect address adjustments performed by the linker. *See* The MASM GROUP Directive below.

Note: Certain older versions of the IBM Macro Assembler wrote segments to the object file in alphabetic order regardless of their order in the source file. These older versions can limit efforts to control segment ordering. Upgrading to a new version of the assembler is the best solution to this problem.

Ordering segments to shrink the .EXE file

Correct segment ordering can significantly decrease the size of a .EXE program as it resides on disk. This size-reduction ordering is achieved by placing all uninitialized data fields in their own segments and then controlling the linker's ordering of the program's segments so that the uninitialized data field segments all reside at the end of the program. When the program modules are assembled, MASM places information in the object modules to tell the linker about initialized and uninitialized areas of all segments. The linker then uses this information to prevent the writing of uninitialized data areas that occur at the end of the program image as part of the resulting .EXE file. To account for the memory space required by these fields, the linker also sets the MINALLOC field in the .EXE file header to represent the data area not written to the file. MS-DOS then uses the MINALLOC field to reallocate this missing space when loading the program.

The MASM GROUP directive

The MASM GROUP directive can also have a strong impact on a .EXE program. However, the GROUP directive has *no* effect on the arrangement of program segments within memory. Rather, GROUP associates program segments for addressing purposes.

The GROUP directive has the following syntax:

grpname GROUP *segname,segname,segname,…*

This directive causes the linker to adjust all address references to labels within any specified *segname* to be relative to the start of the declared group. The start of the group is determined at link time. The group starts with whichever of the segments in the GROUP list the linker places lowest in memory.

That the GROUP directive neither causes nor requires contiguous arrangement of the grouped segments creates some interesting, although not necessarily desirable, possibilities. For instance, it permits the programmer to locate segments not belonging to the declared group between segments that do belong to the group. The only restriction imposed on the declared group is that the last byte of the last segment in the group must occur within 64 KB of the start of the group. Figure 4-7 illustrates this type of segment arrangement:

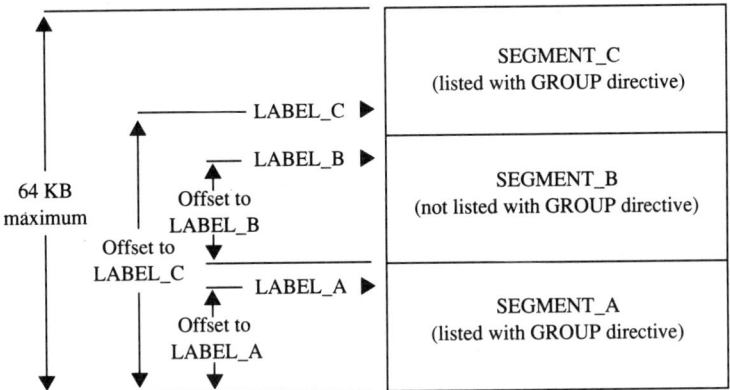

Figure 4-7. Noncontiguous segments in the same GROUP.

Warning: One of the most confusing aspects of the GROUP directive relates to MASM's OFFSET operator. The GROUP directive affects only the offset addresses generated by such direct addressing instructions as

```
MOV     AX,FIELD_LABEL
```

but it has no effect on immediate address values generated by such instructions as

```
MOV     AX,OFFSET FIELD_LABEL
```

Using the OFFSET operator on labels contained within grouped segments requires the following approach:

```
MOV     AX,OFFSET GROUP_NAME:FIELD_LABEL
```

The programmer must *explicitly* request the offset from the group base, because MASM defines the result of the OFFSET operator to be the offset of the label from the start of its segment, not its group.

Structuring a small program with SEGMENT and GROUP

Now that we have analyzed the functions performed by the SEGMENT and GROUP directives, we'll put both directives to work structuring a skeleton program. The program, shown in Figures 4-8, 4-9, and 4-10, consists of three source modules (MODULE_A, MODULE_B, and MODULE_C), each using the following four program segments:

Segment	Definition
_TEXT	The code or program text segment
_DATA	The standard data segment containing preinitialized data fields the program might change
CONST	The constant data segment containing constant data fields the program will not change
_BSS	The "block storage segment/space" segment containing uninitialized data fields*

* Programmers familiar with the IBM 1620/1630 or CDC 6000 and Cyber assemblers may recognize BSS as "block started at symbol," which reflects an equally appropriate, although somewhat more elaborate, definition of the abbreviation. Other common translations of BSS, such as "blank static storage," misrepresent the segment name, because blanking of BSS segments does not occur — the memory contains undetermined values when the program begins execution.

```
;Source Module MODULE_A

;Predeclare all segments to force the linker's segment ordering **************

_TEXT   SEGMENT BYTE PUBLIC 'CODE'
_TEXT   ENDS

_DATA   SEGMENT WORD PUBLIC 'DATA'
_DATA   ENDS

CONST   SEGMENT WORD PUBLIC 'CONST'
CONST   ENDS

_BSS    SEGMENT WORD PUBLIC 'BSS'
_BSS    ENDS
```

Figure 4-8. Structuring a .EXE program: MODULE_A.   (more)

```
STACK    SEGMENT PARA STACK 'STACK'
STACK    ENDS

DGROUP   GROUP    _DATA,CONST,_BSS,STACK


;Constant declarations ***************************************************

CONST    SEGMENT WORD PUBLIC 'CONST'

CONST_FIELD_A    DB       'Constant A'    ;declare a MODULE_A constant

CONST    ENDS


;Preinitialized data fields *********************************************

_DATA    SEGMENT WORD PUBLIC 'DATA'

DATA_FIELD_A     DB       'Data A'        ;declare a MODULE_A preinitialized field

_DATA    ENDS


;Uninitialized data fields **********************************************

_BSS     SEGMENT WORD PUBLIC 'BSS'

BSS_FIELD_A      DB       5 DUP(?)        ;declare a MODULE_A uninitialized field

_BSS     ENDS


;Program text ***********************************************************

_TEXT    SEGMENT BYTE PUBLIC 'CODE'

         ASSUME  CS:_TEXT,DS:DGROUP,ES:NOTHING,SS:NOTHING

         EXTRN   PROC_B:NEAR            ;label is in _TEXT segment (NEAR)
         EXTRN   PROC_C:NEAR            ;label is in _TEXT segment (NEAR)

PROC_A PROC      NEAR

         CALL    PROC_B                 ;call into MODULE_B
         CALL    PROC_C                 ;call into MODULE_C

         MOV     AX,4C00H               ;terminate (MS-DOS 2.0 or later only)
         INT     21H

PROC_A ENDP

_TEXT    ENDS
```

Figure 4-8. Continued.   *(more)*

```
;Stack ************************************************************************

STACK   SEGMENT PARA STACK 'STACK'

        DW        128 DUP(?)                ;declare some space to use as stack
STACK_BASE        LABEL   WORD

STACK   ENDS

        END       PROC_A                    ;declare PROC_A as entry point
```

Figure 4-8. Continued.

```
;Source Module MODULE_B

;Constant declarations ******************************************************

CONST   SEGMENT WORD PUBLIC 'CONST'

CONST_FIELD_B   DB        'Constant B'    ;declare a MODULE_B constant

CONST   ENDS


;Preinitialized data fields *************************************************

_DATA   SEGMENT WORD PUBLIC 'DATA'

DATA_FIELD_B    DB        'Data B'        ;declare a MODULE_B preinitialized field

_DATA   ENDS


;Uninitialized data fields **************************************************

_BSS    SEGMENT WORD PUBLIC 'BSS'

BSS_FIELD_B     DB        5 DUP(?)        ;declare a MODULE_B uninitialized field

_BSS    ENDS


;Program text ***************************************************************

DGROUP  GROUP   _DATA,CONST,_BSS

_TEXT   SEGMENT BYTE PUBLIC 'CODE'

        ASSUME  CS:_TEXT,DS:DGROUP,ES:NOTHING,SS:NOTHING
```

Figure 4-9. Structuring a .EXE program: MODULE_B.   *(more)*

```
        PUBLIC  PROC_B                      ;reference in MODULE_A
PROC_B  PROC    NEAR

        RET

PROC_B  ENDP

_TEXT   ENDS

        END
```

Figure 4-9. Continued.


```
;Source Module MODULE_C

;Constant declarations ********************************************************

CONST   SEGMENT WORD PUBLIC 'CONST'

CONST_FIELD_C   DB      'Constant C'    ;declare a MODULE_C constant

CONST   ENDS


;Preinitialized data fields **************************************************

_DATA   SEGMENT WORD PUBLIC 'DATA'

DATA_FIELD_C    DB      'Data C'        ;declare a MODULE_C preinitialized field

_DATA   ENDS


;Uninitialized data fields ***************************************************

_BSS    SEGMENT WORD PUBLIC 'BSS'

BSS_FIELD_C     DB      5 DUP(?)        ;declare a MODULE_C uninitialized field

_BSS    ENDS


;Program text ****************************************************************

DGROUP  GROUP   _DATA,CONST,_BSS

_TEXT   SEGMENT BYTE PUBLIC 'CODE'

        ASSUME  CS:_TEXT,DS:DGROUP,ES:NOTHING,SS:NOTHING
```

Figure 4-10. Structuring a .EXE program: MODULE_C.   *(more)*

```
            PUBLIC  PROC_C                          ;referenced in MODULE_A
PROC_C  PROC    NEAR

        RET

PROC_C  ENDP

_TEXT   ENDS

        END
```

Figure 4-10. Continued.

This example creates a small memory model program image, so the linked program can have only a single code segment and a single data segment — the simplest standard form of a .EXE program. *See* Using Microsoft's Contemporary Memory Models below.

In addition to declaring the four segments already discussed, MODULE_ A declares a STACK segment in which to define a block of memory for use as the program's stack and also defines the linking order of the five segments. Defining the linking order leaves the programmer free to declare the segments in any order when defining the segment contents — a necessity because the assembler has difficulty assembling programs that use forward references.

With Microsoft's MASM and LINK on the same disk with the .ASM files, the following commands can be made into a batch file:

```
MASM STRUCA;
MASM STRUCB;
MASM STRUCC;
LINK STRUCA+STRUCB+STRUCC/M;
```

These commands will assemble and link all the .ASM files listed, producing the memory map report file STRUCA.MAP shown in Figure 4-11.

```
Start   Stop    Length  Name            Class
00000H  0000CH  0000DH  _TEXT           CODE
0000EH  0001FH  00012H  _DATA           DATA
00020H  0003DH  0001EH  CONST           CONST
0003EH  0004EH  00011H  _BSS            BSS
00050H  0014FH  00100H  STACK           STACK


Origin    Group
0000:0    DGROUP


 Address            Publics by Name

0000:000B       PROC_B
0000:000C       PROC_C
```

Figure 4-11. Structuring a .EXE program: memory map report.

(more)

```
Address           Publics by Value

0000:000B         PROC_B
0000:000C         PROC_C
Program entry point at 0000:0000
```

Figure 4-11. Continued.

The above memory map report represents the memory diagram shown in Figure 4-12.

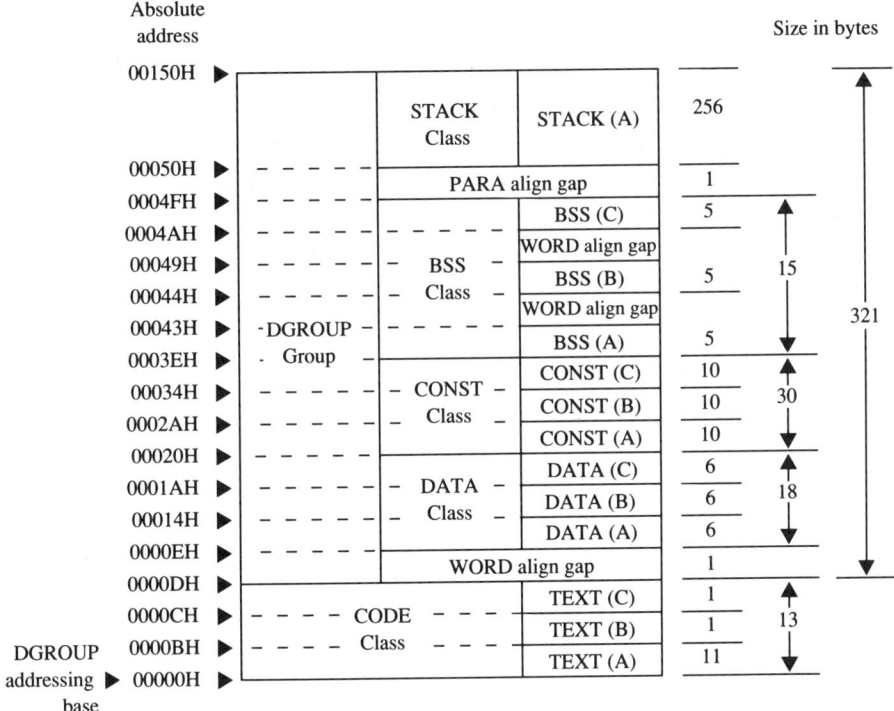

Figure 4-12. Structure of the sample .EXE program.

Using Microsoft's contemporary memory models

Now that we've analyzed the various aspects of designing assembly-language .EXE programs, we can look at how Microsoft's high-level-language compilers create .EXE programs from high-level-language source files. Even assembly-language programmers will find this discussion of interest and should seriously consider using the five standard memory models outlined here.

This discussion is based on the Microsoft C Compiler version 4.0, which, along with the Microsoft FORTRAN Compiler version 4.0, incorporates the most contemporary code generator currently available. These newer compilers generate code based on three to five of the following standard programmer-selectable program structures, referred to as memory models. The discussion of each of these memory models will center on the model's use with the Microsoft C Compiler and will close with comments regarding any differences for the Microsoft FORTRAN Compiler.

Small (C compiler switch /AS) This model, the default, includes only a single code segment and a single data segment. All code must fit within 64 KB, and all data must fit within an additional 64 KB. Most C program designs fall into this category. Data can exceed the 64 KB limit only if the far and huge attributes are used, forcing the compiler to use far addressing, and the linker to place far and huge data items into separate segments. The data-size-threshold switch described for the compact model is ignored by the Microsoft C Compiler when used with a small model. The C compiler uses the default segment name _TEXT for all code and the default segment name _DATA for all non-far/huge data. Microsoft FORTRAN programs can generate a semblance of this model only by using the /NM (name module) and /AM (medium model) compiler switches in combination with the near attribute on all subprogram declarations.

Medium (C and FORTRAN compiler switch /AM) This model includes only a single data segment but breaks the code into multiple code segments. All data must fit within 64 KB, but the 64 KB restriction on code size applies only on a module-by-module basis. Data can exceed the 64 KB limit only if the far and huge attributes are used, forcing the compiler to use far addressing, and the linker to place far and huge data items into separate segments. The data-size-threshold switch described for the compact model is ignored by the Microsoft C Compiler when used with a medium model. The compiler uses the default segment name _DATA for all non-far/huge data and the template *module*_TEXT to create names for all code segments. The *module* element of *module*_TEXT indicates where the compiler is to substitute the name of the source module. For example, if the source module HELPFUNC.C is compiled using the medium model, the compiler creates the code segment HELPFUNC_TEXT. The Microsoft FORTRAN Compiler version 4.0 directly supports the medium model.

Compact (C compiler switch /AC) This model includes only a single code segment but breaks the data into multiple data segments. All code must fit within 64 KB, but the data is allowed to consume all the remaining available memory. The Microsoft C Compiler's optional data-size-threshold switch (/Gt) controls the placement of the larger data items into additional data segments, leaving the smaller items in the default segment for faster access. Individual data items within the program cannot exceed 64 KB under the compact model without being explicitly declared huge. The compiler uses the default segment name _TEXT for all code segments and the template *module*#_DATA to create names for all data segments. The *module* element indicates where the compiler is to substitute the source module's name; the # element represents a digit that the compiler changes for each additional data segment required to hold the module's data. The compiler starts with the digit 5 and counts up. For example, if the name of the source module is HELPFUNC.C, the compiler names the first data segment HELPFUNC5_DATA. FORTRAN programs can generate a semblance of this model only by using the /NM (name module) and /AL (large model) compiler switches in combination with the near attribute on all subprogram declarations.

Large (C and FORTRAN compiler switch /AL) This model creates multiple code and data segments. The compiler treats data in the same manner as it does for the compact model and treats code in the same manner as it does for the medium model. The Microsoft FORTRAN Compiler version 4.0 directly supports the large model.

Huge (C and FORTRAN compiler switch /AH) Allocation of segments under the huge model follows the same rules as for the large model. The difference is that individual data items can exceed 64 KB. Under the huge model, the compiler generates the necessary code to index arrays or adjust pointers across segment boundaries, effectively transforming the microprocessor's segment-addressed memory into linear-addressed memory. This makes the huge model especially useful for porting a program originally written for a processor that used linear addressing. The speed penalties the program pays in exchange for this addressing freedom require serious consideration. If the program actually contains any data structures exceeding 64 KB, it probably contains only a few. In that case, it is best to avoid using the huge model by explicitly declaring those few data items as huge using the huge keyword within the source module. This prevents penalizing all the non-huge items with extra addressing math. The Microsoft FORTRAN Compiler version 4.0 directly supports the huge model.

Figure 4-13 shows an example of the segment arrangement created by a large/huge model program. The example assumes two source modules: MSCA.C and MSCB.C. Each source module specifies enough data to cause the compiler to create two extra data segments for that module. The diagram does not show all the various segments that occur as a result of linking with the run-time library or as a result of compiling with the intention of using the CodeView debugger.

Groups	Classes	Segments	
DGROUP	STACK	STACK	◀ SMCLH: Program stack
	BSS	c_common	◀ SM: All uninitialized global items, CLH: Empty
		_BSS	◀ SMCLH: All uninitialized non-far/huge items
	CONST	CONST	◀ SMCLH: Constants (floating point constraints, segment addresses, etc.)
	DATA	_DATA	◀ SMCLH: All items that don't end up anywhere else
	FAR_BSS	FAR_BSS	◀ SM: Nonexistent, CLH: All uninitialized global items
	FAR_DATA	MSCB6_DATA	◀ From MSCB only: SM: Far/huge items, CLH: Items larger than threshold
		MSCB5_DATA	◀ From MSCB only: SM: Far/huge items, CLH: Items larger than threshold
		MSCA6_DATA	◀ From MSCA only: SM: Far/huge items, CLH: Items larger than threshold
		MSCA5_DATA	◀ From MSCA only: SM: Far/huge items, CLH: Items larger than threshold
	CODE	TEXT	◀ SC: All code, MLH: Run-time library code only
		MSCB_TEXT	◀ SC: Nonexistent, MLH: MSCB.C Code
		MSCA_TEXT	◀ SC: Nonexistent, MLH: MSCA.C Code

S = Small model   L = Large model
M = Medium model   H = Huge model
C = Compact model

Figure 4-13. General structure of a Microsoft C program.

Note that if the program declares an extremely large number of small data items, it can exceed the 64 KB size limit on the default data segment (_DATA) regardless of the memory model specified. This occurs because the data items all fall below the data-size-threshold limit (compiler /Gt switch), causing the compiler to place them in the _DATA segment. Lowering the data size threshold or explicitly using the far attribute within the source modules eliminates this problem.

Modifying the .EXE file header

With most of its language compilers, Microsoft supplies a utility program called EXEMOD. *See* PROGRAMMING UTILITIES: EXEMOD. This utility allows the programmer to display and modify certain fields contained within the .EXE file header. Following are the header fields EXEMOD can modify (based on EXEMOD version 4.0):

MAXALLOC This field can be modified by using EXEMOD's /MAX switch. Because EXEMOD operates on .EXE files that have already been linked, the /MAX switch can be used to modify the MAXALLOC field in existing .EXE programs that contain the default MAXALLOC value of FFFFH, provided the programs do not rely on MS-DOS's allocating all free memory to them. EXEMOD's /MAX switch functions in an identical manner to LINK's /CPARMAXALLOC switch.

MINALLOC This field can be modified by using EXEMOD's /MIN switch. Unlike the case with the MAXALLOC field, most programs do not have an arbitrary value for MINALLOC. MINALLOC normally represents uninitialized memory and stack space the linker has compressed out of the .EXE file, so a programmer should never *reduce* the MINALLOC value within a .EXE program written by someone else. If a program requires some minimum amount of extra dynamic memory in addition to any static fields, MINALLOC can be increased to ensure that the program will have this extra memory before receiving control. If this is done, the program will not have to verify that MS-DOS allocated enough memory to meet program needs. Of course, the same result can be achieved without EXEMOD by declaring this minimum extra memory as an uninitialized field at the end of the program.

Initial SP Value This field can be modified by using the /STACK switch to increase or decrease the size of a program's stack. However, modifying the initial SP value for programs developed using Microsoft language compiler versions earlier than the following may cause the programs to fail: C version 3.0, Pascal version 3.3, and FORTRAN version 3.3. Other language compilers may have the same restriction. The /STACK switch can also be used with programs developed using MASM, provided the stack space is linked at the end of the program, but it would probably be wise to change the size of the STACK segment declaration within the program instead. The linker also provides a /STACK switch that performs the same purpose.

Note: With the /H switch set, EXEMOD displays the current values of the fields within the .EXE header. This switch should not be used with the other switches. EXEMOD also displays field values if no switches are used.

Warning: EXEMOD also functions correctly when used with packed .EXE files created using EXEPACK or the /EXEPACK linker switch. However, it is important to use the EXEMOD version shipped with the linker or EXEPACK utility. Possible future changes in the packing method may result in incompatibilities between EXEMOD and nonassociated linker/EXEPACK versions.

Patching the .EXE program using DEBUG

Every experienced programmer knows that programs always seem to have at least one unspotted error. If a program has been distributed to other users, the programmer will probably need to provide those users with corrections when such bugs come to light. One inexpensive updating approach used by many large companies consists of mailing out single-page instructions explaining how the user can patch the program to correct the problem.

Program patching usually involves loading the program file into the DEBUG utility supplied with MS-DOS, storing new bytes into the program image, and then saving the program file back to disk. Unfortunately, DEBUG cannot load a .EXE program into memory and then save it back to disk in .EXE format. The programmer must trick DEBUG into patching .EXE program files, using the procedure outlined below. *See* PROGRAMMING UTILITIES: DEBUG.

Note: Users should be reminded to make backup copies of their program before attempting the patching procedure.

1. Rename the .EXE file using a filename extension that does not have special meaning for DEBUG. (Avoid .EXE, .COM, and .HEX.) For instance, MYPROG.BIN serves well as a temporary new name for MYPROG.EXE because DEBUG does not recognize a file with a .BIN extension as anything special. DEBUG will load the entire image of MYPROG.BIN, including the .EXE header and relocation table, into memory starting at offset 100H within a .COM-style program segment (as discussed previously).

2. Locate the area within the load module section of the .EXE file image that requires patching. The previous discussion of the .EXE file image, together with compiler/ assembler listings and linker memory map reports, provides the information necessary to locate the error within the .EXE file image. DEBUG loads the file image starting at offset 100H within a .COM-style program segment, so the programmer must compensate for this offset when calculating addresses within the file image. Also, the compiler listings and linker memory map reports provide addresses relative to the start of the program image within the .EXE file, not relative to the start of the file itself. Therefore, the programmer must first check the information contained in the .EXE file header to determine where the load module (the program's image) starts within the file.

3. Use DEBUG's E (Enter Data) or A (Assemble Machine Instructions) command to insert the corrections. (Normally, patch instructions to users would simply give an address at which the user should apply the patch. The user need not know how to determine the address.)

4. After the patch has been applied, simply issue the DEBUG W (Write File or Sectors) command to write the corrected image back to disk under the same filename, provided the patch has not increased the size of the program. If program size has

increased, first change the appropriate size fields in the .EXE header at the start of the file and use the DEBUG R (Display or Modify Registers) command to modify the BX and CX registers so that they contain the file image's new size. Then use the W command to write the image back to disk under the same name.

5. Use the DEBUG Q (Quit) command to return to MS-DOS command level, and then rename the file to the original .EXE filename extension.

.EXE summary

To summarize, the .EXE program and file structures provide considerable flexibility in the design of programs, providing the programmer with the necessary freedom to produce large-scale applications. Programs written using Microsoft's high-level-language compilers have access to five standardized program structure models (small, medium, compact, large, and huge). These standardized models are excellent examples of ways to structure assembly-language programs.

The .COM Program

The majority of differences between .COM and .EXE programs exist because .COM program files are not prefaced by header information. Therefore, .COM programs do not benefit from the features the .EXE header provides.

The absence of a header leaves MS-DOS with no way of knowing how much memory the .COM program requires in addition to the size of the program's image. Therefore, MS-DOS must always allocate the largest free block of memory to the .COM program, regardless of the program's true memory requirements. As was discussed for .EXE programs, this allocation of the largest block of free memory usually results in MS-DOS's allocating all remaining free memory—an action that can cause problems for multitasking supervisor programs.

The .EXE program header also includes the direct segment address relocation pointer table. Because they lack this table, .COM programs cannot make address references to the labels specified in SEGMENT directives, with the exception of SEGMENT AT address directives. If a .COM program did make these references, MS-DOS would have no way of adjusting the addresses to correspond to the actual segment address into which MS-DOS loaded the program. *See* Creating the .COM Program below.

The .COM program structure exists primarily to support the vast number of CP/M programs ported to MS-DOS. Currently, .COM programs are most often used to avoid adding the 512 bytes or more of .EXE header information onto small, simple programs that often do not exceed 512 bytes by themselves.

The .COM program structure has another advantage: Its memory organization places the PSP within the same address segment as the rest of the program. Thus, it is easier to access fields within the PSP in .COM programs.

Giving control to the .COM program

After allocating the largest block of free memory to the .COM program, MS-DOS builds a PSP in the lowest 100H bytes of the block. No difference exists between the PSP MS-DOS builds for .COM programs and the PSP it builds for .EXE programs. Also with .EXE programs, MS-DOS determines the initial values for the AL and AH registers at this time and then loads the entire .COM-file image into memory immediately following the PSP. Because .COM files have no file-size header fields, MS-DOS relies on the size recorded in the disk directory to determine the size of the program image. It loads the program exactly as it appears in the file, without checking the file's contents.

MS-DOS then sets the DS, ES, and SS segment registers to point to the start of the PSP. If able to allocate at least 64 KB to the program, MS-DOS sets the SP register to offset FFFFH + 1 (0000H) to establish an initial stack; if less than 64 KB are available for allocation to the program, MS-DOS sets the SP to 1 byte past the highest offset owned by the program. In either case, MS-DOS then pushes a single word of 0000H onto the program's stack for use in terminating the program.

Finally, MS-DOS transfers control to the program by setting the CS register to the PSP's segment address and the IP register to 0100H. This means that the program's entry point must exist at the very start of the program's image, as shown in later examples.

Figure 4-14 shows the overall structure of a .COM program as it receives control from MS-DOS.

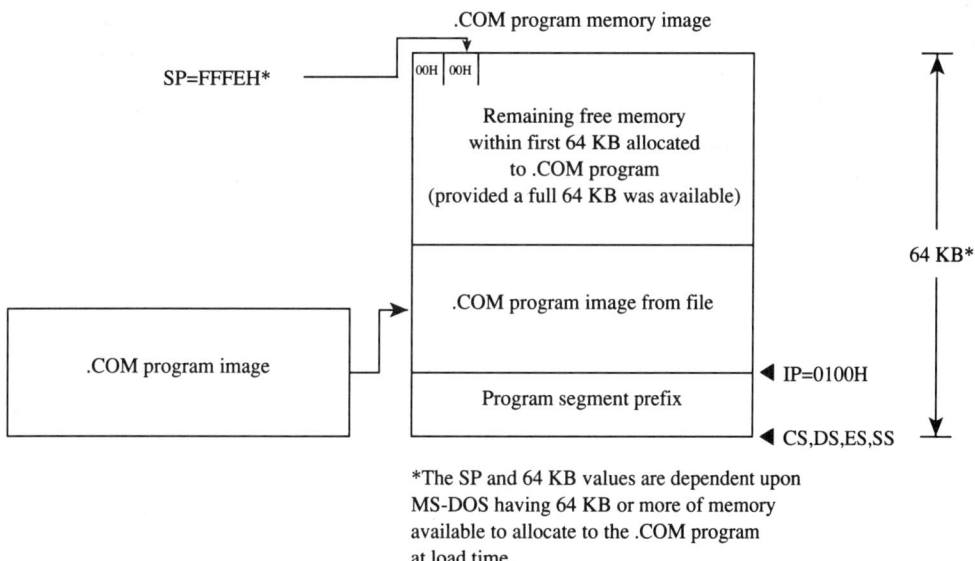

Figure 4-14. The .COM program: memory map diagram with register pointers.

Terminating the .COM program

A .COM program can use all the termination methods described for .EXE programs but should still use the MS-DOS Interrupt 21H Terminate Process with Return Code function (4CH) as the preferred method. If the .COM program must remain compatible with versions of MS-DOS earlier than 2.0, it can easily use any of the older termination methods, including those described as difficult to use from .EXE programs, because .COM programs execute with the CS register pointing to the PSP as required by these methods.

Creating the .COM program

A .COM program is created in the same manner as a .EXE program and then converted using the MS-DOS EXE2BIN utility. *See* PROGRAMMING UTILITIES: EXE2BIN.

Certain restrictions do apply to .COM programs, however. First, .COM programs cannot exceed 64 KB minus 100H bytes for the PSP minus 2 bytes for the zero word initially pushed on the stack.

Next, only a single segment—or at least a single addressing group—should exist within the program. The following two examples show ways to structure a .COM program to satisfy both this restriction and MASM's need to have data fields precede program code in the source file.

COMPROG1.ASM (Figure 4-15) declares only a single segment (*COMSEG*), so no special considerations apply when using the MASM OFFSET operator. *See* The MASM GROUP Directive above. COMPROG2.ASM (Figure 4-16) declares separate code (*CSEG*) and data (*DSEG*) segments, which the GROUP directive ties into a common addressing block. Thus, the programmer can declare data fields at the start of the source file and have the linker place the data fields segment (*DSEG*) after the code segment (*CSEG*) when it links the program, as discussed for the .EXE program structure. This second example simulates the program structuring provided under CP/M by Microsoft's old Macro-80 (M80) macro assembler and Link-80 (L80) linker. The design also expands easily to accommodate COMMON or other additional segments.

```
COMSEG   SEGMENT BYTE PUBLIC 'CODE'
         ASSUME  CS:COMSEG,DS:COMSEG,ES:COMSEG,SS:COMSEG
         ORG     0100H

BEGIN:
         JMP     START            ;skip over data fields
;Place your data fields here.

START:
;Place your program text here.
         MOV     AX,4C00H          ;terminate (MS-DOS 2.0 or later only)
         INT     21H
COMSEG   ENDS
         END     BEGIN
```

Figure 4-15. .COM program with data at start.

```
CSEG    SEGMENT BYTE PUBLIC 'CODE'        ;establish segment order
CSEG    ENDS
DSEG    SEGMENT BYTE PUBLIC 'DATA'
DSEG    ENDS
COMGRP  GROUP   CSEG,DSEG                 ;establish joint address base
DSEG    SEGMENT
;Place your data fields here.
DSEG    ENDS
CSEG    SEGMENT

        ASSUME  CS:COMGRP,DS:COMGRP,ES:COMGRP,SS:COMGRP
        ORG     0100H

BEGIN:
;Place your program text here.  Remember to use
;OFFSET COMGRP:LABEL whenever you use OFFSET.
        MOV     AX,4C00H                  ;terminate (MS-DOS 2.0 or later only)
        INT     21H
CSEG    ENDS
        END     BEGIN
```

Figure 4-16. .COM program with data at end.

These examples demonstrate other significant requirements for producing a functioning .COM program. For instance, the *ORG 0100H* statement in both examples tells MASM to start assembling the code at offset 100H within the encompassing segment. This corresponds to MS-DOS's transferring control to the program at IP = 0100H. In addition, the entry-point label (BEGIN) immediately follows the ORG statement and appears again as a parameter to the END statement. Together, these factors satisfy the requirement that .COM programs declare their entry point at offset 100H. If any factor is missing, the MS-DOS EXE2BIN utility will not properly convert the .EXE file produced by the linker into a .COM file. Specifically, if a .COM program declares an entry point (as a parameter to the END statement) that is at neither offset 0100H nor offset 0000H, EXE2BIN rejects the .EXE file when the programmer attempts to convert it. If the program fails to declare an entry point or declares an entry point at offset 0000H, EXE2BIN assumes that the .EXE file is to be converted to a binary image rather than to a .COM image. When EXE2BIN converts a .EXE file to a non-.COM binary file, it does not strip the extra 100H bytes the linker places in front of the code as a result of the *ORG 0100H* instruction. Thus, the program actually begins at offset 200H when MS-DOS loads it into memory, but all the program's address references will have been assembled and linked based on the 100H offset. As a result, the program — and probably the rest of the system as well — is likely to crash.

A .COM program also must not contain direct segment address references to any segments that make up the program. Thus, the .COM program cannot reference any segment labels or reference any labels as long (FAR) pointers. (This rule does not prevent the program from referencing segment labels declared using the SEGMENT AT address directive.) Following are various examples of direct segment address references that are *not* permitted as part of .COM programs:

```
PROC_A   PROC     FAR
PROC_A   ENDP
         CALL     PROC_A              ;intersegment call
         JMP      PROC_A              ;intersegment jump
```

or

```
         EXTRN    PROC_A:FAR
         CALL     PROC_A              ;intersegment call
         JMP      PROC_A              ;intersegment jump
```

or

```
         MOV      AX,SEG SEG_A    ;segment address
         DD       LABEL_A         ;segment:offset pointer
```

Finally, .COM programs must not declare any segments with the STACK *combine* type. If a program declares a segment with the STACK *combine* type, the linker will insert initial SS and SP values into the .EXE file header, causing EXE2BIN to reject the .EXE file. A .COM program does not have explicitly declared stacks, although it can reserve space in a non-STACK *combine* type segment to which it can initialize the SP register *after* it receives control. The absence of a stack segment will cause the linker to issue a harmless warning message.

When the program is assembled and linked into a .EXE file, it must be converted into a binary file with a .COM extension by using the EXE2BIN utility as shown in the following example for the file YOURPROG.EXE:

```
C>EXE2BIN YOURPROG YOURPROG.COM  <Enter>
```

It is not necessary to delete or rename a .EXE file with the same filename as the .COM file before trying to execute the .COM file as long as both remain in the same directory, because MS-DOS's order of execution is .COM files first, then .EXE files, and finally .BAT files. However, the safest practice is to delete a .EXE file immediately after converting it to a .COM file in case the .COM file is later renamed or moved to a different directory. If a .EXE file designed for conversion to a .COM file is executed by accident, it is likely to crash the system.

Patching the .COM program using DEBUG

As discussed for .EXE files, a programmer who distributes software to users will probably want to send instructions on how to patch in error corrections. This approach to software updates lends itself even better to .COM files than it does to .EXE files.

For example, because .COM files contain only the code image, they need not be renamed in order to read and write them using DEBUG. The user need only be instructed on how to load the .COM file into DEBUG, how to patch the program, and how to write the patched image back to disk. Calculating the addresses and patch values is even easier, because no header exists in the .COM file image to cause complications. With the preceding exceptions, the details for patching .COM programs remain the same as previously outlined for .EXE programs.

.COM summary

To summarize, the .COM program and file structures are a simpler but more restricted approach to writing programs than the .EXE structure because the programmer has only a single memory model from which to choose (the .COM program segment model). Also, .COM program files do not contain the 512-byte (or more) header inherent to .EXE files, so the .COM program structure is well suited to small programs for which adding 512 bytes of header would probably at least double the file's size.

Summary of Differences

The following table summarizes the differences between .COM and .EXE programs.

	.COM program	.EXE program
Maximum size	65536 bytes minus 256 bytes for PSP and 2 bytes for stack	No limit
Entry point	PSP:0100H	Defined by END statement
CS at entry	PSP	Segment containing program's entry point
IP at entry	0100H	Offset of entry point within its segment
DS at entry	PSP	PSP
ES at entry	PSP	PSP
SS at entry	PSP	Segment with STACK attribute
SP at entry	FFFEH or top word in available memory, whichever is lower	End of segment defined with STACK attribute
Stack at entry	Zero word	Initialized or uninitialized, depending on source
Stack size	65536 bytes minus 256 bytes for PSP and size of executable code and data	Defined in segment with STACK attribute
Subroutine calls	NEAR	NEAR or FAR
Exit method	Interrupt 21H Function 4CH preferred; NEAR RET if MS-DOS versions 1.x	Interrupt 21H Function 4CH preferred; indirect jump to PSP:0000H if MS-DOS versions 1.x
Size of file	Exact size of program	Size of program plus header (at least 512 extra bytes)

Which format the programmer uses for an application usually depends on the program's intended size, but the decision can also be influenced by a program's need to address multiple memory segments. Normally, small utility programs (such as CHKDSK and FORMAT) are designed as .COM programs; large programs (such as the Microsoft C Compiler) are designed as .EXE programs. The ultimate decision is, of course, the programmer's.

Keith Burgoyne

Article 5:
Character Device Input and Output

All functional computer systems are composed of a central processing unit (CPU), some memory, and peripheral devices that the CPU can use to store data or communicate with the outside world. In MS-DOS systems, the essential peripheral devices are the keyboard (for input), the display (for output), and one or more disk drives (for nonvolatile storage). Additional devices such as printers, modems, and pointing devices extend the function-ality of the computer or offer alternative methods of using the system.

MS-DOS recognizes two types of devices: block devices, which are usually floppy-disk or fixed-disk drives; and character devices, such as the keyboard, display, printer, and com-munications ports.

The distinction between block and character devices is not always readily apparent, but in general, block devices transfer information in chunks, or blocks, and character devices move data one character (usually 1 byte) at a time. MS-DOS identifies each block device by a drive letter assigned when the device's controlling software, the device driver, is loaded. A character device, on the other hand, is identified by a logical name (similar to a filename and subject to many of the same restrictions) built into its device driver. *See* PROGRAM-MING IN THE MS-DOS ENVIRONMENT: CUSTOMIZING MS-DOS: Installable Device Drivers.

Background Information

Versions 1.x of MS-DOS, first released for the IBM PC in 1981, supported peripheral devices with a fixed set of device drivers loaded during system initialization from the hidden file IO.SYS (or IBMBIO.COM with PC-DOS). These versions of MS-DOS offered application programs a high degree of input/output device independence by allowing character devices to be treated like files, but they did not provide an easy way to augment the built-in set of drivers if the user wished to add a third-party peripheral device to the system.

With the release of MS-DOS version 2.0, the hardware flexibility of the system was tremen-dously enhanced. Versions 2.0 and later support installable device drivers that can reside in separate files on the disk and can be linked into the operating system simply by adding a DEVICE directive to the CONFIG.SYS file on the startup disk. *See* USER COMMANDS: CONFIG.SYS: DEVICE. A well-defined interface between installable drivers and the MS-DOS kernel allows such drivers to be written for most types of peripheral devices without the need for modification to the operating system itself.

The CONFIG.SYS file can contain a number of different DEVICE commands to load sepa-rate drivers for pointing devices, magnetic-tape drives, network interfaces, and so on. Each driver, in turn, is specialized for the hardware characteristics of the device it supports.

When the system is turned on or restarted, the installable device drivers are added to the chain, or linked list, of default device drivers loaded from IO.SYS during MS-DOS initialization. Thus, the need for the system's default set of device drivers to support a wide range of optional device types and features at an excessive cost of system memory is avoided.

One important distinction between block and character devices is that MS-DOS always adds new block-device drivers to the tail of the driver chain but adds new character-device drivers to the head of the chain. Thus, because MS-DOS searches the chain sequentially and uses the first driver it finds that satisfies its search conditions, any existing character-device driver can be superseded by simply installing another driver with an identical logical device name.

This article covers some of the details of working with MS-DOS character devices: displaying text, keyboard input, and other basic character I/O functions; the definition and use of standard input and output; redirection of the default character devices; and the use of the IOCTL function (Interrupt 21H Function 44H) to communicate directly with a character-device driver. Much of the information presented in this article is applicable only to MS-DOS versions 2.0 and later.

Accessing Character Devices

Application programs can use either of two basic techniques to access character devices in a portable manner under MS-DOS. First, a program can use the handle-type function calls that were added to MS-DOS in version 2.0. Alternatively, a program can use the so-called "traditional" character-device functions that were present in versions 1.x and have been retained in the operating system for compatibility. Because the handle functions are more powerful and flexible, they are discussed first.

A handle is a 16-bit number returned by the operating system whenever a file or device is opened or created by passing a name to MS-DOS Interrupt 21H Function 3CH (Create File with Handle), 3DH (Open File with Handle), 5AH (Create Temporary File), or 5BH (Create New File). After a handle is obtained, it can be used with Interrupt 21H Function 3FH (Read File or Device) or Function 40H (Write File or Device) to transfer data between the computer's memory and the file or device.

During an open or create function call, MS-DOS searches the device-driver chain sequentially for a character device with the specified name (the extension is ignored) before searching the disk directory. Thus, a file with the same name as any character device in the driver chain — for example, the file NUL.TXT — cannot be created, nor can an existing file be accessed if a device in the chain has the same name.

The second method for accessing character devices is through the traditional MS-DOS character input and output functions, Interrupt 21H Functions 01H through 0CH. These functions are designed to communicate directly with the keyboard, display, printer, and serial port. Each of these devices has its own function or group of functions, so neither names nor handles need be used. However, in MS-DOS versions 2.0 and later, these function calls are translated within MS-DOS to make use of the same routines that are used by the handle functions, so the traditional keyboard and display functions are affected by I/O redirection and piping.

Use of either the traditional or the handle-based method for character device I/O results in highly portable programs that can be used on any computer that runs MS-DOS. A third, less portable access method is to use the hardware-specific routines resident in the read-only memory (ROM) of a specific computer (such as the IBM PC ROM BIOS driver functions), and a fourth, definitely nonportable approach is to manipulate the peripheral device's adapter directly, bypassing the system software altogether. Although these latter hardware-dependent methods cannot be recommended, they are admittedly sometimes necessary for performance reasons.

The Basic MS-DOS Character Devices

Every MS-DOS system supports at least the following set of logical character devices without the need for any additional installable drivers:

Device	Meaning
CON	Keyboard and display
PRN	System list device, usually a parallel port
AUX	Auxiliary device, usually a serial port
CLOCK$	System real-time clock
NUL	"Bit-bucket" device

These devices can be opened by name or they can be addressed through the "traditional" function calls; strings can be read from or written to the devices according to their capabilities on any MS-DOS system. Data written to the NUL device is discarded; reads from the NUL device always return an end-of-file condition.

PC-DOS and compatible implementations of MS-DOS typically also support the following logical character-device names:

Device	Meaning
COM1	First serial communications port
COM2	Second serial communications port
LPT1	First parallel printer port
LPT2	Second parallel printer port
LPT3	Third parallel printer port

In such systems, PRN is an alias for LPT1 and AUX is an alias for COM1. The MODE command can be used to redirect an LPT device to another device. *See* USER COMMANDS: MODE.

As previously mentioned, any of these default character-device drivers can be superseded by a user-installed device driver — for example, one that offers enhanced functionality or changes the device's apparent characteristics. One frequently used alternative character-device driver is ANSI.SYS, which replaces the standard MS-DOS CON device driver and allows ANSI escape sequences to be used to perform tasks such as clearing the screen, controlling the cursor position, and selecting character attributes. *See* USER COMMANDS: ANSI.SYS.

The standard devices

Under MS-DOS versions 2.0 and later, each program owns five previously opened handles for character devices (referred to as the standard devices) when it begins executing. These handles can be used for input and output operations without further preliminaries. The five standard devices and their associated handles are

Standard Device Name	Handle	Default Assignment
Standard input (*stdin*)	0	CON
Standard output (*stdout*)	1	CON
Standard error (*stderr*)	2	CON
Standard auxiliary (*stdaux*)	3	AUX
Standard printer (*stdprn*)	4	PRN

The standard input and standard output handles are especially important because they are subject to I/O redirection. Although these handles are associated by default with the CON device so that read and write operations are implemented using the keyboard and video display, the user can associate the handles with other character devices or with files by using redirection parameters in a program's command line:

Redirection	Result
< *file*	Causes read operations from standard input to obtain data from *file*.
> *file*	Causes data written to standard output to be placed in *file*.
>> *file*	Causes data written to standard output to be appended to *file*.
p1 ¦ *p2*	Causes data written to standard output by program *p1* to appear as the standard input of program *p2*.

This ability to redirect I/O adds great flexibility and power to the system. For example, programs ordinarily controlled by keyboard entries can be run with "scripts" from files, the output of a program can be captured in a file or on a printer for later inspection, and general-purpose programs (filters) can be written that process text streams without regard to the text's origin or destination. *See* PROGRAMMING IN THE MS-DOS ENVIRONMENT: CUSTOMIZING MS-DOS: Writing MS-DOS Filters.

Ordinarily, an application program is not aware that its input or output has been redirected, although a write operation to standard output will fail unexpectedly if standard output was redirected to a disk file and the disk is full. An application can check for the existence of I/O redirection with an IOCTL (Interrupt 21H Function 44H) call, but it cannot obtain any information about the destination of the redirected handle except whether it is associated with a character device or with a file.

Raw versus cooked mode

MS-DOS associates each handle for a character device with a mode that determines how I/O requests directed to that handle are treated. When a handle is in raw mode, characters are passed between the application program and the device driver without any filtering or buffering by MS-DOS. When a handle is in cooked mode, MS-DOS buffers any data that is read from or written to the device and takes special actions when certain characters are detected.

During cooked mode input, MS-DOS obtains characters from the device driver one at a time, checking each character for a Control-C. The characters are assembled into a string within an internal MS-DOS buffer. The input operation is terminated when a carriage return (0DH) or an end-of-file mark (1AH) is received or when the number of characters requested by the application have been accumulated. If the source is standard input, lone linefeed characters are translated to carriage-return/linefeed pairs. The string is then copied from the internal MS-DOS buffer to the application program's buffer, and control returns to the application program.

During cooked mode output, MS-DOS transfers the characters in the application program's output buffer to the device driver one at a time, checking after each character for a Control-C pending at the keyboard. If the destination is standard output and standard output has not been redirected, tabs are expanded to spaces using eight-column tab stops. Output is terminated when the requested number of characters have been written or when an end-of-file mark (1AH) is encountered in the output string.

In contrast, during raw mode input or output, data is transferred directly between the application program's buffer and the device driver. Special characters such as carriage return and the end-of-file mark are ignored, and the exact number of characters in the application program's request are always read or written. MS-DOS does not break the strings into single-character calls to the device driver and does not check the keyboard buffer for Control-C entries during the I/O operation. Finally, characters read from standard input in raw mode are not echoed to standard output.

As might be expected from the preceding description, raw mode input or output is usually much faster than cooked mode input or output, because each character is not being individually processed by the MS-DOS kernel. Raw mode also allows programs to read characters from the keyboard buffer that would otherwise be trapped by MS-DOS (for example, Control-C, Control-P, and Control-S). (If BREAK is on, MS-DOS will still check for Control-C entries during other function calls, such as disk operations, and transfer control to the Control-C exception handler if a Control-C is detected.) A program can use the MS-DOS IOCTL Get and Set Device Data services (Interrupt 21H Function 44H Subfunctions 00H and 01H) to set the mode for a character-device handle. *See* IOCTL below.

Ordinarily, raw or cooked mode is strictly an attribute of a specific handle that was obtained from a previous open operation and affects only the I/O operations requested by the program that owns the handle. However, when a program uses IOCTL to select raw or cooked mode for one of the standard device handles, the selection has a global effect on the behavior of the system because those handles are never closed. Thus, some of the "traditional" keyboard input functions might behave in unexpected ways. Consequently, programs that change the mode on a standard device handle should save the handle's mode at entry and restore it before performing a final exit to MS-DOS, so that the operation of COMMAND.COM and other applications will not be disturbed. Such programs should also incorporate custom critical error and Control-C exception handlers so that the programs cannot be terminated unexpectedly. *See* PROGRAMMING IN THE MS-DOS ENVIRONMENT: Customizing ms-dos: Exception Handlers.

The keyboard

Among the MS-DOS Interrupt 21H functions are two methods of checking for and receiving input from the keyboard: the traditional method, which uses MS-DOS character input Functions 01H, 06H, 07H, 08H, 0AH, 0BH, and 0CH (Table 5-1); and the handle method, which uses Function 3FH. Each of these methods has its own advantages and disadvantages. *See* SYSTEM CALLS.

Table 5-1. Traditional MS-DOS Character Input Functions.

Function	Name	Read Multiple Characters	Echo	Ctrl-C Check
01H	Character Input with Echo	No	Yes	Yes
06H	Direct Console I/O	No	No	No
07H	Unfiltered Character Input Without Echo	No	No	No
08H	Character Input Without Echo	No	No	Yes
0AH	Buffered Keyboard Input	Yes	Yes	Yes
0BH	Check Keyboard Status	No	No	Yes
0CH	Flush Buffer, Read Keyboard	*	*	*

* Varies depending on function (from above) called in the AL register.

The first four traditional keyboard input calls are really very similar. They all return a character in the AL register; they differ mainly in whether they echo that character to the display and whether they are sensitive to interruption by the user's entry of a Control-C. Both Functions 06H and 0BH can be used to test keyboard status (that is, whether a key has been pressed and is waiting to be read by the program); Function 0BH is simpler to use, but Function 06H is immune to Control-C entries.

Function 0AH is used to read a "buffered line" from the user, meaning that an entire line is accepted by MS-DOS before control returns to the program. The line is terminated when the user presses the Enter key or when the maximum number of characters (to 255) specified by the program have been received. While entry of the line is in progress, the usual editing keys (such as the left and right arrow keys and the function keys on IBM PCs and compatibles) are active; only the final, edited line is delivered to the requesting program.

Function 0CH allows a program to flush the type-ahead buffer before accepting input. This capability is important for occasions when a prompt must be displayed unexpectedly (such as when a critical error occurs) and the user could not have typed ahead a valid response. This function should also be used when the user is being prompted for a critical decision (such as whether to erase a file), to prevent a character that was previously pressed by accident from triggering an irrecoverable operation. Function 0CH is unusual in that it is called with the number of one of the other keyboard input functions in register AL. After any pending input has been discarded, Function 0CH simply transfers to the other specified input function; thus, its other parameters (if any) depend on the function that ultimately will be executed.

The primary disadvantage of the traditional function calls is that they handle redirected input poorly. If standard input has been redirected to a file, no way exists for a program calling the traditional input functions to detect that the end of the file has been reached — the input function will simply wait forever, and the system will appear to hang.

A program that wishes to use handle-based I/O to get input from the keyboard must use the MS-DOS Read File or Device service, Interrupt 21H Function 3FH. Ordinarily, the program can employ the predefined handle for standard input (0), which does not need to be opened and which allows the program's input to be redirected by the user to another file or device. If the program needs to circumvent redirection and ensure that its input is from the keyboard, it can open the CON device with Interrupt 21H Function 3DH and use the handle obtained from that open operation instead of the standard input handle.

A program using the handle functions to read the keyboard can control the echoing of characters and sensitivity to Control-C entries by selecting raw or cooked mode with the IOCTL Get and Set Device Data services (default = cooked mode). To test the keyboard status, the program can either issue an IOCTL Check Input Status call (Interrupt 21H Function 44H Subfunction 06H) or use the traditional Check Keyboard Status call (Interrupt 21H Function 0BH).

The primary advantages of the handle method for keyboard input are its symmetry with file operations and its graceful handling of redirected input. The handle function also allows strings as long as 65535 bytes to be requested; the traditional Buffered Keyboard Input function allows a maximum of 255 characters to be read at a time. This consideration is important for programs that are frequently used with redirected input and output (such as filters), because reading and writing larger blocks of data from files results in more efficient operation. The only real disadvantage to the handle method is that it is limited to MS-DOS versions 2.0 and later (although this is no longer a significant restriction).

Role of the ROM BIOS

When a key is pressed on the keyboard of an IBM PC or compatible, it generates a hardware interrupt (09H) that is serviced by a routine in the ROM BIOS. The ROM BIOS interrupt handler reads I/O ports assigned to the keyboard controller and translates the key's scan code into an ASCII character code. The result of this translation depends on the current state of the NumLock and CapsLock toggles, as well as on whether the Shift, Control, or Alt key is being held down. (The ROM BIOS maintains a keyboard flags byte at address 0000:0417H that gives the current status of each of these modifier keys.)

After translation, both the scan code and the ASCII code are placed in the ROM BIOS's 32-byte (16-character) keyboard input buffer. In the case of "extended" keys such as the function keys or arrow keys, the ASCII code is a zero byte and the scan code carries all the information. The keyboard buffer is arranged as a circular, or ring, buffer and is managed as a first-in/first-out queue. Because of the method used to determine when the buffer is empty, one position in the buffer is always wasted; the maximum number of characters that can be held in the buffer is therefore 15. Keys pressed when the buffer is full are discarded and a warning beep is sounded.

The ROM BIOS provides an additional module, invoked by software Interrupt 16H, that allows programs to test keyboard status, determine whether characters are waiting in the type-ahead buffer, and remove characters from the buffer. *See* Appendix O: IBM PC BIOS Calls. Its use by application programs should ordinarily be avoided, however, to prevent introducing unnecessary hardware dependence.

On IBM PCs and compatibles, the keyboard input portion of the CON driver in the BIOS is a simple sequence of code that calls ROM BIOS Interrupt 16H to do the hardware-dependent work. Thus, calls to MS-DOS for keyboard input by an application program are subject to two layers of translation: The Interrupt 21H function call is converted by the MS-DOS kernel to calls to the CON driver, which in turn remaps the request onto a ROM BIOS call that obtains the character.

Keyboard programming examples

Example: Use the ROM BIOS keyboard driver to read a character from the keyboard. The character is not echoed to the display.

```
        mov     ah,00h          ; subfunction 00H = read character
        int     16h             ; transfer to ROM BIOS
                                ; now AH = scan code, AL = character
```

Example: Use the MS-DOS traditional keyboard input function to read a character from the keyboard. The character is not echoed to the display. The input can be interrupted with a Ctrl-C keystroke.

```
        mov     ah,08h          ; function 08H = character input
                                ;    without echo
        int     21h             ; transfer to MS-DOS
                                ; now AL = character
```

Example: Use the MS-DOS traditional Buffered Keyboard Input function to read an entire line from the keyboard, specifying a maximum line length of 80 characters. All editing keys are active during entry, and the input is echoed to the display.

```
kbuf    db      80              ; maximum length of read
        db      0               ; actual length of read
        db      80 dup (0)      ; keyboard input goes here
        .
        .
        .
        mov     dx,seg kbuf     ; set DS:DX = address of
        mov     ds,dx           ; keyboard input buffer
        mov     dx,offset kbuf
        mov     ah,0ah          ; function 0AH = read buffered line
        int     21h             ; transfer to MS-DOS
                                ; terminated by a carriage return,
                                ; and kbuf+1 = length of input,
                                ; not including the carriage return
```

Example: Use the MS-DOS handle-based Read File or Device function and the standard input handle to read an entire line from the keyboard, specifying a maximum line length of 80 characters. All editing keys are active during entry, and the input is echoed to the display. (The input will not terminate on a carriage return as expected if standard input is in raw mode.)

```
kbuf    db      80 dup (0)      ; buffer for keyboard input
        .
        .
        .
        mov     dx,seg kbuf     ; set DS:DX = address of
        mov     ds,dx           ; keyboard input buffer
        mov     dx,offset kbuf
        mov     cx,80           ; CX = maximum length of input
        mov     bx,0            ; standard input handle = 0
        mov     ah,3fh          ; function 3FH = read file/device
        int     21h             ; transfer to MS-DOS
        jc      error           ; jump if function failed
                                ; otherwise AX = actual
                                ; length of keyboard input,
                                ; including carriage-return and
                                ; linefeed, and the data is
                                ; in the buffer 'kbuf'
```

The display

The output half of the MS-DOS logical character device CON is the video display. On IBM PCs and compatibles, the video display is an "option" of sorts that comes in several forms. IBM has introduced five video subsystems that support different types of displays: the Monochrome Display Adapter (MDA), the Color/Graphics Adapter (CGA), the Enhanced Graphics Adapter (EGA), the Video Graphics Array (VGA), and the Multi-Color Graphics Array (MCGA). Other, non-IBM-compatible video subsystems in common use include the Hercules Graphics Card and its variants that support downloadable fonts.

Two portable techniques exist for writing text to the video display with MS-DOS function calls. The traditional method is supported by Interrupt 21H Functions 02H (Character Output), 06H (Direct Console I/O), and 09H (Display String). The handle method is supported by Function 40H (Write File or Device) and is available only in MS-DOS versions 2.0 and later. *See* SYSTEM CALLS: INTERRUPT 21H: Functions 02H, 06H, 09H, 40H. All these calls treat the display essentially as a "glass teletype" and do not support bit-mapped graphics.

Traditional Functions 02H and 06H are similar. Both are called with the character to be displayed in the DL register; they differ in that Function 02H is sensitive to interruption by the user's entry of a Control-C, whereas Function 06H is immune to Control-C but cannot be used to output the character 0FFH (ASCII rubout). Both calls check specifically for carriage return (0DH), linefeed (0AH), and backspace (08H) characters and take the appropriate action if these characters are detected.

Because making individual calls to MS-DOS for each character to be displayed is inefficient and slow, the traditional Display String function (09H) is generally used in preference to Functions 02H and 06H. Function 09H is called with the address of a string that is terminated with a dollar-sign character ($); it displays the entire string in one operation, regardless of its length. The string can contain embedded control characters such as carriage return and linefeed.

To use the handle method for screen display, programs must call the MS-DOS Write File or Device service, Interrupt 21H Function 40H. Ordinarily, a program should use the predefined handle for standard output (1) to send text to the screen, so that any redirection requested by the user on the program's command line will be honored. If the program needs to circumvent redirection and ensure that its output goes to the screen, it can either use the predefined handle for standard error (2) or explicitly open the CON device with Interrupt 21H Function 3DH and use the resulting handle for its write operations.

The handle technique for displaying text has several advantages over the traditional calls. First, the length of the string to be displayed is passed as an explicit parameter, so the string need not contain a special terminating character and the $ character can be displayed as part of the string. Second, the traditional calls are translated to handle calls inside MS-DOS, so the handle calls have less internal overhead and are generally faster. Finally, use of the handle Write File or Device function to display text is symmetric with the methods the program must use to access its files. In short, the traditional functions should be avoided unless the program must be capable of running under MS-DOS versions 1.x.

Controlling the screen

One of the deficiencies of the standard MS-DOS CON device driver is the lack of screen-control capabilities. The default CON driver has no built-in routines to support cursor placement, screen clearing, display mode selection, and so on.

In MS-DOS versions 2.0 and later, an optional replacement CON driver is supplied in the file ANSI.SYS. This driver contains most of the screen-control capabilities needed by text-oriented application programs. The driver is installed by adding a DEVICE directive to the

CONFIG.SYS file and restarting the system. When ANSI.SYS is active, a program can position the cursor, inquire about the current cursor position, select foreground and background colors, and clear the current line or the entire screen by sending an escape sequence consisting of the ASCII Esc character (1BH) followed by various function-specific parameters to the standard output device. *See* USER COMMANDS: ANSI.SYS.

Programs that use the ANSI.SYS capabilities for screen control are portable to any MS-DOS implementation that contains the ANSI.SYS driver. Programs that seek improved performance by calling the ROM BIOS video driver or by assuming direct control of the hardware are necessarily less portable and usually require modification when new PC models or video subsystems are released.

Role of the ROM BIOS

The video subsystems in IBM PCs and compatibles use a hybrid of memory-mapped and port-addressed I/O. A range of the machine's memory addresses is typically reserved for a video refresh buffer that holds the character codes and attributes to be displayed on the screen; the cursor position, display mode, palettes, and similar global display characteristics are governed by writing control values to specific I/O ports.

The ROM BIOS of IBM PCs and compatibles contains a primitive driver for the MDA, CGA, EGA, VGA, and MCGA video subsystems. This driver supports the following functions:

- Read or write characters with attributes at any screen position.
- Query or set the cursor position.
- Clear or scroll an arbitrary portion of the screen.
- Select palette, background, foreground, and border colors.
- Query or set the display mode (40-column text, 80-column text, all-points-addressable graphics, and so on).
- Read or write a pixel at any screen coordinate.

These functions are invoked by a program through software Interrupt 10H. *See* Appendix O: IBM PC BIOS Calls. In PC-DOS-compatible implementations of MS-DOS, the display portions of the MS-DOS CON and ANSI.SYS drivers use these ROM BIOS routines. Video subsystems that are not IBM compatible either must contain their own ROM BIOS or must be used with an installable device driver that captures Interrupt 10H and provides appropriate support functions.

Text-only application programs should avoid use of the ROM BIOS functions or direct access to the hardware whenever possible, to ensure maximum portability between MS-DOS systems. However, because the MS-DOS CON driver contains no support for bit-mapped graphics, graphically oriented applications usually must resort to direct control of the video adapter and its refresh buffer for speed and precision.

Display programming examples

Example: Use the ROM BIOS Interrupt 10H function to write an asterisk character to the display in text mode. (In graphics mode, BL must also be set to the desired foreground color.)

```
mov     ah,0eh          ; subfunction 0EH = write character
                        ; in teletype mode
mov     al,'*'          ; AL = character to display
mov     bh,0            ; select display page 0
int     10h             ; transfer to ROM BIOS video driver
```

Example: Use the MS-DOS traditional function to write an asterisk character to the display. If the user's entry of a Control-C is detected during the output and standard output is in cooked mode, MS-DOS calls the Control-C exception handler whose address is found in the vector for Interrupt 23H.

```
mov     ah,02h          ; function 02H = display character
mov     dl,'*'          ; DL = character to display
int     21h             ; transfer to MS-DOS
```

Example: Use the MS-DOS traditional function to write a string to the display. The output is terminated by the $ character and can be interrupted when the user enters a Control-C if standard output is in cooked mode.

```
msg     db      'This is a test message','$'
        .
        .
        .
        mov     dx,seg msg      ; DS:DX = address of text
        mov     ds,dx           ; to display
        mov     dx,offset msg
        mov     ah,09h          ; function 09H = display string
        int     21h             ; transfer to MS-DOS
```

Example: Use the MS-DOS handle-based Write File or Device function and the predefined handle for standard output to write a string to the display. Output can be interrupted by the user's entry of a Control-C if standard output is in cooked mode.

```
msg     db      'This is a test message'
msg_len equ     $-msg
        .
        .
        .
        mov     dx,seg msg      ; DS:DX = address of text
        mov     ds,dx           ; to display
        mov     dx,offset msg
        mov     cx,msg_len      ; CX = length of text
        mov     bx,1            ; BX = handle for standard output
        mov     ah,40h          ; function 40H = write file/device
        int     21h             ; transfer to MS-DOS
```

The serial communications ports

Through version 3.2, MS-DOS has built-in support for two serial communications ports, identified as COM1 and COM2, by means of three drivers named AUX, COM1, and COM2. (AUX is ordinarily an alias for COM1.)

The traditional MS-DOS method of reading from and writing to the serial ports is through Interrupt 21H Function 03H for AUX input and Function 04H for AUX output. In MS-DOS versions 2.0 and later, the handle-based Read File or Device and Write File or Device functions (Interrupt 21H Functions 3FH and 40H) can be used to read from or write to the auxiliary device. A program can use the predefined handle for the standard auxiliary device (3) with Functions 3FH and 40H, or it can explicitly open the COM1 or COM2 devices with Interrupt 21H Function 3DH and use the handle obtained from that open operation to perform read and write operations.

MS-DOS support for the serial communications port is inadequate in several respects for high-performance serial I/O applications. First, MS-DOS provides no portable way to test for the existence or the status of a particular serial port in a system; if a program "opens" COM2 and writes data to it and the physical COM2 adapter is not present in the system, the program may simply hang. Similarly, if the serial port exists but no character has been received and the program attempts to read a character, the program will hang until one is available; there is no traditional function call to check if a character is waiting as there is for the keyboard.

MS-DOS also provides no portable method to initialize the communications adapter to a particular baud rate, word length, and parity. An application must resort to ROM BIOS calls, manipulate the hardware directly, or rely on the user to configure the port properly with the MODE command before running the application that uses it. The default settings for the serial port on PC-DOS-compatible systems are 2400 baud, no parity, 1 stop bit, and 8 databits. *See* USER COMMANDS: MODE.

A more serious problem with the default MS-DOS auxiliary device driver in IBM PCs and compatibles, however, is that it is not interrupt driven. Accordingly, when baud rates above 1200 are selected, characters can be lost during time-consuming operations performed by the drivers for other devices, such as clearing the screen or reading or writing a floppy-disk sector. Because the MS-DOS AUX device driver typically relies on the ROM BIOS serial port driver (accessed through software Interrupt 14H) and because the ROM BIOS driver is not interrupt driven either, bypassing MS-DOS and calling the ROM BIOS functions does not usually improve matters.

Because of all the problems just described, telecommunications application programs commonly take over complete control of the serial port and supply their own interrupt handler and internal buffering for character read and write operations. *See* PROGRAMMING IN THE MS-DOS ENVIRONMENT: PROGRAMMING FOR MS-DOS: Interrupt-Driven Communications.

Serial port programming examples

Example: Use the ROM BIOS serial port driver to write a string to COM1.

```
msg       db       'This is a test message'
msg_len equ        $-msg
          .
          .
          .
          mov      bx,seg msg      ; DS:BX = address of message
          mov      ds,bx
          mov      bx,offset msg
          mov      cx,msg_len      ; CX = length of message
          mov      dx,0            ; DX = 0 for COM1
L1:       mov      al,[bx]         ; get next character into AL
          mov      ah,01h          ; subfunction 01H = output
          int      14h             ; transfer to ROM BIOS
          inc      bx              ; bump pointer to output string
          loop     L1              ; and loop until all chars. sent
```

Example: Use the MS-DOS traditional function for auxiliary device output to write a string to COM1.

```
msg       db       'This is a test message'
msg_len equ        $-msg
          .
          .
          .
          mov      bx,seg msg      ; set DS:BX = address of message
          mov      ds,bx
          mov      bx,offset msg
          mov      cx,msg_len      ; set CX = length of message
L1:       mov      dl,[bx]         ; get next character into DL
          mov      ah,04h          ; function 04H = auxiliary output
          int      21h             ; transfer to MS-DOS
          inc      bx              ; bump pointer to output string
          loop     L1              ; and loop until all chars. sent
```

Example: Use the MS-DOS handle-based Write File or Device function and the predefined handle for the standard auxiliary device to write a string to COM1.

```
msg       db       'This is a test message'
msg_len equ        $-msg
          .
          .
          .
          mov      dx,seg msg      ; DS:DX = address of message
          mov      ds,dx
          mov      dx,offset msg
          mov      cx,msg_len      ; CX = length of message
          mov      bx,3            ; BX = handle for standard aux.
          mov      ah,40h          ; function 40H = write file/device
          int      21h             ; transfer to MS-DOS
          jc       error           ; jump if write operation failed
```

The parallel port and printer

Most MS-DOS implementations contain device drivers for four printer devices: LPT1, LPT2, LPT3, and PRN. PRN is ordinarily an alias for LPT1 and refers to the first parallel output port in the system. To provide for list devices that do not have a parallel interface, the LPT devices can be individually redirected with the MODE command to one of the serial communications ports. *See* USER COMMANDS: MODE.

As with the keyboard, the display, and the serial port, MS-DOS allows the printer to be accessed with either traditional or handle-based function calls. The traditional function call is Interrupt 21H Function 05H, which accepts a character in DL and sends it to the physical device currently assigned to logical device name LPT1.

A program can perform handle-based output to the printer with Interrupt 21H Function 40H (Write File or Device). The predefined handle for the standard printer (4) can be used to send strings to logical device LPT1. Alternatively, the program can issue an open operation for a specific printer device with Interrupt 21H Function 3DH and use the handle obtained from that open operation with Function 40H. This latter method also allows more than one printer to be used at a time from the same program.

Because the parallel ports are assumed to be output only, no traditional call exists for input from the parallel port. In addition, no portable method exists to test printer port status under MS-DOS; programs that wish to avoid sending a character to the printer adapter when it is not ready or not physically present in the system must test the adapter's status by making a call to the ROM BIOS printer driver (by means of software Interrupt 17H; *see* Appendix O: IBM PC BIOS Calls) or by accessing the hardware directly.

Parallel port programming examples

Example: Use the ROM BIOS printer driver to send a string to the first parallel printer port.

```
msg      db      'This is a test message'
msg_len  equ     $-msg
         .
         .
         .
         mov     bx,seg msg      ; DS:BX = address of message
         mov     ds,bx
         mov     bx,offset msg
         mov     cx,msg_len      ; CX = length of message
         mov     dx,0            ; DX = 0 for LPT1
L1:      mov     al,[bx]         ; get next character into AL
         mov     ah,00h          ; subfunction 00H = output
         int     17h             ; transfer to ROM BIOS
         inc     bx              ; bump pointer to output string
         loop    L1              ; and loop until all chars. sent
```

Example: Use the traditional MS-DOS function call to send a string to the first parallel printer port.

```
msg      db       'This is a test message'
msg_len equ       $-msg
            .
            .
            .
         mov      bx,seg msg       ; DS:BX = address of message
         mov      ds,bx
         mov      bx,offset msg
         mov      cx,msg_len       ; CX = length of message
L1:      mov      dl,[bx]          ; get next character into DL
         mov      ah,05h           ; function 05H = printer output
         int      21h              ; transfer to MS-DOS
         inc      bx               ; bump pointer to output string
         loop     L1               ; and loop until all chars. sent
```

Example: Use the handle-based MS-DOS Write File or Device call and the predefined handle for the standard printer to send a string to the system list device.

```
msg      db       'This is a test message'
msg_len equ       $-msg
            .
            .
            .
         mov      dx,seg msg       ; DS:DX = address of message
         mov      ds,dx
         mov      dx,offset msg
         mov      cx,msg_len       ; CX = length of message
         mov      bx,4             ; BX = handle for standard printer
         mov      ah,40h           ; function 40H = write file/device
         int      21h              ; transfer to MS-DOS
         jc       error            ; jump if write operation failed
```

IOCTL

In versions 2.0 and later, MS-DOS has provided applications with the ability to communicate directly with device drivers through a set of subfunctions grouped under Interrupt 21H Function 44H (IOCTL). *See* SYSTEM CALLS: INTERRUPT 21H: Function 44H. The IOCTL subfunctions that are particularly applicable to the character I/O needs of application programs are

Subfunction	Name
00H	Get Device Data
01H	Set Device Data
02H	Receive Control Data from Character Device

(more)

Subfunction	Name
03H	Send Control Data to Character Device
06H	Check Input Status
07H	Check Output Status
0AH	Check if Handle is Remote (version 3.1 or later)
0CH	Generic I/O Control for Handles: Get/Set Output Iteration Count

Various bits in the device information word returned by Subfunction 00H can be tested by an application to determine whether a specific handle is associated with a character device or a file and whether the driver for the device can process control strings passed by Subfunctions 02H and 03H. The device information word also allows the program to test whether a character device is the CLOCK$, standard input, standard output, or NUL device and whether the device is in raw or cooked mode. The program can then use Subfunction 01H to select raw mode or cooked mode for subsequent I/O performed with the handle.

Subfunctions 02H and 03H allow control strings to be passed between the device driver and an application; they do not usually result in any physical I/O to the device. For example, a custom device driver might allow an application program to configure the serial port by writing a specific set of control parameters to the driver with Subfunction 03H. Similarly, the custom driver might respond to Subfunction 02H by passing the application a series of bytes that defines the current configuration and status of the serial port.

Subfunctions 06H and 07H can be used by application programs to test whether a device is ready to accept an output character or has a character ready for input. These subfunctions are particularly applicable to the serial communications ports and parallel printer ports because MS-DOS does not supply traditional function calls to test their status.

Subfunction 0AH can be used to determine whether the character device associated with a handle is local or remote — that is, attached to the computer the program is running on or attached to another computer on a local area network. A program should not ordinarily attempt to distinguish between local and remote devices during normal input and output, but the information can be useful in attempts to recover from error conditions. This subfunction is available only if Microsoft Networks is running.

Finally, Subfunction 0CH allows a program to query or set the number of times a device driver tries to send output to the printer before assuming the device is not available.

IOCTL programming examples

Example: Use IOCTL Subfunction 00H to obtain the device information word for the standard input handle and save it, and then use Subfunction 01H to place standard input into raw mode.

```
info    dw      ?                    ; save device information word here
        .
        .
        .
```

(more)

```
mov     ax,4400h        ; AH = function 44H, IOCTL
                        ; AL = subfunction 00H, get device
                        ; information word
mov     bx,0            ; BX = handle for standard input
int     21h             ; transfer to MS-DOS
mov     info,dx         ; save device information word
                        ; (assumes DS = data segment)
or      dl,20h          ; set raw mode bit
mov     dh,0            ; and clear DH as MS-DOS requires
mov     ax,4401h        ; AL = subfunction 01H, set device
                        ; information word
                        ; (BX still contains handle)
int     21h             ; transfer to MS-DOS
```

Example: Use IOCTL Subfunction 06H to test whether a character is ready for input on the first serial port. The function returns AL = 0FFH if a character is ready and AL = 00H if not.

```
mov     ax,4406H        ; AH = function 44H, IOCTL
                        ; AL = subfunction 06H, get
                        ; input status
mov     bx,3            ; BX = handle for standard aux
int     21h             ; transfer to MS-DOS
or      al,al           ; test status of AUX driver
jnz     ready           ; jump if input character ready
                        ; else no character is waiting
```

Jim Kyle
Chip Rabinowitz

Article 6
Interrupt-Driven Communications

In the earliest days of personal-computer communications, when speeds were no faster than 300 bits per second, primitive programs that moved characters to and from the remote system were adequate. The PC had time between characters to determine what it ought to do next and could spend that time keeping track of the status of the remote system.

Modern data-transfer rates, however, are four to eight times faster and leave little or no time to spare between characters. At 1200 bits per second, as many as three characters can be lost in the time required to scroll the display up one line. At such speeds, a technique to permit characters to be received and simultaneously displayed becomes necessary.

Mainframe systems have long made use of hardware interrupts to coordinate such activities. The processor goes about its normal activity; when a peripheral device needs attention, it sends an interrupt request to the processor. The processor interrupts its activity, services the request, and then goes back to what it was doing. Because the response is driven by the request, this type of processing is known as interrupt-driven. It gives the effect of doing two things at the same time without requiring two separate processors.

Successful telecommunication with PCs at modern data rates demands an interrupt-driven routine for data reception. This article discusses in detail the techniques for interrupt-driven communications and culminates in two sample program packages.

The article begins by establishing the purpose of communications programs and then discusses the capability of the simple functions provided by MS-DOS to achieve this goal. To see what must be done to supplement MS-DOS functions, the hardware (both the modem and the serial port) is examined. This leads to a discussion of the method MS-DOS has provided since version 2.0 for solving the problems of special hardware interfacing: the installable device driver.

With the background established, alternate paths to interrupt-driven communications are discussed — one following recommended MS-DOS techniques, the other following standard industry practice — and programs are developed for each.

Throughout this article, the discussion is restricted to the architecture and BIOS of the IBM PC family. MS-DOS systems not totally compatible with this architecture may require substantially different approaches at the detailed level, but the same general principles apply.

Purpose of Communications Programs

The primary purpose of any communications program is communicating — that is, transmitting information entered as keystrokes (or bytes read from a file) in a form suitable for transmission to a remote computer via phone lines and, conversely, converting information received from the remote computer into a display on the video screen (or data in a file).

Some years ago, the most abstract form of all communications programs was dubbed a modem engine, by analogy to Babbage's analytical engine or the inference-engine model used in artificial-intelligence development. The functions of the modem engine are common to all kinds of communications programs, from the simplest to the most complex, and can be described in a type of pseudo-C as follows:

```
The Modem Engine Pseudocode

        DO {  IF (input character is available)
                  send_it_to_remote;
              IF (remote character is available)
                  use_it_locally;
          } UNTIL (told_to_stop);
```

The essence of this modem-engine code is that the absence of an input character, or of a character from the remote computer, does not hang the loop in a wait state. Rather, the engine continues to cycle: If it finds work to do, it does it; if not, the engine keeps looking.

Of course, at times it is desirable to halt the continuous action of the modem engine. For example, when receiving a long message, it is nice to be able to pause and read the message before the lines scroll into oblivion. On the other hand, taking too long to study the screen means that incoming characters are lost. The answer is a technique called flow control, in which a special control character is sent to shut down transmission and some other character is later sent to start it up again.

Several conventions for flow control exist. One of the most widespread is known as XON/XOFF, from the old Teletype-33 keycap legends for the two control codes involved. In the original use, XOFF halted the paper tape reader and XON started it going again. In mid-1967, the General Electric Company began using these signals in its time-sharing computer services to control the flow of data, and the practice rapidly spread throughout the industry.

The sample program named ENGINE, shown later in this article, is an almost literal implementation of the modem-engine approach. This sample represents one extreme of simplicity in communications programs. The other sample program, CTERM.C, is much more complex, but the modem engine is still at its heart.

Using Simple MS-DOS Functions

Because MS-DOS provides, among its standard service functions, the capability of sending output to or reading input from the device named AUX (which defaults to COM1, the first serial port on most machines), a first attempt at implementing the modem engine using MS-DOS functions might look something like the following incomplete fragment of Microsoft Macro Assembler (MASM) code:

```
;Incomplete (and Unworkable) Implementation

LOOP:   MOV     AH,08h          ; read keyboard, no echo
        INT     21h
        MOV     DL,AL           ; set up to send
        MOV     AH,04h          ; send to AUX device
        INT     21h
        MOV     AH,03h          ; read from AUX device
        INT     21h
        MOV     DL,AL           ; set up to send
        MOV     AH,02h          ; send to screen
        INT     21h
        JMP     LOOP            ; keep doing it
```

The problem with this code is that it violates the keep-looking principle both at the keyboard and at the AUX port: Interrupt 21H Function 08H does not return until a keyboard character is available, so no data from the AUX port can be read until a key is pressed locally. Similarly, Function 03H waits for a character to become available from AUX, so no more keys can be recognized locally until the remote system sends a character. If nothing is received, the loop waits forever.

To overcome the problem at the keyboard end, Function 0BH can be used to determine if a key has been pressed before an attempt is made to read one, as shown in the following modification of the fragment:

```
;Improved, (but Still Unworkable) Implementation

LOOP:   MOV     AH,0Bh          ; test keyboard for char
        INT     21h
        OR      AL,AL           ; test for zero
        JZ      RMT             ; no char avail, skip
        MOV     AH,08h          ; have char, read it in
        INT     21h
        MOV     DL,AL           ; set up to send
        MOV     AH,04h          ; send to AUX device
        INT     21h
RMT:
        MOV     AH,03h          ; read from AUX device
        INT     21h
        MOV     DL,AL           ; set up to send
        MOV     AH,02h          ; send to screen
        INT     21h
        JMP     LOOP            ; keep doing it
```

This code permits any input from AUX to be received without waiting for a local key to be pressed, but if AUX is slow about providing input, the program waits indefinitely before checking the keyboard again. Thus, the problem is only partially solved.

MS-DOS, however, simply does not provide any direct method of making the required tests for AUX or, for that matter, any of the serial port devices. That is why communications programs must be treated differently from most other types of programs under MS-DOS and why such programs must be intimately involved with machine details despite all accepted principles of portable program design.

The Hardware Involved

Personal-computer communications require at least two distinct pieces of hardware (separate devices, even though they are often combined on a single board). These hardware items are the serial port, which converts data from the computer's internal bus into a bit stream for transmission over a single external line, and the modem, which converts the bit stream into a form suitable for telephone-line (or, sometimes, radio) transmission.

The modem

The modem (a word coined from MOdulator-DEModulator) is a device that converts a stream of bits, represented as sequential changes of voltage level, into audio frequency signals suitable for transmission over voice-grade telephone circuits (modulation) and converts these signals back into a stream of bits that duplicates the original input (demodulation).

Specific characteristics of the audio signals involved were established by AT&T when that company monopolized the modem industry, and those characteristics then evolved into de facto standards when the monopoly vanished. They take several forms, depending on the data rate in use; these forms are normally identified by the original Bell specification number, such as 103 (for 600 bps and below) or 212A (for the 1200 bps standard).

The data rate is measured in bits per second (bps), often mistermed baud or even "baud per second." A baud measures the number of signals per second; as with knot (nautical miles per hour), the time reference is built in. If one signal change marks one bit, as is true for the Bell 103 standard, then baud and bps have equal values. However, they are not equivalent for more complex signals. For example, the Bell 212A diphase standard for 1200 bps uses two tone streams, each operating at 600 baud, to transmit data at 1200 bits per second.

For accuracy, this article uses bps, rather than baud, except where widespread industry misuse of baud has become standardized (as in "baud rate generator").

Originally, the modem itself was a box connected to the computer's serial port via a cable. Characteristics of this cable, its connectors, and its signals were standardized in the 1960s by the Electronic Industries Association (EIA), in Standard RS232C. Like the Bell standards for modems, RS232C has survived almost unchanged. Its characteristics are listed in Table 6-1.

Table 6-1. RS232C Signals.

DB25 Pin	232	Name	Description
1			Safety Ground
2	BA	TXD	Transmit Data
3	BB	RXD	Receive Data
4	CA	RTS	Request To Send
5	CB	CTS	Clear To Send
6	CC	DSR	Data Set Ready
7	AB	GND	Signal Ground
8	CF	DCD	Data Carrier Detected
20	CD	DTR	Data Terminal Ready
22	CE	RI	Ring Indicator

With the increasing popularity of personal computers, internal modems that plug into the PC's motherboard and combine the modem and a serial port became available.

The first such units were manufactured by Hayes Corporation, and like Bell and the EIA, they created a standard. Functionally, the internal modem is identical to the combination of a serial port, a connecting cable, and an external modem.

The serial port

Each serial port of a standard IBM PC connects the rest of the system to a type INS8250 Universal Asynchronous Receiver Transmitter (UART) integrated circuit (IC) chip developed by National Semiconductor Corporation. This chip, along with associated circuits in the port,

1. Converts data supplied via the system data bus into a sequence of voltage levels on the single TXD output line that represent binary digits.
2. Converts data received as a sequence of binary levels on the single RXD input line into bytes for the data bus.
3. Controls the modem's actions through the DTR and RTS output lines.
4. Provides status information to the processor; this information comes from the modem, via the DSR, DCD, CTS, and RI input lines, and from within the UART itself, which signals data available, data needed, or error detected.

The word *asynchronous* in the name of the IC comes from the Bell specifications. When computer data is transmitted, each bit's relationship to its neighbors must be preserved; this can be done in either of two ways. The most obvious method is to keep the bit stream strictly synchronized with a clock signal of known frequency and count the cycles to identify the bits. Such a transmission is known as synchronous, often abbreviated to synch or sometimes bisync for binary synchronous. The second method, first used with mechanical teleprinters, marks the start of each bit group with a defined start bit and the end with one or more defined stop bits, and it defines a duration for each bit time. Detection of a start bit marks the beginning of a received group; the signal is then sampled at each bit time until the stop bit is encountered. This method is known as asynchronous (or just asynch) and is the one used by the standard IBM PC.

The start bit is, by definition, exactly the same as that used to indicate binary zero, and the stop bit is the same as that indicating binary one. A zero signal is often called SPACE, and a one signal is called MARK, from terms used in the teleprinter industry.

During transmission, the least significant bit of the data is sent first, after the start bit. A parity bit, if used, appears as the most significant bit in the data group, before the stop bit or bits; it cannot be distinguished from a databit except by its position. Once the first stop bit is sent, the line remains in MARK (sometimes called idling) condition until a new start bit indicates the beginning of another group.

In most PC uses, the serial port transfers one 8-bit byte at a time, and the term *word* specifies a 16-bit quantity. In the UART world, however, a word is the unit of information sent by the chip in each chunk. The word length is part of the control information set into the chip during setup operations and can be 5, 6, 7, or 8 bits. This discussion follows UART conventions and refers to words, rather than to bytes.

One special type of signal, not often used in PC-to-PC communications but sometimes necessary in communicating with mainframe systems, is a BREAK. The BREAK is an all-SPACE condition that extends for more than one word time, including the stop-bit time. (Many systems require the BREAK to last at least 150 milliseconds regardless of data rate.) Because it cannot be generated by any normal data character transmission, the BREAK is used to interrupt, or break into, normal operation. The IBM PC's 8250 UART can generate the BREAK signal, but its duration must be determined by a program, rather than by the chip.

The 8250 UART architecture

The 8250 UART contains four major functional areas: receiver, transmitter, control circuits, and status circuits. Because these areas are closely related, some terms used in the following descriptions are, of necessity, forward references to subsequent paragraphs.

The major parts of the receiver are a shift register and a data register called the Received Data Register. The shift register assembles sequentially received data into word-parallel form by shifting the level of the RXD line into its front end at each bit time and, at the same time, shifting previous bits over. When the shift register is full, all bits in it are moved over to the data register, the shift register is cleared to all zeros, and the bit in the status circuits that indicates data ready is set. If an error is detected during receipt of that word, other bits in the status circuits are also set.

Similarly, the major parts of the transmitter are a holding register called the Transmit Holding Register and a shift register. Each word to be transmitted is transferred from the data bus to the holding register. If the holding register is not empty when this is done, the previous contents are lost. The transmitter's shift register converts word-parallel data into bit-serial form for transmission by shifting the most significant bit out to the TXD line once each bit time, at the same time shifting lower bits over and shifting in an idling bit at the low end of the register. When the last databit has been shifted out, any data in the holding register is moved to the shift register, the holding register is filled with idling bits in case no more data is forthcoming, and the bit in the status circuits that indicates the Transmit Holding Register is empty is set to indicate that another word can be transferred. The parity bit, if any, and stop bits are added to the transmitted stream after the last databit of each word is shifted out.

The control circuits establish three communications features: first, line control values, such as word length, whether or not (and how) parity is checked, and the number of stop bits; second, modem control values, such as the state of the DTR and RTS output lines; and third, the rate at which data is sent and received. These control values are established by two 8-bit registers and one 16-bit register, which are addressed as four 8-bit registers. They are the Line Control Register (LCR), the Modem Control Register (MCR), and the 16-bit BRG Divisor Latch, addressed as Baud0 and Baud1.

The BRG Divisor Latch sets the data rate by defining the bit time produced by the Programmable Baud Rate Generator (PBRG), a major part of the control circuits. The PBRG can provide any data speed from a few bits per second to 38400 bps; in the BIOS of the IBM PC, PC/XT, and PC/AT, though, only the range 110 through 9600 bps is supported. How the LCR and the MCR establish their control values, how the PBRG is programmed, and how interrupts are enabled are discussed later.

The fourth major area in the 8250 UART, the status circuits, records (in a pair of status registers) the conditions in the receive and transmit circuits, any errors that are detected, and any change in state of the RS232C input lines from the modem. When any status register's content changes, an interrupt request, if enabled, is generated to notify the rest of the PC system. This approach lets the PC attend to other matters without having to continually monitor the status of the serial port, yet it assures immediate action when something does occur.

The 8250 programming interface

Not all the registers mentioned in the preceding section are accessible to programmers. The shift registers, for example, can be read from or written to only by the 8250's internal circuits. There are 10 registers available to the programmer, and they are accessed by only seven distinct addresses (shown in Table 6-2). The Received Data Register and the Transmit Holding Register share a single address (a read gets the received data; a write goes to the holding register). In addition, both this address and that of the Interrupt Enable Register (IER) are shared with the PBRG Divisor Latch. A bit in the Line Control Register called the Divisor Latch Access Bit (DLAB) determines which register is addressed at any specific time.

In the IBM PC, the seven addresses used by the 8250 are selected by the low 3 bits of the port number (the higher bits select the specific port). Thus, each serial port occupies eight positions in the address space. However, only the lowest address used — the one in which the low 3 bits are all 0 — need be remembered in order to access all eight addresses.

Because of this, any serial port in the PC is referred to by an address that, in hexadecimal notation, ends with either 0 or 8: The COM1 port normally uses address 03F8H, and COM2 uses 02F8H. This lowest port address is usually called the base port address, and each addressable register is then referenced as an offset from this base value, as shown in Table 6-2.

Table 6-2. 8250 Port Offsets from Base Address.

Offset	Name	Description
If DLAB bit in LCR = 0:		
00H	DATA	Received Data Register if read from, Transmit Holding Register if written to
01H	IER	Interrupt Enable Register
If DLAB bit in LCR = 1:		
00H	Baud0	BRG Divisor Latch, low byte
01H	Baud1	BRG Divisor Latch, high byte
Not affected by DLAB bit:		
02H	IID	Interrupt Identifier Register
03H	LCR	Line Control Register
04H	MCR	Modem Control Register
05H	LSR	Line Status Register
06H	MSR	Modem Status Register

The control circuits

The control circuits of the 8250 include the Programmable Baud Rate Generator (PBRG), the Line Control Register (LCR), the Modem Control Register (MCR), and the Interrupt Enable Register (IER).

The PBRG establishes the bit time used for both transmitting and receiving data by dividing an external clock signal. To select a desired bit rate, the appropriate divisor is loaded into the PBRG's 16-bit Divisor Latch by setting the Divisor Latch Access Bit (DLAB) in the Line Control Register to 1 (which changes the functions of addresses 0 and 1) and then writing the divisor into Baud0 and Baud1. After the bit rate is selected, DLAB is changed back to 0, to permit normal operation of the DATA registers and the IER.

With the 1.8432 MHz external UART clock frequency used in standard IBM systems, divisor values (in decimal notation) for bit rates between 45.5 and 38400 bps are listed in Table 6-3. These speeds are established by a crystal contained in the serial port (or internal modem) and are totally unrelated to the speed of the processor's clock.

Table 6-3. Bit Rate Divisor Table for 8250/IBM.

BPS	Divisor
45.5	2532
50	2304
75	1536
110	1047
134.5	857
150	768
300	384
600	192
1200	96
1800	64
2000	58
2400	48
4800	24
9600	12
19200	6
38400	3

The remaining control circuits are the Line Control Register, the Modem Control Register, and the Interrupt Enable Register. Bits in the LCR control the assignment of offsets 0 and 1, transmission of the BREAK signal, parity generation, the number of stop bits, and the word length sent and received, as shown in Table 6-4.

Table 6-4. 8250 Line Control Register Bit Values.

Bit	Name	Binary	Meaning
Address Control:			
7	DLAB	0xxxxxxx	Offset 0 refers to DATA; offset 1 refers to IER
		1xxxxxxx	Offsets 0 and 1 refer to BRG Divisor Latch
BREAK Control:			
6	SETBRK	x0xxxxxx	Normal UART operation
		x1xxxxxx	Send BREAK signal

(more)

Table 6-4. *Continued.*

Bit	Name	Binary	Meaning
Parity Checking:			
5,4,3	GENPAR	xxxx0xxx	No parity bit
		xx001xxx	Parity bit is ODD
		xx011xxx	Parity bit is EVEN
		xx101xxx	Parity bit is 1
		xx111xxx	Parity bit is 0
Stop Bits:			
2	XSTOP	xxxxx0xx	Only 1 stop bit
		xxxxx1xx	2 stop bits (1.5 if WL = 5)
Word Length:			
1,0	WD5	xxxxxx00	Word length = 5
	WD6	xxxxxx01	Word length = 6
	WD7	xxxxxx10	Word length = 7
	WD8	xxxxxx11	Word length = 8

Two bits in the MCR (Table 6-5) control output lines DTR and RTS; two other MCR bits (OUT1 and OUT2) are left free by the UART to be assigned by the user; a fifth bit (TEST) puts the UART into a self-test mode of operation. The upper 3 bits have no effect on the UART. The MCR can be both read from and written to.

Both of the user-assignable bits are defined in the IBM PC. OUT1 is used by Hayes internal modems to cause a power-on reset of their circuits; OUT2 controls the passage of UART-generated interrupt request signals to the rest of the PC. Unless OUT2 is set to 1, interrupt signals from the UART cannot reach the rest of the PC, even though all other controls are properly set. This feature is documented, but obscurely, in the IBM *Technical Reference* manuals and the asynchronous-adapter schematic; it is easy to overlook when writing an interrupt-driven program for these machines.

Table 6-5. 8250 Modem Control Register Bit Values.

Name	Binary	Description
TEST	xxx1xxxx	Turns on UART self-test configuration.
OUT2	xxxx1xxx	Controls 8250 interrupt signals (User2 Output).
OUT1	xxxxx1xx	Resets Hayes 1200b internal modem (User1 Output).
RTS	xxxxxx1x	Sets RTS output to RS232C connector.
DTR	xxxxxxx1	Sets DTR output to RS232C connector.

The 8250 can generate any or all of four classes of interrupts, each individually enabled or disabled by setting the appropriate control bit in the Interrupt Enable Register (Table 6-6). Thus, setting the IER to 00H disables all the UART interrupts within the 8250 without regard to any other settings, such as OUT2, system interrupt masking, or the CLI/STI commands. The IER can be both read from and written to. Only the low 4 bits have any effect on the UART.

Table 6-6. 8250 Interrupt Enable Register Constants.

Binary	Action
xxxx1xxx	Enable Modem Status Interrupt.
xxxxx1xx	Enable Line Status Interrupt.
xxxxxx1x	Enable Transmit Register Interrupt.
xxxxxxx1	Enable Received Data Ready Interrupt.

The status circuits

The status circuits of the 8250 include the Line Status Register (LSR), the Modem Status Register (MSR), the Interrupt Identifier (IID) Register, and the interrupt-request generation system.

The 8250 includes circuitry that detects a received BREAK signal and also detects three classes of data-reception errors. Separate bits in the LSR (Table 6-7) are set to indicate that a BREAK has been received and to indicate any of the following: a parity error (if lateral parity is in use), a framing error (incoming bit = 0 at stop-bit time), or an overrun error (word not yet read from receive buffer by the time the next word must be moved into it).

The remaining bits of the LSR indicate the status of the Transmit Shift Register, the Transmit Holding Register, and the Received Data Register; the most significant bit of the LSR is not used and is always 0. The LSR is a read-only register; writing to it has no effect.

Table 6-7. 8250 Line Status Register Bit Values.

Bit	Binary	Meaning
7	0xxxxxxx	Always zero
6	x1xxxxxx	Transmit Shift Register empty
5	xx1xxxxx	Transmit Holding Register empty
4	xxx1xxxx	BREAK received
3	xxxx1xxx	Framing error
2	xxxxx1xx	Parity error
1	xxxxxx1x	Overrun error
0	xxxxxxx1	Received data ready

The MSR (Table 6-8) monitors the four RS232C lines that report modem status. The upper 4 bits of this register indicate the voltage level of the associated RS232C line; the lower 4 bits indicate that the voltage level has changed since the register was last read.

Table 6-8. 8250 Modem Status Register Bit Values.

Bit	Binary	Meaning
7	1xxxxxxx	Data Carrier Detected (DCD) level
6	x1xxxxxx	Ring Indicator (RI) level
5	xx1xxxxx	Data Set Ready (DSR) level
4	xxx1xxxx	Clear To Send (CTS) level
3	xxxx1xxx	DCD change
2	xxxxx1xx	RI change
1	xxxxxx1x	DSR change
0	xxxxxxx1	CTS change

As mentioned previously, four types of interrupts are generated. The four types are identified by flag values in the IID Register (Table 6-9). These flags are set as follows:

- Change of any bit value in the MSR sets the modem status flag.
- Setting of the BREAK Received bit or any of the three error bits in the LSR sets the line status flag.
- Setting of the Transmit Holding Register Empty bit in the LSR sets the transmit flag.
- Setting of the Received Data Ready bit in the LSR sets the receive flag.

The IID register indicates the interrupt type, even though the IER may be disabling that type of interrupt from generating any request. The IID is a read-only register; attempts to write to it have no effect.

Table 6-9. 8250 Interrupt Identification and Causes.

IID content	Meaning
xxxxxxx1B	No interrupt active
xxxxx000B	Modem Status Interrupt; bit changed in MSR
xxxxx010B	Transmit Register Interrupt; Transmit Holding Register empty, bit set in LSR
xxxxx100B	Received Data Ready Interrupt; Data Register full, bit set in LSR
xxxxx110B	Line Status Interrupt; BREAK or error bit set in LSR

As shown in Table 6-9, an all-zero value (which in most of the other registers is a totally disabling condition) means that a Modem Status Interrupt condition has not yet been serviced. A modem need not be connected, however, for a Modem Status Interrupt condition to occur; all that is required is for one of the RS232C non-data input lines to change state, thus changing the MSR.

Whenever a flag is set in the IID, the UART interrupt-request generator will, if enabled by the UART programming, generate an interrupt request to the processor. Two or more interrupts can be active at the same time; if so, more than one flag in the IID register is set.

The IID flag for each interrupt type (and the LSR or MSR bits associated with it) clears when the corresponding register is read (or, in one case, written to). For example, reading the content of the MSR clears the modem status flag; writing a byte to the DATA register clears the transmit flag; reading the DATA register clears the receive flag; reading the LSR clears the line status flag. The LSR or MSR bit does not clear until it has been read; the IID flag clears with the LSR or MSR bit.

Programming the UART

Each time power is applied, any serial-interface device must be programmed before it is used. This programming can be done by the computer's bootstrap sequence or as a part of the port initialization routines performed when a port driver is installed. Often, both techniques are used: The bootstrap provides default conditions, and these can be modified during initialization to meet the needs of each port driver used in a session.

When the 8250 chip is programmed, the BRG Divisor Latch should be set for the proper baud rate, the LCR and MCR should be loaded, the IER should be set, and all internal interrupt requests and the receive buffer should be cleared. The sequence in which these are done is not especially critical, but any pending interrupt requests should be cleared before they are permitted to pass on to the rest of the PC.

The following sample code performs these startup actions, setting up the chip in device COM1 (at port 03F8H) to operate at 1200 bps with a word length of 8 bits, no parity checking, and all UART interrupts enabled. (In practical code, all values for addresses and operating conditions would not be built in; these values are included in the example to clarify what is being done at each step.)

```
MOV     DX,03FBh        ; base port COM1 (03F8) + LCR (3)
MOV     AL,080h         ; enable Divisor Latch
OUT     DX,AL
MOV     DX,03F8h        ; set for Baud0
MOV     AX,96           ; set divisor to 1200 bps
OUT     DX,AL
INC     DX              ; to offset 1 for Baud1
MOV     AL,AH           ; high byte of divisor
OUT     DX,AL
MOV     DX,03FBh        ; back to the LCR offset
MOV     AL,03           ; DLAB = 0, Parity = N, WL = 8
OUT     DX,AL
MOV     DX,03F9h        ; offset 1 for IER
MOV     AL,0Fh          ; enable all ints in 8250
OUT     DX,AL
MOV     DX,03FCh        ; COM1 + MCR (4)
MOV     AL,0Bh          ; OUT2 + RTS + DTR bits
OUT     DX,AL
```

(more)

```
CLRGS:
        MOV     DX,03FDh        ; clear LSR
        IN      AL,DX
        MOV     DX,03F8h        ; clear RX reg
        IN      AL,DX
        MOV     DX,03FEh        ; clear MSR
        IN      AL,DX
        MOV     DX,03FAh        ; IID reg
        IN      AL,DX
        IN      AL,DX           ; repeat to be sure
        TEST    AL,1            ; int pending?
        JZ      CLRGS           ; yes, repeat
```

Note: This code does not completely set up the IBM serial port. Although it fully programs the 8250 itself, additional work remains to be done. The system interrupt vectors must be changed to provide linkage to the interrupt service routine (ISR) code, and the 8259 Priority Interrupt Controller (PIC) chip must also be programmed to respond to interrupt requests from the UART channels. *See* PROGRAMMING IN THE MS-DOS ENVIRONMENT: CUSTOMIZING MS-DOS: Hardware Interrupt Handlers.

Device Drivers

All versions of MS-DOS since 2.0 have permitted the installation of user-provided device drivers. From the standpoint of operating-system theory, using such drivers is the proper way to handle generic communications interfacing. The following paragraphs are intended as a refresher and to explain this article's departure from standard device-driver terminology. *See* PROGRAMMING IN THE MS-DOS ENVIRONMENT: CUSTOMIZING MS-DOS: Installable Device Drivers.

An installable device driver consists of (1) a driver header that links the driver to others in the chain maintained by MS-DOS, tells the system the characteristics of this specific driver, provides pointers to the two major routines contained in the driver, and (for a character-device driver) identifies the driver by name; (2) any data and storage space the driver may require; and (3) the two major code routines.

The code routines are called the Strategy routine and the Interrupt routine in normal device-driver descriptions. Neither has any connection with the hardware interrupts dealt with by the drivers presented in this article. Because of this, the term Request routine is used instead of Interrupt routine, so that hardware interrupt code can be called an interrupt service routine (ISR) with minimal chances for confusion.

MS-DOS communicates with a device driver by reserving space for a command packet of as many as 22 bytes and by passing this packet's address to the driver with a call to the Strategy routine. All data transfer between MS-DOS and the driver, in both directions, occurs via this command packet and the Request routine. The operating system places a command code and, optionally, a byte count and a buffer address into the packet at the specified locations, then calls the Request routine. The driver performs the command and returns the status (and sometimes a byte count) in the packet.

Two Alternative Approaches

Now that the factors involved in creating interrupt-driven communications programs have been discussed, they can be put together into practical program packages. Doing so brings out not only general principles but also minor details that make the difference between success and failure of program design in this hardware-dependent and time-critical area.

The traditional way: Going it alone

Because MS-DOS provides no generic functions suitable for communications use, virtually all popular communications programs provide and install their own port driver code, and then remove it before returning to MS-DOS. This approach entails the creation of a communications handler for each program and requires the "uninstallation" of the handler on exit from the program that uses it. Despite the extra requirements, most communications programs use this method.

The alternative: Creating a communications device driver

Instead of providing temporary interface code that must be removed from the system before returning to the command level, an installable device driver can be built as a replacement for COMx so that every program can have all features. However, this approach is not compatible with existing terminal programs because it has never been a part of MS-DOS.

Comparison of the two methods

The traditional approach has several advantages, the most obvious being that the driver code can be fully tailored to the needs of the program. Because only one program will ever use the driver, no general cases need be considered.

However, if a user wants to keep communications capability available in a terminate-and-stay-resident (TSR) module for background use and also wants a different type of communications program running in the foreground (not, of course, while the background task is using the port), the background program and the foreground job must each have its own separate driver code. And, because such code usually includes buffer areas, the duplicated drivers represent wasted resources.

A single communications device driver that is installed when the system powers up and that remains active until shutdown avoids wasting resources by allowing both the background and foreground tasks to share the driver code. Until such drivers are common, however, it is unlikely that commercial software will be able to make use of them. In addition, such a driver must either provide totally general capabilities or it must include control interfaces so each user program can dynamically alter the driver to suit its needs.

At this time, the use of a single driver is an interesting exercise rather than a practical application, although a possible exception is a dedicated system in which all software is either custom designed or specially modified. In such a system, the generalized driver can provide significant improvement in the efficiency of resource allocation.

A Device-Driver Program Package

Despite the limitations mentioned in the preceding section, the first of the two complete packages in this article uses the concept of a separate device driver. The driver handles all hardware-dependent interfacing and thus permits extreme simplicity in all other modules of the package. This approach is presented first because it is especially well suited for introducing the concepts of communications programs. However, the package is not merely a tutorial device: It includes some features that are not available in most commercial programs.

The package itself consists of three separate programs. First is the device driver, which becomes a part of MS-DOS via the CONFIG.SYS file. Second is the modem engine, which is the actual terminal program. (A functionally similar component forms the heart of every communications program, whether it is written in assembly language or a high-level language and regardless of the machine or operating system in use.) Third is a separately executed support program that permits changing such driver characteristics as word length, parity, and baud rate.

In most programs that use the traditional approach, the driver and the support program are combined with the modem engine in a single unit and the resulting mass of detail obscures the essential simplicity of each part. Here, the parts are presented as separate modules to emphasize that simplicity.

The device driver: COMDVR.ASM

The device driver is written to augment the default COM1 and COM2 devices with other devices named ASY1 and ASY2 that use the same physical hardware but are logically separate. The driver (COMDVR.ASM) is implemented in MASM and is shown in the listing in Figure 6-1. Although the driver is written basically as a skeleton, it is designed to permit extensive expansion and can be used as a general-purpose sample of device-driver source code.

The code

```
 1 : Title   COMDVR  Driver for IBM COM Ports
 2 : ;       Jim Kyle, 1987
 3 : ;             Based on ideas from many sources......
 4 : ;                 including Mike Higgins, CLM March 1985;
 5 : ;                 public-domain INTBIOS program from BBS's;
 6 : ;                 COMBIOS.COM from CIS Programmers' SIG; and
 7 : ;                 ADVANCED MS-DOS by Ray Duncan.
 8 : Subttl  MS-DOS Driver Definitions
 9 :
10 :         Comment *       This comments out the Dbg macro.....
11 : Dbg     Macro   Ltr1,Ltr2,Ltr3  ; used only to debug driver...
12 :         Local   Xxx
13 :         Push    Es              ; save all regs used
```

Figure 6-1. COMDVR.ASM.   *(more)*

```
14 :          Push    Di
15 :          Push    Ax
16 :          Les     Di,Cs:Dbgptr    ; get pointer to CRT
17 :          Mov     Ax,Es:[di]
18 :          Mov     Al,Ltr1         ; move in letters
19 :          Stosw
20 :          Mov     Al,Ltr2
21 :          Stosw
22 :          Mov     Al,Ltr3
23 :          Stosw
24 :          Cmp     Di,1600         ; top 10 lines only
25 :          Jb      Xxx
26 :          Xor     Di,Di
27 : Xxx:     Mov     Word Ptr Cs:Dbgptr,Di
28 :          Pop     Ax
29 :          Pop     Di
30 :          Pop     Es
31 :          Endm
32 :          *                       ; asterisk ends commented-out region
33 : ;
34 : ;                Device Type Codes
35 : DevChr   Equ     8000h   ; this is a character device
36 : DevBlk   Equ     0000h   ; this is a block (disk) device
37 : DevIoc   Equ     4000h   ; this device accepts IOCTL requests
38 : DevNon   Equ     2000h   ; non-IBM disk driver (block only)
39 : DevOTB   Equ     2000h   ; MS-DOS 3.x out until busy supported (char)
40 : DevOCR   Equ     0800h   ; MS-DOS 3.x open/close/rm supported
41 : DevX32   Equ     0040h   ; MS-DOS 3.2 functions supported
42 : DevSpc   Equ     0010h   ; accepts special interrupt 29H
43 : DevClk   Equ     0008h   ; this is the CLOCK device
44 : DevNul   Equ     0004h   ; this is the NUL device
45 : DevSto   Equ     0002h   ; this is standard output
46 : DevSti   Equ     0001h   ; this is standard input
47 : ;
48 : ;                Error Status BITS
49 : StsErr   Equ     8000h   ; general error
50 : StsBsy   Equ     0200h   ; device busy
51 : StsDne   Equ     0100h   ; request completed
52 : ;
53 : ;                Error Reason values for lower-order bits
54 : ErrWp    Equ     0       ; write protect error
55 : ErrUu    Equ     1       ; unknown unit
56 : ErrDnr   Equ     2       ; drive not ready
57 : ErrUc    Equ     3       ; unknown command
58 : ErrCrc   Equ     4       ; cyclical redundancy check error
59 : ErrBsl   Equ     5       ; bad drive request structure length
60 : ErrSl    Equ     6       ; seek error
61 : ErrUm    Equ     7       ; unknown media
62 : ErrSnf   Equ     8       ; sector not found
63 : ErrPop   Equ     9       ; printer out of paper
64 : ErrWf    Equ     10      ; write fault
```

Figure 6-1. Continued.   *(more)*

```
 65 : ErrRf    Equ    11        ; read fault
 66 : ErrGf    Equ    12        ; general failure
 67 : ;
 68 : ;           Structure of an I/O request packet header.
 69 : ;
 70 : Pack     Struc
 71 : Len      Db     ?         ; length of record
 72 : Prtno    Db     ?         ; unit code
 73 : Code     Db     ?         ; command code
 74 : Stat     Dw     ?         ; return status
 75 : Dosq     Dd     ?         ; (unused MS-DOS queue link pointer)
 76 : Devq     Dd     ?         ; (unused driver queue link pointer)
 77 : Media    Db     ?         ; media code on read/write
 78 : Xfer     Dw     ?         ; xfer address offset
 79 : Xseg     Dw     ?         ; xfer address segment
 80 : Count    Dw     ?         ; transfer byte count
 81 : Sector   Dw     ?         ; starting sector value (block only)
 82 : Pack     Ends
 83 :
 84 : Subttl   IBM-PC Hardware Driver Definitions
 85 : page
 86 : ;
 87 : ;                  8259 data
 88 : PIC_b    Equ    020h      ; port for EOI
 89 : PIC_e    Equ    021h      ; port for Int enabling
 90 : EOI      Equ    020h      ; EOI control word
 91 : ;
 92 : ;                  8250 port offsets
 93 : RxBuf    Equ    0F8h      ; base address
 94 : Baud1    Equ    RxBuf+1   ; baud divisor high byte
 95 : IntEn    Equ    RxBuf+1   ; interrupt enable register
 96 : IntId    Equ    RxBuf+2   ; interrupt identification register
 97 : Lctrl    Equ    RxBuf+3   ; line control register
 98 : Mctrl    Equ    RxBuf+4   ; modem control register
 99 : Lstat    Equ    RxBuf+5   ; line status register
100 : Mstat    Equ    RxBuf+6   ; modem status register
101 : ;
102 : ;                  8250 LCR constants
103 : Dlab     Equ    10000000b ; divisor latch access bit
104 : SetBrk   Equ    01000000b ; send break control bit
105 : StkPar   Equ    00100000b ; stick parity control bit
106 : EvnPar   Equ    00010000b ; even parity bit
107 : GenPar   Equ    00001000b ; generate parity bit
108 : Xstop    Equ    00000100b ; extra stop bit
109 : Wd8      Equ    00000011b ; word length = 8
110 : Wd7      Equ    00000010b ; word length = 7
111 : Wd6      Equ    00000001b ; word length = 6
112 : ;
113 : ;                  8250 LSR constants
114 : xsre     Equ    01000000b ; xmt SR empty
115 : xhre     Equ    00100000b ; xmt HR empty
```

Figure 6-1. Continued.   *(more)*

```
116 : BrkRcv    Equ    00010000b ; break received
117 : FrmErr    Equ    00001000b ; framing error
118 : ParErr    Equ    00000100b ; parity error
119 : OveRun    Equ    00000010b ; overrun error
120 : rdta      Equ    00000001b ; received data ready
121 : AnyErr    Equ    BrkRcv+FrmErr+ParErr+OveRun
122 : ;
123 : ;                8250 MCR constants
124 : LpBk      Equ    00010000b ; UART out loops to in (test)
125 : Usr2      Equ    00001000b ; Gates 8250 interrupts
126 : Usr1      Equ    00000100b ; aux user1 output
127 : SetRTS    Equ    00000010b ; sets RTS output
128 : SetDTR    Equ    00000001b ; sets DTR output
129 : ;
130 : ;                8250 MSR constants
131 : CDlvl     Equ    10000000b ; carrier detect level
132 : RIlvl     Equ    01000000b ; ring indicator level
133 : DSRlvl    Equ    00100000b ; DSR level
134 : CTSlvl    Equ    00010000b ; CTS level
135 : CDchg     Equ    00001000b ; Carrier Detect change
136 : RIchg     Equ    00000100b ; Ring Indicator change
137 : DSRchg    Equ    00000010b ; DSR change
138 : CTSchg    Equ    00000001b ; CTS change
139 : ;
140 : ;                8250 IER constants
141 : S_Int     Equ    00001000b ; enable status interrupt
142 : E_Int     Equ    00000100b ; enable error interrupt
143 : X_Int     Equ    00000010b ; enable transmit interrupt
144 : R_Int     Equ    00000001b ; enable receive interrupt
145 : Allint    Equ    00001111b ; enable all interrupts
146 :
147 : Subttl  Definitions for THIS Driver
148 : page
149 : ;
150 : ;                Bit definitions for the output status byte
151 : ;                      ( this driver only )
152 : LinIdl    Equ    0ffh     ; if all bits off, xmitter is idle
153 : LinXof    Equ    1        ; output is suspended by XOFF
154 : LinDSR    Equ    2        ; output is suspended until DSR comes on again
155 : LinCTS    Equ    4        ; output is suspended until CTS comes on again
156 : ;
157 : ;                Bit definitions for the input status byte
158 : ;                      ( this driver only )
159 : BadInp    Equ    1        ; input line errors have been detected
160 : LostDt    Equ    2        ; receiver buffer overflowed, data lost
161 : OffLin    Equ    4        ; device is off line now
162 : ;
163 : ;                Bit definitions for the special characteristics words
164 : ;                      ( this driver only )
165 : ;                InSpec controls how input from the UART is treated
166 : ;
```

Figure 6-1. Continued.   *(more)*

```
167 : InEpc    Equ    0001h   ; errors translate to codes with parity bit on
168 : ;
169 : ;               OutSpec controls how output to the UART is treated
170 : ;
171 : OutDSR   Equ    0001h   ; DSR is used to throttle output data
172 : OutCTS   Equ    0002h   ; CTS is used to throttle output data
173 : OutXon   Equ    0004h   ; XON/XOFF is used to throttle output data
174 : OutCdf   Equ    0010h   ; carrier detect is off-line signal
175 : OutDrf   Equ    0020h   ; DSR is off-line signal
176 : ;
177 : Unit     Struc          ; each unit has a structure defining its state:
178 : Port     Dw     ?       ; I/O port address
179 : Vect     Dw     ?       ; interrupt vector offset (NOT interrupt number!)
180 : Isradr   Dw     ?       ; offset to interrupt service routine
181 : OtStat   Db     Wd8     ; default LCR bit settings during INIT,
182 :                         ; output status bits after
183 : InStat   Db     Usr2+SetRTS+SetDTR   ; MCR bit settings during INIT,
184 :                         ; input status bits after
185 : InSpec   Dw     InEpc   ; special mode bits for INPUT
186 : OutSpec Dw      OutXon  ; special mode bits for OUTPUT
187 : Baud     Dw     96      ; current baud rate divisor value (1200 b)
188 : Ifirst   Dw     0       ; offset of first character in input buffer
189 : Iavail   Dw     0       ; offset of next available byte
190 : Ibuf     Dw     ?       ; pointer to input buffer
191 : Ofirst   Dw     0       ; offset of first character in output buffer
192 : Oavail   Dw     0       ; offset of next avail byte in output buffer
193 : Obuf     Dw     ?       ; pointer to output buffer
194 : Unit     Ends
195 :
196 : ;
197 : ;               Beginning of driver code and data
198 : ;
199 : Driver   Segment
200 :          Assume  Cs:driver, ds:driver, es:driver
201 :          Org     0               ; drivers start at 0
202 :
203 :          Dw      Async2,-1       ; pointer to next device
204 :          Dw      DevChr + DevIoc ; character device with IOCTL
205 :          Dw      Strtegy         ; offset of Strategy routine
206 :          Dw      Request1        ; offset of interrupt entry point 1
207 :          Db      'ASY1    '      ; device 1 name
208 : Async2:
209 :          Dw      -1,-1           ; pointer to next device: MS-DOS fills in
210 :          Dw      DevChr + DevIoc ; character device with IOCTL
211 :          Dw      Strtegy         ; offset of Strategy routine
212 :          Dw      Request2        ; offset of interrupt entry point 2
213 :          Db      'ASY2    '      ; device 2 name
214 :
215 : ;dbgptr Dd      0b0000000h
216 : ;
217 : ;               Following is the storage area for the request packet pointer
```

Figure 6-1. Continued.   *(more)*

```
218 : ;
219 : PackHd   Dd      0
220 : ;
221 : ;           baud rate conversion table
222 : Asy_baudt Dw          50,2304      ; first value is desired baud rate
223 :           Dw          75,1536      ; second is divisor register value
224 :           Dw         110,1047
225 :           Dw      ∉  134, 857
226 :           Dw         150, 786
227 :           Dw         300, 384
228 :           Dw         600, 192
229 :           Dw        1200,  96
230 :           Dw        1800,  64
231 :           Dw        2000,  58
232 :           Dw        2400,  48
233 :           Dw        3600,  32
234 :           Dw        4800,  24
235 :           Dw        7200,  16
236 :           Dw        9600,  12
237 :
238 : ; table of structures
239 : ;        ASY1 defaults to the COM1 port, INT 0CH vector, XON,
240 : ;        no parity, 8 databits, 1 stop bit, and 1200 baud
241 : Asy_tab1:
242 :        Unit   <3f8h,30h,asy1isr,,,,,,,,,in1buf,,,out1buf>
243 :
244 : ;        ASY2 defaults to the COM2 port, INT 0BH vector, XON,
245 : ;        no parity, 8 databits, 1 stop bit, and 1200 baud
246 : Asy_tab2:
247 :        Unit   <2f8h,2ch,asy2isr,,,,,,,,,in2buf,,,out2buf>
248 :
249 : Bufsiz  Equ    256       ; input buffer size
250 : Bufmsk  =      Bufsiz-1  ; mask for calculating offsets modulo bufsiz
251 : In1buf  Db     Bufsiz DUP (?)
252 : Out1buf Db     Bufsiz DUP (?)
253 : In2buf  Db     Bufsiz DUP (?)
254 : Out2buf Db     Bufsiz DUP (?)
255 : ;
256 : ;           Following is a table of offsets to all the driver functions
257 :
258 : Asy_funcs:
259 :        Dw     Init        ;  0 initialize driver
260 :        Dw     Mchek       ;  1 media check (block only)
261 :        Dw     BldBPB      ;  2 build BPB (block only)
262 :        Dw     Ioctlin     ;  3 IOCTL read
263 :        Dw     Read        ;  4 read
264 :        Dw     Ndread      ;  5 nondestructive read
265 :        Dw     Rxstat      ;  6 input status
266 :        Dw     Inflush     ;  7 flush input buffer
267 :        Dw     Write       ;  8 write
268 :        Dw     Write       ;  9 write with verify
```

Figure 6-1. Continued.   *(more)*

```
269 :          Dw      Txstat         ; 10 output status
270 :          Dw      Txflush        ; 11 flush output buffer
271 :          Dw      Ioctlout       ; 12 IOCTL write
272 : ; Following are not used in this driver.....
273 :          Dw      Zexit          ; 13 open (3.x only, not used)
274 :          Dw      Zexit          ; 14 close (3.x only, not used)
275 :          Dw      Zexit          ; 15 rem med (3.x only, not used)
276 :          Dw      Zexit          ; 16 out until bsy (3.x only, not used)
277 :          Dw      Zexit          ; 17
278 :          Dw      Zexit          ; 18
279 :          Dw      Zexit          ; 19 generic IOCTL request (3.2 only)
280 :          Dw      Zexit          ; 20
281 :          Dw      Zexit          ; 21
282 :          Dw      Zexit          ; 22
283 :          Dw      Zexit          ; 23 get logical drive map (3.2 only)
284 :          Dw      Zexit          ; 24 set logical drive map (3.2 only)
285 :
286 : Subttl   Driver Code
287 : Page
288 : ;
289 : ;          The Strategy routine itself:
290 : ;
291 : Strtegy Proc     Far
292 : ;        dbg     'S','R',' '
293 :          Mov     Word Ptr CS:PackHd,BX     ; store the offset
294 :          Mov     Word Ptr CS:PackHd+2,ES ; store the segment
295 :          Ret
296 : Strtegy Endp
297 : ;
298 : Request1:                        ; async1 has been requested
299 :          Push    Si              ; save SI
300 :          Lea     Si,Asy_tab1     ; get the device unit table address
301 :          Jmp     Short   Gen_request
302 :
303 : Request2:                        ; async2 has been requested
304 :          Push    Si              ; save SI
305 :          Lea     Si,Asy_tab2     ; get unit table two's address
306 :
307 : Gen_request:
308 : ;        dbg     'R','R',' '
309 :          Pushf                   ; save all regs
310 :          Cld
311 :          Push    Ax
312 :          Push    Bx
313 :          Push    Cx
314 :          Push    Dx
315 :          Push    Di
316 :          Push    Bp
317 :          Push    Ds
318 :          Push    Es
319 :          Push    Cs              ; set DS = CS
```

Figure 6-1. Continued.   *(more)*

```
320 :          Pop     Ds
321 :          Les     Bx,PackHd       ; get packet pointer
322 :          Lea     Di,Asy_funcs    ; point DI to jump table
323 :          Mov     Al,es:code[bx]  ; command code
324 :          Cbw
325 :          Add     Ax,Ax           ; double to word
326 :          Add     Di,ax
327 :          Jmp     [di]            ; go do it
328 : ;
329 : ;        Exit from driver request
330 : ;
331 : ExitP    Proc    Far
332 : Bsyexit:
333 :          Mov     Ax,StsBsy
334 :          Jmp     Short   Exit
335 :
336 : Mchek:
337 : BldBPB:
338 : Zexit:   Xor     Ax,Ax
339 : Exit:    Les     Bx,PackHd       ; get packet pointer
340 :          Or      Ax,StsDne
341 :          Mov     Es:Stat[Bx],Ax  ; set return status
342 :          Pop     Es              ; restore registers
343 :          Pop     Ds
344 :          Pop     Bp
345 :          Pop     Di
346 :          Pop     Dx
347 :          Pop     Cx
348 :          Pop     Bx
349 :          Pop     Ax
350 :          Popf
351 :          Pop     Si
352 :          Ret
353 : ExitP    Endp
354 :
355 : Subttl   Driver Service Routines
356 : Page
357 :
358 : ;        Read data from device
359 :
360 : Read:
361 : ;        dbg     'R','d',' '
362 :          Mov     Cx,Es:Count[bx] ; get requested nbr
363 :          Mov     Di,Es:Xfer[bx]  ; get target pointer
364 :          Mov     Dx,Es:Xseg[bx]
365 :          Push    Bx              ; save for count fixup
366 :          Push    Es
367 :          Mov     Es,Dx
368 :          Test    InStat[si],BadInp Or LostDt
369 :          Je      No_lerr         ; no error so far...
370 :          Add     Sp,4            ; error, flush SP
```

Figure 6-1. Continued.   *(more)*

```
371 :           And     InStat[si],Not ( BadInp Or LostDt )
372 :           Mov     Ax,ErrRf        ; error, report it
373 :           Jmp.    Exit
374 : No_lerr:
375 :           Call    Get_in          ; go for one
376 :           Or      Ah,Ah
377 :           Jnz     Got_all         ; none to get now
378 :           Stosb                   ; store it
379 :           Loop    No_lerr         ; go for more
380 : Got_all:
381 :           Pop     Es
382 :           Pop     Bx
383 :           Sub     Di,Es:Xfer[bx]  ; calc number stored
384 :           Mov     Es:Count[bx],Di ; return as count
385 :           Jmp     Zexit
386 :
387 : ;         Nondestructive read from device
388 :
389 : Ndread:
390 :           Mov     Di,ifirst[si]
391 :           Cmp     Di,iavail[si]
392 :           Jne     Ndget
393 :           Jmp     Bsyexit         ; buffer empty
394 : Ndget:
395 :           Push    Bx
396 :           Mov     Bx,ibuf[si]
397 :           Mov     Al,[bx+di]
398 :           Pop     Bx
399 :           Mov     Es:media[bx],al ; return char
400 :           Jmp     Zexit
401 :
402 : ;         Input status request
403 :
404 : Rxstat:
405 :           Mov     Di,ifirst[si]
406 :           Cmp     Di,iavail[si]
407 :           Jne     Rxful
408 :           Jmp     Bsyexit         ; buffer empty
409 : Rxful:
410 :           Jmp     Zexit           ; have data
411 :
412 : ;         Input flush request
413 :
414 : Inflush:
415 :           Mov     Ax,iavail[si]
416 :           Mov     Ifirst[si],ax
417 :           Jmp     Zexit
418 :
419 : ;         Output data to device
420 :
```

Figure 6-1. Continued.   *(more)*

```
421 :  Write:
422 : ;           dbg      'W','r',' '
423 :             Mov      Cx,es:count[bx]
424 :             Mov      Di,es:xfer[bx]
425 :             Mov      Ax,es:xseg[bx]
426 :             Mov      Es,ax
427 :  Wlup:
428 :             Mov      Al,es:[di]       ; get the byte
429 :             Inc      Di
430 :  Wwait:
431 :             Call     Put_out          ; put away
432 :             Cmp      Ah,0
433 :             Jne      Wwait            ; wait for room!
434 :             Call     Start_output     ; get it going
435 :             Loop     Wlup
436 :
437 :             Jmp      Zexit
438 :
439 : ;           Output status request
440 :
441 :  Txstat:
442 :             Mov      Ax,ofirst[si]
443 :             Dec      Ax
444 :             And      Ax,bufmsk
445 :             Cmp      Ax,oavail[si]
446 :             Jne      Txroom
447 :             Jmp      Bsyexit          ; buffer full
448 :  Txroom:
449 :             Jmp      Zexit            ; room exists
450 :
451 : ;           IOCTL read request, return line parameters
452 :
453 :  Ioctlin:
454 :             Mov      Cx,es:count[bx]
455 :             Mov      Di,es:xfer[bx]
456 :             Mov      Dx,es:xseg[bx]
457 :             Mov      Es,dx
458 :             Cmp      Cx,10
459 :             Je       Doiocin
460 :             Mov      Ax,errbsl
461 :             Jmp      Exit
462 :  Doiocin:
463 :             Mov      Dx,port[si]      ; base port
464 :             Mov      Dl,Lctrl         ; line status
465 :             Mov      Cx,4             ; LCR, MCR, LSR, MSR
466 :  Getport:
467 :             In       Al,dx
468 :             Stos     Byte Ptr [DI]
469 :             Inc      Dx
470 :             Loop     Getport
471 :
```

Figure 6-1. Continued.   *(more)*

```
472 :           Mov     Ax,InSpec[si]    ; spec in flags
473 :           Stos    Word Ptr [DI]
474 :           Mov     Ax,OutSpec[si]   ; out flags
475 :           Stos    Word Ptr [DI]
476 :           Mov     Ax,baud[si]      ; baud rate
477 :           Mov     Bx,di
478 :           Mov     Di,offset Asy_baudt+2
479 :           Mov     Cx,15
480 : Baudcin:
481 :           Cmp     [di],ax
482 :           Je      Yesinb
483 :           Add     Di,4
484 :           Loop    Baudcin
485 : Yesinb:
486 :           Mov     Ax,-2[di]
487 :           Mov     Di,bx
488 :           Stos    Word Ptr [DI]
489 :           Jmp     Zexit
490 :
491 : ;        Flush output buffer request
492 :
493 : Txflush:
494 :           Mov     Ax,oavail[si]
495 :           Mov     Ofirst[si],ax
496 :           Jmp     Zexit
497 :
498 : ;        IOCTL request: change line parameters for this driver
499 :
500 : Ioctlout:
501 :           Mov     Cx,es:count[bx]
502 :           Mov     Di,es:xfer[bx]
503 :           Mov     Dx,es:xseg[bx]
504 :           Mov     Es,dx
505 :           Cmp     Cx,10
506 :           Je      Doiocout
507 :           Mov     Ax,errbsl
508 :           Jmp     Exit
509 :
510 : Doiocout:
511 :           Mov     Dx,port[si]      ; base port
512 :           Mov     Dl,Lctrl         ; line ctrl
513 :           Mov     Al,es:[di]
514 :           Inc     Di
515 :           Or      Al,Dlab          ; set baud
516 :           Out     Dx,al
517 :           Clc
518 :           Jnc     $+2
519 :           Inc     Dx               ; mdm ctrl
520 :           Mov     Al,es:[di]
521 :           Or      Al,Usr2          ; Int Gate
522 :           Out     Dx,al
```

Figure 6-1. Continued.   *(more)*

```
523 :          Add    Di,3              ; skip LSR,MSR
524 :          Mov    Ax,es:[di]
525 :          Add    Di,2
526 :          Mov    InSpec[si],ax
527 :          Mov    Ax,es:[di]
528 :          Add    Di,2
529 :          Mov    OutSpec[si],ax
530 :          Mov    Ax,es:[di]        ; set baud
531 :          Mov    Bx,di
532 :          Mov    Di,offset Asy_baudt
533 :          Mov    Cx,15
534 : Baudcout:
535 :          Cmp    [di],ax
536 :          Je     Yesoutb
537 :          Add    Di,4
538 :          Loop   Baudcout
539 :
540 :          Mov    Dl,Lctrl          ; line ctrl
541 :          In     Al,dx             ; get LCR data
542 :          And    Al,not Dlab       ; strip
543 :          Clc
544 :          Jnc    $+2
545 :          Out    Dx,al             ; put back
546 :          Mov    Ax,ErrUm          ; "unknown media"
547 :          Jmp    Exit
548 :
549 : Yesoutb:
550 :          Mov    Ax,2[di]          ; get divisor
551 :          Mov    Baud[si],ax       ; save to report later
552 :          Mov    Dx,port[si]       ; set divisor
553 :          Out    Dx,al
554 :          Clc
555 :          Jnc    $+2
556 :          Inc    Dx
557 :          Mov    Al,ah
558 :          Out    Dx,al
559 :          Clc
560 :          Jnc    $+2
561 :          Mov    Dl,Lctrl          ; line ctrl
562 :          In     Al,dx             ; get LCR data
563 :          And    Al,not Dlab       ; strip
564 :          Clc
565 :          Jnc    $+2
566 :          Out    Dx,al             ; put back
567 :          Jmp    Zexit
568 :
569 : Subttl   Ring Buffer Routines
570 : Page
571 :
572 : Put_out Proc    Near    ; puts AL into output ring buffer
573 :          Push   Cx
```

Figure 6-1. Continued.   *(more)*

```
574 :          Push     Di
575 :          Pushf
576 :          Cli
577 :          Mov      Cx,oavail[si]    ; put ptr
578 :          Mov      Di,cx
579 :          Inc      Cx               ; bump
580 :          And      Cx,bufmsk
581 :          Cmp      Cx,ofirst[si]    ; overflow?
582 :          Je       Poerr            ; yes, don't
583 :          Add      Di,obuf[si]      ; no
584 :          Mov      [di],al          ; put in buffer
585 :          Mov      Oavail[si],cx
586 : ;        dbg      'p','o',' '
587 :          Mov      Ah,0
588 :          Jmp      Short    Poret
589 : Poerr:
590 :          Mov      Ah,-1
591 : Poret:
592 :          Popf
593 :          Pop      Di
594 :          Pop      Cx
595 :          Ret
596 : Put_out Endp
597 :
598 : Get_out Proc      Near     ; gets next character from output ring buffer
599 :          Push     Cx
600 :          Push     Di
601 :          Pushf
602 :          Cli
603 :          Mov      Di,ofirst[si]    ; get ptr
604 :          Cmp      Di,oavail[si]    ; put ptr
605 :          Jne      Ngoerr
606 :          Mov      Ah,-1            ; empty
607 :          Jmp      Short    Goret
608 : Ngoerr:
609 : ;        dbg      'g','o',' '
610 :          Mov      Cx,di
611 :          Add      Di,obuf[si]
612 :          Mov      Al,[di]          ; get char
613 :          Mov      Ah,0
614 :          Inc      Cx               ; bump ptr
615 :          And      Cx,bufmsk        ; wrap
616 :          Mov      Ofirst[si],cx
617 : Goret:
618 :          Popf
619 :          Pop      Di
620 :          Pop      Cx
621 :          Ret
622 : Get_out Endp
623 :
624 : Put_in Proc       Near     ; puts the char from AL into input ring buffer
```

Figure 6-1. Continued.   *(more)*

```
625 :           Push    Cx
626 :           Push    Di
627 :           Pushf
628 :           Cli
629 :           Mov     Di,iavail[si]
630 :           Mov     Cx,di
631 :           Inc     Cx
632 :           And     Cx,bufmsk
633 :           Cmp     Cx,ifirst[si]
634 :           Jne     Npierr
635 :           Mov     Ah,-1
636 :           Jmp     Short    Piret
637 : Npierr:
638 :           Add     Di,ibuf[si]
639 :           Mov     [di],al
640 :           Mov     Iavail[si],cx
641 : ;         dbg     'p','i',' '
642 :           Mov     Ah,0
643 : Piret:
644 :           Popf
645 :           Pop     Di
646 :           Pop     Cx
647 :           Ret
648 : Put_in    Endp
649 :
650 : Get_in    Proc    Near    ; gets one from input ring buffer into AL
651 :           Push    Cx
652 :           Push    Di
653 :           Pushf
654 :           Cli
655 :           Mov     Di,ifirst[si]
656 :           Cmp     Di,iavail[si]
657 :           Je      Gierr
658 :           Mov     Cx,di
659 :           Add     Di,ibuf[si]
660 :           Mov     Al,[di]
661 :           Mov     Ah,0
662 : ;         dbg     'g','i',' '
663 :           Inc     Cx
664 :           And     Cx,bufmsk
665 :           Mov     Ifirst[si],cx
666 :           Jmp     Short    Giret
667 : Gierr:
668 :           Mov     Ah,-1
669 : Giret:
670 :           Popf
671 :           Pop     Di
672 :           Pop     Cx
673 :           Ret
674 : Get_in    Endp
675 :
```

Figure 6-1. Continued.   *(more)*

```
676 :   Subttl  Interrupt Dispatcher Routine
677 :   Page
678 :
679 :   Asy1isr:
680 :           Sti
681 :           Push    Si
682 :           Lea     Si,asy_tab1
683 :           Jmp     Short   Int_serve
684 :
685 :   Asy2isr:
686 :           Sti
687 :           Push    Si
688 :           Lea     Si,asy_tab2
689 :
690 :   Int_serve:
691 :           Push    Ax              ; save all regs
692 :           Push    Bx
693 :           Push    Cx
694 :           Push    Dx
695 :           Push    Di
696 :           Push    Ds
697 :           Push    Cs              ; set DS = CS
698 :           Pop     Ds
699 :   Int_exit:
700 : ;         dbg     'I','x',' '
701 :           Mov     Dx,Port[si]     ; base address
702 :           Mov     Dl,IntId        ; check Int ID
703 :           In      Al,Dx
704 :           Cmp     Al,00h          ; dispatch filter
705 :           Je      Int_modem
706 :           Jmp     Int_mo_no
707 :   Int_modem:
708 : ;         dbg     'M','S',' '
709 :           Mov     Dl,Mstat
710 :           In      Al,dx           ; read MSR content
711 :           Test    Al,CDlvl        ; carrier present?
712 :           Jnz     Msdsr           ; yes, test for DSR
713 :           Test    OutSpec[si],OutCdf   ; no, is CD off line?
714 :           Jz      Msdsr
715 :           Or      InStat[si],OffLin
716 :   Msdsr:
717 :           Test    Al,DSRlvl       ; DSR present?
718 :           Jnz     Dsron           ; yes, handle it
719 :           Test    OutSpec[si],OutDSR    ; no, is DSR throttle?
720 :           Jz      Dsroff
721 :           Or      OtStat[si],LinDSR     ; yes, throttle down
722 :   Dsroff:
723 :           Test    OutSpec[si],OutDrf    ; is DSR off line?
724 :           Jz      Mscts
725 :           Or      InStat[si],OffLin     ; yes, set flag
726 :           Jmp     Short   Mscts
```

Figure 6-1. Continued.   *(more)*

```
727 :   Dsron:
728 :           Test    OtStat[si],LinDSR       ; throttled for DSR?
729 :           Jz      Mscts
730 :           Xor     OtStat[si],LinDSR       ; yes, clear it out
731 :           Call    Start_output
732 :   Mscts:
733 :           Test    Al,CTSlvl       ; CTS present?
734 :           Jnz     Ctson           ; yes, handle it
735 :           Test    OutSpec[si],OutCTS      ; no, is CTS throttle?
736 :           Jz      Int_exit2
737 :           Or      OtStat[si],LinCTS       ; yes, shut it down
738 :           Jmp     Short   Int_exit2
739 :   Ctson:
740 :           Test    OtStat[si],LinCTS       ; throttled for CTS?
741 :           Jz      Int_exit2
742 :           Xor     OtStat[si],LinCTS       ; yes, clear it out
743 :           Jmp     Short   Int_exit1
744 :   Int_mo_no:
745 :           Cmp     Al,02h
746 :           Jne     Int_tx_no
747 :   Int_txmit:
748 : ;         dbg     'T','x',' '
749 :   Int_exit1:
750 :           Call    Start_output    ; try to send another
751 :   Int_exit2:
752 :           Jmp     Int_exit
753 :   Int_tx_no:
754 :           Cmp     Al,04h
755 :           Jne     Int_rec_no
756 :   Int_receive:
757 : ;         dbg     'R','x',' '
758 :           Mov     Dx,port[si]
759 :           In      Al,dx           ; take char from 8250
760 :           Test    OutSpec[si],OutXon  ; is XON/XOFF enabled?
761 :           Jz      Stuff_in        ; no
762 :           Cmp     Al,'S' And 01FH ; yes, is this XOFF?
763 :           Jne     Isq             ; no, check for XON
764 :           Or      OtStat[si],LinXof ; yes, disable output
765 :           Jmp     Int_exit2       ; don't store this one
766 :   Isq:
767 :           Cmp     Al,'Q' And 01FH ; is this XON?
768 :           Jne     Stuff_in        ; no, save it
769 :           Test    OtStat[si],LinXof ; yes, waiting?
770 :           Jz      Int_exit2       ; no, ignore it
771 :           Xor     OtStat[si],LinXof ; yes, clear the XOFF bit
772 :           Jmp     Int_exit1       ; and try to resume xmit
773 :   Int_rec_no:
774 :           Cmp     Al,06h
775 :           Jne     Int_done
776 :   Int_rxstat:
777 : ;         dbg     'E','R',' '
```

Figure 6-1. Continued.   *(more)*

```
778 :          Mov     Dl,Lstat
779 :          In      Al,dx
780 :          Test    InSpec[si],InEpc ; return them as codes?
781 :          Jz      Nocode           ; no, just set error alarm
782 :          And     Al,AnyErr        ; yes, mask off all but error bits
783 :          Or      Al,080h
784 : Stuff_in:
785 :          Call    Put_in           ; put input char in buffer
786 :          Cmp     Ah,0             ; did it fit?
787 :          Je      Int_exit3        ; yes, all OK
788 :          Or      InStat[si],LostDt ; no, set DataLost bit
789 : Int_exit3:
790 :          Jmp     Int_exit
791 : Nocode:
792 :          Or      InStat[si],BadInp
793 :          Jmp     Int_exit3
794 : Int_done:
795 :          Clc
796 :          Jnc     $+2
797 :          Mov     Al,EOI           ; all done now
798 :          Out     PIC_b,Al
799 :          Pop     Ds               ; restore regs
800 :          Pop     Di
801 :          Pop     Dx
802 :          Pop     Cx
803 :          Pop     Bx
804 :          Pop     Ax
805 :          Pop     Si
806 :          Iret
807 :
808 : Start_output   Proc    Near
809 :          Test    OtStat[si],LinIdl ; Blocked?
810 :          Jnz     Dont_start       ; yes, no output
811 :          Mov     Dx,port[si]      ; no, check UART
812 :          Mov     Dl,Lstat
813 :          In      Al,Dx
814 :          Test    Al,xhre          ; empty?
815 :          Jz      Dont_start       ; no
816 :          Call    Get_out          ; yes, anything waiting?
817 :          Or      Ah,Ah
818 :          Jnz     Dont_start       ; no
819 :          Mov     Dl,RxBuf         ; yes, send it out
820 :          Out     Dx,al
821 : ;        dbg     's','o',' '
822 : Dont_start:
823 :          ret
824 : Start_output   Endp
825 :
826 : Subttl  Initialization Request Routine
827 : Page
828 :
```

Figure 6-1. Continued.

(more)

```
829 : Init:    Lea    Di,$              ; release rest...
830 :          Mov    Es:Xfer[bx],Di
831 :          Mov    Es:Xseg[bx],Cs
832 :
833 :          Mov    Dx,Port[si]       ; base port
834 :          Mov    Dl,Lctrl
835 :          Mov    Al,Dlab           ; enable divisor
836 :          Out    Dx,Al
837 :          Clc
838 :          Jnc    $+2
839 :          Mov    Dl,RxBuf
840 :          Mov    Ax,Baud[si]       ; set baud
841 :          Out    Dx,Al
842 :          Clc
843 :          Jnc    $+2
844 :          Inc    Dx
845 :          Mov    Al,Ah
846 :          Out    Dx,Al
847 :          Clc
848 :          Jnc    $+2
849 :
850 :          Mov    Dl,Lctrl          ; set LCR
851 :          Mov    Al,OtStat[si]     ; from table
852 :          Out    Dx,Al
853 :          Mov    OtStat[si],0      ; clear status
854 :          Clc
855 :          Jnc    $+2
856 :          Mov    Dl,IntEn          ; IER
857 :          Mov    Al,AllInt         ; enable ints in 8250
858 :          Out    Dx,Al
859 :          Clc
860 :          Jnc    $+2
861 :          Mov    Dl,Mctrl          ; set MCR
862 :          Mov    Al,InStat[si]     ; from table
863 :          Out    Dx,Al
864 :          Mov    InStat[si],0      ; clear status
865 :
866 : ClRgs:   Mov    Dl,Lstat          ; clear LSR
867 :          In     Al,Dx
868 :          Mov    Dl,RxBuf          ; clear RX reg
869 :          In     Al,Dx
870 :          Mov    Dl,Mstat          ; clear MSR
871 :          In     Al,Dx
872 :          Mov    Dl,IntId          ; IID reg
873 :          In     Al,Dx
874 :          In     Al,Dx
875 :          Test   Al,1              ; int pending?
876 :          Jz     ClRgs             ; yes, repeat
877 :
878 :          Cli
879 :          Xor    Ax,Ax             ; set int vec
```

Figure 6-1. Continued.   *(more)*

```
880 :          Mov      Es,Ax
881 :          Mov      Di,Vect[si]
882 :          Mov      Ax,IsrAdr[si]   ; from table
883 :          Stosw
884 :          Mov      Es:[di],cs
885 :
886 :          In       Al,PIC_e        ; get 8259
887 :          And      Al,0E7h         ; com1/2 mask
888 :          Clc
889 :          Jnb      $+2
890 :          Out      PIC_e,Al
891 :          Sti
892 :
893 :          Mov      Al,EOI          ; now send EOI just in case
894 :          Out      PIC_b,Al
895 :
896 : ;        dbg      'D','I',' '     ; driver installed
897 :          Jmp      Zexit
898 :
899 : Driver   Ends
900 :          End
```

Figure 6-1. Continued.

The first part of the driver source code (after the necessary MASM housekeeping details
in lines 1 through 8) is a commented-out macro definition (lines 10 through 32). This
macro is used only during debugging and is part of a debugging technique that requires
no sophisticated hardware and no more complex debugging program than the venerable
DEBUG.COM. (Debugging techniques are discussed after the presentation of the driver
program itself.)

Definitions

The actual driver source program consists of three sets of EQU definitions (lines 34
through 194), followed by the modular code and data areas (lines 197 through 900). The
first set of definitions (lines 34 through 82) gives symbolic names to the permissible values
for MS-DOS device-driver control bits and the device-driver structures.

The second set of definitions (lines 84 through 145) assigns names to the ports and bit
values that are associated with the IBM hardware — both the 8259 PIC and the 8250 UART.
The third set of definitions (lines 147 through 194) assigns names to the control values and
structures associated with this driver.

The definition method used here is recommended for all drivers. To move this driver from
the IBM architecture to some other hardware, the major change required to the program
would be reassignment of the port addresses and bit values in lines 84 through 145.

The control values and structures for this specific driver (defined in the third EQU set)
provide the means by which the separate support program can modify the actions of each
of the two logical drivers. They also permit the driver to return status information to both

the support program and the using program as necessary. Only a few features are implemented, but adequate space for expansion is provided. The addition of a few more definitions in this area and one or two extra procedures in the code section would do all that is necessary to extend the driver's capabilities to such features as automatic expansion of tab characters, case conversion, and so forth, should they be desired.

Headers and structure tables

The driver code itself starts with a linked pair of device-driver header blocks, one for *ASY1* (lines 201 through 207) and the other for *ASY2* (lines 208 through 213). Following the headers, in lines 215 through 236, are a commented-out space reservation used by the debugging procedure (line 215), the pointer to the command packet (line 219), and the baud-rate conversion table (lines 221 through 236).

The conversion table is followed by structure tables containing all data unique to *ASY1* (lines 239 through 242) and *ASY2* (lines 244 through 247). After the structure tables, buffer areas are reserved in lines 249 through 254. One input buffer and one output buffer are reserved for each port. All buffers are the same size; for simplicity, buffer size is given a name (at line 249) so that it can be changed by editing a single line of the program.

The size is arbitrary in this case, but if file transfers are anticipated, the buffer should be able to hold at least 2 seconds' worth of data (240 bytes at 1200 bps) to avoid data loss during writes to disk. Whatever size is chosen should be a power of 2 for simple pointer arithmetic and, if video display is intended, should not be less than 8 bytes, to prevent losing characters when the screen scrolls.

If additional ports are desired, more headers can be added after line 213; corresponding structure tables for each driver, plus matching pairs of buffers, would also be necessary. The final part of this area is the dispatch table (lines 256 through 284), which lists offsets of all request routines in the driver; its use is discussed below.

Strategy and Request routines

With all data taken care of, the program code begins at the Strategy routine (lines 289 through 296), which is used by both ports. This code saves the command packet address passed to it by MS-DOS for use by the Request routine and returns to MS-DOS.

The Request routines (lines 298 through 567) are also shared by both ports, but the two drivers are distinguished by the address placed into the SI register. This address points to the structure table that is unique to each port and contains such data as the port's base address, the associated hardware interrupt vector, the interrupt service routine offset within the driver's segment, the base offsets of the input and output buffers for that port, two pointers for each of the buffers, and the input and output status conditions (including baud rate) for the port. The only difference between one port's driver and the other's is the data pointed to by SI; all Request routine code is shared by both ports.

Each driver's Request routine has a unique entry point (at line 298 for *ASY1* and at line 303 for *ASY2*) that saves the original content of the SI register and then loads it with the address of the structure table for that driver. The routines then join as a common stream at line 307 (*Gen_request*).

This common code preserves all other registers used (lines 309 through 318), sets DS equal to CS (lines 319 and 320), retrieves the command-packet pointer saved by the Strategy routine (line 321), uses the pointer to get the command code (line 323), uses the code to calculate an offset into a table of addresses (lines 324 through 326), and performs an indexed jump (lines 322 and 327) by way of the dispatch table (lines 256 through 284) to the routine that executes the requested command (at line 336, 360, 389, 404, 414, 421, 441, 453, 500, or 829).

Although the device-driver specifications for MS-DOS version 3.2 list command request codes ranging from 0 to 24, not all are used. Earlier versions of MS-DOS permitted only 0 to 12 (versions 2.x) or 0 to 16 (versions 3.0 and 3.1) codes. In this driver, all 24 codes are accounted for; those not implemented in this driver return a DONE and NO ERROR status to the caller. Because the Request routine is called only by MS-DOS itself, there is no check for invalid codes. Actually, because the header attribute bits are *not* set to specify that codes 13 through 24 are valid, the 24 bytes occupied by their table entries (lines 273 through 284) could be saved by omitting the entries. They are included only to show how nonexistent commands can be accommodated.

Immediately following the dispatch indexed jump, at lines 329 through 353 within the same PROC declaration, is the common code used by all Request routines to store status information in the command packet, restore the registers, and return to the caller. The alternative entry points for BUSY status (line 332), NO ERROR status (line 338), or an error code (in the AX register at entry to *Exit*, line 339) not only save several bytes of redundant code but also improve readability of the code by providing unique single labels for BUSY, NO ERROR, and ERROR return conditions.

All of the Request routines, except for the *Init* code at line 829, immediately follow the dispatching shell in lines 358 through 568. Each is simplified to perform just one task, such as read data in or write data out. The *Read* routine (lines 360 through 385) is typical: First, the requested byte count and user's buffer address are obtained from the command packet. Next, the pointer to the command packet is saved with a PUSH instruction, so that the ES and BX registers can be used for a pointer to the port's input buffer.

Before the *Get_in* routine that actually accesses the input buffer is called, the input status byte is checked (line 368). If an error condition is flagged, lines 370 through 373 clear the status flag, flush the saved pointers from the stack, and jump to the error-return exit from the driver. If no error exists, line 375 calls *Get_in* to access the input buffer and lines 376 and 377 determine whether a byte was obtained. If a byte is found, it is stored in the user's buffer by line 378, and line 379 loops back to get another byte until the requested count has been obtained or until no more bytes are available. In practice, the count is an upper limit and the loop is normally broken when data runs out.

No matter how it happens, control eventually reaches the *Got_all* routine and lines 381 and 382, where the saved pointers to the command packet are restored from the stack. Lines 383 and 384 adjust the count value in the packet to reflect the actual number of bytes obtained. Finally, line 385 jumps to the normal, no-error exit from the driver.

Buffering

Both buffers for each driver are of the type known as circular, or ring, buffers. Effectively, such a buffer is endless; it is accessed via pointers, and when a pointer increments past the end of the buffer, the pointer returns to the buffer's beginning. Two pointers are used here for each buffer, one to put data into it and one to get data out. The *get* pointer always points to the next byte to be read; the *put* pointer points to where the next byte will be written, just past the last byte written to the buffer.

If both pointers point to the same byte, the buffer is empty; the next byte to be read has not yet been written. The full-buffer condition is more difficult to test for: The *put* pointer is incremented and compared with the *get* pointer; if they are equal, doing a write would force a false buffer-empty condition, so the buffer must be full.

All buffer manipulation is done via four procedures (lines 569 through 674). *Put_out* (lines 572 through 596) writes a byte to the driver's output buffer or returns a buffer-full indication by setting AH to 0FFH. *Get_out* (lines 598 through 622) gets a byte from the output buffer or returns 0FFH in AH to indicate that no byte is available. *Put_in* (lines 624 through 648) and *Get_in* (lines 650 through 674) do exactly the same as *Put_out* and *Get_out*, but for the input buffer. These procedures are used both by the Request routines and by the hardware interrupt service routine (ISR).

Interrupt service routines

The most complex part of this driver is the ISR (lines 676 through 806), which decides which of the four possible services for a port is to be performed and where. Like the Request routines, the ISR provides unique entry points for each port (line 679 for *ASY1* and line 685 for *ASY2*); these entry points first preserve the SI register and then load it with the address of the port's structure table. With SI indicating where the actions are to be performed, the two entries then merge at line 690 into common code that first preserves all registers to be used by the ISR (lines 690 through 698) and then tests for each of the four possible types of service and performs each requested action.

Much of the complexity of the ISR is in the decoding of modem-status conditions. Because the resulting information is not used by this driver (although it could be used to prevent attempts to transmit while off line), these ISR options can be removed so that only the Transmit and Receive interrupts are serviced. To do this, *AllInt* (at line 145) should be changed from the OR of all four bits to include only the transmit and receive bits (03H, or 00000011B).

The transmit and receive portions of the ISR incorporate XON/XOFF flow control (for transmitted data only) by default. This control is done at the ISR level, rather than in the using program, to minimize the time required to respond to an incoming XOFF signal. Presence of the flow-control decisions adds complexity to what would otherwise be extremely simple actions.

Flow control is enabled or disabled by setting the *OutSpec* word in the structure table with the Driver Status utility (presented later) via the IOCTL function (Interrupt 21H Function 44H). When flow control is enabled, any XOFF character (11H) that is received halts all outgoing data until XON (13H) is received. No XOFF or XON is retained in the input buffer to be sent on to any program, although all patterns other than XOFF and XON *are* passed through by the driver. When flow control is disabled, the driver passes all patterns in both directions. For binary file transfer, flow control must be disabled.

The transmit action is simple: The code merely calls the *Start_output* procedure at line 750. *Start_output* is described in detail below.

The receive action is almost as simple as transmit, except for the flow-control testing. First, the ISR takes the received byte from the UART (lines 758 and 759) to avoid any chance of an overrun error. The ISR then tests the input specifier (at line 760) to determine whether flow control is in effect. If it is not, processing jumps directly to line 784 to store the received byte in the input buffer with *Put_in* (line 785).

If flow control is active, however, the received byte is compared with the XOFF character (lines 762 through 765). If the byte matches, output is disabled and the byte is ignored. If the byte is not XOFF, it is compared with XON (lines 766 through 768). If it is not XON either, control jumps to line 784. If the byte is XON, output is re-enabled if it was disabled. Regardless, the XON byte itself is ignored.

When control reaches *Stuff_in* at line 784, *Put_in* is called to store the received byte in the input buffer. If there is no room for it, a lost-databit is set in the input status flags (line 788); otherwise, the receive routine is finished.

If the interrupt was a line-status action, the LSR is read (lines 776 through 779). If the input specifier so directs, the content is converted to an IBM PC extended graphics character by setting bit 7 to 1 and the character is stored in the input buffer as if it were a received byte. Otherwise, the Line Status interrupt merely sets the generic *BadInp* error bit in the input status flags, which can be read with the IOCTL Read function of the driver.

When all ISR action is complete, lines 794 through 806 restore machine conditions to those existing at the time of the interrupt and return to the interrupted procedure.

The *Start_output* routine
Start_output (lines 808 through 824) is a routine that, like the four buffer procedures, is used by both the Request routines and the ISR. Its purpose is to initiate transmission of a byte, provided that output is not blocked by flow control, the UART Transmit Holding Register is empty, and a byte to be transmitted exists in the output ring buffer. This routine uses the *Get_out* buffer routine to access the buffer and determine whether a byte is available. If all conditions are met, the byte is sent to the UART holding register by lines 819 and 820.

The Initialization Request routine
The Initialization Request routine (lines 829 through 897) is critical to successful operation of the driver. This routine is placed last in the package so that it can be discarded as soon as it has served its purpose by installing the driver. It is essential to clear each register of the 8250 by reading its contents before enabling the interrupts and to loop through this

action until the 8250 finally shows no requests pending. The strange *Clc jnc $+2* sequence that appears repeatedly in this routine is a time delay required by high-speed machines (6 MHz and up) so that the 8250 has time to settle before another access is attempted; the delay does no harm on slower machines.

Using COMDVR

The first step in using this device driver is assembling it with the Microsoft Macro Assembler (MASM). Next, use the Microsoft Object Linker (LINK) to create a .EXE file. Convert the .EXE file into a binary image file with the EXE2BIN utility. Finally, include the line *DEVICE=COMDVR.SYS* in the CONFIG.SYS file so that COMDVR will be installed when the system is restarted.

Note: The number and colon at the beginning of each line in the program listings in this article are for reference only and should not be included in the source file.

Figure 6-2 shows the sequence of actions required, assuming that EDLIN is used for modifying (or creating) the CONFIG.SYS file and that all commands are issued from the root directory of the boot drive.

Creating the driver:

```
C>MASM COMDVR;  <Enter>
C>LINK COMDVR;  <Enter>
C>EXE2BIN COMDVR.EXE COMDVR.SYS  <Enter>
```

Modifying CONFIG.SYS (^Z = press Ctrl-Z):

```
C>EDLIN CONFIG.SYS  <Enter>
*#I  <Enter>
*DEVICE=COMDVR.SYS  <Enter>
*^Z  <Enter>
*E  <Enter>
```

Figure 6-2. Assembling, linking, and installing COMDVR.

Because the devices installed by COMDVR do not use the standard MS-DOS device names, no conflict occurs with any program that uses conventional port references. Such a program will not use the driver, and no problems should result if the program is well behaved and restores all interrupt vectors before returning to MS-DOS.

Device-driver debugging techniques

The debugging of device drivers, like debugging for any part of MS-DOS itself, is more difficult than normal program checking because the debugging program, DEBUG.COM or DEBUG.EXE, itself uses MS-DOS functions to display output. When these functions are being checked, their use by DEBUG destroys the data being examined. And because MS-DOS always saves its return address in the same location, any call to a function from inside the operating system usually causes a system lockup that can be cured only by shutting the system down and powering up again.

One way to overcome this difficulty is to purchase costly debugging tools. An easier way is to bypass the problem: Instead of using MS-DOS functions to track program operation, write data directly to video RAM, as in the macro *DBG* (lines 10 through 32 of COMDVR.ASM).

This macro is invoked with a three-character parameter string at each point in the program a progress report is desired. Each invocation has its own unique three-character string so that the sequence of actions can be read from the screen. When invoked, *DBG* expands into code that saves all registers and then writes the three-character string to video RAM. Only the top 10 lines of the screen (800 characters, or 1600 bytes) are used: The macro uses a single far pointer to the area and treats the video RAM like a ring buffer.

The pointer, *Dbgptr* (line 215), is set up for use with the monochrome adapter and points to location B000:0000H; to use a CGA or EGA (in CGA mode), the location should be changed to B800:0000H.

Most of the frequently used Request routines, such as *Read* and *Write*, have calls to *DBG* as their first lines (for example, lines 361 and 422). As shown, these calls are commented out, but for debugging, the source file should be edited so that all the calls and the macro itself are enabled.

With *DBG* active, the top 10 lines of the display are overwritten with a continual sequence of reports, such as *RR Tx*, put directly into video RAM. Because MS-DOS functions are not used, no interference with the driver itself can occur.

Although this technique prevents normal use of the system during debugging, it greatly simplifies the problem of knowing what is happening in time-critical areas, such as hardware interrupt service. In addition, all invocations of *DBG* in the critical areas are in conditional code that is executed only when the driver is working as it should.

Failure to display the *pi* message, for instance, indicates that the received-data hardware interrupt is not being serviced, and absence of *go* after an *Ix* report shows that data is not being sent out as it should.

Of course, once debugging is complete, the calls to *DBG* should be deleted or commented out. Such calls are usually edited out of the source code before release. In this case, they remain to demonstrate the technique and, most particularly, to show placement of the calls to provide maximum information with minimal clutter on the screen.

A simple modem engine

The second part of this package is the modem engine itself (ENGINE.ASM), shown in the listing in Figure 6-3. The main loop of this program consists of only a dozen lines of code (lines 9 through 20). Of these, five (lines 9 through 13) are devoted to establishing initial contact between the program and the serial-port driver and two (lines 19 and 20) are for returning to command level at the program's end.

Thus, only five lines of code (lines 14 through 18) actually carry out the bulk of the program as far as the main loop is concerned. Four of these lines are calls to subroutines that get and put data from and to the console and the serial port; the fifth is the JMP that closes the loop. This structure underscores the fact that a basic modem engine is simply a data-transfer loop.

```
 1 :              TITLE    engine
 2 :
 3 : CODE      SEGMENT PUBLIC 'CODE'
 4 :
 5 :              ASSUME   CS:CODE,DS:CODE,ES:CODE,SS:CODE
 6 :
 7 :              ORG      0100h
 8 :
 9 : START:   mov      dx,offset devnm ; open named device (ASY1)
10 :              mov      ax,3d02h
11 :              int      21h
12 :              mov      handle,ax      ; save the handle
13 :              jc       quit
14 : alltim: call     getmdm         ; main engine loop
15 :              call     putcrt
16 :              call     getkbd
17 :              call     putmdm
18 :              jmp      alltim
19 : quit:    mov      ah,4ch         ; come here to quit
20 :              int      21h
21 :
22 : getmdm  proc                    ; get input from modem
23 :              mov      cx,256
24 :              mov      bx,handle
25 :              mov      dx,offset mbufr
26 :              mov      ax,3F00h
27 :              int      21h
28 :              jc       quit
29 :              mov      mdlen,ax
30 :              ret
31 : getmdm  endp
32 :
33 : getkbd  proc                    ; get input from keyboard
34 :              mov      kblen,0        ; first zero the count
35 :              mov      ah,11          ; key pressed?
36 :              int      21h
37 :              inc      al
38 :              jnz      nogk           ; no
39 :              mov      ah,7           ; yes, get it
40 :              int      21h
41 :              cmp      al,3           ; was it Ctrl-C?
42 :              je       quit           ; yes, get out
43 :              mov      kbufr,al       ; no, save it
44 :              inc      kblen
45 :              cmp      al,13          ; was it Enter?
46 :              jne      nogk           ; no
```

Figure 6-3. ENGINE.ASM. *(more)*

```
47 :            mov     byte ptr kbufr+1,10 ; yes, add LF
48 :            inc     kblen
49 : nogk:      ret
50 : getkbd     endp
51 :
52 : putmdm     proc                      ; put output to modem
53 :            mov     cx,kblen
54 :            jcxz    nopm
55 :            mov     bx,handle
56 :            mov     dx,offset kbufr
57 :            mov     ax,4000h
58 :            int     21h
59 :            jc      quit
60 : nopm:      ret
61 : putmdm     endp
62 :
63 : putcrt     proc                      ; put output to CRT
64 :            mov     cx,mdlen
65 :            jcxz    nopc
66 :            mov     bx,1
67 :            mov     dx,offset mbufr
68 :            mov     ah,40h
69 :            int     21h
70 :            jc      quit
71 : nopc:      ret
72 : putcrt     endp
73 :
74 : devnm      db      'ASY1',0          ; miscellaneous data and buffers
75 : handle     dw      0
76 : kblen      dw      0
77 : mdlen      dw      0
78 : mbufr      db      256 dup (0)
79 : kbufr      db      80 dup (0)
80 :
81 : CODE       ENDS
82 :            END     START
```

Figure 6-3. Continued.

Because the details of timing and data conversion are handled by the driver code, each of the four subroutines is — to show just how simple the whole process is — essentially a buffered interface to the MS-DOS Read File or Device or Write File or Device routine.

For example, the *getmdm* procedure (lines 22 through 31) asks MS-DOS to read a maximum of 256 bytes from the serial device and then stores the number actually read in a word named *mdlen*. The driver returns immediately, without waiting for data, so the normal number of bytes returned is either 0 or 1. If screen scrolling causes the loop to be delayed, the count might be higher, but it should never exceed about a dozen characters.

When called, the *putcrt* procedure (lines 63 through 72) checks the value in *mdlen*. If the value is zero, *putcrt* does nothing; otherwise, it asks MS-DOS to write that number of bytes from *mbufr* (where *getmdm* put them) to the display, and then it returns.

Similarly, *getkbd* gets keystrokes from the keyboard, stores them in *kbufr*, and posts a count in *kblen*; *putmdm* checks *kblen* and, if the count is not zero, sends the required number of bytes from *kbufr* to the serial device.

Note that *getkbd* does not use the Read File or Device function, because that would wait for a keystroke and the loop must never wait for reception. Instead, it uses the MS-DOS functions that test keyboard status (0BH) and read a key without echo (07H). In addition, special treatment is given to the Enter key (lines 45 through 48): A linefeed is inserted in *kbufr* immediately behind Enter and *kblen* is set to 2.

A Ctrl-C keystroke ends program operation; it is detected in *getkbd* (line 41) and causes immediate transfer to the *quit* label (line 19) at the end of the main loop. Because ENGINE uses only permanently resident routines, there is no need for any uninstallation before returning to the MS-DOS command prompt.

ENGINE.ASM is written to be used as a .COM file. Assemble and link it the same as COMDVR.SYS (Figure 6-2) but use the extension COM instead of SYS; no change to CONFIG.SYS is needed.

The driver-status utility: CDVUTL.C

The driver-status utility program CDVUTL.C, presented in Figure 6-4, permits either of the two drivers (*ASY1 and ASY2*) to be reconfigured after being installed, to suit different needs. After one of the drivers has been specified (port 1 or port 2), the baud rate, word length, parity, and number of stop bits can be changed; each change is made independently, with no effect on any of the other characteristics. Additionally, flow control can be switched between two types of hardware handshaking — the software XON/XOFF control or disabled — and error reporting can be switched between character-oriented and message-oriented operation.

```
 1 : /* cdvutl.c - COMDVR Utility
 2 : *      Jim Kyle - 1987
 3 : *      for use with COMDVR.SYS Device Driver
 4 : */
 5 :
 6 : #include <stdio.h>              /* i/o definitions      */
 7 : #include <conio.h>              /* special console i/o  */
 8 : #include <stdlib.h>             /* misc definitions     */
 9 : #include <dos.h>                /* defines intdos()     */
10 :
11 : /*      the following define the driver status bits     */
12 :
13 : #define HWINT 0x0800            /* MCR, first word, HW Ints gated */
14 : #define o_DTR 0x0200            /* MCR, first word, output DTR    */
15 : #define o_RTS 0x0100            /* MCR, first word, output RTS    */
16 :
17 : #define m_PG  0x0010            /* LCR, first word, parity ON     */
18 : #define m_PE  0x0008            /* LCR, first word, parity EVEN   */
```

Figure 6-4. CDVUTL.C   (*more*)

```
19 : #define m_XS   0x0004          /* LCR, first word, 2 stop bits  */
20 : #define m_WL   0x0003          /* LCR, first word, wordlen mask */
21 :
22 : #define i_CD   0x8000          /* MSR, 2nd word, Carrier Detect */
23 : #define i_RI   0x4000          /* MSR, 2nd word, Ring Indicator */
24 : #define i_DSR  0x2000          /* MSR, 2nd word, Data Set Ready */
25 : #define i_CTS  0x1000          /* MSR, 2nd word, Clear to Send  */
26 :
27 : #define l_SRE  0x0040          /* LSR, 2nd word, Xmtr SR Empty  */
28 : #define l_HRE  0x0020          /* LSR, 2nd word, Xmtr HR Empty  */
29 : #define l_BRK  0x0010          /* LSR, 2nd word, Break Received */
30 : #define l_ER1  0x0008          /* LSR, 2nd word, FrmErr         */
31 : #define l_ER2  0x0004          /* LSR, 2nd word, ParErr         */
32 : #define l_ER3  0x0002          /* LSR, 2nd word, OveRun         */
33 : #define l_RRF  0x0001          /* LSR, 2nd word, Rcvr DR Full   */
34 :
35 : /*            now define CLS string for ANSI.SYS          */
36 : #define CLS    "\033[2J"
37 :
38 : FILE * dvp;
39 : union REGS rvs;
40 : int iobf [ 5 ];
41 :
42 : main ()
43 : { cputs ( "\nCDVUTL - COMDVR Utility Version 1.0 - 1987\n" );
44 :   disp ();                         /* do dispatch loop        */
45 : }
46 :
47 : disp ()                            /* dispatcher; infinite loop */
48 : { int c,
49 :     u;
50 :   u = 1;
51 :   while ( 1 )
52 :     { cputs ( "\r\n\tCommand (? for help): " );
53 :       switch ( tolower ( c = getche ()))   /* dispatch        */
54 :          {
55 :          case '1' :                 /* select port 1          */
56 :            fclose ( dvp );
57 :            dvp = fopen ( "ASY1", "rb+" );
58 :               u = 1;
59 :            break;
60 :
61 :          case '2' :                 /* select port 2          */
62 :            fclose ( dvp );
63 :            dvp = fopen ( "ASY2", "rb+" );
64 :            u = 2;
65 :            break;
66 :
67 :          case 'b' :                 /* set baud rate          */
68 :            if ( iobf [ 4 ] == 300 )
69 :               iobf [ 4 ] = 1200;
```

Figure 6-4. Continued.   *(more)*

```
 70 :             else
 71 :               if ( iobf [ 4 ] == 1200 )
 72 :                 iobf [ 4 ] = 2400;
 73 :             else
 74 :               if ( iobf [ 4 ] == 2400 )
 75 :                 iobf [ 4 ] = 9600;
 76 :             else
 77 :               iobf [ 4 ] = 300;
 78 :           iocwr ();
 79 :           break;
 80 :
 81 :         case 'e' :                     /* set parity even          */
 82 :           iobf [ 0 ] |= ( m_PG + m_PE );
 83 :           iocwr ();
 84 :           break;
 85 :
 86 :         case 'f' :                     /* toggle flow control      */
 87 :           if ( iobf [ 3 ] == 1 )
 88 :             iobf [ 3 ] = 2;
 89 :           else
 90 :             if ( iobf [ 3 ] == 2 )
 91 :               iobf [ 3 ] = 4;
 92 :           else
 93 :             if ( iobf [ 3 ] == 4 )
 94 :               iobf [ 3 ] = 0;
 95 :           else
 96 :             iobf [ 3 ] = 1;
 97 :           iocwr ();
 98 :           break;
 99 :
100 :         case 'i' :                     /* initialize MCR/LCR to 8N1 : */
101 :           iobf [ 0 ] = ( HWINT + o_DTR + o_RTS + m_WL );
102 :           iocwr ();
103 :           break;
104 :
105 :         case '?' :                     /* this help list           */
106 :           cputs ( CLS );               /* clear the display        */
107 :           center ( "COMMAND LIST \n" );
108 : center ( "1 = select port 1         L = toggle word LENGTH  " );
109 : center ( "2 = select port 2         N = set parity to NONE  " );
110 : center ( "B = set BAUD rate         O = set parity to ODD   " );
111 : center ( "E = set parity to EVEN    R = toggle error REPORTS" );
112 : center ( "F = toggle FLOW control   S = toggle STOP bits    " );
113 : center ( "I = INITIALIZE ints, etc. Q = QUIT                " );
114 :           continue;
115 :
116 :         case 'l' :                     /* toggle word length       */
117 :           iobf [ 0 ] ^= 1;
118 :           iocwr ();
119 :           break;
120 :
```

Figure 6-4. Continued.   *(more)*

```
121 :        case 'n' :                    /* set parity off              */
122 :          iobf [ 0 ] &=~ ( m_PG + m_PE );
123 :          iocwr ();
124 :          break;
125 :
126 :        case 'o' :                    /* set parity odd              */
127 :          iobf [ 0 ] |= m_PG;
128 :          iobf [ 0 ] &=~ m_PE;
129 :          iocwr ();
130 :          break;
131 :
132 :        case 'r' :                    /* toggle error reports        */
133 :          iobf [ 2 ] ^= 1;
134 :          iocwr ();
135 :          break;
136 :
137 :        case 's' :                    /* toggle stop bits            */
138 :          iobf [ 0 ] ^= m_XS;
139 :          iocwr ();
140 :          break;
141 :
142 :        case 'q' :
143 :          fclose ( dvp );
144 :          exit ( 0 );                 /* break the loop, get out     */
145 :          }
146 :        cputs ( CLS );                /* clear the display           */
147 :        center ( "CURRENT COMDVR STATUS" );
148 :        report ( u, dvp );            /* report current status       */
149 :      }
150 : }
151 :
152 : center ( s ) char * s;              /* centers a string on CRT     */
153 : { int i ;
154 :   for ( i = 80 - strlen ( s ); i > 0; i -= 2 )
155 :     putch ( ' ' );
156 :   cputs ( s );
157 :   cputs ( "\r\n" );
158 : }
159 :
160 : iocwr ()                            /* IOCTL Write to COMDVR       */
161 : { rvs . x . ax = 0x4403;
162 :   rvs . x . bx = fileno ( dvp );
163 :   rvs . x . cx = 10;
164 :   rvs . x . dx = ( int ) iobf;
165 :   intdos ( & rvs, & rvs );
166 : }
167 :
168 : char * onoff ( x ) int x ;
169 : { return ( x ? " ON" : " OFF" );
170 : }
171 :
```

Figure 6-4. Continued.   (more)

```
172 : report ( unit ) int unit ;
173 : { char temp [ 80 ];
174 :   rvs . x . ax = 0x4402;
175 :   rvs . x . bx = fileno ( dvp );
176 :   rvs . x . cx = 10;
177 :   rvs . x . dx = ( int ) iobf;
178 :   intdos ( & rvs, & rvs );          /* use IOCTL Read to get data */
179 :   sprintf ( temp, "\nDevice ASY%d\t%d BPS, %d-c-%c\r\n\n",
180 :          unit, iobf [ 4 ],          /* baud rate              */
181 :          5 + ( iobf [ 0 ] & m_WL ),  /* word length           */
182 :          ( iobf [ 0 ] & m_PG ?
183 :             ( iobf [ 0 ] & m_PE ? 'E' : 'O' ) : 'N' ),
184 :             ( iobf [ 0 ] & m_XS ? '2' : '1' )); /* stop bits    */
185 :   cputs ( temp );
186 :
187 :   cputs ( "Hardware Interrupts are" );
188 :   cputs ( onoff ( iobf [ 0 ] & HWINT ));
189 :   cputs ( ", Data Terminal Rdy" );
190 :   cputs ( onoff ( iobf [ 0 ] & o_DTR ));
191 :   cputs ( ", Rqst To Send" );
192 :   cputs ( onoff ( iobf [ 0 ] & o_RTS ));
193 :   cputs ( ".\r\n" );
194 :
195 :   cputs ( "Carrier Detect" );
196 :   cputs ( onoff ( iobf [ 1 ] & i_CD ));
197 :   cputs ( ", Data Set Rdy" );
198 :   cputs ( onoff ( iobf [ 1 ] & i_DSR ));
199 :   cputs ( ", Clear to Send" );
200 :   cputs ( onoff ( iobf [ 1 ] & i_CTS ));
201 :   cputs ( ", Ring Indicator" );
202 :   cputs ( onoff ( iobf [ 1 ] & i_RI ));
203 :   cputs ( ".\r\n" );
204 :
205 :   cputs ( l_SRE & iobf [ 1 ] ? "Xmtr SR Empty, " : "" );
206 :   cputs ( l_HRE & iobf [ 1 ] ? "Xmtr HR Empty, " : "" );
207 :   cputs ( l_BRK & iobf [ 1 ] ? "Break Received, " : "" );
208 :   cputs ( l_ER1 & iobf [ 1 ] ? "Framing Error, " : "" );
209 :   cputs ( l_ER2 & iobf [ 1 ] ? "Parity Error, " : "" );
210 :   cputs ( l_ER3 & iobf [ 1 ] ? "Overrun Error, " : "" );
211 :   cputs ( l_RRF & iobf [ 1 ] ? "Rcvr DR Full, " : "" );
212 :   cputs ( "\b\b.\r\n" );
213 :
214 :   cputs ( "Reception errors " );
215 :   if ( iobf [ 2 ] == 1 )
216 :     cputs ( "are encoded as graphics in buffer" );
217 :   else
218 :     cputs ( "set failure flag" );
219 :   cputs ( ".\r\n" );
220 :
221 :   cputs ( "Outgoing Flow Control " );
222 :   if ( iobf [ 3 ] & 4 )
```

Figure 6-4. Continued.   *(more)*

```
223 :     cputs ( "by XON and XOFF" );
224 :   else
225 :     if ( iobf [ 3 ] & 2 )
226 :       cputs ( "by RTS and CTS" );
227 :   else
228 :     if ( iobf [ 3 ] & 1 )
229 :       cputs ( "by DTR and DSR" );
230 :   else
231 :     cputs ( "disabled" );
232 :   cputs ( ".\r\n" );
233 : }
234 :
235 : /*end of cdvutl.c */
```

Figure 6-4. Continued.

Although CDVUTL appears complicated, most of the complexity is concentrated in the routines that map driver bit settings into on-screen display text. Each such mapping requires several lines of source code to generate only a few words of the display report. Table 6-10 summarizes the functions found in this program.

Table 6-10. CDVUTL Program Functions.

Lines	Name	Description
42–45	*main()*	Conventional entry point.
47–150	*disp()*	Main dispatching loop.
152–158	*center()*	Centers text on CRT.
160–166	*iocwr()*	Writes control string to driver with IOCTL Write.
168–170	*onoff()*	Returns pointer to ON or OFF.
172–233	*report()*	Reads driver status and reports it on display.

The long list of *#define* operations at the start of the listing (lines 11 through 33) helps make the bitmapping comprehensible by assigning a symbolic name to each significant bit in the four UART registers.

The *main()* procedure of CDVUTL displays a banner line and then calls the dispatcher routine, *disp()*, to start operation. CDVUTL makes no use of either command-line parameters or the environment, so the usual argument declarations are omitted.

Upon entry to *disp()*, the first action is to establish the default driver as *ASY1* by setting *u = 1* and opening *ASY1* (line 50); the program then enters an apparent infinite loop (lines 51 through 149).

With each repetition, the loop first prompts for a command (line 52) and then gets the next keystroke and uses it to control a huge *switch()* statement (lines 53 through 145). If no case matches the key pressed, the *switch()* statement does nothing; the program simply displays a report of all current conditions at the selected driver (lines 146 through 148) and then closes the loop back to issue a new prompt and get another keystroke.

However, if the key pressed matches one of the cases in the *switch()* statement, the corresponding command is executed. The digits *1* (line 55) and *2* (line 61) select the driver to be affected. The *?* key (line 105) causes the list of valid command keys to be displayed. The *q* key (line 142) causes the program to terminate by calling *exit(0)* and is the only exit from the infinite loop. The other valid keys all change one or more bits in the IOCTL control string to modify corresponding attributes of the driver and then send the string to the driver by using the MS-DOS IOCTL Write function (Interrupt 21H Function 44H Subfunction 03H) via function *iocwr()* (lines 160 through 166).

After the command is executed (except for the *q* command, which terminates operation of CDVUTL and returns to MS-DOS command level, and the *?* command, which displays the command list), the *report()* function (lines 172 through 233) is called (at line 148) to display all of the driver's attributes, including those just changed. This function issues an IOCTL Read command (Interrupt 21H Function 44H Subfunction 02H, in lines 174 through 178) to get new status information into the control string and then uses a sequence of bit filtering (lines 179 through 232) to translate the obtained status information into words for display.

The special console I/O routines provided in Microsoft C libraries have been used extensively in this routine. Other compilers may require changes in the names of such library routines as *getch* or *dosint* as well as in the names of *#include* files (lines 6 through 9).

Each of the actual command sequences changes only a few bits in one of the 10 bytes of the command string and then writes the string to the driver. A full-featured communications program might make several changes at one time — for example, switching from 7-bit, even parity, XON/XOFF flow control to 8-bit, no parity, without flow control to prevent losing any bytes with values of 11H or 13H while performing a binary file transfer with error-correcting protocol. In such a case, the program could make all required changes to the control string before issuing a single IOCTL Write to put them into effect.

The Traditional Approach

Because the necessary device driver has never been a part of MS-DOS, most communications programs are written to provide and install their own port driver code and remove it before returning to MS-DOS. The second sample program package in this article illustrates this approach. Although the major part of the package is written in Microsoft C, three assembly-language modules are required to provide the hardware interrupt service routines, the exception handler, and faster video display. They are discussed first.

The hardware ISR module

The first module is a handler to service UART interrupts. Code for this handler, including routines to install it at entry and remove it on exit, appears in CH1.ASM, shown in Figure 6-5.

```
 1 :            TITLE   CH1.ASM
 2 :
 3 : ; CH1.ASM -- support file for CTERM.C terminal emulator
 4 : ;       set up to work with COM2
 5 : ;       for use with Microsoft C and SMALL model only...
 6 :
 7 : _TEXT   segment byte public 'CODE'
 8 : _TEXT   ends
 9 : _DATA   segment byte public 'DATA'
10 : _DATA   ends
11 : CONST   segment byte public 'CONST'
12 : CONST   ends
13 : _BSS    segment byte public 'BSS'
14 : _BSS    ends
15 :
16 : DGROUP  GROUP   CONST, _BSS, _DATA
17 :         assume  cs:_TEXT, DS:DGROUP, ES:DGROUP, SS:DGROUP
18 :
19 : _TEXT   segment
20 :
21 :         public  _i_m,_rdmdm,_Send_Byte,_wrtmdm,_set_mdm,_u_m
22 :
23 : bport   EQU     02F8h           ; COM2 base address, use 03F8H for COM1
24 : getiv   EQU     350Bh           ; COM2 vectors, use 0CH for COM1
25 : putiv   EQU     250Bh
26 : imrmsk  EQU     00001000b       ; COM2 mask, use 00000100b for COM1
27 : oiv_o   DW      0               ; old int vector save space
28 : oiv_s   DW      0
29 :
30 : bf_pp   DW      in_bf           ; put pointer (last used)
31 : bf_gp   DW      in_bf           ; get pointer (next to use)
32 : bf_bg   DW      in_bf           ; start of buffer
33 : bf_fi   DW      b_last          ; end of buffer
34 :
35 : in_bf   DB      512 DUP (?)     ; input buffer
36 :
37 : b_last  EQU     $               ; address just past buffer end
38 :
39 : bd_dv   DW      0417h           ; baud rate divisors (0=110 bps)
40 :         DW      0300h           ; code 1 =  150 bps
41 :         DW      0180h           ; code 2 =  300 bps
42 :         DW      00C0h           ; code 3 =  600 bps
43 :         DW      0060h           ; code 4 = 1200 bps
44 :         DW      0030h           ; code 5 = 2400 bps
45 :         DW      0010h           ; code 6 = 4800 bps
46 :         DW      000Ch           ; code 7 = 9600 bps
47 :
48 : _set_mdm proc   near            ; replaces BIOS 'init' function
49 :         PUSH    BP
50 :         MOV     BP,SP           ; establish stackframe pointer
51 :         PUSH    ES              ; save registers
```

Figure 6-5. CH1.ASM   *(more)*

```
 52 :          PUSH    DS
 53 :          MOV     AX,CS           ; point them to CODE segment
 54 :          MOV     DS,AX
 55 :          MOV     ES,AX
 56 :          MOV     AH,[BP+4]       ; get parameter passed by C
 57 :          MOV     DX,BPORT+3      ; point to Line Control Reg
 58 :          MOV     AL,80h          ; set DLAB bit (see text)
 59 :          OUT     DX,AL
 60 :          MOV     DL,AH           ; shift param to BAUD field
 61 :          MOV     CL,4
 62 :          ROL     DL,CL
 63 :          AND     DX,00001110b    ; mask out all other bits
 64 :          MOV     DI,OFFSET bd_dv
 65 :          ADD     DI,DX           ; make pointer to true divisor
 66 :          MOV     DX,BPORT+1      ; set to high byte first
 67 :          MOV     AL,[DI+1]
 68 :          OUT     DX,AL           ; put high byte into UART
 69 :          MOV     DX,BPORT        ; then to low byte
 70 :          MOV     AL,[DI]
 71 :          OUT     DX,AL
 72 :          MOV     AL,AH           ; now use rest of parameter
 73 :          AND     AL,00011111b    ; to set Line Control Reg
 74 :          MOV     DX,BPORT+3
 75 :          OUT     DX,AL
 76 :          MOV     DX,BPORT+2      ; Interrupt Enable Register
 77 :          MOV     AL,1            ; Receive type only
 78 :          OUT     DX,AL
 79 :          POP     DS              ; restore saved registers
 80 :          POP     ES
 81 :          MOV     SP,BP
 82 :          POP     BP
 83 :          RET
 84 : _set_mdm endp
 85 :
 86 : _wrtmdm proc    near            ; write char to modem
 87 : _Send_Byte:                     ; name used by main program
 88 :          PUSH    BP
 89 :          MOV     BP,SP           ; set up pointer and save regs
 90 :          PUSH    ES
 91 :          PUSH    DS
 92 :          MOV     AX,CS
 93 :          MOV     DS,AX
 94 :          MOV     ES,AX
 95 :          MOV     DX,BPORT+4      ; establish DTR, RTS, and OUT2
 96 :          MOV     AL,0Bh
 97 :          OUT     DX,AL
 98 :          MOV     DX,BPORT+6      ; check for on line, CTS
 99 :          MOV     BH,30h
100 :          CALL    w_tmr
101 :          JNZ     w_out           ; timed out
102 :          MOV     DX,BPORT+5      ; check for UART ready
```

Figure 6-5. Continued.   *(more)*

```
103 :           MOV    BH,20h
104 :           CALL   w_tmr
105 :           JNZ    w_out          ; timed out
106 :           MOV    DX,BPORT       ; send out to UART port
107 :           MOV    AL,[BP+4]      ; get char passed from C
108 :           OUT    DX,AL
109 : w_out:    POP    DS             ; restore saved regs
110 :           POP    ES
111 :           MOV    SP,BP
112 :           POP    BP
113 :           RET
114 : _wrtmdm  endp
115 :
116 : _rdmdm   proc    near           ; reads byte from buffer
117 :           PUSH   BP
118 :           MOV    BP,SP          ; set up ptr, save regs
119 :           PUSH   ES
120 :           PUSH   DS
121 :           MOV    AX,CS
122 :           MOV    DS,AX
123 :           MOV    ES,AX
124 :           MOV    AX,0FFFFh      ; set for EOF flag
125 :           MOV    BX,bf_gp       ; use "get" ptr
126 :           CMP    BX,bf_pp       ; compare to "put"
127 :           JZ     nochr          ; same, empty
128 :           INC    BX             ; else char available
129 :           CMP    BX,bf_fi       ; at end of bfr?
130 :           JNZ    noend          ; no
131 :           MOV    BX,bf_bg       ; yes, set to beg
132 : noend:    MOV    AL,[BX]        ; get the char
133 :           MOV    bf_gp,BX       ; update "get" ptr
134 :           INC    AH             ; zero AH as flag
135 : nochr:    POP    DS             ; restore regs
136 :           POP    ES
137 :           MOV    SP,BP
138 :           POP    BP
139 :           RET
140 : _rdmdm   endp
141 :
142 : w_tmr    proc    near
143 :           MOV    BL,1           ; wait timer, double loop
144 : w_tm1:    SUB    CX,CX          ; set up inner loop
145 : w_tm2:    IN     AL,DX          ; check for requested response
146 :           MOV    AH,AL          ; save what came in
147 :           AND    AL,BH          ; mask with desired bits
148 :           CMP    AL,BH          ; then compare
149 :           JZ     w_tm3          ; got it, return with ZF set
150 :           LOOP   w_tm2          ; else keep trying
151 :           DEC    BL             ; until double loop expires
152 :           JNZ    w_tm1
153 :           OR     BH,BH          ; timed out, return NZ
```

Figure 6-5. Continued.   *(more)*

```
154 :  w_tm3:   RET
155 :  w_tmr    endp
156 :
157 :  ; hardware interrupt service routine
158 :  rts_m:   CLI
159 :           PUSH     DS              ; save all regs
160 :           PUSH     AX
161 :           PUSH     BX
162 :           PUSH     CX
163 :           PUSH     DX
164 :           PUSH     CS              ; set DS same as CS
165 :           POP      DS
166 :           MOV      DX,BPORT        ; grab the char from UART
167 :           IN       AL,DX
168 :           MOV      BX,bf_pp        ; use "put" ptr
169 :           INC      BX              ; step to next slot
170 :           CMP      BX,bf_fi        ; past end yet?
171 :           JNZ      nofix           ; no
172 :           MOV      BX,bf_bg        ; yes, set to begin
173 :  nofix:   MOV      [BX],AL         ; put char in buffer
174 :           MOV      bf_pp,BX        ; update "put" ptr
175 :           MOV      AL,20h          ; send EOI to 8259 chip
176 :           OUT      20h,AL
177 :           POP      DX              ; restore regs
178 :           POP      CX
179 :           POP      BX
180 :           POP      AX
181 :           POP      DS
182 :           IRET
183 :
184 :  _i_m     proc     near            ; install modem service
185 :           PUSH     BP
186 :           MOV      BP,SP           ; save all regs used
187 :           PUSH     ES
188 :           PUSH     DS
189 :           MOV      AX,CS           ; set DS,ES=CS
190 :           MOV      DS,AX
191 :           MOV      ES,AX
192 :           MOV      DX,BPORT+1      ; Interrupt Enable Reg
193 :           MOV      AL,0Fh          ; enable all ints now
194 :           OUT      DX,AL
195 :
196 :  im1:     MOV      DX,BPORT+2      ; clear junk from UART
197 :           IN       AL,DX           ; read IID reg of UART
198 :           MOV      AH,AL           ; save what came in
199 :           TEST     AL,1            ; anything pending?
200 :           JNZ      im5             ; no, all clear now
201 :           CMP      AH,0            ; yes, Modem Status?
202 :           JNZ      im2             ; no
203 :           MOV      DX,BPORT+6      ; yes, read MSR to clear
204 :           IN       AL,DX
```

Figure 6-5. Continued.   *(more)*

```
205 :  im2:     CMP      AH,2              ; Transmit HR empty?
206 :           JNZ      im3               ; no (no action needed)
207 :  im3:     CMP      AH,4              ; Received Data Ready?
208 :           JNZ      im4               ; no
209 :           MOV      DX,BPORT          ; yes, read it to clear
210 :           IN       AL,DX
211 :  im4:     CMP      AH,6              ; Line Status?
212 :           JNZ      im1               ; no, check for more
213 :           MOV      DX,BPORT+5        ; yes, read LSR to clear
214 :           IN       AL,DX
215 :           JMP      im1               ; then check for more
216 :
217 :  im5:     MOV      DX,BPORT+4        ; set up working conditions
218 :           MOV      AL,0Bh            ; DTR, RTS, OUT2 bits
219 :           OUT      DX,AL
220 :           MOV      AL,1              ; enable RCV interrupt only
221 :           MOV      DX,BPORT+1
222 :           OUT      DX,AL
223 :           MOV      AX,GETIV          ; get old int vector
224 :           INT      21h
225 :           MOV      oiv_o,BX          ; save for restoring later
226 :           MOV      oiv_s,ES
227 :           MOV      DX,OFFSET rts_m ; set in new one
228 :           MOV      AX,PUTIV
229 :           INT      21h
230 :           IN       AL,21h            ; now enable 8259 PIC
231 :           AND      AL,NOT IMRMSK
232 :           OUT      21h,AL
233 :           MOV      AL,20h            ; then send out an EOI
234 :           OUT      20h,AL
235 :           POP      DS                ; restore regs
236 :           POP      ES
237 :           MOV      SP,BP
238 :           POP      BP
239 :           RET
240 : _i_m      endp
241 :
242 : _u_m      proc     near              ; uninstall modem service
243 :           PUSH     BP
244 :           MOV      BP,SP             ; save registers
245 :           IN       AL,21h            ; disable COM int in 8259
246 :           OR       AL,IMRMSK
247 :           OUT      21h,AL
248 :           PUSH     ES
249 :           PUSH     DS
250 :           MOV      AX,CS             ; set same as CS
251 :           MOV      DS,AX
252 :           MOV      ES,AX
253 :           MOV      AL,0              ; disable UART ints
254 :           MOV      DX,BPORT+1
255 :           OUT      DX,AL
```

Figure 6-5. Continued.   *(more)*

```
256 :        MOV    DX,oiv_o      ; restore original vector
257 :        MOV    DS,oiv_s
258 :        MOV    AX,PUTIV
259 :        INT    21h
260 :        POP    DS            ; restore registers
261 :        POP    ES
262 :        MOV    SP,BP
263 :        POP    BP
264 :        RET
265 : _u_m   endp
266 :
267 : _TEXT  ends
268 :
269 :        END
```

Figure 6-5. Continued.

The routines in CH1 are set up to work only with port COM2; to use them with COM1, the three symbolic constants BPORT (base address), GETIV, and PUTIV must be changed to match the COM1 values. Also, as presented, this code is for use with the Microsoft C small memory model only; for use with other memory models, the C compiler manuals should be consulted for making the necessary changes. *See also* PROGRAMMING IN THE MS-DOS ENVIRONMENT: Programming for ms-dos: Structure of an Application Program.

The parts of CH1 are listed in Table 6-11, as they occur in the listing. The leading underscore that is part of the name for each of the six functions is supplied by the C compiler; within the C program that calls the function, the underscore is omitted.

Table 6-11. CH1 Module Functions.

Lines	Name	Description
1–26		Administrative details.
27–46		Data areas.
48–84	_set_mdm	Initializes UART as specified by parameter passed from C.
86–114	_wrtmdm	Outputs character to UART.
87	_Send_Byte	Entry point for use if flow control is added to system.
116–140	_rdmdm	Gets character from buffer where ISR put it, or signals that no character available.
142–155	w_tmr	Wait timer; internal routine used to prevent infinite wait in case of problems.
157–182	rts_m	Hardware ISR; installed by _i_m and removed by _u_m.
184–240	_i_m	Installs ISR, saving old interrupt vector.
242–265	_u_m	Uninstalls ISR, restoring saved interrupt vector.

For simplest operation, the ISR used in this example (unlike the device driver) services *only* the received-data interrupt; the other three types of IRQ are disabled at the UART. Each time a byte is received by the UART, the ISR puts it into the buffer. The _rdmdm code, when called by the C program, gets a byte from the buffer if one is available. If not, _rdmdm returns the C EOF code (−1) to indicate that no byte can be obtained.

To send a byte, the C program can call either _Send_Byte or _wrtmdm; in the package as shown, these are alternative names for the same routine. In the more complex program from which this package was adapted, _Send_Byte is called when flow control is desired and the flow-control routine calls _wrtmdm. To implement flow control, line 87 should be deleted from CH1.ASM and a control function named Send_Byte() should be added to the main C program. Flow-control tests must occur in Send_Byte(); _wrtmdm performs the actual port interfacing.

To set the modem baud rate, word length, and parity, _set_mdm is called from the C program, with a setup parameter passed as an argument. The format of this parameter is shown in Table 6-12 and is identical to the IBM BIOS Interrupt 14H Function 00H (Initialization).

Table 6-12. *set_mdm()* Parameter Coding.

Binary	Meaning
000xxxxx	Set to 110 bps
001xxxxx	Set to 150 bps
010xxxxx	Set to 300 bps
011xxxxx	Set to 600 bps
100xxxxx	Set to 1200 bps
101xxxxx	Set to 2400 bps
110xxxxx	Set to 4800 bps
111xxxxx	Set to 9600 bps
xxxx0xxx	No parity
xxx01xxx	ODD Parity
xxx11xxx	EVEN Parity
xxxxx0xx	1 stop bit
xxxxx1xx	2 stop bits (1.5 if WL = 5)
xxxxxx00	Word length = 5
xxxxxx01	Word length = 6
xxxxxx10	Word length = 7
xxxxxx11	Word length = 8

The CH1 code provides a 512-byte ring buffer for incoming data; the buffer size should be adequate for reception at speeds up to 2400 bps without loss of data during scrolling.

The exception-handler module

For the ISR handler of CH1 to be usable, an exception handler is needed to prevent return of control to MS-DOS before _u_m restores the ISR vector to its original value. If a program using this code returns to MS-DOS without calling _u_m, the system is virtually certain to crash when line noise causes a received-data interrupt and the ISR code is no longer in memory.

A replacement exception handler (CH1A.ASM), including routines for installation, access, and removal, is shown in Figure 6-6. Like the ISR, this module is designed to work with Microsoft C (again, the small memory model only).

Note: This module does not provide for fatal disk errors; if one occurs, immediate restarting is necessary. *See* PROGRAMMING IN THE MS-DOS ENVIRONMENT: CUSTOMIZING MS-DOS: Exception Handlers.

```
 1 :         TITLE   CH1A.ASM
 2 :
 3 : ; CH1A.ASM -- support file for CTERM.C terminal emulator
 4 : ;       this set of routines replaces Ctrl-C/Ctrl-BREAK
 5 : ;       usage: void set_int(), rst_int();
 6 : ;               int broke();   /* boolean if BREAK      */
 7 : ;       for use with Microsoft C and SMALL model only...
 8 :
 9 : _TEXT   segment byte public 'CODE'
10 : _TEXT   ends
11 : _DATA   segment byte public 'DATA'
12 : _DATA   ends
13 : CONST   segment byte public 'CONST'
14 : CONST   ends
15 : _BSS    segment byte public 'BSS'
16 : _BSS    ends
17 :
18 : DGROUP  GROUP   CONST, _BSS, _DATA
19 :         ASSUME  CS:_TEXT, DS:DGROUP, ES:DGROUP, SS:DGROUP
20 :
21 : _DATA   SEGMENT BYTE PUBLIC 'DATA'
22 :
23 : OLDINT1B DD     0                 ; storage for original INT 1BH vector
24 :
25 : _DATA   ENDS
26 :
27 : _TEXT   SEGMENT
28 :
29 :         PUBLIC  _set_int,_rst_int,_broke
30 :
31 : myint1b:
32 :         mov     word ptr cs:brkflg,1Bh          ; make it nonzero
33 :         iret
```

Figure 6-6. CH1A.ASM.   *(more)*

```
34 :
35 : myint23:
36 :        mov     word ptr cs:brkflg,23h          ; make it nonzero
37 :        iret
38 :
39 : brkflg dw      0                    ; flag that BREAK occurred
40 :
41 : _broke proc    near                 ; returns 0 if no break
42 :        xor     ax,ax                ; prepare to reset flag
43 :        xchg    ax,cs:brkflg         ; return current flag value
44 :        ret
45 : _broke endp
46 :
47 : _set_int proc near
48 :        mov     ax,351bh             ; get interrupt vector for 1BH
49 :        int     21h                  ; (don't need to save for 23H)
50 :        mov     word ptr oldint1b,bx      ; save offset in first word
51 :        mov     word ptr oldint1b+2,es   ; save segment in second word
52 :
53 :        push    ds                   ; save our data segment
54 :        mov     ax,cs                ; set DS to CS for now
55 :        mov     ds,ax
56 :        lea     dx,myint1b           ; DS:DX points to new routine
57 :        mov     ax,251bh             ; set interrupt vector
58 :        int     21h
59 :        mov     ax,cs                ; set DS to CS for now
60 :        mov     ds,ax
61 :        lea     dx,myint23           ; DS:DX points to new routine
62 :        mov     ax,2523h             ; set interrupt vector
63 :        int     21h
64 :        pop     ds                   ; restore data segment
65 :        ret
66 : _set_int endp
67 :
68 : _rst_int proc near
69 :        push    ds                   ; save our data segment
70 :        lds     dx,oldint1b          ; DS:DX points to original
71 :        mov     ax,251bh             ; set interrupt vector
72 :        int     21h
73 :        pop     ds                   ; restore data segment
74 :        ret
75 : _rst_int endp
76 :
77 : _TEXT  ends
78 :
79 :        END
```

Figure 6-6. Continued.

The three functions in CH1A are *_set_int*, which saves the old vector value for Interrupt 1BH (ROM BIOS Control-Break) and then resets both that vector and the one for Interrupt 23H (Control-C Handler Address) to internal ISR code; *_rst_int*, which restores the original value for the Interrupt 1BH vector; and _broke, which returns the present value of an internal flag (and always clears the flag, just in case it had been set). The internal flag is set to a nonzero value in response to either of the revectored interrupts and is tested from the main C program via the _broke function.

The video display module

The final assembly-language module (CH2.ASM) used by the second package is shown in Figure 6-7. This module provides convenient screen clearing and cursor positioning via direct calls to the IBM BIOS, but this can be eliminated with minor rewriting of the routines that call its functions. In the original, more complex program (DT115.EXE, available from DL6 in the CLMFORUM of CompuServe) from which CTERM was derived, this module provided windowing capability in addition to improved display speed.

```
 1 :           TITLE   CH2.ASM
 2 :
 3 : ; CH2.ASM -- support file for CTERM.C terminal emulator
 4 : ;         for use with Microsoft C and SMALL model only...
 5 :
 6 : _TEXT     segment byte public 'CODE'
 7 : _TEXT     ends
 8 : _DATA     segment byte public 'DATA'
 9 : _DATA     ends
10 : CONST     segment byte public 'CONST'
11 : CONST     ends
12 : _BSS      segment byte public 'BSS'
13 : _BSS      ends
14 :
15 : DGROUP    GROUP   CONST, _BSS, _DATA
16 :           assume  CS:_TEXT, DS:DGROUP, ES:DGROUP, SS:DGROUP
17 :
18 : _TEXT     segment
19 :
20 :           public  __cls,_color,_deol,_i_v,__key,_wrchr,__wrpos
21 :
22 : atrib     DB      0               ; attribute
23 : _colr     DB      0               ; color
24 : v_bas     DW      0               ; video segment
25 : v_ulc     DW      0               ; upper left corner cursor
26 : v_lrc     DW      184Fh           ; lower right corner cursor
27 : v_col     DW      0               ; current col/row
28 :
29 : __key     proc    near            ; get keystroke
30 :           PUSH    BP
31 :           MOV     AH,1            ; check status via BIOS
32 :           INT     16h
33 :           MOV     AX,0FFFFh
34 :           JZ      key00           ; none ready, return EOF
35 :           MOV     AH,0            ; have one, read via BIOS
```

Figure 6-7. CH2.ASM.   *(more)*

```
36 :            INT     16h
37 : key00:     POP     BP
38 :            RET
39 : __key      endp
40 :
41 : __wrchr    proc    near
42 :            PUSH    BP
43 :            MOV     BP,SP
44 :            MOV     AL,[BP+4]        ; get char passed by C
45 :            CMP     AL,' '
46 :            JNB     prchr            ; printing char, go do it
47 :            CMP     AL,8
48 :            JNZ     notbs
49 :            DEC     BYTE PTR v_col   ; process backspace
50 :            MOV     AL,byte ptr v_col
51 :            CMP     AL,byte ptr v_ulc
52 :            JB      nxt_c            ; step to next column
53 :            JMP     norml
54 :
55 : notbs:     CMP     AL,9
56 :            JNZ     notht
57 :            MOV     AL,byte ptr v_col       ; process HTAB
58 :            ADD     AL,8
59 :            AND     AL,0F8h
60 :            MOV     byte ptr v_col,AL
61 :            CMP     AL,byte ptr v_lrc
62 :            JA      nxt_c
63 :            JMP     SHORT   norml
64 :
65 : notht:     CMP     AL,0Ah
66 :            JNZ     notlf
67 :            MOV     AL,byte ptr v_col+1     ; process linefeed
68 :            INC     AL
69 :            CMP     AL,byte ptr v_lrc+1
70 :            JBE     noht1
71 :            CALL    scrol
72 :            MOV     AL,byte ptr v_lrc+1
73 : noht1:     MOV     byte ptr v_col+1,AL
74 :            JMP     SHORT   norml
75 :
76 : notlf:     CMP     AL,0Ch
77 :            JNZ     ck_cr
78 :            CALL    __cls            ; process formfeed
79 :            JMP     SHORT   ignor
80 :
81 : ck_cr:     CMP     AL,0Dh
82 :            JNZ     ignor            ; ignore all other CTL chars
83 :            MOV     AL,byte ptr v_ulc       ; process CR
84 :            MOV     byte ptr v_col,AL
85 :            JMP     SHORT   norml
86 :
```

Figure 6-7. Continued.   *(more)*

```
 87 : prchr:   MOV    AH,_colr          ; process printing char
 88 :          PUSH   AX
 89 :          XOR    AH,AH
 90 :          MOV    AL,byte ptr v_col+1
 91 :          PUSH   AX
 92 :          MOV    AL,byte ptr v_col
 93 :          PUSH   AX
 94 :          CALL   wrtvr
 95 :          MOV    SP,BP
 96 : nxt_c:   INC    BYTE PTR v_col    ; advance to next column
 97 :          MOV    AL,byte ptr v_col
 98 :          CMP    AL,byte ptr v_lrc
 99 :          JLE    norml
100 :          MOV    AL,0Dh            ; went off end, do CR/LF
101 :          PUSH   AX
102 :          CALL   __wrchr
103 :          POP    AX
104 :          MOV    AL,0Ah
105 :          PUSH   AX
106 :          CALL   __wrchr
107 :          POP    AX
108 : norml:   CALL   set_cur
109 : ignor:   MOV    SP,BP
110 :          POP    BP
111 :          RET
112 : __wrchr endp
113 :
114 : __i_v    proc   near              ; establish video base segment
115 :          PUSH   BP
116 :          MOV    BP,SP
117 :          MOV    AX,0B000h         ; mono, B800 for CGA
118 :          MOV    v_bas,AX          ; could be made automatic
119 :          MOV    SP,BP
120 :          POP    BP
121 :          RET
122 : __i_v    endp
123 :
124 : __wrpos proc    near              ; set cursor position
125 :          PUSH   BP
126 :          MOV    BP,SP
127 :          MOV    DH,[BP+4]         ; row from C program
128 :          MOV    DL,[BP+6]         ; col from C program
129 :          MOV    v_col,DX          ; cursor position
130 :          MOV    BH,atrib          ; attribute
131 :          MOV    AH,2
132 :          PUSH   BP
133 :          INT    10h
134 :          POP    BP
135 :          MOV    AX,v_col          ; return cursor position
136 :          MOV    SP,BP
137 :          POP    BP
```

Figure 6-7. Continued.   *(more)*

```
138 :           RET
139 : __wrpos endp
140 :
141 : set_cur proc    near            ; set cursor to v_col
142 :           PUSH    BP
143 :           MOV     BP,SP
144 :           MOV     DX,v_col        ; use where v_col says
145 :           MOV     BH,atrib
146 :           MOV     AH,2
147 :           PUSH    BP
148 :           INT     10h
149 :           POP     BP
150 :           MOV     AX,v_col
151 :           MOV     SP,BP
152 :           POP     BP
153 :           RET
154 : set_cur endp
155 :
156 : __color proc    near            ; _color(fg, bg)
157 :           PUSH    BP
158 :           MOV     BP,SP
159 :           MOV     AH,[BP+6]       ; background from C
160 :           MOV     AL,[BP+4]       ; foreground from C
161 :           MOV     CX,4
162 :           SHL     AH,CL
163 :           AND     AL,0Fh
164 :           OR      AL,AH           ; pack up into 1 byte
165 :           MOV     _colr,AL        ; store for handler's use
166 :           XOR     AH,AH
167 :           MOV     SP,BP
168 :           POP     BP
169 :           RET
170 : __color endp
171 :
172 : scrol   proc    near            ; scroll CRT up by one line
173 :           PUSH    BP
174 :           MOV     BP,SP
175 :           MOV     AL,1            ; count of lines to scroll
176 :           MOV     CX,v_ulc
177 :           MOV     DX,v_lrc
178 :           MOV     BH,_colr
179 :           MOV     AH,6
180 :           PUSH    BP
181 :           INT     10h             ; use BIOS
182 :           POP     BP
183 :           MOV     SP,BP
184 :           POP     BP
185 :           RET
186 : scrol   endp
187 :
188 : __cls   proc    near            ; clear CRT
```

Figure 6-7. Continued. *(more)*

```
189 :          PUSH     BP
190 :          MOV      BP,SP
191 :          MOV      AL,0              ; flags CLS to BIOS
192 :          MOV      CX,v_ulc
193 :          MOV      v_col,CX         ; set to HOME
194 :          MOV      DX,v_lrc
195 :          MOV      BH,_colr
196 :          MOV      AH,6
197 :          PUSH     BP
198 :          INT      10h              ; use BIOS scroll up
199 :          POP      BP
200 :          CALL     set_cur          ; cursor to HOME
201 :          MOV      SP,BP
202 :          POP      BP
203 :          RET
204 : __cls    endp
205 :
206 : __deol   proc     near             ; delete to end of line
207 :          PUSH     BP
208 :          MOV      BP,SP
209 :          MOV      AL,' '
210 :          MOV      AH,_colr         ; set up blanks
211 :          PUSH     AX
212 :          MOV      AL,byte ptr v_col+1
213 :          XOR      AH,AH            ; set up row value
214 :          PUSH     AX
215 :          MOV      AL,byte ptr v_col
216 :
217 : deol1:   CMP      AL,byte ptr v_lrc
218 :          JA       deol2            ; at RH edge
219 :          PUSH     AX               ; current location
220 :          CALL     wrtvr            ; write a blank
221 :          POP      AX
222 :          INC      AL               ; next column
223 :          JMP      deol1            ; do it again
224 :
225 : deol2:   MOV      AX,v_col         ; return cursor position
226 :          MOV      SP,BP
227 :          POP      BP
228 :          RET
229 : __deol   endp
230 :
231 : wrtvr    proc     near             ; write video RAM (col, row, char/atr)
232 :          PUSH     BP
233 :          MOV      BP,SP            ; set up arg ptr
234 :          MOV      DL,[BP+4]        ; column
235 :          MOV      DH,[BP+6]        ; row
236 :          MOV      BX,[BP+8]        ; char/atr
237 :          MOV      AL,80            ; calc offset
238 :          MUL      DH
239 :          XOR      DH,DH
```

Figure 6-7. Continued.   *(more)*

```
240 :          ADD    AX,DX
241 :          ADD    AX,AX         ; adjust bytes to words
242 :          PUSH   ES            ; save seg reg
243 :          MOV    DI,AX
244 :          MOV    AX,v_bas      ; set up segment
245 :          MOV    ES,AX
246 :          MOV    AX,BX         ; get the data
247 :          STOSW                ; put on screen
248 :          POP    ES            ; restore regs
249 :          MOV    SP,BP
250 :          POP    BP
251 :          RET
252 : wrtvr    endp
253 :
254 : _TEXT    ends
255 :
256 :          END
```

Figure 6-7. Continued.

The sample smarter terminal emulator: CTERM.C

Given the interrupt handler (CH1), exception handler (CH1A), and video handler (CH2), a simple terminal emulation program (CTERM.C) can be presented. The major functions of the program are written in Microsoft C; the listing is shown in Figure 6-8.

```
 1 : /* Terminal Emulator    (cterm.c)
 2 : *       Jim Kyle, 1987
 3 : *
 4 : *       Uses files CH1, CH1A, and CH2 for MASM support...
 5 : */
 6 :
 7 : #include <stdio.h>
 8 : #include <conio.h>                    /* special console i/o    */
 9 : #include <stdlib.h>                   /* misc definitions       */
10 : #include <dos.h>                      /* defines intdos()       */
11 : #include <string.h>
12 : #define BRK   'C'-'@'                 /* control characters     */
13 : #define ESC   '['-'@'
14 : #define XON   'Q'-'@'
15 : #define XOFF  'S'-'@'
16 :
17 : #define True   1
18 : #define False  0
19 :
20 : #define Is_Function_Key(C) ( (C) == ESC )
21 :
22 : static char capbfr [ 4096 ];          /* capture buffer         */
23 : static int wh,
24 :     ws;
```

Figure 6-8. CTERM.C. (more)

```
25 :
26 : static int I,
27 :      waitchr = 0,
28 :      vflag = False,
29 :      capbp,
30 :      capbc,
31 :      Ch,
32 :      Want_7_Bit = True,
33 :      ESC_Seq_State = 0;          /* escape sequence state variable    */
34 :
35 : int _cx ,
36 :      _cy,
37 :      _atr = 0x07,                       /* white on black             */
38 :      _pag = 0,
39 :      oldtop = 0,
40 :      oldbot = 0x184f;
41 :
42 : FILE * in_file = NULL;         /* start with keyboard input        */
43 : FILE * cap_file = NULL;
44 :
45 : #include "cterm.h"             /* external declarations, etc.      */
46 :
47 : int Wants_To_Abort ()         /* checks for interrupt of script   */
48 : { return broke ();
49 : }
50 : void
51 :
52 : main ( argc, argv ) int argc ; /* main routine                    */
53 :  char * argv [];
54 : { char * cp,
55 :      * addext ();
56 :  if ( argc > 1 )                /* check for script filename       */
57 :     in_file = fopen ( addext ( argv [ 1 ], ".SCR" ), "r" );
58 :  if ( argc > 2 )                /* check for capture filename      */
59 :     cap_file = fopen ( addext ( argv [ 2 ], ".CAP" ), "w" );
60 :  set_int ();                   /* install CH1 module              */
61 :  Set_Vid ();                   /* get video setup                */
62 :  cls ();                       /* clear the screen               */
63 :  cputs ( "Terminal Emulator" ); /* tell who's working            */
64 :  cputs ( "\r\n< ESC for local commands >\r\n\n" );
65 :  Want_7_Bit = True;
66 :  ESC_Seq_State = 0;
67 :  Init_Comm ();                 /* set up drivers, etc.           */
68 :  while ( 1 )                   /* main loop                      */
69 :   { if (( Ch = kb_file ()) > 0 )    /* check local              */
70 :      { if ( Is_Function_Key ( Ch ))
71 :         { if ( docmd () < 0 )       /* command                  */
72 :              break;
73 :         }
74 :        else
75 :           Send_Byte ( Ch & 0x7F );  /* else send it            */
```

Figure 6-8. Continued.   *(more)*

```
 76 :            }
 77 :        if (( Ch = Read_Modem ()) >= 0 )    /* check remote              */
 78 :          { if ( Want_7_Bit )
 79 :              Ch &= 0x7F;                    /* trim off high bit         */
 80 :            switch ( ESC_Seq_State )         /* state machine             */
 81 :              {
 82 :              case 0 :                       /* no Esc sequence           */
 83 :                switch ( Ch )
 84 :                  {
 85 :                  case ESC  :                /* Esc char received         */
 86 :                    ESC_Seq_State = 1;
 87 :                    break;
 88 :
 89 :                  default :
 90 :                    if ( Ch == waitchr )     /* wait if required          */
 91 :                      waitchr = 0;
 92 :                    if ( Ch == 12 )          /* clear screen on FF         */
 93 :                      cls ();
 94 :                    else
 95 :                      if ( Ch != 127 )       /* ignore rubouts            */
 96 :                        { putchx ( (char) Ch );  /* handle all others */
 97 :                          put_cap ( (char) Ch );
 98 :                        }
 99 :                  }
100 :                break;
101 :
102 :              case 1 : /* ESC -- process any escape sequences here      */
103 :                switch ( Ch )
104 :                  {
105 :                  case 'A' :                  /* VT52 up                   */
106 :                    ;                         /* nothing but stubs here    */
107 :                    ESC_Seq_State = 0;
108 :                    break;
109 :
110 :                  case 'B' :                  /* VT52 down                 */
111 :                    ;
112 :                    ESC_Seq_State = 0;
113 :                    break;
114 :
115 :                  case 'C' :                  /* VT52 left                 */
116 :                    ;
117 :                    ESC_Seq_State = 0;
118 :                    break;
119 :
120 :                  case 'D' :                  /* VT52 right                */
121 :                    ;
122 :                    ESC_Seq_State = 0;
123 :                    break;
124 :
125 :                  case 'E' :                  /* VT52 Erase CRT            */
126 :                    cls ();                   /* actually do this one      */
```

Figure 6-8. Continued.

(more)

```
127 :                        ESC_Seq_State = 0;
128 :                        break;
129 :
130 :              case 'H' :                /* VT52 home cursor        */
131 :                 locate ( 0, 0 );
132 :                 ESC_Seq_State = 0;
133 :                 break;
134 :
135 :              case 'j' :                /* VT52 Erase to EOS       */
136 :                 deos ();
137 :                 ESC_Seq_State = 0;
138 :                 break;
139 :
140 :              case '[' :     /* ANSI.SYS - VT100 sequence      */
141 :                 ESC_Seq_State = 2;
142 :                 break;
143 :
144 :             default :
145 :                putchx ( ESC );        /* pass thru all others    */
146 :                putchx ( (char) Ch );
147 :                ESC_Seq_State = 0;
148 :                }
149 :            break;
150 :
151 :          case 2 :                      /* ANSI 3.64 decoder       */
152 :             ESC_Seq_State = 0;         /* not implemented         */
153 :             }
154 :         }
155 :     if ( broke ())                     /* check CH1A handlers     */
156 :        { cputs ( "\r\n***BREAK***\r\n" );
157 :          break;
158 :        }
159 :     }                                  /* end of main loop        */
160 : if ( cap_file )                        /* save any capture        */
161 :    cap_flush ();
162 : Term_Comm ();                          /* restore when done       */
163 : rst_int ();                            /* restore break handlers  */
164 : exit ( 0 );                            /* be nice to MS-DOS       */
165 : }
166 :
167 : docmd ()                               /* local command shell     */
168 : { FILE * getfil ();
169 :   int wp;
170 :   wp = True;
171 :   if ( ! in_file || vflag )
172 :      cputs ( "\r\n\tCommand: " );       /* ask for command         */
173 :   else
174 :      wp = False;
175 :   Ch = toupper ( kbd_wait ());          /* get response            */
176 :   if ( wp )
177 :      putchx ( (char) Ch );
```

Figure 6-8. Continued.   *(more)*

```
178 :     switch  ( Ch )                              /* and act on it              */
179 :     {
180 :     case 'S' :
181 :       if ( wp )
182 :         cputs ( "low speed\r\n" );
183 :       Set_Baud ( 300 );
184 :       break;
185 :
186 :     case 'D' :
187 :       if ( wp )
188 :         cputs ( "elay (1-9 sec): " );
189 :       Ch = kbd_wait ();
190 :       if ( wp )
191 :         putchx ( (char) Ch );
192 :       Delay ( 1000 * ( Ch - '0' ));
193 :       if ( wp )
194 :         putchx ( '\n' );
195 :       break;
196 :
197 :     case 'E' :
198 :       if ( wp )
199 :         cputs ( "ven Parity\r\n" );
200 :       Set_Parity ( 2 );
201 :       break;
202 :
203 :     case 'F' :
204 :       if ( wp )
205 :         cputs ( "ast speed\r\n" );
206 :       Set_Baud ( 1200 );
207 :       break;
208 :
209 :     case 'H' :
210 :       if ( wp )
211 :         { cputs ( "\r\n\tVALID COMMANDS:\r\n" );
212 :           cputs ( "\tD = delay 0-9 seconds.\r\n" );
213 :           cputs ( "\tE = even parity.\r\n" );
214 :           cputs ( "\tF = (fast) 1200-baud.\r\n" );
215 :           cputs ( "\tN = no parity.\r\n" );
216 :           cputs ( "\tO = odd parity.\r\n" );
217 :           cputs ( "\tQ = quit, return to DOS.\r\n" );
218 :           cputs ( "\tR = reset modem.\r\n" );
219 :           cputs ( "\tS = (slow) 300-baud.\r\n" );
220 :           cputs ( "\tU = use script file.\r\n" );
221 :           cputs ( "\tV = verify file input.\r\n" );
222 :           cputs ( "\tW = wait for char." );
223 :         }
224 :       break;
225 :
226 :     case 'N' :
227 :       if ( wp )
```

Figure 6-8. Continued.

(more)

```
228 :            cputs ( "o Parity\r\n" );
229 :          Set_Parity ( 1 );
230 :          break;
231 :
232 :        case 'O' :
233 :          if ( wp )
234 :            cputs ( "dd Parity\r\n" );
235 :          Set_Parity ( 3 );
236 :          break;
237 :
238 :        case 'R' :
239 :          if ( wp )
240 :            cputs ( "ESET Comm Port\r\n" );
241 :          Init_Comm ();
242 :          break;
243 :
244 :        case 'Q' :
245 :          if ( wp )
246 :            cputs ( " = QUIT Command\r\n" );
247 :          Ch = ( - 1 );
248 :          break;
249 :
250 :        case 'U' :
251 :          if ( in_file && ! vflag )
252 :            putchx ( 'U' );
253 :          cputs ( "se file: " );
254 :          getfil ();
255 :          cputs ( "File " );
256 :          cputs ( in_file ? "Open\r\n" : "Bad\r\n" );
257 :          waitchr = 0;
258 :          break;
259 :
260 :        case 'V' :
261 :          if ( wp )
262 :            { cputs ( "erify flag toggled " );
263 :              cputs ( vflag ? "OFF\r\n" : "ON\r\n" );
264 :            }
265 :          vflag = vflag ? False : True;
266 :          break;
267 :
268 :        case 'W' :
269 :          if ( wp )
270 :            cputs ( "ait for: <" );
271 :          waitchr = kbd_wait ();
272 :          if ( waitchr == ' ' )
273 :            waitchr = 0;
274 :          if ( wp )
275 :            { if ( waitchr )
276 :                putchx ( (char) waitchr );
277 :              else
278 :                cputs ( "no wait" );
```

Figure 6-8. Continued.   (more)

```
279 :            cputs ( ">\r\n" );
280 :              }
281 :        break;
282 :
283 :      default :
284 :        if ( wp )
285 :          { cputs ( "Don't know " );
286 :            putchx ( (char) Ch );
287 :            cputs ( "\r\nUse 'H' command for Help.\r\n" );
288 :            }
289 :          Ch = '?';
290 :          }
291 :    if ( wp )                            /* it window open...    */
292 :      { cputs ( "\r\n[any key]\r" );
293 :        while ( Read_Keyboard () == EOF ) /* wait for response     */
294 :          ;
295 :        }
296 :    return Ch ;
297 : }
298 :
299 : kbd_wait ()                            /* wait for input        */
300 : { int c ;
301 :    while (( c = kb_file ()) == ( - 1 ))
302 :      ;
303 :    return c & 255;
304 : }
305 :
306 : kb_file ()                             /* input from kb or file */
307 : { int c ;
308 :    if ( in_file )                       /* USING SCRIPT          */
309 :      { c = Wants_To_Abort ();           /* use first as flag     */
310 :        if ( waitchr && ! c )
311 :          c = ( - 1 );                   /* then for char         */
312 :        else
313 :          if ( c || ( c = getc ( in_file )) == EOF || c == 26 )
314 :            { fclose ( in_file );
315 :              cputs ( "\r\nScript File Closed\r\n" );
316 :              in_file = NULL;
317 :              waitchr = 0;
318 :              c = ( - 1 );
319 :              }
320 :          else
321 :            if ( c == '\n' )             /* ignore LFs in file    */
322 :              c = ( - 1 );
323 :          if ( c == '\\' )               /* process Esc sequence  */
324 :            c = esc ();
325 :          if ( vflag && c != ( - 1 ))    /* verify file char      */
326 :            { putchx ( '{' );
327 :              putchx ( (char) c );
328 :              putchx ( '}' );
329 :              }
```

Figure 6-8. Continued.   *(more)*

```
330 :      }
331 :    else                                 /* USING CONSOLE          */
332 :      c = Read_Keyboard ();              /* if not using file      */
333 :    return ( c );
334 : }
335 :
336 : esc ()                                  /* script translator      */
337 : { int c ;
338 :   c = getc ( in_file );                 /* control chars in file  */
339 :   switch ( toupper ( c ))
340 :     {
341 :     case 'E' :
342 :       c = ESC;
343 :       break;
344 :
345 :     case 'N' :
346 :       c = '\n';
347 :       break;
348 :
349 :     case 'R' :
350 :       c = '\r';
351 :       break;
352 :
353 :     case 'T' :
354 :       c = '\t';
355 :       break;
356 :
357 :     case '^' :
358 :       c = getc ( in_file ) & 31;
359 :       break;
360 :     }
361 :   return ( c );
362 : }
363 :
364 : FILE * getfil ()
365 : { char fnm [ 20 ];
366 :   getnam ( fnm, 15 );                    /* get the name           */
367 :   if ( ! ( strchr ( fnm, '.' )))
368 :     strcat ( fnm, ".SCR" );
369 :   return ( in_file = fopen ( fnm, "r" ));
370 : }
371 :
372 : void getnam ( b, s ) char * b;           /* take input to buffer   */
373 :   int s ;
374 : { while ( s -- > 0 )
375 :     { if (( * b = (char) kbd_wait ()) != '\r' )
376 :         putchx ( * b ++ );
377 :       else
378 :         break ;
379 :     }
380 :   putchx ( '\n' );
```

Figure 6-8. Continued.   *(more)*

```
381 :    * b = 0;
382 : }
383 :
384 : char * addext ( b,                         /* add default EXTension    */
385 :     e ) char * b,
386 :     * e;
387 : { static char bfr [ 20 ];
388 :   if ( strchr ( b, '.' ))
389 :     return ( b );
390 :   strcpy ( bfr, b );
391 :   strcat ( bfr, e );
392 :   return ( bfr );
393 : }
394 :
395 : void put_cap ( c ) char c ;
396 : { if ( cap_file && c != 13 )               /* strip out CRs            */
397 :     fputc ( c, cap_file );                 /* use MS-DOS buffering     */
398 : }
399 :
400 : void cap_flush ()                          /* end Capture mode         */
401 : { if ( cap_file )
402 :     { fclose ( cap_file );
403 :       cap_file = NULL;
404 :       cputs ( "\r\nCapture file closed\r\n" );
405 :     }
406 : }
407 :
408 : /*      TIMER SUPPORT STUFF (IBMPC/MSDOS)        */
409 : static long timr;                          /* timeout register         */
410 :
411 : static union REGS rgv ;
412 :
413 : long getmr ()
414 : { long now ;                               /* msec since midnite       */
415 :   rgv.x.ax = 0x2c00;
416 :   intdos ( & rgv, & rgv );
417 :   now = rgv.h.ch;                          /* hours                    */
418 :   now *= 60L;                              /* to minutes               */
419 :   now += rgv.h.cl;                         /* plus min                 */
420 :   now *= 60L;                              /* to seconds               */
421 :   now += rgv.h.dh;                         /* plus sec                 */
422 :   now *= 100L;                             /* to 1/100                 */
423 :   now += rgv.h.dl;                         /* plus 1/100               */
424 :   return ( 10L * now );                    /* msec value               */
425 : }
426 :
427 : void Delay ( n ) int n ;                   /* sleep for n msec         */
428 : { long wakeup ;
429 :   wakeup = getmr () + ( long ) n;          /* wakeup time              */
430 :   while ( getmr () < wakeup )
431 :     ;                                      /* now sleep                */
```

Figure 6-8. Continued.   *(more)*

```
432 : }
433 :
434 : void Start_Timer ( n ) int n ;          /* set timeout for n sec      */
435 : { timr = getmr () + ( long ) n * 1000L;
436 : }
437 :
438 : Timer_Expired ()         /* if timeout return 1 else return 0         */
439 : { return ( getmr () > timr );
440 : }
441 :
442 : Set_Vid ()
443 : { _i_v ();                              /* initialize video           */
444 :   return 0;
445 : }
446 :
447 : void locate ( row, col ) int row ,
448 :      col;
449 : { _cy = row % 25;
450 :   _cx = col % 80;
451 :   _wrpos ( row, col );                  /* use ML from CH2.ASM         */
452 : }
453 :
454 : void deol ()
455 : { _deol ();                             /* use ML from CH2.ASM         */
456 : }
457 :
458 : void deos ()
459 : { deol ();
460 :   if ( _cy < 24 )                       /* if not last, clear          */
461 :     { rgv.x.ax = 0x0600;
462 :       rgv.x.bx = ( _atr << 8 );
463 :       rgv.x.cx = ( _cy + 1 ) << 8;
464 :       rgv.x.dx = 0x184F;
465 :       int86 ( 0x10, & rgv, & rgv );
466 :     }
467 :   locate ( _cy, _cx );
468 : }
469 :
470 : void cls ()
471 : { _cls ();                              /* use ML                      */
472 : }
473 :
474 : void cursor ( yn ) int yn ;
475 : { rgv.x.cx = yn ? 0x0607 : 0x2607;      /* ON/OFF                      */
476 :   rgv.x.ax = 0x0100;
477 :   int86 ( 0x10, & rgv, & rgv );
478 : }
479 :
480 : void revvid ( yn ) int yn ;
481 : { if ( yn )
482 :     _atr = _color ( 8, 7 );             /* black on white              */
```

Figure 6-8. Continued.   *(more)*

```
483 :    else
484 :       _atr = _color ( 15, 0 );                /* white on black          */
485 : }
486 :
487 : putchx ( c ) char c ;                         /* put char to CRT         */
488 : { if ( c == '\n' )
489 :      putch ( '\r' );
490 :    putch ( c );
491 :    return c ;
492 : }
493 :
494 : Read_Keyboard ()                      /* get keyboard character
495 :                                          returns -1 if none present     */
496 : { int c ;
497 :    if ( kbhit ())                             /* no char at all          */
498 :       return ( getch ());
499 :    return ( EOF );
500 : }
501 :
502 : /*        MODEM SUPPORT                 */
503 : static char mparm,
504 :       wrk [ 80 ];
505 :
506 : void Init_Comm ()                     /* initialize comm port stuff      */
507 : { static int ft = 0;                  /* firstime flag                   */
508 :    if ( ft ++ == 0 )
509 :      i_m ();
510 :    Set_Parity ( 1 );                          /* 8,N,1                   */
511 :    Set_Baud ( 1200 );                         /* 1200 baud               */
512 : }
513 :
514 : #define B1200 0x80                             /* baudrate codes          */
515 : #define B300 0x40
516 :
517 : Set_Baud ( n ) int n ;                         /* n is baud rate          */
518 : { if ( n == 300 )
519 :      mparm = ( mparm & 0x1F ) + B300;
520 :    else
521 :      if ( n == 1200 )
522 :         mparm = ( mparm & 0x1F ) + B1200;
523 :    else
524 :      return 0;                                 /* invalid speed           */
525 :    sprintf ( wrk, "Baud rate = %d\r\n", n );
526 :    cputs ( wrk );
527 :    set_mdm ( mparm );
528 :    return n ;
529 : }
530 :
531 : #define PAREVN 0x18                            /* MCR bits for commands   */
532 : #define PARODD 0x10
533 : #define PAROFF 0x00
```

Figure 6-8. Continued.   *(more)*

```
534 : #define STOP2 0x40
535 : #define WORD8 0x03
536 : #define WORD7 0x02
537 : #define WORD6 0x01
538 :
539 : Set_Parity ( n ) int n ;                      /* n is parity code        */
540 : { static int mmode;
541 :   if ( n == 1 )
542 :     mmode = ( WORD8 | PAROFF );               /* off                     */
543 :   else
544 :     if ( n == 2 )
545 :       mmode = ( WORD7 | PAREVN );             /* on and even             */
546 :   else
547 :     if ( n == 3 )
548 :       mmode = ( WORD7 | PARODD );             /* on and odd              */
549 :   else
550 :     return 0;                                 /* invalid code            */
551 :   mparm = ( mparm & 0xE0 ) + mmode;
552 :   sprintf ( wrk, "Parity is %s\r\n", ( n == 1 ? "OFF" :
553 :                                        ( n == 2 ? "EVEN" : "ODD" )));
554 :   cputs ( wrk );
555 :   set_mdm ( mparm );
556 :   return n ;
557 : }
558 :
559 : Write_Modem ( c ) char c ;                     /* return 1 if ok, else 0  */
560 : { wrtmdm ( c );
561 :   return ( 1 );                                /* never any error         */
562 : }
563 :
564 : Read_Modem ()
565 : { return ( rdmdm ());                          /* from int bfr            */
566 : }
567 :
568 : void Term_Comm ()                    /* uninstall comm port drivers        */
569 : { u_m ();
570 : }
571 :
572 : /* end of cterm.c */
```

Figure 6-8. Continued.

CTERM features file-capture capabilities, a simple yet effective script language, and a number of stub (that is, incompletely implemented) actions, such as emulation of the VT52 and VT100 series terminals, indicating various directions in which it can be developed.

The names of a script file and a capture file can be passed to CTERM in the command line. If no filename extensions are included, the default for the script file is .SCR and that for the capture file is .CAP. If extensions are given, they override the default values. The capture feature can be invoked only if a filename is supplied in the command line, but a script file can be called at any time via the Esc command sequence, and one script file can call for another with the same feature.

The functions included in CTERM.C are listed and summarized in Table 6-13.

Table 6-13. CTERM.C Functions.

Lines	Name	Description
1–5		Program documentation.
7–11		*Include* files.
12–20		Definitions.
22–43		Global data areas.
45		External prototype declaration.
47–49	*Wants_To_Abort()*	Checks for Ctrl-Break or Ctrl-C being pressed.
52–165	*main()*	Main program loop; includes modem engine and sequential state machine to decode remote commands.
167–297	*docmd()*	Gets, interprets, and performs local (console or script) command.
299–304	*kbd_wait()*	Waits for input from console or script file.
306–334	*kb_file()*	Gets keystroke from console or script; returns EOF if no character available.
336–362	*esc()*	Translates script escape sequence.
364–370	*getfil()*	Gets name of script file and opens the file.
372–382	*getnam()*	Gets string from console or script into designated buffer.
384–393	*addext()*	Checks buffer for extension; adds one if none given.
395–398	*put_cap()*	Writes character to capture file if capture in effect.
400–406	*cap_flush()*	Closes capture file and terminates capture mode if capture in effect.
408–411		Timer data locations.
413–425	*getmr()*	Returns time since midnight, in milliseconds.
427–432	*Delay()*	Sleeps *n* milliseconds.
434–436	*Start_Timer()*	Sets timer for *n* seconds.
438–440	*Timer_Expired()*	Checks timer versus clock.
442–445	*Set_Vid()*	Initializes video data.
447–452	*locate()*	Positions cursor on display.
454–456	*deol()*	Deletes to end of line.
458–468	*deos()*	Deletes to end of screen.
470–472	*cls()*	Clears screen.
474–478	*cursor()*	Turns cursor on or off.
480–485	*revvid()*	Toggles inverse/normal video display attributes.
487–492	*putchx()*	Writes char to display using *putch()* (Microsoft C library).

(more)

Table 6-13. *Continued.*

Lines	Name	Description
494–500	*Read_Keyboard()*	Gets keystroke from keyboard.
502–504		Modem data areas.
506–512	*Init_Comm()*	Installs ISR and so forth and initializes modem.
514–515		Baud-rate definitions.
517–529	*Set_Baud()*	Changes bps rate of UART.
531–537		Parity, WL definitions.
539–557	*Set_Parity()*	Establishes UART parity mode.
559–562	*Write_Modem()*	Sends character to UART.
564–566	*Read_Modem()*	Gets character from ISR's buffer.
568–570	*Term_Comm()*	Uninstalls ISR and so forth and restores original vectors.

For communication with the console, CTERM uses the special Microsoft C library functions defined by CONIO.H, augmented with the functions in the CH2.ASM handler. Much of the code may require editing if used with other compilers. CTERM also uses the function prototype file CTERM.H, listed in Figure 6-9, to optimize function calling within the program.

```
/* CTERM.H - function prototypes for CTERM.C */
int Wants_To_Abort(void);
void main(int ,char * *);
int docmd(void);
int kbd_wait(void);
int kb_file(void);
int esc(void);
FILE *getfil(void);
void getnam(char *,int );
char *addext(char *,char *);
void put_cap(char );
void cap_flush(void);
long getmr(void);
void Delay(int );
void Start_Timer(int );
int Timer_Expired(void);
int Set_Vid(void);
void locate(int ,int );
void deol(void);
void deos(void);
void cls(void);
void cursor(int );
void revvid(int );
int putchx(char );
```

Figure 6-9. CTERM.H.

(more)

```
int  Read_Keyboard(void);
void Init_Comm(void);
int  Set_Baud(int );
int  Set_Parity(int );
int  Write_Modem(char );
int  Read_Modem(void);
void Term_Comm(void);

/* CH1.ASM functions - modem interfacing */
void i_m(void);
void set_mdm(int);
void wrtmdm(int);
void Send_Byte(int);
int  rdmdm(void);
void u_m(void);

/* CH1A.ASM functions - exception handlers */
void set_int (void);
void rst_int (void);
int broke (void);

/* CH2.ASM functions - video interfacing */
void _i_v(void);
int  _wrpos(int, int);
void _deol(void);
void _cls(void);
int  _color(int, int);
```

Figure 6-9. Continued.

Program execution begins at the entry to *main()*, line 52. CTERM first checks (lines 56 through 59) whether any filenames were passed in the command line; if they were, CTERM opens the corresponding files. Next, the program installs the exception handler (line 60), initializes the video handler (line 61), clears the display (line 62), and announces its presence (lines 63 and 64). The serial driver is installed and initialized to 1200 bps and no parity (lines 65 through 67), and the program enters its main modem-engine loop (lines 68 through 159).

This loop is functionally the same as that used in ENGINE, but it has been extended to detect an Esc from the keyboard as signalling the start of a local command sequence (lines 70 through 73) and to include a state-machine technique (lines 80 through 153) to recognize incoming escape sequences, such as the VT52 or VT100 codes. To specify a local command from the keyboard, press the Escape (Esc) key, then the first letter of the local command desired. After the local command has been selected, press any key (such as Enter or the spacebar) to continue. To get a listing of all the commands available, press Esc-H.

The *kb_file()* routine of CTERM (called in the main loop at line 69) can get its input from either a script file or the keyboard. If a script file is open (lines 308 through 330), it is used until EOF is reached or until the operator presses Ctrl-C to stop script-file input. Otherwise, input is taken from the keyboard (lines 331 and 332). If a script file is in use, its input is echoed to the display (lines 325 through 329) if the V command has been given.

To permit the Esc character itself to be placed in script files, the backslash (\) character serves as a secondary escape signal. When a backslash is detected (lines 323 and 324) in the input stream, the next character input is translated according to the following rules:

Character	Interpretation
E *or* e	Translates to Esc.
N *or* n	Translates to Linefeed.
R *or* r	Translates to Enter (CR).
T *or* t	Translates to Tab.
^	Causes the *next* character input to be converted into a control character.

Any other character, including another \, is not translated at all.

When the Esc character is detected from either the console or a script file, the *docmd()* function (lines 167 through 297) is called to prompt for and decode the next input character as a command and to perform appropriate actions. Valid command characters, and the actions they invoke, are as follows:

Command Character	Action
D	Delay 0–9 seconds, then proceed. Must be followed by a decimal digit that indicates how long to delay.
E	Set EVEN parity.
F	Set (fast) 1200 baud.
H	Display list of valid commands.
N	Set no parity.
O	Set ODD parity.
Q	Quit; return to MS-DOS command prompt.
R	Reset modem.
S	Set (slow) 300 baud.
U	Use script file (CTERM prompts for filename).
V	Verify file input. Echoes each script-file byte.
W	Wait for character; the next input character is the one that must be matched.

Any other character input after an Esc and the resulting Command prompt generates the message *Don't know X* (where *X* stands for the actual input character) followed by the prompt *Use 'H' command for Help*.

If input is taken from a script and the V flag is off, *docmd()* performs its task quietly, with no output to the screen. If input is received from the console, however, the command letter, followed by a descriptive phrase, is echoed to the screen. Input, detection, and execution of the local commands are accomplished much as in CDVUTL, by way of a large *switch()* statement (lines 178 through 290).

Although the listed commands are only a subset of the features available in CDVUTL for the device-driver program, they are more than adequate for creating useful scripts. The predecessor of CTERM (DT115.EXE), which included the CompuServe B-Protocol file-transfer capability but had no additional commands, has been in use since early 1986 to handle automatic uploading and downloading of files from the CompuServe Information Service by means of script files. In conjunction with an auto-dialing modem, DT115.EXE handles the entire transaction, from login through logout, without human intervention.

All the bits and pieces of CTERM are put together by assembling the three handlers with MASM, compiling CTERM with Microsoft C, and linking all four object modules into an executable file. Figure 6-10 shows the complete sequence and also the three ways of using the finished program.

Compiling:

```
C>MASM CH1;   <Enter>
C>MASM CH1A;  <Enter>
C>MASM CH2;   <Enter>
C>MSC CTERM;  <Enter>
```

Linking:

```
C>LINK CTERM+CH1+CH1A+CH2;  <Enter>
```

Use:
(no files)

```
C>CTERM  <Enter>
```

or
(script only)

```
C>CTERM scriptfile  <Enter>
```

or

```
C>CTERM scriptfile capturefile  <Enter>
```

Figure 6-10. Putting CTERM together and using it.

Jim Kyle
Chip Rabinowitz

Article 7
File and Record Management

The core of most application programs is the reading, processing, and writing of data stored on magnetic disks. This data is organized into files, which are identified by name; the files, in turn, can be organized by grouping them into directories. Operating systems provide application programs with services that allow them to manipulate these files and directories without regard to the hardware characteristics of the disk device. Thus, applications can concern themselves solely with the form and content of the data, leaving the details of the data's location on the disk and of its retrieval to the operating system.

The disk storage services provided by an operating system can be categorized into file functions and record functions. The file functions operate on entire files as named entities, whereas the record functions provide access to the data contained within files. (In some systems, an additional class of directory functions allows applications to deal with collections of files as well.) This article discusses the MS-DOS function calls that allow an application program to create, open, close, rename, and delete disk files; read data from and write data to disk files; and inspect or change the information (such as attributes and date and time stamps) associated with disk filenames in disk directories. *See also* PROGRAMMING IN THE MS-DOS ENVIRONMENT: STRUCTURE OF MS-DOS: MS-DOS Storage Devices; PROGRAMMING FOR MS-DOS: Disk Directories and Volume Labels.

Historical Perspective

Current versions of MS-DOS provide two overlapping sets of file and record management services to support application programs: the handle functions and the file control block (FCB) functions. Both sets are available through Interrupt 21H (Table 7-1). *See* SYSTEM CALLS: INTERRUPT 21H. The reasons for this surprising duplication are strictly historical.

The earliest versions of MS-DOS used FCBs for all file and record access because CP/M, which was the dominant operating system on 8-bit microcomputers, used FCBs. Microsoft chose to maintain compatibility with CP/M to aid programmers in converting the many existing CP/M application programs to the 16-bit MS-DOS environment; consequently, MS-DOS versions 1.x included a set of FCB functions that were a functional superset of those present in CP/M. As personal computers evolved, however, the FCB access method did not lend itself well to the demands of larger, faster disk drives.

Accordingly, MS-DOS version 2.0 introduced the handle functions to provide a file and record access method similar to that found in UNIX/XENIX. These functions are easier to use and more flexible than their FCB counterparts and fully support a hierarchical (tree-like) directory structure. The handle functions also allow character devices, such as the console or printer, to be treated for some purposes as though they were files. MS-DOS version 3.0 introduced additional handle functions, enhanced some of the existing handle functions for use in network environments, and provided improved error reporting for all functions.

The handle functions, which offer far more capability and performance than the FCB functions, should be used for all new applications. Therefore, they are discussed first in this article.

Table 7-1. Interrupt 21H Function Calls for File and Record Management.

Operation	Handle Function	FCB Function
Create file.	3CH	16H
Create new file.	5BH	
Create temporary file.	5AH	
Open file.	3DH	0FH
Close file.	3EH	10H
Delete file.	41H	13H
Rename file.	56H	17H
Perform sequential read.	3FH	14H
Perform sequential write.	40H	15H
Perform random record read.	3FH	21H
Perform random record write.	40H	22H
Perform random block read.		27H
Perform random block write.		28H
Set disk transfer area address.		1AH
Get disk transfer area address.		2FH
Parse filename.		29H
Position read/write pointer.	42H	
Set random record number.		24H
Get file size.	42H	23H
Get/Set file attributes.	43H	
Get/Set date and time stamp.	57H	
Duplicate file handle.	45H	
Redirect file handle.	46H	

Using the Handle Functions

The initial link between an application program and the data stored on disk is the name of a disk file in the form

drive:path\ filename.ext

where *drive* designates the disk on which the file resides, *path* specifies the directory on that disk in which the file is located, and *filename.ext* identifies the file itself. If *drive* and/or *path* is omitted, MS-DOS assumes the default disk drive and current directory. Examples of acceptable pathnames include

C:\PAYROLL\TAXES.DAT
LETTERS\MEMO.TXT
BUDGET.DAT

Pathnames can be hard-coded into a program as part of its data. More commonly, however, they are entered by the user at the keyboard, either as a command-line parameter or in response to a prompt from the program. If the pathname is provided as a command-line parameter, the application program must extract it from the other information in the command line. Therefore, to allow a program to distinguish between pathnames and other parameters when the two are combined in a command line, the other parameters, such as switches, usually begin with a slash (/) or dash (-) character.

All handle functions that use a pathname require the name to be in the form of an ASCIIZ string — that is, the name must be terminated by a null (zero) byte. If the pathname is hard-coded into a program, the null byte must be part of the ASCIIZ string. If the pathname is obtained from keyboard input or from a command-line parameter, the null byte must be appended by the program. *See* Opening an Existing File below.

To use a disk file, a program opens or creates the file by calling the appropriate MS-DOS function with the ASCIIZ pathname. MS-DOS checks the pathname for invalid characters and, if the open or create operation is successful, returns a 16-bit handle, or identification code, for the file. The program uses this handle for subsequent operations on the file, such as record reads and writes.

The total number of handles for simultaneously open files is limited in two ways. First, the per-process limit is 20 file handles. The process's first five handles are always assigned to the standard devices, which default to the CON, AUX, and PRN character devices:

Handle	Service	Default
0	Standard input	Keyboard (CON)
1	Standard output	Video display (CON)
2	Standard error	Video display (CON)
3	Standard auxiliary	First communications port (AUX)
4	Standard list	First parallel printer port (PRN)

Ordinarily, then, a process has only 15 handles left from its initial allotment of 20; however, when necessary, the 5 standard device handles can be redirected to other files and devices or closed and reused.

In addition to the per-process limit of 20 file handles, there is a system-wide limit. MS-DOS maintains an internal table that keeps track of all the files and devices opened with file handles for all currently active processes. The table contains such information as the current file pointer for read and write operations and the time and date of the last write to the file. The size of this table, which is set when MS-DOS is initially loaded into memory, determines the system-wide limit on how many files and devices can be open simultaneously. The default limit is 8 files and devices; thus, this system-wide limit usually overrides the per-process limit.

To increase the size of MS-DOS's internal handle table, the statement *FILES*=nnn can be included in the CONFIG.SYS file. (CONFIG.SYS settings take effect the next time the system is turned on or restarted.) The maximum value for FILES is 99 in MS-DOS versions 2.x and 255 in versions 3.x. *See* USER COMMANDS: CONFIG.SYS: FILES.

Error handling and the handle functions

When a handle-based file function succeeds, MS-DOS returns to the calling program with the carry flag clear. If a handle function fails, MS-DOS sets the carry flag and returns an error code in the AX register. The program should check the carry flag after each operation and take whatever action is appropriate when an error is encountered. Table 7-2 lists the most frequently encountered error codes for file and record I/O (exclusive of network operations).

Table 7-2. Frequently Encountered Error Diagnostics for File and Record Management.

Code	Error
02	File not found
03	Path not found
04	Too many open files (no handles left)
05	Access denied
06	Invalid handle
11	Invalid format
12	Invalid access code
13	Invalid data
15	Invalid disk drive letter
17	Not same device
18	No more files

The error codes used by MS-DOS in versions 3.0 and later are a superset of the MS-DOS version 2.0 error codes. *See* APPENDIX B: CRITICAL ERROR CODES; APPENDIX C: EXTENDED ERROR CODES. Most MS-DOS version 3 error diagnostics relate to network operations, which provide the program with a greater chance for error than does a single-user system.

Programs that are to run in a network environment need to anticipate network problems. For example, the server can go down while the program is using shared files.

Under MS-DOS versions 3.x, a program can also use Interrupt 21H Function 59H (Get Extended Error Information) to obtain more details about the cause of an error after a failed handle function. The information returned by Function 59H includes the type of device that caused the error and a recommended recovery action.

Warning: Many file and record I/O operations discussed in this article can result in or be affected by a hardware (critical) error. Such errors can be intercepted by the program if it contains a custom critical error exception handler (Interrupt 24H). *See* PROGRAMMING IN THE MS-DOS ENVIRONMENT: Customizing ms-dos: Exception Handlers.

Creating a file

MS-DOS provides three Interrupt 21H handle functions for creating files:

Function	Name
3CH	Create File with Handle (versions 2.0 and later)
5AH	Create Temporary File (versions 3.0 and later)
5BH	Create New File (versions 3.0 and later)

Each function is called with the segment and offset of an ASCIIZ pathname in the DS:DX registers and the attribute to be assigned to the new file in the CX register. The possible attribute values are

Code	Attribute
00H	Normal file
01H	Read-only file
02H	Hidden file
04H	System file

Files with more than one attribute can be created by combining the values listed above. For example, to create a file that has both the read-only and system attributes, the value 05H is placed in the CX register.

If the file is successfully created, MS-DOS returns a file handle in AX that must be used for subsequent access to the new file and sets the file read/write pointer to the beginning of the file; if the file is not created, MS-DOS sets the carry flag (CF) and returns an error code in AX.

Function 3CH is the only file-creation function available under MS-DOS versions 2.x. It must be used with caution, however, because if a file with the specified name already exists, Function 3CH will open it and truncate it to zero length, eradicating the previous contents of the file. This complication can be avoided by testing for the previous existence of the file with an open operation before issuing the create call.

Under MS-DOS versions 3.0 and later, Function 5BH is the preferred function in most cases because it will fail if a file with the same name already exists. In networking environments, this function can be used to implement semaphores, allowing the synchronization of programs running in different network nodes.

Function 5AH is used to create a temporary work file that is guaranteed to have a unique name. This capability is important in networking environments, where several copies of the same program, running in different nodes, may be accessing the same logical disk volume on a server. The function is passed the address of a buffer that can contain a drive and/or path specifying the location for the created file. MS-DOS generates a name for the created file that is a sequence of alphanumeric characters derived from the current time and returns the entire ASCIIZ pathname to the program in the same buffer, along with the file's handle in AX. The program must save the filename so that it can delete the file later, if necessary; the file created with Function 5AH is not destroyed when the program exits.

Example: Create a file named MEMO.TXT in the \LETTERS directory on drive C using Function 3CH. Any existing file with the same name is truncated to zero length and opened.

```
fname     db       'C:\LETTERS\MEMO.TXT',0
fhandle dw         ?
          .
          .
          .
          mov      dx,seg fname    ; DS:DX = address of
          mov      ds,dx           ; pathname for file
          mov      dx,offset fname
          xor      cx,cx           ; CX = normal attribute
          mov      ah,3ch          ; Function 3CH = create
          int      21h             ; transfer to MS-DOS
          jc       error           ; jump if create failed
          mov      fhandle,ax      ; else save file handle
          .
          .
          .
```

Example: Create a temporary file using Function 5AH and place it in the \TEMP directory on drive C. MS-DOS appends the filename it generates to the original path in the buffer named *fname*. The resulting file specification can be used later to delete the file.

```
fname     db       'C:\TEMP\'      ; generated ASCIIZ filename
          db       13 dup (0)      ; is appended by MS-DOS

fhandle dw         ?
          .
          .
          .
```

(more)

```
        mov     dx,seg fname    ; DS:DX = address of
        mov     ds,dx           ; path for temporary file
        mov     dx,offset fname
        xor     cx,cx           ; CX = normal attribute
        mov     ah,5ah          ; Function 5AH = create
                                ; temporary file
        int     21h             ; transfer to MS-DOS
        jc      error           ; jump if create failed
        mov     fhandle,ax      ; else save file handle
        .
        .
        .
```

Opening an existing file

Function 3DH (Open File with Handle) opens an existing normal, system, or hidden file in the current or specified directory. When calling Function 3DH, the program supplies a pointer to the ASCIIZ pathname in the DS:DX registers and a 1-byte access code in the AL register. This access code includes the read/write permissions, the file-sharing mode, and an inheritance flag. The bits of the access code are assigned as follows:

Bit(s)	Description
0–2	Read/write permissions (versions 2.0 and later)
3	Reserved
4–6	File-sharing mode (versions 3.0 and later)
7	Inheritance flag (versions 3.0 and later)

The read/write permissions field of the access code specifies how the file will be used and can take the following values:

Bits 0–2	Description
000	Read permission desired
001	Write permission desired
010	Read and write permission desired

For the open to succeed, the permissions field must be compatible with the file's attribute byte in the disk directory. For example, if the program attempts to open an existing file that has the read-only attribute when the permissions field of the access code byte is set to write or read/write, the open function will fail and an error code will be returned in AX.

The sharing-mode field of the access code byte is important in a networking environment. It determines whether other programs will also be allowed to open the file and, if so, what operations they will be allowed to perform. Following are the possible values of the file-sharing mode field:

Bits 4–6	Description
000	Compatibility mode. Other programs can open the file and perform read or write operations as long as no process specifies any sharing mode other than compatibility mode.
001	Deny all. Other programs cannot open the file.
010	Deny write. Other programs cannot open the file in compatibility mode or with write permission.
011	Deny read. Other programs cannot open the file in compatibility mode or with read permission.
100	Deny none. Other programs can open the file and perform both read and write operations but cannot open the file in compatibility mode.

When file-sharing support is active (that is, SHARE.EXE has previously been loaded), the result of any open operation depends on both the contents of the permissions and file-sharing fields of the access code byte and the permissions and file-sharing requested by other processes that have already successfully opened the file.

The inheritance bit of the access code byte controls whether a child process will inherit that file handle. If the inheritance bit is cleared, the child can use the inherited handle to access the file without performing its own open operation. Subsequent operations performed by the child process on inherited file handles also affect the file pointer associated with the parent's file handle. If the inheritance bit is set, the child process does not inherit the handle.

If the file is opened successfully, MS-DOS returns its handle in AX and sets the file read/write pointer to the beginning of the file; if the file is not opened, MS-DOS sets the carry flag and returns an error code in AX.

Example: Copy the first parameter from the program's command tail in the program segment prefix (PSP) into the array *fname* and append a null character to form an ASCIIZ filename. Attempt to open the file with compatibility sharing mode and read/write access. If the file does not already exist, create it and assign it a normal attribute.

```
cmdtail equ     80h             ; PSP offset of command tail
fname   db      64 dup (?)
fhandle dw      ?

        .
        .
        .

                                ; assume that DS already
                                ; contains segment of PSP
```

(more)

```
                          ; prepare to copy filename...
        mov     si,cmdtail        ; DS:SI = command tail
        mov     di,seg fname      ; ES:DI = buffer to receive
        mov     es,di             ; filename from command tail
        mov     di,offset fname
        cld                       ; safety first!

        lodsb                     ; check length of command tail
        or      al,al
        jz      error             ; jump, command tail empty

label1:                           ; scan off leading spaces
        lodsb                     ; get next character
        cmp     al,20h            ; is it a space?
        jz      label1            ; yes, skip it

label2:
        cmp     al,0dh            ; look for terminator
        jz      label3            ; quit if return found
        cmp     al,20h
        jz      label3            ; quit if space found
        stosb                     ; else copy this character
        lodsb                     ; get next character
        jmp     label2

label3:
        xor     al,al             ; store final NULL to
        stosb                     ; create ASCIIZ string

                          ; now open the file...
        mov     dx,seg fname      ; DS:DX = address of
        mov     ds,dx             ; pathname for file
        mov     dx,offset fname
        mov     ax,3d02h          ; Function 3DH = open r/w
        int     21h               ; transfer to MS-DOS
        jnc     label4            ; jump if file found

        cmp     ax,2              ; error 2 = file not found
        jnz     error             ; jump if other error
                          ; else make the file...
        xor     cx,cx             ; CX = normal attribute
        mov     ah,3ch            ; Function 3CH = create
        int     21h               ; transfer to MS-DOS
        jc      error             ; jump if create failed

label4:
        mov     fhandle,ax        ; save handle for file
        .
        .
        .
```

Closing a file

Function 3EH (Close File) closes a file created or opened with a file handle function. The program must place the handle of the file to be closed in BX. If a write operation was performed on the file, MS-DOS updates the date, time, and size in the file's directory entry.

Closing the file also flushes the internal MS-DOS buffers associated with the file to disk and causes the disk's file allocation table (FAT) to be updated if necessary.

Good programming practice dictates that a program close files as soon as it finishes using them. This practice is particularly important when the file size has been changed, to ensure that data will not be lost if the system crashes or is turned off unexpectedly by the user. A method of updating the FAT without closing the file is outlined below under Duplicating and Redirecting Handles.

Reading and writing with handles

Function 3FH (Read File or Device) enables a program to read data from a file or device that has been opened with a handle. Before calling Function 3FH, the program must set the DS:DX registers to point to the beginning of a data buffer large enough to hold the requested transfer, put the file handle in BX, and put the number of bytes to be read in CX. The length requested can be a maximum of 65535 bytes. The program requesting the read operation is responsible for providing the data buffer.

If the read operation succeeds, the data is read, beginning at the current position of the file read/write pointer, to the specified location in memory. MS-DOS then increments its internal read/write pointer for the file by the length of the data transferred and returns the length to the calling program in AX with the carry flag cleared. The only indication that the end of the file has been reached is that the length returned is less than the length requested. In contrast, when Function 3FH is used to read from a character device that is *not* in raw mode, the read will terminate at the requested length or at the receipt of a carriage return character, whichever comes first. *See* PROGRAMMING IN THE MS-DOS ENVIRONMENT: PROGRAMMING FOR MS-DOS: Character Device Input and Output. If the read operation fails, MS-DOS returns with the carry flag set and an error code in AX.

Function 40H (Write File or Device) writes from a buffer to a file (or device) using a handle previously obtained from an open or create operation. Before calling Function 40H, the program must set DS:DX to point to the beginning of the buffer containing the source data, put the file handle in BX, and put the number of bytes to write in CX. The number of bytes to write can be a maximum of 65535.

If the write operation is successful, MS-DOS puts the number of bytes written in AX and increments the read/write pointer by this value; if the write operation fails, MS-DOS sets the carry flag and returns an error code in AX.

Records smaller than one sector (512 bytes) are not written directly to disk. Instead, MS-DOS stores the record in an internal buffer and writes it to disk when the internal buffer is full, when the file is closed, or when a call to Interrupt 21H Function 0DH (Disk Reset) is issued.

Note: If the destination of the write operation is a disk file and the disk is full, the only indication to the calling program is that the length returned in AX is not the same as the length requested in CX. *Disk full* is not returned as an error with the carry flag set.

A special use of the Write function is to truncate or extend a file. If Function 40H is called with a record length of zero in CX, the file size will be adjusted to the current location of the file read/write pointer.

Example: Open the file MYFILE.DAT, create the file MYFILE.BAK, copy the contents of the .DAT file into the .BAK file using 512-byte reads and writes, and then close both files.

```
file1     db      'MYFILE.DAT',0
file2     db      'MYFILE.BAK',0

handle1 dw        ?               ; handle for MYFILE.DAT
handle2 dw        ?               ; handle for MYFILE.BAK

buff      db      512 dup (?)     ; buffer for file I/O
          .
          .
          .
                                  ; open MYFILE.DAT...
          mov     dx,seg file1    ; DS:DX = address of filename
          mov     ds,dx
          mov     dx,offset file1
          mov     ax,3d00h        ; Function 3DH = open (read-only)
          int     21h             ; transfer to MS-DOS
          jc      error           ; jump if open failed
          mov     handle1,ax      ; save handle for file

                                  ; create MYFILE.BAK...
          mov     dx,offset file2 ; DS:DX = address of filename
          mov     cx,0            ; CX = normal attribute
          mov     ah,3ch          ; Function 3CH = create
          int     21h             ; transfer to MS-DOS
          jc      error           ; jump if create failed
          mov     handle2,ax      ; save handle for file

loop:                             ; read MYFILE.DAT
          mov     dx,offset buff  ; DS:DX = buffer address
          mov     cx,512          ; CX = length to read
          mov     bx,handle1      ; BX = handle for MYFILE.DAT
          mov     ah,3fh          ; Function 3FH = read
          int     21h             ; transfer to MS-DOS
          jc      error           ; jump if read failed
          or      ax,ax           ; were any bytes read?
          jz      done            ; no, end of file reached

                                  ; write MYFILE.BAK
          mov     dx,offset buff  ; DS:DX = buffer address
          mov     cx,ax           ; CX = length to write
          mov     bx,handle2      ; BX = handle for MYFILE.BAK
          mov     ah,40h          ; Function 40H = write
          int     21h             ; transfer to MS-DOS
          jc      error           ; jump if write failed
          cmp     ax,cx           ; was write complete?
          jne     error           ; jump if disk full
          jmp     loop            ; continue to end of file
```

(more)

```
done:                           ; now close files...
        mov     bx,handle1      ; handle for MYFILE.DAT
        mov     ah,3eh          ; Function 3EH = close file
        int     21h             ; transfer to MS-DOS
        jc      error           ; jump if close failed

        mov     bx,handle2      ; handle for MYFILE.BAK
        mov     ah,3eh          ; Function 3EH = close file
        int     21h             ; transfer to MS-DOS
        jc      error           ; jump if close failed

            .
            .
            .
```

Positioning the read/write pointer

Function 42H (Move File Pointer) sets the position of the read/write pointer associated with a given handle. The function is called with a signed 32-bit offset in the CX and DX registers (the most significant half in CX), the file handle in BX, and the positioning mode in AL:

Mode	Significance
00	Supplied offset is relative to beginning of file.
01	Supplied offset is relative to current position of read/write pointer.
02	Supplied offset is relative to end of file.

If Function 42H succeeds, MS-DOS returns the resulting absolute offset (in bytes) of the file pointer relative to the beginning of the file in the DX and AX registers, with the most significant half in DX; if the function fails, MS-DOS sets the carry flag and returns an error code in AX.

Thus, a program can obtain the size of a file by calling Function 42H with an offset of zero and a positioning mode of 2. The function returns a value in DX:AX that represents the offset of the end-of-file position relative to the beginning of the file.

Example: Assume that the file MYFILE.DAT was previously opened and its handle is saved in the variable *fhandle*. Position the file pointer 32768 bytes from the beginning of the file and then read 512 bytes of data starting at that file position.

```
fhandle dw      ?               ; handle from previous open
buff    db      512 dup (?)     ; buffer for data from file

            .
            .
            .
```

(more)

```
                                  ; position the file pointer...
        mov     cx,0              ; CX = high part of file offset
        mov     dx,32768          ; DX = low part of file offset
        mov     bx,fhandle        ; BX = handle for file
        mov     al,0              ; AL = positioning mode
        mov     ah,42h            ; Function 42H = position
        int     21h               ; transfer to MS-DOS
        jc      error             ; jump if function call failed

                                  ; now read 512 bytes from file
        mov     dx,offset buff    ; DS:DX = address of buffer
        mov     cx,512            ; CX = length of 512 bytes
        mov     bx,fhandle        ; BX = handle for file
        mov     ah,3fh            ; Function 3FH = read
        int     21h               ; transfer to MS-DOS
        jc      error             ; jump if read failed
        cmp     ax,512            ; was 512 bytes read?
        jne     error             ; jump if partial rec. or EOF
        .
        .
        .
```

Example: Assume that the file MYFILE.DAT was previously opened and its handle is saved in the variable *fhandle*. Find the size of the file in bytes by positioning the file pointer to zero bytes relative to the end of the file. The returned offset, which is relative to the beginning of the file, is the file's size.

```
fhandle dw      ?                 ; handle from previous open

        .
        .
        .
                                  ; position the file pointer
                                  ; to the end of file...
        mov     cx,0              ; CX = high part of offset
        mov     dx,0              ; DX = low part of offset
        mov     bx,fhandle        ; BX = handle for file
        mov     al,2              ; AL = positioning mode
        mov     ah,42h            ; Function 42H = position
        int     21h               ; transfer to MS-DOS
        jc      error             ; jump if function call failed

                                  ; if call succeeded, DX:AX
                                  ; now contains the file size
        .
        .
        .
```

Other handle operations

MS-DOS provides other handle-oriented functions to rename (or move) a file, delete a file, read or change a file's attributes, read or change a file's date and time stamp, and duplicate or redirect a file handle. The first three of these are "file-handle-like" because they use an ASCIIZ string to specify the file; however, they do not return a file handle.

Renaming a file

Function 56H (Rename File) renames an existing file and/or moves the file from one location in the hierarchical file structure to another. The file to be renamed cannot be a hidden or system file or a subdirectory and must not be currently open by any process; attempting to rename an open file can corrupt the disk. MS-DOS renames a file by simply changing its directory entry; it moves a file by removing its current directory entry and creating a new entry in the target directory that refers to the same file. The location of the file's actual data on the disk is not changed.

Both the current and the new filenames must be ASCIIZ strings and can include a drive and path specification; wildcard characters (* and ?) are not permitted in the filenames. The program calls Function 56H with the address of the current pathname in the DS:DX registers and the address of the new pathname in ES:DI. If the path elements of the two strings are not the same and both paths are valid, the file "moves" from the source directory to the target directory. If the paths match but the filenames differ, MS-DOS simply modifies the directory entry to reflect the new filename.

If the function succeeds, MS-DOS returns to the calling program with the carry flag clear. The function fails if the new filename is already in the target directory; in that case, MS-DOS sets the carry flag and returns an error code in AX.

Example: Change the name of the file MYFILE.DAT to MYFILE.OLD. In the same operation, move the file from the \WORK directory to the \BACKUP directory.

```
file1    db       '\WORK\MYFILE.DAT',0
file2    db       '\BACKUP\MYFILE.OLD',0
         .
         .
         .
         mov      dx,seg file1     ; DS:DX = old filename
         mov      ds,dx
         mov      es,dx
         mov      dx,offset file1
         mov      di,offset file2 ; ES:DI = new filename
         mov      ah,56h           ; Function 56H = rename
         int      21h              ; transfer to MS-DOS
         jc       error            ; jump if rename failed
         .
         .
         .
```

Deleting a file

Function 41H (Delete File) effectively deletes a file from a disk. Before calling the function, a program must set the DS:DX registers to point to the ASCIIZ pathname of the file to be deleted. The supplied pathname cannot specify a subdirectory or a read-only file, and the file must not be currently open by any process.

If the function is successful, MS-DOS deletes the file by simply marking the first byte of its directory entry with a special character (0E5H), making the entry subsequently unrecognizable. MS-DOS then updates the disk's FAT so that the clusters that previously belonged to the file are "free" and returns to the program with the carry flag clear. If the delete function fails, MS-DOS sets the carry flag and returns an error code in AX.

The actual contents of the clusters assigned to the file are not changed by a delete operation, so for security reasons sensitive information should be overwritten with spaces or some other constant character before the file is deleted with Function 41H.

Example: Delete the file MYFILE.DAT, located in the \WORK directory on drive C.

```
fname    db       'C:\WORK\MYFILE.DAT',0
         .
         .
         .
         mov      dx,seg fname      ; DS:DX = address of filename
         mov      ds,dx
         mov      dx,offset fname
         mov      ah,41h            ; Function 41H = delete
         int      21h               ; transfer to MS-DOS
         jc       error             ; jump if delete failed
         .
         .
         .
```

Getting/setting file attributes

Function 43H (Get/Set File Attributes) obtains or modifies the attributes of an existing file. Before calling Function 43H, the program must set the DS:DX registers to point to the ASCIIZ pathname for the file. To read the attributes, the program must set AL to zero; to set the attributes, it must set AL to 1 and place an attribute code in CX. *See* Creating a File above.

If the function is successful, MS-DOS reads or sets the attribute byte in the file's directory entry and returns with the carry flag clear and the file's attribute in CX. If the function fails, MS-DOS sets the carry flag and returns an error code in AX.

Function 43H cannot be used to set the volume-label bit (bit 3) or the subdirectory bit (bit 4) of a file. It also should not be used on a file that is currently open by any process.

Example: Change the attributes of the file MYFILE.DAT in the \BACKUP directory on drive C to read-only. This prevents the file from being accidentally deleted from the disk.

```
fname    db       'C:\BACKUP\MYFILE.DAT',0
         .
         .
         .
         mov      dx,seg fname      ; DS:DX = address of filename
         mov      ds,dx
         mov      dx,offset fname
         mov      cx,1              ; CX = attribute (read-only)
         mov      al,1              ; AL = mode (0 = get, 1 = set)
```

(more)

```
mov     ah,43h      ; Function 43H = get/set attr
int     21h         ; transfer to MS-DOS
jc      error       ; jump if set attrib. failed
   .
   .
   .
```

Getting/setting file date and time

Function 57H (Get/Set Date/Time of File) reads or sets the directory time and date stamp of an open file. To set the time and date to a particular value, the program must call Function 57H with the desired time in CX, the desired date in DX, the handle for the file (obtained from a previous open or create operation) in BX, and the value 1 in AL. To read the time and date, the function is called with AL containing 0 and the file handle in BX; the time is returned in the CX register and the date is returned in the DX register. As with other handle-oriented file functions, if the function succeeds, the carry flag is returned cleared; if the function fails, MS-DOS returns the carry flag set and an error code in AX.

The formats used for the file time and date are the same as those used in disk directory entries and FCBs. *See* Structure of the File Control Block below.

The main uses of Function 57H are to force the time and date entry for a file to be updated when the file has *not* been changed and to circumvent MS-DOS's modification of a file date and time when the file *has* been changed. In the latter case, a program can use this function with AL = 0 to obtain the file's previous date and time stamp, modify the file, and then restore the original file date and time by re-calling the function with AL = 1 before closing the file.

Duplicating and redirecting handles

Ordinarily, the disk FAT and directory are not updated until a file is closed, even when the file has been modified. Thus, until the file is closed, any new data added to the file can be lost if the system crashes or is turned off unexpectedly. The obvious defense against such loss is simply to close and reopen the file every time the file is changed. However, this is a relatively slow procedure and in a network environment can cause the program to lose control of the file to another process.

Use of a second file handle, created by using Function 45H (Duplicate File Handle) to duplicate the original handle of the file to be updated, can protect data added to a disk file before the file is closed. To use Function 45H, the program must put the handle to be duplicated in BX. If the operation is successful, MS-DOS clears the carry flag and returns the new handle in AX; if the operation fails, MS-DOS sets the carry flag and returns an error code in AX.

If the function succeeds, the duplicate handle can simply be closed in the usual manner with Function 3EH. This forces the desired update of the disk directory and FAT. The original handle remains open and the program can continue to use it for file read and write operations.

Note: While the second handle is open, moving the read/write pointer associated with either handle moves the pointer associated with the other.

Example: Assume that the file MYFILE.DAT was previously opened and the handle for that file has been saved in the variable *fhandle*. Duplicate the handle and then close the duplicate to ensure that any data recently written to the file is saved on the disk and that the directory entry for the file is updated accordingly.

```
fhandle dw      ?               ; handle from previous open

        .
        .
        .
                                ; duplicate the handle...
        mov     bx,fhandle      ; BX = handle for file
        mov     ah,45h          ; Function 45H = dup handle
        int     21h             ; transfer to MS-DOS
        jc      error           ; jump if function call failed

                                ; now close the new handle...
        mov     bx,ax           ; BX = duplicated handle
        mov     ah,3eh          ; Function 3EH = close
        int     21h             ; transfer to MS-DOS
        jc      error           ; jump if close failed
        mov     bx,fhandle      ; replace closed handle with active handle
        .
        .
        .
```

Function 45H is sometimes also used in conjunction with Function 46H (Force Duplicate File Handle). Function 46H forces a handle to be a duplicate for another open handle — in other words, to refer to the same file or device at the same file read/write pointer location. The handle is then said to be redirected.

The most common use of Function 46H is to change the meaning of the standard input and standard output handles before loading a child process with the EXEC function. In this manner, the input for the child program can be redirected to come from a file or its output can be redirected into a file, without any special knowledge on the part of the child program. In such cases, Function 45H is used to also create duplicates of the standard input and standard output handles before they are redirected, so that their original meanings can be restored after the child exits. *See* PROGRAMMING IN THE MS-DOS ENVIRONMENT: CUSTOMIZING MS-DOS: Writing MS-DOS Filters.

Using the FCB Functions

A file control block is a data structure, located in the application program's memory space, that contains relevant information about an open disk file: the disk drive, the filename and extension, a pointer to a position within the file, and so on. Each open file must have its own FCB. The information in an FCB is maintained cooperatively by both MS-DOS and the application program.

MS-DOS moves data to and from a disk file associated with an FCB by means of a data buffer called the disk transfer area (DTA). The current address of the DTA is under the control of the application program, although each program has a 128-byte default DTA at offset 80H in its program segment prefix (PSP). *See* PROGRAMMING IN THE MS-DOS ENVIRONMENT: PROGRAMMING FOR MS-DOS: Structure of an Application Program.

Under early versions of MS-DOS, the only limit on the number of files that can be open simultaneously with FCBs is the amount of memory available to the application to hold the FCBs and their associated disk buffers. However, under MS-DOS versions 3.0 and later, when file-sharing support (SHARE.EXE) is loaded, MS-DOS places some restrictions on the use of FCBs to simplify the job of maintaining network connections for files. If the application attempts to open too many FCBs, MS-DOS simply closes the least recently used FCBs to keep the total number within a limit.

The CONFIG.SYS file directive FCBS allows the user to control the allowed maximum number of FCBs and to specify a certain number of FCBs to be protected against automatic closure by the system. The default values are a maximum of four files open simultaneously using FCBs and zero FCBs protected from automatic closure by the system. *See* USER COMMANDS: CONFIG.SYS: FCBS.

Because the FCB operations predate MS-DOS version 2.0 and because FCBs have a fixed structure with no room to contain a path, the FCB file and record services do not support the hierarchical directory structure. Many FCB operations can be performed only on files in the current directory of a disk. For this reason, the use of FCB file and record operations should be avoided in new programs.

Structure of the file control block

Each FCB is a 37-byte array allocated from its own memory space by the application program that will use it. The FCB contains all the information needed to identify a disk file and access the data within it: drive identifier, filename, extension, file size, record size, various file pointers, and date and time stamps. The FCB structure is shown in Table 7-3.

Table 7-3. Structure of a Normal File Control Block.

Maintained by	Offset (bytes)	Size (bytes)	Description
Program	00H	1	Drive identifier
Program	01H	8	Filename
Program	09H	3	File extension
MS-DOS	0CH	2	Current block number
Program	0EH	2	Record size (bytes)
MS-DOS	10H	4	File size (bytes)
MS-DOS	14H	2	Date stamp
MS-DOS	16H	2	Time stamp
MS-DOS	18H	8	Reserved
MS-DOS	20H	1	Current record number
Program	21H	4	Random record number

Drive identifier: Initialized by the application to designate the drive on which the file to be opened or created resides. 0 = default drive, 1 = drive A, 2 = drive B, and so on. If the application supplies a zero in this byte (to use the default drive), MS-DOS alters the byte during the open or create operation to reflect the actual drive used; that is, after an open or create operation, this drive will always contain a value of 1 or greater.

Filename: Standard eight-character filename; initialized by the application; must be left justified and padded with blanks if the name has fewer than eight characters. A device name (for example, PRN) can be used; note that there is no colon after a device name.

File extension: Three-character file extension; initialized by the application; must be left justified and padded with blanks if the extension has fewer than three characters.

Current block number: Initialized to zero by MS-DOS when the file is opened. The block number and the record number together make up the record pointer during sequential file access.

Record size: The size of a record (in bytes) as used by the program. MS-DOS sets this field to 128 when the file is opened or created; the program can modify the field afterward to any desired record size. If the record size is larger than 128 bytes, the default DTA in the PSP cannot be used because it will collide with the program's own code or data.

File size: The size of the file in bytes. MS-DOS initializes this field from the file's directory entry when the file is opened. The first 2 bytes of this 4-byte field are the least significant bytes of the file size.

Date stamp: The date of the last write operation on the file. MS-DOS initializes this field from the file's directory entry when the file is opened. This field uses the same format used by file handle Function 57H (Get/Set/Date/Time of File):

Date Format

Bit:	15	14	13	12	11	10	9	8	7	6	5	4	3	2	1	0
Content:	Y	Y	Y	Y	Y	Y	Y	M	M	M	M	D	D	D	D	D

Bits	Contents
0–4	Day of month (1–31)
5–8	Month (1–12)
9–15	Year (relative to 1980)

Time stamp: The time of the last write operation on the file. MS-DOS initializes this field from the file's directory entry when the file is opened. This field uses the same format used by file handle Function 57H (Get/Set/Date/Time of File):

Time Format

Bit:	15	14	13	12	11	10	9	8	7	6	5	4	3	2	1	0
Content:	H	H	H	H	H	M	M	M	M	M	M	S	S	S	S	S

Bits	Contents
0–4	Number of 2-second increments (0–29)
5–10	Minutes (0–59)
11–15	Hours (0–23)

Current record number: Together with the block number, constitutes the record pointer used during sequential read and write operations. MS-DOS does not initialize this field when a file is opened. The record number is limited to the range 0 through 127; thus, there are 128 records per block. The beginning of a file is record 0 of block 0.

Random record pointer: A 4-byte field that identifies the record to be transferred by the random record functions 21H, 22H, 27H, and 28H. If the record size is 64 bytes or larger, only the first 3 bytes of this field are used. MS-DOS updates this field after random block reads and writes (Functions 27H and 28H) but not after random record reads and writes (Functions 21H and 22H).

An extended FCB, which is 7 bytes longer than a normal FCB, can be used to access files with special attributes such as hidden, system, and read-only. The extra 7 bytes of an extended FCB are simply prefixed to the normal FCB format (Table 7-4). The first byte of an extended FCB always contains 0FFH, which could never be a legal drive code and therefore serves as a signal to MS-DOS that the extended format is being used. The next 5 bytes are reserved and must be zero, and the last byte of the prefix specifies the attributes of the file being manipulated. The remainder of an extended FCB has exactly the same layout as a normal FCB. In general, an extended FCB can be used with any MS-DOS function call that accepts a normal FCB.

Table 7-4. Structure of an Extended File Control Block.

Maintained by	Offset (bytes)	Size (bytes)	Description
Program	00H	1	Extended FCB flag = 0FFH
MS-DOS	01H	5	Reserved
Program	06H	1	File attribute byte
Program	07H	1	Drive identifier
Program	08H	8	Filename

(more)

Table 7-4. *Continued.*

Maintained by	Offset (bytes)	Size (bytes)	Description
Program	10H	3	File extension
MS-DOS	13H	2	Current block number
Program	15H	2	Record size (bytes)
MS-DOS	17H	4	File size (bytes)
MS-DOS	1BH	2	Date stamp
MS-DOS	1DH	2	Time stamp
MS-DOS	1FH	8	Reserved
MS-DOS	27H	1	Current record number
Program	28H	4	Random record number

Extended FCB flag: When 0FFH is present in the first byte of an FCB, it is a signal to MS-DOS that an extended FCB (44 bytes) is being used instead of a normal FCB (37 bytes).

File attribute byte: Must be initialized by the application when an extended FCB is used to open or create a file. The bits of this field have the following significance:

Bit	Meaning
0	Read-only
1	Hidden
2	System
3	Volume label
4	Directory
5	Archive
6	Reserved
7	Reserved

FCB functions and the PSP

The PSP contains several items that are of interest when using the FCB file and record operations: two FCBs called the default FCBs, the default DTA, and the command tail for the program. The following table shows the size and location of these elements:

PSP Offset (bytes)	Size (bytes)	Description
5CH	16	Default FCB #1
6CH	20	Default FCB #2
80H	1	Length of command tail
81H	127	Command-tail text
80H	128	Default disk transfer area (DTA)

When MS-DOS loads a program into memory for execution, it copies the command tail into the PSP at offset 81H, places the length of the command tail in the byte at offset 80H, and parses the first two parameters in the command tail into the default FCBs at PSP offsets 5CH and 6CH. (The command tail consists of the command line used to invoke the program minus the program name itself and any redirection or piping characters and their associated filenames or device names.) MS-DOS then sets the initial DTA address for the program to PSP:0080H.

For several reasons, the default FCBs and the DTA are often moved to another location within the program's memory area. First, the default DTA allows processing of only very small records. In addition, the default FCBs overlap substantially, and the first byte of the default DTA and the last byte of the first FCB conflict. Finally, unless either the command tail or the DTA is moved beforehand, the first FCB-related file or record operation will destroy the command tail.

Function 1AH (Set DTA Address) is used to alter the DTA address. It is called with the segment and offset of the new buffer to be used as the DTA in DS:DX. The DTA address remains the same until another call to Function 1AH, regardless of other file and record management calls; it does not need to be reset before each read or write.

Note: A program can use Function 2FH (Get DTA Address) to obtain the current DTA address before changing it, so that the original address can be restored later.

Parsing the filename

Before a file can be opened or created with the FCB function calls, its drive, filename, and extension must be placed within the proper fields of the FCB. The filename can be coded into the program itself, or the program can obtain it from the command tail in the PSP or by prompting the user and reading it in with one of the several function calls for character device input.

MS-DOS automatically parses the first two parameters in the program's command tail into the default FCBs at PSP:005CH and PSP:006CH. It does not, however, attempt to differentiate between switches and filenames, so the pre-parsed FCBs are not necessarily useful to the application program. If the filenames were preceded by any switches, the program itself has to extract the filenames directly from the command tail. The program is then responsible for determining which parameters are switches and which are filenames, as well as where each parameter begins and ends.

After a filename has been located, Function 29H (Parse Filename) can be used to test it for invalid characters and separators and to insert its various components into the proper fields in an FCB. The filename must be a string in the standard form *drive:filename.ext.* Wildcard characters are permitted in the filename and/or extension; asterisk (∗) wildcards are expanded to question mark (?) wildcards.

To call Function 29H, the DS:SI registers must point to the candidate filename, ES:DI must point to the 37-byte buffer that will become the FCB for the file, and AL must hold the parsing control code. *See* SYSTEM CALLS: Interrupt 21h: Function 29H.

If a drive code is not included in the filename, MS-DOS inserts the drive number of the current drive into the FCB. Parsing stops at the first terminator character encountered in the filename. Terminators include the following:

; , = + / " [ ] ¦ < > ¦ space tab

If a colon character (:) is not in the proper position to delimit the disk drive identifier or if a period (.) is not in the proper position to delimit the extension, the character will also be treated as a terminator. For example, the filename C:MEMO.TXT will be parsed correctly; however, ABC:DEF.DAY will be parsed as ABC.

If an invalid drive is specified in the filename, Function 29H returns 0FFH in AL; if the filename contains any wildcard characters, it returns 1. Otherwise, AL contains zero upon return, indicating a valid, unambiguous filename.

Note that this function simply parses the filename into the FCB. It does not initialize any other fields of the FCB (although it does zero the current block and record size fields), and it does not test whether the specified file actually exists.

Error handling and FCB functions

The FCB-related file and record functions do not return much in the way of error information when a function fails. Typically, an FCB function returns a zero in AL if the function succeeded and 0FFH if the function failed. Under MS-DOS versions 2.x, the program is left to its own devices to determine the cause of the error. Under MS-DOS versions 3.x, however, a failed FCB function call can be followed by a call to Interrupt 21H Function 59H (Get Extended Error Information). Function 59H will return the same descriptive codes for the error, including the error locus and a suggested recovery strategy, as would be returned for the counterpart handle-oriented file or record function.

Creating a file

Function 16H (Create File with FCB) creates a new file and opens it for subsequent read/write operations. The function is called with DS:DX pointing to a valid, unopened FCB. MS-DOS searches the current directory for the specifed filename. If the filename is found, MS-DOS sets the file length to zero and opens the file, effectively truncating it to a zero-length file; if the filename is not found, MS-DOS creates a new file and opens it. Other fields of the FCB are filled in by MS-DOS as described below under Opening a File.

If the create operation succeeds, MS-DOS returns zero in AL; if the operation fails, it returns 0FFH in AL. This function will not ordinarily fail unless the file is being created in the root directory and the directory is full.

Warning: To avoid loss of existing data, the FCB open function should be used to test for file existence before creating a file.

Opening a file

Function 0FH opens an existing file. DS:DX must point to a valid, unopened FCB containing the name of the file to be opened. If the specified file is found in the current directory, MS-DOS opens the file, fills in the FCB as shown in the list below, and returns with AL set to 00H; if the file is not found, MS-DOS returns with AL set to 0FFH, indicating an error.

When the file is opened, MS-DOS

- Sets the drive identifier (offset 00H) to the actual drive (01 = A, 02 = B, and so on).
- Sets the current block number (offset 0CH) to zero.
- Sets the file size (offset 10H) to the value found in the directory entry for the file.
- Sets the record size (offset 0EH) to 128.
- Sets the date and time stamp (offsets 14H and 16H) to the values found in the directory entry for the file.

The program may need to adjust the FCB — change the record size and the random record pointer, for example — before proceeding with record operations.

Example: Display a prompt and accept a filename from the user. Parse the filename into an FCB, checking for an illegal drive identifier or the presence of wildcards. If a valid, unambiguous filename has been entered, attempt to open the file. Create the file if it does not already exist.

```
kbuf     db      64,0,64 dup (0)
prompt   db      0dh,0ah,'Enter filename: $'
myfcb    db      37 dup (0)

               .
               .
               .

                              ; display the prompt...
         mov    dx,seg prompt   ; DS:DX = prompt address
         mov    ds,dx
         mov    es,dx
         mov    dx,offset prompt
         mov    ah,09h          ; Function 09H = print string
         int    21h             ; transfer to MS-DOS

                              ; now input filename...
         mov    dx,offset kbuf  ; DS:DX = buffer address
         mov    ah,0ah          ; Function 0AH = enter string
         int    21h             ; transfer to MS-DOS

                              ; parse filename into FCB...
         mov    si,offset kbuf+2 ; DS:SI = address of filename
         mov    di,offset myfcb ; ES:DI = address of fcb
         mov    ax,2900h        ; Function 29H = parse name
         int    21h             ; transfer to MS-DOS
         or     al,al           ; jump if bad drive or
         jnz    error           ; wildcard characters in name
```

(more)

```
                            ; try to open file...
        mov     dx,offset myfcb ; DS:DX = FCB address
        mov     ah,0fh          ; Function 0FH = open file
        int     21h             ; transfer to MS-DOS
        or      al,al           ; check status
        jz      proceed         ; jump if open successful

                            ; else create file...
        mov     dx,offset myfcb ; DS:DX = FCB address
        mov     ah,16h          ; Function 16H = create
        int     21h             ; transfer to MS-DOS
        or      al,al           ; did create succeed?
        jnz     error           ; jump if create failed

proceed:
        .                       ; file has been opened or
        .                       ; created, and FCB is valid
        .                       ; for read/write operations...
```

Closing a file

Function 10H (Close File with FCB) closes a file previously opened with an FCB. As usual, the function is called with DS:DX pointing to the FCB of the file to be closed. MS-DOS updates the directory, if necessary, to reflect any changes in the file's size and the date and time last written.

If the operation succeeds, MS-DOS returns 00H in AL; if the operation fails, MS-DOS returns 0FFH.

Reading and writing files with FCBs

MS-DOS offers a choice of three FCB access methods for data within files: sequential, random record, and random block.

Sequential operations step through the file one record at a time. MS-DOS increments the current record and current block numbers after each file access so that they point to the beginning of the next record. This method is particularly useful for copying or listing files.

Random record access allows the program to read or write a record from any location in the file, without sequentially reading all records up to that point in the file. The program must set the random record number field of the FCB appropriately before the read or write is requested. This method is useful in database applications, in which a program must manipulate fixed-length records.

Random block operations combine the features of sequential and random record access methods. The program can set the record number to point to any record within a file, and MS-DOS updates the record number after a read or write operation. Thus, sequential operations can easily be initiated at any file location. Random block operations with a record length of 1 byte simulate file-handle access methods.

All three methods require that the FCB for the file be open, that DS:DX point to the FCB, that the DTA be large enough for the specified record size, and that the DTA address be previously set with Function 1AH if the default DTA in the program's PSP is not being used.

MS-DOS reports the success or failure of any FCB-related read operation (sequential, random record, or random block) with one of four return codes in register AL:

Code	Meaning
00H	Successful read
01H	End of file reached; no data read into DTA
02H	Segment wrap (DTA too close to end of segment); no data read into DTA
03H	End of file reached; partial record read into DTA

MS-DOS reports the success or failure of an FCB-related write operation as one of three return codes in register AL:

Code	Meaning
00H	Successful write
01H	Disk full; partial or no write
02H	Segment wrap (DTA too close to end of segment); write failed

For FCB write operations, records smaller than one sector (512 bytes) are not written directly to disk. Instead, MS-DOS stores the record in an internal buffer and writes the data to disk only when the internal buffer is full, when the file is closed, or when a call to Interrupt 21H Function 0DH (Disk Reset) is issued.

Sequential access: reading

Function 14H (Sequential Read) reads records sequentially from the file to the current DTA address, which must point to an area at least as large as the record size specified in the file's FCB. After each read operation, MS-DOS updates the FCB block and record numbers (offsets 0CH and 20H) to point to the next record.

Sequential access: writing

Function 15H (Sequential Write) writes records sequentially from memory into the file. The length written is specified by the record size field (offset 0EH) in the FCB; the memory address of the record to be written is determined by the current DTA address. After each sequential write operation, MS-DOS updates the FCB block and record numbers (offsets 0CH and 20H) to point to the next record.

Random record access: reading

Function 21H (Random Read) reads a specific record from a file. Before requesting the read operation, the program specifies the record to be transferred by setting the record size and random record number fields of the FCB (offsets 0EH and 21H). The current DTA address must also have been previously set with Function 1AH to point to a buffer of adequate size if the default DTA is not large enough.

After the read, MS-DOS sets the current block and current record number fields (offsets 0CH and 20H) to point to the same record. Thus, the program is set up to change to sequential reads or writes. However, if the program wants to continue with random record access, it must continue to update the random record field of the FCB before each random record read or write operation.

Random record access: writing

Function 22H (Random Write) writes a specific record from memory to a file. Before issuing the function call, the program must ensure that the record size and random record pointer fields at FCB offsets 0EH and 21H are set appropriately and that the current DTA address points to the buffer containing the data to be written.

After the write, MS-DOS sets the current block and current record number fields (offsets 0CH and 20H) to point to the same record. Thus, the program is set up to change to sequential reads or writes. If the program wants to continue with random record access, it must continue to update the random record field of the FCB before each random record read or write operation.

Random block access: reading

Function 27H (Random Block Read) reads a block of consecutive records. Before issuing the read request, the program must specify the file location of the first record by setting the record size and random record number fields of the FCB (offsets 0EH and 21H) and must put the number of records to be read in CX. The DTA address must have already been set with Function 1AH to point to a buffer large enough to contain the group of records to be read if the default DTA was not large enough. The program can then issue the Function 27H call with DS:DX pointing to the FCB for the file.

After the random block read operation, MS-DOS resets the FCB random record pointer (offset 21H) and the current block and current record number fields (offsets 0CH and 20H) to point to the beginning of the next record not read and returns the number of records actually read in CX.

If the record size is set to 1 byte, Function 27H reads the number of bytes specified in CX, beginning with the byte position specified in the random record pointer. This simulates (to some extent) the handle type of read operation (Function 3FH).

Random block access: writing

Function 28H (Random Block Write) writes a block of consecutive records from memory to disk. The program specifies the file location of the first record to be written by setting the record size and random record pointer fields in the FCB (offsets 0EH and 21H). If the default DTA is not being used, the program must also ensure that the current DTA address is set appropriately by a previous call to Function 1AH. When Function 28H is called, DS:DX must point to the FCB for the file and CX must contain the number of records to be written.

After the random block write operation, MS-DOS resets the FCB random record pointer (offset 21H) and the current block and current record number fields (offsets 0CH and 20H) to point to the beginning of the next block of data and returns the number of records actually written in CX.

If the record size is set to 1 byte, Function 28H writes the number of bytes specified in CX, beginning with the byte position specified in the random record pointer. This simulates (to some extent) the handle type of write operation (Function 40H).

Calling Function 28H with a record count of zero in register CX causes the file length to be extended or truncated to the current value in the FCB random record pointer field (offset 21H) multiplied by the contents of the record size field (offset 0EH).

Example: Open the file MYFILE.DAT and create the file MYFILE.BAK on the current disk drive, copy the contents of the .DAT file into the .BAK file using 512-byte reads and writes, and then close both files.

```
fcb1    db      0                   ; drive = default
        db      'MYFILE  '          ; 8 character filename
        db      'DAT'               ; 3 character extension
        db      25 dup (0)          ; remainder of fcb1
fcb2    db      0                   ; drive = default
        db      'MYFILE  '          ; 8 character filename
        db      'BAK'               ; 3 character extension
        db      25 dup (0)          ; remainder of fcb2
buff    db      512 dup (?)         ; buffer for file I/O
            .
            .
            .
                                    ; open MYFILE.DAT...
        mov     dx,seg fcb1         ; DS:DX = address of FCB
        mov     ds,dx
        mov     dx,offset fcb1
        mov     ah,0fh              ; Function 0FH = open
        int     21h                 ; transfer to MS-DOS
        or      al,al               ; did open succeed?
        jnz     error               ; jump if open failed
                                    ; create MYFILE.BAK...
        mov     dx,offset fcb2      ; DS:DX = address of FCB
        mov     ah,16h              ; Function 16H = create
        int     21h                 ; transfer to MS-DOS
        or      al,al               ; did create succeed?
        jnz     error               ; jump if create failed
                                    ; set record length to 512
        mov     word ptr fcb1+0eh,512
        mov     word ptr fcb2+0eh,512
                                    ; set DTA to our buffer...
        mov     dx,offset buff      ; DS:DX = buffer address
        mov     ah,1ah              ; Function 1AH = set DTA
        int     21h                 ; transfer to MS-DOS
loop:                               ; read MYFILE.DAT
        mov     dx,offset fcb1      ; DS:DX = FCB address
        mov     ah,14h              ; Function 14H = seq. read
        int     21h                 ; transfer to MS-DOS
        or      al,al               ; was read successful?
        jnz     done                ; no, quit
                                    ; write MYFILE.BAK...
```

(more)

```
          mov     dx,offset fcb2   ; DS:DX = FCB address
          mov     ah,15h           ; Function 15H = seq. write
          int     21h              ; transfer to MS-DOS
          or      al,al            ; was write successful?
          jnz     error            ; jump if write failed
          jmp     loop             ; continue to end of file
done:                              ; now close files...
          mov     dx,offset fcb1   ; DS:DX = FCB for MYFILE.DAT
          mov     ah,10h           ; Function 10H = close file
          int     21h              ; transfer to MS-DOS
          or      al,al            ; did close succeed?
          jnz     error            ; jump if close failed
          mov     dx,offset fcb2   ; DS:DX = FCB for MYFILE.BAK
          mov     ah,10h           ; Function 10H = close file
          int     21h              ; transfer to MS-DOS
          or      al,al            ; did close succeed?
          jnz     error            ; jump if close failed
          .
          .
          .
```

Other FCB file operations

As it does with file handles, MS-DOS provides FCB-oriented functions to rename or delete a file. Unlike the other FCB functions and their handle counterparts, these two functions accept wildcard characters. An additional FCB function allows the size or existence of a file to be determined without actually opening the file.

Renaming a file

Function 17H (Rename File) renames a file (or files) in the current directory. The file to be renamed cannot have the hidden or system attribute. Before calling Function 17H, the program must create a special FCB that contains the drive code at offset 00H, the old filename at offset 01H, and the new filename at offset 11H. Both the current and the new filenames can contain the ? wildcard character.

When the function call is made, DS:DX must point to the special FCB structure. MS-DOS searches the current directory for the old filename. If it finds the old filename, MS-DOS then searches for the new filename and, if it finds no matching filename, changes the directory entry for the old filename to reflect the new filename. If the old filename field of the special FCB contains any wildcard characters, MS-DOS renames every matching file. Duplicate filenames are not permitted; the process will fail at the first duplicate name.

If the operation is successful, MS-DOS returns zero in AL; if the operation fails, it returns 0FFH. The error condition may indicate either that no files were renamed or that at least one file was renamed but the operation was then terminated because of a duplicate filename.

Example: Rename all the files with the extension .ASM in the current directory of the default disk drive to have the extension .COD.

```
renfcb  db      0                   ; default drive
        db      '????????'          ; wildcard filename
        db      'ASM'               ; old extension
        db      5 dup (0)           ; reserved area
        db      '????????'          ; wildcard filename
        db      'COD'               ; new extension
        db      15 dup (0)          ; remainder of FCB

          .
          .
          .

        mov     dx,seg renfcb       ; DS:DX = address of
        mov     ds,dx               ; "special" FCB
        mov     dx,offset renfcb
        mov     ah,17h              ; Function 17H = rename
        int     21h                 ; transfer to MS-DOS
        or      al,al               ; did function succeed?
        jnz     error               ; jump if rename failed
          .
          .
          .
```

Deleting a file

Function 13H (Delete File) deletes a file from the current directory. The file should not be currently open by any process. If the file to be deleted has special attributes, such as read-only, the program must use an extended FCB to remove the file. Directories cannot be deleted with this function, even with an extended FCB.

Function 13H is called with DS:DX pointing to an unopened, valid FCB containing the name of the file to be deleted. The filename can contain the ? wildcard character; if it does, MS-DOS deletes all files matching the specified name. If at least one file matches the FCB and is deleted, MS-DOS returns 00H in AL; if no matching filename is found, it returns 0FFH.

Note: This function, if it succeeds, does not return any information about which and how many files were deleted. When multiple files must be deleted, closer control can be exercised by using the Find File functions (Functions 11H and 12H) to inspect candidate filenames. *See* PROGRAMMING IN THE MS-DOS ENVIRONMENT: PROGRAMMING FOR MS-DOS: Disk Directories and Volume Labels. The files can then be deleted individually.

Example: Delete all the files in the current directory of the current disk drive that have the extension .BAK and whose filenames have *A* as the first character.

```
delfcb  db      0                   ; default drive
        db      'A???????'          ; wildcard filename
        db      'BAK'               ; extension
        db      25 dup (0)          ; remainder of FCB
```

(more)

```
        .
        .
        .
mov     dx,seg delfcb    ; DS:DX = FCB address
mov     ds,dx
mov     dx,offset delfcb
mov     ah,13h           ; Function 13H = delete
int     21h              ; transfer to MS-DOS
or      al,al            ; did function succeed?
jnz     error            ; jump if delete failed
        .
        .
        .
```

Finding file size and testing for existence

Function 23H (Get File Size) is used primarily to find the size of a disk file without opening it, but it may also be used instead of Function 11H (Find First File) to simply test for the existence of a file. Before calling Function 23H, the program must parse the filename into an unopened FCB, initialize the record size field of the FCB (offset 0EH), and set the DS:DX registers to point to the FCB.

When Function 23H returns, AL contains 00H if the file was found in the current directory of the specified drive and 0FFH if the file was not found.

If the file was found, the random record field at FCB offset 21H contains the number of records (rounded upward) in the target file, in terms of the value in the record size field (offset 0EH) of the FCB. If the record size is at least 64 bytes, only the first 3 bytes of the random record field are used; if the record size is less than 64 bytes, all 4 bytes are used. To obtain the size of the file in bytes, the program must set the record size field to 1 before the call. This method is not any faster than simply opening the file, but it does avoid the overhead of closing the file afterward (which is necessary in a networking environment).

Summary

MS-DOS supports two distinct but overlapping sets of file and record management services. The handle-oriented functions operate in terms of null-terminated (ASCIIZ) filenames and 16-bit file identifiers, called handles, that are returned by MS-DOS after a file is opened or created. The filenames can include a full path specifying the file's location in the hierarchical directory structure. The information associated with a file handle, such as the current read/write pointer for the file, the date and time of the last write to the file, and the file's read/write permissions, sharing mode, and attributes, is maintained in a table internal to MS-DOS.

In contrast, the FCB-oriented functions use a 37-byte structure called a file control block, located in the application program's memory space, to specify the name and location of the file. After a file is opened or created, the FCB is used by both MS-DOS and the application to hold other information about the file, such as the current read/write file pointer, while that file is in use. Because FCBs predate the hierarchical directory structure that was introduced in MS-DOS version 2.0 and do not have room to hold the path for a file, the FCB functions cannot be used to access files that are not in the current directory of the specified drive.

In addition to their lack of support for pathnames, the FCB functions have much poorer error reporting capabilities than handle functions and are nearly useless in networking environments because they do not support file sharing and locking. Consequently, it is strongly recommended that the handle-related file and record functions be used exclusively in all new applications.

Robert Byers
Code by Ray Duncan

Article 8
Disk Directories and Volume Labels

MS-DOS, being a disk operating system, provides facilities for cataloging disk files. The data structure used by MS-DOS for this purpose is the directory, a linear list of names in which each name is associated with a physical location on the disk. Directories are accessed and updated implicitly whenever files are manipulated, but both directories and their contents can also be manipulated explicitly using several of the MS-DOS Interrupt 21H service functions.

MS-DOS versions 1.x support only one directory on each disk. Versions 2.0 and later, however, support multiple directories linked in a two-way, hierarchical tree structure (Figure 8-1), and the complete specification of the name of a file or directory thus must describe the location in the directory hierarchy in which the name appears. This specification, or path, is created by concatenating a disk drive specifier (for example, A: or C:), the

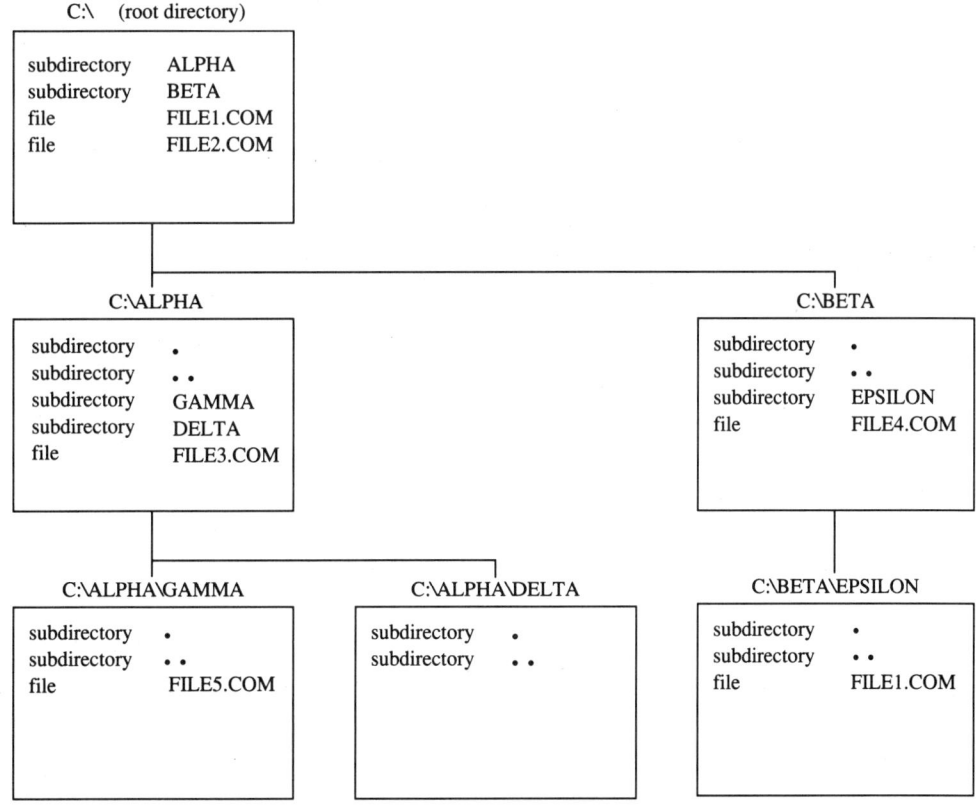

Figure 8-1. *Typical hierarchical directory structure (MS-DOS versions 2.0 and later).*

names of the directories in hierarchical order starting with the root directory, and finally the name of the file or directory. For example, in Figure 8-1, the complete pathname for FILE5.COM is C:\ALPHA\GAMMA\FILE5.COM. The two instances of FILE1.COM, in the root directory and in the directory EPSILON, are distinguished by their pathnames: C:\FILE1.COM in the first instance and C:\BETA\EPSILON\FILE1.COM in the second.

Note: If no drive is specified, the current drive is assumed. Also, if the first name in the specification is not preceded by a backslash, the specification is assumed to be relative to the current directory. For example, if the current directory is C:\BETA\EPSILON, the specification \FILE1.COM indicates the file FILE1.COM in the root directory and the specification FILE1.COM indicates the file FILE1.COM in the directory C:\BETA\EPSILON. *See* Figure 8-1.

Although the casual user of MS-DOS need not be concerned with how this hierarchical directory structure is implemented, MS-DOS programmers should be familiar with the internal structure of directories and with the Interrupt 21H functions available for manipulating directory contents and maintaining the links between directories. This article provides that information.

Logical Structure of MS-DOS Directories

An MS-DOS directory consists of a list of 32-byte directory entries, each of which contains a name and descriptive information. In MS-DOS versions 1.x, each name must be a filename; in versions 2.0 and later, volume labels and directory names can also appear in directory entries.

Directory searches

Directory entries are not sorted, nor are they maintained as a linked list. Thus, when MS-DOS searches a directory for a name, the search must proceed linearly from the first name in the directory. In MS-DOS versions 1.x, a directory search continues until the specified name is found or until every entry in the directory has been examined. In versions 2.0 and later, the search continues until the specified name is found or until a null directory entry (that is, one whose first byte is zero) is encountered. This null entry indicates the logical end of the directory.

Adding and deleting directory entries

MS-DOS deletes a directory entry by marking it with 0E5H in the first byte rather than by erasing it or excising it from the directory. New names are added to the directory by reusing the first deleted entry in the list. If no deleted entries are available, MS-DOS appends the new entry to the list.

The current directory

When more than one directory exists on a disk, MS-DOS keeps track of a default search directory known as the current directory. The current directory is the directory used for all implicit directory searches, such as those occasioned by a request to open a file, if no alternative path is specified. At startup, MS-DOS makes the root directory the current directory, but any other directory can be designated later, either interactively by using the CHDIR command or from within an application by using Interrupt 21H Function 3BH (Change Current Directory).

Directory Format

The root directory is created by the MS-DOS FORMAT program. *See* USER COMMANDS: FORMAT. The FORMAT program places the root directory immediately after the disk's file allocation tables (FATs). FORMAT also determines the size of the root directory. The size depends on the capacity of the storage medium: FORMAT places larger root directories on high-capacity fixed disks and smaller root directories on floppy disks. In contrast, the size of subdirectories is limited only by the storage capacity of the disk because disk space for subdirectories is allocated dynamically, as it is for any MS-DOS file. The size and physical location of the root directory can be derived from data in the BIOS parameter block (BPB) in the disk boot sector. *See* PROGRAMMING IN THE MS-DOS ENVIRONMENT: STRUCTURE OF MS-DOS: MS-DOS Storage Devices.

Because space for the root directory is allocated only when the disk is formatted, the root directory cannot be deleted or moved. Subdirectories, whose disk space is allocated dynamically, can be added or deleted as needed.

Directory entry format

Each 32-byte directory entry consists of seven fields, including a name, an attribute byte, date and time stamps, and information that describes the file's size and physical location on the disk (Figure 8-2). The fields are formatted as described in the following paragraphs.

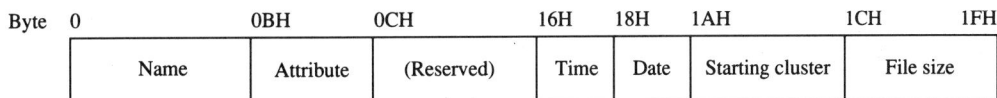

Byte	0	0BH	0CH	16H	18H	1AH	1CH	1FH
	Name	Attribute	(Reserved)	Time	Date	Starting cluster	File size	

Figure 8-2. Format of a directory entry.

The name field (bytes 0–0AH) contains an 11-byte name unless the first byte of the field indicates that the directory entry is deleted or null. The name can be an 11-byte filename (8-byte name followed by a 3-byte extension), an 11-byte subdirectory name (8-byte name followed by a 3-byte extension), or an 11-byte volume label. Names less than 8 bytes and extensions less than 3 bytes are padded to the right with blanks so that the extension always appears in bytes 08-0AH of the name field. The first byte of the name field can contain certain reserved values that affect the way MS-DOS processes the directory entry:

Value	Meaning
0	Null directory entry (logical end of directory in MS-DOS versions 2.0 and later)
5	First character of name to be displayed as the character represented by 0E5H (MS-DOS version 3.2)
0E5H	Deleted directory entry

When MS-DOS creates a subdirectory, it always includes two aliases as the first two entries in the newly created directory. The name . (an ASCII period) is an alias for the name of the current directory; the name .. (two ASCII periods) is an alias for the directory's parent directory — that is, the directory in which the entry containing the name of the current directory is found.

The attribute field (byte 0BH) is an 8-bit field that describes the way MS-DOS processes the directory entry (Figure 8-3). Each bit in the attribute field designates a particular attribute of that directory entry; more than one of the bits can be set at a time.

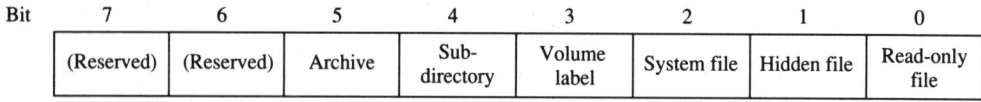

Bit	7	6	5	4	3	2	1	0
	(Reserved)	(Reserved)	Archive	Sub-directory	Volume label	System file	Hidden file	Read-only file

Figure 8-3. Format of the attribute field in a directory entry.

The read-only bit (bit 0) is set to 1 to mark a file read-only. Interrupt 21H Function 3DH (Open File with Handle) will fail if it is used in an attempt to open this file for writing. The hidden bit (bit 1) is set to 1 to indicate that the entry is to be skipped in normal directory searches — that is, in directory searches that do not specifically request that hidden entries be included in the search. The system bit (bit 2) is set to 1 to indicate that the entry refers to a file used by the operating system. Like the hidden bit, the system bit excludes a directory entry from normal directory searches. The volume label bit (bit 3) is set to 1 to indicate that the directory entry represents a volume label. The subdirectory bit (bit 4) is set to 1 when the directory entry contains the name and location of another directory. This bit is always set for the directory entries that correspond to the current directory (.) and the parent directory (..). The archive bit (bit 5) is set to 1 by MS-DOS functions that close a file that has been written to. Simply opening and closing a file is not sufficient to update the archive bit in the file's directory entry.

The time and date fields (bytes 16–17H and 18–19H) are initialized by MS-DOS when the directory entry is created. These fields are updated whenever a file is written to. The formats of these fields are shown in Figures 8-4 and 8-5.

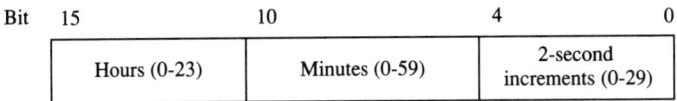

Figure 8-4. *Format of the time field in a directory entry.*

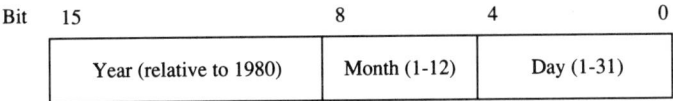

Figure 8-5. *Format of the date field in a directory entry.*

The starting cluster field (bytes 1A–1BH) indicates the disk location of the first cluster assigned to the file. This cluster number can be used as an entry point to the file allocation table (FAT) for the disk. (Cluster numbers can be converted to logical sector numbers with the aid of the information in the disk's BPB.)

For the **.** entry (the alias for the directory that contains the entry), the starting cluster field contains the starting cluster number of the directory itself. For the **..** entry (the alias for the parent directory), the value in the starting cluster field refers to the parent directory unless the parent directory is the root directory, in which case the starting cluster number is zero.

The file size field (bytes 1C–1FH) is a 32-bit integer that indicates the file size in bytes.

Volume Labels

The generic term *volume* refers to a unit of auxiliary storage such as a floppy disk, a fixed disk, or a reel of magnetic tape. In computer environments where many different volumes might be used, the operating system can uniquely identify each volume by initializing it with a volume label.

Volume labels are implemented in MS-DOS versions 2.0 and later as a specific type of directory entry specified by setting bit 3 in the attribute field to 1. In a volume label directory entry, the name field contains an 11-byte string specifying a name for the disk volume. A volume label can appear only in the root directory of a disk, and only one volume label can be present on any given disk.

In MS-DOS versions 2.0 and later, the FORMAT command can be used with the /V switch to initialize a disk with a volume label. In versions 3.0 and later, the LABEL command can be used to create, update, or delete a volume label. Several commands can display a disk's volume label, including VOL, DIR, LABEL, TREE, and CHKDSK. *See* USER COMMANDS.

In MS-DOS versions 2.x, volume labels are simply a convenience for the user; no MS-DOS routine uses a volume label for any other purpose. In MS-DOS versions 3.x, however, the SHARE command examines a disk's volume label when it attempts to verify whether a disk volume has been inadvertently replaced in the midst of a file read or write operation. Removable disk volumes should therefore be assigned unique volume names if they are to contain shared files.

Functional Support for MS-DOS Directories

Several Interrupt 21H service routines can be useful to programmers who need to manipulate directories and their contents (Table 8-1). The routines can be broadly grouped into two categories: those that use a modified file control block (FCB) to pass filenames to and from the Interrupt 21H service routines (Functions 11H, 12H, 17H, and 23H) and those that use hierarchical path specifications (Functions 39H, 3AH, 3BH, 43H, 47H, 4EH, 4FH, 56H, and 57H). *See* PROGRAMMING IN THE MS-DOS ENVIRONMENT: Programming for ms-dos: File and Record Management; SYSTEM CALLS: Interrupt 21h.

The functions that use an FCB require that the calling program reserve enough memory for an extended FCB before the Interrupt 21H function is called. The calling program initializes the filename and extension fields of the FCB and passes the address of the FCB to the MS-DOS service routine in DS:DX. The functions that use pathnames expect all pathnames to be in ASCIIZ format — that is, the last character of the name must be followed by a zero byte.

Names in pathnames passed to Interrupt 21H functions can be separated by either a backslash (\) or a forward slash (/). (The forward slash is the separator character used in pathnames in UNIX/XENIX systems.) For example, the pathnames C:/MSP/SOURCE/ROSE.PAS and C:\MSP\SOURCE\ROSE.PAS are equivalent when passed to an Interrupt 21H function. The forward slash can thus be used in a pathname in a program that must run on both MS-DOS and UNIX/XENIX. However, the MS-DOS comand processor (COMMAND.COM) recognizes only the backslash as a pathname separator character, so forward slashes cannot be used as separators in the command line.

Table 8-1. MS-DOS Functions for Accessing Directories.

Function	Call With	Returns	Comment

Find First File	AH = 11H
	DS:DX = pointer to
	  unopened FCB
	INT 21H
		AL = 0 (directory entry
		  found) or 0FFH (not found)
		DTA updated (if directory
		  entry found)
			If default not satisfactory, DTA must be set before using this function.

Find Next File	AH = 12H
	DS:DX = pointer to
	  unopened FCB
	INT 21H
		AL = 0 (directory entry
		  found) or 0FFH (not found)
		DTA updated (if directory
		  entry found)
			Use the same FCB for Function 11H and Function 12H.

(more)

Table 8-1. *Continued.*

Function	Call With	Returns	Comment

Rename File	AH = 17H
	DS:DX = pointer to
	   modified FCB
	INT 21H
		AL = 0 (file renamed) or
		   0FFH (no directory entry
		   or duplicate filename)	

Get File Size	AH = 23H
	DS:DX = pointer to
	   unopened FCB
	INT 21H
		AL = 0 (directory entry
		   found) or 0FFH (not found)
		FCB updated with number
		   of records in file	

Create Directory	AH = 39H DS:DX = pointer to ASCIIZ pathname INT 21H	Carry flag set (if error) AX = error code (if error)	
Remove Directory	AH = 3AH DS:DX = pointer to ASCIIZ pathname INT 21H	Carry flag set (if error) AX = error code (if error)	
Change Current Directory	AH = 3BH DS:DX = pointer to ASCIIZ pathname INT 21H	Carry flag set (if error) AX = error code (if error)	

Get/Set File
Attributes
	AH = 43H
	AL = 0 (get attributes)
	   1 (set attributes)
	CX = attributes (if AL = 1)
	DS:DX = pointer to
	   ASCIIZ pathname
	INT 21H
		Carry flag set (if error)
		AX = error code (if error)
		CX = attribute field from
		   directory entry (if called
		   with AL = 0)
			Cannot be used to
			modify the volume
			label or subdirectory
			bits.

Get Current
Directory
	AH = 47H
	DS:SI = pointer to
	   64-byte buffer
	DL = drive number
	INT 21H
		Carry flag set (if error)
		AX = error code (if error)
		Buffer updated with
		   pathname of current
		   directory	

Find First File	AH = 4EH
	DS:DX = pointer to
	   ASCIIZ pathname
	CX = file attributes to
	   match
	INT 21H
		Carry flag set (if error)
		AX = error code (if error)
		DTA updated
			If default not satisfac-
			tory, DTA must be
			set before using
			this function.

Find Next File	AH = 4FH INT 21H	Carry flag set (if error) AX = error code (if error) DTA updated	

(more)

Table 8-1. *Continued.*

Function	Call With	Returns	Comment

Rename File	AH = 56H
	DS:DX = pointer to
	  ASCIIZ pathname
	ES:DI = pointer to
	  new ASCIIZ pathname
	INT 21H
		Carry flag set (if error)
		AX = error code (if error)	

Get/Set Date/Time of File	AH = 57H AL = 0 (get date/time) 1 (set date/time) BX = handle CX = time (if AL = 1) DX = date (if AL = 1) INT 21H	Carry flag set (if error) AX = error code (if error) CX = time (if AL = 0) DX = date (if AL = 0)	

Searching a directory

Two pairs of Interrupt 21H functions are available for directory searches. Functions 11H and 12H use FCBs to transfer filenames to MS-DOS; these functions are available in all versions of MS-DOS, but they cannot be used with pathnames. Functions 4EH and 4FH support pathnames, but these functions are unavailable in MS-DOS versions 1.x. All four functions require the address of the disk transfer area (DTA) to be initialized appropriately before the function is invoked. When Function 12H or 4FH is used, the current DTA must be the same as the DTA for the preceding call to Function 11H or 4EH.

The Interrupt 21H directory search functions are designed to be used in pairs. The Find First File functions return the first matching directory entry in the current directory (Function 11H) or in the specified directory (Function 4EH). The Find Next File functions (Functions 12H and 4FH) can be called repeatedly after a successful call to the corresponding Find First File function. Each call to one of the Find Next File functions returns the next directory entry that matches the name originally specified to the Find First File function. A directory search can thus be summarized as follows:

```
call "find first file" function

while ( matching directory entry returned )
    call "find next file" function
```

Wildcard characters

This search strategy is used because name specifications can include the wildcard characters ?, which matches any single character, and * (*see* below). When one or more wildcard characters appear in the name specified to one of the Find First File functions, only the nonwildcard characters in the name participate in the directory search. Thus, for example, the specification FOO? matches the filenames FOO1, FOO2, and so on; the specification FOO?????.??? matches FOO4.COM, FOOBAR.EXE, and FOONEW.BAK, as well as FOO1 and FOO2; the specification ????????.TXT matches all files whose extension is .TXT; the specification ????????.??? matches all files in the directory.

Function 4EH also recognizes the wildcard character *, which matches any remaining characters in a filename or extension. MS-DOS expands the * wildcard character internally to question marks. Thus, for example, the specification FOO* is the same as FOO?????; the specification FOO*.* is the same as FOO?????.???; and, of course, the specification *.* is the same as ????????.???.

Examining a directory entry

All four Interrupt 21H directory search functions return the name, attribute, file size, time, and date fields for each directory entry found during a directory search. The current DTA is used to return this data, although the format is different for the two pairs of functions: Functions 11H and 12H return a copy of the 32-byte directory entry—including the cluster number—in the DTA; Functions 4EH and 4FH return a 43-byte data structure that does not include the starting cluster number. *See* SYSTEM CALLS: INTERRUPT 21H: Function 4EH.

The attribute field of a directory entry can be examined using Function 43H (Get/Set File Attributes). Also, Function 57H (Get/Set Date/Time of File) can be used to examine a file's time or date. However, unlike the other functions discussed here, Function 57H is intended only for files that are being actively used within an application—that is, Function 57H can be called to examine the file's time or date stamp only after the file has been opened or created using an Interrupt 21H function that returns a handle (Function 3CH, 3DH, 5AH, or 5BH).

Modifying a directory entry

Four Interrupt 21H functions can modify the contents of a directory entry. Function 17H (Rename File) can be used to change the name field in any directory entry, including hidden or system files, subdirectories, and the volume label. Related Function 56H (Rename File) also changes the name field of a filename but cannot rename a volume label or a hidden or system file. However, it can be used to move a directory entry from one directory to another. (This capability is restricted to filenames only; subdirectory entries cannot be moved with Function 56H.)

Functions 43H (Get/Set File Attributes) and 57H (Get/Set Date/Time of File) can be used to modify specific fields in a directory entry. Function 43H can mark a directory entry as a hidden or system file, although it cannot modify the volume label or subdirectory bits. Function 57H, as noted above, can be used only with a previously opened file; it provides a way to read or update a file's time and date stamps without writing to the file itself.

Creating and deleting directories

Function 39H (Create Directory) exists only to create directories—that is, directory entries with the subdirectory bit set to 1. (Interrupt 21H functions that create files, such as Function 3CH, cannot assign the subdirectory attribute to a directory entry.) The converse function, 3AH (Remove Directory), deletes a subdirectory entry from a directory. (The subdirectory must be completely empty.) Again, Interrupt 21H functions that delete files from directories, such as Function 41H, cannot be used to delete subdirectories.

Specifying the current directory

A call to Interrupt 21H Function 47H (Get Current Directory) returns the pathname of the current directory in use by MS-DOS to a user-supplied buffer. The converse operation, in which a new current directory can be specified to MS-DOS, is performed by Function 3BH (Change Current Directory).

Programming examples: Searching for files

The subroutines in Figure 8-6 below illustrate Functions 4EH and 4FH, which use path specifications passed as ASCIIZ strings to search for files. Figure 8-7 applies these assembly-language subroutines in a simple C program that lists the attributes associated with each entry in the current directory. Note how the directory search is performed in the WHILE loop in Figure 8-7 by using a global wildcard file specification (*.*) and by repeatedly executing *FindNextFile()* until no further matching filenames are found. (*See* Programming Example: Updating a Volume Label for examples of the FCB-related search functions, 11H and 21H.)

```
                    TITLE    'DIRS.ASM'

;
; Subroutines for DIRDUMP.C
;


ARG1                EQU      [bp + 4]          ; stack frame addressing for C arguments
ARG2                EQU      [bp + 6]


_TEXT               SEGMENT byte public 'CODE'
                    ASSUME  cs:_TEXT

;----------------------------------------------------------------------------
;
; void SetDTA( DTA );
;        char *DTA;
;
;----------------------------------------------------------------------------

                    PUBLIC  _SetDTA
_SetDTA             PROC    near

                    push    bp
                    mov     bp,sp

                    mov     dx,ARG1          ; DS:DX -> DTA
                    mov     ah,1Ah           ; AH = INT 21H function number
                    int     21h              ; pass DTA to MS-DOS
```

Figure 8-6. Subroutines illustrating Interrupt 21H Functions 4EH and 4FH. (more)

```
                  pop     bp
                  ret

_SetDTA           ENDP

;-----------------------------------------------------------------------------
;
; int GetCurrentDir( *path );            /* returns error code */
;       char *path;                      /* pointer to buffer to contain path */
;
;-----------------------------------------------------------------------------

                  PUBLIC  _GetCurrentDir
_GetCurrentDir    PROC    near

                  push    bp
                  mov     bp,sp
                  push    si

                  mov     si,ARG1         ; DS:SI -> buffer
                  xor     dl,dl           ; DL = 0 (default drive number)
                  mov     ah,47h          ; AH = INT 21H function number
                  int     21h             ; call MS-DOS; AX = error code
                  jc      L01             ; jump if error

                  xor     ax,ax           ; no error, return AX = 0

L01:              pop     si
                  pop     bp
                  ret

_GetCurrentDir    ENDP

;-----------------------------------------------------------------------------
;
; int FindFirstFile( path, attribute ); /* returns error code */
;       char *path;
;       int  attribute;
;
;-----------------------------------------------------------------------------

                  PUBLIC  _FindFirstFile
_FindFirstFile    PROC    near

                  push    bp
                  mov     bp,sp

                  mov     dx,ARG1         ; DS:DX -> path
                  mov     cx,ARG2         ; CX = attribute
                  mov     ah,4Eh          ; AH = INT 21H function number
                  int     21h             ; call MS-DOS; AX = error code
                  jc      L02             ; jump if error
```

Figure 8-6. Continued.   *(more)*

```
                  xor      ax,ax           ; no error, return AX = 0

L02:              pop      bp
                  ret


_FindFirstFile    ENDP

;-----------------------------------------------------------------------------
;
; int FindNextFile();                      /* returns error code */
;
;-----------------------------------------------------------------------------

                  PUBLIC   _FindNextFile
_FindNextFile     PROC     near

                  push     bp
                  mov      bp,sp

                  mov      ah,4Fh          ; AH = INT 21H function number
                  int      21h             ; call MS-DOS; AX = error code
                  jc       L03             ; jump if error

                  xor      ax,ax           ; if no error, set AX = 0


L03:              pop      bp
                  ret

_FindNextFile     ENDP

_TEXT             ENDS


_DATA             SEGMENT word public 'DATA'

CurrentDir        DB       64 dup(?)
DTA               DB       64 dup(?)

_DATA             ENDS

                  END
```

Figure 8-6. Continued.

```
/* DIRDUMP.C */

#define AllAttributes   0x3F           /* bits set for all attributes */

main()
{
        static  char CurrentDir[64];
        int     ErrorCode;
        int     FileCount = 0;

        struct
        {
          char    reserved[21];
          char    attrib;
          int     time;
          int     date;
          long    size;
          char    name[13];
        }         DTA;

/* display current directory name */

        ErrorCode = GetCurrentDir( CurrentDir );
        if( ErrorCode )
        {
          printf( "\nError %d:  GetCurrentDir", ErrorCode );
          exit( 1 );
        }

        printf( "\nCurrent directory is \\%s", CurrentDir );


/* display files and attributes */

        SetDTA( &DTA );                 /* pass DTA to MS-DOS */

        ErrorCode = FindFirstFile( "*.*", AllAttributes );

        while( !ErrorCode )
        {
          printf( "\n%12s -- ", DTA.name );
          ShowAttributes( DTA.attrib );
          ++FileCount;

          ErrorCode = FindNextFile( );
        }

/* display file count and exit */

        printf( "\nCurrent directory contains %d files\n", FileCount );
        return( 0 );
}
```

Figure 8-7. The complete DIRDUMP.C program.   *(more)*

```
ShowAttributes( a )
int      a;
{
        int      i;
        int      mask = 1;

        static char *AttribName[] =
        {
          "read-only ",
          "hidden ",
          "system ",
          "volume ",
          "subdirectory ",
          "archive "
        };


        for( i=0; i<6; i++ )               /* test each attribute bit */
        {
          if( a & mask )
            printf( AttribName[i] );   /* display a message if bit is set */
          mask = mask << 1;
        }
}
```

Figure 8-7. Continued.

Programming example: Updating a volume label

To create, modify, or delete a volume-label directory entry, the Interrupt 21H functions that work with FCBs should be used. Figure 8-8 contains four subroutines that show how to search for, rename, create, or delete a volume label in MS-DOS versions 2.0 and later.

```
                TITLE    'VOLS.ASM'

;-------------------------------------------------------------------------
;
; C-callable routines for manipulating MS-DOS volume labels.
; Note: These routines modify the current DTA address.
;
;-------------------------------------------------------------------------

ARG1            EQU      [bp + 4]        ; stack frame addressing

DGROUP          GROUP    _DATA

_TEXT           SEGMENT  byte public 'CODE'
                ASSUME   cs:_TEXT,ds:DGROUP
```

Figure 8-8. Subroutines for manipulating volume labels.   *(more)*

```
;---------------------------------------------------------------------------
;
; char *GetVolLabel();              /* returns pointer to volume label name */
;
;---------------------------------------------------------------------------

              PUBLIC   _GetVolLabel
_GetVolLabel  PROC     near

              push     bp
              mov      bp,sp
              push     si
              push     di

              call     SetDTA            ; pass DTA address to MS-DOS
              mov      dx,offset DGROUP:ExtendedFCB
              mov      ah,11h            ; AH = INT 21H function number
              int      21h               ; Search for First Entry
              test     al,al
              jnz      L01
                                         ; label found so make a copy
              mov      si,offset DGROUP:DTA + 8
              mov      di,offset DGROUP:VolLabel
              call     CopyName
              mov      ax,offset DGROUP:VolLabel ; return the copy's address
              jmp      short L02

L01:          xor      ax,ax             ; no label, return 0 (null pointer)

L02:          pop      di
              pop      si
              pop      bp
              ret

_GetVolLabel  ENDP

;---------------------------------------------------------------------------
;
; int RenameVolLabel( label );          /* returns error code */
;       char *label;                    /* pointer to new volume label name */
;
;---------------------------------------------------------------------------

              PUBLIC   _RenameVolLabel
_RenameVolLabel PROC    near

              push     bp
              mov      bp,sp
              push     si
              push     di
```

Figure 8-8. Continued.   *(more)*

```
            mov     si,offset DGROUP:VolLabel  ; DS:SI -> old volume name
            mov     di,offset DGROUP:Name1
            call    CopyName          ; copy old name to FCB

            mov     si,ARG1
            mov     di,offset DGROUP:Name2
            call    CopyName          ; copy new name into FCB

            mov     dx,offset DGROUP:ExtendedFCB     ; DS:DX -> FCB
            mov     ah,17h            ; AH = INT 21H function number
            int     21h               ; rename
            xor     ah,ah             ; AX = 00H (success) or 0FFH (failure)

            pop     di                ; restore registers and return
            pop     si
            pop     bp
            ret

_RenameVolLabel ENDP

;------------------------------------------------------------------------------
;
; .int NewVolLabel( label );              /* returns error code */
;       char *label;                      /* pointer to new volume label name */
;
;------------------------------------------------------------------------------

            PUBLIC  _NewVolLabel
_NewVolLabel  PROC    near

            push    bp
            mov     bp,sp
            push    si
            push    di

            mov     si,ARG1
            mov     di,offset DGROUP:Name1
            call    CopyName          ; copy new name to FCB

            mov     dx,offset DGROUP:ExtendedFCB
            mov     ah,16h            ; AH = INT 21H function number
            int     21h               ; create directory entry
            xor     ah,ah             ; AX = 00H (success) or 0FFH (failure)

            pop     di                ; restore registers and return
            pop     si
            pop     bp
            ret

_NewVolLabel    ENDP
```

Figure 8-8. Continued.   *(more)*

```
;----------------------------------------------------------------------------
;
; int DeleteVolLabel();                    /* returns error code */
;
;----------------------------------------------------------------------------

               PUBLIC   _DeleteVolLabel
_DeleteVolLabel PROC    near

               push    bp
               mov     bp,sp
               push    si
               push    di

               mov     si,offset DGROUP:VolLabel
               mov     di,offset DGROUP:Name1
               call    CopyName            ; copy current volume name to FCB

               mov     dx,offset DGROUP:ExtendedFCB
               mov     ah,13h              ; AH = INT 21H function number
               int     21h                 ; delete directory entry
               xor     ah,ah               ; AX = 00H (success) or 0FFH (failure)

               pop     di                  ; restore registers and return
               pop     si
               pop     bp
               ret

_DeleteVolLabel ENDP

;----------------------------------------------------------------------------
;
; miscellaneous subroutines
;
;----------------------------------------------------------------------------

SetDTA         PROC    near

               push    ax                  ; preserve registers used
               push    dx

               mov     dx,offset DGROUP:DTA    ; DS:DX -> DTA
               mov     ah,1Ah              ; AH = INT 21H function number
               int     21h                 ; set DTA

               pop     dx                  ; restore registers and return
               pop     ax
               ret

SetDTA         ENDP
```

Figure 8-8. Continued.   *(more)*

```
CopyName        PROC    near            ; Caller:  SI -> ASCIIZ source
                                        ;          DI -> destination
                push   ds
                pop    es               ; ES = DGROUP
                mov    cx,11            ; length of name field

L11:            lodsb                   ; copy new name into FCB ..
                test   al,al
                jz     L12              ; .. until null character is reached
                stosb
                loop   L11

L12:            mov    al,' '           ; pad new name with blanks
                rep    stosb
                ret

CopyName        ENDP

_TEXT           ENDS


_DATA           SEGMENT word public 'DATA'

VolLabel        DB      11 dup(0),0

ExtendedFCB     DB      0FFh            ; must be 0FFH for extended FCB
                DB      5 dup(0)        ; (reserved)
                DB      1000b           ; attribute byte (bit 3 = 1)
                DB      0               ; default drive ID
Name1           DB      11 dup('?')     ; global wildcard name
                DB      5 dup(0)        ; (unused)
Name2           DB      11 dup(0)       ; second name (for renaming entry)
                DB      9 dup(0)        ; (unused)

DTA             DB      64 dup(0)

_DATA           ENDS

                END
```

Figure 8-8. Continued.

Richard Wilton

Article 9
Memory Management

Personal computers that are MS-DOS compatible can be outfitted with as many as three kinds of random-access memory (RAM): conventional memory, expanded memory, and extended memory.

All MS-DOS machines have at least some conventional memory, but the presence of expanded or extended memory depends on the installed hardware options and the model of microprocessor on which the computer is based. Each storage class has its own capabilities, characteristics, and limitations. Each also has its own management techniques, which are the subject of this chapter.

Conventional Memory

Conventional memory is the term for the up to 1 MB of memory that is directly addressable by an Intel 8086/8088 microprocessor or by an 80286 or 80386 microprocessor running in real mode (8086-emulation mode). Physical addresses for references to conventional memory are generated by a 16-bit segment register, which acts as a base register and holds a paragraph address, combined with a 16-bit offset contained in an index register or in the instruction being executed.

On IBM PCs and compatibles, MS-DOS and the programs that run under its control occupy the bottom 640 KB or less of the conventional memory space. The memory space above the 640 KB mark is partitioned among ROM (read-only memory) chips on the system board that contain various primitive device handlers and test programs and among RAM and ROM chips on expansion boards that are used for input and output buffers and for additional device-dependent routines.

The bottom 640 KB of memory administered by MS-DOS is divided into three zones (Figure 9-1):

- The interrupt vector table
- The operating system area
- The transient program area

The interrupt vector table occupies the lowest 1024 bytes of memory (locations 00000–003FFH); its address and length are hard-wired into the processor and cannot be changed. Each doubleword position in the table is called an interrupt vector and contains the segment and offset of an interrupt handler routine for the associated hardware or software interrupt number. Interrupt handler routines are usually built into the operating system,

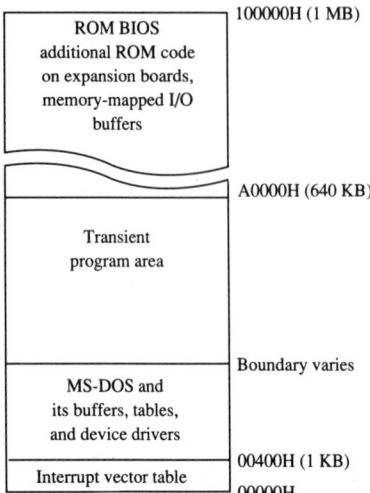

ROM BIOS
additional ROM code
on expansion boards,
memory-mapped I/O
buffers

100000H (1 MB)

A0000H (640 KB)

Transient
program area

Boundary varies

MS-DOS and
its buffers, tables,
and device drivers

00400H (1 KB)

Interrupt vector table

00000H

Figure 9-1. A diagram showing conventional memory in an IBM PC-compatible MS-DOS system. The bottom 1024 bytes of memory are used for the interrupt vector table. The memory above the vector table, up to the 640 KB boundary, is available for use by MS-DOS and the programs that run under its control. The top 384 KB are used for the ROM BIOS, other device-control and diagnostic routines, and memory-mapped input and output.

but in special cases application programs can contain handler routines of their own. Vectors for interrupt numbers that are not used for software linkages or by some hardware device are usually initialized by the operating system to point to a simple interrupt return (IRET) instruction or to a routine that displays an error message.

The operating-system area begins immediately above the interrupt vector table and holds the operating system proper, its tables and buffers, any additional installable device drivers specified in the CONFIG.SYS file, and the resident portion of the COMMAND.COM command interpreter. The amount of memory occupied by the operating-system area varies with the version of MS-DOS being used, the number of disk buffers, and the number and size of installed device drivers.

The transient program area (TPA) is the remainder of RAM above the operating-system area, extending to the 640 KB limit or to the end of installed RAM (whichever is smaller). External MS-DOS commands (such as CHKDSK) and other programs are loaded into the TPA for execution. The transient portion of COMMAND.COM also runs in this area.

The TPA is organized into a structure called the memory arena, which is divided into portions called *arena entries* (or memory blocks). These entries are allocated in paragraph (16-byte) multiples and can be as small as one paragraph or as large as the entire TPA. Each arena entry is preceded by a control structure called an arena entry header, which contains information indicating the size and status of the arena entry.

MS-DOS inspects the arena entry headers whenever a function requesting a memory-block allocation, modification, or release is issued; when a program is loaded and executed with the EXEC function (Interrupt 21H Function 4BH); or when a program is terminated. If any of the arena entry headers appear to be damaged, MS-DOS returns an error to the calling process. If that process is COMMAND.COM, COMMAND.COM then displays the message *Memory allocation error* and halts the system.

MS-DOS support for conventional memory management

The MS-DOS kernel supports three memory-management functions, invoked with Interrupt 21H, that operate on the TPA:

- Function 48H (Allocate Memory Block)
- Function 49H (Free Memory Block)
- Function 4AH (Resize Memory Block)

These three functions (Table 9-1) can be called by application programs, by the command processor, and by MS-DOS itself to dynamically allocate, resize, and release arena entries as they are needed. *See* SYSTEM CALLS: INTERRUPT 21H: Functions 48H; 49H; 4AH.

Table 9-1. MS-DOS Memory-Management Functions.

Function Name	Call With	Returns
Allocate Memory Block	AH = 48H BX = paragraphs needed	AX = segment of allocated 　　block If failed: BX = size of largest available 　　block in paragraphs
Free Memory Block	AH = 49H ES = segment of block to 　　release	nothing
Resize (Allocated) Memory Block	AH = 4AH BX = new size of block in 　　paragraphs ES = segment of block to 　　resize	If failed: BX = maximum size 　　for block in paragraphs
Get/Set Allocation Strategy*	AH = 58H AL = 00H (get strategy) 　　01H (set strategy) If setting: BX = strategy: 　　00H = first fit 　　01H = best fit 　　02H = last fit	If getting: AX = strategy code

* MS-DOS versions 3.x only.

When the MS-DOS kernel receives a memory-allocation request, it inspects the chain of arena entry headers to find a free arena entry that can satisfy the request. The memory manager can use any of three allocation strategies:

- First fit–the arena entry at the lowest address that is large enough to satisfy the request
- Best fit–the smallest available arena entry that satisfies the request, regardless of its position
- Last fit–the arena entry at the highest address that is large enough to satisfy the request

If the arena entry selected is larger than the size needed to fulfill the request, the arena entry is divided and the program is given an arena entry exactly the size it requires. A new arena entry header is then created for the remaining portion of the original arena entry; it is marked "unowned" and can be used to satisfy subsequent allocation calls.

Research on allocation strategies has demonstrated that the first-fit approach is most efficient, and this is the default strategy used by MS-DOS. However, in MS-DOS versions 3.0 and later, an application program can select a different strategy for the memory manager with Interrupt 21H Function 58H (Get/Set Allocation Strategy). *See* SYSTEM CALLS: INTERRUPT 21H: Function 58H.

Using the memory-management functions

When a program begins executing, it already owns two arena entries allocated on its behalf by the MS-DOS EXEC function (Interrupt 21H Function 4BH). The first entry holds the program's environment and is just large enough to contain this information; the second entry (called the program block in this article) contains the program's PSP, code, data, and stack.

The amount of memory MS-DOS allocates to the program block for a newly loaded transient program depends on its type (.COM or .EXE). Under typical conditions, a .COM program is allocated all of the first arena entry that is large enough to hold the contents of its file, plus 256 bytes for the PSP and at least 2 bytes for the stack. Because the TPA is seldom fragmented into more than one arena entry before a program is loaded, a .COM program usually ends up owning all the memory in the system that does not belong to the operating system itself — memory divided between a relatively small environment and a comparatively immense program block.

The amount of memory allocated to a .EXE program, on the other hand, is controlled by two fields called MINALLOC and MAXALLOC in the .EXE program file header. The MINALLOC field tells the MS-DOS loader how many paragraphs of memory, in addition to the memory required to hold the initialized code and the data present in the file, *must* be available for the program to execute at all. The MAXALLOC field contains the maximum number of excess paragraphs, *if available,* to allocate to the program.

The default value placed in MAXALLOC by the Microsoft Object Linker is FFFFH para-graphs, corresponding to 1 MB. Consequently, a .EXE program is typically allocated all of available memory when it is loaded, as is a .COM file. Although it is possible to set the MAXALLOC field to other, smaller values with the linker's /CPARMAXALLOC switch or with the EXEMOD utility supplied with Microsoft language compilers, few programmers bother to do so.

In short, when a program begins executing, it usually owns all of available memory—frequently much more memory than it needs. If the program wants to be well behaved in its use of memory and, possibly, load child programs as well, it should immediately release any extra memory. In assembly-language programs, the extra memory is released by call-ing Interrupt 21H Function 4AH (Resize Memory Block) with the segment of the program's PSP in the ES register and the number of paragraphs of memory to retain for the program's use in the BX register. (*See* Figures 9-2 and 9-3.) In most high-level languages, such as Microsoft C, excess memory is released by the run-time library's startup module.

```
        .
        .
        .
_TEXT   segment para public 'CODE'

        org     100h

        assume  cs:_TEXT,ds:_TEXT,es:_TEXT,ss:_TEXT

main    proc    near            ; entry point from MS-DOS
                                ; CS = DS = ES = SS = PSP

                                ; first move our stack
        mov     sp,offset stk   ; to a safe place...

                                ; now release extra memory...
        mov     bx,offset stk   ; calculate paragraphs to keep
        mov     cl,4            ; (divide offset of end of
        shr     bx,cl           ; program by 16 and round up)
        inc     bx
        mov     ah,4ah          ; Fxn 4AH = resize mem block
        int     21h             ; transfer to MS-DOS
        jc      error           ; jump if resize failed
        .
        .                       ; otherwise go on with work...
        .
main    endp

        .
        .
        .
```

(more)

Figure 9-2. An example of a .COM program releasing excess memory after it receives control from MS-DOS. Interrupt 21H Function 4AH is called with the segment address of the program's PSP in register ES and the number of paragraphs of memory to retain in register BX.

```
        dw      64 dup (?)
stk     equ     $                       ; base of new stack area

_TEXT   ends

        end     main                    ; defines program entry point
```

Figure 9-2. Continued.

```
_TEXT   segment word public 'CODE'      ; executable code segment

        assume  cs:_TEXT,ds:_DATA,ss:STACK

main    proc    far                     ; entry point from MS-DOS
                                        ; CS = _TEXT segment,
                                        ; DS = ES = PSP

        mov     ax,_DATA                ; set DS = our data segment
        mov     ds,ax

                                        ; give back extra memory...
        mov     ax,es                   ; let AX = segment of PSP base
        mov     bx,ss                   ; and BX = segment of stack base
        sub     bx,ax                   ; reserve seg stack - seg psp
        add     bx,stksize/16           ; plus paragraphs of stack
        inc     bx                      ; round up
        mov     ah,4ah                  ; Fxn 4AH = resize memory block
        int     21h                     ; transfer to MS-DOS
        jc      error                   ; jump if resize failed
        .
        .
        .

main    endp

_TEXT   ends

_DATA   segment word public 'DATA'      ; static & variable data
        .
        .
        .

_DATA   ends
```

(more)

Figure 9-3. An example of a .EXE program releasing excess memory after it receives control from MS-DOS. This particular code sequence depends on the segment order shown. When a .EXE program is linked from many different object modules, other techniques may be needed to determine the amount of memory occupied by the program at run time.

```
STACK    segment para stack 'STACK'

         db       stksize dup (?)

STACK    ends

         end      main              ; defines program entry point
```

Figure 9-3. Continued.

Later, if the transient program needs additional memory for a buffer, table, or other work area, it can call Interrupt 21H Function 48H (Allocate Memory Block) with the desired number of paragraphs. If a sufficiently large block of memory is available, MS-DOS creates a new arena entry of the requested size and returns a pointer to its base in the form of a segment address in the AX register. If an arena entry of the requested size cannot be created, MS-DOS returns an error code in the AX register and the size in paragraphs of the largest available block of memory in the BX register. The application program can inspect this value to determine whether it can continue in a degraded fashion with a smaller amount of memory.

When a program finishes using an allocated arena entry, it should promptly call Interrupt 21H Function 49H to release it. This allows MS-DOS to collect small blocks of freed memory into contiguous arena entries and reduces the chance that future allocation requests by the same program will fail because of memory fragmentation. In any case, all arena entries owned by a program are released when the program terminates with Interrupt 20H or with Interrupt 21H Function 00H or 4CH.

A program skeleton demonstrating the use of dynamic memory allocation services is shown in Figure 9-4.

```
         .
         .
         .
         mov     bx,800h         ; 800H paragraphs = 32 KB
         mov     ah,48h          ; Fxn 48H = allocate block
         int     21h             ; transfer to MS-DOS
         jc      error           ; jump if allocation failed
         mov     bufseg,ax       ; save segment of block


                                 ; open working file...
         mov     dx,offset file1 ; DS:DX = filename address
         mov     ax,3d00h        ; Fxn 3DH = open, read only
         int     21h             ; transfer to MS-DOS
         jc      error           ; jump if open failed
         mov     handle1,ax      ; save handle for work file
```

(more)

Figure 9-4. A skeleton example of dynamic memory allocation. The program requests a 32 KB memory block, uses it to copy its working file to a backup file, and then releases the memory block. Note the use of ASSUME directives to force the assembler to generate proper segment overrides on references to variables containing file handles.

```
                                    ; create backup file...
              mov      dx,offset file2 ; DS:DX = filename address
              mov      cx,0            ; CX = attribute (normal)
              mov      ah,3ch          ; Fxn 3CH = create file
              int      21h             ; transfer to MS-DOS
              jc       error           ; jump if create failed
              mov      handle2,ax      ; save handle for backup file

              push     ds              ; set ES = our data segment
              pop      es
              mov      ds,bufseg       ; set DS:DX = allocated block
              xor      dx,dx

              assume   ds:NOTHING,es:_DATA     ; tell assembler

next:                                   ; read working file...
              mov      bx,handle1      ; handle for work file
              mov      cx,8000h        ; try to read 32 KB
              mov      ah,3fh          ; Fxn 3FH = read
              int      21h             ; transfer to MS-DOS
              jc       error           ; jump if read failed
              or       ax,ax           ; was end of file reached?
              jz       done            ; yes, exit this loop

                                       ; now write backup file...
              mov      cx,ax           ; set write length = read length
              mov      bx,handle2      ; handle for backup file
              mov      ah,40h          ; Fxn 40H = write
              int      21h             ; transfer to MS-DOS
              jc       error           ; jump if write failed
              cmp      ax,cx           ; was write complete?
              jne      error           ; no, disk must be full
              jmp      next            ; transfer another record

done:         push     es              ; restore DS = data segment
              pop      ds

              assume   ds:_DATA,es:NOTHING     ; tell assembler

                                       ; release allocated block...
              mov      es,bufseg       ; segment base of block
              mov      ah,49h          ; Fxn 49H = release block
              int      21h             ; transfer to MS-DOS
              jc       error           ; (should never fail)

                                       ; now close backup file...
              mov      bx,handle2      ; handle for backup file
              mov      ah,3eh          ; Fxn 3EH = close
              int      21h             ; transfer to MS-DOS
              jc       error           ; jump if close failed
```

Figure 9-4. Continued.   *(more)*

```
            .
            .
            .

file1   db      'MYFILE.DAT',0  ; name of working file
file2   db      'MYFILE.BAK',0  ; name of backup file

handle1 dw      ?               ; handle for working file
handle2 dw      ?               ; handle for backup file
bufseg  dw      ?               ; segment of allocated block
```

Figure 9-4. Continued.

Expanded Memory

The original Expanded Memory Specification (EMS) version 3.0 was developed as a joint effort of Lotus Development Corporation and Intel Corporation and was announced at the Spring COMDEX in 1985. The EMS was designed to provide a uniform means for applications running on 8086/8088-based personal computers, or on 80286/80386-based computers in real mode, to circumvent the 1 MB limit on conventional memory, thus providing such programs with much larger amounts of fast random-access storage. The EMS version 3.2, modified from 3.0 to add support for multitasking operating systems, was released shortly afterward as a joint effort of Lotus, Intel, and Microsoft.

The EMS is a functional definition of a bank-switched memory subsystem; it consists of user-installable boards that plug into the IBM PC's expansion bus and a resident driver program called the Expanded Memory Manager (EMM) that is provided by the board manufacturer. As much as 8 MB of expanded memory can be installed in a single machine. Expanded memory is made available to application software in 16 KB pages, which are mapped by the EMM into a contiguous 64 KB area called the page frame somewhere above the conventional memory area used by MS-DOS (0–640 KB). An application program can thus access as many as four 16 KB expanded memory pages simultaneously. The location of the page frame is user configurable so that it will not conflict with other hardware options (Figure 9-5).

The Expanded Memory Manager

The Expanded Memory Manager provides a hardware-independent interface between application programs and the expanded memory board(s). The EMM is supplied by the board manufacturer in the form of an installable character-device driver and is linked into MS-DOS by a DEVICE directive added to the CONFIG.SYS file on the system startup disk.

Internally, the EMM is divided into two distinct components that can be referred to as the driver and the manager. The driver portion mimics some of the actions of a genuine installable device driver, in that it includes Initialization and Output Status subfunctions and a valid device header. *See* PROGRAMMING IN THE MS-DOS ENVIRONMENT: CUSTOMIZING MS-DOS: Installable Device Drivers.

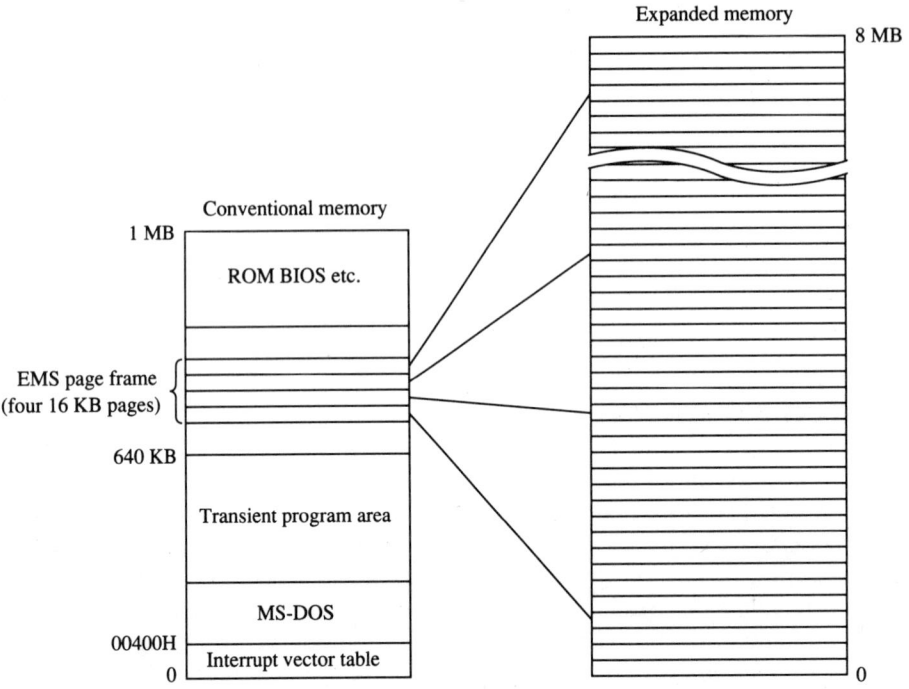

Figure 9-5. A sketch of the relationship of expanded memory to conventional memory; 16 KB pages of expanded memory are mapped into a 64 KB area, called the page frame, above the 640 KB boundary. The location of the page frame can be configured by the user to eliminate conflicts with ROMs or I/O buffers on expansion boards.

The second, and major, element of the EMM is the true interface between application software and the expanded memory hardware. Several classes of services provide

- Status of the expanded memory subsystem
- Allocation of expanded memory pages
- Mapping of logical pages into physical memory
- Deallocation of expanded memory pages
- Support for multitasking operating systems
- Diagnostic routines

Application programs communicate with the EMM directly by means of a software interrupt (Interrupt 67H). The MS-DOS kernel does not take part in expanded memory manipulations and does not use expanded memory for its own purposes.

Checking for expanded memory

Before it attempts to use expanded memory for storage, an application program must establish that the EMM is present and functional, and then it must use the manager portion of the EMM to check the status of the memory boards themselves. There are two methods a program can use to test for the existence of the EMM.

The first method is to issue an Open File or Device request (Interrupt 21H Function 3DH) using the guaranteed device name of the EMM driver: EMMXXXX0. If the open operation succeeds, one of two conditions is indicated — either the driver is present or a file with the same name exists in the current directory of the default disk drive. To rule out the latter possibility, the application can issue IOCTL Get Device Information (Interrupt 21H Function 44H Subfunction 00H) and Check Output Status (Interrupt 21H Function 44H Subfunction 07H) requests to determine whether the handle returned by the open operation is associated with a file or with a device. In either case, the handle that was obtained from the open function should then be closed (Interrupt 21H Function 3EH) so that it can be reused for another file or device.

The second method of testing for the driver is to use the address that is found in the vector for Interrupt 67H to inspect the device header of the presumed EMM. (The contents of the vector can be obtained conveniently with Interrupt 21H Function 35H.) If the EMM is present, the name field at offset 0AH of the device header contains the string *EMMXXXX0*. This method is nearly foolproof, and it avoids the relatively high overhead of an MS-DOS open function. However, it is somewhat less well behaved because it involves inspection of memory that does not belong to the application.

The two methods of testing for the existence of the EMM are illustrated in Figures 9-6 and 9-7.

```
          .
          .
          .
                               ; attempt to "open" EMM...
     mov     dx,seg emm_name  ; DS:DX = address of name
     mov     ds,dx            ; of EMM
     mov     dx,offset emm_name
     mov     ax,3d00h         ; Fxn 3DH, Mode = 00H
                              ; = open, read-only
     int     21h              ; transfer to MS-DOS
     jc      error            ; jump if open failed

                              ; open succeeded, make sure
                              ; it was not a file...
```

(more)

Figure 9-6. Testing for the presence of the Expanded Memory Manager with the MS-DOS Open File or Device (Interrupt 21H Function 3DH) and IOCTL (Interrupt 21H Function 44H) functions.

```
        mov     bx,ax           ; BX = handle from open
        mov     ax,4400h        ; Fxn 44H Subfxn 00H
                                ; = IOCTL Get Device Information
        int     21h             ; transfer to MS-DOS
        jc      error           ; jump if IOCTL call failed
        and     dx,80h          ; Bit 7 = 1 if character device
        jz      error           ; jump if it was a file

                                ; EMM is present, make sure
                                ; it is available...
                                ; (BX still contains handle)
        mov     ax,4407h        ; Fxn 44H Subfxn 07H
                                ; = IOCTL Get Output Status
        int     21h             ; transfer to MS-DOS
        jc      error           ; jump if IOCTL call failed
        or      al,al           ; test device status
        jz      error           ; if AL = 0 EMM is not available

                                ; now close handle ...
                                ; (BX still contains handle)
        mov     ah,3eh          ; Fxn 3EH = Close
        int     21h             ; transfer to MS-DOS
        jc      error           ; jump if close failed
        .
        .
        .

emm_name db     'EMMXXXX0',0    ; guaranteed device name for EMM
```

Figure 9-6. Continued.

```
emm_int equ     67h             ; EMM software interrupt

        .
        .
        .
                                ; first fetch contents of
                                ; EMM interrupt vector...
        mov     al,emm_int      ; AL = EMM int number
        mov     ah,35h          ; Fxn 35H = get vector
        int     21h             ; transfer to MS-DOS
                                ; now ES:BX = handler address

                                ; assume ES:0000 points
                                ; to base of the EMM...
```

(more)

Figure 9-7. Testing for the presence of the Expanded Memory Manager by inspecting the name field in the device driver header.

```
        mov     di,10           ; ES:DI = address of name
                                ; field in device header
        mov     si,seg emm_name ; DS:SI = address of
        mov     ds,si           ; expected EMM driver name
        mov     si,offset emm_name
        mov     cx,8            ; length of name field
        cld
        repz cmpsb              ; compare names...
        jnz     error           ; jump if driver absent
        .
        .
        .


emm_name db     'EMMXXXX0'      ; guaranteed device name for EMM
```

Figure 9-7. Continued.

Using expanded memory

After establishing that the EMM is present, the application program can bypass MS-DOS and communicate with the EMM directly by means of software Interrupt 67H. The calling sequence is as follows:

```
    mov     ah,function     ; AH selects EMM function

    .                       ; Load other registers with
    .                       ; values specific to the
    .                       ; requested service

    int     67h             ; Transfer to EMM
```

In general, the ES:DI registers are used to pass the address of a buffer or an array, and the DX register is used to hold an expanded memory "handle." Some EMM functions also use other registers (chiefly AL and BX) to pass such information as logical and physical page numbers. Table 9-2 summarizes the services available from the EMM.

Upon return from an EMM function call, the AH register contains zero if the function was successful; otherwise, AH contains an error code with the most significant bit set (Table 9-3). Other values are typically returned in the AL and BX registers or in a user-specified buffer.

Table 9-2. Summary of the Software Interface to Application Programs Provided by the EMM.*

Function Name	Action	Call With	Returns	Comments
Get Manager Status	Test whether the expanded memory software and hardware are functional.	AH = 40H	AH = status	This call is used after the program has established, with one of the techniques presented in Figures 9-6 and 9-7, that the EMM is present.
Get Page Frame Segment	Obtain the segment address of the EMM page frame.	AH = 41H	AH = status BX = segment of page frame, if AH = 00H	The page frame is divided into four 16 KB pages that are used to map logical expanded memory pages into the physical memory space of the 8086/8088 processor.
Get Expanded Memory Pages	Obtain the number of logical expanded memory pages present in the system and the number of pages that are not already allocated.	AH = 42H	AH = status BX = unallocated EMM pages, if AH = 00H DX = total EMM pages in system	The application need not have already acquired an EMM handle to use this function.
Allocate Expanded Memory	Obtain an EMM handle and allocate logical pages to be controlled by that handle.	AH = 43H BX = logical pages to allocate	AH = status DX = handle, if AH = 00H	This function is equivalent to a file-open function for the EMM. The handle returned is analogous to a file handle and owns a certain number of EMM pages. The handle must be used with every subsequent request to map memory and must be released by a close operation when the application is finished. This function can fail because either the available EMM handles or the EMM pages have been exhausted. Function 42H can be called by the application to determine the actual number of pages available.
Map Memory	Map one of the logical pages of expanded memory assigned to a handle onto one of the four physical pages within the EMM's page frame.	AH = 44H AL = physical page (0–3) BX = logical page (0...n-1) DX = EMM handle	AH = status	The logical page number must be in the range 0–n-1, where n is the number of logical pages previously allocated to the EMM handle with Function 43H. To access the memory after it has been mapped to a physical page, the application also needs the segment of the EMM's page frame, which can be obtained with Function 41H.

Function Name	Description	Call	Return	Comment
Release Handle and Memory	Deallocate the logical pages of expanded memory currently assigned to a handle and then release the handle itself for reuse.	AH = 45H DX = EMM handle	AH = status	This function is the equivalent of a close operation on a file. It notifies the EMM that the application will not be making further use of the data it may have stored within expanded memory pages.
Get EMM Version	Return the version number of the EMM software.	AH = 46H	AH = status AL = EMM version, if AH = 00H	The returned value is the version of the EMM with which the driver complies. The version number is encoded as BCD, with the integer part in the upper 4 bits and the fractional part in the lower 4 bits.
Save Mapping Context	Save the contents of the expanded memory page-mapping registers on the expanded memory boards, associating those contents with a specific EMM handle.	AH = 47H DX = EMM handle	AH = status	This function is designed for use by interrupt handlers and resident drivers or utilities that must access expanded memory. The handle supplied to the function is the handle that was assigned to the interrupt handler during its initialization sequence, not to the program that was interrupted.
Restore Mapping Context	Restore the contents of all expanded memory hardware page-mapping registers to the values associated with the given handle.	AH = 48H DX = EMM handle	AH = status	Use of this function must be balanced by a previous call to EMM Function 47H. It allows an interrupt handler or a resident driver that used expanded memory to restore the mapping context to its state at the point of interruption.
Get Number of EMM Handles	Return the number of active EMM handles.	AH = 4BH	AH = status BX = number of EMM handles, if AH = 00H	If the number of handles returned is zero, none of the expanded memory is in use. The number of active EMM handles never exceeds 255. A single program can make several allocation requests and therefore own several EMM handles.
Get Pages Owned by Handle	Return the number of logical expanded memory pages allocated to a specific handle.	AH = 4CH DX = EMM handle	AH = status BX = logical pages, if AH = 00H	The number of pages returned if the function is successful is always in the range 1–512. An EMM handle never has zero pages of memory allocated to it.

*EMM Functions 49H and 4AH (not listed) were defined in EMS version 3.0 and are "reserved" in later EMS versions.

(more)

Table 9-2. *Continued.*

Function Name	Action	Call With	Returns	Comments
Get Pages for All Handles	Return an array that contains all the active handles and the number of logical expanded memory pages associated with each handle.	AH = 4DH DI = offset of array to receive information ES = array segment	AH = status BX = number of active EMM handles If AH = 00H, array is filled in as described in comments column	The array is filled in with doubleword entries. The first word of each entry contains a handle; the second word contains the number of pages associated with that handle. The value returned in BX gives the number of valid doubleword entries in the array. Because 255 is the maximum number of EMM handles, the array need not be larger than 1020 bytes.
Get/Set Page Map	Save or set the contents of the EMM page-mapping registers on the expanded memory boards.	AH = 4EH AL = subfunction number DS:SI = array holding mapping information (Subfunctions 01H, 02H) ES:DI = array to receive information (Subfunctions 00H, 02H)	AH = status AL = bytes in page-mapping array (Subfunction 03H) Array pointed to by ES:DI receives mapping information for Subfunctions 00H and 02H	Subfunctions: 00H = get mapping registers into array 01H = set mapping registers from array 02H = get and set mapping registers in one operation 03H = return needed size of page-mapping array This function was added in EMM version 3.2 and is designed to support multitasking. It should not ordinarily be used by application programs. The content of the array is hardware and EMM software dependent. In addition to the contents of the page-mapping registers, it may contain other information that is necessary to restore the expanded memory subsystem to its previous state.

Table 9-3. The Expanded Memory Manager (EMM) Error Codes.

Error Code	Significance
00H	Function was successful.
80H	Internal error in the EMM software. Possible causes include an error in the driver itself or damage to its memory image.
81H	Malfunction in the expanded memory hardware.
82H	EMM is busy.
83H	Invalid expanded memory handle.
84H	Function requested by the application is not supported by the EMM.
85H	No more expanded memory handles available.
86H	Error in save or restore of mapping context.
87H	Allocation request specified more logical pages than are available in the system; no pages were allocated.
88H	Allocation request specified more logical pages than are currently available in the system (the request does not exceed the physical pages that exist, but some are already allocated to other handles); no pages were allocated.
89H	Zero pages cannot be allocated.
8AH	Logical page requested for mapping is outside the range of pages assigned to the handle.
8BH	Illegal physical page number in mapping request (not in the range 0–3).
8CH	Save area for mapping contexts is full.
8DH	Save of mapping context failed because save area already contains a context associated with the requested handle.
8EH	Restore of mapping context failed because save area does not contain a context for the requested handle.
8FH	Subfunction parameter not defined.

An application program that uses expanded memory should regard that memory as a system resource, such as a file or a device, and use only the documented EMM services to allocate, access, and release expanded memory pages. Here is the general strategy that can be used by such a program:

1. Establish the presence of the EMM by one of the two methods demonstrated in Figures 9-6 and 9-7.
2. After the driver is known to be present, check its operational status with EMM Function 40H.
3. Check the version number of the EMM with EMM Function 46H to ensure that all services the application will request are available.
4. Obtain the segment of the page frame used by the EMM with EMM Function 41H.
5. Allocate the desired number of expanded memory pages with EMM Function 43H. If the allocation is successful, the EMM returns a handle in DX that is used by the application to refer to the expanded memory pages it owns. This step is exactly analogous

to opening a file and using the handle obtained from the open function for subsequent read/write operations on the file.

6. If the requested number of pages is not available, query the EMM for the actual number of pages available (EMM Function 42H) and determine whether the program can continue.

7. After successfully allocating the number of expanded memory pages needed, use EMM Function 44H to map logical pages in and out of the physical page frame, to store and retrieve data in expanded memory.

8. When finished using the expanded memory pages, release them by calling EMM Function 45H. Otherwise, the pages will not be available for use by other programs until the system is restarted.

A program skeleton that illustrates this general approach to the use of expanded memory is shown in Figure 9-8.

```
        .
        .
        .
        mov     ah,40h          ; test EMM status
        int     67h
        or      ah,ah
        jnz     error           ; jump if bad status from EMM

        mov     ah,46h          ; check EMM version
        int     67h
        or      ah,ah
        jnz     error           ; jump if couldn't get version
        cmp     al,30h          ; make sure at least ver. 3.0
        jb      error           ; jump if wrong EMM version

        mov     ah,41h          ; get page frame segment
        int     67h
        or      ah,ah
        jnz     error           ; jump if failed to get frame
        mov     page_frame,bx   ; save segment of page frame

        mov     ah,42h          ; get no. of available pages
        int     67h
        or      ah,ah
        jnz     error           ; jump if get pages error
        mov     total_pages,dx  ; save total EMM pages
        mov     avail_pages,bx  ; save available EMM pages
        or      bx,bx
        jz      error           ; abort if no pages available

        mov     ah,43h          ; try to allocate EMM pages
```

(more)

Figure 9-8. A program skeleton for the use of expanded memory. This code assumes that the presence of the Expanded Memory Manager has already been verified with one of the techniques shown in Figures 9-6 and 9-7.

```
mov     bx,needed_pages
int     67h             ; if allocation is successful
or      ah,ah
jnz     error           ; jump if allocation failed

mov     emm_handle,dx   ; save handle for allocated pages

.
.                       ; now we are ready for other
.                       ; processing using EMM pages
.
                        ; map in EMM memory page...
mov     bx,log_page     ; BX <- EMM logical page number
mov     al,phys_page    ; AL <- EMM physical page (0-3)
mov     dx,emm_handle   ; EMM handle for our pages
mov     ah,44h          ; Fxn 44H = map EMM page
int     67h
or      ah,ah
jnz     error           ; jump if mapping error

.
.
.

                        ; program ready to terminate,
                        ; give up allocated EMM pages...
mov     dx,emm_handle   ; handle for our pages
mov     ah,45h          ; EMM Fxn 45H = release pages
int     67h
or      ah,ah
jnz     error           ; jump if release failed
.
.
.
```

Figure 9-8. Continued.

An interrupt handler or resident driver that uses the EMM follows the same general procedure outlined in steps 1 through 8, with a few minor variations. It may need to acquire an EMM handle and allocate pages before the operating system is fully functional; in particular, the MS-DOS services Open File or Device (Interrupt 21H Function 3DH), IOCTL (Interrupt 21H Function 44H), and Get Interrupt Vector (Interrupt 21H Function 35H) cannot be assumed to be available. Thus, such a handler or driver must use a modified version of the "get interrupt vector" technique to test for the existence of the EMM, fetching the contents of the Interrupt 67H vector directly instead of using MS-DOS Interrupt 21H Function 35H.

A device driver or interrupt handler typically owns its expanded memory pages on a permanent basis (until the system is restarted) and never deallocates them. Such a program must also take care to save (EMM Function 47H) and restore (EMM Function 48H) the EMM's page-mapping context (the EMM pages mapped into the page frame at the time the device driver or interrupt handler takes control of the system) so that use of the expanded memory by a foreground program will not be disturbed.

The EMM relies heavily on the good behavior of application software to avoid the corruption of expanded memory. If several applications that use expanded memory are running under a multitasking manager, such as Microsoft Windows, and one or more of those applications does not abide strictly by the EMM's conventions, the data stored in expanded memory can be corrupted.

Extended Memory

Extended memory is that storage at addresses above 1 MB (100000H) that can be accessed by an 80286 or 80386 microprocessor running in protected mode. IBM PC/AT-compatible machines can (theoretically) have as much as 15 MB of extended memory installed, in addition to the usual 1 MB of conventional memory address space. Unlike expanded memory, extended memory is linearly addressable: The address of each memory cell is fixed, so no special manager program is required.

Protected-mode operating systems, such as Microsoft XENIX and MS OS/2, can use extended memory for execution of programs. MS-DOS, on the other hand, runs in real mode on an 80286 or 80386, and programs running under its control cannot ordinarily execute from extended memory or even address that memory for storage of data.

To provide some access to extended memory for real-mode programs, IBM PC/AT-compatible machines contain two routines in their ROM BIOS (Tables 9-4 and 9-5) that allow the amount of extended memory present to be determined (Interrupt 15H Function 88H) and that transfer blocks of data between conventional memory and extended

Table 9-4. IBM PC/AT ROM BIOS Interrupt 15H Functions for Access to Extended Memory.

Interrupt 15H Function	Call With	Returns
Move Extended Memory Block	AH = 87H* CX = length (words) ES:SI = address of block move descriptor table	Carry flag = 0 if successful 1 if error AH = status: 00H no error 01H RAM parity error 02H exception inter- rupt error 03H gate address line 20 failed
Obtain Size of Extended Memory	AH = 88H	AX = kilobytes of memory installed above 1 MB

* Table 9-5 shows the descriptor table format used by Function 87H.

memory (Interrupt 15H Function 87H). These routines can be used by electronic disks (RAMdisks) and by other programs that wish to use extended memory for fast storage and retrieval of information that would otherwise have to be written to a slower physical disk drive.

Table 9-5. Block Move Descriptor Table Format for IBM PC/AT ROM BIOS Interrupt 15H Function 87H (Move Extended Memory Block).

Bytes	Contents
00–0FH	Zero
10–11H	Segment length in bytes (2*CX−1 or greater)
12–14H	24-bit source address
15H	Access rights byte (93H)
16–17H	Zero
18–19H	Segment length in bytes (2*CX−1 or greater)
1A–1CH	24-bit destination address
1DH	Access rights byte (93H)
1E–1FH	Zero
20–2FH	Zero

Note: This data structure actually constitutes a global descriptor table (GDT) to be used by the CPU while it is running in protected mode; the zero bytes at offsets 0–0FH and 20–2FH are filled in by the ROM BIOS code before the mode transition. The supplied 24-bit address is a linear address in the range 000000–FFFFFFH (not a segment and offset), with the least significant byte first and the most significant byte last.

Programmers should use these ROM BIOS routines with caution. Data stored in extended memory is volatile; it is lost if the machine is turned off. The transfer of data to or from extended memory involves a switch from real mode to protected mode and back again. This is a relatively slow process on 80286-based machines; in some cases it is only marginally faster than actually reading the data from a fixed disk. In addition, programs that use the ROM BIOS extended memory functions are not compatible with the MS-DOS 3.x Compatibility Box of MS OS/2, nor are they reliable if used for communications or networking.

Finally, a major deficit in these ROM BIOS functions is that they do not make any attempt to arbitrate between two or more programs or device drivers that are using extended memory for temporary storage. For example, if an application program and an installed RAMdisk driver attempt to put data in the same area of extended memory, no error is returned to either program, but the data belonging to one or both may be destroyed.

Figure 9-9 demonstrates the use of the ROM BIOS routines to transfer a block of data from extended memory to conventional memory.

```
                                      ; block move descriptor table
bmdt     db        8 dup (0)          ; dummy descriptor
         db        8 dup (0)          ; GDT descriptor
         db        8 dup (0)          ; source segment descriptor
         db        8 dup (0)          ; destination segment descriptor
         db        8 dup (0)          ; BIOS CS segment descriptor
         db        8 dup (0)          ; BIOS SS segment descriptor


buff     db        80h dup (0)        ; buffer to receive data


          .
          .
          .
         mov       dx,10h             ; DX:AX = source extended memory
         mov       ax,0               ; address 100000H (1 MB)
         mov       bx,seg buff        ; DS:BX = destination conventional
         mov       ds,bx              ; memory address
         mov       bx,offset buff
         mov       cx,80h             ; CX = length to move (bytes)
         mov       si,seg bmdt        ; ES:SI = block move descriptor table
         mov       es,si
         mov       si,offset bmdt
         call      getblk             ; get block from extended memory
         or        ah,ah              ; test status
         jnz       error              ; jump if block move failed
          .
          .
          .

getblk   proc      near               ; transfer block from extended
                                      ; memory to real memory
                                      ; call with
                                      ; DX:AX = extended memory address
                                      ; DS:BX = destination buffer
                                      ;    CX = length (bytes)
                                      ; ES:SI = block move descriptor table
                                      ; returns
                                      ;    AH = 0 if transfer OK
         mov       es:[si+10h],cx     ; store length in descriptors
         mov       es:[si+18h],cx

                                      ; store access rights bytes
         mov       byte ptr es:[si+15h],93h
         mov       byte ptr es:[si+1dh],93h
```

(more)

Figure 9-9. Demonstration of a block move from extended memory to conventional memory using the ROM BIOS routine. The procedure getblk *accepts a source address in extended memory, a destination address in conventional memory, a length in bytes, and the segment and offset of a block move descriptor table. The extended-memory address is a linear 32-bit address, of which only the lower 24 bits are significant; the conventional-memory address is a segment and offset. The* getblk *routine converts the destination segment and offset to a linear address, builds the appropriate fields in the block move descriptor table, invokes the ROM BIOS routine to perform the transfer, and returns the status in the AH register.*

```
                                    ; source (extended memory) address
        mov     es:[si+12h],ax
        mov     es:[si+14h],dl
                                    ; destination (conv memory) address
        mov     ax,ds               ; segment * 16
        mov     dx,16
        mul     dx
        add     ax,bx               ; + offset -> linear address
        adc     dx,0
        mov     es:[si+1ah],ax
        mov     es:[si+1ch],dl

        shr     cx,1                ; convert length to words
        mov     ah,87h              ; Fxn 87H = block move
        int     15h                 ; transfer to ROM BIOS

        ret                         ; back to caller
```

Figure 9-9. Continued.

Summary

Personal computers that run MS-DOS can support as many as three different types of fast, random-access memory (RAM). Each type has specific characteristics and requires different techniques for its management.

Conventional memory is the term used for the 1 MB of linear address space that can be accessed by an 8086 or 8088 microprocessor or by an 80286 or 80386 microprocessor running in real mode. MS-DOS and the programs that execute under its control run in this address space. MS-DOS provides application programs with services to dynamically allocate and release blocks of conventional memory.

As much as 8 MB of expanded memory can be installed in a PC and used for electronic disks, disk caching, and storage of application program data. The memory is made available in 16 KB pages and is administered by a driver program called the Expanded Memory Manager, which provides allocation, mapping, deallocation, and multitasking support.

Extended memory refers to the memory at addresses above 1 MB that can be accessed by an 80286-based or 80386-based microprocessor running in protected mode; it is not available in PCs based on the 8086 or 8088 microprocessors. As much as 15 MB of extended memory can be installed; however, the ROM BIOS services to access the memory are primitive and slow, and no manager is provided to arbitrate between multiple programs that attempt to use the same extended memory addresses for storage.

Ray Duncan

Article 10
The MS-DOS EXEC Function

The MS-DOS system loader, which brings .COM or .EXE files from disk into memory and executes them, can be invoked by any program with the MS-DOS EXEC function (Interrupt 21H Function 4BH). The default MS-DOS command interpreter, COMMAND.COM, uses the EXEC function to load and run its external commands, such as CHKDSK, as well as other application programs. Many popular commercial programs, such as databases and word processors, use EXEC to load and run subsidiary programs (spelling checkers, for example) or to load and run a second copy of COMMAND.COM. This allows a user to run subsidiary programs or enter MS-DOS commands without losing his or her current working context.

When EXEC is used by one program (called the parent) to load and run another (called the child), the parent can pass certain information to the child in the form of a set of strings called the environment, a command line, and two file control blocks. The child program also inherits the parent program's handles for the MS-DOS standard devices and for any other files or character devices the parent has opened (unless the open operation was performed with the "noninheritance" option). Any operations performed by the child on inherited handles, such as seeks or file I/O, also affect the file pointers associated with the parent's handles. A child program can, in turn, load another program, and the cycle can be repeated until the system's memory area is exhausted.

Because MS-DOS is not a multitasking operating system, a child program has complete control of the system until it has finished its work; the parent program is suspended. This type of processing is sometimes called synchronous execution. When the child terminates, the parent regains control and can use another system function call (Interrupt 21H Function 4DH) to obtain the child's return code and determine whether the program terminated normally, because of a critical hardware error, or because the user entered a Control-C.

In addition to loading a child program, EXEC can also be used to load subprograms and overlays for application programs written in assembly language or in a high-level language that does not include an overlay manager in its run-time library. Such overlays typically cannot be run as self-contained programs; most require "helper" routines or data in the application's root segment.

The EXEC function is available only with MS-DOS versions 2.0 and later. With MS-DOS versions 1.x, a parent program can use Interrupt 21H Function 26H to create a program segment prefix for a child but must carry out the loading, relocation, and execution of the child's code and data itself, without any assistance from the operating system.

How EXEC Works

When the EXEC function receives a request to execute a program, it first attempts to locate and open the specified program file. If the file cannot be found, EXEC fails immediately and returns an error code to the caller.

If the file exists, EXEC opens the file, determines its size, and inspects the first block of the file. If the first 2 bytes of the block are the ASCII characters *MZ*, the file is assumed to contain a .EXE load module, and the sizes of the program's code, data, and stack segments are obtained from the .EXE file header. Otherwise, the entire file is assumed to be an absolute load image (a .COM program). The actual filename extension (.COM or .EXE) is ignored in this determination.

At this point, the amount of memory needed to load the program is known, so EXEC attempts to allocate two blocks of memory: one to hold the new program's environment and one to contain the program's code, data, and stack segments. Assuming that enough memory is available to hold the program itself, the amount actually allocated to the program varies with its type. Programs of the .COM type are usually given all the free memory in the system (unless the memory area has previously become fragmented), whereas the amount assigned to a .EXE program is controlled by two fields in the file header, MINALLOC and MAXALLOC, that are set by the Microsoft Object Linker (LINK). *See* PROGRAMMING IN THE MS-DOS ENVIRONMENT: PROGRAMMING FOR MS-DOS: Structure of an Application Program; PROGRAMMING TOOLS: The Microsoft Object Linker; PROGRAMMING UTILITIES: LINK.

EXEC then copies the environment from the parent into the memory allocated for child's environment, builds a program segment prefix (PSP) at the base of the child's program memory block, and copies into the child's PSP the command tail and the two default file control blocks passed by the parent. The previous contents of the terminate (Interrupt 22H), Control-C (Interrupt 23H), and critical error (Interrupt 24H) vectors are saved in the new PSP, and the terminate vector is updated so that control will return to the parent program when the child terminates or is aborted.

The actual code and data portions of the child program are then read from the disk file into the program memory block above the newly constructed PSP. If the child is a .EXE program, a relocation table in the file header is used to fix up segment references within the program to reflect its actual load address.

Finally, the EXEC function sets up the CPU registers and stack according to the program type and transfers control to the program. The entry point for a .COM file is always offset 100H within the program memory block (the first byte following the PSP). The entry point for a .EXE file is specified in the file header and can be anywhere within the program. *See also* PROGRAMMING IN THE MS-DOS ENVIRONMENT: PROGRAMMING FOR MS-DOS: Structure of an Application Program.

When EXEC is used to load and execute an overlay rather than a child program, its operation is much simpler than described above. For an overlay, EXEC does not attempt to allocate memory or build a PSP or environment. It simply loads the contents of the file at the address specified by the calling program and performs any necessary relocations (if the overlay file has a .EXE header), using a segment value that is also supplied by the caller. EXEC then returns to the program that invoked it, rather than transferring control to the code in the newly loaded file. The requesting program is responsible for calling the overlay at the appropriate location.

Using EXEC to Load a Program

When one program loads and executes another, it must follow these steps:

1. Ensure that enough free memory is available to hold the code, data, and stack of the child program.
2. Set up the information to be passed to EXEC and the child program.
3. Call the MS-DOS EXEC function to run the child program.
4. Recover and examine the child program's termination and return codes.

Making memory available

MS-DOS typically allocates all available memory to a .COM or .EXE program when it is loaded. (The infrequent exceptions to this rule occur when the transient program area is fragmented by the presence of resident data or programs or when a .EXE program is loaded that was linked with the /CPARMAXALLOC switch or modified with EXEMOD.) Therefore, before a program can load another program, it must free any memory it does not need for its own code, data, and stack.

The extra memory is released with a call to the MS-DOS Resize Memory Block function (Interrupt 21H Function 4AH). In this case, the segment address of the parent's PSP is passed in the ES register, and the BX register holds the number of paragraphs of memory the program must retain for its own use. If the prospective parent is a .COM program, it must be certain to move its stack to a safe area if it is reducing its memory allocation to less than 64 KB.

Preparing parameters for EXEC

When used to load and execute a program, the EXEC function must be supplied with two principal parameters:

- The address of the child program's pathname
- The address of a parameter block

The parameter block, in turn, contains the addresses of information to be passed to the child program.

The program name

The pathname for the child program must be an unambiguous, null-terminated (ASCIIZ) file specification (no wildcard characters). If a path is not included, the current directory is searched for the program; if a drive specifier is not present, the default drive is used.

The parameter block

The parameter block contains the addresses of four data items (Figure 10-1):

- The environment block
- The command tail
- The two default file control blocks (FCBs)

The position reserved in the parameter block for the pointer to an environment is only 2 bytes and contains a segment address, because an environment is always paragraph aligned (its address is always evenly divisible by 16); a value of 0000H indicates the parent program's environment should be inherited unchanged. The remaining three addresses are all doubleword addresses in the standard Intel format, with an offset value in the lower word and a segment value in the upper word.

To Call

```
AH      = 4BH
AL      = 00H      load and execute child process
          03H      load overlay
DS:DX   = segment:offset of ASCIIZ pathname for an executable program file
ES:BX   = segment:offset of parameter block
```

Returns

If function is successful:
Carry flag is clear.
Other registers are preserved if MS-DOS version 3.0 or later, destroyed if MS-DOS versions 2.x.

If function is not successful:
Carry flag is set.

```
AX      = error code
```

Parameter Block Format

Offset	Contents
If AL = 00H (load and execute program):	
00H	Segment pointer of the environment to be passed
02H	Offset of command-line tail for the new PSP
04H	Segment of command-line tail for the new PSP
06H	Offset of first file control block, to be copied into new PSP at offset 5CH
08H	Segment of first file control block
0AH	Offset of second file control block, to be copied into new PSP at offset 6CH
0CH	Segment of second file control block
If AL = 03H (load overlay):	
00H	Segment address where overlay is to be loaded
02H	Relocation factor to apply to loaded image

Figure 10-1. Synopsis of calling conventions for the MS-DOS EXEC function (Interrupt 21H Function 4BH), which can be used to load and execute child processes or overlays.

The environment

An environment always begins on a paragraph boundary and is composed of a series of null-terminated (ASCIIZ) strings of the form:

name=variable

The end of the entire set of strings is indicated by an additional null byte.

If the environment pointer in the parameter block supplied to an EXEC call contains zero, the child simply acquires a copy of the parent's environment. The parent can, however, provide a segment pointer to a different or expanded set of strings. In either case, under MS-DOS versions 3.0 and later, EXEC appends the child program's fully qualified pathname to its environment block. The maximum size of an environment is 32 KB, so very large amounts of information can be passed between programs by this mechanism.

The original, or master, environment for the system is owned by the command processor that is loaded when the system is turned on or restarted (usually COMMAND.COM). Strings are placed in the system's master environment by COMMAND.COM as a result of PATH, SHELL, PROMPT, and SET commands, with default values always present for the first two. For example, if an MS-DOS version 3.2 system is started from drive C and a PATH command is not present in the AUTOEXEC.BAT file nor a SHELL command in the CONFIG.SYS file, the master environment will contain the two strings:

PATH=
COMSPEC=C:\COMMAND.COM

These specifications are used by COMMAND.COM to search for executable "external" commands and to find its own executable file on the disk so that it can reload its transient portion when necessary. When the PROMPT string is present (as a result of a previous PROMPT or SET PROMPT command), COMMAND.COM uses it to tailor the prompt displayed to the user.

```
        0  1  2  3  4  5  6  7  8  9  A  B  C  D  E  F  0123456789ABCDEF
0000   43 4F 4D 53 50 45 43 3D 43 3A 5C 43 4F 4D 4D 41   COMSPEC=C:\COMMA
0010   4E 44 2E 43 4F 4D 00 50 52 4F 4D 50 54 3D 24 70   ND.COM.PROMPT=$p
0020   24 5F 24 64 20 20 20 24 74 24 68 24 68 24 68 24   $_$d   $t$h$h$h$
0030   68 24 68 24 68 20 24 71 24 71 24 67 00 50 41 54   h$h$h $q$q$g.PAT
0040   48 3D 43 3A 5C 53 59 53 54 45 4D 3B 43 3A 5C 41   H=C:\SYSTEM;C:\A
0050   53 4D 3B 43 3A 5C 57 53 3B 43 3A 5C 45 54 48 45   SM;C:\WS;C:\ETHE
0060   52 4E 45 54 3B 43 3A 5C 46 4F 52 54 48 5C 50 43   RNET;C:\FORTH\PC
0070   33 31 3B 00 00 01 00 43 3A 5C 46 4F 52 54 48 5C   31;....C:\FORTH\
0080   50 43 33 31 5C 46 4F 52 54 48 2E 43 4F 4D 00      PC31\FORTH.COM.
```

Figure 10-2. Dump of a typical environment under MS-DOS version 3.2. This particular example contains the default COMSPEC parameter and two relatively complex PATH and PROMPT control strings that were set up by entries in the user's AUTOEXEC file. Note the two null bytes at offset 73H, which indicate the end of the environment. These bytes are followed by the pathname of the program that owns the environment.

Other strings in the environment are used only for informational purposes by transient programs and do not affect the operation of the operating system proper. For example, the Microsoft C Compiler and the Microsoft Object Linker look in the environment for INCLUDE, LIB, and TMP strings that specify the location of *include* files, library files, and temporary working files. Figure 10-2 contains a hex dump of a typical environment block.

The command tail

The command tail to be passed to the child program takes the form of a byte indicating the length of the remainder of the command tail, followed by a string of ASCII characters terminated with an ASCII carriage return (0DH); the carriage return is not included in the length byte. The command tail can include switches, filenames, and other parameters that can be inspected by the child program and used to influence its operation. It is copied into the child program's PSP at offset 80H.

When COMMAND.COM uses EXEC to run a program, it passes a command tail that includes everything the user typed in the command line except the name of the program and any redirection parameters. I/O redirection is processed within COMMAND.COM itself and is manifest in the behavior of the standard device handles that are inherited by the child program. Any other program that uses EXEC to run a child program must try to perform any necessary redirection on its own and must supply an appropriate command tail so that the child program will behave as though it had been loaded by COMMAND.COM.

The default file control blocks

The two default FCBs pointed to by the EXEC parameter block are copied into the child program's PSP at offsets 5CH and 6CH. *See also* PROGRAMMING IN THE MS-DOS ENVIRONMENT: Programming for ms-dos: File and Record Management.

Few of the currently popular application programs use FCBs for file and record I/O because FCBs do not support the hierarchical directory structure. But some programs do inspect the default FCBs as a quick way to isolate the first two switches or other parameters from the command tail. Therefore, to make its own identity transparent to the child program, the parent should emulate the action of COMMAND.COM by parsing the first two parameters of the command tail into the default FCBs. This can be conveniently accomplished with the MS-DOS function Parse Filename (Interrupt 21H Function 29H).

If the child program does not require one or both of the default FCBs, the corresponding address in the parameter block can be initialized to point to two dummy FCBs in the application's memory space. These dummy FCBs should consist of 1 zero byte followed by 11 bytes containing ASCII blank characters (20H).

Running the child program

After the parent program has constructed the necessary parameters, it can invoke the EXEC function by issuing Interrupt 21H with the registers set as follows:

AH   = 4BH
AL   = 00H (EXEC subfunction to load and execute program)
DS:DX   = segment:offset of program pathname
ES:BX   = segment:offset of parameter block

Upon return from the software interrupt, the parent must test the carry flag to determine whether the child program did, in fact, run. If the carry flag is clear, the child program was successfully loaded and given control. If the carry flag is set, the EXEC function failed, and the error code returned in AX can be examined to determine why. The usual reasons are

- The specified file could not be found.
- The file was found, but not enough memory was free to load it.

Other causes are uncommon and can be symptoms of more severe problems in the system as a whole (such as damage to disk files or to the memory image of MS-DOS). With MS-DOS versions 3.0 and later, additional details about the cause of an EXEC failure can be obtained by subsequently calling Interrupt 21H Function 59H (Get Extended Error Information).

In general, supplying either an invalid address for an EXEC parameter block or invalid addresses within the parameter block itself does *not* cause a failure of the EXEC function, but may result in the child program behaving in unexpected ways.

Special considerations

With MS-DOS versions 2.x, the previous contents of all the parent registers except for CS:IP can be destroyed after an EXEC call, including the stack pointer in SS:SP. Consequently, before issuing the EXEC call, the parent must push onto the stack the contents of any registers that it needs to preserve, and then it must save the stack segment and offset in a location that is addressable with the CS segment register. Upon return, the stack segment and offset can be loaded into SS:SP with code segment overrides, and then the other registers can be restored by popping them off the stack. With MS-DOS versions 3.0 and later, registers are preserved across an EXEC call in the usual fashion.

Note: The code segments of Windows applications that use this technique should be given the IMPURE attribute.

In addition, a bug in MS-DOS version 2.0 and in PC-DOS versions 2.0 and 2.1 causes an arbitrary doubleword in the parent's stack segment to be destroyed during an EXEC call. When the parent is a .COM program and SS = PSP, the damaged location falls within the PSP and does no harm; however, in the case of a .EXE parent where DS = SS, the affected location may overlap the data segment and cause aberrant behavior or even a crash after the return from EXEC. This bug was fixed in MS-DOS versions 2.11 and later and in PC-DOS versions 3.0 and later.

Examining the child program's return codes

If the EXEC function succeeds, the parent program can call Interrupt 21H Function 4DH (Get Return Code of Child Process) to learn whether the child executed normally to completion and passed back a return code or was terminated by the operating system because of an external event. Function 4DH returns

AH = termination type:

    00H   Child terminated normally (that is, exited via Interrupt 20H or Interrupt 21H Function 00H or Function 4CH).

    01H   Child was terminated by user's entry of a Ctrl-C.

    02H   Child was terminated by critical error handler (either the user responded with *A* to the *Abort, Retry, Ignore* prompt from the system's default Interrupt 24H handler, or a custom Interrupt 24H handler returned to MS-DOS with action code = 02H in register AL).

    03H   Child terminated normally and stayed resident (that is, exited via Interrupt 21H Function 31H or Interrupt 27H).

AL = return code:

    Value passed by the child program in register AL when it terminated with Interrupt 21H Function 4CH or 31H.

    00H if the child terminated using Interrupt 20H, Interrupt 27H, or Interrupt 21H Function 00H.

These values are only guaranteed to be returned once by Function 4DH. Thus, a subsequent call to Function 4DH, without an intervening EXEC call, does not necessarily return any useful information. Additionally, if Function 4DH is called without a preceding successful EXEC call, the returned values are meaningless.

Using COMMAND.COM with EXEC

An application program can "shell" to MS-DOS — that is, provide the user with an MS-DOS prompt without terminating — by using EXEC to load and execute a secondary copy of COMMAND.COM with an empty command tail. The application can obtain the location of the COMMAND.COM disk file by inspecting its own environment for the COMSPEC string. The user returns to the application from the secondary command processor by typing *exit* at the COMMAND.COM prompt.

Batch-file interpretation is carried out by COMMAND.COM, and a batch (.BAT) file cannot be called using the EXEC function directly. Similarly, the sequential search for .COM, .EXE, and .BAT files in all the locations specified in the environment's PATH variable is a function of COMMAND.COM, rather than of EXEC. To execute a batch file or search the system path for a program, an application program can use EXEC to load and execute a secondary copy of COMMAND.COM to use as an intermediary. The application finds the location of COMMAND.COM as described in the preceding paragraph, but it passes a command tail in the form:

/C program parameter1 parameter2 ...

where *program* is the .EXE, .COM, or .BAT file to be executed. When *program* terminates, the secondary copy of COMMAND.COM exits and returns control to the parent.

A parent and child example

The source programs PARENT.ASM in Figure 10-3 and CHILD.ASM in Figure 10-4 illustrate
how one program uses EXEC to load another.

```
        name    parent
        title   'PARENT --- demonstrate EXEC call'
;
; PARENT.EXE --- demonstration of EXEC to run process
;
; Uses MS-DOS EXEC (Int 21H Function 4BH Subfunction 00H)
; to load and execute a child process named CHILD.EXE,
; then displays CHILD's return code.
;
; Ray Duncan, June 1987
;

stdin   equ     0               ; standard input
stdout  equ     1               ; standard output
stderr  equ     2               ; standard error

stksize equ     128             ; size of stack

cr      equ     0dh             ; ASCII carriage return
lf      equ     0ah             ; ASCII linefeed


DGROUP  group   _DATA,_ENVIR,_STACK


_TEXT   segment byte public 'CODE'      ; executable code segment

        assume  cs:_TEXT,ds:_DATA,ss:_STACK


stk_seg dw      ?               ; original SS contents
stk_ptr dw      ?               ; original SP contents


main    proc    far             ; entry point from MS-DOS

        mov     ax,_DATA        ; set DS = our data segment
        mov     ds,ax

                                ; now give back extra memory
                                ; so child has somewhere to run...
```

Figure 10-3. PARENT.ASM, source code for PARENT.EXE.   *(more)*

```
        mov     ax,es                       ; let AX = segment of PSP base
        mov     bx,ss                       ; and BX = segment of stack base
        sub     bx,ax                       ; reserve seg stack - seg psp
        add     bx,stksize/16               ; plus paragraphs of stack
        mov     ah,4ah                      ; fxn 4AH = modify memory block
        int     21h
        jc      main1
                                            ; display parent message ...
        mov     dx,offset DGROUP:msg1       ; DS:DX = address of message
        mov     cx,msg1_len                 ; CX = length of message
        call    pmsg

        push    ds                          ; save parent's data segment
        mov     stk_seg,ss                  ; save parent's stack pointer
        mov     stk_ptr,sp

                                            ; now EXEC the child process...
        mov     ax,ds                       ; set ES = DS
        mov     es,ax
        mov     dx,offset DGROUP:cname      ; DS:DX = child pathname
        mov     bx,offset DGROUP:pars       ; ES:BX = parameter block
        mov     ax,4b00h                    ; function 4BH subfunction 00H
        int     21h                         ; transfer to MS-DOS

        cli                                 ; (for bug in some early 8088s)
        mov     ss,stk_seg                  ; restore parent's stack pointer
        mov     sp,stk_ptr
        sti                                 ; (for bug in some early 8088s)
        pop     ds                          ; restore DS = our data segment

        jc      main2                       ; jump if EXEC failed

                                            ; otherwise EXEC succeeded,
                                            ; convert and display child's
                                            ; termination and return codes...
        mov     ah,4dh                      ; fxn 4DH = get return code
        int     21h                         ; transfer to MS-DOS
        xchg    al,ah                       ; convert termination code
        mov     bx,offset DGROUP:msg4a
        call    b2hex
        mov     al,ah                       ; get back return code
        mov     bx,offset DGROUP:msg4b      ; and convert it
        call    b2hex
        mov     dx,offset DGROUP:msg4       ; DS:DX = address of message
        mov     cx,msg4_len                 ; CX = length of message
        call    pmsg                        ; display it

        mov     ax,4c00h                    ; no error, terminate program
        int     21h                         ; with return code = 0
```

Figure 10-3. Continued.   *(more)*

```
main1:  mov     bx,offset DGROUP:msg2a   ; convert error code
        call    b2hex
        mov     dx,offset DGROUP:msg2    ; display message 'Memory
        mov     cx,msg2_len             ; resize failed...'
        call    pmsg
        jmp     main3


main2:  mov     bx,offset DGROUP:msg3a   ; convert error code
        call    b2hex
        mov     dx,offset DGROUP:msg3    ; display message 'EXEC
        mov     cx,msg3_len             ; call failed...'
        call    pmsg


main3:  mov     ax,4c01h                ; error, terminate program
        int     21h                     ; with return code = 1


main    endp                            ; end of main procedure



b2hex   proc    near                    ; convert byte to hex ASCII
                                        ; call with AL = binary value
                                        ;           BX = addr to store string
        push    ax
        shr     al,1
        shr     al,1
        shr     al,1
        shr     al,1
        call    ascii                   ; become first ASCII character
        mov     [bx],al                 ; store it
        pop     ax
        and     al,0fh                  ; isolate lower 4 bits, which
        call    ascii                   ; become the second ASCII character
        mov     [bx+1],al               ; store it
        ret
b2hex   endp



ascii   proc    near                    ; convert value 00-0FH in AL
        add     al,'0'                  ; into a "hex ASCII" character
        cmp     al,'9'
        jle     ascii2                  ; jump if in range 00-09H,
        add     al,'A'-'9'-1            ; offset it to range 0A-0FH,

ascii2: ret                             ; return ASCII char. in AL
ascii   endp



pmsg    proc    near                    ; displays message on standard output
                                        ; call with DS:DX = address,
                                        ;           CX = length
```

Figure 10-3. Continued.   *(more)*

```
            mov      bx,stdout              ; BX = standard output handle
            mov      ah,40h                 ; function 40H = write file/device
            int      21h                    ; transfer to MS-DOS
            ret                             ; back to caller

pmsg        endp

_TEXT       ends


_DATA       segment para public 'DATA'     ; static & variable data segment

cname       db       'CHILD.EXE',0          ; pathname of child process

pars        dw       _ENVIR                 ; segment of environment block
            dd       tail                   ; long address, command tail
            dd       fcb1                   ; long address, default FCB #1
            dd       fcb2                   ; long address, default FCB #2

tail        db       fcb1-tail-2            ; command tail for child
            db       'dummy command tail',cr

fcb1        db       0                      ; copied into default FCB #1 in
            db       11 dup (' ')           ; child's program segment prefix
            db       25 dup (0)

fcb2        db       0                      ; copied into default FCB #2 in
            db       11 dup (' ')           ; child's program segment prefix
            db       25 dup (0)

msg1        db       cr,lf,'Parent executing!',cr,lf
msg1_len equ        $-msg1

msg2        db       cr,lf,'Memory resize failed, error code='
msg2a       db       'xxh.',cr,lf
msg2_len equ        $-msg2

msg3        db       cr,lf,'EXEC call failed, error code='
msg3a       db       'xxh.',cr,lf
msg3_len equ        $-msg3

msg4        db       cr,lf,'Parent regained control!'
            db       cr,lf,'Child termination type='
msg4a       db       'xxh, return code='
msg4b       db       'xxh.',cr,lf
msg4_len equ        $-msg4

_DATA       ends


_ENVIR   segment para public 'DATA'        ; example environment block
                                           ; to be passed to child
```

Figure 10-3. Continued.   *(more)*

```
        db      'PATH=',0               ; basic PATH, PROMPT,
        db      'PROMPT=$p$_$n$g',0     ; and COMSPEC strings
        db      'COMSPEC=C:\COMMAND.COM',0
        db      0                       ; extra null terminates block

_ENVIR  ends


_STACK  segment para stack 'STACK'

        db      stksize dup (?)

_STACK  ends


        end     main                    ; defines program entry point
```

Figure 10-3. Continued.

```
        name    child
        title   'CHILD process'
;
; CHILD.EXE --- a simple process loaded by PARENT.EXE
; to demonstrate the MS-DOS EXEC call, Subfunction 00H.
;
; Ray Duncan, June 1987
;

stdin   equ     0                       ; standard input
stdout  equ     1                       ; standard output
stderr  equ     2                       ; standard error

cr      equ     0dh                     ; ASCII carriage return
lf      equ     0ah                     ; ASCII linefeed


DGROUP  group   _DATA,STACK


_TEXT   segment byte public 'CODE'      ; executable code segment

        assume  cs:_TEXT,ds:_DATA,ss:STACK

main    proc    far                     ; entry point from MS-DOS

        mov     ax,_DATA                ; set DS = our data segment
        mov     ds,ax

                                        ; display child message ...
```

Figure 10-4. CHILD.ASM, source code for CHILD.EXE.   *(more)*

```
            mov     dx,offset msg         ; DS:DX = address of message
            mov     cx,msg_len            ; CX = length of message
            mov     bx,stdout             ; BX = standard output handle
            mov     ah,40h                ; AH = fxn 40H, write file/device
            int     21h                   ; transfer to MS-DOS
            jc      main2                 ; jump if any error

            mov     ax,4c00h              ; no error, terminate child
            int     21h                   ; with return code = 0

main2:      mov     ax,4c01h              ; error, terminate child
            int     21h                   ; with return code = 1

main        endp                          ; end of main procedure

_TEXT       ends


_DATA       segment para public 'DATA'    ; static & variable data segment

msg         db      cr,lf,'Child executing!',cr,lf
msg_len equ         $-msg

_DATA       ends


STACK       segment para stack 'STACK'

            dw      64 dup (?)

STACK       ends


            end     main                  ; defines program entry point
```

Figure 10-4. Continued.

PARENT.ASM can be assembled and linked into the executable program PARENT.EXE
with the following commands:

```
C>MASM PARENT;   <Enter>
C>LINK PARENT;   <Enter>
```

Similarly, CHILD.ASM can be assembled and linked into the file CHILD.EXE as follows:

```
C>MASM CHILD;   <Enter>
C>LINK CHILD;   <Enter>
```

When PARENT.EXE is executed with the command

```
C>PARENT   <Enter>
```

PARENT reduces the size of its main memory block with a call to Interrupt 21H Function 4AH, to maximize the amount of free memory in the system, and then calls the EXEC function to load and execute CHILD.EXE.

CHILD.EXE runs exactly as though it had been loaded directly by COMMAND.COM. CHILD resets the DS segment register to point to its own data segment, uses Interrupt 21H Function 40H to display a message on standard output, and then terminates using Interrupt 21H Function 4CH, passing a return code of zero.

When PARENT.EXE regains control, it first checks the carry flag to determine whether the EXEC call succeeded. If the EXEC call failed, PARENT displays an error message and terminates with Interrupt 21H Function 4CH, itself passing a nonzero return code to COMMAND.COM to indicate an error.

Otherwise, PARENT uses Interrupt 21H Function 4DH to obtain CHILD.EXE's termination type and return code, which it converts to ASCII and displays. PARENT then terminates using Interrupt 21H Function 4CH and passes a return code of zero to COMMAND.COM to indicate success. COMMAND.COM in turn receives control and displays a new user prompt.

Using EXEC to Load Overlays

Loading overlays with the EXEC function is much less complex than using EXEC to run another program. The main program, called the root segment, must carry out the following steps to load and execute an overlay:

1. Make a memory block available to receive the overlay.
2. Set up the overlay parameter block to be passed to the EXEC function.
3. Call the EXEC function to load the overlay.
4. Execute the code within the overlay by transferring to it with a far call.

The overlay itself can be constructed as either a memory image (.COM) or a relocatable (.EXE) file and need not be the same type as the root program. In either case, the overlay should be designed so that the entry point (or a pointer to the entry point) is at the beginning of the module after it is loaded. This allows the root and overlay modules to be maintained separately and avoids a need for the root to have "magical" knowledge of addresses within the overlay.

To prevent users from inadvertently running an overlay directly from the command line, overlay files should be assigned an extension other than .COM or .EXE. The most convenient method relates overlays to their root segment by assigning them the same filename but an extension such as .OVL or .OV1, .OV2, and so on.

Making memory available

If EXEC is to load a child program successfully, the parent must release memory. In contrast, EXEC loads an overlay into memory that *belongs* to the calling program. If the root segment is a .COM program and has not explicitly released extra memory, the root segment program need only ensure that the system contains enough memory to load the overlay and that the overlay load address does not conflict with its own code, data, or stack areas.

If the root segment program was loaded from a .EXE file, no straightforward way exists for it to determine unequivocally how much memory it already owns. The simplest course is for the program to release all extra memory, as discussed earlier in the section on loading a child program, and then use the MS-DOS memory allocation function (Interrupt 21H Function 48H) to obtain a new block of memory that is large enough to hold the overlay.

Preparing overlay parameters

When it is used to load an overlay, the EXEC function requires two major parameters:

● The address of the pathname for the overlay file
● The address of an overlay parameter block

As for a child program, the pathname for the overlay file must be an unambiguous ASCIIZ file specification (again, no wildcard characters), and it must include an explicit extension. As before, if a path and/or drive are not included in the pathname, the current directory and default drive are used.

The overlay parameter block contains the segment address at which the overlay should be loaded and a fixup value to be applied to any relocatable items within the overlay file. If the overlay file is in .EXE format, the fixup value is typically the same as the load address; if the overlay is in memory-image (.COM) format, the fixup value should be zero. The EXEC function does not attempt to validate the load address or the fixup value or to ensure that the load address actually belongs to the calling program.

Loading and executing the overlay

After the root segment program has prepared the filename of the overlay file and the overlay parameter block, it can invoke the EXEC function to load the overlay by issuing an Interrupt 21H with the registers set as follows:

```
AH       = 4BH
AL       = 03H (EXEC subfunction to load overlay)
DS:DX    = segment:offset of overlay file pathname
ES:BX    = segment:offset of overlay parameter block
```

Upon return from Interrupt 21H, the root segment must test the carry flag to determine whether the overlay was loaded. If the carry flag is clear, the overlay file was located and brought into memory at the requested address. The overlay can then be entered by a far call and should exit back to the root segment with a far return.

If the carry flag is set, the overlay file was not found or some other (probably severe) system problem was encountered, and the AX register contains an error code. With MS-DOS versions 3.0 and later, Interrupt 21H Function 59H can be used to get more information about the EXEC failure. An invalid load address supplied in the overlay parameter block does not (usually) cause the EXEC function itself to fail but may result in the disconcerting message *Memory Allocation Error, System Halted* when the root program terminates.

An overlay example

The source programs ROOT.ASM in Figure 10-5 and OVERLAY.ASM in Figure 10-6 demonstrate the use of EXEC to load a program overlay. The program ROOT.EXE is executable from the MS-DOS prompt; it represents the root segment of an application. OVERLAY is constructed as a .EXE file (although it is named OVERLAY.OVL because it cannot be run alone) and represents a subprogram that can be loaded by the root segment when and if it is needed.

```
        name      root
        title     'ROOT --- demonstrate EXEC overlay'
;
; ROOT.EXE --- demonstration of EXEC for overlays
;
; Uses MS-DOS EXEC (Int 21H Function 4BH Subfunction 03H)
; to load an overlay named OVERLAY.OVL, calls a routine
; within the OVERLAY, then recovers control and terminates.
;
; Ray Duncan, June 1987
;

stdin   equ     0                       ; standard input
stdout  equ     1                       ; standard output
stderr  equ     2                       ; standard error

stksize equ     128                     ; size of stack

cr      equ     0dh                     ; ASCII carriage return
lf      equ     0ah                     ; ASCII linefeed


DGROUP  group   _DATA,_STACK


_TEXT   segment byte public 'CODE'      ; executable code segment

        assume  cs:_TEXT,ds:_DATA,ss:_STACK


stk_seg dw      ?                       ; original SS contents
stk_ptr dw      ?                       ; original SP contents
```

Figure 10-5. ROOT.ASM, source code for ROOT.EXE.   (more)

```
main    proc    far                     ; entry point from MS-DOS

        mov     ax,_DATA                ; set DS = our data segment
        mov     ds,ax

                                        ; now give back extra memory
        mov     ax,es                   ; AX = segment of PSP base
        mov     bx,ss                   ; BX = segment of stack base
        sub     bx,ax                   ; reserve seg stack - seg psp
        add     bx,stksize/16           ; plus paragraphs of stack
        mov     ah,4ah                  ; fxn 4AH = modify memory block
        int     21h                     ; transfer to MS-DOS
        jc      main1                   ; jump if resize failed

                                        ; display message 'Root
                                        ; segment executing...'
        mov     dx,offset DGROUP:msg1   ; DS:DX = address of message
        mov     cx,msg1_len             ; CX = length of message
        call    pmsg

                                        ; allocate memory for overlay
        mov     bx,1000h                ; get 64 KB (4096 paragraphs)
        mov     ah,48h                  ; fxn 48H, allocate mem block
        int     21h                     ; transfer to MS-DOS
        jc      main2                   ; jump if allocation failed

        mov     pars,ax                 ; set load address for overlay
        mov     pars+2,ax               ; set relocation segment for overlay
        mov     word ptr entry+2,ax     ; set segment of entry point

        push    ds                      ; save root's data segment
        mov     stk_seg,ss              ; save root's stack pointer
        mov     stk_ptr,sp

                                        ; now use EXEC to load overlay
        mov     ax,ds                   ; set ES = DS
        mov     es,ax
        mov     dx,offset DGROUP:oname  ; DS:DX = overlay pathname
        mov     bx,offset DGROUP:pars   ; ES:BX = parameter block
        mov     ax,4b03h                ; function 4BH, subfunction 03H
        int     21h                     ; transfer to MS-DOS

        cli                             ; (for bug in some early 8088s)
        mov     ss,stk_seg              ; restore root's stack pointer
        mov     sp,stk_ptr
        sti                             ; (for bug in some early 8088s)
        pop     ds                      ; restore DS = our data segment

        jc      main3                   ; jump if EXEC failed

                                        ; otherwise EXEC succeeded...
```

Figure 10-5. Continued.   *(more)*

```
            push    ds                          ; save our data segment
            call    dword ptr entry             ; now call the overlay
            pop     ds                          ; restore our data segment

                                                ; display message that root
                                                ; segment regained control...
            mov     dx,offset DGROUP:msg5       ; DS:DX = address of message
            mov     cx,msg5_len                 ; CX = length of message
            call    pmsg                        ; display it

            mov     ax,4c00h                    ; no error, terminate program
            int     21h                         ; with return code = 0

main1:      mov     bx,offset DGROUP:msg2a      ; convert error code
            call    b2hex
            mov     dx,offset DGROUP:msg2       ; display message 'Memory
            mov     cx,msg2_len                 ; resize failed...'
            call    pmsg
            jmp     main4

main2:      mov     bx,offset DGROUP:msg3a      ; convert error code
            call    b2hex
            mov     dx,offset DGROUP:msg3       ; display message 'Memory
            mov     cx,msg3_len                 ; allocation failed...'
            call    pmsg
            jmp     main4

main3:      mov     bx,offset DGROUP:msg4a      ; convert error code
            call    b2hex
            mov     dx,offset DGROUP:msg4       ; display message 'EXEC
            mov     cx,msg4_len                 ; call failed...'
            call    pmsg

main4:      mov     ax,4c01h                    ; error, terminate program
            int     21h                         ; with return code = 1

main        endp                                ; end of main procedure


b2hex       proc    near                        ; convert byte to hex ASCII
                                                ; call with AL = binary value
                                                ; BX = addr to store string
            push    ax
            shr     al,1
            shr     al,1
            shr     al,1
            shr     al,1
            call    ascii                       ; become first ASCII character
            mov     [bx],al                     ; store it
            pop     ax
```

Figure 10-5. Continued.   *(more)*

```
              and     al,0fh               ; isolate lower 4 bits, which
              call    ascii                ; become the second ASCII character
              mov     [bx+1],al            ; store it
              ret
    b2hex     endp


    ascii     proc    near                 ; convert value 00-0FH in AL
              add     al,'0'               ; into a "hex ASCII" character
              cmp     al,'9'
              jle     ascii2               ; jump if in range 00-09H,
              add     al,'A'-'9'-1         ; offset it to range 0A-0FH,
    ascii2:   ret                          ; return ASCII char. in AL.
    ascii     endp


    pmsg      proc    near                 ; displays message on standard output
                                           ; call with DS:DX = address,
                                           ;            CX = length

              mov     bx,stdout            ; BX = standard output handle
              mov     ah,40h               ; function 40H = write file/device
              int     21h                  ; transfer to MS-DOS
              ret                          ; back to caller

    pmsg      endp

    _TEXT     ends


    _DATA     segment para public 'DATA'   ; static & variable data segment

    oname     db      'OVERLAY.OVL',0      ; pathname of overlay file

    pars      dw      0                    ; load address (segment) for file
              dw      0                    ; relocation (segment) for file

    entry     dd      0                    ; entry point for overlay

    msg1      db      cr,lf,'Root segment executing!',cr,lf
    msg1_len equ      $-msg1

    msg2      db      cr,lf,'Memory resize failed, error code='
    msg2a     db      'xxh.',cr,lf
    msg2_len equ      $-msg2

    msg3      db      cr,lf,'Memory allocation failed, error code='
    msg3a     db      'xxh.',cr,lf
    msg3_len equ      $-msg3
```

Figure 10-5. Continued.   (more)

```
msg4       db      cr,lf,'EXEC call failed, error code='
msg4a      db      'xxh.',cr,lf
msg4_len equ      $-msg4

msg5       db      cr,lf,'Root segment regained control!',cr,lf
msg5_len equ      $-msg5

_DATA    ends


_STACK   segment para stack 'STACK'

         db      stksize dup (?)

_STACK   ends


         end     main                    ; defines program entry point
```

Figure 10-5. Continued.


```
         name       overlay
         title      'OVERLAY segment'
;
; OVERLAY.OVL --- a simple overlay segment
; loaded by ROOT.EXE to demonstrate use of
; the MS-DOS EXEC call Subfunction 03H.
;
; The overlay does not contain a STACK segment
; because it uses the ROOT segment's stack.
;
; Ray Duncan, June 1987
;

stdin    equ    0               ; standard input
stdout   equ    1               ; standard output
stderr   equ    2               ; standard error

cr       equ    0dh             ; ASCII carriage return
lf       equ    0ah             ; ASCII linefeed


_TEXT    segment byte public 'CODE'      ; executable code segment

         assume  cs:_TEXT,ds:_DATA
ovlay    proc    far                     ; entry point from root segment

         mov     ax,_DATA                ; set DS = local data segment
         mov     ds,ax
```

Figure 10-6. OVERLAY.ASM, source code for OVERLAY.OVL. *(more)*

```
                                      ; display overlay message ...
            mov     dx,offset msg     ; DS:DX = address of message
            mov     cx,msg_len        ; CX = length of message
            mov     bx,stdout         ; BX = standard output handle
            mov     ah,40h            ; AH = fxn 40H, write file/device
            int     21h               ; transfer to MS-DOS

            ret                       ; return to root segment

ovlay       endp                      ; end of ovlay procedure

_TEXT       ends


_DATA       segment para public 'DATA'     ; static & variable data segment

msg         db      cr,lf,'Overlay executing!',cr,lf
msg_len equ         $-msg

_DATA       ends

            end
```

Figure 10-6. Continued.

ROOT.ASM can be assembled and linked into the executable program ROOT.EXE with the following commands:

```
C>MASM ROOT;   <Enter>
C>LINK ROOT;   <Enter>
```

OVERLAY.ASM can be assembled and linked into the file OVERLAY.OVL by typing

```
C>MASM OVERLAY;   <Enter>
C>LINK OVERLAY,OVERLAY.OVL;   <Enter>
```

The Microsoft Object Linker will display the message

```
Warning: no stack segment
```

but this message can be ignored.

When ROOT.EXE is executed with the command

```
C>ROOT   <Enter>
```

it first shrinks its main memory block with a call to Interrupt 21H Function 4AH and then allocates a separate block for the overlay with Interrupt 21H Function 48H. Next, ROOT calls the EXEC function to load the file OVERLAY.OVL into the newly allocated memory block. If the EXEC function fails, ROOT displays an error message and terminates with Interrupt 21H Function 4CH, passing a nonzero return code to COMMAND.COM to indicate an error. If the EXEC function succeeds, ROOT saves the contents of its DS segment register and then enters the overlay through an indirect far call.

The overlay resets the DS segment register to point to its own data segment, displays a message using Interrupt 21H Function 40H, and then returns. Note that the main procedure of the overlay is declared with the far attribute to force the assembler to generate the opcode for a far return.

When ROOT regains control, it restores the DS segment register to point to its own data segment again and displays an additional message, also using Interrupt 21H Function 40H, to indicate that the overlay executed successfully. ROOT then terminates using Interrupt 21H Function 4CH, passing a return code of zero to indicate success, and control returns to COMMAND.COM.

Ray Duncan

Part C
Customizing MS-DOS

Article 11
Terminate-and-Stay-Resident Utilities

The MS-DOS Terminate and Stay Resident system calls (Interrupt 21H Function 31H and Interrupt 27H) allow the programmer to install executable code or program data in a reserved block of RAM, where it resides while other programs execute. Global data, interrupt handlers, and entire applications can be made RAM-resident in this way. Programs that use the MS-DOS terminate-and-stay-resident capability are commonly known as TSR programs or TSRs.

This article describes how to install a TSR in RAM, how to communicate with the resident program, and how the resident program can interact with MS-DOS. The discussion proceeds from a general description of the MS-DOS functions useful to TSR programmers to specific details about certain MS-DOS structural elements necessary to proper functioning of a TSR utility and concludes with two programming examples.

Note: Microsoft cannot guarantee that the information in this article will be valid for future versions of MS-DOS.

Structure of a Terminate-and-Stay-Resident Utility

The executable code and data in TSRs can be separated into RAM-resident and transient portions (Figure 11-1). The RAM-resident portion of a TSR contains executable code and data for an application that performs some useful function on demand. The transient portion installs the TSR; that is, it initializes data and interrupt handlers contained in the RAM-resident portion of the program and executes an MS-DOS Terminate and Stay Resident function call that leaves the RAM-resident portion in memory and frees the memory used by the transient portion. The code in the transient portion of a TSR runs when the .EXE or .COM file containing the program is executed; the code in the RAM-resident portion runs only when it is explicitly invoked by a foreground program or by execution of a hardware or software interrupt.

TSRs can be broadly classified as passive or active, depending on the method by which control is transferred to the RAM-resident program. A passive TSR executes only when another program explicitly transfers control to it, either through a software interrupt or by means of a long JMP or CALL. The calling program is not interrupted by the TSR, so the status of MS-DOS, the system BIOS, and the hardware is well defined when the TSR program starts to execute.

In contrast, an active TSR is invoked by the occurrence of some event external to the currently running (foreground) program, such as a sequence of user keystrokes or a predefined hardware interrupt. Therefore, when it is invoked, an active TSR almost always

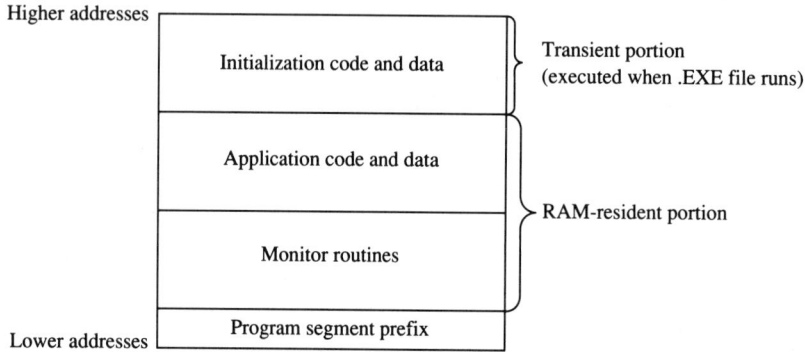

Higher addresses

Initialization code and data — Transient portion (executed when .EXE file runs)

Application code and data

RAM-resident portion

Monitor routines

Program segment prefix

Lower addresses

Figure 11-1. Organization of a TSR program in memory.

interrupts some other program and suspends its execution. To avoid disrupting the interrupted program, an active TSR must monitor the status of MS-DOS, the ROM BIOS, and the hardware and take control of the system only when it is safe to do so.

Passive TSRs are generally simpler in their construction than active TSRs because a passive TSR runs in the context of the calling program; that is, when the TSR executes, it assumes that it can use the calling program's program segment prefix (PSP), open files, current directory, and so on. *See* PROGRAMMING IN THE MS-DOS ENVIRONMENT: PROGRAMMING FOR MS-DOS: Structure of an Application Program. It is the calling program's responsibility to ensure that the hardware and MS-DOS are in a stable state before it transfers control to a passive TSR.

An active TSR, on the other hand, is invoked asynchronously; that is, the status of the hardware, MS-DOS, and the executing foreground program is indeterminate when the event that invokes the TSR occurs. Therefore, active TSRs require more complex code. The RAM-resident portion of an active TSR must contain modules that monitor the operating system to determine when control can safely be transferred to the application portion of the TSR. The monitor routines typically test the status of keyboard input, ROM BIOS interrupt processing, hardware interrupt processing, and MS-DOS function processing. The TSR activates the application (the part of the RAM-resident portion that performs the TSR's main task) only when it detects the appropriate keyboard input and determines that the application will not interfere with interrupt and MS-DOS function processing.

Keyboard input

An active TSR usually contains a RAM-resident module that examines keyboard input for a predetermined keystroke sequence called a "hot-key" sequence. A user executes the RAM-resident application by entering this hot-key sequence at the keyboard.

The technique used in the TSR to monitor keyboard input depends on the keyboard hardware implementation. On computers in the IBM PC and PS/2 families, the keyboard coprocessor generates an Interrupt 09H for each keypress. Therefore, a TSR can monitor user keystrokes by installing an interrupt handler (interrupt service routine, or ISR) for Interrupt 09H. This handler can thus detect a specified hot-key sequence.

ROM BIOS interrupt processing

The ROM BIOS routines in IBM PCs and PS/2s are not reentrant. An active TSR that calls the ROM BIOS must ensure that its code does not attempt to execute a ROM BIOS function that was already being executed by the foreground process when the TSR program took control of the system.

The IBM ROM BIOS routines are invoked through software interrupts, so an active TSR can monitor the status of the ROM BIOS by replacing the default interrupt handlers with custom interrupt handlers that intercept the appropriate BIOS interrupts. Each of these interrupt handlers can maintain a status flag, which it increments before transferring control to the corresponding ROM BIOS routine and decrements when the ROM BIOS routine has finished executing. Thus, the TSR monitor routines can test these flags to determine when non-reentrant BIOS routines are executing.

Hardware interrupt processing

The monitor routines of an active TSR, which may themselves be executed as the result of a hardware interrupt, should not activate the application portion of the TSR if any other hardware interrupt is being processed. On IBM PCs, for example, hardware interrupts are processed in a prioritized sequence determined by an Intel 8259A Programmable Interrupt Controller. The 8259A does not allow a hardware interrupt to execute if a previous interrupt with the same or higher priority is being serviced. All hardware interrupt handlers include code that signals the 8259A when interrupt processing is completed. (The programming interface to the 8259A is described in IBM's *Technical Reference* manuals and in Intel's technical literature.)

If a TSR were to interrupt the execution of another hardware interrupt handler before the handler signaled the 8259A that it had completed its interrupt servicing, subsequent hardware interrupts could be inhibited indefinitely. Inhibition of high-priority hardware interrupts such as the timer tick (Interrupt 08H) or keyboard interrupt (Interrupt 09H) could cause a system crash. For this reason, an active TSR must monitor the status of all hardware interrupt processing by interrogating the 8259A to ensure that control is transferred to the RAM-resident application only when no other hardware interrupts are being serviced.

MS-DOS function processing

Unlike the IBM ROM BIOS routines, MS-DOS is reentrant to a limited extent. That is, there are certain times when MS-DOS's servicing of an Interrupt 21H function call invoked by a foreground process can be suspended so that the RAM-resident application can make an Interrupt 21H function call of its own. For this reason, an active TSR must monitor operating system activity to determine when it is safe for the TSR application to make its calls to MS-DOS.

MS-DOS Support for Terminate-and-Stay-Resident Programs

Several MS-DOS system calls are useful for supporting terminate-and-stay-resident utilities. These are listed in Table 11-1. *See* SYSTEM CALLS.

Table 11-1. MS-DOS Functions Useful in TSR Programs.

Function Name	Call With	Returns	Comment
Terminate and Stay Resident	AH = 31H AL = return code DX = size of resident program (in 16-byte paragraphs) INT 21H	Nothing	Preferred over Interrupt 27H with MS-DOS versions 2.x and later
Terminate and Stay Resident	CS = PSP DX = size of resident program (bytes) INT 27H	Nothing	Provided for compatibility with MS-DOS versions 1.x
Set Interrupt Vector	AH = 25H AL = interrupt number DS:DX = address of interrupt handler INT 21H	Nothing	
Get Interrupt Vector	AH = 35H AL = interrupt number INT 21H	ES:BX = address of interrupt handler	
Set PSP Address	AH = 50H BX = PSP segment INT 21H	Nothing	
Get PSP Address	AH = 51H INT 21H	BX = PSP segment	

Set Extended Error Information	AX = 5D0AH
	DS:DX = address of 11-word data structure:
	    word 0: register AX
	        as returned by Function 59H
	    word 1: register BX
	    word 2: register CX
	    word 3: register DX
	    word 4: register SI
	    word 5: register DI
	    word 6: register DS
	    word 7: register ES
	    words 8–0AH: reserved; should be 0
	INT 21H
		Nothing	MS-DOS versions 3.1 and later

(more)

Table 11-1. *Continued.*

Function Name	Call With	Returns	Comment
Get Extended Error Information	AH = 59H BX = 0 INT 21H	AX = extended error code BH = error class BL = suggested action CH = error locus	
Set Disk Transfer Area Address	AH = 1AH DS:DX = address of DTA INT 21H	Nothing	
Get Disk Transfer Area Address	AH = 2FH INT 21H	ES:BX = address of current DTA	
Get InDOS Flag Address	AH = 34H INT 21H	ES:BX = address of InDOS flag	

Terminate-and-stay-resident functions

MS-DOS provides two mechanisms for terminating the execution of a program while leaving a portion of it resident in RAM. The preferred method is to execute Interrupt 21H Function 31H.

Interrupt 21H Function 31H

When this Interrupt 21H function is called, the value in DX specifies the amount of RAM (in paragraphs) that is to remain allocated after the program terminates, starting at the program segment prefix (PSP). The function is similar to Function 4CH (Terminate Process with Return Code) in that it passes a return code in AL, but it differs in that open files are not automatically closed by Function 31H.

Interrupt 27H

When Interrupt 27H is executed, the value passed in DX specifies the number of bytes of memory required for the RAM-resident program. MS-DOS converts the value passed in DX from bytes to paragraphs, sets AL to zero, and jumps to the same code that would be executed for Interrupt 21H Function 31H. Interrupt 27H is less flexible than Interrupt 21H Function 31H because it limits the size of the program that can remain resident in RAM to 64 KB, it requires that CS point to the base of the PSP, and it does not pass a return code. Later versions of MS-DOS support Interrupt 27H primarily for compatibility with versions 1.x.

TSR RAM management

In addition to the RAM explicitly allocated to the TSR by means of the value in DX, the RAM allocated to the TSR's environment remains resident when the installation portion of the TSR program terminates. (The paragraph address of the environment is found at offset 2CH in the TSR's PSP.) Moreover, if the installation portion of a TSR program has used Interrupt 21H Function 48H (Allocate Memory Block) to allocate additional RAM, this memory also remains allocated when the program terminates. If the RAM-resident program does not need this additional RAM, the installation portion of the TSR program should free it explicitly by using Interrupt 21H Function 49H (Free Memory Block) before executing Interrupt 21H Function 31H.

Set and Get Interrupt Vector functions

Two Interrupt 21H function calls are available to inspect or update the contents of a specified 8086-family interrupt vector. Function 25H (Set Interrupt Vector) updates the vector of the interrupt number specified in the AL register with the segment and offset values specified in DS:DX. Function 35H (Get Interrupt Vector) performs the inverse operation: It copies the current vector of the interrupt number specified in AL into the ES:BX register pair.

Although it is possible to manipulate interrupt vectors directly, the use of Interrupt 21H Functions 25H and 35H is generally more convenient and allows for upward compatibility with future versions of MS-DOS.

Set and Get PSP Address functions

MS-DOS uses a program's PSP to keep track of certain data unique to the program, including command-line parameters and the segment address of the program's environment. *See* PROGRAMMING IN THE MS-DOS ENVIRONMENT: PROGRAMMING FOR MS-DOS: Structure of an Application Program. To access this information, MS-DOS maintains an internal variable that always contains the location of the PSP associated with the foreground process. When a RAM-resident application is activated, it should use Interrupt 21H Functions 50H (Set Program Segment Prefix Address) and 51H (Get Program Segment Prefix Address) to preserve the current contents of this variable and to update the variable with the location of its own PSP. Function 50H (Set Program Segment Prefix Address) updates an internal MS-DOS variable that locates the PSP currently in use by the foreground process. Function 51H (Get Program Segment Prefix Address) returns the contents of the internal MS-DOS variable to the caller.

Set and Get Extended Error Information functions

In MS-DOS versions 3.1 and later, the RAM-resident program should preserve the foreground process's extended error information so that, if the RAM-resident application encounters an MS-DOS error, the extended error information pertaining to the foreground process will still be available and can be restored. Interrupt 21H Functions 59H and 5D0AH provide a mechanism for the RAM-resident program to save and restore this information during execution of a TSR application.

Function 59H (Get Extended Error Information), which became available in version 3.0, returns detailed information on the most recently detected MS-DOS error. The inverse operation is performed by Function 5D0AH (Set Extended Error Information), which can be used only in MS-DOS versions 3.1 and later. This function copies extended error information to MS-DOS from a data structure defined in the calling program.

Set and Get Disk Transfer Area Address functions

Several MS-DOS data transfer functions, notably Interrupt 21H Functions 21H, 22H, 27H, and 28H (the Random Read and Write functions) and Interrupt 21H Functions 14H and 15H (the Sequential Read and Write functions), require a program to specify a disk transfer area (DTA). By default, a program's DTA is located at offset 80H in its program segment prefix. If a RAM-resident application calls an MS-DOS function that uses a DTA, the TSR should save the DTA address belonging to the interrupted program by using Interrupt 21H Function 2FH (Get Disk Transfer Area Address), supply its own DTA address to MS-DOS using Interrupt 21H Function 1AH (Set Disk Transfer Area Address), and then, before terminating, restore the interrupted program's DTA.

The MS-DOS idle interrupt (Interrupt 28H)

Several of the first 12 MS-DOS functions (01H through 0CH) must wait for the occurrence of an expected event such as a user keypress. These functions contain an "idle loop" in which looping continues until the event occurs. To provide a mechanism for other system activity to take place while the idle loop is executing, these MS-DOS functions execute an Interrupt 28H from within the loop.

The default MS-DOS handler for Interrupt 28H is only an IRET instruction. By supplying its own handler for Interrupt 28H, a TSR can perform some useful action at times when MS-DOS is otherwise idle. Specifically, a custom Interrupt 28H handler can be used to examine the current status of the system to determine whether or not it is safe to activate the RAM-resident application.

Determining MS-DOS Status

A TSR can infer the current status of MS-DOS from knowledge of its internal use of stacks and from a pair of internal status flags. This status information is essential to the proper execution of an active TSR because a RAM-resident application can make calls to MS-DOS only when those calls will not disrupt an earlier call made by the foreground process.

MS-DOS internal stacks

MS-DOS versions 2.0 and later may use any of three internal stacks: the I/O stack (*IOStack*), the disk stack (*DiskStack*), and the auxiliary stack (*AuxStack*). In general, *IOStack* is used for Interrupt 21H Functions 01H through 0CH and *DiskStack* is used for the remaining Interrupt 21H functions; *AuxStack* is normally used only when MS-DOS has detected a critical error and subsequently executed an Interrupt 24H. *See* PROGRAMMING IN THE MS-DOS ENVIRONMENT: Customizing ms-dos: Exception Handlers. Specifically, MS-DOS's internal stack use depends on which MS-DOS function is being executed and on the value of the critical error flag.

The critical error flag

The critical error flag (*ErrorMode*) is a 1-byte flag that MS-DOS uses to indicate whether or not a critical error has occurred. During normal, errorless execution, the value of the critical error flag is zero. Whenever MS-DOS detects a critical error, it sets this flag to a nonzero value before it executes Interrupt 24H. If an Interrupt 24H handler subsequently invokes an MS-DOS function by using Interrupt 21H, the nonzero value of the critical error flag tells MS-DOS to use its auxiliary stack for Interrupt 21H Functions 01H through 0CH instead of using the I/O stack as it normally would.

In other words, when control is transferred to MS-DOS through Interrupt 21H, the function number and the critical error flag together determine MS-DOS stack use for the function. Figure 11-2 outlines the internal logic used on entry to an MS-DOS function to select which stack is to be used during processing of the function. As stated above, for Functions 01H through 0CH, MS-DOS uses *IOStack* if the critical error flag is zero and *AuxStack* if the flag is nonzero. For function numbers greater than 0CH, MS-DOS usually uses *DiskStack*, but Functions 50H, 51H, and 59H are important exceptions. Functions 50H and 51H use either *IOStack* (in versions 2.x) or the stack supplied by the calling program (in versions 3.x). In version 3.0, Function 59H uses either *IOStack* or *AuxStack*, depending on the value of the critical error flag, but in versions 3.1 and later, Function 59H always uses *AuxStack*.

MS-DOS versions 2.x

```
if    (FunctionNumber >= 01H and FunctionNumber <= 0CH)
      or
      FunctionNumber = 50H
      or
      FunctionNumber = 51H

then if   ErrorMode = 0
      then use IOStack
      else use AuxStack

else ErrorMode = 0
      use DiskStack
```

MS-DOS version 3.0

```
if    FunctionNumber = 50H
      or
      FunctionNumber = 51H
      or
      FunctionNumber = 62H

then use caller's stack

else if   (FunctionNumber >= 01H and FunctionNumber <= 0CH)
          or
          Function Number = 59H

      then if   ErrorMode = 0
           then use IOStack
           else use AuxStack

      else ErrorMode = 0
           use DiskStack
```

Figure 11-2. Strategy for use of MS-DOS internal stacks.   (more)

MS-DOS versions 3.1 and later

```
if    FunctionNumber = 33H
      or
      FunctionNumber = 50H
      or
      FunctionNumber = 51H
      or
      FunctionNumber = 62H

then use caller's stack

else if      (FunctionNumber >= 01H and FunctionNumber <= 0CH)

      then if    ErrorMode = 0
           then use IOStack
           else use AuxStack

      else if FunctionNumber = 59H
           then use AuxStack
           else ErrorMode = 0
                use DiskStack
```

Figure 11-2. Continued.

This scheme makes Functions 01H through 0CH reentrant in a limited sense, in that a substitute critical error (Interrupt 24H) handler invoked while the critical error flag is nonzero can still use these Interrupt 21H functions. In this situation, because the flag is nonzero, *AuxStack* is used for Functions 01H through 0CH instead of *IOStack*. Thus, if *IOStack* is in use when the critical error is detected, its contents are preserved during the handler's subsequent calls to these functions.

The stack-selection logic differs slightly between MS-DOS versions 2 and 3. In versions 3.x, a few functions — notably 50H and 51H — avoid using any of the MS-DOS stacks. These functions perform uncomplicated tasks that make minimal demands for stack space, so the calling program's stack is assumed to be adequate for them.

The InDOS flag

InDOS is a 1-byte flag that is incremented each time an Interrupt 21H function is invoked and decremented when the function terminates. The flag's value remains nonzero as long as code within MS-DOS is being executed. The value of InDOS does not indicate which internal stack MS-DOS is using.

Whenever MS-DOS detects a critical error, it zeros InDOS before it executes Interrupt 24H. This action is taken to accommodate substitute Interrupt 24H handlers that do not return control to MS-DOS. If InDOS were not zeroed before such a handler gained control, its value would never be decremented and would therefore be incorrect during subsequent calls to MS-DOS.

The address of the 1-byte InDOS flag can be obtained from MS-DOS by using Interrupt 21H Function 34H (Return Address of InDOS Flag). In versions 3.1 and later, the 1-byte critical error flag is located in the byte preceding InDOS, so, in effect, the address of both flags can be found using Function 34H. Unfortunately, there is no easy way to find the critical error flag in other versions. The recommended technique is to scan the MS-DOS segment, which is returned in the ES register by Function 34H, for one of the following sequences of instructions:

```
test    ss:[CriticalErrorFlag],0FFH       ;(versions 3.1 and later)
jne     NearLabel
push    ss:[NearWord]
int     28H
```

or

```
cmp     ss:[CriticalErrorFlag],00         ;(versions earlier than 3.1)
jne     NearLabel
int     28H
```

When the TEST or CMP instruction has been identified, the offset of the critical error flag can be obtained from the instruction's operand field.

The Multiplex Interrupt

The MS-DOS multiplex interrupt (Interrupt 2FH) provides a general mechanism for a program to verify the presence of a TSR and communicate with it. A program communicates with a TSR by placing an identification value in AH and a function number in AL and issuing an Interrupt 2FH. The TSR's Interrupt 2FH handler compares the value in AH to its own predetermined ID value. If they match, the TSR's handler keeps control and performs the function specified in the AL register. If they do not match, the TSR's handler relinquishes control to the previously installed Interrupt 2FH handler. (Multiplex ID values 00H through 7FH are reserved for use by MS-DOS; therefore, user multiplex numbers should be in the range 80H through 0FFH.)

The handler in the following example recognizes only one function, corresponding to AL = 00H. In this case, the handler returns the value 0FFH in AL, signifying that the handler is indeed resident in RAM. Thus, a program can detect the presence of the handler by executing Interrupt 2FH with the handler's ID value in AH and 00H in AL.

```
mov     ah,MultiplexID
mov     al,00H
int     2FH
cmp     al,0FFH
je      AlreadyInstalled
```

To ensure that the identification byte is unique, its value should be determined at the time the TSR is installed. One way to do this is to pass the value to the TSR program as a command-line parameter when the TSR program is installed. Another approach is to place the identification value in an environment variable. In this way, the value can be found in the environment of both the TSR and any other program that calls Interrupt 2FH to verify the TSR's presence.

In practice, the multiplex interrupt can also be used to pass information to and from a RAM-resident program in the CPU registers, thus providing a mechanism for a program to share control or status information with a TSR.

TSR Programming Examples

One effective way to become familiar with TSRs is to examine functional programs. Therefore, the subsequent pages present two examples: a simple passive TSR and a more complex active TSR.

HELLO.ASM

The "bare-bones" TSR in Figure 11-3 is a passive TSR. The RAM-resident application, which simply displays the message *Hello, World*, is invoked by executing a software interrupt. This example illustrates the fundamental interactions among a RAM-resident program, MS-DOS, and programs that execute after the installation of the RAM-resident utility.

```
;
; Name:          hello
;
; Description:   This RAM-resident (terminate-and-stay-resident) utility
;                displays the message "Hello, World" in response to a
;                software interrupt.
;
; Comments:      Assemble and link to create HELLO.EXE.
;
;                Execute HELLO.EXE to make resident.
;
;                Execute  INT 64h  to display the message.
;


TSRInt          EQU     64h
STDOUT          EQU     1

RESIDENT_TEXT   SEGMENT byte public 'CODE'
                ASSUME  cs:RESIDENT_TEXT,ds:RESIDENT_DATA

TSRAction       PROC    far

                sti                     ; enable interrupts

                push    ds              ; preserve registers
                push    ax
                push    bx
                push    cx
                push    dx
```

Figure 11-3. HELLO.ASM, a passive TSR.   (more)

```
                    mov      dx,seg RESIDENT_DATA
                    mov      ds,dx
                    mov      dx,offset Message        ; DS:DX -> message
                    mov      cx,16                    ; CX = length
                    mov      bx,STDOUT                ; BX = file handle
                    mov      ah,40h                   ; AH = INT 21H function 40H
                                                      ; (Write File)
                    int      21h                      ; display the message

                    pop      dx                       ; restore registers and exit
                    pop      cx
                    pop      bx
                    pop      ax
                    pop      ds
                    iret

TSRAction           ENDP

RESIDENT_TEXT       ENDS


RESIDENT_DATA       SEGMENT word public 'DATA'

Message             DB       0Dh,0Ah,'Hello, World',0Dh,0Ah

RESIDENT_DATA       ENDS


TRANSIENT_TEXT      SEGMENT para public 'TCODE'
                    ASSUME   cs:TRANSIENT_TEXT,ss:TRANSIENT_STACK

HelloTSR PROC       far                      ; At entry:    CS:IP -> SnapTSR
                                             ;              SS:SP -> stack
                                             ;              DS,ES -> PSP
; Install this TSR's interrupt handler

                    mov      ax,seg RESIDENT_TEXT
                    mov      ds,ax
                    mov      dx,offset RESIDENT_TEXT:TSRAction
                    mov      al,TSRInt
                    mov      ah,25h
                    int      21h

; Terminate and stay resident

                    mov      dx,cs           ; DX = paragraph address of start of
                                             ; transient portion (end of resident
                                             ; portion)
                    mov      ax,es           ; ES = PSP segment
                    sub      dx,ax           ; DX = size of resident portion
```

Figure 11-3. Continued.   *(more)*

```
                    mov     ax,3100h        ; AH = INT 21H function number (TSR)
                                            ; AL = 00H (return code)
                    int     21h

HelloTSR            ENDP

TRANSIENT_TEXT      ENDS


TRANSIENT_STACK     SEGMENT word stack 'TSTACK'

                    DB      80h dup(?)

TRANSIENT_STACK     ENDS


                    END     HelloTSR
```

Figure 11-3. Continued.

The transient portion of the program (in the segments *TRANSIENT_TEXT* and *TRANSIENT_STACK*) runs only when the file HELLO.EXE is executed. This installation code updates an interrupt vector to point to the resident application (the procedure *TSRAction*) and then calls Interrupt 21H Function 31H to terminate execution, leaving the segments *RESIDENT_TEXT* and *RESIDENT_DATA* in RAM.

The order in which the code and data segments appear in the listing is important. It ensures that when the program is executed as a .EXE file, the resident code and data are placed in memory at lower addresses than the transient code and data. Thus, when Interrupt 21H Function 31H is called, the memory occupied by the transient portion of the program is freed without disrupting the code and data in the resident portion.

The RAM containing the resident portion of the utility is left intact by MS-DOS during subsequent execution of other programs. Thus, after the TSR has been installed, any program that issues the software interrupt recognized by the TSR (in this example, Interrupt 64H) will transfer control to the routine *TSRAction*, which uses Interrupt 21H Function 40H to display a simple message on standard output.

Part of the reason this example is so short is that it performs no error checking A truly reliable version of the program would check the version of MS-DOS in use, verify that the program was not already installed in memory, and chain to any previously installed interrupt handlers that use the same interrupt vector. (The next program, SNAP.ASM, illustrates these techniques.) However, the primary reason the program is small is that it makes the basic assumption that MS-DOS, the ROM BIOS, and the hardware interrupts are all stable at the time the resident utility is executed.

SNAP.ASM

The preceding assumption is a reliable one in the case of the passive TSR in Figure 11-3, which executes only when it is explicitly invoked by a software interrupt. However, the situation is much more complicated in the case of the active TSR in Figure 11-4. This program is relatively long because it makes no assumptions about the stability of the operating environment. Instead, it monitors the status of MS-DOS, the ROM BIOS, and the hardware interrupts to decide when the RAM-resident application can safely execute.

```
;
; Name:          snap
;
; Description:   This RAM-resident (terminate-and-stay-resident) utility
;                produces a video "snapshot" by copying the contents of the
;                video regeneration buffer to a disk file.  It may be used
;                in 80-column alphanumeric video modes on IBM PCs and PS/2s.
;
; Comments:      Assemble and link to create SNAP.EXE.
;
;                Execute SNAP.EXE to make resident.
;
;                Press Alt-Enter to dump current contents of video buffer
;                to a disk file.
;

MultiplexID       EQU     0CAh              ; unique INT 2FH ID value

TSRStackSize      EQU     100h              ; resident stack size in bytes

KB_FLAG           EQU     17h               ; offset of shift-key status flag in
                                            ; ROM BIOS keyboard data area

KBIns             EQU     80h               ; bit masks for KB_FLAG
KBCaps            EQU     40h
KBNum             EQU     20h
KBScroll          EQU     10h
KBAlt             EQU     8
KBCtl             EQU     4
KBLeft            EQU     2
KBRight           EQU     1

SCEnter           EQU     1Ch

CR                EQU     0Dh
LF                EQU     0Ah
TRUE              EQU     -1
FALSE             EQU     0

                  PAGE
;------------------------------------------------------------------------------
;
; RAM-resident routines
;
;------------------------------------------------------------------------------

RESIDENT_GROUP  GROUP    RESIDENT_TEXT,RESIDENT_DATA,RESIDENT_STACK
```

Figure 11-4. SNAP.ASM, a video snapshot TSR.   *(more)*

```
RESIDENT_TEXT   SEGMENT byte public 'CODE'
                ASSUME  cs:RESIDENT_GROUP,ds:RESIDENT_GROUP


;------------------------------------------------------------------------------
; System verification routines
;------------------------------------------------------------------------------


VerifyDOSState  PROC    near            ; Returns:    carry flag set if MS-DOS
                                        ;                  is busy
                push    ds              ; preserve these registers
                push    bx
                push    ax

                lds     bx,cs:ErrorModeAddr
                mov     ah,[bx]         ; AH = ErrorMode flag

                lds     bx,cs:InDOSAddr
                mov     al,[bx]         ; AL = InDOS flag

                xor     bx,bx           ; BH = 00H, BL = 00H
                cmp     bl,cs:InISR28   ; carry flag set if INT 28H handler
                                        ; is running
                rcl     bl,01h          ; BL = 01H if INT 28H handler is running

                cmp     bx,ax           ; carry flag zero if AH = 00H
                                        ; and AL <= BL
                pop     ax              ; restore registers
                pop     bx
                pop     ds
                ret

VerifyDOSState  ENDP


VerifyIntState  PROC    near            ; Returns:    carry flag set if hardware
                                        ;                  or ROM BIOS unstable

                push    ax              ; preserve AX

; Verify hardware interrupt status by interrogating Intel 8259A Programmable
;   Interrupt Controller

                mov     ax,00001011b    ; AH = 0
                                        ; AL = 0CW3 for Intel 8259A (RR = 1,
                                        ; RIS = 1)
                out     20h,al          ; request 8259A's in-service register
                jmp     short L10       ; wait a few cycles
L10:            in      al,20h          ; AL = hardware interrupts currently
                                        ; being serviced (bit = 1 if in-service)
```

Figure 11-4. Continued.   *(more)*

```
                cmp     ah,al
                jc      L11               ; exit if any hardware interrupts still
                                          ; being serviced

; Verify status of ROM BIOS interrupt handlers

                xor     al,al             ; AL = 00H

                cmp     al,cs:InISR5
                jc      L11               ; exit if currently in INT 05H handler

                cmp     al,cs:InISR9
                jc      L11               ; exit if currently in INT 09H handler

                cmp     al,cs:InISR10
                jc      L11               ; exit if currently in INT 10H handler

                cmp     al,cs:InISR13     ; set carry flag if currently in
                                          ; INT 13H handler
L11:            pop     ax                ; restore AX and return
                ret

VerifyIntState  ENDP


VerifyTSRState  PROC    near              ; Returns: carry flag set if TSR
                                          ;          inactive
                rol     cs:HotFlag,1      ; carry flag set if (HotFlag = TRUE)
                cmc                       ; carry flag set if (HotFlag = FALSE)
                jc      L20               ; exit if no hot key

                ror     cs:ActiveTSR,1    ; carry flag set if (ActiveTSR = TRUE)
                jc      L20               ; exit if already active

                call    VerifyDOSState
                jc      L20               ; exit if MS-DOS unstable

                call    VerifyIntState    ; set carry flag if hardware or BIOS
                                          ; unstable
L20:            ret

VerifyTSRState  ENDP

                PAGE
;-------------------------------------------------------------------------------
; System monitor routines
;-------------------------------------------------------------------------------

ISR5            PROC    far               ; INT 05H handler
                                          ; (ROM BIOS print screen)
                inc     cs:InISR5         ; increment status flag
```

Figure 11-4. Continued.   *(more)*

```
                    pushf
                    cli
                    call    cs:PrevISR5     ; chain to previous INT 05H handler

                    dec     cs:InISR5       ; decrement status flag
                    iret

ISR5                ENDP


ISR8                PROC    far             ; INT 08H handler (timer tick, IRQ0)

                    pushf
                    cli
                    call    cs:PrevISR8     ; chain to previous handler

                    cmp     cs:InISR8,0
                    jne     L31             ; exit if already in this handler

                    inc     cs:InISR8       ; increment status flag

                    sti                     ; interrupts are ok
                    call    VerifyTSRState
                    jc      L30             ; jump if TSR is inactive

                    mov     byte ptr cs:ActiveTSR,TRUE
                    call    TSRapp
                    mov     byte ptr cs:ActiveTSR,FALSE

L30:                dec     cs:InISR8

L31:                iret

ISR8                ENDP


ISR9                PROC    far             ; INT 09H handler
                                            ; (keyboard interrupt IRQ1)
                    push    ds              ; preserve these registers
                    push    ax
                    push    bx

                    push    cs
                    pop     ds              ; DS -> RESIDENT_GROUP

                    in      al,60h          ; AL = current scan code

                    pushf                   ; simulate an INT
                    cli
                    call    ds:PrevISR9     ; let previous handler execute
```

Figure 11-4. Continued.   *(more)*

```
                mov     ah,ds:InISR9     ; if already in this handler ..
                or      ah,ds:HotFlag    ; .. or currently processing hot key ..
                jnz     L43              ; .. jump to exit

                inc     ds:InISR9        ; increment status flag
                sti                      ; now interrupts are ok

; Check scan code sequence

                cmp     ds:HotSeqLen,0
                je      L40              ; jump if no hot sequence to match

                mov     bx,ds:HotIndex
                cmp     al,[bx+HotSequence]      ; test scan code sequence
                jne     L41              ; jump if no match

                inc     bx
                cmp     bx,ds:HotSeqLen
                jb      L42              ; jump if not last scan code to match

; Check shift-key state

L40:            push    ds
                mov     ax,40h
                mov     ds,ax            ; DS -> ROM BIOS data area
                mov     al,ds:[KB_FLAG]  ; AH = ROM BIOS shift-key flags
                pop     ds

                and     al,ds:HotKBMask  ; AL = flags AND "don't care" mask
                cmp     al,ds:HotKBFlag
                jne     L42              ; jump if shift state does not match

; Set flag when hot key is found

                mov     byte ptr ds:HotFlag,TRUE

L41:            xor     bx,bx            ; reinitialize index

L42:            mov     ds:HotIndex,bx   ; update index into sequence
                dec     ds:InISR9        ; decrement status flag

L43:            pop     bx               ; restore registers and exit
                pop     ax
                pop     ds
                iret

ISR9            ENDP
```

Figure 11-4. Continued.   *(more)*

```
ISR10           PROC    far             ; INT 10H handler (ROM BIOS video I/O)

                inc     cs:InISR10      ; increment status flag

                pushf
                cli
                call    cs:PrevISR10    ; chain to previous INT 10H handler

                dec     cs:InISR10      ; decrement status flag
                iret

ISR10           ENDP


ISR13           PROC    far             ; INT 13H handler
                                        ; (ROM BIOS fixed disk I/O)
                inc     cs:InISR13      ; increment status flag

                pushf
                cli
                call    cs:PrevISR13    ; chain to previous INT 13H handler

                pushf                   ; preserve returned flags
                dec     cs:InISR13      ; decrement status flag
                popf                    ; restore flags register

                sti                     ; enable interrupts
                ret     2               ; simulate IRET without popping flags

ISR13           ENDP


ISR1B           PROC    far             ; INT 1BH trap (ROM BIOS Ctrl-Break)

                mov     byte ptr cs:Trap1B,TRUE
                iret

ISR1B           ENDP


ISR23           PROC    far             ; INT 23H trap (MS-DOS Ctrl-C)

                mov     byte ptr cs:Trap23,TRUE
                iret

ISR23           ENDP


ISR24           PROC    far             ; INT 24H trap (MS-DOS critical error)

                mov     byte ptr cs:Trap24,TRUE
```

Figure 11-4. Continued.   *(more)*

```
                    xor     al,al           ; AL = 00H (MS-DOS 2.x):
                    cmp     cs:MajorVersion,2 ; ignore the error
                    je      L50

                    mov     al,3            ; AL = 03H (MS-DOS 3.x):
                                            ; fail the MS-DOS call in which
                                            ; the critical error occurred

L50:                iret

ISR24               ENDP


ISR28               PROC    far             ; INT 28H handler
                                            ; (MS-DOS idle interrupt)
                    pushf
                    cli
                    call    cs:PrevISR28    ; chain to previous INT 28H handler

                    cmp     cs:InISR28,0
                    jne     L61             ; exit if already inside this handler

                    inc     cs:InISR28      ; increment status flag

                    call    VerifyTSRState
                    jc      L60             ; jump if TSR is inactive

                    mov     byte ptr cs:ActiveTSR,TRUE
                    call    TSRapp
                    mov     byte ptr cs:ActiveTSR,FALSE

L60:                dec     cs:InISR28      ; decrement status flag

L61:                iret

ISR28               ENDP


ISR2F               PROC    far             ; INT 2FH handler
                                            ; (MS-DOS multiplex interrupt)
                                            ; Caller:  AH = handler ID
                                            ;          AL = function number
                                            ; Returns for function 0:  AL = 0FFH
                                            ; for all other functions:  nothing

                    cmp     ah,MultiplexID
                    je      L70             ; jump if this handler is requested

                    jmp     cs:PrevISR2F    ; chain to previous INT 2FH handler
```

Figure 11-4. Continued.   *(more)*

```
L70:            test    al,al
                jnz     MultiplexIRET   ; jump if reserved or undefined function

; Function 0:  get installed state

                mov     al,0FFh         ; AL = 0FFH (this handler is installed)

MultiplexIRET:  iret                    ; return from interrupt

ISR2F           ENDP

                PAGE
;
;
; AuxInt21--sets ErrorMode while executing INT 21H to force use of the
;       AuxStack instead of the IOStack.
;
;

AuxInt21        PROC    near            ; Caller:    registers for INT 21H
                                        ; Returns:   registers from INT 21H

                push    ds
                push    bx
                lds     bx,ErrorModeAddr
                inc     byte ptr [bx]   ; ErrorMode is now nonzero
                pop     bx
                pop     ds

                int     21h             ; perform MS-DOS function

                push    ds
                push    bx
                lds     bx,ErrorModeAddr
                dec     byte ptr [bx]   ; restore ErrorMode
                pop     bx
                pop     ds
                ret

AuxInt21        ENDP


Int21v          PROC    near            ; perform INT 21H or AuxInt21,
                                        ; depending on MS-DOS version

                cmp     DOSVersion,30Ah
                jb      L80             ; jump if earlier than 3.1

                int     21h             ; versions 3.1 and later
                ret
```

Figure 11-4. Continued. *(more)*

```
L80:            call    AuxInt21        ; versions earlier than 3.1
                ret

Int21v          ENDP

                PAGE
;--------------------------------------------------------------------------
; RAM-resident application
;--------------------------------------------------------------------------

TSRapp          PROC    near

; Set up a safe stack

                push    ds              ; save previous DS on previous stack

                push    cs
                pop     ds              ; DS -> RESIDENT_GROUP

                mov     PrevSP,sp       ; save previous SS:SP
                mov     PrevSS,ss

                mov     ss,TSRSS        ; SS:SP -> RESIDENT_STACK
                mov     sp,TSRSP

                push    es              ; preserve remaining registers
                push    ax
                push    bx
                push    cx
                push    dx
                push    si
                push    di
                push    bp

                cld                     ; clear direction flag

; Set break and critical error traps

                mov     cx,NTrap
                mov     si,offset RESIDENT_GROUP:StartTrapList

L90:            lodsb                   ; AL = interrupt number
                                        ; DS:SI -> byte past interrupt number

                mov     byte ptr [si],FALSE    ; zero the trap flag

                push    ax              ; preserve AX
                mov     ah,35h          ; INT 21H function 35H
                                        ; (get interrupt vector)
                int     21h             ; ES:BX = previous interrupt vector
                mov     [si+1],bx       ; save offset and segment ..
                mov     [si+3],es       ;  .. of previous handler
```

Figure 11-4. Continued.   *(more)*

```
              pop      ax              ; AL = interrupt number
              mov      dx,[si+5]       ; DS:DX -> this TSR's trap
              mov      ah,25h          ; INT 21H function 25H
              int      21h             ; (set interrupt vector)
              add      si,7            ; DS:SI -> next in list

              loop     L90

; Disable MS-DOS break checking during disk I/O

              mov      ax,3300h        ; AH = INT 21H function number
                                       ; AL = 00H (request current break state)
              int      21h             ; DL = current break state
              mov      PrevBreak,dl    ; preserve current state

              xor      dl,dl           ; DL = 00H (disable disk I/O break
                                       ; checking)
              mov      ax,3301h        ; AL = 01H (set break state)
              int      21h

; Preserve previous extended error information

              cmp      DOSVersion,30Ah
              jb       L91             ; jump if MS-DOS version earlier
                                       ; than 3.1
              push     ds              ; preserve DS
              xor      bx,bx           ; BX = 00H (required for function 59H)
              mov      ah,59h          ; INT 21H function 59H
              call     Int21v          ; (get extended error info)

              mov      cs:PrevExtErrDS,ds
              pop      ds
              mov      PrevExtErrAX,ax ; preserve error information
              mov      PrevExtErrBX,bx ; in data structure
              mov      PrevExtErrCX,cx
              mov      PrevExtErrDX,dx
              mov      PrevExtErrSI,si
              mov      PrevExtErrDI,di
              mov      PrevExtErrES,es

; Inform MS-DOS about current PSP

L91:          mov      ah,51h          ; INT 21H function 51H (get PSP address)
              call     Int21v          ; BX = foreground PSP

              mov      PrevPSP,bx      ; preserve previous PSP

              mov      bx,TSRPSP       ; BX = resident PSP
              mov      ah,50h          ; INT 21H function 50H (set PSP address)
              call     Int21v
```

Figure 11-4. Continued.   *(more)*

```
; Inform MS-DOS about current DTA (not really necessary in this application
; because DTA is not used)

                mov     ah,2Fh          ; INT 21H function 2FH
                int     21h             ; (get DTA address) into ES:BX
                mov     PrevDTAoffs,bx
                mov     PrevDTAseg,es

                push    ds              ; preserve DS
                mov     ds,TSRPSP
                mov     dx,80h          ; DS:DX -> default DTA at PSP:0080H
                mov     ah,1Ah          ; INT 21H function 1AH
                int     21h             ; (set DTA address)
                pop     ds              ; restore DS

; Open a file, write to it, and close it

                mov     ax,0E07h        ; AH = INT 10H function number
                                        ; (write teletype)
                                        ; AL = 07H (bell character)
                int     10h             ; emit a beep

                mov     dx,offset RESIDENT_GROUP:SnapFile
                mov     ah,3Ch          ; INT 21H function 3CH
                                        ; (create file handle)
                mov     cx,0            ; file attribute
                int     21h
                jc      L94             ; jump if file not opened

                push    ax              ; push file handle
                mov     ah,0Fh          ; INT 10H function 0FH (get video status)
                int     10h             ; AL = video mode number
                                        ; AH = number of character columns
                pop     bx              ; BX = file handle

                cmp     ah,80
                jne     L93             ; jump if not 80-column mode

                mov     dx,0B800h       ; DX = color video buffer segment
                cmp     al,3
                jbe     L92             ; jump if color alphanumeric mode

                cmp     al,7
                jne     L93             ; jump if not monochrome mode

                mov     dx,0B000h       ; DX = monochrome video buffer segment

L92:            push    ds
                mov     ds,dx
                xor     dx,dx           ; DS:DX -> start of video buffer
                mov     cx,80*25*2      ; CX = number of bytes to write
                mov     ah,40h          ; INT 21H function 40H (write file)
```

Figure 11-4. Continued.   *(more)*

```
                        int     21h
                        pop     ds

L93:                    mov     ah,3Eh          ; INT 21H function 3EH (close file)
                        int     21h

                        mov     ax,0E07h        ; emit another beep
                        int     10h

; Restore previous DTA

L94:                    push    ds              ; preserve DS
                        lds     dx,PrevDTA      ; DS:DX -> previous DTA
                        mov     ah,1Ah          ; INT 21H function 1AH (set DTA address)
                        int     21h
                        pop     ds

; Restore previous PSP

                        mov     bx,PrevPSP      ; BX = previous PSP
                        mov     ah,50h          ; INT 21H function 50H
                        call    Int21v          ; (set PSP address)

; Restore previous extended error information

                        mov     ax,DOSVersion
                        cmp     ax,30Ah
                        jb      L95             ; jump if MS-DOS version earlier than 3.1
                        cmp     ax,0A00h
                        jae     L95             ; jump if MS OS/2-DOS 3.x box

                        mov     dx,offset RESIDENT_GROUP:PrevExtErrInfo
                        mov     ax,5D0Ah
                        int     21h             ; (restore extended error information)

; Restore previous MS-DOS break checking

L95:                    mov     dl,PrevBreak    ; DL = previous state
                        mov     ax,3301h
                        int     21h

; Restore previous break and critical error traps

                        mov     cx,NTrap
                        mov     si,offset RESIDENT_GROUP:StartTrapList
                        push    ds              ; preserve DS

L96:                    lods    byte ptr cs:[si] ; AL = interrupt number
                                                ; ES:SI -> byte past interrupt number

                        lds     dx,cs:[si+1]    ; DS:DX -> previous handler
                        mov     ah,25h          ; INT 21H function 25H
                        int     21h             ; (set interrupt vector)
```

Figure 11-4. Continued.   *(more)*

```
                       add     si,7            ; DS:SI -> next in list
                       loop    L96
                       pop     ds              ; restore DS

; Restore all registers

                       pop     bp
                       pop     di
                       pop     si
                       pop     dx
                       pop     cx
                       pop     bx
                       pop     ax
                       pop     es

                       mov     ss,PrevSS       ; SS:SP -> previous stack
                       mov     sp,PrevSP
                       pop     ds              ; restore previous DS

; Finally, reset status flag and return

                       mov     byte ptr cs:HotFlag,FALSE
                       ret

TSRapp         ENDP

RESIDENT_TEXT  ENDS

RESIDENT_DATA  SEGMENT word public 'DATA'

ErrorModeAddr  DD      ?               ; address of MS-DOS ErrorMode flag
InDOSAddr      DD      ?               ; address of MS-DOS InDOS flag

NISR           DW      (EndISRList-StartISRList)/8 ; number of installed ISRs

StartISRList   DB      05h             ; INT number
InISR5         DB      FALSE           ; flag
PrevISR5       DD      ?               ; address of previous handler
               DW      offset RESIDENT_GROUP:ISR5

               DB      08h
InISR8         DB      FALSE
PrevISR8       DD      ?
               DW      offset RESIDENT_GROUP:ISR8

               DB      09h
InISR9         DB      FALSE
PrevISR9       DD      ?
               DW      offset RESIDENT_GROUP:ISR9

               DB      10h
InISR10        DB      FALSE
```

Figure 11-4. Continued.   *(more)*

```
PrevISR10       DD      ?
                DW      offset RESIDENT_GROUP:ISR10

                DB      13h
InISR13         DB      FALSE
PrevISR13       DD      ?
                DW      offset RESIDENT_GROUP:ISR13

                DB      28h
InISR28         DB      FALSE
PrevISR28       DD      ?
                DW      offset RESIDENT_GROUP:ISR28

                DB      2Fh
InISR2F         DB      FALSE
PrevISR2F       DD      ?
                DW      offset RESIDENT_GROUP:ISR2F


EndISRList      LABEL   BYTE

TSRPSP          DW      ?                     ; resident PSP
TSRSP           DW      TSRStackSize    ; resident SS:SP
TSRSS           DW      seg RESIDENT_STACK
PrevPSP         DW      ?                     ; previous PSP
PrevSP          DW      ?                     ; previous SS:SP
PrevSS          DW      ?

HotIndex        DW      0                     ; index of next scan code in sequence
HotSeqLen       DW      EndHotSeq-HotSequence    ; length of hot-key sequence

HotSequence     DB      SCEnter          ; hot sequence of scan codes
EndHotSeq       LABEL   BYTE

HotKBFlag       DB      KBAlt            ; hot value of ROM BIOS KB_FLAG
HotKBMask       DB      (KBIns OR KBCaps OR KBNum OR KBScroll) XOR 0FFh
HotFlag         DB      FALSE


ActiveTSR       DB      FALSE


DOSVersion      LABEL   WORD
                DB      ?                     ; minor version number
MajorVersion    DB      ?                     ; major version number

; The following data is used by the TSR application:

NTrap           DW      (EndTrapList-StartTrapList)/8    ; number of traps

StartTrapList   DB      1Bh
Trap1B          DB      FALSE
PrevISR1B       DD      ?
                DW      offset RESIDENT_GROUP:ISR1B

                DB      23h
```

Figure 11-4. Continued.   *(more)*

```
Trap23          DB      FALSE
PrevISR23       DD      ?
                DW      offset RESIDENT_GROUP:ISR23


                DB      24h
Trap24          DB      FALSE
PrevISR24       DD      ?
                DW      offset RESIDENT_GROUP:ISR24


EndTrapList     LABEL   BYTE


PrevBreak       DB      ?                   ; previous break-checking flag


PrevDTA         LABEL   DWORD               ; previous DTA address
PrevDTAoffs     DW      ?
PrevDTAseg      DW      ?


PrevExtErrInfo  LABEL   BYTE                ; previous extended error information
PrevExtErrAX    DW      ?
PrevExtErrBX    DW      ?
PrevExtErrCX    DW      ?
PrevExtErrDX    DW      ?
PrevExtErrSI    DW      ?
PrevExtErrDI    DW      ?
PrevExtErrDS    DW      ?
PrevExtErrES    DW      ?
                DW      3 dup(0)


SnapFile        DB      '\snap.img'    ; output filename in root directory


RESIDENT_DATA   ENDS


RESIDENT_STACK  SEGMENT word stack 'STACK'

                DB      TSRStackSize dup(?)


RESIDENT_STACK  ENDS

                PAGE
;---------------------------------------------------------------------------
;
; Transient installation routines
;
;---------------------------------------------------------------------------

TRANSIENT_TEXT  SEGMENT para public 'TCODE'
                ASSUME  cs:TRANSIENT_TEXT,ds:RESIDENT_DATA,ss:RESIDENT_STACK

InstallSnapTSR  PROC    far             ; At entry:  CS:IP -> InstallSnapTSR
                                        ;            SS:SP -> stack
                                        ;            DS,ES -> PSP
```

Figure 11-4. Continued.   *(more)*

```
; Save PSP segment

                mov     ax,seg RESIDENT_DATA
                mov     ds,ax           ; DS  -> RESIDENT_DATA

                mov     TSRPSP,es       ; save PSP segment

; Check the MS-DOS version

                call    GetDOSVersion   ; AH = major version number
                                        ; AL = minor version number

; Verify that this TSR is not already installed
;
;       Before executing INT 2FH in MS-DOS versions 2.x, test whether INT 2FH
;       vector is in use.  If so, abort if PRINT.COM is using it.
;
;       (Thus, in MS-DOS 2.x, if both this program and PRINT.COM are used,
;       this program should be made resident before PRINT.COM.)

                cmp     ah,2
                ja      L101            ; jump if version 3.0 or later

                mov     ax,352Fh        ; AH = INT 21H function number
                                        ; AL = interrupt number
                int     21h             ; ES:BX = INT 2FH vector

                mov     ax,es
                or      ax,bx           ; jump if current INT 2FH vector ..
                jnz     L100            ; .. is nonzero

                push    ds
                mov     ax,252Fh        ; AH = INT 21H function number
                                        ; AL = interrupt number
                mov     dx,seg RESIDENT_GROUP
                mov     ds,dx
                mov     dx,offset RESIDENT_GROUP:MultiplexIRET

                int     21h             ; point INT 2FH vector to IRET
                pop     ds
                jmp     short L103       ; jump to install this TSR

L100:           mov     ax,0FF00h       ; look for PRINT.COM:
                int     2Fh             ; if resident, AH = print queue length;
                                        ; otherwise, AH is unchanged

                cmp     ah,0FFh         ; if PRINT.COM is not resident ..
                je      L101            ; .. use multiplex interrupt

                mov     al,1
                call    FatalError      ; abort if PRINT.COM already installed
```

Figure 11-4. Continued.   *(more)*

```
L101:           mov     ah,MultiplexID   ; AH = multiplex interrupt ID value
                xor     al,al            ; AL = 00H
                int     2Fh              ; multiplex interrupt

                test    al,al
                jz      L103             ; jump if ok to install

                cmp     al,0FFh
                jne     L102             ; jump if not already installed

                mov     al,2
                call    FatalError       ; already installed

L102:           mov     al,3
                call    FatalError       ; can't install

; Get addresses of InDOS and ErrorMode flags

L103:           call    GetDOSFlags

; Install this TSR's interrupt handlers

                push    es               ; preserve PSP segment

                mov     cx,NISR
                mov     si,offset StartISRList

L104:           lodsb                    ; AL = interrupt number
                                         ; DS:SI -> byte past interrupt number
                push    ax               ; preserve AX
                mov     ah,35h           ; INT 21H function 35H
                int     21h              ; ES:BX = previous interrupt vector
                mov     [si+1],bx        ; save offset and segment ..
                mov     [si+3],es        ; .. of previous handler

                pop     ax               ; AL = interrupt number
                push    ds               ; preserve DS
                mov     dx,[si+5]
                mov     bx,seg RESIDENT_GROUP
                mov     ds,bx            ; DS:DX -> this TSR's handler
                mov     ah,25h           ; INT 21H function 25H
                int     21h              ; (set interrupt vector)
                pop     ds               ; restore DS
                add     si,7             ; DS:SI -> next in list
                loop    L104

; Free the environment

                pop     es               ; ES = PSP segment
                push    es               ; preserve PSP segment
                mov     es,es:[2Ch]      ; ES = segment of environment
```

Figure 11-4. Continued.   *(more)*

```
                  mov      ah,49h          ; INT 21H function 49H
                  int      21h             ; (free memory block)

; Terminate and stay resident

                  pop      ax              ; AX = PSP segment
                  mov      dx,cs           ; DX = paragraph address of start of
                                           ; transient portion (end of resident
                                           ; portion)
                  sub      dx,ax           ; DX = size of resident portion

                  mov      ax,3100h        ; AH = INT 21H function number
                                           ; AL = 00H (return code)
                  int      21h

InstallSnapTSR    ENDP

GetDOSVersion     PROC     near            ; Caller:   DS = seg RESIDENT_DATA
                                           ;           ES = PSP
                                           ; Returns:  AH = major version
                                           ;           AL = minor version
                  ASSUME   ds:RESIDENT_DATA

                  mov      ah,30h          ; INT 21H function 30H:
                                           ; (get MS-DOS version)
                  int      21h
                  cmp      al,2
                  jb       L110            ; jump if versions 1.x

                  xchg     ah,al           ; AH = major version
                                           ; AL = minor version
                  mov      DOSVersion,ax   ; save with major version in
                                           ; high-order byte
                  ret

L110:             mov      al,00h          .
                  call     FatalError      ; abort if versions 1.x

GetDOSVersion     ENDP
GetDOSFlags       PROC     near            ; Caller:   DS = seg RESIDENT_DATA
                                           ; Returns:  InDOSAddr -> InDOS
                                           ;           ErrorModeAddr -> ErrorMode
                                           ; Destroys: AX,BX,CX,DI
                  ASSUME   ds:RESIDENT_DATA

; Get InDOS address from MS-DOS

                  push     es

                  mov      ah,34h          ; INT 21H function number
                  int      21h             ; ES:BX -> InDOS
```

Figure 11-4. Continued.   *(more)*

```
                      mov      word ptr InDOSAddr,bx
                      mov      word ptr InDOSAddr+2,es

; Determine ErrorMode address

                      mov      word ptr ErrorModeAddr+2,es      ; assume ErrorMode is
                                                                ; in the same segment
                                                                ; as InDOS

                      mov      ax,DOSVersion
                      cmp      ax,30Ah
                      jb       L120             ; jump if MS-DOS version earlier
                                                ; than 3.1 ..
                      cmp      ax,0A00h
                      jae      L120             ; .. or MS OS/2-DOS 3.x box

                      dec      bx               ; in MS-DOS 3.1 and later, ErrorMode
                      mov      word ptr ErrorModeAddr,bx     ; is just before InDOS
                      jmp      short L125

L120:                                           ; scan MS-DOS segment for ErrorMode

                      mov      cx,0FFFFh        ; CX = maximum number of bytes to scan
                      xor      di,di            ; ES:DI -> start of MS-DOS segment

L121:                 mov      ax,word ptr cs:LF2   ; AX = opcode for INT 28H

L122:                 repne    scasb            ; scan for first byte of fragment
                      jne      L126             ; jump if not found

                      cmp      ah,es:[di]                 ; inspect second byte of opcode
                      jne      L122                       ; jump if not INT 28H

                      mov      ax,word ptr cs:LF1 + 1  ; AX = opcode for CMP
                      cmp      ax,es:[di][LF1-LF2]
                      jne      L123                       ; jump if opcode not CMP

                      mov      ax,es:[di][(LF1-LF2)+2]  ; AX = offset of ErrorMode
                      jmp      short L124                 ; in DOS segment

L123:                 mov      ax,word ptr cs:LF3 + 1  ; AX = opcode for TEST
                      cmp      ax,es:[di][LF3-LF4]
                      jne      L121                       ; jump if opcode not TEST

                      mov      ax,es:[di][(LF3-LF4)+2]  ; AX = offset of ErrorMode

L124:                 mov      word ptr ErrorModeAddr,ax

L125:                 pop      es
                      ret
```

Figure 11-4. Continued.   *(more)*

```
; Come here if address of ErrorMode not found

L126:           mov     al,04h
                call    FatalError

; Code fragments for scanning for ErrorMode flag

LFnear          LABEL   near            ; dummy labels for addressing
LFbyte          LABEL   byte
LFword          LABEL   word
                                        ; MS-DOS versions earlier than 3.1
LF1:            cmp     ss:LFbyte,0     ; CMP ErrorMode,0
                jne     LFnear
LF2:            int     28h
                                        ; MS-DOS versions 3.1 and later
LF3:            test    ss:LFbyte,0FFh  ; TEST ErrorMode,0FFH
                jne     LFnear
                push    ss:LFword
LF4:            int     28h


GetDOSFlags     ENDP

FatalError      PROC    near            ; Caller:  AL = message number
                                        ;          ES = PSP
                ASSUME  ds:TRANSIENT_DATA

                push    ax              ; save message number on stack

                mov     bx,seg TRANSIENT_DATA
                mov     ds,bx

; Display the requested message

                mov     bx,offset MessageTable
                xor     ah,ah           ; AX = message number
                shl     ax,1            ; AX = offset into MessageTable
                add     bx,ax           ; DS:BX -> address of message
                mov     dx,[bx]         ; DS:BX -> message
                mov     ah,09h          ; INT 21H function 09H (display string)
                int     21h             ; display error message

                pop     ax              ; AL = message number
                or      al,al
                jz      L130            ; jump if message number is zero
                                        ; (MS-DOS versions 1.x)

; Terminate (MS-DOS 2.x and later)

                mov     ah,4Ch          ; INT 21H function 4CH
                int     21h             ; (terminate process with return code)
```

Figure 11-4. Continued.   *(more)*

```
; Terminate (MS-DOS 1.x)

L130            PROC    far

                push    es              ; push PSP:0000H
                xor     ax,ax
                push    ax
                ret                     ; far return (jump to PSP:0000H)

L130            ENDP

FatalError      ENDP


TRANSIENT_TEXT  ENDS

                PAGE
;
;
; Transient data segment
;
;

TRANSIENT_DATA  SEGMENT word public 'DATA'

MessageTable    DW      Message0        ; MS-DOS version error
                DW      Message1        ; PRINT.COM found in MS-DOS 2.x
                DW      Message2        ; already installed
                DW      Message3        ; can't install
                DW      Message4        ; can't find flag

Message0        DB      CR,LF,'TSR requires MS-DOS 2.0 or later version',CR,LF,'$'
Message1        DB      CR,LF,'Can''t install TSR:  PRINT.COM active',CR,LF,'$'
Message2        DB      CR,LF,'This TSR is already installed',CR,LF,'$'
Message3        DB      CR,LF,'Can''t install this TSR',CR,LF,'$'
Message4        DB      CR,LF,'Unable to locate MS-DOS ErrorMode flag',CR,LF,'$'

TRANSIENT_DATA  ENDS

                END     InstallSnapTSR
```

Figure 11-4. Continued.

When installed, the SNAP program monitors keyboard input until the user types the hot-key sequence Alt-Enter. When the hot-key sequence is detected, the monitoring routine waits until the operating environment is stable and then activates the RAM-resident application, which dumps the current contents of the computer's video buffer into the file SNAP.IMG. Figure 11-5 is a block diagram of the RAM-resident and transient components of this TSR.

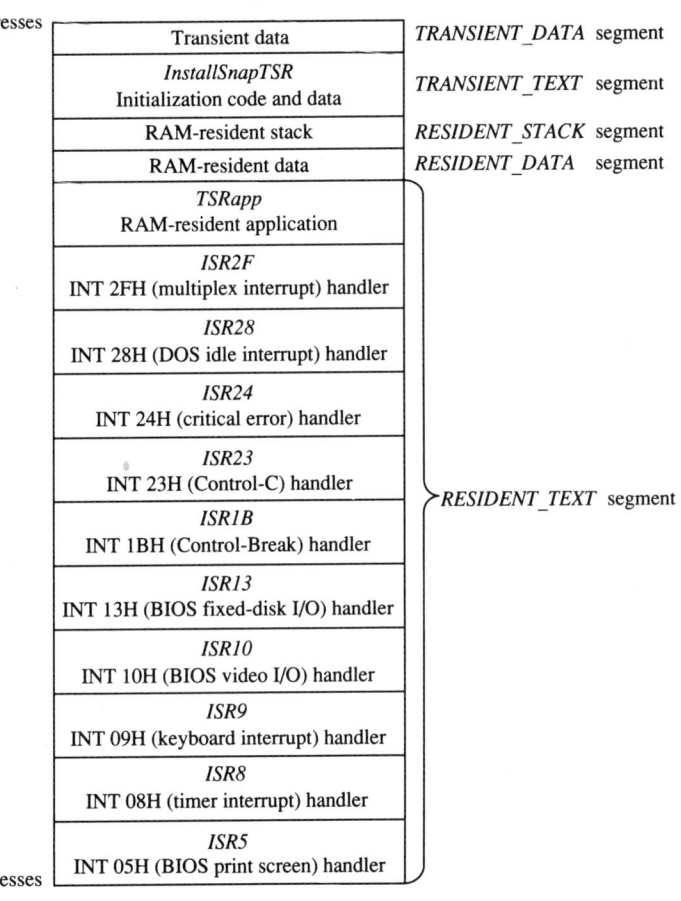

Figure 11-5. Block structure of the TSR program SNAP.EXE when loaded into memory. (Compare with Figure 11-1.)

Installing the program

When SNAP.EXE is run, only the code in the transient portion of the program is executed. The transient code performs several operations before it finally executes Interrupt 21H Function 31H (Terminate and Stay Resident). First it determines which MS-DOS version is in use. Then it executes the multiplex interrupt (Interrupt 2FH) to discover whether the resident portion has already been installed. If an MS-DOS version earlier than 2.0 is in use or if the resident portion has already been installed, the program aborts with an error message.

Otherwise, installation continues. The addresses of the InDOS and critical error flags are saved in the resident data segment. The interrupt service routines in the RAM-resident portion of the program are installed by updating all relevant interrupt vectors. The transient code then frees the RAM occupied by the program's environment, because the resident portion of this program never uses the information contained there. Finally, the transient portion of the program, which includes the *TRANSIENT_TEXT* and *TRANSIENT_DATA* segments, is discarded and the program is terminated using Interrupt 21H Function 31H.

Detecting a hot key

The SNAP program detects the hot-key sequence (Alt-Enter) by monitoring each keypress. On IBM PCs and PS/2s, each keystroke generates a hardware interrupt on IRQ1 (Interrupt 09H). The TSR's Interrupt 09H handler compares the keyboard scan code corresponding to each keypress with a predefined sequence. The TSR's handler also inspects the shift-key status flags maintained by the ROM BIOS Interrupt 09H handler. When the predetermined sequence of keypresses is detected at the same time as the proper shift keys are pressed, the handler sets a global status flag (*HotFlag*).

Note how the TSR's handler transfers control to the previous Interrupt 09H ISR before it performs its own work. If the TSR's Interrupt 09H handler did not chain to the previous handler(s), essential system processing of keystrokes (particularly in the ROM BIOS Interrupt 09H handler) might not be performed.

Activating the application

The TSR monitors the status of *HotFlag* by regularly testing its value within a timer-tick handler. On IBM PCs and PS/2s, the timer-tick interrupt occurs on IRQ0 (Interrupt 08H) roughly 18.2 times per second. This hardware interrupt occurs regardless of what else the system is doing, so an Interrupt 08H ISR a convenient place to check whether *HotFlag* has been set.

As in the case of the Interrupt 09H handler, the TSR's Interrupt 08H handler passes control to previous Interrupt 08H handlers before it proceeds with its own work. This procedure is particularly important with Interrupt 08H because the ROM BIOS Interrupt 08H handler, which maintains the system's time-of-day clock and resets the system's Intel 8259A Programmable Interrupt Controller, must execute before the next timer tick can occur. The TSR's handler therefore defers its own work until control has returned after previous Interrupt 08H handlers have executed.

The only function of the TSR's Interrupt 08H handler is to attempt to transfer control to the RAM-resident application. The routine *VerifyTSRState* performs this task. It first examines the contents of *HotFlag* to determine whether a hot-key sequence has been detected. If so, it examines the state of the MS-DOS InDOS and critical error flags, the current status of hardware interrupts, and the current status of any non-reentrant ROM BIOS routines that might be executing.

If *HotFlag* is nonzero, the InDOS and critical error flags are both zero, no hardware interrupts are currently being serviced, and no non-reentrant ROM BIOS code has been interrupted, the Interrupt 08H handler activates the RAM-resident utility. Otherwise, nothing happens until the next timer tick, when the handler executes again.

While *HotFlag* is nonzero, the Interrupt 08H handler continues to monitor system status until MS-DOS, the ROM BIOS, and the hardware interrupts are all in a stable state. Often the system status is stable at the time the hot-key sequence is detected, so the RAM-resident application runs immediately. Sometimes, however, system activities such as prolonged disk reads or writes can preclude the activation of the RAM-resident utility for several seconds after the hot-key sequence has been detected. The handler could be designed to detect this situation (for example, by decrementing *HotFlag* on each timer tick) and return an error status or display a message to the user.

A more serious difficulty arises when the MS-DOS default command processor (COMMAND.COM) is waiting for keyboard input. In this situation, Interrupt 21H Function 01H (Character Input with Echo) is executing, so InDOS is nonzero and the Interrupt 08H handler can never detect a state in which it can activate the RAM-resident utility. This problem is solved by providing a custom handler for Interrupt 28H (the MS-DOS idle interrupt), which is executed by Interrupt 21H Function 01H each time it loops as it waits for a keypress. The only difference between the Interrupt 28H handler and the Interrupt 08H handler is that the Interrupt 28H handler can activate the RAM-resident application when the value of InDOS is 1, which is reasonable because InDOS must have been incremented when Interrupt 21H Function 01H started to execute.

The interrupt service routines for ROM BIOS Interrupts 05H, 10H, and 13H do nothing more than increment and decrement flags that indicate whether these interrupts are being processed by ROM BIOS routines. These flags are inspected by the TSR's Interrupt 08H and 28H handlers.

Executing the RAM-resident application

When the RAM-resident application is first activated, it runs in the context of the program that was interrupted; that is, the contents of the registers, the video display mode, the current PSP, and the current DTA all belong to the interrupted program. The resident application is responsible for preserving the registers and updating MS-DOS with its PSP and DTA values.

The RAM-resident application preserves the previous contents of the CPU registers on its own stack to avoid overflowing the interrupted program's stack. It then installs its own handlers for Control-Break (Interrupt 1BH), Control-C (Interrupt 23H), and critical error (Interrupt 24H). (Otherwise, the interrupted program's handlers would take control if the user pressed Ctrl-Break or Ctrl-C or if an MS-DOS critical error occurred.) These handlers perform no action other than setting flags that can be inspected later by the RAM-resident application, which could then take appropriate action.

The application uses Interrupt 21H Functions 50H and 51H to update MS-DOS with the address of its PSP. If the application is running under MS-DOS versions 2.x, the critical error flag is set before Functions 50H and 51H are executed so that *AuxStack* is used for the call instead of *IOStack*, to avoid corrupting *IOStack* in the event that InDOS is 1.

The application preserves the current extended error information with a call to Interrupt 21H Function 59H. Otherwise, the RAM-resident application might be activated immediately after a critical error occurred in the interrupted program but before the interrupted program had executed Function 59H and, if a critical error occurred in the TSR application, the interrupted program's extended error information would inadvertently be destroyed.

This example also shows how to update the MS-DOS default DTA using Interrupt 21H Functions 1AH and 2FH, although in this case this step is not necessary because the DTA is never used within the application. In practice, the DTA should be updated only if the RAM-resident application includes calls to Interrupt 21H functions that use a DTA (Functions 11H, 12H, 14H, 15H, 21H, 22H, 27H, 28H, 4EH, and 4FH).

After the resident interrupt handlers are installed and the PSP, DTA, and extended error information have been set up, the RAM-resident application can safely execute any Interrupt 21H function calls except those that use *IOStack* (Functions 01H through 0CH). These functions cannot be used within a RAM-resident application even if the application sets the critical error flag to force the use of the auxiliary stack, because they also use other non-reentrant data structures such as input/output buffers. Thus, a RAM-resident utility must rely either on user-written console input/output functions or, as in the example, on ROM BIOS functions.

The application terminates by returning the interrupted program's extended error information, DTA, and PSP to MS-DOS, restoring the previous Interrupt 1BH, 23H, and 24H handlers, and restoring the previous CPU registers and stack.

Richard Wilton

Article 12
Exception Handlers

Exceptions are system events directly related to the execution of an application program; they ordinarily cause the operating system to abort the program. Exceptions are thus different from errors, which are minor unexpected events (such as failure to find a file on disk) that the program can be expected to handle appropriately. Likewise, they differ from external hardware interrupts, which are triggered by events (such as a character arriving at the serial port) that are not directly related to the program's execution.

The computer hardware assists MS-DOS in the detection of some exceptions, such as an attempt to divide by zero, by generating an internal hardware interrupt. Exceptions related to peripheral devices, such as an attempt to read from a disk drive that is not ready or does not exist, are called *critical* errors. Instead of causing a hardware interrupt, these exceptions are typically reported to the operating system by device drivers. MS-DOS also supports a third type of exception, which is triggered by the entry of a Control-C or Control-Break at the keyboard and allows the user to signal that the current program should be terminated immediately.

MS-DOS contains built-in handlers for each type of exception and so guarantees a minimum level of system stability that requires no effort on the part of the application programmer. For some applications, however, these default handlers are inadequate. For example, if a communications program that controls the serial port directly with custom interrupt handlers is terminated by the operating system without being given a chance to turn off serial-port interrupts, the next character that arrives on the serial line will trigger an interrupt for which a handler is no longer present in memory. The result will be a system crash. Accordingly, MS-DOS allows application programs to install custom exception handlers so that they can shut down operations in an orderly way when an exception occurs.

This article examines the default exception handlers provided by MS-DOS and discusses methods programmers can use to replace those routines with handlers that are more closely matched to specific application requirements.

Overview

Two major exception handlers of importance to application programmers are supported under all versions of MS-DOS. The first, the Control-C exception handler, terminates the program and is invoked when the user enters a Ctrl-C or Ctrl-Break keystroke; the address of this handler is found in the vector for Interrupt 23H. The second, the critical error exception handler, is invoked if MS-DOS detects a critical error while servicing an I/O request. (A critical error is a hardware error that makes normal completion of the request impossible.) This exception handler displays the familiar *Abort, Retry, Ignore* prompt; its address is saved in the vector for Interrupt 24H.

When a program begins executing, the addresses in the Interrupt 23H and 24H vectors usually point to the system's default Control-C and critical error handlers. If the program is a child process, however, the vectors might point to exception handlers that belong to the parent process, if the immediate parent is not COMMAND.COM. In any case, the application program can install its own custom handler for Control-C or critical error exceptions simply by changing the address in the vector for Interrupt 23H or Interrupt 24H so that the vector points to the application's own routine. When the program performs a final exit by means of Interrupt 21H Function 00H (Terminate Process), Function 31H (Terminate and Stay Resident), Function 4CH (Terminate Process with Return Code), Interrupt 20H (Terminate Process), or Interrupt 27H (Terminate and Stay Resident), MS-DOS restores the previous contents of the Interrupt 23H and 24H vectors.

Note that Interrupts 23H and 24H *never* occur as externally generated hardware interrupts in an MS-DOS system. The vectors for these interrupts are used simply as storage areas for the addresses of the exception handlers.

MS-DOS also contains default handlers for the Control-Break event detected by the ROM BIOS in IBM PCs and compatible computers and for some of the Intel microprocessor exceptions that generate actual hardware interrupts. These exception handlers are not replaced by application programs as often as the Control-C and critical error handlers. The interrupt vectors that contain the addresses of these handlers are *not* restored by MS-DOS when a program exits.

The address of the Control-Break handler is saved in the vector for Interrupt 1BH and is invoked by the ROM BIOS whenever the Ctrl-Break key combination is detected. The default MS-DOS handler normally flushes the keyboard input buffer and substitutes Control-C for Control-Break, and the Control-C is later handled by the Control-C exception handler. The default handlers for exceptions that generate hardware interrupts either abort the current program (as happens with Divide by Zero) or bring the entire system to a halt (as for a memory parity error).

The Control-C Handler

The vector for Interrupt 23H points to code that is executed whenever MS-DOS detects a Control-C character in the keyboard input buffer. When the character is detected, MS-DOS executes a software Interrupt 23H.

In response to Interrupt 23H, the default Control-C exception handler aborts the current process. Files that were opened with handles are closed (FCB-based files are not), but no other cleanup is performed. Thus, unsaved data can be left in buffers, some files might not be processed, and critical addresses, such as the vectors for custom interrupt handlers, might be left pointing into free RAM. If more complete control over process termination is wanted, the application should replace the default Control-C handler with custom code. *See* Customizing Control-C Handling below.

The Control-Break exception handler, pointed to by the vector for Interrupt 1BH, is closely related to the Control-C exception handler in MS-DOS systems on the IBM PC and close compatibles but is called by the ROM BIOS keyboard driver on detection of the Ctrl-Break keystroke combination. Because the Control-Break exception is generated by the ROM BIOS, it is present only on IBM PC-compatible machines and is not a standard feature of MS-DOS. The default ROM BIOS handler for Control-Break is a simple interrupt return — in other words, no action is taken to handle the keystroke itself, other than converting the Ctrl-Break scan code to an extended character and passing it through to MS-DOS as normal keyboard input.

To account for as many hardware configurations as possible, MS-DOS redirects the ROM BIOS Control-Break interrupt vector to its own Control-Break handler during system initialization. The MS-DOS Control-Break handler sets an internal flag that causes the Ctrl-Break keystroke to be interpreted as a Ctrl-C keystroke and thus causes Interrupt 23H to occur.

Customizing Control-C handling

The exception handlers most often neglected by application programmers — and most often responsible for major program failures — are the default exception handlers invoked by the Ctrl-C and Ctrl-Break keystrokes. Although the user must be able to recover from a runaway condition (the reason for Ctrl-C capability in the first place), any exit from a complex program must also be orderly, with file buffers flushed to disk, directories and indexes updated, and so on. The default Control-C and Control-Break handlers do not provide for such an orderly exit.

The simplest and most direct way to deal with Ctrl-C and Ctrl-Break keystrokes is to install new exception handlers that do nothing more than an IRET and thus take MS-DOS out of the processing loop entirely. This move is not as drastic as it sounds: It allows an application to check for and handle the Ctrl-C and Ctrl-Break keystrokes at its convenience when they arrive through the normal keyboard input functions and prevents MS-DOS from terminating the program unexpectedly.

The following example sets the Interrupt 23H and Interrupt 1BH vectors to point to an IRET instruction. When the user presses Ctrl-C or Ctrl-Break, the keystroke combination is placed into the keyboard buffer like any other keystroke. When it detects the Ctrl-C or Ctrl-Break keystroke, the executing program should exit properly (if that is the desired action) after an appropriate shutdown procedure.

To install the new exception handlers, the following procedure (*set_int*) should be called while the main program is initializing:

```
_DATA    segment para public 'DATA'
oldint1b dd     0                  ; original INT 1BH vector
oldint23 dd     0                  ; original INT 23H vector
_DATA    ends
_TEXT    segment byte public 'CODE'
         assume cs:_TEXT,ds:_DATA,es:NOTHING
myint1b:                           ; handler for Ctrl-Break
myint23:                           ; handler for Ctrl-C
         iret

set_int proc    near
        mov     ax,351bh           ; get current contents of
        int     21h                ; Int 1BH vector and save it
        mov     word ptr oldint1b,bx
        mov     word ptr oldint1b+2,es
        mov     ax,3523h           ; get current contents of
        int     21h                ; Int 23H vector and save it
        mov     word ptr oldint23,bx
        mov     word ptr oldint23+2,es
        push    ds                 ; save our data segment
        push    cs                 ; let DS point to our
        pop     ds                 ; code segment
        mov     dx,offset myint1b
        mov     ax,251bh           ; set interrupt vector 1BH
        int     21h                ; to point to new handler
        mov     dx,offset myint23
        mov     ax,2523h           ; set interrupt vector 23H
        int     21h                ; to point to new handler
        pop     ds                 ; restore our data segment
        ret                        ; back to caller
set_int endp
_TEXT   ends
```

The application can use the following routine to restore the original contents of the vectors pointing to the Control-C and Control-Break exception handlers before making a final exit back to MS-DOS. Note that, although MS-DOS restores the Interrupt 23H vector to its previous contents, the application *must* restore the Interrupt 1BH vector itself.

```
rest_int proc   near
         push   ds                 ; save our data segment
         mov    dx,word ptr oldint23
         mov    ds,word ptr oldint23+2
         mov    ax,2523h           ; restore original contents
         int    21h                ; of Int 23H vector
         pop    ds                 ; restore our data segment
         push   ds                 ; then save it again
         mov    dx,word ptr oldint1B
         mov    ds,word ptr oldint1B+2
         mov    ax,251Bh           ; restore original contents
         int    21h                ; of Int 1BH vector
         pop    ds                 ; get back our data segment
         ret                       ; return to caller
rest_int endp
```

The preceding example simply prevents MS-DOS from terminating an application when a Ctrl-C or Ctrl-Break keystroke is detected. Program termination is still often the ultimate goal, but after a more orderly shutdown than is provided by the MS-DOS default Control-C handler. The following exception handler allows the program to exit more gracefully:

```
myint1b:                        ; Control-Break exception handler
        iret                    ; do nothing
myint23:                        ; Control-C exception handler
        call    safe_shut_down  ; release interrupt vectors,
                                ; close files, etc.
        jmp     program_exit_point
```

Note that because the Control-Break handler is invoked by the ROM BIOS keyboard driver and MS-DOS is not reentrant, MS-DOS services (such as closing files and terminating with return code) cannot be invoked during processing of a Control-Break exception. In contrast, any MS-DOS Interrupt 21H function call can be used during the processing of a Control-C exception. Thus, the Control-Break handler in the preceding example does nothing, whereas the Control-C handler performs orderly shutdown of the application.

Most often, however, neither a handler that does nothing nor a handler that shuts down and terminates is sufficient for processing a Ctrl-C (or Ctrl-Break) keystroke. Rather than simply prevent Control-C processing, software developers usually prefer to have a Ctrl-C keystroke signal some important action without terminating the program. Using methods similar to those above, the programmer can replace Interrupts 1BH and 23H with a routine like the following:

```
myint1b:                        ; Control-Break exception handler
myint23:                        ; Control-C exception handler
        call    control_c_happened
        iret
```

Notes on processing Control-C

The preceding examples assume the programmer wants to treat Control-C and Control-Break the same way, but this is not always desirable. Control-C and Control-Break are not the same, and the difference between the two should be kept in mind: The Control-Break handler is invoked by a keyboard-input interrupt and can be called at any time; the Control-C handler is called only at "safe" points during the processing of MS-DOS Interrupt 21H functions. Also, even though MS-DOS restores the Interrupt 23H vector on exit from a program, the *application* must restore the previous contents of the Interrupt 1BH vector before exiting. If this interrupt vector is not restored, the next Ctrl-Break keystroke will cause the machine to attempt to execute an undetermined piece of code or data and will probably crash the system.

Although it is generally desirable to take control of the Control-C and Control-Break interrupts, control should be retained only as long as necessary. For example, a RAM-resident pop-up application should take over Control-C and Control-Break handling only when it is activated, and it should restore the previous contents of the Interrupt 1BH and Interrupt 23H vectors before it returns control to the foreground process.

The Critical Error Handler

When MS-DOS detects a critical error—an error that prevents successful completion of an I/O operation—it calls the exception handler whose address is stored in the vector for Interrupt 24H. Information about the operation in progress and the nature of the error is passed to the exception handler in the CPU registers. In addition, the contents of all the registers at the point of the original MS-DOS call are pushed onto the stack for inspection by the exception handler.

The action of MS-DOS's default critical error handler is to present a message such as

```
Error type error action device
Abort, Retry, Ignore?
```

This message signals a hardware error from which MS-DOS cannot recover without user intervention. For example, if the user enters the command

```
C>DIR A:   <Enter>
```

but drive A either does not contain a disk or the disk drive door is open, the MS-DOS critical error handler displays the message

```
Not ready error reading drive A
Abort, Retry, Ignore?
```

I (*Ignore*) simply tells MS-DOS to forget that an error occurred and continue on its way. (Of course, if the error occurred during the writing of a file to disk, the file is generally corrupted; if the error occurred during reading, the data might be incorrect.)

R (*Retry*) gives the application a second chance to access the device. The critical error handler returns information to MS-DOS that says, in effect, "Try again; maybe it will work this time." Sometimes, the attempt succeeds (as when the user closes an open drive door), but more often the same or another critical error occurs.

A (*Abort*) is the problem child of Interrupt 24H. If the user responds with *A*, the application is terminated immediately. The directory structure is not updated for open files, interrupt vectors are left pointing to inappropriate locations, and so on. In many cases, restarting the system is the only safe thing to do at this point.

Note: Beginning with version 3.3, an *F* (*Fail*) option appears in the message displayed by MS-DOS's default critical error handler. When *Fail* is selected, the current MS-DOS function is terminated and an error condition is returned to the calling program. For example, if a program calls Interrupt 21H Function 3DH to open a file on drive A but the drive door is open, choosing *F* in response to the error message causes the function call to return with the carry flag set, indicating that an error occurred but processing continues.

Like the Control-C exception handler, the default critical error exception handler can and should be replaced by an application program when complete control of the system is desired. The program installs its own handler simply by placing the address of the new handler in the vector for Interrupt 24H; MS-DOS restores the previous contents of the Interrupt 24H vector when the program terminates.

Unlike the Control-C handler, however, the critical error handler must be kept within carefully defined limits to preserve the stability of the operating system. Programmers must rigidly adhere to the structure described in the following pages for passing information to and from an Interrupt 24H handler.

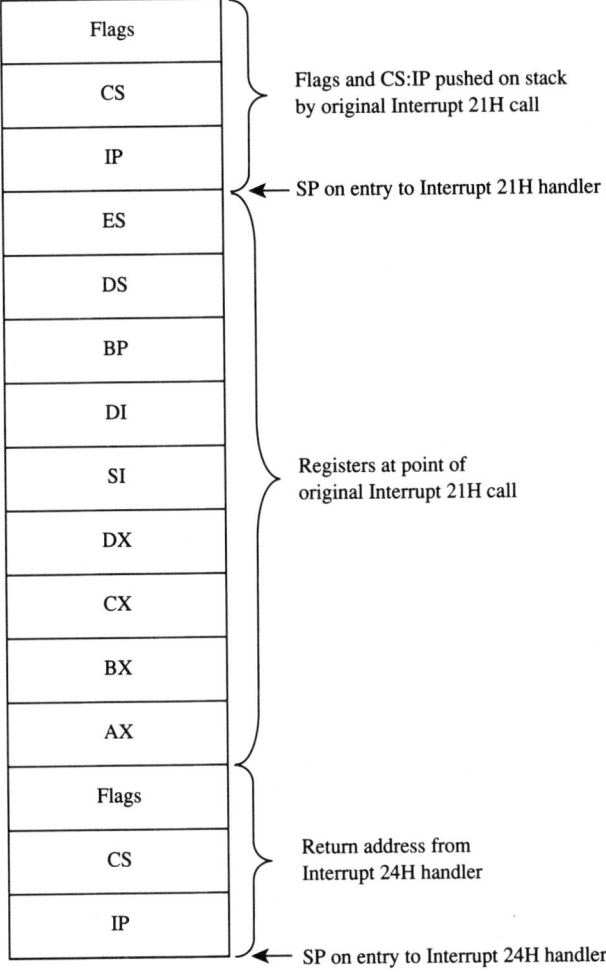

Figure 12-1. The stack contents at entry to a critical error exception handler.

Mechanics of critical error handling

MS-DOS critical error handling has two components: the exception handler, whose address is saved in the Interrupt 24H vector and which can be replaced by an application program; and an internal routine inside MS-DOS. The internal routine sets up the information to be passed to the exception handler on the stack and in registers and, in turn, calls the exception handler itself. The internal routine also responds to the values returned by the critical error handler when that handler executes an IRET to return to the MS-DOS kernel.

Before calling the exception handler, MS-DOS arranges the stack (Figure 12-1 on the preceding page) so the handler can inspect the location of the error and register contents at the point in the original MS-DOS function call that led to the critical error.

When the critical error handler is called by the internal routine, four registers may contain important information: AX, DI, BP, and SI. (With MS-DOS versions 1.x, only the AX and DI registers contain significant information.) The information passed to the handler in the registers differs somewhat, depending on whether a character device or a block device is causing the error.

Block-device (disk-based) errors

If the critical error handler is entered in response to a block-device (disk-based) error, registers BP:SI contain the segment:offset of the device driver header for the device causing the error and bit 7 (the high-order bit) of the AH register is zero. The remaining bits of the AH register contain the following information (bits 3 through 5 apply only to MS-DOS versions 3.1 and later):

Bit	Value	Meaning
0	0	Read operation
	1	Write operation
1-2		Indicate the affected disk area:
	00	MS-DOS
	01	File allocation table
	10	Root directory
	11	Files area
3	0	Fail response not allowed
	1	Fail response allowed
4	0	Retry response not allowed
	1	Retry response allowed
5	0	Ignore response not allowed
	1	Ignore response allowed
6	0	Undefined

The AL register contains the designation of the drive where the error occurred; for example, AL = 00H (drive A), AL = 01H (drive B), and so on.

The lower half of the DI register contains the following error codes (the upper half of this register is undefined):

Error Code	Meaning
00H	Write-protected disk
01H	Unknown unit
02H	Drive not ready
03H	Invalid command
04H	Data error (CRC)
05H	Length of request structure invalid
06H	Seek error
07H	Non-MS-DOS disk
08H	Sector not found
09H	Printer out of paper
0AH	Write fault
0BH	Read fault
0CH	General failure
0FH	Invalid disk change (version 3.0 or later)

Note: With versions 1.x, the only valid error codes are 00H, 02H, 04H, 06H, 08H, 0AH, and 0CH.

Before calling the critical error handler for a disk-based error, MS-DOS tries from one to five times to perform the requested read or write operation, depending on the type of operation. Critical disk errors result only from Interrupt 21H operations, not from failed sector-read and sector-write operations attempted with Interrupts 25H and 26H.

Character-device errors

If the critical error handler is called from the MS-DOS kernel with bit 7 of the AH register set to 1, either an error occurred on a character device or the memory image of the file allocation table is bad (a rare occurrence). Again, registers BP:SI contain the segment and offset of the device driver header for the device causing the critical error. The exception handler can inspect bit 15 of the device attribute word at offset 04H in the device header to confirm that the error was caused by a character device — this bit is 0 for block devices and 1 for character devices. *See also* PROGRAMMING IN THE MS-DOS ENVIRONMENT: CUSTOMIZING MS-DOS: Installable Device Drivers.

If the error was caused by a character device, the lower half of the DI register contains error codes as described above and the contents of the AL register are undefined. The exception handler can inspect the other fields of the device header to obtain the logical name of the character device; to determine whether that device is the standard input, standard output, or both; and so on.

Critical error processing

The critical error exception handler is entered from MS-DOS with interrupts disabled. Because an MS-DOS system call is already in progress and MS-DOS is not reentrant, the handler cannot request any MS-DOS system services other than Interrupt 21H Functions 01 through 0CH (character I/O functions), Interrupt 21H Function 30H (Get MS-DOS Version Number), and Interrupt 21H Function 59H (Get Extended Error Information). These functions use a special stack so that they can be called during error processing.

In general, the critical error handler must preserve all but the AL register. It must not change the contents of the device header pointed to by BP:SI. The handler must return to the MS-DOS kernel with an IRET, passing an action code in register AL as follows:

Value in AL	Meaning
00H	Ignore
01H	Retry
02H	Terminate process
03H	Fail current system call

These values correspond to the options presented by the MS-DOS default critical error handler. The default handler prompts the user for input, places the appropriate return information in the AL register, and immediately issues an IRET instruction.

Note: Although the *Fail* option is displayed by the MS-DOS default critical error handler in versions 3.3 and later, the *Fail* option inside the handler was added in version 3.1.

With MS-DOS versions 3.1 and later, if the handler returns an action code in AL that is not allowed for the error in question (bits 3 through 5 of the AH register at the point of call), MS-DOS reacts according to the following rules:

If *Ignore* is specified by AL = 00H but is not allowed because bit 5 of AH = 0, the response defaults to *Fail* (AL = 03H).

If *Retry* is specified by AL = 01H but is not allowed because bit 4 of AH = 0, the response defaults to *Fail* (AL = 03H).

If *Fail* is specified by AL = 03H but is not allowed because bit 3 of AH = 0, the response defaults to *Abort*.

Custom critical error handlers

Each time it receives control, COMMAND.COM restores the Interrupt 24H vector to point to the system's default critical error handler and displays a prompt to the user. Consequently, a single custom handler cannot terminate and stay resident to provide critical error handling services for subsequent application programs. Each program that needs better critical error handling than MS-DOS provides must contain its own critical error handler.

Figure 12-2 contains a simple critical error handler, INT24.ASM, written in assembly language. In the form shown, INT24.ASM is no more than a functional replacement for the MS-DOS default critical error handler, but it can be used as the basis for more sophisticated handlers that can be incorporated into application programs.

INT24.ASM contains three routines:

Routine	Action
get24	Saves the previous contents of the Interrupt 24H critical error handler vector and stores the address of the new critical error handler into the vector.
res24	Restores the address of the previous critical error handler, which was saved by a call to get24, into the Interrupt 24 vector.
int24	Replaces the MS-DOS critical error handler.

A program wishing to substitute the new critical error handler for the system's default handler should call the *get24* routine during its initialization sequence. If the program wishes to revert to the system's default handler during execution, it can accomplish this with a call to the *res24* routine. Otherwise, a call to *res24* (and the presence of the routine itself in the program) is not necessary, because MS-DOS automatically restores the Interrupt 24H vector to its previous value when the program exits, from information stored in the program segment prefix (PSP).

The replacement critical error handler, *int24*, is simple. First it saves all registers; then it displays a message that a critical error has occurred and prompts the user to enter a key selecting one of the four possible options: *Abort, Retry, Ignore,* or *Fail.* If an illegal key is entered, the prompt is displayed again; otherwise, the action code corresponding to the key is extracted from a table and placed in the AL register, the other registers are restored, and control is returned to the MS-DOS kernel with an IRET instruction.

Note that the handle read and write functions (Interrupt 21H Functions 3FH and 40H), which would normally be preferred for interaction with the display and keyboard, cannot be used in a critical error handler.

```
        name    int24
        title   INT24 Critical Error Handler


;
; INT24.ASM — Replacement critical error handler
; by Ray Duncan, September 1987
;


cr      equ     0dh             ; ASCII carriage return
lf      equ     0ah             ; ASCII linefeed

DGROUP  group   _DATA

_DATA   segment word public 'DATA'

save24  dd      0               ; previous contents of Int 24H
                                ; critical error handler vector
```

Figure 12-2. INT24.ASM, a replacement Interrupt 24H handler.   (more)

```
                              ; prompt message used by
                              ; critical error handler
prompt  db      cr,lf,'Critical Error Occurred: '
        db      'Abort, Retry, Ignore, Fail? $'

keys    db      'aArRiIfF'    ; possible user response keys
keys_len equ    $-keys        ; (both cases of each allowed)

codes   db      2,2,1,1,0,0,3,3 ; codes returned to MS-DOS kernel
                              ; for corresponding response keys

_DATA   ends


_TEXT   segment word public 'CODE'

        assume  cs:_TEXT,ds:DGROUP

        public  get24
get24   proc    near          ; set Int 24H vector to point
                              ; to new critical error handler

        push    ds            ; save segment registers
        push    es

        mov     ax,3524h      ; get address of previous
        int     21h           ; INT 24H handler and save it

        mov     word ptr save24,bx
        mov     word ptr save24+2,es

        push    cs            ; set DS:DX to point to
        pop     ds            ; new INT 24H handler
        mov     dx,offset _TEXT:int24
        mov     ax,2524h      ; then call MS-DOS to
        int     21h           ; set the INT 24H vector

        pop     es            ; restore segment registers
        pop     ds
        ret                   ; and return to caller

get24   endp


        public  res24
res24   proc    near          ; restore original contents
                              ; of Int 24H vector

        push    ds            ; save our data segment
```

Figure 12-2. Continued.   *(more)*

```
        lds     dx,save24       ; put address of old handler
        mov     ax,2524h        ; back into INT 24H vector
        int     21h

       ·pop     ds              ; restore data segment
        ret                     ; and return to caller

res24   endp

;
; This is the replacement critical error handler.  It
; prompts the user for Abort, Retry, Ignore, or Fail and
; returns the appropriate code to the MS-DOS kernel.
;
int24   proc    far             ; entered from MS-DOS kernel

        push    bx              ; save registers
        push    cx
        push    dx
        push    si
        push    di
        push    bp
        push    ds
        push    es

int24a: mov     ax,DGROUP       ; display prompt for user
        mov     ds,ax           ; using function 09H (print string
        mov     es,ax           ; terminated by $ character)
        mov     dx,offset prompt
        mov     ah,09h
        int     21h

        mov     ah,01h          ; get user's response
        int     21h             ; function 01H = read one character

        mov     di,offset keys  ; look up code for response key
        mov     cx,keys_len
        cld
        repne scasb
        jnz     int24a          ; prompt again if bad response

                                ; set AL = action code for MS-DOS
                                ; according to key that was entered:
                                ; 0 = ignore, 1 = retry, 2 = abort, 3 = fail
        mov     al,[di+keys_len-1]

        pop     es              ; restore registers
        pop     ds
        pop     bp
        pop     di
        pop     si
```

Figure 12-2. Continued. *(more)*

```
        pop     dx
        pop     cx
        pop     bx
        iret                        ; exit critical error handler

int24   endp

_TEXT   ends

        end
```

Figure 12-2. Continued.

Hardware-generated Exception Interrupts

Intel reserved the vectors for Interrupts 00H through 1FH (Table 12-1) for exceptions generated by the execution of various machine instructions. Handling of these chip-dependent internal interrupts can vary from one make of MS-DOS machine to another; some such differences are mentioned in the discussion.

Table 12-1. Intel Reserved Exception Interrupts.

Interrupt Number	Definition
00H	Divide by Zero
01H	Single-Step
02H	Nonmaskable Interrupt (NMI)
03H	Breakpoint Trap
04H	Overflow Trap
05H	BOUND Range Exceeded*
06H	Invalid Opcode*
07H	Coprocessor not Available†
08H	Double-Fault Exception†
09H	Coprocessor Segment Overrun†
0AH	Invalid Task State Segment (TSS)†
0BH	Segment not Present†
0CH	Stack Exception†
0DH	General Protection Exception†
0EH	Page Fault‡
0FH	(Reserved)
10H	Coprocessor Error†
11–1FH	(Reserved)

* The 80186, 80286, and 80386 microprocessors only.
† The 80286 and 80386 microprocessors only.
‡ The 80386 microprocessor only.

Note: A number of these reserved exception interrupts generally do not occur in MS-DOS because they are generated only when the 80286 or 80386 microprocessor is operating in protected mode. The following discussions do not cover these interrupts.

Divide by Zero (Interrupt 00H)

An Interrupt 00H occurs whenever a DIV or IDIV operation fails to terminate within a reasonable period of time. The interrupt is triggered by a mathematical anomaly: Division by zero is inherently undefined. To handle such situations, Intel built special processing into the DIV and IDIV instructions to ensure that the condition does not cause the processor to lock up. Although the assumption underlying Interrupt 00H is an attempt to divide by zero (a condition that will never terminate), the interrupt can also be triggered by other error conditions, such as a quotient that is too large to fit in the designated register (AX or AL).

The ROM BIOS handler for Interrupt 00H in the IBM PC and close compatibles is a simple IRET instruction. During the MS-DOS startup process, however, MS-DOS modifies the interrupt vector to point to its own handler — a routine that issues the warning message *Divide by Zero* and aborts the current application. This abort procedure can leave the computer and operating system in an extremely unstable state. If the default handler is used, the system should be restarted immediately and an attempt should be made to find and eliminate the cause of the error. A better approach, however, is to provide a replacement handler that treats Interrupt 00H much as MS-DOS treats Interrupt 24H.

Single-Step (Interrupt 01H)

If the trap flag (bit 8 of the microprocessor's 16-bit flags register) is set, Interrupt 01H occurs at the end of every instruction executed by the processor. By default, Interrupt 01H points to a simple IRET instruction, so the net effect is as if nothing happened. However, debugging programs, which are the only applications that use this interrupt, modify the interrupt vector to point to their own handlers. The interrupt can then be used to allow a debugger to single-step through the machine instructions of the program being debugged, as DEBUG does with its T (Trace) command.

Nonmaskable Interrupt, or NMI (Interrupt 02H)

In the hardware architecture of IBM PCs and close compatibles, Interrupt 02H is invoked whenever a memory parity error is detected. MS-DOS provides no handler, because this error, as a hardware-related problem, is in the domain of the ROM BIOS.

In response to the Interrupt 02H, the default ROM BIOS handler displays a message and locks the machine, on the assumption that bad memory prevents reliable system operation. Many programmers, however, prefer to include code that permits orderly shutdown of the system. Replacing the ROM BIOS parity trap routine can be dangerous, though, because a parity error detected in memory means the contents of RAM are no longer reliable — even the memory locations containing the NMI handler itself might be defective.

Breakpoint Trap (Interrupt 03H)

Interrupt 03H, which is used in conjunction with Interrupt 01H for debugging, is invoked by a special 1-byte opcode (0CCH). During a debugging session, a debugger modifies the vector for Interrupt 03H to point to its own handler and then replaces 1 byte of program opcode with the 0CCH opcode at any location where a breakpoint is needed.

When a breakpoint is reached, the 0CCH opcode triggers Interrupt 03H and the debugger regains control. The debugger then restores the original opcode in the program being debugged and issues a prompt so that the user can display or alter the contents of memory or registers. The use of Interrupt 03H is illustrated by DEBUG and SYMDEB's breakpoint capabilities.

Overflow Trap (Interrupt 04H)

If the overflow bit (bit 11) in the microprocessor's flags register is set, Interrupt 04H occurs when the INTO (Interrupt on Overflow) instruction is executed. The overflow bit can be set during prior execution of any arithmetic instruction (such as MUL or IMUL) that can produce an overflow error.

The ROM BIOS of the IBM PC and close compatibles initializes the Interrupt 04H vector to point to an IRET, so this interrupt becomes invisible to the user if it is executed. MS-DOS does not have its own handler for Interrupt 04H. However, because the Intel microprocessors also include JO (Jump if Overflow) and JNO (Jump if No Overflow) instructions, applications rarely need the INTO instruction and, hence, seldom have to provide their own Interrupt 04H handlers.

BOUND Range Exceeded (Interrupt 05H)

Interrupt 05H is generated on 80186, 80286, and 80386 microprocessors if a BOUND instruction is executed to test the value of an array index and the index falls outside the limits specified by the instruction's operand. The exception handler is expected to alter the index so that it is correct—when the handler performs an interrupt return (IRET), the CPU reexecutes the BOUND instruction that caused the interrupt.

On IBM PC/AT-compatible machines, the ROM BIOS assignment of the PrtSc (print screen) routine to Interrupt 05H is in conflict with the CPU's use of Interrupt 05H for BOUND exceptions.

Invalid opcode (Interrupt 06H)

Interrupt 06H is generated by the 80186, 80286, and 80386 microprocessors if the current instruction is not a valid opcode—for example, if the machine tries to execute a data statement.

On IBM PC/ATs, Interrupt 06H simply points to an IRET instruction. The ROM BIOS routines of some IBM PC/AT-compatibles, however, provide an interrupt handler that reports an unexpected software Interrupt 06H and asks if the user wants to continue. A *Y* response causes the interrupt handler to skip over the invalid opcode. Unfortunately, because the succeeding opcode is often invalid as well, the user may have the feeling of being trapped in a loop.

Extended Error Information

Under MS-DOS versions 1.x, the operating system provided limited information about errors that occurred during calls to the Interrupt 21H system functions. For example, if a program called Function 0FH to open a file, there were only two possible results: On return, the AL register either contained 00H for a successful open or 0FFH for failure. No further detail was available from the operating system. Although some of these early system calls (such as the read and write functions) returned somewhat more information, the 1.x versions of MS-DOS were essentially limited to success/failure return codes.

Beginning with version 2.0 and the introduction of the handle concept, additional error information became available. *See* PROGRAMMING IN THE MS-DOS ENVIRONMENT: PROGRAMMING FOR MS-DOS: File and Record Management. For example, if a program attempts to open a file with Interrupt 21H Function 3DH (Open File with Handle), it can check the status of the carry flag on return to detect whether an error occurred. If the carry flag is not set, the call was successful and the AX register contains the file handle. If the carry flag is set, the AX register contains one of the following possible error codes:

Error Code	Meaning
01H	Invalid function code
02H	File not found
03H	Path not found
04H	Too many open files (no more handles available)
05H	Access denied
0CH	Invalid access code

In some circumstances, however, even these error codes do not provide enough information. Therefore, beginning with version 3.0, MS-DOS made extended error information available through Interrupt 21H Function 59H (Get Extended Error Information). This function can be called after any other Interrupt 21H function fails, or it can be called from a critical error handler. The extended error codes, briefly described below, maintain compatibility with the MS-DOS versions 2.x error returns and are grouped as follows:

Error Code	Error Group
00H	No error encountered.
01–12H	MS-DOS versions 2.x and 3.x Interrupt 21H errors. These error codes are identical to those returned in the AX register by Functions 38H through 57H if the carry flag is set on return from the function call.
13–1FH	MS-DOS versions 2.x and 3.x Interrupt 24H errors. These error codes are 13H (19) greater than the codes passed to a critical error handler in the lower half of the DI register; that is, if the critical error handler receives error code 04H (CRC error), Interrupt 21H Function 59H returns 17H.
20–58H	Extended error codes, many related to networking and file sharing, for MS-DOS versions 3.0 and later.

Note: The contents of the CPU registers (except CS:IP and SS:SP) are destroyed by a call to Function 59H. Also, as mentioned earlier, this function is available only with MS-DOS versions 3.x, even though it maintains compatibility with error returns in versions 2.x.

On return, Function 59H provides the extended error code in the AX register, the error class (type) in the BH register, a code for the suggested corrective action in the BL register, and the locus of the error in the CH register. These values are defined in the following paragraphs. With MS-DOS or PC-DOS versions 3.x, if an error 22H (invalid disk change) occurs and if the capability is supported by the system's block-device drivers, ES:DI points to an ASCIIZ volume label that designates the disk to be inserted in the drive before the operation is retried.

Error Code (AX register). This value is defined as follows:

Value in AX	Meaning
Interrupt 21H errors (MS-DOS versions 2.0 and later):	
01H	Invalid function number
02H	File not found
03H	Path not found
04H	Too many open files (no handles available)
05H	Access denied
06H	Invalid handle
07H	Memory control blocks destroyed
08H	Insufficient memory
09H	Invalid memory-block address
0AH	Invalid environment
0BH	Invalid format
0CH	Invalid access code
0DH	Invalid data
0EH	Reserved
0FH	Invalid disk drive specified
10H	Attempt to remove the current directory
11H	Not same device
12H	No more files
Interrupt 24H errors (MS-DOS versions 2.0 and later):	
13H	Attempt to write on write-protected disk
14H	Unknown unit
15H	Drive not ready
16H	Invalid command
17H	Data error based on cyclic redundancy check (CRC)
18H	Length of request structure invalid
19H	Seek error

(more)

Value in AX	Meaning
Interrupt 24H errors *(continued)*	
1AH	Unknown media type (non-MS-DOS disk)
1BH	Sector not found
1CH	Printer out of paper
10H	Write fault
1EH	Read fault
1FH	General failure

MS-DOS versions 3.x extended errors:	
20H	Sharing violation
21H	Lock violation
22H	Invalid disk change
23H	FCB unavailable
24H	Sharing buffer exceeded
25H–31H	Reserved
32H	Network request not supported
33H	Remote computer not listening
34H	Duplicate name on network
35H	Network name not found
36H	Network busy
37H	Device no longer exists on network
38H	Net BIOS command limit exceeded
39H	Error in network adapter hardware
3AH	Incorrect response from network
3BH	Unexpected network error
3CH	Incompatible remote adapter
3DH	Print queue full
3EH	Queue not full
3FH	Not enough room for print file
40H	Network name deleted
41H	Access denied
42H	Incorrect network device type
43H	Network name not found
44H	Network name limit exceeded
45H	Net BIOS session limit exceeded
46H	Temporary pause
47H	Network request not accepted
48H	Print or disk redirection paused
49H–4FH	Reserved
50H	File already exists
51H	Reserved

(more)

Value in AX	Meaning
MS-DOS versions 3.x extended errors *(continued)*	
52H	Cannot make directory
53H	Failure on Interrupt 24H
54H	Out of structures
55H	Already assigned
56H	Invalid password
57H	Invalid parameter
58H	Network write fault

Locus (CH register). This value provides information on the location of the error:

Value in CH	Meaning
01H	Location unknown
02H	Block device; generally caused by a disk error
03H	Network
04H	Serial device; generally caused by a timeout from a character device
05H	Memory; caused by an error in RAM

Error Class (BH register). This value gives the general category of the error:

Value in BH	Meaning
01H	Out of resource; out of storage space or I/O channels.
02H	Temporary situation; expected to clear, as in a file or record lock — generally occurs only in a network environment.
03H	Authorization; a problem with permission to access the requested device.
04H	Internal error in system software; generally reflects a system software bug rather than an application or system failure.
05H	Hardware failure; a serious hardware-related problem not the fault of the user program.
06H	System failure; a serious failure of the system software, not directly the fault of the application — generally occurs if configuration files are missing or incorrect.
07H	Application-program error; generally caused by inconsistent function requests from the user program.
08H	File or item not found.
09H	File or item of invalid format or type detected, or an otherwise unsuitable or invalid item requested.
0AH	File or item interlocked by the system.

(more)

Value in BH	Meaning
0BH	Media failure; generally occurs with a bad disk in a drive, a bad spot on the disk, or the like.
0CH	Already exists; generally occurs when application tries to declare a machine name or device that already exists.
0DH	Unknown.

Suggested Action (BL register). One of the most useful returns from Function 59H, this value suggests a corrective action to try:

Value in BL	Meaning
01H	Retry a few times before prompting the user to choose *Ignore* for the program to continue or *Abort* to terminate.
02H	Pause for a few seconds between retries and then prompt user as above.
03H	Ask user to reenter the input. In most cases, this solution applies when an incorrect drive specifier or filename was entered. Of course, if the value was hard-coded into the program, the user should not be prompted for input.
04H	Clean up as well as possible, then abort the application. This solution applies when the error is destructive enough that the application cannot safely proceed, but the system is healthy enough to try an orderly shutdown of the application.
05H	Exit from the application as soon as possible, without trying to close files and clean up. This means something is seriously wrong with either the application or the system.
06H	Ignore; error is informational.
07H	Prompt user to perform some action, such as changing floppy disks in a drive and then retry.

Function 59H and older system calls

The Interrupt 21H functions — primarily the FCB-related file and record calls — that return 0FFH in the AL register to indicate that an error has occurred but provide no further information about the type of error include

Function	Name
0FH	Open File with FCB
10H	Close File with FCB
11H	Find First File
12H	Find Next File

(more)

Function	Name
13H	Delete File
16H	Create File with FCB
17H	Rename File
23H	Get File Size

These function calls now exist only to maintain compatibility with MS-DOS versions 1.x. The preferred choices are the handle-style calls available in MS-DOS versions 2.0 and later, which offer full path support and much better error reporting. *See also* SYSTEM CALLS.

If the older calls *must* be used, the program can use Function 59H to obtain more detailed information under MS-DOS version 3.0 or later. For example:

```
myfcb   db      0                 ; drive = default
        db      'MYFILE  '        ; filename, 8 chars
        db      'DAT'             ; extension, 3 chars
        db      25 dup (0)        ; remainder of FCB
        .
        .
        .
        mov     dx,seg myfcb      ; DS:DX = FCB
        mov     ds,dx
        mov     dx,offset myfcb
        mov     ah,0fh            ; function 0FH = Open FCB

        int     21h               ; transfer to MS-DOS
        or      al,al             ; test status
        jz      success           ; jump, open succeeded
                                  ; open failed, get
                                  ; extended error info
        mov     bx,0              ; BX = 00H for ver. 2.x-3.x
        mov     ah,59h            ; function 59H = Get Info
        int     21h               ; transfer to MS-DOS
        or      ax,ax             ; really an error?
        jz      success           ; no error, jump
                                  ; test recommended actions
        cmp     bl,01h
        jz      retry             ; if BL = 01H retry operation
        cmp     bl,04h
        jz      cleanup           ; if BL = 04H clean up and exit
        cmp     bl,05h
        jz      panic             ; if BL = 05H exit immediately
        .
        .
        .
```

Function 59H and newer system calls

The function calls listed below were added in MS-DOS versions 2.0 and later. These calls return with the carry flag set if an error occurs; in addition, the AX register contains an error value corresponding to error codes 01H through 12H of the extended error return codes:

Function	Name
MS-DOS versions 2.0 and later:	
38H	Get/Set Current Country
39H	Create Directory
3AH	Remove Directory
3BH	Change Current Directory
3CH	Create File with Handle
3DH	Open File with Handle
3EH	Close File
3FH	Read File or Device
40H	Write File or Device
41H	Delete File
42H	Move File Pointer
43H	Get/Set File Attributes
44H	IOCTL (I/O Control for Devices)
45H	Duplicate File Handle
46H	Force Duplicate File Handle
47H	Get Current Directory
48H	Allocate Memory Block
49H	Free Memory Block
4AH	Resize Memory Block
4BH	Load and Execute Program (EXEC)
4EH	Find First File
4FH	Find Next File
56H	Rename File
57H	Get/Set Date/Time of File
MS-DOS versions 3.0 and later:	
58H	Get/Set Allocation Strategy
5AH	Create Temporary File
5BH	Create New File
5CH	Lock/Unlock File Region
MS-DOS versions 3.1 and later:	
5EH	Network Machine Name/Printer Setup
5FH	Get/Make Assign List Entry

Although these newer functions have much better error reporting than the older FCB functions, Function 59H is still useful. Regardless of the version of MS-DOS that is running, the error code returned in the AX register from an Interrupt 21H function call is always in the range 0–12H. If a program is running under MS-DOS versions 3.x and wants to obtain one or more of the more specific error codes in the range 20–58H, the program must follow the failed Interrupt 21H call with a subsequent call to Interrupt 21H Function 59H. The program can then use the code returned by Function 59H in the BL register as a guide to the action to take in response to the error. For example:

```
myfile  db      'MYFILE.DAT',0  ; ASCIIZ filename
        .
        .
        .
        mov     dx,seg myfile   ; DS:DX = ASCIIZ filename
        mov     ds,dx
        mov     dx,offset myfile
        mov     ax,3d02h        ; open, read/write
        int     21h             ; transfer to MS-DOS
        jnc     success         ; jump, open succeeded
                                ; open failed, get
                                ; extended error info
        mov     bx,0            ; BX = 00H for ver. 2.x-3.x
        mov     ah,59h          ; function 59H = Get Info
        int     21h             ; transfer to MS-DOS
        or      ax,ax           ; really an error?
        jz      success         ; no error, jump
                                ; test recommended actions
        cmp     bl,01h
        jz      retry           ; if BL = 01H retry operation
        .
        .
        .
```

If the standard critical error handler is replaced with a customized critical handler, Function 59H can also be used to obtain more detailed information about an error inside the handler before either returning control to the application or aborting. The value in the BL register should be used to determine the appropriate action to take or the message to display to the user.

Jim Kyle
Chip Rabinowitz

Article 13
Hardware Interrupt Handlers

Unlike software interrupts, which are service requests initiated by a program, hardware interrupts occur in response to electrical signals received from a peripheral device such as a serial port or a disk controller, or they are generated internally by the microprocessor itself. Hardware interrupts, whether external or internal to the microprocessor, are given prioritized servicing by the Intel CPU architecture.

The 8086 family of microprocessors (which includes the 8088, 8086, 80186, 80286, and 80386) reserves the first 1024 bytes of memory (addresses 0000:0000H through 0000:03FFH) for a table of 256 interrupt vectors, each a 4-byte far pointer to a specific interrupt service routine (ISR) that is carried out when the corresponding interrupt is processed. The design of the 8086 family requires certain of these interrupt vectors to be used for specific functions (Table 13-1). Although Intel actually reserves the first 32 interrupts, IBM, in the original PC, redefined usage of Interrupts 05H to 1FH. Most, but not all, of these reserved vectors are used by software, rather than hardware, interrupts; the redefined IBM uses are listed in Table 13-2.

Table 13-1. Intel Reserved Exception Interrupts.

Interrupt Number	Definition
00H	Divide by zero
01H	Single step
02H	Nonmaskable interrupt (NMI)
03H	Breakpoint trap
04H	Overflow trap
05H	BOUND range exceeded*
06H	Invalid opcode*
07H	Coprocessor not available†
08H	Double-fault exception†
09H	Coprocessor segment overrun†
0AH	Invalid task state segment (TSS)†
0BH	Segment not present†
0CH	Stack exception†
0DH	General protection exception†
0EH	Page fault‡

(more)

Table 13-1. *Continued.*

Interrupt Number	Definition
0FH	(Reserved)
10H	Coprocessor error†

*The 80186, 80286, and 80386 microprocessors only.
†The 80286 and 80386 microprocessors only.
‡The 80386 microprocessor only.

Table 13-2. IBM Interrupt Usage.

Interrupt Number	Definition
05H	Print screen
06H	Unused
07H	Unused
08H	Hardware IRQ0 (timer-tick)*
09H	Hardware IRQ1 (keyboard)
0AH	Hardware IRQ2 (reserved)†
0BH	Hardware IRQ3 (COM2)
0CH	Hardware IRQ4 (COM1)
0DH	Hardware IRQ5 (fixed disk)
0EH	Hardware IRQ6 (floppy disk)
0FH	Hardware IRQ7 (printer)
10H	Video service
11H	Equipment information
12H	Memory size
13H	Disk I/O service
14H	Serial-port service
15H	Cassette/network service
16H	Keyboard service
17H	Printer service
18H	ROM BASIC
19H	Restart system
1AH	Get/Set time/date
1BH	Control-Break (user defined)
1CH	Timer tick (user defined)
1DH	Video parameter pointer
1EH	Disk parameter pointer
1FH	Graphics character table

*IRQ = Interrupt request line.
†*See* Table 13-4.

Nestled in the middle of Table 13-2 are the eight hardware interrupt vectors (08-0FH) IBM implemented in the original PC design. These eight vectors provide the maskable interrupts for the IBM PC-family and close compatibles. Additional IRQ lines built into the IBM PC/AT are discussed under The IRQ Levels below.

The conflicting uses of the interrupts listed in Tables 13-1 and 13-2 have created compatibility problems as the 8086 family of microprocessors has developed. For complete compatibility with IBM equipment, the IBM usage must be followed even when it conflicts with the chip design. For example, a BOUND error occurs if an array index exceeds the specified upper and lower limits (bounds) of the array, causing an Interrupt 05H to be generated. But the 80286 processor used in all AT-class computers will, if a BOUND error occurs, send the contents of the display to the printer, because IBM uses Interrupt 05H for the Print Screen function.

Hardware Interrupt Categories

The 8086 family of microprocessors can handle three types of hardware interrupts. First are the internal, microprocessor-generated exception interrupts (Table 13-1). Second is the nonmaskable interrupt, or NMI (Interrupt 02H), which is generated when the NMI line (pin 17 on the 8088 and 8086, pin 59 on the 80286, pin B8 on the 80386) goes high (active). In the IBM PC family (except the PCjr and the Convertible), the nonmaskable interrupt is designated for memory parity errors. Third are the maskable interrupts, which are usually generated by external devices.

Maskable interrupts are routed to the main processor through a chip called the 8259A Programmable Interrupt Controller (PIC). When it receives an interrupt request, the PIC signals the microprocessor that an interrupt needs service by driving the interrupt request (INTR) line of the main processor to high voltage level. This article focuses on the maskable interrupts and the 8259A because it is through the PIC that external I/O devices (disk drives, serial communication ports, and so forth) gain access to the interrupt system.

Interrupt priorities in the 8086 family

The Intel microprocessors have a built-in priority system for handling interrupts that occur simultaneously. Priority goes to the internal instruction exception interrupts, such as Divide by Zero and Invalid Opcode, because priority is determined by the interrupt number: Interrupt 00H takes priority over all others, whereas the last possible interrupt, 0FFH, would, if present, never be allowed to break in while another interrupt was being serviced. However, if interrupt service is enabled (the microprocessor's interrupt flag is set), any hardware interrupt takes priority over any software interrupt (INT instruction).

The priority sequencing by interrupt number must not be confused with the priority resolution performed by hardware external to the microprocessor. The numeric priority discussed here applies only to interrupts generated within the 8086 family of microprocessor chips and is totally independent of system interrupt priorities established for components external to the microprocessor itself.

Interrupt service routines

For the most part, programmers need not write hardware-specific program routines to service the hardware interrupts. The IBM PC BIOS routines, together with MS-DOS services, are usually sufficient. In some cases, however, MS-DOS and the ROM BIOS do not provide enough assistance to ensure adequate performance of a program. Most notable in this category is communications software, for which programmers usually must access the 8259A and the 8250 Universal Asynchronous Receiver and Transmitter (UART) directly. *See* PROGRAMMING IN THE MS-DOS ENVIRONMENT: Programming for ms-dos: Interrupt-Driven Communications.

Characteristics of Maskable Interrupts

Two major characteristics distinguish maskable interrupts from all other events that can occur in the system: They are totally unpredictable, and they are highly volatile. In general, a hardware interrupt occurs when a peripheral device requires the full attention of the system and data will be irretrievably lost unless the system responds rapidly.

All things are relative, however, and this is especially true of the speed required to service an interrupt request. For example, assume that two interrupt requests occur at essentially the same time. One is from a serial communications port receiving data at 300 bps; the other is from a serial port receiving data at 9600 bps. Data from the first serial port will not change for at least 30 milliseconds, but the second serial port must be serviced within one millisecond to avoid data loss.

Unpredictability

Because maskable interrupts generally originate in response to external physical events, such as the receipt of a byte of data over a communications line, the exact time at which such an interrupt will occur cannot be predicted. Even the timer interrupt request, which by default occurs approximately 18.2 times per second, cannot be predicted by any program that happens to be executing when the interrupt request occurs.

Because of this unpredictability, the system must, if it allows any interrupts to be recognized, be prepared to service all maskable interrupt requests. Conversely, if interrupts cannot be serviced, they must all be disabled. The 8086 family of microprocessors provides the Set Interrupt Flag (STI) instruction to enable maskable interrupt response and the Clear Interrupt Flag (CLI) instruction to disable it. The interrupt flag is also cleared automatically when a hardware interrupt response begins; the interrupt handler should execute STI as quickly as possible to allow higher priority interrupts to be serviced.

Volatility

As noted earlier, a maskable interrupt request must normally be serviced immediately to prevent loss of data, but the concept of immediacy is relative to the data transfer rate of the device requesting the interrupt. The rule is that the currently available unit of data must be processed (at least to the point of being stored in a buffer) before the next such item can arrive. Except for such devices as disk drives, which always require immediate response, interrupts for devices that receive data are normally much more critical than interrupts for devices that transmit data.

The problems imposed by data volatility during hardware interrupt service are solved by establishing service priorities for interrupts generated outside the microprocessor chip itself. Devices with the slowest transfer rates are assigned lower interrupt service priorities, and the most time-critical devices are assigned the highest priority of interrupt service.

Handling Maskable Interrupts

The microprocessor handles all interrupts (maskable, nonmaskable, and software) by pushing the contents of the flags register onto the stack, disabling the interrupt flag, and pushing the current contents of the CS:IP registers onto the stack.

The microprocessor then takes the interrupt number from the data bus, multiplies it by 4 (the size of each vector in bytes), and uses the result as an offset into the interrupt vector table located in the bottom 1 KB (segment 0000H) of system RAM. The 4-byte address at that location is then used as the new CS:IP value (Figure 13-1).

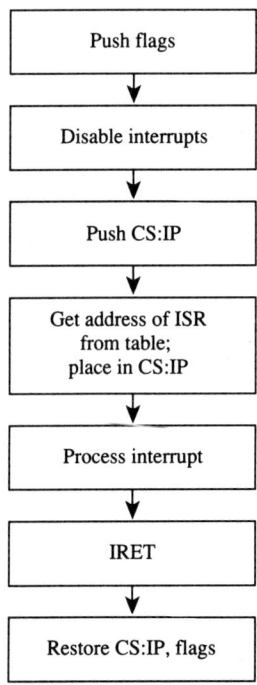

Figure 13-1. General interrupt sequence.

External devices are assigned dedicated interrupt request lines (IRQs) associated with the 8259A. *See* The IRQ Levels below. When a device requires attention, it sends a signal to the PIC via its IRQ line. The PIC, which functions as an "executive secretary" for the external devices, operates as shown in Figure 13-2. It evaluates the service request and, if appropriate, causes the microprocessor's INTR line to go high. The microprocessor then checks whether interrupts are enabled (whether the interrupt flag is set). If they are, the flags are pushed onto the stack, the interrupt flag is disabled, and CS:IP is pushed onto the stack.

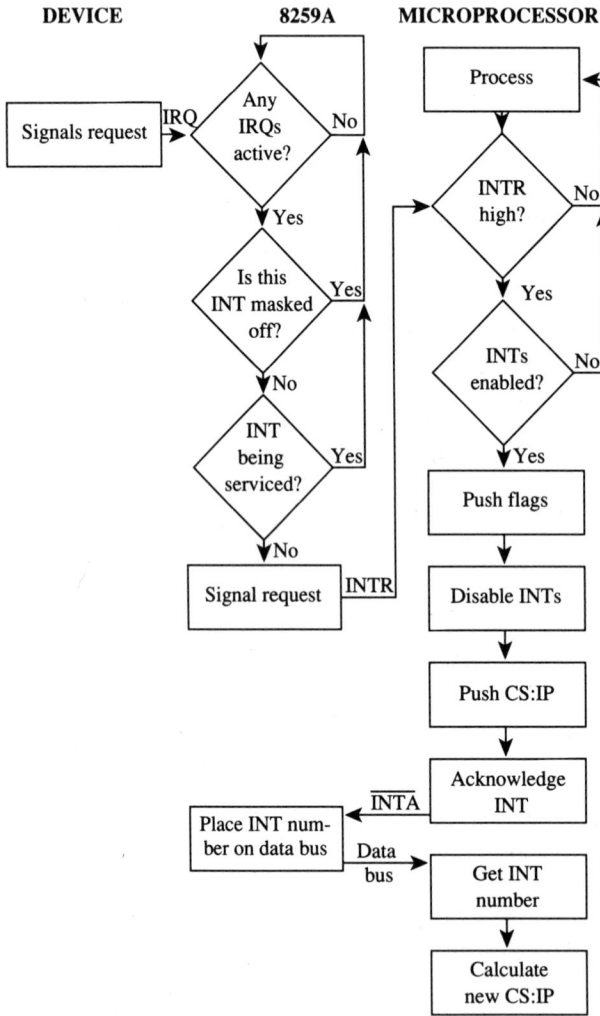

Figure 13-2. Maskable interrupt service.

The microprocessor acknowledges the interrupt request by signaling the 8259A via the interrupt acknowledge (INTA) line. The 8259A then places the interrupt number on the data bus. The microprocessor gets the interrupt number from the data bus and services the interrupt. Before issuing the IRET instruction, the interrupt service routine must issue an end-of-interrupt (EOI) sequence to the 8259A so that other interrupts can be processed. This is done by sending 20H to port 20H. (The similarity of numbers is pure coincidence.) The EOI sequence is covered in greater detail elsewhere. *See* PROGRAMMING IN THE MS-DOS ENVIRONMENT: PROGRAMMING FOR MS-DOS: Interrupt-Driven Communications.

The 8259A Programmable Interrupt Controller

The 8259A (Figure 13-3) has a number of internal components, many of them under software control. Only the default settings for the IBM PC family are covered here.

Three registers influence the servicing of maskable interrupts: the interrupt request register (IRR), the in-service register (ISR), and the interrupt mask register (IMR).

The IRR is used to keep track of the devices requesting attention. When a device causes its IRQ line to go high to signal the 8259A that it needs service, a bit is set in the IRR that corresponds to the interrupt level of the device.

The ISR specifies which interrupt levels are currently being serviced; an ISR bit is set when an interrupt has been acknowledged by the CPU (via INTA) and the interrupt number has been placed on the data bus. The ISR bit associated with a particular IRQ remains set until an EOI sequence is received.

The IMR is a read/write register (at port 21H) that masks (disables) specific interrupts. When a bit is set in this register, the corresponding IRQ line is masked and no servicing for it is performed until the bit is cleared. Thus, a particular IRQ can be disabled while all others continue to be serviced.

The fourth major block in Figure 13-3, labeled *Priority resolver*, is a complex logical circuit that forms the heart of the 8259A. This component combines the statuses of the IMR, the ISR, and the IRR to determine which, if any, pending interrupt request should be serviced and then causes the microprocessor's INTR line to go high. The priority resolver can be programmed in a number of modes, although only the mode used in the IBM PC and close compatibles is described here.

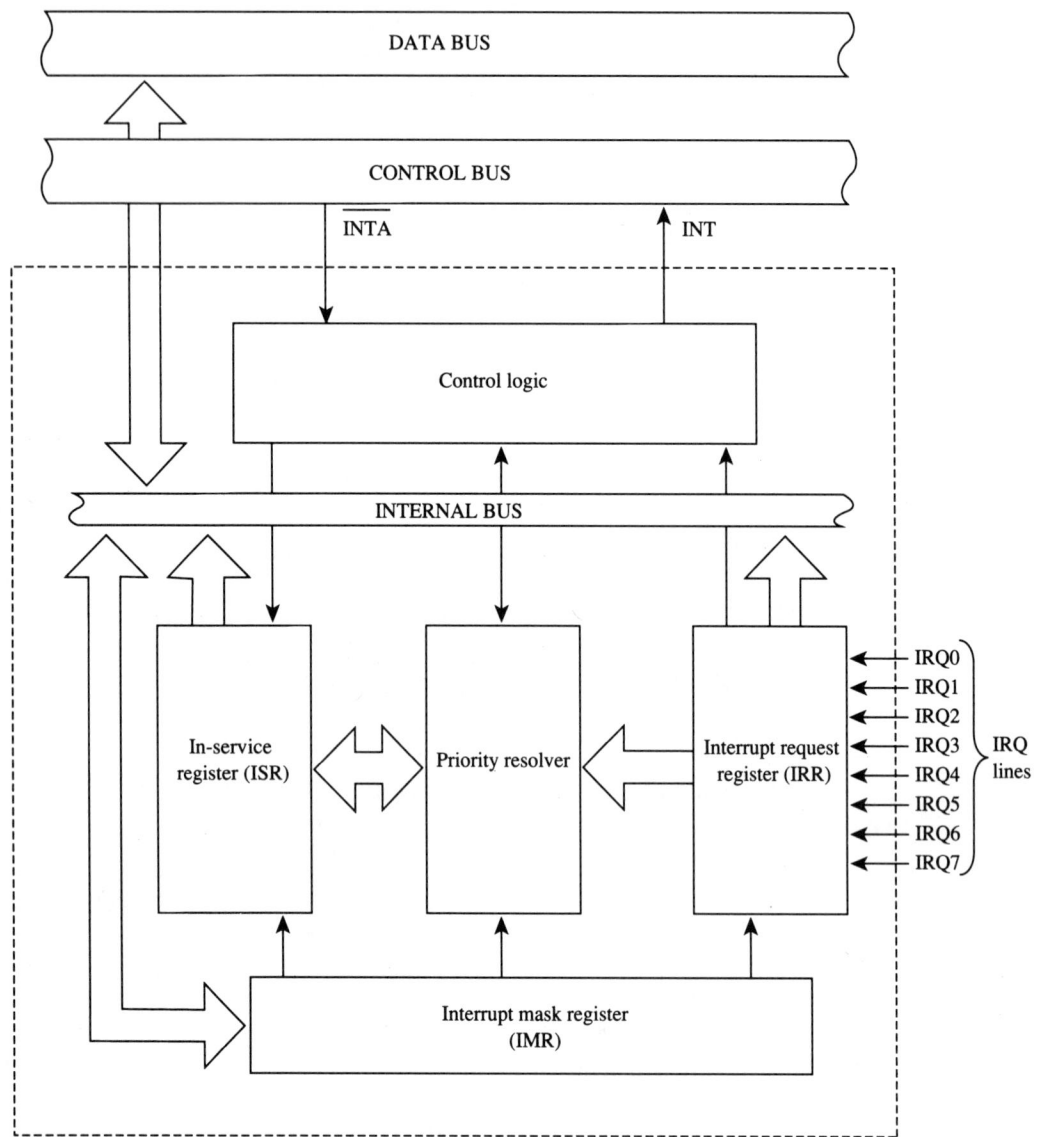

Figure 13-3. Block diagram of the 8259A Programmable Interrupt Controller.

The IRQ levels

When two or more unserviced hardware interrupts are pending, the 8259A determines which should be serviced first. The standard mode of operation for the PIC is the fully nested mode, in which IRQ lines are prioritized in a fixed sequence. Only IRQ lines with higher priority than the one currently being serviced are permitted to generate new interrupts.

The highest priority is IRQ0, and the lowest is IRQ7. Thus, if an Interrupt 09H (signaled by IRQ1) is being serviced, only an Interrupt 08H (signaled by IRQ0) can break in. All other interrupt requests are delayed until the Interrupt 09H service routine is completed and has issued an EOI sequence.

Eight-level designs

The IBM PC, PCjr, and PC/XT (and port-compatible computers) have eight IRQ lines to the PIC chip — IRQ0 through IRQ7. These lines are mapped into interrupt vectors for Interrupts 08H through 0FH (that is, 8 + IRQ level). These eight IRQ lines and their associated interrupts are listed in Table 13-3.

Table 13-3. Eight-Level Interrupt Map.

IRQ Line	Interrupt	Description
IRQ0	08H	Timer tick, 18.2 times per second
IRQ1	09H	Keyboard service required
IRQ2	0AH	I/O channel (unused on IBM PC/XT)
IRQ3	0BH	COM1 service required
IRQ4	0CH	COM2 service required
IRQ5	0DH	Fixed-disk service required
IRQ6	0EH	Floppy-disk service required
IRQ7	0FH	Data request from parallel printer*

* This request cannot be reliably generated by older versions of the IBM Monochrome/Printer Adapter and compatibles. Printer drivers that depend on this signal for operation with these cards are subject to failure.

Sixteen-level designs

In the IBM PC/AT, 8 more IRQ levels have been added by using a second 8259A PIC (the "slave") and a cascade effect, which gives 16 priority levels.

The cascade effect is accomplished by connecting the INT line of the slave to the IRQ2 line of the first, or "master," 8259A instead of to the microprocessor. When a device connected to one of the slave's IRQ lines makes an interrupt request, the INT line of the slave goes high and causes the IRQ2 line of the master 8259A to go high, which, in turn, causes the INT line of the master to go high and thus interrupts the microprocessor.

The microprocessor, ignorant of the second 8259A's presence, simply generates an interrupt acknowledge signal on receipt of the interrupt from the master 8259A. This signal initializes *both* 8259As and also causes the master to turn control over to the slave. The slave then completes the interrupt request.

On the IBM PC/AT, the eight additional IRQ lines are mapped to Interrupts 70H through 77H (Table 13-4). Because the eight additional lines are effectively connected to the master

8259A's IRQ2 line, they take priority over the master's IRQ3 through IRQ7 events. The cascade effect is graphically represented in Figure 13-4.

Table 13-4. Sixteen-Level Interrupt Map.

IRQ Line	Interrupt	Description
IRQ0	08H	Timer tick, 18.2 times per second
IRQ1	09H	Keyboard service required
IRQ2	0AH	INT from slave 8259A:
IRQ8	70H	Real-time clock service
IRQ9	71H	Software redirected to IRQ2
IRQ10	72H	Reserved
IRQ11	73H	Reserved
IRQ12	74H	Reserved
IRQ13	75H	Numeric coprocessor
IRQ14	76H	Fixed-disk controller
IRQ15	77H	Reserved
IRQ3	0BH	COM2 service required
IRQ4	0CH	COM1 service required
IRQ5	0DH	Data request from LPT2
IRQ6	0EH	Floppy-disk service required
IRQ7	0FH	Data request from LPT1

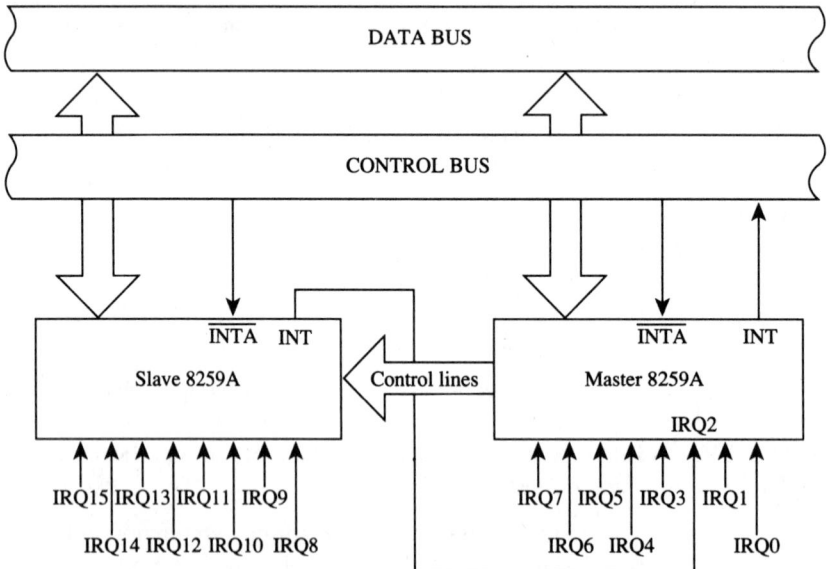

Figure 13-4. A graphic representation of the cascade effect for IRQ priorities.

Note: During the INTA sequence, the corresponding bit in the ISR register of both 8259As is set, so two EOIs must be issued to complete the interrupt service — one for the slave and one for the master.

Programming for the Hardware Interrupts

Any program that modifies an interrupt vector must restore the vector to its original condition before returning control to MS-DOS (or to its parent process). Any program that totally replaces an existing hardware interrupt handler with one of its own must perform all the handshaking and terminating actions of the original — re-enable interrupt service, signal EOI to the interrupt controller, and so forth. Failure to follow these rules has led to many hours of programmer frustration. *See also* PROGRAMMING IN THE MS-DOS ENVIRONMENT: CUSTOMIZING MS-DOS: Exception Handlers.

When an existing interrupt handler is completely replaced with a new, customized routine, the existing vector must be saved so it can be restored later. Although it is possible to modify the 4-byte vector by directly addressing the vector table in low RAM (and many published programs have followed this practice), any program that does so runs the risk of causing system failure when the program is used with multitasking or multiuser enhancements or with future versions of MS-DOS. The only technique that can be recommended for either obtaining the existing vector values or changing them is to use the MS-DOS functions provided for this purpose: Interrupt 21H Functions 25H (Set Interrupt Vector) and 35H (Get Interrupt Vector).

After the existing vector has been saved, it can be replaced with a far pointer to the replacement routine. The new routine must end with an IRET instruction. It should also take care to preserve all microprocessor registers and conditions at entry and restore them before returning.

A sample replacement handler

Suppose a program performs many mathematical calculations of random values. To prevent abnormal termination of the program by the default MS-DOS Interrupt 00H handler when a DIV or IDIV instruction is attempted and the divisor is zero, a programmer might want to replace the Interrupt 00H (Divide by Zero) routine with one that informs the user of what has happened and then continues operation without abnormal termination. The .COM program DIVZERO.ASM (Figure 13-5) does just that. (Another example is included in the article on interrupt-driven communications. *See* PROGRAMMING IN THE MS-DOS ENVIRONMENT: PROGRAMMING FOR MS-DOS: Interrupt-Driven Communications.)

```
        name    divzero
        title   'DIVZERO - Interrupt 00H Handler'
;
; DIVZERO.ASM: Demonstration Interrupt 00H Handler
;
; To assemble, link, and convert to COM file:
;
;       C>MASM DIVZERO;  <Enter>
;       C>LINK DIVZERO;  <Enter>
;       C>EXE2BIN DIVZERO.EXE DIVZERO.COM  <Enter>
;       C>DEL DIVZERO.EXE  <Enter>
;

cr      equ     0dh             ; ASCII carriage return
lf      equ     0ah             ; ASCII linefeed
eos     equ     '$'             ; end of string marker

_TEXT   segment word public 'CODE'

        assume  cs:_TEXT,ds:_TEXT,es:_TEXT,ss:_TEXT

        org     100h

entry:  jmp     start           ; skip over data area

intmsg  db      'Divide by Zero Occurred!',cr,lf,eos

divmsg  db      'Dividing '     ; message used by demo
par1    db      '0000h'         ; dividend goes here
        db      ' by '
par2    db      '00h'           ; divisor goes here
        db      ' equals '
par3    db      '00h'           ; quotient here
        db      ' remainder '
par4    db      '00h'           ; and remainder here
        db      cr,lf,eos

oldint0 dd      ?               ; save old Int 00H vector

intflag db      0               ; nonzero if divide by
                                ; zero interrupt occurred

oldip   dw      0               ; save old IP value


;
; The routine 'int0' is the actual divide by zero
; interrupt handler.  It gains control whenever a
; divide by zero or overflow occurs.  Its action
; is to set a flag and then increment the instruction
; pointer saved on the stack so that the failing
```

(more)

Figure 13-5. The Divide by Zero replacement handler, DIVZERO.ASM. This code is specific to 80286 and 80386 microprocessors. (See Appendix M: 8086/8088 Software Compatibility Issues.)

```
; divide will not be reexecuted after the IRET.
;
; In this particular case we can call MS-DOS to
; display a message during interrupt handling
; because the application triggers the interrupt
; intentionally. Thus, it is known that MS-DOS or
; other interrupt handlers are not in control
; at the point of interrupt.
;

int0:   pop     cs:oldip        ; capture instruction pointer

        push    ax
        push    bx
        push    cx
        push    dx
        push    di
        push    si
        push    ds
        push    es

        push    cs              ; set DS = CS
        pop     ds

        mov     ah,09h          ; print error message
        mov     dx,offset _TEXT:intmsg
        int     21h

        add     oldip,2         ; bypass instruction causing
                                ; divide by zero error

        mov     intflag,1       ; set divide by 0 flag

        pop     es              ; restore all registers
        pop     ds
        pop     si
        pop     di
        pop     dx
        pop     cx
        pop     bx
        pop     ax

        push    cs:oldip        ; restore instruction pointer

        iret                    ; return from interrupt


;
; The code beginning at 'start' is the application
; program.  It alters the vector for Interrupt 00H to
; point to the new handler, carries out some divide
```

Figure 13-5. Continued.   *(more)*

```
; operations (including one that will trigger an
; interrupt) for demonstration purposes, restores
; the original contents of the Interrupt 00H vector,
; and then terminates.
;

start:  mov     ax,3500h        ; get current contents
        int     21h             ; of Int 00H vector

                                ; save segment:offset
                                ; of previous Int 00H handler
        mov     word ptr oldint0,bx
        mov     word ptr oldint0+2,es

                                ; install new handler...
        mov     dx,offset int0  ; DS:DX = handler address
        mov     ax,2500h        ; call MS-DOS to set
        int     21h             ; Int 00H vector

                                ; now our handler is active,
                                ; carry out some test divides.

        mov     ax,20h          ; test divide
        mov     bx,1            ; divide by 1
        call    divide

        mov     ax,1234h        ; test divide
        mov     bx,5eh          ; divide by 5EH
        call    divide

        mov     ax,5678h        ; test divide
        mov     bx,7fh          ; divide by 127
        call    divide

        mov     ax,20h          ; test divide
        mov     bx,0            ; divide by 0
        call    divide          ; (triggers interrupt)

                                ; demonstration complete,
                                ; restore old handler

        lds     dx,oldint0      ; DS:DX = handler address
        mov     ax,2500h        ; call MS-DOS to set
        int     21h             ; Int 00H vector

        mov     ax,4c00h        ; final exit to MS-DOS
        int     21h             ; with return code = 0

;
; The routine 'divide' carries out a trial division,
; displaying the arguments and the results.  It is
```

Figure 13-5. Continued.   *(more)*

```
; called with AX = dividend and BL = divisor.
;

divide  proc    near

        push    ax              ; save arguments
        push    bx

        mov     di,offset par1  ; convert dividend to
        call    wtoa            ; ASCII for display

        mov     ax,bx           ; convert divisor to
        mov     di,offset par2  ; ASCII for display
        call    btoa

        pop     bx              ; restore arguments
        pop     ax

        div     bl              ; perform the division
        cmp     intflag,0       ; divide by zero detected?
        jne     nodiv           ; yes, skip display

        push    ax              ; no, convert quotient to
        mov     di,offset par3  ; ASCII for display
        call    btoa

        pop     ax              ; convert remainder to
        xchg    ah,al           ; ASCII for display
        mov     di,offset par4
        call    btoa

        mov     ah,09h          ; show arguments, results
        mov     dx,offset divmsg
        int     21h

nodiv:  mov     intflag,0       ; clear divide by 0 flag
        ret                     ; and return to caller

divide  endp



wtoa    proc    near            ; convert word to hex ASCII
                                ; call with AX = binary value
                                ;           DI = addr for string
                                ; returns AX, CX, DI destroyed

        push    ax              ; save original value
        mov     al,ah
        call    btoa            ; convert upper byte
        add     di,2            ; increment output address
```

Figure 13-5. Continued.   *(more)*

```
            pop     ax
            call    btoa            ; convert lower byte
            ret                     ; return to caller

    wtoa    endp



    btoa    proc    near            ; convert byte to hex ASCII
                                    ; call with AL = binary value
                                    ;          DI = addr to store string
                                    ; returns AX, CX destroyed

            mov     ah,al           ; save lower nibble
            mov     cx,4            ; shift right 4 positions
            shr     al,cl           ; to get upper nibble
            call    ascii           ; convert 4 bits to ASCII
            mov     [di],al         ; store in output string
            mov     al,ah           ; get back lower nibble

            and     al,0fh          ; blank out upper one
            call    ascii           ; convert 4 bits to ASCII
            mov     [di+1],al       ; store in output string
            ret                     ; back to caller

    btoa    endp



    ascii   proc    near            ; convert AL bits 0-3 to
                                    ; ASCII {0...9,A...F}
            add     al,'0'          ; and return digit in AL
            cmp     al,'9'
            jle     ascii2
            add     al,'A'-'9'-1    ; "fudge factor" for A-F
    ascii2: ret                     ; return to caller

    ascii   endp

    _TEXT   ends

            end     entry
```

Figure 13-5. Continued.

Supplementary handlers

In many cases, a custom interrupt handler augments, rather than replaces, the existing routine. The added routine might process some data before passing the data to the existing routine, or it might do the processing afterward. These cases require slightly different coding for the handler.

If the added routine is to process data before the existing handler does, the routine need only jump to the original handler after completing its processing. This jump can be done indirectly, with the same pointer used to save the original content of the vector for restoration at exit. For example, a replacement Interrupt 08H handler that merely increments an internal flag at each timer tick can look something like the following:

```
        .
        .
        .
myflag  dw      ?                       ; variable to be incremented
                                        ; on each timer-tick interrupt

oldint8 dd      ?                       ; contains address of previous
                                        ; timer-tick interrupt handler

        .                               ; get the previous contents
        .                               ; of the Interrupt 08H vector...
        mov     ax,3508h                ; AH = 35H (Get Interrupt Vector)
        int     21h                     ; AL = Interrupt number (08H)
        mov     word ptr oldint8,bx     ; save the address of
        mov     word ptr oldint8+2,es   ; the previous Int 08H Handler
        mov     dx,seg myint8           ; put address of the new
        mov     ds,dx                   ; interrupt handler into DS:DX
        mov     dx,offset myint8        ; and call MS-DOS to set vector
        mov     ax,2508h                ; AH = 25H (Set Interrupt Vector)
        int     21h                     ; AL = Interrupt number (08H)
        .
        .
        .
myint8:                                 ; this is the new handler
                                        ; for Interrupt 08H

        inc     cs:myflag               ; increment variable on each
                                        ; timer-tick interrupt

        jmp     dword ptr cs:[oldint8]  ; then chain to the
                                        ; previous interrupt handler
```

The added handler must preserve all registers and machine conditions, except those machine conditions it will modify, such as the value of *myflag* in the example (and the flags register, which is saved by the interrupt action), and it must restore those registers and conditions before performing the jump to the original handler.

A more complex situation arises when a replacement handler does some processing *after* the original routine executes, especially if the replacement handler is not reentrant. To allow for this processing, the replacement handler must prevent nested interrupts, so that even if the old handler (which is chained to the replacement handler by a CALL instruction) issues an EOI, the replacement handler will not be interrupted during postprocessing. For example, instead of using the preceding Interrupt 08H example routine, the programmer could use the following code to implement *myflag* as a semaphore and use the XCHG instruction to test it:

```
myint8:                                 ; this is the new handler
                                        ; for Interrupt 08H

        mov     ax,1                    ; test and set interrupt-
        xchg    cs:myflag,ax            ; handling-in-progress semaphore

        push    ax                      ; save the semaphore

        pushf                           ; simulate interrupt, allowing
        call    dword ptr cs:oldint8    ; the previous handler for the
                                        ; Interrupt 08H vector to run

        pop     ax                      ; get the semaphore back
        or      ax,ax                   ; is our interrupt handler
                                        ; already running?

        jnz     myint8x                 ; yes, skip this one

        .                               ; now perform our interrupt
        .                               ; processing here...
        .

        mov     cs:myflag,0             ; clear the interrupt-handling-
                                        ; in-progress flag

myint8x:
        iret                            ; return from interrupt
```

Note that an interrupt handler of this type must simulate the original call to the interrupt routine by first doing a PUSHF, followed by a far CALL via the saved pointer to execute the original handler routine. The flags register pushed onto the stack is restored by the IRET of the original handler. Upon return from the original code, the new routine can preserve the machine state and do its own processing, finally returning to the caller by means of its own IRET.

The flags inside the new routine need not be preserved, as they are automatically restored by the IRET instruction. Because of the nature of interrupt servicing, the service routine should not depend on any information in the flags register, nor can it return any information in the flags register. Note also that the previous handler (invoked by the indirect CALL) will almost certainly have dismissed the interrupt by sending an EOI to the 8259A PIC. Thus, the machine state is not the same as in the first *myint8* example.

To remove the new vector and restore the original, the program simply replaces the new vector (in the vector table) with the saved copy. If the substituted routine is part of an application program, the original vector must be restored for every possible method of exiting from the program (including Control-Break, Control-C, and critical-error *Abort* exits). Failure to observe this requirement invariably results in system failure. Even though the system failure might be delayed for some time after the exit from the offending program, when some subsequent program overlays the interrupt handler code the crash will be imminent.

Summary

Hardware interrupt handler routines, although not strictly a part of MS-DOS, form an integral part of many MS-DOS programs and are tightly constrained by MS-DOS requirements. Routines of this type play important roles in the functioning of the IBM personal computers, and, with proper design and programming, significantly enhance product reliability and performance. In some instances, no other practical method exists for meeting performance requirements.

Jim Kyle
Chip Rabinowitz

Article 14
Writing MS-DOS Filters

A filter is, essentially, a program that operates on a stream of characters. The source and destination of the character stream can be files, another program, or almost any character device. The transformation applied by the filter to the character stream can range from an operation as simple as substituting a character set to an operation as elaborate as generating splines from sets of coordinates.

The standard MS-DOS package includes three simple filters: SORT, which alphabetically sorts text on a line-by-line basis; FIND, which searches a text stream to match a specified string; and MORE, which displays text one screenful at a time. This article describes how filters work and how new ones can be constructed. *See also* USER COMMANDS: FIND; MORE; SORT.

System Support for Filters

The operation of a filter program relies on two features that appeared in MS-DOS version 2.0: standard devices and redirectable I/O.

The standard devices are represented by five handles that are originally established when the system is initialized. Each process inherits these handles from its immediate parent. Thus, the standard device handles are already opened when a process acquires control of the system, and the process can use the handles with Interrupt 21H Functions 3FH and 40H for read and write operations without further preliminaries. The default assignments of the standard device handles are

Handle	Name	Default Device
0	*stdin* (standard input)	CON
1	*stdout* (standard output)	CON
2	*stderr* (standard error)	CON
3	*stdaux* (standard auxiliary)	AUX
4	*stdlst* (standard list)	PRN

The CON device is assigned by default to the system's keyboard and video display. AUX is assigned by default to COM1 (the first physical serial port), and PRN is assigned by default to LPT1 (the first physical parallel printer port); in some systems these assignments can be altered with the MODE command. *See* PROGRAMMING IN THE MS-DOS ENVIRONMENT: PROGRAMMING FOR MS-DOS: Character Device Input and Output; USER COMMANDS: MODE; CTTY.

When a program is executed by entering its name at the system (COMMAND.COM) prompt, the user can redirect either or both of the standard input and standard output handles from their default device (CON) to another file, a character device, or a process. This redirection is accomplished by including one of the special characters <, >, >>, or ¦ in the command line, in the following form:

Redirection	Result
< *file*	Contents of the specified *file* are used instead of the keyboard as the program's standard input.
< *device*	Program takes its standard input from the named *device* instead of from the keyboard.
> *device*	Program sends its standard output to the named *device* instead of to the video display.
> *file*	Program sends its standard output to the specified *file* instead of to the video display.
>> *file*	Program appends its standard output to the current contents of the specified *file* instead of to the video display.
p1 ¦ *p2*	Standard output of program *p1* is routed to become the standard input of program *p2* (output of *p1* is said to be piped to *p2*).

For example, the command

```
C>SORT < MYFILE.TXT > PRN   <Enter>
```

causes the SORT filter to read its input from the file MYFILE.TXT, sort the lines alphabetically, and write resulting text to the character device PRN (the logical name for the system's list device).

The redirection requested by the <, >, >>, or ¦ characters takes place at the level of COMMAND.COM and is invisible to the program it affects. Such redirection can also be put into effect by another process. *See* Using a Filter as a Child Process below.

Note that if a program "goes around" MS-DOS to perform its input and output, either by calling ROM BIOS functions or by manipulating the keyboard or video controller directly, redirection commands placed in the program's command line do not have the expected effect.

How Filters Work

By convention, a filter program reads its text from standard input and writes the results of its operations to standard output. When the end of the input stream is reached, the filter simply terminates, optionally writing an end-of-file mark (1AH) to the output stream. As a result, filters are both flexible and simple.

Filter programs are flexible because they do not know, and do not care, about the source of the data they process or the destination of their output. Any redirection that the user specifies in the command line is invisible to the filter. Thus, any character device that has a logical name within the system (CON, AUX, COM1, COM2, PRN, LPT1, LPT2, LPT3, and so on), any file on any block device (local or network) known to the system, or any other program can supply a filter's input or accept its output. If necessary, several functionally simple filters can be concatenated with pipes to perform very complex operations.

Although flexible, filters are also simple because they rely on their parent process to supply standard input and standard output handles that have already been appropriately redirected. The parent is responsible for opening or creating any necessary files, checking the validity of logical character device names, and loading and executing the preceding or following process in a pipe. The filter need only concern itself with the transformation it will apply to the data; it can leave the I/O details to the operating system and to its parent.

Building a Filter

Creating a new filter for MS-DOS is a straightforward process. In its simplest form, a filter need only use the handle-oriented read (Interrupt 21H Function 3FH) and write (Interrupt 21H Function 40H) functions to get characters or lines from standard input and send them to standard output, performing any desired alterations on the text stream on a character-by-character or line-by-line basis.

Figures 14-1 through 14-4 contain template character-oriented and line-oriented filters in both assembly language and C. The C version of the character filter runs much faster than the assembly-language version, because the C run-time library provides hidden blocking and deblocking (buffering) of character reads and writes; the assembly-language program actually makes two calls to MS-DOS for each character processed. (Of course, if buffering is added to the assembly-language version it will be both faster and smaller than the C filter.) The C and assembly-language versions of the line-oriented filter run at roughly the same speed.

```
        name    protoc
        title   'PROTOC.ASM --- template character filter'
;
; PROTOC.ASM: a template for a character-oriented filter.
;
; Ray Duncan, June 1987
;

stdin   equ     0               ; standard input
stdout  equ     1               ; standard output
stderr  equ     2               ; standard error

cr      equ     0dh             ; ASCII carriage return
lf      equ     0ah             ; ASCII linefeed
```

Figure 14-1. Assembly-language template for a character-oriented filter (file PROTOC.ASM). (more)

```
DGROUP  group   _DATA,STACK     ; 'automatic data group'


_TEXT   segment byte public 'CODE'

        assume  cs:_TEXT,ds:DGROUP,ss:STACK

main    proc    far             ; entry point from MS-DOS

        mov     ax,DGROUP       ; set DS = our data segment
        mov     ds,ax

main1:                          ; read a character from standard input
        mov     dx,offset DGROUP:char    ; address to place character
        mov     cx,1            ; length to read = 1
        mov     bx,stdin        ; handle for standard input
        mov     ah,3fh          ; function 3FH = read from file or device
        int     21h             ; transfer to MS-DOS
        jc      main3           ; error, terminate
        cmp     ax,1            ; any character read?
        jne     main2           ; end of file, terminate program

        call    translt         ; translate character if necessary

                                ; now write character to standard output
        mov     dx,offset DGROUP:char    ; address of character
        mov     cx,1            ; length to write = 1
        mov     bx,stdout       ; handle for standard output
        mov     ah,40h          ; function 40H = write to file or device
        int     21h             ; transfer to MS-DOS
        jc      main3           ; error, terminate
        cmp     ax,1            ; was character written?
        jne     main3           ; disk full, terminate program
        jmp     main1           ; go process another character

main2:  mov     ax,4c00h        ; end of file reached, terminate
        int     21h             ; program with return code = 0

main3:  mov     ax,4c01h        ; error or disk full, terminate
        int     21h             ; program with return code = 1

main    endp                    ; end of main procedure

;
; Perform any necessary translation on character from input,
; stored in 'char'.  Template action: leave character unchanged.
;
translt proc    near

        ret                     ; template action: do nothing

translt endp
```

Figure 14-1. Continued.   *(more)*

```
_TEXT    ends


_DATA    segment word public 'DATA'

char     db      0                    ; temporary storage for input character

_DATA    ends


STACK    segment para stack 'STACK'

         dw      64 dup (?)

STACK    ends


         end     main                 ; defines program entry point
```

Figure 14-1. Continued.

```
/*
        PROTOC.C: a template for a character-oriented filter.

        Ray Duncan, June 1987
*/

#include <stdio.h>

main(argc,argv)
int argc;
char *argv[];
{       char ch;

        while ( (ch=getchar())!=EOF )    /* read a character */
        {       ch=translate(ch);        /* translate it if necessary */
                putchar(ch);             /* write the character */
        }
        exit(0);                         /* terminate at end of file */
}

/*
        Perform any necessary translation on character from
        input file.  Template action just returns same character.
*/

int translate(ch)
char ch;
{       return (ch);
}
```

Figure 14-2. C template for a character-oriented filter (file PROTOC.C).

```
        name    protol
        title   'PROTOL.ASM --- template line filter'
;
; PROTOL.ASM:  a template for a line-oriented filter.
;
; Ray Duncan, June 1987
;

stdin   equ    0              ; standard input
stdout  equ    1              ; standard output
stderr  equ    2              ; standard error

cr      equ    0dh            ; ASCII carriage return
lf      equ    0ah            ; ASCII linefeed


DGROUP  group  _DATA,STACK    ; 'automatic data group'


_TEXT   segment byte public 'CODE'

        assume  cs:_TEXT,ds:DGROUP,es:DGROUP,ss:STACK

main    proc    far            ; entry point from MS-DOS

        mov     ax,DGROUP      ; set DS = ES = our data segment
        mov     ds,ax
        mov     es,ax

main1:                         ; read a line from standard input
        mov     dx,offset DGROUP:input  ; address to place data
        mov     cx,256         ; max length to read = 256
        mov     bx,stdin       ; handle for standard input
        mov     ah,3fh         ; function 3FH = read from file or device
        int     21h            ; transfer to MS-DOS
        jc      main3          ; if error, terminate
        or      ax,ax          ; any characters read?
        jz      main2          ; end of file, terminate program

        call    translt        ; translate line if necessary
        or      ax,ax          ; anything to output after translation?
        jz      main1          ; no, get next line

                               ; now write line to standard output
        mov     dx,offset DGROUP:output ; address of data
        mov     cx,ax          ; length to write
        mov     bx,stdout      ; handle for standard output
        mov     ah,40h         ; function 40H = write to file or device
        int     21h            ; transfer to MS-DOS
        jc      main3          ; if error, terminate
```

Figure 14-3. Assembly-language template for a line-oriented filter (file PROTOL.ASM).   *(more)*

```
        cmp     ax,cx           ; was entire line written?
        jne     main3           ; disk full, terminate program
        jmp     main1           ; go process another line

main2:  mov     ax,4c00h        ; end of file reached, terminate
        int     21h             ; program with return code - 0

main3:  mov     ax,4c01h        ; error or disk full, terminate
        int     21h             ; program with return code = 1

main    endp                    ; end of main procedure


;
; Perform any necessary translation on line stored in
; 'input' buffer, leaving result in 'output' buffer.
;
; Call with:    AX = length of data in 'input' buffer.
;
; Return:       AX = length to write to standard output.
;
; Action of template routine is just to copy the line.
;
translt proc    near

                                ; just copy line from input to output
        mov     si,offset DGROUP:input
        mov     di,offset DGROUP:output
        mov     cx,ax
        rep movsb
        ret                     ; return length in AX unchanged

translt endp


_TEXT   ends


_DATA   segment word public 'DATA'

input   db      256 dup (?)     ; storage for input line
output  db      256 dup (?)     ; storage for output line

_DATA   ends


STACK   segment para stack 'STACK'

        dw      64 dup (?)

STACK   ends


        end     main            ; defines program entry point
```

Figure 14-3. Continued.

```
/*
        PROTOL.C: a template for a line-oriented filter.

        Ray Duncan, June 1987.
*/

#include <stdio.h>

static char input[256];                 /* buffer for input line */
static char output[256];                 /* buffer for output line */

main(argc,argv)
int argc;
char *argv[];
{       while( gets(input) != NULL )     /* get a line from input stream */
                                         /* perform any necessary translation
                                            and possibly write result */
        {       if (translate()) puts(output);
        }
        exit(0);                         /* terminate at end of file */
}


/*
        Perform any necessary translation on input line, leaving
        the resulting text in output buffer.  Value of function
        is 'true' if output buffer should be written to standard output
        by main routine, 'false' if nothing should be written.
*/

translate()
{       strcpy(output,input);            /* template action is copy input */
        return(1);                       /* line and return true flag */
}
```

Figure 14-4. C template for a line-oriented filter (file PROTOL.C).

Each of the four template filters can be assembled or compiled, linked, and run exactly as they are shown in Figures 14-1 through 14-4. Of course, in this form they function like an incredibly slow COPY command.

To obtain a filter that does something useful, a routine that performs some modification of the text stream that is flowing by must be inserted between the reads and writes. For example, Figures 14-5 and 14-6 contain the assembly-language and C source code for a character-oriented filter named LC. This program converts all uppercase input characters (A–Z) to lowercase (a–z) output, leaving other characters unchanged. The only difference between LC and the template character filter is the translation subroutine that operates on the text stream.

```
        name    lc
        title   'LC.ASM --- lowercase filter'
;
; LC.ASM:       a simple character-oriented filter to translate
;               all uppercase {A-Z} to lowercase {a-z}.
;
; Ray Duncan, June 1987
;

stdin   equ     0               ; standard input
stdout  equ     1               ; standard output
stderr  equ     2               ; standard error

cr      equ     0dh             ; ASCII carriage return
lf      equ     0ah             ; ASCII linefeed


DGROUP  group   _DATA,STACK     ; 'automatic data group'


_TEXT   segment byte public 'CODE'

        assume  cs:_TEXT,ds:DGROUP,ss:STACK

main    proc    far             ; entry point from MS-DOS

        mov     ax,DGROUP       ; set DS = our data segment
        mov     ds,ax

main1:                          ; read a character from standard input
        mov     dx,offset DGROUP:char   ; address to place character
        mov     cx,1            ; length to read = 1
        mov     bx,stdin        ; handle for standard input
        mov     ah,3fh          ; function 3FH = read from file or device
        int     21h             ; transfer to MS-DOS
        jc      main3           ; error, terminate
        cmp     ax,1            ; any character read?
        jne     main2           ; end of file, terminate program

        call    translt         ; translate character if necessary

                                ; now write character to standard output
        mov     dx,offset DGROUP:char   ; address of character
        mov     cx,1            ; length to write = 1
        mov     bx,stdout       ; handle for standard output
        mov     ah,40h          ; function 40H = write to file or device
        int     21h             ; transfer to MS-DOS
        jc      main3           ; error, terminate
        cmp     ax,1            ; was character written?
        jne     main3           ; disk full, terminate program
        jmp     main1           ; go process another character
```

Figure 14-5. Assembly-language source code for the LC filter (file LC.ASM).   *(more)*

```
main2:  mov     ax,4c00h        ; end of file reached, terminate
        int     21h             ; program with return code = 0

main3:  mov     ax,4c01h        ; error or disk full, terminate
        int     21h             ; program with return code = 1

main    endp                    ; end of main procedure

;
; Translate uppercase {A-Z} characters to corresponding
; lowercase characters {a-z}.  Leave other characters unchanged.
;
translt proc    near

        cmp     byte ptr char,'A'
        jb      transx
        cmp     byte ptr char,'Z'
        ja      transx
        add     byte ptr char,'a'-'A'
transx: ret

translt endp


_TEXT   ends


_DATA   segment word public 'DATA'

char    db      0                       ; temporary storage for input character

_DATA   ends


STACK   segment para stack 'STACK'

        dw      64 dup (?)

STACK   ends


        end     main            ; defines program entry point
```

Figure 14-5. Continued.

```
/*
        LC:     a simple character-oriented filter to translate
                all uppercase {A-Z} to lowercase {a-z} characters.

        Usage:  LC [< source] [> destination]
```

Figure 14-6. C source code for the LC filter (file LC.C).   *(more)*

```
        Ray Duncan, June 1987

*/

#include <stdio.h>

main(argc,argv)
int argc;
char *argv[];
{       char ch;
                                        /* read a character */
        while ( (ch=getchar() ) != EOF )
        {       ch=translate(ch);       /* perform any necessary
                                           character translation */

                putchar(ch);            /* then write character */
        }
        exit(0);                        /* terminate at end of file */
}

/*
        Translate characters A-Z to lowercase equivalents
*/

int translate(ch)
char ch;
{       if (ch >= 'A' && ch <= 'Z') ch += 'a'-'A';
        return (ch);
}
```

Figure 14-6. Continued.

As another example, Figure 14-7 contains the C source code for a line-oriented filter called FIND. This simple filter is invoked with a command line in the form

FIND "*pattern*" < *source* > *destination*

FIND searches the input stream for lines containing the pattern specified in the command line. The line number and text of any line containing a match is sent to standard output, with any tabs expanded to eight-column tab stops.

```
/*
        FIND.C          Searches text stream for a string.

        Usage:          FIND "pattern" [< source] [> destination]

        by Ray Duncan, June 1987

*/

#include <stdio.h>
```

Figure 14-7. C source code for a new FIND filter (file FIND.C).   *(more)*

```
#define TAB      '\x09'           /* ASCII tab character (^I) */
#define BLANK    '\x20'           /* ASCII space character */

#define TAB_WIDTH 8               /* columns per tab stop */

static char input[256];          /* buffer for line from input */
static char output[256];         /* buffer for line to output */
static char pattern[256];        /* buffer for search pattern */

main(argc,argv)
int argc;
char *argv[];
{      int line=0;                /* initialize line variable */

       if ( argc < 2 )           /* was search pattern supplied? */
       {      puts("find: missing pattern.");
              exit(1);           /* abort if not */
       }
       strcpy(pattern,argv[1]);  /* save copy of string to find */
       strupr(pattern);          /* fold it to uppercase */
       while( gets(input) != NULL )  /* read a line from input */
       {      line++;            /* count lines */
              strcpy(output,input);   /* save copy of input string */
              strupr(input);     /* fold input to uppercase */
                                 /* if line contains pattern */
              if( strstr(input,pattern) )
                                 /* write it to standard output */
                   writeline(line,output);
       }
       exit(0);                  /* terminate at end of file */
}


/*
       WRITELINE: Write line number and text to standard output,
       expanding any tab characters to stops defined by TAB_WIDTH.
*/

writeline(line,p)
int line;
char *p;
{      int i=0;                  /* index to original line text */
       int col=0;                /* actual output column counter */
       printf("\n%4d: ",line);   /* write line number */
       while( p[i]!=NULL )       /* while end of line not reached */
       {      if(p[i]==TAB)      /* if current char = tab, expand it */
              {      do putchar(BLANK);
                     while((++col % TAB_WIDTH) != 0);
              }
              else               /* otherwise just send character */
              {      putchar(p[i]);
                     col++;      /* count columns */
              }
```

Figure 14-7. Continued.   *(more)*

```
            i++;                        /* advance through output line */
      }
}
```

Figure 14-7. Continued.

This sample FIND filter differs from the FIND filter supplied by Microsoft with MS-DOS in several respects. It is not case sensitive, so the pattern "foobar" will match "FOOBAR", "FooBar", and so forth. Second, this filter supports no switches; these are left as an exercise for the reader. Third, unlike the Microsoft version of FIND, this program always reads from standard input; it is not able to open its own files.

Using a Filter as a Child Process

Instead of incorporating all the code necessary to do the job itself, an application program can load and execute a filter as a child process to carry out a specific task. Before the child filter is loaded, the parent must arrange for the standard input and standard output handles that will be inherited by the child to be attached to the files or character devices that will supply the filter's input and receive its output. This redirection is accomplished with the following steps using Interrupt 21H functions:

1. The parent process uses Function 45H (Duplicate File Handle) to create duplicates of its standard input and standard output handles and then saves the duplicates.
2. The parent opens (with Function 3DH) or creates (with Function 3CH) the files or devices that the child process will use for input and output.
3. The parent uses Function 46H (Force Duplicate File Handle) to force its own standard device handles to track the new file or device handles acquired in step 2.
4. The parent uses Function 4B00H (Load and Execute Program [EXEC]) to load and execute the child process. The child inherits the redirected standard input and standard output handles and uses them to do its work. The parent regains control after the child filter terminates.
5. The parent uses the duplicate handles created in step 1, together with Function 46H (Force Duplicate File Handle), to restore its own standard input and standard output handles to their original meanings.
6. The parent closes (with Function 3EH) the duplicate handles created in step 1, because they are no longer needed.

It might seem as though the parent process could just as easily close its own standard input and standard output (handles 0 and 1), open the input and output files needed by the child, load and execute the child, close the files upon regaining control, and then reopen the CON device twice. Because the open operation always assigns the first free handle, this approach would have the desired effect as far as the child process is concerned. However, it would throw away any redirection that had been established for the parent process by its parent. Thus, the need to preserve any preexisting redirection of the parent's standard input and standard output, along with the desire to preserve the parent's usual output channel for informational messages right up to the actual point of the EXEC call, is the reason for the elaborate procedure outlined above in steps 1 through 6.

The program EXECSORT.ASM in Figure 14-8 demonstrates this redirection of input and output for a filter run as a child process. The parent, which is called EXECSORT, saves duplicates of its current standard input and standard output handles and then redirects those handles respectively to the files MYFILE.DAT (which it opens) and MYFILE.SRT (which it creates). EXECSORT then uses Interrupt 21H Function 4BH (EXEC) to run the SORT.EXE filter that is supplied with MS-DOS (this file must be in the current drive and directory for the demonstration to work correctly).

```
        name    execsort
        title   'EXECSORT --- demonstrate EXEC of filter'
        .sall
;
; EXECSORT.ASM --- demonstration of use of EXEC to run the SORT
; filter as a child process, redirecting its input and output.
; This program requires the files SORT.EXE and MYFILE.DAT in
; the current drive and directory.
;
; Ray Duncan, June 1987
;

stdin   equ     0                       ; standard input
stdout  equ     1                       ; standard output
stderr  equ     2                       ; standard error

stksize equ     128                     ; size of stack

cr      equ     0dh                     ; ASCII carriage return
lf      equ     0ah                     ; ASCII linefeed

jerr    macro   target                  ;; Macro to test carry flag
        local   notset                  ;; and jump if flag set.
        jnc     notset                  ;; Uses JMP DISP16 to avoid
        jmp     target                  ;; branch out of range errors
notset:
        endm


DGROUP  group   _DATA,_STACK            ; 'automatic data group'
```

(more)

Figure 14-8. Assembly-language source code demonstrating use of a filter as a child process. This code redirects the standard input and standard output handles to files, invokes the EXEC function (Interrupt 21H Function 4BH) to run the SORT.EXE program, and then restores the original meaning of the standard input and standard output handles (file EXECSORT.ASM).

```
_TEXT   segment byte public 'CODE'      ; executable code segment

        assume  cs:_TEXT,ds:DGROUP,ss:_STACK


stk_seg dw      ?                        ; original SS contents
stk_ptr dw      ?                        ; original SP contents


main    proc    far                      ; entry point from MS-DOS

        mov     ax,DGROUP                ; set DS = our data segment
        mov     ds,ax

                                         ; now give back extra memory so
                                         ; child SORT has somewhere to run...
        mov     ax,es                    ; let AX = segment of PSP base
        mov     bx,ss                    ; and BX = segment of stack base
        sub     bx,ax                    ; reserve seg stack - seg psp
        add     bx,stksize/16            ; plus paragraphs of stack
        mov     ah,4ah                   ; fxn 4AH = modify memory block
        int     21h                      ; transfer to MS-DOS
        jerr    main1                    ; jump if resize block failed

                                         ; prepare stdin and stdout
                                         ; handles for child SORT process

        mov     bx,stdin                 ; dup the handle for stdin
        mov     ah,45h
        int     21h                      ; transfer to MS-DOS
        jerr    main1                    ; jump if dup failed
        mov     oldin,ax                 ; save dup'd handle

        mov     dx,offset DGROUP:infile  ; now open the input file
        mov     ax,3d00h                 ; mode = read-only
        int     21h                      ; transfer to MS-DOS
        jerr    main1                    ; jump if open failed

        mov     bx,ax                    ; force stdin handle to
        mov     cx,stdin                 ; track the input file handle
        mov     ah,46h
        int     21h                      ; transfer to MS-DOS
        jerr    main1                    ; jump if force dup failed

        mov     bx,stdout                ; dup the handle for stdout
        mov     ah,45h
        int     21h                      ; transfer to MS-DOS
        jerr    main1                    ; jump if dup failed
        mov     oldout,ax                ; save dup'd handle

        mov     dx,offset dGROUP:outfile ; now create the output file
```

Figure 14-8. Continued.   *(more)*

```
        mov     cx,0                    ; normal attribute
        mov     ah,3ch
        int     21h                     ; transfer to MS-DOS
        jerr    main1                   ; jump if create failed

        mov     bx,ax                   ; force stdout handle to
        mov     cx,stdout               ; track the output file handle
        mov     ah,46h
        int     21h                     ; transfer to MS-DOS
        jerr    main1                   ; jump if force dup failed

                                        ; now EXEC the child SORT,
                                        ; which will inherit redirected
                                        ; stdin and stdout handles

        push    ds                      ; save EXECSORT's data segment
        mov     stk_seg,ss              ; save EXECSORT's stack pointer
        mov     stk_ptr,sp

        mov     ax,ds                   ; set ES = DS
        mov     es,ax
        mov     dx,offset DGROUP:cname  ; DS:DX = child pathname
        mov     bx,offset DGROUP:pars   ; EX:BX = parameter block
        mov     ax,4b00h                ; function 4BH, subfunction 00H
        int     21h                     ; transfer to MS-DOS

        cli                             ; (for bug in some early 8088s)
        mov     ss,stk_seg              ; restore execsort's stack pointer
        mov     sp,stk_ptr
        sti                             ; (for bug in some early 8088s)
        pop     ds                      ; restore DS = our data segment

        jerr    main1                   ; jump if EXEC failed

        mov     bx,oldin                ; restore original meaning of
        mov     cx,stdin                ; standard input handle for
        mov     ah,46h                  ; this process
        int     21h
        jerr    main1                   ; jump if force dup failed

        mov     bx,oldout               ; restore original meaning
        mov     cx,stdout               ; of standard output handle
        mov     ah,46h                  ; for this process
        int     21h
        jerr    main1                   ; jump if force dup failed

        mov     bx,oldin                ; close dup'd handle of
        mov     ah,3eh                  ; original stdin
        int     21h                     ; transfer to MS-DOS
```

Figure 14-8. Continued.   *(more)*

```
        jerr    main1               ; jump if close failed

        mov     bx,oldout           ; close dup'd handle of
        mov     ah,3eh              ; original stdout
        int     21h                 ; transfer to MS-DOS
        jerr    main1               ; jump if close failed

                                    ; display success message
        mov     dx,offset DGROUP:msg1  ; address of message
        mov     cx,msg1_len         ; message length
        mov     bx,stdout           ; handle for standard output
        mov     ah,40h              ; fxn 40H = write file or device
        int     21h                 ; transfer to MS-DOS
        jerr    main1

        mov     ax,4c00h            ; no error, terminate program
        int     21h                 ; with return code = 0

main1:  mov     ax,4c01h            ; error, terminate program
        int     21h                 ; with return code = 1

main    endp                        ; end of main procedure

_TEXT   ends


_DATA   segment para public 'DATA'  ; static & variable data segment

infile  db      'MYFILE.DAT',0      ; input file for SORT filter
outfile db      'MYFILE.SRT',0      ; output file for SORT filter

oldin   dw      ?                   ; dup of old stdin handle
oldout  dw      ?                   ; dup of old stdout handle

cname   db      'SORT.EXE',0        ; pathname of child SORT process

pars    dw      0                   ; segment of environment block
                                    ; (0 = inherit parent's)
        dd      tail                ; long address, command tail
        dd      -1                  ; long address, default FCB #1
                                    ; (-1 = none supplied)
        dd      -1                  ; long address, default FCB #2
                                    ; (-1 = none supplied)

tail    db      0,cr                ; empty command tail for child

msg1    db      cr,lf,'SORT was executed as child.',cr,lf
msg1_len equ    $-msg1

_DATA   ends
```

Figure 14-8. Continued.   *(more)*

```
_STACK   segment para stack 'STACK'

         db      stksize dup (?)

_STACK   ends


         end     main                    ; defines program entry point
```

Figure 14-8. Continued.

The MS-DOS SORT program reads the file MYFILE.DAT via its standard input handle, sorts the file alphabetically, and writes the sorted data to MYFILE.SRT via its standard output handle. When SORT terminates, MS-DOS closes SORT's inherited handles for standard input and standard output, which forces an update of the directory entries for the associated files. The program EXECSORT then resumes execution, restores its own standard input and standard output handles (which are still open) to their original meanings, displays a success message on standard output, and exits to MS-DOS.

Ray Duncan

Article 15
Installable Device Drivers

The software that runs on modern computer systems is, by convention, organized into layers with varied degrees of independence from the underlying computer hardware. The purpose of this layering is threefold:

- To minimize the impact on programs of differences between hardware devices or changes in the hardware.
- To allow the code for common operations to be centralized and optimized.
- To ease the task of moving programs and their data from one machine to another.

The top and most hardware-independent layer is usually the transient, or application, program, which performs a specific job and deals with data in terms of files and records within those files. Such programs are called transient because they are brought into RAM for execution when needed and are discarded from memory when their job is finished. Examples of such programs are Microsoft Word, various programming tools such as the Microsoft Macro Assembler (MASM) and the Microsoft Object Linker (LINK), and even some of the standard MS-DOS utility programs such as CHKDSK and FORMAT.

The middle layer is the operating-system kernel, which manages the allocation of system resources such as memory and disk storage, provides a battery of services to application programs, and implements disk directories and the other housekeeping details of disk storage. The MS-DOS kernel is brought into memory from the file MSDOS.SYS (or IBMDOS.COM with PC-DOS) when the system is turned on or restarted and remains fixed in memory until the system is turned off. The system's default command processor, COMMAND.COM, and system manager programs such as Microsoft Windows bridge the categories of application program and operating system: Parts of them remain resident in memory at all times, but they rely on the MS-DOS kernel for services such as file I/O. *See* PROGRAMMING IN THE MS-DOS ENVIRONMENT: Structure of ms-dos: Components of MS-DOS.

The modules in the lowest layer are called device drivers. These drivers are the components of the operating system that manage the controller, or adapter, of a peripheral device — a piece of hardware that the computer uses for such purposes as storage or communicating with the outside world. Thus, device drivers are responsible for transferring data between a peripheral device and the computer's RAM memory, where other programs can work on it. Drivers shield the operating-system kernel from the need to deal with hardware I/O port addresses, operating characteristics, and the peculiarities of a particular peripheral device, just as the kernel, in turn, shields application programs from the details of file management.

In MS-DOS versions 1.x, device drivers were integrated into the operating system and could be extended or replaced only by patching the files that contained the operating system itself. Because every third-party peripheral manufacturer evolved a different method of modifying these files to get its product to work, conflicts between products from different manufacturers were frequent and expansion of a PC with new disk drives and other devices (especially fixed disks) was often a chancy proposition.

In MS-DOS versions 2.0 and later, there is a clean separation between device drivers and the MS-DOS kernel. Device drivers have a straightforward structure and are interfaced to the kernel through a simple and clearly defined scheme that consists of far calls, function codes, and data packets. Given adequate information about the hardware, a programmer can write a new device driver that follows this structure and interface for almost any conceivable peripheral device; such a driver can subsequently be installed and used without any changes to the underlying operating system.

This article explains the anatomy, operation, and creation of drivers for MS-DOS versions 2.0 and later. Device drivers for versions 1.x are not discussed further here.

Resident and Installable Drivers

Every MS-DOS system contains built-in device drivers for the console (keyboard and video display), the serial port, the parallel printer port, the real-time clock, and at least one disk storage device (the system boot device). These drivers, known as the resident drivers, are loaded as a set from the file IO.SYS (or IBMBIO.COM with PC-DOS) when the system is turned on or restarted.

Drivers for additional peripheral devices occupy individual files on the disk. These drivers, called installable drivers, are loaded and linked into the system during its initialization as a result of DEVICE directives in the CONFIG.SYS file. *See* PROGRAMMING IN THE MS-DOS ENVIRONMENT: STRUCTURE OF MS-DOS: Components of MS-DOS. Examples of such drivers are the ANSI.SYS and RAMDISK.SYS files included with MS-DOS version 3.2. In all other respects, installable drivers have the same structure and relationship to the MS-DOS kernel as the resident drivers. All drivers in the system are chained together so that MS-DOS can rapidly search the entire set to find a specific block or character device when an I/O operation is requested.

Device drivers as a whole are categorized into two groups: block-device drivers and character-device drivers. A driver's membership in one of these two groups determines how the associated device is viewed by MS-DOS and what functions the driver itself must support.

Character-device drivers

Character-device drivers control peripheral devices, such as a terminal or a printer, that perform input and output one character (or byte) at a time. Each character-device driver ordinarily supports a single hardware unit. The device has a one-character to eight-character logical name that can be used by an application program to "open" the device for input or output as though it were a file. The logical name is strictly a means of identifying the driver to MS-DOS and has no physical equivalent on the device (unlike a volume label for block devices).

The three resident character-device drivers for the console, serial port, and printer carry the logical device names CON, AUX, and PRN, respectively. These three drivers receive special treatment by MS-DOS that allows application programs to address the associated devices in three different ways:

- They can be opened by name for input and output (like any other character device).
- They are supported by special-purpose MS-DOS function calls (Interrupt 21H Functions 01–0CH).
- They are assigned to default handles (standard input, standard output, standard error, standard auxiliary, and standard list) that need not be opened to be used.

See PROGRAMMING IN THE MS-DOS ENVIRONMENT: Programming for ms-dos: Character Device Input and Output.

Other character devices can be supported by simply installing additional character-device drivers. The only significant restriction on the total number of devices that can be supported, other than the memory required to hold the drivers, is that each driver must have a unique logical name. When MS-DOS receives an open request for a character device, it searches the chain of device drivers in order from the last driver loaded to the first. Thus, if more than one driver uses the same logical name, the last driver to be loaded supersedes any others and receives all I/O requests addressed to that logical name. This behavior can be used to advantage in some situations. For example, it allows the more powerful ANSI.SYS display driver to supersede the system's default console driver, which does not support cursor positioning and character attributes.

The MS-DOS kernel's buffering and filtering of the characters that pass between it and a character-device driver are affected by whether MS-DOS regards the device to be in cooked mode or raw mode. During cooked mode input, MS-DOS requests characters one at a time from the driver and places them in its own internal buffer, echoing each character to the screen (if the input device is the keyboard) and checking each character for a Control-C (03H) or a Return (0DH). When either the number of characters requested by the application program has been received or a Return is detected, the input is terminated and the data is copied from MS-DOS's internal buffer into the requesting program's buffer. When a Control-C is detected, MS-DOS aborts the input operation and transfers to the routine whose address is stored in the Interrupt 23H (Control-C Handler Address) vector. *See* PROGRAMMING IN THE MS-DOS ENVIRONMENT: Customizing ms-dos: Exception Handlers. Similarly, during output in cooked mode, MS-DOS checks between each character for a Control-C pending at the keyboard and aborts the output operation if one is detected.

In raw mode, the exact number of bytes requested by the application program is read or written, without regard to any control characters such as Return or Control-C. MS-DOS passes the entire I/O request to the driver in a single operation, instead of breaking the request into single-character reads or writes, and the characters are transferred directly to or from the requesting program's buffer.

The mode for a specific device can be queried by an application program with the IOCTL Get Device Data function (Interrupt 21H Function 44H Subfunction 00H); the mode can be selected with the Set Device Data function (Interrupt 21H Function 44H Subfunction 01H). *See* SYSTEM CALLS: INTERRUPT 21H: Function 44H. The driver itself is not usually aware of its mode and the mode does not affect its operation.

Block-Device Drivers

Block-device drivers control peripheral devices that transfer data in chunks rather than 1 byte at a time. Block devices are usually randomly addressable devices such as floppy- or fixed-disk drives, but they can also be sequential devices such as magnetic-tape drives. A block driver can support more than one physical unit and can also map two or more logical units onto a single physical unit, as with a partitioned fixed disk.

MS-DOS assigns single-letter drive identifiers (A, B, and so forth) to block devices, instead of logical names. The first letter assigned to a block-device driver is determined solely by the driver's position in the chain of all drivers—that is, by the number of units supported by the block drivers loaded before it; the total number of letters assigned to the driver is determined by the number of logical drive units the driver supports.

MS-DOS does not associate a mode (cooked or raw) with block-device drivers. A block-device driver always reads or writes exactly the number of sectors requested (barring hardware or addressing errors) and never filters or otherwise manipulates the contents of the blocks being transferred.

Structure of an MS-DOS Device Driver

A device driver has three major components (Figure 15-1):

- The device header
- The Strategy routine (*Strat*)
- The Interrupt routine (*Intr*)

The device header

The device header (Figure 15-2) always lies at the beginning of the driver. It contains a link to the next driver in the chain, a word (16 bits) of device attribute flags, offsets to the executable Strategy and Interrupt routines for the device, and the logical device name if it is a character device such as PRN or COM1 or the number of logical units if it is a block device.

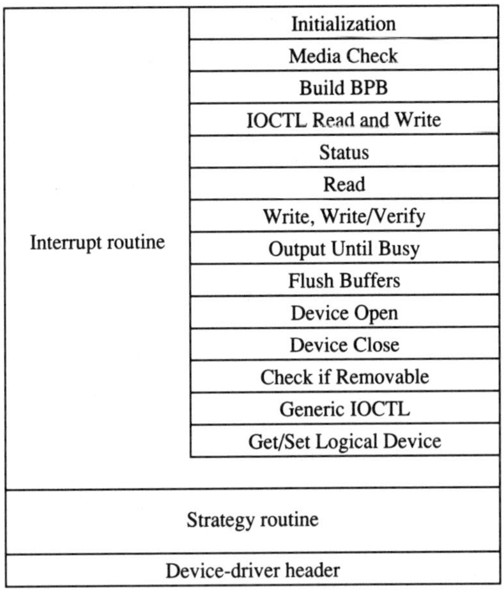

	Initialization
	Media Check
	Build BPB
	IOCTL Read and Write
	Status
	Read
Interrupt routine	Write, Write/Verify
	Output Until Busy
	Flush Buffers
	Device Open
	Device Close
	Check if Removable
	Generic IOCTL
	Get/Set Logical Device
Strategy routine	
Device-driver header	

Figure 15-1. General structure of an MS-DOS installable device driver.

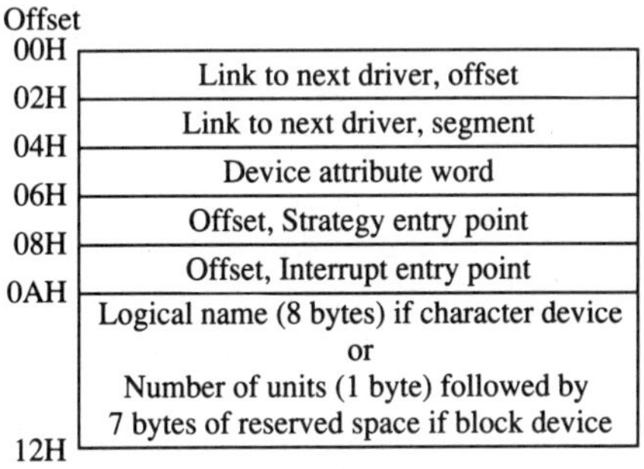

Offset

Offset	
00H	Link to next driver, offset
02H	Link to next driver, segment
04H	Device attribute word
06H	Offset, Strategy entry point
08H	Offset, Interrupt entry point
0AH	Logical name (8 bytes) if character device or Number of units (1 byte) followed by 7 bytes of reserved space if block device
12H	

Figure 15-2. Device header. The offsets to the Strat *and* Intr *routines are offsets from the same segment used to point to the device header.*

The device attribute flags word (Table 15-1) defines whether a driver controls a character or a block device, which of the optional subfunctions added in MS-DOS versions 3.0 and 3.2 are supported by the driver, and, in the case of block drivers, whether the driver supports IBM-compatible disk media. The least significant 4 bits of the device attribute flags word control whether MS-DOS should use the driver as the standard input, standard output, clock, or NUL device; each of these 4 bits should be set on only one driver in the system at a time.

Table 15-1. Device Attribute Word in Device Header.

Bit	Setting
15*	1 if character device, 0 if block device
14*	1 if IOCTL Read and Write supported
13*	1 if non-IBM format (block device)
	1 if Output Until Busy supported (character device)
12	0 (reserved)
11*	1 if Open/Close/Removable Media supported (versions 3.0 and later)
10	0 (reserved)
9	0 (reserved)
8	0 (reserved)
7	0 (reserved)
6*	1 if Generic IOCTL and Get/Set Logical Drive supported (version 3.2)
5	0 (reserved)
4	1 if special fast output function for CON device supported
3	1 if current CLOCK device
2	1 if current NUL device
1	1 if current standard output (*stdout*)
0	1 if current standard input (*stdin*)

* Only bits 6, 11, and 13-15 have significance on block devices; the remainder should be zero.

The information in the device header is ordinarily used only by the MS-DOS kernel and is not available to application programs. However, the IOCTL subfunctions Get and Set Device Data (Interrupt 21H Function 44H Subfunctions 00H and 01H) can be used to inspect or modify some of the bits in the device attribute flags word. Note that there is not a one-to-one correspondence between the bits defined for those functions and the bits in the device header. For example, in the device information word used by the IOCTL subfunctions, bit 7 indicates a block or character device; in the device attribute word of the device header, bit 15 indicates a block or character device.

The Strategy routine (*Strat*)

MS-DOS calls the driver's Strategy routine as the first step of any operation, passing it the segment and offset of a data structure called a request header in registers ES:BX. The Strategy routine saves this pointer for subsequent processing by the Interrupt routine and returns to MS-DOS.

A request header is essentially a small buffer used for private communication between MS-DOS and the device driver. Both MS-DOS and the device driver read and write information in the request header.

The first 13 bytes of a request header are the same for all device-driver functions and are therefore referred to as the static portion of the header. The number and contents of the subsequent bytes vary according to the type of operation being requested by the MS-DOS kernel (Figure 15-3). The request header's most important component is the command code passed in its third byte; this code selects a driver function such as Read or Write. Other information passed to the driver in the request header includes unit numbers, transfer addresses, and sector or byte counts.

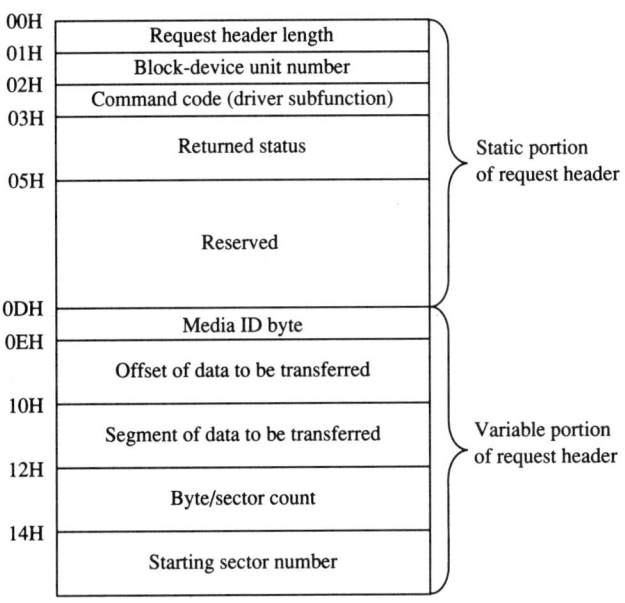

Figure 15-3. A typical driver request header. The bytes following the static portion are the format used for driver Read, Write, Write with Verify, IOCTL Read, and IOCTL Write operations.

The Interrupt routine (*Intr*)

The last and most complex part of a device driver is the Interrupt routine, which is called by MS-DOS immediately after the call to the Strategy routine. The bulk of the Interrupt routine is a collection of functions or subroutines, sometimes called command-code routines, that carry out each of the various operations the MS-DOS kernel requires a driver to support.

When the Interrupt routine receives control from MS-DOS, it saves any affected registers, examines the request header whose address was previously passed in the call to the Strategy routine, determines which command-code routine is needed, and branches to the appropriate function. When the operation is completed, the Interrupt routine stores the status (Table 15-2), error (Table 15-3), and any other applicable information into the request header, restores the previous contents of the affected registers, and returns to the MS-DOS kernel.

Table 15-2. The Request Header Status Word.

Bits	Meaning
15	Error
12-14	Reserved
9	Busy
8	Done
0-7	Error code if bit 15 = 1

Table 15-3. Device-Driver Error Codes. *

Code	Meaning
00H	Write-protect violation
01H	Unknown unit
02H	Drive not ready
03H	Unknown command
04H	CRC error
05H	Bad drive request structure length
06H	Seek error
07H	Unknown media
08H	Sector not found
09H	Printer out of paper
0AH	Write fault
0BH	Read fault
0CH	General failure
0DH	Reserved
0EH	Reserved
0FH	Invalid disk change (versions 3.x)

* Returned in bits 0-7 of the request header status word.

The Interrupt routine's name is misleading in that it is never entered asynchronously as a hardware interrupt. The division of function between the Strategy and Interrupt routines is present for symmetry with UNIX/XENIX and MS OS/2 drivers but is essentially meaningless in single-tasking MS-DOS because there is never more than one I/O request in progress at a time.

The command-code functions

A total of twenty command codes are defined for MS-DOS device drivers. The command codes and the names of their associated Interrupt routines are shown in the following list:

Code	Routine
0	Init (initialization)
1	Media Check (block devices only)
2	Build BIOS Parameter Block (block devices only)
3	IOCTL Read
4	Read (Input)
5	Nondestructive Read (character devices only)
6	Input Status (character devices only)
7	Flush Input Buffers (character devices only)
8	Write (Output)
9	Write with Verify
10	Output Status (character devices only)
11	Flush Output Buffers (character devices only)
12	IOCTL Write
13*	Device Open
14*	Device Close
15*	Removable Media (block devices only)
16*	Output Until Busy (character devices only)
19†	Generic IOCTL Request
23†	Get Logical Device (block devices only)
24†	Set Logical Device (block devices only)

* MS-DOS versions 3.0 and later
† MS-DOS version 3.2

Functions 0 through 12 must be supported by a driver's Interrupt section under all versions of MS-DOS. Drivers tailored for versions 3.0 and 3.1 can optionally support an additional 4 functions defined under those versions of the operating system and drivers designed for version 3.2 can support 3 more, for a total of 20. MS-DOS inspects the bits in the device attribute word of the device header to determine which of the optional version 3.x functions a driver supports, if any.

As noted in the list above, some of the functions are relevant only for character drivers, some only for block drivers, and some for both. In any case, there must be an executable routine present for each function, even if the routine does nothing but set the done flag in the status word of the request header. The general requirements for each function routine are described below.

The Init function

The Init (initialization) function (command code 0) for a driver is called only once, when the driver is loaded (Figure 15-4). Init is responsible for checking that the hardware device controlled by the driver is present and functional, performing any necessary hardware initialization (such as a reset on a printer or a seek to the home track on a disk device), and capturing any interrupt vectors that the driver will need later.

The Init function is passed a pointer in the request header to the text of the DEVICE line in CONFIG.SYS that caused the driver to be loaded — specifically, the address of the next byte after the equal sign (=). The line is read-only and is terminated by a linefeed or carriage-return character; it can be scanned by the driver for switches or other parameters that might influence the driver's operation. (Alphabetic characters in the line are folded to uppercase.) With versions 3.0 and later, block drivers are also passed the drive number that will be assigned to their first unit (0 = A, 1 = B, and so on).

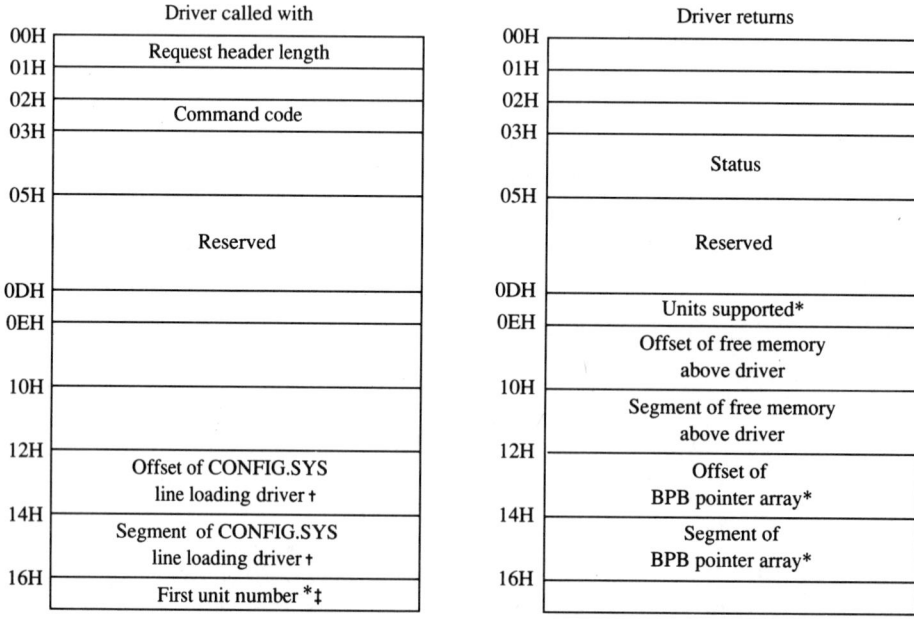

```
                Driver called with                          Driver returns
00H ┌──────────────────────────────┐         00H ┌──────────────────────────────┐
    │      Request header length    │             │                              │
01H ├──────────────────────────────┤         01H ├──────────────────────────────┤
02H ├──────────────────────────────┤         02H ├──────────────────────────────┤
    │        Command code           │             │                              │
03H ├──────────────────────────────┤         03H ├──────────────────────────────┤
    │                               │             │                              │
    │                               │             │           Status             │
    │                               │             │                              │
05H ├──────────────────────────────┤         05H ├──────────────────────────────┤
    │                               │             │                              │
    │          Reserved             │             │          Reserved            │
    │                               │             │                              │
0DH ├──────────────────────────────┤         0DH ├──────────────────────────────┤
0EH ├──────────────────────────────┤         0EH │       Units supported*       │
    │                               │             ├──────────────────────────────┤
    │                               │             │    Offset of free memory     │
10H │                               │             │       above driver           │
    ├──────────────────────────────┤         10H ├──────────────────────────────┤
    │                               │             │   Segment of free memory     │
    │                               │             │       above driver           │
12H ├──────────────────────────────┤         12H ├──────────────────────────────┤
    │     Offset of CONFIG.SYS      │             │       Offset of              │
    │     line loading driver †     │             │   BPB pointer array*         │
14H ├──────────────────────────────┤         14H ├──────────────────────────────┤
    │    Segment of CONFIG.SYS      │             │      Segment of              │
    │    line loading driver †      │             │  BPB pointer array*          │
16H ├──────────────────────────────┤         16H ├──────────────────────────────┤
    │     First unit number *‡      │             │                              │
    └──────────────────────────────┘             └──────────────────────────────┘
```

* Block-device drivers only
† Points to the character after DEVICE=
‡ MS-DOS 3.0 and later only

Figure 15-4. Initialization request header (command code 0).

When it returns to the kernel, the Init function must set the done flag in the status word of the request header and return the address of the start of free memory after the driver (sometimes called the break address). This address tells the kernel where it can build certain control structures of its own associated with the driver and then load the next driver. The Init routine of a block-device driver must also return the number of logical units supported by the driver and the address of a BPB pointer array.

The number of units returned by a block driver is used to assign device identifiers. For example, if at the time the driver is loaded there are already drivers present for four block devices (drive codes 0–3, corresponding to drive identifiers A through D) and the driver being initialized supports four units, it will be assigned the drive numbers 4 through 7 (corresponding to the drive names E through H). (Although there is also a field in the device header for the number of units, it is not inspected by MS-DOS; rather, it is set by MS-DOS from the information returned by the Init function.)

The BPB pointer array is an array of word offsets to BIOS parameter blocks. *See* The Build BIOS Parameter Block Function below; PROGRAMMING IN THE MS-DOS ENVIRON-MENT: Structure of ms-dos: MS-DOS Storage Devices. The array must contain one entry for each unit defined by the driver, although all entries can point to the same BPB to conserve memory. During the operating-system boot sequence, MS-DOS scans all the BPBs defined by all the units in all the resident block-device drivers to determine the largest sector size that exists on any device in the system; this information is used to set MS-DOS's cache buffer size. Thus, the sector size in the BPB of any installable block driver must be no larger than the largest sector size used by the resident block drivers.

If the Init routine finds that its hardware device is missing or defective, it can bypass the installation of the driver completely by returning the following values in the request header:

Item	Value
Number of units	0
Address of free memory	Segment and offset of the driver's own device header

A character-device driver must also clear bit 15 of the device attribute word in the device header so that MS-DOS will load the next driver in the same location as the one that just terminated itself.

The operating-system services that can be invoked by the Init routine are very limited. Only MS-DOS Interrupt 21H Functions 01–0CH (various character input and output services), 25H (Set Interrupt Vector), 30H (Get MS-DOS Version Number), and 35H (Get Interrupt Vector) can be called by the Init code. These functions assist the driver in configuring itself for the version of the host operating system it is to run under, capturing vectors for hardware interrupts, and displaying informational or error messages.

The amount of RAM required by a device driver can be reduced by positioning the Init routine at the end of the driver and returning that routine's starting address as the location of the first free memory.

The Media Check function

The Media Check function (command code 1) is used only in block-device drivers. It is called by the MS-DOS kernel when there is a pending drive access call other than a simple file read or write (for example, a file open, close, rename, or delete), passing the media ID byte (Figure 15-5) for the disk that MS-DOS assumes is in the drive:

Description	Medium
0F9H	5.25-inch double-sided, 15 sectors
0FCH	5.25-inch single-sided, 9 sectors
0FDH	5.25-inch double-sided, 9 sectors
0FEH	5.25-inch single-sided, 8 sectors
0FFH	5.25-inch double-sided, 8 sectors
0F9H	3.5-inch double-sided, 9 sectors
0F0H	3.5-inch double-sided, 18 sectors
0F8H	Fixed disk

The function returns a code indicating whether the medium has been changed since the last transfer:

Code	Meaning
−1	Medium changed
0	Don't know if medium changed
1	Medium not changed

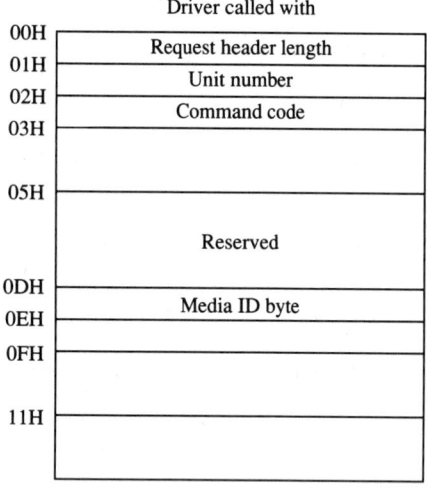
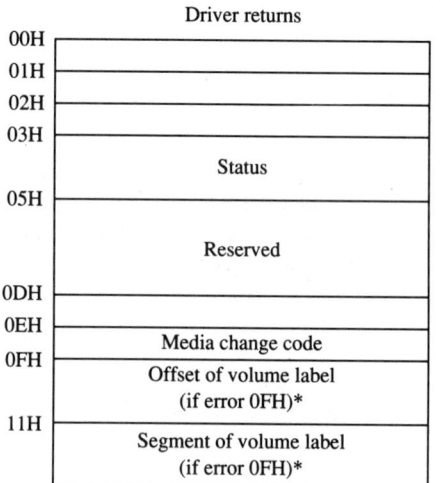

* MS-DOS 3.0 and later only

Figure 15-5. Media Check request header (command code 1).

If the Media Check routine asserts that the disk has not been changed, MS-DOS bypasses rereading the FAT and proceeds with the disk access. If the returned code indicates that the disk has been changed, MS-DOS invalidates all buffers associated with the drive, including buffers containing data waiting to be written (this data is simply lost), performs a Build BPB call, and then reads the disk's FAT and directory.

The action taken by MS-DOS when *Don't know* is returned depends on the state of its internal buffers. If data that needs to be written out is present in the buffers associated with the drive, MS-DOS assumes that no disk change has occurred. If the buffers are empty or have all been previously flushed to the disk, MS-DOS assumes that the disk was changed and proceeds as described above for the *Medium changed* return code.

If bit 11 of the device attribute word is set (that is, the driver supports the optional Open/Close/Removable Media functions), the host system is MS-DOS version 3.0 or later, and the function returns the *Medium changed* code (–1), the function must also return the segment and offset of the ASCIIZ volume label for the previous disk in the drive. (If the driver does not have the volume label, it can return a pointer to the ASCIIZ string *NO NAME*.) If MS-DOS determines that the disk was changed with unwritten data still present in the buffers, it issues a critical error 0FH (Invalid Disk Change). Application programs can trap this critical error and prompt the user to replace the original disk.

In character-device drivers, the Media Change function should simply set the done flag in the status word of the request header and return.

The Build BIOS Parameter Block function

The Build BPB function (command code 2) is supported only on block devices. MS-DOS calls this function when the *Medium changed* code has been returned by the Media Check routine or when the *Don't know* code has been returned and there are no dirty buffers (buffers that have not yet been written to disk). Thus, a call to this function indicates that the disk has been legally changed.

The Build BPB call receives a pointer to a one-sector buffer in the request header (Figure 15-6). If the non-IBM-format bit (bit 13) in the device attribute word in the device header is zero, the buffer contains the first sector of the disk's FAT, with the media ID byte in the first byte of the buffer. In this case, the contents of the buffer should not be modified by the driver. However, if the non-IBM-format bit is set, the buffer can be used by the driver as scratch space.

The Build BPB function must return the segment and offset of a BIOS parameter block (Table 15-4) for the disk format indicated by the media ID byte and set the done flag in the status word of the request header. The information in the BPB is used by the kernel to interpret the disk structure and is also used by the driver itself to translate logical sector addresses into physical track, sector, and head addresses. If bit 11 of the device attribute word is set (that is, the driver supports the optional Open/Close/Removable Media functions) and the host system is MS-DOS version 3.0 or later, this routine should also read the volume label from the disk and save it.

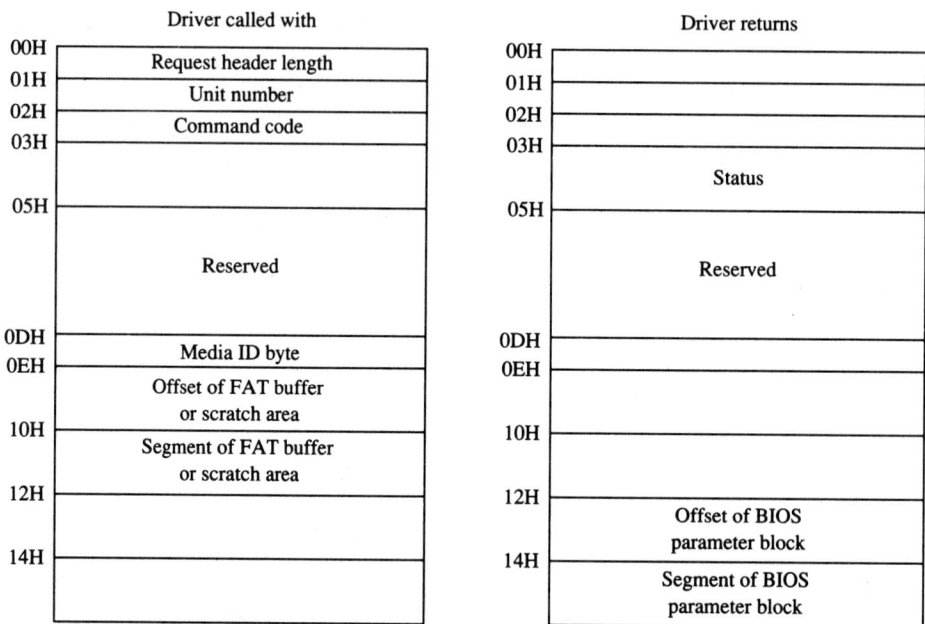

Figure 15-6. Build BPB request header (command code 2).

Table 15-4. Format of a BIOS Parameter Block (BPB).

Bytes	Contents
00–01H	Bytes per sector
02H	Sectors per allocation unit (must be power of 2)
03–04H	Number of reserved sectors (starting at sector 0)
05H	Number of file allocation tables (FATs)
06–07H	Maximum number of root-directory entries
08–09H	Total number of sectors in medium
0AH	Media ID byte
0B–0CH	Number of sectors occupied by a single FAT
0D–0EH	Sectors per track (versions 3.0 and later)
0F–10H	Number of heads (versions 3.0 and later)
11–12H	Number of hidden sectors (versions 3.0 and later)
13–14H	High-order word of number of hidden sectors (version 3.2)
15–18H	If bytes 8–9 are zero, total number of sectors in medium (version 3.2)

In character-device drivers, the Build BPB function should simply set the done flag in the status word of the request header and return.

The Read, Write, and Write with Verify functions

The Read (Input) function (command code 4) transfers data from the device into a specified memory buffer. The Write (Output) function (command code 8) transfers data from a specified memory buffer to the device. The Write with Verify function (command code 9) works like the Write function but, if feasible, also performs a read-after-write verification that the data was transferred correctly. The MS-DOS kernel calls the Write with Verify function, instead of the Write function, whenever the system's global verify flag has been turned on with the VERIFY command or with Interrupt 21H Function 2EH (Set Verify Flag).

All three of these driver functions are called by the MS-DOS kernel with the address and length of the buffer for the data to be transferred. In the case of block-device drivers, the kernel also passes the drive unit code, the starting logical sector number, and the media ID byte for the disk (Figure 15-7).

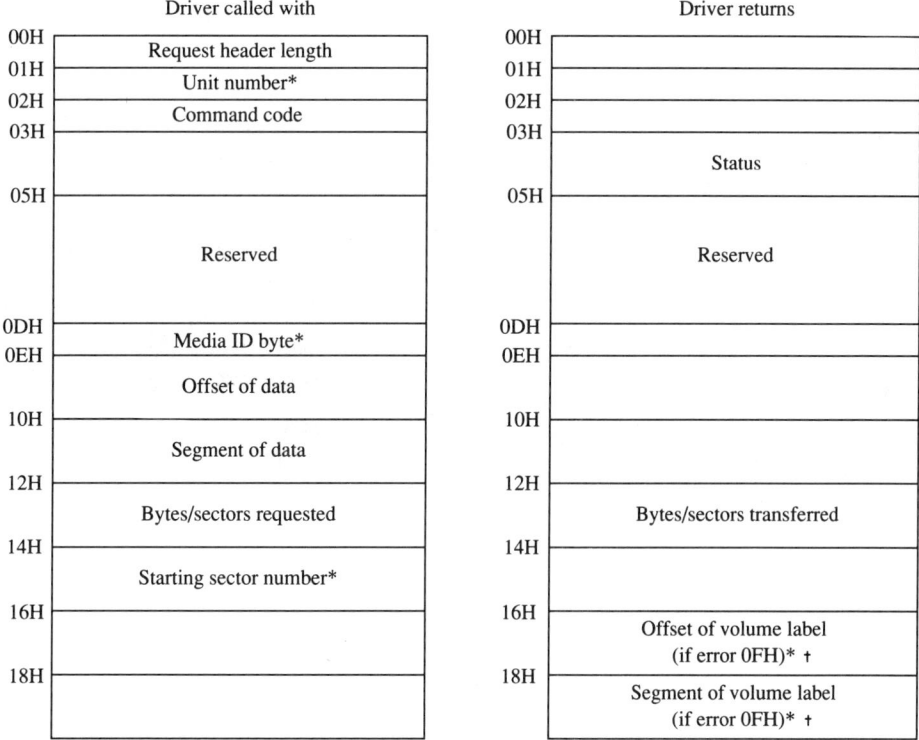

Driver called with		Driver returns
00H Request header length		00H
01H Unit number*		01H
02H Command code		02H
03H		03H
		Status
05H Reserved		05H Reserved
0DH Media ID byte*		0DH
0EH Offset of data		0EH
10H Segment of data		10H
12H Bytes/sectors requested		12H Bytes/sectors transferred
14H Starting sector number*		14H
16H		16H Offset of volume label (if error 0FH)* †
18H		18H Segment of volume label (if error 0FH)* †

* Block-device drivers only
† MS-DOS 3.0 and later, command codes 4, 8, and 9 only

Figure 15-7. The request header for IOCTL Read (command code 3), Read (command code 4), Write (command code 8), Write with Verify (command code 9), IOCTL Write (command code 12), and Output Until Busy (command code 16).

The Read and Write functions must perform the requested I/O, first translating each logical sector number for a block device into a physical track, head, and sector with the aid of the BIOS parameter block. Then the functions must return the number of bytes or sectors actually transferred in the appropriate field of the request header and also set the done flag in the request header status word. If an error is encountered during an operation, the functions must set the done flag, the error flag, and the error type in the status word and also report the number of bytes or sectors successfully transferred before the error; it is not sufficient to simply report the error.

Under MS-DOS versions 3.0 and later, the Read and Write functions can optionally use the reference count of open files maintained by the driver's Device Open and Device Close functions, together with the media ID byte, to determine whether the medium has been illegally changed. If the medium was changed with files open, the driver can return the error code 0FH and the segment and offset of the volume label for the correct disk so that the user can be prompted to replace the disk.

The Nondestructive Read function

The Nondestructive Read function (command code 5) is supported only on character devices. It allows MS-DOS to look ahead in the character stream by one character and is used to check for Control-C characters pending at the keyboard.

The function is called by the kernel with no parameters other than the command code itself (Figure 15-8). It must set the done bit in the status word of the request header and also set the busy bit in the status word to reflect whether the device's input buffer is empty (busy bit = 1) or contains at least one character (busy bit = 0). If the latter, the function must also return the next character that would be obtained by a kernel call to the Read function, without removing that character from the buffer (hence the term nondestructive).

In block-device drivers, the Nondestructive Read function should simply set the done flag in the status word of the request header and return.

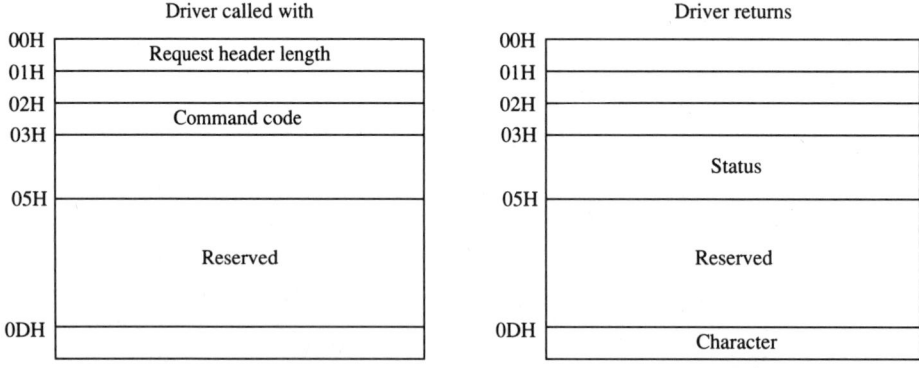

Figure 15-8. The Nondestructive Read request header.

The Input Status and Output Status functions

The Input Status and Output Status functions (command codes 6 and 10) are defined only for character devices. They are called with no parameters in the request header other than the command code itself and return their results in the busy bit of the request header status word (Figure 15-9). These functions constitute the driver-level support for the services the MS-DOS kernel provides to application programs by means of Interrupt 21H Function 44H Subfunctions 06H and 07H (Check Input Status and Check Output Status).

MS-DOS calls the Input Status function to determine whether there are characters waiting in a type-ahead buffer. The function sets the done bit in the status word of the request header and sets the busy bit to 0 if at least one character is already in the input buffer or to 1 if no characters are in the buffer and a read request would wait on a character from the physical device. If the character device does not have a type-ahead buffer, the Input Status routine should always return the busy bit set to 0 so that MS-DOS will not wait for something to arrive in the buffer before calling the Read function.

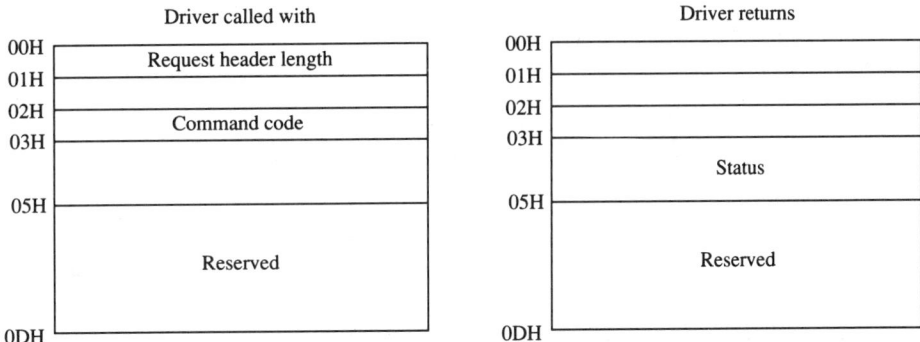

Figure 15-9. The request header for Input Status (command code 6), Flush Input Buffers (command code 7), Output Status (command code 10), and Flush Output Buffers (command code 11).

MS-DOS uses the Output Status function to determine whether a write operation is already in progress for the device. The function must set the done bit and the busy bit (0 if the device is idle and a write request would start immediately; 1 if a write is already in progress and a new write request would be delayed) in the status word of the request header.

In block-device drivers, the Input Status and Output Status functions should simply set the done flag in the status word of the request header and return.

The Flush Input Buffer and Flush Output Buffer functions

The Flush Input Buffer and Flush Output Buffer functions (command codes 7 and 11) are defined only for character devices. They simply terminate any read (for Flush Input) or write (for Flush Output) operations that are in progress and empty the associated buffer. The Flush Input Buffer function is used by MS-DOS to discard characters waiting in the type-ahead queue. This driver action corresponds to the MS-DOS service provided to application programs by means of Interrupt 21H Function 0CH (Flush Buffer, Read Keyboard).

These functions are called with no parameters in the request header other than the command code itself (*see* Figure 15-9) and return only the status word.

In block-device drivers, the Flush Buffer functions have no meaning. They should simply set the done flag in the status word of the request header and return.

The IOCTL Read and IOCTL Write functions

The IOCTL (I/O Control) Read and IOCTL Write functions (command codes 3 and 12) allow control information to be passed directly between a device driver and an application program. The IOCTL Read and Write driver functions are called by the MS-DOS kernel only if the IOCTL flag (bit 14) is set in the device attribute word of the device header.

The MS-DOS kernel passes the address and length of the buffer that contains or will receive the IOCTL information (*see* Figure 15-7). The driver must return the actual count of bytes transferred and set the done flag in the request header status word. Any error code returned by the driver is ignored by the kernel.

IOCTL Read and IOCTL Write operations are typically used to configure a driver or device or to report driver or device status and do not usually result in the transfer of data to or from the physical device. These functions constitute the driver support for the services provided to application programs by the MS-DOS kernel through Interrupt 21H Function 44H Subfunctions 02H, 03H, 04H, and 05H (Receive Control Data from Character Device, Send Control Data to Character Device, Receive Control Data from Block Device, and Send Control Data to Block Device).

The Device Open and Device Close functions

The Device Open and Device Close functions (command codes 13 and 14) are supported only in MS-DOS versions 3.0 and later and are called only if the open/close/removable media flag (bit 11) is set in the device attribute word of the device header. The Device Open and Device Close functions have no parameters in the request header other than the unit code for block devices and return nothing except the done flag and, if applicable, the error flag and number in the request header status word (Figure 15-10).

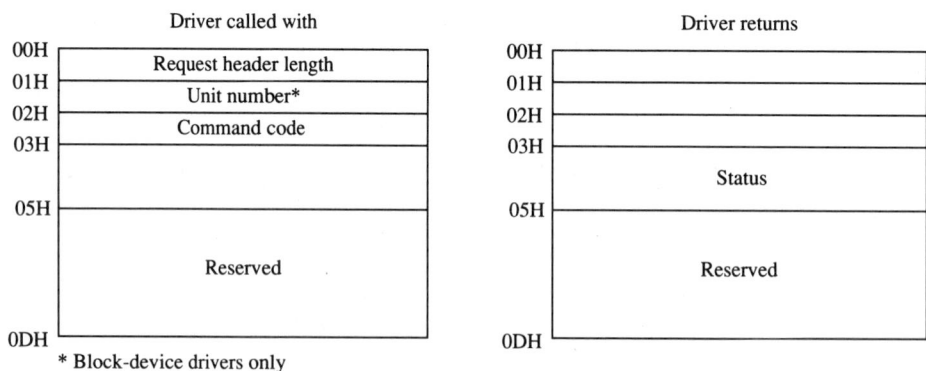

Figure 15-10. *The request header for Device Open (command code 13), Device Close (command code 14), and Removable Media (command code 15).*

Each Interrupt 21H request by an application to open or create a file or to open a character device for input or output results in a Device Open call by the kernel to the corresponding device driver. Similarly, each Interrupt 21H call by an application to close a file or device results in a Device Close call by the kernel to the appropriate device driver. These Device Open and Device Close calls are in addition to any directory read or write calls that may be necessary.

On block devices, the Device Open and Device Close functions can be used to manage local buffering and to maintain a reference count of the number of open files on a device. Whenever this reference count is decremented to zero, all files on the disk have been closed and the driver should flush any internal buffers so that data is not lost, as the user may be about to change disks. The reference count can also be used together with the media ID byte by the Read and Write functions to determine whether the disk has been changed while files are still open.

The reference count should be forced to zero when a Media Check call that returns the *Medium changed* code is followed by a Build BPB call, to provide for those programs that use FCBs to open files and then never close them. This problem does not arise with programs that use the handle functions for file management, because all handles are always closed automatically by MS-DOS on behalf of the program when it terminates. *See* PROGRAMMING IN THE MS-DOS ENVIRONMENT: PROGRAMMING FOR MS-DOS: File and Record Management.

On character devices, the Device Open and Device Close functions can be used to send hardware-dependent initialization and post-I/O strings to the associated device (for example, a reset sequence or formfeed character to precede new output and a formfeed to follow it). Although these strings can be written directly by an application using ordinary write function calls, they can also be previously passed to the driver by application programs with IOCTL Write calls (Interrupt 21H Function 44H Subfunction 05H), which in turn are translated by the MS-DOS kernel into driver command code 12 (IOCTL Write) requests. The latter method makes the driver responsible for sending the proper control strings to the device each time a Device Open or Device Close is executed, but this method can be used only with drivers specifically written to support it.

The Removable Media function

The Removable Media function (command code 15) is defined only for block devices. It is supported in MS-DOS versions 3.0 and later and is called by MS-DOS only if the open/close/removable media flag (bit 11) is set in the device attribute word of the device header. This function constitutes the driver-level support for the service provided to application programs by MS-DOS by means of Interrupt 21H Function 44H Subfunction 08H (Check If Block Device Is Removable).

The only parameter for the Removable Media function is the unit code (*see* Figure 15-10). The function sets the done bit in the request header status word and sets the busy bit to 1 if the disk is not removable or to 0 if the disk is removable. This information can be used by MS-DOS to optimize its accesses to the disk and to eliminate unnecessary FAT and directory reads.

In character-device drivers, the Removable Media function should simply set the done flag in the status word of the request header and return.

The Output Until Busy function

The Output Until Busy function (command code 16) is defined only for character devices under MS-DOS versions 3.0 and later and is called by the MS-DOS kernel only if the corresponding flag (bit 13) is set in the device attribute word of the device header. This function is an optional driver-optimization function included specifically for the benefit of background print spoolers driving printers that have internal memory buffers. Such printers can accept data at a rapid rate until the buffer is full.

The Output Until Busy function is called with the address and length of the data to be written to the device (see Figure 15-7). It transfers data continuously to the device until the device indicates that it is busy or until the data is exhausted. The function then must set the done flag in the request header status word and return the actual number of bytes transferred in the appropriate field of the request header.

For this function to return a count of bytes transferred that is less than the number of bytes requested is not an error. MS-DOS will adjust the address and length of the data passed in the next Output Until Busy function request so that all characters are sent.

In block-device drivers, the Output Until Busy function should simply set the done flag in the status word of the request header and return.

The Generic IOCTL function

The Generic IOCTL function (command code 19) is defined under MS-DOS version 3.2 and is called only if the 3.2-functions-supported flag (bit 6) is set in the device attribute word of the device header. This driver function corresponds to the MS-DOS generic IOCTL service supplied to application programs by means of Interrupt 21H Function 44H Subfunctions 0CH (Generic I/O Control for Handles) and 0DH (Generic I/O Control for Block Devices).

In addition to the usual information in the static portion of the request header, the Generic IOCTL function is passed a category (major) code, a function (minor) code, the contents of the SI and DI registers at the point of the IOCTL call, and the segment and offset of a data buffer (Figure 15-11). This buffer in turn contains other information whose format depends on the major and minor IOCTL codes passed in the request header. The driver must interpret the major and minor codes in the request header and the contents of the additional buffer to determine which operation it will carry out and then set the done flag in the request header status word and return any other applicable information in the request header or the data buffer.

Services that can be invoked by the Generic IOCTL function, if the driver supports them, include configuring the driver for nonstandard disk formats, reading and writing entire disk tracks of data, and formatting and verifying tracks. The Generic IOCTL function has been designed to be open-ended so that it can be used to easily extend the device driver definition in future versions of MS-DOS.

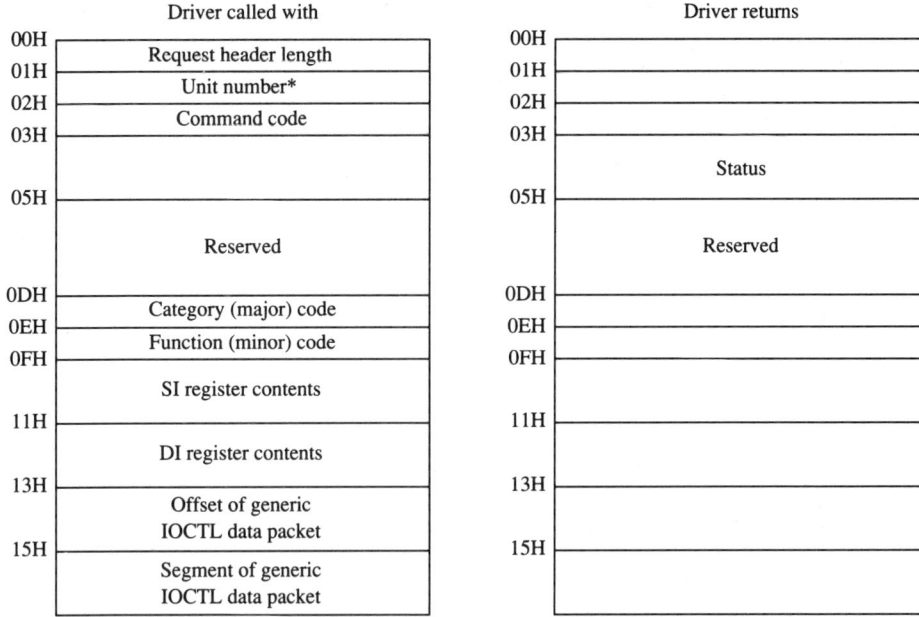

Figure 15-11. *Generic IOCTL request header.*

The Get Logical Device and Set Logical Device functions

The Get and Set Logical Device functions (command codes 23 and 24) are defined only for block devices under MS-DOS version 3.2 and are called only if the 3.2-functions-supported flag (bit 6) is set in the device attribute word of the device header. They correspond to the Get and Set Logical Drive Map services supplied by MS-DOS to application programs by means of Interrupt 21H Function 44H Subfunctions 0EH and 0FH.

The Get and Set Logical Device functions are called with a drive unit number in the request header (Figure 15-12). Both functions return a status word for the operation in the request header; the Get Logical Device function also returns a unit number.

The Get Logical Device function is called to determine whether more than one drive letter is assigned to the same physical device. It returns a code for the last drive letter used to reference the device (1 = A, 2 = B, and so on); if only one drive letter is assigned to the device, the returned unit code should be 0.

The Set Logical Device function is called to inform the driver of the next logical drive identifier that will be used to reference the device. The unit code passed by the MS-DOS kernel in this case is zero based relative to the logical drives supported by this particular driver. For example, if the driver supports two logical floppy-disk-drive units (A and B), only one physical disk drive exists in the system, and Set Logical Device is called with a unit number of 1, the driver is being informed that the next read or write request from the MS-DOS kernel will be directed to drive B.

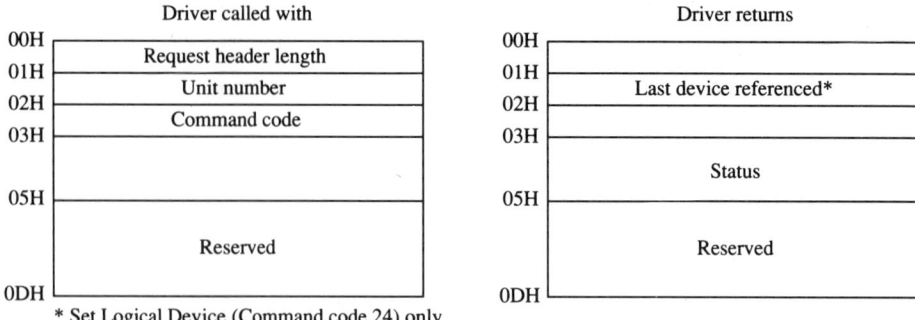

Figure 15-12. *Get Logical Device and Set Logical Device request header.*

In character-device drivers, the Get Logical Device and Set Logical Device functions should simply set the done flag in the status word of the request header and return.

The Processing of a Typical I/O Request

An application program requests an I/O operation from MS-DOS by loading registers with the appropriate values and addresses and executing a software Interrupt 21H. MS-DOS inspects its internal tables, searches the chain of device headers if necessary, and determines which device driver should receive the I/O request.

MS-DOS then creates a request header data packet in a reserved area of memory. Disk I/O requests are transformed from file and record information into logical sector requests by MS-DOS's interpretation of the disk directory and file allocation table. (MS-DOS locates these disk structures using the information returned by the driver from a previous Build BPB call and issues additional driver read requests, if necessary, to bring their sectors into memory.)

After the request header is prepared, MS-DOS calls the device driver's Strategy entry point, passing the address of the request header in registers ES:BX. The Strategy routine saves the address of the request header and performs a far return to MS-DOS.

MS-DOS then immediately calls the device driver's Interrupt entry point. The Interrupt routine saves all registers, retrieves the address of the request header that was saved by the Strategy routine, extracts the command code, and branches to the appropriate function to perform the operation requested by MS-DOS. When the requested function is complete, the Interrupt routine sets the done flag in the status word and places any other required information into the request header, restores all registers to their state at entry, and performs a far return.

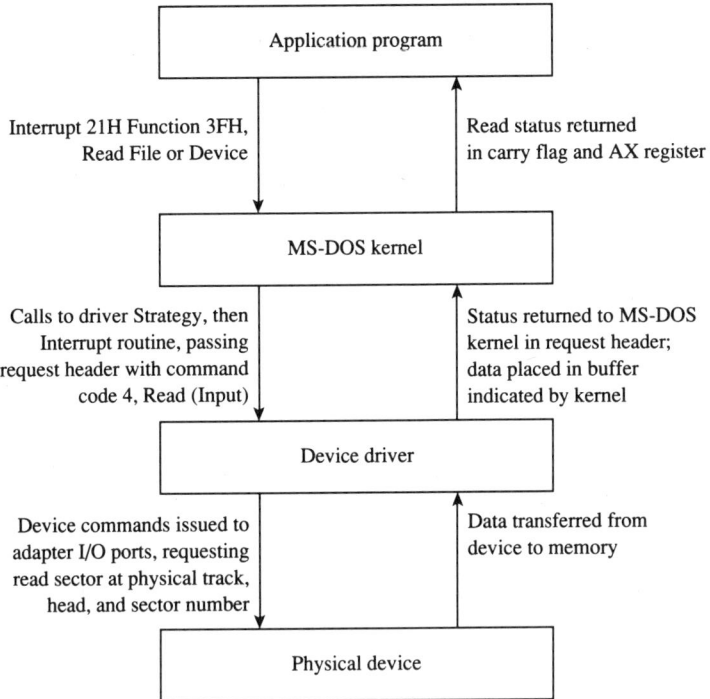

Figure 15-13. The processing of a typical I/O request from an application program.

MS-DOS translates the driver's returned status into the appropriate carry flag status, register values, and (possibly) error code for the MS-DOS Interrupt 21H function that was requested and returns control to the application program. Figure 15-13 sketches this entire flow of control and data.

Note that a single Interrupt 21H function request by an application program can result in many operation requests by MS-DOS to the device driver. For example, if the application invokes Interrupt 21H Function 3DH (Open File with Handle) to open a file, MS-DOS may have to issue multiple sector read requests to the driver while searching the directory for the filename. Similarly, an application program's request to write a string to the screen in cooked mode with Interrupt 21H Function 40H (Write File or Device) will result in a write request to the driver for each character in the string, because MS-DOS filters the characters and polls the keyboard for a pending Control-C between each character output.

Writing Device Drivers

Device drivers are traditionally coded in assembly language, both because of the rigid structural requirements and because of the need to keep driver execution speed high and memory overhead low. Although MS-DOS versions 3.0 and later are capable of loading drivers in .EXE format, versions 2.x can load only pure memory-image device drivers that do not require relocation. Therefore, drivers are typically written as though they were .COM programs with an "origin" of zero and converted with EXE2BIN to .BIN or .SYS files so that they will be compatible with any version of MS-DOS (2.0 or later). *See* PROGRAM-MING IN THE MS-DOS ENVIRONMENT: Programming for ms-dos: Structure of an Application Program.

The device header must be located at the beginning of the file (offset 0). Both words in the header's link field should be set to −1, thus allowing MS-DOS to fix up the link field when the driver is loaded during system initialization so that it points to the next driver in the chain. When a single file contains more than one driver, the offset portion of each header link field should point to the next header in that file, all using the same segment base of zero, and only the link field of the last header in the file should be set to −1, −1.

The device attribute word must reflect the device-driver type (character or block) and the bits that indicate support for the various optional command codes must have appropriate values. The device header's offsets to the Strategy and Interrupt routines must be relative to the same segment base as the device header itself. If the driver is for a character device, the name field should be filled in properly with the device's logical name, which can be any legal eight-character uppercase filename padded with spaces and without a colon. Duplication of existing character-device names or existing disk-file names should be avoided (unless a resident character-device driver is being intentionally superseded).

The Strategy and Interrupt routines for the device are called by MS-DOS by means of an intersegment call (CALL FAR) and must return to MS-DOS with a far return. Both routines must preserve all CPU registers and flags. The MS-DOS kernel's stack has room for 40 to 50 bytes when the driver is called; if the driver makes heavy use of the stack, it should switch to an internal stack of adequate depth.

The Strategy routine is, of course, very simple. It need only save the address of the request header that is passed to it in registers ES:BX and exit back to the kernel.

The logic of the Interrupt routine is necessarily more complex. It must save the CPU registers and flags, extract the command code from the request header whose address was previously saved by the Strategy routine, and dispatch the appropriate command-code function. When that function is finished, the Interrupt routine must ensure that the appropriate status and other information is placed in the request header, restore the CPU registers and flags, and return control to the kernel.

Although the interface between the MS-DOS kernel and the command-code routines is fairly simple, it is also strict. The command-code functions must behave exactly as they are defined or the system will behave erratically. Even a very subtle discrepancy in the action of a driver function can have unexpectedly large global effects. For example, if a block driver Read function returns an error but does not return a correct value for the number of sectors successfully transferred, the MS-DOS kernel will be misled in its attempts to retry the read for only the failing sectors and disk data might be corrupted.

Example character driver: TEMPLATE

Figure 15-14 contains the source code for a skeleton character-device driver called TEMPLATE.ASM. This driver does nothing except display a sign-on message when it is loaded, but it demonstrates all the essential driver components, including the device header, Strategy routine, and Interrupt routine. The command-code functions take no action other than to set the done flag in the request header status word.

```
        name    template
        title   'TEMPLATE --- installable driver template'


;
; TEMPLATE.ASM:  A program skeleton for an installable
;                device driver (MS-DOS 2.0 or later)
;
; The driver command-code routines are stubs only and have
; no effect but to return a nonerror "Done" status.
;
; Ray Duncan, July 1987
;


_TEXT   segment byte public 'CODE'

        assume  cs:_TEXT,ds:_TEXT,es:NOTHING

        org     0

MaxCmd  equ     24              ; maximum allowed command code
                                ; 12 for MS-DOS 2.x
                                ; 16 for MS-DOS 3.0-3.1
                                ; 24 for MS-DOS 3.2-3.3


cr      equ     0dh             ; ASCII carriage return
lf      equ     0ah             ; ASCII linefeed
eom     equ     '$'             ; end-of-message signal



Header:                         ; device driver header
        dd      -1              ; link to next device driver
        dw      c840h           ; device attribute word
        dw      Strat           ; "Strategy" routine entry point
        dw      Intr            ; "Interrupt" routine entry point
        db      'TEMPLATE'      ; logical device name


RHPtr   dd      ?               ; pointer to request header, passed
                                ; by MS-DOS kernel to Strategy routine
```

Figure 15-14. TEMPLATE.ASM, the source file for the TEMPLATE.SYS driver.   *(more)*

```
        Dispatch:                           ; Interrupt routine command-code
                                            ; dispatch table
                dw      Init                ;  0 = initialize driver
                dw      MediaChk            ;  1 = media check on block device
                dw      BuildBPB            ;  2 = build BIOS parameter block
                dw      IoctlRd             ;  3 = I/O control read
                dw      Read                ;  4 = read (input) from device
                dw      NdRead              ;  5 = nondestructive read
                dw      InpStat             ;  6 = return current input status
                dw      InpFlush            ;  7 = flush device input buffers
                dw      Write               ;  8 = write (output) to device
                dw      WriteVfy            ;  9 = write with verify
                dw      OutStat             ; 10 = return current output status
                dw      OutFlush            ; 11 = flush output buffers
                dw      IoctlWt             ; 12 = I/O control write
                dw      DevOpen             ; 13 = device open        (MS-DOS 3.0+)
                dw      DevClose            ; 14 = device close       (MS-DOS 3.0+)
                dw      RemMedia            ; 15 = removable media    (MS-DOS 3.0+)
                dw      OutBusy             ; 16 = output until busy (MS-DOS 3.0+)
                dw      Error               ; 17 = not used
                dw      Error               ; 18 = not used
                dw      GenIOCTL            ; 19 = generic IOCTL      (MS-DOS 3.2+)
                dw      Error               ; 20 = not used
                dw      Error               ; 21 = not used
                dw      Error               ; 22 = not used
                dw      GetLogDev           ; 23 = get logical device (MS-DOS 3.2+)
                dw      SetLogDev           ; 24 = set logical device (MS-DOS 3.2+)


        Strat   proc    far                 ; device driver Strategy routine,
                                            ; called by MS-DOS kernel with
                                            ; ES:BX = address of request header

                                            ; save pointer to request header
                mov     word ptr cs:[RHPtr],bx
                mov     word ptr cs:[RHPtr+2],es

                ret                         ; back to MS-DOS kernel

        Strat   endp


        Intr    proc    far                 ; device driver Interrupt routine,
                                            ; called by MS-DOS kernel immediately
                                            ; after call to Strategy routine

                push    ax                  ; save general registers
                push    bx
                push    cx
                push    dx
                push    ds
```

Figure 15-14. Continued.   *(more)*

```
        push    es
        push    di
        push    si
        push    bp

        push    cs              ; make local data addressable
        pop     ds              ; by setting DS = CS

        les     di,[RHPtr]      ; let ES:DI = request header

                                ; get BX = command code
        mov     bl,es:[di+2]
        xor     bh,bh
        cmp     bx,MaxCmd       ; make sure it's valid
        jle     Intr1           ; jump, function code is ok
        call    Error           ; set error bit, "Unknown Command" code
        jmp     Intr2

Intr1:  shl     bx,1            ; form index to dispatch table
                                ; and branch to command-code routine
        call    word ptr [bx+Dispatch]

        les     di,[RHPtr]      ; ES:DI = address of request header

Intr2:  or      ax,0100h        ; merge Done bit into status and
        mov     es:[di+3],ax    ; store status into request header

        pop     bp              ; restore general registers
        pop     si
        pop     di
        pop     es
        pop     ds
        pop     dx
        pop     cx
        pop     bx
        pop     ax
        ret                     ; return to MS-DOS kernel


; Command-code routines are called by the Interrupt routine
; via the dispatch table with ES:DI pointing to the request
; header. Each routine should return AX = 00H if function was
; completed successfully or AX = 8000H + error code if
; function failed.


MediaChk proc   near            ; function 1 = Media Check

        xor     ax,ax
        ret

MediaChk endp
```

Figure 15-14. Continued.   *(more)*

```
BuildBPB proc    near              ; function 2 = Build BPB

         xor     ax,ax
         ret

BuildBPB endp


IoctlRd  proc    near              ; function 3 = I/O Control Read

         xor     ax,ax
         ret

IoctlRd  endp


Read     proc    near              ; function 4 = Read (Input)

         xor     ax,ax
         ret

Read     endp


NdRead   proc    near              ; function 5 = Nondestructive Read

         xor     ax,ax
         ret

NdRead   endp


InpStat  proc    near              ; function 6 = Input Status

         xor     ax,ax
         ret

InpStat  endp


InpFlush proc    near              ; function 7 = Flush Input Buffers

         xor     ax,ax
         ret

InpFlush endp
```

Figure 15-14. Continued.   *(more)*

```
Write    proc    near            ; function 8 = Write (Output)

         xor     ax,ax
         ret

Write    endp


WriteVfy proc    near            ; function 9 = Write with Verify

         xor     ax,ax
         ret

WriteVfy endp


OutStat  proc    near            ; function 10 = Output Status

         xor     ax,ax
         ret

OutStat  endp


OutFlush proc    near            ; function 11 = Flush Output Buffers

         xor     ax,ax
         ret

OutFlush endp


IoctlWt  proc    near            ; function 12 = I/O Control Write

         xor     ax,ax
         ret

IoctlWt  endp


DevOpen  proc    near            ; function 13 = Device Open

         xor     ax,ax
         ret

DevOpen  endp
```

Figure 15-14. Continued.   *(more)*

```
        DevClose proc    near            ; function 14 = Device Close

                xor      ax,ax
                ret

        DevClose endp


        RemMedia proc    near            ; function 15 = Removable Media

                xor      ax,ax
                ret

        RemMedia endp


        OutBusy proc     near            ; function 16 = Output Until Busy

                xor      ax,ax
                ret

        OutBusy endp


        GenIOCTL proc    near            ; function 19 = Generic IOCTL

                xor      ax,ax
                ret

        GenIOCTL endp


        GetLogDev proc   near            ; function 23 = Get Logical Device

                xor      ax,ax
                ret

        GetLogDev endp


        SetLogDev proc   near            ; function 24 = Set Logical Device

                xor      ax,ax
                ret

        SetLogDev endp
```

Figure 15-14. Continued.

(more)

```
Error   proc    near                ; bad command code in request header

        mov     ax,8003h            ; error bit + "Unknown Command" code
        ret

Error   endp


Init    proc    near                ; function 0 = initialize driver

        push    es                  ; save address of request header
        push    di

        mov     ah,9                ; display driver sign-on message
        mov     dx,offset Ident
        int     21h

        pop     di                  ; restore request header address
        pop     es

                                    ; set address of free memory
                                    ; above driver (break address)
        mov     word ptr es:[di+14],offset Init
        mov     word ptr es:[di+16],cs

        xor     ax,ax               ; return status
        ret

Init    endp

Ident   db      cr,lf,lf
        db      'TEMPLATE Example Device Driver'
        db      cr,lf,eom

Intr    endp


_TEXT   ends

        end
```

Figure 15-14. Continued.

TEMPLATE.ASM can be assembled, linked, and converted into a loadable driver with the following commands:

```
C>MASM TEMPLATE;   <Enter>
C>LINK TEMPLATE;   <Enter>
C>EXE2BIN TEMPLATE.EXE TEMPLATE.SYS   <Enter>
```

The Microsoft Object Linker (LINK) will display the warning message *No Stack Segment*, this message can be ignored. The driver can then be installed by adding the line

```
DEVICE=TEMPLATE.SYS
```

to the CONFIG.SYS file and restarting the system. The fact that the TEMPLATE.SYS
driver also has the logical character-device name TEMPLATE allows the demonstration of
an interesting MS-DOS effect: After the driver is installed, the file that contains it can no
longer be copied, renamed, or deleted. The reason for this limitation is that MS-DOS
always searches its list of character-device names first when an open request is issued,
before it inspects the disk directory. The only way to erase the TEMPLATE.SYS file is to
modify the CONFIG.SYS file to remove the associated DEVICE statement and then restart
the system.

For a complete example of a character-device driver for interrupt-driven serial communications, *See* PROGRAMMING IN THE MS-DOS ENVIRONMENT: PROGRAMMING FOR MS-DOS:
Interrupt-Driven Communications.

Example block driver: TINYDISK

Figure 15-15 contains the source code for a simple 64 KB virtual disk (RAMdisk) called
TINYDISK.ASM. This code provides a working example of a simple block-device driver.
When its Initialization routine is called by the kernel, TINYDISK allocates itself 64 KB of
RAM and maps a disk structure onto the RAM in the form of a boot sector containing a
valid BPB, a FAT, a root directory, and a files area. *See* PROGRAMMING IN THE MS-DOS
ENVIRONMENT: STRUCTURE OF MS-DOS: MS-DOS Storage Devices.

```
        name    tinydisk
        title   TINYDISK example block-device driver

; TINYDISK.ASM --- 64 KB RAMdisk
;
; Ray Duncan, July 1987
; Example of a simple installable block-device driver.

_TEXT   segment public 'CODE'

        assume  cs:_TEXT,ds:_TEXT,es:_TEXT

        org     0

MaxCmd  equ     12              ; max driver command code
                                ; (no MS-DOS 3.x functions)

cr      equ     0dh             ; ASCII carriage return
lf      equ     0ah             ; ASCII linefeed
blank   equ     020h            ; ASCII space code
eom     equ     '$'             ; end-of-message signal

Secsize equ     512             ; bytes/sector, IBM-compatible media
```

Figure 15-15. TINYDISK.ASM, the source file for the TINYDISK.SYS driver.   *(more)*

```
                                ; device-driver header
Header   dd      -1             ; link to next driver in chain
         dw      0              ; device attribute word
         dw      Strat          ; "Strategy" routine entry point
         dw      Intr           ; "Interrupt" routine entry point
         db      1              ; number of units, this device
         db      7 dup (0)      ; reserved area (block-device drivers)

RHPtr    dd      ?              ; segment:offset of request header

Secseg   dw      ?              ; segment base of sector storage

Xfrsec   dw      0              ; current sector for transfer
Xfrcnt   dw      0              ; sectors successfully transferred
Xfrreq   dw      0              ; number of sectors requested
Xfraddr  dd      0              ; working address for transfer

Array    dw      BPB            ; array of pointers to BPB
                                ; for each supported unit


Bootrec  equ     $

         jmp     $              ; phony JMP at start of
         nop                    ; boot sector; this field
                                ; must be 3 bytes

         db      'MS   2.0'     ; OEM identity field

                                ; BIOS Parameter Block (BPB)
BPB      dw      Secsize        ; 00H - bytes per sector
         db      1              ; 02H - sectors per cluster
         dw      1              ; 03H - reserved sectors
         db      1              ; 05H - number of FATs
         dw      32             ; 06H - root directory entries
         dw      128            ; 08H - sectors = 64 KB/secsize
         db      0f8h           ; 0AH - media descriptor
         dw      1              ; 0BH - sectors per FAT

Bootrec_len equ $-Bootrec


Strat    proc    far            ; RAMdisk strategy routine

                                ; save address of request header
         mov     word ptr cs:RHPtr,bx
         mov     word ptr cs:[RHPtr+2],es
         ret                    ; back to MS-DOS kernel

Strat    endp
```

Figure 15-15. Continued.   *(more)*

```
Intr     proc    far                  ; RAMdisk interrupt routine

         push    ax                   ; save general registers
         push    bx
         push    cx
         push    dx
         push    ds
         push    es
         push    di
         push    si
         push    bp

         mov     ax,cs                ; make local data addressable
         mov     ds,ax

         les     di,[RHPtr]           ; ES:DI = request header

         mov     bl,es:[di+2]         ; get command code
         xor     bh,bh
         cmp     bx,MaxCmd            ; make sure it's valid
         jle     Intr1                ; jump, function code is ok
         mov     ax,8003h             ; set Error bit and
         jmp     Intr3                ; "Unknown Command" error code

Intr1:   shl     bx,1                 ; form index to dispatch table and
                                      ; branch to command-code routine
         call    word ptr [bx+Dispatch]
                                      ; should return AX = status

         les     di,[RHPtr]           ; restore ES:DI = request header

Intr3:   or      ax,0100h             ; merge Done bit into status and store
         mov     es:[di+3],ax         ; status into request header

Intr4:   pop     bp                   ; restore general registers
         pop     si
         pop     di
         pop     es
         pop     ds
         pop     dx
         pop     cx
         pop     bx
         pop     ax
         ret                          ; return to MS-DOS kernel

Intr     endp
```

Figure 15-15. Continued.   *(more)*

```
Dispatch:                       ; command-code dispatch table
                                ; all command-code routines are
                                ; entered with ES:DI pointing
                                ; to request header and return
                                ; the operation status in AX
        dw      Init            ;  0 = initialize driver
        dw      MediaChk        ;  1 = media check on block device
        dw      BuildBPB        ;  2 = build BIOS parameter block
        dw      Dummy           ;  3 = I/O control read
        dw      Read            ;  4 = read (input) from device
        dw      Dummy           ;  5 = nondestructive read
        dw      Dummy           ;  6 = return current input status
        dw      Dummy           ;  7 = flush device input buffers
        dw      Write           ;  8 = write (output) to device
        dw      Write           ;  9 = write with verify
        dw      Dummy           ; 10 = return current output status
        dw      Dummy           ; 11 = flush output buffers
        dw      Dummy           ; 12 = I/O control write


MediaChk proc   near            ; command code 1 = Media Check

                                ; return "not changed" code
        mov     byte ptr es:[di+0eh],1
        xor     ax,ax           ; and success status
        ret

MediaChk endp


BuildBPB proc   near            ; command code 2 = Build BPB

                                ; put BPB address in request header
        mov     word ptr es:[di+12h],offset BPB
        mov     word ptr es:[di+14h],cs
        xor     ax,ax           ; return success status
        ret

BuildBPB endp


Read    proc    near            ; command code 4 = Read (Input)

        call    Setup           ; set up transfer variables

Read1:  mov     ax,Xfrcnt       ; done with all sectors yet?
        cmp     ax,Xfrreq
        je      Read2           ; jump if transfer completed
        mov     ax,Xfrsec       ; get next sector number
        call    Mapsec          ; and map it
```

Figure 15-15. Continued.   *(more)*

```
        mov     ax,es
        mov     si,di
        les     di,Xfraddr      ; ES:DI = requester's buffer
        mov     ds,ax           ; DS:SI = RAMdisk address
        mov     cx,Secsize      ; transfer logical sector from
        cld                     ; RAMdisk to requestor
        rep movsb
        push    cs              ; restore local addressing
        pop     ds
        inc     Xfrsec          ; advance sector number
                                ; advance transfer address
        add     word ptr Xfraddr,Secsize
        inc     Xfrcnt          ; count sectors transferred
        jmp     Read1

Read2:                          ; all sectors transferred
        xor     ax,ax           ; return success status
        les     di,RHPtr        ; put actual transfer count
        mov     bx,Xfrcnt       ; into request header
        mov     es:[di+12h],bx
        ret

Read    endp


Write   proc    near            ; command code 8 = Write (Output)
                                ; command code 9 = Write with Verify

        call    Setup           ; set up transfer variables

Write1: mov     ax,Xfrcnt       ; done with all sectors yet?
        cmp     ax,Xfrreq
        je      Write2          ; jump if transfer completed

        mov     ax,Xfrsec       ; get next sector number
        call    Mapsec          ; and map it
        lds     si,Xfraddr
        mov     cx,Secsize      ; transfer logical sector from
        cld                     ; requester to RAMdisk
        rep movsb
        push    cs              ; restore local addressing
        pop     ds
        inc     Xfrsec          ; advance sector number
                                ; advance transfer address
        add     word ptr Xfraddr,Secsize
        inc     Xfrcnt          ; count sectors transferred
        jmp     Write1

Write2:                         ; all sectors transferred
        xor     ax,ax           ; return success status
        les     di,RHPtr        ; put actual transfer count
```

Figure 15-15. Continued.   *(more)*

```
        mov     bx,Xfrcnt       ; into request header
        mov     es:[di+12h],bx
        ret

Write   endp


Dummy   proc    near            ; called for unsupported functions

        xor     ax,ax           ; return success flag for all
        ret

Dummy   endp


Mapsec  proc    near            ; map sector number to memory address
                                ; call with AX = logical sector no.
                                ; return ES:DI = memory address

        mov     di,Secsize/16   ; paragraphs per sector
        mul     di              ; * logical sector number
        add     ax,Secseg       ; + segment base of sector storage
        mov     es,ax
        xor     di,di           ; now ES:DI points to sector
        ret

Mapsec  endp


Setup   proc    near            ; set up for read or write
                                ; call ES:DI = request header
                                ; extracts address, start, count

        push    es              ; save request header address
        push    di
        mov     ax,es:[di+14h]  ; starting sector number
        mov     Xfrsec,ax
        mov     ax,es:[di+12h]  ; sectors requested
        mov     Xfrreq,ax
        les     di,es:[di+0eh]  ; requester's buffer address
        mov     word ptr Xfraddr,di
        mov     word ptr Xfraddr+2,es
        mov     Xfrcnt,0        ; initialize sectors transferred count
        pop     di              ; restore request header address
        pop     es
        ret

Setup   endp
```

Figure 15-15. Continued.   *(more)*

```
Init     proc    near            ; command code 0 = Initialize driver
                                 ; on entry ES:DI = request header

         mov     ax,cs           ; calculate segment base for sector
         add     ax,Driver_len   ; storage and save it
         mov     Secseg,ax
         add     ax,1000h        ; add 1000H paras (64 KB) and
         mov     es:[di+10h],ax  ; set address of free memory
         mov     word ptr es:[di+0eh],0

         call    Format          ; format the RAMdisk

         call    Signon          ; display driver identification

         les     di,cs:RHPtr     ; restore ES:DI = request header
                                 ; set logical units = 1
         mov     byte ptr es:[di+0dh],1
                                 ; set address of BPB array
         mov     word ptr es:[di+12h],offset Array
         mov     word ptr es:[di+14h],cs

         xor     ax,ax           ; return success status
         ret

Init     endp


Format   proc    near            ; format the RAMdisk area

         mov     es,Secseg       ; first zero out RAMdisk
         xor     di,di
         mov     cx,8000h         ; 32 K words = 64 KB
         xor     ax,ax
         cld
         rep stosw

         mov     ax,0            ; get address of logical
         call    Mapsec          ; sector zero
         mov     si,offset Bootrec
         mov     cx,Bootrec_len
         rep movsb               ; and copy boot record to it

         mov     ax,word ptr BPB+3
         call    Mapsec          ; get address of 1st FAT sector
         mov     al,byte ptr BPB+0ah
         mov     es:[di],al      ; put media ID byte into it
         mov     word ptr es:[di+1],-1

         mov     ax,word ptr BPB+3
         add     ax,word ptr BPB+0bh
         call    Mapsec          ; get address of 1st directory sector
```

Figure 15-15. Continued.   (more)

```
            mov     si,offset Volname
            mov     cx,Volname_len
            rep movsb                   ; copy volume label to it

            ret                         ; done with formatting

Format  endp


Signon  proc    near                    ; driver identification message

            les     di,RHPtr            ; let ES:DI = request header
            mov     al,es:[di+22]       ; get drive code from header,
            add     al,'A'              ; convert it to ASCII, and
            mov     drive,al            ; store into sign-on message

            mov     ah,30h              ; get MS-DOS version
            int     21h
            cmp     al,2
            ja      Signon1             ; jump if version 3.0 or later
            mov     Ident1,eom          ; version 2.x, don't print drive

Signon1:                                ; print sign-on message
            mov     ah,09H              ; Function 09H = print string
            mov     dx,offset Ident     ; DS:DX = address of message
            int     21h                 ; transfer to MS-DOS

            ret                         ; back to caller

Signon  endp


Ident   db      cr,lf,lf        ; driver sign-on message
        db      'TINYDISK 64 KB RAMdisk'
        db      cr,lf
Ident1  db      'RAMdisk will be drive '
Drive   db      'X:'
        db      cr,lf,eom


Volname db      'DOSREF_DISK'   ; volume label for RAMdisk
        db      08h             ; attribute byte
        db      10 dup (0)      ; reserved area
        dw      0               ; time = 00:00
        dw      0f01h           ; date = August 1, 1987
        db      6 dup (0)       ; reserved area

Volname_len equ $-volname

Driver_len dw ((($-header)/16)+1 ; driver size in paragraphs

_TEXT   ends

        end
```

Figure 15-15. Continued.

Subsequent driver Read and Write calls by the kernel to TINYDISK function as though they were transferring sectors to and from a physical storage device but actually only copy data from one area in memory to another. A programmer can learn a great deal about the operation of block-device drivers and MS-DOS's relationship to those drivers (such as the order and frequency of Media Change, Build BPB, Read, Write, and Write With Verify calls) by inserting software probes into TINYDISK at appropriate locations and monitoring its behavior.

TINYDISK.ASM can be assembled, linked, and converted into a loadable driver with the following commands:

```
C>MASM TINYDISK;    <Enter>
C>LINK TINYDISK;    <Enter>
C>EXE2BIN TINYDISK.EXE TINYDISK.SYS   <Enter>
```

The linker will display the warning message *No Stack Segment*; this message can be ignored. The driver can then be installed by adding the line

```
DEVICE=TINYDISK.SYS
```

to the CONFIG.SYS file and restarting the system. When it is loaded, TINYDISK displays a sign-on message and the drive letter that it was assigned if it is running under MS-DOS version 3.0 or later. (If the host system is MS-DOS version 2.x, this information is not provided to the driver.) Files can then be copied to the RAMdisk as though it were a small but extremely fast disk drive.

Ray Duncan

Part D
Directions of MS-DOS

Article 16
Writing Applications for
Upward Compatibility

One of the major concerns of the designers of Microsoft OS/2 was that it be backwardly compatible — that is, that programs written to run under MS-DOS versions 2 and 3 be able to run on MS OS/2. A major concern for present application programmers is that their programs run not only on current versions of MS-DOS (and MS OS/2) but also on future versions of MS-DOS. Ensuring such upward compatibility involves both hardware issues and operating-system issues.

Hardware Issues

A basic requirement for ensuring upward compatibility is hardware-independent code. If you bypass system services and directly program the hardware — such as the system interrupt controller, the system clock, and the enhanced graphics adapter (EGA) registers — your application will not run on future versions of MS-DOS.

Protected mode compatibility

The 80286 and the 80386 microprocessors can operate in two incompatible modes: real mode and protected mode. When either chip is operating in real mode, it is perceived by the operating system and programs as a fast 8088 chip. Applications written for the 8086 and 8088 run the same on the 80286 and the 80386 — only faster. They cannot, however, take advantage of 80286 and 80386 features unless they can run in protected mode.

Following the guidelines below will minimize the work necessary to convert a real mode program to protected mode and will also allow a program to use a special subset of the MS OS/2 Applications Program Interface (API) — Family API. A binary program (.EXE) that uses the family API can run in either protected mode or real mode under MS OS/2 and subsequent systems, but it can run only in real mode under MS-DOS version 3.

Family API

The Family API requires that the application use a subset of the MS OS/2 Dynamic Link System API. Special tools link the application with a special library that implements the subset MS OS/2 system services in the MS-DOS version 3 environment. Many of these services are implemented by calling the appropriate Interrupt 21H subfunction; some are implemented in the special library itself.

When a Family API application is loaded under MS OS/2 protected mode, MS OS/2 ignores the special library code and loads only the application itself. MS OS/2 then provides the requested services in the normal fashion. However, MS-DOS version 3 loads the entire package — the application and the special library — because the Family API .EXE file is constructed to look like an MS-DOS 3 .EXE file.

Linear *vs* segmented memory

The protected mode and the real mode of the 80286 and the 80386 are compatible except in the area of segmentation. The 8086 has been described as a segmented machine, but it is actually a linear memory machine with offset registers. When a memory address is generated, the value in one of the "segment" registers is multiplied by 16 and added as a displacement to the offset value supplied by the instruction's addressing mode. No length information is associated with each "segment"; the "segment" register supplies only a 20-bit addressing offset. Programs routinely use this by computing a 20-bit address and then decomposing it into a 16-bit "segment" value and a 16-bit displacement value so that the address can be referenced.

The protected mode of the 80286 and the 80386, however, is truly segmented. A value placed in a segment register selects an entry from a descriptor table; that entry contains the addressing offset, a segment length, and permission bits. On the 8086, the so-called segment component of an address is multiplied by 16 and added to the offset component, producing a 20-bit physical address. Thus, if you take an address in the *segment:offset* form, add 4 to the segment value, and subtract 64 (that is, $4*16$) from the offset value, the new address references exactly the same location as the old address. On the 80286 and the 80386 in protected mode, however, segment values, called segment selectors, have no direct correspondence to physical addresses. In other words, in 8086 mode, the two address forms

$1000_{16}{:}0345_{16}$

and

$1004_{16}{:}0305_{16}$

reference the same memory location, but in protected mode these two forms reference totally different locations.

Creating segment values

This architectural difference gives rise to the most common cause of incompatibility — the program performs addressing arithmetic to compute "segment" values. Any program that uses the 20-bit addressing scheme to create or to compute a value to be loaded in a segment register cannot be converted to run in protected mode. To be protected mode compatible, a program must treat the 8086's so-called segments as true segments.

To create a program that does this, write according to the following guidelines:

1. Do not generate any segment values. Use only the segment values supplied by MS-DOS calls and those placed in the segment registers when MS-DOS loaded your program. The exception is "huge objects" — memory objects larger than 64 KB. In

this case, MS OS/2 provides a base segment number and a "segment offset value." The returned segment number selects the first 64 KB of the object and the segment number, plus the segment offset value address the second 64 KB of the object. Likewise, the returned segment value plus N*(segment offset value) selects the N+1 64 KB piece of the huge object. Write real mode code in this same fashion, using 4096 as the segment offset value. When you convert your program, you can substitute the value provided by MS OS/2.

2. Do not address beyond the allocated length of a segment.

3. Do not use segment registers as scratch registers by placing general data in them. Place only valid segment values, supplied by MS-DOS, in a segment register. The one exception is that you can place a zero value in a segment register, perhaps to indicate "no address." You can place the zero in the segment register, but you cannot reference memory using that register; you can only load/store or push/pop it.

4. Do not use CS: overrides on instructions that store into memory. It is impossible to store into a code segment in protected mode.

CPU speed

Because various microprocessors and machine configurations execute at different speeds, a program should not contain timing loops that depend on CPU speed. Specifically, a program should not establish CPU speed during initialization and then use that value for timing loops because the preemptive scheduling of MS OS/2 and future operating systems can "take away" the CPU at any time for arbitrary and unpredictable lengths of time. (In any case, time should not be wasted in a timing loop when other processes could be using system resources.)

Program timing

Programs must measure the passage of time carefully. They can use the system clock-tick interrupt while directly interfacing with the user, but no clock ticks will be seen by real mode programs when the user switches the screen interface to another program.

It is recommended that applications use the time-of-day system interface to determine elapsed time. To facilitate conversion to MS OS/2 protected mode, programs should encapsulate time-of-day or elapsed-time functions into subroutines.

BIOS

Avoid BIOS interrupt interfaces except for Interrupt 10H (the screen display functions) and Interrupt 16H (the keyboard functions). Interrupt 10H functions are contained in the MS OS/2 VIO package, and Interrupt 16H functions are in the MS OS/2 KBD package. Other BIOS interrupts provide functions that are available under MS OS/2 only in considerably modified forms.

Special operations

Uncommon, or special, operations and instructions can produce varied results, depending on the microprocessor. For example, when a "divide by 0" trap is taken on an 8086, the stack frame points to the instruction after the fault; when such action is taken on the 80286 and 80386, the return address points to the instruction that caused the fault. The effect of pushing the SP register is different between the 80286 and the 80386 as well. *See* Appendix M: 8086/8088 Software Compatibility Issues. Write your program to avoid these problem areas.

Operating-System Issues

Basic to writing programs that will run on future operating systems is writing code that is not version specific. Incorporating special version-specific features in a program will virtually ensure that the program will be incompatible with future versions of MS-DOS and MS OS/2.

Following the guidelines below will not necessarily ensure your program's compatibility, but it will facilitate converting the program or using the Family API to produce a dual-mode binary program.

Filenames

MS-DOS versions 2 and 3 silently truncate a filename that is longer than eight characters or an extension that is longer than three characters. MS-DOS generates no error message when performing this task. In real mode, MS OS/2 also silently truncates a filename or extension that exceeds the maximum length; in protected mode, however, it does not. Therefore, a real mode application program needs to perform this truncating function. The program should check the length of the filenames that it generates or that it obtains from a user and refuse names that are longer than the eight-character maximum. This prevents improperly formatted names from becoming embedded in data and control files — a situation that could cause a protected mode version of the application to fail when it presents that invalid name to the operating system.

When you convert your program to protected mode API, remove the length-checking code; MS OS/2 will check the length and return an error code as appropriate. Future file systems will support longer filenames, so it's important that protected mode programs simply present filenames to the operating system, which is then responsible for judging their validity.

Other MS-DOS version 2 and 3 elements have fixed lengths, including the current directory path. To be upwardly compatible, your program should accept whatever length is provided by the user or returned from a system call and rely on MS OS/2 to return an error message if a length is inappropriate. The exception is filename length in real mode non-Family API programs: These programs should enforce the eight-character maximum because MS-DOS versions 2 and 3 fail to do so.

File truncation

Files are truncated by means of a zero-length write under MS-DOS versions 2 and 3; under MS OS/2 in protected mode, files are truncated with a special API. File truncation operations should be encapsulated in a special routine to facilitate conversion to MS OS/2 protected mode or the Family API.

File searches

MS-DOS versions 2 and 3 never close file-system searches (Find First File/Find Next File). The returned search contains the information necessary for MS-DOS to continue the search later, and if the search is never continued, no harm is done.

MS OS/2, however, retains the necessary search continuation information in an internal structure of limited size. For this reason, your program should not depend on more than about 10 simultaneous searches and it should be able to close searches when it is done. If your program needs to perform more than about 10 searches simultaneously, it should be able to close a search, restart it later, and advance to the place where the program left off, rather than depending on MS OS/2 to continue the search.

MS OS/2 further provides a Find Close function that releases the internal search information. Protected mode programs should use this call at the end of every search sequence. Because MS-DOS versions 2 and 3 have no such call, your program should call a dummy procedure by this name at the appropriate locations. Then you can convert your program to the protected mode API or to the Family API without reexamining your algorithms.

Note: Receiving a "No more files" return code from a search does not implicitly close the search; all search closes must be explicit.

The Family API allows only a single search at a time. To circumvent this restriction, code two different Find Next File routines in your program — one for MS OS/2 protected mode and one for MS-DOS real mode — and use the Family API function that determines the program's current environment to select the routine to execute.

MS-DOS calls

A program that uses only the Interrupt 21H functions listed below is guaranteed to work in the Compatibility Box of MS OS/2 and will be relatively easy to modify for MS OS/2 protected mode.

Function	Name
0DH	Disk Reset
0EH	Select Disk
19H	Get Current Disk
1AH	Set DTA Address
25H	Set Interrupt Vector
2AH	Get Date
2BH	Set Date
2CH	Get Time
2EH	Set/Reset Verify Flag
2FH	Get DTA Address

(more)

Function	Name
30H	Get MS-DOS Version Number
33H	Get/Set Control-C Check Flag
35H	Get Interrupt Vector
36H	Get Disk Free Space
38H	Get/Set Current Country
39H	Create Directory
3AH	Remove Directory
3BH	Change Current Directory
3CH	Create File with Handle
3DH	Open File with Handle
3EH	Close File
3FH	Read File or Device
40H	Write File or Device
41H	Delete File
42H	Move File Pointer
43H	Get/Set File Attributes
44H	IOCTL (all subfunctions)
45H	Duplicate File Handle
46H	Force Duplicate File Handle
47H	Get Current Directory
48H	Allocate Memory Block
49H	Free Memory Block
4AH	Resize Memory Block
4BH	Load and Execute Program (EXEC)
4CH	Terminate Process with Return Code
4DH	Get Return Code of Child Process
4EH	Find First File
4FH	Find Next File
54H	Get Verify Flag
56H	Rename File
57H	Get/Set Date/Time of File
59H	Get Extended Error Information
5AH	Create Temporary File
5BH	Create New File
5CH	Lock/Unlock File Region

FCBs

FCBs are not supported in MS OS/2 protected mode. Use handle-based calls instead.

Interrupt calls

MS-DOS versions 2 and 3 use an interrupt-based interface; MS OS/2 protected mode uses a procedure-call interface. Write your code to accommodate this difference by encapsulating the interrupt-based interfaces into individual subroutines that can then easily be modified to use the MS OS/2 procedure-call interface.

System call register usage

The MS OS/2 procedure-call interface preserves all registers except AX and FLAGS. Write your program to assume that the contents of AX and the contents of any register modified by MS-DOS version 2 and 3 interrupt interfaces are destroyed at each system call, regardless of the success or failure of that call.

Flush/Commit calls

Your program should issue Flush/Commit calls where necessary — for example, after writing out the user's work file — but no more than necessary. Because MS OS/2 is multitasking, the floppy disk that contains the files to be flushed may not be in the drive. In such a case, MS OS/2 prompts the user to insert the proper floppy disk. As a result, too frequent flushes could generate a great many *Insert disk* messages and degrade the system's usability.

Seeks

Seeks to negative offsets and to devices also create compatibility issues.

To negative offsets

Your program should not attempt to seek to a negative file location. A negative seek offset is permissible as long as the sum of the seek offset and the current file position is positive. MS-DOS versions 2 and 3 allow seeking to a negative offset as long as you do not attempt to read or write the file at that offset. MS OS/2 and subsequent systems return an error code for negative net offsets.

On devices

Your program should not issue seeks to devices (such as AUX, COM, and so on). Doing so produces an error under MS OS/2.

Error codes

Because future releases of the operating system may return new error codes to system calls, you should write code that is open-ended about error codes — that is, write your program to deal with error codes beyond those currently defined. You can generally do this by including special handling for any codes that require special treatment, such as "File not found," and by taking a generic course of action for all other errors. The MS OS/2 protected mode API and the Family API have an interface that contains a message describing the error; this message can be displayed to the user. The interface also returns error classification information and a recommended action.

Multitasking concerns

Multitasking is a feature of MS OS/2 and will be a feature of all future versions of MS-DOS. The following guidelines apply to all programs, even to those written for MS-DOS version 3, because they may run in compatibility mode under MS OS/2.

Disabling interrupts

Do not disable interrupts, typically with the CLI instruction. The consequences of doing so depend on the environment.

In real mode programs under MS OS/2, disabling interrupts works normally but has a negative impact on the system's ability to maintain proper system throughput. Communications programs or networking applications might lose data. In a future version of real mode MS OS/2-80386, the operating system will disregard attempts to disable interrupts.

Protected mode programs under MS OS/2 can disable interrupts only in special Ring 2 segments. Disabling interrupts for longer than 100 microseconds might cause communications programs or networking applications to lose data or break connection. A future 80386-specific version of MS OS/2 will ignore attempts to disable interrupts in protected mode programs.

Measuring system resources

Do not attempt to measure system resources by exhausting them, and do not assume that because a resource is available at one time it will be available later. Remember: System resources are being shared with other programs.

For example, it is common for an MS-DOS version 3 application to request 1 MB of memory. The system cannot fulfill this request, so it returns the largest amount of memory available. The application then requests that amount of memory. Typically, applications do not even check for an error code from the second request. They routinely request all available memory because their creators knew that no other application could be in the system at the same time. This practice will work in real mode MS OS/2, although it is inefficient because MS OS/2 must allocate memory to a program that has no effective use for it. However, this practice will *not* work under MS OS/2 protected mode or under the Family API.

Another typical resource-exhaustion technique is opening files until an open is refused and then closing unneeded file handles. All applications, even those that run only in an MS OS/2 real mode environment, must use only the resources they need and not waste system resources; in a multitasking environment, other programs in the system usually need those resources.

Sharing rules

Because multiple programs can run under MS OS/2 simultaneously and because the system can be networked, conflicts can occur when two programs try to access the same file. MS OS/2 handles this situation with special file-sharing support. Although programs ignorant of file-sharing rules can run in real mode, you should explicitly specify file-sharing rules in your program. This will reduce the number of file-access conflicts the user will encounter.

Miscellaneous guidelines

Do not use undocumented features of MS-DOS or undocumented fields such as those in the Find First File buffer. Also, do not modify or store your own values in such areas.

Maintain at least 2048 free bytes on the stack at all times. Future releases of MS-DOS may require extra stack space at system call and at interrupt time.

Print using conventional handle writes to the LPT device(s). For example:

```
fd = open("LPT1");
write(fd, data, datalen);
```

Do not use Interrupt 17H (the IBM ROM BIOS printer services), writes to the *stdprn* handle (handle 3), or special-purpose Interrupt 21H functions such as 05H (Printer Output). These methods are not supported under MS OS/2 protected mode or in the Family API.

Do not use the MS-DOS standard handles *stdaux* and *stdprn* (handles 3 and 4); these handles are not supported in MS OS/2 protected mode. Use only *stdin* (handle 0), *stdout* (handle 1), and *stderr* (handle 2). Do use these latter handles where appropriate and avoid opening the CON device directly. Avoid Interrupt 21H Functions 03H (Auxiliary Input) and 04H (Auxiliary Output), which are polling operations on *stdaux*.

Summary

A tenet of MS OS/2 design was flexibility: Each component was constructed in anticipation of massive changes in a future release and with an eye toward existing versions of MS-DOS. Writing applications that are upwardly and backwardly compatible in such an environment is essential — and challenging. Following the guidelines in this article will ensure that your programs function appropriately in the MS-DOS/OS/2 operating-system family.

Gordon Letwin

Article 17
Windows

Microsoft Windows is an operating environment that runs under MS-DOS versions 2.0 and later. The current version of Windows, version 2.0, requires either a fixed disk or two double-sided floppy-disk drives, at least 320 KB of memory, and a video display board and monitor capable of graphics and a screen resolution of at least 640 (horizontal) by 200 (vertical) pixels. A fixed disk and 640 KB of memory provide the best environment for running Windows; a mouse or other pointing device is optional but recommended.

For the user, Windows provides a multitasking, graphics-based windowing environment for running programs. In this environment, users can easily switch among several programs and transfer data between them. Because programs specially designed to run under Windows usually have a consistent user interface, the time spent learning a new program is greatly diminished. Furthermore, the user can carry out command functions using only the keyboard, only the mouse, or some combination of the two. In some cases, Windows (and Windows applications) provides several different ways to execute the same command.

For the program developer, Windows provides a wealth of high-level routines that make it easy to incorporate menus, scroll bars, and dialog boxes (which contain controls, such as push buttons and list boxes) into programs. Windows' graphics interface is device independent, so programs developed for Windows work with every video display adapter and printer that has a Windows driver (usually supplied by the hardware manufacturer). Windows also includes features that facilitate the translation of programs into foreign languages for international markets.

When Windows is running, it shares responsibility for managing system resources with MS-DOS. Thus, programs that run under Windows continue to use MS-DOS function calls for all file input and output and for executing other programs, but they do not use MS-DOS for display or printer output, keyboard or mouse input, or memory management. Instead, they use functions provided by Windows.

Program Categories

Programs that run under Windows can be divided into three categories:

1. Programs specially designed for the Windows environment. Examples of such programs include Clock and Calculator, which come with Windows. Microsoft Excel is also specially designed for Windows. Other programs of this type (such as Aldus's Pagemaker) are available from software vendors other than Microsoft. Programs in this category cannot run under MS-DOS without Windows.
2. Programs designed to run under MS-DOS but that can usually be run in a window along with programs designed specially for Windows. These programs do not require

large amounts of memory, do not write directly to the display, do not use graphics, and do not alter the operation of the keyboard interrupt. They cannot use the mouse, the Windows application-program interface (such as menus and dialog boxes), or the graphics services that Windows provides. MS-DOS utilities, such as EDLIN and CHKDSK, are examples of programs in this category.

3. Programs designed to run under MS-DOS but that require large amounts of memory, write directly to the display, use graphics, or alter the operation of the keyboard inter-rupt. When Windows runs such a program, it must suspend operation of all other programs running in Windows and allow the program to use the full screen. In some cases, Windows cannot switch back to its normal display until the program termi-nates. Microsoft Word and Lotus 1-2-3 are examples of programs in this category.

The programs in categories 2 and 3 are sometimes called standard applications. To run one of these programs in Windows, the user must create a PIF file (Program Information File) that describes how much memory the program requires and how it uses the com-puter's hardware.

Although the ability to run existing MS-DOS programs under Windows benefits the user, the primary purpose of Windows is to provide an environment for specially designed pro-grams that take full advantage of the Windows interface. This discussion therefore concen-trates almost exclusively on programs written for the Windows 2.0 environment.

The Windows Display

Figure 17-1 shows a typical Windows display running several programs that are included with the retail version of Windows 2.0.

The display is organized as a desktop, with each program occupying one or more rect-angular windows that, unlike the tiled (juxtaposed) windows typical of earlier versions, can be overlapped. Only one program is active at any time — usually the program that is currently receiving keyboard input. Windows displays the currently active program on top of (overlying) the others. Programs such as CLOCK and TERMINAL that are not active continue to run normally, but do not receive keyboard input.

The user can make another program active by pressing and releasing (clicking) the mouse button when the mouse cursor is positioned in the new program's window or by pressing either the Alt-Tab or Alt-Esc key combination. Windows then brings the new active pro-gram to the top.

Most Windows programs allow their windows to be moved to another part of the display or to be resized to occupy smaller or larger areas. Most of these programs can also be max-imized to fill the entire screen or minimized — generally as a small icon displayed at the bottom of the screen — to occupy a small amount of display space.

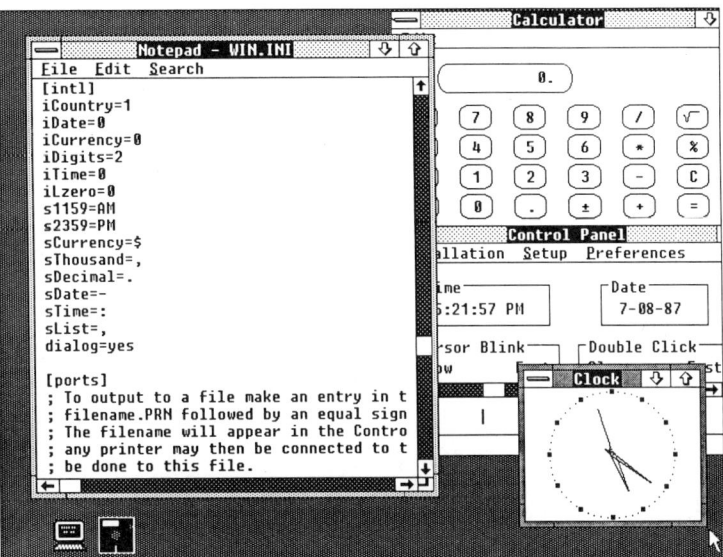

Figure 17-1. A typical Windows display.

Parts of the window

Figure 17-2 shows the Windows NOTEPAD program, with the different parts of the window identified. NOTEPAD is a small ASCII text editor limited to files of 16 KB. The various parts of the NOTEPAD window (similar to all Windows programs) are described in this section.

Title bar (or caption bar). The title bar identifies the program and, if applicable, the data file currently loaded into the program. For example, the NOTEPAD window shown in Figure 17-2 on the next page has the file WIN.INI loaded into memory. Windows uses different title-bar colors to distinguish the active window from inactive windows. The user can move a window to another part of the display by pressing the mouse button when the mouse pointer is positioned anywhere on the title bar and dragging (moving) the mouse while the button is pressed.

System-menu icon. When the user clicks a system-menu icon with the mouse (or presses Alt-Spacebar), Windows displays a system menu like that shown in Figure 17-3. (Most Windows programs have identical system menus.) The user selects a menu item in one of several ways: clicking on the item; moving the highlight bar to the item with the cursor-movement keys and then pressing Enter; or pressing the letter that is underlined in the menu item (for example, *n* for *Mi̱nimize*).

The keyboard combinations (Alt plus function key) at the right of the system menu are keyboard accelerators. Using a keyboard accelerator, the user can select system-menu options without first displaying the system menu.

System-menu icon

Title bar

Minimize icon

Maximize icon

Menu bar

Client area

Window border

Scroll bars

Icons

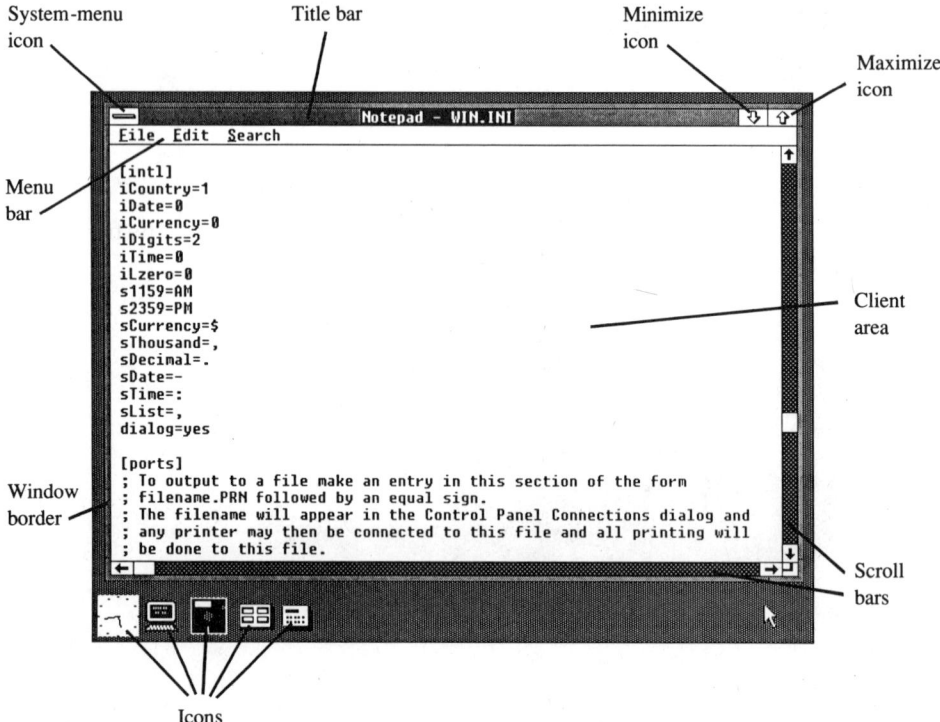

Figure 17-2. The Windows NOTEPAD program, with different parts of the display labeled.

The six options on the standard system menu are

- *Restore*: Return the window to its previous position and size after it has been minimized or maximized.
- *Move*: Allow the window to be moved with the cursor-movement keys.
- *Size*: Allow the window to be resized with the cursor-movement keys.
- *Minimize*: Display the window in its iconic form.
- *Maximize*: Allow the window to occupy the full screen.
- *Close*: End the program.

Windows displays an option on the system menu in grayed text to indicate that the option is not currently valid. In the system menu shown in Figure 17-3, for example, the *Restore* option is grayed because the window is not in a minimized or maximized form.

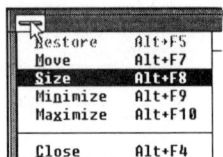

Figure 17-3. A system menu, displayed either when the user clicks the system-menu icon (top left corner) or presses Alt-Spacebar.

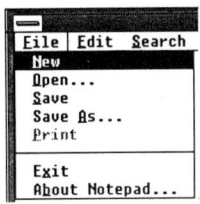———Restore icon

Figure 17-4. The restore icon, which replaces the maximize icon when a window is expanded to fill the entire screen.

Minimize icon. When the user clicks on the minimize icon with the mouse, Windows displays the program in its iconic form.

Maximize icon. Clicking on the maximize icon expands the window to fill the full screen. Windows then replaces the maximize icon with a restore icon (shown in Figure 17-4). Clicking on the restore icon restores the window to its previous size and position.

Programs that use a window of a fixed size (such as the CALC.EXE calculator program included with Windows) do not have a maximize icon.

Menu bar. The menu bar, sometimes called the program's main or top-level menu, displays keywords for several sets of commands that differ from program to program.

When the user clicks on a main-menu item with the mouse or presses the Alt key and the underlined letter in the menu text, Windows displays a pop-up menu for that item. The pop-up menu for NOTEPAD's keyword *File* is shown in Figure 17-5. Items are selected from a pop-up menu in the same way they are selected from the system menu.

A Windows program can display options on the menu in grayed text to indicate that they are not currently valid. The program can also display checkmarks to the left of pop-up menu items to indicate which of several options have been selected by the user.

In addition, items on a pop-up menu can be followed by an ellipsis (...) to indicate that selecting the item invokes a dialog box that prompts the user for additional information— more than can be provided by the menu.

Client area. The client area of the window is where the program displays data. In the case of the NOTEPAD program shown in Figure 17-2, the client area displays the file currently being edited. A program's handling of keyboard and mouse input within the client area depends on the type of work it does.

Scroll bars. Programs that cannot display all the data in a file within the client area of the window often have a horizontal scroll bar across the bottom and a vertical scroll bar down the right edge. Both types of scroll bars have a small, boxed arrow at each end to indicate the direction in which to scroll. In the NOTEPAD window in Figure 17-2, for example, clicking on the up arrow of the vertical scroll bar moves the data within the window down

Figure 17-5. The NOTEPAD program's pop-up file menu.

one line. Clicking on the shaded part of the vertical scroll bar above the thumb (the box near the middle) moves the data within the client area of the window down one screen; clicking below the thumb moves the data up one screen. The user can also drag the thumb with the mouse to move to a relative position within the file.

Windows programs often include a keyboard interface (generally relying on the cursor-movement keys) to duplicate the mouse-based scroll-bar commands.

Window border. The window border is a thick frame surrounding the entire window. It is segmented into eight sections that represent the four sides and four corners of the window. The user can change the size of a window by dragging the window border with the mouse. Dragging a corner section moves two adjacent sides of the border.

When a program is maximized to fill the full screen, Windows does not draw the window border. Programs that use a window of a fixed size do not have a window border either.

Dialog boxes

When a pop-up menu is not adequate for all the command options a program requires, the program can display a dialog box. A dialog box is a pop-up window that contains various controls in the form of push buttons, check boxes, radio buttons, list boxes, and text and edit fields. Programmers can also design their own controls for use in dialog boxes. A user fills in a dialog box and then clicks on a button, such as *OK*, or presses Enter to indicate that the information can be processed by the program.

Most Windows programs use a dialog box to open an existing data file and load it into the program. The program displays the dialog box when the user selects the *Open* option on the *File* pop-up menu. The sample dialog box shown in Figure 17-6 is from the NOTEPAD program.

The list box displays a list of all valid disk drives, the subdirectories of the current directory, and all the filenames in the current directory, including the filename extension used by the program. (NOTEPAD uses the extension .TXT for its data files.) The user can scroll through this list box and change the current drive or subdirectory or select a filename with the keyboard or the mouse. The user can also perform these actions by typing the name directly into the edit field.

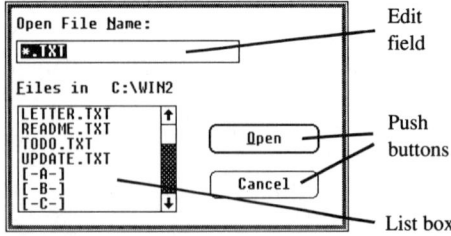

Figure 17-6. A dialog box from the NOTEPAD program, with parts labeled.

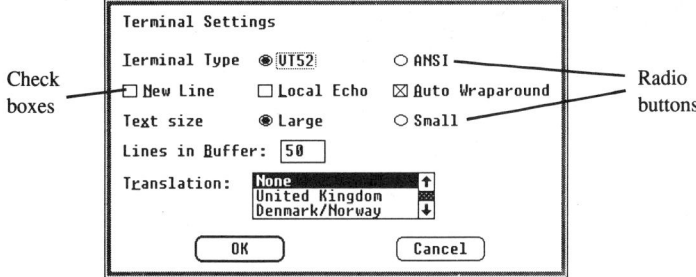

Check boxes

Radio buttons

Figure 17-7. A dialog box from the TERMINAL program, with parts labeled.

Clicking the *Open* button (or pressing Enter) indicates to NOTEPAD that a file has been selected or that a new drive or subdirectory has been chosen (in this case, the program displays the files on the new drive or subdirectory). Clicking the *Cancel* button (or pressing Esc) tells NOTEPAD to close the dialog box without loading a new file.

Figure 17-7 shows a different dialog box — this one from the Windows TERMINAL communications program. The check boxes turn options on (indicated by an *X*) and off. The circular radio buttons allow the user to select from a set of mutually exclusive options.

Another, simple form of a dialog box is called a message box. This box displays one or more lines of text, an optional icon such as an exclamation point or an asterisk, and one or more buttons containing the words *OK, Yes, No,* or *Cancel.* Programs sometimes use message boxes for warnings or error messages.

The MS-DOS Executive

Within Windows, the MS-DOS Executive program (shown in Figure 17-8) serves much the same function as the COMMAND.COM program in the MS-DOS environment.

The top of the MS-DOS Executive client area displays all valid disk drives. The current disk drive is highlighted. Below or to the right of the disk drives is a display of the full path of the current directory. Below this is an alphabetic listing of all subdirectories in the current directory, followed by an alphabetic listing of all files in the current directory. Subdirectory names are displayed in boldface to distinguish them from filenames.

The user can change the current drive by clicking on the disk drive with the mouse or by pressing Ctrl and the key corresponding to the disk drive letter.

To change to one of the parent directories, the user double-clicks (clicks the mouse button twice in succession) on the part of the text string corresponding to the directory name. Pressing the Backspace key moves up one directory level toward the root directory. The user can also change the current directory to a child subdirectory by double-clicking on the subdirectory name in the list or by pressing the Enter key when the cursor highlight is on the subdirectory name. In addition, the menu also contains an option for changing the current directory.

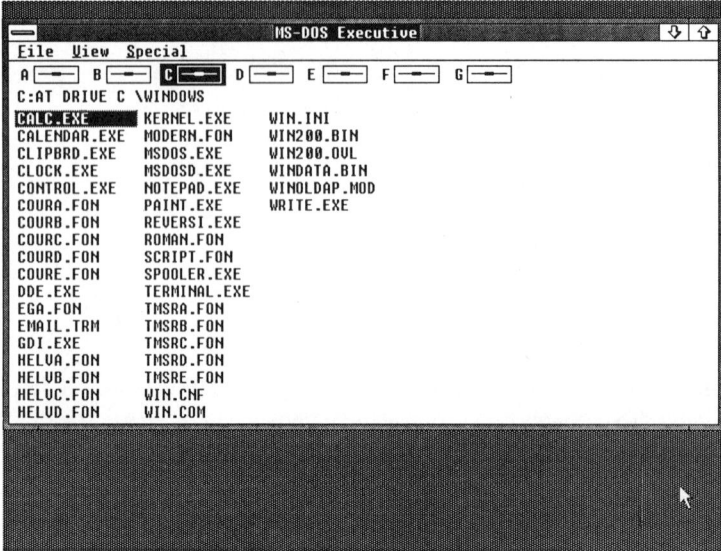

Figure 17-8. The MS-DOS Executive.

The user can run a program by double-clicking on the program filename, by pressing the Enter key when the highlight is on the program name, or by selecting it from a menu.

Other menu options allow the user to display the file and subdirectory lists in a variety of ways. A long format includes the same information displayed by the MS-DOS DIR command, or the user can choose to display a select group of files. Menu options also enable the user to specify whether the files should be listed in alphabetic order by filename, by filename extension, or by date or size.

The remaining options on the MS-DOS Executive menu allow the user to run programs; copy, rename, and delete files; format a floppy disk; change a volume name; make a system disk; create a subdirectory; and print a text file.

Other Windows Programs

Windows 2.0 also includes a number of application and utility programs. The application programs are CALC (a calculator), CALENDAR, CARDFILE (a database arranged as a series of index cards), CLOCK, NOTEPAD, PAINT (a drawing and painting program), REVERSI (a game), TERMINAL, and WRITE (a word processor).

The utility programs include

CLIPBRD. This program displays the current contents of the Clipboard, which is a storage facility that allows users to transfer data from one program to another.

CONTROL. The Control Panel utility allows the user to add or delete font files and printer drivers and to change the following: current printer, printer output port, communications parameters, date and time, cursor blink rate, screen colors, border width, mouse double-click time and options, and country-specific information, such as time and date formats. The Control Panel stores much of this information in the file named WIN.INI (Windows Initialization), so the information is available to other Windows programs.

PIFEDIT. The PIF editor allows the user to create or modify the PIFs that contain information about standard applications that have not been specially designed to run under Windows. This information allows Windows to adjust the environment in which the program runs.

SPOOLER. Windows uses the print-spooler utility to print files without suspending the operation of other programs. Most printer-directed output from Windows programs goes to the print spooler, which then prints the files while other programs run. SPOOLER enables the user to change the priority of print jobs or to cancel them.

The Structure of Windows

When programs run under MS-DOS, they make requests of the operating system through MS-DOS software interrupts (such as Interrupt 21H), through BIOS software interrupts, or by directly accessing the machine hardware.

When programs run under Windows, they use MS-DOS function calls only for file input and output and (more rarely) for executing other programs. Windows programs do not use MS-DOS function calls for memory management, keyboard input, display or printer output, or RS232 communications. Nor do Windows programs use BIOS routines or direct access to the hardware.

Instead, Windows provides application programs with access to more than 450 functions that allow programs to create and manipulate windows on the display; use menus, dialog boxes, and scroll bars; display text and graphics within the client area of a window; use the printer and RS232 communications port; and allocate memory.

The Windows modules

The functions provided by Windows are largely handled by three main modules named KERNEL, GDI, and USER. The KERNEL module is responsible for scheduling and multitasking, and it provides functions for memory management and some file I/O. The GDI module provides Windows' Graphics Device Interface functions, and the USER module does everything else.

The USER and GDI modules, in turn, call functions in various driver modules that are also included with Windows. Drivers control the display, printer, keyboard, mouse, sound, RS232 port, and timer. In most cases, these driver modules access the hardware of the computer directly. Windows includes different driver files for various hardware configurations. Hardware manufacturers can also develop Windows drivers specifically for their products.

A block diagram showing the relationships of an application program, the KERNEL, USER, and GDI modules, and the driver modules is shown in Figure 17-9. The figure shows each of these modules as a separate file — KERNEL, USER, and GDI have the extension .EXE; the driver files have the extension .DRV. Some program developers install Windows with these modules in separate files, as in Figure 17-9, but most users install Windows by running the SETUP program included with Windows.

SETUP combines most of these modules into two larger files called WIN200.BIN and WIN200.OVL. Printer drivers are a little different from the other driver files, however, because the Windows SETUP program does not include them in WIN200.BIN and WIN200.OVL. The name of the driver file identifies the printer. For example, IBMGRX.DRV is a printer driver file for the IBM Personal Computer Graphics Printer.

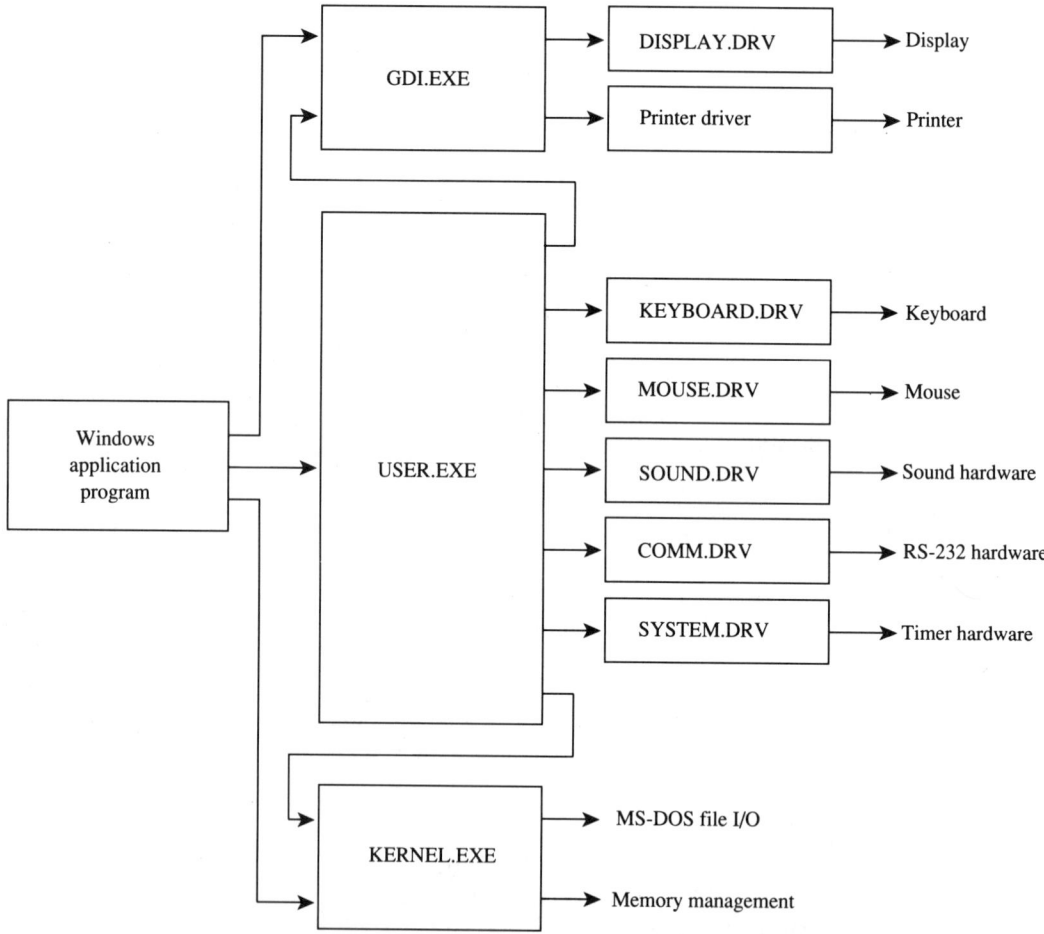

Figure 17-9. A simplified block diagram showing the relationships of an application program, Windows modules (GDI, USER, and KERNEL), driver modules, and system hardware.

The diagram in Figure 17-9 is somewhat simplified. In reality, a Windows application program can also make direct calls to the KEYBOARD.DRV and SOUND.DRV modules, and USER.EXE calls the DISPLAY.DRV and printer driver modules directly. The GDI.EXE module and driver modules can also call routines in KERNEL.EXE, and drivers sometimes call routines in SYSTEM.DRV.

Also, Figure 17-9 omits the various font files provided with Windows, the WIN.INI file that contains Windows initialization information and user preferences, and the files WINOLDAP.MOD and WINOLDAP.GRB, which Windows uses to run standard MS-DOS applications.

Libraries and programs

The USER.EXE, GDI.EXE, and KERNEL.EXE files, all driver files with the extension .DRV, and all font files with the extension .FON are called Windows libraries or, sometimes, dynamic link libraries to distinguish them from Windows programs. Programs and libraries both use a file format called the New Executable format.

From the user's perspective, a Windows program and a Windows library are very different. The user cannot run a Windows library directly: Windows loads a part of a library into memory only when a program needs to use a function that the library provides.

The user can also run multiple instances of the same Windows program. Windows uses the same code segments for the different instances but creates a unique data segment for each. Windows never runs multiple instances of a Windows library.

From the programmer's perspective, a Windows program is a task that creates and manages windows on the display. Libraries are modules that assist the task. A programmer can write additional library modules, which one or more programs can use. For the developer, one important distinction between programs and libraries is that a Windows library does not have its own stack; instead, the library uses the stack of the program that calls the routine in the library.

The New Executable format used for both programs and libraries gives Windows much more information about the module than is provided by the current MS-DOS .EXE format. In particular, the module contains information that allows Windows to make links between program modules and library modules when a program is run.

When a module (such as a library) contains functions that can be called from another module (such as a program), the functions are said to be exported from the module that contains them. Each exported function in a module is identified either by a name (generally the name of the function) or by an ordinal (positive) number. A list of all exported functions in a module is included in the New Executable format header section of the module.

Conversely, when a module (such as a program) contains code that calls a function in another module (such as a library), the function is said to be imported to the module that makes the call. This call appears in the .EXE file as an unresolved reference to an external function. The New Executable format identifies the module and the function name or ordinal number that the call references.

When Windows loads a program or a library into memory, it must resolve all calls the module makes to functions in other modules. Windows does this by inserting the addresses of the functions into the code—a process called dynamic linking.

For example, many Windows programs use the function TextOut to display text in the client area. In the code segment of the program's .EXE file, a call to TextOut appears as an unresolved far (intersegment) call. The code segment's relocation table shows that this call is to an imported function in the GDI module identified by the ordinal number 33. The header section of the GDI module lists TextOut as an exported function with the ordinal number 33. When Windows loads the program, it resolves all references to TextOut by inserting the address of the function into the program's code segment in each place where TextOut is called.

Although Windows programs reference many functions that are exported from the standard Windows libraries, Windows programs also often include at least one exported function, called a window function. While the program is running, Windows calls this function to pass messages to the program's window. *See* The Structure of a Windows Program below.

Memory Management

Windows' memory management is based on the segmented-memory architecture of the Intel 8086 family of microprocessors. The memory space controlled by Windows is divided into segments of various lengths. Windows uses separate segments for nearly everything kept in memory—such as the code and data segments of programs and libraries—and for resources, such as fonts and bitmaps.

Windows programs and libraries contain one or more code segments, which are usually both movable and discardable. Windows can move a code segment in memory in order to consolidate free memory space. It can also discard a code segment from memory and later reload the code segment from the program's or library's .EXE file when it is needed again. This capability is called demand loading.

Windows programs usually contain only one data segment; Windows libraries are limited to one data segment. In most cases, Windows can move data segments in memory. However, it cannot usually discard data segments, because they can contain data that changes after the program begins executing. When a user runs multiple copies of a program, the different instances share the same code segments but have separate data segments.

The use of movable and discardable segments allows Windows to run several large programs in a memory space that might be inadequate for even one of the programs if the entire program were kept in memory, as is typical under MS-DOS without Windows. The ability of Windows to use memory in this way is called memory overcommitment.

The moving and discarding of code segments requires Windows to make special provisions so that intersegment calls continue to reference the correct address when a code segment is moved. These provisions are another part of dynamic linking. When Windows resolves a far call from one code segment to a function in another code segment that is movable and discardable, the call actually references a fixed area of memory. This fixed area of memory contains a small section of code called a thunk. If the code segment containing the function is currently in memory, the thunk simply jumps to the function. If the code segment with the function is not currently in memory, the thunk calls a loader that loads the segment into memory. This process is called dynamic loading. When Windows moves or discards a code segment, it must alter the thunks appropriately.

Windows and Windows programs generally reference data structures stored in Windows' memory space by using 16-bit unsigned integers known as handles. The data structure that a handle references can be movable and discardable, so when Windows or the Windows program needs to access the data directly, it must lock the handle to cause the data to become fixed in memory. The function that locks the segment returns a pointer to the program.

During the time the handle is locked, Windows cannot move or discard the data. The data can then be referenced directly with the pointer. When Windows (or the Windows program) finishes using the data, it unlocks the segment so that it can be moved (or in some cases discarded) to free up memory space if necessary.

Programmers can choose to allocate nonmovable data segments, but the practice is not recommended, because Windows cannot relocate the segments to make room for segments required by other programs.

The Structure of a Windows Program

During development, a Windows program includes several components that are combined later into a single executable file with the extension .EXE for execution under Windows. Although the Windows executable file has the same .EXE filename extension as MS-DOS executable files, the format is different. Among other things, the New Executable format includes Windows-specific information required for dynamic linking and the discarding and reloading of the program's code segments.

Programmers generally use C, Pascal, or assembly language to create applications specially designed to run under Windows. Also required are several header files and development tools, which are included in the Microsoft Windows Software Development Kit.

The Microsoft Windows Software Development Kit

The Windows Software Development Kit contains reference material, a special linker (LINK4), the Windows Resource Compiler (RC), special versions of the SYMDEB and CodeView debuggers, header files, and several programs that aid development and testing. These programs include

- DIALOG: Used for creating dialog boxes.
- ICONEDIT: Used for creating a program's icon, customized cursors, and bitmap images.

- FONTEDIT: Used for creating customized fonts derived from an existing font file with the extension .FNT.
- HEAPWALK: Used for displaying the organization of code and data segments in Windows' memory space and for testing programs under low memory conditions.
- SHAKER: Used for randomly allocating memory to force segment movement and discarding. SHAKER tests a program's response to movement in memory and is useful for exposing program bugs involving pointers to unlocked segments.

The Windows Software Development Kit also provides several *include* and header files that contain declarations of all Windows functions, definitions of many macro identifiers that the programmer can use, and structure definitions. Import libraries included in the kit allow LINK4 to resolve calls to Windows functions and to prepare the program's .EXE file for dynamic linking.

Work with the Windows Software Development Kit requires one of the following compilers or assemblers:

- Microsoft C Compiler version 4.0 or later
- Microsoft Pascal Compiler version 3.31 or later
- Microsoft Macro Assembler version 4.0 or later

Other software manufacturers also provide compilers that are suitable for compiling Windows programs.

Components of a Windows program

The discussion in this section is illustrated by a program called SAMPLE, which displays the word *Windows* in its client area. In response to a menu selection, the program

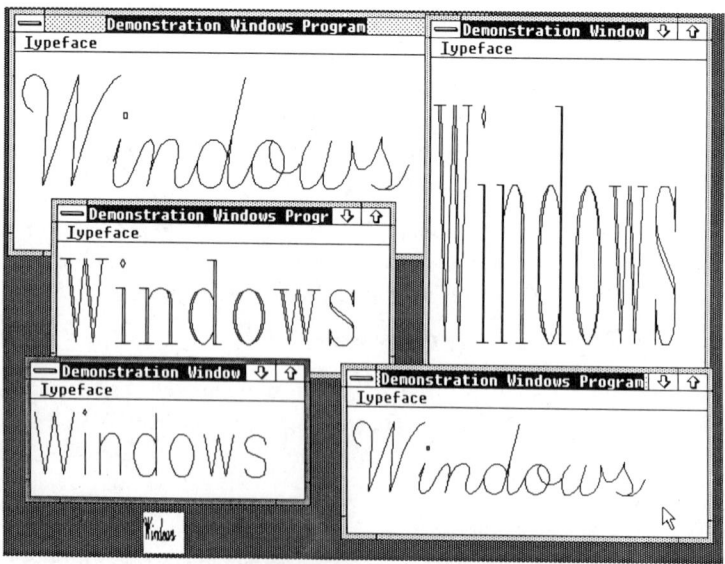

Figure 17-10. A display produced by the example program SAMPLE.

displays this text in any of the three vector fonts — Script, Modern, and Roman — that are included with Windows. Sometimes also called stroke or graphics fonts, these vector fonts are defined by a series of line segments, rather than by the pixel patterns that make up the more common raster fonts. The SAMPLE program picks a font size that fits the client area.

Figure 17-10 shows several instances of this program running under Windows.

Five separate files go into the making of this program:

1. Source-code file: This is the main part of the program, generally written in C, Pascal, or assembly language. The SAMPLE program was written in C, which is the most popular language for Windows programs because of its flexibility in using pointers and structures. The SAMPLE.C source-code file is shown in Figure 17-11.

```
/* SAMPLE.C -- Demonstration Windows Program */

#include <windows.h>
#include "sample.h"

long FAR PASCAL WndProc (HWND, unsigned, WORD, LONG) ;

int PASCAL WinMain (hInstance, hPrevInstance, lpszCmdLine, nCmdShow)
     HANDLE     hInstance, hPrevInstance ;
     LPSTR      lpszCmdLine ;
     int        nCmdShow ;
     {
     WNDCLASS   wndclass ;
     HWND       hWnd ;
     MSG        msg ;
     static char szAppName [] = "Sample" ;

               /*-------------------------*/
               /* Register the Window Class */
               /*-------------------------*/

     if (!hPrevInstance)
         {
         wndclass.style          = CS_HREDRAW ¦ CS_VREDRAW ;
         wndclass.lpfnWndProc    = WndProc ;
         wndclass.cbClsExtra     = 0 ;
         wndclass.cbWndExtra     = 0 ;
         wndclass.hInstance      = hInstance ;
         wndclass.hIcon          = NULL ;
         wndclass.hCursor        = LoadCursor (NULL, IDC_ARROW) ;
         wndclass.hbrBackground  = GetStockObject (WHITE_BRUSH) ;
         wndclass.lpszMenuName   = szAppName ;
         wndclass.lpszClassName  = szAppName ;

         RegisterClass (&wndclass) ;
         }
```

Figure 17-11. The SAMPLE.C source code.   *(more)*

```
                        /*----------------------------------*/
                        /* Create the window and display it */
                        /*----------------------------------*/

        hWnd = CreateWindow (szAppName, "Demonstration Windows Program",
                            WS_OVERLAPPEDWINDOW,
                            (int) CW_USEDEFAULT, 0,
                            (int) CW_USEDEFAULT, 0,
                            NULL, NULL, hInstance, NULL) ;

        ShowWindow (hWnd, nCmdShow) ;
        UpdateWindow (hWnd) ;

                    /*----------------------------------------------*/
                    /* Stay in message loop until a WM_QUIT message */
                    /*----------------------------------------------*/

        while (GetMessage (&msg, NULL, 0, 0))
                {
                TranslateMessage (&msg) ;
                DispatchMessage (&msg) ;
                }
        return msg.wParam ;
        }

long FAR PASCAL WndProc (hWnd, iMessage, wParam, lParam)
        HWND          hWnd ;
        unsigned      iMessage ;
        WORD          wParam ;
        LONG          lParam ;
        {
        PAINTSTRUCT   ps ;
        HFONT         hFont ;
        HMENU         hMenu ;
        static short xClient, yClient, nCurrentFont = IDM_SCRIPT ;
        static BYTE  cFamily [] = { FF_SCRIPT, FF_MODERN, FF_ROMAN } ;
        static char  *szFace [] = { "Script",  "Modern",  "Roman"  } ;

        switch (iMessage)
            {

                    /*----------------------------------------------*/
                    /* WM_COMMAND message: Change checkmarked font */
                    /*----------------------------------------------*/

            case WM_COMMAND:
                    hMenu = GetMenu (hWnd) ;
                    CheckMenuItem (hMenu, nCurrentFont, MF_UNCHECKED) ;
                    nCurrentFont = wParam ;
                    CheckMenuItem (hMenu, nCurrentFont, MF_CHECKED) ;
                    InvalidateRect (hWnd, NULL, TRUE) ;
                    break ;
```

Figure 17-11. Continued.   *(more)*

```
                        /*---------------------------------------------*/
                        /* WM_SIZE message: Save dimensions of window */
                        /*---------------------------------------------*/

               case WM_SIZE:
                    xClient = LOWORD (lParam) ;
                    yClient = HIWORD (lParam) ;
                    break ;

                        /*-----------------------------------------------*/
                        /* WM_PAINT message: Display "Windows" in Script */
                        /*-----------------------------------------------*/

               case WM_PAINT:
                    BeginPaint (hWnd, &ps) ;

                    hFont = CreateFont (yClient, xClient / 8,
                                     0, 0, 400, 0, 0, 0, OEM_CHARSET,
                                     OUT_STROKE_PRECIS, OUT_STROKE_PRECIS,
                                     DRAFT_QUALITY, (BYTE) VARIABLE_PITCH |
                                     cFamily [nCurrentFont - IDM_SCRIPT],
                                     szFace  [nCurrentFont - IDM_SCRIPT]) ;

                    hFont = SelectObject (ps.hdc, hFont) ;
                    TextOut (ps.hdc, 0, 0, "Windows", 7) ;

                    DeleteObject (SelectObject (ps.hdc, hFont)) ;
                    EndPaint (hWnd, &ps) ;
                    break ;

                        /*---------------------------------------*/
                        /* WM_DESTROY message: Post Quit message */
                        /*---------------------------------------*/

               case WM_DESTROY:
                    PostQuitMessage (0) ;
                    break ;

                        /*---------------------------------------*/
                        /* Other messages: Do default processing */
                        /*---------------------------------------*/

               default:
                    return DefWindowProc (hWnd, iMessage, wParam, lParam) ;
               }
          return 0L ;
          }
```

Figure 17-11. Continued.

2. Resource script: The resource script is an ASCII file that generally has the extension .RC. This file contains definitions of menus, dialog boxes, string tables, and keyboard accelerators used by the program. The resource script can also reference other files that contain icons, cursors, bitmaps, and fonts in binary form, as well as other read-only data defined by the programmer. When a program is running, Windows loads resources into memory only when they are needed and in most cases can discard them if additional memory space is required.

SAMPLE.RC, the resource script for the SAMPLE program, is shown in Figure 17-12; it contains only the definition of the menu used in the program.

```
#include "sample.h"

Sample MENU
     BEGIN
          POPUP  "&Typeface"
               BEGIN
                    MENUITEM  "&Script",  IDM_SCRIPT, CHECKED
                    MENUITEM  "&Modern",  IDM_MODERN
                    MENUITEM  "&Roman",   IDM_ROMAN
               END
     END
```

Figure 17-12. The resource script for the SAMPLE program.

3. Header (or *include*) file: This file, with the extension .H, can contain definitions of constants or macros, as is customary in C programming. For Windows programs, the header file also reconciles constants used in both the resource script and the program source-code file. For example, in the SAMPLE.RC resource script, each item in the pop-up menu (*Script, Modern,* and *Roman*) also includes an identifier — IDM_SCRIPT, IDM_MODERN, and IDM_ROMAN, respectively. These identifiers are merely numbers that Windows uses to notify the program of the user's selection of a menu item. The same names are used to identify the menu selection in the C source-code file. And, because both the resource compiler and the source-code compiler must have access to these identifiers, the header file is included in both the resource script and the source-code file.

The header file for the SAMPLE program, SAMPLE.H, is shown in Figure 17-13.

```
#define IDM_SCRIPT 1
#define IDM_MODERN 2
#define IDM_ROMAN  3
```

Figure 17-13. The SAMPLE.H header file.

4. Module-definition file: The module-definition file generally has a .DEF extension. The Windows linker uses this file in creating the executable .EXE file. The module-definition file specifies various attributes of the program's code and data segments, and it lists all imported and exported functions in the source-code file. In large programs that are divided into multiple code segments, the module-definition file allows the programmer to specify different attributes for each code segment.

The module-definition file for the SAMPLE program is named SAMPLE.DEF and is shown in Figure 17-14.

```
NAME            SAMPLE
DESCRIPTION     'Demonstration Windows Program'
STUB            'WINSTUB.EXE'
CODE            MOVABLE
DATA            MOVABLE MULTIPLE
HEAPSIZE        1024
STACKSIZE       4096
EXPORTS         WndProc
```

Figure 17-14. The SAMPLE.DEF module-definition file.

5. Make file: To facilitate construction of the executable file from these different components, Windows programmers often use the MAKE program to compile only those files that have changed since the last time the program was linked. To do this, the programmer first creates an ASCII text file called a make file. By convention, the make file has no extension.

    The make file for the SAMPLE program is named SAMPLE and is shown in Figure 17-15. The programmer can create the SAMPLE.EXE executable file by executing

    ```
    C>MAKE SAMPLE   <Enter>
    ```

    A make file often contains several sections, each beginning with a target filename, followed by a colon and one or more dependent filenames, such as

    ```
    sample.obj : sample.c sample.h
    ```

    If either or both the SAMPLE.C and SAMPLE.H files have a later creation time than SAMPLE.OBJ, then MAKE runs the program or programs listed immediately below. In the case of the SAMPLE make file, the program is the C compiler, and it compiles the SAMPLE.C source code:

    ```
    cl -c -Gsw -W2 -Zdp sample.c
    ```

    Thus, if the programmer changes only one of the several files used in the development of SAMPLE, then running MAKE ensures that the executable file is brought up to date, while carrying out only the required steps.

    ```
    sample.obj : sample.c sample.h
        cl -c -Gsw -W2 -Zdp sample.c

    sample.res : sample.rc sample.h
        rc -r sample.rc

    sample.exe : sample.obj sample.def sample.res
        link4 sample, /align:16, /map /line, slibw, sample
        rc sample.res
        mapsym sample
    ```

Figure 17-15. The make file for the SAMPLE program.

Construction of a Windows program

The make file shows the steps that create a program's .EXE file from the various components:

1.   Compiling the source-code file:

```
cl -c -Gsw -W2 -Zdp sample.c
```

This step uses the CL.EXE C compiler to create a .OBJ object-module file. The command line switches are
   —   -c: Compiles the program but does not link it. Windows programs must be linked with Windows' LINK4 linker, rather than with the LINK program the C compiler would normally invoke.
   —   -Gsw: Includes two switches, -Gs and -Gw. The -Gs switch removes stack checks from the program. The -Gw switch inserts special prologue and epilogue code in all far functions defined in the program. This special code is required for Windows' memory management.
   —   -W2: Compiles with warning level 2. This is the highest warning level, and it causes the compiler to display messages for conditions that may be acceptable in normal C programs but that can cause serious errors in a Windows program.
   —   -Zdp: Includes two switches, -Zd and -Zp. The -Zd switch includes line numbers in the .OBJ file — helpful for debugging at the source-code level. The -Zp switch packs structures on byte boundaries. The -Zp switch is required, because data structures used within Windows are in a packed format.

2.   Compiling the resource script:

```
rc -r sample.rc
```

This step runs the resource compiler and converts the ASCII .RC resource script into a binary .RES form. The -r switch indicates that the resource script should be compiled but the resources should not yet be added to the program's .EXE file.

3.   Linking the program:

```
link4 sample, /align:16, /map /line, slibw, sample
```

This step uses the special Windows linker, LINK4. The first parameter listed is the name of the .OBJ file. The /align:16 switch instructs LINK4 to align segments in the .EXE file on 16-byte boundaries. The /map and /line switches cause LINK4 to create a .MAP file that contains program line numbers — again, useful for debugging source code. Next, slibw is a reference to the SLIBW.LIB file, which is an import library that contains module names and ordinal numbers for all Windows functions. The last parameter, sample, is the program's module-definition file, SAMPLE.DEF.

4.   Adding the resources to the .EXE file:

```
rc sample.res
```

This step runs the resource compiler a second time, using the compiled resource file, SAMPLE.RES. This time, the resource compiler adds the resources to the .EXE file.

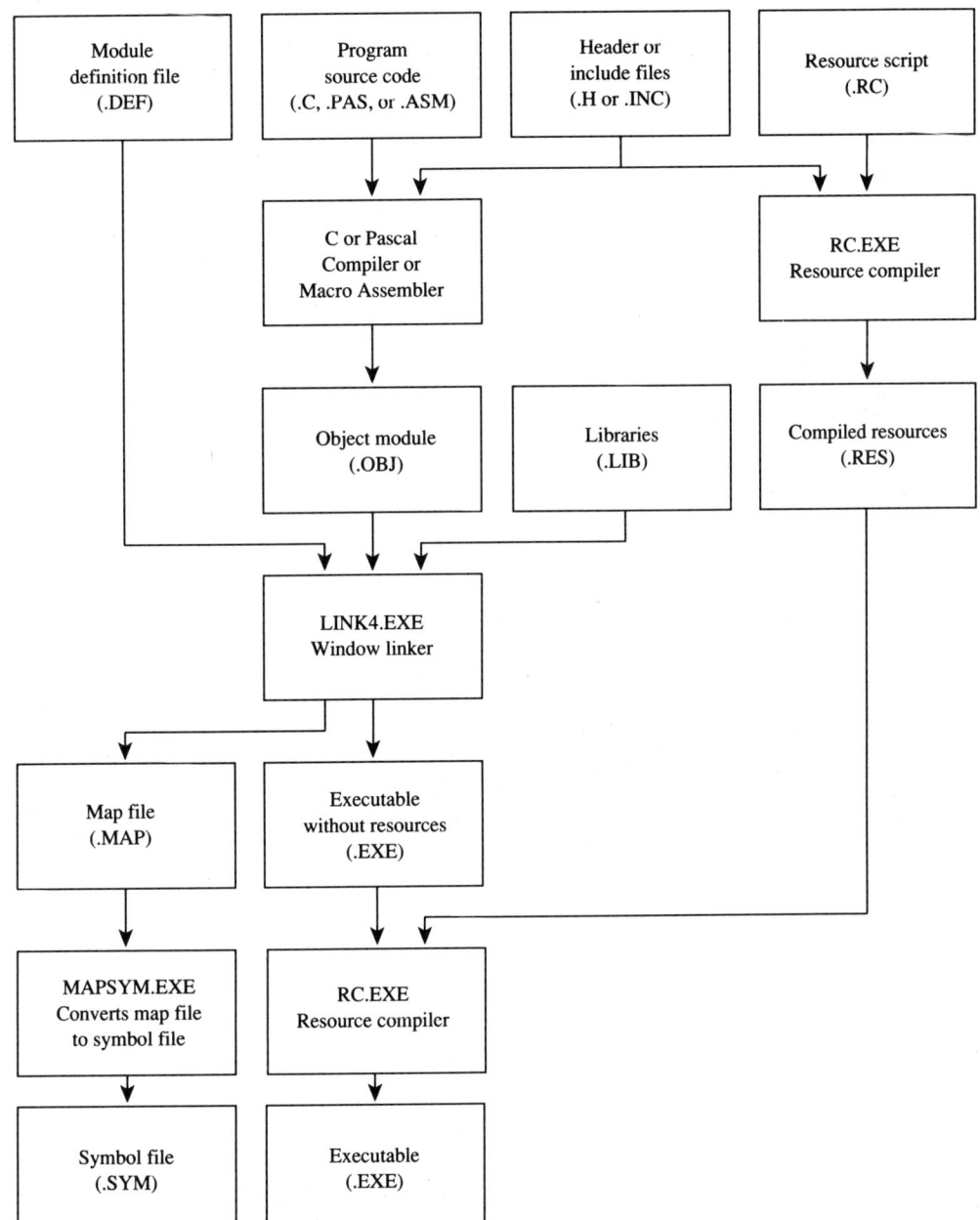

Figure 17-16. A block diagram showing the creation of a Windows .EXE file.

5. Creating a symbol (.SYM) file from the linker's map (.MAP) file:

```
mapsym sample
```

This step is required for symbolic debugging with SYMDEB.

Figure 17-16 on the preceding page shows how the various components of a Windows program fit into the creation of a .EXE file.

Program initialization

The SAMPLE.C program shown in Figure 17-11 contains some code that appears in almost every Windows program. The statement

```
#include <windows.h>
```

appears at the top of every Windows source-code file written in C. The WINDOWS.H file, provided with the Microsoft Windows Software Development Kit, contains templates for all Windows functions, structure definitions, and #define statements for many mnemonic identifiers.

Some of the variable names in SAMPLE.C may look unusual to C programmers because they begin with a prefix notation that denotes the data type of the variable. Windows programmers are encouraged to use this type of notation. Some of the more common prefixes are

Prefix	Data Type
i *or* n	Integer (16-bit signed integer)
w	Word (16-bit unsigned integer)
l	Long (32-bit signed integer)
dw	Doubleword (32-bit unsigned integer)
h	Handle (16-bit unsigned integer)
sz	Null-terminated string
lpsz	Long pointer to null-terminated string
lpfn	Long pointer to a function

The program's entry point (following some startup code) is the WinMain function, which is passed the following parameters: a handle to the current instance of the program (hInstance), a handle to the most recent previous instance of the program (hPrevInstance), a long pointer to the program's command line (lpszCmdLine), and a number (nCmdShow) that indicates whether the program should initially be displayed as a normally sized window or as an icon.

The first job SAMPLE performs in the WinMain function is to register a window class — a structure that describes characteristics of the windows that will be created in the class. These characteristics include background color, the type of cursor to be displayed in the window, the window's initial menu and icon, and the window function (the structure member called lpfnWndProc).

Multiple instances of a program can share the same window class, so SAMPLE registers the window class only for the first instance of the program:

```
if (!hPrevInstance)
        {
        wndclass.style          = CS_HREDRAW | CS_VREDRAW ;
        wndclass.lpfnWndProc    = WndProc ;
        wndclass.cbClsExtra     = 0 ;
        wndclass.cbWndExtra     = 0 ;
        wndclass.hInstance      = hInstance ;
        wndclass.hIcon          = NULL ;
        wndclass.hCursor        = LoadCursor (NULL, IDC_ARROW) ;
        wndclass.hbrBackground  = GetStockObject (WHITE_BRUSH) ;
        wndclass.lpszMenuName   = szAppName ;
        wndclass.lpszClassName  = szAppName ;

        RegisterClass (&wndclass) ;
        }
```

The SAMPLE program then creates a window using the CreateWindow call, displays it to the screen by calling ShowWindow, and updates the client area by calling UpdateWindow:

```
hWnd = CreateWindow (szAppName, "Demonstration Windows Program",
                    WS_OVERLAPPEDWINDOW,
                    (int) CW_USEDEFAULT, 0,
                    (int) CW_USEDEFAULT, 0,
                    NULL, NULL, hInstance, NULL) ;
ShowWindow (hWnd, nCmdShow) ;
UpdateWindow (hWnd) ;
```

The first parameter to CreateWindow is the name of the window class. The second parameter is the actual text that appears in the window's title bar. The third parameter is the style of the window — in this case, the WINDOWS.H identifier WS_OVERLAPPEDWINDOW. The WS_OVERLAPPEDWINDOW is the most common window style. The fourth through seventh parameters specify the initial position and size of the window. The identifier CW_USEDEFAULT tells Windows to position and size the window according to the default rules.

After creating and displaying a Window, the SAMPLE program enters a piece of code called the message loop:

```
while (GetMessage (&msg, NULL, 0, 0))
        {
        TranslateMessage (&msg) ;
        DispatchMessage (&msg) ;
        }
return msg.wParam ;
```

This loop continues to execute until the GetMessage call returns zero. When that happens, the program instance terminates and the memory required for the instance is freed.

The Windows messaging system

Interactive programs written for the normal MS-DOS environment generally obtain user input only from the keyboard, using either an MS-DOS or a ROM BIOS software interrupt to check for keystrokes. When the user types something, such programs act on the keystroke and then return to wait for the next keystroke.

Programs written for Windows, however, can receive user input from a variety of sources, including the keyboard, the mouse, the Windows timer, menus, scroll bars, and controls, such as buttons and edit boxes.

Moreover, a Windows program must be informed of other events occurring within the system. For instance, the user of a Windows program might choose to make its window smaller or larger. Windows must make the program aware of this change so that the program can adjust its screen output to fit the new window size. Thus, for example, if a Windows program is minimized as an icon and the user maximizes its window to fill the full screen, Windows must inform the program that the size of the client area has changed and needs to be re-created.

Windows carries out this job of keeping a program informed of other events through the use of formatted messages. In effect, Windows sends these messages to the program. The Windows program receives and acts upon the messages.

This messaging makes the relationship between Windows and a Windows program much different from the relationship between MS-DOS and an MS-DOS program. Whereas MS-DOS does not provide information until a program requests it through an MS-DOS function call, Windows must continually notify a program of all the events that affect its window.

Window messages can be separated into two major categories: queued and nonqueued.

Queued messages are similar to the keyboard information an MS-DOS program obtains from MS-DOS. When the Windows user presses a key on the keyboard, moves the mouse, or presses one of the mouse buttons, Windows saves information about the event (in the form of a data structure) in the system message queue. Each message is destined for a particular window in a particular instance of a Windows program. Windows therefore determines which window should get the information and then places the message in the instance's own message queue.

A Windows program retrieves information from its queue in the message loop:

```
while (GetMessage (&msg, NULL, 0, 0))
        {
        TranslateMessage (&msg) ;
        DispatchMessage (&msg) ;
        }
```

The *msg* variable is a structure. During the GetMessage call, Windows fills in the fields of this structure with information about the message. The fields are as follows:

- *hwnd*: The handle for the window that is to receive the message.
- *iMessage*: A numeric code identifying the type of message (for example, keyboard or mouse).
- *wParam*: A 16-bit value containing information specific to the message. *See* The Windows Messages below.
- *lParam*: A 32-bit value containing information specific to the message.
- *time*: The time, in milliseconds, that the message was placed in the queue. The time is a 32-bit value relative to the time at which the current Windows session began.
- *pt.x*: The horizontal coordinate of the mouse cursor at the time the event occurred.
- *pt.y*: The vertical coordinate of the mouse cursor at the time the event occurred.

GetMessage always returns a nonzero value except when it receives a quit message. The quit message causes the message loop to end. The program should then terminate and return control to Windows.

Within the message loop, the TranslateMessage function translates physical keystrokes into character-code messages. Windows places these translated messages into the program's message queue.

The DispatchMessage function essentially makes a call to the window function of the window specified by the hwnd field. This window function (WndProc in SAMPLE) is indicated in the lpfnWndProc field of the window class structure.

When DispatchMessage passes the message to the window function, Windows uses the first four fields of the message structure as parameters to the function. The window function can then process the message. In SAMPLE, for instance, the four fields passed to WndProc are *hwnd* (the handle to the window), *iMessage* (the numeric message identifier), *wParam*, and *lParam*. Although Windows does not pass the time and mouse-position information fields as parameters to the window function, this information is available through the Windows functions GetMessageTime and GetMessagePos.

A Windows program obtains only a few specific types of messages through its message queue. These are keyboard messages, mouse messages, timer messages, the paint message that tells the program it must re-create the client area of its window, and the quit message that tells the program it is being terminated.

In addition to the queued messages, however, a program's window function also receives many nonqueued messages. Windows sends these nonqueued messages by bypassing the message loop and calling the program's window function directly.

Many of these nonqueued messages are derived from queued messages. For example, when the user clicks the mouse on the menu bar, a mouse-click message is placed in the program's message queue. The GetMessage function retrieves the message and the DispatchMessage function sends it to the program's window function. However, because this mouse message affects a nonclient area of the window (an area outside the window's client area), the window function normally does not process it. Instead, the function passes the message back to Windows. In this example, the message tells Windows to invoke a pop-up menu. Windows calls up the menu and then sends the window function several nonqueued messages to inform the program of this action.

A Windows program is thus message driven. Once a program reaches the message loop, it acts only when the window function receives a message. And, although a program receives many messages that affect the window, the program usually processes only some of them, sending the rest to Windows for normal default processing.

The Windows messages

Windows can send a window function more than 100 different messages. The WINDOWS.H header file includes identifiers for all these messages so that C programmers do not have to remember the message numbers. Some of the more common messages and the meanings of the *wParam* and *lParam* parameters are discussed here:

WM_CREATE. Windows sends a window function this nonqueued message while processing the CreateWindow call. The *lParam* parameter is a pointer to a creation structure. A window function can perform some program initialization during the WM_CREATE message.

WM_MOVE. Windows sends a window function the nonqueued WM_MOVE message when the window has been moved to another part of the display. The *lParam* parameter gives the new coordinates of the window relative to the upper left corner of the screen.

WM_SIZE. This nonqueued message indicates that the size of the window has been changed. The new size is encoded in the *lParam* parameter. Programs often save this window size for later use.

WM_PAINT. This queued message indicates that a region in the window's client area needs repainting. (The message queue can contain only one WM_PAINT message.)

WM_COMMAND. This nonqueued message signals a program that a user has selected a menu item or has triggered a keyboard accelerator. Child-window controls also use WM_COMMAND to send messages to the parent window.

WM_KEYDOWN. The *wParam* parameter of this queued message is a virtual key code that identifies the key being pressed. The *lParam* parameter includes flags that indicate the previous key state and the number of keypresses the message represents.

WM_KEYUP. This queued message tells a window function that a key has been released. The *wParam* parameter is a virtual key code.

WM_CHAR. This queued message is generated from WM_KEYDOWN messages during the TranslateMessage call. The *wParam* parameter is the ASCII code of a keyboard key.

WM_MOUSEMOVE. Windows uses this queued message to tell a program about mouse movement. The *lParam* parameter contains the coordinates of the mouse relative to the upper left corner of the client area of the window. The *wParam* parameter contains flags that indicate whether any mouse buttons or the Shift or Ctrl keys are currently pressed.

WM_xBUTTONDOWN. This queued message tells a program that a button on the mouse was depressed while the mouse was in the window's client area. The *x* can be either L, R, or M for the left, right, or middle mouse button. The *wParam* and *lParam* parameters are the same as for WM_MOUSEMOVE.

WM_xBUTTONUP. This queued message tells a program that the user has released a mouse button.

WM_xBUTTONDBLCLK. When the user double-clicks a mouse button, Windows generates a WM_*x*BUTTONDOWN message for the first click and a queued WM_*x*BUTTONDBLCLK message for the second click.

WM_TIMER. When a Windows program sets a timer with the SetTimer function, Windows places a WM_TIMER message in the message queue at periodic intervals. The *wParam* parameter is a timer ID. (If the message queue already contains a WM_TIMER message, Windows does not add another one to the queue.)

WM_VSCROLL. A Windows program that includes a vertical scroll bar in its window receives nonqueued WM_VSCROLL messages indicating various types of scroll-bar manipulation.

WM_HSCROLL. This nonqueued message indicates a user is manipulating a horizontal scroll bar.

WM_CLOSE. Windows sends a window function this nonqueued message when the user has selected *Close* from the window's system menu. A program can query the user to determine whether any action, such as saving a file to disk, is needed before the program is terminated.

WM_QUERYENDSESSION. This nonqueued message indicates that the user is shutting down Windows by selecting *Close* from the MS-DOS Executive system menu. A program can request the user to verify that the program should be ended. If the window function returns a zero value from the message, Windows does not end the session.

WM_DESTROY. This nonqueued message is the last message a window function receives before the program ends. A window function can perform some last-minute cleanup while processing WM_DESTROY.

WM_QUIT. This is a queued message that never reaches the window function because it causes GetMessage to return a zero value that causes the program to exit the message loop.

Message processing

Programmers can choose to process some messages and ignore others in the window function. Messages that are ignored are generally passed on to the function Def WindowProc for default processing within Windows.

Because Windows eventually has access to messages that a window function does not process, it can send a program messages that might otherwise be regarded as pertaining to system functions — for example, mouse messages that occur in a nonclient area of the window, or system keyboard messages that affect the menu. Unless these messages are passed on to Def WindowProc, the menu and other system functions do not work properly.

A program can, however, trap some of these messages to override Windows' default processing. For example, when Windows needs to repaint the nonclient area of a window (the title bar, system-menu box, and scroll bars), it sends the window function a WM_NCPAINT (nonclient paint) message. The window function normally passes this message to Def WindowProc, which then calls routines to update the nonclient areas of the window. The program can, however, choose to process the WM_NCPAINT message and paint the nonclient area itself. A program that does this can, for example, draw its own scroll bars.

The Windows messaging system also notifies a program of important events occurring outside its window. For example, if the MS-DOS Executive were simply to end the Windows session when the user selects the *Close* option from its system menu, then applications that were still running would not have a chance to save changed files to disk. Instead, when the user selects *Close* from the last instance of the MS-DOS Executive's system menu, the MS-DOS Executive sends a WM_QUERYENDSESSION message to each currently running application. If any application responds by returning a zero value, the MS-DOS Executive does not end the Windows session.

Before responding, an application can process the WM_QUERYENDSESSION message and display a message box asking the user if a file should be saved. The message box should include three buttons labeled *Yes*, *No*, and *Cancel*. If the user answers *Yes*, the program can save the file and then return a nonzero value to the WM_QUERYENDSESSION message. If the user answers *No*, the program can return a nonzero value without saving the file. But if the user answers *Cancel*, the program should return a zero value so that the Windows session will not be ended. If a program does not process the WM_QUERYENDSESSION message, Def WindowProc returns a nonzero value.

When a user selects *Close* from the system menu of a particular instance of an application, rather than from the MS-DOS Executive's menu, Windows sends the window function a WM_CLOSE message. If the program has an unsaved file loaded, it can query the user with a message box — possibly the same one displayed when WM_QUERYENDSESSION is processed. If the user responds *Yes* to the query, the program can save the file and then call DestroyWindow. If the user responds *No*, the program can call DestroyWindow without saving the file. If the user responds *Cancel*, the window function does not call DestroyWindow and the program will not be terminated. If a program does not process WM_CLOSE messages, Def WindowProc calls DestroyWindow.

Finally, a window function can send messages to other window functions, either within the same program or in other programs, with the Windows SendMessage function. This function returns control to the calling program after the message has been processed. A program can also place messages in a program's message queue with the PostMessage function. This function returns control immediately after posting the message.

For example, when a program makes changes to the WIN.INI file (a file containing Windows initialization information), it can notify all currently running instances of these changes by sending them a WM_WININICHANGE message:

```
SendMessage (-1, WM_WININICHANGE, 0, 0L) ;
```

The -1 parameter indicates that the message is to be sent to all window functions of all currently running instances. Windows calls the window functions with the WM_WININICHANGE message and then returns control to the program that sent the message.

SAMPLE's message processing

The SAMPLE program shown in Figure 17-11 processes only four messages: WM_COMMAND, WM_SIZE, WM_PAINT, and WM_DESTROY. All other messages are passed to Def WindowProc. As is typical with most Windows programs written in C, SAMPLE uses a switch and case construction for processing messages.

The WM_COMMAND message signals the program that the user has selected a new font from the menu. SAMPLE first obtains a handle to the menu and removes the checkmark from the previously selected font:

```
hMenu = GetMenu (hWnd) ;
CheckMenuItem (hMenu, nCurrentFont, MF_UNCHECKED) ;
```

The value of *wParam* in the WM_COMMAND message is the menu ID of the newly selected font. SAMPLE saves that value in a static variable (nCurrentFont) and then places a checkmark on the new menu choice:

```
nCurrentFont = wParam ;
CheckMenuItem (hMenu, nCurrentFont, MF_CHECKED) ;
```

Because the typeface has changed, SAMPLE must repaint its display. The program does not repaint it immediately, however. Instead, it calls the InvalidateRect function:

```
InvalidateRect (hWnd, NULL, TRUE) ;
```

This causes a WM_PAINT message to be placed in the program's message queue. The NULL parameter indicates that the entire client area should be repainted. The TRUE parameter indicates that the background should be erased.

The WM_SIZE message indicates that the size of SAMPLE's client area has changed. SAMPLE simply saves the new dimensions of the client area in two static variables:

```
xClient = LOWORD (lParam) ;
yClient = HIWORD (lParam) ;
```

The LOWORD and HIWORD macros are defined in WINDOWS.H.

Windows also places a WM_PAINT message in SAMPLE's message queue when the size of the client area has changed. As is the case with WM_COMMAND, the program does not have to repaint the client area immediately, because the WM_PAINT message is in the message queue.

SAMPLE can receive a WM_PAINT message for many reasons. The first WM_PAINT message it receives results from calling UpdateWindow in the WinMain function. Later, if the current font is changed from the menu, the program itself causes a WM_PAINT message to be placed in the message queue by calling InvalidateRect. Windows also sends a window function a WM_PAINT message whenever the user changes the size of the window or when part of the window previously covered by another window is uncovered.

Programs begin processing WM_PAINT messages by calling BeginPaint:

```
BeginPaint (hWnd, &ps) ;
```

The SAMPLE program then creates a font based on the current size of the client area and the current typeface selected from the menu:

```
hFont = CreateFont (yClient, xClient / 8,
                    0, 0, 400, 0, 0, 0, OEM_CHARSET,
                    OUT_STROKE_PRECIS, OUT_STROKE_PRECIS,
                    DRAFT_QUALITY, (BYTE) VARIABLE_PITCH |
                    cFamily [nCurrentFont - IDM_SCRIPT],
                    szFace  [nCurrentFont - IDM_SCRIPT]) ;
```

The font is selected into the device context (a data structure internal to Windows that describes the characteristics of the output device); the program also saves the original device-context font:

```
hFont = SelectObject (ps.hdc, hFont) ;
```

And the word *Windows* is displayed:

```
TextOut (ps.hdc, 0, 0, "Windows", 7) ;
```

The original font in the device context is then selected, and the font that was created is now deleted:

```
DeleteObject (SelectObject (ps.hdc, hFont)) ;
```

Finally, SAMPLE calls EndPaint to signal Windows that the client area is now updated and valid:

```
EndPaint (hWnd, &ps) ;
```

Although the processing of the WM_ PAINT message in this program is simple, the method used is common to all Windows programs. The Begin Paint and End Paint functions always occur in pairs, first to get information about the area that needs repainting and then to mark that area as valid.

SAMPLE will display this text even when the program is minimized to be displayed as an icon at the bottom of the screen. Although most Windows programs use a customized icon for this purpose, the window-class structure in SAMPLE indicates that the program's icon is NULL, meaning that the program is responsible for drawing its own icon. SAMPLE does not, however, make any special provisions for drawing the icon. To it, the icon is simply a small client area. As a result, SAMPLE displays the word *Windows* in its "icon," using a small font size.

Windows sends the window function the WM_DESTROY message as a result of the DestroyWindow function that Def WindowProc calls when processing a WM_CLOSE message. The standard processing involves placing a WM_QUIT message in the message queue:

```
PostQuitMessage (0) ;
```

When the GetMessage function retrieves WM_QUIT from the message queue, GetMessage returns 0. This terminates the message loop and the program.

For all other messages, SAMPLE calls Def WindowProc and exits the window function by returning the value from the call:

```
return DefWindowProc (hWnd, iMessage, wParam, lParam) ;
```

This allows Windows to perform default processing on the messages SAMPLE ignores.

Windows' multitasking

Most operating systems or operating environments that allow multitasking use what is called a preemptive scheduler. Generally, the procedure involves use of the computer's ciock to switch rapidly between programs and allow each a small time slice. When switching between programs, the operating system must preserve the machine state.

Windows is different. It is a nonpreemptive multitasking environment. Although Windows allows several programs to run simultaneously, it never switches from one program to allow another to run. It switches between programs only when the currently running program calls the GetMessage function or the related Peek Message and WaitMessage functions.

When a Windows program calls GetMessage and the program's message queue contains a message other than WM_PAINT or WM_TIMER, Windows returns control to the program with the next message. However, if the program's message queue contains only a WM_PAINT or WM_TIMER message and another program's queue contains a message other than WM_PAINT or WM_TIMER, Windows returns control to the other program, which is also waiting for its GetMessage call to return.

(Windows also switches between programs temporarily when a program uses SendMessage to send a message to a window function in another program, but control returns to the calling program after the window function has processed the message sent to it.)

To cooperate with Windows' nonpreemptive multitasking, programmers should try to perform message processing as quickly as possible. Programs can, for example, split a large amount of processing into several smaller pieces to allow other programs to run in the interval. During long processing a program can also periodically call PeekMessage to allow other programs to run.

Graphics Device Interface

Programs receive input through the Windows message system. For program output, Windows provides a device-independent interface to graphics output devices, such as the video display, printers, and plotters. This interface is called the Graphics Device Interface, or GDI.

The device context (DC)

When a Windows program needs to send output to the video screen, the printer, or another graphics output device, it must first obtain a handle to the device's device context, or DC. Windows provides a number of functions for obtaining this device-context handle:

BeginPaint. Used for obtaining a video device-context handle during processing of a WM_PAINT message. This device context applies only to the rectangular section of the client area that is invalid (needs repainting). This region is also a clipping region, meaning that a program cannot paint outside this rectangle. BeginPaint fills in the fields of a PAINTSTRUCT structure. This structure contains the coordinates of the invalid rectangle and a byte that indicates if the background of the invalid rectangle has been erased.

GetDC. Generally used for obtaining a video device-context handle during processing of messages other than WM_PAINT. The handle obtained with this function references only the client area of the window.

GetWindowDC. Used for obtaining a video device-context handle that encompasses the entire window, including the title bar, menu bar, and scroll bars. A Windows program can use this function if it is necessary to paint over areas of the window outside the client area.

CreateDC. Used for obtaining a device-context handle for the entire display or for a printer, a plotter, or other graphics output device.

CreateIC. Used for obtaining an information-context handle, which is similar to a device-context handle but can be used only for obtaining information about the output device, not for drawing.

CreateCompatibleDC. Used for obtaining a device-context handle to a memory device context compatible with a particular graphics output device. This function is generally used for transferring bitmaps to a graphics output device.

CreateMetaFile. Used for obtaining a metafile device-context handle. A metafile is a collection of GDI calls encoded in binary form.

The Windows program uses the device-context handle when calling GDI functions. In addition to drawing, the various GDI functions can change the attributes of the device context, select different drawing objects (such as pens and fonts) into the device context, and determine the characteristics of the device context.

Device-independent programming

Windows supports such a wide variety of video displays, printers, and plotters that programs cannot make assumptions about the size and resolution of the device. Furthermore, because the user can generally alter the size of a program's window, the program must be able to adjust its output appropriately. The SAMPLE program, for example, showed how the window function can use the WM_SIZE message to obtain the current size of a window to create a font that fits text within the window's client area.

Programs can also use other Windows functions to determine the physical characteristics of a device. For instance, a program can use the GetDeviceCaps function to obtain information about the device context, including the resolution of the device, its physical dimensions, and its relative pixel height and width.

Then, too, the GetTextMetrics function returns information about the current font selected in the device context. In the default device context, this is the system font. Many Windows programs base the size of their display output on the size of a system-font character.

Device-context attributes

The device context includes attributes that define how the graphics output functions work on the device. When a program first obtains a handle to a device context, Windows sets these attributes to default values, but the program can change them. Some of these device-context attributes are as follows:

Pen. Windows uses the current pen for drawing lines. The default pen produces a solid black line 1 pixel wide. A program can change the pen color, change to a dotted or dashed line, or make the pen draw a solid line wider than 1 pixel.

Brush. Windows uses the current brush (sometimes called a pattern) for filling areas. A brush is an 8-pixel-by-8-pixel bitmap. The default brush is solid white. Programs can create colored brushes, hatched brushes, and customized brushes based on bitmaps.

Background color. Windows uses the background color to fill the spaces in and between characters when drawing text and to color the open areas in hatched brushstrokes and dotted or dashed pen lines. Windows uses the background color only if the background mode (another attribute of the display context) is opaque. If the background mode is transparent, Windows leaves the background unaltered. The default background color is white.

Text color. Windows uses this color for drawing text. The default is black.

Font. Windows uses the font to determine the shape of text characters. The default is called the system font, a fixed-pitch font that also appears in menus, caption bars, and dialog boxes.

Additional device-context attributes (such as mapping modes) are described in the following sections.

Mapping modes

Most GDI drawing functions in Windows have parameters that specify the coordinates or size of an object. For instance, the Rectangle function has five parameters:

```
Rectangle (hDC, x1, y1, x2, y2) ;
```

The first parameter is the handle to the device context. The others are

- $x1$: horizontal coordinate of the upper left corner of the rectangle.
- $y1$: vertical coordinate of the upper left corner of the rectangle.
- $x2$: horizontal coordinate of the lower right corner of the rectangle.
- $y2$: vertical coordinate of the lower right corner of the rectangle.

In the Rectangle and most other GDI functions, coordinates are logical coordinates, which are not necessarily the same as the physical coordinates (pixels) of the device. To translate logical coordinates into physical coordinates, Windows uses the current mapping mode.

In actuality, the mapping mode defines a transformation of coordinates between a window, which is defined in terms of logical coordinates, and a viewport, which is defined in terms of physical coordinates. For any mapping mode, a program can define separate window and viewport origins. The logical point defined as the window origin is then mapped to the physical point defined as the viewport origin. For some mapping modes, a program can also define window and viewport extents, which determine how the logical coordinates are scaled to the physical coordinates.

Windows programs can select one of eight mapping modes. The first six are sometimes called fully constrained, because the ratio between the window and viewport extents is fixed and cannot be changed.

In MM_TEXT, the default mapping mode, coordinates on the x axis increase from left to right, and coordinates on the y axis increase from the top downward. In the other five fully constrained mapping modes, coordinates on the x axis also increase from left to right, but coordinates on the y axis increase from the bottom upward. The six fully constrained mapping modes are

- *MM_TEXT*: Logical coordinates are the same as physical coordinates.
- *MM_LOMETRIC*: Logical coordinates are in units of 0.1 millimeter.
- *MM_HIMETRIC*: Logical coordinates are in units of 0.01 millimeter.
- *MM_LOENGLISH*: Logical coordinates are in units of 0.01 inch.
- *MM_HIENGLISH*: Logical coordinates are in units of 0.001 inch.
- *MM_TWIPS*: Logical coordinates are in units of $1/1440$ inch. (These units are $1/20$ of a typographic point, which is approximately $1/72$ inch.)

The seventh mapping mode is called partially constrained, because a program can change the window and viewport extents but Windows adjusts the values to ensure that equal horizontal and vertical logical coordinates translate to equal horizontal and vertical physical dimensions:

- *MM_ISOTROPIC*: Logical coordinates represent the same physical distance on both the x and y axes.

The MM_ISOTROPIC mapping mode is useful for drawing circles and squares. The MM_LOMETRIC, MM_HIMETRIC, MM_LOENGLISH, MM_HIENGLISH, and MM_TWIPS mapping modes are also isotropic, because equal logical coordinates map to the same physical dimensions on both axes.

The final mapping mode is sometimes called unconstrained because a program is free to set different window and viewport extents on the x and y axes.

- *MM_ANISOTROPIC*: Logical coordinates are mapped to arbitrarily scaled physical coordinates.

Functions for drawing

Windows includes several functions that programs can use to draw in the client area of a window. The most common of these functions are

SetPixel. Sets a point to a particular color.

LineTo. Draws a line from the current position to a point specified in the LineTo function. The current position is defined in the device context and can be altered before the call to LineTo with the MoveTo function, which changes the current position but does not draw anything. Windows uses the current pen and the current drawing mode (*see* below) for drawing the line.

Polyline. Draws multiple lines much like a series of LineTo calls but does not alter the current position on completion.

Rectangle. Draws a filled rectangle with a border. Parameters to the Rectangle function specify the coordinates of the upper left and lower right corners of the rectangle. Windows draws the border of the rectangle with the current pen and current drawing mode defined in the device context, just as if it were using the Polyline function then Windows fills the rectangle with the current brush defined in the device context.

Ellipse. Uses the same parameters as Rectangle but draws an ellipse within the rectangular area.

RoundRect. Draws a rectangle with rounded corners. Two parameters to this function define the height and width of an ellipse that Windows uses for drawing the rounded corners.

Polygon. Draws a polygon connecting a series of points and fills the enclosed areas in either an alternate or winding mode. The winding mode causes Windows to fill every area within the polygon. The alternate mode fills every other area. For a polygon that defines a five-pointed star, for instance, the center is filled if the mode is winding but is not filled if the mode is alternate.

Arc. Draws a curved line that is part of the circumference of an ellipse.

Chord. Similar to the Arc function, but Windows connects the beginning and ending points of the arc with a straight line. The area is filled with the current brush defined in the device context.

Pie. Similar to the Arc function, but Windows draws lines from the beginning and ending points of the arc to the center of the ellipse. The area is filled with the current brush defined in the device context.

TextOut. Writes text with the current font, text color, background color, and background mode (transparent or opaque).

Windows also includes other drawing functions for filling areas, formatting text, and transferring bitmaps.

Raster operations for pens

When Windows uses a pen to write to a device context, it must first determine which pixels of the destination are to be altered by the pen (the foreground) and which pixels will not be affected (the background). With dotted and dashed pens, the background — the space between the dots or dashes — is left unaltered if the drawing mode is transparent and is filled with the background color if the drawing mode is opaque.

When Windows alters the pixels of the destination that correspond to the foreground of the pen, the most obvious result is that the color of the current pen defined in the display context is used to color the destination. But this is not the only possible result. Windows also generalizes the process by using a logical operation to combine the pixels of the pen and the pixels of the destination.

This logical operation is defined by the drawing mode attribute of the device context. This drawing mode can be set to one of 16 binary raster operations (abbreviated ROP2).

The following table shows the 16 binary raster operation codes defined in WINDOWS.H. The column headed "Resultant Destination" shows how the destination changes, depending on the bit pattern of the pen and the bit pattern of the destination before the line is drawn. The words OR, AND, XOR, and NOT are the logical operations.

Binary Raster Operation	Resultant Destination
R2_BLACK	0
R2_COPYPEN	pen
R2_MERGEPEN	pen OR destination
R2_MASKPEN	pen AND destination
R2_XORPEN	pen XOR destination
R2_NOTCOPYPEN	NOT pen
R2_NOTMERGEPEN	NOT (pen OR destination)
R2_NOTMASKPEN	NOT (pen AND destination)
R2_NOTXORPEN	NOT (pen XOR destination)
R2_MERGEPENNOT	pen OR (NOT destination)
R2_MASKPENNOT	pen AND (NOT destination)
R2_MERGENOTPEN	(NOT pen) OR destination
R2_MASKNOTPEN	(NOT pen) AND destination
R2_NOP	destination
R2_NOT	NOT destination
R2_WHITE	1

The default drawing mode defined in a device context is R2_COPYPEN, which simply copies the pen to the destination. However, if the pen color is blue, the destination is red, and the drawing mode is R2_MERGEPEN, then the drawn line appears as magenta, which results from combining the pen and destination colors. If the pen color is blue, the destination is red, and the drawing mode is R2_ NOTMERGEPEN, then the drawn line is green, because the blue pen and the red destination are combined into magenta, which Windows then inverts to make green.

Bit-block transfers

Windows also uses logical operations when transferring a rectangular pixel pattern (a bit block) from one device context to another or from one area of a device context to another area of the same device context.

While line drawing involves a logical combination of two sets of pixels (the pen and the destination), the bit-block transfer functions perform a logical combination of three sets of pixels: a source bitmap, a destination bitmap, and the brush currently selected in the destination device context. As shown in the preceding section, there are 16 different ROP2 drawing modes for all the possible combinations of two sets of pixels. The tertiary raster operations (abbreviated ROP3) for bit-block transfers require 256 different operations for all possible combinations.

Windows defines three functions for transferring rectangular pixel patterns: BitBlt (bit-block transfer), StretchBlt (stretch-block transfer), and PatBlt (pattern-block transfer). Of these three functions, StretchBlt is the most generalized. StretchBlt transfers a bitmap from a source device context to a destination device context. Function parameters specify the origin, width, and height of the bitmap. If the source and destination widths and heights are different, Windows stretches or compresses the bitmap appropriately. Negative values of widths and heights cause Windows to draw a mirror image of the bitmap.

The BitBlt function transfers a bitmap from a source device context to a destination device context, but the width and height of the source and destination must be the same. If the source and destination device contexts have different mapping modes, Windows uses StretchBlt instead.

In both BitBlt and StretchBlt, Windows performs a bit-by-bit logical operation with the bit block in the source device context, the bit block in the destination area of the destination device context, and the brush currently selected in the destination device context. Although Windows supports all 256 possible raster operations with these three bitmaps, only a few have been given WINDOWS.H identifiers:

Raster Operation	Resultant Destination
BLACKNESS	0
SRCCOPY	source
SRCAND	source AND destination
SRCPAINT	source OR destination

(more)

Raster Operation	Resultant Destination
SRCINVERT	source XOR destination
SRCERASE	source AND (NOT destination)
MERGEPAINT	source OR (NOT destination)
NOTSRCCOPY	NOT source
NOTSRCERASE	NOT (source OR destination)
DSTINVERT	NOT destination
PATCOPY	pattern
MERGECOPY	source AND pattern
PATINVERT	destination XOR pattern
PATPAINT	source OR (NOT destination) OR pattern
WHITENESS	1

The PatBlt function is similar to BitBlt and StretchBlt but performs a logical operation only between the currently selected brush and a destination area of the device context. Thus, only 16 raster operations can be used with PatBlt; these are equivalent to the binary raster operations used with line drawing.

Text and fonts

Windows supports file-based text fonts in two different formats: raster and vector. The raster fonts, such as Courier, Helvetica, and Times Roman, are defined by digital representations of the bit patterns of the characters. Font files usually contain several different sizes for each typeface. The vector fonts, such as Modern, Script, and Roman, are defined by points that are connected to form the letters and can be scaled to different sizes.

When using a device such as a printer, which has built-in fonts, Windows can also use these device-based fonts.

To specify a font, a Windows program uses the CreateFont function to create a logical font—a detailed description of the desired font. When this logical font is selected into a device context, Windows finds the actual font that best fits this description. In many cases, this match is not exact. The program can then call GetTextMetrics to determine the characteristics of the actual font that the device will use to display text.

Windows supports both fixed-width and variable-width fonts, as well as such attributes as italics, underlining, and boldfacing. Programs can also justify text with the GetTextExtent call, which obtains the width of a particular text string. The program can then insert extra spaces between words with SetTextJustification or it can insert extra spaces between letters with SetTextCharacterExtra.

Metafiles

As explained earlier, a metafile is a collection of GDI function calls stored in a binary coded form. A program can create a metafile by calling CreateMetaFile and giving it either an MS-DOS filename or NULL as a parameter. If CreateMetaFile is given an MS-DOS filename, Windows creates a disk-based metafile; if the parameter is NULL, Windows creates a metafile in memory. The CreateMetaFile call returns a handle to a metafile device context. Any GDI calls that reference this device-context handle become part of the metafile.

When the program calls CloseMetaFile, Windows closes the metafile device context and returns a handle to the metafile. The program can then "play" this metafile on another device context (such as the video display) without calling the GDI functions directly.

Metafiles provide a useful way to transfer device-independent pictures between programs.

Data Sharing and Data Exchange

Windows includes a variety of methods by which programs can share and exchange data. These methods are discussed in the following sections.

Sharing local data among instances

Multiple instances of the same program can share data in the static data area of the program's data segment. Later instances of a program can thus call GetInstanceData and copy configuration options established by the user in the first instance. Multiple instances of programs can also share resources, such as dialog-box templates.

The Windows Clipboard

The Windows Clipboard is a general-purpose mechanism that allows a user to transfer data from one program to another. Programs that support the Clipboard generally include a top-level menu item called *Edit,* which invokes a pop-up menu that offers at least these three options:

- *Cut*: Copies the current selection to the Clipboard and deletes the selection from the current program file.
- *Copy*: Copies the current selection to the Clipboard without deleting the selection from the current program file.
- *Paste*: Copies the contents of the Clipboard to the current program file.

The Clipboard can hold only one item at a time. A program can transfer data to the Clipboard through the function call SetClipboardData. With this function, the program passes the Clipboard a handle to a global memory block, which then becomes the property of the Clipboard. A program can access Clipboard data through the complementary function GetClipboardData.

The Clipboard supports several formats:

- Text: ASCII text; each line ends with a carriage return and linefeed, and the text is terminated with a NULL character.
- Bitmap: A collection of bits in the GDI bitmap format.

- Metafile Picture: A structure that contains a handle to a metafile along with other information suggesting the mapping mode and aspect ratio of the picture.
- SYLK: Microsoft's Symbolic Link format.
- DIF: Software Arts' Data Interchange Format.

Programs can also use the Clipboard for storing data in private formats.

Some programs, such as the CLIPBRD program included with Windows, can also become Clipboard viewers. Such programs receive a message whenever the contents of the Clipboard change.

Dynamic Data Exchange (DDE)

Dynamic Data Exchange (DDE) is a protocol that cooperating programs can use to exchange data without user intervention. DDE makes use of the facilities in Windows that enable programs to send messages among themselves.

In DDE, the program that needs data from another program is called the client. The client sends a WM_DDE_INITIATE message either to a dedicated server program or to all currently running programs. Parameters to the WM_DDE_INITIATE message are *atoms*, which are numbers referring to text strings. A server application that has the data the client needs sends a WM_DDE_ACK message back to the client. The client can then be more specific about the data it needs by sending the server a WM_DDE_ADVISE message. The server can then pass global memory handles to the client with the WM_DDE_DATA message.

Internationalization

Windows includes several features that ease the conversion and translation of programs for international markets. Among these features are keyboard drivers appropriate for many European languages and use of the ANSI character set, which provides a richer set of accented letters than does the character set resident in the IBM PC and compatibles.

Windows also includes several functions that assist in language-independent coding. The AnsiUpper and AnsiLower functions translate characters or strings to uppercase or lowercase in the full ANSI character set, rather than the more limited ASCII character set. In addition, the AnsiNext and AnsiPrev functions allow scanning of text strings that may contain 2 or more bytes per character.

Windows programmers can also help in program translation by defining all text strings used within the program as resources contained in the resource script file. Because the resource script file also contains menu templates and dialog-box templates, it thus becomes the only file that needs alteration when a foreign-language version of the program is created.

Charles Petzold

Part E
Programming Tools

Article 18
Debugging in the MS-DOS Environment

It is axiomatic that any program will need debugging at some time in its development cycle, and programs written to run under MS-DOS are no exception. This article provides an introduction to the debugging tools and techniques available to the serious programmer developing code in the MS-DOS environment. Space does not permit a thorough investigation of the philosophy, psychology, and science of debugging computer programs; instead, a brief and practical discussion of the basic debugging approaches is presented, along with some rules-of-thumb for choosing the best approach. Nor are the details of every single utility and command included in this article; these are described in detail in the reference sections of this volume. The commands and utility programs that are most useful for debugging are discussed and illustrated with examples and case histories that also serve as models for the various debugging methods.

The reader of this article is assumed to be a programmer with sufficient experience to understand an assembly-language program. The reader is also assumed to be familiar with MS-DOS — terms like FCB and PSP are not explained. A reader without this background in MS-DOS need not be deterred, however; these terms are thoroughly explained elsewhere in this book. Besides assembly language, examples in this article are written in Microsoft QuickBASIC and Microsoft C. A detailed knowledge of these languages is not required; the examples are short and straightforward.

The reader should also keep in mind that the examples given here are real but not necessarily realistic. To avoid the tedium that accompanies debugging, the examples have been designed to reveal their bugs fairly quickly. All the methods and techniques shown are accurate in detail but not always in scale. Most of the debugging examples presented here would require one-half to one hour of work. It is possible for real debugging sessions to last for hours or days, especially if the wrong approach or tool is chosen. One of the purposes of this article is to help the programmer choose the correct tool and, thus, to reduce the tedium.

The Programs

There are more than a dozen listings in this article. Some of them are correct and others contain errors for use in illustrating debugging techniques. Many of the programs serve as examples in multiple sections of the article. The following summary of the programs (Table 18-1) is given to avoid confusion and to provide a common location to consult for explanations of the programs.

Table 18-1. Summary of Example Programs.

Name:	EXP.BAS
Figure:	18-1
Status:	Incorrect — do not use.
Purpose:	Computes EXP(x) (the exponential of x) to a specified precision using an infinite series.
Compiling:	QB EXP;
	LINK EXP;
Parameters:	Prompts for value for x and a convergence criterion. Enter zero to quit.

Name:	EXP.BAS
Figure:	18-3
Status:	Correct version of Figure 18-1.
Purpose:	Computes EXP(x) (the exponential of x) to a specified precision using an infinite series.
Compiling:	QB EXP;
	LINK EXP;
Parameters:	Prompts for value for x and a convergence criterion. Enter zero to quit.

Name:	COMMSCOP.ASM
Figure:	18-4
Status:	Correct.
Purpose:	Monitors the activity on a specified COM port and places a copy of all transmitted and received data in a RAM buffer. Each entry in the buffer is tagged to indicate whether the byte was sent by or received by the application program under test. Control is provided to start, stop, and resume tracing by means of a control interrupt. When tracing is stopped and resumed, a marker is left in the buffer. COMMSCOP is a terminate-and-stay-resident (TSR) program.
Compiling:	MASM COMMSCOP;
	LINK COMMSCOP;
	EXE2BIN COMMSCOP.EXE COMMSCOP.COM
	DEL COMMSCOP.EXE
Parameters:	Installed by entering *COMMSCOP*; no parameters for installation. The TSR is controlled by passing parameter data in registers with an Interrupt 60H call. The registers can have the following values:

AH:	Command:
00H	STOP
01H	FLUSH AND START
02H	RESUME TRACE
03H	RETURN TRACE BUFFER ADDRESS

(more)

DX:	COM port:
00H	COM1
01H	COM2

Interrupt 60H returns the following in response to function 3:

CX	Buffer count in bytes
DX	Segment address of buffer
BX	Offset address of buffer

Name:	COMMSCMD.C
Figure:	18-5
Status:	Correct.
Purpose:	Controls the COMMSCOP program by issuing Interrupt 60H calls. C version.
COMPILING:	MSC COMMSCMD;
	LINK COMMSCMD;
Parameters:	Commands are issued by

COMMSCMD [[*cmd*][*port*]]

where: *cmd* is the command to be executed:

STOP   Stop trace
START   Flush buffer and start trace
RESUME   Resume a stopped trace

port is the COM port (1 = COM1, 2 = COM2)

If *cmd* is omitted, STOP is assumed; if *port* is omitted, 1 is assumed.

Name:	COMMSCMD.BAS
Figure:	18-6
Status:	Correct.
Purpose:	Controls the COMMSCOP program by issuing Interrupt 60H calls. QuickBASIC version.
Compiling:	QB COMMSCMD;
	LINK COMMSCMD USERLIB;
Parameters:	Commands are issued by

COMMSCMD [[*cmd*][,*port*]]

where: *cmd* is the command to be executed:

STOP   Stop trace
START   Flush buffer and start trace
RESUME   Resume a stopped trace

port is the COM port (1 = COM1, 2 = COM2)

If *cmd* is omitted, STOP is assumed; if *port* is omitted, 1 is assumed.

Name	COMMDUMP.BAS
Figure:	18-7
Status:	Correct.
Purpose:	Produces a formatted dump of the communications trace buffer.

(more)

Compiling:	QB COMMDUMP; LINK COMMDUMP USERLIB;
Parameters:	No parameters. When COMMDUMP is invoked, it formats and dumps the entire buffer.

Name:	TESTCOMM.ASM
Figure:	18-9
Status:	Incorrect — do not use.
Purpose:	Provides test data for the COMMSCOP routine.
Compiling:	MASM TESTCOMM; LINK TESTCOMM;
Parameters:	No parameters. TESTCOMM reads data from the keyboard and writes to COM1 and reads COM1 data and displays it on the screen. Ctrl-C cancels.

Name:	TESTCOMM.ASM
Figure:	18-10
Status:	Correct version of Figure 18-9.
Purpose:	Provides test data for the COMMSCOP routine.
Compiling:	MASM TESTCOMM; LINK TESTCOMM;
Parameters:	No parameters. TESTCOMM reads data from the keyboard and writes to COM1 and reads COM1 data and displays it on the screen. Ctrl-C cancels.

Name:	BADSCOP.ASM
Figure:	18-11
Status:	Incorrect version of Figure 18-4 — do not use.
Purpose:	Monitors the activity on a specified COM port and places a copy of all transmitted and received data in a RAM buffer. Each entry in the buffer is tagged to indicate whether the byte was sent by or received by the application program under test. Control is provided to start, stop, and resume tracing by means of a control interrupt. When tracing is stopped and resumed, a marker is left in the buffer. BADSCOP is a terminate-and-stay-resident (TSR) program.
Compiling:	MASM BADSCOP; LINK BADSCOP; EXE2BIN BADSCOP.EXE BADSCOP.COM DEL BADSCOP.EXE
Parameters:	Installed by entering *BADSCOP*; no parameters for installation. The TSR is controlled by passing parameter data in registers with an Interrupt 60H call. The registers can have the following values:

AH:	Command:
00H	STOP
01H	FLUSH AND START

(more)

02H	RESUME TRACE
03H	RETURN TRACE BUFFER ADDRESS

DX:	COM port:
00H	COM1
01H	COM2

Interrupt 60H returns the following in response to function 3:

CX	Buffer count in bytes
DX	Segment address of buffer
BX	Offset address of buffer

Name:	UPPERCAS.C
Figure:	18-13
Status:	Incorrect — do not use.
Purpose:	Converts a fixed string to uppercase and prints it.
Compiling:	MSC /Zi UPPERCAS;
	LINK UPPERCAS /CO;
Parameters:	No parameters.

Name:	UPPERCAS.C
Figure:	18-14
Status:	Correct version of Figure 18-13.
Purpose:	Converts a fixed string to uppercase and prints it.
Compiling:	MSC /Zi UPPERCAS;
	LINK UPPERCAS /CO;
Parameters:	No parameters.

Name:	ASCTBL.C
Figure:	18-16
Status:	Incorrect — do not use.
Purpose:	Displays a table of all displayable characters.
Compiling:	MSC /Zi ASCTBL;
	LINK ASCTBL /CO;
Parameters:	No parameters.

Name:	ASCTBL.C
Figure:	18-17
Status:	Correct version of Figure 18-16.
Purpose:	Displays a table of all displayable characters.
Compiling:	MSC /Zi ASCTBL;
	LINK ASCTBL /CO;
Parameters:	No parameters.

Debugging Tools and Techniques

MS-DOS provides a wide variety of tools to aid in the debugging process. Some are intended specifically for debugging. For example, the DEBUG program is delivered with MS-DOS and provides basic debugging aid; the more sophisticated SYMDEB is supplied with MASM, Microsoft's macro assembler; CodeView, a debugger for high-order languages, is supplied with Microsoft C, Microsoft Pascal, and Microsoft FORTRAN. Others are general MS-DOS services and features that are also useful in the debugging process.

Debugging, like programming, has aspects of both an art and a craft. The craft—the mechanical details of using the tools—is discussed both here and elsewhere in this volume, but the main subject of this article is the *art* of debugging—the choice of the correct tool, the best techniques to use in various situations, the methods of extracting the clues to the problem from a recalcitrant program.

Debugging a program is a form of puzzle solving. As with most intellectual detective work, the following rule applies:

Gather enough information and the solution will be obvious.

The craft of debugging involves gathering the data; the art lies in deciding which data to gather and in noticing when the solution has become obvious.

The methods of gathering data for debugging, listed in order of increasing difficulty and tediousness, fall into four major categories:

- Inspection and observation
- Instrumentation
- Use of software debugging monitors (DEBUG, SYMDEB, and CodeView)
- Use of hardware debugging aids

As mentioned above, part of the art of debugging is knowing which method to use. This is one of the most difficult aspects of debugging—so difficult, in fact, that even programmers with years of experience make mistakes. Many programmers have spent hours single-stepping through a program with DEBUG only to discover that the cause of the problem would have been obvious if they had given the program's output even a cursory check. The only universal rule for choosing the correct debugging method is

Try them all, starting with the simplest.

Inspection and observation

Inspection and observation is the oldest and, usually, the best method of program debugging. It is also the basis for all the other methods. The first step with this method, as with the others, is to gather all the pertinent materials. Program listings, file layouts, report layouts, and program design materials (such as algorithm descriptions and flowcharts) are all extremely valuable in the debugging process.

Desk-checking

Before a programmer can determine what a program is doing wrong, he or she must know the correct operation of the program. There was a time, when computers were rare and expensive resources, that programmers were encouraged not to run their programs until the programs had been thoroughly desk-checked. The desk-checking process involves sitting down with a listing, a hand calculator, and some sample data. The programmer then "plays computer," executing each line of the program manually and writing down on paper the results of each program step. This process is extremely slow and tedious. When the desk-checking is completed, however, the programmer not only has found most of the bugs in the program but also has become intimately familiar with the execution of the program and the values of the program variables at each step.

The advent of inexpensive yet powerful personal computers, combined with the rising cost of programmer time, has made complete desk-checking nearly obsolete. It is now cheaper to run the program and let the computer find the errors. However, the usefulness of the desk-checking technique remains. Many programmers find it helpful to manually execute those sections of a program that they suspect are causing trouble. Even if they don't find errors in the code, the insight they gain into the workings of the code and the values of the variables at each step can be invaluable when applying other debugging techniques.

The inspection-and-observation methodology

The basic technique of the inspection-and-observation method is simple: After gathering all the required materials, run the program and observe. Observe very carefully; events that seem insignificant may be the very clues needed to discover where the program is going astray. As the program executes, note whether each section performs correctly. Does the program clear the screen when it should? Does it ask for input when it should? Does it produce the correct results? Observable events are the debugger's milestones in the execution of the program. If the program clears the screen but writes purple asterisks instead of requesting input, then the problem lies somewhere after the program issues the Clear Screen command but before it writes the input prompt on the screen. At this point, the program listing and design data become important. Inspect the listing and examine the area after the last successful milestone and before the missing milestone. Look for a logic error in the code that could explain the observed data.

If the program produces printed reports, they may also be useful. Watch the screen and listen to the printer. Clues can sometimes be found in the order in which things happen. The light on the disk drive can be another indication of activity. See how disk activity coordinates with screen and printer events. Try to identify each section of the program from these clues. Then use this information to localize the inspection of the listing to isolate the erroneous code.

The values of data given in reports and on the screen can also give clues to what's going wrong. Examining the data and reconstructing the values used to compute it sometimes leads to inferences about data problems. Perhaps a variable was misspelled in the code or perhaps a data file is in the wrong format or has been corrupted. With this information, the bug can often be isolated. However, a very thorough knowledge of the program and its algorithms is required. *See* Desk-checking above.

MS-DOS provides four commands and filters that are useful in the collection and examination of data for debugging: TYPE, PRINT, FIND, and DEBUG. All these commands display the data in a file in some way. If the data is ASCII (displayable) characters, TYPE and PRINT can be used, with some help from FIND. Binary files can be examined and modified with the DEBUG utility. *See* USER COMMANDS: FIND; PRINT; TYPE; PROGRAMMING UTILITIES: DEBUG.

The TYPE command provides the simplest way to display ASCII data files. This method can be used to examine both input and output files. Checking the input files may uncover some bad (or unexpected) data that causes the program to malfunction; examining the output files will show whether calculations are being performed correctly and may help pinpoint the erroneous calculations if they are not.

The FIND utility is useful in locating specific data in a file. Using FIND is more accurate and definitely less tedious than examining the file manually using the TYPE command. The /N switch causes FIND to also display the relative line number of the matching line — information that is most useful in debugging.

Sometimes the data is too complex to be examined on the screen and printed copy is needed. The PRINT command will produce hard copy of an ASCII file as will the TYPE command if its output is redirected to the printer with the >PRN command-line parameter after the filename.

Not all data files contain pure ASCII data, and displaying such non-ASCII files requires a different approach. The TYPE command can be used, but nonprintable characters will produce garbage on the screen. This technique can still prove useful if the file has a large amount of ASCII data or if the records are regular and the ASCII information always appears at the same location, but no information can be gained about non-ASCII numeric data in such files. Note also that the entire file might not be displayed using TYPE because if TYPE encounters a byte containing 1AH (Control-Z), it assumes it has reached the end of the file and stops.

Clearly, a more useful tool for examining non-ASCII files would be a program that dumps the file in hexadecimal, with an appropriate translation of all displayable characters. Such programs exist in the public domain (through bulletin-board services, for instance) and, in any event, are not difficult to write. MS-DOS does not include a stand-alone file-dumping program among its standard commands and utilities, but the DEBUG program can be used, with minor inconvenience, to display files. This program is discussed in detail later in this article; for now, simply follow these instructions to use DEBUG as a file dumper. To load DEBUG and the program to be debugged, use the form

DEBUG [*drive:*][*path*]*filename.ext*

DEBUG will display a hyphen as a prompt. To see the contents of the file, enter *D* (the DEBUG Display Memory command) and press Enter. DEBUG will display the first 128 (80H) bytes of the file in hexadecimal and will also show any displayable characters.

To see the rest of the file, simply continue entering *D* until the desired area is found. Hard copy of the contents of the display can be made by using the PrtSc key (or Ctrl-PrtSc to print continuously). Note that the offset addresses for the bytes in the file begin at the value in the program's CS:IP registers, which can be viewed by using the Debug R (Display or Modify Registers) command. To obtain the true offsets, subtract CS:IP from the address shown.

The essence of the inspection-and-observation method is careful and thoughtful observation. The computer and the operating system can provide tools to aid in the collection of data, but the most important tool is the programmer's mind. By applying the logical skills they already possess to the observed data, programmers can usually avoid the more complex forms of debugging.

Instrumentation

Debugging by instrumentation is a traditional method that has been popular since programs were holes punched in cards. In general, this method consists of adding something to the program, either internally or externally, to report on the progress of program execution. Programmers call this added mechanism instrumentation because of its resemblance to the measuring instruments used in science and engineering. Instrumentation can be software, hardware, or a combination of both; it can be internal to the program or external to it. Internal instrumentation is always software, but external instrumentation may be either hardware or software.

Internal instrumentation

Internal instrumentation usually consists of display or print statements placed at strategic locations. Other signals to the user can be used if they are available. For instance, the system beeper can be sounded at key locations, perhaps in a coded sequence of beeps; if the device being debugged has lights that can be accessed by the program, these lights can be flashed at important locations in the program. Beeping and flashing do not, however, possess the information content usually required for debugging, so display or print statements are preferred.

The use of display or print statements to display key data and milestones on the screen or printer requires careful planning. First, apply the techniques of inspection and observation described in the previous section to determine the most probable points of failure. Then, if there is some doubt about what path execution is taking through the code, embed messages of the following types after key decision points:

BEGINNING SORT PHASE
ENDING PRINCIPAL CALCULATION
PROCESSING RECORD *XX*

A second way to use display or print statement instrumentation is to embed statements that display the data and interim values used for calculations. This technique can be extremely useful in finding problems related to the data being processed. Consider the QuickBASIC program in Figure 18-1 as an example. The program has no syntax errors and compiles cleanly, but it sometimes produces an incorrect answer.

```
'  EXP.BAS -- COMPUTE EXPONENTIAL WITH INFINITE SERIES
'
'  ***********************************************************************
'  *                                                                     *
'  *   EXP                                                               *
'  *                                                                     *
'  *   This routine computes EXP(x) using the following infinite series: *
'  *                                                                     *
'  *                     x     x^2    x^3    x^4    x^5                   *
'  *         EXP(x) = 1 + --- + --- + --- + --- + --- + ...              *
'  *                     1!     2!     3!     4!     5!                   *
'  *                                                                     *
'  *                                                                     *
'  *   The program requests a value for x and a value for the convergence *
'  *   criterion, C.  The program will continue evaluating the terms of  *
'  *   the series until the difference between two terms is less than C.  *
'  *                                                                     *
'  *   The result of the calculation and the number of terms required to *
'  *   converge are printed.  The program will repeat until an x of 0 is *
'  *   entered.                                                          *
'  *                                                                     *
'  ***********************************************************************


'   Initialize program variables
'
INITIALIZE:
        TERMS = 1
        FACT = 1
        LAST = 1.E35
        DELTA = 1.E34
        EX = 1
'
'   Input user data
'
        INPUT "Enter number:  "; X
        IF X = 0 THEN END
        INPUT "Enter convergence criterion (.0001 for 4 places):  "; C


'   Compute exponential until difference of last 2 terms is < C
'
        WHILE ABS(LAST - DELTA) >= C
            LAST = DELTA
            FACT = FACT * TERMS
            DELTA = X^TERMS / FACT
            EX = EX + DELTA
            TERMS = TERMS + 1
        WEND
```

Figure 18-1. A routine to compute exponentials.   *(more)*

```
'

'  Display answer and number of terms required to converge

'

      PRINT EX
      PRINT TERMS; "elements required to converge"
      PRINT

      GOTO INITIALIZE
```

Figure 18-1. Continued.

The purpose of the EXP.BAS program is to compute the exponential of a given number to a specified precision using an infinite series. The program computes the value of each term in the infinite series and adds it to a running total. To keep from executing forever, the program checks the difference between the last two elements computed and stops when this difference is less than the convergence criterion entered by the user.

When the program is run for several values, the following results are observed:

```
Enter number:   ? 1
Enter convergence criterion (.0001 for 4 places):   ? .0001
 2.718282
 10 elements required to converge

Enter number:   ? 1.5
Enter convergence criterion (.0001 for 4 places):   ? .0001
 4.481686
 11 elements required to converge

Enter number:   ? 2
Enter convergence criterion (.0001 for 4 places):   ? .0001
 5
 3 elements required to converge

Enter number:   ? 2.5
Enter convergence criterion (.0001 for 4 places):   ? .0001
 12.18249
 15 elements required to converge

Enter number:   ? 3
Enter convergence criterion (.0001 for 4 places):   ? .0001
 13
 4 elements required to converge

Enter number:   ? 0
```

Some of these numbers are incorrect. Table 18-2 shows the computed values and the correct values.

Table 18-2. The Computed Values Generated by EXP.BAS and the Expected Values.

x	Computed	Correct
1.0	2.718282	2.718282
1.5	4.481686	4.481689
2.0	5	7.389056
2.5	12.18249	12.18249
3.0	13	20.08554

Applying the methods from the first section of this article and observing the data quickly reveals a pattern. With the exception of 1, all whole numbers give incorrect results, but all numbers with fractions give results that are correct to the specified convergence criterion. Examination of the listing shows no obvious reason for this. The answer is there, but only an exceptionally intuitive numeric analyst would see it. Because no answer is obvious, the next step is to validate the only information available — that whole numbers produce errors and fractional ones do not. Repeating the first experiment with 2 and a number very close to 2 yields the following results:

```
Enter number:   ? 1.999
Enter convergence criterion (.0001 for 4 places):   ? .0001
 7.38167
 13 elements required to converge

Enter number:   ? 2
Enter convergence criterion (.0001 for 4 places):   ? .0001
 5
 3 elements required to converge

Enter number:   ? 0
```

The outcome is the same — repeating the experiment with a number as near to 2 as the convergence criterion permits (1.9999) produces the same result. The error is indeed caused by the fact that the number is an integer.

Because no intuitive way can be found to solve the mystery by inspection, the programmer must turn to the next method in the hierarchy, instrumentation. The problem has something to do with the calculation of the terms of the series. Therefore, the section of the program that performs this calculation should be instrumented by placing PRINT statements inside the WHILE loop (Figure 18-2) to display all the intermediate values of the calculation.

```
WHILE ABS(LAST - DELTA) >= C
      LAST = DELTA
      FACT = FACT * TERMS
      DELTA = X ^ TERMS / FACT
```

Figure 18-2. Instrumenting the WHILE loop.   *(more)*

```
        EX = EX + DELTA
        PRINT "TERMS="; TERMS; "EX="; EX; "FACT="; FACT; "DELTA="; DELTA;
        PRINT "LAST="; LAST
        TERMS = TERMS + 1
    WEND
```

Figure 18-2. Continued.

The print statements used in this WHILE loop are typical of the type used for instrumentation. The program makes no attempt at fancy formatting. The print statements simply identify each value with its variable name, allowing easy correlation of the data and the code in the listing. Repeating the experiment with 1.999 and 2 yields

```
Enter number:  ? 1.999
Enter convergence criterion (.0001 for 4 places):  ? .0001
TERMS= 1 EX= 2.999 FACT= 1 DELTA= 1.999 LAST= 1E+34
TERMS= 2 EX= 4.997001 FACT= 2 DELTA= 1.998 LAST= 1.999
TERMS= 3 EX= 6.328335 FACT= 6 DELTA= 1.331334 LAST= 1.998
TERMS= 4 EX= 6.993669 FACT= 24 DELTA= .6653343 LAST= 1.331334
TERMS= 5 EX= 7.25967 FACT= 120 DELTA= .2660006 LAST= .6653343
TERMS= 6 EX= 7.348292 FACT= 720 DELTA= 8.862254E-02 LAST= .2660006
TERMS= 7 EX= 7.373601 FACT= 5040 DELTA= 2.530806E-02 LAST= 8.862254E-02
TERMS= 8 EX= 7.379924 FACT= 40320 DELTA= 6.323853E-03 LAST= 2.530806E-02
TERMS= 9 EX= 7.381329 FACT= 362880 DELTA= 1.404598E-03 LAST= 6.323853E-03
TERMS= 10 EX= 7.38161 FACT= 3628800 DELTA= 2.807791E-04 LAST= 1.404598E-03
TERMS= 11 EX= 7.381661 FACT= 3.99168E+07 DELTA= 5.102522E-05 LAST= 2.807791E-04
TERMS= 12 EX= 7.38167 FACT= 4.790016E+08 DELTA= 8.499951E-06 LAST= 5.102522E-05
 7.38167
 13 elements required to converge

Enter number:  ? 2
Enter convergence criterion (.0001 for 4 places):  ? .0001
TERMS= 1 EX= 3 FACT= 1 DELTA= 2 LAST= 1E+34
TERMS= 2 EX= 5 FACT= 2 DELTA= 2 LAST= 2
 5
 3 elements required to converge
```

Examination of the instrumentation printout for the two cases shows a drastically different pattern. The fractional number went through 13 iterations following the expected pattern; the whole number, however, quit on the third step. The loop is terminating prematurely. Why? Look at the values calculated for *DELTA* and *LAST* on the last complete step. They are the same, giving a difference of zero. Because this difference will always be less than the convergence criterion, the loop will always terminate early. A moment's reflection shows why. The numerator of the fraction for each term but the first in the infinite series is a power of the number entered; the denominator is a factorial, a product formed by multiplying successive integers. Because $n! = n*(n-1)!$, when an integer is raised to a power equal to itself and divided by the factorial of that integer the result will always be the same as the preceding term. That is what has happened here.

Now that the cause of the problem is found, it must be fixed. How can this problem be prevented? In this case, the problem is caused by a logic error. The programmer misread (or miswrote!) the algorithm and assumed that the criterion for termination was that the difference between the last two terms be less than the specified value. This is incorrect. Actually, the termination criterion should be that the difference between the forming EXP(x) and the last term be less than the criterion. To simplify, the last term itself must be less than the value specified. The correct program listing, including the new WHILE loop, is shown in Figure 18-3.

```
'   EXP.BAS -- COMPUTE EXPONENTIAL WITH INFINITE SERIES
'
' **********************************************************************
' *                                                                    *
' *   EXP                                                              *
' *                                                                    *
' *   This routine computes EXP(x) using the following infinite series: *
' *                                                                    *
' *                    x     x^2    x^3    x^4    x^5                  *
' *         EXP(x) = 1 + --- + --- + --- + --- + --- + ...            *
' *                    1!     2!     3!     4!     5!                  *
' *                                                                    *
' *                                                                    *
' *   The program requests a value for x and a value for the convergence *
' *   criterion, C.  The program will continue evaluating the terms of *
' *   the series until the amount added with a term is less than C.    *
' *                                                                    *
' *   The result of the calculation and the number of terms required to *
' *   converge are printed.  The program will repeat until an x of 0 is *
' *   entered.                                                         *
' *                                                                    *
' **********************************************************************


'
'   Initialize program variables
'
INITIALIZE:
          TERMS = 1
          FACT = 1
          DELTA = 1.E35
          EX = 1
'
'   Input user data
'
          INPUT "Enter number:  "; X
          IF X = 0 THEN END
          INPUT "Enter convergence criterion (.0001 for 4 places):  "; C

'
'   Compute exponential until difference of last 2 terms is < C
'
```

Figure 18-3. Corrected exponential calculation routine.   *(more)*

```
        WHILE DELTA > C
            FACT = FACT * TERMS
            DELTA = X^TERMS / FACT
            EX = EX + DELTA
            TERMS = TERMS + 1
        WEND


'
'  Display answer and number of terms required to converge
'

        PRINT EX
        PRINT TERMS; "elements required to converge"
        PRINT

        GOTO INITIALIZE
```

Figure 18-3. Continued.

The program now produces the correct results within the limits of the specified accuracy:

```
Enter number:   ? 1.999
Enter convergence criterion (.0001 for 4 places):   ? .0001
 7.381661
 12 elements required to converge

Enter number:   ? 2
Enter convergence criterion (.0001 for 4 places):   ? .0001
 7.389047
 12 elements required to converge

Enter number:   ? 0
```

This example illustrates how easy it is to use internal instrumentation in high-order languages. Because these languages usually have simple formatted output commands, they require very little work to instrument. When these output commands are not available, however, more work may be required. For instance, if the program being debugged is in assembly language, it is possible that the code required to format and print internal data will be longer than the program being debugged. For this reason, internal instrumentation is rarely used on small and moderate assembly programs. However, large assembly programs and systems often already have print formatting routines built into them; in these cases, internal instrumentation may be as easy as with high-order languages.

External instrumentation

Sometimes it is difficult to use internal instrumentation with a program. If, for instance, the problem is timing related, adding print statements could cloud the problem or, worse yet, make it go away completely. This leaves the programmer in the frustrating position of having the problem only when the cause can't be seen and not having the problem when it can. A solution to this type of problem can sometimes be found by moving the instrumentation outside the program itself. There are two types of external instrumentation: hardware and software.

Hardware instrumentation consists of whatever logic analyzers, oscilloscopes, meters, lights, bells, or gongs are appropriate to the hardware and software under test. Hardware instrumentation is difficult to set up and tedious to use. It is, therefore, usually reserved for those problems directly associated with hardware. Such problems often arise when new software is being run on new hardware and no one is quite sure where the bugs are. Because most programmers reading this book are developing software on tried-and-true personal computer hardware and because most of those programmers are unlikely to have a logic analyzer costing several thousand dollars, we will skip over the use of hardware instrumentation for software debugging. If a logic analyzer must be used, the programmer should remember that the debugging philosophy and techniques discussed in this article can still be applied effectively.

MS-DOS provides a feature that is very useful in building external instrumentation software: the TSR, or terminate-and-stay-resident routine. *See* PROGRAMMING IN THE MS-DOS ENVIRONMENT: Customizing ms-dos: Terminate-and-Stay-Resident Utilities. This feature of the operating system allows the programmer to build a monitoring routine that is, in essence, a part of the operating system and outside the application program. The TSR is loaded as a normal program, but instead of leaving the system when it is done, it remains intact in memory. The operating system provides no way to reexecute the program after it terminates, so most TSRs are interrupt driven.

Because TSRs exist outside the application program, they can be used to build external instrumentation devices. This independence allows them to perform monitoring functions without disturbing the logic flow of the application program. The only areas where interference is likely are those where the TSR and the program must use common resources. These conflicts typically involve timing but can also involve other resources, such as I/O devices, disk files, and MS-DOS resources, including environment space. Some of these problems are addressed in the next example.

The TSR type of external instrumentation software can prove useful in analyzing serial communications. Such an instrumentation program monitors the serial communication line and records all data. To detect protocol or timing problems, the program tags the recorded data so that transmitted data can be differentiated from received data. Hardware devices exist that plug into the serial port and perform both the monitoring and tagging function, but they are expensive and not always handy. Fortunately, this inexpensive piece of software instrumentation will serve in many cases.

Software interrupt calls are made with the INT instruction. Although their service routines must obey similar rules, these interrupts should not be confused with hardware interrupts caused by external hardware events. Software interrupts in MS-DOS are used by an application program to communicate with the operating system and, by extension in IBM systems, with the ROM BIOS. For example, on IBM PCs and compatibles, application programs can use software Interrupt 14H to communicate with the ROM BIOS serial port driver. The ROM BIOS routine, in turn, manages the hardware interrupts from the actual serial device. Thus, Interrupt 14H does not communicate directly with the hardware. All the programs in this article deal with software interrupts to the ROM BIOS and MS-DOS.

A program to trace the serial data flow must have access to the serial data, so such a program must replace the vector for Interrupt 14H with one that points to itself. The routine can then record all the serial data and pass it along through the serial port. Because the goal is to minimize the effect of this monitoring on the timing of the data, the method used for recording the data should be fast. This requirement rules out writing to a disk file, because unexpected delays can be introduced (and because doing disk I/O from an interrupt service routine under MS-DOS is difficult, if not impossible). Printing the data on paper is clearly too slow, and data displayed on the screen is too ephemeral. Thus, about the only thing that can be done with the data is to write it to RAM. Luckily, memory has become cheap and most personal computers have plenty.

Writing a routine that monitors and records serial data is not enough, however. The data must still flow through the serial port to and from the external serial device. Thus, the monitor program can have only temporary custody of the data and must pass it on to the serial interrupt service routine in the ROM BIOS. This is accomplished by using MS-DOS function calls to extract the address of the serial interrupt handler before the new vector is installed in its place. The process of intercepting interrupts and then passing the data on is known as "daisy-chaining" interrupt handlers. So long as such intercepting programs are careful to maintain the data and conditions upon entrance for subsequent routines (that is, so long as routines are well behaved; *see* PROGRAMMING IN THE MS-DOS ENVIRON-MENT: PROGRAMMING FOR MS-DOS), several interrupt handlers can be daisy-chained together with no detriment to processing. (Woe be unto the person who breaks the daisy chain — the results are annoying at best and unpredictable at worst.)

The serial monitoring program, as described so far, correctly collects and stores serial data and then passes it on to the serial port. This may be intellectually satisfying, but it is not of much use in the real world. Some way must be provided to control the program — to start collection, to stop collection, to pause and resume collection. Also, once data is collected, a control function must be provided that returns the number of bytes collected and their starting location, so that the data can be examined.

From all this, it is clear that a serial communications monitoring instrument must

1. Replace the Interrupt 14H vector with one pointing to itself.
2. Save the address of the old interrupt handler.
3. Collect the serial data, tag it as transmitted or received, and store it in RAM.
4. Pass the data on, in a completely transparent manner, to the old interrupt handler.
5. Provide some way to control data collection.

A program that meets all these criteria is shown in Figure 18-4. The COMMSCOP program has three major parts:

Procedure	Purpose
COMMSCOPE	Monitoring and tagging
CONTROL	External control
VECTOR_INIT	Interrupt vector initialization

The *COMMSCOPE* procedure provides the new Interrupt 14H handler that intercepts the serial I/O interrupts. The *CONTROL* procedure provides the external control needed to make the system work. The *VECTOR_INIT* procedure gets the old interrupt handler address, installs *COMMSCOPE* as the new interrupt handler, and installs the interrupt handler for the control interrupt.

```
        TITLE   COMMSCOP -- COMMUNICATIONS TRACE UTILITY
;******************************************************************
; *                                                              *
; *  COMMSCOP --                                                 *
; *    THIS PROGRAM MONITORS THE ACTIVITY ON A SPECIFIED COMM PORT *
; *    AND PLACES A COPY OF ALL COMM ACTIVITY IN A RAM BUFFER.  EACH *
; *    ENTRY IN THE BUFFER IS TAGGED TO INDICATE WHETHER THE BYTE *
; *    WAS SENT BY OR RECEIVED BY THE SYSTEM.                    *
; *                                                              *
; *    COMMSCOP IS INSTALLED BY ENTERING                         *
; *                                                              *
; *                    COMMSCOP                                  *
; *                                                              *
; *    THIS WILL INSTALL COMMSCOP AND SET UP A 64K BUFFER TO BE USED *
; *    FOR DATA LOGGING.  REMEMBER THAT 2 BYTES ARE REQUIRED FOR *
; *    EACH COMM BYTE, SO THE BUFFER IS ONLY 32K EVENTS LONG, OR ABOUT *
; *    30 SECONDS OF CONTINUOUS 9600 BAUD DATA.  IN THE REAL WORLD, *
; *    ASYNC DATA IS RARELY CONTINUOUS, SO THE BUFFER WILL PROBABLY *
; *    HOLD MORE THAN 30 SECONDS WORTH OF DATA.                 *
; *                                                              *
; *    WHEN INSTALLED, COMMSCOP INTERCEPTS ALL INT 14H CALLS.  IF THE *
; *    PROGRAM HAS BEEN ACTIVATED AND THE INT IS EITHER SEND OR RE- *
; *    CEIVE DATA, A COPY OF THE DATA BYTE, PROPERLY TAGGED, IS PLACED *
; *    IN THE BUFFER.  IN ANY CASE, DATA IS PASSED ON TO THE REAL *
; *    INT 14H HANDLER.                                          *
; *                                                              *
; *    COMMSCOP IS INVOKED BY ISSUING AN INT 60H CALL.  THE INT HAS *
; *    THE FOLLOWING CALLING SEQUENCE:                           *
; *                                                              *
; *        AH -- COMMAND                                         *
; *              0 -- STOP TRACING, PLACE STOP MARK IN BUFFER    *
; *              1 -- FLUSH BUFFER AND START TRACE               *
; *              2 -- RESUME TRACE                               *
; *              3 -- RETURN COMM BUFFER ADDRESSES              *
; *        DX -- COMM PORT (ONLY USED WITH AH = 1 or 2)          *
; *              0 -- COM1                                       *
; *              1 -- COM2                                       *
```

Figure 18-4. Communications trace utility.   *(more)*

```
; *                                                                    *
; *      THE FOLLOWING DATA IS RETURNED IN RESPONSE TO AH = 3:          *
; *                                                                    *
; *              CX -- BUFFER COUNT IN BYTES                           *
; *              DX -- SEGMENT ADDRESS OF THE START OF THE BUFFER      *
; *              BX -- OFFSET ADDRESS OF THE START OF THE BUFFER       *
; *                                                                    *
; *      THE COMM BUFFER IS FILLED WITH 2-BYTE DATA ENTRIES OF THE     *
; *      FOLLOWING FORM:                                               *
; *                                                                    *
; *              BYTE 0 -- CONTROL                                     *
; *                  BIT 0 -- ON FOR RECEIVED DATA, OFF FOR TRANS.     *
; *                  BIT 7 -- STOP MARK -- INDICATES COLLECTION WAS    *
; *                          INTERRUPTED AND RESUMED.                  *
; *              BYTE 1 -- 8-BIT DATA                                  *
; *                                                                    *
; **********************************************************************


CSEG    SEGMENT
        ASSUME  CS:CSEG,DS:CSEG
        ORG     100H                    ;TO MAKE A COMM FILE

INITIALIZE:
        JMP     VECTOR_INIT             ;JUMP TO THE INITIALIZATION
                                        ; ROUTINE WHICH, TO SAVE SPACE,
                                        ; IS IN THE COMM BUFFER


;
;   SYSTEM VARIABLES
;
OLD_COMM_INT    DD      ?               ;ADDRESS OF REAL COMM INT
COUNT           DW      0               ;BUFFER COUNT
COMMSCOPE_INT   EQU     60H             ;COMMSCOPE CONTROL INT
STATUS          DB      0               ;PROCESSING STATUS
                                        ; 0 -- OFF
                                        ; 1 -- ON
PORT            DB      0               ;COMM PORT BEING TRACED
BUFPNTR         DW      VECTOR_INIT     ;NEXT BUFFER LOCATION

        SUBTTL  DATA INTERRUPT HANDLER
PAGE
; **********************************************************************
; *                                                                    *
; *  COMMSCOPE                                                         *
; *      THIS PROCEDURE INTERCEPTS ALL INT 14H CALLS AND LOGS THE DATA *
; *      IF APPROPRIATE.                                               *
; *                                                                    *
; **********************************************************************
COMMSCOPE       PROC    NEAR

        TEST    CS:STATUS,1             ;ARE WE ON?
        JZ      OLD_JUMP                ; NO, SIMPLY JUMP TO OLD HANDLER
```

Figure 18-4. Continued. *(more)*

```
        CMP     AH,00H              ;SKIP SETUP CALLS
        JE      OLD_JUMP            ; .

        CMP     AH,03H              ;SKIP STATUS REQUESTS
        JAE     OLD_JUMP            ; .

        CMP     AH,02H              ;IS THIS A READ REQUEST?
        JE      GET_READ            ; YES, GO PROCESS

;
;   DATA WRITE REQUEST -- SAVE IF APPROPRIATE
;
        CMP     DL,CS:PORT          ;IS WRITE FOR PORT BEING TRACED?
        JNE     OLD_JUMP            ; NO, JUST PASS IT THROUGH

        PUSH    DS                  ;SAVE CALLER'S REGISTERS
        PUSH    BX                  ; .
        PUSH    CS                  ;SET UP DS FOR OUR PROGRAM
        POP     DS                  ; .
        MOV     BX,BUFPNTR          ;GET ADDR OF NEXT BUFFER LOC
        MOV     [BX],BYTE PTR 0     ;MARK AS TRANSMITTED BYTE
        MOV     [BX+1],AL           ;SAVE DATA IN BUFFER
        INC     COUNT               ;INCREMENT BUFFER BYTE COUNT
        INC     COUNT               ; .
        INC     BX                  ;POINT TO NEXT LOCATION
        INC     BX                  ; .
        MOV     BUFPNTR,BX          ;SAVE NEW POINTER
        JNZ     WRITE_DONE          ;ZERO MEANS BUFFER HAS WRAPPED

        MOV     STATUS,0            ;TURN COLLECTION OFF
WRITE_DONE:
        POP     BX                  ;RESTORE CALLER'S REGISTERS
        POP     DS                  ; .
        JMP     OLD_JUMP            ;PASS REQUEST ON TO BIOS ROUTINE
;
;   PROCESS A READ DATA REQUEST AND WRITE TO BUFFER IF APPROPRIATE
;
GET_READ:
        CMP     DL,CS:PORT          ;IS READ FOR PORT BEING TRACED?
        JNE     OLD_JUMP            ; NO, JUST PASS IT THROUGH

        PUSH    DS                  ;SAVE CALLER'S REGISTERS
        PUSH    BX                  ; .
        PUSH    CS                  ;SET UP DS FOR OUR PROGRAM
        POP     DS                  ; .

        PUSHF                       ;FAKE INT 14H CALL
        CLI                         ; .
        CALL    OLD_COMM_INT        ;PASS REQUEST ON TO BIOS
        TEST    AH,80H              ;VALID READ?
        JNZ     READ_DONE           ; NO, SKIP BUFFER UPDATE
```

Figure 18-4. Continued.   *(more)*

```
        MOV     BX,BUFPNTR              ;GET ADDR OF NEXT BUFFER LOC
        MOV     [BX],BYTE PTR 1         ;MARK AS RECEIVED BYTE
        MOV     [BX+1],AL               ;SAVE DATA IN BUFFER
        INC     COUNT                   ;INCREMENT BUFFER BYTE COUNT
        INC     COUNT                   ; .
        INC     BX                      ;POINT TO NEXT LOCATION
        INC     BX                      ; .
        MOV     BUFPNTR,BX              ;SAVE NEW POINTER
        JNZ     READ_DONE               ;ZERO MEANS BUFFER HAS WRAPPED

        MOV     STATUS,0                ;TURN COLLECTION OFF
READ_DONE:
        POP     BX                      ;RESTORE CALLER'S REGISTERS
        POP     DS                      ; .
        IRET


;
;  JUMP TO COMM BIOS ROUTINE
;
OLD_JUMP:
        JMP     CS:OLD_COMM_INT

COMMSCOPE ENDP

        SUBTTL  CONTROL INTERRUPT HANDLER
PAGE
; ****************************************************************
; *                                                              *
; *  CONTROL                                                     *
; *     THIS ROUTINE PROCESSES CONTROL REQUESTS.                 *
; *                                                              *
; ****************************************************************

CONTROL PROC    NEAR
        CMP     AH,00H                  ;STOP REQUEST?
        JNE     CNTL_START              ; NO, CHECK START
        PUSH    DS                      ;SAVE REGISTERS
        PUSH    BX                      ; .
        PUSH    CS                      ;SET DS FOR OUR ROUTINE
        POP     DS
        MOV     STATUS,0                ;TURN PROCESSING OFF
        MOV     BX,BUFPNTR              ;PLACE STOP MARK IN BUFFER
        MOV     [BX],BYTE PTR 80H       ; .
        MOV     [BX+1],BYTE PTR 0FFH    ; .
        INC     BX                      ;INCREMENT BUFFER POINTER
        INC     BX                      ; .
        MOV     BUFPNTR,BX              ; .
        INC     COUNT                   ;INCREMENT COUNT
        INC     COUNT                   ; .
        POP     BX                      ;RESTORE REGISTERS
        POP     DS                      ; .
        JMP     CONTROL_DONE
```

Figure 18-4. Continued.   *(more)*

```
CNTL_START:
        CMP     AH,01H                  ;START REQUEST?
        JNE     CNTL_RESUME             ; NO, CHECK RESUME
        MOV     CS:PORT,DL              ;SAVE PORT TO TRACE
        MOV     CS:BUFPNTR,OFFSET VECTOR_INIT ;RESET BUFFER TO START
        MOV     CS:COUNT,0              ;ZERO COUNT
        MOV     CS:STATUS,1             ;START LOGGING
        JMP     CONTROL_DONE

CNTL_RESUME:
        CMP     AH,02H                  ;RESUME REQUEST?
        JNE     CNTL_STATUS             ; NO, CHECK STATUS
        CMP     CS:BUFPNTR,0            ;END OF BUFFER CONDITION?
        JE      CONTROL_DONE            ; YES, DO NOTHING
        MOV     CS:PORT,DL              ;SAVE PORT TO TRACE
        MOV     CS:STATUS,1             ;START LOGGING
        JMP     CONTROL_DONE

CNTL_STATUS:
        CMP     AH,03H                  ;RETURN STATUS REQUEST?
        JNE     CONTROL_DONE            ; NO, ERROR -- DO NOTHING
        MOV     CX,CS:COUNT             ;RETURN COUNT
        PUSH    CS                      ;RETURN SEGMENT ADDR OF BUFFER
        POP     DX                      ; .
        MOV     BX,OFFSET VECTOR_INIT   ;RETURN OFFSET ADDR OF BUFFER

CONTROL_DONE:
        IRET

CONTROL ENDP


        SUBTTL     INITIALIZE INTERRUPT VECTORS
PAGE
; ***********************************************************************
; *                                                                     *
; *  VECTOR_INIT                                                        *
; *     THIS PROCEDURE INITIALIZES THE INTERRUPT VECTORS AND THEN       *
; *     EXITS VIA THE MS-DOS TERMINATE-AND-STAY-RESIDENT FUNCTION.      *
; *     A BUFFER OF 64K IS RETAINED.  THE FIRST AVAILABLE BYTE          *
; *     IN THE BUFFER IS THE OFFSET OF VECTOR_INIT.                     *
; *                                                                     *
; ***********************************************************************

        EVEN                            ;ASSURE BUFFER ON EVEN BOUNDARY
VECTOR_INIT     PROC    NEAR
;
;  GET ADDRESS OF COMM VECTOR (INT 14H)
;
        MOV     AH,35H
```

Figure 18-4. Continued.   *(more)*

```
            MOV     AL,14H
            INT     21H
;
;   SAVE OLD COMM INT ADDRESS
;
            MOV     WORD PTR OLD_COMM_INT,BX
            MOV     AX,ES
            MOV     WORD PTR OLD_COMM_INT[2],AX
;
;   SET UP COMM INT TO POINT TO OUR ROUTINE
;
            MOV     DX,OFFSET COMMSCOPE
            MOV     AH,25H
            MOV     AL,14H
            INT     21H
;
;   INSTALL CONTROL ROUTINE INT
;
            MOV     DX,OFFSET CONTROL
            MOV     AH,25H
            MOV     AL,COMMSCOPE_INT
            INT     21H
;
;   SET LENGTH TO 64K, EXIT AND STAY RESIDENT
;
            MOV     AX,3100H            ;TERM AND STAY RES COMMAND
            MOV     DX,1000H.           ;64K RESERVED
            INT     21H                 ;DONE
VECTOR_INIT ENDP
CSEG    ENDS
            END     INITIALIZE
```

Figure 18-4. Continued.

The first executable statement of the program is a jump to the *VECTOR_INIT* procedure. The vector initialization code is needed only during installation; after initialization of the vectors, the code can be discarded. In this case, the area where this code resides will become the start of the trace buffer; therefore, it makes sense to put the initialization code at the end of the program where it can be overlaid by the trace buffer. The jump at the start of the program is required because the rules for making .COM files require that the entry point be the first instruction of the program.

The vector initialization routine uses Interrupt 21H Function 35H (Get Interrupt Vector) to get the address of the current Interrupt 14H service routine. The segment and offset address (returned in the ES:BX registers) is stored in the doubleword at *OLD_COMM_INT.* Interrupt 21H Function 25H (Set Interrupt Vector) is then used to vector all Interrupt 14H calls to *COMMSCOPE.* Another Function 25H call sets Interrupt 60H to vector to the *CONTROL* routine. This interrupt, which provides the means to control and interrogate the *COMMSCOPE* routine, was chosen because it is unused by MS-DOS and because some IBM technical materials list 60H through 66H as being available for user interrupts. (If, for some reason, Interrupt 60H is not available, simply change the equated symbol *COMMSCOPE_INT* to an available interrupt.)

When the vector initialization process is complete, the routine exits and stays resident by using Interrupt 21H Function 31H (Terminate and Stay Resident). As part of the termination process, the routine requests 1000H paragraphs, or 64 KB, of storage. A little over 500 bytes of this storage area is used for the code; the rest is available for trace data. If the serial port is running at 2400 baud, a solid stream of data will fill this buffer in about two minutes. However, a solid 32 KB block of data is unusual in asynchronous communications and, in reality, the buffer will usually contain many minutes worth of data. Note that the buffer-handling routines in *COMMSCOPE* require that the buffer be aligned on an even byte boundary, so *VECTOR_INIT* is preceded by the EVEN directive.

The interrupt service routine, *COMMSCOPE*, receives all Interrupt 14H calls. First *COMMSCOPE* checks its own status. If it has not been activated, it immediately passes control to the real service routine. If the tracer is active, *COMMSCOPE* examines the Interrupt 14H function in AH. Setup and status requests (AH = 0 and AH = 3) do not affect tracing, so they are passed on directly to the the real service routine. If the Interrupt 14H call is a write-data request (AH = 1), *COMMSCOPE* moves the byte marking the data as transmitted and the data byte itself to the current buffer location and increments both the byte count and the buffer pointer by 2. If the buffer pointer goes to zero, the buffer has wrapped; data collection is turned off and cannot be turned on again without clearing the trace buffer. Because the buffer, which starts at *VECTOR_INIT*, is always on an even byte boundary, there is no danger of the first byte of the data pair forcing a wrap. After the transmitted data is added to the buffer, *COMMSCOPE* passes control to the real service routine.

A read-data request (AH = 2) must be handled a little differently. In this case, the data to be collected is not yet available. In order to get it, *COMMSCOPE* must pass control to the real service routine and then intercept the results on the way back. The code at *GET_READ* fakes an interrupt to the service routine by pushing the flags onto the stack so that the service routine's IRET will pop them off again. *COMMSCOPE* then calls the service routine and, when it returns, retrieves the incoming serial data character from AL. If the incoming data byte is valid (bit 7 of AH is zero), the byte marking the data as received and the data byte itself are placed in the trace buffer, and both the byte count and the buffer pointer are incremented by 2. The buffer-wrap condition is detected and handled in the same manner as with transmitted data. Because the real service routine has already been called, *COMMSCOPE* exits as if it were the service routine by issuing an IRET.

The *CONTROL* procedure provides the mechanism for external control of the trace procedure. The routine is entered whenever an Interrupt 60H is executed. Commands are sent through the AH register and can cause the routine to STOP (AH = 0), START/FLUSH (AH = 1), RESUME (AH = 2), or RETURN STATUS (AH = 3). This routine also sets the communications port to be traced. The required information is provided in DX using the same format as the Interrupt 14H routine. The port information is used only with START and RESUME requests. The RETURN STATUS command returns data in registers: the byte count (CX), the segment address of the buffer (DX), and the offset of the first byte in the buffer (BX).

The COMMSCOP program is assembled using the Microsoft Macro Assembler (MASM), linked using the Microsoft Object Linker (LINK), and then converted to a .COM file using EXE2BIN (*see* PROGRAMMING UTILITIES):

```
C>MASM COMMSCOP;   <Enter>
C>LINK COMMSCOP;   <Enter>
C>EXE2BIN COMMSCOP.EXE COMMSCOP.COM  <Enter>
C>DEL COMMSCOP.EXE  <Enter>
```

The linker will display the message *Warning: no stack segment*; this message can be ignored because the rules for making a .COM file forbid a separate stack segment.

The program is installed by simply typing *COMMSCOP*. Tracing can then be started and stopped using Interrupt 60H. MS-DOS does not allow resident routines to be removed, so COMMSCOP will be in the system until the system is restarted. Also note that, because COMMSCOP is well behaved, nothing disastrous will happen if multiple copies of it are accidentally installed. As each new copy is installed, it chains to the previous copy. When Interrupt 14H is intercepted, the new routine dutifully passes the data on to the previous routine, which repeats the process until the real service routine is reached. The data is added to the trace buffer of each copy, giving multiple, redundant copies of the same data. Because Interrupt 60H is not chained, only the last copy's buffer can be accessed. Thus, the other copies simply waste 64 KB each.

Two techniques can be used to start or stop a trace. The first is to issue Interrupt 60H calls at strategic locations within the program being debugged. With assembly-language programs, this is easy. The appropriate registers are loaded and an INT 60H instruction is executed. Issuing this INT instruction is not much more difficult with higher-order Microsoft languages — both QuickBASIC and C provide a library routine called INT86 that allows registers to be loaded and INT instructions to be executed. (In QuickBASIC, the INT86 library routine is included in the File USERLIB.OBJ; in Microsoft C, it is included in the file DOS.H.) Embedded Interrupt 60H calls can be convenient because they limit tracing to those areas where processing is suspect. Because COMMSCOP marks the buffer each time the trace is stopped and resumed, the separate pieces of a trace are easy to differentiate.

The second technique is to write a simple routine to start or stop the trace outside the program being debugged. The example in Figure 18-5, COMMSCMD, is a Microsoft C program that can perform these functions using the INT86 library function to issue Interrupt 60H calls.

```
/***********************************************************************
*                                                                     *
*   COMMSCMD                                                          *
*                                                                     *
*   This routine controls the COMMSCOP program that has been in-      *
*   stalled as a resident routine.  The operation performed is de-    *
*   termined by the command line.  The COMMSCMD program is invoked    *
*   as follows:                                                       *
*                                                                     *
*                COMMSCMD [[cmd][ port]]                              *
*                                                                     *
```

Figure 18-5. A serial-trace control routine written in C. (*more*)

```
*    where cmd is the command to be executed                            *
*           STOP    -- stop trace                                        *
*           START   -- flush trace buffer and start trace                *
*           RESUME -- resume a stopped trace                             *
*         port is the COMM port to be traced (1=COM1, 2=COM2, etc.)      *
*                                                                        *
*   If cmd is omitted, STOP is assumed.  If port is omitted, 1 is        *
*   assumed.                                                             *
*                                                                        *
*************************************************************************/

#include <stdlib.h>
#include <stdio.h>
#include <dos.h>
#define COMMCMD 0x60

main(argc, argv)
int argc;
char *argv[];
{
    int cmd, port, result;
    static char commands[3] [10] = {"STOPPED", "STARTED", "RESUMED"};
    union REGS inregs, outregs;

    cmd = 0;
    port = 0;

    if (argc > 1)
        {
        if (0 == stricmp(argv[1], "STOP"))
            cmd = 0;
        else if (0 == stricmp(argv[1], "START"))
            cmd = 1;
        else if (0 == stricmp(argv[1], "RESUME"))
            cmd = 2;
        }

    if (argc == 3)
        {
        port = atoi(argv[2]);
        if (port > 0)
            port = port - 1;
        }

    inregs.h.ah = cmd;
    inregs.x.dx = port;
    result = int86(COMMCMD, &inregs, &outregs);


    printf("\nCommunications tracing %s for port COM%1d:\n",
            commands[cmd], port + 1);
}
```

Figure 18-5. Continued.

COMMSCMD is passed arguments in the command line. The first argument is the command to be performed: STOP, START, or RESUME. If no command is specified, STOP is assumed. The second argument is the port number: 1 (for COM1) or 2 (for COM2). If no port number is specified, 1 is assumed.

The COMMSCMD program uses a simple IF filter to determine the function to be performed. The program tests the number of arguments in the command line to see if a port has been specified. If the argument count (*argc*) is 3 (one for the command name, one for the command, and one for the port number), the port number argument is retrieved and converted to an integer. The Interrupt 60H routine expects port numbers to be specified in the same manner as for Interrupt 14H, so the port number is decremented if it is not already zero. The AH register is loaded with the command (*cmd*), the DX register is loaded with the port number (*port*), and the INT86 library function is then used to execute an Interrupt 60H call. When the interrupt returns, COMMSCMD displays a message showing the function and port.

The same function can be performed by the QuickBASIC program in Figure 18-6.

```
'   **********************************************************************
'   *                                                                    *
'   *   COMMSCMD                                                          *
'   *                                                                    *
'   *   This routine controls the COMMSCOP program that has been in-      *
'   *   stalled as a resident routine.  The operation performed is de-    *
'   *   termined by the command line.  The COMMSCMD program is invoked    *
'   *   as follows:                                                       *
'   *                                                                    *
'   *            COMMSCMD [[cmd][,port]]                                  *
'   *                                                                    *
'   *   where cmd is the command to be executed                          *
'   *            STOP   -- stop trace                                     *
'   *            START  -- flush trace buffer and start trace            *
'   *            RESUME -- resume a stopped trace                         *
'   *        port is the COMM port to be traced (1=COM1, 2=COM2, etc.)   *
'   *                                                                    *
'   *   If cmd is omitted, STOP is assumed.  If port is omitted, 1 is     *
'   *   assumed.                                                          *
'   *                                                                    *
'   **********************************************************************

        '
        ' Establish system constants and variables
        '
        DEFINT A-Z

        DIM INREG(7), OUTREG(7)         'Define register arrays
```

Figure 18-6. A QuickBASIC version of COMMSCMD.   (*more*)

```
        RAX = 0                         'Establish values for 8086
        RBX = 1                         '  registers
        RCX = 2                         '  .
        RDX = 3                         '  .
        RBP = 4                         '  .
        RSI = 5                         '  .
        RDI = 6                         '  .
        RFL = 7                         '  .

        DIM TEXT$(2)

        TEXT$(0) = "STOPPED"
        TEXT$(1) = "STARTED"
        TEXT$(2) = "RESUMED"


        '
        '  Process command-line tail
        '
        C$ = COMMAND$                   'Get command-line data

        IF LEN(C$) = 0 THEN             'If no command line specified
            CMD = 0                     'Set CMD to STOP
            PORT = 0                    'Set PORT to COM1
            GOTO SENDCMD
        END IF

        COMMA = INSTR(C$, ", ")         'Extract operands
        IF COMMA = 0 THEN
            CMDTXT$ = C$
            PORT = 0
        ELSE
            CMDTXT$ = LEFT$(C$, COMMA - 1)
            PORT = VAL(MID$(C$, COMMA + 1)) - 1
        END IF

        IF PORT < 0 THEN PORT = 0

        IF CMDTXT$ = "STOP" THEN
            CMD = 0
        ELSEIF CMDTXT$ = "START" THEN
            CMD = 1
        ELSEIF CMDTXT$ = "RESUME" THEN
            CMD = 2
        ELSE
            CMD = 0
        END IF


        '
        '  Send command to COMMSCOP routine
        '
SENDCMD:
        INREG(RAX) = 256 * CMD
```

Figure 18-6. Continued.   *(more)*

```
INREG(RDX) = PORT
CALL INT86(&H60, VARPTR(INREG(0)), VARPTR(OUTREG(0)))
'
'   Notify user that action is complete
'
PRINT : PRINT
PRINT "Communications tracing "; TEXT$(CMD);
IF CMD <> 0 THEN
    PRINT " for port COM"; MID$(STR$(PORT + 1), 2); ":"
ELSE
    PRINT
END IF

END
```

Figure 18-6. Continued.

Both versions of COMMSCMD accept their commands from the command tail; both are invoked with a STOP, START, or RESUME command and a serial port number (1 or 2). If the operands are omitted, STOP and COM1 are assumed.

After data has been collected and safely placed in the trace buffer, it must be read before it can be useful. Interrupt 60H provides a function (AH = 3) that returns the buffer address and the number of bytes in the buffer. The QuickBASIC routine in Figure 18-7 uses this function to get the address of the data and then formats the data on the screen.

```
' ***********************************************************************
' *                                                                     *
' *   COMMDUMP                                                          *
' *                                                                     *
' *   This routine dumps the contents of the COMMSCOP trace buffer to   *
' *   the screen in a formatted manner.  Received data is shown in      *
' *   reverse video.  Where possible, the ASCII character for the byte  *
' *   is shown; otherwise a dot is shown.  The value of the byte is     *
' *   displayed in hex below the character.  Points where tracing was   *
' *   stopped are shown by a solid bar.                                 *
' *                                                                     *
' ***********************************************************************

        '
        '   Establish system constants and variables
        '
        DEFINT A-Z

        DIM INREG(7), OUTREG(7)          'Define register arrays

        RAX = 0                          'Establish values for 8086
        RBX = 1                          ' registers
        RCX = 2                          '   .
        RDX = 3                          '   .
```

Figure 18-7. Formatted dump routine for serial-trace buffer.   *(more)*

```
RBP = 4                         '  .
RSI = 5                         '  .
RDI = 6                         '  .
RFL = 7                         '  .

'
'   Interrogate COMMSCOP to obtain addresses and count of data in
'   trace buffer
'
INREG(RAX) = &H0300             'Request address data and count
CALL INT86(&H60, VARPTR(INREG(0)), VARPTR(OUTREG(0)))

NUM = OUTREG(RCX)               'Number of bytes in buffer
BUFSEG = OUTREG(RDX)            'Buffer segment address
BUFOFF = OUTREG(RBX)            'Offset of buffer start

IF NUM = 0 THEN END

'
'   Set screen up and display control data
'
CLS
KEY OFF
LOCATE 25, 1
PRINT "NUM ="; NUM;"BUFSEG = "; HEX$(BUFSEG); " BUFOFF = ";
PRINT HEX$(BUFOFF);
LOCATE 4, 1
PRINT STRING$(80,"-")
DEF SEG = BUFSEG

'
'   Set up display control variables
'
DLINE = 1
DCOL = 1
DSHOWN = 0

'
'   Fetch and display each character in buffer
'
FOR I= BUFOFF TO BUFOFF+NUM-2 STEP 2
    STAT = PEEK(I)
    DAT = PEEK(I + 1)

    IF (STAT AND 1) = 0 THEN
        COLOR 7, 0
    ELSE
        COLOR 0, 7
    END IF

    RLINE = (DLINE-1) * 4 + 1
```

Figure 18-7. Continued.   *(more)*

```
IF (STAT AND &H80) = 0 THEN
    LOCATE RLINE, DCOL
    C$ = CHR$(DAT)
    IF DAT < 32 THEN C$ = "."
    PRINT C$;
    H$ = RIGHT$("00" + HEX$(DAT), 2)
    LOCATE RLINE + 1, DCOL
    PRINT LEFT$(H$, 1);
    LOCATE RLINE + 2, DCOL
    PRINT RIGHT$(H$, 1);
ELSE
    LOCATE RLINE, DCOL
    PRINT CHR$(178);
    LOCATE RLINE + 1, DCOL
    PRINT CHR$(178);
    LOCATE RLINE + 2, DCOL
    PRINT CHR$(178);
END IF

DCOL = DCOL + 1
IF DCOL > 80 THEN
    COLOR 7, 0
    DCOL = 1
    DLINE = DLINE + 1
    SHOWN = SHOWN + 1
    IF SHOWN = 6 THEN
        LOCATE 25, 50
        COLOR 0, 7
        PRINT "ENTER ANY KEY TO CONTINUE:   ";
        WHILE LEN(INKEY$) = 0
        WEND
        COLOR 7, 0
        LOCATE 25, 50
        PRINT SPACE$(29);
        SHOWN = 0
    END IF
    IF DLINE > 6 THEN
        LOCATE 24, 1
        PRINT : PRINT : PRINT : PRINT
        LOCATE 24, 1
        PRINT STRING$(80, "-");
        DLINE = 6
    ELSE
        LOCATE DLINE * 4, 1
        PRINT STRING$(80, "-");
    END IF
END IF

NEXT I

END
```

Figure 18-7. Continued.

COMMDUMP is a simple routine. Like most debugging aids, it lacks needless frills. When it is executed, COMMDUMP displays the data in the trace buffer on the screen in the format shown in Figure 18-8.

```
.012832.13205678000100671320567800010067132056780001006713205678000100671320567 80001006713205678
0333333303333333333333333333333333333333333333333333333333333333333333333333333333333333333333333
10128323213205678000100671320567800010067132056780001006713205678000100671320567 8
 
00010067132056780001006713205678000100671320567800010067.#.█.012832.567813200001
33333333333333333333333333333333333333333333333333333302100333333330333333333333
000100671320567800010067132056780001006713205678000100673386101283235678132000 01
 
006756781320000100675678132000010067567813200001006756781320000100675678132000 01
3333333333333333333333333333333333333333333333333333333333333333333333333333333 3
006756781320000100675678132000010067567813200001006756781320000100675678132000 01
 
006756781320000100675678132000010067.#.█.012832.0067132056780001006713205678000 1
33333333333333333333333333333333330210033333330333333333333333333333333333333333 3
006756781320000100675678132000010067338610128323006713205678000100671320567800 01
 
006713205678000100671320567800010067132056780001006713205678000100671320567800 01
3333333333333333333333333333333333333333333333333333333333333333333333333333333 3
006713205678000100671320567800010067132056780001006713205678000100671320567800 01
 
0067132056780001.#.█.012832.13205678000100671320567800010067132056780001006713 20
3333333333333333021003333333033333333333333333333333333333333333333333333333333 3
0067132056780001338610128323132056780001006713205678000100671320567800010067132 0
```

`NUM = 1122 BUFSEG = 1313 BUFOFF = 208           ENTER ANY KEY TO CONTINUE:`

Figure 18-8. Formatted trace dump routine output.

Note that the data for each byte is presented in two forms. If the byte is greater than 1FH, the ASCII character represented by that number is shown; otherwise, a dot is shown. Directly below each character is the hexadecimal representation of the data. The display shows received data in reverse video and transmitted data in normal video. The mark placed in the buffer when collection is stopped and resumed is represented on the screen as a vertical bar one character wide. The display pauses when the screen is full and waits for a key to be pressed.

Data collected and displayed in this way can be invaluable to the programmer trying to debug a program involving a communications protocol. The example shown above is part of an ordered exchange of sales data for a system using blocked transmissions and ACK/NAK protocol. Like all debugging, finding bugs in such a system requires the collection of large amounts of data. With no data, the causes of problems can be almost impossible to find; with sufficiently large amounts of data, the solutions are obvious.

Several things could be done to the COMMSCOP program to increase its usefulness. For instance, there are six unused bits in the tag accompanying each data byte in the trace buffer. These could be used to record the status of the modem control bits, to place timer ticks in the buffer, or to coordinate the data with some outside event. (Such changes to COMMSCOP would require a more complicated COMMDUMP routine to display them.)

Software debugging monitors

Debugging monitors provide the next level of sophistication in the hierarchy of debugging methods. These monitors are coresident in memory with the application being debugged and provide a controlled testing environment — that is, they allow the programmer to control the execution of the program and to monitor the results. They even allow some problems to be fixed directly and the result reexecuted immediately, without the need to reassemble or recompile.

These monitors are analogous to the TSR serial monitor from the previous section. The debugging monitors, however, do not reside permanently in memory and are controlled interactively from the keyboard during the execution of the program under test. Although this level of control is more flexible than instrumentation, it is also more intrusive into program execution. While the debugging monitor sits and waits for input from the keyboard, the application program is also idle. For programs that must run in real time or must respond to external stimuli, long delays can be fatal. Careful planning and a thorough knowledge of the internal workings of the program are required to debug in such an environment.

Other problems with debugging monitors arise from the nature of the monitors themselves. They are programs, no different from the application program being debugged and are therefore limited to those things that can be done with software. For instance, they can break (stop execution to allow investigation of program status) when a specific instruction address is executed (because this can be done with software), but they cannot break when a data address is referenced (because this would require special hardware). Because these monitors reside in RAM, as do the application program and MS-DOS, they are susceptible to damage from a program running wild. Some trial and error is usually involved in locating the problem causing this kind of damage; breakpoints won't work here because the problem kills the monitor (and usually MS-DOS also).

Microsoft provides three debugging monitors, each with greater capabilities than its predecessor. In order of increasing sophistication, these three monitors are

Monitor	Description
DEBUG	A basic debugging monitor with the ability to load files, modify memory and registers, execute programs, set simple breakpoints, trace execution, modify disk files, and enter assembly-language statements into memory.
SYMDEB	A more advanced debugging monitor incorporating all the features of DEBUG plus more sophisticated data display, support for graphics programs, support for the Intel 80186/80286 microprocessors and the Intel 80287 math coprocessor, improved breakpoints, improved tracing, recognition of symbols from the program being debugged, and limited source-line display.
CodeView	The most sophisticated debugging monitor, incorporating the functionality of SYMDEB (with some differences in the details) plus windows, full source-line support, mouse support, and generally more sophistication on all functions.

Although all these debugging monitors will be discussed here, this section is not intended to be a tutorial on all the commands and options of the monitors — those are presented elsewhere in this volume and in the manuals accompanying the monitors. *See* PROGRAMMING UTILITIES: DEBUG; SYMDEB; CODEVIEW. Rather, this section uses case histories and sample programs to illustrate the techniques for solving various types of common debugging problems. The case histories have been chosen to show a wide range of problems, from simple to extremely complex.

DEBUG

Although DEBUG is the least sophisticated of the software debugging monitors, it is quite useful with moderately complex programs and is an effective tool for learning basic techniques.

Basic techniques

The first sample program is written in assembly language. It is a test program that performs serial input and output and was used to debug COMMSCOP, the serial-trace TSR presented earlier. The routine reads from the keyboard and writes to COM1 by means of Interrupt 14H. It also accepts incoming serial data and displays it on the screen. This process continues until Ctrl-C is pressed on the keyboard. A serial terminal is attached to COM1 to serve as a data source. Figure 18-9 shows the erroneous program.

```
              TITLE TESTCOMM — TEST COMMSCOP ROUTINE
; **********************************************************************
; *                                                                  *
; *   TESTCOMM                                                       *
; *      THIS ROUTINE PROVIDES DATA FOR THE COMMSCOP ROUTINE.  IT READS *
; *      CHARACTERS FROM THE KEYBOARD AND WRITES THEM TO COM1 USING   *
; *      INT 14H.  DATA IS ALSO READ FROM INT 14H AND DISPLAYED ON THE *
; *      SCREEN.  THE ROUTINE RETURNS TO MS-DOS WHEN Ctrl-C IS PRESSED *
; *      ON THE KEYBOARD.                                            *
; *                                                                  *
; **********************************************************************

SSEG     SEGMENT PARA STACK 'STACK'
         DW      128 DUP(?)
SSEG     ENDS

CSEG     SEGMENT
         ASSUME  CS:CSEG,SS:SSEG
BEGIN    PROC    FAR
         PUSH    DS                      ;SET UP FOR RET TO MS-DOS
         XOR     AX,AX                   ; .
         PUSH    AX                      ; .
```

Figure 18-9. Incorrect serial test routine.   *(more)*

```
MAINLOOP:
        MOV     AH,6              ;USE MS-DOS CALL TO CHECK FOR
        MOV     DL,0FFH           ; KEYBOARD ACTIVITY
        INT     21                ; IF NO CHARACTER, JUMP TO
        JZ      TESTCOMM          ; COMM ACTIVITY TEST

        CMP     AL,03             ;WAS CHARACTER A Ctrl-C?
        JNE     SENDCOMM          ; NO, SEND IT TO SERIAL PORT
        RET                       ; YES, RETURN TO MS-DOS

SENDCOMM:
        MOV     AH,01             ;USE INT 14H WRITE FUNCTION TO
        MOV     DX,0              ; SEND DATA TO SERIAL PORT
        INT     14H               ; .

TESTCOMM:
        MOV     AH,3              ;GET SERIAL PORT STATUS
        MOV     DX,0              ; .
        INT     14H               ; .
        AND     AH,1              ;ANY DATA WAITING?
        JZ      MAINLOOP          ; NO, GO BACK TO KEYBOARD TEST
        MOV     AH,2              ;READ SERIAL DATA
        MOV     DX,0              ; .
        INT     14H               ; .
        MOV     AH,6              ;WRITE SERIAL DATA TO SCREEN
        INT     21H               ; .
        JMP     MAINLOOP          ;CONTINUE
BEGIN   ENDP
CSEG    ENDS
        END     BEGIN
```

Figure 18-9. Continued.

When executed, this program produces a constant stream of zeros from the serial port. Incoming serial data is not echoed on the screen, but the cursor moves as if it were. Further, the Ctrl-C keystroke is not recognized, so the only way to stop the program is to restart the system.

An examination of the listing should reveal the errors that cause these problems, but things do not always happen that way. For the purposes of this case study, assume that the listing was no help. Instrumentation is more difficult for assembly-language programs than for programs written in higher-order languages, so in this case it is advantageous to go directly to a debugging monitor. The monitor for this example is DEBUG.

The first step in using DEBUG is not to invoke the monitor; rather, it is to gather all pertinent listings, link maps, and program design documentation. In this case, the program is so short that a link map will not be needed; all the design documentation that exists is in the program comments.

Now begin DEBUG by typing

```
C>DEBUG TESTCOMM.EXE   <Enter>
```

The filename must be fully qualified; DEBUG makes no assumptions about the extension. Any type of file can be examined with DEBUG, but only files with an extension of .COM, .EXE, or .HEX are actually loaded and made ready for execution. Since TESTCOMM is a .EXE file, DEBUG loads it and prepares it for execution in a manner compatible with the MS-DOS loader. Type the Display or Modify Registers command, R.

```
-R  <Enter>
AX=0000  BX=0000  CX=0131  DX=0000  SP=0100  BP=0000  SI=0000  DI=0000
DS=1AAD  ES=1AAD  SS=1ABD  CS=1ACD  IP=0000     NV UP EI PL NZ NA PO NC
1ACD:0000 1E             PUSH  DS
```

Notice that the SS and CS registers have been loaded to their correct values and that SP points to the bottom of the stack. DS and ES point to an address 100H bytes (10H paragraphs) before the stack segment. (This is because the system sets these registers to point to the program segment prefix [PSP] when a .EXE program is loaded.) Normally, the program code would be responsible for loading the correct value of DS, but this example does not use the data segment, so the program doesn't bother. The register display also shows the instruction at the current value of CS:IP, 1ACD:0000H. The instruction pointer was set to this address because the END statement in the source program specified the procedure *BEGIN* as the entry point and that procedure begins at CS:IP. Note that the instruction displayed below the register information has not yet been executed. This condition is true for all register displays in DEBUG — IP always points to the *next* instruction to be executed, so the instruction at IP has not been executed.

From the symptoms observed during program execution, it is clear that the keyboard data is not reaching the serial port. The failure could be in the keyboard read routine or in the serial port write routine. This code is compact and fairly linear, so the easiest way to find out what is going on is to trace through the first few instructions of the program. Executing five instructions with the Trace Program Execution command, T, will do this.

```
-T5  <Enter>

AX=0000  BX=0000  CX=0131  DX=0000  SP=00FE  BP=0000  SI=0000  DI=0000
DS=1AAD  ES=1AAD  SS=1ABD  CS=1ACD  IP=0001     NV UP EI PL NZ NA PO NC
1ACD:0001 33C0           XOR   AX,AX

AX=0000  BX=0000  CX=0131  DX=0000  SP=00FE  BP=0000  SI=0000  DI=0000
DS=1AAD  ES=1AAD  SS=1ABD  CS=1ACD  IP=0003     NV UP EI PL ZR NA PE NC
1ACD:0003 50             PUSH  AX

AX=0000  BX=0000  CX=0131  DX=0000  SP=00FC  BP=0000  SI=0000  DI=0000
DS=1AAD  ES=1AAD  SS=1ABD  CS=1ACD  IP=0004     NV UP EI PL ZR NA PE NC
1ACD:0004 B406           MOV   AH,06

AX=0600  BX=0000  CX=0131  DX=0000  SP=00FC  BP=0000  SI=0000  DI=0000
DS=1AAD  ES=1AAD  SS=1ABD  CS=1ACD  IP=0006     NV UP EI PL ZR NA PE NC
1ACD:0006 B2FF           MOV   DL,FF

AX=0600  BX=0000  CX=0131  DX=00FF  SP=00FC  BP=0000  SI=0000  DI=0000
DS=1AAD  ES=1AAD  SS=1ABD  CS=1ACD  IP=0008     NV UP EI PL ZR NA PE NC
1ACD:0008 CD15           INT   15
```

The Trace command shows the contents of the registers as each instruction is executed. The register contents are *after* the execution of the instruction listed above the registers and the instruction shown with the registers is the *next* instruction to be executed. The first register display in this example represents the state of affairs after the execution of the PUSH DS instruction, as indicated by SP. The first three instructions set up the stack so that the far return issued at the end of the program will pass control to the PSP for termination. The next two instructions set the registers for a Direct Console I/O MS-DOS call (AH = 060, DL = HFFH for input). After these registers are set up, the program should execute the MS-DOS call INT 21H. However, the next instruction to be executed is INT 15H. This is the reason the keyboard data is not being read. The code requests INT 21, not 21H. This mistake is a common one. The assembler's default radix is decimal, so it converted 21 into 15H. This error can be corrected in memory from within DEBUG and, because the instruction hasn't executed yet, the fix can be tested immediately. To make the correction, use the Assemble Machine Instructions command, A.

```
-A 8  <Enter>
1ACD:0008 int 21  <Enter>
1ACD:000A  <Enter>
```

The *A 8* code instructs DEBUG to begin assembling at CS:0008H. DEBUG prompts with the address and waits for an instruction to be entered. The letter *H* is not needed after the 21 this time because DEBUG assumes all numbers entered with the Assemble command are in hexadecimal form. In general, any valid 8086/8087/8088 assembly-language statement can be entered this way and translated into executable machine code. *See* PROGRAMMING UTILITIES: DEBUG: A. Within its restrictions, the Assemble command is a handy way of making changes. The Enter Data command, E, could also have been used to change the 15H to a 21H, but the Assemble command is safer, especially for complex instructions. After the new instruction has been entered, press Enter again to stop the assembly process.

There is a danger associated with making changes in memory during debugging: The memory copy of the program is temporary; the changes exist only in memory and when DEBUG exits, they are lost. Changes made to .EXE and .HEX files cannot be written back to disk. To avoid forgetting the changes, write them down. When DEBUG exits, edit the source file *immediately*. Changes made to other files can be written back to disk with DEBUG's Write File or Sectors command, W.

To be sure that the change was made correctly, use the Disassemble (Unassemble) Program command, U, to show the instructions starting at CS:0004H.

```
-U 4  <Enter>
1ACD:0004 B406        MOV    AH,06
1ACD:0006 B2FF        MOV    DL,FF
1ACD:0008 CD21        INT    21
1ACD:000A 740C        JZ     0018
1ACD:000C 3C03        CMP    AL,03
1ACD:000E 7501        JNZ    0011
1ACD:0010 CB          RETF
```

```
1ACD:0011 B401          MOV   AH,01
1ACD:0013 BA0000        MOV   DX,0000
1ACD:0016 CD14          INT   14
1ACD:0018 B403          MOV   AH,03
1ACD:001A BA0000        MOV   DX0000
1ACD:001D CD14          INT   14
1ACD:001F 80E401        AND   AH,01
1ACD:0022 74E0          JZ    0004
```

The change has been correctly made. Now, to test the change, start the program to see if characters make it out the serial port. The problem of data from the serial port not making it to the screen remains, however, so instead of simply starting the program, set a breakpoint at the location in the program that handles incoming serial data (CS:0024H). This technique allows the output section of the code to be tested separately. The breakpoint is set using the Go command, G.

```
-G 24   <Enter>

AX=0130  BX=0000  CX=0131  DX=0000  SP=00FC  BP=0000  SI=0000  DI=0000
DS=1AAD  ES=1AAD  SS=1ABD  CS=1ACD  IP=0024    NV UP EI PL NZ NA PO NC
1ACD:0024 B402          MOV   AH,02
-U  <Enter>
1ACD:0024 B402          MOV   AH,02
1ACD:0026 BA0000        MOV   DX,0000
1ACD:0029 CD14          INT   14
1ACD:002B B406          MOV   AH,06
1ACD:002D CD21          INT   21
1ACD:002F EBD3          JMP   0004
1ACD:0031 0000          ADD   [BX+SI],AL
1ACD:0033 0000          ADD   [BX+SI],AL
1ACD:0035 0000          ADD   [BX+SI],AL
1ACD:0037 0000          ADD   [BX+SI],AL
1ACD:0039 0000          ADD   [BX+SI],AL
1ACD:003B 0000          ADD   [BX+SI],AL
1ACD:003D 0000          ADD   [BX+SI],AL
1ACD:003F 0000          ADD   [BX+SI],AL
1ACD:0041 0000          ADD   [BX+SI],AL
1ACD:0043 0000          ADD   [BX+SI],AL
```

As stated earlier, the serial port is attached to a serial terminal. After execution of the program is started with the Go command, all keys typed on the keyboard are displayed correctly on the terminal, thus confirming the fix made to the INT 21H instruction. To test serial input, a key must be pressed on the terminal, causing the breakpoint at CS:0024H to be executed.

The fact that location CS:0024H was reached indicates that Interrupt 14H is detecting the presence of an input character. To test if the character is now making it to the screen, a breakpoint is needed after the write to the screen. The Disassemble command shows the instructions starting at the current IP value. The program ends at CS:002FH; the instructions shown after that are whatever happened to be in memory when the program was loaded. A good place to set the next breakpoint is CS:002FH, just after the Interrupt 21H call.

```
-G 2f  <Enter>

AX=0600  BX=0000  CX=0131  DX=0000  SP=00FC  BP=0000  SI=0000  DI=0000
DS=1AAD  ES=1AAD  SS=1ABD  CS=1ACD  IP=002F    NV UP EI PL NZ NA PO NC
1ACD:002F EBD3        JMP   0004
```

DEBUG shows that the breakpoint was reached and the character did not print (it should have been on the line after -*G 2f*), so something must be wrong with the Interrupt 21H call. A breakpoint just before the MS-DOS call at CS:002DH should reveal the cause of the problem.

```
-G 2d  <Enter>

AX=0662  BX=0000  CX=0131  DX=0000  SP=00FC  BP=0000  SI=0000  DI=0000
DS=1AAD  ES=1AAD  SS=1ABD  CS=1ACD  IP=002D    NV UP EI PL NZ NA PO NC
1ACD:002D CD21        INT   21
```

The key that was entered on the serial terminal (b) is in AL, where it was returned by Interrupt 14H. Unfortunately, it is not in DL, where it is expected by the Direct Console I/O function (06H) of the MS-DOS command. The MS-DOS function was simply printing a null (00H) and then moving the cursor. An instruction (MOV DL,AL) is missing.

Fixing this problem requires the insertion of a line of code, which is usually difficult to do inside DEBUG. The Move (Copy) Data command, M, can be used to move the code located below the point where the insertion is to be made down 2 bytes, but this will probably throw any subsequent addressing off. It is usually easier to exit DEBUG, edit the source file, and then reassemble. In this case, however, because the instruction to be added is near the last instruction, a patch can easily be made by entering only three instructions: the new one and the two it destroys.

```
-A 2d  <Enter>
1ACD:002D mov dl,al  <Enter>
1ACD:002F int 21  <Enter>
1ACD:0031 jmp 4  <Enter>
1ACD:0033  <Enter>
-U 2b  <Enter>
1ACD:002B B406        MOV   AH,06
1ACD:002D 88C2        MOV   DL,AL
1ACD:002F CD21        INT   21
1ACD:0031 EBD1        JMP   0004
1ACD:0033 0000        ADD   [BX+SI],AL
1ACD:0035 0000        ADD   [BX+SI],AL
1ACD:0037 0000        ADD   [BX+SI],AL
1ACD:0039 0000        ADD   [BX+SI],AL
1ACD:003B 0000        ADD   [BX+SI],AL
1ACD:003D 0000        ADD   [BX+SI],AL
1ACD:003F 0000        ADD   [BX+SI],AL
1ACD:0041 0000        ADD   [BX+SI],AL
1ACD:0043 0000        ADD   [BX+SI],AL
1ACD:0045 0000        ADD   [BX+SI],AL
1ACD:0047 0000        ADD   [BX+SI],AL
1ACD:0049 0000        ADD   [BX+SI],AL
```

The new line of code has been inserted and verified with the Disassemble command. The fix is ready to test. The Trace command could be used to single-step through the program to verify execution. A word of warning is in order, however: The DEBUG Trace command should never be used to trace an Interrupt 21H call. Once the trace enters the MS-DOS call, it will wander around for a while and then lock the machine, requiring a restart. Avoid this problem either by setting a breakpoint just beyond the Interrupt 21H call or by using the Proceed Through Loop or Subroutine command, P. The Proceed command operates in a similar manner to the Trace command but does not trace loops, calls, and interrupts.

Because the fix is fairly certain, use the Go command in its simple form with no breakpoints. The program will execute without further intervention from DEBUG.

```
-G  <Enter>
lasdfgh
Program terminated normally
-Q  <Enter>
```

The *lasdfgh* text entered on the serial terminal is displayed correctly. When a Ctrl-C is entered from the keyboard, the program terminates properly and DEBUG displays the message *Program terminated normally.* Now exit DEBUG with the Quit command, Q.

The source code of TESTCOMM should be edited immediately so that it reflects the two changes made temporarily under DEBUG. Figure 18-10 shows the corrected listing.

```
        TITLE TESTCOMM — TEST COMMSCOP ROUTINE
; *********************************************************************
; *                                                                   *
; *   TESTCOMM                                                        *
; *     THIS ROUTINE PROVIDES DATA FOR THE COMMSCOP ROUTINE.  IT READS *
; *   CHARACTERS FROM THE KEYBOARD AND WRITES THEM TO COM1 USING       *
; *   INT 14H.  DATA IS ALSO READ FROM INT 14H AND DISPLAYED ON THE    *
; *   SCREEN.  THE ROUTINE RETURNS TO MS-DOS WHEN Ctrl-C IS PRESSED    *
; *   ON THE KEYBOARD.                                                 *
; *                                                                   *
; *********************************************************************

SSEG    SEGMENT PARA STACK 'STACK'
        DW      128 DUP(?)
SSEG    ENDS

CSEG    SEGMENT
        ASSUME  CS:CSEG,SS:SSEG
BEGIN   PROC    FAR
        PUSH    DS                      ;SET UP FOR RET TO MS-DOS
        XOR     AX,AX                   ; .
        PUSH    AX                      ; .
```

Figure 18-10. Correct serial test routine.   *(more)*

```
MAINLOOP:
        MOV     AH,6            ;USE DOS CALL TO CHECK FOR
        MOV     DL,0FFH         ; KEYBOARD ACTIVITY
        INT     21H             ; IF NO CHARACTER, JUMP TO
        JZ      TESTCOMM        ; COMM ACTIVITY TEST

        CMP     AL,03           ;WAS CHARACTER A Ctrl-C?
        JNE     SENDCOMM        ; NO, SEND IT TO SERIAL PORT
        RET                     ; YES, RETURN TO MS-DOS

SENDCOMM:
        MOV     AH,01           ;USE INT 14H WRITE FUNCTION TO
        MOV     DX,0            ; SEND DATA TO SERIAL PORT
        INT     14H             ; .

TESTCOMM:
        MOV     AH,3            ;GET SERIAL PORT STATUS
        MOV     DX,0            ; .
        INT     14H             ; .
        AND     AH,1            ;ANY DATA WAITING?
        JZ      MAINLOOP        ; NO, GO BACK TO KEYBOARD TEST
        MOV     AH,2            ;READ SERIAL DATA
        MOV     DX,0            ; .
        INT     14H             ; .
        MOV     AH,6            ;WRITE SERIAL DATA TO SCREEN
        MOV     DL,AL           ; .
        INT     21H             ; .
        JMP     MAINLOOP        ;CONTINUE

BEGIN   ENDP
CSEG    ENDS
        END     BEGIN
```

Figure 18-10. Continued.

DEBUG has a rich set of commands and features. The preceding case study shows the more common ones in their most straightforward aspect. Some of the other commands and some useful techniques are described below. *See* PROGRAMMING UTILITIES: DEBUG.

Establishing initial conditions

When a program is loaded for testing, four areas may require initialization:

- Registers
- Data areas
- Default file-control blocks (FCBs)
- Command tail

These areas may also require changes during testing, especially when the programmer is working around bugs or establishing different test conditions.

Registers. Registers are ordinarily set when the program is loaded. The values in them depend on whether a .EXE, .COM, or .HEX file was loaded. Generally, the segment registers, the IP register, and the SP register are set to appropriate values; with the exception of AX, BX, and CX, the rest of the registers are set to zero. BX and CX contain the length of the loaded file. By MS-DOS convention, when a program is loaded, the contents of AL and AH indicate the validity of the drive specifiers in the first and second DEBUG command-line parameters, respectively. Each register contains zero if the corresponding drive was valid, 01H if the drive was valid and wildcards were used, or 0FFH if the drive was invalid.

To change the value of any register, use an alternate form of the Register command. Enter R followed by the two-letter register name. Only 16-bit registers can be changed, so use the X form of the general-purpose registers:

```
-R AX   <Enter>
```

DEBUG will respond with the current contents of the register and prompt for a new value. Either enter a new hexadecimal value or press Enter to keep the current value:

```
AX 0000
:FFFF   <Enter>
```

In this example, the new value of AX is FFFFH.

When changing registers, exercise caution modifying the segment registers. These registers control the execution of the program and should be changed only after careful and thoughtful consideration.

The Register command can also be used to modify the CPU flags.

Data areas. Initializing or changing data areas is easy, and several methods are provided. The Fill Memory command, F, can be used to initialize areas of RAM. For instance,

```
-F 0 L400 0   <Enter>
```

fills DS:0000H through DS:03FFH with zero. (The absence of a segment override causes the Fill command to use its default segment, DS.) Entering

```
-F CS:100 200 1B "[Hello" 0D   <Enter>
```

fills CS:0100H through CS:0200H with many repetitions of the string 1B 5B 48 65 6C 6C 6F 0D. (Note that an address range was specified, not a length.)

When the wholesale changing of memory is not appropriate, the Enter command can be used to edit a small number of locations. The Enter command has two forms: One enters a list of bytes into the specified memory location; the other prompts with the contents of each location and waits for input. Either form can be used as appropriate.

Default file-control blocks and the command tail. The setting of the default FCBs and of the command tail are related functions. When DEBUG is entered, the first parameter following the command DEBUG is the name of the file to be loaded into memory for debugging. If the next two parameters are filenames, FCBs for these files are formatted at

DS:005CH and DS:006CH in the PSP. *See* PROGRAMMING IN THE MS-DOS ENVIRON-MENT: Programming for ms-dos: File and Record Management. If either parameter contains a pathname, the corresponding FCB will contain only a valid drive number; the filename field will not be valid. All filenames and switches following the name of the file to be debugged are considered the command tail and are saved in memory starting at DS:0081H. The length of the command tail is in DS:0080H. For example, entering

```
C>DEBUG COMMDUMP.EXE FILE1.DAT FILE2.DAT  <Enter>
```

results in the first FCB (5CH), the second FCB (6CH), and the command tail (81H) being loaded as follows:

```
-D 50  <Enter>
42C9:0050  CD 21 CB 00 00 00 00 00-00 00 00 00 00 46 49 4C   .!...........FIL
42C9:0060  45 31 20 20 20 44 41 54-00 00 00 00 00 46 49 4C   E1   DAT.....FIL
42C9:0070  45 32 20 20 20 44 41 54-00 00 00 00 00 00 00 00   E2   DAT........
42C9:0080  15 20 66 69 6C 65 31 2E-64 61 74 20 66 69 6C 65   . file1.dat file
42C9:0090  32 2E 64 61 74 20 0D 74-20 66 69 6C 65 32 2E 64   2.dat .t file2.d
42C9:00A0  61 74 20 0D 00 00 00 00-00 00 00 00 00 00 00 00   at .............
42C9:00B0  00 00 00 00 00 00 00 00-00 00 00 00 00 00 00 00   ................
42C9:00C0  00 00 00 00 00 00 00 00-00 00 00 00 00 00 00 00   ................
```

In this example, location DS:005CH contains an unopened FCB for file FILE1.DAT on the current drive. Location DS:006CH contains an unopened FCB for FILE2.DAT on the current drive. (The second FCB cannot be used where it is and must be moved to another location before the first FCB is opened.) Location DS:0080H contains the length of the command tail, 15H (21) bytes. The next 21 bytes are the command tail prepared by DEBUG; they correspond exactly to what the command tail would be if the program had been loaded by COMMAND.COM instead of by DEBUG.

The default FCBs and the command tail can also be set after the program has been loaded, by using the Name File or Command-Tail Parameters command, N. DEBUG treats the string of characters that follow the Name command as the command tail: If the first two parameters are filenames, they become the first and second FCBs, respectively. The Name command also places the string at DS:0081H, with the length of the string at DS:0080H. Entering the DEBUG command

```
-N FILE1.DAT FILE2.DAT  <Enter>
```

produces the same results as specifying the filenames in the command line. When employed in this manner, the Name command is useful for initializing command-tail data that was not in the command line or for changing the command-tail data to test different aspects of a program. (If files are named in this manner, they are not validated until the Load File or Sectors command, L, is used.) Note that the data following the Name command need not be filenames; it can be any parameters, data, or switches that the application program expects to see.

More on breakpoints

The case study at the beginning of this section used breakpoints in their simplest form: Only a single breakpoint was specified at a time and the execution address was considered to be the current IP. The Go command is also capable of setting multiple breakpoints and of beginning execution at any address in memory. The more general form of the Go command is

G [=*address*] [*address* [*address*...]]

If Go is used with no operands, execution begins at the current value of CS:IP and no breakpoints are set. If the =*address* operand is used, DEBUG sets IP to the address specified and execution then begins at the new CS:IP. The other optional addresses are breakpoints. When execution reaches one of these breakpoints, DEBUG stops and displays the system's registers. As many as 10 breakpoints can be set on one Go command, and they can be in any order.

The breakpoint addresses must be on instruction boundaries because DEBUG replaces the instruction at each breakpoint address with an INT 03H instruction (0CCH). DEBUG saves the replaced instructions internally. When any breakpoint is reached, DEBUG stops execution and restores the instructions at *all* the breakpoints; if no breakpoint is reached, the instructions are not restored and the Load command must be used to reload the original program.

The multiple-breakpoint feature of the Go command allows the tracing of program execution when branches exist in the code. When a program contains, for instance, a conditional jump on the zero flag, a breakpoint can be placed in each of the two possible branches. When the branch is reached, one of the two breakpoints will be encountered shortly thereafter. When DEBUG displays the breakpoint, the programmer knows which branch was taken. Moving through a program with breakpoints at key locations is faster than using the Trace command to execute each and every instruction.

Multiple breakpoints can also be used to home in on a bad piece of code. This technique is particularly useful in those nasty situations when there are no symptoms except that the system locks up and must be restarted. When debugging a problem such as this, set breakpoints at each of the major sections of the program and then note those breakpoints that are executed successfully, continuing until the system locks up. The problem lies somewhere between the last successful breakpoint and the next breakpoint set. Now repeat the processes, setting breakpoints between the last breakpoint and the one that was never reached. By progressively narrowing the gap between breakpoints, the exact offending instruction can be isolated.

Some general comments about the Go command and breakpoints:

- After a program has reached completion and returned to MS-DOS, it must be reloaded with the Load command before it can be executed again. (DEBUG intercepts this return and displays *Program terminated normally.*)
- Because DEBUG replaces program instructions with an INT 03H instruction to form breakpoints, the break address must be on an instruction boundary. If it is not, the INT 03H will be stuck in the middle of an instruction, causing strange and sometimes entertaining results.

- Breakpoints cannot be set in data, because data is not executed.
- The target program's SS:SP registers must point to a valid stack that has at least 6 bytes of stack space available. When the Go command is executed, it pushes the target program's flags and CS and IP registers onto the stack and then transfers control to the program with an IRET instruction. Thus, if the target program's stack is not valid or is too small, the system may crash.
- Finally, and obviously, breakpoints cannot be set in read-only memory (the ROM BIOS, for instance).

Using the Write commands

After a program has been debugged, fixed, and tested with DEBUG, the temptation exists to write the patched program directly back to the disk as a .COM file. This action is sometimes legitimate, but only rarely. The technique will be explained in a moment, but first a sermon:

DON'T DO IT.

One of the greatest sadnesses in a programmer's life comes when, after a program has been running wonderfully, enhancements are made to the source code and the recompiled program suddenly has bugs in it that haven't been seen for months. Always make any debugging patches permanent in the source file immediately.

Unless, of course, the source code is not available. This is the only time saving a patched program is permissible. For example, sometimes commercial programs require patching because the program does not quite fit the hardware it must run on or because bugs have been found in the program. The source of these patches is sometimes word-of-mouth, sometimes a bulletin-board service, and sometimes the program's manufacturer.

Even when legitimate reasons exist to save patched code, precautions should be taken. Be very careful, meticulous, and alert as the patches are applied. Understand each step before undertaking it. Most important of all, always have a backup of the original unpatched program safely on a floppy disk.

Use the Write command to write the program image to disk. A starting address can optionally be specified; otherwise the write starts at CS:0100H. The name of the file will be either the name specified in the last Name command or the name of the program from the DEBUG command line if the Name command has not been used. The number of bytes to be written is in BX and CX, with the most significant half in BX. These registers will have been loaded correctly when the program was loaded, but they should be checked if the program has executed since it was loaded.

The .EXE and .HEX file types cannot be written to disk with the Write command. The command performs no formatting and only writes the binary image of memory to the disk file. Thus, all programs written with Write must be .COM files. The image of a .EXE or .HEX file can still be written as a .COM file provided no segment fixups are required and provided the other rules for a .COM file are followed. *See* PROGRAMMING IN THE MS-DOS ENVIRONMENT: PROGRAMMING FOR MS-DOS: Structure of an Application Program. (A segment fixup is a segment address that must be provided by the loader when the

program is originally loaded. *See* PROGRAMMING IN THE MS-DOS ENVIRONMENT: PRO-
GRAMMING TOOLS: Object Modules.) If a .EXE file containing a segment fixup is written as a
.COM file, the new file will execute correctly only when loaded at exactly the same address
as the original file, and this is difficult to ensure for programs running under MS-DOS.

If it is necessary to patch a .EXE or .HEX file and the exact addresses relative to the start of
the file are known, use the following procedure:

1. Rename (or better yet, copy) the file to an extension other than .EXE or .HEX.
2. Load the program image into memory by placing the new name on DEBUG's com-
    mand line. Note that the loaded file is an image of the disk file and is not executable.
3. Modify the program image in memory, but *never* try to execute the program. Results
    would be unpredictable and the program image could be damaged.
4. Write the modified image back to disk using a simple *w*. No other action is needed,
    because the original load will have set the filename and the correct length in BX
    and CX.
5. Rename the file to a name with the correct .EXE or .HEX extension. The new name
    need not be the same as the original, but it should have the same extension.

The same technique can be used to load, modify, and save data files. Simply make sure
that the file does not have an extension of .COM, .EXE, or .HEX. The data file will be
loaded at address CS:0100H. (DEBUG treats the file much the same as a .COM file.) After
patching the data (the Enter command works best), use the Write command to write it
back to the disk.

SYMDEB

SYMDEB is an extension of DEBUG; virtually all the DEBUG commands and techniques
still work as expected. The major new feature, and the source of the name SYMDEB, is
symbolic debugging: SYMDEB can use all public labels in a program for reference, instead
of using hexadecimal offset addresses. In addition, SYMDEB allows the use of line numbers for reference in compatible high-order languages; source-line display within SYMDEB
is also possible for these languages. Currently, the languages supporting these options are
Microsoft FORTRAN versions 3.0 and later, Microsoft Pascal versions 3.0 and later, and
Microsoft C versions 2.0 and later. Versions 4.0 and earlier of the Microsoft Macro Assembler (MASM) do not generate the data needed for line-number display and source-line
debugging.

In addition to symbolic debugging, SYMDEB has added several other new features and has
expanded existing DEBUG features:

● Breakpoints have been made more sophisticated with the addition of "sticky"
  breakpoints. Unlike the breakpoints set with the Go command, sticky breakpoints
  remain attached to the program throughout a SYMDEB session until they are explicitly removed. Specific commands are supplied for listing, removing, enabling, and
  disabling sticky breakpoints.
● DEBUG's Display Memory command, D, has been extended so that data can be
  displayed in different formats.

- Full redirection is supported.
- A stack trace feature has been added.
- Terminate-and-stay-resident programs are supported.
- A shell escape command has been added to allow the execution of MS-DOS commands and programs without leaving SYMDEB and the debugging session.

These additions allow more sophisticated debugging techniques to be used and, in some cases, also simplify locating problems. To see the advantages of using symbols and sticky breakpoints in debugging, consider a type of program that is one of the most difficult to debug—the TSR.

Debugging TSRs with SYMDEB

Terminate-and-stay-resident routines can be difficult to debug. They exist in two worlds and can have bugs associated with each. At the outset, they are usually simple programs that perform some initialization task and then exit. At this point, they are transformed into another type of beast entirely—resident routines that are more a part of the operating system than of any application program. Each form of the program must be debugged separately, using different techniques.

The TSR routine used for this case study is the same one created previously to serve as external instrumentation to trace serial communications. The program was called COMMSCOP, but to avoid confusion of that working program with the broken one presented here, the name has been changed to BADSCOP. BADSCOP was assembled and linked in the usual manner and then converted to a .COM file using EXE2BIN. When it was installed, it returned normally, but at the first attempt to issue an Interrupt 14H, the system locked up completely. Warm booting was not sufficient to restore it, and a power-on cold boot was required to get the system working again.

Figure 18-11 is a listing of BADSCOP. The only difference from COMMSCOP, aside from the errors, is the addition of two PUBLIC statements to make all the procedure names and the important data names available to SYMDEB.

```
        TITLE   BADSCOP — BAD VERSION OF COMMUNICATIONS TRACE UTILITY
; ************************************************************************
; *                                                                    *
; *  BADSCOP —                                                         *
; *    THIS PROGRAM MONITORS THE ACTIVITY ON A SPECIFIED COMM PORT     *
; *    AND PLACES A COPY OF ALL COMM ACTIVITY IN A RAM BUFFER.  EACH    *
; *    ENTRY IN THE BUFFER IS TAGGED TO INDICATE WHETHER THE BYTE      *
; *    WAS SENT BY OR RECEIVED BY THE SYSTEM.                          *
; *                                                                    *
; *    BADSCOP IS INSTALLED BY ENTERING                                *
; *                                                                    *
; *                   BADSCOP                                          *
; *                                                                    *
```

Figure 18-11. An incorrect version of the serial trace utility.   *(more)*

```
;  *   THIS WILL INSTALL BADSCOP AND SET UP A 64K BUFFER TO BE USED     *
;  *   FOR DATA LOGGING.  REMEMBER THAT 2 BYTES ARE REQUIRED FOR        *
;  *   EACH COMM BYTE, SO THE BUFFER IS ONLY 32K EVENTS LONG, OR ABOUT  *
;  *   30 SECONDS OF CONTINUOUS 9600 BAUD DATA.  IN THE REAL WORLD,     *
;  *   ASYNC DATA IS RARELY CONTINUOUS, SO THE BUFFER WILL PROBABLY     *
;  *   HOLD MORE THAN 30 SECONDS WORTH OF DATA.                         *
;  *                                                                    *
;  *   WHEN INSTALLED, BADSCOP INTERCEPTS ALL INT 14H CALLS.  IF THE    *
;  *   PROGRAM HAS BEEN ACTIVATED AND THE INT IS EITHER SEND OR RE-     *
;  *   CEIVE DATA, A COPY OF THE DATA BYTE, PROPERLY TAGGED, IS PLACED  *
;  *   IN THE BUFFER.  IN ANY CASE, DATA IS PASSED ON TO THE REAL       *
;  *   INT 14H HANDLER.                                                 *
;  *                                                                    *
;  *   BADSCOP IS INVOKED BY ISSUING AN INT 60H CALL.  THE INT HAS      *
;  *   THE FOLLOWING CALLING SEQUENCE:                                  *
;  *                                                                    *
;  *       AH - COMMAND                                                 *
;  *             0 - STOP TRACING, PLACE STOP MARK IN BUFFER            *
;  *             1 - FLUSH BUFFER AND START TRACE                       *
;  *             2 - RESUME TRACE                                       *
;  *             3 - RETURN COMM BUFFER ADDRESSES                       *
;  *       DX - COMM PORT (ONLY USED WITH AH = 1 or 2)                  *
;  *             0 - COM1                                               *
;  *             1 - COM2                                               *
;  *                                                                    *
;  *   THE FOLLOWING DATA IS RETURNED IN RESPONSE TO AH = 3:            *
;  *                                                                    *
;  *       CX - BUFFER COUNT IN BYTES                                   *
;  *       DX - SEGMENT ADDRESS OF THE START OF THE BUFFER              *
;  *       BX - OFFSET ADDRESS OF THE START OF THE BUFFER               *
;  *                                                                    *
;  *   THE COMM BUFFER IS FILLED WITH 2-BYTE DATA ENTRIES OF THE        *
;  *   FOLLOWING FORM:                                                  *
;  *                                                                    *
;  *       BYTE 0 - CONTROL                                             *
;  *             BIT 0 - ON FOR RECEIVED DATA, OFF FOR TRANS.           *
;  *             BIT 7 - STOP MARK - INDICATES COLLECTION WAS           *
;  *                     INTERRUPTED AND RESUMED.                       *
;  *       BYTE 1 - 8-BIT DATA                                          *
;  *                                                                    *
; ***********************************************************************

        PUBLIC   INITIALIZE,CONTROL,VECTOR_INIT,COMMSCOPE
        PUBLIC   OLD_COMM_INT,COUNT,STATUS,PORT,BUFPNTR

CSEG    SEGMENT
        ASSUME   CS:CSEG,DS:CSEG
        ORG      100H                    ;TO MAKE A COM FILE
```

Figure 18-11. Continued. *(more)*

```
INITIALIZE:
        JMP     VECTOR_INIT              ;JUMP TO THE INITIALIZATION
                                         ; ROUTINE WHICH, TO SAVE SPACE,
                                         ; IS IN THE COMM BUFFER


;
;   SYSTEM VARIABLES
;
OLD_COMM_INT    DD      ?                ;ADDRESS OF REAL COMM INT
COUNT           DW      0                ;BUFFER COUNT
COMMSCOPE_INT   EQU     60H              ;COMMSCOPE CONTROL INT
STATUS          DB      0                ;PROCESSING STATUS
                                         ; 0 — OFF
                                         ; 1 — ON
PORT            DB      0                ;COMM PORT BEING TRACED
BUFPNTR         DW      VECTOR_INIT      ;NEXT BUFFER LOCATION


        SUBTTL  DATA INTERRUPT HANDLER
PAGE
; **************************************************************************
; *                                                                        *
; *  COMMSCOPE                                                             *
; *  THIS PROCEDURE INTERCEPTS ALL INT 14H CALLS AND LOGS THE DATA        *
; *  IF APPROPRIATE.                                                      *
; *                                                                        *
; **************************************************************************
COMMSCOPE       PROC    NEAR

        TEST    CS:STATUS,1              ;ARE WE ON?
        JZ      OLD_JUMP                 ; NO, SIMPLY JUMP TO OLD HANDLER

        CMP     AH,00H                   ;SKIP SETUP CALLS
        JE      OLD_JUMP                 ; .

        CMP     AH,03H                   ;SKIP STATUS REQUESTS
        JAE     OLD_JUMP                 ; .

        CMP     AH,02H                   ;IS THIS A READ REQUEST?
        JE      GET_READ                 ; YES, GO PROCESS

;
;   DATA WRITE REQUEST — SAVE IF APPROPRIATE
;
        CMP     DL,CS:PORT               ;IS WRITE FOR PORT BEING TRACED?
        JNE     OLD_JUMP                 ; NO, JUST PASS IT THROUGH

        PUSH    DS                       ;SAVE CALLER'S REGISTERS
        PUSH    BX                       ; .
        PUSH    CS                       ;SET UP DS FOR OUR PROGRAM
        POP     DS                       ; .
        MOV     BX,BUFPNTR               ;GET ADDRESS OF NEXT BUFFER LOCATION
```

Figure 18-11. Continued.   *(more)*

```
          MOV    [BX],BYTE PTR 0      ;MARK AS TRANSMITTED BYTE
          MOV    [BX+1],AL            ;SAVE DATA IN BUFFER
          INC    COUNT                ;INCREMENT BUFFER BYTE COUNT
          INC    COUNT                ; .
          INC    BX                   ;POINT TO NEXT LOCATION
          INC    BX                   ; .
          MOV    BUFPNTR,BX           ;SAVE NEW POINTER
          JNZ    WRITE_DONE           ;ZERO INDICATES BUFFER HAS WRAPPED

          MOV    STATUS,0             ;TURN COLLECTION OFF - BUFFER FULL
WRITE_DONE:
          POP    BX                   ;RESTORE CALLER'S REGISTERS
          POP    DS                   ; .
          JMP    OLD_JUMP             ;PASS REQUEST ON TO BIOS ROUTINE
;
;   PROCESS A READ DATA REQUEST AND WRITE TO BUFFER IF APPROPRIATE
;
GET_READ:
          CMP    DL,CS:PORT           ;IS READ FOR PORT BEING TRACED?
          JNE    OLD_JUMP             ; NO, JUST PASS IT THROUGH

          PUSH   DS                   ;SAVE CALLER'S REGISTERS
          PUSH   BX                   ; .
          PUSH   CS                   ;SET UP DS FOR OUR PROGRAM
          POP    DS                   ; .

          PUSHF                       ;FAKE INT 14H CALL
          CLI                         ; .
          CALL   OLD_COMM_INT         ;PASS REQUEST ON TO BIOS
          TEST   AH,80H               ;VALID READ?
          JNZ    READ_DONE            ; NO, SKIP BUFFER UPDATE

          MOV    BX,BUFPNTR           ;GET ADDRESS OF NEXT BUFFER LOCATION
          MOV    [BX],BYTE PTR 1      ;MARK AS RECEIVED BYTE
          MOV    [BX+1],AL            ;SAVE DATA IN BUFFER
          INC    COUNT                ;INCREMENT BUFFER BYTE COUNT
          INC    COUNT                ; .
          INC    BX                   ;POINT TO NEXT LOCATION
          INC    BX                   ; .
          MOV    BUFPNTR,BX           ;SAVE NEW POINTER
          JNZ    READ_DONE            ;ZERO INDICATES BUFFER HAS WRAPPED

          MOV    STATUS,0             ;TURN COLLECTION OFF - BUFFER FULL
READ_DONE:
          POP    BX                   ;RESTORE CALLER'S REGISTERS
          POP    DS                   ; .
          IRET


;
;   JUMP TO COMM BIOS ROUTINE
;
OLD_JUMP:
          JMP    OLD_COMM_INT

COMMSCOPE ENDP
```

Figure 18-11. Continued.   *(more)*

```
        SUBTTL  CONTROL INTERRUPT HANDLER
PAGE
; **********************************************************************
; *                                                                    *
; *  CONTROL                                                           *
; *      THIS ROUTINE PROCESSES CONTROL REQUESTS.                       *
; *                                                                    *
; **********************************************************************

CONTROL PROC    NEAR
        CMP     AH,00H                  ;STOP REQUEST?
        JNE     CNTL_START              ; NO, CHECK START
        PUSH    DS                      ;SAVE REGISTERS
        PUSH    BX                      ; .
        PUSH    CS                      ;SET DS FOR OUR ROUTINE
        POP     DS
        MOV     STATUS,0                ;TURN PROCESSING OFF
        MOV     BX,BUFPNTR              ;PLACE STOP MARK IN BUFFER
        MOV     [BX],BYTE PTR 80H       ; .
        MOV     [BX+1],BYTE PTR 0FFH    ; .
        INC     COUNT                   ;INCREMENT COUNT
        INC     COUNT                   ; .
        POP     BX                      ;RESTORE REGISTERS
        POP     DS                      ; .
        JMP     CONTROL_DONE

CNTL_START:
        CMP     AH,01H                  ;START REQUEST?
        JNE     CNTL_RESUME             ; NO, CHECK RESUME
        MOV     CS:PORT,DL              ;SAVE PORT TO TRACE
        MOV     CS:BUFPNTR,OFFSET VECTOR_INIT   ;RESET BUFFER TO START
        MOV     CS:COUNT,0              ;ZERO COUNT
        MOV     CS:STATUS,1             ;START LOGGING
        JMP     CONTROL_DONE

CNTL_RESUME:
        CMP     AH,02H                  ;RESUME REQUEST?
        JNE     CNTL_STATUS             ; NO, CHECK STATUS
        CMP     CS:BUFPNTR,0            ;END OF BUFFER CONDITION?
        JE      CONTROL_DONE            ; YES, DO NOTHING
        MOV     CS:PORT,DL              ;SAVE PORT TO TRACE
        MOV     CS:STATUS,1             ;START LOGGING
        JMP     CONTROL_DONE

CNTL_STATUS:
        CMP     AH,03H                  ;RETURN STATUS REQUEST?
        JNE     CONTROL_DONE            ; NO, ERROR — DO NOTHING
        MOV     CX,CS:COUNT             ;RETURN COUNT
        PUSH    CS                      ;RETURN SEGMENT ADDR OF BUFFER
        POP     DX                      ; .
        MOV     BX,OFFSET VECTOR_INIT   ;RETURN OFFSET ADDR OF BUFFER
```

Figure 18-11. Continued.   *(more)*

```
CONTROL_DONE:
        IRET

CONTROL ENDP


        SUBTTL  INITIALIZE INTERRUPT VECTORS
PAGE
; **********************************************************************
; *                                                                    *
; *  VECTOR_INIT                                                        *
; *  THIS PROCEDURE INITIALIZES THE INTERRUPT VECTORS AND THEN         *
; *  EXITS VIA THE MS-DOS TERMINATE-AND-STAY-RESIDENT FUNCTION.        *
; *  A BUFFER OF 64K IS RETAINED.  THE FIRST AVAILABLE BYTE            *
; *  IN THE BUFFER IS THE OFFSET OF VECTOR_INIT.                       *
; *                                                                    *
; **********************************************************************

        EVEN                            ;ASSURE BUFFER ON EVEN BOUNDARY
VECTOR_INIT     PROC    NEAR
;
;   GET ADDRESS OF COMM VECTOR (INT 14H)
;
        MOV     AH,35H
        MOV     AL,14H
        INT     21H
;
;   SAVE OLD COMM INT ADDRESS
;
        MOV     WORD PTR OLD_COMM_INT,BX
        MOV     AX,ES
        MOV     WORD PTR OLD_COMM_INT[2],AX
;
;   SET UP COMM INT TO POINT TO OUR ROUTINE
;
        MOV     DX,OFFSET COMMSCOPE
        MOV     AH,25H
        MOV     AL,14H
        INT     21H

;
;   INSTALL CONTROL ROUTINE INT
;
        MOV     DX,OFFSET CONTROL
        MOV     AH,25H
        MOV     AL,COMMSCOPE_INT
        INT     21H
;
;   SET LENGTH TO 64K, EXIT AND STAY RESIDENT
;
        MOV     AX,3100H                ;TERM AND STAY RES COMMAND
        MOV     DX,1000H                ;64K RESERVED
        INT     21H                     ;DONE
```

Figure 18-11. Continued.   *(more)*

```
VECTOR_INIT ENDP

CSEG    ENDS
        END     INITIALIZE
```

Figure 18-11. Continued.

In order to use the symbolic debugging features of SYMDEB, a symbol file must be built in a specific format. The SYMDEB utility MAPSYM performs this function, using the contents of the .MAP file built by LINK. MAPSYM is easy to use because it has only two parameters: the .MAP file and the /L switch (which triggers verbose mode). The symbol table for BADSCOP is built as follows:

```
C>MAPSYM BADSCOP  <Enter>
```

This operation produces a symbol file called BADSCOP.SYM.

Armed with the .SYM file and the usual collection of listing and design notes, the programmer can begin the debugging process using SYMDEB.

The first task is to discover if the BADSCOP TSR is installing correctly. To test this, run the .COM file under SYMDEB by typing

```
C>SYMDEB BADSCOP.SYM BADSCOP.COM  <Enter>
```

Note the order in which operands are passed to SYMDEB — it is not the order that would be expected. All switches (none were used here) must immediately follow the word *SYMDEB*. These switches must be followed in turn by the fully qualified names of any symbol files (in this case, BADSCOP.SYM). Only then is the name of the file to be debugged given. If BADSCOP expected any parameters in the command tail, they would be last. This potential need for command-tail data is the reason the name of the file to be debugged follows the name of the symbol file. SYMDEB knows that the first non-.SYM file it encounters is the file to be loaded; the parameters that follow the filename may be of any form and number.

When SYMDEB begins, it displays

```
Microsoft (R) Symbolic Debug Utility  Version 4.00
Copyright (C) Microsoft Corp 1984, 1985. All rights reserved.

Processor is [80286]
```

The debugger identifies itself and then notes the type of CPU it is running on — in this case, an Intel 80286. The Display or Modify Registers command, R, gives the same display that DEBUG gives, with one exception.

```
-R  <Enter>
AX=0000  BX=0000  CX=0133  DX=0000  SP=FFFE  BP=0000  SI=0000  DI=0000
DS=1FD0  ES=1FD0  SS=1FD0  CS=1FD0  IP=0100   NV UP EI PL NZ NA PO NC
CSEG:INITIALIZE:
1FD0:0100 E90701          JMP   VECTOR_INIT
```

The instruction at CS:IP, JMP, is now preceded by the information that the instruction is at label *INITIALIZE* within segment *CSEG*. An examination of Figure 18-11 shows that this is indeed the case.

To check that all the symbols requested with the PUBLIC statement are present, use the X?* form of the Examine Symbol Map command.

```
-X?*   <Enter>

CSEG: (1FD0)
0100 INITIALIZE    0103 OLD_COMM_INT 0107 COUNT        0109 STATUS
010A PORT          010B BUFPNTR      010D COMMSCOPE     018F CONTROL
020A VECTOR_INIT
```

The display shows that the value of *CSEG* (1FD0H) matches the current value of CS. The offset values shown for the procedure names and data names match the numbers from an assembled listing. Because this is a .COM file, there is only one segment. If there had been other segments — a data segment, for instance — they would have been shown with their values and associated labels and offsets.

The purpose of this test is to determine whether the problems this program is having are caused by an incorrect installation. First, use the Trace Program Execution command, T, to trace through the first few steps.

```
-T7   <Enter>
AX=0000  BX=0000  CX=0133  DX=0000  SP=FFFE  BP=0000  SI=0000  DI=0000
DS=1FD0  ES=1FD0  SS=1FD0  CS=1FD0  IP=020A  NV UP EI PL NZ NA PO NC
CSEG:VECTOR_INIT:
1FD0:020A B435             MOV  AH,35                          ;'5'
AX=3500  BX=0000  CX=0133  DX=0000  SP=FFFE  BP=0000  SI=0000  DI=0000
DS=1FD0  ES=1FD0  SS=1FD0  CS=1FD0  IP=020C  NV UP EI PL NZ NA PO NC
1FD0:020C B014             MOV  AL,14
AX=3514  BX=0000  CX=0133  DX=0000  SP=FFFE  BP=0000  SI=0000  DI=0000
DS=1FD0  ES=1FD0  SS=1FD0  CS=1FD0  IP=020E  NV UP EI PL NZ NA PO NC
1FD0:020E CD21             INT  21  ;Get Interrupt Vector
AX=3514  BX=1375  CX=0133  DX=0000  SP=FFFE  BP=0000  SI=0000  DI=0000
DS=1FD0  ES=1567  SS=1FD0  CS=1FD0  IP=0210  NV UP EI PL NZ NA PO NC
1FD0:0210 891E0301         MOV  [OLD_COMM_INT],BX              DS:0103=0000
AX=3514  BX=1375  CX=0133  DX=0000  SP=FFFE  BP=0000  SI=0000  DI=0000
DS=1FD0  ES=1567  SS=1FD0  CS=1FD0  IP=0214  NV UP EI PL NZ NA PO NC
1FD0:0214 8CC0             MOV  AX,ES
AX=1567  BX=1375  CX=0133  DX=0000  SP=FFFE  BP=0000  SI=0000  DI=0000
DS=1FD0  ES=1567  SS=1FD0  CS=1FD0  IP=0216  NV UP EI PL NZ NA PO NC
1FD0:0216 A30501           MOV  [OLD_COMM_INT+02 (0105)],AX    DS:0105=0000
AX=1567  BX=1375  CX=0133  DX=0000  SP=FFFE  BP=0000  SI=0000  DI=0000
DS=1FD0  ES=1567  SS=1FD0  CS=1FD0  IP=0219  NV UP EI PL NZ NA PO NC
1FD0:0219 BA0D01           MOV  DX,010D
```

This part of the program uses Interrupt 21H Function 35H to obtain the current vector for Interrupt 14H. Note that, unlike DEBUG, SYMDEB coasts right through an Interrupt 21H call with no problems. It not only knows enough not to make the call but also displays the type of function call being made, based on the value in AH.

To make sure that the correct vector for the old Interrupt 14H handler has been stored, use the Display Doublewords command, DD, in conjunction with a symbol name.

```
-DD OLD_COMM_INT L1  <Enter>
1FD0:01030  1567:1375
```

This is the correct vector address (1567:1375H). Now trace through the next part of the program, which establishes the new vectors for interrupts.

```
-T8   <Enter>
AX=1567  BX=1375  CX=0133  DX=010D  SP=FFFE  BP=0000  SI=0000  DI=0000
DS=1FD0  ES=1567  SS=1FD0  CS=1FD0  IP=021C   NV UP EI PL NZ NA PO NC
1FD0:021C B425          MOV  AH,25                          ;'%'
AX=2567  BX=1375  CX=0133  DX=010D  SP=FFFE  BP=0000  SI=0000  DI=0000
DS=1FD0  ES=1567  SS=1FD0  CS=1FD0  IP=021E   NV UP EI PL NZ NA PO NC
1FD0:021E B014          MOV  AL,14
AX=2514  BX=1375  CX=0133  DX=010D  SP=FFFE  BP=0000  SI=0000  DI=0000
DS=1FD0  ES=1567  SS=1FD0  CS=1FD0  IP=0220   NV UP EI PL NZ NA PO NC
1FD0:0220 CD21          INT  21  ;Set Vector
AX=2514  BX=1375  CX=0133  DX=010D  SP=FFFE  BP=0000  SI=0000  DI=0000
DS=1FD0  ES=1567  SS=1FD0  CS=1FD0  IP=0222   NV UP EI PL NZ NA PO NC
1FD0:0222 BA8F01        MOV  DX,018F
AX=2514  BX=1375  CX=0133  DX=018F  SP=FFFE  BP=0000  SI=0000  DI=0000
DS=1FD0  ES=1567  SS=1FD0  CS=1FD0  IP=0225   NV UP EI PL NZ NA PO NC
1FD0:0225 B425          MOV  AH,25                          ;'%'
AX=2514  BX=1375  CX=0133  DX=018F  SP=FFFE  BP=0000  SI=0000  DI=0000
DS=1FD0  ES=1567  SS=1FD0  CS=1FD0  IP=0227   NV UP EI PL NZ NA PO NC
1FD0:0227 B060          MOV  AL,60                          ;'`'
AX=2560  BX=1375  CX=0133  DX=018F  SP=FFFE  BP=0000  SI=0000  DI=0000
DS=1FD0  ES=1567  SS=1FD0  CS=1FD0  IP=0229   NV UP EI PL NZ NA PO NC
1FD0:0229 CD21          INT  21  ;Set Vector
AX=2560  BX=1375  CX=0133  DX=018F  SP=FFFE  BP=0000  SI=0000  DI=0000
DS=1FD0  ES=1567  SS=1FD0  CS=1FD0  IP=022B   NV UP EI PL NZ NA PO NC
1FD0:022B B80031        MOV  AX,3100
```

Examination of these trace steps shows that all went normally. The new Interrupt 14H vector has been established at *COMMSCOPE*; the vector for the new Interrupt 60H has also been correctly installed. Use the Go command, G, to allow the program to continue to termination and then use the Quit command, Q, to exit SYMDEB.

```
-G   <Enter>

Program terminated and stayed resident (0)
-Q   <Enter>
```

SYMDEB displays the information that the program terminated with a completion code of zero and stayed resident. This is as it should be, and the conclusion is that the installation portion of this TSR is running properly. The problem must be in the real-time execution of the program.

Debugging the resident portion of a TSR is complicated but not especially difficult. A simple program is used to exercise the TSR, and it is this program that is debugged. As this driver program exercises the TSR, the tracing process continues into the resident routine.

Because symbol tables exist for the TSR, symbolic debugging can be used to follow its execution.

The driver program will be TESTCOMM, shown in Figure 18-10. To make the program more easily usable by SYMDEB, one line has been added before the first SEGMENT statement:

```
PUBLIC    BEGIN,MAINLOOP,SENDCOMM,TESTCOMM
```

Using the .MAP file produced by LINK, the MAPSYM routine creates TESTCOMM.SYM. TESTCOMM can now be invoked with two symbol files:

```
C>SYMDEB TESTCOMM.SYM BADSCOP.SYM TESTCOMM.EXE  <Enter>
```

SYMDEB will load both symbol files and then load TESTCOMM.EXE. Because the name of the TESTCOMM.SYM file matches the name of the program being loaded, SYMDEB makes TESTCOMM.SYM the active symbol file.

Use the Register command to show that the test program was properly loaded.

```
-R  <Enter>
AX=0000  BX=0000  CX=0133  DX=0000  SP=0100  BP=0000  SI=0000  DI=0000
DS=38EE  ES=38EE  SS=38FE  CS=390E  IP=0000    NV UP EI PL NZ NA PO NC
CSEG:BEGIN:
390E:0000 1E          PUSH    DS
```

Then use the Examine Symbol Map command to determine whether the symbol files were loaded correctly. The form X* lists all the symbol maps and their segments; the form X?* lists all the symbols for the current symbol map and segment.

```
-X*  <Enter>
[38FE TESTCOMM]
     [390E CSEG]
 0000 BADSCOP
     0000 CSEG
-X?*  <Enter>

CSEG: (390E)
0000 BEGIN    0004 MAINLOOP 0011 SENDCOMM 0018 TESTCOMM
```

The current symbol map and segment are shown in square brackets. The symbol map for BADSCOP is also present but not selected. Note that there are no values associated with BADSCOP in the listing produced by the X?* command, because all the symbols currently available to SYMDEB are shown and only the symbols in TESTCOMM's *CSEG* are available (that is, TESTCOMM.SYM is the only active symbol file).

Recall that the BADSCOP TSR loaded normally but locked the system up at the first attempt to issue an Interrupt 14H. This behavior indicates that the problem is associated with an Interrupt 14H call. TESTCOMM repeatedly makes the system fail, but which of the Interrupt 14H calls within TESTCOMM is causing the trouble is not known. The most straightforward approach would be to put a breakpoint just before each Interrupt 14H instruction. Use the Disassemble (Unassemble) command, U, to find the location of all Interrupt 14H calls.

```
-U MAINLOOP L19  <Enter>
CSEG:MAINLOOP:
390E:0004 B406          MOV    AH,06
390E:0006 B2FF          MOV    DL,FF
390E:0008 CD21          INT    21
390E:000A 740C          JZ     TESTCOMM
390E:000C 3C03          CMP    AL,03
390E:000E 7501          JNZ    SENDCOMM
390E:0010 CB            RETF
CSEG:SENDCOMM:
390E:0011 B401          MOV    AH,01
390E:0013 BA0000        MOV    DX,BADSCOP!CSEG
390E:0016 CD14          INT    14
CSEG:TESTCOMM:
390E:0018 B403          MOV    AH,03
390E:001A BA0000        MOV    DX,BADSCOP!CSEG
390E:001D CD14          INT    14
390E:001F 80E401        AND    AH,01
390E:0022 74E0          JZ     MAINLOOP
390E:0024 B402          MOV    AH,02
390E:0026 BA0000        MOV    DX,BADSCOP!CSEG
390E:0029 CD14          INT    14
390E:002B B406          MOV    AH,06
390E:002D 8AD0          MOV    DL,AL
390E:002F CD21          INT    21
390E:0031 EBD1          JMP    MAINLOOP
```

The Disassemble request starts at *MAINLOOP* and acts on the next 25 (19H) instructions. SYMDEB displays symbol names instead of numbers whenever it can. However, it does get confused from time to time, so a grain of salt might be needed when reading the disassembly. Notice, for instance, the MOV DX,0 instructions at offsets 13H, 1AH, and 26H. SYMDEB has decided that what is being moved is not zero, but BADSCOP!CSEG. (The ! identifies a mapname in the same way a : defines a segment.) In this case, SYMDEB searched its map tables for an address of zero and found one at *CSEG* in BADSCOP. This segment has the address of zero because it has not been initialized.

Ignoring the name confusions, the disassembly clearly shows the three INT 14H instructions at offsets 16H, 1DH, and 29H. Use the Set Breakpoints command, BP, to set a sticky, or permanent, breakpoint at each of these locations. In this way, any Interrupt 14H call issued by TESTCOMM will be intercepted before it executes. Use the List Breakpoints command, BL, to verify the breakpoints.

```
-BP 16  <Enter>
-BP 1D  <Enter>
-BP 29  <Enter>
-BL  <Enter>
0 e 390E:0016 [CSEG:SENDCOMM+05 (0016)]
1 e 390E:001D [CSEG:TESTCOMM+05 (001D)]
2 e 390E:0029 [CSEG:TESTCOMM+11 (0029)]
```

The List Breakpoints command shows that breakpoint 0 is enabled and set to
SENDCOMM+05, or CS:0016H. Likewise, breakpoint 1 is at CS:001DH and breakpoint 2 is at
CS:0029H. It is important to trap on an Interrupt 14H so that the subsequent actions of the
Interrupt 14H service routine can be traced. Now allow the program to execute until it
encounters a breakpoint.

```
-G  <Enter>
AX=0300  BX=0000  CX=0133  DX=0000  SP=00FC  BP=0000  SI=0000  DI=0000
DS=38EE  ES=38EE  SS=38FE  CS=390E  IP=001D   NV UP EI PL ZR NA PE NC
390E:001D CD14          INT     14                                  ;BR1
```

The first Interrupt 14H encountered is the one at the second breakpoint, breakpoint 1, as
can be seen from the address at which execution broke. Also, SYMDEB was kind enough
to include the comment *;BR1* on the disassembled line, indicating that this is Break Request 1. The instruction at this location is a request for serial port status (AH = 3) and the
registers are loaded correctly. Execution can now be passed to the TSR by simply executing the current instruction. (Remember that the instruction displayed at a breakpoint
has not yet been executed.)

```
-T  <Enter>
AX=0300  BX=0000  CX=0133  DX=0000  SP=00F6  BP=0000  SI=0000  DI=00Q0
DS=38EE  ES=38EE  SS=38FE  CS=1FD0  IP=010D   NV UP DI PL ZR NA PE NC
1FD0:010D 2EF606090101   TEST      Byte Ptr CS:[0109],01             CS:0109=00
```

The single Trace command has moved execution into the TSR. Note that the Interrupt
14H has changed the value of CS and jumped to location 10DH off the new CS. This location contains the first instruction of the *COMMSCOPE* procedure in the TSR. SYMDEB
does not know that a different segment is being executed and must be instructed to use a
different map table. Use the Open Symbol Map command, XO, to do this, instructing
SYMDEB to set the active map table to BADSCOP!.

```
-XO BADSCOP!  <Enter>
-X?*  <Enter>

CSEG: (0000)
0100 INITIALIZE   0103 OLD_COMM_INT 0107 COUNT      0109 STATUS
010A PORT         010B BUFPNTR      010D COMMSCOPE   018F CONTROL
020A VECTOR_INIT
```

The X?* command shows that the BADSCOP symbols are now the current map. They are
not usable, however, because the value of *CSEG*— zero — needs to be changed to the current CS register. To correct this, use the SYMDEB Set Symbol Value command, Z. This
command can set any symbol in the current map table to any value; the value can be a
number, another symbol, or the contents of a register. In this case, set the value of *CSEG*
in BADSCOP! to the current contents of the CS register.

```
-Z CSEG CS  <Enter>
-X*  <Enter>
 38FE TESTCOMM
      390E CSEG
[0000 BADSCOP]
     [1FD0 CSEG]
```

The X* command confirms that BADSCOP! is now the selected symbol map and that the *CSEG* within it has the value 1FD0H. The *CSEG* segment in TESTCOMM is an entirely different entity and still has its correct value, which will be valid when the TSR returns.

With the symbols set, the debugging can begin by tracing the first few instructions. Because *COMMSCOPE* is not currently active, the routine should quickly pass the processing on to the old interrupt handler.

```
-T5  <Enter>
AX=0300  BX=0000  CX=0133  DX=0000  SP=00F6  BP=0000  SI=0000  DI=0000
DS=38EE  ES=38EE  SS=38FE  CS=1FD0  IP=0113   NV UP DI PL ZR NA PE NC
1FD0:0113 7476          JZ   COMMSCOPE+7E (018B)
AX=0300  BX=0000  CX=0133  DX=0000  SP=00F6  BP=0000  SI=0000  DI=0000
DS=38EE  ES=38EE  SS=38FE  CS=1FD0  IP=018B   NV UP DI PL ZR NA PE NC
1FD0:018B FF2E0301      JMP  FAR [0103]                      DS:0103=0000
AX=0300  BX=0000  CX=0133  DX=0000  SP=00F6  BP=0000  SI=0000  DI=0000
DS=38EE  ES=38EE  SS=38FE  CS=0000  IP=0000   NV UP DI PL ZR NA PE NC
0000:0000 381E6715      CMP  [1567],BL                       DS:1567=00
AX=0300  BX=0000  CX=0133  DX=0000  SP=00F6  BP=0000  SI=0000  DI=0000
DS=38EE  ES=38EE  SS=38FE  CS=0000  IP=0004   NV UP DI PL ZR NA PE NC
0000:0004 BC2CE1        MOV  SP,E12C
AX=0300  BX=0000  CX=0133  DX=0000  SP=E12C  BP=0000  SI=0000  DI=0000
DS=38EE  ES=38EE  SS=38FE  CS=0000  IP=0007   NV UP DI PL ZR NA PE NC
0000:0007 2F            DAS
```

STATUS is tested with a mask of 01H at CS:010DH; the test sets the zero flag, indicating that tracing is disabled. The JZ to *COMMSCOPE+7E* (CS:018BH) is taken. At this address is a far jump to the old Interrupt 14H handler at 1567:1375H. The jump is taken and then disaster strikes. Instead of going to the correct address, processing is suddenly at 0000:0000H. Any wild jump is dangerous, but a far jump into low memory is exceptionally so. This explains the system's locking up and requiring a cold boot to recover.

Now that the bug has been caught in the act, it should be a simple matter to determine what went wrong. When the BADSCOP TSR installed itself, it was seen to place the correct offset address at 0103H. Yet whenever the resident portion of the TSR tries to use the value at that address, it finds all zeros. The initialization routine placed the address at the symbol *OLD_COMM_INT* (1FD0:0103H). If that location is examined, the following is found:

```
-DD OLD_COMM_INT L1   <Enter>
1FD0:0103  1567:1375
```

This is the correct address. Why, then, did the programs find zero there? Use the Display Doublewords command to look at the same memory location again, this time using the specific address 0103H rather than a program symbol.

```
-DD 103 L1   <Enter>
38EE:0103  0000:0000
```

The dump of *OLD_COMM_INT* looked at 1FD0:0103H, but the simple dump looked at 38EE:0103H. The explanation is clear when the values of the registers just before the far jump are examined. The CS register contains 1FD0H and the DS register contains 38EEH.

This is the problem—there is a missing CS override on the indirect jump command. When the TSR installed itself, CS and DS were the same because it was a .COM file. When the TSR is entered as the result of an interrupt call, only CS is set; DS remains what it was in the calling program. Without an override, the CPU assumed that the address of the destination of the far call was located at offset 103H from the DS register. This offset, unfortunately, contained zeros, and the program locked up the system.

The problem is now easily corrected. Exit SYMDEB with the Quit command and edit the program source so that the offending line reads

```
OLD_JUMP:
        JMP     CS:OLD_COMM_INT
```

Debugging C programs with SYMDEB

One of SYMDEB's finest features is the ability to debug with source-line data from programs written in Microsoft C, Pascal, and FORTRAN. The actual lines of C or FORTRAN can be included in the debugging display, and the addresses for breakpoints show which line of code the breakpoints are in. Combined with symbolic debugging, these features provide a powerful tool that can significantly reduce debugging time for programs written in a supported language.

The following rather complicated case illustrates SYMDEB at its best. The program BADSCOP from the previous example was not completely debugged. Although the patch to the BADSCOP code at *OLD_JUMP:* did correct the disastrous problem that caused the system to lock up, running the program in a realistic test situation reveals that a subtle problem still remains that might be in either BADSCOP or one of the support programs.

Before we investigate the problem, a quick review of the programs in the COMMSCOP system is in order. At the heart of the system is the Interrupt 14H intercept program COMMSCOP. When executed, this program installs itself as a TSR and intercepts all Interrupt 14H calls. (The incorrect version of the COMMSCOP program is called BADSCOP.) The installed COMMSCOP TSR passes all Interrupt 14H calls on to the real service routine in the ROM BIOS until it is commanded to start tracing. The COMMSCMD routine controls tracing. This control routine can request that COMMSCOP start, stop, or resume tracing for a specific serial port. These commands are facilitated through Interrupt 60H, which is recognized by the COMMSCOP TSR as a command request. When tracing is started, the trace buffer is emptied by zeroing the trace count and setting the buffer pointer to the first buffer location. When tracing is stopped by COMMSCMD's STOP command, a marker is placed in the buffer to indicate the end of a trace segment. Tracing can be resumed with COMMSCMD's RESUME command. Resuming a trace preserves collected data and places new trace data after the marker in the trace buffer. The RESUME command differs from the START command in that the buffer is not emptied.

Now the problem: When the serial data tracing is started with COMMSCMD (*see* Figure 18-5), data is collected normally. When COMMSCMD issues a STOP command and the data is displayed with COMMDUMP (*see* Figure 18-7), the data appears normal. The traced data ends with a stop mark just as it should. However, the RESUME command of

COMMSCMD causes the stop mark to be overwritten with collected data. After this, whenever COMMDUMP displays data an extra byte appears at the end of the data. The problem could be with either BADSCOP or COMMSCMD. SYMDEB has the facilities to debug both the routines at once.

The first step in the debugging process is, as usual, to gather all the listings and design documentation. As a part of this process, the symbol tables needed for SYMDEB must be prepared. The process of preparing a symbol table for BADSCOP has already been explained; however, preparing the SYMDEB input and supporting listings for a C program is slightly more complicated.

First, when the C program is compiled, three switches must be specified. (C switches are case sensitive and must be entered exactly as shown.)

```
C>MSC /Fc /Zd /Od COMMSCMD;   <Enter>
```

The /Zd switch produces an object file containing line-number information that corresponds to the line numbers of the source file. The /Od switch disables optimization that involves complex code rearrangement; localized optimization, peephole optimization, and other simple forms of optimization are still performed. The /Od switch is not required, but code rearrangement can make the resulting object code more difficult to debug.

The /Fc switch invokes a feature of C that is especially important for debugging with SYMDEB: a listing that contains the C source lines and the generated assembler code intermixed. The file is a .COD file; the command line shown above would produce the file COMMSCMD.COD. Figure 18-12 shows the contents of COMMSCMD.COD.

```
;       Static Name Aliases
;
;       $S142_commands  EQU       commands
        TITLE   commscmd
;       NAME    commscmd.C

        .287
_TEXT   SEGMENT  BYTE PUBLIC 'CODE'
_TEXT   ENDS
_DATA   SEGMENT  WORD PUBLIC 'DATA'
_DATA   ENDS
CONST   SEGMENT  WORD PUBLIC 'CONST'
CONST   ENDS
_BSS    SEGMENT  WORD PUBLIC 'BSS'
_BSS    ENDS
DGROUP  GROUP    CONST, _BSS,  _DATA
        ASSUME  CS: _TEXT, DS: DGROUP, SS: DGROUP, ES: DGROUP
EXTRN   _int86:NEAR
EXTRN   _printf:NEAR
EXTRN   _stricmp:NEAR
EXTRN   _atoi:NEAR
EXTRN   __chkstk:NEAR
_DATA        SEGMENT
```

Figure 18-12. COMMSCMD.COD.   *(more)*

```
$SG148    DB        'STOP',  00h
$SG151    DB        'START',  00h
$SG154    DB        'RESUME',  00h
$SG157    DB        0ah, 'Communications tracing %s for port COM%1d:',  0ah,  00h
$S142_commands  DB      'STOPPED',  00h
          ORG       $+2
          DB        'STARTED',  00h
          ORG       $+2
          DB        'RESUMED',  00h
          ORG       $+2
_DATA     ENDS
_TEXT     SEGMENT
;¦*** /*******************************************************************
;¦*** *                                                                 *
;¦*** *   COMMSCMD                                                      *
;¦*** *                                                                 *
;¦*** *   This routine controls the COMMSCOP program that has been in- *
;¦*** *   stalled as a resident routine.  The operation performed is de- *
;¦*** *   termined by the command line.  The COMMSCMD program is invoked *
;¦*** *   as follows:                                                   *
;¦*** *                                                                 *
;¦*** *                 COMMSCMD [[cmd][ port]]                         *
;¦*** *                                                                 *
;¦*** *   where cmd is the command to be executed                      *
;¦*** *           STOP   -- stop trace                                 *
;¦*** *           START  -- flush trace buffer and start trace         *
;¦*** *           RESUME -- resume a stopped trace                     *
;¦*** *       port is the COMM port to be traced (1=COM1, 2=COM2, etc.) *
;¦*** *                                                                 *
;¦*** *   If cmd is omitted, STOP is assumed.  If port is omitted, 1 is *
;¦*** *   assumed.                                                      *
;¦*** *                                                                 *
;¦*** ********************************************************************/
;¦***
;¦*** #include <stdlib.h>
;¦*** #include <stdio.h>
;¦*** #include <dos.h>
;¦*** #define COMMSCMD 0x60
;¦***
;¦*** main(argc, argv)
;¦*** int argc;
; Line 29
          PUBLIC _main
_main     PROC NEAR
          *** 000000      55                      push    bp
          *** 000001      8b ec                   mov     bp,sp
          *** 000003      b8 22 00                mov     ax,34
          *** 000006      e8 00 00                call    _chkstk
          *** 000009      57                      push    di
          *** 00000a      56                      push    si
```

Figure 18-12. Continued.   *(more)*

```
; ¦*** char *argv[];
; ¦*** {
; Line 31
;        argc = 4
;        argv = 6
;        cmd = -4
;        port = -6
;        result = -2
;        inregs = -34
;        outregs = -20
; ¦***    int cmd, port, result;
; ¦***    static char commands[3] [10] = {"STOPPED", "STARTED", "RESUMED"};
; ¦***    union REGS inregs, outregs;
; ¦***
; ¦***    cmd = 0;
; Line 36
        *** 00000b    c7 46 fc 00 00         mov    WORD PTR [bp-4],0    ;cmd
; ¦***    port = 0;
; Line 37
        *** 000010    c7 46 fa 00 00         mov    WORD PTR [bp-6],0    ;port
; ¦***
; ¦***    if (argc > 1)
; Line 39
        *** 000015    83 7e 04 01            cmp    WORD PTR [bp+4],1    ;argc
        *** 000019    7f 03                  jg     $JCC25
        *** 00001b    e9 5d 00               jmp    $I145
                              $JCC25:
; ¦***        {
; Line 40
; ¦***        if (0 == stricmp(argv[1], "STOP"))
; Line 41
        *** 00001e    b8 00 00               mov    ax,OFFSET DGROUP:$SG148
        *** 000021    50                     push   ax
        *** 000022    8b 5e 06               mov    bx,[bp+6]           ;argv
        *** 000025    ff 77 02               push   WORD PTR [bx+2]
        *** 000028    e8 00 00               call   _stricmp
        *** 00002b    83 c4 04               add    sp,4
        *** 00002e    3d 00 00               cmp    ax,0
        *** 000031    74 03                  je     $JCC49
        *** 000033    e9 08 00               jmp    $I147
                              $JCC49:
; ¦***            cmd = 0;
; Line 42
        *** 000036    c7 46 fc 00 00         mov    WORD PTR [bp-4],0    ;cmd
; ¦***        else if (0 == stricmp(argv[1], "START"))
```

Figure 18-12. Continued.   *(more)*

```
; Line 43
        *** 00003b    e9 3d 00                         jmp     $I149
                                        $I147:
        *** 00003e    b8 05 00                         mov     ax,OFFSET DGROUP:$SG151
        *** 000041    50                               push    ax
        *** 000042    8b 5e 06                         mov     bx,[bp+6]      ;argv
        *** 000045    ff 77 02                         push    WORD PTR [bx+2]
        *** 000048    e8 00 00                         call    _stricmp
        *** 00004b    83 c4 04                         add     sp,4
        *** 00004e    3d 00 00                         cmp     ax,0
        *** 000051    74 03                            je      $JCC81
        *** 000053    e9 08 00                         jmp     $I150
                                        $JCC81:
;¦***              cmd = 1;
; Line 44
        *** 000056    c7 46 fc 01 00                   mov     WORD PTR [bp-4],1      ;cmd
;¦***         else if (0 == stricmp(argv[1], "RESUME"))
; Line 45
        *** 00005b    e9 1d 00                         jmp     $I152
                                        $I150:
        *** 00005e    b8 0b 00                         mov     ax,OFFSET DGROUP:$SG154
        *** 000061    50                               push    ax
        *** 000062    8b 5e 06                         mov     bx,[bp+6]      ;argv
        *** 000065    ff 77 02                         push    WORD PTR [bx+2]
        *** 000068    e8 00 00                         call    _stricmp
        *** 00006b    83 c4 04                         add     sp,4
        *** 00006e    3d 00 00                         cmp     ax,0
        *** 000071    74 03                            je      $JCC113
        *** 000073    e9 05 00                         jmp     $I153
                                        $JCC113:
;¦***              cmd = 2;
; Line 46
        *** 000076    c7 46 fc 02 00                   mov     WORD PTR [bp-4],2      ;cmd
;¦***         }
; Line 47
                                        $I153:
                                        $I152:
                                        $I149:
;¦***
;¦***     if (argc == 3)
; Line 49
                                        $I145:
        *** 00007b    83 7e 04 03                      cmp     WORD PTR [bp+4],3      ;argc
        *** 00007f    74 03                            je      $JCC127
        *** 000081    e9 1b 00                         jmp     $I155
                                        $JCC127:
;¦***         {
; Line 50
;¦***              port = atoi(argv[2]);
```

Figure 18-12. Continued.   *(more)*

```
; Line 51
        *** 000084      8b 5e 06                    mov     bx,[bp+6]           ;argv
        *** 000087      ff 77 04                    push    WORD PTR [bx+4]
        *** 00008a      e8 00 00                    call    _atoi
        *** 00008d      83 c4 02                    add     sp,2
        *** 000090      89 46 fa                    mov     [bp-6],ax           ;port
;|***        if (port > 0)
; Line 52
        *** 000093      83 7e fa 00                 cmp     WORD PTR [bp-6],0   ;port
        *** 000097      7f 03                       jg      $JCC151
        *** 000099      e9 03 00                    jmp     $I156
                                    $JCC151:
;|***                port = port-1;
; Line 53
        *** 00009c      ff 4e fa                    dec     WORD PTR [bp-6]     ;port
;|***        }
; Line 54
                                    $I156:
;|***
;|***        inregs.h.ah = cmd;
; Line 56
                                    $I155:
        *** 00009f      8a 46 fc                    mov     al,[bp-4]           ;cmd
        *** 0000a2      88 46 df                    mov     [bp-33],al
;|***        inregs.x.dx = port;
; Line 57
        *** 0000a5      8b 46 fa                    mov     ax,[bp-6]           ;port
        *** 0000a8      89 46 e4                    mov     [bp-28],ax
;|***        result = int86(COMMCMD, &inregs, &outregs);
; Line 58
        *** 0000ab      8d 46 ec                    lea     ax,[bp-20]          ;outregs
        *** 0000ae      50                          push    ax
        *** 0000af      8d 46 de                    lea     ax,[bp-34]          ;inregs
        *** 0000b2      50                          push    ax
        *** 0000b3      b8 60 00                    mov     ax,96
        *** 0000b6      50                          push    ax
        *** 0000b7      e8 00 00                    call    _int86
        *** 0000ba      83 c4 06                    add     sp,6
        *** 0000bd      89 46 fe                    mov     [bp-2],ax           ;result
;|***
;|***
;|***        printf("\nCommunications tracing %s for port COM%1d:\n",
;|***                commands[cmd], port + 1);
; Line 62
        *** 0000c0      8b 46 fa                    mov     ax,[bp-6]           ;port
        *** 0000c3      40                          inc     ax
        *** 0000c4      50                          push    ax
        *** 0000c5      8b 46 fc                    mov     ax,[bp-4]           ;cmd
        *** 0000c8      8b c8                       mov     cx,ax
        *** 0000ca      d1 e0                       shl     ax,1
        *** 0000cc      d1 e0                       shl     ax,1
        *** 0000ce      03 c1                       add     ax,cx
        *** 0000d0      d1 e0                       shl     ax,1
```

Figure 18-12. Continued.   *(more)*

```
        *** 0000d2    05 40 00              add    ax,OFFSET DGROUP:$S142_commands
        *** 0000d5    50                    push   ax
        *** 0000d6    b8 12 00              mov    ax,OFFSET DGROUP:$SG157
        *** 0000d9    50                    push   ax
        *** 0000da    e8 00 00              call   _printf
        *** 0000dd    83 c4 06              add    sp,6
;|*** }
; Line 63
                                $EX138:
        *** 0000e0    5e                    pop    si
        *** 0000e1    5f                    pop    di
        *** 0000e2    8b e5                 mov    sp,bp
        *** 0000e4    5d                    pop    bp
        *** 0000e5    c3                    ret

_main       ENDP
_TEXT       ENDS
END
```

Figure 18-12. Continued.

After the C program is compiled, it must be linked using the /LI switch to indicate that the line number information is to be maintained:

```
C>LINK COMMSCMD /MAP /LI;  <Enter>
```

The /MAP switch is still required to generate a map file of public names for use in building the symbol file, which is created in the usual manner:

```
C>MAPSYM COMMSCMD  <Enter>
```

Everything needed to debug COMMSCMD and BADSCOP is now available. The first test is an attempt to start tracing. To invoke SYMDEB, type

```
C>SYMDEB COMMSCMD.SYM BADSCOP.SYM COMMSCMD.EXE START 1  <Enter>
```

SYMDEB first loads the symbol files for COMMSCMD and BADSCOP and then loads the .EXE file for COMMSCMD. BADSCOP is already in memory, having been loaded by simply running it. (It then stays resident.) The last two entries in the command line load the command tail for COMMSCMD with a start request for COM1. SYMDEB responds with

```
Microsoft (R) Symbolic Debug Utility  Version 4.00
Copyright (C) Microsoft Corp 1984, 1985. All rights reserved.

Processor is [80286]
```

Use the Register and Examine Symbol Map commands to display the initial register values and symbol table information.

```
-R  <Enter>
AX=0000  BX=0000  CX=1928  DX=0000  SP=0800  BP=0000  SI=0000  DI=0000
DS=2CA0  ES=2CA0  SS=2E85  CS=2CB0  IP=010F    NV UP EI PL NZ NA PO NC
_TEXT:__astart:
2CB0:010F B430        MOV  AH,30                          ;'0'
-X*  <Enter>
[2CB0 COMMSCMD]
     [2CB0 _TEXT]
       2E08 DGROUP
 0000 BADSCOP
       0000 CSEG
-X?*  <Enter>
9876 __acrtused    9876 __acrtmsg
_TEXT: (2CB0)
0010 _main         00F6 _atoi
00F9 __chkstk      010F __astart     01AB __cintDIV    01AE __amsg_exit
01B9 _int86        023A _printf      0270 _strcmpi     0270 _stricmp
02C2 __stbuf       0361 __ftbuf      03E7 __catox      043C __nullcheck
0458 __cinit       0507 _exit        051E __exit       054A __ctermsub
0572 __dosret0     057A __dosretax   0586 __maperror   05BA __NMSG_TEXT
05EA __NMSG_WRITE  0613 __output     0E22 __setargv    0F07 __setenvp
0F6D __flsbuf      1098 __fassign    1098 __cropzeros  1098 __positive
1098 __forcdecpt   1098 __cfltcvt    109B _fflush      1103 _isatty
1125 __myalloc     1167 _strlen      1182 _ultoa       118C __fptrap
1192 _flushall     11C3 _free        11C3 __nfree      11D1 _malloc
11D1 __nmalloc     1217 _write       12F1 __cltoasub   12FD __cxtoa
1351 __amalloc     1432 __amexpand   146C __amlink     148E __amallocbrk
14AD _brkctl
DGROUP: (2E08)
0094 STKHQQ        0096 __asizds     0098 __atopsp
009A __abrktb      00EA __abrktbe    00EA __abrkp      00EC __iob
018C __iob2        0204 __lastiob    0212 __aintdiv    0216 __fac
021E _errno        0220 __umaskval   0222 __pspadr     0224 __psp
0226 __osmajor     0226 __dosvermajor 0227 __osminor  0227 __dosverminor
0228 __oserr       0228 __doserrno   022A __osfile     023E ___argc
0240 ___argv       0242 _environ     0244 __child      0246 __csigtab
0278 __cflush      027A __asegds     0286 __aseg1      0288 __asegn
028A __asegr       028C __amblksiz   0292 __fpinit     03A8 __edata
03D0 __bufout      05D0 __bufin      07D0 _end
```

The Register command shows that the first instruction to be executed will be at symbol __*astart* in the _TEXT segment. (Note that C puts a single underscore in front of all public library and routine names; a double underscore indicates routines for C's internal use.) The Examine Symbol Map command reveals that the symbol map COMMSCMD! has two segments, _*TEXT* and *DGROUP*, with _*TEXT* currently selected. The segment in BADSCOP!, *CSEG*, has no value assigned to it because SYMDEB doesn't know where it is; one of the debugging tasks is to determine the location of *CSEG*.

C places initialization and preamble code at the front of its object modules. This code can be skipped during debugging, so this example begins at the label _ *main*. Examination of the code at this label using the Disassemble command reveals the following:

```
-U _main  <Enter>
commscmd.C
29:  int argc;
_TEXT:_main:
2CB0:0010 55              PUSH     BP
2CB0:0011 8BEC            MOV      BP,SP
2CB0:0013 B82200          MOV      AX,0022
2CB0:0016 E8E000          CALL     __chkstk
2CB0:0019 57              PUSH     DI
```

This disassembly shows the way source-line information is displayed. These instructions are generated by line 29 of COMMSCMD.C. When the disassembly is compared with the listing in Figure 18-12, the same instructions are seen. However, their addresses are different. The addresses in the disassembly are relative to the start of the segment _TEXT, but the addresses in the listing are relative to the start of _main. SYMDEB allows address references to be made relative to a symbol, so breakpoints can be set as displacements from _main and the addresses shown in the listing can be used.

Because the location of the problem being debugged is not known, breakpoints must be placed strategically throughout COMMSCMD to trace the execution of the program. Use the Set Breakpoints command to set the breakpoints.

```
-BP _main+1e   <Enter>
-BP _main+36   <Enter>
-BP _main+56   <Enter>
-BP _main+76   <Enter>
-BP _main+7b   <Enter>
-BP _main+9c   <Enter>
-BP _main+b7   <Enter>
-BP _main+e5   <Enter>
-BL  <Enter>
0 e 2CB0:002E [_TEXT:_main+1E (002E)] commscmd.C:41
1 e 2CB0:0046 [_TEXT:_main+36 (0046)] commscmd.C:42
2 e 2CB0:0066 [_TEXT:_main+56 (0066)] commscmd.C:44
3 e 2CB0:0086 [_TEXT:_main+76 (0086)] commscmd.C:46
4 e 2CB0:008B [_TEXT:_main+7B (008B)] commscmd.C:49
5 e 2CB0:00AC [_TEXT:_main+9C (00AC)] commscmd.C:53
6 e 2CB0:00C7 [_TEXT:_main+B7 (00C7)] commscmd.C:58
7 e 2CB0:00F5 [_TEXT:_main+E5 (00F5)] commscmd.C:63
```

The List Breakpoints command shows the breakpoint addresses in three ways: first the absolute segment:offset address, then the displacement from the label _main, and finally the line number in COMMSCMD.C.

The first part of the COMMSCMD program decodes the arguments and sets the appropriate values for cmd and port. If there are no arguments, this decoding is skipped; if there are arguments, the decoding begins at line 41, so the first breakpoint is set there. If the criterion of line 41 is met (the first argument is STOP), then line 42 is executed. The second breakpoint is set there. Reaching the second breakpoint means that a STOP command was properly decoded. If the command was not STOP, execution continues at line 43. If this test is passed, line 44 is executed. This is the location of the third breakpoint. If the test at line 44 fails but the one at line 45 is passed, then the breakpoint at line 46 is executed. Whether or not one of the tests passes, execution ends up at line 49. At this point, the program tests for the presence of a second operand. If there is a second operand, execution traps at line 53, where the program decrements the port number to put it in the proper form for the Interrupt 60H handler. Execution will then always stop in line 58, just before the call to _int86. (_int86 is a library routine that loads registers and executes INT instructions.)

When the program is run with *START 1* in the command tail, it gives the following results:

```
-G  <Enter>
AX=0022  BX=0F82  CX=0019  DX=0098  SP=0F7E  BP=0FA4  SI=0089  DI=1065
DS=2E08  ES=2E08  SS=2E08  CS=2CB0  IP=002E   NV UP EI PL NZ NA PO NC
41:            if (0 == stricmp(argv[1],"STOP"))
2CB0:002E B83600        MOV      AX,0036                  ;BR0
-G  <Enter>
AX=0000  BX=415A  CX=0000  DX=0098  SP=0F7E  BP=0FA4  SI=0089  DI=1065
DS=2E08  ES=2E08  SS=2E08  CS=2CB0  IP=0066   NV UP EI PL ZR NA PE NC
44:                cmd = 1;
2CB0:0066 C746FC0100     MOV      Word Ptr [BP-04],0001     ;BR2 SS:0FA0=0000
-G  <Enter>
AX=0000  BX=415A  CX=0000  DX=0098  SP=0F7E  BP=0FA4  SI=0089  DI=1065
DS=2E08  ES=2E08  SS=2E08  CS=2CB0  IP=008B   NV UP EI PL ZR NA PE NC
49:          if (argc == 3)
2CB0:008B 837E0403       CMP      Word Ptr [BP+04],+03      ;BR4 SS:0FA8=0003
-G  <Enter>
AX=0001  BX=00D0  CX=0000  DX=0000  SP=0F7E  BP=0FA4  SI=0089  DI=1065
DS=2E08  ES=2E08  SS=2E08  CS=2CB0  IP=00AC   NV UP EI PL NZ NA PO NC
5            port = port-1;
2CB0:00AC FF4EFA         DEC      Word Ptr [BP-06]          ;BR5 SS:0F9E=0001
-G  <Enter>
AX=0060  BX=00D0  CX=0000  DX=0000  SP=0F78  BP=0FA4  SI=0089  DI=1065
DS=2E08  ES=2E08  SS=2E08  CS=2CB0  IP=00C7   NV UP EI PL ZR NA PE NC
2CB0:00C7 E8EF00         CALL     _int86                    ;BR6
```

The first break occurs at line 41, indicating that one or more arguments were present in the command line. The next break is at line 44, where the program sets the *cmd* code for Interrupt 60H to 1, the correct value for a start request. The next break occurs at line 49, where the program checks the number of arguments. If this number is 3, then there is a second argument in the command line. (Remember that, in C, the first argument is the name of the routine, so an argument count of 3 actually means that there are 2 arguments present.) The number of arguments is at BP+04, or SS:0FA8H, and it is indeed 3. Therefore, the next break is at line 53. The program decrements the current value of *port*, leaving a value of 0, which is what Interrupt 60H expects to see for COM1.

Continuing execution causes a break just before the call to _int86. To validate that the Interrupt 60H call is being made correctly, set a breakpoint just before the INT 60H instruction is issued. Unfortunately, no listing of _int86 is available, so no alternative exists but to trace the execution of the routine until the INT instruction is issued. The details of the processing are of no interest to this debugging session, so they can be ignored until an INT 60H is seen. (The trace offers a great deal of information about how C interfaces with subroutines. Studying the trace would be educational but is beyond the scope of this example.)

```
-T 5  <Enter>
AX=0060  BX=00D0  CX=0000  DX=0000  SP=0F76  BP=0FA4  SI=0089  DI=1065
DS=2E08  ES=2E08  SS=2E08  CS=2CB0  IP=01B9   NV UP EI PL ZR NA PE NC
_TEXT:_int86:
2CB0:01B9 55            PUSH    BP
AX=0060  BX=00D0  CX=0000  DX=0000  SP=0F74  BP=0FA4  SI=0089  DI=1065
DS=2E08  ES=2E08  SS=2E08  CS=2CB0  IP=01BA   NV UP EI PL ZR NA PE NC
2CB0:01BA 8BEC          MOV     BP,SP
AX=0060  BX=00D0  CX=0000  DX=0000  SP=0F74  BP=0F74  SI=0089  DI=1065
DS=2E08  ES=2E08  SS=2E08  CS=2CB0  IP=01BC   NV UP EI PL ZR NA PE NC
2CB0:01BC 56            PUSH    SI
AX=0060  BX=00D0  CX=0000  DX=0000  SP=0F72  BP=0F74  SI=0089  DI=1065
DS=2E08  ES=2E08  SS=2E08  CS=2CB0  IP=01BD   NV UP EI PL ZR NA PE NC
2CB0:01BD 57            PUSH    DI
AX=0060  BX=00D0  CX=0000  DX=0000  SP=0F70  BP=0F74  SI=0089  DI=1065
DS=2E08  ES=2E08  SS=2E08  CS=2CB0  IP=01BE   NV UP EI PL ZR NA PE NC
2CB0:01BE 83EC0A        SUB     SP,+0A
-T 5  <Enter>
AX=0060  BX=00D0  CX=0000  DX=0000  SP=0F66  BP=0F74  SI=0089  DI=1065
DS=2E08  ES=2E08  SS=2E08  CS=2CB0  IP=01C1   NV UP EI PL NZ AC PE NC
2CB0:01C1 C646F6CD      MOV     Byte Ptr [BP-0A],CD            SS:0F6A=BE
AX=0060  BX=00D0  CX=0000  DX=0000  SP=0F66  BP=0F74  SI=0089  DI=1065
DS=2E08  ES=2E08  SS=2E08  CS=2CB0  IP=01C5   NV UP EI PL NZ AC PE NC
2CB0:01C5 8B4604        MOV     AX,[BP+04]                    SS:0F78=0060
AX=0060  BX=00D0  CX=0000  DX=0000  SP=0F66  BP=0F74  SI=0089  DI=1065
DS=2E08  ES=2E08  SS=2E08  CS=2CB0  IP=01C8   NV UP EI PL NZ AC PE NC
2CB0:01C8 8846F7        MOV     [BP-09],AL                    SS:0F6B=01
AX=0060  BX=00D0  CX=0000  DX=0000  SP=0F66  BP=0F74  SI=0089  DI=1065
DS=2E08  ES=2E08  SS=2E08  CS=2CB0  IP=01CB   NV UP EI PL NZ AC PE NC
2CB0:01CB 3C25          CMP     AL,25                  ;'%'
AX=0060  BX=00D0  CX=0000  DX=0000  SP=0F66  BP=0F74  SI=0089  DI=1065
DS=2E08  ES=2E08  SS=2E08  CS=2CB0  IP=01CD   NV UP EI PL NZ AC PO NC
2CB0:01CD 740A          JZ      _int86+20 (01D9)
-T 5  <Enter>
AX=0060  BX=00D0  CX=0000  DX=0000  SP=0F66  BP=0F74  SI=0089  DI=1065
DS=2E08  ES=2E08  SS=2E08  CS=2CB0  IP=01CF   NV UP EI PL NZ AC PO NC
2CB0:01CF 3C26          CMP     AL,26                  ;'&'
AX=0060  BX=00D0  CX=0000  DX=0000  SP=0F66  BP=0F74  SI=0089  DI=1065
DS=2E08  ES=2E08  SS=2E08  CS=2CB0  IP=01D1   NV UP EI PL NZ AC PE NC
2CB0:01D1 7406          JZ      _int86+20 (01D9)
AX=0060  BX=00D0  CX=0000  DX=0000  SP=0F66  BP=0F74  SI=0089  DI=1065
DS=2E08  ES=2E08  SS=2E08  CS=2CB0  IP=01D3   NV UP EI PL NZ AC PE NC
2CB0:01D3 C646F8CB      MOV     Byte Ptr [BP-08],CB           SS:0F6C=B0
AX=0060  BX=00D0  CX=0000  DX=0000  SP=0F66  BP=0F74  SI=0089  DI=1065
DS=2E08  ES=2E08  SS=2E08  CS=2CB0  IP=01D7   NV UP EI PL NZ AC PE NC
```

(more)

```
2CB0:01D7 EB0C          JMP     _int86+2C (01E5)
AX=0060  BX=00D0  CX=0000  DX=0000  SP=0F66  BP=0F74  SI=0089  DI=1065
DS=2E08  ES=2E08  SS=2E08  CS=2CB0  IP=01E5   NV UP EI PL NZ AC PE NC
2CB0:01E5 8C56F4          MOV     [BP-0C],SS                      SS:0F68=0F74
-T 5 <Enter>
AX=0060  BX=00D0  CX=0000  DX=0000  SP=0F66  BP=0F74  SI=0089  DI=1065
DS=2E08  ES=2E08  SS=2E08  CS=2CB0  IP=01E8   NV UP EI PL NZ AC PE NC
2CB0:01E8 8D46F6          LEA     AX,[BP-0A]                      SS:0F6A=60CD
AX=0F6A  BX=00D0  CX=0000  DX=0000  SP=0F66  BP=0F74  SI=0089  DI=1065
DS=2E08  ES=2E08  SS=2E08  CS=2CB0  IP=01EB   NV UP EI PL NZ AC PE NC
2CB0:01EB 8946F2          MOV     [BP-0E],AX                      SS:0F66=0060
AX=0F6A  BX=00D0  CX=0000  DX=0000  SP=0F66  BP=0F74  SI=0089  DI=1065
DS=2E08  ES=2E08  SS=2E08  CS=2CB0  IP=01EE   NV UP EI PL NZ AC PE NC
2CB0:01EE 8B7E06          MOV     DI,[BP+06]                      SS:0F7A=0F82
AX=0F6A  BX=00D0  CX=0000  DX=0000  SP=0F66  BP=0F74  SI=0089  DI=0F82
DS=2E08  ES=2E08  SS=2E08  CS=2CB0  IP=01F1   NV UP EI PL NZ AC PE NC
2CB0:01F1 8B05            MOV     AX,[DI]                         DS:0F82=0100
AX=0100  BX=00D0  CX=0000  DX=0000  SP=0F66  BP=0F74  SI=0089  DI=0F82
DS=2E08  ES=2E08  SS=2E08  CS=2CB0  IP=01F3   NV UP EI PL NZ AC PE NC
2CB0:01F3 8B5D02          MOV     BX,[DI+02]                      DS:0F84=0000
-T 5 <Enter>
AX=0100  BX=0000  CX=0000  DX=0000  SP=0F66  BP=0F74  SI=0089  DI=0F82
DS=2E08  ES=2E08  SS=2E08  CS=2CB0  IP=01F6   NV UP EI PL NZ AC PE NC
2CB0:01F6 8B4D04          MOV     CX,[DI+04]                      DS:0F86=0000
AX=0100  BX=0000  CX=0000  DX=0000  SP=0F66  BP=0F74  SI=0089  DI=0F82
DS=2E08  ES=2E08  SS=2E08  CS=2CB0  IP=01F9   NV UP EI PL NZ AC PE NC
2CB0:01F9 8B5506          MOV     DX,[DI+06]                      DS:0F88=0000
AX=0100  BX=0000  CX=0000  DX=0000  SP=0F66  BP=0F74  SI=0089  DI=0F82
DS=2E08  ES=2E08  SS=2E08  CS=2CB0  IP=01FC   NV UP EI PL NZ AC PE NC
2CB0:01FC 8B7508          MOV     SI,[DI+08]                      DS:0F8A=0000
AX=0100  BX=0000  CX=0000  DX=0000  SP=0F66  BP=0F74  SI=0000  DI=0F82
DS=2E08  ES=2E08  SS=2E08  CS=2CB0  IP=01FF   NV UP EI PL NZ AC PE NC
2CB0:01FF 8B7D0A          MOV     DI,[DI+0A]                      DS:0F8C=0000
AX=0100  BX=0000  CX=0000  DX=0000  SP=0F66  BP=0F74  SI=0000  DI=0000
DS=2E08  ES=2E08  SS=2E08  CS=2CB0  IP=0202   NV UP EI PL NZ AC PE NC
2CB0:0202 55             PUSH    BP
-T 5 <Enter>
AX=0100  BX=0000  CX=0000  DX=0000  SP=0F64  BP=0F74  SI=0000  DI=0000
DS=2E08  ES=2E08  SS=2E08  CS=2CB0  IP=0203   NV UP EI PL NZ AC PE NC
2CB0:0203 83ED0E          SUB     BP,+0E
AX=0100  BX=0000  CX=0000  DX=0000  SP=0F64  BP=0F66  SI=0000  DI=0000
DS=2E08  ES=2E08  SS=2E08  CS=2CB0  IP=0206   NV UP EI PL NZ AC PE NC
2CB0:0206 FF5E00          CALL    FAR [BP+00]                     SS:0F66=0F6A
AX=0100  BX=0000  CX=0000  DX=0000  SP=0F60  BP=0F66  SI=0000  DI=0000
DS=2E08  ES=2E08  SS=2E08  CS=2E08  IP=0F6A   NV UP EI PL NZ AC PE NC
2E08:0F6A CD60            INT     60
AX=0100  BX=0000  CX=0000  DX=0000  SP=0F5A  BP=0F66  SI=0000  DI=0000
DS=2E08  ES=2E08  SS=2E08  CS=1313  IP=0190   NV UP DI PL NZ AC PE NC
1313:0190 80FC00          CMP     AH,00
AX=0100  BX=0000  CX=0000  DX=0000  SP=0F5A  BP=0F66  SI=0000  DI=0000
DS=2E08  ES=2E08  SS=2E08  CS=1313  IP=0193   NV UP DI PL NZ NA PO NC
1313:0193 7521            JNZ     01B6
```

When the Interrupt 60H call is encountered at offset 0F6AH, the values passed to it can be checked. AH contains 1 and DX contains 0 — the correct values for START COM1.

In order to use the symbols for BADSCOP, use the Open Symbol Map command, XO, to switch to the correct symbol map. Then, because the value of *CSEG* is not defined in the map, use the Set Symbol Value command to set *CSEG* to the current value of CS. (CS was changed to the correct value for BADSCOP when the program executed the INT 60H instruction.)

```
-XO BADSCOP!  <Enter>
-Z CSEG CS    <Enter>
-X?*          <Enter>

CSEG: (1313)
0100 INITIALIZE    0103 OLD_COMM_INT 0107 COUNT       0109 STATUS
010A PORT          010B BUFPNTR      010D COMSCOPE     0190 CONTROL
020A VECTOR_INIT
```

Because the BADSCOP symbols now have meaning, a great deal of trouble can be avoided by setting a breakpoint at *CONTROL*, the entry point for Interrupt 60H, so that it will no longer be necessary to trace the *_int86* routine to find the INT 60H command. Execution will automatically stop when the Interrupt 60H handler is entered.

```
-BP CONTROL   <Enter>
-BL   <Enter>
0 e 2CB0:002E [COMMSCMD!_TEXT:_main+1E (002E)] commscmd.C:41
1 e 2CB0:0046 [COMMSCMD!_TEXT:_main+36 (0046)] commscmd.C:42
2 e 2CB0:0066 [COMMSCMD!_TEXT:_main+56 (0066)] commscmd.C:44
3 e 2CB0:0086 [COMMSCMD!_TEXT:_main+76 (0086)] commscmd.C:46
4 e 2CB0:008B [COMMSCMD!_TEXT:_main+7B (008B)] commscmd.C:49
5 e 2CB0:00AC [COMMSCMD!_TEXT:_main+9C (00AC)] commscmd.C:53
6 e 2CB0:00C7 [COMMSCMD!_TEXT:_main+B7 (00C7)] commscmd.C:58
7 e 2CB0:00F5 [COMMSCMD!_TEXT:_main+E5 (00F5)] commscmd.C:63
8 e 1313:0190 [CSEGS:CONTROL]
```

With the housekeeping tasks done, the business of debugging BADSCOP can begin. The first thing *CONTROL* does is check for a stop request. If no stop request is present, the routine jumps to the check for a start request. (The first test and jump were already complete when the trace ended above.) The test for a start request is passed. *CONTROL* places the port number in a local variable, resets the buffer pointer and the buffer count, and turns tracing status on. With all this complete, *CONTROL* returns.

```
-T 5  <Enter>
AX=01BB   BX=E81E   CX=3F48   DX=0000   SP=0F5A   BP=0F66   SI=1CE7   DI=7400
DS=2E08   ES=2E08   SS=2E08   CS=1313   IP=01B6    NV UP DI PL NZ NA PO NC
1313:01B6 80FC01          CMP     AH,01
AX=01BB   BX=E81E   CX=3F48   DX=0000   SP=0F5A   BP=0F66   SI=1CE7   DI=7400
DS=2E08   ES=2E08   SS=2E08   CS=1313   IP=01B9    NV UP DI PL ZR NA PE NC
1313:01B9 751C            JNZ     CONTROL+47 (01D7)
AX=01BB   BX=E81E   CX=3F48   DX=0000   SP=0F5A   BP=0F66   SI=1CE7   DI=7400
DS=2E08   ES=2E08   SS=2E08   CS=1313   IP=01BB    NV UP DI PL ZR NA PE NC
1313:01BB 2E88160A01      MOV     CS:[PORT],DL                      CS:010A=00
```

(more)

```
AX=01BB  BX=E81E  CX=3F48  DX=0000  SP=0F5A  BP=0F66  SI=1CE7  DI=7400
DS=2E08  ES=2E08  SS=2E08  CS=1313  IP=01C0   NV UP DI PL ZR NA PE NC
1313:01C0 2EC7060B010202 MOV     Word Ptr CS:[BUFPNTR],VECTOR_INIT (0209) CS:010B=0202
AX=01BB  BX=E81E  CX=3F48  DX=0000  SP=0F5A  BP=0F66  SI=1CE7  DI=7400
DS=2E08  ES=2E08  SS=2E08  CS=1313  IP=01C7   NV UP DI PL ZR NA PE NC
1313:01C7 2EC70607010000 MOV     Word Ptr CS:[COUNT],0000        CS:0107=0002
-T 5  <Enter>
AX=01BB  BX=E81E  CX=3F48  DX=0000  SP=0F5A  BP=0F66  SI=1CE7  DI=7400
DS=2E08  ES=2E08  SS=2E08  CS=1313  IP=01CE   NV UP DI PL ZR NA PE NC
1313:01CE 2EC606090101  MOV     Byte Ptr CS:[STATUS],01         CS:0109=01
AX=01BB  BX=E81E  CX=3F48  DX=0000  SP=0F5A  BP=0F66  SI=1CE7  DI=7400
DS=2E08  ES=2E08  SS=2E08  CS=1313  IP=01D4   NV UP DI PL ZR NA PE NC
1313:01D4 EB2B          JMP       CONTROL+71 (0201)
AX=01BB  BX=E81E  CX=3F48  DX=0000  SP=0F5A  BP=0F66  SI=1CE7  DI=7400
DS=2E08  ES=2E08  SS=2E08  CS=1313  IP=0201   NV UP DI PL ZR NA PE NC
1313:0201 CF            IRET
AX=01BB  BX=E81E  CX=3F48  DX=0000  SP=0F60  BP=0F66  SI=1CE7  DI=7400
DS=2E08  ES=2E08  SS=2E08  CS=2E08  IP=0F6C   NV UP EI PL NZ AC PE NC
2E08:0F6C CB            RETF
AX=01BB  BX=E81E  CX=3F48  DX=0000  SP=0F64  BP=0F66  SI=1CE7  DI=7400
DS=2E08  ES=2E08  SS=2E08  CS=2CB0  IP=0209   NV UP EI PL NZ AC PE NC
2CB0:0209 5D            POP       BP
```

As can be seen from the trace, *CONTROL* performed correctly, so execution of the routine can continue.

```
-G  <Enter>
Communications tracing STARTED for port COM1:
AX=002F  BX=0001  CX=0C13  DX=0000  SP=0FA6  BP=0000  SI=0089  DI=1065
DS=2E08  ES=2E08  SS=2E08  CS=2CB0  IP=00F5   NV UP EI PL NZ NA PE NC
2CB0:00F5 C3            RET                              ;BR7
```

COMMSCMD has written the message to the user and trapped at the breakpoint set at the end of *_main*. The Examine Symbol Map command now shows that SYMDEB has automatically switched to the symbol map for COMMSCMD.

```
-X*  <Enter>
[2CB0 COMMSCMD]
    [2CB0 _TEXT]
     2E08 DGROUP
 0000 BADSCOP
     1313 CSEG
```

No problems have been encountered with the START command; now the same process of checking COMMSCMD and BADSCOP must be repeated for the STOP command. (Even if problems had been found with the START command, it would be imprudent not to test the other commands — they could have errors, too.) SYMDEB could be exited and restarted with new commands, but this would mean the loss of the painfully created set of breakpoints. Instead, a new copy of COMMSCMD is loaded without leaving SYMDEB. One problem with this, however, is that when SYMDEB loads an .EXE file, it adds the value of the initial CS register to the addresses of the segments in the symbol map whose name matches the .EXE file. This is fine the first time the program loads, but the second time, all the values are doubled and therefore incorrect. To avoid this error, the addresses must be adjusted before the load. Use the Set Symbol Value command to subtract CS from each segment name in COMMSCMD!. The Examine Symbol Map command shows the new values.

```
-Z _TEXT _TEXT-CS  <Enter>
-Z DGROUP DGROUP-CS  <Enter>
-X*  <Enter>
[2CB0 COMMSCMD]
      [0000 _TEXT]
        0158 DGROUP
  0000 BADSCOP
      1313 CSEG
```

The Name File or Command-Tail Parameters command, N, and the Load File or Sectors command, L, can now be used to load a new copy of COMMSCMD.EXE.

```
-N COMMSCMD.EXE  <Enter>
-L  <Enter>
-X*  <Enter>
[2CB0 COMMSCMD]
      [2CB0 _TEXT]
        2E08 DGROUP
  0000 BADSCOP
      1313 CSEG
```

Notice that the segment values inside COMMSCMD! are the same as they were when the program was first loaded. Use the Name command again, this time to set the command tail to contain a STOP command for COM1. The breakpoint table from the first execution is still set, so the program can now be traced in the same way.

```
-N STOP 1  <Enter>
-G  <Enter>
AX=0022  BX=0F84  CX=0019  DX=0098  SP=0F80  BP=0FA6  SI=0089  DI=1065
DS=2E08  ES=2E08  SS=2E08  CS=2CB0  IP=002E   NV UP EI PL NZ NA PO NC
41:            if (0 == stricmp(argv[1],"STOP"))
2CB0:002E B83600      MOV    AX,0036                    ;BR0
-G  <Enter>
AX=0000  BX=415A  CX=0000  DX=0098  SP=0F80  BP=0FA6  SI=0089  DI=1065
DS=2E08  ES=2E08  SS=2E08  CS=2CB0  IP=0046   NV UP EI PL ZR NA PE NC
42:            cmd = 0;
2CB0:0046 C746FC0000      MOV    Word Ptr [BP-04],0000      ;BR1 SS:0FA2=0000
-G  <Enter>
AX=0000  BX=415A  CX=0000  DX=0098  SP=0F80  BP=0FA6  SI=0089  DI=1065
DS=2E08  ES=2E08  SS=2E08  CS=2CB0  IP=008B   NV UP EI PL ZR NA PE NC
49:      if (argc == 3)
2CB0:008B 837E0403      CMP    Word Ptr [BP+04],+03      ;BR4 SS:0FAA=0003
-G  <Enter>
AX=0001  BX=00D0  CX=0000  DX=0000  SP=0F80  BP=0FA6  SI=0089  DI=1065
DS=2E08  ES=2E08  SS=2E08  CS=2CB0  IP=00AC   NV UP EI PL NZ NA PO NC
53:            port = port-1;
```

(more)

```
2CB0:00AC FF4EFA          DEC      Word Ptr [BP-06]                ;BR5 SS:0FA0=0001
-G  <Enter>
AX=0060  BX=00D0  CX=0000  DX=0000  SP=0F7A  BP=0FA6  SI=0089  DI=1065
DS=2E08  ES=2E08  SS=2E08  CS=2CB0  IP=00C7    NV UP EI PL ZR NA PE NC
2CB0:00C7 E8EF00          CALL     _int86                          ;BR6
```

COMMSCMD detected that this is a stop request for COM1 and set the arguments for
_int86 correctly. Because a breakpoint is now set at *CONTROL*, tracing until the Interrupt
60H call is found is not necessary. Simply executing the program will cause it to stop at
CONTROL.

```
-G  <Enter>
AX=001E  BX=3F48  CX=0000  DX=0000  SP=0F5C  BP=0F68  SI=7400  DI=E903
DS=2E08  ES=2E08  SS=2E08  CS=1313  IP=0190    NV UP DI PL NZ AC PO NC
CSEG:CONTROL:
1313:0190 80FC00          CMP      AH,00                           ;BR8
```

The registers are set correctly for a stop request on COM1 (AH = 0, DX = 0). The routine
can now be traced to check for correct operation. First, however, a quick look at the symbol maps shows that SYMDEB has automatically switched to BADSCOP's symbols.

```
-X*  <Enter>
 2CB0 COMMSCMD
      2CB0 _TEXT
      2E08 DGROUP
[0000 BADSCOP]
      [1313 CSEG]
-T 5  <Enter>
AX=001E  BX=3F48  CX=0000  DX=0000  SP=0F5C  BP=0F68  SI=7400  DI=E903
DS=2E08  ES=2E08  SS=2E08  CS=1313  IP=0193    NV UP DI PL ZR NA PE NC
1313:0193 7521            JNZ      CONTROL+26 (01B6)
AX=001E  BX=3F48  CX=0000  DX=0000  SP=0F5C  BP=0F68  SI=7400  DI=E903
DS=2E08  ES=2E08  SS=2E08  CS=1313  IP=0195    NV UP DI PL ZR NA PE NC
1313:0195 1E              PUSH     DS
AX=001E  BX=3F48  CX=0000  DX=0000  SP=0F5A  BP=0F68  SI=7400  DI=E903
DS=2E08  ES=2E08  SS=2E08  CS=1313  IP=0196    NV UP DI PL ZR NA PE NC
1313:0196 53              PUSH     BX
AX=001E  BX=3F48  CX=0000  DX=0000  SP=0F58  BP=0F68  SI=7400  DI=E903
DS=2E08  ES=2E08  SS=2E08  CS=1313  IP=0197    NV UP DI PL ZR NA PE NC
1313:0197 0E              PUSH     CS
AX=001E  BX=3F48  CX=0000  DX=0000  SP=0F56  BP=0F68  SI=7400  DI=E903
DS=2E08  ES=2E08  SS=2E08  CS=1313  IP=0198    NV UP DI PL ZR NA PE NC
1313:0198 1F              POP      DS
-T 5  <Enter>
AX=001E  BX=3F48  CX=0000  DX=0000  SP=0F58  BP=0F68  SI=7400  DI=E903
DS=1313  ES=2E08  SS=2E08  CS=1313  IP=0199    NV UP DI PL ZR NA PE NC
1313:0199 C606090100      MOV      Byte Ptr [STATUS],00             DS:0109=01
AX=001E  BX=3F48  CX=0000  DX=0000  SP=0F58  BP=0F68  SI=7400  DI=E903
DS=1313  ES=2E08  SS=2E08  CS=1313  IP=019E    NV UP DI PL ZR NA PE NC
1313:019E 8B1E0B01        MOV      BX,[BUFPNTR]                     DS:010B=0202
AX=001E  BX=0202  CX=0000  DX=0000  SP=0F58  BP=0F68  SI=7400  DI=E903
DS=1313  ES=2E08  SS=2E08  CS=1313  IP=01A2    NV UP DI PL ZR NA PE NC
```

(more)

```
1313:01A2 C60780        MOV     Byte Ptr [BX],80                    DS:0202=80
AX=001E  BX=0202  CX=0000  DX=0000  SP=0F58  BP=0F68  SI=7400  DI=E903
DS=1313  ES=2E08  SS=2E08  CS=1313  IP=01A5   NV UP DI PL ZR NA PE NC
1313:01A5 C64701FF      MOV     Byte Ptr [BX+01],FF                 DS:0203=FF
AX=001E  BX=0202  CX=0000  DX=0000  SP=0F58  BP=0F68  SI=7400  DI=E903
DS=1313  ES=2E08  SS=2E08  CS=1313  IP=01A9   NV UP DI PL ZR NA PE NC
1313:01A9 FF060701      INC     Word Ptr [COUNT]                    DS:0107=0000
-T 5  <Enter>
AX=001E  BX=0202  CX=0000  DX=0000  SP=0F58  BP=0F68  SI=7400  DI=E903
DS=1313  ES=2E08  SS=2E08  CS=1313  IP=01AD   NV UP DI PL NZ NA PO NC
1313:01AD FF060701      INC     Word Ptr [COUNT]                    DS:0107=0001
AX=001E  BX=0202  CX=0000  DX=0000  SP=0F58  BP=0F68  SI=7400  DI=E903
DS=1313  ES=2E08  SS=2E08  CS=1313  IP=01B1   NV UP DI PL NZ NA PO NC
1313:01B1 5B            POP     BX
AX=001E  BX=3F48  CX=0000  DX=0000  SP=0F5A  BP=0F68  SI=7400  DI=E903
DS=1313  ES=2E08  SS=2E08  CS=1313  IP=01B2   NV UP DI PL NZ NA PO NC
1313:01B2 1F            POP     DS
AX=001E  BX=3F48  CX=0000  DX=0000  SP=0F5C  BP=0F68  SI=7400  DI=E903
DS=2E08  ES=2E08  SS=2E08  CS=1313  IP=01B3   NV UP DI PL NZ NA PO NC
1313:01B3 EB4C          JMP     CONTROL+71 (0201)
AX=001E  BX=3F48  CX=0000  DX=0000  SP=0F5C  BP=0F68  SI=7400  DI=E903
DS=2E08  ES=2E08  SS=2E08  CS=1313  IP=0201   NV UP DI PL NZ NA PO NC
1313:0201 CF            IRET
```

CONTROL correctly detected that this was a stop request. It then saved the user's registers and established a DS equal to CS. (Remember that BADSCOP is a .COM file and CS = DS = SS.) Having done this, the routine moves a zero to *STATUS*, which turns the trace off. It then moves 80H FFH to the buffer to indicate the end of a trace session, increments *COUNT* to allow for the new entry, and restores the user's registers. What it does *not* do is increment the buffer pointer to allow for the stop marker. This behavior is entirely consistent with the observed phenomena: When a trace is stopped and resumed, the stop marker is missing and the count is one too high. The fix is to add

```
INC     BX              ;INCREMENT BUFFER POINTER
INC     BX              ; .
MOV     BUFPNTR,BX      ; .
```

to the *CONTROL* procedure before the registers are restored. (Insert these lines later with your favorite editor.)

Even though the bug has been found, the rest of the routine should be checked for other possible bugs.

```
-G  <Enter>
Communications tracing STOPPED for port COM1:
AX=002F  BX=0001  CX=0C13  DX=0000  SP=0FA8  BP=0000  SI=0089  DI=1065
DS=2E08  ES=2E08  SS=2E08  CS=2CB0  IP=00F5   NV UP EI PL NZ AC PO NC
2CB0:00F5 C3            RET                                    ;BR7
```

Loading a new copy of COMMSCMD, setting the command tail to *RESUME 1*, and monitoring program execution yields the following:

```
-N COMMSCMD.EXE  <Enter>
-Z _TEXT _TEXT-CS  <Enter>
-Z DGROUP DGROUP-CS  <Enter>
-X*  <Enter>
[2CB0 COMMSCMD]
      [0000 _TEXT]
       0158 DGROUP
 0000 BADSCOP
       1313 CSEG
-L  <Enter>
-X*  <Enter>
[2CB0 COMMSCMD]
      [2CB0 _TEXT]
       2E08 DGROUP
 0000 BADSCOP
       1313 CSEG
-N RESUME 1  <Enter>
-G  <Enter>
AX=0022  BX=0F82  CX=0019  DX=0098  SP=0F7E  BP=0FA4  SI=0089  DI=1065
DS=2E08  ES=2E08  SS=2E08  CS=2CB0  IP=002E   NV UP EI PL NZ NA PO NC
41:             if (0 == stricmp(argv[1],"STOP"))
2CB0:002E B83600        MOV     AX,0036                     ;BR0
-G  <Enter>
AX=0000  BX=415A  CX=0000  DX=0098  SP=0F7E  BP=0FA4  SI=0089  DI=1065
DS=2E08  ES=2E08  SS=2E08  CS=2CB0  IP=0086   NV UP EI PL ZR NA PE NC
46:             cmd = 2;
2CB0:0086 C746FC0200     MOV     Word Ptr [BP-04],0002       ;BR3 SS:0FA0=0000
-G  <Enter>
AX=0000  BX=415A  CX=0000  DX=0098  SP=0F7E  BP=0FA4  SI=0089  DI=1065
DS=2E08  ES=2E08  SS=2E08  CS=2CB0  IP=008B   NV UP EI PL ZR NA PE NC
49:        if (argc == 3)
2CB0:008B 837E0403       CMP     Word Ptr [BP+04],+03        ;BR4 SS:0FA8=0003
-G  <Enter>
AX=0001  BX=00D0  CX=0000  DX=0000  SP=0F7E  BP=0FA4  SI=0089  DI=1065
DS=2E08  ES=2E08  SS=2E08  CS=2CB0  IP=00AC   NV UP EI PL NZ NA PO NC
53:             port = port-1;
2CB0:00AC FF4EFA         DEC     Word Ptr [BP-06]            ;BR5 SS:0F9E=0001
-G  <Enter>
AX=0060  BX=00D0  CX=0000  DX=0000  SP=0F78  BP=0FA4  SI=0089  DI=1065
DS=2E08  ES=2E08  SS=2E08  CS=2CB0  IP=00C7   NV UP EI PL ZR NA PE NC
2CB0:00C7 E8EF00         CALL    _int86                      ;BR6
-G  <Enter>
AX=0265  BX=001E  CX=3F48  DX=0000  SP=0F5A  BP=0F66  SI=0000  DI=7400
DS=2E08  ES=2E08  SS=2E08  CS=1313  IP=0190   NV UP DI PL NZ AC PE NC
CSEG:CONTROL:
1313:0190 80FC00         CMP     AH,00                       ;BR8
-T 5  <Enter>
AX=0265  BX=001E  CX=3F48  DX=0000  SP=0F5A  BP=0F66  SI=0000  DI=7400
DS=2E08  ES=2E08  SS=2E08  CS=1313  IP=0193   NV UP DI PL NZ NA PO NC
1313:0193 7521           JNZ     CONTROL+26 (01B6)
AX=0265  BX=001E  CX=3F48  DX=0000  SP=0F5A  BP=0F66  SI=0000  DI=7400
DS=2E08  ES=2E08  SS=2E08  CS=1313  IP=01B6   NV UP DI PL NZ NA PO NC
1313:01B6 80FC01         CMP     AH,01
```

(more)

```
AX=0265  BX=001E  CX=3F48  DX=0000  SP=0F5A  BP=0F66  SI=0000  DI=7400
DS=2E08  ES=2E08  SS=2E08  CS=1313  IP=01B9   NV UP DI PL NZ NA PO NC
1313:01B9 751C          JNZ     CONTROL+47 (01D7)
AX=0265  BX=001E  CX=3F48  DX=0000  SP=0F5A  BP=0F66  SI=0000  DI=7400
DS=2E08  ES=2E08  SS=2E08  CS=1313  IP=01D7   NV UP DI PL NZ NA PO NC
1313:01D7 80FC02        CMP     AH,02
AX=0265  BX=001E  CX=3F48  DX=0000  SP=0F5A  BP=0F66  SI=0000  DI=7400
DS=2E08  ES=2E08  SS=2E08  CS=1313  IP=01DA   NV UP DI PL ZR NA PE NC
1313:01DA 7516          JNZ     CONTROL+62 (01F2)
-T 5  <Enter>
AX=0265  BX=001E  CX=3F48  DX=0000  SP=0F5A  BP=0F66  SI=0000  DI=7400
DS=2E08  ES=2E08  SS=2E08  CS=1313  IP=01DC   NV UP DI PL ZR NA PE NC
1313:01DC 2E833E0B0100  CMP     Word Ptr CS:[BUFPNTR],+00      CS:010B=0202
AX=0265  BX=001E  CX=3F48  DX=0000  SP=0F5A  BP=0F66  SI=0000  DI=7400
DS=2E08  ES=2E08  SS=2E08  CS=1313  IP=01E2   NV UP DI PL NZ NA PO NC
1313:01E2 741D          JZ      CONTROL+71 (0201)
AX=0265  BX=001E  CX=3F48  DX=0000  SP=0F5A  BP=0F66  SI=0000  DI=7400
DS=2E08  ES=2E08  SS=2E08  CS=1313  IP=01E4   NV UP DI PL NZ NA PO NC
1313:01E4 2E88160A01    MOV     CS:[PORT],DL                  CS:010A=00
AX=0265  BX=001E  CX=3F48  DX=0000  SP=0F5A  BP=0F66  SI=0000  DI=7400
DS=2E08  ES=2E08  SS=2E08  CS=1313  IP=01E9   NV UP DI PL NZ NA PO NC
1313:01E9 2EC606090101  MOV     Byte Ptr CS:[STATUS],01       CS:0109=00
AX=0265  BX=001E  CX=3F48  DX=0000  SP=0F5A  BP=0F66  SI=0000  DI=7400
DS=2E08  ES=2E08  SS=2E08  CS=1313  IP=01EF   NV UP DI PL NZ NA PO NC
1313:01EF EB10          JMP     CONTROL+71 (0201)
-T 5  <Enter>
AX=0265  BX=001E  CX=3F48  DX=0000  SP=0F5A  BP=0F66  SI=0000  DI=7400
DS=2E08  ES=2E08  SS=2E08  CS=1313  IP=0201   NV UP DI PL NZ NA PO NC
1313:0201 CF            IRET
AX=0265  BX=001E  CX=3F48  DX=0000  SP=0F60  BP=0F66  SI=0000  DI=7400
DS=2E08  ES=2E08  SS=2E08  CS=2E08  IP=0F6C   NV UP EI PL NZ AC PE NC
2E08:0F6C CB            RETF
AX=0265  BX=001E  CX=3F48  DX=0000  SP=0F64  BP=0F66  SI=0000  DI=7400
DS=2E08  ES=2E08  SS=2E08  CS=2CB0  IP=0209   NV UP EI PL NZ AC PE NC
2CB0:0209 5D            POP     BP
AX=0265  BX=001E  CX=3F48  DX=0000  SP=0F66  BP=0F74  SI=0000  DI=7400
DS=2E08  ES=2E08  SS=2E08  CS=2CB0  IP=020A   NV UP EI PL NZ AC PE NC
2CB0:020A 57            PUSH    DI
AX=0265  BX=001E  CX=3F48  DX=0000  SP=0F64  BP=0F74  SI=0000  DI=7400
DS=2E08  ES=2E08  SS=2E08  CS=2CB0  IP=020B   NV UP EI PL NZ AC PE NC
2CB0:020B 8B7E08        MOV     DI,[BP+08]                    SS:0F7C=0F90
-G  <Enter>
Communications tracing RESUMED for port COM1:
AX=002F  BX=0001  CX=0C13  DX=0000  SP=0FA6  BP=0000  SI=0089  DI=1065
DS=2E08  ES=2E08  SS=2E08  CS=2CB0  IP=00F5   NV UP EI PL NZ NA PE NC
2CB0:00F5 C3            RET                                   ;BR7
-Q  <Enter>
```

The processing of a resume request is correct. Thus, the problem with stop processing in BADSCOP was the only problem. The corrected BADSCOP, which is actually COMMSCOP, is shown in Figure 18-4.

CodeView

CodeView is the most sophisticated debugging monitor produced by Microsoft. It combines the philosophy and many of the commands of its predecessors, DEBUG and SYMDEB, with true source-code debugging. The availability of source lines and symbols allows CodeView to rival the convenience of program development and debugging previously available only in interpreters such as Microsoft GW-BASIC. However, this high level of interaction with the source program is also the root of its problems for advanced debugging.

In order to provide the debugger with the tools to debug at the source-line level and to interrogate program variables, CodeView is required to have a detailed knowledge of how high-order languages work and of their internal conventions. This is not a problem for languages like C, Pascal, and FORTRAN, versions of which are produced by the same company that created CodeView. The object code generated by these compilers obeys a stringent set of rules and conventions. Assembly-language programs, however, tend to follow their own rules and traditions, making them quite different from C programs, with their own separate debugging needs.

C, Pascal, and FORTRAN programmers will find CodeView a dream to use. Assembly-language programmers using versions of MASM earlier than 5.0 will find CodeView cumbersome and will have to weigh its advantages over its disadvantages. All users will, however, appreciate the good design and programming that have gone into CodeView. It is pleasing to know that someone understands the programmer's debugging needs and is trying to ease the burden.

CodeView has added several welcome functions to the debugger's repertoire, but one of these new features towers above the rest — watchpoints. The debugger can watch the values of program variables or expressions and set breakpoints on them, making it possible to stop execution if an expression evaluates to zero or if a location changes. Previous debugging monitors have been limited to tracing and breaking on instructions. This new facet of debugging changes, somewhat, the approach to resolving a bug.

In the previous discussion of debugging techniques, an orderly application of techniques from inspection and observation through instrumentation to debugging monitors was recommended. This sequence is still recommended with CodeView, but now the instrumentation features have been integrated into the debugging monitor.

A simple example

The following example shows how CodeView uses the instrumentation approach to isolate a problem and then uses the debugging monitor functions to solve it. The example is also an introduction to CodeView commands and techniques. The commands are, for the most part, similar to those used by SYMDEB. Those commands that differ greatly are indicated. This example, like all the examples and demonstrations in this article, is not intended to be a complete tutorial — CodeView commands are summarized elsewhere in this book and explained in detail in the manual accompanying the product. *See* PROGRAMMING UTILITIES: codeview. The example simply shows some of the more common CodeView commands and demonstrates debugging techniques using them.

UPPERCAS.C (Figure 18-13) is a simple program whose sole function is to convert a canned string to uppercase. When executed, the program prints a few of the characters from the string and some that aren't in the string. Inspecting the listing doesn't reveal the cause of the problem. (Some readers with experience writing C programs will see the cause of the problem, because it is quite common; pretend, for now, that the listing is of no help and enjoy the wonders of CodeView.)

```
/***********************************************************************
 *                                                                     *
 * UPPERCAS.C                                                           *
 *    This routine converts a fixed string to uppercase and prints it. *
 *                                                                     *
 ***********************************************************************/

#include <ctype.h>
#include <string.h>
#include <stdio.h>

main(argc,argv)

int argc;
char *argv[];

{
char    *cp,c;

        cp = "a string\n";

        /*  Convert *cp to uppercase and write to standard output  */

        while (*cp != '\0')
                {
                c = toupper(*cp++);
                putchar(c);
                }

}
```

Figure 18-13. An erroneous C program to convert a string to uppercase.

Like SYMDEB, CodeView requires some special preparation to produce a suitable executable file. CodeView, however, makes the job much simpler. Using the Microsoft C Compiler, compile the program with

```
C>MSC /Zi UPPERCAS;  <Enter>
```

(Remember that C is case sensitive when interpreting switches, so the /Zi switch should be entered exactly as shown.) The /Zi switch instructs the compiler to generate the symbol tables and line-number information needed by CodeView. Other options appropriate to the program can also be included, but /Zi is required.

To form an executable file, use the Microsoft Object Linker (LINK) as follows:

```
C>LINK /CO UPPERCAS;  <Enter>
```

This command line instructs LINK to build an executable file with the information needed for CodeView. Other options can be used as needed or desired. The output of LINK, UPPERCAS.EXE, will be larger than a .EXE file built without /CO (about 2600 bytes larger in this case), but the program will run correctly when executed without CodeView.

Starting CodeView is straightforward. Simply type

```
C> CV UPPERCAS   <Enter>
```

CodeView loads UPPERCAS.EXE. It locates UPPERCAS.C, the source file, and loads that too. It then presents a full-screen display similar to this:

```
 File  View  Search  Run  Watch  Options  Language  Calls  Help | F8=Trace F5=Go
                            uppercas.C
1:
2:    /*********************************************************************
3:     *
4:     * UPPERCAS.C
5:     *     This routine converts a fixed string to uppercase and prints it.
6:     *
7:     *********************************************************************
8:
9:    #include <ctype.h>
10:   #include <string.h>
11:   #include <stdio.h>
12:
13:   main(argc,argv)
14:
15:   int argc;
16:   char *argv[];
17:
18:   {

Microsoft (R) CodeView (R)  Version 2.0
(C) Copyright Microsoft Corp. 1986, 1987.  All rights reserved.
>
```

This display has two windows open: the display window, which shows the program being debugged, and the the dialog window, which currently contains only the copyright notice and a prompt (>) for input. The F6 function key moves the cursor back and forth between the two windows.

CodeView can be instructed from either window to go to a specific line (that is, to execute until a specific line is reached). If the cursor is in the display window, use the arrow keys to select a line and press the F7 key. Execution will proceed until the selected line (or the end of the program) is reached. To start execution without specifying a stop line, press F5.

The same functions can be performed from the dialog window using typed commands, which may seem more familiar. Enter the Go Execute Program command, G, optionally followed by an address. Execution will continue until the specified address is reached or until stopped by something else, such as the end of the program. In this sense, the CodeView Go command is the same as that of DEBUG and SYMDEB. Unlike those routines, however, CodeView's Go command does not allow an equals operator (=).

The address for the Go command can be specified in several ways. Because the display window is currently showing only source lines, it is appropriate to set the stop location in terms of line numbers. The syntax of a line-number specification is the same as in SYMDEB — simply enter the line number preceded by a period:

```
>G .27  <Enter>
```

Note that the line number is specified in decimal. This seemingly innocent statement uncovers one of the problem areas in CodeView, especially for assembly-language programmers. The default radix for CodeView is decimal. This convention works well for things associated with the C program, such as line numbers, but is very inconvenient for addresses and other similar items, which are usually in hexadecimal. Hexadecimal numbers must be specified using the cumbersome C notation. Thus, the number FF3EH would be entered as 0xff3e. The radix can be changed using the Change Current Radix command, N (different from the DEBUG and SYMDEB N command). (The problems associated with hexadecimal numbers in early versions of CodeView are no longer present in versions 2.0 and later.)

The radix problem can be avoided, for the moment, by using labels. Issue

```
>G _main  <Enter>
```

to cause CodeView to execute until the main routine is reached. CodeView then shows

```
 File   View   Search   Run   Watch   Options   Language   Calls   Help  | F8=Trace F5=Go
                            ╡ uppercas.C ╞
9:         #include <ctype.h>
10:        #include <string.h>
11:        #include <stdio.h>
12:
13:        main(argc,argv)
14:
15:        int argc;
16:        char *argv[];
17:
18:        {
19:        char    *cp,c;
20:
21:                cp = "a string\n";
22:
23:                /*  Convert *cp to uppercase and write to standard output  */
24:
25:                while (*cp != '\0')
26:                    {
───────────────────────────────────────────────────────────────────
Microsoft (R) CodeView (R)  Version 2.0
(C) Copyright Microsoft Corp. 1986, 1987.  All rights reserved.
>g _main
>
```

The display shows line 15 in reverse video, indicating that CodeView has stopped there. This is the first line of the *main()* module, but it is not executable. Press the F10 key, which has the same effect as entering the Step Through Program command, P, in the dialog window, to cause line 19 to be executed. The reverse video line is then 21, which is the next line to be executed.

To see the changes to *cp*, *∗cp*, and *c*, establish a watch on these three variables. To use the Watch Word command, WW, for the word *cp*, type

```
>WW cp  <Enter>
```

When entered from the dialog window, this command opens the watch window at the top of the screen and displays the current value of *cp*. To display the expression at *∗cp*, use the Watch Expression command, W?, as follows:

```
>W? cp,s  <Enter>
```

This expression will display the null-delimited string at *∗cp*. Finally, to see the ASCII character value of *c*, use the Watch ASCII command, WA:

```
>WA c  <Enter>
```

The results of these watch commands are shown in the following screen:

```
 File   View   Search   Run   Watch   Options   Language   Calls   Help | F8=Trace F5=Go
                                   uppercas.C
0)  cp   :  55C4:0FF0  5527
1)  cp,s :    ""
2)  c    :  55C4:0FF2  .

9:        #include <ctype.h>
10:       #include <string.h>
11:       #include <stdio.h>
12:
13:       main(argc,argv)
14:
15:       int argc;
16:       char *argv[];
17:
18:       {
19:       char    *cp,c;
20:
21:                    cp = "a string\n";
22:

>ww cp
>w? cp,s
>wa c
>
```

The values displayed in the watch window are not yet defined because line 21, which initialized *cp*, has not been executed. Press F8 to rectify this. Press it again to bring the execution of the program into the main loop.

```
 File   View   Search   Run   Watch   Options   Language   Calls   Help │ F8=Trace F5=Go
                                  ═╡ uppercas.C ╞═
0)   cp  :  55C4:0FF0   0036
1)   cp,s  :  "a string
2)   c   :  55C4:0FF2   .

18:     {
19:     char    *cp,c;
20:
21:             cp = "a string\n";
22:
23:             /*  Convert *cp to uppercase and write to standard output  */
24:
25:             while (*cp != '\0')
26:                     {
27:                       c = toupper(*cp++);
28:                       putchar(c);
29:                     }
30:
31:     }

>ww cp
>w? cp,s
>wa c
>
```

The pointer *cp* now contains the correct address. The Display Memory command, D, could be used to display the contents of DS:0036H, just as in DEBUG and SYMDEB. (This step is not necessary, however, because there is a formatted display of memory in the watch window at 1). The variable *c* has not yet been initialized.

Press the F8 key to execute line 27. A curious and unexpected thing happens, as shown in the next screen:

```
File   View   Search   Run   Watch   Options   Language   Calls   Help │ F8=Trace F5=Go
                                  ┤ uppercas.C ├
0)   cp   :   55C4:0FF0   0038
1)   cp,s  :   "string
2)   c   :   55C4:0FF2

18:        {
19:        char     *cp,c;
20:
21:                cp = "a string\n";
22:
23:                /*  Convert *cp to uppercase and write to standard output  */
24:
25:                while (*cp != '\0')
26:                        {
27:                        c = toupper(*cp++);
28:                        putchar(c);
29:                        }
30:
31:        }

>ww cp
>w? cp,s
>wa c
>
```

Notice that the value of *cp* has changed from 0036H to 0038H. The line of code, however, indicates that the pointer should have been incremented by only one (*cp++*). The second character of the string, a blank, has been loaded into *c*. This could explain the apparent random selection of characters being displayed (actually every other character) and the garbage characters displayed (the zero at the end of the string might be skipped, causing the routine to continue converting until a zero is encountered somewhere in memory).

Source-line debugging does not reveal enough about what is happening in this case. To look more closely at the mechanism of the program, the program must be restarted. Before doing this, set a breakpoint at line 27:

```
>BP  .27   <Enter>
```

Then restart (actually, reload) the program with the Reload Program command, L. Note that watch commands and breakpoints are preserved when a program is restarted. Executing the restarted program with G yields

```
 File  View  Search  Run  Watch  Options  Language  Calls  Help | F8=Trace F5=Go
                           =| uppercas.C |=
0)  cp  :  55C4:0FF0  0036
1)  cp,s  :  "a string
2)  c  :  55C4:0FF2  .

18:    {
19:    char    *cp,c;
20:
21:            cp = "a string\n";
22:
23:            /* Convert *cp to uppercase and write to standard output  */
24:
25:            while (*cp != '\0')
26:                    {
27:                        c = toupper(*cp++);
28:                        putchar(c);
29:                    }
30:
31:    }

>bp .27
>l
>g
>
```

The display shows line 27 in reverse video, indicating that it is the next line to be executed. The pointer *cp* has the correct value, as shown in the watch window. Now Press the F2 key to turn on the register display and press F3 to show the assembly code.

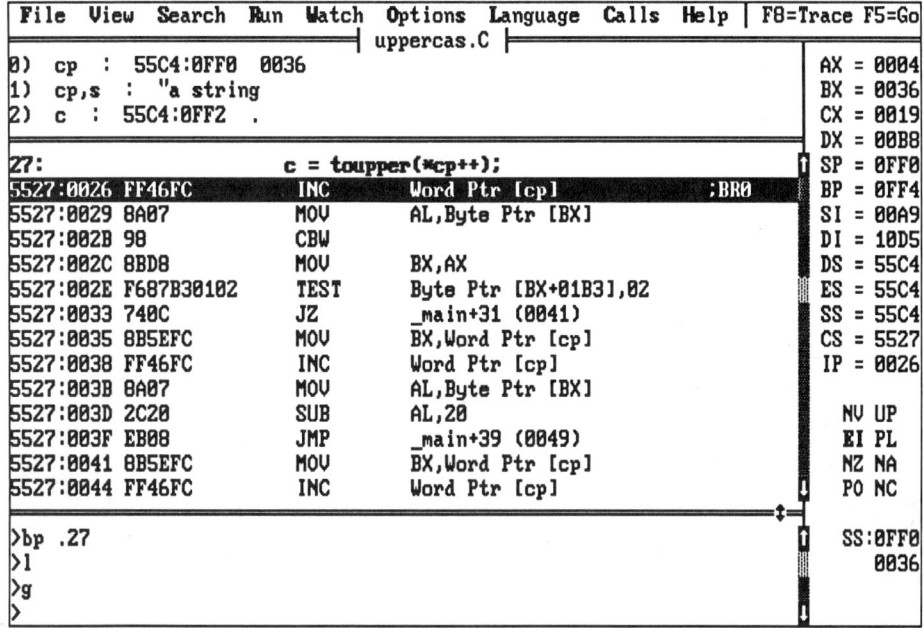

```
 File  View  Search  Run  Watch  Options  Language  Calls  Help │ F8=Trace F5=Go
                                 ┤ uppercas.C ├
0) cp   :  55C4:0FF0   0036                                          AX = 0004
1) cp,s :  "a string                                                 BX = 0036
2) c    :  55C4:0FF2   .                                             CX = 0019
                                                                     DX = 00B8
27:                      c = toupper(*cp++);                         SP = 0FF0
5527:0026 FF46FC        INC       Word Ptr [cp]            ;BR0      BP = 0FF4
5527:0029 8A07          MOV       AL,Byte Ptr [BX]                   SI = 00A9
5527:002B 98            CBW                                          DI = 10D5
5527:002C 8BD8          MOV       BX,AX                              DS = 55C4
5527:002E F687B30102    TEST      Byte Ptr [BX+01B3],02              ES = 55C4
5527:0033 740C          JZ        _main+31 (0041)                    SS = 55C4
5527:0035 8B5EFC        MOV       BX,Word Ptr [cp]                   CS = 5527
5527:0038 FF46FC        INC       Word Ptr [cp]                      IP = 0026
5527:003B 8A07          MOV       AL,Byte Ptr [BX]
5527:003D 2C20          SUB       AL,20                              NV UP
5527:003F EB08          JMP       _main+39 (0049)                    EI PL
5527:0041 8B5EFC        MOV       BX,Word Ptr [cp]                   NZ NA
5527:0044 FF46FC        INC       Word Ptr [cp]                      PO NC

>bp .27                                                             SS:0FF0
>1                                                                    0036
>g
>
```

The display highlights line 27, indicating that a breakpoint exists at this line. The line of code at CS:0026H is in reverse video, indicating that it is the next line to be executed.

The previous instruction has loaded BX with *[cp]*. The first thing the code for line 27 does is increment the word at memory location *[cp]*. The initial value of *cp* is in BX, so the *cp++* request can now be executed. Use the F8 key to single-step through the lines of code. Notice that when only source lines are on the screen, F8 steps one source line at a time, but when assembly code is shown, F8 steps one assembly line at a time. Single-stepping through the code, note how the registers and watch window change. Everything appears normal until CS:0038H is executed.

```
 File   View   Search   Run   Watch   Options   Language   Calls   Help │ F8=Trace F5=Go
                                   ┤ uppercas.C ├
0)  cp   :  55C4:0FF0   0038                                            AX = 0061
1)  cp,s :  "string                                                     BX = 0037
2)  c    :  55C4:0FF2   .                                               CX = 0019
                                                                        DX = 00B8
27:                           c = toupper(*cp++);                       SP = 0FF0
5527:0026 FF46FC       INC        Word Ptr [cp]              ;BR0       BP = 0FF4
5527:0029 8A07         MOV        AL,Byte Ptr [BX]                      SI = 00A9
5527:002B 98           CBW                                              DI = 10D5
5527:002C 8BD8         MOV        BX,AX                                 DS = 55C4
5527:002E F687B30102   TEST       Byte Ptr [BX+01B3],02                 ES = 55C4
5527:0033 740C         JZ         _main+31 (0041)                       SS = 55C4
5527:0035 8B5EFC       MOV        BX,Word Ptr [cp]                      CS = 5527
5527:0038 FF46FC       INC        Word Ptr [cp]                         IP = 003B
5527:003B 8A07         MOV        AL,Byte Ptr [BX]
5527:003D 2C20         SUB        AL,20                                 NV UP
5527:003F EB08         JMP        _main+39 (0049)                       EI PL
5527:0041 8B5EFC       MOV        BX,Word Ptr [cp]                      NZ NA
5527:0044 FF46FC       INC        Word Ptr [cp]                         PO NC
                                                                   ‡
>bp .27                                                                 DS:0037
>l                                                                          20
>g
>
```

Notice that the value of *cp* in the watch window has incremented again. The line of C code has two increments hidden in it, not the expected single increment. Why is this?

To find the answer, examine the *toupper()* macro. The following definition, extracted from CTYPE.H, explains what is happening:

```
#define _UPPER          0x1        /* uppercase letter */
#define _LOWER          0x2        /* lowercase letter */
#define isupper(c)      ( (_ctype+1)[c] & _UPPER )
#define islower(c)      ( (_ctype+1)[c] & _LOWER )

#define _tolower(c)     ( (c)-'A'+'a' )
#define _toupper(c)     ( (c)-'a'+'A' )

#define toupper(c)      ( (islower(c)) ? _toupper(c) : (c) )
#define tolower(c)      ( (isupper(c)) ? _tolower(c) : (c) )
```

The argument to *toupper()*, *c*, is used twice, once in the macro that checks for lowercase, *islower()*, and once in *_toupper()*. The argument is replaced in this case with *cp++*, which has the famous C unexpected side effects. Because the unary post-increment is the handiest way to perform the function desired in the program, fixing the problem by changing the code in the main loop is undesirable. Another solution to the problem is to use the function version of *toupper()*. Because *toupper()* is defined as a function in STDIO.H, simply deleting *#include <ctype.h>* would solve the problem. Unfortunately, this would also deprive the program of the other useful definitions in CTYPE.H. (Admittedly, the features are not currently used by the program, but little programs sometimes grow into mighty systems.) So to keep CTYPE.H but still remove the macro definition of *toupper()*, use the #undef command. (Because *tolower()* has the same problem, it should also be undefined.) The corrected listing is shown in Figure 18-14.

```
/************************************************************************
 *                                                                      *
 * UPPERCAS.C                                                           *
 *     This routine converts a fixed string to uppercase and prints it. *
 *                                                                      *
 ************************************************************************/

#include <ctype.h>
#undef toupper
#undef tolower
#include <string.h>
#include <stdio.h>

main(argc,argv)

int argc;
char *argv[];

{
char    *cp,c;

        cp = "a string\n";

        /*  Convert *cp to uppercase and write to standard output  */

        while (*cp != '\0')
                {
                c = toupper(*cp++);
                putchar(c);
                }

}
```

Figure 18-14. The corrected version of UPPERCAS.C.

An example using screen output

A problem with DEBUG is that it writes to the same screen as the program does. Both SYMDEB and CodeView, however, allow the debugger to switch back and forth between the screen containing the program's output and the screen containing the debugger's output. This feature is a special option with SYMDEB and is sometimes clumsy to use, but with CodeView, keeping a separate program output screen is automatic and switching back and forth involves simply pressing a function key (F4).

The following example program is intended to display an ASCII lookup table with all the displayable characters available on an IBM PC. The expected output is shown in Figure 18-15.

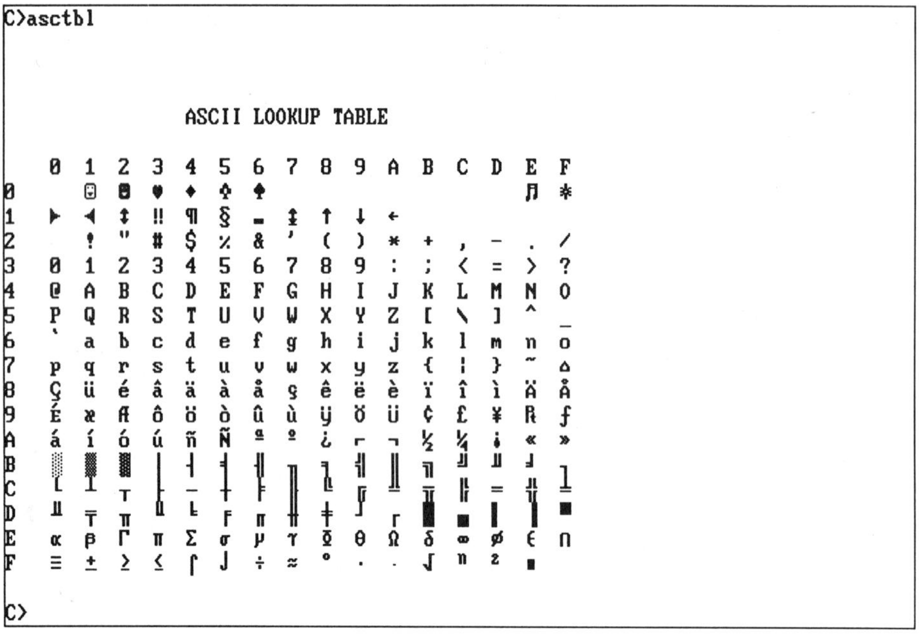

Figure 18-15. The output expected from ASCTBL.C.

The program that should produce this display, ASCTBL.C, is shown in Figure 18-16.

```
/**************************************************************************
 *                                                                      *
 *   ASCTBL.C                                                           *
 *     This program generates an ASCII lookup table for all displayable *
 *     ASCII and extended IBM PC codes, leaving blanks for nondisplayable *
 *     codes.                                                           *
 *                                                                      *
 **************************************************************************/

#include <ctype.h>
#include <stdio.h>

main()
{
int i, j, k;
        /* Print table title. */
        printf("\n\n\n                   ASCII LOOKUP TABLE\n\n");

        /* Print column headers. */
        printf("     ");
        for (i = 0; i < 16; i++)
                printf("%X  ", i);
        fputchar("\n");
```

Figure 18-16. An erroneous program to display ASCII characters.   (more)

```
/* Print each line of the table. */
for (i = 0, k = 0; i < 16; i++)
        {
        /* Print first hex digit of symbols on this line. */
        printf("%X   ", i);
        /* Print each of the 16 symbols for this line. */
        for (j = 0; j < 16; j++)
                {
                /* Filter nonprintable characters. */
                if ((k >= 7 && k <= 13) || (k >= 28 && k <= 31))
                        printf("   ");
                else
                        printf("%c  ", k);
                k++;
                }
        fputchar("\n");
        }
}
```

Figure 18-16. Continued.

The problem to be debugged in this example is evident when the program in Figure 18-16 is compiled, linked, and executed. Here is the resulting display:

Something is clearly wrong. The output is jumbled and no pattern is immediately obvious. To locate the problem, first prepare a .EXE file and start CodeView as follows:

```
C>MSC /Zi ASCTBL;   <Enter>
C>LINK /CO ASCTBL;   <Enter>
C>CV ASCTBL   <Enter>
```

CodeView starts and displays the following screen:

```
 File   View   Search   Run   Watch   Options   Language   Calls   Help | F8=Trace F5=Go
                                  ┤ asctbl.C ├
1:                                                                                       ↑
2:       /********************************************************************
3:        *
4:        *  ASCTBL.C
5:        *    This program generates an ASCII lookup table for all displayable
6:        *    ASCII and extended IBMPC codes, leaving blanks for nondisplayable
7:        *    codes.
8:        *
9:        ********************************************************************
10:
11:       #include <ctype.h>
12:       #include <stdio.h>
13:
14:       main()
15:       {
16:       int i, j, k;
17:              /* Print table title. */
18:              printf("\n\n\n                    ASCII LOOKUP TABLE\n\n");        ↓
                                                                                    ‡
Microsoft (R) CodeView (R)   Version 2.0                                             ↑
(C) Copyright Microsoft Corp. 1986, 1987.  All rights reserved.
>                                                                                   ↓
```

The start of the source program is shown in the display window and the dialog window contains an input prompt. Press the F10 key three times to bring execution to line 21. (Remember that the line indicated in reverse video has not yet been executed.)

```
  File  View  Search  Run  Watch  Options  Language  Calls  Help │ F8=Trace F5=Go
 ══════════════════════════════════╡ asctbl.C ╞═══════════════════════════════
9:       *****************************************************************↑
10:
11:      #include <ctype.h>
12:      #include <stdio.h>
13:
14:      main()
15:      {
16:      int  i, j, k;
17:              /* Print table title. */
18:              printf("\n\n\n                    ASCII LOOKUP TABLE\n\n");
19:
20:              /* Print column headers. */
21:              printf("    ");
22:              for (i = 0; i < 16; i++)
23:                      printf("%X  ", i);
24:              fputchar("\n");
25:
26:              /* Print each line of the table. */                        ↓
 ═══════════════════════════════════════════════════════════════════════╪═╡
Microsoft (R) CodeView (R)  Version 2.0
(C) Copyright Microsoft Corp. 1986, 1987.  All rights reserved.
>
```

The display heading has been printed at line 18. Press the F4 key to display what the program has written on the screen.

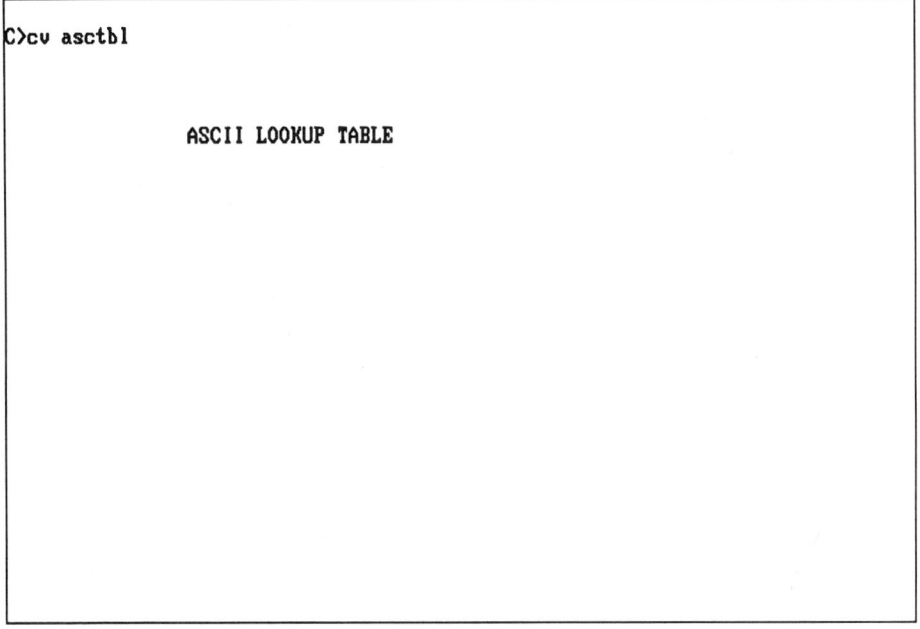

```
C)cv asctbl


            ASCII LOOKUP TABLE
```

Note: Any information on the screen when you started CodeView will remain on the virtual output screen until program execution clears it or forces it to scroll off.

The table heading has been properly written to the screen. Press the F4 key again to return to the CodeView display. Continue executing the program with the F10 key to bring the program to line 24.

```
 File   View   Search   Run   Watch   Options   Language   Calls   Help │ F8=Trace F5=Go
                            ┤ asctbl.C ├
9:      *********************************************************************
10:
11:     #include <ctype.h>
12:     #include <stdio.h>
13:
14:     main()
15:     {
16:     int i, j, k;
17:             /* Print table title. */
18:             printf("\n\n\n                        ASCII LOOKUP TABLE\n\n");
19:
20:             /* Print column headers. */
21:             printf("     ");
22:             for (i = 0; i < 16; i++)
23:                     printf("%X  ", i);
24:             fputchar("\n");
25:
26:             /* Print each line of the table. */

Microsoft (R) CodeView (R)  Version 2.0
(C) Copyright Microsoft Corp. 1986, 1987.  All rights reserved.
>
```

At this point in program execution, the column headings have been written on the screen. Press the F4 key again to see the results.

```
C>cv asctbl



            ASCII LOOKUP TABLE

    0  1  2  3  4  5  6  7  8  9  A  B  C  D  E  F
```

The output of the program is still correct, so allow execution to continue by pressing F4 to return to the CodeView screen and then pressing the F10 key. This will execute the call to the *fputchar()* function to write a newline character.

```
File  View  Search  Run  Watch  Options  Language  Calls  Help | F8=Trace F5=Go
                                 asctbl.C
21:            printf("    ");
22:            for (i = 0; i < 16; i++)
23:                   printf("%X  ", i);
24:            fputchar("\n");
25:
26:            /* Print each line of the table. */
27:            for ( i = 0, k = 0; i < 16; i++)
28:                   {
29:                   /* Print first hex digit of symbols on this line. */
30:                   printf("%X   ", i);
31:                   /* Print each of the 16 symbols for this line. */
32:                   for (j = 0; j < 16; j++)
33:                          {
34:                          /* Filter non-printable characters. */
35:                          if ((k >= 7 && k <= 13) || (k >= 28 && k <= 31)
36:                                 printf("   ");
37:                          else
38:                                 printf("%c  ", k);

Microsoft (R) CodeView (R)  Version 2.0
(C) Copyright Microsoft Corp. 1986, 1987.  All rights reserved.
>
```

Examination of the output screen shows that the display is now incorrect.

```
C>cv asctbl


                ASCII LOOKUP TABLE

     0  1  2  3  4  5  6  7  8  9  A  B  C  D  E  F  h
```

A lowercase *h* has been written to the screen instead of a newline character. Further execution demonstrates that newline characters written with *fputchar()* are not working. A
closer inspection of the *fputchar()* function is needed.

To see what is happening, use the Reload Program command to restart execution at
the top of the program. Change the cursor window with the F6 key, use the arrow keys
to place the cursor on line 24, and press F7. This brings execution back to line 24, where
fputchar() is called. Press the F3 key to place the display in assembly mode and the F2
key to show the CPU registers and flags. The first assembly instruction of the *fputchar()*
function call is about to be executed.

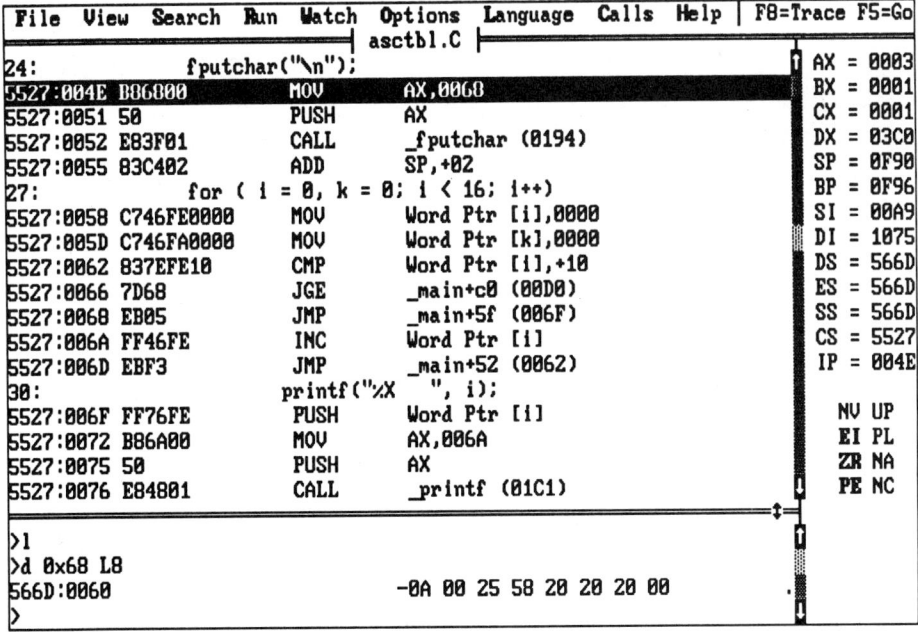

```
 File  View  Search  Run  Watch  Options  Language  Calls  Help │ F8=Trace F5=Go
                              asctbl.C
24:                fputchar("\n");                                          ▲ AX = 0003
5527:004E B86800          MOV         AX,0068                                BX = 0001
5527:0051 50              PUSH        AX                                     CX = 0001
5527:0052 E83F01          CALL        _fputchar (0194)                       DX = 03C0
5527:0055 83C402          ADD         SP,+02                                 SP = 0F90
27:                for ( i = 0, k = 0; i < 16; i++)                          BP = 0F96
5527:0058 C746FE0000      MOV         Word Ptr [i],0000                      SI = 00A9
5527:005D C746FA0000      MOV         Word Ptr [k],0000                      DI = 1075
5527:0062 837EFE10        CMP         Word Ptr [i],+10                       DS = 566D
5527:0066 7D68            JGE         _main+c0 (00D0)                        ES = 566D
5527:0068 EB05            JMP         _main+5f (006F)                        SS = 566D
5527:006A FF46FE          INC         Word Ptr [i]                           CS = 5527
5527:006D EBF3            JMP         _main+52 (0062)                        IP = 004E
30:                printf("%X    ", i);
5527:006F FF76FE          PUSH        Word Ptr [i]                           NV UP
5527:0072 B86A00          MOV         AX,006A                                EI PL
5527:0075 50              PUSH        AX                                     ZR NA
5527:0076 E84801          CALL        _printf (01C1)                       ▼ PE NC

Microsoft (R) CodeView (R)  Version 2.0
(C) Copyright Microsoft Corp. 1986, 1987.  All rights reserved.
>1
>
```

Notice that the parameter being passed to the function by means of the stack is 0068H. Use the Display Memory command to display DS:0068H. (Note the hexadecimal notation.)

```
 File  View  Search  Run  Watch  Options  Language  Calls  Help │ F8=Trace F5=Go
                              asctbl.C
24:                fputchar("\n");                                          ▲ AX = 0003
5527:004E B86800          MOV         AX,0068                                BX = 0001
5527:0051 50              PUSH        AX                                     CX = 0001
5527:0052 E83F01          CALL        _fputchar (0194)                       DX = 03C0
5527:0055 83C402          ADD         SP,+02                                 SP = 0F90
27:                for ( i = 0, k = 0; i < 16; i++)                          BP = 0F96
5527:0058 C746FE0000      MOV         Word Ptr [i],0000                      SI = 00A9
5527:005D C746FA0000      MOV         Word Ptr [k],0000                      DI = 1075
5527:0062 837EFE10        CMP         Word Ptr [i],+10                       DS = 566D
5527:0066 7D68            JGE         _main+c0 (00D0)                        ES = 566D
5527:0068 EB05            JMP         _main+5f (006F)                        SS = 566D
5527:006A FF46FE          INC         Word Ptr [i]                           CS = 5527
5527:006D EBF3            JMP         _main+52 (0062)                        IP = 004E
30:                printf("%X    ", i);
5527:006F FF76FE          PUSH        Word Ptr [i]                           NV UP
5527:0072 B86A00          MOV         AX,006A                                EI PL
5527:0075 50              PUSH        AX                                     ZR NA
5527:0076 E84801          CALL        _printf (01C1)                       ▼ PE NC

>1
>d 0x68 L8
566D:0060                          -0A 00 25 58 20 20 20 00              .
>
```

The contents of memory at this address consist of a null-delimited string containing a newline character. The representation of \n is correct. To see how the string is handled, use the trace key, F8, to single-step through *fputchar()* and subordinate functions. These functions are complicated; nearly 100 steps are required to reach the MS-DOS Interrupt 21H call that actually writes the screen.

```
 File  View  Search  Run  Watch  Options  Language  Calls  Help │ F8=Trace F5=Go
                                 │ asctbl.C │
 5527:10E9 51             PUSH    CX                              ▯ AX = 400A
 5527:10EA 8BCF           MOV     CX,DI                             BX = 0001
 5527:10EC 2BCA           SUB     CX,DX                             CX = 0001
▌5527:10EE CD21           INT     21                              ▌ DX = 0F84
 5527:10F0 9C             PUSHF                                     SP = 0F68
 5527:10F1 03F0           ADD     SI,AX                             BP = 0F6E
 5527:10F3 9D             POPF                                      SI = 0000
 5527:10F4 7304           JNB     _write+82 (10FA)                  DI = 0F85
 5527:10F6 B409           MOV     AH,09                             DS = 566D
 5527:10F8 EB1A           JMP     _write+9c (1114)                  ES = 566D
 5527:10FA 0BC0           OR      AX,AX                             SS = 566D
 5527:10FC 7516           JNZ     _write+9c (1114)                  CS = 5527
 5527:10FE F687120240     TEST    Byte Ptr [BX+__osfile],40         IP = 10EE
 5527:1103 740B           JZ      _write+98 (1110)
 5527:1105 8B5E06         MOV     BX,Word Ptr [BP+06]               NV UP
 5527:1108 803F1A         CMP     Byte Ptr [BX],1A                  EI PL
 5527:110B 7503           JNZ     _write+98 (1110)                  NZ NA
 5527:110D F8             CLC                                       PO NC
─────────────────────────────────────────────────────────────╪─
 566D:0060                      -0A 00 25 58 20 20 20 00         .▯
>d 0xf84 L8
 566D:0F80              68 00 DC 00-A9 00 96 0F              h....▯
>
```

The AH register's contents, 40H, indicate that the Interrupt 21H call is a request for a write to a device. The BX register has the handle of the device, 1, which is the special file handle for standard output (*stdout*). For this program as it was invoked, standard output is the screen. The CX register indicates that 1 byte is to be written; DS:DX points to the data to be written. The contents of memory at DS:0F84H finally reveal the cause of the problem: This memory location contains the *address* of the data to be written, not the data. The *fputchar()* function was called with the wrong level of indirection.

Examination of the listing shows that all the newline requests were made with

```
fputchar("\n");
```

Strings specified with double quotes are replaced in C functions with the address of the string, but the function expected the actual character and not its address. The problem can be corrected by replacing the *fputchar()* calls with

```
fputchar('\n');
```

The newline character will now be passed directly to the function.

This kind of problem can be avoided. C provides the ability to check the type of each parameter passed to a function against the expected type. If the following definition is included at the top of the C program, incorrect types will generate error messages:

```
#define LINT_ARGS
```

The corrected listing is shown in Figure 18-17. This new program produces the correct output.

```
/*************************************************************************
 *                                                                       *
 *   ASCTBL.C                                                            *
 *   This program generates an ASCII lookup table for all displayable    *
 *   ASCII and extended IBM PC codes, leaving blanks for nondisplayable  *
 *   codes.                                                              *
 *                                                                       *
 *************************************************************************/

#define LINT_ARGS
#include <ctype.h>
#include <stdio.h>

main()
{
int i, j, k;
        /* Print table title. */
        printf("\n\n\n                      ASCII LOOKUP TABLE\n\n");

        /* Print column headers. */
        printf("      ");
        for (i = 0; i < 16; i++)
                printf("%X  ", i);
        fputchar('\n');

        /* Print each line of the table. */
        for (i = 0, k = 0; i < 16; i++)
                {
                /* Print first hex digit of symbols on this line. */
                printf("%X   ", i);
                /* Print each of the 16 symbols for this line. */
                for (j = 0; j < 16; j++)
                        {
                        /* Filter nonprintable characters. */
                        if ((k >= 7 && k <= 13) || (k >= 28 && k <= 31))
                                printf("   ");
                        else
                                printf("%c  ", k);
                        k++;
                        }
                fputchar('\n');
                }
}
```

Figure 18-17. The correct ASCII table generation program.

CodeView is a good choice for debugging C, Pascal, BASIC, and FORTRAN programs. The fact that versions of MASM earlier than 5.0 do not generate data for CodeView makes CodeView a poorer choice for these assembly-language programs. These disadvantages must be weighed against the ability to set watchpoints and to trap nonmaskable interrupts (NMIs). CodeView is also not as well suited as SYMDEB for debugging programs that interact with TSRs and device drivers, because CodeView does not provide any mechanism for including symbol tables for routines not linked together.

Hardware debugging aids

Hardware debuggers are a combination of hardware and software designed to be installed in a PC system. The software provides features much like those available with SYMDEB and CodeView. The advantages of hardware debuggers over purely software debuggers can be summarized in three points:

- Crash protection
- Manual execution break
- Hardware breakpoints

A hardware debugger can provide program crash protection because of its independence from the PC software. If the program being debugged goes wild and destroys the operating system of the PC, the hardware debugger is protected by virtue of being a separate hardware system and is capable of recovering enough control to allow the user to find out what happened.

All hardware debuggers offer a means of breaking into the program under test from some external source — usually a push button in the hands of the programmer. The mechanism used to get the attention of the PC's CPU is the nonmaskable interrupt (NMI). This interrupt provides a more reliable means of interrupting program execution than the Break key because its operation is independent of the state of interrupts and other conditions.

Hardware debuggers usually have access to the address and data lines on the PC bus, allowing them to set *hardware* breakpoints. Thus, these debuggers can be set to break when specific addresses are referenced. They execute the breakpoint code from a debugging monitor, which generally runs from their own memory. This memory is usually protected from the regular operating system and the application program.

Although hardware debuggers can be used to instrument a program, they should not be confused with the external hardware instrumentation discussed earlier in this article. The logic analyzers and in-circuit emulators mentioned there are general-purpose test instruments; the hardware debuggers are highly specific devices intended to do only one thing on one type of hardware — provide debugging monitor functions at a hardware level to IBM PC-type machines. It is this specialization that makes hardware debuggers so much easier to use for programmers trying to get a piece of code running.

Because this volume deals only with MS-DOS and associated Microsoft software, a detailed discussion of hardware debuggers and debugging would not be appropriate. Instead, a few popular hardware products that work with MS-DOS utilities are mentioned and a general discussion of debugging with hardware is presented.

Several manufacturers make hardware products that can be used for debugging. These products vary in the features offered and in their suitability for various kinds of debugging. Three of these products that can be used with SYMDEB are

- IBM Professional Debug Utility
- PC Probe and AT Probe from Atron Corporation
- Periscope from The Periscope Company, Inc.

These boards can be used with SYMDEB by specifying the /N switch when the program is started. When used in this way, however, the hardware provides little more than a source of NMIs to interrupt program execution; otherwise, SYMDEB runs as usual. This restriction may not be acceptable to a programmer who wants to use the sophisticated debugging software that accompanies these products and makes use of their hardware features. For this reason, these boards are rarely used with SYMDEB.

The general techniques of debugging with hardware aids will already be familiar to the reader—they are the same techniques discussed at length earlier in this article. The techniques of inspection and observation should still be applied; instrumentation is facilitated by hardware; a debugging monitor accompanies all hardware debuggers and the same techniques discussed for DEBUG, SYMDEB, and CodeView apply. No new techniques are needed to use these devices. The changes in the details of the techniques come with the added features available with the hardware debuggers. (Remember that all these features are not universally available on all hardware debuggers.)

The manual interrupt feature of hardware debuggers is useful in a system crash. Every programmer, especially assembly-language programmers, has had the situation where the program runs wild, destroys the operating system, and locks up the system. The techniques described in previous sections of this article show that about the only way to solve these problems without hardware help is to set breakpoints at strategic locations in the program and see how many are passed before the system locks up. The breakpoints are placed at finer and finer increments until the instruction causing the crash is located.

This long and ugly procedure can sometimes be shortened with a hardware debugger. When the system crashes, the programmer can push the manual interrupt button, suspend program execution, and give control to the debugger card. At this point, the programmer can use the debugging monitor software supplied with the card to sniff around memory looking for something suspicious. Clues can sometimes be found by examining the program's stack and data areas—provided, of course, that they are still in memory and haven't been destroyed, along with the operating system, by the rampaging program. This approach is not always an immediate solution to the problem, however; often, the start-and-set-breakpoints process has to be repeated even with a hardware debugger. The hardware will, however, possibly shed some light on the causes of the problem and shorten the procedure.

Another feature offered by many of the debugging boards is the ability to set breakpoints on events other than the execution of a line of code. Often, these boards will allow the programmer to break on a reference to a specific memory location, to a range of memory locations, or to an I/O port. This feature allows a watch to be set on data, analogous to the watchpoint feature of CodeView. This technique is almost always useful, as it is with CodeView, but there is one class of problems where it is *essential* to reaching a solution.

Consider the case of a program that seems to be running well. Every so often, however, an ampersand appears in the middle of a payroll amount, or occasionally the program makes an erroneous branch and executes the wrong path. Suppose that, after painstaking investigation, the programmer discovers that these problems are being caused by a change in a specific location in memory sometime during the execution of the program. In debugging, the discovery of the cause of a problem usually leads almost instantly to a fix. Not so in this case. That byte of memory could be changed by an error in the program, by a glitch in the operating system or in a device driver, or by cosmic rays from outer space. Discovering the culprit in a case like this is almost impossible without the help of hardware breakpoints. Setting a breakpoint on the affected memory location and running the program will solve the problem. As soon as the memory location is changed, the breakpoint will be executed and the state of the system registers will point a clear finger at the instruction that caused the problem.

Hardware debuggers can provide significant aid to the serious programmer. They are especially helpful in debugging operating systems and operating-system services such as device drivers. They are also helpful in complicated situations where many programs may be running at the same time. The consensus among programmers who have hardware debuggers is that they are well worth the money.

Summary

Although Microsoft and others have provided an impressive array of technology to aid in program debugging, the most important tool a programmer has is his or her native wit and talent. As the examples in this article have illustrated, the technology makes the task easier, but never easy. In all cases, however, it is the programmer who debugs the program and solves the problems.

Technology will never be able to replace the person for solving the problem of a bug-ridden program. (This is an area where artificial intelligence will undoubtedly fail.) Therefore, it is the skills discussed in the first part of this article — debugging by inspection and observation — that deserve the greatest attention and practice. All the other techniques and technologies, with their ever-increasing sophistication, are only extensions of these basic techniques. A programmer who can debug effectively at the lowest level of technology will always be ready to use whatever advanced technology is available.

Therefore, as a final word, remember the rule that opened this article:

Gather enough information and the solution will be obvious.

All the rest of this article was merely a discussion of ways to gather the information.

Steve Bostwick

Article 19
Object Modules

Object modules are used primarily by programmers. The end user of an MS-DOS application need never be concerned with object code, object modules, and object libraries because application programs are almost always distributed as .EXE or .COM files that can be executed with a simple startup command.

An application programmer writing in a high-level language can use object modules and object libraries without knowing either the format of object code or the details of what the utilities that process object modules, such as the Microsoft Library Manager (LIB) and the Microsoft Object Linker (LINK), are actually doing. Most application programmers simply regard the contents of an object module as a "black box" and trust their compilers and object module utility programs to do the right thing.

A programmer using assembly language or an assembly-language debugger such as DEBUG or SYMDEB, however, might want to know more about the content and function of object modules. The use of assembly language gives the programmer more control over the actual contents of object modules, so knowing how the modules are constructed and examining their contents can sometimes help with program debugging.

Finally, a programmer writing a compiler, an assembler, or a language translator must know the details of object module format and processing. To take advantage of LIB and LINK, a language translator must construct object modules that conform to the format and usage conventions specified by Microsoft.

Note: This article assumes some background knowledge of the process by which source code is converted into an executable file in the MS-DOS environment. *See* PROGRAMMING IN THE MS-DOS ENVIRONMENT: PROGRAMMING FOR MS-DOS: Structure of an Application Program; PROGRAMMING TOOLS: The Microsoft Object Linker; PROGRAMMING UTILITIES.

The Use of Object Modules

Although some MS-DOS language translators generate executable 8086-family machine code directly from source code, most produce object code instead. Typically, a translator processes each file of source code individually and leaves the resulting object module in a separate file bearing a .OBJ extension. The source-code files themselves remain unchanged. After all of a program's source-code modules have been translated, the resulting object modules can be linked into a single executable program. Because object modules frequently represent only a portion of a complete program, each source-code module usually contains instructions that indicate how its corresponding object code is to be combined with the object code in other object modules when they are linked.

The object code contained in each object module consists of a binary image of the program plus program structure information. This object code is not directly executable. The binary image corresponds to the executable code that will ultimately be loaded into memory for execution; it contains both machine code and program data. The program structure information includes descriptions of logical groupings defined in the source code (such as named subroutines or segments) and symbolic references to addresses in other object modules.

The program structure information is used by a linkage editor, or linker, such as Microsoft LINK to edit the binary image of the program contained in the object module. The linker combines the binary images from one or more object modules into a complete executable program.

The linker's output is a .EXE file — a file containing executable machine code that can be loaded into RAM and executed (Figure 19-1). The linker leaves intact all of the object modules it processes.

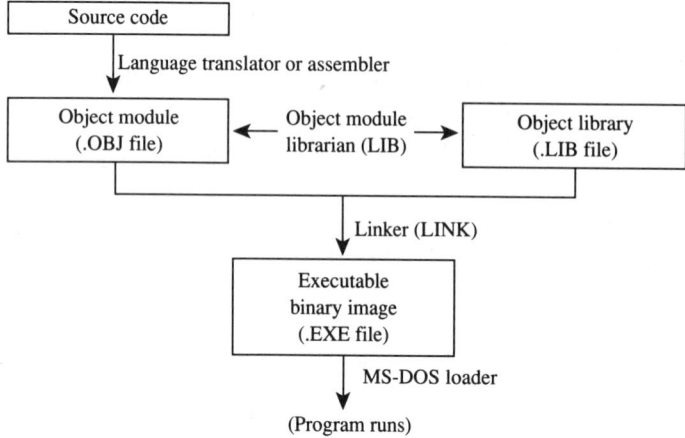

Figure 19-1. Generation of an executable (.EXE) file.

Object code thus serves as an intermediate form for compiled programs. This form offers two major advantages:

- Modular intermediate code. The use of object modules eliminates the overhead of repeated compilation of an entire program whenever changes are made to parts of its source code. Instead, only those object modules affected by source-code revisions need be recompiled.
- Shareable format. Object module format is well defined, so object modules can be linked even if they were produced by different translators. Many high-level-language compilers take advantage of this commonality of object-code format to support "interlanguage" linkage.

Contents of an object module

Object modules contain five basic types of information. Some of this information exists explicitly in the source code (and is subsequently passed on to the object module), but much is inferred by the program translator from the structure of the source code and the way memory is accessed by the 8086.

Binary Image. As described earlier, the binary image comprises executable code (such as opcodes and addresses) and program data. When object modules are linked, the linker builds an executable program from the binary image in each object module it processes. The binary image in each object module is always associated with program structure information that tells the linker how to combine it with related binary images in other object modules.

External References. Because an object module generally represents only a small portion of a larger program that will be constructed from several object modules, it usually contains symbols that allow it to be linked to the other modules. Such references to corresponding symbols in other object modules are resolved when the modules are linked.

For example, consider the following short C program:

```
main()
{
        puts("Hello, world\n");
}
```

This program calls the C function *puts()* to display a character string, but *puts()* is not defined in the source code. Rather, the name *puts* is a reference to a function that is external to the program's *main()* routine. When the C compiler generates an object module for this program, it will identify *puts* as an external reference. Later, the linker will resolve the external reference by linking the object module containing the *puts()* routine with the module containing the *main()* routine.

Address References. When a program is built from a group of object modules, the actual values of many addresses cannot be computed until the linker combines the binary image of executable code and the program data from each of the program's constituent object modules. Object modules contain information that tells the linker how to resolve the values of such addresses, either symbolically (as in the case of external references) or relatively, in terms of some other address (such as the beginning of a block of executable code or program data).

Debugging Information. An object module can also contain information that relates addresses in the executable program to the corresponding source code. After the linker performs its address fixups, it can use the object module's debugging information to relate a line of source code in a program module to the executable code that corresponds to it.

Miscellaneous Information. Finally, an object module can contain comments, lists of symbols defined in or referenced by the module, module identification information, and information for use by an object library manager or a linker (for example, the names of object libraries to be searched by default).

Object module terminology

When the linker generates an executable program, it organizes the structural components of the program according to the information contained in the object modules. The layout of the executable program can be conceptually described as a run-time memory map after it has been loaded into memory.

The basic structure of every executable program for the 8086 family of microprocessors must conform to the segmented architecture of the microprocessor. Thus, the run-time memory map of an executable program is partitioned into segments, each of which can be addressed by using one of the microprocessor's segment registers. This segmented structure of 8086-based programs is the basis for most of the following terminology.

Frames. The memory address space of the 8086 is conceptually divided into a sequence of paragraph-aligned, overlapping 64 KB regions called frames. Frame 0 in the 8086's address space is the 64 KB of memory starting at physical address 00000H (0000:0000 in segment:offset notation), frame 1 is the 64 KB of memory starting at 00010H (0001:0000), and so on. A frame number thus denotes the beginning of any paragraph-aligned 64 KB of memory. For example, the location of a 64 KB buffer that starts at address B800:0000 can be specified as frame 0B800H.

Logical Segments. The run-time memory map for every 8086 program is partitioned into one or more logical segments, which are groupings of logically related portions of the program. Typically, an MS-DOS program includes at least one code segment (that contains all of the program's executable code), one or more data segments (that contain program data), and one stack segment.

When a program is loaded into RAM to be executed, each logical segment in the program can be addressed with a frame number — that is, a physical 8086 segment address. Before the MS-DOS loader transfers control to a program in memory, it initializes the CS and SS registers with the segment addresses of the program's executable code and stack segments. If an MS-DOS program has a separate logical segment for program data, the program itself usually stores this segment's address in the DS register.

Relocatable Segments. In MS-DOS programs, most logical segments are relocatable. The loader determines the physical addresses of a program's relocatable segments when it places the program into memory to be executed. However, this address determination poses a problem for the MS-DOS loader, because a program may contain references to the address of a relocatable segment even though the address value is not determined until the program is loaded. The problem is solved by indicating where such references occur within the program's object modules. The linker then extracts this information from the object modules and uses it to build a list of such address references into a segment relocation table in the header of executable files. After the loader copies a program into memory for execution, it uses the segment relocation table to update, or fix up, the segment address references within the program.

Consider the following example, in which a program loads the starting addresses of two data segments into the DS and ES segment registers:

```
mov     ax,seg _DATA
mov     ds,ax                 ; make _DATA segment addressable through DS
mov     ax,seg FAR_DATA
mov     es,ax                 ; make FAR_DATA segment addressable through ES
```

The actual addresses of the _DATA and FAR_DATA segments are unknown when the source code is assembled and the corresponding object module is constructed. The assembler indicates this by including segment fixup information, instead of actual segment addresses, in the program's object module. When the object module is linked, the linker builds this segment fixup information into the segment relocation table in the header of the program's .EXE file. Then, when the .EXE file is loaded, the MS-DOS loader uses the information in the .EXE file's header to patch the actual address values into the program.

Absolute Segments. Sometimes a program needs to address a predetermined segment of memory. In this case, the program's source code must declare an absolute segment so that a reference to the corresponding frame number can be built into the program's object module.

For example, a program might need to address a video display buffer located at a specific physical address. The following assembler directive declares the name of the segment and its frame number:

```
VideoBufferSeg    SEGMENT at 0B800h
```

Segment Alignment. When a program is loaded, the physical address of each logical segment is constrained by the segment's alignment. A segment can be page aligned (aligned on a 256-byte boundary), paragraph aligned (aligned on a 16-byte paragraph boundary), word aligned (aligned on an even-byte boundary), or byte aligned (not aligned on any particular boundary). A specification of each segment's alignment is part of every object module's program structure information.

High-level-language translators generally align segments according to the type of data they contain. For example, executable code segments are usually byte aligned; program data segments are usually word aligned. With an assembler, segment alignment can be specified with the SEGMENT directive and the assembler will build this information into the program's object module.

Concatenated Segments. The linker can concatenate logical segments from different object modules when it builds the executable program. For example, several object modules may each contain part of a program's executable code. When the linker processes these object modules, it can concatenate the executable code from the different object modules into one range of contiguous addresses.

The order in which the linker concatenates logical segments in the executable program is determined by the order in which the linker processes its input files and by the program structure information in the object modules. With a high-level-language translator, the translator infers which segments can be concatenated from the structure of the source code and builds appropriate segment concatenation information into the object modules it generates. With an assembler, the segment class type can be used to indicate which segments can be concatenated.

Groups of Segments. Segments with different names may also be grouped together by the linker so that they can all be addressed within the same 64 KB frame, even though they are not concatenated. For example, it might be desirable to group program data segments and a stack segment within the same 64 KB frame so that program data items and data on the stack can be addressed with the same 8086 segment register.

In high-level languages, it is up to the translator to incorporate appropriate segment grouping information into the object modules it generates. With an assembler, groups of segments can be declared with the GROUP directive.

Fixups. Sometimes a compiler or an assembler encounters addresses whose values cannot be determined from the source code. The addresses of external symbols are an obvious example. The addresses of relocatable segments and of labels within those segments are another example.

A fixup is a language translator's way of passing the buck about such addresses to the linker. Typically, a translator builds a zero value in the binary image at locations where it cannot store an actual address. Accompanying each such location is fixup information, which allows the linker to determine the correct address. The linker then completes the fixup by calculating the correct address value and adding it to the value in the corresponding location in the binary image. The only fixups the linker cannot fully resolve are those that refer to the segment address of a relocatable segment. Such addresses are not known until the program is actually loaded, so the linker, in turn, passes the responsibility to the MS-DOS loader by creating a segment relocation table in the header of the executable file.

To process fixups properly, the linker needs three pieces of information: the LOCATION of the value in the object module, the nature of the TARGET (the address whose value is not yet known), and the FRAME in which the address calculations are to take place. Object modules contain the LOCATION, TARGET, and FRAME information the linker uses to calculate the appropriate address for any given fixup.

Consider the "program" in Figure 19-2. The statement:

```
start:  call    far ptr FarProc
```

contains a reference to an address in the logical segment *FarSeg2*. Because the assembler does not know the address of *FarSeg2*, it places fixup information about the address into the object module. The LOCATION to be fixed up is 1 byte past the label *start* (the 4-byte pointer following the *call* opcode 9AH). The TARGET is the address referenced in the *call* instruction — that is, the label *FarProc* in the segment *FarSeg2*. The FRAME to which the fixup relates is designated by the group *FarGroup* and is inferred from the statement

```
ASSUME  cs:FarGroup
```

in the *FarSeg2* segment.

```
                               title     fixups


                     FarGroup GROUP   FarSeg1,FarSeg2

0000                 CodeSeg SEGMENT byte public 'CODE'
                             ASSUME  cs:CodeSeg

0000  9A 0000 ---- R  start:  call    far ptr FarProc

0005                 CodeSeg ENDS


0000                 FarSeg1 SEGMENT byte public    ;part of FarGroup

0000                 FarSeg1 ENDS


0000                 FarSeg2 SEGMENT byte public
                             ASSUME  cs:FarGroup

0000                 FarProc PROC    far
0000  CB                     ret                    ;a FAR return
                     FarProc ENDP

0001                 FarSeg2 ENDS

                             END
```

Figure 19-2. A sample "program" containing statements from which the assembler derives fixup information.

There are several different ways for a language translator to identify a fixup. For example, the LOCATION might be a single byte, a 16-bit offset, or a 32-bit pointer, as in Figure 19-2. The TARGET might be a label whose offset is relative either to the base (beginning) of a particular segment or to the LOCATION itself. The FRAME might be a relocatable segment, an absolute segment, or a group of segments.

Taken together, all the information in an object module that concerns the alignment and grouping of segments can be regarded as a specification of a program's run-time memory map. In effect, the object module specifies what goes where in memory when a program is loaded. The linker can then take the program structure information in the object modules and generate a file containing an executable program with the corresponding structure.

The Structure of an Object Module

Although object modules contain the information that ultimately determines the structure of an executable program, they bear little structural resemblance to the resulting executable program. Each object module is made up of a sequence of variable-length object records. Different types of object records contain different types of program information.

Each object record begins with a 1-byte field that identifies its type. This is followed by a 2-byte field containing the length (in bytes) of the remainder of the record. Next comes the actual structural or program information, represented in one or more fields of varied lengths. Finally, each record ends with a 1-byte checksum.

The sequence in which object records appear in an object module is important. Because the records vary in length, each object module must be constructed linearly, from start to end. More important, however, is the fact that some types of object records contain references to preceding object records. Because the linker processes object records sequentially, the position of each object record within an object module depends primarily on the type of information each record contains.

Types of object records

Microsoft LINK currently recognizes 14 types of object records, each of which carries a specific type of information within the object module. Each type of object record is assigned an identifying six-letter abbreviation, but these abbreviations are used only in documentation, not within an object module itself. As already mentioned, the first byte of each object record contains a value that indicates its type. In a hexadecimal dump of the contents of an object module, these identifying bytes identify the start of each object record.

Table 19-1 lists the types of object records supported by LINK. The value of each record's identifying byte (in hexadecimal) is included, along with the six-letter abbreviation and a brief functional description. The functions of the 14 types of object records fall into six general categories:

- Binary data (executable code and program data) is contained in the LEDATA and LIDATA records.
- Address binding and relocation information is contained in FIXUPP records.
- The structure of the run-time memory map is indicated by SEGDEF, GRPDEF, COMDEF, and TYPDEF records.
- Symbol names are declared in LNAMES, EXTDEF, and PUBDEF records.
- Debugging information is in the LINNUM record.
- Finally, the structure of the object module itself is determined by the THEADR, COMENT, and MODEND records.

Table 19-1. Types of 8086 Object Records Supported by Microsoft LINK.

ID byte	Abbreviation	Description
80H	THEADR	Translator Header Record
88H	COMENT	Comment Record
8AH	MODEND	Module End Record
8CH	EXTDEF	External Names Definition Record
8EH	TYPDEF	Type Definition Record
90H	PUBDEF	Public Names Definition Record
94H	LINNUM	Line Number Record
96H	LNAMES	List of Names Record
98H	SEGDEF	Segment Definition Record
9AH	GRPDEF	Group Definition Record
9CH	FIXUPP	Fixup Record
0A0H	LEDATA	Logical Enumerated Data Record
0A2H	LIDATA	Logical Iterated Data Record
0B0H	COMDEF	Communal Names Definition Record

Object record order

The sequence in which the types of object records appear in an object module is fairly flexible in some respects. Several record types are optional, and if the type of information they carry is unnecessary, they are omitted from an object module. In addition, most object record types can occur more than once in the same object module. And, because object records are variable in length, it is often possible to choose, as a matter of convenience, between combining information into one large record or breaking it down into several smaller records of the same type.

As stated previously, an important constraint on the order in which object records appear is the need for some types of object records to refer to information contained in other records. Because the linker processes the records sequentially, object records containing such information must precede the records that refer to it. For example, two types of object records, SEGDEF and GRPDEF, refer to the names contained in an LNAMES record. Thus, an LNAMES record must appear before any SEGDEF or GRPDEF records that refer to it so that the names in the LNAMES record are known to the linker by the time it processes the SEGDEF or GRPDEF records.

A typical object module

Figure 19-3 contains the source code for HELLO.ASM, an assembly-language program that displays a short message. Figure 19-4 is a hexadecimal dump of HELLO.OBJ, the object module generated by assembling HELLO.ASM with the Microsoft Macro Assembler. Figure 19-5 isolates the object records within the object module.

```
          NAME      HELLO

_TEXT     SEGMENT byte public 'CODE'

          ASSUME  cs:_TEXT,ds:_DATA

start:                                ;program entry point
          mov       ax,seg msg
          mov       ds,ax
          mov       dx,offset msg     ;DS:DX -> msg
          mov       ah,09h
          int       21h               ;perform int 21H function 09H
                                      ;(Output character string)

          mov       ax,4C00h
          int       21h               ;perform int 21H function 4CH
                                      ;(Terminate with return code)
_TEXT     ENDS


_DATA     SEGMENT word public 'DATA'

msg       DB        'Hello, world',0Dh,0Ah,'$'

_DATA     ENDS


_STACK    SEGMENT stack 'STACK'

          DW        80h dup(?)        ;stack depth = 128 words

_STACK    ENDS

          END       start
```

Figure 19-3. The source code for HELLO.ASM.

```
           0  1  2  3  4  5  6  7  8  9  A  B  C  D  E  F
0000      80 07 00 05 48 45 4C 4C 4F 00 96 25 00 00 04 43    ....HELLO..%...C
0010      4F 44 45 04 44 41 54 41 05 53 54 41 43 4B 05 5F    ODE.DATA.STACK._
0020      44 41 54 41 06 5F 53 54 41 43 4B 05 5F 54 45 58    DATA._STACK._TEX
0030      54 8B 98 07 00 28 11 00 07 02 01 1E 98 07 00 48    T....(.........H
0040      0F 00 05 03 01 01 98 07 00 74 00 01 06 04 01 E1    .........t......
0050      A0 15 00 01 00 00 B8 00 00 8E D8 BA 00 00 B4 09    ................
0060      CD 21 B8 00 4C CD 21 D5 9C 0B 00 C8 01 04 02 02    .!..L.!.........
0070      C4 06 04 02 02 B6 A0 13 00 02 00 00 48 65 6C 6C    ............Hell
0080      6F 2C 20 77 6F 72 6C 64 0D 0A 24 A8 8A 07 00 C1    o, world..$.....
0090      00 01 01 00 00 AC                                  ......
```

Figure 19-4. A hexadecimal dump of HELLO.OBJ.

```
                  0   1   2   3   4   5   6   7   8   9   A   B   C   D   E   F

THEADR
0000   80  07  00  05  48  45  4C  4C  4F  00                            ....HELLO.

LNAMES
0000                                           96  25  00  00  04  43          .%...C
0010   4F  44  45  04  44  41  54  41  05  53  54  41  43  4B  05  5F    ODE.DATA.STACK._
0020   44  41  54  41  06  5F  53  54  41  43  4B  05  5F  54  45  58    DATA._STACK._TEX
0030   54  8B                                                           T.

SEGDEF
0030       98  07  00  28  11  00  07  02  01  1E                        ...(......

SEGDEF
0030                                       98  07  00  48                ...H
0040   0F  00  05  03  01  01                                           ......

SEGDEF
0040                   98  07  00  74  00  01  06  04  01  E1            ...t......

LEDATA
0050   A0  15  00  01  00  00  B8  00  00  8E  D8  BA  00  00  B4  09    ...............
0060   CD  21  B8  00  4C  CD  21  D5                                   .!..L.!.

FIXUPP
0060                               9C  0B  00  C8  01  04  02  02        ........
0070   C4  06  04  02  02  B6                                           ......

LEDATA
0070                       A0  13  00  02  00  00  48  65  6C  6C        ......Hell
0080   6F  2C  20  77  6F  72  6C  64  0D  0A  24  A8                    o, world..$.

MODEND
0080                                       8A  07  00  C1                ....
0090   00  01  01  00  00  AC                                           ......
```

Figure 19-5. The object records in HELLO.OBJ.

As shown most clearly in Figure 19-5, each of the object records begins with the single byte value identifying the record's type. The second and third bytes of each record contain a single 16-bit value, stored with its low-order byte first, that represents the length (in bytes) of the remainder of the object record.

The first record, THEADR, identifies the object module and the last record, MODEND, terminates the object module. The second record, LNAMES, contains a list of segment names and segment class names that LINK will use to lay out the run-time memory map. The three succeeding SEGDEF records describe the three corresponding segments defined in the source code.

The order in which the object records appear reflects both the structure of the source code and the record order constraints already mentioned. The LNAMES record appears before the three SEGDEF records because each SEGDEF record contains a reference to a name in the LNAMES record.

The binary data representing each of the two segments in the source code is contained in the two LEDATA records. The first LEDATA record represents the _TEXT_ segment; the second specifies the data in the _ DATA_ segment. The FIXUPP record following the first LEDATA record contains information about the address references in the _TEXT_ segment. Again, the order in which the records appear is important: the FIXUPP record refers to the LEDATA record preceding it.

References between object records

Object records can refer to information in other records either indirectly, by means of implicit references, or directly, by means of indexed references to names or other records.

Implicit References. Some types of object records implicitly reference another record in the same object module. The most important example of such implicit referencing is in the FIXUPP record, which always contains fixup information for the preceding LEDATA or LIDATA record in the object module. Whenever an LEDATA or LIDATA record contains a value that needs to be fixed up, the next record in the object module is always a FIXUPP record containing the actual fixup information.

Indexed References to Names. An object record that refers to a symbolic name, such as the name of a segment or an external routine, uses an index into a list of names contained in a previous object record. (The LNAMES record in Figure 19-5 is an example.) The first name in such a list has the index number 1, the second name has index number 2, the third has index number 3, and so on. Altogether, a list of as many as 32,767 (7FFFH) names can be incorporated into an object module — generally adequate for even the most verbose programmer. (LINK does, however, impose its own version-specific limits.)

Indexed References to Object Records. An object record can also refer to a previous object record by using the same type of index. In this case, the index number refers to one of a list of object records of a particular type. For example, a FIXUPP record might refer to a segment by referencing one of several preceding SEGDEF records in the object module. In that case, a value of 1 would indicate the first SEGDEF record in the object module, a value of 2 would indicate the second, and so on.

The _index-number_ field in an object record can be either 1 or 2 bytes long. If the number is in the range 0–7FH, the high-order bit (bit 7) is 0 and the low-order 7 bits contain the index number, so the field is only 1 byte long:

If the index number is in the range 80–7FFFH, the field is 2 bytes long. The high-order bit of the first byte in the field is set to 1, and the high-order byte of the index number (which must be in the range 0–7FH) fits in the remaining 7 bits. The low-order byte of the index number is specified in the second byte of the field:

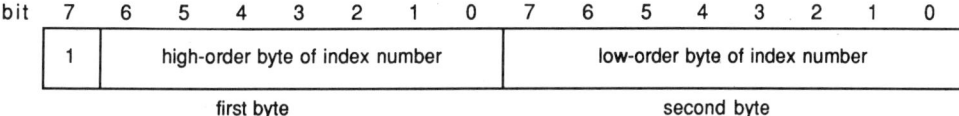

The same format is used whether an index refers to a list of names or to a previous object record.

Microsoft 8086 Object Record Formats

Just as the design of the Intel 8086 microprocessor reflects the design of its 8-bit predecessors, 8086 object record formats are reminiscent of the 8-bit software tradition. In 8-bit systems, disk space and RAM were often at a premium. To minimize the space consumed by object records, information is packed into bit fields within bytes and variable-length fields are frequently used.

Microsoft LINK recognizes a major subset of Intel's original 8086 object module specification (Intel Technical Specification 121748-001). Intel also proposed a six-letter name for each type of object record and symbolic names for fields. These names are documented in the following descriptions, which appear in the order shown earlier in Table 19-1.

The Intel record types that are not recognized by LINK provide information about an executable program that MS-DOS obtains in other ways. (For example, information about run-time overlays is supplied in LINK's command line rather than being encoded in object records.) Because they are ignored by LINK, they are not included here.

All 8086 object records conform to the following format:

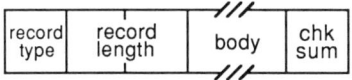

The *record type* field is a 1-byte field containing the hexadecimal number that identifies the type of object record (*see* Table 19-1).

The *record length* is a 2-byte field that gives the length of the remainder of the object record in bytes (excluding the bytes in the *record type* and *record length* fields). The record length is stored with the low-order byte first.

The *body* field of the record varies in size and content, depending on the record type.

The *checksum* is a 1-byte field that contains the negative sum (modulo 256) of all other bytes in the record. In other words, the checksum byte is calculated so that the low-order byte of the sum of all the bytes in the record, including the checksum byte, equals zero.

Note: As shown in the preceding example, the boxes used to depict the fields vary in size. The square boxes used for *record type* and *chksum* indicate a single byte, the rectangular box used for *record length* indicates 2 bytes, and the diagonal lines used for *body* indicate a variable-length field.

80H THEADR Translator Header Record

The THEADR record contains the name of the object module. This name identifies an object module within an object library or in messages produced by the linker.

Record format

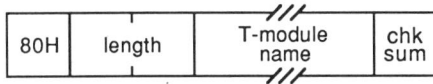

T-module name

The *T-module name* field is a variable-length field that contains the name of the object module. The first byte of the field contains the number of subsequent bytes that contain the name itself. The name can be uppercase or lowercase and can be any string of characters.

The *T-module name* is used by LIB and LINK within error messages. Language translators frequently derive the *T-module name* from the name of the file that contains a program's source code. Assembly-language programmers can specify the *T-module name* explicitly with the assembler NAME directive.

Location in object module

As its name implies, the THEADR record must be the first record in every object module generated by a language translator.

Example

The following THEADR record was generated by the Microsoft C Compiler:

```
        0  1  2  3  4  5  6  7  8  9  A  B  C  D  E  F
0000   80 09 00 07 68 65 6C 6C 6F 2E 63 CB              ....hello.c.
```

- Byte 00H contains 80H, indicating a THEADR record.
- Bytes 01–02H contain 0009H, the length of the remainder of the record.
- Bytes 03–0AH contain the *T-module name*. Byte 03H contains 07H, the length of the name, and bytes 04H through 0AH contain the name itself (*hello.c*). (In object modules generated by the Microsoft C Compiler, the THEADR record indicates the filename that contained the C source code for the module.)
- Byte 0BH contains the checksum, 0CBH.

88H COMENT Comment Record

The COMENT record contains a character string that may represent a plain text comment, a symbol meaningful to a program such as LIB or LINK, or even binary-encoded identification data. An object module can contain any number of COMENT records.

Record format

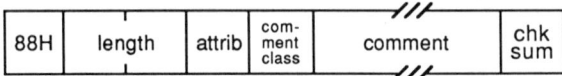

Attrib

Attrib is a 1-byte field in which only the first 2 bits are meaningful:

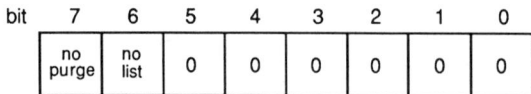

- If bit 7 (*no purge*) is set to 1, utility programs that manipulate object modules should not delete the comment record from the object module. Bit 7 can thus protect an important comment, such as a copyright message, from deletion.
- If bit 6 (*no list*) is set to 1, utility programs that can list the contents of object modules are directed not to list the comment. Bit 6 can thus hide a comment.
- Bits 5 through 0 are unused and should be set to 0.

Microsoft LIB ignores the *attrib* field.

Comment class

Comment class is a 1-byte field whose value provides information about the type of comment. The original Intel specification provided for the following possible *comment class* values:

Value	Use
00H	Language-translator comment (the name of the translator that generated the object module).
01H	Copyright comment.
02–9BH	Reserved for Intel proprietary software.

Microsoft language translators can generate several other classes of COMENT record that communicate specific information about the object module to LINK:

Value	Use
81H	Obsolete; replaced by *comment class* 9FH.
9CH	MS-DOS version number. Some language translators create a COMENT record with a 2-byte binary value in the *comment* field indicating the MS-DOS version under which the module was created. This record is ignored by LINK.
9DH	Memory model. The *comment* field contains a string that indicates the memory model used by the language translator. The string contains one of the lowercase letters s, c, m, l, and h to designate small, compact, medium, large, and huge memory models. Microsoft language translators generate COMENT records with this *comment class* only for compatibility with the XENIX version of LINK. The MS-DOS version of LINK ignores these COMENT records.
9EH	Sets Microsoft LINK's DOSSEG switch.
9FH	Default library search name. LINK interprets the contents of the *comment* field as the name of a library to be searched in order to resolve external references within the object module. The default library search can be overridden with LINK's NODEFAULTLIBRARYSEARCH switch.
0A1H	Indicates that Microsoft extensions to the Intel object record specification are used in the object module. For example, when COMDEF records are used within an object module, a COMENT record with *comment class* 0A1H must appear in the object module at some point before the first COMDEF record. LINK ignores the *comment* string in COMENT records with this *comment class*.
0C0H– 0FFH	Reserved for user-defined comment classes.

Comment

The *comment* field is a variable-length string of bytes that represent the comment. The length of the string is inferred from the length of the object record.

Location in object module

A COMENT record can appear almost anywhere in an object module. Only two restrictions apply:

- A COMENT record cannot be placed between a FIXUPP record and the LEDATA or LIDATA record to which it refers.
- A COMENT record cannot be the first or last record in an object module. (The first record must always be a THEADR record and the last must always be MODEND.)

Examples

The following three examples are typical COMENT records taken from an object module generated by the Microsoft C Compiler.

This first example is a language-translator comment:

```
       0  1  2  3  4  5  6  7  8  9  A  B  C  D  E  F
0000   88 07 00 00 00 4D 53 20 43 6E                      .....MS Cn
```

- Byte 00H contains 88H, indicating that this is a COMENT record.
- Bytes 01–02H contain 0007H, the length of the remainder of the record.
- Byte 03H (the *attrib* field) contains 00H. Bit 7 (*no purge*) is set to 0, indicating that this COMENT record may be purged from the object module by a utility program that manipulates object modules. Bit 6 (*no list*) is set to 0, indicating that this comment need not be excluded from any listing of the module's contents. The remaining bits are all 0.
- Byte 04H (the *comment class* field) contains 00H, indicating that this COMENT record contains the name of the language translator that generated the object module.
- Bytes 05H through 08H contain the name of the language translator, MS C.
- Byte 09H contains the checksum, 6EH.

The second example contains the name of an object library to be searched by default when LINK processes the object module containing this COMENT record:

```
       0  1  2  3  4  5  6  7  8  9  A  B  C  D  E  F
0000   88 09 00 00 9F 53 4C 49 42 46 50 10               .....SLIBFP.
```

- Byte 04H (the *comment class* field) contains 9FH, indicating that this record contains the name of a library for LINK to use to resolve external references.
- Bytes 05–0AH contain the library name, SLIBFP. In this example, the name refers to the Microsoft C Compiler's floating-point function library, SLIBFP.LIB.

The last example indicates that the object module contains Microsoft-defined extensions to the Intel object module specification:

```
       0  1  2  3  4  5  6  7  8  9  A  B  C  D  E  F
0000   88 06 00 00 A1 01 43 56 37                         .....CV7
```

- Byte 04H indicates the *comment class*, 0A1H.
- Bytes 05–07H, which contain the *comment* string, are ignored by LINK.

8AH MODEND Module End Record

The MODEND record denotes the end of an object module. It also indicates whether the object module contains the main routine in a program, and it can, optionally, contain a reference to a program's entry point.

Record format

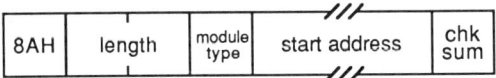

| 8AH | length | module type | start address | chk sum |

Module type

The *module type* field is an 8-bit (1-byte) field:

bit	7	6	5	4	3	2	1	0
	main	start	0	0	0	0	0	1

- Bit 7 (*main*) is set to 1 if the module is a main program module.
- Bit 6 (*start*) is set to 1 if the MODEND record contains an entry point (*start address*).
- Bit 0 is set to 1 if the *start address* field contains a relocatable address reference that LINK must fix up. If bit 6 is set to 1, bit 0 must also be set to 1. (The Intel specification allows bit 0 to be set to 0, to indicate that *start address* is an absolute physical address, but this capability is not supported by LINK.)

Start address

The *start address* field appears in the MODEND record only when bit 6 is set to 1:

| end dat | frame datum | target datum | target displacement |

The format and interpretation of the *start address* field corresponds to the *fixup* field of the FIXUPP record. The *end dat* field corresponds to the *fix dat* field in the FIXUPP record. Bit 2 of the *end dat* field, which corresponds to the *P* bit in a *fix dat* field, must be zero.

Location in object module

A MODEND record can appear only as the last record in an object module.

Example

Consider the *MODEND* record of the HELLO.ASM example:

```
        0  1  2  3  4  5  6  7  8  9  A  B  C  D  E  F
0000   8A 07 00 C1 00 01 01 00 00 AC                     . . . . . . . . . .
```

- Byte 00H contains 8AH, indicating a MODEND record.
- Bytes 01–02H contain 0007H, the length of the remainder of the record.
- Byte 03H contains 0C1H (11000001B). Bit 7 is set to 1, indicating that this module is the main module of the program. Bit 6 is set to 1, indicating that a *start address* field is present. Bit 0 is set to 1, indicating that the address referenced in the *start address* field must be fixed up by LINK.
- Byte 04H (*end dat* in the *start address* field) contains 00H. As in a FIXUPP record, bit 7 indicates that the frame for this fixup is specified explicitly, and bits 6 through 4 indicate that a SEGDEF index specifies the frame. Bit 3 indicates that the target reference is also specified explicitly, and bits 2 through 0 indicate that a SEGDEF index also specifies the target. *See also* FIXUPP 9CH Fixup Record below.
- Byte 05H (*frame datum* in the *start address* field) contains 01H. This is a reference to the first SEGDEF record in the module, which in this example corresponds to the _TEXT segment. This reference tells LINK that the start address lies in the _TEXT segment of the module.
- Byte 06H (*target datum* in the *start address* field) contains 01H. This too is a reference to the first SEGDEF record in the object module, which corresponds to the _TEXT segment. LINK uses the following *target displacement* field to determine where in the _TEXT segment the address lies.
- Bytes 07–08H (*target displacement* in the *start address* field) contain 0000H. This is the offset (in bytes) of the *start address*.
- Byte 09H contains the checksum, 0ACH.

8CH EXTDEF External Names Definition Record

The EXTDEF record contains a list of symbolic external references — that is, references to symbols defined in other object modules. The linker resolves external references by matching the symbols declared in EXTDEF records with symbols declared in PUBDEF records.

Record format

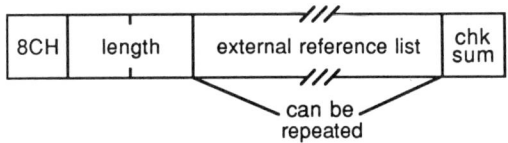

External reference list

The *external reference list* is a variable-length field containing a list of names and name types, each formatted as follows:

- The *name length* is a 1-byte field containing the length of the *name* field that follows it. (LINK restricts *name length* to a value between 01H and 7FH.)
- The *type index* is a 1-byte reference to the TYPDEF record in the object module that describes the type of symbol the name represents. A *type index* value of zero indicates that no TYPDEF record is associated with the symbol. A nonzero value indicates which TYPDEF record is associated with the external name. Microsoft LINK recognizes TYPDEF records only for the purpose of declaring communal variables. *See* 8EH TYPDEF Type Definition Record below.

LINK imposes a limit of 1023 external names.

Location in object module

Any EXTDEF records in an object module must appear before the FIXUPP records that reference them. Also, if an EXTDEF record contains a nonzero *type index*, the indexed TYPDEF record must precede the EXTDEF record.

Example

Consider this EXTDEF record generated by the Microsoft C Compiler:

```
        0   1   2   3   4   5   6   7   8   9   A   B   C   D   E   F
0000   8C  25  00  0A  5F  5F  61  63  72  74  75  73  65  64  00  05    .%.._acrtused..
0010   5F  6D  61  69  6E  00  05  5F  70  75  74  73  00  08  5F  5F    _main.._puts.._
0020   63  68  6B  73  74  6B  00  A5                                    chkstk..
```

- Byte 00H contains 8CH, indicating that this is an EXTDEF record.
- Bytes 01–02H contain 0025H, the length of the remainder of the record.
- Bytes 03–26H contain a list of external references. The first reference starts in byte 03H, which contains 0AH, the length of the name __acrtused. The name itself follows in bytes 04–0DH. Byte 0EH contains 00H, which indicates that the symbol's type is not defined by any TYPDEF record in this object module. Bytes 0F–26H contain similar references to the external symbols _main, _puts, and __chkstk.
- Byte 27H contains the checksum, 0A5H.

8EH TYPDEF Type Definition Record

The TYPDEF record contains details about the type of data represented by a name declared in a PUBDEF or an EXTDEF record. This information may be used by the linker to validate references to names, or it may be used by a debugger to display data according to type.

Starting with Microsoft LINK version 3.50, the COMDEF record should be used for declaration of communal variables. For compatibility, however, later versions of LINK recognize TYPDEF records as well as COMDEF records.

Record format

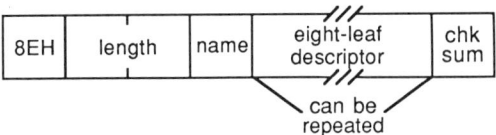

Although the original Intel specification allowed for many different type specifications, such as scalar, pointer, and mixed data structure, LINK uses TYPDEF records to declare only communal variables. Communal variables represent globally shared memory areas — for example, FORTRAN common blocks or uninitialized public variables in C.

The size of a communal variable is declared explicitly in the TYPDEF record. If a communal variable has different sizes in different object modules, LINK uses the largest declared size when it generates an executable module.

Name

The *name* field of a TYPDEF record is a 1-byte field that is always null; that is, it contains a single zero byte.

Eight-leaf descriptor

The *eight-leaf descriptor* field, in the original Intel specification, was a variable-length field that contained as many as eight "leaves" that could be used to describe mixed data structures.

Microsoft uses a stripped-down version of the *eight-leaf descriptor*, because the field's only function is to describe communal variables:

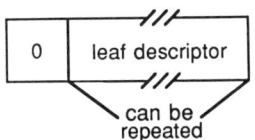

- The first field in the *eight-leaf descriptor* is a 1-byte field that contains a zero byte.
- The *leaf descriptor* field is a variable-length field that is itself divided into four fields ("leaves") that describe the size and type of a variable. The two possible variable types are NEAR and FAR.

  If the field describes a NEAR variable (one that can be referenced as an offset within a default data segment), the format is

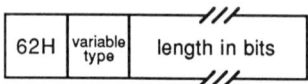

  - The 1-byte field containing 62H signifies a NEAR variable.
  - The *variable type* field is a 1-byte field that specifies the variable type:

77H	Array
79H	Structure
7BH	Scalar

    This field is ignored by LINK.
  - The *length in bits* field is a variable-length field that indicates the size of the communal variable. Its format depends on the size it represents. If the size is less than 128 (80H) bits, *length in bits* is a 1-byte field containing the actual size of the field:

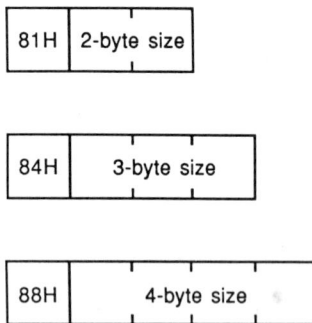

  If the size is 128 bits or greater, it cannot be represented in a single byte value, so the *length in bits* field is formatted with an extra initial byte that indicates whether the size is represented as a 2-, 3-, or 4-byte value:

If the *leaf descriptor* field describes a FAR variable (one that must be referenced with an explicit segment and offset), the format is

```
+------+--------+-----------+-----------+
|      |variable| number of |element type|
| 61H  | type   | elements  |  index    |
+------+--------+-----------+-----------+
```

- The 1-byte field containing 61H signifies a FAR variable.
- The 1-byte *variable type* for a FAR communal variable is restricted to 77H (array). (As with the NEAR *variable type* field, LINK ignores this field.)
- The *number of elements* is a variable-length field that contains the number of elements in the array. It has the same format as the *length in bits* field in the *leaf descriptor* for a NEAR variable.
- The *element type index* is an index field that references a previous TYPDEF record. A value of 1 indicates the first TYPDEF record in the object module, a value of 2 indicates the second TYPDEF record, and so on. The TYPDEF record referenced must describe a NEAR variable. This way, the data type and size of the elements in the array can be determined.

Location in object module

Any TYPDEF records in an object module must precede the EXTDEF or PUBDEF records that reference them.

Examples

The following three examples of TYPDEF records were generated by the Microsoft C Compiler version 3.0. (Later versions use COMDEF records.)

The first sample TYPDEF record corresponds to the public declaration

```
int     foo;              /* 16-bit integer */
```

The TYPEDEF record is

```
      0  1  2  3  4  5  6  7  8  9  A  B  C  D  E  F
0000  8E 06 00 00 00 62 7B 10 7F                        .....b{..
```

- Byte 00H contains 8EH, indicating that this is a TYPDEF record.
- Bytes 01–02H contain 0006H, the length of the remainder of the record.
- Byte 03H (the *name* field) contains 00H, a null name.
- Bytes 04–07H represent the *eight-leaf descriptor* field. The first byte of this field (byte 04H) contains 00H. The remaining bytes (bytes 05–07H) represent the *leaf descriptor* field:
  - Byte 05H contains 62H, indicating this TYPDEF record describes a NEAR variable.
  - Byte 06H (the *variable type* field) contains 7BH, which describes this variable as a scalar.
  - Byte 07H (the *length in bits* field) contains 10H, the size of the variable in bits.

- Byte 08H contains the checksum, 7FH.

The next example demonstrates how the variable size contained in the *length in bits* field of the *leaf descriptor* is formatted:

```
char    foo2[32768];              /* 32 KB array */

        0  1  2  3  4  5  6  7  8  9  A  B  C  D  E  F
0000   8E 09 00 00 00 62 7B 84 00 00 04 04              .....b{.....
```

- The *length in bits* field (bytes 07–0AH) starts with a byte containing 84H, which indicates that the actual size of the variable is represented as a 3-byte value (the following 3 bytes). Bytes 08–0AH contain the value 040000H, the size of the 32 KB array in bits.

This third C statement, because it declares a FAR variable, causes two TYPDEF records to be generated:

```
char    far     foo3[10][2][20];        /* 400-element FAR array */
```

The two TYPDEF records are

```
        0  1  2  3  4  5  6  7  8  9  A  B  C  D  E  F
0000   8E 06 00 00 00 62 7B 08 87 8E 09 00 00 00 61 77   .....b{.......aw
0010   81 90 01 01 7E                                    ....|
```

- Bytes 00–08H contain the first TYPDEF record, which defines the data type of the elements of the array (NEAR, scalar, 8 bits in size).
- Bytes 09–14H contain the second TYPDEF record. The *leaf descriptor* field of this record declares that the variable is FAR (byte 0EH contains 61H) and an array (byte 0FH, the *variable type*, contains 77H).
  - Because this TYPDEF record describes a FAR variable, bytes 10–12H represent a *number of elements* field. The first byte of the field is 81H, indicating a 2-byte value, so the next 2 bytes (bytes 11–12H) contain the number of elements in the array, 0190H (400D).
- Byte 13H (the *element type index*) contains 01H, which is a reference to the first TYPDEF record in the object module — in this example, the one in bytes 00–08H.

90H PUBDEF Public Names Definition Record

The PUBDEF record contains a list of public names. When object modules are linked, the linker uses these names to resolve external references in other object modules.

Record format

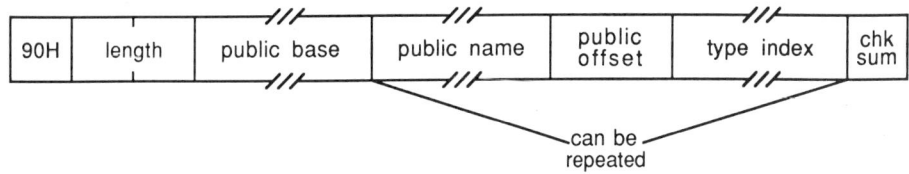

Public base

Each name in the PUBDEF record refers to a location (a 16-bit offset) in a particular segment or group. The *public base*, a variable-length field that specifies the segment or group, is formatted as follows:

- *Group index* is an index field that references a previous GRPDEF record in the object module. If the *group index* value is 0, no group is associated with this PUBDEF record.
- *Segment index* is also an index field. It associates a particular segment with this PUBDEF record by referencing a previous SEGDEF record. A value of 1 indicates the first SEGDEF record in the object module, a value of 2 indicates the second, and so on. If the *segment index* value is 0, the *group index* must also be 0 — in this case, the *frame number* appears in the *public base* field.
- The 2-byte *frame number* appears in the *public base* field only when the *group index* and *segment index* are both 0. In other words, the *frame number* specifies the start of an absolute segment. If present, the value in the *frame number* field indicates the number of the frame containing the public name.

Public name

Public name is a variable-length field containing a public name. The first byte specifies the length of the name; the remainder is the name itself. (The Intel specification allows names of 1 to 255 bytes. Microsoft LINK restricts the maximum length of a public name to 127 bytes.)

Public offset

Public offset is a 2-byte field containing the offset of the location referred to by the *public name*. This offset is assumed to lie within the segment, group, or frame specified in the *public base* field.

Type index

Type index is an index field that references a previous TYPDEF record in the object module. A value of 1 indicates the first TYPDEF record in the module, a value of 2 indicates the second, and so on. The *type index* value can be 0 if no data type is associated with the public name.

The *public name*, *public offset*, and *type index* fields can be repeated within a single PUBDEF record. Thus, one PUBDEF record can declare a list of public names.

Location in object module

Any PUBDEF records in an object module must appear after the GRPDEF and SEGDEF records to which they refer. Because PUBDEF records are not themselves referenced by any other type of object record, they are generally placed near the end of an object module.

Examples

The following two examples show PUBDEF records created by the Microsoft Macro Assembler.

The first example is the record for the statement

```
PUBLIC  GAMMA
```

The PUBDEF record is

```
      0  1  2  3  4  5  6  7  8  9  A  B  C  D  E  F
0000  90 0C 00 00 01 05 47 41 4D 4D 41 02 00 00 F9     ......GAMMA....
```

- Byte 00H contains 90H, indicating a PUBDEF record.
- Bytes 01–02H contain 000CH, the length of the remainder of the record.
- Bytes 03–04H represent the *public base* field. Byte 03H (the *group index*) contains 0, indicating that no group is associated with the name in this PUBDEF record. Byte 04H (the *segment index*) contains 1, a reference to the first SEGDEF record in the object module. This is the segment to which the name in this PUBDEF record refers.
- Bytes 05–0AH represent the *public name* field. Byte 05H contains 05H (the length of the name), and bytes 06–0AH contain the name itself, *GAMMA*.
- Bytes 0B–0CH contain 0002H, the *public offset*. The name *GAMMA* thus refers to the location that is offset 2 bytes from the beginning of the segment referenced by the *public base*.
- Byte 0DH is the *type index*. The value of the *type index* is 0, indicating that no data type is associated with the name *GAMMA*.
- Byte 0EH contains the checksum, 0F9H.

The next example is the PUBDEF record for the following absolute symbol declaration:

```
        PUBLIC    ALPHA
ALPHA   EQU       1234h
```

The PUBDEF record is

```
      0  1  2  3  4  5  6  7  8  9  A  B  C  D  E  F
0000  90 0E 00 00 00 00 00 05 41 4C 50 48 41 34 12 00   ......ALPHA4....
0010  B1
```

- Bytes 03–06H (the *public base* field) contain a *group index* of 0 (byte 03H) and a *segment index* of 0 (byte 04H). Since both the *group index* and *segment index* are 0, a *frame number* also appears in the *public base* field. In this instance, the *frame number* (bytes 05–06H) also happens to be 0.
- Bytes 07–0CH (the *public name* field) contain the name *ALPHA*, preceded by its length.
- Bytes 0D–0EH (the *public offset* field) contain 1234H. This is the value associated with the symbol *ALPHA* in the assembler EQU directive. If *ALPHA* is declared in another object module with the declaration

```
        EXTRN     ALPHA:ABS
```

any references to *ALPHA* in that object module are fixed up as absolute references to offset 1234H in frame 0. In other words, *ALPHA* would have the value 1234H.
- Byte 0FH (the *type index*) contains 0.

94H LINNUM Line Number Record

The LINNUM record relates line numbers in source code to addresses in object code.

Record format

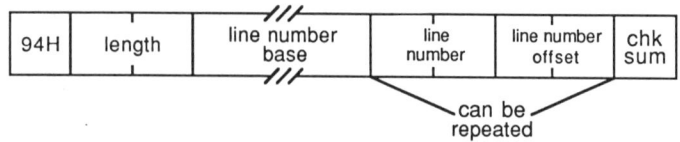

Line number base

The *line number base* describes the segment to which the line number refers. Although the complete Intel specification allows the line number base to refer to a group or to an absolute segment as well as to a relocatable segment, Microsoft restricts references in this field to relocatable segments. The format of the *line number base* field is

- The *group index* field always contains a single zero byte.
- The *segment index* is an index field that references a previous SEGDEF record. A value of 1 indicates the first SEGDEF record in the object module, a value of 2 indicates the second, and so on.

Line number

Line number is a 2-byte field containing a line number between 0 and 32,767 (0–7FFFH).

Line number offset

The *line number offset* is a 2-byte field that specifies the offset of the executable code (in the segment specified in the *line number base* field) to which the line number in the *line number* field refers.

The *line number* and *line number offset* fields can be repeated, so a single LINNUM record can specify multiple line numbers in the same segment.

Location in object module

Any LINNUM records in an object module must appear after the SEGDEF records to which they refer. Because LINNUM records are not themselves referenced by any other type of object record, they are generally placed near the end of an object module.

Example

The following LINNUM record was generated by the Microsoft C Compiler:

```
      0  1  2  3  4  5  6  7  8  9  A  B  C  D  E  F
0000  94 0F 00 00 01 02 00 00 00 03 00 08 00 04 00 0F  ................
0010  00 3C                                            ..
```

- Byte 00H contains 94H, indicating that this is a LINNUM record.
- Bytes 01–02H contain 000FH, the length of the remainder of the record.
- Bytes 03–04H represent the *line number base* field. Byte 03H (the *group index* field) contains 00H, as it must. Byte 04H (the *segment index* field) contains 01H, indicating that the line numbers in this LINNUM record refer to code in the segment defined in the first SEGDEF record in this object module.
- Bytes 05–06H (a *line number* field) contain 0002H, and bytes 07–08H (a *line number offset* field) contain 0000H. Together, they indicate that source-code line number 0002 corresponds to offset 0000H in the segment indicated in the *line number base* field.

  Similarly, the two pairs of *line number* and *line number offset* fields in bytes 09–10H specify that line number 0003 corresponds to offset 0008H and that line number 0004 corresponds to offset 000FH.
- Byte 11H contains the checksum, 3CH.

96H LNAMES List of Names Record

The LNAMES record is a list of names that can be referenced by subsequent SEGDEF and GRPDEF records in the object module.

Record format

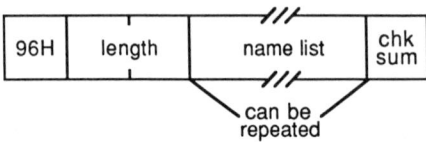

Name list

Name list is a variable-length field that contains the list of names. Each name is preceded by 1 byte that defines its length, which can be a value between 0 and 255 (0–0FFH).

The names in the list are indexed implicitly in the order they appear: The first name in the list has an index of 1, the second name has an index of 2, and so forth. References to the names contained in *name list* by subsequent object records, such as SEGDEF, are accomplished by using this index number. LINK imposes a limit of 255 logical names per object module.

Location in object module

Any LNAMES records in an object module must appear before the GRPDEF or SEGDEF records that refer to them. Because it does not refer to any other type of object records, an LNAMES record usually appears near the start of an object module.

Example

The following LNAMES record contains the segment and class names specified in all three of the assembler statements:

```
_TEXT    SEGMENT byte public 'CODE'
_DATA    SEGMENT word public 'DATA'
_STACK   SEGMENT para public 'STACK'
```

The LNAMES record is

```
       0  1  2  3  4  5  6  7  8  9  A  B  C  D  E  F
0000  96 25 00 00 04 43 4F 44 45 04 44 41 54 41 05 53   .%...CODE.DATA.S
0010  54 41 43 4B 05 5F 44 41 54 41 06 5F 53 54 41 43   TACK._DATA._STAC
0020  4B 05 5F 54 45 58 54 8B                           K._TEXT.
```

- Byte 00H contains 96H, indicating that this is an LNAMES record.
- Bytes 01–02H contain 0025H, the length of the remainder of the record.

- Byte 03H contains 00H, a zero-length name.
- Byte 04H contains 04H, the length of the class name CODE, which is found in bytes 05–08H. Bytes 09–26H contain the class names DATA and STACK and the segment names _DATA, _STACK, and _TEXT, each preceded by 1 byte giving its length.
- Byte 27H contains the checksum, 8BH.

98H SEGDEF Segment Definition Record

The SEGDEF record describes a logical segment in an object module. It defines the segment's name, length, and alignment, and the way the segment can be combined with other logical segments. LINK imposes a limit of 255 SEGDEF records per object module.

Object records that follow a SEGDEF record can refer to it to identify a particular segment.

Record format

98H	length	segment attributes	segment length	segment name index	class name index	overlay name index	chk sum

Segment attributes

Segment attributes is a variable-length field:

ACBP byte	frame number	offset

The ACBP byte

The contents and size of the *segment attributes* field depend on the first byte of the field, the ACBP byte:

bit   7   6   5   4   3   2   1   0

A	C	B	P

The bit fields in the ACBP byte describe the following characteristics of the segment:

A   **A**lignment in the run-time memory map
C   **C**ombination with other segments
B   **B**ig (a segment of exactly 64 KB)
P   **P**age-resident (not used in MS-DOS)

The A field. Bits 7–5 of the ACBP byte, the *A* field, describe the logical segment's alignment:

$A = 0$ (000B)   Absolute (located at a specified frame address)
$A = 1$ (001B)   Relocatable, byte aligned
$A = 2$ (010B)   Relocatable, word aligned
$A = 3$ (011B)   Relocatable, paragraph aligned
$A = 4$ (100B)   Relocatable, page aligned

The original Intel specification includes two additional segment-alignment values not supported in MS-DOS.

The following examples of Microsoft assembler SEGMENT directives show the resulting values for the A field in the corresponding SEGDEF object record:

```
aseg    SEGMENT at 400h                 ; A = 0
bseg    SEGMENT byte public 'CODE'      ; A = 1
cseg    SEGMENT para stack 'STACK'      ; A = 3
```

The C field. Bits 4–2 of the ACBP byte, the C field, describe how the linker can combine the segment with other segments. Under MS-DOS, segments with the same name and class can be combined in two ways. They can be concatenated to form one logical segment, or they can be overlapped. In the latter case, they have either the same starting address or the same end address and they describe a common area of memory.

The value in the C field corresponds to one of these two methods of combining segments. Meaningful values, however, also depend on whether the segment is absolute ($A = 0$) or relocatable ($A = 1, 2, 3,$ or 4). If $A = 0$, then C must also be 0, because absolute segments cannot be combined. Values for the C field are

$C = 0$ (000B)	Cannot be combined; used for segments whose combine type is not explicitly specified (private segments).
$C = 1$ (001B)	Not used by Microsoft.
$C = 2$ (010B)	Can be concatenated with another segment of the same name; used for segments with the *public* combine type.
$C = 3$ (011B)	Undefined.
$C = 4$ (100B)	As defined by Microsoft, same as C = 2.
$C = 5$ (101B)	Can be concatenated with another segment with the same name; used for segments with the *stack* combine type.
$C = 6$ (110B)	Can be overlapped with another segment with the same name; used for segments with the *common* combine type.
$C = 7$ (111B)	As defined by Microsoft, same as C = 2.

The following examples of assembler SEGMENT directives show the resulting values for the C field in the corresponding SEGDEF object record:

```
aseg    SEGMENT at 400H                 ; C = 0
bseg    SEGMENT public 'DATA'           ; C = 2
cseg    SEGMENT stack 'STACK'           ; C = 5
dseg    SEGMENT common 'COMMON'         ; C = 6
```

See PROGRAMMING IN THE MS-DOS ENVIRONMENT: PROGRAMMING TOOLS: The Microsoft Object Linker.

The B and P fields. Bit 1 of the ACBP byte, the B field, is set to 1 (and the *segment length* field is set to 0) only if the segment is exactly 64 KB long.

Bit 0 of the ACBP byte, the P field, is unused in MS-DOS. Its value should always be 0.

Frame number and offset

The *frame number* and *offset* fields of the *segment attributes* field are present only if the segment is an absolute segment (A = 0 in the ACBP byte). Taken together, the *frame number* and *offset* indicate the starting address of the segment.

- *Frame number* is a 2-byte field that contains the frame number of the start of the segment.
- *Offset* is a 1-byte field that contains an offset between 00H and 0FH within the specified frame. LINK ignores the *offset* field.

Segment length

Segment length is a 2-byte field that specifies the length of the segment in bytes. The length can be from 00H to FFFFH. If a segment is exactly 64 KB (10000H) in size, *segment length* should be 0 and the *B* field in the ACBP byte should be 1.

Segment name index, class name index, and overlay name index

Each of the *segment name index*, *class name index*, and *overlay name index* fields contains an index into the list of names defined in previous LNAMES records in the object module. An index value of 1 indicates the first name in the LNAMES record, a value of 2 the second, and so on.

- The *segment name index* identifies the segment with a unique name. The name may have been assigned by the programmer, or it may have been generated by a compiler.
- The *class name index* identifies the segment with a class name (such as CODE, FAR_DATA, and STACK). The linker places segments with the same class name into a contiguous area of memory in the run-time memory map.
- The *overlay name index* identifies the segment with a run-time overlay. Starting with version 2.40, however, LINK ignores the *overlay name index*. In versions 2.40 and later, command-line parameters to LINK, rather than information contained in object modules, determine the creation of run-time overlays.

Location in object module

SEGDEF records must follow the LNAMES record to which they refer. In addition, SEGDEF records must precede any PUBDEF, LINNUM, GRPDEF, FIXUPP, LEDATA, or LIDATA records that refer to them.

Examples

In this first example, the segment is byte aligned:

```
      0  1  2  3  4  5  6  7  8  9  A  B  C  D  E  F
0000  98 07 00 28 11 00 07 02 01 1E                    ...(......
```

- Byte 00H contains 98H, indicating that this is a SEGDEF record.
- Bytes 01–02H contain 0007H, the length of the remainder of the record.

- Byte 03H contains 28H (00101000B), the ACBP byte. Bits 7–5 (the *A* field) contain 1 (001B), indicating that this segment is relocatable and byte aligned. Bits 4–2 (the *C* field) contain 2 (010B), which represents a *public* combine type. (When this object module is linked, this segment will be concatenated with all other segments with the same name.) Bit 1 (the *B* field) is 0, indicating that this segment is smaller than 64 KB. Bit 0 (the *P* field) is ignored and should be zero, as it is here.
- Bytes 04–05H contain 0011H, the size of the segment in bytes.
- Bytes 06–08H index the list of names defined in the module's LNAMES record. Byte 06H (*the segment name index*) contains 07H, so the name of this segment is the seventh name in the LNAMES record. Byte 07H (the *class name index*) contains 02H, so the segment's class name is the second name in the LNAMES record. Byte 08H (the *overlay name index*) contains 1, a reference to the first name in the LNAMES record. (This name is usually null, as MS-DOS ignores it anyway.)
- Byte 09H contains the checksum, 1EH.

The second SEGDEF record declares a word-aligned segment. It differs only slightly from the first.

```
      0  1  2  3  4  5  6  7  8  9  A  B  C  D  E  F
0000  98 07 00 48 0F 00 05 03 01 01                    ...H......
```

- Bits 7–5 (the *A* field) of byte 03H (the ACBP byte) contain 2 (010B), indicating that this segment is relocatable and word aligned.
- Bytes 04–05H contain the size of the segment, 000FH.
- Byte 06H (the *segment name index*) contains 05H, which refers to the fifth name in the previous LNAMES record.
- Byte 07H (the *class name index*) contains 03H, a reference to the third name in the LNAMES record.

9AH GRPDEF Group Definition Record

The GRPDEF record defines a group of segments, all of which lie within the same 64 KB frame in the run-time memory map. LINK imposes a limit of 21 GRPDEF records per object module.

Record format

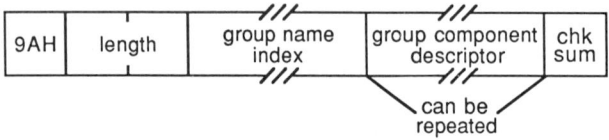

Group name index

Group name index is an index field whose value refers to a name in the *name list* field of a previous LNAMES record.

Group component descriptor

The *group component descriptor* consists of two fields:

- *Type* is a 1-byte field whose value is always 0FFH, indicating that the following field contains a *segment index* value. The original Intel specification defines four other types of *group component descriptor* with the values 0FEH, 0FDH, 0FBH, and 0FAH. LINK ignores these other *type* values, however, and assumes that the *group component descriptor* contains a *segment index* value.
- The *segment index* field contains an index number that refers to a previous SEGDEF record. A value of 1 indicates the first SEGDEF record in the object module, a value of 2 indicates the second, and so on.

The *group component descriptor* field is usually repeated within the GRPDEF record, so all segments constituting the group can be included in one GRPDEF record.

Location in object module

GRPDEF records must follow the LNAMES and SEGDEF records to which they refer. They must also precede any PUBDEF, LINNUM, FIXUPP, LEDATA, or LIDATA records that refer to them.

Example

The following example of a GRPDEF record corresponds to the assembler directive:

```
tgroup  GROUP seg1,seg2,seg3
```

The GRPDEF record is

```
        0  1  2  3  4  5  6  7  8  9  A  B  C  D  E  F
0000   9A 08 00 06 FF 01 FF 02 FF 03 55                   .........U
```

- Byte 00H contains 9AH, indicating that this is a GRPDEF record.
- Bytes 01–02H contain 0008H, the length of the remainder of the record.
- Byte 03H contains 06H, the *group name index*. In this instance, the index number refers to the sixth name in the previous LNAMES record in the object module. That name is the name of the group of segments defined in the remainder of the record.
- Bytes 04–05H contain the first of three *group component descriptor* fields. Byte 04H contains the required 0FFH, indicating that the subsequent field is a *segment index*. Byte 05H contains 01H, a *segment index* that refers to the first SEGDEF record in the object module. This SEGDEF record declared the first of three segments in the group.
- Bytes 06–07H represent the second *group component descriptor*, this one referring to the second SEGDEF record in the object module.
- Similarly, bytes 08–09H are a *group component descriptor* field that references the third SEGDEF record.
- Byte 0AH contains the checksum, 55H.

9CH FIXUPP Fixup Record

The FIXUPP record contains information that allows the linker to resolve (fix up) addresses whose values cannot be determined by the language translator. FIXUPP records describe the LOCATION of each address value to be fixed up, the TARGET address to which the fixup refers, and the FRAME relative to which the address computation is performed.

Record format

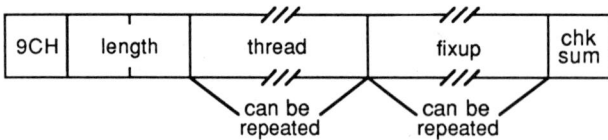

Thread and fixup fields

A FIXUPP record can contain zero or more *thread* fields and zero or more *fixup* fields. Each *fixup* field describes the method to be used by the linker to compute the TARGET address to be placed at a particular location in the executable image, relative to a particular FRAME. The information that determines the LOCATION, TARGET, and FRAME can be specified explicitly in the *fixup* field. It can also be specified within the *fixup* field by a reference to a previous *thread* field.

A *thread* field describes only the method to be used by the linker to refer to a particular TARGET or FRAME. Because the same *thread* field can be referenced in several subsequent *fixup* fields, a FIXUPP record that uses *thread* fields may be smaller than one in which *thread* fields are not used.

Thread and *fixup* fields are distinguished from one another by the high-order bit of the first byte in the field. If the high-order bit is 0, the field is a *thread* field. If the high-order bit is 1, the field is a *fixup* field.

The thread field

A *thread* field contains information that can be referenced in subsequent *thread* or *fixup* fields in the same or subsequent FIXUPP records. It has the following format:

The *thread data* field is a single byte comprising five subfields:

bit	7	6	5	4	3	2	1	0
	0	D	0	method			thread number	

- Bit 7 of the *thread data* byte is 0, indicating the start of a *thread* field.
- The *D* field (bit 6) indicates whether the *thread* field specifies a FRAME or a TARGET. The *D* bit is set to 1 to indicate a FRAME or to 0 to indicate a TARGET.
- Bit 5 of the *thread data* byte is not used. It should always be set to 0.
- Bits 4 through 2 represent the *method* field. If $D = 1$, the *method* field contains 0, 1, 2, 4, or 5. Each of these numbers corresponds to one method of specifying a FRAME (*see* Table 19-2). If $D = 0$, the *method* field contains 0, 1, 2, 4, 5, or 6, each of which corresponds to one of the methods of specifying a TARGET (*see* Table 19-3).

  In the case of a TARGET address, only bits 3 and 2 of the *method* field are used. When $D = 0$, the high-order bit of the value in the *method* field is derived from the *P* bit in the *fix dat* field of any subsequent *fixup* field that refers to this *thread* field. Thus, if $D = 0$, bit 4 of the *method* field is also 0, and the only meaningful values for the *method* field are 0, 1, and 2.

- The *thread number* field (bits 1 and 0) contains a number between 0 and 3. This number is used in subsequent *fixup* or *thread* fields to refer to this particular *thread* field.

  The *thread number* is implicitly associated with the *D* field by the linker, so as many as eight different *thread* fields (four FRAMEs and four TARGETs) can be referenced at any time. A *thread number* can be reused in an object module and, if it is, always refers to the *thread* field in which it last appeared.

Table 19-2. FRAME Fixup Methods.

Method	Description
0	The FRAME is specified by a segment index.
1	The FRAME is specified by a group index.
2	The FRAME is indicated by an external index. LINK determines the FRAME from the external name's corresponding PUBDEF record in another object module, which specifies either a logical segment or a group.
3	The FRAME is identified by an explicit frame number. (Not supported by LINK.)
4	The FRAME is determined by the segment in which the LOCATION is defined. In this case, the largest possible frame number is used.
5	The FRAME is determined by the TARGET's segment, group, or external index.

Table 19-3. TARGET Fixup Methods.

Method	Description
0	The TARGET is specified by a segment index and a displacement. The displacement is given in the *target displacement* field of the FIXUPP record.
1	The TARGET is specified by a group index and a *target displacement*.
2	The TARGET is specified by an external index and a *target displacement*. LINK adds the displacement to the address it determines from the external name's corresponding PUBDEF record in another object module.
3	The TARGET is identified by an explicit frame number. (Not supported by LINK.)
4*	The TARGET is specified by a segment index only.
5*	The TARGET is specified by a group index only.
6*	The TARGET is specified by an external index. The TARGET is the address associated with the external name.
7*	The TARGET is identified by an explicit frame number. (Not supported by LINK.)

*TARGET methods 4–7 are analogous to the preceding four, except that methods 4–7 do not use an explicit displacement to identify the TARGET. Instead, a displacement of 0 is assumed.

The *index* field either contains an index value that refers to a previous SEGDEF, GRPDEF, or EXTDEF record, or it contains an explicit frame number. The interpretation of the index value depends on the value of the *method* field of the *thread data* field:

method = 0	Segment index (reference to a previous SEGDEF record)
method = 1	Group index (reference to a previous GRPDEF record)
method = 2	External index (reference to a previous EXTDEF record)
method = 3	Frame number (not supported by LINK; ignored)

The fixup field

The *fixup* field provides the information needed by the linker to resolve a reference to a relocatable or external address. The *fixup* field has the following format:

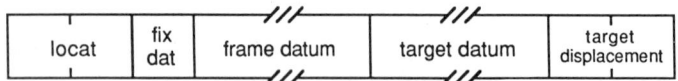

locat	fix dat	frame datum	target datum	target displacement

The 2-byte *locat* field has an unusual format. Contrary to the usual byte order in Intel data structures, the most significant bits of the *locat* field are found in the low-order, rather than the high-order, byte:

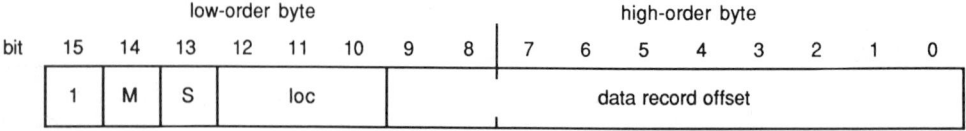

	low-order byte							high-order byte							
bit	15	14	13	12	11	10	9	8	7	6	5	4	3	2	1	0
	1	M	S	loc					data record offset							

- Bit 15 (the high-order bit of the *locat* field) contains 1, indicating that this is a *fixup* field.
- Bit 14 (the *M* bit) is 1 if the fixup is segment relative and 0 if the fixup is self-relative.
- Bit 13 (the *S* bit) is currently unused and should always be set to 0.
- Bits 12 through 10 represent the *loc* field. This field contains a number between 0 and 5 that indicates the type of LOCATION to be fixed up:

loc = 0	Low-order byte
loc = 1	Offset
loc = 2	Segment
loc = 3	Pointer (segment:offset)
loc = 4	High-order byte (not recognized by LINK)
loc = 5	Loader-resolved offset (treated as *loc* = 1 by the linker)

- Bits 9 through 0 (the *data record offset*) indicate the position of the LOCATION to be fixed up in the LEDATA or LIDATA record immediately preceding the FIXUPP record. This offset indicates either a byte in the *data* field of an LEDATA record or a data byte in the *content* field of an *iterated data block* in an LIDATA record.

The *fix dat* field is a single byte comprising five fields:

bit	7	6	5	4	3	2	1	0
	F	frame			T	P	targt	

- Bit 7 (the *F* bit) is set to 1 if the FRAME for this fixup is specified by a reference to a previous *thread* field. The *F* bit is 0 if the FRAME method is explicitly defined in this *fixup* field.
- The interpretation of the *frame* field in bits 6 through 4 depends on the value of the *F* bit. If *F* = 1, the *frame* field contains a number between 0 and 3 that indicates the *thread* field containing the FRAME method. If *F* = 0, the *frame* field contains 0, 1, 2, 4, or 5, corresponding to one of the methods of specifying a FRAME listed in Table 19-2.
- Bit 3 (the *T* bit) is set to 1 if the TARGET for the fixup is specified by a reference to a previous *thread* field. If the *T* bit is 0, the TARGET is explicitly defined in this *fixup* field.
- Bit 2 (the *P* bit) and bits 1 and 0 (the *targt* field) can be considered a 3-bit field analogous to the *frame* field.
- If the *T* bit indicates that the TARGET is specified by a previous *thread* reference (*T* = 1), the *targt* field contains a number between 0 and 3 that refers to a previous *thread* field containing the TARGET method. In this case, the *P* bit, combined with the 2 low-order bits of the *method* field in the *thread* field, determines the TARGET method.

If the *T* bit is 0, indicating that the target is explicitly defined, the *P* and *targt* fields together contain 0, 1, 2, 4, 5, or 6. This number corresponds to one of the TARGET fixup methods listed in Table 19-3. (In this case, the *P* bit can be regarded as the high-order bit of the method number.)

Frame datum is an index field that refers to a previous SEGDEF, GRPDEF, or EXTDEF record, depending on the FRAME method.

Similarly, the *target datum* field contains a segment index, a group index, or an external index, depending on the TARGET method.

The *target displacement* field, a 2-byte field, is present only if the *P* bit in the *fixdat* field is set to 0, in which case the *target displacement* field contains the 16-bit offset used in methods 0, 1, and 2 of specifying a TARGET.

Location in object module

FIXUPP records must appear after the SEGDEF, GRPDEF, or EXTDEF records to which they refer. In addition, if a FIXUPP record contains any *fixup* fields, it must immediately follow the LEDATA or LIDATA record to which the fixups refer.

Examples

Although crucial to the proper linking of object modules, FIXUPP records are terse: Almost every bit is meaningful. For these reasons, the following three examples of FIXUPP records are particularly detailed.

A good way to understand how a FIXUPP record is put together is to compare it to the corresponding source code. The Microsoft Macro Assembler is helpful in this regard, because it marks in its source listing address references it cannot resolve. The "program" in Figure 19-6 is designed to show how some of the most frequently encountered fixups are encoded in FIXUPP records.

```
                             TITLE   fixupps
                     _TEXT   SEGMENT byte public 'CODE'
                             ASSUME  cs:_TEXT
                             EXTRN   NearLabel:near
                             EXTRN   FarLabel:far

0000                 NearProc          PROC      near

0000  E9 0000 E                        jmp       NearLabel       ;relocatable word offset
0003  EB 00 E                          jmp       short NearLabel ;relocatable byte offset
0005  EA 0000 ---- R                   jmp       far ptr FarProc ;far jump to a known seg
000A  EA 0000 ---- E                   jmp       FarLabel        ;far jump to an unknown seg

000F  BB 0015 R                        mov       bx,offset LocalLabel ;relocatable offset
0012  B8 ---- R                        mov       ax,seg LocalLabel    ;relocatable seg
```

Figure 19-6. A sample "program" showing how some common fixups are encoded in FIXUPP records.   (more)

```
0015   C3                    LocalLabel:     ret

                             NearProc        ENDP

0016                         _TEXT    ENDS


0000          .              FAR_TEXT        SEGMENT byte public 'FAR_CODE'
                                     ASSUME  cs:FAR_TEXT

0000                         FarProc PROC    far

0000   CB                            ret

                             FarProc ENDP

0001                         FAR_TEXT        ENDS

                                     END
```

Figure 19-6. Continued.

The assembler generates one LEDATA record for this program:

```
       0  1  2  3  4  5  6  7  8  9  A  B  C  D  E  F
0010   A0 1A 00 01 00 00 E9 00 00 EB 00 EA 00 00 00 00   ................
0020   EA 00 00 00 00 BB 00 00 B8 00 00 C3 67            ...........g
```

Bytes 06–2BH (the *data* field) of this LEDATA record contain 8086 opcodes for each of the instruction mnemonics in the source code. The gaps (zero values) in the *data* field correspond to address values that the assembler cannot resolve. The linker will fix up the address values in the gaps by computing the correct values and adding them to the zero values in the gaps. The FIXUPP record that tells the linker how to do this immediately follows the LEDATA record in the object module:

```
       0  1  2  3  4  5  6  7  8  9  A  B  C  D  E  F
0000   9C 21 00 84 01 06 01 02 80 04 06 01 02 CC 06 04   .!..............
0010   02 02 CC 0B 06 01 01 C4 10 00 01 01 15 00 C8 13   ................
0020   04 01 01 A3                                        ....
```

- Byte 00H contains 9CH, indicating this is a FIXUPP record.
- Bytes 01–02H contain 0021H, the length of the remainder of the record.
- Bytes 03–07H represent the first of the six *fixup* fields in this record:

```
       0  1  2  3  4  5  6  7  8  9  A  B  C  D  E  F
0000   9C 21 00 84 01 06 01 02 80 04 06 01 02 CC 06 04   .!..............
0010   02 02 CC 0B 06 01 01 C4 10 00 01 01 15 00 C8 13   ................
0020   04 01 01 A3                                        ....
```

The information in this *fixup* field will allow the linker to resolve the address reference in the statement

```
jmp     NearLabel
```

- Bytes 03–04H (the *locat* field) contain 8401H (1000010000000001B). (Recall that this field does not conform to the usual Intel byte order.) Bit 15 is 1, signifying that this is a *fixup* field, not a *thread* field. Bit 14 (the *M* bit) is 0, so this fixup is self-relative. Bit 13 is unused and should be set to 0, as it is here. Bits 12–10 (the *loc* field) contain 1 (001B), so the LOCATION to be fixed up is a 16-bit offset. Bits 9–0 (the *data record offset*) contain 1 (0000000001B), which informs the linker that the LOCATION to be fixed up is at offset 1 in the *data* field of the LEDATA record immediately preceding this FIXUPP record—in other words, the 2 bytes immediately following the first opcode 0E9H.
- Byte 05H (the *fix dat* field) contains 06H (00000110B). Bit 7 (the *F* bit) is 0, meaning the FRAME for this fixup is explicitly specified in this *fixup* field. Bits 6–4 (the *frame* field) contain 0 (000B), indicating that FRAME method 0 specifies the FRAME. Bit 3 (the *T* bit) is 0, so the TARGET for this fixup is also explicitly specified. Bits 2–0 (the *P* bit) and the *targt* field contain 6 (110B), so TARGET method 6 specifies the TARGET.
- Byte 06H is a *frame datum* field, because the FRAME is explicitly specified (the *F* bit of the *fix dat* field = 0). And, because method 0 is specified, the *frame datum* is an index field that refers to a previous SEGDEF record. In this example, the *frame datum* field contains 1, which indicates the first SEGDEF record in the object module: the _TEXT segment.
- Similarly, byte 07H is a *target datum*, because the TARGET is also explicitly specified (the *T* bit of the *fix dat* field = 0). The *fix dat* field also indicates that TARGET method 6 is used, so the *target datum* is an index field that refers to the *external reference list* in a previous EXTDEF record. The value of this index is 2, so the TARGET is the second external reference declared in the EXTDEF record: *NearLabel* in this object module.

- Bytes 08–0CH represent the second *fixup* field:

```
      0  1  2  3  4  5  6  7  8  9  A  B  C  D  E  F
0000  9C 21 00 84 01 06 01 02 80 04 06 01 02 CC 06 04   .!..............
0010  02 02 CC 0B 06 01 01 C4 10 00 01 01 15 00 C8 13   ................
0020  04 01 01 A3                                        ....
```

This *fixup* field corresponds to the statement

```
jmp     short NearLabel
```

The only difference between this statement and the first is that the jump uses an 8-bit, rather than a 16-bit, offset. Thus, the *loc* field (bits 12–10 of byte 08H) contains 0 (000B) to indicate that the LOCATION to be fixed up is a low-order byte.

- Bytes 0D–11H represent the third *fixup* field in this FIXUPP record:

```
      0  1  2  3  4  5  6  7  8  9  A  B  C  D  E  F
0000  9C 21 00 84 01 06 01 02 80 04 06 01 02 CC 06 04   .!..............
0010  02 02 CC 0B 06 01 01 C4 10 00 01 01 15 00 C8 13   ................
0020  04 01 01 A3                                        ....
```

This *fixup* field corresponds to the statement

```
jmp     far ptr FarProc
```

In this case, both the TARGET's frame (the segment *FAR_TEXT*) and offset (the label *FarProc*) are known to the assembler. Both the segment address and the label offset are relocatable, however, so in the FIXUPP record the assembler passes the responsibility for resolving the addresses to the linker.

- Bytes 0D–0EH (the *locat* field) indicate that the field is a *fixup* field (bit 15 = 1) and that the fixup is segment relative (bit 14 — the *M* bit = 1). The *loc* field (bits 12–10) contains 3 (011B), so the LOCATION being fixed up is a 32-bit (FAR) pointer (segment and offset). The *data record offset* (bits 9–0) is 6 (0000000110B); the LOCATION is the 4 bytes following the first far jump opcode (EAH) in the preceding LEDATA record.
- In byte 0FH (the *fix dat* field), the *F* bit and the *frame* field are 0, indicating that method 0 (a segment index) is used to specify the FRAME. The *T* bit is 0 (meaning the *target* is explicitly defined in the *fixup* field); therefore, the *P* bit and *targt* fields together indicate method 4 (a segment index) to specify the TARGET.
- Because the FRAME is specified with a segment index, byte 10H (the *frame datum* field) is a reference to the second SEGDEF record in the object module, which in this example declared the *FAR_TEXT* segment. Similarly, byte 11H (the *target datum* field) references the *FAR_TEXT* segment. In this case, the FRAME is the same as the TARGET segment; had *FAR_TEXT* been one of a group of segments, the FRAME could have referred to the group instead.

- The fourth assembler statement is different from the third because it references a segment not known to the assembler:

```
jmp     FarLabel
```

Bytes 12–16H contain the corresponding *fixup* field:

```
       0  1  2  3  4  5  6  7  8  9  A  B  C  D  E  F
0000  9C 21 00 84 01 06 01 02 80 04 06 01 02 CC 06 04   .!..............
0010  02 02 CC 0B 06 01 01 C4 10 00 01 01 15 00 C8 13   ................
0020  04 01 01 A3                                       ....
```

The significant difference between this and the preceding *fixup* field is that the *P* bit and *targt* field of the *fix dat* byte (byte 14H) specify TARGET method 6. In this *fixup* field, the *target datum* (byte 16H) refers to the first EXTDEF record in the object module, which declares *FarLabel* as an external reference.

- The fifth *fixup* field (bytes 17–1DH) is

```
       0  1  2  3  4  5  6  7  8  9  A  B  C  D  E  F
0000  9C 21 00 84 01 06 01 02 80 04 06 01 02 CC 06 04   .!..............
0010  02 02 CC 0B 06 01 01 C4 10 00 01 01 15 00 C8 13   ................
0020  04 01 01 A3                                       ....
```

This *fixup* field contains information that enables the linker to calculate the value of the relocatable offset *LocalLabel*:

```
mov     bx,offset LocalLabel
```

- Bytes 17–18H (the *locat* field) contain C410H (1100010000010000B). Bit 15 is 1, denoting a *fixup* field. The *M* bit (bit 14) is 1, indicating that this fixup is segment relative. The *loc* field (bits 12–10) contains 1 (001B), so the LOCATION is a 16-bit offset. The *data record offset* (bits 9–0) is 10H (0000010000B), a reference to the 2 bytes in the LEDATA record following the opcode 0BBH.
- Byte 19H (the *fix dat* byte) contains 00H. The *F* bit, *frame* field, *T* bit, *P* bit, and *targt* field are all 0, so FRAME method 0 and TARGET method 0 are explicitly specified in this *fixup* field.
- Because FRAME method 0 is used, byte 1AH (the *frame datum* field) is an index field. It contains 01H, a reference to the first SEGDEF record in the object module, which declares the segment _TEXT.

    Similarly, byte 1BH (the *target datum* field) references the _TEXT segment.
- Because TARGET method 0 is specified, an offset, in addition to a segment, is required to define the TARGET. This offset appears in the *target displacement* field in bytes 1C–1DH. The value of this offset is 0015H, corresponding to the offset of the TARGET (*LocalLabel*) in its segment (_TEXT).

● The sixth and final *fixup* field in this FIXUPP record (bytes 1E–22H) is

```
        0  1  2  3  4  5  6  7  8  9  A  B  C  D  E  F
0000   9C 21 00 84 01 06 01 02 80 04 06 01 02 CC 06 04   .!..............
0010   02 02 CC 0B 06 01 01 C4 10 00 01 01 15 00 C8 13   ................
0020   04 01 01 A3                                       ....
```

This corresponds to the segment of the relocatable address *LocalLabel*:

```
mov     ax,seg LocalLabel
```

- Bytes 1E–1FH (the *locat* field) contain C813H (1100100000010011B). Bit 15 is 1, so this is a *fixup* field. The *M* bit (bit 14) is 1, so the fixup is segment relative. The *loc* field (bits 12–10) contains 2 (010B), so the LOCATION is a 16-bit segment value. The *data record offset* (bits 9–0) indicates the 2 bytes in the LEDATA record following the opcode 0B8H.
- Byte 20H (the *fix dat* byte) contains 04H, so FRAME method 0 and TARGET method 4 are explicitly specified in this *fixup* field.
- Byte 21H (the *frame datum* field) contains 01H. Because FRAME method 0 is specified, the *frame datum* is an index value that refers to the first SEGDEF record in the object module (corresponding to the _TEXT segment).
- Byte 22H (the *target datum* field) contains 01H. Because TARGET method 4 is specified, the *target datum* also references the _TEXT segment.

● Finally, byte 23H contains this FIXUPP record's checksum, 0A3H.

The next two FIXUPP records show how *thread* fields are used. The first of the two contains six *thread* fields that can be referenced by both *thread* and *fixup* fields in subsequent FIXUPP records in the same object module:

```
        0  1  2  3  4  5  6  7  8  9  A  B  C  D  E  F
0000   9C 0D 00 00 03 01 02 02 01 03 04 40 01 45 01 C0   ...........@....
```

Bytes 03–04H, 05–06H, 07–08H, 09–0AH, 0B–0CH, and 0D–0EH represent the six *thread* fields in this FIXUPP record. The high-order bit of the first byte of each of these fields is 0, indicating that they are, indeed, *thread* fields and not *fixup* fields.

- Byte 03H, which contains 00H, is the *thread data* byte of the first *thread* field. Bit 7 of this byte is 0, indicating this is a *thread* field. Bit 6 (the *D* bit) is 0, so this field specifies a TARGET. Bit 5 is 0, as it must always be. Bits 4 through 2 (the *method* field) contain 0 (000B), which specifies TARGET method 0. Finally, bits 1 and 0 contain 0 (00B), the *thread number* that identifies this *thread* field.

  Byte 04H represents a segment *index* field, because method 0 of specifying a TARGET references a segment. The value of the index, 3, is a reference to the third SEGDEF record defined in the object module.

- Bytes 05–06H, 07–08H, and 09–0AH contain similar *thread* fields. In each, the *method* field specifies TARGET method 0. The three *thread* fields also have *thread numbers* of 1, 2, and 3. Because TARGET method 0 is specified for each *thread* field, bytes 06H, 08H, and 0AH represent segment *index* fields, which reference the second, first, and fourth SEGDEF records, respectively.

- Byte 0BH (the *thread data* byte of the fifth *thread* field in this FIXUPP record) contains 40H (01000000B). The *D* bit (bit 6) is 1, so this *thread* field specifies a FRAME. The *method* field (bits 4 through 2) contains 0 (000B), which specifies FRAME method 0. Byte 0CH (which contains 01H) is therefore interpreted as a segment *index* reference to the first SEGDEF record in the object module.

- Byte 0DH is the *thread data* byte of the sixth *thread* field. It contains 45H (01000101B). Bit 6 is 1, which indicates that this *thread* specifies a FRAME. The *method* field (bits 4 through 2) contains 1 (001B), which specifies FRAME method 1. Byte 0EH (which contains 01H) is therefore interpreted as a group *index* to the first preceding GRPDEF record.

  The *thread number* fields of the fifth and sixth *thread* fields contain 0 and 1, respectively, but these *thread numbers* do not conflict with the ones used in the first and second *thread* fields, because the latter represent TARGET references, not FRAME references.

The next FIXUPP example appears after the preceding record, in the same object module. This FIXUPP record contains a *fixup* field in bytes 03–05H that refers to a *thread* in the previous FIXUPP record:

```
        0  1  2  3  4  5  6  7  8  9  A  B  C  D  E  F
0000   9C 04 00 C4 09 9D F6                              . . . . . . .
```

- Bytes 03–04H represent the 16-bit *locat* field, which contains C409H (1100010000001001B). Bit 15 of the *locat* field is 1, indicating a *fixup* field. The *M* bit (bit 14) is 1, so this fixup is relative to a particular segment, which is specified later in the *fixup* field. Bit 13 is 0, as it should be. Bits 12–10 (the *loc* field) contain 1 (001B), so the LOCATION to be fixed up is a 16-bit offset. Bits 9–0 (the *data record offset* field) contain 9 (0000001001B), so the LOCATION to be fixed up is represented at an offset of 9 bytes into the data field of the preceding LEDATA or LIDATA record.

- Byte 05H (the *fix dat* byte) contains 9DH (10011101B). The *F* bit (bit 7) is 1, so this *fixup* field references a *thread* field that, in turn, defines the method of specifying the FRAME for the fixup. Bits 6–4 (the *frame* field) contain 1 (001B), the number of the *thread* that contains the FRAME method. This *thread* contains a *method* number of 1, which references the first GRPDEF record in the object module, thus specifying the FRAME.

  The *T* bit (bit 3 in the *fix dat* byte) is 1, so the TARGET method is also defined in a preceding *thread* field. The *targt* field (bits 1 and 0 in the *fix dat* byte) contains 1 (01B), so the TARGET *thread* field whose *thread number* is 1 specifies the TARGET. The *P* bit (bit 3 in the *fix dat* byte) contains 1, which is combined with the low-order bits of the *method* field in the *thread* field that describes the target to obtain TARGET method number 4 (100B). The TARGET *thread* references the second SEGDEF record to specify the TARGET.

The last FIXUPP example illustrates that the linker performs a fixup by adding the calculated address value to the value in the LOCATION being fixed up. This function of the linker can be exploited to use fixups to modify opcodes or program data, as well as to resolve address references.

Consider how the following assembler instruction might be fixed up:

```
lea  bx,alpha+10h   ; alpha is an external symbol
```

Typically, this instruction is translated into an LEDATA record with zero in the LOCATION (bytes 08–09H) to be fixed up:

```
     0  1  2  3  4  5  6  7  8  9  A  B  C  D  E  F
0000 A0 08 00 01 00 00 8D 1E 00 00 AC            ..........
```

The corresponding FIXUPP record contains a *target displacement* of 10H bytes (bytes 08–09H):

```
     0  1  2  3  4  5  6  7  8  9  A  B  C  D  E  F
0000 9C 08 00 C4 02 02 01 01 10 00 82            ..........
```

This FIXUPP record specifies TARGET method 2, which is indicated by the *targt* field (bits 2–0) of the *fixdat* field (byte 05H). In this case, the linker adds the *target displacement* to the address it has determined for the TARGET (*alpha*) and then completes the fixup by adding this calculated address value to the zero value in the LOCATION.

The same result can be achieved by storing the displacement (10H) directly in the LOCATION in the LEDATA record:

```
     0  1  2  3  4  5  6  7  8  9  A  B  C  D  E  F
0000 A0 08 00 01 00 00 8D 1E 10 00 9C            ..........
```

Then, the *target displacement* can be omitted from the FIXUPP record:

```
     0  1  2  3  4  5  6  7  8  9  A  B  C  D  E  F
0000 9C 06 00 C4 02 06 01 01 90                  .........
```

This FIXUPP record specifies TARGET method 6, which does not use a *target displacement*. The linker performs this fixup by adding the address of *alpha* to the value in the LOCATION, so the result is identical to the preceding one.

The difference between the two techniques is that in the latter the linker does not perform error checking when it adds the calculated fixup value to the value in the LOCATION. If this second technique is used, the linker will not flag arithmetic overflow or underflow errors when it adds the displacement to the TARGET address. The first technique, then, traps all errors; the second can be used when overflow or underflow is irrelevant and an error message would be undesirable.

0A0H LEDATA Logical Enumerated Data Record

The LEDATA record contains contiguous binary data — executable code or program data — that is eventually copied into the program's executable binary image.

The binary data in an LEDATA record can be modified by the linker if the record is followed by a FIXUPP record.

Record format

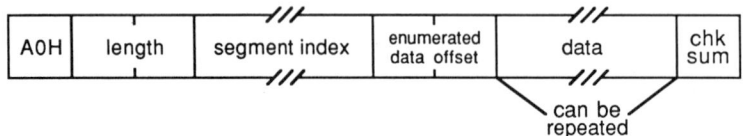

Segment index

The *segment index* is a variable-length index field. The index number in this field refers to a previous SEGDEF record in the object module. A value of 1 indicates the first SEGDEF record, a value of 2 the second, and so on. That SEGDEF record, in turn, indicates the segment into which the data in this LEDATA record is to be placed.

Enumerated data offset

The *enumerated data offset* is a 2-byte offset into the segment referenced by the *segment index*, relative to the base of the segment. Taken together, the *segment index* and the *enumerated data offset* fields indicate the location where the enumerated data will be placed in the run-time memory map.

Data

The *data* field contains the actual data, which can be either executable 8086 instructions or program data. The maximum size of the *data* field is 1024 bytes.

Location in object module

Any LEDATA records in an object module must be preceded by the SEGDEF records to which they refer. Also, if an LEDATA record requires a fixup, a FIXUPP record must immediately follow the LEDATA record.

Example

The following LEDATA record contains a simple text string:

```
        0  1  2  3  4  5  6  7  8  9  A  B  C  D  E  F
0000   A0 13 00 02 00 00 48 65 6C 6C 6F 2C 20 77 6F 72    ......Hello, wor
0010   6C 64 0D 0A 24 A8                                  ld..$.
```

- Byte 00H contains 0A0H, which identifies this as an LEDATA record.
- Bytes 01–02H contain 0013H, the length of the remainder of the record.

- Byte 03H (the *segment index* field) contains 02H, a reference to the second SEGDEF record in the object module.
- Bytes 04–05H (the *enumerated data offset* field) contain 0000H. This is the offset, from the base of the segment indicated by the *segment index* field, at which the data in the *data* field will be placed when the program is linked. Of course, this offset is subject to relocation by the linker because the segment declared in the specified SEGDEF record may be relocatable and may be combined with other segments declared in other object modules.
- Bytes 06–14H (the *data* field) contain the actual data.
- Byte 15H contains the checksum, 0A8H.

0A2H LIDATA Logical Iterated Data Record

Like the LEDATA record, the LIDATA record contains binary data — executable code or program data. The data in an LIDATA record, however, is specified as a repeating pattern (iterated), rather than by explicit enumeration.

The data in an LIDATA record may be modified by the linker if the LIDATA record is followed by a FIXUPP record.

Record format

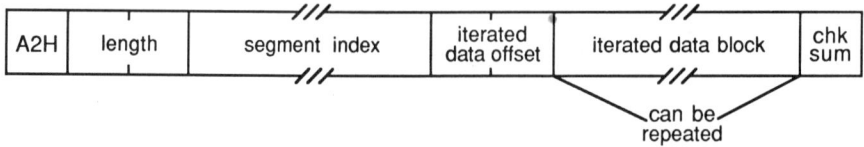

Segment index

The *segment index* is a variable-length index field. The index number in this field refers to a previous SEGDEF record in the object module. A value of 1 indicates the first SEGDEF record, 2 indicates the second, and so on. That SEGDEF record, in turn, indicates the segment into which the data in this LIDATA record is to be placed when the program is executed.

Iterated data offset

The *iterated data offset* is a 2-byte offset into the segment referenced by the *segment index*, relative to the base of the segment. Taken together, the *segment index* and the *iterated data offset* fields indicate the location where the iterated data will be placed in the run-time memory map.

Iterated data block

The *iterated data block* is a variable-length field containing the actual data — executable code and program data. *Iterated data blocks* can be nested, so one *iterated data block* can contain one or more other *iterated data blocks*. Microsoft LINK restricts the maximum size of an *iterated data block* to 512 bytes.

The format of the *iterated data block* is

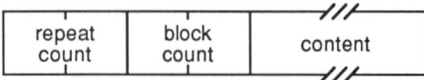

- *Repeat count* is a 2-byte field indicating the number of times the *content* field is to be repeated.
- *Block count* is a 2-byte field indicating the number of *iterated data blocks* in the *content* field. If the *block count* is 0, the *content* field contains data only.

- *Content* is a variable-length field that can contain either nested *iterated data blocks* (if the *block count* is nonzero) or data (if the *block count* is 0). If the *content* field contains data, the field contains a 1-byte count of the number of data bytes in the field, followed by the actual data.

Location in object module

Any LIDATA records in an object module must be preceded by the SEGDEF records to which they refer. Also, if an LIDATA record requires a fixup, a FIXUPP record must immediately follow the LIDATA record.

Example

This sample LIDATA record corresponds to the following assembler statement, which declares a 10-element array containing the strings *ALPHA* and *BETA*:

```
db      10 dup('ALPHA','BETA')
```

The LIDATA record is

```
     0  1  2  3  4  5  6  7  8  9  A  B  C  D  E  F
0000 A2 1B 00 01 00 00 0A 00 02 00 01 00 00 00 05 41   ..............A
0010 4C 50 48 41 01 00 00 00 04 42 45 54 41 A9         LPHA.....BETA.
```

- Byte 00H contains 0A2H, identifying this as an LIDATA record.
- Bytes 01–02H contain 1BH, the length of the remainder of the record.
- Byte 03H (the *segment index*) contains 01H, a reference to the first SEGDEF record in this object module, indicating that the data declared in this LIDATA record is to be placed into the segment described by the first SEGDEF record.
- Bytes 04–05H (the *iterated data offset*) contain 0000H, so the data in this LIDATA record is to be located at offset 0000H in the segment designated by the *segment index*.
- Bytes 06–1CH represent an *iterated data block*:
  - Bytes 06–07H contain the *repeat count*, 000AH, which indicates that the *content* field of this *iterated data block* is to be repeated 10 times.
  - Bytes 08–09H (the *block count* for this *iterated data block*) contain 0002H, which indicates that the *content* field of this *iterated data block* (bytes 0A–1CH) contains two nested *iterated data block* fields (bytes 0A–13H and bytes 14–1CH).
  - Bytes 0A–0BH contain 0001H, the *repeat count* for the first nested *iterated data block*. Bytes 0C–0DH contain 0000H, indicating that the *content* field of this nested *iterated data block* contains data, rather than more nested *iterated data blocks*. The *content* field (bytes 0E–13H) contains the data: Byte 0EH contains 05H, the number of subsequent data bytes, and bytes 0F–13H contain the actual data (the string *ALPHA*).
  - Bytes 14–1CH represent the second nested *iterated data block*, which has a format similar to that of the block in bytes 0A–13H. This second nested *iterated data block* represents the 4-byte string *BETA*.
- Byte 1DH is the checksum, 0A9H.

0B0H COMDEF Communal Names Definition Record

The COMDEF record is a Microsoft extension to the basic set of 8086 object record types defined by Intel that declares a list of one or more communal variables. The COMDEF record is recognized by versions 3.50 and later of LINK. Microsoft encourages the use of the COMDEF record for declaration of communal variables.

Record format

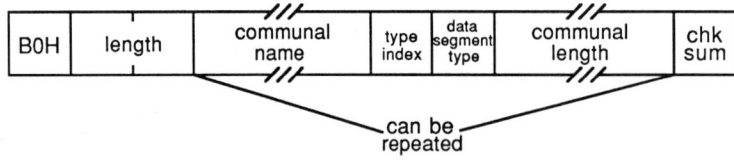

Communal name

The *communal name* field is a variable-length field that contains the name of a communal variable. The first byte of this field indicates the length of the name contained in the remainder of the field.

Type index

The *type index* field is an index field that references a previous TYPDEF record in the object module. A value of 1 indicates the first TYPDEF record in the module, a value of 2 indicates the second, and so on. The *type index* value can be 0 if no data type is associated with the public name.

Data segment type

The *data segment type* field is a single byte that indicates whether the communal variable is FAR or NEAR. There are only two possible values for *data segment type*:

61H   FAR variable
62H   NEAR variable

Communal length

The *communal length* is a variable-length field that indicates the amount of memory to be allocated for the communal variable. The contents of this field depend on the value in the *data segment type* field. If the *data segment type* is NEAR (62H), the *communal length* field contains the size (in bytes) of the communal variable:

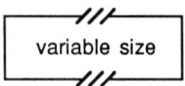

If the *data segment type* is FAR (61H), the *communal length* field is formatted as follows:

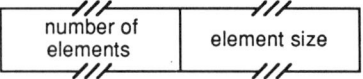

A FAR communal variable is viewed as an array of elements of a specified size. Thus, the *number of elements* field is a variable-length field representing the number of elements in the array, and the *element size* field is a variable-length field that indicates the size (in bytes) of each element. The amount of memory required for a FAR communal variable is thus the product of the *number of elements* and the *element size*.

The format of the *variable size*, *number of elements*, and *element size* fields depends upon the magnitude of the values they contain:

● If the value is less than 128 (80H), the field is formatted as a 1-byte field containing the actual value:

● If the value is 128 (80H) or greater, the field is formatted with an extra initial byte that indicates whether the value is represented in the subsequent 2, 3, or 4 bytes:

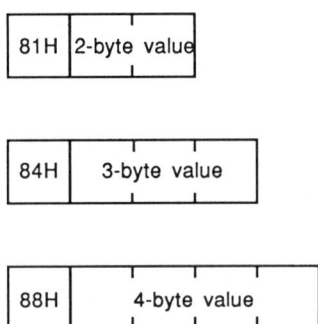

Groups of *communal name*, *type index*, *data segment type*, and *communal length* fields can be repeated so that more than one communal variable can be declared in the same COMDEF record.

Location in object module

Any object module that contains COMDEF records must also contain one COMENT record with the *comment class* 0A1H, indicating that Microsoft extensions to the Intel object record specification are included in the object module. This COMENT record must appear before any COMDEF records in the object module.

Example

The following COMDEF record was generated by the Microsoft C Compiler version 4.0 for these public variable declarations:

```
int     foo;                    /* 2-byte integer */
char    foo2[32768];            /* 32768-byte array */
char    far foo3[10][2][20];    /* 400-byte array */
```

The COMDEF record is

```
        0  1  2  3  4  5  6  7  8  9  A  B  C  D  E  F
0000   B0 20 00 04 5F 66 6F 6F 00 62 02 05 5F 66 6F 6F    . .._foo.b.._foo
0010   32 00 62 81 00 80 05 5F 66 6F 6F 33 00 61 81 90    2.b...._foo3.a..
0020   01 01 99                                           ...
```

- Byte 00H contains 0B0H, indicating that this is a COMDEF record.
- Bytes 01–02H contain 0020H, the length of the remainder of the record.
- Bytes 03–0AH, 0B–15H, and 16–21H represent three declarations for the communal variables *foo*, *foo2*, and *foo3*. The C compiler prepends an underscore to each of the names declared in the source code, so the symbols represented in this COMDEF record are _foo, _foo2, and _foo3.
  - Byte 03H contains 04H, the length of the first *communal name* in this record. Bytes 04–07H contain the name itself (_foo). Byte 08H (the *type index* field) contains 00H, as required. Byte 09H (the *data segment type* field) contains 62H, indicating this is a NEAR variable. Byte 0AH (the *communal length* field) contains 02H, the size of the variable in bytes.
  - Byte 0BH contains 05H, the length of the second *communal name*. Bytes 0C–10H contain the name, _foo2. Byte 11H is the *type index* field, which again contains 00H as required. Byte 12H (the *data segment type* field) contains 62H, indicating that _foo2 is a NEAR variable.

    Bytes 13–15H (the *communal length* field) contain the size in bytes of the variable. The first byte of the *communal length* field (byte 13H) is 81H, indicating that the size is represented in the subsequent 2 bytes of data — bytes 14–15H, which contain the value 8000H.
  - Bytes 16–1BH represent the *communal name* field for _foo3, the third communal variable declared in this record. Byte 1CH (the *type index* field) again contains 00H as required. Byte 1DH (the *data segment type* field) contains 61H, indicating this is a FAR variable. This means the *communal length* field is formatted as a *number of elements* field (bytes 1E–20H, which contain the value 0190H) and an *element size* field (byte 21H, which contains 01H). The total size of this communal variable is thus 190H times 1, or 400 bytes.
- Byte 22H contains the checksum, 99H.

Richard Wilton

Article 20
The Microsoft Object Linker

MS-DOS object modules can be processed in two ways: They can be grouped together in object libraries, or they can be linked into executable files. All Microsoft language translators are distributed with two utility programs that process object modules: The Microsoft Library Manager (LIB) creates and modifies object libraries; the Microsoft Object Linker (LINK) processes the individual object records within object modules to create executable files.

The following discussion focuses on LINK because of its crucial role in creating an executable file. Before delving into the complexities of LINK, however, it is worthwhile reviewing how object modules are managed.

Object Files, Object Libraries, and LIB

Compilers and assemblers translate source-code modules into object modules (Figure 20-1). *See* PROGRAMMING IN THE MS-DOS ENVIRONMENT: PROGRAMMING TOOLS: Object Modules. An object module consists of a sequence of object records that describe the form and content of part of an executable program. An MS-DOS object module always starts with a THEADR record; subsequent object records in the module follow the sequence discussed in the Object Modules article.

Object modules can be stored in either of two types of MS-DOS files: object files and object libraries. By convention, object files have the filename extension .OBJ and object libraries have the extension .LIB. Although both object files and object libraries contain one or

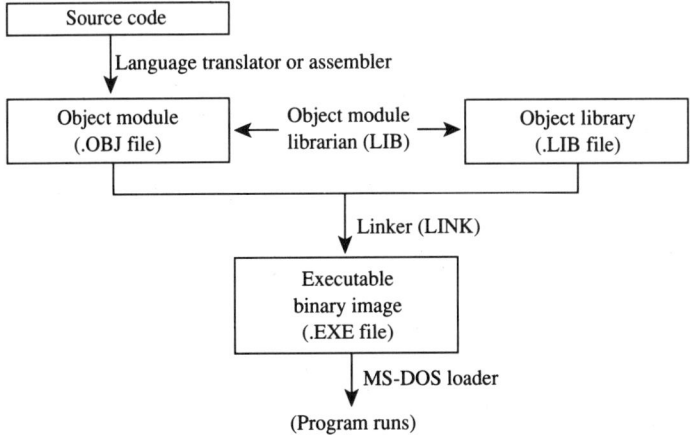

Figure 20-1. Object modules, object libraries, LIB, and LINK.

more object modules, the files and the libraries have different internal organization. Furthermore, LINK processes object files and libraries differently.

The structures of object files and libraries are compared in Figure 20-2. An object file is a simple concatenation of object modules in any arbitrary order. (Microsoft discourages the use of object files that contain more than one object module; Microsoft language translators never generate more than one object module in an object file.) In contrast, a library contains a hashed dictionary of all the public symbols declared in each of the object modules, in addition to the object modules themselves. Each symbol in the dictionary is associated with a reference to the object module in which the symbol was declared.

LINK processes object files differently than it does libraries. When LINK builds an executable file, it incorporates all the object modules in all the object files it processes. In contrast, when LINK processes libraries, it uses the hashed symbol dictionary in each library to extract object modules selectively — it uses an object module from a library only when the object module contains a symbol that is referenced within some other object module. This distinction between object files and libraries is important in understanding what LINK does.

(a)
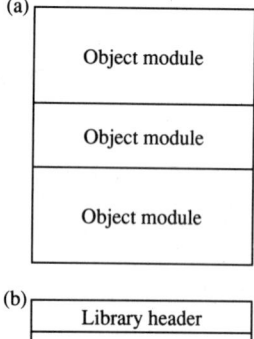

(b)
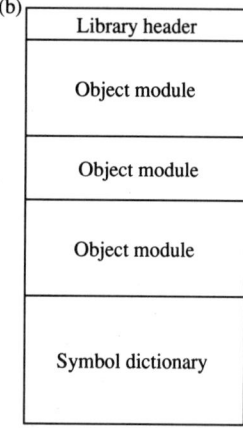

Figure 20-2. Structures of an object file and an object library. (a) An object file contains one or more object modules. (Microsoft discourages using more than one object module per object file.) (b) An object library contains one or more object modules plus a hashed symbol dictionary indicating the object modules in which each public symbol is defined.

What LINK Does

The function of LINK is to translate object modules into an executable program. LINK's input consists of one or more object files (.OBJ files) and, optionally, one or more libraries (.LIB files). LINK's output is an executable file (.EXE file) containing binary data that can be loaded directly from the file into memory and executed. LINK can also generate a symbolic address map listing (.MAP file) — a text file that describes the organization of the .EXE file and the correspondence of symbols declared in the object modules to addresses in the executable file.

Building an executable file

LINK builds two types of information into a .EXE file. First, it extracts executable code and data from the LEDATA and LIDATA records in object modules, arranges them in a specified order according to its rules for segment combination and relocation, and copies the result into the .EXE file. Second, LINK builds a header for the .EXE file. The header describes the size of the executable program and also contains a table of load-time segment relocations and initial values for certain CPU registers. *See* Pass 2 below.

Relocation and linking

In building an executable image from object modules, LINK performs two essential tasks: relocation and linking. As it combines and rearranges the executable code and data it extracts from the object modules it processes, LINK frequently adjusts, or relocates, address references to account for the rearrangements (Figure 20-3). LINK links object modules by resolving address references among them. It does this by matching the symbols declared in EXTDEF and PUBDEF object records (Figure 20-4). LINK uses FIXUPP records to determine exactly how to compute both address relocations and linked address references.

Object Module Order

LINK processes input files from three sources: object files and libraries specified explicitly by the user (in the command line, in response to LINK's prompts, or in a response file) and object libraries named in object module COMENT records.

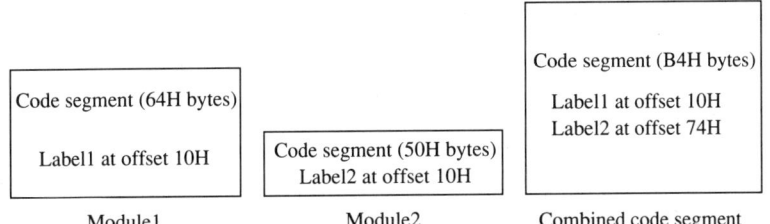

Figure 20-3. A simple relocation. Both object modules contain code that LINK combines into one logical segment. In this example, LINK appends the 50H bytes of code in Module2 to the 64H bytes of code in Module1. LINK relocates all references to addresses in the code segment so that they apply to the combined segment.

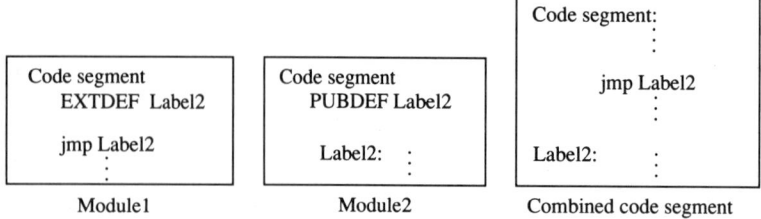

Figure 20-4. *Resolving an external reference. LINK resolves the external reference in* Module1 *(declared in an EXTDEF record) with the address of* Label2 *in* Module2 *(declared in a PUBDEF record).*

LINK always uses all the object modules in the object files it processes. In contrast, it extracts individual object modules from libraries — only those object modules needed to resolve references to public symbols are used. This difference is implicit in the order in which LINK reads its input files:

1. Object files specified in the command line or in response to the *Object Modules* prompt
2. Libraries specified in the command line or in response to the *Libraries* prompt
3. Libraries specified in COMENT records

The order in which LINK processes object modules influences the resulting executable file in three ways. First, the order in which segments appear in LINK's input files is reflected in the segment structure of the executable file. Second, the order in which LINK resolves external references to public symbols depends on the order in which it finds the public symbols in its input files. Finally, LINK derives the default name of the executable file from the name of the first input object file.

Segment order in the executable file

In general, LINK builds named segments into the executable file in the order in which it first encounters the SEGDEF records that declare the segments. (The /DOSSEG switch also affects segment order. *See* Using the /DOSSEG Switch below.) This means that the order in which segments appear in the executable file can be controlled by linking object modules in a specific order. In assembly-language programs, it is best to declare all the segments used in the program in the first object module to be linked so that the segment order in the executable file is under complete control.

Order in which references are resolved

LINK resolves external references in the order in which it encounters the corresponding public declarations. This fact is important because it determines the order in which LINK extracts object modules from libraries. When a public symbol required to resolve an external reference is declared more than once among the object modules in the input libraries, LINK uses the first object module that contains the public symbol. This means that the actual executable code or data associated with a particular external reference can be varied by changing the order in which LINK processes its input libraries.

For example, imagine that a C programmer has written two versions of a function named *myfunc()* that is called by the program MYPROG.C. One version of *myfunc()* is for debugging; its object module is found in MYFUNC.OBJ. The other is a production version whose object module resides in MYLIB.LIB. Under normal circumstances, the programmer links the production version of *myfunc()* by using MYLIB.LIB (Figure 20-5). To use the debugging version of *myfunc()*, the programmer explicitly includes its object module (MYFUNC.OBJ) when LINK is executed. This causes LINK to build the debugging version of *myfunc()* into the executable file because it encounters the debugging version in MYFUNC.OBJ before it finds the other version in MYLIB.LIB.

To exploit the order in which LINK resolves external references, it is important to know LINK's library search strategy: Each individual library is searched repeatedly (from first library to last, in the sequence in which they are input to LINK) until no further external references can be resolved.

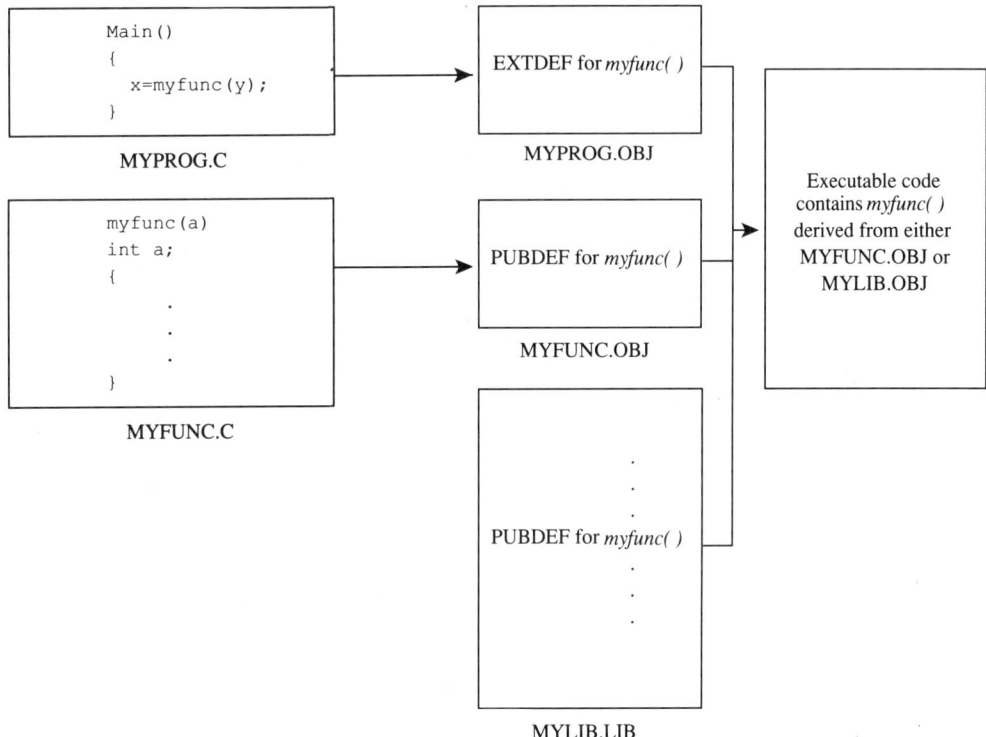

Figure 20-5. Ordered object module processing by LINK. (a) With the command LINK MYPROG,,,MYLIB, *the production version of* myfunc() *in MYLIB.LIB is used. (b) With the command* LINK MYPROG+ MYFUNC,,,MYLIB, *the debugging version of* myfunc() *in MYFUNC.OBJ is used.*

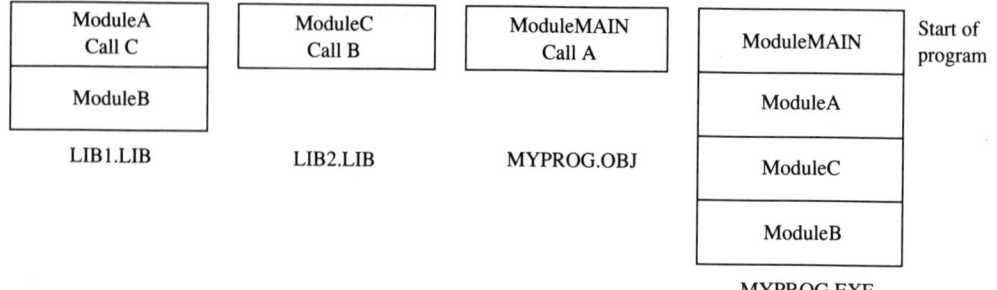

Figure 20-6. Library search order. Modules are incorporated into the executable file as LINK extracts them from the libraries to resolve external references.

The example in Figure 20-6 demonstrates this search strategy. Library LIB1.LIB contains object modules *A* and *B*, library LIB2.LIB contains object module *C*, and the object file MYPROG.OBJ contains the object module *MAIN*; modules *MAIN*, *A*, and *C* each contain an external reference to a symbol declared in another module. When this program is linked with

```
C>LINK MYPROG,,,LIB1+LIB2  <Enter>
```

LINK starts by incorporating the object module *MAIN* into the executable program. It then searches the input libraries until it resolves all the external references:

1. Process MYPROG.OBJ, find unresolved external reference to *A*.
2. Search LIB1.LIB, extract *A*, find unresolved external reference to *C*.
3. Search LIB1.LIB again; reference to *C* remains unresolved.
4. Search LIB2.LIB, extract *C*, find unresolved external reference to *B*.
5. Search LIB2.LIB again; reference to *B* remains unresolved.
6. Search LIB1.LIB again, extract *B*.
7. No more unresolved external references, so end library search.

The order in which the modules appear in the executable file thus reflects the order in which LINK resolves the external references; this, in turn, depends on which modules were contained in the libraries and on the order in which the libraries are input to LINK.

Name of the executable file

If no filename is specified in the command line or in response to the *Run File* prompt, LINK derives the name of the executable file from the name of the first object file it processes. For example, if the object files PROG1.OBJ and PROG2.OBJ are linked with the command

```
C>LINK PROG1+PROG2;  <Enter>
```

the resulting executable file, PROG1.EXE, takes its name from the first object file processed by LINK.

Segment Order and Segment Combinations

LINK builds segments into the executable file by applying the following sequence of rules:

1. Segments appear in the executable file in the order in which their SEGDEF declarations first appear in the input object modules.
2. Segments in different object modules are combined if they have the same name and class and a *public, memory, stack,* or *common* combine type. All address references within the combined segments are relocated relative to the start of the combined segment.
    - Segments with the same name and either the *public* or the *memory* combine type are combined in the order in which they are processed by LINK. The size of the resulting segment equals the total size of the combined segments.
    - Segments with the same name and the *stack* combine type are overlapped so that the data in each of the overlapped segments ends at the same address. The size of the resulting segment equals the total size of the combined segments. The resulting segment is always paragraph aligned.
    - Segments with the same name and the *common* combine type are overlapped so that the data in each of the overlapped segments starts at the same address. The size of the resulting segment equals the size of the largest of the overlapped segments.
3. Segments with the same class name are concatenated.
4. If the /DOSSEG switch is used, the segments are rearranged in conjunction with DGROUP. *See* Using the /DOSSEG Switch below.

These rules allow the programmer to control the organization of segments in the executable file by ordering SEGMENT declarations in an assembly-language source module, which produces the same order of SEGDEF records in the corresponding object module, and by placing this object module first in the order in which LINK processes its input files.

A typical MS-DOS program is constructed by declaring all executable code and data segments with the *public* combine type, thus enabling the programmer to compile the program's source code from separate source-code modules into separate object modules. When these object modules are linked, LINK combines the segments from the object modules according to the above rules to create logically unified code and data segments in the executable file.

Segment classes

LINK concatenates segments with the same class name after it combines segments with the same segment name and class. For example, Figure 20-7 shows the following compiling and linking:

```
C>MASM MYPROG1;   <Enter>
C>MASM MYPROG2;   <Enter>
C>LINK MYPROG1+MYPROG2;   <Enter>
```

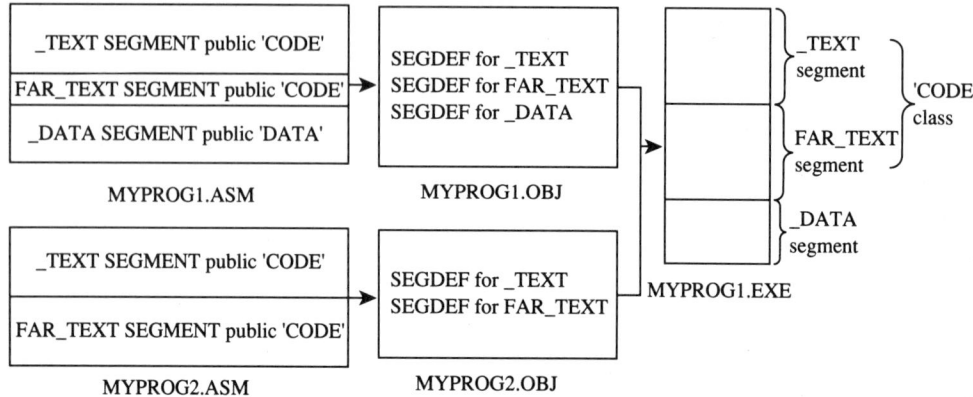

Figure 20-7. Segment order and concatenation by LINK. The start of each file, corresponding to the lowest address, is at the top.

After MYPROG1.ASM and MYPROG2.ASM have been compiled, LINK builds the *_TEXT* and *FAR_TEXT* segments by combining segments with the same name from the different object modules. Then, *_TEXT* and *FAR_TEXT* are concatenated because they have the same class name ('CODE'). *_TEXT* appears before *FAR_TEXT* in the executable file because LINK encounters the SEGDEF record for *_TEXT* before it finds the SEGDEF record for *FAR_TEXT*.

Segment alignment

LINK aligns the starting address of each segment it processes according to the alignment specified in each SEGDEF record. It adjusts the alignment of each segment it encounters regardless of how that segment is combined with other segments of the same name or class. (The one exception is *stack* segments, which always start on a paragraph boundary.)

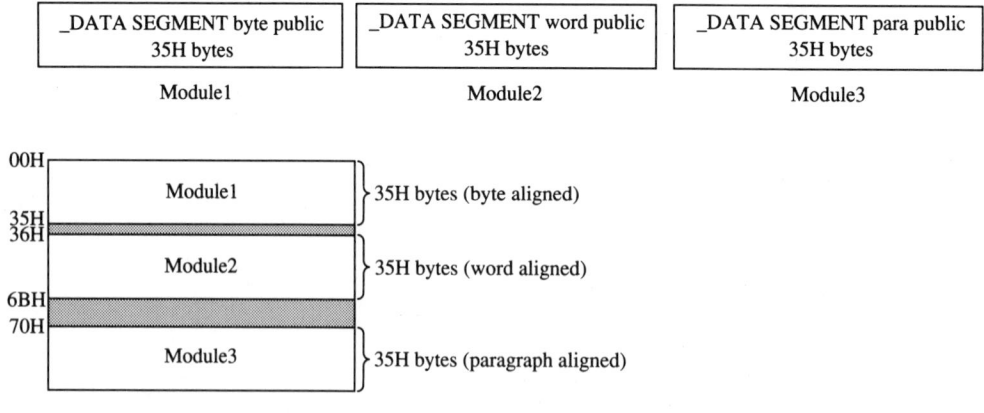

Figure 20-8. Alignment of combined segments. LINK enforces segment alignment by padding combined segments with uninitialized data bytes.

Segment alignment is particularly important when public segments with the same name and class are combined from different object modules. Note what happens in Figure 20-8, where the three concatenated _DATA segments have different alignments. To enforce the word alignment and paragraph alignment of the _DATA segments in Module2 and Module3, LINK inserts one or more bytes of padding between the segments.

Segment groups

A segment group establishes a logical segment address to which all offsets in a group of segments can refer. That is, all addresses in all segments in the group can be expressed as offsets relative to the segment value associated with the group (Figure 20-9). Declaring segments in a group does not affect their positions in the executable file; the segments in a group may or may not be contiguous and can appear in any order as long as all address references to the group fall within 64 KB of each other.

```
DataGroup      GROUP      DataSeg1,DataSeg2
CodeSeg        SEGMENT    byte public 'CODE'
               ASSUME     cs:CodeSeg

               mov        ax,offset DataSeg2:TestData
               mov        ax,offset DataGroup:TestData

CodeSeg        ENDS

DataSeg1       SEGMENT    para public 'DATA'
               DB         100h dup(?)
DataSeg1       ENDS

DataSeg2       SEGMENT    para public 'DATA'
TestData       DB         ?
DataSeg2       ENDS
               END
```

Figure 20-9. Example of group addressing. The first MOV loads the value 00H into AX (the offset of TestData *relative to* DataSeg2*); the second MOV loads the value 100H into AX (the offset of* TestData *relative to the group* DataGroup*).*

LINK reserves one group name, DGROUP, for use by Microsoft language translators. DGROUP is used to group compiler-generated data segments and a default stack segment. *See* DGROUP below.

LINK Internals

Many programmers use LINK as a "black box" program that transforms object modules into executable files. Nevertheless, it is helpful to observe how LINK processes object records to accomplish this task.

LINK is a two-pass linker; that is, it reads all its input object modules twice. On Pass 1, LINK builds an address map of the segments and symbols in the object modules. On Pass 2, it extracts the executable code and program data from the object modules and builds a memory image — an exact replica — of the executable file.

The reason LINK builds an image of the executable file in memory, instead of simply copying code and data from object modules into the executable file, is that it organizes the executable file by segments and not by the order in which it processes object modules. The most efficient way to concatenate, combine, and relocate the code and data is to build a map of the executable file in memory during Pass 1 and then fill in the map with code and data during Pass 2.

In versions 3.52 and later, whenever the /I (/INFORMATION) switch is specified in the command line, LINK displays status messages at the start of each pass and as it processes each object module. If the /M (/MAP) switch is used in addition to the /I switch, LINK also displays the total length of each segment declared in the object modules. This information is helpful in determining how the structure of an executable file corresponds to the contents of the object modules processed by LINK.

Pass 1

During Pass 1, LINK processes the LNAMES, SEGDEF, GRPDEF, COMDEF, EXTDEF, and PUBDEF records in each input object module and uses the information in these object records to construct a symbol table and an address map of segments and segment groups.

Symbol table

As each object module is processed, LINK uses the symbol table to resolve external references (declared in EXTDEF and COMDEF records) to public symbols. If LINK processes all the object files without resolving all the external references in the symbol table, it searches the input libraries for public symbols that match the unresolved external references. LINK continues to search each library until all the external references in the symbol table are resolved.

Segments and groups

LINK processes each SEGDEF record according to the segment name, class name, and attributes specified in the record. LINK constructs a table of named segments and updates it as it concatenates or combines segments. This allows LINK to associate each public symbol in the symbol table with an offset into the segment in which the symbol is declared.

LINK also generates default segments into which it places communal variables declared in COMDEF records. Near communal variables are placed in one paragraph-aligned public segment named c_common, with class name BSS (block storage space) and group

DGROUP. Far communal variables are placed in a paragraph-aligned segment named FAR_BSS, with class name FAR_BSS. The combine type of each far communal variable's FAR_BSS segment is private (that is, not *public, memory, common,* or *stack*). As many FAR_BSS segments as necessary are generated.

After all the object files have been read and all the external references in the symbol table have been resolved, LINK has a complete map of the addresses of all segments and symbols in the program. If a .MAP file has been requested, LINK creates the file and writes the address map to it. Then LINK initiates Pass 2.

Pass 2

In Pass 2, LINK extracts executable code and program data from the LEDATA and LIDATA records in the object modules. It builds the code and data into a memory image of the executable file. During Pass 2, LINK also carries out all the address relocations and fixups related to segment relocation, segment grouping, and resolution of external references, as well as any other address fixups specified explicitly in object module FIXUPP records.

If it determines during Pass 2 that not enough RAM is available to contain the entire image, LINK creates a temporary file in the current directory on the default disk drive. (LINK versions 3.60 and later use the environment variable TMP to find the directory for the temporary scratch file.) LINK then uses this file in addition to all the available RAM to construct the image of the executable file. (In versions of MS-DOS earlier than 3.0, the temporary file is named VM.TMP; in versions 3.0 and later, LINK uses Interrupt 21H Function 5AH to create the file.)

LINK reads each of the input object modules in the same order as it did in Pass 1. This time it copies the information from each object module's LEDATA and LIDATA records into the memory image of each segment in the proper sequence. This is when LINK expands the iterated data in each LIDATA record it processes.

LINK processes each LEDATA and LIDATA record along with the corresponding FIXUPP record, if one exists. LINK processes the FIXUPP record, performs the address calculations required for relocation, segment grouping, and resolving external references, and then stores binary data from the LEDATA or LIDATA record, including the results of the address calculations, in the proper segment in the memory image. The only exception to this process occurs when a FIXUPP record refers to a segment address. In this case, LINK adds the address of the fixup to a table of segment fixups; this table is used later to generate the segment relocation table in the .EXE header.

When all the data has been extracted from the object modules and all the fixups have been carried out, the memory image is complete. LINK now has all the information it needs to build the .EXE header (Table 20-1). At this point, therefore, LINK creates the executable file and writes the header and all segments into it.

Table 20-1. How LINK Builds a .EXE File Header.

Offset	Contents	Comments
00H	'MZ'	.EXE file signature
02H	Length of executable image MOD 512	Total size of all segments plus .EXE file header
04H	Length of executable image in 512-byte pages, including last partial page (if any)	
06H	Number of run-time segment relocations	Number of segment fixups
08H	Size of the .EXE header in 16-byte paragraphs	Size of segment relocation table
0AH	MINALLOC: Minimum amount of RAM to be allocated above end of the loaded program (in 16-byte paragraphs)	Size of uninitialized data and/or stack segments at end of program (0 if /HI switch is used)
0CH	MAXALLOC: Maximum amount of RAM to be allocated above end of the loaded program (in 16-byte paragraphs)	0 if /HI switch is used; value specified with /CP switch; FFFFH if /CP and /HI switches are not used
0EH	Stack segment (initial value for SS register); relocated by MS-DOS when program is loaded	Address of stack segment relative to start of executable image
10H	Stack pointer (initial value for register SP)	Size of stack segment in bytes
12H	Checksum	One's complement of sum of all words in file, excluding checksum itself
14H	Entry point offset (initial value for register IP)	MODEND object record that specifies program start address
16H	Entry point segment (initial value for register CS); relocated by MS-DOS when program is loaded	
18H	Offset of start of segment relocation table relative to start of .EXE header	
1AH	Overlay number	0 for resident segments; >0 for overlay segments
1CH	Reserved	

Using LINK to Organize Memory

By using LINK to rearrange and combine segments, a programmer can generate an executable file in which segment order and addressing serve specific purposes. As the following examples demonstrate, careful use of LINK leads to more efficient use of memory and simpler, more efficient programs.

Segment order for a TSR

In a terminate-and-stay-resident (TSR) program, LINK must be used carefully to generate segments in the executable file in the proper order. A typical TSR program consists of a resident portion, in which the TSR application is implemented, and a transient portion, which executes only once to initialize the resident portion. *See* PROGRAMMING IN THE MS-DOS ENVIRONMENT: Customizing ms-dos: Terminate-and-Stay-Resident Utilities.

Because the transient portion of the TSR program is executed only once, the memory it occupies should be freed after the resident portion has been initialized. To allow the MS-DOS Terminate and Stay Resident function (Interrupt 21H Function 31H) to free this memory when it leaves the resident portion of the TSR program in memory, the TSR program must have its resident portion at lower addresses than its transient portion.

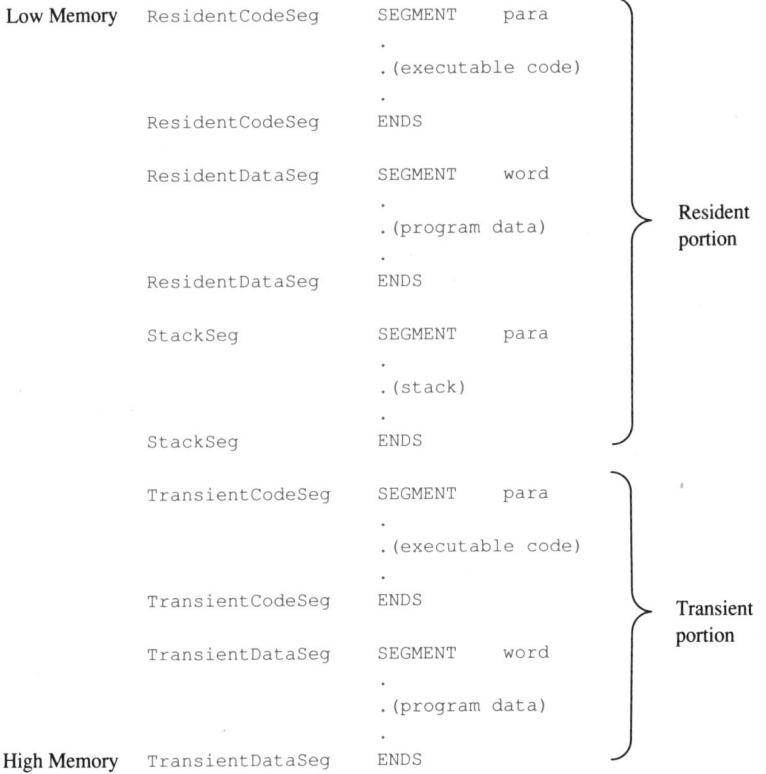

Figure 20-10. Segment order for a terminate-and-stay-resident program.

In Figure 20-10, the segments containing the resident code and data are declared before the segments that represent the transient portion of the program. Because LINK preserves this segment order, the executable program has the desired structure, with resident code and data at lower addresses than transient code and data. Moreover, the number of paragraphs in the resident portion of the program, which must be computed before Interrupt 21H Function 31H is called, is easy to derive from the segment structure: This value is the difference between the segment address of the program segment prefix, which immediately precedes the first segment in the resident portion, and the address of the first segment in the transient portion of the program.

Groups for unified segment addressing

In some programs it is desirable to maintain executable code and data in separate logical segments but to address both code and data with the same segment register. For example, in a hardware interrupt handler, using the CS register to address program data is generally simpler than using DS or ES.

In the routine in Figure 20-11, code and data are maintained in separate segments for program clarity, yet both can be addressed using the CS register because both code and data segments are included in the same group. (The SNAP.ASM listing in the Terminate-and-Stay-Resident Utilities article is another example of this use of a group to unify segment addressing.)

```
ISRgroup       GROUP     CodeSeg,DataSeg
CodeSeg        SEGMENT   byte public 'CODE'
               ASSUME    cs:ISRgroup
               mov       ax,offset ISRgroup:CodeLabel
CodeLabel:     mov       bx,ISRgroup:DataLabel
CodeSeg        ENDS

DataSeg        SEGMENT   para public 'DATA'
DataLabel      DW        ?
DataSeg        ENDS
               END
```

Figure 20-11. Code and data included in the same group. In this example, addresses within both CodeSeg *and* DataSeg *are referenced relative to the CS register by grouping the segments (using the assembler GROUP directive) and addressing the group through CS (using the assembler ASSUME directive).*

Uninitialized data segments

A segment that contains only uninitialized data can be processed by LINK in two ways, depending on the position of the segment in the program. If the segment is not at the end of the program, LINK generates a block of bytes initialized to zero to represent the segment in the executable file. If the segment appears at the end of the program, however, LINK does not generate a block of zeroed bytes. Instead, it increases the minimum runtime memory allocation by increasing MINALLOC (specified at offset 0AH in the .EXE header) by the amount of memory required for the segment.

Therefore, if it is necessary to reserve a large amount of uninitialized memory in a segment, the size of the .EXE file can be decreased by building the segment at the end of a program (Figure 20-12). This is why, for example, Microsoft high-level-language translators always build BSS and STACK segments at the end of compiled programs. (The loader does not fill these segments with zeros; a program must still initialize them with appropriate values.)

```
(a)        CodeSeg     SEGMENT     byte public 'CODE'
                       ASSUME      cs:CodeSeg,ds:DataSeg
                       ret
           CodeSeg     ENDS

           DataSeg     SEGMENT     word public 'DATA'
           BigBuffer   DB          10000 dup(?)
           DataSeg     ENDS
                       END

(b)        DataSeg     SEGMENT     word public 'DATA'
           BigBuffer   DB          10000 dup(?)
           DataSeg     ENDS

           CodeSeg     SEGMENT     byte public 'CODE'
                       ASSUME      cs:CodeSeg,ds:DataSeg
                       ret
           CodeSeg     ENDS
                       END
```

Figure 20-12. LINK processing of uninitialized data segments. (a) When DataSeg, *which contains only uninitialized data, is placed at the end of this program, the size of the .EXE file is only 513 bytes. (b) When* DataSeg *is not placed at the end of the program, the size of the .EXE file is 10513 bytes.*

Overlays

If a program contains two or more subroutines that are mutually independent — that is, subroutines that do not transfer control to each other — LINK can be instructed to build each subroutine into a separately loaded portion of the executable file. (This instruction is indicated in the command line when LINK is executed by enclosing each overlay subroutine or group of subroutines in parentheses.) Each of the subroutines can then be overlaid as it is needed in the same area of memory (Figure 20-13). The amount of memory required to run a program that uses overlays is, therefore, less than the amount required to run the same program without overlays.

A program that uses overlays must include the Microsoft run-time overlay manager. The overlay manager is responsible for copying overlay code from the executable file into memory whenever the program attempts to transfer control to code in an overlay. A program that uses overlays runs slower than a program that does not use them, because it takes longer to extract overlays separately from the .EXE file than it does to read the entire .EXE file into memory at once.

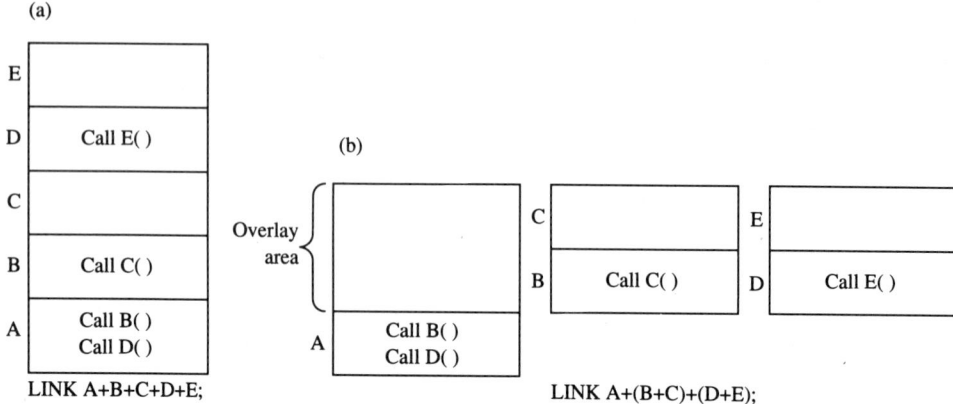

(a)

(b)

LINK A+B+C+D+E;

LINK A+(B+C)+(D+E);

Figure 20-13. Memory use in a program linked (a) without overlays and (b) with overlays. In (b), either modules (B+C) or modules (D+E) can be loaded into the overlay area at run time.

The default object libraries that accompany Microsoft high-level-language compilers contain object modules that support the Microsoft run-time overlay manager. The following description of LINK's relationship to the run-time overlay manager applies to versions 3.00 through 3.60 of LINK; implementation details may vary in future versions.

Overlay format in a .EXE file

An executable file that contains overlays has a .EXE header preceding each overlay (Figure 20-14). The overlays are numbered in sequence, starting at 0; the overlay number is stored in the word at offset 1AH in each overlay's .EXE header. When the contents of the .EXE file are loaded into memory for execution, only the resident, nonoverlaid part of the program is copied into memory. The overlays must be read into memory from the .EXE file by the run-time overlay manager.

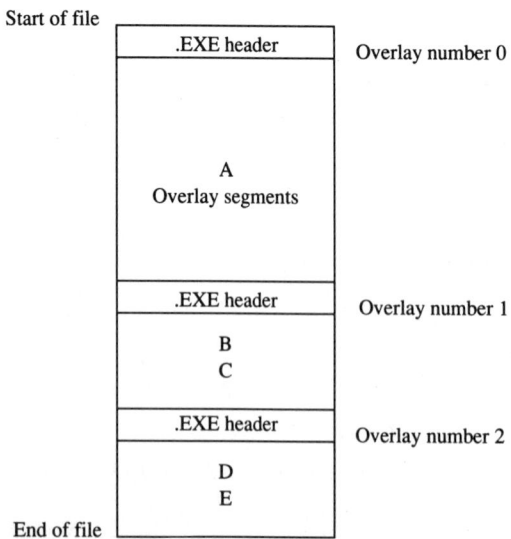

Figure 20-14. .EXE file structure produced by LINK A + (B+C) + (D+E).

Segments for overlays

When LINK produces an executable file that contains overlays, it adds three segments to those defined in the object modules: OVERLAY_AREA, OVERLAY_END, and OVERLAY_DATA. LINK assigns the segment class name 'CODE' to OVERLAY_AREA and OVERLAY_END and includes OVERLAY_DATA in the default group DGROUP.

OVERLAY_AREA is a reserved segment into which the run-time overlay manager is expected to load each overlay as it is needed. Therefore, LINK sets the size of OVERLAY_AREA to fit the largest overlay in the program. The OVERLAY_END segment is declared immediately after OVERLAY_AREA, so a program can determine the size of the OVERLAY_AREA segment by subtracting its segment address from that of OVERLAY_END. The OVERLAY_DATA segment is initialized by LINK with information about the executable file, the number of overlays, and other data useful to the run-time overlay manager.

LINK requires the executable code used in overlays to be contained in segments whose class names end in *CODE* and whose segment names differ from those of the segments used in the resident (nonoverlaid) portion of the program. In assembly language, this is accomplished by using the SEGMENT directive; in high-level languages, the technique of ensuring unique segment names depends on the compiler. In Microsoft C, for example, the /A switch in the command line selects the memory model and thus the segment naming defaults used by the compiler; in medium, large, and huge memory models, the compiler generates a unique segment name for each C function in the source code. In Microsoft FORTRAN, on the other hand, the compiler always generates a uniquely named segment for each SUBROUTINE and FUNCTION in the source code, so no special programming is required.

LINK substitutes all far CALL instructions from root to overlay or from overlay to overlay with a software interrupt followed by an overlay number and an offset into the overlay segment (Figure 20-15). The interrupt number can be specified with LINK's /OVERLAYINTERRUPT switch; if the switch is omitted, LINK uses Interrupt 3FH by default. By replacing calls to overlay code with a software interrupt, LINK provides a mechanism for the run-time overlay manager to take control, load a specified overlay into memory, and transfer control to a specified offset within the overlay.

```
(a)          EXTRN      OverlayEntryPoint:far
             call       OverlayEntryPoint   ; far CALL

(b)          int        IntNo               ; interrupt number
                                            ;   specified with /OVERLAYINTERRUPT
                                            ;   switch (default 3FH)
             DB         OverlayNumber       ; overlay number
             DW         OverlayEntry        ; offset of overlay entry point
                                            ;   (the address to which
                                            ;   the overlay manager transfers
                                            ;   control)
```

Figure 20-15. Executable code modification by LINK for accessing overlays. (a) Code as written. (b) Code as modified by LINK.

Run-time processing of overlays

The resident (nonoverlaid) portion of a program that uses overlays initializes the overlay interrupt vector specified by LINK with the address of the run-time overlay manager. (The OVERLAY_DATA segment contains the interrupt number.) The overlay manager then takes control wherever LINK has substituted a software interrupt for a far call in the executable code.

Each time the overlay manager executes, its first task is to determine which overlay is being called. It does this by using the return address left on the stack by the INT instruction that invoked the overlay manager; this address points to the overlay number stored in the byte after the interrupt instruction that just executed. The overlay manager then determines whether the destination overlay is already resident and loads it only if necessary. Next, the overlay manager opens the .EXE file, using the filename in the OVERLAY_DATA segment. It locates the start of the specified overlay in the file by examining the length (offset 02H and offset 04H) and overlay number (offset 1AH) in each overlay's .EXE header.

The overlay manager can then read the overlay from the .EXE file into the OVERLAY_AREA segment. It uses the overlay's segment relocation table to fix up any segment references in the overlay. The overlay manager transfers control to the overlay with a far call to the OVERLAY_AREA segment, using the offset stored by LINK 1 byte after the interrupt instruction (*see* Figure 20-15).

Interrupt 21H Function 4BH

LINK's protocol for implementing overlays is not recognized by Interrupt 21H Function 4BH (Load and Execute Program). This MS-DOS function, when called with AL = 03H, loads an overlay from a .EXE file into a specified location in memory. *See* SYSTEM CALLS: INTERRUPT 21H: Function 4BH. However, Function 4BH does not use an overlay number, so it cannot find overlays in a .EXE file formatted by LINK with multiple .EXE headers.

DGROUP

LINK always includes DGROUP in its internal table of segment groups. In object modules generated by Microsoft high-level-language translators, DGROUP contains both the default data segment and the stack segment. LINK's /DOSSEG and /DSALLOCATE switches both affect the way LINK treats DGROUP. Changing the way LINK manages DGROUP ultimately affects segment order and addressing in the executable file.

Using the /DOSSEG switch

The /DOSSEG switch causes LINK to arrange segments in the default order used by Microsoft high-level-language translators:

1. All segments with a class name ending in *CODE*. These segments contain executable code.
2. All other segments outside DGROUP. These segments typically contain far data items.

3.   DGROUP segments. These are a program's near data and stack segments. The order
     in which segments appear in DGROUP is
     – Any segments of class BEGDATA. (This class name is reserved for Microsoft use.)
     – Any segments not of class BEGDATA, BSS, or STACK.
     – Segments of class BSS.
     – Segments of class STACK.

This segment order is necessary if programs compiled by Microsoft translators are to run
properly. The /DOSSEG switch can be used whenever an object module produced by an
assembler is linked ahead of object modules generated by a Microsoft compiler, to ensure
that segments in the executable file are ordered as in the preceding list regardless of the
order of segments in the assembled object module.

When the /DOSSEG switch is in effect, LINK always places DGROUP at the end of the
executable program, with all uninitalized data segments at the end of the group. As discussed above, this placement helps to minimize the size of the executable file. The
/DOSSEG switch also causes LINK to restructure the executable program to support
certain conventions used by Microsoft language translators:

●   Compiler-generated segments with the class name BEGDATA are placed at the begin-
    ning of DGROUP.
●   The public symbols _edata and _end are generated to point to the beginning of the
    BSS and STACK segments.
●   Sixteen bytes of zero are inserted in front of the _TEXT segment.

Microsoft compilers that rely on /DOSSEG conventions generate a special COMENT object
record that sets the /DOSSEG switch when the record is processed by LINK.

Using the /HIGH and /DSALLOCATE switches

When a program has been linked without using LINK's /HIGH switch, MS-DOS loads
program code and data segments from the .EXE file at the lowest address in the first available block of RAM large enough to contain the program (Figure 20-16). The value in the
.EXE header at offset 0CH specifies the maximum amount of extra RAM MS-DOS must
allocate to the program above what is loaded from the .EXE file. Above that, all unused
RAM is managed by MS-DOS. With this memory allocation strategy, a program can use
Interrupt 21H Functions 48H (Allocate Memory Block) and 4AH (Resize Memory Block)
to increase or decrease the amount of RAM allocated to it.

When a program is linked with LINK's /HIGH switch, LINK zeros the words it stores in
the .EXE header at offset 0AH and 0CH. Setting the words at 0AH and 0CH to zero indicates that the program is to be loaded into RAM at the highest address possible (Figure
20-16). With this memory layout, however, a program can no longer change its memory
allocation dynamically because all available RAM is allocated to the program when it is
loaded and the uninitialized RAM between the program segment prefix and the program
itself cannot be freed.

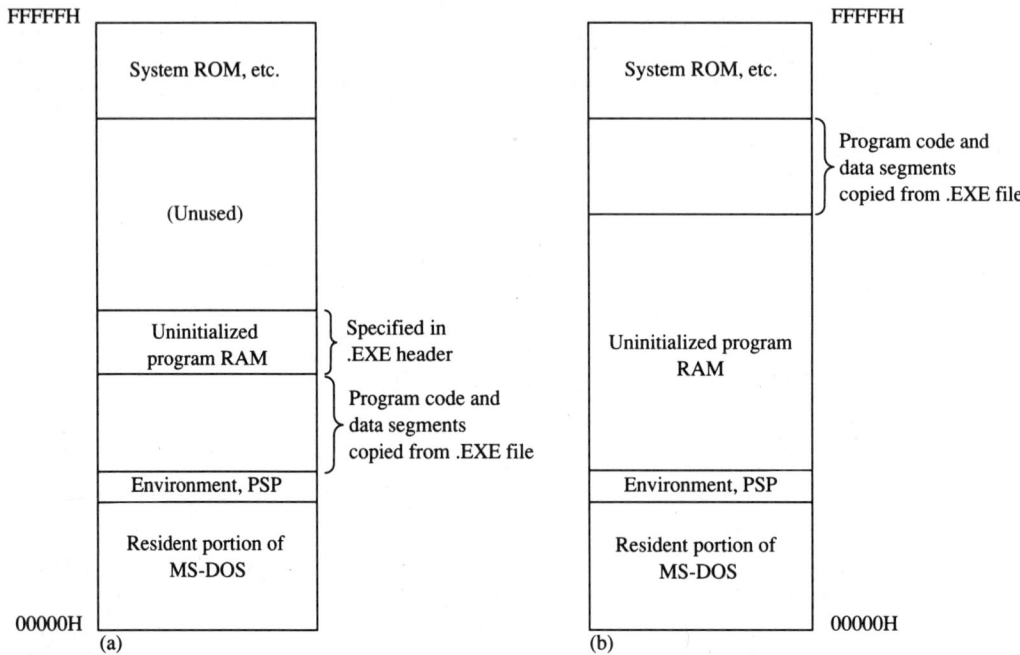

Figure 20-16. Effect of the /HIGH switch on run-time memory use. (a) The program is linked without *the /HIGH switch. (b) The program is linked* with *the /HIGH switch.*

The only reason to load a program with this type of memory allocation is to allow a program data structure to be dynamically extended toward lower memory addresses. For example, both stacks and heaps can be implemented in this way. If a program's stack segment is the first segment in its memory map, the stack can grow downward without colliding with other program data.

To facilitate addressing in such a segment, LINK provides the /DSALLOCATE switch. When a program is linked using this switch, all addresses within DGROUP are relocated in such a way that the last byte in the group has offset FFFFH. For example, if the program in Figure 20-17 is linked without the /DSALLOCATE and /HIGH switches, the value of offset *DGROUP:DataItem* would be 00H; if these switches are used, the linker adjusts the segment value of DGROUP downward so that the offset of *DataItem* within DGROUP becomes FFF0H.

Early versions of Microsoft Pascal (before version 3.30) and Microsoft FORTRAN (before version 3.30) generated object code that had to be linked with the /DSALLOCATE switch. For this reason, LINK sets the /DSALLOCATE switch by default if it processes an object module containing a COMENT record generated by one of these compilers. (Such a COMENT record contains the string *MS PASCAL* or *FORTRAN 77*. *See* PROGRAMMING IN THE MS-DOS ENVIRONMENT: PROGRAMMING TOOLS: Object Modules.) Apart from this special requirement of certain language translators, however, the use of /DSALLOCATE and /HIGH should probably be avoided because of the limitations they place on run-time memory allocation.

```
DGROUP          GROUP      _DATA
_DATA           SEGMENT    word public 'DATA'
DataItem        DB         10h dup (?)
_DATA           ENDS

_TEXT           SEGMENT    byte public 'CODE'
                ASSUME     cs:_TEXT,ds:DGROUP
                mov        bx,offset DGROUP:DataItem
_TEXT           ENDS
                END
```

Figure 20-17. The value of offset DGROUP:DataItem *in this program is FFF0H if the program is linked with the /DSALLOCATE switch or 00H if the program is linked without using the switch.*

Summary

LINK's characteristic support for segment ordering, for run-time memory management, and for dynamic overlays has an impact in many different situations. Programmers who write their own language translators must bear in mind the special conventions followed by LINK in support of Microsoft language translators. Application programmers must be familiar with LINK's capabilities when they use assembly language or link assembly-language programs with object modules generated by Microsoft compilers. LINK is a powerful program development tool and understanding its special capabilities can lead to more efficient programs.

Richard Wilton

Section III
User Commands

Introduction

This section of *The MS-DOS Encyclopedia* describes the standard internal and external MS-DOS commands available to the user who is running MS-DOS (versions 1.0 through 3.2). System configuration options, special batch-file directives, the line editor (EDLIN), and the installable device drivers normally included with MS-DOS are also covered.

Entries are arranged alphabetically by the name of the command or driver. The configuration, batch-file, and line-editor directives appear alphabetically under the headings CONFIG.SYS, BATCH, and EDLIN, respectively. Each entry includes

- Command name
- Version dependencies and network information
- Command purpose
- Prototype command and summary of options
- Detailed description of command
- One or more examples of command use
- Return codes (where applicable)
- Informational and error messages

The experienced user can find information with a quick glance at the first part of a command entry; a less experienced user can refer to the detailed explanation and examples in a more leisurely fashion. The next two pages contain an example of a typical entry from the User Commands section, with explanations of each component. This example is followed by listings of the commands by functional group.

The following terms are used for command-line variables in the sample syntax:

drive	a letter in the range A–Z, followed by a colon, indicating a logical disk drive.
path	a specific location in a disk's hierarchical directory structure; can include the special directory names . and ..; elements are separated by backslash characters (\).
pathname	a file specification that can include a path and/or drive and/or filename extension.
filename	the name of a file, generally with its extension; cannot include a drive or path.

Note: PC-DOS, though not an official product name, is used in this section to indicate IBM's version of the disk operating system originally provided by Microsoft. Commands sometimes have slightly different options or appear for the first time in different versions of MS-DOS and PC-DOS. When a command appears only in the IBM versions, the abbreviation IBM appears in the heading area. Significant differences between MS-DOS and PC-DOS versions of a command are indicated in the *Syntax* and *Description* portions of the entry.

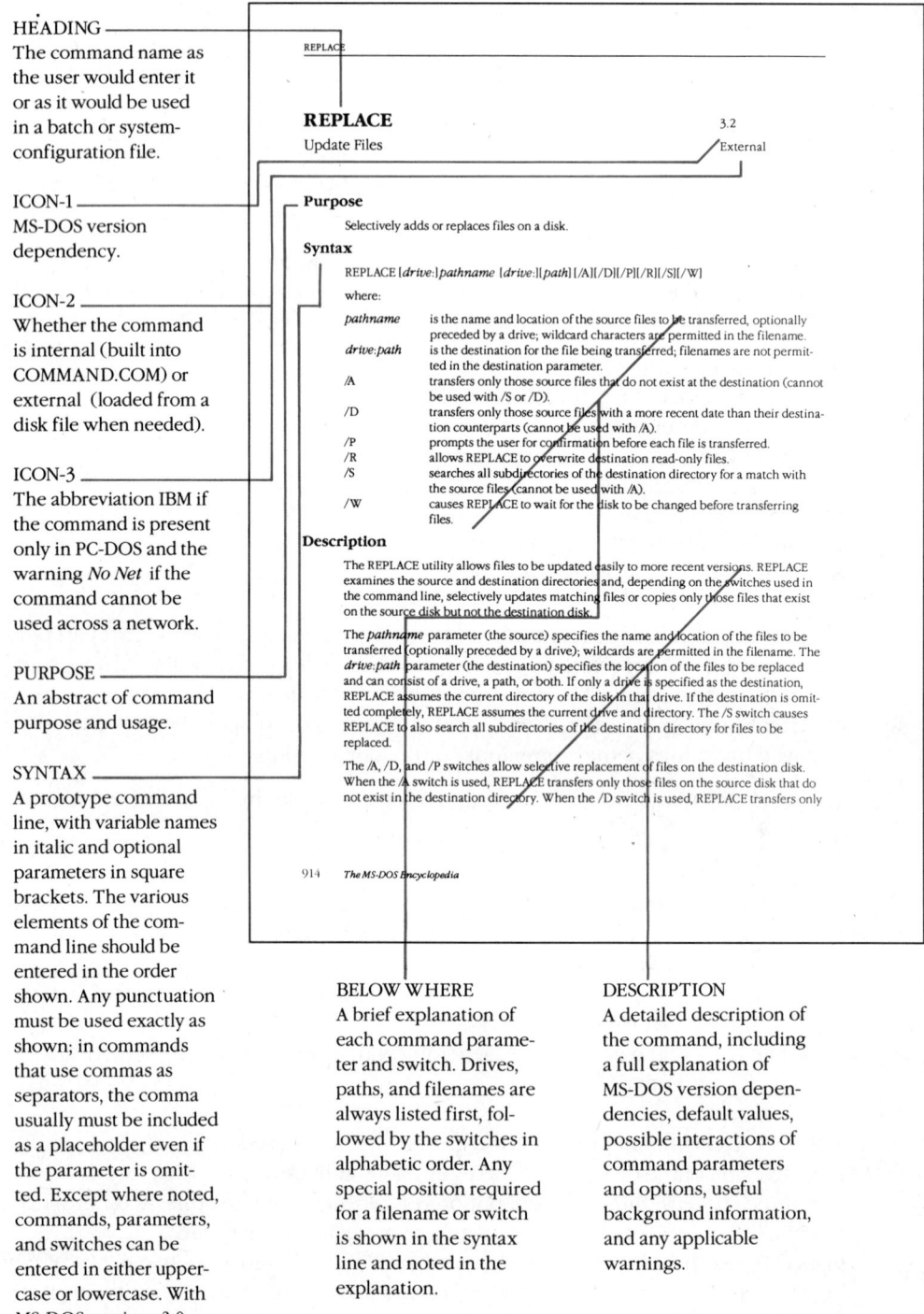

HEADING
The command name as the user would enter it or as it would be used in a batch or system-configuration file.

ICON-1
MS-DOS version dependency.

ICON-2
Whether the command is internal (built into COMMAND.COM) or external (loaded from a disk file when needed).

ICON-3
The abbreviation IBM if the command is present only in PC-DOS and the warning *No Net* if the command cannot be used across a network.

PURPOSE
An abstract of command purpose and usage.

SYNTAX
A prototype command line, with variable names in italic and optional parameters in square brackets. The various elements of the command line should be entered in the order shown. Any punctuation must be used exactly as shown; in commands that use commas as separators, the comma usually must be included as a placeholder even if the parameter is omitted. Except where noted, commands, parameters, and switches can be entered in either uppercase or lowercase. With MS-DOS versions 3.0 and later, external commands can be preceded by a drive and/or path.

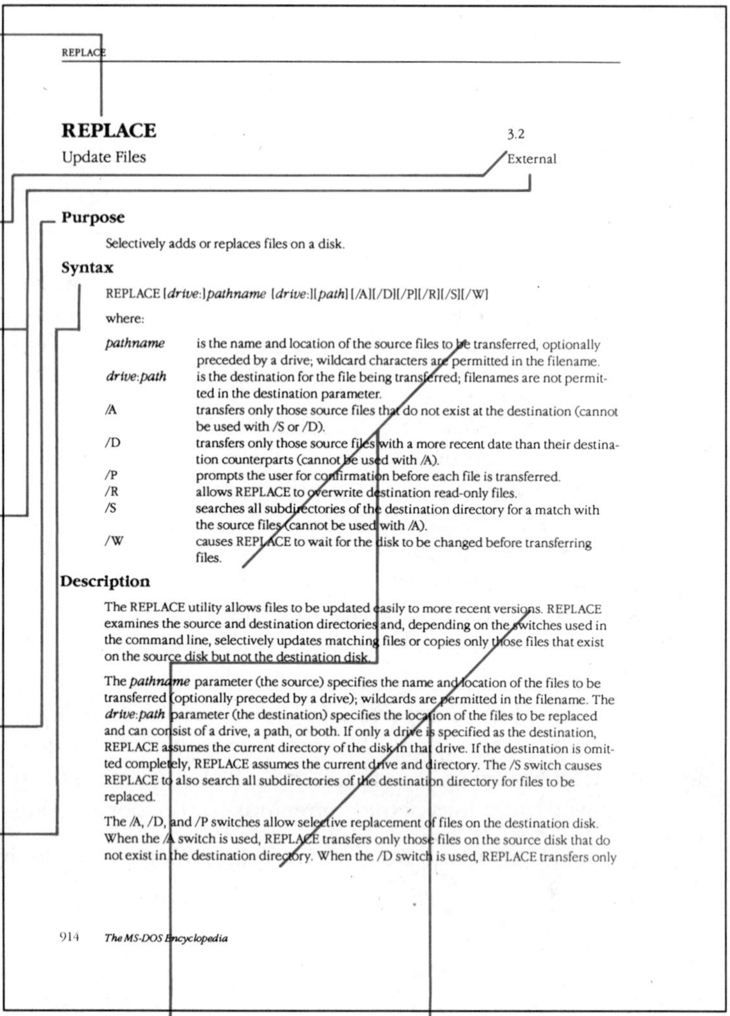

REPLACE

REPLACE 3.2
Update Files External

Purpose

Selectively adds or replaces files on a disk.

Syntax

REPLACE [*drive*:]*pathname* [*drive*:][*path*] [/A][/D][/P][/R][/S][/W]

where:

pathname	is the name and location of the source files to be transferred, optionally preceded by a drive; wildcard characters are permitted in the filename.
drive:path	is the destination for the file being transferred; filenames are not permitted in the destination parameter.
/A	transfers only those source files that do not exist at the destination (cannot be used with /S or /D).
/D	transfers only those source files with a more recent date than their destination counterparts (cannot be used with /A).
/P	prompts the user for confirmation before each file is transferred.
/R	allows REPLACE to overwrite destination read-only files.
/S	searches all subdirectories of the destination directory for a match with the source files (cannot be used with /A).
/W	causes REPLACE to wait for the disk to be changed before transferring files.

Description

The REPLACE utility allows files to be updated easily to more recent versions. REPLACE examines the source and destination directories and, depending on the switches used in the command line, selectively updates matching files or copies only those files that exist on the source disk but not the destination disk.

The *pathname* parameter (the source) specifies the name and location of the files to be transferred (optionally preceded by a drive); wildcards are permitted in the filename. The *drive:path* parameter (the destination) specifies the location of the files to be replaced and can consist of a drive, a path, or both. If only a drive is specified as the destination, REPLACE assumes the current directory of the disk in that drive. If the destination is omitted completely, REPLACE assumes the current drive and directory. The /S switch causes REPLACE to also search all subdirectories of the destination directory for files to be replaced.

The /A, /D, and /P switches allow selective replacement of files on the destination disk. When the /A switch is used, REPLACE transfers only those files on the source disk that do not exist in the destination directory. When the /D switch is used, REPLACE transfers only

914 *The MS-DOS Encyclopedia*

BELOW WHERE
A brief explanation of each command parameter and switch. Drives, paths, and filenames are always listed first, followed by the switches in alphabetic order. Any special position required for a filename or switch is shown in the syntax line and noted in the explanation.

DESCRIPTION
A detailed description of the command, including a full explanation of MS-DOS version dependencies, default values, possible interactions of command parameters and options, useful background information, and any applicable warnings.

REPLACE

those source files that match the destination filenames but have a more recent date than their destination counterparts. (The /D switch is not available with the PC-DOS version of REPLACE.) The /P switch causes REPLACE to prompt the user for confirmation before each file is transferred.

The /R switch allows the replacement of read-only as well as normal files. If the /R switch is not used and one of the destination files that would otherwise be replaced is marked read-only, the REPLACE program terminates with an error message. (REPLACE cannot be used to update hidden or system files.)

The /W switch causes REPLACE to pause and wait for the user to press any key before beginning the transfer of files. This allows the user to change disks in floppy-disk systems with no fixed disk and in those cases where the REPLACE program itself is present on neither the source nor the destination disk.

Return Codes

0	The REPLACE operation was successful.
1	An error was found in the REPLACE command line.
2	No matching files were found to replace.
3	The source or destination path was invalid or does not exist.
5	One of the files to be replaced was marked read-only and the /R switch was not included in the command line.
8	Memory was insufficient to run the REPLACE command.
15	An invalid drive was specified in the command line.
Other	Standard MS-DOS error codes (returned on a failed Interrupt 21H file-function request).

Examples

To replace the files in the directory \SOURCE on the current drive with all matching files on the disk in drive A that have a more recent date, type

C>REPLACE A:*.* \SOURCE /D <Enter>

To transfer from the disk in drive A only those files that are not already present in the current directory, type

C>REPLACE A:*.* /A <Enter>

Messages

n File(s) added
After the replacement operation is completed, if the /A switch was used in the command line, REPLACE displays the total number of files added.

n File(s) replaced
After the replacement operation is completed, REPLACE displays the total number of files processed.

Section III: User Commands 915

RETURN CODES
Exit codes returned by the command (if any) that can be tested in a batch file or by another program.

EXAMPLES
One or more examples of the command at work, including examples of the resulting output where appropriate. User entry appears in color; do not type the prompt, which appears in black. Press the Enter key (labeled Return on some keyboards) as directed at the end of each command line.

MESSAGES
An alphabetic list of messages that may be displayed when the command is used in MS-DOS version 3.2 (may vary slightly in earlier versions). Both messages generated by the command itself and applicable messages generated by MS-DOS are included. Following each message is a brief explanation of the condition that produces the message and, where appropriate, any action that should be taken.

Contents by Functional Group

The MS-DOS commands can be divided into several distinct groups according to the functions they perform. These are listed on the following pages.

Command	Action
System Configuration and Control	
BREAK	Set Control-C check.
COMMAND	Install secondary copy of command processor.
DATE	Set date.
EXIT	Terminate command processor.
PROMPT	Define system prompt.
SELECT	Configure system disk for a specific country.
SET	Set environment variable.
SHARE	Install file-sharing support.
TIME	Set system time.
VER	Display version.
Character-Device Management	
CLS	Clear screen.
CTTY	Assign standard input/output.
GRAFTABL	Load graphics character set.
GRAPHICS	Print graphics screen-dump program.
KEYB*xx*	Define keyboard.
MODE	Configure device.
PRINT	Print file (background print spooler).
File Management	
ATTRIB	Change file attributes.
BACKUP	Back up files.
COMP	Compare files.
COPY	Copy file or device.
DEL/ERASE	Delete file.
EDLIN	Create or modify text file (see also commands below).
FC	Compare files.
RECOVER	Recover files.
RENAME	Change filename.
REPLACE	Update files.
RESTORE	Restore backup files.
TYPE	Display file.
XCOPY	Copy files.

(more)

Command	Action
Filters	
FIND	Find string.
MORE	Display by screenful.
SORT	Sort file or character stream alphabetically.
Directory Management	
APPEND	Set data-file search path.
CHDIR	Change current directory.
DIR	Display directory.
MKDIR	Make directory.
PATH	Define command search path.
RMDIR	Remove directory.
TREE	Display directory structure.
Disk Management	
ASSIGN	Assign drive alias.
CHKDSK	Check disk status.
DISKCOMP	Compare floppy disks.
DISKCOPY	Copy floppy disks.
FORMAT	Initialize disk.
FDISK	Configure fixed disk.
JOIN	Join disk to directory.
LABEL	Display volume label.
SUBST	Substitute drive for subdirectory.
SYS	Transfer system files.
VERIFY	Set verify flag.
VOL	Display disk name.
Installable Device Drivers	
ANSI.SYS	ANSI console driver.
DRIVER.SYS	Configurable external-disk-drive driver.
RAMDRIVE.SYS	Virtual disk.
VDISK.SYS	Virtual disk.
System-Configuration File Directives	
BREAK	Configure Control-C checking.
BUFFERS	Configure internal disk buffers.
COUNTRY	Set country code.
DEVICE	Install device driver.
DRIVPARM	Set block-device parameters.
FCBS	Set maximum open files using File Control Blocks (FCBs).

(more)

Command	Action
System-Configuration File Directives *(continued)*	
FILES	Set maximum open files using handles.
LASTDRIVE	Set highest logical drive.
SHELL	Specify command processor.
STACKS	Configure internal stacks.
Batch-File Directives	
AUTOEXEC.BAT	System startup batch file.
ECHO	Display text.
FOR	Execute command on file set.
GOTO	Jump to label.
IF	Perform conditional execution.
PAUSE	Suspend batch-file execution.
REM	Include comment line.
SHIFT	Shift replaceable parameters.
EDLIN Commands	
linenumber	Edit line.
A	Append lines from disk.
C	Copy lines.
D	Delete lines.
E	End editing session.
I	Insert lines.
L	List lines.
M	Move lines.
P	Display in pages.
Q	Quit.
R	Replace text.
S	Search for text.
T	Transfer another file.
W	Write lines to disk.

ANSI.SYS

ANSI Console Driver

2.0 and later

External

Purpose

Allows the user to employ a subset of the American National Standards Institute (ANSI) standard escape sequences for control of the console.

Syntax

DEVICE=[*drive:*][*path*]ANSI.SYS

where:

drive:path   is the drive and/or path to search for ANSI.SYS if it is not in the root directory of the startup disk.

Description

The ANSI.SYS file contains an installable character-device driver that supersedes the system's default driver for the console device (video display and keyboard). After ANSI.SYS is installed by means of a *DEVICE=ANSI.SYS* command in the CONFIG.SYS file of the disk used to start the system, programs can use a subset of the ANSI 3.64-1979 standard escape sequences to erase the display, set the display mode and attributes, and control the cursor in a hardware-independent fashion. (A supplementary set of escape sequences that are not part of the ANSI standard allows reprogramming of the keyboard.)

Programs that use ANSI.SYS for control of the screen can run on any MS-DOS machine without modification, regardless of its hardware configuration. However, most popular application programs for the IBM PC and compatibles circumvent ANSI.SYS and manipulate the video controller and its video buffer directly to achieve maximum performance.

The ANSI.SYS device driver detects ANSI escape sequences in a character stream and interprets them as commands to control the keyboard and display. An ANSI escape sequence is a sequence of ASCII characters, the first two of which must be the Escape character (1BH) and the left-bracket character (5BH). The characters following the Escape and left-bracket characters vary with the type of control function being performed; most consist of an alphanumeric code followed by a letter. In some cases this code is a single character; in others it is more than one character or a two-part string separated by a semicolon. Each ANSI escape sequence ends in a unique letter character that identifies the sequence; case is significant for these letters. The escape sequences supported by the ANSI.SYS driver are summarized in the tables on the following pages.

An escape sequence cannot be entered directly at the system prompt because each ANSI escape sequence must begin with an Escape character, and pressing the Esc key (or Alt-27 on the numeric keypad) causes MS-DOS to cancel the command line. There are three methods of executing ANSI escape sequences that do not require writing a program:

- Include the escape sequences in a PROMPT command.
- Enter the escape sequences into a word processor or text editor, save the file as an ASCII text file, and then execute the file by using the TYPE or COPY command (specifying CON as the destination for COPY) from the MS-DOS system prompt. (If the escape sequences are echoed on the screen when the file is executed, a *DEVICE=ANSI.SYS* command was not included in the CONFIG.SYS file when the system was turned on.)
- Place the escape sequences in a batch (.BAT) file as part of an ECHO command. When the batch file is executed, the sequences are sent to the console.

When escape sequences are entered using the PROMPT command, the Escape character is entered as $e. When escape sequences are entered using a word processor to create an ASCII text or batch file, the Escape character is usually entered by pressing the Esc key or by holding down the Alt key while typing 27 on the numeric keypad. (See the documentation provided with the word-processor for specific instructions.) In most cases, the escape character will appear in the word processor or text editor as a back-arrow character (←) or a caret–left bracket combination (^[).

Note: When the escape character is represented as ^[(as it is in EDLIN, for example), an additional left-bracket character must still be added to properly begin an ANSI escape sequence. Thus, the beginning of a valid ANSI escape sequence in EDLIN appears as ^[[.

The tables in this section use the abbreviation ESC to show where the ASCII escape character 27 (1BH) appears in the string.

Note: Case is significant for the terminal character in the string.

The following escape sequences control cursor movement:

Operation	Escape Sequence	Effect
Cursor Up	ESC[*number*A	Moves the cursor up *number* rows (1–24, default = 1). Has no effect if cursor is on the top row.
Cursor Down	ESC[*number*B	Moves the cursor down *number* rows (1–24, default = 1). Has no effect if cursor is on the bottom row.
Cursor Right	ESC[*number*C	Moves the cursor right *number* rows (1–79, default = 1). Has no effect if cursor is in the far right column.
Cursor Left	ESC[*number*D	Moves the cursor left *number* rows (1–79, default = 1). Has no effect if cursor is in the far left column.
Position Cursor	ESC[*row;column*H	Moves the cursor to the specified row (1–25, default = 1) and column (1–80, default = 1). If *row* is omitted, the semicolon before *column* must be specified.

(more)

Operation	Escape Sequence	Effect
Position Cursor	ESC[*row*;*column*f	Same as above.
Save Cursor Position	ESC[s	Stores the current row and column position of the cursor. Cursor can be restored to this position later with a Restore Cursor Position escape sequence.
Restore Cursor Position	ESC[u	Moves the cursor to the position of the most recent Save Cursor Position escape sequence.

The following two escape sequences are used to erase all or part of the display:

Operation	Escape Sequence	Effect
Erase Display	ESC[2J	Clears the screen and places the cursor at the home position.
Erase Line	ESC[K	Erases from the cursor position to the end of the same row.

The following escape sequences control the width and the color capability of the display. The use of any of these sequences clears the screen.

Operation	Escape Sequence	Effect
Set Mode	ESC[=0h	Sets display to 40 x 25 monochrome (text).
	ESC[=1h	Sets display to 40 x 25 color (text).
	ESC[=2h	Sets display to 80 x 25 monochrome (text).
	ESC[=3h	Sets display to 80 x 25 color (text).
	ESC[=4h	Sets display to 320 x 200 4-color (graphics).
	ESC[=5h	Sets display to 320 x 200 4-color (graphics, color burst disabled).
	ESC[=6h	Sets display to 640 x 200 2-color (graphics).

The following escape sequences control whether characters will wrap around to the first column of the next row after the rightmost column in the current row has been filled:

Operation	Escape Sequence	Effect
Enable Character Wrap	ESC[=7h	Sets character wrap.
Disable Character Wrap	ESC[=7l	Disables character wrap. (Note that the terminating letter is a lowercase L.)

The following escape sequence controls specific graphics attributes such as intensity, blinking, superscript, and subscript, as well as the foreground and background colors:

ESC[*attrib*;...;*attrib*m

where:

attrib   is one or more of the following values. Multiple values must be separated by semicolons.

Value	Attribute	Value	Foreground Color	Value	Background Color
0	All attributes off	30	Black	40	Black
1	High intensity (bold)	31	Red	41	Red
2	Normal intensity	32	Green	42	Green
4	Underline (mono-chrome only)	33	Yellow	43	Yellow
5	Blink	34	Blue	44	Blue
7	Reverse video	35	Magenta	45	Magenta
8	Concealed (invisible)	36	Cyan	46	Cyan
		37	White	47	White

Note: Values 30 through 47 meet the ISO 6429 standard.

The following escape sequence allows redefinition of keyboard keys to a specified *string*:

ESC[*code*;*string*;...p

where:

code   is one or more of the following values that represent keyboard keys. Semicolons shown in this table must be entered in addition to the required semicolons in the command line.

string   is either the ASCII code for a single character or a string contained in quotation marks. For example, both 65 and "A" can be used to represent an uppercase A.

Key	Code			
	Alone	Shift-	Ctrl-	Alt-
F1	0;59	0;84	0;94	0;104
F2	0;60	0;85	0;95	0;105
F3	0;61	0;86	0;96	0;106
F4	0;62	0;87	0;97	0;107
F5	0;63	0;88	0;98	0;108
F6	0;64	0;89	0;99	0;109

(more)

Key	Code			
	Alone	**Shift-**	**Ctrl-**	**Alt-**
F7	0;65	0;90	0;100	0;110
F8	0;66	0;91	0;101	0;111
F9	0;67	0;92	0;102	0;112
F10	0;68	0;93	0;103	0;113
Home	0;71	55	0;119	–
Up Arrow	0;72	56	–	–
Pg Up	0;73	57	0;132	–
Left Arrow	0;75	52	0;115	–
Down Arrow	0;77	54	0;116	–
End	0;79	49	0;117	–
Down Arrow	0;80	50	–	–
Pg Dn	0;81	51	0;118	–
Ins	0;82	48	–	–
Del	0;83	46	–	–
PrtSc	–	–	0;114	–
A	97	65	1	0;30
B	98	66	2	0;48
C	99	67	3	0;46
D	100	68	4	0;32
E	101	69	5	0;18
F	102	70	6	0;33
G	103	71	7	0;34
H	104	72	8	0;35
I	105	73	9	0;23
J	106	74	10	0;36
K	107	75	11	0;37
L	108	76	12	0;38
M	109	77	13	0;50
N	110	78	14	0;49
O	111	79	15	0;24
P	112	80	16	0;25
Q	113	81	17	0;16
R	114	82	18	0;19
S	115	83	19	0;31
T	116	84	20	0;20
U	117	85	21	0;22
V	118	86	22	0;47
W	119	87	23	0;17
X	120	88	24	0;45

(more)

Key	Code			
	Alone	**Shift-**	**Ctrl-**	**Alt-**
Y	121	89	25	0;21
Z	122	90	26	0;44
1	49	33	–	0;120
2	50	64	–	0;121
3	51	35	–	0;122
4	52	36	–	0;123
5	53	37	–	0;124
6	54	94	–	0;125
7	55	38	–	0;126
8	56	42	–	0;127
9	57	40	–	0;128
0	48	41	–	0;129
–	45	95	–	0;130
=	61	43	–	0;131
Tab	9	0;15	–	–
Null	0;3	–	–	–

Examples

The following examples use ESC or $e to show where the ASCII escape character 27 (1BH) appears in the string. The PROMPT examples can be typed as shown, but for the examples that use ESC to denote the escape character, the actual escape character should be typed in its place.

To move the cursor to row 10, column 30 and display the string *Main Menu*, use the escape sequence

```
ESC[10;30fMain Menu
```

or

```
ESC[10;30HMain Menu
```

To move the cursor to row 5, column 10 and display the letter A (*ESC[5;10fA*), move the cursor down one row (*ESC[B*), move the cursor back one space and display the letter B (*ESC[DB*), move the cursor down one row (*ESC[B*), and move the cursor back one space and display the letter C (*ESC[DC*), use the escape sequence

```
ESC[5;10fAESC[BESC[DBESC[BESC[DC
```

To use ANSI escape sequences with the PROMPT command to save the current cursor position (*$e[s*), move the cursor to row 1, column 69 (*$e[1;69f*), display the current time using the PROMPT command's $t function, restore the cursor position (*$e[u*), and then display the current path using the PROMPT command's $p function and display a greater-than sign using the PROMPT command's $g function, use the escape sequence

```
C>PROMPT $e[s$e[1;69f$t$e[u$p$g  <Enter>
```

To erase the display (*ESC[2J*), then move the cursor to row 10, column 30 and display the string *Main Menu* (*ESC[10;30fMain Menu*), use the escape sequence

```
ESC[2JESC[10;30fMain Menu
```

To move the cursor to row 5, column 40 (*ESC[5;40f*) and erase the remainder of the row starting at the current cursor position (*ESC[K*), use the escape sequence

```
ESC[5;40fESC[K
```

To move the cursor to row 3 (*ESC[3;f*), erase the entire row (*ESC[K*), move the cursor down one row (*ESC[B*), erase that entire row (*ESC[K*), move the cursor down one row and erase that entire row, use the escape sequence

```
ESC[3;fESC[KESC[BESC[KESC[BESC[K
```

To set the display mode to 25 rows of 80 columns in color (*ESC[=3h*) and disable character wrap (*ESC[=7l*), use the escape sequence

```
ESC[=3hESC[=7l
```

Note that ESC[=3h will also clear the screen.

To enable character wrap, use the escape sequence

```
ESC[=7h
```

To set the foreground color to black and the background color to blue (*ESC[30;44m*), clear the display (*ESC[2J*), then position the cursor at row 10, column 30 and display the string *Main Menu* (*ESC[10;30fMain Menu*), use the escape sequence

```
ESC[30;44mESC[2JESC[10;30fMain Menu
```

To (effectively) exchange the backslash and question-mark keys using literal strings to denote the keys, use the escape sequence

```
ESC["\";"?"pESC["?";"\"p
```

To exchange the backslash and question-mark keys using each key's ASCII value to denote the key, use the escape sequence

```
ESC[92;63pESC[63;92p
```

To restore the backslash and question-mark keys to their original meanings, use the escape sequence

```
ESC["\";"\"pESC["?";"?"p
```

or

```
ESC[92;92pESC[63;63p
```

To redefine the Alt-F9 key combination (*ESC[0;112*) so that it issues a CLS command (*;"CLS"*) plus a carriage return (*;13*) to execute the CLS command, then issues a DIR command piped through the SORT filter starting at column 24 (*;"DIR | SORT /+24"*) followed by another carriage return, use the escape sequence

```
ESC[0;112;"CLS";13;"DIR | SORT /+24";13p
```

To restore the Alt-F9 key combination to its original meaning, use the escape sequence

```
ESC[0;112;0;112p
```

APPEND

Set Data-File Search Path

3.2

External

Purpose

Specifies a search path for open operations on data files. (Also supported with some implementations of version 3.1, for use with networks.)

Syntax

APPEND [[*drive:*]*path*] [;[*drive:*]*path* ...]

or

APPEND ;

where:

path   is the name of a valid directory, optionally preceded by a drive.

Description

APPEND is a terminate-and-stay-resident program that is used to specify a path or paths to be searched for data files (in contrast with the PATH command, which specifies a path to be searched for executable or batch files). The search path can include a network drive. If a program attempts to open a file and the file is not found in the current or specified directory, each path given in the APPEND command is searched.

If the APPEND command is entered with a path consisting of only a semicolon character (;), a "null" search path for data files is set; that is, no directory other than the current or specified directory is searched. This effectively cancels any search paths previously set with an APPEND command but does not free the memory used by APPEND.

An APPEND command without any parameters displays the current search path(s) for data files.

Note that a program cannot detect whether an opened file was found where it was expected (in the current or specified directory) or in some other directory specified in the APPEND command.

Warning: When an assigned drive is to be part of the search path, the ASSIGN command must be used before the APPEND command. Use of the ASSIGN command should be avoided whenever possible because it hides drive characteristics from those programs that require detailed knowledge of the drive size and format.

Examples

To cause the directories C:\SYSTEM and C:\SOURCE to be searched for a file during an open operation if the file is not found in the current or specified directory, type

```
C>APPEND C:\SYSTEM;C:\SOURCE  <Enter>
```

To display the current search path for data files, type

```
C>APPEND  <Enter>
```

MS-DOS then displays

```
APPEND=C:\SYSTEM;C:\SOURCE
```

To ensure that no directories other than the current or specified directory are searched during a file open operation, type

```
C>APPEND ;  <Enter>
```

Messages

APPEND / ASSIGN Conflict
APPEND was used before ASSIGN.

Incorrect DOS version
The version of APPEND is not compatible with the version of MS-DOS that is running.

No appended directories
The APPEND command had no parameters and no APPEND search path is active.

ASSIGN

Assign Drive Alias

Purpose

Redirects requests for disk operations on one drive to a different drive. (Available with PC-DOS beginning with version 2.0.)

Syntax

ASSIGN [*x*=*y* [...]]

where:

x   is a valid designator (A, B, C, etc.) for a disk drive that physically exists in the system.

y   is a valid designator for the drive to be accessed by references to *x*.

Description

ASSIGN is a terminate-and-stay-resident program that redirects all references to drive *x* or files on drive *x* to drive *y*. The ASSIGN command is intended for use with application programs that require files to reside on drive A or B and have no provision within the program for changing those drives.

Multiple drive assignments can be requested in the same ASSIGN command line; the drive pairs must be separated with spaces, commas, or semicolons. Unlike the form in most other MS-DOS commands, the drive letters are not followed by colon characters (:). When a single drive is assigned, the equal sign is optional.

ASSIGN commands are not incremental. Each new ASSIGN command replaces assignments made with the previous ASSIGN command and cancels any assignments not specifically replaced. Entering ASSIGN with no parameters cancels all current drive assignments.

Warning: Use of the ASSIGN command should be avoided whenever possible because it hides drive characteristics from those programs that require detailed knowledge of the drive size and format; in particular, drives redirected with an ASSIGN statement should never be used with a BACKUP, RESTORE, LABEL, JOIN, SUBST, or PRINT command. ASSIGN can also defeat the checking performed by the COPY command to prevent a file from being copied onto itself. The FORMAT, SYS, DISKCOPY, and DISKCOMP commands ignore any drive reassignments made with ASSIGN.

With MS-DOS versions 3.1 and later, the SUBST command should be used instead of ASSIGN. For example, the command

```
C>ASSIGN A=C  <Enter>
```

should be replaced with the command

```
C>SUBST A: C:\  <Enter>
```

Examples

To redirect all requests for drive A to drive C, type

```
C>ASSIGN A=C  <Enter>
```

To redirect all requests for drives A and B to drive C, type

```
C>ASSIGN A=C B=C  <Enter>
```

To cancel all drive redirections currently in effect, type

```
C>ASSIGN  <Enter>
```

Messages

Incorrect DOS version
The version of ASSIGN is not compatible with the version of MS-DOS that is running.

Invalid parameter
One of the specified drive designators refers to a drive that does not exist in the system.

ATTRIB

Change File Attributes

Purpose

Sets, removes, or displays a file's read-only and/or archive attributes.

Syntax

ATTRIB [+R¦–R] [+A¦–A] [*drive:*]*pathname*

where:

+R	marks the file read-only.
–R	removes the read-only attribute.
+A	sets the file's archive flag (version 3.2).
–A	removes the file's archive flag (version 3.2).
pathname	is the name and location, optionally preceded by a drive, of the file whose attributes are to be changed or displayed; wildcard characters are permitted in the filename.

Description

Each file has an entry in the disk's directory that contains its name, location, and size; the date and time it was created or last modified; and an attribute byte. For normal files, bits 0, 1, 2, and 5 in the attribute byte designate, respectively, whether the file is read-only, hidden, or system and whether it has been changed since it was last backed up.

The ATTRIB command provides a way to alter the read-only and archive bits from the MS-DOS command level. If a file is marked read-only, it cannot be deleted or modified; thus, crucial programs or data can be protected from accidental erasure. A file's archive flag can be used together with the /M switch of the BACKUP command or the /M or /A switch of the XCOPY command to allow an incremental or selective backup of files from one disk to another.

If the ATTRIB command is entered with only a pathname, the current attributes of the selected file are displayed. An R is displayed next to the name of a file that is marked read-only and an A is displayed if the file has the archive flag set.

Examples

To make the file MENUMGR.C in the current directory of the current drive a read-only file, type

```
C>ATTRIB +R MENUMGR.C  <Enter>
```

To display the attributes of the file LETTER.DOC in the directory \SOURCE on the disk in drive D, type

```
C>ATTRIB D:\SOURCE\LETTER.DOC  <Enter>
```

Section III: User Commands 743

MS-DOS then displays

```
R A      D:\SOURCE\LETTER.DOC
```

to indicate that the file is marked read-only and the archive flag has been set.

To set the archive flag on all files in the directory \SYSTEM on drive C and mark them as read-only, type

```
C>ATTRIB +A +R C:\SYSTEM\*.*   <Enter>
```

Messages

Access denied
ATTRIB cannot be used to alter or replace the attributes of a file in use across a network.

DOS 2.0 or later required
ATTRIB does not work with versions of MS-DOS earlier than 2.0.

Incorrect DOS version
The version of ATTRIB is not compatible with the version of MS-DOS that is running.

Invalid number of parameters
More than two attributes were used before the pathname.

Invalid path or file not found
The file named in the command line or one of the directories in the given path does not exist.

Syntax error
An invalid attribute was supplied or the attribute was not properly placed before the pathname in the command line.

BACKUP

Back Up Files

Purpose

Creates backup copies of files, along with the associated directory information necessary to restore the files to their original locations.

Syntax

BACKUP *source destination* [/A] [/D:*date*] [/L:*filename*] [/M] [/P] [/S] [/T:*time*]

where:

source	is the location (drive and/or path) and, optionally, the name of the files to be backed up; wildcard characters are permitted in the filename.
destination	is the drive to receive the backup files.
/A	adds the files to existing files on the destination disk without erasing the destination disk.
/D:*date*	backs up only those files modified on or after *date*.
/L:*filename*	creates a log file with the specified name in the root directory of the disk being backed up. If *filename* is not specified, BACKUP creates a file named BACKUP.LOG and places the log entries there. Use of the /L:*filename* switch may cause loss of IBM compatibility.
/M	backs up only those files modified since the last backup.
/P	packs the destination disk with as many files as possible, creating sub-directories, if necessary, to hold some of the files. Use of the /P switch causes loss of IBM compatibility.
/S	backs up the contents of all subdirectories of the source directory.
/T:*time*	backs up only those files modified on or after *time*.

Note: Not all switches are supported by all implementations of MS-DOS.

Description

The BACKUP command creates a backup copy of the specified file or files, transferring them from either a floppy disk or a fixed disk to another removable or fixed disk. The backup file is in a special format that includes information about the original file's location in the directory structure. Files created by BACKUP can be restored to their original form only with the RESTORE command.

BACKUP can back up a single file or many files in the same operation. If only a drive letter is given as the source, all the files in the current directory of that disk are backed up. If only a path is given as the source, all the files in the specified directory are backed up. If the /S switch is used, all the files in the current or specified directory are backed up, and the files in all its subdirectories as well. If both a path and a filename are entered as the source, the specified file or files in the named directory are backed up.

If the source file is marked read-only, the resulting backup file will also be marked read-only. If the source file's archive bit is set, it will be cleared for both the source and the destination files. BACKUP also backs up hidden files; the files will remain hidden on the destination disk.

If the destination disk is a floppy disk, its previous contents are erased as part of the backup operation (unless the /A switch is included in the command line and the destination disk has already been used as a backup disk — that is, the disk contains a valid BACKUPID.@@@ file). If the files being backed up do not fit onto a single floppy disk, the user will be prompted to insert additional disks until the backup operation is complete.

If the destination disk is a fixed disk, the backed-up files are placed in a directory named \BACKUP. If a \BACKUP directory already exists on the fixed disk, any files previously contained in it are erased as part of the backup operation (unless the /A switch is included in the command line and the destination disk has already been used as a backup disk — that is, the \BACKUP directory contains a valid BACKUPID.@@@ file). Other files on the destination fixed disk are not disturbed.

A control file named BACKUPID.@@@ is placed on every floppy disk onto which files are backed up or in the /BACKUP directory if the files are backed up onto a fixed disk. The BACKUPID.@@@ file has the following format:

Byte	Value	Use
00H	00 or FFH	Not last floppy disk/last floppy disk
01–02H	*nn*	Floppy disk number in low-byte/high-byte decimal format
03–04H	*nnnn*	Full year in low-byte/high-byte order
05H	1–31	Day of the month
06H	1–12	Month of the year
07–0AH	*nnnn*	Standard MS-DOS system time if the /T:*time* switch was used; otherwise 0
0B–7FH	00	Not used

Each backed-up file also has a 128-byte header added to it when it is created. The header has the following format:

Byte	Value	Use
00H	00 or FFH	Not last floppy disk/last floppy disk on which this file resides
01H	*nn*	Floppy disk number
02–04H	00	Not used

(more)

Byte	Value	Use
05–44H	*nn*	File's full pathname, except for drive designator
45–52H	00	Not used
53H	*nn*	Length of the file's pathname plus one
54–7FH	00	Not used

The /T:*time*, /D:*date*, and /M switches allow incremental or partial backups. The /T:*time* switch excludes files modified or created before a certain time and should be used in the form of the COUNTRY command in effect. For the USA, the format is /T:*hh:mm:ss*. (The /T:*time* switch is not supported in all implementations of BACKUP.) The /D:*date* switch excludes files modified or created before a certain date and should be used in the form of the COUNTRY command in effect. For the USA, the format is /D:*mm-dd-yy*. The /M switch selects only those files that have been modified since the last backup operation.

The /L:*filename* switch causes a log file to be created on the source disk. This file includes the name of each file backed up, the time and date, and the number of the destination disk that received that backup file. If *filename* is omitted, the name defaults to BACKUP.LOG. Use of the /L:*filename* switch can cause compatibility problems between MS-DOS and PC-DOS because the backup log file may match the search pattern and be backed up, too, resulting in an extra file on the backup disk.

The /P switch causes backup files to be packed as densely as possible on the destination disk. When many short files are being backed up to floppy disks, the number of files that fit on the destination disk may exceed the number of entries that will fit in the destination's root directory. If the /P switch is included in the command line, subdirectories are created on the destination disk as needed to use the disk space more effectively. The /P switch is not supported under PC-DOS; backup disks created with the /P switch will not be compatible with IBM's BACKUP and RESTORE commands.

Warning: BACKUP should not be used on disk directories or drives that have been redirected with an ASSIGN, JOIN, or SUBST command.

Return Codes

0 Backup operation was successful.
1 No files were found to back up.
2 Some files were not backed up because of sharing conflicts (versions 3.0 and later).
3 Backup operation was terminated by user.
4 Backup operation was terminated because of error.

Examples

To back up the file REPORT.TXT in the current directory on the current drive, placing the backup file on the disk in drive A, type

```
C>BACKUP REPORT.TXT A:  <Enter>
```

To back up all the files in the subdirectory B:\V2\SOURCE, placing the backup files on the disk in drive A, type

```
C>BACKUP B:\V2\SOURCE A:   <Enter>
```

To back up all the files with extension .C in the directory \V2\SOURCE on the current drive, placing the backup files on the disk in drive A, type

```
C>BACKUP \V2\SOURCE\*.C A:   <Enter>
```

To back up all the files with the extension .ASM from the current directory on the current drive and from all its subdirectories, placing the backup files on the disk in drive A, type

```
C>BACKUP *.ASM A: /S   <Enter>
```

To back up all the files that have been modified since the last backup from all the sub-directories on drive C, placing the backup files on the disk in drive A, type

```
C>BACKUP C:\ A: /S /M   <Enter>
```

To back up all the files with the extension .C from the directory C:\V2\SOURCE that were modified on or after October 16, 1985, placing the backup files on the disk in drive A, type

```
C>BACKUP C:\V2\SOURCE\*.C A: /D:10-16-85   <Enter>
```

Messages

•••Backing up files to drive X: •••
Diskette Number: n
This informational message informs the user of the progress of the BACKUP command.

•••Last file not backed up •••
The destination drive does not have enough space to back up the last file.

•••Not able to back up file •••
One of the system calls used by BACKUP failed unexpectedly; for example, a file could not be opened, read, or written.

Cannot create Subdirectory BACKUP on drive X:
Drive X is full or its root directory is full.

DOS 2.0 or later required
BACKUP does not work with versions of MS-DOS earlier than 2.0.

Error trying to open backup log file
Continuing without making log entries
The /L switch was used and BACKUP is unable to create the backup log file.

**Files cannot be added to this diskette
unless the PACK (/P) switch is used
Set the switch (Y/N)?**
The root directory of the destination disk is full and a subdirectory must be created to hold the remaining files. Respond with *Y* to cause BACKUP to create a subdirectory and continue backing up files into it; respond with *N* to return to MS-DOS.

Incorrect DOS version
The version of BACKUP is not compatible with the version of MS-DOS that is running.

**Insert backup diskette in drive *X*:
Strike any key when ready**
This message prompts the user to insert a disk to receive the backup files into the specified destination drive.

**Insert backup diskette *n* in drive *X*:
Strike any key when ready**
The files being backed up will not fit onto a single floppy disk; this message prompts the user to insert the next floppy disk. Multiple-floppy-disk backup disks should be labeled and numbered to match the number displayed in this message.

**Insert backup source diskette in drive *X*:
Strike any key when ready**
This message prompts the user to insert the floppy disk to be backed up into the specified source drive.

**Insert last backup diskette in drive *X*:
Strike any key when ready**
This message prompts the user to insert the final disk that will receive the backup files into the specified destination drive.

Insufficient memory
Available system memory is insufficient to run the BACKUP program.

Invalid argument
One of the switches specified in the command line is invalid or is not supported in the version of BACKUP being used.

Invalid Date/Time
An invalid date or time was given with the /D:*date* or /T:*time* switch.

Invalid drive specification
The source or destination drive specified in the command line is not available or is not valid.

Invalid number of parameters
At least two parameters, the source and the destination, must be specified in the command line; a maximum of seven switches can be specified after the source and destination.

Invalid parameter

One of the switches supplied in the command line is invalid.

Invalid path

The path specified as the source is invalid or does not exist.

Last backup diskette not inserted
Insert last backup diskette in drive *X*:
Strike any key when ready

The backup disk inserted as the last backup disk was not the correct disk. Insert the correct disk.

No space left on device

The destination disk is full.

No such file or directory

The source specified is invalid or does not exist.

Source and target drives are the same

The disks specified as the source and destination disks are identical.

Source disk is Non-removable

The disk containing the files to be backed up is a fixed disk.

Target can not be used for backup

The disk specified as the destination disk is damaged or the /A switch was used in the command line and the disk does not contain a valid BACKUPID.@@@ file.

Target disk is Non-removable

The disk that will contain the backed-up files is a fixed disk.

Target is a floppy disk

or

Target is a hard disk

This informational message indicates which type of disk was specified as the destination disk.

Too many open files

Too many files are open. Increase the value of the FILES command in the CONFIG.SYS file.

Unable to erase *filename*

BACKUP is unable to erase an older version of a backed-up file because the file is read-only or is in use by another program.

Warning! Files in the target drive
X:**root directory will be erased**
Strike any key when ready
The destination is a floppy-disk drive and this message warns the user that all files in its
root directory will be erased before the backup operation.

Warning! Files in the target drive
C:\BACKUP directory will be erased
Strike any key when ready
BACKUP is ready to begin backing up files to the \BACKUP directory on drive C. All exist-
ing files in the \BACKUP directory will be deleted. Press Crtl-Break to terminate the
backup operation or press any key to continue.

Warning! No files were found to back up
No files were found on the source disk in the current or specified directory or no files were
found matching the filename supplied.

BATCH

System Batch-File Interpreter

1.0 and later

Internal

Purpose

Sequentially executes commands stored in a batch file (a text-only file with a .BAT extension).

Syntax

filename [[*parameter1* [*parameter2* [...]]]]

where:

filename	is the name of the batch file to be executed, without the .BAT extension. (The filename is always %0 in the list of replaceable parameters.)
parameter1	is the filename, switch, or string that is the value of the first replaceable parameter (%1).
parameter2	is the filename, switch, or string that is the value of the second replaceable parameter (%2). As many additional replaceable parameters can be specified as the command line will hold.

Description

A batch file is an ASCII text file that contains one or more MS-DOS commands. It is a useful way to perform sequences of frequently used commands without having to type them all each time they are needed. When a batch file is invoked by entering its name, the commands it contains are carried out in sequence by a special batch-file interpreter built into COMMAND.COM. Additional information entered in the batch-file command line can be passed to other programs by means of replaceable parameters (*see below*).

A batch file must always have the extension .BAT. The file can contain any number of lines of ASCII text; each line can contain a maximum of 128 characters. Batch files can be created with EDLIN or another text editor or with a word processor in nondocument mode. (Formatted document files cannot be used as batch files because they contain special control codes or escape sequences that cannot be processed by the batch-file interpreter.) Batch files can also be created with the MS-DOS COPY command by specifying the CON device (keyboard) as the source file and the desired batch-file name as the destination file. For example, after the command

```
C>COPY CON MYFILE.BAT  <Enter>
```

each line that is typed will be placed into MYFILE.BAT. This form of the COPY command is terminated by pressing Ctrl-Z or the F6 key, followed by the Enter key.

The commands in a batch file can be any combination of internal MS-DOS commands (such as DIR or COPY), external MS-DOS commands (such as CHKDSK or BACKUP), the names of other programs or batch files, or the following special batch-file directives:

Command	Action
ECHO	Displays a message on standard output (versions 2.0 and later).
FOR	Executes a command on each of a set of files (versions 2.0 and later).
GOTO	Transfers control to another point in a batch file (versions 2.0 and later).
IF	Conditionally executes a command based on the existence of a file, the equality of two strings, or the return code of a previously run program (versions 2.0 and later).
PAUSE	Waits for the user to press a key before executing the remainder of the batch file.
REM	Allows comment lines to be placed in batch files for internal documentation.
SHIFT	Provides access to more than 10 command-line parameters (versions 2.0 and later).

These special batch commands are discussed individually, with examples, in the following pages.

A batch file is executed by entering its name, without the .BAT extension, in response to the MS-DOS prompt. The system's command processor, COMMAND.COM, searches the current directory and then each directory named in the PATH environment variable for a file with the specified name and the extension .COM, .EXE, or .BAT, in that order. If a .COM or .EXE file is found, it is loaded into memory and receives control; if a .BAT file is found, it is assumed to be a text file and is passed to the batch-file interpreter. (If two files with the same name exist in the same directory, one with a .COM or .EXE extension and the other with a .BAT extension, it is not possible to execute the .BAT file — the .COM or .EXE file is always loaded instead.)

If the disk that contains a batch file is removed before all the commands in the batch file are executed, COMMAND.COM will prompt the user to replace the disk so that the batch file can be completed. Execution of a batch file can be terminated by pressing Ctrl-C or Ctrl-Break, causing COMMAND.COM to issue the message *Terminate batch job? (Y/N)*. If the user responds with *Y*, the batch file is abandoned and COMMAND.COM displays its usual prompt.

The input redirection (<), output redirection (> or >>), and piping (¦) characters have no effect when they are used in a command line that invokes a batch file. However, they can be used in individual command lines *within* the file.

Ordinarily, if a batch file includes the name of another batch file, control passes to the second batch file and never returns. That is, when the commands in the second batch file are completed, the batch-file interpreter terminates and any remaining commands in the first batch file are not processed. However, a batch file can execute another batch file without itself being terminated by first loading a secondary copy of the system's command processor. To accomplish this, the first batch file must contain a command of the form

COMMAND /C *batch2*

where *batch2* is the name of the second batch file. When all the commands in the second batch file have been processed, the secondary copy of COMMAND.COM exits and the first batch file continues where it left off. (*See* USER COMMANDS: COMMAND for details on the use of the /C switch with COMMAND.COM.)

A batch file can be made more flexible by including replaceable parameters inside the file. A replaceable parameter takes the form *%n*, where *n* is a numeral in the range 0 through 9. Replaceable parameters simply hold places in the batch file for filenames or other information that the user will supply in the command line when the batch file is invoked.

When a batch file is interpreted and a command containing a replaceable parameter is encountered, the corresponding value specified in the batch-file command line is substituted for the replaceable parameter and the command is then executed. The %0 replaceable parameter is replaced by the name of the batch file itself; parameters %1 through %9 are replaced sequentially with the remaining values specified in the command line. If a replaceable parameter references a command-line entry that does not exist, the parameter is replaced with a null (zero-length) string.

For example, if the batch file MYBATCH.BAT contains the single line

```
COPY %1.COM %2.SAV
```

and is executed by entry of

```
C>MYBATCH FILE1 FILE2   <Enter>
```

the actual command that is carried out is

```
COPY FILE1.COM FILE2.SAV
```

(The SHIFT batch command makes it possible to use more than 10 replaceable parameters. *See* USER COMMANDS: BATCH:SHIFT)

An environment variable is a special case of a replaceable parameter. If the SET command is used in the form

SET *name=value*

to add an environment variable to the system's environment block, the string *value* will be substituted for the string %*name*% wherever the latter is encountered during the interpretation of a batch file. This capability is available only in versions 2.x, 3.1, and 3.2.

BATCH: AUTOEXEC.BAT

1.0 and later

System Startup Batch File

Description

The AUTOEXEC.BAT file is an optional batch file containing a series of MS-DOS commands that automatically execute when the system is turned on or restarted.

When the system's default command processor, COMMAND.COM, is first loaded, it looks in the root directory of the current drive for a file named AUTOEXEC.BAT. If AUTOEXEC.BAT is not found, COMMAND.COM prompts the user to enter the current time and date and then displays the MS-DOS copyright notice and command prompt. If AUTOEXEC.BAT is found, COMMAND.COM sequentially executes the commands within the file. No prompts to enter the time and date are issued unless the TIME and DATE commands are explicitly included in the batch file; no copyright notice is displayed.

Typical uses of the AUTOEXEC.BAT file include

- Running a program to set the system time and date from a real-time clock/calendar located on a multipurpose expansion board (IBM PC, PC/XT, or compatibles only)
- Using the MODE command to configure a serial port or to redirect printing
- Executing SET commands to configure environment variables
- Setting display colors on a color monitor (if the command *DEVICE=ANSI.SYS* has been included in the CONFIG.SYS file)
- Installing terminate-and-stay-resident (TSR) utilities
- Using the PATH command to tell COMMAND.COM where to find executable program files if they are not in the current drive and/or directory
- Defining a custom prompt using the PROMPT command
- Invoking an application program such as a database, spreadsheet, or word processor

A secondary copy of the command processor can also be loaded from within the AUTOEXEC.BAT file. If this copy of COMMAND.COM is loaded with the /P switch, it too searches for an AUTOEXEC.BAT file on the current drive and processes the file if it is found. This feature can be useful for performing special operations. For example, on very old PCs that are unable to start from a fixed disk, a secondary copy of the command processor can be used to make the fixed disk's copy of COMMAND.COM the copy used by the system from that point on (at the expense of some system memory). If the AUTOEXEC.BAT file containing the lines

```
C:
COMMAND C:\ /P
```

is stored on the floppy disk in drive A when the system is turned on or restarted, the first line of the file causes drive C to become the current drive; then the second line permanently loads a secondary copy of COMMAND.COM from drive C and instructs COMMAND.COM to reload its transient portion from the root directory of drive C when necessary. This in turn triggers the execution of the AUTOEXEC.BAT file on the fixed disk to perform the actual system configuration. Because the transient part of COMMAND.COM will be reloaded from the fixed disk when necessary, rather than from the floppy disk, system performance is improved considerably.

Example

The following example illustrates several common uses of the AUTOEXEC.BAT file to configure the MS-DOS system at startup time. (The line numbers are included for reference and are not part of the actual file.)

```
1    ECHO OFF
2    SETCLOCK
3    PROMPT $p$g
4    MD D:\BIN
5    COPY C:\SYSTEM\*.* D:\BIN > NUL
6    PATH=D:\BIN;C:\WP\WORD;C:\MSC\BIN;C:\ASM
7    APPEND D:\BIN;C:\WP\WORD;C:\ASM
8    SET INCLUDE=C:\MSC\INCLUDE
9    SET LIB=C:\MSC\LIB
10   SET TMP=C:\TEMP
11   MODE COM1:9600,n,8,1,p
12   MODE LPT1:=COM1:
```

Line 1 causes the batch-file processor to operate silently; that is, the commands in the batch file are not displayed on the screen as they are executed.

Line 2 runs a utility program called SETCLOCK, which reads the current time and date from a real-time clock chip on a multifunction board and sets the system time and date accordingly.

Line 3 configures COMMAND.COM's user prompt so that it displays the current drive and directory.

Line 4 creates a directory named \BIN on drive D, which in this case is a RAMdisk that was created by an entry in the system's CONFIG.SYS file.

Line 5 copies all the programs in the \SYSTEM directory on drive C to the \BIN directory on drive D. The normal output of this COPY command is redirected to the NUL device — in effect, the output is thrown away — to avoid cluttering the screen.

Line 6 sets the search path for executable files and line 7 sets the search path for data files. Note that the RAMdisk directory D:\BIN is specified as the first directory in the PATH command; therefore, if the name of a program is entered and it cannot be found in the current directory, COMMAND.COM will look next in the directory D:\BIN. This strategy allows commonly used programs (in this example, the programs in the \SYSTEM directory that were copied into D:\BIN) to be located and loaded quickly.

Lines 8 through 10 add the environment variables INCLUDE, LIB, and TMP to the system's environment. These variables are used by the Microsoft C Compiler and the Microsoft Object Linker.

Line 11 configures the first serial communications port (COM1) and line 12 causes program output to the system's first parallel port (LPT1) to be redirected to the first serial port. This pair of commands allows a serial-interface Hewlett Packard LaserJet printer to be used as the system list device.

Note: Depending on the version of MS-DOS in use, some commands in this example may not be available or may support different options. See the individual command entries for more detailed information.

BATCH: ECHO
Display Text

2.0 and later

Internal

Purpose

Displays a message during the execution of a batch file and controls whether or not batch-file commands are listed on the screen as they are executed.

Syntax

ECHO [ON¦OFF¦ *message*]

where:

ON   enables the display of all subsequent batch-file commands as they are executed.

OFF   disables the display of all subsequent batch-file commands as they are executed.

message   is a text string to be displayed on standard output.

Description

Each command line of a batch file is ordinarily displayed on the screen as it is executed. The ECHO command has a dual usage: to control the display of these commands and to display a message to the user.

ECHO is used with ON or OFF to enable or disable the display of commands during batch-file processing. If the ECHO command is used with no parameter, the current status of the batch processor's ECHO flag is displayed. Note that the ECHO flag is always forced on at the start of any batch-file processing, even if that batch file was invoked by another batch file.

The ECHO command is not limited to batch files; an ECHO command can also be issued at the command prompt. ECHO OFF entered at the command prompt prevents the prompt from subsequently being displayed. ECHO ON entered interactively restores the display. If ECHO is entered interactively without a parameter, the current status of the ECHO flag is displayed.

ECHO can also be followed by a message to be sent to standard output regardless of the status of the ECHO flag (on or off). Note that if ECHO is on, two copies of the message are actually displayed, the first copy preceded by the word *ECHO*. ECHO *message* is frequently used to display prompts and informative text during the execution of a batch file because text following REM or PAUSE commands is not displayed if ECHO is off.

ECHO *message* can also be used to build lists or other batch files dynamically while the batch file is executing. For example, the messages in the following ECHO commands are used to build the file STARTUP.BAT:

```
ECHO CHKDSK > STARTUP.BAT
ECHO DIR /W >> STARTUP.BAT
ECHO PROMPT $p$g >> STARTUP.BAT
```

The first ECHO command causes the message *CHKDSK* to be redirected to the file STARTUP.BAT. The second and third ECHO commands cause the messages *DIR/W* and *PROMPT pg* to be appended to the existing contents of STARTUP.BAT. The completed STARTUP.BAT file contains the following:

```
CHKDSK
DIR /W
PROMPT $p$g
```

Note: When the pipe symbol (¦) is used in *message*, the symbol and any characters following it are ignored until a redirection symbol (<, >, or >>) is encountered, at which point the redirection symbol and the remaining characters are recognized. For example, if the line

```
ECHO DIR ¦ SORT > STARTUP.BAT
```

was placed in a batch file and subsequently executed, the only characters echoed to the file STARTUP.BAT would be *DIR*; the pipe symbol and the characters between it and the redirection symbol > would be ignored.

Examples

To disable the display of each batch-file command as it is executed, include the following line as the first line in the batch file:

```
ECHO OFF
```

To display the message *Now formatting disk* on standard output, include the following line in the batch file:

```
ECHO Now formatting disk
```

To display the current status of the ECHO flag, include the following line in the batch file:

```
ECHO
```

If the ECHO flag is currently off, MS-DOS displays:

```
ECHO is off
```

To echo a blank line to the screen with versions 2.x, type a space after the ECHO command and press Enter. To echo a blank line with versions 3.x, type the ECHO command and a space, then hold down Alt and type 255 on the numeric keypad; finally, release the Alt key and press Enter.

Messages

ECHO is off

or

ECHO is on

If the ECHO command is entered without a parameter, one of these lines is displayed to give the current status of the batch processor's ECHO flag.

BATCH: FOR

Execute Command on File Set

2.0 and later

Internal

Purpose

Executes a command or program for each file in a set of files.

Syntax

FOR %%*variable* IN (*set*) DO *command*   (batch processing)

or

FOR %*variable* IN (*set*) DO *command*   (interactive processing)

where:

variable   is a variable name that can be any single character except the numerals 0
            through 9, the redirection symbols (<, >, and >>), and the pipe symbol (¦);
            case is significant.

set   is one or more filenames, pathnames, character strings, or metacharacters,
            separated by spaces, commas, or semicolons; wildcard characters are per-
            mitted in filenames.

command   is any MS-DOS command or program except the FOR command; the vari-
            able name %%*variable* (or %*variable* in interactive mode) can be part of
            the command.

Description

The FOR command allows sequential execution of the same command or program on
each member of a set of files.

The *set* parameter can contain multiple filenames (including wildcards), pathnames, character strings, or metacharacters such as the replaceable parameters %0 through %9. Each of
the following lines is an example of a valid set:

```
(FILE1.TXT %1 %2 B:\PROG\LISTING?.TXT)
(A:\%1 A:\%2 C:\LETTERS\*.TXT C:MEMO?.*)
(%PATH%)
```

Each filename from *set* is assigned in turn to %*variable* and then the specified command
or program is executed. (When the FOR command line is executed in a batch file, the
leading percent sign of %%*variable* is removed, leaving %*variable*.) If a filename in *set*
contains wildcards, each matching file is used before the batch processor goes on to the
next member of *set*.

Note: In versions 2.x, *set* can consist only of a list of single filenames, a single filename with wildcard characters, or a combination of single filenames and metacharacters. In versions 3.x, however, all combinations of these are allowed in the same set.

The FOR command can also be used interactively at the MS-DOS prompt to perform a single command on several files without entering the same command for each file. When FOR is used in this manner, only one percent sign (%) should be used before the dummy alphabetic variable; in this case, the percent sign is not removed during processing. When the FOR command is used interactively, environment variables such as %PATH% cannot be used as part of the filename set.

Examples

To view all the files with the extension .TXT in the current directory, include the following line in the batch file:

```
FOR %%X IN (*.TXT) DO TYPE %%X
```

To perform the same function interactively, type

```
C>FOR %X IN (*.TXT) DO TYPE %X   <Enter>
```

To copy up to nine files to the disk in drive A, specifying the names of the files in the batch-file command line, include the following line in the batch file:

```
FOR %%Y IN (%1 %2 %3 %4 %5 %6 %7 %8 %9) DO COPY %%Y A:
```

(Recall that %0 is the name of the batch file.)

To execute successive batch files under the control of one batch file, use the /C switch with COMMAND, as in the following batch-file line:

```
FOR %%Z IN (BAT1 BAT2 BAT3) DO COMMAND /C %%Z
```

Message

FOR cannot be nested
The command or program performed by a FOR command cannot be another FOR command.

BATCH: GOTO

Jump to Label

2.0 and later

Internal

Purpose

Transfers program control to the batch-file line following the specified label.

Syntax

GOTO *name*

where:

name   is a batch-file label declared elsewhere in the file in the form *:name.*

Description

The GOTO command causes the batch-file processor to transfer its point of execution to the line following the specified label. If the label does not exist in the file, execution of the batch file is terminated with the message *Label not found.*

A batch-file label is defined as a line with a colon character (:) in the first column, followed by any text (including spaces but not other separator characters such as semicolons or equal signs). Only the first eight characters following the colon are significant; spaces are not counted in the eight characters.

Examples

The GOTO command is frequently used in combination with the IF and SHIFT batch commands to perform some action based on the return code from a program. For example, the following batch file will back up a variable number of files or directories, whose names are specified in the batch-file command line, to a floppy disk in drive A. The batch file accomplishes this by executing the BACKUP program with successive pathnames specified in the command line until BACKUP returns a nonzero (error) code. Control is then transferred to the label *:DONE*, and the batch file is terminated.

```
1    ECHO OFF
2    :START
3    BACKUP %1 A:
4    IF ERRORLEVEL 1 GOTO DONE
5    SHIFT
6    GOTO START
7    :DONE
```

Note that the batch file includes two labels, *:START* and *:DONE*, in lines 2 and 7, respectively. It also includes two GOTO commands, in lines 4 and 6. (The line numbers in the listing above are included only for reference and are not present in the actual batch file.) If the condition in line 4 is true (the BACKUP program returned an exit code of 1 or higher), the remainder of line 4 is executed and program control passes to the *:DONE* label in line 7. If the condition is false, program control passes to line 5, the SHIFT command is executed, and program control goes to line 6, where the GOTO statement returns program control to line 2.

Message

Label not found
The specified label does not exist in the batch file.

BATCH: IF

Perform Conditional Execution

2.0 and later

Internal

Purpose

Tests a condition and executes a command or program if the condition is met.

Syntax

IF [NOT] *condition command*

where:

condition   is one of the following:

ERRORLEVEL *number*
The condition is true if the exit code of the program last executed by
COMMAND.COM was equal to or greater than *number*. Note that not all
MS-DOS commands return explicit exit codes.

string1==*string2*
The condition is true if *string1* and *string2* are identical after parameter
substitution; case is significant. The strings cannot contain separator characters such as commas, semicolons, equal signs, or spaces.

EXIST *pathname*
The condition is true if the specified file exists. The pathname can include
metacharacters.

command   is the command or program to be executed if the condition is true.

Description

The IF command provides conditional execution of a command or program in a batch file.
When *condition* is true, IF executes the specified command, which can be another IF
command, any other MS-DOS internal command, or a program. When *condition* is not
true, MS-DOS ignores *command* and proceeds to the next line in the batch file. The sense
of any condition can be reversed by preceding the test or expression with NOT.

Examples

To branch to the label *:ERROR* if the file LEDGER.DAT does not exist, include the following line in the batch file:

```
IF NOT EXIST LEDGER.DAT GOTO ERROR
```

To branch to the label :*ONEPAR* if the batch-file command line does not contain at least two parameters, include the following line in the batch file:

```
IF "%2"==""GOTO ONEPAR
```

or

```
IF %2~==~ GOTO ONEPAR
```

Note that the existence of a replaceable parameter can be determined by concatenating it to another string. In the first example, quotation marks are concatenated on either side of the replaceable parameter; if %2 doesn't exist, *"%2"==""* evaluates to *""==""*, which is true and will allow *GOTO ONEPAR* to be executed. In the second example, a tilde character is concatenated to the end of the replaceable parameter; if %2 doesn't exist, the argument becomes ~==~.

To copy the file specified by the first replaceable batch-file parameter to drive A only if it does not already exist on the disk in drive A, include the following line in the batch file:

```
IF NOT EXIST A:%1 COPY %1 A:
```

To branch to the label :*DONE* if the first replaceable batch-file parameter exists in the \PROG directory on drive C *and* in the \BACKUP directory on drive C, include the following line in the batch file:

```
IF EXIST C:\PROG\%1 IF EXIST C:\BACKUP\%1 GOTO DONE
```

Messages

Bad command or filename
The command following the condition in the IF statement was misspelled, does not exist, or was represented by a replaceable parameter that was not supplied in the command line that invoked the batch file.

Syntax error
The condition specified in the IF statement cannot be tested.

BATCH: PAUSE

Suspend Batch-File Execution

1.0 and later

Internal

Purpose

Displays a message, suspends execution of a batch file, and waits for the user to press a key.

Syntax

PAUSE [*message*]

where:

message   is a text string to be displayed on standard output.

Description

The PAUSE command displays the message *Strike a key when ready...* and suspends execution of a batch file until the user presses a key. This command can be used to allow time for the operator to change disks, change the type of forms on the printer, or take some other action that is necessary before the batch file can continue.

If the batch processor's ECHO flag is on when the PAUSE command is executed, the entire line containing the PAUSE statement is displayed on the screen so that the optional message is visible to the user. The message *Strike a key when ready...* is then displayed on a new line and the system waits. Note that *Strike a key when ready...* is *always* displayed, even if the ECHO flag is off. When the user presses a key, execution of the batch file resumes.

Note: Redirection symbols should not be used within *message*. They prevent the message *Strike a key when ready...* from being displayed on the screen.

If the user presses Ctrl-C or Ctrl-Break while a PAUSE command is waiting for a key to be pressed, a prompt is displayed that gives the user the opportunity to terminate the execution of the batch file. This same message is displayed whenever the user presses Ctrl-C or Ctrl-Break during the execution of a batch file; however, using PAUSE commands supplemented by appropriate ECHO commands at strategic points within a batch file provides the user with clearly defined breakpoints for terminating the file.

Examples

To display the message *Put an empty disk in drive A* and then wait until the user has pressed a key, include the following line in the batch file:

```
PAUSE Put an empty disk in drive A
```

When this line of the batch file is executed, if the ECHO flag is on, the user sees the following messages on the screen:

```
C>PAUSE Put an empty disk in drive A
Strike a key when ready . . .
```

If the ECHO flag is off, only the message *Strike a key when ready...* appears.

To display the message without the prompt and command, the PAUSE command can be used immediately after an ECHO command, as follows:

```
ECHO OFF
CLS
ECHO Put an empty disk in drive A
PAUSE
```

This batch file will display the following message on the screen:

```
Put an empty disk in drive A
Strike a key when ready . . .
```

Note that the message must be included in an ECHO command. With ECHO off, a PAUSE message is not displayed.

BATCH: REM

Include Comment Line

1.0 and later

Internal

Purpose

Designates a remark, or comment, line in a batch file.

Syntax

REM [*message*]

where:

message   is any text.

Description

The REM command allows inclusion of remarks, or comments, within a batch file. Remarks are often used to document the purpose of other commands within the file for the benefit of those who may wish to modify the file later.

If the ECHO flag is on, remarks are displayed on the screen during the execution of a batch file. Thus, remarks can also be used to provide information, guidance, or prompts to the user; however, the ECHO and PAUSE commands are more suitable for these purposes.

REM can also be used alone to insert blank lines in a batch file to improve readability. (If ECHO is on, the word *REM* will still be displayed.)

Note: The redirection symbols (<, >, and >>) and piping character (¦) produce no meaningful results with the REM command and should not be used.

Example

To document a batch file's revision history with the internal comment *This batch file last modified on 6/18/87*, include the following line in the batch file:

```
REM This batch file last modified on 6/18/87
```

BATCH: SHIFT

Shift Replaceable Parameters

2.0 and later

Internal

Purpose

Changes the position of the replaceable parameters in a batch-file command line, thereby allowing more than 10 replaceable parameters.

Syntax

SHIFT

Description

Ordinarily only 10 replaceable parameters (%0 through %9, where %0 is the name of the batch file) can be referenced within a batch file. The SHIFT command allows access to additional parameters specified in the command line by shifting the contents of each of the previously assigned parameters to a lower number (%1 becomes %0, %2 becomes %1, and so on). The previous contents of %0 are lost and are not recoverable. The eleventh parameter in the batch-file command line is then moved into %9. This allows more than 10 parameters to be specified in the batch-file command line and subsequently processed in the batch file.

Example

The following batch file will copy a variable number of files, whose names are entered in the batch-file command line, to the disk in drive A:

```
ECHO OFF
:NEXT
IF "%1"=="" GOTO DONE
COPY %1 A:
SHIFT
GOTO NEXT
:DONE
```

BREAK

Set Control-C Check

2.0 and later

Internal

Purpose

Sets or clears MS-DOS's internal flag for Control-C checking.

Syntax

BREAK [ON¦OFF]

Description

Pressing Ctrl-C or Ctrl-Break while a program is running ordinarily terminates the program, unless the program itself contains instructions that disable MS-DOS's Control-C handling. As a rule, MS-DOS checks the keyboard for a Control-C only when a character is read from or written to a character device (keyboard, screen, printer, or auxiliary port). Therefore, if a program executes for long periods without performing such character I/O, detection of the user's entry of a Control-C may be delayed. The BREAK ON command causes MS-DOS to also check the keyboard for a Control-C at the time of each system call (which slows the system somewhat); the BREAK OFF command disables such extended Control-C checking. The default setting for BREAK is off.

If the BREAK command is entered alone, the current status of MS-DOS's internal BREAK flag is displayed.

Examples

To display the current status of the MS-DOS internal flag for extended Control-C checking, type

```
C>BREAK  <Enter>
```

MS-DOS displays

```
BREAK is off
```

or

```
BREAK is on
```

depending on the status of the BREAK flag.

To enable extended checking for Control-C during disk operations, type

```
C>BREAK ON  <Enter>
```

Messages

BREAK is on

or

BREAK is off

Extended Control-C checking is enabled or disabled, respectively. These messages occur in response to a BREAK status check.

Must specify ON or OFF

An invalid parameter was supplied in a BREAK command.

CHDIR or CD

Change Current Directory

2.0 and later

Internal

Purpose

Changes the current directory or displays the current path of the specified or default disk drive.

Syntax

CHDIR [*drive*:][*path*]

or

CD [*drive*:][*path*]

where:

drive   is the letter of the drive for which the current directory will be changed or displayed, followed by a colon. Note that use of the *drive* parameter does not change the currently active drive.

path   is one or more directory names, separated by backslash characters (\), that define an existing path.

Description

The CHDIR command, when followed by an existing path, is used to set the working directory for the default or specified disk drive.

The *path* parameter consists of the name of an existing directory, optionally followed by the names of existing subdirectories, each separated from the next by a backslash character. If *path* begins with a backslash, CHDIR assumes that the first named directory is a subdirectory of the root directory; otherwise, CHDIR assumes that the first named directory is a subdirectory of the current directory. The special directory name .. , which is an alias for the parent directory of the current directory, can be used as the path.

When CHDIR is entered alone or with only a drive letter followed by a colon, the full path of the current directory for the default or specified drive is displayed.

CD is simply an alias for CHDIR; the two commands are identical.

Examples

To change the current directory for the current (default) disk drive to the path \V2\SOURCE, type

```
C>CD \V2\SOURCE  <Enter>
```

To display the name of the current directory for the disk in drive D, type

```
C>CD D:  <Enter>
```

To return to the parent directory of the current directory, type

```
C>CD ..  <Enter>
```

Messages

Invalid directory
One of the directories in the specified path does not exist.

Invalid drive specification
An invalid drive letter was given or the named drive does not exist in the system.

CHKDSK

Check Disk Status

1.0 and later

External

Purpose

Analyzes the allocation of storage space on a disk and displays a summary report of the space occupied by files and directories.

Syntax

CHKDSK [*drive*:][*pathname*] [/F] [/V]

where:

drive   is the letter of the drive containing the disk to be analyzed, followed by a colon.

pathname   is the location and, optionally, the name of the file(s) to be checked for fragmentation; wildcard characters are permitted in the filename.

/F   repairs errors (versions 2.0 and later).

/V   "verbose mode," reports the name of each file as it is checked (versions 2.0 and later).

Description

The CHKDSK command analyzes the disk directory and file allocation table for consistency and reports any errors. If the /V switch is included in the command line, the name of each file processed is displayed as the disk is being analyzed.

After analyzing the disk, CHKDSK displays a summary of the disk and RAM space used and available. The disk-space report includes

- Total disk space in bytes
- Number of bytes allocated to hidden files
- Number of bytes contained in directories
- Number of bytes contained in user files
- Number of bytes contained in bad (unusable) sectors
- Number of available bytes on the disk

(Hidden files are files that do not appear in a directory listing. A bootable MS-DOS or PC-DOS disk always contains two hidden files — MSDOS.SYS and IO.SYS or IBMDOS.COM and IBMBIO.COM, respectively — that contain the operating system. A volume label, if present, counts as a hidden file. In addition, some application programs create hidden files for copy protection or other purposes.)

Directory errors detected by CHKDSK include

- Invalid pointers to data areas
- Bad file attributes in directory entries

- Damage to a portion of the directory that makes it impossible to check one or more paths
- Damage to an entire directory that makes the files contained in that directory inaccessible

File allocation table (FAT) errors detected by CHKDSK include

- Defective disk sectors in the FAT
- Invalid cluster (disk allocation unit) numbers in the FAT
- Lost clusters
- Cross-linking of files on the same cluster

If the /F switch is included in the command line, CHKDSK will attempt to repair errors in disk allocation and recover as much data as possible. Because repairs usually involve changes to the disk's file allocation table that may cause a loss of information, the user is prompted for confirmation. Lost clusters are collected into files in the root directory with names of the form FILE*nnnn*.CHK.

If the command line contains a file specification, CHKDSK will examine all files that match the specification and report on their fragmentation — that is, on whether or not their sectors are contiguous on the disk. (Fragmented files can degrade the performance of the system because of the time required to move the drive head back and forth across the disk to reach the various parts of the file.) Files on a floppy disk can be collected into contiguous sectors by copying them to an empty floppy disk. Files on a fixed disk can be collected into contiguous sectors by backing them all up to floppy disks, erasing all files and subdirectories on the fixed disk, and then restoring the files from the floppy disk.

Warning: CHKDSK should not be used on a network drive or on a drive created or affected by an ASSIGN, JOIN, or SUBST command.

Examples

To check the disk in the current drive, type

```
C>CHKDSK  <Enter>
```

If CHKDSK finds no errors, a report such as the following is displayed:

```
Volume HARDDISK    created Jun 8, 1986 9:34a

 21204992 bytes total disk space
    38912 bytes in 3 hidden files
   116736 bytes in 53 directories
 17055744 bytes in 715 user files
    20480 bytes in bad sectors
  3973120 bytes available on disk

   655360 bytes total memory
   566576 bytes free
```

Note that the line containing the volume name and creation date does not appear if the disk has not been assigned a volume name.

If CHKDSK finds errors, a message such as the following is displayed:

```
Errors found, F parameter not specified.
Corrections will not be written to disk.

10 lost clusters found in 3 chains.
Convert lost chains to files  (Y/N)?
```

A *Y* response at this point does not convert the lost chains to files; to do this, enter the CHKDSK command again with the /F switch specified.

To correct any allocation errors found by the CHKDSK command, type

```
C>CHKDSK /F  <Enter>
```

In this example, CHKDSK displays its usual report, followed by an error message:

```
Volume HARDDISK    created Jun 8, 1986 9:34a

 21204992 bytes total disk space
    38912 bytes in 3 hidden files
   116736 bytes in 53 directories
 17055744 bytes in 715 user files
    20480 bytes in bad sectors
  3973120 bytes available on disk

   655360 bytes total memory
   566576 bytes free

10 lost clusters found in 3 chains.
Convert lost chains to files (Y/N) ?
```

A *Y* response causes CHKDSK to recover the lost chains of clusters into files in the root directory, giving the files the names FILE0000.CHK, FILE0001.CHK, FILE0002.CHK, and so on. An *N* response causes CHKDSK to free the lost chains of clusters without saving the contents to files.

To check all files in the directory C:\SYSTEM with the extension .COM for fragmentation, type

```
C>CHKDSK C:\SYSTEM\*.COM  <Enter>
```

CHKDSK displays its usual report, followed by a list of fragmented files:

```
Volume HARDDISK    created Jun 8, 1986 9:34a

 21204992 bytes total disk space
    38912 bytes in 3 hidden files
   116736 bytes in 53 directories
 17055744 bytes in 715 user files
    20480 bytes in bad sectors
  3973120 bytes available on disk

   655360 bytes total memory
   566576 bytes free

C:\SYSTEM\ALUSQ.COM
    Contains 2 non-contiguous blocks.

C:\SYSTEM\EJECT.COM
    Contains 4 non-contiguous blocks.
```

Messages

. Does not exist.

or

.. Does not exist.

The **.** (alias for the current directory) or the **..** (alias for the parent directory) entry is missing.

filename Is cross linked on cluster *n*

Two or more files have been assigned the same cluster. Make a copy of both files on another disk and then delete them from the disk containing the error. One or both of the resulting files may contain information belonging to the other file.

x lost clusters found in *y* chains.
Convert lost chains to files (Y/N)?

Clusters have been identified that are not assigned to any existing file. If the /F switch was included in the original command line, respond with *Y* to convert the lost clusters to files in the root directory of the disk with names of the form FILE*nnnn*.CHK. If desired, the recovered clusters can then be returned to the free-disk-space pool by erasing the .CHK files.

Allocation error, size adjusted.

The size of the file indicated in the disk directory is not consistent with the number of clusters allocated to the file. If the /F switch was included in the command line, the file is truncated to the size indicated in the disk directory.

All specified file(s) are contiguous.

The clusters belonging to the specified file(s) are allocated contiguously (without fragmentation).

Cannot CHDIR to *pathname*
tree past this point not processed.
The tree directory structure of the disk being checked cannot be traveled to the specified directory. This message indicates severe damage to the disk's directories or files.

Cannot CHDIR to root
Processing cannot continue.
In traversing the tree directory structure of the disk being checked, CHKDSK was unable to return to the root directory. This message indicates severe damage to the disk's directories or files.

Cannot CHKDSK a Network drive
The drive containing the disk to be checked has been assigned to a network.

Cannot CHKDSK a SUBSTed or ASSIGNed drive
The drive containing the disk to be checked has been substituted or assigned.

Cannot recover . entry, processing continued.
The special directory entry **.** (alias for the current directory) is defective.

Cannot recover .. entry,
Entry has a bad attribute

or

Cannot recover .. entry,
Entry has a bad link

or

Cannot recover .. entry,
Entry has a bad size
The special directory entry **..** (alias for the parent directory of the current directory) is defective due to a bad attribute, link, or size.

CHDIR .. failed, trying alternate method.
While checking the tree structure, CHKDSK was unable to return to the parent directory of the current directory. It will attempt to return to that directory by starting over at the root directory and searching again.

Contains *n* **non-contiguous blocks.**
The clusters assigned to the specified file are not allocated contiguously on the disk.

Directory is joined
CHKDSK cannot process directories that have been joined using the JOIN command. Use the JOIN /D command to unjoin the directories, then run CHKDSK again.

Directory is totally empty, no . or ..
The specified directory does not contain the usual aliases for the current and parent directories. This message indicates severe damage to the disk's directories or files. Delete the directory and recreate it.

Disk error reading FAT *n*

or

Disk error writing FAT *n*

One of the file allocation tables for the disk being checked contains a defective sector. MS-DOS will use the alternate FAT if one is available. It is advisable to copy all the files on the disk containing the defective sector to another disk.

Errors found, F parameter not specified.
Corrections will not be written to disk.

Errors were found on the disk being checked, but the /F switch was not included in the command line.

File allocation table bad drive *X*:

The disk is not an MS-DOS disk. Repeat CHKDSK with the /F option; if this message is displayed again, reformat the disk.

File not found.

CHKDSK was unable to find the specified file.

First cluster number is invalid, entry truncated.

The directory entry for the specified file contains an invalid pointer to the disk's data area. If the /F switch was included in the command line, the file is truncated to a zero-length file.

General Failure error reading drive *X*:

The format of the disk being checked is not compatible with MS-DOS or the disk has not been formatted for use by MS-DOS.

Has invalid cluster, file truncated.

The file directory contains an invalid pointer to the disk's data area. If the /F switch was included in the command line, the file is truncated to a zero-length file.

Incorrect DOS version

The version of CHKDSK is not compatible with the version of MS-DOS that is running.

Insufficient memory
Processing cannot continue.

The computer does not have enough memory to contain the tables necessary for CHKDSK to process the specified disk.

Insufficient room in root directory.
Erase files in root and repeat CHKDSK.

The root directory is full and does not have room for the entries for recovered files. Delete some files from the root directory of the disk being checked and rerun the CHKDSK program.

Invalid current directory
Processing cannot continue.
The directory structure of the disk is so badly damaged that the disk is unusable.

Invalid drive specification
The CHKDSK command contained an invalid disk drive.

Invalid parameter
One of the switches in the command line is invalid.

Invalid sub-directory entry.
The directory name specified in the command line does not exist or is invalid.

Path not found.
One of the directories in the path specified in the command line does not exist or is invalid.

Probable non-DOS disk
Continue (Y/N) ?
The disk being checked was not formatted by MS-DOS or the file allocation table has been severely damaged or destroyed.

Unrecoverable error in directory.
Convert directory to file (Y/N)?
The specified directory is damaged and unusable. If the /F switch was included in the original command line, respond with *Y* to convert the damaged directory to a file in the root directory of the disk with a name of the form FILE*nnnn*.CHK. If desired, the .CHK file can then be deleted. Any files that were previously reached through the damaged directory will be lost.

CLS
Clear Screen

2.0 and later
Internal

Purpose

Clears the video display.

Syntax

CLS

Description

The CLS command clears the video display and displays the current prompt.

In some implementations of MS-DOS, proper operation of the CLS command may require installation of the ANSI.SYS console driver with a *DEVICE=ANSI.SYS* command in the CONFIG.SYS file.

Examples

To clear the screen, type

```
C>CLS  <Enter>
```

To save the ANSI escape sequence used by the CLS command (ESC[2J) into a file named CLEAR.TXT, type

```
C>CLS > CLEAR.TXT  <Enter>
```

COMMAND

1.0 and later

Command Processor

External

Purpose

Loads a secondary copy of the MS-DOS default command processor.

Syntax

COMMAND [*drive*:][*path*] [*device*] [/E:*n*] [/P] [/C *string*]

where:

path	is the name of the directory to be searched for COMMAND.COM when the transient portion needs to be reloaded; a drive letter can be included with versions 2.0 and later.
device	is the name of a character device to be used instead of CON for the command processor's input and output (versions 2.0 and later).
/E:*n*	is the initial size, in bytes, of the command processor's environment block (160–32768, default = 160) (version 3.2).
/P	fixes the newly loaded command processor permanently in memory (versions 2.0 and later).
/C *string*	causes the command processor to behave as a transient program and execute the command or program specified by *string* (versions 2.0 and later).

Description

The command processor is the module of the operating system that is responsible for issuing prompts to the user, interpreting commands, loading and executing transient application programs, and interpreting batch files. The file COMMAND.COM contains the MS-DOS default command processor, or shell. It is ordinarily loaded from the root directory of the system disk when the system is turned on or restarted, unless the SHELL command is used in the CONFIG.SYS file to specify another command processor or an alternate location for COMMAND.COM.

With versions 1.x, COMMAND.COM is invoked by the COMMAND command in response to a shell prompt or within a batch file. A second copy of the resident portion of COMMAND.COM is loaded and the memory occupied by the original resident portion is lost. The second copy of the transient portion simply overlays the original transient portion. (Versions 1.x of COMMAND support no switches or other parameters and any specified in the command line are ignored.) With versions 2.0 and later, the new copy of COMMAND.COM is loaded *in addition to* the parent command processor and serves as a secondary command processor.

The *path* parameter specifies the location of the COMMAND.COM file that is used to reload the transient part of the command processor if it is overlaid by application programs. If absent, *path* defaults to the root directory of the system (startup) disk.

The *device* parameter allows a character device other than CON to be used by the command processor for input and output. For example, use of AUX as the *device* parameter allows a personal computer to be controlled from a terminal attached to a serial port, instead of from the usual built-in keyboard and memory-mapped video display.

The secondary copy of COMMAND.COM ordinarily remains in memory and serves as the active command processor until an EXIT command is entered. If a /P switch is used with the COMMAND command, the new copy of COMMAND.COM is fixed in memory and the EXIT command is disabled. In such cases, the memory occupied by previously loaded copies of COMMAND.COM is simply lost.

The /E:n switch controls the size of the environment block initially allocated for the command processor. The default size of the block is 160 bytes, but the /E:n switch allows the initial allocation to be as large as 32768 bytes. This switch is frequently used when *COMMAND.COM* is included in the SHELL command in the CONFIG.SYS file.

When the /C *string* switch is included in the command line, followed by a string designating a command or program name, the new copy of COMMAND.COM carries out the operation specified by *string* and then exits, returning control to its parent command processor or other program. This option allows a batch file to invoke another batch file and then resume its own execution. (If a batch file names another batch file directly without using COMMAND /C *string* as an intermediary, the first batch file is terminated.) Note that when the /C *string* switch is used in combination with other switches, it must be the last switch in the command line.

A secondary copy of COMMAND.COM always inherits a copy of the environment of the command processor or other program that loaded it. Changes made to the new COMMAND.COM's environment with a SET, PROMPT, or PATH command do not affect the environment of any previously loaded program or command processor.

Examples

To execute the batch file MENU2.BAT from the batch file MENU1.BAT and then resume execution of MENU1.BAT, include the following line in MENU1.BAT:

```
COMMAND /C MENU2
```

To cause COMMAND.COM to be loaded from the directory \SYSTEM on drive C rather than from the root directory and to allocate an initial environment block of 1024 bytes, include the following line in the CONFIG.SYS file:

```
SHELL=C:\SYSTEM\COMMAND.COM C:\SYSTEM /P /E:1024
```

Messages

Bad or missing command interpreter
The file COMMAND.COM is not present in the root directory of the system disk and no SHELL command is present to specify an alternate command processor file or location, or the location specified for COMMAND.COM in a SHELL command is not correct. This message may also be seen if COMMAND.COM is moved from its original location after the system is booted.

Invalid device
The character device specified in the command line is not valid or does not exist.

Invalid environment size specified
The value supplied with the /E:n switch was less than 160 bytes or greater than 32768 bytes.

COMP

IBM

External

Compare Files

Purpose

Compares two files or sets of files. This command is available only with PC-DOS.

Syntax

COMP [*primary*] [*secondary*]

where:

primary   is the name of the file to be compared against and can be preceded by a drive and/or path; wildcard characters are permitted in the filename.

secondary   is the name of the file to be compared with *primary* and can be preceded by a drive and/or path; wildcard characters are permitted in the filename.

Description

The COMP command compares one file or set of files with another. As each pair of files is compared, the program reports whether the files are identical, different in size, or the same size but different in content.

The *primary* and *secondary* parameters can be any combination of drive, path, and filename, optionally including wildcards to allow sets of files to be compared. (With versions 1.x, using wildcards does not cause multiple file comparisons — only the first secondary file whose name matches the first primary filename is compared.) The *primary* parameter generally designates the specific files to be compared; the *secondary* parameter is usually only a drive and/or path, except when the files being compared have different names or extensions.

If both *primary* and *secondary* are omitted from the command line, the COMP program prompts for them interactively. If *primary* is given as a drive or path only, COMP assumes *.* to be the primary file. If *secondary* is given as a drive or path only, COMP compares all files on that drive or path whose filenames match those of the primary files.

The COMP command is included only with PC-DOS. MS-DOS versions 2.0 and later provide a similar function in the FC command, which also displays the differences between files.

Examples

To compare the file MYFILE.DAT on the disk in drive A with the file LEDGER.DAT on the disk in drive B, type

```
C>COMP A:MYFILE.DAT B:LEDGER.DAT  <Enter>
```

To compare all the files in the current directory of the disk in drive A with the corresponding files in the current directory of the disk in drive D, type

```
C>COMP A:*.* D:  <Enter>
```

To compare all the files with the extension .ASM in the directory C:\SOURCE with the corresponding files with extension .BAK on the disk in drive B, type

```
C>COMP C:\SOURCE\*.ASM B:*.BAK  <Enter>
```

Messages

10 mismatches - ending compare
The primary and secondary files are the same size but have more than 10 internal differences. The compare operation on this pair of files is aborted and COMP proceeds to the next pair of files, if any.

filename and *filename*
This informational message shows the full filenames of the two files currently being compared.

Access Denied
An attempt was made to compare a locked file.

Cannot compare file to itself
An attempt was made to compare a file with itself.

Compare error at OFFSET *nn*
File 1 = *nn*
File 2 = *nn*
This informational message itemizes the first 10 differences in data between the two files being compared (if the files are the same size), displaying the file offset and the differing bytes from each file as hexadecimal values.

Compare more files (Y/N)?
After all specified pairs of files have been compared, the COMP program allows the entry of another pair of file specifications. Respond with *Y* or press Enter to continue; respond with *N* to terminate the COMP program.

Enter 2nd file name or drive id
If the secondary filename was not specified in the COMP command, this message prompts the user to enter it (or a path, if the secondary file has the same name as the primary file).

Enter primary file name
If no parameter was entered after COMP, this message prompts the user to enter the primary filename. If a drive or path is specified, COMP assumes *.* for the primary filename.

EOF mark not found
The last byte at the logical end of the file was not a Control-Z character (^Z, or 1AH). This message is commonly seen during comparison of two files that are not ASCII text files, such as executable program files.

Files compare OK

The files being compared were the same length and contained identical data.

File not found

The specified filename was invalid or the file does not exist.

Files are different sizes

The two files being compared have different sizes recorded in the directory. No comparison on the data within the files is attempted.

File sharing conflict

COMP is unable to compare the two current files because one of the files is in use by another process.

Incorrect DOS version

The version of COMP is not compatible with the version of PC-DOS that is running.

Insufficient memory

The available system memory is insufficient to run the COMP program.

Invalid drive specification

The drive specification in *primary* or *secondary* is invalid or does not exist.

Invalid path

The path or directory in *primary* or *secondary* is invalid or does not exist.

Too many files open

No more system file handles are available. Increase the value of the FILES command in the CONFIG.SYS file and restart the system.

CONFIG.SYS

System Configuration File

2.0 and later

Purpose

Allows the user to configure the operating system.

Description

The CONFIG.SYS file is an ASCII text file that MS-DOS processes during initialization (when the system is turned on or restarted). It allows the user to configure certain aspects of the operating system, such as the number of internal disk buffers allocated, the number of files that can be open at one time, the formats for date and currency, and the name and location of the executable file containing the command processor. CONFIG.SYS can also contain commands that extend the system with installable device drivers for terminal emulation, virtual disks or RAMdisks, extended or expanded memory, and other special peripheral devices.

The CONFIG.SYS file can be created or modified with EDLIN or with any other editor or word processor that can produce ordinary ASCII text files (nondocument files) and save them to disk. The CONFIG.SYS file must be in the root directory of the disk that is used to start the operating system in order for it to be processed during system initialization. When changes are made to the CONFIG.SYS file, they do not take effect until the system is restarted.

Commands in the CONFIG.SYS file take the form

command [=] *value*

(Note that the equal sign is optional; any other valid MS-DOS separator [semicolon, tab, or space] can be used instead.) The commands supported are

Command	Action
BREAK	Controls extended checking for Control-C.
BUFFERS	Specifies the number of internal disk-sector buffers available for use by MS-DOS when reading from or writing to a disk.
COUNTRY	Controls date, time, and currency formatting.
DEVICE	Specifies the filename of an installable device driver.
DRIVPARM	Redefines the default characteristics of the resident MS-DOS block device(s) (version 3.2).
FCBS	Specifies the maximum number of simultaneously open file control blocks (versions 3.0 and later).

(more)

Command	Action
FILES	Specifies the maximum number of simultaneously open files controlled by handles.
LASTDRIVE	Sets the highest valid drive letter (versions 3.0 and later).
SHELL	Specifies the filename (and optionally the drive and/or path) of the system command processor.
STACKS	Sets the number and size of stack frames for the system.

Each of these commands is discussed in detail on the following pages.

Message

Unrecognized command in CONFIG.SYS
A command in the CONFIG.SYS file was misspelled, an invalid parameter was used, or a command was included that is not compatible with the version of MS-DOS that is running. Correct the CONFIG.SYS file and restart the system.

CONFIG.SYS: BREAK
Configure Control-C Checking

2.0 and later

Purpose

Sets or clears MS-DOS's internal flag for Control-C checking.

Syntax

BREAK=ON ¦OFF

Description

Pressing Ctrl-C or Ctrl-Break while a program is running ordinarily terminates the program, unless the program itself contains instructions that disable MS-DOS's Control-C handling. As a rule, MS-DOS checks the keyboard for a Control-C only when a character is read from or written to a character device (keyboard, screen, printer, or auxiliary port). Therefore, if a program executes for long periods without performing such character I/O, detection of the user's entry of a Control-C may be delayed. The BREAK=ON command causes MS-DOS to also check the keyboard for a Control-C at the time of each system call (which slows the system somewhat); the BREAK=OFF command disables such extended Control-C checking. The default setting for BREAK is off.

Extended Control-C checking can also be enabled or disabled at the command prompt with the interactive form of the BREAK command whenever the system is running.

Example

To enable extended Control-C checking during MS-DOS disk operations, insert the line

```
BREAK=ON
```

into the CONFIG.SYS file and restart the system.

Message

Unrecognized command in CONFIG.SYS
The setting supplied for the BREAK command was not ON or OFF. Correct the CONFIG.SYS file and restart the system.

CONFIG.SYS: BUFFERS

2.0 and later

Configure Internal Disk Buffers

Purpose

Sets the number of MS-DOS's internal disk buffers.

Syntax

BUFFERS=*nn*

where:

nn   is the number of buffers (1–99, default = 2; default = 3 for IBM PC/AT and compatibles).

Description

MS-DOS maintains a set of internal buffers (sometimes referred to as a disk cache) in which it keeps copies of the sectors most recently read from or written to the disk. Whenever a program requests a disk read, MS-DOS first searches the disk buffers to determine whether a copy of the disk sector containing the required data is already present in RAM. If the sector is found, the actual disk access is bypassed. This technique can significantly improve the overall performance of the disk operating system.

By using the BUFFERS command in the CONFIG.SYS file, the user can control the number of buffers in MS-DOS's disk cache. The default number of buffers is 2 for an IBM PC, PC/XT, or compatible and 3 for an IBM PC/AT or compatible. The optimum number of buffers varies, depending in part on the characteristics and types of the system disk drives, the types of application programs used on the system, the number and levels of subdirectories in the file structure, and the amount of RAM in the system.

If the system has only floppy-disk drives, the default setting of 2 buffers is sufficient. If the system includes a fixed disk, increasing the number of buffers to 10 or so typically speeds up overall system operation. Configuring the system for too many buffers, however, can actually degrade the performance of the system.

Increases in the number of buffers should be tailored to the type of application most frequently used. For example, allocation of extra disk buffers will not improve the performance of programs that use primarily sequential file access but may considerably enhance the execution times of programs that perform random access on a relatively small number of disk records (such as the index for a database file). In addition, if the system has many subdirectories organized in several levels, increasing the number of buffers can significantly increase the speed of disk operations.

The ideal number of buffers for a given system is difficult to predict because of the interactions between the access time of the disk, the speed of the central processing unit, and the

RAM requirements and disk access behavior of the mix of application programs. However, a reasonably optimal number of buffers can be quickly estimated experimentally by increasing the number of buffers in increments of five or so, restarting the system, performing some simple timing tests on the most frequently used application programs, and observing at what number of buffers system performance begins to degrade.

Example

To allocate 20 internal disk buffers, insert the line

```
BUFFERS=20
```

into the CONFIG.SYS file and restart the system.

Message

Unrecognized command in CONFIG.SYS
The value supplied for the BUFFERS command was not a number in the range 1 through 99.

CONFIG.SYS: COUNTRY

2.1 and later

Set Country Code

Purpose

Configures MS-DOS's internationalization support for a specific country.

Syntax

COUNTRY=*nnn*

where:

nnn   is the international telephone dialing prefix for the country (001–999, default = 001):

Australia	061
Belgium	032
Denmark	045
Finland	358
France	033
Israel	972
Italy	039
Netherlands	031
Norway	047
Spain	034
Sweden	046
Switzerland	041
United Kingdom	044
USA	001
West Germany	049

Note: In versions 2.x (except 2.0), *nnn* is 01 through 99. Individual computer manufacturers determine the specific codes supported by their versions of MS-DOS.

Description

The COUNTRY command enables the user to tailor MS-DOS's date, time, and currency displays for a specific country. This capability, termed internationalization support, is achieved through use of a country code that controls the contents of the table MS-DOS uses to format these displays (including numeric separators). (The internationalization table is made available to application programs through Interrupt 21H Function 38H.) Beginning with version 3.0, PC-DOS also supports the COUNTRY command.

Example

In West Germany, the format for the date is *dd.mm.yy*. To configure MS-DOS to use this date format, insert the line

```
COUNTRY=049
```

into the CONFIG.SYS file and restart the system.

Message

Invalid country code
The specified country code is not supported by the version of MS-DOS that is running.

CONFIG.SYS: DEVICE

2.0 and later

Install Device Driver

Purpose

Loads and links an installable device driver into the operating system during initialization.

Syntax

DEVICE=[*drive*:][*path*]*filename* [*options*]

where:

filename   is the name of the device-driver file, optionally preceded by a drive and/or path.

options   specifies any switches or other parameters needed by the device driver; the DEVICE command itself has no switches.

Description

Device drivers are the modules of the operating system that control the interface between the operating system and peripheral devices such as disk drives, magnetic-tape drives, CRT terminals, and printers.

As supplied, MS-DOS already contains device drivers for the keyboard, video display, serial port, printer, real-time clock, and disk devices. Device drivers for additional peripheral devices can be linked into the operating system by adding a DEVICE command to the CONFIG.SYS file, placing the file containing the device driver on the system startup disk (or at the location specified by the *drive*: and/or *path* parameter), and restarting the computer.

If a drive other than the one containing the system disk is named as the location of the device driver, that drive must either be accessible via the system's default disk driver or be a drive configured with a previous DEVICE command.

Most OEM implementations of version 3.2 provide three installable device drivers: ANSI.SYS, which allows the video display and keyboard to be controlled by ANSI standard escape sequences; DRIVER.SYS, which supports external disk drives; and RAMDRIVE.SYS (VDISK.SYS with PC-DOS), which uses a portion of the machine's RAM to emulate a disk drive. *See* USER COMMANDS: ANSI.SYS; DRIVER.SYS; RAMDRIVE.SYS; VDISK.SYS.

Many manufacturers of add-on products for MS-DOS machines (such as network interfaces or Lotus/Intel/Microsoft Expanded Memory boards) also supply installable device drivers for use with their hardware. For information concerning these drivers, see the product manufacturer's user's manual.

Examples

To load the ANSI standard console driver, insert the line

```
DEVICE=ANSI.SYS
```

into the CONFIG.SYS file, place the file ANSI.SYS in the root directory of the system disk, and restart the system.

To load the RAMDRIVE.SYS driver located in the \DRIVERS directory on the disk in drive A, configuring it for 1024 KB in extended memory, insert the line

```
DEVICE=A:\DRIVERS\RAMDRIVE.SYS 1024 /E
```

into the CONFIG.SYS file and restart the system.

Messages

Bad or missing *filename*

The filename specified in the DEVICE command is invalid or does not exist or the file does not contain a valid MS-DOS installable device driver.

Sector size too large in file *filename*

The specified installable device driver uses a sector size that is larger than the sector size used by any of the system's default disk drivers. Such a driver cannot be used because MS-DOS's internal disk buffers will not be large enough to hold a sector read from the device.

CONFIG.SYS: DRIVPARM

3.2

Set Block-Device Parameters

Purpose

Alters the system's list of characteristics for an existing block device.

Syntax

DRIVPARM=/D:n [/C] [/F:n] [/H:n] [/N] [/S:n] [/T:n]

where:

/D:n	is the drive number (0–255; 0 = A, 1 = B, etc.) and must always be the first switch in the command line.
/C	indicates that the device provides door-lock-status support.
/F:n	is a form-factor index from the following table (default = 2 if the DRIVPARM command is present but this switch is omitted):

0	320 KB or 360 KB
1	1.2 MB
2	720 KB
3	8-inch single-density floppy disk
4	8-inch double-density floppy disk
5	Fixed disk
6	Tape drive
7	Other

/H:n	is the number of read/write heads (1–99).
/N	indicates that the block device is not removable.
/S:n	is the number of sectors per track (1–99).
/T:n	is the number of tracks per side (1–999).

Note: The DRIVPARM command must not be used to specify device characteristics that the device driver is not capable of supporting.

Description

Whenever the device driver for a block device such as a disk drive or magnetic-tape drive performs input or output, it refers to an internal table of characteristics for the device that allows it to convert logical addresses to physical addresses. The DRIVPARM command modifies the default MS-DOS values in the table of characteristics for a particular block device during system initialization (when the computer is turned on or restarted). Multiple DRIVPARM commands, each modifying the characteristics of a different block device, can be included in the same CONFIG.SYS file. Any characteristics not specifically altered in the DRIVPARM command for a particular device retain their original values, except for /F:*n*, which defaults to 2.

DRIVPARM commands that alter the characteristics for block devices controlled by *installable* device drivers must follow the DEVICE command that loads the device driver itself.

Example

Assume that drive B is a floppy-disk drive originally configured for 40 tracks with 8 sectors per track. To reconfigure the drive to read or write 80 tracks of 9 sectors each, insert the line

```
DRIVPARM=/D:1 /S:9 /T:80
```

into the CONFIG.SYS file and restart the system. For this command to be valid the drive must be capable of supporting these parameters.

Message

Unrecognized command in CONFIG.SYS
An invalid parameter was specified in a DRIVPARM command.

CONFIG.SYS: FCBS

3.0 and later

Set Maximum Open Files Using File Control Blocks (FCBs)

Purpose

Configures the maximum number of files that can be open concurrently using file control blocks (FCBs). This command has no practical effect unless either the file-sharing support module SHARE.EXE or networking support has been loaded.

Syntax

FCBS=m,p

where:

m is the maximum number of files that can be open concurrently using FCBs (1–255, default = 4).

p is the number of files opened with FCBs that are protected against automatic closure (0– m, default = 0).

Description

MS-DOS supports two methods of file access: file control blocks and file handles. A file control block is a data structure that stores information about an open file. It resides inside an application program's memory space and is accessed by both MS-DOS and the application. (*See* USER COMMANDS: CONFIG.SYS: FILES for information on file handles.)

In a network environment, a large number of active FCBs or improper use of FCBs by an application can seriously degrade the performance of the network as a whole. Consequently, MS-DOS versions 3.0 and later provide the FCBS command to enable the user to limit the number of files that can be open concurrently using FCBs if either the file-sharing support module SHARE.EXE (*see* USER COMMANDS: SHARE) or network support has been loaded. If an application program attempts to exceed the specified number of files, MS-DOS closes the file with the least recently used FCB.

The p parameter in the FCBS command line allows the user to protect files from unilateral closure by MS-DOS. The value of p is the number of files, counting from the first file opened using an FCB, that cannot be closed automatically.

If the current value of FCBS is *4,0* (the default) when the file-sharing module SHARE.EXE or network support is loaded, MS-DOS automatically increases the maximum number of files that can be open concurrently to 16 and the number of files protected against automatic closure to 8. (When multiple FCBs refer to the same file, the file is counted only once.)

Examples

To set the maximum number of files that can be concurrently open using FCBs to 10 and protect none of the FCB-opened files against automatic closure by MS-DOS, insert the line

```
FCBS=10,0
```

into the CONFIG.SYS file and restart the system.

To set the maximum number of files that can be concurrently open using FCBs to 8 but protect the first 4 FCB-opened files against automatic closure by MS-DOS, insert the line

```
FCBS=8,4
```

into the CONFIG.SYS file and restart the system.

Message

Unrecognized command in CONFIG.SYS
An invalid number was specified as one of the parameters in the FCBS command.

CONFIG.SYS: FILES

2.0 and later

Set Maximum Open Files Using Handles

Purpose

Configures the maximum number of files and/or devices that can be open concurrently using file handles.

Syntax

FILES=*n*

where:

n   is the maximum number of files and devices that can be open concurrently using file handles (8–255, default = 8).

Description

MS-DOS supports two methods of file access: file handles and file control blocks (FCBs). During initialization, MS-DOS allocates a data structure that holds information about files and/or devices opened with the handle, or extended-file-management, function calls. This structure resides inside the operating system's memory space and is accessed only by MS-DOS. (*See* USER COMMANDS: CONFIG.SYS: FCBS.) The default size of this data structure allows 8 files and/or devices to be open concurrently using the file-handle functions. The FILES command enables the user to change the size of the data structure. (Note that increasing the size of the data structure decreases the amount of RAM available to application programs.)

The FILES command controls the maximum number of files and/or devices opened with handles for *all* active processes in the system combined. The limit on the number of files and/or devices opened for a single process using handles is 20 or the number of entries in the allocated data structure, whichever is less. Five of the 20 possible handles for a given process are automatically assigned to standard input, standard output, standard error, standard auxiliary, and standard list. However, since standard input, standard output, and standard error all default to the same device (CON), only three of the allocated data-structure entries are actually expended. In addition, the preassigned standard device handles for a process can be closed and reused for other files and devices, if necessary.

Example

To set the maximum number of files and/or devices that can be concurrently open using the handle functions to 20, insert the line

```
FILES=20
```

into the CONFIG.SYS file and restart the system.

Message

Unrecognized command in CONFIG.SYS
An invalid number was specified in the FILES command.

CONFIG.SYS: LASTDRIVE
3.0 and later

Set Highest Logical Drive

Purpose

Defines the highest letter that MS-DOS will recognize as a disk-drive code.

Syntax

LASTDRIVE=*drive*

where:

drive   is a single letter (A–Z).

Description

MS-DOS block devices (floppy-disk drives, fixed-disk drives, and magnetic-tape drives) are referred to by logical drive codes consisting of a single letter from A through Z. In most MS-DOS systems, drives A and B are floppy-disk drives, drive C is a fixed disk, and drives D and above are such devices as additional fixed disks, RAMdisks, or network volumes. In some cases, a single physical drive (such as a very large fixed disk) is partitioned into two or more logical drives, each of which is assigned a drive letter.

MS-DOS validates the drive code in a command or filename before carrying out a command. In the default case, MS-DOS recognizes a maximum of five drives (A–E), depending on the total number of default devices and devices incorporated into the system using installable device drivers. (MS-DOS does not consider a drive letter valid unless it refers to a physical or logical device.) The LASTDRIVE command configures MS-DOS to accept additional drive codes, to a total of 26 (A–Z). This also makes it possible to use fictitious drive letters with the SUBST command to assign a drive letter to a subdirectory.

If the letter code for a LASTDRIVE command specifies fewer drives than are physically present in the system (including installed device drivers), MS-DOS uses the actual number of physical drives.

Example

To configure MS-DOS to recognize a maximum of eight logical disk drives, insert the line

```
LASTDRIVE=H
```

into the CONFIG.SYS file and restart the system.

Message

Unrecognized command in CONFIG.SYS
An illegal value was specified in the LASTDRIVE command.

CONFIG.SYS: SHELL

Specify Command Processor

Purpose

Defines the name and, optionally, the location of the file that contains the operating system's command processor.

Syntax

SHELL=[*drive*:][*path*]*filename* [*options*]

where:

filename	is the name of the file containing the command processor, optionally preceded by a drive and/or path.
options	specifies any switches and other parameters needed by the designated command processor; the SHELL command itself has no switches.

Description

The command processor, or shell, is the user's interface to the operating system. It is responsible for parsing and carrying out the user's commands, including the loading and execution of other programs from the disk. MS-DOS uses the SHELL command in the CONFIG.SYS file to locate and load the command interpreter for the system during its initialization process.

The default shell for MS-DOS is the file COMMAND.COM. This file is loaded by MS-DOS from the root directory of the system disk if no SHELL command is found in the CONFIG.SYS file or if no CONFIG.SYS file exists.

The most common use of the SHELL command is simply to advise MS-DOS that COMMAND.COM is stored in a location other than the root directory; MS-DOS then sets the COMSPEC variable in the environment block to COMMAND.COM, preceded by the location specified in the SHELL command. (This can be verified by typing the SET command at the command prompt.) Another common use of SHELL is to specify switches or other parameters for COMMAND.COM itself (*see* USER COMMANDS: COMMAND).

Example

To specify the file VISUAL.COM in the root directory of drive C as the system's command processor, insert the line

```
SHELL=C:\VISUAL.COM
```

into the CONFIG.SYS file and restart the system.

Message

Bad or missing command interpreter
The path or filename in the SHELL command is invalid or the file does not exist.

CONFIG.SYS: STACKS

3.2

Configure Internal Stacks

Purpose

Defines the number and size of stacks for system interrupt handlers.

Syntax

STACKS=*number,size*

where:

number   is the number of stacks allocated for use by interrupt handlers (8–64, default = 9).

size   is the size of each stack in bytes (32–512, default = 128).

Description

Each time certain hardware interrupts occur (02H, 08–0EH, 70H, and 72–77H), MS-DOS version 3.2 switches to an internal stack before transferring control to the handler that will service the interrupt. In the case of nested interrupts, MS-DOS checks to ensure that both interrupts do not get the same stack. After the interrupt has been processed, the stack is released. This protects the stacks owned by application programs or system device drivers from overflowing when several interrupts occur in rapid succession.

The STACKS command configures the number and size of internal stacks available for interrupt handling and thus controls the number of interrupts that can exist only partially processed while still allowing another interrupt to occur.

The *number* parameter sets the number of internal stacks to be allocated; *number* must be in the range 8 through 64. The *size* parameter is the number of bytes allocated per stack frame; *size* must be in the range 32 through 512.

If too many interrupts occur too quickly and the pool of internal stack frames is exhausted, the system halts with the message *Internal Stack Error.* Increasing the *number* parameter in the STACKS command usually corrects the problem.

Example

To configure 10 stacks of 256 bytes each for use by interrupt handlers, insert the line

```
STACKS=10,256
```

into the CONFIG.SYS file and restart the system.

Message

Unrecognized command in CONFIG.SYS
An invalid number was specified in the STACKS command.

COPY
Copy File or Device

1.0 and later

Internal

Purpose

Copies one or more files from one disk, directory, or filename to another. Can also copy files to or from character devices.

Syntax

COPY *source* [/A] [/B] [+*source* [/A] [/B]...] [*destination*] [/A] [/B] [/V]

where:

source   is the names of the file(s) to be copied, optionally preceded by a drive and/or path; wildcard characters are permitted in filenames. The source can also be a device.

destination   is the location and, optionally, the name(s) for the copied file(s) and can be preceded by a drive; wildcard characters are permitted in the filename. The destination can also be a device.

/A   indicates that the previous file is an ASCII text file.

/B   indicates that the previous file is a binary file.

/V   performs read-after-write verification of destination file(s).

Description

The COPY command copies one or more source files to one or more destination files. When multiple files are copied, the name of each source file is displayed as it is processed. The COPY command can also be used to send the contents of a file to a character device or to copy input from a character device into a file.

The *source* parameter identifies the file or files to be copied. It can consist of any combination of drive, path, and filename or it can be a device name. If a path without a filename is specified, all files in the named directory are copied. Several source files can be concatenated into a single destination file by placing a + operator between their names; if the source filename contains a wildcard but the destination name does not, all the source files are concatenated into the specified destination.

Warning: When multiple source files are concatenated into a destination file with the same name as one of the source files, that filename should be specified as the *first* source file. Otherwise, the contents of the source file will be destroyed before the file is copied.

When a device is specified as the source, it is usually the console (CON), for copying keyboard input to a file or another device. Keyboard input is terminated by pressing Ctrl-Z or F6 (on IBM PCs or compatibles) and then the Enter key.

The *destination* parameter also can consist of any combination of drive, path, and filename or be a device name. Unless the source files are being renamed as part of the operation, *destination* is usually simply a drive and/or path specifying where to place the copied files. If no destination is specified, the source file is copied to a file with the same name in the current directory of the default disk drive; if the source file in this case is itself in the current directory of the current drive, an error message is displayed and the copy operation is aborted. If files are being concatenated and no destination is specified, the source files are copied sequentially into one file in the current directory with the same name as the first source file. If the first source file already exists, the second file and any additional specified files are appended sequentially to the first source file.

The /A and /B switches control the manner in which the COPY command operates on a file. Both switches affect the file specification immediately preceding them and any subsequent file specifications in the command until another /A or /B switch is encountered, at which point the new /A or /B switch takes effect for the file immediately preceding it and for any subsequent files.

The /A switch indicates that a file is an ASCII text file. When the /A switch is applied to a source file, the file is copied up to, but not including, the first Control-Z (^Z) character in the file. When the /A switch is applied to a destination file, a Control-Z character is appended by the COPY command as the last character of the new file.

The /B switch indicates a binary file. When /B is applied to a source file, the exact number of bytes in the original file are copied without regard to Control-Z or any other control characters. When the /B switch is applied to a destination file, no Control-Z character is appended to the newly created file.

The default values for the /A and /B switches for file-to-file copies are /A when source files are being concatenated and /B otherwise. When a file is being copied to or from a character device, the /A switch is the default.

The /V switch causes a read-after-write verification of each block of the destination file. Its effect is equivalent to that of the VERIFY ON command. No comparison is made between the source and destination files — the /V switch simply causes MS-DOS to verify that the destination file has been written correctly.

Examples

To copy the file REPORT.TXT from the root directory of the disk in drive B to a file named FINAL.RPT in the \WP\DOCS directory on the current drive, type

```
C>COPY B:\REPORT.TXT \WP\DOCS\FINAL.RPT  <Enter>
```

To make a copy of the file A:\V2\SOURCE\MENUMGR.C in the current directory of the current drive, type

```
C>COPY A:\V2\SOURCE\MENUMGR.C  <Enter>
```

To copy all files with the extension .DOC in the current directory of the disk in drive A to files with the same filenames but a .TXT extension in the current directory of the current drive, type

```
C>COPY A:*.DOC *.TXT  <Enter>
```

To combine the files PROLOG.C, MENUMGR.C, and EPILOG.C in the current directory of the current drive into a single file named VISUAL.C in the current directory of the current drive, type

```
C>COPY PROLOG.C+MENUMGR.C+EPILOG.C VISUAL.C  <Enter>
```

To append the files MENUMGR.C and EPILOG.C to an existing file named PROLOG.C in the current directory of the current drive, type

```
C>COPY PROLOG.C+MENUMGR.C+EPILOG.C  <Enter>
```

To copy the file MENUMGR.MAP in the current directory of the current drive to the system printer, type

```
C>COPY MENUMGR.MAP PRN  <Enter>
```

To copy input from the keyboard (CON) to a file named MENU.BAT in the current directory of the current drive, type

```
C>COPY CON MENU.BAT  <Enter>
```

Text subsequently entered from the keyboard is placed into the file MENU.BAT until a Ctrl-Z or F6 is pressed.

To copy all files in the \MEMOS directory on the current drive to the \ARCHIVE directory on the disk in drive B, type

```
C>COPY \MEMOS\*.* B:\ARCHIVE  <Enter>
```

or

```
C>COPY \MEMOS B:\ARCHIVE  <Enter>
```

Messages

n File(s) copied
This informational message is displayed at the completion of a COPY command and indicates the total number of source files processed.

Cannot do binary reads from a device
The COPY command specified a copy from a character device in binary mode. Reenter the command without a /B switch.

Content of destination lost before copy
One of the source files specified as a destination file was overwritten prior to completion of the copy. When the destination name is the same as one of the source names, that file should be specified as the first source file.

File cannot be copied onto itself
The source directory and filename of a file being copied are the same as the destination directory and filename.

File not found
A file specified in the COPY command is invalid or does not exist.

Invalid directory
A directory specified in the COPY command is invalid or does not exist.

CTTY

Assign Standard Input/Output Device

Purpose

Specifies the character device to be used as standard input and output.

Syntax

CTTY *device*

where:

device   is the logical character-device name.

Description

MS-DOS ordinarily uses the computer's built-in keyboard and screen (CON) as standard input and output. The CTTY command allows another character device to be assigned instead.

CTTY allows MS-DOS commands to be issued from a terminal attached to the computer's serial port or from another custom device with a screen and keyboard. Although PRN and NUL are valid MS-DOS device names, they should not be used with this command, as they have no input capability.

Programs that do not use MS-DOS function calls to perform their input and output will not be affected by the CTTY command. Microsoft BASIC is an example of such a program.

Examples

To use a terminal connected to the serial port as standard input and output for programs, type

```
C>CTTY AUX   <Enter>
```

To reinstate the normal keyboard and video display (CON) as standard input and output for programs, type

```
C>CTTY CON   <Enter>
```

on the currently assigned console device.

Message

Invalid device
The specified device is not a legal character-device name or does not exist in the system.

DATE

Set Date

Purpose

Sets or displays the system date.

Syntax

DATE *mm-dd-yy*

or

DATE *mm/dd/yy*

or

DATE *mm.dd.yy*   (versions 3.0 and later)

where:

mm	is the month (1–12).
dd	is the day (1–31).
yy	is the year (80–99 or 1980–1999; 80–79 or 1980–2079 with versions 3.0 and later).

Description

All computers that run MS-DOS have as part of their hardware configuration a timer, or clock, that maintains the current system date and time. Among other uses, the current date and time are inserted into a file's directory entry when the file is created or modified.

The DATE command allows the user to display or modify the current date that is being maintained by the system's real-time clock. The command is executed automatically by MS-DOS when the system is initialized, unless there is an AUTOEXEC.BAT file on the system disk, in which case DATE is executed only if it is included in the file.

A date entered using the DATE command does not permanently change the system date; the newly entered date will be lost when the system is turned off or reset. On IBM PC/ATs and compatibles, which have a built-in battery-backed clock/calendar, the system setup program (found on the Diagnostics for IBM Personal Computer AT disk or equivalent) must be used to permanently alter the date stored in the machine. On IBM PCs, PC/XTs, and compatibles equipped with add-on cards containing battery-backed clock/calendar circuitry, it is generally necessary to run a time/date installation program (included with the card) when the system is turned on to set the system date and time from the clock/calendar on the card. The DATE command usually has no effect on these card-mounted clock/calendars.

The order of the day, month, and year in the DATE command depends on the country code, which is set with the COUNTRY command in the CONFIG.SYS file. The format shown here is for the USA.

Examples

To set the system date to October 15, 1987, type

```
C>DATE 10-15-87  <Enter>
```

or

```
C>DATE 10/15/87  <Enter>
```

or

```
C>DATE 10.15.87  <Enter>
```

To display the current system date, type

```
C>DATE  <Enter>
```

and MS-DOS will respond in the form

```
Current date is Thu 10-15-1987
Enter new date (mm-dd-yy):
```

To leave the date unchanged, press the Enter key.

Messages

Current date is *day mm-dd-yyyy*
Enter new date (mm-dd-yy):
This informational message and prompt are displayed when MS-DOS is started and there is no AUTOEXEC.BAT file on the system disk, when the DATE command is entered alone, or when the DATE command is included in the AUTOEXEC.BAT file.

Invalid date
Enter new date (mm-dd-yy):
The date entered in the command line or in response to the prompt from the DATE command was not formatted properly or was invalid.

DEL or ERASE

Delete File

1.0 and later

Internal

Purpose

Deletes a file or set of files. DEL and ERASE are synonymous.

Syntax

DEL [*drive*:][*path*] *filename*

or

ERASE [*drive*:][*path*] *filename*

where:

filename   is the name of the file(s) to be deleted, optionally preceded by a drive and/or path; wildcard characters are permitted in the filename.

Description

The DEL command marks the directory entry for the specified file as deleted and frees the disk sectors occupied by the file. If the command line ends with *.* or a directory name (including the special directory names . and ..), MS-DOS prompts the user for confirmation before deleting all the files in the current or specified directory. Note that in the case of a directory name, the directory itself is not removed; only the files within it are deleted.

Warning: If the filename specification begins with an * wildcard and the extension is also * (for example, *xyz.*), DEL interprets the specification as *.* and prompts the user for confirmation before deleting all files from the current or specified directory.

Examples

To delete the file HELLO.C from the current directory on the current drive, type

```
C>DEL HELLO.C  <Enter>
```

To delete all files with the extension .OBJ from the \SOURCE directory on the disk in drive D, type

```
C>DEL D:\SOURCE\*.OBJ  <Enter>
```

To delete all files from the current directory on the current drive, type

```
C>DEL *.*  <Enter>
```

or

```
C>DEL .  <Enter>
```

In this case, MS-DOS will prompt for confirmation that all files should be deleted.

To delete all files from the directory \WORD\LETTERS on the current drive, type

```
C>DEL \WORD\LETTERS  <Enter>
```

Again, MS-DOS will prompt for confirmation that all files should be deleted.

Messages

Access denied
The specified file is read-only. Use the ATTRIB command with the –R switch to remove the file's read-only status.

Are you sure (Y/N)?
This message prompts the user for confirmation if the command would delete all files in a directory (if the command line ends with a directory name or *.*). Respond with *Y* to delete all files in the directory; respond with *N* to terminate the command.

File not found
The filename in the command is invalid or the file does not exist in the specified directory.

Invalid directory
One of the directories named in the file specification is invalid or does not exist.

Invalid drive specification
The drive code in the file specification is invalid or the named drive does not exist in the system.

DIR

Display Directory

1.0 and later

Internal

Purpose

Displays a list of a directory's files and subdirectories.

Syntax

DIR [*drive*:][*path*][*filename*] [/P] [/W]

where:

filename   is the name of the file, optionally preceded by a drive and/or path, whose
directory entry is to be displayed; wildcard characters are permitted.
/P   causes a pause after each screen page of display.
/W   causes a wide display of filenames formatted five across.

Description

The DIR command displays information about the files in a directory. It also displays information about the volume name of the disk that contains the directory, the total number of files and subdirectories in the directory, and the amount of free space remaining on the disk.

The normal format of the DIR command's output is

```
Volume in drive C is HARDDISK
 Directory of  C:\ASM
.            <DIR>      9-19-85   7:09p
..           <DIR>      9-19-85   7:09p
LIB          <DIR>      9-17-86  11:31p
SOURCE       <DIR>      9-17-86  11:31p
AT86     EXE    41146   5-13-85   5:18p
CREF     EXE    15028  10-16-85   4:00a
DEBUG    COM    15552   3-07-85   1:43p
EXE2BIN  EXE     2816   3-07-85   1:43p
EXEMOD   EXE    11034  10-16-85   4:00a
EXEPACK  EXE    10848  10-16-85   4:00a
LIB      EXE    28716  10-16-85   4:00a
LINK     EXE    43988  10-16-85   4:00a
MAKE     EXE    24300  10-16-85   4:00a
MAPSYM   EXE    18026  10-16-85   4:00a
MASM     EXE    85566  10-16-85   4:00a
SYMDEB   EXE    37021  10-16-85   4:00a
T86      EXE    49024  12-06-84   4:03p
       17 File(s)   4022272 bytes free
```

The first line shows the volume label of the disk that contains the directory being displayed; the second line gives the full pathname of the directory. The subsequent lines are the names of the files and subdirectories within the current or specified directory. Each entry includes the time and date the file or subdirectory was created or last modified.

Files are shown with their exact size in bytes; directories are shown with the symbol <DIR>. If the directory being listed is not the root directory of the disk, it always contains the two special directory entries . and .., which are aliases for the current directory and the parent directory, respectively. These aliases are included in the total file count in the last line of the display.

Subsets of the files and subdirectories in the current or specified directory of the current or specified drive can be listed by including a filename with wildcards in the command line. For example, the filename *.DOC will cause DIR to list only the files with a .DOC extension.

If the command line ends with a drive or path, DIR automatically appends an *.*, causing all files and subdirectories in the current or specified directory of the current or specified drive to be listed. If a filename is included but no extension is given, DIR appends a .* to the filename, causing all files with that name to be listed, regardless of their extension. If a filename ending with a . is included, nothing is appended and all matching subdirectories and filenames without extensions are listed.

The /P switch causes a pause in the display after each screen page (23 lines plus a message). The listing resumes when the user presses a key.

The /W switch causes the list to be in a more compact format by omitting size and date/time information and by displaying the filenames five across:

```
Volume in drive C is HARDDISK
Directory of  C:\ASM
.              ..             LIB            SOURCE         AT86      EXE
CREF     EXE   DEBUG   COM   EXE2BIN  EXE   EXEMOD   EXE   EXEPACK   EXE
LIB      EXE   LINK    EXE   MAKE     EXE   MAPSYM   EXE   MASM      EXE
SYMDEB   EXE   T86     EXE
        17 File(s)   4022272 bytes free
```

When the /W form of the listing is displayed, subdirectories are not easily distinguished from files because the <DIR> symbol is not shown.

Examples

To list all files in the current directory on the current drive, type

```
C>DIR   <Enter>
```

To list all files in the current directory on the disk in drive B, type

```
C>DIR B:   <Enter>
```

or

```
C>DIR B:*.*   <Enter>
```

To list all files in the directory \SOURCE on the current drive, type

```
C>DIR \SOURCE  <Enter>
```

or

```
C>DIR \SOURCE\*.*  <Enter>
```

To list all files with the extension .OBJ in the \LIB directory on the disk in drive D, type

```
C>DIR D:\LIB\*.OBJ  <Enter>
```

To list all files in the parent directory of the current directory on the current drive, type

```
C>DIR ..  <Enter>
```

To list all files in the current directory on the current drive, sorted by filename and extension, type

```
C>DIR ¦ SORT  <Enter>
```

To list all files in the current directory on the current drive, sorted by extension, type

```
c>DIR ¦ SORT /+10  <Enter>
```

The */+10* instructs SORT to sort the directory entries starting at the tenth column, which is the first column of the filename extension.

To list the subdirectories and files without extensions in the current directory, type

```
C>DIR *.  <Enter>
```

To print the directory on an attached printer instead of displaying it on the screen, type

```
C>DIR > PRN  <Enter>
```

To make a copy of the directory in a file called FILES.TXT, type

```
C>DIR > FILES.TXT  <Enter>
```

Messages

File not found
A filename was included in the command line and no matching files were found.

Invalid directory
An element of the path included in the command line does not exist.

Invalid drive specification
The specified drive is invalid or is not present in the system.

Strike a key when ready...
If the DIR command includes the /P switch, the display is suspended after each 23 lines and this message prompts the user to press a key to see the next screenful of entries.

DISKCOMP

Compare Floppy Disks

3.2

External

Purpose

Compares two entire floppy disks on a sector-by-sector basis and reports any differences. This command was included with PC-DOS beginning with version 1.0. To compare individual files, *see* USER COMMANDS: COMP; FC.

Syntax

DISKCOMP [*drive1*:] [*drive2*:] [/1] [/8]

where:

drive1	is the drive containing the first disk to be compared.
drive2	is the drive containing the second disk to be compared.
/1	compares only the first sides of the disks.
/8	compares only the first eight sectors of each track.

Description

The DISKCOMP command compares the physical sectors of one floppy disk with those of another. The *drive1* and *drive2* parameters designate the drives holding the two disks to be compared; the drives should always be of the same type. If *drive2* is omitted, DISKCOMP uses the current drive. If both *drive1* and *drive2* are omitted or are identical, DISKCOMP performs the comparison using a single drive, prompting the user to swap disks as required.

Ordinarily, DISKCOMP determines the disk format by inspecting the disk in *drive1*. The /1 and /8 switches override this check so that only one side of the disks or only the first eight sectors of each track are compared, regardless of the actual format of the disks.

If all the sectors on all the tracks are identical, DISKCOMP displays the message *Compare OK.* If differences are found, DISKCOMP reports them by issuing a message that includes the numbers of the track and disk side (read/write head) where the differences occur. Because DISKCOMP works at the level of the disks' physical sectors and is ignorant of the control areas and file structures imposed on a disk by MS-DOS, it also reports as errors bad sectors that were marked during the FORMAT process.

When DISKCOMP finishes comparing two disks, it displays a prompt that allows the user to choose between comparing another pair of disks and returning to the MS-DOS command level.

DISKCOMP cannot be used with a network drive or with a drive created or affected by an ASSIGN, JOIN, or SUBST command, nor can it be used with fixed disks.

Return Codes

0   Compared disks were identical.
1   Differences were found between the compared disks.
2   DISKCOMP was terminated with a Control-C.
3   Bad sector was found on one of the disks being compared.
4   Initialization error was encountered: not enough memory, syntax error in command line, or invalid drive specified in command line.

Note: Return codes are not present in the PC-DOS version of DISKCOMP.

Examples

To compare the disk in drive A with the disk in drive B, type

```
C>DISKCOMP A: B:   <Enter>
```

To compare two disks using only drive A, type

```
C>DISKCOMP A: A:   <Enter>
```

To compare only the first side of the disk in drive A with the first side of the disk in drive B, type

```
C>DISKCOMP A: B: /1   <Enter>
```

To compare only the first eight sectors of each track on one side of one disk with the first eight sectors of each track on one side of another disk using only drive A, type

```
C>DISKCOMP A: A: /1 /8   <Enter>
```

Messages

**Cannot DISKCOMP to or from
an ASSIGNed or SUBSTed drive**
One of the specified drives has been affected by an ASSIGN or SUBST command.

**Cannot DISKCOMP to or from
a network drive**
One of the specified drives is a network device.

Compare another diskette (Y/N) ?
This prompt allows comparison of another pair of disks. Respond with *Y* to cause DISKCOMP to prompt for insertion of the next pair of disks to be compared; respond with *N* to exit to MS-DOS.

Compare error on side *n*, track *n*
A difference was detected between the two disks being compared.

Compare OK
The two disks being compared are identical.

Compare process ended
The disk comparison was terminated as the result of a fatal error.

Comparing *n* tracks,
***n* sectors per track, *n* side(s)**
This informational message specifies the format of the two disks being compared.

DEVICE Support Not Present
The disk drive does not support MS-DOS 3.2 device control.

Drive *X* not ready
Make sure a diskette is inserted into
the drive and the door is closed
DISKCOMP was unable to read the disk in the specified drive.

Drive types or diskette types
not compatible
Single-sided disks cannot be compared with double-sided disks, nor high-density disks with double-density disks.

FIRST diskette bad or incompatible
DISKCOMP is unable to determine the format of the first disk.

Incorrect DOS version
The version of DISKCOMP is not compatible with the version of MS-DOS that is running.

Insert diskette with directory that contains
COMMAND.COM in drive *X* and strike any key when ready
If the system was booted from a floppy disk and the system disk was then removed in order to use DISKCOMP, the user must replace the system disk after the compare operation is complete.

Insert FIRST diskette in drive *X*:
Press any key when ready...
This message prompts the user to insert the first disk of a pair to be compared.

Insert SECOND diskette in drive *X*:
Press any key when ready...
This message prompts the user to insert the second disk of a pair to be compared.

Insufficient memory
The available system memory is insufficient to load and execute the DISKCOMP program.

Invalid drive specification
Specified drive does not exist
or is non-removable
One of the drives specified in the command line is invalid or does not exist.

Invalid parameter
Do not specify filename(s)
Command format: DISKCOMP d: d: [/1][/8]
A syntax error was detected in the command line, usually caused by an incorrect switch.

SECOND diskette bad or incompatible
The second disk of a pair to be compared does not have the same format as the first disk or has bad sectors preventing DISKCOMP from determining its format.

Unrecoverable read error on drive *X*:
The disk in the specified drive contains an unreadable sector.

DISKCOPY

Copy Floppy Disks

2.0 and later

External

Purpose

Performs a sector-by-sector copy of one entire floppy disk to another floppy disk. This command was included with PC-DOS beginning with version 1.0. To copy individual files, *see* USER COMMANDS: COPY.

Syntax

DISKCOPY [*drive1*:] [*drive2*:] [/1]

where:

drive1	is the drive containing the disk to be copied.
drive2	is the drive containing the disk that will become the copy.
/1	copies only the first side of the disk in *drive1* (MS-DOS version 3.2).

Description

The DISKCOPY command duplicates a floppy disk, performing the copy on a physical sector-by-sector basis. The *drive1* parameter specifies the location of the disk to be copied (the source disk). The *drive2* parameter specifies the location of the disk that will become the copy (the destination disk). If *drive2* is omitted, the current drive is used as the destination drive; if both *drive1* and *drive2* parameters are omitted or are the same, DISKCOPY performs the copy operation using a single drive, prompting the user to swap the disks as necessary.

DISKCOPY examines the destination disk before writing any information and terminates with an error message if it does not have the same format as the source disk. If the destination disk is not formatted, DISKCOPY formats it with the same format as the source disk, as part of the DISKCOPY operation.

Note: With MS-DOS versions 2.0 through 3.1, the destination disk must be formatted using the FORMAT command before DISKCOPY can be used. All PC-DOS versions of DISKCOPY will automatically format the destination disk, if necessary.

When DISKCOPY finishes copying a disk, it displays a prompt that allows the user to choose between copying another disk and returning to the MS-DOS command level.

Because DISKCOPY creates an exact duplicate of the source disk, any file fragmentation present on the source disk is also present on the destination disk after the DISKCOPY process is complete. To eliminate fragmentation of the source files, they should be copied to the destination disk individually using COPY or XCOPY.

The DISKCOPY command cannot be used with a network drive or with a drive created or affected by an ASSIGN, JOIN, or SUBST command, nor can it be used with fixed disks.

Return Codes

    0   Disk was copied successfully.
    1   Nonfatal but unrecoverable read or write error occurred (no Interrupt 24H generated).
    2   DISKCOPY was terminated with a Control-C.
    3   Fatal error was encountered: unreadable source disk or unformattable destination disk.
    4   Initialization error was encountered: not enough memory, syntax error in command line, or invalid drive specified in command line.

Note: Return codes are not present in the PC-DOS version of DISKCOPY.

Examples

To copy the contents of the disk in drive A to the disk in drive B, type

```
C>DISKCOPY A: B:  <Enter>
```

To copy the contents of the disk in drive A using only one drive, type

```
C>DISKCOPY A: A:  <Enter>
```

To copy only the first side of the disk in drive A to the first side of the disk in drive B, type

```
C>DISKCOPY A: B: /1  <Enter>
```

Messages

**Cannot DISKCOPY to or from
an ASSIGNed or SUBSTed drive**
One of the specified drives has been affected by an ASSIGN or SUBST command.

**Cannot DISKCOPY to or from
a network drive**
One of the specified drives is a network device.

Copy another diskette (Y/N) ?
This prompt allows copying of another disk. Respond with *Y* to cause DISKCOPY to prompt for insertion of the next set of disks; respond with *N* to exit to MS-DOS.

**Copying *n* tracks
n sectors per track, *n* side(s)**
This informational message specifies the format of the source disk being copied.

Copy process ended
The DISKCOPY process has been successfully completed or has been terminated by a fatal error. In the latter case, this message is preceded by another message explaining the error.

DEVICE Support Not Present
The disk drive does not support MS-DOS version 3.2 device control.

Disk error while reading drive X:
Abort, Retry, Ignore?
A bad sector was detected on the source disk. This does not necessarily invalidate the disk copy; the bad sector may originally have been detected and flagged by the FORMAT program and therefore not included in any file. One solution is to copy the files individually using the COPY command.

Drive X: not ready
Make sure a diskette is inserted into
the drive and the door is closed
DISKCOPY was unable to read the disk in the specified drive.

Drive types or diskette types
not compatible
Single-sided disks cannot be copied to or from double-sided disks, nor high-density disks to or from double-density disks.

Formatting while copying
The destination disk was not previously formatted. It is given the same format as the source disk as part of the DISKCOPY operation (MS-DOS version 3.2).

Incorrect DOS version
The version of DISKCOPY is not compatible with the version of MS-DOS that is running.

Insert diskette with directory that contains
COMMAND.COM in drive X and strike any key when ready
If the system was booted from a floppy disk and the system disk was then removed in order to use DISKCOPY, the user must replace the system disk after the copy operation is complete.

Insert SOURCE diskette in drive X:
Press any key when ready...

or

Insert TARGET diskette in drive X:
Press any key when ready...
These messages prompt the user to insert the source and destination disks before beginning the copy operation.

Insufficient memory
The available system memory is insufficient to load and execute the DISKCOPY program.

Invalid drive specification
Specified drive does not exist,
or is non-removable
One of the drives specified in the command line is invalid or does not exist. A fixed disk cannot be the source or destination disk for a DISKCOPY operation.

Invalid parameter
Do not specify filename(s)
Command Format: DISKCOPY d: d: [/1]
A syntax error was detected in the command line, usually caused by an incorrect switch or by the use of a filename instead of (or in addition to) a disk drive.

SOURCE diskette bad or incompatible

or

TARGET diskette bad or incompatible
The source disk could not be read or the destination disk could not be formatted.

Target diskette is write protected
The destination disk has a write-protect tab on it.

Target diskette may be unusable
Unrecoverable read or write errors were encountered while copying the source disk to the destination disk. The newly copied disk may not be an accurate copy.

Unrecoverable read error on drive X:
side n, track n

or

Unrecoverable write error on drive X:
side n, track n
The disk in the specified drive contained a sector that could not be successfully read or written.

DRIVER.SYS

Configurable External-Disk-Drive Driver

3.2

External

Purpose

Installs and configures external disk drives or assigns logical drive letters to existing floppy-disk drives.

Syntax

DEVICE=DRIVER.SYS /D:n [/C] [/F:n] [/H:n] [/N] [/S:n] [/T:n]

where:

/D:n	is the drive number (0–127 for floppy disks, 128–255 for fixed disks) and must always be the first switch in the command line.
/C	specifies that door-lock-status support is available.
/F:n	is the form-factor index for the device (default = 2):

0	320/360 KB
1	1.2 MB
2	720 KB
3	8" single-density floppy disk
4	8" double-density floppy disk
5	fixed disk
6	magnetic-tape drive
7	other

/H:n	is the number of heads supported by the disk drive (1–99).
/N	specifies a nonremovable block device.
/S:n	is the number of sectors per track (1–40).
/T:n	is the tracks per read/write head (1–999).

Description

When the computer is turned on or restarted, MS-DOS assigns numbers to all existing internal disk drives. The DRIVER.SYS file — an installable, configurable block-device driver for external disk drives and other mass-storage devices — allows installation of peripheral devices that are not supported by the resident drivers in the MS-DOS BIOS module. DRIVER.SYS can also assign a logical drive letter to an existing disk drive, thus giving the device two drive letters. (This allows such activities as copying files between like media — for example, copying files from one 1.2 MB 5.25-inch disk to another — using the same drive.)

The /D:n switch assigns a unit number to the additional disk drive or specifies the number of the existing disk drive that is to be assigned a logical drive letter. (Floppy-disk unit numbers begin at 0; fixed-disk numbers begin at 80H.) For example, if the system contains two floppy-disk drives (0 and 1), an external floppy-disk drive requiring DRIVER.SYS would be assigned the value 2; MS-DOS would then assign that drive the next available drive letter. If the number used with the /D:n switch references an existing drive (for example, 0, the first floppy-disk drive), MS-DOS assigns the drive the next available drive letter, allowing the one drive unit to be referenced by two drive letters. The /D:n switch is not optional and must precede all other switches in the command line.

The /C, /F:n, and /N switches describe characteristics of the disk drive that is being selected for use with DRIVER.SYS. The /C switch is included only if the device has a status line indicating whether the disk in the drive has been changed. (This information is used by the driver to optimize disk accesses to the directory and file allocation table.) If the device does not have a status line, /C will have no effect. The /F:n option describes the form-factor index used by the device. The permissible values for n are given in the preceding table; the default type is a 720 KB disk. The /N switch indicates that the block device is nonremovable. Access to such devices is more efficient than access to removable media because MS-DOS can eliminate calls to the driver for a media-change check.

The /H:n, /S:n, and /T:n switches describe the physical layout of the recording medium. /H:n specifies the number of recording surfaces, or read-write heads, supported by the drive (1–99). /S:n is the number of sectors per track (1–40) and /T:n is the tracks per side (1–999). (The total number of physical sectors on a given disk is found by multiplying the number of heads by the tracks per side and the sectors per track.)

Note: The values used with these switches must be supported by the device being installed. If DRIVER.SYS is used to assign a logical drive letter to an existing physical device, the values used with the switches must be identical to the characteristics imposed by the default device driver.

Examples

To install a driver for an external 720 KB disk drive in a system that already has two 5.25-inch floppy-disk drives, insert the line

```
DEVICE=DRIVER.SYS /D:02
```

into the CONFIG.SYS file and restart the system.

Assume that an IBM PC/AT or compatible has three disk drives installed: Drive A is a 1.2 MB 5.25-inch floppy-disk drive; drive B is a 360 KB 5.25-inch floppy-disk drive; drive C is a 30 MB fixed-disk drive. To assign the logical drive letter D to the existing drive A, effectively giving the one drive two drive letters, insert the line

```
DEVICE=DRIVER.SYS /D:0 /F:1 /H:2 /S:15 /T:80 /C
```

into the CONFIG.SYS file and restart the system.

Messages

Bad or missing DRIVER.SYS
The file DRIVER.SYS could not be found in the root or specified directory or has been damaged.

ERROR - Incorrect DOS version
The version of DRIVER.SYS is not compatible with the version of MS-DOS that is running.

ERROR - No drive specified
The /D:*n* switch was not included in the command line.

Loaded External Disk Driver for Drive *X*
The device driver has been successfully installed and this message informs the user of the drive letter assigned to the device.

Sector size too large in file DRIVER.SYS
DRIVER.SYS uses a sector size that is larger than the sector size used by any of the system's default disk drivers. The driver cannot be used because MS-DOS's internal disk buffers will not be large enough to hold a sector read from the device.

EDLIN
Line Editor

and later

External

Purpose

Creates and changes ASCII text files.

Syntax

EDLIN [*drive*:][*path*] *filename* [/B]

where:

filename   is the name of an ASCII text file to be created or edited, optionally preceded by a drive and/or path.

/B   causes logical end-of-file marks within the file to be ignored (versions 2.0 and later).

Description

The EDLIN program is a simple line-oriented editor that can be used to create or maintain short text files. The user references and edits text by line number; EDLIN displays these numbers for convenience but they do not become part of the file. Each line of the file being edited can be a maximum of 253 characters.

The *filename* parameter specifies a plain ASCII text file; if the file does not already exist, EDLIN creates it. (EDLIN cannot be used on most files created by word-processing programs because such document files have embedded formatting codes and other formatting information that EDLIN cannot interpret.) EDLIN does not assume any extensions; the user must type the complete filename. (EDLIN does not permit editing of a .BAK file.)

If *filename* is a previously existing text file, EDLIN loads lines from the file into memory until the editing buffer is 75 percent full or until a logical end-of-file mark or the physical end of the file is reached. The /B switch forces EDLIN to ignore any logical end-of-file marks (1AH, or Control-Z) the file may contain. If the file is too large for the edit buffer, the Write Lines to Disk (W) and Append Lines from Disk (A) commands are used during the edit session to process the remaining portions of the file.

Once the file is created or loaded into the editing buffer, EDLIN displays its asterisk prompt (∗) and the user can begin entering editing commands.

EDLIN commands consist of a single character, in either uppercase or lowercase, usually preceded by one or more line numbers. More than one command can be entered on a single line by separating the commands with semicolons. EDLIN does not execute a command until the Enter key is pressed.

The EDLIN commands are

Command	Action
linenumber	Edit line.
A	Append lines from disk.
C	Copy lines (versions 2.0 and later).
D	Delete lines.
E	End editing session.
I	Insert lines.
L	List lines.
M	Move lines (versions 2.0 and later).
P	Display in pages (versions 2.0 and later).
Q	Quit without saving changes.
R	Replace text.
S	Search for text.
T	Transfer another file into the edit buffer (versions 2.0 and later).
W	Write lines to disk.

Each of these commands is discussed in detail in the following pages.

All EDLIN commands that accept a line number or range of line numbers can also recognize the following symbolic references:

Symbol	Meaning
#	The line after the last line in the edit buffer
.	The current line
+*n* or −*n*	A line number relative to the current line (for example, +5 = five lines past the current line)

When the user terminates the editing session with the E command, EDLIN gives the new file the same name as the original file and renames the original (unchanged) file with the extension .BAK. Any previous file with the same name and the extension .BAK is lost. When the user terminates the editing session with the Q command, the original filename remains unchanged.

Example

To edit the file AUTOEXEC.BAT in the root directory of the current drive, type

```
C>EDLIN \AUTOEXEC.BAT   <Enter>
```

Messages

Cannot edit .BAK file — rename file

Files with the extension .BAK cannot be edited with EDLIN. Rename the file or copy it to a file with the same name but a different extension.

End of input file
The entire file has been read into memory.

File is READ-ONLY
Files marked with the read-only attribute cannot be edited. Remove the read-only attribute with the ATTRIB command or copy the file to a file with a different name.

File name must be specified
The command line did not include a filename.

File not found
The file named in the command line could not be found or does not exist.

Incorrect DOS version
The version of EDLIN is not compatible with the version of MS-DOS that is running.

Insufficient memory
Not enough memory is available to carry out the requested command.

Invalid drive or file name
The command line included a drive that is invalid or does not exist in the system or the filename is not valid.

Invalid Parameter
The command line contained an illegal switch or other invalid parameter.

New file
The file named in the command line did not previously exist. The file is created and the edit buffer is emptied.

Read error in: *filename*
MS-DOS was unable to read the entire file. Run CHKDSK to determine whether the file or disk has been damaged.

EDLIN: *linenumber*

Edit Line

1.0 and later

Purpose

Selects a line of text for editing.

Syntax

linenumber

where:

linenumber   is the number assigned by EDLIN to the text line to be edited (1–65534).

Description

The command to edit a particular line of text is simply the line's number or one of the special symbols or expressions that evaluate to a line number, followed by the Enter key. EDLIN displays the current contents of the specified line and copies them to a special editing buffer called the template, then moves the cursor to a new line and displays a prompt in the form of the line number followed by a colon and an asterisk. If a line number is not specified (that is, if the Enter key alone is pressed in response to the EDLIN prompt), EDLIN displays the line following the current line and makes it the current line.

The user can change the text of the specified line by simply entering new text followed by a press of the Enter key, leave the text unchanged by pressing Enter alone, or modify the text by using special editing keys to change a portion of the text that has been placed in the template. These editing keys and their actions are

Key	Action
F1	Copies one character from the template to the new line.
F2*char*	Copies all characters up to the specified character from the template to the new line.
F3	Copies all remaining characters in the template to the new line.
Del	Does not copy (skips over) one character.
F4*char*	Does not copy (skips over) all characters up to the specified character.
Esc	Restarts editing for the current line, leaving the template unchanged.
Ins	Enters/exits character-insert mode.
F5	Makes the newly edited line the new template.
→	Copies one character from the template to the new line.
←	Deletes one character from the new line.
Backspace	Deletes one character from the new line.

Note: Computers that are not IBM-compatible may use a different set of editing keys to perform these actions.

Control characters (those characters with ASCII codes in the range 0–1FH) cannot be inserted into text with the usual Control-key combinations. Instead, the user must press the sequence Ctrl-V, followed by an uppercase character or symbol. For example, Ctrl-C (ASCII code 03H) is entered into text by pressing Ctrl-V followed by a capital C; the Escape character (ASCII code 1BH) is generated by pressing Ctrl-V followed by a left square-bracket character ([).

Examples

To edit line 4, type

```
*4  <Enter>
```

To edit the line two lines ahead of the current line, type

```
*+2  <Enter>
```

EDLIN: A

Append Lines from Disk

Purpose

Reads lines from the file being edited into the edit buffer.

Syntax

[*n*]A

where:

n　　　is the number of lines to be read from the file.

Description

If the file being edited is too large to fit into the edit buffer, EDLIN ordinarily reads only enough text to fill 75 percent of the buffer when it opens the file, reserving 25 percent of the buffer for additions and changes to the text. The user must then employ the Write Lines to Disk (W) and Append Lines from Disk (A) commands to write and read successive blocks of text until the entire file has passed through the edit buffer.

The A command alone has no effect if the edit buffer is 75 percent or more full. The W command must be used to write lines to the output file and delete them from the buffer; then the A command can read new lines from the input file and append them to the end of the text remaining in the buffer.

The *n* parameter specifies the number of lines to be read from the file. If *n* is omitted or is too large, EDLIN reads only enough lines to fill the editing buffer to 75 percent of its capacity.

Examples

To append 200 lines from the disk file to the edit buffer, type

```
*200A  <Enter>
```

To append as many lines from the file as possible (until the edit buffer is 75 percent full), type

```
*A  <Enter>
```

Message

End of input file
The last section of the file being edited has been read into the edit buffer.

EDLIN: C

Copy Lines

Purpose

Copies one or more lines from one location in the edit buffer to another.

Syntax

[*first*],[*last*],*destination*[,*count*]C

where:

first	is the number of the first line to be copied.
last	is the number of the last line to be copied.
destination	is the number of the line before which the copied lines are to appear.
count	is the number of times to execute the copy operation.

Description

The Copy Lines (C) command copies one or more text lines, inserting the copied lines at another location in the edit buffer. The original lines that were copied are unchanged. EDLIN then renumbers the edit buffer and makes the first copied line at the destination the new current line.

The *first* and *last* line-number parameters define the block of lines to be copied. (Note that the first line number must be less than or equal to the last line number.) Either or both of these numbers can be omitted (in which case the current line number is used), but the commas must still be entered as placeholders. The *destination* parameter specifies the line before which the copied lines are to be inserted; it is not optional and must not fall within the range of line numbers specified by *first* and *last*. One of the special symbols . (current line) or # (end of buffer) or an expression relative to the current line number (+*n* or −*n*) can be used instead of absolute line numbers.

To replicate the line or lines multiple times, the copy operation can be repeated automatically with the optional parameter *count*. The default value for *count* is one.

Examples

If the current line is line 10, to copy lines 10 through 15 and place the copied lines before line 5, type

```
*10,15,5C  <Enter>
```

or

```
*,15,5C  <Enter>
```

or

```
*,+5,-5C  <Enter>
```

If the current line is line 10, to place three copies of lines 10 through 15 before line 1, type

```
* 10,15,1,3C   <Enter>
```

or

```
* ,15,1,3C   <Enter>
```

or

```
* ,+5,1,3C   <Enter>
```

Messages

Entry error
The command line contained an error such as a first line number that was greater than the last line number or a destination line number that fell within the range *first,last*.

Insufficient memory
The edit buffer does not have sufficient room for EDLIN to carry out the specified command.

Must specify destination line number
No destination line number was specified in the command line; therefore, no changes were made to the edit buffer.

EDLIN: D

Delete Lines

Purpose

Deletes one or more lines from the edit buffer.

Syntax

[*first*][,*last*]D

where:

first   is the number of the first line to delete.
last   is the number of the last line to delete.

Description

The Delete Lines (D) command removes one or more text lines from the edit buffer. The line after the last line deleted becomes the new current line.

The *first* and *last* line-number parameters define the block of lines to be deleted. (Note that the first line number must be less than or equal to the last line number.) Either or both of these numbers can be omitted (in which case the current line number is used), but a leading comma is required as a placeholder if *first* is omitted when *last* is present. One of the special symbols . (current line) or # (end of buffer) or an expression relative to the current line number (+*n* or −*n*) can be used instead of absolute line numbers.

Examples

If the current line is line 10, to delete the current line, type

```
*10D  <Enter>
```

or

```
*D  <Enter>
```

If the current line is line 10, to delete lines 10 through 15, type

```
*10,15D  <Enter>
```

or

```
*,15D  <Enter>
```

or

```
*,+5D  <Enter>
```

If the current line is line 10, to delete all lines from the current line to the end of the buffer, type

```
*10,#D   <Enter>
```

or

```
*,#D   <Enter>
```

Message

Entry error

The command line contained an error such as a first line number that was greater than the last line number.

EDLIN: E

1.0 and later

End Editing Session

Purpose

Saves the edited file to disk and exits from EDLIN.

Syntax

E

Description

The End Editing Session (E) command writes the contents of the edit buffer to the current directory of the disk in the current drive. If a previously existing file was being edited and there is any text remaining in the original file that has not yet passed through the edit buffer, EDLIN copies this text to the output file. EDLIN gives the newly edited file the same name as the original file and renames the original (unchanged) file with the extension .BAK. Any previous file with the same name and the extension .BAK is lost. EDLIN then returns to MS-DOS.

If the disk does not have enough space to hold the edited file in addition to the original file, EDLIN writes as much of the edited file as possible into a file with the extension .$$$; the remainder of the edited text is lost. The name and contents of the original file are left unchanged.

Example

To end an editing session, type

```
*E  <Enter>
```

Messages

Disk full. Edits lost.
The disk does not contain enough free space for the edited file. A partial file may have been created with the extension .$$$.

File Creation Error
The .BAK file is marked read-only, the root directory is full or cannot contain any more files, or the filename is the same as a volume label or directory name.

No room in directory for file
The file could not be saved because its destination was the root directory and the root directory is full.

Too many files open
MS-DOS was unable to open the .BAK file due to a lack of available system file handles. Increase the value of the FILES command in the CONFIG.SYS file.

EDLIN: I

1.0 and later

Insert Lines

Purpose

Inserts new lines into the edit buffer.

Syntax

[*destination*]I

where:

destination   is the number of the line before which text is to be inserted.

Description

The Insert Lines (I) command enables insert mode and allows new text to be placed between previously existing lines of text. When insert mode is terminated, the first line following the inserted lines becomes the new current line.

EDLIN places the new text before the line specified by the *destination* parameter. If *destination* is omitted, EDLIN assumes the current line; if *destination* is larger than the number of lines in the edit buffer, EDLIN simply appends the new text after the actual last line. One of the special symbols . (current line) or # (end of buffer) or an expression relative to the current line number (+n or −n) can be used instead of an absolute line number.

After an I command, EDLIN issues a prompt consisting of the line number for the inserted text followed by a colon and an asterisk and continues to issue such prompts each time the Enter key is pressed until the user terminates insert mode by pressing Ctrl-C or Ctrl-Break.

Examples

If the current line is line 10, to insert text before line 7, type

```
*7I   <Enter>
```

or

```
*-3I   <Enter>
```

To insert lines at the beginning of the buffer, type

```
*1I   <Enter>
```

To insert lines at the end of the buffer, type

```
*#I   <Enter>
```

Message

Insufficient memory
The edit buffer does not have sufficient room for EDLIN to complete the specified command.

EDLIN: L

List Lines

1.0 and later

Purpose

Displays one or more lines from the edit buffer.

Syntax

[*first*][,*last*]L

where:

first   is the number of the first line to be displayed.
last   is the number of the last line to be displayed.

Description

The List Lines (L) command displays text lines on standard output. If the current line lies within the range of lines listed, EDLIN displays an asterisk next to its number. The current line is not changed.

The *first* and *last* line-number parameters define the block of lines to be listed. (Note that the first line number must be less than or equal to the last line number.) Either or both of these numbers can be omitted, but a leading comma is required as a placeholder if *first* is omitted when *last* is present. One of the special symbols . (current line) and # (end of buffer) or an expression relative to the current line number (+*n* or −*n*) can be used instead of absolute line numbers.

If only the first line number is specified, EDLIN displays text in 23-line increments starting with that number. If only the last line number is specified, EDLIN displays text beginning 11 lines before the current line and continuing to the specified last line. If no line numbers are specified in the command, EDLIN lists the 23 lines centered around the current line; if the current line number is less than 13, EDLIN lists the first 23 lines in the buffer.

Examples

To display lines 20 through 30, type

```
*20,30L  <Enter>
```

If the current line is 20, to display the 23 lines centered around the current line, type

```
*L  <Enter>
```

EDLIN displays lines 9 through 31.

Message

Entry error

The command line contained an error such as a first line number that was greater than the last line number.

EDLIN: M

2.0 and later

Move Lines

Purpose

Moves lines from one place in the edit buffer to another.

Syntax

[*first*],[*last*],*destination*M

where:

first	is the number of the first line to be moved.
last	is the number of the last line to be moved.
destination	is the number of the line before which the moved lines are to be inserted.

Description

The Move Lines (M) command transfers one or more text lines from one location in the edit buffer to another. EDLIN then deletes the original lines and renumbers the edit buffer. The first moved line becomes the new current line.

The *first* and *last* line-number parameters define the block of lines to be moved. (Note that the first line number must be less than or equal to the last line number.) Either or both of these numbers can be omitted (in which case the current line number is used), but the commas must still be entered as placeholders. The *destination* parameter specifies the line before which the moved lines are to be inserted; it is not optional and must not fall within the range of line numbers specified by *first* and *last*. One of the special symbols . (current line) or # (end of buffer) or an expression relative to the current line number (+*n* or −*n*) can be used instead of absolute line numbers.

Example

If the current line is line 10, to move lines 10 through 15 and place them before line 5, type

```
*10,15,5M  <Enter>
```

or

```
*,15,5M  <Enter>
```

or

```
*,+5,-5M  <Enter>
```

Messages

Entry error

The command line contained an error such as a first line number that was greater than the last line number or a destination line number that fell within the range *first,last.*

Must specify destination line number

No destination line number was specified in the command line; therefore, no changes were made to the edit buffer.

EDLIN: P

2.0 and later

Display in Pages

Purpose

Displays lines for viewing in successive screenfuls (pages).

Syntax

[*first*][,*last*]P

where:

first	is the number of the first line to be displayed.
last	is the number of the last line to be displayed.

Description

The Display in Pages (P) command displays text lines on standard output one screenful at a time. Unlike the List Lines (L) command, which has no effect on the current line, P causes the last line displayed to become the new current line. Thus, although the edit buffer is not actually organized into pages, the user can employ repeated P commands to sequentially view successive groups of lines.

The *first* and *last* line-number parameters define the block of lines to be listed; the display starts with the line specified by *first*. (Note that the first line number must be less than or equal to the last line number.) Either or both of these numbers can be omitted, but a leading comma is required as a placeholder if *first* is omitted when *last* is present. If omitted, *first* defaults to the line after the current line and *last* defaults to the line 23 lines after the current line. One of the special symbols . (current line) or # (end of buffer) or an expression relative to the current line number ($+n$ or $-n$) can be used instead of absolute line numbers.

Examples

If the current line is 20, to view the next page of lines in the edit buffer, type

```
*P  <Enter>
```

EDLIN displays 23 lines, beginning with line 21, and changes the current line to line 43.

To view successive pages of 23 lines, repeatedly type

```
*P  <Enter>
```

Message

Entry error
The command line contained an error such as a first line number that was greater than the last line number.

EDLIN: Q
Quit

Purpose

Terminates the editing session without saving the revised file.

Syntax

Q

Description

The Quit (Q) command causes EDLIN to exit without saving any of the changes made to the edited file during the session. The original file's name and contents are left unchanged and no new file is created.

To reduce the danger of accidentally losing the contents of the edit buffer, EDLIN prompts the user for confirmation before carrying out the Q command.

Example

To quit an editing session, type

```
*Q  <Enter>
```

EDLIN issues a prompt for confirmation and, if the response from the user is *Y*, exits to MS-DOS without saving any changes made to the file during the session.

Message

Abort edit (Y/N)?
This prompt is displayed in response to the Q command. Respond with *Y* to exit to MS-DOS without saving changes made to the file; respond with *N* to continue the editing session.

EDLIN: R

Replace Text

Purpose

Replaces one string in the edit buffer with another.

Syntax

[*first*][,*last*][?]R[*string1*][^Z*string2*]

where:

first	is the number of the first line to be searched.
last	is the number of the last line to be searched.
?	causes the user to be prompted for confirmation before each replacement is made.
string1	is the sequence of characters to be searched for.
^Z	is a Control-Z character.
string2	is the sequence of characters to be substituted for *string1*.

Note: The character limit for the Replace Text command is 127 characters, including both strings and all other parameters.

Description

The Replace Text (R) command substitutes one character string for another within a specified range of lines. The last line in which a replacement occurs becomes the new current line.

The *first* and *last* line-number parameters define the range of lines to be searched for strings to replace. (Note that the first line number must be less than or equal to the last line number.) Either or both of these numbers can be omitted, but a leading comma is required as a placeholder if *first* is omitted when *last* is present. If omitted, *first* defaults to the line after the current line and *last* defaults to the last line in the buffer. One of the special symbols . (current line) or # (end of buffer) or an expression relative to the current line number (+*n* or −*n*) can be used instead of absolute line numbers.

If *string1* is omitted, EDLIN uses the *string1* from the preceding R command; if there was no preceding R command, EDLIN displays an error message. If *string2* is omitted, EDLIN deletes all occurrences of *string1*. *string1* must be separated from *string2* by a Control-Z (^Z) character. If *string1* is omitted, a Control-Z character must still be included to mark the beginning of *string2*, but if *string2* is omitted when *string1* is present, the Control-Z character has no effect and is therefore optional. (The Control-Z character is entered by pressing Ctrl-Z or the F6 key.)

If the ? option is not included in the command line, EDLIN displays each line that contains a match *after* the replacement is carried out. If the ? option is used, EDLIN displays each line containing a match as it is found and prompts the user for confirmation *before* the string is replaced.

The matching operation is case sensitive; EDLIN carries out the substitution only on sequences of characters that match *string1* exactly. Wildcards are not permitted.

Examples

If the current line is line 10, to replace all occurrences of the string *logical* with the string *bitwise* in lines 11 through 20, type

```
*11,20Rlogical^Zbitwise  <Enter>
```

or

```
*,20Rlogical^Zbitwise  <Enter>
```

To cause EDLIN to prompt for confirmation before replacing each string, type

```
*11,20?Rlogical^Zbitwise  <Enter>
```

or

```
*,20?Rlogical^Zbitwise  <Enter>
```

To delete all occurrences of the string *00H* in line 20, type

```
*20,20R00H^Z  <Enter>
```

Messages

Entry error
The command line contained an error such as a first line number that was greater than the last line number.

Insufficient memory
The edit buffer has insufficient room for EDLIN to carry out the specified Replace Text command.

Line too long
The replacement would cause the line being edited to expand beyond 253 characters.

Not found
No occurrence or further occurrences of the string to be replaced were found in the specified range of lines.

O.K.?
If the ? option is used in the command line, this prompt is displayed each time a matching string is found. Respond with *Y* or press the Enter key to replace the string and continue searching; press any other key to leave the string unchanged and continue searching.

EDLIN: S

1.0 and later

Search for Text

Purpose

Searches the edit buffer for a character string.

Syntax

[*first*][,*last*][?]S[*string*]

where:

first   is the number of the first line to be searched.
last   is the number of the last line to be searched.
?   causes the user to be prompted for confirmation before the search is terminated.
string   is the sequence of characters to be searched for (maximum 126 characters).

Description

The Search for Text (S) command searches for a character string within a specified range of lines. When a match is found, EDLIN displays the line containing the match and that line becomes the new current line. If no lines containing the specified string are found, EDLIN displays the message *Not found* and the current line number remains unchanged.

The *first* and *last* line-number parameters define the block of lines to be searched for strings. (Note that the first line number must be less than or equal to the last line number.) Either or both of these numbers can be omitted, but a leading comma is required as a placeholder if *first* is omitted when *last* is present. If omitted, *first* defaults to the line after the current line and *last* defaults to the last line in the buffer. One of the special symbols . (current line) or # (end of buffer) or an expression relative to the current line number (+*n* or −*n*) can be used instead of absolute line numbers.

If *string* is omitted, EDLIN uses the *string* from the last S command or *string1* from the last Replace Text (R) command instead.

If the ? option is not included in the command line, EDLIN displays the first line that contains a match for *string,* makes this the new current line, and terminates the search. If the ? option is used, EDLIN displays each line containing a match for *string* as it is found, followed by an *O.K.?* prompt. If the user responds with *Y* or presses the Enter key, EDLIN terminates the search; if the user presses any other key, the search continues.

The matching operation is case sensitive; EDLIN reports only sequences of characters that match *string* exactly. Wildcards are not permitted.

Examples

If the current line is line 10, to find the first occurrence of the string *xyz* in lines 11 through 20, type

```
*11,20Sxyz   <Enter>
```

or

```
*,20Sxyz   <Enter>
```

To find a particular occurrence of *proc* in the edit buffer, type

```
*1,#?Sproc   <Enter>
```

EDLIN displays the first line containing *proc* and prompts with

```
O.K.?
```

Type *Y* or press Enter to stop the search; press any other key to continue the search.

Messages

Entry error
The command line contained an error such as a first line number that was greater than the last line number.

Not found
No match or no further matches for *string* were found in the specified range of lines.

O.K.?
If the ? option is used in the command line, this prompt is displayed each time a matching string is found. Respond with *Y* or press the Enter key to stop searching; press any other key to continue searching.

EDLIN: T

2.0 and later

Transfer Another File

Purpose

Merges the contents of another file with the file in the edit buffer.

Syntax

[*destination*]T[*drive*:][*path*]*filename*

where:

destination	is the number of the line before which the text from *filename* is to be inserted.
path	is the location of the file to be merged (versions 3.0 and later).
filename	is the name of the disk file from which text is to be merged.

Description

The Transfer Another File (T) command merges the contents of a text file with the current contents of the edit buffer and then renumbers the contents of the edit buffer. The first line of the merged text becomes the current line.

The *destination* parameter specifies the line before which the transferred lines are to be inserted. If omitted, *destination* defaults to the current line. One of the special symbols . (current line) or # (end of buffer) or an expression relative to the current line number (+*n* or −*n*) can be used instead of an absolute line number.

The *filename* parameter specifies the file from which text is to be merged and can include a drive and, in versions 3.0 and later, a path. If a drive or path is not specified, the file to be merged into the edit buffer with the T command *must* be in the current directory of the current drive.

Example

If the current line is line 10, to merge the contents of the file named KEYDEFS.C before line 10 of the edit buffer, type

```
*10Tkeydefs.c  <Enter>
```

or

```
*Tkeydefs.c  <Enter>
```

Messages

File not found
The specified filename does not exist in the current or specified location.

Not enough room to merge the entire file
The space available in the edit buffer is not sufficient to hold the entire file named in the T command. Use the Write Lines to Disk (W) command to partially empty the edit buffer.

EDLIN: W

1.0 and later

Write Lines to Disk

Purpose

Writes lines from the edit buffer to the disk.

Syntax

[*n*]W

where:

n   is the number of lines to be written to the file.

Description

If the file being edited is too large to fit into the edit buffer, EDLIN ordinarily reads only enough text to fill 75 percent of the buffer when it opens the file, reserving 25 percent of the buffer for changes and additions to the text. The user must then employ the Write Lines to Disk (W) command and the Append Lines from Disk (A) command to transfer successive blocks of text from the disk until the entire file has passed through the edit buffer. The W command causes EDLIN to write lines to the disk file and delete them from the buffer; then the A command can read new lines from the input file, placing them after the end of the text remaining in the buffer.

The *n* parameter specifies the number of lines to be written to the output file; if *n* is omitted or is larger than the number of lines in the edit buffer, EDLIN writes only enough lines to leave the edit buffer about 25 percent full. EDLIN then renumbers the lines remaining in the edit buffer so that the first remaining line becomes line number one.

Examples

To write 200 lines from the edit buffer to disk (effectively deleting those lines from the buffer), type

```
*200W  <Enter>
```

To write lines from the edit buffer to the disk until the edit buffer is only 25 percent full, type

```
*W  <Enter>
```

EXIT

Terminate Command Processor

2.0 and later

Internal

Purpose

Terminates a secondary copy of the command processor.

Syntax

EXIT

Description

Many communications programs, word processors, database managers, and other application programs load and execute a secondary copy of the system's command processor (COMMAND.COM) to let the user carry out MS-DOS commands without losing the context of the work in progress. Secondary copies of the command processor are also commonly used to execute one batch file under the control of another. (For more information about secondary copies of the command processor, *see* USER COMMANDS: COMMAND.)

The EXIT command cancels a secondary command processor. The terminating processor displays no message and control returns directly to the parent program or command processor.

EXIT has no effect on the currently executing command processor if it was loaded with the /P (permanent) switch or if it is the original command processor (the one loaded during system initialization, when the computer was turned on or restarted).

The EXIT command also allows the user to choose Close from the system menu if a COMMAND window is open under Microsoft Windows.

Example

To terminate the currently executing command processor, type

```
C>EXIT  <Enter>
```

Message

Bad command or filename
The EXIT command did not exist in versions earlier than 2.0, so MS-DOS attempted to execute a nonexistent program named EXIT instead.

FC

Compare Files

2.0 and later

External

Purpose

Compares two files and lists the differences on standard output.

Syntax

FC [/A] [/C] [/L] [/LB*n*] [/N] [/*nnnn*] [/T] [/W] [*drive:*]*pathname1* [*drive:*]*pathname2*

or

FC [/B] [*drive:*]*pathname1* [*drive:*]*pathname2*

where:

pathname1	is the name and location of the first file to be compared, optionally preceded by a drive; wildcard characters are not permitted.
pathname2	is the name and location of the second file to be compared, optionally preceded by a drive; wildcard characters are not permitted.
/A	causes FC to abbreviate the output when comparing ASCII text files (version 3.2).
/B	causes a byte-by-byte (binary) comparison; may not be used with any other switch (default when file extension is .EXE, .COM, .SYS, .OBJ, .LIB, or .BIN).
/C	causes FC to ignore case when comparing alphabetic characters.
/L	causes a line-by-line comparison of two ASCII text files (default when file extension is not .EXE, .COM, .SYS, .OBJ, .LIB, or .BIN) (version 3.2).
/LB*n*	sets the size of the internal line buffer to *n* lines (default = 100) (version 3.2).
/N	includes line numbers on the output of an ASCII file comparison (version 3.2).
/*nnnn*	is the number of lines that must match to resynchronize during an ASCII file comparison (default = 2; in versions 2.0 through 3.1, range = 1–9, default = 3).
/T	causes FC to compare tabs in text files literally (default = tabs expanded to spaces, with stops at each eighth character position) (version 3.2).
/W	causes FC to ignore spaces, tabs, and blank lines in text files.

Description

The FC utility compares two text files containing lines of ASCII text delimited by new-line characters or two binary files containing data of any type (such as executable programs).

FC

The differences between the two files are listed on standard output, which defaults to the video display but can be redirected to another character device or a file or can be piped to another program.

The FC program first examines the extensions of the two files being compared and, in most cases, selects the appropriate type of comparison automatically. However, the /B switch can be used to force a binary, or byte-by-byte, comparison of the two files named; the /L switch can be used to force a line-by-line comparison. When the /B switch is present, use of the /L, /N, and /nnnn switches causes an error message to be displayed; any other switches in the command line are ignored.

When comparing ASCII text files, FC loads a buffer with sequential sets of lines from each file and compares the two sets. The size of this buffer defaults to 100 lines but can be modified by including the /LB*n* switch in the command line. If differences are found, the name of the first file, the last matched line, and any mismatched lines from that file are displayed, followed by the first rematched line; then the name of the second file, the last matched line, and any mismatched lines are displayed, followed by the first rematched line from that file. The number of consecutive matching lines that must be detected in order for FC to consider the files resynchronized is controlled with the /*nnnn* switch; the default is 2.

If no lines match, if no lines match after the first mismatch, or if the number of mismatched lines exceeds the size of the line buffer, FC displays the message *Resynch failed. Files are too different* (or ***Files are different*** in versions 2.x and 3.0) and terminates.

The /C, /T, and /W switches modify the way in which two text files are compared. The /C switch causes FC to ignore case when comparing alphabetic characters. The /T switch causes FC to compare tab characters (ASCII code 09H) literally, rather than expand them to spaces before comparing corresponding lines. Finally, the /W, or whitespace, switch causes FC to ignore spaces, tabs, and blank lines during the comparison.

The /A and /N switches control the format of the listing of differences between the two text files. The /A switch causes FC to compress the listing of each mismatched set of lines to the first and last lines of each set, separated by ellipsis points. The /N switch causes FC to include the line numbers of the mismatched lines in the display.

During a binary comparison of two files, FC's buffer is reloaded as many times as is necessary to compare the complete files. Unlike the procedure with text-file comparisons, no attempt is made to resynchronize the data if a mismatch is detected and, regardless of the number of mismatches, the comparison process is not terminated. Any differences are displayed with the offset from the start of the file and the actual data from each file. If one file is shorter than the other, FC also displays a warning message at the end of the comparison.

The FC command is present only in MS-DOS. PC-DOS versions 1.0 and later provide a similar function in the COMP command.

Examples

Assume that FILE1.TXT and FILE2.TXT are in the current directory on the disk in the current drive and that they contain the following lines:

FILE1.TXT	FILE2.TXT
First line.	First line.
Second line.	Second line.
Third line.	Third line.
Fourth line.	Fourth line.
Fifth line.	Sixth line.
Sixth line.	Fifth line.
Seventh line.	Seventh line.
Eighth line.	Eighth line.
Ninth line.	Ninth line.
Tenth line.	Tenth line.

To compare these files line by line, type

```
C>FC FILE1.TXT FILE2.TXT  <Enter>
```

This will result in the following display:

```
***** file1.txt
Fourth line.
Fifth line.
Sixth line.
Seventh line.
***** file2.txt
Fourth line.
Sixth line.
Fifth line.
Seventh line.
*****
```

To compare the same two files and produce an abbreviated listing of differences that includes line numbers, type

```
C>FC /A /N FILE1.TXT FILE2.TXT  <Enter>
```

This will result in the following display:

```
***** file1.txt
    4:   Fourth line.
...
    7:   Seventh line.
***** file2.txt
    4:   Fourth line.
...
    7:   Seventh line.
*****
```

Assume that two binary files, FILE1.BIN and FILE2.BIN, are the same length and contain only the following three differences:

Offset	FILE1.BIN	FILE2.BIN
19H	04H	03H
33H	4AH	4BH
42H	52H	51H

To compare these two binary files, type

C>FC /B FILE1.BIN FILE2.BIN <Enter>

This will result in the following display:

```
00000019: 04 03
00000033: 4A 4B
00000042: 52 51
```

Note: The use of the /B switch in this example is optional; binary comparison is the default when .BIN files are compared.

Messages

filename longer than _filename_
After all the corresponding data in the two files was compared, data remained in one of the files.

cannot open _filename_ - No such file or directory
The specified file cannot be found or does not exist.

DOS 2.0 or later required
FC does not work with versions of MS-DOS earlier than 2.0.

Incompatible switches
The /B switch was used in combination with one or more of the other switches.

Incorrect DOS version
The version of FC is not compatible with the version of MS-DOS that is running.

no differences encountered
The two files being compared are identical.

out of memory
The available memory in the transient program area is insufficient to compare the two files.

Resynch failed. Files are too different
The number of mismatched lines in an ASCII file comparison exceeded the number of lines that can be loaded into FC's comparison buffer (which by default is 100 lines). Rerun the comparison using the /LB*n* switch to allocate a larger buffer.

usage: fc [/a] [/b] [/c] [/l] [/lbNN] [/w] [/t] [/n] [/NNNN] file1 file2
The command line included an invalid switch or FC was entered without any switches or other parameters.

FDISK

Configure Fixed Disk

3.2

External   No Net

Purpose

Configures an MS-DOS partition on a fixed disk. This command is included with PC-DOS beginning with version 2.0.

Syntax

FDISK

Description

A fixed disk can be divided into areas of contiguous tracks, or partitions, that are used by different operating systems. A master control record (partition table) on the disk specifies the ID number and the starting and ending disk tracks for each partition. Each fixed disk can have as many as four partitions, but only one partition can be active (bootable) at any given time.

The FDISK utility is a menu-driven program that adds or deletes an MS-DOS partition on a fixed disk, selects one partition as active, and displays the size and status of all partitions. With most implementations of MS-DOS, each fixed disk can contain only *one* MS-DOS partition.

After an MS-DOS partition is created, the FORMAT command must be used to initialize the partition's directory structure. To make it possible to start the computer from the MS-DOS partition on the fixed-disk drive, the /S switch must be used with FORMAT to transfer the operating-system files and the MS-DOS partition must be the active partition.

Warning: If the MS-DOS partition is deleted, any files stored in the partition are irretrievably lost.

Examples

To display the current partitioning of the fixed disk, type

```
C>FDISK <Enter>
```

The FDISK utility then displays the following menu:

```
Fixed Disk Setup Program Version 0.02
(C) Copyright Microsoft, 1985.

FDISK Options

Choose one of the following:

    1.   Create DOS Partition
    2.   Change Active Partition

    3.   Delete DOS Partition
    4.   Display Partition Data

Enter choice:[1]

Press ESC to return to DOS
```

Note: A fifth option, *Select Next Fixed Drive*, will appear if more than one fixed disk is installed in the system.

Choose option 4 (*Display Partition Data*). FDISK then displays the partition data for the disk in the following form:

```
Display Partition Information

Partition Status  Type   Start  End  Size
    1        A     DOS      0    613  614
Total disk space is 614 cylinders.

Press ESC to return to FDISK Options
```

Assume that the low-level (hardware) formatting for fixed-disk drive C has just been completed by using the drive manufacturer's setup utility. To establish a bootable MS-DOS partition on the disk, type

```
A>FDISK  <Enter>
```

When the menu is displayed, press Enter to choose option 1 (*Create DOS Partition*). FDISK responds with the following message:

```
Create DOS Partition

Do you wish to use the entire fixed
disk for DOS (Y/N) . . . . . . . . . . . . . . . .?[Y]

Press ESC to return to FDISK Options
```

To partition the entire fixed disk for MS-DOS, press Enter to select *Y* (the default). When the FDISK main menu is again displayed, choose option 4 (*Display Partition Data*) to verify that the MS-DOS partition has in fact been established on the fixed disk.

Messages

n is not a choice. Please enter Y or N.
The response to an FDISK prompt requiring a yes or no answer was not *Y* or *N*.

n is not a choice. Please enter a choice
The response to an FDISK prompt requiring a number was not in the proper range or was not a number.

DOS partition created
A new MS-DOS partition has been established on the fixed disk. Use the FORMAT utility to create a directory structure in that partition.

DOS partition deleted
The previously existing MS-DOS partition on the fixed disk has been deleted. Any files contained in the partition are irretrievably lost.

DOS 2.0 or later required
FDISK does not work with versions of MS-DOS earlier than 2.0.

**Do you wish to use the entire fixed
disk for DOS (Y/N) . . . . ?[Y]**
Option 1, *Create DOS Partition*, has been chosen from the main menu. Respond with *Y* or press Enter to use all available cylinders for a single DOS partition; respond with *N* to specify that only part of the fixed disk should be used.

Enter starting cylinder number . . :[n]
Option 1, *Create DOS Partition*, has been chosen from the main menu and the user has responded *N* to the *Do you wish to use the entire fixed disk for DOS?* prompt. This message then prompts for the starting cylinder number of the DOS partition being created.

**Enter the number of the partition you
want to make active . . . . :[n]**
Option 2, *Change Active Partition*, has been chosen from the main menu and this message prompts the user to enter the number of the partition that will become the active partition.

Error loading operating system
An error occurred while attempting to start the system from the fixed disk. Attempt to restart the system. If that fails, start the system from a floppy disk and use the SYS command to copy a new set of the operating-system files to the fixed disk.

Error reading fixed disk
An unrecoverable hardware error was encountered while FDISK was reading data from the fixed disk. The disk may require a low-level (hardware) formatting operation before FDISK can be used; this is usually performed with a special utility program provided by the drive manufacturer.

Error writing fixed disk
An unrecoverable hardware error was encountered while FDISK was writing the new partition control record to the fixed disk. Test the fixed disk with hardware diagnostics before further use.

Fixed disk already has a DOS partition.
The specified fixed disk already contains an MS-DOS partition. Be sure that the correct fixed disk has been selected before proceeding.

Incorrect DOS version
The version of FDISK is not compatible with the version of MS-DOS that is running.

Invalid partition table
The fixed disk's partition table is invalid and the operating system could not be loaded from the fixed disk during system initialization. Restart the computer using a floppy disk and rerun FDISK to determine and correct the problem.

Missing operating system
The DOS partition is the active partition, but it does not contain the operating system. (This message occurs only during system startup.) Use the SYS command to install the operating system.

No DOS partition to delete.
The fixed disk does not contain an MS-DOS partition.

No fixed disks present
FDISK cannot detect a fixed disk in the system. This may reflect a hardware problem with the fixed disk or its controller.

No partitions defined.
This informational message is displayed after the user has chosen option 4, *Display Partition Data*, to indicate that no partitions are currently defined.

No partitions to make active
The fixed disk has not been previously partitioned using FDISK; therefore, an active partition cannot be selected.

No space for a *nnn* cylinder partition.
The fixed disk does not have enough free cylinders to create the desired partition.

No space to create a DOS partition.
The fixed disk does not have enough free cylinders to create an MS-DOS partition.

Partition *n* is already active
The selected partition is already active (bootable); therefore, no action was taken.

Partition *n* made active
This informational message indicates that the selected partition has been made the active partition.

System will now restart
Insert DOS diskette in drive A:
Press any key when ready...
The DOS partition has successfully been created. Strike any key and the system will restart
from the disk in drive A.

The current active partition is _n_.
This informational message indicates which partition is currently bootable.

The table partition can't be made active.
The master partition record cannot be made bootable.

Total disk space is _nnn_ cylinders.
This informational message indicates the total number of cylinders on the fixed disk.

Total disk space is _nnn_ cylinders.
Maximum available space is _nnn_
cylinders at _n_.
The user has responded _N_ to the _Do you wish to use the entire fixed disk for DOS?_ prompt
and this informational message indicates how much space is available for the DOS
partition.

Warning: Data in the DOS partition
will be lost. Do you wish to
continue . . . . ?[N]
If the MS-DOS partition is deleted, all files within the partition are lost. Be sure that the
files are backed up to another disk before proceeding. Respond with _N_ to return to the
FDISK main menu; respond with _Y_ to delete the DOS partition and lose any files within it.

FIND

Find Character String

Purpose

Searches the character stream from a file or from standard input for a string and displays any lines that contain the string on standard output.

Syntax

FIND [/C] [/N] [/V] *"string"* [[*drive:*][*path*]*filename*] [[*drive:*][*path*]*filename* ...]

where:

string	is the character string to be searched for, always enclosed in quotation marks; case is significant.
filename	is the name of the file to be searched, optionally preceded by a drive and/or path; wildcard characters are not permitted.
/C	displays only the count of the lines containing *string*.
/N	includes the relative line number with each line.
/V	displays only those lines that do *not* contain *string*.

Description

The FIND command searches for all occurrences of a specified string in one or more files (or from standard input). Normally, FIND copies each line in which the string is found to standard output, which defaults to the video display but can be redirected to a file or another character device or can be piped to another program.

The string to be searched for must be enclosed in quotation marks. If the search string itself contains sets of quotation marks, each of those sets of quotation marks must be surrounded by an additional set of quotation marks. FIND's string search is case sensitive.

The search string can be followed by the names of one or more source files; these filenames cannot include wildcards. If no filename is supplied, FIND reads lines from standard input; unless input has been redirected from a file or from the output of another program, this means that FIND reads input from the keyboard. (Keyboard input is terminated by pressing Ctrl-Z or F6 followed by Enter.)

The /C switch counts the total number of lines in which the string appears and sends the count, rather than the lines themselves, to standard output. If the /C switch is used with /V, only the total count of lines that do *not* contain the specified search string is displayed. If both /C and /N are included in the same FIND command, the /N is ignored.

The /N switch includes a relative line number with each line sent to standard output. This is especially helpful when the output of FIND is to be used as a guide to editing the files.

The /V switch reverses the action of FIND so that it copies to standard output all lines that do *not* include the specified string.

Examples

To find and display all lines in the files BREAK.ASM, TALK.ASM, and SHELL.ASM that contain the string *es:*, type

```
C>FIND "es:" BREAK.ASM TALK.ASM SHELL.ASM  <Enter>
```

To find and display all lines in the file STORY.TXT that contain the string *he said "no"*, type

```
C>FIND "he said ""no"""" STORY.TXT  <Enter>
```

To search the file \SOURCE\MENUMGR.ASM on the current drive and display all lines that do not contain the string *Error*, type

```
C>FIND /V "Error" \SOURCE\MENUMGR.ASM  <Enter>
```

To obtain a listing on the printer of the lines in the file SHELL.ASM in the current directory of the current drive that contain the string *proc*, including line numbers, type

```
C>FIND /N "proc" SHELL.ASM > PRN  <Enter>
```

To search for all lines that contain two strings, pipe the output of one FIND command to be the input of another. For example, to find only those lines in the file MENUMGR.ASM in the current directory of the current drive that contain both the strings *MOV* and *AX*, type

```
C>FIND "MOV" MENUMGR.ASM ¦ FIND "AX"  <Enter>
```

Messages

---------- *filename*
This informational message gives the name of the file that is currently being searched.

FIND: Access denied
The specified file is locked or being accessed by another application.

FIND: File not found *filename*
The specified file does not exist or the path or drive is not correct.

FIND: Invalid number of parameters
The command line did not include a search string.

FIND: Invalid Parameter *option*
The command line included an invalid switch.

FIND: Read error in *filename*
A disk error occurred during processing of the specified file.

FIND: Syntax error
The command line included an invalid search string. The string must be enclosed in quotation marks.

Incorrect DOS version
The version of FIND is not compatible with the version of MS-DOS that is running.

FORMAT

Initialize Disk

Purpose

Prepares a disk for use by initializing the directory and file allocation table (FAT).

Syntax

FORMAT [*drive*:] [/S]   (versions 1.x)

or

FORMAT [*drive*:] [/O] [/V] [/S]   (versions 2.0–3.1)

or

FORMAT *drive*: [/1] [/4] [/8] [/N:*n*] [/T:*n*] [/V] [/S]   (version 3.2)

or

FORMAT *drive*: [/1] [/B] [/N:*n*] [/T:*n*]   (version 3.2)

where:

drive	is the location of the disk to be formatted.
/1	formats a single-sided disk in a double-sided disk drive.
/4	formats a standard double-sided, double-density disk (360 KB) on a quad-density disk drive.
/8	formats a disk with 8 sectors per track.
/B	formats a disk with 8 sectors per track and preallocates space for the hidden operating-system files.
/N:*n*	formats a disk with *n* sectors per track.
/O	formats a disk that is compatible with PC-DOS versions 1.x.
/S	creates a system (bootable) disk; for most implementations of FORMAT, this must be the last switch in the command line.
/T:*n*	formats a disk with *n* tracks.
/V	allows a volume label to be assigned to the disk after formatting.

Note: Each OEM determines which switches will be supported by the FORMAT utility included with the versions of MS-DOS sold with its computers.

Description

The FORMAT command effectively erases any existing data on a disk and creates a new root directory and file allocation table. Each sector of the disk is checked for defects and unusable sectors are marked so that they will not be assigned to files.

If the *drive* parameter is not supplied, the current or default drive is formatted. (A drive letter *must* be specified with version 3.2.) With versions 3.0 and later, the FORMAT program displays a warning if the drive to be formatted is a fixed disk and asks for confirmation before continuing.

When the formatting operation is complete, FORMAT displays the total amount of disk space, the number of bytes lost to defective sectors, the space reserved for or occupied by the hidden operating-system files (if the /B or /S switch was used), and the remaining free disk space. If a floppy disk was formatted, FORMAT then prompts the user to select between formatting another disk and returning to MS-DOS.

Normally, the type of disk drive determines the format that is given to a disk. For example, if a disk is formatted in a standard double-sided, double-density drive, the format defaults to double-sided, 40 tracks per side, 9 sectors per track. The version-specific default formats are 9 or 15 sectors per track with versions 3.0 and later, depending on the drive type; 9 sectors per track with versions 2.x; and 8 sectors per track with versions 1.x. The /1, /4, /8, /N:n, and /T:n switches can be used to override the default format in some cases. (Not all combinations of /N:n and /T:n are supported on all hardware.)

Note: A disk formatted with the /4 switch might not be reliably read on a single- or double-sided double-density drive.

The /S switch creates a system (bootable) disk that contains a copy of the operating system. After the format operation is complete, the two hidden files IO.SYS and MSDOS.SYS (or IBMBIO.COM and IBMDOS.COM in PC-DOS) and the nonhidden file COMMAND.COM are copied to the newly formatted disk. Most implementations of FORMAT require that the /S switch, if used, be the last switch in the command line.

The /V switch allows a volume label to be assigned to the new disk. After formatting is complete, FORMAT prompts the user for a volume name, which can be as many as 11 characters. (The characters * ? / ¦ . , ; : + = < > [ ] and tab are not permitted in a volume label.) Volume labels are displayed by the DIR, CHKDSK, TREE, and VOL commands and, with MS-DOS versions 3.1 and later and PC-DOS versions 3.0 and later, can be modified with the LABEL command after the disk has been formatted.

The /O switch causes FORMAT to write an 0E5H byte at the start of each directory entry so that the resulting disk is compatible with MS-DOS and PC-DOS versions 1.x.

The /B switch formats a disk for 8 sectors per track and reserves room on the disk for the operating-system files. The operating system can then be transferred to the disk with the SYS command to make the disk bootable. The /B switch cannot be used in the same FORMAT command line as the /V or /S switch.

Warning: Disks in drives affected by an ASSIGN, JOIN, or SUBST command should not be formatted. Disks cannot be formatted over a network.

Return Codes

0   The FORMAT operation was successful.

3   The program was terminated by entry of a Ctrl-C or Ctrl-Break.

4   The program was terminated because of a fatal system error (any error other than 0, 3, or 5).

5   The program was terminated by an *N* response to the fixed-disk prompt *Proceed with FORMAT (Y/N)?*

Note: Return codes are available with MS-DOS version 3.2.

Examples

To format the disk in drive B, type

```
C>FORMAT B:  <Enter>
```

In response, FORMAT displays the following message:

```
Insert new diskette for drive B:
and strike ENTER when ready
```

With versions earlier than 3.2, FORMAT then displays the message

```
Formatting ...
```

after the Enter key is pressed, to show that the formatting operation is in progress. With version 3.2, FORMAT displays the message

```
Head: n Cylinder: nn
```

instead, to show the progress of the formatting operation. With all versions, FORMAT displays the following messages if the formatting operation is successful:

```
Format complete
    362496 bytes total disk space
    362496 bytes available on disk

Format another (Y/N)?
```

The byte values may vary depending on the drive type or the switches used in the command line. If bad sectors were encountered during the format operation, FORMAT also displays the number of bytes in bad sectors.

Note: The *Format complete* message overwrites the head/cylinder status line but is appended to the *Formatting ...* status line.

To format and assign a volume label to the disk in drive B, type

```
C>FORMAT B: /V  <Enter>
```

After the usual formatting messages, FORMAT prompts as follows:

```
Volume label (11 characters, ENTER for none) ?
```

The user can then enter a volume name of as many as 11 characters (except * ? / ¦ . , ; : + = < > [ ] or tab), followed by a press of the Enter key.

To format the disk in drive B and make it a system (bootable) disk, type

```
C>FORMAT B: /S  <Enter>
```

FORMAT initializes the disk in the usual manner and then copies the two files containing the operating system (IO.SYS and MSDOS.SYS or IBMBIO.COM and IBMDOS.COM) and the file COMMAND.COM onto the disk. When the formatting operation is completed on a 360 KB floppy disk, the following messages appear:

```
Format complete
System transferred

    362496 bytes total disk space
     62464 bytes used by system
    300032 bytes available on disk


Format another (Y/N)?
```

The number of bytes used by the system will vary with the version of MS-DOS in use.

Messages

n bytes total disk space
n bytes used by system
n bytes in bad sectors
n bytes available on disk

When formatting is complete, FORMAT displays this message with information about space available on the disk. The *bytes used by system* line will not appear if the /S switch was not specified; the *bytes in bad sectors* line will not appear if no bad sectors were found.

Attempted write-protect violation

The disk to be formatted is write protected. Remove the write-protect tab and respond with a *Y* to the *Format another (Y/N)?* prompt.

Cannot find System Files

The /S switch was used and FORMAT was unable to find the necessary system files in the default drive or in drive A.

Cannot FORMAT a Network drive

An attempt was made to format a disk in a drive that has been assigned to a network.

Cannot format an ASSIGNed or SUBSTed drive.

An attempt was made to format a disk in a drive affected by an ASSIGN or SUBST command.

Disk unsuitable for system disk

Defective sectors were detected on the tracks where the operating-system files would normally reside on a bootable disk. Such a disk should be used only for data files, if at all.

Drive letter must be specified
A drive letter must be specified when using version 3.2.

Drive not ready
The floppy-disk drive is empty or the drive door is not closed.

Enter current Volume Label for drive X:
The specified drive is a fixed disk, so FORMAT prompts the user to enter the current volume label for verification.

Error in IOCTL call
An internal system error occurred when a pre-version-3.2 block-device driver was used with version 3.2 of FORMAT.

Error reading partition table
FORMAT was unable to read the fixed disk's partition table. Use FDISK on the fixed disk and then try the FORMAT command again.

Error writing directory
FORMAT was unable to create a directory on the disk it is attempting to format. The disk is defective.

Error writing FAT
FORMAT was unable to create the FAT on the disk it is attempting to format. The disk is defective.

Error writing partition table
FORMAT was unable to write the fixed disk's partition table. Use FDISK on the fixed disk and then try the FORMAT command again.

Format another (Y/N)?
At the end of a successful formatting operation or after a nonfatal error, this prompt offers the user the opportunity to format another disk using the same switches specified in the original FORMAT command. Respond with *Y* to format another disk; respond with *N* to return to MS-DOS.

Format complete
The formatting operation has ended. This message contains a number of space characters after it and is printed over the top of the head/cylinder status message, effectively erasing it.

Format failure
The formatting operation was not successful. (This message is usually preceded by another message telling the user why the format failed.) This message contains a number of space characters after it and is printed over the top of the head/cylinder status message, effectively erasing it.

Format not supported on drive X:
Device parameters that the computer cannot support were specified in the FORMAT command line.

Formatting...
This informational message indicates that the FORMAT operation is in progress (versions 1.0 through 3.1).

Head: *n* Cylinder: *nn*
This informational message indicates the progress of the FORMAT command during the formatting operation (version 3.2).

Incorrect DOS version
The version of FORMAT is not compatible with the version of MS-DOS that is running.

Insert DOS disk in drive *X*:
and strike ENTER when ready
The /S switch was specified in the FORMAT command line and the disk containing the FORMAT command does not also contain the hidden system files.

Insert new diskette for drive *X*:
and strike ENTER when ready
This prompt allows the user to change disks before the FORMAT operation continues.

Insufficient memory for system transfer
The command line included the /S switch, but available RAM is insufficient to hold the system files during the FORMAT operation.

Invalid characters in volume label
Certain characters (* ? / ¦ . , ; : + = < > [ ] and tab) are not allowed in a volume name.

Invalid device parameters from device driver
The DEVICE or DRIVPARM device-driver parameters in the CONFIG.SYS file were incorrectly set or the fixed disk specified in the command line was formatted using MS-DOS versions 2.x without first running FDISK. FORMAT displays this message when the number of hidden sectors is not evenly divisible by the number of sectors per track (meaning that the partition does not start on a track boundary).

Invalid drive specification
The drive specified after the FORMAT command is not a valid drive.

Invalid media or Track 0 bad - disk unusable
One of the switches supplied in the command line is not valid for the drive containing the disk to be formatted (for example, the /8 switch for a quad-density floppy disk) or track 0 of the disk being formatted is unusable to the point that FORMAT is unable to create a directory or file allocation table (FAT).

Invalid parameter
One of the switches supplied in the command line is not valid or is not supported by the version of FORMAT being used.

Invalid volume ID
The volume label entered in response to the *Enter current Volume Label for drive X:* prompt was not the same as the current volume label. Use the VOL command to determine the current volume label.

Non-System disk or disk error
Replace and strike any key when ready
The command line contained a /S or /B switch, but the source disk does not contain the operating-system files.

Not a block device
The drive containing the disk to be formatted is not recognized by MS-DOS as a valid block device.

Parameters not compatible
Switches that cannot be used together were specified in the command line.

Parameters not compatible with fixed disk
One of the switches specified in the command line is not compatible with the specified drive.

Parameters not supported
One of the parameters specified in the command line is not supported by the version of FORMAT being used.

Parameters not Supported by Drive
The device driver for the specified drive does not support generic IOCTL function requests.

Re-insert diskette for drive X:
This message prompts the user to reinsert the disk being formatted into the specified drive.

System transferred
The system files IO.SYS and MSDOS.SYS (or IBMBIO.COM and IBMDOS.COM in PC-DOS) and the file COMMAND.COM have been successfully transferred to the newly formatted disk.

Too many open files
FORMAT was unable to write the volume label because insufficient system file handles were available. Increase the value of FILES in the CONFIG.SYS file.

Volume label (11 characters, ENTER for none)?
After formatting a disk with the /V option, FORMAT offers the user the opportunity to enter a volume label for the disk.

Unable to write BOOT
The first track of the disk or MS-DOS partition is bad and cannot be made bootable.

WARNING, ALL DATA ON NON-REMOVABLE DISK
DRIVE X: WILL BE LOST!
Proceed with Format (Y/N)?
If a fixed disk is specified as the disk to be formatted, FORMAT warns the user and gives the opportunity to cancel the FORMAT command (versions 3.0 and later).

GRAFTABL

Load Graphics Character Set

3.0 and later

External

Purpose

Installs a RAM-resident table of bitmaps that defines the screen appearance of character codes 128 through 255 in graphics mode.

Syntax

GRAFTABL

Description

On IBM PCs and compatibles in graphics display modes, the video-display BIOS routines (Interrupt 10H) display characters by writing bitmapped matrices of dots to the display. The dot pattern of each screen character's matrix is defined by an entry in a table of bitmaps. The table of bitmaps for the regular ASCII characters, coded 0 through 7FH (0–127), is permanently located in ROM and is always available for use by the system's video driver. The GRAFTABL utility contains a similar table of bitmaps for the upper (extended) characters, coded 80H through 0FFH (128–255). The GRAFTABL command loads this table into RAM and places the address of the table in the vector for Interrupt 1FH.

The GRAFTABL command is not needed for the IBM PCjr or for an enhanced graphics adapter; their ROM BIOS already contains tables of bitmaps for the extended character set.

GRAFTABL is a terminate-and-stay-resident (TSR) program; therefore, its installation reduces the amount of RAM available for use by application programs.

The GRAFTABL command can be executed only once after the computer has been turned on or restarted. An attempt to execute it again will result in an informational message stating that the graphics characters are already loaded.

Example

To load the table of bitmaps for characters 80H through 0FFH (128–255) for use in graphics mode, type

```
C>GRAFTABL  <Enter>
```

Messages

DOS 2.0 or later required
GRAFTABL does not work with versions of MS-DOS earlier than 2.0.

Graphics characters already loaded
The GRAFTABL command has already been executed since the system was turned on or restarted.

Graphics characters loaded
The table of bitmaps has been successfully loaded into RAM and the interrupt vector that points to the table has been initialized.

Incorrect DOS version
The version of GRAFTABL is not compatible with the version of MS-DOS that is running.

GRAPHICS

3.2

Load Graphics Screen-Dump Program

External

Purpose

Installs a resident program that can dump screen contents to the printer in graphics mode. This command is also available with PC-DOS versions 2.0 and later.

Syntax

GRAPHICS   (PC-DOS 2.x)

or

GRAPHICS [*printer*] [/B] [/R]   (PC-DOS 3.0 and above)

or

GRAPHICS [*printer*] [/B] [/C] [/F] [/P *port*] [/R]   (MS-DOS 3.2)

where:

printer   is the type of printer to be supported, from the following list:

        COLOR1   IBM Personal Computer Color Printer with black ribbon

        COLOR4   IBM Personal Computer Color Printer with red-green-blue-black (RGB) ribbon

        COLOR8   IBM Personal Computer Color Printer with cyan-magenta-yellow-black (CMY) ribbon

        COMPACT   IBM Personal Computer Compact Printer

        GRAPHICS IBM Personal Computer Graphics Printer or compatible (the default)

/B   prints the background in color; valid only with the COLOR4 and COLOR8 printers.

/C   centers the printout on the page.

/F   flips (rotates) the printout 90 degrees.

/P *port* specifies which port the printer is attached to (1–3, where 1 = LPT1, 2 = LPT2, and 3 = LPT3).

/R   prints the image as it appears on the screen (white characters on a black background) rather than reversed (the default, black characters on a white background).

Description

The default system routine for dumping the screen to the printer (invoked by Shift-PrtSc) cannot interpret the display in graphics modes. The GRAPHICS command loads a more sophisticated routine that can dump CGA-compatible graphics displays to several models of IBM graphics printers or compatibles.The GRAPHICS command is not compatible with the Hercules monochrome graphics card or with an enhanced graphics adapter in its enhanced display modes.

If the display is in 640 x 200 graphics mode, the screen dump is printed sideways (rotated 90 degrees). A 320 x 200 graphic can be rotated manually by specifying the /F switch in the command line; however, the image will be elongated horizontally. A rotated image is printed along the left side of the page, which is actually the top of the page in terms of image orientation. The /C option can be used to center a rotated 320 x 200 image on the page.

When used with a printer with a black ribbon, GRAPHICS produces screen dumps with as many as four shades of gray to represent the colors. When used with a printer with a color ribbon (type COLOR4 or COLOR8), GRAPHICS prints all the colors except the background color. With printer types COLOR4 and COLOR8, the /B switch can be used to print the background color also.

Ordinarily, the screen image being dumped is reversed from its appearance on the screen; that is, the light areas on the screen are dark on the printed output and vice versa. The /R switch produces a screen dump that is not reversed in this manner.

If the *printer* parameter is not included in the command line, the GRAPHICS program assumes an IBM Personal Computer Graphics Printer or compatible.

If two or more printers are attached to the system, the /P switch can be used to specify which printer GRAPHICS should use.

The GRAPHICS command is a terminate-and-stay-resident (TSR) program; therefore, its installation reduces the amount of RAM available for use by application programs.

Examples

To load the graphics printing program for use with an IBM Personal Computer Graphics Printer or compatible connected to LPT2, type

```
C>GRAPHICS /P 2  <Enter>
```

Note: A tab, a semicolon character (;), or an equal sign (=) can be used between the /P and the port number instead of a space.

To load the graphics printing program for use with the IBM Personal Computer Color Printer with an RGB ribbon and specify that the background color be printed, type

```
C>GRAPHICS COLOR4 /B  <Enter>
```

To load the graphics printing program for use with the IBM Personal Computer Compact Printer and specify that the images be printed sideways and centered on the page, type

```
C>GRAPHICS COMPACT /F /C  <Enter>
```

Messages

DOS 2.0 or later required

GRAPHICS does not work with versions of MS-DOS earlier than 2.0.

Incorrect DOS version

The version of GRAPHICS is not compatible with the version of MS-DOS that is running.

Unrecognized printer

The printer type specified in the command line is invalid or the printer is not supported.

Unrecognized printer port

The port specified with the /P switch is not a number in the range 1 through 3 or an invalid separator character was used.

JOIN

Join Disk to Directory

3.0 and later

External   No Net

Purpose

Joins the directory structure of a disk drive to a subdirectory on another drive.

Syntax

JOIN [*drive1*: *drive2*:*path*]

or

JOIN *drive1*: /D

where:

drive1	is the drive whose directory structure will be joined to a subdirectory of another drive.
drive2:*path*	is the drive and directory that will be used to reference files on *drive1*.
/D	cancels the effect of a previous JOIN command on *drive1*.

Description

The JOIN command allows the directory structure of a disk in one drive to be joined, or spliced, into an empty subdirectory of a disk in another drive. After a JOIN, the entire directory structure of the disk in *drive1*, starting at the root, together with all the files that it contains, appears to be the directory structure of the specified subdirectory on the disk in *drive2*; the drive letter for *drive1* is no longer available. If the directory at the end of the path on *drive2* already exists, it must not contain any files; if it does not exist, JOIN will attempt to create it.

The current directory status of *drive1* has no effect on the JOIN operation. Regardless of which directory or subdirectory is active when the JOIN command is entered, the entire directory structure, including the root directory, is joined to the subdirectory on the disk in *drive2*.

The /D switch cancels any previous JOIN command for a specific drive.

If the JOIN command is entered without parameters, it displays a list of all joins currently in effect.

Warning: The JOIN command should not be used on drives affected by a SUBST or ASSIGN command. Similarly, the BACKUP, RESTORE, FORMAT, DISKCOPY, and DISKCOMP commands should not be used on drives affected by the JOIN command. Drives that have been redirected over a network cannot be joined.

Examples

To join drive B to the subdirectory \DRIVEB on drive C, type

```
C>JOIN B: C:\DRIVEB  <Enter>
```

A subsequent JOIN command without parameters displays

```
B: => C:\DRIVEB
```

To then list the files in the root directory of the disk in drive B, type

```
C>DIR C:\DRIVEB  <Enter>
```

To cancel a previous JOIN command affecting drive B, type

```
C>JOIN B: /D  <Enter>
```

Messages

Cannot JOIN a network drive
A drive assigned to a network cannot be joined to another drive.

Directory not empty
A drive cannot be joined to a directory that already contains files.

DOS 2.0 or later required
JOIN does not work with versions of MS-DOS earlier than 2.0.

Incorrect DOS version
The version of JOIN is not compatible with the version of MS-DOS that is running.

Incorrect number of parameters
There were missing, extra, or incorrect parameters in the command line.

Invalid parameter
A drive cannot be joined to the root directory of any drive.

Not enough memory
The available system memory is insufficient for MS-DOS to run the JOIN command.

KEYB*xx*

Define Keyboard

3.2

External

Purpose

Installs a table that defines the translation of keys to the extended character codes, replacing the default table in the ROM BIOS. This command is included with PC-DOS beginning with version 3.0.

Syntax

KEYB*xx*

where:

xx is a code that selects a keyboard configuration:

DV	Dvorak keyboard (MS-DOS only)
FR	French
GR	German
IT	Italian
SP	European Spanish
UK	United Kingdom English

Note: KEYB*xx* is hardware dependent; therefore, implementation of this command may vary for different OEM versions of MS-DOS.

Description

The KEYB*xx* utility configures the keyboard for use with a language other than United States English, making available special characters that are appropriate for the specified country's language and currency. These special characters are represented by the extended character codes (128–255) that correspond to the characters implemented on the OEM's display adapter. (Both the KEYB*xx* and the GRAFTABL commands must be used to make these characters available in graphics modes on a color/graphics adapter.)

After KEYB*xx* is loaded, special accented characters not part of the language in use are also available through the use of dead keys—keys that are pressed and released before the letter key is pressed. The following dead keys are available on a United States English keyboard for an IBM PC, PC/XT, PC/AT, or strict compatible:

Keyboard Program	Dead Key	Resulting Accent
KEYBGR (Germany)	+	`
	=	´
KEYBFR (France)	[	^
	{	¨
KEYBSP (Spain)	[	´
	]	`
	{	¨
	}	^
KEYBUK (United Kingdom)	Not supported	
KEYBIT (Italy)	Not supported	

The dead-key combinations supported are

Keyboard Program	Combinations Supported
Germany	á é É í ó ú à è ì ò ù
France	ä Ä ë ï ö Ö ü Ü ÿ â ê î ô û
Spain	ä Ä ë ï ö Ö ü Ü ÿ á é É í ó ú
	à è ì ò ù â ê î ô û
United Kingdom	Dead key not supported
Italy	Dead key not supported

On an IBM PC, PC/XT, PC/AT, or strict compatible, the key sequence Ctrl-Alt-F1 can be used at any time to return the keyboard to the default (United States English) configuration; the sequence Ctrl-Alt-F2 then returns the keyboard to the selected configuration.

KEYB*xx* should be loaded only once during an MS-DOS session; the computer should be restarted if KEYB*xx* is loaded for use with a different language.

KEYB*xx* is a terminate-and-stay-resident (TSR) utility and therefore reduces the amount of memory available to transient application programs (by approximately 2 KB). The only way to reclaim this memory is to restart the system.

Example

To configure the keyboard for Germany, type

```
C>KEYBGR  <Enter>
```

Messages

Bad command or filename

The selected keyboard does not exist or the program that configures the keyboard is not present on the disk.

Incorrect DOS version

The version of KEYB*xx* is not compatible with the version of MS-DOS that is running.

LABEL

Modify Volume Label

Purpose

Adds, alters, or deletes a volume label on a disk. This command is included with PC-DOS beginning with version 3.0.

Syntax

LABEL [*drive:*][*label*]

where:

drive   is any valid disk drive.
label   is a name up to 11 characters long.

Description

With MS-DOS versions 2.0 and later, each disk can have a name called a volume label, which is implemented as a special type of entry in the disk's root directory. With MS-DOS versions 2.x, this volume label can be assigned to a disk only at the time the disk is formatted, using the FORMAT command's /V switch. However, with PC-DOS versions 3.0 and later and MS-DOS versions 3.1 and later, the volume label can be added, modified, or deleted at any time using the LABEL command. (A disk's volume label can be displayed with the VOL command; the label is also included as part of the output from the CHKDSK, DIR, and TREE commands.)

If a new volume name is included in the LABEL command line, the disk's label is changed immediately. If LABEL is entered alone or with only a drive letter, a message is displayed giving the current volume label of the disk in the specified drive (or the default drive, if no drive letter is given) and prompting the user for a new label. (A volume label can be from 1 to 11 characters; it cannot contain any of the characters $* ? / \ | . , ; : + = < > [ ]$ or tab.) If no new volume name is supplied (the user did not type a volume label before pressing Enter), LABEL prompts the user to indicate whether the previous volume label should be deleted. Existing files on the disk are in no way affected by the LABEL command.

The LABEL command cannot be used on a network drive. With MS-DOS version 3.2, the LABEL command also cannot be used on a disk in a drive that is affected by an ASSIGN or SUBST command.

Examples

To give the volume label PAYROLL to the disk in drive B, type

```
C>LABEL B:PAYROLL   <Enter>
```

Note that LABEL immediately overwrites any existing volume label on drive B with the new name; no warning of an existing volume label is given.

To remove the volume label LEDGER from the disk in drive A, type

```
C>LABEL A:  <Enter>
```

The LABEL command displays

```
Volume in drive A is LEDGER
Volume label (11 characters, ENTER for  none)?
```

Press the Enter key to receive the additional prompt

```
Delete current volume label (Y/N)?
```

Then respond with *Y* and Enter to remove the volume label from the disk in drive A.

Messages

Cannot LABEL a Network drive
The disk drive specified in the command line cannot be a network drive.

Cannot LABEL a SUBSTed or ASSIGNed drive
The disk drive specified in the command line is currently affected by a SUBST or ASSIGN command (MS-DOS version 3.2).

Delete current volume label (Y/N)?
No volume label was entered in response to the volume-label prompt and a volume label already exists on the disk. Respond with *Y* to delete the current label; respond with *N* to terminate the command.

Incorrect DOS version
The version of LABEL is not compatible with the version of MS-DOS that is running.

Invalid characters in volume label
The characters * ? / \ | . , ; : + = < > [ ] and tab cannot be part of a volume label.

Invalid drive specification
The drive specified in the command line is not valid or does not exist in the system.

No room in root directory
The root directory of the disk in the designated drive is full and a volume label cannot be added. Delete a file or subdirectory from the root directory to make room for the label.

Too many files open
LABEL was unable to write the volume label because no system file handles were available. Increase the value of FILES in the CONFIG.SYS file.

Volume in drive *X* has no label
Volume label (11 characters, ENTER for none)?

or

Volume in drive *X* is *xxxxxxxxxx*
Volume label (11 characters, ENTER for none)?
This informational message informs the user of the current volume label and prompts the user to add, change, or delete it.

MKDIR or MD

Make Directory

2.0 and later

Internal

Purpose

Creates a new directory.

Syntax

MKDIR [*drive*:][*path*] *new_directory*

or

MD [*drive*:][*path*] *new_directory*

where:

new_directory   is a valid directory name, optionally preceded by an existing path and/or a disk drive.

Description

The MKDIR command creates a directory, adding a branch to the hierarchical directory structure of the disk. If the name of the new directory is preceded by a path, indicating that the new directory is to be a subdirectory of that path, the specified path must already exist.

If *new_directory* is not preceded by an existing path or a backslash character (\), it is presumed to be relative to the current directory. If *new_directory* is preceded by a backslash alone, the directory created will be a subdirectory of the root directory, regardless of the current directory. The length of the full path (including *new_directory*) must not exceed 63 characters.

Warning: The MKDIR command should not be used to create new directories on drives affected by an ASSIGN, JOIN, or SUBST command.

Examples

To create a directory named SOURCE in the current directory of the disk in the current drive, type

```
C>MKDIR SOURCE  <Enter>
```

or

```
C>MD SOURCE  <Enter>
```

To create a directory named LETTERS in the existing directory named WORD (which is a subdirectory of the root directory) on the disk in drive D, type

```
C>MKDIR D:\WORD\LETTERS   <Enter>
```

or

```
C>MD D:\WORD\LETTERS   <Enter>
```

Messages

Invalid drive specification
The drive specified in the command line is not valid or does not exist in the system.

Invalid number of parameters
The name of the new directory was not included in the MKDIR command line.

Unable to create directory
The specified directory cannot be created. This may be caused by a full disk (if the new directory would cause the current directory to be extended), a full root directory (if the new directory's parent is the root directory), the existence of a file or directory with the same name, or an invalid *new_directory* name.

MODE

Configure Device

3.2

External

Purpose

The MODE command has four distinct uses:

- To reconfigure a printer attached to a parallel port (LPT1, LPT2, or LPT3) for printing at 80 or 132 characters per line, 6 or 8 lines per inch, or both (if the printer supports these features). In this form, MODE can also be used to select a parallel printer other than the one attached to LPT1 for use as the default printer.
- To select another display or reconfigure the current display. Reconfiguration includes changing between 40-column and 80-column display, changing between monochrome and color display, centering the display on the screen, or any combination of these.
- To configure the baud rate, parity, and number of databits and stop bits of a serial communications port (COM1 or COM2) for use with a specific printer, modem, or other serial device.
- To redirect printer output from a parallel port to one of the serial ports, so that the serial port becomes the system's default printer port.

Because the syntax for each of these uses of MODE is different, they are discussed separately on the following pages.

Although each form of the MODE command can be issued at the system prompt, MODE commands are commonly used within the AUTOEXEC.BAT file to automatically perform any necessary reconfiguration each time the system is turned on or restarted.

The MODE command is included with PC-DOS beginning with version 1.0.

Message

Incorrect Version of MODE
The version of MODE is not compatible with the version of MS-DOS that is running.

MODE

Configure Printer

3.2

External

Purpose

Sets characteristics for IBM-compatible printers connected to a parallel printer port (LPT1, LPT2, or LPT3). This form of the MODE command is included with PC-DOS beginning with version 1.0.

Syntax

MODE LPT*n*[:][*cpl*] [,[*lpi*][,P]]

where:

LPT*n*	is the parallel printer port (*n* = 1, 2, or 3).
cpl	is the number of characters per line (80 or 132, default = 80).
lpi	is the number of lines per inch (6 or 8, default = 6).
P	causes continuous retries when the printer is not ready.

Description

This form of the MODE command configures an IBM or compatible printer connected to parallel port *n*. Its effect on other printer types may vary. The command has the side effect of canceling any redirection that was previously applied to the specified port with a Redirect Printing MODE command.

The first parameter, LPT*n*, designates the parallel printer port to be configured (LPT1, LPT2, or LPT3). All the other parameters are optional.

The *cpl* parameter selects between printing 80 characters on a line (the default) and 132 characters on a line. The *lpi* parameter selects between 6 lines per inch (the default) and 8 lines per inch. (Note that the attached printer must be capable of printing 132 characters per line or 8 lines per inch and of understanding IBM-compatible printer-control codes; otherwise, specifying these values will have no effect.)

The last parameter in the command line, P, configures the system to retry output continuously (or until Ctrl-Break is pressed) if the printer is not ready or not on line (interpreted by the computer as a time-out error), rather than display an error message. (Note that if P is used and *lpi* is omitted, the comma preceding *lpi* must be specified.) Use of the P option causes part of the MODE program to become permanently resident in memory. (This option is not available in PC-DOS version 1.0.)

Examples

To configure the printer on the first parallel port to print 132 characters per line, with 8 lines per inch, type

```
C>MODE LPT1:132,8  <Enter>
```

To configure the system to continually send output to the printer on the second parallel port if a time-out error occurs but to leave the other values at their defaults, type

```
C>MODE LPT2:,,P   <Enter>
```

Messages

DOS 2.0 or later required
MODE does not work with versions of MS-DOS earlier than 2.0.

Incorrect DOS version
The version of MODE is not compatible with the version of MS-DOS that is running.

Infinite retry of parallel printer timeout
The P option was included in the command line and the system will continuously retry to send output to the printer attached to the specified port if it is not ready or not on line.

INTERNAL ERROR in MODE application
An internal error occurred in the MODE utility and the requested reconfiguration was not carried out.

Invalid parameters
The command line included an incorrect parallel-port specification or one of the configuration parameters was not correct.

LPT*n*: set for 80
The specified printer has been configured for 80 characters per line.

LPT*n*: set for 132
The specified printer has been configured for 132 characters per line.

Printer error
The configuration command could not be carried out because the printer is turned off, not ready, or not on line.

Printer lines per inch set
The printer has successfully been configured for the specified 6 or 8 lines per inch.

Resident portion of MODE loaded
The P option was specified in the command line and part of the MODE command has become permanently resident in memory, decreasing slightly the amount of memory available to other programs.

MODE

Set Display Mode

3.2

External

Purpose

Selects the active video adapter and its display mode or reconfigures the current display. This form of the MODE command is included with PC-DOS beginning with version 2.0.

Syntax

MODE *display*

or

MODE [*display*],*shift*[,T]

where:

display   is a video adapter and display mode from the following list:

40	Color/graphics adapter, 40 characters per line
80	Color/graphics adapter, 80 characters per line
BW40	Color/graphics adapter, 40 characters per line, color disabled from composite output
BW80	Color/graphics adapter, 80 characters per line, color disabled from composite output
CO40	Color/graphics adapter, 40 characters per line, color enabled
CO80	Color/graphics adapter, 80 characters per line, color enabled
MONO	Monochrome adapter

shift   is R or L, to shift the display left or right one (40-column display) or two (80-column display) character positions.

T   causes a test pattern to be displayed for screen alignment.

Description

This form of the MODE command has two uses. The first is to select the active video adapter and its display mode (if more than one adapter is present in the system) or to reconfigure the current adapter. The second is to shift the screen display to the left or right to center it. In both cases, the screen is cleared as a side effect of the command.

The *display* parameter selects the active video adapter and mode or reconfigures the current adapter. If a display adapter that is not available is specified, MODE displays an error message.

The *shift* parameter is simply the single character R or L preceded by a comma. Each shift command causes the screen image to be shifted by two characters if the display adapter is in 80-column mode or by one character if it is in 40-column mode. When the T option is also included in the command line, the screen image is shifted, a test pattern is displayed, and the user is prompted to indicate whether the screen should be shifted again. Note that use of *shift* causes part of the MODE program to become permanently resident in memory.

Examples

In a system with both a color/graphics adapter and a monochrome display adapter, to select the monochrome display as the active display, type

```
C>MODE MONO  <Enter>
```

To select a color 80-column text mode on the color/graphics adapter, shift the screen image two characters to the left, and display a test pattern, type

```
C>MODE CO80,L,T  <Enter>
```

Messages

DOS 2.0 or later required
MODE does not work with versions of MS-DOS earlier than 2.0.

Do you see the leftmost 0? (Y/N)

or

Do you see the rightmost 9? (Y/N)
When the *shift* and T options are used together, this message allows the user to shift the test-pattern display successive positions until it is properly centered.

Incorrect DOS version
The version of MODE is not compatible with the version of MS-DOS that is running.

INTERNAL ERROR in MODE application
An internal error occurred in the MODE utility and the requested reconfiguration was not carried out.

Invalid parameter
The specified display adapter or mode is not available.

Requested Screen Shift out of range
The display cannot be shifted any further.

Unable to shift Screen left
The screen has already been shifted as far left as possible or the active display adapter cannot be shifted (monochrome or enhanced graphics adapter).

Unable to shift Screen right
The screen has already been shifted as far right as possible or the active display adapter cannot be shifted (monochrome or enhanced graphics adapter).

MODE

3.2

Configure Serial Port

External

Purpose

Controls the configuration of the serial communications adapter. This form of the MODE command is included with PC-DOS beginning with version 1.1.

Syntax

MODE COM*n*[:]*baud*[,*parity*[,*databits*[,*stopbits*[,P]]]]

where:

COM*n*   is the serial port (*n* = 1 or 2).
baud   is the baud rate (110, 150, 300, 1200, 2400, 4800, or 9600).
parity   is the type of parity checking (N = none, O = odd, E = even, default = E).
databits is the number of bits per character (7 or 8, default = 7).
stopbits is the number of stop bits (1 or 2, default = 1, except with 110 baud where default = 2).
P   causes continuous retries when the output device is not ready.

Description

This form of the MODE command configures the specified serial port for communication with an external device such as a printer, a terminal, or a modem.

The first parameter, COM*n*, designates the serial port to be configured (COM1 or COM2). Except for the port number and the baud rate, which are required, a parameter can be left unchanged by entering a comma without a value in its position in the command line. (If *all* optional parameters are to be left unchanged and P is not used in the command line, no commas are required.)

The baud rate must be one of the values 110, 150, 300, 600, 1200, 2400, 4800, or 9600. The first two digits can be used as an abbreviation for the full value.

The *parity* parameter specifies the type of parity checking to be done on each character and must be one of the characters N, O, or E (for none, odd, or even, respectively); the default is even parity. The *databits* parameter specifies the length of a character and must be either 7 or 8; the default is 7. The *stopbits* parameter is either 1 or 2. If *baud* is set for 110, the default number of *stopbits* is 2; otherwise, the default is 1.

The last parameter in the command line, P, configures the system to retry output continuously (or until Ctrl-Break is pressed) if the device interfaced to the serial port is not ready or not on line, rather than display an error message. Use of the P option causes part of the MODE program to become permanently resident in memory.

Consult the user's manual for the specific printer, modem, terminal, or other device to determine the proper settings for the MODE parameters.

If a serial printer is to be used instead of LPT1 as the system's default printer, the Redirect Printing MODE command must be specified *after* the Configure Serial Port MODE command.

Example

To configure the first serial port for 9600 baud, no parity, 8 databits, and 1 stop bit, type

```
C>MODE COM1:9600,N,8,1  <Enter>
```

Messages

COM*n: baud, parity, databits, stopbits, timeout*
After the serial port is configured successfully, MODE displays an advisory message confirming the settings. If the P option was not used in the command line, a hyphen character (-) is displayed for *timeout*, to indicate no continuous retries if the printer is not ready or is not on line.

COM port does not exist
The serial port specified in the command line does not exist in the system.

DOS 2.0 or later required
MODE does not work with versions of MS-DOS earlier than 2.0.

Incorrect DOS version
The version of MODE is not compatible with the version of MS-DOS that is running.

INTERNAL ERROR in MODE application
An internal error occurred in the MODE utility and the requested reconfiguration was not carried out.

Invalid baud rate specified
The baud rate included in the command line was not one of the allowed values or was abbreviated incorrectly.

Invalid parameters
The command line specified a COM port that does not exist in the system or one of the configuration parameters for the COM port was not valid.

No COM: ports
The computer does not have any serial ports installed.

Resident portion of MODE loaded
The P option was specified in the command line and part of the MODE command has become permanently resident in memory, decreasing slightly the amount of memory available to other programs.

MODE

Redirect Printing

3.2

External

Purpose

Redirects output from a parallel port to a serial communications port. This form of the MODE command is included with PC-DOS beginning with version 1.1.

Syntax

MODE LPT*n*[:][=COM*n*[:]]

where:

LPT*n*   is the parallel port to be redirected (*n* = 1, 2, or 3).
COM*n*   is the serial port (*n* = 1 or 2) to be used for output instead of LPT*n*.

Description

This form of the MODE command redirects any output for the specified parallel port, sending it to the specified serial communications port instead. The parallel port can be LPT1, LPT2, or LPT3; the serial port can be either COM1 or COM2. A Configure Serial Port MODE command is required *before* the Redirect Printing MODE command, to configure the serial port for the proper baud rate, parity, word length, and stop bits.

Redirection can be canceled by entering *MODE LPT*n alone.

Use of MODE to redirect printer output causes part of the MODE program to become permanently resident in memory. Canceling the redirection will not remove this resident portion from memory.

Example

To cause all output to the first parallel port (LPT1) to be redirected to the first serial port (COM1), type

```
C>MODE LPT1:=COM1:  <Enter>
```

Messages

DOS 2.0 or later required
MODE does not work with versions of MS-DOS earlier than 2.0.

Illegal device name
Either the parallel port or the serial port specified in the command line does not exist in the system.

Incorrect DOS version

The version of MODE is not compatible with the version of MS-DOS that is running.

INTERNAL ERROR in MODE application

An internal error occurred in the MODE utility and the requested reconfiguration was not carried out.

LPT*n*: not redirected

No serial port was specified and any previous redirection from the specified parallel port was canceled.

LPT*n*: redirected to COM*n*:

The MODE command has successfully redirected the output for the specified parallel port to the specified serial port.

Resident portion of MODE loaded

Part of the MODE command has become permanently resident in memory, decreasing slightly the amount of memory available to other programs.

MORE
Display by Screenful

2.0 and later

External

Purpose

Displays output one screenful at a time on standard output.

Syntax

MORE

Description

The MORE filter reads lines of text from standard input and sends them to standard output one screenful (23 lines) at a time. At the end of each screenful, MORE displays the message -- *More* -- and then waits for any key to be pressed before it continues. (Pressing Crtl-C or Ctrl-Break terminates the MORE filter.)

The default input device is the keyboard; the default output device is the video display. Because standard input can be redirected, the MORE filter can also accept input from another character device or a file or from the piped output of another program or filter. Similarly, the output of MORE can be redirected to any character device or file or can be piped to another program (however, the message -- *More* -- will be included with the redirected or piped output).

Examples

To display the file SHELL.C one screenful at a time, type

```
C>MORE < SHELL.C  <Enter>
```

To display the directory of \MASM\SOURCE in the current drive one screenful at a time, pipe the output of the DIR command to the MORE filter by typing

```
C>DIR \MASM\SOURCE ¦ MORE  <Enter>
```

Messages

-- More --
This informational message is displayed at the end of each screenful of text. Press any key to resume output.

MORE: Incorrect DOS version
The version of MORE is not compatible with the version of MS-DOS that is running.

PATH

Define Command Search Path

Purpose

Specifies one or more additional drives and/or directories to be searched for a program or batch file if the file cannot be found in the current or specified drive and directory.

Syntax

PATH [*drive*:][*path*][;[*drive*:][*path*]...]

or

PATH ;

where:

drive   is the drive containing the disk to be searched for the executable file.
path   is the name of the directory to be searched for the executable file.

Description

When a command line is entered at the MS-DOS system prompt, the command processor first checks to see if the specified command is one of its internal commands. If it is not, the command processor searches the current directory of the current drive for a file with the same name and the extension .COM, .EXE, or .BAT, in that order. If found, the file is loaded into memory and executed (if the extension is .COM or .EXE) or interpreted by the resident batch-file processor (if the extension is .BAT); otherwise, MS-DOS displays the message *Bad command or file name,* followed by the system prompt. In versions 3.0 and later, a path can precede the command name, causing MS-DOS to make the initial search for a program or batch file under the specified path.

The PATH command designates one or more disk drives and/or directory paths to be searched sequentially for a program or batch file if the file cannot be found in the current or specified drive and directory. The drives and/or directory paths are searched in the order they appear in the PATH command. Multiple *drive:path* pairs can be specified, separated by semicolons. A copy of the PATH string is passed to each executing process as a part of the process's environment.

If the *drive* parameter is specified without an associated path, MS-DOS assumes the root directory of *drive.* If the PATH command is followed only by a semicolon, MS-DOS deletes the existing path. If the PATH command is entered with no parameters, MS-DOS displays the existing path.

Invalid or nonexistent drives and/or paths in the PATH command do not result in an error message but are ignored when the PATH string is inspected later during a search for a program or batch file.

The PATH command is generally placed in the AUTOEXEC.BAT file on the system disk so that the search order will be defined each time the system is turned on or restarted.

Examples

To define the directory \BIN on the disk in drive A as the directory to be searched for a program or batch file if the file is not found in the current or specified directory, type

```
C>PATH A:\BIN  <Enter>
```

Subsequent entry of the command

```
C>PATH  <Enter>
```

results in the display

```
PATH=A:\BIN
```

To define the root, \BIN, \DOS, and \DATA directories on drive C and the \UTIL directory on the disk in drive B as the locations to be searched for a program or batch file if the file is not found in the current or specified directory, type

```
C>PATH C:\;C:\BIN;C:\DOS;C:\DATA;B:\UTIL  <Enter>
```

To delete the current search path, type

```
C>PATH ;  <Enter>
```

Message

No Path
The PATH command was entered without parameters and no search path is currently in effect.

PRINT

Print Spooler

2.0 and later

External

Purpose

Loads and configures the background print spooler or adds or deletes files from the print spooler's queue.

Syntax

PRINT [/D:*device*] [/B:*n*] [/M:*n*] [/Q:*n*] [/S:*n*] [/U:*n*] [[*drive:*][*path*]*filename*] [/C][/P] [[[*drive:*][*path*]*filename*] [/C][/P]...]

or

PRINT /T

where:

filename	is the name of the file to be added to or deleted from the print queue, optionally preceded by a drive (and a path with versions 3.0 and later); wildcard characters are permitted.
/B:*n*	sets the print-buffer size in bytes (1–32767, default = 512) (versions 3.0 and later).
/C	deletes the immediately preceding file and all subsequent files from the print queue (until a /P switch is encountered).
/D:*device*	is the character device to be used for printing (default = PRN); must be the first switch, if used (versions 3.0 and later).
/M:*n*	is the length of time in timer ticks that PRINT keeps control during each of its time slices (1–255, default = 2) (versions 3.0 and later).
/P	adds the immediately preceding file and all subsequent files to the print queue (until a /C switch is encountered).
/Q:*n*	is the maximum number of files allowed in the print queue (1–32, default = 10) (versions 3.0 and later).
/S:*n*	is the number of time slices per second that PRINT gives control to the foreground process (1–255, default = 8) (versions 3.0 and later).
/T	terminates printing and empties the print queue.
/U:*n*	is the number of timer ticks that PRINT waits for a busy or unavailable printer or for a disk access or MS-DOS function call to terminate before giving up the time slice (1–255, default = 1) (versions 3.0 and later).

Description

The PRINT utility is a terminate-and-stay-resident (TSR) program that can print files from disk while other programs are running. PRINT maintains a first-in, first-out (FIFO) queue that can hold the names of as many as 32 files. PRINT does not attempt to interpret the contents of a file, except to expand tab characters (ASCII code 09H) with spaces to the next eight-column boundary and to interpret 1AH characters as end-of-file marks. (A program such as PRINT that can transfer files to a printer without any special knowledge of their contents or origin is called a print spooler.)

Note: The PRINT utility continues printing a file until it encounters an end-of-file character (1AH). Therefore, if PRINT is used with nontext files, it may encounter a 1AH character before reaching the end of the file and terminate printing before the entire file has been processed. In such cases, files should be printed using the COPY command, with PRN as the destination.

The PRINT program employs a technique called time-slicing, which is based on its use of the timer-tick interrupt and its detailed knowledge of MS-DOS. PRINT uses this interrupt, which occurs 18.2 times per second on IBM PC-compatible machines, to divide the processor's time between an application or utility program (such as a word processor or a spreadsheet) and the print spooler. Because the application program typically controls the display screen and the keyboard and receives most of the CPU time, it is called the foreground program. The print spooler, which receives a lesser part of the CPU time and usually operates without indicating its status or progress to the operator, is called the background program.

The /B:n, /D:*device*, /Q:n, /M:n, /S:n, and /U:n switches configure the PRINT utility. These switches are used only the first time the PRINT command is entered after the system has been turned on or restarted.

The /D:*device* switch, which must be the first switch in the command line if used, specifies the peripheral device the print spooler is to use for output. This can be any legal character-output device that is present in the system. If /D:*device* is not included in the first PRINT command, PRINT prompts the user to select an output device (default = PRN). Once an output device has been assigned, a new device cannot be selected without restarting the system.

The /B:n switch sets the size of PRINT's file buffer, which controls the amount of data that is read from a file at one time for printing. The value of n must be between 1 and 32767 bytes (default value = 512). Large file buffers reduce the amount of extra disk activity caused by the print spooler, but they also reduce the amount of memory available for use by other programs. The /Q:n switch controls the size of PRINT's queue — that is, the number of files that can be held in the buffer pending printing. The queue can be configured to hold 1 to 32 files (default = 10).

The /S:n, /M:n, and /U:n switches, available only with versions 3.0 and later, control the time-slicing behavior of PRINT. The /S:n switch sets the number of time slices per second — that is, how many times per second — PRINT will be given control; n is in the range 1 through 255 (default = 8). The /M:n switch sets the length of time (in timer ticks) that PRINT will keep control during each of its time slices; n is in the range 1 through 255 (default = 2). The /U:n switch specifies how long (in timer ticks) PRINT should wait for a busy or unavailable printer or for a disk access or MS-DOS function call to terminate before giving up its time slice; again, n is in the range 1 through 255 (default = 1). Unless there are special circumstances, the default values for these switches will give acceptable performance.

Files are added to the print queue by entering PRINT followed by one or more pathnames. Files are printed in the order they are placed in the queue. At the end of each file, the print spooler advances the paper to the top of the next page. If a filename containing wildcards is used, all matching files are added to the queue in the order in which they appear in the directory. After a file is queued for printing, it should not be renamed or erased, nor should the disk containing the file be removed, until the printing is complete.

Note: Each print queue entry can be a maximum of 63 characters, including the drive and path.

The /P and /C switches allow files to be added to and deleted from the print queue in the same command line. The /P switch (the default) adds to the print queue the immediately preceding file in the command line and all subsequent files until a /C switch is encountered. Conversely, the /C switch cancels printing for the immediately preceding file in the command line and for all subsequent files until a /P switch is encountered. If a canceled file is currently being printed, PRINT prints the message *File* filename *canceled by operator* on the listing, sounds the printer's alarm (if it has one), and advances the paper to the top of the next page.

The /T switch terminates printing by deleting all files from the print queue. If a file is currently being printed, PRINT prints the message *All files canceled by operator* on the listing, sounds the printer's alarm (if it has one), and advances the paper to the top of the next page.

If PRINT encounters a disk error while attempting to print a particular file, it cancels that file, prints an error message on the printer, sounds the printer's alarm (if it has one), advances the paper to the top of the next page, and goes to the next file in the print queue.

If the PRINT command is entered with no parameters, the contents of the print queue are displayed.

Because PRINT is a TSR utility, it reduces the amount of memory available for use by other programs. The only way to recover the memory occupied by PRINT, even after printing is complete, is to restart the system.

Examples

To install and configure the PRINT program and specify the auxiliary device (AUX) as the printing device, with a print queue that can hold as many as 32 filenames and with a buffer size of 2048 bytes, type

```
C>PRINT /D:AUX /Q:32 /B:2048  <Enter>
```

To add the file DOC.TXT in the current directory of the current drive to the print spooler's queue, type

```
C>PRINT DOC.TXT  <Enter>
```

To delete the file READY.TXT from the print queue and simultaneously add the files FINAL.TXT and REPORT.TXT to the queue, type

```
C>PRINT READY.TXT /C FINAL.TXT /P REPORT.TXT  <Enter>
```

To cancel the file being printed and remove all pending files from the print queue, type

```
C>PRINT /T  <Enter>
```

Messages

filename **File not found**
A disk was changed or the file was renamed or erased after the PRINT command was entered but before the file was actually printed.

filename **File not in print queue**
A command line with a /C switch specified a file that is not in the print queue.

filename **is currently being printed**
This informational message shows which file PRINT is currently printing.

filename **is in queue**
This informational message shows which file is in the queue waiting to be printed.

filename **Pathname too long**
The pathname of a file to be printed exceeded 63 characters.

Access denied
An attempt was made to print a locked file.

All files canceled by operator
The /T switch was included in the command line. PRINT terminates printing of the current file, empties the print queue, sounds the printer alarm (if it has one), and advances the paper to the top of the next page.

Cannot use PRINT - Use NET PRINT
If network support has been installed, the NET PRINT command must be used to print files.

Errors on list device indicate that it may be off-line. Please check it.
The printer has been turned off or placed off line while files are still in the print queue.

File *filename* canceled by operator
A PRINT command was entered with the /C switch to cancel a specific file. If the specified file is currently being printed, PRINT terminates printing of the file, sounds the printer alarm (if it has one), advances the paper to the top of the next page, and resumes printing with the next file in the queue.

Incorrect DOS version
The version of PRINT is not compatible with the version of MS-DOS that is running.

Invalid drive specification
A drive letter specified in the command line is invalid or does not exist in the system.

Invalid parameter
The command line included an invalid switch or configuration switches were used after the first time the PRINT command was used.

List output is not assigned to a device
An invalid destination device was previously entered. Restart the system and specify a valid device in the PRINT command.

Name of list device [PRN]:
This message is displayed in response to the first PRINT command line if the /D:*device* switch was not included. Specify any valid character-output device (default = PRN).

No paper error writing device *device*
An out-of-paper device error was detected while printing on the specified device.

PRINT queue is empty
No files are waiting to be printed.

PRINT queue is full
No additional files can be added to the print queue until the current file is printed. To increase the size of the print queue, restart the system and use the /Q:n switch in the PRINT command.

Resident part of PRINT installed
This informational message is displayed on the first entry of a PRINT command to indicate that the PRINT utility is now resident in memory. The amount of memory available to application programs is reduced accordingly.

PROMPT

Define System Prompt

2.0 and later

Internal

Purpose

Defines the form of the command processor's prompt. This command is included in PC-DOS beginning with version 2.1.

Syntax

PROMPT [*string*]

where:

string   is a combination of ordinary printable characters and the following special display codes:

Code	Meaning
$b	¦ character
$d	Current date (in the form *Day mm-dd-yyyy*)
$e	Escape character (1BH)
$g	> character
$h	Backspace character (erases the previous character)
$l	< character
$n	Current drive
$p	Current drive and path
$q	= character
$t	Current time (in the form *hh:mm:ss.hh*)
$v	MS-DOS version number
$_	Carriage return/linefeed pair (starts a new line)
$$	$ character

Description

The system's default command processor, COMMAND.COM, displays a prompt on the screen whenever it is ready to accept a command from the user. The command processor determines the format of the prompt from the PROMPT environment variable, if it exists. Otherwise, it uses the default format, which in most OEM implementations of MS-DOS is the letter of the current drive followed by a greater-than sign (for example, C>).

The PROMPT command allows the user to customize the system prompt. This command is usually included in the AUTOEXEC.BAT file so that MS-DOS displays the custom prompt when the system is turned on or restarted.

The *string* parameter can be any combination of printable characters and the special $ control codes listed in the preceding table. The special $ codes allow certain variable information, such as the date and time, to be obtained from the operating system and displayed as part of the prompt. Such system information can be edited in the prompt with the backspace function, which is invoked with the code $h.

Note: When the time is displayed as part of a prompt, it is updated only when the command processor redisplays the prompt.

The escape character, invoked with the code $e, can be used to include standard ANSI escape sequences in *string* to control the appearance of text or its position on the screen. *See* USER COMMANDS: ANSI.SYS for further information on the ANSI escape sequences and the ANSI device driver.

If PROMPT is entered with no parameters, the system prompt is reset to the default format.

The PROMPT command works by modifying the PROMPT environment variable. The same result can be obtained using the SET command with *PROMPT*=string as its argument. *See* USER COMMANDS: SET for further discussion of the environment block and environment variables.

Examples

To define the system prompt as the word *Command* followed by a colon, type

```
C>PROMPT Command:  <Enter>
```

On fixed-disk-based systems it is desirable to display the current drive and path as part of the prompt. To define such a prompt followed by a > character, type

```
C>PROMPT $p$g  <Enter>
```

To define the system prompt to display the time, date, and current drive and path followed by a > character, each on a separate line, type

```
C>PROMPT $t$_$d$_$p$g  <Enter>
```

The system will respond with a display in the following form:

```
16:07:31.56
Thu  6-18-1987
C:\BIN\DOS>
```

To create a prompt that displays the time without the seconds and hundredths of a second, followed by a space and the date without the year, followed by a space and the current drive and a > character, type

```
C>PROMPT $t$h$h$h$h$h$h $d$h$h$h$h$h $n$g  <Enter>
```

The system will respond with

```
16:07 Thu  6-18 C>
```

To define a prompt that always displays the current time and date in the upper right corner of the screen before displaying the current drive and the > character on the current line, type

```
C>PROMPT $e[s$e[0;60H$t$h$h$h$h$h$h $d$e[u$n$g  <Enter>
```

The escape sequence *$e[s* saves the current cursor position; the sequence *$e[0;60H* positions the cursor at row 0, column 60; the next several codes format the date and time; the sequence *$e[u* restores the original cursor position. (This example requires that the ANSI driver be loaded to interpret the escape sequences.)

RAMDRIVE.SYS

Virtual Disk

3.2

External

Purpose

Creates a virtual disk in memory.

Syntax

DEVICE=[*drive*:][*path*]RAMDRIVE.SYS [*size*] [*sector*] [*directory*] [/A¦/E]

where:

size	is the size of the virtual disk in kilobytes (minimum = 16, default = 64).
sector	is the sector size in bytes (128, 256, 512, or 1024; default = 128).
directory	is the maximum number of entries in the virtual disk's root directory (3–1024, default = 64).
/A	causes RAMDRIVE to use Lotus/Intel/Microsoft Expanded Memory for storage (cannot be used with /E).
/E	causes RAMDRIVE to use extended memory for storage (cannot be used with /A).

Note: Unless a /A or /E switch is used, the virtual disk is created in conventional memory.

Description

The RAMDRIVE.SYS installable device driver allows the configuration of one or more virtual disks (sometimes referred to as electronic disks or RAMdisks). A virtual disk is implemented by mapping a disk's structure — directory, file allocation table, and files area — onto an area of random-access memory, rather than onto actual sectors located on a magnetic recording medium. Access to files stored on a virtual disk is very fast, because no moving parts are involved and the "disk" operates at the speed of the system's memory.

Warning: Because a RAMdisk resides entirely in RAM and is therefore volatile, any information stored there is irretrievably lost when the computer loses power or is restarted.

RAMDRIVE.SYS can create a virtual disk in conventional memory, extended memory, or Lotus/Intel/Microsoft Expanded Memory. Conventional memory is the term for the up-to-640 KB of RAM that contain MS-DOS and any application programs. Extended memory is the term for the memory at addresses above 1 MB (100000H) that is available on 80286-based personal computers such as the IBM PC/AT. Expanded memory is the term for a subsystem of bank-switched memory boards (and a driver to manage them) that is compatible with the Lotus/Intel/Microsoft Expanded Memory Specification (LIM EMS).

A virtual disk can be installed in conventional memory by simply inserting the line *DEVICE=RAMDRIVE.SYS* into the system's CONFIG.SYS file and restarting the system. A new "drive" then becomes available in the system, with a default size of 64 KB, 128-byte sectors, and 64 available directory entries (assuming memory is sufficient). The virtual disk is assigned the next available drive letter (which is displayed in RAMDRIVE's sign-on message). The drive letter assigned depends on the number of other physical and virtual disks in the system and also on the position of the *DEVICE=RAMDRIVE.SYS* line in the CONFIG.SYS file relative to other installed block devices. Available memory permitting, multiple virtual disks can be created by using multiple *DEVICE=RAMDRIVE.SYS* lines. Several optional parameters allow the user to customize the size and configuration of the virtual disk and to use extended memory or expanded memory if it is available.

The *size* parameter specifies the amount of RAM, in kilobytes, to be allocated to the virtual disk. The default is 64 KB, but any size from 16 KB to the total amount of available memory can be specified.

The *sector* parameter sets the virtual sector size used within the virtual disk. The *sector* value can be 128, 256, 512, or 1024 bytes (default = 128 bytes). Selection of the smallest sector size results in a minimum of wasted virtual disk space per file but also results in a somewhat slower transfer of data. Physical disk devices on IBM PC-compatible systems always use 512-byte sectors.

Warning: The 1024-byte sector size is not supported in most implementations of MS-DOS and will terminate the installation of RAMDRIVE.SYS if it is used. Check the documentation included with the computer to see if this value is supported.

The *directory* parameter sets the number of available entries in the virtual disk's root directory. The allowed range is 3 to 1024 (default = 64). Each directory entry requires 32 bytes. RAMDRIVE rounds the number of available directory entries up, if necessary, so that an integral number of sectors are assigned to the root directory.

The /A switch causes Lotus/Intel/Microsoft Expanded Memory to be used for the virtual disk, rather than conventional memory; the /E switch causes extended memory to be used. Either option allows very large virtual disks to be configured while still leaving the maximum amount of conventional memory available for use by application programs. The /A and /E switches cannot be used together.

Note: If RAMDRIVE uses conventional memory for virtual disk storage, the memory cannot be reclaimed except by modifying the CONFIG.SYS file and restarting the system.

Examples

To create a virtual disk drive with the default values of 64 KB disk size, 128-byte sectors, and 64 available directory entries, include the following command

```
DEVICE=RAMDRIVE.SYS
```

in the CONFIG.SYS file and restart the system.

To create a 4 MB virtual disk drive in Lotus/Intel/Microsoft Expanded Memory, with 512-byte sectors and 224 available directory entries, when RAMDRIVE.SYS is located in a directory named \DRIVERS on drive C, include the command

```
DEVICE=C:\DRIVERS\RAMDRIVE.SYS 4096 512 224 /A
```

in the CONFIG.SYS file and restart the system.

Messages

Microsoft RAMDrive version *n.nn* virtual disk *X*:
    Disk size: *nn*k
    Sector size: *nnn* bytes
    Allocation unit: *n* sectors
    Directory entries: *nnn*
RAMDRIVE.SYS was successfully installed and this message informs the user of the version of RAMDRIVE.SYS that created the virtual disk, the drive letter assigned to the disk, and the characteristics of the disk.

RAMDrive: Above Board Memory Manager not present
The /A switch was used in the command line and the Lotus/Intel/Microsoft Expanded Memory Manager is not present in the system. Place the DEVICE command that loads the memory manager *before* the *DEVICE=RAMDRIVE.SYS* command in the CONFIG.SYS file.

RAMDrive: Above Board Memory Status shows errors
The Above Board device driver is bad or damaged or the board itself is defective. Consult the Above Board manual or the manufacturer.

RAMDrive: Computer must be PC-AT, or PC-AT compatible.
The /E switch was used in the command line and the computer is not an 80286-based IBM PC/AT or compatible.

RAMDrive: Incorrect DOS version
The version of RAMDRIVE.SYS is not compatible with the version of MS-DOS that is running.

RAMDrive: Insufficient memory
Available memory is insufficient for RAMDRIVE.SYS to create a virtual drive.

RAMDrive: Invalid parameter
One of the parameters supplied in the command line is incorrect or is not supported by the computer.

RAMDrive: I/O error accessing drive memory
The Expanded Memory Manager device driver is bad or damaged or the board itself is defective. Consult the board's manual or contact the manufacturer.

RAMDrive: No extended memory available
The /E switch was specified but the system does not contain extended memory.

RECOVER

Recover Files

2.0 and later

External   No Net

Purpose

Reconstructs files from a disk that has developed unreadable sectors or has a damaged directory.

Syntax

RECOVER *drive*:

or

RECOVER [*drive*:][*path*]*filename*

where:

drive   is the letter of the drive holding the disk with a damaged directory.
filename is the name of the file that will be reconstructed, optionally preceded by a drive and/or path; wildcard characters are not permitted.

Description

The RECOVER command partially rescues a file on a disk that has developed bad sectors by deleting the bad sectors from the file. RECOVER can also reconstruct files (including files stored in subdirectories) from a disk that has a damaged directory.

When RECOVER is used with a filename, the file is read allocation unit by allocation unit; unreadable allocation units are marked as bad and are no longer allocated to the file. The resulting file is usable, although the data contained in the bad allocation units is lost. (The recovered file may or may not be reusable by the specific application that created it.) The directory entry for *filename* is also adjusted to reflect the sectors that were lost and the bad sectors are marked in the disk's file allocation table so that they are not reused for another file.

If a disk's directory is damaged, it still may be possible to recover all the files on the disk and build a new directory by using RECOVER with *drive* as the only command-line parameter. RECOVER completely erases the previous contents of the damaged directory and constructs new directory entries for each of the original files by inspecting the disk's file allocation table. The recovered files receive names of the form FILE*nnnn*.REC, starting with FILE0001.REC. Each recovered file's size is always a multiple of the disk cluster size, so recovered files may require editing to eliminate spurious data at the ends of the files.

RECOVER restores each subdirectory as an individual file that contains the names of the files originally stored in it. The actual files contained within those subdirectories are also reconstructed, although they are no longer associated with the subdirectory in which they originally resided. Restored files and subdirectories, regardless of their location on the damaged disk, are placed in the new root directory. If there are more files on the damaged disk than can be contained in the new root directory (for example, more than 112 for a 5.25-inch, 360 KB floppy disk), the user must repeat the RECOVER command after copying the already-recovered files to another disk and deleting them from the damaged disk.

Examples

To recover the file MENUMGR.C in the current directory of the current drive, type

```
C>RECOVER MENUMGR.C  <Enter>
```

To recover all files on the disk in drive B, which has a damaged directory, type

```
C>RECOVER B:  <Enter>
```

Messages

n file(s) recovered
When RECOVER is used on a disk with a damaged directory, this informational message is displayed at the conclusion of processing to indicate how many files of the form FILE*nnnn*.REC were constructed.

n of *n* bytes recovered
When RECOVER is used on a damaged file, this informational message is displayed at the conclusion of processing to advise how many bytes of the file were recovered.

Cannot RECOVER a Network drive
Files on a drive assigned to a network cannot be recovered.

File not found
The file specified in the command line cannot be found or does not exist.

Incorrect DOS version
The version of RECOVER is not compatible with the version of MS-DOS that is running.

Invalid drive or file name
An invalid drive letter was specified or the filename contains a wildcard.

Invalid number of parameters
More than one drive letter or filename was specified in the command line.

Press any key to begin recovery of the
file(s) on drive *X*
This prompt message gives the user the opportunity to change disks after the RECOVER program is loaded but before processing begins.

Warning - directory full
New directory entries for the reconstructed files cannot be created because the root directory is full. Copy the recovered files to another disk, delete them from the damaged disk, and then repeat the RECOVER command on the damaged disk.

RENAME or REN

Change Filename

1.0 and later

Internal

Purpose

Changes the name of a file or set of files.

Syntax

RENAME [*drive*:][*path*]*oldname newname*

or

REN [*drive*:][*path*]*oldname newname*

where:

oldname   is the name of an existing file or set of files, optionally preceded by a drive
and/or path; wildcard characters are permitted.

newname   is the new name to be assigned to *oldname*; wildcard characters are permitted, but a drive and/or path cannot be specified.

Description

The RENAME command changes the name of an existing file or set of files. It does not
make copies of files or move files from one location in the disk's directory structure to
another or from one drive to another.

The *oldname* parameter can refer to a single file or can include wildcards to specify a set
of files; a drive and path can be included as part of *oldname*.

The *newname* parameter specifies the new name to be given to the file or files; it cannot
include a drive or path. A wildcard in *newname* causes that portion of the original filename to be left unchanged. If the new name for a file is the same as the name of an existing file, RENAME terminates with an error message.

Examples

To rename the file REVS.DOC, located in the current directory of the current drive, to
CHANGES.TXT, type

```
C>RENAME REVS.DOC CHANGES.TXT  <Enter>
```

or

```
C>REN REVS.DOC CHANGES.TXT  <Enter>
```

To rename all files with a .DOC extension in the \SOURCE directory on the disk in drive D
to have a .TXT extension, type

```
C>REN D:\SOURCE\*.DOC *.TXT  <Enter>
```

Messages

Duplicate file name or File not found
The new name specified for a file already exists or a file with the old name cannot be found or does not exist.

Invalid directory
The command line included a reference to a directory that is invalid or does not exist.

Invalid drive specification
The command line included a reference to a disk drive that is invalid or does not exist in the system.

Invalid number of parameters
The command line included too few or too many filenames.

Invalid parameter
The *newname* parameter in the command line included a drive and/or path.

REPLACE

3.2

Update Files

External

Purpose

Selectively adds or replaces files on a disk.

Syntax

REPLACE [*drive:*]*pathname* [*drive:*][*path*] [/A][/D][/P][/R][/S][/W]

where:

pathname	is the name and location of the source files to be transferred, optionally preceded by a drive; wildcard characters are permitted in the filename.
drive:path	is the destination for the file being transferred; filenames are not permitted in the destination parameter.
/A	transfers only those source files that do not exist at the destination (cannot be used with /S or /D).
/D	transfers only those source files with a more recent date than their destination counterparts (cannot be used with /A).
/P	prompts the user for confirmation before each file is transferred.
/R	allows REPLACE to overwrite destination read-only files.
/S	searches all subdirectories of the destination directory for a match with the source files (cannot be used with /A).
/W	causes REPLACE to wait for the disk to be changed before transferring files.

Description

The REPLACE utility allows files to be updated easily to more recent versions. REPLACE examines the source and destination directories and, depending on the switches used in the command line, selectively updates matching files or copies only those files that exist on the source disk but not the destination disk.

The *pathname* parameter (the source) specifies the name and location of the files to be transferred (optionally preceded by a drive); wildcards are permitted in the filename. The *drive:path* parameter (the destination) specifies the location of the files to be replaced and can consist of a drive, a path, or both. If only a drive is specified as the destination, REPLACE assumes the current directory of the disk in that drive. If the destination is omitted completely, REPLACE assumes the current drive and directory. The /S switch causes REPLACE to also search all subdirectories of the destination directory for files to be replaced.

The /A, /D, and /P switches allow selective replacement of files on the destination disk. When the /A switch is used, REPLACE transfers only those files on the source disk that do not exist in the destination directory. When the /D switch is used, REPLACE transfers only those source files that match the destination filenames but have a more recent date than their destination counterparts. (The /D switch is not available with the PC-DOS version of REPLACE.) The /P switch causes REPLACE to prompt the user for confirmation before each file is transferred.

The /R switch allows the replacement of read-only as well as normal files. If the /R switch is not used and one of the destination files that would otherwise be replaced is marked read-only, the REPLACE program terminates with an error message. (REPLACE cannot be used to update hidden or system files.)

The /W switch causes REPLACE to pause and wait for the user to press any key before beginning the transfer of files. This allows the user to change disks in floppy-disk systems with no fixed disk and in those cases where the REPLACE program itself is present on neither the source nor the destination disk.

Return Codes

0	The REPLACE operation was successful.
1	An error was found in the REPLACE command line.
2	No matching files were found to replace.
3	The source or destination path was invalid or does not exist.
5	One of the files to be replaced was marked read-only and the /R switch was not included in the command line.
8	Memory was insufficient to run the REPLACE command.
15	An invalid drive was specified in the command line.
Other	Standard MS-DOS error codes (returned on a failed Interrupt 21H file-function request).

Examples

To replace the files in the directory \SOURCE on the current drive with all matching files on the disk in drive A that have a more recent date, type

```
C>REPLACE A:*.* \SOURCE /D  <Enter>
```

To transfer from the disk in drive A only those files that are not already present in the current directory, type

```
C>REPLACE A:*.* /A  <Enter>
```

Messages

n File(s) added
After the replacement operation is completed, if the /A switch was used in the command line, REPLACE displays the total number of files added.

n File(s) replaced
After the replacement operation is completed, REPLACE displays the total number of files processed.

Access denied *'pathname'*
One of the files to be replaced on the destination disk is marked read-only and the /R switch was not included in the command line.

Add *pathname*? **(Y/N)**
The /A and /P switches were specified in the command line and REPLACE prompts the user for confirmation before adding each file.

Adding *pathname*
The /A switch was specified in the command line and REPLACE displays the name of each file it adds.

File cannot be copied onto itself *'pathname'*
The source and destination command-line parameters specified the same file in the same location.

Incorrect DOS Version
The version of REPLACE is not compatible with the version of MS-DOS that is running.

Insufficient disk space
The destination disk does not have enough available space to hold the files being added or replaced.

Insufficient memory
The system does not have enough RAM available to process the REPLACE command.

Invalid drive specification *'X:'*
The command line specified a disk drive that is invalid or does not exist in the system.

Invalid parameter *'switch'*
The command line included a switch that is not supported by the REPLACE command.

No files added
The /A switch was used and the specified file(s) already exist on the destination disk.

No files found *'pathname'*
The files to be added or replaced on the destination disk were not found on the source disk.

No files replaced
The files at the destination are identical with the files on the source disk or do not meet the criteria specified by the switches.

Parameters not compatible
The command line included two or more switches that cannot be used together.

Path not Found *'pathname'*
The source or destination parameter included a nonexistent path or directory.

Path too long

The source or destination parameter included a path element that is too large (probably because of a missing backslash character [\]).

Press any key to begin adding file(s)

The /W and /A switches were specified in the command line and REPLACE waits for the user to press a key before proceeding, allowing disks to be changed.

Press any key to begin replacing file(s)

The /W switch was specified in the command line and REPLACE waits for the user to press a key before proceeding, allowing disks to be changed.

Replace *pathname*? **(Y/N)**

The /P switch was specified in the command line and REPLACE prompts the user for confirmation before replacing the file.

Replacing *pathname*

This informational message indicates the progress of the REPLACE command by displaying the name of each file as it is being replaced.

Source path required

Although the destination parameter can usually be omitted and defaults to the current drive and directory, the source location for the files to be replaced must always be specified.

Unexpected DOS Error *n*

This message usually indicates a bad or damaged disk. Use the CHKDSK command to determine the problem.

RESTORE

Restore Backup Files

2.0 and later

External

Purpose

Restores files from a disk created with the BACKUP command.

Syntax

RESTORE *drive1*: [*drive2*:][*pathname*] [/A:*date*] [/B:*date*] [/E:*time*] [/L:*time*][/M][/N] [/S][/P]

where:

drive1	is the drive that contains the backup files created by the BACKUP command.
drive2	is the drive to which the backup files will be restored.
pathname	is the name of the file(s) to be restored from *drive1*; wildcard characters are permitted in the filename. If a path is used, a filename must be specified.
/A:*date*	restores files that were modified on or after *date*.
/B:*date*	restores files that were modified on or before *date*.
/E:*time*	restores files modified at or before *time*.
/L:*time*	restores files modified at or after *time*.
/M	restores only files modified since the last backup.
/N	restores only files that no longer exist on the destination disk.
/P	prompts the user for confirmation before restoring hidden or read-only files or before overwriting files that have changed since they were last backed up .
/S	restores all files in the subdirectories of the specified directory, in addition to the files in the specified directory.

Note: The PC-DOS version of RESTORE supports only the /P and /S switches.

Description

The RESTORE command restores files from a backup disk or directory created with the BACKUP command to their original location in a directory structure. Before version 3.1, the RESTORE command could restore files only from one floppy disk to another or from a floppy disk to a fixed disk. With later versions, RESTORE can also restore files from one fixed disk to another or from a fixed disk to a floppy disk.

The *drive1* parameter specifies the source for the backed-up files. If the source disk is a fixed disk, the backup files are always obtained from the directory \BACKUP. If multiple floppy disks were used to hold the backed-up files, RESTORE prompts the user for each disk as it is required.

The destination can be any combination of a drive, a path, and a filename; the filename can include wildcards. If the destination drive is omitted, MS-DOS assumes the current drive. If a path is not specified, the files are restored to the current directory. (Note that files must be restored to the same directory they were backed up from.) If a path is specified, a filename must be specified as well. If neither a path nor a filename is included in the command line, all directories, subdirectories, and files on the backup disk(s) are restored to the destination disk. The /S switch can be used to force restoration of the files in all the subdirectories of a named directory.

Files are restored in the order they were backed up, regardless of their current order on the destination disk. If files with the same name and location already exist on the destination disk, they are replaced by the backup copies.

The RESTORE program supports a number of switches that allow selective restoration of files from the backup disk. The /A:*date*, /B:*date*, /E:*time*, and /L:*time* switches allow files to be restored based on the time and/or date they were backed up. The /M switch restores only those files that have been changed on the destination disk since the backup disk was created. The /P switch prompts the user before restoring a hidden or read-only file or a file that has been changed since it was last backed up.

The MS-DOS and PC-DOS RESTORE programs are compatible except when a /A:*date*, /B:*date*, /E:*time*, /L:*time*, /M, or /N switch is used. These switches are not supported in the PC-DOS version.

Warning: The RESTORE command should not be used on a disk drive affected by an ASSIGN, SUBST, or JOIN command.

Return Codes

0   The restore operation was successful.
1   No files were found to restore.
2   Some files were not restored because of a file-sharing conflict (versions 3.0 and later).
3   The restore operation was terminated by the user.
4   The program was terminated by an unrecoverable (critical) hardware error.

Examples

To restore the file named MENUMGR.C from the backup disk in drive A to the directory named \SOURCE on the disk in drive B, type

```
C>RESTORE A: B:\SOURCE\MENUMGR.C  <Enter>
```

To restore all the files on the backup disk in drive A to their original locations in the directory structure of drive C, type

```
C>RESTORE A: C:\*.* /S  <Enter>
```

To restore all the files with the extension .C from the backup disk in drive A to the directory named \SOURCE on drive C, requesting confirmation for those files that are read-only or hidden, type

```
C>RESTORE A: C:\SOURCE\*.C /P   <Enter>
```

Messages

*** Files were backed up at *time* on *date* ***
This informational message shows when the BACKUP command was used on the backed-up files.

*** Not able to restore file ***
The backup file or the destination disk contains an error. Use the CHKDSK command to determine the problem.

*** Restoring files from drive *X*: ***
Diskette: *n*
This informational message indicates the progress of the RESTORE command.

DOS 2.0 or later required
RESTORE does not work with versions of MS-DOS earlier than 2.0.

File creation error
The destination directory is full. This usually occurs only if the destination is the root directory but can also happen if a file is being restored to a subdirectory and the disk itself is full.

Incorrect DOS version
The version of RESTORE is not compatible with the version of MS-DOS that is running.

Insert backup diskette *n* in drive *X*:
Strike any key when ready
This message prompts the user to insert the next backup disk in sequence. Disks used in multidisk backups should always be labeled and numbered during a BACKUP operation.

Insert restore target diskette in drive *X*:
Strike any key when ready
This prompt is displayed when files are being restored to a floppy disk.

Insufficient memory
Available memory is not sufficient for the RESTORE program to execute.

Invalid drive specification
The command line included a drive that is invalid or does not exist in the system.

Invalid number of parameters
The command line included too many or too few parameters.

Invalid parameter
The command line included an invalid switch or other parameter.

Invalid path
The destination parameter included a path that is invalid or does not exist.

Restore file sequence error
Files are being restored from a multidisk set of backup disks and a floppy disk was used out of order.

Source and target drives are the same
Files cannot be restored from a drive to the same drive.

Source does not contain backup files
The files on the backup disk are not in the special format used by the BACKUP and RESTORE programs.

System files restored
Target disk may not be bootable
The backup disk included copies of the hidden operating-system files MSDOS.SYS and IO.SYS (or IBMDOS.COM and IBMBIO.COM in PC-DOS) and these files were restored to the destination disk. The destination disk is bootable only if these two files are the first files on the disk and IO.SYS (or IBMBIO.COM) is written into contiguous clusters.

Target is full
The destination disk is full and no further files can be restored.

Target is Non-Removable
The disk to which files are being restored is not removable.

The last file was not restored
The destination disk is full or the last file on the backup disk was bad.

Warning!   Diskette is out of sequence
Replace diskette or continue if okay
Files are being restored from a multidisk set of backup disks and a floppy disk was used out of order.

Warning! File *filename*
is a hidden file
Replace the file (Y/N)?
The backed-up file has the same filename as a hidden file on the destination disk, which may be overwritten. (This message appears only if the /P switch was used.) Respond with *Y* to overwrite the file on the destination disk; respond with *N* to leave the destination file unchanged and continue the RESTORE operation.

Warning! File *filename*
is a read-only file
Replace the file (Y/N)?
The backed-up file has the same name as a read-only file on the destination disk, which may be overwritten. (This message appears only if the /P switch was used.) Respond with

Y to overwrite the file on the destination disk; respond with *N* to leave the destination file unchanged and continue the RESTORE operation.

Warning! File *filename*
was changed after it was backed up
Replace the file (Y/N)?
Data has been changed or added to the destination file since the backup disk was created and this data will be lost if the file is restored. (This message appears only if the /P switch was used.) Respond with *Y* to restore the backed-up file; respond with *N* to leave the destination file unchanged and continue the RESTORE operation.

Warning! No files were found to restore
No files were found on the backup disk that matched the destination file specification.

RMDIR or RD

Remove Directory

2.0 and later

Internal

Purpose

Removes an empty directory from the hierarchical file structure.

Syntax

RMDIR [*drive:*][*path*]*directory_name*

or

RD [*drive:*][*path*]*directory_name*

where:

directory_name   is the name of the directory to be removed, optionally preceded by a drive and/or path.

Description

The RMDIR command removes an empty directory from a disk's hierarchical file structure. The directory being deleted cannot contain any files or subdirectories (except for the special **.** and **..** entries). The root directory or current directory of a disk cannot be deleted.

If the *path* parameter is used, it must specify a valid existing path. If no path is specified and *directory_name* is not preceded by a backslash (\), MS-DOS assumes that the directory to be removed is a subdirectory of the current directory. If no path is specified and *directory_name* is preceded by a backslash, MS-DOS assumes that the directory is a subdirectory of the root directory. The length of the full path (including the drive designator and directory name) must not exceed 63 characters.

The RMDIR command should not be used to remove subdirectories from drives affected by an ASSIGN or JOIN command. A directory affected by the SUBST command cannot be removed.

Note: If a directory contains files marked as hidden or system, that directory cannot be removed even though no files appear to exist when the directory contents are viewed using the DIR command.

Example

To remove the empty directory \LIB, which is a subdirectory of the \MSC directory on the disk in drive A, type

```
C>RMDIR A:\MSC\LIB  <Enter>
```

or

```
C>RD A:\MSC\LIB  <Enter>
```

Message

Invalid path, not directory, or directory not empty

The named directory cannot be deleted because it does not exist, some element of the path to the directory does not exist, or the directory contains files or subdirectories.

SELECT

Configure System Disk for a Specific Country

IBM

External

Purpose

Creates a system disk with time, date, and keyboard configured for a selected country. This command is available only with PC-DOS.

Syntax

SELECT [[*drive1:*] *drive2:[path]*] *country keyboard*

where:

drive1   is a floppy-disk drive (A or B) containing the distribution disk or, at a minimum, the PC-DOS system files, COMMAND.COM, and the FORMAT and XCOPY utilities (default = drive A) (version 3.2).

drive2   is the drive containing the disk to receive the PC-DOS system files and country information and can include a path (default = drive B) (version 3.2).

country   is a code from the table below that controls the time, date, and currency formats.

keyboard   is a code from the table below that controls the keyboard configuration.

Country	Country Code	Keyboard Code
Australia	061	*
Belgium	032	*
Canadian French	002	*
Denmark	045	*
Finland	358	*
France	033	FR
West Germany	049	GR
Israel	972	*
Italy	039	IT
Middle East	785	*
Netherlands	031	*
Norway	047	*
Portugal	351	*
Spain	034	SP
Sweden	046	*
Switzerland	041	*

(more)

Country	Country Code	Keyboard Code
United Kingdom	044	UK
United States	001	US

*Available only in version 3.2 and may be supplied on a separate floppy disk.

Description

The SELECT utility allows the user to create a bootable system disk configured for a particular country's keyboard layout and date, time, and currency formats without performing these steps separately.

Version 3.2 of SELECT uses the FORMAT command to format the disk in *drive2*, then uses the XCOPY command to copy all files on the disk in *drive1* (including the hidden system files) to *drive2*. If a country configuration other than one of the six KEYB*xx* utilities supplied on the distribution disk is specified, SELECT prompts the user to insert the disk containing the appropriate file.

Versions 3.0 and 3.1 of SELECT use the DISKCOPY program to copy all files on the disk in drive A (including the hidden system files) to the disk in drive B, formatting the disk if necessary.

All versions then add the appropriate CONFIG.SYS and AUTOEXEC.BAT files to the new disk to configure PC-DOS for use with the specified keyboard and country configuration. The specified configuration does not take effect until the computer is turned on or restarted using the new disk.

Examples

To create a PC-DOS system disk configured for West Germany using version 3.0 or 3.1, place a copy of the original PC-DOS distribution disk in drive A and a blank disk in drive B; then type

```
A>SELECT 049 GR  <Enter>
```

During the copy operation, the usual DISKCOPY prompts and messages are displayed. When the copy operation is complete, the two disks are compared using DISKCOMP, producing the usual DISKCOMP prompts and messages. The resulting disk includes all the files from the distribution disk (including the hidden system files), a CONFIG.SYS file that contains the line

```
COUNTRY=049
```

and an AUTOEXEC.BAT file that contains the following lines:

```
KEYBGR
ECHO OFF
CLS
DATE
TIME
VER
```

To create a PC-DOS system disk configured for West Germany using version 3.2, place a copy of the original PC-DOS distribution disk in drive A and a blank disk in drive B; then type

```
A>SELECT 049 GR  <Enter>
```

SELECT first uses the FORMAT command to format the disk in drive B, then uses XCOPY to copy all files on the distribution disk (including the system files), and finally creates a CONFIG.SYS file that contains the line

```
COUNTRY=049
```

and an AUTOEXEC.BAT file that contains the following lines:

```
PATH \;
KEYBGR
ECHO OFF
CLS
DATE
TIME
VER
```

Messages

Cannot execute X: *filename*
One of the files needed by SELECT (FORMAT, DISKCOPY, DISKCOMP, or XCOPY) is not on the source disk or is a version that is not compatible with the version of PC-DOS that is running.

File creation error
The root directory of the destination disk is full or unable to contain any more files or one of the files being created has the same name as a directory already on the destination disk.

Incorrect DOS version
The version of SELECT is not compatible with the version of PC-DOS that is running (version 3.2).

Incorrect number of parameters
Too many or too few parameters were specified in the command line or a separator character was omitted between two parameters (version 3.2).

Insert DOS diskette in drive A:
Strike any key when ready
This message prompts the user to insert the distribution disk containing the system files and COMMAND.COM into drive A (version 3.2).

Insert KEYBxx.COM diskette in drive X:
Strike any key when ready
The user responded *Y* to a previous prompt asking if KEYBxx is on another disk. This message prompts the user to insert that disk into the specified drive (version 3.2).

Insert target diskette in drive A:
Strike any key when ready
This message prompts the user to insert the disk that will become the country-specific system disk into drive A (versions 3.0 and 3.1).

Insert target diskette in drive B:
Strike any key when ready
This message prompts the user to insert the disk that will become the country-specific system disk into drive B (version 3.2).

Invalid country code
The country code given in the command line is not supported by this version of PC-DOS or is not a valid country code.

Invalid drive specification
One of the drives specified in the command line is invalid or does not exist in the system (version 3.2).

Invalid keyboard code
The keyboard code given in the command line is not supported by this version of PC-DOS or is not a valid keyboard code.

Invalid parameter
One of the parameters specified in the command line is invalid or is not supported by the version of SELECT that is running (version 3.2).

Invalid path
The path specified for *drive2* is invalid, contains invalid characters, or is longer than 63 characters (version 3.2).

Is KEYB*xx*.COM on another
diskette (Y/N)?
The keyboard reconfiguration file for the specified country is not on the source disk. Respond with *Y* to cause SELECT to prompt for the disk containing the keyboard file after the FORMAT operation is completed; respond with *N* to terminate the SELECT command (version 3.2).

Keyboard routine not found.
The user responded *N* to a previous prompt asking if KEYB*xx* is on another disk (version 3.2).

SELECT is used to install DOS the first
time. Select erases everything on the
specified target and then installs DOS.
Do you want to continue (Y/N)?
This message warns the user that the specified disk will be formatted and all files on the source disk will be copied over. Respond with *Y* to continue; respond with *N* to terminate the SELECT command (version 3.2).

Unable to copy keyboard routine

An error occurred while the KEYBxx.COM program was being copied. Use the CHKDSK command to check the keyboard program on the source disk for damage (version 3.2).

Unable to create directory

The directory specified in the command line was not created because a directory with the same name already exists on the destination disk, the root directory of the destination disk is full, one of the directory names specified in the path does not exist, or a file with the same name already exists (version 3.2).

SET
Set Environment Variable

2.0 and later

Internal

Purpose

Defines an environment variable and a string that is its value.

Syntax

SET [*name=value*]

or

SET *name=*

where:

name   is a string of characters that defines an environment variable; lowercase letters are automatically converted to uppercase.

value   is a string of characters, a pathname, or a filename that defines the current value of *name*; no case conversion is made for *value*.

Description

The environment is a series of null-terminated ASCII (ASCIIZ) strings that contains environment variables and their values. (An environment variable associates a string consisting of a filename, a pathname, or other literal data with a symbolic name that can be referenced by programs. The form of the association is *name=value*.) The original, or master, environment belongs to the command processor and is established when the system is turned on or restarted. When a program is subsequently executed by the command processor or by another program, the new program inherits a private copy of its parent's environment.

The SET command enables the user to add, change, or delete an environment variable from the command processor's environment. If *value* is not included in the SET command, MS-DOS deletes the environment variable *name* from the environment. If the SET command is issued with no parameters, MS-DOS displays the values of all the variables in the environment.

With MS-DOS versions 2.x and 3.x, two particular variables are always found in an environment: PATH and COMSPEC. These variables are initialized during the system startup process and tell COMMAND.COM which subdirectories to search for executable files and where to find the transient portion of COMMAND.COM for reloading (versions 3.0 and later). (By default, PATH is a null string and therefore searches only the current or specified directory.) These special environment variables are influenced by the PATH and SHELL commands, respectively, but can also be changed with SET commands. Note, however, that changing the value of COMSPEC with SET will serve no useful purpose — changing to a different command processor must be done using an appropriate SHELL command in the CONFIG.SYS file (the system must be restarted for it to take effect). Note also that it is not necessary to use the SET command with the PATH or PROMPT commands — MS-DOS will automatically add their new values to the environment if they are changed.

The environment, which can be as large as 32 KB, can be an effective source of global configuration information to executing programs. For instance, the Microsoft C Compiler and Microsoft Object Linker use environment variables to locate *include* and object library files. Environment variables can also be referenced as replaceable parameters in batch files, using the form %*name*%.

Under normal circumstances, MS-DOS expands the environment as necessary when SET commands are entered. However, when a batch file is being interpreted or when terminate-and-stay-resident (TSR) utilities have been loaded, the size of the command processor's environment becomes fixed. Under these circumstances, a SET command may result in the error message *Out of environment space.*

With version 3.2, the initial size of the environment can be increased either by using the COMMAND command with the /P and /E:*nnnn* switches at the system prompt or by including a SHELL command specifying COMMAND.COM followed by the /E:*nnnn* switch in the CONFIG.SYS file. *See* USER COMMANDS: COMMAND; CONFIG.SYS: SHELL.

Examples

To define the environment variable *USER* and set its value to *FRED*, type

```
C>SET USER=FRED   <Enter>
```

To change the value of the environment variable *USER* to *SALLY*, type

```
C>SET USER=SALLY   <Enter>
```

To delete the environment variable *USER* and its value from the environment, type

```
C>SET USER=   <Enter>
```

To display all the environment variables, type

```
C>SET   <Enter>
```

The output of this command will be in the following form:

```
COMSPEC=C:\DOS3\COMMAND.COM
PROMPT=$p$_$n$g
PATH=D:\BIN;C:\DOS3;C:\WP\WORD;C:\ASM;C:\MSC\BIN
INCLUDE=c:\msc\include;c:\windows\lib
LIB=c:\msc\lib;c:\windows\lib
TMP=c:\temp
PCF32=c:\forth\pc32
PROCOMM=c:\procomm\
```

Message

Out of environment space

The command processor's environment is full and cannot be expanded (usually because the SET command was issued from a batch file or the system has terminate-and-stay-resident [TSR] utilities installed).

SHARE

Install File-Sharing Support

3.0 and later
External

Purpose

Loads the resident file-sharing support module required by Microsoft Networks.

Syntax

SHARE [/F:*n*] [/L:*n*]

where:

/F:*n*	allocates *n* bytes of memory to hold file-sharing information (default = 2048).
/L:*n*	configures support for *n* simultaneous file-region locks (default = 20).

Description

The code that supports file sharing and locking in a networking environment is isolated in the user-installable SHARE module. After SHARE is loaded, MS-DOS checks all read and write requests against the file-sharing module. On personal computers that do not utilize network services, the SHARE module need not be loaded, leaving more memory for application programs.

The /F:*n* switch controls the amount of buffer space allocated for file-sharing information. Each open file requires the length of its full name, including the path, plus some overhead; the average pathname is approximately 20 bytes long. If the /F:*n* switch is not included in the command line, the buffer size defaults to 2048 bytes (sufficient for approximately 100 files with pathnames of average length).

The /L:*n* switch controls the number of entries to be allocated for an internal table containing file-locking information. Each active lock on a region of a file occupies one entry in the table. If the /L:*n* switch is absent, the default is support for 20 simultaneously active locks.

Example

To install the file-sharing support module, allocating 4096 bytes of space for file-sharing information and 40 file-region locks, type

```
C>SHARE /F:4096 /L:40  <Enter>
```

Messages

Incorrect DOS version
The version of SHARE is not compatible with the version of MS-DOS that is running.

Incorrect parameter
The command line included an invalid switch.

Not enough memory
System memory is insufficient to load the SHARE module or to reserve the designated file-sharing information space or file-region locks.

SHARE already installed
The SHARE command has already been executed since the system was turned on or restarted; additional executions have no effect.

SORT

Alphabetic Sort Filter

Purpose

Reads records from standard input, sorts them alphabetically, and writes the sorted records to standard output.

Syntax

SORT [/R][/+*column*]

where:

/R	specifies a reverse, or descending, alphabetic sort.
/+*column*	specifies the first column to be used for sorting each line (default = 1).

Description

The SORT program is a filter that reads lines from standard input until an end-of-file marker is reached, sorts the lines into alphabetic order, and writes the sorted lines to standard output.

Standard input defaults to the keyboard; standard output defaults to the video display. Because standard input can be redirected, the SORT filter can also accept input from another character device, a file, or the piped output of another program or filter. (The most common use of SORT is to sort the redirected input from an ASCII text file.) Similarly, the output of SORT can be redirected to any character device or file or can be piped to another program.

SORT normally orders the lines of the input text stream alphabetically using the entire line, starting with column 1 as the sort key. Tab characters are not expanded to spaces. If the character in the sort-key column of one line is identical with the character in the sort-key column of the next line, SORT checks the next column to the right to determine which line will go before the other. If the second columns are also identical, the search continues to the right until a differing column is found. The maximum amount of data that can be sorted is 63 KB.

The /R switch causes SORT to arrange the set of lines in reverse alphabetic order. The /+*column* switch lets the user specify a column other than column 1 as the first sort key.

With versions 2.x, SORT arranges the input lines based on the ASCII value of the character in each line's sort-key column; the sort operation is therefore case sensitive. With versions 3.0 and later, SORT assigns lowercase letters the same ASCII value as uppercase letters; hence, case is effectively ignored. Depending on the COUNTRY command in effect (*see* USER COMMANDS: config.sys: country), versions 3.0 and later map accented characters with ASCII codes in the range 80H through 0E1H (128–225) to their unaccented equivalents for sorting.

Warning: If the output of the SORT command is redirected to a file with the same name as the input file, the contents of the input file may be destroyed.

Examples

The examples in this entry operate on an ASCII text file named RECORDS.TXT that contains the following lines:

```
Smith     Seattle
Adams     New York
Zoole     Bellevue
Jones     Boston
```

Each line of the file contains a person's surname, starting in column 1, and a city name, starting in column 10.

To sort the file RECORDS.TXT by surname and display the sorted lines on standard output, type

```
C>SORT < RECORDS.TXT  <Enter>
```

This will result in the following display:

```
Adams     New York
Jones     Boston
Smith     Seattle
Zoole     Bellevue
```

To sort the file RECORDS.TXT by surname and write the sorted lines into the file READY.DOC, type

```
C>SORT < RECORDS.TXT > READY.DOC  <Enter>
```

To sort the file RECORDS.TXT by surname in reverse alphabetic order and display the sorted lines on standard output, type

```
C>SORT /R < RECORDS.TXT  <Enter>
```

This will result in the following display:

```
Zoole     Bellevue
Smith     Seattle
Jones     Boston
Adams     New York
```

To sort the file RECORDS.TXT by city name and display the sorted lines on standard output, type

```
C>SORT /+10 < RECORDS.TXT  <Enter>
```

This will result in the following display:

```
Zoole     Bellevue
Jones     Boston
Adams     New York
Smith     Seattle
```

To use SORT as a filter to arrange a directory listing alphabetically, type

```
C>DIR ¦ SORT  <Enter>
```

To use SORT as a filter to arrange a directory listing alphabetically based on the first character of each file's extension, type

```
C>DIR ¦ SORT /+10  <Enter>
```

Messages

Invalid parameter
One of the parameters specified in the command line is invalid or the syntax is incorrect.

SORT: Incorrect DOS version
The version of SORT is not compatible with the version of MS-DOS that is running.

SORT: Insufficient disk space
The output of the SORT filter has been redirected to a file and the disk is full.

SORT: Insufficient memory
The available system memory is insufficient to run the SORT program.

SUBST

Substitute Drive for Subdirectory

3.1 and later

External   No Net

Purpose

Causes a drive letter to be substituted for a directory name. SUBST is present in MS-DOS to support older application programs that do not accept pathnames.

Syntax

SUBST [*drive1*: [*drive2*:]*path*]

or

SUBST *drive1*: /D

where:

drive1	is the drive letter to be used to reference the files in *path*.
drive2	is a drive letter other than *drive1* that can optionally precede the name of the subdirectory being substituted.
path	is the subdirectory to be accessed when *drive1* is referenced, optionally preceded by *drive2*.
/D	cancels the effect of a previous SUBST command for *drive1*.

Description

The SUBST command allows a drive letter to be substituted for a subdirectory name.

The *drive1* parameter can be any valid drive letter except the current drive or *drive2*. Drive letters A through E are always available; drive letters beyond E require that an appropriate LASTDRIVE command be added to the CONFIG.SYS file and the system be restarted (*see* USER COMMANDS: CONFIG.SYS: LASTDRIVE).

After a SUBST command, the files on the disk normally referenced by *drive1* are no longer accessible. However, the files in the location specified by *path* can still be referenced by the usual methods (using their actual drive and path) as well as by the substituted drive designator.

If the SUBST command is entered without parameters, MS-DOS displays the substitutions currently in effect.

Warning: The SUBST command masks the actual disk-drive characteristics from commands that perform critical disk operations. Therefore, ASSIGN, BACKUP, CHKDSK, DISKCOMP, DISKCOPY, FDISK, FORMAT, JOIN, LABEL, and RESTORE should not be used on a drive affected by a SUBST command. CHDIR, MKDIR, RMDIR, and PATH commands that include the affected drive should be used with caution. A network drive cannot be named in a SUBST command.

Examples

To substitute drive B for the directory C:\ASM\SOURCE, type

```
C>SUBST B: C:\ASM\SOURCE  <Enter>
```

To display the substitutions currently in effect, type

```
C>SUBST  <Enter>
```

In this case, the SUBST command displays

```
B: => C:\ASM\SOURCE
```

To cancel the effect of a previous SUBST command that substituted drive B for a subdirectory, type

```
C>SUBST B: /D  <Enter>
```

Messages

Cannot SUBST a network drive
One or both of the drive parameters in the command line referred to a drive that is assigned to a network.

DOS 2.0 or later required
SUBST does not work with versions of MS-DOS earlier than 2.0.

Incorrect DOS version
The version of SUBST is not compatible with the version of MS-DOS that is running.

Incorrect number of parameters
The command line included too many or too few parameters.

Invalid parameter
The drive named in the command line is invalid, does not exist, is the default drive, or is the same as the drive in the path to be substituted.

Not enough memory
The available system memory is insufficient to run the SUBST command.

Path not found
An element of the path included in the command line is invalid or does not exist.

SYS

Transfer System Files

1.0 and later

External   No Net

Purpose

Copies the hidden files that contain the operating system from the disk in the current drive to another formatted disk.

Syntax

SYS *drive*:

where:

drive   is the location of the disk that will receive the system files. This parameter is required.

Description

An MS-DOS system disk must contain three files to be bootable: the two operating-system files and the command processor. The operating system itself is contained in the files IO.SYS and MSDOS.SYS (or IBMBIO.COM and IBMDOS.COM in PC-DOS), which must always be the first two files in the disk's directory. Both have file attributes set for system and hidden (all versions) and read-only (versions 2.0 and later). IO.SYS (or IBMBIO.COM) contains the default set of device drivers for the system; it must occupy contiguous sectors in the disk's files area. MSDOS.SYS (or IBMDOS.COM) contains the kernel of the operating system proper. The third required file is the shell, or command processor, which by default is COMMAND.COM. This is an unrestricted file and can be located anywhere on the disk.

The SYS command transfers the two operating-system files from the default drive to the specified destination disk. The destination disk that receives the files must meet one of the following requirements:

- The disk is formatted but completely empty.
- The disk currently contains hidden MS-DOS system files that are large enough to allow replacement by the new system files.
- The disk has been formatted with the /B switch to reserve room for the system files. (Note that /B produces a disk with only eight sectors per track.)

If the disk already contains the two hidden system files, the SYS command can be used to transfer an equivalent or later version of MS-DOS.

After the two hidden operating-system files are installed with the SYS command, the COMMAND.COM file (or another command processor) must be transferred to the destination disk with the COPY command. The resulting disk is a bootable system disk.

Note: Because the two system files have the hidden attribute, they do not appear on a directory listing produced by the DIR command. The CHKDSK command does report the presence of hidden files on a disk and will list their names if the /V switch is used but will not list such information as the file size or date and time of creation.

Example

To transfer a copy of the system files to the disk in drive B, type

```
C>SYS B:  <Enter>
```

Messages

Cannot SYS to a Network drive
The drive specified in the command line is currently assigned to a network.

Destination disk cannot be booted
The hidden operating-system files were transferred to the destination disk but could not be placed in contiguous sectors.

Incompatible system size
The destination disk already contains operating-system files and they are smaller than those being copied.

Incorrect DOS version
The version of SYS is not compatible with the version of MS-DOS that is running.

Insert destination disk in drive *X*
and strike any key when ready
This message prompts the user to insert the disk onto which the operating-system files will be copied into the specified drive.

Insert system disk in drive *X*
and strike any key when ready
This message prompts the user to insert a disk containing the operating-system files into the specified drive.

Invalid drive specification
The drive specified in the command line is invalid or does not exist in the system.

Invalid parameter
The command line contained an invalid drive letter.

No room for system on destination disk
Contiguous space at the beginning of the destination disk is insufficient for the operating-system files. This can occur when files already exist on the destination disk or when sections of the disk are marked as unusable by the FORMAT command.

No system on default drive
The disk in the default drive does not contain the two hidden system files. Replace the disk with a bootable system disk.

System transferred
The operating-system files have been successfully transferred to the destination disk.

TIME

Set System Time

1.0 and later

Internal

Purpose

Sets or displays the system time. TIME is an external command with PC-DOS version 1.0.

Syntax

TIME [*hh*:*mm*[:*ss*[.*xx*]]]

where:

hh	is hours (0-23).
mm	is minutes (0-59).
ss	is seconds (0-59).
xx	is hundredths of a second (0–99).

Note: No spaces are allowed between any of the time parameters.

Description

All computers that run MS-DOS have as part of their hardware configuration a timer, or clock, that maintains the current system date and time. One use of this clock, among others, is to insert the current date and time into a file's directory entry when the file is created or modified.

The TIME command allows the user to display or modify the current time that is being maintained by the system's real-time clock. TIME is also executed by MS-DOS when the system is turned on or restarted, unless an AUTOEXEC.BAT file is on the system disk, in which case the command is executed only if it is included in the AUTOEXEC.BAT file.

On IBM PC/ATs and compatibles, the TIME command does not permanently change the system time stored in the built-in battery-backed clock/calendar; the newly entered time is lost when the system is turned off or restarted. On these machines, the SETUP program (found on the *Diagnostics for IBM Personal Computer AT* disk or equivalent) must be used to permanently alter the clock/calendar's current time.

On IBM PCs, PC/XTs, and compatibles equipped with add-on cards containing battery-backed clock/calendar circuitry, it is usually necessary to run a time/date installation program (included with the card) to set the system date and time from the clock/calendar on the card. The TIME command generally has no effect on these card-mounted clock/calendars.

The format of times displayed by the system depends on the current country code, which is determined by the optional COUNTRY command in the CONFIG.SYS file (*see* USER COMMANDS: config.sys: country). The default display format is the 24-hour format (00:00–23:59).

Examples

To display the current time, type

```
C>TIME  <Enter>
```

This results in output of the following form:

```
Current time is 12:49:04.93
Enter new time:
```

To leave the time unchanged, press the Enter key.

To set the system time to 8:30 P.M., type

```
C>TIME 20:30  <Enter>
```

Messages

Current time is *hh:mm:ss.xx*
This informational message is displayed in response to any valid TIME command.

Invalid parameter
The delimiter in the time parameter included in the command line was not a colon (:) or a period (.).

Invalid time
Enter new time:
An invalid time, time format, or delimiter was specified in the command line or in response to the *Enter new time:* prompt. Note that no spaces are allowed around delimiters.

TREE

Display Directory Structure

3.2

External

Purpose

Displays the hierarchical directory structure of a disk and, optionally, the names of the files in each subdirectory. This command is included with PC-DOS beginning with version 2.0.

Syntax

TREE [*drive*:][/F]

where:

drive   is the location of the disk whose directory structure is to be displayed.
/F   displays the filenames in each directory in addition to the directory names.

Description

The TREE command displays on standard output the pathname of each directory on the disk in the specified drive, beginning with the subdirectories of the root directory. If a disk drive is not designated, TREE assumes the current, or default, drive. The name of each directory is followed by a list of its subdirectories. If the /F switch is included in the command line, the names of the files in each subdirectory are also displayed. (Prior to version 3.1, the PC-DOS TREE command does not list the files in the root directory if /F is used.)

The output of the TREE command can be redirected to another output device or a file or can be piped to another program.

Examples

Assume that the root directory of the disk in drive B contains three subdirectories: \SOURCE, \LIBS, and \DOC. The subdirectory \SOURCE in turn contains two subdirectories: \ASM and \PASCAL. To display the directory structure of this disk, type

```
C>TREE B:   <Enter>
```

The TREE command displays the following list:

```
DIRECTORY PATH LISTING FOR VOLUME MYDISK

Path: B:\SOURCE

Sub-directories:   ASM
                   PASCAL


Path: B:\SOURCE\ASM

Sub-directories:   None


Path: B:\SOURCE\PASCAL

Sub-directories:   None


Path: B:\LIBS

Sub-directories:   None


Path: B:\DOC

Sub-directories:   None
```

To display the directory structure of the disk in drive B and also display all files in each directory, type

```
C>TREE B: /F   <Enter>
```

To print the directory-structure listing of the disk in drive B on an attached printer, type

```
C>TREE B: > PRN   <Enter>
```

To display the directory structure of the disk in drive B one screenful at a time, type

```
C>TREE B: ¦ MORE   <Enter>
```

For a more compressed listing of all subdirectories on the disk in drive B, type

```
C>TREE B: ¦ FIND "Path:"   <Enter>
```

The output appears in the following form:

```
Path: B:\SOURCE
Path: B:\SOURCE\ASM
Path: B:\SOURCE\PASCAL
Path: B:\LIBS
Path: B:\DOC
```

Messages

DOS 2.0 or later required
TREE does not work with versions of MS-DOS earlier than 2.0.

Incorrect DOS version
The version of TREE is not compatible with the version of MS-DOS that is running.

Invalid drive specification
The drive specified in the command line is invalid or does not exist in the system.

Invalid parameter
The command line contained a path or filename in addition to a disk drive or contained an invalid switch.

No sub-directories exist
The specified drive has no subdirectories.

TYPE

Display File

1.0 and later

Internal

Purpose

Sends the contents of an ASCII text file to standard output.

Syntax

TYPE [*drive*:][*path*]*filename*

where:

filename   is the name of the text file to be displayed, optionally preceded by a drive and/or path; wildcard characters are not permitted.

Description

The TYPE command displays the contents of a text file on standard output (usually the video display) until it encounters an end-of-file character (ASCII code 1AH). Tab characters in the file are expanded to spaces with tab stops at each eighth character position. If a file contains characters with ASCII values less than 32 or greater than 127, the resulting display includes graphics characters and other unintelligible information.

The output of the TYPE command can be redirected to another file or character device or can be piped to another program.

Examples

To display the file SHELL.C in the directory \SOURCE on the disk in drive A, type

```
C>TYPE A:\SOURCE\SHELL.C  <Enter>
```

To direct the output of the same file to the printer, type

```
C>TYPE A:\SOURCE\SHELL.C > PRN  <Enter>
```

The TYPE command can be used with the MORE filter to paginate output. For example, to display the contents of the file MENU.ASM one screenful at a time, type

```
C>TYPE MENU.ASM | MORE  <Enter>
```

Messages

File not found
The file specified in the command line cannot be found or does not exist.

Invalid drive specification
The drive specified in the command line is invalid or does not exist in the system.

Invalid path or file name
The path specified in the command line is invalid or does not exist.

VDISK.SYS

IBM

Virtual Disk

External

Purpose

Creates a virtual disk in memory. This installable driver is available only with PC-DOS.

Syntax

DEVICE=[*drive:*][*path*]VDISK.SYS [*size*] [*sector*] [*directory*] [/E]   (version 3.0)

or

DEVICE=[*drive:*][*path*]VDISK.SYS [*size*] [*sector*] [*directory*] [/E[:*max*]]   (version 3.1)

or

DEVICE=[*drive:*][*path*]VDISK.SYS [*comment*] [*size*] [*comment*] [*sector*] [*comment*]
[*directory*] [/E[:*max*]]   (version 3.2)

where:

comment	is a string of ASCII characters in the range 32 through 126, excluding the slash character (/) (version 3.2).
size	is the size of the virtual disk in kilobytes (minimum = 1, default = 64).
sector	is the sector size in bytes (128, 256, or 512; default = 128).
directory	is the maximum number of entries in the virtual disk's root directory (2–512, default = 64).
/E	causes VDISK to use extended memory.
/E:*max*	causes VDISK to use extended memory and sets the maximum number of sectors (1–8, default = 8) to transfer from extended memory at one time (versions 3.1 and later).

Note: Unless the /E switch is used, the virtual disk is created in conventional memory.

Description

The VDISK.SYS installable device driver allows the configuration of one or more virtual disks (sometimes referred to as electronic disks or RAMdisks). A virtual disk is implemented by mapping a disk's structure — directory, file allocation table, and files area — onto an area of random-access memory, rather than onto actual sectors located on a magnetic recording medium. Access to files stored in a virtual disk is very fast, because no moving parts are involved and the "disk" operates at the speed of the system's memory. (The VDISK driver is available only with PC-DOS; a similar program named RAMDRIVE.SYS is included with MS-DOS.)

Warning: Because a RAMdisk resides entirely in RAM and is therefore volatile, any information stored there is irretrievably lost when the computer loses power or is restarted.

VDISK can create a virtual disk in either conventional memory or extended memory. Conventional memory is the term for the up-to-640 KB of RAM that contain PC-DOS and any application programs. Extended memory is the term for the memory at addresses above 1 MB (100000H) that is available on 80286-based personal computers such as the IBM PC/AT.

A virtual disk can be installed in conventional memory by simply inserting the line *DEVICE=VDISK.SYS* into the system's CONFIG.SYS file and restarting the system. (If the file VDISK.SYS is not in the root directory of the startup disk, it may be preceded by a drive and/or path.) A new "drive" then becomes available in the system, with default values of 64 KB disk size, 128-byte sectors, and 64 available directory entries (assuming there is sufficient memory). The virtual disk is assigned the next available drive letter (which is displayed in VDISK's sign-on message). The drive letter assigned depends on the number of other physical and virtual disks in the system and also on the position of the *DEVICE=VDISK.SYS* line in the CONFIG.SYS file relative to other installed block devices. Available memory permitting, multiple virtual disks can be created by using multiple *DEVICE=VDISK.SYS* lines. Several optional parameters allow the user to customize the size and configuration of the virtual disk and to use extended memory if it is available.

The *size* parameter specifies the amount of RAM, in kilobytes, to be allocated to the virtual disk. The default is 64 KB, but any size from 1 KB to the total amount of available memory can be specified. If the size specified is greater than available memory or less than 1 KB, VDISK ignores it and creates a virtual disk of 64 KB. If necessary, VDISK also adjusts the *size* value to ensure that at least 64 KB of memory remain available in the system.

The *sector* parameter sets the virtual sector size used within the virtual disk. The *sector* value may be 128, 256, or 512 bytes (default = 128 bytes). Selection of the smallest sector size results in a minimum of wasted virtual disk space per file but also results in somewhat slower transfer of data.

Note: Physical disk devices in IBM PC-compatible systems always use 512-byte sectors.

The *directory* parameter sets the number of available entries in the virtual disk's root directory. The allowed range is 2 through 512 (default = 64). Each directory entry requires 32 bytes. VDISK rounds the number of available directory entries up, if necessary, so that an integral number of sectors are assigned to the root directory.

The /E switch causes VDISK to use extended memory for the virtual disk, rather than conventional memory. This allows very large virtual disks to be configured while still leaving the maximum amount of conventional memory available for use by application programs. If the /E switch is used and extended memory is not present in the system, the VDISK driver will not install itself.

When /E is used in the form /E:*max*, the variable *max* controls how many virtual sectors can be transferred at a time from extended memory. The value of *max* must be in the range 1 through 8 (default = 8). If VDISK operation appears to conflict with the communications port or other interrupt-driven peripheral devices, the *max* variable should be set to a smaller number. The *max* option is available only with versions 3.1 and 3.2.

Note: If VDISK uses conventional memory for virtual disk storage, the memory cannot be reclaimed except by modifying the CONFIG.SYS file and restarting the system.

Examples

To create a virtual disk drive with the default values of 64 KB disk size, 128-byte sectors, and 64 available directory entries, include the command

```
DEVICE=VDISK.SYS
```

in the CONFIG.SYS file and restart the system.

To create a 360 KB virtual disk with 512-byte sectors and 112 available directory entries when the file VDISK.SYS is located in a directory named \BIN on drive C, include the command

```
DEVICE=C:\BIN\VDISK.SYS 360 512 112
```

in the CONFIG.SYS file and restart the system. The directory for this virtual disk requires 3584 bytes (112 entries * 32 bytes), or 7 sectors.

With version 3.2, comments can be inserted between the values to identify them. For example, to create a 1 MB virtual disk drive in extended memory with 256-byte sectors and 128 directory entries, placing comments before the values to identify them, include the command

```
DEVICE=VDISK.SYS DISK_SIZE: 1024 SECTOR_SIZE: 256 DIR_ENTRIES: 128 /E
```

in the CONFIG.SYS file and restart the system.

Messages

Buffer size adjusted
No *size* value was specified or the specified value was larger than the amount of available memory.

Directory entries adjusted
No *directory* value was specified, VDISK adjusted the *directory* value up to the nearest sector-size boundary, or the *size* value was too small to hold the file allocation table, the directory, and two additional sectors, in which case VDISK adjusted *directory* downward until these conditions were met.

Invalid switch character
A slash character (/) was included in a comment or the /E switch was entered incorrectly.

Sector size adjusted
The *sector* value was missing from the command line or an incorrect value was entered; therefore, VDISK used the default value of 128 bytes.

Transfer size adjusted
A value outside the range 1 through 8 was specified with the /E:*max* switch; therefore, VDISK used the default value of 8.

VDISK not installed - Extender Card switches
do not match the system memory size
The switch settings on the extender card are not correct or the extended memory exists in an expansion unit, which VDISK is not capable of using.

VDISK not installed - insufficient memory
Less than 64 KB of system memory remained after attempted installation, the /E switch was specified and the system does not contain extended memory, or the amount of available extended memory was too small to support the installation of VDISK.

VDISK Version *n.nn* virtual disk *X*:
    Buffer size: *nn* KB
    Sector size: *nnn*
    Directory size: *nnn*
    Transfer size: *n*
VDISK was successfully installed and this message informs the user of the drive letter assigned to the virtual disk, the version of VDISK that created the disk, and the characteristics of the disk. The *Transfer size:* message appears only in versions 3.1 and 3.2 and only if the /E switch was used.

VER

Display Version

Purpose

Displays the MS-DOS version number.

Syntax

VER

Description

The VER command displays on standard output (usually the video display) the number of the MS-DOS version that is running. The version number is also displayed as part of the copyright notice when the system is turned on or restarted, unless an AUTOEXEC.BAT file is on the system disk. (The VER command can be included in the AUTOEXEC.BAT file to display the version number, but it will not display the copyright information.)

Examples

To display the MS-DOS version number, type

```
C>VER   <Enter>
```

On a system that is running MS-DOS version 3.2, the following message is displayed:

```
MS-DOS Version 3.2
```

To print the MS-DOS version number on an attached printer instead of displaying it on the screen, type

```
C>VER > PRN   <Enter>
```

VERIFY

Set Verify Flag

2.0 and later

Internal

Purpose

Sets the system's internal flag controlling verification of disk writes.

Syntax

VERIFY [ON¦OFF]

Description

The VERIFY command sets or clears an internal MS-DOS flag that controls verification of data written to disks. (The actual verification process is usually carried out by the device driver and the disk-drive controller.) The VERIFY ON command has the same effect on a global basis as the /V switch has on COPY operations. (When VERIFY is on, use of the /V switch with COPY has no additional effect.) VERIFY ON remains in effect until a program turns it off with a Set Verify system call or until the user types *VERIFY OFF* at the command prompt. The VERIFY command does not affect the operation of character devices.

When the VERIFY command is entered without an ON or OFF, MS-DOS displays the current state of the system's internal verify flag. The default setting of the verify flag is off.

Examples

To turn on verification of disk writes, type

```
C>VERIFY ON  <Enter>
```

To display the current status of the verify flag, type

```
C>VERIFY  <Enter>
```

Messages

Must specify ON or OFF
The command line contained an invalid parameter.

VERIFY is off

or

VERIFY is on
No setting was specified in the command line and VERIFY displays this informational message indicating the current status of the verify flag.

VOL

2.0 and later

Display Disk Name

Internal

Purpose

Displays a disk's volume label if one exists.

Syntax

VOL [*drive*:]

where:

drive   is the location of the disk whose volume label is to be displayed.

Description

The VOL command displays a disk's name, or volume label. If *drive* is not included in the command line, the volume label of the disk in the current drive is displayed.

A volume label can be assigned to a disk when it is formatted by using the /V switch with the FORMAT command. A volume label can be added, changed, or deleted *after* a disk has already been formatted by using the LABEL command (PC-DOS versions 3.0 and later, MS-DOS versions 3.1 and later). The CHKDSK, DIR, and TREE commands also display a disk's volume label as part of their output.

Example

To display the volume label for the disk in the current drive, type

```
C>VOL  <Enter>
```

If the disk's name is HARDDISK, the VOL command produces the following output:

```
Volume in drive C is HARDDISK
```

Messages

Invalid drive specification
The drive specified in the command line is invalid or does not exist in the system.

Volume in drive *X* has no label
The disk in the current or specified drive was not previously assigned a volume label with the FORMAT or LABEL command.

XCOPY

Copy Files

Purpose

Copies files and directories, optionally also copying subdirectories and the files they contain.

Syntax

XCOPY *source* [*destination*][/A] [/D:*mm-dd-yy*] [/E] [/M] [/P] [/S] [/V] [/W]

where:

source	is the name of the file(s) to be copied, optionally preceded by a drive and/or path; wildcard characters are permitted in the filename. If the path is omitted, a drive letter must be specified; this parameter is not optional.
destination	is the destination location and, optionally, the name for the copied files, and can be preceded by a drive; wildcard characters are permitted in the filename.
/A	copies only those source files with the archive bit set.
/D:*mm-dd-yy*	copies only files modified on or after the specified date. (The date format depends on the COUNTRY command in effect, if any.)
/E	copies empty subdirectories; if this switch is used, the /S switch must also be specified.
/M	copies only those files with the archive bit set; also turns off the archive bit of each source file after it is copied.
/P	prompts the user for confirmation before copying each file.
/S	copies all nonempty subdirectories of *source* and the files they contain.
/V	performs read-after-write verification of destination file(s).
/W	waits for the user to press a key before copying any files, allowing disks to be changed.

Description

The XCOPY command copies one or more source files to one or more destination files. Unlike the COPY command, however, a single XCOPY command can copy *all* files contained in the entire hierarchical file structure of the source disk to the destination disk, creating a corresponding set of directories and subdirectories at the destination to hold the copied files.

The *source* parameter identifies the file or files to be copied. It can consist of any combination of a drive, path, and filename (optionally including wildcards) but *must* include either a drive or a pathname. If only a drive is specified, all files in the current directory of that drive are copied. If a path without a drive or filename is specified, all files in the named directory are copied from the current drive.

The *destination* parameter can also consist of any combination of drive, path, and filename. Unless only a single file is being copied and it is also being renamed as part of the XCOPY operation, *destination* is usually simply a drive and/or path specifying where to place the copied file. If *destination* includes a filename, XCOPY displays a message asking if the specified destination is a file or a directory. Depending on the user's response, XCOPY then either copies the source file to a destination file with the specified name or creates a directory with the specified name and copies the source files into it. (Note that if the user responds that the destination is to be a file and multiple source files were specified in the command line, only the last source file is copied to the specified destination.) If no destination is specified, the source file is copied to a file with the same name in the current directory of the current drive.

The /A, /D:*mm-dd-yy*, /M, and /P switches allow selective copying of files. The /A switch is used to copy only source files with the archive bit set; the /M switch also copies only source files with the archive bit set but turns off each source file's archive bit after the file is copied. The /D:*mm-dd-yy* switch is used to copy files that were modified on or after a selected date; the date must be entered in one of the formats discussed in the entry for the system's DATE command or in the format of the COUNTRY command currently in effect (*see* USER COMMANDS: CONFIG.SYS: COUNTRY). The /P switch causes XCOPY to prompt the user for confirmation before transferring each file.

The /E and /S switches allow an entire branch of the source disk's hierarchical directory structure to be copied. If the /S switch is specified, XCOPY copies all nonempty subdirectories of *source*, creating equivalent destination subdirectories, if necessary, to hold the files. If the /E switch is specified, XCOPY also duplicates empty source subdirectories in the equivalent destination locations. If the /E switch is used, the /S switch must also be specified.

The /V switch causes a Verify call to be issued on the destination file(s) to ensure that the data was written correctly. Its effect is equivalent to that of the VERIFY ON command.

Finally, the /W switch causes XCOPY to wait for the user to press a key before copying any files, thus allowing an exchange of disks before the files are transferred. This is useful in systems without a fixed disk, because it allows XCOPY to be used when the program itself is not on either the source or the destination disk.

Note: With MS-DOS versions of XCOPY, the related program MCOPY can be created by simply copying the file XCOPY.EXE to a file named MCOPY.EXE using the following command:

```
C>COPY /B XCOPY.EXE MCOPY.EXE  <Enter>
```

What distinguishes MCOPY from XCOPY is the program name; when either program is loaded, it looks at the name under which it was invoked and reconfigures itself accordingly. MCOPY's behavior is similar to XCOPY's, except that MCOPY automatically determines whether the name specified as the destination is a file or a directory according to the following rules:

- If the source is a directory, the specified destination is a directory.
- If the source includes multiple files, the specified destination is a directory.
- If the destination name ends with a backslash character (\), the specified destination is a directory.

MCOPY supports all the XCOPY switches.

Not all implementations of XCOPY can be renamed to MCOPY and function accordingly. The PC-DOS version of XCOPY, for example, does not support this feature.

Return Codes

0   No errors were detected during the copy operation.
1   No files were found to copy.
2   The copy operation was terminated by a Ctrl-C or Ctrl-Break.
4   Initialization error occurred: not enough memory, file not found, or command-line syntax error.
5   The copy operation was terminated by an *A* response to an *Abort, Retry, Ignore?* prompt.

Examples

To copy all files in the directory C:\SOURCE to the directory C:\SOURCE\BACKUP, type

```
C>XCOPY C:\SOURCE\*.* C:\SOURCE\BACKUP   <Enter>
```

To copy all files and directories on drive C to the disk in drive D, type

```
C>XCOPY C:\*.* D: /S /E   <Enter>
```

Messages

nn File(s) copied
This informational message is displayed at the completion of an XCOPY command and indicates the total number of source files processed.

filename File not found
The source file specified in the command line is invalid or does not exist.

X:pathname (Y/N)?
The /P switch was specified in the command line. XCOPY displays the name of each file, preceded by a drive (and path, if one was specified), and asks for confirmation before copying the file.

Access denied
A destination file could not be overwritten because it was marked read-only.

Cannot COPY from a reserved device
A character device such as AUX or COM1 cannot be the source of an XCOPY operation.

Cannot COPY to a reserved device
A character device such as PRN cannot be the destination of an XCOPY operation.

Cannot perform a cyclic copy
The command line included a /S switch and the destination directory is a subdirectory of the source directory. A subdirectory cannot be copied onto itself.

Does *name* specify a file name
or directory name on the target
(F = file, D = directory)?
The specified destination directory does not already exist; the user is prompted to determine whether it should be created. Respond with *F* to copy the source file to a file named *name*; respond with *D* to create a subdirectory named *name* and copy the source file into it.

File cannot be copied onto itself
The name and location of the source file are the same as the name and location of the destination file.

File creation error
A destination file or directory could not be created. The destination disk may be full.

Incorrect DOS version
The version of XCOPY is not compatible with the version of MS-DOS that is running.

Insufficient disk space
The disk does not contain enough available space to perform the specified XCOPY operation.

Insufficient memory
The available system memory is insufficient to perform the XCOPY operation.

Invalid date
The command included a /D switch and the date was not formatted properly.

Invalid drive specification
The source or destination drive specified in the command line is not valid or does not exist in the system.

Invalid number of parameters
The command line contained too many or too few filenames or other parameters.

Invalid parameter
A switch supplied in the command line is not valid.

Invalid path
A directory specified in the command line is invalid or does not exist.

Lock Violation

XCOPY attempted to access a file in use by another program. Respond with *A* to the error-message prompt and try XCOPY later or wait for a few minutes and respond with *R*.

Path not found

One of the pathnames specified in the command line is invalid or does not exist.

Path too long

The path element of the source or destination parameter was longer than 63 characters.

Press any key to begin copying file(s)

The /W switch was specified in the command line and XCOPY waits for the user to press a key before beginning the copy process.

Reading source file(s)...

This informational message is displayed during the XCOPY operation.

Sharing violation

XCOPY attempted to access a file in use by another program. Respond with *A* to the error-message prompt and try XCOPY later or wait a few minutes and respond with *R*.

Too many open files

XCOPY failed due to a lack of available system file handles. Increase the size of the FILES command in the CONFIG.SYS file, restart the system, and attempt the XCOPY command again.

Unable to create directory

A destination directory cannot have the same name as an existing file in the prospective parent directory.

Section IV
Programming Utilities

Introduction

This section of *The MS-DOS Encyclopedia* describes the Microsoft utilities, documentation aids, and debuggers that can be used with the Microsoft C, FORTRAN, Pascal, and BASIC compilers and with the Microsoft Macro Assembler (MASM). Included are operating instructions for MASM, the Macro Assembler; LIB, the Library Manager; LINK, the Microsoft Object Linker; the DEBUG, SYMDEB, and CodeView program debuggers; MAKE, which automates maintenance of programs; CREF, which produces a cross-reference listing of symbols; and EXE2BIN, EXEMOD, and EXEPACK, which modify executable files.

Entries (except for the program debuggers) are arranged alphabetically by the name of the programming utility. The three Microsoft debuggers are listed at the end of the section in the following order: DEBUG, SYMDEB, CodeView. Individual DEBUG and SYMDEB commands appear alphabetically under the headings DEBUG and SYMDEB.

Each utility entry includes

- Utility name
- Utility purpose
- Prototype command line and summary of options
- Detailed description of utility
- One or more examples of utility use
- Return codes (where applicable)
- Error messages and warnings (where applicable)

The experienced user can find information with a quick glance at the first part of a utility entry; a less experienced user can refer to the detailed explanation and examples in a more leisurely fashion. The next two pages contain an example of a typical entry from the Programming Utilities section, with explanations of each component.

HEADING —
The utility name.

PURPOSE —
An abstract of utility purpose and usage plus a statement of which Microsoft products the utility is supplied with and the utility version described in the entry.

SYNTAX —
A prototype command line, with variable names in italic and optional parameters in square brackets. The various elements of the command line should be entered in the order shown. Any punctuation must be used exactly as shown; in commands that use commas as separators, the comma usually must be included as a placeholder even if the parameter is omitted. Except where noted, commands, parameters, and switches can be entered in either uppercase or lowercase. Utility names can be preceded by a drive and/or path.

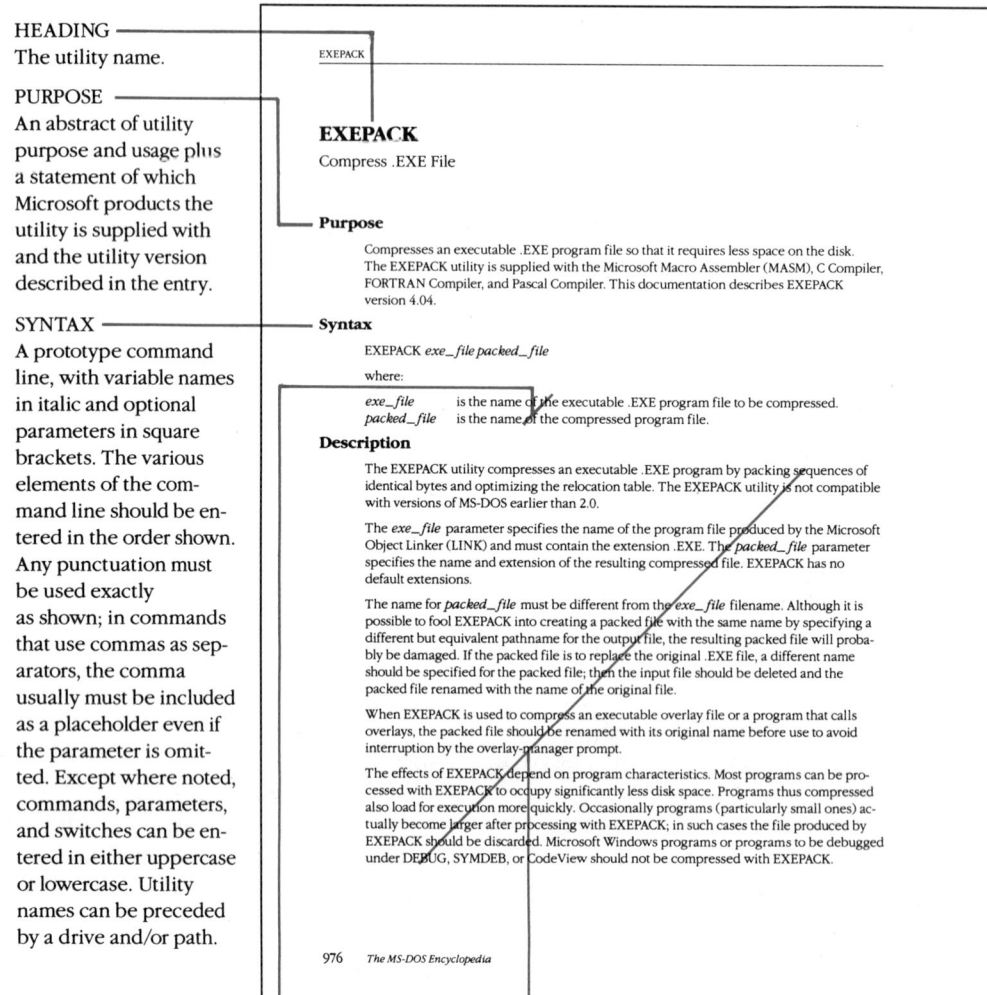

EXEPACK

EXEPACK
Compress .EXE File

Purpose

Compresses an executable .EXE program file so that it requires less space on the disk. The EXEPACK utility is supplied with the Microsoft Macro Assembler (MASM), C Compiler, FORTRAN Compiler, and Pascal Compiler. This documentation describes EXEPACK version 4.04.

Syntax

EXEPACK *exe_file packed_file*

where:

exe_file   is the name of the executable .EXE program file to be compressed.
packed_file is the name of the compressed program file.

Description

The EXEPACK utility compresses an executable .EXE program by packing sequences of identical bytes and optimizing the relocation table. The EXEPACK utility is not compatible with versions of MS-DOS earlier than 2.0.

The *exe_file* parameter specifies the name of the program file produced by the Microsoft Object Linker (LINK) and must contain the extension .EXE. The *packed_file* parameter specifies the name and extension of the resulting compressed file. EXEPACK has no default extensions.

The name for *packed_file* must be different from the *exe_file* filename. Although it is possible to fool EXEPACK into creating a packed file with the same name by specifying a different but equivalent pathname for the output file, the resulting packed file will probably be damaged. If the packed file is to replace the original .EXE file, a different name should be specified for the packed file; then the input file should be deleted and the packed file renamed with the name of the original file.

When EXEPACK is used to compress an executable overlay file or a program that calls overlays, the packed file should be renamed with its original name before use to avoid interruption by the overlay-manager prompt.

The effects of EXEPACK depend on program characteristics. Most programs can be processed with EXEPACK to occupy significantly less disk space. Programs thus compressed also load for execution more quickly. Occasionally programs (particularly small ones) actually become larger after processing with EXEPACK; in such cases the file produced by EXEPACK should be discarded. Microsoft Windows programs or programs to be debugged under DEBUG, SYMDEB, or CodeView should not be compressed with EXEPACK.

BELOW WHERE
A brief explanation of each command parameter and switch. Filenames are always listed first, followed by the switches in alphabetic order. Any special position required for a filename or switch is shown in the syntax line and noted in the explanation.

DESCRIPTION
A detailed description of the utility, including a full explanation of default values, possible interactions of command parameters and options, useful background information, and any applicable warnings.

Programming Utilities Introduction/Key

EXEPACK

Using EXEPACK on a previously linked program is equivalent to specifying LINK's /EXEPACK switch while linking that program.

Note: When using the EXEMOD utility with packed .EXE files created with EXEPACK or the /EXEPACK linker switch, use the EXEMOD version shipped with LINK or with the EXEPACK utility to ensure compatibility.

Return Codes

0   No error; the EXEPACK operation was successful.
1   An error was encountered that terminated execution of the EXEPACK utility.

Example

To compress the file BUILD.EXE into a file named BUILDX.EXE, type

```
C>EXEPACK BUILD.EXE BUILDX.EXE  <Enter>
```

Messages

fatal error U1100: out of space on output file
The destination disk has insufficient space for the output file, or the root directory is full.

fatal error U1101: *filename* **: file not found**
The .EXE file specified in the command line cannot be found.

fatal error U1102: *filename* **: permission denied**
A file with the same name as the specified output file already exists and is read-only.

fatal error U1103: cannot pack file onto itself
The file cannot be compressed because the name specified for the packed file is the same as the name of the source .EXE file.

fatal error U1104: usage : exepack <infile> <outfile>
The command line contained a syntax error, or the output filename was not specified.

fatal error U1105: invalid .EXE file; bad header
The file is not an executable file or has an invalid file header.

fatal error U1106: cannot change load-high program
The file cannot be compressed because the minimum allocation value and the maximum allocation value are both zero. *See also* PROGRAMMING UTILITIES: EXEMOD.

fatal error U1107: cannot pack already-packed file
The file specified has already been packed with EXEPACK.

fatal error U1108: invalid .EXE file; actual length less than reported
The file size indicated in the .EXE file header does not match the size recorded in the disk directory.

fatal error U1109: out of memory
The EXEPACK utility did not have enough memory to operate.

Section IV: Programming Utilities 977

RETURN CODES
Exit codes returned by the utility (if any) that can be tested in a batch file or by another program.

EXAMPLES
One or more examples of the utility at work, including examples of the resulting output where appropriate. User entry appears in color; do not type the prompt, which appears in black. Press the Enter key (labeled Return on some keyboards) as directed at the end of each command line.

MESSAGES
An alphabetic list of messages that may be displayed when the utility is used. Following each message is a brief explanation of the condition that produces the message and, where appropriate, any action that should be taken.

Section IV: Programming Utilities   965

CREF
Generate Cross-Reference Listing

Purpose

Produces a cross-reference listing of all symbols in an assembly-language program. The CREF utility is supplied with the Microsoft Macro Assembler (MASM). This documentation describes CREF version 4.0.

Syntax

CREF

or

CREF *crf_file*[;]

or

CREF *crf_file,ref_file*

where:

crf_file is the input file previously produced by MASM (default extension = .CRF).
ref_file is the output ASCII text file to be created (default extension = .REF).

Description

The CREF utility processes a file produced by MASM and generates an ASCII cross-reference listing in a file on disk or directly on a character device (such as a printer). The output file contains an alphabetic list of the symbols in the assembled program, including the line number of each reference to the symbol and the total number of symbols in the program. A pound sign (#) follows the line number of the reference that defines the symbol.

The *crf_file* has the default extension .CRF. It is produced by providing MASM with a filename other than NUL in the cross-reference position in the command line, by responding to the *Cross-reference:* prompt, or by including the /C switch in the MASM command line or at any MASM prompt. An assembly source listing file (.LST) must also be requested in the MASM command line or in response to the MASM prompts in order to generate a valid .CRF file.

If a semicolon follows the *crf_file* parameter in the CREF command, the resulting *ref_file* containing the cross-reference listing is given the same drive and pathname as *crf_file*, with a .REF extension. If the optional *ref_file* parameter is present, it can consist of any pathname with an optional extension (default is .REF). The cross-reference listing can be sent directly to a character device, rather than to a file, by specifying a valid character device name (such as PRN) in the *ref_file* position.

If the CREF utility is run without any parameters or with some parameters missing, the CREF utility prompts the operator for the necessary information.

Return Codes

0   No error; the CREF operation was successful.
1   An error was encountered that terminated execution of the CREF utility.

Examples

To process the file MENUMGR.CRF (created during assembly of MENUMGR.ASM) into the cross-reference file MENUMGR.REF, type

```
C>CREF MENUMGR;   <Enter>
```

To process the file MENUMGR.CRF and assign the name MENU.REF to the resulting cross-reference file, type

```
C>CREF MENUMGR,MENU   <Enter>
```

To process the file MENUMGR.CRF and send the cross-reference listing directly to the printer, type

```
C>CREF MENUMGR,PRN   <Enter>
```

To run the CREF program in interactive mode, type

```
C>CREF   <Enter>
```

The following is an example of an interactive CREF session:

```
C>CREF   <Enter>
Microsoft (R) Cross Reference Utility  Version 4.00
Copyright (C) Microsoft Corp 1981, 1983, 1984, 1985.  All rights reserved.

Cross-reference [.CRF]: MENUMGR  <Enter>
Listing [MENUMGR.REF]:  <Enter>

9 Symbols

C>
```

The following sequence of commands produces the cross-reference listing HELLO.REF from the assembly-language source file HELLO.ASM:

```
C>MASM HELLO,HELLO,HELLO,HELLO  <Enter>
C>CREF HELLO;  <Enter>
```

Contents of the file HELLO.ASM:

```
        name    hello
        page    55,132
        title   HELLO.ASM - print Hello on terminal
;
; HELLO.COM utility to demonstrate CREF listing
;
cr      equ     0dh                 ;ASCII carriage return
lf      equ     0ah                 ;ASCII linefeed


cseg    segment para public "CODE"

        org     100h

        assume  cs:cseg,ds:cseg,es:cseg,ss:cseg

print   proc    near
        mov     dx,offset message
        mov     ah,9                ;print the string "Hello"
        int     21h
        mov     ax,4c00h            ;exit to MS-DOS
        int     21h                 ;with "return code" of zero
print   endp

message db      cr,lf,'Hello!',cr,lf,'$'

cseg    ends

        end     print
```

Contents of the file HELLO.REF:

```
Microsoft Cross-Reference  Version 4.00           Mon Sep 07 23:31:21 1987
HELLO.ASM - print Hello on terminal

   Symbol Cross-Reference       (# is definition)                Cref-1

CODE . . . . . . . . . . . . .  10
CR . . . . . . . . . . . . . .   7      7#    24    25
CSEG . . . . . . . . . . . . .  10     10#    14    14    14    14    27

LF . . . . . . . . . . . . . .   8      8#    24    25

MESSAGE. . . . . . . . . . . .  17     24    24#

PRINT. . . . . . . . . . . . .  16     16#    29


  6 Symbols
```

Messages

can't open cross-reference file for reading
The pathname or drive specified for the input .CRF file is invalid or does not exist.

can't open listing file for writing
A write error has halted the creation of the .REF listing file. This indicates that the disk is full or write-protected, that the specified output file is read-only, or that the specified device is not available.

cref has no switches
A switch was specified in the command line; CREF has no optional switches.

DOS 2.0 or later required
CREF does not work with versions of MS-DOS earlier than 2.0.

extra file name ignored
More than two filenames were specified in the command line. The CREF utility generates the cross-reference listing using the first two filenames specified.

line invalid, start again
No .CRF file was specified in the command line or at the prompt. Specify a valid .CRF file at the prompt following this message.

out of heap space
Memory is insufficient to process the .CRF file. Remove memory-resident programs and shells or add more memory.

premature eof
The input file specified is damaged or is not a valid .CRF file.

read error on stdin
A Control-Z was received from the keyboard or a redirected file and has halted CREF.

EXE2BIN

Convert .EXE File to Binary-Image File

Purpose

Converts an executable file in the .EXE format to a memory-image file in binary format. The EXE2BIN utility is supplied with the MS-DOS distribution disks.

Syntax

EXE2BIN *exe_file* [*bin_file*]

where:

exe_file	is the .EXE-format file to be converted (default extension = .EXE).
bin_file	is the name to be given to the converted file (default extension = .BIN).

Description

The .EXE executable program files produced by the Microsoft Object Linker (LINK) contain a special header and a relocation table as well as the program code and data. The EXE2BIN utility can be used to convert a .EXE file to a .COM executable file, which is an absolute memory image of the program to be executed and does not contain a special header or relocation table. The EXE2BIN utility can also be used to convert .EXE files with an origin of zero (such as installable MS-DOS device drivers) to pure memory-image files. Files in memory-image format (a common format for device drivers and for programs to be placed in ROM for execution) usually have a .BIN or .SYS extension.

To convert a .EXE program to a binary-image file, the following are required:

- The program must be a valid .EXE file produced by LINK.
- The program can contain only one segment and cannot contain a declared stack segment.
- The program code and data portion of the .EXE file must be less than 64 KB.

To convert a .EXE program to an executable .COM file, the following are required:

- The origin of the program must be 0100H, which must also be specified as the entry point.
- The program code and data portion of the .EXE file must be less than 65227 bytes (64 KB minus 256 bytes used by the program segment prefix minus 2 bytes initially placed on the stack).
- The program must not include any FAR references.

Note: Many compilers cannot create programs that can be converted to .COM files. Check the compiler documentation for specific information concerning executable .COM files.

The *exe_file* parameter in the command line can have any filename and can include a drive and path; the default extension is .EXE. The optional *bin_file* parameter can also contain any filename and a drive and path; the default extension is .BIN. If no path is specified with the *bin_file* parameter, the output file is given the same drive and path as the *exe_file*. If no *bin_file* parameter is supplied, the output file is given the same name as the *exe_file*, with the extension .BIN.

If the program in the .EXE file requires segment fixups (that is, if the program contains instructions requiring segment relocation, which would ordinarily be done by the MS-DOS loader using the .EXE file's relocation table), EXE2BIN prompts for a base segment address. When segment fixups are necessary, the resulting program is not relocatable and must be loaded at the given location to be executed; the MS-DOS loader cannot load the program.

Examples

To convert the file HELLO.EXE to the file HELLO.BIN, type

```
C>EXE2BIN HELLO  <Enter>
```

To convert the file CLEAN.EXE, which has an origin of 0100H and meets the requirements for an executable .COM file, to the file CLEAN.COM, type

```
C>EXE2BIN CLEAN.EXE CLEAN.COM  <Enter>
```

To convert the file ASYNCH.EXE, produced by assembling and linking the device-driver source file ASYNCH.ASM, to the installable device-driver file ASYNCH.SYS, type

```
C>EXE2BIN ASYNCH.EXE ASYNCH.SYS  <Enter>
```

Messages

File cannot be converted
The program to be converted has one of the following problems: The program has an origin of 0100H but a different entry point; the program requires segment fixups; the program code and data are larger than 64 KB; the program has more than one declared segment; or the file is not a valid .EXE-format file.

File creation error
EXE2BIN cannot create the output file because a read-only file with the same name already exists, because the specified directory is full, or because the specified disk is full, write-protected, or unreadable.

File not found
The file does not exist or the incorrect path was given.

Fixups needed - base segment (hex):
The .EXE-format file contains segment references that would ordinarily be relocated by the .EXE file loader. Specify the absolute segment address at which the converted module will be executed.

Incorrect DOS version
The version of EXE2BIN is not compatible with the version of MS-DOS that is running.

Insufficient disk space
The destination disk has insufficent space to create the memory-image output file.

Insufficient memory
Not enough memory is available to run EXE2BIN.

WARNING - Read error in EXE file.
       Amount read less than size in header.
The file size given in the .EXE header is inconsistent with the actual size of the file.

EXEMOD
Modify .EXE File Header

Purpose

Allows inspection or modification of the fields in a .EXE file header. The EXEMOD utility is supplied with the Microsoft Macro Assembler (MASM), C Compiler, FORTRAN Compiler, and Pascal Compiler. This documentation describes EXEMOD version 4.02.

Syntax

EXEMOD *exe_file*[/H]

or

EXEMOD *exe_file*[/STACK *n*][/MAX *n*][/MIN *n*]

where:

exe_file	is the name of an executable program in .EXE format (the extension .EXE is assumed).
/H	displays the values in the file's header.
/STACK *n*	modifies the size of the program's stack segment to *n* (hexadecimal) bytes.
/MAX *n*	sets the maximum memory allocation for the program to *n* (hexadecimal) paragraphs.
/MIN *n*	sets the minimum memory allocation for the program to *n* (hexadecimal) paragraphs.

Note: Switches can be either uppercase or lowercase and can be preceded by a dash (-) instead of a forward slash (/).

Description

Programs that are executable under MS-DOS can be in one of two file formats: .COM, which is an absolute image of the file to be executed and limits the program size to 65227 bytes (64 KB minus 256 bytes used by the program segment prefix minus 2 bytes initially placed on the stack); or .EXE, which allows a program of any size to be loaded and has a special header containing information about the program's entry point, stack size, and memory requirements, plus a relocation table.

The EXEMOD utility can be used to display or modify those fields of a .EXE program header that control the size of the stack segment and the amount of memory allocated to the program when MS-DOS loads the program into the transient program area for execution.

The /STACK*n* switch controls the number of bytes in the program's STACK segment by setting the initial SP to the hexadecimal value specified. The minimum paragraph allocation value is adjusted if necessary. The EXEMOD /STACK*n* switch should be used only with programs compiled by Microsoft C version 3.0 or later, Microsoft Pascal version 3.3

or later, or Microsoft FORTRAN version 3.0 or later. Use of the /STACK*n* switch with a program developed with another compiler can cause the program to fail or cause EXEMOD to return an error message.

The /MAX*n* switch specifies the maximum number of additional paragraphs of memory to allocate for use by the program. The /MIN*n* switch specifies the minimum number of paragraphs of memory, in addition to the size of the program itself and its stack and data segments, that are required for the program to execute. If enough memory exists to satisfy the minimum additional paragraphs requested but not enough exists to satisfy the maximum, MS-DOS allocates all available memory to the program.

To display the current memory allocation and stack size values from a .EXE file's header, the /H switch can be used or the file's name can be entered as the only parameter in the command line.

When EXEMOD is used on a previously packed .EXE file (a file that was processed by EXEPACK or linked with the /EXEPACK switch), the values set or displayed in the file's header are the values that will apply after the file is expanded at load time. EXEMOD displays a message advising the user that the file being modified was previously packed.

The EXEMOD switches /MAX*n* and /STACK*n* correspond to the Microsoft Object Linker's /CPARMAXALLOC:*n* and /STACK:*n* switches, respectively. *See* PROGRAMMING UTILITIES: LINK.

Return Codes

0   No error; EXEMOD operation was successful.
1   An error was encountered that terminated execution of the EXEMOD program.

Examples

To display the values in the file header of the DUMP.EXE program, type

```
C>EXEMOD DUMP.EXE   <Enter>
```

or

```
C>EXEMOD DUMP.EXE /H   <Enter>
```

The EXEMOD utility displays the following:

```
Microsoft (R) EXE File Header Utility  Version 4.02
Copyright (C) Microsoft Corp 1985.  All rights reserved.
DUMP.EXE                          (hex)          (dec)

.EXE size (bytes)                  580           1408
Minimum load size (bytes)          383            899
Overlay number                       0              0
Initial CS:IP                0000:0000
Initial SS:SP                0034:0040             64
Minimum allocation (para)            5              5
Maximum allocation (para)         FFFF          65535
Header size (para)                  20             32
Relocation table offset             20             32
Relocation entries                   1              1
```

To change the size of the STACK segment for the DUMP.EXE program to 400H (1024) bytes, type

```
C>EXEMOD DUMP.EXE /STACK 400   <Enter>
```

EXEMOD displays the message

```
EXEMOD : warning U4051: minimum allocation less than stack; correcting minimum
```

Messages

error U1050: usage : exemod file [-/h] [-/stack n] [-/max n] [-/min n]
An error was detected in the EXEMOD command line.

error U1051: invalid .EXE file : bad header
The file is not an executable file or has an invalid file header.

error U1052: invalid .EXE file : actual length less than reported
The file size indicated in the .EXE file header does not match the size recorded in the disk directory.

error U1053: cannot change load-high program
The header of the file cannot be modified because the minimum allocation value and the maximum allocation value are both zero.

error U1054: file not .EXE
The file specified does not have a .EXE extension.

error U1055: *filename* : cannot find file
The .EXE file specified in the command line cannot be found.

error U1056: *filename* : permission denied
The .EXE file specified in the command line is read-only.

warning U4050: packed file
The specified file is a packed file; that is, it was previously processed with the EXEPACK utility or was linked with the /EXEPACK switch. This is an informational message only; EXEMOD still modifies the file. The header values displayed are the values that will apply after the packed value is expanded at load time.

warning U4051: minimum allocation less than stack; correcting minimum
The minimum allocation value is not large enough to accommodate the stack; the minimum allocation value is adjusted. This is an informational message only.

warning U4052: minimum allocation greater than maximum; correcting maximum
If the minimum allocation value is greater than the maximum allocation value, the maximum value is adjusted. This is an informational message only.

EXEPACK
Compress .EXE File

Purpose

Compresses an executable .EXE program file so that it requires less space on the disk. The EXEPACK utility is supplied with the Microsoft Macro Assembler (MASM), C Compiler, FORTRAN Compiler, and Pascal Compiler. This documentation describes EXEPACK version 4.04.

Syntax

EXEPACK *exe_file packed_file*

where:

exe_file   is the name of the executable .EXE program file to be compressed.
packed_file   is the name of the compressed program file.

Description

The EXEPACK utility compresses an executable .EXE program by packing sequences of identical bytes and optimizing the relocation table. The EXEPACK utility is not compatible with versions of MS-DOS earlier than 2.0.

The *exe_file* parameter specifies the name of the program file produced by the Microsoft Object Linker (LINK) and must contain the extension .EXE. The *packed_file* parameter specifies the name and extension of the resulting compressed file. EXEPACK has no default extensions.

The name for *packed_file* must be different from the *exe_file* filename. Although it is possible to fool EXEPACK into creating a packed file with the same name by specifying a different but equivalent pathname for the output file, the resulting packed file will probably be damaged. If the packed file is to replace the original .EXE file, a different name should be specified for the packed file; then the input file should be deleted and the packed file renamed with the name of the original file.

When EXEPACK is used to compress an executable overlay file or a program that calls overlays, the packed file should be renamed with its original name before use to avoid interruption by the overlay-manager prompt.

The effects of EXEPACK depend on program characteristics. Most programs can be processed with EXEPACK to occupy significantly less disk space. Programs thus compressed also load for execution more quickly. Occasionally programs (particularly small ones) actually become larger after processing with EXEPACK; in such cases the file produced by EXEPACK should be discarded. Microsoft Windows programs or programs to be debugged under DEBUG, SYMDEB, or CodeView should not be compressed with EXEPACK.

Using EXEPACK on a previously linked program is equivalent to specifying LINK's /EXEPACK switch while linking that program.

Note: When using the EXEMOD utility with packed .EXE files created with EXEPACK or the /EXEPACK linker switch, use the EXEMOD version shipped with LINK or with the EXEPACK utility to ensure compatibility.

Return Codes

0   No error; the EXEPACK operation was successful.
1   An error was encountered that terminated execution of the EXEPACK utility.

Example

To compress the file BUILD.EXE into a file named BUILDX.EXE, type

```
C>EXEPACK BUILD.EXE BUILDX.EXE  <Enter>
```

Messages

fatal error U1100: out of space on output file
The destination disk has insufficient space for the output file, or the root directory is full.

fatal error U1101: *filename* : file not found
The .EXE file specified in the command line cannot be found.

fatal error U1102: *filename* : permission denied
A file with the same name as the specified output file already exists and is read-only.

fatal error U1103: cannot pack file onto itself
The file cannot be compressed because the name specified for the packed file is the same as the name of the source .EXE file.

fatal error U1104: usage : exepack <infile> <outfile>
The command line contained a syntax error, or the output filename was not specified.

fatal error U1105: invalid .EXE file; bad header
The file is not an executable file or has an invalid file header.

fatal error U1106: cannot change load-high program
The file cannot be compressed because the minimum allocation value and the maximum allocation value are both zero. *See also* PROGRAMMING UTILITIES: EXEMOD.

fatal error U1107: cannot pack already-packed file
The file specified has already been packed with EXEPACK.

fatal error U1108: invalid .EXE file; actual length less than reported
The file size indicated in the .EXE file header does not match the size recorded in the disk directory.

fatal error U1109: out of memory
The EXEPACK utility did not have enough memory to operate.

fatal error U1110: error reading relocation table

The file cannot be compressed because the relocation table cannot be found or is invalid.

fatal error U1111: file not suitable for packing

The file could not be packed because the packed load image of the specified file was larger than the unpacked load image.

fatal error U1112: *filename* **: unknown error**

An unknown system error occurred while the specified file was being processed.

warning U4100: omitting debug data from output file

EXEPACK has stripped all symbolic debug information from the output file.

LIB

Library Manager

Purpose

Creates or modifies an object module library file. The LIB utility is supplied with the Microsoft Macro Assembler (MASM), C Compiler, FORTRAN Compiler, and Pascal Compiler. This documentation describes LIB version 3.06.

Syntax

LIB

or

LIB *library_file* [/PAGESIZE:*n*] [*operation*][,[*list_file*][,[*new_library_file*]]] [;]

or

LIB @*response_file*

where:

library_file	is the name of the object module library file to be created or modified (default extension = .LIB).
/PAGESIZE:*n*	is the page size of the library file and must immediately follow *library_file* if used; *n* is a power of 2 between 16 and 32768, inclusive (default = 16). Can be abbreviated /P:*n*.
operation	is one or more library manipulations to be performed. Each *operation* is specified as a code followed by an object module name (case is not significant):

+*name*	Add object module or another library to library.
−*name*	Delete object module from library.
−+*name*	Replace object module in library.
name	Copy object module from library to object file.
−*name*	Copy object module to object file and then delete object module from library.

list_file	is the name of the file or character device to receive the cross-reference listing for the library file (default = NUL device).
new_library_file	is the name to be assigned to the modified object module library file. (The default name is the same as *library_file*; if the default is used, the original *library_file* is renamed with the extension .BAK.)
response_file	is the name of a text file containing LIB parameters in the same order in which they are supplied if entered interactively. The name of the response file must be preceded by the @ symbol.

Description

The Microsoft Library Manager (LIB) creates and modifies library files, checks existing library files for consistency, and prints listings of the contents of library files. The LIB utility does not work with versions of MS-DOS earlier than 2.0.

A library file consists of relocatable object modules that are indexed by their names and public symbols. The Microsoft Object Linker (LINK) uses these files during the creation of an executable (.EXE) program to resolve external references to routines and variables contained in other object modules.

The *library_file* parameter specifies the name of the object module library file to be created or modified. This parameter is required; if it is not included, LIB prompts for it. The default extension for a library file is .LIB.

The /PAGESIZE:n switch (abbreviated /P:n) sets the page size (in bytes) for a new library file or changes the page size of an existing library file. The value of n must be a power of 2 between 16 and 32768, inclusive. The default is 16 for a new library file; for an existing library file, the default is the current page size. Because the index to a library file is contained in a fixed number of pages, setting a larger page size increases the number of index entries (and thus the number of object modules) that a library file can contain but results in more wasted disk space (an average of half a library page per object module).

The *operation* parameter specifies one or more relocatable object modules to add to, replace in, copy from, move from, or delete from *library_file*. Each operation is represented by a code specifying the type of operation, followed by the object module name. When an object module is copied or moved from the library file, the drive and pathname of the object module are set to the default drive, current directory, and specified module name, and the extension of the object module defaults to .OBJ. When an object module is added or replaced, LIB assumes a default extension of .OBJ.

The operation +*name* adds the object module in the file *name*.OBJ to the library file. This operation can also be used to add the contents of another entire object module library file to the library file being updated, in which case the extension .LIB must be included in *name*. The operation −*name* deletes the object module *name* from the library. The operation −+*name* deletes the object module *name* from the library file and replaces it with the contents of the file *name*.OBJ. The operation *name copies the object module *name* from the library file into the file *name*.OBJ, which LIB creates in the current directory. The operation −*name* also copies the object module *name* from the library file into a .OBJ file but then deletes the module from the library file. (Although *name* must have exactly the same spelling as the name in the library's reference listing, case is not significant.)

Note: LIB does not actually delete object modules from the specified library file. Instead, it marks the selected object modules for deletion, creates a new library file, and copies only the modules not marked for deletion into the new file. Thus, if LIB is terminated for any reason, the original file is not lost. Enough space must be available on the disk for both the original library file and the copy.

The *list_file* parameter specifies the file or character device to receive a reference listing for the library file. Any valid drive, pathname, and extension or any valid character device, such as PRN, is permitted (default = NUL). If this parameter is omitted, no listing is generated.

The reference listing consists of two tables. The first table contains all the public symbols in the object modules in the library, listed alphabetically, with each symbol followed by the name of the object module in which it is referenced. The second table contains the names of all the object modules, listed alphabetically, with each name followed by the offset from the start of the library file, the code and data size, and an alphabetic listing of the public symbols in that object module.

The *new_library_file* parameter specifies the name for the modified library file that is created. If this parameter is omitted, LIB gives the modified library file the same name as the original library file, and the original library file is renamed with a .BAK extension. When a new library file is being created, this parameter is not necessary.

When the command line is used to supply LIB with filenames and switches, typing a semicolon character (;) after any parameter (except *library_file*) causes LIB to use the default values for the remaining parameters. If a semicolon is entered after *library_file*, LIB simply checks the file for consistency and usability. (This is seldom necessary, because LIB checks each object module for consistency before adding it to the library.)

If the LIB command is entered without any parameters, LIB prompts the user for each parameter needed. If there are too many operations to fit on one line, the line can be ended with the ampersand character (&), causing LIB to repeat the *Operations:* prompt. If any response except *library_file* is terminated with a semicolon character, LIB uses the default values for the remaining filenames. When the *library_file* parameter is followed by a semicolon or a semicolon is entered at the *Operations:* prompt, LIB takes no action except to verify that the contents of the specified file are consistent and usable.

The *response_file* parameter allows the automation of complex LIB sessions involving many files. A response file contains ASCII text that corresponds line for line to the responses that are entered in a normal interactive LIB session, in the form

library_file [/P:*n*]
[Y]
[*operations*]
[*list_file*]
[*new_library_file*] [;]

The response file name must be preceded in the command line by the at symbol (@) and can also be preceded by a path and/or drive letter. If *library_file* is a new file, the letter *Y* must appear by itself on the second line of the response file to approve the creation of a library file. The last line of the response file must end with a semicolon or a carriage return. (LIB ignores any lines following a semicolon.) If all the parameters required by LIB are not present in the response file or the response file does not end with a semicolon, LIB prompts the user for the missing information.

Return Codes

0   No error; LIB operation was successful.
1   An error that terminated execution of the LIB utility was encountered.

Examples

To create a library file named MYLIB.LIB and insert the object files VIDEO.OBJ, COMM.OBJ, and DOSINT.OBJ, type

```
C>LIB MYLIB +VIDEO +COMM +DOSINT;   <Enter>
```

To print a listing of the object modules in the library file MYLIB.LIB, type

```
C>LIB MYLIB,PRN   <Enter>
```

If the LIB command is entered without parameters, the user is prompted for the necessary information. For example, if the user wanted to add the module VIDEO.OBJ to the library file SLIBC.LIB, produce a reference listing in the file SLIBC.LST, and produce a new output library file named SLIBC2.LIB, the following dialogue would take place:

```
C>LIB   <Enter>

Microsoft (R) Library Manager  Version 3.06
Copyright (C) Microsoft Corp 1983, 1984, 1985, 1986.  All rights reserved.

Library name: SLIBC   <Enter>
Operations: +VIDEO   <Enter>
List file: SLIBC.LST   <Enter>
Output library: SLIBC2   <Enter>
```

Messages

filename: cannot access file.
LIB is unable to access an object module specified in a response file, in the command line, or at the *Operations:* prompt.

filename: cannot create extract file
The object module cannot be copied or moved from the library file into a separate disk file called *filename* because the root directory or disk is full or because *filename* already exists and is read-only.

filename: cannot create listing
The list file specified in the response file, in the command line, or at the *List file:* prompt cannot be created because the root directory or disk is full or because *filename* already exists and is read-only.

filename: invalid format (_xxxx_); file ignored.

The hexadecimal signature byte or word _xxxx_ of the specified file was not one of the following recognized types: Microsoft library, Intel library, Microsoft object, or XENIX archive.

filename: invalid library header.

The input library file either is not a library file or is damaged.

filename: invalid library header; file ignored.

The input library file is in the wrong format.

modulename: invalid object module near _location_

The specified object module has an invalid format near the hexadecimal offset indicated.

modulename: module not in library; ignored

The object module specified in the response file, in the command line, or at the _Operations:_ prompt is not in the specified input library file.

modulename: module redefinition ignored

An object module was specified to be added to a library file but an object module with the same name was already in the library file, or the same object module was specified twice in an add operation in the command line.

number: page size too small; ignored

The size specified with a /P:_n_ switch must be a power of 2 between 16 and 32768 bytes, inclusive.

symbol (_modulename_) : symbol redefinition ignored

The specified symbol was defined in more than one module. Only the first definition of a symbol is accepted. All redefinitions are ignored.

cannot create new library

The root directory is full, or a library file with the same name already exists and is read-only.

cannot open response file

The specified response file cannot be found or does not exist.

cannot rename old library

The old library file cannot be renamed with a .BAK extension because such a file already exists and is read-only.

cannot reopen library

The old library file could not be reopened after it was renamed with the .BAK extension. This error usually indicates damage to the operating system or to the disk directory structure.

comma or new line missing

A comma or carriage return was expected in the command line but was not found.

Do not change diskette in drive X:
LIB may have placed important temporary files on the specified disk. Do not remove the disk until the LIB operation is complete or these files may be lost.

error writing to cross-reference file
The disk or root directory is full.

error writing to new library
The new library file cannot be created because the disk is full.

free: not allocated
This is a serious problem. Note the circumstances of the failure and notify Microsoft Corporation.

insufficient memory
Not enough memory is available in the transient program area for LIB to successfully perform the requested operations.

internal failure
This is a serious problem. Note the circumstances of the failure and notify Microsoft Corporation.

Library does not exist. Create?
The specified *library_file* does not exist on disk. Respond with *Y* to create the library file; respond with *N* to terminate the LIB utility.

mark: not allocated
This is a serious problem. Note the circumstances of the failure and notify Microsoft Corporation.

option unknown
The command line included a switch other than /P:*n*.

output-library specification ignored
An output library file was specified in addition to a new library file. This is only a warning. The output library file specification will be disregarded.

page size too small
The page size of an input library file was less than 16 bytes, indicating a damaged or otherwise invalid .LIB file. *See* LIB message *number*: page size too small; ignored.

syntax error
The command line included an invalid parameter or switch.

syntax error: illegal file specification
A command operator (such as *, −, or +) was given without an object module name.

syntax error: illegal input
The command line included an invalid parameter or switch.

syntax error: option name missing
The command line included a forward slash (/) that was not followed by P:*n*.

syntax error: option value missing
The /P switch was not followed by the page size value in bytes.

terminator missing
Either a control character (such as Control-Z) was specified at the *Output library:* prompt or the response file line that corresponds to LIB's *Output library:* prompt was not terminated by a carriage return or semicolon.

too many symbols
The maximum number of public symbols allowed in a library file has been exceeded. The limit for all object modules (combined) is 4609.

unexpected end-of-file on command input
The response file did not include all the necessary LIB parameters.

write to extract file failed
The destination disk has insufficient space for the complete object module, or the root directory is full.

write to library file failed
The destination disk has insufficient space to create the new library file, or the root directory is full.

LINK

Create .EXE File

Purpose

Combines relocatable object modules into an executable (.EXE) file. The Microsoft Object Linker (LINK) is supplied with the Microsoft Macro Assembler (MASM), C Compiler, Pascal Compiler, and FORTRAN Compiler. This documentation describes LINK version 3.50.

Syntax

LINK

or

LINK *obj_file*[+*obj_file*...][,[*exe_file*]][,[*map_file*]][,[*library*[+*library*...]]] [*options*] [;]

or

LINK @*response_file*

where:

obj_file	is the name of a file containing a relocatable object module produced by MASM or by a high-level-language compiler (default extension = .OBJ).
exe_file	is the name of the executable file to be produced by LINK (default extension = .EXE).
map_file	is the name of the file or character device to receive a listing of the names, load addresses, and lengths of the segments in *exe_file* (default = NUL device; default extension = .MAP).
library	is the name of an object module library to be searched to resolve external references in the object file(s) (default extension = .LIB).
response_file	is the name of a text file containing LINK parameters in the order in which they are supplied during an interactive LINK session.
options	specifies one or more of the following switches. Switches can be either uppercase or lowercase.

	/CP:*n*	(/CPARMAXALLOC:*n*) Sets the maximum number of extra memory paragraphs required by *exe_file* (default = 65535).
	/DS	(/DSALLOCATE) Loads the data in DGROUP at the high end of the data segment.
	/DO	(/DOSSEG) Arranges segments according to the Microsoft language segment-ordering convention.
	/E	(/EXEPACK) Compresses repetitive sequences of bytes and optimizes *exe_file*'s relocation table.

(more)

LINK

/HI	(/HIGH) Causes *exe_file* to be loaded as high as possible in memory when *exe_file* is executed.
/HE	(/HELP) Lists LINK options on the screen. No other switches or filenames should be used with this switch.
/LI	(/LINENUMBERS) Copies line-number information (if available) from *obj_file* to *map_file*. If a map file was not specified, this switch creates one.
/M	(/MAP) Copies a list of all public symbols declared in *obj_file* to *map_file*. If a map file was not specified, this switch creates one.
/NOD	(/NODEFAULTLIBRARYSEARCH) Causes LINK to ignore any library names inserted in the object file by the language compiler.
/NOG	(/NOGROUPASSOCIATION) Causes LINK to ignore GROUP associations when assigning addresses.
/NOI	(/NOIGNORECASE) Causes LINK to be case sensitive when resolving external names.
/O:*n*	(/OVERLAYINTERRUPT:*n*) Overrides the interrupt number used by the overlay manager (0–255, default = 63, or 3FH). This switch should be used only when linking with a run-time module from a language compiler that supports overlays.
/P	(/PAUSE) Causes LINK to pause and prompt the user to change disks before writing the *exe_file*.
/SE:*n*	(/SEGMENTS:*n*) Sets the maximum number of segments that can be processed (1–1024, default = 128).
/ST:*n*	(/STACK:*n*) Sets the size of the *exe_file*'s stack segment to *n* bytes (1–65535).

Description

LINK combines relocatable object modules into an executable file in the .EXE format. LINK can be used with object files produced by any high-level-language compiler or assembler that supports the Microsoft object module format. *See* PROGRAMMING IN THE MS-DOS ENVIRONMENT: PROGRAMMING TOOLS: Object Modules; The Microsoft Object Linker.

The *obj_file* parameter, which is required, specifies one or more files containing relocatable object modules. If multiple object files are linked, their names should be separated by a plus operator (+) or a space. If an extension is not specified for an object file, LINK supplies the extension .OBJ. Some high-level-language compilers support partitioning of the executable program into a root segment and one or more overlay segments and include a special overlay manager in their libraries; when these compilers are used, the object modules that compose each overlay segment should be surrounded with parentheses in the LINK command line.

The *exe_file* parameter specifies the name of the executable file that is created by LINK. The default is the same filename as the first object file, but with the extension .EXE.

The *map_file* parameter designates the file or character device to receive LINK's listing of the name, load address, and length of each of *exe_file*'s segments. The map file also includes the names and load addresses of any groups in the program, the program entry point, and, if the /M switch is used, all public symbols and their addresses. If the /LI switch is used and if line numbers were inserted into *obj_file* by the compiler, the starting address of each *obj_file* program line is also copied to *map_file*. The default extension for a map file is .MAP. If the /M or /LI switch is used, a map file is created using the name of the specified .EXE file even if *map_file* is not specified. If neither the /M nor the /LI switch is used and *map_file* is not specified, no listing is created.

The *library* parameter specifies the object module library or libraries that will be searched to resolve external references after all the object files are processed. The default extension for library files is .LIB. Multiple library names should be separated by plus operators (+) or spaces. A maximum of 16 search paths can be specified in the LINK command line. If a library name is preceded by a drive and/or path, LINK searches only the specified location. If no drive or path precedes a library name, LINK searches for library files in the following order:

1.   Current drive and directory
2.   Any other library search paths specified in the command line, in the order they were entered
3.   Directories specified in the LIB= environment variable, if one exists

In the following example, LINK searches only the \ALTLIB directory on drive A to find the library MATH.LIB. To find the library COMMON.LIB, LINK searches the current directory on the current drive, then the current directory on drive B, then directory \LIB on drive D, and finally, any directories named in the LIB environment variable.

```
C>LINK TEST,,TEST,A:\ALTLIB\MATH.LIB+COMMON+B:+D:\LIB\  <Enter>
```

If default libraries are specified within the object files through special records inserted by certain high-level-language compilers, those libraries will be searched *after* the libraries named in the command line or response file.

If the LINK command is entered without parameters, LINK prompts the user for each filename needed. The default response for each prompt (except the *obj_file* prompt) is displayed in square brackets and can be selected by pressing the Enter key. If there are too many *obj_file* or *library* names to fit on one line, the line can be terminated by entering a plus operator (+) and pressing the Enter key; LINK then repeats the prompt. If the user ends any response with a semicolon character (;), LINK uses the default values for the remaining fields.

When the command line contains filenames and switches, commas must be used to separate the *obj_file, exe_file, map_file,* and *library* parameters. If a filename is not supplied, a comma must be used to mark its place. If the user places a semicolon after any parameter in the command line, LINK terminates the command line at the semicolon and uses the default values for any remaining parameters.

The user can automate complex LINK sessions involving multiple files by creating a response file. The *response_file* parameter must be the name of an ASCII file that corresponds line for line to the responses that are entered in a normal interactive LINK session. The last line of the response file must end with a semicolon character (;) or a carriage return. If all parameters required by LINK are not present in the response file and the response file does not end with a semicolon or carriage return, LINK prompts the user for the missing information.

LINK supports many options that can be invoked by including a switch in the command line, as part of the response to a LINK prompt, or in a response file. To simplify this description, these switches are grouped according to their functions.

The /E, /HE, /NOD, /NOI, /P, and /SE:n switches affect LINK's general operation. The /E switch compresses repetitive sequences of bytes in *exe_file* and optimizes certain parts of the relocation table in *exe_file*'s header. The /E switch functions exactly like the EXEPACK utility.

Note: The /E switch does not always save a significant amount of disk space and may even increase file size when used with small programs that have few load-time relocations or repeated characters. The Microsoft Symbolic Debugger (SYMDEB) utility cannot be used with packed files.

The /HE switch displays the available options on the screen. No other switches or filenames should be specified if the /HE switch is used. The /NOD switch causes LINK to ignore any default libraries that have been added to the object modules by the high-level-language compiler that produced the modules, thus restricting searches to those libraries specified in the command line or response file. The /NOI switch causes LINK to be case sensitive when resolving external references to symbols between object modules. The /NOI switch is typically used with object files created by high-level-language compilers that differentiate between uppercase and lowercase letters.

The /P switch causes LINK to pause and prompt the user before writing *exe_file* to disk, thus allowing the user to exchange the disk used during the linking operation for another that has more space available. The /SE:n switch controls the number of program segments processed by LINK. The n must be a decimal, octal, or hexadecimal number from 1 through 1024, inclusive (default = 128). Octal numbers must have a leading zero; hexadecimal numbers must begin with 0x.

The /M and /LI switches affect the production and contents of the optional map file. The /M switch creates a map file with the same name as *exe_file* or, if *exe_file* is not specified, with the same name as the first object file and the extension .MAP. The resulting map file includes a list of all public symbols and their addresses. The /LI switch also creates a map file and includes line-number information if available in the object file. (MASM and some high-level-language compilers do not insert line-number information into object files.)

The /D, /DO, /NOG, and /O:n switches affect the structure of the code in *exe_file*. Use of the /D switch places the data in DGROUP at the top (highest address) of the memory segment pointed to by the DS register, rather than at the bottom (the default). The /DO switch arranges the program segments according to a convention expected by all Microsoft language compilers: All segments with the class name CODE are placed first in the executable file; any other segments that do not belong to DGROUP are placed immediately after the CODE segments; all segments belonging to DGROUP are placed at the end of the file. The /NOG switch causes LINK to ignore group associations specified in the object modules when assigning addresses to data and code items; that is, segments that would ordinarily have been collected into the same physical memory segment because of their association within a GROUP are decoupled. The /NOG switch provides compatibility with LINK versions 2.02 and earlier and with early versions of Microsoft language compilers. The /O:n switch controls the interrupt number used by the resident overlay manager if the linked program includes overlays. The number n can be any decimal, octal, or hexadecimal number in the range 0 through 255 (default = 63, or 3FH). Octal numbers must have a leading zero; hexadecimal numbers must begin with 0x.

Note: MASM and many high-level-language compilers do not include overlay managers in their libraries. Users should check their compiler documentation to determine if the /O:n switch can be used.

Warning: Interrupt numbers that conflict with the software interrupts used to obtain MS-DOS or ROM BIOS services or with hardware interrupts assigned to peripheral device controllers should not be used in the /O:n switch.

The /C:n, /H, and /ST:n switches control the information in *exe_file*'s header that affects the behavior of the MS-DOS system loader when the file is read from the disk into RAM for execution. The /C:n switch sets the maximum number of 16-byte paragraphs of memory to be made available to the program when it is loaded into memory, in addition to the memory required to hold the program's code, data, and stacks; the default is 65535, which causes the program to be allocated all available memory. The /H switch causes the program to be loaded as high as possible in the transient program area (free memory), rather than as low as possible (the default). The /ST:n switch sets the stack size (in bytes) to be allocated for the program when it is loaded and overrides any stack segment size declarations in the original source code. The number n can be any decimal, octal, or hexadecimal number from 1 through 65535; however n must be large enough to accommodate any initialized data in the stack segment. Octal numbers must have a leading zero; hexadecimal numbers must begin with 0x. If the /ST:n switch is not used, LINK calculates a program's stack size, basing the size on the size of any stack segments given in the object files. The /C:n and /ST:n values in the *exe_file* header can be altered after linking by using the EXEMOD utility.

If LINK is unable to hold in RAM all the data it is processing, it creates a temporary disk file named VM.TMP (Virtual Memory) in the current directory of the default disk drive. If a floppy disk is in the default drive, LINK issues a warning message to prevent the user from changing disks until the LINK session is completed. After LINK finishes processing, it deletes the temporary file.

Warning: Any file named VM.TMP that is already on the disk will be destroyed if LINK creates the temporary disk file.

Return Codes

0	No errors or unresolved refcrences were encountered during creation of *exe_file*.
1	A miscellaneous LINK error occurred that was not covered by the other return codes.
16	A data record was too large to process.
32	No object files were specified in the command line or response file.
33	The map file could not be created.
66	A COMMON area was declared that is larger than 65535 (one segment).
96	Too many libraries were specified.
144	An invalid object module (*obj_file*) was detected.
145	Too many TYPDEFs were found in the specified object modules.
146	Too many group, segment, or class names were found in one object module.
147	Too many segments were found in all the object modules combined, or too many segments were found in one object module.
148	Too many overlays were specified.
149	The size of a segment exceeded 65535.
150	Too many groups or GRPDEFs were found in one object module.
151	Too many external symbols were found in one object module.
177	The size of a group exceeded 65535.

Examples

The simplest use of LINK is to process a single object file to produce an executable file, using all the default values. For example, to process the file SHELL.OBJ, create an executable file named SHELL.EXE, and search only the default libraries, type

```
C>LINK SHELL;   <Enter>
```

The semicolon after the filename causes LINK to use the default values for all other parameters.

To link three object files named SHELL.OBJ, VIDEO.OBJ, and DOSINT.OBJ into an executable file named SHELL.EXE and search the library DEVLIB.LIB on drive B before searching any default libraries, type

```
C>LINK SHELL+VIDEO+DOSINT,,,B:DEVLIB   <Enter>
```

If the LINK command is entered without parameters, LINK prompts the user for the necessary information. For example, the following interactive session links the file

MENUMGR.OBJ into the executable file MENUMGR.EXE, creates a map file named
MENUMGR.MAP, and searches the math floating-point emulator library EM.LIB before
any default libraries:

```
C>LINK  <Enter>


Microsoft (R) 8086 Object Linker  Version 3.05
Copyright (C) Microsoft Corp 1983,1984,1985.  All rights reserved.

Object Modules [.OBJ]: MENUMGR  <Enter>
Run File [MENUMGR.EXE]:  <Enter>
List File [NUL.MAP]: MENUMGR  <Enter>
Libraries [.LIB]: EM  <Enter>
```

Messages

filename is not a valid library
The file specified as an object module library either is corrupt or is not a library in the
format created by the Microsoft LIB utility.

About to generate .EXE file
Change diskette in drive *X* and press <ENTER>
The /P switch was used in the command line. LINK is prompting the user to change disks
before LINK creates the file containing the executable program.

Ambiguous switch error: *"option"*
A valid switch was not entered after a forward slash (/) in the command line.

Array element size mismatch
A FAR communal array was declared with two or more different array-element sizes (for
example, once as an array of characters and once as an array of real numbers). This error
occurs only with programs produced by the Microsoft C Compiler or other compilers that
support FAR communal arrays; it does not occur with object files produced by MASM.

Attempt to access data outside segment bounds
A data record in an object module specified data extending beyond the end of a segment.
This is a translator error. Note which compiler or assembler produced the invalid object
module and notify Microsoft Corporation.

Attempt to put segment *name* in more than one group in file *filename*
A segment was declared to be a member of two groups. Correct the source code and re-
create the object modules.

Bad value for cparMaxAlloc
The value specified using the /C:*n* option is not in the range 1 through 65535.

Cannot create temporary file
The destination disk has insufficient space for the temporary file, or the root directory is
full.

Cannot find file *filename*
Change diskette and press <ENTER>
The specified object file cannot be found in the current drive.

Cannot find library: *filename*
Enter new file spec:
The specified library file cannot be found or does not exist. Enter the correct drive letter, check the spelling of the filename and path, or make sure that the LIB environment variable has been set up properly.

Cannot nest response files
A response file was named within a response file. Revise the response file to eliminate the nested file.

Cannot open list file
The destination disk has insufficient space for the listing, or the root directory is full.

Cannot open response file: *filename*
LINK cannot find the specified response file.

Cannot open run file
The destination disk has insufficient space for the .EXE file, or the root directory is full.

Cannot open temporary file
The destination disk has insufficient space for the temporary file, or the root directory is full.

Cannot reopen list file
The original disk was not replaced when requested. Restart LINK.

Common area longer than 65536 bytes
The program has more than 64 KB of communal variables. This error occurs only with programs produced by the Microsoft C Compiler or other compilers that support communal variables.

Data record too large
An LEDATA record (in an object module) contains more than 1024 bytes of data. This is a symptom of an error in the compiler used to generate the object module. Document the circumstances and contact Microsoft Corporation.

Dup record too large
An LIDATA record (in an object module) contains more than 512 bytes of data. This error may be caused by a complex structure definition or by a series of deeply nested DUP operators.

File not suitable for /EXEPACK, relink without
The file linked with the /E switch would have been smaller if it had not been compressed. Relink without the /E switch.

Fixup overflow near *number* in segment *name* in *filename* offset *number*
A group is larger than 64 KB, the original source file contains an intersegment short jump or intersegment short call, the name of a data item conflicts with that of a library sub-routine, or an EXTRN declaration is placed inside the wrong segment.

Incorrect DOS version, use DOS 2.0 or later
LINK uses the extended file management calls to provide path support and, thus, does not work with versions of MS-DOS earlier than 2.0.

Insufficient stack space
Not enough memory is available to run LINK.

Interrupt number exceeds 255
The number specified in the /O:*n* switch is not in the range 0 through 255.

Invalid numeric switch specification
An incorrect value was entered with one of the LINK options.

Invalid object module
One of the object modules is invalid. Recompile the source file. If the error persists after recompiling, document the circumstances and contact Microsoft Corporation.

NEAR/HUGE conflict
Conflicting NEAR and HUGE definitions were given for a communal variable. This error occurs only with programs produced by the Microsoft C Compiler or other compilers that support communal variables.

Nested left parentheses
An opening (left) parenthesis is needed on the left side of an overlay module.

Nested right parentheses
A closing (right) parenthesis is needed on the right side of an overlay module.

No object modules specified
No object file names were specified in the command line or response file.

Object not found
One of the object files specified in the command line was not found.

Out of space on list file
The destination disk has insufficient space for the listing.

Out of space on run file
The destination disk has insufficient space for the .EXE file.

Out of space on scratch file
The disk in the default drive has insufficient space for temporary files.

Overlay manager symbol already defined: *name*
A symbol name was defined that conflicts with one of the special overlay manager names. Use another symbol name.

**Please replace original diskette
in drive X and press <ENTER>**
The /P switch was specified in the command line and the disk to receive the .EXE file produced by LINK has already been inserted. This message indicates that the .EXE file was successfully created and that the original disk should again be placed in the drive.

Relocation table overflow
More than 32768 long calls, long jumps, or other long pointers were found in the program. The program may need to be restructured to reduce the number of FAR references. (Pascal and FORTRAN users should try turning off the debugging option before restructuring the program.)

Response line too long
A line in a response file had more than 127 characters.

Segment limit set too high
The number specified in the /SE:n switch was not in the range 1 through 1024.

Segment limit too high
Not enough memory is available for LINK to allocate tables to describe the number of segments requested (default = 128 or the number specified in the /SE:n switch). Use the /SE:n switch to specify a smaller number of segments, or alter the system configuration to increase the amount of free memory.

Segment size exceeds 64K
The program is a small-model program with more than 64 KB of code or data, a compact-model program with more than 64 KB of code, or a medium-model program with more than 64 KB of data. Selection of a different model or alteration of the program code may be required to successfully complete the LINK process.

Stack size exceeds 65536 bytes
The size specified for the stack in the /ST:n switch was too large, or the combined length of multiple declared stack segments exceeded 64 KB.

Symbol already defined: "*symbol*"
One of the special overlay symbols required for overlay support was previously defined.

Symbol defined more than once: "*symbol*" in file
A symbol has been defined more than once in the object module. Remove the extra symbol definition.

Symbol table overflow
The program has more than 256 KB of symbolic information (publics, externals, segments, groups, classes, files, and so on). Eliminate as many public symbols as possible, combine modules and/or segments, and recreate the object files.

Terminated by user
Ctrl-C or Ctrl-Break was pressed, causing the LINK session to be terminated prematurely.

Too many external symbols in one module
An object module contains more than the limit of 1023 external symbols.

Too many group-, segment-, and class-names in one module
One of the object modules for the program contains too many group, segment, and class names. The source file for the object module may need to be divided or restructured.

Too many groups
The program defines more than nine groups (including DGROUP). Groups must be combined or eliminated.

Too many GRPDEFs in one module
LINK encountered more than nine group definitions (GRPDEFs) in a single object module. Reduce the number of GRPDEFs or split the object module.

Too many libraries
More than 16 libraries were specified. Combine libraries or use object modules that require fewer libraries.

Too many overlays
The program defines more than 63 overlays. Reduce the number of overlays.

Too many segments
The program has more than the maximum number of segments as specified by the default of 128 or with the /SE:n switch. Use the /SE:n switch to specify a greater number of segments.

Too many segments in one module
An object module has more than 255 segments. Split the module or combine segments.

Too many TYPDEFs
An object module contains too many TYPDEF records (these records describe communal variables). This error occurs only with programs produced with the Microsoft C Compiler or other compilers that support communal variables.

Unexpected end-of-file on library
This message may indicate that the disk containing the library in use was removed prematurely.

Unexpected end-of-file on scratch file
The disk containing VM.TMP was removed.

Unmatched left parenthesis
A syntax error was detected in the specification of an overlay structure. Refer to the language compiler manual for instructions on specifying overlays to LINK.

Unmatched right parenthesis
A syntax error was detected in the specification of an overlay structure. Refer to the language compiler manual for instructions on specifying overlays to LINK.

Unrecognized switch error: "*option*"

An unrecognized character was entered after a forward slash (/) in the command line.

Unresolved COMDEF; Microsoft internal error

This is a serious problem. Note the circumstances of the failure and contact Microsoft Corporation.

Unresolved externals: *list*

A symbol was declared external (EXTRN) in one object module but was not declared PUBLIC in the object module in which it was defined, or a necessary library specification was omitted from the command line or response file.

**VM.TMP is an illegal file name
and has been ignored**

VM.TMP was specified as an object file name. If an object file named VM.TMP exists, rename it.

Warning: load-high disables exepack

The /H and /E switches cannot be used at the same time.

Warning: no stack segment

The program contains no segment with the STACK combine type. This message can be ignored if there is a specific reason for not defining a stack (for example, if the .EXE file will subsequently be converted to a .COM file) or for defining one without the STACK combine type.

WARNING: Segment longer than reliable size

Although code segments can be as long as 65536 bytes, code segments longer than 65500 bytes can be unreliable on the Intel 80286 microprocessor. Reduce all code segments to 65500 bytes or less.

Warning: too many public symbols

The /M switch was used to request a sorted listing of public symbols in the map file, but there are too many symbols to sort. LINK will produce an unsorted listing instead.

MAKE

Maintain Programs

Purpose

Interprets a text file of commands to compare dates of files and carry out other operations on the basis of the comparison. MAKE is customarily used to update the executable version of a program after a change to one or more of its source files. The MAKE utility is supplied with the Microsoft Macro Assembler (MASM), C Compiler, and FORTRAN Compiler. This documentation describes MAKE version 4.05.

Syntax

MAKE [/D] [/I] [/N] [/S] [*name=value* ...] *filename*

where:

filename	is an ASCII text file that contains MAKE dependency statements, commands, macro definitions, and inference rules.
name=value	declares a MAKE macro, associating a specific value with the dummy parameter *name*.
/D	displays the last modification date of each file as it is scanned.
/I	causes MAKE to ignore exit codes returned by programs called by *filename*.
/N	displays but does not execute the commands in *filename*.
/S	selects "silent" mode (commands are not displayed as they are executed).

Note: Switches can be either uppercase or lowercase and can be preceded by a dash (-) instead of a forward slash (/). Versions of MAKE earlier than 4.0 have no switches.

Description

The MAKE utility allows maintenance of complex programs to be automated. Its basic operation is to compare the dates of files and to carry out, or not carry out, an associated list of commands on the basis of the comparison.

The *filename* parameter specifies an ASCII text file often referred to as a make file. By convention, *filename* is the same as the name of the executable program being maintained, but without an extension. A make file can contain the following types of entries:

- Dependency statements
- Commands
- Macro definitions
- Inference rules
- Comments

The basic form of a make file is a dependency statement followed by one or more valid MS-DOS command lines:

targetfile: *dependentfile1* [*dependentfile2*...]
    command1
    [*command2*]

    ...

where *targetfile* designates the file that may need updating, *dependentfile* is a source file or files on which *targetfile* depends, and *command1*, *command2*, and so forth are any valid MS-DOS internal commands or external programs. These commands or programs are executed only if the date and time stamps of any dependent file are more recent than those of the target file or if the target file does not exist. Only one target file can be specified. Any number of dependent files can be included; each dependent filename must be separated from the next by at least one space. If too many dependent files are included to fit on a single line, the line can be terminated with a backslash character (\) and the list continued on the next line.

Any number of MS-DOS command lines can follow a dependency statement. The last command line should be followed by a blank line to set it off from the next MAKE entry. It is recommended that each command line include a leading space or tab character for compatibility with future versions of MAKE and existing versions of XENIX MAKE.

A macro definition takes the form

name=value

where both *name* and *value* are any string. Whenever *name* is referenced in the make file in the form $(*name*), *name* is replaced by the string *value* before the statement that contains it is evaluated or executed. Macro definitions can be nested, although very complex macro definitions can result in the premature termination of the MAKE process because of lack of memory. If *name* is not defined in the file but is defined in the system environment block by a previous SET command, $(*name*) is replaced by the string following the equal sign (=) in the environment block. If the command line contains a parameter of the form *name=value*, the command line overrides any definition of *name* in the make file or in the environment block. Thus, the precedence for macro definitions with the same *name* is

1. Command line
2. Make file
3. Environment block

MAKE contains several special macros that make it more convenient to form commands:

Macro	Action
$*	Substitutes as the base portion of *targetfile* (the filename without the extension).
$@	Substitutes as the complete *targetfile* name.
$**	Substitutes as the complete *dependentfile* list.

An inference rule specifies a series of commands to be carried out for a matching dependency statement that is not followed by its own list of commands. Inference rules allow a set of commands to be applied to more than one *targetfile: dependentfile* description, eliminating repetition of the same set of commands for several descriptions. An inference rule takes the form

.dependentextension.targetextension:
    command1
    [*command2*]

    . . .

Whenever MAKE finds a dependency statement not followed by any commands, the utility first searches the make file for an inference rule. If MAKE doesn't find an inference rule in the make file, the utility then searches the current drive and directory (or any directories specified with the MS-DOS PATH command) for the tools initialization file (TOOLS.INI) and searches the *[make]* section of TOOLS.INI for an inference rule that matches the extensions of the target file and dependent files in the dependency statement.

A make file can contain any number of comment lines. If a comment is placed where MAKE expects to find a command, the comment must be on a separate line and must have the pound character (#) as the first character of the line. Elsewhere, a pound character and following comment text can be placed either on a line alone or after the last dependent file or command listed on a line. Characters appearing on a line after the pound character are ignored during execution.

The /D, /N, and /S switches affect MAKE's output to the display while MAKE is executing. The /D switch causes the last modification date of each file to be displayed as the file is scanned. The /N switch causes the commands in the make file to be expanded and displayed, but not executed; this is useful for determining the result of a specific MAKE process without first examining the file dates and without recompiling or relinking files. The /S switch selects "silent" mode, in which commands are not displayed as they are executed.

The /I switch causes MAKE to ignore error codes returned by the compilers, assemblers, linkers, or other programs called by the make file. When the /I switch is used, the MAKE process proceeds to completion regardless of errors instead of terminating immediately as it ordinarily would, but the resulting files may not be executable.

Return Codes

0   No error; the MAKE process was successful.
1   Processing was terminated because of a fatal error by MAKE or by one of the programs called by MAKE.

Example

Assume that the file SHELL contains the following MAKE dependency statements and commands:

```
video.obj: video.asm
        masm video;

shell.obj: shell.c
        msc shell;

shell.exe: shell.obj video.obj
        link /map shell+video,shell,shell,slibc2
```

The SHELL file asserts that the executable program SHELL.EXE is composed of the files SHELL.OBJ and VIDEO.OBJ, which are in turn compiled or assembled from the source files SHELL.C and VIDEO.ASM. To update the file SHELL.EXE if either of the source files for its constituent modules has been changed, type

```
C>MAKE SHELL  <Enter>
```

Messages

fatal error U1001: macro definition larger than 512
A single macro was defined to have a value string longer than the 512-byte maximum. Rewrite the make file to use two or more short lines instead of one long line.

fatal error U1002: infinitely recursive macro
The macros defined in the make file form a circular chain.

fatal error U1003: out of memory
The make file cannot be processed because insufficient memory is available in the transient program area. Split the make file into two make files or reconfigure the system to increase available memory.

fatal error U1004: syntax error : macro name missing
A macro name is missing from the left side of the equal sign (=).

fatal error U1005: syntax error : colon missing
A line that should be a dependency statement lacks the colon that separates a target file from its dependent files. MAKE expects any line that follows a blank line to be a dependency statement.

fatal error U1006: *targetname* : macro expansion larger than 512
A single macro expansion, plus the length of any string to which it may be concatenated, is longer than 512 bytes. Rewrite the make file to use two or more short lines instead of one long line.

fatal error U1007: multiple sources
An inference rule has been defined more than once in the make file.

fatal error U1008: *filename* **: cannot find file**
The specified file does not exist.

fatal error U1009: *command* **: argument list too long**
A command line in the make file is longer than 128 characters (the maximum MS-DOS allows).

fatal error U1010: *filename* **: permission denied**
The specified file is read-only.

fatal error U1011: not enough memory
Memory is insufficient in the transient program area to execute a program listed in the make file. Reconfigure the system to increase available memory, if necessary.

fatal error U1012: *filename* **: unknown error**
This is a serious problem. Note the circumstances of the failure and notify Microsoft Corporation.

fatal error U1013: *command* **: error** *returncode*
One of the programs or commands called by MAKE was not able to execute correctly. MAKE terminates and displays the error code from the program that failed.

warning U4000: *filename* **: target does not exist**
The target file does not already exist. The dependency statement is evaluated as though the target file exists and has a date earlier than that of any of the dependent files.

warning U4001: dependent *filename* **does not exist;**
target *filename* **not built**
One of the dependent files does not exist or could not be found, so MAKE terminated without creating a new target file.

warning U4013: *command* **: error** *returncode* **(ignored)**
One of the programs or commands called by MAKE did not execute successfully and has returned the specified return code. Because MAKE was run with the /I switch, MAKE ignores the error and continues processing the make file.

warning U4014: usage : make [/n] [/d] [/i] [/s] [name=value ...] file
An error was detected in the MAKE command line.

MAPSYM
Create Symbol File for SYMDEB

Purpose

Processes a map file generated by the Microsoft Object Linker (LINK) to create a special symbol file for use with SYMDEB, the symbolic debugging program. The MAPSYM utility is supplied with the Microsoft Macro Assembler (MASM). This documentation describes MAPSYM version 4.0.

Syntax

MAPSYM [/L] *map_file*

where:

map_file	is a map file produced by LINK (default extension = .MAP).
/L	causes information about the symbol file to be displayed as it is created.

Note: The /L switch can be either uppercase or lowercase and can be preceded by a dash (-) instead of a forward slash (/).

Description

LINK combines relocatable object records (produced by MASM or a high-level-language compiler) into an executable program, which is stored in a specially formatted file with a .EXE extension. LINK can also produce an optional map file that contains information about public symbols and addresses in the linked program. The map file is an ordinary ASCII text file and has a default extension of .MAP.

To create a map file to use with MAPSYM, the LINK command line should include the /MAP switch, which creates the file, and the /LINENUMBERS switch, which includes line numbers. *See* PROGRAMMING UTILITIES: LINK.

The MAPSYM utility processes a map file into a special symbol file that can be used by SYMDEB. A drive and pathname can be specified if the map file is not in the current directory. If a file extension is not specified, .MAP is assumed.

The symbol file created by MAPSYM is placed in the current directory and has the same name as the map file but has the extension .SYM. It can contain a maximum of 1024 segments (or as many segments as can fit into available memory) and 10,000 symbols per segment. *See* PROGRAMMING UTILITIES: SYMDEB.

When the /L switch precedes *map_file* in the command line, MAPSYM displays the names of groups defined in the program described by the map and symbol files, plus the program's starting address. The /L switch does not affect the format of the symbol file that is generated.

Return Codes

0   No error; the MAPSYM process was successful.

1   Processing was terminated because of a write failure, because the map file specified does not exist, or because the symbol file could not be created.

4   Processing was terminated because an unexpected end-of-file mark was detected, because too many segments exist in the map file, because no public symbols exist in the map file, or because not enough memory is available to create the symbol file.

Example

To convert the file HELLO.MAP, which was produced by assembling and linking the file HELLO.ASM, to a symbol file that can be used by SYMDEB, type

```
C>MAPSYM /L HELLO   <Enter>
```

MAPSYM displays the following:

```
Microsoft (R) Symbol File Generator   Version 4.00
Copyright (C) Microsoft Corp 1984, 1985.  All rights reserved.
Building: HELLO.SYM
HELLO.MAP
        Program entry point at 0000:0100
HELLO    0 segment
```

The symbol file produced by MAPSYM symbol has the name HELLO.SYM.

Messages

Can't create: <*filename*>
The drive specified does not exist, the current disk or directory is full, or the output file already exists and is read-only.

Can't open MAP file: <*filename*>
The file named in the command line does not exist.

DOS 2.0 or later required
MAPSYM does not work with versions of MS-DOS earlier than 2.0.

mapsym: out of memory
System memory is insufficient to process the map file.

mapsym: segment table (*n*) exceeded.
More than 1024 segments have been used in the map file. The number displayed is the total number of segments in the map file.

No public symbols
Re-link file with the /M switch!
The map file created by LINK does not include a list of public names. The .EXE file must be relinked using the /MAP switch to generate a map file that can be used with MAPSYM.

Unexpected eof reading: *<filename>*
The map file contains no symbols, is corrupt, or is otherwise invalid. The .EXE file must be relinked and a new map file generated.

usage: MAPSYM [/l] maplist
A syntax error was detected in the command line.

Write fail on: *<filename>*
An error occurred during the creation of the output file.

MASM
Microsoft Macro Assembler

Purpose

Translates an assembly-language source program into a relocatable object module. MASM is part of the Microsoft Macro Assembler (MASM) retail package. This documentation describes MASM version 4.0.

Syntax

MASM

or

MASM *source_file* [,[*object_file*][,[*list_file*][,[*cref_file*]]]] [*options*] [;]

where:

source_file	is the name of the file containing the assembly-language source code (default extension = .ASM).
object_file	is the name of the file to receive the assembled object module (default extension = .OBJ).
list_file	is the name of the file or device to receive the assembly listing (default = NUL). (If destination = file, default extension = .LST.)
cref_file	is the name of the cross-reference file to receive information for later processing by the CREF utility (default = NUL). (If destination = file, default extension = .CRF.)
options	is one or more switches from the list below.

/A	Writes the program segments in alphabetic order.
/B*n*	Sets the size of the source-file buffer in kilobytes (1–63, default = 32).
/C	Creates a cross-reference (.CRF) file.
/D	Adds a first-pass program listing to *list_file* if a list file was specified (default = second-pass listing only).
/D*symbol*	Defines *symbol* as a null text string.
/E	Assembles code for an 8087/80287 emulator.
/I*path*	Defines a directory to be searched for *include* files.
/L	Creates a list (.LST) file with line-number information.
/ML	Preserves case sensitivity in all symbol names.

(more)

/MU	Converts all lowercase names to uppercase names.
/MX	Preserves lowercase in public and external names only.
/N	Suppresses generation of tables of macros, structures, records, groups, segments, and symbols at the end of the list file.
/P	Checks for impure code in 80286 protected mode; has no effect unless the .286P directive is included in the source file.
/R	Assembles code for an 8087/80287 math coprocessor.
/S	Arranges program segments in order of occurrence.
/T	Selects terse mode, suppressing all messages generated during assembly except error messages.
/V	Selects verbose mode, displaying the number of lines and symbols at the end of assembly.
/X	Includes false conditionals in the list file.
/Z	Displays source lines with errors during assembly.

Note: Switches can be either uppercase or lowercase and can be preceded by a dash (-) instead of a forward slash (/).

Description

MASM translates assembly-language source code into relocatable object modules. The object modules can then be placed in a library file or processed by the Microsoft Object Linker (LINK) to create an executable program.

The *source_file* parameter is the only required filename. It specifies a file containing the assembly-language source code in ASCII text. If no extension is specified, MASM uses .ASM. If no source file is entered in the command line, MASM prompts for a source file name.

The *object_file* parameter specifies the file that will contain the assembled relocatable object code. If this parameter is not supplied, MASM uses the same filename as *source_file* but substitutes the extension .OBJ.

The *list_file* parameter specifies a destination file or device for the optional program listing. The listing contains the original source code, the assembled machine code, macro definitions and expansions, and other useful information, formatted into pages with titles, dates, and page numbers. If the destination of the listing is a file, the file's default extension is .LST. If the *list_file* parameter is not included in the command line, MASM sends the listing to NUL (that is, a listing is not produced).

The *cref_file* parameter specifies the name of a cross-reference file to receive information to be processed by the CREF utility. If a file extension is not specified, MASM uses .CRF. If the *cref_file* parameter is not included in the command line, MASM sends the file to NUL (that is, no cross-reference file is generated).

If the MASM command is entered without parameters, MASM prompts the user for each filename. The default response for each prompt (except the source file prompt) is displayed in square brackets and can be selected by pressing the Enter key.

After the source file is specified, if MASM encounters a semicolon character (;) in the command line or at any prompt, it uses default values for the remaining parameters. MASM ignores any parameters specified after the semicolon.

MASM does two passes to translate the assembly-language code in the source file into relocatable object code. Any errors detected during translation are displayed on standard output and included in the program listing (if one is requested). Two types of errors may be detected: warning errors and severe errors. If MASM encounters a warning error, it still creates the object file, although the resulting file may be unusable. If MASM encounters a severe error, it does not create the object file. After a file has been successfully assembled without errors, the LINK utility can be used to convert the resulting object file into an executable program file.

MASM supports a wide variety of options that can be selected by including switches in the command line or by responding to any prompt.

The /A and /S switches determine the order of segments in the resulting object module file. The /A switch places the segments into the object file in alphabetic order. The /S switch (the default) arranges the segments in the same order they occur in the source file.

The /B*n*, /D*symbol*, and /I*path* switches have rather general effects on the behavior of MASM. The /B*n* switch sets the size (in kilobytes) of the source file's RAM buffer; the value of *n* must be between 1 and 63, inclusive (default = 32). If the RAM buffer is large enough, the entire source file can be kept resident in memory, reducing disk activity during passes. The /D*symbol* switch defines a null text-string symbol from the command line. This symbol can be referenced inside the program with the IFDEF directive to control the conditional assembly of portions of the program. The /I*path* switch specifies a directory that will be searched for files named in assembler INCLUDE statements if those statements do not include an explicit directory. As many as 10 such search paths can be specified with individual /I*path* switches.

The /E and /R switches affect the generation of code for the 8087/80287 emulator or 8087/80287 math coprocessor. (Support for the 80287 is included with MASM versions 3.0 and later.) The /E switch generates software interrupts to floating-point-processor emulator routines. A subprogram assembled with the /E switch can be linked to C, Pascal, and FORTRAN programs and can use the emulator libraries. The /R switch produces in-line machine instructions for the math coprocessor when floating-point mnemonics are used.

The /ML, /MU, and /MX switches control MASM's handling of uppercase and lowercase names. The /ML switch makes MASM case sensitive; that is, it makes MASM differentiate a name in uppercase letters from the same name in lowercase letters. (The /ML switch should not be used if the source file contains 8087 WAIT instructions and MASM 4.0 is being used to translate the file.) The /MU switch (the default) makes MASM case insensitive; all lowercase letters are converted to uppercase for purposes of assembly. The /MX switch makes MASM case sensitive for public and external names only (names defined with PUBLIC or EXTRN directives). The /MX switch is often used to process assembly-language functions for C programs.

The /P switch checks for impure code segments that will cause problems if the assembled program is run in 80286 protected mode. The switch checks by flagging any instruction that will change a memory location addressed through the processor's CS register. The /P switch has no effect unless the assembly-language source file includes the .286P directive.

The /C, /D, /L, /N, and /X switches control the contents of the program listing and other optional files that are generated as a result of assembly. The /C switch causes the creation of a cross-reference (.CRF) file and the addition of line numbers to the list (.LST) file (if one exists). The /C switch should be included in the command line if the cross-reference file will be used later with the CREF utility to produce a cross-reference listing. The /D switch includes a listing from the first pass as well as a listing from the second pass in the list file if a list file was specified (default = second-pass listing only). By comparing the two listings, the user can isolate an instruction causing a phase error. (A phase error occurs when MASM makes assumptions about addresses, values, or data types on the first pass that are not valid in the second pass.) The /L switch creates a list file with line-number information and gives it the same name as the source file, with the extension .LST. The /N switch suppresses generation of tables — symbols, segments, groups, structures, records, and macros — at the end of a program listing. The /X switch includes statements inside false conditional statements in the list file, allowing conditionals that do not generate code to be displayed. /X has no effect if the .SFCOND or the .LFCOND directive is used in the source file; if the .TFCOND directive is used, the effects of /X are reversed.

Note: The effects of /X are also reversed in MASM version 1.2. In that version, statements within a false conditional are included in the list file by default, and /X will suppress them.

The /T, /V, and /Z switches affect MASM's display on standard output. The /T (terse) switch suppresses messages to standard output, except for messages indicating warning errors or severe errors. The /V (verbose) switch displays information about the number of source lines and symbols at the end of the assembly, in addition to displaying the normal error and symbol space information. The /Z switch displays the actual source lines producing assembly errors (rather than displaying just the error type and line number).

Note: Versions of MASM earlier than 4.0 always show both the source line and the error message.

Return Codes

0   No errors were found during assembly.
1   An error was detected in one of the command-line parameters.
2   The assembly-language source file could not be opened.
3   The list file could not be created.
4   The object file could not be created.
5   The cross-reference file could not be created.
6   An *include* file could not be opened.
7   At least one severe error was detected during assembly. (MASM deletes the invalid object file.)
8   The assembly was terminated because a memory allocation error occurred.
10 An error occurred in defining a symbol (with the /D*symbol* switch) from the command line.
11 Assembly was interrupted by the user's pressing Ctrl-C or Ctrl-Break.

Examples

To assemble the source file CLEAN.ASM in the current drive and directory and place the resulting relocatable object module in the file CLEAN.OBJ without producing a listing or a cross-reference file, type

```
C>MASM CLEAN;   <Enter>
```

The semicolon after the first parameter causes MASM to use the default values for the rest of the parameters.

To assemble the source file CLEAN.ASM, put the object code in a file named CLEAN.OBJ, create a list file named CLEAN.LST, and place information for later processing by the CREF utility in the cross-reference file CLEAN.CRF, type

```
C>MASM CLEAN,CLEAN,CLEAN,CLEAN   <Enter>
```

or

```
C>MASM CLEAN,,CLEAN,CLEAN   <Enter>
```

To use MASM interactively, enter its name without parameters:

```
C>MASM   <Enter>
```

MASM then prompts for all the necessary information. For example, the interactive session on the next page assembles the file HELLO.ASM into the file HELLO.OBJ, producing no listing or .CRF file.

```
C>MASM  <Enter>
Microsoft (R) Macro Assembler  Version 4.00
Copyright (C) Microsoft Corp 1981, 1983, 1984, 1985.  All rights reserved.

Source filename: [.ASM]: HELLO  <Enter>
Object filename: [HELLO.OBJ]:  <Enter>
Source listing [NUL.LST]:  <Enter>
Cross-reference [NUL.CRF]:  <Enter>

  51004 Bytes symbol space free

    0 Warning Errors
    0 Severe Errors
```

Messages

8087 opcode can't be emulated
An 8087 opcode or the operands used with it produced an instruction the emulator cannot support.

Already defined locally
An attempt was made to define a symbol as EXTRN that had already been defined locally.

Already had ELSE clause
An attempt was made to define an ELSE clause within an existing ELSE clause. (ELSE cannot be nested without nesting IF...ENDIF.)

Already have base register
More than one base register was specified within an operand.

Already have index register
More than one index register was specified within an operand.

Block nesting error
A segment, structure, macro, IRC, IRP, REPT, or nested procedure was not terminated properly.

Byte register is illegal
A byte register was used incorrectly in an instruction.

Can't override ES segment
An attempt was made to override the ES segment in an instruction in which this override is invalid.

Can't reach with segment reg
No ASSUME directive was given to make the variable reachable.

Can't use EVEN on BYTE segment
An EVEN directive was used on a segment declared to be a byte segment.

Circular chain of EQU aliases
An alias EQU ultimately points to itself.

Constant was expected
A constant was expected, but an item was received that does not evaluate to a constant.

CS register illegal usage
The CS register was used incorrectly in one of the instructions.

Data emitted with no segment
Code that is not located within a segment attempted to generate data.

Directive illegal in STRUC
All statements within STRUC blocks must be either comments preceded by a semicolon character (;) or one of the define directives (DB, DW, and so on).

Division by 0 or overflow
An expression was encountered that resulted in either a division by 0 or a number too large to be represented.

DUP is too large for linker
Nesting of DUP operators was such that a record too large for LINK was created.

End of file, no END directive
No END statement was encountered, or a nesting error occurred.

Extra characters on line
Superfluous characters were detected on a line after sufficient information to define an instruction was interpreted.

extra file name ignored
The command line contained more than four filename parameters.

Field cannot be overridden
An attempt was made to give a value to a field that cannot be overridden with a STRUC initialization statement.

Forced error
An error was forced with the .ERR directive.

Forced error - expression equals 0
An error was forced with the .ERRE directive.

Forced error - expression not equal 0
An error was forced with the .ERRNZ directive.

Forced error - pass1
An error was forced with the .ERR1 directive.

Forced error - pass2
An error was forced with the .ERR2 directive.

Forced error - string blank
An error was forced with the .ERRB directive.

Forced error - string not blank
An error was forced with the .ERRNB directive.

Forced error - strings different
An error was forced with the .ERRDIF directive.

Forced error - strings identical
An error was forced with the .ERRIDN directive.

Forced error - symbol defined
An error was forced with the .ERRDEF directive.

Forced error - symbol not defined
An error was forced with the .ERRNDEF directive.

Forward reference is illegal
An item was referenced in the operand of an EQU or equal-sign (=) directive before it was defined.

Illegal register value
A specified register value does not fit into the *reg* field (that is, the value is greater than 7).

Illegal size for item
The size of the referenced item is invalid. This error also frequently occurs when an attempt is made to assemble source code written for assemblers with less strict type-checking than that of the Microsoft Macro Assembler (such as early versions of the IBM assembler). The problem can usually be solved by overriding the type of the operand with the PTR operator.

Illegal use of external
A variable that was declared external was used incorrectly.

Illegal use of register
An attempt was made to use a register with an instruction in which a register cannot be used.

Illegal value for DUP count
The DUP count was not a constant that evaluates to a positive integer greater than zero.

Improper operand type
An operand was used in a way that prevents opcode generation.

Improper use of segment register
An attempt was made to use a segment register in an instruction in which use of a segment register is not permitted.

Impure memory reference
An attempt was made to store data in the code segment when the .286P directive and the /P switch were in effect.

Index displ. must be constant

An index displacement was used incorrectly or did not evaluate to an absolute number or memory address.

Internal error

An internal logic error was detected in the assembler. Document the circumstances and contact Microsoft Corporation.

Label can't have seg. override

A segment override was used incorrectly.

Left operand must have segment

The content of the right operand requires that a segment be specified in the left operand.

Line too long expanding *symbol*

A symbol defined by an EQU or equal-sign (=) directive is so long that expanding it will cause the assembler's internal buffers to overflow. This message may indicate a recursive text macro.

Missing data; zero assumed

An operand is missing from a statement and MASM assumes its value is zero. This is a warning error; the object file is not deleted as it is with severe errors.

More values than defined with

Too many initial values were given when defining a variable using a REC or STRUC type.

Must be associated with code

A data-related item was used where a code-related item was expected.

Must be associated with data

A code-related item was used where a data-related item was expected.

Must be AX or AL

A register other than AX or AL was specified where only these are acceptable.

Must be in segment block

An attempt was made to generate code by instructions that were not contained within a segment.

Must be index or base register

An instruction requires a base or index register, and some other register was specified within square brackets ([]).

Must be record field name

A record field name was expected, but something else was encountered.

Must be record or fieldname

A record name or field name was expected, but something else was encountered.

Must be register

A register was expected as the operand, but something else was encountered.

Must be segment or group

A segment or group was expected, but something else was encountered.

Must be structure field name

A structure field name was expected, but something else was encountered.

Must be symbol type

A BYTE, WORD, DWORD, or similar designation was expected, but something else was encountered.

Must be var, label or constant

A variable, label, or constant was expected, but something else was encountered.

Must have opcode after prefix

A REP, REPE, REPNE, REPZ, or REPNZ instruction was not followed by the mnemonic for a string operation.

Near JMP/CALL to different CS

An attempt was made to do a NEAR jump or call to a location in a code segment defined with a different ASSUME:CS.

No immediate mode

Immediate data was supplied as an operand for an instruction that cannot use immediate data. For example, immediate data cannot be moved directly with a MOV instruction to a segment register; it must first be moved into a general register and then copied to the segment register.

No or unreachable CS

An attempt was made to jump to a label that is unreachable.

Normal type operand expected

A STRUC, BYTE, WORD, or some other invalid operand was encountered when a variable label was expected.

Not in conditional block

An ENDIF or ELSE statement was encountered, and no previous conditional-assembly directive was active.

Not proper align/combine type

The SEGMENT parameters are incorrect. Check the align and combine types to be sure they are valid.

One operand must be const

The addition operator was used incorrectly.

Only initialize list legal

An attempt was made to use a STRUC name without angle brackets (<>).

Operand combination illegal

A two-operand instruction was specified and the combination specified was invalid.

Operand must have segment
A SEG directive was used incorrectly.

Operand must have size
An operand was encountered that needed a specified size, but none had been provided. Often this error can be remedied by using the PTR operator to specify a size type.

Operand not in IP segment
An operand cannot be accessed because it is not in the segment last assigned to CS with an ASSUME directive.

Operand types must match
MASM encountered different kinds or sizes of arguments in a case where they must match.

Operand was expected
MASM expected an operand, but an operator was encountered.

Operands must be same or 1 abs
The subtraction operator was used incorrectly.

Operator was expected
MASM expected an operator, but an operand was encountered.

Out of memory
System memory is insufficient to complete the assembly. If a listing (.LST) or cross-reference (.CRF) file was being generated, retry the assembly, generating only an object file. It may also be necessary to modify the source program to reduce the load on the symbol table (by shortening names or reducing the number of EQU statements or macros, for example).

Override is of wrong type
An attempt was made to use a data item of incorrect size in a STRUC initialization statement.

Override value is wrong length
The override value for a structure field is too large to fit in the field.

Override with DUP is illegal
An attempt was made to use DUP to override in a STRUC initialization statement.

Phase error between passes
The program has ambiguous instruction directives that caused the location of a label in the program to change in value between the first and second passes of MASM. A common cause is a forward reference to a typed data item in the instructions preceding the label that generated the phase error message. Use the /D switch to produce a first-pass listing to aid in resolving phase errors between passes.

Redefinition of symbol
This message is displayed during first pass upon the second declaration of a symbol that has been defined in more than one place.

Reference to mult defined
The instruction references a symbol that has been defined more than once.

Register already defined
An internal error was detected. Note the circumstances of the failure and contact Microsoft Corporation.

Relative jump out of range
A conditional jump references a label that is out of the allowed range of −128 to +127 bytes relative to the current instruction. The problem usually can be corrected by reversing the condition of the jump and using an unconditional jump (JMP) to the out-of-range label.

Segment parameters are changed
The list of parameters encountered for a SEGMENT was not identical to the list specified the first time the segment was used.

Shift count is negative
A shift expression was generated that resulted in a negative shift count.

Should have been group name
A group name was expected, but something else was encountered.

Symbol already different kind
An attempt was made to redefine an already defined symbol.

Symbol has no segment
An attempt was made to use a variable with SEG that has no known segment.

Symbol is already external
An attempt was made to redefine a symbol as local that has already been defined as external.

Symbol is multi-defined
This message is displayed during the second pass upon each declaration of a symbol that has been defined in more than one place.

Symbol is reserved word
An attempt was made to use a reserved MASM word as a symbol.

Symbol not defined
A symbol that had not been defined was used.

Symbol type usage illegal
A PUBLIC symbol was used incorrectly.

Syntax error
The syntax of the statement does not match any recognizable syntax.

Type illegal in context
The type specified is of an unacceptable size.

Unable to open input file *filename*
The specified source file cannot be found.

unknown switch *letter*
The command line included an invalid switch.

Unknown symbol type
MASM does not recognize the size type specified in a label or external declaration. Rewrite with a valid type such as BYTE, WORD, or NEAR.

Value is out of range
A value is too large for its expected use.

Wrong type of register
A directive or instruction expected one type of register, but another type was encountered.

DEBUG

Program Debugger

Purpose

Allows the controlled execution of a program for debugging purposes or the alteration of the binary contents of any file. The DEBUG utility is supplied with the MS-DOS distribution disks.

Syntax

DEBUG

or

DEBUG *filename* [*parameter*...]

where:

filename   is the name of the file that contains data to be modified or a program to be debugged. If *filename* includes an extension, it must be specified.

parameter... is one or more filenames or switches required by a program being debugged.

Description

The DEBUG program allows a file to be loaded, examined, and altered. If the file is not a .EXE file or a .HEX file, it may also be written back to disk. If the file contains a program, the program can be disassembled, modified, traced one instruction at a time, or executed at full speed with preset breakpoints. DEBUG can also be used to read from and write to input/output (I/O) ports and to read, modify, and write absolute disk sectors.

The command line typically includes the *filename* parameter, which is the name of an executable program (with the extension .COM or .EXE) to be loaded into DEBUG's memory buffer. Files with the extension .EXE are loaded in a manner compatible with the MS-DOS loader; if necessary, the contents of the file are relocated so that the program is ready to execute. Files with the extension .HEX are converted to binary images and loaded at the internally specified address. All other files are assumed to be direct memory images and are read directly into memory starting at offset 100H.

An appropriate program segment prefix (PSP) is synthesized at the head of DEBUG's buffer for use by the target program (the program being debugged). The PSP includes a command tail at offset 80H and default file control blocks (FCBs) at offsets 5CH and 6CH, constructed from the optional parameters following *filename*.

After DEBUG is loaded and the first file named in the command line is also located and loaded, DEBUG displays its special prompt character, a hyphen (-), and awaits a command. DEBUG commands consist of a single letter, usually followed by one or more parameters. Uppercase and lowercase characters are treated the same except when they are contained in strings enclosed within single or double quotation marks. All commands are executed by pressing the Enter key.

The DEBUG commands are

Command	Action
A	Assemble machine instructions (versions 2.0 and later).
C	Compare memory areas.
D	Display memory.
E	Enter data.
F	Fill memory.
G	Go execute program.
H	Perform hexadecimal arithmetic.
I	Input from port.
L	Load file or sectors.
M	Move (copy) data.
N	Name file or command-tail parameters.
O	Output to port.
P	Proceed through loop or subroutine (versions 3.0 and later).
Q	Quit debugger.
R	Display or modify registers.
S	Search memory.
T	Trace program execution.
U	Disassemble (unassemble) program.
W	Write file or sectors.

The parameters for a DEBUG command include addresses, ranges, 8-bit or 16-bit hexadecimal values, and lists. Multiple parameters can be separated by spaces, tabs, or commas, but separators are *required* only between hexadecimal values.

An address can be a simple offset or a complete address in the form *segment:offset*. The offset is always a hexadecimal number in the range 00H through FFFFH; the segment can be either a hexadecimal value in the same range or a two-character segment register name (CS, DS, ES, or SS). If the segment portion of an address is absent, DEBUG uses DS unless an A, G, L, T, U, or W command is used, in which case DEBUG uses CS.

A range specifies an area of memory and can be expressed as either two addresses or a starting address and a length. A segment can be included only in the first element of a range; an error message is displayed if a segment is found in the second address. A length is represented by the letter L, followed by a hexadecimal value between 00H and FFFFH that indicates the number of bytes following the starting address that the command should operate on.

Note: Any length that causes an address to exceed 16 bits will generate an error.

A byte, or 8-bit, value is entered as one or two hexadecimal digits, whereas a word, or 16-bit, value is entered as one to four hexadecimal digits. Leading zeros can be omitted.

A list is composed of one or more byte values or strings, separated by spaces, commas, or tabs. A string is one or more ASCII characters enclosed within single or double quotation marks. Case is significant within a string. If the same type of quote character that is used to delimit the string occurs inside the string itself, the character must be doubled inside the string in order to be interpreted correctly. For example:

```
"This ""string"" is OK."
```

When used, a list must be the last parameter in the command line.

DEBUG responds to an invalid command by pointing to the approximate location of the error with a caret character (^) and displaying the word *Error.* For example:

```
-D CS:0100,CS:0200  <Enter>
                ^ Error
```

DEBUG maintains a set of virtual CPU registers for a program being debugged. These registers can be examined and modified with DEBUG commands. When a program is first loaded for debugging, the virtual registers are initialized with the following values:

Register	.COM Program	.EXE Program
AX	Valid drive error code	Valid drive error code
BX	Upper half of program size	Upper half of program size
CX	Lower half of program size	Lower half of program size
DX	Zero	Zero
SI	Zero	Zero
DI	Zero	Zero
BP	Zero	Zero
SP	FFFEH or top of available memory minus 2	Size of stack segment
IP	100H	Offset of entry point within target program's code segment
CS	PSP	Base of target program's code segment
DS	PSP	PSP
ES	PSP	PSP
SS	PSP	Base of target program's stack segment

Note: DEBUG checks the first three parameters in the command line. If the second and third parameters are filenames, DEBUG checks any drive specifications with those filenames to verify that they designate valid drives. Register AX contains one of the following codes:

Code	Meaning
0000H	The drives specified with the second and third filenames are both valid, or only one filename was specified in the command line.
00FFH	The drive specified with the second filename is invalid.
FF00H	The drive specified with the third filename is invalid.
FFFFH	The drives specified with the second and third filenames are both invalid.

DEBUG also maintains a set of virtual flags, which may be set or cleared. The flags are

Flag Name	Value If Set (1)	Value If Clear (0)
Overflow	OV (Overflow)	NV (No Overflow)
Direction	DN (Down)	UP (Up)
Interrupt	EI (Enabled)	DI (Disabled)
Sign	NG (Minus)	PL (Plus)
Zero	ZR (Zero)	NZ (Not Zero)
Aux Carry	AC (Aux Carry)	NA (No Aux Carry)
Parity	PE (Even)	PO (Odd)
Carry	CY (Carry)	NC (No Carry)

Before DEBUG transfers control to the target program, it saves the actual CPU registers and then loads them with the current values of the virtual registers. Conversely, when control reverts to DEBUG from the target program, the returned register contents are stored back in the virtual register set for inspection and alteration by the user.

Examples

To load the file SHELL.EXE in the current directory for execution under the control of DEBUG, type

```
C>DEBUG SHELL.EXE   <Enter>
```

To use the DEBUG program to inspect or modify memory or to read, modify, and write absolute disk sectors, simply type

```
C>DEBUG   <Enter>
```

Message

File not found
The filename supplied as the first parameter in the DEBUG command line cannot be found.

DEBUG: A

Assemble Machine Instructions

Purpose

Allows entry of assembler mnemonics and translates them into executable machine code.

Syntax

A [*address*]

where:

address   is the starting location for the assembled machine code.

Description

The Assemble Machine Instructions (A) command accepts assembly-language statements, rather than hexadecimal values, for the Intel 8086/8088 microprocessors and the Intel 8087 math coprocessor and then assembles each statement into executable machine code.

The *address* parameter specifies the location where entry of assembly-language mnemonics will begin. If *address* is omitted, DEBUG uses the address following the last instruction generated the last time the A command was used. If the A command has not been used, DEBUG uses the current value of the target program's CS:IP registers.

After an A command is entered, DEBUG prompts for each assembly-language statement by displaying the address, in the form of a segment and an offset, in which the assembled code will be stored. When the Enter key is pressed, the assembly-language statement is translated, and each byte of the resulting machine instruction is stored sequentially in memory (overwriting existing information), beginning at the displayed address. The address following the last byte of the machine instruction is then displayed so that the user can enter the next assembly-language statement. Pressing the Enter key alone in response to the address prompt terminates the A command.

The syntax of assembly-language statements accepted by the DEBUG A command differs slightly from that of the usual Microsoft Macro Assembler programming statements. The differences can be summarized as follows:

- All numbers are assumed to be hexadecimal integers and should be entered without a trailing H character.
- Segment overrides must be specified by preceding the entire instruction with CS:, DS:, ES:, or SS:.
- File control directives (NAME, PAGE, TITLE, and so forth), macro definitions, record structures, and conditional assembly directives are not supported by DEBUG.
- Specific hexadecimal values, rather than program labels, must be included.

- When the data type (word or byte) is not implicit in the instruction, the type must be specified by preceding the operand with BYTE PTR (or BY) or WORD PTR (or WO).
- The size of the string in a string operation must be specified by adding a B (byte) or W (word) to the string instruction mnemonic (for example, LODSB or LODSW).
- The DB and DW instructions accept a parameter of the type *list* and assemble byte and word values directly.
- The WAIT or FWAIT opcodes for 8087 assembler statements are not generated by default, so they must be coded explicitly.
- Memory locations are differentiated from immediate operands by enclosing memory addresses in square brackets.
- Repeat prefixes, such as REP, REPZ, or REPNZ, can be entered either alone on the line preceding the statement they affect or immediately preceding the statement on the same line.
- Although the assembler generates the optimal form (SHORT, NEAR, or FAR) for jumps or calls, depending on the destination address, these designations can be overridden by preceding the operand with a NEAR (or NE) or FAR (no abbreviation) prefix.
- The mnemonic for a FAR RETURN is RETF.

Examples

To begin assembling code at address CS:0100H, type

```
-A 100  <Enter>
```

To assemble the instruction sequence

```
LODS  WORD PTR [SI]
XCHG  BX,AX
JMP   [BX]
```

beginning at address CS:0100H, the following dialogue would take place:

```
-A 100  <Enter>
1983:0100  LODSW  <Enter>
1983:0101  XCHG BX,AX  <Enter>
1983:0103  JMP [BX]  <Enter>
1983:0105  <Enter>
```

To continue assembling at the location following the last instruction generated by a previous A command, type

```
-A  <Enter>
```

DEBUG: C

Compare Memory Areas

Purpose

Compares two areas of memory and reports any differences.

Syntax

C *range address*

where:

range is the starting and ending addresses or the starting address and length of the first area of memory to be compared.

address is the starting address of the second area of memory to be compared.

Description

The Compare Memory Areas (C) command compares the contents of two areas of memory. The location and contents of any differing bytes are displayed in the following format:

address1 byte1 byte2 address2

If no differences are found, the DEBUG prompt returns.

The *range* parameter specifies the starting and ending addresses or the starting address and length in bytes of the first area of memory to be compared. The *address* parameter specifies the beginning address of the second area of memory to be compared. If a segment is not included in *range* or *address*, DEBUG uses DS.

Example

To compare the 64 bytes beginning at CS:CE00H with the 64 bytes beginning at CS:CF0AH, type

```
-C CS:CE00 CE3F CS:CF0A  <Enter>
```

or

```
-C CS:CE00 L40 CS:CF0A  <Enter>
```

If any differences are found, DEBUG displays them in the following format:

```
2124:CE06  00  FF  2124:CF10
```

DEBUG: D

Display Memory

Purpose

Displays the contents of an area of memory in hexadecimal and ASCII format.

Syntax

D [*range*]

where:

range   is the starting and ending addresses or the starting address and length of the area to be displayed.

Description

The Display Memory (D), or Dump, command displays the contents of a specified range of memory addresses in hexadecimal and ASCII format.

The *range* parameter gives the starting and ending addresses or the starting address and length in bytes of the memory to be displayed. If *range* does not include a segment, DEBUG uses DS.

If *range* is omitted the first time the D command is used, the display starts at the target program's CS:IP registers. If *range* was specified in a preceding D command, the memory address following the last address displayed by that command is used. If a length is not explicitly stated in a D command, 128 bytes are displayed.

Each line displays a segment and offset, followed by the contents of 16 bytes of memory represented as hexadecimal values and separated by spaces (except the eighth and ninth values, which are separated by a dash), followed by the ASCII character equivalents (if any) of the same 16 bytes. In the ASCII portion, nonprinting characters are displayed as periods.

Examples

To display the contents of the 128 bytes of memory beginning at 7F00:0100H, type

```
-D 7F00:0100   <Enter>
```

The contents of the memory addresses are displayed in the following format:

```
7F00:0100   20 64 65 76 69 63 65 0D-0A 00 60 39 0D 0A 00 7C    device...'9...¦
7F00:0110   39 08 20 08 00 81 39 04-1B 5B 32 4A 42 BD 11 44    9. ...9..[2JB=.D
7F00:0120   2E 26 45 AF 11 47 B3 11-48 A5 11 4C B8 11 4E D3    .&E/.G3.H%.L8.NS
7F00:0130   11 50 DF 11 51 AB 11 54-DF 1E 56 37 11 5F 9F 16    .P_.Q+.T_.V7._..
7F00:0140   24 C0 11 00 03 4E 4F 54-C1 07 0A 45 52 52 4F 52    $@...NOTA..ERROR
7F00:0150   4C 45 56 45 4C 85 08 05-45 58 49 53 54 18 08 00    LEVEL...EXIST...
7F00:0160   03 44 49 52 03 91 0C 06-52 45 4E 41 4D 45 01 C0    .DIR....RENAME.@
7F00:0170   0F 03 52 45 4E 01 C0 0F-05 45 52 41 53 45 01 68    ..REN.@..ERASE.h
```

To view the next 128 bytes of memory, type

```
-D   <Enter>
```

In this case, the contents of memory addresses 7F00:0180H through 7F00:01FFH are displayed.

DEBUG: E

Enter Data

Purpose

Enters data into memory.

Syntax

E *address* [*list*]

where:

address   is the first memory location for data entry.

list   specifies the data to be entered into successive bytes of memory, starting at *address*.

Description

The Enter Data (E) command allows data to be entered into successive memory locations. The data can be entered in either hexadecimal or ASCII format. Data previously stored in the specified locations is lost.

The *address* parameter specifies the first byte to be modified. If *address* does not include a segment, DEBUG uses DS. The address is incremented for each byte of data stored.

The *list* parameter is one or more hexadecimal byte values and/or strings, separated by spaces, commas, or tab characters. Strings must be enclosed within single or double quotation marks, and case is significant within a string.

If *list* is included in the command line, the changes to memory are made unless an error is detected in the command line, in which case an error message is displayed and the E command is terminated. If *list* is omitted from the command line, the user is prompted byte by byte for data to be entered into memory, starting at *address*. The current contents of a byte are displayed, followed by a period. A new value for that byte can be entered as one or two hexadecimal digits (extra characters are ignored) or the contents can be left unchanged. Pressing the spacebar displays the contents of the next byte. Entering a minus sign or hyphen character (-) instead of pressing the spacebar displays the contents of the previous byte. A maximum of 8 bytes can be entered on each input line; a new line is begun each time an 8-byte boundary is crossed. Pressing the Enter key without pressing the spacebar or entering any data terminates data entry.

Text strings can be entered only by using the *list* parameter; they cannot be entered in response to an address prompt.

Examples

To store the byte values 00H, 0DH, and 0AH in the three bytes beginning at DS:1FB3H, type

```
-E 1FB3 00 0D 0A  <Enter>
```

To store the string *MAIN MENU* into memory beginning at address ES:0C14H, type

```
-E ES:C14 "MAIN MENU"  <Enter>
```

DEBUG: F

Fill Memory

Purpose

Stores a repetitive data pattern in an area of memory.

Syntax

F *range list*

where:

range   is the starting and ending addresses or starting address and length of the memory to be filled.

list   is the data to be entered.

Description

The Fill Memory (F) command fills an area of memory with the data from a list. The data can be entered in either hexadecimal or ASCII format. Any data previously stored at the specified locations is lost. If an error message is displayed, the original values in memory remain unchanged.

The *range* parameter specifies the starting and ending addresses or the starting address and hexadecimal length in bytes of the area of memory to be filled. If *range* does not specify a segment, DEBUG uses DS.

The *list* parameter specifies one or more hexadecimal byte values and/or strings, separated by spaces, commas, or tab characters. Strings must be enclosed in single or double quotation marks, and case is significant within a string.

If the area to be filled is larger than the data list, the list is repeated as often as necessary to fill the area. If the data list is longer than the area of memory to be filled, it is truncated to fit into the area.

Examples

To fill the area of memory from DS:0B10H through DS:0B4FH with the value 0E8H, type

```
-F B10 B4F E8   <Enter>
```

or

```
-F B10 L40 E8   <Enter>
```

To fill the 16 bytes of memory beginning at address CS:1FA0H by replicating the 2-byte sequence 0DH 0AH, type

```
-F CS:1FA0 1FAF 0D 0A   <Enter>
```

or

```
-F CS:1FA0 L10 0D 0A   <Enter>
```

To fill the area of memory from ES:0B00H through ES:0BFFH by replicating the text string *BUFFER*, type

```
-F ES:B00 BFF "BUFFER"   <Enter>
```

or

```
-F ES:B00 L100 "BUFFER"   <Enter>
```

DEBUG: G

Go

Purpose

Transfers control from DEBUG to the program being debugged.

Syntax

G [=*address*] [*break0* [... *break9*]]

where:

address   is the location DEBUG begins execution.
break0...break9   specify from 1 to 10 temporary breakpoints.

Description

The Go (G) command transfers control from DEBUG to the program being debugged. If no breakpoints are set, the program executes until it crashes or finishes, in which latter case the message *Program terminated normally* is displayed and control returns to DEBUG. (After this message is displayed, the program may need to be reloaded before it can be executed again.)

The *address* parameter can specify any location in memory. If no segment is specified, DEBUG uses the target program's CS register. If *address* is omitted, DEBUG transfers to the current address in the target program's CS:IP registers. An equal sign (=) must precede *address* to distinguish it from the breakpoints *break0...break9*.

The parameters *break0...break9* are addresses that represent from 1 to 10 temporary breakpoints that can be set as part of the G command. A breakpoint is an address at which execution stops. Breakpoints can be placed in any order, because execution stops at the first breakpoint address encountered, regardless of the position of that breakpoint in the list. Each breakpoint address must contain the first byte of an 8086 opcode. DEBUG installs breakpoints by replacing the first byte of the machine instruction at each breakpoint address with an INT 03H instruction (opcode 0CCH). If the program encounters a breakpoint, execution is suspended and control returns to DEBUG. DEBUG then restores the original machine code to the breakpoint addresses; displays the contents of the registers, the status of the flags, and the instruction pointed to by CS:IP; and displays the DEBUG prompt. If the program executes to completion without encountering any of the breakpoints or stops for any reason other than because it encountered a breakpoint, DEBUG does not replace the INT 03H instructions with the original machine code, and the Load File or Sectors (L) command must be used to reload the original program.

The G command requires that the target program's SS:SP registers point to a valid stack that has at least 6 bytes of stack space available. When the G command is executed, it pushes the target program's flags and CS and IP registers onto the stack and then transfers control to the target program with an IRET instruction. Thus, if the target program's stack is not valid or is too small, the system may crash.

Examples

To begin execution of the program in DEBUG's buffer at location CS:110AH and set breakpoints at CS:12FCH and CS:1303H, type

```
-G =110A 12FC 1303  <Enter>
```

To resume execution of the program after a breakpoint has been encountered and control has been returned to DEBUG, type

```
-G  <Enter>
```

Messages

bp Error

More than 10 breakpoints were specified in a G command. The command must be entered again with 10 or fewer breakpoints.

Program terminated normally

No breakpoints were encountered and the target program executed to completion. If breakpoints were set, the original program should be restored with the L command.

DEBUG: H

Perform Hexadecimal Arithmetic

Purpose

Displays the sum and difference of two hexadecimal numbers.

Syntax

H *value1 value2*

where:

value1 and *value2* are any two hexadecimal numbers from 0 through FFFFH.

Description

The Perform Hexadecimal Arithmetic (H) command displays the sum and the difference of two 16-bit hexadecimal numbers — that is, the result of the operations *value1+value2* and *value1−value2*. If *value2* is greater than *value1*, the difference of the two values is displayed as a two's complement number. This command is convenient for quickly calculating addresses and other values during an interactive debugging session.

Examples

To display the sum and the difference of the values 4B03H and 104H, type

```
-H 4B03 104  <Enter>
```

This produces the following display:

```
4C07  49FF
```

If the addition produces an overflow, the four least significant digits are displayed. For example, the command line

```
-H FFFF 2  <Enter>
```

produces the following display:

```
0001 FFFD
```

If the second number is bigger than the first, the difference is displayed in two's complement form. For example, the command line

```
-H 1 2  <Enter>
```

produces the following display:

```
0003 FFFF
```

DEBUG: I

Input from Port

Purpose

Reads and displays 1 byte from an input/output (I/O) port.

Syntax

I *port*

where:

port   is an I/O port address from 0 through FFFFH.

Description

The Input from Port (I) command reads the specified I/O port address and displays the data as a two-digit hexadecimal number.

Warning: The I command should be used with caution because it directly accesses the computer hardware and no error checking is performed. Input operations directed to the ports assigned to some peripheral device controllers may interfere with the proper operation of the system. If no device has been assigned to the specified I/O port or if the port is write-only, the value displayed by an I command is unreliable.

Example

To read and display the contents of I/O port 10AH, type

```
-I 10A  <Enter>
```

An example of the output of this command is

```
FF
```

DEBUG: L

Load File or Sectors

Purpose

Loads a file or individual sectors from a disk into DEBUG's memory.

Syntax

L [*address*]

or

L *address drive start number*

where:

address   is the memory location for the data to be read from the disk.
drive   is the number of the disk drive to read (0 = drive A, 1 = drive B, 2 = drive C, and so on).
start   is the hexadecimal number of the first logical sector to load (0–FFFFH).
number   is the hexadecimal number of consecutive sectors to load (0–FFFFH).

Description

The Load File or Sectors (L) command loads a file or individual sectors from a disk. When the L command is entered without parameters or with only an address, the file specified in the DEBUG command line or the one in the most recent Name File or Command-Tail Parameters (N) command line is loaded from the disk into memory. If no segment is specified in *address*, DEBUG uses CS. If the file's extension is .EXE, the file is placed in DEBUG's target program buffer at the load address specified in the .EXE file's header. If the file's extension is .COM, the file is loaded at offset 100H. (If for some reason an address other than 100H is entered for a .EXE or .COM file, an error message is displayed; if the address is 100H, the specification is ignored.) The length of the file or, in the case of a .EXE file, the actual length of the program (the length of the file minus the header) is placed in the target program's BX and CX registers, with the most significant 16 bits in register BX.

The L command can also be used to bypass the MS-DOS file system and directly access logical sectors on the disk. The memory address (*address*), disk drive number (*drive*), starting logical sector number (*start*), and number of sectors to load (*number*) must all be specified in the command line.

Note: The L command should not be used to access logical sectors on network drives.

Examples

To load the file specified in the DEBUG command line or in the most recent N command into DEBUG's target program buffer, type

```
-L  <Enter>
```

To load eight sectors from drive B, starting at logical sector 0, to memory location CS:0100H, type

```
-L 100 1 0 8  <Enter>
```

Messages

Disk error reading drive X
The specified drive does not exist or the disk in the specified drive is defective.

File not found
The file specified in the most recent N command cannot be found.

DEBUG: M

Move (Copy) Data

Purpose

Copies the contents of one area of memory to another.

Syntax

M *range address*

where:

range specifies the starting and ending addresses or the starting address and length of the area of memory to be copied.

address is the first byte in which the copied data will be placed.

Description

The Move (Copy) Data (M) command copies data from one memory location to another without altering the data in the original location. If the source and destination areas overlap, the data is copied so that the resulting copy is correct; the data in the *original* location is changed where the two areas overlap.

The *range* parameter specifies either the starting and ending addresses or the starting address and length of the memory to be copied. The *address* parameter is the first byte in which the copy will be placed. If *range* does not contain an explicit segment, DEBUG uses DS; if *address* does not contain a segment, DEBUG uses the segment used for *range*.

Example

To copy the data in locations DS:0800H through DS:08FFH to locations DS:0900H through DS:09FFH, type

```
-M 800 8FF 900  <Enter>
```

or

```
-M 800 L100 900  <Enter>
```

DEBUG: N

Name File or Command-Tail Parameters

Purpose

Inserts filenames and/or switches into the simulated program segment prefix (PSP).

Syntax

N *parameter* [*parameter*...]

where:

parameter   is one or more filenames or switches to be placed in the simulated PSP.

Description

The Name File or Command-Tail Parameters (N) command is used to enter one or more parameters into the simulated PSP that is built at the base of the buffer holding the program to be debugged. The N command can also be used before the Load File or Sectors (L) and Write File or Sectors (W) commands to name the file to be read from or written to a disk.

The count of the characters following the N command is placed at DS:0080H in the simulated PSP, and the characters themselves are copied into the PSP starting at offset 81H. The string is terminated by a carriage return (0DH), which is not included in the count. If the first and second parameters follow the naming conventions for MS-DOS files, they are parsed into the default file control blocks (FCBs) in the simulated PSP at offsets 5CH and 6CH, respectively. (Switches specified as parameters are stored in the PSP starting at offset 81H along with the rest of the command line but are not included in the FCBs.)

If the N command line contains only one filename, any parameters placed in the default FCBs by a previous N command are destroyed. If the drive specified with the first filename parameter is invalid, the AL register is set to 0FFH. If the drive specified with the second filename parameter is invalid, the AH register is set to 0FFH. The existence of a file specified with the N command is not verified until it is loaded with the L command.

Examples

Assume that DEBUG was started without specifying the name of a target program in the command line. To load the program CLEAN.COM for execution under the control of DEBUG, use the N and L commands together as follows:

```
-N CLEAN.COM  <Enter>
-L  <Enter>
```

Then, to place the parameter MYFILE.DAT in the simulated PSP's command tail and parse MYFILE.DAT into the first default FCB, type

```
-N MYFILE.DAT  <Enter>
```

Finally, to execute the program CLEAN.COM, type

```
-G  <Enter>
```

The result is the same as if the CLEAN.COM program had been run from the MS-DOS command level with the entry

```
C>CLEAN MYFILE.DAT  <Enter>
```

except that the program is executing under the control of DEBUG and within DEBUG's memory buffer.

DEBUG: O

Output to Port

Purpose

Writes 1 byte to an input/output (I/O) port.

Syntax

O *port byte*

where:

port   is an I/O port address from 0 through FFFFH.
byte   is a value from 0 through 0FFH to be written to the I/O port.

Description

The Output to Port (O) command writes 1 byte of data to the specified I/O port address. The data value must be in the range 00H through 0FFH.

Warning: The O command should be used with caution because it directly accesses the computer hardware and no error checking is performed. Attempts to write to some port addresses, such as those for ports connected to peripheral device controllers, timers, or the system's interrupt controller, may cause the system to crash or damage data stored on disk.

Example

To write the value C8H to I/O port 10AH, type

```
-O 10A C8   <Enter>
```

DEBUG: P
Proceed Through Loop or Subroutine

Purpose

Executes a loop, repeated string instruction, software interrupt, or subroutine call to completion.

Syntax

P [=*address*] [*number*]

where:

address   is the location of the first instruction to be executed.
number   is the number of instructions to execute.

Description

The Proceed Through Loop or Subroutine (P) command transfers control from DEBUG to the target program. The program executes without interruption until the loop, repeated string instruction, software interrupt, or subroutine call at *address* is completed or until the specified number of machine instructions have been executed. Control then returns to DEBUG, and the contents of the target program's registers and the status of the flags are displayed.

If the *address* parameter does not include an explicit segment, DEBUG uses the target program's CS register; if *address* is omitted entirely, execution begins at the address specified by the target's CS:IP registers. The *address* parameter must be preceded by an equal sign (=) to distinguish it from *number*.

If the instruction at *address* is not a loop, repeated string instruction, software interrupt, or subroutine call, the P command functions just like the Trace Program Execution (T) command. The optional *number* parameter specifies the number of instructions to be executed before control returns to DEBUG. If *number* is omitted, DEBUG executes only one instruction. After each instruction is executed, DEBUG displays the contents of the target program's registers, the status of the flags, and the next instruction to be executed.

Warning: The P command cannot be used to trace through ROM.

Example

Assume that the target program's location CS:143FH contains a CALL instruction. To execute the subroutine that is the destination of CALL and then return control to DEBUG, type

```
-P =143F  <Enter>
```

DEBUG: Q
Quit

Purpose

Ends a DEBUG session.

Syntax

Q

Description

The Quit (Q) command terminates the DEBUG program and returns control to MS-DOS or
the command shell that invoked DEBUG. Any changes to a program or other file that were
not saved on disk with the Write File or Sectors (W) command are lost.

Example

To exit DEBUG, type

```
-Q  <Enter>
```

DEBUG: R

Display or Modify Registers

Purpose

Displays the contents of one or all registers and the status of the CPU flags and allows them to be modified.

Syntax

R [*register*]

where:

register   is the two-character name of an Intel 8086/8088 register from the following list:

```
AX BX CX DX SP BP SI DI
DS ES SS CS IP PC
```

or the character F, which specifies the CPU flags.

Description

The Display or Modify Registers (R) command displays the target program's register contents and the status of the CPU flags and allows them to be modified.

If R is entered without a *register* parameter, the contents of all registers and the status of the CPU flags are displayed, followed by a disassembly of the machine instruction currently pointed to by the target program's CS:IP registers.

If *register* is included in the R command line, the contents of the specified register are displayed; then DEBUG prompts with a colon character (:) for a new value. The value is entered by typing one to four hexadecimal digits and then pressing the Enter key. Pressing the Enter key without entering any values leaves the register contents unchanged.

Note: The register name PC is not fully supported in some versions of DEBUG, so the register name IP should be used instead.

Specifying the character F instead of a register name causes DEBUG to display the status of the program's CPU flags as two-character codes from the following list:

Flag Name	Value If Set (1)	Value If Clear (0)
Overflow	OV (Overflow)	NV (No Overflow)
Direction	DN (Down)	UP (Up)
Interrupt	EI (Enabled)	DI (Disabled)

(more)

Flag Name	Value If Set (1)	Value If Clear (0)
Sign	NG (Minus)	PL (Plus)
Zero	ZR (Zero)	NZ (Not Zero)
Aux Carry	AC (Aux Carry)	NA (No Aux Carry)
Parity	PE (Even)	PO (Odd)
Carry	CY (Carry)	NC (No Carry)

After displaying the flag values, DEBUG displays a hyphen (-) prompt on the same line. Any or all flags can then be altered by typing one or more codes (in any order and optionally separated by spaces) from the list above and pressing the Enter key. Pressing the Enter key without entering any codes leaves the status of the flags unchanged.

Examples

To display the contents of the target program's CPU registers and the status of the CPU flags, followed by the disassembled mnemonic for the next instruction to be executed (pointed to by CS:IP), type

```
-R   <Enter>
```

This produces a display in the following format:

```
AX=0000   BX=0000  CX=00A1  DX=0000   SP=FFFE   BP=0000 SI=0000   DI=0000
DS=19A5   ES=19A5  SS=19A5  CS=19A5   IP=0100    NV UP EI PL NZ NA PO NC
19A5:0100 BF8000       MOV   DI,0080
```

To display the value of the target program's BX register, type

```
-R BX   <Enter>
```

If BX contains 0200H, for example, DEBUG displays that value and then issues a prompt in the form of a colon:

```
BX 0200
:
```

The contents of BX can then be altered by typing a new value and pressing the Enter key or left unchanged by pressing the Enter key alone.

To set the direction and carry flags, first type

```
-R F   <Enter>
```

DEBUG displays the flag values, followed by a hyphen (-) prompt:

```
NV UP EI PL NZ NA PO NC   -
```

The direction and carry flags can then be set by entering

```
-DN CY   <Enter>
```

Messages

bf Error
Bad flag: An invalid code for a CPU flag was entered.

br Error
Bad register: An invalid register name was entered.

df Error
Double flag: Two values for the same CPU flag were entered in the same command.

DEBUG: S

Search Memory

Purpose

Searches memory for a pattern of 1 or more bytes.

Syntax

S *range list*

where:

range   specifies the starting and ending addresses or the starting address and length of the area to be searched.

list   is 1 or more consecutive byte values and/or a string to be searched for.

Description

The Search Memory (S) command searches a designated range of memory for a specified list of consecutive byte values and/or a text string. The starting address of each set of matching bytes is displayed. The contents of the searched area are not altered.

The *range* parameter specifies the starting and ending addresses or the starting address and length in bytes of the area to be searched. If a segment is not included in *range*, DEBUG uses DS. If a segment is specified for the starting address, DEBUG uses the same segment for the ending address. If a starting address and length in bytes is specified, the starting address plus the length minus 1 cannot exceed FFFFH.

The *list* parameter specifies one or more consecutive hexadecimal byte values and/or a string to be searched for, separated by spaces, commas, or tab characters. Strings must be enclosed within single or double quotation marks, and case is significant within a string.

Examples

To search for the string *Copyright* in the area of memory from DS:0000H through DS:1FFFH, type

```
-S 0 1FFF 'Copyright'  <Enter>
```

or

```
-S 0 L2000 "Copyright"  <Enter>
```

If matches are found, DEBUG displays the starting address of each:

```
20A8:0910
20A8:094F
20A8:097C
```

To search for the byte sequence *3BH 06H* in the area of memory from CS:0100H through CS:12A0H, type

```
-S CS:100 12A0 3B 06   <Enter>
```

or

```
-S CS:100 L11A1 3B 06   <Enter>
```

DEBUG: T

Trace Program Execution

Purpose

Executes one or more instructions, displaying the CPU status after each instruction.

Syntax

T [=*address*] [*number*]

where:

address   is the location of the first instruction to be executed.
number   is the number of machine instructions to be executed.

Description

The Trace Program Execution (T) command executes one or more instructions, starting at the specified address, and after each instruction displays the contents of the CPU registers, the status of the flags, and the instruction pointed to by CS:IP.

Warning: The T command should not be used to execute any instructions that change the contents of the Intel 8259 interrupt mask (ports 20H and 21H on the IBM PC and compatibles) or to trace calls made to MS-DOS through Interrupt 21H. The Go (G) command should be used instead.

The *address* parameter points to the first instruction to be executed. If *address* does not include a segment, DEBUG uses the target program's CS register; if *address* is omitted entirely, execution begins at the address specified by the target program's CS:IP registers. If *address* is included, it must be preceded by an equal sign (=) to distinguish it from *number.*

The *number* parameter specifies the hexadecimal number of instructions to be executed before the DEBUG prompt is redisplayed (default = 1). Pressing Ctrl-C or Ctrl-Break interrupts execution of a sequence of T instructions. Consecutive instructions can then be executed individually by entering T commands with no parameters. Pressing Ctrl-S suspends execution and pressing any key then resumes the trace.

Note: The T command can be used to trace through ROM.

Example

To execute one instruction at location CS:1A00H and then return control to DEBUG, displaying the contents of the CPU registers and the status of the flags, type

```
-T =1A00   <Enter>
```

DEBUG: U

Disassemble (Unassemble) Program

Purpose

Disassembles machine instructions into assembly-language mnemonics.

Syntax

U [*range*]

where:

range   specifies the starting and ending addresses or the starting address and length
of the machine code to be disassembled.

Description

The Disassemble (Unassemble) Program (U) command translates machine instructions
into assembly-language mnemonics.

The *range* parameter specifies the starting and ending addresses or starting address and
length in bytes of the machine instructions to be disassembled. If *range* does not specify a
segment, DEBUG uses CS. Note that if the starting address does not fall on an 8086 instruction boundary, the disassembly will be incorrect.

If *range* does not include a length or ending address, 32 (20H) bytes of memory are disassembled beginning at the specified starting address. If *range* is omitted, 32 bytes of
memory are disassembled, starting at the address following the last instruction disassembled by the previous U command. If a U command has not been used before
and *range* is omitted, disassembly begins at the address specified by the target
program's CS:IP registers.

Note: The actual number of bytes displayed may vary slightly from the amount specified
in *range* or from the default of 32 bytes because the length of instructions may vary. Also,
the U command does not understand instructions specific to the 80186, 80286, and 80386
microprocessors. It displays such instructions as DBs.

Successive 32-byte fragments of code can be disassembled by entering additional U commands without parameters.

Example

To disassemble 8 bytes of machine instructions starting at CS:0100H, type

```
-U 100 107  <Enter>
```

or

```
-U 100 L8  <Enter>
```

DEBUG: W

Write File or Sectors

Purpose

Writes a file or individual sectors to disk.

Syntax

W [*address*]

or

W *address drive start number*

where:

address	is the first memory location of the data to be written.
drive	is the number of the destination disk drive (0 = drive A, 1 = drive B, 2 = drive C, and so on).
start	is the number of the first logical sector to write (0–FFFFH).
number	is the number of consecutive sectors to be written (0–FFFFH).

Description

The Write File or Sectors (W) command transfers a file or individual sectors from memory to the disk.

When the W command is entered without parameters or with only an address, the number of bytes specified by the contents of registers BX:CX is written from memory into the file named in the most recently used Name File or Command-Tail Parameters (N) command or the first file specified in the DEBUG command line if the N command has not been used. Files with a .EXE or .HEX extension cannot be written with the DEBUG W command.

Note: If a Trace Program Execution (T), Go (G), or Proceed Through Loop or Subroutine (P) command has been used or the contents of the BX or CX registers have been changed, the contents of BX:CX must be restored before the W command is used.

When *address* is not included in the command line, the target program's CS:0100H is assumed.

The W command can also be used to bypass the MS-DOS file system and directly access logical sectors on the disk. The memory address (*address*), disk drive number (*drive*), starting logical sector number (*start*), and number of sectors to be written (*number*) must all be provided in the command line in hexadecimal format. The W command should not be used to write sectors on network drives.

Warning: Extreme caution must be used with the W command. The disk's file structure can easily be damaged if the wrong parameters are entered.

Example

Assume that the interactive Assemble Machine Instructions (A) command was used to create a program in DEBUG's memory buffer that is 32 (20H) bytes long, beginning at offset 0100H. This program can be written to the file QUICK.COM by using the DEBUG Name File or Command-Tail Parameters (N), Display or Modify Registers (R), and Write File or Sectors (W) commands sequentially. First, use the N command to specify the name of the file to be written:

```
-N QUICK.COM  <Enter>
```

Next, use the R command to set registers BX and CX to the length to be written. Register BX contains the upper, or most significant half, of the length, whereas register CX contains the lower, or least significant half. Type

```
-R CX  <Enter>
```

DEBUG displays the contents of register CX and prompts with a colon (:). Enter the length after the prompt:

```
:20  <Enter>
```

To use the R command again to set register BX to zero, type

```
-R BX  <Enter>
```

followed by

```
:0  <Enter>
```

Finally, to create the disk file QUICK.COM and write the program into it, type

```
-W  <Enter>
```

DEBUG responds:

```
Writing 0020 bytes
```

Messages

EXE and HEX files cannot be written
Files with a .EXE or .HEX extension cannot be written to disk with the W command.

Writing *nnnn* bytes
After a successful write operation, DEBUG displays in hexadecimal format the number of bytes written to disk.

SYMDEB
Symbolic Debugger

Purpose

The Symbolic Debugger (SYMDEB) allows a file to be loaded, examined, altered, and written back to disk. If the file contains a program, the program can be disassembled, modified, traced one instruction at a time, or executed at full speed with breakpoints. SYMDEB can also be used to read, modify, and write absolute disk sectors.

The SYMDEB utility is supplied with the Microsoft Macro Assembler (MASM) versions 4.0 and earlier. This documentation describes SYMDEB version 4.0.

Syntax

SYMDEB

or

SYMDEB [options] [symfile[symfile...]] [filename[parameter...]]

where:

symfile	is the name of a symbol file created with the MAPSYM utility (extension = .SYM).
filename	is the name of the binary or executable program file to be debugged.
parameter	is a command-line parameter required by the program being debugged.
options	is one or more of the following switches. Switches can be either uppercase or lowercase and can be preceded by a dash (-) instead of a forward slash (/).

/I	(IBM) specifies that the computer is IBM compatible.
/K	enables the interactive breakpoint key (Scroll Lock).
/N	enables the use of nonmaskable interrupt break systems on IBM-compatible computers (requires special hardware).
/S	enables the Screen Swap (\) command on IBM-compatible computers (the /I switch is also required).
/"commands"	specifies one or more SYMDEB commands, separated by semicolons and enclosed in quotation marks.

Description

The SYMDEB commands and capabilities are a superset of those in DEBUG. SYMDEB is also able to load and interpret special symbol files that correlate line numbers, symbols, and memory addresses. With the aid of such files, SYMDEB enables the user to specify addresses with labels, variable names, and expressions, rather than only with absolute hexadecimal addresses. SYMDEB's command repertoire also includes I/O redirection commands, floating-point number entry and display commands, and source-code display capabilities that are not present in DEBUG.

The SYMDEB command line typically includes the *filename* parameter, which is the name of an executable program (with the extension .COM or .EXE) to be loaded into SYMDEB's memory buffer. Files with the extension .EXE are loaded in a manner compatible with the MS-DOS loader. Files with the extension .HEX are converted to binary images and loaded at the internally specified address. All other files are assumed to be direct memory images and are read directly into memory starting at offset 100H. If SYMDEB is entered by itself, no file information is read into memory. An appropriate program segment prefix (PSP) is synthesized at the head of SYMDEB's buffer for use by the target program; the PSP includes a command tail at offset 80H and default file control blocks (FCBs) at offsets 5CH and 6CH, constructed from the optional parameters following *filename*. If necessary, contents of the file are relocated so that the file is ready to execute.

The command line can also contain the names of one or more *symfiles*, symbol files that contain symbol and line-number information for the object modules that constitute the program being debugged. A symbol file is created with the MAPSYM utility from a map file produced by the Microsoft Object Linker (LINK). A symbol file always has the extension .SYM. *See* PROGRAMMING UTILITIES: MAPSYM; LINK.

The four command-line switches /I, /K, /N, and /S provide SYMDEB with information about the computer on which the utility is running. The /I switch is used when the computer is IBM compatible; this causes SYMDEB to take full advantage of special hardware features such as the 8259 Programmable Interrupt Controller or the memory-mapped video display. The /K switch enables the interactive breakpoint key (Scroll Lock), which can then be pressed at any time to interrupt a program that is being traced under the control of SYMDEB.

Note: The /K switch is not necessary on an IBM PC/AT, because the Sys Req key is always active as an interactive break key.

The /N switch enables the use of the nonmaskable interrupt as a breakpoint signal on IBM-compatible computers; this interrupt is triggered by hardware-assisted debugging packages such as Periscope and Atron Corporation's Software Probe. The /S switch enables the Screen Swap (\) command, which allows the output from the program being traced to be maintained and displayed on demand on a virtual screen separate from the SYMDEB commands and messages.

Note: The /I, /N, and /S switches are unnecessary on personal computers built by IBM Corporation; SYMDEB automatically enables the capabilities provided by those switches when SYMDEB finds the IBM copyright notice in the machine's ROM.

After SYMDEB and any files named in the command line are loaded, SYMDEB displays its special prompt character, a hyphen (-), and awaits a command. SYMDEB commands consist of one or two letters, usually followed by one or more parameters. SYMDEB treats uppercase and lowercase characters equivalently except when they are contained in strings enclosed within single or double quotation marks. SYMDEB does not execute commands until the Enter key is pressed.

The SYMDEB commands discussed in this section are

Command	Action
A	Assemble machine instructions.
BC	Clear breakpoints.
BD	Disable breakpoints.
BE	Enable breakpoints.
BL	List breakpoints.
BP	Set breakpoints.
C	Compare memory areas.
D	Display memory.
DA	Display ASCII.
DB	Display bytes.
DD	Display doublewords.
DL	Display long reals.
DS	Display short reals.
DT	Display 10-byte reals.
DW	Display words.
E	Enter data.
EA	Enter ASCII string.
EB	Enter bytes.
ED	Enter doublewords.
EL	Enter long reals.
ES	Enter short reals.
ET	Enter 10-byte reals.
EW	Enter words.
F	Fill memory.
G	Go execute program.
H	Perform hexadecimal arithmetic.
I	Input from port.
K	Perform stack trace.
L	Load file or sectors.
M	Move (copy) data.
N	Name file or command-tail parameters.
O	Output to port.
P	Proceed through loop or subroutine.
Q	Quit debugger.
R	Display or modify registers.
S	Search memory.

(more)

Command	Action
S+	Enable source display mode.
S−	Disable source display mode.
S&	Enable source and machine code display mode.
T	Trace program execution.
U	Disassemble (unassemble) program.
V	View source code.
W	Write file or sectors.
X	Examine symbol map.
XO	Open symbol map.
Z	Set symbol value.
<	Redirect SYMDEB input.
>	Redirect SYMDEB output.
=	Redirect SYMDEB input and output.
{	Redirect target program input.
}	Redirect target program output.
~	Redirect target program input and output.
\	Swap screen.
.	Display source line.
?	Help or evaluate expression.
!	Escape to shell.
*	Enter comment.

One or more SYMDEB commands, separated by semicolons and enclosed in double quotation marks, can be included in the original SYMDEB command line in the form /"*commands*" (for example, /"r;d;q"). These commands, which must precede the filename of the program being debugged, are carried out immediately when SYMDEB is loaded. (This is a convenient way to invoke SYMDEB and execute a series of batch commands.)

The parameters for a SYMDEB command include symbols; line numbers; addresses; ranges; and 8-bit, 16-bit, 32-bit, or floating-point values, expressions, and lists. Multiple parameters can be separated by spaces, tabs, or commas.

A symbol is a name that represents a register, an absolute value, a segment address, or a segment offset. A symbol consists of one or more characters but always begins with a letter, an underscore (_), a question mark (?), an at sign (@), or a dollar sign ($). The names of the various 8086/8088/80286 registers and CPU flags are built into SYMDEB and can be used at any time. Other symbols can be used only when one or more symbol files have been loaded in conjunction with the program to be debugged.

Note: SYMDEB regards symbols whose spellings differ only in case as the same symbol. A unique symbol name that does not conflict with programming instructions, register names, or hexadecimal numbers should always be used.

In MASM programs, symbols must be declared PUBLIC in the source code in order to be accessible during debugging (except for segment and group names, which are PUBLIC by default). In programs compiled with the current versions of Microsoft C, FORTRAN, and Pascal, all symbols are passed through for debugging if the proper compilation switch is used; however, familiarity with the compiler's particular naming conventions is necessary (for example, the Microsoft C Compiler adds an underscore character to the beginning of every symbol).

A line number is a combination of decimal numbers, filenames, and symbols that specifies a unique line of text in a program source file. Line numbers always start with a dot character (.) and take one of the following forms:

.[*filename:*]*linenumber*
.+*displacement*
.−*displacement*
.*symbol*[+*displacement*]
.*symbol*[−*displacement*]

The second and third variations specify a line relative to the current line number; the fourth and fifth specify a line number relative to a designated symbol. Line numbers can be used only with programs developed with compilers that generate line-number information. Programs developed with MASM or an incompatible compiler cannot generate line numbers.

An address identifies a unique location in memory. An address can be a simple offset or a complete address consisting of two 16-bit values in the form segment:offset. Each component can be a valid symbol (including CS, DS, ES, or SS, in the case of segments), a 16-bit hexadecimal number in the range 0 through FFFFH, or a symbol plus or minus a displacement. When the segment portion of an address is absent, the segment specified in the previous instance of the same command is used; if no segment was previously specified, SYMDEB uses DS unless an A, G, L, P, T, U, or W command is used, in which case SYMDEB uses CS.

A range specifies an area of memory or a number of data items and can be expressed as either two addresses or a starting address and a length. A length is represented by the letter L followed by a hexadecimal value in the range 0 through FFFFH. The meaning of the length varies with the SYMDEB command used: The length can signify a number of bytes, words, doublewords, real numbers, machine instructions, or source-code lines. If a command requires a range and the ending address is not supplied, SYMDEB usually assumes 128 bytes.

A value represents an integral number and is a combination of one or more digits. The default base for values is hexadecimal, except in the case of floating-point numbers, but other bases can be used by appending a radix character (Y for binary, O or Q for octal, T for decimal, H for hexadecimal) in either uppercase or lowercase. For example, the following values are equivalent:

0040	0100Q
0040H	0100O
0064t	1000000Y

Doubleword (32-bit) values are entered as two hexadecimal integers separated by a colon character (:). Real numbers are always entered in decimal radix, with or without a decimal point or exponent. Leading zeros can be omitted.

An expression is a combination of symbols, numeric constants, and operators that evaluates to an 8-, 16-, or 32-bit value. An expression can be used in place of a simple value in any command. Unary address operators use DS as the default segment for addresses. Expressions are evaluated in order of operator precedence; operators with equal precedence are evaluated from left to right. Parentheses can be used to override the normal operator precedence.

The available unary operators, listed in order of precedence from highest to lowest, are

Operator	Meaning
+	Unary plus
–	Unary minus
NOT	One's (bitwise) complement
SEG	Segment address of operand
OFF	Offset of operand
BY	Low-order byte from specified address
WO	Low-order word from specified address
DW	Doubleword from specified address
POI	Pointer from specified address (same as DW)
PORT	Byte input from specified port
WPORT	Word input from specified port

The available binary operators, listed in order of precedence from highest to lowest, are

Operator	Meaning
*	Multiplication
/	Integer division
MOD	Modulus
:	Segment override
+	Addition
–	Subtraction
AND	Bitwise Boolean AND
XOR	Bitwise Boolean Exclusive OR
OR	Bitwise Boolean Inclusive OR

A list is composed of one or more values, expressions, or strings, separated by spaces or commas. A string is one or more ASCII characters, enclosed within single or double quotation marks. Case is significant within a string. If the same type of quote character that is used to delimit the string occurs inside the string, the character must be doubled inside the string in order to be interpreted correctly (for example,"A ""quoted"" word").

In a few cases, SYMDEB displays a specific and informative error message in response to an invalid command. In general, though, SYMDEB responds in a generic fashion, pointing to the approximate location of the error with a caret character (^), followed by the word *Error.* For example:

```
-D CS:100,CS:80  <Enter>
                ^ Error
```

SYMDEB maintains a set of virtual CPU registers and flags for a program being debugged. These registers can be examined and modified with SYMDEB commands. When a program is first loaded for debugging, the virtual registers are initialized with the following values:

Register	.COM Program	.EXE Program
AX	Valid drive code	Valid drive code
BX	Upper half of program size	Upper half of program size
CX	Lower half of program size	Lower half of program size
DX	Zero	Zero
SI	Zero	Zero
DI	Zero	Zero
BP	Zero	Zero
SP	FFFEH or top of available memory minus 2	Size of stack segment
IP	100H	Offset of entry point within target program's code segment
CS	PSP	Base of target program's code segment
DS	PSP	PSP
ES	PSP	PSP
SS	PSP	Base of target program's stack segment

Note: SYMDEB checks the first three parameters in the command line. If the second and third parameters are filenames, SYMDEB checks any drive specifications with those filenames to verify that they designate valid drives. Register AX contains one of the following codes:

Code	Meaning
0000H	The drives specified with the second and third filenames are both valid, or only one filename was specified in the command line.
00FFH	The drive specified with the second filename is invalid.
FF00H	The drive specified with the third filename is invalid.
FFFFH	The drives specified with the second and third filenames are both invalid.

Before SYMDEB transfers control to the target program, it saves the actual CPU registers and then loads them with the current values of the virtual registers; conversely, when control reverts to SYMDEB from the target program, the returned register contents are stored back into the virtual register set for inspection and alteration by the SYMDEB user.

Examples

To prepare the program CLEAN.ASM for debugging with SYMDEB, declare all vital labels, procedures, and variable names in the source program PUBLIC. To assemble the program, type

```
C>MASM CLEAN;   <Enter>
```

This produces the relocatable object module CLEAN.OBJ. Then, to link the object module, type

```
C>LINK /MAP CLEAN;   <Enter>
```

This results in the executable program file CLEAN.EXE and the map file CLEAN.MAP.

Note: The /MAP switch must be used even if a map file is specified in the command line. Finally, to create the symbol information file required by SYMDEB, type

```
C>MAPSYM CLEAN   <Enter>
```

At this point, begin symbolic debugging by typing

```
C>SYMDEB CLEAN.SYM CLEAN.EXE   <Enter>
```

Any run-time command-line parameters required by the CLEAN program may be placed in the SYMDEB command line after the filename CLEAN.EXE.

To prepare the program SHELL.C for debugging with SYMDEB, first compile the program with the switches that disable optimization and cause line-number information to be written to the relocatable object module:

```
C>MSC /Zd /Od SHELL;   <Enter>
```

Next, to convert the object module to an executable program and create a map file with line-number information, type

```
C>LINK /MAP /LI SHELL;   <Enter>
```

To create the symbol information file required by SYMDEB for symbolic debugging, type

```
C>MAPSYM SHELL   <Enter>
```

To begin debugging, type

```
C>SYMDEB SHELL.SYM SHELL.EXE   <Enter>
```

To use the SYMDEB utility to inspect or modify memory or to read, modify, and write absolute disk sectors, type

```
C>SYMDEB  <Enter>
```

Message

File not found

The filename supplied as the first parameter in the SYMDEB command line cannot be found.

SYMDEB: A

Assemble Machine Instructions

Purpose

Allows entry of assembler mnemonics and translates them into executable machine code.

Syntax

A [*address*]

where:

address   is the starting location for the assembled machine code.

Description

The Assemble Machine Instructions (A) command accepts assembly-language statements, rather than hexadecimal values, for the Intel 8086/8088, 80186, and 80286 (running in real mode) microprocessors and the Intel 8087 and 80287 math coprocessors and assembles each statement into executable machine language.

The *address* parameter specifies the location where entry of assembly-language mnemonics will begin. If *address* is omitted, SYMDEB uses the last address generated by the previous A command; if there was no previous A command, SYMDEB uses the current value of the target program's CS:IP registers.

After the user enters an A command, SYMDEB prompts for each assembly-language statement by displaying the address (a segment and an offset) in which the assembled code will be stored. When the user presses the Enter key, SYMDEB translates the assembly-language statement and stores each byte of the resulting machine instruction sequentially in memory (overwriting any existing information), beginning at the displayed address. SYMDEB then displays the address following the last byte of the machine instruction to prompt the user to enter the next assembled instruction. The user can terminate assembly mode by pressing the Enter key in response to the address prompt.

The assembly-language statements accepted by the SYMDEB A command have some slight syntactic differences and restrictions compared with the Microsoft Macro Assembler programming statements. These differences can be summarized as follows:

- All numbers are assumed to be hexadecimal integers unless otherwise specified with a radix character suffix.
- Segment overrides must be specified by preceding the entire instruction with CS:, DS:, ES:, or SS:.
- File control directives (NAME, PAGE, TITLE, and so forth), macro definitions, record structures, and conditional assembly directives are not supported by SYMDEB.

- When the data type (word or byte) is not implicit in the instruction, the type must be specified by preceding the operand with BYTE PTR (or BY), WORD PTR (or WO), DWORD PTR (or DW), QWORD PTR (or QW), or TBYTE PTR (or TB).
- In a string operation, the size of the string must be specified with a B (byte) or W (word) added to the string instruction mnemonic (for example, LODSB or LODSW).
- The DB and DW instructions accept a parameter of the type *list* and assemble byte and word values directly into memory.
- The WAIT or FWAIT opcodes for 8087/80287 assembler statements are not generated by the system and must be coded explicitly. (Note: 8087/80287 instructions can be assembled if the system is not equipped with a math coprocessor, but the system will crash if an attempt is made to execute them.)
- Addresses must be enclosed in square brackets to be differentiated from immediate operands.
- Repeat prefixes such as REP, REPZ, and REPNZ can be entered either alone on a line preceding the statement they affect or on the same line immediately preceding the statement.
- The assembler will generate the optimal form (SHORT, NEAR, or FAR) for jumps or calls, depending on the destination address, but these can be overridden if the operand is preceded with a NEAR (or NE) or FAR prefix.
- The mnemonic for a FAR RETURN is RETF.

Examples

To begin assembling code at address CS:0100H, type

```
-A 100   <Enter>
```

To assemble the instruction sequence

```
LODS WORD PTR [SI]
XCHG BX,AX
JMP [BX]
```

beginning at address CS:0100H, the following dialogue would take place:

```
-A 100   <Enter>
1983:0100   LODSW   <Enter>
1983:0101   XCHG BX,AX   <Enter>
1983:0103   JMP [BX]   <Enter>
1983:0105   <Enter>
```

To continue assembling at the last address generated by a previous A command (1983:0105H in the preceding example), type

```
-A   <Enter>
```

SYMDEB: BC

Clear Breakpoints

Purpose

Permanently removes sticky breakpoints.

Syntax

BC *

or

BC *list*

where:

*	represents all sticky breakpoints.
list	is one or more integers (sticky breakpoint numbers) in the range 0 through 9.

Description

The Clear Breakpoints (BC) command permanently clears the sticky breakpoints previously set with the Set Breakpoints (BP) command. A sticky breakpoint remains in memory throughout a SYMDEB session, unlike a breakpoint set with the Go (G) command, which remains in effect only while the G command executes.

If an asterisk character (*) follows the BC command, SYMDEB deletes all sticky breakpoints. If a *list* parameter containing one or more sticky breakpoint numbers in the range 0 through 9 follows the BC command, SYMDEB selectively deletes sticky breakpoints. Each sticky breakpoint is assigned a number when the breakpoint is created with the BP command. The List Breakpoints (BL) command can be used to display all current sticky breakpoint locations and numbers. Breakpoint numbers should be separated by spaces.

Sticky breakpoints can be temporarily disabled with the Disable Breakpoints (BD) command and subsequently re-enabled with the Enable Breakpoints (BE) command.

Examples

To clear sticky breakpoints 0, 4, and 8, type

```
-BC 0 4 8  <Enter>
```

To clear all sticky breakpoints, type

```
-BC *  <Enter>
```

Messages

Bad breakpoint number! (0–9)
A sticky breakpoint number in the command line was not an integer in the range 0 through 9.

Breakpoint list or '*' expected!
The BC command was entered without parameters.

SYMDEB: BD

Disable Breakpoints

Purpose

Temporarily disables sticky breakpoints.

Syntax

BD *

or

BD *list*

where:

*	represents all sticky breakpoints.
list	is one or more integers (sticky breakpoint numbers) in the range 0 through 9.

Description

The Disable Breakpoints (BD) command temporarily disables the sticky breakpoints previously set with the Set Breakpoints (BP) command. A sticky breakpoint remains in memory throughout a SYMDEB session, unlike a breakpoint set with the Go (G) command, which remains in effect only while the G command executes.

If an asterisk character (*) follows the BD command, SYMDEB disables all sticky breakpoints. If a *list* parameter containing one or more sticky breakpoint numbers in the range 0 through 9 follows the BD command, SYMDEB selectively disables sticky breakpoints. Each sticky breakpoint is assigned a number when the breakpoint is created with the BP command. The List Breakpoints (BL) command can be used to display all current sticky breakpoint locations and numbers. Breakpoint numbers should be separated by spaces.

Sticky breakpoints disabled with the BD command can be re-enabled with the Enable Breakpoints (BE) command. The Clear Breakpoints (BC) command can be used to permanently delete a sticky breakpoint.

Examples

To disable sticky breakpoints 0, 4, and 8, type

```
-BD 0 4 8  <Enter>
```

To disable all sticky breakpoints, type

```
-BD *  <Enter>
```

Messages

Bad breakpoint number! (0–9)

A sticky breakpoint number in the command line was not an integer in the range 0 through 9.

Breakpoint list or '*' expected!

The BD command was entered without parameters.

SYMDEB: BE

Enable Breakpoints

Purpose

Enables disabled sticky breakpoints.

Syntax

BE *

or

BE *list*

where:

*	represents all sticky breakpoints.
list	is one or more integers (sticky breakpoint numbers) in the range 0 through 9.

Description

The Enable Breakpoints (BE) command enables the sticky breakpoints disabled with the Disable Breakpoints (BD) command. A sticky breakpoint remains in memory throughout a SYMDEB session, unlike a breakpoint set with the Go (G) command, which remains in effect only while the G command executes.

If an asterisk (*) character follows the BE command, SYMDEB enables all sticky breakpoints. If a *list* parameter containing one or more sticky breakpoint numbers in the range 0 through 9 follows the BE command, SYMDEB selectively enables sticky breakpoints. Each sticky breakpoint is assigned a number when the breakpoint is created with the Set Breakpoints (BP) command. The List Breakpoints (BL) command can be used to display all current sticky breakpoint locations and numbers. Breakpoint numbers should be separated by spaces.

Examples

To enable sticky breakpoints 0, 4, and 8, type

```
-BE 0 4 8  <Enter>
```

To enable all sticky breakpoints, type

```
-BE *  <Enter>
```

Messages

Bad breakpoint number! (0–9)
A sticky breakpoint number in the command line was not an integer in the range 0 through 9.

Breakpoint list or '+' expected!
The BE command was entered without parameters.

SYMDEB: BL

List Breakpoints

Purpose

Displays information about all sticky breakpoints.

Syntax

BL

Description

The List Breakpoints (BL) command lists the current status of each sticky breakpoint created with the Set Breakpoints (BP) command. A sticky breakpoint remains in memory throughout a SYMDEB session, unlike a breakpoint set with the Go (G) command, which remains in effect only while the G command executes.

The BL command lists each sticky breakpoint number, its status code, its address in the target program, the number of passes remaining, and the initial number of passes specified with the BP command (in parentheses). If source display mode was selected with the Enable Source Display Mode (S+) command, SYMDEB also displays the source-file name and the line number that corresponds to each breakpoint location. Breakpoint status codes are

e   Enabled
d   Disabled
v   Virtual

(A virtual breakpoint is a sticky breakpoint set at a symbol contained in a .EXE file that has not yet been loaded into SYMDEB.)

Example

To view the current status of all breakpoints, type

```
-BL  <Enter>
```

If the BP commands

```
-BP0 _TEXT:_main  <Enter>
-BP1 _TEXT:_printf  <Enter>
```

were previously entered, the BL command displays

```
0 e 456E:0010 [_TEXT:_main] dump.C:32
1 e 456E:0612 [_TEXT:_printf]
```

SYMDEB: BP

Set Breakpoints

Purpose

Sets sticky breakpoint locations within the program being debugged.

Syntax

BP[*n*] *address* [*passcount*] ["*commands*"]

where:

n	is the sticky breakpoint number (0–9).
address	is the location of the breakpoint in the target program.
passcount	is the number of times the instruction at *address* should be executed before the breakpoint is taken.
"*commands*"	is one or more SYMDEB commands, separated by semicolons. The entire list must be enclosed in double quotation marks. (Limit = 30 characters.)

Description

The Set Breakpoints (BP) command sets a sticky breakpoint in the program being debugged. A sticky breakpoint remains in memory throughout a SYMDEB session, unlike a breakpoint set with the Go (G) command, which remains in effect only while the G command executes. When the target program reaches the breakpoint, execution of the program is suspended and control returns to SYMDEB. SYMDEB displays the contents of the registers and flags, followed by a prompt so that the user can enter more commands.

The optional *n* parameter associates an integer in the range 0 through 9, called the breakpoint number, with the sticky breakpoint location. If *n* is omitted, the next available breakpoint number is used. No space is allowed between BP and *n*.

The *address* parameter must point to the first byte of a machine instruction in the program. This parameter may be a symbol, a literal address, or a source-code line number. If a segment is not included, SYMDEB uses the target program's CS register.

The optional *passcount* parameter is the number of times execution should pass through the specified location before the break is taken and control is returned to SYMDEB. The value of *passcount* must be a hexadecimal number in the range 0 through FFFFH (default = 0).

The optional "*commands*" parameter is one or more SYMDEB commands with their associated parameters. Each command must be separated from the others by a semicolon character (;) and the entire list enclosed in double quotation marks ("). A maximum of 30 characters can be specified within the quotation marks. The commands are executed whenever the break is taken.

Examples

To set a sticky breakpoint at location *next_file* in the target program and dump the contents of memory locations DS:0000H through DS:00FFH when the breakpoint is reached, type

```
-BP NEXT_FILE "DB DS:0 L100"  <Enter>
```

To associate the breakpoint number 4 with the location CS:4230H in the program being debugged and pass the breakpoint 16 (10H) times before suspending execution of the program, type

```
-BP4 CS:4230 10  <Enter>
```

Messages

Bad breakpoint number! (0–9)
A sticky breakpoint number in the command line was not an integer in the range 0 through 9.

Breakpoint command too long!
The "*commands*" parameter exceeded 30 characters.

Breakpoint error!
The BP command was entered without an *address* parameter.

Breakpoint redefined!
A new address was assigned to an existing breakpoint number, or an attempt was made to create a breakpoint with the same address as an existing breakpoint.

Duplicate breakpoint ignored!
An attempt was made to change an existing breakpoint to a breakpoint already specified in the breakpoint list.

Too many breakpoints!
No more sticky breakpoints are available.

SYMDEB: C

Compare Memory Areas

Purpose

Compares two areas of memory and reports any differences.

Syntax

C *range address*

where:

range   specifies the starting and ending addresses or the starting address and length of the first area of memory to be compared.

address   points to the beginning of the second area of memory to be compared.

Description

The Compare Memory Areas (C) command compares the contents of two areas of memory. The location and contents of any differing bytes are listed in the following form:

address1 byte1 byte2 address2

If no differences are found, the SYMDEB prompt returns.

The *range* parameter specifies the first through last addresses or the starting address and length in bytes of the first area of memory to be compared.

The *address* parameter points to the beginning of the second area of memory to be compared, which is the same size as *range*. If a segment is not included in either *range* or *address*, SYMDEB uses DS.

Example

To compare the 64 bytes beginning at CS:CE00H with the 64 bytes beginning at CS:CF0AH, type

```
-C CS:CE00,CE3F CS:CF0A  <Enter>
```

or

```
-C CS:CE00 L40 CS:CF0A  <Enter>
```

If any differences are found, SYMDEB displays them in the following format:

```
2124:CE06  00  FF  2124:CF10
```

SYMDEB: D

Display Memory

Purpose

Displays the contents of an area of memory.

Syntax

D [*range*]

where:

range   specifies the starting and ending addresses or the starting address and length
of the area of memory to be displayed.

Description

The Display Memory (D) command displays the contents of a specified range of memory
addresses in the same format used in the most recent Display command (DA, DB, DD, DL,
DS, DT, or DW). If no Display command has previously been entered, the memory is displayed in hexadecimal bytes and their ASCII equivalents (the DB format).

The *range* parameter specifies the starting and ending addresses of the memory area to
be displayed or the starting address followed by the length of the area, expressed by an L
and the hexadecimal number of data items to be displayed. When *range* does not include
a segment, SYMDEB uses DS.

The size in bytes of each item and the default value for the length depend on the type of
Display command used: the Display Byte (DB), Display Doubleword (DD), and Display
Word (DW) commands default to a length of 128 (80H) bytes; Display ASCII (DA) displays
128 bytes or up to a null byte, whichever is smaller; Display Short Reals (DS), Display Long
Reals (DL), and Display 10-Byte Reals (DT) default to the display of one floating-point
number.

If a Display command has not previously been used and *range* is omitted from a D command, the display starts at the address specified in the target program's CS:IP registers. If a
Display command has previously been used and *range* is omitted from a D command, the
display starts at the memory address following the last address displayed by the most recent Display command.

Examples

Assume that the only Display commands used during this SYMDEB session are D and DB.
To display the contents of the 128 bytes of memory beginning at offset 100H in the program's DGROUP, type

```
-D DGROUP:0100  <Enter>
```

SYMDEB displays the contents of the range of memory addresses in the following format:

```
7F00:0100   20 64 65 76 69 63 65 0D-0A 00 60 39 0D 0A 00 7C    device...'9...¦
7F00:0110   39 08 20 08 00 81 39 04-1B 5B 32 4A 42 BD 11 44    9. ...9..[2JB=.D
7F00:0120   2E 26 45 AF 11 47 B3 11-48 A5 11 4C B8 11 4E D3    .&E/.G3.H%.L8.NS
7F00:0130   11 50 DF 11 51 AB 11 54-DF 1E 56 37 11 5F 9F 16    .P_.Q+.T_.V7._..
7F00:0140   24 C0 11 00 03 4E 4F 54-C1 07 0A 45 52 52 4F 52    $@...NOTA..ERROR
7F00:0150   4C 45 56 45 4C 85 08 05-45 58 49 53 54 18 08 00    LEVEL...EXIST...
7F00:0160   03 44 49 52 03 91 0C 06-52 45 4E 41 4D 45 01 C0    .DIR....RENAME.@
7F00:0170   0F 03 52 45 4E 01 C0 0F-05 45 52 41 53 45 01 68    ..REN.@..ERASE.h
```

To view the next 128 bytes of memory, type

```
-D   <Enter>
```

SYMDEB displays the contents of memory addresses 7F00:0180H through 7F00:01FFH.

SYMDEB: DA

Display ASCII

Purpose

Displays the contents of memory in ASCII format.

Syntax

DA [*range*]

where:

range   specifies the starting and ending addresses or the starting address and length
            of the area of memory to be displayed.

Description

The Display ASCII (DA) command displays the contents of a specified range of memory
addresses in ASCII format.

The *range* parameter specifies the starting and ending addresses of the memory area to
be displayed in ASCII format or the starting address followed by the length of the area, expressed by an L and a hexadecimal number of bytes. When *range* does not include a
segment, SYMDEB uses DS.

If a Display command has not previously been used and *range* is omitted from a DA command, the display starts at the address specified in the target program's CS:IP registers. If a
Display command has previously been used and *range* is omitted from a DA command,
the display starts at the memory address following the last address displayed by the most
recent Display command.

When a range is not explicit in a DA command, the display terminates after 128 bytes or
when a null (zero) byte is encountered. If a range is specified, the entire range is displayed, including any null bytes, with nonprinting characters displayed as period (.)
characters.

Each line of the display is formatted as a segment and offset, followed by the contents of
16 bytes of memory (or less if a null byte was encountered) represented as an ASCII string.

See also PROGRAMMING UTILITIES: SYMDEB:EA.

Examples

If memory beginning at location 7F00:0100H contains the characters *This is a test string*
followed by a null (zero) byte, the command

```
-DA 7F00:0100  <Enter>
```

produces the following display:

```
7F00:0100  This is a test string
```

To view additional memory in the same format, type

```
-D  <Enter>
```

SYMDEB: DB

Display Bytes

Purpose

Displays the contents of memory as hexadecimal bytes and their equivalent ASCII characters.

Syntax

DB [*range*]

where:

range   specifies the starting and ending addresses or the starting address and length of the area of memory to be displayed.

Description

The Display Bytes (DB) command displays the contents of a specified range of memory addresses as hexadecimal bytes and their ASCII character equivalents. This is the default format for the Display Memory (D) command.

The *range* parameter specifies the starting and ending addresses of the memory area to be displayed or the starting address followed by the length of the area, expressed by an L and a hexadecimal number of bytes. When *range* does not include a segment, SYMDEB uses DS.

If a Display command has not previously been used and *range* is omitted from a DB command, the display starts at the address specified in the target program's CS:IP registers. If a Display command has previously been used and *range* is omitted from a DB command, the display starts at the memory address following the last address displayed by the most recent Display command. When a range is not explicit in a DB command, the display terminates after 128 bytes.

Each line of the display is formatted as a segment and offset, followed by the contents of 16 bytes of memory represented as hexadecimal values separated by spaces (except the eighth and ninth values, which are separated by a dash), followed by their ASCII character equivalents (if any). In the ASCII section, nonprinting characters are displayed as periods.

See also PROGRAMMING UTILITIES: SYMDEB:EB.

Examples

To display the contents of the 128 bytes of memory beginning at 7F00:0100H, type

```
-DB 7F00:0100  <Enter>
```

The contents of the range of memory addresses are displayed in the following format:

```
7F00:0100   20 64 65 76 69 63 65 0D-0A 00 60 39 0D 0A 00 7C    device...'9...¦
7F00:0110   39 08 20 08 00 81 39 04-1B 5B 32 4A 42 BD 11 44    9. ...9..[2JB=.D
7F00:0120   2E 26 45 AF 11 47 B3 11-48 A5 11 4C B8 11 4E D3    .&E/.G3.H%.L8.NS
7F00:0130   11 50 DF 11 51 AB 11 54-DF 1E 56 37 11 5F 9F 16    .P_.Q+.T_.V7._..
7F00:0140   24 C0 11 00 03 4E 4F 54-C1 07 0A 45 52 52 4F 52    $@...NOTA..ERROR
7F00:0150   4C 45 56 45 4C 85 08 05-45 58 49 53 54 18 08 00    LEVEL...EXIST...
7F00:0160   03 44 49 52 03 91 0C 06-52 45 4E 41 4D 45 01 C0    .DIR....RENAME.@
7F00:0170   0F 03 52 45 4E 01 C0 0F-05 45 52 41 53 45 01 68    ..REN.@..ERASE.h
```

To view the next 128 bytes of memory, type

```
-D   <Enter>
```

SYMDEB displays the contents of memory addresses 7F00:0180H through 7F00:01FFH.

SYMDEB: DD
Display Doublewords

Purpose

Displays the contents of memory in hexadecimal doubleword format.

Syntax

DD [*range*]

where:

range   specifies the starting and ending addresses or the starting address and length
of the area of memory to be displayed.

Description

The Display Doublewords (DD) command displays the contents of a specified range of
memory addresses 4 bytes at a time, as if they were FAR memory pointers (offset followed
by segment in reverse byte order).

The *range* parameter specifies the starting and ending addresses of the memory to be displayed or the starting address followed by the length of the area, expressed by an L and a
hexadecimal number of doublewords. When *range* does not include a segment, SYMDEB
uses DS.

If a Display command has not previously been used and *range* is omitted from a DD command, the display starts at the address specified in the target program's CS:IP registers. If a
Display command has previously been used and *range* is omitted from a DD command,
the display starts at the memory address following the last address displayed by the most
recent Display command. When a range is not explicit in a DD command, 32 doublewords
(128 bytes) are displayed.

Each line of the display is formatted as a segment and offset, followed by the contents of
16 bytes of memory represented as 4 paired 16-bit segments and offsets. The 4 bytes that
make up the segment and offset of each doubleword pointer are displayed in reverse order
from their actual storage in memory.

See also PROGRAMMING UTILITIES: SYMDEB:ED.

Examples

To see how DD represents the 4 bytes that make up a doubleword, first type

```
-DB 100  <Enter>
```

This produces the following output:

```
3929:0100  CF 0B 9D 0D 33 0E C3 0E-F2 0E 06 0F 39 0F 49 0F  0...3.C.r...9.I.
```

Then type

```
-DD 100  <Enter>
```

This produces the following output:

```
3929:0100  0D9D:0BCF 0EC3:0E33 0F06:0EF2 0F49:0F39
```

Notice that DD switches the order of the first 2 bytes in a 4-byte set and designates them as the offset; then it switches the order of the second 2 bytes in the 4-byte set and designates them as the segment address.

To display the contents of the first 128 (80H) bytes of the system interrupt vector table, which is based at address 0000:0000H, type

```
-DD 0:0  <Enter>
```

This produces the following output:

```
0000:0000  2075:03D2 0070:01F0 16F3:2C1B 0070:01F0
0000:0010  0070:01F0 F000:FF54 F000:9805 F000:9805
0000:0020  0AE3:0395 16F3:2BAD F000:9805 F000:9805
0000:0030  0972:0D40 F000:9805 F000:EF57 0070:01F0
0000:0040  0AE3:03D6 F000:F84D F000:F841 0070:0D43
0000:0050  F000:E739 F000:F859 F000:E82E F000:EFD2
0000:0060  F000:E76C 0070:0ADD F000:FE6E 1078:3BEC
0000:0070  F000:FF53 F000:F0E4 0000:0522 F000:0000
```

To view the next 128 bytes of memory in the same format, type

```
-D  <Enter>
```

SYMDEB displays the contents of memory addresses 0000:0080H through 0000:00FFH.

SYMDEB: DL

Display Long Reals

Purpose

Displays the contents of memory as long (64-bit) floating-point numbers.

Syntax

DL [*range*]

where:

range   specifies the starting and ending addresses or the starting address and length
of the area of memory to be displayed.

Description

The Display Long Reals (DL) command displays the contents of a specified range of memory addresses 8 bytes at a time, as hexadecimal values and their decimal equivalents. The hexadecimal values are formatted as 64-bit floating-point numbers. The decimal values have the form

+¦−0.*decimaldigits*E+¦−*mantissa*

The sign of the number (+ or −) is followed by a zero, a decimal point, and a maximum of 16 *decimaldigits*; this, in turn, is followed by the designator of the mantissa (E) and the mantissa's sign (+ or −) and digits.

The *range* parameter specifies the starting and ending addresses of the memory to be displayed or the starting address followed by the length of the area, expressed by an L and a hexadecimal number of 8-byte values. When *range* does not include a segment, SYMDEB uses DS.

If a Display command has not previously been used and *range* is omitted from a DL command, the display starts at the address specified in the target program's CS:IP registers. If a Display command has previously been used and *range* is omitted from a DL command, the display starts at the memory address following the last address displayed by the most recent Display command. When a range is not explicit in a DL command, one 64-bit floating-point number is displayed.

Each line of the display is formatted as a segment and offset, followed by the contents of 8 bytes of memory represented as a hexadecimal value, followed by its decimal floating-point equivalent.

See also PROGRAMMING UTILITIES: SYMDEB:EL.

Examples

Assume that the memory beginning at location DS:0100H contains the value $6.624*10^{-27}$ (Planck's constant, in erg-seconds) as a 64-bit floating-point number. The command

```
-DL 100   <Enter>
```

produces the following output:

```
43E8:0100   5F A2 20 73 75 66 80 3A   +0.6624E-26
```

To view the next 8 bytes of memory in the same format, type

```
-D   <Enter>
```

SYMDEB: DS

Display Short Reals

Purpose

Displays the contents of memory as short (32-bit) floating-point numbers.

Syntax

DS [*range*]

where:

range specifies the starting and ending addresses or the starting address and length
of the area of memory to be displayed.

Description

The Display Short Reals (DS) command displays the contents of a specified range of memory addresses 4 bytes at a time, as hexadecimal values and their decimal equivalents. The hexadecimal values are formatted as 32-bit floating-point numbers. The decimal values have the form

+¦–0.*decimaldigits*E+¦–*mantissa*

The sign of the number (+ or –) is followed by a zero, a decimal point, and a maximum of 16 *decimaldigits* (only the first 7 digits are significant); this, in turn, is followed by the designator of the mantissa (E) and the mantissa's sign (+ or –) and digits.

The *range* parameter specifies the starting and ending addresses of the area of memory to be displayed or the starting address followed by the length of the area, expressed by an L and a hexadecimal number of 4-byte values. When *range* does not include a segment, SYMDEB uses DS.

If a Display command has not previously been used and *range* is omitted from a DS command, the display starts at the address specified in the target program's CS:IP registers. If a Display command has previously been used and *range* is omitted from a DS command, the display starts at the memory address following the last address displayed by the most recent Display command. When a range is not explicit in a DS command, one 32-bit floating-point number is displayed.

Each line of the display is formatted as a segment and offset, followed by the contents of 4 bytes of memory represented as a hexadecimal value, followed by its decimal floating-point equivalent.

See also PROGRAMMING UTILITIES: SYMDEB:ES.

Examples

Assume that the memory beginning at location 43E8:0100H contains the value $6.02*10^{+23}$ (Avogadro's number) as a 32-bit floating-point number. The command

```
-DS 43E8:100  <Enter>
```

produces the following output:

```
43E8:0100  F9 F4 FE 66  +0.6020000172718952E+24
```

To view the next 4 bytes of memory in the same format, type

```
-D  <Enter>
```

SYMDEB: DT

Display 10-Byte Reals

Purpose

Displays the contents of memory as 10-byte (80-bit) floating-point numbers.

Syntax

DT [*range*]

where:

range   specifies the starting and ending addresses or the starting address and length of the area of memory to be displayed.

Description

The Display 10-Byte Reals (DT) command displays the contents of a specified range of memory addresses 10 bytes at a time, as hexadecimal values and their decimal equivalents. The hexadecimal values are formatted as 80-bit floating-point numbers. (This format is ordinarily used by the Intel 8087 math coprocessor only for intermediate results during chained floating-point calculations.) The decimal value has the form

+¦−0.*decimaldigits*E+¦−*mantissa*

The sign of the number (+ or −) is followed by a zero, a decimal point, and a maximum of 16 *decimaldigits*; this, in turn, is followed by the designator of the mantissa (E) and the mantissa's sign (+ or −) and digits.

The *range* parameter specifies the starting and ending addresses of the area of memory to be displayed or the starting address followed by the length of the area, expressed by an L and a hexadecimal number of 10-byte values. When *range* does not include a segment, SYMDEB uses DS.

If a Display command has not previously been used and *range* is omitted from a DT command, the display starts at the address specified in the target program's CS:IP registers. If a Display command has previously been used and *range* is omitted from a DT command, the display starts at the memory address following the last address displayed by the most recent Display command. When a range is not explicit in a DT command, one 10-byte floating-point number is displayed.

Each line of the display is formatted as a segment and offset, followed by the contents of 10 bytes of memory represented as a hexadecimal value, followed by its decimal floating-point equivalent.

See also PROGRAMMING UTILITIES: SYMDEB:ET.

Examples

Assume that the memory beginning at location DS:0100H contains the value $2.99*10^{+10}$ (the speed of light in centimeters per second) as an 80-bit floating-point number. The command

```
-DT 100  <Enter>
```

produces the following output:

```
43E8:0100  00 00 00 00 60 B9 C5 DE 21 40  +0.299E+11
```

To view the next 10 bytes of memory in the same format, type

```
-D  <Enter>
```

SYMDEB: DW
Display Words

Purpose

Displays the contents of memory as 2-byte (16-bit) words.

Syntax

DW [*range*]

where:

range   specifies the starting and ending addresses or the starting address and length of the area of memory to be displayed.

Description

The Display Word (DW) command displays the contents of a specified range of memory addresses 2 bytes at a time, as 16-bit hexadecimal integers.

The *range* parameter specifies the starting and ending addresses of the area of memory to be displayed or the starting address followed by the length of the area, expressed by an L and a hexadecimal number of words of memory to be displayed. When *range* does not include a segment, SYMDEB uses DS.

If a Display command has not previously been used and *range* is omitted from a DW command, the display starts at the address specified in the target program's CS:IP registers. If a Display command has previously been used and *range* is omitted from a DW command, the display starts at the memory address following the last address displayed by the most recent Display command. When a range is not explicit in a DW command, 64 words are displayed.

Each line of the display is formatted as a segment and offset, followed by the contents of 16 bytes of memory represented as eight 4-digit hexadecimal numbers. The 2 bytes that make up each word are displayed in reverse order from their actual storage in memory. That is, the first byte in a 2-byte word is displayed after the second byte.

See also PROGRAMMING UTILITIES: SYMDEB:EW.

Examples

To display the contents of the 64 words of memory beginning at DS:0080H in word format, type

```
-DW 80  <Enter>
```

This produces the following output:

```
1FEE:0080   6977  646E  776F  5C73  696C  0062  494C  3D42
1FEE:0090   3A63  6D5C  6373  6C5C  6269  633B  5C3A  6977
1FEE:00A0   646E  776F  5C73  696C  0062  4D54  3D50  3A63
1FEE:00B0   745C  6D65  0070  4554  504D  633D  5C3A  6574
1FEE:00C0   706D  4400  4149  3D4C  3A63  645C  6169  006C
1FEE:00D0   4350  3346  3D32  3A63  665C  726F  6874  705C
1FEE:00E0   3363  0032  4350  3350  3D32  3A63  665C  726F
1FEE:00F0   6874  705C  756C  3373  0032  5255  3146  3D30
```

To view the next 64 words of memory in the same format, type

```
-D   <Enter>
```

SYMDEB displays the contents of memory addresses 1FEE:0100H through 1FEE:017FH.

SYMDEB: E

Enter Data

Purpose

Enters data into memory.

Syntax

E *address* [*list*]

where:

address   is the first memory location for storage.
list   is the data to be placed into successive bytes of memory, starting at *address*.

Description

The Enter Data (E) command enters into memory one or more data items, using the same format as the most recent Enter command (EA, EB, ED, EL, ES, ET, or EW). If no Enter command has previously been used, the data can be entered as either hexadecimal values or ASCII strings (the EA or EB format). Any data previously stored at the specified locations is lost. If SYMDEB displays an error message, no changes are made.

The *address* parameter specifies the first byte to be modified. If *address* does not include a segment, SYMDEB uses DS. SYMDEB increments the address for each byte of data stored.

The *list* parameter must meet the requirements of the last Enter command used. All SYMDEB Enter commands are described in alphabetic order on the following pages. If *list* is included in the command line, the changes are made unless an error is detected in the command line. If *list* is omitted from the command line, the current contents of *address* are displayed, followed by a period (.), and the user is prompted for new data. If no value is entered and the Enter key is pressed, the original value remains unchanged and the Enter command is terminated.

Examples

The following two examples assume that no previous Enter commands have been used or that the most recent Enter command was EA or EB.

To store the byte values 00H, 0DH, and 0AH into the 3 bytes beginning at DS:1FB3H, type

```
-E 1FB3 00 0D 0A  <Enter>
```

If the command

```
-E 2C3 ABC   <Enter>
```

is entered and the last Enter command used was EA or EB, the value BCH is stored at DS:2C3H, and the leading 'A' character on the hexadecimal number 'ABC' is ignored.

SYMDEB: EA

Enter ASCII String

Purpose

Enters an ASCII string or hexadecimal byte values into memory.

Syntax

EA *address* [*list*]

where:

address   is the first memory location for storage.
list   is one or more ASCII strings or hexadecimal byte values.

Description

The Enter ASCII String (EA) command enters data into successive memory bytes. The data can be entered as either hexadecimal byte values or ASCII strings. Any data previously stored at the specified locations is lost. If SYMDEB displays an error message, no changes are made. The EA command functions exactly like the Enter Bytes (EB) command.

The *address* parameter specifies the first byte to be modified. If *address* does not include a segment, SYMDEB uses DS. SYMDEB increments the address for each byte of data stored.

The *list* parameter is one or more ASCII strings and/or hexadecimal byte values, separated by spaces, commas, or tab characters. Extra or trailing characters are ignored. Strings must be enclosed within single or double quotation marks, and case is significant within a string.

If *list* is included in the command line, the changes are made unless an error is detected in the command line. If *list* is omitted from the command line, the user is prompted byte by byte for new data, starting at *address*. The current contents of a byte are displayed, followed by a period. A new value for that byte can be entered as one or two hexadecimal digits (extra characters are ignored), or the contents can be left unchanged. To display the next byte, the user presses the spacebar. If the user enters a minus sign, or hyphen character (-), instead of pressing the spacebar, SYMDEB backs up to the previous byte. A maximum of 8 bytes can be entered on each input line; a new line is begun each time an 8-byte boundary is crossed. Data entry is terminated by pressing the Enter key without pressing the spacebar or entering any data.

Text strings can be used only as part of the *list* parameter in an EA command line; they cannot be entered in response to an address prompt.

Example

To store the string *MAIN MENU* into memory beginning at address ES:0C14H, type

```
-EA ES:C14 "MAIN MENU"  <Enter>
```

SYMDEB: EB

Enter Bytes

Purpose

Enters hexadecimal byte values or ASCII strings into memory.

Syntax

EB *address* [*list*]

where:

address   is the first memory location for storage.
list   is one or more hexadecimal byte values or ASCII strings.

Description

The Enter Bytes (EB) command enters data into successive memory bytes. The data can be entered as either hexadecimal byte values or ASCII strings. Any data previously stored at the specified locations is lost. If SYMDEB displays an error message, no changes are made. The EB command functions exactly like the Enter ASCII String (EA) command.

The *address* parameter specifies the first byte to be modified. If *address* does not include a segment, SYMDEB uses DS. SYMDEB increments the address for each byte of data stored.

The *list* parameter is one or more hexadecimal byte values and/or ASCII strings, separated by spaces, commas, or tab characters. Extra or trailing characters are ignored. Strings must be enclosed within single or double quotation marks, and case is significant within a string.

If *list* is included in the command line, the changes are made unless an error is detected in the command line. If *list* is omitted from the command line, the user is prompted byte by byte for new data, starting at *address*. The current contents of a byte are displayed, followed by a period. A new value for the byte can be entered as one or two hexadecimal digits (extra characters are ignored), or the contents can be left unchanged. To display the next byte, the user presses the spacebar. If the user enters a minus sign, or hyphen character (-), instead of pressing the spacebar, SYMDEB backs up to the previous byte. A maximum of 8 bytes can be entered on each input line; a new line is begun each time an 8-byte boundary is crossed. Data entry is terminated by pressing the Enter key without pressing the spacebar or entering any data.

Text strings can be used only as part of the *list* parameter in an EB command line; they cannot be entered in response to an address prompt.

Examples

To store the byte values 00H, 0DH, and 0AH into the 3 bytes beginning at DS:1FB3H, type

```
-EB 1FB3 00 0D 0A   <Enter>
```

To store the string *MAIN MENU* into memory beginning at address ES:0C14H, type

```
-EB ES:C14 "MAIN MENU"   <Enter>
```

SYMDEB: ED

Enter Doublewords

Purpose

Enters hexadecimal doubleword values into memory.

Syntax

ED *address*[*value*]

where:

address   is the first memory location for storage.
value   is a doubleword (32-bit) hexadecimal value.

Description

The Enter Doublewords (ED) command enters into memory 32-bit hexadecimal double-word values in the form of FAR memory pointers (offset followed by segments in reverse byte order). Any data previously stored at the specified locations is lost. If SYMDEB displays an error message, no changes are made.

The *address* parameter specifies the first memory location to be modified. If *address* does not include a segment, SYMDEB uses DS.

The *value* parameter is one doubleword value, entered as two 16-bit hexadecimal words separated by a colon character (:). Each value is entered in the form segment:offset. The offset portion is stored at *address*, and the segment portion is stored at *address+2*, both in reverse byte order. For example, a value of AABB:CCDDH would be stored in memory as DDH, CCH, BBH, and AAH, starting at *address*. Multiple values cannot be used in an ED command line; SYMDEB ignores any values after the first value.

If *value* is omitted from the command line, SYMDEB prompts the user for new data, starting at *address*. The current contents of the location are displayed, followed by a period. The user can then enter a new doubleword value and press the Enter key or leave the contents unchanged by pressing the Enter key alone, which also terminates the ED command. If a new value is entered, SYMDEB increments *address* and displays the next doubleword value.

Example

To store the doubleword value F000:1392H at the address DS:0200H, type

```
-ED 200 F000:1392  <Enter>
```

SYMDEB: EL

Enter Long Reals

Purpose

Enters 64-bit floating-point numbers into memory.

Syntax

EL *address*[*value*]

where:

address   is the first memory location for storage.
value   is a 64-bit floating-point decimal number.

Description

The Enter Long Reals (EL) command enters into memory 64-bit floating-point numbers in decimal format. Any data previously stored at the specified memory locations is lost. If SYMDEB displays an error message, no changes are made.

The *address* parameter specifies the first byte to be modified. If *address* does not include a segment, SYMDEB uses DS.

The *value* parameter is a floating-point number entered in decimal radix, with or without a decimal point and/or exponent. Multiple values cannot be used in an EL command line; SYMDEB ignores any values after the first value.

The 64-bit floating-point decimal value must be entered in the form

[+¦−]*decimaldigits*[E[+¦−]*mantissa*]

where:

+¦−   is the sign of the long floating-point value or the mantissa.
decimaldigits is a decimal number. A maximum of 16 digits is allowed, including digits before and after a decimal point.
E   denotes the beginning of the mantissa.
mantissa   is the decimal mantissa value.

If *value* is omitted from the command line, SYMDEB prompts the user for new data, starting at *address*. The current contents of the location are displayed. The user can enter a new value and press the Enter key or leave the contents unchanged by pressing the Enter key alone, which also terminates the EL command. If a new value is entered and the Enter key is pressed, SYMDEB increments *address* and displays the next long real number.

Example

To store an approximation of the value *pi* (π) in the form of a 64-bit floating-point number at address DS:0020H, type

```
-EL 20 +0.3141592653589793E+1  <Enter>
```

or

```
-EL 20 3.141592653589793  <Enter>
```

SYMDEB: ES

Enter Short Reals

Purpose

Enters 32-bit floating-point numbers into memory.

Syntax

ES *address* [*value*]

where:

address   is the first memory location for storage.
value   is a 32-bit floating-point decimal number.

Description

The Enter Short Reals (ES) command enters into memory 32-bit floating-point numbers in decimal format. Any data previously stored at the specified locations is lost. If SYMDEB displays an error message, no changes are made.

The *address* parameter specifies the first byte to be modified. If *address* does not include a segment, SYMDEB uses DS.

The *value* parameter is a floating-point number entered in decimal radix, with or without a decimal point and/or exponent. Multiple values cannot be used in an ES command line; SYMDEB ignores any values after the first value.

The 32-bit floating-point decimal value must be entered in the form

[+¦−]*decimaldigits*[E[+¦−]*mantissa*]

where:

+¦−   is the sign of the short floating-point value or the mantissa.
decimaldigits is a decimal number. A maximum of 16 digits is allowed, including digits before and after a decimal point.
E   denotes the beginning of the mantissa.
mantissa   is the decimal mantissa value.

Note: For short floating-point values, the last nine *decimaldigits* are not significant. This can be demonstrated by using the Display Short Reals (DS) command to check the new value in memory.

If *value* is omitted from the command line, SYMDEB prompts the user for new data, starting at *address*. The current contents of the location are displayed. The user can then enter a new value and press the Enter key or leave the contents unchanged by pressing the

Enter key alone, which also terminates the ES command. If a new value is entered and the Enter key is pressed, SYMDEB increments *address* and displays the next short floating-point number.

Example

To store an approximation of the value *pi* (π) in the form of a 32-bit floating-point number at address DS:0020H, type

```
-ES 20 +0.31415927E+1   <Enter>
```

or

```
-ES 20 3.1415927   <Enter>
```

SYMDEB: ET

Enter 10-Byte Reals

Purpose

Enters 10-byte (80-bit) floating-point numbers into memory.

Syntax

ET *address* [*value*]

where:

address   is the first memory location for storage.
value   is an 80-bit floating-point decimal number.

Description

The Enter 10-Byte Reals (ET) command enters into memory 10-byte (80-bit) floating-point numbers in decimal format. Any data previously stored at the specified locations is lost. If SYMDEB displays an error message, no changes are made. (This 10-byte format is ordinarily used by the Intel 8087 math coprocessor only for intermediate results during chained floating-point calculations.)

The *address* parameter specifies the first memory location to be modified. If *address* does not include a segment, SYMDEB uses DS.

The *value* parameter is a floating-point number entered in decimal radix, with or without a decimal point and/or exponent. Multiple values cannot be used in an ET command line; SYMDEB ignores any values after the first value.

The 10-byte floating-point decimal value must be entered in the form

[+¦–]*decimaldigits*[E[+¦–]*mantissa*]

where:

+¦–   is the sign of the 10-byte floating-point value or the mantissa.
decimaldigits   is a decimal number. A maximum of 16 digits is allowed, including digits before and after a decimal point.
E   denotes the beginning of the mantissa.
mantissa   is the decimal mantissa value.

If *value* is omitted from the command, SYMDEB prompts the user for new data, starting at *address*. The current contents are displayed. The user can enter a new value and press the Enter key or leave the contents unchanged by pressing the Enter key alone, which also terminates the ET command. If a new value is entered and the Enter key is pressed, SYMDEB increments *address* and displays the next 10-byte floating-point number.

Example

To store an approximation of the value *pi* (π) in the form of an 80-bit floating-point number at address DS:0020H, type

```
-ET 20 +0.3141592635897932384E+1   <Enter>
```

or

```
-ET 20 3.1415926535897932384   <Enter>
```

SYMDEB: EW

Enter Words

Purpose

Enters word values into memory.

Syntax

EW *address* [*value*]

where:

address   is the first memory location for storage.
value   is a word (16-bit) hexadecimal value.

Description

The Enter Words (EW) command enters into memory 16-bit hexadecimal word values. Any data previously stored at the specified locations is lost. If SYMDEB displays an error message, no changes are made.

The *address* parameter specifies the first memory location to be modified. If *address* does not include a segment, SYMDEB uses DS.

The *value* parameter is one word value in the range 0 through FFFFH. The value is stored in reverse byte order. For example, a value of AABBH would be stored in memory as BBH and AAH, starting at *address*. Multiple values cannot be used in an EW command line; SYMDEB ignores any values after the first value.

If *value* is omitted from the command line, SYMDEB prompts the user word by word for new data, starting at *address*. The current contents are displayed, followed by a period. The user can enter a new word value as one to four hexadecimal digits and press the Enter key or leave the contents unchanged by pressing the Enter key alone, which also terminates the EW command. If a new value is entered, SYMDEB increments *address* and displays the next word value.

Example

To store the word value 1355H at the address DS:1C00H, type

```
-EW 1C00 1355 <Enter>
```

SYMDEB: F

Fill Memory

Purpose

Stores a repetitive data pattern into an area of memory.

Syntax

F *range list*

where:

range specifies the starting and ending addresses or the starting address and length of memory to be filled.

list is the data to be used to fill memory.

Description

The Fill Memory (F) command fills an area of memory with the data from a list. The data can be entered in either hexadecimal or ASCII format. Any data previously stored at the specified locations is lost. If SYMDEB displays an error message, no changes are made.

The *range* parameter specifies the starting and ending addresses or the starting address and hexadecimal length in bytes of the area of memory to be filled. If *range* does not include an explicit segment, SYMDEB uses DS.

The *list* parameter is one or more hexadecimal byte values and/or strings, separated by spaces, commas, or tab characters. Strings must be enclosed in single or double quotation marks, and case is significant within a string.

If the area to be filled is larger than the data list, the list is repeated as often as necessary to fill the area. If the data list is longer than the area of memory to be filled, the list is truncated to fit.

Examples

To fill the area of memory from DS:0B10H through DS:0B4FH with the value 0E8H, type

```
-F B10 B4F E8   <Enter>
```

or

```
-F B10 L40 E8   <Enter>
```

To fill the 16 bytes of memory beginning at address CS:1FA0H by replicating the 2-byte sequence 0DH 0AH, type

```
-F CS:1FA0 1FAF 0D 0A   <Enter>
```

or

```
-F CS:1FA0 L10 0D 0A   <Enter>
```

To fill the area of memory from ES:0B00H through ES:0BFFH by replicating the text string *BUFFER*, type

```
-F ES:B00 BFF "BUFFER"   <Enter>
```

or

```
-F ES:B00 L100 "BUFFER"   <Enter>
```

SYMDEB: G

Go

Purpose

Transfers execution control from SYMDEB to the target program being debugged.

Syntax

G[=*address*] [*break0* [... *break9*]]

where:

address	is the location at which to begin execution.
break0 ... break9	specify from 1 to 10 breakpoints.

Description

The Go (G) command transfers control from SYMDEB to the target program. If no breakpoints are set, the program will execute until it crashes or until it reaches a normal termination, in which case the message *Program terminated normally* is displayed and control returns to SYMDEB. (After this message has been displayed, it may be necessary to reload the program before it can be executed again.)

The *address* parameter can be any location in memory. If no segment is specified, SYMDEB uses the target program's CS register. If *address* is omitted, SYMDEB transfers to the current address in the target program's CS:IP registers. An equal sign (=) must precede *address* to distinguish it from the breakpoints *break0 ... break9*.

The parameters *break0 ... break9* specify from 1 to 10 breakpoints that can be set as part of the G command. Breakpoints can be placed in any order, because execution stops at the first breakpoint address encountered, regardless of the position of that breakpoint in the list. Each of the breakpoint addresses must contain the first byte of an 8086 opcode. SYMDEB installs breakpoints by replacing the first byte of the machine instruction at each breakpoint address with an Interrupt 03H instruction (opcode 0CCH). If the program encounters a breakpoint, program execution is suspended and control returns to SYMDEB. SYMDEB then restores the original machine code in the breakpoint locations, displays the contents of the current registers and flags and the instruction pointed to by CS:IP, and issues the standard SYMDEB prompt. If the target program executes to completion and terminates without encountering any of the breakpoints or is halted by some means other than a breakpoint, the Interrupt 03H instructions are not replaced with the original machine code and the Load File or Sectors (L) command must be used to reload the original program.

The G command requires that the target program's SS:SP registers point to a valid stack that has at least 6 bytes of stack space available. When the G command is executed, it pushes the target program's flags and CS and IP registers onto the stack and then transfers control to the program with an IRET instruction. Thus, if the target program's stack is not valid or is too small, the system may crash.

The G command also recognizes any sticky breakpoints set with the Set Breakpoint (BP) command. These sticky breakpoints are not counted as part of the transient breakpoints specified in the G command line and are not removed after a breakpoint has been encountered.

Examples

To begin execution of the program in SYMDEB's buffer at location CS:110AH, setting breakpoints at CS:12FCH and CS:1303H, type

```
-G =110A 12FC 1303  <Enter>
```

To resume execution of the program following a breakpoint, type

```
-G  <Enter>
```

To begin execution at the label *main,* setting breakpoints at the procedures *fopen()* and *printf()*, type

```
-G =_main _fopen _printf  <Enter>
```

Messages

Program terminated normally
The program being debugged executed successfully without encountering any breakpoints and performed a normal termination with Interrupt 20H, Interrupt 21H Function 00H, or Interrupt 21H Function 4CH. If any breakpoints were set, the original program should be reloaded with the Load File or Sectors (L) command.

Too many breakpoints!
More than 10 breakpoints were specified in a Go (G) command. Enter the command again with 10 or fewer breakpoints.

SYMDEB: H

Perform Hexadecimal Arithmetic

Purpose

Displays the sum and difference of two hexadecimal numbers.

Syntax

H *value1 value2*

where:

value1 and *value2*   are any two hexadecimal numbers in the range 0 through FFFFH.

Description

The Perform Hexadecimal Arithmetic (H) command displays the sum and difference of two 16-bit hexadecimal numbers — that is, the result of the operations *value1+value2* and *value1–value2*. If *value2* is greater than *value1*, SYMDEB displays their difference as a two's complement hexadecimal number. This command is convenient for performing quick calculations of addresses and other values during an interactive debugging session.

Examples

To display the sum and difference of the values 4B03H and 104H, type

```
-H 4B03 104  <Enter>
```

This produces the following display:

```
4C07  49FF
```

If the addition produces an overflow, the four least significant digits are displayed. For example, the command line

```
-H FFFF 2  <Enter>
```

produces the following display:

```
0001 FFFD
```

If *value2* is greater than *value1*, the difference is displayed in two's complement form. For example, the command line

```
-H 1 2  <Enter>
```

produces the following display:

```
0003 FFFF
```

SYMDEB: I

Input from Port

Purpose

Reads and displays 1 byte from an input/output (I/O) port.

Syntax

I *port*

where:

port   is a 16-bit I/O port address in the range 0 through FFFFH.

Description

The Input from Port (I) command performs a read operation on the specified I/O port address and displays the data as a two-digit hexadecimal number.

Warning: This command must be used with caution because it involves direct access to the computer hardware and no error checking is performed. Input operations directed to the ports assigned to some peripheral device controllers may interfere with the proper operation of the system. If no device has been assigned to the specified I/O port or if the port is write-only, the value that will be displayed by an I command is unpredictable.

Example

To read and display the contents of I/O port 10AH, type

```
-I 10A  <Enter>
```

An example of the result of this command is

```
FF
```

SYMDEB: K

Perform Stack Trace

Purpose

Displays the current stack frame.

Syntax

K [*number*]

where:

number   is the number of parameters supplied to the current procedure.

Description

The Perform Stack Trace (K) command displays the contents of the current stack frame. The first line of the display shows the name of the current procedure, parameters to the procedure, and the filename and line number of the call to the procedure. The subsequent lines trace the flow of execution that led to the current procedure.

In cases where SYMDEB cannot determine the number of parameters for a procedure by inspection of the stack frame (for example, if the number of parameters sent to a procedure varies), the *number* option can be used in the command to force the display of one or more parameters.

The K command can be used only on procedures that follow the calling conventions used by Microsoft high-level-language compilers.

Examples

Assume that a breakpoint has been set within the C library *printf()* routine, that the breakpoint has been reached, and that the SYMDEB prompt has reappeared. The command

```
-K  <Enter>
```

produces the following output:

```
_TEXT:_printf(00D4,0000,0000) from .dump.C:108
_TEXT:_dump_para(0000,0000,0FB8) from .dump.C:92
_TEXT:_dump_rec(0FB8,0001,0000,0000) from .dump.C:61
_TEXT:_main(?)
```

In this example, the breakpointed procedure *printf()* was called by the routine *dump_para()* with three parameters. *Dump_para()* was called by *dump_rec()*, which in turn was called by *main()*. Because SYMDEB cannot determine the depth of the stack frame for the routine *main()*, it displays no parameters for it. The display of at least two parameters for every procedure can be forced by the command

```
-K 2  <Enter>
```

which produces the following example display:

```
_TEXT:_printf(00D4,0000,0000) from .dump.C:108
_TEXT:_dump_para(0000,0000,0FB8) from .dump.C:92
_TEXT:_dump_rec(0FB8,0001,0000,0000) from .dump.C:61
_TEXT:_main(0002,1044)
```

From a knowledge of C conventions, it follows that the first parameter for *main()* is *argc*, or the number of tokens in the command line that invoked the program being debugged; the second parameter is the offset within DGROUP of *argv*, or an array of pointers to each token.

SYMDEB: L

Load File or Sectors

Purpose

Loads a file or individual sectors from a disk.

Syntax

L [*address*]

or

L *address drive start number*

where:

address	is the starting address in memory that data read from a disk is placed into.
drive	is the decimal number (0-3) of the disk to read (0 = drive A, 1 = drive B, 2 = drive C, 3= drive D).
start	is the hexadecimal number of the first sector to load (0–FFFFH).
number	is the hexadecimal number of consecutive sectors to load (0–FFFFH).

Description

The Load File or Sectors (L) command loads a file or individual sectors from a disk.

When the L command is entered without parameters or with an address alone, the file specified in the SYMDEB command line or with the most recent Name File or Command-Tail Parameters (N) command is loaded from the disk into memory. If no segment is specified in *address*, SYMDEB uses CS. If the file's extension is .EXE, the file is placed in SYMDEB's target program buffer at the load address specified in the .EXE file's header; if the file's extension is .COM, the file is loaded at offset 100H. (If for some reason an address is entered for a .EXE or .COM file and the address is anything but 100H, an error message is displayed; if the address is 100H, it will be ignored.) If the file has a .HEX extension, the .HEX file's starting address is added to *address* before loading the file. If *address* is not specified, the .HEX file is placed at its own starting address. The length of the file or, in the case of a .EXE file, the actual length of the program (the length of the file minus the header) is placed in the target program's BX and CX registers, with the most significant 16 bits in register BX.

The L command can also be used to bypass the MS-DOS file system and obtain direct access to logical sectors on the disk. The memory address (*address*), disk drive number (*drive*), starting logical sector number (*start*), and number of sectors to read (*number*) must all be specified in the command line.

Note: The L command should not be used to access logical sectors on network drives.

Examples

To load the file specified in the SYMDEB command line or in the most recent N command into SYMDEB's target program buffer, type

```
-L   <Enter>
```

To load eight sectors from drive B, starting at logical sector 0, to memory location CS:0100H in SYMDEB's memory buffer, type

```
-L 100  1  0  8   <Enter>
```

Messages

Disk error reading disk *X*

A hardware-related disk error, such as a checksum error or seek incomplete, was encountered during the execution of an L command.

File not found

The file specified in the most recent N command cannot be found.

SYMDEB: M

Move (Copy) Data

Purpose

Copies the contents of one area of memory to another.

Syntax

M *range address*

where:

range specifies the starting and ending addresses or the starting address and length of the area of memory to be copied.

address is the first byte of the destination of the copy operation.

Description

The Move (Copy) Data (M) command copies data from one location in memory to another without altering the data in the original location. If the source and destination areas overlap, the data is copied in the correct order so that the resulting copy is correct; the data in the original location is changed only when the two areas overlap.

The *range* parameter specifies the starting and ending addresses or the starting address and length of the memory to be copied. The *address* parameter is the first byte in which the copy will be placed. If *range* does not contain an explicit segment, SYMDEB uses DS; if *address* does not contain a segment, SYMDEB uses the same segment used for *range*.

Example

To copy the data in locations DS:0800H through DS:08FFH to locations DS:0900H through DS:09FFH, type

```
-M 800 8FF 900  <Enter>
```

or

```
-M 800 L100 900  <Enter>
```

SYMDEB: N
Name File or Command-Tail Parameters

Purpose

Inserts parameters into the simulated program segment prefix (PSP).

Syntax

N *parameter*[*parameter...*]

where:

parameter   is a filename or switch to be placed into the simulated PSP.

Description

The Name File or Command-Tail Parameters (N) command is used to enter one or more parameters into the simulated PSP that is built at the base of the buffer holding the program to be debugged. The N command can also be used before the Load File or Sectors (L) and Write File or Sectors (W) commands to name a file to be read from a disk or written to a disk.

The count of the characters following the N command is placed at DS:0080H in the simulated PSP and the characters themselves are copied into the PSP starting at DS:0081H. The string is terminated by a carriage return (0DH), which is not included in the count. If the second and third parameters follow the naming conventions for MS-DOS files, they are parsed into the default file control blocks (FCBs) in the simulated PSP, at offset 5CH and offset 6CH, respectively. Note that this is different from the N command in DEBUG, which loads the first and second parameters into the default FCBs. (Switches and other filenames specified as parameters are stored in the PSP starting at offset 81H along with the rest of the command line but are not parsed into the default FCBs.)

If the N command line contains only one filename, any parameters placed in the default FCBs by a previous N command are destroyed. If the drive included with the second filename parameter is invalid, the AL register is set to 0FFH. If the drive included with the third filename parameter is invalid, the AH register is set to 0FFH. The existence of a file specified with the N command is not verified until it is loaded with the L command.

The filename at DS:0081H specifies the file that is read or written by a subsequent L or W command.

Example

Assume that SYMDEB was started without specifying the name of a target program in the command line. To load the program CLEAN.COM for execution under the control of

SYMDEB and include the parameter MYFILE.DAT in the simulated PSP's command tail and FCB, use the N and L commands together as follows:

```
-N CLEAN.COM  MYFILE.DAT  <Enter>
-L  <Enter>
```

To execute the program CLEAN.COM, type

```
-G  <Enter>
```

The net effect is the same as if the CLEAN.COM program had been run from the MS-DOS command level with the command line

```
C>CLEAN MYFILE.DAT  <Enter>
```

except that the program is executing under the control of SYMDEB and within SYMDEB's memory buffer.

SYMDEB: O

Output to Port

Purpose

Writes 1 byte to an input/output (I/O) port.

Syntax

O *port byte*

where:

port   is a 16-bit I/O port address in the range 0 through FFFFH.
byte   is a value to be written to the I/O port (0–0FFH).

Description

The Output to Port (O) command writes 1 byte of data to the specified I/O port address. The data value must be in the range 00H through 0FFH.

Warning: This command must be used with caution because it involves direct access to the computer hardware and no error checking is performed. Attempts to write to some port addresses, such as those for ports connected to peripheral device controllers, timers, or the system's interrupt controller, may cause the system to crash or may even result in damage to data stored on disk.

Example

To write the value C8H to I/O port 10AH, type

```
─O 10A C8  <Enter>
```

SYMDEB: P

Proceed Through Loop or Subroutine

Purpose

Executes a loop, string instruction, software interrupt, or subroutine to completion.

Syntax

P[=*address*] [*number*]

where:

address   is the location of the first instruction to be executed.
number   is the number of instructions to execute.

Description

The Proceed Through Loop or Subroutine (P) command transfers control to the target program. The program executes without interruption until the loop, repeated string instruction, software interrupt, or subroutine call at *address* is completed or until the specified number of machine instructions have been executed. Control then returns to SYMDEB and the current contents of the target program's registers and flags are displayed.

Warning: The P command should not be used to execute any instruction that changes the contents of the Intel 8259 interrupt mask (ports 20H and 21H on the IBM PC and compatibles) and cannot be used to trace through ROM. Use the Go (G) command instead.

If the *address* parameter does not contain a segment, SYMDEB uses the target program's CS register; if *address* is omitted, execution begins at the current address specified by the target's CS:IP registers. The *address* parameter must be preceded by an equal sign (=) to distinguish it from *number*.

The *number* parameter specifies the number of instructions to be executed before control returns to SYMDEB. If *number* is omitted, one instruction is executed.

When the Enable Source Display Mode (S+) command is selected, the P command operates directly on source-code lines, passing over function or procedure calls. (The S+ command can be used only with programs created by high-level-language compilers that insert line-number information into object modules.)

When source display mode is disabled with the S– command or when the program being debugged does not have a .SYM file or has been created with the Microsoft Macro Assembler (MASM) or with a compiler that does not support line numbers in relocatable object modules, the P command behaves like the Trace Program Execution (T) command except that when P encounters a loop, repeated string instruction, software interrupt, or subroutine call, it executes it to completion and then returns to the instruction following the call. For example, if the user wants to trace the first three instructions in a program and if the second instruction is a subroutine call, a P3 command executes the first instruction, goes to the second instruction, identifies it as a CALL instruction, jumps to the subroutine and executes the entire subroutine, comes back and executes the third instruction, and then stops. A T3 command, on the other hand, executes the first instruction, executes the second, executes the first instruction of the subroutine as its third instruction, and then stops. If the instruction at *address* is not a loop, repeated string instruction, software interrupt, or subroutine call, the P command functions just like the T command. After each instruction is executed, SYMDEB displays the current contents of the target program's registers and flags and the next instruction to be executed.

Examples

Assume that the program being debugged was compiled with Microsoft C, a .SYM file was loaded with the executable program to provide line-number information, and source-code display has been enabled with the S+ command. To execute the machine instructions corresponding to the next four lines of source code, type

```
-P 4  <Enter>
```

Assume that the target program was created with MASM and location CS:143FH contains a CALL instruction. To execute the subroutine that is the destination of CALL at full speed and then return control to SYMDEB, type

```
-P =143F  <Enter>
```

SYMDEB: Q

Quit

Purpose

Ends a SYMDEB session.

Syntax

Q

Description

The Quit (Q) command terminates the SYMDEB program and returns control to MS-DOS or the command shell that invoked SYMDEB. Any changes made to a program or other file that were not previously saved to disk with the Write File or Sectors (W) command are lost when the Q command is used.

Example

To exit SYMDEB, type

```
-Q   <Enter>
```

SYMDEB: R

Display or Modify Registers

Purpose

Displays one or all registers and allows a register to be modified.

Syntax

R

or

R *register*[[=] *value*]

where:

register   is the two-character name of an Intel 8086/8088 register from the following list:

```
AX BX CX DX SP BP SI DI
DS ES SS CS IP PC
```

or the character F, to indicate the CPU flags.

=   is an optional equal sign preceding *value*.

value   is a 16-bit integer (0–FFFFH) that will be assigned to the specified register.

Description

The Display or Modify Registers (R) command allows the target program's register contents and CPU flags to be displayed and modified.

If R is entered without a *register* parameter, the current contents of all registers and CPU flags are displayed, followed by a disassembly of the machine instruction currently pointed to by the target program's CS:IP registers.

A register can be assigned a new value in a single command by entering both *register* and *value* parameters, optionally separated by an equal sign (=). If a register is named but no value is supplied, SYMDEB displays the current contents of the specified register and then prompts with a colon character (:) for a new value to be placed in the register. The user can enter the value in any valid radix or as an expression and then press the Enter key. If no radix is appended to the new value, hexadecimal is assumed. If the user presses the Enter key alone in response to the prompt, no changes are made to the register contents.

Note: The PC register name is not supported properly in some versions of SYMDEB, so the IP register name should always be used instead.

Flag Name	Value If Set (1)	Value If Clear (0)
Overflow	OV (Overflow)	NV (No Overflow)
Direction	DN (Down)	UP (Up)
Interrupt	EI (Enabled)	DI (Disabled)
Sign	NG (Minus)	PL (Plus)
Zero	ZR (Zero)	NZ (Not Zero)
Aux Carry	AC (Aux Carry)	NA (No Aux Carry)
Parity	PE (Even)	PO (Odd)
Carry	CY (Carry)	NC (No Carry)

After displaying the current flag values, SYMDEB again displays its prompt (-). Any or all of the individual flags can then be altered by typing one or more two-character flag codes (in any order and optionally separated by spaces) from the list above and then pressing the Enter key. If the user responds to the prompt by pressing the Enter key without entering any codes, no changes are made to the status of the flags.

Examples

To display the current contents of the target program's CPU registers and flags, followed by the disassembled mnemonic for the next instruction to be executed (pointed to by CS:IP), type

```
-R  <Enter>
```

This produces the following display:

```
AX=0000  BX=0000  CX=00A1  DX=0000  SP=FFFE  BP=0000 SI=0000  DI=0000
DS=19A5  ES=19A5  SS=19A5  CS=19A5  IP=0100   NV UP EI PL NZ NA PO NC
19A5:0100 BF8000        MOV   DI,0080
```

If the source display mode is enabled, the R command displays the following:

```
AX=0000  BX=1044  CX=0000  DX=0102  SP=103C  BP=0000  SI=00EA  DI=115E
DS=2143  ES=2143  SS=2143  CS=1F6E  IP=0010   NV UP EI PL ZR NA PE NC
32:    int   argc;
_TEXT:_main:
1F6E:0010 55            PUSH    BP                              ;BR0
```

This format includes the source code that corresponds to the next instruction to be executed.

To set the contents of register AX to FFFFH without displaying its current value, type

```
-R AX=FFFF  <Enter>
```

or

```
-R AX -1  <Enter>
```

To display the current value of the target program's BX register, type

```
-R BX   <Enter>
```

If BX contains 200H, for example, SYMDEB displays that value and then issues a prompt in the form of a colon:

```
BX 0200
:
```

The contents of BX can then be altered by typing a new value and pressing the Enter key, or the contents can be left unchanged by pressing the Enter key alone.

To set the direction and carry flags, first type

```
-R F   <Enter>
```

SYMDEB displays the current flag values, followed by a prompt in the form of a hyphen character (-). For example:

```
NV UP EI PL NZ NA PO NC   -
```

The direction and carry flags can then be set by entering

```
-DN CY   <Enter>
```

on the same line as the prompt.

Messages

Bad Flag!
An invalid code for a CPU flag was entered.

Bad Register!
An invalid register name was entered.

Double Flag!
Two values for the same CPU flag were entered in the same command.

SYMDEB: S

Search Memory

Purpose

Searches memory for a pattern of one or more bytes.

Syntax

S *range list*

where:

range   is the starting and ending address or the starting address and length in bytes of the area to be searched.

list   is one or more byte values or a string to be searched for.

Description

The Search Memory (S) command searches a designated range of memory for a sequence of byte values or text strings and displays the starting address of each set of matching bytes. The contents of the searched area are not altered.

The *range* parameter specifies the starting and ending address or the starting address and length in bytes of the area to be searched. If a segment is not included in *range*, SYMDEB uses DS. If a segment is specified only for the starting address, SYMDEB uses the same segment for the ending address. If a starting address and length in bytes are specified, the starting address plus the length less 1 cannot exceed FFFFH.

The *list* parameter is one or more hexadecimal byte values and/or strings separated by spaces, commas, or tab characters. Strings must be enclosed in single or double quotation marks, and case is significant within a string.

Examples

To search for the string *Copyright* in the area of memory from DS:0000H through DS:1FFFH, type

```
-S 0 1FFF 'Copyright'  <Enter>
```

or

```
-S 0 L2000 "Copyright"  <Enter>
```

If a match is found, SYMDEB displays the address of each occurrence:

```
20A8:0910
20A8:094F
20A8:097C
```

To search for the byte sequence *3BH 06H* in the area of memory from CS:0100H through CS:12A0H, type

```
-S CS:100 12A0 3B 06   <Enter>
```

or

```
-S CS:100 L11A1 3B 06   <Enter>
```

SYMDEB: S+

Enable Source Display Mode

Purpose

Displays source-code lines, rather than machine instructions.

Syntax

S+

Description

The Enable Source Display Mode (S+) command affects the display format of certain SYMDEB commands: Proceed Through Loop or Subroutine (P), Trace Program Execution (T), and Display or Modify Registers (R). The S+ command causes source code, rather than disassembled machine instructions, to be displayed by those commands.

The S+ command is useful only if the program being debugged was created with a high-level-language compiler capable of placing line-number information into the relocatable object modules processed by the Microsoft Object Linker (LINK). When debugging Microsoft Macro Assembler (MASM) programs or programs generated by language compilers that do not pass line-number information to LINK, the S+ command has no effect.

Example

To enable the display of source-code statements during debugging, type

```
-S+  <Enter>
```

SYMDEB: S–

Disable Source Display Mode

Purpose

Displays disassembled machine instructions, rather than source-code lines.

Syntax

S–

Description

The Disable Source Display Mode (S–) command affects the display format of certain
SYMDEB commands: Proceed Through Loop or Subroutine (P), Trace Program Execution
(T), and Display or Modify Registers (R). The S– command causes disassembled machine
instructions, rather than source code, to be displayed by those commands. By default,
SYMDEB displays disassembled machine instructions when debugging Microsoft Macro
Assembler (MASM) programs or programs generated by language compilers that do not
pass line-number information to the Microsoft Object Linker (LINK).

Example

To disable the display of source-code statements during debugging, type

```
-S-   <Enter>
```

SYMDEB: S&

Enable Source and Machine Code Display Mode

Purpose

Displays both source-code lines and disassembled machine instructions.

Syntax

S&

Description

The Enable Source and Machine Code Display Mode (S&) command affects the display format of certain SYMDEB commands: Proceed Through Loop or Subroutine (P), Trace Program Execution (T), and Display or Modify Registers (R). The S& command causes both the disassembled machine instructions and the corresponding source-code lines to be displayed by those commands.

The S& command is useful only if the program being debugged was created with a high-level-language compiler capable of placing line-number information into the relocatable object modules processed by the Microsoft Object Linker (LINK). When debugging Microsoft Macro Assembler (MASM) programs or programs generated by language compilers that do not pass line-number information to LINK, the S& command has no effect.

Example

To enable the display of both source-code statements and disassembled machine-code statements during debugging, type

```
_S&  <Enter>
```

SYMDEB: T

Trace Program Execution

Purpose

Executes one or more machine instructions in single-step mode.

Syntax

T[=*address*] [*number*]

where:

address   is the location of the first instruction to be executed.
number   is the number of machine instructions to be executed.

Description

The Trace Program Execution (T) command executes one or more machine instructions, starting at the specified address. If source display mode has been enabled with the S+ command, each trace operation executes the machine code corresponding to one source statement and displays the lines from the source code. If source display mode has been disabled with the S− command, each trace operation executes an individual machine instruction and displays the contents of the CPU registers and flags after execution.

Warning: The T command should not be used to execute any instruction that changes the contents of the Intel 8259 interrupt mask (ports 20H and 21H on the IBM PC and compatibles). Use the Go (G) command instead.

The *address* parameter points to the first instruction to be executed. If *address* does not include a segment, SYMDEB uses the target program's CS register; if *address* is omitted entirely, execution is begun at the current address specified by the target program's CS:IP registers. The *address* parameter must be preceded by an equal sign (=) to distinguish it from *number*.

The *number* parameter specifies the hexadecimal number of source-code statements or machine instructions to be executed before the SYMDEB prompt is displayed again (default = 1). If source display mode is enabled, the *number* parameter is required. Execution of a sequence of instructions using the T command can be interrupted at any time by pressing Ctrl-C or Ctrl-Break and can be paused by pressing Ctrl-S (pressing any key resumes the trace).

Examples

To execute one instruction at location CS:1A00H and then return control to SYMDEB, displaying the contents of the CPU registers and flags, type

```
-T =1A00   <Enter>
```

Consecutive instructions can then be executed by entering repeated T commands with no parameters.

If source display mode has been enabled with a previous S+ command, to begin execution at the label *main* and continue through the machine code corresponding to four source-code statements, type

```
-T =_main 4   <Enter>
```

SYMDEB: U

Disassemble (Unassemble) Program

Purpose

Disassembles machine instructions into assembly-language mnemonics.

Syntax

U [*range*]

where:

range   specifies the starting and ending addresses or the starting address and the number of instructions of the machine code to be disassembled.

Description

The Disassemble (Unassemble) Program (U) command translates machine instructions into their assembly-language mnemonics.

The *range* parameter specifies the starting and ending addresses or the starting address and number of machine instructions to be disassembled. If *range* does not include an explicit segment, SYMDEB uses CS. Note that the resulting disassembly will be incorrect if the starting address does not fall on an 8086 instruction boundary.

If *range* does not include the number of machine instructions to be executed or an ending address, eight instructions are disassembled. If *range* is omitted completely, eight instructions are disassembled starting at the address following the last instruction disassembled by the previous U command, if a U command has been used; if no U command has been used, eight instructions are disassembled starting at the address specified by the current value of the target program's CS:IP registers.

The display format for the U command depends on the current source display mode setting and on whether the program was developed with a compatible high-level-language compiler. If the source display mode setting is S− or the program was developed with the Microsoft Macro Assembler (MASM) or a noncompatible high-level-language compiler, the display contains only the address and the disassembled equivalent of each instruction within *range*. (For 8-bit immediate operands, SYMDEB also displays the ASCII equivalent as a comment following a semicolon.) If the setting is S+ or S& and a compatible symbol file containing line-number information was loaded with the program being debugged, the display contains both the source-code lines and their corresponding disassembled machine instructions.

Note: The 80286 instructions that are considered privileged when the microprocessor is running in protected mode are not supported by SYMDEB's disassembler.

Examples

To disassemble four machine instructions starting at CS:0100H, type

```
-U 100 L4  <Enter>
```

This produces the following display:

```
44DC:0100 EC            IN    AL,DX
44DC:0101 B80200        MOV   AX,0002
44DC:0104 E86102        CALL  0368
44DC:0107 57            PUSH  DI
```

Successive eight-instruction fragments of machine code can be disassembled by entering additional U commands without parameters.

When a program is being debugged with a symbol file that contains line-number information and source display mode has been enabled, disassembled machine code is accompanied by the corresponding source code:

```
43:        if (argc != 2)
28A5:0031 837E0402      CMP   Word Ptr [BP+04],+02
28A5:0035 7503          JNZ   _main+2A (003A)
28A5:0037 E91400        JMP   _main+3E (004E)
44:            {  fprintf(stderr,"\ndump: wrong number of parameters\n");
28A5:003A B83600        MOV   AX,0036
28A5:003D 50            PUSH  AX
28A5:003E B8F600        MOV   AX,00F6
28A5:0041 50            PUSH  AX
28A5:0042 E8AC04        CALL  _fprintf
28A5:0045 83C404        ADD   SP,+04
45:        return(1);
28A5:0048 B80100        MOV   AX,0001
28A5:004B E9AA00        JMP   _main+E8 (00F8)
```

SYMDEB: V

View Source Code

Purpose

Displays lines from the source-code file for the program being debugged.

Syntax

V *address* [*length*]

or

V [.*sourcefile*:*linenumber*]

where:

address	is the location of an executable instruction in the target program.
length	is an ending address or the number of source-code lines.
.*sourcefile*	is the base name of the source file of the program being debugged, preceded by a period (.).
linenumber	is the first literal line number of .*sourcefile* to be displayed.

Description

The View Source Code (V) command displays lines of source code for the program being debugged, beginning at the location specified by *address*. If *address* does not include a segment, SYMDEB uses the target program's CS register.

The optional *length* parameter can be an ending address or an L followed by a hexadecimal number of source-code lines. If *length* is not specified, eight lines of source code are displayed.

If the .*sourcefile* parameter is specified, followed by a colon character (:) and a line number, eight lines of source code are displayed, starting at *linenumber*. If the V command is entered without parameters after the .*sourcefile*:*linenumber* parameter has been specified, eight lines are displayed from the current source file, beginning with the line after the last line displayed with the V command. The .*sourcefile* parameter must be the name of a high-level-language source file in the current directory. Pathnames and extensions are not supported. The *length* option cannot be used with the .*sourcefile* parameter.

Warning: Specifying a file that does not exist in the current directory may cause the system to crash.

The V command can be used only with programs created by a high-level-language compiler that is capable of placing line-number information into the relocatable object modules processed by the Microsoft Object Linker (LINK). The current source display mode setting (S−, S+, or S&) has no effect on the V command.

Examples

Assume that the program DUMP.EXE is being debugged with the aid of the symbol file DUMP.SYM and that the source file DUMP.C is available in the current directory. To display eight lines of source code beginning at the label _main, type

```
-V _main  <Enter>
```

This produces the following output:

```
32:         int   argc;
33:         char  *argv[];
34:
35:    {    FILE *dfile;                     /* control block for input file */
36:         int status = 0;                  /* status returned from file read */
37:         int file_rec = 0;                /* file record number being dumped */
38:         long file_ptr = 0L;              /* file byte offset for current rec */
39:         char file_buf[REC_SIZE];         /* data block from file */
```

To view eight lines of source code from the file DUMP.C, beginning with line 20, type

```
-V .DUMP:20  <Enter>
```

Message

Source file for *filename* (cr for none)?

The current directory does not contain the source file specified with the *.sourcefile* parameter. Enter the correct filename or press Enter to indicate no source file.

SYMDEB: W

Write File or Sectors

Purpose

Writes a file or individual sectors to disk.

Syntax

W [*address*]

or

W *address drive start number*

where:

address   is the first location in memory of the data to be written.
drive   is the number of the destination disk drive (0 = drive A, 1 = drive B, 2 = drive C, 3 = drive D).
start   is the number of the first logical sector to be written (0 – FFFFH).
number   is the number of consecutive sectors to be written (0 – FFFFH).

Description

The Write File or Sectors (W) command transfers a file or individual sectors from memory to disk.

When the W command is entered without parameters or with an address alone, the number of bytes specified by the contents of registers BX:CX are written from memory to the file named by the most recent Name File or Command-Tail Parameters (N) command or to the first file specified in the SYMDEB command line if the N command has not been used.

Note: If a Go (G), Proceed Through Loop or Subroutine (P), or Trace Program Execution (T) command was previously used or the contents of the BX or CX registers were changed, BX:CX must be restored before the W command is used.

When *address* is not included in the command line, SYMDEB uses the target program's CS:0100H. Files with a .EXE or .HEX extension cannot be written with the W command.

The W command can also be used to bypass the MS-DOS file system and obtain direct access to logical sectors on the disk. To use the W command in this way, the memory address (*address*), disk unit number (*drive*), starting logical sector number (*start*), and number of sectors to be written (*number*) must all be provided in the command line in hexadecimal format.

Warning: Extreme caution should be used with the W command. The disk's file structure can easily be damaged if the command is entered incorrectly. The W command should not be used to write logical sectors to network drives.

Example

Assume that the interactive Assemble Machine Instructions (A) command was used to create a program in SYMDEB's memory buffer that is 32 (20H) bytes long, beginning at offset 100H. This program can be written into the file QUICK.COM by sequential use of the Name File or Command-Tail Parameters (N), Display or Modify Registers (R), and Write File or Sectors (W) commands. First, use the N command to specify the name of the file to be written:

```
-N QUICK.COM  <Enter>
```

Next, use the R command to set registers BX and CX to the length to be written. Register BX contains the upper half or most significant part of the length; register CX contains the lower half or least significant part. Type

```
-R CX  <Enter>
```

SYMDEB displays the current contents of register CX and issues a colon character (:) prompt . Enter the length after the prompt:

```
:20  <Enter>
```

To use the R command again to set the BX register to zero, type

```
-R BX  <Enter>
```

Then type

```
:0  <Enter>
```

To create the disk file QUICK.COM and write the program into it, type

```
-W  <Enter>
```

SYMDEB responds:

```
Writing 0020 bytes
```

Messages

EXE and HEX files cannot be written
Files with a .EXE or .HEX extension cannot be written to disk with the W command.

Writing *nnnn* bytes
After a successful write operation, SYMDEB displays in hexadecimal format the number of bytes written to disk.

SYMDEB: X

Examine Symbol Map

Purpose

Displays names and addresses in the symbol maps.

Syntax

X[∗]

or

X? [*map*!] [*segment*:] [*symbol*]

where:

map!	is the name of a symbol file, without the .SYM extension, followed by an exclamation point (!).
segment:	is the name of a segment within the currently open or specified *map*, followed by a colon character (:).
symbol	is a symbol name within the specified *segment*.

Description

The Examine Symbol Map (X) command displays the addresses and names of symbols in the currently open symbol maps. (SYMDEB maintains a symbol map for each symbol file specified in the SYMDEB command line.)

If the X command is followed by the asterisk wildcard character (∗), the map names, segment names, and segment addresses for all currently loaded symbol maps are displayed. If X is entered alone, the information is displayed only for the active symbol map.

Information from the symbol maps can be displayed selectively by following the X? command with the *map*!, *segment*:, and *symbol* parameters. The three parameters may be used individually or in combination, but at least one parameter must be specified.

The *map*! parameter must be terminated by an exclamation point and consists of the name, without the extension, of a previously loaded symbol file. If *map*! is omitted, SYMDEB uses the currently open symbol map. If more than one .SYM file is specified in the command line, the one with the same name as the program being debugged is opened first.

The *segment*: parameter must be terminated with a colon; it is the name of a segment declared within the specified or currently open symbol map.

The *symbol* parameter is the name of a label, variable, or other object within the specified *segment*.

Any or all parameters can consist of or include the asterisk wildcard character. For example, X?∗ displays everything in the current map.

Examples

Assume that the program DUMP.EXE is being debugged with the symbol file DUMP.SYM. If the following is typed

```
-X  <Enter>
```

SYMDEB displays:

```
[456E DUMP]
     [456E _TEXT]
       4743 DGROUP
```

This indicates that the program contains one executable code segment (named _TEXT), which is loaded at segment 456EH, and one NEAR DATA group and segment (named DGROUP), which is loaded at segment 4743H.

To display the addresses of all procedures in the same example program whose names begin with the character f, type

```
-X? _TEXT:_F*  <Enter>
```

This produces the following listing:

```
_TEXT: (456E)
0428 _fclose        04CB _fopen         04F1 _fprintf
0528 _fread         0ACB _fflush        0BC2 _free
19AD _flushall
```

Note: Unlike the Microsoft C Compiler, SYMDEB is not case sensitive.

SYMDEB: XO

Open Symbol Map

Purpose

Selects the active symbol map and/or segment.

Syntax

XO [*map*!] [*segment*]

where:

map!	is the name of a symbol file, without the .SYM extension, followed by an exclamation point (!).
segment	is the name of the segment that will become the active segment in the current symbol map.

Description

The Open Symbol Map (XO) command selects the active symbol map and/or the active segment within the current symbol map to be used during debugging.

The optional *map*! parameter must be terminated by an exclamation point and must be the name, without the extension, of a symbol file specified in the original SYMDEB command line. If *map*! is omitted, no changes are made to the active symbol map.

The optional *segment* parameter must be the name of a segment within the current or specified symbol map. All segments in the active symbol map are accessible; the active segment is searched first for symbols specified in other SYMDEB commands. If *segment* is omitted and a new active symbol map is specified, the segment with the smallest address in the new active symbol map will become the active segment.

Examples

Assume that the program SHELL.EXE has been loaded with the two symbol files SHELL.SYM and VIDEO.SYM. To use the information loaded from VIDEO.SYM as the active symbol map for debugging, type

```
-XO VIDEO!  <Enter>
```

Subsequent entry of the command

```
-XO _TEXT  <Enter>
```

causes the segment _TEXT within the symbol map VIDEO to be searched first for symbol names.

Message

Symbol not found
The specified symbol map or segment does not exist.

SYMDEB: Z

Set Symbol Value

Purpose

Assigns a value to a symbol.

Syntax

Z [*map!*] *symbol value*

where:

map!   is the name of a symbol file, without the .SYM extension, followed by an exclamation point (!).

symbol   is an existing symbol name in the active symbol map or in the symbol map specified by *map!*.

value   is the new address of *symbol* (0 – FFFFH).

Description

The Set Symbol Value (Z) command allows the address associated with a name in one of the loaded symbol maps to be overridden by a new value.

Note that altering the address of a symbol at debugging time will not affect other addresses or values that were derived from the value of the same symbol at compilation or assembly time.

The optional *map!* parameter must be terminated by an exclamation point and must be the name, without the extension, of a symbol file specified in the original SYMDEB command line. If *map!* is omitted, SYMDEB uses the active symbol map.

The *symbol* parameter specifies the name of a label, variable, or other object in *map!* or the active symbol map.

The *value* parameter specifies a new address to be associated with *symbol*.

To debug programs created with older versions of FORTRAN and Pascal (Microsoft versions earlier than 3.3 or IBM versions earlier than 2.0), the user must start SYMDEB, locate the first procedure of the program being debugged, and then use the Z command to set the address of DGROUP to the current value of the DS register. (Later versions of FORTRAN and Pascal do this by default.)

Examples

To change the segment address for the symbol DGROUP to 5000H, type

```
-Z DGROUP 5000  <Enter>
```

The actual data associated with the label DGROUP must be moved to the new address before debugging can continue.

To change the segment address for the symbol CODE in the inactive symbol map COUNT to 0F00H, type

```
-Z COUNT! CODE F00  <Enter>
```

SYMDEB: <

Redirect SYMDEB Input

Purpose

Redirects input to SYMDEB.

Syntax

< *device*

where:

device   is the name of any MS-DOS device or file.

Description

The Redirect SYMDEB Input (<) command causes SYMDEB to read its commands from the specified text file or character device, rather than from the keyboard (CON).

The *device* parameter specifies the name of any MS-DOS device or file from which commands will be read. If the *device* parameter is a filename, the file must be an ASCII text file and each command in the file must be on a separate line.

If input will be taken from a terminal attached to one of the serial communications ports (AUX, COM1, or COM2), the port must be properly configured with the MODE command before the SYMDEB session is started.

When SYMDEB commands are redirected from a file, the last entry in the file must be either the < CON command, which restores the keyboard as the input device, or the Quit (Q) command. Otherwise, SYMDEB will lock and the system will have to be restarted.

Examples

Assume that the text file FILL.TXT contains the following SYMDEB commands:

```
F CS:0100 L100 00
D CS:0100 L100
R
Q
```

To process FILL.TXT during a SYMDEB session (which in turn exits SYMDEB with the Quit [Q] command), type

```
-< FILL.TXT  <Enter>
```

Assume that the text file SEARCH.TXT contains the following SYMDEB commands:

```
S BUFFER L2000 "error"
< CON
```

To process SEARCH.TXT during a SYMDEB session and return control to the console, type

```
-< SEARCH.TXT   <Enter>
```

SYMDEB: >

Redirect SYMDEB Output

Purpose

Redirects SYMDEB's output to a device or file.

Syntax

> *device*

where:

device   is the name of any MS-DOS device or file.

Description

The Redirect SYMDEB Output (>) command causes SYMDEB to send all its messages to the specified device or file, rather than to the video display (CON). This is useful for creating a record of a debugging session that can be viewed later with an editor or listed on a printer.

After SYMDEB output is redirected, commands typed on the keyboard are not echoed to the video display. Therefore, the user must know in advance which commands to use and which parameters to supply.

The *device* parameter specifies the name of an MS-DOS device or file to receive SYMDEB's output. If output will be redirected to one of the serial communications ports (AUX, COM1, or COM2), the port must be properly configured with the MODE command before the SYMDEB session is started.

Output can be restored to the video display by entering the > CON command or by terminating SYMDEB with the Quit (Q) command.

Examples

To cause SYMDEB to send all prompts and messages to the file SESSION.TXT, type

```
-> SESSION.TXT  <Enter>
```

After this command, new commands are still accepted by SYMDEB, but the keypresses are not echoed to the screen until the command

```
-> CON  <Enter>
```

is entered or SYMDEB is terminated with the Quit (Q) command.

To cause SYMDEB to send all its prompts and messages to the standard printing device, PRN, type

```
-> PRN  <Enter>
```

SYMDEB: =

Redirect SYMDEB Input and Output

Purpose

Redirects both input and output for SYMDEB.

Syntax

= *device*

where:

device   is the name of any MS-DOS device.

Description

The Redirect SYMDEB Input and Output (=) command causes SYMDEB to read its commands from and send its output to the specified device, rather than reading from the keyboard and sending output to the video display (CON). This command is especially useful for debugging programs that run in graphics mode; the SYMDEB commands can be entered on a terminal attached to the computer's serial port while the graphics program has the full use of the system's video display.

The *device* parameter specifies the name of any MS-DOS device. If input and output will be redirected to one of the serial communications ports (AUX, COM1, or COM2), the port must be properly configured with the MODE command before the SYMDEB session is started.

Input and output can be restored to the standard settings with the = CON command.

Example

To redirect SYMDEB's input and output to the first serial communications port (COM1), type

```
-= COM1  <Enter>
```

SYMDEB: ~
Redirect Target Program Input and Output

Purpose

Redirects both input and output for the program being debugged.

Syntax

~ *device*

where:

device   is the name of any MS-DOS device.

Description

The Redirect Target Program Input and Output (~) command causes all read and write operations by the program being debugged to be redirected to the specified character device.

The *device* parameter specifies the name of an MS-DOS device that the target program will read from and write to. If input and output are redirected to one of the serial communications ports (AUX, COM1, or COM2), the port must be properly configured with the MODE command before the SYMDEB session is started.

Example

To redirect input and output for the program being debugged to the first serial communications port (COM1), type

```
-~ COM1   <Enter>
```

SYMDEB: \

Swap Screen

Purpose

Exchanges the SYMDEB display for the target program's display.

Syntax

\

Description

The Swap Screen (\) command causes the SYMDEB status display to be exchanged for the virtual screen used by the program being debugged. After the program's output has been inspected on the virtual screen, the SYMDEB display can be restored by pressing any key. This command is useful for debugging programs that perform direct screen access or run in graphics mode.

Note: Any information on the display when SYMDEB was invoked will also appear on the virtual screen. When SYMDEB is terminated, the current display is set to match the virtual screen.

The Swap Screen command is available only if the /S switch (or the /I switch, if the computer is IBM compatible) preceded the names of the symbol and program files in the original SYMDEB command line.

Example

To exchange the SYMDEB status display for the virtual screen of the program being debugged, type

```
-\   <Enter>
```

To restore the SYMDEB display, press any key.

SYMDEB: .

Display Source Line

Purpose

Displays the current source-code line.

Syntax

.

Description

The Display Source Line (.) command displays the line from the source-code file that corresponds to the machine instruction currently pointed to by the target program's CS:IP registers.

The . command is independent of the current Source Display Mode status (S+, S−, or S&). However, if the program being debugged was not created with a high-level-language compiler that inserts line numbers into the object modules, the . command has no effect.

Example

To display the source-code line corresponding to the next instruction to be executed, type

```
-.  <Enter>
```

This produces output in the following form:

```
56:        printf( '\nDump of file: %s ', argv[1] );
```

SYMDEB: ?

Help or Evaluate Expression

Purpose

Displays the help screen or the value of an expression.

Syntax

? [*expression*]

where:

expression   is any valid combination of symbols, addresses, numbers, and operators.

Description

When ? is entered alone, a help screen summarizing all valid SYMDEB commands, operators, and types is displayed.

When ? is followed by the *expression* parameter, *expression* is evaluated and the value is displayed. The *expression* parameter can include any valid combination of symbols, addresses, numbers, and operators.

The form and content of the resulting display depends on the type of expression entered. If *expression* is a symbol or an address (optionally including operators), the value is shown first as a FAR address pointer in the form segment:offset, then as a 32-bit hexadecimal number representing the value's physical location in memory (followed by its decimal equivalent in parentheses), and finally as the physical location's ASCII character equivalents displayed as a string enclosed in quotation marks (which have no practical value if *expression* is an address or symbol).

If *expression* includes numbers (interpreted as signed hexadecimal values unless a radix is specified) and operators, the resulting value is shown first as a 16-bit hexadecimal value, then as a 32-bit hexadecimal value (followed by its decimal equivalent in parentheses), and finally as the value's ASCII character equivalents displayed as a string enclosed in quotation marks.

(The ASCII characters within the string are displayed as dots if their value is less than 20H [32] or greater than 7EH [126].)

Examples

Assume that the pointer array *argv* in the program DUMP.C is located at address 4743:029CH. The command

```
-? _argv+4  <Enter>
```

produces the following display:

```
4743:02A0h  000476D0  (292560)
```

To display the result of an exclusive OR operation between the values 0FCH and 14H, type

```
-? FC XOR 14  <Enter>
```

SYMDEB displays

```
00E8h  000000E8  (232)
```

SYMDEB: !

Escape to Shell

Purpose

Invokes the MS-DOS command processor.

Syntax

!\[*command*\]

where:

command   is the name of any MS-DOS command, program, or batch file and its required parameters.

Description

The Escape to Shell (!) command loads a copy of the system's command processor (COMMAND.COM), optionally passing it the name of a program or batch file to be executed. This allows MS-DOS functions such as listing or copying files to be carried out without losing the context of the debugging session.

If the ! command is entered alone, an additional copy of COMMAND.COM gains control and displays the system prompt. Control can be returned to SYMDEB by leaving the new shell with the EXIT command.

If the ! character is followed by a *command* parameter that specifies any valid MS-DOS command, program name, or batch-file name, the specified command is executed immediately and control returns directly to SYMDEB.

The SYMDEB statement connector (;) cannot be used on the same line as the ! command; all text encountered after this command is passed to COMMAND.COM and is interpreted as an MS-DOS command line.

Example

To list the files in the current directory, type

```
-! DIR /W  <Enter>
```

Messages

COMMAND.COM not found!

SYMDEB could not find COMMAND.COM because it was not present in the directory location specified in the environment block's COMSPEC variable.

Not enough memory!

Free memory in the transient program area (TPA) is insufficient to execute the requested command or program. This is a common occurrence when debugging a large program with symbol files.

SYMDEB: *

Enter Comment

Purpose

Allows insertion of a comment that will be ignored by SYMDEB's command interpreter.

Syntax

text

where:

text   is any ASCII text up to and including a carriage return.

Description

The Enter Comment (*) command causes the remainder of the text on that line to be ignored, thereby providing a means of commenting a SYMDEB debugging session. SYMDEB echoes any text following the asterisk to the screen or redirected output device, providing the user with a convenient way to comment program output redirected to a file or a printer. A maximum of 78 characters can be included on each comment line. Comment lines are also useful for documenting lines within a text file that SYMDEB will use as redirected input for the program being debugged.

Example

To echo the reminder *Errors in program output start here:* to the screen or redirected output device, type

```
-*Errors in program output start here:   <Enter>
```

A line in a text file that will be used by SYMDEB for redirected input to the program being debugged may be "commented out" by inserting an asterisk at the beginning of the line. For example:

```
*EB CS:1200 90
```

CodeView

Window-Oriented Debugger

Purpose

Allows the controlled execution of an assembly-language program or high-level-language program for debugging purposes. Both source code and the corresponding unassembled machine code can be displayed as program execution is traced. In addition, watch variables, CPU registers and flags, and program output can be examined in separate debugging windows. CodeView is supplied with the Microsoft Macro Assembler (MASM), C Compiler, Pascal Compiler, and FORTRAN Compiler. This documentation describes CodeView version 2.0.

Syntax

CV [*options*] *exe_file* [*parameters*]

where:

exe_file	is the name of the executable file containing the program to be debugged (default extension = .EXE).
parameters	is one or more filenames or switches required by the program being debugged.
options	is one or more switches from the following list. Switches can be either uppercase or lowercase and can be preceded by a dash (–) instead of a forward slash (/).

/2	Allows the use of two video displays for debugging.
/43	Enables 43-line display mode. (An IBM-compatible computer with an enhanced graphics adapter [EGA] and an enhanced color display is required for this option.)
/B	Forces the attached monitor to use two shades of color when displaying information.
/C*commands*	Executes the specified list of startup commands when CodeView is invoked. If the list of startup commands contains any spaces, the entire list must be enclosed in double quotation marks ("). Commands in the list must be separated by a semicolon character (;).
/D	Turns off nonmaskable interrupt trapping and Intel 8259 interrupt trapping. (This switch prevents system crashes on some IBM-compatible machines that do not support certain IBM-specific interrupt trapping functions.)

(more)

/E	Stores the symbolic information of the program in expanded memory.
/F	Enables the screen-flipping method of switching between the debugging display and the virtual output display. Screen flipping is the default method for IBM-compatible computers with color/graphics adapters.
/I	Enables nonmaskable interrupt trapping and Intel 8259 interrupt trapping on computers that are not IBM-compatible.
/M	Disables mouse support within CodeView.
/P	Enables palette register restore mode, which allows non-IBM EGAs to restore the proper colors upon return from the virtual output screen.
/R	Enables Intel 80386 debugging registers.
/S	Enables the screen-swapping method of switching between the debugging display and the virtual output display. Screen swapping is the default method for IBM-compatible computers with monochrome adapters.
/T	Disables window mode. This switch is necessary for some non-IBM computers or when a sequential debugging session is desired.
/W	Enables window mode. This switch allows CodeView to operate in multiple windows on the same screen. (This option is not the default for some computers.)

Description

CodeView is a window-oriented menu-driven debugger that allows tracing and debugging of high-level-language programs and assembly-language programs. In general, any valid C, FORTRAN, BASIC, Pascal, or MASM source code can be debugged with CodeView.

To prepare a program for debugging under CodeView, the program must be compiled and linked so that the resulting executable file has the extension .EXE and contains line-number information, a symbol table, and executable code. (To a limited extent, text files and .COM files can also be examined under CodeView.) During the debugging session, the program source file must remain in the current directory if source-code display is desired.

The CodeView screen contains four windows that display information about the program being debugged: the display window, which contains program source code and (if requested) the unassembled machine code corresponding to the source code; the dialog window, where line-oriented commands similar (and in some cases identical) to SYMDEB can be entered and viewed (see PROGRAMMING UTILITIES: SYMDEB); the register window (optional), which contains the current status of the microprocessor's registers and flags; and the watch window (optional), which contains program variables or memory locations to be examined during program execution. CodeView also provides a virtual output screen (stored internally) that contains all display output generated during the CodeView session.

A typical CodeView debugging screen looks like this:

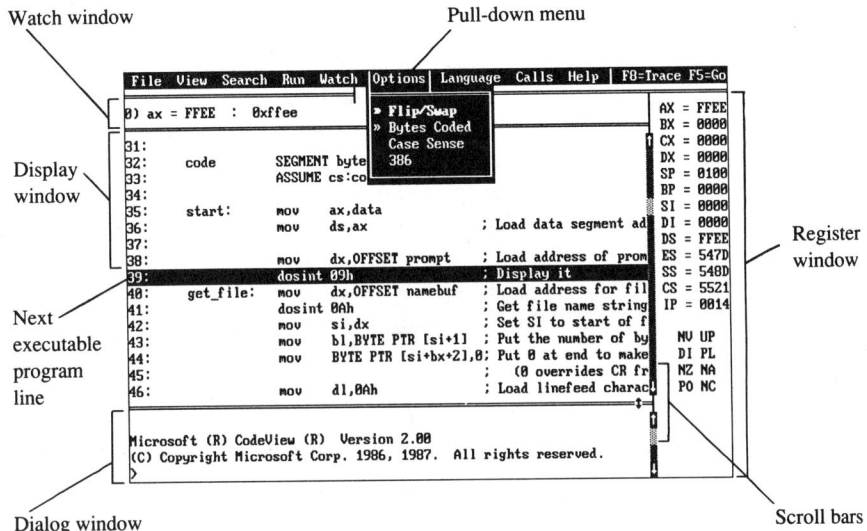

The CodeView display.

Display window commands

Commands that control the display window are available in nine pull-down menus whose names appear in a menu bar near the top of the screen. Commands can be selected with the keyboard or the mouse. Commands are selected with the keyboard by pressing the Alt key, pressing the first letter in the menu name, and then pressing the first letter of the command. Commands are selected with the mouse by pulling down the menu with the mouse pointer, highlighting the command, and then releasing the mouse button. Commands with small double arrows to the left of the command name are currently active. The CodeView menus and commands are described below.

File menu

The File menu includes commands that manipulate the current source or program file. To select the File menu with the keyboard, press Alt-F.

Command	Action
Open...	Opens the specified source file, *include* file, or text file in the display window.
DOS Shell	Exits to the shell temporarily. Type *exit* to return to CodeView.
Exit	Ends the current CodeView session.

View menu

The View menu includes commands that select source or assembly modes and commands that select the debugging screen or the virtual output screen. To select the View menu with the keyboard, press Alt-V.

Command	Action
Source	Displays only the high-level-language or assembly-language source code corresponding to the program being debugged.
Mixed	Displays both the unassembled machine code and the source code corresponding to the program being debugged.
Assembly	Displays only the unassembled machine code corresponding to the program being debugged.
Registers	Displays or removes the optional register window.
Output	Replaces the debugging screen with the virtual output screen. Press any key to return to the debugging screen.

Search menu

The Search menu includes commands that search through text files for text strings and through executable code for labels. To select the Search menu with the keyboard, press Alt-S.

Command	Action
Find...	Searches the current source file or other text file for the specified expression.
Next	Searches forward through the file for the next match of the last expression specified with the Find... command.
Previous	Searches backward through the file for the next match of the last expression specified with the Find... command.
Label...	Searches the executable code for the specified procedure name or program label.

Run menu

The Run menu includes commands that run the program being debugged. To select the Run menu with the keyboard, press Alt-R.

Command	Action
Start	Runs the program at full speed from the first instruction.
Restart	Reloads the program and moves to the first instruction.
Execute	Runs the program at reduced speed from the current instruction.
Clear Breakpoints	Clears all breakpoints.

Watch menu

The Watch menu includes commands that add watch statements to and delete watch statements from the watch window. Watch statements describe expressions or areas of memory to be examined during program execution. To select the Watch menu with the keyboard, press Alt-W.

Command	Action
Add Watch...	Adds the specified watch-expression statement to the watch window.
Watchpoint...	Adds the specified watchpoint statement to the watch window. A watchpoint is a conditional breakpoint that is taken when the expression becomes nonzero (true).
Tracepoint...	Adds the specified tracepoint statement to the watch window. A tracepoint is a conditional breakpoint that is taken when a given expression or range of memory changes.
Delete Watch...	Deletes the specified statement from the watch window.
Delete All Watch	Deletes all statements from the watch window.

Options menu

The Options menu contains commands that affect the general behavior of CodeView. To select the Options menu with the keyboard, press Alt-O.

Command	Action
Flip/Swap	When on (the default), enables screen swapping or screen flipping (whichever option CodeView was started with); when off, disables swapping or flipping. Either method can be used to display the CodeView virtual output screen.
Bytes Coded	When on (the default), displays the instructions, instruction addresses, and the bytes for each instruction; when off, displays only the instructions.
Case Sense	When on, causes CodeView to assume that symbol names are case sensitive; when off, causes CodeView to assume that symbol names are not case sensitive. This option is on by default for C programs and off by default for FORTRAN, BASIC, and assembly programs.
386	When on, allows instructions that reference 32-bit instructions to be assembled and executed and the register window to display 32-bit values. When off, does not allow Intel 80386 instructions and registers to be supported.

Language menu

The Language menu contains commands that select the language-dependent expression evaluator or instruct CodeView to select it for you. To select the Language menu with the keyboard, press Alt-L.

Command	Action
Auto	Forces CodeView to select the expression evaluator of the source file being loaded, based on the extension of the source file.
Basic	Uses a BASIC expression evaluator to determine the value of source-level expressions.
C	Uses a C expression evaluator to determine the value of source-level expressions.
Fortran	Uses a FORTRAN expression evaluator to determine the value of source-level expressions.

Calls menu

The Calls menu is different from other menus in that its contents vary depending on the status of the program. The Calls menu lists the names of specific routines that will be displayed on the screen when that routine name is selected. Routine names in the Calls menu can be selected by typing the number displayed immediately to the left of a routine name. The cursor will move to the line at which the selected routine was last executing.

The current value of each parameter, if any, is shown in parentheses following the name of the routine in the Calls menu. The menu expands to accommodate the parameters of the widest line. Parameters are shown in the current radix (default = decimal). If the program contains more active routines than will fit on the screen or if the routine parameters are too wide, the menu expands to the left and right.

To select the Calls menu with the keyboard, press Alt-C.

Help menu

The Help menu lists the major topics in the CodeView "linked-list" help system. For help, pull down the Help menu and then select the topic of interest. To select the Help menu with the keyboard, press Alt-H.

Command	Action
Intro to Help	Displays information about the "linked-list" help system.
Keyboard/Mouse	Displays information about keyboard and mouse commands.
Run commands	Displays information about Run commands.
Display cmds.	Displays information about Display commands.
Watch/Break	Displays information about setting, listing, and deleting watchpoints and breakpoints.
Memory Ops	Displays information about viewing and modifying memory.
System cmds.	Displays information about system and environment commands.
About CodeView	Displays information about the current CodeView version, time, and date.

Key commands

CodeView supports a variety of function keys and key combinations that modify the active window.

Key	Action
F1	Displays the introductory help screen.
F2	Displays or removes the register window.
F3	Changes the display in the display window to source, mixed, or assembly mode.
F4	Displays the virtual output screen (press any key to return).
F5	Executes to the next breakpoint or to the end of the program if no breakpoint is encountered.
F6	Toggles between the display window and the dialog window.
F7	Sets a temporary breakpoint on the line containing the cursor and executes to that line (or the next breakpoint).
F8	Executes a trace command, stepping through program calls if present.
F9	Sets or clears a breakpoint on the line containing the cursor.
F10	Executes the next source line (in source mode) or the next instruction (in assembly mode), stepping over program calls if present.
Ctrl+G	Increases the size of the display window or the dialog window, whichever is active.
Ctrl+T	Decreases the size of the display window or the dialog window, whichever is active.

Dialog window commands

After CodeView and the specified executable file are loaded, CodeView displays its special prompt character (>) at the bottom of the dialog window and awaits a dialog command. CodeView dialog commands consist of one, two, or three characters, usually followed by one or more parameters. CodeView treats uppercase and lowercase characters the same except when they are contained in strings enclosed within single or double quotation marks. The default radix for dialog command parameters is 10 (decimal). Dialog commands are executed when the Enter key is pressed.

A detailed explanation of CodeView dialog commands and parameters is not presented in this entry. CodeView dialog commands and parameters are similar to SYMDEB commands and parameters. See PROGRAMMING UTILITIES: SYMDEB. Additional information about using CodeView dialog commands and parameters can be found in the CodeView documentation supplied with the Microsoft Macro Assembler (MASM), C Compiler, Pascal Compiler, and FORTRAN Compiler. A sample debugging session using CodeView dialog commands and window commands is documented in this book. See PROGRAMMING IN THE MS-DOS ENVIRONMENT: PROGRAMMING TOOLS: Debugging in the MS-DOS Environment.

The dialog commands available with CodeView are as follows:

Command	Syntax	Action
!	! [*command*]	Escape to shell.
"	"	Pause redirected file execution.
#	#*number*	Set display window tabs.
*	*comment*	Echo comment to output device.
.	.	Display current source line.
/	/[*searchtext*]	Search for regular expression.
7	7	Display 8087 registers.
:	:[:] . . . [:]	Delay redirected file execution.
<	< *device*	Redirect dialog window input.
=	= *device*	Redirect dialog window input and output.
>	[T] > [>] device	Redirect dialog window output.
?	? *expression*[, *format*]	Evaluate expression.
@	@	Redraw screen.
A	A [*address*]	Assemble machine instructions.
BC	BC [*] [*list*]	Clear breakpoints.
BD	BD [*] [*list*]	Disable breakpoints.
BE	BE [*] [*list*]	Enable breakpoints.
BL	BL	List breakpoints.
BP	BP [*address* [*passcount*] ["*cmds*"]]	Set breakpoints.
C	C *range address*	Compare memory areas.
D	D [*range*]	Display (dump) memory.
DA	DA [*range*]	Display ASCII.
DB	DB [*range*]	Display bytes.
DD	DD [*range*]	Display doublewords.
DI	DI [*range*]	Display integers.
DL	DL [*range*]	Display long reals.
DS	DS [*range*]	Display short reals.
DT	DT [*range*]	Display 10-byte reals.
DU	DU [*range*]	Display unsigned integers.
DW	DW [*range*]	Display words.
E	E *address* [*list*]	Enter data.
EA	EA *address* [*list*]	Enter ASCII string.
EB	EB *address* [*list*]	Enter bytes.
ED	ED *address* [*value*]	Enter doublewords.
EI	EI *address* [*list*]	Enter integers.
EL	EL *address* [*value*]	Enter long reals.
ES	ES *address* [*value*]	Enter short reals.
ET	ET *address* [*value*]	Enter 10-byte reals.

(more)

Command	Syntax	Action
EU	EU *address* [*value*]	Enter unsigned integers.
EW	EW *address* [*value*]	Enter words.
F	F *range list*	Fill memory.
G	G [*breakpoint*]	Go execute program.
H	H	Display help screen.
I	I *port*	Input from port.
K	K [*number*]	Perform stack trace.
L	L [*parameters*]	Reload program.
M	M *range address*	Move (copy) data.
N	N [*radix*]	Change current radix.
O	O *port byte*	Output to port.
O	O	Display all options.
O3	O3[+¦-]	Toggle Intel 80386 option.
OB	OB[+¦-]	Toggle bytes coded option.
OC	OC[+¦-]	Toggle case-sense option.
OF	OF[+¦-]	Toggle flip/swap option.
P	P [*count*]	Step through program (over calls).
Q	Q	Quit debugger.
R	R [*register* [*value*]]	Display or modify registers.
RF	RF [*flags*]	Display or modify flags.
S	S *range list*	Search memory.
S	S	Display current display mode.
S+	S+	Display source code.
S−	S−	Display assembly language.
S&	S&	Display source code and assembly language.
T	T [*count*]	Trace program execution (through calls).
TP	TP [*type*] *range*	Set memory-tracepoint statement.
TP?	TP? *expression*[,*format*]	Set tracepoint-expression statement.
U	U [*range*]	Disassemble (unassemble) program.
USE	USE [*language*]	Switch expression evaluators.
V	V [.[*filename:*]*linenumber*]	View source code.
W	W	List watchpoints and tracepoints.
W	W [*type*] *range*	Set memory-watch statement.
W?	W? *expression*[,*format*]	Set watch-expression statement.
WP?	WP? *expression*[,*format*]	Set watchpoint.
X	X[?[*module!*] [*routine.*]*symbol*¦*]	Examine program symbols.
Y	Y [*] [*list*]	Delete watch statements.
\	\	Display virtual output screen.

Examples

To prepare the source file SHELL.C for debugging with CodeView, first compile the source file with the switches that disable optimization and cause symbol-table and line-number information to be written to the relocatable object module:

```
C>MSC /Zi /Od SHELL;   <Enter>
```

Next, to convert the object module to an executable program and prepare it for CodeView, type

```
C>LINK /CO SHELL;   <Enter>
```

To begin debugging, type

```
C>CV SHELL   <Enter>
```

To start CodeView in 43-line mode with TEST.EXE as the executable file and INFO.DAT as the command-tail parameter, type

```
C>CV /43 TEST INFO.DAT   <Enter>
```

In both examples the source file corresponding to the specified executable file must be in the current directory if source-code display is desired.

Messages

Argument to IMAG/DIMAG must be simple type
An invalid parameter to an IMAG or DIMAG function, such as an array with no subscripts, was specified.

Array must have subscript
An array without any subscripts was specified in an expression, such as *IARRAY+2*. A correct example is *IARRAY[1]+2*.

Bad address
An invalid address was specified. For example, an address containing hexadecimal characters might have been specified when the radix is decimal.

Bad breakpoint command
An invalid breakpoint number was specified with the BC, BD, or BE dialog command. The breakpoint number must be in the range 0 through 19.

Bad flag
An invalid flag mnemonic was specified with the RF dialog command.

Bad format string
An invalid format specifier was used following an expression. Expressions used with the ?, W?, WP?, and TP? dialog commands can have format specifiers set off from the expression by a comma. The valid format specifiers are c, d, e, E, f, g, G, i, o, s, u, x, and X. Some format specifiers can be preceded by the prefix h (to specify a 2-byte integer) or l (to specify a 4-byte integer).

Bad integer or real constant
An invalid numeric constant was specified in an expression.

Bad intrinsic function
An invalid intrinsic function name was specified in an expression.

Badly formed type
The type information in the symbol table of the file being debugged is incorrect. This is a serious problem. Note the circumstances of the failure and notify Microsoft Corporation.

Bad radix (use 8, 10, or 16)
An invalid radix was specified with the N dialog command. Use an octal, decimal, or hexadecimal radix.

Bad register
An invalid register name was specified with the R dialog command. Use AX, BX, CX, DX, SP, BP, SI, DI, DS, ES, SS, CS, or IP. If your machine is equipped with an Intel 80386 microprocessor, use EAX, EBX, ECX, EDX, ESP, EBP, ESI, EDI, DS, ES, FS, GS, SS, CS, or IP.

Bad subscript
An invalid subscript expression was specified for an array, such as *IARRAY (3.3)* or *IARRAY ((3,3))*. The correct expression for this example (in BASIC or FORTRAN) is *IARRAY (3,3)*.

Bad type cast
Incompatible types of operands were specified in an expression.

Bad type (use one of 'ABDILSTUW')
An invalid type was used in a Display (D, DA, DB, DF, DU, DW, DD, DS, DL, or DT) dialog command. The valid types are ASCII (A), byte (B), integer (I), unsigned (U), word (W), doubleword (D), short real (S), long real (L), and 10-byte real (T).

Breakpoint # or '*' expected
The BC, BD, or BE dialog command was entered without a parameter.

Cannot cast complex constant component into REAL
An incompatible real or imaginary component was specified in a COMPLEX constant. Both real and imaginary components must be compatible with type REAL.

Cannot cast IMAG/DIMAG argument to COMPLEX
An invalid parameter was specified with an IMAG or DIMAG function. IMAG and DIMAG parameters must be simple numeric types.

Cannot use struct or union as scalar
A struct or union variable was used as a scalar value in a C expression. Such variables must be followed by a file specifier or preceded by the address-of (&) operator.

Can't find *filename*
CodeView could not find the executable file specified in the command line.

Character constant too long
A character constant that is too long for the FORTRAN expression evaluator was specified. The limit is 126 bytes.

Character too big for current radix
A radix that is larger than the current CodeView radix was specified in a constant. Use the N dialog command to change the radix.

Constant too big
An unsigned constant number larger than 4,294,967,295 (FFFFFFFFH) was specified.

CPU not an 80386
The 386 option was selected but a machine without an Intel 80386 microprocessor is being used.

Divide by zero
An expression in a parameter of a dialog command attempted to divide by zero.

EMM error
CodeView failed to use the Expanded Memory Manager (EMM) correctly. This is a serious problem. Note the circumstances of the failure and notify Microsoft Corporation.

EMM hardware error
The Expanded Memory Manager (EMM) routines reported a hardware error. Check your expanded memory board for defects.

EMM memory not found
The /E option was used but expanded memory has not been installed. Install software that accesses the memory according to the Lotus/Intel/Microsoft Expanded Memory Specification (LIM EMS).

EMM software error
The Expanded Memory Manager (EMM) routines reported a software error. Reinstall the EMM software.

Expression too complex
An expression given as a dialog-command parameter is too complex.

Extra input ignored
Too many parameters were specified with a command. CodeView evaluates the valid parameters and ignores the rest. In this situation, CodeView often does not evaluate the parameters as intended.

Flip/Swap option off — application output lost
The program being debugged is writing to the screen, but the output cannot be displayed because the flip/swap option has been disabled.

Floating point error
This is a serious problem. Note the circumstances of the failure and notify Microsoft Corporation.

Illegal instruction
This message usually indicates that a machine instruction attempted to divide by zero.

Index out of bound
A subscript value was specified that is outside the bounds declared for the array.

Insufficient EMM memory
Expanded memory is insufficient to hold the program's symbol table.

Internal debugger error
This is a serious problem. Note the circumstances of the failure and notify Microsoft Corporation.

Invalid argument
An invalid CodeView expression was specified as a parameter.

Invalid executable file format — please relink
The executable file was not linked with the version of LINK released with this version of the CodeView debugger. Relink with the appropriate version of LINK.

Invalid option
An invalid switch was specified with the O command.

Missing ' " '
A string specified as a parameter to a dialog command did not have a closing double quotation mark.

Missing '('
A parameter to a dialog command was specified as an expression containing a right parenthesis but no left parenthesis.

Missing ')'
A parameter to a dialog command was specified as an expression containing a left parenthesis but no right parenthesis.

Missing ']'
A parameter to a dialog command was specified as an expression containing a left bracket but no right bracket, or a regular expression was specified with a right bracket but no left bracket.

Missing '(' in complex constant
An opening parenthesis of a complex constant in an expression was expected but was not found.

Missing ')' in complex constant
A closing parenthesis of a complex constant in an expression was expected but was not found.

Missing ')' in substring
A closing parenthesis of a substring expression was expected but was not found.

Missing '(' to intrinsic
An opening parenthesis for an intrinsic function was expected but was not found.

Missing ')' to intrinsic
A closing parenthesis for an intrinsic function was expected but was not found.

No closing single quote
A character was specified in an expression used as a dialog-command parameter, but the closing single quotation mark is missing.

No code at this line number
A breakpoint was set on a source line that does not correspond to machine code. (In other words, the source line does not contain an executable statement.) For example, the line might be a data declaration or a comment.

No free EMM memory handles
CodeView could not find an available EMM handle. Expanded Memory Manager (EMM) software allocates a fixed number of memory handles (usually 256) to be used for specific tasks.

No match of regular expression
No match was found for the regular expression specified with the Search (S) dialog command or with the Find... command from the Search menu.

No previous regular expression
The Previous command was selected from the Search menu, but CodeView found no previous match for the last regular expression specified.

No source lines at this address
The address specified as a parameter for the V dialog command does not have any source lines. For example, it could be an address in a library routine or an assembly-language module.

No such file/directory
The specified file or directory does not exist.

No symbolic information
The executable file specified is not in the CodeView format. The program cannot be debugged in source mode unless the file is created in the CodeView format. The program can be debugged in assembly mode.

Not an executable file
The file specified to be debugged when CodeView started is not an executable file with a .EXE or .COM extension.

Not a text file
An attempt was made to load a file with the Open... command from the File menu or with the V dialog command, but the file is not a text file. CodeView determines if a file is a text file by checking the first 128 bytes for characters that are not in the ASCII ranges 9 through 13 and 20 through 126.

Not enough space
The ! dialog command or the DOS Shell command from the File menu was chosen, but free memory is insufficient to execute COMMAND.COM. Because memory is released by code in the FORTRAN startup routines, this error always occurs if the ! command is used before executing any code. Use any of the code-execution dialog commands (T, P, or G) to execute the FORTRAN startup code; then try the ! command again. This message also occurs with assembly-language programs that do not specifically release memory.

Object too big
A TP? dialog command was entered with a data object (such as an array) that is larger than 128 bytes.

Operand types incorrect for this operation
An operand in a FORTRAN expression had a type incompatible with the operation applied to it. For example, if P is declared as *CHARACTER P (10)*, then *? P+5* would produce this error, because a character array cannot be an operand of an arithmetic operator.

Operator must have a struct/union type
One of the C member-selection operators (–, >, or .) was used in an expression that does not reference an element of a structure or union.

Operator needs lvalue
An expression was specified that does not evaluate to a memory location in an operation that requires one. (An lvalue is an expression that refers to a memory location.) For example, *buffer (count)* is correct; it represents a symbol in memory. However, *I .EQV. 10* is invalid because it evaluates to TRUE or FALSE instead of to a single memory location.

Overlay not resident
An attempt was made to unassemble machine code from a function that is currently not in memory.

Program terminated normally (*exitcode*)
The program terminated execution normally. The number displayed in parentheses is the exit code returned to MS-DOS by the program.

Radix must be between 2 and 36 inclusive
A radix that is outside the allowable range was specified.

Register variable out of scope
An attempt was made to specify a register variable by using the period (.) operator and a routine name.

Regular expression too complex
The regular expression specified is too complex for CodeView to evaluate.

Regular expression too long
The regular expression specified is too long for CodeView to evaluate.

Restart program to debug
The program being debugged has executed to the end.

Simple variable cannot have argument

A parameter to a simple variable was specified in an expression. For example, given the declaration *INTEGER NUM*, the expression *NUM(1)* is not allowed.

Substring range out of bound

A character expression exceeded the length specified in the CHARACTER statement.

Syntax error

An invalid command line was specified for a dialog command, or an invalid assembly-language instruction was entered with the A dialog command.

Too few array bounds given

The bounds specified in an array subscript do not match the array declaration. For example, given the array declaration *INTEGER IARRAY(3,4)*, the expression *IARRAY(1)* would produce this error message.

Too many array bounds given

The bounds specified in an array subscript do not match the array declaration. For example, given the array declaration *INTEGER IARRAY(3,4)*, the expression *IARRAY (1,3,J)* would produce this error message.

Too many breakpoints

An attempt was made to specify more than 20 breakpoints; CodeView permits only 20.

Too many files

Too few file handles were specified for CodeView to operate correctly. Specify more files in your CONFIG.SYS file.

Type clash in function argument

The type of an actual parameter does not match the corresponding formal parameter, or a subroutine that uses alternate returns was called and the values of the return labels in the actual parameter list are not 0.

Type conversion too complex

An attempt was made to typecast an element of an expression in a type other than the simple types or with more than one level of indirection. An example of a complex type would be typecasting to a struct or union type. An example of two levels of indirection is *char ***.

Unable to open file

A file specified in a command parameter or in response to a prompt cannot be opened.

Unknown symbol

An identifier that is not in CodeView's symbol table was specified, or a local variable was used in a parameter when not in the routine where the variable is defined, or a subroutine that uses alternate returns was called and the values of the return labels in the parameter list are not 0.

Unrecognized option *option*
Valid options: /B /C<command> /D /E /F /I /M /P /R /S /T /W /43 /2

An invalid switch was entered when starting CodeView.

Usage: cv [options] file [arguments]
An executable file was not specified when starting CodeView.

Video mode changed without /S option
The program changed video modes (either to or from graphics modes) when screen swapping was not specified. Use the /S option to specify screen swapping when debugging graphics programs. Debugging can be continued after receiving this message, but the output screen of the debugged program may be damaged.

Warning: packed file
CodeView was started with a packed file as the executable file. The program cannot be debugged in source mode because all symbolic information is stripped from a file when it is packed with LINK's /EXEPACK option or the EXEPACK utility. Try to debug the program in assembly mode. (The packing routines at the start of the program might make this difficult.)

Wrong number of function arguments
An incorrect number of parameters was specified when evaluating a function in a CodeView expression.

Section V
System Calls

Introduction

All versions of MS-DOS include operating-system services that provide the programmer with hardware-independent tools for handling such tasks as file management, device input and output, memory allocation, and getting and setting system-management information such as the date and time. The majority of these services, collectively called the MS-DOS system calls, are invoked through Interrupt 21H. A few others are called using Interrupts 20H through 27H and 2FH. This section includes descriptions of these system-management services, with details relevant to all releases of MS-DOS through version 3.2.

Use of the Interrupt 21H system calls, rather than hardware-specific routines, helps ensure that a program will run on any computer running an appropriate version of MS-DOS. Likewise, because new releases of MS-DOS attempt to maintain compatibility with earlier versions, use of the calls increases the likelihood that a program will remain usable for more than a single major or minor release of the operating system.

The MS-DOS Interrupt 21H system calls are invoked as follows:

AH = function number
AL = subfunction code (if required)
Other registers = additional function-specific information
Execute Interrupt 21H

Version Differences

With MS-DOS versions 2.0 and later, considerable overlap occurs in the way in which many system services, such as file and character device I/O, can be carried out. This overlap is a result of the manner in which MS-DOS has developed since it was first released.

The earliest version of MS-DOS, 1.0, included a relatively small set of Interrupt 21H system calls designed primarily for CP/M compatibility. These calls, numbered 00H through 2DH, relied on the use of file control blocks (FCBs) in an application's memory space for information on open files. *See* PROGRAMMING IN THE MS-DOS ENVIRONMENT: Programming for ms-dos: File and Record Management; Appendix G: File Control Block (FCB) Structure. The FCB-based system calls in MS-DOS do not support hierarchical file structures, nor do they support redirection of input and output. As a result, many of these system calls have been superseded in later releases of MS-DOS. The CP/M-style calls are no longer recommended and should not be used unless program compatibility with versions 1.x is required.

Beginning with version 2.0, MS-DOS introduced the concept of handles—16-bit numbers returned by the operating system after a successful open or create call. The handles can subsequently be used by an application program to reference an open file or device, eliminating redundancy and unnecessary overhead. These handles are also used internally by MS-DOS to keep track of open files and devices. The operating system keeps all such handle-related information in its own memory space. Handles offer full support for the hierarchical file system introduced in version 2.0 of MS-DOS and thus allow the programmer to access any file stored in any directory or subdirectory on a block device. Because of the increased flexibility offered by the handle-related system function calls, these services are recommended over the earlier FCB-based calls, which perform similar tasks but for the current directory only. *See* PROGRAMMING IN THE MS-DOS ENVIRON-MENT: PROGRAMMING FOR MS-DOS: File and Record Management.

Another advantage of using the system calls introduced in versions 2.0 and later is that these calls set the carry flag when an operational error occurs and return an error code in AX that indicates the nature of the error; the error can then be investigated further by calling Function 59H (Get Extended Error Information). The earlier system calls (00H through 2DH) generally simply return 0FFH (255) in AL to indicate an error or 00H to indicate that the call was completed successfully.

Format of Entries

Entries in this section are arranged in hexadecimal order, with decimal equivalents in parentheses. Each entry is organized as follows:

- Hexadecimal interrupt and/or function number (decimal equivalent in parentheses)
- Interrupt or function name (similar to, but not always the same as, the name used in MS-DOS documentation)
- Version dependencies
- Interrupt or function purpose
- Register contents needed to call
- Register contents on return
- Notes for programmers
- Related functions
- Program example

The format of these entries is designed to give programmers ready reference to specific information, such as register contents, as well as more detailed notes on the use and application of each system call. For further information on the use of the system calls, *see* PROGRAMMING IN THE MS-DOS ENVIRONMENT.

The assembly-language examples in this section use the Cmacros capability introduced with the Windows Software Development Kit. Cmacros, a set of assembly-language macros defined in the file CMACROS.INC, are useful because they provide a simplified interface to the function and segment conventions of high-level languages such as Microsoft C and Microsoft Pascal.

Advantages to using Cmacros for assembly-language programming include transparent support for memory models and symbolic names for function arguments and local variables. Cmacros exist for code and data segment declarations (*sBegin* and *sEnd*), storage allocation (*staticX, globalX, externX,* and *labelX*), function declarations (*cProc, parmX, localX, cBegin* and *cEnd*), function calls (*cCall, Save,* and *Arg*), special definitions (*DefX, RegPtr,* and *FarPtr*), and error control (*errnz* and *errn$*). Of these, only *sBegin, sEnd, cProc, parmX, localX, cBegin,* and *cEnd* are used in the examples in this section.

Two additional macros that support functions not found in CMACROS.INC are *loadCP* and *loadDP*. These macros, included in the file CMACROSX.INC listed below, allow pointers previously declared with *staticX, globalX, parmX, DefX* and *localX* to be loaded into registers without regard to the memory model in use — *loadCP* and *loadDP* generate code to load either the offset portion or the full segment:offset of the address, depending on the memory model.

```
;       CMACROSX.INC
;
;       This file includes supplemental macros for two macros included
;       in CMACROS.INC: parmCP and parmDP. When these macros are used,
;       CMACROS.INC allocates either 1 or 2 words to the variables
;       associated with these macros, depending on the memory model in
;       use. However, parmCP and parmDP provide no support for automatically
;       adjusting for different memory models—additional program code
;       needs to be written to compensate for this. The loadCP and loadDP
;       macros included in this file can be used to provide additional
;       flexibility for overcoming this limit.
;
;       For example, "parmDP pointer" will make space (1 word in small
;       and middle models and 2 words in compact, large, and huge models)
;       for the data pointer named "pointer". The statement
;       "loadDP ds,bx,pointer" can then be used to dynamically place the
;       value of "pointer" into DS:BX, depending on the memory model.
;       In small-model programs, this macro would generate the instruction
;       "mov dx,pointer" (it is assumed that DS already has the right
;       segment value); in large-model programs, this macro would generate
;       the statements "mov ds,SEG_pointer" and "mov dx,OFF_pointer".


checkDS macro           segmt
        diffcount = 0
        irp d,<ds,DS,Ds,dS>                     ; Allow for all spellings
           ifdif <segmt>,<d>                    ; of "ds".
               diffcount = diffcount+1
           endif
        endm
        if diffcount EQ 4
           it_is_DS = 0
        else
           it_is_DS = 1
        endif
        endm
```

(more)

```
checkES macro        segmt
          diffcount = 0
          irp d,<es,ES,Es,eS>                    ; Allow for all spellings
              ifdif <segmt>,<d>                   ; of "es".
                  diffcount = diffcount+1
              endif
          endm
          if diffcount EQ 4
              it_is_ES = 0
          else
              it_is_ES = 1
          endif
        endm

loadDP  macro        segmt,offst,dptr
          checkDS segmt
          if sizeD                                ; <-- Large data model
              if it_is_DS
                  lds  offst,dptr
              else
                  checkES segmt
                  if it_is_ES
                      les  offst,dptr
                  else
                      mov  offst,OFF_&dptr
                      mov  segmt,SEG_&dptr
                  endif
              endif
          else
              mov  offst,dptr                     ; <-- Small data model
              if it_is_DS EQ 0
                  push ds                         ; If "segmt" is not DS,
                  pop  segmt                      ; move ds to segmt.
              endif
          endif
        endm

loadCP  macro        segmt,offst,cptr
          if sizeC                                ; <-- Large code model
              checkDS segmt
              if it_is_DS
                  lds offst,cptr
              else
                  checkES
                  if it_is_ES
                      les  offst,cptr
                  else
                      mov  segmt,SEG_&cptr
                      mov  offst,OFF_&cptr
                  endif
              endif
          else
```

(more)

```
            push  cs                            ; <-- Small code model
            pop   segmt
            mov   offst,cptr
         endif
      endm
```

The following example program demonstrates the use of Cmacros in an assembly-language program:

```
memS    =       0               ;Small memory model
?PLM    =       0               ;C calling conventions
?WIN    =       0               ;Disable Windows support


include cmacros.inc
include cmacrosx.inc


sBegin  CODE                    ;Start of code segment
assumes CS,CODE                 ;Required by MASM


        ;Microsoft C function syntax:
        ;
        ;     int addnums(firstnum, secondnum)
        ;          int firstnum, secondnum;
        ;
        ;Returns firstnum + secondnum


cProc   addnums,PUBLIC          ;Start of addnums functions
parmW   firstnum                ;Declare parameters
parmW   secondnum
cBegin
        mov     ax,firstnum
        add     ax,secondnum
cEnd
sEnd    CODE
        end
```

A simple C program to call this function would be

```
main()
{
        printf("The sum is %d",addnums(12,33));
}
```

Contents by Functional Group

Although distinguishing between FCB-based and handle-based system calls provides a broad and very generalized means of categorizing these services, the more common and useful approach is to group the calls by the type of task they perform. The following list groups the Interrupt 21H system calls and Interrupts 20H, 22H through 27H, and 2FH by type of service.

Function	Purpose
Character Input	
01H	Character Input with Echo
03H	Auxiliary Input
06H	Direct Console I/O
07H	Unfiltered Character Input Without Echo
08H	Character Input Without Echo
0AH	Buffered Keyboard Input
0BH	Check Keyboard Status
0CH	Flush Buffer, Read Keyboard
Character Output	
02H	Character Output
04H	Auxiliary Output
05H	Print Character
06H	Direct Console I/O
09H	Display String
Disk Management	
0DH	Disk Reset
0EH	Select Disk
19H	Get Current Disk
1BH	Get Default Drive Data
1CH	Get Drive Data
2EH	Set/Reset Verify Flag
36H	Get Disk Free Space
54H	Get Verify Flag
File Management	
0FH	Open File with FCB
10H	Close File with FCB
11H	Find First File
12H	Find Next File
13H	Delete File
16H	Create File with FCB
17H	Rename File
1AH	Set DTA Address
23H	Get File Size
2FH	Get DTA Address
3CH	Create File with Handle
3DH	Open File with Handle
3EH	Close File

(more)

Function	Purpose
File Management *(continued)*	
41H	Delete File
43H	Get/Set File Attributes
45H	Duplicate File Handle
46H	Force Duplicate File Handle
4EH	Find First File
4FH	Find Next File
56H	Rename File
57H	Get/Set Date/Time of File
5AH	Create Temporary File
5BH	Create New File
5CH	Lock/Unlock File Region
Information Management	
14H	Sequential Read
15H	Sequential Write
21H	Random Read
22H	Random Write
24H	Set Relative Record
27H	Random Block Read
28H	Random Block Write
3FH	Read File or Device
40H	Write File or Device
42H	Move File Pointer
Interrupt 25H	Absolute Disk Read
Interrupt 26H	Absolute Disk Write
Directory Management	
39H	Create Directory
3AH	Remove Directory
3BH	Change Current Directory
47H	Get Current Directory
Process Management	
00H	Terminate Process
31H	Terminate and Stay Resident
4BH	Load and Execute Program (EXEC)
4CH	Terminate Process with Return Code
4DH	Get Return Code of Child Process
59H	Get Extended Error Information
Interrupt 20H	Terminate Program
Interrupt 27H	Terminate and Stay Resident

(more)

Function	Purpose
Memory Management	
48H	Allocate Memory Block
49H	Free Memory Block
4AH	Resize Memory Block
58H	Get/Set Allocation Strategy
Miscellaneous System Management	
25H	Set Interrupt Vector
26H	Create New Program Segment Prefix
29H	Parse Filename
2AH	Get Date
2BH	Set Date
2CH	Get Time
2DH	Set Time
30H	Get MS-DOS Version Number
33H	Get/Set Control-C Check Flag
34H	Return Address of InDOS Flag
35H	Get Interrupt Vector
38H	Get/Set Current Country
44H	IOCTL
5EH	Network Machine Name/Printer Setup
5FH	Get/Make Assign List Entry
62H	Get Program Segment Prefix Address
63H	Get Lead Byte Table (version 2.25 only)
Interrupt 22H	Terminate Routine Address
Interrupt 23H	Control-C Handler Address
Interrupt 24H	Critical Error Handler Address
Interrupt 2FH	Multiplex Interrupt

Interrupt 20H (32)

1.0 and later

Terminate Program

Interrupt 20H is one of several methods that a program can use to perform a final exit. It informs the operating system that the program is completely finished and that the memory the program occupied can be released.

To Call

CS = segment address of program segment prefix (PSP)

Returns

Nothing

Programmer's Notes

- In response to an Interrupt 20H call, MS-DOS takes the following actions:
  - Restores the termination handler vector (Interrupt 22H) from PSP:000AH.
  - Restores the Control-C vector (Interrupt 23H) from PSP:000EH.
  - With MS-DOS versions 2.0 and later, restores the critical error handler vector (Interrupt 24H) from PSP:0012H.
  - Flushes the file buffers.
  - Transfers to the termination handler address.

  The termination handler releases all memory blocks allocated to the program, including its environment block and any dynamically allocated blocks that were not previously explicitly released; closes any files opened with handles that were not previously closed; and returns control to the parent process (usually COMMAND.COM).
- If the program is returning to COMMAND.COM, control transfers first to COMMAND.COM's resident portion, which reloads COMMAND.COM's transient portion (if necessary) and passes control to it. If a batch file is in progress, the next line of the batch file is then fetched and interpreted; otherwise, a prompt is issued for the next user command.
- Any files that have been written by the program using FCBs should be closed before using Interrupt 20H; otherwise, data may be lost.
- For those programmers who have been with MS-DOS since its earliest incarnations, Interrupt 20H is the traditional way to exit from an application program. However, under versions 2.0 and later, the preferred methods of termination are Interrupt 21H Function 31H (Terminate and Stay Resident) and Interrupt 21H Function 4CH (Terminate Process with Return Code).

Example

```
;************************************************************;
;                                                          ;
;                    Perform a final exit.                 ;
;                                                          ;
;************************************************************;
        int     20H     ; Transfer to MS-DOS.
```

Interrupt 21H (33)
Function 00H (0)

1.0 and later

Terminate Process

Function 00H flushes all file buffers to disk, terminates the current process, and releases the memory used by the process.

To Call

AH = 00H
CS = segment of program's program segment prefix (PSP)

Returns

Nothing

Programmer's Notes

- The following interrupt vectors are restored from the PSP of the terminated program:

PSP Offset	Vector for Interrupt
0AH	Interrupt 22H (terminate routine)
0EH	Interrupt 23H (Control-C handler)
12H	Interrupt 24H (critical error handler) (versions 2.0 and later.)

- All file buffers are written to disk and all handles are closed. Control is then transferred to Interrupt 22H (Terminate Routine Address).
- Any file that has changed in length and was opened with an FCB should be closed before Function 00H is called. If such a file is not closed, its length, date, and time are not recorded correctly in the directory.
- With versions 3.x of MS-DOS, restoring the default memory-allocation strategy used by MS-DOS is advisable if that strategy has been changed with Function 58H (Get/Set Allocation Strategy). Any global flags, such as the break and verify flags, that affect system behavior and that have been changed by the process should also be restored to their original values.
- Function 00H performs exactly the same processing as Interrupt 20H (Terminate Program).
- Function 00H is obsolete with MS-DOS versions 2.0 and later. Function 31H (Terminate and Stay Resident) and Function 4CH (Terminate Process with Return Code) are preferred; both enable the terminating process to pass a return code to the calling process and do not require that CS contain the PSP address.

Related Functions

31H (Terminate and Stay Resident)
4CH (Terminate Process with Return Code)

Example

None

Interrupt 21H (33) Function 01H (1)

1.0 and later

Character Input with Echo

Function 01H waits for a character from standard input, echoes it to standard output, and returns the character in the AL register.

To Call

AH = 01H

Returns

AL = 8-bit character code

Programmer's Notes

- With versions 1.x of MS-DOS, Function 01H reads input from the keyboard. With versions 2.0 and later, Function 01H reads a character from standard input, which defaults to the keyboard but can be redirected to another device or to a file. Whether or not input has been redirected, the character is echoed to standard output.

- Function 01H waits for input if a character is not available. A wait can be avoided by calling Function 0BH (Check Keyboard Status), which checks whether a character is available from standard input, and then calling Function 01H if a character is ready.

- On IBM PCs and compatibles, extended characters, such as those produced by the Alt-O and F8 keys, are returned as 2 bytes. The first byte, 00H, signals an extended character; the second byte completes the key code. To read these characters, Function 01H must be called twice.

  With MS-DOS versions 2.0 and later, if standard input has been redirected, the value 00H can also represent a null character from a file and, in that case, might not represent valid data. A program can use Function 44H (IOCTL) Subfunction 00H (Get Device Data) to determine whether standard input has been redirected.

- The carriage-return character (0DH) echoes a carriage return but not a linefeed. Likewise, the linefeed character (0AH) does not echo a carriage return.

- With MS-DOS versions 2.0 and later, Function 01H cannot detect an end-of-file condition if input has been redirected.

- Interrupt 23H (Control-C Handler Address) is called if Control-C (03H) is the input character and (with versions 2.0 and later) input is not redirected.

- With MS-DOS version 2.0 and later, if standard input has been redirected to come from a file, Break must be enabled for Interrupt 23H to be called when Control-C (03H) is the input character.

- Alternative character input functions are 06H (Direct Console I/O), 07H (Unfiltered Character Input Without Echo), and 08H (Character Input Without Echo). The four functions are related as follows:

Function	Waits for Input	Echoes to Std Output	Acts on Control-C
01H	yes	yes	yes
06H	no	no	no
07H	yes	no	no
08H	yes	no	yes

Depending on whether Control-C needs to be filtered, Function 06H, 07H, or 08H can be used to handle character display separately from character input.

• With MS-DOS versions 2.0 and later, Function 3FH (Read File or Device) should be used in preference to Function 01H.

Related Functions

06H (Direct Console I/O)
07H (Unfiltered Character Input Without Echo)
08H (Character Input Without Echo)
0AH (Buffered Keyboard Input)
0CH (Flush Buffer, Read Keyboard)
3FH (Read File or Device)

Example

```
;****************************************************************;
;                                                                ;
;             Function 01H: Character Input with Echo            ;
;                                                                ;
;             int read_kbd_echo()                                ;
;                                                                ;
;             Returns a character from standard input            ;
;             after sending it to standard output.               ;
;                                                                ;
;****************************************************************;

cProc    read_kbd_echo,PUBLIC
cBegin
         mov      ah,01h          ; Set function code.
         int      21h             ; Wait for character.
         mov      ah,0            ; Character is in AL, so clear high
                                  ; byte.
cEnd
```

Interrupt 21H (33)
Function 02H (2)

1.0 and later

Character Output

Function 02H sends a character to standard output.

To Call

AH = 02H
DL = 8-bit code for character to be output

Returns

Nothing

Programmer's Notes

- With versions 1.x of MS-DOS, Function 02H sends a character to the active display. With MS-DOS versions 2.0 and later, Function 02H sends the character to standard output. By default, the output is sent to the active display, but it can be redirected to another device or to a file.
- With all versions of MS-DOS, displaying a backspace (08H) moves the cursor back one position but does not erase the character at the new position.
- If a Control-C is detected after the character is sent, Interrupt 23H (Control-C Handler Address) is called.
- With MS-DOS versions 2.0 and later, Function 40H (Write File or Device) should be used in preference to Function 02H.

Related Functions

06H (Direct Console I/O)
09H (Display String)
40H (Write File or Device)

Example

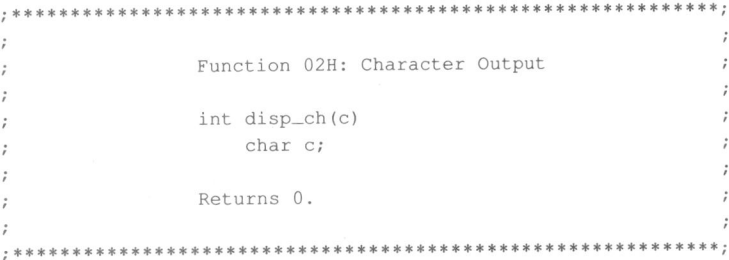

```
;**************************************************************;
;                                                              ;
;              Function 02H: Character Output                  ;
;                                                              ;
;              int disp_ch(c)                                  ;
;                   char c;                                    ;
;                                                              ;
;              Returns 0.                                      ;
;                                                              ;
;**************************************************************;
```

(more)

```
cProc   disp_ch,PUBLIC
parmB   c
cBegin
        mov     dl,c            ; Get character into DL.
        mov     ah,02h          ; Set function code.
        int     21h             ; Send character.
        xor     ax,ax           ; Return 0.
cEnd
```

Interrupt 21H (33)
Function 03H (3)

1.0 and later

Auxiliary Input

Function 03H waits for a character from the standard auxiliary device and returns the character in the AL register.

To Call

AH = 03H

Returns

AL = 8-bit character code

Programmer's Notes

- With versions 1.x of MS-DOS, Function 03H reads a character from the first serial port. With versions 2.0 and later, Function 03H reads from the standard auxiliary device (AUX), which defaults to COM1.
- Function 03H waits for input until a character is available from the standard auxiliary device.
- Function 03H is not interrupt driven and does not buffer characters received from the standard auxiliary device. As a result, it may not be fast enough for some telecommunications applications and data may be lost.
- A program cannot perform error detection using Function 03H. On IBM PCs and compatibles, error detection is available through the ROM BIOS Interrupt 14H. Another option is to drive the communications controller directly.
- Function 03H does not ensure that auxiliary input is connected and working, nor does it perform any error checking or set up the auxiliary input device. On IBM PCs and compatibles, the standard auxiliary device, normally COM1, is set to 2400 baud, no parity, 1 stop bit, and 8 databits at startup. These parameters can be changed with the MS-DOS MODE command.
- Some auxiliary input devices do not support 8-bit data transmission. This transmission parameter is a characteristic of the device and the communication parameters to which it is set; it is independent of Function 03H.
- If a Control-C is detected at the console, Interrupt 23H (Control-C Handler Address) is called.
- With MS-DOS versions 2.0 and later, Function 3FH (Read File or Device), which handles strings as well as single characters, should be used in preference to Function 03H.

Related Functions

04H (Auxiliary Output)
3FH (Read File or Device)

Example

```
;*************************************************************;
;                                                             ;
;               Function 03H: Auxiliary Input                 ;
;                                                             ;
;                    int aux_in()                             ;
;                                                             ;
;               Returns next character from AUX device.       ;
;                                                             ;
;*************************************************************;

cProc   aux_in,PUBLIC
cBegin
        mov     ah,03h          ; Set function code.
        int     21h             ; Wait for character from AUX.
        mov     ah,0            ; Character is in AL
                                ; so clear high byte.
cEnd
```

Interrupt 21H (33)
Function 04H (4)

Auxiliary Output

Function 04H sends a character to the standard auxiliary device.

To Call

AH = 04H
DL = 8-bit code for character to be output

Returns

Nothing

Programmer's Notes

- With versions 1.x of MS-DOS, Function 04H sends a character to the first serial port. With versions 2.0 and later, Function 04H sends the character to the standard auxiliary device (AUX), which defaults to COM1.
- Function 04H does not ensure that auxiliary output is connected and working, nor does it perform any error checking or set up the auxiliary output device. On IBM PCs and compatibles, the standard auxiliary device, normally COM1, is set to 2400 baud, no parity, 1 stop bit, and 8 databits at startup. These parameters can be changed with the MS-DOS MODE command.
- Function 04H does not return the status of auxiliary output, nor does it return an error code if the auxiliary output device is not ready for data. If the device is busy, Function 04H waits until it is available.
- Interrupt 23H (Control-C Handler Address) is called if a Control-C is detected at the console.
- With MS-DOS versions 2.0 and later, Function 40H (Write File or Device), which manages strings as well as single characters, should be used in preference to Function 04H.

Related Functions

03H (Auxiliary Input)
40H (Write File or Device)

Example

```
;***************************************************************;
;                                                             ;
;                Function 04H: Auxiliary Output               ;
;                                                             ;
;                int aux_out(c)                               ;
;                     char c;                                 ;
;                                                             ;
;                Returns 0.                                   ;
;                                                             ;
;***************************************************************;

cProc   aux_out,PUBLIC
parmB   c
cBegin
        mov     dl,c            ; Get character into DL.
        mov     ah,04h          ; Set function code.
        int     21h             ; Write character to AUX.
        xor     ax,ax           ; Return 0.
cEnd
```

Interrupt 21H (33)
Function 05H (5)

1.0 and later

Print Character

Function 05H sends a character to the standard printer.

To Call

AH = 05H
DL = 8-bit code for character to be output

Returns

Nothing

Programmer's Notes

- With versions 1.x of MS-DOS, Function 05H sends a character to the first parallel port (LPT1). With versions 2.0 and later, Function 05H sends the character to the standard printer (PRN), which defaults to LPT1 unless LPT1 has been reassigned with the MS-DOS MODE command. If redirection is in effect, calls to this function send output to the device currently assigned to LPT1.
- Function 05H does not return the status of the standard printer, nor does it return an error code if the standard printer is not ready for characters. If the printer is busy or off line, Function 05H waits until it is available. MS-DOS does, however, perform error checking during the print operation and send any error messages to the standard error device (normally the display).
- If a Control-C is detected at the console, Interrupt 23H (Control-C Handler Address) is called.
- With MS-DOS versions 2.0 and later, Function 40H (Write File or Device) should be used in preference to Function 05H.

Related Function

40H (Write File or Device)

Example

```
;**************************************************************;
;                                                              ;
;               Function 05H: Print Character                  ;
;                                                              ;
;               int print_ch(c)                                ;
;                       char c;                                ;
;                                                              ;
;               Returns 0.                                     ;
;                                                              ;
;**************************************************************;
```

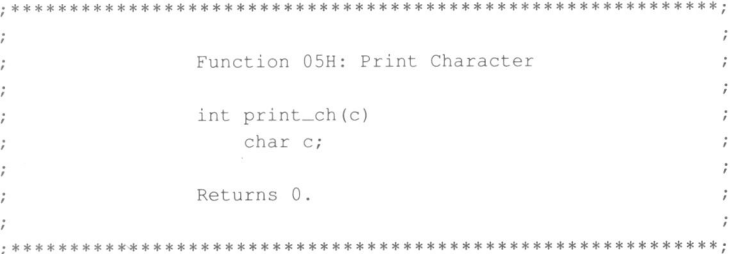

(more)

```
cProc    print_ch,PUBLIC
parmB    c
cBegin
         mov     dl,c              ; Get character into DL.
         mov     ah,05h            ; Set function code.
         int     21h               ; Write character to standard printer.
         xor     ax,ax             ; Return 0.
cEnd
```

Interrupt 21H (33)
Function 06H (6)

Direct Console I/O

Function 06H reads a character from standard input or writes a character to standard output.

To Call

AH = 06H

For character input:

DL = FFH

For character output:

DL = 00–FEH (8-bit character code)

Returns

If DL was 0FFH on call and a character was ready:

Zero flag is clear.

AL = 8-bit character code

If DL was 0FFH on call and no character was ready:

Zero flag is set.

Programmer's Notes

- With MS-DOS versions 1.x, Function 06H reads a character from the keyboard or sends a character to the display. With versions 2.0 and later, input and output can be redirected; Function 06H reads from the device currently assigned to standard input or sends to the device currently assigned to standard output.
- Function 06H allows all possible characters and control codes with values between 00H and 0FEH to be read or written with standard input and output and with no filtering by the operating system. The rubout character (0FFH, 255 decimal), however, cannot be output with Function 06H; Function 02H (Character Output) should be used instead.
- On IBM PCs and compatibles, extended characters, such as those produced by the Alt-O and F8 keys, are returned as 2 bytes. The first byte, 00H, signals an extended character; the second byte completes the key code. To read these characters, Function 06H must be called twice.

With MS-DOS versions 2.0 and later, if standard input has been redirected, the value 00H can also represent a null character from a file and, in that case, might not represent valid data. A program can use Function 44H (IOCTL) Subfunction 00H (Get Device Data) to determine whether standard input has been redirected.

- If Function 06H is an input request and a Control-C is read, the character is returned as any other character would be. Interrupt 23H (Control-C Handler Address) is not called.

- With MS-DOS versions 2.0 and later, Function 3FH (Read File or Device) and Function 40H (Write File or Device) should be used in preference to Function 06H.

Related Functions

01H (Character Input with Echo)
02H (Character Output)
07H (Unfiltered Character Input Without Echo)
08H (Character Input Without Echo)
09H (Display String)
0AH (Buffered Keyboard Input)
0CH (Flush Buffer, Read Keyboard)
3FH (Read File or Device)
40H (Write File or Device)

Example

```
;************************************************************;
;                                                            ;
;            Function 06H: Direct Console I/O                ;
;                                                            ;
;            int con_io(c)                                   ;
;                char c;                                     ;
;                                                            ;
;            Returns meaningless data if c is not 0FFH,      ;
;            otherwise returns next character from           ;
;            standard input.                                 ;
;                                                            ;
;************************************************************;

cProc   con_io,PUBLIC
parmB   c
cBegin
        mov     dl,c            ; Get character into DL.
        mov     ah,06h          ; Set function code.
        int     21h             ; This function does NOT wait in
                                ; input case (c = 0FFH)!
        mov     ah,0            ; Return the contents of AL.
cEnd
```

Interrupt 21H (33)
Function 07H (7)

Unfiltered Character Input Without Echo

Function 07H waits for a character from standard input. It does not echo the character to standard output, and it ignores Control-C characters.

To Call

AH = 07H

Returns

AL = 8-bit character code

Programmer's Notes

- With versions 1.x of MS-DOS, Function 07H reads input from the keyboard. With versions 2.0 and later, Function 07H reads a character from standard input. Standard input defaults to the keyboard but can be redirected to another device or to a file.
- Function 07H waits for input if a character is not available. A wait can be avoided by calling Function 0BH (Check Keyboard Status), which checks whether a character is available from standard input, and then calling Function 07H if a character is ready.
- On IBM PCs and compatibles, extended characters, such as those produced by the Alt-O and F8 keys, are returned as 2 bytes. The first byte, 00H, signals an extended character; the second byte completes the key code. To read these characters, Function 07H must be called twice.

  With MS-DOS versions 2.0 and later, if standard input has been redirected, the value 00H can also represent a null character from a file and, in that case, might not represent valid data. A program can use Function 44H (IOCTL) Subfunction 00H (Get Device Data) to determine whether standard input has been redirected.
- Interrupt 23H (Control-C Handler Address) is not called if a Control-C is read. Function 07H simply passes the character back through the AL register. If Control-C checking is required, Function 08H (Character Input Without Echo) should be used instead.
- With MS-DOS versions 2.0 and later, Function 3FH (Read File or Device) should be used in preference to Function 07H.

Related Functions

01H (Character Input with Echo)
06H (Direct Console I/O)
08H (Character Input Without Echo)
0AH (Buffered Keyboard Input)
0CH (Flush Buffer, Read Keyboard)
3FH (Read File or Device)

Example

```
;***************************************************************;
;                                                               ;
;            Function 07H: Unfiltered Character Input           ;
;                           Without Echo                        ;
;                                                               ;
;               int con_in()                                    ;
;                                                               ;
;            Returns next character from standard input.        ;
;                                                               ;
;***************************************************************;

cProc   con_in,PUBLIC
cBegin
        mov     ah,07h          ; Set function code.
        int     21h             ; Wait for character, no echo.
        mov     ah,0            ; Clear high byte.
cEnd
```

Interrupt 21H (33)
Function 08H (8)

1.0 and later

Character Input Without Echo

Function 08H waits for a character from standard input. The character is not echoed to standard output.

To Call

AH = 08H

Returns

AL = 8-bit character code

Programmer's Notes

- With versions 1.x of MS-DOS, Function 08H reads input from the keyboard. With versions 2.0 and later, Function 08H reads a character from standard input. Standard input defaults to the keyboard but can be redirected to another device or to a file.
- Function 08H waits for input if a character is not available. A wait can be avoided by calling Function 0BH (Check Keyboard Status), which checks whether a character is available, and then calling Function 08H if a character is ready.
- On IBM PCs and compatibles, extended characters, such as those produced by the Alt-O and F8 keys, are returned as 2 bytes. The first byte, 00H, signals an extended character; the second byte completes the key code. To read these characters, Function 08H must be called twice.

  With MS-DOS versions 2.0 and later, if standard input has been redirected, the value 00H can also represent a null character from a file and, in that case, might not represent valid data. A process can use Function 44H (IOCTL) Subfunction 00H (Get Device Data) to determine whether standard input has been redirected.
- If a Control-C is read and (with versions 2.0 and later) input has not been redirected, Interrupt 23H (Control-C Handler Address) is called. To read the Control-C character as data, Function 07H (Unfiltered Character Input Without Echo) should be used.
- Interrupt 23H (Control-C Handler Address) is called if Control-C is the input character, Break is enabled, and (with versions 2.0 and later) standard input has been redirected to come from a file.
- With MS-DOS versions 2.0 and later, Function 3FH (Read File or Device) should be used in preference to Function 08H.

Related Functions

01H (Character Input with Echo)
06H (Direct Console I/O)
07H (Unfiltered Character Input Without Echo)
0AH (Buffered Keyboard Input)
0CH (Flush Buffer, Read Keyboard)
3FH (Read File or Device)

Example

```
;************************************************************;
;                                                          ;
;       Function 08H:  Unfiltered Character Input Without Echo   ;
;                                                          ;
;       int read_kbd()                                     ;
;                                                          ;
;       Returns next character from standard input.        ;
;                                                          ;
;************************************************************;

cProc   read_kbd,PUBLIC
cBegin
        mov     ah,08h          ; Set function code.
        int     21h             ; Wait for character, no echo.
        mov     ah,0            ; Clear high byte.
cEnd
```

Interrupt 21H (33)
Function 09H (9)

1.0 and later

Display String

Function 09H sends a string of characters to standard output. The string must end with the dollar-sign character ($). All characters up to, but not including, the $ are displayed.

To Call

AH   = 09H
DS:DX   = segment:offset of string to display

Returns

Nothing

Programmer's Notes

- With MS-DOS versions 1.x, Function 09H sends the string to the display. With versions 2.0 and later, the string is written to standard output. By default, standard output is sent to the display, but it can be redirected to another device or to a file.
- The string can include any valid ASCII characters, including control codes. Sending a dollar sign with this function, however, is not possible.
- Depending on the device currently serving as standard output, characters other than the normally displayable ASCII characters (20H to 7FH) may or may not be displayed. On IBM PCs and most compatibles, extensions to the displayable ASCII character set (character codes 80H to FFH) appear as foreign or graphics characters.
- Display begins at the current cursor position on standard output. After the string is completely displayed, the cursor position is updated to the location immediately following the string.

  On IBM PCs and compatibles, if the end of a line is reached before the string is completely displayed, a carriage return and linefeed are issued and the next character is displayed in the first position of the following line. If the cursor reaches the bottom right corner of the display before the complete string has been sent, the display is scrolled up one line.
- Control characters are often included in the string to be sent. The following sample fragment of code contains carriage returns and linefeeds:

```
msg     db      'Resident part of TSR.COM installed'
        db      0dh, 0ah
        db      'Copyright (c) 19xx Foo Software, Inc.'
        db      0dh, 0ah, 0ah, 0ah
        db      '$'
```

- If a Control-C is detected, Interrupt 23H (Control-C Handler Address) is called.

- With MS-DOS versions 2.0 and later, Function 40H (Write File or Device) should be used in preference to Function 09H.

Related Functions

02H (Character Output)
06H (Direct Console I/O)
40H (Write File or Device)

Example

```
;**************************************************************;
;                                                            ;
;                 Function 09H: Display String               ;
;                                                            ;
;                    int disp_str(pstr)                       ;
;                         char *pstr;                         ;
;                                                            ;
;                      Returns 0.                             ;
;                                                            ;
;**************************************************************;

cProc    disp_str,PUBLIC,<ds,di>
parmDP   pstr
cBegin
         loadDP  ds,dx,pstr      ; DS:DX = pointer to string.
         mov     ax,0900h        ; Prepare to write dollar-terminated
                                 ; string to standard output, but
                                 ; first replace the 0 at the end of
                                 ; the string with '$'.
         push    ds              ; Set ES equal to DS.
         pop     es              ; (MS-C does not require ES to be
                                 ; saved.)
         mov     di,dx           ; ES:DI points at string.
         mov     cx,0ffffh       ; Allow string to be 64KB long.
         repne   scasb           ; Look for 0 at end of string.
         dec     di              ; Scasb search always goes 1 byte too
                                 ; far.
         mov     byte ptr [di],'$' ; Replace 0 with dollar sign.
         int     21h             ; Have MS-DOS print string.
         mov     [di],al         ; Restore 0 terminator.
         xor     ax,ax           ; Return 0.
cEnd
```

Interrupt 21H (33)
Function 0AH (10)

Buffered Keyboard Input

Function 0AH collects characters from standard input and places them in a user-specified memory buffer. Input is accepted until either a carriage return (0DH) is encountered or the buffer is filled to one character less than its capacity. The characters are echoed to standard output.

To Call

AH   = 0AH
DS:DX   = segment:offset of input buffer

Returns

Nothing

Programmer's Notes

- With MS-DOS versions 1.x, Function 0AH reads a string from the keyboard. With versions 2.0 and later, calls to this function read a string from standard input, which defaults to the keyboard but can be redirected to another device or to a file. The MS-DOS editing keys are active during input with this function.
- The buffer pointed to by DS:DX must have the following format:

Byte	Contents
0	Maximum number of characters to read (1–255); this value must be set by the process before Function 0AH is called.
1	Count of characters read (does not include the carriage return); this value is set by Function 0AH before returning to the process.
2–(n+2)	Actual string of characters read, including the carriage return; n = number of bytes read.

- The first byte of the buffer must contain the maximum number of characters the program will accept, including the carriage return at the end. Because the last byte must be a carriage return, the maximum number of bytes this function will actually read is 254. The carriage return is not included in the character count returned by MS-DOS in the second byte of the buffer.
- If the buffer fills to 1 byte less than its capacity, succeeding characters are ignored and a beep is sounded for each keypress until a carriage return is received.
- If a Control-C is detected and (with versions 2.0 and later) input has not been redirected, Interrupt 23H (Control-C Handler Address) is called.
- With versions 2.0 and later, if standard input has been redirected to come from a file, Break must be enabled for Interrupt 23H (Control-C Handler Address) to be called when Control-C is the input character.

- With MS-DOS versions 2.0 and later, if input is redirected, an end-of-file condition goes undetected by Function 0AH.

Related Functions

01H (Character Input with Echo)
06H (Direct Console I/O)
07H (Unfiltered Character Input Without Echo)
08H (Character Input Without Echo)
0CH (Flush Buffer, Read Keyboard)
3FH (Read File or Device)

Example

```
;*************************************************************;
;                                                           ;
;          Function 0AH: Buffered Keyboard Input            ;
;                                                           ;
;          int read_str(pbuf,len)                           ;
;              char *pbuf;                                   ;
;              int len;                                     ;
;                                                           ;
;          Returns number of bytes read into buffer.        ;
;                                                           ;
;          Note: pbuf must be at least len+3 bytes long.    ;
;                                                           ;
;*************************************************************;

cProc   read_str,PUBLIC,<ds,di>
parmDP  pbuf
parmB   len
cBegin
        loadDP  ds,dx,pbuf      ; DS:DX = pointer to buffer.
        mov     al,len          ; AL = len.
        inc     al              ; Add 1 to allow for CR in buf.
        mov     di,dx
        mov     [di],al         ; Store max length into buffer.
        mov     ah,0ah          ; Set function code.
        int     21h             ; Ask MS-DOS to read string.
        mov     al,[di+1]       ; Return number of characters read.
        mov     ah,0
        mov     bx,ax
        mov     [bx+di+2],ah    ; Store 0 at end of buffer.
cEnd
```

Interrupt 21H (33)
Function 0BH (11)

1.0 and later

Check Keyboard Status

Function 0BH returns a value in AL that indicates whether a character is available from standard input.

To Call

AH = 0BH

Returns

AL = 00H   no character available
     FFH   one or more characters available

Programmer's Notes

- With MS-DOS versions 1.x, Function 0BH checks the type-ahead buffer for a character. With versions 2.0 and later, if input has been redirected, Function 0BH checks standard input for a character. If input has not been redirected, the function checks the type-ahead buffer.
- Function 0BH does not indicate how many characters are available; it merely indicates whether at least one character is available.
- If the available character is Control-C, Interrupt 23H (Control-C Handler Address) is called.
- Function 0BH does not remove characters from standard input. Thus, if a character is present, repeated calls return 0FFH in AL until all characters in the buffer are read, either with one of the character-input functions (01H, 06H, 07H, 08H, or 0AH) or with Function 3FH (Read File or Device) using the handle for standard input (0).

Related Functions

06H (Direct Console I/O)
44H Subfunction 06H (IOCTL: Check Input Status)

Example

```
;***********************************************************;
;                                                          ;
;            Function 0BH: Check Keyboard Status           ;
;                                                          ;
;            int key_ready()                               ;
;                                                          ;
;            Returns 1 if key is ready, 0 if not.          ;
;                                                          ;
;***********************************************************;
```

(more)

```
        cProc    key_ready,PUBLIC
        cBegin
                mov      ah,0bh            ; Set function code.
                int      21h               ; Ask MS-DOS if key is available.
                and      ax,0001h          ; Keep least significant bit only.
        cEnd
```

Interrupt 21H (33)
Function 0CH (12)

1.0 and later

Flush Buffer, Read Keyboard

Function 0CH clears the standard-input buffer and then performs one of the other keyboard input functions (01H, 06H, 07H, 08H, 0AH).

To Call

AH   = 0CH
AL   = input function number to execute

If AL is 06H:

DL   = FFH

If AL is 0AH:

DS:DX   = segment:offset of buffer to receive input

Returns

If AL was 01H, 06H, 07H, or 08H on call:

AL   = 8-bit ASCII character from standard input

If AL was 0AH on call:

Nothing

Programmer's Notes

- With versions 1.x of MS-DOS, Function 0CH empties the type-ahead buffer before executing the input function specified in AL. With versions 2.0 and later, if input has been redirected to a file, Function 0CH does nothing before carrying out the input function specified in AL; if input was not redirected, the type-ahead buffer is flushed.
- A function number other than 01H, 06H, 07H, 08H, or 0AH in AL simply flushes the standard-input buffer and returns control to the calling program.
- If AL contains 0AH, DS:DX must point to the buffer in which MS-DOS is to place the string read from the keyboard.
- Because the buffer is flushed before the input function is carried out, any Control-C characters pending in the buffer are discarded. If subsequent input is a Control-C, however, Interrupt 23H (Control-C Handler Address) is called if (in versions 2.0 and later) standard input has not been redirected to come from a file.
- With versions 2.0 and later, if standard input has been redirected to come from a file and, after the buffer is flushed, subsequent input is a Control-C character, Interrupt 23H (Control-C handler address) is called only if Break is enabled.
- This function exists to defeat the type-ahead feature if necessary — for example, to obtain input at a critical prompt the user may not have anticipated.

Related Functions

01H (Character Input with Echo)
06H (Direct Console I/O)
07H (Unfiltered Character Input Without Echo)
08H (Character Input Without Echo)
0AH (Buffered Keyboard Input)
3FH (Read File or Device)

Example

```
;**************************************************************;
;                                                              ;
;           Function 0CH: Flush Buffer, Read Keyboard          ;
;                                                              ;
;                  int flush_kbd()                             ;
;                                                              ;
;                  Returns 0.                                  ;
;                                                              ;
;**************************************************************;

cProc   flush_kbd,PUBLIC
cBegin
        mov     ax,0c00h        ; Just flush type-ahead buffer.
        int     21h             ; Call MS-DOS.
        xor     ax,ax           ; Return 0.
cEnd
```

Interrupt 21H (33)
Function 0DH (13)

Disk Reset

Function 0DH writes to disk all internal MS-DOS file buffers in memory that have been modified since the last write. All buffers are then marked as "free."

To Call

AH = 0DH

Returns

Nothing

Programmer's Notes

- Function 0DH ensures that the information stored on disk matches changes made by write requests to file buffers in memory.
- Function 0DH does not update the disk directory. The application must issue Function 10H (Close File with FCB) or Function 3EH (Close File) to update directory information correctly.
- Function 0DH should be part of Control-C interrupt-handling routines so that the system is left in a known state when an application is terminated.
- Disk Reset calls can be issued after particularly important disk write calls, such as transactions in an accounting application. Repeated use of this function, however, degrades system performance by defeating the MS-DOS buffering scheme.

Related Functions

10H (Close File with FCB)
3EH (Close File)

Example

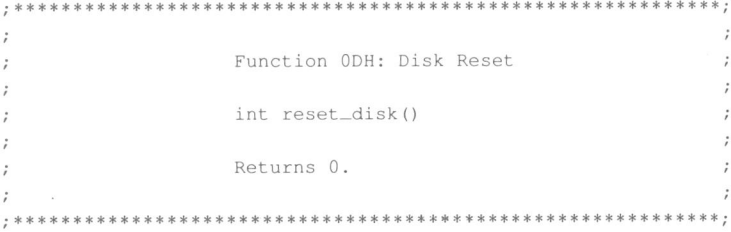

```
;*************************************************************;
;                                                           ;
;               Function 0DH: Disk Reset                    ;
;                                                           ;
;               int reset_disk()                            ;
;                                                           ;
;               Returns 0.                                  ;
;                                                           ;
;*************************************************************;
```

(more)

```
cProc   reset_disk,PUBLIC
cBegin
        mov     ah,0dh          ; Set function code.
        int     21h             ; Ask MS-DOS to write all dirty file
                                ; buffers to the disk.
        xor     ax,ax           ; Return 0.
cEnd
```

Interrupt 21H (33)
Function 0EH (14)

1.0 and later

Select Disk

Function 0EH sets the default disk drive to the drive specified in the DL register. The default is the disk drive MS-DOS chooses for file access when a filename is specified without a drive designator. A successful call to this function returns the number of logical (not physical) drives in the system.

To Call

AH = 0EH
DL = drive number (0 = drive A, 1 = drive B, 2 = drive C, and so on)

Returns

AL = number of logical drives in the system

Programmer's Notes

- The value used as a drive number is the ASCII value of the uppercase drive letter minus the ASCII value of the uppercase letter A (41H); thus, 0 = drive A, 1 = drive B, and so on.
- A logical drive is defined as any block-oriented device; this category includes floppy-disk drives, RAMdisks, tape devices, fixed disks (which can be partitioned into more than one logical drive), and network drives.
- The maximum numbers of drive designators available for each MS-DOS version are as follows:

MS-DOS Version	Number of Designators	Values
1.x	16	0 through 0FH
2.x	63	0 through 3FH
3.x	26	0 through 19H

Drive letters should be limited to A through P (0 through 0FH) to ensure that an application runs on all versions of MS-DOS.
- With versions of MS-DOS earlier than 3.0 running on IBM PCs and compatibles with one floppy-disk drive, Function 0EH returns 02H as the drive count, because the single physical drive is equivalent to the two logical drives A and B. MS-DOS versions 3.0 and later return a minimum value of 05H in AL.
- On IBM PCs and compatibles, the number of physical floppy-disk drives in a system can be obtained from the ROM BIOS with Interrupt 11H (Equipment Determination).

Related Function

19H (Get Current Disk)

Example

```
;**************************************************************;
;                                                              ;
;       Function 0EH: Select Disk                              ;
;                                                              ;
;       int select_drive(drive_ltr)                            ;
;           char drive_ltr;                                    ;
;                                                              ;
;       Returns number of logical drives present in system.    ;
;                                                              ;
;**************************************************************;

cProc   select_drive,PUBLIC
parmB   drive_ltr
cBegin
        mov     dl,drive_ltr      ; Get new drive letter.
        and     dl,not 20h        ; Make sure letter is uppercase.
        sub     dl,'A'            ; Convert drive letter to number,
                                  ; 'A' = 0, 'B' = 1, etc.
        mov     ah,0eh            ; Set function code.
        int     21h               ; Ask MS-DOS to set default drive.
        cbw                       ; Clear high byte of return value.
cEnd
```

Interrupt 21H (33)
Function 0FH (15)

1.0 and later

Open File with FCB

Function 0FH opens the file named in the file control block (FCB) pointed to by DS:DX.

To Call

AH = 0FH
DS:DX = segment:offset of an unopened FCB

Returns

If function is successful:

AL = 00H

If function is not successful:

AL = FFH

Programmer's Notes

- MS-DOS provides several types of file services: FCB file services, which are relatively compatible with the CP/M methods of file handling; extended FCB file services, which take advantage of both CP/M compatibility and MS-DOS extensions; and handle, or "stream-oriented," file services, which are more compatible with UNIX/XENIX and support pathnames (MS-DOS versions 2.0 and later).
- Function 0FH does not support pathnames and so is capable of opening files only in the current directory of the specified drive.
- Function 0FH does not create a new file if the specified file does not already exist. Function 16H (Create File with FCB) is used to create new files with FCBs.
- Function 0FH must use an unopened FCB — that is, one in which all but the drive-designator, filename, and extension fields are zero. If the call is successful, the function fills in the file size and date fields from the file's directory entry. In MS-DOS versions 2.0 and later, the function also fills in the time field.
- If the file is opened on the default drive (the drive number in the FCB is set to 0), MS-DOS fills in the actual drive code. Thus, at some later point in processing, the default drive can be changed and MS-DOS will still have the drive number in the FCB for use in accessing the file. It will therefore continue to use the correct drive.
- If Function 0FH is successful, MS-DOS sets the current-block field to 0; that is, the file pointer is at the beginning of the file. It also sets the record size to 128 bytes (the system default).
- If a record size other than 128 is needed, the record size field of the FCB should be changed after the file is successfully opened and before attempting any I/O.

- In a network running under MS-DOS version 3.1 or later, files are opened by Function 0FH with the share code set to compatibility mode and the access code set to read/ write.
- If Function 0FH returns an error code (0FFH) in the AL register, the attempt to open the file was not successful. Possible causes for the failure are
  - File was not found.
  - File has the hidden or system attribute and a properly formatted extended FCB was not used.
  - Filename was improperly specified in the FCB.
  - SHARE is loaded and the file is already open by another process in a mode other than compatibility mode.
- With MS-DOS versions 3.0 and later, Function 59H (Get Extended Error Information) can be used to determine why the attempt to open the file failed.
- MS-DOS passes the first two command-tail parameters into default FCBs located at offsets 5CH and 6CH in the program segment prefix (PSP). Many applications designed to run as .COM files take advantage of one or both of these default FCBs.
- With MS-DOS versions 2.0 and later, Function 3DH (Open File with Handle) should be used in preference to Function 0FH.

Related Functions

10H (Close File with FCB)
16H (Create File with FCB)
3CH (Create File with Handle)
3DH (Open File with Handle)
3EH (Close File)
59H (Get Extended Error Information)
5AH (Create Temporary File)
5BH (Create New File)

Example

```
;***************************************************************;
;                                                               ;
;          Function 0FH: Open File, FCB-based                   ;
;                                                               ;
;          int FCB_open(uXFCB,recsize)                          ;
;               char *uXFCB;                                    ;
;               int recsize;                                    ;
;                                                               ;
;          Returns 0 if file opened OK, otherwise returns -1.   ;
;                                                               ;
;          Note: uXFCB must have the drive and filename         ;
;          fields (bytes 07H through 12H) and the extension     ;
;          flag (byte 00H) set before the call to FCB_open      ;
;          (see Function 29H).                                  ;
;                                                               ;
;***************************************************************;
```

(more)

```
        cProc   FCB_open,PUBLIC,ds
        parmDP  puXFCB
        parmW   recsize
        cBegin
                loadDP  ds,dx,puXFCB    ; Pointer to unopened extended FCB.
                mov     ah,0fh          ; Ask MS-DOS to open an existing file.
                int     21h
                add     dx,7            ; Advance pointer to start of regular
                                        ; FCB.
                mov     bx,dx           ; BX = FCB pointer.
                mov     dx,recsize      ; Get record size parameter.
                mov     [bx+0eh],dx     ; Store record size in FCB.
                xor     dx,dx
                mov     [bx+20h],dl     ; Set current-record
                mov     [bx+21h],dx     ; and relative-record
                mov     [bx+23h],dx     ; fields to 0.
                cbw                     ; Set return value to 0 or -1.
        cEnd
```

Interrupt 21H (33)
Function 10H (16)

1.0 and later

Close File with FCB

Function 10H flushes file-related information to disk, closes the file named in the file control block (FCB) pointed to by DS:DX, and updates the file's directory entry.

To Call

AH   = 10H
DS:DX   = segment:offset of previously opened FCB

Returns

If function is successful:

AL   = 00H

If function is not successful:

AL   = FFH

Programmer's Notes

- A successful call to Function 10H flushes to disk all MS-DOS internal buffers associated with the file and updates the directory entry and file allocation table (FAT). The function thus ensures that correct information is contained in the copy of the file on disk.
- Because MS-DOS versions 1.x and 2.x do not always detect a disk change, an error can occur if the user changes disks between the time the file is opened and the time it is closed. In the worst case, the FAT and the directory of the newly inserted disk may be damaged.
- With MS-DOS versions 2.0 and later, Function 3EH (Close File) should be used in preference to Function 10H.

Related Functions

0FH (Open File with FCB)
3EH (Close File)

Example

```
;*************************************************************;
;                                                             ;
;            Function 10H: Close file, FCB-based              ;
;                                                             ;
;            int FCB_close(oXFCB)                             ;
;                 char *oXFCB;                                ;
;                                                             ;
;            Returns 0 if file closed OK, otherwise           ;
;            returns -1.                                       ;
;                                                             ;
;*************************************************************;

cProc   FCB_close,PUBLIC,ds
parmDP  poXFCB
cBegin
        loadDP  ds,dx,poXFCB    ; Pointer to opened extended FCB.
        mov     ah,10h          ; Ask MS-DOS to close file.
        int     21h
        cbw                     ; Set return value to 0 or -1.
cEnd
```

Interrupt 21H (33)
Function 11H (17)

1.0 and later

Find First File

Function 11H searches the current directory for the first file that matches a specified name and extension.

To Call

AH   = 11H
DS:DX   = segment:offset of unopened file control block (FCB)

Returns

If function is successful:

AL   = 00H

Disk transfer area (DTA) contains unopened FCB of same type (normal or extended) as search FCB.

If function is not successful:

AL   = FFH

Programmer's Notes

- If necessary, Function 1AH (Set DTA Address) should be used before Function 11H is called, to set the location of the DTA in which the results of the search will be placed.
- With MS-DOS versions 1.0 and later, the wildcard character ? is allowed in the filename. With MS-DOS versions 3.0 and later, both wildcard characters (? and *) are allowed in filenames. Pathnames are not supported.
- With MS-DOS versions 2.0 and later, the attribute field of an extended FCB can be used to search for files with the hidden, system, subdirectory, or volume-label attributes. In such a search, specifying either the normal (00H) or volume-label (08H) attribute restricts MS-DOS to files with the given attribute. Specifying any combination of the hidden (02H), system (04H), and subdirectory (10H) attributes, however, causes MS-DOS to search both for normal files and for those that match the specified attributes.
- For a normal FCB, Function 11H places the drive number in the first byte of the DTA and fills the succeeding 32 bytes with the directory entry.

  For an extended FCB, Function 11H fills in the first 7 bytes of the DTA as follows: the first byte contains 0FFH, indicating an extended FCB; the second through sixth bytes contain 00H, as required by MS-DOS; the seventh byte contains the value of the attribute byte in the search FCB. The next 33 bytes contain the drive number and directory information, as for a normal FCB.

- As with other FCB functions, the number 0 can be used to indicate the default drive. MS-DOS fills in the actual drive number and continues to use that drive for calls to Function 12H (Find Next File) that use the same FCB, regardless of any subsequent selection of a different default drive.
- The FCB with the initial file specifications must remain unmodified if Function 12H is used to continue the search.
- Error reporting in Function 11H is incomplete. An error return (0FFH in the AL register) does not always mean that the file does not exist. Other possibilities include
  - Filename in the FCB was improperly specified.
  - If an extended FCB was used, no files match the attributes given.

  With MS-DOS versions 3.0 and later, Function 59H (Get Extended Error Information) can be used to obtain additional information about the error.
- With MS-DOS versions 2.0 and later, Functions 4EH (Find First File) and 4FH (Find Next File) should be used in preference to Functions 11H and 12H.

Related Functions

12H (Find Next File)
1AH (Set DTA Address)
4EH (Find First File)
4FH (Find Next File)

Example

```
;***********************************************************;
;                                                         ;
;        Function 11H: Find First File, FCB-based         ;
;                                                         ;
;        int FCB_first(puXFCB,attrib)                     ;
;            char *puXFCB;                                ;
;            char  attrib;                                ;
;                                                         ;
;        Returns 0 if match found, otherwise returns -1.  ;
;                                                         ;
;        Note: The FCB must have the drive and            ;
;        filename fields (bytes 07H through 12H) and       ;
;        the extension flag (byte 00H) set before         ;
;        the call to FCB_first (see Function 29H).        ;
;                                                         ;
;***********************************************************;
```

(more)

```
cProc    FCB_first,PUBLIC,ds
parmDP   puXFCB
parmB    attrib
cBegin
         loadDP  ds,dx,puXFCB    ; Pointer to unopened extended FCB.
         mov     bx,dx           ; BX points at FCB, too.
         mov     al,attrib       ; Get search attribute.
         mov     [bx+6],al       ; Put attribute into extended FCB
                                 ; area.
         mov     byte ptr [bx],0ffh ; Set flag for extended FCB.
         mov     ah,11h          ; Ask MS-DOS to find 1st matching
                                 ; file in current directory.
         int     21h             ; If match found, directory entry can
                                 ; be found at DTA address.
         cbw                     ; Set return value to 0 or -1.
cEnd
```

Interrupt 21H (33)
Function 12H (18)

1.0 and later

Find Next File

Function 12H searches the current directory for the next file that matches a specified filename and extension. The function assumes a previous successful call to Function 11H (Find First File) with the same file control block (FCB).

To Call

AH   = 12H
DS:DX   = segment:offset of search FCB

Returns

If function is successful:

AL   = 00H

Disk transfer area (DTA) contains unopened FCB of same type (normal or extended) as search FCB.

If function is not successful:

AL   = FFH

Programmer's Notes

- Function 12H assumes that a successful call to Function 11H (Find First File) has been completed with the same FCB. The FCB specifies the search pattern. This function also assumes that the wildcard character ? appears at least once in the filename or extension specified.
- An error (indicated by 0FFH returned in register AL) does not necessarily mean that a file matching the file specification does not exist in the current directory. MS-DOS relies on certain information that appears in the search FCB initialized by Function 11H, so it is important not to alter that FCB either between calls to Functions 11H and 12H or between subsequent calls to Function 12H.
- If drive code 0 (the default drive) was used in the call to Function 11H, MS-DOS has already filled in the actual drive number for the current directory. MS-DOS continues to use that drive for all calls to Function 12H that use the same FCB, regardless of the default drive in effect at the time of the call.
- With MS-DOS versions 2.0 and later, Functions 4EH (Find First File) and 4FH (Find Next File) should be used in preference to Functions 11H and 12H.

Related Functions

11H (Find First File)
1AH (Set DTA Address)
4EH (Find First File)
4FH (Find Next File)

Example

```
;*************************************************************;
;                                                           ;
;          Function 12H: Find Next File, FCB-based          ;
;                                                           ;
;          int FCB_next(puXFCB)                             ;
;               char *puXFCB;                               ;
;                                                           ;
;          Returns 0 if match found, otherwise returns -1.  ;
;                                                           ;
;          Note: The FCB must have the drive and            ;
;          filename fields (bytes 07H through 12H) and       ;
;          the extension flag (byte 00H) set before         ;
;          the call to FCB_next (see Function 29H).          ;
;                                                           ;
;*************************************************************;

cProc   FCB_next,PUBLIC,ds
parmDP  puXFCB
cBegin
        loadDP  ds,dx,puXFCB    ; Pointer to unopened extended FCB.
        mov     ah,12h          ; Ask MS-DOS to find next matching
                                ; file in current directory.
        int     21h             ; If match found, directory entry can
                                ; be found at DTA address.
        cbw                     ; Set return value to 0 or -1.
cEnd
```

Interrupt 21H (33)
Function 13H (19)

Delete File

Function 13H deletes all files matching a specified name and extension from the current directory.

To Call

AH   = 13H

DS:DX   = segment:offset of an unopened file control block (FCB)

Returns

If function is successful:

AL   = 00H

If function is not successful:

AL   = FFH

Programmer's Notes

- The wildcard character ? can be used to match any character or sequence of characters in specifying the filename and extension.
- Open files must not be deleted.
- Function 13H does not support pathnames.
- An error (indicated by 0FFH returned in register AL) does not necessarily mean that the filename specified does not exist in the current directory. Other possible causes for an error include
  - Filename in the FCB is improperly specified.
  - File is a read-only, hidden, or system file and an extended FCB with the appropriate attribute byte was not used.
  - Program attempted to delete a volume label and the label does not exist or a properly formatted extended FCB was not used.
  - In networking environments, file is locked or access rights are insufficient for deletion.
- MS-DOS removes file allocation table (FAT) mapping for the file or files deleted by this function and flushes the FAT to disk to ensure that the disk contains a correct table. The first character of the filename in the directory entry is replaced by the value 0E5H, indicating a deleted file.
- Because the function does not physically erase data, use of Function 13H alone is not sufficient in security-critical applications that strictly prohibit viewing the data.

- On networks running under MS-DOS versions 3.1 and later, the user must have Create access rights to the directory containing the file to be deleted.
- Because Function 13H deletes all files matching a given file specification, a conservative approach is to use a combination of Functions 11H (Find First File) and 12H (Find Next File) to build a list of files matching the file specification and then obtain confirmation from the user before deleting the files in the list.
- With MS-DOS versions 2.0 and later, Function 41H (Delete File) should be used in preference to Function 13H.

Related Function

41H (Delete File)

Example

```
;****************************************************************;
;                                                                ;
;           Function 13H: Delete File(s), FCB-based              ;
;                                                                ;
;           int FCB_delete(uXFCB)                                ;
;               char *uXFCB;                                     ;
;                                                                ;
;           Returns 0 if file(s) were deleted OK, otherwise      ;
;           returns -1.                                          ;
;                                                                ;
;           Note: uXFCB must have the drive and                  ;
;           filename fields (bytes 07H through 12H) and          ;
;           the extension flag (byte 00H) set before             ;
;           the call to FCB_delete (see Function 29H).           ;
;                                                                ;
;****************************************************************;

cProc   FCB_delete,PUBLIC,ds
parmDP  puXFCB
cBegin
        loadDP  ds,dx,puXFCB    ; Pointer to unopened extended FCB.
        mov     ah,13h          ; Ask MS-DOS to delete file(s).
        int     21h
        cbw                     ; Return value of 0 or -1.
cEnd
```

Interrupt 21H (33)
Function 14H (20)

1.0 and later

Sequential Read

Function 14H reads the next sequential block of data from a file and places the data in the current disk transfer area (DTA).

To Call

AH   = 14H
DS:DX   = segment:offset of a previously opened file control block (FCB)

Returns

AL   = 00H   read successful
              01H   end of file encountered; no data in record
              02H   DTA too small (segment wrap error); read canceled
              03H   end of file; partial record read

If AL = 00H or 03H:

DTA contains data read from file.

Programmer's Notes

- If necessary, Function 1AH (Set DTA Address) should be used to set the base address of the DTA before Function 14H is called. The default DTA is 128 bytes and is located at offset 80H of the program segment prefix (PSP). If record sizes larger than 128 bytes will be used, the program must change the DTA address to point to a buffer of adequate size.
- The read process begins at the current position in the file. When the read is complete, Function 14H increments the current-block and current-record fields of the FCB.
- The size of the record loaded into the DTA is specified in the record size field of the FCB. The default is 128 bytes, set by Function 0FH (Open File with FCB) or Function 16H (Create File with FCB). If the record size is not 128 bytes, the application must set the record size correctly before issuing any reads.
- Function 0FH does not fill in the current-record field of the FCB when opening a file, so this field must be explicitly set (usually to zero) before the first call to Function 14H. The record pointer, which includes the current-block and current-record fields of the FCB, is incremented when Function 14H is successfully completed.
- Function 14H deals with fixed-length records only. Buffering logic must be added to an application if variable-length records are to be manipulated.
- The block of data to be read can be chosen by changing the current-block and current-record fields of the FCB.

- Partial records read at the end of a file are padded with zeros to the requested record length.
- On networks running under MS-DOS version 3.1 or later, the user must have Read access rights to the directory containing the file to be read.
- With MS-DOS versions 2.0 and later, Function 3FH (Read File or Device) should be used in preference to Function 14H.

Related Functions

15H (Sequential Write)
1AH (Set DTA Address)
21H (Random Read)
27H (Random Block Read)
3FH (Read File or Device)

Example

```
;************************************************************;
;                                                          ;
;          Function 14H: Sequential Read, FCB-based         ;
;                                                          ;
;          int FCB_sread(oXFCB)                             ;
;               char *oXFCB;                                ;
;                                                          ;
;          Returns 0 if record read OK, otherwise          ;
;          returns error code 1, 2, or 3.                  ;
;                                                          ;
;************************************************************;

cProc    FCB_sread,PUBLIC,ds
parmDP   poXFCB
cBegin
         loadDP  ds,dx,poXFCB    ; Pointer to opened extended FCB.
         mov     ah,14h          ; Ask MS-DOS to read next record,
                                 ; placing it at DTA.
         int     21h
         cbw                     ; Clear high byte for return value.
cEnd
```

Interrupt 21H (33)
Function 15H (21)

1.0 and later

Sequential Write

Function 15H writes the next sequential block of data from the disk transfer area (DTA) to a specified file.

To Call

AH   = 15H
DS:DX   = segment:offset of a previously opened file control block (FCB)

DTA contains data to write.

Returns

AL   = 00H   block written successfully
        01H   disk full; write canceled
        02H   DTA too small (segment wrap error); write canceled

Programmer's Notes

- If necessary, the calling process should set the DTA address with Function 1AH (Set DTA Address) to point to the data to be written before issuing a call to Function 15H. The default address of the DTA is offset 80H in the program segment prefix (PSP).
- The FCB must already have been filled in by a call to Function 0FH (Open File with FCB) before Function 15H is called.
- The location of the block to be written is given by the current-block and current-record fields of the FCB. If the write is successful, Function 15H increments the current-block and current-record fields.
- The size of the record written by Function 15H is determined by the value in the record size field of the FCB. The default value is 128, set by Function 0FH (Open File with FCB) or Function 16H (Create File with FCB). A process must set the record size in the FCB correctly before issuing any writes.
- Function 15H deals with fixed-length records only. Buffering logic must be added to an application if variable-length records are to be manipulated.
- Function 15H performs a logical, but not necessarily physical, write operation. If less than one sector is being written, MS-DOS moves the record from the DTA to an appropriate MS-DOS internal buffer. When a full sector of data has been buffered, MS-DOS flushes the buffer to disk. Function 0DH (Disk Reset) or Function 10H (Close File with FCB) can be used to flush data to disk before a full sector is buffered.
- On networks running under MS-DOS versions 3.1 and later, the user must have Write access to the directory containing the file to be written to.
- With MS-DOS versions 2.0 and later, Function 40H (Write File or Device) should be used in preference to Function 15H.

Related Functions

14H (Sequential Read)
1AH (Set DTA Address)
22H (Random Write)
28H (Random Block Write)
40H (Write File or Device)

Example

```
;***************************************************************;
;                                                             ;
;          Function 15H: Sequential Write, FCB-based          ;
;                                                             ;
;          int FCB_swrite(oXFCB)                              ;
;              char *oXFCB;                                   ;
;                                                             ;
;          Returns 0 if record read OK, otherwise            ;
;          returns error code 1 or 2.                         ;
;                                                             ;
;***************************************************************;

cProc   FCB_swrite,PUBLIC,ds
parmDP  poXFCB
cBegin
        loadDP  ds,dx,poXFCB    ; Pointer to opened extended FCB.
        mov     ah,15h          ; Ask MS-DOS to write next record
                                ; from DTA to disk file.
        int     21h
        cbw                     ; Clear high byte for return value.
cEnd
```

Interrupt 21H (33)
Function 16H (22)

1.0 and later

Create File with FCB

Function 16H creates a directory entry in the current directory for a specified file and opens the file for use. If the file already exists, it is opened and truncated to zero length.

To Call

AH   = 16H
DS:DX   = segment:offset of an unopened file control block (FCB)

Returns

If function is successful:

AL   = 00H

If function is not successful:

AL   = FFH

Programmer's Notes

- Before creating a new directory entry for the specified file, Function 16H searches the current directory for a matching filename. If a match is found, the existing file is opened, but its length is set to 0. In effect, this action erases an existing file and replaces it with a new, empty file of the same name.

  If a matching filename is not found and the directory has room for a new entry, the file is created and opened, and its length is set to 0.

- An extended file control block (FCB) can be used to create a file with a special attribute, such as hidden. Before the Create File call is issued, the attribute byte must be set appropriately.

- A value of 0FFH returned in the AL register can indicate one of several errors:
  - Filename was improperly specified in the FCB.
  - File with the same name exists but is a read-only, hidden, system, or (in MS-DOS versions 3.x and networks) locked file.
  - Disk is full.
  - Current working directory is the root directory, and it is full.
  - User does not have the appropriate access rights to create a file in this directory (in MS-DOS versions 3.x and networks).

  With MS-DOS versions 3.0 and later, Function 59H (Get Extended Error Information) can be used to obtain additional information about an error.

- Upon successful completion of Function 16H, MS-DOS has
  - Created and opened the file specified in the FCB.

- Filled in the date and time fields of the FCB with the current date and time.
- Set file size to zero.

All other changes made to the FCB are similar to those made by Function 0FH (Open File with FCB).

● Pathnames and wildcard characters (? and *) are not supported by Function 16H.

● With MS-DOS versions 2.0 and later, Function 16H has been superseded by Functions 3CH (Create File with Handle), 5AH (Create Temporary File), and 5BH (Create New File).

Related Functions

0FH (Open File with FCB)
3CH (Create File with Handle)
3DH (Open File with Handle)
5AH (Create Temporary File)
5BH (Create New File)

Example

```
;*****************************************************************;
;                                                               ;
;              Function 16H: Create File, FCB-based             ;
;                                                               ;
;              int FCB_create(uXFCB,recsize)                    ;
;                   char *uXFCB;                                ;
;                   int recsize;                                ;
;                                                               ;
;              Returns 0 if file created OK, otherwise          ;
;              returns -1.                                      ;
;                                                               ;
;              Note: uXFCB must have the drive and filename     ;
;              fields (bytes 07H through 12H) and the           ;
;              extension flag (byte 00H) set before the         ;
;              call to FCB_create (see Function 29H).           ;
;                                                               ;
;*****************************************************************;

cProc    FCB_create,PUBLIC,ds
parmDP   puXFCB
parmW    recsize
cBegin
         loadDP  ds,dx,puXFCB    ; Pointer to unopened extended FCB.
         mov     ah,16h          ; Ask MS-DOS to create file.
         int     21h
         add     dx,7            ; Advance pointer to start of regular
                                 ; FCB.
         mov     bx,dx           ; BX = FCB pointer.
         mov     dx,recsize      ; Get record size parameter.
         mov     [bx+0eh],dx     ; Store record size in FCB.
         xor     dx,dx
         mov     [bx+20h],dl     ; Set current-record
         mov     [bx+21h],dx     ; and relative-record
         mov     [bx+23h],dx     ; fields to 0.
         cbw                     ; Set return value to 0 or -1.
cEnd
```

Interrupt 21H (33)
Function 17H (23)

Rename File

Function 17H renames one or more files in the current directory.

To Call

AH   = 17H

DS:DX = segment:offset of modified file control block (FCB) in the following nonstandard format:

Byte(s)	Contents
00H	Drive number
01–08H	Old filename (padded with blanks, if necessary)
09–0BH	Old file extension (padded with blanks, if necessary)
0CH–10H	Zeroed out
11H–18H	New filename (padded with blanks, if necessary)
19H–1BH	New file extension (padded with blanks, if necessary)
11CH–24H	Zeroed out

Returns

If function is successful:

AL   = 00H

If function is not successful:

AL   = FFH

Programmer's Notes

- The wildcard character ? can be used in specifying both the old and the new filenames, but its meaning differs in each case. A wildcard character in the old filename matches any single character or sequence of characters in the directory entry. A wildcard character in the new filename, however, indicates that the corresponding character or characters in the original filename are not to change.
- With MS-DOS versions 2.0 and later, Function 17H views subdirectory entries as files. These subdirectory entries can be renamed using this function and an extended FCB with the appropriate attribute byte.
- A value of 0FFH returned in the AL register can indicate one of several errors:
  - Old filename is improperly specified in the FCB.
  - File with the new filename already exists in the current directory.

- Old file is a read-only file.
- With MS-DOS versions 3.1 and later in a networking environment, the user has insufficient access rights to the directory.

With MS-DOS versions 3.0 and later, Function 59H (Get Extended Error Information) can be used to obtain additional information about the cause of an error.

● With MS-DOS versions 2.0 and later, Function 56H (Rename File) should be used in preference to Function 17H.

Related Function

56H (Rename File)

Example

```
;**************************************************************;
;                                                              ;
;            Function 17H: Rename File(s), FCB-based           ;
;                                                              ;
;            int FCB_rename(uXFCBold,uXFCBnew)                 ;
;                char *uXFCBold,*uXFCBnew;                     ;
;                                                              ;
;            Returns 0 if file(s) renamed OK, otherwise        ;
;            returns -1.                                       ;
;                                                              ;
;            Note: Both uXFCB's must have the drive and        ;
;            filename fields (bytes 07H through 12H) and       ;
;            the extension flag (byte 00H) set before          ;
;            the call to FCB_rename (see Function 29H).         ;
;                                                              ;
;**************************************************************;

cProc    FCB_rename,PUBLIC,<ds,si,di>
parmDP   puXFCBold
parmDP   puXFCBnew
cBegin
         loadDP  es,di,puXFCBold ; ES:DI = Pointer to uXFCBold.
         mov     dx,di           ; Save offset in DX.
         add     di,7            ; Advance pointer to start of regular
                                 ; FCBold.
         loadDP  ds,si,puXFCBnew ; DS:SI = Pointer to uXFCBnew.
         add     si,8            ; Advance pointer to filename field
                                 ; FCBnew.
                                 ; Copy name from FCBnew into FCBold
                                 ; at offset 11H:
         add     di,11h          ; DI points 11H bytes into old FCB.
         mov     cx,0bh          ; Copy 0BH bytes, moving new
         rep     movsb           ; name into old FCB.
         push    es              ; Set DS to segment of FCBold.
         pop     ds
         mov     ah,17h          ; Ask MS-DOS to rename old
         int     21h             ; file(s) to new name(s).
         cbw                     ; Set return flag to 0 or -1.
cEnd
```

Interrupt 21H (33)
Function 19H (25)

1.0 and later

Get Current Disk

Function 19H returns the code for the current disk drive.

To Call

AH = 19H

Returns

AL = drive code (0 = drive A, 1 = drive B, 2 = drive C, and so on)

Programmer's Note

- The drive code returned by Function 19H is zero-based, meaning that drive A = 0, drive B = 1, and so on. This value is unlike the drive code used in file control blocks (FCBs) and in some other MS-DOS functions, such as 1CH (Get Drive Data) and 36H (Get Disk Free Space), in which 0 indicates the default rather than the current drive.

Related Function

0EH (Select Disk)

Example

```
;************************************************************;
;                                                            ;
;             Function 19H: Get Current Disk                 ;
;                                                            ;
;                 int cur_drive()                            ;
;                                                            ;
;             Returns letter of current "logged" disk.       ;
;                                                            ;
;************************************************************;

cProc   cur_drive,PUBLIC
cBegin
        mov     ah,19h          ; Set function code.
        int     21h             ; Get number of logged disk.
        add     al,'A'          ; Convert number to letter.
        cbw                     ; Clear the high byte of return value.
cEnd
```

Interrupt 21H (33)
Function 1AH (26)

1.0 and later

Set DTA Address

Function 1AH specifies the location of the disk transfer area (DTA) to be used for file control block (FCB) disk I/O operations.

To Call

AH = 1AH
DS:DX = segment:offset of DTA

Returns

Nothing

Programmer's Notes

- If an application does not specify a disk transfer area, MS-DOS uses a default buffer at offset 80H in the program segment prefix (PSP).
- The DTA specified must be large enough to accommodate the amount of data to be transferred in a single block. The default record size for FCB file operations is 128 bytes; this value can be changed after a file is successfully opened or created by altering the record size field in the FCB. If the DTA is too small for the record size used by the program, other code or data may be damaged.
- The location of the DTA must be far enough from the top of the segment that contains it to avoid errors caused by segment wrap (data wrapping from the end of the segment to the beginning), which will cause the disk transfer to be terminated. Thus, for example, if records of 128 bytes are to be read, the highest location acceptable for the DTA is DS:FF80H.
- The DTA is used by all FCB-based read and write functions. In addition, any application using the following functions must also set up a DTA for use as a scratch area in directory searches:
  - 11H (Find First File)
  - 12H (Find Next File)
  - 4EH (Find First File)
  - 4FH (Find Next File)

Related Function

2FH (Get DTA Address)

Example

```
;***************************************************************;
;                                                               ;
;                Function 1AH: Set DTA Address                  ;
;                                                               ;
;                int set_DTA(pDTAbuffer)                        ;
;                     char far *pDTAbuffer;                     ;
;                                                               ;
;                Returns 0.                                     ;
;                                                               ;
;***************************************************************;

cProc   set_DTA,PUBLIC,ds
parmD   pDTAbuffer
cBegin
        lds     dx,pDTAbuffer    ; DS:DX = pointer to buffer.
        mov     ah,1ah           ; Set function code.
        int     21h              ; Ask MS-DOS to change DTA address.
        xor     ax,ax            ; Return 0.
cEnd
```

Interrupt 21H (33)
Function 1BH (27)

1.0 and later

Get Default Drive Data

Function 1BH returns information about the disk in the default drive.

To Call

AH   = 1BH

Returns

If function is successful:

AL   = number of sectors per cluster (allocation unit)
CX   = number of bytes per sector
DX   = number of clusters
DS:BX = segment:offset of the file allocation table (FAT) identification byte

If function is not successful:

AL   = FFH

Programmer's Notes

- If Function 1BH returns 0FFH in the AL register, the current drive was invalid or a disk error occurred. The most likely causes of the latter are
  - Drive door was open.
  - Disk was not ready.
  - Medium was bad.
  - Disk was unformatted.

  If any of these situations arises, MS-DOS issues Interrupt 24H (critical error). If Interrupt 24H has not been revectored to a critical error handler controlled by the program and the user responds *Ignore* to the MS-DOS *Abort, Retry, Ignore?* message, the error code 0FFH is returned to the program. An application should check the AL register for a value of 0FFH before assuming it has information on the default drive.

- Possible values of the FAT ID byte (for IBM-compatible media) are the following:

Value	Medium
0FFH	Double-sided, 8 sectors/track, 40 tracks/side
0FEH	Single-sided, 8 sectors/track, 40 tracks/side
0FDH	Double-sided, 9 sectors/track, 40 tracks/side
0FCH	Single-sided, 9 sectors/track, 40 tracks/side

(more)

Value	Medium
0F9H	Double-sided, 15 sectors/track, 40 tracks/side or double-sided, 9 sectors/ track, 80 tracks/side
0F8H	Fixed disk
0F0H	Others

- With MS-DOS versions 1.x, Function 1BH returns a pointer in DS:BX for the actual memory image of the FAT. In MS-DOS versions 2.0 and later, the function returns a pointer in DS:BX for a copy of the FAT identification byte; the contents of memory beyond the identification byte are not necessarily the FAT memory image. If access to the FAT is necessary, Interrupt 25H (Absolute Disk Read) can be used to read it into memory.
- The FAT ID byte is not enough to identify a drive completely in MS-DOS versions 2.0 and later. In these versions of MS-DOS, Function 36H (Get Disk Free Space) should be used in preference to Function 1BH to avoid the ambiguity caused by the FAT identification byte.
- With MS-DOS versions 3.2 and later, additional drive information can be obtained by inspecting the BIOS parameter block (BPB) obtained with Function 44H (IOCTL) Subfunction 0DH (Generic I/O Control for Block Devices) minor code 60H (Get Device Parameters).
- With MS-DOS versions 2.0 and later, Function 1CH (Get Drive Data) provides the same types of information as Function 1BH, but for a disk in a drive other than the default drive.

Related Functions

1CH (Get Drive Data)
36H (Get Disk Free Space)
44H (IOCTL)

Example

See SYSTEM CALLS: INTERRUPT 21H: Function ICH.

Interrupt 21H (33)
Function 1CH (28)

2.0 and later

Get Drive Data

Function 1CH returns information about the disk in a specified drive.

To Call

AH = 1CH
DL = drive code (0 = default drive, 1 = drive A, 2 = drive B,
      3 = drive C, and so on)

Returns

If function is successful:

AL = number of sectors per cluster (allocation unit)
CX = number of bytes per sector
DX = number of clusters
DS:BX = segment:offset of the file allocation table (FAT) identification byte

If function is not successful:

AL = FFH

Programmer's Notes

- Function 1CH is not available with MS-DOS versions 1.x.
- If the function returns 0FFH in the AL register, the drive code was invalid or a disk
  error occurred. The most likely causes of the latter are
  - Drive door was open.
  - Disk was not ready.
  - Medium was bad.
  - Disk was unformatted.

  If any of these situations arises, MS-DOS issues Interrupt 24H (critical error). If Interrupt 24H has not been revectored to a critical error handler controlled by the program
  and the user responds *Ignore* to the MS-DOS *Abort, Retry, Ignore?* message, the error
  code 0FFH is returned to the program. An application should check the AL register
  for a value of 0FFH before assuming it has information on the specified drive.
- Possible values of the FAT ID byte (for IBM-compatible media) are the following:

Value	Medium
0FFH	Double-sided, 8 sectors/track, 40 tracks/side
0FEH	Single-sided, 8 sectors/track, 40 tracks/side

(more)

Value	Medium
0FDH	Double-sided, 9 sectors/track, 40 tracks/side
0FCH	Single-sided, 9 sectors/track, 40 tracks/side
0F9H	Double-sided, 15 sectors/track, 40 tracks/side or double-sided, 9 sectors/ track, 80 tracks/side
0F8H	Fixed disk
0F0H	Others

● The contents of memory beyond the identification byte pointed to by DS:BX are not necessarily the FAT memory image. If access to the FAT is necessary, Interrupt 25H (Absolute Disk Read) can be used to read it into memory.

● The FAT ID byte is not enough to identify a drive completely. To avoid the ambiguity caused by the FAT identification byte, Function 36H (Get Disk Free Space) should be used in preference to Function 1CH.

● With MS-DOS versions 3.2 and later, additional drive information can be obtained by inspecting the BIOS parameter block (BPB) obtained with Function 44H (IOCTL) Subfunction 0DH (Generic I/O Control for Block Devices) minor code 60H (Get Device Parameters).

Related Functions

1BH (Get Default Drive Data)
36H (Get Disk Free Space)
44H (IOCTL)

Example

```
;**************************************************************;
;                                                              ;
;   Function 1CH: Get Drive Data                               ;
;                                                              ;
;   Get information about the disk in the specified            ;
;   drive.  Set drive_ltr to binary 0 for default drive info.  ;
;                                                              ;
;   int get_drive_data(drive_ltr,                              ;
;        pbytes_per_sector,                                    ;
;        psectors_per_cluster,                                 ;
;        pclusters_per_drive)                                  ;
;      int  drive_ltr;                                         ;
;      int *pbytes_per_sector;                                 ;
;      int *psectors_per_cluster;                              ;
;      int *pclusters_per_drive;                               ;
;                                                              ;
;   Returns -1 for invalid drive, otherwise returns            ;
;   the disk's type (from the 1st byte of the FAT).            ;
;                                                              ;
;**************************************************************;
```

(more)

```
        cProc    get_drive_data,PUBLIC,<ds,si>
        parmB    drive_ltr
        parmDP   pbytes_per_sector
        parmDP   psectors_per_cluster
        parmDP   pclusters_per_drive
        cBegin
                 mov     si,ds              ; Save DS in SI to use later.
                 mov     dl,drive_ltr       ; Get drive letter.
                 or      dl,dl              ; Leave 0 alone.
                 jz      gdd
                 and     dl,not 20h         ; Convert letter to uppercase.
                 sub     dl,'A'-1           ; Convert to drive number: 'A' = 1,
                                            ; 'B' = 2, etc.
        gdd:
                 mov     ah,1ch             ; Set function code.
                 int     21h                ; Ask MS-DOS for data.
                 cbw                        ; Extend AL into AH.
                 cmp     al,0ffh            ; Bad drive letter?
                 je      gddx               ; If so, exit with error code -1.
                 mov     bl,[bx]            ; Get FAT ID byte from DS:BX.
                 mov     ds,si              ; Get back original DS.
                 loadDP  ds,si,pbytes_per_sector
                 mov     [si],cx            ; Return bytes per sector.
                 loadDP  ds,si,psectors_per_cluster
                 mov     ah,0
                 mov     [si],ax            ; Return sectors per cluster.
                 loadDP  ds,si,pclusters_per_drive
                 mov     [si],dx            ; Return clusters per drive.
                 mov     al,bl              ; Return FAT ID byte.
        gddx:
        cEnd
```

Interrupt 21H (33)
Function 21H (33)

1.0 and later

Random Read

Function 21H reads a selected record from disk into memory.

To Call

AH   = 21H
DS:DX   = segment:offset of previously opened file control block (FCB)

Returns

AL	= 00H	record read successfully
	01H	end of file; no record read
	02H	DTA too small (segment wrap error); read canceled
	03H	end of file; partial record transferred

If AL = 00H or 03H:

DTA contains data read from file.

Programmer's Notes

- Function 21H reads the record into the current disk transfer area (DTA). Unless the 128-byte default DTA (at offset 80H in the program segment prefix) is adequate, Function 1AH (Set DTA Address) should be used to set the DTA address before Function 21H is called. The program must ensure that the buffer pointed to by the DTA address is large enough to hold the records to be transferred.
- The relative-record field in the FCB must be set to the record number to be read. Numbering begins with record 00H; thus, the value 06H in the relative-record field would indicate the seventh record, not the sixth.
- Function 21H sets the current-block and current-record fields to match the relative-record field before transferring the data to the DTA.
- Unlike Function 27H (Random Block Read), Function 21H does not increment the current-block, current-record, or relative-record fields.
- The record length read is determined by the record size field of the FCB.
- If a partial record is read and the end of file is encountered, the remainder of the record is filled out to the requested length with zero bytes.
- On networks running under MS-DOS version 3.1 or later, the user must have Read access rights to the directory containing the file to be read.
- With MS-DOS versions 2.0 and later, Function 3FH (Read File or Device) should be used in preference to Function 21H.

Related Functions

14H (Sequential Read)
1AH (Set DTA Address)
22H (Random Write)
24H (Set Relative Record)
27H (Random Block Read)
3FH (Read File or Device)

Example

```
;***********************************************************;
;                                                          ;
;          Function 21H: Random File Read, FCB-based       ;
;                                                          ;
;          int FCB_rread(oXFCB,recnum)                     ;
;              char *oXFCB;                                 ;
;              long recnum;                                 ;
;                                                          ;
;          Returns 0 if record read OK, otherwise          ;
;          returns error code 1, 2, or 3.                  ;
;                                                          ;
;***********************************************************;

cProc   FCB_rread,PUBLIC,ds
parmDP  poXFCB
parmD   recnum
cBegin
        loadDP  ds,dx,poXFCB    ; Pointer to opened extended FCB.
        mov     bx,dx           ; BX points at FCB, too.
        mov     ax,word ptr (recnum)    ; Get low 16 bits of record
        mov     [bx+28h],ax             ; number and store in FCB.
        mov     ax,word ptr (recnum+2)  ; Get high 16 bits of record
        mov     [bx+2ah],ax             ; number and store in FCB.
        mov     ah,21h          ; Ask MS-DOS to read recnum'th
                                ; record, placing it at DTA.
        int     21h
        cbw                     ; Clear high byte of return value.
cEnd
```

Interrupt 21H (33)
Function 22H (34)

1.0 and later

Random Write

Function 22H writes data from the current disk transfer area (DTA) to a specified record location in a file.

To Call

```
AH      = 22H
DS:DX   = segment:offset of previously opened file control block (FCB)
```

DTA contains data to write.

Returns

```
AL      = 00H    record written successfully
          01H    disk full
          02H    DTA too small (segment wrap error); write canceled
```

Programmer's Notes

- Before calling Function 22H, the program must set the disk transfer area (DTA) address appropriately with a call to Function 1AH (Set DTA Address), if necessary, and place the data to be written in the DTA.
- The relative-record field in the FCB must be set to the record number that is to be written. Numbering begins with record 00H; thus, the value 06H in the relative-record field would indicate the seventh record, not the sixth.
- Function 22H sets the current-block and current-record fields to match the relative-record field before writing the data from the DTA.
- Unlike Function 28H (Random Block Write), Function 22H does not increment the current-block, current-record, or relative-record fields.
- The record size field determines the record length written by the function.
- If a record is written beyond the current end of file, the data between the old end of file and the beginning of the new record is uninitialized.
- The file that is written to cannot have the read-only attribute.
- Information is written logically, but not always physically, to disk at the time Function 22H is called. The contents of the DTA are written immediately to disk only if they constitute a sector's worth of information. If less than a sector is written, it is transferred from the DTA to an MS-DOS buffer and is not physically written to disk until one of the following occurs:
  - A full sector of information is ready.
  - The file is closed.
  - Function 0DH (Disk Reset) is issued.

- On networks running under MS-DOS version 3.1 or later, the user must have Write access rights to the directory containing the file to be written to.
- With MS-DOS versions 2.0 and later, Function 40H (Write File or Device) should be used in preference to Function 22H.

Related Functions

15H (Sequential Write)
1AH (Set DTA Address)
21H (Random Read)
24H (Set Relative Record)
28H (Random Block Write)
40H (Write File or Device)

Example

```
;**************************************************************;
;                                                            ;
;          Function 22H: Random File Write, FCB-based        ;
;                                                            ;
;          int FCB_rwrite(oXFCB,recnum)                      ;
;               char *oXFCB;                                 ;
;               long recnum;                                 ;
;                                                            ;
;          Returns 0 if record read OK, otherwise            ;
;          returns error code 1 or 2.                        ;
;                                                            ;
;**************************************************************;

cProc     FCB_rwrite,PUBLIC,ds
parmDP    poXFCB
parmD     recnum
cBegin
          loadDP  ds,dx,poXFCB    ; Pointer to opened extended FCB.
          mov     bx,dx           ; BX points at FCB, too.
          mov     ax,word ptr (recnum)    ; Get low 16 bits of record
          mov     [bx+28h],ax             ; number and store in FCB.
          mov     ax,word ptr (recnum+2)  ; Get high 16 bits of record
          mov     [bx+2ah],ax             ; number and store in FCB.
          mov     ah,22h          ; Ask MS-DOS to write DTA to
          int     21h             ; recnum'th record of file.
          cbw                     ; Clear high byte for return value.
cEnd
```

Interrupt 21H (33)
Function 23H (35)

Get File Size

Function 23H searches the current directory for a specified file and returns the size of the file in records.

To Call

AH = 23H
DS:DX = segment:offset of unopened file control block (FCB) with record size field set appropriately

Returns

If function is successful:

AL = 00H

FCB relative-record field contains number of records, rounded upward if necessary.

If function is not successful:

AL = FFH

Programmer's Notes

- The record size field in the FCB can be set to 1 to find the number of bytes in the file.
- The number of records is the file size divided by the record size. If there is a remainder, the record count is rounded upward. The result stored in the relative-record field may, therefore, contain a value that is 1 larger than the number of complete records in the file.
- Because record numbers are zero based and this function returns the number of records in a file in the relative-record field of the FCB, Function 23H can be used to position the file pointer to the end of file.
- With MS-DOS versions 2.0 and later, Function 42H (Move File Pointer) should be used in preference to Function 23H.

Related Function

42H (Move File Pointer)

Example

```
;**************************************************************;
;                                                            ;
;         Function 23H: Get File Size, FCB-based             ;
;                                                            ;
;         long FCB_nrecs(uXFCB,recsize)                      ;
;              char *uXFCB;                                  ;
;              int recsize;                                  ;
;                                                            ;
;         Returns a long -1 if file not found, otherwise     ;
;         returns the number of records of size recsize.     ;
;                                                            ;
;         Note: uXFCB must have the drive and                ;
;         filename fields (bytes 07H through 12H) and        ;
;         the extension flag (byte 00H) set before           ;
;         the call to FCB_nrecs (see Function 29H).          ;
;                                                            ;
;**************************************************************;

cProc   FCB_nrecs,PUBLIC,ds
parmDP  puXFCB
parmW   recsize
cBegin
        loadDP  ds,dx,puXFCB    ; Pointer to unopened extended FCB.
        mov     bx,dx           ; Copy FCB pointer into BX.
        mov     ax,recsize      ; Get record size
        mov     [bx+15h],ax     ; and store it in FCB.
        mov     ah,23h          ; Ask MS-DOS for file size (in
                                ; records).
        int     21h
        cbw                     ; If AL = 0FFH, set AX to -1.
        cwd                     ; Extend to long.
        or      dx,dx           ; Is DX negative?
        js      nr_exit         ; If so, exit with error flag.
        mov     [bx+2bh],al     ; Only low 24 bits of the relative-
                                ; record field are used, so clear the
                                ; top 8 bits.
        mov     ax,[bx+28h]     ; Return file length in DX:AX.
        mov     dx,[bx+2ah]
nr_exit:
cEnd
```

Interrupt 21H (33)
Function 24H (36)

1.0 and later

Set Relative Record

Function 24H sets the relative-record field of a file control block (FCB) to match the file position indicated by the current-block and current-record fields of the same FCB.

To Call

AH = 24H
DS:DX = segment:offset of previously opened FCB

Returns

AL = 00H

Relative-record field is modified in FCB.

Programmer's Notes

- The AL register is always set to 00H by Function 24H. Thus, any preexisting information in the AL register is lost.
- Before Function 24H is called, the program must open the FCB with Function 0FH (Open File with FCB) or with Function 16H (Create File with FCB).
- The entire relative-record field (4 bytes) of the FCB must be initialized to zeros before calling Function 24H. If this is not done, any value in the high-order byte of the high-order word remaining from previous reads or writes might not be overwritten and the resulting relative-record number will be invalid.
- Function 24H is normally used in changing from sequential to random I/O. Sequential I/O, performed by Functions 14H (Sequential Read) and 15H (Sequential Write), sets the current-block and current-record fields of the FCB. Random I/O uses the relative-record field, which is set by Function 24H to match the current file position as recorded in the current-block and current-record fields.

  After the file pointer is set, any of the following functions can be used to access data at the record pointed to by the relative-record field:
  - 21H (Random Read)
  - 22H (Random Write)
  - 27H (Random Block Read)
  - 28H (Random Block Write)
- With MS-DOS versions 2.0 and later, Function 42H (Move File Pointer) should be used in preference to Function 24H.

Related Function

42H (Move File Pointer)

Example

```
;************************************************************;
;                                                          ;
;               Function 24H: Set Relative Record          ;
;                                                          ;
;                    int FCB_set_rrec(oXFCB)               ;
;                         char *oXFCB;                     ;
;                                                          ;
;               Returns 0.                                 ;
;                                                          ;
;************************************************************;

cProc    FCB_set_rrec,PUBLIC,ds
parmDP   poXFCB
cBegin
         loadDP  ds,dx,poXFCB    ; Pointer to opened extended FCB.
         mov     bx,dx           ; BX points at FCB, too.
         mov     byte ptr [bx+2bh],0 ; Zero high byte of high word of
                                 ;   relative-record field.
         mov     ah,24h          ; Ask MS-DOS to set relative record
                                 ;   to current record.
         int     21h
         xor     ax,ax           ; Return 0.
cEnd
```

Interrupt 21H (33)
Function 25H (37)

Set Interrupt Vector

1.0 and later

Function 25H sets an address in the interrupt vector table to point to a specified interrupt handler.

To Call

AH   = 25H
AL   = interrupt number
DS:DX   = segment:offset of interrupt handler

Returns

Nothing

Programmer's Notes

- When Function 25H is called, the 4-byte address in DS:DX is placed in the correct position in the interrupt vector table.
- Function 25H is the recommended method for initializing or changing an interrupt vector. A vector in the interrupt vector table should never be changed directly.
- Before Function 25H is used to change an interrupt vector, the address of the current interrupt handler should be read with Function 35H (Get Interrupt Vector) and then saved for restoration before the program terminates.

Related Function

35H (Get Interrupt Vector)

Example

```
;**************************************************************;
;                                                            ;
;              Function 25H: Set Interrupt Vector            ;
;                                                            ;
;              typedef void (far *FCP)();                    ;
;              int set_vector(intnum,vector)                 ;
;                   int intnum;                              ;
;                   FCP vector;                              ;
;                                                            ;
;              Returns 0.                                    ;
;                                                            ;
;**************************************************************;
```

(more)

```
cProc    set_vector,PUBLIC,ds
parmB    intnum
parmD    vector
cBegin
         lds      dx,vector       ; Get vector segment:offset into
                                  ; DS:DX.
         mov      al,intnum       ; Get interrupt number into AL.
         mov      ah,25h          ; Select "set vector" function.
         int      21h             ; Ask MS-DOS to change vector.
         xor      ax,ax           ; Return 0.
cEnd
```

Interrupt 21H (33)
Function 26H (38)

1.0 and later

Create New Program Segment Prefix

Function 26H creates a new program segment prefix (PSP) at a specified segment address.

To Call

AH = 26H
DX = segment address of the PSP to create

Returns

Nothing

Programmer's Notes

- Function 26H copies the current PSP to the address indicated by DX. Note that DX contains a segment address, not an absolute address.
- After the copy is made, the memory size information located at offset 06H in the new PSP is adjusted to match the amount of memory available to the new PSP. In addition, the current contents of the interrupt vectors for Interrupt 22H (Terminate Routine Address), Interrupt 23H (Control-C Handler Address), and Interrupt 24H (Critical Error Handler Address) are saved starting at offset 0AH of the new PSP.
- A .COM file can be loaded into memory immediately after the new PSP and execution can begin at that location. A .EXE file cannot be loaded and executed in this manner.
- With MS-DOS versions 2.0 and later, Function 4BH (Load and Execute Program) should be used in preference to Function 26H. Function 4BH can be used to load .COM files, .EXE files, or overlays.

Related Function

4BH (Load and Execute Program)

Example

```
;************************************************************;
;                                                          ;
;        Function 26H: Create New Program Segment Prefix   ;
;                                                          ;
;        int create_psp(pspseg)                            ;
;            int  pspseg;                                  ;
;                                                          ;
;        Returns 0.                                        ;
;                                                          ;
;************************************************************;
```

(more)

```
cProc    create_psp,PUBLIC
parmW    pspseg
cBegin
         mov     dx,pspseg        ; Get segment address of new PSP.
         mov     ah,26h           ; Set function code.
         int     21h              ; Ask MS-DOS to create new PSP.
         xor     ax,ax            ; Return 0.
cEnd
```

Interrupt 21H (33)
Function 27H (39)

1.0 and later

Random Block Read

Function 27H reads one or more records into memory, placing the records in the current disk transfer area (DTA).

To Call

AH = 27H
CX = number of records to read
DS:DX = segment:offset of previously opened file control block (FCB)

Returns

AL = 00H read successful
01H end of file; no record read
02H DTA too small (segment wrap error); no record read
03H end of file; partial record read

If AL is 00H or 03H:

CX = number of records read

DTA contains data read from file.

Programmer's Notes

- The DTA address should be set with Function 1AH (Set DTA Address) before Function 27H is called. If the DTA address has not been set, MS-DOS uses a default 128-byte DTA at offset 80H in the program segment prefix (PSP).
- Function 27H reads the number of records specified in CX sequentially, starting at the file location indicated by the relative-record and record size fields in the FCB. If CX = 0, no records are read.
- The record length used by Function 27H is the value in the record size field of the FCB. Unless a new value is placed in this field after a file is opened or created, MS-DOS uses a default record length of 128 bytes.
- Function 27H is similar to Function 21H (Random Read); however, Function 27H can read more than one record at a time and updates the relative-record field of the FCB after each call. Successive calls to this function thus read sequential groups of records from a file, whereas successive calls to Function 21H repeatedly read the same record.
- Possible alternative causes for end-of-file (01H) errors include
  - Disk removed from drive since file was opened.
  - Previous open failed.

  With MS-DOS versions 3.0 and later, more detailed information on the error can be obtained by calling Function 59H (Get Extended Error Information).

- On networks running under MS-DOS version 3.1 or later, the user must have Read access rights to the directory containing the file to be read.
- With MS-DOS versions 2.0 and later, Function 3FH (Read File or Device) should be used in preference to Function 27H.

Related Functions

14H (Sequential Read)
1AH (Set DTA Address)
21H (Random Read)
24H (Set Relative Record)
28H (Random Block Write)
3FH (Read File or Device)

Example

```
;**************************************************************;
;                                                              ;
;         Function 27H: Random File Block Read, FCB-based      ;
;                                                              ;
;         int FCB_rblock(oXFCB,nrequest,nactual,start)         ;
;              char *oXFCB;                                    ;
;              int   nrequest;                                 ;
;              int  *nactual;                                  ;
;              long  start;                                    ;
;                                                              ;
;         Returns read status 0, 1, 2, or 3 and sets           ;
;         nactual to number of records actually read.          ;
;                                                              ;
;         If start is -1, the relative-record field is         ;
;         not changed, causing the block to be read starting   ;
;         at the current record.                               ;
;                                                              ;
;**************************************************************;

cProc    FCB_rblock,PUBLIC,<ds,di>
parmDP   poXFCB
parmW    nrequest
parmDP   pnactual
parmD    start
cBegin
         loadDP  ds,dx,poXFCB    ; Pointer to opened extended FCB.
         mov     di,dx           ; DI points at FCB, too.
         mov     ax,word ptr (start) ; Get long value of start.
         mov     bx,word ptr (start+2)
         mov     cx,ax           ; Is start = -1?
         and     cx,bx
         inc     cx
         jcxz    rb_skip         ; If so, don't change relative-record
                                 ; field.
         mov     [di+28h],ax     ; Otherwise, seek to start record.
```

(more)

```
        mov     [di+2ah],bx
rb_skip:
        mov     cx,nrequest     ; CX = number of records to read.
        mov     ah,27h          ; Get MS-DOS to read CX records,
        int     21h             ; placing them at DTA.
        loadDP  ds,bx,pnactual  ; DS:BX = address of nactual.
        mov     [bx],cx         ; Return number of records read.
        cbw                     ; Clear high byte.
cEnd
```

Interrupt 21H (33)
Function 28H (40)

1.0 and later

Random Block Write

Function 28H writes one or more records from the current disk transfer area (DTA) to a file.

To Call

AH   = 28H
CX   = number of records to write
DS:DX   = segment:offset of previously opened file control block (FCB)

DTA contains data to write.

Returns

AL   = 00H   write successful
           01H   disk full
           02H   DTA too small (segment wrap error); write canceled

If AL is 00H or 01H:

CX   = number of records written

Programmer's Notes

- Data to be written must be placed in the DTA before Function 28H is called. Unless the DTA address has been set with Function 1AH (Set DTA Address), MS-DOS uses a default 128-byte DTA at offset 80H in the program segment prefix (PSP).
- Function 28H writes the number of records indicated in CX, beginning at the location specified in the relative-record field of the file control block (FCB). If Function 28H is called with CX = 0, the file is truncated or extended to the size indicated by the record-size and relative-record fields of the FCB.
- The record length used by Function 28H is the value in the record size field of the FCB. Unless a new value is assigned after a file is opened or created, MS-DOS uses a default record length of 128 bytes.
- Function 28H is similar to Function 22H (Random Write); however, Function 28H can write more than one record at a time and updates the relative-record field of the FCB after each call. Successive calls to this function thus write sequential groups of records to a file, whereas successive calls to Function 22H repeatedly write the same record.

- Possible alternative causes for disk full (01H) errors include
  - Disk removed from drive since file was opened.
  - Previous open failed.

  In MS-DOS versions 3.0 and later, more detailed information on the error can be obtained by calling Function 59H (Get Extended Error Information).
- Information is written logically, but not always physically, to disk at the time Function 28H is called. The contents of the DTA are written immediately to disk only if they constitute a full sector of information. If less than a sector is written, it is transferred from the DTA to an MS-DOS buffer and is not physically written to disk until one of the following occurs:
  - A full sector of information is ready.
  - The file is closed.
  - Function 0DH (Disk Reset) is issued.
- On networks running under MS-DOS version 3.1 or later, the user must have Write access rights to the directory containing the file to be written to.
- With MS-DOS versions 2.0 and later, Function 40H (Write File or Device) should be used in preference to Function 28H.

Related Functions

15H (Sequential Write)
1AH (Set DTA Address)
22H (Random Write)
24H (Set Relative Record)
27H (Random Block Read)
40H (Write File or Device)

Example

```
;**************************************************************;
;                                                              ;
;        Function 28H: Random File Block Write, FCB-based      ;
;                                                              ;
;        int FCB_wblock(oXFCB,nrequest,nactual,start)          ;
;            char *oXFCB;                                       ;
;            int   nrequest;                                   ;
;            int  *nactual;                                    ;
;            long  start;                                      ;
;                                                              ;
;        Returns write status of 0, 1, or 2 and sets           ;
;        nactual to number of records actually written.        ;
;                                                              ;
;        If start is -1, the relative-record field is          ;
;        not changed, causing the block to be written          ;
;        starting at the current record.                       ;
;                                                              ;
;**************************************************************;
```

(more)

```
        cProc   FCB_wblock,PUBLIC,<ds,di>
        parmDP  poXFCB
        parmW   nrequest
        parmDP  pnactual
        parmD   start
        cBegin
                loadDP  ds,dx,poXFCB    ; Pointer to opened extended FCB.
                mov     di,dx           ; DI points at FCB, too.
                mov     ax,word ptr (start) ; Get long value of start.
                mov     bx,word ptr (start+2)
                mov     cx,ax           ; Is start = -1?
                and     cx,bx
                inc     cx
                jcxz    wb_skip         ; If so, don't change relative-record
                                        ; field.
                mov     [di+28h],ax     ; Otherwise, seek to start record.
                mov     [di+2ah],bx
        wb_skip:
                mov     cx,nrequest     ; CX = number of records to write.
                mov     ah,28h          ; Get MS-DOS to write CX records
                int     21h             ; from DTA to file.
                loadDP  ds,bx,pnactual  ; DS:BX = address of nactual.
                mov     ds:[bx],cx      ; Return number of records written.
                cbw                     ; Clear high byte.
        cEnd
```

Interrupt 21H (33)
Function 29H (41)

1.0 and later

Parse Filename

Function 29H examines a string for a valid filename in the form *drive:filename.ext*. If the string represents a valid filename, the function creates an unopened file control block (FCB) for it.

To Call

AH = 29H

AL = code to control parsing, as follows (bits 0–3 only):

Bit	Value	Meaning
0	0	Stop parsing if file separator is found.
	1	Ignore leading separators (parse off white space).
1	0	Set drive number field in FCB to 0 (current drive) if string does not include a drive identifier.
	1	Set drive as specified in the string; leave unaltered if string does not include a drive identifier.
2	0	Set filename field in the FCB to blanks (20H) if string does not include a filename.
	1	Leave filename field unaltered if string does not include a filename.
3	0	Set extension field in FCB to blanks (20H) if string does not include a filename extension.
	1	Leave extension field unaltered if string does not include a filename extension.

DS:SI = segment:offset of string to parse
ES:DI = segment:offset of buffer for unopened FCB

Returns

AL = 00H string does not contain wildcard characters
01H string contains wildcard characters
FFH drive specifier invalid

DS:SI = segment:offset of first byte following the parsed string
ES:DI = segment:offset of unopened FCB

Programmer's Notes

- Bits 0 through 3 of the byte in the AL register control the way the text string is parsed; bits 4 through 7 are not used and must be 0.
- After MS-DOS parses the string, DS:SI points to the first byte following the parsed string. If DS:SI points to an earlier byte, MS-DOS did not parse the entire string.
- If Function 29H encounters the MS-DOS wildcard character * (match all remaining characters) in a filename or extension, the remaining bytes in the corresponding FCB field are set to the wildcard character ? (match one character). For example, the string DOS*.D* would be converted to DOS????? in the filename field and D?? in the extension field of the FCB.
- With MS-DOS versions 1.x, the following characters are filename separators:

  : . ; , = + space tab / " [ ]

  With MS-DOS versions 2.0 and later, the following characters are filename separators:

  : . ; , = + space tab

- The following characters are filename terminators:

  / " [ ] < > |
  All filename separators
  Any control character

- If the string does not contain a valid filename, ES:DI+1 points to an ASCII blank character (20H).
- Function 29H cannot parse pathnames.

Related Functions

None

Example

```
;**************************************************************;
;                                                            ;
;           Function 29H: Parse Filename into FCB            ;
;                                                            ;
;           int FCB_parse(uXFCB,name,ctrl)                   ;
;                char *uXFCB;                                ;
;                char *name;                                 ;
;                int ctrl;                                   ;
;                                                            ;
;           Returns -1 if error,                            ;
;                    0 if no wildcards found,               ;
;                    1 if wildcards found.                  ;
;                                                            ;
;**************************************************************;
```

(more)

```
cProc     FCB_parse,PUBLIC,<ds,si,di>
parmDP    puXFCB
parmDP    pname
parmB     ctrl
cBegin
          loadDP  es,di,puXFCB      ; Pointer to unopened extended FCB.
          push    di                ; Save DI.
          xor     ax,ax             ; Fill all 22 (decimal) words of the
                                    ; extended FCB with zeros.
          cld                       ; Make sure direction flag says UP.
          mov     cx,22d
          rep     stosw
          pop     di                ; Recover DI.
          mov     byte ptr [di],0ffh ; Set flag byte to mark this as an
                                        ; extended FCB.
          add     di,7              ; Advance pointer to start of regular
                                    ; FCB.
          loadDP  ds,si,pname       ; Get pointer to filename into DS:SI.
          mov     al,ctrl           ; Get parse control byte.
          mov     ah,29h            ; Parse filename, please.
          int     21h
          cbw                       ; Set return parameter.
cEnd
```

Interrupt 21H (33)
Function 2AH (42)

1.0 and later

Get Date

Function 2AH returns the current system date — year, month, day, and day of the week — in binary form.

To Call

AH = 2AH

Returns

AL = day of the week (0 = Sunday, 1 = Monday, 2 = Tuesday, and so on;
MS-DOS versions 1.10 and later)
CX = year (1980 through 2099)
DH = month (1 through 12)
DL = day (1 through 31)

Programmer's Note

- Years outside the range 1980–2099 cannot be returned by Function 2AH.

Related Functions

2BH (Set Date)
2CH (Get Time)
2DH (Set Time)

Example

```
;**********************************************************;
;                                                          ;
;           Function 2AH: Get Date                         ;
;                                                          ;
;           long get_date(pdow,pmonth,pday,pyear)          ;
;                char *pdow,*pmonth,*pday;                 ;
;                int *pyear;                               ;
;                                                          ;
;           Returns the date packed into a long:           ;
;                low byte  = day of month                  ;
;                next byte = month                         ;
;                next word = year.                         ;
;                                                          ;
;**********************************************************;
```

(more)

```
cProc    get_date,PUBLIC,ds
parmDP   pdow
parmDP   pmonth
parmDP   pday
parmDP   pyear
cBegin
         mov      ah,2ah              ; Set function code.
         int      21h                 ; Get date info from MS-DOS.
         loadDP   ds,bx,pdow          ; DS:BX = pointer to dow.
         mov      [bx],al             ; Return dow.
         loadDP   ds,bx,pmonth        ; DS:BX = pointer to month.
         mov      [bx],dh             ; Return month.
         loadDP   ds,bx,pday          ; DS:BX = pointer to day.
         mov      [bx],dl             ; Return day.
         loadDP   ds,bx,pyear         ; DS:BX = pointer to year.
         mov      [bx],cx             ; Return year.
         mov      ax,dx               ; Pack day, month, ...
         mov      dx,cx               ; ... and year into return value.
cEnd
```

Interrupt 21H (33)
Function 2BH (43)

1.0 and later

Set Date

Function 2BH accepts binary values for the year, month, and day of the month and stores them in the system's date counter as the number of days since January 1, 1980.

To Call

AH = 2BH
CX = year (1980 through 2099)
DH = month (1 through 12)
DL = day (1 through 31)

Returns

AL = 00H   system date updated
     FFH   invalid date specified

Programmer's Note

- The year must be a 16-bit value in the range 1980 through 2099. Values outside this range are not accepted. In addition, supplying only the last two digits of the year causes an error.

Related Functions

2AH (Get Date)
2CH (Get Time)
2DH (Set Time)

Example

```
;**************************************************************;
;                                                              ;
;               Function 2BH: Set Date                         ;
;                                                              ;
;               int set_date(month,day,year)                   ;
;                   char month,day;                            ;
;                   int year;                                  ;
;                                                              ;
;               Returns 0 if date was OK, -1 if not.           ;
;                                                              ;
;**************************************************************;
```

(more)

```
cProc    set_date,PUBLIC
parmB    month
parmB    day
parmW    year
cBegin
         mov    dh,month      ; Get new month.
         mov    dl,day        ; Get new day.
         mov    cx,year       ; Get new year.
         mov    ah,2bh        ; Set function code.
         int    21h           ; Ask MS-DOS to change date.
         cbw                  ; Return 0 or -1.
cEnd
```

Interrupt 21H (33)
Function 2CH (44)

1.0 and later

Get Time

Function 2CH reports the current system time — hours (based on a 24-hour clock), minutes, seconds, and hundredths of a second — in binary form.

To Call

AH = 2CH

Returns

CH = hours (0 through 23)
CL = minutes (0 through 59)
DH = seconds (0 through 59)
DL = hundredths of second (0 through 99)

Programmer's Note

- The accuracy of the time returned by Function 2CH depends on the accuracy of the system's timekeeping hardware. On systems unable to resolve time to the hundredth of a second, the DL register may contain either 00H or an approximate value calculated by an MS-DOS algorithm.

Related Functions

2AH (Get Date)
2BH (Set Date)
2DH (Set Time)

Example

```
;*************************************************************;
;                                                             ;
;              Function 2CH: Get Time                         ;
;                                                             ;
;              long get_time(phour,pmin,psec,phund)           ;
;                   char *phour,*pmin,*psec,*phund;           ;
;                                                             ;
;              Returns the time packed into a long:           ;
;                   low byte  = hundredths                    ;
;                   next byte = seconds                       ;
;                   next byte = minutes                       ;
;                   next byte = hours.                        ;
;                                                             ;
;*************************************************************;
```

(more)

```
        cProc   get_time,PUBLIC,ds
        parmDP  phour
        parmDP  pmin
        parmDP  psec
        parmDP  phund
        cBegin
                mov     ah,2ch          ; Set function code.
                int     21h             ; Get time from MS-DOS.
                loadDP  ds,bx,phour     ; DS:BX = pointer to hour.
                mov     [bx],ch         ; Return hour.
                loadDP  ds,bx,pmin      ; DS:BX = pointer to min.
                mov     [bx],cl         ; Return min.
                loadDP  ds,bx,psec      ; DS:BX = pointer to sec.
                mov     [bx],dh         ; Return sec.
                loadDP  ds,bx,phund     ; DS:BX = pointer to hund.
                mov     [bx],dl         ; Return hund.
                mov     ax,dx           ; Pack seconds, hundredths, ...
                mov     dx,cx           ; ... minutes, and hour into
                                        ; return value.
        cEnd
```

Interrupt 21H (33)
Function 2DH (45)

Set Time

Function 2DH accepts binary values for the hour (based on a 24-hour clock), minute, second, and hundredths of a second and stores them in the operating system's time counter.

To Call

AH = 2DH
CH = hours (0 through 23)
CL = minutes (0 through 59)
DH = seconds (0 through 59)
DL = hundredths of second (0 through 99)

Returns

AL = 00H   time successfully updated
    FFH   invalid time specified

Programmer's Note

- On systems that are unable to resolve the time to the hundredth of a second, the DL register should be set to 00H before Function 2DH is called.

Related Functions

2AH (Get Date)
2BH (Set Date)
2CH (Get Time)

Example

```
;****************************************************************;
;                                                                ;
;                  Function 2DH: Set Time                        ;
;                                                                ;
;              int set_time(hour,min,sec,hund)                   ;
;                  char hour,min,sec,hund;                       ;
;                                                                ;
;              Returns 0 if time was OK, -1 if not.              ;
;                                                                ;
;****************************************************************;
```

(more)

```
cProc    set_time,PUBLIC
parmB    hour
parmB    min
parmB    sec
parmB    hund
cBegin
         mov     ch,hour        ; Get new hour.
         mov     cl,min         ; Get new minutes.
         mov     dh,sec         ; Get new seconds.
         mov     dl,hund        ; Get new hundredths.
         mov     ah,2dh         ; Set function code.
         int     21h            ; Ask MS-DOS to change time.
         cbw                    ; Return 0 or -1.
cEnd
```

Interrupt 21H (33)
Function 2EH (46)

1.0 and later

Set/Reset Verify Flag

Function 2EH turns the internal MS-DOS verify flag on or off, thus determining whether MS-DOS verifies disk write operations.

To Call

```
AH = 2EH
AL = 00H      turn verify off
     01H      turn verify on
DL = 00H (MS-DOS versions 1.x and 2.x only)
```

Returns

Nothing

Programmer's Notes

- If the verify flag is on, MS-DOS requests any block-device driver to verify each sector written. If the driver does not support read-after-write verification, the verify flag has no effect.
- Function 54H (Get Verify Flag) can be used to check the current setting of the verify flag.
- Verifying data slows disk access during write operations. Because disk errors are rare, the default setting of the verify flag is off.
- Verification can be controlled at the user level with the MS-DOS VERIFY command.

Related Function

54H (Get Verify Flag)

Example

```
;***********************************************************;
;                                                         ;
;            Function 2EH: Set/Reset Verify Flag          ;
;                                                         ;
;            int set_verify(newvflag)                     ;
;                char newvflag;                           ;
;                                                         ;
;            Returns 0.                                   ;
;                                                         ;
;***********************************************************;
```

(more)

```
cProc    set_verify,PUBLIC
parmB    newvflag
cBegin
         mov     al,newvflag      ; Get new value of verify flag.
         mov     ah,2eh           ; Set function code.
         int     21h              ; Ask MS-DOS to store flag.
         xor     ax,ax            ; Return 0.
cEnd
```

Interrupt 21H (33)
Function 2FH (47)

2.0 and later

Get DTA Address

Function 2FH returns the current disk transfer area (DTA) address.

To Call

AH   = 2FH

Returns

ES:BX   = segment:offset of current DTA address

Programmer's Notes

- Function 2FH returns the base address of the current DTA. MS-DOS has no way of knowing the size of the buffer at that address; the program must ensure that the buffer pointed to by the DTA address is large enough to hold any records transferred to it.
- The current DTA address can be set with Function 1AH (Set DTA Address). If the DTA address is not set, MS-DOS uses a default buffer of 128 bytes located at offset 80H in the program segment prefix (PSP).

Related Function

1AH (Set DTA Address)

Example

```
;***********************************************************;
;                                                         ;
;            Function 2FH: Get DTA Address                ;
;                                                         ;
;            char far *get_DTA()                          ;
;                                                         ;
;            Returns a far pointer to the DTA buffer.     ;
;                                                         ;
;***********************************************************;

cProc    get_DTA,PUBLIC
cBegin
         mov     ah,2fh          ; Set function code.
         int     21h             ; Ask MS-DOS for current DTA address.
         mov     ax,bx           ; Return offset in AX.
         mov     dx,es           ; Return segment in DX.
cEnd
```

Interrupt 21H (33)
Function 30H (48)

2.0 and later

Get MS-DOS Version Number

Function 30H returns the major and minor version numbers for MS-DOS versions 2.0 and later.

To Call

AH	= 30H
AL	= 00H

Returns

AL	= major version number (for example, 3 for MS-DOS version 3.x)
AH	= minor version number (for example, 0AH for MS-DOS version x.10)
BH	= original equipment manufacturer's (OEM's) serial number (OEM dependent — usually 00H for PC-DOS, 0FFH or other values for MS-DOS)
BL:CX	= 24-bit user serial number (optional; OEM dependent)

Programmer's Notes

- With MS-DOS versions 1.x, Function 30H returns 00H in the AL register; the value returned in AH is variable and not representative of the actual 1.x minor version number.
- Function 30H supplies the MS-DOS version number to an application program that might require features of the operating system that are not available in all versions. If an application attempts to use such features with the wrong version of MS-DOS, the results are unpredictable.

   Applications requiring MS-DOS version 2.0 or later should use Function 30H to check for versions 1.x. Because versions 1.x do not contain predefined handles for displaying error messages, Function 02H (Character Output) or Function 09H (Display String) must be used with those versions. Similarly, applications running under versions 1.x cannot terminate through a call to Function 4CH (Terminate Process with Return Code).

Related Functions

None

Example

```
;****************************************************************;
;                                                              ;
;              Function 30H: Get MS-DOS Version Number         ;
;                                                              ;
;                 int DOS_version()                            ;
;                                                              ;
;              Returns number of MS-DOS version, with          ;
;                 major version in high byte,                  ;
;                 minor version in low byte.                   ;
;                                                              ;
;****************************************************************;

cProc   DOS_version,PUBLIC
cBegin
        mov     ax,3000H        ; Set function code and clear AL.
        int     21h             ; Ask MS-DOS for version number.
        xchg    al,ah           ; Swap major and minor numbers.
cEnd
```

Interrupt 21H (33)
Function 31H (49)

2.0 and later

Terminate and Stay Resident

Function 31H terminates a program and returns control to the parent process (usually COMMAND.COM) but keeps the terminated program resident in memory.

To Call

AH = 31H
AL = return code
DX = number of paragraphs of memory to be reserved for current process

Returns

Nothing

Programmer's Notes

- The following interrupt vectors are restored from the program segment prefix (PSP) of the terminated program:

PSP Offset	Vector for Interrupt
0AH	Interrupt 22H (terminate routine)
0EH	Interrupt 23H (Control-C handler)
12H	Interrupt 24H (critical error handler) (versions 2.0 and later.)

- The minimum amount of memory a process can reserve is 6 paragraphs (60H bytes), which constitutes the initial portion of the process's PSP (including the reserved areas).
- The amount of memory required by the program is not necessarily the same as the size of the file that holds the program on disk. The program must allow for its PSP and stack in the amount of memory reserved; on the other hand, the memory occupied by code and data used only during program initialization frequently can be discarded as a side effect of the Function 31H call.

  Before Function 31H is called, memory allocated to the terminating process's environment block should be released by loading ES with the segment value at offset 2CH in the PSP (the segment address of the environment) and calling Function 49H (Free Memory Block).
- The terminating process should return a completion code in the AL register. If the program terminates normally, the return code should be 00H. A return code of 01H or greater usually indicates that termination was caused by an error encountered by the process.

The parent process can retrieve the return code with Function 4DH (Get Return Code of Child Process). If control returns to COMMAND.COM, the return code can be tested with an ERRORLEVEL statement in a batch file.

- After terminating the current process, MS-DOS attempts to set the program's memory allocation to the amount specified in DX.
- Function 31H is most often used for memory-resident utilities and subroutine libraries that can be accessed using interrupts.
- This function is preferable to Interrupt 27H (Terminate and Stay Resident) because it allows programs that are larger than 64 KB to remain resident, allows the terminating program to pass a return code to the parent process, and does not require that the CS register contain the PSP address.

Related Functions

48H (Allocate Memory Block)
49H (Free Memory Block)
4AH (Resize Memory Block)
4BH (Load and Execute Program)
4CH (Terminate Process with Return Code)
4DH (Get Return Code of Child Process)

Example

```
;**************************************************************;
;                                                            ;
;           Function 31H: Terminate and Stay Resident        ;
;                                                            ;
;           void keep_process(exit_code,nparas)              ;
;                 int exit_code,nparas;                       ;
;                                                            ;
;           Does NOT return!                                  ;
;                                                            ;
;**************************************************************;

cProc    keep_process,PUBLIC
parmB    exit_code
parmW    nparas
cBegin
         mov     al,exit_code    ; Get return code.
         mov     dx,nparas       ; Set DX to number of paragraphs the
                                 ; program wants to keep.
         mov     ah,31h          ; Set function code.
         int     21h             ; Ask MS-DOS to keep process.
cEnd
```

Interrupt 21H (33)
Function 33H (51)

Get/Set Control-C Check Flag

Function 33H gets or sets the status of the Control-C check flag.

To Call

AH = 33H
AL = 00H   get current Control-C check flag
     01H   set Control-C check flag to value in DL

If AL is 01H:

DL = 00H   set Control-C check flag to off
     01H   set Control-C check flag to on

Returns

AL = 00H   flag set successfully
     FFH   code in AL on call not 00H or 01H

If AL was 00H on call:

DL = 00H   Control-C check flag off
     01H   Control-C check flag on

Programmer's Notes

- If the Control-C check flag is off, MS-DOS checks for a Control-C entered at the keyboard only during servicing of the character I/O functions, 01H through 0CH. If the Control-C check flag is on, MS-DOS also checks for user entry of a Control-C during servicing of other functions, such as file and record operations.
- The state of the Control-C check flag affects all programs. If a program needs to change the state of Control-C checking, it should save the original flag and restore it before terminating.

Related Functions

None

Example

```
;*************************************************************;
;                                                           ;
;            Function 33H: Get/Set Control-C Check Flag      ;
;                                                           ;
;                int controlC(func,state)                   ;
;                     int func,state;                       ;
;                                                           ;
;            Returns current state of Control-C flag.       ;
;                                                           ;
;*************************************************************;

cProc     controlC,PUBLIC
parmB     func
parmB     state
cBegin
          mov     al,func       ; Get set/reset function.
          mov     dl,state      ; Get new value if present.
          mov     ah,33h        ; MS-DOS ^C check function.
          int     21h           ; Call MS-DOS.
          mov     al,dl         ; Return current state.
          cbw                   ; Clear high byte of return value.
cEnd
```

Interrupt 21H (33)
Function 34H (52)

2.0 and later

Return Address of InDOS Flag

Function 34H returns the address of the InDOS flag, which reflects the current state of Interrupt 21H function processing.

Note: Microsoft cannot guarantee that the information in this entry will be valid for future versions of MS-DOS.

To Call

AH   = 34H

Returns

ES:BX   = segment:offset of InDOS flag

Programmer's Notes

- The InDOS flag is a byte within the MS-DOS kernel. The value in InDOS is incremented when MS-DOS begins execution of an Interrupt 21H function and decremented when MS-DOS's processing of that function is completed. Thus, the value of InDOS is zero only when no Interrupt 21H processing is occurring.
- The InDOS flag is one of the elements used in terminate-and-stay-resident (TSR) programs to determine when the TSR can be executed safely.

Related Functions

None

Example

```
;**************************************************************;
;                                                            ;
;        Function 34H: Get Return Address of InDOS Flag      ;
;                                                            ;
;        char far *inDOS_ptr()                               ;
;                                                            ;
;        Returns a far pointer to the MS-DOS inDOS flag.     ;
;                                                            ;
;**************************************************************;

cProc   inDOS_ptr,PUBLIC
cBegin
        mov     ah,34h          ; InDOS flag function.
        int     21h             ; Call MS-DOS.
        mov     ax,bx           ; Return offset in AX.
        mov     dx,es           ; Return segment in DX.
cEnd
```

Interrupt 21H (33)
Function 35H (53)

2.0 and later

Get Interrupt Vector

Function 35H returns the address stored in the interrupt vector table for the handler associated with the specified interrupt.

To Call

AH = 35H
AL = interrupt number

Returns

ES:BX = segment:offset of handler for interrupt specified in AL

Programmer's Note

- Interrupt vectors should always be read with Function 35H and set with Function 25H (Set Interrupt Vector). Programs should never attempt to read or change interrupt vectors directly in memory.

Related Function

25H (Set Interrupt Vector)

Example

```
;*************************************************************;
;                                                           ;
;           Function 35H: Get Interrupt Vector              ;
;                                                           ;
;           typedef void (far *FCP)();                      ;
;           FCP get_vector(intnum)                          ;
;               int intnum;                                 ;
;                                                           ;
;           Returns a far code pointer that is the          ;
;           segment:offset of the interrupt vector.         ;
;                                                           ;
;*************************************************************;

cProc   get_vector,PUBLIC
parmB   intnum
cBegin
        mov     al,intnum       ; Get interrupt number into AL.
        mov     ah,35h          ; Select "get vector" function.
        int     21h             ; Call MS-DOS.
        mov     ax,bx           ; Return vector offset.
        mov     dx,es           ; Return vector segment.
cEnd
```

Interrupt 21H (33)
Function 36H (54)

2.0 and later

Get Disk Free Space

Function 36H returns disk-storage information for the specified drive.

To Call

AH = 36H
DL = drive specification (0 = default drive, 1 = drive A, 2 = drive B, and so on)

Returns

If function is successful:

AX = number of sectors per cluster
BX = number of clusters available
CX = number of bytes per sector
DX = number of clusters on drive

If function is not successful:

AX = FFFFH   invalid drive number in DL

Programmer's Notes

- The AX register should be checked for a value of FFFFH (error) before information returned by this function is used.
- The number of bytes of free storage remaining on the disk can be calculated by multiplying available clusters times sectors per cluster times bytes per sector (BX ∗ AX ∗ CX).
- Function 36H regards "lost" clusters (clusters that are allocated in the file allocation table [FAT] but do not belong to a file) as being in use and subtracts them from the amount of available storage, exactly as if they were allocated to a file.
- With MS-DOS versions 2.0 and later, Function 36H should be used in preference to the FCB Functions 1BH (Get Default Drive Data) and 1CH (Get Drive Data).

Related Functions

1BH (Get Default Drive Data)
1CH (Get Drive Data)

Example

```
;*************************************************************;
;                                                             ;
;               Function 36H: Get Disk Free Space            ;
;                                                             ;
;               long free_space(drive_ltr)                   ;
;                    char drive_ltr;                         ;
;                                                             ;
;               Returns the number of bytes free as          ;
;               a long integer.                              ;
;                                                             ;
;*************************************************************;

cProc   free_space,PUBLIC
parmB   drive_ltr
cBegin
        mov     dl,drive_ltr    ; Get drive letter.
        or      dl,dl           ; Leave 0 alone.
        jz      fsp
        and     dl,not 20h      ; Convert letter to uppercase.
        sub     dl,'A'-1        ; Convert to drive number: 'A' = 1,
                                ; 'B' = 2, etc.
fsp:
        mov     ah,36h          ; Set function code.
        int     21h             ; Ask MS-DOS to get disk information.
        mul     cx              ; Bytes/sector * sectors/cluster
        mul     bx              ; * free clusters.
cEnd
```

Interrupt 21H (33)
Function 38H (56)

2.0 and later

Get/Set Current Country: Get Current Country

Function 38H includes two subfunctions that either get or set country data, depending on the value in the DX register when the function is called.

With MS-DOS versions 2.0 and later, if DX contains any value other than FFFFH, the Get Current Country subfunction is invoked. Information on date, currency, and other country-specific formats is then returned in a buffer specified by the calling program. The country code is usually the same as the country's international telephone prefix.

To Call

AH = 38H

With MS-DOS versions 2.x:

AL = 00H   current country
DS:DX = segment:offset of 32-byte buffer

With MS-DOS versions 3.x:

AL = 00H   current country
     01–FEH   country code between 1 and 254
     FFH   country code of 255 or greater, specified in BX
BX = country code if AL = FFH
DS:DX = segment:offset of 34-byte buffer

Returns

If function is successful:

Carry flag is clear.

BX = country code (MS-DOS version 3.x only)
DS:DX = segment:offset of buffer containing country information

If function is not successful:

Carry flag is set.

AX = error code:
     02H   invalid country code

Programmer's Notes

- With MS-DOS versions 2.x, the Get Current Country subfunction returns the following information for the current country in the 32-byte country-data buffer (ASCIIZ format is an ASCII character string ending in a zero byte):

Offset	Type	Description
00H	Word	Date format: 　　　0 = United States (m/d/y) 　　　1 = Europe (d/m/y) 　　　2 = Japan (y/m/d)
02H	ASCIIZ	Currency symbol
04H	ASCIIZ	Character used as thousands separator
06H	ASCIIZ	Character used as decimal separator
08H	24 bytes	Reserved

- With MS-DOS versions 3.x, the Get Current Country subfunction returns the following information for the specified country in the 34-byte country-data buffer:

Offset	Type	Description
00H	Word	Date format: 　　　0 = United States (m/d/y) 　　　1 = Europe (d/m/y) 　　　2 = Japan (y/m/d)
02H	ASCIIZ	Currency symbol (5 bytes, as opposed to 2 in versions 2.x of MS-DOS)
07H	ASCIIZ	Character used as thousands separator
09H	ASCIIZ	Character used as decimal separator
0BH	ASCIIZ	Character used as date separator
0DH	ASCIIZ	Character used as time separator
0FH	Byte	Position of currency symbol; possible values are 　　00H　Currency symbol precedes value with no space 　　01H　Currency symbol follows value with no space 　　02H　Currency symbol precedes value with one space 　　03H　Currency symbol follows value with one space
10H	Byte	Number of decimal places in currency

(more)

Offset	Type	Description
11H	Byte	Time format (00H = 12-hour clock; 01H = 24-hour clock)
12H	Dword	Case-mapping call address (*See* Programmer's Notes below.)
16H	ASCIIZ	Character used as separator in data lists
18H	10 bytes	Reserved

● The case-mapping call address (MS-DOS versions 3.x only) is the segment:offset of a FAR procedure that performs country-specific mapping on ASCII characters in the range 80H through 0FFH. The character to be mapped must be placed in the AL register before the call is made. If the character has an uppercase value, that value is returned in AL. If the character has no such value, AL is unchanged.

● Function 59H (Get Extended Error Information) provides further information on any error — in particular, the code, class, recommended corrective action, and locus of the error.

Related Function

38H (Set Current Country subfunction)

Example

```
;**************************************************************;
;                                                            ;
;            Function 38H: Get/Set Current Country Data       ;
;                                                            ;
;            int country_info(country,pbuffer)                ;
;                 char country,*pbuffer;                      ;
;                                                            ;
;            Returns -1 if the "country" code is invalid.     ;
;                                                            ;
;**************************************************************;

cProc    country_info,PUBLIC,ds
parmB    country
parmDP   pbuffer
cBegin
         mov     al,country       ; Get country code.
         loadDP  ds,dx,pbuffer    ; Get buffer pointer (or -1).
         mov     ah,38h           ; Set function code.
         int     21h              ; Ask MS-DOS to get country
                                  ; information.
         jnb     cc_ok            ; Branch if country code OK.
         mov     ax,-1            ; Else return -1.
cc_ok:
cEnd
```

Interrupt 21H (33)
Function 38H (56)

3.0 and later

Get/Set Current Country: Set Current Country

Function 38H includes two subfunctions that either get or set country data, depending on the value in the DX register when the function is called.

With MS-DOS versions 3.0 and later, the Set Current Country subfunction is invoked if Function 38H is called with DX = FFFFH (−1). This subfunction selects the country for which subsequent calls to Get Current Country will return information. The country code used with this function is usually the same as the country's international telephone prefix.

To Call

```
AH  = 38H
AL  = country code      for a code less than 255
      FFH               for country code of 255 or greater, specified in BX
BX  = country code if AL = FFH
DX  = FFFFH (−1)
```

Returns

If function is successful:

Carry flag is clear.

If function is not successful:

Carry flag is set.

```
AX  = error code:
      02H               invalid country code
```

Programmer's Notes

- MS-DOS normally uses the country code associated with the current KEYBxx keyboard driver file, if any. Otherwise, the default country code is OEM dependent.
- Function 59H (Get Extended Error Information) provides further information on any error — in particular, the code, class, recommended corrective action, and locus of the error.

Related Function

38H (Get Current Country subfunction)

Example

See Function 38H Subfunction Get Current Country for example.

Interrupt 21H (33)
Function 39H (57)

Create Directory

Function 39H creates a subdirectory using the specified path.

To Call

AH   = 39H
DS:DX   = segment:offset of ASCIIZ path

Returns

If function is successful:

Carry flag is clear.

If function is not successful:

Carry flag is set.

AX   = error code:
      03H   path not found
      05H   access denied

Programmer's Notes

- The path must be a null-terminated ASCII string (ASCIIZ).
- MS-DOS places the current directory (.) and parent directory (..) entries in all new directories.
- Function 39H returns error code 05H (access denied) in the following cases:
  - File or directory with the same name already exists in the specified path.
  - Parent directory is the root directory and the root directory is full.
  - Path specifies a device.
  - Program is running on a network under MS-DOS version 3.1 or later and the user does not have Create access to the parent directory.
- Function 59H (Get Extended Error Information) provides further information on any error — in particular, the code, class, recommended corrective action, and locus of the error.

Related Functions

3AH (Remove Directory)
3BH (Change Current Directory)
47H (Get Current Directory)

Example

```
;************************************************************;
;                                                            ;
;                  Function 39H: Create Directory            ;
;                                                            ;
;                    int make_dir(pdirpath)                  ;
;                         char *pdirpath;                    ;
;                                                            ;
;                    Returns 0 if directory created OK,      ;
;                    otherwise returns error code.           ;
;                                                            ;
;************************************************************;

cProc    make_dir,PUBLIC,ds
parmDP   pdirpath
cBegin
         loadDP  ds,dx,pdirpath  ; Get pointer to pathname.
         mov     ah,39h          ; Set function code.
         int     21h             ; Ask MS-DOS to make new subdirectory.
         jb      md_err          ; Branch on error.
         xor     ax,ax           ; Else return 0.
md_err:
cEnd
```

Interrupt 21H (33)
Function 3AH (58)

2.0 and later

Remove Directory

Function 3AH removes (deletes) the specified subdirectory.

To Call

AH   = 3AH
DS:DX   = segment:offset of ASCIIZ path

Returns

If function is successful:

Carry flag is clear.

If function is not successful:

Carry flag is set.

AX   = error code:

    03H   path not found
    05H   access denied
    10H   current directory was specified

Programmer's Notes

- The path must be a null-terminated ASCII string (ASCIIZ).
- Function 3AH returns error code 05H (access denied) in the following cases:
  - Directory is not empty.
  - Root directory was specified.
  - Current directory was specified.
  - Path does not specify a valid directory.
  - Directory is malformed (. and .. not first two entries).
  - User has insufficient access rights on a network running under MS-DOS version 3.1 or later.
- Function 59H (Get Extended Error Information) provides further information on any error — in particular, the code, class, recommended corrective action, and locus of the error.

Related Functions

39H (Create Directory)
3BH (Change Current Directory)
47H (Get Current Directory)

Example

```
;************************************************************;
;                                                          ;
;              Function 3AH: Remove Directory              ;
;                                                          ;
;              int remove_dir(pdirpath)                    ;
;                  char *pdirpath;                         ;
;                                                          ;
;              Returns 0 if directory was removed,         ;
;              otherwise returns error code.               ;
;                                                          ;
;************************************************************;

cProc   remove_dir,PUBLIC,ds
parmDP  pdirpath
cBegin
        loadDP  ds,dx,pdirpath  ; Get pointer to pathname.
        mov     ah,3ah          ; Set function code.
        int     21h             ; Ask MS-DOS to delete subdirectory.
        jb      rd_err          ; Branch on error.
        xor     ax,ax           ; Else return 0.
rd_err:
cEnd
```

Interrupt 21H (33)
Function 3BH (59)

2.0 and later

Change Current Directory

Function 3BH changes the current directory to the specified path.

To Call

AH   = 3BH
DS:DX   = segment:offset of ASCIIZ path

Returns

If function is successful:

Carry flag is clear.

If function is not successful:

Carry flag is set.

AX   = error code:
      03H   path not found

Programmer's Notes

- The path must be a null-terminated ASCII string (ASCIIZ).
- Before a call to Function 3BH, Function 47H (Get Current Directory) can be used to determine the current directory so that the original directory can be restored later (for example, on termination of the program).
- Function 3BH can be used with programs that rely on either FCB-based or handle-based calls. It is the only method of changing the current directory that is supported by MS-DOS.
- The path string is limited to a total of 64 characters, including separators.
- Function 59H (Get Extended Error Information) provides further information on any error — in particular, the code, class, recommended corrective action, and locus of the error.

Related Functions

39H (Create Directory)
3AH (Remove Directory)
47H (Get Current Directory)

Example

```
;**************************************************************;
;                                                              ;
;                Function 3BH: Change Current Directory        ;
;                                                              ;
;                int change_dir(pdirpath)                      ;
;                     char *pdirpath;                          ;
;                                                              ;
;                Returns 0 if directory was changed,           ;
;                otherwise returns error code.                 ;
;                                                              ;
;**************************************************************;

cProc   change_dir,PUBLIC,ds
parmDP  pdirpath
cBegin
        loadDP  ds,dx,pdirpath  ; Get pointer to pathname.
        mov     ah,3bh          ; Ask MS-DOS to move to
        int     21h             ; different directory.
        jb      cd_err          ; Branch on error.
        xor     ax,ax           ; Else return 0.
cd_err:
cEnd
```

Interrupt 21H (33)
Function 3CH (60)

Create File with Handle

Function 3CH creates a file, assigns it the attributes specified, and returns a 16-bit handle for the file. If the named file already exists, Function 3CH opens it and truncates it to zero length.

To Call

AH	= 3CH
CX	= attribute
DS:DX	= segment:offset of ASCIIZ pathname

Returns

If function is successful:

Carry flag is clear.

AX   = handle number

If function is not successful:

Carry flag is set.

AX   = error code:

03H	path not found
04H	too many open files
05H	access denied

Programmer's Notes

- Function 3CH is preferable to Function 16H (Create File with FCB) for creating a file because it supports full pathnames. Function 16H should be used only if compatibility with versions 1.x of MS-DOS is required.
- The pathname must be a null-terminated ASCII string (ASCIIZ).
- Bits 0 through 2 of the 2-byte file attribute in CX determine whether the file is normal, read-only, hidden, or system. The attribute codes are
  - 00H   normal file
  - 01H   read-only file
  - 02H   hidden file
  - 04H   system file

  Bits 3 through 5 are associated with volume labels, subdirectories, and archive files. The volume and subdirectory bits are invalid for Function 3CH and must be set to 0. Bits 6 through 15 should be set to 0 to ensure future compatibility.

Values can be combined to set several file attributes. For example, if Function 3CH is called with CX = 0003H, the file created is a read-only hidden file.

- Because Function 3CH truncates an existing file to zero length, any information previously in the file is lost. Alternative functions that protect against such loss include the following:
  - Function 3DH (Open File with Handle) or Function 4EH (Find First File), which can be used to check for the previous existence of the file before Function 3CH is called
  - Function 5AH (Create Temporary File), which creates a file in the specified subdirectory and gives it a unique name assigned by MS-DOS
  - Function 5BH (Create New File), which is similar to Function 3CH but fails if it finds a file that matches the specified pathname
- After creating a file, Function 3CH sets the position of the file pointer to 0. Thus, the next read or write operation takes place at the beginning of the file.
- Function 3CH returns error code 04H (too many open files) if no handle is currently available. With MS-DOS versions 3.2 and earlier, a single process can have no more than 20 files open at one time, 5 of which are normally assigned to the standard devices.

  Error code 05H (access denied) is returned if the file is to be created in the root directory and the root is full or if a read-only file with the same name already exists in the specified subdirectory.
- On networks running under MS-DOS version 3.1 or later, the user must have Create access to the directory containing the file specified.
- Function 59H (Get Extended Error Information) provides further information on any error — in particular, the code, class, recommended corrective action, and locus of the error.

Related Functions

16H (Create File with FCB)
43H (Get/Set File Attributes)
5AH (Create Temporary File)
5BH (Create New File)

Example

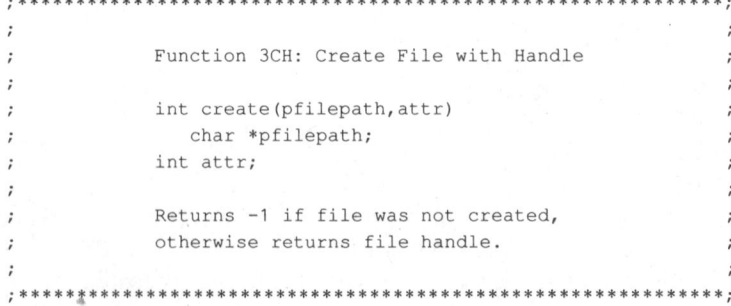

```
;************************************************************;
;                                                            ;
;            Function 3CH: Create File with Handle           ;
;                                                            ;
;            int create(pfilepath,attr)                      ;
;                char *pfilepath;                            ;
;            int attr;                                       ;
;                                                            ;
;            Returns -1 if file was not created,             ;
;            otherwise returns file handle.                  ;
;                                                            ;
;************************************************************;
```

(more)

```
cProc     create,PUBLIC,ds
parmDP    pfilepath
parmW     attr
cBegin
          loadDP  ds,dx,pfilepath ; Get pointer to pathname.
          mov     cx,attr         ; Get new file's attribute.
          mov     ah,3ch          ; Ask MS-DOS to make a new file.
          int     21h
          jnb     cr_ok           ; Branch if MS-DOS returned handle.
          mov     ax,-1           ; Else return -1.
cr_ok:
cEnd
```

Interrupt 21H (33)
Function 3DH (61)

2.0 and later

Open File with Handle

Function 3DH opens the specified file and returns a 16-bit handle number for subsequent access to the file.

To Call

AH   = 3DH

With versions 2.x of MS-DOS:

AL   = file-access code:

Bits	Value	Meaning
3–7	00000	Reserved
0–2	000	Read-only access
	001	Write-only access
	010	Read/write access

DS:DX   = segment:offset of ASCIIZ pathname

With versions 3.x of MS-DOS:

AL   = file-access, file-sharing, and inheritance codes:

Bits	Value	Meaning
7 (inherit bit)	0	Child process inherits file
	1	Child process does not inherit file
4–6 (sharing mode;	000	Compatibility mode
file access granted	001	Deny read/write access
to other processes)	010	Deny write access
	011	Deny read access
	100	Deny none
3	0	Reserved
0–2 (access code;	000	Read-only access
file usage)	001	Write-only access
	010	Read/write access

DS:DX   = segment:offset of ASCIIZ pathname

Returns

If function is successful:

Carry flag is clear.

AX   = handle number

If function is not successful:

Carry flag is set.

AX   = error code:
02H	file not found
03H	path not found
04H	too many open files
05H	access denied
0CH	invalid access code

Programmer's Notes

- Function 3DH is preferable to Function 0FH (Open File with FCB) because it allows the use of pathnames. Function 0FH should be used only if compatibility with versions 1.x of MS-DOS is required.
- Function 3DH opens any file matching the pathname in DS:DX, including hidden and system files.
- The pathname must be a null-terminated ASCII string (ASCIIZ).
- Function 3DH returns error code 04H (too many open files) if no handle is currently available. With MS-DOS versions 3.2 and earlier, a single process can have no more than 20 files open at one time, 5 of which are normally assigned to the standard devices.

  Function 3DH returns error code 05H (access denied) if the pathname specifies a directory or volume label or if read/write access was requested for a read-only file.

  Function 3DH returns error code 0CH (invalid access code) if bits 0–2 in AL contain any value other than 000, 001, or 010.
- With MS-DOS versions 2.x, only bits 0–2 of the byte in AL are meaningful; they should contain the type of access allowed for the file. Bits 3–7 should always be zero.

  With MS-DOS versions 3.0 and later, networking capabilities require bits 4–7, as well as 0–2, to be set. (Bit 3 is reserved and should be 0.)

  Bit 7, the inherit bit, should be set to indicate whether child processes created by the current process with Function 4BH (Load and Execute Program) either can (0) or cannot (1) inherit the file. When a process inherits a file, it also inherits the access and sharing modes.

Bits 4–6 are called the "sharing code"; they indicate the type of access other users on the network can have to the file. The five sharing modes and the conditions under which they pertain are as follows:

- mode 000 (compatibility). Allows other programs running on the same machine unlimited access to the file. Programs running on other machines cannot access the file across the network unless it has the read-only attribute. An attempt to open the file in compatibility mode fails if the file has already been opened with any other sharing mode.

- 001 (deny read and write access). Provides exclusive access to the file. Any subsequent attempts by others (including the current process) to open the file fail. This mode fails if the file has already been opened in compatibility mode or for read or write access, even by the current process.

- 010 (deny write access). Allows other processes to open the file for read-only access. This mode fails if the file has already been opened in compatibility mode or for write access by any other process.

- 011 (deny read access). Allows other processes to open the file for write-only access. This mode fails if the file has already been opened in compatibility mode or for read access by any other process.

- 100 (deny none). Similar to compatibility mode, but does not allow other processes to open the file in compatibility mode. This mode fails if the file has already been opened in compatibility mode by any other process.

- When the file is opened, the position of the file pointer is set to 0. Function 42H (Move File Pointer) can be used to change its position.

- With MS-DOS versions 3.0 and later, if this function fails because of a file-sharing error, the operating system issues an Interrupt 24H (Critical Error Handler Address) with error code 02H (drive not ready). Function 59H (Get Extended Error Information) must be used to find the extended error code specifying the type of sharing violation that occurred.

Related Functions

0FH (Open File with FCB)
3EH (Close File)
3FH (Read File or Device)
40H (Write File or Device)
42H (Move File Pointer)
43H (Get/Set File Attributes)
57H (Get/Set Date/Time of File)

Example

```
;*************************************************************;
;                                                             ;
;              Function 3DH: Open File with Handle            ;
;                                                             ;
;              int open(pfilepath,mode)                       ;
;                  char *pfilepath; int mode;                 ;
;                                                             ;
;              Modes:                                         ;
;                      0: Read                                ;
;                      1: Write                               ;
;                      2: Read/Write                          ;
;                                                             ;
;              Returns -1 if file was not opened,             ;
;              otherwise returns file handle.                 ;
;                                                             ;
;*************************************************************;

cProc   open,PUBLIC,ds
parmDP  pfilepath
parmB   mode
cBegin
        loadDP  ds,dx,pfilepath ; Get pointer to pathname.
        mov     al,mode         ; Get read/write mode.
        mov     ah,3dh          ; Request MS-DOS to open the
        int     21h             ; existing file.
        jnb     op_ok           ; Branch if MS-DOS returned handle.
        mov     ax,-1           ; Else return -1.
op_ok:
cEnd
```

Interrupt 21H (33)
Function 3EH (62)

2.0 and later

Close File

Function 3EH closes the file referenced by the specified handle.

To Call

AH = 3EH
BX = handle number

Returns

If function is successful:

Carry flag is clear.

If function is not successful:

Carry flag is set.

AX = error code:
    06H   invalid handle number

Programmer's Notes

- The handle in BX must be one that was returned by a successful call to one of the following functions:
  - 3CH (Create File with Handle)
  - 3DH (Open File with Handle)
  - 5AH (Create Temporary File)
  - 5BH (Create New File)
- If the file has been modified, truncated, or extended, Function 3EH updates the current date, time, and file size in the directory entry.
- All internal MS-DOS buffers for the file, including directory and file allocation table (FAT) buffers, are flushed to disk.
- With MS-DOS versions 3.0 and later, a program must remove all file locks in effect before it closes a file. The result of closing a file with active locks is unpredictable.
- Function 59H (Get Extended Error Information) provides further information on any error — in particular, the code, class, recommended corrective action, and locus of the error.

Related Functions

10H (Close File with FCB)
3CH (Create File with Handle)
3DH (Open File with Handle)
5AH (Create Temporary File)
5BH (Create New File)

Example

```
;************************************************************;
;                                                          ;
;                 Function 3EH: Close File                 ;
;                                                          ;
;                 int close(handle)                        ;
;                     int handle;                          ;
;                                                          ;
;                 Returns -1 if file was not closed,       ;
;                 otherwise returns 0.                     ;
;                                                          ;
;************************************************************;

cProc    close,PUBLIC
parmW    handle
cBegin
         mov     bx,handle       ; Get handle.
         mov     ah,3eh          ; Set function codes.
         int     21h             ; Ask MS-DOS to close handle.
         mov     al,0
         jnb     cl_ok           ; Branch if no error.
         mov     al,-1           ; Else return -1.
cl_ok:
         cbw                     ; Extend result.
cEnd
```

Interrupt 21H (33)
Function 3FH (63)

2.0 and later

Read File or Device

Function 3FH reads from the file or device referenced by a handle.

To Call

AH = 3FH
BX = handle number
CX = number of bytes to read
DS:DX = segment:offset of data buffer

Returns

If function is successful:

Carry flag is clear.

AX = number of bytes read from file
DS:DX = segment:offset of data read from file

If function is not successful:

Carry flag is set.

AX = error code:
   05H access denied
   06H invalid handle

Programmer's Notes

- Data is read from the file beginning at the current location of the file pointer. After a successful read, the file pointer is updated to point to the byte following the last byte read.
- If Function 3FH returns 00H in the AX register, the function attempted to read when the file pointer was at the end of the file. If AX is less than CX, a partial record at the end of the file was read.
- Function 3FH can be used with all handles, including standard input (normally the keyboard). When reading from standard input, this function normally reads characters only to the first carriage-return character. Thus, the number of bytes read in AX will not necessarily match the length requested in CX.
- On networks running under MS-DOS version 3.1 or later, the user must have Read access to the directory and file containing the information to be read.
- Function 59H (Get Extended Error Information) provides further information on any error — in particular, the code, class, recommended corrective action, and locus of the error.

Related Functions

40H (Write File or Device)
42H (Move File Pointer)
59H (Get Extended Error Information)

Example

```
;***********************************************************;
;                                                         ;
;             Function 3FH: Read File or Device           ;
;                                                         ;
;             int read(handle,pbuffer,nbytes)             ;
;                   int handle,nbytes;                    ;
;                   char *pbuffer;                        ;
;                                                         ;
;             Returns -1 if there was a read error,       ;
;             otherwise returns number of bytes read.     ;
;                                                         ;
;***********************************************************;

cProc   read,PUBLIC,ds
parmW   handle
parmDP  pbuffer
parmW   nbytes
cBegin
        mov     bx,handle       ; Get handle.
        loadDP  ds,dx,pbuffer   ; Get pointer to buffer.
        mov     cx,nbytes       ; Get number of bytes to read.
        mov     ah,3fh          ; Set function code.
        int     21h             ; Ask MS-DOS to read CX bytes.
        jnb     rd_ok           ; Branch if read worked.
        mov     ax,-1           ; Else return -1.
rd_ok:
cEnd
```

Interrupt 21H (33)
Function 40H (64)

2.0 and later

Write File or Device

Function 40H writes the specified number of bytes to a file or device referenced by a handle.

To Call

AH	= 40H
BX	= handle
CX	= number of bytes to write
DS:DX	= segment:offset of data buffer

Returns

If function is successful:

Carry flag is clear.

AX   = number of bytes written to file or device

If function is not successful:

Carry flag is set.

AX   = error code:
  05H   access denied
  06H   invalid handle

Programmer's Notes

- Data is written to the file or device beginning at the current location of the file pointer. After writing the specified data, Function 40H updates the position of the file pointer and returns the actual number of bytes written in AX.
- Function 40H returns error code 05H (access denied) if the file was opened as read-only with Function 3CH (Create File with Handle), 3DH (Open File with Handle), 5AH (Create Temporary File), or 5BH (Create New File). On networks running under MS-DOS version 3.1 or later, access is also denied if the file or record has been locked by another process.
- The handle number in BX must be one of the predefined device handles (0 through 4) or a handle obtained through a previous call to open or create a file (such as Function 3CH, 3DH, 5AH, or 5BH).
- If CX = 0, the file is truncated or extended to the current file pointer location. Clusters are allocated or released in the file allocation table (FAT) as required to fulfill the request.

- If the handle parameter for Function 40H refers to a disk file and the number of bytes written (returned in AX) is less than the number requested in CX, the destination disk is full. The carry flag is *not* set in this situation.
- Function 59H (Get Extended Error Information) provides further information on any error — in particular, the code, class, recommended corrective action, and locus of the error.

Related Functions

3FH (Read File or Device)
42H (Move File Pointer)

Example

```
;*************************************************************;
;                                                             ;
;            Function 40H: Write File or Device               ;
;                                                             ;
;            int write(handle,pbuffer,nbytes)                 ;
;                 int handle,nbytes;                          ;
;                 char *pbuffer;                              ;
;                                                             ;
;            Returns -1 if there was a write error,           ;
;            otherwise returns number of bytes written.       ;
;                                                             ;
;*************************************************************;

cProc   write,PUBLIC,ds
parmW   handle
parmDP  pbuffer
parmW   nbytes
cBegin
        mov     bx,handle       ; Get handle.
        loadDP  ds,dx,pbuffer   ; Get pointer to buffer.
        mov     cx,nbytes       ; Get number of bytes to write.
        mov     ah,40h          ; Set function code.
        int     21h             ; Ask MS-DOS to write CX bytes.
        jnb     wr_ok           ; Branch if write successful.
        mov     ax,-1           ; Else return -1.
wr_ok:
cEnd
```

Interrupt 21H (33)
Function 41H (65)

2.0 and later

Delete File

Function 41H deletes the directory entry of the specified file.

To Call

AH   = 41H
DS:DX   = segment:offset of ASCIIZ pathname

Returns

If function is successful:

Carry flag is clear.

If function is not successful:

Carry flag is set.

AX   = error code:
        02H   file not found
        03H   path not found
        05H   access denied

Programmer's Notes

- The pathname must be a null-terminated ASCII string (ASCIIZ). Unlike Function 13H (Delete File), Function 41H does not allow wildcard characters in the pathname.
- Because Function 41H supports the use of full pathnames, it is preferable to Function 13H.
- Function 41H returns error code 05H (access denied) and fails if the file has either a directory or volume attribute or if it is a read-only file.

  A directory can be deleted (if it is empty) with Function 3AH (Remove Directory). A read-only file can be deleted if its attribute is changed to normal with Function 43H (Get/Set File Attributes) before Function 41H is called.
- On networks running under MS-DOS version 3.1 or later, the user must have Create access to the directory containing the file to be deleted.
- Function 59H (Get Extended Error Information) provides further information on any error — in particular, the code, class, recommended corrective action, and locus of the error.

Related Functions

3AH (Remove Directory)
43H (Get/Set File Attributes)

Example

```
;***********************************************************;
;                                                           ;
;                Function 41H: Delete File                  ;
;                                                           ;
;                int delete(pfilepath)                      ;
;                     char *pfilepath;                      ;
;                                                           ;
;                Returns 0 if file deleted,                 ;
;                otherwise returns error code.              ;
;                                                           ;
;***********************************************************;

cProc   delete,PUBLIC,ds
parmDP  pfilepath
cBegin
        loadDP  ds,dx,pfilepath ; Get pointer to pathname.
        mov     ah,41h          ; Set function code.
        int     21h             ; Ask MS-DOS to delete file.
        jb      dl_err          ; Branch if MS-DOS could not delete
                                ; file.
        xor     ax,ax           ; Else return 0.
dl_err:
cEnd
```

Interrupt 21H (33)
Function 42H (66)

2.0 and later

Move File Pointer

Function 42H sets the position of the file pointer (for the next read/write operation) for the file associated with the specified handle.

To Call

AH	= 42H
AL	= method code:
	00H byte offset from beginning of file
	01H byte offset from current location of file pointer
	02H byte offset from end of file
BX	= handle number
CX:DX	= offset value to move pointer:
	CX most significant half of a doubleword value
	DX least significant half of a doubleword value

Returns

If function is successful:

Carry flag is clear.

DX:AX   = new file pointer position (absolute byte offset from beginning of file)

If function is not successful:

Carry flag is set.

AX	= error code:
	01H invalid function (AL not 00H, 01H, or 02H)
	06H invalid handle

Programmer's Notes

- The value in CX:DX is an offset specifying how far the file pointer is to be moved. With method code 00H, the value in CX:DX is always interpreted as a positive 32-bit integer, meaning the file pointer is always set relative to the beginning of the file.

  With method codes 01H and 02H, the value in CX:DX can be either a positive or negative 32-bit integer. Thus, method 1 can move the file pointer either forward or backward from its current position; method 2 can move the file pointer either forward or backward from the end of the file.

● Specifying method code 00H with an offset of 0 positions the file pointer at the beginning of the file. Similarly, specifying method code 02H with an offset of 0 conveniently positions the file pointer at the end of the file. With method code 02H offset 0, the size of the file can also be determined by examining the pointer position returned by the function.

● Depending on the offset specified in CX:DX, methods 1 and 2 may move the file pointer to a position before the start of the file. Function 42H does not return an error code if this happens, but later attempts to read from or write to the file will produce unexpected errors.

● Function 59H (Get Extended Error Information) provides further information on any error — in particular, the code, class, recommended corrective action, and locus of the error.

Related Functions

3FH (Read File or Device)
40H (Write File or Device)

Example

```
;***************************************************************;
;                                                               ;
;            Function 42H: Move File Pointer                    ;
;                                                               ;
;            long seek(handle,distance,mode)                    ;
;                 int handle,mode;                              ;
;                 long distance;                                ;
;                                                               ;
;            Modes:                                             ;
;                   0: from beginning of file                   ;
;                   1: from the current position                ;
;                   2: from the end of the file                 ;
;                                                               ;
;            Returns -1 if there was a seek error,              ;
;            otherwise returns long pointer position.           ;
;                                                               ;
;***************************************************************;

cProc   seek,PUBLIC
parmW   handle
parmD   distance
parmB   mode
cBegin
        mov     bx,handle       ; Get handle.
        les     dx,distance     ; Get distance into ES:DX.
        mov     cx,es           ; Put high word of distance into CX.
        mov     al,mode         ; Get move method code.
        mov     ah,42h          ; Set function code.
```

(more)

```
            int     21h             ; Ask MS-DOS to move file pointer.
            jnb     sk_ok           ; Branch if seek successful.
            mov     ax,-1           ; Else return -1.
            cwd
sk_ok:
cEnd
```

Interrupt 21H (33)
Function 43H (67)

2.0 and later

Get/Set File Attributes

Function 43H gets or sets the attributes of the specified file.

To Call

AH   = 43H

To get file attributes:

AL   = 00H
DS:DX   = segment:offset of ASCIIZ pathname

To set file attributes:

AL   = 01H
CX   = attributes to set:

Bit	Attribute
0	Read-only file
1	Hidden file
2	System file
5	Archive

DS:DX   = segment:offset of ASCIIZ pathname

Returns

If function is successful:

Carry flag is clear.

CX   = attribute

If function is not successful:

Carry flag is set.

AX   = error code:
           01H   invalid function (AL not 00H or 01H)
           02H   file not found
           03H   path not found
           05H   access denied

Programmer's Notes

- The pathname must be a null-terminated ASCII string (ASCIIZ).
- Function 43H cannot be used to set or change either a volume-label or directory attribute (bits 3 and 4 of the attribute byte). With MS-DOS versions 3.x, Function 43H can be used to make a directory hidden or read-only.
- On networks running under MS-DOS version 3.1 or later, the user must have Create access to the directory containing the file in order to change the read-only, hidden, or system attribute. The archive bit, however, can be changed regardless of access rights.
- Function 59H (Get Extended Error Information) provides further information on any error — in particular, the code, class, recommended corrective action, and locus of the error.

Related Functions

None

Example

```
;************************************************************;
;                                                            ;
;              Function 43H: Get/Set File Attributes         ;
;                                                            ;
;              int file_attr(pfilepath,func,attr)            ;
;                   char *pfilepath;                         ;
;                   int func,attr;                           ;
;                                                            ;
;              Returns -1 for all errors,                    ;
;              otherwise returns file attribute.             ;
;                                                            ;
;************************************************************;

cProc    file_attr,PUBLIC,ds
parmDP   pfilepath
parmB    func
parmW    attr
cBegin
         loadDP  ds,dx,pfilepath ; Get pointer to pathname.
         mov     al,func         ; Get/set flag into AL.
         mov     cx,attr         ; Get new attr (if present).
         mov     ah,43h          ; Set code function.
         int     21h             ; Call MS-DOS.
         jnb     fa_ok           ; Branch if no error.
         mov     cx,-1           ; Else return -1.
fa_ok:
         mov     ax,cx           ; Return this value.

cEnd
```

Interrupt 21H (33)
Function 44H (68)

2.0 and later

IOCTL

Function 44H is a collection of subfunctions that provide a process a direct path of communication with a device driver. As such, this function is the most flexible means of gaining access to the full capabilities of an installed device.

An IOCTL subfunction is called with 44H in AH and the value for the subfunction in AL. If a subfunction has minor functions, those values are specified in CL. Otherwise, the BX, CX, and DX registers are used for such information as handles, drive identifiers, buffer addresses, and so on.

The subfunctions and the versions of MS-DOS with which they are available are

Subfunction	Name	MS-DOS Versions
00H	Get Device Data	2.0 and later
01H	Set Device Data	2.0 and later
02H	Receive Control Data from Character Device	2.0 and later
03H	Send Control Data to Character Device	2.0 and later
04H	Receive Control Data from Block Device	2.0 and later
05H	Send Control Data to Block Device	2.0 and later
06H	Check Input Status	2.0 and later
07H	Check Output Status	2.0 and later
08H	Check If Block Device Is Removable	3.0 and later
09H	Check If Block Device Is Remote	3.1 and later
0AH	Check If Handle Is Remote	3.1 and later
0BH	Change Sharing Retry Count	3.1 and later
0CH	Generic I/O Control for Handles	3.2
	Minor Code 45H: Set Iteration Count	
	Minor Code 65H: Get Iteration Count	
0DH	Generic I/O Control for Block Devices	3.2
	Minor Code 40H: Set Device Parameters	
	Minor Code 60H: Get Device Parameters	
	Minor Code 41H: Write Track on Logical Drive	
	Minor Code 61H: Read Track on Logical Drive	
	Minor Code 42H: Format and Verify Track on Logical Drive	
	Minor Code 62H: Verify Track on Logical Drive	

(more)

Subfunction	Name	MS-DOS Versions
0EH	Get Logical Drive Map	3.2
0FH	Set Logical Drive Map	3.2

These subfunctions are documented, either individually or in related pairs, in the entries that follow.

Interrupt 21H (33)
Function 44H (68) Subfunction 00H

2.0 and later

IOCTL: Get Device Data

Function 44H Subfunction 00H gets information about a character device or file referenced by a handle.

To Call

AH = 44H
AL = 00H
BX = handle number

Returns

If function is successful:

Carry flag is clear.

DX contains information on file or device:

Bit	Value	Meaning
For a file (bit 7 = 0):		
8–15	0	Reserved.
7	0	Handle refers to a file.
6	0	File has been written.
0–5		Drive number (0 = A, 1 = B, 2 = C, and so on).
For a device (bit 7 = 1):		
15	0	Reserved.
14	1	Processes control strings transferred by IOCTL Subfunctions 02H (Receive Control Data from Character Device) and 03H (Send Control Data to Character Device), set by MS-DOS.
8–13	0	Reserved.
7	1	Handle refers to a device.
6	0	End of file on input.
5	0	Checks for control characters (cooked mode).
	1	Does not check for control characters (raw mode).

(more)

Bit	Value	Meaning
4	0	Reserved.
3	1	Clock device.
2	1	Null device.
1	1	Standard output device.
0	1	Standard input device.

If function is not successful:

Carry flag is set.

AX = error code:
  01H invalid IOCTL subfunction
  05H access denied
  06H invalid handle

Programmer's Notes

- Bits 8–15 of DX correspond to the upper 8 bits of the device-driver attribute word.
- The handle in BX must reference an open device or file.
- Bit 5 of the device data word for character-device handles defines whether that handle is in raw mode or cooked mode. In cooked mode, MS-DOS checks for Control-C, Control-P, Control-S, and Control-Z characters and transfers control to the Control-C exception handler (whose address is saved in the vector for Interrupt 23H) when a Control-C is detected. In raw mode, MS-DOS does not check for such characters when I/O is performed to the handle; however, it will still check for a Control-C entered at the keyboard on other function calls unless such checking has been turned off with Function 33H, the BREAK=OFF directive in CONFIG.SYS, or a BREAK OFF command at the MS-DOS prompt.
- Function 59H (Get Extended Error Information) provides further information on any error — in particular, the code, class, recommended corrective action, and locus of the error.

Related Functions

33H (Get/Set Control-C Check Flag)
3CH (Create File with Handle)
3DH (Open File with Handle)

Example

```
;*************************************************************;
;                                                             ;
;           Function 44H, Subfunctions 00H,01H:               ;
;                      Get/Set IOCTL Device Data              ;
;                                                             ;
;           int ioctl_char_flags(setflag,handle,newflags)     ;
;                int setflag;                                 ;
;                int handle;                                  ;
;                int newflags;                                ;
;                                                             ;
;           Set setflag = 0 to get flags, 1 to set flags.     ;
;                                                             ;
;           Returns -1 for error, else returns flags.         ;
;                                                             ;
;*************************************************************;

cProc   ioctl_char_flags,PUBLIC
parmB   setflag
parmW   handle
parmW   newflags
cBegin
        mov     al,setflag      ; Get setflag.
        and     al,1            ; Save only lsb.
        mov     bx,handle       ; Get handle to character device.
        mov     dx,newflags     ; Get new flags (they are used only
                                ; by "set" option).
        mov     ah,44h          ; Set function code.
        int     21h             ; Call MS-DOS.
        mov     ax,dx           ; Assume success - prepare to return
                                ; flags.
        jnc     iocfx           ; Branch if no error.
        mov     ax,-1           ; Else return error flag.
iocfx:
cEnd
```

Interrupt 21H (33)
Function 44H (68) Subfunction 01H

2.0 and later

IOCTL: Set Device Data

Function 44H Subfunction 01H, the complement of IOCTL Subfunction 00H, sets information about a character device — but not a file — referenced by a handle.

To Call

AH = 44H
AL = 01H
BX = handle number
DX = device data word:

Bit	Value	Meaning
8–15	0	Reserved.
7	1	Handle refers to a device.
6	0	End of file on input.
5	0	Check for control characters (cooked mode).
	1	Do not check for control characters (raw mode).
4	0	Reserved.
3	1	Clock device.
2	1	Null device.
1	1	Standard output device.
0	1	Standard input device.

Returns

If function is successful:

Carry flag is clear.

If function is not successful:

Carry flag is set.

AX = error code:
    01H   invalid IOCTL subfunction
    05H   access denied
    06H   invalid handle

Programmer's Notes

- The handle in BX must reference an open device.
- DH must be 00H. If it is not, the carry flag is set and error code 01H (invalid function) is returned.
- Bit 5 of the device data word for character-device handles selects raw mode or cooked mode for the handle. In cooked mode, MS-DOS checks for Control-C, Control-P, Control-S, and Control-Z characters and transfers control to the Control-C exception handler (whose address is saved in the vector for Interrupt 23H) when a Control-C is detected. In raw mode, MS-DOS does not check for such characters when I/O is performed to the handle; however, it will still check for a Control-C entered at the keyboard on other function calls unless such checking has been turned off with Function 33H, the BREAK=OFF directive in CONFIG.SYS, or a BREAK OFF command at the MS-DOS prompt.
- Function 59H (Get Extended Error Information) provides further information on any error — in particular, the code, class, recommended corrective action, and locus of the error.

Related Functions

33H (Get/Set Control-C Check Flag)
3CH (Create File with Handle)
3DH (Open File with Handle)

Example

See SYSTEM CALLS: INTERRUPT 21H: Function 44H Subfunction 00H.

Interrupt 21H (33)
Function 44H (68) Subfunctions 02H and 03H

2.0 and later

IOCTL: Receive Control Data from Character Device; Send Control Data to Character Device

Function 44H Subfunctions 02H and 03H respectively receive and send control strings from and to a character-oriented device driver.

To Call

AH	= 44H	
AL	= 02H	receive control strings
	03H	send control strings
BX	= handle number	
CX	= number of bytes to transfer	
DS:DX	= segment:offset of data buffer	

Returns

If function is successful:

Carry flag is clear.

AX   = number of bytes transferred

If AL was 02H on call:

Buffer at DS:DX contains data read from device driver.

If function is not successful:

Carry flag is set.

AX   = error code:

01H	invalid function
05H	access denied
06H	invalid handle
0DH	invalid data (bad control string)

Programmer's Notes

- Subfunctions 02H and 03H provide a means of transferring control information of any type or length between an application program and a character-device driver. They do not necessarily result in any input to or output from the physical device itself.
- Subfunction 02H can be used to read control information about such features as device status, availability, and current output location. Subfunction 03H is often used to configure the driver or device for subsequent I/O; for example, it may be used to set the baud rate, word length, and parity for a serial communications adapter or to initialize a printer for a specific font, page length, and so on. The format of the control data passed by these subfunctions is driver specific and does not follow any standard.

- Character-device drivers are not required to support IOCTL Subfunctions 02H and 03H. Therefore, Subfunction 00H (Get Device Data) should be called before either Subfunction 02H or 03H to determine whether a device can process control strings. If bit 14 of the device data word returned by Subfunction 00H is set, the device driver supports IOCTL Subfunctions 02H and 03H.
- Function 59H (Get Extended Error Information) provides further information on any error — in particular, the code, class, recommended corrective action, and locus of the error.

Related Functions

44H Subfunction 00H (Get Device Data)
44H Subfunction 04H (Receive Control Data from Block Device)
44H Subfunction 05H (Send Control Data to Block Device)

Example

```
;**************************************************************;
;                                                              ;
;       Function 44H, Subfunctions 02H,03H:                    ;
;                      IOCTL Character Device Control          ;
;                                                              ;
;       int ioctl_char_ctrl(recvflag,handle,pbuffer,nbytes)    ;
;           int   recvflag;                                    ;
;           int   handle;                                      ;
;           char *pbuffer;                                     ;
;           int   nbytes;                                      ;
;                                                              ;
;       Set recvflag = 0 to receive info, 1 to send.           ;
;                                                              ;
;       Returns -1 for error, otherwise returns number of      ;
;       bytes sent or received.                                ;
;                                                              ;
;**************************************************************;

cProc   ioctl_char_ctrl,PUBLIC,<ds>
parmB   recvflag
parmW   handle
parmDP  pbuffer
parmW   nbytes
cBegin
        mov     al,recvflag     ; Get recvflag.
        and     al,1            ; Keep only lsb.
        add     al,2            ; AL = 02H for receive, 03H for send.
        mov     bx,handle       ; Get character-device handle.
        mov     cx,nbytes       ; Get number of bytes to receive/send.
        loadDP  ds,dx,pbuffer   ; Get pointer to buffer.
        mov     ah,44h          ; Set function code.
        int     21h             ; Call MS-DOS.
        jnc     iccx            ; Branch if no error.
        mov     ax,-1           ; Return -1 for all errors.
iccx:
cEnd
```

Interrupt 21H (33)
2.0 and later
Function 44H (68) Subfunctions 04H and 05H

IOCTL: Receive Control Data from Block Device; Send Control Data to Block Device

Function 44H Subfunctions 04H and 05H respectively receive and send control strings from and to a block-oriented device driver.

To Call

AH	= 44H	
AL	= 04H	receive block-device data
	05H	send block-device data
BL	= drive number (0 = default drive, 1 = drive A, 2 = drive B, and so on)	
CX	= number of bytes to transfer	
DS:DX	= segment:offset of data buffer	

Returns

If function is successful:

Carry flag is clear.

AX   = number of bytes transferred

If AL was 04H on call:

Buffer at DS:DX contains control data read from device driver.

If function is not successful:

Carry flag is set.

AX	= error code:	
	01H	invalid function
	05H	access denied
	06H	invalid handle
	0DH	invalid data (bad control string)

Programmer's Notes

- Subfunctions 04H and 05H provide a means of transferring control information of any type or length between an application program and a block-device driver. They do not necessarily result in any input to or output from the physical device itself.
- Control strings can be used to request driver operations that are not file oriented, such as tape rewind or disk eject (if hardware supported). The contents of such control strings are specific to individual device drivers and do not follow any standard format.

- Subfunction 04H can be used to obtain a code from the driver indicating device availability or status. Block devices that might use this subfunction include magnetic tape or tape cassette, CD ROM, and Small Computer Standard Interface (SCSI) devices.
- Block-device drivers are not required to support IOCTL Subfunctions 04H and 05H. If the driver does not support these subfunctions, error code 01H (Invalid Function) is returned.
- Function 59H (Get Extended Error Information) provides further information on any error — in particular, the code, class, recommended corrective action, and locus of the error.

Related Functions

44H Subfunction 00H (Get Device Data)
44H Subfunction 02H (Receive Control Data from Character Device)
44H Subfunction 03H (Send Control Data to Character Device)

Example

```
;************************************************************;
;                                                          ;
;    Function 44H, Subfunctions 04H,05H:                   ;
;              IOCTL Block Device Control                  ;
;                                                          ;
;    int ioctl_block_ctrl(recvflag,drive_ltr,pbuffer,nbytes) ;
;        int   recvflag;                                   ;
;        int   drive_ltr;                                  ;
;        char *pbuffer;                                    ;
;        int   nbytes;                                     ;
;                                                          ;
;    Set recvflag = 0 to receive info, 1 to send.          ;
;                                                          ;
;    Returns -1 for error, otherwise returns number of     ;
;    bytes sent or received.                               ;
;                                                          ;
;************************************************************;

cProc   ioctl_block_ctrl,PUBLIC,<ds>
parmB   recvflag
parmB   drive_ltr
parmDP  pbuffer
parmW   nbytes
cBegin
        mov     al,recvflag     ; Get recvflag.
        and     al,1            ; Keep only lsb.
        add     al,4            ; AL = 04H for receive, 05H for send.
        mov     bl,drive_ltr    ; Get drive letter.
        or      bl,bl           ; Leave 0 alone.
        jz      ibc
        and     bl,not 20h      ; Convert letter to uppercase.
        sub     bl,'A'-1        ; Convert to drive number: 'A' = 1,
                                ; 'B' = 2, etc.
```

(more)

```
ibc:
        mov     cx,nbytes        ; Get number of bytes to receive/send.
        loadDP  ds,dx,pbuffer    ; Get pointer to buffer.
        mov     ah,44h           ; Set function code.
        int     21h              ; Call MS-DOS.
        jnc     ibcx             ; Branch if no error.
        mov     ax,-1            ; Return -1 for all errors.
ibcx:
cEnd
```

Interrupt 21H (33)
Function 44H (68) Subfunctions 06H and 07H

2.0 and later

IOCTL: Check Input Status; Check Output Status

Function 44H Subfunctions 06H and 07H respectively determine whether a device or file associated with a handle is ready for input or output.

To Call

AH = 44H
AL = 06H   get input status
      07H   get output status
BX = handle number

Returns

If function is successful:

Carry flag is clear.

AL = input or output status:
    00H   not ready
    FFH   ready

If function is not successful:

Carry flag is set.

AX = error code:
    01H   invalid function
    05H   access denied
    06H   invalid handle
    0DH   invalid data (bad control string)

Programmer's Notes

- The status returned in AL has the following meanings:

Status	Device	Input File	Output File
00H	Not ready	Pointer at EOF	Ready
0FFH	Ready	Ready	Ready

- Output files always return a ready condition, even if the disk is full or no disk is in the drive.
- Function 59H (Get Extended Error Information) provides further information on any error — in particular, the code, class, recommended corrective action, and locus of the error.

Related Functions

None

Example

```
;*************************************************************;
;                                                           ;
;    Function 44H, Subfunctions 06H,07H:                    ;
;                  IOCTL Input/Output Status                ;
;                                                           ;
;    int ioctl_char_status(outputflag,handle)              ;
;         int outputflag;                                   ;
;         int handle;                                       ;
;                                                           ;
;    Set outputflag = 0 for input status, 1 for output status. ;
;                                                           ;
;    Returns -1 for all errors, 0 for not ready,            ;
;    and 1 for ready.                                        ;
;                                                           ;
;*************************************************************;

cProc    ioctl_char_status,PUBLIC
parmB    outputflag
parmW    handle
cBegin
         mov     al,outputflag    ; Get outputflag.
         and     al,1             ; Keep only lsb.
         add     al,6             ; AL = 06H for input status, 07H for output
                                  ; status.
         mov     bx,handle        ; Get handle.
         mov     ah,44h           ; Set function code.
         int     21h              ; Call MS-DOS.
         jnc     isnoerr          ; Branch if no error.
         mov     ax,-1            ; Return error code.
         jmp     short isx
isnoerr:
         and     ax,1             ; Keep only lsb for return value.
isx:
cEnd
```

Interrupt 21H (33)
Function 44H (68) Subfunction 08H

3.0 and later

IOCTL: Check If Block Device Is Removable

Function 44H Subfunction 08H checks whether the specified block device contains a removable storage medium, such as a floppy disk.

To Call

AH = 44H
AL = 08H
BL = drive number (0 = default drive, 1 = drive A, 2 = drive B, and so on)

Returns

If function is successful:

Carry flag is clear.

AX = 00H   storage medium removable
    01H   storage medium not removable

If function is not successful:

Carry flag is set.

AX = error code:
    01H   invalid function
    0FH   invalid drive

Programmer's Notes

- This subfunction exists to allow an application to check for a removable disk so that the user can be prompted to change disks if a required file is not found.
- When the carry flag is set, error code 01H normally means that MS-DOS did not recognize the function call. However, this error can also mean that the device driver does not support Subfunction 08H. In this case, MS-DOS assumes that the storage medium is not removable.
- Function 59H (Get Extended Error Information) provides further information on any error — in particular, the code, class, recommended corrective action, and locus of the error.

Related Functions

None

Example

```
;**************************************************************;
;                                                            ;
;       Function 44H, Subfunction 08H:                       ;
;                       IOCTL Removable Block Device Query    ;
;                                                            ;
;       int ioctl_block_fixed(drive_ltr)                     ;
;           int drive_ltr;                                   ;
;                                                            ;
;       Returns -1 for all errors, 1 if disk is fixed (not   ;
;       removable), 0 if disk is not fixed.                  ;
;                                                            ;
;**************************************************************;

cProc   ioctl_block_fixed,PUBLIC
parmB   drive_ltr
cBegin
        mov     bl,drive_ltr     ; Get drive letter.
        or      bl,bl            ; Leave 0 alone.
        jz      ibch
        and     bl,not 20h       ; Convert letter to uppercase.
        sub     bl,'A'-1         ; Convert to drive number: 'A' = 1,
                                 ; 'B' = 2, etc.
ibch:
        mov     ax,4408h         ; Set function code, Subfunction 08H.
        int     21h              ; Call MS-DOS.
        jnc     ibchx            ; Branch if no error, AX = 0 or 1.
        cmp     ax,1             ; Treat error code of 1 as "disk is
                                 ; fixed."
        je      ibchx
        mov     ax,-1            ; Return -1 for other errors.
ibchx:
cEnd
```

Interrupt 21H (33)
Function 44H (68) Subfunction 09H

3.1 and later

IOCTL: Check If Block Device Is Remote

Function 44H Subfunction 09H checks whether the specified block device is local (attached to the computer running the program) or remote (redirected to a network server).

To Call

AH = 44H
AL = 09H
BL = drive number (0 = default drive, 1 = drive A, 2 = drive B, and so on)

Returns

If function is successful:

Carry flag is clear.

DX = device attribute word:
    bit 12 = 1   drive is remote
    bit 12 = 0   drive is local

If function is not successful:

Carry flag is set.

AX = error code:
    01H   invalid function
    0FH   invalid drive

Programmer's Notes

- This subfunction should be avoided. Application programs should not distinguish between files on local and remote devices.
- When the carry flag is set, error code 01H can mean either that the function number is invalid or that the network has not been started.
- Function 59H (Get Extended Error Information) provides further information on any error — in particular, the code, class, recommended corrective action, and locus of the error.

Related Functions

None

Example

```
;*************************************************************;
;                                                             ;
;            Function 44H, Subfunction 09H:                   ;
;                      IOCTL Remote Block Device Query        ;
;                                                             ;
;            int ioctl_block_redir(drive_ltr)                 ;
;                int drive_ltr;                               ;
;                                                             ;
;            Returns -1 for all errors, 1 if disk is remote   ;
;            (redirected), 0 if disk is local.                ;
;                                                             ;
;*************************************************************;

cProc   ioctl_block_redir,PUBLIC
parmB   drive_ltr
cBegin
        mov     bl,drive_ltr    ; Get drive letter.
        or      bl,bl           ; Leave 0 alone.
        jz      ibr
        and     bl,not 20h      ; Convert letter to uppercase.
        sub     bl,'A'-1        ; Convert to drive number: 'A' = 1,
                                ; 'B' = 2, etc.
ibr:
        mov     ax,4409h        ; Set function code, Subfunction 09H.
        int     21h             ; Call MS-DOS.
        mov     ax,-1           ; Assume error.
        jc      ibrx            ; Branch if error, returning -1.
        inc     ax              ; Set AX = 0.
        test    dh,10h          ; Is bit 12 set?
        jz      ibrx            ; If not, disk is local: Return 0.
        inc     ax              ; Return 1 for remote disk.
ibrx:
cEnd
```

Interrupt 21H (33)   3.1 and later
Function 44H (68) Subfunction 0AH

IOCTL: Check If Handle Is Remote

Function 44H Subfunction 0AH checks whether the handle in BX refers to a file or device that is local (on the computer running the program) or remote (redirected to a network server).

To Call

AH = 44H
AL = 0AH
BX = handle

Returns

If function is successful:

Carry flag is clear.

DX = attribute word for file or device:
       bit 15 = 1   remote
       bit 15 = 0   local

If function is not successful:

Carry flag is set.

AX = error code:
       01H   invalid function
       06H   invalid handle

Programmer's Notes

- Application programs should not distinguish between files on local and remote devices.
- When the carry flag is set, error code 01H can mean either that the function number is invalid or that the network has not been started.

Related Functions

None

Example

```
;**************************************************************;
;                                                              ;
;       Function 44H, Subfunction 0AH:                         ;
;                       IOCTL Remote Handle Query              ;
;                                                              ;
;       int ioctl_char_redir(handle)                           ;
;           int handle;                                        ;
;                                                              ;
;       Returns -1 for all errors, 1 if device/file is remote  ;
;       (redirected), 0 if it is local.                        ;
;                                                              ;
;**************************************************************;

cProc   ioctl_char_redir,PUBLIC
parmW   handle
cBegin
        mov     bx,handle       ; Get handle.
        mov     ax,440ah        ; Set function code, Subfunction 0AH.
        int     21h             ; Call MS-DOS.
        mov     ax,-1           ; Assume error.
        jc      icrx            ; Branch on error, returning -1.
        inc     ax              ; Set AX = 0.
        test    dh,80h          ; Is bit 15 set?
        jz      icrx            ; If not, device/file is local:
                                ; Return 0.
        inc     ax              ; Return 1 for remote.
icrx:
cEnd
```

Interrupt 21H (33)
Function 44H (68) Subfunction 0BH

3.1 and later

IOCTL: Change Sharing Retry Count

Function 44H Subfunction 0BH sets the number of times MS-DOS retries a disk operation after a failure caused by a file-sharing violation before it returns an error to the requesting process.

To Call

AH = 44H
AL = 0BH
CX = pause between retries
DX = number of retries

Returns

If function is successful:

Carry flag is clear.

If function is not successful:

Carry flag is set.

AX = error code:
    01H   invalid function

Programmer's Notes

- The pause between retries is a machine-dependent value determined by the CPU and CPU clock speed. MS-DOS performs a delay loop that consists of 65,536 machine instructions for each iteration specified by the value in CX. The actual code is as follows:

```
xor     cx,cx
loop    $
```

The default number of retries is 3, with a pause of one loop between retries — equivalent to calling this subfunction with DX = 3 and CX = 1.
- When the carry flag is set, error code 01H indicates either that the function code is invalid or that file sharing (SHARE.EXE) is not loaded.
- Subfunction 0BH can be used to tune the system if file-contention problems are likely to arise with shared files but are expected to last only a short while.
- If file contention is expected and if some applications will lock regions of the file for an appreciable period of time, the user may need to be informed. The best procedure is to set an initial small number of retries with a short pause period. After notifying the user, the application can wait a reasonable amount of time for file access by adjusting the retry or pause-period values.

- If a process uses this subfunction, it should restore the original default values for the pause and number of retries before terminating, to avoid unwanted effects on the behavior of subsequent processes.
- Function 59H (Get Extended Error Information) provides further information on any error — in particular, the code, class, recommended corrective action, and locus of the error.

Related Functions

None

Example

```
;***************************************************************;
;                                                               ;
;       Function 44H, Subfunction 0BH:                          ;
;                       IOCTL Change Sharing Retry Count        ;
;                                                               ;
;       int ioctl_set_retry(num_retries,wait_time)             ;
;           int num_retries;                                    ;
;           int wait_time;                                      ;
;                                                               ;
;       Returns 0 for success, otherwise returns error code.    ;
;                                                               ;
;***************************************************************;

cProc   ioctl_set_retry,PUBLIC,<ds,si>
parmW   num_retries
parmW   wait_time
cBegin
        mov     dx,num_retries   ; Get parameters.
        mov     cx,wait_time
        mov     ax,440bh         ; Set function code, Subfunction 0BH.
        int     21h              ; Call MS-DOS.
        jc      isrx             ; Branch on error.
        xor     ax,ax
isrx:
cEnd
```

Interrupt 21H (33)   3.2
Function 44H (68) Subfunction 0CH

IOCTL: Generic I/O Control for Handles

Function 44H Subfunction 0CH sets or gets the output iteration count for character-oriented devices. *See also* APPENDIX A: MS-DOS Version 3.3.

To Call

AH	= 44H
AL	= 0CH
BX	= handle
CH	= category code:
	05H printer
CL	= function (minor) code:
	45H set iteration count
	65H get iteration count
DS:DX	= segment:offset of 2-byte buffer receiving or containing iteration-count word

Returns

If function is successful:

Carry flag is clear.

If CL was 65H on call:

DS:DX	= segment:offset of iteration-count word

If function is not successful:

Carry flag is set.

AX	= error code:
	01H invalid function
	06H invalid handle

Programmer's Notes

- The iteration count controls the number of times the device driver tries to send output to the printer before assuming that the device is busy.
- With MS-DOS version 3.2, only category code 05H (printer) is supported by this subfunction.
- Function 59H (Get Extended Error Information) provides further information on any error—in particular, the code, class, recommended corrective action, and locus of the error.

Related Functions

None

Example

```
;**************************************************************;
;                                                            ;
;     Function 44H, Subfunction 0CH:                         ;
;                  Generic IOCTL for Handles                 ;
;                                                            ;
;     int ioctl_char_generic(handle,category,function,pbuffer) ;
;          int    handle;                                    ;
;          int    category;                                  ;
;          int    function;                                  ;
;          int    *pbuffer;                                  ;
;                                                            ;
;     Returns 0 for success, otherwise returns error code.   ;
;                                                            ;
;**************************************************************;

cProc    ioctl_char_generic,PUBLIC,<ds>
parmW    handle
parmB    category
parmB    function
parmDP   pbuffer
cBegin
         mov      bx,handle        ; Get device handle.
         mov      ch,category      ; Get category
         mov      cl,function      ; and function.
         loadDP   ds,dx,pbuffer    ; Get pointer to data buffer.
         mov      ax,440ch         ; Set function code, Subfunction 0CH.
         int      21h              ; Call MS-DOS.
         jc       icgx             ; Branch on error.
         xor      ax,ax
icgx:
cEnd
```

Interrupt 21H (33)
Function 44H (68) Subfunction 0DH

3.2

IOCTL: Generic I/O Control for Block Devices

Function 44H Subfunction 0DH includes six input/output tasks, or minor functions, related to block-oriented devices. The tasks perform the following operations: set or get device parameters; write, read, format and verify, or verify tracks on a logical drive.

This entry covers general information on Subfunction 0DH. Details on each minor code are presented in subsequent entries.

To Call

AH	= 44H
AL	= 0DH
BL	= drive number (0 = default drive, 1 = drive A, 2 = drive B, and so on)
CH	= category code:
	08H disk drive
CL	= function (minor) code:
	40H set parameters for block device
	41H write track on logical drive
	42H format and verify track on logical drive
	60H get parameters for block device
	61H read track on logical drive
	62H verify track on logical drive
DS:DX	= segment:offset of parameter block

Returns

If function is successful:

Carry flag is clear.

If CL was 60H or 61H on call:

DS:DX   = segment:offset of parameter block

If function is not successful:

Carry flag is set.

AX	= error code:
	01H invalid function
	02H invalid drive

Programmer's Notes

- Set Device Parameters (minor code 40H) must be used before an attempt to write, read, format, or verify a track on a logical drive. In general, the following sequence applies to any of these operations:

1. Get the current parameters (minor code 60H). Examine and save them.
2. Set the new parameters (minor code 40H).
3. Perform the task.
4. Retrieve the original parameters and restore them (minor code 40H).

- With version 3.2 of MS-DOS, only category code 08H is supported by this subfunction.
- Parameter blocks in the data buffer vary with the task being performed.

Related Functions

None

Example

```
;*****************************************************************;
;                                                                 ;
;       Function 44H, Subfunction 0DH:                            ;
;                    Generic IOCTL for Block Devices              ;
;                                                                 ;
;       int ioctl_block_generic(drv_ltr,category,func,pbuffer)    ;
;           int    drv_ltr;                                       ;
;           int    category;                                      ;
;           int    func;                                          ;
;           char *pbuffer;                                        ;
;                                                                 ;
;       Returns 0 for success, otherwise returns error code.      ;
;                                                                 ;
;*****************************************************************;

cProc   ioctl_block_generic,PUBLIC,<ds>
parmB   drv_ltr
parmB   category
parmB   func
parmDP  pbuffer
cBegin
        mov     bl,drv_ltr      ; Get drive letter.
        or      bl,bl           ; Leave 0 alone.
        jz      ibg
        and     bl,not 20h      ; Convert letter to uppercase.
        sub     bl,'A'-1        ; Convert to drive number: 'A' = 1,
                                ; 'B' = 2, etc.
ibg:
        mov     ch,category     ; Get category
        mov     cl,func         ; and function.
        loadDP  ds,dx,pbuffer   ; Get pointer to data buffer.
        mov     ax,440dh        ; Set function code, Subfunction 0DH.
        int     21h             ; Call MS-DOS.
        jc      ibgx            ; Branch on error.
        xor     ax,ax
ibgx:
cEnd
```

Interrupt 21H (33)
Function 44H (68) Subfunction 0DH
Minor Code 40H

IOCTL: Generic I/O Control for Block Devices: Set Device Parameters

Function 44H Subfunction 0DH minor code 40H sets device parameters in the parameter block pointed to by DS:DX.

To Call

AH	= 44H
AL	= 0DH
BL	= drive number (0 = default drive, 1 = drive A, 2 = drive B, and so on)
CH	= category code:
	08H disk drive
CL	= 40H
DS:DX	= segment:offset of parameter block

Returns

If function is successful:

Carry flag is clear.

If function is not successful:

Carry flag is set.

AX	= error code:
	01H invalid function
	02H invalid drive

Programmer's Notes

* The parameter block is formatted as follows:

Special-functions field: offset 00H, length 1 byte

Bit	Value	Meaning
0	0	Device BIOS parameter block (BPB) field contains a new default BPB.
	1	Use current BPB.
1	0	Use all fields in parameter block.
	1	Use track layout field only.

(more)

Special-functions field: offset 00H, length 1 byte *(continued)*

Bit	Value	Meaning
2	0	Sectors in track may be different sizes. (This setting should not be used.)
	1	Sectors in track are all same size; sector numbers range from 1 to the total number of sectors in the track. (This setting should always be used.)
3–7	0	Reserved.

Device type field: offset 01H, length 1 byte

Value	Meaning
00H	320/360 KB 5.25-inch disk
01H	1.2 MB 5.25-inch disk
02H	720 KB 3.5-inch disk
03H	Single-density 8-inch disk
04H	Double-density 8-inch disk
05H	Fixed disk
06H	Tape drive
07H	Other type of block device

Device attributes field: offset 02H, length 1 word

Bit	Value	Meaning
0	0	Removable storage medium
	1	Nonremovable storage medium
1	0	Door lock not supported
	1	Door lock supported
2–15	0	Reserved

Number of cylinders field: offset 04H, length 1 word

Meaning: Maximum number of cylinders supported; set by device driver

Media type field: offset 06H, length 1 byte

Value	Meaning
00H (default)	1.2 MB 5.25-inch disk
01H	320/360 KB 5.25-inch disk

Device BPB field: offset 07H, length 31 bytes.

Meaning: *See* Programmer's Note below.

If bit 0 = 0 in special-functions field, this field contains the new default BPB for the device.

If bit 0 = 1 in special-functions field, BPB in this field is returned by the device driver in response to subsequent Build BPB requests.

Track layout field: offset 26H, variable-length table

Length	Meaning
Word	Number of sectors in track
Word	Number of first sector in track*
Word	Size of first sector in track*
	.
	.
	.
Word	Number of last sector in track
Word	Size of last sector in track

*Sector number and sector size fields are repeated for each sector on the track. If bit 2 of the special-functions field is set, all sector sizes in the track layout field must be the same.

- The device BPB field is a 31-byte data structure. Information contained in the device BPB field describes the current disk and disk control areas. The device BPB field is formatted as follows:

Byte	Meaning
00–01H	Number of bytes per sector
02H	Number of sectors per allocation unit
03–04H	Number of sectors reserved, beginning at sector 0
05H	Number of file allocation tables (FATs)
06–07H	Maximum number of root-directory entries
08–09H	Total number of sectors
0AH	Media descriptor
0B–0CH	Number of sectors per FAT
0D–0EH	Number of sectors per track
0F–10H	Number of heads
11–14H	Number of hidden sectors
15–1FH	Reserved

- When Set Device Parameters (minor code 40H) is used, the number of cylinders should not be reset — some or all of the volume may become inaccessible.
- Subfunction 0DH minor code 60H performs the complementary action, Get Device Parameters.
- Function 59H (Get Extended Error Information) provides further information on any error — in particular, the code, class, recommended corrective action, and locus of the error.

Related Functions

None

Example

None

Interrupt 21H (33)
Function 44H (68) Subfunction 0DH
Minor Code 60H

IOCTL: Generic I/O Control for Block Devices: Get Device Parameters

Function 44H Subfunction 0DH minor code 60H gets device parameters in the parameter block pointed to by DS:DX.

To Call

AH	= 44H
AL	= 0DH
BL	= drive number (0 = default drive, 1 = drive A, 2 = drive B, and so on)
CH	= category code:
	08H disk drive
CL	= 60H
DS:DX	= segment:offset of parameter block

Returns

If function is successful:

Carry flag is clear.

If function is not successful:

Carry flag is set.

AX	= error code:
	01H invalid function
	02H invalid drive

Programmer's Notes

- The parameter block is formatted as follows:

Special-functions field: offset 00H, length 1 byte		
Bit	**Value**	**Meaning**
0	0	Returns default BIOS parameter block (BPB) for the device.
	1	Returns BPB that the Build BPB device driver call would return.
1–7	0	Reserved (must be zero).

Device type field: offset 01H, length 1 byte

Value	Meaning
00H	320/360 KB 5.25-inch disk
01H	1.2 MB 5.25-inch disk
02H	720 KB 3.5-inch disk
03H	Single-density 8-inch disk
04H	Double-density 8-inch disk
05H	Fixed disk
06H	Tape drive
07H	Other type of block device

Device attributes field: offset 02H, length 1 word

Bit	Value	Meaning
0	0	Removable storage medium
	1	Nonremovable storage medium
1	0	Door lock not supported
	1	Door lock supported
2–15	0	Reserved

Number of cylinders field: offset 04H, length 1 word

Meaning: Maximum number of cylinders supported; set by device driver

Media type field: offset 06H, length 1 byte

Value	Meaning
00H (default)	1.2 MB 5.25-inch disk
01H	320/360 KB 5.25-inch disk

Device BPB field: offset 07H, length 31 bytes

Meaning: *See* Programmer's Note below.

If bit 0 = 0 in special-functions field, this field contains the new default BPB for the device.

If bit 0 = 1 in special-functions field, BPB in this field is returned by the device driver in response to subsequent Build BPB requests.

Track layout field: offset 26H

Unused

- The device BPB field is a 31-byte data structure. Information contained in the device BPB field describes the current disk and disk control areas. The device BPB field is formatted as follows:

Byte	Meaning
00–01H	Number of bytes per sector
02H	Number of sectors per allocation unit
03–04H	Number of sectors reserved, beginning at sector 0
05H	Number of file allocation tables (FATs)
06–07H	Maximum number of root-directory entries
08–09H	Total number of sectors
0AH	Media descriptor
0B–0CH	Number of sectors per FAT
0D–0EH	Number of sectors per track
0F–10H	Number of heads
11–14H	Number of hidden sectors
15–1FH	Reserved

- Subfunction 0DH minor code 40H performs the complementary action, Set Device Parameters.
- Function 59H (Get Extended Error Information) provides further information on any error — in particular, the code, class, recommended corrective action, and locus of the error.

Related Functions

None

Example

None

Interrupt 21H (33)
Function 44H (68) Subfunction 0DH
Minor Codes 41H and 61H

IOCTL: Generic I/O Control for Block Devices: Write Track on Logical Drive;
Read Track on Logical Drive

Function 44H Subfunction 0DH minor code 41H writes a track on the logical drive specified in BL and minor code 61H reads a track on the logical drive specified in BL, using information in the parameter block pointed to by DS:DX.

To Call

AH	= 44H
AL	= 0DH
BL	= drive number (0 = default drive, 1 = drive A, 2 = drive B, and so on)
CH	= category code:
	08H disk drive
CL	= function (minor) code:
	41H write a track
	61H read a track
DS:DX	= segment:offset of parameter block

Returns

If function is successful:

Carry flag is clear.

If function is not successful:

Carry flag is set.

AX	= error code:
	01H invalid function
	02H invalid drive

Programmer's Notes

- The parameter block is formatted as follows:

Offset	Size	Meaning
00H	Byte	Special-functions field; must be 0.
01H	Word	Head field; contains number of disk head used for read/write.
03H	Word	Cylinder field; contains number of disk cylinder used for read/write.
05H	Word	First-sector field; contains number of first sector to read or write (first sector on track = sector 0).
07H	Word	Number-of-sectors field; contains number of sectors to transfer.
09H	Dword	Transfer address field; contains address of buffer to use for data transfer.

- Function 59H (Get Extended Error Information) provides further information on any error—in particular, the code, class, recommended corrective action, and locus of the error.

Related Functions

None

Example

None

Interrupt 21H (33)
Function 44H (68) Subfunction 0DH
Minor Codes 42H and 62H

IOCTL: Generic I/O Control for Block Devices: Format and Verify Track on Logical Drive; Verify Track on Logical Drive

Function 44H Subfunction 0DH minor code 42H formats and verifies a track on the specified logical drive and minor code 62H verifies a track on the specified logical drive, using information in the parameter block pointed to by DS:DX.

To Call

AH	= 44H
AL	= 0DH
BL	= drive number (0 = default drive, 1 = drive A, 2 = drive B, and so on)
CH	= category code:
	08H disk drive
CL	= function (minor) code:
	42H format and verify
	62H verify
DS:DX	= segment:offset of parameter block

Returns

If function is successful:

Carry flag is clear.

If function is not successful:

Carry flag is set.

AX	= error code:
	01H invalid function
	02H invalid drive

Programmer's Notes

- The parameter block is formatted as follows:

Offset	Size	Meaning
00H	Byte	Special-functions field; must be 0.
01H	Word	Head field; contains number of disk head used for format/verify.
03H	Word	Cylinder field; contains number of cylinder used for format/verify.

- This driver subfunction allows the writing of generic formatting programs that are minimally hardware dependent.
- Function 59H (Get Extended Error Information) provides further information on any error — in particular, the code, class, recommended corrective action, and locus of the error.

Related Functions

None

Example

None

Interrupt 21H (33)
Function 44H (68) Subfunctions 0EH and 0FH

3.2

IOCTL: Get Logical Drive Map; Set Logical Drive Map

Function 44H Subfunction 0EH allows a process to determine whether more than one logi-cal drive is assigned to a block device. Subfunction 0FH sets the next logical drive number that will be used to reference a block device.

To Call

```
AH = 44H
AL = 0EH          get logical drive map
     0FH          set logical drive map
BL = drive number (0 = default drive, 1 = drive A, 2 = drive B, and so on)
```

Returns

If function is successful:

Carry flag is clear.

```
AL = mapping code:
     00H          only one letter assigned to the block device
     01–1AH       logical drive letter (A through Z) mapped to block device
```

If function is not successful:

Carry flag is set.

```
AX = error code:
     01H          invalid function
     0FH          invalid drive
```

Programmer's Notes

- If a drive has not been assigned a logical mapping with Function 44H Subfunction 0FH, the logical and physical drive references are the same. (The default is that logical drive A and physical drive A both refer to physical drive A.)
- If this function is used to map logical drives to physical drives, the result is similar to MS-DOS's treatment of a single physical drive as both A and B on a system with one floppy-disk drive. With MS-DOS version 3.2, however, the installable device driver DRIVER.SYS extends this type of physical/logical referencing to other drives. There-fore, processes can prompt for disks themselves, instead of using the prompt provided by MS-DOS.
- Function 59H (Get Extended Error Information) provides further information on any error — in particular, the code, class, recommended corrective action, and locus of the error.

Related Functions

None

Example

```
;**************************************************************;
;                                                              ;
;          Function 44H, Subfunctions 0EH, 0FH:                ;
;                    IOCTL Get/Set Logical Drive Map           ;
;                                                              ;
;          int ioctl_drive_owner(setflag, drv_ltr)             ;
;               int setflag;                                   ;
;               int drv_ltr;                                   ;
;                                                              ;
;          Set setflag = 1 to change drive's map, 0 to get     ;
;          current map.                                        ;
;                                                              ;
;          Returns -1 for all errors, otherwise returns        ;
;          the block device's current logical drive letter.    ;
;                                                              ;
;**************************************************************;

cProc   ioctl_drive_owner,PUBLIC
parmB   setflag
parmB   drv_ltr
cBegin
        mov     al,setflag      ; Load setflag.
        and     al,1            ; Keep only lsb.
        add     al,0eh          ; AL = 0EH for get, 0FH for set.
        mov     bl,drv_ltr      ; Get drive letter.
        or      bl,bl           ; Leave 0 alone.
        jz      ido
        and     bl,not 20h      ; Convert letter to uppercase.
        sub     bl,'A'-1        ; Convert to drive number: 'A' = 1,
                                ; 'B' = 2, etc.
ido:
        mov     bh,0
        mov     ah,44h          ; Set function code.
        int     21h             ; Call MS-DOS.
        mov     ah,0            ; Clear high byte.
        jnc     idox            ; Branch if no error.
        mov     ax,-1-'A'       ; Return -1 for errors.
idox:
        add     ax,'A'          ; Return drive letter.
cEnd
```

Interrupt 21H (33)
Function 45H (69)

2.0 and later

Duplicate File Handle

Function 45H obtains an additional handle for a currently open file or device.

To Call

AH = 45H
BX = handle for open file or device

Returns

If function is successful:

Carry flag is clear.

AX = new handle number

If function is not successful:

Carry flag is set.

AX = error code:
    04H   too many open files
    06H   invalid handle

Programmer's Notes

- The file pointer for the new handle is set to the same position as the pointer for the original handle. Any subsequent changes to the file are reflected in both handles. Thus, using either handle for a read or write operation moves the file pointer associated with both.
- Function 45H is often used to duplicate the handle assigned to standard input (0) or standard output (1) before a call to Function 46H (Force Duplicate File Handle). The handle forced by Function 46H can then be used for redirected input or output from or to a file or device.
- Another use for Function 45H is to keep a file open while its directory entry is being updated to reflect a change in length. If a new handle is obtained with Function 45H and then closed with Function 3EH (Close File), the directory and FAT entries for the file are updated. At the same time, because the original handle remains open, the file need not be reopened for additional read or write operations.
- Function 59H (Get Extended Error Information) provides further information on any error — in particular, the code, class, recommended corrective action, and locus of the error.

Related Function

46H (Force Duplicate File Handle)

Example

```
;**********************************************************;
;                                                         ;
;              Function 45H: Duplicate File Handle        ;
;                                                         ;
;              int dup_handle(handle)                     ;
;                  int handle;                            ;
;                                                         ;
;              Returns -1 for errors,                     ;
;              otherwise returns new handle.              ;
;                                                         ;
;**********************************************************;

cProc    dup_handle,PUBLIC
parmW    handle
cBegin
         mov    bx,handle        ; Get handle to copy.
         mov    ah,45h           ; Set function code.
         int    21h              ; Ask MS-DOS to duplicate handle.
         jnb    dup_ok           ; Branch if copy was successful.
         mov    ax,-1            ; Else return -1.
dup_ok:
cEnd
```

Interrupt 21H (33)
Function 46H (70)

2.0 and later

Force Duplicate File Handle

Function 46H forces the open handle specified in CX to track the same file or device specified by the handle in BX.

To Call

AH = 46H
BX = open handle to be duplicated
CX = open handle to be forced

Returns

If function is successful:

Carry flag is clear.

If function is not successful:

Carry flag is set.

AX = error code:
    04H   too many open files
    06H   invalid handle

Programmer's Notes

- The handle in BX must refer either to an open file or to any of the five standard handles reserved by MS-DOS: standard input, standard output, standard error, standard auxiliary, or standard printer.
- If the handle in CX refers to an open file, the file is closed.
- The file pointer for the duplicate handle is set to the same position as the pointer for the original handle. Changing the position of either file pointer moves the pointer associated with the other handle as well.
- When used with Function 45H (Duplicate File Handle), Function 46H can be used to redirect input and output as follows:

  1. Duplicate the handle from which input or output will be redirected with Function 45H (Duplicate File Handle). Save the duplicated handle for later reference (Step 3).
  2. Call Function 46H, with the handle to be redirected from in the CX register and the handle to be redirected to in the BX register.
  3. To restore I/O redirection to its original state, call Function 46H again, with the redirected file handle from Step 2 in the CX register and the duplicated file handle from Step 1 in the BX register.

This procedure is normally used to redirect a standard device, but it can redirect any device referenced by handles.

● Function 59H (Get Extended Error Information) provides further information on any error — in particular, the code, class, recommended corrective action, and locus of the error.

Related Function

45H (Duplicate File Handle)

Example

```
;*************************************************************;
;                                                             ;
;              Function 46H: Force Duplicate File Handle      ;
;                                                             ;
;              int dup_handle2(existhandle,newhandle)         ;
;                   int existhandle,newhandle;                ;
;                                                             ;
;              Returns -1 for errors,                         ;
;              otherwise returns newhandle unchanged.         ;
;                                                             ;
;*************************************************************;

cProc      dup_handle2,PUBLIC
parmW      existhandle
parmW      newhandle
cBegin
           mov     bx,existhandle   ; Get handle of existing file.
           mov     cx,newhandle     ; Get handle to copy into.
           mov     ah,46h           ; Close handle CX and then
           int     21h              ; duplicate BX's handle into CX.
           mov     ax,newhandle     ; Prepare return value.
           jnb     dup2_ok          ; Branch if close/copy was successful.
           mov     ax,-1            ; Else return -1.
dup2_ok:
cEnd
```

Interrupt 21H (33)
Function 47H (71)

Get Current Directory

Function 47H returns the path, excluding the drive and leading backslash, of the current directory for the specified drive.

To Call

AH	= 47H
DL	= drive number (0 = default drive, 1 = drive A, 2 = drive B, and so on)
DS:SI	= segment:offset of 64-byte buffer

Returns

If function is successful:

Carry flag is clear.

Buffer is filled in with ASCIIZ pathname.

If function is not successful:

Carry flag is set.

AX	= error code:
	0FH invalid drive

Programmer's Notes

- The string representing the pathname is returned as a null-terminated ASCII string (ASCIIZ).
- This function does not return an error if the buffer is too small or is incorrectly identified. MS-DOS pathnames can be as long as 64 characters; if the buffer is less than 64 bytes, MS-DOS can overwrite sections of memory outside the buffer.
- The path returned by Function 47H starts at the root directory and fully specifies the path to the current directory but does not include a drive code or a leading backslash (\) character.
- Function 59H (Get Extended Error Information) provides further information on any error—in particular, the code, class, recommended corrective action, and locus of the error.

Related Function

3BH (Change Current Directory)

Example

```
;**************************************************************;
;                                                            ;
;              Function 47H: Get Current Directory           ;
;                                                            ;
;              int get_dir(drive_ltr,pbuffer)                ;
;                   int drive_ltr;                           ;
;                   char *pbuffer;                           ;
;                                                            ;
;              Returns -1 for bad drive,                     ;
;              otherwise returns pointer to pbuffer.         ;
;                                                            ;
;**************************************************************;

cProc   get_dir,PUBLIC,<ds,si>
parmB   drive_ltr
parmDP  pbuffer
cBegin
        loadDP  ds,si,pbuffer   ; Get pointer to buffer.
        mov     dl,drive_ltr    ; Get drive number.
        or      dl,dl           ; Leave 0 alone.
        jz      gdir
        and     dl,not 20h      ; Convert letter to uppercase
        sub     dl,'A'-1        ; Convert to drive number: 'A' = 1,
                                ; 'B' = 2, etc.
gdir:
        mov     ah,47h          ; Set function code.
        int     21h             ; Call MS-DOS.
        mov     ax,si           ; Return pointer to buffer ...
        jnb     gd_ok
        mov     ax,-1           ; ... unless an error occurred.
gd_ok:
cEnd
```

Interrupt 21H (33)
Function 48H (72)

2.0 and later

Allocate Memory Block

Function 48H allocates a block of memory, in paragraphs (1 paragraph = 16 bytes), to the requesting process.

To Call

AH = 48H
BX = number of paragraphs to allocate

Returns

If function is successful:

Carry flag is clear.

AX = segment address of base of allocated block

If function is not successful:

Carry flag is set.

AX = error code:
     07H   memory control blocks damaged
     08H   insufficient memory to allocate as requested
BX = size of largest available block (paragraphs)

Programmer's Notes

- If the allocation succeeds, the address returned in AX is the segment of the base of the block. This address would be copied to a segment register (usually DS or ES) to access the memory within the block.
- If the amount of memory requested is greater than the amount in any available contiguous block of memory, the number of paragraphs in the largest available memory block is returned in the BX register.
- The default memory-management strategy in MS-DOS is to choose the first contiguous block of memory that fits the request, no matter how good the fit. With MS-DOS versions 3.0 and later, however, the memory-management strategy can be altered with Function 58H (Get/Set Allocation Strategy).
- If a process actively allocates and frees blocks of memory, the transient program area (TPA) can become fragmented — that is, small blocks of memory can be orphaned because the memory-management strategy seeks contiguous blocks of memory.
- If a process writes to memory outside the limits of the allocated block, it can destroy control structures for other memory blocks. This could result in failure of subsequent memory-management functions, and it will cause MS-DOS to print an error message and halt when the process terminates.

- Initially, the MS-DOS loader allocates all available memory to .COM programs. Function 4AH (Resize Memory Block) can free memory for dynamic reallocation by a process or by its children.
- Function 59H (Get Extended Error Information) provides further information on any error—in particular, the code, class, recommended corrective action, and locus of the error.

Related Functions

49H (Free Memory Block)
4AH (Resize Memory Block)
58H (Get/Set Allocation Strategy)

Example

```
;************************************************************;
;                                                            ;
;            Function 48H: Allocate Memory Block             ;
;                                                            ;
;            int get_block(nparas,pblocksegp,pmaxparas)      ;
;                int nparas,*pblockseg,*pmaxparas;           ;
;                                                            ;
;            Returns 0 if nparas are allocated OK and        ;
;            pblockseg has segment address of block,         ;
;            otherwise returns error code with pmaxparas      ;
;            set to maximum block size available.            ;
;                                                            ;
;************************************************************;

cProc    get_block,PUBLIC,ds
parmW    nparas
parmDP   pblockseg
parmDP   pmaxparas
cBegin
         mov     bx,nparas        ; Get size request.
         mov     ah,48h           ; Set function code.
         int     21h              ; Ask MS-DOS for memory.
         mov     cx,bx            ; Save BX.
         loadDP  ds,bx,pmaxparas
         mov     [bx],cx          ; Return result, assuming failure.
         jb      gb_err           ; Exit if error, leaving error code
                                  ; in AX.
         loadDP  ds,bx,pblockseg
         mov     [bx],ax          ; No error, so store address of block.
         xor     ax,ax            ; Return 0.
gb_err:
cEnd
```

Interrupt 21H (33)
Function 49H (73)

2.0 and later

Free Memory Block

Function 49H releases a block of memory previously allocated with Function 48H (Allocate Memory Block).

To Call

AH = 49H
ES = segment address of memory block to release

Returns

If function is successful:

Carry flag is clear.

If function is not successful:

Carry flag is set.

AX = error code:
    07H   memory control blocks damaged
    09H   incorrect memory segment specified

Programmer's Notes

- The memory segment pointed to by ES:0000H must have been allocated by Function 48H (Allocate Memory Block).
- If a program has inadvertently damaged any of the system's memory control blocks by writing outside an allocated block, an attempt to free allocated memory results in error code 07H (memory control blocks damaged).
- Function 59H (Get Extended Error Information) provides further information on any error — in particular, the code, class, recommended corrective action, and locus of the error.

Related Functions

48H (Allocate Memory Block)
4AH (Resize Memory Block)
58H (Get/Set Allocation Strategy)

Example

```
;**************************************************************;
;                                                              ;
;                Function 49H: Free Memory Block               ;
;                                                              ;
;                int free_block(blockseg)                      ;
;                     int blockseg;                            ;
;                                                              ;
;                Returns 0 if block freed OK,                  ;
;                otherwise returns error code.                 ;
;                                                              ;
;**************************************************************;

cProc   free_block,PUBLIC
parmW   blockseg
cBegin
        mov     es,blockseg     ; Get block address.
        mov     ah,49h          ; Set function code.
        int     21h             ; Ask MS-DOS to free memory.
        jb      fb_err          ; Branch on error.
        xor     ax,ax           ; Return 0 if successful.
fb_err:
cEnd
```

Interrupt 21H (33)
Function 4AH (74)

2.0 and later

Resize Memory Block

Function 4AH adjusts the size of a previously allocated block of memory.

To Call

AH = 4AH
BX = new size of memory block, in paragraphs
ES = segment address of previously allocated memory block

Returns

If function is successful:

Carry flag is clear.

If function is not successful:

Carry flag is set.

AX = error code:
    07H   memory control blocks damaged
    08H   insufficient memory to allocate as requested
    09H   incorrect memory segment specified
BX = maximum number of paragraphs available (if an increase was requested)

Programmer's Notes

- Function 4AH can be used to change the size of a memory block previously allocated with Function 48H (Allocate Memory Block) or to modify the amount of memory originally allocated to a process by MS-DOS.
- If a process is denied an increase in the amount of memory it has been allocated, MS-DOS places the size of the largest contiguous block available in the BX register. The process can then notify the user of the problem and exit, or it can continue to operate in a reduced memory environment.
- Because the MS-DOS loader allocates all available memory to .COM programs, such a program should use Function 4AH immediately (with the segment address of its program segment prefix, or PSP) to release any memory that is not needed. This is mandatory if the .COM program will either allocate memory dynamically or use Function 4BH (Load and Execute Program) to load a child process or overlay.

  In addition, if Function 4AH is used to adjust the amount of memory allocated to a .COM program, the stack pointer must be adjusted so that it is within the limits of the program's revised memory allocation.

- If this function is used to shrink an allocated block, any memory above the new limit is not owned by the process and should never be used. If this function is used to expand an allocated block, the contents of memory above the old boundary are unpredictable and the memory should be initialized before use.
- Although it is not possible to predict how much memory-resident software and how many installable device drivers will be used on a computer system, Function 4AH can reliably determine the amount of memory available to an application.
- Function 59H (Get Extended Error Information) provides further information on any error — in particular, the code, class, recommended corrective action, and locus of the error.

Related Functions

48H (Allocate Memory Block)
49H (Free Memory Block)
58H (Get/Set Allocation Strategy)

Example

```
;*************************************************************;
;                                                             ;
;         Function 4AH: Resize Memory Block                   ;
;                                                             ;
;         int modify_block(nparas,blockseg,pmaxparas)         ;
;              int nparas,blockseg,*pmaxparas;                ;
;                                                             ;
;         Returns 0 if modification was a success,            ;
;         otherwise returns error code with pmaxparas         ;
;         set to max number of paragraphs available.          ;
;                                                             ;
;*************************************************************;

cProc   modify_block,PUBLIC,ds
parmW   nparas
parmW   blockseg
parmDP  pmaxparas
cBegin
        mov     es,blockseg         ; Get block address.
        mov     bx,nparas           ; Get nparas.
        mov     ah,4ah              ; Set function code.
        int     21h                 ; Ask MS-DOS to change block size.
        mov     cx,bx               ; Save BX.
        loadDP  ds,bx,pmaxparas
        mov     [bx],cx             ; Set pmaxparas, assuming failure.
        jb      mb_exit             ; Branch if size change error.
        xor     ax,ax               ; Return 0 if successful.
mb_exit:
cEnd
```

Interrupt 21H (33)
Function 4BH (75)

Load and Execute Program (EXEC)

Function 4BH, often called EXEC, loads a program file into memory and, optionally, executes the program. This function can also be used to load a program overlay.

To Call

AH	= 4BH	
AL	= 00H	load and execute program
	03H	load overlay
DS:DX	= segment:offset of ASCIIZ pathname for an executable program file	
ES:BX	= segment:offset of parameter block	

Returns

If function is successful:

Carry flag is clear.

With MS-DOS versions 2.x, all registers except CS and IP can be destroyed; with MS-DOS versions 3.x, registers are preserved.

If function is not successful:

Carry flag is set.

AX	= error code:	
	01H	invalid function (AL did not contain 00H or 03H)
	02H	file not found
	03H	path not found
	05H	access denied
	08H	insufficient memory
	0AH	bad environment
	0BH	bad format (AL = 00H only)

Programmer's Notes

- The pathname must be a null-terminated ASCII string (ASCIIZ).
- The handles for any files opened by the parent process before the call to Function 4BH are inherited by the child process, unless the parent specified otherwise in calling Function 3DH (Open File with Handle).

  All standard devices also remain open and available to the child process. Thus, the parent process can control the files used by the child process and control redirection for the child process.

● If AL = 00H, the parameter block is 14 bytes long and formatted in four parts, as follows:

Offset	Length	Meaning
00H	Word	Segment address of environment to be passed; 00H indicates child program inherits environment of the current process.
02H	Dword	Segment:offset address of command tail for the new program segment prefix (PSP). Command tail must be 128 bytes or fewer and formatted as a count byte followed by an ASCII string and terminated by a carriage return, as follows:


```
db      7,'a:mydoc',0Dh
```

> The carriage return is not included in the count; the command tail is placed at offset 80H in the new process's PSP.

Offset	Length	Meaning
06H	Dword	Segment:offset address of an FCB to be copied to the default FCB position at offset 5CH in the new process's PSP.
0AH	Dword	Segment:offset address of an FCB to be copied to the default FCB position at offset 6CH in the new process's PSP.

If AL = 03H, the parameter block is 4 bytes long and formatted in two parts, as follows:

Offset	Length	Meaning
00H	Word	Segment address where the overlay is to be loaded.
02H	Word	Relocation factor to be applied to the code image (.EXE files only); not needed if the file is a .COM program or is data.

● The first 2 bytes of the parameter block for Function 4BH Subfunction 00H contain either the segment address for an environment block to be passed to the new process or zero. If the value is zero, the child process inherits an exact copy of the parent process's environment.

The environment block must be aligned on a paragraph boundary (a multiple of 16 bytes). It can be as large as 32 KB, and it consists of a block of ASCIIZ strings, each in the following form:

parameter=value

For example:

```
db      'VERIFY=ON',0
```

The final string in the environment block is followed by a second zero byte. With MS-DOS versions 3.0 and later, the second zero is followed by a word containing a count and an ASCIIZ string containing the drive and pathname of the program file.

The environment passed to the child process allows the parent process to send it messages regarding the system state or control parameters. The pathname included with MS-DOS versions 3.0 and later enables the child process to determine where it was loaded from.

- If AL = 00H, MS-DOS creates a PSP for the new process and sets the terminate and Control-C addresses to the instruction in the parent process that follows the call to Function 4BH. If AL = 03H, no PSP is created.

- Before AL = 00H is used to load and execute a process, the system must contain enough free memory to accommodate the new process. Function 4AH (Resize Memory Block) should be used, if necessary, to reduce the amount of memory allocated to the parent process. If the parent is a .COM program, allocated memory *must* be reduced, because a .COM program is given ownership of all available memory when it is executed.

  If Function 4BH is called with AL = 03H, free memory is not a factor, because MS-DOS assumes the new process is being loaded into the calling process's own address space.

- If Function 4BH is called with AL = 00H, the child process remains in control until it executes an exit request, such as Function 4CH (Terminate Process with Return Code), or until Control-C or Control-Break is received or a critical error occurs and the user responds *Abort* to the *Abort, Retry, Ignore?* message.

- With MS-DOS versions 2.x, SS and SP must be saved in the current code segment before Function 4BH is invoked with AL = 00H. When the parent process regains control, all registers other than CS:IP and the stack will most likely have been changed by loading and executing the child process.

- Function 4BH with AL = 03H is useful for loading program overlays or for loading data to be used by the parent process (if that data requires relocation).

- If the child process that is executed attempts to remain resident through either Interrupt 27H or Interrupt 21H Function 31H (Terminate and Stay Resident), system memory becomes permanently fragmented and subsequent processes can fail because of lack of memory.

- The EXEC function (with AL = 00H) is commonly used to load a new copy of COMMAND.COM and then execute an MS-DOS command from within another program.

- Function 59H (Get Extended Error Information) provides further information on any error — in particular, the code, class, recommended corrective action, and locus of the error.

Related Functions

31H (Terminate and Stay Resident)
4CH (Terminate Process with Return Code)
4DH (Get Return Code of Child Process)

Examples

```
;***************************************************;
;                                                   ;
;           Function 4BH: Load and Execute Program  ;
;                                                   ;
;           int execute(pprogname,pcmdtail)         ;
;               char *pprogname,*pcmdtail;          ;
;                                                   ;
;           Returns 0 if program loaded, ran, and   ;
;           terminated successfully, otherwise returns ;
;           error code.                             ;
;                                                   ;
;***************************************************;

sBegin  data
$cmdlen =       126
$cmd    db      $cmdlen+2 dup (?) ; Make space for command line, plus
                                 ; 2 extra bytes for length and
                                 ; carriage return.

$fcb    db      0                ; Make dummy FCB.
        db      'dummy   fcb'
        db      0,0,0,0

                                 ; Here's the EXEC parameter block:
$epb    dw      0                ; 0 means inherit environment.
        dw      dataOFFSET $cmd ; Pointer to cmd line.
        dw      seg dgroup
        dw      dataOFFSET $fcb ; Pointer to FCB #1.
        dw      seg dgroup
        dw      dataOFFSET $fcb ; Pointer to FCB #2.
        dw      seg dgroup
sEnd    data
sBegin  code

$sp     dw      ?                ; Allocate space in code seg
$ss     dw      ?                ; for saving SS and SP.

Assumes ES,dgroup

cProc   execute,PUBLIC,<ds,si,di>
parmDP  pprogname
parmDP  pcmdtail
cBegin
        mov     cx,$cmdlen      ; Allow command line this long.
        loadDP  ds,si,pcmdtail  ; DS:SI = pointer to cmdtail string.
```

(more)

```
              mov      ax,seg dgroup:$cmd     ; Set ES = data segment.
              mov      es,ax
              mov      di,dataOFFSET $cmd+1   ; ES:DI = pointer to 2nd byte of
                                              ; our command-line buffer.
copycmd:
              lodsb                           ; Get next character.
              or       al,al                  ; Found end of command tail?
              jz       endcopy                ; Exit loop if so.
              stosb                           ; Copy to command buffer.
              loop     copycmd
endcopy:
              mov      al,13
              stosb                           ; Store carriage return at
                                              ; end of command.
              neg      cl
              add      cl,$cmdlen             ; CL = length of command tail.
              mov      es:$cmd,cl             ; Store length in command-tail buffer.

              loadDP   ds,dx,pprogname ; DS:DX = pointer to program name.
              mov      bx,dataOFFSET $epb ; ES:BX = pointer to parameter
                                           ; block.

              mov      cs:$ss,ss             ; Save current stack SS:SP (because
              mov      cs:$sp,sp             ; EXEC function destroys stack).
              mov      ax,4b00h              ; Set function code.
              int      21h                   ; Ask MS-DOS to load and execute
                                              ; program.
              cli                            ; Disable interrupts.
              mov      ss,cs:$ss             ; Restore stack.
              mov      sp,cs:$sp
              sti                            ; Enable interrupts.
              jb       ex_err                ; Branch on error.
              xor      ax,ax                 ; Return 0 if no error.
ex_err:
cEnd
sEnd    code


        ;*************************************************************;
        ;                                                           ;
        ;    Function 4BH: Load an Overlay Program                  ;
        ;                                                           ;
        ;    int load_overlay(pfilename,loadseg)                    ;
        ;        char *pfilename;                                   ;
        ;        int  loadseg;                                      ;
        ;                                                           ;
        ;    Returns 0 if program has been loaded OK,               ;
        ;    otherwise returns error code.                          ;
        ;                                                           ;
        ;    To call an overlay function after it has been          ;
        ;    loaded by load_overlay(), you can use                  ;
        ;    a far indirect call:                                   ;
```

(more)

```
;                                                              ;
;   1. FTYPE (far *ovlptr)();                                  ;
;   2. *((unsigned *)&ovlptr + 1) = loadseg;                   ;
;   3. *((unsigned *)&ovlptr) = offset;                        ;
;   4. (*ovlptr)(arg1,arg2,arg3,...);                          ;
;                                                              ;
;   Line 1 declares a far pointer to a                         ;
;   function with return type FTYPE.                           ;
;                                                              ;
;   Line 2 stores loadseg into the segment                     ;
;   portion (high word) of the far pointer.                    ;
;                                                              ;
;   Line 3 stores offset into the offset                       ;
;   portion (low word) of the far pointer.                     ;
;                                                              ;
;   Line 4 does a far call to offset                           ;
;   bytes into the segment loadseg                             ;
;   passing the arguments listed.                              ;
;                                                              ;
;   To return correctly, the overlay  must end with a far      ;
;   return instruction.  If the overlay is                     ;
;   written in Microsoft C, this can be done by                ;
;   declaring the overlay function with the                    ;
;   keyword "far".                                             ;
;                                                              ;
;**************************************************************;

sBegin  data
                                ; The overlay parameter block:
$lob    dw      ?               ; space for load segment;
        dw      ?               ; space for fixup segment.
sEnd    data


sBegin  code

cProc   load_overlay,PUBLIC,<ds,si,di>
parmDP  pfilename
parmW   loadseg
cBegin
        loadDP  ds,dx,pfilename ; DS:DX = pointer to program name.
        mov     ax,seg dgroup:$lob ; Set ES = data segment.
        mov     es,ax
        mov     bx,dataOFFSET $lob ; ES:BX = pointer to parameter
                                ; block.
        mov     ax,loadseg      ; Get load segment parameter.
        mov     es:[bx],ax      ; Set both the load and fixup
        mov     es:[bx+2],ax    ; segments to that segment.

        mov     cs:$ss,ss       ; Save current stack SS:SP (because
        mov     cs:$sp,sp       ; EXEC function destroys stack).
        mov     ax,4b03h        ; Set function code.
        int     21h             ; Ask MS-DOS to load the overlay.
        cli                     ; Disable interrupts.
```

(more)

```
        mov     ss,cs:$ss       ; Restore stack.
        mov     sp,cs:$sp
        sti                     ; Enable interrupts.
        jb      lo_err          ; Branch on error.
        xor     ax,ax           ; Return 0 if no error.
lo_err:
cEnd
sEnd    code
```

Interrupt 21H (33)
Function 4CH (76)

2.0 and later

Terminate Process with Return Code

Function 4CH terminates the current process with a return code and returns control to the calling (parent) process.

To Call

AH = 4CH
AL = return code

Returns

Nothing

Programmer's Notes

- When a process is terminated with Function 4CH, MS-DOS restores the termination-handler (Interrupt 22H), Control-C handler (Interrupt 23H), and critical error handler (Interrupt 24H) addresses from the program segment prefix, or PSP (offsets 0AH, 0EH, and 12H). MS-DOS also flushes the file buffers to disk, updates the disk directory, closes all files with open handles belonging to the terminated process, and then transfers control to the termination-handler address.
- On termination with Function 4CH, all memory owned by the process is freed.
- Function 4CH is the recommended method for terminating all processes — particularly sizable .EXE files — that do not stay resident. This function should be used in preference to the other termination methods (Interrupt 20H, Interrupt 21H Function 00H, near RET for .COM files, or a jump to PSP:0000H). Memory-resident programs should be terminated with Function 31H (Terminate and Stay Resident).
- A return code of 00H is customarily used to indicate that the process executed successfully; a nonzero return code is used to indicate that the process terminated because of an error or lack of resources — for example, the file could not be opened, the process could not be allocated sufficient memory, and so on.
- If the terminated process was invoked by a command line or batch file, control returns to COMMAND.COM and the transient portion of the command interpreter is reloaded, if necessary. If a batch file was in progress, execution continues with the next line of the file and the return code can be tested with an IF ERRORLEVEL statement. Otherwise, the command prompt is issued.

  If the terminated process was loaded by a process other than COMMAND.COM, the parent process can retrieve the child's return code with Function 4DH (Get Return Code of Child Process).
- In a networking environment running under MS-DOS version 3.1 or later, all file locks should be removed by the process before it calls Function 4CH to terminate.

Related Functions

00H (Terminate Process)
31H (Terminate and Stay Resident)
4DH (Get Return Code of Child Process)

Example

```
;**************************************************************;
;                                                            ;
;         Function 4CH: Terminate Process with Return Code   ;
;                                                            ;
;         int terminate(returncode)                          ;
;              int returncode;                               ;
;                                                            ;
;         Does NOT return at all!                            ;
;                                                            ;
;**************************************************************;

cProc   terminate,PUBLIC
parmB   returncode
cBegin
        mov     al,returncode   ; Set return code.
        mov     ah,4ch          ; Set function code.
        int     21h             ; Call MS-DOS to terminate process.
cEnd
```

Interrupt 21H (33)
Function 4DH (77)

2.0 and later

Get Return Code of Child Process

Function 4DH retrieves the return code of a child process that was invoked with Function 4BH (Load and Execute Program) and terminated with either Function 31H (Terminate and Stay Resident) or Function 4CH (Terminate Process with Return Code).

To Call

AH = 4DH

Returns

AH = termination method:

00H	normal termination (Interrupt 20H, or Interrupt 21H Function 00H or Function 4CH)
01H	terminated by entry of Control-C
02H	terminated by critical error handler (for example, user responded *Abort* to *Abort, Retry, Ignore?* prompt)
03H	terminated and stayed resident (Interrupt 27H or Interrupt 21H Function 31H)

AL = return code passed by child process

If terminated with Interrupt 20H, Interrupt 21H Function 00H, or Interrupt 27H:

AL = 00H

Programmer's Notes

- Function 4DH can be used only once to retrieve the return code of a terminated process. Subsequent calls do not yield meaningful results.
- Function 4DH does not set the carry flag to indicate an error. If no previous child process exists, the information returned in AH and AL is undefined.

Related Functions

31H (Terminate and Stay Resident)
4CH (Terminate Process with Return Code)

Example

```
;*************************************************************;
;                                                             ;
;            Function 4DH: Get Return Code of Child Process   ;
;                                                             ;
;                int child_ret_code()                         ;
;                                                             ;
;            Returns the return code of the last              ;
;            child process.                                   ;
;                                                             ;
;*************************************************************;

cProc   child_ret_code,PUBLIC
cBegin
        mov     ah,4dh          ; Set function code.
        int     21h             ; Ask MS-DOS to return code.
        cbw                     ; Convert AL to a word.
cEnd
```

Interrupt 21H (33)
Function 4EH (78)

Find First File

Function 4EH searches the specified directory for the first matching entry.

To Call

AH	= 4EH
CX	= attribute word
DS:DX	= segment:offset of ASCIIZ pathname

Returns

If function is successful:

Carry flag is clear.

Current disk transfer area (DTA) contains the following information about the file:

Offset	Length (bytes)	Value
00H	21	Reserved for use by MS-DOS in subsequent call to Function 4FH (Find Next File)
15H	1	File attribute
16H	2	Time of last write
18H	2	Date of last write
1AH	2	Low word of file size
1CH	2	High word of file size
1EH	13	Filename and extension in ASCIIZ form with blanks removed and period inserted between filename and extension

If function is not successful:

Carry flag is set.

AX	= error code:	
	02H	file not found
	03H	path not found
	12H	no more files; no match found

Programmer's Notes

- The pathname must be a null-terminated ASCII string (ASCIIZ).

- The filename and extension portions of the pathname can contain the MS-DOS wild-cards ? (match any character) and * (match all remaining characters).
- The DTA should be set with Function 1AH (Set DTA Address) before Function 4EH is called. If no DTA address is set, MS-DOS uses a default 128-byte buffer at offset 80H in the program segment prefix (PSP).
- The attribute word in CX controls the search as follows:
  - If the attribute word is 00H, only normal files are included in the search.
  - If the attribute word has any combination of bits 1, 2, and 4 (hidden, system, and subdirectory bits) set, the search includes normal files as well as files with any of the attributes specified.
  - If the attribute word has bit 3 set (volume-label bit), only a matching volume label is returned.
  - Bits 0 and 5 (read-only and archive bits) are ignored by Function 4EH.
- If Function 4FH (Find Next File) is used in conjunction with Function 4EH, the DTA must be preserved, because the first 21 bytes contain information needed by Function 4FH.
- The time at which the file was last written is returned as a binary value in a word formatted as follows:

Bits	Meaning
0–4	Number of seconds divided by 2
5–10	Minutes (0 through 59)
11–15	Hours, based on a 24-hour clock (0 through 23).

- The date on which the file was last written is returned as a binary value in a word formatted as follows:

Bits	Meaning
0–4	Day of the month
5–8	Month (1 = January, 2 = February, 3 = March, and so on)
9–15	Number of the year minus 1980

- Function 4EH is preferred to Function 11H (Find First File) because it fully supports pathnames.
- Function 59H (Get Extended Error Information) provides further information on any error — in particular, the code, class, recommended corrective action, and locus of the error.

Related Functions

11H (Find First File)
12H (Find Next File)
1AH (Set DTA Address)
4FH (Find Next File)

Example

```
;************************************************************;
;                                                            ;
;                Function 4EH: Find First File               ;
;                                                            ;
;                int find_first(ppathname,attr)              ;
;                     char *ppathname;                       ;
;                      int  attr;                            ;
;                                                            ;
;                Returns 0 if a match was found,             ;
;                otherwise returns error code.               ;
;                                                            ;
;************************************************************;

cProc   find_first,PUBLIC,ds
parmDP  ppathname
parmW   attr
cBegin
        loadDP  ds,dx,ppathname ; Get pointer to pathname.
        mov     cx,attr         ; Get search attributes.
        mov     ah,4eh          ; Set function code.
        int     21h             ; Ask MS-DOS to look for a match.
        jb      ff_err          ; Branch on error.
        xor     ax,ax           ; Return 0 if no error.
ff_err:
cEnd
```

Interrupt 21H (33)
Function 4FH (79)

2.0 and later

Find Next File

Function 4FH continues a search initiated by a previously successful call to Function 4EH (Find First File). The search is based on the pathname and attributes specified in the call to Function 4EH and uses information left in the current disk transfer area (DTA) by the call to Function 4EH or by a preceding call to Function 4FH.

To Call

AH = 4FH

DTA contains information from prior search with Function 4EH or Function 4FH.

Returns

If function is successful:

Carry flag is clear.

DTA is filled in as for a call to Function 4EH:

Offset	Length (bytes)	Value
00H	21	Reserved for use by MS-DOS in subsequent call to Function 4FH
15H	1	File attribute
16H	2	Time of last write
18H	2	Date of last write
1AH	2	Low word of file size
1CH	2	High word of file size
1EH	13	Filename and extension in ASCIIZ form with blanks removed and period inserted between filename and extension

If function is not successful:

Carry flag is set.

AX = error code:
12H   no more files, no match found, or no previous call to Function 4EH

Programmer's Notes

- If multiple calls to Function 4FH are used to find more than one matching file, the DTA setting (Function 1AH) and contents must be preserved because they provide information needed for continuing the search.
- The time at which the file was last written is returned as a binary value in a word formatted as follows:

Bits	Meaning
0–4	Number of seconds divided by 2
5–10	Minutes (0 through 59)
11–15	Hours, based on a 24-hour clock (0 through 23).

- The date on which the file was last written is returned as a binary value in a word formatted as follows:

Bits	Meaning
0–4	Day of the month
5–8	Month (1 = January, 2 = February, 3 = March, and so on)
9–15	Number of the year minus 1980

- Function 4FH is preferred to Function 12H (Find Next File) because it fully supports pathnames.
- Function 59H (Get Extended Error Information) provides further information on any error — in particular, the code, class, recommended corrective action, and locus of the error.

Related Functions

11H (Find First File)
12H (Find Next File)
1AH (Set DTA Address)
4EH (Find First File)

Example

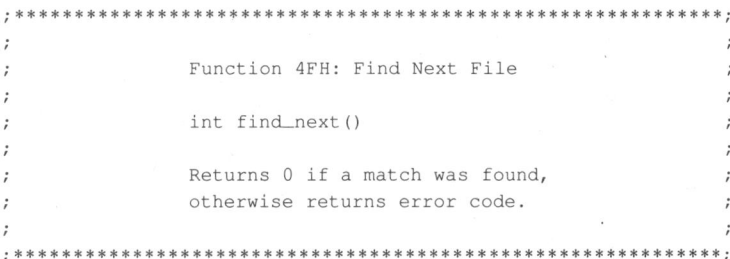

```
;*************************************************************;
;                                                             ;
;           Function 4FH: Find Next File                      ;
;                                                             ;
;           int find_next()                                   ;
;                                                             ;
;           Returns 0 if a match was found,                   ;
;           otherwise returns error code.                     ;
;                                                             ;
;*************************************************************;
```

(more)

```
cProc    find_next,PUBLIC
cBegin
         mov     ah,4fh          ; Set function code.
         int     21h             ; Ask MS-DOS to look for the next
                                 ; matching file.
         jb      fn_err          ; Branch on error.
         xor     ax,ax           ; Return 0 if no error.
fn_err:
cEnd
```

Interrupt 21H (33)
Function 54H (84)

2.0 and later

Get Verify Flag

Function 54H returns the current value of the MS-DOS verify flag.

To Call

AH = 54H

Returns

AL = verify flag:

00H   verify off; no read after write operation
01H   verify on; read after write operation

Programmer's Notes

- The default state of the verify flag is 00H (off).
- The state of the verify flag can be changed either through a call to Function 2EH (Set/Reset Verify Flag) or by the user with the VERIFY ON and VERIFY OFF commands.

Related Function

Function 2EH (Set/Reset Verify Flag)

Example

```
;************************************************************;
;                                                           ;
;              Function 54H: Get Verify Flag                ;
;                                                           ;
;                  int get_verify()                         ;
;                                                           ;
;              Returns current value of verify flag.        ;
;                                                           ;
;************************************************************;

cProc   get_verify,PUBLIC
cBegin
        mov     ah,54h          ; Set function code.
        int     21h             ; Read flag from MS-DOS.
        cbw                     ; Clear high byte of return value.

cEnd
```

Interrupt 21H (33)
Function 56H (86)

2.0 and later

Rename File

Function 56H renames a file and/or moves it to a new location in the hierarchical directory structure.

To Call

AH	= 56H
DS:DX	= segment:offset of existing ASCIIZ pathname for file
ES:DI	= segment:offset of new ASCIIZ pathname for file

Returns

If function is successful:

Carry flag is clear.

If function is not successful:

Carry flag is set.

AX	= error code:	
	02H	file not found
	03H	path not found
	05H	access denied
	11H	not the same device

Programmer's Notes

- The pathnames must be null-terminated ASCII strings (ASCIIZ).
- The directory paths specified in DS:DX and ES:DI need not be identical. Thus, specifying different directory paths effectively moves a file from one directory to another.
- Function 56H cannot be used to move a file to a different drive. Both the existing pathname and the new one must either contain the same drive identifier or default to the same drive.
- If Function 56H returns error code 05H, the cause can be any of the following:
  - The new pathname would move the file to the root directory, but the root directory is full.
  - A file with the new pathname already exists.
  - The user is on a network and has insufficient access to either the existing file or the new subdirectory.
- Unlike Function 17H (Rename File), Function 56H does not support the use of MS-DOS wildcard characters (? and *).

- Function 56H should not be used to rename open files. An open file should be closed with Function 10H (Close File with FCB) or 3EH (Close File) before Function 56H is called to rename it.
- Function 59H (Get Extended Error Information) provides further information on any error — in particular, the code, class, recommended corrective action, and locus of the error.

Related Function

17H (Rename File)

Example

```
;**************************************************************;
;                                                              ;
;                    Function 56H: Rename File                 ;
;                                                              ;
;                    int rename(poldpath,pnewpath)             ;
;                        char *poldpath,*pnewpath;             ;
;                                                              ;
;                    Returns 0 if file moved OK,               ;
;                    otherwise returns error code.             ;
;                                                              ;
;**************************************************************;

cProc   rename,PUBLIC,<ds,di>
parmDP  poldpath
parmDP  pnewpath
cBegin
        loadDP  es,di,pnewpath  ; ES:DI = pointer to newpath.
        loadDP  ds,dx,poldpath  ; DS:DX = pointer to oldpath.
        mov     ah,56h          ; Set function code.
        int     21h             ; Ask MS-DOS to rename file.
        jb      rn_err          ; Branch on error.
        xor     ax,ax           ; Return 0 if no error.
rn_err:
cEnd
```

Interrupt 21H (33)
Function 57H (87)

2.0 and later

Get/Set Date/Time of File

Function 57H retrieves or sets the date and time of a file's directory entry.

To Call

AH = 57H
AL = 00H   get date and time
     01H   set date and time
BX = handle number

If AL = 01H:

CX = time; binary value formatted as follows:

Bits	Meaning
0–4	Number of seconds divided by 2
5–10	Minutes (0 through 59)
11–15	Hours, based on a 24-hour clock (0 through 23)

DX = date; binary value formatted as follows:

Bits	Meaning
0–4	Day of the month (1 through 31)
5–8	Month (1 = January, 2 = February, 3 = March, and so on)
9–15	Year minus 1980

Returns

If function is successful:

Carry flag is clear.

If AL was 00H on call:

CX = time file was last modified; format as described above
DX = date file was last modified; format as described above

If function is not successful:

Carry flag is set.

AX = error code:
    01H   invalid function (AL not 00H or 01H)
    06H   invalid handle

Programmer's Notes

- Before the date and time in a file's directory entry can be retrieved or changed with Function 57H, a handle must be obtained by opening or creating the file using one of the following functions:
  - 3CH (Create File with Handle)
  - 3DH (Open File with Handle)
  - 5AH (Create Temporary File)
  - 5BH (Create New File)
- Use of Function 57H to retrieve the date and time of a file is preferable to examining the fields of an open FCB directly.
- Function 59H (Get Extended Error Information) provides further information on any error — in particular, the code, class, recommended corrective action, and locus of the error.

Related Functions

2AH (Get Date)
2BH (Set Date)
2CH (Get Time)
2DH (Set Time)

Example

```
;*************************************************************;
;                                                             ;
;        Function 57H: Get/Set Date/Time of File              ;
;                                                             ;
;        long file_date_time(handle,func,packdate,packtime)   ;
;             int handle,func,packdate,packtime;              ;
;                                                             ;
;        Returns a long -1 for all errors, otherwise packs    ;
;        date and time into a long integer,                   ;
;        date in high word, time in low word.                 ;
;                                                             ;
;*************************************************************;

cProc   file_date_time,PUBLIC
parmW   handle
parmB   func
parmW   packdate
parmW   packtime
cBegin
        mov     bx,handle       ; Get handle.
        mov     al,func         ; Get function: 0 = read, 1 = write.
        mov     dx,packdate     ; Get date (if present).
        mov     cx,packtime     ; Get time (if present).
        mov     ah,57h          ; Set function code.
        int     21h             ; Call MS-DOS.
```

(more)

```
        mov     ax,cx           ; Set DX:AX = date/time, assuming no
                                ; error.
        jnb     dt_ok           ; Branch if no error.
        mov     ax,-1           ; Return -1 for errors.
        cwd                     ; Extend the -1 into DX.
dt_ok:
cEnd
```

Interrupt 21H (33)
Function 58H (88)

3.0 and later

Get/Set Allocation Strategy

Function 58H retrieves or sets the method MS-DOS uses to allocate memory blocks for a process that issues a memory-allocation request.

To Call

AH = 58H
AL = 00H   get allocation strategy
       01H   set allocation strategy

If AL = 01H:

BX = allocation strategy:
     00H   use first (lowest available) block that fits
     01H   use block that fits best
     02H   use last (highest available) block that fits

Returns

If function is successful:

Carry flag is clear.

If AL was 00H on call:

AX = allocation-strategy code:
     00H   first fit
     01H   best fit
     02H   last fit

If function is not successful:

Carry flag is set.

AX = error code:
     01H   invalid function (AL not 00H or 01H)

Programmer's Notes

- Allocation strategies determine how MS-DOS finds and allocates a block of memory to an application that issues a memory-allocation request with either Function 48H (Allocate Memory Block) or Function 4AH (Resize Memory Block).

  The three strategies are carried out as follows:
  - First fit (the default): MS-DOS works upward from the lowest available block and allocates the first block it encounters that is large enough to satisfy the request for memory. This strategy is followed consistently, even if the block allocated is much larger than required.

- Best fit: MS-DOS searches all available memory blocks and then allocates the smallest block that satisfies the request, regardless of its location in the empty-block chain. This strategy maximizes the use of dynamically allocated memory at a slight cost in speed of allocation.
- Last fit (the reverse of first fit): MS-DOS works downward from the highest available block and allocates the first block it encounters that is large enough to satisfy the request for memory. This strategy is followed consistently, even if the block allocated is much larger than required.

● Function 59H (Get Extended Error Information) provides further information on any error — in particular, the code, class, recommended corrective action, and locus of the error.

Related Functions

48H (Allocate Memory Block)
4AH (Resize Memory Block)

Example

```
;**************************************************************;
;                                                              ;
;            Function 58H: Get/Set Allocation Strategy         ;
;                                                              ;
;            int alloc_strategy(func,strategy)                 ;
;                 int func,strategy;                           ;
;                                                              ;
;            Strategies:                                       ;
;                    0: First fit                              ;
;                    1: Best fit                               ;
;                    2: Last fit                               ;
;                                                              ;
;            Returns -1 for all errors, otherwise              ;
;            returns the current strategy.                     ;
;                                                              ;
;**************************************************************;

cProc    alloc_strategy,PUBLIC
parmB    func
parmW    strategy
cBegin
         mov     al,func           ; AL = get/set selector.
         mov     bx,strategy       ; BX = new strategy (for AL = 01H).
         mov     ah,58h            ; Set function code.
         int     21h               ; Call MS-DOS.
         jnb     no_err            ; Branch if no error.
         mov     ax,-1             ; Return -1 for all errors.
no_err:
cEnd
```

Interrupt 21H (33)
Function 59H (89)

3.0 and later

Get Extended Error Information

Function 59H returns extended error information, including a suggested response, for the function call immediately preceding it.

To Call

AH = 59H
BX = 00H

Returns

AX = extended error code:

00H	no error encountered
01H	invalid function number
02H	file not found
03H	path not found
04H	too many files open; no handles available
05H	access denied
06H	invalid handle
07H	memory control blocks destroyed
08H	insufficient memory
09H	invalid memory-block address
0AH	invalid environment
0BH	invalid format
0CH	invalid access code
0DH	invalid data
0EH	reserved
0FH	invalid disk drive
10H	attempt to remove current directory
11H	device not the same
12H	no more files
13H	write-protected disk
14H	unknown unit
15H	drive not ready
16H	invalid command
17H	data error based on cyclic redundancy check (CRC)
18H	length of request structure invalid
19H	seek error
1AH	non-MS-DOS disk
1BH	sector not found

1CH	printer out of paper
1DH	write fault
1EH	read fault
1FH	general failure
20H	sharing violation
21H	lock violation
22H	invalid disk change
23H	FCB unavailable
24H	sharing buffer exceeded
25–31H	reserved
32H	unsupported network request
33H	remote machine not listening
34H	duplicate name on network
35H	network name not found
36H	network busy
37H	device no longer exists on network
38H	net BIOS command limit exceeded
39H	error in network adapter hardware
3AH	incorrect response from network
3BH	unexpected network error
3CH	remote adapt incompatible
3DH	print queue full
3EH	queue not full
3FH	not enough room for print file
40H	network name deleted
41H	access denied
42H	incorrect network device type
43H	network name not found
44H	network name limit exceeded
45H	net BIOS session limit exceeded
46H	temporary pause
47H	network request not accepted
48H	print or disk redirection paused
49–4FH	reserved
50H	file already exists
51H	reserved
52H	cannot make directory
53H	failure on Interrupt 24H (critical error)
54H	out of structures
55H	already assigned
56H	invalid password
57H	invalid parameter
58H	net write fault

BH = error class:

01H	out of resource (such as storage)
02H	temporary situation, expected to end; not an error
03H	authorization problem
04H	internal error in system software
05H	hardware failure
06H	system-software failure, such as missing or incorrect configuration files; not the fault of the active process
07H	application-program error
08H	file or item not found
09H	file or item of invalid format or type or otherwise unsuitable
0AH	file or item interlocked
0BH	drive contains wrong disk, disk has bad spot, or other problem with storage medium
0CH	already exists
0DH	unknown

BL = suggested action:

01H	perform a reasonable number of retries before prompting user to choose Abort or Ignore in response to error message
02H	perform a reasonable number of retries, with pauses between, before prompting user to choose Abort or Ignore in response to error message
03H	prompt user to enter corrected information, such as drive letter or filename
04H	clean up and exit application
05H	exit immediately without cleanup
06H	ignore; informational error
07H	prompt user to remove cause of error (for example, change disks) and then retry

CH = location of error:

01H	unknown
02H	block device
03H	network
04H	serial device
05H	memory related

Programmer's Notes

- The extended error codes returned by Function 59H correspond to the error values returned in AX by functions in MS-DOS versions 2.0 and later that set the carry flag on error. Versions 2.x of MS-DOS, however, provide a smaller set of error codes (01H through 12H) than do later versions.

  Thus, although Function 59H itself is not available in versions of MS-DOS earlier than 3.0, the matching of error codes to earlier versions helps ensure downward compatibility. Function 59H was also designed to be open-ended so that additional error codes could be incorporated as needed. As a result, processes should remain flexible in their use of this function and should not rely on a fixed set of code numbers for error detection.

- Function 59H is useful in the following situations:
  - When MS-DOS encounters a hardware-related error condition and shifts control to an Interrupt 24H handler that has been created by the programmer
  - When a handle-related function sets the carry flag to indicate an error or when an FCB-related function indicates an error by returning 0FFH in the AL register
- If a function call results in an error, Function 59H returns meaningful information only if it is the next call to MS-DOS. An intervening call to another MS-DOS function, whether explicit or indirect, causes the error value for the unsuccessful function to be lost.
- Unlike most MS-DOS functions, Function 59H alters some registers that are not used to return results: CL, DX, SI, DI, ES, and DS. These registers must be preserved before a call to Function 59H if their contents are needed later.

Related Functions

None

Example

```
;***************************************************************;
;                                                             ;
;          Function 59H: Get Extended Error Information        ;
;                                                             ;
;          int extended_error(err,class,action,locus)         ;
;               int *err;                                      ;
;               char *class,*action,*locus;                    ;
;                                                             ;
;          Return value is same as err.                        ;
;                                                             ;
;***************************************************************;

cProc   extended_error,PUBLIC,<ds,si,di>
parmDP  perr
parmDP  pclass
parmDP  paction
parmDP  plocus
cBegin
        push    ds                ; Save DS.
        xor     bx,bx
        mov     ah,59h            ; Set function code.
        int     21h               ; Request error info from MS-DOS.
        pop     ds                ; Restore DS.
        loadDP  ds,si,perr        ; Get pointer to err.
        mov     [si],ax           ; Store err.
        loadDP  ds,si,pclass      ; Get pointer to class.
        mov     [si],bh           ; Store class.
        loadDP  ds,si,paction     ; Get pointer to action.
        mov     [si],bl           ; Store action.
        loadDP  ds,si,plocus      ; Get pointer to locus.
        mov     [si],ch           ; Store locus.
cEnd
```

Interrupt 21H (33) Function 5AH (90)

3.0 and later

Create Temporary File

Function 5AH uses the system clock to create a unique filename, appends the filename to the specified path, opens the temporary file, and returns a file handle that can be used for subsequent file operations.

To Call

AH   = 5AH
CX   = file attribute:

00H	normal file
01H	read-only file
02H	hidden file
04H	system file

DS:DX   = segment:offset of ASCIIZ path, ending with a backslash character (\) and followed by 13 bytes of memory (to receive the generated filename)

Returns

If function is successful:

Carry flag is clear.

AX   = handle
DS:DX   = segment:offset of full pathname for temporary file

If function is not successful:

Carry flag is set.

AX   = error code:

03H	path not found
04H	too many open files; no handle available
05H	access denied

Programmer's Notes

- Only the drive and path to use for the new file should be specified in the buffer pointed to by DS:DX. The function appends an eight-character filename that is generated from the system time.
- Function 5AH is valuable in such situations as print spooling on a network, where temporary files are created by many users.
- The input string representing the path for the temporary file must be a null-terminated ASCII string (ASCIIZ).
- In networking environments running under MS-DOS version 3.1 or later, MS-DOS opens the temporary file in compatibility mode.

- MS-DOS does not delete temporary files; applications must do this for themselves.
- Function 59H (Get Extended Error Information) provides further information on any error—in particular, the code, class, recommended corrective action, and locus of the error.

Related Functions

16H (Create File with FCB)
3CH (Create File with Handle)
5BH (Create New File)

Example

```
;***************************************************************;
;                                                               ;
;              Function 5AH: Create Temporary File              ;
;                                                               ;
;              int create_temp(ppathname,attr)                  ;
;                  char *ppathname;                             ;
;                  int attr;                                    ;
;                                                               ;
;              Returns -1 if file was not created,              ;
;              otherwise returns file handle.                   ;
;                                                               ;
;***************************************************************;

cProc    create_temp,PUBLIC,ds
parmDP   ppathname
parmW    attr
cBegin
         loadDP  ds,dx,ppathname ; Get pointer to pathname.
         mov     cx,attr         ; Set function code.
         mov     ah,5ah          ; Ask MS-DOS to make a new file with
                                 ; a unique name.
         int     21h             ; Ask MS-DOS to make a tmp file.
         jnb     ct_ok           ; Branch if MS-DOS returned handle.
         mov     ax,-1           ; Else return -1.
ct_ok:
cEnd
```

Interrupt 21H (33)
Function 5BH (91)

3.0 and later

Create New File

Function 5BH creates a new file with the specified pathname. This function operates like Function 3CH (Create File with Handle) but fails if the pathname references a file that already exists.

To Call

AH   = 5BH
CX   = file attribute:
        00H   normal file
        01H   read-only file
        02H   hidden file
        04H   system file
DS:DX   = segment:offset of ASCIIZ pathname

Returns

If function is successful:

Carry flag is clear.

AX   = handle

If function is not successful:

Carry flag is set.

AX   = error code:
        03H   path not found
        04H   too many open files; no handle available
        05H   access denied
        50H   file already exists

Programmer's Notes

- The pathname must be a null-terminated ASCII string (ASCIIZ).
- In networking environments running under MS-DOS version 3.1 or later, the file is opened in compatibility mode. Function 5BH fails, however, if the user does not have Create access to the directory that is to contain the file.
- Function 5BH can be used to implement semaphores in the form of files across a local area network or in a multitasking environment. If the function succeeds, the semaphore has been acquired. To release the semaphore, the application simply deletes the file.

- Function 59H (Get Extended Error Information) provides further information on any error — in particular, the code, class, recommended corrective action, and locus of the error.

Related Functions

16H (Create File with FCB)
3CH (Create File with Handle)
5AH (Create Temporary File)

Example

```
;************************************************************;
;                                                          ;
;              Function 5BH: Create New File               ;
;                                                          ;
;              int create_new(ppathname,attr)              ;
;                   char *ppathname;                       ;
;                    int attr;                             ;
;                                                          ;
;              Returns -2 if file already exists,          ;
;                      -1 for all other errors,            ;
;                      otherwise returns file handle.      ;
;                                                          ;
;************************************************************;

cProc   create_new,PUBLIC,ds
parmDP  ppathname
parmW   attr
cBegin
        loadDP  ds,dx,ppathname ; Get pointer to pathname.
        mov     cx,attr         ; Get new file's attribute.
        mov     ah,5bh          ; Set function code.
        int     21h             ; Ask MS-DOS to make a new file.
        jnb     cn_ok           ; Branch if MS-DOS returned handle.
        mov     bx,-2
        cmp     al,80           ; Did file already exist?
        jz      ae_err          ; Branch if so.
        inc     bx              ; Change -2 to -1.
ae_err:
        mov     ax,bx           ; Return error code.
cn_ok:
cEnd
```

Interrupt 21H (33)
Function 5CH (92)

3.0 and later

Lock/Unlock File Region

Function 5CH enables a process running in a networking or multitasking environment to lock or unlock a range of bytes in an open file.

To Call

AH = 5CH
AL = 00H lock region
   01H unlock region
BX = handle
CX:DX = 4-byte integer specifying beginning of region to be locked or unlocked
   (offset in bytes from beginning of file)
SI:DI = 4-byte integer specifying length of region (measured in bytes)

Returns

If function is successful:

Carry flag is clear.

If function is not successful:

Carry flag is set.

AX = error code:
  01H invalid function (AL not 00H or 01H or file sharing not loaded)
  06H invalid handle
  21H lock violation
  24H sharing buffer exceeded

Programmer's Notes

- A process that either closes a file containing a locked region or terminates with the file open leaves the file in an undefined state. Under either condition, MS-DOS might handle the file erratically. If the process can be terminated by Interrupt 23H (Control-C) or 24H (critical error), these interrupts should be trapped so that any locked regions in files can be unlocked before the process terminates.
- Locking a portion of a file with Function 5CH denies all other processes both read and write access to the specified region of the file. This restriction also applies when open file handles are passed to a child process with Function 4BH (Load and Execute Program). Duplicate file handles created with Function 45H (Duplicate File Handle) and 46H (Force Duplicate File Handle), however, are allowed access to locked regions of a file within the current process.
- Locking a region that goes beyond the end of a file does not cause an error.

- Function 5CH is useful primarily in ensuring that competing programs or processes do not interfere while a record is being updated. Locking at the file level is provided by the sharing parameter in Function 3DH (Open File with Handle).
- Function 5CH can also be used to check the lock status of a file. If an attempt to lock a needed portion of a file fails and error code 21H is returned in the AX register, the region is already locked by another process.
- Any region locked with a call to Function 5CH must also be unlocked, and the same 4-byte integer values must be used for each operation. Two adjacent regions of a file cannot be locked separately and then be unlocked with a single unlock call. If the region to unlock does not correspond exactly to a locked region, Function 5CH returns error code 21H.
- The length of time needed to hold locks can be minimized with the transaction-oriented programming model. This concept requires defining and performing an update in a uniform manner: Assert lock, read data, change data, remove lock.
- If file sharing is not loaded, an application receives a 01H (function number invalid) error status when it attempts to lock a file. An immediate call to Function 59H returns the error locus as an unknown or a serial device.
- Function 59H (Get Extended Error Information) provides further information on any error — in particular, the code, class, recommended corrective action, and locus of the error.

Related Functions

45H (Duplicate File Handle)
46H (Force Duplicate File Handle)
4BH (Load and Execute Program) [EXEC]

Example

```
;**************************************************************;
;                                                            ;
;            Function 5CH: Lock/Unlock File Region           ;
;                                                            ;
;            int  locks(handle,onoff,start,length)           ;
;                  int handle,onoff;                         ;
;                  long start,length;                        ;
;                                                            ;
;            Returns 0 if operation was successful,          ;
;            otherwise returns error code.                   ;
;                                                            ;
;**************************************************************;

cProc   locks,PUBLIC,<si,di>
parmW   handle
parmB   onoff
parmD   start
parmD   length
```

(more)

```
cBegin
        mov     al,onoff        ; Get lock/unlock flag.
        mov     bx,handle       ; Get file handle.
        les     dx,start        ; Get low word of start.
        mov     cx,es           ; Get high word of start.
        les     di,length       ; Get low word of length.
        mov     si,es           ; Get high word of length.
        mov     ah,5ch          ; Set function code.
        int     21h             ; Make lock/unlock request.
        jb      lk_err          ; Branch on error.
        xor     ax,ax           ; Return 0 if no error.
lk_err:
cEnd
```

Interrupt 21H (33)
Function 5EH (94) Subfunction 00H

Network Machine Name/Printer Setup: Get Machine Name

If Microsoft Networks is running, Function 5EH Subfunction 00H retrieves the network name of the local computer.

To Call

AH	= 5EH
AL	= 00H
DS:DX	= segment:offset of 16-byte buffer

Returns

If function is successful:

Carry flag is clear.

CH	= validity of machine name:
	00H invalid
	nonzero valid
CL	= NETBIOS number assigned to machine name
DS:DX	= segment:offset of ASCIIZ machine name

If function is not successful:

Carry flag is set.

AX	= error code:
	01H invalid function; Microsoft Networks not running

Programmer's Notes

- The NETBIOS number in CL and the name at DS:DX are valid only if the value returned in CH is nonzero.
- Function 59H (Get Extended Error Information) provides further information on any error — in particular, the code, class, recommended corrective action, and locus of the error.

Related Function

5FH (Get/Make Assign List Entry)

Example

None

Interrupt 21H (33)
Function 5FH (95) Subfunction 03H

3.1 and later

Get/Make Assign-List Entry: Make Assign-List Entry

Function 5FH Subfunction 03H redirects a local printer or disk drive to a network device and establishes an assign-list index number for the redirected device. Microsoft Networks must be running with file sharing loaded for this subfunction to operate successfully.

To Call

AH	= 5FH
AL	= 03H
BL	= device type:

03H	printer
04H	drive

CX	= user data
DS:SI	= segment:offset of 16-byte ASCIIZ local device name
ES:DI	= segment:offset of 128-byte ASCIIZ remote (network) device name and password in the form

machine name\pathname,null,password,null

For example:

```
string  db      '\\mymach\wp',0,'blibbet',0
```

Returns

If function is successful:

Carry flag is clear.

If function is not successful:

Carry flag is set.

AX	= error code:

01H	invalid function or Microsoft Networks not running
03H	path not found
05H	access denied
08H	insufficient memory
0FH	redirection paused on server
12H	no more files

Programmer's Notes

- The strings used by this subfunction must be null-terminated ASCII strings (ASCIIZ). The ASCIIZ string pointed to by ES:DI (the destination, or remote, device) cannot be more than 128 bytes including the password, which can be a maximum of 8 characters. If the password is omitted, the pathname must be followed by 2 null bytes.

- If BL = 03H, the string pointed to by DS:SI must be one of the following printer names: PRN, LPT1, LPT2, or LPT3. If the call is successful, output is redirected to a network print spooler, which must be named in the destination string. For printer redirection, MS-NET intercepts Interrupt 17H (BIOS Printer I/O). When redirection for a printer is canceled, all printing is sent to the first local printer (LPT1).

  If BL = 04H, the string pointed to by DS:SI can be a drive letter followed by a colon, such as E:, or it can be a null string. If the string represents a valid drive, a successful call redirects drive requests to the network directory named in the destination string. If DS:SI points to a null string, MS-DOS attempts to provide access to the network directory named in the destination string without redirecting any device.

- Only printer and disk devices are supported in MS-DOS versions 3.1 and later. COM1 and COM2 are not supported for network redirection, nor are the standard output or standard error devices supported.

- Function 59H (Get Extended Error Information) provides further information on any error — in particular, the code, class, recommended corrective action, and locus of the error.

Related Function

5EH Subfunction 00H (Get Machine Name)

Example

```
;**************************************************************;
;                                                            ;
;       Function 5FH Subfunction 03H:                        ;
;               Make Assign-List Entry                       ;
;       int add_alist_entry(psrcname,pdestname,uservalue,type) ;
;           char *psrcname,*pdestname;                       ;
;           int  uservalue,type;                             ;
;                                                            ;
;       Returns 0 if new assign-list entry is made, otherwise ;
;       returns error code.                                  ;
;                                                            ;
;**************************************************************;

cProc   add_alist_entry,PUBLIC,<ds,si,di>
parmDP  psrcname
parmDP  pdestname
parmW   uservalue
parmW   type
cBegin
        mov     bx,type         ; Get device type.
        mov     cx,uservalue    ; Get uservalue.
        loadDP  ds,si,psrcname  ; DS:SI = pointer to source name.
        loadDP  es,di,pdestname ; ES:DI = pointer to destination name.
        mov     ax,5f03h        ; Set function code.
        int     21h             ; Make assign-list entry.
        jb      aa_err          ; Exit if there was some error.
        xor     ax,ax           ; Else return 0.
aa_err:
cEnd
```

Int 21H (33)
Function 5FH (95) Subfunction 04H

3.1 and later

Get/Make Assign-List Entry: Cancel Assign-List Entry

Function 5FH Subfunction 04H cancels the redirection of a local device to a network device previously established with Function 5FH Subfunction 03H (Make Assign-List Entry). Microsoft Networks must be running with file sharing loaded for this subfunction to operate successfully.

To Call

AH   = 5FH
AL   = 04H
DS:SI = segment:offset of ASCIIZ device name or path

Returns

If function is successful:

Carry flag is clear.

If function is not successful:

Carry flag is set.

AX   = error code:

01H	invalid function or Microsoft Networks not running
03H	path not found
05H	access denied
08H	insufficient memory
0FH	redirection paused on server
12H	no more files

Programmer's Notes

- The string pointed to by DS:SI must be a null-terminated ASCII string (ASCIIZ). This string can be any one of the following:
  - The letter, followed by a colon, of a redirected local drive. This function restores the drive letter to its original, physical meaning.
  - The name of a redirected printer: PRN, LPT1, LPT2, LPT3, or its machine-specific equivalent. This function restores the printer name to its original, physical meaning at the local workstation.
  - A string, beginning with two backslashes (\\) followed by the name of a network directory. This function terminates the connection between the local workstation and the directory specified in the string.

- Function 59H (Get Extended Error Information) provides further information on any error — in particular, the code, class, recommended corrective action, and locus of the error.

Related Function

5EH Subfunction 00H (Get Machine Name)

Example

```
;************************************************************;
;                                                          ;
;       Function 5FH Subfunction 04H:                      ;
;                 Cancel Assign-List Entry                 ;
;                                                          ;
;       int cancel_alist_entry(psrcname)                   ;
;           char *psrcname;                                ;
;                                                          ;
;       Returns 0 if assignment is canceled, otherwise returns ;
;       error code.                                        ;
;                                                          ;
;************************************************************;

cProc   cancel_alist_entry,PUBLIC,<ds,si>
parmDP  psrcname
cBegin
        loadDP  ds,si,psrcname  ; DS:SI = pointer to source name.
        mov     ax,5f04h        ; Set function code.
        int     21h             ; Cancel assign-list entry.
        jb      ca_err          ; Exit on error.
        xor     ax,ax           ; Else return 0.
ca_err:
cEnd
```

Interrupt 21H (33)
Function 62H (98)

3.0 and later

Get Program Segment Prefix Address

Function 62H gets the segment address of the program segment prefix (PSP) for the current process.

To Call

AH = 62H

Returns

BX = segment address of PSP for current process

Programmer's Notes

- The PSP is constructed by MS-DOS at the base of the memory allocated for a .COM or .EXE program being loaded into memory by the EXEC function, 4BH (Load and Execute Program). The PSP is 100H bytes and contains information useful to an executing program, including
  - The command tail
  - Default file control blocks (FCBs)
  - A pointer to the program's environment block
  - Previous addresses for MS-DOS Control-C, critical error, and terminate handlers
- Function 59H (Get Extended Error Information) provides further information on any error — in particular, the code, class, recommended corrective action, and locus of the error.

Related Functions

None

Example

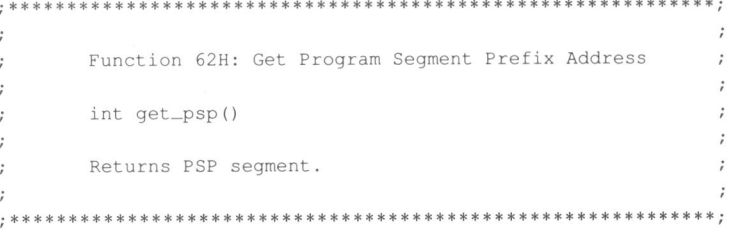

```
;***************************************************************;
;                                                             ;
;        Function 62H: Get Program Segment Prefix Address     ;
;                                                             ;
;        int get_psp()                                        ;
;                                                             ;
;        Returns PSP segment.                                 ;
;                                                             ;
;***************************************************************;
```

(more)

```
        cProc   get_psp,PUBLIC
        cBegin
                mov     ah,62h          ; Set function code.
                int     21h             ; Get PSP address.
                mov     ax,bx           ; Return it in AX.
        cEnd
```

Interrupt 21H (33)
Function 63H (99)

2.25

Get Lead Byte Table

Function 63H, available only in MS-DOS version 2.25, includes three subfunctions that support 2-byte-per-character alphabets such as Kanji and Hangeul (Japanese and Korean characters sets). Subfunction 00H obtains the address of the legal lead byte ranges for the character sets; Subfunctions 01H and 02H set or obtain the value of the interim console flag, which determines whether interim characters are returned by certain console system calls.

To Call

AH	= 63H	
AL	= 00H	get lead byte table address
	01H	set or clear interim console flag
	02H	get interim console flag

If AL = 01H:

DL	= interim console flag:	
	00H	clear
	01H	set

Returns

If function is successful:

Carry flag is clear.

If AL was 00H on call:

DS:SI   = segment:offset of lead byte table

If AL was 02H on call:

DL   = value of interim console flag

If function is not successful:

Carry flag is set.

AX	= error code:	
	01H	invalid function

Programmer's Notes

- Function 63H does not necessarily preserve any registers other than SS:SP, so register values should be saved before a call to this function. To avoid saving registers repeatedly, a process can either copy the table or save the pointer to the table for later use.

- The lead byte table contains pairs of bytes that represent the inclusive boundary values for the lead bytes of the specified alphabet. Because of the way bytes are ordered by the 8086 microprocessor family, the values must be read as byte values, not as word values.
- If the interim console flag is set (DL = 01H) by a program through a call to Function 63H, the following functions return interim character information on request:
  - 07H (Character Input Without Echo)
  - 08H (Unfiltered Character Input Without Echo)
  - 0BH (Check Keyboard Status)
  - 0CH (Flush Buffer, Read Keyboard), if Function 07H or 08H is requested in AL

Related Functions

None

Example

```
;***************************************************************;
;                                                             ;
;    Function 63H: Get Lead Byte Table                        ;
;                                                             ;
;    char far *get_lead_byte_table()                          ;
;                                                             ;
;    Returns far pointer to table of lead bytes for multibyte ;
;    characters.  Will work only in MS-DOS 2.25!              ;
;                                                             ;
;***************************************************************;

cProc   get_lead_byte_table,PUBLIC,<ds,si>
cBegin
        mov     ax,6300h        ; Set function code.
        int     21h             ; Get lead byte table.
        mov     dx,ds           ; Return far pointer in DX:AX.
        mov     ax,si
cEnd
```

Interrupt 22H (34)

Terminate Routine Address

The machine interrupt vector for Interrupt 22H (memory locations 0000:0088H through 0000:008BH) contains the address of the routine that receives control when the currently executing program terminates by means of Interrupt 20H, Interrupt 27H, or Interrupt 21H Function 00H, 31H, or 4CH.

To Call

This interrupt should never be issued directly.

Returns

Nothing

Programmer's Note

● The address in this vector is copied into offsets 0AH through 0DH of the program segment prefix (PSP) when a program is loaded but before it begins executing. The address is restored from the PSP (in case it was modified by the application) as part of MS-DOS's termination handling.

Example

None

Interrupt 23H (35)

Control-C Handler Address

The machine interrupt vector for Interrupt 23H (memory locations 0000:008CH through 0000:008FH) contains the address of the routine that receives control when a Control-C (also Control-Break on IBM PC compatibles) is detected during any character I/O function and, if the Break flag is on, during most other MS-DOS function calls.

To Call

This interrupt should never be issued directly.

Returns

Nothing

Programmer's Notes

- The address in this vector is copied into offsets 0EH through 11H of the program segment prefix (PSP) when a program is loaded but before it begins executing. The address is restored from the PSP (in case it was modified by the application) as part of MS-DOS's termination handling.
- The initialization code for an application can use Interrupt 21H Function 25H (Set Interrupt Vector) to reset the Interrupt 23H vector to point to its own routine for Control-C handling. By installing its own Control-C handler, the program can avoid being terminated as a result of keyboard entry of a Control-C or Control-Break.
- When a Control-C is detected and the program's Interrupt 23H handler receives control, MS-DOS sets all registers to the original values they had when the function call that is being interrupted was made. The program's interrupt handler can then do any of the following:
  - Set a local flag for later inspection by the application (or take any other appropriate action) and then perform a return from interrupt (IRET) to return control to MS-DOS. (All registers must be preserved.) The MS-DOS function in progress is then restarted and proceeds to completion, and control finally returns to the application in the normal manner.
  - Take appropriate action and then perform a far return (RET FAR) to give control back to MS-DOS. MS-DOS uses the state of the carry flag to determine what action to take: If the carry flag is set, the application is terminated; if the carry flag is clear, the application continues in the normal manner.
  - Retain control by transferring to an error-handling routine within the application and then resume execution or take other appropriate action, never performing a RET FAR or IRET to end the interrupt-handling sequence. This option causes no harm to the system.
- Any MS-DOS function call can be used within the body of an Interrupt 23H handler.

Example

None

Interrupt 24H (36)

Critical Error Handler Address

The machine interrupt vector for Interrupt 24H (memory locations 0000:0090H through 0000:0093H) contains the address of the routine that receives control when a critical error (usually a hardware error) is detected.

To Call

This interrupt should never be issued directly.

Returns

Nothing

Programmer's Notes

- The address of this vector is copied into offsets 12H through 15H of the program segment prefix (PSP) when a program is loaded but before it begins executing. The address is restored from the PSP (in case it was modified by the application) as part of MS-DOS's termination handling.
- On entry to the critical error interrupt handler, bit 7 of register AH is clear (0) if the error was a disk I/O error; otherwise, it is set (1). BP:SI contains the address of a device-header control block from which additional information can be obtained. Interrupts are disabled. MS-DOS sets up the registers for a retry operation and one of the following error codes is in the lower byte of the DI register (the upper byte is undefined):

Code	Meaning
00H	Write-protect error
01H	Unknown unit
02H	Drive not ready
03H	Unknown command
04H	Data error (bad CRC)
05H	Bad request structure length
06H	Seek error
07H	Unknown media type
08H	Sector not found
09H	Printer out of paper
0AH	Write fault
0BH	Read fault
0CH	General failure
0FH	Invalid disk change

These are the same error codes returned by the device drivers in the request header.

- On a disk error, MS-DOS retries the operation three times before transferring to the Interrupt 24H handler.
- On entry to the Interrupt 24H handler, the stack is set up as follows:

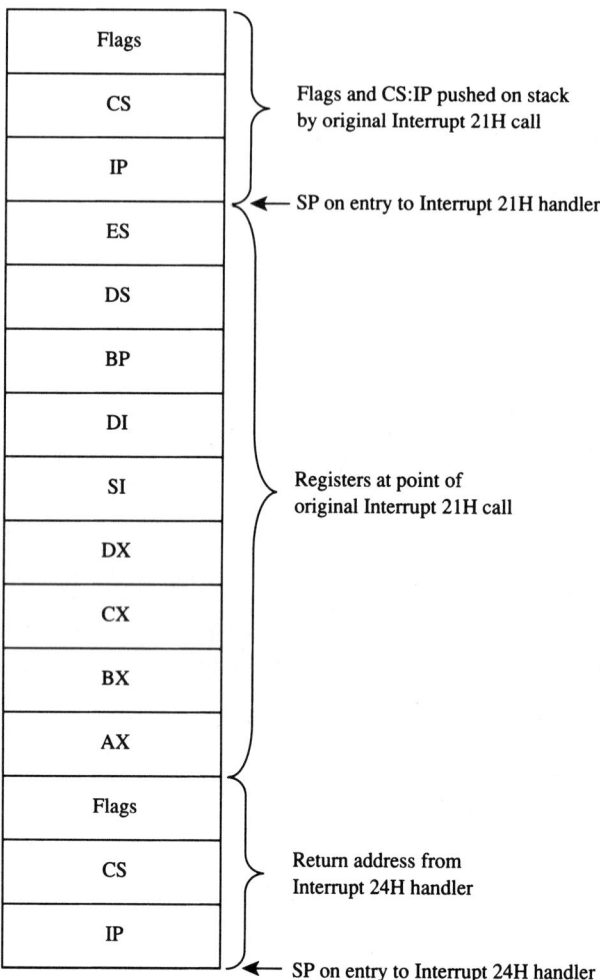

- Interrupt 24H handlers must preserve the SS, SP, DS, ES, BX, CX, and DX registers. Only Interrupt 21H Functions 01H through 0CH, 30H, and 59H can be used by an Interrupt 24H handler; other calls will destroy the MS-DOS stack and its ability to re-try or ignore an error.

- Before issuing a RETURN FROM INTERRUPT (IRET), the Interrupt 24H handler should place an action code in AL that will be interpreted by MS-DOS as follows:

Code	Meaning
00H	Ignore error.
01H	Retry operation.
02H	Terminate program through Interrupt 23H.
03H	Fail system call in progress (versions 3.1 and later).

- If an Interrupt 24H routine returns to the user program rather than to MS-DOS, it must restore the user program's registers, removing all but the last three words from the stack, and issue an IRET. Control returns to the instruction immediately following the Interrupt 21H function call that resulted in an error. This leaves MS-DOS in an unstable state until a call is made to an Interrupt 21H function higher than 0CH.

Example

None

Interrupt 25H (37)

1.0 and later

Absolute Disk Read

Interrupt 25H provides direct linkage to the MS-DOS BIOS module to read data from a logical disk sector into a specified memory location.

To Call

AL	= drive number (0 = drive A, 1 = drive B, and so on)
CX	= number of sectors to read
DX	= starting relative (logical) sector number
DS:BX	= segment:offset of disk transfer area (DTA)

Returns

If operation is successful:

Carry flag is clear.

If operation is not successful:

Carry flag is set.

AX   = error code

Programmer's Notes

- Interrupt 25H might destroy all registers except the segment registers.
- When Interrupt 25H returns, the CPU flags originally pushed onto the stack by the INT 25H instruction are still on the stack. The stack must be cleared by a POPF or ADD SP,2 instruction to prevent uncontrolled stack growth and to make accessible any other values that were pushed onto the stack before the call to Interrupt 25H.
- Logical sector numbers are zero based and are obtained by numbering each disk sector sequentially from track 0, head 0, sector 1 and continuing until the last sector on the disk is counted. The head number is incremented before the track number. Because of interleaving, logically adjacent sectors might not be physically adjacent for some types of disks.
- The lower byte of the error code (AL) is the same error code that is returned in the lower byte of DI when an Interrupt 24H is issued. The upper byte (AH) contains one of the following codes:

Code	Meaning
80H	Device failed to respond
40H	Seek operation failure
20H	Controller failure

(more)

Code	Meaning
10H	Data error (bad CRC)
08H	Direct memory access (DMA) failure
04H	Requested sector not found
03H	Write-protect fault
02H	Bad address mark
01H	Bad command

● **Warning:** Interrupt 25H bypasses the MS-DOS file system. This function must be used with caution to avoid damaging the disk structure.

Example

```
;****************************************************************;
;                                                              ;
;       Interrupt 25H: Absolute Disk Read                      ;
;                                                              ;
;       Read logical sector 1 of drive A into the memory area  ;
;       named buff. (On most MS-DOS floppy disks, this sector  ;
;       contains the beginning of the file allocation table.)  ;
;                                                              ;
;****************************************************************;

        mov     al,0            ; Drive A.
        mov     cx,1            ; Number of sectors.
        mov     dx,1            ; Beginning sector number.
        mov     bx,seg buff     ; Address of buffer.
        mov     ds,bx
        mov     bx,offset buff
        int     25h             ; Request disk read.
        jc      error           ; Jump if read failed.
        add     sp, 2           ; Clear stack.
        .
        .
        .
error:                          ; Error routine goes here.
        .
        .
        .
buff    db      512 dup (?)
```

Interrupt 26H (38)

1.0 and later

Absolute Disk Write

Interrupt 26H provides direct linkage to the MS-DOS BIOS module to write data from a specified memory buffer to a logical disk sector.

To Call

AL	= drive number (0 = drive A, 1 = drive B, and so on)
CX	= number of sectors to write
DX	= starting relative (logical) sector number
DS:BX	= segment:offset of disk transfer area (DTA)

Returns

If operation is successful:

Carry flag is clear.

If operation is not successful:

Carry flag is set.

AX   = error code

Programmer's Notes

- When Interrupt 26H returns, the CPU flags originally pushed onto the stack by the INT 26H instruction are still on the stack. The stack must be cleared by a POPF or ADD SP,2 instruction to prevent uncontrolled stack growth and to make accessible any other values that were pushed on the stack before the call to Interrupt 26H.
- Logical sector numbers are zero based and are obtained by numbering each disk sector sequentially from track 0, head 0, sector 1 and continuing until the last sector on the disk is counted. The head number is incremented before the track number. Because of interleaving, logically adjacent sectors might not be physically adjacent for some types of disks.
- The lower byte of the error code (AL) is the same error code that is returned in the lower byte of DI when an Interrupt 24H is issued. The upper byte (AH) contains one of the following codes:

Code	Meaning
80H	Device failed to respond
40H	Seek operation failure
20H	Controller failure
10H	Data error (bad CRC)

(more)

Code	Meaning
08H	Direct memory access (DMA) failure
04H	Requested sector not found
03H	Write-protect fault
02H	Bad address mark
01H	Bad command

● **Warning:** Interrupt 26H bypasses the MS-DOS file system. This function must be used with caution to avoid damaging the disk structure.

Example

```
;**************************************************************;
;                                                              ;
;       Interrupt 26H: Absolute Disk Write                     ;
;                                                              ;
;       Write the contents of the memory area named buff       ;
;       into logical sector 3 of drive C.                      ;
;                                                              ;
;       WARNING: Verbatim use of this code could damage        ;
;       the file structure of the fixed disk. It is meant      ;
;       only as a general guide. There is, unfortunately,      ;
;       no way to give a really safe example of this interrupt.;
;                                                              ;
;**************************************************************;

        mov     al,2            ; Drive C.
        mov     cx,1            ; Number of sectors.
        mov     dx,3            ; Beginning sector number.
        mov     bx,seg buff     ; Address of buffer.
        mov     ds,bx
        mov     bx,offset buff
        int     26h             ; Request disk write.
        jc      error           ; Jump if write failed.
        add     sp,2            ; Clear stack.
        .
        .
        .
error:                          ; Error routine goes here.
        .
        .
        .
buff    db      512 dup (?)     ; Data to be written to disk.
```

Interrupt 27H (39)

1.0 and later

Terminate and Stay Resident

Interrupt 27H terminates execution of the currently executing program but reserves part or all of its memory so that it will not be overlaid by the next transient program to be loaded.

To Call

DX = offset of last byte plus 1 (relative to the program segment prefix, or PSP) of program to be protected

CS = segment address of PSP

Returns

Nothing

Programmer's Notes

- In response to an Interrupt 27H call, MS-DOS takes the following actions:
  - Restores the termination vector (Interrupt 22H) from PSP:000AH.
  - Restores the Control-C vector (Interrupt 23H) from PSP:000EH.
  - With MS-DOS versions 2.0 and later, restores the critical error handler vector (Interrupt 24H) from PSP:0012H.
  - Transfers to the termination handler address.
- If the program is returning to COMMAND.COM rather than to another program, control transfers first to COMMAND.COM's resident portion, which reloads COMMAND.COM's transient portion (if necessary) and passes it control. If a batch file is in progress, the next line of the file is then fetched and interpreted; otherwise, a prompt is issued for the next user command.
- This interrupt is typically used to allow user-written drivers or interrupt handlers to be loaded as ordinary .COM or .EXE programs and then remain resident. Subsequent entrance to the code is by means of a hardware or software interrupt.
- The maximum amount of memory that can be reserved with this interrupt is 64 KB. Therefore, Interrupt 27H should be used only for applications that must run under MS-DOS versions 1.x.

  With versions 2.0 and later, the preferred method to terminate and stay resident is to use Interrupt 21H Function 31H, which allows the program to reserve more than 64 KB of memory and does not require CS to contain the PSP address.
- Interrupt 27H should not be called by .EXE programs that are loaded into the high end of memory (that is, linked with the /HIGH switch), because this would reserve the memory that is ordinarily used by the transient portion of COMMAND.COM. If COMMAND.COM cannot be reloaded, the system will fail.

- Because execution of Interrupt 27H results in the restoration of the terminate routine (Interrupt 22H), Control-C (Interrupt 23H), and critical error (Interrupt 24H) vectors, it cannot be used to permanently install a user-written critical error handler.
- Interrupt 27H does not work correctly when DX contains values in the range FFF1H through FFFFH. In this case, MS-DOS discards the high bit of the contents of DX, resulting in 32 KB less resident memory than was actually requested by the program.

Example

```
;****************************************************************;
;                                                              ;
;       Interrupt 27H: Terminate and Stay Resident             ;
;                                                              ;
;       Exit and stay resident, reserving enough memory        ;
;       to protect the program's code and data.                ;
;                                                              ;
;****************************************************************;

Start:  .
        .
        .
        mov     dx,offset pgm_end  ; DX = bytes to reserve.
        int     27h                ; Terminate, stay resident.
        .
        .
        .
pgm_end equ     $
        end     start
```

Interrupt 2FH (47)

Multiplex Interrupt

2.0 and later

Interrupt 2FH with AH = 01H submits a file to the print spooler, removes a file from the print spooler's queue of pending files, or obtains the status of the printer. Other values for AH are used by various MS-DOS extensions, such as APPEND.

To Call

AH	= 01H	print spooler call
AL	= 00H	get installed status
	01H	submit file to be printed
	02H	remove file from print queue
	03H	cancel all files in queue
	04H	hold print jobs for status read
	05H	end hold for status read

If AL is 01H:

DS:DX	= segment:offset of packet address

If AL is 02H:

DS:DX	= segment:offset of ASCIIZ file specification

Returns

If operation is successful:

Carry flag is clear.

If AL was 00H on call:

AL	= status:	
	00H	not installed, OK to install
	01H	not installed, not OK to install
	FFH	installed

If AL was 04H on call:

DX	= error count
DS:SI	= segment:offset of print queue

If operation is not successful:

Carry flag is set.

AX	= error code:	
	01H	function invalid
	02H	file not found
	03H	path not found

(more)

04H	too many open files
05H	access denied
08H	queue full
09H	spooler busy
0CH	name too long
0FH	drive invalid

Programmer's Notes

- For Subfunction 01H, the packet consists of 5 bytes. The first byte contains the level (must be zero), the next 4 bytes contain the doubleword address (segment and offset) of an ASCIIZ file specification. (The filename cannot contain wildcard characters.) If the file exists, it is added to the end of the print queue.
- For Subfunction 02H, wildcard characters (* and ?) are allowed in the file specification, making it possible to delete multiple files from the print queue with one call.
- For Subfunction 04H, the address returned for the print queue points to a series of filename entries. Each entry in the queue is 64 bytes and contains an ASCIIZ file specification. The first file specification in the queue is the one currently being printed. The last slot in the queue has a null (zero) in the first byte.

Example

None

Appendixes

Appendix A
MS-DOS Version 3.3

For the MS-DOS user, version 3.3 incorporates some long-awaited capabilities, runs faster in places, and requires about 9 KB more memory than version 3.2. Its most apparent changes, however, relate to a new, more flexible method of supporting different national languages. For the MS-DOS programmer, version 3.3 offers several enhancements in the areas of file management and internationalization support. This appendix offers an overview of these new features.

Version 3.3 User Considerations

MS-DOS version 3.3 has introduced several changes at the user level. A new external command, FASTOPEN, speeds up the filing system by keeping file locations in memory. A new batch command, CALL, lets a batch file call another batch file and, when that file terminates, continue execution with the next command in the original batch file rather than return to MS-DOS as in previous versions. Two commands previously present only in PC-DOS, COMP and SELECT, have been added to MS-DOS. Five commands have additional capabilities: APPEND, ATTRIB, BACKUP, FDISK, and MODE. In addition, the TIME and DATE commands automatically set the CMOS clock-calendar on the IBM PC/AT and PS/2 machines, making use of the separate SETUP program unnecessary for these functions. Changes to the national language support involve four new commands, three new options to the MODE command, two new or modified system information files, and two new device drivers. Each of these new or modified commands is discussed individually below.

The FASTOPEN command

When MS-DOS searches for a program file, it searches each directory specified in the PATH search path. A lengthy path that has to search many levels of a directory structure can make this a slow process. The FASTOPEN command loads a terminate-and-stay-resident (TSR) program that caches the locations of the most recently accessed directories and files on one or more fixed disks in the system. The number of files and directories to be cached is under the user's control; the default is 10. When it needs a file, MS-DOS looks first in the FASTOPEN list; if the file is found in the list, MS-DOS can bypass inspection of the search path specified by PATH. When the FASTOPEN list is filled and a new file is opened, the new file replaces the least recently used file on the FASTOPEN list.

The improvement in file-system performance depends on the number of open files and the frequency of file access. The FASTOPEN command can be entered only once during a session and, if desired, can be placed in the AUTOEXEC.BAT file.

The FASTOPEN command has two parameters:

FASTOPEN *drive*:[=*entries*][...]

The *drive* parameter is the drive letter, followed by a colon, of a fixed disk for which FASTOPEN is to keep track of the most recently accessed directories and files. More than one drive can be specified by separating the drive identifiers with spaces; the maximum is four drives. A drive associated with a JOIN, SUBST, or ASSIGN command cannot be specified, nor can a drive assigned to a network.

The optional *entries* parameter is the number of directory entries FASTOPEN is to keep in memory. The value of *entries* can be from 10 through 999; the default is 34. If more than one *entries* value is specified, their sum cannot exceed 999. Each entry subtracts 40 bytes from the RAM normally available to run application programs.

Examples: The following command tells MS-DOS to keep track of the last 50 directories and files on drive C:

```
C>FASTOPEN C:=50  <Enter>
```

The next command tells MS-DOS to keep track of the last 34 files on drives C and D:

```
C>FASTOPEN C: D:  <Enter>
```

Changes to batch-file processing

Batch-file processing also gains power in MS-DOS version 3.3. The user can now suppress the echo of all batch commands and call one batch file from another without terminating the first batch file.

With MS-DOS version 3.3, any line in a batch file preceded by @ is not echoed to the screen when the batch file is executed.

CALL

A batch file no longer needs to load an additional copy of COMMAND.COM in order to execute another batch file and return control to the calling batch file. The CALL command executes a batch file and returns to the next command in the calling batch file.

CALL commands can be nested. If an exit condition is provided, a batch file can even call itself; however, the input or output of a called batch file cannot be redirected or piped.

The CALL command has two parameters:

CALL *batch-file* [*parameters*]

The *batch-file* parameter is the name of the batch file to be executed. The file must be in the current drive and directory or in a drive and/or directory specified in the command path.

The optional *parameters* parameter represents any parameters that may be required by *batch-file*.

Example: Suppose the batch file SORTFILE.BAT accepts one parameter. The following command calls SORTFILE.BAT, specifying NAMES.TXT as the parameter:

```
CALL SORTFILE NAMES.TXT
```

If NAMES.TXT was specified as a command-line parameter to the *calling* batch file, the CALL command could be

```
CALL SORTFILE %1
```

Commands from PC-DOS

Two commands have been added to MS-DOS from earlier versions of PC-DOS: COMP, present in PC-DOS version 1.0, and SELECT, present in PC-DOS version 2.0.

COMP

The COMP command compares two files or sets of files and reports any differences encountered. FC, a similar file-comparison command present in MS-DOS versions 2.0 and later, is still included with MS-DOS 3.3. *See* USER COMMANDS: COMP; FC.

Syntax for the COMP command is

COMP [*drive*:][*filename1*] [*drive*:][*filename2*]

The optional *drive* parameter is the drive letter, followed by a colon, of the drive containing the file to be compared. The *filename1* parameter is the name and location of the file to compare to *filename2*; *filename2* is the name and location of the file to be compared against. Both filenames can be preceded by a path; wildcard characters are permitted in either filename.

Example: The following command tells MS-DOS to compare the file NEWFILE.TXT in the current drive and directory to the file OLDFILE.TXT in the \ARCHIVE directory on drive D and report any differences encountered:

```
C>COMP NEWFILE.TXT D:\ARCHIVE\OLDFILE.TXT  <Enter>
```

SELECT

The SELECT command creates a system disk with the time format, date format, and keyboard layout configured for a selected country. The syntax for SELECT is

SELECT [[*drive1*:] [*drive2*:][*path*]] [*country*][*keyboard*]

The optional *drive1* parameter is the drive containing a disk with the MS-DOS operating-system files, the FORMAT program, and the country configuration files. The *drive2* parameter is the drive containing the disk to be formatted with the country-specific information; this drive specifier can be followed by a path. The *country* parameter is a code that selects the date and time format; the information is taken from the COUNTRY.SYS system file. The *keyboard* parameter is a code that selects the desired keyboard layout. *See* KEYB below.

The SELECT command

- Formats the target disk.
- Creates CONFIG.SYS and AUTOEXEC.BAT files on the target disk.
- Copies the contents of the source disk to the destination disk.

Example: The following command, which assumes drive A contains a valid system disk and drive B contains the disk to be formatted, creates a bootable system disk that includes country-specific information and keyboard layout for Germany:

```
C>SELECT A: B: 049 GR  <Enter>
```

Enhanced commands

Several existing MS-DOS user commands have been given expanded capabilities in version 3.3. These are presented alphabetically in the next few pages. *See* USER COMMANDS: APPEND; ATTRIB; BACKUP; FDISK; MODE.

APPEND

The APPEND command specifies a search path for data files—files whose extensions are neither .COM, .EXE, nor .BAT—similar to the command path specified by the PATH command, which searches only for executable files *with* those extensions. APPEND has three forms, depending on whether it is being entered for the first time. When it is entered the first time, the APPEND command now has two optional switches:

APPEND [/E] [/X]

The /E switch makes the data path part of the environment, like the command path. The data path can then be displayed or changed with both the SET and APPEND commands and is inherited by child processes. (However, any changes made to the data path by the child process are lost when the child returns to its parent process.)

The /X switch causes calls to the Find First File functions (Interrupt 21H Functions 11H and 4EH) and the EXEC function (Interrupt 21H Function 4BH) to search the data path. If /X is not specified, only Interrupt 21H Function 0FH (Open File with FCB), Interrupt 21H Function 23H (Get File Size), and Interrupt 21H Function 3DH (Open File with Handle) system calls search the data path.

If either /X or /E is specified the first time APPEND is entered, a pathname cannot be included.

Subsequent uses of the command must take the form

APPEND [[*drive:*]*path*] [;[*drive:*]*path* ...]

or

APPEND ;

The *path* parameter is the name of a directory that is to be made part of the data path. The user can specify as many directory names as will fit in the 128 characters of the command line. Entries must be separated by semicolons. If APPEND is followed only by a semicolon, any previous APPEND paths are deleted.

Example: The following two APPEND commands make the data path part of the environment and put the directories C:\WORD\PROPOSAL, C:\WORD\REPORTS, and C:\123\BUDGET in the data path:

```
C>APPEND /E   <Enter>
C>APPEND C:\WORD\PROPOSAL;C:\WORD\REPORTS;C:\123\BUDGET   <Enter>
```

Because the data path usually involves frequently used directories, the APPEND command ordinarily is placed in the AUTOEXEC.BAT file.

Note: APPEND is a new command in PC-DOS version 3.3.

ATTRIB

The /S switch has been added to the ATTRIB command so that any attribute changes can be applied to all files in subdirectories contained in the specified directory.

Example: The following command sets the read-only attribute of all files in the directory C:\DOS and in all its subdirectories:

```
C>ATTRIB +R C:/DOS /S   <Enter>
```

BACKUP

A formatting parameter has been added to the BACKUP command in MS-DOS version 3.3. The /F switch tells MS-DOS to format the backup diskette if it hasn't been formatted. The /F switch formats the backup diskette to the maximum capacity of the backup drive, so a disk of lower capacity, such as a 360 KB diskette in a 1.2M drive, should not be used. If this switch is used, FORMAT.COM must be available in the current drive and directory or in one of the directories named in the environment's PATH string.

Performance of the BACKUP command has also been improved. Instead of storing each file separately on the backup disk, BACKUP stores only two files: BACKUP.*nnn*, which contains all the backed-up files, and CONTROL.*nnn*, which contains the pathnames of the backed-up files.

FDISK

FDISK can now create a new type of MS-DOS partition called an extended partition on a fixed disk. An extended partition can contain multiple logical drives and allows the use of very large fixed disks. Each logical drive is still limited to 32 MB.

An extended partition is not bootable. In order for the fixed disk to be bootable, it must also contain a primary MS-DOS partition that has been formatted using the FORMAT command with the /S switch so that it contains a system boot record and the operating-system files.

MODE

The MODE command now supports two additional serial ports (COM3 and COM4) and increases the maximum serial transmission rate to 19,200 baud.

Some additional options have been added to MODE to support code-page switching. *See* MODE Command Changes below.

New national language support

The new national language support in MS-DOS version 3.3 replaces the methods used in previous versions to change the keyboard layout and the display and printer character sets so that more than one language could be used. These changes are extensive: four new or modified system files, three new commands, four new options for the MODE command, a new parameter for the GRAFTABL command, and a new parameter for the COUNTRY and DEVICE configuration commands.

Code pages and code-page switching

The key element of the new national language support is the code page, a table of 256 character correspondence codes. MS-DOS recognizes both a hardware code page, which is the character correspondence table built into a device, and a prepared code page, which is an alternate character correspondence table available through MS-DOS. The current code page is the code page most recently selected.

The hardware code page for a device is determined by the country for which the device was manufactured. The user selects a prepared code page, from a list of five included with MS-DOS version 3.3, by using the new CP PREPARE option of the MODE command. *See* MODE Command Changes below.

The new national language support is often referred to as code-page switching because, after the devices and code pages required by the system have been defined, the only commands the user must deal with simply switch from one code page to another. In order to use the new national language support, device drivers must support code-page switching and the devices must be able to display the full character sets.

Code pages are numbered. The identifying numbers have no relationship to the country code introduced with previous versions of MS-DOS and used by the COUNTRY configuration command. Five code pages are included with version 3.3:

Page Number	Configuration
437	United States
850	Multilingual
860	Portugal
863	Canadian French
865	Norway/Denmark

Code page 437 is the character correspondence table used in previous versions of MS-DOS. Its character set supports United States English and includes many accented characters used in other languages. It is the hardware code page for most countries.

Code page 850 replaces two of the four box-drawing sets and some of the mathematical symbols in code page 437 with additional accented characters. It supports English and most Latin-based European languages.

Code page 860 is for Portuguese, code page 863 is for Canadian French, and code page 865 is for Norwegian/Danish. These pages are the hardware code pages for the specified countries.

Setting up the system for code-page switching

Although several commands are required to manage national language support, the process is fairly straightforward. Setting up the system requires the following:

- A DEVICE configuration command in CONFIG.SYS to load a driver for each device that supports code-page switching.
- An NLSFUNC command in AUTOEXEC.BAT to load the memory-resident national language support functions.
- A MODE CP PREPARE command in AUTOEXEC.BAT to prepare code pages for each device that supports code-page switching.
- A CHCP command in AUTOEXEC.BAT to select the initial code page.
- Optionally, a KEYB command in AUTOEXEC.BAT to select the initial keyboard layout.

After starting the system with these commands in CONFIG.SYS and AUTOEXEC.BAT, only a MODE CP SELECT command is required to change to a different language during an MS-DOS session.

The COUNTRY configuration command is still used to control country-specific characteristics such as the time and date format and currency symbol. An added parameter in the COUNTRY command lets the user also specify a code page. *See* Modified National Language Support Commands below.

The system files

MS-DOS version 3.3 includes four system files that support the national language functions: two device drivers and two system information files.

The device drivers are PRINTER.SYS and DISPLAY.SYS. These drivers implement code-page switching for the IBM Proprinter Model 4201 and Quietwriter III Model 5202 printers and for the EGA, PC Convertible LCD, and PS/2 display adapters. They also support all display adapters compatible with the EGA.

The information files are COUNTRY.SYS, which contains information such as time and date formats and currency symbols, and KEYBOARD.SYS, which contains the scan-code-to-ASCII translation tables for the various keyboard layouts.

The new support commands

The new national language support in MS-DOS version 3.3 adds three MS-DOS commands: Change Code Page (CHCP), Keyboard (KEYB), and National Language Support Functions (NLSFUNC).

CHCP

The Change Code Page (CHCP) command tells MS-DOS which code page to use for all devices that support code-page switching.

The NLSFUNC command must be executed before the CHCP command can be used.

CHCP is a system-wide command: It specifies the code page used by MS-DOS and each device attached to the system that supports code-page switching. The CP SELECT option of the MODE command, on the other hand, specifies the code page for a single device.

If the code page specified with CHCP is not compatible with a device, CHCP responds

```
Code page nnn not prepared for all devices
```

If the code page specified with CHCP was not first identified with the CP PREPARE option of the MODE command, CHCP responds

```
Code page nnn not prepared for system
```

The CHCP command has one optional parameter:

CHCP [*code-page*]

The *code-page* parameter is the three-digit number that specifies the code page MS-DOS is to use. If *code-page* is omitted, CHCP displays the current MS-DOS code page.

Examples: The following command changes the system code page to 850:

```
C>CHCP 850  <Enter>
```

If the current code page is 850 and CHCP is entered without parameters, MS-DOS responds:

```
Active code page: 850
```

KEYB

The Keyboard (KEYB) command selects a keyboard layout by changing the scan-code-to-ASCII translation table used by the keyboard driver. It replaces the KEYBxx commands used in earlier versions of MS-DOS to select keyboard layouts.

The first time KEYB is executed, it loads the memory-resident keyboard driver and the translation table, thereby increasing the size of MS-DOS by slightly more than 7 KB. Subsequent executions simply load a different translation table, which replaces the previously loaded translation table and accommodates a different country-specific keyboard layout.

The KEYB command has three optional parameters:

KEYB [*country*[,[*code-page*],*kbdfile*]]

The *country* parameter is one of the following two-character country codes:

Country	Code	Country	Code
Australia	US	Netherlands	NL
Belgium	BE	Norway	NO
Canada		Portugal	PO
English	US	Spain	SP
French	CF	Sweden	SV
Denmark	DK	Switzerland	
Finland	SU	French	SF
France	FR	German	SG
Germany	GR	United Kingdom	UK
Italy	IT	United States	US
Latin America	LA		

The *code-page* parameter is the three-digit number that specifies the code page defining the character set that MS-DOS is to use.

If the specified country code and code page aren't compatible, KEYB responds:

```
Code page requested nnn is not valid for given keyboard code
```

If KEYB is entered with no parameters, MS-DOS displays the currently active keyboard country code, keyboard code page, and console device code page.

Examples: The following command selects the French keyboard layout, code page 850, and the keyboard definition file named C:\DOS\KEYBOARD.SYS:

```
C>KEYB FR,850,C:\DOS\KEYBOARD.SYS  <Enter>
```

If the code page is omitted but the keyboard definition file is specified, the comma must be included to show the missing parameter:

```
C>KEYB FR,,C:\DOS\KEYBOARD.SYS  <Enter>
```

NLSFUNC

The National Language Support Function (NLSFUNC) command loads a memory-resident program that implements code-page switching. It also allows the user to name the file that contains country-specific information — such as date format, time format, and currency symbol — if there is no COUNTRY configuration command in CONFIG.SYS. NLSFUNC must be used before the Change Code Page (CHCP) command.

If national language support is needed for every session, NLSFUNC should be placed in the AUTOEXEC.BAT file.

The NLSFUNC command has one optional parameter:

NLSFUNC [*country-file*]

The *country-file* parameter is the name of the country information file (in most imple-mentations of MS-DOS, COUNTRY.SYS). If *country-file* is omitted, MS-DOS defaults to the name of the country information file specified in the COUNTRY configuration command in CONFIG.SYS; if there is no COUNTRY configuration command in CONFIG.SYS, MS-DOS looks for a file named COUNTRY.SYS in the root directory of the current drive.

Example: The following command loads the NLSFUNC program and specifies C:\DOS\COUNTRY.SYS as the country information file:

```
C>NLSFUNC C:\DOS\COUNTRY.SYS  <Enter>
```

The modified support commands

The new national language support changes two configuration commands — COUNTRY and DEVICE — and two general MS-DOS commands — GRAFTABL and MODE.

COUNTRY

The COUNTRY configuration command now has three parameters:

COUNTRY=*country-code,[code-page],[country-file]*

The *country-code* parameter is one of the following three-digit country codes (identical to the specified country's international telephone prefix):

Country	Code	Country	Code
Arabia	785	Latin America	003
Australia	061	Netherlands	031
Belgium	032	Norway	047
Canada		Portugal	351
English	001	Spain	034
French	002	Sweden	046
Denmark	045	Switzerland	
Finland	358	French	041
France	033	German	041
Germany	049	United Kingdom	044
Israel	972	United States	001
Italy	039		

The *code-page* parameter is the three-digit number that specifies the code page defining the character set that MS-DOS is to use.

The *country-file* parameter is the name of the file that contains the country-specific information; the name of the file can be preceded by a drive and/or path. If *country-file* is omitted, MS-DOS defaults to the file COUNTRY.SYS, which it looks for in the root direc-tory of the current drive.

The COUNTRY command is not required; if it is not included in CONFIG.SYS, MS-DOS defaults to country 001 (US), code page 437, and country information file COUNTRY.SYS in the root directory of the current drive.

Example: The following CONFIG.SYS command specifies the French country code, code page 850, and C:\DOS\COUNTRY.SYS as the country information file:

```
COUNTRY=033,850,C:\DOS\COUNTRY.SYS
```

DEVICE
Two options have been added to the DEVICE configuration command that allow the user to specify the display and printer drivers that support code-page switching.

The display driver that supports code-page switching is DISPLAY.SYS. It supports the IBM Enhanced Graphics Adapter (EGA), the IBM Personal System/2 display adapter, and all display adapters compatible with either of these. The Monochrome Display Adapter (MDA) and the Color/Graphics Adapter (CGA) do not support code-page switching.

If the ANSI.SYS display driver is also used, the DEVICE command that defines it must precede the DEVICE command that defines DISPLAY.SYS.

When used to specify the display driver, the DEVICE command has five parameters:

DEVICE=*driver* CON=(*type*[,[*hwcp*][,*prepcp*[,*sub-fonts*]]])

The *driver* parameter is the name of the file that contains the display driver; the filename can be preceded by a drive and/or path. If *driver* is omitted, MS-DOS defaults to the file DISPLAY.SYS, which it looks for in the root directory of the current drive.

The *type* parameter defines the type of display adapter attached to the system. It must be one of the following:

Code	Adapter
MONO	Monochrome display/printer adapter
CGA	Color/graphics adapter
EGA	Enhanced graphics adapter or IBM Personal System/2 display adapter
LCD	IBM PC Convertible liquid crystal display

The *hwcp* parameter is the three-digit number that specifies the hardware code page supported by the display adapter:

Code	Configuration
437	United States (default)
850	Multilingual
860	Portugal
863	Canadian French
865	Norway/Denmark

The *prepcp* parameter is the number of additional code pages the display can support. These are referred to as prepared code pages and must be defined by the CP PREPARE option of the MODE command. If *type* is either MONO or CGA, *prepcp* must be 0; the default is 0. If *type* is either EGA or LCD, *prepcp* can be any value from 1 through 12; the default is 1. If *hwcp* is 437, *prepcp* should be allowed to default to 1; if *hwcp* is not 437, *prepcp* should be set to 2.

The *sub-fonts* parameter is the number of subfonts supported for each code page. If *type* is either MONO or CGA, *sub-fonts* must be 0; the default is 0. If *type* is EGA, *sub-fonts* can be 1 or 2; the default is 2. If *type* is LCD, *sub-fonts* can be 1 or 2; the default is 1.

Example: The following CONFIG.SYS command specifies C:\DOS\DISPLAY.SYS as the display driver for an EGA whose hardware code page is 437. The parameter for prepared code pages is allowed to default to 1 and the parameter for subfonts is allowed to default to 2.

```
DEVICE=C:\DOS\DISPLAY.SYS CON=(EGA,437)
```

The printer driver that supports code-page switching is PRINTER.SYS. It supports the IBM Proprinter Model 4201, the IBM Quietwriter III Printer Model 5202, and all printers compatible with either of these.

When used to specify the printer driver, the DEVICE configuration command has five parameters:

DEVICE=*driver port*=(*type*[,[*hwcp*][,*prepcp*]])

The *driver* parameter is the name of the file that contains the printer driver; the filename can be preceded by a drive and/or path. If *driver* is omitted, MS-DOS defaults to the file PRINTER.SYS, which it looks for in the root directory of the current drive.

The *port* parameter is the MS-DOS device name of the printer port being defined: LPT1 (or PRN), LPT2, or LPT3. A different set of *type*, *hwcp*, and *prepcp* parameters can be specified for each of the three printer ports.

The *type* parameter defines the type of printer attached to the printer port. It must be one of the following:

Code	Printer
4201	IBM Proprinter Model 4201
5202	IBM Quietwriter III Printer Model 5202

The *hwcp* parameter is a three-digit number that specifies the hardware code page supported by the hardware:

Code	Configuration
437	United States (default)
850	Multilingual
860	Portugal
863	Canadian French
865	Norway/Denmark

If *type* is 5202, two hardware code-page numbers can be specified, enclosed in parentheses and separated by a comma. If two hardware code pages are specified, *prepcp* must be 0.

The *prepcp* parameter is the number of additional code pages (referred to as prepared code pages) for which MS-DOS must reserve buffer space; its value can be from 0 through 12. These additional code pages must be defined by the CP PREPARE option of the MODE command. If *hwcp* is 437, *prepcp* should be set to 1; if *hwcp* is not 437 and only one *hwcp* value is specified, *prepcp* should be set to 2.

Examples: The following CONFIG.SYS command defines C:\DOS\PRINTER.SYS as the printer driver for the PRN device. The printer is an IBM Proprinter Model 4201 whose hardware code page is 437, and MS-DOS is instructed to allow for one prepared code page:

```
DEVICE=C:\DOS\PRINTER.SYS PRN=(4201,437,1)
```

The next CONFIG.SYS command defines C:\DOS\PRINTER.SYS as the printer driver for ports LPT1 and LPT2. The printer attached to LPT1 is the same as in the previous command; the printer attached to LPT2 is an IBM Quietwriter III Printer Model 5202 with two hardware code pages (437 and 850). For the second printer, MS-DOS is instructed to allow for no prepared code pages.

```
DEVICE=C:\DOS\PRINTER.SYS LPT1=(4201,437,1) LPT2=(5202,(437,850),0)
```

GRAFTABL
The GRAFTABL command now has two forms:

GRAFTABL [*code-page*]

or

GRAFTABL /STATUS

The first form of the command loads a code page for the color/graphics adapter (CGA) so that its character set matches that used by MS-DOS and other devices when displaying the upper 128 characters. The *code-page* parameter is the three-digit number that specifies the code page defining the character set that GRAFTABL is to use.

The /STATUS switch causes GRAFTABL to display the name of the graphics character set table currently in use.

MODE
National language support adds four options to the MODE command:

Option	Action
CODEPAGE	Displays the code pages available and active.
CODEPAGE PREPARE	Defines the code pages selected for use.
CODEPAGE REFRESH	Restores code-page contents damaged by hardware error or other causes.
CODEPAGE SELECT	Selects a code page for a particular device.

(CODEPAGE can be abbreviated to CP in the command line.)

When used to display the status of the code pages, the MODE command has one parameter:

MODE *device* CP

The *device* parameter is the name of the device whose code-page status is to be displayed. It can be CON, PRN, LPT1, LPT2, or LPT3.

Example: The following command displays the status of the console device:

```
C>MODE CON CP  <Enter>
```

When used to define the code page or pages to be used with a device, the MODE command has three parameters:

MODE *device* CP PREPARE=(*code-page font-file*)

The *device* parameter is the name of the device for which the code page or pages are to be prepared. It can be CON, PRN, LPT1, LPT2, or LPT3.

The *code-page* parameter is one or more of the three-digit numbers, enclosed in parentheses, that specify the code page to be used with *device*. If more than one code-page number is specified, the numbers must be separated with spaces.

The *font-file* parameter is the name of the code-page file that contains the font information for *device*. The files provided for IBM devices include

File	Device
EGA.CPI	IBM Enhanced Graphics Adapter (EGA) and EGA-compatible display adapters
4201.CPI	IBM Proprinter Model 4201
5202.CPI	IBM Quietwriter III Printer Model 5202
LCD.CPI	IBM Convertible liquid crystal display

Example: Assume the display is attached to an EGA. The following command prepares code pages 437 and 850 for the console, specifying C:\DOS\EGA.CPI as the code-page information file:

```
C>MODE CON CP PREPARE=((437 850) C:\DOS\EGA.CPI)   <Enter>
```

When used to select a code page for a device, the MODE command has two parameters:

MODE *device* CP SELECT=*code-page*

The *device* parameter is the name of the device for which the code page is to be selected. Permissible values are CON, PRN, LPT1, LPT2, and LPT3.

The *code-page* parameter is the three-digit number that specifies the code page to be used with *device.*

Example: The following command selects code page 850 for the console:

```
C>MODE CON CP SELECT=850   <Enter>
```

Setting up code-page switching for an EGA-only system

Figure A-1 shows the commands required to implement the new national language support for a system that includes only a display attached to an EGA or EGA-compatible adapter. The hardware code page of the EGA is 437 (United States English) and the system is set up to handle code pages 437 and 850. All MS-DOS files are assumed to be in the directory \DOS on the disk in drive C. If the ANSI.SYS driver is not used, the configuration command DEVICE=C:\DOS\ANSI.SYS should be omitted from CONFIG.SYS; if ANSI.SYS is used, however, the DEVICE configuration command that defines it must precede the DEVICE configuration command that defines DISPLAY.SYS.

Commands in CONFIG.SYS:

```
COUNTRY=001,437,C:\DOS\COUNTRY.SYS
DEVICE=C:\DOS\ANSI.SYS
DEVICE=C:\DISPLAY.SYS CON=(EGA,437,1)
```

Commands in AUTOEXEC.BAT:

```
NLSFUNC C:\DOS\COUNTRY.SYS
MODE CON CP PREPARE=((437 850) C:\DOS\EGA.CPI)
MODE CON CP SELECT=437
KEYB US,437,C:\DOS\KEYBOARD.SYS
```

Figure A-1. Setup commands for a system with an EGA only.

When the system is started, code page 437 is selected for MS-DOS, the display, and the keyboard. To change to code page 850 during the session, simply type

```
C>CHCP 850   <Enter>
```

Setting up code-page switching for a PS/2 and printer

Figure A-2 shows the commands required to implement the new national language support for an IBM Personal System/2 or compatible system that includes both a PS/2, EGA, or EGA-compatible display adapter and an IBM Proprinter Model 4201. The hardware code page of both devices is 437 (United States English) and the system is set up to handle code pages 437 and 850.

Commands in CONFIG.SYS:

```
COUNTRY=001,437,C:\DOS\COUNTRY.SYS
DEVICE=C:\DOS\ANSI.SYS
DEVICE=C:\DISPLAY.SYS CON=(EGA,437,1)
DEVICE=C:\DOS\PRINTER.SYS PRN=(4201,437,1)
```

Commands in AUTOEXEC.BAT:

```
NLSFUNC C:\DOS\COUNTRY.SYS
MODE CON CP PREPARE=((437 850) C:\DOS\EGA.CPI)
MODE PRN CP PREPARE=((437 850) C:\DOS\4202.CPI)
MODE CON CP SELECT=850
MODE PRN CP SELECT=850
KEYB US,850,C:\DOS\KEYBOARD.SYS
```

Figure A-2. Setup commands for a PS/2 with display and printer.

Again, all MS-DOS files are assumed to be in the directory \DOS on the disk in drive C. If the ANSI.SYS driver is not used, the configuration command DEVICE=C:\DOS\ANSI.SYS should be omitted from CONFIG.SYS; if ANSI.SYS is used, however, the DEVICE configuration command that defines it must precede the DEVICE configuration command that defines DISPLAY.SYS.

Version 3.3 Programming Considerations

The changes introduced in MS-DOS version 3.3 that are of primary interest to the programmer include

- New Interrupt 21H function calls for file management and internationalization support
- An extension to the definition of the MS-DOS IOCTL function for code-page switching, plus the addition of the underlying device-driver support
- Support for extended MS-DOS partitions on fixed disks

Each of these areas is discussed in detail below.

New file-management functions

MS-DOS version 3.3 includes two new Interrupt 21H file-management functions: Set Handle Count (Function 67H) and Commit File (Function 68H).

Set Handle Count

The Set Handle Count function (Interrupt 21H Function 67H) allows a single process to have more than 20 handles for files or devices open simultaneously. Function 67H is invoked by issuing a software Interrupt 21H with

AH = 67H
BX = number of desired handles

On return,

If function is successful:

Carry flag is clear.

If function is not successful:

Carry flag is set.

AX = error code

For each process, the operating system maintains a table that relates handle numbers for the process to MS-DOS's internal global table for all open files in the system. In MS-DOS versions 3.0 and later, the per-process table is ordinarily stored within the reserved area of the program segment prefix (PSP) and has only enough room for 20 handle entries. If 20 or fewer handles are requested in register BX, Function 67H takes no action and returns a success signal. If more than 20 handles are requested, however, Function 67H allocates on behalf of the calling program a new block of memory that is large enough to hold the expanded table of handle numbers and then copies the process's old handle table to the new table. Because the function will fail if the system does not have sufficient free memory to allocate the new block, most programs need to make a call to Interrupt 21H Function 4AH (Resize Memory Block) to "shrink" their initial memory block allocations before calling Function 67H.

Function 67H does not fail if the number requested is larger than the available entries in the system's global table for file and device handles. However, a subsequent attempt to open a file or device or to create a new file will fail if all the entries in the system's global file table are in use, even if the requesting process has not used up all its own handles. (The size of the global table is controlled by the FILES entry in the CONFIG.SYS file. *See* USER COMMANDS: config.sys: files; PROGRAMMING IN THE MS-DOS ENVIRONMENT: Programming for ms-dos: File and Record Management.)

Example: Set the maximum handle count for the current process to 30, so that the process can have as many as 25 files or devices open simultaneously (5 of the handles are already expended by the MS-DOS standard devices when the process starts up). Note that a FILES=30 (or greater value) entry in the CONFIG.SYS file also is required for the process to successfully open 30 files or devices.

```
                  .
                  .
                  .
     mov    ah,67h        ; Function 67H = set handle count.
     mov    bx,30         ; Maximum number of handles.
     int    21h           ; Transfer to MS-DOS.
     jc     error         ; Jump if function failed.
                  .
                  .
                  .
```

Commit File

The Commit File function (Interrupt 21H Function 68H) forces all data in MS-DOS's internal buffers that is associated with a given handle to be written to disk and forces the corresponding disk directory and file allocation table (FAT) information to be updated. By calling this function at appropriate points within its execution, a program can ensure that newly entered data will not be lost if there is a power failure, if the program crashes, or if the user fails to terminate the program properly before turning off the machine. Function 68H is called by issuing a software Interrupt 21H with

AH = 68H
BX = handle for previously opened file.

On return,

If function is successful:

Carry flag is clear.

If function is not successful:

Carry flag is set.

AX = error code

The effect of Function 68H is equivalent to closing and reopening the file or to duplicating a file handle with Interrupt 21H Function 45H (Duplicate File Handle) and then closing the duplicate. *See* PROGRAMMING IN THE MS-DOS ENVIRONMENT: PROGRAMMING FOR MS-DOS: File and Record Management. However, Function 68H has the advantages that the application will not lose control of the file (as could happen with the close-open sequence in a networking environment) and that it will not fail because of a lack of handles (as the duplicate handle method might).

Note: Function 68H operations requested on a handle associated with a character device return a success flag but have no effect.

Example: Assume that the file MYFILE.DAT has been opened previously and that the handle for the file is stored in the variable *fhandle*. Call Function 68H to ensure that any data in MS-DOS's internal buffers associated with the handle is written out to disk and that the directory and FAT are up-to-date.

```
fname    db      'MYFILE.DAT',0  ; ASCIIZ filename.
fhandle dw       ?               ; Handle from Open operation.
         .
         .
         .
         mov     ah,68h          ; Function 68H = commit file.
         mov     bx,fhandle      ; Handle from previous open.
         int     21h             ; Transfer to MS-DOS.
         jc      error           ; Jump if function failed.
         .
         .
         .
```

New internationalization support functions

MS-DOS version 3.3 includes two new Interrupt 21H internationalization support functions: Get Extended Country Information (Function 65H) and Select Code Page (Function 66H).

Get Extended Country Information

The Get Extended Country Information function (Interrupt 21H Function 65H) returns a superset of the internationalization information obtained with Interrupt 21H Function 38H (Get/Set Current Country). Function 65H is called by issuing a software Interrupt 21H with

AH   = 65H
AL   = information ID code:
       01H   get general internationalization information
       02H   get pointer to uppercase table
       04H   get pointer to filename uppercase table
       06H   get pointer to collating sequence table
BX   = code page of interest (active CON device = −1)
CX   = length of buffer to receive information (error returned if less than 5)
DX   = country ID (default = −1)
ES:DI   = address of buffer to receive information

On return,

If function is successful:

Carry flag is clear.

Requested data is in calling program's buffer.

If function is not successful:

Carry flag is set.

AX   = error code

Function 65H may fail if either the country code or the code-page number is invalid or if the code page does not match the country code. If the buffer to receive the information is at least 5 bytes but is too short for the requested information, the data is truncated and no error is returned.

The format of the data returned by Subfunction 01H in the calling program's buffer is

Field	Size
Information ID code (01H)	Byte
Length of following buffer (38 or less)	Word
Country ID	Word
Code-page number	Word
Date format	Word
Currency symbol	5 bytes
Thousands separator	Word
Decimal separator	Word
Date separator	Word
Time separator	Word
Currency format flags	Byte
Digits in currency	Byte
Time format	Byte
Monocase routine entry point	Doubleword
Data list separator	Word
Reserved	10 bytes

See SYSTEM CALLS: INTERRUPT 21H: Function 38H.

The format of the data returned by Subfunctions 02H, 04H, and 06H is

Field	Size
Information ID code (02H, 04H, or 06H)	Byte
Pointer to table	Doubleword

The uppercase and filename uppercase tables are 130 bytes. The first 2 bytes contain the size of the table; the subsequent 128 bytes contain the uppercase equivalents, if any, for character codes 80H through 0FFH. The main use of these tables is to map accented or otherwise modified vowels to their plain vowel equivalents. Text translated using these tables can be sent to devices that do not support the IBM graphics character set or can be used to create filenames that do not require a special keyboard configuration for entry.

The collating table is 258 bytes. The first 2 bytes contain the table length and the next 256 bytes contain the values to be used for the corresponding character codes (0–0FFH) during a sort operation. Among other things, this table maps uppercase and lowercase ASCII characters to the same collating codes (so that sorts will be case insensitive) and maps accented vowels to their plain vowel equivalents.

Note: In some cases, a truncated translation table might be presented to the program by MS-DOS. Applications should always check the length specified at the beginning of the table to be sure the table contains a translation code for the character of interest.

Example: Obtain the extended country information associated with the default country and code page 437.

```
buffer  db      41 dup (0)       ; Receives country information.
        .
        .
        .
        mov     ax,6501h         ; Function = get extended info.
        mov     bx,437           ; Code page.
        mov     cx,41            ; Length of buffer.
        mov     dx,-1            ; Default country.
        mov     di,seg buffer    ; ES:DI = buffer address.
        mov     es,di
        mov     di,offset buffer
        int     21h              ; Transfer to MS-DOS.
        jc      error            ; Jump if function failed.
        .
        .
        .
```

In this case, MS-DOS fills the following extended country information into the buffer:

```
buffer  db      1                ; Information ID code
        dw      38               ; Length of following buffer
        dw      1                ; Country ID (USA)
        dw      437              ; Code-page number
        dw      0                ; Date format
        db      '$',0,0,0,0      ; Currency symbol
        db      ',',0            ; Thousands separator
        db      '.',0            ; Decimal separator
        db      '-',0            ; Date separator
        db      ':',0            ; Time separator
        db      0                ; Currency format flags
        db      2                ; Digits in currency
        db      0                ; Time format
        dd      026ah:176ch      ; Monocase routine entry point
        db      ',',0            ; Data list separator
        db      10 dup (0)       ; Reserved
```

Example: Obtain the pointer to the uppercase table associated with the default country and code page 437.

```
buffer  db      5 dup (0)        ; Receives pointer information.
        .
        .
        .
        mov     ax,6502h         ; Function = get pointer to
                                 ; uppercase table.
```

(more)

```
        mov     bx,437          ; Code page.
        mov     cx,5            ; Length of buffer.
        mov     dx,-1           ; Default country.
        mov     di,seg buffer   ; ES:DI = buffer address.
        mov     es,di
        mov     di,offset buffer
        int     21h             ; Transfer to MS-DOS.
        jc      error           ; Jump if function failed.
        .
        .
        .
```

In this case, MS-DOS fills the following values into the buffer:

```
buffer  db      2               ; Information ID code
        dw      0204h           ; Offset of uppercase table
        dw      1140h           ; Segment of uppercase table
```

The table at 1140:0204H contains the following data:

```
            0  1  2  3  4  5  6  7  8  9  A  B  C  D  E  F   0123456789ABCDEF
1140:0200                  80 00 80 9A 45 41 8E 41 8F 80 45 45    ....EA.A..EE
1140:0210   45 49 49 49 8E 8F 90 92 92 4F 99 4F 55 55 59 99   EIII.....O.OUUY.
1140:0220   9A 9B 9C 9D 9E 9F 41 49 4F 55 A5 A5 A6 A7 A8 A9   ......AIOU......
1140:0230   AA AB AC AD AE AF B0 B1 B2 B3 B4 B5 B6 B7 B8 B9   ................
1140:0240   BA BB BC BD BE BF C0 C1 C2 C3 C4 C5 C6 C7 C8 C9   ................
1140:0250   CA CB CC CD CE CF D0 D1 D2 D3 D4 D5 D6 D7 D8 D9   ................
1140:0260   DA DB DC DD DE DF E0 E1 E2 E3 E4 E5 E6 E7 E8 E9   ................
1140:0270   EA EB EC ED EE EF F0 F1 F2 F3 F4 F5 F6 F7 F8 F9   ................
1140:0280   FA FB FC FD FE FF                                 ......
```

Select Code Page

The Select Code Page function (Interrupt 21H Function 66H) queries or selects the current code page. Function 66H is called by issuing a software Interrupt 21H with

AH = 66H
AL = subfunction:
    01H   get code page
    02H   select code page
BX = code page to select if AL = 02H

On return,

If function is successful:

Carry flag is clear.

If AL was 01H on call:

BX = active code page
DX = default code page

If function is not successful:

Carry flag is set.

AX = error code

When Subfunction 02H is used, MS-DOS gets the new code page from the COUNTRY.SYS file. The device must be previously prepared for code-page switching by including the appropriate DEVICE command in the CONFIG.SYS file and by issuing the NLSFUNC and MODE CP PREPARE commands (usually by placing them in the AUTOEXEC.BAT file).

Example: Force the active code page to be the same as the system's default code page — that is, return to the code page that was active when the system was first booted.

```
        .
        .
        .
mov     ax,6601h        ; Function = get code page.
int     21h             ; Transfer to MS-DOS.
jc      error           ; Jump if function failed.

mov     bx,dx           ; Force active page = default.

mov     ax,6602h        ; Function = set code page.
int     21h             ; Transfer to MS-DOS.
jc      error           ; Jump if function failed.
        .
        .
        .
```

Extension of IOCTL

The MS-DOS IOCTL service (Interrupt 21H Function 44H) and its device-driver underpinnings have been extended to support code-page switching by the interactive CHCP and MODE commands or by application programs. The relevant IOCTL subfunction is 0CH (Generic IOCTL for Handles). An MS-DOS utility or application program gains access to this subfunction by executing a software Interrupt 21H with

AH   = 44H
AL   = 0CH
BX   = handle for character device
CH   = category code:
    00H   unknown
    01H   COM1, COM2, COM3, or COM4
    03H   CON (keyboard and video display)
    05H   LPT1, LPT2, or LPT3

(more)

CL   = function (minor) code:
      4AH   select code page
      4CH   start code-page preparation
      4DH   end code-page preparation
      6AH   query selected code page
      6BH   query prepare list
DS:DX   = pointer to Generic IOCTL parameter block

On return,

If function is successful:

Carry flag is clear.

If function is not successful:

Carry flag is set.

AX   = error code:
      01H   invalid function number
      19H   bad data read from font file
      22H   unknown command
      26H   code page not prepared or selected
      27H   code page conflict or device or code page not found in file
      29H   device error
      31H   file contents not a valid font or no previous "start code-page preparation" call

Additional information about the cause of the error can be obtained with a call to Interrupt 21H Function 59H (Get Extended Error Information).

The parameter blocks for minor codes 4AH, 4DH, and 6AH have the following format:

Field	Size
Length of following data	Word
Code page ID	Word

The parameter block for minor code 4CH has the following format:

Field	Size
Flags	Word
Length of remainder of parameter block ($2[n+1]$)	Word
Number of code pages in the following list (n)	Word

(more)

Field	Size
Code page 1	Word
Code page 2	Word
.	
.	
.	
Code page n	Word

The parameter block for minor code 6BH has the following format, assuming n hardware code pages and m prepared code pages ($n <= 12$, $m <= 12$):

Field	Size
Length of following data ($2[n+m+2]$)	Word
Number of hardware code pages (n)	Word
Hardware code page 1	Word
Hardware code page 2	Word
.	
.	
.	
Hardware code page n	Word
Number of prepared code pages (m)	Word
Prepared code page 1	Word
Prepared code page 2	Word
.	
.	
.	
Prepared code page m	Word

After a Start Code-Page Preparation (minor code 4CH) call, the program must write the data defining the code-page font to the driver using one or more IOCTL Send Control Data to Character Device (Interrupt 21H Function 44H Subfunction 03H) calls. The format of the data is both device-specific and driver-specific. After the font data has been written to the driver, the program must issue an End Code-Page Preparation (minor code 4DH) call. If no data is written to the driver between the start and end calls, the driver interprets the newly prepared code pages as hardware code pages.

A special variation of Start Code-Page Preparation, called "refresh," is required to actually load the peripheral device with the prepared code pages. The refresh operation is obtained by calling minor code 4CH with each code-page position in the parameter block set to −1 and then immediately calling minor code 4DH.

The device-driver support that corresponds to IOCTL Subfunction 0CH is invoked by the MS-DOS kernel via the Generic IOCTL function (driver command code 19). The category (major) and function (minor) codes described above, along with a pointer to the parameter block, are passed to the driver in the request header. *See* PROGRAMMING IN THE MS-DOS ENVIRONMENT: Customizing ms-dos: Installable Device Drivers.

Extended MS-DOS partitions

An extended MS-DOS partition is indicated by a system indicator byte value of 05 in the partition table of the fixed disk's master boot record. *See* PROGRAMMING IN THE MS-DOS ENVIRONMENT: Structure of ms-dos: MS-DOS Storage Devices. An extended partition is not bootable and can be created on a bootable fixed-disk drive only if that drive already contains a primary MS-DOS partition (system indicator type 01 or 04). Fixed disks that are not bootable can contain an extended partition without a primary partition.

An extended partition is subdivided into extended logical disk volumes, each consisting of an extended boot record and a logical block device. The extended boot record is analogous in structure to the partition table for the fixed disk as a whole; it contains a logical drive table describing the volume and a pointer to the next extended logical volume. The logical block device is an image of a normal MS-DOS disk, including a master block (logical sector 0 containing the BPB describing the device), root directory, FAT, and files area. Each extended volume must start and end on a cylinder boundary.

Van Wolverton
Ray Duncan

Appendix B
Critical Error Codes

Critical errors are returned via Interrupt 24H. If register AL bit 7 is 0, then the error was a disk error; if register AL bit 7 is 1, then the error was a nondisk error. The upper half of DI is undefined; the lower half of DI contains one of the following error-condition codes:

Code	Description
00H	Attempt to write on write-protected disk
01H	Unknown drive or unit
02H	Drive not ready
03H	Invalid command
04H	Data error (CRC failed)
05H	Bad request structure length
06H	Seek error
07H	Unknown media type
08H	Sector not found
09H	Printer out of paper
0AH	Write fault
0BH	Read fault
0CH	General failure
0FH	Invalid disk change

Appendix C
Extended Error Codes

The extended error codes used by Interrupt 21H functions consist of four separate codes in the AX, BH, BL, and CH registers. These codes give as much detail as possible about the error and suggest how the issuing program should respond.

AX — Extended Error Code

If an error condition occurs in response to an Interrupt 21H function call, the carry flag is set and one of the following error codes is returned in AX:

Error	Description	Error	Description
01H	Invalid function code	16H	Invalid disk command
02H	File not found	17H	CRC error
03H	Path not found	18H	Invalid length (disk operation)
04H	Too many open files (no handles left)	19H	Seek error
		1AH	Not an MS-DOS disk
05H	Access denied	1BH	Sector not found
06H	Invalid handle	1CH	Out of paper
07H	Memory control blocks destroyed	1DH	Write fault
		1EH	Read fault
08H	Insufficient memory	1FH	General failure
09H	Invalid memory block address	20H	Sharing violation
0AH	Invalid environment	21H	Lock violation
0BH	Invalid format	22H	Wrong disk
0CH	Invalid access code	23H	FCB unavailable
0DH	Invalid data	24H	Sharing buffer overflow
0EH	Reserved	25–31H	Reserved
0FH	Invalid drive	32H	Network request not supported
10H	Attempt to remove the current directory	33H	Remote computer not listening
		34H	Duplicate name on network
11H	Not same device	35H	Network path not found
12H	No more files	36H	Network busy
13H	Disk is write-protected	37H	Network device no longer exists
14H	Bad disk unit	38H	Net BIOS command limit exceeded
15H	Drive not ready		

(more)

Error	Description	Error	Description
39H	Network adapter hardware error	45H	Net BIOS session limit exceeded
3AH	Incorrect response from network	46H	Sharing temporarily paused
		47H	Network request not accepted
3BH	Unexpected network error	48H	Print or disk redirection paused
3CH	Incompatible remote adapter	49–4FH	Reserved
3DH	Print queue full	50H	File exists
3EH	Print queue not full	51H	Reserved
3FH	Print file was canceled (not enough space)	52H	Cannot make directory entry
		53H	Fail on Interrupt 24H
40H	Network name was deleted	54H	Out of network structures
41H	Access denied	55H	Device already assigned
42H	Network device type incorrect	56H	Invalid password
43H	Network name not found	57H	Invalid parameter
44H	Network name limit exceeded	58H	Network data fault

BH — Error Class

BH returns a code that describes the class of error that occurred:

Class	Description
01H	Out of a resource, such as storage or channels
02H	Not an error, but a temporary situation (such as a locked region in a file) that can be expected to end
03H	Authorization problem
04H	An internal error in system software
05H	Hardware failure
06H	A system software failure not the fault of the active process (could be caused by missing or incorrect configuration files, for example)
07H	Application program error
08H	File or item not found
09H	File or item of invalid format or type or otherwise invalid or unsuitable
0AH	File or item interlocked
0BH	Wrong disk in drive, bad spot on disk, or other problem with storage medium
0CH	Other error

BL — Suggested Action

BL returns a code that suggests how the program should respond to the error:

Action	Description
01H	Retry, then prompt user.
02H	Retry after a pause.
03H	If the user entered data such as a drive letter or filename, prompt for it again.
04H	Terminate with cleanup.
05H	Terminate immediately. The system is so unhealthy that the program should exit as soon as possible without taking the time to close files and update indexes.
06H	Error is informational.
07H	Prompt the user to perform some action, such as changing disks, then retry the operation.

CH — Locus

CH returns a code that provides additional information to help locate the area involved in the failure. This code is particularly useful for hardware failures (BH = 05H).

Locus	Description
01H	Unknown
02H	Related to random-access block devices, such as a disk drive
03H	Related to network
04H	Related to serial-access character devices, such as a printer
05H	Related to random-access memory

Procedure

Programs should handle errors by noting the error returned in AX from the original system call and then invoking Interrupt 21H Function 59H to get the extended error information. If no extended error information is provided, the program should respond to the original error code.

The Function 59H system call is available during Interrupt 24H.

Appendix D
ASCII Character Set and
IBM Extended Character Set

Char	Dec	Hex	Control		Char	Dec	Hex	Control
	0	00	NUL (Null)		#	35	23	
☺	1	01	SOH (Start of heading)		$	36	24	
☻	2	02	STX (Start of text)		%	37	25	
♥	3	03	ETX (End of text)		&	38	26	
♦	4	04	EOT (End of transmission)		’	39	27	
					(	40	28	
♣	5	05	ENQ (Enquiry)		)	41	29	
♠	6	06	ACK (Acknowledge)		*	42	2A	
•	7	07	BEL (Bell)		+	43	2B	
◘	8	08	BS (Backspace)		,	44	2C	
○	9	09	HT (Horizontal tab)		-	45	2D	
◉	10	0A	LF (Linefeed)		.	46	2E	
♂	11	0B	VT (Vertical tab)		/	47	2F	
♀	12	0C	FF (Formfeed)		0	48	30	
♪	13	0D	CR (Carriage return)		1	49	31	
♫	14	0E	SO (Shift out)		2	50	32	
☼	15	0F	SI (Shift in)		3	51	33	
►	16	10	DLE (Data link escape)		4	52	34	
◄	17	11	DC1 (Device control 1)		5	53	35	
↕	18	12	DC2 (Device control 2)		6	54	36	
‼	19	13	DC3 (Device control 3)		7	55	37	
¶	20	14	DC4 (Device control 4)		8	56	38	
§	21	15	NAK (Negative acknowledge)		9	57	39	
					:	58	3A	
▬	22	16	SYN (Synchronous idle)		;	59	3B	
↨	23	17	ETB (End transmission block)		<	60	3C	
					=	61	3D	
↑	24	18	CAN (Cancel)		>	62	3E	
↓	25	19	EM (End of medium)		?	63	3F	
→	26	1A	SUB (Substitute)		@	64	40	
←	27	1B	ESC (Escape)		A	65	41	
∟	28	1C	FS (File separator)		B	66	42	
↔	29	1D	GS (Group separator)		C	67	43	
▲	30	1E	RS (Record separator)		D	68	44	
▼	31	1F	US (Unit separator)		E	69	45	
<space>	32	20			F	70	46	
!	33	21			G	71	47	
”	34	22			H	72	48	

(more)

Char	Number Dec	Hex	Char	Number Dec	Hex	Control	Char	Number Dec	Hex
I	73	49	z	122	7A		½	171	AB
J	74	4A	{	123	7B		¼	172	AC
K	75	4B	¦	124	7C		¡	173	AD
L	76	4C	}	125	7D		«	174	AE
M	77	4D	~	126	7E		»	175	AF
N	78	4E	Δ	127	7F	DEL	░	176	B0
O	79	4F	Ç	128	80		▒	177	B1
P	80	50	ü	129	81		▓	178	B2
Q	81	51	é	130	82		│	179	B3
R	82	52	â	131	83		┤	180	B4
S	83	53	ä	132	84		╡	181	B5
T	84	54	à	133	85		╢	182	B6
U	85	55	å	134	86		╖	183	B7
V	86	56	ç	135	87		╕	184	B8
W	87	57	ê	136	88		╣	185	B9
X	88	58	ë	137	89		║	186	BA
Y	89	59	è	138	8A		╗	187	BB
Z	90	5A	ï	139	8B		╝	188	BC
[	91	5B	î	140	8C		╜	189	BD
\	92	5C	ì	141	8D		╛	190	BE
]	93	5D	Ä	142	8E		┐	191	BF
^	94	5E	Å	143	8F		└	192	C0
—	95	5F	É	144	90		┴	193	C1
`	96	60	æ	145	91		┬	194	C2
a	97	61	Æ	146	92		├	195	C3
b	98	62	ô	147	93		—	196	C4
c	99	63	ö	148	94		┼	197	C5
d	100	64	ò	149	95		╞	198	C6
e	101	65	û	150	96		╟	199	C7
f	102	66	ù	151	97		╚	200	C8
g	103	67	ÿ	151	98		╔	201	C9
h	104	68	Ö	152	99		╩	202	CA
i	105	69	Ü	154	9A		╦	203	CB
j	106	6A	¢	155	9B		╠	204	CC
k	107	6B	£	156	9C		=	205	CD
l	108	6C	¥	157	9D		╬	206	CE
m	109	6D	₧	158	9E		╧	207	CF
n	110	6E	ƒ	159	9F		╨	208	D0
o	111	6F	á	160	A0		╤	209	D1
p	112	70	í	161	A1		╥	210	D2
q	113	71	ó	162	A2		╙	211	D3
r	114	72	ú	163	A3		╘	212	D4
s	115	73	ñ	164	A4		╒	213	D5
t	116	74	Ñ	165	A5		╓	214	D6
u	117	75	ª	166	A6		╫	215	D7
v	118	76	º	167	A7		╪	216	D8
w	119	77	¿	168	A8		┘	217	D9
x	120	78	⌐	169	A9		┌	218	DA
y	121	79	¬	170	AA		█	219	DB

(more)

Char	Number Dec	Hex	Char	Number Dec	Hex	Char	Number Dec	Hex
■	220	DC	Φ	232	E8	⌠	244	F4
▌	221	DD	Θ	233	E9	⌡	245	F5
▐	222	DE	Ω	234	EA	÷	246	F6
■	223	DF	δ	235	EB	≈	247	F7
α	224	E0	∞	236	EC	°	248	F8
β	225	E1	φ	237	ED	•	249	F9
Γ	226	E2	ε	238	EE	·	250	FA
π	227	E3	∩	239	EF	√	251	FB
Σ	228	E4	≡	240	F0	η	252	FC
σ	229	E5	±	241	F1	²	253	FD
μ	230	E6	≥	242	F2	•	254	FE
τ	231	E7	≤	243	F3		255	FF

Appendix E
EBCDIC Character Set

Char	Dec	Hex		Char	Dec	Hex		Char	Dec	Hex
NUL	0	00			41	29			82	52
SOH	1	01		SM	42	2A			83	53
STX	2	02		CU2	43	2B			84	54
ETX	3	03			44	2C			85	55
PF	4	04		ENQ	45	2D			86	56
HT	5	05		ACK	46	2E			87	57
LC	6	06		BEL	47	2F			88	58
DEL	7	07			48	30			89	59
GE	8	08			49	31		!	90	5A
RLF	9	09		SYN	50	32		$	91	5B
SMM	10	0A			51	33		*	92	5C
VT	11	0B		PN	52	34		)	93	5D
FF	12	0C		RS	53	35		;	94	5E
CR	13	0D		UC	54	36		¬	95	5F
SO	14	0E		EOT	55	37		-	96	60
SI	15	0F			56	38		/	97	61
DLE	16	10			57	39			98	62
DC1	17	11			58	3A			99	63
DC2	18	12		CU3	59	3B			100	64
TM	19	13		DC4	60	3C			101	65
RES	20	14		NAK	61	3D			102	66
NL	21	15			62	3E			103	67
BS	22	16		SUB	63	3F			104	68
IL	23	17		Sp	64	40			105	69
CAN	24	18			65	41		¦	106	6A
EM	25	19			66	42		,	107	6B
CC	26	1A			67	43		%	108	6C
CU1	27	1B			68	44		_	109	6D
IFS	28	1C			69	45		>	110	6E
IGS	29	1D			70	46		?	111	6F
IRS	30	1E			71	47			112	70
IUS	31	IF			72	48			113	71
DS	32	20			73	49			114	72
SOS	33	21		¢	74	4A			115	73
FS	34	22		.	75	4B			116	74
	35	23		<	76	4C			117	75
BYP	36	24		(	77	4D			118	76
LF	37	25		+	78	4E			119	77
ETB	38	26		|	79	4F			120	78
ESC	39	27		&	80	50			121	79
	40	28			81	51			122	7A

Char	Number Dec	Hex	Char	Number Dec	Hex	Char	Number Dec	Hex
#	123	7B	y	168	A8	N	213	D5
@	124	7C	z	169	A9	O	214	D6
'	125	7D		170	AA	P	215	D7
=	126	7E		171	AB	Q	216	D8
"	127	7F		172	AC	R	217	D9
	128	80		173	AD		218	DA
a	129	81		174	AE		219	DB
b	130	82		175	AF		220	DC
c	131	83		176	B0		221	DD
d	132	84		177	B1		222	DE
e	133	85		178	B2		223	DF
f	134	86		179	B3	\	224	E0
g	135	87		180	B4		225	E1
h	136	88		181	B5	S	226	E2
i	137	89		182	B6	T	227	E3
	138	8A		183	B7	U	228	E4
	139	8B		184	B8	V	229	E5
	140	8C		185	B9	W	230	E6
	141	8D		186	BA	X	231	E7
	142	8E		187	BB	Y	232	E8
	143	8F		188	BC	Z	233	E9
	144	90		189	BD		234	EA
j	145	91		190	BE		235	EB
k	146	92		191	BF	ꓶ	236	EC
l	147	93	{	192	C0		237	ED
m	148	94	A	193	C1		238	EE
n	149	95	B	194	C2		239	EF
o	150	96	C	195	C3	0	240	F0
p	151	97	D	196	C4	1	241	F1
q	152	98	E	197	C5	2	242	F2
r	153	99	F	198	C6	3	243	F3
	154	9A	G	199	C7	4	244	F4
	155	9B	H	200	C8	5	245	F5
	156	9C	I	201	C9	6	246	F6
	157	9D		202	CA	7	247	F7
	158	9E		203	CB	8	248	F8
	159	9F	♪	204	CC	9	249	F9
	160	A0		205	CD	|	250	FA
~	161	A1	Ψ	206	CE		251	FB
s	162	A2		207	CF		252	FC
t	163	A3	}	208	D0		253	FD
u	164	A4	J	209	D1		254	FE
v	165	A5	K	210	D2	EO	255	FF
w	166	A6	L	211	D3			
x	167	A7	M	212	D4			

Appendix F
ANSI.SYS Key and Extended Key Codes

The following escape sequence allows redefinition of keyboard keys to a specified *string*:

ESC[*code*;*string*;...p

where:

string   is either the ASCII code for a single character or a string contained in quotation marks. For example, both 65 and "A" can be used to represent an uppercase A.

code   is one or more of the following values that represent keyboard keys. Semicolons shown in this table must be entered in addition to the required semicolons in the command line.

Key	Code			
	Alone	**Shift-**	**Ctrl-**	**Alt-**
F1	0;59	0;84	0;94	0;104
F2	0;60	8;85	0;95	0;105
F3	0;61	0;86	0;96	0;106
F4	0;62	0;87	0;97	0;107
F5	0;63	0;88	0;98	0;108
F6	0;64	0;89	0;99	0;109
F7	0;65	0;90	0;100	0;110
F8	0;66	0;91	0;101	0;111
F9	0;67	0;92	0;102	0;112
F10	0;68	0;93	0;103	0;113
Home	0;71	55	0;119	–
Up Arrow	0;72	56	–	–
Pg Up	0;73	57	0;132	–
Left Arrow	0;75	52	0;115	–
Down Arrow	0;77	54	0;116	–
End	0;79	49	0;117	–
Down Arrow	0;80	50	–	–
Pg Dn	0;81	51	0;118	–
Ins	0;82	48	–	–
Del	0;83	46	–	–
PrtSc	–	–	0;114	–
A	97	65	1	0;30

(more)

Key	Code			
	Alone	Shift-	Ctrl-	Alt-
B	98	66	2	0;48
C	99	67	3	0;46
D	100	68	4	0;32
E	101	69	5	0;18
F	102	70	6	0;33
G	103	71	7	0;34
H	104	72	8	0;35
I	105	73	9	0;23
J	106	74	10	0;36
K	107	75	11	0;37
L	108	76	12	0;38
M	109	77	13	0;50
N	110	78	14	0;49
O	111	79	15	0;24
P	112	80	16	0;25
Q	113	81	17	0;16
R	114	82	18	0;19
S	115	83	19	0;31
T	116	84	20	0;20
U	117	85	21	0;22
V	118	86	22	0;47
W	119	87	23	0;17
X	120	88	24	0;45
Y	121	89	25	0;21
Z	122	90	26	0;44
1	49	33	–	0;120
2	50	64	–	0;121
3	51	35	–	0;122
4	52	36	–	0;123
5	53	37	–	0;124
6	54	94	–	0;125
7	55	38	–	0;126
8	56	42	–	0;127
9	57	40	–	0;128
0	48	41	–	0;129
–	45	95	–	0;130
=	61	43	–	0;131
Tab	9	0;15	–	–
Null	0;3	–	–	–

Appendix G
File Control Block (FCB) Structure

Figures G-1 and G-2 (memory block diagrams) and Tables G-1 and G-2 describe the structure of normal and extended file control blocks (FCBs).

Offset

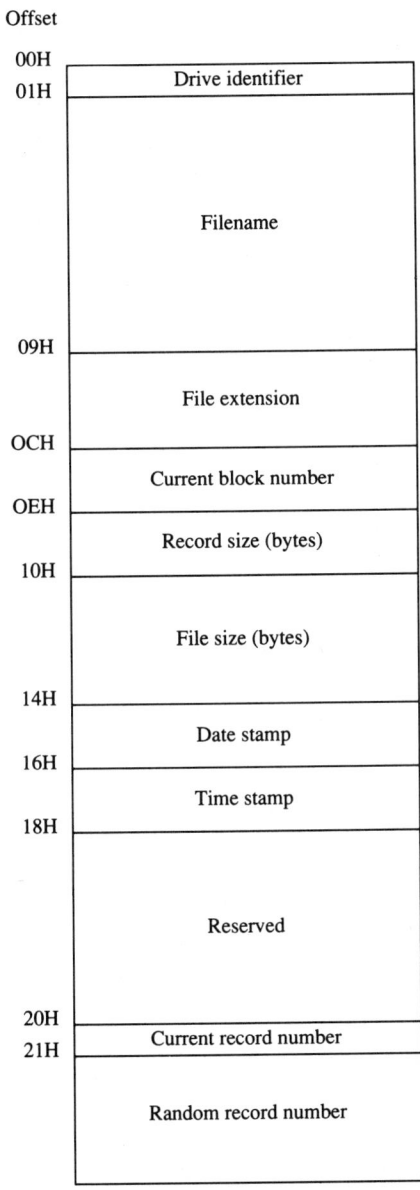

Figure G-1. Structure of a normal file control block.

Table G-1. Elements of a Normal File Control Block.

Element	Maintained by	Comments
Drive identifier	Program	Designates the drive on which the file to be opened or created resides (0 = default drive, 1 = drive A, 2 = drive B, and so on). If the application supplies a zero in this byte, MS-DOS alters the byte during the open or create operation to reflect the actual drive used.
Filename	Program	Standard eight-character filename; must be left justified and must be padded with blanks if fewer than eight characters. A device name (for example, PRN) can be used; there is no colon after a device name.
File extension	Program	Three-character file extension; must be left justified and must be padded with blanks if fewer than three characters.
Current block number	Program	Zero when the file is opened; the current block number and the current record number combined make up the record pointer during sequential file access.
Record size	Program	Set to 128 when the file is opened or created; the program can modify the field afterward to any desired record size.*
File size	MS-DOS	The size of the file in bytes; the first 2 bytes of this 4-byte field are the least significant bytes of the file size.
Date stamp	MS-DOS	The date of the last write operation on the file; follows the same format used by Interrupt 21H file handle Function 57H (Get/Set Time and Date):

Bits	Contents
9–15	Year (relative to 1980)
5–8	Month (1–12)
0–4	Day of month (1–31)

Time stamp	MS-DOS	The time of the last write operation on the file; follows the same format used by Interrupt 21H file handle Function 57H (Get/Set Time and Date):

Bits	Contents
11–15	Hours (0–23)
5–10	Minutes (0–59)
0–4	Number of 2-second increments (0–29)

(more)

Table G-1. *Continued.*

Element	Maintained by	Comments
Current record number	Program	Limited to the range 0 through 127; there are 128 records per block. The beginning of a file is record 0 of block 0. Together with the current block number, this field constitutes the record pointer used during sequential read and write operations. MS-DOS does not automatically initialize this field when a file is opened.
Random record pointer	Program	Identifies the record to be transferred by the Interrupt 21H random record functions 21H, 22H, 27H, and 28H; if the record size is 64 bytes or larger, only the first 3 bytes of this field are used. MS-DOS updates this field after random block reads and writes (Functions 27H and 28H) but not after random record reads and writes (Functions 21H and 22H).

* If the record size is made larger than 128 bytes, the default data transfer area (DTA) in the program segment prefix (PSP) cannot be used because it will collide with the program's own code or data.

Table G-2. Additional Elements of an Extended File Control Block.

Element	Maintained by	Comments
Extended FCB flag	Program	0FFH tells MS-DOS this is an extended (44-byte) FCB.
File attribute byte	Program	Must be initialized by the application when an extended FCB is used to open or create a file. The bits of this field have the following significance:

Bit	Meaning
0	Read-only
1	Hidden
2	System
3	Volume label
4	Directory
5	Archive
6	Reserved
7	Reserved

Offset

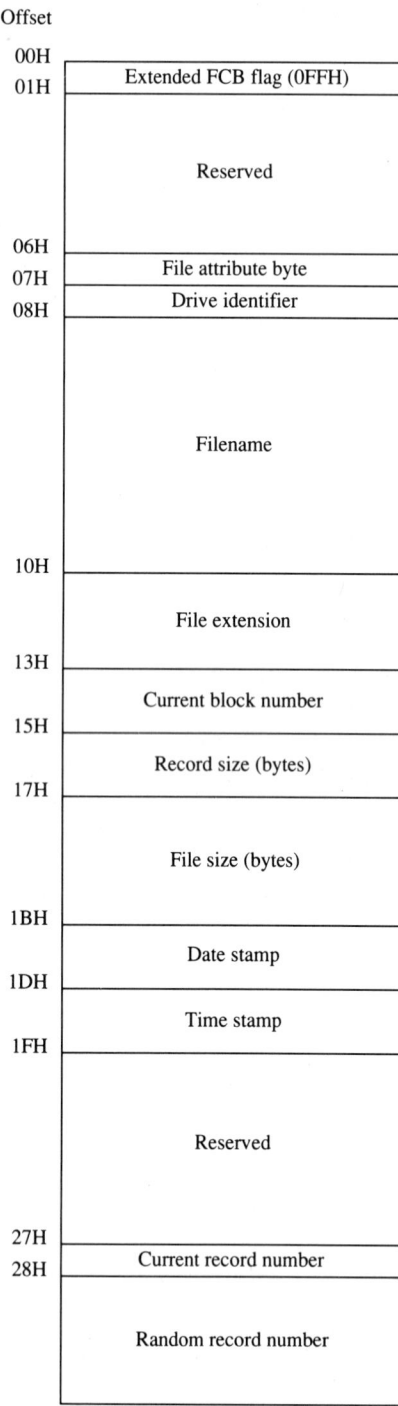

Offset	
00H	
01H	Extended FCB flag (0FFH)
	Reserved
06H	
07H	File attribute byte
08H	Drive identifier
	Filename
10H	
	File extension
13H	
	Current block number
15H	
	Record size (bytes)
17H	
	File size (bytes)
1BH	
	Date stamp
1DH	
	Time stamp
1FH	
	Reserved
27H	
28H	Current record number
	Random record number

Figure G-2. Structure of an extended file control block.

Appendix H
Program Segment Prefix (PSP) Structure

Offset	Size (in bytes)	Contents
00H (0)	2	INT 20H instruction
02H (2)	2	Address of last segment allocated to program
04H (4)	1	Reserved; normally 0
05H (5)	5	Long call to MS-DOS function dispatcher
0AH (10)	4	Terminate program interrupt vector (Interrupt 22H)
0EH (14)	4	Ctrl-C handler interrupt vector (Interrupt 23H)
12H (18)	4	Critical error handler interrupt vector (Interrupt 24H)
16H (22)	22	Reserved
2CH (44)	2	Segment address of environment
2EH (46)	34	Reserved
50H (80)	3	INT 21H, RETF instructions
53H (83)	9	Reserved
5CH (92)	16	Default file control block 1
6CH (108)	20	Default file control block 2 (overlaid if FCB 1 opened)
80H (128)	127	Command tail and default DTA
FFH (255)		

Figure H-1 (memory block diagram) illustrates the structure of the program segment prefix (PSP).

Figure H-1. Structure of the program segment prefix.

Appendix I
8086/8088/80286/80386 Instruction Sets

The 8086/8088 Instruction Set

Mnemonic	Description	Mnemonic	Description
AAA	ASCII adjust after addition	JB	Jump on below
AAD	ASCII adjust before division	JBE	Jump on below or equal
AAM	ASCII adjust after multiplication	JC	Jump on carry
AAS	ASCII adjust after subtraction	JCXZ	Jump on CX zero
ADC	Add with carry	JE	Jump on equal
ADD	Add	JG	Jump on greater
AND	Logical AND	JGE	Jump on greater or equal
CALL	Call procedure	JL	Jump on less than
CBW	Convert byte to word	JLE	Jump on less than or equal
CLC	Clear carry flag	JMP	Jump unconditionally
CLD	Clear direction flag	JNA	Jump on not above
CLI	Clear interrupt flag	JNAE	Jump on not above or equal
CMC	Complement carry flag	JNB	Jump on not below
CMP	Compare	JNBE	Jump on not below or equal
CMPS	Compare string	JNC	Jump on no carry
CMPSB	Compare byte string	JNE	Jump on not equal
CMPSW	Compare word string	JNG	Jump on not greater
CWD	Convert word to doubleword	JNGE	Jump on not greater or equal
DAA	Decimal adjust for addition	JNL	Jump on not less than
DAS	Decimal adjust for subtraction	JNLE	Jump on not less than or equal
DEC	Decrement by 1	JNO	Jump on not overflow
DIV	Unsigned divide	JNP	Jump on not parity
ESC	Escape	JNS	Jump on not sign
HLT	Halt	JNZ	Jump on not zero
IDIV	Integer divide	JO	Jump on overflow
IMUL	Integer multiply	JP	Jump on parity
IN	Input from port	JPE	Jump on parity even
INC	Increment by 1	JPO	Jump on parity odd
INT	Call to interrupt procedure	JS	Jump on sign
INTO	Interrupt on overflow	JZ	Jump on zero
IRET	Interrupt on return	LAHF	Load AH with flags
JA	Jump on above	LDS	Load pointer into DS
JAE	Jump on above or equal	LEA	Load effective address

(more)

Mnemonic	Description	Mnemonic	Description
LES	Load pointer into ES	REPNE	Repeat while not equal
LOCK	Lock the bus	REPNZ	Repeat while not zero
LODS	Load string	REPZ	Repeat while zero
LODSB	Load byte (string)	RET	Return
LODSW	Load word (string)	ROL	Rotate left
LOOP	Loop	ROR	Rotate right
LOOPE	Loop while equal	SAHF	Store AH into flags
LOOPNE	Loop while not equal	SAL	Shift arithmetic left
LOOPNZ	Loop while not zero	SAR	Shift arithmetic right
LOOPZ	Loop while zero	SBB	Subtract with borrow
MOV	Move data	SCAS	Scan string
MOVS	Move data from string to string	SCASB	Scan byte (string)
MOVSB	Move byte (string)	SCASW	Scan word (string)
MOVSW	Move word (string)	SHL	Shift logical left
MUL	Multiply	SHR	Shift logical right
NEG	Negate	STC	Set carry flag
NOP	No operation	STD	Set direction flag
NOT	Logical NOT	STI	Set interrupt flag
OR	Logical OR	STOS	Store string
OUT	Output to port	STOSB	Store byte (string)
POP	Pop top of stack	STOSW	Store word (string)
POPF	Pop stack into flags	SUB	Subtract
PUSH	Push onto stack	TEST	Logical compare
PUSHF	Push flags onto stack	WAIT	Enter wait state
RCL	Rotate through carry left	XCHG	Exchange
RCR	Rotate through carry right	XLAT	Translate
REP	Repeat	XOR	Exclusive OR
REPE	Repeat while equal		

The 80286 Instruction Set

Mnemonic	Description	Mnemonic	Description
AAA	ASCII adjust after addition	AND	Logical AND
AAD	ASCII adjust before division	ARPL	Adjust RPL field of selector
AAM	ASCII adjust after multiplication	BOUND	Check array index against bounds
AAS	ASCII adjust after subtraction	CALL	Call procedure
ADC	Add with carry	CBW	Convert byte to word
ADD	Add	CLC	Clear carry flag

(more)

Mnemonic	Description	Mnemonic	Description
CLD	Clear direction flag	JNE	Jump on not equal
CLI	Clear interrupt flag	JNG	Jump on not greater
CLTS	Clear task switched flag	JNGE	Jump on not greater or equal
CMC	Complement carry flag	JNL	Jump on not less than
CMP	Compare	JNLE	Jump on not less than or equal
CMPS	Compare string	JNO	Jump on not overflow
CMPSB	Compare byte string	JNP	Jump on not parity
CMPSW	Compare word string	JNS	Jump on not sign
CWD	Convert word to doubleword	JNZ	Jump on not zero
DAA	Decimal adjust for addition	JO	Jump on overflow
DAS	Decimal adjust for subtraction	JP	Jump on parity
DEC	Decrement by 1	JPE	Jump on parity even
DIV	Unsigned divide	JPO	Jump on parity odd
ENTER	Make stack frame	JS	Jump on sign
	(for procedure parameters)	JZ	Jump on zero
ESC	Escape	LAHF	Load AH with flags
HLT	Halt	LAR	Load access-rights byte
IDIV	Integer divide	LDS	Load pointer into DS
IMUL	Integer multiply	LEA	Load effective address
IN	Input from port	LEAVE	High-level procedure exit
INC	Increment by 1	LES	Load pointer into ES
INS	Input string from port	LGDT	Load global descriptor table
INT	Call to interrupt procedure	LIDT	Load interrupt descriptor table
INTO	Interrupt on overflow	LLDT	Load local descriptor table
IRET	Interrupt on return	LMSW	Load machine status word
JA	Jump on above	LOCK	Lock the bus
JAE	Jump on above or equal	LODS	Load string
JB	Jump on below	LODSB	Load byte (string)
JBE	Jump on below or equal	LODSW	Load word (string)
JC	Jump on carry	LOOP	Loop
JCXZ	Jump on CX zero	LOOPE	Loop while equal
JE	Jump on equal	LOOPNE	Loop while not equal
JG	Jump on greater	LOOPNZ	Loop while not zero
JGE	Jump on greater or equal	LOOPZ	Loop while zero
JL	Jump on less than	LSL	Load segment limit
JLE	Jump on less than or equal	LTR	Load task register
JMP	Jump unconditionally	MOV	Move data
JNA	Jump on not above	MOVS	Move data from string to string
JNAE	Jump on not above or equal	MOVSB	Move byte (string)
JNB	Jump on not below	MOVSW	Move word (string)
JNBE	Jump on not below or equal	MUL	Multiply
JNC	Jump on no carry	NEG	Negate

(more)

Mnemonic	Description	Mnemonic	Description
NOP	No operation	SCAS	Scan string
NOT	Logical NOT	SCASB	Scan byte (string)
OR	Logical OR	SCASW	Scan word (string)
OUT	Output to port	SGDT	Store global descriptor table
OUTS	Output string to port	SHL	Shift logical left
POP	Pop top of stack	SHR	Shift logical right
POPA	Pop eight 16-bit registers	SIDT	Store interrupt descriptor table
POPF	Pop stack into flags	SLDT	Store local descriptor table
PUSH	Push onto stack	SMSW	Store machine status word
PUSHA	Push eight 16-bit registers	STC	Set carry flag
PUSHF	Push flags onto stack	STD	Set direction flag
RCL	Rotate through carry left	STI	Set interrupt flag
RCR	Rotate through carry right	STOS	Store string
REP	Repeat	STOSB	Store byte (string)
REPE	Repeat while equal	STOSW	Store word (string)
REPNE	Repeat while not equal	STR	Store task register
REPNZ	Repeat while not zero	SUB	Subtract
REPZ	Repeat while zero	TEST	Logical compare
RET	Return	VERR	Verify a segment for reading
ROL	Rotate left	VERW	Verify a segment for writing
ROR	Rotate right	WAIT	Enter wait state
SAHF	Store AH into flags	XCHG	Exchange
SAL	Shift arithmetic left	XLAT	Translate
SAR	Shift arithmetic right	XOR	Exclusive OR
SBB	Subtract with borrow		

The 80386 Instruction Set

Mnemonic	Description	Mnemonic	Description
AAA	ASCII adjust after addition	BSF	Bit scan forward
AAD	ASCII adjust before division	BSR	Bit scan reverse
AAM	ASCII adjust after multiplication	BT	Bit test
AAS	ASCII adjust after subtraction	BTC	Bit test and complement
ADC	Add with carry	BTR	Bit test and reset
ADD	Add	BTS	Bit test and set
AND	Logical AND	CALL	Call procedure
ARPL	Adjust RPL field of selector	CBW	Convert byte to word
BOUND	Check array index against bounds	CDQ	Convert doubleword to quad word

(more)

Mnemonic	Description	Mnemonic	Description
CLC	Clear carry flag	JMP	Jump unconditionally
CLD	Clear direction flag	JNA	Jump on not above
CLI	Clear interrupt flag	JNAE	Jump on not above or equal
CLTS	Clear task switched flag	JNB	Jump on not below
CMC	Complement carry flag	JNBE	Jump on not below or equal
CMP	Compare	JNC	Jump on no carry
CMPS	Compare string	JNE	Jump on not equal
CMPSB	Compare byte string	JNG	Jump on not greater
CMPSD	Compare doubleword string	JNGE	Jump on not greater or equal
CMPSW	Compare word string	JNL	Jump on not less than
CWD	Convert word to doubleword	JNLE	Jump on not less than or equal
DAA	Decimal adjust for addition	JNO	Jump on not overflow
DAS	Decimal adjust for subtraction	JNP	Jump on not parity
DEC	Decrement by 1	JNS	Jump on not sign
DIV	Unsigned divide	JNZ	Jump on not zero
ENTER	Make stack frame	JO	Jump on overflow
	(for procedure parameters)	JP	Jump on parity
ESC	Escape	JPE	Jump on parity even
HLT	Halt	JPO	Jump on parity odd
IDIV	Integer divide	JS	Jump on sign
IMUL	Integer multiply	JZ	Jump on zero
IN	Input from port	LAHF	Load AH with flags
INC	Increment by 1	LAR	Load access-rights byte
INS	Input string from port	LDS	Load pointer into DS
INSD	Input doubleword from port	LEA	Load effective address
INT	Call to interrupt procedure	LEAVE	High-level procedure exit
INTO	Interrupt on overflow	LES	Load pointer into ES
IRET	Interrupt on return	LFS	Load pointer into FS
IRETD	Interrupt return to	LGDT	Load global descriptor table
	virtual 8086 mode	LGS	Load pointer into GS
JA	Jump on above	LIDT	Load interrupt descriptor table
JAE	Jump on above or equal	LLDT	Load local descriptor table
JB	Jump on below	LMSW	Load machine status word
JBE	Jump on below or equal	LOCK	Lock the bus
JC	Jump on carry	LODS	Load string
JCXZ	Jump on CX zero	LODSB	Load byte (string)
JE	Jump on equal	LODSD	Load doubleword (string)
JECXZ	Jump on ECX zero	LODSW	Load word (string)
JG	Jump on greater	LOOP	Loop
JGE	Jump on greater or equal	LOOPE	Loop while equal
JL	Jump on less than	LOOPNE	Loop while not equal
JLE	Jump on less than or equal	LOOPNZ	Loop while not zero

(more)

Mnemonic	Description	Mnemonic	Description
LOOPZ	Loop while zero	ROL	Rotate left
LSL	Load segment limit	ROR	Rotate right
LSS	Load pointer into SS	SAHF	Store AH into flags
LTR	Load task register	SAL	Shift arithmetic left
MOV	Move data	SAR	Shift arithmetic right
MOVS	Move data from string to string	SBB	Subtract with borrow
MOVSB	Move byte (string)	SCAS	Scan string
MOVSD	Move doubleword (string)	SCASB	Scan byte (string)
MOVSW	Move word (string)	SCASD	Scan doubleword (string)
MOVSX	Move with sign extend	SCASW	Scan word (string)
MOVZX	Move with zero extend	SET	Byte set on condition
MUL	Multiply	SGDT	Store global descriptor table
NEG	Negate	SHL	Shift logical left
NOP	No operation	SHLD	Double precision shift left
NOT	Logical NOT	SHR	Shift logical right
OR	Logical OR	SHRD	Double precision shift right
OUT	Output to port	SIDT	Store interrupt descriptor table
OUTS	Output string to port	SLDT	Store local descriptor table
POP	Pop top of stack	SMSW	Store machine status word
POPA	Pop eight 16-bit registers	STC	Set carry flag
POPAD	Pop eight 32-bit registers	STD	Set direction flag
POPF	Pop stack into flags	STI	Set interrupt flag
POPFD	Loads doubleword into EFLAGS	STOS	Store string
PUSH	Push onto stack	STOSB	Store byte (string)
PUSHA	Push eight 16-bit registers	STOSD	Store doubleword (string)
PUSHAD	Push eight 32-bit registers	STOSW	Store word (string)
PUSHED	Push EFLAGS	STR	Store task register
PUSHF	Push flags onto stack	SUB	Subtract
RCL	Rotate through carry left	TEST	Logical compare
RCR	Rotate through carry right	VERR	Verify a segment for reading
REP	Repeat	VERW	Verify a segment for writing
REPE	Repeat while equal	WAIT	Enter wait state
REPNE	Repeat while not equal	XCHG	Exchange
REPNZ	Repeat while not zero	XLAT	Translate
REPZ	Repeat while zero	XOR	Exclusive OR
RET	Return		

Appendix J
Common MS-DOS Filename Extensions

The Microsoft systems programs and language products commonly use the following file-name extensions:

Extension	Program/System	Description
.@@@	MS-DOS	Backup ID file
.$$$	EDLIN	Backup filename if out of disk space; error condition
.ASC	Generic	ASCII text file
.ASM	MASM	Assembly-language source code
.BAK	Generic	Backup file
.BAS	BASIC	BASIC language source code
.BAT	MS-DOS	Batch file (contains MS-DOS command lines)
.BIN	Generic	Binary file
.C	C	C language source code
.CAL	Windows	Calendar file
.COB	COBOL	COBOL language source code
.COD	Generic	Object listing file
.COM	MS-DOS	Executable program file
.CRD	Windows	Cardfile file
.CRF	MASM	Cross-reference file
.DAT	Generic	Data file
.DBG	COBOL	Debug file
.DEF	Windows	Module definition file
.DOC	Generic	Documentation or document file
.DRV	Generic	Driver file
.ERR	Generic	Error file
.EXE	MS-DOS	Executable program file
.FNT	Generic	Font file
.FON	Generic	Font file
.FOR	FORTRAN	FORTRAN language source code
.GRB	Windows	Grab file (snapshot)
.H	C	Include file
.HEX	MS-DOS	INTEL hexadecimal format file
.HLP	Generic	Help file
.INC	Generic	Include file
.INI	Windows	Initialization file

(more)

Extension	Program/System	Description
.INT	COBOL	Object file
.LIB	Generic	Library file
.LST	Generic	List file
.MAP	Generic	Address map file
.MOD	Generic	Module file
.MSG	COBOL	Message file
.MSP	Windows	Windows Paint file
.OBJ	Generic	Relocatable object module
.OVL	Generic	Overlay file
.OVR	COBOL	Compiler overlay file
.PAS	PASCAL	PASCAL language source code
.PIF	Windows	Program information file
.QLB	Generic	Library file for Microsoft's Quick products
.RC	Windows	Resource script file
.REF	CREF	Cross-reference listing file
.RES	Windows	Compiled resource file
.SCR	Generic	Script file
.SYM	Generic	Symbol file
.SYS	Generic	System file or device driver
.TMP	Generic	Temporary file
.TRM	Windows	Terminal file
.TXT	Generic	Text file or Windows Notepad file
.WRI	Windows	Write file

Appendix K
Segmented (New) .EXE File Header Format

Microsoft Windows requires much more information about a program than is available in the format of the .EXE executable file supported by MS-DOS. For example, Windows needs to identify the various segments of a program as code segments or data segments, to identify exported and imported functions, and to store the program's resources (such as icons, cursors, menus, and dialog-box templates). Windows must also support dynamically linkable library modules containing routines that programs and other library modules can call. For this reason, Windows programs use an expanded .EXE header format called the New Executable file header format. This format is used for Windows programs, Windows library modules, and resource-only files such as the Windows font resource files.

The Old Executable Header

The New Executable file header format incorporates the existing MS-DOS executable file header format. In fact, the beginning of a New Executable file is simply a normal MS-DOS .EXE header. The 4 bytes at offset 3CH are a pointer to the beginning of the New Executable header. (Offsets are from the beginning of the Old Executable header.)

Offset	Length (bytes)	Contents
00H	1	Signature byte *M*
01H	1	Signature byte *Z*
3CH	4	Offset of New Executable header from beginning of file

This normal MS-DOS .EXE header can contain size and relocation information for a non-Windows MS-DOS program that is contained within the .EXE file along with the Windows program. This program is run when the .EXE file is executed from the MS-DOS command line. Most Windows programmers use a standard program that simply prints the message *This program requires Microsoft Windows.*

The New Executable Header

The beginning of the New Executable file header contains information about the location and size of various tables within the header. (Offsets are from the beginning of the New Executable header.)

Offset	Length (bytes)	Contents
00H	1	Signature byte *N*
01H	1	Signature byte *E*
02H	1	LINK version number
03H	1	LINK revision number
04H	2	Offset of beginning of entry table relative to beginning of New Executable header
06H	2	Length of entry table
08H	4	32-bit checksum of entire contents of file, using zero for these 4 bytes
0CH	2	Module flag word (*see* below)
0EH	2	Segment number of automatic data segment (0 if neither SINGLEDATA nor MULTIPLEDATA flag is set in flag word)
10H	2	Initial size of local heap to be added to automatic data segment (0 if there is no local heap)
12H	2	Initial size of stack to be added to automatic data segment (0 for library modules)
14H	2	Initial value of instruction pointer (IP) register on entry to program
16H	2	Initial segment number for setting code segment (CS) register on entry to program
18H	2	Initial value of stack pointer (SP) register on entry to program (0 if stack segment is automatic data segment; stack should be set above static data area and below local heap in automatic data segment)

(more)

Offset	Length (bytes)	Contents
1AH	2	Segment number for setting stack segment (SS) register on entry to program (0 for library modules)
1CH	2	Number of entries in segment table
1EH	2	Number of entries in module reference table
20H	2	Number of bytes in nonresident names table
22H	2	Offset of beginning of segment table relative to beginning of New Executable header
24H	2	Offset of beginning of resource table relative to beginning of New Executable header
26H	2	Offset of beginning of resident names table relative to beginning of New Executable header
28H	2	Offset of beginning of module reference table relative to beginning of New Executable header
2AH	2	Offset of beginning of imported names table relative to beginning of New Executable header
2CH	4	Offset of nonresident names table relative to beginning of file
30H	2	Number of movable entry points listed in entry table
32H	2	Alignment shift count (0 is equivalent to 9)
34H	12	Reserved for expansion

The module flag word at offset 0CH in the New Executable header is defined as shown in Figure K-1.

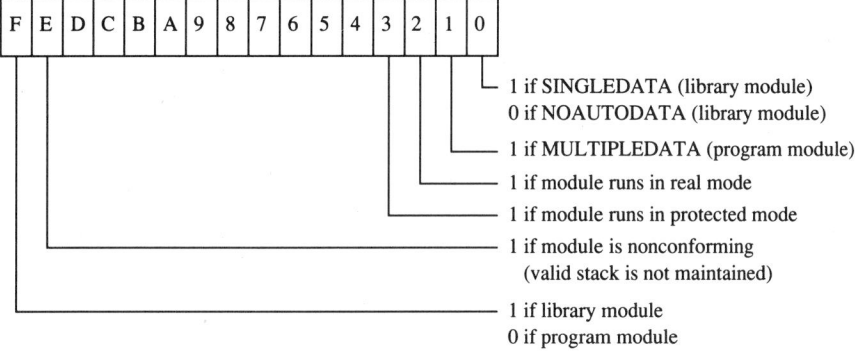

Figure K-1. The module flag word.

The segment table

This table contains one 8-byte record for every code and data segment in the program or library module. Each segment has an ordinal number associated with it. For example, the first segment has an ordinal number of 1. These segment numbers are used to reference the segments in other sections of the New Executable file. (Offsets are from the beginning of the record.)

Offset	Length (bytes)	Contents
00H	2	Offset of segment relative to beginning of file after shifting value left by alignment shift count
02H	2	Length of segment (0000H for segment of 65536 bytes)
04H	2	Segment flag word (*see* below)
06H	2	Minimum allocation size for segment; that is, amount of space Windows reserves in memory for segment (0000H for minimum allocation size of 65536 bytes)

The segment flag word is defined as shown in Figure K-2.

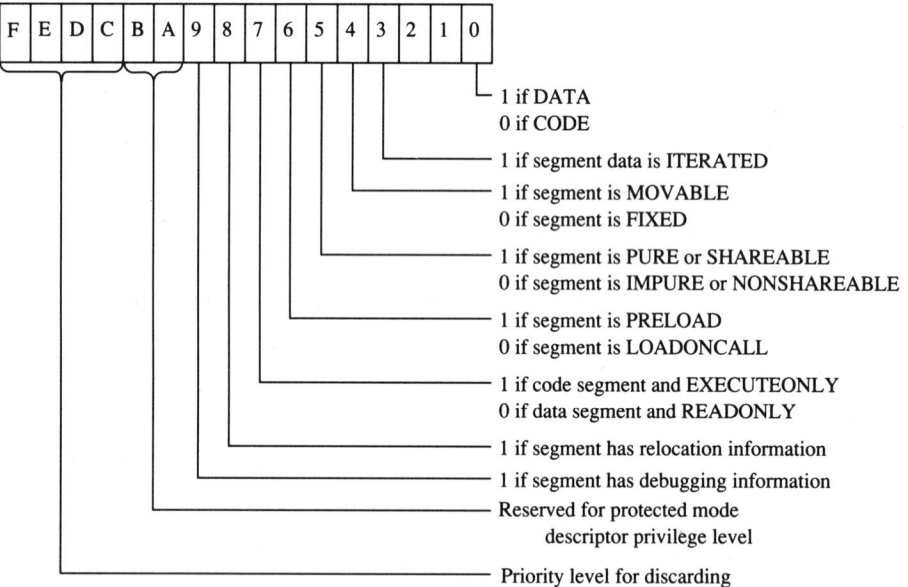

Figure K-2. The segment flag word.

The resource table

Resources are segments that contain data but are not included in a program's normal data segments. Resources are commonly used in Windows programs to store menus, dialog-box templates, icons, cursors, and text strings, but they can also be used for any type of read-only data. Each resource has a type and a name, both of which can be represented by either a number or an ASCII name.

The resource table begins with a resource shift count used for adjusting other values in the table. (Offsets are from the beginning of the table.)

Offset	Length (bytes)	Contents
00H	2	Resource shift count

This is followed by one or more resource groups, each defining one or more resources. (Offsets are from the beginning of the group.)

Offset	Length (bytes)	Contents
00H	2	Resource type (0 if end of table)
		If high bit set, type represented by predetermined number (high bit not shown):
		1 Cursor
		2 Bitmap
		3 Icon
		4 Menu template
		5 Dialog-box template
		6 String table
		7 Font directory
		8 Font
		9 Keyboard-accelerator table
		If high bit not set, type is ASCII text string and this value is offset from beginning of resource table, pointing to 1-byte value with number of bytes in string followed by string itself.
02H	2	Number of resources of this type
04H	4	Reserved for run-time use
08H	12 each	Resource description

Each resource description requires 12 bytes. (Offsets are from the beginning of the description.)

Offset	Length (bytes)	Contents
00H	2	Offset of resource relative to beginning of file after shifting left by resource shift count
02H	2	Length of resource after shifting left by resource shift count
04H	2	Resource flag word (*see* below)
06H	2	Resource name
		If high bit set, represented by a number; otherwise, type is ASCII text string and this value is offset from beginning of resource table, pointing to 1-byte value with number of bytes in string followed by string itself.
08H	4	Reserved for run-time use

The resource flag word is defined as shown in Figure K-3.

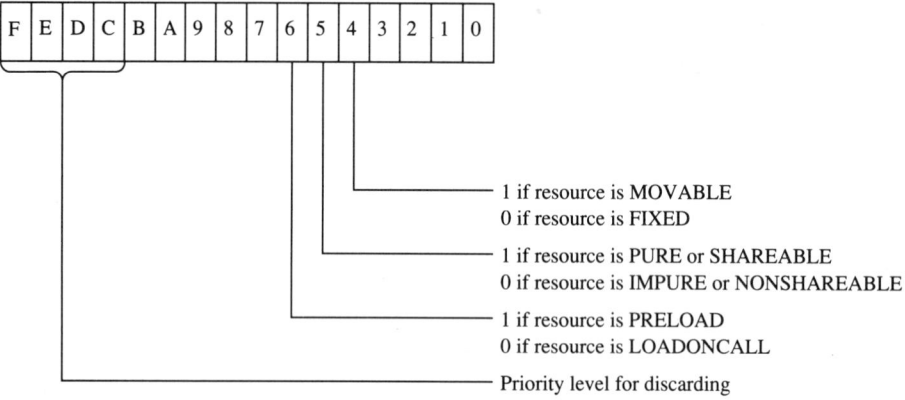

Figure K-3. The resource flag word.

The resident names table

This table contains a list of ASCII strings. The first string is the module name given in the module definition file. The other strings are the names of all exported functions listed in the module definition file that were not given explicit ordinal numbers or that were explicitly specified in the file as resident names. (Exported functions with explicit ordinal numbers in the module definition file are listed in the nonresident names table.)

Each string is prefaced by a single byte indicating the number of characters in the string and is followed by a word (2 bytes) referencing an element in the entry table, beginning at 1. The word that follows the module name is 0. (Offsets are from the beginning of the record.)

Offset	Length (bytes)	Contents
00H	1	Number of bytes in string (0 if end of table)
01H	n	ASCII string, not null-terminated
$n+1$	2	Index into entry table

The module reference table

The module reference table contains 2 bytes for every external module the program uses. These 2 bytes are an offset into the imported names table.

The imported names table

The imported names table contains a list of ASCII strings. These strings are the names of all other modules that are referenced through imported functions. The strings are prefaced with a single byte indicating the length of the string.

For most Windows programs, the imported names table includes KERNEL, USER, and GDI, but it can also include names of other modules, such as KEYBOARD and SOUND. (Offsets are from the beginning of the record.)

Offset	Length (bytes)	Contents
00H	1	Number of bytes in name string
01H	n	ASCII name string, not null-terminated

These strings do not necessarily start at the beginning of the imported names table; the names are referenced by offsets specified in the module reference table.

The entry table

This table contains one member for every entry point in the program or library module. (Every public FAR function or procedure in a module is an entry point.) The members in the entry table have ordinal numbers beginning at 1. These ordinal numbers are referenced by the resident names table and the nonresident names table.

LINK versions 4.0 and later bundle the members of the entry table. Each bundle begins with the following information. (Offsets are from the beginning of the bundle.)

Offset	Length (bytes)	Contents
00H	1	Number of entry points in bundle (0 if end of table)
01H	1	Segment number of entry points if entry points in bundle are in single fixed segment; 0FFH if entry points in bundle are in movable segments

For a bundle containing entry points in fixed segments, each entry point requires 3 bytes. (Offsets are from the beginning of the entry description.)

Offset	Length (bytes)	Contents
00H	1	Entry-point flag byte (*see* below)
01H	2	Offset of entry point in segment

For bundles containing entry points in movable segments, each entry point requires 6 bytes. (Offsets are from the beginning of the entry description.)

Offset	Length (bytes)	Contents
00H	1	Entry-point flag byte (*see* below)
01H	2	Interrupt 3FH instruction: CDH 3FH
03H	1	Segment number of entry point
04H	2	Offset of entry-point segment

The entry-point flag byte is defined as shown in Figure K-4.

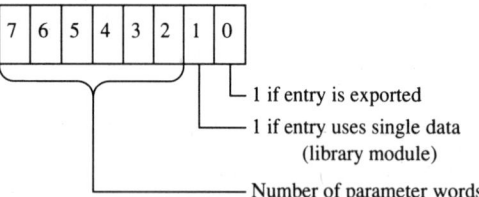

Figure K-4. The entry-point flag.

The nonresident names table

This table contains a list of ASCII strings. The first string is the module description from the module definition file. The other strings are the names of all exported functions listed in the module definition file that have ordinal numbers associated with them. (Exported functions without ordinal numbers in the module definition file are listed in the resident names table.)

Each string is prefaced by a single byte indicating the number of characters in the string and is followed by a word (2 bytes) referencing a member of the entry table, beginning at 1. The word that follows the module description string is 0. (Offsets are from the beginning of the table.)

Offset	Length (bytes)	Contents
00H	1	Number of bytes in string (0 if end of table)
01H	n	ASCII string, not null-terminated
$n+1$	2	Index into entry table

The code and data segment

Following the various tables in the New Executable file header are the code and data segments of the program or library module.

If the code or data segment is flagged in the segment flag word as ITERATED, the segment is organized as follows. (Offsets are from the beginning of the segment.)

Offset	Length (bytes)	Contents
00H	2	Number of iterations of data
02H	2	Number of bytes of data
04H	n	Data

Otherwise, the size of the segment data is given by the length of the segment field in the segment table.

If the segment is flagged in the segment flag word as containing relocation information, then the relocation table begins immediately after the segment data. Windows uses the relocation table to resolve references within the segments to functions in other segments in the same module and to imported functions in other modules. (Offsets are from the beginning of the table.)

Offset	Length (bytes)	Contents
00H	2	Number of relocation items

Each relocation item requires 8 bytes. (Offsets are from the beginning of the relocation item.)

Offset	Length (bytes)	Contents
00H	1	Type of address to insert in segment: 01H Offset only 02H Segment only 03H Segment and offset

(more)

Offset	Length (bytes)	Contents
01H	1	Relocation type: 00H Internal reference 01H Imported ordinal 02H Imported name If bit 2 set, relocation type is additive (*see* below)
02H	2	Offset of relocation item within segment

The next 4 bytes depend on the relocation type. If the relocation type is an internal reference to a segment in the same module, these bytes are defined as follows. (Offsets are from the beginning of the relocation item.)

Offset	Length (bytes)	Contents
04H	1	Segment number for fixed segment; 0FFH for movable segment
05H	1	0
06H	2	If MOVABLE segment, ordinal number referenced in entry table; if FIXED segment, offset into segment

If the relocation type is an imported ordinal to another module, then these bytes are defined as follows. (Offsets are from the beginning of the relocation item.)

Offset	Length (bytes)	Contents
04H	2	Index into module reference table
06H	2	Function ordinal number

Finally, if the relocation type is an imported name of a function in another module, these bytes are defined as follows. (Offsets are from the beginning of the relocation item.)

Offset	Length (bytes)	Contents
04H	2	Index into module reference table
06H	2	Offset within imported names table to name of imported function

If the ADDITIVE flag of the relocation type is set, the address of the external function is added to the contents of the address in the target segment. If the ADDITIVE flag is not set, then the target contains an offset to another target within the same segment that requires the same relocation address. This defines a chain of target addresses that get the same address. The chain is terminated with a −1 entry.

Charles Petzold

Appendix L
Intel Hexadecimal Object File Format

The MCS-86 hexadecimal object file format provides a means of recording a program's binary (compiled or assembled) image in a text-only (printable) file format. This format makes it easy to transfer the program between computers over telephone lines without using special communications software. More important, it provides a ready means of transferring programs between computers and the various types of laboratory equipment typically used during the development of specialized programs.

The MCS-86 hexadecimal file format is a superset of Intel's older Intellec-8 hexadecimal object file format. Intel originally designed the Intellec-8 format for use with its 8-bit microprocessor line. The format rapidly gained acceptance among other microprocessor manufacturers. When Intel subsequently developed the MCS-86 microprocessor family, it also expanded the Intellec-8 hexadecimal file format into the MCS-86 hexadecimal file format to support the new microprocessors' extended addressing capabilities.

The MCS-86 hexadecimal object file format should not be confused with the object (.OBJ) files produced by the Microsoft Macro Assembler (MASM) and language compilers. The MCS-86 hexadecimal object file format is referred to as an *absolute* object file format because the code contained within the file has been completely linked and all address references have already been resolved. The object modules produced by the assembler and compilers (.OBJ files) are referred to as *relocatable* object modules because they contain the information necessary to relocate the enclosed code to any memory address for execution.

The MCS-86 hexadecimal object file format consists of four types of ASCII text records:

- Data record
- End-of-file record
- Extended-address record
- Start-address record

All records begin with a *record mark* consisting of a single ASCII colon character (:). The remainder of the record consists of a variable number of ASCII hexadecimal digit pairs (00–0FH), each representing an unsigned byte value (0–255 decimal). The first digit represents the value of the high nibble (bits 7–4) of the byte; the second digit represents the value of the low nibble (bits 3–0). These digit pairs begin immediately after the record mark and continue through the end of the record without any separation between them.

All records have the following fields, in the order listed:

- A fixed-length *record length* field
- A fixed-length *address* field (optional)
- A fixed-length *record type* field

- A fixed-length or variable-length *data* field
- A fixed-length *checksum* field

The fixed-length *record length* field consists of the first digit pair following the record mark and gives the length of the record-type-dependent variable-length data field.

The optional fixed-length *address* field consists of the second and third digit pairs following the record mark. The first digit pair of this field (second digit pair of the record) gives the high byte of a word address value (bits 15–8); the second digit pair (third digit pair of the record) gives the low byte of a word address value (bits 7–0). If the record type does not use the address field, then the field contains a fill-in value consisting of the four-character ASCII string *0000.*

The fixed-length *record type* field consists of the fourth digit pair of the record and indicates the type of data the record contains. The valid record-type values are

Value	Type
00H	Data record
01H	End-of-file record
02H	Extended-address record
03H	Start-address record

All records end with a fixed-length *checksum* field. This field contains the negative of the sum of all byte values represented by the digit pairs in the record, from the record length field through the last digit pair before the checksum field. The checksum field is used to determine whether an error occurred during the transmission of a record between computers or other pieces of equipment.

(The receiving equipment can easily perform this error checking as each record is received. It only has to add all digit pairs of the record, including the checksum, and ignore any overflow beyond 8 bits. The total should be 00H, because the checksum is the negative of the summation of all preceding digit pairs.)

The variable-length *data* field of the data record contains the actual data bytes of the program's image. In data records, the record length field indicates the number of bytes, each represented as a digit pair, contained within the data field; the address field gives the offset within the current memory segment at which to load the record's data into memory.

The fixed-length data field of the extended-address record establishes the memory segment into which subsequent data records are to be loaded. In extended-address records, the data field consists of a single field identical to the address field. The address field of an extended-address record always contains the ASCII 0000 filler, and the record length field always contains ASCII 02, which reflects the fixed length of the data field. The memory segment (also known as the memory frame) established by an extended-address record remains in effect until the next extended-address record is encountered; thus, all data records following the most recent extended-address record are loaded in the established memory segment. *See* PROGRAMMING IN MS-DOS: PROGRAMMING TOOLS: The Microsoft Object Linker.

Figures L-1 and L-2 show how the extended-address record and the data record combine to load the byte values 0FDH, 0B9H, 75H, 31H, 0ECH, 0A8H, 64H, and 20H into memory starting at address 9A6EH:429FH.

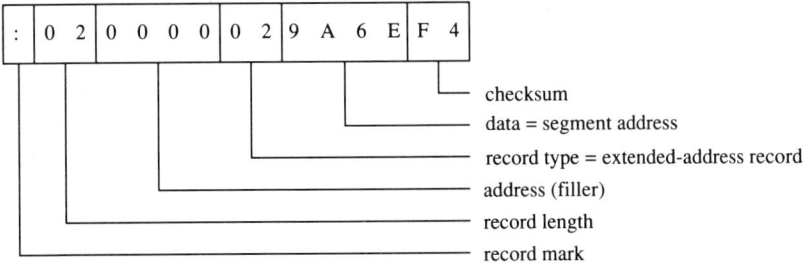

Figure L-1. The extended-address record.

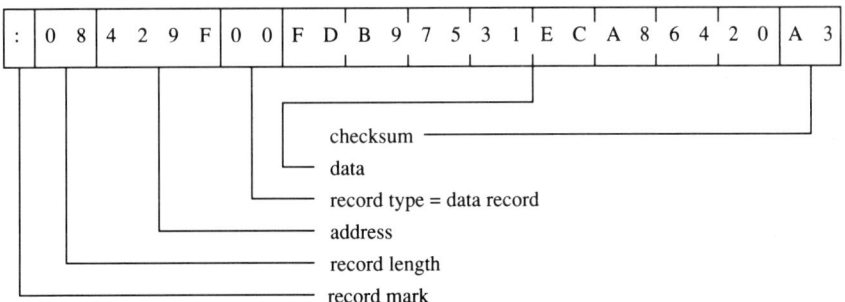

Figure L-2. The data record.

The start-address record provides the CS and IP register values at which program execution begins. This record contains the register values within the fixed-length data field. The address field of a start-address record always contains the ASCII 0000 filler, and the record length field always contains ASCII 04, which reflects the fixed length of the data field. The example in Figure L-3 shows a CS:IP setting (program entry point) of F924H:E69AH.

The end-of-file record marks the end of an MCS-86 hexadecimal file. Under the MCS-86 hexadecimal file definition, the end-of-file record does not contain any variable-value fields; the record always appears as shown in Figure L-4.

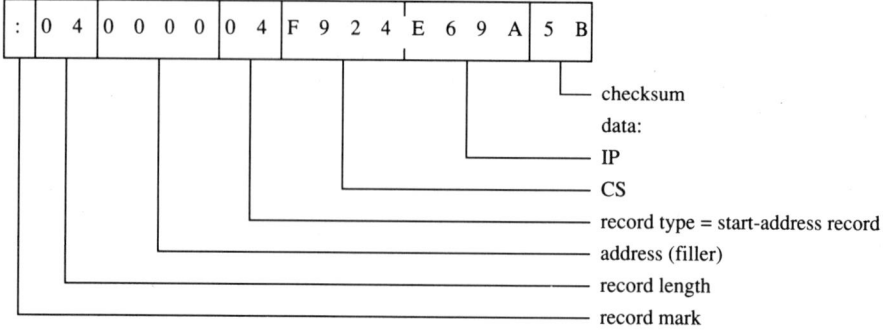

Figure L-3. The start-address record.

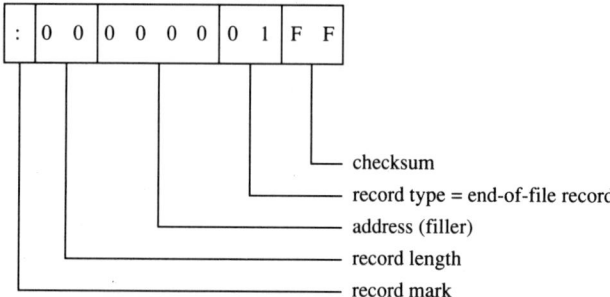

Figure L-4. The end-of-file record.

Traditionally, development equipment and programs that accept the MCS-86 hexadecimal file format as input also recognize an alternate end-of-file record. The alternate record consists of a data record that contains no data; therefore, its record length field contains 00. Figure L-5 shows this alternate end-of-file record.

DEBUG is the only program supplied with MS-DOS that accepts the MCS-86 hexadecimal file format. Even then, DEBUG only loads hexadecimal files into memory; it does not save a program back to disk as a hexadecimal file. (The same applies for SYMDEB and for CodeView.)

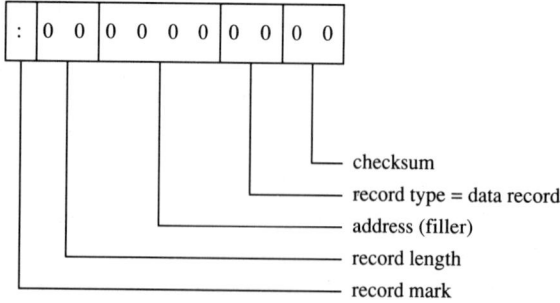

Figure L-5. The alternate end-of-file record.

While loading a hexadecimal file, DEBUG actually processes only data records and end-of-file records; it ignores both start-address records and any extended-address records. Thus, DEBUG actually supports only the older Intellec-8 hexadecimal file format but will not reject the file if it also contains the newer MCS-86 hexadecimal file records.

DEBUG does not support MCS-86 records because it must operate within the MS-DOS environment and MS-DOS does not support the loading of programs into absolute memory locations — a restriction imposed by most general-purpose operating systems. Because DEBUG cannot load the data records into the absolute segments indicated by the extended-address records, it simply loads the program image contained within the data records in a manner similar to that in which a .COM program is loaded. *See* PROGRAMMING IN THE MS-DOS ENVIRONMENT: PROGRAMMING FOR MS-DOS: Structure of an Application Program. DEBUG uses the address field for the data records as the offset into the .COM program segment at which to load the contents of the records.

The sample QuickBASIC (versions 3.0 and later) program shown in Figure L-6 converts binary files, including .COM files, into limited MCS-86 hexadecimal files that DEBUG can load. Examining this program can provide additional understanding of the structure of Intel hexadecimal files.

```
'Binary-to-Hex file conversion utility.
'Requires Microsoft QuickBASIC version 3.0 or later.

DEFINT A-Z                                  ' All variables are integers
                                            ' unless otherwise declared.
CONST FALSE = 0                             ' Value of logical FALSE.
CONST TRUE = NOT FALSE                      ' Value of logical TRUE.

DEF FNHXB$(X) = RIGHT$(HEX$(&H100 + X), 2)  ' Return 2-digit hex value for X.
DEF FNHXW$(X!) = RIGHT$("000" + HEX$(X!), 4) ' Return 4-digit hex value for X!.
DEF FNMOD(X, Y) = X! - INT(X!/Y) * Y        ' X! MOD Y (the MOD operation is
                                            ' only for integers).
CONST SRCCNL = 1                            ' Source (.BIN) file channel.
CONST TGTCNL = 2                            ' Target (.HEX) file channel.

LINE INPUT "Enter full name of source .BIN file      : ";SRCFIL$
OPEN SRCFIL$ FOR INPUT AS SRCCNL            ' Test for source (.BIN) file.
SRCSIZ! = LOF(SRCCNL)                       ' Save file's size.
CLOSE SRCCNL
IF (SRCSIZ! > 65536) THEN                   ' Reject if file exceeds 64 KB.
    PRINT "Cannot convert file larger than 64 KB."
    END
END IF

LINE INPUT "Enter full name of target .HEX file      : ";TGTFIL$
OPEN TGTFIL$ FOR OUTPUT AS TGTCNL           ' Test target (.HEX) filename.
CLOSE TGTCNL
```

Figure L-6. QuickBASIC binary-to-hexadecimal file conversion utility.   *(more)*

```
    DO
        LINE INPUT "Enter starting address of .BIN file in HEX :  ";L$
        ADRBGN! = VAL("&H" + L$)                    ' Convert ASCII HEX address value
                                                    ' to binary value.
        IF (ADRBGN! < 0) THEN                       ' HEX values 8000-FFFFH convert
          ADRBGN! = 65536 + ADRBGN!                 ' to negative values.
        END IF
        ADREND! = ADRBGN! + SRCSIZ! - 1             ' Calculate resulting end address.
        IF (ADREND! > 65535) THEN                   ' Reject if address exceeds FFFFH.
          PRINT "Entered start address causes end address to exceed FFFFH."
        END IF
    LOOP UNTIL (ADRFLD! >= 0) AND (ADRFLD! <= 65535) AND (ADREND! <= 65535)

    DO
        LINE INPUT "Enter byte count for each record in HEX    :  ";L$
        SRCRLN = VAL("&H" + L$)                     ' Convert ASCII HEX max record
                                                    ' length value to binary value.
        IF (SRCRLN < 0) THEN                        ' HEX values 8000-FFFFH convert
          SRCRLN = 65536 + SRCRLN                   ' to negative values.
        END IF
    LOOP UNTIL (SRCRLN > 0) AND (SRCRLN < 256)      ' Ask again if not 1-255.

    OPEN SRCFIL$ AS SRCCNL LEN = SRCRLN             ' Reopen source for block I/O.
    FIELD#SRCCNL,SRCRLN AS SRCBLK$
    OPEN TGTFIL$ FOR OUTPUT AS TGTCNL               ' Reopen target for text output.
    SRCREC = 0                                      ' Starting source block # minus 1.

    FOR ADRFLD! = ADRBGN! TO ADREND! STEP SRCRLN    ' Convert one block per loop.
        SRCREC = SRCREC + 1                         ' Next source block.
        GET SRCCNL,SRCREC                           ' Read the source block.
       'IF (ADRFLD! + SRCRLN > ADREND!) THEN        ' If last block less than full
          BLK$=LEFT$(SRCBLK$,ADREND!-ADRFLD!+1)     ' size:  trim it.
        ELSE                                        ' Else:
            BLK$ = SRCBLK$                          ' Use full block.
        END IF

        PRINT#TGTCNL, ":";                          ' Write record mark.

        PRINT#TGTCNL, FNHXB$(LEN(BLK$));            ' Write data field size.
        CHKSUM = LEN(BLK$)                          ' Initialize checksum accumulate
                                                    ' with first value.
        PRINT#TGTCNL,FNHXW$(ADRFLD!);               ' Write record's load address.

    ' The following "AND &HFF" operations limit CHKSUM to a byte value.
        CHKSUM = CHKSUM + INT(ADRFLD!/256) AND &HFF    ' Add hi byte of adrs to csum.
        CHKSUM = CHKSUM + FNMOD(ADRFLD!,256) AND &HFF ' Add lo byte of adrs to csum.

        PRINT#TGTCNL,FNHXB$(0);                     ' Write record type.
```

Figure L-6. Continued.   *(more)*

```
' Don't bother to add record type byte to checksum since it's 0.
     FOR IDX = 1 TO LEN(BLK$)                    ' Write all bytes.
       PRINT#TGTCNL,FNHXB$(ASC(MID$(BLK$,IDX,1)));       ' Write next byte.
       CHKSUM = CHKSUM + ASC(MID$(BLK$,IDX,1)) AND &HFF ' Incl byte in csum.
     NEXT IDX

     CHKSUM = 0 - CHKSUM AND &HFF                 ' Negate checksum then limit
                                                  ' to byte value.
     PRINT #TGTCNL,FNHXB$(CHKSUM)                 ' End record with checksum.

NEXT ADRFLD!

PRINT#TGTCNL, ":00000001FF"                       ' Write end-of-file record.

CLOSE TGTCNL                                      ' Close target file.
CLOSE SRCCNL                                      ' Close source file.

END
```

Figure L-6. Continued.

Keith Burgoyne

Appendix M
8086/8088 Software Compatibility Issues

In general, the Intel 80286 microprocessor running in real mode executes 8086/8088 software correctly. The following is a list of the actions to take to compensate for the minor differences between the 8086/8088 and real mode of the 80286.

- *Do not rely on 8086/8088 instruction clock counts.* The 80286 takes fewer clocks for most instructions than the 8086/8088. The areas to look into are delays between I/O operations and assumed delays when the 8086/8088 is operating in parallel with an 8087 coprocessor.
- *Note that divide exceptions point to the DIV instruction.* Any interrupt on the 80286 always leaves the saved CS:IP value pointing to the instruction that failed. On the 8086/8088, the CS:IP value saved for a divide exception points to the next instruction.
- *Set up numeric exception handlers to allow prefixes.* The saved CS:IP value in the NPX environment save area points to any ESC instruction prefixes. On 8086/8088 systems, this value points only to the ESC instruction.
- *Do not attempt undefined 8086/8088 operations.* 8086/8088 instructions like POP CS or MOV CS,op either invoke exception 06H (Invalid Opcode) or perform a protection setup operation like LIDT on the 80286. Undefined bit encodings for bits 5–3 of the second byte of POP MEM or PUSH MEM invoke exception 13H on the 80286.
- *Do not rely on the value written by PUSH SP.* The 80286 pushes a different value on the stack for PUSH SP than does the 8086/8088. If the value pushed is important, replace PUSH SP instructions with the following instructions:

```
PUSH    BP
MOV     BP,SP
XCHG    BP,[BP]
```

This code functions like the 8086/8088 PUSH SP instruction on the 80286.
- *Do not shift or rotate by more than 31 bits.* The 80286 masks all SHIFT/ROTATE counts to the low 5 bits. This MOD 32 operation limits the count to a maximum of 31 bits. With this change, the longest SHIFT/ROTATE instruction is 39 clocks. Without this change, the longest SHIFT/ROTATE instruction is 264 clocks, which delays interrupt response until the instruction completes execution.
- *Do not duplicate prefixes.* The 80286 sets an instruction-length limit of 10 bytes. The only way to exceed this limit is to include the same prefix two or more times before an instruction. Exception 06H occurs if the instruction-length limit is violated. The 8086/8088 has no instruction-length limit.
- *Do not rely on odd 8086/8088 LOCK characteristics.* The LOCK prefix and its corresponding output signal should be used only to prevent other bus masters from interrupting a data movement operation. The 80286 always asserts LOCK during an XCHG instruction with memory (even if the LOCK prefix was not used). LOCK should be

used only with the XCHG, MOV, MOVS, INS, and OUTS instructions. The 80286 LOCK signal will *not* go active during an instruction prefetch.

- *Do not rely on IDIV exceptions for quotients of 80H or 8000H.* The 80286 can generate the largest negative number as a quotient for IDIV instructions. The 8086/8088 generates exception 00H (Divide by Zero) instead.
- *Do not rely on address space wraparound.*
- *Do not use I/O ports 0F8–0FFH.* These are reserved for controlling the 80287 and future microprocessor extensions.

Appendix N
An Object Module Dump Utility

The program OBJDUMP.C displays the contents of an object file as individual object records. It can be used to study the structure of object modules as well as to verify the output of a language translator. The program recognizes all of the object record types discussed in PROGRAMMING IN THE MS-DOS ENVIRONMENT: PROGRAMMING TOOLS: Object Modules.

OBJDUMP.C should be executed with the following syntax:

OBJDUMP *filename*

where *filename* is a complete filename specification. For example, to dump the contents of the object file MYPROG.OBJ, the user would type

```
C>OBJDUMP MYPROG.OBJ  <Enter>
```

The following is a typical object record as displayed by OBJDUMP:

```
Record 9:   96h LNAMES
96 002Eh 00 06 44 47 52 4F 55 50 05 5F 54 45 58 54 04 43    ..DGROUP._TEXT.C
         4F 44 45 05 5F 44 41 54 41 04 44 41 54 41 05 43    ODE._DATA.DATA.C
         4F 4E 53 54 04 5F 42 53 53 03 42 53 53 3F          ONST._BSS.BSS?
```

This sample LNAMES record defines a null name and eight names used in subsequent SEGDEF and GRPDEF records. The first 3 bytes of the record (the identifying byte and the 2-byte record length) are displayed to the left of the hexadecimal and ASCII listings of the contents of the record.

```
/*****************************************************************************
*                                                                           *
* OBJDUMP.C -- display contents of an object file                           *
*                                                                           *
*                                                                           *
*     Compile:  msc objdump;   (Microsoft C version 4.0 or later)           *
*     Link:     link objdump;                                               *
*     Execute:  objdump <filename>                                          *
*                                                                           *
*****************************************************************************/

#include      <fcntl.h>

#define       TRUE    1
#define       FALSE   0
```

(more)

```
main( argc, argv )
int       argc;
char      **argv;
{
        unsigned char       CurrentByte;
        int       ObjFileHandle;
        int       CurrentLineLength;                    /* length of output line */
        int       ObjRecordNumber = 0;
        int       ObjRecordLength;
        int       ObjRecordOffset = 0;   /* offset into current object record */
        char      ASCIIEquiv[17];
        char      FormatString[24];
        char      *ObjRecordName();
        char      *memset();


/* open the object file */

        ObjFileHandle = open( argv[1],O_BINARY );

        if( ObjFileHandle == -1 )
        {
          printf( "\nCan't open object file\n" );
          exit( 1 );
        }

/* process the object file character by character */

        while( read( ObjFileHandle, &CurrentByte, 1 ) )
        {
          switch( ObjRecordOffset ) /* action depends on offset into record */
          {
            case(0):                                 /* start of object record */
              printf( "\n\nRecord %d:  %02Xh %s",
                ++ObjRecordNumber, CurrentByte, ObjRecordName(CurrentByte) );
              printf( "\n%02X ", CurrentByte );
              ++ObjRecordOffset;
              break;

            case(1):                                 /* first byte of length field */
              ObjRecordLength = CurrentByte;
              ++ObjRecordOffset;
              break;

            case(2):                                 /* second byte of length field */
              ObjRecordLength += CurrentByte << 8; /* compute record length */
              printf( "%04Xh ", ObjRecordLength );          /* show length */
              CurrentLineLength = 0;
              memset( ASCIIEquiv, '\0' , 17 );               /* zero this string */
              ++ObjRecordOffset;
              break;
```

(more)

```
        default:                    /* remaining bytes in object record */
          printf( "%02X ", CurrentByte );                        /* hex */

          if( CurrentByte < 0x20 || CurrentByte > 0x7F )      /* ASCII */
            CurrentByte = '.';
          ASCIIEquiv[CurrentLineLength++] = CurrentByte;

          if( CurrentLineLength == 16 ||    /* if end of output line ... */
            ObjRecordOffset == ObjRecordLength+2 )
          {                                           /* ... display it */
            sprintf( FormatString, "%%%ds%%s\n          ",
              3*(16-CurrentLineLength)+2 );
            printf( FormatString, " ", ASCIIEquiv );
            memset( ASCIIEquiv, '\0', 17 );
            CurrentLineLength = 0;
          }

          if( ++ObjRecordOffset == ObjRecordLength+3 )   /* if done ... */
            ObjRecordOffset = 0;          /* ... process another record */
          break;
      }
    }

    if( CurrentLineLength )    /* display remainder of last output line */
      printf( "  %s", ASCIIEquiv );

    close( ObjFileHandle );

    printf( "\n%d object records\n", ObjRecordNumber );

    return( 0 );
}


char *ObjRecordName( n )                    /* return object record name */
int      n;                                      /* n = record type */
{
    int       i;

    static    struct
    {
      int       RecordNumber;
      char      *RecordName;
    }         RecordStruct[] =
              {
                0x80,"THEADR",
                0x88,"COMENT",
                0x8A,"MODEND",
                0x8C,"EXTDEF",
                0x8E,"TYPDEF",
                0x90,"PUBDEF",
```

(more)

```
                        0x94,"LINNUM",
                        0x96,"LNAMES",
                        0x98,"SEGDEF",
                        0x9A,"GRPDEF",
                        0x9C,"FIXUPP",
                        0xA0,"LEDATA",
                        0xA2,"LIDATA",
                        0xB0,"COMDEF",
                        0x00,"******"
                        };

    int     RecordTableSize = sizeof(RecordStruct)/sizeof(RecordStruct[0]);


    for( i=0; i<RecordTableSize-1; i++ )            /* scan table for name */
      if ( RecordStruct[i].RecordNumber == n )
        break;

    return( RecordStruct[i].RecordName );
}
```

Richard Wilton

Appendix O
IBM PC ROM BIOS Calls

To invoke an IBM PC BIOS routine, set register AH to the desired function and execute the software interrupt (INT) for the desired routine.

Graphics pixel coordinates and cursor row and column coordinates are always zero based.

Interrupt 10H: Video Services

Function 00H: Set Video Mode

To call:

AH	= 00H			
AL	= mode:			
	00H	16-shade gray text EGA: 64-color	40 by 25	B000:8000H
	01H	16/8-color text EGA: 64-color	40 by 25	B000:8000H
	02H	16-shade gray text EGA: 64-color	80 by 25	B000:8000H
	03H	16/8-color text EGA: 64-color	80 by 25	B000:8000H
	04H	4-color graphics	320 by 200	B000:8000H
	05H	4-shade gray graphics	320 by 200	B000:8000H
	06H	2-shade gray graphics	640 by 200	B000:8000H
	07H	monochrome text	80 by 25	B000:0000H
	08H	16-color graphics	160 by 200	B000:0000H
	09H	16-color graphics	320 by 200	B000:0000H
	0AH	4-color graphics	640 by 200	B000:0000H
	0BH	Reserved		
	0CH	Reserved		
	0DH	16-color graphics	320 by 200	A000:0000H
	0EH	16-color graphics	640 by 200	A000:0000H
	0FH	monochrome graphics	640 by 350	A000:0000H
	10H	16/64-color graphics	640 by 350	A000:0000H

Returns:

Nothing

Function 01H: Set Cursor Size and Shape

To call:

AH	= 01H
CH	= starting scan line
CL	= ending scan line

Note: CH < CL gives normal one-part cursor; CH > CL gives two-part cursor; CH = 20H gives no cursor.

Returns:

Nothing

Function 02H: Set Cursor Position

To call:

AH	= 02H
BH	= display page (0 in graphics)
DH	= row number
DL	= line number

Returns:

Nothing

Function 03H: Read Cursor Position, Size, and Shape

To call:

AH	= 03H
BH	= display page

Returns:

CH	= starting scan line
CL	= ending scan line
DH	= row number
DL	= column number

Function 04H: Read Light-Pen Position

To call:

AH	= 04H

Returns:

AH	= status:
	01H pen triggered
	00H not triggered
BX	= pixel column number
CH	= pixel line number
CX	= pixel line number for some EGA modes
DH	= character row number
DL	= character column number

Function 05H: Select Active Page

To call:

AH	= 05H
AL	= page number:
	00–07H 40-column text modes
	00–03H 80-column text modes
	varies EGA graphics modes

Note: Each page = 2 KB in 40-column text mode, 4 KB in 80-column text mode.

Returns:

Nothing

Function 06H: Scroll Window Up
Function 07H: Scroll Window Down

To call:

AH	= 06H scroll up
	= 07H scroll down
AL	= number of lines to scroll (00H blanks screen)
BH	= display attributes for blank lines
CH	= row number of upper left corner
CL	= column number of upper left corner
DH	= row number of lower right corner
DL	= column number of lower right corner

Returns:

Nothing

Function 08H: Read Character and Attribute at Cursor

To call:

AH	= 08H
BH	= display page (for text mode only)

Returns:

If text mode:

AH   = color attributes of character
AL   = ASCII character from current location

If graphics mode:

AL   = ASCII character (00H if unmatched)

Function 09H: Write Character and Attribute

To call:

AH   = 09H
AL   = ASCII character to write
BH   = display page
BL   = text attribute or graphics foreground color
CX   = number of times to write character (must be > 0)

Returns:

Nothing

Note: Cursor position unchanged.

Function 0AH: Write Character Only

To call:

AH   = 0AH
AL   = ASCII character to write
BH   = display page
BL   = graphics foreground color (unused in text modes)
CX   = number of times to write character (must be > 0)

Returns:

Nothing

Note: Cursor position unchanged.

Function 0BH: Select Color Palette

To call:

AH   = 0BH
BH   = palette color ID
BL   = color or palette value

Returns:

Nothing

Function 0CH: Write Pixel Dot

To call:

AH	= 0CH
AL	= color attribute of pixel
CX	= pixel column number
DX	= pixel raster line number

Returns:

Nothing

Function 0DH: Read Pixel Dot

To call:

AH	= 0DH
CX	= pixel column number (0-based)
DX	= pixel raster line number (0-based)

Returns:

AL	= pixel color attribute

Function 0EH: Write Character as TTY

To call:

AH	= 0EH
AL	= ASCII character
BH	= display page
BL	= foreground color of character (unused in text mode)

Returns:

Nothing

Note: Cursor position advanced; beep, backspace, linefeed, and carriage return active; all other characters displayed.

Function 0FH: Get Current Video Mode

To call:

AH	= 0FH

Returns:

AH	= characters per line (20, 40, or 80)
AL	= current video mode (*see* Interrupt 10H Function 00H)
BH	= active display page

Function 13H: Write Character String

To call:

AH	= 13H
AL	= subfunction number:

        00H   string shares attribute in BL, cursor unchanged
        01H   string shares attribute in BL, cursor advanced
        02H   each character has attribute, cursor unchanged
        03H   each character has attribute, cursor advanced

BH	= active display page
BL	= string attribute (for AL = 00H or 01H only)
CX	= length of character string
DH	= starting row number
DL	= starting column number
ES:BP	= address of string to be displayed

Note: For AL = 00H or 01H, string = (*char, char, char, ...*). For AL = 02H or 03H, string = (*char, attr, char, attr, ...*).

Returns:

Nothing

Note: For AL = 01H or 03H, cursor position set to location following last character output.

Interrupt 11H: Get Peripheral Equipment List

Returns:

AX	= equipment list code word (bit settings PPMURRRUFFVVUUCI):

     PP   number of printers installed
     M   1 if internal modem installed
     RRR   number of RS-232 ports installed
     U   unused
     FF   number of floppy-disk drives minus 1 (0 = one drive)
     VV   initial video mode:
            00 = reserved
            01 = 40-by-25 color
            10 = 80-by-25 color
            11 = 80-by-25 monochrome
     U   unused
     C   1 if math coprocessor installed
     I   1 if IPL (Initial Program Load) diskette installed

Interrupt 12H: Get Usable Memory Size (KB)

Returns:

AX   = available memory size in KB

Interrupt 13H: Disk Services

Function 00H: Reset Disk System

To call:

AH	= 00H
AL	= drive number:

        00–7FH   floppy disk
        80–FFH   fixed disk

Returns:

CF	= 0	no error
	1	error
AH	= error code (*see* Interrupt 13H Function 01H)	

Function 01H: Get Disk Status

To call:

AH   = 01H

Returns:

AH	= 00H	
AL	= disk status of previous disk operation:	
	00H	no error
	01H	invalid command
	02H	address mark not found
	03H	write attempt on write-protected disk (F)
	04H	sector not found
	05H	reset failed (H)
	06H	floppy disk removed (F)
	07H	bad parameter table (H)
	08H	DMA overflow (F)
	09H	DMA crossed 64 KB boundary
	0AH	bad sector flag (H)
	10H	uncorrectable CRC or ECC data error
	11H	ECC corrected data error (H)
	20H	controller failed

(more)

40H	seek failed	
80H	time out	
AAH	drive not ready (H)	
BBH	undefined error (H)	
CCH	write fault (H)	
E0H	status error (H)	

Note: H = fixed disk only, F = floppy disk only.

Function 02H: Read Disk Sectors
Function 03H: Write Disk Sectors
Function 04H: Verify Disk Sectors
Function 05H: Format Disk Tracks

To call:

AH	= 02H	read disk sectors
	03H	write disk sectors
	04H	verify disk sectors
	05H	format disk track
AL	= number of sectors	
CH	= cylinder number	
CL	= sector number (unused if AH = 05H)	
DH	= head number	
DL	= drive number	
ES:BX	= buffer address (unused if AH = 04H)	

Returns:

CF	= 0	no error
	1	error
AH	= error code (*see* Interrupt 13H Function 01H)	

If AH was 05H on call:

ES:BX	= 4-byte address field entries, 1 per sector:	
	byte 0	cylinder number
	byte 1	head number
	byte 2	sector number
	byte 3	sector-size code:
	00H	128 bytes per sector
	01H	256 bytes per sector
	02H	512 bytes per sector (standard)
	03H	1024 bytes per sector

Function 08H: Get Current Drive Parameters

To call:

AH	= 08H
DL	= drive number

Returns:

AX	= 00H
BH	= 00H
BL	= drive type
CH	= low-order 8 bits of 10-bit maximum number of cylinders
CL	= bits 7 and 6 high-order 2 bits of 10-bit maximum number of cylinders
	bits 5–0 maximum number of sectors/track
DH	= maximum head number
DL	= number of drives installed
ES:DI	= address of floppy-disk-drive parameter table

Function 09H: Initialize Hard-Disk Parameter Table

To call:

AH   = 09H

Returns:

Nothing

Function 0AH: Read Long

Reads 512-byte sector plus 4-byte ECC code.

To call:

See Interrupt 13H Function 02H.

Returns:

See Interrupt 13H Function 02H.

Function 0BH: Write Long

Writes 512-byte sector plus 4-byte ECC code.

To call:

See Interrupt 13H Function 03H.

Returns:

See Interrupt 13H Function 03H.

Function 0CH: Seek to Head

Positions head but does not transfer data.

To call:

See Interrupt 13H Functions 02H and 03H.

Returns:

See Interrupt 13H Functions 02H and 03H.

Function 0DH: Alternate Disk Reset

To call:

AH   = 0DH
DL   = drive number

Returns:

Nothing

Function 10H: Test for Drive Ready

To call:

AH   = 10H
DL   = drive number

Returns:

AH   = status

Function 11H: Recalibrate Drive

To call:

AH   = 11H
DL   = drive number

Returns:

AH   = status

Function 14H: Controller Diagnostic

To call:

AH   = 14H

Returns:

AH   = status

Function 15H: Get Disk Type

To call:

AH   = 15H
DL   = drive number

Returns:

AH   = drive type code:
                        00H   no drive present
                        01H   cannot sense when floppy disk is changed

(more)

            02H   can sense when floppy disk is changed
            03H   fixed disk

   If AH = 03H:

   CX:DX   = number of sectors

Function 16H: Check for Change of Floppy Disk Status

To call:

    AH   = 16H
    DL   = drive number to check

Returns:

    AH   = 00H   no change
                  06H   floppy-disk change

Function 17H: Set Disk Type

To call:

    AH   = 17H
    DL   = drive number
    AL   = floppy-disk type code

Returns:

    Nothing

Interrupt 14H: Serial Port Services

Function 00H: Initialize Port Parameters

To call:

    AH   = 00H
    AL   = serial port parameters (bit settings BBBPPSCC):
                  BBB   baud rate:
                         000   110 baud
                         001   150 baud
                         010   300 baud
                         011   600 baud
                         100   1200 baud
                         101   2400 baud
                         110   4800 baud
                         111   9600 baud

(more)

	PP	parity code:	
		00	none
		01	odd
		10	none
		11	even
	S	number of stop bits code:	
		0	one stop bit
		1	two stop bits
	CC	character size:	
		00	unused
		01	unused
		10	7-bit character size
		11	8-bit character size
	DX	= serial port number (0 = first port)	

Returns:

Nothing

Function 01H: Send One Character

To call:

AH	= 01H
AL	= character to send
DX	= serial port number (0 = first port)

Returns:

AH	= error status (*see* Interrupt 14H Function 03H):
	00H no error

Function 02H: Receive One Character

To call:

AH	= 02H
DX	= serial port number (0 = first port)

Returns:

AL	= character received
AH	= error status (*see* Interrupt 14H Function 03H):
	00H no error

Function 03H: Get Port Status

To call:

AH	= 03H
DX	= serial port number (0 = first port)

Returns:

AX   = serial port status:

8000H	time out
4000H	transfer shift register empty
2000H	transfer holding register empty
1000H	break detect
0800H	framing error
0400H	parity error
0200H	overrun error
0100H	data ready
0080H	received line signal detect
0040H	ring indicator
0020H	data set ready
0010H	clear to send
0008H	delta receive line signal detect
0004H	trailing edge ring detector
0002H	delta data set ready
0001H	delta clear to send

Note: Multiple conditions can be active simultaneously.

Interrupt 15H: Miscellaneous System Services

Function 00H: Turn On Cassette Motor
Function 01H: Turn Off Cassette Motor

To call:

AH	= 00H	turn on cassette motor
	01H	turn off cassette motor

Returns:

Nothing

Function 02H: Read Data from Cassette

To call:

AH	= 02H
CX	= number of bytes to read
ES:BX	= buffer address

Returns:

CF	= 0		no error
	1		error
AH	= error status (if needed):		
	01H		CRC error
	02H		bit signals scrambled
	03H		no data found
DX	= number of bytes read		
ES:BX	= location following last byte read		

Function 03H: Write Data to Cassette

To call:

AH	= 03H
CX	= number of bytes to write
ES:BX	= buffer address

Note: Blocking factor = 256 bytes/block.

Returns:

CX	= 00H
ES:BX	= location following last byte written

Interrupt 16H: Keyboard Services

Function 00H: Read Next Character

To call:

AH	= 00H

Returns:

If ASCII characters:

AH	= standard PC keyboard scan code
AL	= ASCII character

If extended ASCII codes:

AH	= extended ASCII code
AL	= 00H

Note: Does not return until character is read; removes character from keyboard buffer.

Function 01H: Report If Character Ready

To call:

AH	= 01H

Returns:

ZF	= 0	character ready
	1	character not ready
AH	= *see* Interrupt 16H Function 00H	
AL	= *see* Interrupt 16H Function 00H	

Note: Returns immediately; does not remove character from keyboard buffer.

Function 02H: Get Shift Status

To call:

AH	= 02H

Returns:

AL	= shift status:	
	01H	right shift active
	02H	left shift active
	04H	Ctrl active
	08H	Alt active
	10H	Scroll Lock active
	20H	Num Lock active
	40H	Caps Lock active
	80H	insert state active

Note: Multiple states can be active simultaneously.

Interrupt 17H: Printer Services

Function 00H: Send Byte to Printer

To call:

AH	= 00H
AL	= character to be printed
DX	= printer number

Returns:

AH	= status (*see* Interrupt 17H Function 02H)

Function 01H: Initialize Printer

To call:

    AH   = 01H
    DX   = printer number

Returns:

    AH   = status (*see* Interrupt 17H Function 02H)

Function 02H: Get Printer Status

To call:

    AH   = 02H
    DX   = printer number

Returns:

    AH   = status:

01H	time out
02H	unused
04H	unused
08H	I/O error
10H	printer selected
20H	out of paper
40H	printer acknowledgment
80H	printer not busy (bit off, 0, = busy)

Note: Multiple states can be active simultaneously.

Interrupt 18H: Transfer Control to ROM-BASIC

Interrupt 19H: Reboot Computer (Warm Start)

Interrupt 1AH: Get/Set Time/Date

Function 00H: Read Current Clock Count

To call:

    AH   = 00H

Returns:

AL	= midnight signal
CX	= high-order word of tick count
DX	= low-order word of tick count

Function 01H: Set Current Clock Count

To call:

AH	= 01H
CX	= high-order word of tick count
DX	= low-order word of tick count

Returns:

Nothing

Function 02H: Read Real-Time Clock

To call:

AH	= 02H

Returns:

CF	= 0	clock running
	1	clock stopped
CH	= hours in BCD	
CL	= minutes in BCD	
DH	= seconds in BCD	

Function 03H: Set Real-Time Clock

To call:

AH	= 03H	
CH	= hours in BCD	
CL	= minutes in BCD	
DH	= seconds in BCD	
DL	= 00H	standard time
	01H	daylight saving time

Returns:

Nothing

Function 04H: Read Date from Real-Time Clock

To call:

AH	= 04H

Returns:

CF	= 0	clock running
	1	clock stopped
CH	= century in BCD (19 or 20)	
CL	= year in BCD	
DH	= month in BCD	
DL	= day in BCD	

Function 05H: Set Date in Real-Time Clock

To call:

AH	= 05H
CH	= century in BCD (19 or 20)
CL	= year in BCD
DH	= month in BCD
DL	= day in BCD

Returns:

Nothing

Function 06H: Set Alarm

To call:

AH	= 06H
CH	= hours in BCD
CL	= minutes in BCD
DH	= seconds in BCD

Returns:

CF	= status:	
	0	operation successful
	1	alarm already set or clock stopped

Function 07H: Reset Alarm (Turn Alarm Off)

To call:

AH	= 07H

Returns:

Nothing

Indexes

Subject

Flush Buffer, Read Keyboard. *See* Interrupt 21H
Function 0CH
Flux reversal 86
Force Duplicate File Handle. *See* Interrupt 21H
Function 46H
FOR command (BATCH) 66, 753, 760–61
Foreground program 900
Format and Verify Track on Logical Drive. *See*
Interrupt 21H Function 44H
Subfunction 0DH
FORMAT command 44, 865–71
ASSIGN and 741
directory format 281–83
DISKCOPY and 822
FDISK and 858
JOIN and 877–78
Format Disk Tracks. *See* Interrupt 13H Function 05H
FORTRAN (language) 8, 14
FORTRAN Compiler, Microsoft
memory models using 137–40
utilities with 974, 977, 980, 987, 999
Free Memory Block. *See* Interrupt 21H Function 49H
Frequency modulation (FM) recording 86
Function calls. *See* System calls

G

Gates, Bill 8(fig.), 16(fig.)
in the development of early BASIC 3–8, 11
in the development of MS-DOS 14–15, 20
General Protection exception. *See* Interrupt 0DH
Generate Cross-Reference Listing (CREF) 967–70
Generic I/O Control for Block Devices. *See* Interrupt
21H Function 44H Subfunction 0DH
Generic I/O Control for Handles. *See* Interrupt 21H
Function 44H Subfunction 0CH
Get and Set Time. *See* Interrupt 1AH
Get Assign-List Entry. *See* Interrupt 21H Function
5FH Subfunction 02H
Get Current Country. *See* Interrupt 21H Function 38H
Get Current Directory. *See* Interrupt 21H
Function 47H
Get Current Disk. *See* Interrupt 21H Function 19H
Get Current Drive Parameters. *See* Interrupt 13H
Function 08H
Get Current Video Mode. *See* Interrupt 10H
Function 0FH
Get Date. *See* Interrupt 21H Function 2AH
Get Default Drive Data. *See* Interrupt 21H
Function 1BH
Get Device Data. *See* Interrupt 21H Function 44H
Subfunction 00H

Get Disk Free Space. *See* Interrupt 21H Function 36H
Get Disk Status. *See* Interrupt 13H Function 01H
Get Disk Type. *See* Interrupt 13H Function 15H
Get Drive Data. *See* Interrupt 21H Function 1CH
Get DTA Address. *See* Interrupt 21H Function 2FH
Get Extended Country Information. *See* Interrupt
21H Function 65H
Get Extended Error Information. *See* Interrupt 21H
Function 59H
Get File Size. *See* Interrupt 21H Function 23H
Get Interrupt Vector. *See* Interrupt 21H Function 35H
Get Lead Byte Table. *See* Interrupt 21H Function 63H
Get Logical Drive Map. *See* Interrupt 21H Function
44H Subfunction 0EH
Get Machine Name. *See* Interrupt 21H Function 5EH
Subfunction 00H
Get MS-DOS Version Number. *See* Interrupt 21H
Function 30H
Get Peripheral Equipment List. *See* Interrupt 11H
Get Port Status. *See* Interrupt 14H Function 03H
Get Printer Setup. *See* Interrupt 21H Function 5EH
Subfunction 03H
Get Printer Status. *See* Interrupt 17H Function 02H
Get Program Segment Prefix Address. *See* Interrupt
21H Function 51H; Interrupt 21H
Function 62H
Get Return Code of the Child Process. *See* Interrupt
21H Function 4DH
Get/Set Allocation Strategy. *See* Interrupt 21H
Function 58H
Get/Set Control-C Check Flag. *See* Interrupt 21H
Function 33H
Get/Set Date/Time of File. *See* Interrupt 21H
Function 57H
Get/Set File Attributes. *See* Interrupt 21H
Function 43H
Get Shift Status. *See* Interrupt 16H Function 02H
Get Time. *See* Interrupt 21H Function 2CH
Get/Set Time/Date. *See* Interrupt 1AH
Get Usable Memory Size (KB). *See* Interrupt 12H
Get Verify Flag. *See* Interrupt 21H Function 54H
Gilbert, Paul 5–6
Global descriptor table (GDT) 317
Go
DEBUG G 584–85, 1033–34
SYMDEB G 1107–8
GOTO command (BATCH) 67, 753, 762–63
GRAFTABL command 872–73
MS-DOS version 3.3 1445
Graphics
loading character set 872–73
loading screen-dump program 874–76
screen-display attributes 734
Graphics Character Table. *See* Interrupt 1FH

N

O

OBJDUMP.C program 1509–12
Object files 701–2
    hexadecimal files format 1499–1505
Object Linker (LINK) 701–21, 757, 981, 993–98, 1004
    building a .EXE file header 712(table)
    combine parameters 127–28
    converting .EXE files produced by, with
        EXE2BIN 971–73
    creating .EXE files 620–21
    creating map files with 1004
    description of 988–92
    environmental variables in 931
    functions of 703
    LINK intervals 709–12
    messages 993–98
    object files, object libraries, and LIB 701–2
    object module order 703–6
    operating in .EXE program 111, 113
    organizing memory with 713–21
    return codes 992–93
    segment order/combinations 707–9
Object module(s) 643–700
    contents of 645–46
    dump utility 1509–12
    linking (*see* Object Linker)
    object record formats 655–56
    object records listed 657–700
    order of 703–6
    structure of 650–55
      object record order 651
      references between records 654–55
    terminology 646–49
    translation of assembly programs into
        relocatable (*see* Microsoft Macro
        Assembler)
    types of 650, 651(fig.)
    typical 651–54
    use of 643–44
Object module library file 701–2
    creating/modifying 980–86
Object records
    formats 655–56
    listed 657–700
    order 651
    references between 654–55
    types 650, 651(fig.)
Obtain Size of Extended Memory. *See* Interrupt 15H
    Function 88H
OFFSET operator (MASM), using on labels in
    grouped segments 131–32

Open File with FCB. *See* Interrupt 21H Function 0FH
Open File with Handle. *See* Interrupt 21H
    Function 3DH
Open-loop servomechanism 89
Open Symbol Map (SYMDEB XO) 1140
Operating system
    compatibility issues, MS-DOS and MS OS/2
        492–97
      error codes 495
      filenames 492–93
      MS-DOS function calls 493–94
      multitasking concerns 496–97
      seeks 495
    in conventional memory 298
    three types of 51(table), 52
    transfer 940
Operating-system loader 52, 72
Options menu (CodeView) 1161
O'Rear, Bob 8(fig.), 15–19
OS/2 operating system. *See* MS OS/2 operating
    system
Output to Port
    DEBUG O 1042
    SYMDEB O 1118
Overflow Trap exception. *See* Interrupt 04H
OVERLAY.ASM program 342
Overlays, program 122–23
    EXEC function and 321, 322–23, 335–43
      example program 337–42
      loading and executing 336–37
      making memory available 335–36
      preparing parameters 336–37
    LINK memory organization using 715–18

P

PAGE alignment 126–27
Page Fault exception. *See* Interrupt 0EH
Panners, Nancy 34
PARA alignment 126
Parallel port, input/output 163
PARENT.ASM program 330–34
Parent program, use of EXEC by 321
    sample program 330–36
Parity parameters 892
Parse Filename. *See* Interrupt 21H Function 29H
Partition(s)
    block device 90–92, 858
    extended, in MS-DOS version 3.3 1458
Partition table 91, 92
Pascal (language) 14

X

Z

Commands and System Calls

This index lists only primary command and system call entries. Please use the Subject Index for related entries.

SYMBOLS

@ (BATCH) 1434

A

ANSI.SYS 731–38
APPEND 739–40, 1436–37
ASSIGN 741–42
ATTRIB 743–44, 1437
AUTOEXEC.BAT (BATCH) 755–57

B

BACKUP 745–51, 1437
BATCH 752–69, 1434–35
BREAK 770–71
BREAK (CONFIG.SYS) 790
BUFFERS (CONFIG.SYS) 791–92

C

CALL (BATCH) 1434–35
CD 772–73
CHCP 1440
CHDIR 772–73
CHKDSK 774–80
CLS 781
CodeView utility 1157–73
COMMAND 782–84
COMP 785–87, 1435
CONFIG.SYS 788–805
COPY 806–9
COUNTRY (CONFIG.SYS) 793–94, 1442–43
CREF utility 967–70
CTTY 810

D

DATE 811–12
DEBUG, general 1020–23
DEBUG utility 1020–53
    A command 1024–25
    C command 1026
    D command 1027–28
    E command 1029–30
    F command 1031–32
    G command 1033–34
    H command 1035
    I command 1036
    L command 1037–38
    M command 1039
    N command 1040–41
    O command 1042
    P command 1043
    Q command 1044
    R command 1045–47
    S command 1048–49
    T command 1050
    U command 1051
    W command 1052–53
DELETE 813–14
DEVICE (CONFIG.SYS) 795–96, 1443–45
DIR 815–17
DISKCOMP 818–21
DISKCOPY 822–25
DRIVER.SYS 826–28
DRIVPARM (CONFIG.SYS) 797–98

E

ECHO (BATCH) 758–59
EDLIN, general 829–31
EDLIN line editor 829–52
    A command 834
    C command 835–36
    D command 837–38
    E command 839

J, K, L

M

Book Design by The NBBJ Group, Seattle, Washington

Cover Design by Greg Hickman

Principal Typography by Carol L. Luke

The manuscript for this book was prepared and submitted to Microsoft Press in electronic form. Text files were processed and formatted using Microsoft Word.

Text composition by Microsoft Press in Garamond with display in Garamond Bold using the Magna composition system and the Linotronic 300 laser imagesetter.

ISBN 1-55615-049-0

90000

9 781556 150494

Special Companion Disk Offer

In addition to the comprehensive technical information presented throughout *The MS-DOS Encyclopedia*, you'll find a wealth of programming examples, handy code fragments, and complete utilities that you'll turn to again and again — literally thousands of lines of code written to make your MS-DOS programming more efficient and more reliable. Included on the companion disks are:

- a complete serial-communications program ▪ two working TSR utilities ▪ examples for each of the more than 100 system function calls ▪ instructive debugging exercises ▪ installable device drivers ▪ two complete skeleton filters ▪ replacement interrupt handlers ▪ hundreds of working code fragments ▪ a .OBJ Module Format Utility ▪ and much, much more.

Save time, avoid those inevitable typing errors, and start using the code immediately. The disks are available in 5.25" or 3.5" format. To order, fill out the postpaid order card below. If the order card has already been used, refer to the ordering instructions on page xvi.

ORDER CARD

YES... please send me *The MS-DOS Encyclopedia* Companion Disks indicated below:

_____ set(s) of 5.25" disks at $49.95 per set . . . . $_____

_____ set(s) of 3.5" disks at $49.95 per set . . . . $_____

Postage and Handling Charges. $2.50 per set for domestic postage and handling;
$5.00 per set for international postage and handling . . . . $_____

TOTAL (U.S. funds only) $_____

Name_____
                                            Please Print

Address_____
(Please no p.o. boxes)

_____ Daytime Phone #: (_____)_____

City_____ State_____ ZIP_____

Payment: ☐ Check/Money Order ☐ VISA ☐ MasterCard ☐ American Express
                                                (13 or 16 numbers)   (16 Numbers)   (15 numbers)

Credit Card No.   [ ][ ][ ][ ][ ][ ][ ][ ][ ][ ][ ][ ][ ][ ][ ][ ] Exp. Date_____

Signature_____
                              Please allow 4 weeks for delivery, all orders shipped UPS

☐ Please send me information on receiving updates to *The MS-DOS Encyclopedia.*

Updates to The MS-DOS Encyclopedia

Periodically, the staff of *The MS-DOS Encyclopedia* will publish updates containing clarifications or corrections to the information presented in this current edition. If you would like information about receiving these updates, please check the appropriate box on the other side of this card when ordering your companion disks, or send your name and address to: MS-DOS Encyclopedia Update Information, c/o Microsoft Press, 16011 NE 36th Way, Box 97017, Redmond, WA 98073-9717.

Student's
Manual of

Student's
Manual of Auditing

The Guide to UK Auditing Practice

SIXTH EDITION

Executive Editors
Diane Walters and John Dunn

THOMSON
TM
LEARNING

Australia Canada Mexico Singapore Spain United Kingdom United States

Student's Manual of Auditing: 6th Edition

Copyright © 2000 Gee

The Thomson Learning logo is a registered trademark used herein under licence.

For more information, contact Thomson Learning, Berkshire House, 168–173 High Holborn, London, WC1V 7AA or visit us on the World Wide Web at: http://www.thomsonlearning.co.uk

British Library Cataloguing-in-Publication Data

A catalogue record for this book is available from the British Library

ISBN 1-86152-496-X

First published 2001 by Thomson Learning. The *Student's Manual of Accounting* is the student's edition of the loose-leaf *Manual of Auditing*, published by Gee Publishing Ltd.

Typeset by Multiplex Techniques Ltd, Orpington, Kent

Printed in Great Britain TJ International, Padstow, Cornwall

Dedicated to Gerard and Flora Cassels.

Contents

Contents

Introduction

    Introduction to the Manual of Auditing

    Terminology

    Statements of Auditing Standards

Contributors

How to Use this Book

Introduction

Introduction to the Manual of Auditing

Objectives, scope and contents
UK Statements of Auditing Standards
International Standards on Auditing
Ethical guidance
Statute and case law
Audits of small businesses
Efficiency
Client service
Terminology
Audit stationery

Terminology

Introduction
The audit firm
The audit team
The client
Computers

Statements of Auditing Standards

Introduction
Scope of Statements of Auditing Standards
Auditing Standards
Other guidance for auditors

Introduction to the Manual of Auditing

Objectives, scope and contents

This Manual is intended primarily for use on audits of the financial statements of limited companies under the Companies Act 1985. However, its use will be appropriate in all circumstances where audits are performed in accordance with Auditing Standards.

The Manual comprises the following chapters:

Chapter 1 – The audit approach

Chapter 2 – Fundamental concepts

Chapter 3 – Before the audit

Chapter 4 – Planning the audit

Chapter 5 – Controlling the audit

Chapter 6 – Recording audit work

Chapter 7 – Involvement of others in the audit

Chapter 8 – Systems and controls

Chapter 9 – Detailed testing

Chapter 10 – Audit completion

Chapter 11 – Group audits

Chapter 12 – Audit reporting to management

Chapter 13 – Audit reporting to members

Chapter 14 – Cessation as auditor

After setting the scene and covering the background to auditing in the first two chapters, the Manual follows the different phases of the audit in the order in which they will normally be carried out.

This Manual does not contain guidance on accounting matters, except where it is specifically relevant to the auditor's duties. An understanding of financial accounting and reporting is assumed. Guidance on accounting matters is contained in separate publications:

- PricewaterhouseCoopers, *Manual of Accounting*

  (published by GEE Publishing)

- Statements of Standard Accounting Practice (SSAPs)

  (published by ICAEW, ICAS, ICAI, ACCA, CIMA, and CIPFA. These are gradually being withdrawn and replaced by FRSs)

• Financial Reporting Standards (FRSs)

(published by the Accounting Standards Board (ASB))

UK Statements of Auditing Standards

The Auditing Practices Board (APB) was established in 1991 by the Consultative Committee of Accountancy Bodies to advance standards of auditing and associated review activities in the United Kingdom and Republic of Ireland and to provide a framework of practice for the exercise of the auditor's role. The pronouncements of the Auditing Practices Board fall into three principal categories: Statements of Auditing Standards (SASs), Practice Notes and Bulletins. SASs contain basic principles and essential procedures with which auditors are required to comply in the conduct of any audit. Practice Notes are indicative of good practice, even though they may be developed without the full process of consultation and exposure used for SASs and hence are persuasive rather than prescriptive and have a lower level of authority than SASs. Bulletins provide auditors with timely guidance on new or emerging issues.

The Statements of Auditing Standards **contain basic principles and essential procedures (Auditing Standards) with which auditors are required to comply in the conduct of any audit of financial statements**. The Standards are indicated in bold type and are numbered (e.g., SAS 100.1 is the first Auditing Standard in SAS 100 – Objective and General Principles Governing an Audit of Financial Statements). **SASs also include explanatory and other material which, rather than being prescriptive, is designed to assist auditors in interpreting and applying Auditing Standards.**

The SASs are quoted and referred to in this Manual where relevant, but are not reproduced at length. The procedures given in this Manual comply with SASs and also cover situations and items where there is, as yet, no published guidance.

International Standards on Auditing

International Standards on Auditing are issued by the International Federation of Accountants (IFAC). **The APB supports IFAC in its aim of improving the harmonisation of auditing practices throughout the world. SASs are formulated with due regard to international developments, in particular the International Standards on Auditing (ISAs) issued by IFAC. Each SAS explains its relationship to the ISA dealing with the same topic. In most cases, complying with the Auditing Standards in an SAS ensures compliance with the basic principles and essential procedures identified in the relevant ISA. Where the provisions of an SAS and an ISA differ, the Auditing Standards contained in the SAS should be complied with in respect of audits of entities reporting within the United Kingdom and the Republic of Ireland**. Several International Standards have no equivalent UK document at present. In all cases the guidance in this Manual is in accordance with best practice internationally, and will remain relevant as and when UK documents are published to incorporate the international equivalents.

Ethical guidance

The rules of conduct laid down for members of the Institutes of Chartered Accountants in England and Wales (ICAEW), in Scotland (ICAS) and in Ireland (ICAI) are principally contained in the *Guide to Professional Ethics*. In addition, reference should be made to Sections 1.3 and 1.4 of the Handbook, which contain general guidance for members in practice, and also the financial and accounting responsibilities of directors. It is not proposed to repeat in this Manual the guidance on professional ethics published by those bodies, but those which are of particular relevance to the auditor are discussed. The most important procedures in practice are those which relate to professional independence and to changes in a professional appointment. Other ethical considerations are referred to in the text when relevant, but reference should be made to the Guide for detailed guidance.

Statute and case law

This Manual is intended as a practical guide to carrying out audits and audit work, rather than a study textbook. The legal basis for the work has, therefore, been referred to where necessary, but has not been covered in detail.

Audits of small businesses

It is widely recognised that the conduct of audits of small, owner-managed businesses will necessarily be different from the conduct of audits of larger businesses with formal and well-developed systems of control on which the auditor can place reliance. However, the fundamental objectives of the audit remain the same, and most of the procedures in this Manual are equally applicable to audits of large and small businesses. Most of the differences in procedure are explained in the introduction to each chapter. Further guidance on the audit of small businesses can be found in the APB, Note 13, 'The Audit of Small Businesses'.

Efficiency

Auditing is a professional service, which must by law be carried out to a high technical standard. The guidance in this Manual is intended to encourage that high technical standard. However, the Manual also puts auditing in its commercial context, and includes guidance on how to deliver the required standard efficiently as one of a range of services offered by firms of accountants.

Client service

Auditors can offer positive benefits from audits going beyond statutory and professional obligations without compromising the standard of the work or incurring significant extra costs. The Manual, therefore, includes ways for the auditor to provide a constructive service to clients as part of the audit. These are summarised in **Section 1:5**, 'Adding value to the audit'.

Terminology

Different auditing firms use different expressions for forms, files and audit personnel. Where the terms in this Manual are initially unfamiliar, their meaning can usually be taken from the context and description. However, a brief glossary of some of the terms in common usage in the Manual is included in the next section, 'Terminology', to explain any which may be unfamiliar or capable of different interpretations. This section also describes the assumptions made in the Manual about the roles of the different members of the audit team, and how these can be related to teams made up of different combinations of staff.

Audit stationery

In an established practice standardised working papers contribute to the efficiency of audit work and audit review. Many of the procedures in this Manual are carried out in practice by completing such pre-prepared schedules. These should be amended to suit the circumstances of particular clients, e.g. by keeping the master programs in word processing files or other electronic format, and 'customising' them to increase efficiency. Examples of some working papers relevant to each section are given in the appendices to the sections; in most cases their contents, structure and purpose are described in the text so that the reader may design a comprehensive set of documents.

Terminology

Introduction

Different audit firms have different terms for their personnel employed on audits, for audit approach stationery and for procedures. This section explains the assumptions that have been made in the Manual about the 'standard' audit, so that readers from different firms can adapt the content to their own situation.

The audit firm

This Manual refers to departments of the firm separate from this main audit function, in particular:

- tax specialists;
- systems specialists; and
- those with specialist knowledge about particular industries.

Firms may be organised in different ways. Those with specialist knowledge in the above fields may be employed in the main audit function. In all cases references in this Manual to consultation with such a specialist highlight a special need to make sure that the auditor is competent to come to an appropriate conclusion, because there is a risk that this may not be the case. However the firm is organised, the engagement partner should ensure that there is adequate consultation with in-house specialists (whether or not in separate departments) when necessary to support the core engagement team.

The audit team

The 'standard', or core, audit team envisaged by this Manual comprises:

(a)   An engagement partner, who takes overall responsibility for the audit opinion. The engagement partner will ensure that there is an appropriate process for managing the detailed audit plan, within the team and with the client. The partner will be available to the team to discuss progress, help resolve issues and improve communication with the client and will be available to the client to discuss issues as they arise.

(b)   A field team leader, who takes responsibility for the administration of the audit, and will normally review the work of the audit team in detail, and will ensure that the summary for the partner includes all matters that could affect the audit opinion. The manager will sometimes perform audit work in the most sensitive areas.

(c)   An 'in-charge' accountant, who is responsible for the day-to-day conduct of the audit, supervision of junior staff and carrying out the more difficult audit work. This person will normally be a qualified senior.

(d)   Team members.

This Manual uses the expression 'the auditor' to mean any of the above. The member of staff who carries out specific procedures is a matter for each firm to decide, and also to be planned on individual audits. Where it is more appropriate for a specific member of staff to carry out a procedure, the Manual uses 'the engagement partner', 'the manager' or 'the in-charge', as appropriate.

The roles described above should be regarded as 'typical' rather than prescriptive. There can be flexibility when allocating roles and responsibilities within an engagement team, taking account of the engagement circumstances and the knowledge and experience of the individuals. In the audit of a smaller business the team leader may report directly to the partner, or there may be no junior staff. The audit of a very large business may require more than one partner, manager or team leader for different sections of the work. Where the responsibilities of each member of the audit team are to be combined or divided, the allocation should be a matter for audit planning.

The client

The term 'the client' is used throughout this Manual to indicate the company whose financial statements are being audited. The company itself should be distinguished from:

(a) the proprietors (usually shareholders);

(b) the board of directors, being the most senior level of management;

(c) management, including all line management in the business.

There may be an overlap between these three categories. In a small business they may be identical. However, their interests, and the responsibilities of the auditor to each, are different, and should be distinguished.

Computers

This Manual assumes that most clients will have accounting systems which are heavily reliant on computers. It does not draw any distinction between procedures required for manual and computerised systems and sets out an audit approach which will be appropriate for either.

Statements of Auditing Standards

Introduction

Registered auditors are expected to follow the basic principles and practices prescribed in the Statements of Auditing Standards (SASs) issued by the Auditing Practices Board. The full texts of the Standards and Guidelines are publicly available and are not repeated in this Manual.

Scope of Statements of Auditing Standards

The scope and authority of SASs are set out in the Explanatory Foreword, which states:

Auditors who do not comply with Auditing Standards when performing company or other audits in Great Britain make themselves liable to regulatory action by the Recognised Supervisory Body with whom they are registered which may include the withdrawal of registration and hence of eligibility to perform company audits.

Auditing Standards

The current SASs are:

Responsibility

100 Objective and General Principles Governing an Audit of Financial Statements

110 Fraud and Error

120 Consideration of Law and Regulations

130 The Going Concern Basis in Financial Statements

140 Engagement Letters

150 Subsequent Events

160 Other Information in Documents Containing Audited Financial Statements

Planning, controlling and recording

200 Planning

210 Knowledge of the Business

220 Materiality and the Audit

230 Working Papers

240 Quality Control for Audit Work

Accounting systems and internal control

300 Accounting and Internal Control Systems and Audit Risk Assessments

Evidence

400 Audit Evidence

410 Analytical Procedures

420 Audit of Accounting Estimates

430 Audit Sampling

440 Management Representations

450 Opening Balances and Comparatives

460 Related Parties

470 Overall Review of Financial Statements

480 Service Organisations

Using the work of others

500 Considering the Work of Internal Audit

510 The Relationship Between Principal Auditors and Other Auditors

520 Using the Work of an Expert

Reporting

Auditors' Reports on Financial Statements

601 Imposed Limitation of Audit Scope

610 Reports to Directors or Management

620 The Auditors' Right and Duty to Report to Regulators in the Financial Sector

Other guidance for auditors

Other guidance for auditors can be found in:

APB Practice Notes

1. Investment Businesses

5. The Auditors' Right and Duty to Report to the SIB and Other Regulators of Investment Business

7. The Auditors' Right and Duty to Report to the Friendly Societies Commission

8. Reports by Auditors Under Company Legislation in the United Kingdom.

9. Reports by Auditors Under Company Legislation in the Republic of Ireland

10. Audit of Central Government Financial Statements in the United Kingdom

11. The Audit of Charities

APB Bulletins

Contributors

Diane Walters qualified as a chartered accountant with Thomson McLintock (now KPMG) and practised as a financial controller in industry before moving to Heriot-Watt University in 1989 where she lectured in auditing and financial accounting. Her research interests centred on accounting for the environment.

Ms Walters currently runs her own training and consultancy business, specialising in accountancy education using her extensive experience of training auditors both in the UK and overseas. She is a member of the Institute of Chartered Accountants of Scotland.

John Dunn is a chartered accountant and a lecturer in the Department of Accounting and Finance at the University of Strathclyde in Glasgow where he teaches auditing and financial accounting on undergraduate courses and short courses for practitioners. He is an examiner in financial accounting for the Chartered Institute of Management Accountants. Mr Dunn is the author of a number of works on auditing and financial accounting.

1 INDEX

To refer to a particular subject you can use the index. Entries and sub entries are in alphabetical order with the chapter reference in bold followed by the section number.

Therefore in the example, information on auditors responsibilities in accountancy work can be found in chapter 1, paragraph 2.10.

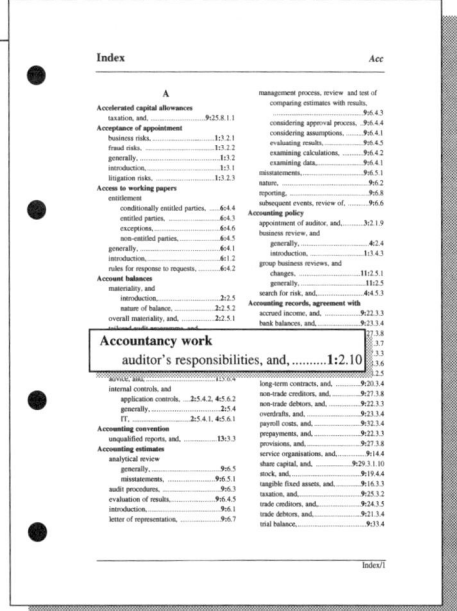

2 CONTENTS PAGES

There are main contents pages at the front of your book listing chapter titles and main headings; all references are to page numbers.

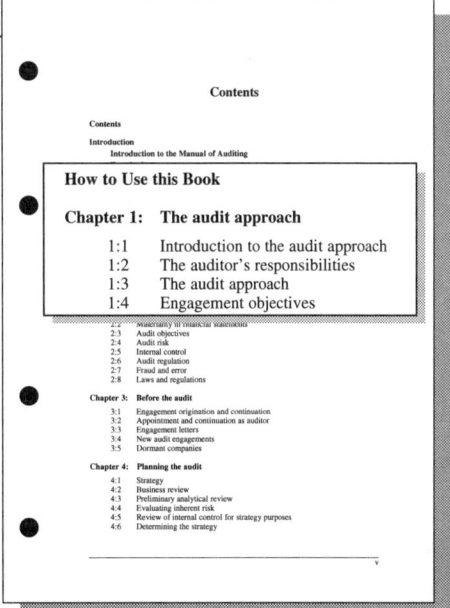

3 CROSS REFERENCES

Within the text there are cross references to other chapters and paragraphs within the book. These are highlighted in bold for ease of use.

A further concern to group management is to be made aware of accounting and reporting issues in different locations before they become major problems. Senior management at clients does not like surprises in its own business. Again the auditor can provide a valuable link for helping to identify such issues and, in consultation with local management, ensuring that they are promptly reported to group management.

Central management will often be most interested in the auditor's views on the quality of individuals in management teams. Clearly this is a matter which needs to be handled sensitively and the auditor should not provide views about individuals without substantiating them. But, if asked, the auditor can be of value in arriving at an objective assessment of the quality of management on the basis of the results of thorough consideration of factors of the type set out in the preceding paragraphs.

The external auditor's role in providing intelligence to corporate management in this way will be particularly useful where there is no internal audit or where its annual coverage is not comprehensive. In other cases, the external auditor's role will be useful in complementing that of the internal auditor and in reinforcing internal audit recommendations.

1:5.8 Constructive reporting to management

So far this section has dealt with the ways in which the auditor can use, and build on, his audit work to provide clients with more value from the audit. Each of these involves

Section 12:1, 'Audit reporting to the board and to management', deals in detail with reporting of all matters relating to the audit. The form and style of reporting will particularly affect the client's perception of value. It is obvious that professional advisers who do not effectively get their message across have wasted some or all of the work which has led up to it.

The auditor has long provided clients with 'management letters' setting out weaknesses found and, usually, making recommendations for improvement.

Management letters have too often been framed negatively and have appeared overcritical and unhelpful and failed to focus on the matters of principal concern to management. In short, they appear too much as *by-products*, which is how they are often described.

Whereas the auditor's aim has been to provide clients with more value from the audit, the client's perception can be far from this; management letters are often unwelcome and create a defensive reaction by the client. It is much better to work with management to develop a framework for communication which meets the needs of both the auditor and the client.

4 PAGE NUMBERING

At the foot of every page we give the chapter number, followed by the actual page number.

1:5.3 Objective of this section

The aim of this section is to suggest how the auditor might contribute positively to clients' businesses from the work necessarily undertaken for the purposes of the published opinion. There are occasions when a modest addition to scope can produce disproportionately large benefits to clients, e.g. when the auditor's statutory audit work on a particular function of the business, tailored to the opinion on the financial statements as a whole, needs only a small 'top-up' to enable the auditor to express a view on that function itself.

1:5.4 The potential for adding value

In assessing how the auditor can contribute more, the principle should be to derive greater value for clients from the work the auditor already undertakes and from the natural skills and independent perspective of the auditor. The potential derives from the following:

(a) **The auditor's objectivity**: The auditor's independence from the client puts the auditor in a position to stand back and take a detached view of the business. The auditor should aim to be clear and unambiguous in any comments and recommendations made.

(b) **The auditor's understanding of the client's business and industry**: To provide the basis for an effective audit the auditor has to gain a good understanding of the client's business and the industry in which it operates. This understanding forms a sound basis for additional commentary and recommendations.

(c) **The auditor's breadth of experience**: Whereas a good understanding of the client's business is crucial in order to be able to offer advice and comment, it is the auditor's breadth of experience that allows a unique perspective to be offered to clients. In many ways the auditor offers a perspective that client management cannot easily achieve from within its own ranks. (Non-executive directors assist but in practice they are unlikely to investigate what is happening in the business in the same depth as the auditor.)

(d) **The auditor's technical skills**: The particular technical skills of the auditor are:

   (i) the expertise and experience of the assembly, presentation and articulation of information on business activity (planned and actual);

   (ii) the interpretation of financial information;

   (iii) knowledge of the best use of systems to derive and to handle the necessary data; and

   (iv) experience of the essential elements of good corporate administration which are common to all businesses.

1:5.5 Advice on published corporate information

It is the auditor's responsibility to express a professional opinion on the truth and fairness of financial statements presented by the directors. But in reality the auditor can,

Chapter 1

The audit approach

1:1   Introduction to the audit approach

       1:1.1   Importance of a consistent audit approach
       1:1.2   The auditor's responsibilities
       1:1.3   The audit approach
       1:1.4   Engagement objectives

1:2   The auditor's responsibilities

       1:2.1   Introduction
       1:2.2   SAS 100
       1:2.3   The Companies Act 1985
       1:2.4   Specific regulations
       1:2.5   True and fair view
       1:2.6   Audit reports
       1:2.7   Internal control
       1:2.8   Subsidiaries or branches of overseas companies
       1:2.9   Partnerships and sole traders
       1:2.10 Accountancy work for audit clients

1:3   The audit approach

       1:3.1   Introduction
       1:3.2   Acceptance and continuance
       1:3.3   Engagement objectives
       1:3.4   Business review
       1:3.5   Evaluating inherent risk
       1:3.6   Review of internal control for strategy purposes
       1:3.7   Determining the audit strategy
       1:3.8   Assessment of control risk
       1:3.9   Tailored audit programme
       1:3.10 Audit programmes
       1:3.11 Substantive testing
       1:3.12 Audit completion
       1:3.13 Reporting
       1:3.14 Debriefing

1:4   Engagement objectives

       1:4.1   Introduction
       1:4.2   Technical achievement
       1:4.3   Client service
       1:4.4   Best use of audit personnel
       1:4.5   Commercial efficiency
       1:4.6   Use of technology

1:5   Adding value to the audit

1:1   Introduction to the audit approach

1:1.1   Importance of a consistent audit approach

Every audit should be carried out in a planned and controlled manner, to achieve specific objectives leading to the overall audit opinion. Audit firms should aim to achieve audits of consistent quality, guiding their staff to carry out their work to the required standard. **Chapter 1** explains and outlines the audit approach which underlies the detailed procedures described in the later chapters.

1:1.2   The auditor's responsibilities

Section 1:2, 'The auditor's responsibilities', sets out the overall statutory and professional responsibilities of the auditor. These include the forming of the audit opinion on the truth and fairness of the financial statements, and carrying out the audit in accordance with SAS 100. The rest of this Manual sets out how these responsibilities should be fulfilled in practice.

1:1.3   The audit approach

Section 1:3, 'The audit approach', provides a detailed explanation of the audit approach. The major stages in any audit are identified, to provide the framework for the detailed procedures described in later chapters.

The audit approach in this Manual is 'top-down', in that it starts with the identification of strategic issues affecting the audit (materiality, audit objectives, audit risk, the control environment), uses them to determine an overall strategy for the audit and arrives at the detailed work on the basis of the strategy. This Manual adopts the same structure, beginning with strategic issues and the determination of the strategy, setting out the testing plan and describing the detailed work which should be carried out as a result. The relationship between this outline of the underlying concepts and the explanation of the procedures in other chapters of this Manual is as follows:

Chapter 1   Outline of the audit approach
Chapter 2   Explanation of fundamental concepts, such as audit risk, audit objectives, internal controls
Chapter 4   Use of these fundamental concepts in planning the audit
Chapter 8   Detailed audit work on accounting systems and internal controls
Chapter 9   Substantive audit work based on the results of the work set out in Chapters 4 and 8

1:1.4   Engagement objectives

The Manual puts the auditor's work in the context of running a professional practice. In order for the audit to meet the client's needs it should be seen to be constructive. In order for the audit firm to continue to provide the service demanded by clients, it should define its own service objectives for carrying out audits, and should direct its efforts to achieving those objectives. **Section 1:4**, 'Engagement objectives', suggests objectives to promote good practice and commercial efficiency. Suggestions of ways to add value to the audit are included in **Section 1:5**, 'Adding value to the audit'.

1:2 The auditor's responsibilities

1:2.1 Introduction

The UK Auditing Practices Board has defined the audit of financial statements as:

> *an exercise whose objective is to enable auditors to express an opinion whether the financial statements give a true and fair view … of the entity's affairs at the period end and of its profit or loss … for the period then ended and have been properly prepared in accordance with the applicable reporting framework (e.g., relevant legislation and applicable accounting standards) or, where statutory or other specific requirements prescribe the term, whether the financial statements 'present fairly'.*

1:2.2 SAS 100, 'Objective and General Principles Governing an Audit of Financial Statements'

SAS 100 applies whenever an audit is carried out. It is reproduced below:

> *In undertaking an audit of financial statements auditors should:*
>
> *(a) carry out procedures designed to obtain sufficient appropriate audit evidence, in accordance with Auditing Standards contained in SASs, to determine with reasonable confidence whether the financial statements are free of material misstatement;*
>
> *(b) evaluate the overall presentation of the financial statements, in order to ascertain whether they have been prepared in accordance with relevant legislation and accounting standards; and*
>
> *(c) issue a report containing a clear expression of their opinion on the financial statements. (SAS 100.1)*
>
> *In the conduct of any audit of financial statements auditors should comply with the ethical guidance issued by their relevant professional bodies. (SAS 100.2)*

The term 'audit' normally applies where:

(a) there is a statutory requirement for the auditor to express an opinion in terms of whether the financial statements give a true and fair view;

(b)   there is a statutory requirement for the auditor to express an opinion in terms other than whether the financial statements give a true and fair view (e.g., audits of local authorities).

However, the term can also apply to other situations where a professional accountant undertakes to carry out an examination of financial statements with a view to expressing an opinion on them, for example, when requested by a partnership to carry out a full examination of its financial statements. The principles and procedures described in this Manual apply whenever the term 'audit' is used in an engagement letter or opinion report. Many of the same principles and procedures will also be relevant and useful in carrying out other types of work, for example in reporting on management accounts in support of a loan application to a bank. However, the term 'audit' should only be used when a full audit of financial statements has been carried out.

1:2.3 The Companies Act 1985

Most audits are of the annual financial statements of limited companies prepared by management for presentation to the members under the Companies Act 1985.

Section 235 of the Act provides that an auditor is required to report whether:

(a)   the balance sheet gives a true and fair view of the state of the company's affairs;

(b)   the profit and loss account gives a true and fair view of the profit or loss for the year;

(c)   in the case of group financial statements, the group financial statements give a true and fair view of the state of affairs and the profit or loss of the undertakings included in the consolidation as a whole, so far as concerns the members of the company;

(d)   the financial statements have been properly prepared in accordance with the Companies Act 1985.

These requirements are modified for banking and insurance companies, to which less onerous accounting disclosure rules apply.

In addition, the auditor is required by s. 237 of the Act to report whether:

(a)   proper accounting records have been kept by the company and proper returns adequate for the audit have been received from branches not visited by the auditor;

(b)   the company's individual accounts are in agreement with the accounting records and returns.

If the auditor fails to obtain all the information and explanations considered necessary for the audit, that fact should be stated in the report. Also, if the requirements of Sch. 6 to the Act (disclosure of information: emoluments and other benefits of directors and others) have not been complied with in the financial statements, the auditor must, as far as possible, include the necessary information.

1:2.4 Specific regulations

Where appropriate the auditor should take into account specific regulations applicable to the entity subject to audit. For example, when auditing solicitors' accounts the auditor should refer to the Solicitors' Accounts Rules and the Accountants' Report Rules for the time being in force. When auditing certain types of investment businesses, reference should be made to the rules of the relevant self-regulating organisation (SRO) authorised under the Financial Services Act 1986. Specific regulations also apply to organisations such as building societies, pension schemes, registered friendly societies and industrial and provident societies, trade unions, employers' associations, charities, local authorities and businesses carrying on estate agency work.

1:2.5 True and fair view

There is no authoritative definition or interpretation of the term 'a true and fair view'. Moreover, because there can be more than one 'true and fair view' of any given situation, it is the auditor's informed professional judgement which is of overriding importance in applying the concept to the particular facts and circumstances of each client.

The presentation of a true and fair view in financial statements requires that those statements comply both with:

(a)   generally accepted accounting practices that are applied consistently from year to year; and

(b)   all relevant legislation.

A true and fair view may not be given, for example, where:

(a)   the figures given in the financial statements are overstated or understated by a material amount;

(b)   the description of the figures in the financial statements does not fully and properly disclose their substance or is misleading or ambiguous;

(c)   the financial statements are prepared on a basis that is not consistent with previous periods unless there is adequate disclosure;

(d)   the financial statements do not conform with accounting policies required by the Companies Act 1985, relevant accounting standards, or those acceptable to the auditor;

(e)   relevant information is not given;

(f)   the presentation of the figures in the financial statements is so obscure or complicated that they are difficult to interpret or understand.

Accordingly, for the purpose of reaching an opinion as to whether the financial statements give a true and fair view, the auditor should be satisfied that:

(a) regarding the presentation of the financial statements:

   (i)   all information materially affecting the view given by the financial statements is properly disclosed and is unambiguous;

   (ii) a proper balance is achieved between completeness of disclosure and the degree of summarisation that is necessary if the financial statements are to be clear and readily understandable;

   (iii) the information in the financial statements ensures that the conclusions which a reader might draw from it would be justified and consistent with the circumstances of the entity's business;

   (iv) the financial statements fairly reflect the commercial effect of the underlying transactions and balances and not merely their legal form;

   (v)   the presentation adopted in the financial statements has not been unduly influenced by management's desire to present facts in an unreasonably favourable or unfavourable light;

(b) regarding the assets:

   (i)   they exist and they are the property of the entity;

   (ii) they have not been charged or pledged or, if so, the position is properly disclosed in the financial statements;

   (iii) they are stated at amounts which are in accordance with accounting policies which are required by the Companies Act 1985 (or other relevant legislation) and by relevant Accounting Standards, or are otherwise acceptable to the auditor, and which have been consistently applied;

(c) regarding the liabilities and any contingent liabilities:

   (i)   all material liabilities of the company at the balance sheet date have been included in the financial statements;

   (ii) adequate provision for known or expected losses has been made;

   (iii) all material contingent liabilities have been referred to in the notes to the financial statements unless either the possibility of losses is remote or adequate provision has been made where losses are considered to be probable;

   (vi) they are stated at amounts which are in accordance with accounting policies which are required by the Companies Act 1985 (or other relevant legislation) and by relevant Accounting Standards, or are otherwise acceptable to the auditor, and which have been consistently applied;

(d) regarding the results shown by the profit and loss account:

   (i)   they represent profits or losses properly attributable to the period;

   (ii) they are stated at amounts which have been arrived at in accordance with accounting policies which are required by the Companies Act 1985 (or other relevant legislation) and by relevant Accounting Standards, or are otherwise acceptable to the auditor, and which have been consistently applied.

Where the auditor is not satisfied that the financial statements give a true and fair view, the audit opinion given to the members should be qualified, and the audit report should include a statement of the matters which are not satisfactory. Guidance on qualified reports is given in **Chapter 13**.

1:2.6 Audit reports

The principles that form the basis of audit reporting to members have evolved from the requirements placed on auditors by successive Companies Acts. In addition, guidance is provided by Statements of Auditing Standards.

Statements of Auditing Standards are not intended to override any statutory exemptions which have been granted. In other respects, however, they should be applied to audit reports relating to enterprises benefiting from such exemptions. The principles of reporting to members are dealt with more fully in **Chapter 13**.

1:2.7 Internal control

Management has the primary responsibility for safeguarding assets, maintaining proper records and preventing and detecting errors and fraud. These objects are best achieved by means of a proper internal control system, which normally comprises a hierarchy of elements covering the control environment, the accounting systems and internal financial controls.

The auditor should consider these elements individually and collectively, to enable effective audit work to be performed (by relying on internal controls where it is appropriate to do so) and to establish whether proper accounting records have been maintained.

The ordinary examination of the accounting records which the auditor undertakes to form an opinion as to whether the financial statements give a true and fair view is not primarily nor specifically designed, and cannot be relied upon, to disclose all frauds and other irregularities that may exist. However, audit procedures should be planned, performed and evaluated so that they have a reasonable expectation of detecting material misstatements in the financial statements, whether they are caused by fraud, other irregularities or errors. If the auditor's suspicions are aroused, legal precedent imposes a clear duty to investigate the circumstances and, if material fraud or other irregularities are discovered, to report them as appropriate to senior management and/or to the members and, in certain circumstances, to third parties.

1:2.8 Subsidiaries or branches of overseas companies

UK audit firms may be asked by overseas companies to perform audit work on their UK subsidiaries or branches. In such situations, it is important to establish clearly the reporting requirements applicable:

(a) For a UK subsidiary of a foreign holding company, a full audit of UK statutory accounts in accordance with UK Statements of Auditing Standards should be conducted, and the principles set out in this Manual should be followed. However, the subsidiary auditor should also take account of the requirements of the parent company and the parent company auditor, and should clarify such requirements with them at the planning stage of the audit. Such requirements might include the provision of extra information for the consolidation under foreign accounting rules, or particular attention being paid to audit areas where the foreign auditor foresees a specific audit risk.

(b)   For a UK branch of a foreign company, there will not normally be any statutory requirement for audited accounts to be produced in the UK. The audit is therefore carried out in accordance with the instructions received from the client appointing the auditor. However, whenever the term 'audit' is to be used in the engagement letter or the report, UK Statements of Auditing Standards should be applied, and the principles set out in this Manual will be relevant.

Guidance on the duties of an auditor in these circumstances is set out in **Section 11:9**, 'Responsibilities of a performing office'.

1:2.9 Partnerships and sole traders

The principles and procedures set out in this Manual have particular relevance to limited companies, in relation to which the rights and duties of auditors are laid down by statute. In the case of partnerships or sole traders the scope of audit work will, in the absence of specific regulations, be determined by instructions from the client, and these instructions should be confirmed in the engagement letter. However, if required to express an opinion, the auditor should ensure that the audit is conducted in accordance with the principles contained in this Manual.

1:2.10 Accountancy work for audit clients

Where accountants assist in writing up the financial records of a client and are also responsible for the audit, the writing up of the records does not in any way constitute an audit and it is preferable that it should not be carried out by audit staff. This area is considered in more detail in **Section 7:2**, 'Accountancy work for audit clients'.

1:3 The audit approach

1:3.1 Introduction

The audit approach described in this Manual is based on a 'top-down' assessment of inherent risks and the effectiveness of the client's internal control, carried out in relation to specified audit objectives. The 'top-down' approach begins with an overview of the client's business and systems, identifying areas of particular concern, and uses this to direct attention to critical aspects of the audit. The approach is described in this and other chapters of this Manual under the following headings, which broadly correspond to the different phases of the audit. The detailed procedures are explained in the sections stated.

(a) **Acceptance and continuance (Section 1:3.2)**. The auditor should consider the commercial and professional issues associated with accepting every appointment.

(b) **Engagement objectives (Section 1:3.3)**. Every audit should be carefully planned to ensure the highest technical standards, provide a high standard of client service, make best use of audit personnel and achieve commercial efficiency.

(c) **Business review (Section 1:3.4)**. The first step in the 'top-down' risk assessment is the gathering or updating of knowledge of the client. The auditor should also consider the likely effect of new legislation and professional standards, as well as events in the business world, on the client and the audit.

(d) **Evaluating inherent risk (Section 1:3.5)**. Using knowledge of the client and a structured approach to risk identification, the auditor should identify major risks of fraud and error and evaluate their significance.

(e) **Review of internal control for strategy purposes (Section 1:3.6)**. To assist in forming the appropriate audit strategy, the auditor makes a preliminary assessment of internal control. This assessment is 'top-down' because it starts with a consideration of the control environment, including the controls operated by management to run the business, then the accounting systems and, finally, the related internal accounting controls. At this stage of the audit the auditor should concentrate on gathering only the information that is necessary to help in determining the overall strategy, i.e., whether to use a systems-based or substantive testing audit strategy.

(f) **Determining the strategy (Section 1:3.7)**. The auditor should bring together the evaluation of major inherent risks and the preliminary assessment of the likely effectiveness of control in reducing such risks. In the light of this, the auditor can decide whether to carry out an extended assessment of controls for one or more systems and determine, in broad terms, the substantive responses to the major risks. The strategy should be discussed with the client.

(g) **Assessing control risk (Sections 1:3.8 to 1:3.8.4)**. The auditor should complete the work on assessing control risk required by the strategy. Where appropriate, this work will include an extended assessment of internal financial controls for one or more systems. In other cases the purpose will be to obtain a sufficient understanding to develop the substantive testing plan. The auditor should report findings to the client.

(h) **The tailored audit programme (Section 1:3.9)**. The auditor's purpose at this stage is to develop the audit programme. This programme can then describe the nature, extent and timing of the tests which, in the auditor's judgement, will be the most effective response to the risks of material misstatement.

(i) **Substantive testing (Chapter 9)**. The auditor should record and complete a detailed testing audit programme. The results of tests will be evaluated. The appropriateness of judgements about materiality, and risks of misstatement, should be reconsidered in the light of this evaluation.

(j) **Audit completion (Chapter 10)**. The auditor should review the financial statements and draw final conclusions from the audit. Significant findings should be discussed with the client.

(k) **Reporting (Chapters 12** and **13).** The auditor should report to the client on the financial statements in accordance with these conclusions, reporting both the opinion on the financial statements and audit findings.

Although the audit is summarised above in terms of separate phases many of the steps are interrelated. Planning will not necessarily make clear-cut divisions between these stages.

Audit can be viewed as a continuous process from year to year. This approach is designed to take maximum credit from prior years' experience of the client and from previous audits. The experience of the engagement partner and the engagement manager of the client is particularly important.

The following paragraphs of this section of the Manual describe the approach in more detail. Firms may wish to summarise the approach for distribution to partners, managers and staff in an 'easy reference' form.

1:3.2 Acceptance and continuance

Auditors should evaluate the reliability and reputation of both current and prospective clients. Acting for a company whose management lacks integrity or which is not financial viable may leave the auditor open to criticism or loss of revenue. The auditor should also ensure that there are no professional impediments such as doubts about independence of the firm's ability to provide an acceptable quality of service. Audit firms need not accept appointments which are not in their commercial interests and should not accept work compromises their professional integrity.

The commercial and professional issues are partly related. Management will have a greater incentive to compromise the auditor's integrity if they are under pressure to make the business appear viable.

1:3.2.1 Business risks

The auditor should review all matters which might affect either management's motivation or the viability of the company. This review should include the company's operating environment to identify problems affecting its industry or its potential markets.

The auditor should also consider the risks affecting the company itself, such as its competitive position within the market, its financial strength and the competence and experience of the senior management team.

1:3.2.2 Fraud risks

Management's commitment to high ethical standards and proper working practices is an important aspect of the business' culture. The auditor should form an opinion on the values of senior management and of the extent to which these are communicated to their subordinates.

The auditor should also decide whether there are any circumstances which indicate that management might, under certain conditions, override internal control or intentionally misstate the entity's financial statements.

The auditor should also form an opinion as to whether there are any particular risks arising as a result of management's methodologies for and attention given to financial reporting judgements and estimates.

In the case of continuing engagements, the auditor should consider the implications of any problems which have arisen in the past, such as the nature of any disagreements over accounting matters or a lack of openness on the part of senior management.

1:3.2.3 Litigation risks

The auditor is more likely to be criticised if the client fails or is taken over by a third party. The implications of any concerns about the company's viability or the interests of any potential bidders should be considered carefully.

1:3.3 Engagement objectives

It is important for audit firms to define clear objectives for carrying out audits, in order to assist staff in providing a high-quality, consistent service in accordance with the firm's policies and quality control objectives. The audit approach may be planned to deliver additional benefits to clients as a result of the audit work. The following four objectives may be considered:

(a)   High-quality technical achievement.

(b)   A high standard of client service.

(c)   Best use of audit personnel.

(d)   Commercial efficiency from the firm's perspective.

The audit team should be selected carefully to meet the particular requirements of the engagement, taking into account the need for specialist skills. Proper audit planning, continuing effective contact with the client and, in particular, determining the audit strategy most appropriate to the circumstances of the client also help to meet these objectives. These requirements should be kept in mind at all stages of the audit to ensure a properly balanced, high-quality approach.

1:3.4 Business review

The business review comprises:

(a)   developing or updating the auditor's understanding of the client's business;

(b)   carrying out preliminary analytical reviews;

(c)   reviewing the client's accounting policies;

(d)   assessing materiality.

These procedures provide the basis for the subsequent risk assessment. They may also help to develop client service objectives, if the firm has decided that this should be part of the strategy.

1:3.4.1 Understanding the business

The auditor should gain an understanding of the business by considering important factors which affect the client. Possible procedures include discussions with key client personnel, visits to principal locations and reviews of internally and externally published material. The auditor may consider the political and economic influences on the industry in which the client operates and important internal factors such as the structure of the organisation, management's strategy, finance, marketing and personnel policies. Each year the auditor can build on existing knowledge gained in prior years.

1:3.4.2 Preliminary analytical reviews

The auditor should apply preliminary analytical reviews to high-level aggregations of data, often using the client's management accounts. Examples of such high-level aggregations include total or divisional turnover and gross profit margins, and major categories of expenditure. The purpose of this review is to establish familiarity with the client's cash flows, operating results and financial position. The auditor should consider whether there are any unusual or unexpected relationships or balances.

1:3.4.3 Accounting policies

The auditor should review whether the client's significant accounting policies are appropriate in the light of legislation, accounting standards, industry norms and requirements as to good practice.

1:3.4.4 Materiality

Statement of Auditing Standards 220, 'Materiality and the Audit', requires that 'auditors should consider materiality and its relationship with audit risk when conducting an audit'.

To plan audit work effectively, the auditor should make preliminary judgements concerning materiality – both overall and for individual account balances or classes of transactions. These initial judgements may be affected by subsequent matters. In drawing conclusions from audit work, the auditor should compare the results to preliminary judgements of materiality to establish whether adjustments are needed in the financial statements.

1:3.5 Evaluating inherent risk

The risk of material misstatement is a combination of the inherent risk that items in the financial statements will be misstated through fraud or error, and the risk that the client's controls will not be effective in detecting or preventing those misstatements. Accordingly, the identification and evaluation of the inherent risk of fraud and error are essential to the audit approach, and help to determine both the audit strategy and the substantive testing plan.

The objective is to assess the risk of material misstatement for all significant audit objectives for each individual account balance and class of transactions. This assessment is used as the basis for designing substantive tests aimed at giving the amount of assurance the auditor needs that the financial statements are not materially misstated.

The procedures the auditor should carry out are:

(a)   searching for inherent risks;

(b)   evaluating the significance of such risks;

(c)   relating the significance of identified risks to account balances, classes of transactions and audit objectives.

1:3.5.1 Searching for inherent risk

The auditor should search for inherent risk by considering:

(a)   the findings of the business review, including preliminary analytical reviews and a review of significant accounting policies;

(b)   the characteristics of account balances or classes of transactions;

(c)   the history of fraud and error.

1:3.5.2 Evaluating the significance of identified risks

The auditor should consider the potential significance of each identified risk. This requires an appreciation of the following:

(a)   the client's operating environment and the external factors that affect it;

(b)   whether there is any particular motivation for management to distort the financial statements;

(c)   whether the risk is of fraud or error;

(d)   the number of risks affecting the audit objectives concerned;

(e)   the likely materiality of any misstatement.

1:3.5.3 Relating identified risks to account balances, classes of transactions and audit objectives

Audit objectives are those matters on which the auditor needs to be satisfied to reach a conclusion on an account balance or class of transactions. They comprise: completeness, accuracy, existence, cut-off, valuation, rights and obligations and presentation and disclosure. For example, the auditor would wish to know that an account balance was complete and that it was valued correctly.

The auditor should relate the precise consequences of each material risk of fraud or error to significant audit objectives for each account balance and class of transactions. It should be recognised that different types of risk will affect some audit objectives rather than others. This linkage of the risk to specific accounts and audit objectives enables the auditor to concentrate substantive tests on higher-risk areas and minimise tests on lower-risk areas.

1:3.5.4 Risk of fraud

Statement of Auditing Standards 110, 'Fraud and Error', requires that 'Auditors should plan and perform their audit procedures and evaluate and report the results thereof, recognising that fraud or error may materiality affect the financial statements'.

The knowledge obtained from evaluation of inherent risks, taken in conjunction with the assessment of the effectiveness of control in reducing such risks, is normally sufficient to allow the auditor to reach a conclusion about the risk of material fraud for the purposes of the audit opinion.

In addition, many clients may be concerned about the risks of fraud that they face. Accordingly, as an additional service to clients, the auditor may carry out a specific assessment of the risk of fraud.

1:3.5.5 Risk to the auditor and to the firm

Risk to the auditor and to the firm is the risk that they might suffer damage to their reputations through adverse publicity, deterioration of client relationships and litigation. Although such risks are always present, the auditor may seek to identify factors which might lead to an increase in them. If such factors are present, they may be taken into account when determining the strategy and testing plan, and when carrying out the work. In extreme cases the auditor should consider whether or not to accept appointment or reappointment.

1:3.6 Review of internal control for strategy purposes

A favourable assessment of control risk enables the auditor to reduce substantive testing for the relevant audit objectives. For many audits, this is the most cost-effective way of obtaining assurance.

The preliminary assessment of the control structure should be 'top-down' in that the auditor should consider the control environment first, then the accounting systems and, finally, the internal accounting controls. The adequacy of the accounting system should be considered at an overview level on all audits, whether or not the auditor intends to place reliance on internal accounting controls.

The auditor should assess control risk in two stages. For determining the audit strategy, it is necessary to obtain a sufficient understanding of the control structure to facilitate a conclusion as to whether it will be efficient to make an extended assessment of controls for one or more systems. As discussed in **Sections 1:3.8 to 1:3.8.4**, it is necessary to obtain further information about the control structure and to assess control effectiveness including, if appropriate, making an extended assessment of internal accounting controls.

1:3.7 Determining the audit strategy

The audit strategy describes, in broad terms, the principal features of the auditor's proposed approach to the audit. Accordingly, it is developed from an understanding of the client's business, from the evaluation of inherent risks and from the review of internal control for strategy purposes.

Professional judgement is needed to determine the strategy. Therefore, the participation of the engagement partner and the engagement manager is essential. They should normally hold a strategy meeting involving the in-charge and, where appropriate, in-house specialists and other members of the audit team.

At the strategy meeting, the following key judgements and decisions are made:

(a)   The effect of changes in the regulatory environment, the client's business, industry and financial arrangements.

(b)   Preliminary assessments of materiality.

(c)   Responses, in broad terms, to major risks identified, including risks of fraud and risks to the auditor and the firm.

(d)   The system(s) for which the auditor proposes to make an extended assessment of control effectiveness.

(e)   Principal engagement objectives, including key client service objectives.

The strategy should be supported by a budget and timetable and it should be communicated to the engagement team and others involved. The auditor should consult the client's senior management to ensure that its requirements and concerns are being addressed and that the auditor has fully understood the features of the business that can help in the audit work. Fee and billing arrangements may be planned at this stage.

1:3.8 Assessment of control risk

In practice, a significant amount of control assessment work is normally carried out after the strategy has been determined. Such work will involve completing the assessment of the control environment, evaluating the internal accounting controls in more detail than is required for strategy purposes and obtaining evidence that control procedures have operated as intended.

1:3.8.1 Control environment

The auditor should assess the attitudes, abilities, awareness and actions of client personnel, and particularly management, in relation to control. The assessment of the control environment initially helps the auditor to determine the audit strategy and subsequently helps to assess control effectiveness, as a whole, as a basis for the substantive testing plan.

Favourable features of the control environment can help to reduce substantive tests for particular account balances, classes of transactions and audit objectives. The assessment of the control environment also helps the auditor to understand significant reports, key performance indicators and procedures that management uses to control the business. This information can be useful in developing the substantive testing plan, particularly the design of substantive analytical procedures.

1:3.8.2 Accounting systems

Statement of Auditing Standards 300, 'Accounting and Internal Control Systems and Audit Risk Assessments', requires that auditors should 'obtain an understanding of the accounting and internal control systems sufficient to plan the audit and develop an effective audit approach; and use professional judgement to assess the components of audit risk and to design audit procedures to ensure it is reduced to an acceptably low level'.

The auditor should obtain sufficient knowledge of the accounting systems to facilitate the determination of the audit strategy, the assessment of control effectiveness and the design and performance of substantive tests. This understanding also provides a basis for conclusions on whether proper accounting records have been kept.

1:3.8.3 Internal financial controls

The auditor should obtain sufficient knowledge of the internal financial controls, both information technology (IT) controls and application controls, to facilitate the determination of the audit strategy and the carrying out of subsequent steps. The work required to determine the strategy will depend on the circumstances and may involve making the following assessments:

(a) **Control environment**: The auditor should obtain sufficient knowledge of the control environment to understand the attitudes of management and the board of directors, their awareness of risks and their actions concerning the control environment.

(b) **Risk assessment**: The auditor should obtain sufficient knowledge of the client's risk assessment process to understand how management considers risks relevant to financial reporting objectives and how it decides about actions to address those risks.

(c) **Control activities**: These are the policies and procedures that help ensure management directives are carried out. The auditor should obtain an understanding of those control activities which are relevant to planning the audit.

(d) **Information and communication**: The auditor should obtain sufficient knowledge of the means that management uses to communicate financial reporting roles and responsibilities and significant matters relating to financial reporting. Effective communication is a prerequisite for the implementation of the control procedures designed by management.

(d) **Monitoring**: The auditor should obtain sufficient knowledge of the major types of activities that management uses to monitor internal control relevant to the audit, including how those activities are used to initiate corrective actions.

1:3.8.4 Conclusions on control risk

The auditor's conclusions on the effectiveness of control in reducing risks of material misstatement are a matter of judgement taking into account all aspects of the internal control structure. The more assurance the auditor wishes to take from the evaluation control risk, the higher the quality of the evidence that is needed.

There is less benefit in carrying out a thorough assessment of internal accounting controls for non-systems-derived accounts, but the auditor may still be justified in obtaining some assurance from effective control. If desired, it is possible to rely on an identified strength in the control environment (e.g., a budgetary control) or on a specific internal accounting control.

1:3.9 Tailored audit programme

The auditor should prepare an audit programme which:

(a) Shows responses to the risks identified in the evaluations of inherent and control risk.

(b) Provides a basis for the individual plans that will control the implementation of the overall audit strategy.

(c) Provides members of the audit team with clear instructions as to the nature, extent and timing of audit procedures.

(d) Provides a structure for recording the audit work done and the conclusions drawn.

1:3.10 Audit programmes

The auditor should prepare an audit programme for each significant account balance or class of transactions. Audit programmes are designed to:

(a) assist in planning audit work, so that procedures applied in implementing the substantive testing plan are efficient and effective;

(b) provide clear instructions as to the nature, extent and timing of the procedures;

(c) provide a record of the work done and the conclusions drawn.

The auditor may prepare or update audit programmes at any time after the substantive testing plan has been agreed, and before substantive testing begins. For efficiency and quality control, the form of audit programmes is often standardised, but the auditor should adapt the content to the requirements of the substantive testing plan.

1:3.10.1 Early substantive testing

Early substantive testing, e.g. at an interim audit visit, often improves efficiency. It may also be beneficial for client service reasons. For example, early substantive testing may:

(a) make it possible to complete the audit soon after the balance sheet date;

(b) give early warning of potential final audit problems.

1:3.10.2 Interim clearance

If the auditor carries out interim fieldwork (which may include early substantive testing) and has completed the substantive testing plan, the engagement partner and the engagement manager should consider the audit's progress and findings, including any need to revise the strategy. If significant matters have arisen, these should be regarded as 'critical matters'.

The auditor should consider reporting to management, either orally or in writing, any findings from the interim fieldwork. It is important to report internal control weaknesses that could cause significant error or loss. The auditor may also recommend improvements in the client's systems that will contribute to a more cost-efficient final audit.

1:3.11 Substantive testing

Substantive tests comprise substantive analytical review and tests of details. The auditor may apply them separately or in combination.

Substantive analytical review involves comparing recorded amounts with the auditor's expectations of what such amounts should be. These expectations are developed by identifying relationships between data and using such relationships to estimate the likely amount of the account balance or class of transactions. The auditor should investigate any significant difference between the recorded amount and the expectations.

Tests of details may involve direct tests of account balances or transactions, or other general procedures such as a review of board minutes. They often involve a combination of techniques, such as observation and enquiry, reperformance and recomputation, third party confirmation, physical inspection and examining documentary evidence. Tests of details will tend to be concentrated on balance sheet accounts.

Substantive tests of profit and loss account items will often be limited because of the generally lower risks of material misstatement that are involved.

1:3.11.1 *Evaluating the results of substantive tests*

If the auditor finds misstatements as a result of substantive tests, they should be evaluated:

(a)   qualitatively, by reassessing risks in the light of their nature, cause and potential for further misstatement; and

(b)   quantitatively, by estimating the likely amount of the total misstatement.

If the auditor finds misstatements, it is necessary to consider the implications for the original assessment of inherent risk and control effectiveness. The auditor should do this in case it is necessary to revise the strategy and substantive testing plan. The auditor should also consider the results of substantive tests in the light of preliminary judgements of materiality to establish whether the financial statements should be adjusted, or whether the audit opinion may be affected.

1:3.12 Audit completion

Before signing the audit report the auditor should:

(a)   complete the fieldwork and review it for quality;

(b)   carry out a subsequent events review;

(c)   obtain representations from management and consider whether they are acceptable; and

(d)   carry out a final review of the financial statements, including a review of the credibility of the information presented and a review of compliance with legislation and relevant accounting standards.

Significant matters that could affect the audit opinion or which need to be reported to the engagement partner should be recorded in the issues documentation. Before the auditor finalises the audit opinion, findings should be discussed with the client to ensure that all the relevant information and explanations have been obtained, and any concerns arising from the audit have been explained to management. Issues documentation should be reviewed and cleared by the engagement partner, after consultation with other partners on major issues if necessary.

1:3.13 Reporting

1:3.13.1 The audit opinion

The principal end-product of audit work is the audit report on the financial statements. If the auditor has achieved sufficient audit assurance, and is satisfied that the client has met the appropriate legal and accounting requirements, the standard unqualified report should be given. If the auditor is not satisfied with the audit outcome, and intends to qualify the opinion, it may be necessary to consult with other partners in order to ensure that quality control objectives are met.

1:3.13.2 Reporting to the board and to management

An important product of the audit is the regular flow of information and reports to the board. This should set out in a positive and constructive way the main recommendations arising from the audit.

   The auditor should also report findings to other levels of management to ensure that action is taken by those directly responsible. Doing this also ensures that the report to the board is confined to the most important matters.

1:3.14 Debriefing

After the audit report is signed, and earlier if possible, the partner and manager should debrief the audit team so that they can identify matters relevant to the following year's audit. They should also analyse the time and costs of the audit and make the final billing arrangements.

1:4 Engagement objectives

1:4.1 Introduction

To ensure efficiency and effectiveness as a firm and as an auditor, it is important to set overall objectives for performance, and to communicate them to all those involved in planning, controlling and carrying out audits. The auditor may seek to meet five principal objectives on each audit engagement:

(a)   high-quality technical achievement;

(b) high standards of client service;

(c) best use of audit personnel;

(d) commercial efficiency;

(e) effective use of technology.

1:4.2 Technical achievement

Other sections of this Manual set out policies and procedures which are designed to ensure that audits meet the highest technical standards. This section of the Manual discusses some of the issues which should be considered in seeking to meet other engagement objectives.

1:4.3 Client service

The following broad client service objectives may be appropriate:

(a) Meeting the present needs of clients, with the right services at the right time.

(b) Anticipating clients' future needs, through the development of new services.

(c) Ensuring that high-quality service is delivered consistently across practice areas and in each location.

The provision of additional benefits and services as part of the audit strategy is discussed in **Section 1:5**, 'Adding value to the audit'.

1:4.4 Best use of audit personnel

Clients expect their auditors to demonstrate an understanding of their business, to provide a cost-effective audit, to be sensitive to their needs and to maintain independence. To do this, the auditor needs to recruit and retain the best people and to use them as effectively and efficiently as possible. Therefore, there are three main objectives with regard to staff:

(a) To make best operational use of partners, managers and staff.

(b) To attract and retain the best people, developing and equipping them to provide the high-quality audit service that clients need and want.

(c) To ensure that the individuals assigned to each audit team have the appropriate level of professional skill and experience for the various tasks allocated to them.

Accordingly, the firm should seek to develop the skills of its people and to maintain their motivation on every engagement. This is discussed below under the following headings:

- assignment
- communication

- coaching
- assessment

1:4.4.1 Assignment

The engagement manager, in consultation with the engagement partner, is normally responsible for assigning staff to the audit team. The manager should ensure that the team's qualifications, ability, experience, time availability and their prospective continuity are appropriate to the engagement. The engagement manager should, therefore, take account of factors such as: the size and complexity of the client; the industry in which it operates; the history of particular audit or accounting problems or of complex or contentious matters; and the existence of any significant increase in risks to the firm. In addition, the engagement manager should, as far as possible, take account of the personal development objectives of the individuals involved.

Once an in-charge is assigned to an audit, it may be useful for this person to have a continuing role in the engagement beyond each separate audit visit, e.g. by being available to assist the engagement manager in dealing with the client throughout the year.

The engagement manager and in-charge should ensure that the particular audit work assigned to team members is challenging but commensurate with their ability to handle efficiently and responsibly. If the work assigned is too demanding it will result in a loss of audit efficiency (largely because of extra supervision time and the possible need to perform the work again) and, at worst, in an increase in audit risk. Conversely, assigning work which is not demanding may demotivate the individual concerned.

Clients normally consider continuity of the audit team to be important. The audit firm should seek to ensure continuity between the interim and final audits and, as far as possible, from one year to the next, so that the knowledge of the client gained at each audit visit maximises the efficiency of subsequent work. However, the auditor should also consider the need to bring fresh blood into the team from time to time, to bring in new ideas and help avoid complacency.

1:4.4.2 Communication

To ensure effective teamwork, there should be appropriate communication within the audit team at all levels. This will ensure that all members of the team, including partners and managers, have the information necessary for them to carry out their audit work effectively and efficiently. Communication should be a continuous process and should be both downwards and upwards.

The engagement team should therefore be properly briefed before the start of the audit work. The way this is achieved will necessarily vary according to the size and complexity of each engagement. However, briefing meetings should be held involving the engagement partner, the engagement manager, the in-charge and other members of the team before the start of audit work and before the final audit. In many cases the audit strategy meeting (discussed in **Section 4:6**, 'Determining the strategy') will serve this purpose, either wholly or in part.

At the completion of the audit the team members should be properly debriefed in accordance with the guidance set out in **Section 10:1**, 'Audit completion'.

1:4.4.3 Coaching

Coaching plays an important part in the development of an individual's skills and in maintaining motivation. It therefore can have significant influence on the quality of audit work. All members of the audit team responsible for supervising the work of other team members should monitor that work and provide coaching to enhance their efficiency and effectiveness. An increase in time allocated to supervision and to on-the-job coaching will often mean the firm can use less experienced individuals on an engagement, who are cheaper for the client.

The in-charge has a particular responsibility to ensure that other members of the audit team receive adequate coaching. The engagement manager should assess the performance of the in-charge in this respect. In addition, the engagement partner can contribute to the development of the engagement manager and the in-charge by including them in client meetings.

When the work has been assigned, the individual members of the team are responsible for the quality of their work. In particular, they should ensure they complete the tasks for which they are responsible, including clearing review notes.

1:4.4.4 Assessment

Honest, clear and constructive feedback on performance is essential for the development and motivation of members of the audit team at all levels. Feedback immediately after performance has much more positive impact than comments made, say, six months later.

Accordingly, time should be budgeted in the planning process both for writing assessment reports and for discussing them with members of the audit team. The process should involve the following:

(a) Providing immediate feedback to individuals on their performance on the engagement.

(b) Taking account of the development objectives set for individuals before the engagement began, and considering those that should be carried forward.

(c) Identifying further experience, training and development needs for immediate follow-up.

(d) Providing supporting information for the assessment of individuals in connection with, e.g., performance rating.

(e) Providing information for the regular appraisal process.

The immediate supervisor (whether the in-charge or the engagement manager) should be responsible for the assignment reporting on individual members of the audit team and for completing the related documentation. Following discussion with the individual being assessed, and the recording of any comments made, the reports should be passed to the team member at the next level up (e.g., the engagement manager or engagement partner) for review, and for action on any specific matters identified.

1:4.5 Commercial efficiency

It is important for the auditor and the firm not only to be seen to provide value for money, but also – for their own credibility as an auditor – to be recognised as skilled in business. On every engagement, therefore, they should seek to adopt the most cost-effective audit strategy for the particular client's circumstances and ensure that this is mirrored by cost control and billing arrangements that are commercial and timely.

The following are examples of commercial efficiency points for each audit:

(a)   Appropriate time and cash cost budgeting.

(b)   Awareness of the factors affecting the agreement of fees with the client.

(c)   Billing arrangements that suit the audit circumstances and maintain working capital control.

(d)   Monitoring of the budget and disposing of matters arising, including those that might affect fee and billing on account proposals.

(e)   Efficient audit completion and control of related costs.

(f)   Prompt final billing and collection.

Setting and agreeing fee levels with the client should normally be the responsibility of the engagement partner. Subject to this, the engagement manager may be primarily responsible for most of the matters listed in the preceding paragraph, in consultation with the engagement partner. Day-to-day time and expenditure control is normally the responsibility of the in-charge.

Efficiency can frequently be increased by thorough planning of the audit so as to identify, and eliminate, areas which in prior years have been inefficient. Ways in which efficiency might be increased include:

(a)   changing the mix of staff;

(b)   changing the timing of the work, e.g. by carrying out early substantive testing;

(c)   using computer software to promote more efficient work;

(d)   encouraging the client to prepare many of the working papers.

1:4.6 Use of technology

Technology can be used throughout the audit to improve communication, decision making and efficiency through better information management and accessibility.

For example, microcomputers can be used in the following ways to improve efficiency;

(a)   rolling forward prior year audit work relevant to the current period;

(b)   devising and recording the audit strategy, including the assessment of the control environment, identification of inherent risks, and the creation of a testing plan and tailored audit programmes for each audit area;

(c)   recording and classifying critical matters in the electronic audit file and, possibly, communicating these to senior members of the audit team by electronic mail;

(d)   producing reports to facilitate review;

(e)   copying and sharing information between team members so that each member of the audit team has an up-to-date version of the audit work carried out by the rest of the team; and

(f)   documenting the assessment of control risks.

Many of these benefits can be obtained from the use of standard groupware and communication packages, possible adapted for audit purposes.

1:5 Adding value to the audit

1:5.1 Introduction

Auditing is no different from any other industry in that a key measure of its output is the **added value** it brings to clients and to the wider business community. It is also not immune from the increasing competitive pressures on all industries to reduce costs.

1:5.2 Background

Auditing is not a commodity to be traded but a complex service which needs to be carefully tailored to the needs of the business. Although the audit fee is undoubtedly an important consideration to many clients, it will not necessarily be the only consideration.

The growing number of audit committees, charged by boards of directors with responsibility for liaising with the auditor, has meant a greater focus on the scope and value from the audit.

1:5.3 Objective of this section

The aim of this section is to suggest how the auditor might contribute positively to clients' businesses from the work necessarily undertaken for the purposes of the published opinion. There are occasions when a modest addition to scope can produce disproportionately large benefits to clients, e.g. when the auditor's statutory audit work on a particular function of the business, tailored to the opinion on the financial statements as a whole, needs only a small 'top-up' to enable the auditor to express a view on that function itself.

1:5.4 The potential for adding value

In assessing how the auditor can contribute more, the principle should be to derive greater value for clients from the work the auditor already undertakes and from the natural skills and independent perspective of the auditor. The potential derives from the following:

(a) **The auditor's objectivity**: The auditor's independence from the client puts the auditor in a position to stand back and take a detached view of the business. The auditor should aim to be clear and unambiguous in any comments and recommendations made.

(b) **The auditor's understanding of the client's business and industry**: To provide the basis for an effective audit the auditor has to gain a good understanding of the client's business and the industry in which it operates. This understanding forms a sound basis for additional commentary and recommendations.

(c) **The auditor's breadth of experience**: Whereas a good understanding of the client's business is crucial in order to be able to offer advice and comment, it is the auditor's breadth of experience that allows a unique perspective to be offered to clients. In many ways the auditor offers a perspective that client management cannot easily achieve from within its own ranks. (Non-executive directors assist but in practice they are unlikely to investigate what is happening in the business in the same depth as the auditor.)

(d) **The auditor's technical skills**: The particular technical skills of the auditor are:

    (i)   the expertise and experience of the assembly, presentation and articulation of information on business activity (planned and actual);

    (ii)   the interpretation of financial information;

    (iii)   knowledge of the best use of systems to derive and to handle the necessary data; and

    (iv)   experience of the essential elements of good corporate administration which are common to all businesses.

1:5.5 Advice on published corporate information

It is the auditor's responsibility to express a professional opinion on the truth and fairness of financial statements presented by the directors. But in reality the auditor can, and frequently does, make a valuable contribution to shareholders by objectively advising management what information to present and how best to present it. This in no way diminishes the responsibility of the directors for the financial statements, but it can help them, in a practical way, to fulfil that responsibility.

The auditor has skills and experience in the communication of information, particularly financial information, and can therefore advise clients on the best methods of presenting this information. This is particularly important as business activity grows more complex, and accounting and legal rules struggle to keep pace. The auditor's experience of how similar companies are facing similar problems, and of the latest trends in accounting practice and disclosure, can be invaluable to clients. Tailoring accounting policies to specific industries, and adopting industry best practice, is of growing importance. Further, the increasing *globalisation* of business is increasingly forcing the need to consider accounting policies and practices across the world.

The auditor's advice can extend beyond the financial statements themselves, to the chairman's statement, the directors' report, the review of operations and any other information which it is useful to provide to shareholders. The auditor can also provide a useful contribution by reviewing and reporting on interim statements and preliminary announcements.

Information technology (IT) can be used to enhance the auditor's contribution. It provides opportunities for pooling the auditor's experience of accounting practices and enhancing internal databases so that they can more readily be turned to the benefit of clients.

Annual reports now tend to go much further than is required by statute and are used as an increasingly important public relations tool. They also provide a major focus in hostile takeover situations. It is therefore vital that the right message is conveyed about the company objectively and in the right way. Tables, charts, graphs and other pictorial representations all have an important part to play.

1:5.6 Advice on business controls

The following paragraphs look at the areas in which the auditor can contribute to management a wide experience of corporate and financial stewardship, by offering an objective perspective based on that experience.

It is not suggested that the auditor should seek to force advice on management on all of these topics, nor that many managements will need it. Different clients will have different strengths and areas of expertise. But it is rare for clients not to seek the auditor's views on at least some of the areas suggested in the following paragraphs. The suggestions given should at least help the auditor to be prepared to respond to questions. They may also help management or audit committees in suggesting questions they might ask of their auditor. This is not management consultancy, which involves systematic, subjective and specialist appraisal of management processes and techniques; it is more about a high-level overall view on management controls as part of the audit.

The most important starting point for improving the value of audit to clients is to discuss at a planning meeting the audit scope. This gives the client the opportunity to suggest areas which it would like emphasised or any work additional to the normal statutory work it would like to have carried out and which it would be efficient to carry out at the same time as the audit work. Decisions on audit scope are the auditor's not the client's.

The main areas where the auditor is best positioned to contribute to management advice on business controls are:

(a)   overall corporate and financial administration;

(b)   management information;

(c)   financial management and control;

(d)   accounting control; and

(e)   computer security.

These are, however, not the only areas of control where the auditor may be able to contribute. For example, the auditor may advise on compliance with rules for corporate conduct or ethics. Many larger companies have established codes of conduct and the auditor's understanding of the business, together with the work necessarily carried out for the audit, provides a good basis for commenting on whether codes of conduct are being complied with.

1:5.6.1 Overall corporate and financial administration

Effective corporate governance and administration is the starting point for a well-run and well-controlled business. It is also the auditor's usual starting point in assessing the control environment as part of risk assessment for audit purposes. Corporate governance and administration involves such matters as the constitution of the board, the overall management structure, whether there is a clear statement of the company's direction and objectives, the documentation of corporate and financial policies and the key management information received by the board and senior corporate management.

Given professional experience the auditor should be in a position to advise clients, at least if called upon to do so.

In considering the overall corporate administration the auditor may consider the following:

(a)   the board (and board committees);

(b)   objectivity in the direction of the business;

(c)   effective control by the board and senior management;

(d)   management and organisational structure of the business;

(e)   statements of the business's direction and objectives;

(f)   effective discharge of directors' responsibilities;

(g)   internal procedures designed to protect the client against fraud and illegal acts; and

(h)   relationship with the auditor and internal auditors.

1:5.6.2 *Management information*

The greater the complexity of business the more speedy, relevant, reliable and unambiguous management information is needed for effective planning and control. And good information systems can offer a competitive edge.

This need provides the auditor with another important opportunity to enhance the value of audit, by commenting to the board and senior corporate management on whether in overall terms they are receiving reliable, up-to-date information, and at the right time, on which to base important decisions. Management information is essential for proper control of the business and therefore it is usually essential for the auditor to address it in assessing audit risk.

In addressing management information the auditor may consider the following:

(a)   budgeting;

(b)   the relevance of performance measures;

(c)   the extent to which management information is presented in an informative way to facilitate action; and

(d)   the reliability of management information.

Work on the truth and fairness of financial statements for publication will usually give the auditor a good insight into the *reliability* of internal financial information. An audit which produces few *audit adjustments* will generally indicate that management is receiving reliable information. But errors of principle or application revealed by the statutory audit will equally be indicative of unreliable management information. For example, what effect does an *audit adjustment* have on the product profitability or unit cost analysis used by the board?

The auditor should therefore be well placed to advise on shortcomings in the quality of management information, by mere extension of the thought processes used in the audit. The auditor should review the quality of the information provided to management on a regular basis and should discuss the results of this review with the board. One of the main reasons for doing so is to ensure that the board is equipped to manage the control environment in an effective way.

Of course, management information goes much wider than statutory financial information; e.g., unit cost information and product or service quality statistics. These are often of as much concern in the management of the business as the traditional financial performance indicators. However, whereas they are probably subject to at least the same vulnerability to error or misstatement, they are often less subject to internal control and critical review.

To report on non-statutory information such as this demands a sound understanding of the business and industry, and of the overall control environment. This the auditor has gained from the work carried out as part of the statutory audit. Further, the auditor may have specifically reviewed important non-financial indicators as part of analytical review work. All of this work provides a good starting point for reporting to management on non-financial information.

To provide a comprehensive report on the reliability of management information it may well be necessary to carry out work on information additional to that needed to report on the published financial statements. But the basic procedures for doing so should be precisely the same as for reporting on financial information and thus come naturally to the auditor. The additional cost of doing so should be proportionally small, given the factors set out in the preceding paragraph. And, if quantified non-financial information did not lend itself to such independent examination, that would question its usefulness.

1:5.6.3 *Financial management and control*

The auditor can also contribute valuable experience to the broader criteria for financial management and control of the business. A distinction needs to be drawn between day-to-day financial management *techniques and decisions*, which are not the province nor necessarily within the expertise of the auditor, and the financial management *policies* where, for example, advice on how other companies are tackling similar issues is something the auditor is well placed to give. This need in no way contravene the auditor's bond of confidentiality with clients. Any advice will be based on general trends and practice rather than on individual cases.

To illustrate the principle, most larger companies have at least some degree of foreign currency exposure and need to determine how it should be managed. The degree of exposure and hedging techniques range widely between companies and industries. But the basic criteria for exposure management remain largely common, and the potential costs to the company of lack of a clear policy, or of non-compliance with the policy, can be substantial. The auditor knows the criteria for current good practice, needs to consider them as part of the audit risk assessment and can advise management accordingly. But deciding the establishment of actual policy and the financial instruments used is of course a management task.

The auditor often needs to consider whether there are reasonably comprehensive financial management policies, and information against which to measure performance.

The auditor may consider management's practices in the following areas:

(a)   procurement;

(b)   inventory management;

(c)   sales order processing;

(d)   credit control and debtor management;

(e)   cash management;

(f)   product/market profitability;

(g)   foreign currency management;

(h)   project expenditure control (including R&D);

(i)   financial strategy; and

(j)   investment appraisal.

Thus the auditor, from breadth of experience, should be able to advise management on how well the policies, in general, measure up to good management practice.

The auditor may also need to consider whether there is adequate management information to judge compliance with the policies and their effectiveness.

Further, if there is no internal audit, the auditor could, with the agreement of the client, extend the audit to determine compliance with the policies; the additional work might only be marginal to what has been undertaken for statutory purposes.

Beyond these broad criteria, whereas financial management processes and techniques themselves would not normally be examined in detail, this does not mean that the auditor has nothing potentially to contribute. In particular the auditor may well be able to highlight where, and why, they are not effective. For example, the auditor naturally considers provisions against redundant stocks or potential bad debts. In doing so the auditor will tend to be aware of *why* the provisions have been necessary. A few additional enquiries if necessary should elucidate more precisely *what* went wrong. For example, was there a failure to comply with procurement or inventory management policies or credit control procedures; and/or do the policies and procedures need review? The auditor does not need necessarily to be expert in the subjects to reach a common-sense conclusion.

Thus it is quite easy to adopt relatively simple diagnostic techniques drawing on the auditor's wide experience of good financial management practice, so that an effective contribution to the determination of good financial management policy can be made. This can comprise simple statements of good practice supported by the auditor's database of practical examples of good, and not so good, practice.

The essence is that the auditor draws thoughtfully and systematically on the experience gained from all other clients in areas which naturally need to be considered in any event in assessing, first, audit risk and, second, the results of the audit for each of the auditor's clients.

1:5.6.4 *Accounting control*

The Statement of Auditing Standards 300 defines an internal control system as being:

> *all the policies and procedures (internal controls) adopted by the directors and management of an entity to assist in achieving their objective of ensuring, as far*

as practicable, the orderly and efficient conduct of its business, including adherence to internal policies, the safeguarding of assets, the prevention and detection of fraud and error, the accuracy and completeness of the accounting records, and the timely preparation of reliable financial information.

Accounting controls are those whose purpose is principally to *safeguard the assets and secure as far as possible the completeness and accuracy of the records* and to comply with the provisions on accounting records in the Companies Acts. (The other aspects of internal controls, as defined above, underline much of what has been said above.)

It is natural for the auditor to take account of accounting control in planning audit work. There is also a statutory duty to report to shareholders if proper accounting records have not been kept.

It is not the purpose of this section to consider specifically how the auditor adds value by pointing to deficiencies in accounting control. However, it is suggested that it is most valuable to report deficiencies in the context of an overall assessment of the totality of the audit results. Clients can then see the significance of the matters reported and are more likely to take corrective action.

At the end of the audit, taking stock of all information gathered to date, the auditor should usually be in a position to assess whether or not, in general terms, the accounting systems appear to be functioning effectively. Examples of the broader matters that the auditor would wish to consider are post year-end adjustments required to management accounts, adjustments to control accounts resulting from year-end confirmation procedures, audit adjustments required in relation to deviations from approved policies or methods and significant breakdowns in the system, missing records, unsatisfactory explanations or other exceptions indicating system breakdowns or control weaknesses.

The auditor also needs to recognise in advising clients that well-run companies have different cultural attitudes to control, none of which is exclusively right or best. Some, for example, rely heavily on approval of paperwork; others more on supervisory accountability of individual managers. In fact the auditor can be of value in advising the client on current trends in control style; and how its systems compare with latest practice.

1:5.6.5 Computer security

Today most businesses not only use computers to handle accounting and other business systems but would find it virtually impossible to operate their businesses if deprived of their computers. The large volumes and values passing through, and held on, computers pose increasing risk of theft, hacking, strikes and sabotage. Computer security is therefore a concern to businesses of all sizes, whether they have large mainframe installations or use mini or microcomputers, which increasingly store and process vital or confidential information.

The adequacy of *computer security* is a key consideration from the auditor's point of view. The auditor will assess the steps taken by management to ensure the complete and accurate processing of data. The auditor cannot cover every aspect of computer security, particularly in operational fields, but should be able to determine whether, overall, management appears to have the right attitude and approach. This need not entail an in- depth review, but will involve considering the main elements of computer security, including matters such as those below. The degree to which each applies will depend on the nature and size of computer operations.

The auditor may review computer security in respect to the following:

(a)   management commitment to security;

(b)   appropriateness of the computer department size and organisation;

(c)   development procedures;

(d)   selection and implementation procedures;

(e)   computer operations;

(f)   prevention of unauthorised access; and

(g)   contingency plan.

Consideration of these key elements of computer security, as part of the audit, will put the auditor in an ideal position to make a valuable contribution by advising management on their overall approach in an area of control that is increasingly becoming vital to all businesses.

1:5.7 The auditor as a source of intelligence to management

As part of the work in gathering audit evidence to support the opinion on the financial statements, the auditor carries out considerable investigative work into the client's business. This usually involves holding discussions with various levels of management and other personnel, visiting the company's various locations and observing the operations of the business. This work gives the auditor a powerful insight into the business, often built up over several years. Much of the information obtained will frequently be useful to senior financial management who may value the auditor's independent perspective. The audit can therefore provide a useful source of information to client management about the business.

This particular source of additional value to clients will usually be of most use in groups of companies and other businesses where there are several locations, particularly in decentralised businesses. Senior client management will often seek the views of the auditor on the types of issues described in the paragraphs above at different locations and on such matters as compliance with group policies and interpretation of results.

A further concern to group management is to be made aware of accounting and reporting issues in different locations before they become major problems. Senior management at clients does not like surprises in its own business. Again the auditor can provide a valuable link for helping to identify such issues and, in consultation with local management, ensuring that they are promptly reported to group management.

Central management will often be most interested in the auditor's views on the quality of individuals in management teams. Clearly this is a matter which needs to be handled sensitively and the auditor should not provide views about individuals without substantiating them. But, if asked, the auditor can be of value in arriving at an objective assessment of the quality of management on the basis of the results of thorough consideration of factors of the type set out in the preceding paragraphs.

The external auditor's role in providing intelligence to corporate management in this way will be particularly useful where there is no internal audit or where its annual coverage is not comprehensive. In other cases, the external auditor's role will be useful in complementing that of the internal auditor and in reinforcing internal audit recommendations.

1:5.8 Constructive reporting to management

So far this section has dealt with the ways in which the auditor can use, and build on, his audit work to provide clients with more value from the audit. Each of these involves providing the client with a commentary on aspects of his business. An important consideration is therefore the way in which the auditor's findings and opinions are reported to clients.

Section 12:1, 'Audit reporting to the board and to management', deals in detail with reporting of all matters relating to the audit. The form and style of reporting will particularly affect the client's perception of value. It is obvious that professional advisers who do not effectively get their message across have wasted some or all of the work which has led up to it.

Reporting to management on controls and other aspects of the business is not new. The auditor has long provided clients with 'management letters' setting out weaknesses found and, usually, making recommendations for improvement.

Management letters have too often been framed negatively and have appeared overcritical and unhelpful and failed to focus on the matters of principal concern to management. In short, they appear too much as *by-products*, which is how they are often described.

Whereas the auditor's aim has been to provide clients with more value from the audit, the client's perception can be far from this; management letters are often unwelcome and create a defensive reaction by the client. It is much better to work with management to develop a framework for communication which meets the needs of both the auditor and the client.

Communication with clients should be frequent and ongoing. One possible strategy is to build a series of meetings into the annual audit cycle. The auditor might present the findings of the business risk assessment at the planning stage of the audit. Any findings from the systems stage could be presented at an interim stage during the year. A final meeting could be held at the conclusion of the audit to discuss any matters arising from the fieldwork and also to receive any feedback from management on the audit. These meetings can be structured around a formal written report.

The traditional management letter was largely concerned with creating a formal written record of the problems that had been communicated to the client. The approach described above goes beyond this by making information which has been collected for audit purposes much more visible and useful to the client.

1:5.9 Value from people

The main source of added value for clients is the individuals who form part of the audit team; particularly the engagement partner and the more experienced staff, with whom client management deals directly. Clients frequently look to them for general advice and views on current business concerns. The better the people, the more likely they are to be able to do so.

To be able to meet this need, and give clients the value they are seeking, the auditor needs to ensure that the audit team is properly organised. The primary aim is to establish a dialogue with key members of the client's management team. This means maintaining regular contact throughout the year, not just visiting the client at the year-end, the busiest time, when there may not be sufficient time to discuss all important business issues. It also means being approachable and accessible so that the client is encouraged to contact the auditor to discuss matters of concern.

The auditor should ensure that the audit team has sufficient expertise in specialist areas in which the client operates. This may need to be considered in relation to specialised industries, such as financial services, or specialised transactions, such as a client who operates an in-house treasury operation dealing in foreign currency hedges and options. Some clients could require specialised accounting knowledge e.g. because they are accounting in accordance with International Accounting Standards or other overseas GAAP.

Audit firms can develop specialised knowledge of specific industry issues and regulations e.g. by involvement with other clients in the industry, attendance at internal and external specialist training courses, and subscription to industry specific journals. Such expertise and resources can be best utilised by keeping a central register of industry specific knowledge.

Perhaps just as important is the need to choose an engagement partner and team members who, while remaining professional and objective have personal chemistry that matches that of the client contacts with whom they will deal. Without that it is unlikely that a constructive, open and honest relationship can develop.

The skills and attributes required of financial managers in audit clients are developing rapidly. So too must the skills and attributes of the auditor if real value is to continue to be provided from the audit, beyond the audit opinion. The auditor must be able to talk to clients with at least their level of general knowledge of business and financial management. The implications for continuing professional education and development are obvious.

Chapter 2

Fundamental concepts and professional issues

2:1 Fundamental concepts for auditing

2:1.1 Introduction

It is important to understand the fundamental concepts underlying the audit before considering the procedures which should be adopted to carry out an audit. This chapter describes these concepts, and explains their effect on the audit procedures described in later chapters.

2:1.2 Materiality in financial statements

The audit report should be qualified if there is a 'material' error in the financial statements. The auditor therefore needs an understanding of what *may be* material in order to plan audit work effectively to look for what *is* material (and not to over-audit what is not material); and an understanding of what *is* material in order to assess whether errors found should affect the audit report. **Section 2:2**, 'Materiality in financial statements', discusses the determination of materiality. **Sections 4:2**, 'Business review', and **4:6**, 'Determining the strategy', describe the procedure of making judgements about materiality in planning the audit. **Sections 9:5**, 'Evaluating the results of substantive testing', and **10:3**, 'Reviewing the financial statements', discuss the procedure of assessing whether errors found are, in fact, material.

2:1.3 Audit objectives

The possible types of material error need to be analysed, so that they can be eliminated by individual audit tests. **Section 2:3**, 'Audit objectives', sets out the seven general audit objectives which should be satisfied by testing in each area of the financial statements, to deal with the different possible types of error which may occur. These objectives form the basis for the guidance on substantive testing of the individual areas in **Chapter 9**. The approach can therefore be described as 'objectives driven'.

2:1.4 Audit risk

The audit approach in this Manual is 'risk-based'. This simply means that it is necessary to identify risks of error, so that attention can be directed to the most important aspects of the audit. Similarly, it will be inefficient to carry out extensive audit procedures where there is a minimal risk of material error. This is discussed in **Section 2:4**, 'Audit risk'. **Section 4:4**, 'Evaluating inherent risk', describes the procedure of evaluating the inherent risk of a particular audit at the planning stage.

2:1.5 Internal control and control effectiveness

The audit approach in this Manual is based on a top-down assessment of the internal control structure of a business, to assist in determining the most efficient and effective strategy and detailed audit procedures. The concepts of internal control and control effectiveness, and their effect on the audit strategy and procedures, are discussed in **Section 2:5**, 'Internal control'. **Section 4:5**, 'Review of internal control for strategy purposes', and **Chapter 8**, 'Systems and controls', describe the audit work which should be carried out on controls.

The audit strategy and detailed audit procedures for large and small businesses may differ. However, the fundamental concepts are exactly the same. It will still be the most efficient and effective approach to adopt a *risk-based, objective-driven* approach which concentrates on searching for material errors.

Section 2:6, 'Audit regulation', sets out the regulatory framework for auditor firms that are registered by a supervisory body recognised by the Department of Trade and Industry.

Section 2:7, 'Fraud and error', provides guidance on the auditor's responsibility in relation to fraud and error in respect of:

(a)   the impact of the risk of fraud, error and non-compliance with law or regulations on the auditor's work; and

(b)   how any such items which the auditor discovers should be reported.

2:2 Materiality in financial statements

2:2.1 Introduction

Materiality is important to the auditor because the assessment of materiality is used:

(a)   to help to establish the extent of substantive tests;

(b)   to evaluate potential and actual misstatements. Materiality defines the threshold at which the auditor would require the client to make an adjustment to the financial statements.

2:2.1.1 Background

The Statement of Auditing Standards 220 describes materiality as follows:

> 'Materiality' is an expression of the relative significance or importance of a particular matter in the context of financial statements as a whole. A matter is material if its omission would reasonably influence the decisions of an addressee of the auditors' report; likewise a misstatement is material if it would have a similar influence.

In the UK and in other countries, the courts, in deciding whether misstatements were material, have generally applied definitions similar to that quoted above. In such cases the user has normally been considered to be a hypothetical 'average prudent investor'. Because materiality depends on the judgement of a user and because users differ there is no single 'correct' amount for what is material in particular circumstances.

Materiality can only be considered in relation to context. On the question of disclosure, those responsible for preparing accounts have to decide which, out of the many facts available to them, are the ones which are likely to influence users of these accounts. On the question of the required degree of accuracy, a difference of 10 per cent or more might be acceptable in some circumstances, but in other circumstances any difference might be unacceptable. While appropriate percentage comparisons can constitute useful broad guides, they should not be applied indiscriminately without regard to the particular circumstances.

2:2.2 Quantitative guidelines on materiality

For the reasons described in the preceding paragraphs, no definitive pronouncements setting out quantitative criteria or guidelines have so far been issued by professional bodies either in the UK or overseas. It would be inappropriate to do so in this Manual. Instead, the determination of materiality in specific situations requires the application of professional judgement and experience and is, ultimately, the responsibility of the engagement partner.

2:2.3 Determining materiality

During audit planning, the auditor should make preliminary judgements concerning:

(a) overall materiality; and

(b) materiality for individual account balances or classes of transactions and audit objectives.

2:2.3.1 The timing of the assessment of materiality

The auditor should assess overall materiality and individual materialities for account balances or classes of transaction as part of the process of determining the strategy, in particular in the light of the business review. However, initial judgements may be affected by matters that arise subsequently, and the auditor should consider the effect of audit findings on preliminary assessments of materiality. Thus, if the initial assessment of materiality is based on budgeted or estimated figures, the auditor should consider whether it is necessary to modify this assessment when the actual figures are known. If the assessment is modified after the auditor has started the audit fieldwork, it is necessary to consider whether additional work is required to be able to conclude at the desired level of materiality. The auditor should deal with changes to the audit strategy or to the substantive testing plan in accordance with the guidance given in **Sections 4:6**, 'Determining the strategy', and **4:7**, 'The audit programme'.

2:2.4 Setting an overall materiality

2:2.4.1 Determining overall materiality by reference to key components

The auditor should determine overall materiality by reference to *key components* of the financial statements. Key components are those figures, accounts or groups of accounts that may be considered essential to a user's proper understanding of the financial statements.

Because the auditor's determination of materiality is made with the judgement of the users in mind, it will frequently concentrate on the key components that are of more interest to such users. In many cases their interest will include profit (either before or after tax) and shareholders' funds or net assets. Other key components might be, e.g.:

- total assets
- total liabilities
- net tangible assets
- working capital

The auditor should make a preliminary judgement about the amounts that would be material for each key component. **Section 2:2.7** explains how to use these assessments of materiality when determining whether any misstatements found might be material to the users.

When determining overall materiality (which helps to establish the extent of substantive testing), the auditor should normally use the lowest materiality which has been established in relation to the identified key components. This is because any misstatement that exists might affect more than one key component. For example, an error of £100,000 might be immaterial in the context of debtors but it might be material as regards the profit before tax. To continue the example, if the auditor sets overall materiality at a level that is appropriate to debtors, but which is too high as regards profit and loss, there will be a risk that an error which is material in profit and loss terms, and which arises from a non-existent debtor, might go undetected. Therefore, the auditor should set the materiality level at an amount which is appropriate for all key components that would be affected by a misstatement. **Section 2:2.5.1** considers the circumstances when it might be appropriate to use a materiality level that is higher than the overall materiality level.

2:2.4.2 Profit as a key component

Current literature and research indicate that the users of the financial statements of a listed entity are usually primarily interested in the results of its operations.

However, the absolute amount of the profit or loss from continuing operations becomes of little or no significance to the user when an entity is at or near break-even point. Consequently, in such a situation, the auditor needs to identify an alternative profit measure as a key component which will be relevant to users. Such an alternative could be the trend of profits or losses from continuing operations for recent years, or it could be the rate of return on current sales, or investment, achieved by other entities in the client's industry.

Similarly, where profit before tax and extraordinary items is unusually high or low in a particular year, it might be more appropriate to assess materiality of this key component either on the basis of the recent profit trend (say, the average profits of the past five years) or on the basis of turnover for the year.

2:2.4.3 *Other key components*

If the principal users of the financial statements are the present or prospective creditors, which is normally the case for a private entity, their primary interest is likely to be in the entity's financial position. The owners of a private entity are likely to have a similar primary interest.

If liquidity or solvency is the principal matter of concern, the primary interest of creditors and owners is likely to centre, respectively, on their claims and their equity. However, creditors are also likely to be interested in shareholders' equity as one measure of the margin of security for their claims, and creditors and owners are both also likely to be interested in current assets as a primary source of funds to provide liquidity.

For entities such as non-profit-making organisations, the primary interest of the users of the financial statements might be in key components other than the results of operations, current assets or the owners' equity. Sometimes, the users' primary interest will be in gross turnover and gross expenditure. In some other businesses, such as financial institutions, the interest will centre either on total assets and total liabilities or on shareholders' equity.

2:2.4.4 *Special factors*

The auditor may become aware of special factors that influence the assessment of materiality and which will often represent a risk to the auditor and to the firm. For example, if aware that the audited financial statements are likely to have a special significance for other parties (such as a potential purchaser), the auditor should consider whether the situation is such that the key components differ from normal expectations or that a lower threshold of materiality exists because of user expectations. Consultation with other partners is recommended in cases of difficulty, to ensure that quality control objectives are met.

2:2.4.5 *Determining materiality levels for a subsidiary undertaking*

It is not acceptable to adopt group and subsidiary audit strategies that reduce audit work on a wholly-owned subsidiary simply because of materiality factors within the group as a whole. The materiality for each subsidiary should be set in relation to that entity's financial statements, taking into account all relevant factors.

If the auditor does not report on the subsidiary's financial statements (e.g., in the case of an overseas subsidiary, where local laws do not require an audit) materiality levels for the subsidiary should normally, for audit efficiency reasons, be determined by reference to the circumstances of the group and not by reference to the circumstances of the subsidiary itself. The auditor should discuss with the client management the implications of doing this, so that it is aware of the restricted extent of the examination of the subsidiary's financial statements. Sometimes the client's management might wish the auditor to extend the examination of the subsidiary's financial statements.

2:2.4.6 Determining materiality levels for multi-location clients

The client's financial statements might represent the aggregation of a number of branches or divisions often, although not necessarily, reporting from several different locations. In these circumstances, the auditor should normally determine materiality levels in relation to the key components of the client's financial statements, irrespective of the number of branches, divisions or locations it has. However, because management might want a report on the locations as if each were a separate entity, the auditor should in such cases discuss the desired scope of the audit of each location with the client. It may be necessary, as a result of these discussions, to set materiality levels specifically related to each location's financial statements. Because these would be lower than materiality levels based on the whole of the client's operations, the auditor would need to carry out more audit work and it would be appropriate to negotiate an extra fee.

2:2.4.7 Consolidations

When reporting on group financial statements the auditor should use group-based materiality levels to audit any consolidation adjustments and to evaluate the total unadjusted errors of all subsidiaries and the parent company. However, when carrying out the review of subsequent events on a group basis, the auditor should ensure that each subsidiary is reviewed on the basis of its materiality levels taking into account the factors described in **Section 2:2.4.5**.

2:2.5 Materiality for account balances or classes of transaction and audit objectives

The materiality levels for individual account balances or classes of transactions and audit objectives should be set taking into consideration the following factors:

(a)   overall materiality;

(b)   nature of the account balance or class of transaction and audit objective.

2:2.5.1 Overall materiality

Individual materiality levels for account balances and classes of transactions should normally be no higher than the overall materiality established for the financial statements as a whole. Sometimes it may be possible to set individual materiality levels higher than the overall level of materiality. This is most likely to apply to balance sheet accounts. However, the auditor should consider carefully whether sufficient 'corollary assurance' will be obtained from audit work in these areas. 'Corollary assurance' is the assurance about one audit area gained from the audit work on another audit area. In this case, considerable assurance about the profit and loss account can be gained by audit work on balance sheet areas. This is discussed further in **Section 4:7**, 'The audit programme'.

2:2.5.2 *Nature of the account balance or class of transaction and audit objective*

If the Companies Act 1985 or standard accounting practice require an item to be accounted for or disclosed in a particular manner, any misstatement in that item is more likely to be regarded as material than a similar misstatement in an item for which there is no such requirement. Furthermore, a misstatement in a transaction that affects only the balance sheet classification (e.g., cut-off of receipts from debtors) is less likely to be material than a misstatement that affects the determination of profit (e.g., bad debts).

2:2.6 Recording preliminary judgements about materiality

Preliminary judgements of materiality should be included in the audit strategy memorandum. The auditor may need to supplement the strategy memorandum with supporting working papers which record the basis for those judgements.

2:2.7 Materiality in relation to misstatements

The auditor should consider whether actual or potential misstatements which have been identified are, either individually or in aggregate, material in relation to the relevant key component(s) and/or the particular account balance or class of transaction in which the misstatement was found. In doing this, the auditor should also consider whether amounts which are themselves lower than the materiality level might be considered significant by the users of the financial statements.

When considering the materiality of *detected* misstatements, the auditor should remember that the nature of audit testing will normally result in the possibility of *undetected* misstatements. Accordingly, as the quantity of detected misstatements increases, the risk that the combined total of detected and undetected misstatements might be material also increases. If this risk is unacceptably high, the auditor should carry out additional procedures, or propose that the client adjusts the financial statements for the detected misstatements, to reduce the risk of material misstatement to an acceptable level. Further guidance on the appropriate response to misstatements and drawing conclusions on substantive tests is contained in **Section 9:5**, 'Evaluating the results of substantive testing'.

2:3 Audit objectives

2:3.1 Introduction

The principal overall purpose of an audit is to add credibility to the financial statements by the expression of an independent opinion thereon. Management is responsible for the preparation of those financial statements and, in compiling them, makes certain assertions regarding the information given therein (e.g., that stocks as stated in the balance sheet actually exist, are owned by the entity and are stated at a proper value).

The auditor needs to assess the risk of material misstatement and to develop audit procedures to deal with that risk. This process is facilitated by identifying specific objectives which contribute to overall assurance, breaking down the overall risk into specific subdivisions which can be dealt with one by one. The seven audit objectives, which are applicable to all account balances and classes of transactions, are as follows:

(a)   Completeness.

(b)   Accuracy.

(c)   Existence.

(d)   Cut-off.

(e)   Accuracy.

(f)   Rights and obligations.

(g)   Presentation and disclosure.

2:3.2 Definitions and examples

The audit objectives are defined in **Table 2:1** and illustrated by their application to trade debtors and sales.

Table 2:1 *Audit objectives: definitions and examples*

Definitions	Examples
Completeness: all account balances and transactions that should be included in the financial statements are included.	Trade debtors represent all amounts due to the entity in respect of trading transactions at the balance sheet date. All shipments or services rendered during the period under audit are included in the financial statements.
Accuracy: a transaction or event is recorded at the proper amount and revenue or expense is allocated to the proper period.	Debtor balances reflect sales transactions that are based on correct prices and quantities and are accurately computed and allocated to the appropriate general ledger and debtors ledger accounts. Invoice summarisations and postings to the debtors ledger and sales account are correct. The debtors ledger is mathematically correct and agrees with the general ledger.
Existence: recorded assets and liabilities exist as at the balance sheet date; recorded transactions have occurred and are not fictitious.	Recorded trade debtors represent amounts owed to the entity at the balance sheet date. Recorded sales transactions represent actual goods shipped or services rendered.
Cut-off: a transaction or event took place which pertains to the entity during the relevant period.	Sales transactions are recorded in the correct period.
Valuation: appropriate accounting measurement and recognition principles are properly selected and applied.	Debtors are stated at net collectible amounts. Allowances for doubtful accounts, discounts, returns and similar items are appropriately determined. Revenue is recognised only when appropriate recognition and measurement criteria are met.
Rights and obligations: recorded assets are rights of the entity and recorded liabilities are obligations of the entity at the balance sheet date.	Debtors are legal rights of the entity at the balance sheet date. The client is entitled to substantially all the risks and rewards arising from the amounts receivable and all debts that have been assigned have been properly excluded.
Presentation and disclosure: account balances and classes of transactions are properly classified and described; appropriate disclosures are made.	Debtors and sales are properly described and classified in the financial statements (e.g., as between current and non-current). Debtors pledged as collateral are properly disclosed. Significant credit balances have been classified as creditors. Changes in the measurement and recognition of revenue have been properly presented and disclosed.

2:3.3 Audit objectives and the tailored audit programme

Audit objectives are used to link together all audit procedures and develop an appropriate response to the risks of material misstatement. For each significant account balance and class of transactions the tailored audit programme may set out, in terms of the audit objective(s) involved, the auditor's assessment of inherent risk, the effectiveness of controls and the substantive audit response. In this way, the effectiveness and efficiency of audit work is maximised.

Although the seven audit objectives remain the same from engagement to engagement, they are not equally relevant to all account balances or classes of transactions (e.g., valuation is not normally relevant to cash). Materiality judgements and risk assessment will affect the emphasis the auditor gives to particular objectives for an individual account balance or class of transactions and thus the nature, extent and timing of the audit procedures used to achieve those objectives.

2:4 Audit risk

2:4.1 Introduction

2:4.1.1 Definition of audit risk

This section discusses the general nature of audit risk and its principal elements. Guidance on how the auditor can identify risks and the means by which audit risk can be reduced to an acceptable level is contained in other sections which are referred to below.

The term 'audit risk' is used to describe the risk that the auditor will issue an incorrect opinion on the financial statements. In practice, audit risk is the risk that the auditor will issue an unqualified opinion when the financial statements taken as a whole are materially misstated. The auditor should design and execute audit procedures that result in an acceptably low risk that the opinion expressed on the financial statements will be inappropriate. These procedures comprise:

(a)   identifying and evaluating inherent risks;

(b)   assessing the control risk;

(c)   designing and carrying out substantive tests of account balances and classes of transactions.

2:4.1.2 The components of audit risk

At the account balance or class of transactions level, audit risk has two major components:

(a)   **The risk of material misstatement**: This is a combination of the inherent risk that items in the financial statements will be materially misstated, either individually or in aggregate, and the risk that the client's controls will not be effective in preventing or detecting those misstatements.

(b)   **Detection risk**: This is the risk that misstatements contained in the financial statements will not be detected by audit work.

The risk of misstatement differs from detection risk in that the auditor can assess it, but cannot control it. In other words, the auditor's assessment of inherent risk and control effectiveness will give a better understanding of the risk of material misstatement in the financial statements, but it does not reduce or otherwise change that risk. However, the auditor can control detection risk by varying the nature, extent and timing of specific substantive tests.

The auditor's assessment of inherent risk and control risk determines the acceptable level of detection risk and, thereby, affects the nature and extent of substantive testing. As the risk of material misstatement decreases, the level of detection risk that the auditor can accept from substantive testing increases. As a result, the amount of assurance needed from substantive tests decreases. Conversely, the greater the risk that a material misstatement is contained in the financial statements, the lower the acceptable level of detection risk, and the greater the assurance needed from substantive testing.

2:4.2 Inherent risk

2:4.2.1 Definitions

Inherent risk is the susceptibility of an account balance or class of transactions to material misstatement through fraud or error, before taking into account the effectiveness of controls.

The term 'fraud' encompasses:

(a)   the use of deception to obtain an unjust or illegal financial advantage;

(b)   intentional misstatements in, or omissions of amounts or disclosures from, an entity's accounting records or financial statements; and

(c)   theft (whether or not accompanied by misstatements of accounting records or financial statements).

Fraud may be perpetrated by proprietors, by one or more members of management, by employees or by third parties.

The term 'error' denotes unintentional misstatements in, or omissions from, an entity's accounting records or financial statements.

The auditor should search for and evaluate inherent risk to identify potential sources of material misstatement and to assist in planning the nature, extent and timing of substantive auditing procedures. The search for risk should concentrate on identifying inherent risk 'conditions' that exist at the macroeconomic, industry and company level (whether external or internal) and inherent risk 'characteristics' which apply at the level of account balances or classes of transactions.

2:4.2.2 Inherent risk conditions

The auditor can identify inherent risk conditions through the business review, including preliminary analytical procedures, and by having regard to certain aspects of the control environment. Some inherent risk conditions are pervasive, in that they affect more than one account balance or audit objective (e.g., a risk relating to whether the client remains a going concern will affect many account balances), but they can, nevertheless, be analysed to individual account balances and audit objectives.

The nature of inherent risk conditions is that they may change from year to year. Accordingly, risk identification and evaluation procedures reflect the need to review them in detail at the beginning of every audit.

Inherent risk conditions are not normally addressed by systems of internal accounting control. However, special procedures may be performed by the client in response to inherent risk conditions. Examples of such procedures include special reviews of stock obsolescence and doubtful debts.

2:4.2.3 Inherent risk characteristics

Inherent risk characteristics are attributable to specific account balances or classes of transactions and they may affect all audit objectives. Examples of inherent risk characteristics include:

(a) **Assets susceptible to theft**: Theft may include misappropriation of cash and other readily convertible assets, deliberate underpricing of sales or payment for goods not received.

(b) **Risks associated with the accounting process**: There is an inherent risk associated with every accounting process, although this will often be reduced by internal controls. Risks associated with systems-derived accounts are generally lower than those for non-systems-derived accounts.

(c) **Account balances derived from estimates**: Because calculation of such amounts involves the use of judgement, estimates generally have a relatively high risk of fraud (e.g., through management manipulation of the estimate to distort profits). Also, estimates are frequently applied in situations where there is uncertainty as to the outcome of future events (e.g., the ultimate realisable value of obsolescent stock) and, as a result, are particularly prone to both fraud and error.

(d) **Unsettled transactions** (e.g., sales for which cash is yet to be received) are generally subject to a higher risk than settled transactions (e.g., sales where the cash has been received).

(e) **Unusual or complex transactions**: Unusual transactions are prone to error because they are often not systems derived, and there may not be established procedures for dealing with them, or because normal procedures, including internal controls, may be overridden. In addition, because such transactions occur infrequently, it is less likely that there will be personnel with adequate experience of dealing with them. Complex transactions are, by their nature, prone to the risk of error. In addition, unusual and complex transactions may both involve fraud. For example, complex accounting policies are sometimes used as a means of disguising recognition of income before it is properly due.

(f) **Cut-offs or accruals** can have the risk characteristics of systems-derived accounts (in which case they may have a low risk of error) or estimates, or (as is frequently the case) they may exhibit the risk characteristics of both. Accordingly, the auditor's response to such items should reflect the characteristics that they display.

(g) **The history of fraud or error** is a key indicator of possible misstatement in the current year. A pattern of continuing fraud or error affecting particular account balances and classes of transactions often emerges over time.

The identification and evaluation of inherent risk characteristics are discussed in **Section 4:4**, 'Evaluating inherent risk'.

2:4.2.4 Risk of fraud

The Statement of Auditing Standards 110, 'The Auditing Guideline: Fraud and error', requires the auditor to plan and conduct the audit so as to have a reasonable expectation of detecting material misstatements in the financial statements resulting from fraud. Accordingly, the risk of fraud may need to be assessed separately from the risk of error.

In addition, there may be concern among many clients about the risks of fraud that they face. The audit approach described in this Manual aims to recognise client concerns and helps to identify and to limit such risks wherever practicable.

2:4.2.5 Risk to the auditor and to the firm

Although risks to the auditor and to the firm (defined in **Section 1:3**, 'The audit approach') are always present, the auditor may identify an increased risk caused by, e.g., doubts about management's attitude to reporting which might lead to the firm being associated with deliberately misstated financial statements.

When an increased risk to the firm is identified, the auditor should respond to it. However, if the auditor does not identify increased risk to the firm this does not, in itself, justify a restriction of the audit response. Risk to the firm is discussed further in **Section 4:4**, 'Evaluating inherent risk'.

2:4.3 Control risk

Control risk may be defined as the risk that a material misstatement which could occur in an account balance or class or transactions would not be prevented, or detected and corrected on a timely basis, by the accounting and internal control systems. The auditor should assess this risk to assist in developing an appropriate response to the inherent risks identified and in planning the nature, extent and timing of substantive testing. In practice this involves:

(a)   assessing strengths and weaknesses of the control environment;

(b)   obtaining an understanding of the accounting systems and related internal accounting controls;

(c)   deciding whether the auditor can, by relying on the client's internal control, reduce the extent of substantive tests of account balances and audit objectives;

(d)   assessing whether the effectiveness of control, taken as a whole, is such that the risks of material misstatement are reduced, thus limiting the range of substantive tests of account balances and audit objectives the auditor needs to carry out.

Guidance on drawing conclusions on control effectiveness for the purpose of determining the audit strategy is given in **Section 4:6**, 'Determining the strategy', and, in relation to the substantive testing plan, in **Section 4:7**, 'The audit programme'.

2:4.4 Detection risk

2:4.4.1 Definitions

Detection risk is the risk that the auditor's substantive tests will not detect material misstatements in the financial statements. The auditor should aim to keep detection risk to an acceptably low level by designing an effective programme of substantive tests, tailored to the client's circumstances and having regard to the risks assessed, and by carrying out the tests thoroughly and effectively.

There is always a risk that the auditor will reach an inappropriate conclusion in performing and evaluating the results of audit procedures. That risk has two components, namely sampling risk, which is present only when tests involving sampling are performed, and non-sampling risk, which is present when any auditing procedures (whether they be substantive analytical review or tests of details) are carried out.

2:4.4.2 Sampling risk

When the auditor carries out substantive tests of details of transactions or balances, it is often impracticable or inefficient to perform them on all or substantially all of the items that make up a population. In such cases, the auditor can often accomplish the objective of the test more efficiently by sampling. In deciding to sample, the auditor accepts the risk that the results of the sample will lead to a conclusion that would have been different had the entire population been examined. The auditor's objective should be to reduce sampling risk to an acceptably low level by designing the sample properly.

2:4.4.3 Non-sampling risk

Non-sampling risk is the risk that any factor other than the sample selected will cause the auditor to draw an incorrect conclusion about an account balance or about the effectiveness of a control. Examples of non-sampling risk are:

(a) omitting essential audit procedures (e.g., failing to review minutes of management or board meetings);

(b) setting an inappropriate threshold for a substantive analytical review;

(c) applying audit procedures improperly (e.g., by giving confirmation requests to the client for mailing);

(d) applying audit procedures to an inappropriate or incomplete population (e.g., excluding an entire class of purchases from the process of selecting a sample and then concluding that the relevant audit objective has been met for all classes of purchase transactions).

2:5 Internal control

2:5.1 Introduction

The internal control system is defined in the Statement of Auditing Standards 300, 'Accounting and Internal Control Systems and Audit Risk Assessments', as:

> *all the policies and procedures (internal controls) adopted by the directors and management of an entity to assist in achieving their objective of ensuring, as far as practicable, the orderly and efficient conduct of its business, including adherence to internal policies, the safeguarding of assets, the prevention and detection of fraud and error, the accuracy and completeness of the accounting records, and the timely preparation of reliable financial information.*

In most businesses, it is possible to identify an 'internal control environment' which comprises the following three 'tiers' or elements:

(a) Management organisation, roles and responsibilities.

(b) Management's risk assessment.

(c) Management's monitoring of the system.

2:5.2 The control environment

The control environment encompasses the overall attitudes, abilities, awareness and actions of the personnel of an entity, and particularly those of its management, concerning the importance of control and the emphasis attached to it. The leadership and support of senior management are essential if a favourable control environment is to be established and maintained. The key elements of the control environment are:

(a) the effectiveness of the organisational structure;

(b) the role of the board of directors and key management;

(c) the role of the audit committee and internal audit;

(d) the reasonableness of management plans and budgets;

(e) the relevance and reliability of management information;

(f) the reliability of management estimates;

(g) the existence of adequate policies and procedures for controlling the business;

(h) the risk that management might override internal controls or intentionally misstate the financial statements;

(i) the effectiveness of management control over computer operations;

(j) the effectiveness of management control, excluding computer operations.

Favourable or unfavourable features of the control environment have a significant effect on the quality of an entity's internal accounting controls, on the degree of control exercised by management over the business operations and, ultimately, on the fair presentation of its financial statements. An unfavourable control environment can indicate the presence of particular inherent risk conditions.

The control environment is discussed more fully in **Section 8:1.3**, 'Assessing the control environment'.

2:5.3 Accounting systems

Accounting systems normally comprise the financially significant computer applications and the computer environment(s) in which these are developed, implemented, maintained and operated. These systems will form the basis for the preparation of periodic financial statements and other information required by management to control the business. They consist of a series of procedures for recording, processing and controlling transactions and for recording resources and their use.

Such procedures may be performed manually (e.g., the recording of goods received) or by computer (e.g., the automatic generation of cheques to pay suppliers). In this Manual, computerised accounting procedures are called 'programmed procedures'.

It is increasingly rare for accounting systems to be wholly or mainly prepared without the use of computers. This Manual concentrates on the problems posed by computerised accounting systems, and the auditing procedures which deal with those problems. Where significant parts of an accounting system are manual, or involve the use of accounting machines other than computers, the principles of understanding and assessing the system and the control environment are the same as for computer systems. However, it is likely that an audit strategy based mainly on substantive testing will be indicated, because the volume of transactions is likely to be low, and the system and controls are likely to be unsophisticated.

An accounting system should be designed in the light of factors such as the nature of the business, its size and organisational structure, the types and volumes of transactions and whether it is subject to the requirements of any regulatory bodies. It should take into account any relevant inherent risk characteristics of the account balances and classes of transactions.

Effective accounting systems should:

(a)   ensure that all valid, but only valid, transactions are identified and recorded on a timely basis;

(b)   ensure that details of transactions recorded are accurate;

(c)   determine the time period in which transactions occur, to permit recording of the transaction in the proper accounting period;

(d)   permit realistic measurement of the amount of the transactions in the financial statements;

(e)   describe the type of transaction in sufficient detail to facilitate the proper presentation of the transaction and related disclosure in the financial statements;

(f)   limit the opportunity for fraud and other irregularities.

An understanding of the accounting systems is necessary as the basis for the assessment of control effectiveness and for the design and performance of substantive tests. Obtaining an understanding of accounting systems is discussed in **Section 8:2**, 'Accounting systems'.

2:5.4 Internal accounting controls

Internal accounting controls are the specific procedures established by management to ensure, as far as possible, that:

(a)   transactions are completely and accurately processed;

(b)   transactions are recorded in accordance with management's authorisation;

(c)   assets are safeguarded;

(d)   the accounting systems are reliable and the account balances are correct.

Internal accounting controls consist of:

(a)   information technology (IT) controls; and

(b)   application controls.

The design of internal accounting controls is influenced by the size, complexity and nature of the business, as well as the nature of its control environment, its accounting systems and its methods of data processing. For example, IT controls will be more important in a large business with a complex data-processing environment. For a small business, with simple data processing, formal procedures may not be necessary to control the business and safeguard its assets, although application controls will still be desirable.

2:5.4.1 IT controls

IT controls ensure that the programmed procedures within a computer system are appropriately designed, implemented, maintained and operated, and that only authorised changes are made to programs and data.

IT controls can be classified under the following headings:

(a)   Implementation controls.

(b)   File conversion controls.

(c)   Maintenance controls.

(d)   Computer operations controls.

(e)   Data file security controls.

(f)   Program security controls.

(g)   System software controls.

Although both types of application control discussed in **Section 2:5.4.2** are ultimately manual controls carried out in user departments, many control techniques are based on the correct operation of programmed procedures. It is the combination of programmed procedure and user control that makes the application controls effective. IT controls, which ensure the proper and continued operation of programmed procedures, are therefore normally necessary to the effective operation of application controls involving programmed procedures.

Because IT controls apply to the entire IT environment, rather than to specific applications or transactions, they assist in ensuring the effectiveness of application controls in all systems in that environment. Accordingly, an assessment of the effective operation of these common IT controls is a particularly important element in the extended assessment of application controls, which may provide evidence about controls in several audit areas at once.

2:5.4.2 *Application controls*

Application controls can be further classified into *file controls* (controls over the files from which figures in the financial statements are derived) and *transaction controls* (controls over the transactions that update those files).

(a) **File controls** are designed to ensure that the data are properly maintained between transaction updates. The objectives of file controls are:

   (i)   file continuity, to ensure that, once data are updated to a file, the data remain correct and current on the file;

   (ii) asset protection, to ensure that the assets represented by the balances on the file are secure, by ensuring that movements are properly approved and recorded, and that records are adequately protected from unauthorised or incorrect amendment.

(b) **Transaction controls** have the following objectives:

   (i)   completeness, to ensure that all transactions are recorded and remain complete through each stage of processing;

   (ii) accuracy, to ensure that transactions are accurately processed at each stage;

   (iii) authorisation, to ensure that only authorised transactions are processed.

Completeness and accuracy relate primarily to the audit objectives of completeness, accuracy and cut-off. Authorisation relates primarily to the audit objective of existence.

Separate transaction controls normally exist in relation to the processing of standing data and transaction data. Standing data are defined as data of a permanent or semi-permanent nature held on files and referred to repeatedly during processing (e.g., rates of pay). Transaction data are data concerning individual transactions (e.g., hours worked during the week). Controls over standing data are likely to be of greater significance than those over transaction data because standing data are used many times. In addition, standing data are usually verified only when they are originally input and not each time they are used. However, controls over the processing of transaction data are important for significant transactions (i.e., those that could have a material impact on the account balance).

2:5.5 Division of duties

If internal control is to be effective, there should be an adequate division of duties in the performance of accounting procedures and related internal accounting controls. Adequate division of duties reduces the risk of error and, particularly, fraud. The fundamental principle underlying adequate division of duties is that employees who, as part of their normal duties, have access to an entity's assets should not also have uncontrolled access to the records that establish accountability for those assets. Consequently, adequate division of duties will restrict the opportunity to conceal the misappropriation of assets.

2:5.6 Assessing control risk

Assessing the risk of internal control for audit purposes is the process of evaluating strengths and weaknesses of the client's internal control structure, and concluding whether the operation of internal control is effective in reducing the risk of material misstatement in the financial statements. Internal control can be effective either by preventing a misstatement occurring, or in detecting it in a reasonable time after it has occurred.

Where there is a risk of material misstatement, a favourable assessment of control effectiveness allows the auditor to reduce the extent of substantive testing in respect of relevant audit objectives for particular account balances and classes of transactions.

2:5.6.1 The process of assessing control risk

The auditor should assess control risk for each transaction cycle of audit significance. This assessment will depend on the strength of the control procedures applicable to the applications (including related monitoring controls) as well as the related computer controls and the control environment. The results of the control risk assessment will affect a number of audit objectives for each cycle.

On all audits the auditor should assess the control environment and obtain and record an understanding of the accounting system. The degree to which each of the types of control procedures needs to be assessed, and tested, for the purposes of the control risk assessment is a judgement that depends on the apparent quality of internal control, the relative efficiency of obtaining audit evidence from the operation of internal control and from substantive tests, optimum timing of work, the skills of the engagement team and client expectations.

Taking into account prior year experience and knowledge obtained in the current year, the auditor will often presume the level of control risk for purposes of determining the audit strategy, before control procedures have been documented completely or tests of controls performed.

For purposes of planning the audit, control risk can be assessed for each significant transaction cycle as:

(a) Maximum – no assurance to be taken from internal control;

(b) Below the maximum – some assurance to be obtained from internal control; or

(c) Low – high assurance to be obtained from internal control.

In practice, control risk is a continuum from non-existent control (maximum control risk – high risk of misstatement through error or fraud) to very good control (low control risk), where we can obtain high assurance of the reliability of financial information generated by the system by testing controls. Particularly in below the maximum it will be efficient to assess control risk at points on the continuum.

2:6 Audit regulation

2:6.1 Introduction

Under the Companies Act 1989, an auditor of a UK registered company must usually be a member of a recognised supervisory body (RSB) and eligible for the appointment under the rules of that body. The supervisory bodies recognised by the Department of Trade and Industry are:

- The Institute of Chartered Accountants in England and Wales (ICAEW)
- The Institute of Chartered Accountants of Scotland (ICAS)
- The Institute of Chartered Accountants in Ireland (ICAI)
- The Chartered Association of Certified Accountants (ACCA)
- The Association of Authorised Public Accountants (AAPA)
- The Association of International Accountants (AIA)

Members of other bodies may act as a reporting accountant for smaller companies. A main change introduced by the Companies Act 1989 is that a partnership or incorporated body may be appointed as auditor provided it is controlled or appointed by qualifying people.

2:6.1.1 *Role of the supervisory body*

Under the Companies Act 1989 a supervisory body must maintain and enforce rules as to:

(a)   the eligibility of persons to seek appointment as a company auditor; and

(b)   the conduct of company audit work

   which are binding on persons seeking appointment or acting as a company auditor.

2:6.2 Regulations

ICAEW, ICAS and ICAI have jointly published *Audit Regulations and Guidance*. These rules for registered auditors cover various matters, including:

(a)   eligibility and registration;

(b)   conduct of regulated audit work;

(c)   fit and proper status;

(d)   maintenance of competence;

(e)   monitoring compliance with the audit regulations.

The objectives of the Institutes in issuing these audit regulations are to make sure that:

(a)   auditors registered with the Institutes maintain high standards of work;

(b)   the reputation of registered auditors with the public is maintained;

(c)   the application of the regulations is fair but firm;

(d)   the regulations are clear; and

(e)   the regulations apply to all sizes of firm.

2:6.2.1 Registration

The regulations provide for a Registration Committee to be responsible for:

(a)   granting applications for registration subject to or without restrictions or conditions or rejecting applications for registration;

(b)   withdrawing or suspending registration;

(c)   imposing such restrictions or conditions on the undertaking of audits by a registered auditor as it may consider appropriate;

(d)   granting or refusing dispensation from the requirements for eligibility;

(e)   reviewing the returns and reports made under these regulations, and investigating any failure to make such returns or reports;

(f)   making such enquiries (in writing, by way of visit to the office or offices of a registered auditor or otherwise) as it may consider appropriate to ascertain the eligibility of an applicant for registration or to confirm the compliance of a registered auditor with these regulations;

(g)   publishing such of its orders or decisions under these regulations as it may consider appropriate in such manner as it shall determine; and

(h)   compiling and maintaining the register.

2:6.2.1.1 Regulations

The regulations regarding registration are set out in the *Audit Regulations and Guidance* (**Chapter 2**). The principal eligibility requirements for a firm applying for registration are that:

(a)   the firm is fit and proper (*see* **Section 2:6.3, Appendix A**, for the criteria as to what constitutes 'fit and proper');

(b)   the firm has professional indemnity insurance (*see* **Section 2:6.2.4**);

(c)   the individuals responsible for company audit work (partners or directors) in the firm are qualified individuals; and

(d)   the firm has appointed an audit compliance principal.

A registered auditor is required to establish and maintain procedures designed to ensure that:

(a)   any individual who is or will be employed by or associated with it for the purposes of or in connection with audit work is a fit and proper person;

(b)   in making a decision to accept appointment or reappointment as auditor, consideration is given to its own independence, the availability of the resources required and its ability properly to perform the audit;

(c)   all partners and staff adhere to the principles of independence and confidentiality set out in the ethical statements from time to time issued by the ICAEW;

(d)   all partners and staff consult at the appropriate professional level on ethical, technical or practical issues as appropriate; and

(e)   it maintains the appropriate level of competence in the conduct of audits.

2:6.2.2 Conduct of auditors

There are two main elements to the guidance on conduct of auditors:

(a)   Professional integrity and independence.

(b)   Technical standards.

2:6.2.2.1 Professional integrity and independence

Independence is a fundamental characteristic for the registered auditor. It is an attitude of mind characterised by integrity and an objective approach to professional work. All partners and staff must ensure, by their conduct, that they both *are* independent and *are seen to be so*.

SAS 100 requires that in the conduct of any audit of financial statements, auditors should comply with the ethical guidance issued by their relevant professional bodies. Each professional body has published detailed guidance on maintaining professional independence. Each publication is broadly similar, and it is not appropriate to repeat the guidance in full in this Manual. Particular reference should be made to the relevant ethical statements when further guidance is needed. This section describes the principal procedures which should be instituted to protect the independence of partners and staff within a firm.

Each firm should take appropriate steps to ensure that all partners and staff understand the requirement for independence and follow it. In addition to setting a requirement for independence and conflicts of interest to be considered before accepting new clients, firms may also:

(a)   prepare and distribute a rulebook;

(b)   distribute lists of client companies and other prohibited investments or activities;

(c)   require partners and staff to sign a declaration of independence;

(d)   monitor compliance with independence rules, with disciplinary procedures if necessary.

2:6.2.2.2 *Undue dependence on an audit client*

Objectivity may be threatened or appear to be threatened by undue dependence on any audit client or group of connected clients. Whether objectivity is threatened will depend on a variety of factors including the size and nature of the practice and the size and nature of the audit client and its relationship with the practice.

The public perception of an auditor's objectivity is likely to be in jeopardy where the fees for audit and other recurring work paid by one client or group of connected clients exceed 15 per cent of the gross practice income. Where the public interest is involved it is particularly important that objectivity is seen to be preserved, and in the case of listed and other public interest companies the appropriate figure should be 10 per cent of the gross practice income.

A new practice seeking to establish itself or an established practice reducing its activities may not be able to comply with these criteria. Such practices therefore should take particular care to safeguard their independence.

The figures given above indicate only the extremes beyond which the public perception of a member's objectivity is likely to be at risk. It is the duty of the firm to satisfy itself that it is not open to criticism in respect of any audit engagement, having regard to all the circumstances of the case. Before accepting an audit appointment and as part of its annual review, a practice should carefully consider each case where for a client or group of associated clients the fees from audit and from other recurring work represent 10 per cent or more of the gross practice income. In the case of a listed company or other public interest company a figure of not more than 5 per cent is the appropriate point to initiate a review.

The fees from a number of non-recurring assignments could, if taken together with recurring work, give rise to a problem of undue dependence on an audit client. Any such dependency should be assessed and, if necessary, action taken to reduce this dependence.

In circumstances where the auditor is dependent for income on the profits of any one office within a practice and the gross income of that office is regularly dependent on one client or a group of connected clients for more than 15 per cent of its gross fees (in the case of listed or other public interest companies, 10 per cent), a partner from another office of the practice should take final responsibility for any report made by the practice on the affairs of the client. The same considerations apply to every partner whose income from the practice depends significantly on the retention of a specific audit client or group of clients.

2:6.2.2.3 *Beneficial interests in shares and other investments*

Partners and their dependants should not own beneficial interests in shares or other investments in audit clients. Beneficial 'interests in shares and other investments' is widely drawn. It would include a beneficial interest in a trust where the trustees might reasonably be expected to act in accordance with the wishes of a beneficiary or where the partner is a trustee. It will also include debentures, loan stock, and options to buy or sell shares and unit trusts where the trust itself is an audit client. It is not possible to avoid this rule by having holdings managed by a nominee, under a blind trust or through a Personal Equity Plan. Staff should not work on an audit client where they or their dependants own a beneficial interest in shares or other investments in that client. Some firms may wish to prohibit investment in audit clients by all staff and their dependants. Depending on the size of the firm, it might be appropriate to prepare a list of 'prohibited investments' for distribution to partners and staff.

Shares and other investments in audit clients which are 'involuntarily' acquired, e.g. by marriage, inheritance or as a result of the firm gaining a new audit client, should be disposed of at the earliest practicable date at which the transaction would not amount to insider dealing.

A firm is allowed to audit a company where a partner acts as trustee of a trust or trusts which hold(s) shares in the company. In these circumstances the guidance on disclosure of the holdings in the financial statements and the 10 per cent limits for listed and other public interest companies should be noted. A trustee partner should not act as audit partner of a company in which the trust is a shareholder. A sole practitioner wishing to continue an audit appointment in such circumstances should be satisfied it is appropriate to do so and have made arrangements for external consultation.

2:6.2.2.4 *Loans to or from a client*

Partners and staff should only have loans, mortgages or overdrafts from, or make deposits with or loans to, an audit client if this is in the ordinary course of the client's business and entered into on normal commercial terms. No partner should borrow from an audit client, even in the ordinary course of business, in order to subscribe to partnership capital. An engagement partner should not have a loan from his/her client. Similar conditions apply where there are significant overdue fees from a client. In this case, a principal not involved in the audit should review the situation to ascertain whether the overdue fees, together with the fees for the current audit, could be regarded as a significant loan.

2:6.2.2.5 *Goods, services and hospitality*

Social relationships with clients' officers and employees should be kept within reasonable limits of courtesy. Goods, services or hospitality should not be accepted by a firm, its partners and staff, or anyone closely connected with them, unless the value of any benefit is modest.

The purchase of client goods and services is permissible. In order to limit any benefits, firms may wish to stipulate that the price paid for such goods and services should generally be no lower than that charged by the client to the public. An engagement partner should not take out a **new** insurance or pension policy with his/her client insurance company or society.

2:6.2.2.6 *Other situations where independence could be impaired*

The guidance highlights certain other situations that could threaten a firm's objectivity or the appearance of objectivity. These include:

(a)   When a principal or senior employee of the audit firm leaves to join the audit client.

(b)   When a firm is involved in or threatened with litigation in relation to an audit client.

(c)   As a result of pressures arising from associated practices or external sources such as bankers or solicitors, or those introducing business.

(d)   A family, business or personal relationship with a client.

(e)   Where an auditor acts for a client company over a long period of time.

2:6.2.2.7 *Other services*

Potential independence problems can also arise when a firm provides other services in addition to the audit. Clients expect a full range of professional services from their auditor, but this should not be allowed to compromise the independence, or the appearance of independence, of the audit.

Problems may arise from, e.g.:

(a)   preparation of accounting records and financial statements (*see* **Section 7:2**, 'Accounting work for audit clients');

(b)   design and implementation of accounting systems and internal controls;

(c)   past or present employment of a partner or employee by the client;

(d)   appointment as liquidator, administrator or receiver of an audit client;

(e)   provision of corporate finance advice, e.g. on takeovers and mergers;).

In each case, the engagement partner should consider the guidance contained in the guidance for professional conduct, and that included in **Section 3:2**, 'Appointment and continuation as an auditor', and take whatever action appears to be necessary to protect independence. If necessary, the engagement partner should follow the consultation procedures in **Section 5:5**, 'Consultation and concurring reviews'.

2:6.2.2.8 *Undue influence*

A registered auditor must ensure that individuals who are not qualified individuals, or persons who are not partners, directors or shareholders, are not able to exert any influence over the independence or integrity of the audit.

2:6.2.2.9 *Conflicts of interest*

Partners should consider the appropriate course of action whenever there is a possibility of a conflict of interest between the firm and the client, or between different clients of the firm. Problems may arise, e.g. where clients are in competition or in dispute.

A firm should not accept or continue an engagement where a significant conflict of interest between the firm and its client arises or could arise.

Where a firm has two or more clients whose interests may be in conflict, the work of the firm may be managed in a way that avoids the interests of one client's prejudicing those of another. If, even with appropriate safeguards in place, accepting or continuing an engagement would materially prejudice the interests of any client, the appointment should not be accepted or continued, or the firm should cease to act in one or more cases. For further guidance, *see* the statements contained in the guidance on professional ethics which specifically deal with conflicts of interest and corporate finance advice.

2:6.2.3 *Technical standards*

The *Audit Regulations and Guidance* require a registered auditor to comply with Statements of Auditing Standards (SASs). Compliance with the guidance in this Manual and the establishment and maintenance of quality control procedures (*see* **Section 5:6**, 'Quality assurance inspections') will assist the registered auditor in complying with standards.

2:6.2.4 *Professional indemnity insurance regulations*

One of the criteria which a firm must satisfy on applying for registration is that it has taken such steps as may reasonably be expected of it to secure that it is able to meet claims against it arising out of professional business. The firm must also arrange professional indemnity insurance (PII) to meet the required criteria.

Firms must comply with PII regulations or by-laws which are issued separately by each of the Chartered Institutes. The PII regulations are contained in Volume 1 of the ICAEW Members' Handbook, or the ICAI's Members' Handbook, and the PII by-laws are in the Council statements of ICAS.

The PII regulations and by-laws include details of:

(a)   the annual minimum limit of indemnity;

(b)   limits of the self-insured excess.

Firms should have proper procedures for assessing and mitigating risk including:

(a)   considering the impact of the economic climate on clients;

(b)   evaluating new and existing clients on a regular basis; and

(c)   procedures for identifying and monitoring claims or potential claims and to enable them to learn from experience.

2:6.2.5 Fit and proper status

The Companies Act 1989 requires RSBs to have adequate rules and practices designed to ensure that registered auditors are fit and proper persons to accept appointment as company auditor.

2:6.2.5.1 The firm

As part of the criteria for registration, the *Audit Regulations and Guidelines* require a firm to be fit and proper. Set out in **Appendix A** (*see* **Section 2:6.3**) is the fit and proper questionnaire for a firm, as contained in the *Audit Regulations and Guidelines*.

2:6.2.5.2 Individuals

For a firm to be fit and proper, all partners and those staff involved in audit work must also be fit and proper. The guidance suggests that firms require individuals to complete a 'fit and proper' questionnaire and to update this information once every three years. Set out in **Appendix B** (*see* **Section 2:6.4**) is the fit and proper questionnaire for individuals. Firms should consult the relevant Institute if they are in any doubt about whether specific disclosures would render an individual unsuitable to participate in audit work.

2:6.2.6 Maintenance of competence

Maintaining competence falls into four main sections:

(a)   recruitment;

(b)   technical training and updating;

(c)   on-the-job training and professional development;

(d)   information technology.

2:6.2.6.1 Recruitment

Each firm should ensure that it recruits staff with suitable qualifications, including any necessary expertise in specialised areas. The recruitment criteria should ensure that the firm recruits audit staff who have individually, and in aggregate, the experience and ability to exercise the appropriate level of judgement. When planning for staffing needs the firm should consider:

(a)   volume of practice work;

(b)   types of work at all levels;

(c)   existing staff structure;

(d)   methods of work and staff management; and

(e)   expected changes from the current situation.

2:6.2.6.2 *Technical training and updating*

All principals and staff should be required to keep themselves technically up to date on matters that are relevant to their work. Each firm should establish guidelines and/or requirements for continuing professional education for personnel at each level within the firm and communicate them to personnel.

A firm's procedures to assist personnel to keep up to date may include:

(a)   circulating digests or full texts of accounting and auditing standards, relevant legislation, and relevant pronouncements by regulatory bodies and pronouncements on accounting and auditing matters;

(b)   maintaining a technical library;

(c)   issuing technical circulars and memoranda on professional developments as they affect the firm; and

(d)   requiring attendance on appropriate professional courses, e.g. in-house courses, Institute courses, industry-led courses.

A firm should identify expertise required in specialised areas and industries and develop and maintain that expertise by:

(a)   encouraging attendance at external courses, meetings and conferences;

(b)   encouraging membership and participation in organisations concerned with specialised areas and industries; and

(c)   providing relevant technical literature.

2:6.2.6.3 *On-the-job training and professional development*

The firm should ensure that, in assigning staff to particular audits, the assignment provides, where appropriate, the opportunity for on-the-job training and professional development. This should provide staff with exposure to different types of audits and the opportunity to work with more experienced members of the team. The latter should be made responsible for the supervision and review of the work of junior staff.

The performance of staff on audits should be evaluated and the results of the assessments should be communicated to the staff concerned, giving staff the opportunity to respond to comments made and to agree to any proposed action.

2:6.2.6.4 Information technology

If an audit client has computer-based accounting systems, principals and employees involved in the audit should have an appropriate level of theoretical knowledge and experience of information technology (IT). The level of competence required will depend on the sophistication of the client's computer system. The principal responsible for the audit should understand enough about IT to understand the concepts and objectives of the audit work being done, and to decide whether or not these have been achieved.

2:6.3 Appendix A Fit and proper questionnaire for a firm

For each of the following questions, the answers will be 'yes' or 'no', but a 'yes' answer will need further explanation.

2:6.3.1 Financial integrity and reliability

In the last ten years, has the firm made any compromise or arrangement with its creditors, or otherwise failed to satisfy creditors in full?

2:6.3.2 Civil liabilities

In the last five years, has the firm been the subject of any civil action relating to its professional or business activities which resulted in a finding against it by a court, or a settlement being agreed?

2:6.3.3 Good reputation and character

In the last ten years has the firm been:

(a)   refused or restricted in the right to carry on any trade, business or profession for which a specific licence, registration or other authority is required?

(b)   refused entry to any professional body or trade association, or decided not to continue with an application?

(c)   reprimanded, warned about future conduct, disciplined or publicly criticised by any professional or regulatory body?

(d)   made the subject of a court order at the instigation of any professional or regulatory body?

(e)   investigated on allegations of misconduct or malpractice in connection with its professional or business activities which resulted in a formal complaint being proved but no disciplinary order being made?

2:6.4 Appendix B Fit and proper questionnaire for individuals

To be completed by each principal and member of staff or other individual involved in or connected with audit work.

For each of the following questions, the answers will be 'yes' or 'no', but a 'yes' answer will need further explanation.

2:6.4.1 Financial integrity and reliability

In the last ten years has a court, in the United Kingdom or elsewhere, given any judgement against you about a debt?

In the last ten years have you made any compromise arrangement with your creditors?

Have you ever been declared bankrupt or been the subject of a bankruptcy court order in the United Kingdom or elsewhere or has a bankruptcy petition ever been served on you?

Have you ever signed a trust deed for a creditor, made an assignment for the benefit of creditors or made any arrangement for the payment of a composition to creditors?

2:6.4.2 Convictions or civil liabilities

(*Note*: There is no need to mention offences committed before the age of 17, unless committed within the last ten years, and road traffic offences that did not lead to a disqualification or prison sentence.)

Have you at any time pleaded guilty to or been found guilty of any offence? If so, give particulars of the court which convicted you, the offence, the penalty imposed and date of conviction.

In the last five years have you, in the United Kingdom or elsewhere, been the subject of any civil action relating to your professional or business activities which has resulted in a finding against you by a court, or a settlement being agreed?

Have you ever been disqualified by a court from being a director, or from acting in the management or conduct of the affairs of any company?

2:6.4.3 Good reputation and character

Have you, in the United Kingdom or elsewhere, ever been:

(a) refused the right or been restricted in the right to carry on any trade, business or profession for which a specific licence, registration or other authority is required?

(b) investigated in relation to allegations of misconduct or malpractice in connection with your professional activities which resulted in a formal complaint being proved but no disciplinary order made?

(c) the subject of disciplinary procedures by a professional body or employer resulting in a finding against you?

(d) reprimanded, excluded, disciplined or publicly criticised by any professional body to which you belong or have belonged?

(e) refused entry to or excluded from membership of any profession or vocation?

(f) dismissed from any office (other than as auditor) or employment or requested to resign from any office, employment or partnership?

(g) reprimanded, warned about future conduct, disciplined, or publicly criticised by any regulatory body, or any officially appointed inquiry concerned with the regulation of a financial, professional or other business activity?

(h) the subject of a court order at the instigation of any regulatory body, or any officially appointed inquiry concerned with the regulation of a financial, professional or other business activity?

Are you currently undergoing investigation or disciplinary procedure as described in the above list?

2:7 Fraud and other irregularities

2:7.1 Introduction

SAS 110 'Fraud and error' defines fraud as comprising 'both the use of deception to obtain an unjust or illegal financial advantage and intentional misrepresentations affecting the financial statements by one or more individuals among management, employees, or third parties. Fraud may involve:

(a) falsification or alteration of accounting records or other documents;

(b) misappropriation of assets or theft;

(c) suppression or omission of the effects of transactions from records or documents;

(d) recording of transactions without substance;

(e) intentional misapplication of accounting policies; or

(f) wilful misrepresentations of transactions or of the entity's state of affairs.'

SSA 110 refers to 'error' as 'unintentional mistakes in financial statement, such as:

(a) mathematical or clerical mistakes in the underlying records and accounting date;

(b) oversight or misinterpretation of facts; or

(c) unintentional misapplication of accounting policies'.

This section discusses the auditor's responsibilities concerning the detection and reporting of material misstatements caused by fraud or error in financial statements upon which the auditor is reporting. In practices, because the lawfulness of an act is only determined following a decision by the courts, the auditor will normally be concerned with suspected, rather than proven, frauds.

The auditor should be alert to conduct which may be dishonest before considering whether it may be fraudulent. For example, the auditor should consider 'questionable' payments made by the client which may be illegal or involve doubtful ethics or fraud. In particular circumstances, conduct may be dishonest in some respect but no fraudulent, e.g. conduct which breaches an undertaking to follow a specified course of conduct required by a regulator. Where specific breaches of laws or regulations are concerned, the guidance in **Section 2:8**, 'Laws and regulations', should be followed.

2:7.2 Responsibilities for the prevention and detection of fraud and error

2:7.2.1 Directors' responsibilities

It is the responsibility of the directors to take steps as are reasonably open to them to prevent and detect fraud. This includes:

(a) Taking steps to provide reasonable assurance that the activities of the entity are conducted honestly and that its assets are safeguarded.

(b) Establishing arrangements designed to deter fraudulent or other dishonest conduct and to detect any that occurs.

(c) Ensuring that, to the best of their knowledge and belief, financial information, whether used in the entity or for financial reporting, is reliable.

They are also responsible for preparing financial statements that give true and fair view of the state of affairs of a company or group and of its profit or loss for the financial year. Neither the assignment of particular responsibilities to management nor the audit process relieves the directors of these fundamental responsibilities.

In addition, directors and officers of companies have responsibility to provide information required by the auditors, to which they have a legal right of access under s. 389A of the Companies Act 1985. That section also provides that it is a criminal offence to give the auditor information or explanations which are misleading, false or deceptive.

The following steps, among others, may assist the directors in discharging their responsibilities for the prevention and detection of fraud and error:

(a) The practices contemplated in the document 'Internal control and financial reporting' giving guidance for directors of listed companies developed in response to the recommendation of the Cadbury Committee;

(b)   The steps taken to develop within the entity an appropriate control environment, which is itself dependent upon the attitude, awareness and actions of directors;

(c)   The development of a Code of Conduct, ensuring employees are properly trained in and understand its provisions, monitoring compliance and taking appropriate disciplinary action in cases of non-compliance;

(d)   The institution and operation of appropriate systems of internal control including monitoring their effectiveness and taking corrective action where necessary.

In order to assist them in achieving the above objectives, directors of larger entities will often assign particular responsibilities to:

(a)   an internal audit function;

(b)   a legal department;

(c)   a compliance function; and/or

(d)   an audit committee.

In certain sectors activities (e.g. financial services), there are detailed laws and regulations that specifically require directors to have systems to safeguard the entity's assets and to ensure the reliability of financial reporting.

Given the responsibility of directors to prepare financial statements that give a true and fair view of the state of affairs of a company and of its profit or loss for the financial year, it is necessary, where material error or fraud has occurred, for them to correct the accounting records and to ensure that the matter is appropriately reflected and/or disclosed in the financial statements.

2:7.2.2 *Responsibilities of auditors*

Although the audit may act as a deterrent, the auditor is not responsible for preventing fraud or errors. If the auditor identifies weaknesses in the client's accounting systems and internal controls which might result in fraud not being detected, the auditor should report these to management. *See* **Sections 2:7.4** and **2:7.5**.

At SAS 110.1 it is stated that 'Auditors should plan and perform their audit procedures and evaluate and report the results thereof, recognising that fraud or error may materially affect the financial statements.'

The auditor must plan, perform and evaluate the audit work in order to have a reasonable expectation of detecting material misstatements in the financial statements arising from error or fraud. However, the audit cannot be expected to detect all errors or instances of fraudulent or dishonest conduct. The likelihood of detecting errors is higher than that of detecting fraud, because fraud is usually accompanied by acts specifically designed to conceal its existence, such as management introducing transactions without substance, collusion between employees or falsification of records. Consequently, 'reasonably expectation' in the context of fraud must be construed having regard to nature of the fraud and, in particular, the degree of collusion, the seniority of those involved and the level of deception concerned.

2:7.3 Limitations of an audit in relation to detecting fraud and error

An audit is subject to the unavoidable risk that some material misstatements of the financial statements will not be detected, even though the audit is properly planned and performed in accordance with Auditing Standards. The risk is higher with regard to misstatements resulting from dishonest or fraudulent conduct. The reasons for this include:

(a)   The effectiveness of audit procedures is affected by the inherent limitations of the accounting and internal control systems and by the use of selective testing rather than the examination of all transactions.

(b)   Much of the evidence obtained by the auditors is persuasive rather than conclusive in nature.

(c)   Dishonest or fraudulent conduct may take place over a number of years but may only be discovered in a later year (e.g. because a fictitious asset become material to the financial statements).

(d)   Dishonest or fraudulent conduct may involve conduct designed to conceal it, such as collusion, forgery, override of controls or intentional misrepresentations being made to the auditors.

   While the existence of effective accounting and internal control systems may reduce the probability of misstatement of financial statements resulting from fraud and error, there is always some risk of internal controls failing to operate as designed. Furthermore, any accounting and internal control systems may be ineffective against fraud committed by management, particularly if it involves collusion, internally or with third parties.

   The detection of fraud committed by management poses particular difficulties for auditors because management can be in a strong position to commit a fraud and conceal it from others within the entity and from the auditors. Actions that management may take to commit and conceal fraud include:

(a)   introducing complexity into the corporate structure, commercial arrangements with third parties, transactions or internal systems;

(b)   collusive acts with employees or third parties, whether related parties or otherwise;

(c)   the override of internal controls set up to prevent or detect fraud;

(d)   influencing accounting policies, financial statement presentation and accounting estimates affecting financial information used within the business or for external reporting; and

(e)   manipulating evidence available to, or reposes to evidence requested by, the auditors, delaying the provision of evidence or making representations and responses to audit enquiries that lack integrity or are deliberately untruthful.

2:7.4 Audit considerations

2:7.4.1 Engagement letter

As stated in **Section 3:3** 'Engagement letters', the auditor must send a letter to all audit clients setting out the terms of the engagement. This letter must include a paragraph regarding fraud and error. For example:

> **The responsibility for safeguarding the assets of the company and for the prevention and detection of fraud, error and non-compliance with law or regulations rests with yourselves. However, the auditor shall endeavour to plan the audit so that the auditor has a reasonable expectation of detecting material misstatements in the financial statements or accounting records (including those resulting from fraud, error or non-compliance with law or regulations), but the examination should not be relied upon to disclose all such material misstatement or frauds, errors or instances on non-compliance as may exist.**

2:7.4.2 Planning

SAS 110.2 states: 'When planning the audit the auditors should assess the risk that fraud or error may cause the financial statements to contain material misstatements.' In developing the audit strategy and testing plan the auditor must assess the risk that fraud or error may cause the financial statements to contain material misstatements, including:

(a) assessing fraud and error risk as part of the assessment of the risk to the firm;

(b) considering fraud risk at planning meetings, so that staff on the audit are briefed;

(c) using the understanding of the business, its organisational and commercial arrangements and the nature of its transactions (focusing on the substance of the arrangements and transactions, not just the form) to identify any significant risks;

(d) assessing the control environment, including assessments of:

　　(i)   the risk of employing fraudsters or individuals whose behaviour is considered unacceptable;

　　(ii) management and staff integrity and ethical values; and

　　(iii) the possible motivation and opportunities for management fraud and any indications of possible fraud; and

(e) considering monitoring, application and computer controls as part of the initial assessment of control risk.

The auditor should, as part of the normal audit, assess the risk of fraud separately from the risk of error, because:

(a)   the assessment of the significance of a risk fraud may differ from that for a risk of error, and

(b)   the appropriate audit response to a risk of fraud will often be different in nature and extent to that for a risk of error.

As part of determining the audit strategy, the auditor should ask management to provide details of any dishonest or fraudulent conduct which has come to its attention during the reporting period, any material weaknesses or breakdowns in the accounting records or controls, or of risks of which it is aware. The audit should record in the working papers any significant matter notified by management, together with the planned audit response.

Conditions or events which increase the risk of fraud and error are set out in **Appendix A** to this Section.

> *'Based on their risk assessment, the auditors should design audit procedures so as to have a reasonable expectation of detecting misstatements arising from fraud or error which are material to the financial statements (SAS 110.3).'*

The audit procedures must:

(a)   Ensure that the skill and experience of the audit team is appropriate to the size and complexity of the client concerned and to the industry in which the client operates. Where appropriate the auditor should consider specialist involvement.

(b)   Design responses to specific risks identified from the understanding of the business and the assessment of the control environment.

(c)   Where the auditor is placing reliance on controls to reduce the extent of the substantive procedures, evaluate the strengths and weaknesses of internal control, including any internal audit department;

(d)   Be alert throughout the conduct of the audit to audit evidence indicating unusual events or actions such as:

    (i)   control overrides

    (ii)   unusual transactions

    (iii) insubstantial responses to audit enquiries, delays or vague representations

    (iv) unusual accounting judgements; and

(e)   Obtain sufficient reliable audit evidence that puts appropriate emphasis on external evidence or evidence which the auditor create. The auditor should pay particular attention to the quality of audit evidence generated by the client or by third parties with whom the client has a relationship.

The auditor must document that he or she has assessed fraud risk, recorded in the working papers any fraud risks identified and planned an adequate response.

Unless the audit reveals evidence to the contrary, the auditor may accept representations as truthful and records and documents as genuine. However, the auditor should plan and perform the audit with an attitude of professional scepticism, recognising that the auditor might find conditions or events that indicate fraud or error may exist.

When the risk assessment or audit evidence obtained suggests that there may be fraudulent or dishonest conduct by directors or senior management, the auditor should increase the level of professional scepticism and the degree to which evidence independent of the client is sought. In such circumstances, the auditor should place less emphasis on management representations and documents generated or provided by the client.

2:7.4.3 Overseas activities

SAS 110.3 states: 'Where any of the activities of a company or group are carried on outside the United Kingdom or the Republic of Ireland, the auditors should take steps to ensure that the audit work in relation to the detection and reporting of any fraud and error is planned and carried out in accordance with the requirements of this SAS.'

These apply requirements apply irrespective of whether the overseas activities are carried on by a subsidiary of a UK or Irish parent, a division of the company based overseas or employees operating from the UK or the Republic of Ireland.

On group audits, the auditor should include in group audit instructions issued to other firms of auditors involved in the audit of significant business units:

(a)   an instruction to comply with UK Auditing Standards, including SAS 110; and

(b)   a request that issues documentation or equivalent confirm that the requirement has been met and identify any significant issues arising.

2:7.5 Other fraud services

In addition to work that the auditor undertakes as part of the normal audit, the auditor may undertake:

(a)   fraud limitation reviews, based on high levels interviews; and

(b)   other fraud services, including detailed fraud limitation audits of specific areas, involving the use of specialists from other practice areas.

The auditor will carry out these services to specific terms of reference.

2:7.6 Procedures when there is an indication that fraud or error may exist

SAS 110.4 states:

> 'When auditors become aware of information which indicates that fraud or error may exist, they should obtain an understanding of the nature of the event and the circumstances in which it has occurred, and sufficient other information to evaluate the possible effect on the financial statements. If the auditors believe that the indicated fraud or error could have a material effect on the financial statements, they should perform appropriate modified or additional procedures.'

Where the auditor identifies possible fraud or error the auditor should:

(a)   evaluate the possible effect on the financial statements;

(b)   document the findings and where appropriate discuss them with management; and

(c)   consider the implications for the audit.

2:7.6.1 Evaluating the possible effects on the financial statements

When the auditor becomes aware of information which indicates that fraud or error may exist, the auditor should obtain an understanding of the nature of the event and the circumstances in which it has occurred.

Where the auditor considers that the fraud or error could have a material effect on the financial statements, the auditor should perform appropriate modified or additional procedures. The auditor should design such procedures based on the judgement as to the:

(a)   types of fraud or error indicated;

(b)   identify of the persons involved;

(c)   likelihood of the occurrence of fraud or error;

(d)   likelihood that a particular type of fraud or error have a material effect on the financial statements, possible including those of prior years; and

(e)   extent to which it is realistic to expect that further procedures are likely to clarify the position.

Unless circumstances clearly indicate otherwise, the auditor should not assume that an instance of fraud or error is an isolated occurrence. If necessary, the auditor should adjust the nature, timing and extent of the substantive procedures.

The auditor should evaluate the possible effect of dishonest or fraudulent conduct on the financial statements. The auditor should consider its potential materiality, including an evaluation of:

(a)   the potential financial consequences, such as fines, penalties, damages, threat of expropriation of assets, enforced discontinuance of operations and litigation;

(b)   whether the potential financial consequences require disclosure, and if so, the adequacy of any disclosure;

(c)   whether breaches of laws and regulations may be involved; or

(d)   whether the potential financial consequences are so serious as to call into question the view given by the financial statements.

Such an evaluation may require the assistance of the client's directors, legal advisers, bankers or other advisors.

As the assessment of the effect of dishonest or fraudulent conduct may involve consideration of matters which do not lie within the competence and experience as auditors, the auditor may need to obtain appropriate expert advice (whether through the client or independently) in order to make the assessment of the possible effect on the client's financial statements. Where this is the case, the auditor should follow the guidance in **Section 7:6** 'Using the work of an expert'.

2:7.6.2 Documenting the findings

SAS 110.5 states:

> 'When the auditors become aware of, or suspect that there may be, instances of error or fraudulent conduct, they should document their findings and, subject to any requirement to report them direct to a third party, discuss them with the appropriate level of management.'

Depending on the circumstances, the auditor may document the findings by, e.g., taking copies of records and documents and making minutes of conversations. When the auditor discusses with management findings which indicate the possibility of fraud, the auditor should ensure so far as possible that there is no communication with any person who may be implicated in the events which the auditor are investigating.

If the directors do not provide sufficient information to satisfy the concerns in relation to the suspected or actual error or fraudulent conduct, the auditor should obtain legal advice about the application of law or regulations to the particular circumstances (including e.g., s. 389A of Companies Act 1985) and the possible effects on the financial statements.

The auditor should normally, with the client's permission, consult the client's lawyer as to the possible legal consequences of any fraudulent conduct. However, the auditor should obtain the own legal advice where it is not:

(a)   possible to consult the client's own lawyer;

(b)   appropriate to rely on the client's lawyer's opinion; or

(c)   clear what further action, if any the auditor should take.

When the auditor cannot obtain adequate information about the suspected or actual error or fraud, the auditor should ensure that the board of directors is aware of the position, and consider the implications of the lack of audit evidence for the report on the financial statements and whether any obligation arises to report to third parties.

2:7.6.3 Implications for other aspects of the audit

> 'The auditors should consider the implications of suspected or actual error or fraudulent conduct in relation to other aspects of the audit, particularly the reliability of management representation'. (SAS 110.6)

In particular, the auditor should:

(a)   re-evaluate the assessment of audit risk;

(b)   reconsider whether the other audit procedures have been performed with an appropriate degree of professional scepticism; and

(c)   consider the validity of management representations.

In maintaining an appropriate degree of professional scepticism the auditor should consider the following factors:

(a)   It's not a witchhunt, but don't necessarily assume the honesty of management.

(b)   Be alert to fraud risk indicators. Probe to the bottom if put on enquiry.

(c)   Don't over-rely on management representations, or on faxes and photocopies.

(d)   Seek good qualify independent audit evidence, especially if put on enquiry.

(e)   Be alert to attempts to break down the objectivity or hamper the audit.

(f)   Get basic disciplines right (e.g. stock sheet and debtor confirmation procedures).

In re-evaluating the assessment of audit risk, the auditor should take into account the following:

(a)   any apparent failure of specific control procedures;

(b)   the level of management or employees involved; and

(c)   the concealment, if any, of the act.

For example, a series of suspected or actual instances of error or fraudulent conduct which are financially immaterial may be symptomatic of management's probity and hence may throw doubt on the integrity of the financial statements and perhaps even the future prospect of the client.

2:7.7 Reporting fraud and error

The action the auditor should take to report an event will vary in relation to its nature and the gravity of its consequences. For example, the suspected or actual error or fraud is likely to have a substantial effect on the financial statements but there is little firm evidence yet available, the auditor should nevertheless consider whether the matter requires inclusion in the report concerning either fundamental uncertainties or circumstances in which a qualified opinion is to be expressed. If the matter is fully documented but the effect is not material, then unless the auditor concludes that an apparently isolated incidence is part of a wider pattern calling into question the probity of the client's management no references need be made in the financial statements or in the report.

The auditor should consider the implications for reporting:

(a)   to management;

(b)   within the audit firm;

(c)   to addressees of the audit report; and

(d)   to third parties.

2:7.7.1 Reporting to management

SAS 110.7 instructs that:

> The auditors should as soon as practicable communicate their findings to the appropriate level of management, the board of directors or the audit committee if they suspect or discover fraud, even if:

(a)   the potential effect on the financial statements is immaterial (save where SAS 110.12 applies), or

(b)   material error is actually found to exist.

The auditor should deal with suspected fraud with due regard to the impact that it might have on the relationship with the client and on the individuals who might be involved. The auditor should report the findings to an appropriately senior level of client management. This should normally be the board of directors or those within the client who have been authorised to receive such reports on behalf of the board (e.g. an audit committee).

If the auditor believes that senior management, including members of the board are involved in a suspected fraud, the auditor should seek legal advice. Legal advice should also be sought if the auditor:

(a)   is precluded by the client from obtaining sufficient appropriate audit evidence to evaluate whether fraud (or error) which is material to the financial statements has, or is likely to have, occurred;

(b)   is unsure to whom the auditor should report; or

(c)   believes that the report may not be acted upon.

The auditor should establish what action management takes when the auditor reports a suspected fraud or other irregularity. Appropriate action might include one or more of the following:

(a)   Investigating the circumstances.

(b)   Taking measures to ensure that the fraud or other irregularity ceases and/or does not recur.

(c)   Taking appropriate disciplinary action against the individual(s) responsible.

(d)   Taking appropriate steps for recovery and for dealing with any other consequences of the fraud (for example, the correction of inaccurate returns).

(e)   Ensuring proper classification of any loss in the financial statements, and other proper disclosures as required.

Where the auditor determines that the matter involves error rather than suspected fraud, the auditor should request the directors to make appropriate amendments to the financial statements. If such amendments are not made, the auditor should consider whether the opinion on the financial statements should be qualified. Guidance on qualified audit reports is given in **Section 13:16**, 'Qualified and modified reports to the members of limited companies and other organisations in Great Britain'.

2:7.7.2 *Reporting within the audit firm*

When a fraud is either discovered or reported to the auditor, the engagement partner must follow the consultation procedures set out in **Section 5:5**, 'Consultation and concurring reviews'.

2:7.7.3 *Reporting to addressees of the audit report on the financial statements*

SAS 110.8 states that:

> *Where the auditors conclude that the view given by the financial statements could be affected by a level of uncertainty concerning the consequences of a*

*suspected or actual error or fraud which, in their opinion, is fundamental, they
should include an explanatory paragraph referring to the matter in their report.*

This explanatory paragraph should be included in the 'Basis of Opinion' section of the
audit report.

SAS 110.9 states that:

*'If the auditor concludes that a fraud or error is material and disagrees with the
accounting treatment or with the extent, or the lack of, disclosure, in the
financial statements, the auditor should qualify the audit report'.*

In these circumstances, the qualification may need to extend to the following:

(a)   that the financial statements have not been properly prepared in accordance with the
Companies Act 1985, and/or

(b)   that proper accounting records have not been kept; and/or

(c)   that the financial statements are not in agreement with the accounting records.

Often, the circumstances surrounding the fraud (suspected or otherwise) will be such
that the auditor will not have sufficient audit evidence to be able to reach a conclusion
concerning the amounts involved. This will constitute a limitation on the scope of the
audit and the auditor should therefore qualify the report using an 'except for' qualification
in relation to adjustments which might have been necessary had the necessary evidence
been available and report that the auditor has not received all the information and
explanations necessary for the purposes of the audit (*see* SAS 110.9).

In considering an explanatory paragraph or a qualification, the auditor should consider
matters such as:

(a)   materiality;

(b)   the length of time during which the accounting records have been incorrect;

(c)   whether the client has suffered loss; and

(d)   whether the fraud was detected by the client's control procedures.

Steps taken to regularise the position, or the possible consequences of qualification, are
not, on their own, grounds on which the auditor may refrain from qualifying the opinion
or from including an explanatory paragraph reflecting a fundamental uncertainty.

When considering whether the financial statements reflect the possible consequences of
any suspected or actual dishonest or fraudulent conduct, the auditor should consider the
requirements of SSAP 18 'Accounting for contingencies'. Suspected or actual dishonest
or fraudulent conduct may require disclosure in the financial statements because, although
the immediate financial effect on the client may not be material, there could be future
material consequences such as fines or litigation.

When determining whether the directors have appropriately treated a possible or actual instance of dishonesty or fraud that may require disclosure in the financial statements, the auditor should consider whether:

(a)   the financial statements are free of material misstatements;

(b)   shareholders require the information to enable them to assess the performance of the client; and

(c)   there are any potential implications for its future operations or standing.

Corrections to the financial statements need to be made in respect of errors identified. Where suspected or actual instances of dishonest or fraudulent conduct needs to be reflected in the financial statements, a true and fair view will require that sufficient particulars are provided to enable users of the financial statements to appreciate the significance of the information disclosed. This would usually require the full potential consequences to be disclosed and, in some cases, it may be necessary for this purpose that the financial statements indicate that dishonest or fraudulent conduct is or may be involved.

2:7.7.4 *Reporting to third parties*

Where the auditors become aware of a suspected or actual instance of fraud they should;

a)   consider whether the matter may be one that ought to be reported to a proper authority in the public interest; and where this is the case

b)   except in the circumstances covered in SAS 110.12, discuss the matter with the board of directors, including any audit committee (SAS 110.10).

Where, having considered any views expressed on behalf of the entity and in the light of any legal advice obtained, the auditors conclude that the matter ought to be reported to an appropriate authority in the public interest, they should notify the directors in writing of their view and, if the entity does not voluntarily do so itself or is unable to provide evidence that the matter has been reported, they should report it themselves (SAS 110.11).

When a suspected or actual or instance of fraud casts doubt on the integrity of the directors auditors should make a report direct to a proper authority in the public interest without delay and without informing the directors in advance (SAS 110.12).

In certain circumstances, the auditor should consider reporting fraud or other irregularities outside the client, without necessarily informing management of this intention. The auditor may disclose matters to a proper authority in the public interest or for other specific reasons. Confidentiality is an implied term of the contract with the client. The duty of confidentiality, however, is not absolute. In certain exceptional circumstances the auditor is not bound by the duty of confidentiality and has the right or duty to report matters to a proper authority in the public interest. The auditor should weigh the public interest in maintaining confidential client relationships against the public interest in disclosure to a proper authority. Determination of where the balance of public interest lies requires careful consideration. Where the suspicions have been aroused the auditor should use professional judgement to determine whether the misgivings justify carrying the matter further or are too insubstantial to deserve reporting.

The auditor is protected from the risk of liability for breach of confidence or defamation provided that:

(a)   In the case of breach of confidence:

    (i)   disclosure is made in the public interest;

    (ii) such disclosure is made to an appropriate body or person; and

    (iii) there is no malice motivating the disclosure.

In the case of defamation:

    (i)   disclosure is made in their capacity as auditors of the entity concerned, and

    (ii) there is no malice motivating the disclosure.

In addition, the auditor is protected from such risks where the auditor is expressly permitted or required by legislation to disclose information.

The auditor should take the following matters into account when considering whether disclosure to third parties is justified in the public interest:

(a)   The weight of evidence, and the assessment of the likelihood that a fraud has been committed.

(b)   The extent to which the fraud is likely to affect members of the public.

(c)   The extend to which non-disclosure of the suspected or actual fraud is likely to enable it to be repeated with impunity.

(d)   The gravity of the matter.

(e)   Whether the directors have rectified the matter or are taking, or a likely to take, effective remedial action.

(f)   Whether there is a general management ethos within the entity of flouting the law and regulations.

The engagement partner, after appropriate consultation within the audit firm and with the legal advisors, is responsible for determining whether the auditor should make a report in the public interest. The auditor should normally do so only if he or she concludes that there is no appropriate level in the client to which the auditor can report, possibly because the fraud affects senior management and the board of directors.

In the case of clients subject to specific regulations (e.g., financial services or public sector clients), the engagement partner should consult the appropriate specialist partner(s).

When reporting to proper authorities in the public interest it is important that the auditor only report to one which has a proper interest to receive the information. Which body or person is the proper authority in a particular instance depends on the nature of the suspected or actual fraud. Proper authorities could include:

- Serious Fraud Office
- Crown Prosecution Service
- Police forces
- Securities and Investments Board and the Self Regulating Organisations it has recognised
- Recognised Professional Bodies recognised by the SIB under the Financial Services Act 1986
- International Stock Exchange
- Panel on Takeover and Mergers
- Society of Lloyd's
- Bank of England
- Local authorities
- Charity Commission for England and Wales
- Scottish Office for Scottish Charities
- Inland Revenue
- HM Customs and Excise
- Department of Trade and Industry

In cases of doubt as to the appropriate authority, the audit firm may consult their professional accountancy body. Also, the audit firm may refer the facts to the Investigations Division of the Department of Trade and Industry with a view to investigation by that Division.

The auditor receives the same protection even if he or she only has a reasonable suspicion that fraud has occurred. If the auditor could demonstrate that the he or she acted reasonably and in good faith in informing an authority of an instance of fraud which he or she thought had been committed the auditor would not be held by the court to be in breach of duty to the client even if, an investigation or prosecution having occurred, it were found that there had been no offence.

When the auditor decides whether to report, and if so to whom, the decision may be called into question at a future date for example on the basis of:

(a)   what the auditor knew at the time;

(b)   what the auditor ought to have known in the course of the audit;

(c)   what the auditor ought to have concluded; and

(d)   what the auditor ought to have done.

The auditor should therefore ensure that the working papers contain an appropriate record of the nature of the fraud and the basis for the decision whether or not to report.

The auditor should also consider the possible consequences if financial loss is occasioned as a result of fraud which the auditor suspect (or ought to suspect) has occurred but decide not to report.

The auditor may no longer have confidence in the integrity of the directors in situations such as:
(a)   where the auditor suspects or has evidence of the involvement or intended involvement of the directors in possible fraud which could have a material effect on the financial statements; or

(b)   where the auditor suspects or has evidence that the directors are aware of such fraud and, contrary to regulatory requirements or the public interest, have not reported it to a proper authority within a reasonably period.

2:7.7.5 *Statutory duty to report to third parties*

Where the client is a financial institution subject to statutory regulation, the auditor must report certain information direct to the relevant regulator.

The auditor must also, as a statutory duty, take the initiative to report to the appropriate authorities suspected money-laundering related to drug trafficking and terrorism. A failure to report in these circumstances is itself a criminal offence.

2:7.8 Audit completion

In relation to all suspected fraud which the auditor has identified, the auditor must document that the audit firm has:

(a)   recorded them in the working papers;

(b)   reported them to the client/authorities as necessary; and

(c)   evaluated them for their impact on the financial statements.

2:7.9 Withdrawal from the engagement

The auditor may conclude that withdrawal from the engagement is necessary in certain circumstances, e.g. if the auditor considers that the shareholders have not been given the information they require and the auditor sees no opportunity for reporting such information to the shareholders whilst continuing as auditor. Factors that may affect the conclusion include the implications if the client's directors are suspected of involvement with the suspected or actual fraud, which may affect the reliability of management representations, and the effects on continuing association with the client. In reaching a conclusion, the auditor may need to seek legal advice.

Resignation should be seen as a last resort. However, there are circumstances where there may be no alternative e.g., where the client's directors refuse to issue its financial statements or the auditor wishes to inform the shareholders or creditors of the client of the concerns and there is no immediate occasion to do so.

If the auditor decides to withdraw from the engagement, he or she must follow the professional procedures set in out in **Chapter 14**, 'Cessation as auditor'.

If the auditor is removed from office before issuing the audit report, the points which the auditor would have made in the qualified audit report should be made in the communication to the client concerning the removal from office or resignation, and in the communication with successor auditors. The auditor should also consider whether in accordance with s. 391A CA 1985, to make representations at a general meeting.

2:7.10 Compliance with International Standards on Auditing

Compliance with the Auditing Standards contained in SAS 120 and with relevant ethical guidance ensure compliance in all material respects with the requirements of the basic principles and essential procedures identified in the ISA 120 'Fraud and error'.

2:7.11 Appendix A Examples of conditions or events which may increase the risk of fraud or error occurring

Examples of conditions or events which may increase the risk of either fraud or error, or in some cases both follow. This is not an exhaustive checklist of such conditions or events.

(a) Previous experience or incidents which call into question the integrity or competence of management:

   (i)   Management dominated by one person (or a small group) and no effective oversight board or committee.

   (ii) Complex corporate structure where complexity does not seem to be warranted.

   (ii) High turnover over rate of key accounting and financial personnel.

   (iv) Personnel (key or otherwise) not taking holidays.

   (v)   Significant and prolonged under-staffing of the accounting department.

   (vi) Frequent changes of legal advisors or auditors.

(b) Particular financial reporting pressures within an entity:

   (i)   Industry volatility.

    (ii)   Inadequate working capital as a result of declining profits or too rapid expansion.

    (iii) Deteriorating quality of earnings, e.g. increased risk taking with respect to credit sales, changes in business practice or selection of accounting policy alternatives that improve income.

    (iv) The entity needs a rising profit trend to support the market price of its shares because of a contemplated public offering, a takeover or other reason.

    (v)   Significant investment in an industry or product line noted for rapid change.

    (vii) Pressure on accounting personnel to complete financial statements in an unreasonably short period of time.

    (vii) Dominant owner-management.

    (viii) Performance-based remuneration.

(c) Weaknesses in the design and operation of the accounting and internal controls system:

    (i)   A weak control environment within the entity.

    (ii)   Systems that, in their design, are inadequate to give reasonable assurance of preventing or detecting error or fraud.

    (iii) Inadequate segregation of responsibilities in relation to functions involving the handling, recording or controlling of the entity's assets.

    (iv) Indications that internal financial information is unreliable.

    (v)   Evidence that internal controls have been overridden by management.

    (vi) Ineffective monitoring of the operation of the system which allows control overrides, breakdown or weakness to continue without proper corrective action.

    (vii) Continuing failure to correct major weakness in internal controls where such corrections are practicable and cost effective.

(d)   Unusual transactions:

    (i)   Unusual transactions, especially near the year end, that have a significant effect on earnings.

    (ii)   Complex transactions or accounting treatments.

    (iii) Unusual transactions with related parties.

    (iv) Payments for services (e.g. to lawyers, consultants or agents) that appear excessive in relation to the services provided.

(e)   Problems in obtaining sufficient appropriate audit evidence:

    (i)   Inadequate records, e.g. incomplete files, excessive adjustments to accounting records, transactions not recorded in accordance with normal procedures and out-of-balance control accounts.

(ii) Inadequate documentation or transactions, such as a lack of proper authorisation, supporting documents not available and alteration to documents (any of these documentation problems assume greater significance when they relate to large or unusual transactions).

(iii) An excessive number of differences between accounting records and third party confirmations, conflicting audit evidence and unexplainable changes in operating ratios.

(iv) Evasive, delayed or unreasonable responses by management to audit inquiries.

(v) Inappropriate attitude of management to the conduct of the audit, e.g. time pressure, scope limitation and other constraints.

(f)   Some factors unique to an information systems environment which relate to the conditions and events described above:

(i) Inability to extract information from computer files because of a lack of, or non-current, documentation of record contents or programs.

(ii) Large numbers or program changes that are not documented, approved and tested.

(iii) Inadequate overall balancing of computer transactions and data bases to the financial accounts.

2:8 Laws and regulations

2:8.1 Introduction

SAS 120, 'Consideration of law and regulations' defines 'non-compliance with law or regulations' as:

> *acts of omission or commission by the entity being audited, either intentional or unintentional, which are contrary to law (comprising common law and statute) or regulations. Such acts include transactions entered into by, or in the name of, the entity or on its behalf by its directors or employees.*

This Section discusses the issues the auditor should consider and the procedures the auditor should carry out to meet the responsibility to consider law and regulations in an audit of financial statements as set out in SAS 120. The scope of SAS 120 does not include personal misconduct (unrelated to the business activities of the entity) by the entity's directors or employees. Nor does it include civil wrongs, e.g., breaches of duties in contract or tort.

Whether an act constitutes non-compliance with law or regulations is a legal determination that is ordinarily beyond the auditors' professional competence. However, auditors' training, experience and understanding of the entity and its industry may enable them to recognise that some acts coming to their attention may constitute non-compliance with law or regulations. The determination as to whether a particular act constitutes or is likely to constitute non-compliance with law or regulations is generally based on the advice of an informed expert qualified to practise law, but ultimately can be determined only by a court of law.

2:8.2 Nature of laws and regulations

Laws and regulations vary considerably in their relation to the financial statements. Some laws and regulations relate directly to the preparation of, or the inclusion or disclosure of specific items in, the financial statements. Examples of such laws and regulations are given in **Section 2:8.2.1**. Other laws and regulations provide a legal framework within which the client conducts its business, and may be central to its ability to carry out its business (*see* **Sections 2:8.2.1** and **2:8.2.2** below).

Thus, while some clients operate in heavily regulated industries (such as banks and chemical companies), others are subject only to the many laws and regulations that generally relate to the operating aspects of the business (such as those relating to occupational safety and health, and equal opportunities). Therefore, when the auditor determines the type of procedures necessary in a particular instance the auditor should take account of the particular client concerned and the complexity of the regulations with which it is required to comply. In general, a small company which does not operate in a regulated area will require few specific procedures compared with a large multinational corporation carrying on complex, regulated business.

2:8.2.1 Laws and regulations directly affecting the financial statements

Those laws and regulations which relate directly to the preparation of, or the inclusion or disclosure of specific items in, the financial statements include:

(a)   Those which specify the form and content of financial statements, such as Sch. 4 to the Companies Act 1985.

(b)   Those which determine the circumstances under which a company is prohibited from making a distribution except out of profits available for the purpose, such as s. 263 of the Companies Act 1985.

(c)   Those laws which require auditors expressly to report non-compliance, such as the requirements of the Companies Act 1985 relating to the maintenance of proper accounting records or the disclosure of particulars of directors' remuneration in a company's financial statements.

(d)   Financial reporting requirements for particular industries.

2:8.2.2 *Laws and regulations indirectly affecting the financial statements*

Laws and regulations are central to a client's ability to carry out its business when either:

(a) compliance is a prerequisite of obtaining a licence to operate in the business concerned (e.g., compliance with regulations for financial resources in the case of an entity authorised under the Financial Services Act 1986, or clients in the public transport business which need an appropriate safety certificate); or

(b) non-compliance may reasonably be expected to result in the entity ceasing operations, or otherwise call into question the client's continuance as a going concern (e.g., where the non-compliance accounts for a substantial proportion of profits, or through the level of fines or damages which could result).

Following are some risk indicators in relation to laws and regulations included within the scope of (b):

(a) Clients dependent upon a single product or line of business e.g.:

    (i) property companies subject to planning regulations;

    (ii) high technology companies subject to patent laws;

    (iii) publishing companies subject to copyright or libel laws.

(b) Clients operating in businesses subject to risk of damage to their reputation or substantial losses or liabilities because of public safety or environmental issues, e.g.:

    (i) mining, heavy manufacturing, chemical, pharmaceutical and public transport entities;

    (ii) professional firms subject to the risk of negligence claims;

    (iii) food or household product-related businesses where non-compliance in environmental health areas could cause damaging loss of custom or closure.

(c) Clients operating in regulated markets or where there are few major players. Such clients could be subject to substantial fines or other penalties by regulatory agencies such as the European Commission where anti-competitive practices are identified.

2:8.3 Responsibilities for the prevention and detection of non-compliance with law and regulations

2:8.3.1 *Directors' responsibilities*

It is the responsibility of the directors to:

(a) Take appropriate steps to provide reasonable assurance that the client complies with law and regulations applicable to its activities.

(b)   Establish arrangements for preventing any non-compliance with law or regulations and detecting any that occur.

(c)   Prepare financial statements that give a true and fair view of the state of affairs of a company or group and of its profit or loss for the financial year.

In addition, directors and officers of companies have a responsibility to provide information required by the auditors, to which they have a legal right of access under s. 389A of the Companies Act 1985. That section also provides that it is a criminal offence to give to the auditors information or explanations which are misleading, false or deceptive.

The following steps, among others, may assist the directors in discharging their responsibilities for the prevention and detection of non-compliance with law or regulations:

(a)   Maintaining an up-to-date register of significant laws and regulations with which the entity has to comply within its particular industry.

(b)   Monitoring legal requirements and any changes therein and ensuring that operating procedures are designed to meet these requirements.

(c)   Instituting and operating appropriate systems of internal control.

(d)   Developing a Code of Conduct, ensuring employees are properly trained in and understand its provisions, monitoring compliance and taking appropriate disciplinary action in cases of non-compliance.

(e)   Engaging legal advisers to assist in monitoring legal requirements.

(f)   Maintaining a record of complaints.

In larger entities, these policies and procedures may be supplemented by assigning appropriate responsibilities to:

(a)   an internal audit function;

(b)   a legal department;

(c)   a compliance function; and/or

(d)   an audit committee.

In certain sectors or activities (e.g., financial services), there are detailed laws and regulations that specifically require directors to have systems in place to ensure compliance. These laws and regulations could, if breached, have a material effect on the financial statements. In addition, the directors are required to report certain instances of non-compliance to the appropriate authorities on a timely basis.

Given the responsibility of the directors to prepare financial statements that give a true and fair view of the state of affairs of a company and of its profit or loss for the financial year, where possible non-compliance with law or regulations has occurred which may result in a material misstatement in the financial statements, it is necessary for them to ensure that the matter is appropriately reflected and/or disclosed in the financial statements.

2:8.3.2 Auditor's responsibilities

Although the audit may act as a deterrent, the auditor is not responsible for preventing non-compliance with law or regulations. If the auditor identifies weaknesses in the client's accounting systems and internal controls which might result in non-compliance not being detected, the auditor should report these to management (*see* **Sections 2:8.7.2 to 2:8.8.3** below).

SAS 120.1 states:

> *Auditors should plan and perform their audit procedures, and evaluate and report on the results thereof, recognising that non-compliance by the entity with law or regulations may materially affect the financial statements.*

The auditor must plan, perform and evaluate the audit work in order to have a reasonable expectation of detecting material misstatements in the financial statements. When doing so, the auditor should recognise that material misstatements may arise from non-compliance with law or regulations. However, an audit cannot be expected to detect all possible non-compliance with law and regulations.

2:8.4 Limitations of an audit in relation to detecting non-compliance with law and regulations

An audit is subject to the unavoidable risk that some material misstatements of the financial statements will not be detected, even though the audit is properly planned and performed in accordance with Auditing Standards. This risk is higher with regard to misstatements resulting from non-compliance with law or regulations because of such factors as:

(a)   There are many laws and regulations, relating principally to the operating aspects of the entity, that typically do not have a material effect on the financial statements and where the consequences of any non-compliance are not captured by the accounting and internal financial control systems.

(b)   The effectiveness of audit procedures is affected by the inherent limitations of the accounting and internal control systems and by the use of selective testing rather than by the examination of all transactions.

(c)   Much of the evidence obtained by auditors is persuasive rather than conclusive in nature.

(d)   Non-compliance with law or regulations may involve conduct designed to conceal it, such as collusion, forgery, and override of controls or intentional misrepresentations being made to the auditors.

2:8.5 Audit considerations

2:8.5.1 Engagement letter

As stated in **Section 3:3**, 'Engagement letters', the auditor must send a letter to all audit clients setting out the terms of the engagement. This letter must include a paragraph relating to non-compliance with law and regulations. For example:

> **The responsibility for safeguarding the assets of the company and for the prevention and detection of fraud, error and non-compliance with law or regulations rests with yourselves. However, the auditor shall endeavour to plan the audit so that the auditor have a reasonable expectation of detecting material misstatements in the financial statements or accounting records (including those resulting from fraud, error or non-compliance with law or regulations), but the examination should not be relied upon to disclose all such material misstatements or frauds, errors or instances of non-compliance as may exist.**

2:8.5.2 Planning

In developing the audit strategy and testing plan, the auditor must assess that the client's non-compliance with law and regulations may cause the financial statements to contain material misstatement, including:

(a) assessment of the risk of non-compliance as part of the assessment of the risk to the audit firm;

(b) consideration of law and regulations at planning meetings so that the engagement partner, manager and team leader consider the implications for the audit, including what other information the auditor should obtain at the planning stage;

(c) consideration of the need to involve industry specialists; and

(d) assessment of the client's control environment in relation to law and regulations, including consideration of management's own risk assessment and compliance procedures.

The auditor should discuss the implications with the client. The auditor should include significant issues in the presentation to the client of the audit strategy and plan and follow up those issues in subsequent reports.

The auditor should plan and perform the audit with an attitude of professional scepticism. The auditor should recognise that the audit may reveal conditions or events that could lead to questioning whether an entity is complying with law and regulations. For audit purposes, laws and regulations relevant to the audit can be regarded as falling into two main categories:

(a)   Those which relate directly to the preparation of, or the inclusion or disclosure of specific items in, the financial statements of the entity.

(b)   Those which provide a legal framework within which the entity conducts its business and which are central to the entity's ability to conduct its business and where non-compliance may reasonably be expected to result in the entity ceasing operations, or call into question its continuance as a going concern.

The auditor should identify the key risks in relation to possible non-compliance by the client and develop appropriate responses. Where risks are identified the auditor must record the nature of the risk and plan an adequate response. The auditor must document that he or she has:

(a)   assessed the risk of the client's non-compliance;

(b)   recorded where such a risk is identified; and

(c)   planned an adequate response.

2:8.5.3 Overseas activities

SAS 120.16 states that:

> *Where any of the activities of a company or group are carried on outside the United Kingdom or the Republic of Ireland, the auditors should take steps to ensure that the audit work in relation to the detection and reporting of any non-compliance with local law and regulations is planned and carried out in accordance with the requirements of this SAS.*

The requirements of this section apply irrespective of whether the overseas activities are carried on by a subsidiary of a UK *or* Irish parent company, a division of the company based overseas or employees operating from the UK or the Republic of Ireland. On group audits, the auditor should include in group audit instructions issued to other firms involved in the audit of significant business units:

(a)   an instruction to comply with UK Auditing Standards, including SAS 120; and

(b)   a request that issues documentation confirms that the requirement has been met and identifies any significant issues arising.

2:8.5.4 Audit procedures

The nature and extent of the audit procedures the auditor should carry out depends on whether the laws and regulations:

(a)   directly affect the financial statements; or

(b)   provide a legal framework within which the client conducts its business and which are central to the client's ability to conduct its business and hence to its financial statements.

The auditor should develop and complete an audit programme tailored to the client's circumstances and the results of the risk assessment.

SAS 120.2 states that:

The auditors should obtain sufficient appropriate audit evidence about compliance with those laws and regulations which relate directly to the preparation of, or the inclusion or disclosure of specific items in, the financial statements.

Where the auditor is required by statute to report, as part of the audit of the financial statements, whether the entity complies with certain provisions of laws or regulations, the auditor should:

(a)   have a sufficient understanding of such laws and regulations in order to consider them when auditing the assertions related to the determination of the amounts to be recorded and the disclosures to be made; and

(b)   test for compliance with such provisions.

The auditor may obtain much of the assurance he or she requires by completing a UK GAAP Checklist. However, where the client operates in an industry where specific laws and regulations apply, the auditor should use a checklist tailored to that particular industry. Guidance is given in SAS 120.3:

The auditors should perform procedures to help identify possible or actual instances of non-compliance with those laws and regulations which provide a legal framework within which the entity conducts its business and which are central to the entity's ability to conduct its business and hence to its financial statements, by:

(a) obtaining a general understanding of the legal and regulatory framework applicable to the entity and the industry, and of the procedures followed to ensure compliance with that framework;

(b) inspecting correspondence with relevant licensing or regulatory authorities;

(c) enquiring of the directors as to whether they are on notice of any such possible instances of non-compliance with law or regulations; and

(d) obtaining written confirmation from the directors that they have disclosed to the auditors all those events of which they are aware which involve possible non-compliance, together with the actual or contingent consequences which may arise therefrom.

The auditor should obtain a general understanding of those laws and regulations which provide a legal framework within which the client conducts its business. This includes a general understanding of those laws and regulations which are specific to an industry, such as:

(a)   in a client in which a major activity is the development of a single property, the planning regulations or consents;

(b)   in a waste disposal company, the terms of licences held by the client under which it is allowed to dispose of hazardous waste; and

(c)   those laws and regulations in relation to which the client is required to provide financial information to regulatory or other authorities and where non-compliance may affect the client's ability to continue trading.

To obtain this general understanding, the auditor should:

(a)   Enquire of management as to the laws or regulations (and any changes therein) that may be central to the entity's ability to conduct its business.

(b)   Enquire of management concerning the entity's policies and procedures regarding compliance with laws and regulations, in particular those which may be central to its ability to conduct its business (*see* **Section 2:8.2.2** above).

(c)   Discuss with management the policies or procedures adopted for identifying, evaluating and accounting for litigation, claims and assessments.

(d)   Use the existing knowledge of the entity's industry and business and of its regulatory environment.

(e)   Where applicable discuss the legal and regulatory framework with auditors of subsidiaries in other countries (e.g., if the subsidiary is required to adhere to the securities regulations of the parent company).

The auditor should inspect correspondence, where relevant, with authorities responsible for regulation or licensing in industries subject to regulation.

The auditor should enquire of management concerning whether the client organisation has been subject to investigations by regulatory authorities or to fines and penalties for non-compliance or whether management has any other reason to believe that there are instances of non-compliance.

2:8.5.5 *Representations from management*

The auditor should obtain written confirmation from client management that they have disclosed to the auditor all those events of which they are aware which involve possible non-compliance with law and regulations, together with the actual or contingent consequences which may arise therefrom.

2:8.6 Maintaining an awareness of potential non-compliance

SAS 120.4 states that:

When carrying out their procedures for the purpose of forming an opinion on the financial statements, the auditors should in addition be alert for instances of possible or actual non-compliance with law or regulations which might affect the financial statements.

Other than as set out in **Sections 2:8.5.2** and **2:8.5.4** above, the auditor is not required, within the scope of SAS 120, to plan and perform other procedures to identify possible instances of non-compliance with law or regulations, because to do so is outside the scope of an audit of financial statements.

There is a wide range of laws and regulations falling into this category, many of which fall outside the competence and experience as auditors. There can therefore be no assurance that the auditor will detect all material breaches of such laws and regulations. However, when the auditor suspects the existence of breaches which could be material, the auditor should consider whether and how the matter ought to be reported, as set out later in this Section.

Procedures that may bring such non-compliance to the attention of the auditor include:

(a)   reading minutes of board and management meetings;

(b)   enquiring of the entity's directors and legal counsel concerning litigation, claims and assessments; and

(c)   performing substantive tests of details of transactions or balances.

2:8.7 Responsibilities in specific areas

2:8.7.1 Money laundering

When, in the course of the work, the auditor becomes aware of evidence which leads him or her to suspect the laundering of money which either derives from drug trafficking or is related to terrorist offences, the auditor must, under the Criminal Justice Act 1993, report those suspicions to the appropriate authority.

Under the terms of the Act, it is a criminal offence to disclose the reporting of such suspicions to any other party where this may prejudice a criminal investigation. The auditor must not therefore disclose the matter to the directors if the latter may be implicated in the laundering. Further guidance is given in Technical Release AUDIT 1/96 *The Laundering of the Proceeds of Criminal Conduct. A Discussion of the Audit Implications* issued by the Audit Faculty of the ICAEW in June 1996.

2:8.7.2 Compliance with the Taxes Acts

The responsibility to express an opinion on a client's financial statements does not extend to determining whether the client has complied in every respect with applicable tax legislation. The auditor should, however, obtain sufficient appropriate evidence to give reasonable assurance that the amounts included in the financial statements in respect of taxation are not materially misstated. This will usually include making appropriate enquiries of those advising the client on taxation matters.

Where the audit firm is not responsible for computing and agreeing the client's tax liabilities, the auditor should seek to obtain assurance that the amounts included in the financial statements in respect of tax liabilities are not materially misstated. At the time the auditor expresses the opinion on the financial statements, those amounts are often estimates yet to be agreed with the Inland Revenue. If the auditor becomes aware that the client has failed to comply with the requirements of tax legislation, the auditor should follow the procedures for reporting set out later in this Section.

Frequently, an audit firm acts as both auditors and as the client's tax advisers and in this capacity is responsible for computing the client's tax liabilities and agreeing them with the tax authority on the client's behalf. In such cases where the audit team becomes aware of any apparent non-compliance with the Taxes Acts in the course of its work, the engagement partner or manager should make the details known to the partner responsible for tax matters, so that appropriate action can be taken. The auditor should also assess the effect of the matter on the opinion on the financial statements (*see* **Sections 2:8.9.2** and **2:8.9.3** below). However, where appropriate action is taken by the tax partner responsible for taxation services to the client, the auditor will not normally need to follow the other reporting requirements of this Section.

2:8.8 Procedures when possible non-compliance with law or regulations is discovered

Appendix A to this Section sets out examples of the types of information that may come to the attention of the auditor and which may indicate non-compliance with law or regulations. Where the auditor identifies possible non-compliance the auditor should:

(a) evaluate the possible effect on the financial statements;

(b) document the findings and where appropriate discuss them with management; and

(c) consider the implications for the audit.

2:8.8.1 Evaluating the possible effect on the financial statements

SAS 120.5 guides that:

> When the auditors become aware of information which indicates that non-compliance with law or regulations may exist, they should obtain an understanding of the nature of the act and the circumstances in which it has

occurred and sufficient other information to evaluate the possible effect on the financial statements.

When evaluating the possible effect on the financial statements, the auditor should consider:

(a) the potential financial consequences, such as fines, penalties, damages, threat of expropriation of assets, enforced discontinuance of operations and litigation;

(b) whether the potential financial consequences require disclosure, and if so, the adequacy of any disclosure; and

(c) whether the potential financial consequences are sufficiently serious as to call into question the view by the financial statements.

As the assessment of compliance with laws and regulations may involve consideration of matters outside the competence and experience as auditors, the auditor may need to obtain appropriate expert advice (whether through the client or independently) in order to make the assessment of the possible effect on the client's financial statements. Where this is the case, the auditor should follow the guidance in **Section 7:6**, 'Using the work of an expert'.

2:8.8.2 *Documenting the findings*

SAS 120.6 states that:

> *When the auditors become aware of or suspect that there may be non-compliance with law or regulations, they should document their findings and, subject to any requirement to report them direct to a third party, discuss them with the appropriate level of management.*

The auditor should document the findings of the investigation into possible non-compliance. Depending on the circumstances, the auditor may do this, e.g. by taking copies of records and documents and making minutes of conversations.

If the directors do not provide sufficient information to satisfy the concerns in relation to the suspected non-compliance to show that the client is in fact in compliance, the auditor should obtain legal advice about the application of law or regulations to the particular circumstances, e.g. including s. 389A of the Companies Act 1985) and the possible effects on the financial statements.

The auditor should normally, with the client's permission, consult the client's lawyer as to whether non-compliance with a law or regulation is involved and the possible legal consequences. However, the auditor should obtain his or her own legal advice where:

(a) it is not possible to consult the client's own lawyer;

(b)   it is not appropriate to rely on the client lawyer's opinion; or

(c)   it is not clear what further action, if any, the auditor should take.

When the auditor cannot obtain adequate information about the suspected non-compliance with law or regulations, or where the client has no procedures to ensure compliance with laws and regulations, the auditor should:

(a)   ensure that the board of directors is aware of the position;

(b)   consider the implications of the lack of audit evidence for the report on the financial statements (*see* **Sections 2:8.9.2** and **2:8.9.3** below); and

(c)   consider whether any obligation arises to report to third parties (*see* **Section 2:8.9.4** below).

2:8.8.3 *Implications for other aspects of the audit*

SAS 120.7 states that:

> *The auditors should consider the implications of suspected or actual non-compliance with law or regulations in relation to other aspects of the audit, particularly the reliability of management representations.*

If the auditor considers that non-compliance with law or regulations may have or has occurred, the auditor should consider the implications for other aspects of the audit. In particular, the auditor should:

(a)   re-evaluate the assessment of audit risk; and

(b)   consider the validity of management representations.

In re-evaluating the assessment of audit risk, the auditor should take into account the following:

(a)   any apparent failure of specific control procedures;

(b)   the level of management or employees involved; and

(c)   the concealment, if any, of the act.

A series of suspected or actual instances of non-compliance with law or regulations which are financially immaterial may be symptomatic of management's general disregard for the law and therefore may throw doubt on the integrity of the financial statements and perhaps even the future prospects of the client.

2:8.9 Reporting non-compliance with law or regulations

The action the auditor should take to report suspected or actual non-compliance with law or regulations varies in relation to its nature and the gravity of its consequences. The auditor should consider the implications for reporting:

(a)   to management;

(b)   within the audit firm;

(c)   to addressees of the audit report; and

(d)   to third parties.

2:8.9.1 Reporting to management

At SAS 120.8 it is stated that:

> *The auditors should, as soon as practicable (save where SAS 120.15 applies), either*
>
> *(a) communicate with management, the board of directors or the audit committee, or*
>
> *(b) obtain evidence that they are appropriately informed,*
>
> *regarding any suspect or actual non-compliance with law or regulations that comes to the auditor's attention.*

and SAS 120.9 states that:

> *If, in the auditors' judgement, the suspected or actual non-compliance with the law or regulations is material or is believed to be intentional, the auditors should communicate the finding without delay.*

If the auditor suspects that there has been an instance of possible non-compliance with the law or regulations, the auditor should report the matter to an appropriately senior level of client management. This should normally be the board of directors, or those within the client organisation who have been authorised to receive such reports on behalf of the board (e.g. an audit committee). If the auditor suspects that members of senior management, including members of the board of directors, are involved, it may be appropriate to report the matter to the audit committee or, in the case of suspected money laundering, direct to the appropriate authority. Where no higher authority exists within the client organisation, or if the auditor believes that the report may not be acted upon or is unsure as to the person to whom to report, the auditor should obtain legal advice.

2:8.9.2 *Reporting within the audit firm*

When significant non-compliance with law and regulations is either discovered or reported to the auditor, the engagement partner must follow the consultation procedures set out in **Section 5:5**, 'Consultation and concurring reviews'.

2:8.9.3 *Reporting to addressees of the audit report*

The auditor should consider the implications of suspected or actual non-compliance with law and regulations for the auditor report, for example:

(a) If the non-compliance is likely to have a substantial effect on the financial statements but there is little firm evidence yet available, the auditor should consider whether the matter should be included in the report as either an explanatory paragraph referring to a fundamental uncertainty or whether the auditor should express a qualified opinion.

(b) If the matter is fully documented but the effect is not material, then unless the auditor concludes that an apparently isolated incidence is part of a wider pattern aimed at circumventing a major element of the laws and regulations which apply to the client concerned, no reference need be made in the financial statements or in the audit report.

Further guidance on the reporting implications is given in **Section 13:16**, 'Qualified and modified reports to the members of limited companies and other organisations in Great Britain.'

2:8.9.4 *Reporting to third parties*

SAS 120.12 states that:

> *When the auditors become aware of a suspected or actual non-compliance with law and regulations which gives rise to a statutory duty to report, they should make a report to the appropriate authority without undue delay.*

SAS 120.13 guides that:

> *Where the auditors become aware of a suspected or actual instance of non-compliance with law or regulations which does not give rise to a statutory duty to report to an appropriate authority they should:*
>
> *(a) consider whether the matter may be one that ought to be reported to a proper authority in the public interest; and where this is the case*
>
> *(b) except in the circumstances covered in SAS 120.15, discuss the matter with the board of directors, including any audit committee.*

SAS 120.14 directs that:

Where, having considered any views expressed on behalf of the entity and in the light of any legal advice obtained, the auditors conclude that the matter ought to be reported to an appropriate authority in the public interest, they should notify the directors in writing of their view and, if the entity does not voluntarily do so itself or is unable to provide evidence that the matter has been reported, they should report it themselves.

SAS 120.15 states that:

Auditors should report a matter direct to a proper authority in the public interest and without discussing the matter with the entity if they conclude that the suspected or actual instance of non-compliance has caused them no longer to have confidence in the integrity of the directors.

In certain circumstances the auditor should consider reporting non-compliance with law and regulations outside the client organisation, without necessarily informing management that the auditor intends to do so. The auditor may disclose matters to an appropriate authority in the public interest or for other specific reasons. Confidentiality is an implied term of the contract with the client organisation. The duty of confidentiality, however, is not absolute. In certain exceptional circumstances the auditor is not bound by the duty of confidentiality and has the right or duty to report matters to an appropriate authority in the public interest. The auditor should weigh the public interest in maintaining confidential client relationships against the public interest in disclosure to an appropriate authority. Determination of where the balance of public interest lies requires careful consideration. Where the suspicions have been aroused the auditor should use professional judgement to determine whether the misgivings provide justification for carrying the matter further or are too insubstantial to deserve reporting.

The auditor is protected from the risk of liability for breach of confidence or defamation provided that:

(a) In the case of breach of confidence:

  (i)   disclosure is made in the public interest;

  (ii) such disclosure is made to an appropriate body or person; and

  (iii) there is no malice motivating the disclosure;

(b) In the case of defamation:

  (i)   disclosure is made in the capacity as auditor of the entity concerned; and

  (ii) there is no malice motivating the disclosure.

In addition, the auditor is protected from such risks where he or she is expressly permitted or required by legislation to disclose information.

The auditor should take the following into account when considering whether or not disclosure to third parties is justified in the public interest:

(a)   The extent to which the suspect or actual non-compliance with law or regulations is likely to affect members of the public;

(b)   Whether the directors have rectified the matter or are taking, or are likely to take, effective corrective action;

(c)   The extent to which non-disclosure is likely to enable the suspected or actual non-compliance with law or regulations to recur with impunity;

(d)   The gravity of the matter;

(e)   Whether there is a general management ethos within the entity of disregarding law or regulations; and

(f)   The weight of evidence and the degree of the auditor's suspicion that there has been an instance of non-compliance with law or regulations.

When reporting to appropriate authorities in the public interest it is important that, in order to retain the protection of qualified privilege, the auditor report only to one which has a proper interest to receive the information. The appropriate authority in a particular instance depends on the nature of the suspected or actual non-compliance. Appropriate authorities could include:

- Serious Fraud Office
- Crown Prosecution Service
- Police forces
- Securities and Investments Board and the Self-Regulating Organisations it has recognised
- Recognised Professional Bodies recognised by the SIB under the Financial Services Act 1986
- International Stock Exchange
- Panel on Takeovers and Mergers
- Society of Lloyd's
- Bank of England
- Local authorities
- Charity Commission for England and Wales
- Scottish Office for Scottish Charities
- Inland Revenue
- HM Customs & Excise
- Department of Trade and Industry

In cases of doubt as to the appropriate authority, the audit firm may consult the appropriate professional accountancy body. The audit firm may also refer to the Investigations Division of the Department of Trade and Industry with a view to investigation by that Division.

The auditor receives the same protection even if the auditor has only a reasonable suspicion that non-compliance with law or regulations has occurred. If the auditor can demonstrate that he or she acted reasonably and in good faith in informing an authority of a breach of law or regulations which he or she thought had been committed, the auditor will not be held by the court to be in breach of duty to the client even if an investigation or prosecution finds that there has been no offence.

The auditor may need to take legal advice before making a decision whether the matter should be reported to an appropriate authority in the public interest.

When the auditor decides whether to report, and if so to whom, the decision may be called into question at a future date, for example on the basis of:

(a)   what the auditor knew at the time;

(b)   what the auditor ought to have known in the course of the audit;

(c)   what the auditor ought to have concluded; and

(d)   what the auditor ought to have done.

The auditor should therefore ensure that the working papers contain an appropriate record of the nature of the non-compliance with law and regulations and the basis for the decision whether or not to report.

The auditor should also consider the possible consequences if financial loss is occasioned by non-compliance with law or regulations which the auditor suspects (or ought to suspect) has occurred but which the auditor decides not to report.

The auditor may no longer have confidence in the integrity of the directors in situations such as:

(a)   where the auditor suspects or has evidence of the involvement or intended involvement of the directors in possible non-compliance with law or regulations which could have a material effect of the financial statements; or

(b)   where the auditor is aware that the directors are aware of such non-compliance and, contrary to regulatory requirements or the public interest, have not reported it to an appropriate authority within a reasonable period.

2:8.10 Statutory duty to report to third parties

Where the client is a financial institution subject to statutory regulation, the auditor must report certain information direct to the relevant regulator.

The auditor must also, as a statutory duty, take the initiative to report to the appropriate authorities suspected non-compliance with law or regulations related to drug trafficking, money laundering and terrorism. A failure to report in these circumstances is itself a criminal offence.

2:8.11 Audit completion

In relation to all suspected non-compliance with law and regulations (including suspected money laundering) which the auditor have identified, the auditor must document that he or she has:

(a)   recorded them in the working papers;

(b)   reported them to the client/authorities as necessary; and

(c)   evaluated them for their impact on the financial statements.

2:8.12 Withdrawal from the engagement

The auditor may conclude that withdrawal from the engagement is necessary in certain circumstances e.g., if the auditor considers that the shareholders have not been given information they require and the auditor sees no opportunity for reporting such information to the shareholders whilst continuing as auditor. The conclusion may be affected by the implications if the directors within the client organisation are suspected of involvement with the suspected or actual non-compliance, which may affect the reliability of management representations, and also affect in continuing the association with the entity. In reaching such conclusions, the auditor may need to seek legal advice.

Resignation should be seen as a last resort. However, there are circumstances where there may be no alternative to resignation e.g., where the client's directors refuse to issue the financial statements or the auditor wishes to inform the shareholders or creditors of the client of the concerns and there is no immediate occasion to do so.

If the auditor concludes that he or she should withdraw from the engagement, the auditor must follow the professional procedures set out in **Chapter 14** 'Cessation as auditor'.

2:8.13 Consultation

Where the auditor identifies material suspected or actual non-compliance with laws and regulations which relate directly to the preparation of, or the inclusion or disclosure of specific items in, the financial statements of the client, the engagement partner must follow the consultation procedures set out in **Section 5:5** 'Consultation and concurring reviews'. This should include consultation with industry specialists where relevant.

Where there is suspected or actual non-compliance with other laws and regulations falling within the scope of SAS 120, in addition to the normal consultation procedures, where it is concluded that legal advice is required, the matter should be referred to legal advisers. Such advice must be sought if public interest reporting to an appropriate authority is being considered.

2:8.14 Compliance with International Standards on Auditing

Compliance with the Auditing Standards contained in SAS 120 reproduced in this section and with relevant ethical guidance ensures compliance in all material respects with the requirements of the basic principles and essential procedures identified in **Section 2:7** 'Fraud and error'.

2:8.15 Appendix A Indications that non-compliance with law or regulations may have occurred

Listed below are examples of the type of information that may come to the auditors' attention and may indicate that non-compliance with law or regulations has occurred:

(a)   Investigation by government department or payment of fines or penalties.

(b)   Payments for unspecified services or loans to consultants, related parties, employees or government employees.

(c)   Sales commissions or agents' fees that appear excessive in relation to those normally paid by the entity or in its industry or to the services actually received.

(d)   Purchasing at prices significantly above or below market price.

(e)   Unusual payments in cash, purchases in the form of cashiers' cheques payable to bearer or transfers to numbered bank accounts.

(f)   Unusual transactions with companies registered in tax havens.

(g)   Payments for good or services made other than to the country from which the goods or services originated.

(h)   Existence of an accounting system that fails, whether by design or by accident, to provide adequate audit trail or sufficient evidence.

(i)   Unauthorised transactions or improperly recorded transactions.

(j)   Media comment.

Chapter 3

Before the audit

3:1 Engagement origination and continuation

3:1.1 Appointment as auditor

Section 3:2, 'Appointment and continuation as auditor', provides guidance on the matters that firms should consider before accepting an audit appointment and before agreeing to continue as auditor. It also sets out the professional procedures that should be followed on accepting a new appointment.

3:1.2 Engagement letters

Section 3:3, 'Engagement letters', explains the purpose of letters of engagement and gives guidance on tailoring the standard letter.

3:1.3 New engagements

Section 3:4, 'New audit engagements', provides guidance on the administration and other procedures an auditor should follow after accepting a new audit engagement.

3:1.4 Dormant companies

Section 3:5, 'Dormant companies', sets out the guidance on the administrative and audit implications of dormant companies.

3:2 Appointment and continuation as auditor

3:2.1 Accepting appointment as auditor

It is normal to welcome new work, but sometimes it can cause additional risk to the auditor and to the firm. This section sets out the matters that should be considered in each case as to whether it is appropriate to accept an audit engagement for a prospective client.

It is important regularly to review appointments to existing clients. Therefore, the procedures set out in **Sections 3:2.1.2** to **3:2.1.11** also apply to all existing audit clients. Usually this will only involve a brief annual review in the light of any changes in circumstances, but if the client's activities or management undergo major change it will be necessary to carry out a more extensive review, and more frequently.

The acceptance or continuance of an audit engagement is ultimately determined by the engagement partner. If the level of risk to the firm is so high that serious doubts exist about the wisdom of accepting or continuing an engagement, the engagement partner should follow the consultation procedures set out in **Section 5:5**, 'Consultation and concurring reviews'.

3:2.1.1 Acceptance of new work

For the purpose of this section, a new client is one for which the audit firm has not previously performed audit services. If audit services have been performed in the past, it may be possible to gain some assurance from the acceptance procedures carried out in respect of the previous engagement. This can be done by means of discussions between the previous engagement partner and the prospective engagement partner, and/or reviewing the papers relating to the previous appointment. However, it is essential to investigate the reasons for the termination of a previous engagement and to consider any changes to the prospective client's circumstances and to professional standards.

The professional conditions that should be present before a new engagement should be accepted are the following:

(a) The firm will not be exposed to undue risk either from damage to professional reputation or from financial loss (e.g., litigation or uncollected fees).

(b) The firm will have competent personnel available to perform services when they are required and no matter will prevent the firm from performing the work.

(c) The independence requirements will be met.

(d) There is no conflict of interest likely to affect the firm's conduct of the audit or adequate safeguards are in place.

(e) The firm has adequately identified the client to comply with money laundering regulations.

3:2.1.2 The reputation of the auditor and the firm

The prospective engagement partner should consider the following matters when deciding whether to accept a new client:

(a) The integrity both of the prospective client's management and of its principal owners.

(b) The legality of the entity's activities, and the entity's reputation.

(c) The entity's business environment and who will use its financial statements.

(d) The entity's financial position and prospects.

(e) The likelihood that the scope of the audit will be restricted or subject to an unacceptable time constraint.

(f) Accounting issues.

These matters are discussed in more detail in the following paragraphs. **Section 3:2.5 (Appendix A)** sets out a list of conditions that may present an unusual level of risk to the firm.

3:2.1.3 *Integrity of management and the principal owners*

The auditor should attempt to ascertain the reputation of the management and principal owners of the prospective client either by enquiring directly of knowledgeable third parties (including, where appropriate, by making personal contact with the retiring auditor) or by using other appropriate means. The engagement should not normally be accepted if, after making these enquiries, the auditor believes that the integrity of the entity's management and principal owners is such that an association with the entity will adversely affect the auditor's professional reputation. Particular care should be taken where the identity of the principal owner is hidden, and it is not normally advisable to accept the appointment in such circumstances.

3:2.1.4 *Legality of activities and reputation*

The auditor should not accept an engagement with an entity that is engaged in activities that are or appear to be either illegal or potentially illegal, or are of a nature that could result in adverse publicity that might reflect badly on the auditor and the firm.

3:2.1.5 *Identifying the client*

There are a number of regulatory requirements which arise mainly from money laundering regulations.

The auditor must obtain evidence of the client's identity. The auditor should obtain a certificate of incorporation for a UK or overseas company. The auditor should verify the identity of one or more of the principal directors and shareholders if the company is unlisted and is not a subsidiary of a listed company.

Additional care should be taken over overseas companies, especially those not listed on recognised, designated or other established investment exchanges. It may be possible to obtain a Certificate of Legal Validity from a company's foreign lawyers.

The evidence collected for this purpose should be retained for at least five years after the end of the auditor's relationship with the client.

3:2.1.6 *The entity's business environment and use of financial statements*

As part of client acceptance and continuance procedures the auditor should understand the risks associated with the client's business environment and the expected uses of the financial statements. To understand these risks, it is important to obtain knowledge of:

(a)   the entity's organisational structure;

(b)   industry environment;

(c)   ownership;

(d)   financial resources;

(e) obligations;

(f) related parties;

(g) customers; and

(h) suppliers and products.

The auditor should obtain this knowledge from a variety of sources including:

(a) prior knowledge or experience of the prospective client;

(b) discussions with the prospective client's owners, management, directors or other personnel;

(c) enquiry of third parties, such as solicitors and bankers;

(d) reading of articles or research reports on the prospective client's business;

(e) consultation with industry specialists; and

(f) reading prior years' financial statements.

Guidance on carrying out the above procedures is also contained in **Section 4:2**, 'Business review'.

3:2.1.7 *Financial position and prospects*

If in doubt whether a prospective client's financial position will enable it to continue as a going concern, the auditor should not normally accept the audit engagement. However, if the appointment is specifically related to helping the client, and if the reason for the firm's involvement is known and accepted by all concerned, it may be possible, after the prospective engagement partner has consulted other partners, to accept the appointment.

An invitation from a prospective client should not normally be refused merely because it is either a new venture or one engaged in high-risk operations. But if the auditor considers that the prospective client is unlikely to succeed, it may be best not to accept the engagement. Before making a decision in such a situation, the following factors should be considered:

(a) The reputation of, and the personal investment of funds by, the organisers of the new venture.

(b) The nature and the results of the feasibility studies of the new venture (such as engineering, geological, scientific, economic, or market research reports and financial projections).

(c) The recent operating results of similar ventures.

(d) The business experience of the entity's management.

3:2.1.8 The potential for scope and time constraints

It is desirable for a single audit firm to act as auditor to all the companies in a group of companies that are under common control.

There may, however, be valid business reasons why it is not possible to act in this way. Therefore, the auditor should not necessarily refuse to act for one or more companies or divisions in a group solely because the same firm does not act for all of them. However, it is important to consider the effect that intra-group transactions and relationships will have on audit work.

It is also important to consider management's attitude and intentions and the environment in which the audit will be carried out. In particular, the auditor should ascertain whether management wishes to restrict the scope of the audit, and whether it will place unreasonable time or fee constraints on the audit.

SAS 601.1 contains guidance for the situation where the auditor is aware, before accepting an audit engagement, that the directors will impose a limitation on the scope of the audit work. If this is likely to result in the need to issue a disclaimer of opinion on the financial statements, the auditor should not accept the appointment, unless required to do so by statute.

3:2.1.9 Accounting issues

The auditor should discuss with a prospective client the principal accounting policies it has adopted. If the client operates in a specialised industry it may be useful, where necessary, to discuss these policies with a specialist in that industry. If after discussion the auditor considers that the prospective client is following a policy or policies that would not be acceptable, the prospective client should be advised of these views before the engagement is accepted. It is particularly important to be satisfied with the accounting policies of a prospective client which intends to raise finance in the near future.

3:2.1.10 Sufficient competent personnel

The auditor's ability both to discharge professional responsibilities to clients and others, and to maintain the professional reputation of the firm, depends on the ability to provide high-quality services to clients. The quality of service depends, to a large extent, on the professional competence of personnel and on the availability of those personnel to perform the services. Consequently, before accepting a new engagement, the auditor should determine that a sufficient number of competent staff (including those who have the necessary specialist experience) will be available to provide the services that the client has requested.

3:2.1.11 Independence and conflicts of interest

Before commencing any services on an engagement for a new client, the auditor should determine whether the firm is independent with respect to that client. The standards that should be applied are laid down in the ICAEW's *Audit Regulations and Guidance*, and in the Handbook, *Guide to Professional Ethics*. Members of other professional bodies should refer to the standards laid down by their supervisory body. It should also be confirmed that the firm has no potential conflict of interest or that adequate safeguards are in place. The prospective engagement partner should consider whether the appointment might be in conflict with either the ICAEW's Handbook or in-house rules, and in cases of doubt should follow the consultation procedures in 'Consultation and concurring reviews'. The main considerations are described in, 'Audit regulation'.

3:2.1.12 Corporate practices

Where a registered auditor is a corporate practice it should obtain written confirmation from a potential audit client that the client or associated undertaking holds no interests in the firm, before accepting the audit appointment.

3:2.1.13 Professional procedures on accepting appointment as auditor

After considering the matters described above in **Sections 3:2.1** to **3:2.1.11**, the firm should follow the correct professional procedures before it can accept nomination as auditor. These procedures are set out in the *Guide to Professional Ethics*, Sections 1.206 and 1.309, and their application is set out in the remaining paragraphs of **Section 3:2.1.12** below.

When a firm is invited to accept nomination to be appointed as auditor to an established company, it is necessary to write a letter to the directors of the proposed new client in which the auditor should do the following:

(a) Indicate that the rules of professional conduct require that the auditor has a professional duty, if asked to act or be nominated, to communicate with the existing auditor or adviser.

(b) When nominated or asked to act the auditor should ask the client to inform the existing auditor or adviser of the proposed change and, at the same time, to give the latter written authority to discuss the client's affairs with the member.

(c) If the client fails or refuses to grant the existing auditor or adviser permission to discuss the client's affairs with the proposed successor the existing auditor or adviser should report that fact to the prospective auditor or adviser who should not accept nomination or appointment.

A specimen of a formal letter to the directors of the prospective client is set out in **Section 3:2.6 (Appendix B)**.

The prospective auditor should then write to the existing auditor, seeking information which could influence the decision as to whether or not it would be proper to accept appointment. The existing auditor has no responsibility for that decision, and there is no 'professional clearance' which can be given or withheld.

If the existing auditor either is being removed or is resigning, the letter should ask for a copy of the resolution and of any representations made under s. 391A of the Companies Act 1985, or for a copy of the notice of resignation under s. 392 of the Companies Act 1985, as appropriate.

In all cases where the existing auditor is ceasing to hold office, the letter should also ask for a copy of the statement made under s. 394 of the Companies Act 1985 (statement of any circumstances connected with the auditor ceasing to hold office which the auditor considers should be brought to the attention of members or creditors, or a negative statement). A specimen letter is set out in **Section 3:2.7 (Appendix C)** to this section.

It is important to consider whether it is appropriate to meet the existing auditor, if the prospective auditor believes that the existing auditor might have reasons which require detailed explanation. If there is a meeting, a note should be made for the files, of the matters discussed with the existing auditor.

When these steps have been carried out, and provided that the previous auditor has not raised any matters that would prevent the firm from accepting the proposed appointment, the auditor should send a letter to the client accepting appointment. A specimen letter is set out in **Section 3:2.8 (Appendix D)** to this section.

3:2.1.14 Documentation

When the decision is taken to accept an appointment as auditor, the engagement partner should record the factors which were considered and the reasons why the decision was taken to accept the engagement. If the engagement partner has consulted with other partners, a record of the results of that consultation should be retained.

The engagement partner should then send an engagement letter in accordance with **Section 3:3**, 'Engagement letters', and should follow the procedures for new engagements laid down in **Section 3:4**, 'New audit engagements'.

3:2.1.15 Rotation of audit partners

An audit firm's objectivity may be threatened or appear to be threatened if senior audit staff and the audit engagement partner in particular continue to act in relation to the same audit client for a prolonged period of time. Section 1.201 of the *Guide to Professional Ethics* requires that audit firms should ensure that no engagement partner remains in charge of the audit of a listed company for a period exceeding seven consecutive years. An audit engagement partner who has ceased under the above provision to act as such should not return to that role in relation to that audit until a minimum of five years has passed but is not precluded from other involvement with the client.

The same principles apply in respect of unquoted companies, although there is no formal requirement for partner rotation to take place within any particular period. Instead, firms should review annually the possible need for rotation of an audit engagement partner.

3:2.2 Continuation as auditor

3:2.2.1 Introduction

It is necessary to consider the circumstances of an existing client to ensure that they have not changed in such a way as to make it unacceptable for the firm to continue to act as the client's auditor. It is also necessary to consider whether any change in either the firm's own circumstances or the client's circumstances has increased the risk to the auditor and to the firm to an unacceptable level. The auditor should, therefore, at all times be alert for conditions, such as an undue risk of damage to the firm's professional reputation, that might have caused a rejection of a client if they had existed when this engagement was initially accepted.

3:2.2.2 Considerations for continuing as auditor

It is necessary to consider annually, at the debriefing stage before being reappointed, matters which might make it undesirable to continue as auditor. It is also important to consider them annually at the planning stage of the audit, and on the other specific occasions set out below. All the members of the audit team on an engagement should consider the matters, and where there is doubt the engagement partner should consult with other partners.

Each year, as part of the business review, the auditor should consider the risk attached to each client. Both the normal business review procedures in **Section 4:2**, 'Business review', and the risk criteria set out in **Section 3:2.5 (Appendix A)** to this section, should be used for this purpose. If, for whatever reason, these procedures indicate an increase in risk to the auditor and to the firm, it is necessary to consider whether this risk is so high that the firm should not continue to act as auditor. Also, before starting the audit, it is necessary to reconsider whether the criteria relating to independence are still being complied with. If not, the engagement partner should consider whether it is necessary to resign from the audit appointment. Where the review indicates that it may be necessary to resign, the engagement partner should follow the consultation procedures in **Section 5:5**, 'Consultation and concurring reviews'. Where the review indicates that the appointment should continue only if appropriate safeguards are put in place to guard against loss of independence, a partner not concerned with the engagement should review the decision to continue and the safeguards implemented.

Whenever there is a significant change in the client's management or the directors or the principal owners, the auditor should consider the personal and business reputations of the new individuals. This should be done by using first-hand knowledge, by enquiring of knowledgeable third parties or by other appropriate means.

If there is reason to believe that a client's management is making misrepresentations, or is less than honest about matters relating to audit work, the auditor should review the position to decide whether the increase in risk to the auditor, and to the firm, has become unacceptable.

If, for whatever reason, the decision is taken not to seek reappointment, the auditor should follow the procedures set out in **Chapter 14**, 'Cessation as auditor'.

The consideration of the matters set out in the necessary paragraphs of **Section 3:2.2.2** should be recorded in the working papers.

3:2.3 Directors' and officers' liability insurance

Some clients take out liability insurance for their officers and directors. If the client has such insurance then the auditor should understand its nature and extent including the exclusion clauses in place and procedures for allocation in the event of a settlement. The provision of such insurance does not mitigate the auditor's assessment of engagement risk, and therefore should not result in a reduction of the risk class. However, it may be a factor in any decision on whether a client assessed as high risk is taken on or retained.

3:2.4 Practice economics

Quite apart from the risks associated with the individual engagement, the auditor should consider the wider implications for the firm as a whole.

The auditor should be satisfied that the fees recovered from the client will be sufficient to justify the hours charged to the audit. This would include both the client's attitude towards budgeted costs at the planning stage and also to variations in fee arising from unforeseen problems.

Accepting a new client will also have implications for the firm's investment in working capital. The client should be willing to accept a reasonable billing schedule for work in progress and should arrange for invoices to be settled promptly.

The auditor should also be satisfied that any additional work will arise at a time when resources are available, particularly specialist resources such as staff with any necessary industry expertise.

3:2.5 Appendix A Conditions that may present an unusual level of risk to the firm

The examples of risks which follow are intended for guidance only. They will normally be considered during the review of the control environment. Many of the risks are encountered regularly in practice in relation to existing as well as new clients. The acceptance or continuance of an appointment is ultimately determined by the judgement of the engagement partner. However, where the incidence of specific risks detailed below is so high that real doubts exist about the wisdom of accepting or continuing an engagement, the engagement partner should follow the consultation procedures set out in **Section 5:5**, 'Consultation and concurring reviews'.

3:2.5.1 Examples of unusual risks relating to management and the principal owners

(a)   There is information (e.g., a person's conviction for a criminal offence, suspension or sanction by a regulatory body) that calls into question the integrity of one or more members of senior management or otherwise raises serious questions as to the auditor's ability to rely on management's representations.

(b)   An individual with no apparent ownership interest in, or executive position with, the client appears to exercise substantial influence over its affairs.

(c)   A significant or unexpected change of management has recently occurred or is likely to occur in the next year.

(d)   There is reason to question the ethics or business methods of the client.

(e)   Management has become unreasonably demanding of audit personnel and has become difficult to work with or has placed unreasonable time constraints on the issue of audit reports.

(f)   A single individual dominates the management in a manner that inhibits or precludes the effectiveness of others (e.g., other board members or audit committee members) in performing their duties.

(g)   There has been an unusual turnover rate of individuals in key positions.

(h)   There has been a high turnover rate of professional advisers and/or there is evidence of disputes with professional advisers.

(i)   Management places undue emphasis on achieving planned results or issues over-optimistic forecasts.

(j)   Management is willing to take unusually high risks in areas affecting the financial position (e.g., credit control policies, R&D projects, compliance with laws and regulations).

(k)   A significant part of directors' remuneration is derived from bonuses or share options or other remuneration linked to earnings or share price.

(l)   Management has disposed of a large part of its shares in the client in the past year or plans to do so.

(m) Management has failed to appoint reputable professional advisers appropriate to the client's needs (e.g., lawyers, investment bankers, actuaries).

(n)   The client has made a significant acquisition in the past year of another entity whose operations are in an industry in which management has little or no prior expertise.

(o)   Management is not addressing or implementing significant internal control recommendations.

(p)   There is a lack of concern by senior management over a weak internal accounting control system.

(q)   One or more members of management appear to be having personal financial difficulties or maintaining lifestyles inconsistent with their earnings.

3:2.5.2 Examples of unusual risks relating to the legality of activities and reputation

(a)   A substantial part of the client's income and expenses comprise commissions or fees for which there is little or no supporting documentation.

(b)   There are significant unexplained cash flows between the client and other entities incorporated abroad from which the client itself does not profit.

(c)   The client's management appears to act on instructions from persons whose identities are deliberately kept secret.

(d)   The client is unduly secretive about the nature of its trading with politically sensitive countries.

3:2.5.3 Examples of unusual risks relating to the business environment

(a)   The client operates in an industry that is experiencing, or is likely to experience, an abnormal number of business failures or other conditions (e.g., bid rumours) that could cause its accounting and reporting practices to be scrutinised by third parties at a later date.

(b)   The client is in the process of going public by means of a listing or a quotation on one of the over-the-counter markets.

(c)   The client is proposing to raise finance from the public in some other way, e.g. under the business expansion scheme or from venture capitalists.

(d)   The price of the client's shares has changed significantly in comparison with those of similar entities in the same industry, or there has been an unusually high trading volume.

(e)   There are matters such as significant litigation between this entity and another client of the firm that could cause the firm to have a conflict of interest.

(f)   The client has recently taken legal action against other advisers.

(g)   It is likely that the client's financial statements to be reported on will be involved in litigation or other claims.

(h)   The client has been criticised by a regulatory authority in respect of its activities or its accounting and reporting standards.

(i)   The auditor has had significant disagreements with management about accounting policies or auditing matters which have not been satisfactorily resolved.

3:2.5.4 Examples of unusual risks relating to the financial position and prospects

(a)   The client has experienced, or expects to experience, a severe adverse business development that could result in audit and business risks that would be unacceptable risks to the firm.

(b)   It is unlikely that the client will be able to meet its financial obligations as they become due.

(c)   The client has substantial debt from unusual sources, e.g. related parties, or on unusual terms.

(d)   The client has employed creative accounting policies to improve earnings and/or gearing.

(e)   The client's performance has been significantly better or worse than that of its industry as a whole and the reason is not apparent.

(f)   The client has grown by making acquisitions and is dependent on making further acquisitions to meet the market's expectations of future growth.

(g)   The client's method of accounting for acquisitions has enabled it to show high growth when real growth is low.

(h)   A major portion of the client's revenue is dependent on a single customer or group of customers whose continued business is in doubt because of adverse business conditions or competition from others.

(i)   The client has significant joint venture agreements with third parties which may be in financial difficulties.

3:2.5.5 *Examples of unusual risks relating to the audit environment*

(a)   The client engages in transactions with entities under common control, or with other related parties that are not (and will not become) clients of the firm and which can be expected to present significant unusual risks to the firm.

(b)   Formal or informal restrictions have been placed on the auditor limiting effective communication with the audit committee, non-executive directors or other directors having responsibilities for overseeing the client's operations.

(c)   Fee pressures will be encountered because of the effects of adverse business conditions in circumstances where third parties can be expected to place significant reliance on the client's financial statements.

(d)   The last audit report was not an unqualified opinion.

(e)   The previous audit led to significant adjustments to the financial statements or significant weaknesses in systems being reported to management.

(f)   The auditor would be relying on other auditors for material parts of the work on consolidated subsidiaries.

(g)   There are significant related parties or associated companies with which significant transactions may occur, and which the auditor will not audit or which have different year-ends.

(h)   There is reason to believe that it will not be possible to render an unqualified report because of such matters as scope limitations, going concern problems, significant litigation or accounting or disclosure issues.

(i)   The auditor is aware of recent 'opinion shopping' by the client.

(j)   There are restrictions on the disclosure of ownership or identity of shareholders.

(k)   The client's accounting records or internal control systems are inadequate or in poor condition.

(l)   The client's directors include persons who also act for the entity in a professional capacity, e.g. stockbrokers or solicitors, and this could lead to conflicts of interest for the directors.

(m)   The client maintains banking relationships with a number of different banks for no apparent reason.

(n)   There has been a significant change in the ownership of the client during the year.

3:2.5.6 *Examples of unusual risks relating to significant accounting issues*

(a)   The client engages in unique, highly complex and material transactions that pose difficult questions of substance over form.

(b)   Management has a history of completing significant or unusual transactions late in the entity's financial year.

(c)   During the past year a relatively small number of transactions have had a material effect on results and such transactions were designed to meet the minimum criteria that have to be met in order to permit revenue to be recognised (creative accounting).

(d)   There are special problems relating to accounting estimates or measurements that are of unusual significance because of the nature of the industry or the relative importance of the financial statements.

(e)   The client uses accounting policies that are inconsistent with predominant industry practice or which are otherwise questionable.

(f)   A change to what might be a less preferable accounting policy has recently been made or is under active consideration (particularly where the client is contemplating a public offering of its shares or is raising money by other means).

(g)   There are significant non-monetary transactions.

(h)   The financial statements include assets that have been written up in value in connection with a purchase from a related party or a management buyout in which management continues to hold an ownership interest.

(i)   The client carries significant 'off balance sheet' finance.

3:2.6 Appendix B Specimen letter to the directors of a proposed new client when the firm has been invited to accept nomination for appointment as auditor

Dear Sirs,

Thank you for your letter of [*date*] informing us of your proposal to nominate/appoint* us as auditors of [*name of proposed client*].

Before we can accept nomination/appointment*, our rules of professional conduct require us to write to your existing auditors seeking information which could influence our decision whether or not we may properly accept appointment. If you have not already done so, please inform your existing auditors of the proposed change and provide them with written authority to discuss the affairs of the company with us.

[*Would you please send us a copy of the resolution that will be put at a general meeting of the company proposing that the existing auditors be removed before their term of office expires/or the resolution proposing our appointment in place of the existing auditors who are not seeking reappointment.*]*

Until we have obtained the necessary response to our professional enquiries, please do not take any further action regarding our nomination/appointment.*

Yours faithfully,

*Delete as appropriate.

3:2.7 Appendix C Specimen letter to the existing auditor of a proposed new client when the firm has been invited to accept nomination for appointment as auditor

Dears Sirs,

[*Name of proposed client*]

We understand that the directors of the above company have recently informed you that they have invited us to accept appointment/nomination to be appointed* as auditors of the company. We also understand that the directors have given you written authorisation to discuss the company's affairs with us.

Before we accept appointment/nomination* as auditors, please confirm whether there are any matters of which we should be aware including, in particular, any matters which could influence our decision as to whether or not to accept appointment/nomination* as auditors of the company.

In addition, please send copies of the notice of resignation and statement deposited at the company's registered office under Sections 392 and 394 of the Companies Act 1985 [*or other relevant industry specific (UK) legislation*]*, or let us have copies when they are finalised.

Please also send a copy of any representations you have made, or intend to make, to the company under Section 391A of the Companies Act 1985 [*or other relevant (UK) industry specific legislation*]*.

Yours faithfully,

*Delete as appropriate.

3:2.8 Appendix D Specimen letter to a proposed new client when all enquiries to the preceding auditor have been completed and the firm is accepting appointment

Dear Sirs,

We have now completed our professional enquiries and are delighted to be able formally to accept your invitation to become the auditors of [*name of proposed client*]

Yours faithfully,

3:3 Engagement letters

3:3.1 Introduction

Statement of Auditing Standards 140, 'Engagement Letters', states that 'The auditors and the client should agree on the terms of the engagement, which should be recorded in writing.' The purpose of an audit engagement letter is to define clearly the nature and extent of the auditor's responsibilities that have been agreed with the client, and so to minimise the possibility that any misunderstanding will arise between the auditor and the client's management. Both the auditor and the client should clearly understand that the engagement letter, when agreed between both parties, will give rise to contractual obligations.

3:3.2 New clients

The engagement partner should send an engagement letter to all new clients soon after the appointment as auditor, and in any event before the start of the first audit engagement.

3:3.3 Existing clients

Statement of Auditing Standards 140.2 states that:

> *Auditors should agree the terms of their engagement with new clients in writing. Thereafter auditors should regularly review the terms of engagement and if appropriate agree any updating in writing.*

It is common practice to update and reissue the engagement letter annually. The auditor should always reissue the letter when there is a significant change in ownership or directors of the company or there is another significant change in audit circumstances.

3:3.4 Procedures

3:3.4.1 *Addressee*

For clients incorporated under the Companies Act 1985, the auditor should address the engagement letter to the directors of the company. For a client that is not incorporated, the auditor should address the letter to the governing body or to the proprietor, as appropriate.

3:3.4.2 *Agreeing the terms of the engagement*

The auditor should always discuss the scope of the engagement with the client's management, and should then confirm the matters agreed in the engagement letter. In the case of a new engagement, the auditor should normally discuss and agree the contents of the engagement letter with the client's management before accepting the audit appointment. Usually the auditor will discuss these matters with the directors, but the directors may assign this responsibility to other members of management, or to an audit committee.

The auditor should obtain the client's confirmation of the terms of the engagement by sending an additional copy of the engagement letter and asking the client to sign and return this. This request may be contained in a less formal covering letter from the engagement partner. The covering letter should also, where appropriate, refer to the matters discussed at the meetings with (named) directors or members of senior management.

In the case of a company, the auditor should request that the letter be tabled at a board meeting or, where the board delegates this responsibility, at a meeting of a suitable committee of the board (e.g., the audit committee), and for the approval of the letter to be minuted.

3:3.4.3 Filing

A copy of the engagement letter should be filed with the audit working papers.

3:3.5 Contents of the letter

Firms may wish to send their corporate clients an engagement letter covering additional services (e.g., corporate tax advice and assistance in preparing tax computations). **Section 3:3.13 (Appendix)** covers those matters the engagement letter should include concerning audit.

3:3.6 Investment business

If the firm is authorised to carry on investment business by one of the Recognised Professional Bodies (RPBs) it should consider the nature of the services to be provided under the engagement letter and whether any might fall within the definition of investment business in Sch. 1 to the Financial Services Act 1986. If that is the case (note that a pure audit service is not investment business) then the firm must comply with any rules issued by its RPB.

Firms authorised by the ICAEW may wish to include an investment business paragraph in their engagement letter. This paragraph will cover any investment business services provided as an integral part of the general professional services supplied under the engagement letter.

If the client requires specific investment business services, these should be covered in a separate engagement letter.

3:3.6.1 Corporate finance clients

If the only incidental investment business the firm is likely to undertake for the client consists of corporate finance type activities, and the client has agreed that it is appropriate for the firm to treat the client as a 'corporate finance' client, the engagement letter should include a paragraph on the following lines:

> **This Firm is regulated in its carrying on of Investment Business by The Institute of Chartered Accountants in England and Wales. Under the Institute's Investment Business Regulations, Investment Business carried on for a Corporate Finance Client in the course of Corporate Finance Activities is subject to a system of regulation which differs in certain material respects from that for Investment Business generally. Accordingly, if a client agrees to be treated as a Corporate Finance Client, it will enjoy the general protection afforded to a Corporate Finance Client rather than the protection that may be appropriate for individual investors. We may undertake Investment Business on your behalf arising out of the**

normal professional services we provide for you, and will treat you as a Corporate Finance Client.

3:3.6.2 *Other clients*

If the client does not agree to be treated as a corporate finance client, or the investment business anticipated would not be a corporate finance activity, the engagement letter should include a paragraph on the following lines:

Investment business services

We may, in the course of the other professional services set out in this engagement letter, advise you on the acquisition and disposal of investments. If, as a result of such advice, you require us to arrange or effect a transaction, we will require a written statement of your instructions.

Please bear in mind that we may not undertake any more extensive investment business on your behalf without specifically agreeing with you the terms and conditions that will apply.

We may give you oral or written advice. To enable us to provide a proper service to you, there may be occasions when we will need to contact you without your express invitation. For example, it may be in your interests to buy or sell a particular investment and we would wish to be able to inform you of that fact. We therefore may contact you in such circumstances. We would, however, only do so between [*8 a.m.*] and [*7 p.m.*] on weekdays and [*8 a.m.*] and [*1 p.m.*] on Saturdays. We shall, of course, comply with any restrictions you may wish to impose with regard to the timing of such contacts or otherwise and which you notify to us in writing.

3:3.7 Groups

The auditor should consider sending a separate letter to each company in a group that the firm audits, particularly in respect of any subsidiary authorised to carry on investment business under the Financial Services Act 1986. However, the auditor may also send one letter relating to the group as a whole, provided that:

(a)   the terms of the engagement are common and all the subsidiaries are audited by one firm;

(b)   the letter to the parent company relates to both the parent and its subsidiaries;

(c)   the auditor requests that a copy of the letter be forwarded by the parent company to the boards of the subsidiaries;

(d)   each board confirms to the auditor that the terms of the engagement are accepted;

(e)   the subsidiary is not authorised to carry on investment business; and

(f)   the auditor forwards a copy of the letter to each office that audits a subsidiary.

3:3.8 Overseas parent company

The auditor should normally send an engagement letter to the client even if it is the UK subsidiary of an overseas parent company.

3:3.9 Joint audits

Guidance on engagement letters for joint audits is given in **Section 7:7**, 'Joint audits'.

3:3.10 Specialised industries

If the client operates in a specialised industry such as financial services, banking or insurance, the engagement partner or the engagement manager should consult an industry specialist or appropriate industry guidance to confirm any specific requirements relating to engagement letters.

3:3.11 Greenbury/Corporate governance

Following recent changes to the Listing Rules, the directors of listed companies are required to agree with their auditors that the scope of the audit includes the requirements of Listing Rule 12.43(x) regarding directors' emoluments. APB Bulletin 1997/2, 'Disclosure of directors' remuneration', recommended that these terms of the auditors' engagement be reflected in the audit engagement letter.

3:3.12 Reporting to third parties

Auditors are sometimes requested to issue reports to banks and other third parties, e.g., in connection with banking and financial covenants entered into by clients. Such reports will establish a duty of care to a bank or other third party, and for risk-management purposes it is essential that the auditor agrees satisfactory terms before undertaking to provide such reports, including, e.g., obtaining appropriate limitation of liability. This should be made clear in the engagement letter by including the following paragraph referring to the provision by the auditor of reports to third parties.

Reporting to third parties

There may be situations, for example in relation to loan agreements, where a third party seeks to request us, in our capacity as auditors, to report to them. Any contractual arrangements between you and a third party which may seek to impose such requirements upon us will not, as a matter of law, be binding upon us. However, depending on the circumstances, we may agree to provide reports to third parties, but not in our capacity as auditors. Any such possible requirements must be discussed with us at the earliest

opportunity and well before the loan agreement or other arrangement is finalised.

3:3.13 Appendix A Specimen engagement letter for company audits

An engagement letter for a company might follow the wording given below. The wording is based closely on the example contained in the Statement of Auditing Standards 140, 'Engagement Letters'. Specific changes, other than those indicated in the text, may be needed to suit individual requirements and circumstances.

The Directors

Dear Sirs

The purpose of this letter is to set out the basis on which we are to act as auditor of the company [*and its subsidiaries*] and the respective areas of responsibility of the company and of ourselves.

Audit

As directors of the above-named company, you are responsible for maintaining proper accounting records and for preparing financial statements which give a true and fair view and comply with the Companies Act 1985. You are also responsible for making available to us, as and when required, all of the company's accounting records and all other records and related information, including minutes of directors' and shareholders' meetings and of all relevant management meetings. We are also entitled to attend all general meetings of the company and to receive notice of all such meetings.

We have a statutory responsibility to report to the members whether in our opinion the financial statements give a true and fair view of the state of the company's affairs and of the profit or loss for the year, and whether they are properly prepared in accordance with the Companies Act. In arriving at our opinion, we are required to consider the following matters, and to report on any in respect of which we are not satisfied:

(a) Whether proper accounting records have been kept by the company and proper returns adequate for our audit have been received from branches not visited by us.

(b) Whether the company's balance sheet and profit and loss account are in agreement with the accounting records and returns.

(c) Whether we have obtained all the information and explanations which we consider necessary for the purpose of our audit.

(d) Whether the information in the directors' report is consistent with that in the audited financial statements.

In addition, there are certain other matters which, according to the circumstances, may need to be dealt with in our report. For example, where the financial statements do not give full details of directors' remuneration or of directors' transactions with the company, the Companies Act 1985 [*and the Listing Rules of the London Stock Exchange*] requires us to disclose such matters in our report. [*Our report on corporate governance matters will be the subject of a separate engagement.*]

We have a professional responsibility to report if financial statements do not comply in any material respect with Accounting Standards, unless in our opinion the non-compliance is justified in the circumstances.

Our audit will be conducted in accordance with Auditing Standards and will have regard to relevant Auditing Guidelines. Furthermore, it will be conducted in such a manner as we consider necessary to fulfil our responsibilities as auditor and it will include such tests of transactions and of the existence, ownership and valuation of assets and liabilities as we consider necessary. We shall obtain an understanding of the accounting system to assess its adequacy as a basis for the preparation of the financial statements, and to establish whether proper accounting records have been maintained. We shall expect to obtain such relevant and reliable evidence as we consider sufficient to enable us to draw reasonable conclusions therefrom. The nature and extent of our tests will vary according to our assessment of what is material in the context of the company's financial statements, our assessment of the company's accounting system and, where we wish to place reliance on it, the system of internal control, and they may cover any aspect of the business operations.

[*Include a paragraph along the following lines unless it has been agreed with the client that the scope in respect of certain units or divisions will be increased beyond that required to express an opinion on the financial statements on the company as a whole. Where this is agreed with the client, the increase in the scope of work should be described and it should be stated that the fees for the additional work will be separately identified and billed in addition to the audit fee.*] Because our responsibilities are to report on the financial statements as a whole, rather than those of individual units or divisions, the nature and extent of our tests and enquiries at each unit or division will vary according to our assessment of its circumstances. Thus we will carry out limited work at certain units or divisions, rather than the full audit that would be necessary if we were to report on the separate financial statements of the unit or division concerned.

Reporting to directors/management

We shall report to you and if necessary to management also, normally in writing, any significant weaknesses in, or our observations on, the company's systems and other areas which come to our notice, and which we consider should be brought to your attention.

Representations by directors/management

As part of our normal audit procedures, we may request you/management to provide written confirmation of oral representations which we have received from you/them during the course of the audit.

Documents issued with the financial statements

To assist us with the examination of your financial statements, we shall request sight of all documents or statements, including the chairman's statement and the directors' report, which are due to be issued with the financial statements. [*We will need to satisfy ourselves that they are consistent with and do not undermine the credibility of the audited accounts. If it is proposed that any documents or statements which refer to our name, other than the audited financial statements, are to be circulated to third parties, please consult us before they are issued.*]

Irregularities, including fraud

The responsibility for the prevention and detection of irregularities, including fraud, rests with yourselves. However, we shall endeavour to plan our audit so that we have a reasonable expectation of detecting material misstatements in the financial statements or accounting records resulting from such irregularities, but our examination should not be relied upon to disclose those which may exist.

Other auditors

[*A paragraph along the following lines should be included where the letter is addressed to a parent company and it has subsidiaries audited by other auditors.*] Our reporting responsibilities in connection with the financial statements of the group are identical to those set out above in respect of the company. Other duties and powers in connection with subsidiaries audited by other auditors are contained in the Companies Act 1985. In carrying out our duties under this heading, we shall make such enquiries of the other auditors, and review their work to such an extent, as we consider necessary to form our opinion on the group financial statements. However, the responsibility to your company, as shareholder, for the audits of such subsidiaries remains with the auditors of the subsidiaries concerned.

Internal audit

[*If the auditor plans to make use of work done by an internal audit department it will be necessary to agree the arrangements in writing with the company, including the chief internal auditor. Such agreement may need to be made anew each year. The detail will generally best be dealt with in a separate letter. Guidance on using the work of internal audit is discussed in Section 7:5, 'Using the work of internal audit'*].

Fiduciary responsibilities

[*This paragraph may be omitted if the client does not hold assets on behalf of others. It would need to be adapted if the client is subject to Client Money Rules under the Financial Services Act 1986 or if for other reasons the audit enquiries are to be extended thereto. This will be necessary if the client or third parties could suffer loss as a result of the assets concerned being lost, damaged or misappropriated, or if the client specifically requests the firm to extend the audit in this way. Examples of clients that may hold assets on behalf of others are dealers in securities, commodity dealers and brokers, warehousing and transport businesses and any business buying goods on consignment.*] Because our audit is directed at forming an opinion on the company's financial statements our audit tests will not normally extend to assets, or documents of title in respect of assets, that are in the company's possession but owned by others.

Reporting to third parties

There may be situations, e.g. in relation to loan agreements, where a third party seeks to request us, in our capacity as auditors, to report to them. Any contractual arrangements between you and a third party which may seek to impose such requirements upon us will not, as a matter of law, be binding upon us. However, depending on the circumstances, we may agree to provide reports to third parties, but not in our capacity as auditors. Any such possible requirements must be discussed with us at the earliest opportunity and well before the loan agreement or other arrangement is finalised.

Access to working papers

The Companies Act 1985 requires us as auditors of the subsidiary undertaking to give the auditors of the parent company such information and explanations as those auditors may reasonably require for their audit. This could include our giving them access to our working papers and discussing relevant matters with them. We may [*also*] be required to give access to our audit working papers for regulatory purposes or because of other statutory obligations.

Confidentiality and conflicts of interest

We provide a wide range of services for a large number of clients and may be in a position where we are providing services to companies and organisations which you might regard as giving rise to a conflict of interest. Although we have established procedures to identify such situations we cannot be certain that we will identify all of those which exist or may develop, in part because it is difficult for us to anticipate what you might perceive to be a conflict. We request that you notify us of any conflicts affecting this assignment of which you are, or become, aware. Where the above circumstances are identified and we believe that your interests can be properly safeguarded by the implementation of appropriate procedures, we will discuss and agree with you the arrangements which we will put in place to preserve confidentiality and to ensure that the advice and opinions which you receive from us are wholly independent. Just as we will not use information confidential to you for the advantage of a third party, we will not use confidential information obtained from any other party for your advantage.

Investment business

[*In relation to corporate finance clients: If the only incidental investment business the firm is likely to undertake for a client consists of corporate finance type activities and the auditor is satisfied the client can be properly treated as a corporate finance client the auditor should, with the client's agreement, insert the following paragraph in the engagement letter. Many corporate clients will fall within this definition but, before the auditor asks an individual or the directors of an owner-managed company to sign a letter including this paragraph, the auditor should be satisfied that the client has sufficient investment experience.*]

This Firm is regulated in its carrying on of Investment Business by The Institute of Chartered Accountants in England and Wales. Under the Institute's Investment Business Regulations, Investment Business carried on for a Corporate Finance Client in the course of Corporate Finance Activities is subject to a system of regulation which differs in certain material respects from that for Investment Business generally. Accordingly, if a client agrees to be treated as a Corporate Finance Client, it will enjoy the general protection afforded to a Corporate Finance Client rather than the protection that may be appropriate for individual investors. We may undertake Investment Business on your behalf arising out of the normal professional services we provide for you, and will treat you as a Corporate Finance Client.

Partner roles on the engagement

One partner in this Firm, the audit engagement partner, will have overall responsibility for the conduct of the audit and for the issue of our opinion on the financial statements. In practice we adopt a number of both formal and informal consultation and concurring review procedures involving other partners in order that the advice we give and the opinions we express represent the breadth of knowledge and collective experience of the Firm. Other partners may also be assigned either to help ensure the quality of our service or to assist with aspects of the audit. We will change the audit engagement partner from time to time [*Insert the following words in the case of a listed company: in accordance with ethical requirements at least every seven years on this audit*]. We believe this will enhance the quality of our audit and our service by introducing a fresh, objective view without sacrificing the Firm's knowledge and experience of your business. Other partner roles may also change periodically.

Fees

Our fees are computed on the basis of the time spent on your affairs by the partners and our staff, and on the levels of skill and responsibility involved. Our fees will be billed at appropriate intervals during the course of the year and will be due on presentation. Any queries concerning an invoice must be raised within 30 days of the invoice date.

Law and jurisdiction

The contract formed by this engagement letter when accepted by you shall be governed by, and construed in accordance with, English law and it is hereby irrevocably agreed and accepted that the Courts of England and Wales shall have exclusive jurisdiction to settle any claim, difference or dispute (including, without limitation claims for set-off or counterclaims) which may arise out of or in connection with such contract. Each party irrevocably waives any right it may have to object to an action being brought in such Courts, to claim that the action has been brought in an inconvenient forum or to claim that such Courts do not have jurisdiction.

Agreement of terms

Once it has been agreed, this letter will remain effective from one audit appointment to another until it is replaced. We shall be grateful if you could confirm in writing your agreement to the terms of this letter, either by acknowledging it or by signing and returning the enclosed copy, or let us know if they are not in accordance with your understanding of our terms of appointment.

Yours faithfully,

3:4 New audit engagements

3:4.1 Introduction

This section discusses the administrative and other procedures the auditor should follow after accepting a new audit engagement. The legal and professional procedures the auditor should follow before accepting an audit engagement are discussed in **Section 3:2**, 'Appointment and continuation as auditor'.

3:4.2 Timing of work

The auditor should carry out as much as possible of the work discussed in this section immediately after the firm is appointed, so that the auditor is aware of any errors or changes in policies that might have an effect on the financial statements which the auditor is auditing, and so that they can be discussed with the client in good time before the end of the financial period.

At the conclusion of the interim audit work the engagement manager should document how the procedures discussed below have been carried out. This issues documentation should state whether the accounting policies and the opening balances to be used for the current year are acceptable. If there are errors, or the accounting policies are to be changed, the engagement manager should record the potential effect on the financial statements.

3:4.3 Administration procedures

The engagement partner should appoint an engagement manager. Together they will appoint other members of the core audit team. The engagement manager and in-charge should:

(a) follow the procedures necessary for the time and other costs associated with this audit engagement to be recorded in the firm's own accounting records;

(b) obtain background information about the client's management, the client's business, and the industry in which the client operates;

(c) liaise with computer and other specialists where necessary to supplement the knowledge and experience of the core audit team;

(d) if the firm is to be responsible for taxation work for the client, liaise with tax specialists and ensure that all necessary and relevant client information is passed to them as discussed in **Section 7:4**, 'Tax specialists';

(e) draft an appropriate engagement letter in accordance with **Section 3:3**, 'Engagement letters'.

3:4.4 Record of acceptance procedures

The auditor will have considered the existence of any conditions which might present an unusual level of risk to the firm before accepting appointment as auditor. These are set out in **Section 3:2.5 (Appendix A)**. The engagement partner or the engagement manager should ensure that the working papers contain the information obtained from the enquiries into the matters discussed in that section.

3:4.5 Standing data

The engagement manager should visit the client before the planning stage of the audit and obtain copies of 'standing data' to assist with the planning process. Examples are:
(a) Incorporation documents and Articles of Association, or the partnership agreement.

(b) Agreements such as major leases, trust deeds and contracts.

(c) Financial statements, tax returns, tax assessments and management letters for the previous two years.

Relevant extracts from the documents referred to above may be retained on the audit file as carry-forward material.

The engagement manager should also arrange to inspect the company's file kept by the Registrar of Companies.

3:4.6 Initial planning

The engagement partner, the engagement manager and the in-charge should discuss, jointly with relevant specialists, the planning of the first audit and the use of other specialist services, and record their decisions in the audit strategy memorandum. These arrangements should be agreed with the client and confirmed in the engagement letter.

3:4.7 Audit procedures

3:4.7.1 Previous financial statements

For all audits of a client's financial statements, the auditor should consider the accounting policies of the preceding period and the balances brought forward to the current year. Guidance on the effect of an audit qualification on the prior period's financial statements is provided in **Section 13:16**, 'Qualified and modified reports to members of limited companies and other organisations in Great Britain'.

3:4.7.2 Accounting policies

The auditor should establish whether the accounting policies adopted by the client for the current period are both consistent with those of the previous period and also appropriate in the circumstances. Where the client has been acquired as a group by the firm, the auditor should also ensure their consistency with the policies of fellow group companies.

If the auditor considers the accounting policies to be unacceptable, the auditor should discuss with the client how the policies might be changed. If the client initiates any changes to its accounting policies, the auditor should review the proposed policies for acceptability.

3:4.7.3 Opening balances

Statement of Auditing Standards 450 'Opening Balances and Comparatives' requires that:

> *Auditors should obtain sufficient appropriate audit evidence that amounts derived from the preceding period's financial statements are free from material misstatements and are appropriately incorporated in the financial statements for the current period. (SAS 450.1)*

Auditors should obtain sufficient appropriate audit evidence that:

(a)   opening balances have been appropriately brought forward;

(c)   opening balances do not contain errors or misstatements which materially affect the current period's financial statements; and

(c)   appropriate accounting policies are consistently applied or changes in accounting policies have been properly accounted for and adequately disclosed (SAS 450.2).

If the preceding auditors issued an unqualified report on the preceding period's financial statements and the audit of the current period has not revealed any matters which cast doubt on those financial statements, the procedures regarding opening balances need not extend beyond ensuring that opening balances have been appropriately brought forward and that current accounting policies have been consistently applied.

If a qualified report was issued on the preceding period's financial statements the auditor should consider whether the matter which gave rise to the qualification has been resolved and properly dealt with in the current period's financial statements.

Other procedures which incoming auditors might perform include the following:

(a) Consultations with management and review of records, working papers and accounting and control procedures for the preceding period.

(b) Substantive testing of any opening balances in respect of which the results of other procedures are considered unsatisfactory. Particular emphasis may need to be given to such testing where the previous financial statements were unaudited, e.g. if a company has taken advantage in the previous year of the exemptions from audit conferred under ss. 249A to 249E of the Companies Act 1985. If in these circumstances it is not possible for auditors to obtain sufficient appropriate audit evidence, they must consider the implications for their report.

3:4.7.4 Prior period amounts

Auditors should obtain sufficient appropriate audit evidence that:

(a) the accounting policies used for the comparatives are consistent with those of the current period and appropriate adjustments and disclosures have been made where this is not the case;

(b) the comparatives agree with the amounts and other disclosures presented in the preceding period and are free from errors in the context of the financial statements of the current period; and

(c) where comparatives have been adjusted as required by relevant legislation and accounting standards, appropriate disclosures have been (SAS 450.3).

To express an opinion on the current period's profit or loss and cash flow, the auditor should obtain assurance on the opening balance sheet.

The auditor should review the comparative figures for credibility, and consider what further audit work is required. Financial statements of companies prepared under the Companies Act 1985 are required to disclose corresponding amounts for all items in the balance sheet, the profit and loss account and, with a few exceptions, the notes to the financial statements. In other cases, financial statements usually contain corresponding amounts as a matter of law, regulation or good practice. Their purpose, unless stated otherwise, is to complement the amounts relating to the current period and not to represent the complete financial statements for the preceding period. Appropriate audit work will normally include the following:

(a) Discussions with the client's management.

(b) Reviewing the client's records, working papers and accounting and control procedures for the preceding period, particularly in so far as they affect the opening position.

(c) Enquiry of the predecessor auditor.

(d) Performing audit work on the current period to provide assurance regarding opening balances. For example, the auditor might extend the scope of the preliminary analytical review, particularly in relation to account balances which have a significant risk of misstatement. Thus, if stocks were material to the financial statements, the auditor might compare the stock sheets and summaries of the preceding year with those for the current year.

In those (exceptional) circumstances where the auditor does not consider that the results of the procedures in (a) to (d) are satisfactory, the auditor may need to carry out substantive tests on the opening balances.

3:4.7.5 *Review of client's working papers*

The amounts included in the preceding period's financial statements should be supported by the accounting records together with working papers and instructions issued by the client. The auditor should review the supporting material to confirm that the financial statements agree with the accounting records. The auditor should confirm that the client carried out important procedures such as counting stocks and reviewing debtors for recoverability.

3:4.7.6 *Enquiry of a predecessor auditor*

The auditor should seek to meet the predecessor auditor. The auditor would usually expect to receive reasonable co-operation with any requests made, either for information to enable the auditor to examine areas that contain a risk of misstatement, or to clarify any significant accounting matters that are not adequately dealt with in the client's records. However, there are no professional statements or legal requirements in the UK that place a predecessor auditor under any obligation to make its working papers or any other information available to the auditor.

Enquiries of a predecessor auditor should principally take the form of discussion, but the auditor may need to seek agreement to refer to the predecessor auditor's working papers. Some firms will only respond to requests for specific information or to a meeting, and will not allow a successor auditor general access to their working papers.

3:4.7.7 *Problems with prior period amounts*

If the results of the procedures described in **Section 3:4.7.4** (second paragraph) are unsatisfactory, and if the predecessor auditor refuses to co-operate, the engagement partner should follow the consultation procedures set out in **Section 5:5**, 'Consultation and concurring reviews'. If sufficient audit evidence is not available from these sources or from additional audit work (e.g., by carrying out substantive tests of the relevant opening balances), the auditor may have to qualify the audit report in respect of the allocation of results between the current year and prior years.

When the financial statements of the preceding period were unaudited, e.g. if a company has taken advantage in the previous year of the exemption from audit conferred by ss. 249A to 249E of the Companies Act 1985, the incoming auditors must consider whether there is clear disclosure in the financial statements that the comparatives are unaudited.

3:5 Dormant companies

3:5.1 Definition

A company is regarded as being dormant only if there were no accounting transactions, other than the initial issue of shares to the subscribers, required to be entered in the accounting records during the year.

3:5.2 Reasons for dormant companies

Many parent companies have subsidiaries which are dormant for the following or other reasons:

(a) A subsidiary company has been formed as a vehicle for future operations, but for one reason or another the time is not yet ripe for it to start business.

(b) A subsidiary company has been formed and is retained in existence in order to protect the use of a particular name.

(c) A company has been acquired by the parent company and the latter has taken over all its assets, but the subsidiary company is retained in existence in case the parent company should require to use the subsidiary company at some time in the future and in order to retain the benefit of the stamp duty paid on the capital of the company.

(d) The subsidiary company's name includes some registered trade mark and, although the company is not trading to its own name, it is trading through another company as agent as described in **Section 3:5.3**.

(e) Taxation reasons, for example:

  (i)   The benefit of rollover provisions for chargeable gains.

  (ii) The maximisation of allowable losses.

  (iii) The use of capital losses in the company.

(f) In order that legal action may be taken if necessary to recover debts which arose when the now dormant company carried on a trade which has been transferred to another group company and to avoid precipitating claims in connection with the trade formerly carried on by the now dormant company.

Where a group has a large number of dormant companies, the client should be recommended to centralise the control of, and the responsibility for, the statutory books and accounts of such companies in order to reduce administrative costs.

In appropriate circumstances clients should be advised to investigate the possibility of eliminating dormant companies which do not appear to be required for a specific purpose.

However, care should be taken before any dormant company is liquidated or struck off the register by the Registrar of Companies under s. 652 of the Companies Act 1985, to ensure that there will be no adverse tax effects.

3:5.3 Dormant agency companies

It is frequently the practice for one or more main trading companies in a group to take over the trades of other group companies though such trades continue to be carried on in the names of the companies which formerly owned them. In such cases the legal position is that the company formerly owning the trade ('the agency company') should not be regarded as having become dormant but rather as acting as managing agent for the trading company and as carrying on the trade in its own name but on behalf of and for the account of the trading company.

Under normal circumstances, provided the conditions set out in the next paragraph are observed, there is no need for the agency company to keep accounting records to record any of the transactions relating to the trade which may be recorded in the accounting records of the trading company. Additionally, under normal circumstances the agency company need not prepare a profit and loss account provided that it receives no remuneration for its services and has no other receipts, and makes no payments, for its own account. It is necessary to ensure that appropriate group VAT arrangements have been made. *See* **Section 9:26**, 'Value added tax'.

The conditions to be observed are as follows:

(a)   The arrangements should be recorded, preferably in a formal agreement, but as an alternative in a board minute. If a board minute is relied on instead of a formal agreement, the wording of the minute should be in the same terms as an agreement. However, it should be noted that a board minute does not amount to an agreement but can constitute evidence of an informal agreement.

(b)   There should be a note to the financial statements in one of the two forms suggested in **Section 3:5.5**.

(c)   A statement in the same form as the note to the financial statements should be included in the directors' report.

(d)   The trading company should fully indemnify the agency company against any obligations that it may incur so that the trading company bears any losses of the business.

3:5.4 Statutory requirements

Under s. 652 of the Companies Act 1985 the Registrar of Companies may strike the name of a company off the register and dissolve the company if there is cause to believe that the company is not carrying on business or is not in operation. It is understood that the Registrar of Companies will strike off the register any companies which have in fact ceased to exist, but that it is not intended to treat in this manner the dormant companies referred to above, for whose continued existence there are valid reasons. It is suggested that, if any such companies receive an enquiry from the Registrar of Companies as to whether they are trading or in operation, a letter to the Registrar explaining the reasons for their continued existence would probably meet the case.

Dormant companies of the character referred to above still have to comply with the provisions of the Companies Act and for this purpose they must:

(a)   either appoint an auditor or pass a special resolution that an auditor shall not be appointed (*see* **Section 3:5.6**);

(b)   prepare financial statements;

(c)   cause one director to sign the financial statements and where an auditor is not appointed include the statement that the company was dormant (*see* **Section 3:5.6**) immediately above the signature;

(d)   hold an annual general meeting;

(e)   file an annual return with the Registrar of Companies together with the financial statements of the company.

3:5.5 Financial statements and directors' report

A dormant company's financial statements should follow the normal pattern insofar as this is applicable, but usually only a balance sheet and a few notes will be needed, together with a directors' report.

In the year in which a company which has previously been active becomes dormant, the financial statements need not include a profit and loss account but in order to state corresponding figures as required by the Companies Acts 1985 should include a note explaining the circumstances and including the key figures of the previous year's profit and loss account. A profit and loss account will not normally be required in subsequent years, but a statement should be made explaining why there is no profit and loss account, for example, 'The company has not traded during the period and has made neither profits nor losses'. This wording should be appropriately amended where the company has operated on an agency basis, and one of the two following forms should be used:

(a)   'The company has not traded on its own account and has made neither profits nor losses'.

(b)   'All trading transactions are entered into as agent for X Limited, the records thereof being incorporated in the books and accounts of that company'.

If preferred, a combination of (a) and (b) could be used.

3:5.6 Auditor not appointed

Section 250 of the Companies Act 1985 permits dormant companies not to appoint an auditor. Such companies, other than ones required to prepare group financial statements, may pass a special resolution resolving that an auditor shall not be appointed at any general meeting at which copies of the company's financial statements are laid, provided that:

(a)   the directors are entitled under s. 246 to deliver, in respect of that financial year, accounts modified or for a small company (or would be so entitled but for the company being, or having been at any time in the financial year, a member of an ineligible group within s. 248(2)); and

(b)   it has been dormant since the end of the previous financial year.

In addition, following the formation of a dormant company it may be resolved, by passing a special resolution at any time before the first annual general meeting, that an auditor shall not be appointed, provided that the company has been dormant since formation.

Where a company has resolved not to appoint an auditor, unaudited financial statements may be prepared and filed with the Registrar of Companies provided that the company remains dormant. Section 250 of the Companies Act 1985 requires that the balance sheet contain a statement by the directors immediately above the signature of the director that the company was dormant throughout the financial year ending with the date of the balance sheet. An appropriate statement in the first year would be:

> **At the annual general meeting on ... the company resolved by special resolution not to appoint an auditor. The company was dormant, within the meaning of Section 250 of the Companies Act 1985, throughout the financial year ended on**

In subsequent years the first sentence is unnecessary and should be omitted.

For the purposes of s. 250 of the Companies Act 1985 a company is regarded as dormant if there were no transactions required by s. 221 to be entered in the accounting records. Transactions arising from the initial issue of shares to the subscribers to the memorandum may be ignored for this purpose.

It is understood that provisions for depreciation would not constitute 'transactions' and thus if they are the only entries in the accounting records the company can still be regarded as dormant. However, items such as the receipt or payment of dividends would be regarded as transactions and would preclude the company from claiming exemption from appointing an auditor. As indicated in paragraph 07 a dormant agency company need not record the transactions relating to the trade in its accounting records, provided the conditions set out in **Section 3:5.3** are observed. A dormant agency company, as such, can be regarded as dormant within the meaning of s. 250 of the Companies Act 1985.

3:5.7 Audit approach

Where an audit of a dormant company is required the audit work to be carried out is usually limited to the following aspects:

(a) Comparison of the balance sheet with the general ledger in order to see that it is in accordance therewith.

(b) Verification of the issued share capital and inter-company balance or bank account.

(c) Ensuring that the statutory requirements have been complied with, including those applicable to the directors' report.

Chapter 4

Planning the audit

4:1 Strategy

4:1.1 Introduction

This chapter describes the stages that the auditor should complete in preparing an audit strategy that suits the particular circumstances of the engagement. These are:

(a) Business review (*see* **Section 4:2**);

(b) Preliminary analytical review (*see* **Section 4:3**);

(c) Evaluating inherent risk (*see* **Section 4:4**);

(d) Review of internal control for strategy purposes (*see* **Section 4:5**);

(e) Determining the strategy (*see* **Section 4:6**).

4:1.2 Developing the audit programme

The audit programme should be developed in response to the risks of misstatement. The objective of this is to ascertain the best combination of work that will enable the auditor to arrive at a sufficiently low level of audit risk at minimum cost. Guidance on tailoring audit programmes is included in **Section 4:7**, 'The audit programme'.

4:1.3 Planning and control

Section 4:8, 'Planning and control', includes guidance on planning and control matters that should be considered at the strategy stage.

4:2 Business review

4:2.1 Introduction

Statement of Auditing Standards 210, 'Knowledge of the Business', states:

> *Auditors should have or obtain a knowledge of the business of the entity to be audited which is sufficient to enable them to identify and understand the events, transactions and practices that may have a significant effect on the financial statements or the audit thereof*

In order to plan the audit effectively, the auditor should carry out a review of the business and obtain a thorough understanding of all its business processes. The information and understanding that is obtained through the business review forms, jointly with the assessment of control, the foundation of the risk assessment process and the subsequent audit response. In addition, gathering information for the business review enables the auditor to obtain insights into the client's operations which enhance the ability to act as a business adviser to management.

The business review should comprise:

(a) **Developing or updating the auditor's understanding of the client's business:** This understanding helps the auditor to understand the concerns of senior management and to assess both the risk of material misstatement in the financial statements and the risk to the auditor and to the firm.

(b) **Carrying out preliminary analytical reviews** to establish familiarity with the client's current financial position and results of operations. This helps to identify unusual or unexpected balances.

(c) **Reviewing and obtaining an understanding of the client's significant accounting policies.**

(d) **Making a preliminary assessment of materiality**, to help in determining the extent of audit work and to assess its results.

4:2.1.1 *Extent and timing of the business review*

The extent and timing of business review procedures will vary according to existing knowledge of the client and its industry. Often, members of the engagement team will have had regular contact with the client during the year. The knowledge gained from such contact is an important contribution to the conclusions that the auditor seeks to draw from the business review. If meetings with the client have not occurred during the year, the auditor should arrange to meet management to get up to date.

For existing clients, the business review is principally concerned with gaining an understanding of any changes that affect the auditor's base of knowledge. For a new client, it will be necessary to do more extensive work. The phases of the review will not necessarily be carried out in the order described below. Often they will overlap and the auditor may, in practice, carry out several phases at the same time.

4:2.1.2 *Role of the engagement partner*

As part of the business review, and before the audit team carries out any extensive procedures, the engagement partner or the engagement manager should meet members of the engagement team to discuss significant matters relevant to the business review.

In addition, the engagement partner or manager should be actively involved in:

(a) determining the nature and extent of the information gathering process;

(b) establishing engagement objectives (discussed in **Section 1:4**, 'Engagement objectives'); and

(c) assessing the implications of the information gathered, as part of the strategy process (discussed in **Section 4:6**, 'Determining the strategy').

4:2.1.3 *Involving other specialists*

Sometimes the auditor should involve in-house specialists (e.g., computer auditors, industry and tax specialists, and management consultants) in the business review. This is important if the process of determining the strategy will require specialist knowledge.

4:2.2 Developing or updating the auditor's understanding of the business

The main categories of information the auditor should obtain are discussed below under the following headings:

(a)   External factors affecting the business.

(b)   Internal factors affecting the business.

(c)   Sources of information.

    The appendices to this section (*see* **Sections 4:2.6 (Appendix A)** and **4:2.7 (Appendix B)**) contain a list of factors that the auditor might consider. Not all factors will apply to every engagement and a detailed knowledge of each one is not necessary. The auditor should concentrate on those matters that affect the ability to assess inherent risk, perform substantive procedures and meet client service objectives. An 'audit risk questionnaire' may be designed to incorporate these risks, and so assist audit staff in the assessment and identification of risks. However, such a questionnaire should not be used as an exhaustive checklist. It may be used as an *aide-mémoire*, to remind audit staff to consider some of the more common audit risks, but staff should use judgement in deciding whether there are any other risks which are not included on the form.

4:2.2.1 *External factors affecting the business*

Information about the external environment provides a useful perspective on the client, can provide corroborating evidence about factors affecting operations and may indicate areas of risk. The auditor should focus on aspects of the external environment which significantly affect the client's business.

    The auditor should consider the following:

(a) **Macroeconomic factors**, including the direct effects of government and fiscal policies, as well as social and environmental considerations.

(b) **Industry factors**, including information about the market, the main competitors in the industry, industry practices with audit implications and specialised reporting, accounting and regulatory matters.

(c) **Multinational clients**, including the significant local conditions affecting the various operating units of multinational clients, to ensure that the auditor has sufficient knowledge to plan the scope of the audit, to evaluate the implications of information for the client's operations in other countries and to provide knowledgeable input to senior management. The auditor may need to liaise with overseas offices of the same firm, or correspondent firms.

A list of external factors that may be relevant to the auditor's understanding of the business is set out in Appendix A (*see* **Section 4:2.6 (Appendix A)**). It is unlikely that many of the items on the list will be relevant to any one client.

4:2.2.2 Internal factors affecting the business

The auditor should gain an understanding of key factors in the client's business that affect the way it operates. The auditor needs this understanding to facilitate a proper evaluation of inherent risk. Further, by gaining this understanding, the auditor can be more effective in developing an appropriate response to risk and in identifying constructive recommendations that address the key concerns of management. The auditor should consider the following:

(a) **General matters**, including the location and size of the operations, major capital and research projects, and management's concerns, plans and expectations.

(b) **Operations**, including the nature of the products and production methods.

(c) **Finance**, including the financial structure, the key cash flows, investments and the need, if any, for financing.

(d) **Personnel**, including the remuneration structure.

A list of internal factors that may be relevant to the auditor's understanding of the business is set out in Appendix B (*see* **Section 4:2.7 (Appendix B)**). It is unlikely that many of the items on the list will be relevant to any one client.

4:2.2.3 Sources of information

Although the way the auditor obtains the information discussed in **Sections 4:2.2.1** and **4:2.2.2** will vary according to the nature, size and complexity of each individual client, the sources of information available are usually:

(a) discussions with management;

(b) visits to principal locations;

(c) external and internal reports and other publications.

If the client operates in a specialist industry, the auditor may need to consult industry specialists to identify significant matters and current developments.

4:2.2.3.1 Discussions with management

The auditor should meet senior management to obtain information that is not otherwise available and to gain an understanding of key issues and management's major business concerns. In addition to meeting officials responsible for finance and accounting, the auditor should seek to meet executives with responsibility for other significant areas. For example, senior management from production, distribution and marketing might provide useful information about their plans for under-utilised facilities, or the marketing director might provide an explanation of significant changes in the competitive environment.

The auditor may need to have several discussions with management at various points in the information gathering process. The first step should be to develop a general base of knowledge, including recent business results and major trends. Then the auditor should meet management to address specific areas of concern and to identify the areas where further information may be needed. For an existing client, the emphasis of meetings with management will normally be on updating the auditor's base of knowledge. For smaller and less complex clients, the understanding of the business may be based on less formal discussions with appropriate members of management and will rely more on existing knowledge of the industry and the client.

4:2.2.3.2 *Visits to principal locations*

The auditor's understanding of the client's operations will often be substantially enhanced by visits to principal operating units. Such visits provide an opportunity to meet local management and to consider significant business and financial factors as they relate to each unit. They are especially important for multi-location and multinational clients that have decentralised management.

The auditor's ability to consider individual operations in the context of the client as a whole is often enhanced when the auditor is accompanied on any visit by key management personnel. Visits should include meetings with representatives of local offices of the firm (or of other firms) to ensure that 'central' audit requirements are understood and met, and to enhance the 'central' auditor's understanding of the local operations and the significant factors that affect the client.

If the 'central' auditor does not visit principal locations, local offices (or other firms) should be asked to provide information on significant matters affecting the client's business.

4:2.2.3.3 *External and internal reports and other publications*

The auditor can find information about external factors in:

(a)   trade periodicals and newspapers;

(b)   analysts' reports on the industry;

(c)   external databases that allow comparison with major competition and indicate industry averages;

(d)   information provided by local offices or correspondent firms;

(e)   relevant publications, including any internally produced publications about this industry;

(f)   government and tax authority legislation and regulations;

(g)   new or revised auditing and accounting pronouncements.

The auditor can find information about internal factors in:

(h)   published financial statements, including interim reports;

(i)   monthly financial data;

(j)   strategic plans;

(k)   minutes of board, executive committee and shareholders' meetings;

(l)   management reports, including budgets, forecasts and projections;

(m) internal audit reports;

(n)   consultants' reports;

(o)   tax returns and correspondence;

(p)   policy and procedure manuals, including those for accounting matters.

4:2.3 Preliminary analytical reviews

The auditor should carry out preliminary analytical reviews as part of the process of understanding the business. They help to establish familiarity with the client's current cash flows, operating results and financial position. These reviews can also assist in identifying matters which might raise questions about the client's ability to continue as a going concern. This subject is considered in more detail in **Section 4:3**, 'Preliminary analytical review'.

4:2.4 Understanding the significant accounting policies

The auditor should acquire an understanding of the significant accounting policies used by the client, and should consider whether they are appropriate in relation to the nature of the business and to the economic substance of the client's transactions. The auditor should identify any policies that are likely to increase the risk of misstatement, e.g. policies that are:

(a)   not the predominant industry practice;

(b)   complex by nature;

(c)   controversial (e.g., certain revenue recognition or cost deferral policies).

4:2.5 Preliminary assessment of materiality

In the light of the results of the preliminary analytical reviews the auditor should make a preliminary assessment of materiality. Materiality is discussed in **Section 2:2**, 'Materiality in financial statements'.

4:2.6 Appendix A External factors that may be relevant to the auditor's understanding of the business

4:2.6.1 Macroeconomic factors

- Economic factors outside the client's control:
  - general economic activity (e.g., recession, growth);
  - international trade or tariff barriers.

- Changes in taxation:
  - company;
  - other.

- Dependence on foreign markets experiencing economic problems.
- Fluctuating foreign currency exchange rates.
- Exchange control.
- Changes in UK government policies.
- Financial incentives (e.g., regional aid).
- Impact of interest rates in view of company's gearing.
- Impact of economic factors on consumer liquidity.
- Effects of inflation, in the UK or overseas.
- Movements in stock market indices or developments in capital markets affecting availability of finance.

4:2.6.2 Industry factors

4:2.6.2.1 Regulatory environment

- recent or pending legislation (e.g., relating to price controls or pollution controls);
- environmental issues.

4:2.6.2.2 Economic conditions

- Declining or expanding industry.
- High-risk industry susceptible to economic pressures, or with high rate of business failure.
- Recent industry studies reporting adverse conditions.
- High technology or high fashion environment.

- Newly developed technology affecting client's operations, including inroads from other industries.

- Serious price competition, either domestic or from imports.

- Market saturation, or declining demand.

- Excess capacity.

- Activity cyclical or showing seasonal patterns.

4:2.6.2.3 Labour

- Industry-wide labour relations problems.

- Unusual labour practices.

- High industry unemployment.

- General level of salaries and wages within industry.

- Shortage of appropriate labour.

4:2.7 Appendix B Internal factors that may be relevant to the auditor's understanding of the business

4:2.7.1 General

- History of the client.

- The structure of the business (e.g., whether operations and controls are centralised or decentralised).

- Significant operating units or business activities in other countries.

- Rapid expansion of business which has overextended management and administration.

- The role and effect of computers in the business.

- Significant existing and likely litigation.

- The role of the governing board and audit committee, if any, in overseeing the management and control of the client.

- The information on which management relies to monitor the business and to make operating or other decisions.

- Management's view of the entity and the industry in which it operates.

- Management's view of the results and trends in the current year.

- Management's major business concerns.

- Management's attitude to, and expectations of, the audit.

4:2.7.2 Ownership

- The nature and diversity of the ownership of the client.
- Trading in the client's shares.
- Contest for control of the client.
- Unusual trading in the client's shares.
- Pressure on management to increase or support share price:
  - contemplated issue;
  - possible takeover;
  - other reason.

4:2.7.3 The client's principal business strategies

- Major planned or proposed acquisitions, disposals or mergers.
- Expected changes in product lines.
- Significant R&D projects, including assessment of product life cycle.
- Major planned capital expenditure, including new manufacturing plants.
- Planned expansion into new markets and/or geographical areas.
- Enhancements of computer systems and likely changes in the use of information technology.
- Tax planning strategies.
- Proposed amendments to existing labour agreements, including renegotiation of employment contracts.

4:2.7.4 The board of directors and senior management

- Independence from executive management.
- High turnover of non-executive directors.
- Board meetings infrequent.
- Board unable to constrain management from entering into illegal acts:
  - subjecting company to unduly risky transactions;
  - failing to act in interests of all the shareholders;
  - disregarding normal business ethics;
  - materially misstating financial statements;
  - failing to maintain effective system of internal control.
- The management structure and the responsibilities of senior executives.

- Management's relationships with relevant government regulators.
- Key factors affecting management compensation (e.g., whether a significant portion of compensation is tied to financial performance).

4:2.7.5 Executive management

- Dominated by one person (or a small group) without effective oversight by non-executive directors.
- Unwarranted complex corporate structure.
- High senior staff turnover:
  - key financial personnel;
  - others.
- Bonuses or incentives based on profit.
- Unrealistic forecasts that put management under undue pressure.
- Forecasts, whether published or otherwise, not met.
- Results announced prematurely.
- Excessive secrecy.
- Unusual transactions near the year-end affecting earnings:
  - large year-end shipments;
  - 'window dressing'.
- Creative accounting.
- Client operates on crisis or day-to-day basis.

4:2.7.6 Operations

- The nature and principal uses of the products or services provided by the client.
- The various stages and methods of production or delivery of products or services.
- Risks associated with the client's methods of manufacture or services.
- The character and location of production facilities.
- The level of head office control over decentralised operations.
- Cost factors affecting products or services.
- Availability of credit from suppliers.
- Purchases subject to special terms or credit arrangements.
- Sources and availability of raw material including the lead time for delivery and dependence on one supplier.
- Sources and availability of services (e.g., power and fuel supplies), including dependence on one supplier.

- Restrictions or problems associated with the movements of goods between countries or locations.

- Purchase commitments (particularly long-term ones) at fixed prices or for minimum quantities.

- Operational capacity.

- Technical operating problems.

- Difficulties associated with meeting production schedules.

- The condition of the client's plant and equipment.

- Types of scrap or residue arising and manner of disposal.

- The client's quality control procedures and warranty experience.

- Length and flexibility of production cycle.

4:2.7.7 *Finance*

- The nature and timing of significant funds flows.

- The client's cash management practices.

- The client's investment policies and procedures.

- Past and planned sources of long- and short-term capital and funds, e.g.: public offerings; stock options; revolving credit facilities; and refinancing options.

- Growth and the extent to which this has been generated internally or by business combinations.

- Past profitability.

- The existence of significant foreign currency exposures.

- Restrictions over repatriation of funds invested in other countries.

- Principal banking relationships.

- Restrictions imposed by loan agreements.

- The extent to which the client has entered into leasing agreements.

- Guarantees and other financial commitments.

- The client's tax status and any unresolved matters raised by the tax authorities.

- Significant funding considerations related to employee pension plans or other obligations.

4:2.7.8 *Marketing*

- Major customers or markets served, including concentration in geographic or social sectors.

- Reliance on a few customers, products, projects or transactions.

- Limited number of potential customers.

- Financial position of customers.

- Significant related-party transactions.

- Significant competitors and the client's position in the market.

- Key competitive advantages and the client's plans to exploit them.

- Extension of credit period to attract customers from competitors.

- Market stability (demand and prices) and patterns of seasonal trends.

- The current phase of the 'life cycle' (i.e., whether new, mature, or declining) of the client's products or services and their expected future market.

- Marketing of certain lines discontinued.

- Product obsolescence.

- Dependence on revocable franchise, licence or patent.

- New products with dubious potential.

- Changing customer preferences.

- Significant employee incentives tied to marketing objectives.

- Major distribution costs and methods (e.g., direct sale or agent), together with any associated risks.

- Terms of distribution (e.g., volume incentives, returns policies, delivery problems or other related risks).

- Credit policies and significant product-financing arrangements.

- Pricing and discount policies.

- Advertising and how its effectiveness is measured.

- Activities subject to cycles or seasonal patterns.

- Deteriorating trend:
  - declining sales;
  - rising costs;
  - pressure on margins;
  - sales at fixed prices;
  - reduction in market share.

- Results worse than industry average.

- Sales order book or trend unhealthy.

- Extension of credit period to attract customers from competitors.

- Change in pattern of customer settlement, e.g. cash to credit.

- Risks taken to achieve sales:

- – special credit arrangements;
- – other incentives;
- – future quantity or price commitments;
- – consignment sales;
- – excessive discounting;
- – bulk sale arrangements;
- – waiver of escalation clauses;
- – acceptance of bills;
- – price concessions on slow moving goods;
- – unlimited returns.

- Risks associated with:
  - – product warranty arrangements;
  - – service or maintenance contracts;
  - – unusual marketing or distribution arrangements.

4:2.7.9 Personnel

- The qualifications, experience and competence of key personnel.
- The adequacy of training programmes and demonstrated employee performance.
- Employee relations and any significant contractual arrangements with employees or their unions.
- Significant policies for recruitment and promotion of employees.
- Employee pay and benefits, including the terms and conditions of employee pension plans, health benefits and holiday entitlements.
- Management incentive plans, including commissions, bonuses and profit-sharing plans.
- Turnover of senior management and other key employees.

4:2.7.10 Going concern problems

Factors which may indicate increased risk that the entity will be unable to meet its debts as they fall due include:

- Inadequate cash flow/working capital.
- Low liquidity ratios.
- Recurring operating losses.
- Excessive or obsolete stock.

- Long overdue debtors.

- Whether restrictions have been placed on usual supplier trade terms.

- Excessive 'off-balance-sheet' financing or special-purpose transactions.

- Trade creditors not being paid.

- Other creditors not being paid, e.g. VAT, PAYE or social security.

- Bonus payments delayed.

- Unusual intercompany transfers of funds.

- Short-term borrowing financing long-term assets.

- Terms of loan agreements violated, waived or at risk.

- Borrowing limits, whether set internally (e.g., articles) or externally (e.g., loan agreement or debenture trust deed) exceeded or at risk.

- Dividends in arrears.

- Burden of interest charges.

- Gearing unsatisfactory, e.g. high or increasing debt–equity ratios.

- Deterioration of relationships with bankers.

- Demands for new capital.

- Potential significant losses on long-term contracts.

- Future projects that could cause financing difficulties.

- Plans to restructure share capital or debt, or raise finance on capital markets.

Mitigating factors relating to alternative means of maintaining adequate cash flows include:

- Disposal of assets or postponement of asset replacement without adversely affecting operations.

- Leasing of assets rather than purchasing them outright.

- Obtaining new sources of finance.

- Renewal and extension of existing sources of finance.

- Restructuring of debt.

Further guidance on going concerns is given in **Section 9:8**, 'Considerations in respect of going concern'.

4:3 Preliminary analytical review

4:3.1 Introduction

Statement of Auditing Standards 410, 'Analytical Procedures', states that analytical review means the 'analysis of relationships:

(a) between items of financial data, or items of financial and non-financial data, deriving from the same period; or

(b) between comparable financial information deriving from different periods or different entities,

to identify consistencies and predicted patterns or significant fluctuations and unexpected relationships, and the results of investigations thereof'. These procedures would encompass the following:

(a) Analysing the relationship between items of financial data (e.g., between sales and cost of sales), or between financial and non-financial information (e.g., between payroll costs and the size of the workforce).

(b) Comparing actual data with predictions derived from the analysis of known or expected relationships between items of data.

(c) Comparing information for the latest period with corresponding information for earlier periods, other comparable enterprises or industry averages.

(d) Investigating unexpected variations which are identified by such analysis and comparison.

(e) Obtaining and substantiating explanations for those variations.

(f) Evaluating the results of such analysis, comparison and investigation in the light of other audit evidence obtained to support the auditor's opinion on the financial statements.

4:3.2 Types of analytical review

Because the general term 'analytical review' describes such a wide variety of procedures, 'analytical review' is carried out at various stages of the audit. However, the extent of the procedures varies according to the stage at which they are carried out.

To reduce confusion in the terminology, analytical review procedures are categorised in this Manual into three distinct types, as follows:

(a) **Preliminary analytical review**: Preliminary analytical review procedures are carried out at two levels:

    (i)   in developing the strategy (see **Section 4:3.3.1** and **Section 4:6**, 'Determining the strategy');

(ii) in developing an audit programme (see **Section 4:3.3.2** and **Section 4:7**, 'The audit programme').

(b) **Analytical procedures**: The auditor uses analytical procedures to obtain evidence about specific audit objectives, for account balances and classes of transactions where a significant risk of material misstatement has been identified (*see* **Section 9:3**, 'Analytical procedures').

(c) **Final analytical review**: The auditor should carry out final analytical reviews to obtain assurance that the conclusions drawn from the results of other audit work remain valid and that the financial statements are internally consistent and are compatible with the understanding of the business gained from the audit (*see* **Section 10:3**, 'Reviewing the financial statements'). In many ways the final analytical review is similar to the preliminary analytical review.

4:3.3 Preliminary analytical review

4:3.3.1 Strategy stage

The preliminary analytical review should be carried out initially as part of the business review. The primary objective is to identify risks of fraud or error that might affect the strategy. In addition, the auditor will be seeking to extend or confirm the understanding of the business, because the review will help to establish familiarity with the client's current cash flows, operating results and financial position. The review may also help to identify matters which might raise questions about the client's ability to continue as a going concern.

Review procedures should normally be directed towards high-level aggregations of data. The auditor should review key 'performance indicators' at the financial statement level, relating to profitability, return on assets, liquidity and gearing. The performance indicators would normally be evaluated by reference to balance sheets and results from interim or management accounts.

Preliminary analytical reviews should be conducted in the light of previous experience of the client and an understanding of its business. Therefore, for continuing clients, it should not normally be necessary to carry out extensive procedures. For example, although the relative performance of different operating units might be identified, it is not necessary, at this stage, to disaggregate their results on to a monthly basis. The auditor might, however, need to carry out more extensive procedures for a new client or one that is undergoing significant changes to its business.

4:3.3.2 Detailed planning stage

When the strategy has been determined, the auditor may carry out preliminary analytical review procedures in greater detail.

(a) **Considering performance indicators at the account balance or class of transactions level**: The auditor may do this even where the high-level review for strategy purposes has not indicated specific risks. This will confirm that, in looking at high-level aggregations and financial statement level performance indicators, the auditor has not overlooked unusual fluctuations in particular figures.

(b) **Analysing the component parts of an account for which a risk has been identified**: For example, if sales appeared unusually high in the last three months of the year the auditor might analyse the sales by location, or by product, or by period, or by sales representative, so as to identify more precisely the likely cause of the fluctuation and the most appropriate response thereto.

The nature and extent of detailed preliminary analytical review procedures will depend upon matters such as:

(a)   the results of the preliminary analytical review for strategy purposes;

(b)   the evaluation of control effectiveness;

(c)   the extent of any substantive testing which the auditor might have already decided to carry out when the strategy was determined.

4:3.4 Performance indicators

Performance indicators are ratios, trends or other statistics which the auditor, or management, uses to assess and review the client's financial position and performance when carrying out preliminary and final analytical reviews. **Sections 4:3.4.1** to **4:3.7** discuss the use of performance indicators and the appendix to this section (**Section 4:3.10**) provides examples of performance indicators.

4:3.4.1 Validity of the performance indicator

To provide a useful insight into the client's financial position and performance, sufficient to identify risks of misstatement, performance indicators need to have certain characteristics, as follows:

(a)   The relationship's underlying performance indicators should be plausible.

(b)   Data used to calculate performance indicators should be sufficiently reliable.

4:3.4.1.1 Plausible relationships

A plausible relationship is one which can be explained logically, either from its existence in previous years or from an understanding of the business. The auditor should not use a performance indicator in analytical reviews if it is inconsistent with this understanding of the business, or if it is not possible to explain why a historical trend should continue into the period being audited.

4:3.4.1.2 Reliability of data

The evidence as to the reliability of information used in analytical review procedures varies with the extent of the assurance sought from the procedure. Accordingly, it should not normally be necessary to carry out significant work to establish the reliability of the data used for preliminary and final analytical reviews because:

(a)   the work is principally directed towards the identification of unusual balances and relationships, rather than providing a source of substantive assurance; and

(b)   other procedures are normally also carried out on the relevant account balances and classes of transactions which provide further evidence of the reliability of the data.

When a substantive analytical review is carried out, however, because the procedure is the response to a risk of misstatement, the auditor should obtain assurance that the underlying data are reliable. This should be done by establishing either that they are independent or that they have been audited, as discussed in **Section 9:3**, 'Analytical procedures'.

4:3.5 Reviewing performance indicators

In the light of the understanding of the client's business the auditor should identify appropriate performance indicators for review. A change in a performance indicator may take a number of different forms, e.g. a difference between:

(a)   management's budgeted or forecast figures and the actual results;

(b)   the actual results and the figure which the auditor would expect based on a previous year's results;

(c)   a particular indicator and the same indicator calculated for other units in a group of companies with similar businesses.

The auditor should investigate unusual or unexpected changes identified by this review.

4:3.6 Investigating changes in performance indicators

A basic premise underlying the use of these performance indicators for preliminary and final analytical review is that relationships between the underlying financial and non-financial data may be expected to exist and continue into the future in the absence of changes caused by:

(a)   changes in the business;

(b)   changes in accounting methods;

(c)   specific unusual transactions or events;

(d)   random (i.e., unpredictable) fluctuations;

(e)   misstatements.

4:3.6.1 *Random fluctuations*

The auditor should consider the extent to which there are likely to be random (i.e., unpredictable) fluctuations in the light of the following:

(a) Relationships in a stable environment are more predictable than those in a dynamic or unstable environment.

(b) Relationships for profit and loss accounts tend to be more predictable because they represent transactions over a period of time, whereas relationships for balance sheet accounts tend to be less predictable because a balance at a point in time is subject to short-term influences.

(c) Relationships involving transactions undertaken at management's discretion are usually less predictable. For example, advertising or maintenance expenditure can vary considerably.

If there are likely to be random variations in a performance indicator large enough to obscure variations due to material misstatement, the ability to obtain positive evidence from a review of that indicator will be limited. However, the auditor should still consider reviewing such performance indicators because they may improve the understanding of the business. Also, if there are variations which are too large to be explained as random, this would strongly indicate the risk of misstatement.

For example, it is common to review 'debtor days' as a performance indicator. However, random variations in debtor days can often be of the same magnitude as those which would be caused by a material misstatement in debtors. Hence such a review cannot be relied upon to provide positive evidence that debtors are not misstated. However, the review of debtor days is usually important for understanding the business. Also, a very significant unexplained change in debtor days would indicate potential misstatement.

4:3.6.2 *Other factors*

As well as considering the likelihood of random variation, the auditor should consider whether any performance indicators which are in line with previous years should, in fact, have changed because of changes in the other factors referred to in **Section 4:3.6**. The auditor should consider:

(a) Knowledge of the client's business and of the environment in which it operates, obtained during the business review. For example, an understanding of changes in macroeconomic factors, such as significant fluctuations in exchange rates, will help to predict the trend of results in a company with significant export sales.

(b) Knowledge of significant management decisions, e.g. a change in accounting policy.

(c) Knowledge of significant events or transactions.

(d) The results of other audit work.

4:3.7 Evaluating a review of performance indicators

Where unusual changes in performance indicators are identified, the auditor should attempt to identify the cause of the change in the light of the factors discussed in **Sections 4:3.6** to **4:3.6.2**. If the difference remains unexplained, it might be concluded that an increased risk has been identified that one or more of the amounts in the financial statements were misstated. For example, unexplained changes in the ratio of the cost of raw materials used to the total cost of production might indicate cut-off errors.

Where evidence of adverse or deteriorating business circumstances is obtained, this might indicate that the value of an asset or the adequacy of a provision should be the subject of particular audit attention. For example, declining selling prices might indicate that the auditor should be careful when reviewing the net realisable value of specific stocks.

When risks are identified, the auditor should design substantive tests to reflect this identified risk of misstatement and record the intended response in the substantive testing plan (STP). This should be done even when the risks are identified during the final analytical review. In this situation the auditor should reconsider the original STP and the results of substantive tests, and consider whether substantive testing should be extended or reperformed.

4:3.8 Engagement considerations

The effective performance of analytical review procedures requires:
(a) a thorough knowledge of the client's business and financial position, and the factors that might affect it;

(b) a full appreciation of the relationships between the various financial accounts and the sources of information for the selection of the review procedures; and

(c) an ability to draw the proper conclusions and understand the implications for subsequent audit procedures.

The procedures should be performed by staff with the necessary degree of experience, judgement and skill. Sometimes the engagement manager should carry out some of the work. However, it is important to encourage the delegation of such work to the in-charge and other members of the audit team. When analytical review procedures are delegated in this way, the engagement manager should ensure that responsibilities are clear, that team members have adequate guidance and coaching and that there are effective monitoring and review procedures.

4:3.9 Working papers

The following details should be recorded in the working papers:
(a) The performance indicators used in analytical reviews, and how they were calculated.

(b)   Comparable amounts including, where relevant, prior year indicators and budgets.

(c)   Unusual or unexpected fluctuations identified.

(d)   Explanations of the fluctuations, including re-calculations of the indicators reflecting the explanations, and the work carried out to corroborate these explanations.

(e)   The effect of findings on the audit programme, if any, and on the strategy. It will normally be sufficient to record the comments in one working paper and cross-refer the audit programme to it.

Certain analytical review information can, if computed on a consistent basis from year to year and monitored over a number of years, give a valuable indication of the trend of the business, e.g. by the identification of a gradual deterioration in profitability or liquidity ratios. However, it is not normally necessary to keep information that is more than five years old.

4:3.10 Appendix Performance indicators *aide-mémoire*

4:3.10.1 *Introduction*

The following pages suggest the appropriate design of an *aide-mémoire* to help the auditor carry out preliminary and final analytical review procedures. They contain examples of performance indicators which may be used in audit reviews.

4:3.10.2 *Structure of an* aide-mémoire

The structure of the *aide-mémoire* assumes a 'top-down' approach to analytical review, whereby a financial statement level review will normally be carried out at the strategy stage and a more detailed review during the development of the audit programme.

Accordingly, the *aide-mémoire* may usefully be organised as follows:

- **Financial statement level**
  - Business performance.
  - Capital structure and liquidity.
- Detailed level
  - Sales.
  - Production costs.
  - Operating costs.
  - Fixed assets.
  - Investments.
  - Stock.
  - Stock provisions.

- – Trade debtors.

- – Bad debt provision and expense.

- – Trade creditors.

These main headings for review at a detailed level are arranged in the same order as they would appear in a profit and loss account and balance sheet prepared in accordance with the Companies Act 1985 (format 1). The detailed content of an *aide-mémoire* for the first heading is included in this appendix.

4:3.10.3 Using an aide-mémoire

The suggested order of this *aide-mémoire* provides a simple, logical sequence in which to carry out the review, and this will often be appropriate in practice. For example, it would be normal first to review the financial statement level indicators relating to business performance, capital structure and liquidity, because these might suggest how more detailed indicators should be reviewed. Subject to this, at the detailed level, sales should normally be reviewed before trade debtors, because errors or fluctuations in the level of sales will have an effect on the level of trade debtors and the calculation of trade debtors performance indicators.

Although the lists of performance indicators may be made as comprehensive as possible, it is important to remember the following:

(a)   Lists cannot be exhaustive and the auditor should consider whether there are other performance indicators and explanations specific to the client's operations and circumstances.

(b)   Many clients carry out their own review procedures, which may include the calculation of performance indicators which are specific to that client. The auditor should consider the usefulness and applicability of such indicators to preliminary analytical reviews. Where client indicators are available and the auditor is satisfied that they are reliable, they normally provide the most efficient approach to preliminary analytical review.

(c)   Not all indicators will be relevant to every client. The auditor should, therefore, select only the relevant indicators.

(d)   Some performance indicators relate to the same audit objectives and differ only in the way they are calculated. For example, the debtors turnover ratio and the average collection period ratio both relate to the time taken to collect debtors. Where a choice is available, the auditor should usually select the indicator which is most appropriate in the specific circumstances of the client.

(e)   Information required to calculate certain indicators may not be readily available. In these circumstances, it is important to weigh the benefits of using the indicator against the time and costs of obtaining the necessary information.

(f)   Published performance indicators may not be calculated in the same manner as those described in this *aide-mémoire*. When calculating the client's indicators and comparing them to, e.g., industry norms, the auditor should take care to make sure that like is compared with like.

Changes in performance indicators may be caused by several factors, and it is important to ensure that all relevant factors are considered to an appropriate extent. The auditor should be particularly aware of the possibility of compensating effects. Also, when considering performance indicators which express relationships between account balances or transactions dealt with in different sections of the *aide-mémoire*, it is important to take into account findings from earlier sections when referring to later sections. A change in one indicator might mean that a change in another should be expected.

4:3.10.4 *Extracts from an* aide-mémoire

Set out below are the detailed ratios that might be calculated for the assessment of business performance, together with categories of ratios which might be calculated under the other main headings.

BUSINESS PERFORMANCE

Profit/(loss) on ordinary activities before/after tax

(a)   By month, quarter or year.

(b)   By business activity/division.

(c)   By geographical area.

Return on capital/assets employed

(a)
$$\frac{\text{Profit/(loss) after interest and tax}}{\text{Equity share capital + reserves}}$$

(b)
$$\frac{\text{Profit/(loss) before interest and tax}}{\text{Equity share capital + reserves + longer-term liabilities}}$$

(c)
$$\frac{\text{Profit/(loss) before interest and tax}}{\text{Total assets}}$$

Analysis of return on capital/assets employed

(a) Profit margin:

$$\frac{\text{Profit/(loss) after interest and tax}}{\text{Sales}}$$

and

(b) Turnover on capital/assets:

$$\frac{Sales}{Equity\ share\ capital + reserves}$$

(*Note:* This analysis is of version (a) of the return on capital calculation. Where versions (b) and (c) are used the analysis would be adjusted accordingly.)

Equity earnings

(a) Earnings per share:

$$\frac{Profit\ after\ corporation\ tax\ and\ preference\ dividends}{Number\ of\ ordinary\ shares}$$

(b) Earnings yield:

$$\frac{Equity\ earnings\ per\ share\ (grossed\ up\ at\ the\ standard\ rate\ of\ tax) \times 100}{Market\ value\ per\ ordinary\ share}$$

(c)P/E ratio:

$$\frac{Market\ value\ per\ ordinary\ share}{Earnings\ per\ share}$$

Dividends

(a) Gross dividends paid.

(b) Gross dividend per share:

$$\frac{Gross\ dividend\ (net\ dividend\ grossed\ up\ at\ the\ standard\ rate\ of\ tax)}{Number\ of\ ordinary\ shares}$$

(c) Dividend yield:

$$\frac{Gross\ dividend\ per\ share \times 100}{Market\ value\ per\ ordinary\ share}$$

(d) Dividend cover:

$$\frac{Profits\ attributable\ to\ ordinary\ shareholders\ (refer\ note)}{Net\ ordinary\ dividends}$$

(*Note:* Profits are calculated after tax, extraordinary items, minority interests and preference dividends.)

(e)   Dividends in arrears.

Market value

(a) Market price per share.

(b) Market capitalisation:

$$\frac{\text{Market capitalisation}}{\text{Net assets}}$$

(c) Price multiple of net assets:

$$\frac{\text{Market price per share}}{\text{Net assets value per share}}$$

Gross profit

(a) Gross profit:

    (i) by week, month or quarter

    (ii) by geographical area

    (iii) by business activity/division

    (iv) by major products or services

(b) Gross profit percentage:

$$\frac{\text{Gross profit}}{\text{Sales}}$$

(*Note:* This can be calculated by category, as above.)

Value added

Value added is calculated as sales value less cost of materials and services purchased:

(a) By business activity/division.

(b) By major products or services.

(c) As a percentage of turnover (by category, as above).

Research and development expenditure

(a) By business activity/division.

(b) By major products or services.

(c) As a percentage of turnover (by category, as above).

Employee numbers

This is calculated by business activity/division.

These are other areas where ratios may be useful. These are listed below.

Capital structure and liquidity

- Capital maintenance (net assets/capital) ratio.
- Long-term borrowings.
- Interest costs.
- Gearing (debt/equity) ratio.
- Working capital (movements).
- Working capital ratios.
- Liquidity ratios.
- Cash flow ratios.
- Financing requirements compared to cash flow, credit limits and loan facilities.

Sales

- Sales (value or units).
- Market share.
- Analysis between cash and credit sales.
- Order book.
- Average selling price of major products or services   .
- Sales returns, discounts and allowances.
- Sales per employee (by appropriate category).

Production costs

- Production (costs or units).
- Analysis by major type of cost (value and percentage of total).
- Production costs per unit.
- Labour productivity.
- Utilisation of capacity.

Operating expenses

- Operating costs.
- Ratio to turnover.
- Administration cost ratios.
- Distribution cost ratios.
- Marketing and selling cost ratios.
- Staff cost ratios.

Fixed assets

- Balance sheet amounts: cost, valuation, net book value (NBV).
- Additions.
- Disposals.
- Depreciation charge for period by category.
- Other related costs.
- Utilisation/Productivity of fixed assets.

Investments (held as fixed assets)

- Fixed asset investments analysed by major category (book value and/or market value).
- Comparison of change in market value with change in a relevant index (e.g., FT indices).
- Investment yield.

Stock

- Analysis by business activity, major product line or location.
- Analysis by type of stock (for analyses above).
- Analysis of costs in stocks (for analyses/types above).
- Age analysis (for analyses/types as above).
- Stock turnover.
- Days stock held.
- Estimated percentage of next periods sales held (by product line).
- Closing stock compared with actual sales in the following period.
- Level of physical stock count adjustments (for analyses/types above).

- Analysis of standard cost variances included in stock values.
- Use of stockholding capacity.

Stock provisions

- Stock provision (value and percentage of stock before provision).
- Analysis of cause of stock provisions.
- Comparison of stock provisions with age analysis of stock.
- Stock write-offs (value and percentage of average stock).
- Level of stock write-offs to provision.
- Stock valuation ratios (by product).

Trade debtors

- Trade debtors analysed by value, geographical area, major customer.
- Age analysis into age bands.
- Days sales uncollected.
- Average collection period.
- Debtors turnover.
- Comparison of trade debtors with post period-end receipts.
- Proportion of credit balances.
- Proportion of unmatched cash.
- Bills receivable.

Bad debt provision and expense

- Closing provision analysed by value, geographical area, major customer.
- Percentage of trade debtors provided.
- Bad debt expense.
- Bad debt recoveries.

Trade creditors

- Trade creditors analysed by value, geographical area, major supplier.
- Age analysis into age bands.
- Days purchases unpaid.
- Percentage of stock financed by creditors.

- Percentage of debtors financed by creditors.

- Unmatched goods received notes.

- Unprocessed invoices not posted to purchase ledger.

- Bills payable.

4:4 Evaluating inherent risk

4:4.1 Introduction

As discussed in **Section 2:4**, 'Audit risk', the risk of material misstatement is a combination of the inherent risk that items in the financial statements will be misstated, either through fraud or error, and the risk that the client's controls will not be effective in detecting or preventing those misstatements. Statement of Auditing Standards 300, 'Accounting and Internal Control Systems and Audit Risk Assessments', states that:

> *In developing their audit approach and detailed procedures, auditors should assess inherent risk in relation to financial statement assertions about material account balances and classes of transactions, taking account of factors relevant both to the entity as a whole and to the specific assertions.*

4:4.2 Timing of work

The extent and timing of procedures relating to inherent risk will vary from client to client and are a matter for the judgement of the engagement partner and manager. The following general considerations apply:

(a) For an existing client the auditor will normally be able to gain a sufficient understanding of most new or changed inherent risks that affect the strategy from the business review.

(b) For a new client the auditor will often need to carry out more extensive procedures to identify and evaluate inherent risks for strategy purposes.

(c) The extent of the inherent risk identification and evaluation procedures required to determine the strategy will increase with the size and complexity of the client's business and its systems. It may also vary from industry to industry. For example, risks in a stable, mature industry will frequently be less extensive than in a new, high-growth industry such as electronics.

(d) The auditor should normally consider risks associated with characteristics of account balances or classes of transactions when developing substantive tests.

During the process of developing the substantive tests, the auditor should update the preliminary evaluation of inherent risk that was reflected in the strategy. Any significant changes to the strategy should be recorded in the issues documentation and brought to the attention of the partner or manager.

4:4.3 Involvement of the partner and manager

Understanding the client's business and the industry in which it operates are the key elements in identifying inherent risk. Partners and managers, because of their experience and general business knowledge, provide the most significant contribution to the identification process.

4:4.4 Procedures for identifying and evaluating inherent risk

Procedures relating to inherent risk are as follows:

(a) Searching for inherent risks.

(b) Evaluating the significance of identified risks.

(c) Relating such risks to account balances, classes of transactions and audit objectives.

The strategy and audit programme are developed by assessing the effectiveness of controls in reducing the risks the auditor has evaluated and by drawing conclusions about the most efficient responses to those risks. Further guidance is set out in **Sections 4:6**, 'Determining the strategy', and **4:7**, 'The audit programme'.

4:4.5 Searching for inherent risks

The search for inherent risks should be made in the light of the auditor's understanding of the client's business, its control environment (including an assessment of management's motivation to distort the financial statements) and its accounting systems. The auditor should consider the risks associated with each of the following areas:

(a) The auditor's understanding of the client's business.

(b) Preliminary analytical review.

(c) Significant accounting policies.

(d) The characteristics of account balances or transactions.

(e) The history of fraud or error.

The procedures listed in the preceding paragraph may identify risks of fraud and of error and some of them might reveal increased risk to the auditor and to the firm.

4:4.5.1 Risks identified from the auditor's understanding of the client's business

When searching for, and evaluating, inherent risk the auditor should consider the implications of information obtained from an understanding of the client's business. Extensive examples of the types of risk the auditor might identify are set out in the appendices to **Section 4:2**, 'Business review'.

4:4.5.2 Risks identified during preliminary analytical review

The auditor should consider the results of preliminary analytical review in the light of an understanding of the business. For example, if during the business review the auditor noted that a significant proportion of management's remuneration was directly tied to profitability and analytical review showed that profitability had substantially improved in the last part of the year, with debtors increasing disproportionately to sales, this might indicate a risk that sales and debtors were overstated. Similarly, if an unusual or unexpected balance was identified in the preliminary analytical review the auditor might conclude that there was a significant risk of that balance being misstated.

4:4.5.3 Risks associated with significant accounting policies

An important part of the search for inherent risks is the review of the client's significant accounting policies. An increased risk of fraud or error will normally be indicated by the use of policies that are new, significantly affected by changes in the client's business, not the predominant industry practice, controversial, or complex by nature. For example, the auditor might establish that a client's accounting policy for income was less prudent than the industry norm and this might lead to the conclusion that there was a risk that income could be overstated.

4:4.5.4 Risks associated with characteristics of account balances or classes of transactions

Section 2:4, 'Audit risk', outlines the nature of risks associated with characteristics of account balances or classes of transactions. Although the significance of such inherent risks will vary from client to client, most or all of them will be present in each client. They should be considered under the following headings:

(a)   Account balances relating to assets susceptible to theft.

(b)   Risks associated with the accounting process.

(c)   Types of transactions, being:

  (i)   Account balances derived from estimates.

  (ii)   Unsettled and settled transactions.

  (iii) Unusual and complex transactions.

  (iv)   Cut-offs and accruals.

4:4.5.4.1 Assets susceptible to theft

The prevention and detection of fraud are not, in themselves, audit objectives. Fraud could, however, create an incentive to manipulate the financial statements. Furthermore, the possibility of theft by means of computer through electronic funds transfers might be so material as to threaten the client's viability.

The auditor should also pay particular attention to assets of high value that are easily moved, because the risk of misappropriation is greater than for other assets. In addition, assets that are readily convertible into cash (e.g., marketable securities) are generally subject to a higher risk of theft than stocks consisting of low-value or relatively large items, or items for which there is not a ready market.

Other risks that the auditor may consider under this heading include:

(a)   The theft of information.

(b)   Unusual investment of funds held in a fiduciary capacity.

(c)   Payments for goods not received, or received but not required, or received and paid for at excessive prices.

(d)   The risk of disposal at less than fair value, by means of low pricing, excessive discounts, failure to invoice and writing off debts.

(e)   Illicit use of the client's assets for private benefit. This risk frequently arises in respect of computers, office services and cars.

It may be appropriate for the audit firm to design and use a practice aid to assist in the identification and evaluation of these risks. The importance of the evaluation of the risk of fraud, both as an audit objective and as a client service, is discussed further in **Section 2:7**, 'Fraud and error'.

4:4.5.4.2 The accounting process

There is an inherent risk associated with every accounting process, although such risk will often be reduced by internal controls. The extent of the inherent risk can vary significantly according to a number of factors and, in particular, it will depend upon whether an account balance is systems derived.

Systems-derived account balances are those that derive from a transaction-processing system involving significant volumes of similar transactions. Examples of systems-derived accounts include cash, debtors, stocks, creditors, purchases and sales.

In general, accounts that are not systems derived are subject to a higher inherent risk of error than systems-derived accounts. This is because the former typically involve transactions that may be complex or unusual and which are therefore likely to involve a higher risk of processing error. However, when systems-derived accounts are new, or have significantly changed, they may be subject to an increased risk of fraud or error.

If there is an established computerised accounting system, the risk of material misstatement will normally be low for the objectives of completeness and accuracy, provided that the client has an effective system of control.

4:4.5.4.3 *Types of transactions*

Estimates involve the use of judgement, frequently applied in situations where there is uncertainty as to the outcome of future events (e.g., the ultimate realisable value of obsolescent stock). Consequently, estimates may be incorrect because of invalid assumptions about the future and/or because they are subject to management manipulation. Accordingly, when searching for risks associated with estimates, the auditor should consider both the inherent risks in making accurate estimates and management's motivation to override the control system and/or manipulate the financial statements. When there is motivation for management to distort the financial results, the distortion is frequently concealed in estimates which, because of their subjective element, may be difficult to challenge.

The following matters are relevant:

(a) **Management's attitude towards financial reporting**: A casual attitude towards financial reporting significantly increases the risk of error because, in such circumstances, management's judgement and experience of the business are not brought to bear on the estimates. An aggressive attitude will result in a generally consistent pattern of bias in the estimates, normally towards over-optimism.

(b) **The client's prior experience**: An estimate developed on the basis of prior experience is less likely to be susceptible to error than estimates which have no relevant history. For example, the estimate of the stock obsolescence provision for a product in a rapidly changing area of technology will normally have a greater risk of error than a similar estimate for a stable product.

(c) **The availability of relevant data and the adequacy of the systems for collecting such data**: Both of these have a significant effect upon the inherent risk of an estimate. For example, a client with a detailed credit-rating policy and a systems-derived debtors' aged analysis will be able to develop a better estimate of bad debts than a client with a less sophisticated approach.

(d) **The process used to develop the estimate**: There is a greater inherent risk in estimates based primarily on the client's judgement or on a loosely defined formula which cannot be recomputed.

Unsettled transactions (e.g., sales for which cash is yet to be received) are generally subject to a higher inherent risk than **settled transactions** (e.g., sales where the cash has been received). This is because a settled transaction generally involves a third party which, by accepting the transaction, provides some independent assurance as to its validity. For example, subject to the assessment of the risk of fraud in such accounts, a receipt in respect of a debt and a payment in respect of a creditor or payroll indicates that the income or expense falls properly to the account of the client.

However, in assessing settled transactions as having a low inherent risk, the auditor should consider the possibility that such transactions may be used to conceal a fraud. For example, cash payments might be fraudulently diverted and the record concealed in an account comprising settled transactions. Accordingly, the auditor will often need to identify controls that reduce the risk of fraud as it relates to such transactions.

Unusual transactions are prone to error because they are often not systems derived and there may not be established procedures for dealing with them, or because normal procedures, including internal controls, may be overridden. In addition, because such transactions occur infrequently there are less likely to be personnel with adequate experience of dealing with them.

Unusual transactions may reflect management motivation to distort the results, often by accounting for the form of the transaction rather than its substance. Accordingly, when considering unusual transactions, the auditor should take into account an assessment of management's motivation to distort the financial statements.

Complex transactions are, by their nature, prone to the risk of error. For example, a risk factor arising in a complex transaction might be the application of percentage-of-completion accounting for long-term contracts. Complex transactions may also be used as a means of concealing a fraud. For example, complex accounting policies are sometimes used as a means of disguising recognition of income before it is properly due.

Cut-offs and accruals can have the risk characteristics of systems-derived accounts (in which case they may have a low risk of error), or of estimates, or (as is frequently the case) they may exhibit the risk characteristics of both.

In addition to having the risk characteristics associated with the judgements implicit in estimates, as discussed above, cut-offs and accruals are frequently subject to a relatively high inherent risk because:

(a) they are dealt with infrequently and therefore client staff may have little experience or competence in this regard;

(b) they are often developed under time-reporting pressures;

(c) they are susceptible to manipulation by the client.

Consequently, in assessing the inherent risk associated with cut-offs and accruals the auditor should have regard to an assessment of management's motivation to manipulate the financial statements.

4:4.5.5 *The history of fraud or error*

The auditor should consider whether prior experience of the client indicates that any accounts have a history of proposed or actual audit adjustments. For many clients where significant fraud or error occurs, a pattern of continuing fraud or error affecting particular account balances and classes of transactions will emerge over time.

Accordingly, consideration of the history of fraud or error is a key indicator of likely misstatement in the current year.

In considering the history of fraud or error, the auditor should review points forward, management letters and schedules of significant matters arising, from previous audits. In addition, such problems will often be indicated by an unusually large number or value of late adjustments in prior years.

If clients have a history of making frequent or significant correcting entries, it might indicate that systems are not functioning properly, with a consequent effect on the auditor's assessment of control effectiveness. Frequently, it will be necessary to obtain most of the required assurance in such areas from substantive tests.

4:4.6 The risk of fraud

As explained in **Section 4:4.1**, the risk of material misstatement includes the risk that items in the financial statements will be misstated through fraud and that the client's systems will not be effective in preventing or detecting such misstatements. The auditor should, as part of normal audit work, assess the risk of fraud separately from the risk of error; see the guidance in **Section 2:7**, 'Fraud and error'.

4:4.7 Risk to the auditor and to the firm

Risk to the auditor and to the firm is defined in **Section 2:4**, 'Audit risk'. Although such risks are always present, the auditor may identify factors that lead to an increase in the risk to the firm through:

(a) **Information gathering and search for risk**: For example, the following factors are likely to increase risk to the firm:

  (i)   Management's attitude towards financial reporting: The auditor might identify a concern relating to management's motivation to distort the financial statements through the review of the matters set out in **Section 8:1.3**, 'Assessing the control environment'.

  (ii) The client is operating in an unstable industry or is experiencing deteriorating financial conditions: This might indicate a possibility of going concern problems and the associated risk that, in the event of failure of the client, others might expect the auditor to have reflected the matter in the audit report.

(b) **Procedures relating to acceptance of new clients**: A significant proportion of risks to the firm will probably arise from new clients, especially when there is evidence of unusual or controversial circumstances associated with the client's decision to change auditors. These risks should be taken into consideration when deciding whether to accept a new client or, indeed, whether to continue with an existing client.

(c) **Consideration of the engagement objectives**: The auditor might identify that the audit working papers are to be reviewed by another firm of auditors in connection with a proposed transfer of interest in which the purchase price had regard to the financial statements. These risks should be taken into consideration when deciding whether to accept a new client or, indeed, whether to continue with an existing client.

Increased risk to the firm may or may not also represent a risk of fraud or error. For example, the possibility of a third party review of the audit work might represent a risk to the auditor's reputation but would not represent a risk of error. On the other hand, a client that is operating in an unstable industry might have an increased risk of error (because assets may be stated at amounts that subsequently prove to be irrecoverable) but would not necessarily have an increased risk of fraud.

If there is increased risk to the firm the engagement partner should consult other partners to ensure that quality control objectives are met. The auditor should also increase professional scepticism. In extreme cases, it may be necessary to consider whether to resign from the audit engagement, in accordance with the principles set out in **Section 3:2**, 'Appointment and continuation as an auditor'.

The absence of increased risk to the firm does not indicate a reduced risk of error and does not, of itself, justify a restriction of the audit response.

4:4.8 Evaluating the significance of inherent risks

Although the auditor may find it helpful to categorise identified inherent risks as 'high', 'medium' or 'low', such descriptions are, of themselves, insufficient. Instead, such inherent risks should be evaluated by considering:

(a)   the likelihood that the risk will crystallise into a fraud or error, before taking any controls into account;

(b)   the likely materiality of any consequent misstatement.

4:4.8.1 Assessing the likelihood that the risk will crystallise

Considering the likelihood that an identified risk will crystallise is a matter of professional judgement. However, the auditor will normally find it helpful to take into account the following factors:

(a)   **An appreciation of the client's operating environment and the external factors that affect it**: For example, in the case of a software development company, the auditor might conclude, on the basis of an understanding of the industry trends, that there was a higher than normal inherent risk of stock obsolescence.

(b)   **The history of fraud or error.**

(c)   **Motivation**: The auditor should seek to identify whether any particular motivation might exist to distort the financial statements. For example, management might be more likely to manipulate the annual financial statements if results were falling short of a publicly announced profit forecast than if the forecast were for internal purposes only.

(d)   **The number of risks affecting the audit objective**: These will affect the auditor's assessment of the likelihood that the account balance will be misstated. For example, the inherent risk normally associated with calculating a stock obsolescence estimate would be greater if the product were new and the client had little experience of developing such estimates; it would increase further if the client had a history of error in developing other estimates.

4:4.8.2 Assessing the likely materiality of possible fraud or error

The auditor should consider the likelihood of any error or fraud being material. In some cases, the risk of fraud or error may appear to be remote but, were the risk to crystallise, the consequences would be material. For example, the risk of a major theft of a client's stocks might be judged to be remote, even before taking controls into account. However, the consequences to the client of such a theft might be so serious that, in such circumstances, the auditor would normally modify the audit response accordingly.

4:4.9 Relating identified risks to audit objectives for account balances and classes of transactions

The auditor should relate the precise consequences of each material risk of fraud or error identified to significant audit objectives for each account balance and class of transactions. At the same time it is important, for completeness, to consider for each significant account balance and class of transactions and for each significant audit objective whether all the significant inherent risks have been identified and evaluated. In doing so, the auditor should use knowledge of the risks so far identified and have regard to the guidance about the classes of risk discussed above.

The different classes of risk discussed above will normally affect some audit objectives rather than others. For example, the risks associated with estimates will generally affect the audit objectives of **valuation**, **rights and obligations**, **cut-off** and **presentation and disclosure**. In addition, the audit objective of **existence** is most affected by the risk of fraud because it is the objective affected by assets susceptible to theft and because employee frauds are often concealed by overstating expenses and assets.

Some audit objectives will tend to be subject to a lower inherent risk. For example, systems-derived accounts will normally have a lower risk of random error and this will consequently reduce the inherent risks affecting the audit objectives of **accuracy** and, to a lesser extent, **completeness**.

4:4.10 Documenting the results of risk assessment procedures

The auditor should document the results of risk assessment procedures. The strategy should set out the nature of major identified inherent risks indicating, in broad terms, the planned response. Risks that are not of major significance need not be included.

An audit programme may contain, for each relevant audit objective, details of the nature of each material risk identified, its possible consequences and the response. Such response might, for example, be to carry out substantive tests alone, or a combination of an extended assessment of control effectiveness and reduced substantive tests. This is discussed further in **Section 4:7**, 'The audit programme'.

4:5 Review of internal control for strategy purposes

4:5.1 Introduction

Section 2:5, 'Internal control', explains the purpose of understanding and assessing internal control and outlines the effect on the audit.

This section discusses the information the auditor needs about the client's control environment, accounting systems and internal accounting controls to determine the audit strategy. Guidance is also provided on how this information is used in determining the strategy.

4:5.2 Objectives of gathering information

The information the auditor obtains for strategy purposes will normally help to:

(a) make preliminary judgements on control effectiveness;

(b) decide whether an extended assessment of controls is likely to be effective;

(c) develop engagement objectives, including identifying matters which should be investigated for inclusion in the report to the board;

(d) assess the feasibility and cost-effectiveness of applying computer-assisted audit techniques.

4:5.3 Obtaining or updating information

The extent of information gathering will depend on factors such as:

(a) whether the auditor is dealing with a new or existing client;

(b) existing knowledge of the client and the degree to which conditions have changed;

(c) the number and complexity of the systems;

(d) the likely engagement objectives.

The decision whether to rely on, and make an extended assessment of, controls will often be immediately apparent. For example, for a small client with unsophisticated systems the auditor might need very little investigation to establish that the assurance needed to support the audit opinion would be obtained most efficiently from substantive tests. Similarly, the auditor would normally restrict the information to be gathered about controls and concentrate audit work on identifying the most efficient means of carrying out substantive testing if:

(a) the control environment were unfavourable;

(b) the previous year's audit or subsequent information indicated that the client's internal accounting controls or IT controls were not effective;

(c) the volume of transactions were low, or the nature of the assets, liabilities or operations (or the composition of the account balance) made substantive testing relatively cost effective.

However, before deciding to obtain all the required assurance from substantive tests, the auditor should consider whether this will satisfy all the engagement objectives. For example, the client might wish the auditor to report in detail on controls, even when it would be more efficient for audit purposes to obtain all the required assurance from substantive testing.

4:5.4 Control environment

The auditor's assessment of the control environment is crucial to the decision on whether to make an extended assessment of controls. This is because a good control environment is conducive to the maintenance of a reliable system of accounting and control procedures.

For strategy purposes the auditor should obtain a sufficient understanding of the control environment. This is discussed in **Section 8:1.3**, 'Assessing the control environment'. If the issues described in that section are not fully addressed in determining the strategy, the assessment of the control environment should be completed before the substantive tests are determined.

4:5.5 Accounting systems

The auditor needs an understanding of the accounting systems, regardless of whether the audit strategy will involve an extended assessment of internal accounting controls. This should be done by:

(a) documenting the extent to which the system is computerised; and

(b) preparing or updating overview flowcharts to record the files and transactions relating to significant systems-derived account balances.

Guidance on these two areas can be found in **Section 8:2**, 'Accounting systems'.

The extent of work necessary prior to determining the strategy will depend on the circumstances. For a new client where the strategy is uncertain, it might be necessary to obtain an understanding of all the accounting systems to decide, for systems-derived account balances, whether it would be efficient to make an extended assessment of controls. For a continuing client, the information should already be available unless there have been significant changes in the accounting systems.

4:5.6 *Internal accounting controls*

4:5.6.1 *IT controls*

If there are significant computer systems, the auditor should obtain an understanding of the IT controls to decide whether to make an extended assessment of monitoring controls. Whether it is necessary to carry out any preliminary work for strategy purposes to ascertain whether IT controls are likely to be satisfactory will depend on the auditor's previous knowledge about IT controls. For an existing audit, the objective will normally be to carry out the minimum work necessary to update this previous understanding. If more information is needed, or if the engagement is new or substantially changed, the auditor should carry out an overview assessment of IT controls as described in **Section 8:3.5**, 'Computer controls'.

It is not necessary to make an overview assessment of IT controls for strategy purposes if it is clear, at the outset, that the strategy will involve an extended assessment of internal accounting controls, or if, e.g., the auditor has no intention of carrying out an extended assessment, or because programmed procedures are not significant.

However, even if the auditor has not carried out an overview assessment of the IT controls for strategy purposes, it may be necessary to do so later, to help design and perform substantive tests and draw conclusions on whether proper accounting records have been kept. Whether this work is done before determining the strategy or subsequently as part of the fieldwork is a matter of audit efficiency.

4:5.6.2 *Application controls*

In many cases, it will be clear at the outset that an extended assessment of application controls is likely to be effective in relation to significant audit objectives for particular account balances or classes of transactions. This might be because either the auditor has past experience of the client, or the initial information gathered about the control environment, accounting systems and IT controls suggests that they are strong enough to support the assumption, for strategy purposes, that extended assessment will justify a significant reduction in levels of substantive testing. In these cases, it will be unnecessary to obtain further information about the application controls to determine the audit strategy.

However, if unsure whether controls exist in relation to a particular account balance or class of transactions (and therefore the audit strategy is not evident), the auditor should carry out an overview assessment of the relevant controls. This should be done to determine whether making an extended assessment is likely to be an effective strategy. Guidance on obtaining an overview understanding of application controls is contained in **Section 8:3.4**, 'Application controls'. Obtaining an overview of the application controls may be important to the strategy decision as to which systems-derived account balances or classes of transaction will be subject to an extended assessment.

If it is clear that the strategy will not be to make an extended assessment of controls, the auditor should nevertheless consider the need to carry out an overview assessment of the internal accounting controls. This may be necessary:

(a) to ensure that substantive tests properly reflect the client's control procedures;

(b) to help to assess whether proper accounting records have been kept.

Even if the auditor does not intend to reduce levels of substantive testing by carrying out an extended assessment of internal accounting controls, in exceptional circumstances it may be appropriate to record the systems and controls in detail to help in designing and performing substantive tests and to help draw conclusions on whether proper accounting records have been kept. This will be a strategy decision.

4:5.7 Sources of information

Much of the information the auditor needs when considering internal control for strategy purposes can be obtained from:

(a) discussions with management;

(b) discussions with IT and user department personnel and with senior IT and user management;

(c) reviewing the client's documentation of the systems; and

(d) the work performed, if any, by the internal audit function on the computer environment and systems.

4:6 Determining the strategy

4:6.1 Introduction

The audit strategy describes, in broad terms, the principal features of the auditor's proposed approach to the audit. It should contain sufficient detail to provide a proper basis for planning and controlling the subsequent audit work (including briefing the audit team) and to assist in the development of the detailed budget and the timetable.

The auditor should develop the strategy by:

(a) considering the results of gathering or updating information about the client; and

(b) making preliminary judgements about materiality, inherent risk and control effectiveness. These will include identification of the system(s) the auditor proposes to subject to an extended assessment of controls.

4:6.2 Developing the strategy

The extent and timing of the work necessary to determine the strategy will vary according to the circumstances of each client and may vary from year to year. Nevertheless, as a minimum the auditor should:

(a)   carry out the business review (*see* **Section 4:2**, 'Business review');

(b)   consider the client's requirements and the engagement objectives (*see* **Section 1:4**, 'Engagement objectives');

(c)   make a preliminary assessment of the inherent risk of fraud and error (*see* **Section 4:4**, 'Evaluating inherent risk');

(d)   carry out a sufficient assessment (or update an existing assessment) of the control environment (*see* **Section 8:1.3**, 'Assessing the control environment');

(e)   obtain or update an understanding of the client's accounting systems (*see* **Section 8:2**, 'Accounting systems').

The initial assessment of the quality and complexity of the client's systems will affect the amount of the information the auditor needs to gather. Sometimes, on a new engagement, the appropriate strategy may be obvious from a limited amount of investigative work. In other cases, the necessary information gathering will be extensive. The auditor should consider the following matters:

(a)   For many existing clients, the majority of the information the auditor needs will already exist in the prior year's strategy and in the audit programme. Accordingly, it will often be possible to restrict the work to updating existing knowledge, considering whether there are any significant new or changed risks and confirming that there are no new or substantially changed significant systems.

(b)   On a new, large or complex engagement the auditor may be uncertain about the extent of information that should be gathered. Accordingly, in such cases the engagement partner, the engagement manager and the in-charge should consider together their knowledge of the matters listed in the preceding paragraph before undertaking further information gathering. This will ensure that the information-gathering process is carried out in as efficient and effective a manner as possible.

(c)   If the auditor determines that there have been significant changes to risks, systems and other client circumstances, it may be necessary to gather extensive information before determining the strategy. For example, more information would be required for a client with an acquisition or a significant new system than for a client with a stable, unchanging business and accounting environment.

(d)   If the auditor has had substantial contact with the client in the current period it may be possible to determine the strategy without gathering additional information.

4:6.3 Strategy meeting

When sufficient information has been gathered to make it possible to determine the strategy, the engagement manager should arrange a strategy meeting. The engagement partner, the engagement manager, senior specialists involved in the audit, the in-charge and, where appropriate, some or all of the other members of the audit team should attend the meeting.

The engagement manager or the in-charge should prepare a list of the matters to be considered at the strategy meeting, as well as essential (but not excessive) supporting papers. Matters that should normally be considered include:

(a)   The engagement objectives.

(b)   The results of the business review, including major developments in the client's business and industry, significant operating results and financial arrangements.

(c)   Preliminary judgements as to materiality.

(d)   Identified inherent risks. The team should also consider the risk of fraud and, in particular, any evidence of a high level of risk to the firm. They should take into account the results of procedures for the acceptance and continuation of clients.

(e)   The degree to which the team should carry out further assessment of controls as a means of reducing substantive tests.

(f)   The broad nature, extent and timing of substantive tests, or changes to the previous year's strategy for substantive testing.

(g)   Main points relating to planning and controlling the audit, or comments on the adequacy of the existing arrangements.

These matters are discussed further in the following paragraphs.

4:6.4 Engagement objectives

At the strategy meeting the team should consider the engagement objectives and determine whether, in the light of information so far gathered, they remain appropriate. In particular, the possibility of adding value to the audit may be considered. The procedures the audit team carries out to help to add value to the audit should not be significantly more extensive than those necessary for the purposes of the statutory opinion.

4:6.5 Results of the business review

At the strategy meeting the team should consider the results of the business review and their effect on the strategy. For example, the review might have identified that the client had entered a new market and that the team needed to develop additional procedures to respond to the new business. Alternatively, if there had been changes in tax legislation the team might require the early involvement of a tax specialist in the audit.

4:6.6 Risk of material misstatement

At the strategy meeting, the team should reach initial conclusions about identified risks for each significant account balance and class of transactions, and appropriate responses thereto. They do this by bringing together and considering the following:

(a)   The evaluation of significant inherent risks (discussed in **Section 4:4**, 'Evaluating inherent risk'). It is important that the engagement partner and the engagement manager bring their experience to bear to help to ensure that all significant inherent risks are identified and properly evaluated.

(b)   The judgement of materiality (discussed in **Section 2:2**, 'Materiality in financial statements').

(c)   Preliminary conclusions about the effectiveness of internal control in reducing inherent risks (discussed in **Section 2:5**, 'Internal control').

Using their understanding of the client's internal control structure, the team should decide whether it is likely to be efficient to identify one or more systems for which to make an extended assessment of control. If they can do so, they will be able to place reliance on the effectiveness of controls that reduce inherent risks in systems-derived accounts.

4:6.7 Extended assessment of controls for selected systems

In taking the decision whether to make an extended assessment of controls the team should consider the following matters:

(a)   **The systems that the team is likely to wish to rely on to reduce substantive testing:** In deciding which systems and controls to test the auditor will take into account the results of work on the control environment and IT controls. The engagement partner should be involved in the decision.

(b)   **Comparing the cost-effectiveness of the proposed strategy with an alternative strategy of not seeking to rely on the effectiveness of control:** This has the consequence that all the assurance required will have to be obtained from substantive testing.

4:6.8 Nature, extent and timing of substantive tests

Central to the audit strategy are decisions concerning the broad nature, extent and timing of substantive tests. These decisions are taken in the light of the assessment of the risk of material misstatement and after taking into account whether the auditor intends to carry out an extended assessment of control for one or more systems. Detailed information should not be included in the strategy memorandum, because it is the purpose of the audit programme to record such detail in the light of any further risk assessment required by the strategy. However, at the strategy stage the auditor should normally determine:

(a) whether it will be efficient to carry out early substantive testing and the extent to which this will cover the profit and loss account;

(b) the relative efficiencies of carrying out substantive analytical review or tests of details, or a combination of both;

(c) the broad time allocation between assessment of control and substantive testing;

(d) any particular features of the substantive response to risks, e.g. procedures that will require specialist assistance or a significant amount of audit time.

4:6.9 Main points relating to the administration of the audit

The auditor should consider the adequacy of the administrative arrangements and communications for the audit. For existing clients, the previous year's arrangements should be reviewed to identify how they might be improved and consider how subsequent changes in the client's business, systems and structure affect such arrangements. The administrative matters that should be considered include:

(a) specific matters arising if the client is a member of a group or has multiple locations, e.g. the collation of a group report for management;

(b) liaison with, and instructions to, other auditors, other offices, and correspondent firms;

(c) liaison with internal audit;

(d) proposed involvement of specialists, e.g. computer or tax specialists and consultants.

4:6.10 Recording the audit plan

The auditor should compile a record of strategy decisions in the audit working papers. The engagement partner and the engagement manager should decide the format and the amount of detail in the record. It should be as brief as possible. It may need to address the following matters:

4:6.10.1 Briefing material

(a) Important changes in the client since the previous audit. In the first year of an audit, the memorandum might include a brief description of the nature of the client's business and any significant matters that affect the financial statements.

(b) New or significantly changed accounting policies and particulars of policies that are non-standard for the industry.

(c) Significant changes in applicable auditing and regulatory standards.

(d) Key financial data identified through preliminary analytical procedures, including significant changes in operating results and trends, and recent financing and investment activities.

(d)   Preliminary judgements as to materiality.

(e)   Major inherent risks, including any sensitive auditing and accounting matters continuing from prior years. These might include, e.g., areas where the auditor has disagreed with the client over the correct treatment of an item, or has accepted a treatment on the grounds that its effect is not material but expects that it will eventually become material. It will normally be helpful to relate the major inherent risks to the relevant account balance or audit objective.

(f)   Significant changes in the control environment.

(g)   A preliminary assessment of new and substantially changed significant systems.

4:6.10.2 Identified tasks

(a)   The engagement objectives, including the client's requirements and the auditor's client service objectives. These should be as specific as possible, e.g. to perform a review of the security over electronic funds transfers, rather than a general statement such as 'render a constructive report to management'.

(b)   Responses, in broad terms, to the major inherent risks of fraud or error that have been identified. These should also cover responses to increased risk to the auditor and to the firm.

(c)   The system(s) for which the auditor will rely on the evaluation of control risk to support the audit opinion, and particulars of any systems that are to be included to meet client expectations.

(d)   Regardless of whether the auditor intends to evaluate internal financial controls, the amount of any further control assessment work required on the audit to help complete the assessment of the control environment.

(e)   Significant matters to be taken into account in developing the substantive tests, e.g. whether to perform early substantive testing and the extent of substantive testing of profit and loss account items.

   The engagement partner should approve the memorandum before the identified tasks are started.

4:6.11 Communicating with clients

The engagement partner and the engagement manager will normally discuss relevant parts of the strategy and related implementation plans with the client. They should consider whether it would be helpful to provide the client with a copy of the strategy memorandum or, if the memorandum is not suitable for this purpose, with a suitably amended version. This can be a valuable way of building relationships with the client and it serves the additional purpose of ensuring that the client's expectations are met and that the strategy takes full account of significant management concerns. The auditor may also obtain valuable input from the client that helps to improve audit efficiency.

4:6.12 Monitoring the strategy

The auditor may need to reconsider the judgements and decisions reached during the development of the audit strategy in the light of further information that becomes available during the audit. Accordingly, during the assessment of controls, or the development of the substantive tests and the subsequent testing, it is necessary to remain alert for matters that might require a change in the strategy. In particular, evidence that systems are not as reliable as expected, or the discovery of an unexpected incidence of errors, will normally lead the auditor to reconsider the strategy and, consequently, the substantive tests. The in-charge or the engagement manager should bring important changes to the attention of the engagement partner.

4:7 The audit programme

4:7.1 Introduction

The audit programme is a proposed detailed response to the risks of material misstatement that have been identified. It is intended to be recorded in sufficient detail to enable audit strategy decisions to be translated into individual audit programme steps.

4:7.2 How the tailored audit programme fits into the planning process

Tailored audit programmes are the end product, in a technical sense, of the audit planning process.

A properly tailored programme is the key to an efficient and effective audit because it:

(a)   Shows responses to the risks identified in the audit strategy.

(b)   Provides a basis for the task plan and individual work plans that will control the implementation of the plan.

(c)   Provides clear instructions as to the nature, extent and timing of procedures for staff doing the work.

(d)   Provides a structure for recording the audit work done and the conclusions drawn, which should lead to quality documentation, cost-effective review procedures and timely completion.

Preparing a task plan and individual work plans uses the same information as is included in the tailored audit programme but in a different way.

4:7.3 The need for an audit strategy

An audit strategy should be developed to help ensure that the auditor meets the goal of providing high quality, value-added service in an effective and efficient manner that focuses on the client's issues, risk, needs and expectations.

This process will include gathering and analysing relevant data, identifying adequate responses to risks, determining the broad approach to the detailed work required for each cycle or other main audit area and recording the agreed on strategy.

4:7.4 Developing the strategy

The engagement partner, manager and other key members of the engagement team should meet to develop the audit strategy. This could be based on a review of the effectiveness and efficiency of the previous year's engagement.

The development of the audit strategy should be a dynamic and interactive process, involving discussion between members of the audit team, to arrive at the most effective and efficient strategy for the engagement.

During the planning meeting the audit implications of the following matters should be discussed as a basis for determining the strategy:

- Client background:
  - engagement objectives;
  - significant developments and factors about the client's business and industry, including external factors such as regulatory, economic, social, technological, environmental and legal;
  - recent financing and investment activities and significant changes in the client's organisation or business activities;
  - significant changes in applicable accounting, auditing or regulatory standards affecting the business;
- Engagement management:
  - work that will require specialist assistance;
  - list of audit deliverables, e.g., presentations to the client;
  - proposed timetable, reflecting scope for reducing work during peak periods;
  - staffing and allocation of roles and responsibilities;
  - fees and client billing schedule;
  - planning the efficient use of technology;
  - approach where client is a group or has multiple locations, e.g., instructions to other auditors;
  - liaison with internal audit.

- Risk assessment and response:

  - significant business and inherent risks;

  - sensitive accounting and auditing matters (including significant management estimates) from prior years such as the nature and cause of prior year adjusted and unadjusted differences;

  - preliminary control risk assessment for system-derived accounts and related transaction cycles and other audit implications.

- Audit approach

  - broad approach to audit areas;

  - significant matters arising from preliminary analytical procedures;

  - list of client deliverables;

  - preliminary assessment of materiality.

4:7.5 Recording the strategy

The nature of the records to be kept depends on the complexity of the audit e.g., the audit of a group of companies will create the need for communication of group audit instructions. As a minimum there should be a record of the:

(a)   preliminary control risk assessment for each significant cycle;

(b)   overall approach to the audit of other significant accounts; and

(c)   critical matters that need to be resolved and the planned approach to resolving them.

4:7.6 Obtaining agreement and finalising the strategy

To finalise the planning phase of the audit it is important to ensure the following:

(a)   The auditor has designed the most effective and efficient audit approach for the engagement and obtained adequate approval.

(b)   The auditor has clearly communicated the approach to the client at an appropriate level of detail and has received the client's agreement and commitment to the plan sufficient to:

  (i)   represent a 'contract' on deliverables, and

  (ii)   be a reliable basis for future possible variation orders.

4:7.6.1 Meeting the audit objectives

It is essential to communicate the whole strategy to the engagement team. This is fundamental to good engagement management and will help to ensure that each member of the engagement team understands the reasons behind each individual task.

If information comes to light during the audit that affects previous risk assessments and planned responses, the auditor should:

(a)   consider the audit implications;

(b)   suggest amendments to the audit strategy and audit approach;

(c)   record all changes to the audit strategy; and

(d)   obtain manager or partner approval of the revisions.

To gain further assurance as to the quality and efficiency of the proposed audit approach and plan, an independent review of the proposed audit strategy could be carried out prior to the initiation of fieldwork. This procedure may be performed by the independent review partner, where appointed. The auditor should appoint an independent review partner for all high risk clients.

The auditor should ensure the client's understanding of the plan by presenting the audit strategy to the client and eliciting feedback. Agreed on changes to the plan resulting from the independent review and client presentation should be included in the final plan and communicated to the engagement team.

4:7.7 Preparing the tailored audit programme

4:7.7.1 *Responding to risks of misstatement*

Before preparing the tailored audit programme, the auditor should consider, for relevant audit objectives, the planned response to detailed risks of material misstatement covering as necessary:

- Tests of controls
- Analytical procedures
- Tests of detail

The objective is to ascertain the best combination of work that will enable the auditor to arrive at a sufficiently low level of audit risk at minimum cost. This should be considered for each significant account balance or class of transactions that is both relevant and material to the audit of the financial statements.

Matters to consider include the results of the control risk assessment and their effect on our audit objectives. Other matters to consider include:

(a)   assessing materiality;

(b)   the nature and composition of the account balance; and

(c)   specific risks for the account balance in relation to audit objectives.

4:7.7.2 *Assessing materiality*

The results of the preliminary analytical procedures can be used as a basis for assessing 'planning materiality'. This helps target subsequent audit work to where it is most needed – areas of higher risk of material misstatement. Judgements on materiality will be refined as the audit progresses.

It is important for 'planning materiality' to be discussed and agreed on at the strategy meeting. If planning materiality is too high, then audit procedures might fail to detect a misstatement that users of the financial statements consider material. If materiality is set too low, the auditor may tend to perform too much work and be inefficient.

Agreement across the team at this early stage is vital to avoiding under- and over-auditing, which can be caused by team members having different views on what is material.

4:7.7.3 *Nature and composition of the account balance*

Identifying and analysing the composition of an account balance (e.g. by, number, value, location or product line) will help the auditor understand better the factors influencing risk assessment and response and what is likely to be the most cost-effective plan.

4:7.7.4 *Specific risks for the account balance in relation to audit objectives*

The auditor should identify whether the client's controls address the inherent risk. It may be possible to obtain evidence of the effectiveness of the controls and the auditor should consider this when assessing control risk and developing tests of controls. If they do not, the auditor should carry out substantive testing focused on the risk.

It may be helpful to cross-reference tailored audit programme steps to the key risks and responses identified in the audit strategy.

4:7.7.5 *The appropriate timing for substantive testing*

Some work can normally be done early, e.g., analytical procedures on the completeness and accuracy of sales for the first nine months of the year. Where control risk is assessed below the maximum or at low, controls testing, income statement work and some balance sheet work will often be cost-effectively performed before the balance sheet date.

Points to remember in carrying out early testing are:

(a)   The efficiency and effectiveness of early testing will depend mainly on the auditor's assessment of risk. It is unlikely to be cost-effective if there is a significant risk of material misstatement arising in the intervening period or affecting the year end balances. This is because it will usually be necessary to repeat some of the tests of detail at the balance sheet date (or test transactions in the intervening period between the substantive testing date and the balance sheet date) to obtain sufficient assurance that the financial statements are not materially misstated.

(b) If control risk is assessed below the maximum, updating the tests of monitoring controls in the intervening period will often be an efficient way of gaining assurance that the year end balances are reliable. If tests of controls at the interim stage were mainly of application and computer controls the assurance gained could be 'rolled forward' by further tests of them. Alternatively tests of monitoring controls only in the intervening period will likely be more efficient.

4:8 Planning and control

4:8.1 Introduction

The audit approach set out in this Manual is outlined in **Section 1:3**, 'The audit approach', and described in more detail in other sections. Audit firms should plan and control all audits, to ensure that they are carried out efficiently and promptly, in accordance with the policies of the firm, with Auditing Standards, and with any other policies and standards that are relevant.

The methods used to plan and control audit work will vary according to the nature and size of the audit and the personal styles of the people involved. The audit firm should implement procedures to ensure that:

(a) the audit is carried out as planned, and that the audit work carried out and the service given to the client is of the high quality required;

(b) all decisions and judgements relating to the audit are made by those competent and authorised to do so, at the appropriate time and with the necessary facts available to them;

(c) all decisions are promptly communicated to the individuals who are expected to implement them;

(d) best use is made of the skills and experience of people in the audit practice, to develop their careers and to benefit clients and the firm. On-the-job coaching and development of people is an important part of all stages of an audit.

The engagement partner is ultimately responsible for the audit opinion and, therefore, the effective conduct of the audit. However, the engagement partner will usually delegate many aspects of planning and control to the engagement manager who may in turn delegate aspects of this work to the in-charge.

Audit planning and control is a continuous process. The principal planning and control issues which the auditor should consider are discussed in the following paragraphs.

4:8.1.1 Initial steps

For a new client, the engagement manager should ensure that all the necessary steps in connection with the firm's appointment as auditor are carried out.

The engagement manager should consider for each engagement what information is needed before the current year strategy can be set. It will often be appropriate for the engagement partner, the engagement manager and possibly the in-charge to meet and consider various matters arising out of correspondence, direct contact with the client and instructions from other offices or from other auditors.

The engagement partner and the engagement manager should agree at this stage which key team members should be assigned to the audit in order to gather the information needed to set the strategy. This work will usually be carried out by the in-charge and relevant specialist staff. When they select the other members of the audit team, the engagement partner and the engagement manager should ensure that the experience and abilities of the individuals concerned are appropriate to the client's needs and to the engagement objectives. The personal career development of each member of the team should also be considered.

4:8.2 Planning the implementation of the audit strategy

After the audit strategy has been approved by the engagement partner, the engagement manager should carry out the planning necessary to implement it. The detail of planning that is required will depend on the complexity and size of the audit. It should, however, be in sufficient detail to enable the approved audit strategy to be properly implemented. The matters which should normally be addressed in the audit strategy are set out in **Section 4:6**, 'Determining the strategy'.

The planning should allow the progress of the audit to be monitored effectively. This will involve:

(a) Setting timetables.

(b) Preparing time and fee budgets and discussing them with the client.

(c) Allocating tasks and responsibilities to team members.

(d) Identifying and briefing the members of the engagement team.

(e) Liaising with other departments in the firm.

(f) Discussing strategy and audit arrangements with the client.

The proposed audit timetable, together with a time and fee budget and a note of staff assigned to the engagement, should be discussed and agreed with the engagement partner during the audit strategy meeting or shortly after the strategy has been approved.

4:8.2.1 Setting timetables

Before setting the audit timetable the auditor should hold preliminary discussions with those members of the client's staff responsible for preparing the financial statements. The client's ability to produce the information required by the intended commencement date should be taken into account. Wherever possible, arrangements should be made for the client to prepare information in a form which will be most appropriate for an efficient audit. The timing of audit work should take account of the client's requirements, the timetable adopted by the client for the completion of its financial statements and the availability of suitable audit staff.

The timetable should be both realistic and phased in a way that will ensure that audit work is carried out in efficient manner. An important element in planning the timing of the audit is the need to divert work, where possible, away from peak periods. The auditor should therefore seek to:

(a)   make maximum use of early substantive testing, as discussed in **Section 4:7**, 'The audit programme', and

(b)   identify potential audit problems at an early stage so that they can be settled at the interim clearance.

Computer software is available to assist in the planning and controlling of a series of tasks, such as those involved in an audit. Such programmes allow key deadlines to be set and the progress of the audit to be monitored through various timetable reports. The software can list tasks such as those which need to be carried out by a particular date, those which were not completed until after the deadline, and those which are still outstanding.

4:8.2.2 Preparing time and fee budgets

(a)   **Objectives**: The objectives of time budgets are to assist in:

    (i)   planning work so that the audit can be completed efficiently;

    (ii)   monitoring actual costs, using the results to identify at an early stage the possibility that the time required will exceed the time planned and analysing the reasons for that overrun;

    (iii)   negotiating and monitoring payments on account and audit fees.

(b)   **Preparation of budgets**: A budget should be prepared for all engagements, taking into account the planned audit strategy. Therefore, for new clients, budgets should be prepared by the engagement manager after the business review has been carried out. For existing clients, it may be helpful to prepare an outline budget for the following year as soon as the audit is completed. The actual budget for the following year's audit should then be set when the auditor considers the strategy for that audit.

(c)   **Monitoring against budget**: During the audit, the in-charge should advise the engagement manager of any material discrepancies that are likely to arise between the budget and the expected time costs, preferably before the time is actually incurred. The engagement manager should discuss these discrepancies with the engagement partner. Where appropriate, the auditor should advise the client and negotiate a revised fee as soon as possible.

4:8.3 Assignment of staff

The auditor should plan the mix of the various members of the audit team properly in the light of the resources available, the audit roles that need to be filled and the needs of the client. The engagement manager should assign more experienced individuals to engagements where their experience and abilities are necessary and will be used to the best advantage. However, as much work as possible should be delegated to more junior members of the audit team, to give them further responsibility in a planned way, to develop their knowledge and experience and to meet the firm's general engagement objectives (*see* 'Best use of audit personnel', **Section 1:4.4**). Work should not be delegated to individuals who do not have the experience to carry it out properly, unless an increase in time is allocated to allow for extra supervision, including on-the-job coaching. The engagement manager should discuss and agree the composition of the audit team with the engagement partner.

4:8.4 Communication of the audit strategy and plan

Once assigned to the audit, individuals to whom work is delegated should be informed of the audit strategy, their responsibilities, the objectives of the procedures they are to perform and the completion dates for their work.

4:8.5 Liaison with internal audit

Where the auditor intends to rely on the work of the client's internal audit function as part of the audit strategy, the engagement manager should liaise with the client's internal audit department and make arrangements to review their work. Further guidance on reliance on the work of internal audit is set out in **Section 7:5**, 'Using the work of internal audit'.

4:8.6 Liaison with the client

Good liaison with the client is essential if the audit is to be conducted efficiently and effectively. The engagement partner and the engagement manager should normally discuss the audit strategy and audit arrangements with the client. Each member of the audit team has a role to play in ensuring that the firm maintains effective communication with the client throughout the engagement.

4:8.7 Further guidance

Further guidance on specific issues relevant to planning and controlling audit work is set out in **Chapters 5**, 'Controlling the audit', **6**, 'Recording audit work', and **7**, 'Involvement of others in the audit'.

Chapter 5

Controlling the audit

5:1 Engagement control and review

5:1.1 Introduction

Statement of Auditing Standards 240, 'Quality control for audit work', states that 'quality control policies and procedures should be implemented both at the level of the audit firm, and on individual audits'.

5:1.1.1 Roles of partners and managers

Section 5:2 explains the need for partners and managers to provide proper supervision and direction on all audits.

5:1.1.2 Supervision and review

Section 5:3 provides guidance on the basic disciplines that will assist the auditor to meet the requirements to control the audit.

5:1.2 Changes of personnel

Section 5:4, 'Changes of personnel assigned to engagements', explains the benefits to both the firm and the client of periodic changes in personnel assigned to engagements.

5:1.3 Consultation

Section 5:5, 'Consultation and concurring reviews', provides guidance on circumstances where formal consultation is appropriate between the engagement partner and other partners in the firm. For smaller firms and particularly for sole practitioners, consultation in the firm may not be possible. In these cases the most appropriate action for the auditor may be to consult with another practitioner, or with any relevant professional advisory service, provided that confidentiality of the client's affairs is maintained.

5:1.4 Quality assurance inspections

SAS 240, 'Quality control for audit work', requires each firm to monitor the effectiveness of its quality control procedures; this is covered by **Section 5:6**, 'Quality assurance inspections'.

5:1.5 Controlling audit costs

Section 5:7 provides guidance on a system to control audit costs.

5:1.6 Audit technology

Section 5:8 provides guidance on some of the control issues that arise from the use of computer technology in an audit.

5:1.7 Proposed revision of SAS 240

The APB has recently issued an exposure draft of a revision to SAS 240 'Quality Control for Audit Work'. It is broader in scope than the existing SAS, and there are additional standards covering leadership, resources, acceptance and continuation of engagements, consultation and monitoring.

5:2 Roles of partners and managers

5:2.1 Introduction

To ensure that engagement objectives are met all audit engagements need to be properly supervised and directed. Although the exact form of this supervision and direction will need to be flexible, as it depends on a number of factors, such as the size of the audit firm and the audit client, geographic dispersion, organisation and appropriate cost/benefit considerations, the audit team will normally comprise the following senior members:

(a) the engagement partner;

(b) the engagement manager;

(c) partners and managers from other practice areas, as determined by the engagement partner.

The audit team may also include a 'review' partner and a 'second' partner. The roles of these partners are discussed further in **Section 5:5**, 'Consultation and concurring reviews', and in **Section 5:2.3**.

Each firm should develop procedures for appointing engagement partners. The engagement partner will normally be responsible for appointing the engagement manager.

This section provides guidance on the role of partners and managers in the team, based primarily on procedures contained elsewhere in this Manual. However, these procedures do not cover all aspects of client service, use of personnel and commercial efficiency objectives, and partners and managers should therefore treat the guidance as a starting point rather than as a definitive list of tasks.

5:2.2 The engagement partner

The engagement partner has overall responsibility for the conduct of the engagement, including the quality of service delivery and the achievement of the auditor's other engagement objectives. However, a significant part of that responsibility may be delegated to the engagement manager.

5:2.3 The second partner

It is desirable that a second partner is appointed for each client. The role of the second partner is to:

(a) be known to the senior management of the client and, in the absence of the engagement partner, discharge the responsibilities of the engagement partner;

(b) remain informed about the major matters relating to the engagement; and

(c) on larger engagements, assist the engagement partner on discrete parts of the work (e.g., subsidiaries in a group).

5:2.4 The engagement manager

The engagement manager is responsible for all aspects of the engagement that are delegated by the engagement partner. These will generally include:

(a) Planning and review of work of the audit team.

(b) Regular monitoring of progress of all aspects of the audit.

(c) Briefing the engagement partner on progress of the audit and on any problems identified.

(d) Preparation of issues documentation.

(e) Review of all financial statements and reports.

5:2.5 Specialist partners and managers

The need for participation from specialist partners and managers will be determined by the engagement partner, in consultation with the specialists.

The factors that should be considered in determining whether computer specialists and tax specialists should be involved are discussed in **Section 7:3**, 'Specialist computer staff', and **Section 7:4**, 'Tax specialists'.

5:2.6 Signing letters and reports

5:2.6.1 Partners

Because partners are jointly and severally liable for all actions of the firm, they should sign the following written communications:

(a) **Any audit opinion given by the firm.** This includes audit opinions on statutory financial statements and consolidation packages, and also other opinions addressed to shareholders, other offices in the UK (in respect of group audits), auditors of parent companies and any other parties.

(b) **Any letter of engagement.**

(c) **Any report or letter of professional advice** to clients or others which contains an expression of opinion by the firm.

(d) **Any letter containing commitments** in respect of billing or fees.

If such communications are made to clients or other third parties in the form of fax or telex, a partner should authorise them before they are sent.

5:2.6.2 *Managers*

Managers may sign the communications referred to in (c) or (d) of **Section 5:2.6.1** if they have received specific authority from the engagement partner, and the report or letter has been reviewed by that partner or another partner. In these circumstances the letter should clearly state the name and title of the signatory, and should not be signed in the name of the firm.

Managers may sign letters acknowledging receipt of documents, confirming dates of audit visits, and those relating to other similar administrative matters, without the specific authority or review of a partner.

5:3 Supervision and review

5:3.1 Introduction

SAS 240 requires that 'any work delegated to assistants should be directed, supervised and reviewed in a manner which provides reasonable assurance that such work is performed competently'. Supervision and review are an integral part of a firm's audit procedures. They are required to ensure that:

(a) the audit complies with the firm's standards and professional standards;

(b) the work undertaken is sufficient to support the opinion;

(c) the work is carried out in accordance with the audit strategy, taking into account the engagement objectives;

(d) the work is performed efficiently within the timetable and the budget;

(e) the client values the quality of the service provided; and

(f) members of the audit team receive support in the development of their career.

On-the-job coaching is fundamental to these objectives.

5:3.2 Supervision

The engagement manager and other senior members of the engagement team should provide effective on-the-job coaching to those reporting to them. A person in a supervisory position should be available when needed to give advice, guidance or other help to the staff concerned.

The team leader (who may be given another title by different audit firms, such as senior, supervisor or in-charge) will have day-to-day responsibility for controlling the progress of the audit, and should notify the engagement manager of any significant accounting and auditing problems that have been identified and, as soon as they become apparent, any significant variations from the timetable. The team leader is also responsible day to day for the quality of work performed by members of the audit team.

The engagement manager should plan and monitor the progress of the audit regularly, and ascertain the reasons for any departures from the planned timetable. The manager should, as they occur, inform the engagement partner of significant accounting and auditing problems identified during the audit, and provide an assessment of their effect. The engagement manager is primarily responsible for ensuring that the objectives set out in **Section 5:3.1** are met, and in particular that the client values the service provided and that the engagement objectives are met.

5:3.3 Reviews

5:3.3.1 Policies and guidelines applicable to all reviews

Working papers are an essential part of all audits. SAS 230, 'Working Papers', states that 'working papers should record the auditors' planning, the nature, timing and extent of the audit procedures performed, and the conclusions drawn from the audit evidence obtained'. The working papers form the basis of audit reviews.

The following policies and guidance should be applied to all reviews of audit work:

(a) Whenever possible, audit team members should be present when their work is being reviewed. In any event, the person who has carried out the work, rather than another member of the team, should resolve queries raised by the review.

(b) The reviewer should carry out the review in a positive manner and use it to coach other members of the audit team.

(c) The review should take place as soon as possible after the work has been completed.

(d) The review should normally take place at the client's premises. In general, face to face reviews are to be preferred over remote reviews.

(e) Matters raised during the review should be promptly followed up and cleared without delay. The auditor should give the highest priority to those that affect the audit opinion.

(f)   The reviewer should consider the implications for other areas of the audit of points arising during the review.

(g)   The reviewer should ensure that exceptions identified by the member of the audit team who has carried out the work are disposed of satisfactorily and, in the case of significant exceptions, recorded in interim or final issues documentation.

(h)   The team leader should ensure that comments and notes made by the engagement partner and engagement manager from their working paper reviews are cleared by correction or improvement of the appropriate working paper. The comments sheets should be removed from working paper files after they have been cleared or resolved to the reviewer's satisfaction. The audit files should only retain comments on matters of substance that have a bearing on the audit report or that are to be raised by the engagement partner or the engagement manager with the client's management.

(i)   Each working paper should be initialled by the reviewer as evidence of review.

In addition to being guided by the policies listed above the various reviews will depend, in terms of their extent, on a number of factors, including the level of experience, training and competence of the staff involved.

The achievement of the objectives discussed in **Section 5:3.1** will not necessarily be clear from the working papers. The engagement partner and the engagement manager should, therefore, assess the quality of work done, and in particular the quality of the service provided to the client, by adopting other measures, e.g. observation, enquiry and discussion with the client. If there is evidence that the firm is not providing a high-quality service, the engagement partner and the engagement manager should take immediate steps to rectify the position, involving the team leader and other team members as necessary.

5:3.3.2 Team leader review

The purpose of the team leader review is to ensure that:

(a)   the members of the team have carried out their assigned tasks properly, in accordance with the audit strategy; and

(b)   the work done has been adequately recorded in the audit programmes and other working papers.

The team leader should ensure that the audit files presented for the engagement manager review are complete and that, except as reported in the issues documentation, all significant matters have been resolved and the files are free of outstanding queries.

5:3.3.3 Engagement manager review

The engagement manager should review the working papers, financial statements and reports to establish that:

(a)   the audit work has been adequately and properly executed in accordance with the agreed audit strategy;

(b)   the audit work complies with the firm's standards and with professional standards;

(c)   the working papers adequately record the work performed, provide the basis for the opinion expressed in the audit report and comply with the requirements of **Section 6:2**, 'Audit working papers';

(d)   the working papers provide adequate information about the audit, and constitute a basis on which the engagement manager and partner can ask and answer questions at meetings with the client;

(e)   all matters that require the engagement partner's attention are recorded in issues documentation;

(f)   the financial statements comply with appropriate accounting policies, and with relevant legislation and accounting standards; and

(g)   the audit report is clearly expressed, complies with the firm's guidelines and relevant auditing standards and is appropriate in the circumstances.

The extent of the manager's review will depend on what the team leader has received and found.

5:3.3.4 Engagement partner review

The engagement partner should, as a minimum, review the following:

(a)   Issues documentation and working papers supporting any contentious matters dealt with in issues documentation.

(b)   To the extent considered appropriate, any working papers that have been prepared by the engagement manager.

(c)   Evidence that the engagement manager has properly completed and recorded the detailed review.

(d)   The draft audit report to the board and to management.

The review should be sufficient to enable the engagement partner to conclude whether the audit evidence is sufficient to enable the firm to form an opinion on the financial statements, and whether the working papers support the other objectives listed in **Section 5:3.1**.

5:3.3.5 Timing

The timing of review procedures will be determined by the dates of completion of the various stages of the audit as set out in the audit timetable. All reviews should take place in good time to enable appropriate action to be taken before any subsequent audit procedures are adversely affected. For example, review of the work done on internal controls should normally take place at an interim stage, because the nature, extent and timing of later audit procedures may depend on the results of this work; accordingly, the engagement manager should not leave this detailed review until the end of the audit.

5:4 Changes of personnel assigned to engagements

5:4.1 Introduction

The quality of audits and the service to clients may be enhanced if the partners and managers assigned to engagements are changed from time to time. The client benefits from receiving a fresh, objective view of the enterprise and of the firm's service to it, without sacrificing all the knowledge and understanding of the business that the firm has acquired that would be lost through changing auditing firms. Also, changes can promote the continuing impartial attitude that an auditor must maintain on all matters relating to audit engagements. For the firm, the policy of periodic change offers partners and managers greater opportunities for personal development. Changes often occur naturally because of promotion or for other reasons. In the case of listed companies, the engagement partner must be rotated every seven years. However, where changes of the partner and manager on an engagement do not occur in the normal course of events it is desirable to arrange for reassignment to take place to obtain the benefits of change. If there is a change, for whatever reason, changes in both the engagement partner and engagement manager in the same year should preferably be avoided.

5:4.2 Regular review

The audit firm should adopt a policy for the rotation of audit partners, having regard to professional requirements in force or best practice, e.g. that engagement partners and engagement managers should not serve a client for more than a certain length of time consecutively in the same role. The partner in charge of the firm or office should carry out a review each year to consider, in the light of such a policy, the assignment of partners and managers to engagements. If the circumstances of the client require it, the partner in charge should consider the need to change the engagement partner, review partner or the engagement manager at any time before the formal review. When the audit firm is considering a change in the engagement partner or manager, other than for reasons of promotion, retirement or resignation the client should be informed in advance. The auditor should explain to the board or to management the benefits that a change brings.

5:5 Consultation and concurring reviews

5:5.1 Introduction

It is the essence of professional partnership that the auditor should consult others in the firm to take advantage of the firm's collective breadth of knowledge. The auditor should do this on an informal basis to obtain objective and informed views about accounting and auditing issues. However, where the engagement partner needs to form an opinion on matters of particular importance, complexity or sensitivity, the engagement partner should follow formal consultation procedures, and record the results of that process. This section discusses the general application of formal consultation procedures. Brief reference is made to consultation procedures that apply to clients in certain specialised industries. The Manual assumes that partners will be able to consult other partners within the firm. Sole practitioners should establish consulting arrangements outside their firm and small firms may also need to set up appropriate consultation arrangements.

5:5.2 Circumstances requiring formal consultation

The engagement partner should follow formal consultation procedures in the following circumstances:

(a)   Whenever there are circumstances which suggest a qualified or otherwise modified audit report may need to be issued.

(b)   If a material issue concerns the application of accounting standards, the Companies Act, or other generally accepted accounting practices which are subject to varying interpretations.

(c)   If an accounting or auditing issue is not covered by existing practice or stated firm's policy.

(d)   If the client wishes to invoke the 'true and fair' override to justify departure from the application of accounting standards or the Companies Act.

(e)   If there are ethical considerations, e.g. a matter possibly affecting the auditor's professional independence and objectivity, or a significant risk to the firm.

(f)   When the firm ceases to act as auditor.

5:5.3 Appointment of review partner

In addition to the engagement partner, a 'review partner' might be appointed for all clients which fall into the categories listed below. It should also be considered whether a review partner needs to be appointed for all new audit clients.

The formal consultation procedures that should be followed depend on the size and nature of the client, in particular on whether there is a significant public interest involved, and on whether there is significant risk to the firm because, for some other reason, the engagement is difficult. The suggested categories are as follows:

(a) **Public interest**

    (i)   Listed and AIM companies, and clients whose financial statements are being audited in connection with a public offering of securities.

    (ii)   Major public sector clients (including Government or quasi-government entities, monopolies, duopolies, local authorities and health authorities).

    (iii) Large charitable organisations and trusts or non-profit organisations, e.g., that obtain significant resources from the public and/or whose financial statements are widely distributed.

    (iv) Major industrial and provident societies or credit unions.

    (v)   Banks, insurance companies, building societies, and other financial services clients where there is a significant public interest or significant risk to the audit firm, e.g. those holding significant investment business client money. More specific guidance on entities falling into this category may need to be developed.

    (vi) Major pension funds.

(b) **Significant risk to the firm for other reasons**

    (i)   Clients known to be aggressive in their accounting and reporting practices.

    (ii)   Those with material amounts of deferred costs to be recovered from future revenues.

    (iii) Those with going concern problems.

    (iv) Clients in industries subject to significant audit risk because of economic downturn.

    (v)   Those where the auditor lacks confidence in the completeness or accuracy of disclosure by the client.

    (vi) Where there has been a serious breakdown in the internal control or accounting systems during the period.

    (vii) Clients in specialised industry sectors where the engagement partner is relatively new to the industry.

5:5.4 Role of the review partner

The review partner is intended as the first point for consultation throughout the audit, and should:

(a)   discuss significant matters relating to the audit with the engagement partner, and review, to the extent considered necessary, the audit strategy and other critical working papers;

(b)   before the financial statements and the audit report are released, and before any preliminary announcement is made, carry out a concurring review, covering, e.g.:

(i) either the draft issues documentation or a summary of it; and

(ii) the draft financial statements, proposed audit report and the other parts of the client's annual report; and

(c) provide additional assurance that:

(i) significant matters relating to the conduct of the audit are satisfactorily dealt with; and

(ii) the financial statements, and related audit report, are appropriate for issue.

A memorandum should be prepared of the matters arising from the concurring review, or the review partner should sign-off the critical issues. The engagement partner should inform the review partner of the final decisions that were taken on the matters raised by the review partner.

5:5.5 Qualified or otherwise modified audit reports

All qualified or otherwise modified audit reports should be reviewed, before they are signed, by a partner other than the engagement partner.

If there are circumstances which suggest the firm may need to issue a qualified or otherwise modified audit report on a client in which there is a significant public interest, as defined in the list in **Section 5:5.3** (categories (a)(i) to (a)(vi)), the engagement partner should consult the review partner. If the review partner confirms that the firm may need to issue a qualified or otherwise modified report, the engagement partner should immediately provide a copy of the draft audit report, the draft financial statements and a briefing memorandum (e.g., the relevant issues documentation) to appropriate senior partner for consultation.

Firms may consider it appropriate to identify a 'panel of consultant partners' to whom such matters should be referred. This panel should decide whether one of its members should formally concur with the proposed report.

If a member of this panel is asked to review the draft report, that partner should discuss the matter with the engagement partner and the review partner at a meeting of the partners concerned. A memorandum of the result of the discussion should be prepared, a copy of which should be referred to in the issues documentation and kept as part of the audit working papers.

If the report is to be reviewed only by the review partner, the engagement partner should discuss the circumstances with the review partner. A memorandum of the result of the discussion should be prepared, a copy of which should be referred to in the issues documentation and kept as part of the audit working papers.

5:5.6 Other matters

Engagement partners should consult formally one or more of the following sources on any matter arising from the circumstances identified in **Section 5:5.2**, points (b) to (f):

(a)   the review partner, if one has been appointed;

(b)   a senior audit partner;

(c)   for matters arising from a specialised industry, a designated specialist for that industry.

5:5.7 Disagreements

5:5.7.1 Between the engagement partner and members of the audit team

Audit personnel in a firm are normally, or are training to be, professionally qualified. They therefore possess a high level of personal integrity and dedication to professional standards, and occasionally hold differing views on matters arising from audit work. Each firm should seek to maintain an environment in which any member of the audit practice can express his or her own point of view within the audit team on any audit matter, in a controlled manner.

Through the processes of consultation, supervision and review at successively higher levels during an audit, each individual's point of view is considered at the appropriate level, and all controversial issues are exposed to the differing points of view. As a result, tentative decisions are fully explored by all concerned before they are finally agreed.

Most differences of opinion that arise during the progressive reviews during an audit are resolved without difficulty. Occasionally, however, the auditor needs to undertake additional research or investigation to resolve the particular issues to the satisfaction of all concerned.

In those rare cases where the engagement partner disagrees with a member of the audit team on the need to qualify the audit report on an issue which that individual considers is material, the engagement partner should follow the consultation procedures set out above. The member of the audit team who disagrees with the engagement partner should participate in the consultation.

5:5.7.2 Working papers

The engagement partner should ensure that the working papers support the firm's conclusions. The engagement partner should, therefore, make a full note of disposal in respect of any dissenting views of a member of the audit team, and indicate the reasons that form the basis of the firm's opinion. A copy of the note should be given to the individual concerned.

5:5.7.3 Between the engagement and other partners

The engagement partner has the final responsibility for the firm's audit report and for other decisions relating to the client. However, if as a result of a concurring review or consultation there is disagreement, the matter should be referred to the chairman of the 'panel of consultant partners', who should attempt to resolve the matter with the partners concerned. If the disagreement cannot be resolved in this way it may need to be considered at a full or representative meeting of that panel.

5:5.8 Roles of the engagement partners and review partner in respect of non-audit services

The engagement partner has an obligation to ensure that independence and objectivity are not compromised by the provision of other services to an audit client. Also, where it is considered that an audit should be accepted or continued only with additional safeguards against loss of independence, the engagement partner's decision and the range of safeguards proposed should be subject to independent review. Accordingly, as part of the engagement partner's review of matters that could affect independence and objectivity explicit consideration is needed of the nature of any non-audit services supplied to the client and the safeguards in place to prevent any impairment of independence and objectivity. For those jobs where a review partner is appointed, the review partner should consider the position with the engagement partner and, based on information provided by the engagement partner, specifically conclude as to whether or not independence and objectivity have been safeguarded.

5:5.9 Evidence of review

When seeking formal consultation on specific issues the engagement partner and manager should:

(a)   provide background information, together with supporting papers;

(b)   indicate the nature and results of any previous research and consultation; and

(c)   state the alternatives identified, the tentative conclusions reached and the supporting arguments.

After the consultation the engagement partner or manager should annotate the relevant papers or prepare a note of the matter and the decision made and this must be referred to in issues documentation.

The engagement partner should inform the review partner of decisions taken on the matters raised by the review partner. The review partner's signature on relevant documentation indicates completion of the concurring review of the financial statements to the review partner's satisfaction and that from his or her perspective:

(a)   all significant matters relating to the review of the audit have been satisfactorily dealt with;

(b)   the financial statements, and related audit report, are appropriate for issue; and

(c)   all the significant matters in the issues documentation and relevant notes related to the review have been appropriately resolved and recorded and no other significant related questions remain open.

5:6 Quality assurance inspections

5:6.1 Introduction

Each Registered Auditor is required by the *Audit Regulations and Guidance* to establish and maintain quality control procedures appropriate to the firm's circumstances. This section sets out guidance on such procedures. A firm's programme of quality assurance inspections has, as its main objective, to monitor whether audits are conducted in accordance with the relevant policies and procedures. The programme also seeks to encourage accountability for quality. As the majority of audits are conducted annually it is appropriate for inspections to be carried out as part of an annual programme.

Annual quality assurance inspections (or 'quality reviews') have the following benefits:

(a)   They confirm that general professional standards, and the firm's standards where higher, have been met.

(b)   They confirm that audit working papers have been subjected to the necessary reviews by engagement managers, engagement partners and, where appropriate, review partners.

(c)   They provide constructive comments for enhancing the efficiency and effectiveness of future engagements.

(d)   They highlight important issues in respect of which the firm's policies may need to be specified or redefined.

(e)   They review the performance of people assigned on the engagement.

(f)   They identify possibilities for improvement in the services provided to clients.

5:6.2 Selection of audits for review

Selection of the engagements for review and maintenance of the historical records of the reviews carried out should be the responsibility of a central department or person. The selection should be made from engagements completed during the 12 months preceding the date of the review.

5:6.3 Composition of review teams

A review team might consist of:

(a)   a chairman, being an experienced audit partner;

(b)   a review partner, being any other audit partner;

(c)   one or more audit managers of appropriate seniority and experience.

Where possible the chairman should be appointed from a practice unit other than that subject to review. The chairman should assemble the review team who, at the chairman's discretion, may be drawn from the practice unit subject to review. However, none of the review team should have been directly involved with the engagements selected for review.

5:6.4 Involvement of the partners in charge

Partners in charge of the practice unit should ensure that:

(a) dates are fixed for the reviews;

(b) briefing papers are prepared for the review team in good time;

(c) reviews are concluded and minutes of review meetings agreed promptly; and

(d) matters arising are communicated properly to those concerned.

5:6.5 Scope

In addition to considering the technical standards applied to an engagement, the review team might consider the commercial efficiency of the engagement, the quality of service to the client and the effectiveness of the use of people.

Accordingly, each review might:

(a) provide constructive advice for increasing the effectiveness and efficiency of the audit;

(b) assess whether the audit meets the firm's standards and complies with the firm's policies and procedures;

(c) consider whether the quality of the service to the client is satisfactory; and

(d) make recommendations in respect of any shortcomings identified.

Firms may consider preparing detailed checklists to assist in the conduct of the reviews.

5:6.6 Reporting

The initial findings on individual engagements should be discussed and agreed with the engagement partner and the engagement manager to allow them to correct any misunderstandings, consider the independent views the review team has expressed and develop proposals for improving the effectiveness and/or the efficiency of the audit.

In addition to reporting on the individual engagements reviewed, review teams might report on common features arising from the reviews, and on any other matters which they consider should be brought to the attention of the partner in charge.

The results of all the reviews should be summarised and important findings considered by the appropriate professional standards body in the firm.

5:6.7 Retention of documents

Review schedules and notes prepared as part of the quality assurance inspections of individual engagements are confidential and should not be placed on audit files. Following completion of the quality assurance inspections the detailed records of the engagements examined may be destroyed with only the report summarising the findings kept as a record.

5:7 Controlling audit costs

5:7.1 Introduction

Control of audit costs may be achieved by the use of the following:

(a) Time accounts, which record the time actually incurred on the audit for the purposes of the firm's internal management accounting system.

(b) Budgets, which set up an initial plan of the cost of the audit.

(c) Time summaries, which record time spent on individual audit areas on a daily basis during the audit.

5:7.2 Time accounts

The engagement manager should open a separate time account for each individual engagement and all time and expenditure incurred on an engagement should be included in it. Further time accounts may be opened for larger audits, or in cases where this is a useful way of monitoring costs.

5:7.3 Budgets

5:7.3.1 Objective

The objective of preparing budgets is to assist in:

(a) planning the work so that the audit team can complete the audit efficiently;

(b) monitoring actual costs and, as a consequence, identifying:

   (i)   any likelihood that the time required will exceed the time planned; and

   (ii) the reasons for any such variance;

(c) agreeing audit fees and payments on account; and

(d) forward staff planning.

5:7.3.2 Preparation

The auditor should prepare a budget for every audit engagement as part of the audit strategy. Firms may wish to develop audit software to help the budgeting process.

At the conclusion of each audit, the team leader should prepare an outline budget for the following year's audit, taking account of experience gained in the current year. The outline budget should be reviewed and a firm budget approved by the engagement manager when developing the strategy for the next audit. For new clients, the budget should reflect the audit strategy, and be drawn up after the auditor has an adequate preliminary understanding of the client's business and circumstances. In all cases, the engagement partner should finally approve the budget at the same time as approving the strategy.

When preparing budgets, the auditor should take account of the following:

(a) If the engagement manager considers that detailed analysis would be of limited value, totals only may be included for the budgeting and recording of time spent on determining audit strategy and developing the substantive testing plan. However, a detailed analysis of time to be spent on substantive testing procedures will be helpful.

(b) The auditor should list separately any work of a specific nature that is not covered by the normal time analysis.

(c) The auditor should budget adequate time for internal planning and control meetings, for meetings with the client at key stages of the audit, and for developing reports to management and to the board.

(d) The auditor should normally evaluate budgeted units using hourly rates in force at the time the budget is prepared.

(e) The auditor may wish to include a contingency provision to allow for such factors as expected changes in scale rates or staff promotions and any unforeseen excess over budget.

The budget might also include the following information:

(a) The cumulative amount of budgeted work-in-progress by time and value at the end of each month.

(b) The proposed amounts of bills on account and the final bill, entered under the month in which the bills are expected to be issued to the client.

5:7.3.3 Expenses

When expenses form a significant element of the total charge to the client, the auditor should prepare an expenses budget and include it in the overall audit budget.

5:7.3.4 *Tax specialists*

The auditor should include in the audit budget any time to be charged by tax specialists to the audit in respect of the audit of the taxation provision. The auditor should not include in the audit budget time relating to separate services provided by the firm in connection with the client's tax affairs.

5:7.3.5 *Computer and other specialists*

Where appropriate the engagement manager should ensure that adequate allowance for computer and other specialists is included in the overall budget for the client. The engagement manager should liaise with the specialists when preparing the budget to ensure that all planned or likely work is taken into account, including proper allowance for assistance in determining the audit strategy and substantive tests, systems or other work. Further guidance is given in **Section 7:3**, 'Specialist computer staff'.

5:7.4 Time summaries

On every engagement, the team leader should keep a record on a daily basis of the time spent, analysed over the various audit areas. The team leader should advise the engagement manager of any material differences which appear likely to arise between budgeted and expected performance, before the time is actually incurred. In some cases the audit strategy or substantive tests may require revision (as discussed in **Sections 4:6**, 'Determining the strategy', and **4:7**, 'The audit programme'). If necessary, the engagement manager should prepare a revised budget and submit it, together with a separate memorandum recording the reasons, to the engagement partner for approval and discussion with the client, as necessary.

Once the engagement is completed, the team leader should reconcile the total hours analysed on the time records with the hours charged to that engagement in the firm's management accounting system. The total reconciled time so determined should then be compared with the budget and all significant variances accounted for.

The engagement manager should review the reconciliation and any variances that arise, and should review with the engagement partner the proposed final fee for the engagement. This recommendation should cover fees for additional work that the audit team has carried out (e.g., accountancy work) even if such work was not included in the original budget or in the original fee estimate to the client. Fees for any additional work should not be described as audit fees, unless they are directly audit related.

5:8 Audit technology

5:8.1 Introduction

This section is primarily concerned with setting out policies for the use of microcomputers to assist in the planning, controlling and recording of audit work. It does not cover liaison with computer specialists, which is discussed in **Section 7:3**, 'Specialist computer staff'. It is also not significantly concerned with the use of microcomputers for performing audit procedures, the design of software for which is discussed in **Section 9:7**, 'Computer-assisted audit techniques'.

Using software is frequently more efficient than carrying out equivalent manual procedures, and it may also improve the effectiveness of the audit. Audit teams should, therefore, use computer software whenever practicable.

5:8.2 Audit working papers

SAS 230, 'Working Papers', states that 'auditors should document in their working papers matters which are important in supporting their report'.

Audit working papers can be prepared using a combination of software. Firms may buy appropriate word processing and spreadsheet packages and issue standard instructions to their audit staff or may issue standard templates, together with brief user instructions as needed. Alternatively, firms may develop their own software applications tailored to their requirements using available software platforms. Audit staff can adapt the standard working paper templates in less time than it takes to start from scratch. The templates will normally need to be accompanied by programmed routines (often known as 'macros'), e.g. to print out the finished working paper, or to put the client name and the key dates at the head of every working paper in the set. These measures, templates and macros help to maximise audit productivity.

Audit working papers prepared using software are subject to the same policies and considerations as those discussed in **Section 6:2**, 'Audit working papers'. In particular, each working paper should show the preparer's initials or signature. This is necessary to enable the auditor to identify who produced a working paper, in order to:

(a) be satisfied that the work has been carried out by a suitably experienced member of the audit team;

(b) consider, if the work is challenged, whether the person who carried out the work can provide any additional information that may assist in answering the specific questions.

If the initials of the preparer are omitted from a manuscript working paper, it will usually still be possible to identify the preparer from handwriting. This is not the case when working papers are produced electronically. Accordingly, the auditor should apply the following procedures for electronically produced working papers:

(a) When the system allows for an 'electronic signature', protected by appropriate passwords, the electronic signature should be used. Users should not sign in another's name.

(b) When the system does not allow for an electronic signature, the working paper should be printed out and the hard copy signed by the principal preparer and the reviewer.

(c) Material changes by another person to an electronically produced working paper will normally need to be identified.

In addition, the auditor should safeguard the working papers from deliberate or inadvertent change. Accordingly, the audit firm should apply the data security procedures set out in **Sections 5:8.5** to **5:8.5.3**.

5:8.3 Security over hardware

Microcomputers and printers are expensive and readily marketable. Therefore, to guard against theft or loss, the auditor should safeguard hardware when it is left unattended, whether at a client's premises or in the firm's offices, by a combination of physical security and administrative procedures.

Each firm might establish procedures for the following:

(a) **Authorising the removal of microcomputers from the office**: For example, when a microcomputer is taken from the office, a designated individual should be responsible for it, and for its safe keeping and return.

(b) **Keeping an inventory of hardware**, showing the location of all equipment belonging to the firm. Counts should be carried out at intervals appropriate to the value and number of the firm's microcomputers.

(c) **Storing the hardware** in areas which are free from excessive heat, sunlight, dust and other potential hazards.

5:8.4 Security over software

Master copies of the firm's audit software and back-up copies of internally distributed software should be available centrally.

Each firm should establish procedures for storing the master program diskettes for third party software such as spreadsheet, word processing or accounts production packages in a secure location in the office as back-up. Working copies for day-to-day use should be installed on the hard disk. However, to avoid infringing the licence agreements, each firm should have procedures in place to ensure that only one of these copies is used at any one time. Special arrangements in respect of copyright may be required in cases where proprietary software is being used on a network. Firms should take care to meet software copyright requirements.

Each firm should also keep records of the number of copies of each program that it owns. This helps to ensure that new versions are installed as they become available, as well as providing a readily available master source in the event of the working copy's being accidentally deleted or corrupted.

5:8.5 Data security

Information held on microcomputers will, in many cases, be confidential, and it should be subject to the same security procedures as confidential documents and audit working papers. The auditor should therefore adopt measures to ensure the confidentiality of client data stored in electronic form.

The auditor should prevent unauthorised access to data by maintaining physical security over microcomputers (especially if they are portable) and storage media, and by software security mechanisms such as passwords.

5:8.5.1 Physical security as a means of data security

The most effective data security is achieved by restricting access to the microcomputers, diskettes or other storage media holding client data. Therefore, whenever possible, each firm should provide lockable rooms or cupboards for portable microcomputers and for diskettes containing client data, and should arrange with their clients for suitable secure storage overnight and at weekends when portable microcomputers are being used at clients' premises. Firms should institute procedures to control the keys to such rooms or cupboards. The auditor should ensure that microcomputers and diskettes are not left unattended while they are in transit (e.g., in cars).

Individuals to whom microcomputers are allocated should be made responsible for the physical security of their microcomputer and diskettes. Where data security is achieved by means of physical control over the microcomputer, the machines should be locked away outside normal working hours. Users should also lock away stored data on diskettes or tapes when not in use, including during lunch-breaks.

The auditor should store particularly sensitive data only on diskettes and apply suitable physical security arrangements to them. Where it is necessary to hold such sensitive data temporarily on a hard disk, the auditor should overwrite the data as soon as possible thereafter, using a utility that wipes all data rather than using a standard delete command that leaves much of the original data on the disk.

Data stored in the firm's offices (e.g., back-up copies) should also be subject to physical controls, and only authorised users should be allowed access to the data.

5:8.5.2 Software access controls as a means of data security

Regardless of whether a firm applies physical control as a means of data security, it should apply software access controls. The nature and extent of such controls should vary according to the sensitivity of the data.

Password controls should be used for all machines, whether used alone or on a network. Where passwords are used to restrict access to data, the auditor should ensure that such passwords are not made available to unauthorised persons. However, they should be readily ascertainable by members of the firm (who will not normally be restricted from having access).

Where an office network is in use, the password system should incorporate a time-lapse lock-out, so that an unauthorised user is much less likely to be able to access sensitive data by using a temporarily unattended terminal still logged on to the network.

5:8.5.3 *Other data security considerations*

Client data stored on the fixed disk of a portable computer should be backed up and deleted before the computer is taken to a different client. The auditor should make regular checks to ensure that data files are not being left on the hard disks of portable audit machines.

If microcomputers are hired from an external supplier, the auditor should remove all software (other than the programs that were on the machine when delivered) and overwrite (as discussed in **Section 5:8.5.1**) all data before they are returned.

Before allowing engineers access to a microcomputer for maintenance purposes, the auditor should confirm that they are authorised to carry out repairs on a microcomputer (e.g., by checking their identity). When it is necessary for an engineer to remove a microcomputer or its hard disk from the premises, the auditor should remove all client data.

Some engineers provide a fast replacement service by substituting a working machine for the one that is damaged. This practice, while efficient, introduces the risk that data on the original machine could fall into the wrong hands. Firms should take steps to ensure their engineers will not pass their machines to any third party.

5:8.6 Data integrity

Data stored in electronic form are subject to corruption by magnetic fields and improper storage. Therefore, to ensure that the auditor may rely on such data when expressing the audit opinion, proper care should be taken of the hardware and of the diskettes used to store and transport the data.

5:8.7 Viruses

Firms should take precautions to avoid computer viruses which can corrupt or destroy data without warning. Such viruses are normally introduced by the use of diskettes from third parties, even clients, or by downloading programs from external 'bulletin board' services. For this reason, the auditor should ensure that only software from reliable sources is loaded on to the firm's microcomputers. In particular, firms should prohibit the use of public domain software, or programs from external bulletin board services. Viruses which infect a client's machine may be blamed on the audit machines if they are infected.

Firms should invest in one or more copies of a suitable proprietary virus-checking software package. Where the use of diskettes from third parties is unavoidable, which is often the case if, for example, data from clients are to be used on audit machines, it will probably be worth while to use one or more microcomputers for the sole purpose of checking such diskettes for viruses before such diskettes are to be used on any other audit microcomputers.

The proprietary virus-checking software packages should also be capable of checking hard disks, for use before an audit microcomputer goes out to a client site and as soon as it is brought back.

The auditor should take account of the following matters relating to the integrity of data:

(a) **Care of diskettes**: Diskettes and other removable storage media should be handled with care to prevent damage and consequent loss of data. In particular, they should be protected from dust, heat or direct sunlight and magnetic fields.

(b) **Labelling diskettes**: All diskettes should be labelled clearly, informatively and promptly. Labels should be kept up to date so as to reflect, as far as possible, the contents of the diskette. Failure to do so may result in data being mislaid or incorrect versions being used.

(c) **Filing diskettes**: Each firm should maintain a filing system for back-up copies of diskettes in a safe location.

5:8.8 Back-up copies of data

Individuals should take back-up copies of data regularly. Each firm should set out its detailed policies for taking back-up and should make sure that individuals in charge of microcomputers are aware of them. The policies should deal with:

(a) frequency of back-up;

(b) the number of generations of back-up to be stored;

(c) where the back-up is to be kept;

(d) required labelling and identification of diskettes;

(e) necessary records to be kept by the users.

In the case of particularly valuable data, the loss of which would result in significant restoration costs, firms should store back-up copies in a fireproof safe or, preferably, in a separate building. In determining whether such procedures are appropriate, the costs should be weighed against the risk of data loss and the resultant adverse consequences for the firm. In addition, such data should be subject to the data security considerations set out in **Sections 5:8.5** to **5:8.5.3**.

5:8.9 Distribution of the firm's software

Most of the software developed by a firm is for internal use only. Therefore the auditor should not, without the approval of the appropriate partner, give, nor disclose, to other parties software that is distributed for use by members of the firm only.

5:8.10 Documentation of applications

Where a firm's standard package is used, the user guide should provide sufficient evidence of the method of processing, and the reports produced should provide the means to show evidence of the audit work carried out.

Where a specific application has been developed (e.g., if a spreadsheet has been designed for use on an audit), the audit team should ensure that documentation of microcomputer applications is adequate to allow a person new to the application to use it properly, and to modify it if necessary. The documentation should, as a minimum, include the following:

(a)   Planning documentation, showing the purpose of the application and how it has been achieved.

(b)   An adequate explanation of each data element and each formula or programmed process.

(c)   Annotated program or macro listings.

(d)   A record of testing that has been carried out.

(e)   Details of changes made to the application.

(f)   The version number of the package, if applicable.

Each firm should set development standards to be followed for the design, development and testing of all applications. The more complex the application the more the time that should be spent testing. A systematic approach is essential to ensure that all data entered will be processed as intended and that the correct result will be produced. It is important that testing is repeated each time a change is made to the application.

Generally, the engagement partner is responsible for ensuring that applications are properly developed and tested. However, in practice such responsibility will normally be delegated to the engagement manager or to the team leader.

5:8.11 Data Protection Act 1984

Certain data, when held on computer, are subject to the Data Protection Act 1984. The auditor should take care to ensure that data are only stored for the specified purposes. People about whom data are stored have the right to be provided with details of such data, on request.

Chapter 6

Recording audit work

6:1 Recording audit work

6:1.1 Introduction

All audit work must be documented to provide tangible evidence of the work carried out in support of the audit opinion. This documentation is the subject of SAS 230, 'Working Papers'. **Section 6:2**, 'Audit working papers', and **Section 6:3**, 'Notes of meetings and related matters', provide guidance on the basic disciplines that assist the auditor to meet the standard's requirement for work to be adequately recorded.

6:1.2 Access to working papers and other material

Section 6:4, 'Access to audit working papers', provides guidance on general procedures to be followed when requests are received for working papers and other material to be made available to clients or third parties.

6:2 Audit working papers

6:2.1 Introduction

Audit working papers comprise all those documents that contain information relating to the audit of a client's financial statements. Working papers may be in the form of data stored on paper, film, electronic media or other media. The special considerations relating to working papers and other records of work which are prepared using computer software are discussed in **Section 5:8**, 'Audit technology'.

The objectives of audit working papers are to:

(a)   assist in the efficient conduct of work;

(b)   enable the work carried out to be independently reviewed; and

(c)   demonstrate that the auditor has properly performed all the audit work necessary to enable an opinion to be formed on the financial statements.

The quantity, type and content of audit working papers will vary with the circumstances. They must meet the overall objectives listed above, but should not be so extensive that their preparation is an inefficient use of time.

Unlike communications between legal advisers and their clients, those between accountants and their clients are generally not privileged. It is prudent, therefore, to assume that in the event of litigation all working papers, correspondence, memoranda and other similar items relating to the engagement will be made available to, and will be used by, the litigants. Furthermore, in the event of an administration, receivership or liquidation, the auditor has a duty to co-operate with the office-holder, which may mean disclosing information from the audit files.

Anybody who challenges audit work after it has been completed has the benefit of hindsight. Any indication on the working papers of apparent inconclusiveness or incompleteness might be seized upon as evidence that the auditor did not have an adequate basis for forming the opinion expressed. If the auditor's judgement is subsequently questioned, particularly by a third party who has the benefit of hindsight, it is important to be able to identify what facts the auditor knew at the time of reaching the conclusion, and also that, based on those facts, the conclusion was reasonable. For these reasons, the following procedures are important:

(a) The auditor should not make comments on analyses and schedules that are incomplete or only preliminary or which might later be construed as indicating that the auditor considered a matter in a careless or superficial manner.

(b) The auditor should remove all lists of outstanding work, and all queries and comments arising from the detailed working paper reviews during an engagement, once these have been resolved.

(c) If difficult questions of principle or of judgement arise, the auditor should record the relevant information received and the source of the information, and should summarise both management's and the auditor's conclusions.

(d) Before the audit report is signed, the auditor should ensure that there are no open items, unfinished procedures, unexplained tick marks, and unanswered questions in the working papers. The working papers should be consistent in all respects with the report and the financial information to which the report relates.

(e) If the work is challenged, the auditor may need to consider whether the person who performed the relevant work can provide any additional information to assist the firm in answering the specific questions put. Therefore, each working paper should contain the preparer's initials.

(f) Similarly, the firm may need to know when the work was done. Accordingly, each working paper should indicate the date when it was prepared.

(g) If the auditor includes in the working papers suggestions for modifying procedures for future audits, the auditor should make it clear that the procedures applied were adequate, and that the suggestions made for the future are made either in the interests of efficiency or in recognition of changed conditions.

(h) All documentation accumulated in the working papers during the audit that either is beyond the level required for audit purposes or has subsequently been superseded should be removed and destroyed.

6:2.2 General

SAS 230 states that 'working papers should record the auditors' planning, the nature, timing and extent of the audit procedures performed, and the conclusions drawn from the audit evidence obtained'. The auditor should plan and organise audit working papers in a manner that aids the most efficient and most economical execution of the audit. The auditor should avoid preparing or accumulating unnecessary working papers, and should not make extensive copies of accounting records.

   Section 6:2.4 provides details of what constitutes a good working paper. It is important that the auditor places emphasis on the quality of the working papers, ensuring that they contain the right material, rather than on quantity for quantity's sake.

6:2.3 Avoiding unnecessary papers

Before deciding to prepare a particular audit working paper the auditor should ensure that:

(a)   it is necessary to prepare the working paper, either because it will serve an essential or useful purpose in support of the report, or because it will provide information needed for tax purposes; and

(b)   it is not practicable for the client's staff to prepare the working paper, or for the auditor to make use of copies of papers that the client's staff (including internal auditors) have prepared as part of their regular duties.

For a particular audit working paper, the auditor should consider the following:

(a)   Whether the auditor can adapt last year's working paper or photocopy it and carry it forward to the current year.

(b)   Whether the working paper can be designed so that it can be used for both interim and final work.

(c)   What information might be useful in future years.

6:2.4 Contents

Each audit working paper should be headed with the following information:

(a)   The name of the client.

(b)   The period covered by the audit.

(c)   The subject matter.

(d)   The file reference (*see also* **Section 6:2.7**).

(e)   The initials of the member of the audit team who prepared it, and the date on which it was prepared.

(f)   In the case of a working paper prepared by the client, the date received and the initials of the audit team member who carried out the audit work thereon.

(g)   The initials of the member of the audit team who reviewed the working paper.

The quantity, nature, and content of the working papers will vary from one audit engagement to another. SAS 230 points out that the form of working papers will be affected by matters such as:

(a) the nature of the engagement;

(b) the form of the auditors' report;

(c) the nature and complexity of the entity's business;

(d) the nature and condition of the entity's accounting and internal control systems;

(e) the needs in the particular circumstances for direction, supervision and review of the work of members of the audit team; and

(f) the specific methodology and technology the auditors use.

6:2.5 Recording the results of audit work

When the auditor records conclusions on a working paper, the following should be considered:

(a) If the auditor has completed the audit procedures satisfactorily with no exceptions, this should be recorded on the working paper.

(b) If the auditor finds exceptions, these should be explained on the working paper so that the auditor can consider their implications both for the financial statements and for management.

(c) The audit opinion is expressed on the financial statements taken as a whole. Opinions in the working papers on individual assets and liabilities are not necessary and may not be appropriate.

6:2.6 Using working papers prepared by the client

Certain working papers that the auditor requires may already be prepared by the client's staff. The auditor should make arrangements, wherever possible, for copies of these to be made available. If clients prepare working papers that the auditor retains, their form should be agreed with the client at an early stage in the audit and this information included in the audit timetable.

When the client prepares working papers for the audit, the auditor should take care to ensure that they will give all the information required. All such working papers should be clearly identified as having been prepared by the client.

6:2.7 Filing and referencing

Audit working papers should be designed to suit the particular circumstances of each engagement. However, the same general approach to the arrangement of working papers is desirable to ensure uniformity of presentation. This applies whether papers are held manually or using technology.

A firm may find it useful to use standard audit working paper dividers or sections, numbering completed working papers serially in each section of the file and cross-referencing them. If working papers are intended to agree with, or support items appearing in, the financial statements or other working papers on the file, the auditors should prepare them so as to make agreement obvious without the necessity of further investigation and reconciliation.

6:2.8 Carrying forward

Whenever there is an advantage in doing so, the auditor should carry forward working papers from one audit to the next. Whenever an auditor adds information to analyses or memoranda, the auditor should do so in a manner that leaves no doubt about what was added and on what date.

The auditor should not bring working papers forward from a previous audit without reconsidering their contents in relation to the current work. The auditor should provide space on analyses carried forward for the initials of each person who updated or reviewed them.

Because the firm might need to refer to a working paper several years after an engagement has been completed, the auditor should maintain the files in a manner that makes this possible.

6:2.9 Physical control

SAS 230 requires auditors to adopt appropriate procedures for maintaining the confidentiality and safe custody of their working papers. Because they are confidential, audit working papers should be kept under the auditor's control at all times, both on the client's premises and in the firm's offices. The auditor should safeguard any confidential client information (e.g., directors' emoluments). It is also important that the auditor safeguards any information concerning the precise nature, extent and timing of the audit procedures (e.g., the detailed work programme) from client's staff. Special arrangements may be made in order to co-ordinate with the work of an internal audit department (refer to **Section 7:5**, 'Using the work of internal audit').

6:2.10 Subsequent changes

The auditor should ensure that all working papers are complete and in a proper condition for filing before the report is issued. Except as set out below the auditor should not, after the report is issued, change the working papers that relate to the auditing procedures performed and the conclusions reached.

It may be alleged after the report is issued that the working papers do not adequately support the opinion given in the report. This may be as a result of, e.g.:

(a)   a review of the working papers by another firm of auditors;

(b)   an investigation for a special purpose, such as a takeover bid;

(c)   an alleged misstatement of the reported figures; or

(d)   an investigation by, or disciplinary procedures of, the auditors' supervisory body.

If it appears that the working papers may be deficient, the engagement partner should consider whether this is because the auditor performed the relevant procedures but evidenced them insufficiently in the working papers. The auditor should consider obtaining legal advice on whether the working papers should be amended to reflect the work that was actually carried out or to explain if the engagement partner concludes that it would not have affected the decision to refer the report.

6:2.11 Retention

Working papers are the property of the auditors. All the working papers discussed in this section should be retained for a specified number of years from the date of the audit report to which they relate. After that period the working papers should be destroyed after the engagement partner has confirmed that they may be. The partner may issue instructions that they are to be retained for a longer period.

6:3 Notes of meetings and related matters

6:3.1 Policy

The auditor should make a proper file note of any meeting with clients, their advisers or other parties at which matters of significance in relation to the audit or other engagement objectives are discussed. This also applies to telephone conversations.

Normally, with the engagement partner's consent, the auditor should send a copy or summary of the note to the client or other representatives with whom the meeting was held. This will confirm what was discussed and agreed at the meeting, and serve as a reminder if action was agreed to be taken on a particular matter.

6:3.2 Content and approval

The following matters may need to be recorded:

(a)   The date of the meeting, where it took place and who was present.

(b)   The purpose of the meeting.

(c)   A summary of the principal points discussed, and a reference to any documents exchanged.

(d)   If contentious issues were discussed, and decisions made, the arguments advanced by the parties which led up to those decisions.

(e)   The conclusions of the meeting, and the nature of, and responsibility for further action.

Equivalent information should be recorded for telephone conversations.

The note should be clear and concise, and preferably written up immediately after the meeting or telephone conversation. The member of the firm who prepares the note should sign and date it. If significant matters were discussed, the other members of the firm present at the meeting should also review the note and, if they agree that it is a correct record, they should also sign and date it. The note should be initialled as approved by the senior representative of the firm present at the meeting. If the meeting was attended by the engagement manager in the absence of the engagement partner, a copy of the note should be passed immediately to the engagement partner.

6:3.3 Need to make the firm's position clear

If the auditor disagrees on a matter with a client or a client's advisers or another party, the records should show this. For example, if the auditor attends a meeting at which a document proposed to be published is discussed, and the auditor is not satisfied with the document, this should be made clear at the meeting. Sometimes others present at the meeting may ignore these views and state that they intend to publish the document anyway. In such circumstances, in addition to making the firm's attitude clear at the meeting, the auditor should:

(a)   make a full note of what took place, and of the view expressed by the auditor, as discussed above;

(b)   consider sending a letter to those concerned immediately after the meeting, confirming the views expressed at the meeting; and

(c)   in exceptional cases, and after having followed the consultation procedures set out in **Section 5:5**, 'Consultation and concurring reviews', consider whether anything further should be done (e.g., by means of an announcement to the press) to make the firm's position clear to the public.

6:4 Access to audit working papers

6:4.1 Introduction

Requests for access to audit files or working papers should be treated as falling into one of three categories:

(a)   third parties with a statutory or regulatory right of access, where the auditor should assist to the extent necessary;

(b)   those where the auditor has a practice generally to grant access, subject to conditions; and

(c)   others who are denied access.

This section summarises the general rules for responding to such requests and the key policy requirements and issues in each situation, and explains the limited exceptions possible in respect of (b) and (c) above.

6:4.2   General rules for responding to requests for access

(a)   **General policy on access.** The firm's general policy in response to third party requests for access should be not to give access unless the third party has enforceable rights or the firm can adopt appropriate risk management procedures.

(b)   **Oral representations.** The firm's policy should be that it must not give oral representations, statements or warranties about the work, audit report or matters arising after the date of the report – including any statement at a later date that the auditor stands by the audit report. Oral representations can be as damaging as providing access to working papers.

(c)   **Partner approval and consultation.** In all cases the engagement partner should approve access, only after reviewing the particular circumstances and applying the firm's policy. The following consultation procedures apply:

   (i)   where the policy is normally to grant access and there is no added risk, the engagement partner may grant access, subject to the appropriate conditions;

   (ii)   where the policy is normally to grant access but there is potentially added risk, the engagement partner should consult the review partner, or, where a review partner has not been appointed, another independent partner. Where the added risk is regarded as acceptable, the engagement partner may then decide to grant access. Where the risk is considered high the engagement partner should additionally seek legal advice;

   (iii) where the general policy is not to grant access, but where the auditor might consider an exception, legal advice should be sought;

   (iv)   legal advice should be sought where there is an enforceable right to access, to ensure the firm assists only to the extent that is necessary.

(d)   **Authorisation letters.** Unless there is an enforceable right of access/court order or it is a matter addressed in an engagement letter or a written agreement, e.g. a joint audit, the auditor should obtain the client's authorisation in writing before allowing third party access or rendering assistance.

(e)   **Timing of access.** Access to the audit files or working papers should normally only be allowed after all audit work has been completed. In a group audit the timing of access should be in line with that agreed in the group instructions. Possible exceptions to the general rule will be joint audits or due diligence, where there is a letter referring to the circumstances.

(f) **Prior review of audit files and working papers.** When access is granted the audit file and working papers should be reviewed by the engagement manager to remove information to which access should not be given. Where there is an enforceable right of access, the only documents that the auditor is entitled to remove are those that are privileged or do not fall within the specific enforceable right.

(g) **Copying information.** The third party can make notes during their review but should *not* copy the audit file or working papers. For this reason the third party's access should always be under the auditor's control. Those with an enforceable right of access may have a legal right to copies.

6:4.3 Third parties with an enforceable right of access

Third parties who in certain circumstances will have a statutory or regulatory right of access (an 'enforceable right') are:

- Department of Trade and Industry inspectors
- Police
- Serious Fraud Office (SFO)
- National Criminal Intelligence Service (NCIS)
- Customs & Excise
- Joint Monitoring Unit (JMU)
- Joint Disciplinary Scheme (JDS)
- Liquidators and receivers

The firm's policy should be that such parties should be given access to the audit file and working papers but only to the extent that the audit firm is obliged to assist and after consultation with legal advisers. Where possible, access should be limited and/or carefully controlled.

6:4.4 Third parties where the auditor's practice is to grant conditional access

(a) **Joint auditors.** The legal responsibilities of each firm are both joint and several and in order for each firm to form its own opinion on the financial statements reasonable access is required to the other firm's audit file and working papers. Conditions as to what constitutes reasonable access will usually be set out in writing, e.g. in the engagement letter or in a letter of arrangements.

(b) **Parent company auditors.** Subsidiary auditors have a legal and professional obligation to give parent company auditors 'information and explanations as they may reasonably require'. However, it may be possible to achieve this by means of attending a meeting or responding to a questionnaire. Access to the auditors audit file or working papers will not always be necessary. Where giving access could increase risk, the rules for consultation should be applied. Access should preferably be restricted to those audit working papers that the parent company auditors have requested, and that the manager has reviewed and that are approved for release.

(c) **Reporting accountants.** There are no legal or professional requirements for an auditor to make audit files or working papers in respect of a client or former client available to the reporting accountant of a third party. However, where there is involvement of reporting accountants for Stock Exchange of due diligence purposes, generally the auditor should, subject to obtaining the appropriate authorisation and release letters, comply with such requests. This is because the ICAEW, in an effort to help companies and their advisers, has established conditions in which this can be done. These conditions involve obtaining a release letter counter-signed by the third party and, where relevant, its accountants, stating that the auditor has no duty to them and, as far as the third party is concerned, indemnifying the auditor against any claim that might result from allowing such access.

6:4.5 Third parties who are denied access

In the following three situations there are no legal or professional requirements about access and accordingly the firm's policy should be that access should, except as explained below, be denied:

(a) **Successor auditors.** If the client cannot provide accounting information the partner may allow access to working papers providing accounting information but *not* those relating to audit work. Where the successor auditor requires a meeting the partner should be aware that the firm can be equally liable for an oral statement made at a meeting.

(b) **Investing company auditors** (where the client is treated as an associated undertaking). If the client cannot provide accounting information the partner may allow access to papers providing accounting information but *not* those relating to audit work.

(c) **Representatives of the client/any other third party.** The auditor's response to requests from representatives of the client/any other third party for access or to attend meetings must, in all cases, be that they should contact the client or former client for the information that they require.

Access to accounting information provided to successor auditors or investing company auditors should be accompanied by a letter stating that ownership of the working papers remains with the firm.

6:4.6 Exceptions

There will be occasions when even though the firm's general policy is to allow access with conditions, the engagement partner is concerned at the risks involved. The rules for consultation must be followed. Where the firm retains the discretion to do so, the firm may decide that access will not be granted.

There will also be occasions when there may be a perceived advantage to the firm in granting access to third parties who would generally be met with a rebuttal. The advantage may, for example, be a client relationship benefit or from enabling the client or the third party to be better informed. However, in all such cases, the risks must be weighed carefully and consideration given to other ways in which appropriate information can be provided. There must also be appropriate release letters in instances where s. 310 of Companies Act 1985 does not apply. The consultation procedures must be followed.

Chapter 7

Involvement of others in the audit

7:1 Involvement of others in the audit

7:1.1 Introduction

As explained in the Introduction to this work, under the heading 'Terminology', the Manual refers to departments of the audit firm separate from the main audit function. This chapter provides guidance on the matters to be considered when liaising with specialist departments within the firm and, if necessary, with experts from outside the firm. Firms may be organised in different ways and there may be no need for liaison with specialists outside the audit department.

7:1.2 Accountancy work for audit clients

Section 7:2, 'Accountancy work for audit clients', describes the procedures that a firm should follow to ensure that, when the firm undertakes accountancy work for audit clients, the audit work is independent.

7:1.3 Specialist computer staff

Section 7:3, 'Specialist computer staff', describes the relationship which should exist between the auditor and computer specialists.

7:1.4 Tax specialists

Section 7:4 discusses the role of the tax specialist in relation to the auditor.

7:1.5 Using the work of internal audit

Section 7:5 describes the relationship which should exist between the auditor and the client's own internal audit department, where this exists.

7:1.6 Using the work of an expert

The guidance in **Section 7:6**, 'Using the work of an expert', applies to experts both within the firm and from outside.

7:1.7 Joint audits

Section 7:7, 'Joint audits', sets out the guidance on the procedures to be followed on joint audits, where each firm's responsibility is joint and several.

7:2 Accountancy work for audit clients

7:2.1 Introduction

This section discusses matters that affect audit work when the firm undertakes accountancy services for audit clients, whether incorporated or unincorporated, in particular the need to retain independence.

7:2.2 Ethical guidance on independence

One of the fundamental principles in the ethical guidance issued by the professional bodies, is that a member should:

> *strive for objectivity in all professional and business judgements. Objectivity is the state of mind which has regard to all considerations relevant to the task in hand but no other.*

The guidance goes on to point out that:

> *The need for objectivity is particularly evident in the case of a practising accountant carrying out an audit or some other reporting role where his professional opinion is likely to affect rights between parties and the decisions they take.*

There is also guidance for occasions when objectivity may be threatened or appear to be threatened when a firm provides other services, including accounting services for audit clients.

7:2.3 Accountancy work and audit independence

To comply with the guidance in the case of a listed company or other public interest company, a firm should not participate in the preparation of the client's accounts and accounting records save in relation to assistance of a routine clerical nature or in emergency situations. Such assistance might include, e.g., work on the finalisation of statutory accounts, including consolidations and tax provisions. The scale and nature of such work should be regularly reviewed. However, a firm will frequently be asked by private company audit clients to provide a much broader accounting service than is appropriate for a public company audit client, and this may include preparing the accounting records. Such accounting assistance does not in any way constitute an audit. Accordingly, when a firm carries out accountancy work for audit clients, it should ensure that:

(a)   the client accepts full responsibility for all accounting records and documentation;

(b)   the firm does not assume the role of management conducting the operations of an enterprise;

(c)   the firm's objectivity in carrying out the audit work is not impaired; and

(d)   the accountancy work used to support the audit opinion is reviewed by a manager or partner sufficiently independent of the preparation of the financial statements.

The engagement partner should decide who is to perform the accountancy work and the audit work and how this is to be co-ordinated in order that the work carried out to enable the firm to express an audit opinion is adequate but not excessive. If there are significant risks to the firm associated with the audit engagement, it will be preferable for the staff engaged in the accountancy work not to be employed on the audit.

Normally, it will be possible for the review of both the accountancy and audit work to be conducted by the same manager. The engagement partner should, however, consider whether the involvement, if any, of the manager in the performance or review of the accountancy work means that the audit work, or aspects of it, needs to be reviewed in detail by another manager, or the engagement partner, who is not so involved. A separate review may be necessary if there are significant risks to the firm.

To assess the risk to the firm the engagement partner should take into account the client's circumstances, including, e.g., the extent of any minority interests and external finance. An owner-managed company without significant external finance will normally not pose particular risk to the firm for this purpose.

7:2.3.1 Documentation

Each firm should develop its own procedures for controlling the quality of the accounting services provided. Such procedures are outside the scope of this Manual but may well include special work programmes.

7:2.4 Consultation

If a firm is asked by a client, or by a prospective client, to carry out work which might call the firm's independence into question, the engagement partner should consider carefully whether the engagement should be declined. This may warrant following the consultation procedures set out in **Section 5:5**, 'Consultation and concurring reviews' before a decision is taken on acceptance, or otherwise.

7:2.5 Audit procedures

If the auditor is required to form an opinion on financial statements that the firm has prepared, the detailed work performed in preparing them will, in most cases, provide the auditor with some audit assurance, and reduce the degree of assurance required from substantive audit procedures, e.g.:

(a)   re-performance, as part of the accountancy work, of a calculation that was originally performed by a member of the firm's staff; or

(b)   examining documentation, if the relevant evidence has already been examined, and that examination recorded, by a member of the firm as part of the accountancy work.

7:2.5.1 Working papers

Before taking audit assurance from accountancy work that the firm has undertaken, the auditor should ensure that:

(a)   a complete file of audit working papers that adequately supports the audit opinion is prepared and independently reviewed, as discussed in **Section 7:2.3**, list item (d); and

(b)   the accountancy working papers contain sufficient evidence to justify that reliance.

7:2.6   Preparation of periodic management accounts

A firm may be asked to prepare periodic management accounts for an audit client's own internal use. These management accounts may not always include all the disclosures that might otherwise be desirable. The firm should draw this fact to the attention of readers of the accounts either by way of note to the management accounts or in the report on them. The accounts should include the following wording:

> **These accounts are for internal management purposes only and they do not include all disclosures that may be required to comply with generally accepted accounting principles.**

If the client requests that a firm does not report on the management accounts which the firm has been asked to prepare, the firm should ensure that the terms of the work and the responsibilities of both the client and the firm are clearly set out in the engagement letter. Accounts to which no report is to be attached should state clearly at the foot of each page:

> **Unaudited accounts prepared for management purposes.**

7:3   Specialist computer staff

7:3.1   Introduction

Whenever a client has computer-based systems the audit partner should ensure that the audit team includes staff, or has access to staff, with appropriate knowledge of such systems. Where this expertise is held in a separate computer audit group the audit team should liaise with computer specialists to ensure that the audit is conducted in the most effective and efficient manner, that the client receives a high quality of client service and that opportunities for adding value are identified. This liaison should normally start before the audit strategy is determined. Depending on the strategy, the audit team may need to liaise further with computer specialists to:

(a)   assess computer security;

(b)   assess control risk;

(c)   develop the substantive test programme;

(d)   carry out substantive testing; and

(e)   report findings to management.

7:3.2 Division of responsibilities

When determining the strategy, the auditor should consider the extent of use and the complexity of the client's computer systems. The engagement partner and engagement manager should therefore also determine, at this stage, the probable nature and extent of involvement of computer specialists. If computer specialists are to be involved, they should attend the relevant strategy meetings.

The engagement manager and the computer specialist manager should discuss the extent to which audit staff or computer specialists should be responsible for obtaining information on the computer environment and the systems. Computer specialists should normally be involved in more complex situations, and where the client is new or there have been major changes in the systems.

However, the engagement manager should consider whether to consult computer specialists in less complex situations (e.g., where the client service objectives include addressing computer security, implementation of systems or use of microcomputers, or where the client has an expectation of the involvement of computer specialists).

If computer specialists are involved, the engagement manager should ensure that the extent of the work, the budget and an appropriate timetable are agreed. The audit team should work closely with the computer specialists during the assignment.

When part of the audit work is carried out by computer specialists, the specialists are responsible for the technical aspects of that work and for drawing conclusions relevant to the task performed. However, because the engagement partner and the engagement manager are ultimately responsible for the audit and therefore should be satisfied with all conclusions drawn by computer specialists, they should:

(a)   agree that part of the work to be carried out by computer specialists;

(b)   agree with a computer specialist partner whether the work carried out by the computer specialists should be supervised by a computer specialist partner;

(c)   apply the conclusions drawn by computer specialists from the work they have carried out to the remaining audit work to be performed.

7:3.3 Reporting to management

If a computer specialist is involved in work that gives rise to matters that should be reported to the client, the policy set out in **Section 12:1**, 'Audit reporting to the board and to management', applies. Matters to be reported should be discussed with the engagement manager as soon as possible and should be reviewed and approved by the engagement partner before they are presented to the client.

7:3.4 Control of time

If computer specialists are involved in significant amounts of audit work, a budget for that work should be prepared, and approved by the engagement partner. The engagement manager should ensure that the budget is included in the overall audit budget and that the computer audit costs are taken into account when billing the work.

Once a budget is set for significant work to be carried out by computer specialists, the computer specialist manager should inform the engagement manager of any significant variations from estimated costs that arise during the course of the work. The computer specialists should prepare a report for the engagement manager describing the work carried out, and the actual costs, and explaining any significant variances from the agreed budget.

7:4 Tax specialists

7:4.1 Introduction

The auditor's responsibility extends to all aspects of a client's financial statements, including taxation matters. The objective should be to gain an adequate understanding of the client's tax position and carry out the audit of taxation as effectively and efficiently as possible.

It is the client's responsibility to prepare financial statements in which the tax liabilities and related disclosures are accurate and complete. However, the client will often engage a firm to calculate the tax charge and provisions for inclusion in the financial statements. A firm is also often engaged to prepare, submit and agree tax computations on behalf of audit clients.

Consideration of tax matters will often call for the expertise of tax specialists, and it is therefore important that there should be effective liaison between the audit team and tax specialists. This is particularly important when audit clients have engaged the firm to perform taxation services.

Additionally, the auditor should always be conscious of the possible tax effect of the client's business plans and of any other client matters which come to the auditor's notice through the audit work. The audit team should therefore ensure that the tax specialists are kept up to date on these matters. Similarly, specialist tax partners and managers should keep the audit practice informed of any tax-planning discussions or other matters relevant to the client's affairs that come to their notice.

7:4.2 Planning the audit of taxation

The engagement manager and the tax manager should consider at the strategy stage the division of responsibilities for the audit of taxation and, if appropriate, for the collection of information for, and the preparation of, the tax computations. This should be approved by the engagement partner and, if necessary, the tax partner.

The specific matters to be considered at the strategy stage include the following:

(a) Whether there are any particular matters relating to the client's tax affairs that might affect the audit strategy and the substantive tests.

(b) Agreeing the allocation of individual responsibilities between the members of the audit team and tax staff in relation to the audit of tax provisions.

(c) Ascertaining any other information that will be required by the tax specialists, and determining how this will be obtained.

(d) Setting the timetable for the tax specialists to review the tax provisions in the financial statements.

(e) Ensuring that the client will be providing taxation schedules and detailed analyses of profit and loss account items, as a basis for the preparation of the computations, within the proposed timescale.

If the audit team carries out the work to audit the tax provisions, that work should be reviewed by a tax manager.

7:4.3 VAT and customs duties

Whereas the auditor is expected to have a knowledge of VAT and customs regulations sufficient to plan and perform the audit, members of the audit team may not know detailed rules concerning, e.g., special partial exemption methods. To help the auditor identify situations where specialist knowledge is needed either for the purposes of the audit or to assist the client, firms may find it helpful to prepare a suitable VAT audit risk checklist. Guidance on the audit of VAT is given in **Section 9:26**, 'Value added tax'.

7:4.4 PAYE

Similarly the auditor may need for audit purposes to carry out audit work on the PAYE account and will in the event of matters arising bear in mind the conditions that might give rise to an adverse finding on a PAYE inspection. In cases of doubt the engagement manager should consult a PAYE specialist.

7:5 Using the work of internal audit

7:5.1 Introduction

SAS 500 states that 'external auditors should consider the activities of internal audit, and their effect, if any, on external audit procedures'.

Many audit clients have an internal audit function, the responsibilities and effectiveness of which vary according to the professional competence of the internal auditors, the scope of their duties and the standing of the persons to whom they report. At the one extreme, an internal audit department might operate with few or no restrictions and report to the chief executive or to the board of directors on a wide range of matters. At the other extreme, internal audit might be restricted to routine duties and report to management responsible for the preparation of financial statements, without any access to the board.

Viewed from the perspective of the external auditor, an internal audit function can be an important part of a client's internal control. It can provide assurance to management that the accounting systems, internal accounting controls and management review procedures are operating effectively and that reliable financial information is generated. Internal audit may also provide assurance as to the effectiveness of operating controls exercised by management.

The auditor should assess the effectiveness of internal audit as part of the assessment of the control environment and take the conclusions into account when determining the audit strategy and the substantive testing plan. Effective co-operation with a properly organised internal audit function can often result in significant reductions in the extent of the audit work as well as improving client service. The guidance in this section complements that set out in SAS 500, 'Considering the work of internal audit'.

7:5.2 Definition

For the purpose of this section the terms 'internal audit' and 'internal auditors' are used to describe those persons employed by the client's management to perform some or all of the following functions:

(a) **Internal control**: In this role internal audit determines and reports on whether systems and controls are appropriately designed and are functioning effectively, having regard to the risks. This will normally involve carrying out tests of controls and substantive testing on a routine basis. Many clients, in both the public and private sectors, consider this function to be the main responsibility of their internal audit department.

(b) **Review of budgetary control and management information systems**: The effectiveness of management depends to a large extent on the adequacy and reliability of its budgetary control and management information systems. This is particularly the case where management relies heavily on systems for day-to-day control of business operations because of dynamic and fast changing business conditions (e.g., in financial or capital markets) or because a high volume of transactions is processed daily.

Therefore, management needs to ensure that adequate information systems are in place at appropriate levels for decision-making purposes. Internal audit can be used to examine these systems and ascertain whether management is receiving relevant and reliable information, at the right time, to monitor the business and on which to base important decisions.

(c) **Compliance with policies, plans, procedures, laws and regulations**: Management is responsible for establishing systems designed to ensure compliance with policies, plans, procedures, laws and regulations which could have a significant impact on operations. Internal auditors are sometimes made responsible for determining whether the organisation is in compliance with such matters and for ensuring that exceptions are identified and followed up. This function often assumes greater importance in clients which are regulated and operate, e.g., under financial services legislation and rules.

(d) **Operational and 'value for money' audits**: In some clients management routinely uses internal audit to enquire into certain aspects of operations. This usually involves an assessment of whether established objectives and goals conform with those of the organisation and whether they have been met. Often, operational audit extends to reviewing the economy and efficiency with which resources are employed, to identify such conditions as under-utilised facilities, non-productive work, procedures which are not cost justified, and overstaffing or understaffing.

(e) **Special audits or investigations**: Internal audit may also be required to carry out special investigations on behalf of management. For example, internal audit can be used as a resource for the board of directors and senior management to perform special audits in confidential areas such as potential acquisitions, asset disposals and suspected fraud, and to carry out other special investigations.

For the purposes of this section internal audit does not include those persons who, although described as internal auditors, only perform, as part of their normal duties, routine internal accounting control procedures, such as reconciliations.

The mix of internal audit responsibilities is properly determined by the board, a board committee or senior management in the light of the needs of the client, senior management's style and the resources allocated to the internal audit function. In some clients, operating efficiency will be the first priority; e.g., in a large manufacturing group it is more likely that internal audit will concern itself primarily with operational matters. In other clients, ensuring the proper performance of procedures for the prevention and detection of fraud will be more important. In financial services clients, internal audit is more likely to concentrate on security and control procedures. The nature and scope of internal audit should always reflect the requirements of senior management and the expected benefits and costs.

7:5.3 Co-ordination with internal auditors

There are a number of different ways in which the auditor can work effectively with internal audit to improve audit efficiency and client service. For the purpose of the guidance that follows it is helpful to distinguish broadly between two principal ways:

(a)   Internal auditors' work may help to improve control effectiveness and thus reduce the risk of material misstatement. By using their work the auditor may be able to change the nature and extent of the work of the external audit team on assessing control effectiveness and on substantive testing.

(b)   Internal auditors may work under the auditor's direct supervision on portions of the overall audit coverage.

Both these methods of co-ordination may be used on a particular engagement and in practice there can be overlaps between the two. The objective when the auditor determines the audit strategy should be to maximise the extent to which the auditor can co-ordinate the external and internal auditors' work to provide the maximum service to the client.

7:5.4 Assessing the internal auditors

SAS 500 states that 'the external auditors should obtain a sufficient understanding of internal audit activities to assist in planning the audit and developing an effective audit approach'.

Before deciding to use the work of internal auditors, the auditor should assess the following factors that contribute to its overall quality:

(a)   The internal auditors' independence and objectivity.

(b)   The attitude of management to their reports.

(c)   Their technical knowledge and professional competence.

(d)   The professional standards, including quality control procedures, applied in their work.

This is particularly important on new audit engagements where the auditor does not have prior knowledge of, or experience in, using the work of the internal auditors concerned, or on engagements where there have been significant changes in the internal audit function. As a minimum, on each audit the auditor should reassess previous findings in the light of up-to-date knowledge.

In groups of companies, internal audit will normally be organised as a central function and it will therefore be necessary for the preliminary assessment to be carried out wholly or primarily by the parent company auditor. The auditor should set out arrangements for liaison with internal audit in the group audit instructions.

Certain organisations subcontract their internal audit functions to third parties. In these circumstances the auditor should still consider the matters set out in **Sections 7:5.4.1** to **7:5.4.3.2** if proposing to use the work of internal audit. If internal audit work is carried out by members of the firm, the auditor should ensure that professional requirements are complied with, e.g. they do not form part of the audit engagement team, and should subject their work to the same assessment as that of any other internal auditors.

7:5.4.1 Independence and objectivity

The level within the organisation to which the internal auditors report the results of their work, and the level to which they report administratively, are indications of the importance the client attaches to the internal audit function.

For maximum effectiveness, the internal audit function should have direct access to, and freedom to report to, senior management, including the chief executive, the board of directors and, where one exists, the audit committee.

To determine the extent to which the internal audit function is independent and objective, the auditor should consider the following:

(a) **Autonomy**: The auditor should ascertain the extent to which the internal auditors have the authority to carry out such work as they consider necessary (with access to all relevant records) without first obtaining the permission of senior management.

(b) **Groups**: In groups, internal auditors will often be independent of subsidiary company management, reporting to group management. Although this might appear to increase the independence of internal audit when viewed in the context of the subsidiary audit, the actual independence of the internal audit will depend on the circumstances, and the auditor will need to assess it.

(c) **Operating responsibilities**: The independence and objectivity of the internal auditors may be impaired if they are involved in carrying out routine control tasks, such as reconciliation procedures or the authorising of transactions, which are part of the system of internal accounting controls. In some clients, internal auditors are used to dealing with problems such as breakdowns in accounting systems. This could, but will not necessarily, impair the independence and objectivity of those so engaged.

(d) **Development of systems**: Internal audit can have a valuable role in reviewing and commenting on systems as they are being developed and the auditor may find its systems documentation and review comments useful. The auditor should nevertheless assess whether, in relation to particular systems changes, internal audit's independence and objectivity are impaired.

The auditor should obtain evidence of internal audit's independence and objectivity by talking to the internal auditors, by discussion with management and by observation.

7:5.4.2 Management attitudes

Internal audit reports should be sent to managers who have a direct responsibility for the unit or function being audited and who have the authority to take action on internal audit recommendations. The auditor should carefully consider management's attitude to internal audit reports, including whether the action taken in response to those reports is both timely and appropriate. The internal audit reports will often acknowledge the action taken, or proposed, by management. Failure to act upon important findings in reports may not preclude the auditor from using the work of the internal auditors, but it could cast doubt upon their value in improving control effectiveness.

7:5.4.3 Technical knowledge and professional competence

7:5.4.3.1 Personnel and awareness of company policy

The way in which the internal audit function is staffed will vary in practice. For example, it might be comprised of:

(a)   a permanent team of professional internal auditors; or

(b)   a group largely dependent on internal transfers of line management, not necessarily with a financial background; or

(c)   management trainees who will move into management after a period in internal audit.

The auditor should determine whether there are sufficient suitably qualified and experienced auditors to meet the objectives of the internal audit function. The auditor should consider matters such as: the level of education attained; relevant work experience; specialised skills (e.g., computer auditing or industry expertise); participation in training programmes; and professional qualifications.

The auditor should review relevant company policy and procedures manuals, internal audit manuals and other technical guidance, and assess the internal auditors' awareness of such material. This awareness might be obtained through training programmes and by attendance at regular staff meetings. The internal auditors' knowledge of the systems of control and the business generally will be indicative of their knowledge and competence.

7:5.4.3.2 Professional standards and quality control procedures

The auditor should review the scope and objectives of the internal auditors' work, and consider whether it is carried out with due professional care (e.g., whether it is subjected to adequate standards of planning, control, recording and review). The auditor might obtain further evidence of appropriate standards from, e.g., the existence of internal audit manuals, internal audit plans, quality control reviews and follow-up arrangements.

Quality control procedures operated by internal audit should cover matters such as:

(a)   Recruitment and training of staff.

(b)   Assignment of staff to projects.

(c)   Supervision of work.

(d)   Post-project reviews of work.

Reports issued by the internal auditors are normally a good indication of the extent to which the internal auditors are effective in carrying out their work. Consequently, the auditor should ascertain whether the reports:

(a)   state the scope, purpose, extent and conclusions of each internal audit assignment;

(b)   contain all the recommendations of substance arising from the audit; and

(c)   are of a quality that evidences the competence of the internal auditors and the extent of the quality control procedures operated.

7:5.5 Planning

The objective in working with internal audit should be to develop an effective working relationship with sufficient understanding of each other's working practices and requirements. The auditor should encourage internal audit to adopt working practices similar to those of the auditor and to codify its procedures in an internal audit manual, but should recognise that it may have different priorities.

It will often be advantageous to liaise on a regular basis and to plan together to help ensure that internal audit's schedule is as helpful as possible to the external audit strategy. This might, e.g., include keeping up to date with internal audit reports and action taken by management, and agreeing a common timetable for the completion and review of audit-related work. However, there may be circumstances where only limited liaison is possible, even though internal audit's effectiveness as a part of the control environment is unimpaired.

The auditor should consider at both the strategy and the detailed planning stages whether:

(a)   the work of internal auditors can be used when assessing control risk; and/or

(b)   arrangements should be made for internal auditors to work under the auditor's direct supervision.

The auditor should assess the potential for using the work of internal audit when determining audit strategy, in conjunction with consideration of the extent to which the auditor needs to obtain assurance from the effectiveness of the client's controls to reduce substantive testing. Regardless of whether the auditor decides that it is possible to use their work, it should be considered whether the internal auditors can assist the audit process through working under direct supervision of the external auditor, either on tests of the effectiveness of controls or on substantive tests.

7:5.5.1 Audit strategy

When developing the strategy for a client with an internal audit function, the auditor should normally:

(a)   discuss with senior management and the chief internal auditor the overall purpose of the internal audit function and the scope of its work;

(b)   consider the potential effectiveness of the internal audit function in enhancing control;

(c)   subject to (a) and (b) above, make a preliminary assessment of the audit areas where the auditor will be able either to use the internal auditors' work or to have internal auditors assist with the auditor's work, and consider the audit arrangements that will be necessary;

(d)   read all the significant internal audit reports to obtain information on matters of audit interest, e.g. in relation to the different functions set out in the listing in **Section 7:5.2**, as appropriate. Examples of such matters include:

  (i)   conditions that might indicate the existence of risks of fraud or error;

  (ii)   problem areas and unresolved matters which might require audit adjustment or disclosure;

  (iii)   comments made by internal auditors on the operations of the client, or on other business matters that might assist the auditor in assessing the control environment, in carrying out analytical reviews, or in reporting any findings to management.

The auditor should also consider the following matters:

(a)   The existence of factors indicating an increased risk to the firm.

(b)   The number, size and distribution of accounting locations and the location of internal control functions.

(c)   The audit tasks which may have been carried out by the internal auditors in the previous year, and whether the auditor needs to rotate such tasks between the external and the internal auditors (this could also apply at the STP level).

(d)   The degree of the external auditor's control over the internal auditors' work.

(e)   The client's expectation that the external auditor's work will be co-ordinated with that of the internal auditors.

The engagement partner should approve all decisions to make significant use of the internal auditors' work or have them work under direct supervision of the external auditor as part of the strategy. The former is dealt with in more detail in **Sections 7:5.5.2** and **7:5.6** and the latter is dealt with in more detail in **Section 7:5.7**.

7:5.5.2 *Control risk*

The auditor should assess internal audit's contribution to enhancing control risk in relation to each relevant control objective, in conjunction with other applicable controls. The auditor should in particular consider the following:

(a)   Sometimes the auditor may decide that the control environment, including the internal audit function, is so strong that the auditor can obtain all of the evidence on the effectiveness of control from assessing the quality of internal audit and from reviewing their work. Conversely, a weak internal audit function means that the auditor is unable to take credit for its contribution to control effectiveness, and will have to test the effectiveness of control or rely on substantive testing to gain the assurance required.

(b)   The effectiveness of internal audit might be important when obtaining assurance for the application(s) subjected to a more detailed assessment of control risk. The auditor should, however, consider whether the internal auditors' work is adequate to support the general conclusions on the effectiveness of control. If, for example, significant control objectives have not been adequately addressed by the internal auditors, the auditor may have to perform additional procedures concerning those objectives.

(c)   When the auditor develops substantive tests for a particular audit area, including on a multi-location audit, the auditor should establish internal audit's coverage of the audit area, taking into account the risk of misstatement and the risk of breakdown or change in control since internal audit's last work on the area. If internal audit has not audited an area in the current period or has not done so for some time the auditor might still be able to take some credit for their work. However, the assessment will also have to take into account other aspects of the control environment and the auditor's prior-year experience, including knowledge from substantive testing in prior years.

(d)   In areas where there is a high inherent risk of material misstatement, the auditor may still be able to make use of the work of internal audit provided that the auditor is satisfied with the quality of work carried out. However, the auditor should also carry out substantive tests to enable a conclusion to be formed.

7:5.6 Audit evidence

Where the auditor takes credit for the work of internal audit in assessing control effectiveness the auditor should obtain sufficient reliable evidence of the quality of its work. The extent of evidence required is a matter of professional judgement and it might vary from, e.g., reviewing internal audit reports and observation and enquiry as to internal audit's quality, to detailed examination of its working papers and even re-performance of part of its work.

The auditor should consider the following specific factors:

(a)   The risk of material misstatement of the relevant account balance or class of transactions.

(b)   The level of judgement required to perform the planned audit work.

(c)   The results of the preliminary assessment of internal audit.

(d)   The evidence obtained of the effective operation of internal audit's own quality control procedures.

(e)   The extent to which internal audit's findings and conclusions correlate with the auditor's own findings and conclusions in other areas.

If the auditor considers it necessary to examine evidence of the work carried out by internal audit, the objectives should be to determine whether:

(a)   the scope of the work was relevant to the audit objectives;

(b)   sufficient reliable audit evidence was obtained to provide a reasonable basis for the conclusions reached;

(c)   reported conclusions were consistent with the results of the work carried out.

In circumstances where the auditor wishes to make some use of the work of internal audit, but has reservations from the preliminary assessment of internal audit, the auditor should consider whether it is necessary to re-perform some of the tests of controls over transactions or account balances that internal audit examined (or, alternatively, examine similar transactions or account balances) and compare the results of these tests with the results of its work. The auditor should then compare these conclusions with the conclusions recorded by the internal auditors and, if their conclusions cannot be supported, extend the substantive testing accordingly.

7:5.7 Internal auditors working under direct supervision of the auditor

In addition to using the work of internal audit as a part of the assessment of control risk, the auditor may use internal auditors to carry out work that the auditor would otherwise have to do in accordance with the audit strategy. In this case, the internal auditors will be acting primarily as individuals rather than as members of the client's internal audit function. Accordingly, the policies and procedures of internal audit and its status within the organisation are of less significance than the assessment of the qualifications, competence and objectivity of each individual assigned to the auditor.

The extent to which the auditor makes use of the internal auditors' work in this way might vary in practice from individuals joining the audit team and, for example, reporting to the team leader on a daily basis, to carrying out segments of the audit work on a semi-autonomous basis (e.g., performing a circularisation or attending a stock count). Where the auditor uses internal auditors in this way, it is preferable that they should use the firm's techniques and programmes. If the auditor agrees with management and with the internal auditors that they use their own techniques and programmes, the auditor should be satisfied that such techniques and programmes will provide sufficient relevant and reliable audit evidence.

If the internal auditors' work is carried out initially under their own supervisory and quality control function, the auditor should consider whether these procedures are adequate (e.g., whether the individuals concerned are adequately versed in the details of auditing techniques used by the auditor and attach appropriate significance to the inter-relationships of various procedures in the audit approach). The auditor should ensure that important judgements regarding the scope of audit work, the evaluation of findings and the conclusions are reviewed and concurred with by members of the external auditor's audit team. Ultimately the internal auditors should work under the auditor's supervision and the auditor will be responsible for the quality of their work.

The auditor should not normally arrange for this form of assistance from internal auditors on substantive testing in the following cases:

(a)   Where there is a significant risk of misstatement arising from the possibility of distortion by management.

(b)   When carrying out tests to confirm management representations.

(c)   In sensitive areas, such as related-party transactions, or 'questionable' payments.

When internal auditors work under the auditor's direct supervision the auditor should:

(a)   instruct them on the application of audit procedures, if appropriate;

(b)   normally provide them with copies of standard documentation, and, if necessary, with specimen working papers;

(c)   ensure that they are properly briefed as to the specified objectives of the work assigned to them and the matters which they should bring to the auditor's attention;

(d)   review their completed working papers to determine whether these adequately document the work performed and conclusions reached, and whether the audit tests, audit evidence, evaluation of errors, and other matters are sufficient and appropriate in the circumstances; and

(e)   consider the need to examine some of the transactions or balances that they examined, and compare these results with theirs to satisfy the auditor that their work has been properly performed. This will not normally be necessary. If the auditor has reservations about the work carried out or if the audit area is of such significance that it is considered necessary to carry out some re-performance, the auditor should reconsider whether to use internal auditors on other important work on the same audit and in future years.

7:5.8 Reporting to the board and to management

The existence of an internal audit department does not absolve the auditor from the responsibility to report to the board and to management significant findings from the audit. Therefore, the guidance set out in **Section 12:1**, 'Audit reporting to the board and to management', still applies.

Where there is an internal audit function, the auditor should consider adapting the reporting procedures, in consultation with senior management and with internal audit, to ensure that the auditor addresses the client's requirements and concerns and achieves an effective working relationship with internal audit. The auditor should consider the need to discuss findings initially with the internal auditors and to give them copies of reports. Often internal audit will consider this an important courtesy, but in some cases management may require the auditor to report to it direct without reference to internal audit.

If internal audit has reported weaknesses in internal controls which are relevant to the accounting period being audited, the auditor should consider whether there is a need to draw management's attention to the report of the internal auditors and/or whether to explain the weaknesses in the auditor's report. The action to be taken in such cases should be agreed in advance with management and internal audit. However, the auditor should normally report a matter if there is a significant weakness and if the auditor considers management's response to internal audit's report is inadequate. The auditor should also report if it is part of internal audit's role to follow up reports of weaknesses and ensure effective action, and it is not doing this properly.

7:5.9 Working papers

In all cases where internal audit has a significant impact on the audit strategy, the auditor should record this for the file, and in the engagement letter or in a separate letter to the client. In particular, the working papers should normally include:

(a) A sufficient summary of the internal audit department's activities and responsibilities.

(b) The preliminary assessment of the internal audit department.

(c) The audit planning discussions with the chief internal auditor and the arrangements for co-ordinating the work of the external and internal auditors.

(d) Matters of audit interest in internal audit reports and the conclusions concerning them.

(e) Evidence of the work assessing the effectiveness of internal audit as a part of internal control, together with a record of its work for which the auditor is taking specific credit.

(f) Evidence of any work performed by internal auditors under the external auditor's direct supervision, and the review of their work and conclusions thereon, including any further work carried out to re-perform their work. Normally this can conveniently be recorded on the auditor's own copies of the working papers prepared by the internal auditors.

It may be helpful to obtain copies of internal audit working papers that are considered relevant to the audit work. The auditor should ensure that the name of the preparer is clearly recorded on each working paper, and should add the date it was received and the name of the audit team member who reviewed it, together with its audit significance.

The engagement partner may agree that the internal auditors establish 'common user' files. These are files maintained by internal audit and to which both external and internal auditors have access. They should be subject to the following conditions:

(a) Internal audit should agree not to make the common user files available to others within the client, without the external auditor's prior consent.

(b) The only working papers of the firm included in the common user files should normally be those relating to the understanding and assessment of accounting systems. However, the common user files may contain copies, if appropriate, of client documents, such as documents of incorporation, trust deeds and contracts, or extracts thereof.

(c) The auditor's own working papers should explain the audit work performed with regard to the working papers in the common user files.

Where common user files are not maintained, the auditor may, with the prior approval of the engagement partner, allow the internal auditors access to the firm's working papers and files, provided that these are directly relevant to their work. A member of the firm's staff should normally be present whenever such documents are made available to internal audit.

7:6 Using the work of an expert

7:6.1 Introduction

This section discusses the auditor's responsibilities when using the work of an expert as audit evidence. Reference should also be made to SAS 520, 'Using the work of an expert'.

Although education and experience enable the auditor to be knowledgeable about business matters in general, the auditor is not expected to have the expertise of a person trained for, or qualified to engage in, the practice of another profession or occupation (e.g., an actuary, valuer or engineer).

The term 'expert', for the purpose of this section, refers to a person or organisation possessing special skills, knowledge and experience in a particular field other than accounting and auditing. Such an expert, or 'specialist', may be employed, or specially engaged, either by the client or by the firm.

7:6.2 Determining the need to use the work of an expert

During the audit the auditor may seek to obtain audit evidence in the form of reports, opinions, valuations, and statements of an expert. For example, the auditor may need:

(a) Valuations of certain types of assets such as land and buildings, plant and machinery, works of art, precious stones or intangibles.

(b) Corroboration of quantities or physical condition of assets (e.g., minerals stored in stockpiles, underground ore or petroleum reserves and the remaining useful lives of plant and machinery).

(c) Confirmation of amounts using specialised techniques or methods (e.g., accounting for pension costs based on actuarial calculations).

(d) Measurement of work completed, and to be completed, on contracts in progress for the purpose of revenue recognition.

(e) Legal opinions concerning interpretations of agreements, statutes and regulations, and pending or threatened litigation.

The expert may be engaged either by management, or by the auditor, with the consent of management. If management is unable or unwilling to appoint (or allow the auditor to appoint) an expert, the auditor does not have a responsibility to seek that evidence independently by engaging an expert. Accordingly, in circumstances where the auditor requires expert evidence, and there is insufficient alternative audit evidence to enable the auditor to draw reasonable conclusions that the audit objectives have been achieved, the auditor's responsibility may be properly discharged by qualifying the audit report.

When determining whether to use the work of an expert as audit evidence, the auditor should consider the following:

(a)   The nature and complexity of the item(s) of audit interest.

(b)   The risk of material misstatement of the account balance or class of transactions and the audit objective.

(c)   The other audit evidence available with respect to the item(s).

7:6.3 Skills and competence of the expert

SAS 520 states that 'when planning to use the work of an expert, the auditors should assess the objectivity and professional qualifications, experience and resources of the expert'.

When planning to use an expert's work as audit evidence, the auditor should be satisfied as to the expert's skills and competence by considering:

(a)   the expert's professional certification, licence or membership of an appropriate professional body; and

(b)   the experience and reputation of the expert in the field in which evidence is sought.

7:6.4 Independence and objectivity of the expert

The auditor should consider the independence and objectivity of the expert. The risk that an expert's objectivity will be impaired increases when the expert is:

(a)   employed by the client; and/or

(b)   related in some other manner to the client (e.g., by being financially dependent on, or having an investment in, the client).

If the auditor doubts whether the expert will be sufficiently independent or objective to provide reliable audit evidence to support the audit objectives, the auditor should discuss these reservations with the client's management.

7:6.5 Communication with the expert

Before using the work of an expert, the auditor should consult the expert and the client to establish the terms of the expert's engagement. These terms should be documented and should include the following:

(a)   The objectives and scope of the expert's work.

(b)   A general outline of the specific matters which the auditor expects the expert's report to cover.

(c)   The intended use of the expert's work, including the possible communication to third parties of the expert's identity and extent of involvement.

(d)   The extent of the expert's access to appropriate records and files.

(e)   Clarification of the expert's relationship, if any, with the client.

(f)   Confidentiality of the client's information.

(g)   Information on the assumptions and methods intended to be used by the expert and, if appropriate, on their consistency with those used in prior periods.

(h)   Documentation or further information required as audit evidence.

Sometimes it will not be practicable for consultation to take place before the work is carried out by the expert. The auditor should, however, obtain an understanding of the expert's terms of reference and of the work the expert has been instructed to carry out.

7:6.6 Evaluating the work of the expert

SAS 520 states that 'the auditors should assess the appropriateness of the expert's work as audit evidence regarding the financial statement assertions being considered'.

The auditor should seek reasonable assurance that the expert's work constitutes appropriate audit evidence by considering the results of the work in the light both of the overall knowledge of the business and of the results of the audit procedures. In particular, the auditor should consider the following:

(a)   The source data used by the expert.

(b)   The assumptions and methods used and, if appropriate, their consistency with preceding periods.

The auditor should also confirm that the substance of the expert's findings is properly reflected in the financial statements.

7:6.6.1 *Source data*

The auditor should consider whether the expert has used appropriate source data. The procedures to be applied include:

(a)   making enquiries of the expert to determine how the expert has become satisfied that the source data are sufficient, relevant and reliable; and

(b)   conducting audit procedures on the data provided by the client to the expert to obtain reasonable assurance that the data are appropriate.

7:6.6.2 *Assumptions and methods*

The appropriateness and reasonableness of assumptions and methods used by the expert are the responsibility of the expert. Not having the same expertise the auditor cannot normally challenge those assumptions and methods. However, the auditor should obtain an understanding of them to determine that they appear to be reasonable, based on the auditor's knowledge of the client's business, and consistent with the results of the other audit procedures.

7:6.6.3 *Conclusions*

Normally, completion of the procedures discussed in **Sections 7:6.6** to **7:6.6.2** will provide reasonable assurance that the auditor has obtained appropriate audit evidence to support the specific audit objectives. However, if the work of the expert does not support the information presented in the financial statements, the auditor should attempt to resolve the inconsistency by discussions with the client and the expert. Sometimes the auditor may need to obtain the opinion of another expert.

7:6.7 **Reporting**

In the following cases the auditor may need to qualify the expert's report on the grounds that not all the information necessary for the audit has been obtained:

(a)   If the auditor concludes that:

  (i)   the work of the expert is inconsistent with the information in the financial statements; or

  (ii)   the work of the expert does not constitute sufficient appropriate audit evidence.

(b)   If the client is unable or unwilling to appoint an expert, as referred to in **Section 7:6.2** (second paragraph).

If as a result of the work of an expert the auditor decides to express a qualified opinion, it may help the reader of the audit report if, when explaining the nature of the qualification, the auditor refers to or describes the work of the expert. In such circumstances, the auditor should consider including the identity of the expert in the report and noting the extent of the expert's involvement. Before making such a reference, the auditor should, if this has not already been done (as discussed in **Section 7:6.5**, list point (c)), obtain the permission of the expert, preferably in writing. If permission is refused, and the auditor believes a reference is necessary, the engagement partner should consult with other partners as discussed in **Section 5:5**, 'Consultation and concurring reviews', and should consider seeking legal advice.

When an unqualified opinion is given, the auditor should not normally refer to the work of an expert in the audit report because such a reference might be misunderstood as a qualification of the opinion or as a division of responsibility.

7:7 Joint audits

7:7.1 Introduction

Joint audit appointments normally arise when:

(a) the parent company auditor is appointed jointly with the existing auditor of a subsidiary; or

(b) a transitional arrangement is made for a newly appointed firm to act jointly for (say) one year before the existing auditor resigns.

Whatever the reason for the joint appointment, the auditor's responsibility remains the same as with a sole audit. The legal responsibilities of each firm are joint and several. Each firm should therefore form its own opinion on the financial statements on which it is reporting. Each auditor should ensure that the audit is completed to the normal standards, and that the audit work is evidenced by appropriate working papers.

7:7.2 Appointment

7:7.2.1 Procedures prior to acceptance

Before an appointment as joint auditor is accepted, the considerations set out in **Section 3:2**, 'Appointment and continuation as an auditor', apply, except that the specimen letters set out in Appendices B, C and D to that section (*see* **Sections 3:2.6, 3:2.7** and **3:2.8**) should be amended accordingly.

Also, in addition to considering the acceptability of the client, the auditor should decide whether the proposed joint audit arrangement is likely to give rise to an unacceptable level of risk to the firm for reasons such as:

(a) the professional reputation of the joint auditor;

(b) the proposed terms of the joint audit agreement, including the division of work and the arrangements for review of the joint auditor's working papers.

The auditor will wish to consider whether an appointment can be accepted if there are doubts about the willingness or ability of the joint auditor to co-operate effectively.

If it is proposed that a joint auditor should become a client's sole auditor the auditor should follow the procedures set out in **Section 3:2**, 'Appointment and continuation as an auditor', except that the auditor should, in place of the specimen letter set out in Appendix C (*see* **Section 3:2.7**), write to the joint auditor in terms of the specimen letter in Appendix A to this section (**Section 7:7.8**).

7:7.2.2 *Engagement letters*

Whenever appointed as a joint auditor, the auditor should issue an engagement letter in accordance with **Section 3:3**, 'Engagement letters'.

The engagement letter should refer both to the firm and to the other joint auditor, with whom the auditor should agree whether joint or separate letters will be sent to the client. It may be appropriate to send separate letters where either firm is providing other services. However, in such circumstances it is important that, to avoid any subsequent misunderstanding or difficulty, the audit engagement is explained in similar terms by both firms.

7:7.3 Division of work

On the occasion of the first joint audit, or when there is a significant change in the audit strategy, the engagement partner should agree with the joint auditor the arrangements for the division of the work and the other matters relating to the conduct of the audit, as discussed in **Sections 7:7.4.1** to **7:7.6.** The way the work is divided between the two firms may range from the one extreme where one firm 'leads' and the other firm 'follows', to the other extreme where the audit areas are divided equally between them. The most appropriate method depends partly on the reason for the joint appointment and partly on the relationship between the two firms.

Both firms need to understand the basis on which the work is to be divided, and the reasons for the division, well in advance of the start of the audit. Irrespective of the method of allocating work the auditor should write to the other firm to obtain confirmation that its understanding of the arrangements is the same. The auditor should notify the particulars of the division of work to the client's management.

If the auditor is satisfied that the joint auditor's work will be properly carried out in accordance with Auditing Standards and will have regard to Auditing Guidelines, the audit work may be split evenly. In other cases the auditor should ensure that the firm carries out the majority of the audit work, and should ask the joint auditor to use the firm's audit documentation and programmes.

If the firm is not 'leading' the joint audit, the auditor should endeavour to rotate, from time to time, the sections of the work covered by each firm. The advantage of rotation is that it ensures that all areas of the client's activities become familiar to both firms.

7:7.4 Specific audit procedures

7:7.4.1 *Audit strategy and risk assessment*

Because of the joint and several liability associated with joint audits the auditor should obtain assurance that the risk assessment procedures have identified all relevant risks for the audit as a whole and that the audit strategy has been appropriately designed to address these risks. However, the means by which the auditor obtains assurance is a matter of judgement, depending on the degree of risk to the firm arising from the acceptance of the joint audit arrangement.

7:7.4.2 *Substantive testing*

The auditor should carry out sufficient substantive audit procedures to be satisfied that the overall audit risk is acceptable. Where the joint auditor has performed the audit work the auditor should review the joint auditor's working papers. Sometimes (e.g., in the case of a material and highly subjective matter involving the exercise of professional judgement) the auditor should also carry out or re-perform substantially all the joint auditor's work.

7:7.4.3 *Communication with the joint auditor*

The auditor should communicate with the joint auditor to ensure that:

(a)   both firms have a sufficient understanding of the audit strategy and detailed plans, including the nature, extent and timing of each other's audit procedures; and

(b)   the audit procedures are planned, performed and controlled in an efficient and satisfactory manner.

In particular, both firms should recognise the need to inform each other of discussions with the client and of significant audit issues as they arise.

7:7.4.4 *Differences of opinion*

If significant differences of opinion arise, the auditor should discuss with the joint auditor whether the same information and assumptions are being used. If the differences of opinion persist, the engagement partner should follow the consultation procedures set out in **Section 5:5**, 'Consultation and concurring reviews'.

7:7.4.5 *Issues documentation*

The auditor should prepare issues documentation covering the engagement as a whole for review by the engagement partner and the review partner (where applicable) in accordance with **Section 10:2**, 'Issues documentation'. Sometimes one integrated set of issues documentation may be prepared and used by both joint auditors. However, because the firm is jointly and severally responsible for the audit report (and, therefore, needs to be independently satisfied as to the appropriate treatment of all matters), the joint auditor need not sign the other firm's issues documentation.

7:7.4.6 *Audit working papers*

The auditor should complete and review the audit working papers in the same way as applies to a sole audit. In addition, the engagement manager or the engagement partner should review the joint auditor's working papers. The auditor should make and retain copies of the joint auditor's working papers so that the copies taken, together with the papers prepared by the auditor, provide adequate support for the opinion. The auditor should make working papers available to the joint auditor in the manner described in **Section 6:4**, 'Access to audit working papers'.

Both firms should keep separate working paper files. Wherever possible, the auditor should file the working papers in accordance with normal procedures. However, it may not be either appropriate or economic for the auditor to re-file or re-number the working papers that the other auditor has prepared, depending upon their method of working. In such a case the auditor should pay particular attention to the various programmes, checklists and contents of files to ensure that all the working papers (from both firms) are complete. The auditor should make it clear on the copies of the joint auditor's working papers that they have been prepared by them.

7:7.5 Letter of representation

The provisions of **Section 10:4**, 'Representations from management', apply to joint audits. The letter of representation should be agreed by both the firm and the joint auditor, and it should be addressed to both audit firms jointly.

7:7.6 Reporting to management

The provisions of **Section 12:1**, 'Audit reporting to the board and to management', apply to joint audits. A joint report may be issued.

7:7.7 Fees

The auditor should normally discuss fees with the joint auditor before submission to the client's management. Because both firms have to form their own opinion, and have joint and several liability, the total fees will be higher than if one firm were sole auditors. The auditor should explain this fact, and the reasons for it, to the client's management.

7:7.8 Appendix A Specimen letter to the existing joint auditor when it is proposed that the auditor should become a company's sole auditor

Dear Sirs,

XYZ Company Limited

As discussed at our meeting with   on we are writing to you formally in connection with the proposed change in audit arrangements.

We understand that you (have resigned/will be retiring) as joint auditor of XYZ Limited (at the conclusion of the annual general meeting) on and that the company proposes to ask us to continue in office as its sole auditor.

We are writing to you with the authority of the directors to ask you whether there are any matters of which we should be aware including, in particular, any matters which could influence our decision whether or not to accept nomination/appointment as auditors of the company.

[*Include the following paragraphs as applicable.*]

Please also send us a copy of any representations you have made to the company under s. 391A of the Companies Act 1985 [*or other relevant (UK) industry-specific legislation*].

In addition please send us copies of the notice of resignation and statement deposited at the company's registered office under ss. 392 and 394 of the Companies Act 1985 [*or other relevant (UK) industry-specific legislation*] or let us have copies when they are finalised.

Yours faithfully,

Chapter 8

Systems and controls

8:1 Control environment

8:1.1 Definition

SAS 300.3, 'Accounting And Internal Control Systems And Audit Risk Assessments' requires that:

> *In planning the audit, auditors should obtain and document an understanding of the accounting system and control environment sufficient to determine their audit approach.*

The control environment encompasses the attitudes, awareness and actions of an entity's directors, management and other personnel regarding internal controls and their importance in the entity.

An understanding of the control environment enables auditors to assess the likely effectiveness of control procedures. A strong control environment, i.e. one with strong budgetary controls and an effective internal audit function, increases the effectiveness of control procedures. A favourable control environment requires the support and leadership of senior management.

Based on their understanding of the accounting system and control environment, auditors can make a preliminary assessment of the adequacy of the system as a basis for the preparation of the financial statements, and of the likely mix of tests of control and substantive procedures.

8:1.2 Reasons for assessing the control environment

Understanding the control environment provides a basis for determining whether the environment appears to be conducive to the maintenance of an effective accounting system and control procedures and whether it minimises the incentives and opportunities for management to override control procedures or intentionally misrepresent the financial statements.

The auditor should assess the control environment in order to identify the impact of particular control environment factors, both favourable and unfavourable, on the risk of material misstatement in the financial statements. In particular in assessing the control environment, the auditor will:

(a)   Consider management's ability to make the informed judgements and estimates that are necessary to prepare financial statements.

(b)   Assess the incentives and opportunities for intentional misrepresentation or distortion of the financial statements by management.

(c)   Assess whether management has a proper understanding of the key risks facing the business.

(d) Assess whether management has sufficient reliable information for the effective control of the business and is using such information effectively.

Understanding how senior management runs the business as a whole will help us subsequently to identify monitoring controls at the cycle level.

Some aspects of the control environment should be assessed in conjunction with the performance of client acceptance and continuance procedures.

An effective control environment is a necessary prerequisite for effective internal control. If the control environment is not conducive to the maintenance of a reliable system of accounting and control procedures or does not minimise sufficiently the risk of intentional misrepresentations in the financial statements then the auditor consider whether to should accept or continue the engagement. If the engagement is accepted or continued then appropriate substantive procedures will have to be designed to address the increased risk of both error and fraud, in particular the possibility of management fraud.

8:1.3 Assessing the control environment

Assessment of the control environment is carried out primarily through enquiry, observation and, on recurring engagements, knowledge obtained in prior years.

The assessment of the control environment should be undertaken by those with the experience necessary to make the relevant judgements. Often this will be the engagement partner and manager, who should, however, take into account information gathered by others on the engagement team, particularly assigned specialists and the field team leader.

In assessing the control environment, the auditor should look beyond the form of control measures and management actions and should concentrate on their substance. An environment may appear to be favourable but in reality may not be. For instance, a system may provide adequate reports for the board or senior management, but if the information is not analysed and acted on, the system does not contribute to the control environment. Similarly, appropriate policies can only be effective if they are enforced by management. For example, although a client may have a formal code of conduct, management may have a record of condoning actions that violate it. By not reprimanding such actions, management sends a clear message undermining the code of conduct.

The auditor should also consider circumstances that negate the effectiveness of factors that appear to contribute to a favourable control environment. For example, unrealistic performance standards may influence managers to report inaccurate data through an otherwise satisfactory internal reporting system, or individuals may engage in actions in the belief that they are not 'really' illegal or wrong and that the activity is in the client's best interests.

Identifying strengths in the control environment should lead the auditor to consider reducing the assessment of the overall amount of assurance needed from other work, as part of our overall assessment of control risk. Appropriate evidence will be needed that control environment procedures are in operation if it is planned to reduce substantive tests by testing controls and if that assessment of control risk is partly dependent on a favourable assessment of the control environment. This will normally involve inquiry of client personnel responsible for the procedures together with examination of applicable supporting documentation.

The understanding and assessment of the control environment, including the audit implications, should be recorded. The conclusions should be approved by the engagement partner and manager.

8:1.3.1 Risk of management fraud

Any factors which indicate that there is a risk of management fraud should be thoroughly investigated and documented. Any substantial doubt about the honesty or integrity of the directors will require a much greater reliance on substantive testing. Alternatively, the auditor might feel that it is not in the firm's interests to accept or continue with that appointment.

Examples of risk factors include:

(a)   A lack of encouragement of ethical and moral behaviour from senior management. This could be accomplished by codes of conduct and other policies regarding acceptable business practices. Management could also set an example by being forthright in its dealings with employees, suppliers, customers, insurers and competitors.

(b)   Doubt regarding integrity as a result of employee allegations, regulatory or outside inquiries, adverse publicity, or a past record of unethical behaviour.

(c)   Past attempts to circumvent or coerce the engagement team or otherwise unduly influence the performance of the audit.

(d)   Management attempts to sanitise the presentation of the audit results through excessive rehearsal or challenging of the audit findings.

(e)   Past attempts or evidence that management has attempted to distort or hide information relevant to the company's financial condition or results of operations.

(f)   The client is experiencing core business problems such as shrinking margins, declining sales or unusually heavy competition or, conversely, rapid growth is placing stress on the resources of management or the business.

(g)   Unusually heavy pressure to achieve accounting-based performance objectives.

(h)   Members of senior management have a significant proportion of their net worth invested in the company.

(i)   Evidence that past management estimates have been unrealistic.

(j)   Accounting policies are unusual, difficult, imprudent or very aggressive.

8:1.3.2 *Other control environment areas*

The auditor's evaluation of the control environment should include:

- The role of the board of directors
- Effectiveness of the organisation and key management
- Human resource policies and procedures
- Management's risk assessment process
- Compliance with laws and regulations
- Reasonableness of management plans and budgetary control
- Reliability of overall financial reporting
- Role of the audit committee
- Internal audit

The auditor should address each area for assessment. However, they are not equally relevant to all engagements. The applicability and importance of each should be judged in the context of the particular engagement.

The key issues for these areas are listed in **Section 8:1.3.3**.

8:1.3.3 *Points of focus for control environment areas*

8:1.3.3.1 *Organisation, roles and responsibilities*

(a) Role of the board of directors.

   (i)   Balance of power and authority at the head of the client, including:

      – directors' independence from management and controlling shareholders,

      – calibre and number of non-executive directors.

   (ii) Reasons for the resignations of directors.

   (iii) Timeliness and sufficiency of information provided to the board for monitoring:

      – management's goals, strategies and plans,

      – the client's financial position and operating results,

      – the terms of material transactions, contracts and other agreements,

      – significant business risks.

   (iv) The board's role in establishing the appropriate 'tone at the top', including involvement in monitoring management's interpretation of and compliance with the code of conduct.

(v)   The board's involvement in:

–   determining the annual remuneration of the directors and senior management and, where appropriate, the head of internal audit,

–   appointing and removing directors and senior management, including where appropriate the company secretary and head of internal audit,

–   material, non routine transactions (e.g., the acquisition or disposal of major assets).

(vi) Manner of board operations, including:

–   frequency of board meetings,

–   use of board committees,

–   procedures for reserving significant decisions for the full board.

(b)   Effectiveness of the organisation and key management.

(i)   Appropriateness of structure of the client and ability to provide for the necessary flow of information.

(ii) Definition of key areas of senior management responsibility and control.

(iii) Appropriate numbers of people, particularly with respect to management and supervisory functions, with the requisite skill levels relative to the size of the client and complexity of activities and skills.

(iv) Knowledge, experience and capacity for effective action of key management.

(v)   Nature of control that senior management has over operating management.

(vi) Management's attitude toward computer operations and accounting functions.

(vii) Assignment of responsibility and delegation of authority to deal with organisational goals and objectives.

(viii) Standards and procedures governing the control of the activities of the client, such as procedures and accounting policies manuals.

(ix) Rapid growth or continued change in products or services.

(x)   Extent to which modifications to organisational structure are made in light of changed conditions.

(xi) Frequency of emergency or 'crisis' conditions.

(xii) Where there is owner-management the nature, extent and impact of the owner's involvement.

(c)   Human resource policies and procedures.

(i)   The extent to which policies and procedures for hiring, training, evaluating, promoting and remunerating employees are in place.

(ii) The extent to which people are made aware of their responsibilities and expectations of them.

(iii) Personnel turnover in key functions affecting financial management, e.g., operating, accounting, computer operations, internal audit.

(iv) The adequacy of employee background checks, particularly with regard to prior actions or activities considered unacceptable by the client.

(v) The level or frequency of unplanned overtime.

8:1.3.3.2 Risk assessment

(a) Management's risk assessment process.

  (i) Existence of business-wide objectives providing sufficiently broad statements and guidance that are specific to the business.

  (ii) Relevance of objectives to all significant business processes.

  (iii) Thoroughness and evidence of the risk analysis process, including:

  - procedures in place to identify key business risks in a timely manner,

  - procedures to identify changes that have taken, or will take, place in any material conditions affecting the business, and

  - consideration of the likelihood of risks crystallising and the significance of the consequent financial impact on the business.

  (iv) The level of personnel responsible for the procedures.

  (v) The establishment of priorities for the allocation of resources available for control and the setting and communicating of clear control objectives.

(b) Compliance with laws and regulations.

  (i) The extent to which management has in place procedures to identify applicable laws and regulations.

  (ii) The knowledge and experience of personnel responsible for the procedures.

  (iii) The extent to which a code of conduct is developed and employees are properly trained in and understand its provisions.

  (iv) In regulated industries, the terms of reference and competence of the compliance function.

  (v) Past attempts by directors or senior management to contravene laws and regulations.

  (vi) Indications of particular pressures on individuals or groups of individuals to breach laws and regulations.

  (vii) Evidence that management have failed to condone cases of non compliance resulting from the actions of staff.

  (viii) The availability of appropriate legal advice.

  (ix) The extent of any complaints from customers, suppliers or other third parties.

8:1.3.3.3 Monitoring

(a)   Reasonableness of management plans and budgetary control.

   (i)   Information produced is sufficient, timely and reliable enough to review, evaluate and if necessary take executive action on the business' operations and financial position.

   (ii)   The level of detail and value of plans and budgets and of financial, statistical or other information used by management with respect to its relevance, its sufficiency, the frequency and timeliness with which it is received and its reliability.

   (iii) Appropriate involvement of personnel.

   (iv)   The comparison of current conditions or results with appropriate benchmarks (e.g., the preceding year's conditions or results, or a practicably achievable budget or plan).

   (v)   The intended purpose of plans and budgets (e.g., to reflect management's reasonable expectations or to serve as 'motivational' tools reflecting unrealistic targets).

   (vi)   The assumptions underlying strategic plans and budgets.

   (vii) The past record of the client in meeting plans and budgets.

   (viii) The effectiveness of monitoring performance with respect to:

       – documentation of significant departures from plans, with explanations,

       – evaluation of explanations by the appropriate levels of management or the board of directors,

       – implementation of corrective actions by appropriate levels of management and follow-up by senior management,

       –- timeliness of consideration of the effect of changes in the economy, industry and competition,

       – identification and timeliness of corrective actions, and

       – timeliness of modification and communication of plans when warranted.

(b)   Reliability of overall financial reporting.

   (i)   Staffing levels and the related skill levels within the finance function in relation to the size and complexity of the business.

   (ii)   Organisation of, and degree of supervision within, the finance function.

   (iii) Management's procedures for ensuring that all economic activity of the entity for the period is reflected in the financial statements.

   (iv)   Management's processes for periodic review of financial reports.

   (v)   Frequency of unusual, nonrecurring, or correcting journal entries, and management's review of them.

    (vi) Extent to which the accrual basis is adopted in regular financial reports.

    (vii) Maturity of the accounting systems and control procedures used by the entity.

    (viii) Timeframe for closing the general ledger and preparing the financial statements.

    (ix) Extent of reconciling items resulting from exception reports generated by the accounting system.

(c)   Role of the audit committee.

    (i)   The committee's independence from management.

    (ii)   The frequency and timeliness of the committee's meetings with the:

        – external auditors and

        – client's internal auditors.

    (iii) The adequacy with which the committee monitors:

        – the scope of our audit of the client's financial statements,

        – our findings and management's response thereto,

        – unaudited client financial information issued externally by management,

        – professional competence and performance of internal audit, and

        – the scope of internal audit's work.

    (iv) Authority of the committee to investigate any matters within its terms of reference, resources available (including internal audit) and access to information or professional advice.

    (v)   Actions the committee takes as a result of its findings.

(d)   Internal audit

    (i)   The goals and objectives of the internal audit function, including a formal charter, mission statement or corporate directive.

    (ii)   The accessibility to the board of directors or audit committee.

    (iii) Internal audit's responsibilities regarding testing and evaluating the client's internal control.

    (iv) Internal audit's use of standards developed by professional internal audit associations.

    (v)   The breadth of skills available in the internal audit group, including computer audit skills.

    (vi) The assignments undertaken by the internal audit group and the types of reports and recommendations generated.

    (vii) Our initial assessment of the quality of internal audit's work.

    (viii) The importance given by the client to addressing issues raised in internal audit reports.

    (ix) Limitations on internal audit's access to records or scope of activities.

8:2 Accounting systems

8:2.1 Definition

The accounting system is part of the client's internal control, although for audit purposes understanding it should be seen as distinct from understanding the related controls. Understanding the accounting system includes understanding the computer environment, or environments, in which accounting applications operate.

A client's accounting system comprises the procedures established to identify, assemble, classify, analyse and record transactions and the documents produced by the system. An effective accounting system includes appropriate consideration to establishing methods and records that will:

(a)   Identify and record all valid transactions.

(b)   Describe on a timely basis the type of transaction in sufficient detail to permit proper classification of the transaction for financial reporting.

(c)   Measure the value of the transaction in a manner that permits recording its monetary value in the financial statements.

(d)   Generate sufficient information to enable management to monitor the financial performance and the effective operation of financial control.

(e)   Determine the time period in which the transaction occurred to permit recording of the transaction in the proper accounting period.

(f)   Present properly the transaction and related disclosure in the financial statements.

(g)   Assist in the effective operation of the business.

8:2.1.1 Manual versus programmed accounting procedures

Such procedures may be performed manually (e.g., the recording of goods received) or by computer (e.g., the automatic generation of cheques to pay vendors). Computerised accounting procedures are called 'programmed accounting procedures'. In a computer environment, the extent and complexity of computer processing will be affected by the hardware and computer networks in use, and by the nature of the computerised applications.

8:2.1.2 Transaction/systems cycle

An accounting system usually comprises a combination of manual and programmed accounting procedures to record transactions and process the flow of transactions from their inception to their entry in the general ledger. This can be described as a 'transaction cycle' or 'systems cycle', e.g., the revenue cycle will record sales transactions, cash receipts, and sales and credit adjustments, and will result in receivable balances and summarised sales transactions in the general ledger. Account balances and classes of transactions related to a transaction or systems cycle are referred to as 'systems-derived'.

8:2.1.3 Transaction/standing/accumulated data

The three principal types of data that are used in the accounting system are 'standing data', 'transaction data' and 'accumulated data'.

Standing data Data of a permanent or semi-permanent nature that is used repeatedly during processing, e.g., rates of pay used for calculating salaries.

Transaction data Relates to an individual transaction, e.g., the number of hours worked by an individual employee in a particular week, which is used to calculate that person's salary.

Accumulated data The accumulated results of transactions, not necessarily capable of direct analysis by individual transaction.

Errors in standing data are likely to be of greater significance than errors in transaction data because they will apply to many transactions until corrected.

8:2.2 Documenting the accounting system

8:2.2.1 Reasons for documenting the accounting system

The preparation or updating of systems documents will help the audit team to:

(a) Understand the client's business.

(b) Identify inherent risks and understand control procedures, assess control risk and consider the audit implications.

(c) Understand how misstatements might occur and their significance.

(d) Design effective tests of controls and substantive tests for systems-derived accounts.

(e) Identify significant reports used to prepare the financial statements or monitor the business and how they are generated.

(f) Discuss transactions and reports with client management and staff that process the transactions or generate the reports.

(g) Discuss the computer environment with client management and staff responsible for the information technology (IT) function.

(h) Identify opportunities for improved client service through proactive reporting to management on areas where the client can improve its business and accounting controls.

(i) If applicable, meet any statutory reporting obligations concerning accounting records.

(j) Meet reporting obligations in regulated clients such as banks and investment businesses.

The auditor should obtain and document an understanding of the accounting system sufficient to determine the audit approach. This will require an appropriate understanding of:

(a) The accounting records and the major transactions input and information flows through the system.

(b) The nature of the computer environment (the hardware and software used to process data).

The study of the system should be organised around the principal transaction cycles. These cycles may include the treasury, revenue, purchasing, payroll, inventory and property plant and equipment cycles. Other cycles may need to be understood, depending on the client's circumstances and the industry in which it operates.

The auditor should consider the impact of the transaction on the client's financial statements, e.g., the trial balance accounts affected. It is only necessary to obtain an overview of the accounting system at this stage.

It will be unnecessary to document the accounting system extensively, particularly if the client's control procedures are properly documented. The understanding of control procedures will help demonstrate that the auditor has a sufficient understanding of the accounting system.

8.2.2.2 *Methods of documenting the accounting system*

It is unnecessary to understand and document every detail of systems processing for every application; the evaluation of controls should focus on what is material and necessary for the audit strategy and audit programme and keep to an overview level.

The accounting system can be documented via a diagram, narrative or a combination of the two. In more complex systems a diagram is usually preferable to narrative notes because more information can be given clearly in one diagram than in a page of narrative notes.

There are various diagrammatic methods that can be used to document the accounting system; however, it is helpful to create diagrams consistently that reviewers and staff in subsequent years can understand. Guidance on two useful methods is given below.

Recording a sufficient understanding of the accounting system is necessary on all audits, whatever the strategy. If a wholly substantive approach is to be followed, the record can be confined to what is necessary to design a substantive testing programme addressing all significant audit risks related to the accounting system. Overview flowcharts or equivalent narrative normally will still be needed.

8.2.2.2.1 Overview systems diagrams

This form of systems documentation is particularly useful in showing how the applications produce the balances in the financial accounts. An example of an overview system diagram is shown below. **Figure 8:1** shows:

(a)   Which applications the information passes through from input to the general ledger.

(b)   The information flows between applications.

(c)   Whether the information flows electronically, on diskette or manually.

(d)   How the major transactions are input.

Figure 8.1 *Understanding internal control and its audit implications*

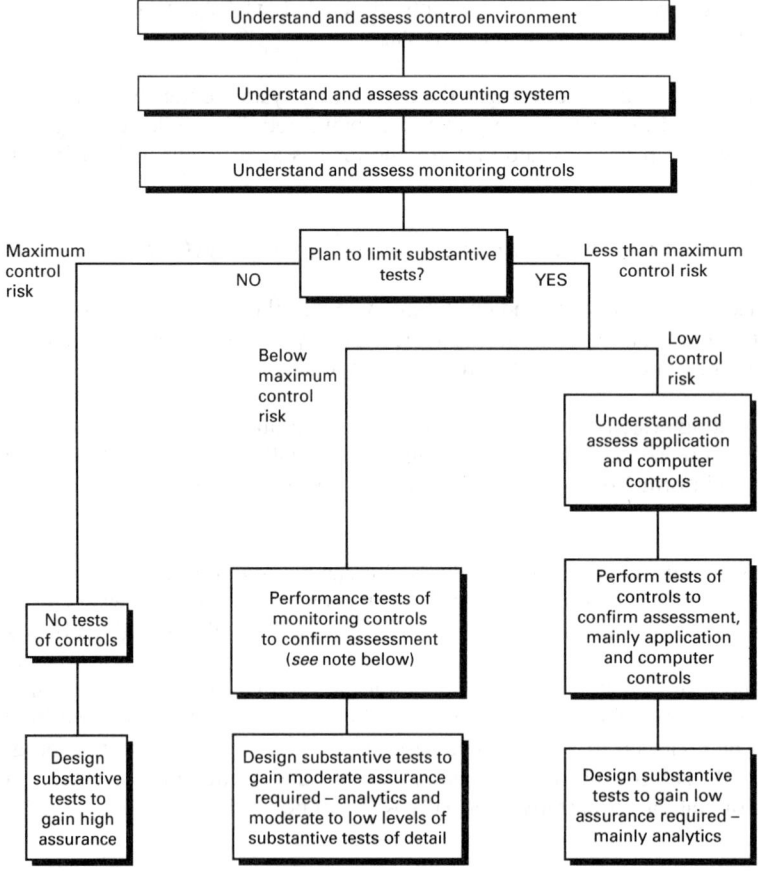

Note: Where control risk is below the maximum, understanding and testing application and computer controls may be a cost-effective response in certain circumstances.

8:2.2.2.2 *Overview flowcharts*

Overview flowcharts are useful if reliance is going to be placed on application controls because they identify the key transactions, standing data and accumulated data that are covered within the control objectives for application controls. However, overview flowcharts would probably be unnecessary if control risk is to be assessed at maximum for a cycle. It will depend on whether the audit file can demonstrate knowledge of the accounting system in designing and performing the audit work.

The overview flowchart, **Figure 8:2**, summarises diagrammatically the main inputs, data updated and referred to and outputs of a process. This process can be the entire accounting system, a cycle, an application, or a particular operation within an application.

In simple cases one overview flowchart may be sufficient to provide an adequate understanding of a whole application. However, in more complex situations it may be necessary to prepare a summary flowchart of a whole application, supported by more detailed flowcharts of key processing steps.

The information necessary to prepare an overview flowchart is obtained primarily through inquiry of client personnel. This information consists of the principal features of the accounting system, including:

(a)   The nature, source and estimated volumes and values of transactions.

(b)   The key processes and flow of significant transactions.

(c)   Principal files or ledgers supporting account balances, and the related balances, and the processes by which they are updated.

(d)   The reports of accounting significance produced, their frequency, distribution and the files from which they are derived.

Figure 8.2 Example of overview flowchart: revenue cycle

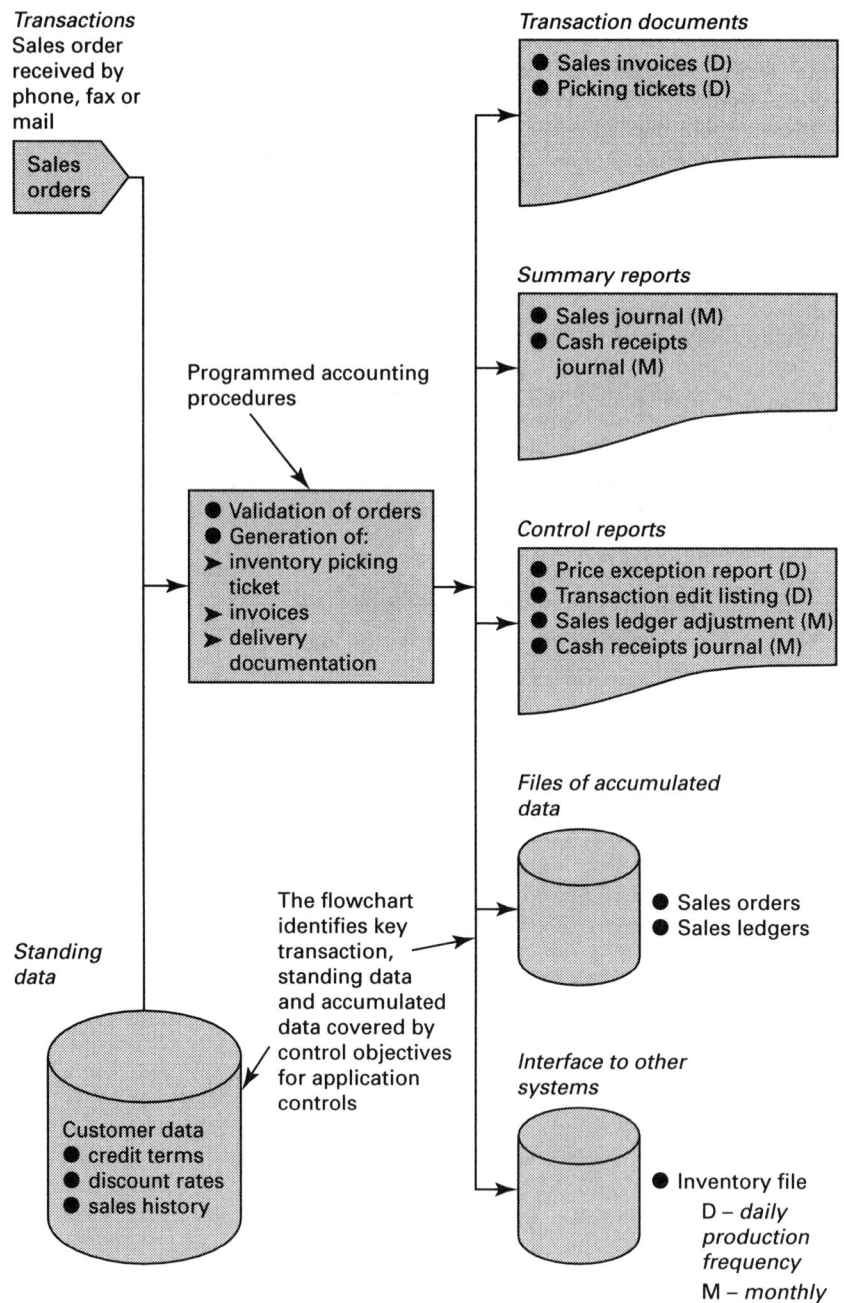

Alternatively, the estimated volumes and values of significant transactions as well as the relative average size and values of principal files or ledgers supporting account balances may be attached to the overview flowchart on a supplementary schedule. We should obtain copies of, or extracts from, the client's accounting instructions and completed specimen documents if these are necessary to obtain an understanding of the client's system. Such supporting documentation can be cross-referenced to, and filed with, the flowcharts if necessary.

8:2.2.2.3 Updating systems notes

The documented understanding of the client's accounting system should be updated on each audit and the audit implications of significant changes should be considered. Diagrams and flowcharts should only be redrawn if the underlying processes have changed or the clarity of the flowcharts has become impaired as a result of previous amendments. Photocopies of the old flowcharts should be taken before changes are made to maintain a permanent record of the previous systems.

8:2.2.2.4 Flowcharting methodology

Examples of flowcharts are shown above. The principal direction of flow in a flowchart is from left to right.

Clarity and simplicity of presentation are important, and unduly elaborate flowcharts should be avoided.

The flowcharting symbols described in **Figure 8:3** may be used when preparing an overview flowchart.

Figure 8.3 Symbols to be used in preparing flowcharts

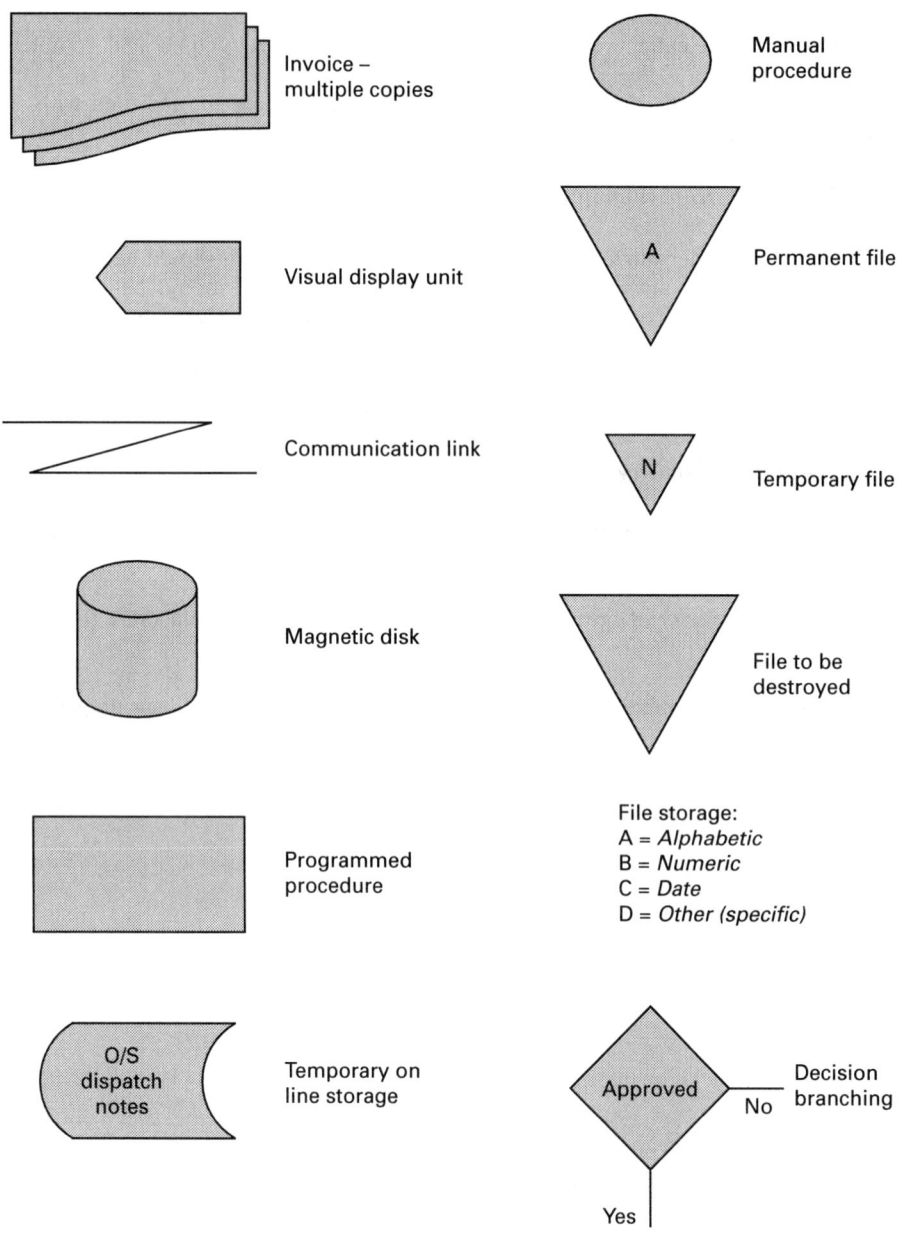

Invoice –
multiple copies

Manual
procedure

Visual display unit

Permanent file

Communication link

Temporary file

Magnetic disk

File to be
destroyed

Programmed
procedure

File storage:
A = *Alphabetic*
B = *Numeric*
C = *Date*
D = *Other (specific)*

O/S
dispatch
notes

Temporary on
line storage

Approved

Yes

No

Decision
branching

8:2.3 Understanding and documenting the computer environment

Where a client's accounting system or other significant systems producing information of financial significance are computerised, the auditor should understand and document the computer environment in which these significant applications operate.

The size and type of hardware, and the complexity and age of the applications, all have an impact on the controls likely to be in place, and hence on the assessment of control risk.

8:2.3.1 Audit-significant applications

The applications that are essential to the operation of the client's business need to be identified. While all of these key applications are business-significant applications, only some of them may be of audit significance. Any applications that generate monitoring information are audit significant.

Both business-significant and audit-significant applications need to be identified in order to:

(a)   Assist in understanding how important the computer environment is to the successful running of the client's business.

(b)   Help identify client service opportunities.

In general, the information required will be obtained by discussion with Information Technology (IT) function management.

The following information will normally be recorded:

(a)   Details of client contacts within the IT function and user departments.

(b)   Structure of the IT department.

(c)   Details of significant IT responsibilities located in other departments (e.g. stand-alone processing based on PCs).

(d)   Overall operation of the IT function:

- Clearly defined IT roles and responsibilities, appropriate to the size of the organisation

- Appropriate number of IT personnel

- Changes in staffing, particularly turnover

- Adequacy of IT staff skills

- Clear IT strategy, consistent with the business strategy

- Users' perception of the quality of the service provided.

(e)   Key applications and background, for each major transaction cycle:

- Source of software (e.g. written in-house or purchased package)
- Programming language
- Hardware
- Original implementation date
- Most recent modification date
- Any known problems or limitations, along with their audit implications
- Any plans for significant modifications
- Application level security facilities

(f)   Computer environment:

- Hardware manufacturer and model number
- Operating system and version
- Other relevant systems software and version
- Arrangements for maintenance of system software (e.g. maintenance agreement with a support company).

(g)   Overview of network links:

- Main processing and user sites, and the links between them
- External network connections

(h)   Connection details:

- Business purpose (e.g. electronic mail, EDI, Internet, etc)
- Approach to control.

This information should normally be obtained by inquiry of management of the computer function. For clients where the processing of key applications is not controlled by a centralised computer department, it may be necessary to consider several parts of the client's organisation in order to gather the necessary information.

8:2.3.2 Audit implications arising from review of the IT system

There are a number of factors which determine whether the auditor should collect further information about computer controls in order to conduct the control risk assessment.

8:2.3.2.1 Changes to applications

If the client can make changes to the program code related to audit-significant computer programmes then controls to prevent unauthorised changes must be evaluated.

If there have there been any changes to any audit-significant computer programs during the period other than vendor installed updates then the controls to ensure that these have been adequately implemented must be evaluated.

8:2.3.2.2 Development and implementation

The development or implementation of any audit-significant computer programs during the period, including new vendor packages, would require further investigation.

8:2.3.2.3 Computer security and operations

The following would require further investigation:

(a)   Authorisation controls depend on computer security (e.g., user IDs and passwords).

(b)   Controls over restricted access to assets and records depend on computer security.

(c)   Computer systems contain confidential data whose disclosure could pose an audit risk.

(d)   Audit reliance is being placed on controls over changes to application programs which depend on restricted access to the live/production system.

(e)   Network connections pose an audit risk.

(f)   Significant operational problems have arisen during the period.

(g)   The client can make changes to end of day, end of month, or end of year processes within the computer system.

(h)   Permanent loss of systems or data could cause a significant risk of misstatement in the financial statements or a potential going concern problem.

8:2.3.3 Use of client documentation

Clients can help compile most of the information about the computer environment and can provide other accounting systems documentation.

Client documentation will usually be too detailed for audit purposes, but having access to it can avoid having to record information or save time. Copies of, or extracts from, the client's accounting instructions and completed specimen documents may be included in the audit files. Alternatively, the audit team should refer on the file to what client information is available and where it can readily be found. Client documentation should be cross-referenced to, and filed with, the other audit documentation.

8:3 Assessment of control risk

SAS 300.4, 'Accounting and Internal Control Systems and Audit Risk Assessments', states that:

> *If auditors, after obtaining an understanding of the accounting system and control environment, expect to be able to rely on their assessment of control risk to reduce the extent of their substantive procedures, they should make a preliminary assessment of control risk for material financial statement assertions, and should plan and perform tests of control to support that assessment.*

8:3.1 Understanding and assessing control procedures

Figure 8.4 shows the basic 'steps' in the process of reaching a control risk assessment. This section contains guidance on the nature of the control procedures referred to, on the extent of understanding and assessment of each type of control necessary according to the control risk assessment, and on tests of controls.

Figure 8.4 Understanding internal control and its audit implications

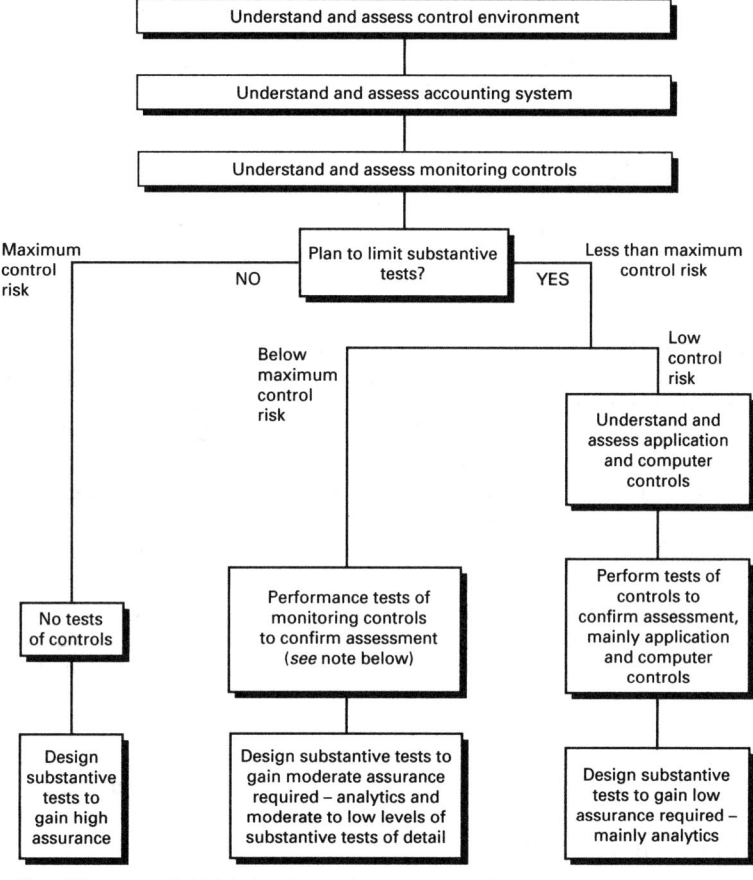

Note: Where control risk is below the maximum, understanding and testing application and computer controls may be a cost-effective response in certain circumstances.

8:3.2 Nature of control procedures

Control procedures are part of the client's internal control. They can be instituted to achieve control objectives covering any aspect of a company's activities. The auditor will focus mainly on financial controls, i.e., control procedures designed to achieve a company's financial control and financial reporting objectives. Such procedures will also help to ensure the safeguarding of assets as well as the maintenance of proper accounting records and the reliability of financial information within the business.

The different types of control procedures of particular audit significance are illustrated in **Figure 8:5**.

Figure 8:5 *Types of control procedures*

Monitoring controls relevant to:	
Applications Cycle level	Computer environment Can cover more than one cycle

Application controls
Transaction level Cycle level

Computer controls
Computer environment level

Monitoring controls are those procedures that management uses to meet its business objectives and run the business in a controlled fashion, taking into account those objectives and the key business opportunities and risks the company faces. They should also provide management (and therefore the auditor) with assurance as to the reliability of financial information. The fact that managers are familiar with the activities of the business means that they should know whether the information being reviewed corresponds with expectations, or needs to be investigated further. This provides indirect assurance that application and computer controls are in place and operating effectively.

Application controls are those procedures designed to ensure that valid transactions, and only valid transactions, are recorded completely and accurately in the accounting records and that data on files from which the financial statements are derived is properly maintained between updates.

Computer controls are those procedures that ensure the proper development, implementation, maintenance, security and operation of computer programs.

8:3.3 Monitoring controls

Monitoring controls are often a form of detection rather than prevention – controls after the event that indirectly provide assurance that systems are working or detect whether problems have occurred. Understanding monitoring controls is an efficient way of helping to identify and assess the risk of material misstatements in the financial statements. Monitoring controls also provide a good indication of the quality of internal control and can be a source of constructive, business-related issues that should be reported to management. They are not expected to provide more than moderate assurance because they are not directly concerned with the application and computer controls.

An internal audit function can form an important part of management's overall monitoring controls. For audit purposes, however, the use that can be made of internal audit's work should be separately assessed as part of the development of the audit strategy and audit programme.

Monitoring of the accounting or financial information systems within a business by internal audit will normally be different in character from the monitoring controls to be assessed in the external audit. Internal audit's work may enable us to assess control risk at low if a significant amount of assurance is obtained directly about the reliability of the accounting system.

8:3.3.1 Monitoring controls relevant to applications

Monitoring controls include reviews of information by management. They should be capable of detecting material misstatements and provide indirect evidence that underlying application controls have operated effectively. They are much like an analytical procedure that indicates that a problem may exist, but its cause, if any, and their effects require further investigation. For a monitoring control to be effective, management should be able to identify if there is a potential error, or fraud, in the underlying data, or at least institute an investigation that will establish if there is.

Examples of monitoring controls relevant to applications include:

(a)   Reviewing a report of revenue with overall knowledge of the volume of goods shipped.

(b)   Monitoring capital expenditure via a quarterly report that analyses expenditure by department with comparisons to budgeted levels.

(c)   Monitoring payroll expense via a report analysing costs by department compared with prior year and budget and commenting on significant changes in head count from prior period.

8:3.3.2 Monitoring controls relevant to the computer environment

Other monitoring controls are concerned with ensuring the ongoing effectiveness of the computer processes and the controls put in place over those processes. In other words, they would alert senior management to problems with the company's computer systems which could cause the data to be unreliable or other control objectives to be at risk.

Monitoring controls relevant to the computer environment are considered in terms of categories rather than cycles: changes to applications, development and implementation, computer security and computer operations. They relate to IT environments that generally cover a number of applications. For example, the controls used to monitor systems security will generally be the same for the purchasing cycle as for the revenue cycle.

The question of whether to consider each category depends on whether the auditor's understanding of the computer environment indicates that they are significant to the control risk assessment.

Examples of monitoring controls relevant to the computer environment include:

(a)   Management review of problem log analysis.

(b)   Steering committee monitoring and controlling development activities.

(c)   Monitoring the backlog of user change requests.

(d) Performing quality assurance reviews and monitoring actual delivery dates of new systems against milestones and deadlines.

8:3.4 Application controls

Application controls are controls and procedures designed to ensure that valid transactions, and only valid transactions, are recorded completely and accurately in the accounting records and that data on files from which the financial statements are derived is properly maintained between updates. They may be manual procedures carried out by users, but will often rely on procedures performed by computer programs. Some controls are specific to individual types of transactions in the cycle. Other control objectives and controls will be the same for all transactions within that cycle.

8:3.4.1 Transaction-level application controls

Controls over authorisation of input are designed to ensure that transactions are not fictitious and that they relate to the client (by ensuring that transactions are approved and that only authorised transactions are processed). For example, authorisation of credit notes by a responsible official prior to issue to customer.

Controls over completeness of input are designed to ensure that all transactions are recorded, input and accepted for processing once and only once. For example, matching goods received notes to outstanding purchase orders.

Controls over accuracy of input are designed to ensure that key data elements, e.g. quantities, prices and account codes are recorded accurately and input to the computer. For example, matching cash receipts to specific invoices on the receivables ledger.

8:3.4.2 Cycle-level application controls

Controls over the integrity of standing data are designed to ensure that changes to standing data are authorised and accurately input and that standing data, once input, is not changed without authorisation. For example, periodic checking of standing data to independently maintained records of authorised data, such as checking salary rates on the payroll system to personnel records.

Controls over completeness and accuracy of updating are designed to ensure that all transactions input and accepted for processing are updated to the appropriate data file and that the update is accurate. For example, reconciliation between general ledger control accounts and other ledgers.

Controls over accumulated data are designed to ensure that once data is updated to a file, that data remains correct and current on the file and represents balances that exist. For example, reconciliations between independent documents and client records, such as bank reconciliations.

Controls to restrict access are designed to protect against unauthorised amendment of data, ensure confidentiality of data and protect physical assets such as cash and inventory.

For example, passwords can be used to restrict access to data held on computer to certain specified users; the ability to amend that data can be further restricted.

8:3.4.3   Controls carried out by programmed procedures

Some application controls are performed manually, e.g. the manual authorisation of an invoice for payment or the manual performance of a bank reconciliation. Other controls are carried out by computer programs, e.g. the computer matching of purchase invoices with goods received records and the preparation of an exception report; these are called programmed control procedures.

Many application controls will be performed by people but will be computer-dependent, being a combination of programmed control procedures and user controls. For example, a review by a purchasing supervisor of a computer-generated list of unfilled purchase orders (an exception report) to identify shipments that may have been received but not recorded. Because many application controls are dependent on programmed accounting or control procedures and the related computer processing, the effectiveness of the application controls, and the resultant achievement of the application control objectives, will often depend on the effectiveness of computer controls.

8:3.5   Computer controls

8:3.5.1   Link between computer and application controls

The auditor assesses and tests computer controls because there is a direct link between satisfaction of the computer control objectives and the audit assurance that can be obtained from programmed procedures within the accounting systems. If controls rely on programmed procedures, then the main impact is in the way in which their effective operation is tested. Normally, rather than directly testing the programmed control procedure, we test the corresponding computer controls.

Audit work on accounting systems and application controls will include the documentation of the information input to and recorded on the system, the programmed procedures that operate on that information and the outputs from the programmed procedures. The control objectives in evaluating computer controls are to ensure that the programmed procedures important to the processing of transactions and the related application controls have been developed, implemented, maintained and operated as intended. The auditor must also be sure that the information held on the computer can be relied upon, so procedures need to be in place to ensure that only authorised personnel can amend data, and that amendments can only be made through the applications.

Computer controls relate to the whole computer environment in which applications are operated. Where more than one computer environment is identified, each one that has applications with an audit impact should be assessed. Control over transaction processing is often achieved by manual procedures that operate in conjunction with, or depend on, programmed procedures. Computer controls are needed to ensure that these programmed procedures continue to operate properly.

8:3.5.2 *Control objectives of computer controls*

Controls over the maintenance of existing applications are designed to ensure that changes to programmed procedures are designed appropriately and implemented effectively. These controls relate to programme amendments, rather than to entire applications and should ensure that amendments are properly designed, tested and implemented. For example, all change requests are raised on a change request form, which is reviewed and approved before development starts.

Controls over the development and implementation of new or significantly enhanced applications are also designed to ensure that programmed procedures are appropriately designed and effectively implemented. They include controls over the original design of systems, the testing and documentation of programmes and systems and procedures for putting approved programmes into use and transferring data held in prior applications. For example, new systems are tested to ensure correct interaction with existing systems, and that the original design requirements are met.

Controls over computer security are designed to restrict access to the computer system, programs and data. Restricted access is generally accomplished through a combination of system-level, application-level, and physical access controls. Computer security management should ensure appropriate access controls through definition of risks, requirements and responsibilities. For example, user profiles restrict users to the system functions appropriate to their job functions.

Controls over computer operations are designed to ensure that data are processed to the correct file, recovery from processing failures is possible and programmes are properly scheduled, set up and executed. For example, changes to job control statements can be made only by appropriate personnel, and such changes are checked.

8:4 Control risk assessment

Control risk is the risk that the client's internal control will not prevent or detect material misstatements on a timely basis.

The auditor should assess control risk for each transaction cycle of audit significance. This assessment will depend on the strength of the control procedures applicable to the applications (including related monitoring controls) as well as the related computer controls and the control environment. The results of the control risk assessment will affect a number of audit objectives for each cycle. For practical purposes, it is normally convenient to divide the seven audit objectives into two groups:

Completeness, accuracy and existence/occurrence: The audit programme for these will often be similar or have a number of points in common.

Cut-off, valuation, rights and obligations and presentation and disclosure: The audit programme for these will to a greater extent need to be different according to the objective and the specific risks identified.

Table 8.1 highlights the likely impact of the client's internal control and the assessment of material misstatement for each group.

Table 8.1: *Control risk*

	Completeness; accuracy; existence/occurrence	Cut-off; valuation; rights and obligations; presentation and disclosure
Affected by control environment and monitoring controls?	Yes	Yes
Affected by management's subjective judgements and estimates?	No	Management's judgements and estimates, particularly in relation to the valuation and presentation and disclosure objectives, can be complex and may not be free from bias. Many clients do not have the professional expertise internally to deal completely with issues arising.
Affected by control procedures within established accounting systems?	Normally. In particular the degree of discipline necessarily involved in processing data by computer reduces risks.	Not normally. However, cut-off may be subject to controls, and data that provides the basis for management's judgements may also be derived from the accounting system.
Likely assessment of risk of material misstatement	A controls-oriented audit will aim to assess control risk at below the maximum or at low. Even if controls can be improved the auditor often might conclude that the risk of material misstatement will be lower than for other audit objectives.	Even in large, well-man aged clients, the auditor will rarely be able to assess the risk of material mis statement as low. The auditor may be able to derive some assurance from controls.

On all audits we should assess the control environment and obtain and record an understanding of the accounting system. The degree to which each of the types of control procedures needs to be assessed, and tested, for the purposes of the control risk assessment is a judgement that depends on the apparent quality of internal control, the relative efficiency of obtaining audit evidence from the operation of internal control and from substantive tests, optimum timing of work, the skills of the engagement team and client expectations.

Taking into account prior-year experience and knowledge obtained in the current year, the auditor will often presume the level of control risk for purposes of determining the audit strategy, before control procedures have been documented completely or tests of controls performed.

For purposes of planning the audit, control risk can be assessed for each significant transaction cycle as:

Maximum: no assurance to be taken from internal control;

Below the maximum: some assurance to be obtained from internal control; or

Low: high assurance to be obtained from internal control.

In practice, control risk is a continuum from non-existent control (maximum control risk – high risk of misstatement through error or fraud) to very good control (low control risk) – where we can obtain high assurance of the reliability of financial information generated by the system by testing controls. Particularly in below the maximum it will be efficient to assess control risk at points on the continuum.

For systems-derived account balances, our assessment of control risk will be a major factor in determining the audit programme. However, some control risk will always exist; therefore, control risk cannot reasonably be assessed below low. This is because even though properly designed computer procedures should eliminate random processing errors, human error in applying manual procedures, deliberate override of controls for legitimate purposes or fraud by management or employees means that for audit purposes we should never rely wholly on tests of controls. Management may be in a position to render monitoring controls ineffective and override application and computer controls. Therefore, if we suspect management fraud, a significant level of substantive testing will be necessary.

There may also be controls, particularly monitoring controls, over non systems-derived account balances, and therefore the auditor may be able to assess control risk at less than maximum for those account balances.

8:4.1 Maximum control risk

The auditor should gain and record an understanding of monitoring controls for each audit-significant transaction cycle and the related computer environment(s). When control risk is assessed at the maximum, no tests of controls are required.

The auditor will perform analytical procedures and, primarily, tests of detail designed to give high assurance. The tests of detail needed may include work in the nature of re-performance of control procedures, e.g., checking the bank reconciliation. The purpose is to establish whether there is a misstatement rather than to confirm that a procedure is operating. Any substantive audit programme will provide evidence of the effective operation of client procedures, which is why a report of control weaknesses should still be given even though a substantive audit is performed.

8:4.2 Below maximum control risk

The auditor should gain and record an understanding of monitoring controls for each audit-significant transaction cycle and the related computer environment(s).

The auditor does not generally need a detailed understanding of application or computer controls. However, sufficient information should be collected about application and computer controls to effectively design substantive tests for the current year. The following factors should be considered:

(a)   Whether understanding and testing monitoring controls alone will be sufficient to design, and support the planned level of, substantive tests.

(b)   Risks that have been identified during our acceptance/continuance procedures, assessment of the control environment or other planning activities, e.g., employee fraud, that require increased understanding of specific controls.

(c)   Client service expectations and needs.

Tests of controls will normally comprise tests of monitoring controls. However, tests of application and computer controls may be a cost-effective response to some of the factors described above.

Assessing control risk below the maximum requires considering where on the continuum the assessment lies.

Substantive testing where control risk is assessed below the maximum should comprise analytical procedures and medium to low levels of tests of detail (*see* **Figure 8.6** 'Control risk continuum', later in this section). Below the maximum represents a continuum between maximum and low. Therefore the extent of assurance necessary from substantive tests of detail will depend on where we assess control risk along the continuum, based on our professional judgement. **Table 8.2** provides guidance on matters to consider.

Table 8.2: *Assessing control risk along the continuum*

Matters to consider	Indicators suggesting higher end of continuum	Indicators suggesting lower end of continuum
Prior experience with the client	Prior years' audits revealed control weaknesses	Errors generally detected and corrected by the client
Strength of control environment	Weaknesses identified in control environment, e.g., board of directors not closely involved in operations	Effective organisation/ management Strong internal audit function
Finance and computer functions	Systems new or significantly changed	Well-established systems
	Inexperienced staff /high staff turnover	Qualified, knowledgeable and experienced staff
	Adjustments to figures common at month end	Regular accounting routines, ensuring, e.g., books are closed promptly at month ends
	Staff changes or other events affecting effectiveness of controls during accounting period	
Monitoring controls	Unmet control objectives because of inadequate design of controls	Monitoring controls strong

8:4.3 Low control risk

The auditor should gain and record an understanding of the monitoring controls for each audit-significant transaction cycle and the related computer environment.

Additionally the auditor should record an understanding of the relevant application controls for each transaction cycle and of the categories of computer controls relevant to the control risk assessment. It normally is not necessary to record all application controls that may exist, nor in the case of computer controls is it always necessary to address all objectives, but the auditor should identify those key procedures that address the specific control objectives that have audit significance.

Tests of controls to support a control risk assessment at low will be mainly of application and computer controls. These controls together can provide high assurance that material misstatements in the accounting records will be prevented, whereas monitoring controls will generally only detect whether there has been a failure. Also, monitoring controls are higher level controls that are not directed primarily to transaction cycle control objectives. For this reason it will normally not be possible to assess control risk for a cycle at low on the basis of testing monitoring controls alone. When application and computer controls are tested to support a low control risk assessment it will not be efficient for tests of monitoring controls to be performed as well. If it is efficient the auditor may, however, design tests of controls combining appropriate tests of monitoring, application and computer controls when monitoring controls and computer controls are strong enough, in combination with key application controls, to permit significantly restricting substantive tests.

Assessing control risk at low means that the risk of material misstatement arising from the functioning of internal control is sufficiently low that the level of assurance required from substantive tests is also low, after taking into account the presence or absence of inherent risk.

Where control risk is low, substantive tests directed at the objectives of completeness, accuracy and existence/occurrence should be designed to provide low assurance only. These tests may comprise analytical procedures and restricted, or no, tests of detail.

8:4.4 Summary of control risk assessment

The key is to arrive at the appropriate combination of tests of controls (monitoring, application and computer controls), analytical procedures and tests of detail for the client's circumstances. **Figure 8.6**, 'Control risk continuum', shows how the combination of tests varies with the assessment of control risk.

Figure 8.6: *Control risk continuum*

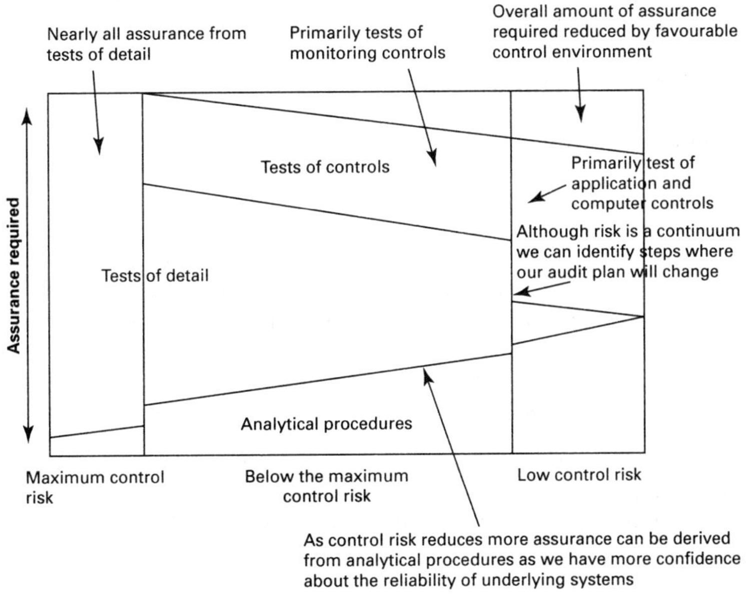

8:5 Audit implications of unmet control objectives

8:5.1 Effect of unmet application control objectives

An unmet control objective arises where a control has not been properly designed or is not in use for a significant systems-derived account balance or class of transactions. Such an omission could result in a material misstatement of the financial statements. When an unmet control objective has been discovered it might be appropriate to:

(a)   Inform the client.

(b)   Consider whether the problem could result in a material misstatement in the financial statements.

(c)   If a material misstatement might have occurred, through either error or fraud, design a specific auditing procedure, or consider whether other planned auditing procedures will result in sufficient assurance.

(d)   Ensure that the audit programme properly reflects the conclusion about the system.

Unmet control objectives also represent additional service opportunities in that the auditor can assist the client in developing action plans to improve controls.

The identification of an unmet application control objective does not necessarily make it necessary to change the control risk assessment over the whole cycle under consideration. The problem may either not be material or, if it could be, it may be possible to respond by designing a specific auditing procedure, either controls-related or substantive in nature. If, however, there are a number of unmet objectives or the problems are individually serious, the control risk assessment will be significantly affected, e.g., low becomes below the maximum.

8:5.2 Effect of unmet computer control objectives

In principle there is no difference between the response to an unmet computer control objective and an unmet application control objective. However, the pervasive nature of any computer control weakness means that its potential effect must be considered carefully.

Where there are weaknesses in computer controls the auditor should consider whether they are so significant as to prevent overall reliance on computer controls or whether their impact may be isolated to certain types of transactions or records. Breakdowns identified in the operation of programmed procedures may indicate weaknesses in computer controls. For example, many computer systems have powerful programs (utilities) that allow a user to amend data or programs without leaving an audit trail. In a well-controlled environment regular users will not have access to the utilities, and programmers, who often need to use utilities, will not have access to programs or data. If the security controls are not adequately set up, then it may be possible to use a utility on live data or programs.

There are two risks that arise in this circumstance, fraud and systematic error. The risk of systematic error is common to all businesses and would often arise from a well-intentioned action to amend a program or standing data. The auditor should look for monitoring or other direct controls that would detect or prevent such actions. Where such controls cannot be found, the proper functioning of the programmed procedures during the period should be tested directly.

The risk of fraud differs between businesses. In a financial institution, where the only record of the asset is electronic, it may not be possible to rely on programmed procedures for audit evidence and it may be necessary to design substantive audit procedures. In a retail or manufacturing organisation controls over assets mean that there would probably have to be collusion to conceal a fraud. It should therefore be possible to identify alternative control procedures, such as segregation of duties, that will permit reliance on the information produced by the systems. In both types of organisation the auditor should consider the risks arising from the control weakness and perform specific fraud assessment or detection procedures as appropriate.

8:6 Assessing whether control procedures are in place

Recording an understanding of controls includes being satisfied that the control procedures identified meet the objective and are in use. This is not as rigorous as testing a control (*see* **Section 8:7**) and will normally involve little more that a brief discussion with those members of staff who operate the control, together with a brief inspection of any relevant documents. For example, a member of the management team might be asked to explain how a particular monthly report is used and to provide a copy of a recent report.

8:7 Testing controls

SAS 400.2, 'Audit evidence', states that:

> *In seeking to obtain audit evidence from tests of control, auditors should consider the sufficiency and appropriateness of the audit evidence to support the assessed level of control risk.*

Testing the continued effective operation of a control procedure includes determining that:

(a)   The control has been appropriately designed to achieve its objective. For example, if application controls are based on computer-produced reports, the relevant programmed procedures should be properly designed.

(b) The control operates as prescribed. The person carrying out control procedures should understand how to perform them and be diligent in doing so. If application control procedures are based on the operation of computer programs, the relevant programmed procedures should operate as intended.

Computer controls are designed to ensure that programmed procedures are appropriately designed, implemented, maintained and operated. Effective operation of computer controls is therefore normally necessary to ensure the effectiveness of application controls involving programmed procedures.

The principles of obtaining evidence when testing monitoring, application and computer controls are the same.

In designing tests of controls we should consider the factors set out below:

- Observation and in-depth enquiry
- Examination of evidence
- Re-performance

8:7.1 Observation and in-depth enquiry

In order to be satisfied that a procedure is satisfactorily performed what the person actually does has to be probed. The auditor should ask open questions and should look out for evasive or incomplete answers. Inquiry alone generally does not provide sufficient evidence that controls are effective.

For example, a manager reviews a report for exceptions. If an exception comes to his or her attention another department is contacted to explain the circumstances and help establish if corrective action is needed. The auditor should enquire not only how the manager performs the review and responds to exceptions but also of the other department about the circumstances giving rise to exceptions, whether the manager picks them up and whether appropriate corrective action is taken when the manager does find an exception. This corroborative inquiry will provide further evidence of how effectively the control is performed.

8:7.2 Examination of evidence

The auditor should examine evidence of the performance of a control procedure when it might reasonably be expected to exist. Absence of evidence may indicate that the control procedure is not operating as prescribed and further inquiries will be necessary to determine whether there is in fact an effective control. In some cases the control may be absent and either there is no obvious evidence of the review or the data reviewed is transitory and cannot be precisely reproduced.

8:7.3 Re-performance

We should normally consider re-performance only when observation and enquiry, supported by examination of evidence, does not provide sufficient assurance that the control is operating effectively. This might be because there is no adequate evidence to examine, e.g. because the control is based on a review of information on a computer screen, or because the control is of such significance that the auditor should obtain further evidence of its effective operation.

8:7.4 Extent of examination of evidence

The procedures required to test whether a control has been operating effectively are more rigorous than those required to determine whether a control is in use.

In continuing audits where the system is reasonably stable, it will often be effective to test controls at the same time as updating the systems information in the audit files.

Obtaining an updated understanding of the system involves finding out if there have been any changes in the control procedures. Where there have been changes the auditor should consider whether the current procedure achieves the objective, in which case our audit programme need not be affected and the work can proceed to establish that the controls in place have continued to operate effectively.

When testing controls, the extent of examination of evidence should be decided by considering the importance of the control procedure, the degree to which it is cumulative and also the risk that observation of controls and answers to limited enquiries may not accurately represent the proper and continued operation of controls. The auditor should also base this assessment partly on the quality of the answers received to audit inquiries and whether, in the circumstances, such answers appear sound and credible.

If tests of controls will require examination of documentation that will also need to be examined for substantive testing purposes, it may be efficient and practicable to combine the work, or ensure that individual work plans make clear the need to consider both tests of controls and substantive testing.

8:7.5 Testing controls during the period

It may be possible to obtain specific evidence that controls operated continuously throughout the period, by spreading tests of controls. Observation and enquiry should be sufficiently thorough to enable a conclusion as to whether controls have operated effectively and continuously until the date when the observation and enquiry were carried out. Reviews of control procedures carried out by the client may provide evidence of the continuous operation of the underlying manually performed control procedures. Evidence of performance of controls might include, e.g., consideration of control procedures which have cumulative effect such as the reconciliation of control accounts.

SAS 300.5, 'Accounting and Internal Control Systems and Audit Risk Assessments' requires that:

> *If intending to rely on tests of control performed in advance of the period end,*
> *auditors should obtain sufficient appropriate audit evidence as to the nature and*

extent of any changes in design or operation of the entity's accounting and internal control systems within the accounting period since such procedures were performed.

The auditor should consider the intervening period from the date of the observation, enquiry and examination of evidence until the end of the financial period under audit. This should take into account:

(a)   the results of the interim procedures;

(b)   the length of the intervening period;

(c)   whether any changes have occurred to systems and controls during the intervening period;

(d)   the quality of the control environment and monitoring controls (which will often need to be tested); and

(e)   any other relevant factors, such as the results of current year substantive testing.

8:7.6 Documentation of tests of controls

The nature, extent and timing of tests of controls performed to support an assessment of control risk below the maximum or at low should be recorded in the working papers.

The recording requirement applies whatever the nature of the tests. The working papers should describe:

(a)   The tests performed.

(b)   The observations made.

(c)   The client personnel interviewed and their significant responses.

(d)   Any documents examined.

(e)   Any other evidence obtained to corroborate the enquiries.

(f)   Any exceptions and how they were cleared or the audit implications.

It is unnecessary for the working paper to repeat information contained in the record of understanding of the controls.

Chapter 9

Substantive testing

9:1 Substantive testing

9:1.1 Introduction

The sections in this chapter describe the steps to be taken in designing and completing substantive tests in accordance with the audit strategy. The sections are grouped as follows.

- **Sections 9:2** to **9:5** General guidance on audit programmes and substantive tests.
- **Sections 9:6** to **9:14** Guidance on audit areas not covered by specific balances in financial statements.
- **Sections 9:15** to **9:23** Guidance on substantive tests of assets.
- **Sections 9:24** to **9:29** Guidance on substantive tests of liabilities.
- **Sections 9:30** to **9:33** Guidance on substantive tests on profit and loss account balances and the trial balance and general ledger.

The extent of assurance required from substantive tests will be decided in audit planning (*see* **Section 4:6**, 'Determining the strategy', and may also be recorded on a detailed substantive testing plan (*see* **Section 4:7**, 'The audit programme'). These should provide sufficient guidance to allow the preparation of detailed audit programmes, or the amendment of standard programmes, for use by audit staff.

9:1.2 Small businesses

The suggested substantive tests in **Sections 9:6** to **9:33** are extensive and it may not be appropriate or necessary to follow all of the tests for small businesses with straightforward business transactions. Choice of tests is a matter of professional judgement.

9:2 Audit programmes

9:2.1 Objectives

The objectives of preparing audit programmes are as follows:

(a)   To assist in planning the audit, so that efficient and effective procedures are applied in accordance with the audit strategy and where prepared, the substantive testing plan.

(b)   To provide clear instructions to staff as to the nature, extent and timing of procedures.

(c)   To provide a record of the work done and the conclusions drawn, as a basis for effective quality control and to meet audit evidence requirements.

9:2.2 Form of audit programmes

For the purposes of efficiency and quality control each firm will wish to consider specifying procedures in relation to the form and content of audit programmes. The following may be considered appropriate:

(a)   Programmes should describe the nature of procedures in sufficient detail to provide adequate instruction to members of the audit team carrying out the work.

(b)   Programmes should indicate the extent of testing and the intended timing of the work.

(c)   Programmes should show against each procedure the following:

   (i)   A cross-reference to the related working papers recording the evidence obtained.

   (ii)   The initials of the member of the audit team carrying out the work.

   (iii)   The date on which the work was completed.

   (iv)   Whether any exceptions were found in carrying out the test and whether they were satisfactorily cleared. Any matters for Issues documentation should be clearly identified.

An audit programme should be prepared for each account balance or class of transaction where significant substantive procedures are to be carried out. The procedures specified in the programme should be designed to provide the requisite degree of substantive assurance in relation to each audit objective. This will vary according to the risk and materiality of the matter under consideration.

Audit programmes should be prepared or updated every year to ensure that they reflect the assessments of inherit risk and control risk. The engagement manager should review and approve each audit programme, ensuring that the nature, extent and timing of procedures are appropriate to the audit strategy. It is preferable for the engagement manager's approval to be given before procedures are carried out, as well as on completion of work.

9:2.3 Preparation

To help control the completion, approval and review of the programme, each programme produced might have a standard declaration by the manager and the in-charge. A standard declaration is adequate.

9:2.3.1 Link to the strategy and testing plan

As discussed in **Section 4:7**, 'The audit programme', the tailored audit programme should be cross-referenced to the individual work plans. To assist this process the audit objectives to which each step relates can be indicated on the work plan.

Usually a particular step will provide evidence relating to more than one objective, but the evidence obtained will be stronger in relation to some objectives than in relation to others. For example, a circularisation of debtors will provide strong evidence of existence but weaker evidence on accuracy, cut-off and rights and obligations.

9:2.4 Essential audit objectives

Later sections of this chapter provide guidance on the design of substantive procedures for inclusion in audit programmes. The guidance is presented in those sections under the heading, 'Essential audit objectives', and tailors the seven general audit objectives (*see* **Section 2:3**, 'Audit objectives') to each principal area of the financial statements. Such guidance, combined with the auditor's own experience, will usually provide sufficient basis for designing and drafting audit programmes.

9:2.5 Tailoring specimen steps

'Standard' programmes of specimen tests are widely available for each main category of asset and liability in the balance sheet and for the profit and loss account, and many firms will have their own programmes on pre-printed stationery or on computer disk. These specimen programmes set out typical procedures which might be carried out. However, they should be tailored to the specific requirements of the audit programme and the circumstances of the client. For audits of clients in specialised industry sectors, the extent of changes necessary will normally be so great that attempting to amend the specimen test steps will not be an efficient approach. In these cases firms should arrange for in-house industry specialists to help in preparing specimen audit programmes for the industry and/or the auditor should consult industry specialists to help in tailoring the specimen programmes.

If specimen programmes are used as a basis for producing audit programmes, amendments should involve the following (where applicable):

(a) **Additions, changes or deletions of audit steps** for the following reasons:

    (i) To comply with the audit programme.

    (ii) To respond to risks of material misstatements.

    (iii) To take account of the results of work done on controls.

    (iv) To take account of any special year-end procedures instituted by the client.

    (v) To take account of any exceptions noted during other audit procedures.

    (vi) To remove steps not relevant to the client's business.

    (vii) To add steps relevant to specialised aspects of the client's business.

(viii) To recognise the use of computer-assisted audit techniques, by deleting steps covered by the software and adding appropriate follow-up procedures in relation to reports produced by the software.

(b) **Reordering of steps, or combining of steps from different sections of the programme, for reasons of efficiency**: The object should be to structure the steps in such a way that:

(i)   duplication of selection or examination of documents is avoided;

(ii) members of the audit team will be able, as much as possible, to perform at one time all related aspects of work with which they are concerned; and

(iii) conclusions on one aspect of the work which may have an impact on related areas are recognised at an early stage.

9:2.6 Impact of computer-assisted audit techniques

The auditor may need to liaise with specialist computer audit staff when designing audit programmes. However, responsibility for the audit programme should normally remain with the engagement manager, who should ascertain that all necessary steps are included.

9:2.7 Completion and review of programmes

On completion of each step in an audit programme, the individual who has carried out the work should note the incidence of any exceptions and their clearance in accordance with the guidance in **Section 9:5**, 'Evaluating the results of substantive testing', and then initial and enter the date in the appropriate columns or make the necessary entry in the computerised working papers. This should only be done if the work completed conforms with that in the programme. If the step in the programme cannot be completed in the form set out, or it could be improved, the matter should be brought to the attention of the in-charge or the engagement manager. An appropriate amendment should be made to the programme step before the work is completed and the programme signed off.

The in-charge should review and approve the completion of each programme and sign off the programme to confirm that:

(a)   all procedures have been completed (except as noted) and working papers have been properly prepared and reviewed;

(b)   the results of testing have been properly evaluated and appropriate conclusions reached; and

(c)   appropriate matters have been identified and draft points drawn up for reporting in the issues documentation.

The engagement manager should review the completion of the programme and the overall conclusions, and should ensure appropriate matters are reported in the issues documentation.

9:3 Substantive analytical review

9:3.1 Introduction

This section discusses the use of analytical review as a substantive test to support audit objectives for individual account balances and classes of transactions. Preliminary analytical review procedures used in the assessment of risk and analytical review procedures appropriate in the final review of financial statements are discussed in **Sections 4:2**, 'Business review', and **4:3**, 'Preliminary analytical review'.

9:3.2 Nature and rigour of substantive analytical review

The basic premise underlying the use of substantive analytical review procedures is that relationships between data may be expected to exist and continue into the future in the absence of changes caused by:

- changes in the business;
- changes in accounting methods;
- specific unusual transactions or events;
- random fluctuations;
- misstatements.

Effective substantive analytical procedures involve review of recorded amounts against expectations developed from such relationships between data, combined with investigation of significant differences. Hence it is possible to identify the following three elements of a substantive analytical review:

(a)   Developing an expectation of the recorded amount.

(b)   Determining the amount of variation between the expectation and the recorded amount that is acceptable without explanation (the 'threshold').

(c)   Investigating variations that cannot be accepted without explanation.

These elements need not be viewed as consecutive steps.

Analytical review procedures can be an effective and efficient source of substantive assurance in relation to some or all of the audit objectives for an account balance or class of transactions. They may therefore substitute for tests of details as a means of obtaining significant audit assurance. Before carrying out substantive analytical review procedures, the auditor should clarify the audit objectives for which evidence is sought, and the degree of assurance desired, since these are factors influencing the nature and rigour of the review procedures required.

Effective substantive analytical reviews should involve the three general elements of a substantive analytical review described above. However, the greater the assurance required from the procedures, the more rigorous should be the development of expectations and the investigation of variations. Examples of procedures which might be appropriate in particular circumstances are included in this section.

9:3.3   Developing an expectation

9:3.3.1   Validity of the expectation

To provide valid substantive evidence, the expectation the auditor develops should be such that, when compared to the recorded amount, it can reasonably be expected to highlight differences caused by significant errors. Accordingly:

(a)   The relationship on which the expectation is based should be plausible (**Section 9:3.3.2**).

(b)   The data used to develop the expectation should be reliable (**Section 9:3.3.3**).

9:3.3.2   Plausible relationships

A plausible relationship for audit purposes is one which can be explained logically either from its existence in previous years or from an understanding of the business. However, the auditor should not rely on a 'historical' trend's continuing unless able to explain why it should do so. A relationship should not be used if the auditor cannot understand or explain it, because this could lead to erroneous conclusions. Accordingly, if it is not possible to explain the basis for the expectations, variations or lack of variation between the expectations and the recorded amount cannot provide positive audit evidence.

The auditor should consider the extent to which there are likely to be random (i.e., unpredictable) fluctuations in the relationship, and hence the likely efficiency and effectiveness of the review, in the light of the following:

(a)   Relationships in a stable environment are more predictable than in a dynamic or unstable environment.

(b)   Relationships for profit and loss accounts tend to be more predictable because they represent transactions over a period of time, whereas relationships for balance sheet accounts tend to be less predictable because a balance at any one time might be subject to random or short-term influences.

(c)   Relationships involving transactions undertaken at management's discretion are usually less predictable. For example, advertising or maintenance expenditure can vary considerably.

The auditor should also consider whether any information has already come to light regarding the other factors identified in **Section 9:3.2** which might indicate that a change in the relationship should be expected. Information relating to these factors might come from:

(a)   knowledge of the client's business and the environment in which it operates;

(b)   knowledge obtained of significant management decisions (e.g., a change in accounting policy);

(c)   knowledge of significant events or transactions;

(d)   the results of other audit work.

9:3.3.3 Reliable information

The auditor needs to be satisfied that the data used to develop the expectation are reliable. The extent of evidence required as to the reliability of information used in analytical review procedures varies with the assurance sought from the procedure. Also, if information from a variety of sources is used, the auditor normally requires less evidence of reliability in relation to each individual source than would be needed if one source alone were used. Professional judgement should be used to decide whether sufficient evidence has been obtained as to reliability of the underlying information for the level of assurance that it is intended to take from the review.

The auditor may obtain assurance that the underlying data used in developing the expectation are reliable by establishing either that the data are independent, or that they have been audited. Sources of reliable data include both external and internal data:

(a)   **External data**: Data from external sources are normally, by their nature, independent for audit purposes. The auditor should, however, consider the reliability of the source of the external data as well as any influence the client may have upon such data. External data such as industry statistics may not be independent if the client represents a large share of the market. The auditor should also consider the timeliness of the data, because data from external sources are often not recent enough to be relevant.

(b)   **Internal data**: Data from internal sources are independent if they are derived from records maintained by persons who are not in a position to manipulate, directly or indirectly, the accounting records that affect the account balance or class of transactions being audited. For example, employment records kept by a personnel department will normally be independent for the purpose of testing payroll. However, the auditor should be aware that data maintained by persons outside the accounting department can be subject to manipulation (e.g., certain production statistics may be important performance criteria for production managers).

If internal data are not independent because they are generated by persons who are in a position to manipulate the accounting records that affect the amount being audited, the auditor should consider the extent of testing necessary to obtain assurance as to the data's reliability. The following should be taken into account:

(i)   knowledge obtained during previous audits;

(ii)   the results of other substantive testing; and, in particular:

(iii) the results of the assessment of the control environment, accounting systems and internal accounting controls.

If analytical review procedures are based on information from interim financial statements or management accounts, the auditor will need to consider its quality before obtaining assurance from the conclusions drawn from reviewing it. For example, information from interim statements will not be so useful if routine adjusting entries are not made. It is also necessary to consider the possibility that estimated figures or even artificial entries might have been made in the management accounts, or accounting records, to produce the 'normal' or expected ratios or relationships.

If underlying data have not been subject to tests of details as part of the audit process and the other factors discussed above do not provide sufficient assurance, the auditor may need to carry out specific tests to confirm the data's reliability.

An example of establishing reliability of data concerns an analytical review of payroll for a small client with few classes of employee. Procedures designed to provide low assurance might involve developing an expectation based on the prior year's total annual payroll adjusted for changes in wage rates, assuming that the number of employees was constant. The reliability of the assumption as to the number of employees might be corroborated by discussions with operating management and by examining evidence that the client's level of operations was essentially equivalent to that of the prior year. Information about pay increases might be obtained by enquiry or by review of board minutes or other documentation authorising the pay scale adjustment.

If the auditor required more assurance from analytical review, employee numbers might be corroborated by examining statistics in the personnel department. In addition, the reliability of this information might be established by detailed enquiry in the personnel department as to how the records were kept accurate and up to date.

9:3.3.4 Basis of the expectation

The auditor's expectation will be developed on the basis of one or more of the following:

(a)   Information used by management to monitor the business.

(b)   Prior-year amounts adjusted for known changes.

(c)   Relationships between elements of financial data.

(d)   Relationships between financial and non-financial data.

When choosing the most efficient and effective procedures, the auditor should consider the information available within the business, because management often uses key performance indicators and other management information to monitor the business. This information can be used to develop an appropriate expectation. Indeed, the ease with which it is possible to perform analytical reviews will often be related to the extent of direct involvement by senior management in reviewing and evaluating the performance of the entity. The assessment of the control environment will help identify the scope for effective analytical review procedures.

9:3.3.4.1 Information used by management to monitor the business

Effective budgeting involves the consideration of previous results and management's expectation of current results, based on known relationships between operating and financial data. Consequently a review of client budgets supported by discussions with the people responsible for their preparation will often help the auditor to develop expectations more efficiently and effectively.

The auditor should carefully consider whether management regards the budget as a realistic expectation, or whether the budget reflects aggressive or unrealistic targets. In the latter case, the budget should not be used as the expectation. If the auditor concludes that the client's budget is itself an appropriate expectation, it is still necessary to obtain assurance that the data the client uses to develop the budget meet the same standards of plausibility and reliability as the auditor would require when developing expectations independently.

If management carries out analytical review procedures, using budgets or other management information, as part of its management controls over the business, the auditor may, as an alternative to performing detailed reviews independently, assess the relevance and reliability of management's procedures, and management's response when it identifies fluctuations requiring explanations. Using the client's review procedures (with re-performance where appropriate) is likely to be more efficient. It may be efficient to consider the nature and extent of such work at the strategy stage, in relation to the assessment of the effective operation of control.

If the auditor chooses to perform detailed reviews independently, it will, nevertheless, often be effective to design procedures around the relationships identified by the performance indicators that management uses for controlling the business.

9:3.3.4.2 Prior-year amounts adjusted for known changes

There will often be a plausible relationship between the recorded amount and the prior-period amount. Consequently, the auditor might develop an expectation of the monthly sales for the current year by, e.g., adjusting prior-year amounts for changes in the level of activity and price rises. In such cases, however, it is also necessary to consider any changes in underlying relationships that might cause the expectation to be invalid.

9:3.3.4.3 Relationships between elements of financial data

An example of an expectation based on a relationship between elements of financial data would be an expectation of commission expense developed in relation to sales. The relationship could be based either on the client's stated policies or, if still valid, on the recorded relationship in the past.

The auditor should avoid imputing validity to two accounts simply because the relationship between them appears reasonable. One of the accounts forms part of the data used in developing the expectation. For example, the auditor may conclude that sales appear to be reasonably stated from a review of an apparent relationship between sales and cost of sales, but only if the validity of cost of sales has been established by other audit procedures.

If there is a direct relationship between income and expenses and assets and liabilities, it is usually efficient to perform analytical review procedures on the income or expense accounts at the same time as the auditor tests the related balance sheet accounts. Examples of these relationships are: dividends receivable and investments; interest payable and loans outstanding; rent receivable and property held; and hire fees receivable and plant available for hire.

9:3.3.4.4 Relationships between financial and non-financial data

Because non-financial data are usually maintained independently of the accounting records, relationships between financial and non-financial data can be particularly effective. Examples of relationships which the auditor could use to develop an expectation are: sales and production volumes or quantities in a manufacturing organisation; sales and square footage in a retail organisation; rental income and square footage; payroll cost and staff numbers. In process industries, in particular, it is often possible to develop a relationship based on overall reconciliation of physical quantities flowing into and out of the process.

9:3.3.5 Precision of the expectation

In general, the less precise the expectation the less possible it is to distinguish variations caused by material misstatements from random variations, or variations caused by the other factors discussed in **Section 9:3.2**. This reduces the effectiveness of the analytical review, decreasing the assurance the auditor can obtain from the procedure. It might also decrease the efficiency of the review since variations which have arisen from purely random fluctuations are more likely to be identified for investigation.

The auditor can increase precision by performing some or all of the following procedures:

(a) Increasing the extent of disaggregation of data, so that, e.g., the expectation is determined on a month-by-month basis rather than annually, or it is developed separately for different categories of item within the account balance or class of transactions.

(b) Considering additional data which might affect the expectation.

(c) Examining relevant data in greater detail.

To continue the **example** in **Section 9:3.3.3**, the precision might be increased by using monthly employee number statistics to develop a month-by-month expectation. The auditor might also consider changes in the mix of grades of employee and look in more detail at the analysis of pay rises by grade, and might further consider whether more disaggregation or weighting of the pay rise calculation would increase precision.

9:3.4 Identifying variations which require investigation

SAS 410.4, *'Analytical Procedures'*, states that:

> *When significant fluctuations or unexpected relationships are identified that are inconsistent with other relevant information or that deviate from predicted patterns, auditors should investigate and obtain adequate explanations and appropriate corroborative evidence.*

The auditor should decide whether any variations between the expectation and the recorded amount require investigation. This can be done by determining the amount of variation that is acceptable without investigation (the 'threshold'). The threshold should be an amount that is sufficiently small to detect potential misstatements which could be material either individually or when aggregated with other misstatements. Variations in excess of the threshold are indicators of potential material misstatement and therefore require investigation.

9:3.4.1 Determining the threshold for investigation

The threshold cannot be precisely computed without employing sophisticated mathematical techniques. Accordingly, the auditor should use professional judgement to determine the acceptable amount of variation between the expectation and the recorded amount. This judgement will be based on the following factors:

- materiality;
- the size of the amount being audited;
- the effect of disaggregation;
- the precision of the expectation.

These factors are examined in turn.

(a) **Materiality**: The threshold for an entire account balance or class of transactions should not normally be set at an amount as high as the overall materiality level for the audit. This is because a variation between the auditor's expectation and the recorded amount which is equal to, or slightly less than, materiality could represent a material misstatement that has, in fact, been offset by a fluctuation due to other factors. Materiality is dealt with in **Section 2:2**.

(b) **Size of the amount being audited**: As the total amount of the account balance or class of transactions decreases the auditor should decrease the threshold to allow for the possibility that non-material errors in several accounts might aggregate to a material amount. A variation that is significant in relation to the account balance might represent a misstatement, even though it was not, in itself, material. Alternatively it might indicate a significant deficiency in the expectation. Thus, for example, if certain operating expenses were £4 million the auditor might want to investigate a total difference greater than £250,000, even though materiality was £500,000.

(c) **The effect of disaggregation**: The threshold applied at a disaggregated level should generally be smaller than the threshold for an entire account balance or class of transactions, to allow for the fact that smaller misstatements in the disaggregated amounts might be material in aggregate. However, the amount of difference acceptable without investigation does not decrease proportionately to the extent of disaggregation. This is mainly because misstatements are unlikely to occur in all of the disaggregated amounts. In any case, the auditor should not normally use a threshold less than 10-20 per cent of the overall level of materiality because further reduction does not substantially increase the likelihood of identifying material misstatements.

(d) **Precision of the expectation**: If a precise expectation has been developed, a difference is more likely to represent misstatement than a similar difference in a less precise expectation. For example, the auditor might expect an estimate of interest expense to be very close to the actual amount if it were based on weighted average debt balances and interest rates; consequently, if even a small difference were found, a detailed investigation into the possibility of misstatement might be indicated.

9:3.5 Investigating significant variations

When an expectation has been developed at the appropriate level of disaggregation and the appropriate threshold has been determined, the auditor should investigate and evaluate all differences between the expectation and the recorded amount that exceed the threshold. This should be done by means of the following:

(a) Identifying plausible reasons for differences. As discussed in **Section 9:3.2**, these might include business or accounting changes, unusual transactions or events or random fluctuations due to simplifications of data used in developing the expectation.

(b) Corroborating these reasons.

(c) Quantifying the effect of the reasons.

The auditor should be alert for a consistent pattern of differences from expectations. Such a pattern might indicate either a deficiency in the expectations or a misstatement in the recorded amount. Thus, if (for example) expectations of monthly balances were consistently less than the recorded amount, the auditor should investigate the reasons for such differences even if none of the individual differences exceeded the threshold.

Unexplained differences are a potential danger signal and they indicate an increased risk of misstatement. Accordingly, in those rare cases where analytical review procedures disclose differences that cannot be adequately explained, the auditor should regard the difference as an indication of misstatement.

9:3.5.1 *Identifying plausible reasons for the difference*

Plausible reasons for differences in excess of the threshold can be identified in a number of ways. The auditor will generally start by reconsidering information about the client obtained from the business review and other procedures, and its impact on the expectation. For example, if the initial expectation was based on comparison of prior and current-year financial data, the investigation might begin with a more thorough consideration of key factors that would be expected to influence the account, and by further disaggregation of the data.

The auditor might identify plausible reasons for differences from discussions with appropriate client personnel, including the financial controller and those directly responsible for operations. If budgeting is used to monitor and control a client's operations the auditor can take advantage of the client's investigation of significant fluctuations by discussing them with individuals responsible for explaining variances from budgeted amounts.

9:3.5.2 *Corroborating explanations*

The auditor should corroborate explanations for significant differences. The procedures used will depend on the nature of the explanation, the type of account and the results of other substantive auditing procedures. In some cases the auditor's understanding of the business and the knowledge gained from other procedures will be sufficient to corroborate an explanation. In most cases, however, an explanation should be corroborated by performing one or more of the following:

(a) **Examining documentation**: Examining documentation to corroborate plausible reasons for significant differences will generally be efficient when the difference is caused by a small number of unusual or infrequently occurring transactions. Thus, if the identified difference from the expectation is attributed to an unusual transaction, such as a large expenditure for a major advertising campaign to launch a new product line, the auditor could examine underlying documents such as contracts, invoices or minutes of meetings.

(b) **Extending the analytical review procedures**: This is appropriate when additional factors are identified from which it is possible to develop a more precise expectation. The reliability of such additional factors should be corroborated in the same manner as that used for those factors employed to develop the initial expectation. The auditor might also consider further disaggregation of the data (e.g., by product line) to develop an expectation likely to have less variance from recorded amounts.

(c) **Making independent enquiries**: This should involve discussions with independent individuals either inside or outside the client's organisation. For example, an explanation for an increase in advertising expense from the Financial Controller might be substantiated through discussions with the Marketing Director. The auditor might also make enquiries of individuals outside the client's organisation. For example, a change in revenue recognition practices might be corroborated through discussions with significant customers regarding sales terms such as the right of return.

Tests of details may also be specifically designed to corroborate explanations. For example, an increase in sales might be attributed to a general 5 per cent increase in prices. The auditor might choose to corroborate this explanation by selecting sales of comparable products from the current and prior year and comparing the relevant sales prices. However, because the expectation is developed from logical relationships that can reasonably be expected to exist, the auditor should not respond to unexplained differences by carrying out unfocused tests of details.

9:3.5.3 *Quantifying the reasons for the difference*

The auditor should attempt to quantify that portion of the difference from the expectation for which explanations have been obtained and ensure that such amount is sufficient to support the conclusion that there is no material misstatement.

9:3.6 Concluding on the results of substantive analytical review procedures

The substantive analytical review procedures discussed in this section are designed and carried out to determine whether there is material misstatement in a recorded amount. If it is not possible to reduce the unexplained difference between the expectation and the recorded amount to an acceptable level by the investigations described above, the conclusion should be drawn that the amount of such unexplained difference represents a misstatement, and the auditor should consider whether the assumptions made in connection with the risk assessment continue to be appropriate.

If a potential material misstatement is identified the auditor should request that the client perform additional work to justify the account balance. If, as a result of this work, it is possible to conclude that the account balance or class of transaction is not materially misstated, this should be stated in the working papers. If, however, this conclusion is not possible, the client should be asked to make an appropriate adjustment.

9:3.6.1 *Reporting to management*

The auditor should also be aware that analytical review procedures often identify matters which could be reported to management, e.g.:

(a)   Weaknesses in management or business controls or in management processes.

(b)   Unsatisfactory budgeting and management information systems.

(c)   Findings that have an impact on the overall assessment of the control environment, in that it appears that the quality of financial and non-financial information available to senior management does not match up to good practice.

Where appropriate significant matters should be included in the issues documentation.

9:3.7 Use of software

The audit firm may wish to consider whether audit software could improve the efficiency or effectiveness of analytical review procedures. Generalised software packages can be used to carry out calculations in developing expectations and to compare figures in both disaggregated and aggregated form. Most such packages can also provide comparisons in the form of graphs.

It is also possible to develop more specialised software to apply statistical techniques in the performance of substantive analytical review. The use of a statistical model enables the program to build a more precise expectation, and also to identify more clearly those variations which require investigation.

9:3.8 Engagement considerations

The effective performance of analytical review requires:

(a) a thorough knowledge of the client's business and the factors that might affect it;

(b) an adequate appreciation of the relationships between the various accounts;

(c) an ability to draw the proper conclusions and understand the implications for subsequent audit procedures.

Accordingly, the members of the audit team involved in developing analytical review procedures should have appropriate levels of experience, judgement and skill, and at times it may be necessary for the in-charge or above to carry out the review. However, the auditor should take advantage of opportunities to delegate some or all aspects of the analytical procedures adopted for a particular account balance or class of transactions to other members of the audit team provided they have appropriate skills and experience.

9:3.9 Audit programmes

The auditor should record appropriate details of the substantive analytical review procedures to be carried out in the substantive testing plan and audit programmes. These or the working papers should explain the basis for the expectation and threshold. The audit programme should be clear as to expectations, the level of fluctuation that should be investigated and how follow up work will be performed. These decisions should be made at the end of the planning stage rather than during the fieldwork as it reduces the risk of over-auditing.

9:3.10 Working papers

The auditor should record the results of the substantive analytical review procedures in sufficient detail to provide evidence of the work done, the conclusions drawn and the evidence obtained to support those conclusions. This should include:

(a) The explanations obtained from the client's officials and the means used to corroborate the explanations.

(b) The estimated amount of any misstatement indicated by significant unexplained variations.

9:4 Tests of details

9:4.1 Nature and extent of tests of details

Tests of details are carried out to obtain substantive audit evidence to support audit objectives for individual account balances and classes of transactions.

The nature and amount of the evidence required, and hence the choice or combination of procedures and the extent of testing, is a matter of professional judgement which the auditor exercises in the light of the circumstances of each case and the evidence obtained from other auditing procedures. For this reason, it is not appropriate to lay down definitive rules specifying levels of tests. Instead, this Manual provides general guidance on the amount of testing that might be appropriate. The engagement manager and the engagement partner should be satisfied with the extent of tests in individual cases that are critical to the audit opinion.

Tests of details may involve the following procedures:

(a)   Observation and enquiry.

(b)   Reperformance and recomputation.

(c)   Confirmation.

(d)   Physical inspection.

(e)   Examination of documentary evidence.

(f)   Review of minutes.

(g)   Letters of enquiry to solicitors.

These procedures are often combined in carrying out a particular test. For example, observing client stock counts will normally be combined with physical inspection of stock items. The procedures are generally equally applicable whether accounting records are computerised or maintained manually. However, in computerised systems, the auditor may consider using audit software to assist in testing, as described in **Sections 9:4.2 to 9:4.2.5**.

9:4.1.1 Observation and enquiry

The auditor will normally use observation and enquiry to obtain substantive testing evidence where management itself carries out specific procedures to validate financial information. Examples are:

(a)   Observing client stock counts.

(b)   Establishing by enquiry that regular reconciliations of debtors and bank balances are performed.

(c)   Reviewing with the client the basis upon which provisions for bad debts, warranties or obsolete stock have been made.

When carrying out observation and enquiry procedures, the auditor should adopt an appropriate level of professional scepticism. In the case of enquiry, it is important to be alert for vague and glib answers and for client staff confusing hearsay with fact. It will normally be necessary to corroborate enquiries. When observation is used, it is important to be wary of drawing conclusions from client procedures or routines which might have been modified because of the auditor's presence.

Although sometimes observation or enquiry may provide all the substantive audit evidence needed, the auditor should normally combine them with other procedures such as reperformance, recomputation or inspection of documentary evidence.

9:4.1.2 Reperformance and recomputation

Reperformance involves reperformance of client procedures or computations, in part or in full. For example, where the client carries out a bank reconciliation, the auditor might test the reconciling items by rechecking the compilation of those reconciling items, either on a test basis or, in a simple situation, by reperforming the reconciliation.

Where an account balance represents the result of a computation or an accumulation of computations (e.g., depreciation), it may be efficient to substantiate such account balances by recomputation, either in detail or on a total basis.

If judgement is the basis of a computation, reperformance of the computation should also include evaluating the reasoning process supporting the judgement. For example, if the client's determination of the provision for doubtful debts, giving due regard to past experience, is based on a formula related to the age of the debtors, the auditor should, in addition to checking the mathematical calculations, also evaluate the reasonableness of the formula.

9:4.1.3 Confirmation

Confirmation consists of obtaining audit evidence from a third party in support of a fact or condition. Confirmations obtained externally from persons who are independent of the client provide strong support for the existence, accuracy and rights of items making up an account balance. Thus, they often serve as the principal substantive tests of details for these audit objectives.

Using confirmation can be a useful supplement to other audit procedures, even in the absence of complete independence of the third party. For example, although confirmation of a group company balance would normally 'produce a lower degree of audit assurance because the company is not independent, the confirmation would, nevertheless, supplement other procedures (such as examination of unmatched purchase orders and goods received notes) performed to substantiate the balance.

Confirmation procedures are most commonly applied in relation to the verification of trade debtors, and reference should be made to the 'Trade debtors', **Section 9:21**. Use of confirmations is also discussed in relation to trade creditors, investments, stocks and bank and cash.

The normal means of confirmation is by letter. However, the auditor may also use electronic means such as telex or facsimile copier (fax), e.g., to communicate with banks and commodity brokers (who use these means extensively), or when there may be insufficient time for an exchange of letters. If telex or fax are used, the auditor should perform additional procedures to ensure the electronic confirmation can be regarded as acceptable evidence. These are described in **Section 9:21**, 'Trade debtors'.

9:4.1.4 Physical inspection

Inspection involves examining and, frequently, counting the physical assets underlying the amounts in an account (e.g., cash, securities, fixed assets, or stocks). The procedures are often most cost effective when they are combined with observation and enquiry.

For any inspection procedure, auditors should not assume a responsibility inconsistent with their professional qualifications. Thus, although it is appropriate to exercise common sense when concluding whether the items being inspected are what they are represented to be, the auditor should not assume the role of a valuer, lawyer or other expert outside the field of auditing. Sometimes the inspection procedure should be supplemented by a report by such outside experts, e.g. the report of a metallurgist in relation to the composition of metal alloys.

9:4.1.5 Examining documentary evidence

This will normally involve examining (on a test basis where appropriate) documents which support the existence or validity of a recorded item or balance. To do this, the auditor should normally ascertain whether there is evidence that the client's required approval procedures have been performed, and determine whether any aspects of the transaction appear unreasonable (e.g., a supplier's invoice not addressed to the client). When examining a document, the auditor should consider what further steps are necessary to obtain assurance as to its authenticity if there are any signs of erasure or alteration, or if the document is not in its original form (e.g., because it has been copied or microfilmed). Documents generated wholly or in part by persons outside the client (e.g., suppliers' invoices, customers' orders, signed contracts) are normally more conclusive than internal evidence (such as purchase orders, goods received notes and marketing plans).

9:4.1.6 Reviewing minutes of meetings

Reading the minutes of general meetings of the client and of meetings of the directors and important committees makes it possible to examine the members' or the board's approval of significant corporate actions. This will help to determine whether significant decisions taken that affect and/or require disclosure in the financial statements have been dealt with properly. The auditor should obtain assurance that copies of minutes of all important meetings during the period have been made available for audit examination.

9:4.1.7 Letters of enquiry to solicitors

Obtaining letters from the client's solicitors regarding legal matters provides additional assurance as to active, pending or expected litigation. **Section 9:10**, 'Enquiry of a client's solicitors concerning lawsuits, claims and other actions', provides guidance on the factors to consider when deciding whether to obtain such letters and the matters that should be taken into account when corresponding with solicitors.

9:4.2 Using audit software in substantive tests

In computerised systems, the auditor may be able to improve audit quality and efficiency by using general-purpose file interrogation software, or an application-specific package. Typical objectives achieved by audit software are as follows:

(a) **Reperformance of significant programmed procedures** within the client's system, e.g. checking the client's stock pricing or the totals and age analysis of the debtors file.

(b) **Analysing and summarising information** to help to determine audit procedures, e.g. the stratifying of a stock file to help in selecting samples and determining levels of tests.

(c) **Selection of items for audit testing either on an exception basis (because they meet particular criteria) or by sampling**, e.g. selecting a sample of debtor balances for circularisation, or selecting debtor balances in excess of their credit limits for follow-up. The ability to examine a complete file and report unusual items makes software an effective audit tool.

(d) **Checking for consistency and reasonableness**: Software can efficiently compare large volumes of information from separate but related files. For example, actual costs used for pricing stocks might be compared to standard costs held on a separate file, and with current sales prices on another file.

9:4.2.1 Application-specific packages

An audit firm may develop application-specific packages to achieve standard sets of typical audit objectives in specific applications. These packages should still provide the flexibility to select particular options from the standard procedures, to determine the specific reports to be produced and to specify selection criteria. When these packages can be used they are more efficient than general-purpose audit software.

The applications that may usefully be covered include:

- Accounts payable
- Accounts receivable
- Inventories
- General ledger

In addition, certain industry application packages are available.

9:4.2.2 General-purpose audit software

Where it is not possible to use an application-specific package, general-purpose audit software may be used. It will normally permit the auditor to specify audit objectives, and will:

(a)   read and analyse information stored in a single data file or two logically related data files;

(b)   select information for review on the basis of given criteria;

(c)   perform all arithmetic functions;

(d)   sort, resequence and summarise data;

(e)   produce easily read reports.

9:4.2.3 Other query languages and interrogation packages

In addition to general-purpose audit software and application-specific packages, the auditor may use 'query languages' available on the client's computer or may write special programs. It may also be possible to use proprietary microcomputer-based interrogation packages to assist in audit work.

9:4.2.4 Client software

Although the use of the audit firm's software is preferable, sometimes, particularly where it is difficult to run this software economically, the auditor may consider using client software. However, it is necessary to take specific steps to establish the reliability of client software. This is particularly necessary if the software is to be used to reperform significant year-end programmed procedures to provide audit evidence (e.g., reperformance of stock ageing), since the auditor is effectively using one of the client's programs to verify another. The audit firm's software would be independent of the client and for this reason would usually be preferred (if available and compatible with the client's computer system).

The auditor should consult specialist computer audit staff before using client software.

9:4.2.5 Effect on other substantive tests

The auditor will normally need to combine the use of audit software with other manual substantive testing procedures. This is either because the software only provides evidence in respect of some of the audit objectives, or because it does not provide all the evidence required in relation to an objective. For example, although software can provide some evidence relevant to the completeness and accuracy of stock quantities by checking the arithmetical accuracy of stock summaries, the auditor should normally obtain further evidence on these objectives, and on the existence objective, by observing and testing physical count procedures.

The auditor should plan the work to ensure that, if audit software is to be used, other substantive tests are modified to make effective use of that software. This can be achieved, e.g., by ensuring that the reports produced by audit software are properly followed up and that tasks performed by the audit software are not duplicated with manual procedures.

In addition, if software is used, the auditor should obtain assurance as to the reliability of the information extracted from the client's system and included in computer reports. Such assurance may be obtained through an extended assessment of internal accounting controls or through specific substantive tests.

9:4.3 Selecting items to be tested

9:4.3.1 Procedures involving selecting items

Tests of details involving confirmation, recomputation, physical inspection or examining documentary evidence involve selecting items for testing. **Sections 9:4.3.2** to **9:4.3.2.3** discuss the matters that should be considered in making the selection.

9:4.3.2 Defining the test objective and population from which to select

The auditor should carefully consider the primary objective of each test of details to ensure that the population from which the items are to be selected is appropriate. For example, tests directed towards establishing the existence and accuracy of recorded amounts are normally carried out on different populations from those used when the primary objective is to substantiate the completeness of recorded amounts.

9:4.3.2.1 Existence and accuracy

When carrying out tests with the primary purpose of gaining evidence as to existence and accuracy, the auditor normally selects items from the recorded amounts, e.g.:

(a)   Because the primary objective of a circularisation of trade debtors is to verify the existence and accuracy of the particular accounts, the auditor should select items from the listing of all trade debtors. Completeness of the listing should be confirmed by other procedures.

(b)   Because the primary purpose of testing expenses charged to the profit and loss account is to ensure the accuracy, existence and appropriate classification of the amounts charged to the various expense accounts, the auditor should select the items for testing from the recorded population of expenses.

9:4.3.2.2 Completeness

When carrying out tests of details primarily to provide evidence with respect to completeness, the auditor should not normally select items from the recorded amounts. Rather, testing should be carried out on items selected from some other 'reciprocal' population, e.g.:

(a)   To establish the completeness of recorded amounts of trade creditors, the auditor might decide to select and test the inclusion of amounts on statements from known suppliers, unmatched goods received notes, or subsequent payments.

(b)   If the auditor wished to test completeness of sales by tests of details, items might be selected from the despatch records, sales order records or similar; the relevant test would be to ensure that corresponding sales had been invoiced and recorded in the sales account.

In the course of carrying out these tests to establish completeness, the auditor will gather some evidence of the existence and accuracy of the recorded amounts. It should be recognised that this is a secondary objective of performing such tests.

9:4.3.3 *Options for selecting items*

Before considering how to select items for testing, the auditor should consider first whether the account can be more efficiently and effectively tested using substantive analytical review procedures. For those parts of an account and audit objectives where tests of details are needed in place of, or in combination with, analytical review, the following options are available:

(a)   One hundred per cent testing of:

    (i)   all items in the population, or sufficient items that the risk of misstatement in the remaining amount untested is insignificant;

    (ii)   items which exceed a particular size, or which have a particular characteristic. In this case the auditor might apply analytical review or other procedures, including selecting a representative sample, to the remaining items.

(b)   Testing a representative sample drawn from the entire population.

9:4.3.4 *Testing of 100 per cent of items*

There will often be individual items in an account balance or class of transactions which the auditor should examine because they are individually material, or because their inherent risk characteristics render them particularly susceptible to misstatement. Such items might be identified in developing the audit strategy or the substantive testing plan by considering the general inherent risk characteristics of accounts or transactions. (These are discussed in **Section 4:4**, 'Evaluating inherent risk'.) Additionally, items may be identified by preliminary analytical review procedures, by account analysis or by scrutiny. Examples of such items include:

(a)   Trade debtor and trade creditor accounts which are not made up of specific unpaid invoices because of payments on account (indicating the existence of disputed invoices).

(b)   Trade debtor credit balances and trade creditor debit balances.

(c)   Items reported on software exception report printouts.

(d) Items that are individually material to the account balance, or the financial statements as a whole, or that are larger than would ordinarily be expected for the particular type of account balance.

Sometimes (e.g., when a relatively small number of items represent a significant part of an account balance) it might be efficient to carry out 100 per cent testing of all items larger than a particular size, even if they are not individually material. Where the auditor intends to test 100 per cent of the items above a particular value and sample from the remainder, Appendix B (*see* **Section 9:4.8**) provides a quick method of identifying the cut-off value which will provide the most efficient combination of 100 per cent testing and sampling.

9:4.3.5 Sampling

SAS 430.1, *'Audit Sampling'*, states that:

> *When using either statistical or non-statistical sampling methods, auditors should design and select an audit sample, perform audit procedures thereon and evaluate sample results so as to obtain appropriate audit evidence.*

If the auditor is selecting items on a basis other than 100 per cent testing of all items having a particular characteristic or size, a suitable form of representative sampling should be used to make it possible to draw conclusions about the population. SAS 430, 'Audit sampling', requires that auditors should consider the specific audit objectives, the nature of the population from which they wish to sample and the sampling and selection methods.

9:4.3.5.1 Sample selection methods

Selection may be based on value-weighted, systematic or haphazard methods.

(a) **Value-weighted selection** gives greater emphasis to high-value items. Statistical methods can be used to achieve this result. However, as discussed in **Section 9:4.3.5.3** (first paragraph), such sampling is normally most efficiently carried out using non-statistical selection methods.

(b) **Systematic selection** involves a sampling interval expressed in terms of number of items, without reference to size. For example, if there were 600 trade debtors to sample and the auditor wished to select 12 balances, every fiftieth balance might be selected.

(c) **Haphazard sampling** describes the situation where the auditor attempts to select items randomly (i.e., avoiding any bias), without using any formal selection techniques.

The SAS does not recommend any particular selection strategy. It does, however, suggest that all items in the population are required to have an equal or known probability of being selected for a sample to be representative.

9:4.3.5.2 *Appropriateness of selection method*

One consideration in determining the selection method is the primary audit objective addressed by the test. If the auditor is primarily concerned with detecting existence and accuracy (e.g., trade debtor confirmations), a value-weighted sample might be most appropriate, because misstatements that are likely to be material, even in aggregate, are more probable in the higher-value items.

Conversely, different considerations apply if the auditor is primarily concerned about detecting understatement. Material monetary understatement is equally likely to be found in small value or 'no-value' recorded amounts, as well as in high ones. Thus, a systematic or haphazard selection method will be more appropriate. However, the auditor can 'value-weight' the selection when sampling from a suitable reciprocal population. For example, for tests of completeness of trade creditors, payments after the date at which completeness is being tested might be used as the population from which the selection was made; in this case, value-weighting would ensure that larger suppliers were selected rather than large creditor balances. It is more likely that material monetary understatement of liabilities will be found in the accounts of larger suppliers or by testing larger subsequent payments, regardless of the amount of the creditor balance.

9:4.3.5.3 *Sampling methods*

The objectives of sampling can be achieved by either non-statistical or statistical methods. Virtually all the principles, procedures and matters relevant to the planning and performance of audit samples can be applied equally to either method. The differences between the two methods are in the formality of the selection techniques used (hence the time taken to perform the work) and the ability to quantify the sampling risk associated with the procedure in reaching a conclusion. A properly thought out method of non-statistical sampling will generally be the most cost effective method of audit sampling.

Statistical sampling methods can be cost effective where some of the following conditions apply:

(a)   The population under examination is very large.

(b)   The auditor can use audit software to select the sample items.

(c)   A significant portion of the total evidence concerning an account balance or class of transactions is derived from a single sample, particularly where there is a high risk of misstatement.

(d)   The perceived benefit of quantifying the sample risk associated with the sample exceeds any extra costs in selection.

(e)   It is desirable to quantify precisely the size of the sample to achieve a specific quantified degree of assurance.

The auditor needs, at the planning stage of the audit, to be alert to the possible existence of these conditions. The Auditing Practices Board has not recommended either statistical or non-statistical sampling. Statement of Auditing Standards 430 does, however, impose the same requirement that the auditor should obtain appropriate audit evidence regardless of the method used.

9:4.3.5.4 Determining sample size

The determination of sample sizes for substantive tests of details depends on the interrelation of a number of factors as described in **Appendix A** to this section (*see* **Section 9:4.7**). Sample sizes are a matter for professional judgement considering all the relevant circumstances.

If the proposed sample size is unduly large (e.g., more than 150 items), the auditor should ensure, before proceeding, that the effect of other procedures has been fully assessed and taken into account in determining the sample size.

Appendix A (**Section 9:4.7**) explains how a simple sampling formula or tables can be used to generate sample sizes. The formula and tables are based on the statistical theory used in monetary unit sampling, where value-weighted samples are selected on the 'probability proportional to size basis'. The formula or tables should not be followed slavishly. Nor is it necessary to know the details of the statistical calculations that underlie them, although the auditor should have a reasonable understanding of when and how they should be used.

Because of the judgemental processes involved there is no 'absolutely accurate' sample size and the auditor should not be concerned if the sample size determined judgementally differs from that indicated by the formula or tables. Where judgement suggests a significantly different sample size from that given by the formula or tables, this does not mean that the judgement is incorrect, nor that the auditor should necessarily revise that judgement. However, the auditor should review and confirm judgements on the factors affecting sample size in the particular client's circumstances.

The audit approach in this Manual is such that the audit opinion on the financial statements is the culmination of a wide range of procedures. The auditor examines many different forms of audit evidence and gathers information and obtains explanations from many different sources. The audit opinion is the expression of professional judgement having regard to all the information at the auditor's disposal. It states in overall terms whether the financial statements give a true and fair view of the results and financial position. The opinion is not expressed in terms of a confidence level or specific degree of assurance.

9:4.4 Evaluating the results of tests of details

SAS 430.5, 'Audit Sampling', requires that the results of the sample should be evaluated. In particular, this requires that the audit team should:

(a) *analyse any errors detected in the sample; and*

(b) *draw inferences for the population as a whole.*

The auditor should evaluate any misstatements in both qualitative and quantitative terms. However, if the testing has been on an 'accept or reject' basis, quantitative evaluation will not usually be appropriate, as discussed in **Section 9:4.4.2**.

9:4.4.1 Qualitative evaluation

Qualitative evaluation involves considering the nature and causes of the misstatement and assessing the potential for further misstatement. The auditor should assess the potential for further misstatement not only within the population tested, but also by relating the misstatements to other phases of the audit and to other account balances. In particular, it is important to consider whether the nature, frequency or amount of misstatement is such that the assessment of risk for the purpose of the substantive testing plan should be reconsidered in relation to this or other accounts.

Examples of the considerations which might apply are:

(a) Misstatements which are the result of the incorrect application of procedures in systematically processed transactions are more likely to be repeated. A misstatement caused by an incorrect computer program will usually be repeated every time that program is run.

(b) Misstatements arising from infrequent procedures or unusual circumstances have a lower potential for further error.

(c) Misstatements (e.g., in cut-off or accruals) might indicate management bias, and hence indicate an increased inherent risk of such management bias in other areas.

(d) Misstatements identified in reconciliations of a subsidiary ledger to the general ledger, although probably directly affecting only one account, might be indicative of a failure in accounting controls and might cause a reassessment of the control environment.

In some cases the nature of, and reasons for, the misstatement might be a cause of audit concern, regardless of the monetary amount of the actual or potential misstatement. For example, misstatements that are the result of fraud or breaches of statute or government regulation require a response by the auditor, regardless of the amount involved.

9:4.4.2 Tests performed on an 'accept or reject' basis

Sometimes, the objective in performing tests is to obtain assurance as to whether certain procedures were properly performed to provide evidence in relation to the completeness, accuracy or existence of a particular transaction or account. Accordingly, the conclusion is either that the procedure was adequate (hence the auditor is satisfied that there are only negligible misstatements, or none) or that the client (or, in exceptional cases, the auditor) will have to reperform it. For this reason, although it would be theoretically possible to quantify the likely amount of misstatement indicated by those misstatements found, this will not be efficient or appropriate in practice. Examples of tests on such an 'accept or reject' basis include:

(a) **Independent test counts of stock during the observation of the client's physical stock count procedures**: Discrepancies uncovered as a result of taking independent test counts would normally lead to an extension of audit procedures to prove the adequacy of the physical count and/or to have the client's count-teams recount the stock until the adequacy of the count can be established.

(b) **Cut-off tests, such as the examination of records of goods despatched and related sales invoices for periods before and after the substantive test date**: If exceptions are discovered, the auditor would normally carry out additional work either to conclude that the cut-off was adequate or to determine the total monetary effect of the cut-off errors.

(c) **Tests of additions of, e.g., printouts or ledger account**: If these were incorrect, it might indicate a pervasive problem. In any event it would not be practicable to project a monetary result.

(d) **Tests of profit and loss account transactions where the main concern is an indication of fraud**: If invalid payments are being made, or sales recorded in respect of non-existent transactions, the auditor should be concerned regardless of the monetary amounts involved, and should perform additional work to gain the necessary assurance.

As these examples illustrate, the formality of determining a likely amount of misstatement by some form of projection is unnecessary, as well as impractical. This is because the auditor will almost always want to 'reject' the sample result and conduct additional procedures (possibly 100 per cent examination of all items in the population) to determine more accurately the extent of the errors in the total population.

  The concept of sampling may, however, be helpful when items are being chosen for examination. In addition to providing a framework for setting the extent of the examination, concepts such as weighting may further assist in effectively meeting audit objectives. For example, in cut-off tests the auditor might wish to ensure that periods closer to the cut-off date receive a higher sampling intensity than periods further away from the cut-off date.

9:4.4.3 Estimating the amount of likely misstatement

To evaluate the likely aggregate amount of misstatement, the auditor should consider both the actual misstatement found from 100 per cent testing and tests of samples, and the likely misstatement indicated by the results from testing samples. It is possible to quantify the likely misstatement indicated by the sample testing by projecting the monetary result of the sample tested to the population from which the sample was drawn. If the sample was taken from different strata in a population, the projected errors from each stratum should be calculated separately.

9:4.4.3.1 Projecting the monetary result

Although there are a number of methods available for projecting the result of procedures applied to sample items to the whole population, the most common are the ratio method and the average difference method.

(a) **The Ratio method**: In the ratio method, the aggregate value of the misstatements found in the sample is first expressed as a percentage of the value of the sample. Then this percentage is applied to the value of the total population from which the sample was drawn, to determine the projected misstatement amount in that population. This method is theoretically most suitable if the amount of the misstatement relates closely to the size of the item (i.e., large items contain the large misstatements), but it may also be more suitable than the average difference method if, as will often be the case, there is no clear pattern between the size of the errors and the sizes of the items.

(b) **The Average difference method**: Under the average difference approach, the aggregate value of the errors found in the sample is divided by the number of items examined to produce an average misstatement amount for each item. This average misstatement is then multiplied by the total number of items in the population from which the sample was selected to give the projected misstatement in that population. This method is suitable if the misstatement amounts are relatively constant and do not vary much with the size of the item.

9:4.4.3.2 Client adjustments

If errors have been found in sample items, but the client has detected and corrected them in the proper period before the auditor drew them to management's attention, then these items would not need to be included as errors to be projected to the whole population. If, however, the client adjusts the errors as a result of audit findings, the auditor should still project the errors to the whole population, but then deduct any adjustments made by the client for these or any other errors.

9:4.4.4 Concluding on whether there is material misstatement

The auditor should consider whether the aggregate of the known and projected misstatements is material in relation to the account balance or class of transaction concerned. If the aggregate amount is close to being material, it is necessary to consider the margin of imprecision inherent in projections of likely amounts and the risk that the true monetary misstatement exceeds this aggregate. Whether this is acceptable will depend on the degree of assurance required from the test.

When the aggregate error amount indicates a material misstatement of an item in the financial statements, it is necessary to consider the need for additional audit evidence. The auditor should first consider the possibility that there are offsetting errors in other components of the balance sheet or profit and loss account category, or that the results of other procedures might, when aggregated, provide adequate assurance that the item is not materially misstated. When this appears unlikely, the auditor should explain the situation to the client and follow one of the following courses:

(a) Request the client to adjust for the known errors, both those in the sample and those in the items covered by 100 per cent testing.

(b) Request the client to examine those remaining items that have similar characteristics to the known errors and to adjust for any further errors found or to justify the account balance.

(c)   Request the client to perform other additional work to justify the account balance.

(d)   Consider whether additional procedures might efficiently demonstrate that the account balance or class of transactions is not materially misstated.

(e)   Consider whether extended sampling might demonstrate that the account balance or class of transactions is not misstated; however, this is unlikely to be cost effective.

If, as a result of these procedures, it is possible to conclude that the account balance or class of transactions is not materially misstated, this should be stated in the working papers. If, however, the auditor cannot accept the recorded amount, the effect on the audit opinion should be considered.

9:4.5 Audit programmes

Appropriate information about the tests of details to be carried out should be provided in audit programmes (discussed in **Section 9:2**, 'Audit programmes'), including:

(a)   A description of the work performed.

(b)   The extent and timing of the test.

(c)   An explanation of the basis for selection of items.

9:4.6 Working papers

The results of tests of details should be recorded in sufficient detail to provide evidence of the work done, the evidence obtained and the conclusions drawn. In particular, working papers should show:

(a)   sufficient information in relation to items selected to permit these to be reselected if necessary;

(b)   evidence of observations made, the results of the discussions and the reasons for conclusions from those procedures where these are significant;

(c)   the aggregate of known and likely misstatement in the population, showing separately the projection from the sample and the known misstatement found in any components of the account balance examined 100 per cent; the aggregate of known and projected misstatements is often referred to as the 'score sheet', or the 'overs and unders' found on the audit;

(d)   conclusions on the results of tests of details.

9:4.7 Appendix A Guidance on appropriate sample sizes

9:4.7.1 Introduction

This appendix gives practical guidance to assist in determining sample sizes. It should be emphasised, however, that levels of test are a matter of judgement having regard to all relevant circumstances. The guidance should not therefore be used as a substitute for professional judgement.

9:4.7.2 General comments on use of judgement

The determination of sample sizes is a matter of professional judgement, based on certain key factors. **Table 9.1** illustrates how the impact of those factors can be expressed (the terms used are defined in **Section 9:4.7.3**):

Table 9.1 *Impact of factors affecting sample size*

	Conditions leading to:	
	Smaller sample size	**Larger sample size**
Tolerable error	Larger	Smaller
Expected error	Lower	Higher
Degree of assurance required	Lower	Higher
Number of items in population	Little effect on sample size unless there are fewer than 250 items in the population, in which case the sample size is likely to be smaller, all other factors being equal.	

It might appear that the formula and tables discussed in the remainder of this appendix introduce an element of precision into this highly judgmental process. This is not so. The formula and tables merely indicate an appropriate sample size for a given set of judgemental decisions, and allow the effects of these decisions to be understood more easily. The formula and tables can never be used as a substitute for professional judgement, and for this reason they should only be used to assist the auditor in judging the appropriateness of sample sizes.

Because of the judgemental processes involved there is no such thing as an 'absolutely accurate' sample size and the auditor should not be concerned if the sample size determined judgementally differs from that indicated by the formula or tables. Where judgement suggests a significantly different sample size from that given by the formula or tables, this does not mean the judgement is incorrect, nor that the auditor should necessarily revise that judgement. However, the auditor should review and confirm judgements on the factors affecting sample size in the particular client's circumstances.

9:4.7.3 Definition of terms

(a) **Tolerable error amount**: The tolerable error amount is defined as the maximum misstatement for the account balance or class of transactions that the auditor is ultimately willing to accept in the context of the overall strategy. The term 'error' as used in this appendix relates to misstatements from both fraud and error. The tolerable error amount should not normally exceed the materiality limit for the financial statements as a whole, otherwise the evidence the auditor obtains of the lack of misstatement in the account might not be adequate to support the audit opinion on the financial statements as a whole.

(b) **Expected error amount**: The expected error amount is the estimated misstatement likely to exist in the population to be sampled. The assessment of the expected error amount will be based on the results of the previous year's testing and the risk assessment in developing the testing plan.

For many clients, the amount of expected error will be negligible or very low and the effect on sample size can in effect be ignored. If, however, there is evidence that some significant error will be found, this will need to be taken into account and the sample size increased. This will enable the auditor to make a more precise evaluation of the sample result and the auditor will, therefore, be less likely to decide that an account balance is possibly materially misstated when it is not.

(c)   **Degree of assurance required**: The degree of assurance required from the sample is a key factor in determining the sample size. Decisions on assurance required will be taken in developing the testing plan based on:

(i)   the assessment of the risk of misstatement;

(ii)   the assessment of the effectiveness of internal controls; and

(iii) corollary assurance (if applicable) from tests on related areas.

Where items in an account are subject to varying risks of misstatement, it is often efficient to stratify the items to permit different intensities of sampling for different strata.

9:4.7.4 Sampling formula

A straightforward way of generating a potential sample size as an aid to judgement is to use a simple formula using 'factors' to represent the degree of assurance required. The possible sample size is derived thus:

$$\frac{\text{Value of population}}{\text{Tolerable error}} \times \text{'Factor'} = \text{Possible sample size}$$

where the 'factor' is a number that varies according to the degree of assurance required. The less assurance required, the smaller the factor. Appropriate factors to use are discussed in **Sections 9:4.7.4.1** and **9:4.7.4.2**.

This formula assumes that the expected error is nil or negligible. If an error is expected, sampling theory suggests that the auditor should increase significantly the sample size. However, the theory also suggests that further adjustments to the sample size, which the auditor might make as the amount of error expected to be found increases, become less significant. Therefore, if the auditor expects to find error a reasonable adjustment is simply to double the sample size produced by the formula.

If the formula is used, it is necessary to appreciate the following:

(a)   As with all methods derived from the laws of probability, a large population is assumed ('large', in this context, for convenience, may be taken as greater than 250 items). If the population is smaller than this the formula will produce conservative sample sizes and the smaller the population the more conservative the sample sizes become. Accordingly, for small populations the sample size produced by the formula should be reduced (or 100 per cent testing should be considered).

(b)   This particular formula is based on theory which assumes that the sample has been selected on a 'probability proportional to size' basis. The non-statistical sampling method described in **Appendix B** (*see* **Section 9:4.8**) approximates this basis very closely.

9:4.7.4.1 Appropriate factors for balance sheet testing

There is such variability in the nature of balance sheet accounts that the range of sample sizes that might be appropriate in particular circumstances is very wide. However, for the purposes of generating a possible sample size, the auditor might use, for low assurance a factor of around one-half (0.5), and for high assurance a factor of 3, with intermediate factors for intermediate levels of assurance.

9:4.7.4.2 Appropriate factors for profit and loss testing

The determination of sample sizes for profit and loss account substantive tests is also a matter of professional judgement, but there are certain general factors relating to profit and loss account testing which suggest that sample sizes will generally be smaller than those for balance sheet testing. These are discussed more fully in **Section 4:7**, 'The audit programme'.

Therefore, if the auditor requires only a low level of assurance from tests of details of profit and loss items the auditor might base sample sizes on a factor of one-third (0.35). If the auditor requires additional assurance the factor may be increased. However, it is unlikely that the auditor would require additional assurance greater than that equivalent to using a factor of two-thirds (0.7). For convenience this might commonly be referred to as 'high' in relation to profit and loss account testing, even though such a level might be regarded as 'low' in relation to balance sheet testing.

There is a further common feature of profit and loss account substantive testing, namely that the expected error is usually nil or negligible. Hence the formula result will not usually need any adjustment.

9:4.7.5 *Effect of testing 100 per cent of the larger items*

The number of items the auditor needs to test to obtain the particular level of assurance will often be lower than the sample sizes derived from the sample formula or tables by considering testing 100 per cent of the larger items (even if these are not individually material), and then selecting a revised number of items from the remainder. The guidance on sample selection techniques in **Appendix B** (**Section 9:4.8**) describes a quick method of identifying the most efficient cut-off level for 100 per cent testing.

9:4.7.6 *Use of tables*

The tables that follow (*see* **Tables 9.2** to **9.4**) provide an alternative means of arriving at a possible sample size. The numbers in the tables and the numbers obtained by the formula method are approximately the same and the tables are not intended to be any more precise than the numbers generated by the formula. The possible sample size can be obtained from the tables by reading the number corresponding to the tolerable error percentage and expected error percentage that the auditor has determined are appropriate. The 'tolerable error percentage' is the tolerable error amount divided by the population value. The 'expected error percentage' is the expected error amount divided by population value.

Where the expected error percentage is between those shown in the tables, the auditor normally reads the figure for the next higher percentage in the table. Where the tolerable error percentage is between those for which sample sizes are shown in the tables, the auditor normally estimates a number between the table figures for the next higher and next lower percentage using interpolation.

Where the expected error percentage is higher than that shown in the tables for the particular tolerable error required, a very large sample size would be indicated. The reason for this is that the expected error rate is high in relation to the tolerable error rate. In other words, there is an expectation that error in the account balance is almost at an unacceptable level before testing commences. These circumstances will be rare, but where they occur it is unlikely that sampling will be cost-effective. Examining a few items only is likely to support the belief that the error rate is exceptionally high and thus the auditor should persuade the client that further work is required by his staff to correct the errors in the population before the detailed audit work is performed.

9:4.7.6.1 Balance sheet substantive tests

Tables 9.2 to **9.4** provide tables for balance sheet substantive tests.

Table 9.2 *Low degree of assurance**

Expected error (%)	Tolerable error (%)									
	2	3	4	5	8	10	14	20	30	50
0	25	20	15	10	10	5	5	5	5	5
1		40	25	20	20	10	10	5	5	5
2			25	20	20	10	10	5	5	5
3				30	20	10	10	5	5	5
5					25	10	10	5	5	5
8						30	15	5	5	
10							15	10	5	5

*Equivalent to a factor of 0.5 in the formula.

Table 9.3 *Moderate degree of assurance**

Expected error (%)	\ Tolerable error (%) 2	3	4	5	8	10	14	20	30	50
0	80	55	40	35	20	15	15	10	5	5
1		100	75	60	40	30	25	15	10	5
2			140	85	40	30	25	15	10	5
3				160	55	30	25	15	10	5
5					100	55	30	15	10	5
8							50	25	10	5
10							80	30	10	5

*Equivalent to a factor of 1.5 in the formula.

Table 9.4 *High degree of assurance**

Expected error (%)	\ Tolerable error (%) 2	3	4	5	8	10	14	20	30	50
0	150	100	75	60	40	30	20	15	10	5
1			160	95	60	50	35	25	15	10
2			190	90	50		35	25	15	10
3				95	65		35	25	15	10
5					120		55	30	15	10
8							100	40	20	10
10								50	25	10

*Equivalent to a factor of 3 in the formula.

9:4.7.6.2 *Profit and loss account tests*

Table 9.5 provides tables on profit and loss account tests.

Table 9.5 *Low, moderate and high degrees of assurance*

*Low degree of assurance**

Tolerable error (%)	0.5	1	2	5	10
Sample size	70	35	20	10	5

*Equivalent to a factor of 0.35 in the formula.

*Moderate degree of assurance**

Tolerable error (%)	0.5	1	2	5	10
Sample size	100	50	25	10	5

*Equivalent to a factor of 0.5 in the formula.

High degree of assurance*

Tolerable error (%)	0.5	1	2	5	10
Sample size	140	70	35	15	10

*Equivalent to a factor of 0.7 in the formula.

9:4.8 Appendix B Non-statistical sample selection

9:4.8.1 Introduction

This appendix provides practical guidance on selection of items by non-statistical means. The guidance applies only to **value weighted sampling**, since the other methods require the auditor to avoid any type of bias or weighting, and do not therefore require any particular method. Although the auditor usually uses non-statistical methods for efficiency, it is useful to relate the non-statistical approach to the statistical, to illustrate how the two methods achieve the same end.

Statistical methods attempt to give items a probability of selection proportional to the size of item, by using the concept that the population is made up of notional £1 units, and individual items are just aggregations of these £1 units. The method identifies the notional £1 units to be selected, and it is the items containing those £1 units that are actually tested.

The notional £1 units are selected using a regular sampling interval (e.g., every one-hundred-thousandth £1). The sampling interval is calculated thus:

$$\text{Sampling interval} = \frac{\text{Population}}{\text{No. of items}}$$

This method has the following effects:

(a)   All individual items larger than the sampling interval are automatically selected (i.e., tests cover 100 per cent of these items). Such items are called 'top-stratum' items. If they are sufficiently large they may count for more than one selection. Hence the final number of items examined will be reduced from the original estimate of the number required. This is illustrated by the example in **Section 9:4.8.3**.

(b)   Of the remaining items the larger items are more likely to be selected than the smaller.

9:4.8.2 Non-statistical sampling method

The auditor can efficiently select a sample which approximates closely to that which would be produced by the more time-consuming statistical method, and which automatically produces the most efficient combination of 100 per cent testing and sampling, as follows:

(a)   Decide in the usual way the number of items appropriate to the size of the total population and assurance required (discussed in **Appendix A** – *see* **Section 9:4.7**).

(b) Calculate the sampling interval that would be used in the statistical method described above.

(c) Select all items larger than this amount (i.e., all top-stratum items).

(d) Decide in the usual way how many items should be selected from the remaining population (discussed in **Appendix A** – *see* **Section 9:4.7**) and select that number of items using judgement, giving more emphasis to larger items.

9:4.8.3 *Illustrative example*

Table 9.6 presents an analysis of the year-end stock of a company on which the auditor intends to perform pricing tests.

Table 9.6 Example of year-end and stock analysis

Stock lines	Number	Value £
Line value over £600,000	5	3,500,000
Line value between £250,001 and £600	10	4,850,000
Line value between £100,001 and £250,000	20	3,600,000
Line value between £25,001 and £100,000	70	2,800,000
Line value under £25,000	300	2,050,000
TOTAL	405	£16,800,000

The following assumptions are made:

(a) The overall materiality for the engagement is £600,000, and as errors in stock pricing could directly affect profit the auditor has decided that the tolerable error for this test is £600,000.

(b) In each of the past few years a very small number of minor pricing errors have been made, never exceeding about 0.1 per cent of the total value of stock. The expected error is therefore negligible.

(c) The auditor has concluded from the risk assessment procedures that a moderate degree of assurance is needed from the substantive tests of prices.

The initial estimate of sample size is quickly derived using the formula:

$$\frac{\text{Total value of population}}{\text{Tolerable error}} \times \text{'Factor'} = \text{Possible sample size}$$

$$\frac{£16,800,000}{£600,000} \times 1.5 = 42 \text{ selections}$$

Notes:

(a) If the auditor had expected to find error, the number of selections would have been considerably increased (to approximately double the level).

(b)   The figure could equally have been taken from the tables in **Appendix A** (*see* **Section 9:4.7**), by interpolation between the values given for 3% and 4% tolerable error. (£600,000/£16,800,000 is a tolerable error percentage of 3.6%).

The sampling interval to select 42 items is derived thus:

$$\frac{\text{Total value of population}}{\text{Tolerable error}} = \text{Sampling interval}$$

$$\frac{£16,800,000}{42} = £400,000$$

£400,000 is now the cut-off point to mark 'top-statum' items.

The most efficient sampling method will then be to select all items greater than £400,000 and to select an appropriate number of items from the remainder, which (assuming that all 10 items in the second band are greater than £400,000) might be calculated using the formula thus:

$$\frac{\text{Value of remaining population (after selectinf 'top-stratum' items}}{\text{Samplings interval}}$$

or:

$$\frac{£8,450,00}{£400,000} = 21 \text{ items}$$

The total number of individual items the auditor would actually select is thus 15 'top-stratum' items plus a representative sample of 21 items which equals 36 items (as compared to the original figure of 42, which took no account of 100 per cent testing of top-stratum items).

9:5 Evaluating the results of substantive testing

9:5.1 Qualitative and quantitative evaluation

When a misstatement is found as a result of substantive tests, it should be evaluated:

(a) **qualitatively**, by reassessing risks in the light of the nature and cause of the misstatement and the potential for further misstatement; and

(b) **quantitatively**, by estimating its likely total amount.

Guidance on the evaluation of the results from tests of details is given in **Section 9:4**, 'Tests of details', and from substantive analytical review, in **Section 9:3**, 'Analytical procedures'.

9:5.2 Reassessing risks

Because of misstatements identified, the auditor may need to change the preliminary assessment of risk and, consequently, the strategy and the substantive testing plan. For example, a misstatement in a transaction processed through a systems-derived account might cause a reassessment of the degree of planned reliance on the system concerned.

It is also important to take into account items that do not individually represent misstatement but which, taken together, may increase the risk of a material misstatement. For example, the auditor might conclude that an estimate of stock obsolescence was optimistic but supportable and therefore not a misstatement. However, if several estimates were found in the financial statements that fell within acceptable ranges but indicated a pattern of bias, it would be necessary to consider whether there were implications for the estimates in the financial statements.

9:5.3 Fraud and other irregularities

The auditor should consider whether misstatements could be caused by fraud or other irregularity, rather than error, and endeavour to clarify whether a fraud has occurred. If fraud is suspected, reference should be made to the more detailed guidance contained in **Section 2:7**, 'Fraud and error'. In rare circumstances (e.g., if misstatements are detected that were apparently known to client personnel but not disclosed to the auditor), it may be necessary to reassess the scope of the entire audit. If senior management is involved, the auditor should reconsider the need to report the matter to the authorities and the appropriateness of continuing to serve the client. Accordingly, all such cases should immediately be brought to the attention of the engagement partner who should consult other partners as necessary.

9:5.4 Known and likely misstatement

The likely amounts of misstatement determined by the evaluation in accordance with the sections referred to in **Section 9:5.1** represent the auditor's best estimates of misstatement. Accordingly, those estimates should be considered in the same manner as actual misstatements identified. Those sections give guidance on the initial action which should be taken when evaluation indicates the possibility of significant misstatement in the account balance or in related account balances.

Because it is the client's responsibility to produce accurate financial statements, the auditor should encourage management to carry out any additional investigation work required. If this is not possible, the auditor will need to undertake the necessary work, but the cost of this work should be monitored carefully and it may be appropriate to consider seeking an additional fee from the client. The client should be advised to adjust the records and financial statements for known errors.

9:5.5 Recording and reporting on issues documentation

The auditor should note misstatements and their evaluation in the working papers. In addition, because unadjusted misstatements, which in themselves might not be material, can in aggregate be material, it is necessary to summarise estimates of the likely misstatement in each account in the form of a 'score sheet' so that the aggregate effect can be readily ascertained at the end of the audit. The summary should include the effect of misstatements detected in prior periods which have an effect in the current year, and all amounts should be presented on a consistent tax-effect assumption (i.e., either before tax or after tax). Where significant, the summary should be drawn to the partner's attention on issues documentation.

As well as discussing known errors with the client the auditor should propose that adjustment is made for likely significant error amounts. The measurement of what represents a significant amount in relation to some account balances or classes of transaction may differ from the overall materiality for the financial statements. For example, a likely error in expenses charged to a government-sponsored cost reimbursement project might be more significant than a similar misclassification between internal projects, because of the potential for lost revenues, penalties and public embarrassment.

Sometimes it may not be possible to quantify a misstatement in the financial statements, even by alternative or extended procedures. Accordingly, adjustment is not possible. This might arise, for example, where it was not possible to complete the substantive tests of particular transactions because appropriate documentation was not available, or if there was reason to doubt its validity or completeness.

The auditor may need to consider qualifying the audit report because of the uncertainty caused by such misstatements.

9:5.6 Reporting to the board and to management

The auditor should normally comment, in communications with management, on significant misstatements noted during the performance of substantive tests, even if such misstatements do not indicate weaknesses in internal control. Examples of such misstatements might be matters of judgement which, after consultation with management, were seen to be incorrect, or breakdowns in the client's year-end procedures.

The following, if they occur, may be of particular interest to the board and to management and the auditor should consider their impact on the 'Audit report to the board' (*see* **Section 12:1**, 'Audit reporting to the board and to management'):

(a)   Late adjustments required to management accounts.

(b)   Adjustments to control accounts resulting from year-end confirmation procedures.

(c)   Audit adjustments in relation to deviations from approved policies or methods.

(d)   Significant breakdowns in the system, missing records, unsatisfactory explanations or other exceptions indicating systems breakdown or control weaknesses.

9:6 Audit of accounting estimates

9:6.1 Introduction

Statement of Auditing Standards 420, 'Audit of Accounting Estimates', requires that 'Auditors should obtain sufficient appropriate audit evidence regarding accounting estimates'. Directors and management are responsible for making accounting estimates for inclusion in financial statements. Such estimates are often made when the outcome of events that have occurred, or are likely to occur, is uncertain, and they involve the use of judgement. As a result, audit evidence obtained is generally less conclusive when accounting estimates are involved and the risk of material misstatement in financial statements increases when they are significantly dependent on estimates rather than historical facts. Consequently, in assessing the sufficiency and appropriateness of audit evidence on which to base the audit opinion, auditors are more likely to exercise judgement in considering accounting estimates than in other areas of the audit.

This section describes the procedures the auditor should consider when auditing accounting estimates. It should be read in conjunction with other sections which discuss the application of these procedures to specific accounts.

9:6.2 The nature of accounting estimates

An accounting estimate is an approximation of the amount of an item, made in the absence of a precise means of measurement. Examples are:

(a)   Allowances to reduce current assets to their estimated realisable value, e.g., provisions for bad and doubtful debts, warranties, losses on long-term contracts and obsolete stocks.

(b)   Depreciation provisions to allocate the cost of fixed assets over their estimated useful lives.

(c)   Provisions for losses which may arise from pending litigation.

The determination of an accounting estimate may be simple or complex depending upon the nature of the item. For example, accruing a charge for an overhead expense might be a simple calculation involving the apportionment of a periodic charge on the basis of estimated consumption, whereas estimating a provision for slow-moving stock might involve considerable analyses of current data and a forecast of future sales. In complex estimates, a high degree of special knowledge and judgement may be required.

Accounting estimates may be determined as part of the routine accounting system operating on a continuing basis, or they may be non-routine, and determined only at the end of the financial period. Often, accounting estimates are made by using a formula based on historical experience, such as the use of standard rates for depreciating each category of fixed assets, or a standard percentage of sales revenue for computing a warranty provision. In such cases, the formulae need to be reviewed periodically by management, e.g. by reassessing the remaining useful lives of assets or by monitoring subsequent actual results for comparison with the estimate and adjusting the formulae when necessary.

If the uncertainty associated with an item, or the lack of objective data, makes reasonable estimation impossible, the auditor should consider the implications for the audit report.

9:6.3 Audit procedures

The objective when auditing accounting estimates is to obtain sufficient relevant and reliable evidence to be able to conclude whether the estimates are:

- necessary;
- reasonable in the circumstances;
- appropriately disclosed.

The auditor should recognise that the evidence available to support accounting estimates will often be more difficult to obtain and less conclusive than evidence available to support other items in the financial statements.

The auditor should obtain an understanding of the procedures and methods used by management in making material accounting estimates, including an understanding of the control structure relating to such procedures and methods. This understanding helps to determine the extent and nature of the procedures required to evaluate such estimates. To obtain this understanding the auditor should consider the following:

(a) The methods used by management to identify circumstances for which accounting estimates are required.

(b) The knowledge and experience of client staff responsible for developing estimates.

(c) The knowledge and experience of the management personnel who participate in or oversee the development of estimates.

(d) The procedures for adequate review and approval of estimates by the appropriate levels of authority.

(e) The conscientiousness of management and non-management personnel who play important roles in developing estimates.

(f) The relevance, reliability, timeliness and sufficiency of historical and prospective financial, statistical and other information used to develop estimates.

(g) The development and review of the reasonableness of the assumptions used in developing estimates.

(h) The reliability of the client's past history in developing estimates.

Statement of Auditing Standards 420, 'Audit of Accounting Estimates', suggests that auditors should adopt one or a combination of the following approaches in the audit of an accounting estimate:

(a) Review and test the process used by management or the directors to develop the estimate.

(b) Use an independent estimate for comparison with that prepared by management or the directors.

(c) Review subsequent events.

These procedures should be used in the light of the business review and the assessment of the control environment, particularly as regards management's commitment to accurate financial reporting and in the light of the matters listed in the preceding paragraph.

9:6.4 Reviewing and testing the process used by management

9:6.4.1 Examination of data and consideration of assumptions

The auditor should obtain reasonable assurance that the data on which the estimate is based are accurate, complete and relevant. If non-accounting data are used, they should be consistent with the data processed through the accounting system. For example, to audit a warranty provision, the auditor should obtain reasonable assurance that data relating to products sold which are still within the warranty period at the balance sheet date agree with the sales information in the accounting system.

The auditor may also wish to seek corroborating evidence from sources outside the client. For example, when examining a provision for stock obsolescence calculated by reference to anticipated future turnover, it might be considered appropriate, in addition to examining internal data such as past levels of sales, orders in hand and marketing trends, to seek corroborative evidence from industry-produced sales projections and market analyses.

The auditor should ascertain how management has determined that the data collected are properly analysed and projected to form a reasonable basis for determining the estimate. If such analytical and projection procedures are computerised, the auditor must ensure that the results are reliable by applying appropriate audit procedures. Such procedures might include testing the procedures for developing and operating the computer program and using computer-assisted audit techniques.

The auditor should review the continuing appropriateness of formulae used by management in the preparation of accounting estimates. Such a review should reflect knowledge of the financial results of the client in previous periods, the practices used by other entities in the industry and the future plans of management.

To evaluate the assumptions on which the estimate is based, the auditor should first consider whether the client has an adequate basis for the principal assumptions used in the estimate. Sometimes, the assumptions will be based on industry or government statistics, such as future inflation rates, interest rates, employment rates and anticipated market growth. In other cases, the assumptions will be specific to the client and will be based on internally generated data.

The auditor should also determine whether the assumptions are:

(a)   reasonable in the light of actual results in previous accounting periods, except when changes can be justified;

(b)   consistent with those made for other relevant accounting estimates; and

(c)   consistent with management's plans which themselves appear reasonable.

The auditor should pay particular attention to assumptions that are sensitive to variation and those that appear to be subjective or susceptible to material misstatement.

In the case of complex estimating processes involving specialised techniques, the auditor may need to use the work of an expert, e.g. engineers for estimating quantities in stockpiles of mineral ores. In such cases, the auditor should refer to **Section 7:6**, 'Using the work of an expert'.

9:6.4.2 Examination of calculations

The auditor should test the calculation procedures used by management. The nature and extent of tests will depend on the complexity involved in determining the estimate, and on an evaluation of the procedures and methods used by the client in producing the estimate.

9:6.4.3 Comparison of previous estimates with actual results

Whenever possible, the auditor should compare estimates made for a prior period with actual results of that period to help to:

(a)   obtain evidence about the general reliability of the client's estimating procedures;

(b)   establish where adjustments to estimating formulae may be required; and

(c)   ensure that differences between actual results and previous estimates have been quantified and that, where necessary, appropriate accounting action has been taken.

9:6.4.4 Consideration of management's procedures for approving estimates

Material accounting estimates should be reviewed and approved by management. The auditor should ensure that such review and approval is performed by the appropriate level of management and that there is evidence of such approval in the documentation supporting the accounting estimate.

9:6.4.5 Evaluation of results of audit procedures on management processes

The auditor should determine whether reasonable assurance has been obtained about the appropriateness of the assumptions and the accuracy of the calculation of the accounting estimate. The auditor should also assess the reasonableness of the estimate based on knowledge of the client and industry and the degree of consistency with other evidence obtained during the audit. If the assumptions do not appear to be reasonable, the auditor should test the sensitivity of the estimate to the use of different assumptions, and the engagement partner and the engagement manager should discuss the matter with the client.

9:6.5 Substantive analytical review

The auditor will often be able to use substantive analytical review procedures to audit accounting estimates cost effectively. Using the data discussed in **Section 9:6.4.1** (first three paragraphs) and the other relevant information, such as the reasonable assumptions used by management, the auditor should develop an expectation of the amount of the estimate and compare this with management's estimate. These procedures will be particularly helpful when an estimate is sensitive to different assumptions. Further guidance on substantive analytical review procedures is given in **Section 9:3**, 'Analytical procedures'.

9:6.5.1 Evaluation of likely misstatement

The auditor should consider whether there are any significant subsequent transactions or events which affect the data and the assumptions used in determining the accounting estimate.

Because of the approximation inherent in accounting estimates, evaluating misstatement can be more difficult than in other areas of the audit. If the results of substantive analytical review produce a difference between the auditor's estimate (based on available audit evidence) and the estimated amount included in the financial statements, it is necessary to form an opinion as to whether such a difference constitutes a material misstatement.

If the auditor is unable to reduce the difference between the expectation and the recorded amount to an acceptable level by carrying out investigations, the appropriate conclusion is that the amount of such difference represents a misstatement.

The auditor should also consider whether individual differences which have been accepted as reasonable are consistently biased in one direction, so that, on a cumulative basis, they may have a material impact on the financial statements. In such circumstances, the auditor should reconsider the estimates taken as a whole.

If the auditor believes the difference is unreasonable then management or the directors should be asked to revise the estimate. If they refuse to revise the estimate, the difference is considered a misstatement and is considered with all other misstatements in assessing whether the affect on the financial statements is material.

9:6.6 Review of subsequent events

The auditor should consider whether there are any significant subsequent events or transactions which help to establish the reasonableness of the estimate or which affect the data and corroborate or otherwise the assumptions used for the accounting estimate.

9:6.7 Letter of representation

The auditor should consider asking management to confirm in its letter of representation that accounting estimates have been properly determined. Guidance on letters of representation is given in **Section 10:4**, 'Representations from management'.

9:6.8 Reporting

If the auditor is unable to obtain sufficient assurance as to the appropriateness of an accounting estimate and is also unable to obtain audit evidence to support a different estimate, it will be necessary to consider whether a significant limitation of scope exists and whether this will affect the audit opinion.

9:7 Computer-assisted audit techniques

9:7.1 Introduction

For the purpose of this Manual a computer-assisted audit technique (CAAT) involves writing programs or using application program packages or test data to perform, or assist in the performance of, audit procedures. CAATs may include programs developed by a firm for use in the audit of different clients, or may be developed specifically for a single client or computer application.

This section discusses when the auditor might use a CAAT and gives examples of the types of application that might be appropriate. It also deals with:

(a) Matters to consider when developing and running CAATs.

(b) When computer audit specialist staff should be involved.

(c) Reliance on the client or internal auditors.

(d) Review procedures.

9:7.2 When to use CAATs

9:7.2.1 Introduction

CAATs may be effective in the following situations:

(a)   If planned substantive tests involve the re-performance of a calculation or processing function.

(b)   Where a hard copy audit trail does not exist, or output is not available in a usable form.

(c)   Where the auditor wishes to reduce audit time at the year-end.

(d)   If there is a large volume of data.

(e)   When the auditor wishes to identify unusual items in a large population.

(f)   When the auditor wishes to present summarised information for review in a standard format.

(g)   When the auditor requires a high level of assurance, because CAATs can include all items of a population and produce a quantified result.

CAATs can also provide some assurance concerning the effective operation of IT controls.

9:7.2.2 Performing or re-performing analyses, re-computations and processing functions

CAATs may be used to perform detailed analyses of complete populations or to re-compute amounts involving complex calculations. Re-computation of an amount using a CAAT will frequently provide all the assurance the auditor requires for that amount in relation to a number of audit objectives.

Once they have been developed, CAATs can be efficient when used in this way, because it is often easy to change the format or structure of the application. For example, where there are changes to tax rates or indices that the auditor uses to re-compute an amount, these changes can be easily incorporated into an existing CAAT.

CAATs may be used to perform analyses and re-computations, and to re-perform processing functions as follows:

(a)   Debtors age analyses.

(b)   Stock obsolescence provisions.

(c)   Summaries of demographic data used in actuarial calculations.

(d)   Calculations of unearned interest on instalment loans.

(e)   Testing that payment records include appropriate cross-references to purchase orders, receiving reports and invoice data.

(f)   Re-performing depreciation calculations in a fixed-asset register.

(g)   Summarising data from the general ledger.

9:7.2.3 *Using CAATs in the absence of a suitable hard copy audit trail*

In many clients, the computer system will perform some processes without producing audit evidence that the process has occurred. An example is an automated ordering system in which suppliers are notified electronically of required quantities and the system automatically selects a supplier after the electronic receipt of price quotes, and also generates the purchase order and the related payments. To test accruals at such a client, the auditor might develop a CAAT that selected all unmatched receipts records at the year-end and compared them with the related purchase orders. The CAAT could produce a summary of valid year-end purchases for comparison with the client's accrual. Sometimes the auditor may develop test data to re-perform programmed procedures where there is no audit evidence of their operation.

9:7.2.4 *Using CAATs to reduce audit time*

CAATs may be effective when the auditor wishes to reduce audit time. An application can be specified, developed, tested and debugged before the audit visit, so that the work can be completed quickly. Examples of such applications include final tax computations and analyses for inclusion in the notes to the financial statements.

9:7.2.5 *Using CAATs when there is a large volume of data*

When performing substantive tests the auditor will often need to manipulate client data to assist in analyses or to select items for testing. However, it is often not possible to do this manually because of the volume of data. In such cases, the auditor should consider developing a CAAT, because CAATs can perform such tasks quickly and efficiently. Examples of such applications include:

(a)   Preparing confirmation letters and the associated control lists and summaries.

(b)   Selecting samples.

(c)   Disaggregating data for analytical review purposes.

(d)   Sorting, aggregating and summarising data.

(e)   Preparing age analyses.

9:7.2.6 *Identifying unusual items*

If clients do not provide exception reports, CAATs may be used to identify unusual items for further investigation. Examples include identifying:

(a)   billings at unusually high or low prices;

(b)   items for which set approval procedures have not been applied;

(c)   credits in the trade debtors account;

(d)   payments of salary outside normal boundaries;

(e)   overdue loans;

(f)   slow-moving stock items;

(g)   negative stock amounts.

9:7.3 Matters to consider when developing and running a CAAT

To ensure that CAATs achieve the relevant audit objective(s) as efficiently and effectively as possible, the auditor should exercise effective control over:

(a)   developing a CAAT (**Sections 9:7.3.1.1** to **9:7.3.1.3**); and

(b)   running a CAAT (**Sections 9:7.3.2** to **9:7.3.2.3**).

9:7.3.1 Developing a CAAT

9:7.3.1.1 Initial considerations

The auditor should take account of the following matters before deciding to develop a CAAT:

(a)   **Cost-effectiveness**: The auditor should consider the following matters:

   (i)   The availability of an existing application that meets the audit requirements. Such an application may already have been developed elsewhere in the firm.

   (ii)   The cost of developing the program compared with the cost of equivalent manual procedures. Because the marginal cost of running a CAAT is likely to be significantly lower in subsequent years the auditor should consider the likely useful life of the application, in the light of knowledge of the client's plans for computer developments.

(b)   **Client expectations**: A benefit of using CAATs is that they often help to meet client expectations both as regards the auditor's computer expertise and as regards the auditor's understanding of the systems. CAATs may also produce information that will be of use to the client.

(c)   **The nature of the system to be interrogated and the most appropriate files to interrogate**: The auditor may need to supplement the knowledge of the client's systems obtained prior to determining the audit strategy.

(d)   **The extent to which developing and running a CAAT will provide evidence of the effective operation of IT controls and application controls**: The use of CAATs is one of the ways in which the auditor can obtain evidence of the effective operation of IT controls and application controls.

9:7.3.1.2 Detailed planning

If the auditor decides to develop a CAAT, a specification of the application should be prepared. Depending on the type of software used, this should deal with matters such as the following:

(a)   **The objectives for the CAAT and the audit objectives it is intended to address**: For example, to address the valuation objective for debtors the auditor might wish to interrogate a client's sales ledger master file to identify balances over 60 days old.

(b)   **The files or data to be addressed by the CAAT**: To continue the example in (a) above, these would be the sales ledger master file and a parameter indicating the age above which balances would be reported.

(c)   **The processing steps to be performed on the data by the CAAT**: The specification should detail the fields to be processed, the processing that is required and the nature of the output required.

(d)   **The format of the output.**

(e)   **The computer on which the auditor intends to run the CAAT**: This might be the client's computer, a computer bureau or a computer owned by the audit firm.

(f)   **A budget for developing the CAAT**: This should include an estimate of the recurring costs of maintaining and running the CAAT.

The auditor should reappraise the audit effectiveness and the cost-effectiveness of the CAAT when the specification of the requirements and the budget have been completed. The engagement partner or the engagement manager should review and agree the specification and budget before development proceeds.

9:7.3.1.3 Development

When developing a CAAT the auditor should:

(a)   design and develop the CAAT as defined in the audit specification;

(b)   test the CAAT to ensure that it works as intended;

(c)   record the work performed to develop the CAAT to comply with the requirements for audit evidence and to facilitate the future maintenance of the CAAT; and

(d)   record the operational procedures relevant to running the CAAT in subsequent years, including the dates during the year when action is required (e.g., when to ask the client to keep a copy of a particular data file).

9:7.3.2 Running a CAAT

To ensure that a CAAT runs effectively and efficiently the auditor should carry out certain procedures. These are discussed below under the following headings:

(a) Procedures before running the CAAT.

(b) Procedures when the CAAT is run.

(c) Procedures after the CAAT has been run.

9:7.3.2.1 Procedures before running the CAAT

Before running a CAAT the auditor should carry out the following procedures:

(a) **Determine whether there have been any changes to the system since the application was last run**: Generally, the auditor will already have obtained this information before determining the audit strategy. The auditor should document any consequential changes which are made to the CAAT.

(b) **Define the relevant parameters for the application**: These include matters such as: the periods for which the application is to be run; date of the file to be processed; company numbers; and period numbers.

(c) **Controls over the output from the CAAT**: These include, e.g., determining who is responsible for reconciling the output to the client's records and to whom the output should be given.

(d) **Making arrangements to run the application**: These include: determining when the auditor can run interrogations; whether the application will be run by the audit team or a computer audit specialist; and who to contact at the client before running the CAAT.

9:7.3.2.2 Procedures when the CAAT is run

(a) **Validity of the data**: When the CAAT is run the auditor should obtain assurance that the data processed by the application are the data of audit interest and are not invalid, e.g. because the wrong versions of data files have been used. The auditor should obtain assurance that the data are valid by carrying out tests such as:

  (i) completeness tests, to provide assurance that the correct version of the data was completely processed;

  (ii) tests of the details on the file, to provide assurance that it contains the correct data in the intended format;

The auditor may do this by, e.g.:

  (i) reconciling a control total produced by the program to the relevant control account;

  (ii) selecting some records from the file and comparing the data to independent records.

(b) **Independent performance**: The auditor should obtain reasonable assurance that the CAAT was not adversely affected, either directly or indirectly, by client personnel or others. A CAAT may be intentionally or unintentionally affected in many ways, of which the following are examples:

(i)   Alteration or substitution of the program before processing.

(ii) Alteration or substitution of data files.

(iii) Alteration or circumvention of the computer's operating system controls (e.g., bypassing security systems).

(iv) Alteration or substitution of output files or reports.

Depending on an assessment of the risk that the CAAT will be adversely affected, the auditor should perform appropriate procedures, which may include one or more of the following:

(i)   Maintaining control over the reports and computer files relating to the application.

(ii) Limiting the extent to which client personnel can gain a detailed understanding of the program by restricting access to all printed copies of specifications and program code.

(iii) Disclosing to as few client personnel as possible the nature and timing of audit computer processing.

(iv) Maintaining the program and specifications in a library that is either secure or physically independent (e.g., on a removable disk) from other users of the computer. If the auditor plans to maintain the program or specifications on the client's system, reasonable assurance should be obtained that system security procedures are adequate and functioning properly. The auditor should also periodically reload and recompile the audit program to override any undisclosed alterations to the CAAT.

(v)   Obtaining printed reports immediately after the data have been processed.

(vi) Testing the output of the program by independent means.

If the auditor cannot obtain reasonable assurance that the CAAT can be run securely on the client's system, running the CAAT on an independent system should be considered.

9:7.3.2.3 Procedures after the CAAT has been run

After running the CAAT the auditor should carry out the following procedures:

(a)   Reconcile the output to the amount of audit interest and investigate any material differences.

(b)   Record any changes made to the program as a consequence of changes to the client's system and/or problems encountered.

(c)   Record particulars of the run details, including:

(i)   when the run was made;

(ii) the period covered by the run; and

(iii) conclusions concerning the adequacy of results.

9:7.4 Taking data from the client's premises

Sometimes the auditor needs to take data from the client's premises to run a CAAT at a different location. If this is done, the auditor should ensure that:

(a)   the necessary agreement is obtained from the client;

(b)   the correct versions of the data and the correct files have been obtained;

(c)   the client's data are safeguarded; and

(d)   the security of audit software is maintained.

9:7.5 Involving computer audit specialists

Whether the auditor involves a computer audit specialist to help develop and run a CAAT will depend on the nature and complexity of the application. Some audit programs can be used without involving specialists. However, the auditor should normally obtain assistance from a computer audit specialist in the following circumstances:

(a)   If the auditor develops a new application, or tailors an existing package.

(b)   When the auditor transfers client data on to a PC.

(c)   If the application is extensive or complex.

In such cases the CAAT application should normally be developed under the supervision of a computer audit specialist manager.

A specialist who has been involved in the development of a CAAT should normally be present when the application is run for the first time. Subsequently, provided the client's systems have not changed significantly, the audit team may be able to run the application without a specialist being present.

9:7.6 Reliance on the client or internal auditors

If the auditor uses a CAAT which has been developed by the client, or if the client's system is used to process the CAAT, it is necessary to obtain assurance that the appropriate audit and quality control objectives for the application are achieved.

The auditor may rely on internal auditors to perform certain procedures relating to the use of computer programs. For instance, internal auditors may process an entire CAAT application. In such circumstance the external auditor should supervise, test and review their work to obtain reasonable assurance that quality control and processing objectives are met. For example, the external auditor might reprocess selected applications, test reconciliations of data to client records, or review program outputs for evidence that the work of the internal auditors is of an acceptable standard.

9:7.7 Reliance on third party software

The auditor should involve a computer audit specialist when planning to use third party software for audit purposes, to ensure that any risks associated with its use are addressed.

9:7.8 Working papers

The auditor should record details of the work undertaken in relation to the CAAT because it represents audit evidence and also because it may assist in carrying out the work in subsequent years. These details might include the following:

(a) The proposal, showing software to be used and objectives to be achieved.

(b) Program source listings, if a proprietary computer language has been used to develop the software.

(c) Evidence of the date of the run and files used, normally in the form of an extract from the computer system log.

(d) The parameters used for the run.

(e) The final reports produced as audit working papers, giving details of audit work carried out.

(f) Copies of software as used on the audit, job control statements and final run parameters held on disk or tape.

(g) Instructions adequate to enable the CAAT to be run for later audits.

9:7.9 Review procedures

The engagement partner should consider whether the work performed should be reviewed by a computer audit specialist partner and manager, to determine that reasonable assurance has been obtained that the processing objectives of the audit have been achieved.

9:8 Considerations in respect of going concern

9:8.1 Introduction

SAS 130, 'The going concern basis in financial statements', states that:

> When forming an opinion as to whether financial statements give a true and fair view, the auditors should consider the entity's ability to continue as a going concern, and any relevant disclosures in the financial statements. (SAS 130.1)

When the directors prepare financial statements it is both a requirement of the Companies Act 1985 and a fundamental accounting concept that, in the absence of information to the contrary, the financial statements should be prepared on the going concern basis of accounting. The Companies Act specifies certain accounting principles which should normally be adopted in preparing the financial statements of a company. One of these principles is that 'the company shall be presumed to be carrying on in business as a going concern'. The going concern basis assumes that 'the entity will continue in operational existence for the foreseeable future'. Accordingly, in the financial statements, assets and liabilities are treated in the following ways:

(a) Assets are recognised and measured on the basis that the entity expects to recover (through use or realisation) the recorded amounts in the normal course of business. Assets are included in the balance sheet at book values, representing historical cost or a valuation (as opposed to estimated realisable values, except for items such as stocks which should be reported at the lower of cost and net realisable value).

(b) Liabilities are recognised and measured on the basis that they will be discharged in the normal course of business; liabilities, such as realisation expenses and redundancy pay, which would be incurred if operations were discontinued or significantly curtailed are omitted.

(c) Assets and liabilities are classified as either current or non-current.

The going concern basis of accounting is therefore not appropriate when there is an intention or a necessity either:

(a) to liquidate an enterprise in the foreseeable future; or

(b) to discontinue, or curtail significantly, operations in the foreseeable future.

It follows from the preceding paragraph that where the going concern basis is not appropriate, adjustments may have to be made to the values at which balance sheet assets and liabilities are recorded and to the headings under which they are classified, and provision made for further liabilities.

An important consequence of the legal and professional accounting requirements is that, when preparing financial statements, the directors should satisfy themselves as to whether the going concern basis is appropriate. Even if it is appropriate, it may still be necessary for the financial statements to contain additional disclosures, e.g. relating to the adoption of that basis, in order to give a true and fair view.

Audit procedures in relation to going concern are intended to provide assurance that:

(a) the going concern basis used in the preparation of the financial statements as a whole is appropriate; and

(b) there are adequate disclosures regarding that basis in the financial statements in order that they give a true and fair view.

Audit procedures necessarily involve a consideration of the client's ability to continue in operational existence for the foreseeable future. In turn, that necessitates consideration of both the current and the possible future circumstances of the business and the environment in which it operates.

9:8.2 Foreseeable future

In defining the going concern accounting concept, Statement of Standard Accounting Practice (SSAP) 2 uses the term 'foreseeable future' without further elaboration. Neither the Act nor accounting standards expand on that term in the context of going concern. Any consideration involving the foreseeable future involves making a judgement, at a particular time, about future events which are inherently uncertain. The following factors are relevant:

(a)   In general terms, the degree of uncertainty increases significantly the further into the future the consideration is taken. The manner in which the uncertainty increases with time depends on the circumstances of each particular client.

(b)   Any judgement about the future is based on information available at the time at which it is made. Subsequent events can overturn a judgement which was reasonable at the time it was made.

Accordingly, the foreseeable future depends on the specific circumstances at a point in time, including the nature of the entity's business, its associated risks and external influences.

As a consequence, it is not possible to give any certainty in relation to going concern. Any judgement made, whether by directors or by auditors, although reasonable at the time, can be valid only at that time and can be overturned by subsequent events.

9:8.3 Consideration of going concern by directors and auditors

In assessing going concern, directors should take account of all relevant information of which they are aware at the time. The nature of the exercise requires the directors to look forward, and there will be some future period to which they will pay particular attention in assessing going concern. It is not possible to specify a minimum length for this period: it is recognised in any case that any such period would be artificial and arbitrary since in reality there is no 'cut-off point' after which there should be a sudden change in the approach adopted by the directors. The length of the period is likely to depend upon such factors as:

- the client's reporting and budgeting systems; and
- the nature of the client, including its size or complexity.

Where the period considered by the directors has been limited, e.g., to a period of less than one year from the date of approval of the financial statements, the directors will have determined whether, in their opinion, the financial statements require any additional disclosure to explain adequately the assumptions that underlie the adoption of the going concern basis.

Audit procedures are based on the information upon which the directors have based their assessment and the directors' reasoning. The auditor must assess whether this constitutes sufficient appropriate audit evidence for this purpose and whether to concur with the directors' judgement about the need for additional disclosures. The following factors in particular may affect the information available for audit purposes and whether that information constitutes sufficient audit evidence for the purposes of the audit.

(a)   The nature of the client (e.g., its size and the complexity of its circumstances). The larger or more complex the client, the more sophisticated is likely to be the information available and needed to support the assessment of whether it is appropriate to adopt the going concern basis.

(b)   Whether the information relates to future events, and if so how far into the future those events lie. The information relating to the period falling after one year from the balance sheet date is often prepared in far less detail and subject to a greater degree of estimation than the information relating to earlier periods.

9:8.4 Audit evidence

SAS 130 states:

> *The auditors should assess the adequacy of the means by which the directors have satisfied themselves that:*
>
> *(a) It is appropriate for them to adopt the going concern basis in preparing the financial statements; and*
>
> *(b) the financial statements include such disclosures, if any, relating to going concern as are necessary for them to give a true and fair view.*
>
> *For this purpose:*
>
> *(i) the auditors should make enquiries of the directors and examine appropriate available financial information; and*
>
> *(ii) having regard to the future period to which the directors have paid particular attention in assessing going concern, the auditors should plan and perform procedures specifically designed to identify any material matters which could indicate concern about the entity's ability to continue as a going concern. (SAS 130.2)*

The evidence collected to support these steps should be recorded in the audit working papers and should be reviewed by the audit manager and engagement partner.

9:8.5 Preliminary enquiries in all cases

9:8.5.1 Initial risk assessment

As part of the business review the auditor should carry out preliminary analytical review procedures to consider the client's financial position and its ability to continue in business. Use of software for analytical review can be useful in this. It may identify indicators, such as abnormal gearing or declining liquidity or profitability, which cast doubt on a client's ability to continue in business, and that require further examination.

9:8.5.2 Discussions with directors

The auditor should ask the directors or management what evidence they have to support their conclusion that it is appropriate to prepare the financial statements on a going concern basis and enquire whether they have any concerns over the entity's ability to continue as a going concern.

The evidence provided by the directors should be reviewed in order to determine whether the evidence supports the directors' assertion that the going concern basis is appropriate. It is not necessary to examine the cash or other forecasts in detail at this stage.

The auditor should discuss with management its future intentions for the business and its view of its financial position. The auditor should also:

(a)   identify key assumptions adopted by management in drawing up cash and other forecasts and review the assumptions for reasonableness in the light of discussions with management, comparison with prior periods and knowledge of the business under review;

(b)   form a commercial view of the reliability of management forecasts, avoiding reliance on over-optimistic representations from management and taking a view on the capability of management, assessing its judgements;

The work should involve discussions with management and examination of correspondence with the client's banks to form a view whether there is a risk that existing borrowing facilities might not be renewed. In particular the auditor should look for indications that:

(a)   the company is not meeting its bankers' expectations;

(b)   there has been difficulty renewing facilities; or

(c)   the company's relationships with its banks have deteriorated.

9:8.5.3 Reliance on bankers

Bank overdraft or credit facilities are normally reviewed by the lenders annually and there is no automatic right of renewal by the borrower. However, in practice an established business will normally be able to renew its facilities provided it has not breached the terms of any borrowing agreements or covenants and provided its trading position has not deteriorated to the extent that the lender considers it is unlikely to get its money back in the foreseeable future. Similarly, a bank will normally be sympathetic to a request for an increase in facilities to an established customer if it can be reasonably assured that the money will eventually be repaid.

The auditor should compare the borrowing requirements disclosed by the cash flow projections with the client's borrowing powers in its Articles, with available facilities, any related covenants and/or sources of additional capital. As part of this review the auditor should check particulars of current borrowing facilities on the replies to the standard bank confirmation requests and:

(a)   ensure that all banking covenants are being met, and are forecast to be met (i.e., the company should have some procedures for monitoring future periods), especially in relation to asset cover, interest cover and any material adverse changes in financial position;

(b)   examine correspondence to establish whether credit facilities are committed or uncommitted (uncommitted banking lines cannot be relied on if a serious problem arises); and

(c)   if the borrowing facilities expire during the period of the review, the auditor may need to obtain confirmation that facilities of sufficient amount will be renewed, as discussed in **Section 9:8.6.3**.

9:8.5.4 *Review of the period considered by directors*

SAS 130 states:

> *If the period to which the directors have paid particular attention in assessing going concern is less than one year from the date of approval of the financial statements, and the directors have not disclosed that fact, the auditors should do so within the section of their report setting out the basis of their opinion, unless the fact is clear from any other references in their report. They should not qualify their opinion on the financial statements on these grounds alone.* (SAS 130.7)

9:8.5.5 *Analytical procedures*

Analytical procedures are part of the process of developing an understanding of the entity's business. This will include consideration of the client's financial position and its ability to continue in business. The analytical procedures could include some or all of the points detailed in **Appendix A** (*see* **Section 9:8.13**). As part of the review the auditor should:

(a)   form a view on the quality of current and prospective earnings;

(b)   keep alert to manipulation of profits;

(c)   consider whether the client's accounting policies are sufficiently prudent.

The auditor should be alert for conditions which might provide early warning of business failure which become apparent during other audit work. Examples of such conditions are given in Appendix B (*see* **Section 9:8.14**).

9:8.5.6 Audit of groups

SAS 130 states that it may be appropriate, on the grounds of materiality, for the group financial statements to be prepared on the going concern basis even though it is inappropriate for the individual financial statements of one or more members of the group to be prepared on this basis.

Where the company is a member of a group the auditor should:

(a)   consider whether there are any indications of going concern problems within the group;

(b)   investigate the position of liabilities within the group, e.g. check whether:

    (i)   liabilities of other group companies that might have to be assumed by the company are fully recorded;

    (ii)   intra-group transactions are properly accounted for;

    (iii)   any obligations, undertakings or contingencies between the company and other group members are identified; and

    (iv)   there are significant cross-guarantees within the group;

(c)   consider whether the company relies for finance on the support of its parent company or a fellow subsidiary.

9:8.5.7 UK-listed and unlisted securities market companies – impact of the Cadbury Report

Any matters identified in the completion of the work on going concern should be reflected in the work on compliance with the recommendations of the Cadbury Report. This topic is discussed in **Section 9:15**.

9:8.5.8 Early conclusion that the going concern basis is appropriate

The evidence obtained from the audit work described in **Sections 9:8.4** to the end of the present section, together with discussions with the client's management and knowledge of the business, may enable the auditor to conclude that the client is a going concern. In other cases, the adoption of realisable values for the assets and the inclusion of additional liabilities related to closure might not result in any material adjustments to the financial statements, although the basis of accounting would need to be disclosed.

No further audit evidence needs to be obtained if discussions with the client's management and the evidence obtained from the results of the audit work above enable the auditor to make an early conclusion that the basis adopted for the preparation of the financial statements is not inappropriate.

The auditor should consider whether either:

(a)   There is sufficient evidence to support an early conclusion that the going concern basis is appropriate for the preparation of the financial statements and there are no matters requiring disclosure. This will be the case if:

　　(i)   even though the period considered by the directors is less than one year from the date of the approval of the financial statements, this is disclosed and it does not cause the auditor concern; or

　　(ii)   the directors have made comments on going concern in the annual report and the auditor is satisfied that the comments are not appropriate; or

　　(iii) there are no other concerns about the appropriateness of the going concern basis and no other matters that require disclosure.

　　or

(b)   The adoption of realisable values for the assets and the inclusion of additional liabilities related to closure will not result in any material adjustments to the financial statements, even though the alternative basis of accounting will need to be disclosed.

9:8.6 Further procedures

SAS 130 states:

> *The auditors should determine and document the extent of their concern (if any) about the entity's ability to continue as a going concern. In determining the extent of their concern, the auditors should take account of all relevant information of which they have become aware during their audit.* (SAS 130.3)

The review partner should be consulted at an early stage if significant issues affecting the financial position or the going concern status have been identified.

In addition to considering information obtained having regard to the future period and to which the directors have paid particular attention, the auditor should take into account:

(a)   any information relating to the period thereafter which has been collected; and

(b)   other audit evidence (such as knowledge of the client, its industry and possible developments therein).

9:8.6.1 Review of budgets and forecasts

It is prudent for clients to prepare cash flow forecasts for at least a year ahead, usually on a rolling basis. Realistically, however, they may not forecast in as much detail beyond one year from the balance sheet date.

The auditor should assess the reliability of the company's budgets and forecasts and in particular examine the cash flow forecast, taking into account the points detailed in the *aide-mémoire* in Appendix C (*see* **Section 9:8.15**).

Where there is doubt about the client's ability to continue as a going concern and there are no formal forecasting procedures the auditor should:

(a)   discuss with senior management its plans for the future;

(b)   assess the level of assurance that can be gained from alternative sources of audit evidence;

(c)   request that cash flow projections based on reasonable assumptions are drawn up.

The auditor should consider the directors' plans for resolving any matters giving rise to the concern about the appropriateness of the going concern basis and in particular, should consider whether:

(a)   the plans are realistic;

(b)   the period to which the directors have paid particular attention is appropriate;

(c)   there is a reasonable expectation that the plans are likely to resolve any problems foreseen; and

(d)   the directors are likely to put the plans into practice effectively.

Taking account of all information obtained that relates to the period after that to which the directors have paid particular attention, the auditor should assess whether the period considered by the directors in their review should be extended. The period should normally be extended in the following circumstances:

(a)   Where the client's normal business cycle extends beyond the review period referred to. The review should be extended to the end of the cycle.

(b)   When substantial repayments of borrowing fall due for repayment soon after the end of the review period. The review should be extended to cover the effects of such repayments.

(c)   When the client is making a loss. The review should be extended until the date that the losses are expected to cease.

When carrying out these reviews the auditor should carry out the following procedures:

(a)   Compare projected cash flows with available borrowing facilities and/or sources of additional capital.

(b)   Discuss with management its future intentions and record such discussions in the working papers.

(c)   Review board and management committee minutes for indications of funding or trading problems.

9:8.6.2 *Reviewing projected cash flows*

When reviewing projections of future cash flows, the auditor should establish whether management has made a reasonable attempt to determine the consequences, in cash terms, of future trading activities and other material transactions. Although the auditor should not try to form an audit opinion on the projections it is necessary to:

(a)   identify the assumptions adopted by management in drawing up the forecasts; and

(b)   review the assumptions for reasonableness in the light of discussions with management, comparison with prior periods (including the period under audit), and knowledge of the business and the industry gained from, among other things, the auditor's understanding of the business and business risk assessment.

In many clients the headroom between the financial resources required in the foreseeable future and the facilities available is large. In others, it will often be marginal. The nature and scope of audit procedures depends on the circumstances. The extent of the procedures is influenced primarily by the excess of the financial resources available to the client over the financial resources that it requires. Neither the client's procedures nor the auditor's need always be elaborate in order to provide sufficient appropriate audit evidence. For example, it is not always necessary to examine budgets and forecasts for this purpose. This is particularly likely to be the case in respect of clients with uncomplicated circumstances. Many smaller companies fall into this category. Thus the auditor might encounter the following situations:

(a)   With regard to the systems or other means for timely identification of warnings of future risks and uncertainties, the directors might consider it appropriate simply to keep abreast of developments within their individual business and their business sector. In the circumstances, the auditor might concur with the directors.

(b)   The directors might not, as a matter of course, prepare periodic cash flow and other budgets, forecasts or other management accounts information apart from the accounting records required by law and outline plans for the future. In the directors' view, this might be acceptable where the business is stable. In the circumstances the auditor might concur with the directors. Hence audit procedures regarding budgets, forecasts and related issues might comprise discussion of the directors' outline plans in the light of other information available to the auditors.

The extent of the work which should be carried out will vary according to the auditor's assessment of the risk that the going concern basis is not appropriate. In most cases where the client is reporting profits and a positive cash flow, and has shareholders' funds and liquidity adequate for the scale of the business, it is not necessary to carry out a detailed cash flow review. If, however, a significant risk has been identified, the auditor should consider consulting colleagues who specialise in such work. The auditor should consider the points detailed in Appendix C (*see* **Section 9:8.15**).

9:8.6.3 *Renewal of bank facilities*

If audit work indicates that there is a satisfactory level of cash flow which maintains the client's borrowing requirements within the present level of facilities then the auditor should examine correspondence with the bank(s) and check that the facilities will be continued at the same level.

If the client is dependent on the annual renewal of its existing overdraft facilities then the auditor should consider the need to obtain confirmation of the existence and terms of bank facilities and assess the intentions of the bankers with respect to the facilities. Where there is no reason to believe that their renewal is in doubt, such formality is probably unnecessary.

If borrowing facilities expire during the period under review and it is unreasonable to assume that the present facilities will be renewed, or if the review indicates that the existing facilities provide insufficient headroom, or if relationships with the company's bankers have deteriorated the auditor should carry out the following procedures:

(a)   Discuss with management how it intends to arrange the necessary resources, assess management's awareness of the risks and form an opinion as to whether management is justified in assuming that the necessary finance will be forthcoming.

(b)   Consider asking the client to obtain confirmation from the company's bankers of the duration of the current facility and whether facilities of sufficient amount will be renewed at the end of that period. The auditor should ask the bank to send a copy of any confirmation letter direct to the firm's office. The auditor should investigate any arrangements made with banks, including their formality and what written evidence there is. Confirmation might be required in instances where:

(i)   there is a low margin of financial resources available to the client;

(ii)   the client is dependent on borrowing facilities shortly due for renewal;

(iii) correspondence between the bankers and the client reveals that the last renewal of facilities was agreed with difficulty, or that, since the last review of facilities, the bankers have imposed additional conditions as a prerequisite of continued lending;

(iv)   a significant deterioration in cash flow is projected;

(v)   the value of assets granted as security for the borrowing is declining;

(vi)   the client has breached the terms of borrowing covenants, or there are indications of potential breaches.

(c)   Consider attending a meeting with the company's bankers to assess the intentions of the bankers with respect to the facilities.

Examples of arrangements which may be made are:

(a)   agreeing with bankers either to review the existing facilities or to provide additional facilities;

(b) replacing short-term borrowings with longer-term borrowings;

(c) agreeing with a parent or other related company to make good the cash shortfall.

Any such arrangements should be formalised and the auditor should examine the written evidence, rather than rely solely on oral assurances from the client. If the renewal of the facilities is in doubt, the auditor should request the client's bankers to confirm the duration of the current facility and whether they have any reason not to renew it at the end of that period.

Where there is a problem with the renewal of bank facilities and bank exposure is substantial it is strongly recommended that at an early stage the engagement and/or review partner should consult a partner in insolvency, to ensure there is a full understanding of the banking issues involved and the best advice is given to clients.

In accordance with SAS 600, 'Auditors' report on financial statements', the auditor should consider whether any lack of evidence regarding the existence and terms of borrowing facilities and the intentions of the lender relating thereto, and/or the factors giving rise to this inability, should be:

(a) disclosed in the financial statements in order that they give a true and fair view; and/or

(b) referred to (by way of an explanatory paragraph or a qualified opinion) in the audit report.

9:8.6.4 *Partial curtailment*

The auditor should consider taking expert adivce on whether the business could be partially curtailed to enable it to continue on a reduced scale, and should take one of the following steps:

(a) If the business can continue within its available financial resources and the partial curtailment can be effected within the necessary time scale, give an unqualified audit opinion.

(b) If the partial curtailment would result in a material loss on disposal of assets and/or significant closure costs, refer in the audit report to the need for additional finance without which assets might need to be realised at a loss and the need for further provisions.

9:8.6.5 *Audit of groups*

Where there are indications of going concern problems within the group the auditor should carry out the following procedures:

(a) Review the need for provisions against subsidiaries or associates in parent company financial statements.

(b)   Review the significance of going concern problems in subsidiaries and assess their materiality to the group financial statements.

(c)   Check that adjustments made on consolidation that affect the financial position and could affect the going concern status are properly reflected in subsidiaries' financial statements.

Where the company relies on the finance or support of its parent company or a fellow subsidiary the auditor should carry out the following procedures:

(a)   Confirm that the parent company or fellow subsidiary is capable (in terms of both its own financial position and any legal or commercial restrictions) of offering the necessary support.

(b)   Obtain suitable evidence of the intention to support which might include an appropriate letter of support (which may need to be legally binding).

9:8.6.6 Results of the review

Audit work on projected cash flows and available facilities should lead to one of the following conclusions:

(a)   Adequate funds are available or can be obtained with reasonable probability.

(b)   The client might not be a going concern, but another entity (normally the holding company) will continue to provide financial support to the client or to subordinate its loans and advances (referred to in **Section 9:8.6.5** (second paragraph)).

(c)   The client will be able to continue in business within the limits of its existing facilities only by reducing the scale of its operations through the closure of factories, abandonment of branches or disposal of parts of the undertaking, and this will either involve, or not involve, material losses on disposal of assets.

(d)   The client has no prospect of raising adequate finance to continue as a going concern.

(e)   It is uncertain whether adequate funds are likely to be available, because either:

  (i)   negotiations for additional finance are in progress and their outcome is uncertain; or

  (ii)   negotiations have not yet started and the client's trading and financial position is such that it is not reasonably probable that the facilities will be renewed.

In these cases the auditor will normally have to issue a qualified or modified audit report referring to the uncertainty.

9:8.7 Assessing disclosure in the financial statements

SAS 130 states that 'The auditors should consider whether the financial statements are required to include disclosures relating to going concern in order to give a true and fair view'. (SAS 130.5)

Where there is significant level of concern about the entity's ability to continue as a going concern, the auditor should check that the following matters are disclosed in the financial statements:

(a)   A statement that the financial statements have been prepared on the going concern basis.

(b)   A statement of the pertinent facts.

(c)   The nature of the concern.

(d)   A statement of the assumptions adopted by the directors, which should be clearly distinguishable from the pertinent facts.

(e)   Where appropriate and practicable, a statement regarding the directors' plans for resolving the matters giving rise to the concern.

(f)   Details of any relevant actions by the directors.

In addition, it is preferable for there to be a statement of the effects that would be felt as a result, if the going concern basis were not appropriate.

  Where the going concern basis is inappropriate at the balance sheet date or significantly uncertain in the foreseeable future, this affects the manner in which the other fundamental accounting concepts are applied in the financial statements. It is thus important where there is concern as to the entity's ability to continue as a going concern, that readers of the financial statements have a proper understanding of the context in which the directors have satisfied themselves that the financial statements prepared on the going concern basis show a true and fair view. Therefore, in such cases, if the financial statements do not include disclosures relating to the entity's ability to continue as a going concern the auditor should:

(a)   consider whether the financial statements give a true and fair view; and hence

(b)   consider whether the audit opinion requires to be qualified in respect of disagreement with the disclosure of this matter in the financial statements.

In particular, if the future period to which the directors have paid particular attention is, as described in **Section 9:8.5.4**, not very long, the directors will have determined whether, in their opinion, the financial statements require any additional disclosures to explain adequately the assumptions that underlie the adoption of the going concern basis. The auditors assess whether they concur with the directors' judgements regarding the need for additional disclosures and their adequacy. Disclosure, however, does not eliminate the need to make appropriate judgements about the suitability of the future period as an adequate basis for assessing the position.

To avoid repetition, the text in the financial statements might refer readers to specific disclosures located elsewhere in the annual report (for instance in the Operating and Financial Review). The auditors take account of such specified disclosures in considering the adequacy of disclosures in the financial statements.

9:8.8 Trading while insolvent

Whenever the conclusion is drawn that a company is not a going concern the auditor should draw the directors' attention to the consequences of trading while insolvent and suggest that they may want to obtain legal advice.

9:8.9 Maintenance of capital

The Companies Act 1985 requires the directors of a public company to convene an extraordinary general meeting within 28 days of their becoming aware that there has been a 'serious loss of capital', namely when the company's net assets represent less than 50 per cent of its called-up capital. The auditor should advise the directors of their duties in this respect if a serious loss of capital has taken place.

9:8.10 Reliance by banks on auditors

The auditor should review carefully whether any confirmations received from banks indicate that the banks propose to place reliance on the audited financial statements. Where there are such indications the auditor should write to the bank following the guidance in Practice Note 4, 'Reliance by banks on audited financial statements'.

9:8.11 Letter of representation

SAS 130 states:

> The auditors should consider the need to obtain written confirmations of representations from the directors regarding:
>
> (a) the directors' assessment that the company is a going concern; and
>
> (b) any relevant disclosures in the financial statements. (SAS 130.4)

The auditor should obtain written confirmations from the directors in respect of matters material to the financial statements when those representations are critical to obtaining sufficient appropriate audit evidence.

On all clients where there is doubt on the validity of the going concern basis and how the financial statements should be presented, whether or not the auditor qualified or modifies the report, the auditor should ensure that the board has fully addressed the main areas of vulnerability and that the directors have specifically minuted their approval of the following matters:

(a)   The basis on which the financial statements are drawn up.

(b)   The key assumptions.

(c)   Commitments to bankers or other lenders.

(d)   The relevant disclosures in the financial statements.

The auditor should consider, in light of SAS 600, 'Auditors' report on financial statements', any inability to obtain from the directors such written confirmation of representations as are considered necessary. The lack of such confirmations may constitute a limitation on the scope of the audit work which requires a qualified opinion in 'except for' or 'disclaimer' terms.

9:8.12 Consultation

The auditor should follow the consultation procedures (as discussed in **Section 5:5**, 'Consultation and concurring reviews') before issuing a modified audit report. Reference to the going concern basis in the financial statements or in the audit report might have a significant effect on the future viability of the company, including the possibility that it might stimulate a collapse, and consultation should take place as soon as possible.

9:8.13 Appendix A Points to consider when performing analytical review procedures

When performing analytical procedures to assess the client's financial position and its ability to continue in business the auditor should consider the following points:

- The systems, or other means (formal or informal), for timely identification of warnings of future risks and uncertainties the entity might face.

- Budget and/or forecast information (cash flow information in particular) produced by the entity, and the quality of the systems (or other means, formal or informal) in place for producing this information and keeping it up to date.

- Whether the key assumptions underlying the budgets and/or forecasts appear appropriate in the circumstances.

- The sensitivity of budgets and/or forecasts to variable factors both within and outside the control of the directors.

- Whether there is a mismatch in the liquidities of assets and liabilities.

- Any obligations, undertakings or guarantees arranged with other entities (in particular, lenders, suppliers and group companies) for the giving or receiving of support.

- The existence, adequacy and terms of borrowing facilities, and supplier credit.

- The possible financial impact of significant trading relationships with third parties, e.g. partnerships, joint ventures.

- The financial structure and financial ratios.

- The nature and possible impact of financial commitments and contingencies, including guarantees to third parties.

- The nature and timing of significant expected cash flows.
- The financial management practices and track record.
- Board and management committee minutes indicating funding or trading problems.
- Arrears or discontinuance of dividends.

9:8.14 Appendix B Examples of conditions which might provide early warning of business failure

(*Note*: This is not intended to be an exhaustive list. Audit staff should continually be alert to relevant conditions.)

When assessing the client's financial position and its ability to continue in business, the auditor should consider the following examples of conditions which might provide early warning of business failure.

9:8.14.1 *Operations or profitability indicators*

- Marked decline in sales volumes during the year or subsequently, or over-capacity or fierce competition in the industry, or significant proportion of customers operating in depressed market sectors.
- Susceptibility to declining demand (e.g., retailers or suppliers thereto, advertising, construction and property, estate agents, travel agents and other companies in the leisure industry).
- Fundamental changes in the market or technology to which the entity is unable to adapt adequately, e.g. technical developments which render a key product obsolete.
- Externally forced reductions in operations (e.g., as a result of legislation or regulatory action).
- Loss of key management or staff, labour difficulties, redundancies, failure to replace natural wastage of personnel.
- Excessive dependence on few product lines where market is depressed, or loss of key suppliers or customers.
- Substantial and/or recurring operating losses or adverse key financial ratios.
- Major losses or cash flow problems arising since the balance sheet date that threaten the entity's continued existence.

9:8.14.2 *Debt-related issues or banking relationships*

- High debt-servicing costs or a poor ratio of profit before interest to interest expense.
- Significant liquidity or cash flow problems, i.e., significant and/or consistent rise in bank overdrafts or other forms of short-term finance, or over-gearing in the form of high or increasing debt-to-equity ratios.

- Deterioration of relationships with bankers, e.g. default on terms of loan agreements, potential breaches of loan covenants or failure to meet bankers' expectations of performance.

- Inability to obtain new financing, necessary borrowing facilities have not been agreed or major restructuring of debt.

- Complex banking relationships, e.g., use of significant number of UK and overseas banks to provide funding.

- Borrowing in excess of, or close to, the limits imposed by debenture trust deeds or Articles of Association.

- Imminent maturity of debt without adequate means of replacement, where refinancing is necessary for entity's continued existence.

- Inability to pay debts as they fall due, or withdrawal of credit facilities.

- An excess of liabilities over assets; net current liabilities.

9:8.14.3 *Working capital*

- Denial of or reduction in normal credit terms by suppliers, or significant reliance on overdue creditors as source of finance.

- Significant amounts of long-overdue debtors; or a recent general increase in the collection period for debtors.

- Significant amounts of unsecured debts from private individuals, small businesses or entities which are themselves vulnerable.

- Indications of excessive or obsolete stock or of any increase in stocks of finished goods (i.e., decline in stock turnover ratios).

9:8.14.4 *Other indicators*

- A significant increase in the use of off-balance-sheet finance.

- Major litigation in which an adverse judgement would imperil the entity's continued existence.

- Issues which involve a range of possible outcomes so wide that an unfavourable result could affect the appropriateness of the going concern basis.

- Press comment on particular industry segments or forms of debt.

- Over-aggressive accounting policies, i.e., early booking of sales or non-compliance with relevant financial requirements.

- Continuing use of old fixed assets (in the absence of available funds to replace them) and/or deferral of planned capital investment programmes; substantial sales of fixed assets not intended to be replaced.

9:8.15 Appendix C Points to consider when examining cash flow forecasts

(*Note*: This is not intended to be an exhaustive list. Audit staff should adapt their approach to the particular client circumstances.)

When assessing the reliability of the client's cash flow forecast, the auditor should examine the forecast in detail and in particular consider the following questions:

- Are the forecast profit, and the levels of stocks, debtors and creditors realistic?

- Are the assumptions reasonable, mutually compatible and consistent?

- Has projected necessary capital expenditure been allowed for in the forecast?

- Does the forecast take into account all payments (including taxation, dividends and borrowing) falling due within the period of the forecast (or thereafter, if any known significant borrowings due for repayment after the period under review are likely to have a significant effect on the client's ability to continue in business)?

- Has management identified the critical periods when cash requirements are greatest, and also estimated the maximum cash requirements during those periods?

- Are any significant payments planned to be met by cash held in other countries from which remittances might be blocked?

- Is sufficient cash available to fund necessary capital investment?

- Has sensitivity analysis highlighted any problems?

- Has the client a history of reliable cash flow forecasting?

- Is the client a member of a group, and in particular is it itself a parent company? If this is the case the auditor should identify guarantees and known commitments to other group companies and check that they are reflected to the extent necessary in the cash flow projections.

- Is there any degree of reliance on asset disposals? If this is the case the auditor should form a view of their distress sale value.

- For significant borrowings repayable in a foreign currency, do projections include a sensitivity analysis of the effect of any fluctuations in the sterling exchange rate?

- Is other currency exposure properly assessed and reflected?

9:9 Directors' emoluments, transactions and loans

9:9.1 Essential audit objective

The auditor should obtain assurance that directors' emoluments have been accurately determined and properly disclosed in accordance with relevant legislation, and that any transactions and loans favouring directors have also been properly disclosed.

9:9.2 Directors' emoluments

The disclosure of directors' emoluments is of particular interest to the users of financial statements and involves an increased level of risk to audit firms. If the financial statements do not disclose the information required by the Companies Act 1985, as amended by the Companies Act 1989, the auditor must include in the audit report a statement that gives the necessary particulars. Directors' emoluments should be audited with particular care and the calculations should normally be tested in detail. It is important to ensure that members of the audit team who are involved in the work have adequate experience and knowledge. Any difficulties arising from this work should be referred to the engagement manager or the engagement partner.

9:9.2.1 Audit procedures

A schedule setting out full particulars of the directors' emoluments should be obtained. The auditor should ensure, by referring to board minutes, directors' service contracts, and the Articles of Association, that all salaries, bonuses and commissions have been properly authorised. If a remuneration committee represents the board the auditor should see its minutes. It is also necessary for the auditor to check that the amounts have been properly calculated and have been paid to the director concerned.

   The auditor should check that the total directors' emoluments include benefits in kind (discussed in **Section 9:9.2.3**), any amounts paid by the company to a pension scheme on behalf of a director (but not employers' national insurance contributions) and payments to third parties (not a group company) for the services of a director. It is also necessary for the auditor to check that the disclosure of the directors' emoluments in bandings, and of the chairman's and the highest paid director's emoluments, **exclude** pension contributions.

9:9.2.2 Completeness

The auditor should check that the schedule of directors' emoluments includes any and all directors in office at any time during the year and also check this schedule with the Register of Directors, the minutes of directors' and shareholders' meetings and the previous year's published report and working papers. The auditor should also scan payroll records input to identify any salaries and pension contributions that might have been paid on behalf of directors.

   The auditor should identify other sources of emoluments by discussions with the appropriate client personnel or by a review of the minutes of meetings of directors or management. These might include, e.g., amounts received in respect of a person accepting office as a director, amounts paid by connected companies, pension fund contributions, compensation for loss of office and *ex gratia* payments.

9:9.2.3 Benefits in kind

The auditor should carry out procedures to identify benefits in kind received by directors, including the following:

(a)   Discussion with the client.

(b)   Review of directors' expense reports.

(c)   Use of audit work generally.

Benefits in kind may include loans at below market rates, free accommodation, goods provided free or at a material discount, cars, meals, household expenses and subsidised travel arrangements. The auditor should consider carefully the value at which the benefits are disclosed. The estimated money value of a benefit in kind should be taken as the market value of the facility provided for the director's private benefit, less any contribution the director pays. The taxable amount may give a useful indication of the market value of the benefit.

The auditor should consider whether benefits in kind have been properly approved under the constitution of the company and are not prohibited by the Companies Act. For example, a loan to a director on beneficial terms is a disclosable benefit but would only be permitted by the Companies Act in certain circumstances.

Transactions with directors, particularly those conferring some form of benefit, are a highly sensitive matter and the auditor should, in the case of any transactions identified but which were not disclosed to the auditor, bring these to the attention of the engagement partner or the engagement manager after ascertaining the facts in a discreet and tactful manner.

9:9.2.4 Past directors

Payments to former directors are normally pensions, compensation for loss of office, and *ex gratia* payments. The auditor should check that such payments are properly disclosed by referring to:

(a)   the preceding year's working papers;

(b)   minutes of the directors' and shareholders' meetings of the company and its subsidiaries;

(c)   correspondence with persons who have served as directors during the past few years;

(d)   audit work in other areas such as salaries, wages and expenses.

9:9.3 Directors' transactions and loans

9:9.3.1 Disclosure

The Companies Act 1985, as amended by the Companies Act 1989, requires that loans to and transactions favouring directors should be disclosed in the financial statements. The Act also provides that if a company does not make adequate disclosure of such transactions and loans in the financial statements the auditors must provide that information in their report.

9:9.3.2 Audit procedures

Although it is a relatively straightforward matter to examine recorded particulars of directors' transactions, it is more difficult to test them for omitted items. The auditor should, therefore, be alert to the possible existence of such transactions during work on other audit areas such as staff loans, salaries and expenses. When carrying out this work, the auditor should also consider directors' interests in other companies with which the client has transactions.

The auditor should make enquiries to ensure that all potentially disclosable transactions have been found where, for example:

(a)   the transaction is between a subsidiary company and the director, or between the company and a director of the parent company; or

(b)   directors have other business or professional interests in related companies that might enter into transactions with the company; or

(c)   a director uses the company's funds to meet personal expenditure with subsequent reimbursement; or

(d)   there are doubts as to the completeness or accuracy of the directors' disclosure to the auditor.

The auditor should review for adequacy the company's procedures for:

(a)   notifying and explaining to its directors their obligations under the Companies Act;

(b)   ensuring that directors provide the company with details of all their disclosable transactions and with the identities of persons connected with them;

(c)   recording the details of transactions with directors of either the company or its parent company (including transactions with persons connected with those directors).

The auditor should also review the board minutes that sanctioned transactions with the directors of either the company or its parent company (including connected persons). The auditor may need to consider:

(a)   Inspecting agreements and contracts with directors and connected persons and checking details of transactions to source documents;

(b)   Whether amounts due from directors or connected persons are recoverable;

(c)   The legality or otherwise of the transactions disclosed. If there are doubts about the legality of the transactions the engagement partner should follow the consultation procedures set out in **Section 5:5**, 'Consultation and concurring reviews', and may need to obtain legal advice.

Any sensitive disclosure items or potential breaches of the Companies Act with respect to transactions with directors and officers should be brought to the attention of the engagement partner on issues documentation.

9:9.4 Representations

The auditor should arrange with the company secretary for the company to obtain a representation from all directors in which they should disclose the amounts of their emoluments and benefits in kind and also full particulars of their transactions and loans, and the auditors should inspect these representations. If the engagement partner considers it appropriate, it may be acceptable to obtain only a summary representation containing the required information from the company.

   Directors may be reluctant to complete or sign a representation form. In such cases, the engagement partner should explain that the director has a statutory obligation to provide the company with the information, and if it is not disclosed there is a statutory duty to report this in the audit report.

9:10   Enquiry of a client's solicitors concerning lawsuits, claims and other actions

9:10.1 Accounting considerations

It is the duty of management to ensure that proper account is taken of all liabilities and contingent liabilities when the client's financial statements are prepared. Management, therefore, is responsible for adopting policies and procedures to identify, evaluate and account for lawsuits, claims and all other actions against the client. In the case of companies incorporated under the Companies Act 1985 there is a specific legal obligation to this effect placed upon the directors.

9:10.2 Auditing considerations

With respect to lawsuits, claims and other actions the auditor should obtain evidence about the following matters:

(a)   The existence of a condition, situation or set of circumstances which indicates that there is a potential loss to the client.

(b)   The period in which the underlying cause for legal action occurred.

(c)   The degree of probability that there will be an unfavourable outcome.

(d)   The amount or the range of potential loss.

9:10.3 Audit procedures

Management is the primary source of information about legal actions against the client. Accordingly, the auditor should carry out the following procedures:

(a)   Enquire of, and discuss with, management the policies and procedures adopted for identifying, evaluating and accounting for legal actions against the client.

(b)   Obtain from management a description and an evaluation of all lawsuits, claims and other legal actions that existed at the balance sheet date, and also of those that existed during the period from the balance sheet date to the date the information is provided. The auditor should ask management to indicate those matters that have been referred to the client's solicitors.

(c)   Obtain assurances from management that, as of the date that the financial statements are approved in writing, it has disclosed all matters that are required to be disclosed.

(d)   Examine documents in the client's possession concerning lawsuits, claims and other legal actions, including correspondence and bills from solicitors.

The auditor might also carry out the following procedures because they may also disclose legal actions:

(a)   Read minutes of meetings of shareholders, directors and management committees held during, and subsequent to, the period being audited.

(b)   Read contracts, loan agreements, leases and other similar documents.

(c)   Read correspondence with the Board of Inland Revenue and other government bodies.

(d)   Obtain information concerning guarantees from bank confirmations and other documents.

9:10.4 Letters of audit enquiry

The request to the client's solicitors should be kept within the solicitor/client relationship. The auditor should therefore request management to send a letter of enquiry to the client's solicitors, to obtain corroboration of the information provided by management concerning lawsuits, claims and other legal actions.

It should be requested that a copy of the reply to the client is sent direct to the auditor.

The auditor should arrange that at least the following matters are covered in a letter of audit enquiry:

(a)   Identification of the client, its subsidiaries and the period of the audit.

(b)   A list prepared by management that describes and evaluates pending or threatened lawsuits, claims and other legal actions with which the solicitors have been involved. This list should include:

>   (i)   a description of the nature of the matter, the progress of the case to date and the action the client intends to take (e.g., whether to contest the matter in court or to seek an out-of-court settlement);

>   (ii)   an evaluation of the likelihood that there will be an unfavourable outcome and an estimate (if one can be made) of the amount, or the range, of the potential loss.

(c)   A request that the solicitors comment on each matter listed by the client and state their views concerning the description or the evaluation of the matter where these views differ from those stated by management.

(d)   A request that the solicitors either identify any material omissions from the client's list referred to above on which they have received instructions, or else state that they have no material matters in hand which are not included on the list (but *see* the discussion below).

(e)   A request that the solicitors specifically identify the nature of, and the reasons for, any limitation their response contains.

(f)   A request that the solicitors provide an estimate of costs incurred but not yet billed to the client.

If audit enquiries lead to the discovery of significant matters not previously identified, the auditor should extend these enquiries and request the client to send a further letter of enquiry to, or arrange a meeting with, the solicitors, at which the engagement partner should be present.

In relation to specific enquiries, the following form of wording has to date been agreed between the Councils of the Law Society and the Institute of Chartered Accountants in England and Wales as one which may be properly addressed by management to, and answered by, solicitors:

>   **In connection with the preparation and audit of our accounts for the year ended . . . the directors have made estimates of the amounts of ultimate liabilities (including costs) which might be incurred, and are regarded as material, in relation to the following matters on which you have been consulted. We should be obliged if you would confirm that in your opinion these estimates are reasonable.**

>   **Matter**   **Estimated liability including costs**

The Council of the Law Society has advised solicitors that it is unable to recommend them to comply with non-specific requests for information such as that described in the list above **(point (d))**.

However, the Council of the ICAEW 'nevertheless believes that there may be circumstances in which it is necessary as an audit procedure for an enquiry of a general nature to be addressed to the solicitors in order to confirm that the information provided by the directors is complete in all material particulars' (Statement 3.906, paragraph 7).

The auditor should, therefore, normally arrange that the client's letter of audit enquiry includes a non-specific request such as that referred to in the listing above (**point (d)**). If the solicitors decline to comply with the request, they should be asked to explain the reasons for their refusal.

If the solicitors decline to respond to a non-specific request this does not, of itself, constitute a limitation in the scope of the audit sufficient to warrant qualification of the opinion. However, there may be circumstances where the auditor has some evidence concerning the existence of lawsuits, claims or other actions that are not included or otherwise dealt with in the financial statements and where it has not been possible to obtain from the solicitors positive evidence of whether such lawsuits, claims or other actions exist. In those circumstances there may be a restriction in scope which would lead to a modification in the audit report.

If solicitors are not willing to discuss the nature or possible outcome of pending matters, but they do give an estimate of their outstanding costs, this amount can give some indication of the extent (but not the nature) of matters in hand.

9:10.5 Letter of representation

The auditor should ask management to confirm in its letter of representation that there is no pending lawsuit, claim or other action or that adequate provision and proper disclosure has been made in respect of them. Guidance on letters of representation is given in **Section 10:4**, 'Representations from management'.

9:11 'Questionable' transactions

9:11.1 Introduction

9:11.1.1 'Questionable' payments

'Questionable' payments are defined as amounts paid, or material benefits provided, by a client which either are possibly illegal or involve doubtful ethics. They can include: 'kickbacks' (payments made to staff or executives of potential or existing customers to ensure that business is obtained or retained); bribes; certain political contributions; payments in respect of share support operations; and 'commissions' paid to 'off-shore' bank accounts. A characteristic of such transactions is that the payer and the payee are both anxious to avoid disclosure.

An example of a 'questionable' payment is made for 'rights' or 'licences' (frequently ill defined) to an entity based in a country where it is not possible to identify the ownership of the recipient. In such circumstances it is often difficult to establish whether the 'rights' or 'licences' actually exist and whether any laws have, in fact, been breached. In some countries to make such payments is regarded as a precondition of doing business.

Questionable payments may involve fraud and/or non-compliance with law and regulations and therefore reference should also be made to Statement of Auditing Standards 110, 'Fraud and error', and 120, 'Consideration of law and regulations'.

9:11.1.2 *'Questionable' receipts*

'Questionable' receipts are defined as amounts or material benefits received by a client which either are possibly illegal or involve doubtful ethics. They can include the receipt by a third party of a 'questionable' payment, either for the benefit of the recipient or to provide a conduit to facilitate a questionable payment by the third party; or they may occur when connected parties attempt to inflate the results or the financial position of a company by over-generous payments for goods or services.

9:11.2 **Identifying and following up 'questionable' transactions**

Subject to any specific overriding requirements laid down in the engagement letter, the auditor does not have a specific legal or professional responsibility to design or extend audit procedures to seek out 'questionable' transactions. However, all members of the audit team should be aware that such transactions may arise and that the likelihood of their arising in certain clients, particularly (for example) construction companies operating overseas, may be high.

'Questionable' transactions are usually identified during audit fieldwork. When this occurs, the particulars should immediately be brought to the attention of the engagement manager and the engagement partner **before** being discussed any further with management.

The engagement partner should ensure that the matter is thoroughly investigated. The auditor should:

(a) consider whether there is any evidence that benefit appears actually to have accrued to the client in the form of, e.g., contracts or sales orders that can be related to the 'questionable' payments;

(b) establish the reason for the 'questionable' receipt and whether the terms of the transaction can be considered as arm's length;

(c) attempt to establish the beneficial ownership of any overseas companies or firms involved in the 'questionable' transactions;

(d) attempt to establish whether the payments (or provision of benefits) were legal under the laws of the countries in which they were made and received.

It will normally be necessary for the engagement partner to discuss each item with the directors to establish the answers to the following questions:

(a)   Whether all the directors of the company (and the parent company, if the item relates to a subsidiary or associate) were aware of, and approved, the transaction; and, for 'questionable' receipts, confirm the explanation of the terms of the transaction given to the auditor. It is not usually sufficient for the matter to be approved by only a committee of the board.

(b)   Whether the directors (as defined in (a) above) are satisfied that none of the company's employees or directors obtained any improper undisclosed benefits or advantage, pecuniary or otherwise, from the arrangement.

(c)   Whether the transaction was entered into wholly in connection with the furtherance of the client's business operations.

To confirm these matters the auditor should consider asking each director of the parent company (and, as applicable, the subsidiary or associate company) to sign a representation. For 'questionable' receipts the representation should set out the nature of the transactions and confirm, if appropriate, that the terms were arm's length. For 'questionable' payments the representation should be along the following lines:

> **I confirm that the payment of £xxx made on [*date*] to [*name of recipient*] was made wholly in connection with the furtherance of the company's business operations in the XYZ land.**
>
> **Yours faithfully,**
>
> **(A. Director)**

Alternatively, if the engagement partner considers it more appropriate, the partner may attend a meeting of the audit committee of a meeting of the board at which all non-executive directors should be present. At that board meeting the partner should present the audit findings, confirm that all the directors are aware of their responsibilities, and seek formal assurances from all board members as to the matters for investigation set out above. The partner should ensure either that a full board minute is made of the proceedings, or that a detailed file note is made of the discussion and of the oral representations received from the directors present. The partner may also consider it appropriate to record an understanding of the meeting in a letter to the board.

Some clients which operate in export markets where the payment of commissions is customary have developed procedures for the proper authorisation and payment of commissions. The auditor should carry out tests to obtain evidence that the procedures have been followed and report accordingly to the board.

If the auditor does not obtain adequate representations from the directors, whether written or oral, and is unable to obtain sufficient evidence concerning the matters for investigation referred to above, it will be necessary to write to all members of the board explaining the position. It will also be necessary to consider qualifying the audit report.

9:12 Transactions with related parties

9:12.1 Introduction

Financial statements are generally prepared on the basis that enterprises are distinct and separate from their owners and other entities, and that transactions reflected in the financial statements have been made on an arm's length basis between independent parties. However, transactions between related parties are common in business. Financial Reporting Standard 8, 'Related Party Disclosures' (FRS 8), requires that all such transactions are disclosed in the financial statements. A parallel Statement of Auditing Standards, 460, 'Related Parties', was published at around the same time.

9:12.2 Definition of related parties

Two or more parties are related parties when at any time during the financial period:

(a)   one party has direct or indirect control of the other party; or

(b)   the parties are subject to common control from the same source; or

(c)   one party has influence over the financial and operating policies of the other party to an extent that that other party might be inhibited from pursuing at all times its own separate interests; or

(d)   the parties, in entering a transaction, are subject to influence from the same source to such an extent that one of the parties to the transaction has subordinated its own separate interests.

The following are examples of parties that are normally 'related' to a company:

(a)   A parent company, subsidiary or fellow subsidiary company.

(b)   A related or associated company.

(c)   The directors, senior management and their immediate families.

(d)   Companies or businesses owned or controlled by the directors or their immediate families.

(e)   Major providers of finance.

(f)   Any company or person owning, or able to exercise effective control over, 10 per cent or more of the voting rights of the company, and members of the immediate families of such a person.

(g)   Any other party who has the ability to prevent the company from fully pursuing its own separate interests.

When the reporting entity is controlled by another party, there should be disclosure of the related party relationship and the name of that party and, if different, that of the ultimate controlling party. If the controlling party or ultimate controlling party of the reporting entity is not known, that fact should be disclosed. This information should be disclosed irrespective of whether any transactions have taken place between the controlling parties and the reporting entity.

Financial statements should disclose material transactions undertaken by the reporting entity with a related party. Disclosure should be made irrespective of whether a price is charged. The disclosure should include:

(a)   The names of the transacting related parties.

(b)   A description of the relationship between the parties.

(c)   A description of the transactions.

(d)   The amounts involved.

(e)   Any other elements of the transactions necessary for an understanding of the financial statements.

(f)   The amounts due to or from related parties at the balance sheet date and provisions for doubtful debts due from such parties at that date.

(g)   Amounts written off in the period in respect of debts due to or from related parties.

FRS 8 does not, however, require disclosure of the following:

(a)   In consolidated financial statements, of any transactions or balances between group entities that have been eliminated on consolidation.

(b)   In a parent's own financial statements when those statements are presented together with its consolidated financial statements.

(c)   In the financial statements of subsidiary undertakings, 90 per cent or more of whose voting rights are controlled within the group, of transactions with entities that are part of the group or investees of the group qualifying as related parties, provided that the consolidated financial statements in which that subsidiary is included are publicly available.

(d)   Of pension contributions paid to a pension fund.

(e)   Of emoluments in respect of services as an employee of the reporting entity.

Certain related-party transactions, such as loans to directors, may be illegal or may require disclosure under the Companies Act 1985. Transactions with directors are discussed in **Section 9:9**, 'Directors' emoluments, transactions and loans'. Some related-party transactions may require disclosure to comply with The London Stock Exchange's Continuing Obligations for listed companies or the General Undertaking for unlisted securities market (USM) companies.

9:12.3 Audit objective

Statement of Auditing Standards 460 requires that: 'the auditors should plan and perform the audit with the objective of obtaining sufficient audit evidence regarding the adequacy of the disclosure of related party transactions and control of the entity in the financial statements'. For these purposes, the auditor should:

(a)　consider, during the business review, which parties are related;

(b)　determine what material transactions, if any, have taken place between the client and the related parties;

(c)　obtain evidence as to the purpose, nature and extent of the transactions, and their effect on the financial statements.

9:12.4　Identification of related parties during the business review

To identify related parties during the business review the auditor should first consider whether the client's own procedures for identifying transactions with related parties are likely to be adequate and, if so, whether they can be used as the basis for audit enquiries. The auditor should also consider carrying out the following:

(a)　Enquiry of management.

(b)　Reviewing the client's annual return to ascertain the directors' other directorships.

(c)　Reviewing the register of shareholders to identify significant shareholders.

(d)　Identifying the pension and trust funds connected with the client, including those for the benefit of employees, and the names of the managers of such funds.

(e)　Referring to the prior year's working papers and to the carry-forward schedules for previously identified related parties.

(f)　Carrying out company searches on debtors or creditors that appear to be unusual.

If it appears that the true identity of significant shareholders, customers, suppliers or business partners may be concealed by the use of devices such as nominees or 'offshore' companies, the auditor should normally assume the existence of a risk of undisclosed related-party transactions. If the directors are unable or unwilling to identify the ultimate owners of the parties concerned, the auditor should carefully consider the risks involved in forming an audit opinion without such knowledge. In such circumstances, the engagement partner should follow the consultation procedures set out in **Section 5:5**, 'Consultation and concurring reviews'.

All members of the audit team should be provided with the names of related parties to assist them in identifying any relevant transactions when carrying out their audit work. They should also remain alert for other related parties not identified during the business review.

9:12.5 Specific procedures to identify transactions with related parties

In addition to the business review the auditor should consider carrying out the following procedures to identify related-party transactions during audit work:

(a)   Review the minutes of all meetings of directors and management committees to identify material transactions that have been authorised or discussed.

(b)   Consider whether free, or discounted, management or other services have been provided or received, or whether a major shareholder has paid company expenses.

(c)   Review bills received from solicitors who have performed regular or special services for the client.

(d)   Examine confirmations of loans receivable and payable for indications of guarantees received or made. When such guarantees are identified the auditor should determine the relationship to the client of the parties concerned.

(e)   Consider whether there are any material transactions which might indicate the existence of previously unidentified relationships, e.g.:

  (i)   borrowing at rates of interest above or below market rates;

  (ii)   sales of fixed assets at above or below the market price;

  (iii) exchanges of assets;

  (iv)   loans made in the absence of scheduled repayment terms;

  (v)   transactions with suppliers or customers at rates or volumes significantly different from those of normal business transactions.

  (vi)   transactions processed other than in the normal manner for similar transactions.

The auditor should consider the tax implications of any related-party transactions encountered, if necessary (as will generally be the case) consulting tax specialists. Such transactions might attract additional duties or penalties, e.g., where tax is payable on the market value of goods or services that have been obtained from a related party at below that value.

9:12.6 Disclosure of transactions with related parties

Transactions with related parties which take place on normal commercial terms are unlikely to have a distorting effect upon the financial statements of an individual client. Many transactions between related parties are made on this basis. For example management charges might properly reflect the cost to a parent company of its directors or officers who act for a subsidiary. Similarly, intra-group purchases and sales might be made at the same price as external purchases and sales, or they might be made with a discount which is commercially acceptable.

It is, however, common for groups of companies to transfer materials and goods and services between one company and another at non-market prices for the purpose of manipulating the reported earnings of the companies concerned. This might be done where high profits could cause difficulties in negotiating with employees or in dealing with suppliers; profits may also be 'transferred' for tax purposes (e.g., to ensure that all group relief is utilised, or to delay payment of tax if certain group companies have later payment dates). Other examples of related-party transactions which might be made at abnormal or preferential terms include:

(a)   a transfer of assets between companies at net book value or other amount that differs from market prices;

(b)   goods and services provided free of charge or via a management fee that is not based on normal commercial terms;

(c)   outright gifts and capital contributions.

Where related-party transactions of the types referred to in the preceding paragraph are encountered, the auditor should consider whether:

(a)   full disclosure will ensure that the financial statements give a true and fair view of the client's financial position and results;

(b)   the transactions are of such significance and/or so artificial that the truth and fairness of the financial statements will still be affected even though full disclosure is made;

(c)   the transactions indicate the possibility of false accounting or fraud, in as much as they appear to be dishonestly intended to mislead or to evade tax.

In these cases the auditor should carry out the following procedures:

(a)   Ascertain and record the amounts concerned, the nature of the transactions, the names of the related parties involved and, if possible, the reasons for the transactions.

(b)   Consider the effects of the transactions on any third parties. For example the auditor should consider whether any minority shareholders are affected, whether creditors' rights are affected and whether there is a possible infringement of the anti-avoidance provisions in tax legislation.

(c)   Consider whether the client has taken into account all the accounting implications of the transactions, e.g. the effect on stock valuations of any surcharges for materials.

(d)   Consider taking legal advice.

(e)   Consider whether it is necessary to qualify the audit report.

9:13 Window dressing and off-balance-sheet finance

9:13.1 Introduction

'Window dressing' and the use of 'off-balance-sheet' financing schemes are two common ways in which management may attempt to distort the financial statements.

'Window dressing' is the process by which transactions are recorded before the year-end but then reverse or mature soon after the balance sheet date. The purpose and substance of such transactions is to alter the appearance of the balance sheet.

'Off-balance-sheet' financing is the funding or refinancing of an entity's operations in such a way that assets and the related liabilities are not shown on the balance sheet. This enables entities to increase their borrowings and assets without the substance of these transactions being reflected in the financial statements.

A balance sheet that has been window dressed or which has been distorted by an off-balance-sheet financing scheme may show the strict legal form of the client's transactions, but not the substance of the transactions. In the absence of adequate disclosure in the financial statements, therefore, such a balance sheet might not give a true and fair view.

9:13.2 Examples of window dressing

The following are examples of transactions that management might enter into with the intention of window dressing the balance sheet. Such transactions will often be reversed soon after the year-end:

(a) Obtaining deposits just before the year-end from a 'friendly' or related source. These deposits are then re-deposited either with the same source or with a related company. This may be done directly or through an intermediate third party. The effect of the transaction is to increase the apparent size of deposits in the balance sheet.

(b) Using a bank loan or overdraft facility just before the balance sheet date and placing the funds with other banks, thereby increasing current assets and current liabilities by an equal amount, but improving the liquidity ratio.

(c) Including in the bank balance monies received after the balance sheet date. This has the effect of inflating balances in the cash records.

(d) Sending cheques to creditors before the balance sheet date but not entering them in the cash records until the following period.

(e) Entering cheques in the cash records before the balance sheet date but not sending them to payees until the following period.

(f) Drawing cheques and making deposits on a number of different bank accounts to create the impression of trading activity and to gain temporary credit because of timing differences between deposits and withdrawals being entered in the bank's records.

(g) 'Overnight' sale and repurchase of assets except for legitimate reasons such as 'bed and breakfasting' investments to establish tax losses.

Statement of Standard Accounting Practice 17, 'Post Balance Sheet Events', requires the disclosure of the reversal or maturity of any transaction which was entered into before the year-end, the substance of which was primarily to alter the appearance of the balance sheet.

9:13.3 Examples of off-balance-sheet financing

The following are some examples of off-balance-sheet financing schemes:

(a) **A company sets up another company which is not legally a subsidiary but is effectively under its control**: Assets and liabilities are then transferred from the 'parent' to the new (non-subsidiary) company with the intention of excluding them from the consolidated financial statements. The Companies Act 1989 definition of a subsidiary has made these schemes more difficult to establish.

(b) **A company sells stocks or other assets with the option to buy back, the option being reasonably certain to be exercised**: The arrangement may not necessarily be short term and might even last for several years, during which time the company which sold the assets will use the sale proceeds as a form of finance. The assets and related repurchase obligation (i.e., the 'finance' provided by the temporary holder of the assets) have sometimes been excluded from the balance sheet.

(c) **A manufacturer provides stocks on consignment to dealerships, the purchase price for which is payable either immediately on resale or after a set period of time and normally is calculated to take account of the length of time for which the stocks have been held**: The manufacturer thereby effectively finances the trading stocks of the dealership, but neither the stocks nor the 'loan' are reflected in the dealer's balance sheet.

Any scheme which appears to take assets or liabilities off the balance sheet should be investigated to determine whether it has commercial substance or whether its purpose is simply to distort the balance sheet. FRS 5, 'Substance of Transactions', requires that the economic substance of transactions and relationships should be disclosed rather than their legal form.

9:13.4 Audit procedures

Window dressing and off-balance-sheet finance schemes are often complex and involve a high level of risk to the auditor and to the audit firm. The auditor should seek to identify the existence of such schemes, or the possibility of their existence, during the business review and take account of them in determining the audit strategy.

Such schemes are normally carried out with the full knowledge of management. Accordingly, if the auditor encounters either of these types of scheme it will be necessary to exercise a heightened degree of scepticism in considering management's explanations and representations. Senior, experienced members of the audit team should be involved in dealing with them.

In addition to the business review the auditor may identify transactions that might be window dressing or off-balance-sheet finance schemes at various stages of the audit, e.g.:

(a)   While carrying out analytical reviews the auditor might identify significant movements in assets and liabilities caused by management's attempts to distort the balance sheet.

(b)   When checking intra-group transactions, especially between group companies with differing accounting dates, the auditor should be alert for entries intended to support window dressing.

(c)   During the audit of bank and cash balances, by carrying out the following procedures the auditor might identify large cash payments or receipts around the balance sheet date which could indicate window dressing:

    (i)   Reviewing material receipts and payments in the final month of the period and for a reasonable period after the balance sheet date to assess whether they appear unusual in terms of the type of transaction or the amount.

    (ii)   Investigating undue delays in depositing amounts shown on the bank reconciliations as outstanding lodgements which might indicate that the records of receipts of cash were kept open after the balance sheet date.

    (iii)   Ascertaining when un-presented cheques on the bank reconciliation were presented and assessing whether the time seems reasonable or indicates that cheques were held back.

    (iv)   Identifying and investigating high bank balances when equivalent overdrafts or borrowings exist, to determine whether they reflect transactions of the sort described in **Section 9:13.2** (second paragraph), or whether a right of set-off is being deliberately suppressed.

(c)   During audit work on associated companies and joint ventures the auditor might need to question the client's relationship with the associate or joint venture, particularly if the associate or joint venture has been formed in the year or if the client has guaranteed its borrowings.

(d)   During the review of events subsequent to the date of the balance sheet the auditor should be alert for the reversal of window-dressing transactions. The procedures which should be adopted in such reviews are discussed further in **Section 10:5**, 'Subsequent events'.

Window dressing or off-balance-sheet financing are sensitive matters and they can be an indication of financial strain particularly affecting liquidity. Accordingly, any evidence of them should always be brought to the attention of the engagement partner or manager **before** they are discussed with client management.

9:14 Service organisations

9:14.1 Introduction

It has become increasingly commonplace for organisations to outsource a variety of basic functions, ranging from office cleaning and catering to bookkeeping and other major administrative functions. The delegation of such tasks to an outside entity could affect the approach taken to the audit. It could, for example, become more difficult for the auditor to observe the operation of internal control procedures if they are conducted externally. This does not, however, affect the auditor's duties and responsibilities in any way.

SAS 480, 'Service Organisations', was published in 1999.

9.14.2 Audit planning

SAS 480.2 requires that:

> *In planning the audit, user entity auditors should determine whether activities undertaken by service organisations are relevant to the audit.*

Apart from obvious areas such as the maintenance of bookkeeping records, the service organisation might be involved in managing assets belonging to the company and could, say, be involved in making decisions which might have implications for the carrying values of assets in the balance sheet. An example of this might the maintenance of the debtors' ledger and provision of credit control facilities.

The auditor should review the contractual terms of such arrangements. These could affect the auditor's right of access to evidence held by the service organisation. If access to such evidence is necessary for audit purposes and cannot be granted then the auditor is likely to be forced to qualify the audit report. The contract might also detail indemnities provided by the service organisation. These are not likely to provide any audit assurance in themselves; the auditor cannot, for example, accept an assurance that the records are being kept properly.

The auditor should consider the manner in which the client monitors the effectiveness of the service organisation and the accuracy and reliability of any information that it provides.

9.14.3 Audit risk

The auditor should consider the risk implications of using a service organisation (**SAS 480.4**). Both inherent risk and control risk might be affected.

9.14.3.1 Inherent risk

Indicators of higher inherent risk associated with the use of a service organisation include:

(a) complex activities undertaken by the organisation (e.g., outsourcing of the treasury function);

(b) delegation of significant levels of authority to the organisation (e.g., discretionary powers over the management of an investment portfolio);

(c) limited opportunity for the client to monitor the quality of the service provided;

(d) delegation of control over assets that are susceptible to loss or misappropriation; and

(e) a lack of an established reputation for integrity or quality of service on the part of he service provider.

9.14.3.2 *Control risk*

The fact that a service organisation is involved need not prevent the auditor from placing reliance on internal control. Doing so would, however, require the documentation of controls and testing of operations to the same standards as is required for controls which are operated directly by the client.

9.14.4 Accounting records

SAS 480.5 requires the auditor to consider the extent to which the use of the service organisation affects the reporting responsibilities with respect to the maintenance of proper accounting records.

The duties imposed on both the auditor and the client are not reduced in any way by the fact that a third party has been employed. The auditor must ensure that all of the statutory requirements have been met.

The terms of the agreement with the service organisation should make it clear that ownership of all books and records remains with the client and that the client has full and unrestricted access to these at all times. This is because the statutory duty to keep proper accounting records remains with the company and cannot be delegated in any way to a third party.

9.14.5 Obtaining audit evidence

The auditor should see the most efficient combination of testing procedures and should ensure that sufficient evidence has been obtained to support the full range of audit assertions. This may involve obtaining access to documents and records maintained by the service organisation, in either physical or electronic form.

In some cases it may be sufficient to rely on assurances from the service organisation. If the client maintains independent records of certain transactions or balances (e.g., stock held by a distributor) then it may be possible to rely on corroborations from the organisation. The auditor might also be able to ask for some specific tests to be carried out by the service organisation's internal or external auditors.

If the service organisation cannot or will not provide access to any evidence required for audit purposes then the auditor should follow the normal reporting procedures which are appropriate to a limitation of scope of audit work (SAS 480.8).

9:15 Corporate governance considerations

9:15.1 Introduction

A series of statements on corporate governance matters was published in the course of the 1990s. This culminated in the publication in 1998 of a 'Combined Code' which brought together the requirements of the Hampel, Greenbury and Cadbury reports. This document recommends a number of courses of action for quoted companies. The London Stock Exchange's listing rules require quoted companies to disclose how they have applied the principles set out in the Combined Code. The same rules require certain aspects of this report to be reviewed by the company's auditor.

The auditor of a quoted company will have different levels of responsibility for different parts of the audit report:

- The **financial statements** themselves should be **audited**.

- **Compliance with the Combined Code** should be **reviewed**.

- **Other information** should be **read** for consistency with the audited financial statements.

9:15.2 Internal controls

Code Provision D.2.1 of the Combined Code states:

> *The directors should, at least annually, conduct a review of the effectiveness of the group's system of internal control and should report to the shareholders that they have done so. The review should cover all controls, including financial, operational and compliance controls and risk management.*

The Institute of Chartered Accountants in England and Wales has published a supplementary report entitled 'Internal Control: Guidance for Directors on the Combined Code' (known colloquially as the 'Turnbull Report').

The APB has released **Bulletin 1999/5, The Combined Code: Requirements of Auditors under the Listing Rules of the London Stock Exchange**, which includes guidance for auditors when reviewing companies' internal control disclosures. The objective of the auditors' review of companies' internal control disclosures is to assess whether the company's summary of the process the board has adopted in reviewing the effectiveness of the system of internal control is both supported by the documentation prepared by the company and appropriately reflects that process.

Auditors report on their review by exception only. The Bulletin provides guidance for auditors in drafting their audit opinion when they conclude, for example, that the board's disclosures arising from the requirements of Code provision D.2.1 do not reflect the auditors' understanding of the process undertaken.

9:15.3 Audit committees

Code Provision D.3.1 of the Combined Code states:

> *The board should establish an audit committee of at least three directors, all non-executive, with written terms of reference which deal clearly with its authority and duties. The members of the committee, a majority of whom should be independent non-executive directors, should be named in the report and accounts.*

The APB Bulletin 1999/5 does not require the auditor to undertake a great deal of work in respect of the disclosures relating to audit committees. The auditor's review should be limited to establishing that an audit committee has been formed, has written terms of reference and the majority comprise independent non-executive directors as identified in the annual report. It is not the auditors' responsibility to consider whether directors are properly described as being 'independent' non-executives.

9:15.4 Going concern

The directors are required to report that the company is a going concern, with supporting assumptions or qualifications as necessary.

The auditor should not make any direct report on going concern, but should highlight any inconsistency between the directors' statement and any information that the auditor has collected in the course of audit work.

9:15.5 Directors' remuneration

Quoted companies are required to provide additional information in respect of directors' emoluments. The auditor is required to review these disclosures and should report on any omissions or inconsistencies in this information.

9:16   Tangible fixed assets

9:16.1   Introduction

This section provides guidance for the development of a programme of substantive tests for fixed assets in accordance with the audit strategy and substantive testing plan (STP), if prepared. The strategy for fixed assets should specify the planned response to the assessment of the risk of material misstatement, including the nature, extent and timing of substantive tests.

    This section should be read in conjunction with the general guidance on substantive testing in the following sections:

(a)   **Section 9:3**, 'Analytical procedures'

(b)   **Section 9:4**, 'Tests of details'

(c)   **Section 9:5**, 'Evaluating the results of substantive testing'

The accounting treatment of tangible fixed assets is covered by FRS 15, which applies to accounting periods ending on or after 23 March 2000. FRS 15 superseded SSAP 12.

9:16.1.1   Essential audit objectives

The specific audit objectives for tangible fixed assets are set out below for each of the seven general audit objectives. The auditor should obtain sufficient evidence to achieve these specific objectives:

●   **Completeness**   All tangible fixed assets have been recorded in the financial statements.

●   **Accuracy**   Tangible fixed assets have been accurately identified, summarised and recorded.

                            Depreciation has been correctly calculated in accordance with one of the generally accepted methods.

                            The amounts reported in the financial statements are in agreement with the accounting records.

●   **Existence**   The recorded tangible fixed assets exist at the balance sheet date.

●   **Cut-off**   Additions and disposals of tangible fixed assets have been recorded in the correct accounting period.

●   **Valuation**   Re-valued tangible fixed assets are supported by proper valuations.

                            Tangible fixed assets affected by a permanent diminution in value have been written down to an appropriate carrying value.

- **Rights and**   The client has valid title to all tangible fixed assets at the
  obligations   balance sheet date. It is responsible for substantially all the risks
                        and is entitled to substantially all the rewards of ownership
                        therefrom.

- **Presentation**   Tangible fixed assets have been properly classified,
  and disclosure   described and disclosed in the financial statements.

Sometimes the auditor may conclude that there is a negligible risk of material misstatement in relation to one or more of these audit objectives, and that consequently no specific substantive procedures are necessary.

9:16.1.2 Early substantive testing

The auditor should consider carrying out some of the procedures discussed in this section at an interim date, as part of early substantive testing (discussed in **Section 4:7**, 'The audit programme'). The audit programme for tangible fixed assets should set out the procedures to be performed in respect of the intervening period.

9:16.2 Completeness

The required assurance in relation to completeness should normally be obtained from the corollary effect of direct tests of creditors and of repairs and maintenance. If, however, further assurance is required, the auditor should consider carrying out appropriate direct tests. For example, the auditor might select items of plant and equipment by physical inspection and trace them to the client's accounting records.

9:16.3 Accuracy

9:16.3.1 Assets at cost

Assets stated at cost will comprise brought forward balances plus additions, less disposals. It is not normally necessary to audit the cost brought forward because this will have been subject to audit in prior years. Audit work in this area should therefore concentrate on additions and disposals in the accounting period.

9:16.3.1.1 Additions

The auditor should consider carrying out the following tests of details on additions:

(a)   Testing the arithmetical accuracy of the invoice or completion statement.

(b)   Verifying the asset details with the invoice or (in the case of freehold or leasehold property) the contract or title document.

(c)   Checking the details to the goods received note or other supporting documentation, including (e.g.):

　　(i)   in the case of property, a completion statement from the client's solicitor;

(ii)   for assets in the course of construction, an architect's or engineer's certificate.

(d)   Inspecting the paid cheque (or other payment advice) if the risk assessment indicates a possible fraud risk associated with payments.

(e)   Checking, by reference to the capitalisation policy, that the purchase is correctly classified as capital expenditure and that it has been allocated to the correct fixed asset account.

(f)   Checking by reference to requisition documents and board minutes that the purchase was authorised.

(g)   Checking that the asset has been recorded in the fixed asset register.

(h)   If the asset was also disposed of in the accounting period, testing the disposal in accordance with the list in **Section 9:16.3.1.3** (first paragraph).

9:16.3.1.2 Other considerations

Other matters that it may be necessary to consider in relation to additions include:

(a)   **Leased assets**: The auditor should ensure that finance leases have been classified in accordance with SSAP 21 and that the amounts capitalised, together with the related liabilities, have been calculated correctly. It may be possible to use software to help in this work. The auditor should also check that the lease transaction was properly authorised, and that the asset was received, and should review some of the leases to ensure that the lease conditions have been complied with (e.g., the terms of a lease might require that the asset is insured).

(b)   **Capitalisation of interest**: If the client capitalises interest on funds borrowed to finance a purchase, the auditor should check the calculation. If the borrowing cannot be directly related to the asset, but merely represents an increase in overall funding, the auditor should check that the client capitalises only the proportion of the interest charge relating to the financing of the purchase. It is also important to check that the client does not continue to capitalise interest after the asset has been brought into use.

(c)   **Assets constructed or installed by the client**: The auditor should carry out the following procedures:

    (i)   Inspect supporting documents for labour cost (time-sheets, clock-cards, departmental summaries), materials (requisition notes), and overheads (management accounts, standard costing documents).

    (ii)   Check that only expenditure relating to the design, construction or installation of the relevant asset is capitalised and that no profit has been included.

    (iii)   Check that assets completed and brought into use have been transferred out of construction in progress accounts, and that the transfers are made in a timely fashion because failure to do so may result in a misstatement of the depreciation charge.

    (iv)   Obtain explanations where expenditure varies significantly from that planned.

    (v)   Check that the correct distinction between capital and revenue items has been made.

(d) **Government grants**: The auditor should check that any grants obtained have been credited to a deferred income account. There are particular VAT problems relating to assets funded by grants and, accordingly, it may be appropriate to consider consulting a VAT specialist. Further guidance on potential VAT problems in respect of tangible fixed assets is given in **Section 9:16.3.1.4**.

(e) **Intra-group transfers**: The auditor should check that intra-group transfers are identified and reported to the parent company for consolidation purposes.

(f) **Tax**: As a matter of audit efficiency, and also as a potential client service, the auditor should consider the following matters:

(i) *Repairs and maintenance*: Additions and repairs and maintenance should be reviewed for material misallocations of expenditure between capital and revenue.

(ii) *Interest*: Capitalised interest is not eligible for capital allowances but is a charge on income. The auditor should therefore check that such interest is identified.

(iii) *Capital allowances*: The auditor should identify expenditure that is not eligible for capital allowances. It is also important for the auditor to consider whether any expenditure should, for tax purposes, be reanalysed between plant and machinery and buildings to ensure that appropriate allowances are claimed.

It should be a matter of agreement between the audit team and the tax team what should be done in this area.

9:16.3.1.3 Disposals

The following tests of details might be carried out on selected disposals:

(a) Check that the items have been deleted from both the fixed asset register and the general ledger in the correct accounting period.

(b) Ascertain whether the proceeds seem reasonable in relation to the items sold, particularly if the purchaser was a related party.

(c) Check that the calculation of the profit or loss is correct and has been accounted for properly. For items on finance lease, the auditor should check any profits or losses arising from rental rebate or termination clauses with the terms of the lease.

(d) Agree the details with supporting documentation (e.g., sales agreements or correspondence), checking that the disposal was properly authorised.

(e) Establish whether the client has made a reasonable recovery in the case of an asset which has been scrapped.

(f) If the disposal is to a group company, check that the particulars have been reported for consolidation purposes, and that VAT has been correctly treated.

These tests should cover any additions which were selected for testing but found to have been disposed of in the same accounting period (referred to in **Section 9:16.3.1.1** (point (h))).

It is important to remember the following points:

(a)   Machine spares may become obsolete if a related machine is sold.

(b)   A potential corporation tax liability on the chargeable gain may need to be recognised if the client decides to sell a re-valued asset, even though the sale has not actually taken place. This is because the potential deferred tax, previously not provided, must be accrued when it is likely to be payable in the foreseeable future.

(c)   There may be an obligation to repay a grant if an asset disposal is in breach of the grant terms.

If a risk has been identified that disposals have not been properly recorded, the auditor should carry out the following procedure:

(a)   Ascertain whether additions should have resulted in other assets being disposed of.

(b)   Read minutes and relevant correspondence with this in mind.

(c)   Make enquiries of appropriate client personnel.

(d)   Ascertain whether any changes in the business, such as discontinued product lines or rationalisation of production or distribution facilities, have given rise to any disposals that might not have been recorded.

9:16.3.1.4 Value added tax

The value added tax (VAT) implications relating to the acquisition and disposal of fixed assets can be complex. In addition, events that are not recorded in the financial records may result in a VAT liability. Accordingly, it may be appropriate to seek specialist advice on significant transactions or events affecting fixed assets. The following are of particular importance:

(a)   The acquisition or disposal of land and buildings, and extensions or alterations to buildings.

(b)   The construction or alteration of a building for occupation by the client or an associate.

(c)   The grant of permission to a tenant to develop any land or extend any buildings.

(d)   The acquisition or disposal of any individual item of computer equipment (hardware only) costing £50,000 or more.

(e)   Any change in the use a client makes of a property, including a change of group company occupying it as tenant.

(f) The acquisition or disposal of any part of the business as a 'going concern' – the VAT legislation contains its own definition of what comprises a going concern.

(g) The acquisition of assets funded, wholly or in part, by government grants.

9:16.3.2 Depreciation

When auditing depreciation, the auditor should carry out the following procedures:

(a) Ascertain the method that the client adopts for calculating depreciation (e.g., straight line, reducing balance, output or usage related) and whether it:

    (i) complies with FRS 15 and the Companies Act 1985; and

    (ii) is consistently applied.

(b) Determine whether the rates of depreciation are reasonable based on the estimated useful economic lives and the estimated residual values of the assets. The rates should take into account any special circumstances that would shorten the useful life of the asset, such as a franchise or licence for a period shorter than the expected useful life.

(c) Establish that the amounts of depreciation have been correctly calculated in accordance with (a) and (b) above.

(d) Determine whether the depreciation method and rates are consistent with the general practice in that industry and, if applicable, with the group policy.

9:16.3.2.1 Reasonableness of depreciation rates

The auditor might consider the following matters:

(a) **Does the client consistently make gains or losses when the assets are disposed of?** This may indicate that inappropriate rates are being used.

(b) **If there has been a change in the rate of depreciation for an asset or asset class, can this be justified in terms of re-estimation of its expected useful economic life?** If there has been a change, there is a risk that the asset's useful life might expire before it has been fully depreciated, or that fully depreciated assets will continue in use. In either case this will result in the cost of the asset not being properly allocated over its life.

(c) **Are there substantial numbers of fully depreciated assets still in use?** If there are, this might indicate that assets are being written off too quickly.

(d) **Is there a policy of replacing assets after a fixed period?** If so, the auditor should ensure that the depreciation rate is consistent with this.

(e) **In respect of leasehold property and related improvements, is the depreciable life no longer than the remaining lease period (unless there is reasonable expectation that the lease will be renewed)?**

(f) **As regards a finance lease, is the depreciable life the shorter of the lease term or the economic life of the asset?** The auditor should remember that the lease term is not necessarily the same as the rental term. The lease term is normally the primary rental term plus the secondary rental term, if it is likely that the client will take up the option to extend the lease into the second term. Consequently, rental payments may cover a different period from the asset life adopted for depreciation purposes.

(g)   **Is depreciation provided on re-valued assets?** If the assets are revalued as at the balance sheet date, depreciation should still be charged for the year.

(h)   **If grants are taken to a deferred income account, are they released over the life of the related asset?**

9:16.3.2.2 Re-computation in total

Re-computation in total can be an efficient method of auditing depreciation. However, it is not usually practicable if depreciation is calculated on the straight line basis and there are fully depreciated assets (unless the client maintains detailed records of fully depreciated items).

The fixed asset register or records are usually computerised and the depreciation is therefore calculated automatically.

Sometimes it may be possible to use software to re-compute the depreciation charge. If this is done, the auditor should consider designing the reports to print out an exception report of unusually low or high rates of depreciation on individual assets, or of depreciation charged on fully depreciated assets.

9:16.3.2.3 Substantive analytical review

It may be possible to develop an expectation of the depreciation charge based on the gross cost of the fixed assets and the depreciation rates. It may also be possible to develop an expectation by applying the previous year's ratio of depreciation to cost or valuation to the current year's cost or valuation.

9:16.3.2.4 Tests of details

If tests of details are carried out on the items selected for existence testing (referred to in **Section 9:16.4.1** (first paragraph)) this should make it possible to conclude whether the accumulated depreciation (and related charge for the year) is understated. To obtain substantive assurance that the depreciation is not overstated, however, it is necessary to select and check items from the charge for the year.

In testing items selected the auditor might check that:

(a)   the authorised depreciation rate has been used, particularly as regards the charge for depreciation in the year of addition or disposal;

(b)   the calculation is correct;

(c)   depreciation is not provided on fully depreciated assets.

The auditor should also test the additions of the depreciation accounts.

9:16.3.3 *Agreement with accounting records*

The tangible fixed asset balances reported in the financial statements should be checked to the general ledger, normally by tracing the amounts via the trial balance to the financial statements. If the client maintains a fixed asset register, the auditor should also check that the general ledger agrees with the fixed asset register, and should test the arithmetical accuracy of the register.

9:16.4 Existence

Often it may be possible to conclude that the continuation of business operations up to, and after, the balance sheet date provides audit assurance that assets exist. Sometimes the business review will provide sufficient knowledge of production levels, capacity and operating results to conclude that assets exist. A review of the repairs and maintenance account may also provide relevant evidence.

Additional evidence can be obtained by, e.g., reviewing production figures and reports and relating them to the asset groups or production units involved, or by reviewing production by reference to output from similar units, prior years, budgets and knowledge of the business.

9:16.4.1 *Tests of details*

If tests of details are carried out, items for testing may be selected from the opening balances of fixed assets and from the additions, or from the closing balances only. In the former case, tests for existence may be combined with the work carried out under **Section 9:16.3.1.**

The most effective way to verify the existence of fixed assets is physical inspection. This may often be conveniently done in conjunction with observation of physical stock counts. By inspecting an asset the auditor should obtain evidence of whether it is controlled by the client and whether there are any apparent indications of obsolescence or under-utilisation.

9:16.4.1.1 *Early substantive testing*

If assets are inspected prior to the balance sheet date, the auditor should consider whether it is necessary to reconfirm their existence at that date. If the asset is not held at the balance sheet date, the auditor should check whether its disposal has been properly accounted for (referred to in **Section 9:16.3.1.3** (first paragraph)).

9:16.4.1.2 *Absence of detailed records*

If the client does not keep detailed records of plant and equipment, it may be difficult to verify the existence of assets purchased in previous years. This may be overcome by one or more of the following procedures:

(a)   Relying on the auditor's own information (e.g., records of additions included as carry-forward information in the audit files) to identify items for testing.

(b)   Using alternative procedures such as those referred to in **Section 9:16.4.1.3** (point (b)).

It is, however, unlikely that audit files will retain such information. If the client does not maintain detailed records, this is likely to present the auditor with a significant problem, which may impact upon the audit opinion.

   The audit staff should bring to the attention of the engagement manager all cases where adequate detailed records are not available, or where the client is unable properly to reconcile the detailed records with the general ledger. The engagement manager should decide whether the matter should be reported in issues documentation.

9:16.4.1.3 Difficulties with physical inspection

The auditor may encounter the following problems when making physical inspections of fixed assets:

(a)   The asset might not be separately identified from those of a similar type because there are no distinguishing plant numbers. In these circumstances, and if the assets are of high value, the auditor should inspect all items of that type or group recorded in the asset register. If the assets are of low value it may be appropriate to recommend that they are no longer capitalised. If the assets are valuable the auditor should recommend that the client carries out regular inventories and maintains records to ensure that the assets are properly controlled.

(b)   The asset may not be available for inspection (e.g., ships or freight vehicles) or it might not be accessible (e.g., mining equipment or undersea cables). In these circumstances, it may be possible to reach a reasonable conclusion that an asset exists by reference to evidence such as:

   (i)   reports by plant engineers;

   (ii)   insurance policies;

   (iii) valuations by third parties;

   (iv)   analysis of repair and maintenance expenditure;

   (v)   income generated by the asset.

(c)   The asset may be in the possession of a third party. In this case it may be necessary to carry out a circularisation or check the receipt of rental income.

9:16.4.2 Leased assets

If an asset is leased the auditor should check (where possible by reference to audit work in earlier years) that the asset is correctly capitalised and that the secondary period has not expired.

9:16.5 Cut-off

Normally, tests of additions and disposals discussed in **Sections 9:16.3.1.1** to **9:16.3.1.3** will provide sufficient evidence that fixed asset movements have been recorded in the correct accounting period. However, it may be necessary to supplement that work if, e.g., there were significant movements at or near the balance sheet date, particularly if such movements involved transfers out of construction in progress. The auditor should remember that cut-off errors in fixed assets may have adverse tax consequences.

9:16.6 Valuation

9:16.6.1 Revaluations

Many clients account for land and buildings at a valuation. Such valuations, or revaluations, should be carried out by a qualified valuer (except in the case of investment properties). Qualified valuers include corporate members of the Royal Institution of Chartered Surveyors (RICS) or the Incorporated Society of Valuers and Auctioneers (ISVA). The valuer may be a director or employee of the client. Further guidance on the auditor's responsibilities when using the work of an expert as audit evidence is given in **Section 7:6**, 'Using the work of an expert'.

The RICS has issued guidance on valuation of assets and, if necessary, the auditor should refer to this guidance.

In the intervals between asset re-valuations, the auditor should not accept a carrying value without question. It is necessary to consider whether any events have occurred which might call into question the carrying value. The auditor should bring any doubts to the attention of the engagement manager.

9:16.6.1.1 Auditing the valuation

The auditor might carry out the following procedures:

(a)   Confirm that the valuer is suitably qualified, and establish the extent of the valuer's independence from the client (discussed in **Section 9:16.6.1.2**).

(b)   Review the objectives and scope of the valuation, and obtain particulars of the assets to be valued. The auditor should check that all assets in the same category are to be re-valued, either currently or in accordance with a revaluation programme. If this is not the case, it is necessary to review the available evidence (including relevant indices and minutes) to ensure that any assets that are not re-valued do not have values materially different from their book value.

(c)   Review the assumptions and bases of valuations on which the valuer's report will depend. This will normally mean an 'existing use' or 'depreciated replacement cost' basis. 'Existing use' has regard both to current open market transactions in similar assets and to the use of the asset for its existing purposes. 'Depreciated replacement cost' is used for assets that are rarely sold except by way of the sale of the whole business (e.g., garages or hotels); it is the current cost of constructing or acquiring the asset, less a deduction for its present condition. Any expenses or liabilities to completion should be incorporated into the basis.

(d)   Establish that the valuer's report will cover all the matters necessary for both the client's and the auditor's purposes, including the remaining useful life of the asset.

(e)   Obtain a copy of the client's instructions to the valuer and check that they deal adequately with the matters referred to in (b), (c) and (d) above.

(f)   Check that the information given to the valuer is consistent with that used for the preparation of the financial statements, is complete and is not misleading.

(g)   Check that the information provided by the valuer, and the work carried out, is in accordance with the client's instructions.

(h)   Review the valuation to establish whether it is complete and generally reasonable (auditors are not, however, required to be experts in the matter of property valuation).

Other points which might be considered include the following:

(a)   Certain items (e.g., heating and ventilation plant, and lifts) should not be included both in the property valuation and under the heading 'plant and machinery'.

(b)   The property valuation should be analysed into the separate values of land and buildings, so as to identify the depreciable amount.

(c)   If the valuer's name is to be disclosed in the financial statements, the auditor should check that permission has been given.

9:16.6.1.2 Internal valuations

When a property valuation has been carried out internally (by a director or employee of the client), the auditor should consider whether the internal valuer, even with a suitable professional qualification, possesses the experience and the independence of an external valuer. It may be necessary to perform additional work or to consult an expert to check that the assumptions used appear reasonable, that the supporting evidence is valid and appropriate and that the calculations have been made correctly.

9:16.6.1.3 Re-valuation surpluses and deficits

The auditor should check that the amount of any re-valuation surplus or deficit is correctly calculated and accounted for in accordance with relevant legislation and standard accounting practice. In particular, for companies preparing financial statements in accordance with Sch. 4 to the Companies Act 1985, it is necessary to ensure that the client makes a separate valuation of each asset.

9:16.6.1.4 Other matters

Because companies are required to disclose the historical cost equivalent of both the re-valued assets and the depreciation charge for the year, the auditor should check whether the records are adequate for the purpose. The auditor might either:

(a)   review the overall figures by reference to previous years, adjusted for known additions, disposals and re-valuations in the year; or

(b)   check the original cost of a sample of re-valued assets, trace these to the client's summary, and test the additions of the summary.

9:16.6.2 *Impairment of assets*

If any of the client's tangible fixed assets has become worth less than its written down value (WDV) in an accounting period, the asset should be written down to that lower value. Provision may also be required when future income generated from the use of the asset is likely to be insufficient to cover the depreciation charge. Accounting procedures to be followed in such cases are detailed in FRS 11 *Impairment of fixed assets and goodwill* . Impairment is measured by comparing the comparing the WDV with the recoverable amount, where the recoverable amount is the higher of:

(a)   The amount which could be realised by selling the asset; and

(b)   The value determined by the asset's income generation

There is no requirement to consider every asset for impairment every year. Consideration of impairment must be triggered by some indication that the value may be impaired. The auditor might identify such assets by undertaking the following procedures:

(a)   Ascertaining whether there has been a significant change in the level of production or in the range of products. This might indicate that particular fixed assets were no longer in use or had become under-utilised.

(b)   Reviewing levels of expenditure on repairs and maintenance. Abnormally high levels might indicate that fixed assets were approaching the end of their useful economic lives and should be written down.

(c)   Making appropriate enquiries of members of the client's staff such as the production manager or the plant engineer.

(d)   Considering, when inspecting fixed assets, whether there is any evidence that they are idle or under-utilised.

(e)   Considering, for marketable properties, whether the current market value is substantially below book value.

(f)   In the case of industrial or other land, the presence of erosion or contamination.

If the client has constructed an asset for its own use, it is necessary to consider, by reference either to the cost of an equivalent asset (if any) on the open market or to the likely profits that the asset will generate, whether its carrying value is reasonable. This should also be done for construction in progress.

The auditor might check that the written-down value or the recoverable amount is reasonable by reference to trade journals, valuers' reports or subsequent sale proceeds.

The auditor should ensure that the calculation of any impairment is correct and is accounted for in accordance with relevant legislation and accepted accounting practice.

9:16.7 Rights and obligations

9:16.7.1 Property

When seeking to verify that freehold and leasehold property is owned by the client at the balance sheet date, the auditor is not expected to express an authoritative legal view on whether the client has a valid title to a particular property. However, it is necessary to obtain satisfactory evidence that, *prima facie*, the client has good title to it. Because the law relating to title is complex expert legal advice should be obtained in the event of any uncertainty.

The nature and extent of verification procedures on freehold and leasehold property will depend on the auditor's assessment of the risk of material misstatement in these areas of the client's financial statements. The verification of the client' title to property is strictly a matter for a solicitor, although for normal purposes the auditor may rely on evidence in the form of minutes, title deeds ,land registry certificates, leases and other documentation.

Because the transfer of legal title to property will usually be recorded by special minute, the auditor may accept a review of the minute book and representations by a duly authorised member of management (e.g., the company secretary), in the absence of specific risks, to provide sufficient evidence that the property is still owned by the client.

However, if greater assurance is required, the auditor should consider verifying ownership by inspecting title deeds or leases, or by writing to appropriate third parties. This should be done because property can be sold or mortgaged with no obvious change in the way the client uses it. Tests should normally be carried out on the same sample that was selected for existence testing.

9:16.7.2 Other assets

Although direct evidence of ownership of other assets (e.g., plant and equipment) is obtained when testing additions, that evidence does not necessarily establish ownership **at the balance sheet date**. Generally, however, the asset's physical presence and its continuing use and control by the client will be sufficient evidence of the continuing ownership by the client.

Further evidence as to whether any assets have been pledged may be obtained from loan agreements or contracts into which the client has entered. It is also important to enquire of management whether there are any encumbrances over fixed assets. The auditor might consider whether to include this matter in management's formal written representations.

9:16.7.3 Sale and leaseback

Certain fixed assets, usually property, may be sold by the client and leased back from the purchaser. The auditor should obtain evidence of such transactions by reviewing minutes and correspondence and, if concerned that such a transaction has not been minuted, by scrutinising the cash records for significant receipts. If a sale and leaseback transaction is identified, the auditor should confirm that it has been accounted for in accordance with FRS 5, 'Reporting the substance of transactions'.

9:16.8 Presentation and disclosure

To help achieve the objective of presentation and disclosure the auditor should, at the end of the audit, review the financial statements and consider the matters set out in a UK GAAP (generally accepted accounting principles) checklist. Also, it is important for the auditor to be alert for any matters that require disclosure which can be more efficiently identified during fieldwork. These include:

- fixed assets that the client intends to dispose of
- capitalised interest
- fixed assets charged to secure liabilities
- disposals to directors
- movements on fixed assets for use in the cash flow statement
- capital commitments
- fixed assets pledged as security

9:17 Intangible fixed assets

9:17.1 Introduction

This section is designed to help to develop a programme of substantive tests for intangible fixed assets, as defined below, in accordance with the assessment of the risk of material misstatement including the nature, extent and timing of substantive tests.

This section should be read in conjunction with FRS 10, 'Goodwill and intangible assets', as well as the general guidance on substantive testing in the following sections:

- **Section 9:3**, 'Analytical procedures'
- **Section 9:4**, 'Tests of details'
- **Section 9:5**, 'Evaluating the results of substantive testing'

For the purposes of this section, intangible fixed assets comprise:

(a) Goodwill, including amounts written off in the year.

(b) Development costs.

(c)   Patents, licences and copyrights.

(d)   Brands, trade marks, registered designs, newspaper titles and similar rights.

9:17.1.1 Essential audit objectives

The specific audit objectives for intangible fixed assets are set out below for each of the seven general audit objectives. The auditor should obtain sufficient evidence to achieve these specific objectives:

- **Completeness**   All intangible fixed assets have been recorded in the financial statements.

- **Accuracy**   The cost of intangible fixed assets has been correctly recorded on the basis of the client's accounting policies, consistently applied.

  Amortisation has been correctly calculated on an acceptable basis.

  The amounts reported in the financial statements are in agreement with the accounting records.

- **Existence;**   Intangible fixed assets exist at the balance sheet date.
  Rights and
  obligations   The client has valid title to all intangible fixed assets at the balance sheet date. It is responsible for substantially all the risks and is entitled to substantially all the rewards of ownership therefrom.

- **Cut-off**   Additions and disposals of intangible fixed assets have been recorded in the correct accounting period.

- **Valuation**   Assets affected by a permanent diminution in value have been written down to an appropriate carrying value.

- **Presentation**   Intangible fixed assets have been properly classified, described
  and disclosure   and disclosed in the financial statements.

Sometimes the auditor may conclude that there is a negligible risk of material misstatement in relation to one or more of these audit objectives, and that consequently no specific substantive procedures are necessary.

9:17.1.2 Early substantive testing

The auditor should consider carrying out some of the procedures discussed in this section at an interim date, as part of early substantive testing (discussed in **Section 4:7**, 'The audit programme'). The strategy for intangible fixed assets should specify which procedures will be carried out at an interim date, and whether it is expected that it will be necessary to repeat or extend them as at the balance sheet date. The audit programme for intangible fixed assets should set out the procedures to be performed in respect of the intervening period.

9:17.2 Completeness

The nature of intangible fixed assets is such that the auditor is likely to obtain little assurance concerning the completeness objective from the corollary effects of direct tests of creditors and expenses. Instead, the required assurance should normally be derived from an understanding of the business (e.g., by considering whether any of the client's processes or products may be protected by a patent and checking if it is included as an intangible fixed asset).

If a risk of material misstatement is identified which affects the completeness of intangible fixed assets, the auditor might consider the following procedures:

(a)   Discussing the scope of the assets with the client's in-house or external lawyers.

(b)   Reviewing the research and development (R&D) expense account to ascertain if any development costs written off should instead have been capitalised.

9:17.3 Accuracy

9:17.3.1 Assets stated at cost

Assets stated at cost will comprise brought forward balances plus additions less disposals. The auditor should not normally need to audit the costs brought forward because they will have been subject to audit in prior years. Tests should therefore concentrate on additions and disposals. In many cases, there will be few movements in intangible assets and it will normally be appropriate to test them all.

9:17.3.1.1 Additions

Audit work should vary according to the nature of the asset, but it might normally include some of the following tests of details:

(a)   Checking the particulars of the assets with the supporting documentation, and testing the arithmetical accuracy of that documentation.

(b)   Checking that the expenditure has been correctly capitalised in accordance with the accounting policy, which should have been applied consistently.

(c)   Checking by reference to requisition documents and board minutes that purchases have been properly authorised.

(d)   If there is a risk of fraud, inspecting the paid cheques or other evidence of payments.

(e)   If the asset was also disposed of in the accounting period, testing its disposal in accordance with **Section 9:17.3.1.2 (first paragraph)**.

The evidence to support an addition will vary according to the nature of the asset and whether it was purchased externally (e.g., goodwill) or generated internally (e.g., deferred development expenditure). Examples of documentation include:

(a)   in the case of goodwill, the agreement to purchase the business;

(b)   for internally generated assets, labour costs allocations, materials requisitions, and schedules of overheads.

9:17.3.1.2 Disposals

For all disposals selected for testing the auditor should check that:

(a)   the item has been deleted both from the asset register (or other such record maintained by the client) and from the general ledger in the correct accounting period;

(b)   the proceeds seem reasonable in relation to the nature of the asset sold, particularly if the purchaser was a related party;

(c)   the profit or loss on disposal has been calculated correctly and accounted for properly;

(d)   the supporting documentation (e.g., minutes, invoices and correspondence) indicates that the disposal was properly authorised. If the disposal was to a related party, the auditor should check that the particulars have been reported for consolidation purposes, and that VAT has been correctly treated.

If a risk has been identified that disposals have not been properly recorded, the auditor should carry out the following procedures:

(a)   Ascertain whether additions initiate disposals.

(b)   Check minutes, correspondence or other relevant documentation for evidence of disposals.

(c)   Make enquiries of appropriate client personnel.

Sometimes, a client will allow a patent to lapse by not renewing it. The auditor might inspect the authority, such as board minutes, for this and discuss with management the reasons therefor.

9:17.3.2 Amortisation

To audit amortisation the auditor might carry out the following steps:

(a)   Ascertain the method that the client adopts for calculating amortisation, and whether it is acceptable and consistently applied. A basis of amortisation other than straight line will only normally be acceptable if it is systematic and more conservative in nature.

(b)   Determine whether the rates of amortisation are based on reasonable useful economic lives of the assets, and that such rates are applied from an appropriate date (e.g., the date that commercial production begins). Specific considerations in respect of goodwill are discussed in **Section 9:17.3.2.1**.

(c) Establish that the amounts of amortisation have been correctly calculated in accordance with (a) and (b) above.

Some intangible assets may have indefinite lives, and the auditor should consider only reviewing them for permanent diminution in value, as discussed in **Section 9:17.6.2.**

9:17.3.2.1 Goodwill

In order to amortise goodwill, the client will need to determine the useful economic life of the goodwill in respect of each acquisition. The following factors may be relevant:

(a) Expected changes in products, markets or technology.

(b) The expected period of future service of certain employees.

(c) Expected future demand, competition or other economic factors which may affect current advantages.

It is not possible to specify general rules regarding the useful economic lives of goodwill. The auditor should discuss the basis of amortisation with management at an early stage and should encourage the adoption of a prudent approach.

9:17.3.2.2 Re-computation in total

Re-computation will generally be the most efficient method of testing amortisation. However, it may not be practicable in all circumstances (e.g., where the individual assets each have different amortisation rates).

9:17.3.2.3 Substantive analytical review

Substantive analytical review might include, e.g., reconciling the charge for the year with that of the previous year, or estimating the charge for each major category by applying, to the current year's cost, the previous year's ratio of cost to amortisation (adjusted for significant additions and disposals).

9:17.3.2.4 Tests of details

If the auditor carries out tests of details on amortisation of the items selected for existence testing, this will make it possible to conclude whether the related accumulated amortisation (and the charge for the year), is understated. To obtain assurance that the amortisation is not overstated, however, it is necessary to select and check items from the charge for the year.

   In testing items selected the auditor should check that:

(a) the authorised amortisation rate has been used, particularly as regards the charge for amortisation in the year of addition or disposal;

(b)   the calculation is correct;

(c)   amortisation is not provided on fully amortised assets.

The auditor should also test the additions and postings of the amortisation accounts.

9:17.3.3 Agreement with accounting records

The auditor should check the intangible fixed asset balances reported in the financial statements to the general ledger and trial balance. It is also necessary to check that the general ledger agrees with any supporting detailed records of intangible fixed assets, and test the additions of such records.

9:17.4 Existence; Rights and obligations

Because of the nature of most intangible fixed assets, the procedures discussed in **Sections 9:17.4.1.1** and **9:17.4.1.2** will normally provide relevant audit evidence both for the existence and the rights and obligations objectives.

9:17.4.1 Audit evidence

9:17.4.1.1 Patents and trade marks

In the case of patents the auditor might carry out one of the following procedures:

(a)   Inspect the register at the Patent Office which gives the name of the proprietor of the patent and details of any licences or mortgages that have been notified to the office.

(b)   Request the Patent Office to send a certified copy of the register entry direct to the auditor (the appropriate form must be obtained and completed and a small fee is payable).

(c)   Instruct a firm of patent agents to obtain the information.

Because changes in proprietorship or other interests in patents are not always notified to the Patent Office, the auditor should consider whether it is necessary to make further enquiries. If a client claims to own a patent but the proprietorship is not recorded at the Patent Office, the auditor should inspect the assignment or agreement transferring the title from the previous registered owner.

In the case of trade marks, the auditor might take the following steps:

(a)   Ensure (by reference to original documentation) that the registration period of a trade mark has not yet lapsed.

(b)   Check the payment of a renewal fee in the year to confirm that a trade mark has been renewed.

9:17.4.1.2 Other intangible fixed assets

For those assets where there are no documents of title, the auditor may obtain evidence of existence and ownership from other sources. Examples of such evidence are as follows:

(a)   Receipt of related income, e.g., from royalties.

(b)   Evidence of expenditure by the client. Many intangible assets (e.g., development expenditure) 'exist' and are 'owned' only to the extent that they represent monies expended by the client. Accordingly, it is not normally necessary to seek to obtain evidence of the existence and ownership of such assets if they represent balances properly brought forward from prior years. However, the auditor should consider whether a diminution in value has occurred (referred to in **Section 9:17.6.2**) and whether the client has, for any reason, ceased to be entitled to future benefits of the expenditure. It is also important to test any additions as described in **Section 9:17.3.1.1** (first paragraph).

(c)   Confirmation that a business on which purchased goodwill arose has not been sold or closed down.

9:17.5 Cut-off

Normally the tests of additions and disposals discussed in **Sections 9:17.3.1.1** and **9:17.3.1.2** should provide sufficient evidence that intangible fixed asset movements have been recorded in the correct accounting period. However, the auditor might decide to supplement that work if, e.g., there were significant movements at or near the balance sheet date.

9:17.6 Valuation

9:17.6.1 Valuations

In respect of any intangible assets which are valued, the auditor should ensure that the basis of valuation is appropriate. It is also necessary to review carefully any instructions to, or reports from, valuers to ensure that the auditor understands the basis on which the valuation has been made.

9:17.6.1.1 Goodwill

The auditor should be careful when 'fair values' are attributed to assets after acquisitions have occurred and, in particular, where values are attributed to separable net assets in accordance with standard accounting practice. It is necessary to examine evidence that the fair values are correctly apportioned and justified. This might include valuer's reports, indices and the client's calculations.

9:17.6.1.2 Brands or publishing rights

If intangible assets such as brands or publishing rights have been recognised in the financial statements, the auditor will need to consider the following factors:

(a) Accounting for such assets.

(b) The basis of valuation.

(c) The marketability of such assets.

(d) The amortisation policy to be adopted.

The engagement manager should consider consulting recent technical publications or specialists to establish the latest developments in accounting and valuing intangible assets.

9:17.6.2 Assets affected by a loss of value

The auditor should compare the carrying value of individual intangible assets with the future benefits to be earned by those assets. If the future benefits are uncertain, and it is probable that the effect will be more than temporary, the asset should be written down to an appropriate amount. In the case of goodwill, the auditor should ensure that the requirements of FRS 11 Impairment of fixed assets and goodwill have been complied with. In particular, the auditor should consider whether or not the goodwill has been impaired, and if so, whether it has been adequately accounted for and disclosed in the financial statements.

9:17.6.2.1 Development costs

Where development costs are deferred and carried as an intangible fixed asset, the auditor should determine that the criteria necessary for deferral are fulfilled. Of these criteria, the most difficult to establish are usually the technical feasibility of a project and whether sufficient future income will be earned to justify the carry-forward. In assessing the value of the capitalised expenditure it may be necessary for the auditor to carry out some or all of the following procedures:

(a) Reviewing the client's records regarding the outcome of the development projects.

(b) Reviewing the controls set up by management to minimise the likelihood of technically unsound projects either being started or continuing once they have been appraised as such.

(c) Reading the minutes of any relevant committees to establish the key factors affecting the feasibility and viability of the project and whether there have been any disagreements.

(d) Reviewing expenditure and marketing forecasts and other management plans to ensure that they are not unrealistically optimistic, and to confirm that the resources required to finance the plans will be available.

(e) Discussing the position with management and obtaining formal representations that the project is technically feasible and that the forecasts of future income have been properly prepared after careful consideration of all relevant information. If it is necessary to review an expert's report on the feasibility the auditor should consider the matters discussed in **Section 7:6**, 'Using the work of an expert'.

(f)   Considering whether income has, in fact, materialised to match expenditure carried forward in past years in the expectation of future income.

(g)   Considering the possibility that the future benefits expected to be derived will not materialise (e.g., because of termination of, or a change in, a contract).

Sometimes it may be necessary for the auditor to consult specialists in the firm to help assess the criteria relevant to the outcome of a project.

9:17.6.2.2 *Other intangible fixed assets*

When assessing the future benefits expected to be derived from the assets, the auditor should consider the possibility that they might not materialise because of the following:

(a)   The operation of law (e.g., expiry of a patent).

(b)   The termination of or a change in a contract (e.g., a licence agreement).

(c)   Changes in the client's circumstances (e.g., the disposal of part of its business to which goodwill related).

(d)   Any failure by the client to maintain the value of the asset (e.g., by abandoning advertising).

9:17.6.3 *Representations from management*

If intending to rely on representations made by management concerning the value of an intangible fixed asset the auditor should consider requesting confirmation of the representation in writing. Guidance on letters of representation is given in **Section 10:4**, 'Representations from management'.

9:17.7 **Presentation and disclosure**

To help to achieve the objective of presentation and disclosure the auditor should, at the end of the audit, review the financial statements and consider the matters set out in a UK GAAP checklist. Also, it is important for the auditor to be alert for any matters that require disclosure and can be more efficiently identified during fieldwork. These include:

(a)   Research and development projects which may give rise to deferred expenditure.

(b)   Restrictions on distributable reserves which may arise following the capitalisation of development costs.

(c)   Goodwill arising on acquisitions.

Because of the controversial nature of some intangible fixed assets, the auditor should encourage clients to disclose fully the nature of such assets included in the balance sheet, and to give details of how they have been valued.

9:18 Investments (including investment income)

9:18.1 Introduction

This section is designed to help to develop a programme of substantive tests for investments (as defined below) and their related income in accordance with the strategy, and, if prepared, the substantive testing plan (STP).

  This section should be read in conjunction with the general guidance on substantive testing in the following sections:

- **Section 9:3**, 'Analytical procedures'
- **Section 9:4**, 'Tests of details'
- **Section 9:5**, 'Evaluating the results of substantive testing'

Investments are defined as equity or fixed interest investments, either listed or unlisted, held as either fixed assets or current assets, and including holdings in subsidiaries and related or associated companies.

9:18.1.1 Essential audit objectives

The specific audit objectives for investments are set out below for each of the seven general audit objectives. The auditor should obtain sufficient evidence to achieve these specific objectives:

• **Completeness**	All investments have been recorded in the financial statements.
	Investment income to which the client is entitled has been recorded in full.
• **Accuracy**	Carrying values have been correctly calculated based on correct particulars of investment holdings.
	Investment income has been accurately determined, summarised and recorded in the financial statements.
	Profits and losses on disposals have been accurately determined, summarised and recorded in the financial statements.
	Amounts reported in the financial statements are in agreement with the accounting records.
• **Existence; Rights and obligations**	Recorded investments represent rights in respect of genuine underlying entities.
	The client has title to all identified investments and to all rights arising from investments (including rights and scrip issues).
	All encumbrances to title (e.g., legal charges) have been identified.

- **Cut-off**   All purchases and sales of investments, and all income from investments, have been accounted for in the correct accounting period.

- **Valuation**   Fixed asset investments affected by a permanent diminution in value have been written down by an appropriate amount.

                        Provision has been made against all current asset investments whose book value exceeds net realisable value.

- **Presentation**   Investments have been properly classified, described and
  and disclosure   disclosed in the financial statements.

Sometimes the auditor may conclude that there is a negligible risk of material misstatement in relation to one or more of these audit objectives, and that consequently no specific substantive procedures are necessary.

9:18.1.2 Early substantive testing

The auditor should consider carrying out some of the procedures discussed in this section at an interim date, as part of early substantive testing (discussed in **Section 4:7**, 'The audit programme'). The strategy, or, if prepared, the STP, for investments should specify which procedures will be carried out at an interim date and whether it is expected that it will be necessary to repeat or extend them as at the balance sheet date. The audit programme for investments should set out the procedures to be performed in respect of the intervening period.

The procedures which should normally be repeated or extended include:

(a) Confirming, by assessing the risk of fraud and error and the effectiveness of controls, that the risk of material misstatement in the intervening period is low.

(b) Reviewing the control accounts for the intervening period to identify unusual items.

(c) Inspecting documents of title as at the balance sheet date.

(d) Comparing schedules of investments with the investments registers to obtain assurance that the schedules are in agreement with the investment control accounts at the year-end.

(e) Testing the carrying value of a small number of individual items to confirm the accuracy of the year-end amounts.

If the audit work in the preceding paragraph indicates that the risk of material misstatement in the intervening period is not low, the auditor should extend these procedures and, in addition, perform specific tests in response to the risk identified. Thus, e.g., if the auditor had identified a breakdown in the safe custody controls, it would be necessary to perform additional tests to confirm the existence of investments as at the balance sheet date. If the auditor identifies a risk of material misstatement in relation to investments when completing the audit strategy and STP, if prepared, this should not normally involve, for efficiency reasons, carrying out early substantive testing in respect of the audit objective(s) affected by the risk.

9:18.2 Completeness

9:18.2.1 Investments

The auditor will normally obtain sufficient assurance on the completeness objectives for investments from work in connection with other objectives, particularly that relating to existence and to rights and obligations. However, if the auditor concludes that further assurance is required, specific tests should be carried out, such as, e.g., extending confirmation procedures to include the client's known stockbrokers, or reviewing board and management committee minutes.

9:18.2.2 Investment income

9:18.2.2.1 Re-computation in total

Re-computation in total is an efficient method of auditing income on fixed interest investments such as loans, debentures, fixed-rate preference shares and government securities. The auditor should re-compute the total income by using the principal amount and the known interest rate.

9:18.2.2.2 Substantive analytical review

A substantive analytical review may, e.g., be based on a comparison of the average recorded yield on the investment portfolio (or outstanding loans) with prior years and with budget. Alternatively, the auditor may develop an estimate by applying an average yield to the average market value of investments held.

9:18.2.2.3 Tests of details

The auditor should base tests of details on the sample of investments selected to test for existence and rights and obligations, as discussed in **Section 9:18.4.1.2** (first paragraph).

For each investment sampled the auditor should check that all related income has been accounted for. For fixed interest investments, this can be done by reference to the specified date. In the case of equities, dividends can be checked with:

(a)   EXTEL (or a similar reference service) or stock exchange lists (if listed); or

(b)   the financial statements of the company concerned (if unlisted).

The procedures discussed in **Sections 9:18.2.2.1** to **9:18.2.2.3** (first paragraph) should also provide some assurance in relation to the specific audit objectives for accuracy, existence, cut-off and presentation and disclosure.

9:18.3 Accuracy

9:18.3.1 Sources of assurance

The auditor will obtain part of the required assurance concerning the accuracy objective from work on the other objectives. For example, the work carried out to verify the existence and ownership of investments (discussed in **Sections 9:18.4.1** to **9:18.4.3**) should provide secondary assurance that those investments have been accurately recorded. However, it is necessary to check the following:

(a)   The control account reconciliation.

(b)   The carrying values of investments.

(c)   The classification of investments in subsidiaries and associates.

(d)   Any foreign currency calculations.

(e)   That the amounts in the financial statements agree with the accounting records.

9:18.3.2 Control account reconciliation

Where there is an investments control account in the general ledger, the auditor should check the reconciliation of the control account with the total of the individual investment balances by carrying out the following steps:

(a)   Tracing the totals to the general ledger.

(b)   Testing individual balances with the investment ledger (or equivalent records).

(c)   Checking the additions of the reconciliation.

(d)   Investigating contras, adjustments and unusual entries in the reconciliation.

(e)   Examining supporting documents, and reviewing the subsequent clearance of reconciling items.

9:18.3.2.1 Problems with reconciliations

If the client is unable to reconcile the control account with the total of the underlying balances, or has difficulty in doing so, the auditor should consider whether the records are reliable. Any failure by the client to reconcile the control account, or significant and repeated delays in doing so, should be brought to the attention of the engagement manager.

9:18.3.3 Carrying values

9:18.3.3.1 Accounting policy

As part of the business review, the auditor should review the client's accounting policies for determining the carrying value of investments. This should include checking that such policies conform with relevant legislation and Accounting Standards, that they are appropriate to the particular circumstances and that they have been consistently applied.

9:18.3.3.2 Verification of cost

Investments comprise balances brought forward, plus additions, less disposals. Except in the case of a new client, the balances brought forward will have been audited in earlier years and accordingly audit work on the current period may be restricted to testing the cost of additions and disposals. To do this, the auditor may use the same selections that were made for testing existence and rights and obligations referred to in **Section 9:18.4.1.2** (first paragraph).

9:18.3.3.3 Additions

The auditor should examine supporting documents for additions (e.g., brokers' contract notes), ascertain that the transaction was properly authorised and approved and trace the acquisition to the investment ledger or equivalent detailed records. It is also important to confirm that the acquisition complies with the client's investment policy.

    The auditor should also check, e.g. by reference to EXTEL cards (or, in the case of unlisted investments, to the companies' financial statements), that all reported capital changes such as bonus or rights issues and capital repayments have been recorded in respect of securities held during the period.

9:18.3.3.4 Disposals

The auditor should examine supporting documents such as brokers' contract notes, ensuring that the disposal has been authorised and approved. The disposal should be checked to the investment ledger or equivalent detailed records. The correct calculation and recording of any gain or loss on disposal should also be checked. If only part of the investment has been sold, the auditor should check that the unsold balance is recorded correctly.

    It is not normally necessary to investigate the selling price if it is possible to rely on the independence of the broker who originated the contract note. However, if there is any doubt about the independence of the broker, or if the investment is not listed, it is important to consider whether the sale price appears reasonable. If necessary the auditor should refer to a stock exchange official list (if the investment is listed), or to audited financial statements or P/E ratios of similar companies (if the investment is not listed).

    When a company sells subsidiary or associated companies to other group companies, the auditor should consider whether its purpose in doing so might be to 'realise' profits with the intention of distributing them. If this appears to be the case the auditor should inform the engagement manager or the engagement partner.

9:18.3.3.5 Investments carried at a valuation

The auditor can check investments carried at a valuation by sampling from the closing balances, as discussed in **Section 9:18.4.1.2** (first paragraph), and carrying out the following procedures:

(a) **Listed investments**: If the investments are listed on the London Stock Exchange, the auditor should check the market value in the Stock Exchange Daily Official List (SEDOL) or the *Financial Times*. If the client itself uses one of these sources of establishing market values, the auditor might consider using the alternative to provide an additional cross-check against inaccuracies. Special arrangements should be made to test the market values of securities listed on an overseas stock exchange. If a reliable source is not available in the UK, it is necessary for the auditor to consider obtaining confirmation of the quoted prices from a correspondent or other professional firm in the country concerned.

(b) **Unlisted investments**: For unlisted investments, the valuation by the directors is often based on the underlying net assets or P/E ratios of similar companies using reports or valuations made by experts. The auditor should discuss the basis of the valuation with the client, review the available financial statements and inspect any reports of the experts on whom the directors have relied. This Manual does not deal with techniques and procedures that the auditor should follow when reviewing the methods used in arriving at valuations of unlisted companies. The auditor may need to refer to specialists with experience of such valuations. The objective is to conclude whether the valuation has been made on the basis of reasonable criteria in the light of all relevant factors.

9:18.3.4 Classification of subsidiaries and associates

The auditor should check, normally by reference to the investee's financial statements or EXTEL cards, that the client's percentage shareholding in subsidiaries and associates is correct. It is also necessary to ensure that any investments treated as subsidiary or associated companies have been classified in accordance with standard accounting practice and relevant legislation.

9:18.3.5 Foreign exchange

Where investments are denominated in foreign currencies, it is necessary to check the accuracy of the foreign currency translation into sterling. The auditor should ensure that the investments have been translated into sterling either at the closing exchange rate or at the historic exchange rate, in accordance with the client's stated accounting policy.

9:18.3.6 *Agreement with accounting records*

The auditor should check that the investments and investment income balances in the general ledger agree with the financial statements, by tracing the general ledger accounts to the trial balance and then to the financial statements.

9:18.4 Existence; Rights and obligations

9:18.4.1 *Inspection or confirmation*

The principal substantive test for the existence and ownership of investments is the inspection of documents of title, or confirmation from third parties (normally independent, reliable authorised custodians) that they are holding such documents on behalf of the client. The auditor should obtain direct confirmation of loans.

9:18.4.1.1 *Timing*

Confirmation and inspection procedures may be carried out either as part of early substantive testing, discussed in **Section 9:18.1.2**, or as at the balance sheet date.

When documents of title have been inspected before the balance sheet date, if the risk of material misstatement is high because of lack of controls, the auditor should arrange for them to be put in sealed envelopes. It will not then be necessary to inspect the documents at the balance sheet date if the seals are unbroken. Similarly, it will not be necessary to inspect them in subsequent years, although the auditor should still carry out periodic inspections. To ensure that a seal cannot be broken and replaced without the auditor's knowledge, it should be clearly marked (e.g., by signing across it).

9:18.4.1.2 *Selecting items for testing*

The selection of items for testing may normally be made in one of the following ways:

(a) **From the opening balances and additions during the period**: This sample may also be used to test additions and profits or losses on disposals (discussed in **Section 9:18.3.3.4**), and to test investment income (discussed in **Section 9:18.2.2.3**). The selected items should be followed through to the year-end listing or to a disposal. If the client maintains an investment ledger, the sample should normally be selected from it.

(b) **From the closing balances**: This method of selection is appropriate to the existence and rights and obligations objectives, but it will not be possible to test profits or losses on disposals and the completeness of investment income. In this case, therefore, the auditor should identify and sample from an appropriate reciprocal population.

If selections are taken from investment records that are based on the acquisition cost of investments, the auditor should consider including in the sample those investments with a market value significantly greater than cost.

9:18.4.1.3 Inspecting documents of title

Audit work should involve one or more of the following procedures:

(a) Examining the certificate or warrant to establish that it is a proper document of title (e.g., a share certificate or letter of allotment), and that it is:

 (i)   complete and apparently in order; and

 (ii) if registered, in the name of the client or an authorised nominee (referred to in (d) below).

(b) If the document inspected is of a temporary nature (e.g., a transfer receipt), following up and inspecting the formal document of title, issued later, when it becomes available.

(c) For bearer warrants, checking that the coupon next due is attached. The auditor should record the date or other identification (such as the number) of such coupon in the working papers.

(d) If securities are held in the names of nominees, inspecting signed blank transfers and letters of trust, and recording the names of the nominees in the working papers. If the nominees are companies controlled by the client, the auditor should ensure that the investments are held on behalf of the client and not third parties.

9:18.4.1.4 Confirmation from third parties

If documents of title are held by the client's independent clearing or other major bankers, the bank confirmation (discussed in **Section 9:23**, 'Bank and cash balances', should state in whose name the investments are registered, and that they are held for safe custody, 'free from lien' (or alternatively for what other purpose they are held). If the bank confirmation does not specifically state that the investments are held free from lien, or for what purposes they are held, the auditor should obtain written confirmation to this effect from the bank. If the bank is holding documents of title which are registered in the name of nominees, the bank confirmation should state that the bank also holds signed blank transfers and declarations of trust.

In certain specialist industries there are trade organisations for the custody of securities (e.g., Euroclear) which may be accepted for audit purposes. In these cases the auditor should request confirmation in the same way as for investments held by a clearing or other major bank.

If the documents of title are held by any party other than a clearing or other major bank or similar institution independent of the client or any other independent institution whose normal business includes the holding of securities (e.g., a stockbroker or solicitor), the auditor should not normally rely on a confirmation because the holding of securities is not a normal part of their business. Accordingly, unless the investments are held by such a third party in respect of a transaction awaiting settlement at the balance sheet date (referred to in the next paragraph), the auditor should ask that the client obtain possession of the documents of title to make it possible to inspect them, or alternatively that they are placed in safe custody in a major bank or similar independent institution from which confirmation should be obtained. If this is not done, the auditor should, with the client's permission, inspect the relevant documents at the third party's premises.

If investments are held by a broker at the balance sheet date pending settlement of a purchase or sale transaction, it is possible to rely on a confirmation from the broker that the documents of title were held on behalf of the client. In such cases, however, the auditor should check either that the securities were subsequently delivered (by inspecting the share certificate or the deposit receipt from the client's bankers), or that the sales proceeds were subsequently received (by tracing the receipt of cash to the bank statement and inspecting the contract note).

9:18.4.2 Pledged assets

To ascertain whether investments have been pledged as collateral or security for liabilities (either of the client or of third parties), the auditor should enquire of client management, and review board minutes, loan agreements and other appropriate documentation.

9:18.4.3 Loans

The auditor should obtain direct confirmation from the borrowers following the procedures set out in **Section 9:21**, 'Trade debtors', by selecting from the recorded balances.

In the case of loans made during the year the auditor should:

(a)   ensure that the loan was properly authorised;

(b)   inspect the loan agreement to confirm the rate of interest and terms of repayment;

(c)   obtain and check particulars of any security. (For secured loans, the auditor should ensure that charges were notified to the Registrar of Companies within 21 days.)

9:18.5 Cut-off

The auditor will normally obtain sufficient assurance relating to the cut-off objective from work carried out on the completeness, accuracy, existence and rights and obligations objectives. e.g., work on additions and disposals discussed in **Sections 9:18.3.3.3** and **9:18.3.3.4** will also provide evidence that purchases and sales of investments and income from investments have been recorded in the appropriate period. Where a client trades actively in investments the auditor may need to design specific tests to obtain assurance relating to the cut-off objective.

9:18.6 Valuation

9:18.6.1 Diminution in value

Clients may classify investments as either fixed or current assets and the treatment of any diminution in value will vary accordingly. In the case of fixed asset investments, the procedures discussed in the next paragraph and in **Sections 9:18.6.1.1** to **9:18.6.1.3** should normally be used to identify any permanent diminution in value requiring a provision. For current asset investments carried at cost, the same procedures should be used, but the auditor should also check that any diminution in value (whether permanent or temporary) is provided for so that the current asset is carried at the lower of cost and net realisable value.

There are two complementary procedures that may be used:

(a)   Selecting individual investments and making specific enquiries into their current status and prospects.

(b)   Reviewing the investment portfolio in the light of background knowledge of the client acquired during the business review, and discussing the portfolio with members of management who possess an adequate level of knowledge and seniority.

9:18.6.1.1 Listed investments

For listed investments carried at cost, a significant decrease in the market value may suggest a permanent diminution in value. However, market value might not be an appropriate indicator if the market in the shares is small or infrequent, or if the dealings have been suspended. In these cases the auditor may need to follow the procedures relating to unlisted investments.

9:18.6.1.2 Unlisted investments

Unlisted investments should be examined by reference to all the available information, such as recent financial statements, reports by independent accountants or investment advisors, and operating forecasts and budgets produced by the investee. The auditor should consider the marketability of the investment and, in the case of overseas investments, any restrictions on the remittance of funds to the UK.

Management is frequently reluctant to recognise that an apparent reduction in the value of an investment is permanent, particularly if the client is committed to some form of continuing support to the investee. Although it is important to recognise that decisions concerning permanent impairment of value involve judgement, the auditor should not accept unrealistic optimism on the part of management. Accordingly, if there is a material investment that appears to have suffered a diminution in value, and where a material write-down may therefore be necessary, the auditor should inform the engagement manager or the engagement partner.

For significant unlisted investments, the working papers should contain a summary of the net assets of the investments as shown by their latest financial statements, together with details of profits earned and dividends declared in recent years, and the other information that has been used to assess the value of the investments.

9:18.6.1.3 Investments in subsidiaries

The relevant factors in deciding whether amounts should be provided for diminution in value of subsidiaries include:

(a)   Post-acquisition losses in the subsidiary.

(b)   Apparently insolvent subsidiaries where provisions may be needed against the parent company's investment (including loans due to the parent company).

(c)   Subsidiaries where the parent company's share of the underlying net assets is less than the book value of the investment.

Accordingly, the auditor should review the financial statements (and any other relevant information such as cash flow forecasts) of subsidiaries and consider whether a provision should be made.

9:18.6.1.4 Loans

The work carried out on loans should be broadly similar to that set out in **Section 9:18.6.1.2** (first and second paragraphs). In particular, the auditor should:

(a)   review the financial statements of the borrower;

(b)   check that the loan agreement is being complied with and that repayments are being made on time;

(c)   ascertain whether interest payments are being made promptly. Failure to make such payments may indicate that the recoverability of the loan is doubtful;

(d)   consider whether other factors (e.g., remittance problems in the case of a foreign loan) cast doubt on the recoverability of the loan;

(e)   check that any security for the loan is effective and that the value of the security is adequate to cover the loan;

(f)   discuss with management the recoverability of the loan.

9:18.7 Write-back of provisions

If an investment was written down in prior years and the reasons for the write-down no longer apply, the auditor should check that the provision has been released.

9:18.7.1 Presentation and disclosure

To help achieve the objective of presentation and disclosure the auditor should, at the end of the audit, review the financial statements and consider the matters set out in a UK GAAP checklist. Also, it is important to be alert for any matters that require disclosure and which can more efficiently be identified during fieldwork. These include the following:

(a) Correct classification of investments as fixed or current assets.

(b) Separate disclosure of investments in subsidiaries and associates.

(c) Restrictions, such as exchange controls, on the realisation of investments or investment income.

(d) Uncalled capital which should be disclosed as a contingent liability.

(e) Options to purchase shares that may require disclosure as a contingent liability.

(f) Investments representing holdings in excess of 10 per cent of the allotted share capital of a body corporate.

(g) Income from group companies, fixed asset investments and current asset investments for which separate disclosure is required.

(h) The market value of any listed investment which exceeds the stock exchange value (usually if a client holds a large number of shares because stock exchange prices reflect the values of a small holding of shares).

9:19 Stocks

9:19.1 Introduction

This section is designed to help to develop a programme of substantive tests for stocks, as defined below, in accordance with the strategy. The strategy or the approved substantive testing plan (STP), if prepared, for stocks should specify the planned response to the assessment of the risk of material misstatement, including the nature, extent and timing of substantive tests.

This section should be read in conjunction with the general guidance on substantive testing in the following sections:

- **Section 9:3**, 'Analytical procedures'
- **Section 9:4**, 'Tests of details'
- **Section 9:5**, 'Evaluating the results of substantive testing'

For the purposes of this section, stocks are defined as comprising:

(a) goods or other assets purchased for resale;

(b) consumable stores;

(c) raw materials and components purchased for incorporation into products for resale;

(d) products and services in intermediate stages of production; and

(e) finished goods.

Long-term contracts are discussed in **Section 9:20**, 'Long-term contracts'.

9:19.1.1 Essential audit objectives

The specific audit objectives for stocks are set out below for each of the seven general audit objectives. The auditor should obtain sufficient evidence to achieve these specific objectives:

- **Completeness**

  All items or quantities of stocks owned by the client at the balance sheet date have been identified for costing, valuation and summarisation purposes.

- **Accuracy**

  Stock items or quantities have been correctly identified, measured, costed and summarised.

  Cost has been accurately determined according to one of the recognised methods.

  The amounts reported in the financial statements are in agreement with the accounting records.

- **Existence**

  The stock amounts shown in the balance sheet only include items or quantities of stock represented by physical stock or work-in-progress.

- **Cut-off**

  All movements of stock items and quantities into within and out of stock up to the balance sheet date have been reflected in the financial statements.

- **Valuation**

  All slow-moving, damaged or obsolete stock has been properly identified and compared with its estimated net realisable value, and written down where necessary.

- **Rights and obligations**

  The client is responsible for substantially all the risks and is entitled to substantially all the rewards arising from ownership of stocks.

- **Presentation and disclosure**

  Stocks have been properly classified, described and disclosed in the financial statements.

Sometimes the auditor may conclude that there is a negligible risk of material misstatement in relation to one or more of these audit objectives, and that consequently no specific substantive procedures are necessary.

9:19.1.2 Early substantive testing

The auditor should consider carrying out some of the procedures discussed in this section at an interim date, as part of early substantive testing (discussed in **Section 4:7**, 'The audit programme'). The strategy, or STP if prepared, for stocks should specify which procedures will be carried out at an interim date and whether it is expected that it will be necessary to repeat or extend them as at the balance sheet date. The audit programme for stocks should set out the procedures to be performed in respect of the intervening period.

9:19.2 Audit software

General purpose audit software may be used for the audit of stock. It may also be desirable to develop an application-specific package. The procedures which may be carried out by software include:

(a) Re-performing the evaluation of stock at unit cost.

(b) Selecting items for physical counting or other purposes.

(c) Identifying significant movements in unit costs and quantities on hand of different stocks.

(d) Comparing unit costs with selling prices.

(e) Identifying slow-moving stocks by examining past usage and date of last movement.

(f) Reporting stock lines deleted or added in the period.

9:19.3 Completeness

The auditor should ascertain how the client determines the stock quantities that form the basis of the amounts included in the financial statements. It is necessary to consider whether the client's procedures provide reasonable assurance that stock quantities will be accurately determined. Accordingly, the auditor should determine whether:

(a) the client's stocktaking procedures are adequate to arrive at an accurate record of stock quantities; and

(b) the count procedures are applied effectively.

Because of the importance of stock in the balance sheet of most clients and of the difficulties that can arise in accurately quantifying stock, the auditor should attend a client's stocktake unless the amounts of stocks are immaterial.

9:19.3.1 Adequacy of the stocktaking procedures

The frequency, timing, extent and method of physical stock counts should be adequate to provide the client with reasonable assurance that the recorded quantities of stocks are an accurate measurement of all stocks which it owns at the balance sheet date, and that all other items are excluded. This applies irrespective of whether the client relies on periodic (e.g., annual) stocktakes of all stocks to determine the quantities, or on a system of continuous stock counting.

The auditor should review the stocktaking instructions before they are issued and obtain assurance that they are likely to lead to an accurate count. Some of the more important matters which should be considered when assessing the stocktaking instructions, and the client's procedures generally, are set out in **Appendix A** (*see* **Section 9:19.10**). The auditor should check that the instructions have been reviewed and approved by a member of management, and that the stocktaking personnel have been properly briefed.

If it appears that the client's proposed stocktaking procedures are unsatisfactory, the auditor should discuss the deficiencies immediately with the client and explain their significance. It is necessary to attempt to persuade the client to correct the deficiencies before the count takes place. If this is not possible, the auditor should consider carefully their likely effects on the reliability of the stocktaking.

If the deficiencies in the proposed stocktaking procedures are likely to be so fundamental that the count(s) will not be a reliable basis for stating stocks in the financial statements, their possible effect on the audit opinion should be explained to the client. If the deficiencies are less fundamental, it may be possible to obtain assurance that there have been no material errors by modifying the nature, extent and timing of one or more of the audit stocktaking observation procedures.

If the client's staff participating in the count(s) do not receive adequate written instructions, the auditor should assess the risk that they do not fully understand their duties. This might be done by discussion beforehand, or during the observation of the count. If the risk is considered significant, it will be necessary to increase the level of observation, enquiry and, if necessary, reperformance of their work.

9:19.3.2 *Testing that the stocktaking procedures have been applied effectively*

The effectiveness of the stocktaking procedures should be tested by direct observation, supported by inspection of documents and re-performance of test counts. Therefore the auditor should attend while counts are in progress and observe their conduct. The procedures which should be carried out are discussed in Appendix B (*see* **Section 9:19.11**).

The nature, extent and timing of stocktake attendance will depend on the circumstances of each case, and in particular on:

(a)   the assessment of the risk of misstatement as recorded in the strategy, or, if prepared, the STP;

(b)   the review of the adequacy of the stocktaking procedures as discussed in **Section 9:19.3.1**;

(c)   whether the client carries out periodic or continuous stocktaking.

9:19.3.3 *Periodic stocktakes*

When the client performs annual or other periodic stocktakes, and counts most or all of the stocks at one time, the auditor should attend the count and carry out the procedures discussed in **Appendix B** (*see* **Section 9:19.11**).

The auditor should test for completeness by taking the following steps:

(a)   Checking that all count records, such as stock sheets or tags, have been incorporated in the stocks summary.

(b)   Tracing the items that were test-counted into the stocks summary. If the summary does not contain sufficient detail for identification of test counts, the client should be asked to analyse which stock sheets are incorporated in the summary, and the auditor should ensure that the sample selected has been included. The remaining sheets should be scrutinised to ensure that no other amounts of that item have been excluded from the summary.

(c)   Testing the additions of the stock sheets and the stocks summary.

9:19.3.4 Continuous or cyclical stocktaking

If the client carries out continuous or cyclical stocktaking, the auditor should, prior to the substantive testing date, consider the results of counts during the period to ascertain the extent of any errors revealed to date. It is important to consider whether such errors indicate significant deficiencies in stock recording or the occurrence of consistent stock losses (which might indicate inadequacies in the physical security of stocks).

It may not be necessary to attend every stocktake. However, the auditor should observe at least one stocktake and check that the count procedures are applied effectively. It is also necessary to check that any differences revealed by the count are subsequently adjusted in the stock records.

9:19.3.5 Auditing stocks at an interim date

When a periodic stocktake is carried out before the balance sheet date, it may be necessary to perform one or more of the following procedures. It may also be necessary to carry out similar procedures where the client carries out continuous stocktaking:

(a)   In respect of the intervening period between the stocktake date and the balance sheet date:

    (i)   Selecting issues or receipts of stock from the stock records and checking with supporting documentation.

    (ii)   Selecting from issues and receipts documents such as despatch notes or goods received notes, and tracing the details to the stock records.

    (iii)   Reviewing the sequence of pre-numbered issues and receipts documents.

(b)   Performing test counts of stock at the balance sheet date.

The choice and extent of such additional procedures will depend on the assessment of the risk of material misstatement in the intervening period, taking into account (among other things) the results of the interim stocktake(s) and the effectiveness of internal control.

9:19.3.6 Stocks held by third parties

The auditor should ascertain whether all stocks belonging to the client and held by third parties at the balance sheet date have been identified and included in the balance sheet. The extent to which the client uses third parties to hold stock should normally be identified during the business review.

   The procedures that should be applied in respect of such stocks should, for efficiency, normally be combined with audit work on existence, and they are discussed in **Section 9:19.5.2**.

9:19.4 Accuracy

The accuracy of the stock figure in the balance sheet will depend upon the following:

(a)   The correct identification of different types of stock and of different stock lines.

(b)   The accurate recording and measurement of stock quantities, and their correct summarisation.

(c)   The determination of costs in accordance with suitable accounting policies.

(d)   The application of the correct costs to individual stock items or lines, and their accurate extension, addition and summarisation.

9:19.4.1 Identification, recording, and measurement

The work on completeness discussed in **Sections 9:19.3** to **9:19.3.6** and in Appendix B (*see* **Section 9:19.11**) should normally provide sufficient assurance concerning the correct identification, measurement and recording of stock quantities. The following **Sections 9:19.4.2.1** to **9:19.4.2.3** discuss how the auditor might obtain the required assurance concerning the determination of unit costs and their accurate application to the stock quantities.

9:19.4.2 Determination and application of unit costs

9:19.4.2.1 Accounting policies

During the business review the auditor should identify the policies that the client applies to determine the cost of stocks, and consider whether the policies:

(a)   are appropriate to the particular nature of the stocks;

(b)   comply with relevant legislation, and Accounting Standards; and

(c)   are consistent with prior years.

The auditor should particularly consider the following:

(a)   The inclusion of import duties, transport and handling costs.

(b)   The exclusion of trade discounts and rebates.

(c)   In manufacturing companies, the inclusion of direct labour, direct expenses and an appropriate proportion of production and other overheads.

(d)   The exclusion of selling and distribution overheads and inter-branch profits.

Under generally accepted accounting practice in the United Kingdom, the client may use any of the following bases to arrive at cost:

● actual unit cost

● average cost

● FIFO

The use of standard costs or adjusted selling prices may be accepted provided that the resulting evaluation approximates one of the foregoing bases.

9:19.4.2.2 Checking the cost of stock

Items for testing should be selected from:

(a)   those items which were test-counted at the stocktake; and

(b)   the final evaluated stock listing.

The auditor should re-perform the additions of each page or sub-total of the final listing which contains a selection, and prove that the final total represents the sum of all the sub-totals. The stock sheets should also be reviewed generally for obvious anomalies or errors.

In respect of the items selected the auditor should:

(a)   trace the unit costs to the client's costing records;

(b)   check the arithmetical accuracy of the extensions;

(c)   check the calculation of the unit costs to establish whether they have been accurately determined in accordance with the client's accounting policies. To do this, the auditor should normally examine;

    (i)   suppliers' invoices;

    (ii)   labour analyses;

    (iii) overhead allocation records.

The auditor should confirm that the allocation of production overheads reflects the client's normal level of activity. One way of doing this is to compare the relationship between the total overhead content of stock and the material and labour content of stock with that between total overheads, materials and labour costs for the period in which the stocks were produced.

If the unit costs have been obtained from standard cost records, the auditor should review, and enquire into, the variance reports over the period in which the stock was produced. If the variances indicate that actual costs differ materially from the standards used to price the stocks, it is necessary to investigate the reasons.

9:19.4.2.3 Inclusion of costs

If the cost of work-in-progress and finished goods includes specific outside costs (e.g., machining or painting carried out on a contract basis), the auditor should ensure that those costs incurred in the accounting period are completely and accurately accounted for. In the absence of an integrated accounting system, this may be done by ascertaining the names of the contractors and determining that invoices or accruals are recorded for all the work they have done up to the balance sheet date.

9:19.4.3 Control account reconciliation

The auditor should check the reconciliation between the general ledger stock control account and the subsidiary stock ledger (or the stock listing).

If the amounts cannot be reconciled, or if the client has difficulty doing so, the auditor should consider whether the records are reliable. The auditor should bring to the attention of the engagement manager any failure by the client to maintain a control account properly.

9:19.4.4 Agreement with accounting records

The auditor should check the amounts reported in the financial statements to the stock control account in the general ledger, normally by tracing them via the trial balance. Where the client has made late adjustments, e.g. because of stock provisions, it is important to ensure that they are recorded in the accounting records.

9:19.5 Existence

9:19.5.1 Sources of assurance

The auditor should obtain most of the required assurance in relation to this objective from the procedures relating to periodic or continuous stocktakes discussed in **Sections 9:19.3.3** and **9:19.3.4** and in Appendix B (*see* **Section 9:19.11**).

These procedures should be supplemented by:

(a)   selecting items from the final evaluated stock listing, checking the particulars to a stock sheet or tag, and ensuring, by reference to details noted during the stock count (referred to in **Appendix B** – *see* **Section 9:19.11.4** last point (f)) that the stock sheet or tag is valid and that no items have been added since the count;

(b) reviewing the final stock sheets and summaries and checking that any amendments are properly authorised and valid. If the explanation is not satisfactory it may be necessary for the auditor to recount the item that was amended and reconcile the recorded quantity to that at the count date by reference to goods despatched and received documents.

9:19.5.2 Stocks held by third parties

The auditor should obtain assurance that the possession of any stocks by other parties is reasonable in the circumstances. It is important to enquire carefully into any cases which do not seem to be in the normal course of business.

The auditor should assess the adequacy of the client's records of such stocks, and of the procedures operated by the client for confirming them. If the accuracy of the client's records is supported by regular and recent confirmations of quantities held, and if a custodian is independent and of good repute, it may not be necessary to obtain direct confirmation in person.

If a decision is taken to seek direct confirmation from external custodians, the auditor should apply procedures similar to those discussed in **Section 9:21**, 'Trade debtors', and request the custodian to confirm that the stocks are the property of the client and are held free from charge or lien. However, for efficiency, the confirmations may be structured to provide assurance concerning the completeness objective also. Accordingly:

(a) Rather than seeking confirmation of a specific recorded amount, custodians may be requested to provide particulars of **all** stocks held on behalf of the client.

(b) The auditor should obtain assurance, in the light of knowledge of the business and other audit procedures, that all the external custodians of the client's stocks have been identified and covered by the confirmations.

(c) The auditor may also consider writing to all other parties who are known to hold material amounts of stocks from time to time even if they are recorded as holding none at the substantive testing date.

If unable to obtain confirmation, the auditor should carry out alternative procedures. Normally, in the absence of suspicious circumstances, these will involve inspecting evidence that the client bought or manufactured the stocks, that they were delivered to the custodian and that there is no indication from correspondence, despatch records or invoices that they have been sold. However, if a higher level of assurance is required concerning such stocks the auditor should request the client to arrange for an audit inspection of them with test counts. It may be necessary to do this if, e.g., a risk of fraud or error has been identified, or if individual external holdings of stocks are particularly significant.

9:19.6 Cut-off

9:19.6.1 Sources of assurance

Stock cut-off can be defined as the procedures to ensure that movements into, within and out of stock up to the balance sheet date are reflected in the financial statements for the period. The procedures are also intended to ensure:

(a)   in conjunction with creditors cut-off, that the liability for all items included in stocks is taken up in the financial statements; and

(b)   in conjunction with debtors cut-off, that the sales which are included in the financial statements are matched by the corresponding cost of such sales, which has been excluded from stocks.

For these reasons, work on the despatch element of stocks cut-off should normally be combined with the debtors cut-off (discussed in **Section 9:21**, 'Trade debtors'), and work on the goods received element of stocks cut-off with the creditors cut-off (discussed in **Section 9:24**, 'Trade creditors').

   The nature and extent of testing will depend upon:

(a)   The methods the client uses to record transactions.

(b)   The special cut-off procedures adopted by the client.

(c)   The timing of the stocktake.

(d)   The potential materiality of any cut-off errors.

(e)   The length of time before and after the substantive testing date in which undetected cut-off errors are likely or possible.

If the stock count was carried out at an interim date the cut-off should be tested both at that date and at the balance sheet date.

9:19.6.2 Tests of details

Using the cut-off details noted during stocktake attendance, the auditor should carry out the following procedures:

(a)   Select items from the goods inwards and goods outwards documents each side of the stocktaking/balance sheet date and trace these to the relevant stock records. Tests should include the last goods inwards, outwards and returns documents noted during the stocktake.

(b)   Select items from the stock records each side of the stocktaking/balance sheet date and trace these to the relevant goods inwards and goods outwards records (including records of goods returned by, or to, the client).

Some high-value stock items should be selected.

   The sequence of pre-numbered despatch and goods received documents should be checked, and also that:

(a)   numbers earlier than those recorded at the stocktake have been included in the transactions for the period; and

(b)   later numbers have been excluded.

Where necessary, the auditor should also test the cut-off on internal movements of stock, e.g. where there are movements between different locations, between different departments within a location, between raw materials and work-in-progress, and between work-in-progress and finished goods.

9:19.7 Valuation

Work on valuation should cover the following:

(a)   The client's procedures for identifying stocks against which provisions might be required.

(b)   The methods used by the client to determine net realisable values for such stocks.

(c)   The calculation of the provisions based on (a) and (b).

9:19.7.1 Identifying stocks against which provisions are required

The auditor should review the client's procedures for identifying stocks with a net realisable value below cost. These procedures might take into account factors such as:

(a)   Sales projections which might indicate excess stock levels.

(b)   New products rendering current stock obsolete.

(c)   Discontinuation of existing stock lines.

(d)   Known shelf-lives of perishable goods.

(e)   Elimination of inter-department profit.

To test these procedures work should include the following:

(a)   **Finished goods**:

    (i)   Comparing stock levels with budgets and prior years.

    (ii) Calculating, by reference to known orders or recent sales, how many weeks or months of sales the stock levels represent.

    (iii) Using the information noted during stocktake attendance to identify stocks that are obsolete, damaged or otherwise unsaleable at the normal price.

(b)　**Work-in-progress**: Reviewing the saleability of work-in-progress in the light of levels of finished goods held and known orders or recent sales.

(c)　**Raw materials**:

(i)　Comparing stock levels with prior years and budgets.

(ii)　Considering whether any raw materials are obsolescent, damaged, or surplus to requirements. This can be done by referring to the results of the stock count as in (a) (iii) above, by considering the known orders or projected sales, and by ascertaining whether there have been any significant recent changes in product lines.

9:19.7.2　Methods of determining net realisable values

The auditor should ascertain how the client calculates the estimated net realisable values of the items requiring provision. The appropriateness of the client's methods should be assessed by the following methods:

(a)　Reviewing them in the light of the work carried out in **Section 9:19.7.1** and above and of discussions with members of management. When provisions are based on the application of a formula, the auditor should review the formula critically, checking that it is consistent with that used in prior years, and/or that it has been appropriately modified in the light of current trading experience.

(b)　Testing selected items as follows:

(i)　**Finished goods**: comparing estimated sales proceeds with cost plus likely disposal costs.

(ii)　**Work-in-progress**: estimating the total costs to completion and comparing them with the sales or net contract price, less disposal costs.

(iii)　**Raw materials**: checking defective or damaged items by reference to scrap or salvage recoveries.

9:19.7.3　Calculating the provisions

The auditor should check that the provisions have been accurately calculated in accordance with the client's procedures for identifying stocks requiring provision and the methods used to determine net realisable values of such stocks. This should be done by:

(a)　testing the computation of the provisions; or

(b)　developing an independent estimate of the provisions, based on the work carried out in **Sections 9:19.7.1** and **9:19.7.2**.

9:19.7.4　Timing of work

If the procedures discussed in **Sections 9:19.7.1** to **9:19.7.3** above are carried out as part of early substantive testing, the work should be updated as at the balance sheet date by:

(a)   reviewing the procedures adopted by the client to identify the need for further provisions;

(b)   obtaining explanations for significant movements in the provision(s) between the early substantive testing date and balance sheet date; and

(c)   determining whether further provisions are required as a result of:

    (i)   increased costs of purchase or production that have not been fully reflected in selling prices;

    (ii)   falling selling prices;

    (iii) any decision, as part of the client's marketing strategy, to manufacture and sell products at a loss; or

    (iv)   a surplus of stocks over foreseeable requirements.

9:19.8 Rights and obligations

Sufficient assurance in relation to rights and obligations is normally gained from:

(a)   the work on completeness and existence of stock discussed above; and

(b)   the corollary effect of testing of creditors.

9:19.9 Presentation and disclosure

To help achieve the objective of the presentation and disclosure the auditor should, at the end of the audit, review the financial statements and consider the matters set out in a UK GAAP checklist. Also, it is important to be alert for any matters that require disclosure which could be more efficiently identified during fieldwork. These include the following:

(a)   The correct classification of stocks between raw materials, work-in-progress and finished goods, and the correct treatment of payments on account.

(b)   Inter-company stocks which may include unrealised profits that should be identified and excluded on consolidation.

(c)   Stocks purchased subject to a reservation of title clause, which should be disclosed in the financial statements.

(d)   Stocks pledged as security for liabilities of the client or third parties.

(e)   The replacement cost of stocks (when this is materially different from the carrying value).

9:19.10 Appendix A Matters to consider when reviewing stocktaking instructions and procedures

The matters to consider when receiving stocktaking instructions and procedures are as follows. They are referred to in **Section 9:19.3.1** (second paragraph of the text).

(a)   The independence of the counters from stock control functions.

(b)   Procedures for collecting and checking count data and ensuring that they are complete.

(c)   Cut-off procedures before and during the counts.

(d)   Procedures for ensuring that all stocks owned by the client are counted, and that stocks held for customers or third parties are excluded.

(e)   Procedures for investigating differences exposed by the stock counts including, where necessary, subsequent adjustment of the records.

(f)   Procedures for identifying and, if necessary, segregating obsolete, slow-moving and damaged stocks.

(g)   Procedures for ensuring that stock records (if any) are up to date.

(h)   Control over movements of stock between areas and locations during the count.

(i)   Lay out of the stock to facilitate an accurate count.

(j)   Procedures for ensuring that there is no double counting of stocks held at several locations.

(k)   In the case of continuous or cyclical stocktaking, the extent of coverage of the stock counts during the accounting period. (Although it is not essential that the client counts 100 per cent of all stocks, the stocktaking should cover a significant proportion by number and/or value of the total stocks during the period, and those items/areas where there is a history of error or stock losses.)

9:19.11 Appendix B Attendance at stocktaking

9:19.11.1 Introduction

The procedures discussed below are designed to provide relevant audit evidence in support of the specific objectives of completeness, existence, and accuracy. They are referred to in **Sections 9:19.3** to **9:19.5.2** of the text.

Members of the audit team who attend the stocktake should have adequate experience and be fully briefed. Therefore, before attendance, it is important for them to establish familiarity with the location of the stocks and the layout of the factory, works, warehouse or store. The team should also ensure that they have a working knowledge of the appearance, purpose and approximate value of various items of stock, together with an understanding of the manufacturing or other processes involved.

9:19.11.2 Stock held at more than one location

Where the client holds stocktakes at more than one location, it may not be necessary to attend them all. Locations for attendance should be selected by reference to the following criteria:

(a)   The materiality of estimated stock levels at each location.

(b)   The extent to which different locations are covered by the same procedures and overall control.

(c)   Unusual stock levels, gross margins or operating results at a particular location.

(d)   The nature and reliability of supporting stock records and the results of stocktaking both in previous years and during the current period.

(e)   The findings of any internal audit reports.

(f)   Client expectations of external audit attendance.

9:19.11.3 Internal auditors

Provided that the external auditor is satisfied with the independence and competence of the internal auditors, they may be relied on to attend certain of the locations. However, the external auditor should attend all material locations over a number of audits. Where the auditor wishes to rely on the work of internal auditors the general procedures discussed in **Section 7:5**, 'Using the work of internal audit', should be followed. In particular, it is important to:

(a)   discuss the internal auditors' work programme with them in advance to ensure that it is consistent with external audit requirements; and

(b)   review their working papers and conclusions.

9:19.11.4 General procedures

Before the count starts the auditor should:

(a)   note the nature, location and layout of the stocks to be counted;

(b)   establish that any weighbridge or weighing machine to be used in the count gives accurate results;

(c)   determine whether stocks are marked, labelled or otherwise described so that they can be identified by the count team(s).

The auditor should attend the start of the count (and any briefing by the client) to ensure that it is orderly, well-controlled and methodical from the outset.

   During the count, the auditor should carry out the following procedures:

(a)   Observe and enquire whether stocks are adequately safeguarded and protected against deterioration.

(b)   Confirm that the procedures for segregating stock not owned by the client, or to be otherwise excluded from the count, have been followed.

(c)   In the case of work-in-progress, ensure by observation that each production stage has been segregated and the stage of completion has been identified.

(d)   Confirm, by touring the location and observing the work of the counting teams, that the instructions are carried out effectively so that:

(i)   all stocks owned by the client are counted;

(ii)   all other stocks are excluded from the results of the count (clients frequently count all stocks present in a particular location, identifying third party goods to ensure their subsequent exclusion);

(iii) stock sheets, tags or other means used to record quantities are adequately controlled;

(iv)   movements of goods during the count are properly controlled to avoid double counting or omission;

(v)   slow-moving, obsolete or damaged stocks are clearly identified.

(e)   Record details of despatch and receipts records, for cut-off purposes. These might include, e.g., the last pre-numbered despatch notes or goods received notes issued prior to the stocktake date, or the last entries in goods inwards/outwards registers. Also for cut-off purposes, it is important to identify and note:

(i)   items which appear to have been recently delivered (e.g., in the goods inwards bay but not unpacked); and

(ii)   items which appear ready for despatch (e.g., stocks in the despatch bay or packed and addressed).

(f)   Obtain details, at the conclusion of the count, of all records used in the count, so that it is possible to check later for suppression, manipulation, addition or substitution of records after the count. If it is not practicable to retain copies of the count records, the auditor should note details of, and take extracts from, the records used. It may be necessary to authenticate the records by, e.g., initialling them.

9:19.11.5 Test counts

Test counts should be carried out. To obtain evidence in respect of both completeness and existence (as well as accuracy), the auditor should select items for testing from two sources:

(a)   The count records, verifying the existence and quantity of the stocks (existence and accuracy).

(b)   The physical stocks, ensuring that the amounts are accurately included in the count records (completeness and accuracy).

9:19.11.6 Inadequacies in the stocktaking procedures

If the stocktaking procedures in operation are unsatisfactory, the auditor should increase testing of the results of those procedures by observation, enquiry and test-counting to assess the risk that errors have in fact arisen.

If the stocktake is inadequately supervised, or it is not carried out by persons with an adequate degree of independence, the auditor should increase the extent of observation and enquiry to determine whether the count procedures operated satisfactorily throughout the stocktake. This is because the relevant supervision which would otherwise have been relied on is absent. In such cases it may be necessary to attend the entire stocktake, because there will be no assurance that the count procedures were satisfactory while the auditor was absent.

Where the completeness of the count records is in doubt, the auditor should increase the number and value of count totals recorded for subsequent tracing to the final stock sheets.

9:19.11.7 Working papers

A summary should be prepared to record:

(a)   the nature and extent of the substantive tests performed;

(b)   any exceptions found during attendance.

The summary should be prepared immediately after the stocktake, so that any problems are identified and followed up without delay.

9:19.11.8 Independent stocktakers

In some trades it is common practice to employ firms of independent specialist stocktakers and valuers. Provided the auditor is satisfied as to the professional competence and objectivity of such persons, and the procedures which they adopt, their stock counts may be accepted as reliable. Accordingly, it is necessary to confirm that the stocktaking was organised and carried out to give the specific assurance needed in relation to the audit objectives, and to make enquiries as to the stocktakers' terms of reference and the methods and procedures used. The latter might best be done by visiting the client's premises from time to time when the independent stocktakers are in attendance. If it appears that the specialist stocktakers' work may not be reliable, the auditor should make arrangements, through the client, to extend observations of the independent stocktakes so that steps can be taken to overcome any shortcomings.

9:20 Long-term contracts

9:20.1 Introduction

This section is designed to help to develop a programme of substantive tests in accordance with the strategy for long-term contracts, as defined below. The strategy or substantive testing plan (STP), if prepared, for long-term contracts should specify the planned response to the assessment of the risk of material misstatement, including the nature, extent and timing of substantive tests.

This section should be read in conjunction with the general guidance on substantive testing in the following sections:

- **Section 9:3**, 'Analytical procedures'
- **Section 9:4**, 'Tests of details'
- **Section 9:5**, 'Evaluating the results of substantive testing'

For the purposes of this section, long-term contracts are those contracts which are defined as such by SSAP 9 (Revised) and which are included in the balance sheet heading of stocks, together with the related sales and cost of sales.

9:20.1.1 Essential audit objectives

The specific audit objectives for long-term contracts are set out below for each of the seven general audit objectives. The auditor should obtain sufficient evidence to achieve these specific objectives:

- **Completeness**

  All the client's long-term contracts have been recorded in the financial statements.

  Sales represent the total amounts chargeable to customers under long-term contracts, and cost of sales represents all the costs associated with them.

- **Accuracy**

  Amounts accumulated in long-term contract accounts have been accurately determined, summarised and recorded in accordance with the client's accounting policies, consistently applied.

  The amounts reported in the financial statements are in agreement with the accounting records.

- **Existence**

  Amounts attributed to long-term contracts in the balance sheet represent actual contracts for which work has been performed and costs incurred.

  All reported sales and costs of sales are valid.

- **Cut-off**

  Costs and income associated with long-term contracts have been recorded in the correct accounting period.

  The related costs of all sales up to the balance sheet date have been removed from the carrying value of long-term contracts.

- **Valuation**

  Appropriate adjustments have been made to the carrying value of long-term contracts to reflect attributable profits and foreseeable losses.

- **Rights and obligations**   The client is responsible for substantially all the obligations risks and is entitled to substantially all the rewards arising from the long-term contracts included in the balance sheet.

- **Presentation and disclosure**   Long-term contracts have been properly classified, described and disclosed in the financial statements.

Sometimes the auditor may conclude that there is a negligible risk of material misstatement in relation to one or more of these audit objectives, and that consequently no specific substantive procedures are necessary.

9:20.1.2 Early substantive testing

The auditor should consider carrying out some of the procedures discussed in this section at an interim date, as part of early substantive testing (discussed in **Section 4:7**, 'The audit programme'). The strategy for long-term contracts should specify which procedures will be carried out at an interim date and whether it is expected that it will be necessary to repeat or extend them as at the balance sheet date. The audit programme for long-term contracts should set out the procedures to be performed in respect of the intervening period.

9:20.2 Completeness

9:20.2.1 Contracts in progress

To confirm that all relevant contracts have been included in the listing that supports the balance sheet amount, the auditor should carry out the following procedures:

(a)   Check that all uncompleted contracts at the previous year-end have been correctly brought forward and either are still in progress at the balance sheet date or have been completed during the year and transferred to cost of sales.

(b)   Ascertain (e.g., by reference to contract records, correspondence and minutes) that all additional contracts have been accounted for.

In addition to this, some assurance may be obtained from the corollary effect of testing of the completeness of creditors and the existence of debtors. However, because of the nature of long-term contracts, particular attention should be paid to the understatement of sub-contractors' costs. The auditor may do this by identifying all significant sub-contractors and requesting them to provide details of costs incurred up to the balance sheet date.

9:20.2.2 Sales and cost of sales

9:20.2.2.1 Completed contracts

To obtain assurance that all completed contracts have been invoiced and the attributable costs charged to cost of sales, it is necessary to carry out tests of details on those contracts which have been identified as complete from the work described in **Section 9:20.2.1** (first paragraph).

The auditor's work may include the following:

(a)   Checking the descriptions and amounts on the related invoices (and contracts of sale) with the contract information recorded in the working papers and listed in the **Appendix** (*see* **Section 9:20.9**).

(b)   Tracing the selected invoices into the sales summary, and then to the general ledger.

(c)   Ascertaining that the contracts were, in fact, complete and ready for billing in accordance with the contract terms.

(d)   Checking the transfer of cost from the cost ledger to cost of sales.

9:20.2.2.2 Contracts in progress

To confirm whether interim billings due on these contracts have been raised, the auditor should review the uncompleted contracts selected for valuation testing (discussed in **Section 9:20.6.2.1** (second paragraph). In each case the auditor should carry out the following procedures:

(a)   Refer to the contract terms to ascertain whether any amounts are due for billing, examine the related invoices and trace these through to the general ledger.

(b)   Check that the amounts of work-in-progress transferred to cost of sales in respect of such interim billings represent an appropriate proportion of the total contract costs.

When the selection for valuation testing has been made at an interim date, the auditor should follow this up by reviewing the contracts still uncompleted at the balance sheet date to identify amounts that should have been invoiced at that date. The auditor should check that appropriate amounts, less retentions where applicable, have been billed.

9:20.3 Accuracy

9:20.3.1 Testing contract costs

The auditor should select items charged to the contracts ledger during the accounting period, and test the selected items as follows:

(a)   If the item is an amount charged directly to the contracts ledger, the auditor should carry out the tests described in **Section 9:31**, 'Purchases and expenses'.

(b)   If the selected item is an amount transferred by journal entry, the auditor should check that the corresponding credit has been posted to the appropriate account. For example, if the transfer represents raw materials, the credit should be traced to the stock account. If the debits to these accounts have already been tested, it is not necessary to examine the selected item any further.

(c)   For journal transfers allocating labour or overheads, the auditor should check that calculations are in accordance with the client's accounting policy. It is also important to trace the credits to the appropriate accounts as in (b) above. The auditor should review the labour and overhead recovery rates to see that they adequately reflect the client's normal level of activity and include all applicable expenditure.

(d)   If the selected item is a transfer between contracts (e.g., materials moved from one contract to another), the auditor should check the validity of the transfer by examining supporting documentation and checking any calculations.

The auditor should check that the selected items have been allocated to the correct contract. This may be done by comparing the details with underlying documentation such as purchase orders, goods received notes and time records.

9:20.3.2 'Questionable' payments

It is important to remain alert for any 'commissions' or other 'questionable' payments by the client to secure contracts, particularly if a risk of such payments has been identified through the risk-assessment procedures. These matters are highly sensitive. Accordingly, if the auditor finds evidence that such payments have been made, the auditor should inform the engagement manager and the engagement partner **before** raising the matter with management. Guidance on the auditor's response to such payments is given in **Section 9:11**, ' "Questionable" transactions'.

9:20.3.3 Control account reconciliation

If the client maintains a control account for long-term contracts, the auditor should check the reconciliation between the control account and the total of the long-term contracts balances in the subsidiary records.

If the client is unable to reconcile the control account, or has difficulty in doing so, the reliability of the records should be considered. The auditor should inform the engagement manager of any failure by the client to reconcile the control account, or of significant and repeated delays in doing so. The engagement manager should decide whether the position should be brought to the engagement partner's attention in the issues documentation.

9:20.3.4 Agreement with accounting records

The auditor should check the amounts for long-term contracts and related income and cost of sales reported in the financial statements to the control account in the general ledger, normally by tracing the amounts via the trial balance. If the client has made late adjustments, e.g. because of loss provisions, the auditor should check that they have been entered into the ledger.

9:20.4 Existence

Most of the procedures appropriate to the existence objectives are discussed elsewhere in this section, as follows:

(a)　Testing items from the contract ledger for accuracy of contract costs, as described in **Section 9:20.3.1**.

(b)　Physical inspection procedures, as discussed in **Section 9:20.6.2.8**.

(c)　As regards the validity of sales, the work discussed in **Section 9:20.2.2.1** to **9:20.3.1**.

However, in addition to this, items debited to the cost of sales account should be selected and checked for validity by reference to the related invoice, the costs incurred to date, and other relevant supporting documentation. This is because the verification of cost transfers referred to in **Section 9:20.2.2.2** (first paragraph, point (b)) above is done by first identifying a sale and then tracing the related cost of sale, which will not necessarily identify invalid debits to the cost of sales account.

9:20.5 Cut-off

9:20.5.1 Contract costs

To confirm that costs have been recorded in the correct accounting period, the auditor should select items recorded in the long-term contracts accounts either side of the balance sheet date (or the substantive testing date, if carrying out early substantive testing) in respect of the following:

(a)　Issues of materials to, and returns from, long-term contracts accounts.

(b)　Labour and overheads charged to long-term contracts.

(c)　Other direct costs and charges.

(d)　Transfers and adjustments.

The auditor should check the selected items to appropriate supporting documentation to confirm that they were recorded in the correct accounting period.

9:20.5.2 Sales and cost of sales

To confirm that sales have been recorded in the correct accounting period, and that the cost of sales has been removed from the contracts ledger in the correct accounting period, the auditor should select from billings either side of the balance sheet date (or the early substantive testing date) and carry out the following procedures:

(a)　Confirm, by reference to contract documentation, and architects' or engineers' certificates, that the billing was recorded in the correct period.

(b)　Identify the related transfer of costs out of the contracts ledger.

(c)   Review the amounts of such transfers for inclusion of all costs by reference to the contract documentation, architects' or engineers' certificates, and similar evidence.

(d)   Trace the transfers into cost of sales.

9:20.6 Valuation

9:20.6.1 Accounting policies

During the business review the auditor should determine the client's policies for accounting for long-term contracts and, in particular, those relating to the attribution of profit and provision for losses and those dealing with accounting for overheads. It is necessary to check that the accounting policies are:

(a)   acceptable in the particular circumstances of the client's business;

(b)   consistent with previous years; and

(c)   in accordance with relevant legislation and Accounting Standards.

9:20.6.2 Attributable profits and expected losses

9:20.6.2.1 Basis of selection

Adjustments made to reflect attributable profits or to provide for known or expected losses are accounting estimates and, as such, involve the use of judgement to a significant degree (as discussed in **Section 9:6**, 'Audit of accounting estimates'). Also, the calculations involved are frequently complex (e.g., percentage of completion adjustments). Consequently, such adjustments are prone to misstatement.

The auditor should, therefore, apply procedures to a selection of contracts which is biased towards the high-risk and material contracts. These should include the following types:

(a)   Contracts with unusual profits or losses, including contracts with low margins or with unusual or disadvantageous financing terms which might have been entered into to boost production and recover fixed overheads.

(b)   Contracts larger than those the client is used to taking. Large contracts not only bring with them more severe technical problems, but also demand a higher level of management expertise and experience which might not be available to the client.

(c)   Contracts whose profit, loss and liquidity requirements materially affect the client.

(d)   Contracts entered into in politically sensitive or volatile areas overseas, or in countries outside the client's experience, where difficulties might arise as a result of the following:

  (i)   The effect of climatic differences on technical performance.

  (ii)   The effect of climatic and social differences on employee performance.

 (iii) Differences in, and problems arising from, commercial, political, legal and tax practices.

 (iv) High costs and logistical difficulties in carrying out erection and remedial work.

 (v) Exposure to currency exchange risks, or difficulties in remitting funds.

(e) Contracts with a large difference between the gross balance sheet value and any internal or external valuation.

(f) Contracts whose costs to date, plus costs to completion, are likely to exceed the original tendered price.

(g) Contracts where the work is behind schedule and there are significant penalties for late delivery.

(h) Contracts with a poor ratio of cash collected to costs incurred.

(i) Contracts whose costs in the year are low but costs brought forward are high.

(j) Contracts which are heavily dependent on sub-contractors (or, if the client is a sub-contractor, on the main contractor).

(k) Contracts demanding engineering or other skills different from those of which the client has experience.

(l) Contracts with new customers of different types.

The selection should be made from the contracts in progress at the substantive testing date. Relevant particulars of the contracts should be recorded in the working papers (discussed in the **Appendix** – (*see* **Section 9:20.9**).

9:20.6.2.2 *Reviewing selected contracts*

The auditor should carry out the following procedures on the selected contracts:

(a) Consider the adequacy of the client's reviews and reports on work-in-progress, and the effectiveness of any corrective action taken.

(b) Test the accuracy of the projections, forecasts and estimates of costs of completion. In particular, the auditor should:

 (i) check their arithmetical accuracy;

 (ii) review the assumptions;

 (iii) consider whether all known costs to completion (including adjustments for inflation) have been included;

 (iv) review the accuracy of forecasts and estimates made in previous years.

(c) Determine whether the amounts provided for foreseeable losses are adequate but not excessive.

(d) Consider inspecting the work-in-progress.

9:20.6.2.3 General

The auditor should assess the prudence of the client's basis of recognising profits or losses on long-term contracts by considering the accuracy of previous forecasts. This may be done by comparing the profit calculations made at previous year-ends with the actual results.

When doing this, the auditor should take into account any indications that client management tends towards undue optimism or caution in assessing the expected out-turn on contracts. We should consider the results of the assessment of the control environment. For example, management will sometimes tend to assume that contracts will be finished on time, thereby avoiding extra costs (and, possibly, penalty payments or liquidated damages for delays). Management will often also assume that extra income possibly receivable but still to be negotiated will duly be received even where such assumptions are not realistic. Also, management sometimes has a tendency to be over-optimistic in years when the overall results of the business are poor, but to take an attitude of pessimism in years when the overall results of the business are good.

9:20.6.2.4 Costs to completion

The auditor should examine the estimate of costs to completion to ensure, as far as possible, that they include all the labour, materials and overheads which have still to be expended before the jobs are finished and accepted by the customers. The estimates should incorporate suitable margins for contingencies including (where appropriate) allowances for:

(a) future increases in wage rates not covered by an escalation clause in the contract;

(b) the cost of materials not yet purchased; and

(c) provision for any penalties or liquidated damages that may become payable.

9:20.6.2.5 Calculation of attributable profit

When assessing the calculation of attributable profit on a particular contract, the auditor should consider whether:

(a) the estimate is based on an internal or an external valuation;

(b) the estimate has been made close to the substantive testing date;

(c) the estimate is significantly different from the gross carrying value;

(d) the contract is standard (and consequently the client has well-developed estimation procedures) or non-standard, and therefore subject to greater uncertainty (in which case particular attention should be paid to the prudence of the client's profit assessment)

(e) the specific terms of the contract affect the estimate (e.g., whether the price is fixed or on a cost plus a percentage basis);

(f)   the basis of allocating profit is appropriate. For example, if the profit is calculated by reference to the amount billed to date, the auditor should consider whether (as is often the case) the client has 'front-end loaded' the billings and consequently overstated the profit.

9:20.6.2.6 Discussions with client management

The auditor should discuss the status of each contract selected for examination with appropriate client management such as contract managers, surveyors, engineers and site foremen, as well as financial and Head Office staff. The matters discussed, and the names of the members of management, should be recorded in the working papers. Significant matters should be recorded in the issues documentation. In addition to matters arising directly from audit work, the following matters should be discussed at this point in relation to each contract examined:

(a)   Whether there are any technical or other construction problems.

(b)   The likelihood of problems arising from labour relations (e.g., because of current pay negotiations).

(c)   Estimated completion dates, including the possibility of performance bonds or delay penalties falling due following a delay.

(d)   Whether there are any other matters likely to affect the profitability of the contract.

9:20.6.2.7 Valuations

Certain types of contract (e.g., civil engineering) are assessed by means of a valuation by an expert. The auditor should review any valuations of the work-in-progress, paying particular attention to any valuations that have not been incorporated in the financial statements, because this may indicate profit-smoothing. When reviewing valuations, the auditor should consider the following:

(a)   The independence and competence of the valuer (e.g., whether the valuer is a member of a recognised professional body).

(b)   Whether the information supplied to the valuer was adequate, accurate and complete.

(c)   The bases and assumptions used by the valuer and whether they are consistent with those of prior years.

(d)   Whether, by reference to the final out-turn of the contracts, valuations in previous years proved to be accurate.

(e)   The results of the valuation in the light of other available evidence.

Guidance on using the work of a valuer is given in **Section 7:6**, 'Using the work of an expert'.

If risks of material misstatement have been identified, the auditor should consider using an industry specialist to assist in reviewing the valuations. Such a person might be either a member of the audit firm who has detailed knowledge of the industry, or an external specialist.

9:20.6.2.8 Physical inspection of work on long-term contracts

If the client's staff who are responsible for the day-to-day control of the contracts are based at the accounting centre, and there is sufficient alternative evidence of the existence of the contract or the stage of completion, it may not be necessary to inspect the work-in-progress on all contracts selected for testing. However, the auditor may still wish to visit sites as part of the process of understanding the business. Physical inspection may be necessary where alternative evidence of the existence of the contract and of the stage of completion is not practicable or reliable, e.g. where the contract is located overseas or the work is a secret defence contract. The auditor should obtain evidence from physical inspection in the case of particularly significant amounts.

If the audit strategy or the STP, if prepared, requires that physical inspections should be carried out, the auditor should arrange to make the visit accompanied by an appropriate member of management. If the nature of the contract makes it particularly difficult to measure the stage of completion, or if significant risks of misstatement have been identified, it may be appropriate to request the assistance of industry specialists, as discussed in the last paragraph of **Section 9:20.6.2.7**. If the contract is overseas it may be appropriate to ask a local or correspondent firm to make the inspection.

9:20.6.3 Tender costs

Clients that incur tender costs may include them in the amount of long-term contracts. If so, the auditor should review the basis used to arrive at the costs and consider carefully the likelihood of the tender's being successful. Generally, unless there is a reasonable certainty that the tender will succeed, such costs should be written off.

9:20.6.4 Retentions

The auditor should consider whether retentions (which may be in either long-term contracts or debtors) are valid and recoverable. It may be possible to do this by inspecting correspondence or by reviewing receipts after the balance sheet date. This work should be co-ordinated with tests on cost reserves (discussed in **Section 9:20.6.6**) because indications of high rectification costs might indicate a risk of non-recoverability.

9:20.6.5 Unagreed claims

Clients are often entitled to revenue additional to the contract price because of changes in the scope of the work, delays or extra costs caused by the customer, or the operation of price escalation clauses. Frequently, such items are disputed in principle or amount and are only agreed (sometimes at compromise figures) after long negotiation. The auditor should check the validity of any claims that are included in the value of long-term contracts (or in debtors). It is important to ensure that the customer has accepted liability for the additional work. In the absence of such acceptance other evidence should be inspected to support the inclusion of the claim. Unless there is a reasonable certainty that the claim will succeed, such amounts should be written off.

9:20.6.6 Cost reserves

When the client provides cost reserves on completion of a contract to allow for tidying up and rectification work, the auditor should ensure that the reserves are adequate but not excessive. This should be done by reference to the client's previous experience, the nature of the work, discussions with relevant employees and any minutes or correspondence. Reserves set up in earlier years should also be tested to establish whether they are no longer needed or whether the extent of rectification work to date indicates that they need to be increased.

9:20.6.7 Progress payments

If amounts received or receivable as progress payments exceed the costs to date plus attributable profits, the auditor should check that such excess is disclosed as a liability.

9:20.6.8 Other matters

(a) **Fixed assets**: Sometimes fixed assets are purchased specifically for use on a particular contract. When a contract is complete, or approaching completion, the auditor should consider whether any such assets should be written down to their residual values.

(b) **Debtors**: The review of the valuation of particular long-term contracts may provide additional evidence regarding the collectability of debts associated with these contracts. The auditor should therefore link the work to the review of doubtful debts.

(c) **Guarantees, performance bonds and warranties**: The auditor should co-ordinate work on guarantees with the review of contingent liabilities. It may be appropriate to use the particulars of contracts selected for testing (as discussed in **Section 9:20.6.2.1** (second and third paragraphs)) to help to identify whether the client has any contingent, or actual, liabilities arising from guarantees, performance bonds and warranties given to customers or other parties, such as government agencies.

9:20.6.9 Post-balance-sheet events review

Before signing the audit report, the auditor should contact management responsible for all contracts on which specific risks of material misstatement have been identified, and ensure that up-to-date information has been obtained about any developments which might affect the audit opinion. The auditor should also discuss with the contract managers the overall position up to the date of the report.

9:20.7 Rights and obligations

The auditor should inspect the contracts selected for valuation testing (discussed in **Section 9:20.6.2.1** (second and third paragraphs)) and should carry out the following procedures:

(a)   Check that the terms of the contract confer the rights and benefits of the contracts to the client.

(b)   Ascertain that the contract has been properly executed by both parties. (It will normally be sufficient to ascertain from inspection that this is apparently the case; however, if in any doubts the auditor should consider taking legal advice.) The auditor should confirm that the client's signatory is duly authorised.

(c)   Review correspondence and minutes, and make enquiries of client officials as to whether any of the client's rights under the contract have been assigned. The auditor should do this in the light of knowledge of the client and its business and trading practices.

9:20.8 Presentation and disclosure

To help to achieve the objective of presentation and disclosure the auditor should, at the end of the audit, review the financial statements and consider the matters set out in a UK GAAP checklist. Also, it is important to be alert for any matters that require disclosure and which can more efficiently be identified during fieldwork. These include:

(a)   inter-company contracts (which may include unrealised profits) that need to be identified for consolidation purposes;

(b)   payments that exceed costs to date and which should therefore be classified as creditors (as discussed in **Section 9:20.6.7**).

9:20.9 Appendix Recording particulars of contracts

The following particulars may be recorded in the working papers for contracts selected for testing:

(a)   The nature and subject of the contract (e.g., the client, location, description of work and duration).

(b)   The original tendered value.

(c)   Any procedures for amendments to the contracts.

(d)   Any agreement or terms for billings or retentions.

(e)   The nature and amounts of delay penalties.

(f)   The source of valuations.

(g)   The approximate stage of completion (where not complete).

(h)   Total amounts of retentions.

(i)   Any contract price adjustment (CPA) claims made.

(j)   Details of any guarantees and warranties.

(k)   The amount of costs to date and estimated costs of completion.

(l)   The amount of profits or losses recognised.

(m) The amount of any payments on account.

Because these particulars of contracts will usually be of use for more than one audit, the auditor should consider including them as part of the material to be carried forward.

9:21 Trade debtors

9:21.1 Introduction

This section is designed to help to develop a programme of substantive tests in accordance with the strategy for trade debtors. The strategy, or approved substantive testing plan (STP), if prepared, for trade debtors should specify the planned response to the assessment of the risk of material misstatement, including the nature, extent and timing of substantive tests.

   This section should be read in conjunction with the general guidance on substantive testing in the following sections:

   ● **Section 9:3**, 'Analytical procedures'

   ● **Section 9:4**, 'Tests of details'

   ● **Section 9:5**, 'Evaluating the results of substantive testing'

For the purposes of this section, trade debtors are defined as those debtors arising from:

(a)   sales of goods and services invoiced; and

(b)   completed transactions for the sale of goods and services for which invoices have not yet been prepared.

9:21.1.1 Essential audit objectives

The specific audit objectives for trade debtors are set out below for each of the seven general audit objectives. The auditor should obtain sufficient evidence to achieve these specific objectives:

• **Completeness**	All trade debtors have been included in the balance sheet.
• **Accuracy**	Trade debtors have been accurately determined, summarised and recorded.
	The amounts reported in the financial statements are in agreement with the accounting records.
• **Existence**	Trade debtors exist at the balance sheet date.
• **Cut-off**	Transactions relating to trade debtors, sales, credit notes and cash receipts have been recorded in the correct accounting period.
• **Valuation**	Trade debtors have been stated at net collectible amounts. Allowances for doubtful accounts, discounts, returns and similar items are adequate but not excessive.
• **Rights and obligations**	Recorded trade debtors represent amounts owed to the client at the balance sheet date, and the client is subject to substantially all the risks and is entitled to substantially all the rewards arising therefrom.
• **Presentation and disclosure**	Debtors have been properly classified, described and disclosed in the financial statements.

Sometimes the auditor may conclude that there is a negligible risk of material misstatement in relation to one or more of these audit objectives, and that consequently no specific substantive procedures are necessary.

9:21.1.2 Early substantive testing

The auditor should consider carrying out some of the procedures discussed in this section at an interim date, as part of early substantive testing (discussed in **Section 4:7**, 'The audit programme'). The strategy, or STP if prepared, for trade debtors should specify which procedures should be carried out at an interim date and whether it is expected that it will be necessary to repeat or extend them as at the balance sheet date. The audit programme for trade debtors should set out the procedures to be performed in respect of the intervening period.

9:21.2 Completeness

The auditor will normally obtain sufficient assurance concerning the completeness objective from the corollary effect of tests on the completeness of sales. If further assurance is required (because, e.g., specific risks of misstatement have been identified) it will be necessary to carry out tests such as:

(a)   Direct confirmation of total sales in the period to selected customers.

(b) Extension of cut-off procedures.

(c) Tests of details on individual debtor balances selected from a 'reciprocal' population which the auditor has assessed to be complete.

9:21.3 Accuracy

9:21.3.1 Sources of assurance

The auditor will normally obtain sufficient assurance that the trade debtors records are accurate from the following sources:

(a) Confirmation procedures, as discussed in **Sections 9:21.4.3** to **9:21.4.6**.

(b) Tests of invoice pricing as part of substantive testing of sales, discussed in **Section 9:30**, 'Turnover and other income'.

If further assurance is required, the auditor should respond accordingly. For example, if a risk had been identified that individual invoices were understated, it might be necessary to test the accuracy of the pricing of confirmed balances, because customer confirmations will not necessarily disclose an **understatement** of amounts due.

9:21.3.1.1 Control account reconciliation

The auditor should check the reconciliation between the general ledger trade debtors control account and the total of the individual amounts in the subsidiary debtors records. To do this, it is necessary to carry out the following procedures:

(a) Trace amounts on the listing of debtor balances to individual accounts.

(b) Test the additions of the reconciliation and of the listing.

(c) Investigate contra-adjustments and unusual items in the reconciliation.

(d) Review the subsequent clearance of reconciling items.

If the reconciliation has been checked at an interim date, the auditor should normally carry out the following procedures with respect to the intervening period, in addition to any tests on the reconciliation itself which might need to be repeated or extended as at the balance sheet date:

(a) Examine the control account for the period between the substantive testing date and the balance sheet date to confirm that no recurring entries have been omitted, and to identify any unusual items.

(b) Test the additions of the control account.

(c) Test significant postings in the control account from the records of prime entry.

(d) Test the additions in the records of prime entry.

9:21.3.1.2 Problems with reconciliations

If the client is unable to reconcile the control account, or has difficulty in doing so, the auditor should consider whether the records are reliable. The auditor should inform the engagement manager of failure by the client to reconcile the control account, or significant and repeated delays in doing so.

9:21.3.2 Amounts owed by group companies

The principal audit procedure on amounts owed by group companies is to ensure that the inter-company balances have been properly agreed by the client. It is important that such amounts are properly reconciled, and the auditor should consider obtaining written confirmation of the balances from the local auditors.

The auditor should review the reconciliations and test the reconciling items, particularly when there are transactions in foreign currencies or where there is a history of error, because of the risk that differences caused by errors or disputed items might be written off by the client without investigation (e.g., by classifying them as 'differences on exchange').

These procedures will provide assurance in relation to the completeness and existence of amounts owed by group companies as well as the accuracy of those amounts.

9:21.3.3 Foreign exchange

If any trade debtors are denominated in foreign currencies, the auditor should check that they have been correctly translated into sterling at an appropriate exchange rate.

9:21.3.4 Agreement with accounting records

The auditor should check the figure for trade debtors reported in the financial statements to the reconciled control account in the general ledger, normally by tracing the amounts via the trial balance to the financial statements.

9:21.4 Existence

9:21.4.1 Sources of assurance

The auditor should normally achieve the existence objective by obtaining confirmation of balances directly from the debtors. Although the alternative procedures discussed in **Section 9:21.4.6** are an acceptable procedure, confirmation of the debt with an independent third party (the customer) provides more assurance than it is possible to obtain from alternative procedures and is often more efficient.

9:21.4.2 *Selecting balances for confirmation*

When items are selected for confirmation, the auditor should take into account the nature of the population of debtors. For example, it might be efficient to carry out 100 per cent testing of a particular category of balances (e.g., balances in excess of a particular monetary amount) and, if the auditor considered that there was a risk of material misstatement in the remaining balances, to select a representative sample of those balances. However, if the trade debtors population is relatively homogeneous it will often be most efficient to obtain the required assurance from a representative sample of the entire population of trade debtors. **Section 9:4**, 'Tests of details', provides further guidance on selecting items for testing.

The basis of the selection should be recorded in the working papers, including:

(a)   The portion of the total balance of trade debtors selected for 100 per cent testing, the number of items so selected and the criteria for selecting them (e.g., balances over a set amount).

(b)   The portion of the total balance of trade debtors subject to sampling, and the resulting sample size.

(c)   The amount of any remaining balance, with an indication of how the auditor will obtain any required audit assurance from substantive testing.

The auditor should ensure there is agreement between the total of the listing, from which the selections are made, and the trade debtors control account, and test the additions of the listing.

9:21.4.3 *Confirmation procedures*

Requests for confirmation should be sent as soon as possible after the confirmation date.

Confirmation of the selected amount should be requested in the currency in which the amount is receivable. If the balance includes unmatched items, the auditor should consider sending a full statement.

Because debtors are more likely to respond to requests for confirmation of individual invoices, the auditor should consider selecting individual outstanding invoices for confirmation, rather than the entire balance. However, confirming invoices is a less effective procedure than confirming balances because it will not identify any invoices omitted or any discrepancies relating to cash receipts or adjustments. Therefore, it will not provide secondary assurance on the accuracy, completeness and cut-off of trade debtors.

Selections for confirmation should be approved by the client. If the client is unwilling to allow the auditor to confirm a particular debtor, the auditor should inform the engagement manager or the engagement partner and, if they are satisfied with the client's reasons, the alternative procedures discussed in **Section 9:21.4.6** should be carried out. In such cases the auditor should consider asking the client to record its reasons in the formal written representations obtained before the end of the audit. Guidance on letters of representation is given in **Section 10:4**, 'Representations from management'.

Difficulties may be encountered in obtaining confirmations from government departments, from some overseas debtors and from entities which pay individual invoices and ignore statements. In such cases, the auditor should consider whether the debtor will respond to requests to confirm outstanding invoices, as discussed above. For government departments, it may be possible to overcome the difficulty by contacting the department concerned in advance to establish what information should be provided to enable it to respond.

9:21.4.3.1 Mailing

When sending confirmation requests, the auditor should ensure that they comply with the following points:

(a)   Requests should be clear and concise and they should be prepared in a form that makes replying easy. The response to confirmation requests is greatest if they are sent on the client's headed stationery.

(b)   The account balances and other information included in the requests should be checked against the client's accounting records.

(c)   The names and addresses should be checked against the client's records.

(d)   A reply-paid envelope should be enclosed (with the engagement manager's reference on it) or an airmail voucher.

(e)   All letters should be posted by the auditor or under the auditor's control. The requests should not merely be delivered to the client's post room.

Although the normal means of confirmation is by letter, the auditor may use electronic means such as facsimile copier (fax) or telex, particularly when there may be insufficient time for an exchange of letters. When using fax or telex, it is necessary to comply with the following further requirements:

(a)   The fax or telex should be sent by the auditor's own operators, and should request the confirming party to reply direct to the auditor.

(b)   The auditor should take appropriate steps to obtain positive identification of the respondent, e.g. by verifying that the telex or fax number of the confirming party corresponds to their listed number.

(c)   A written follow up to a fax should always be requested.

9:21.4.3.2 Follow-up

All replies should be examined to check that each debtor has agreed the balance, or the specified invoice, and has signed the reply. All discrepancies should be investigated, as discussed in **Section 9:21.4.4**. The auditor should note, and investigate, any relevant remarks made by the debtor on the reply.

Non-replies should be followed up by a second letter or, with the client's approval, by fax, telex and/or telephone. Second requests should be sent under the auditor's control, and any telephone calls involving confirmation should be made personally by the auditor, except where they are merely reminders to send the confirmation in writing.

9:21.4.4 Investigation of discrepancies

The investigation of discrepancies disclosed by confirmations may be carried out in conjunction with the client's staff. If the client's staff investigate discrepancies, the auditor should maintain a record of the accounts being investigated and should check the explanations given by the client.

If discrepancies of a particular type appear to be widespread, the auditor should consider modifying the substantive testing plan to respond to the risk of misstatement which this may indicate.

The following are some of the more common reasons for discrepancies:

(a)   Sales might have been incorrectly recorded by the client before the substantive testing date, the charge not being recognised as a debt by the customer until later. It may be necessary to extend cut-off tests.

(b)   Goods might have been returned by the debtor but the returns not recorded by the client. Again, it may be necessary to extend cut-off tests.

(c)   Payment might have been made by the debtor before the substantive testing date, but not received or not recorded by the client until after that date. It may be necessary to examine remittances in transit recorded in the bank reconciliation to ensure that receipts around the substantive testing date are entered in the cash and debtors records in the correct accounting period.

(d)   The relevant debtor account might not have been identified at the time of receipt of cash, the cash being posted to a suspense account. The auditor should consider reviewing the size of any such suspense account, and the client's procedures for regularly investigating and clearing items posted thereto.

(e)   There might be other sales ledger accounts for the customer (or connected persons or companies), and items such as sales, cash or adjustments might have been posted to one of these other accounts. If this is the case, there might be deficiencies in the procedure for controlling the postings to debtors' subsidiary records. The auditor should review the client's procedures, and, if appropriate, carry out tests of postings to the subsidiary records.

(f)   If the debtor is also a supplier, sales and purchase ledger balances might have been offset. If so, the auditor should confirm whether the arrangements with the customer/supplier permit such offset.

(g) There may be evidence of a dispute between the client and the debtor, or the response might indicate unwillingness or inability to pay. The auditor should consider the need for provision against the debt.

(h) The difference may have been caused by 'teeming and lading' to conceal one or more defalcations. Teeming and lading of debtor balances is a method of concealing the theft of a remittance from a particular debtor by incorrectly posting remittances (or parts of remittances) from other debtors so that no particular debtor's account falls significantly into arrears and thus attracts attention. By this method, the defalcation will not come to light from a debtor account apparently falling into arrears, and differences identified (either by the client sending statements or by audit confirmation procedures) might be attributed to a slight delay in recording the cash receipt against the account. If the auditor has identified a specific fraud risk, it is important to examine the controls over cash receipts for debtors and check the cash receipts records.

9:21.4.5 *Summary and evaluation of errors*

The results of confirmation procedures should be summarised and evaluated, and the nature and effect of exceptions found should be reviewed carefully. The auditor should:

(a) request the client to adjust them;

(b) consider whether, in the case of an interim confirmation, it will be necessary to repeat any procedures as at the balance sheet date. This may be necessary if the nature of the exceptions found in an interim confirmation casts doubt on the reliability of the accounting system;

(c) record details of any errors which have been found on the score sheet.

9:21.4.6 *Alternative procedures to direct confirmation*

If it is decided not to seek direct confirmation of the selected debtors or if, having tried, the auditor has found it not possible to obtain direct confirmation either in writing, or by fax, telex or telephone, the auditor should carry out alternative procedures to test the existence of the debt.

In the absence of direct confirmation, the most persuasive evidence of the existence of a debt is its subsequent settlement. However, a credit to the customer's account after the confirmation date is not, of itself, evidence of existence at the date of the confirmation. Usually it will be necessary to see evidence that the debt was settled **by the recorded debtor**. Accordingly, tests of remittances received after the substantive testing date should normally include comparison of the credit in the debtors accounts with the entries in the cash receipts records, the bank paying-in records and other available evidence.

Wherever possible, the auditor should inspect the customer's remittance advice, because this will provide evidence that the debt existed at the substantive testing date. If a remittance advice or equivalent evidence is not available, it might be necessary to consider other evidence. For example, if a remittance corresponded exactly to the amount of one or several invoices, this would be persuasive, and the nearer the date of receipt was to the substantive testing date, the more persuasive would be the evidence that the debt existed at that date.

If it is not possible to obtain satisfactory evidence of settlement of a selected balance or invoice, or if it is not clear that the selected item(s) can be identified with a remittance, the auditor should seek evidence of the sale. Appropriate evidence will normally include a combination of goods despatched records, service records, customer purchase orders or contracts or other supporting documents. Externally generated evidence, such as correspondence relating to the sale, generally provides greater assurance than internal documents and this should be taken into account in deciding whether adequate evidence has been obtained.

In general, the auditor should exercise an appropriate level of professional scepticism when examining the evidence that the debt existed at the verification date. For example, if a debt has not been paid by the date the audit work is carried out, the auditor should find out whether more recent invoices have been paid. If so, this might indicate either that the amount has already been paid and the payment has not been recorded correctly, or that its recoverability is doubtful.

9:21.4.7 Additional procedures

The auditor should be placed on enquiry by the existence of balances which are not made up of specific unsettled transactions, and/or the presence of partial or round-sum receipts and transfers between accounts. They may indicate:

(a)   the existence of disputes on the amounts concerned; and/or

(b)   the presence of an unusually high level of posting errors; and/or

(c)   the possible misappropriation of customers' remittances concealed by teeming and lading; and/or

(d)   that the customer is in financial difficulty and the debt is doubtful.

Accordingly, the auditor should test round-sum receipts by examining correspondence and customer remittance advices, tracing them to the cash records, and identifying them on the bank paying-in slip. Transfers between accounts should be tested to supporting correspondence.

9:21.4.8 Bills receivable

If it is necessary to check the existence of bills receivable held by the client in settlement of debts, the auditor should select some of the bills, using the approach outlined in **Section 9:21.4.2** (first paragraph), and:

(a)   inspect the bill to confirm that it is properly drawn (and, if relevant, trace the subsequent proceeds); or

(b)   if the client does not hold the bill, obtain confirmation of the client's title to the bill from the bank or other independent custodians, using the confirmation procedures described either in this section or in **Section 9:23**, 'Bank and cash balances'.

If the client has sold any bills with recourse, the auditor should check that any resulting contingent liabilities have been properly disclosed.

9:21.5 Cut-off

Cut-off, in this context, can be defined as the procedures instituted to ensure that the financial statements reflect only those sales, customer returns and cash receipts made or received up to the balance sheet date, and that post-balance-sheet despatches and cash receipts are not reflected.

In conjunction with stocks cut-off, the procedures are also intended to ensure that the cost of items recorded as sales during the year is duly excluded from stocks and included in cost of sales. Because of their close relationship, the substantive tests for sales cut-off should normally be combined with those for the despatch element of stocks cut-off and with bank and cash balances cut-off.

9:21.5.1 Tests of details

The auditor should normally carry out the following procedures:

(a)   Check a sample of entries in the debtors control account (or other appropriate record) in the last few days of the period with evidence that the goods were despatched, or services rendered, before the end of the reporting period. Where possible the customer's acknowledgement of receipt of the goods or services should be inspected or, failing that, evidence of despatch.

(b)   Select major debits in the sales returns account or sales account in the last few days of the period and inspect supporting documentation such as goods returned notes, correspondence and sales invoices, to ensure that amounts were both valid and recorded in the correct accounting period.

(c)   Select credits to the sales account for the first few days after the balance sheet date, and determine, by inspecting original evidence of despatches or services rendered, that sales were recorded in the correct period.

(d)   Select major despatches (e.g., from despatch notes) or evidence of services rendered in the last few days of the period, and ensure that the relevant sales and debtors were recorded prior to the balance sheet date.

(e)   Select major items from evidence of sales returns and allowances (such as goods returned records) for the last few days of the period and in the period after the balance sheet date, and trace them to the credit of the debtors control account.

(f)   Compare credit notes issued in the period after the balance sheet date with relevant supporting evidence, and ensure that all amounts that should have been provided were provided.

(g)   Examine evidence of cash receipts from customers (e.g., remittance advices) in the last few days of the period, trace them to the debtors control account, and ensure that they were posted in the correct accounting period.

(h)   Examine any unprocessed invoices to ascertain whether any relate to the current period and have not been recorded.

If specific risks of misstatement have been identified (e.g., from the results of the confirmation procedure discussed in **Sections 9:21.4.3** to **9:21.4.6**), the nature and/or extent of audit tests should be designed to respond to such risks. Possible responses to provide higher assurance include:

(a)   Reviewing goods despatch or service records for completeness.

(b)   Analysing the level of activity immediately before and after the balance sheet date, and comparing it with an expectation based on, e.g., the previous year's level.

(c)   Inspecting sales terms for major sales to ensure that there are no terms that affect the recognition of sales or likely level of sales.

(d)   Obtaining confirmation from customers of significant recorded sales or returns transactions around the balance sheet date.

9:21.6 Valuation

9:21.6.1 Provision for bad and doubtful debts

9:21.6.1.1 Checking the client's aged analysis

Whenever possible, audit procedures should be based on the client's aged analysis. The auditor should therefore test that the aged analysis is properly prepared by carrying out the following procedures:

(a)   Selecting amounts from the debtor listing and checking the analysis with the dates on the underlying invoices. The auditor should normally use some or all of the amounts selected for confirmation, if this is being conducted at the same date as the work on the provision. If the customer confirmed the specific invoice details as part of the confirmation exercise, that will normally be sufficient for this purpose.

(b)   Testing the additions of the analysis and checking that the total agrees with the control account.

(c)   Checking for significant unapplied credits or unallocated cash. The existence of any such items may indicate that the aged analysis is inaccurate and that the items should be investigated.

If the client does not produce adequate aged analyses, or if the analysis is not up to date, the auditor should ask management to produce a listing of all debts over a certain age which should be specified by reference to the client's normal credit collection period.

9:21.6.1.2 *Reviewing individual old or large items*

The best evidence of a debtor's collectability is the subsequent receipt of cash. However, if the auditor believes there is a risk of fraud, such as deliberate distortion of the financial statements or concealment of a defalcation by teeming and lading, the cash receipts records should be checked to verify that receipts are authentic. In such cases, that work should be co-ordinated with the alternative procedures discussed in **Section 9:21.4.6** because the audit procedures are similar and the same audit evidence may be required.

If a debt has not been settled by the date of testing, the auditor should discuss its collectability with the officials responsible for credit control, and review any relevant correspondence with the customer. If there is reason to question the customer's ability to pay, the auditor should consider carrying out one or more of the following:

(a) Establishing whether the debt is secured or guaranteed. The procedures which should be adopted are discussed in **Sections 9:21.6.1.3** and **9:21.6.1.4**.

(b) Reviewing the client's most recent independent check on the customer's creditworthiness or, if no recent data are available, requesting a check specifically for the test.

(c) Reviewing the customer's most recent financial statements (this will be particularly important if the client has only a few, material debtors).

(d) Comparing the amount due with the credit limit allocated by the client.

(e) Reviewing the customer's payment record to ascertain whether the number of days of credit taken appears to be increasing.

9:21.6.1.3 *Secured debts*

Where a client has a doubtful debt that is secured, the auditor should ascertain whether:

(a) there is evidence that the charge on the secured assets has been properly registered (where possible) in accordance with the agreement between the parties and, where relevant, is not void under the Companies Act;

(b) the entity offering the security is financially sound; and

(c) the security offered is of sufficient value to cover the doubtful debt.

If any of these matters is in doubt the auditor should:

(a) consider the need to obtain further information (e.g., by carrying out a company search of the company offering the security); and

(b) ascertain whether any guarantees have also been given in respect of the doubtful debt.

If any guarantees have been given, the auditor should consider them as discussed in **Section 9:21.6.1.4**. If no guarantees have been given, the auditor should consider the amount at which the debt should be stated, after taking into account the amount the customer can repay and the value, if any, of the security.

9:21.6.1.4 Guaranteed debts

If a client has a doubtful debt in respect of which guarantees have been given, regardless of whether these are in addition to the provision of security, the auditor should, if the guarantor is a company, ascertain whether:

(a)   the guarantor company has the power under its Memorandum to give guarantees;

(b)   the directors of the guarantor company have the power under the company's Articles to commit the company to such contingent liabilities; and

(c)   the directors signing the guarantee have the authority of the board of directors to sign.

If these matters are in doubt, the auditor should consider:

(a)   the need to obtain further information; and

(b)   the amount at which the debt should be stated after taking into account:

   (i)   the amount the customer can repay;

   (ii)   where relevant, the value of any security provided; and

   (iii) the amount recoverable from the guarantors.

9:21.6.1.5 Estimating the amount of general provisions

The auditor should develop an estimate of the likely provision for doubtful debts by taking account of:

(a)   The client's past experience of bad debts, and the adequacy of previous provisions.

(b)   The age of debtors at the substantive testing date.

(c)   The effectiveness of the client's credit control procedures.

(d)   Changes in the client's provision policies.

(e)   Trends in the industry as regards debt collection.

If these procedures and calculations result in an estimate that is outside an acceptable range of the client's recorded amount the auditor should discuss the matter with the client and, in the absence of a satisfactory resolution, regard the amount as an error, as discussed in **Section 9:6**, 'Audit of accounting estimates'.

9:21.6.2 Post-balance-sheet events

The auditor should enquire whether any debtor has gone into liquidation, administration or bankruptcy since the balance sheet date because this will normally indicate that the value of its debt was impaired at that date. It is also necessary to consider whether any events (e.g., the receipt of cash) since the balance sheet date indicate that the provision for bad debts was excessive.

9:21.6.3 Provision for credit notes

Generally, assurance concerning the adequacy of the provision for credit notes will be obtained from tests of cut-off (as discussed in **Section 9:21.5.1** (first paragraph)). However, when there is a risk that sales and debtors may be overstated, the auditor might consider obtaining further assurance by, e.g.:

(a) extending the period over which to search for returned goods or evidence of customer disputes;

(b) developing an estimate of the current year's provision (as, e.g., a percentage of sales) by reference to the client's history of credit notes issued;

(c) discussing the level of returns with production and warehouse staff.

9:21.6.4 Allowances, rebates and claims

The preliminary analytical review will help to indicate whether a provision for allowances, rebates or claims should be made. Also, general knowledge of the client's affairs should be used (e.g., by making enquiries of management and by reviewing the client's experience in past years), and the auditor should consider whether there is:

(a) a significant recurring level of allowances or claims, including credits given under guarantee or warranty agreements; and

(b) the incidence and likelihood of any large individual item.

9:21.7 Rights and obligations

The work in relation to the existence objective (**Sections 9:21.4.1** to **9:21.4.8**) will normally provide sufficient evidence in respect of the audit objective or rights and obligations. However, if further assurance is required, procedures may include one or more of the following:

(a) Reviewing the client's terms of sale and major agreements or contracts.

(b) Consulting or involving an industry or other specialists within the audit firm.

(c) Reviewing correspondence with, or obtaining confirmation from, parties who collect debts on the client's behalf.

(d)   Contacting the client's significant customers and confirming the client's sales terms with them. This should only be done with the prior approval of the engagement partner and the client.

If the client has sold its trade debts to a banking or finance company with recourse, there will be a contingent liability at the balance sheet date, the amount of which might be material.

9:21.8 Presentation and disclosure

To help achieve the objective of presentation and disclosure the auditor should, at the end of the audit, review the financial statements and consider the matters set out in a UK GAAP checklist. Also, it is important to be alert for any matters that require disclosure or reclassification and which can be more efficiently identified during fieldwork. These include:

(a)   Any part of a debtor balance that is not receivable within 12 months from the balance sheet date.

(b)   Trade debtors which have been replaced by bills receivable.

(c)   Amounts due from group and related companies.

(d)   Any debts which are pledged.

(e)   Credit balances incorrectly deducted from trade debtors.

(f)   Contingencies in respect of trade debts sold with recourse.

9:22 Prepayments, accrued income and other debtors

9:22.1 Introduction

This section is designed to help to develop a programme of substantive tests for prepayments, accrued income and other (non-trade) debtors in accordance with the strategy. The strategy or substantive testing plan (STP), if prepared, for these items should specify the planned response to the assessment of the risk of material misstatement, including the nature, extent and timing of substantive tests. Loans to directors and officers have important disclosure implications and are discussed separately in **Section 9:9**, 'Directors' emoluments, transactions and loans'.

This section should be read in conjunction with the general guidance on substantive testing in the following sections:

● **Section 9:3**, 'Analytical procedures'

● **Section 9:4**, 'Tests of details'

● **Section 9:5**, 'Evaluating the results of substantive testing'

9:22.1.1 Essential audit objectives

The specific audit objectives for prepayments, accrued income and other debtors are set out below for each of the seven general audit objectives. The auditor should obtain sufficient evidence that these specific objectives have been achieved:

● **Completeness**	All prepayments, accrued income and other debtors have been recorded in the financial statements.
● **Accuracy; Existence; Rights and obligations**	Prepayments, accrued income and other debtors have been accurately determined, summarised and recorded.
	The amounts reported in the financial statements are in agreement with the accounting records.
	Prepayments, accrued income and other debtors included in the balance sheet represent future benefits or cash to be received.
● **Cut-off**	Prepayments have been calculated so that expenditure falls into the correct accounting period.
	Other debtors and accrued income have been recorded in the correct accounting period.
● **Valuation**	Adequate provision has been made against all items whose recoverability is doubtful.
● **Presentation and disclosure**	Prepayments, accrued income and other debtors have been properly classified, described and disclosed in the financial statements.

Sometimes the auditor may conclude that there is a negligible risk of material misstatement in relation to one or more of these audit objectives, and that consequently no specific substantive procedures are necessary.

9:22.2 Completeness

In the absence of specific risks of misstatement, the auditor will normally obtain sufficient evidence concerning this objective from the following sources:

(a) A substantive analytical review of prepayments and/or accrued income, based on prior period amounts adjusted for relevant changes in the business. (This procedure will also provide evidence concerning the accuracy, existence and rights and obligations objectives.)

(b)   The corollary effect of direct tests on purchases and expenses, trade debtors, and turnover and other income.

If further evidence is required, the auditor should identify the client's major items of income and expenditure from which prepayments, accrued income and other debtors might arise and carry out appropriate direct tests.

9:22.3 Accuracy; Existence; Rights and obligations

9:22.3.1 Prepayments and accrued income

A substantive analytical review, based on prior period amounts, adjusted for relevant changes in the client's business is often effective as a means of obtaining sufficient assurance with respect to the objectives of accuracy, existence and rights and obligations (as well as the completeness objective, as discussed in **Section 9:22.2**).

If the auditor carries out tests of details, items for testing should be selected from the recorded amounts, and tests should involve:

(a)   examining supporting documents to confirm the period covered by the charge or credit;

(b)   checking the calculation of the prepayment or accrual.

9:22.3.2 Other debtors

Work on other debtors will normally consist of tests of details on the recorded amounts based on similar procedures to those discussed in **Section 9:21**, 'Trade debtors'.

If any items are denominated in foreign currencies, the auditor should check that they have been translated into sterling at the closing exchange rate or, if applicable, at the rate of exchange at which the transaction is contracted to be settled in the future.

If any security has been given in respect of amounts due from debtors, the appropriate evidence should be examined. For example, the auditor should inspect investments or title deeds, or obtain confirmation from banks or similar institutions holding them. It is also important to confirm, where appropriate, that signed transfer forms in favour of the client are in the client's possession.

9:22.3.3 Agreement with accounting records

The auditor should check the figure for prepayments, accrued income and other debtors against the general ledger, normally doing this by tracing the amounts via the trial balance to the ledger.

9:22.4 Cut-off

The assurance required in relation to the specific cut-off objectives will normally be obtained from work on other objectives, particularly completeness and existence. Accordingly, it will not normally be necessary to carry out specific procedures.

9:22.5 Valuation

Tests for valuation should consist of the following:

(a) **Prepayments**: The auditor should be satisfied that the costs carried forward will be covered by a related stream of income. For example, it would not be appropriate to defer the prepaid element of shop rental on a shop which either had been, or was intended to be, closed.

(b) **Other debtors**: The auditor should follow similar procedures to those discussed in **Section 9:21**, 'Trade debtors'.

9:22.6 Presentation and disclosure

The auditor will normally achieve the objective of presentation and disclosure at the end of the audit by reviewing the financial statements and considering the matters set out in a UK GAAP checklist. Also, it is important to be alert for any matters that require disclosure and which can be more efficiently identified during fieldwork. In particular, the auditor should ensure that:

(a) items are correctly analysed between categories (prepayments, accrued income and other debtors);

(b) any balances not receivable within 12 months from the balance sheet date are separately identified;

(c) any debtors pledged as security have been identified.

9:23 Bank and cash balances

9:23.1 Introduction

This section is designed to help to develop a programme of substantive tests in accordance with the strategy for all bank and cash balances (including short-term deposits, bank overdrafts and short-term bank borrowing). The strategy or substantive testing plan (STP), if prepared, for bank and cash balances should specify the planned response to the assessment of the risk of material misstatement, including the nature, extent and timing of substantive tests.

This section should be read in conjunction with the general guidance on substantive testing included in the following sections:

- **Section 9:3**, 'Analytical procedures'
- **Section 9:4**, 'Tests of details'
- **Section 9:5**, 'Evaluating the results of substantive testing'

9:23.1.1 Essential audit objectives

The specific audit objectives for bank and cash balances are set out below for each of the seven general audit objectives. The auditor should obtain sufficient evidence that these specific objectives have been achieved:

- **Completeness** — All bank and cash balances have been recorded in the financial statements.

- **Accuracy** — Bank and cash balances have been accurately determined, summarised and recorded.

  The amounts reported in the financial statements are in agreement with the accounting records.

- **Existence** — Bank and cash balances exist at the balance sheet date.

- **Cut-off** — Bank and cash transactions have been recorded in the correct accounting period.

  Bank and cash balances have not been distorted by 'window dressing'.

- **Valuation** — Adequate provision has been made against bank balances whose recoverability is in doubt.

- **Rights and obligations** — The client has title to bank and cash deposits, and overdrafts and short-term borrowings represent obligations of the client, at the balance sheet date.

- **Presentation and disclosure** — Bank and cash balances have been properly classified, described and disclosed in the financial statements.

In some cases the auditor may conclude that there is a negligible risk of material misstatement in relation to one or more of these audit objectives and that consequently no specific substantive procedures are necessary.

9:23.1.2 Early substantive testing

The auditor should consider carrying out some of the procedures discussed in this section at an interim date, as part of early substantive testing (discussed in **Section 4:7**, 'The audit programme'). Sometimes, depending principally on the assessment of control effectiveness, it may be necessary to repeat or extend these procedures as at the balance sheet date. The strategy or STP, if prepared, for bank and cash balances should specify which procedures should be carried out at an interim date and whether it is expected that it will be necessary to repeat or extend them at the balance sheet date. The audit programme for bank and cash balances should set out the procedures to be performed in respect of the intervening period.

9:23.2 Completeness

The auditor should principally derive the required assurance that all bank balances have been identified and accounted for from the understanding of the business acquired through the business review. In particular, the auditor should consider whether the number of bank accounts appears adequate for the level of business. An expansion of the business, such as the opening of new branches, may indicate that there are new accounts.

Additionally, the following procedures may be appropriate:

(a)   Reviewing the list of balances at the previous balance sheet date and enquiring into any changes.

(b)   Scrutinising bank confirmations, cash books, bank statements and board minutes for evidence of accounts opened during the period.

(c)   Enquiring into foreign currency accounts, particularly for clients with frequent dealings overseas.

(d)   Investigating whether the client has opened separate bank accounts for petty cash and payrolls and whether these have all been accounted for.

9:23.3 Accuracy

9:23.3.1 *Bank reconciliations*

Detailed checking of the client's bank reconciliations should normally provide sufficient assurance that bank and cash transactions have been accurately processed. This work should also provide assurance concerning cut-off objectives. The auditor should normally check the bank reconciliations as at the date confirmation of balances is obtained from the bank.

The auditor should carry out the following work:

(a)   Checking the balances on the reconciliations to the general ledger (or, where appropriate, the cash records), the bank confirmations and the bank statements.

(b)   Testing the additions of the reconciliations, and of the lists of un-presented cheques and outstanding lodgements.

(c)   Tracing entries in the cash records before the substantive testing date to bank statements or reconciliations (referred to in **Section 9:23.3.2**).

(d)   Checking un-presented cheques and outstanding lodgements recorded on the bank reconciliation to the cash records and the bank statements (referred to in **Section 9:23.3.1.2**).

(e)   Investigating and verifying any other reconciling items.

9:23.3.1.1 Entries in the cash records

The auditor should select from the receipts and payments recorded in the cash records for a period (as specified by the strategy or STP, if prepared), before the substantive testing date, and should ensure that the items selected are:

(a)   recorded on bank statements prior to the substantive testing date; or

(b)   included in the bank reconciliation as un-presented cheques or outstanding lodgements (as appropriate).

9:23.3.1.2 Outstanding items on the bank reconciliation

Unless outstanding items on the bank reconciliation are adequately covered by the work described in the preceding paragraph, the auditor should carry out the following procedures:

(a)   Trace un-presented cheques and outstanding lodgements recorded on the bank reconciliation to the cash records and the bank statements.

(b)   Check that such items were recorded:

  (i)   in the cash records prior to the substantive testing date; and

  (ii)   on the bank statements after the substantive testing date.

In deciding whether items have been adequately covered by the work described in **Section 9:23.3.1.1**, the auditor should (among other things) bear in mind that a shortage of cash can be concealed by overstating outstanding lodgements. Where the number of reconciling items is small they should normally all be tested.

   The auditor should check that the paying-in date for outstanding lodgements is no later than the reconciliation date, and should investigate any unusual delay in the recording of lodgements on the bank statement. Such a delay might be caused by a client's holding open the cash receipts records and including monies received subsequent to the balance sheet date.

   The auditor should check that any material payments to creditors, identified in work on creditors' reconciliations as not recorded on the creditors' statements at the reconciliation date, are traced to the un-presented cheque list. It is also important to check that any discrepancies have been investigated as these might cast doubt on the validity of the reconciling items.

The auditor should review the detailed list of un-presented cheques for all large amounts (particularly large round sums) that have not been cleared by the bank since the substantive testing date, and should trace these back to original documentation and discuss with the client why they have not cleared. For un-presented cheques not cleared by the time the work is carried out, the auditor should:

(a) obtain explanations for any large or unusual items; and

(b) investigate any cheques which have been outstanding for more than six months and consider whether they should be added back to the bank balance.

The auditor should also scrutinise bank statements for a period subsequent to the substantive testing date for dishonoured cheques, and investigate any such items.

9:23.3.1.3 Problems with reconciliations

If the client either does not perform regular bank reconciliations, or has difficulty in reconciling the bank accounts, the auditor should consider whether the records are reliable. The auditor should inform the engagement manager of failure by the client to carry out regular and proper bank reconciliations, or significant and repeated delays in doing so, and the engagement partner should decide whether the matter should be reported in issues documentation.

9:23.3.1.4 Following up interim reconciliations

If a detailed check of the bank reconciliations has been carried out as part of early substantive testing, it may be necessary to carry out the following further procedures as at the balance sheet date:

(a) Trace the balances recorded on the reconciliations to the cash records, bank statements and bank confirmations.

(b) Check the additions of the reconciliations.

(c) Ascertain that outstanding items included on the reconciliations tested at the early substantive testing date have been cleared.

9:23.3.2 Foreign exchange

The auditor should check that all bank balances denominated in foreign currencies have been translated into sterling at appropriate exchange rates.

9:23.3.3 Risk of fraud

If the auditor has identified a risk of fraud relating to payments, the auditor should verify payments by obtaining the paid cheques (or copies kept by the bank) and checking that the payee corresponds to the payee recorded in the cash records, and that the cheque has not been altered or endorsed. In assessing the risk of fraudulent endorsement of cheques the auditor should take into account the provisions of the Cheques Act 1992.

Where payment is made by other means, such as bank transfer, the auditor should inspect the supporting documentation, checking that the transfer has been made to the correct account.

9:23.3.4 *Agreement with accounting records*

The auditor should obtain sufficient evidence that the bank and cash balances in the general ledger agree with the financial statements, by tracing the general ledger account balances to the financial statements via the trial balance.

9:23.4 Existence

The auditor should normally obtain sufficient evidence that recorded bank and cash balances exist by obtaining direct confirmation from the client's bankers. If for any reason it is decided not to confirm a particular balance, the reasons should be noted in the strategy.

9:23.4.1 *Confirmation of balances*

The auditor should consider whether it is necessary to confirm balances as at the balance sheet date, regardless of whether confirmations were also obtained as part of early substantive testing. The confirmation should, save in exceptional circumstances that might apply on the audits of banking industry clients where there are good controls, cover all banks with which the client held an account during any part of the period under audit, including payroll and dividend accounts, even though the account might have been closed before the balance sheet date. This should be done to identify possible unrecorded bank borrowings and contingent liabilities.

Guidance on correspondence between an auditor and bank is given in APB Practice Note 16. The text has been agreed with the British Bankers Association. Bank confirmation requests should be sent, using a standard letter, at least two weeks before the confirmation date..

There are additional questions an auditor may ask if the banking arrangements . are complex, such as when the bank handles commodity trading for the client.

The letter to the bank should state:

(a) The names of the companies covered by the request.

(b) Whether the auditors are requesting standard information, or, if not, what supplementary information is required.

(c) The date for providing this information.

(d) A statement that providing this information will not create any contractual relationship between the bank and auditor.

(e) A contact name and telephone number.

9:23.4.2 *Procedures on receipt of confirmations*

On receipt of bank confirmations the auditor should carry out the following procedures:

(a)   Check that the bank has answered all the questions on the bank letter in full. It is important to ensure that all relevant matters appear to have been disclosed. Additionally, the auditor should consider the significance of **all** matters reported in the reply and ensure that the bank's response deals **specifically** with each point on the request. If supplementary or amended information is required, it is unsatisfactory to rely on information obtained by telephone or via the client. The auditor should ask the bank to confirm it in writing directly to the auditor.

(b)   If a confirmation provides details of a balance or of other information of which the auditor was not aware (e.g., in relation to a previously unknown contingent liability), bring the matter to the attention of the client and the engagement manager.

(c)   Check that a reply has been received for all requests.

9:23.4.3 *Use of software*

Software packages may be designed to assist in confirmation procedures. A microcomputer database can help to produce bank confirmation letters, and to control, summarise and report the results of confirmation procedures.

9:23.4.4 *Cash balances*

Many clients' cash balances are immaterial and, depending on the assessment of the risk of misstatement, the auditor may decide not to carry out any substantive testing on them. However, it is important to remember that, because cash is a sensitive area, the client may expect the auditor to count cash balances and report any weaknesses in cash systems. If there is any doubt about client expectations and the in-charge does not intend to count cash or review the systems, the auditor should discuss the matter with the engagement partner or manager at the audit strategy stage.

9:23.4.5 *Cash counts*

Cash counts should be carried out unannounced. To prevent cash being transferred between accounts to disguise discrepancies, the auditor might count all cash funds at a particular location simultaneously. To avoid any possibility that a shortfall could be blamed on the audit staff, it is essential to count cash in the custodian's presence, insist that he or she stays until the count is completed, and ask the custodian to sign the record of the amount counted to confirm acceptance of the findings. The auditor should check the amount counted to the general ledger and to the petty cash records.

Cash funds often include cheques that have been cashed (quite properly) for directors or employees. However, shortages of cash are often concealed by the inclusion of fictitious, forged or worthless cheques and IOUs in the funds. The auditor should therefore carry out the following procedures:

(a)   Examine cheques carefully and ensure that they bear a recent date and are not post-dated.

(b)   Check that they are subsequently banked and cleared.

(c)   Check that there is authority for the issue of IOUs and test that they are repaid subsequently.

If payment vouchers make up part of the balance of a cash float, the auditor should carry out the following procedures:

(a)   Check that they are genuine and have not already been used to support previous payments.

(b)   Check that the vouchers represent recent expenditure and are recorded in the cash payment records.

(c)   If they have not yet been recorded, check that they are subsequently recorded.

The auditor should also check, by subsequent examination of the copy paying-in slips, that any un-banked cash receipts found in the cash funds are banked promptly, and that the last cheque drawn to replenish the cash funds has been recorded in the petty cash records.

9:23.5 Cut-off

9:23.5.1 Sources of assurance

The auditor should normally obtain much of the required assurance concerning the correct cut-off of bank and cash balances from the work on bank reconciliations discussed in **Sections 9:23.3.1** to **9:23.3.1.2**. However, if a risk of 'window dressing' has been identified, the additional tests below should be considered.

9:23.5.1.1 Window dressing

The actions that relate to window dressing are likely to be contentious. Accordingly, audit staff should report suspicions to the engagement manager **before** discussing them with the client.

Further guidance on window dressing can be found in **Section 9:13**, 'Window dressing and off-balance-sheet finance'. The most common methods of window dressing bank balances are:

(a)   Including monies received after the balance sheet date.

(b)   Utilising bank borrowing facilities immediately before the year-end to place money on deposit, thereby improving liquidity ratios. This can be particularly difficult to detect when the funds are transferred to other group companies.

(c)   Sending cheques to creditors before the balance sheet date but not entering them in the cash book until the following period.

(d)   Entering cheques in the cash book before the balance sheet date but not sending them to payees until the following period.

9:23.5.1.2 Transfers of funds

The auditor should identify any significant transfers of funds occurring near to the balance sheet date which involve the following:

(a)   Two or more accounts held by the client with the same bank, or with different banks.

(b)   One of the client's bank accounts and the bank account of another company for which records are maintained by the client.

In respect of such transfers the auditor should check that:

(a)   respective receipts and payments were recording in the accounting records in the same accounting period; and

(b)   any such items not reflected by the bank in the same accounting period appear in the appropriate bank reconciliation.

9:23.5.1.3 Outstanding lodgements

The auditor should review the accounting records for evidence of the inclusion of lodgements which were physically received after the balance sheet date. If such items are identified, the possible need for reversing entries should be considered.

9:23.5.1.4 Un-presented cheques

The auditor should review the lapse of time between the date of issue of un-presented cheques as recorded in the accounting records and the date of their subsequent presentation at the bank, and determine whether this was longer than would be expected. If it appears that any un-presented cheques on the bank reconciliations might not have been released by the client until after the balance sheet date, it is necessary to:

(a)   ascertain whether there was any delay in issuing such cheques;

(b)   consider whether any reversing entries are required.

9:23.6 Valuation

If balances are held with reputable banks (e.g. a UK clearing bank), the auditor should not need to question their recoverability. However, if a balance is held with a small bank or with an institution of uncertain standing, the recoverability of the balance should be considered.

If there are substantial balances in other countries or currencies, the auditor should determine whether there are any restrictions on transferability of funds which could affect the value of the asset or which, for any other reason, should be disclosed in the financial statements.

The auditor should review loan agreements, minutes or other relevant documentation to determine whether there are any restrictions on the availability or use of bank balances or cash.

9:23.7 Rights and obligations

The rights and obligations objective should normally be accomplished through the confirmation procedures discussed in **Sections 9:23.4.1** and **9:23.4.2**. However, if the auditor has identified a risk that the bank accounts in the client's name may include the property of others (e.g., an employees association or employees' savings) it may be necessary to carry out the following procedures:

(a) Review bank statements or cheques to ensure that they are in the name of the client.

(b) Read correspondence with the bank.

(c) Obtain specific confirmation from the bank concerning the status of any suspected trust accounts.

9:23.8 Presentation and disclosure

The auditor will normally achieve the objective of presentation and disclosure at the end of the audit by reviewing the financial statements and considering the matters set out in a UK GAAP checklist. Also, it is important to be alert for any matters that require disclosure or reclassification and which can more efficiently be identified during fieldwork. These include the following:

(a) Overdrafts and other liabilities which should be classified as creditors.

(b) Bank accounts where withdrawal of funds or remittance to the UK may be restricted.

(c) Bank accounts having the right of set-off.

(d) Offsetting of balances where no such right exists.

(e) The existence of window dressing.

(f) Secured overdrafts and borrowings.

(g) The existence of group banking arrangements.

(h)   Balances which are not held with authorised institutions under the Banking Act 1987, and which should not, therefore, be included as bank balances (e.g., a petrol deposit with a garage).

(i)   Cash subject to restrictions (e.g., deposits with the International Air Transport Association (IATA) or other regulatory bodies).

(j)   Contingent liabilities such as discounted bills, guarantees, and outstanding forward exchange contracts.

9:24 Trade creditors

9:24.1 Introduction

This section is designed to help to develop a programme of substantive tests of trade creditors, as defined below, in accordance with the strategy. The strategy or substantive testing plan (STP), if prepared, for trade creditors should specify the planned response to the assessment of the risk of material misstatement, including the nature, extent and timing of substantive tests.

This section should be read in conjunction with the general guidance on substantive testing in the following sections:

- **Section 9:3**, 'Analytical procedures'
- **Section 9:4**, 'Tests of details'
- **Section 9:5**, 'Evaluating the results of substantive testing'

For the purposes of this section, trade creditors are defined as liabilities (including amounts owing to group or related companies) related to the client's business for which:

(a)   invoices have been received but not paid; or

(b)   goods and services have been received but the related invoices had not been received at the balance sheet date.

9:24.1.1 Essential audit objectives

The specific audit objectives for trade creditors are set out below for each of the seven general audit objectives. The auditor should obtain sufficient evidence to achieve these specific objectives:

- **Completeness**   All amounts owed to trade creditors at the balance sheet date have been included in the balance sheet.

- **Accuracy**   Trade creditor balances have been accurately determined, summarised and recorded.

                                The amounts reported in the financial statements are in agreement with the accounting records.

- **Existence**   Only valid trade creditors have been included in the financial statements.

- **Cut-off**   Proper account has been taken for all liabilities relating to goods and services rendered or delivered up to the balance sheet date.

                                Liabilities for goods and services rendered or delivered after the balance sheet date have been excluded.

- **Valuation**   Adequate provision has been made in relation to debit balances.

                                Adequate provision has been made for potential losses arising from purchase commitments.

- **Rights and obligations**   Trade creditors represent amounts payable by the client at the balance sheet date.

- **Presentation and disclosure**   Trade creditors have been properly classified, described and disclosed in the financial statements.

Sometimes the auditor may conclude that there is a negligible risk of material misstatement in relation to one or more of these audit objectives, and that consequently no specific substantive procedures are necessary.

9:24.1.2 Early substantive testing

The auditor should consider carrying out some of the procedures discussed in this section at an interim date, as part of early substantive testing (discussed in **Section 4:7**, 'The audit programme'). The strategy, or STP if prepared, for trade creditors should specify which procedures will be carried out at an interim date and whether it is expected that it will be necessary to repeat or extend them as at the balance sheet date. The audit programme for trade creditors should set out the procedures to be performed in respect of the intervening period.

9:24.2 Completeness

9:24.2.1 Inspection and reconciliation of suppliers' statements

In addition to meeting the completeness objective, the inspection and reconciliation of selected suppliers' statements (which may be obtained either directly from the suppliers or from the client) will provide evidence concerning the accuracy, existence, cut-off and rights and obligations objectives. It is, therefore, the principal substantive test of trade creditors. Where possible, the auditor should carry out the procedures as at the stock count date.

In the absence of identified risks of fraud or error the auditor need not normally request statements from suppliers, and may use the suppliers' statements retained by the client. If statements are not available, it is necessary to establish the reasons therefor and request a copy directly from the supplier, using the procedures referred to in **Section 9:24.2.1.4**. Audit work should not be based on the inspection of suppliers' invoices, as an alternative to inspecting statements, because this will not provide sufficient evidence that all invoices have been recorded.

9:24.2.1.1 Inspection

Accounts should be selected for inspection and reconciliation from the sources which are most likely to identify all suppliers with whom the client has, or had, a substantial amount of business. One source could be the list of creditors from the previous balance sheet date. The auditor might also consider selecting from the suppliers identified during tests of purchases and fixed assets during the latter part of the period and from the cash payments records. Because material amounts are more likely to be omitted from major suppliers, the aim should be to select major suppliers, even though the current recorded balance may be small.

The auditor should also review the names of suppliers on the listing of individual balances for omissions, e.g. by reference to knowledge of the client's main suppliers gained from the business review, and by reviewing the previous period's listing.

9:24.2.1.2 Reconciliation with the client's records

The client should be asked to reconcile the balance shown by each selected supplier's statement with its own records as at the substantive testing date, and to investigate any differences. The auditor should examine the reconciliations and check the details to supporting documentation. When the reconciling items are material, unusual or suspicious the auditor should consider requesting the supplier to confirm the particulars directly to the auditor.

The following are the items for which reconciliation is normally required:

(a) **Invoices for goods included on a supplier's statement but not in the client's records**: In these cases the auditor should check the date that the goods were received to determine whether a liability should have been recorded. If the goods were received prior to the substantive testing date and the invoice is not in the ledger, it is necessary to ensure that an amount has been included in the accruals.

(b) **Payments made by the client which do not appear on the supplier's statement**: In these cases the auditor should check the date the cheque was cleared through the bank to confirm when payment was made.

(c) **Purchase returns debited to the supplier's account in the client's ledger but which do not appear on the supplier's statement**: The auditor should check evidence, such as despatch records and correspondence, that the goods have been returned, and should also check that the goods were returned for a valid reason and whether there is any evidence of dispute by the supplier which might cast doubt on the client's treatment of the item.

9:24.2.1.3 Unusual items and discrepancies

To identify any invalid transactions, the auditor should investigate unmatched items, unusual items in the reconciliations, and other discrepancies. In particular:

(a)   The existence of balances not comprising specific unsettled transactions and of transfers between accounts may indicate the existence of fraud or error.

(b)   The existence of old unpaid invoices or round-sum payments may indicate either disputes with suppliers or the inclusion of invalid invoices, or that the client is unable to pay its debts as they fall due.

9:24.2.1.4 Requesting statements from suppliers

If the auditor decides to request statements directly from suppliers, the confirmation procedures described in **Section 9:21**, 'Trade debtors', should be followed, except that the request should be for a statement rather than the confirmation of a balance. The requests should, if possible, be sent out a few days before the substantive testing date, because the suppliers are more likely to reply if they receive the audit letter while preparing their statements. The auditor should use follow-up procedures for non-replies that are similar to those described in **Section 9:21**, 'Trade debtors'.

9:24.2.1.5 Alternative procedures to the inspection of suppliers' statements

If suppliers' statements are not available from the client and it is not possible to obtain them directly from the suppliers, the auditor should perform the following alternative procedures on the selected accounts:

(a)   Check the opening balance on the account with the list of creditors at the previous year-end.

(b)   Check the additions of the account.

(c)   Examine a sample of debit entries to the account (payments, returns or discounts) and establish their validity by comparing them with supporting documentation such as paid cheques or credit notes.

In addition, the auditor should identify the most suitable reciprocal population (e.g., goods received records), select items from that population, and trace them to invoices for goods and services received and into the relevant creditors ledger account.

9:24.2.1.6 *Following up interim reconciliations*

If the auditor has reviewed suppliers' statement reconciliations as part of early substantive testing, the auditor may need to carry out further work as at the balance sheet date including the following:

(a) Examining invoices or other supporting documentation in the intervening period.

(b) Enquiring into any unusual delay in discharging liabilities and investigating any unusual items.

(c) Examining the reconciliations of suppliers' statements carried out by the client to ensure that the reconciliations appear to be properly completed, investigating any unusual items and re-performing a small number of reconciliations.

(d) Reviewing the movements on debit balances and performing appropriate steps on significant new debit balances.

The choice and extent of these procedures will depend on the circumstances of each case and, in particular, on the assessment of the risk of material misstatement in the intervening period. As discussed in **Section 9:24.1.2**, they should be specified in the strategy for trade creditors, or the STP, if prepared.

9:24.2.2 *Unrecorded liabilities*

The auditor should design cut-off tests (as discussed in **Section 9:24.5.1**) to detect understated liabilities within a short period of the balance sheet date. These should be supplemented with the following procedures:

(a) Enquiring of management and other client officials as to any unrecorded liabilities of which they are aware.

(b) Selecting items from the purchases and expense records (including the cash records) after the balance sheet date and examining them to see whether they should have been recorded as creditors at that date. The auditor should enquire whether any significant invoices have been received after the balance sheet date but not processed at the date of the audit.

9:24.2.3 *Examination of debit balances*

Debit balances in the creditors ledger may indicate unrecorded purchase invoices or cut-off problems. All material debit balances should be examined to ascertain the appropriate treatment of the amount. If debit balances are material they should be classified as debtors in the balance sheet.

Tests of debit balances should normally include:

(a) Identifying any individual debit entries forming a significant part of the debit balances.

(b) Ascertaining, by inspection of correspondence or other evidence, the reason for the larger individual debit entries and, where appropriate, considering their recoverability.

(c) Where relevant, identifying and substantiating the credit which the debit entry was apparently designed to pay or cancel, and considering the risk of unrecorded invoices.

(d) Where there remains doubt as to the nature or existence of a debit balance, confirming debit balances directly with suppliers.

In addition to satisfying the completeness objective, investigation of debit balances will provide some or all of the required assurance in relation to the specific accuracy, existence, cut-off and valuation objectives.

9:24.2.4 Bills payable

The auditor should enquire whether the client settles any liabilities by using bills of exchange. If so, a list of the bills payable as at the balance sheet date should be obtained and tested for completeness by reference to correspondence, the bills register and bank confirmations. It is also important to carry out the following procedures:

(a) Check that any material bills of exchange maturing after the year-end were met on their due dates.

(b) Inspect the cancelled bills.

(c) Test the additions of the list.

If the substitution of bills for trade debts is a change in the client's business practice, this may indicate that the client is having difficulty in meeting its debts as they fall due. The auditor should, therefore, enquire into the circumstances behind the change. Similarly, if the bills have been renewed or renegotiated since the balance sheet date, the reasons should be ascertained. If there is any indication that the client is in financial difficulties, the auditor should inform the engagement manager.

In addition to satisfying the completeness objective, the examination of bills payable will provide some assurance in relation to the accuracy, existence, cut-off and rights and obligations objectives.

9:24.3 Accuracy

Much of the required assurance concerning the specific accuracy objectives will normally be obtained from work carried out on the other objectives. For example, work on suppliers' statements to verify the completeness of trade creditors (discussed in **Sections 9:24.2.1** to **9:24.2.4**) will provide secondary assurance that the creditors have been accurately recorded.

The auditor should, however, carry out the following procedures:

(a) Test the control account reconciliation.

(b) Where appropriate, test the accuracy of the accruals listing.

(c) Perform tests of any inter-company balances.

(d) Check any foreign exchange translations.

(e) Check that the amounts reported in the financial statements agree with the accounting records.

9:24.3.1 Control account reconciliation

The auditor should test the reconciliation between the amount recorded in the general ledger trade creditors control account and the listing of individual accounts in the subsidiary creditors ledger. To do this, it is necessary to carry out the following procedures:

(a) Trace amounts on the listing to individual accounts.

(b) Test the additions of the reconciliation and of the listing.

(c) Investigate contra-adjustments and unusual items in the reconciliation.

(d) Review the subsequent clearance of reconciling items.

If this work is done as part of early substantive testing, the auditor may need to carry out the following further procedures:

(a) Examine the control account for the period between the substantive testing date and the balance sheet date to confirm that no recurring entries have been omitted, and to identify any unusual items.

(b) Review the reconciliation at the balance sheet date and investigate any unusual reconciling items.

(c) Test the additions of the control account.

(d) Test significant postings in the control account from the records of prime entry.

(e) Test the additions in the records of prime entry.

(f) Test the additions of the subsidiary creditors ledger balances.

The choice and extent of these procedures will depend on the assessment of the risk of material misstatement in the intervening period and they should be specified in the strategy or STP, if prepared, for trade creditors.

9:24.3.1.1 Problems with reconciliations

If the client is unable to reconcile the control account with the total of the individual underlying balances, or has difficulty in doing so, the auditor should consider whether the records are reliable. The auditor should bring to the attention of the engagement manager failure by the client to reconcile the control account, or significant and repeated delays in doing so. The engagement manager should decide whether the matter should be reported in issues documentation.

9:24.3.2 Accruals listing

Where there is a separate trade creditors accruals listing which is not systems derived and which has no control account in the general ledger the auditor should test the additions of the listing and agree the total to the trial balance.

9:24.3.3 Amounts owed to group companies

The principal audit procedure on amounts owed to group companies is intended to ensure that the inter-company balances have been properly agreed by the client. It is important that such amounts are properly reconciled, and the auditor should consider obtaining written confirmation of the balances from the local auditors.

The auditor should review the reconciliations and test the reconciling items, particularly when there are transactions in foreign currencies or where there is a history of error, because of the risk that differences caused by errors or disputed items might be written off by the client without investigation (e.g., by classifying them as 'differences on exchange').

These procedures will provide assurance in relation to the completeness and existence of amounts owed to group companies as well as the accuracy of those amounts.

9:24.3.4 Foreign exchange

If the client has transactions with overseas suppliers, the auditor should carrying out the following procedures:

(a)   Determine whether the transactions are payable in sterling or in another currency.

(b)   Enquire whether the client has procedures to ensure that liabilities denominated in foreign currencies are accurately translated into sterling.

(c)   Test the translations.

9:24.3.5 Agreement with accounting records

The auditor should check the amount for trade creditors reported in the financial statements against the reconciled control account in the general ledger. This should normally be done by agreeing the figures via the trial balance.

9:24.4 Existence

9:24.4.1 Sources of assurance

The auditor will often obtain much of the required assurance relating to the existence objective from the work carried out on other objectives and other audit areas. For example, inspection and reconciliation of suppliers' statements to confirm the completeness of trade creditors (discussed in **Sections 9:24.2.1** to **9:24.2.4**) will provide assurance in respect of the existence objective, as will the corollary effect of work in respect of the existence objectives for purchases.

If the strategy, or STP if prepared, requires specific additional testing in relation to the existence of trade creditors, the auditor should normally select recorded balances from the trade creditors listing (or items from a separate accruals listing), as discussed in **Section 9:24.4.2**. Such work will also provide assurance concerning the accuracy and the rights and obligations objectives.

9:24.4.2 Specific tests

The auditor should select a number of creditor balances and, for those items not settled at the substantive testing date, examine the invoices or other supporting documentation and ensure that the balance is made up of specific and recent invoices subject to approval in accordance with the client's procedures. In respect of the balances selected the auditor should enquire into any unusual items, and should also consider enquiring into any unusual delays in discharging liabilities.

Where there is a separate accruals listing the auditor should review the listing and obtain explanations for long outstanding items. A number of items on the list should also be selected, and the originating documentation should be examined. This will normally consist of goods received notes supported by subsequent purchase invoices or, if the items remain uninvoiced, available price lists, recent invoices for the same goods or other supporting documentation.

9:24.5 Cut-off

Clients frequently receive significant amounts of goods which will not have been processed through the trade creditors ledger at the date the auditor carries out tests. Because incorrect cut-off can directly affect the profit, it is necessary to obtain evidence that cut-off procedures have been applied effectively. Such procedures should ensure that payments, purchases and returns to suppliers made up to the substantive testing date are reflected in the financial statements for the period. In conjunction with stocks cut-off, the trade creditors cut-off procedures are also intended to ensure that the liability for all such items included in stocks is included in the financial statements.

Although both aspects are important, it is important to remember that failure to **match** transactions properly in the financial statements (e.g., including stock but omitting the liability for its purchase) is likely to have a greater effect on the financial statements than the recording of all aspects of a few transactions in the wrong accounting period (e.g., omitting stocks in transit together with the corresponding liability). Because of their close relationship, the auditor should normally combine substantive tests for trade creditors cut-off with those for the 'inwards' cut-off of stocks. Although the nature and extent of cut-off testing will depend on the assessment of the risk of misstatement, the greatest emphasis should normally be placed on high-value items and on items closer to the cut-off date.

9:24.5.1 Tests of details

The auditor should normally carry out the following procedures:

(a)   Test the sequence of goods received records, and select items immediately before the creditors substantive testing date to check that the stock and the related liability were both recorded in the correct period. The liability may be recorded either in the individual suppliers' accounts or, if the invoice has not been received, on a trade creditors accruals listing.

(b)   Select amounts debited to the creditors control account immediately before the creditors substantive testing date and check their validity by inspecting evidence of payments, purchase returns and other significant entries. If the level of purchase returns is abnormally high the auditor should consider whether the client may be 'window dressing' by returning excessive stocks rather than genuinely faulty or damaged goods.

(c)   Select entries from the purchases records in the last few days of the period, check goods received notes to ensure that the goods were delivered in the period, and ensure that the liability has been taken up as in (a) above.

(d)   Select from debit entries in the stock accounts after the substantive testing date and check that, if the item related to goods received **before** the substantive testing date, they were included in stocks and creditors.

(e)   Select payments after the substantive testing date and, if payments are related to liabilities at the substantive testing date, check that the liabilities were properly recorded at that date.

(f)   Review invoices received but not processed for evidence of unrecorded liabilities. Where applicable the auditor should select items from the purchase invoice register (or equivalent record).

(g)   Select items from goods received records after the substantive testing date to check that the liability has been recorded in the correct period.

(h)   Review credit notes from suppliers dated after the substantive testing date to check that they were accounted for in the correct period.

9:24.6 Valuation

9:24.6.1 Debit balances

The auditor will obtain the required assurance regarding the recoverability of any debit balances on suppliers' accounts from the work discussed in **Section 9:24.2.3** (second paragraph).

9:24.6.2 Purchase commitments

If material losses could arise from unfulfilled purchase commitments, the auditor might identify such commitments by some or all of the following procedures:

(a) Examination, where possible, of open purchase order records.

(b) Enquiry of employees who make purchase commitments.

(c) Requests to selected major suppliers (with the client's prior agreement) to provide details of any purchase commitments outstanding as at the balance sheet date.

(d) In respect of dealing transactions, enquiry into and examination of the following aspects:

>   (i) The extent to which purchase and sale contracts are matched in amount and timing.

>   (ii) Changes in the market price after the substantive testing date, and the difference between spot and forward prices.

>   (iii) Changes in currency exchange rates, where relevant.

If uncertain whether all commitments have been identified, the auditor should review suppliers' invoices for a period after the balance sheet date for evidence of:

(a) purchases above prevailing prices;

(b) quantities purchased in excess of current requirements; or

(c) goods that are slow moving or obsolete.

Any of these conditions might indicate onerous purchase commitments outstanding at the balance sheet date.

9:24.7 Rights and obligations

The auditor will normally obtain sufficient evidence in relation to the rights and obligations objective from work carried out in relation to the completeness and existence objectives. However, if the strategy or STP, if prepared, for trade creditors requires specific additional procedures, these should normally involve examining, or extending the examination of, supporting documentation as discussed in **Section 9:24.4.2**.

9:24.8 Presentation and disclosure

The auditor will normally achieve the presentation and disclosure objective at the end of the audit by reviewing the financial statements and considering the matters set out in a UK GAAP checklist. Also, it is important to be alert for any matters that require disclosure or reclassification and which may more efficiently be identified during fieldwork. These include:

(a) **Reservation of title**: When creditors which supply goods under reservation of title are identified, the auditor should consider whether the amounts are material at the balance sheet date. It may be necessary to investigate the validity of the reservation of title and to request disclosure of the amounts involved. However, the auditor should first bring the matter to the attention of the engagement manager or the engagement partner.

(b) Any part of a creditor balance which is not payable within 12 months from the balance sheet date.

(c) Amounts due to group and related companies.

(d) Net amounts which should be disclosed gross.

(e) Creditors for capital purchases (which should be classified as 'other' creditors and not trade creditors).

(f) Bills of exchange payable.

(g) Payment periods for creditors.

9:25 Taxation

9:25.1 Introduction

This section is designed to help to develop a programme of substantive tests in accordance with the testing plan for taxation. This should specify the planned response to the assessment of the risk of material misstatement, including the nature, extent and timing of substantive tests.

This section should be read in conjunction with the general guidance on substantive testing in the following sections:

- **Section 9:3**, 'Analytical procedures'
- **Section 9:4**, 'Tests of details'
- **Section 9:5**, 'Evaluating the results of substantive testing'

This section covers all types of taxation in the financial statements, with the exception of Value Added Tax (VAT), PAYE and Customs & Excise duties. The section applies to UK resident companies. If the client is resident outside the UK, the auditor should consult a tax specialist.

The relevant accounting standards which should be complied with are FRS 16 *Current tax* (which replaced SSAP8) and SSAP 15 *Accounting for deferred tax.*

9:25.1.1 *Essential audit objectives*

The application of the seven audit objectives to the audit of taxation results in the specific objectives listed below. The auditor should obtain sufficient evidence to be satisfied that:

(a)   contentious matters are identified and their treatment is considered by a tax specialist (**all objectives**);

(b)   the tax figures are generated from reliable accounting records (**accuracy**);

(c)   the amounts reported in the financial statements are in agreement with the accounting records (**accuracy**);

(d)   the charge and provision for current corporation tax have been properly computed and accounted for (**all objectives**);

(e)   withholding tax and tax credits have been accounted for correctly (**all objectives**);

(f)   the total potential deferred tax has been correctly computed and provided in the financial statements to the extent that it is probable a liability will crystallise (**all objectives**);

(g)   tax charges and provisions are properly classified, described and disclosed in the financial statements (**presentation and disclosure**).

9:25.2 Consideration of contentious matters

The possible existence of contentious matters should normally be identified during the business review, by enquiry of management and by reviewing correspondence with the Inspector of Taxes. Such matters, which should immediately be discussed with a tax specialist, include:

(a)   The commencement of a new trade, the expansion or alteration of the existing trade or the proposed cessation or transfer of part of the trade. The auditor should remember that the definition of a new trade for tax purposes may be wider than that used for the financial statements.

(b)   Any significant changes in accounting policy.

(c)   Any transactions which appear to be artificial, or part of a scheme which might be interpreted as a tax reduction or avoidance device.

(d)   The sale and leaseback of an asset.

(e)   Any area in which it is known that the Inspector of Taxes is in dispute with the client, particularly for prior years where time limits may be due to expire.

(f)   The tax status of the client, where it is covered by specific provisions (e.g., close companies, unit trusts and investment companies).

(g)   A proposed change of year-end.

9:25.2.1 *Management representations*

If the treatment of taxation in the financial statements is significantly dependent on the intentions of management, the auditor should consider whether to obtain written representations as to those intentions. Such matters are:

(a) Proposed group relief arrangements.

(b) For groups with overseas subsidiaries, the policy regarding distribution or repatriation of overseas profits.

(c) Whether losses are to be carried back to relieve past profits from tax, or forward to relieve future profits.

(d) Investment intentions and budgets supporting decisions on any deferred tax provision.

Guidance on representations from management is given in **Section 10:4**, 'Representations from management'. In particular we should ensure that:

(a)   Where deferred tax has been calculated on the partial provision basis and the liability method approach, the assumptions upon which the provision is based are included in the letter of representation; and

(b)   with reference to the representations *aide-mémoire* any other matters noted during the audit of taxation which require specific mention in the letter of representation are identified and the proposed paragraphs for inclusion in the letter drafted.

9:25.3 Reliable accounting records

Before it is possible to conclude on the accuracy of the tax figures, it is necessary to assess the reliability of the information produced. The matters that the auditor should consider include:

(a)   The expertise (including knowledge of recent developments) of the client's staff responsible for preparing either the necessary information for the computations or the computations themselves.

(b)   The reliability of the procedures for classifying expenditure between revenue and capital.

(c)   The reliability of the procedures for analysing expenditure between allowable or disallowable amounts.

(d)   The procedures for making returns, for corresponding with the Inspector of Taxes and for agreeing computations and liabilities.

(e)   The procedures for identifying matters which should be the subject of a claim for tax purposes, and the timely submission of these claims.

(f)   Adjustments to previous years' provisions which indicate unreliable procedures.

(g)   The reliability of procedures for identifying other relevant information.

9:25.3.1 Groups

If the client is a member of a group for tax purposes there will normally be significant scope for tax planning, as well as an increased risk that individual subsidiaries' claims may be overlooked. The auditors of the holding company should assess the effectiveness of the group's procedures for reporting tax information, including the calculation and submission of group relief.

9:25.3.2 Agreement with accounting records

Taxation provisions or charges are normally made after the trial balance has been produced and are consequently a 'late' adjustment. The auditor should check that any such adjustments are subsequently made in the accounting records.

9:25.4 Taxation schedules

The auditor should obtain from the client, or prepare, a lead schedule for the taxation section of the audit file that reconciles the opening and closing balances and shows in detail debits and credits for each corporation tax and other account. The analysis should be by each tax year, showing the amount of the brought forward balance, movement for the year and carried forward balance that the attributable to prior years.

The auditor should obtain or prepare a statement in columnar form reconciling the balance sheet figures of the current year with those at the previous balance sheet date and showing in detail the debits or credits in the current year's financial statements for the following:

(a)   Payments of and charges for mainstream and advance corporation tax in the period, including payments and receipts for group relief.

(b)   Other United Kingdom taxes relating to:

    (i)   dividends paid and received

    (ii)   other payments and receipts.

(c)   Any other relevant UK taxes.

(d)   Foreign taxes on income and related UK tax relief.

(e)   Deferred tax.

The auditor should identify on the statement any over on under-provision on tax provisions made in the previous year(s).

Working on the statement obtained in the paragraph above the auditor should:

(a) Agree the opening figures on the statement to the previous year's financial statements and working papers.

(b) Investigate balances outstanding from previous years to confirm their continued validity and accuracy, and inquire into the progress made in the agreement of computations. The auditor should bring any material areas of dispute or serious lack of progress to the attention of the engagement and tax managers and check any prior year adjustments.

(c) Obtain an analysis of any recoverable advance corporation tax (ACT) carried forward under the shadow ACT system.

(d) Check transactions arising on the tax accounts during the year to the cash book or equivalent.

(e) Check the additions of the statement.

(f) Agree the balances on the statement to the relevant figures in the general ledger.

(g) Ensure that the financial statement properly reflect the charge for taxation and taxation balances.

(h) Agree taxation figures on the lead schedule to the financial statements, including comparative figures.

(i) Ensure that the comparative figures agree with the financial statements of the previous period.

9:25.5 Use of software packages

For efficiency reasons, where the auditor prepares and submits computations on the client's behalf, the schedules in support of the provision should normally be prepared by tax staff using an appropriate taxation software package at the client's premises. In certain instances audit staff who have been properly trained in its use and have current experience of corporation tax can use the software during the audit. Use of such software will not however be cost-efficient in some simple situations, and the tax managers or partner should assess this. Where accounting practice staff do the work the computation should be reviewed by a manager from the tax practice.

9:25.6 Current corporation tax

It is important to remember that the estimates made for audit purposes may be used as the basis for the preparation of submissions to the Inland Revenue. Accordingly, there may be an increase in risk to the auditor and to the firm, because failures in audit work might lead to penalties being charged or reliefs being lost. This risk is in addition to the risks of misstatement that arise from the complexity of the computations.

Consequently, audit work should involve the review and testing of the tax accounts and the underlying computations, as well as the use of tax specialists to review the audit work and to discuss any contentious issues.

To prepare or check a tax computation the auditor should obtain the following:

(a) A detailed profit and loss account, balance sheet, notes, directors' report and chairman's statement.

(b) Analyses of accounts in which there may be an element of disallowable expenditure and other relevant accounts, e.g. commission and rents.

(c) Analyses of income accounts which might include non-trading receipts.

(d) Details of movements on: asset accounts which qualify for capital allowances; reserves; provisions; debtors; creditors; and other balance sheet items.

The auditor should inspect correspondence with the Inspector of Taxes agreeing such computations as have been agreed, and file copes of important letters (normally those dealing with the most recently agreed tax assessment) on the audit file.

9:25.6.1 *Nature of audit work*

The auditor should carry out the following work:

(a) Unless the firm prepares the analyses referred to in the preceding paragraph, the auditor should test that they have been properly prepared and that they include all late adjustments to the trial balance. This should be done by reviewing the method of preparation and carrying out tests of details on selected items.

(b) Review copies of the tax computations and calculations of deferred tax provision;

  (i)   scrutinise for points of principle; and

  (ii) check significant figures from their sources.

(c) Ensure that the provisions already made in respect of prior year computations not yet agreed appear to be reasonable.

(d) Check that items treated differently for tax purposes and financial statements purposes are correctly treated. Examples include depreciation, profits and losses on the disposal of fixed assets, general provisions and interest accruals.

(e) Check that items disallowable for tax purposes are added back to the profit.

(f) Check that capital allowances have been claimed only on eligible assets. Any repairs should be identified and deducted as expenses.

(g) Check that all remuneration has been paid within nine months of the year-end.

(h) Check that non-trading income has been identified and treated as taxed under the appropriate schedule or case. Such items may include interest received, foreign income, rent received and royalties receivable. The auditor should also check that franked and un-franked investment income is properly treated in the computation.

(i) Ensure that charges on income are identified and treated correctly. Such charges will normally be paid gross to UK companies (provided the necessary election has been made) and often to foreign companies, but otherwise they should be paid net of tax. The auditor should also check that charitable gifts, whether or not under gift aid, have been properly treated.

(j) Check that any chargeable gains have been brought into the computation, and that available capital losses brought forward have been utilised.

(k) Ensure that all reliefs to be claimed are valid and that the correct amount is recorded in the computation (e.g., that losses brought forward are offset against profits from the same continuing trade).

(l) Check the arithmetical accuracy of the computation, unless a reliable taxation software package has been used to prepare it.

(m) Check that appropriate adjustments to interest income have been made.

(n) Agree the figures which have been used/input to the relevant figures in the audit file to ensure that the amounts are in agreement with the accounting records and have been subject to audit (i.e. be satisfied that movements, including prior year adjustments, are valid and properly presented and disclosed).

Work on other audit areas may help to identify items relating to (b), (c) and (d) above (e.g., **Section 9:16**, 'Tangible fixed assets', refers to matters that might be considered).

Additionally, where another firm of accountants is responsible for the tax work, the auditor should obtain a letter from the other firm stating the amount to be set aside for tax (including information on deferred tax) and how it is made up.

9:25.6.2 Calculation of the tax charge

The auditor should check that the tax charge has been calculated on the basis of the appropriate tax rates, taking into account, where appropriate, small companies' rates. It is important to remember that the small companies rate does not apply if the client is a close investment holding company. Also, if the client has any associated (for tax purposes) companies, the small companies benefit will be apportioned. The auditor should ensure that taxable income for all relevant schedules and cases has been included and that any double taxation relief (DTR) has been properly applied. A tax specialist should normally be consulted on all matters relating to DTR.

9:25.6.3 Calculation of the tax liability

The calculation of the tax liability should be checked by re-computation. The auditor should also check other deductions such as income tax suffered on unfranked investment income or on building society interest, and the validity of any group relief claims.

9:25.6.4 Tax reconciliation

The auditor should ask the client to prepare (or the auditor should prepare) a tax reconciliation which analyses any difference between the 'normal' tax charge (at the ordinary rate on the pre-tax profit per the financial statements) and the actual charge. The reconciling items will normally include timing differences not provided as deferred tax, disallowable expenditure, non-taxable income and adjustments to prior years' provisions (also shown in the tax account).

The auditor should check the arithmetical accuracy of the reconciliation and trace the reconciling amounts to the tax working papers.

9:25.6.5 *Testing the tax account*

The validity of each entry in the tax account during the year should normally be checked, and the additions of the account should be tested. The auditor should also normally obtain or prepare a tax account in a standard format.

The auditor should review the correspondence with the Inspector of Taxes. Matters that should be considered include:

(a) **The agreement of any computations**, to identify over- and under-provisions for tax in earlier periods. The auditor should check that these are correctly accounted for, and should also review the computations, and check that any losses or other balances have been correctly brought forward.

(b) **Computations not yet agreed**, especially those where there has been no movement in the provisions. The auditor should discuss the status of such computations with management or their tax advisers. If there is a significant amount in dispute, it is necessary to consider whether the client would be liable for interest on any liability that is finally agreed.

9:25.6.5.1 *Debit entries to the tax account*

Debit entries to the tax account should be checked as follows:

(a) **Payments to the Collector of Taxes**: The auditor should check the payment by inspection of assessment notices, correspondence with the tax authorities agreeing assessments and receipts where available. If the payment is for an agreed computation, the treatment of any consequent adjustments for under- or over-provisions should be checked. If the payment is in respect of an estimated assessment, the auditor should check whether it is materially different from the client's estimate of the probable liability. It is also necessary to check that the correct amount has been paid on the due date to ensure that no penalty for late payment is payable. If interest has been charged for late payment of tax, the auditor should verify the period of charge and check the calculations. The payment should be checked with the relevant correspondence or assessment, including any payments of foreign tax.

(b) **Previous years' over-provisions written back**: The auditor should check the calculation of the adjustment, either by inspecting the correspondence with the Inspector of Taxes or by testing the client's revised provision. In the latter case, explanations should be obtained for the earlier over-provision as these may provide evidence of a history of error in the tax computation.

(c) **Tax recoverable**: This will normally arise from losses in the current year that can be carried back to reclaim tax paid for a previous period. The auditor should check that the losses are eligible for carry-back and that the client has actually paid tax for the preceding period.

(d) **Entries arising from losses surrendered by other group companies**: These will arise when the client's liability for tax is reduced or extinguished by losses surrendered by another group company. The auditor should:

  (i)   check that the surrendering company is eligible to surrender the losses;

  (ii) check that Inland Revenue agreement has been obtained;

  (iii) request confirmation from its directors that they intend to surrender the losses; and

  (iv) check the payment or the credit to the inter-company account (if the losses are to be paid for).

9:25.6.5.2 Credit entries to the tax account

The auditor should identify the possible sources of credit entries to the tax account and check that all relevant items are correctly accounted for. These include:

  (a) **The liability arising from the charge for the year**: This should be checked with the tax computation.

  (b) **Previous years' under-provisions**: These should be checked in the same way as previous years' over provisions written back (described in **Section 9:25.6.5.1**).

  (c) **Payments from the Inland Revenue for tax recoverable**: The auditor should check the amounts with the correspondence. It is also important to consider whether the client should have received an interest supplement on the repayment, and check the amount of any supplement received.

  (d) **Entries arising from losses surrendered to other group companies**: The auditor should confirm that the losses may properly be transferred to the other companies. It may be considered necessary to ask the directors to confirm in writing that they intend to surrender the losses. The surrender notices for earlier periods should be checked.

9:25.7 Advance corporation tax and income tax

9:25.7.1 ACT

In April 1999, the system whereby companies were required to pay ACT on dividends paid during the year was abolished. There are transitional arrangements (outlined in FRS 16) whereby companies can carry forward recoverable ACT which can be set off against a future corporation tax liability. This is known as the shadow ACT scheme. There are restrictions on the use of ACT for set-off, and the auditor should ensure that any ACT carried forward is recoverable. If ACT that was previously regarded as recoverable becomes irrecoverable, it should be charged in the profit and loss account as a separately disclosed component of the tax charge.

9:25.7.2 Income tax

The auditor should identify income that is received under deduction of income tax and check that the income has not been grossed up for presentation and disclosure in the financial statements, but is included net of any attributable tax credit. (This is a reversal of the treatment under SSAP 8, which required dividends to be recognised at an amount that included the attributable tax credit). Income shown should include any withholding taxes.

If a company makes payments under deduction of tax the auditor should check that tax has been deducted for all appropriate payments and reported in the CT61.

If a risk of fraud has been identified in respect of payments, it is necessary to inspect paid cheques to verify that all income tax has been paid over. At the year-end the auditor should check that the last period's net income tax has, as appropriate, been deducted from or added to the tax payable.

9:25.8 Deferred tax

There are two stages in checking deferred tax. It is necessary first to check whether the client has correctly calculated the total potential liability to deferred tax for all timing differences. The auditor should then obtain evidence that the client has correctly calculated and provided for those deferred tax liabilities that are likely to crystallise.

9:25.8.1 Potential deferred tax

9:25.8.1.1 Accelerated capital allowances

The auditor should check whether the potential liability arising from accelerated capital allowances is the excess of the book written-down value over the tax written-down value for assets qualifying for capital allowances, charged at the appropriate rate of tax (discussed further in **Section 9:25.6.4**). To do this it is necessary to test the analysis of fixed assets into those that qualify for capital allowances and those that do not. The analysis of the depreciation charge between the two categories should also be tested.

Because the potential deferred tax is calculated by reference to the written down values referred to in the preceding paragraph, the accuracy of that calculation should be checked by reconciling the movements on potential deferred tax in the year. This should be done by calculating the opening potential deferred tax and proving the closing balance by adjusting the former amount by such items as capital allowances, balancing charges, depreciation and profits and losses on disposals.

9:25.8.1.2 Effect of government grants

Certain grants, such as Regional Development Grants, are not taxable and capital allowances are available on the full original cost of the asset. Consequently, if a client deducts the grant from the cost of the asset, the amount eligible for capital allowances will exceed the net cost recorded in the books. In such cases the auditor should check that the potential deferred tax is calculated after adding back the unamortised element of the grant.

9:25.8.1.3 Potential capital gains

Potential deferred tax liabilities may also arise when:

(a)   fixed assets (normally land and buildings) are re-valued above their cost for tax purposes;

(b)   the client holds an asset whose cost is reduced by, e.g., the 'roll-over' of a gain on a previous sale.

The auditor should check the calculation of such potential liabilities by computing the gain in accordance with the provisions of the Taxes Acts.

9:25.8.1.4 Other short-term timing differences

Other short-term timing differences include interest receivable and payable, general bad debt provisions, finance leases and pension fund accruals. The auditor should check that the potential deferred tax liability has been calculated by applying the appropriate tax rate to the closing balances of the relevant accounts.

9:25.8.2 Deductions from potential deferred tax liabilities

Two deductions are permitted from the total potential deferred tax liabilities:

(a)   The tax benefit of unrelieved losses.

(b)   Recoverable ACT.

9:25.8.2.1 Losses

The auditor should check that any losses offset against potential deferred tax liabilities are eligible for offset. For example, any trading losses utilised must arise from the same trade as the potential liability and they cannot be offset against a potential capital gain. Similarly, capital losses must only be offset against deferred tax on capital gains. It is also important to check that the amount of these losses is correct.

9:25.8.2.2 ACT

ACT carried forward under the shadow ACT scheme (*see* **Section 9:25.7.1**) should be offset against a credit balance on the deferred tax account only if, in the period in which the underlying timing differences are expected to reverse, the reversal will create sufficient taxable profits to enable ACT to be recovered.

9:25.8.3 *Provisions for deferred tax liabilities*

To obtain assurance that the client has correctly calculated and provided for deferred tax liabilities that are likely to crystallise, the auditor should examine each type of timing difference separately and consider whether it is probable that the liability will crystallise.

The auditor should review plans or projections that the client has made covering a period of years sufficient to enable an assessment to be made of the likely pattern of future tax liabilities.

9:25.8.3.1 *Accelerated capital allowances*

The auditor should examine the client's forecasts of capital expenditure and expected future capital allowances for at least three years, and longer if they are available. It is important to check that all such forecasts have been approved by the directors. Where possible, this work should be co-ordinated with the 'going concern' review (described in **Section 9:8**, 'Considerations in respect of going concern'). If the client does not provide forecasts, the audit staff should discuss this with the engagement manager or the engagement partner.

When reviewing the forecasts, the auditor should consider whether:

(a)   the forecasts are based on reasonable assumptions;

(b)   the assumptions are consistent with the auditor's knowledge of the business and with other information and forecasts available within the client;

(c)   the forecasts are arithmetically accurate, and amounts such as future depreciation charges that can be predicted with reasonable certainty have been calculated accurately;

(d)   the client has adequate cash resources to support the forecast capital expenditure (if this is in doubt, the auditor should examine any cash flow forecasts produced);

(e)   the forecast is reasonable in relation to the information upon which it is based and to the reliability of previous forecasts;

(f)   the forecast is consistent with the client's known intentions for expansion, contraction and diversification, taking into account the economic situation and the client's trading position;

(g)   the client has any intention to lease assets rather than purchase them.

9:25.8.3.2 *Capital gains*

To determine whether any liability will crystallise, the auditor should review appropriate correspondence, plans and minutes to identify the following:

(a)   The likelihood of sales of assets being carried at a valuation for which no provision for deferred tax on the potential gain has been provided.

(b)   Whether the client intends to sell an asset whose cost is reduced by the roll-over of a gain on a previous sale or for any other reason.

(c)   Whether, where gains have been held over into depreciating assets, the gains will crystallise on the tenth anniversary of the hold-over occurring during the year.

(d)   Plans for further investment which will qualify for relief.

9:25.8.3.3 *Other short-term timing differences*

The auditor should check that deferred tax has been provided on short-term timing differences only to the extent that they will reverse without replacement.

9:25.8.4 *Applicable tax rates*

Deferred tax should be provided at the rates expected to be in force in the periods in which the timing differences are forecast to reverse. Potential deferred tax should be calculated at the best estimate of the rate likely to be in force after those periods.

9:25.9 Presentation and disclosure

To help achieve the presentation and disclosure objective the auditor should, at the end of the audit, review the financial statements and consider the matters set out in a UK GAAP checklist. Also, it is important to be alert for any matters that require disclosure and which can be more efficiently identified during fieldwork.

9:25.10 Appendix A Checklist of information required for tax purposes

Information required for the preparation of and review of the tax computation will be obtained when carrying out the audit steps on the various items in the financial statements. Give the working paper references where the information is applicable.

Account balance/ class of transactions	Information
Debentures and long term loans	Interest accrued at the beginning and end of the period, and amounts charged and paid during the period.

| Accrual, provisions for liabilities and charges and other creditors | Accrued interest. Details (including nature, basis of calculation and movements during the period) of sums included in creditors for known liabilities (including reserves and general provisions). Unpaid pension contributions. |

Tangible fixed assets — Record of additions and disposals giving sufficient information to enable capital allowances to be computed. In this connection the following information will normally

(a) Additions and disposals should be analysed between and, buildings and plant for capital allowances purposes and reconciled to the figures in the tangible fixed asset analysis shown in the financial statements.

(b) Plant included in the cost of buildings should be identified (including expenditure in compliance with fire safety certificates).

(c) The following categories of buildings should be separately identified:

    (i) buildings ranking for industrial buildings allowances (giving date and amount of expenditure originally incurred if the building is not new)

    (ii) agricultural buildings;

    (iii) scientific research expenditure; and

    (iv) hotel buildings (after 11 April 1978).

(d) Additions to motor vehicles should be analysed between

    (i) commercial vehicles and hire car; and

    (ii) other vehicles.

(e) Purchases and sales between companies under common control should be separately identified.

Intangible fixed assets — Details of any asset disposed of where the net sales proceeds exceed cost.

Details of patents and 'know how' acquired during the year.

Investments — Is a rebasing election in place?

Details of investments sold during this year, including date of purchase, date of sale, cost, proceeds of sale, value at 31 March 1982 and where no rebasing election is made in respect of investments acquired before 6 April 1965, valuation for capital gains tax purposes at that date.

Stocks	Details of any round sum or percentage deductions from stock values which are not allocated to specific items, together with any information which may indicate that the deductions are allowable for tax purposes.
	Details of any change in the basis of valuation of stocks.
	The basis on which profits and losses on long-term contracts are included in the financial statements.
	Details of progress payment received.
Trade debtors	Analysis of provisions between general and specific amounts.
Other debtors	Details of amounts which are allowable for tax purposes although not yet charged in the profit and loss account (e.g. interest prepayments).

Profit and loss account

Account balance/ class of transactions	Information

- income other than trading income (e.g. dividends, group income, interest) showing any tax credit and tax deducted at source
- repairs in excess of a specified sum
- subscriptions and donations
- expenditure on entertaining and gifts
- interest on overdue tax and VAT penalties
- royalties, loan interest and other changes on income (e.g. covenanted donations to charities)
- professional charges
- expenses relating to let properties
- exceptional and extraordinary items
- any repayment supplement received
- miscellaneous expenses in excess of a specified sum
- directors' remuneration
- profits and losses on disposals of tangible fixed assets
- hire charges for leased cars by individual car, with details of cars' original market values

9:26 Value added tax

9:26.1 Introduction

This section discusses the audit of Value Added Tax (VAT) and contains guidance designed to assist in developing a programme of substantive tests for VAT. In many cases, this work will often be performed in conjunction with audit work on other areas including purchases, sales, fixed assets, investments and stocks.

VAT is charged on goods and services *supplied* in the UK. It is important to note that VAT may be due on *events* that are not recorded in the financial records of a business. Examples include stock loans and swaps and a change in the use to which a building is put. From 1 January 1993, special rules applied to goods acquired (whether by purchase or otherwise) from a business, including a branch, established elsewhere in the European Union. Similarly, special rules were introduced for goods despatched to such businesses from the UK.

9:26.1.1 Basic knowledge

This section assumes a basic knowledge of VAT. However, the audit of VAT includes certain matters that may require specialist knowledge. The members of the audit team are not expected to know the detailed rules concerning, e.g., special partial exemption methods. They should, however, know the basic principles of VAT, and be able to appreciate the possible problems which may arise. To assist staff in this, an *aide-mémoire* could usefully be designed to help in the identification of situations in which specialist knowledge is likely to be necessary for the audit, or may be of assistance to the client.

9:26.1.2 Essential audit objectives

The application of the seven audit objectives to the audit of VAT results in the specific objectives listed below. The auditor should obtain sufficient evidence to be satisfied that:

(a)   the existence of any risks of misstatement arising from the client's method of accounting for VAT is ascertained (**all objectives**);

(b)   contentious matters are identified and their treatment is considered by a VAT specialist (**all objectives**);

(c)   registration has been effected where required (**all objectives**);

(d)   VAT on all sales, purchases and expenses is properly accounted for (**completeness, accuracy, existence, cut-off**);

(e)   VAT payable or receivable at the balance sheet date is properly recorded and represents the total payable or total receivable for VAT (**completeness, accuracy, existence, cut-off, rights and obligations**);

(f)   the amounts reported in the financial statements are in agreement with the accounting records (**accuracy**);

(g) VAT is properly classified, described and disclosed in the financial statements (**presentation and disclosure**).

This section deals with UK VAT. However, similar VAT rules apply in other EU member states. In addition, other states throughout the world have introduced VAT systems of their own. Where appropriate the steps outlined in this section should be modified and applied to the audit of international transactions (e.g., foreign branches or mail order sales).

9:26.1.3 General

Most clients are affected by VAT. It is a complex and changing tax. The consequences of departures from VAT regulations in terms of additional tax liabilities and penalties can be severe. Also the auditor may often identify areas for improvement and cost savings (including cash flow savings) in the way that clients deal with VAT.

   The audit of VAT is unusual for the following reasons:

(a) The VAT on the total value of transactions in an accounting period is likely to be material even though the amount outstanding at the balance sheet date might be immaterial.

(b) Because VAT incurred is often fully recoverable and VAT on outputs will be charged to customers, it might appear that there is no VAT cost to a business and therefore little VAT risk. This conclusion is, however, only true where there has been proper compliance with the rules. For example, input tax can only be reclaimed by a taxpayer in possession of adequate evidence of entitlement.

(c) VAT due to or from Customs & Excise is calculated by the taxpayer and is the subject of only irregular checks by Customs & Excise. A client error in interpretation or application of VAT law (particularly in relation to an unusual or 'one-off' transaction) may, therefore, go undetected for long enough for the cumulative effect to be sufficiently material for management to expect the auditor to have identified it. It is important to remember that Customs & Excise can levy assessments for tax and penalties retrospectively for up to six years (or more in some cases) and that the assessment may be estimated.

(d) Although each transaction will have VAT implications, the actual liability to VAT is determined in total. The auditor should therefore consider, when examining transactions, not only the VAT implications of the transaction being examined but also how it impacts on the overall liability calculation.

(e) The transactions that need to be recognised for VAT purposes may differ, both in nature and in timing, from those required to be recognised for financial accounting and other tax purposes. For example, VAT may be due on the cash received from a customer where this event precedes the issue of an invoice.

9:26.1.4 Planning considerations

Because VAT is a tax on transactions and, in some cases, events, it is useful to consider at the planning stage the extent to which the work should be carried out in conjunction with work on other areas. For example, tests of output tax on sales may be best carried out at the same time as tests on turnover. **Section 9:30**, 'Turnover and other income', therefore includes audit steps in relation to the VAT on sales. Similarly, VAT should also be considered when auditing purchases and expenses, fixed assets, stock, debtors and creditors.

As in other audit areas, the nature and extent of the work carried out on VAT will vary according to the assessment of the risk of material misstatement and it should be specified in the strategy or the substantive testing plan (STP), if prepared. However, it is important to remember that Customs & Excise operates, for VAT purposes, on levels of materiality lower than those which would normally be used for audit purposes.

It is also important to remember that failure to comply with the VAT regulations may lead not only to civil penalties but, in some cases, to criminal prosecution and possible imprisonment. Although these risks might not have a material impact on the financial statements, it is important to consider both client expectation and any risk to the auditor and to the firm in such circumstances.

9:26.1.5 VAT regulations

Any questions and issues concerning the application or interpretation of the VAT Act, and the regulations made thereunder, should normally be referred to a VAT specialist within the firm.

Only certain Customs & Excise leaflets have any force in law. Although the others may have some value in illustrating Customs & Excise's view of the law, they should not be used to settle matters of interpretation of VAT law, except as directed by the audit firm's VAT specialists.

9:26.2 Risks of misstatement

9:26.2.1 Management awareness

The auditor should consider the extent to which management is aware of VAT issues generally, and of their specific application to the client's business. Apart from a review of the control environment, it will usually be useful to design a checklist of the more common indicators of both good and bad control of VAT to assist staff to complete this exercise.

9:26.2.2 VAT overview

The auditor should obtain an overview of the way the client manages VAT by carrying out the following steps:

(a)   Examining the records of correspondence with Customs & Excise on VAT to determine whether there is evidence of any control visits and of resulting assessments made by Customs & Excise. In a well-managed system, the auditor should expect to find a record of all dealings with Customs & Excise, including a record of questions asked by the officers at control visits and the answers given. Also, Customs & Excise's written views on liability matters should be recorded and circulated to persons dealing with such matters.

(b)   Reviewing the dates shown on returns to ensure that returns are submitted on a timely basis. Returns must normally be submitted to be received by Customs & Excise by the end of the month following the end of the VAT accounting period. However, a further week is allowed where payment is made to Customs & Excise by direct debit. There are severe penalties for late submission of VAT returns.

(c)   Reviewing the VAT accounts kept by the client to ascertain whether there are adequate references to the source data to enable entries to the account to be traced. Records should also be examined to ensure compliance with VAT law relating to VAT accounting.

(d)   Enquiring whether the client carries out overall credibility tests on VAT at all levels within the business. For example, Customs & Excise will normally attempt to reconcile turnover disclosed in VAT returns with the turnover shown in the annual financial statements of a business. An assessment may be issued if there is an unexplained shortfall. Where practicable, clients should carry out similar tests in relation both to outputs and to inputs (this is discussed further in the last two paragraphs of **Section 9:26.4**).

(e)   Testing the client's procedures for analysing and identifying disallowable VAT, e.g. VAT on motor cars and entertainment expenses, VAT which is not deductible under the partial exemption rules and VAT which is not deductible under the Tour Operators Margin Scheme and the various second-hand schemes.

9:26.2.3 VAT groups

If the client is a member of a group and there is a group VAT registration in force the auditor should carry out the following procedures:

(a)   Examine the procedures for accumulating the necessary information from the various group members. These should preferably be reported on specially designed input documents.

(b)   Establish what checks are applied at all levels in the supply chain to ensure that such procedures are free from error.

(c)   Determine whether the correct procedures have been followed when, for example, a member has left the group or there are other changes to the group structure.

(d)   Establish whether the staff responsible for VAT at each group location are aware of those transactions which should be ignored for VAT purposes, e.g. transactions between VAT group members.

(e)   If the group is partly exempt, establish what procedures exist for identifying VAT incurred in one group company which is attributable to activities in another group company. For example, if a property company in a group rents its properties to other group companies, the input tax incurred in the property company will be regarded as being attributable to whatever activities are undertaken in the companies occupying the properties.

(f)   Ensure that there is evidence that management reviews the composition of any VAT group registrations when appropriate, e.g. when new companies are acquired or disposals or reorganisations carried out.

9:26.3 Proper accounting

The VAT balance on the account will be included in the financial statements as a balance due to or from Customs & Excise. However, audit work should not be limited to subsequent payments or receipts and to a comparison of the balance with VAT returns. The auditor should also carry out the following procedures:

(a)   Check that the VAT returns are an accurate account of the client's VAT liability or refund entitlement. The fact that Customs & Excise has carried out a control visit and not challenged the client's returns should not be regarded as conclusive evidence that the client has complied with all VAT requirements. Customs & Excise can and will issue assessments for tax and penalties if a later inspection indicates that the client's original returns were incorrect.

(b)   Test tax points (the date when VAT is brought to account) to ensure that any output tax is accounted for, and that any input tax is claimed as a deduction from output tax, in the correct period. Failure to account for output and input tax in the correct period may result in penalties, adverse cash flow or the possible loss of an input tax deduction.

(c)   Examine payments of VAT to Customs & Excise and other appropriate evidence to check that the VAT return and any payment due were submitted to Customs & Excise in the correct period. Late returns may result in the application of the default surcharge provisions.

(d)   Determine whether the client has carried out any significant activities, which may be classed as supplies for VAT purposes, but which may not have been recorded in the accounting records. Consider whether VAT should have been brought to account. The following activities are particularly relevant:

   (i)   A change in the use to which a property is applied, e.g. from manufacturing to letting.

   (ii)   Any movement of goods across EU borders for which no consideration is received and no invoice issued, e.g. goods sent on sale or return, samples sent to potential customers and fixed assets transferred to an overseas branch.

   (iii)   Transactions for a consideration other than money, e.g. a swap of stocks.

   (iv)   Consent to a tenant carrying out significant improvements to a property. In certain cases, such leases will be regarded as a 'development tenancy' and VAT will have to be charged on that part of the rent that is referable to the improvements.

It may be appropriate to consult a specialist in regard to these transactions.

Because the client's records might be arithmetically correct but based on an incorrect understanding of the principles involved, the auditor should, when testing VAT accounting, pay particular attention to the following:

(a)   The application of the partial exemption rules, where a business makes exempt supplies (e.g., if it receives income from investments).

(b)   The manner in which the 'tour operators scheme' has been implemented by tour operators.

(c)   The use of the 'special retail schemes' by retailers.

(d)   The records kept by second-hand goods dealers.

(e)   Other complex areas including:

    (i)   property transactions;

    (ii)   agency transactions and disbursements;

    (iii) the importation or export of goods from outside the EU;

    (iv) the movement of goods within the EU.

The VAT accounting regulations require that separate VAT accounts are kept for each VAT accounting period in respect of both output and input tax. Errors which are subsequently discovered by the client must be separately disclosed, unless the amount of the net error (understatements less overstatements) adjusted in the period is low. The auditor should check whether the client has complied with the accounting requirements of the VAT regulations.

In addition, it may be useful to carry out specific tests to confirm that the client's procedures for controlling the specific risks which have been identified are operating satisfactorily.

9:26.3.1 Re-computation in total

The auditor should attempt to test output tax in total by re-computation. It should usually be possible to do this in a business whose total turnover is subject to VAT at the standard rate, but it may also be possible to do this in other cases. Re-computation of input tax in total will rarely be practicable, but the auditor might nevertheless consider it in appropriate circumstances.

When attempting a re-computation in total, the auditor should consider the following factors:

(a)   VAT is due on capital as well as on revenue items. Therefore, capital items should be included in turnover potentially subject to VAT.

(b)   Some netting will take place where VAT is due on the margin rather than on the gross sales amount (e.g., second-hand goods and tour operators margin scheme supplies).

(c)   VAT is charged on the value of sales net of any settlement discounts claimable, regardless of whether they are taken.

(d)   VAT may be due both on debits and credits to an account (e.g., on disbursements by agents). If the accounting system nets these items for reporting purposes, they will have to be adjusted in any re-computation.

(e)   VAT may be due on events which are not recorded in the financial records (*see* the first paragraph of **Section 9:26.3**). Events giving rise to a VAT charge can include gifts, a change in use of fixed property and the supply of goods and services for non-monetary consideration.

(f)   The 'acquisition from', or 'despatch to', an EU destination.

9:26.3.2 Tests of details

9:26.3.2.1 Debit entries

Items for testing may be selected by using either of the following methods:

(a)   **Selecting from the VAT account in the general ledger**: If the strategy or STP, if prepared, requires tests of details on purchases and expenses, while selecting items for testing from the purchase and expense accounts in the general ledger, the VAT account should be sampled at the same time (discussed in **Section 9:31**, 'Purchases and expenses'). If items are only sampled from the purchase records, the auditor should check the calculation of VAT on specific invoices, and trace the figures to the VAT account. The possible overstatement of recorded VAT debits will not be tested because the sample has not been selected from the VAT account in the general ledger.

(b)   **Selecting from the cash records and tracing the total cash postings to the general ledger**: This method may be more efficient with a small client where the cash book is the principal or only detailed record of transactions. The auditor should also review the general ledger accounts for any unusual items not posted from the cash records.

The auditor should reconcile the population from which samples are taken with the amount claimed as input tax.

In relation into the testing of selected items, debit entries to the VAT account will normally fall into one of the following categories:

(a)   **Payments of VAT to Customs & Excise**: For selected items the auditor should carry out the following procedures:

  (i)   Trace payments from the VAT account in the ledger to the relevant VAT return and to the VAT account kept in accordance with the requirements of VAT legislation.

  (ii)   Examine the date shown on the return and determine whether it was completed in sufficient time for it to reach Customs & Excise by the due date.

(iii) If a risk of fraud relating to payments has been identified, examine the paid cheque or other advice of payment. When doing this, it is important to consider the date that it was processed by the bank with a view to deciding whether it provides evidence that the payment reached Customs & Excise by the due date.

(b) **VAT on purchases and expenses**: The auditor should carry out the following procedures:

(i) Examine the supporting VAT invoice (or, in respect of imported goods and services, other input documentation) and check that it complies with VAT regulations (e.g. that the VAT registration number is included).

(ii) Establish that VAT should be charged on the items supplied.

(iii) Check that the tax point (usually the delivery date or date of the tax invoice) falls within the correct VAT period. Special tax point rules apply to certain types of transactions including:

- deposits and advance payments;

- continuous (i.e., periodic) supplies of goods or services, e.g. water or rentals of equipment;

- progress payments under building or engineering contracts.

One way of ensuring that audit staff are aware of the rules is to design flowcharts setting out the tax point rules.

(iv) Check whether the VAT is charged on the correct taxable amount. The taxable value of a supply will normally be the amount charged less any prompt payment discount that may be claimed by the client, regardless of whether the client does in fact do so. When a client is partially exempt, the method authorised by Customs & Excise might require any input tax to be identified as being attributable to taxable supplies, exempt supplies, or both taxable and exempt supplies. If this is the case, the auditor should check the allocation of the input tax at the same time as testing the input tax debit.

(v) Check that all invoices bear the name of the client. The auditor should consider whether the client is incorrectly reclaiming VAT on, e.g., motor cars used in the business, petrol used by employees for private motoring, business entertainment, director's accommodation (excluding business travel) and invoices where no VAT is charged. The auditor should check whether the goods or services supplied are for business purposes and not for the private use of an employee, director or any other individual. Separate charges for delivery and packaging shown on the invoice should have VAT charged at the standard rate, regardless of the VAT status of the goods supplied unless the contract with the customer is for 'delivered goods' (e.g., mail order sales), or when the goods are exported.

(c) **VAT on sales credit notes**: The auditor should check the details on the credit note with the original sales invoice and check the calculation of VAT. It is also necessary to check whether the entry in the VAT account has been made in the VAT accounting period in which the credit note was raised and not the period when the original sales invoice was issued. Credit notes may only be issued for *bona fide* commercial reasons, and not as a device for recovering VAT on bad debts.

9 Substantive testing

(d) **Adjustments to VAT recovered on 'capital items'**: This refers to individual computers having a high value, and certain acquisitions of, or services in respect of, land. Questions in regard to the application of the capital items rules should be referred to a VAT specialist within the audit firm.

9:26.3.2.2 Credit entries

In selecting items for testing, if tests of details of sales and purchase returns have been carried out, the samples selected for testing should be used to check the credit entries to the VAT control account. If such tests have been carried out, testing for VAT purposes may be restricted to approximately one in six of the sales and purchase returns selections (100 per cent divided by the rate of VAT, currently 17.5 per cent). If tests of details of sales have not been carried out, it will be necessary to select a sample of items for VAT testing.

Even where it has been possible to re-compute the VAT charge as discussed in **Section 9:26.3.1**, the auditor should test some credit entries for the correct determination and calculation of the VAT liability and the correct application of the tax point and disclosure rules.

In relation to the testing of selected items, credit entries to the VAT account will normally fall into one of the following categories:

(a) **VAT on sales**: The auditor should examine the relevant sales invoices, ascertain whether the required details for tax invoices are present, and also ensure that VAT has been correctly charged and calculated. If the invoice selected relates to an export sale, the client should have the required evidence of the export, such as shipping/airport documents, to support the zero-rating.

(b) **Repayments of VAT from Customs & Excise**: The auditor should check repayments with the supporting documentation such as the VAT return or the notification of repayment from Customs & Excise.

(c) **VAT on credit notes for purchases and expenses**: The auditor should trace the details on the credit note to the original invoice, and should also check the calculation of VAT. Only the original VAT claimed is eligible for adjustment.

(d) **Adjustments to VAT claimed on 'capital items'**: This refers to items discussed in **Section 9:26.3.2.1** (last paragraph, point (d)), for which adjustments may be credits or debits to the VAT account.

9:26.3.3 VAT invoices

The auditor should check that VAT invoices are issued for all standard-rated supplies (other than retail sales) and that the invoices comply with VAT regulations. However, a VAT invoice must not be issued for certain specialist transactions, such as sales made under the second-hand sales schemes. A VAT invoice should also not be issued for any supply between members of a VAT group.

9:26.3.4 *Tax point*

The auditor should check whether the tax point has been correctly determined by examining delivery notes (in the case of goods) or job or time records (in the case of services), and comparing the dates of delivery/completion with the invoice date and the date that payment was received. Special rules apply for retailers, small businesses and tour operators margin scheme supplies, and it may be necessary to consult a VAT specialist in respect of these matters.

9:26.3.5 *Adjustments to the VAT account*

9:26.3.5.1 *Partial exemption and other non-deductible input tax*

If a client makes any exempt supplies it will be unable to reclaim all of its input tax unless the input tax attributable to the exempt supplies either is within the *de minimis* limits or can be ignored because it relates to one or more of the transactions described in Customs & Excise Notice 706 (*see* **Section 9:26.3**). VAT may also be deductible where it is attributable to 'non-business income', e.g. donations received by a charity. If a business incurs significant irrecoverable input tax, the following matters should be considered:

(a) **Partial exemption method**: The auditor should examine any Customs & Excise correspondence dealing with the method to be used to determine exempt input tax and check that the client's accounting arrangements ensure that the method is correctly applied. Most methods will require that the client distinguishes between tax which is directly attributable to taxable supplies and tax attributable to exempt supplies, the latter being non-deductible. Any input tax which is not directly attributable to either must be apportioned using an agreed basis between taxable and exempt supplies.

(b) **Treatment of non-deductible input tax**: Input tax which is non-deductible will normally be treated as follows:

(i)   If it relates to expenditure written off to the profit and loss account, it should be similarly treated.

(ii)   If it relates to capital expenditure it should, where significant, be capitalised as part of the cost of the asset.

(iii) If it is recoverable from a third party, it should be charged to a debtors account (e.g., where it represents part of the expenditure which can be passed on by a landlord to a tenant under a lease).

(c) **Annual adjustment**: The irrecoverable input tax is calculated on a provisional basis during the VAT accounting year and adjusted at the end of that year. If large amounts of exempt input tax are incurred, the auditor should test any adjustment to the VAT account to ensure that the client has correctly applied the regulations.

9:26.3.5.2 *Bad debt relief*

If an adjustment has been made to the VAT account for bad debt relief, the auditor should ensure that the client has complied with the conditions for claiming bad debt relief. It may be appropriate to ensure that the client claims relief at the earliest possible time where large bad debts are experienced.

9:26.4 VAT payable or receivable

Sections 9:26.3 to **9:26.3.5.2** above describe the testing which should be carried out on VAT transactions. Tests should make it possible to conclude whether the amounts posted to the VAT account in the period of audit interest are misstated.

At the balance sheet date work may therefore be restricted to checking that the final balance on the VAT control account is reconciled by the client to the underlying records and that the reconciling items appear to be reasonable. Any unusual items should be investigated and explanations corroborated.

If the VAT returns show a net payment due to Customs & Excise, the auditor should trace the subsequent payments to the returned paid cheques (or other advice of payment) if a risk of fraud relating to payments has been identified.

If the VAT returns show a net receipt due from Customs & Excise, the auditor should check that the amount has subsequently been received. Payment is normally made within about two weeks of submission of the return. It may be appropriate to consider whether cash flow could be improved by speeding up the processing of VAT returns showing a repayment due.

In addition, the total output and input values on VAT returns should be reviewed by reference to the turnover and the appropriate purchases figures in the financial statements. To do so the auditor should allow for:

(a) transactions of a non-revenue nature, such as purchases and disposals of fixed assets; and

(b) differences arising because the periods covered by the returns differ from the client's financial reporting period.

This work will be made easier if it is possible to obtain from the client a reconciliation that relates turnover to the VAT amounts.

9:26.5 Agreement with accounting records

The auditor should check that this presentation and disclosure VAT balance in the general ledger agrees with the financial statements, by tracing the general ledger account balance to the financial statements via the trial balance.

9:26.6 Presentation and disclosure

To help achieve the presentation and disclosure objective the auditor should, at the end of the audit, review the financial statements and consider the matters set out in a UK GAAP checklist. Also, it is important to be alert for any matters that require disclosure and which can more efficiently be identified during fieldwork.

9:27 Other creditors, provisions and contingencies

9:27.1 Introduction

This section is designed to help in developing a programme of substantive tests in accordance with the strategy for other creditors (including accruals and deferred income), provisions and contingencies and commitments. The strategy or substantive testing (STP), if prepared, should specify the planned response to the assessment of the risk of material misstatement, including the nature, extent and timing of substantive tests.

This section should be read in conjunction with the general guidance on substantive testing in the following sections:

- **Section 9:3**, 'Analytical procedures'

- **Section 9:4**, 'Tests of details'

- **Section 9:5**, 'Evaluating the results of substantive testing'

Liabilities are discussed in the following sections:

• Bank loans and overdrafts	**Section 9:23**
• Trade creditors	**Section 9:24**
• Corporation tax and deferred tax	**Section 9:25**
• Value added tax	**Section 9:26**
• Long-term borrowings	**Section 9:28**

9:27.1.1 Essential audit objectives

The specific audit objectives for other creditors are set out below for each of the seven general audit objectives. The auditor should obtain sufficient evidence to achieve these specific objectives:

Completeness	All amounts owed to other creditors at the balance sheet date have been recorded in the financial statements.
	All contingent liabilities have been identified.
Accuracy; Existence; Cut-off; Valuation; Rights and obligations	Other creditors have been accurately determined, summarised and recorded.
	Contingencies and commitments have been correctly identified and appropriate monetary values ascribed.
	Only valid creditors and known or expected liabilities have been included in the financial statements.

The amounts reported in the financial statements are in agreement with the accounting records.

● **Presentation and disclosure** Other creditors and contingent liabilities have been properly classified, described and disclosed in the financial statements.

Sometimes, the auditor may conclude that there is a negligible risk of material misstatement in relation to one or more of these audit objectives, and that consequently no specific substantive procedures are necessary.

9:27.2 Completeness

To conclude whether all amounts owed to other creditors have been included or accrued in the financial statements, the auditor should review the client's detailed schedules of other creditors and accruals in the light of:

(a) Knowledge of the business acquired through the business review.

(b) A comparison with the corresponding amounts at the previous year-end.

(c) The detailed profit and loss account, in which the different categories of expense are disclosed.

The following are the more common categories of expenditure which are likely to give rise to liabilities classified as 'other creditors' (rather than 'trade creditors'):

(a) Personnel costs:

    (i) Accrued payrolls.

    (ii) Bonuses and commissions.

    (iii) Holiday pay.

    (iv) Pension fund costs.

    (v) PAYE and NI.

    (vi) Other payroll deductions.

(b) Rent, including equipment hire and leasing, and hire purchase costs.

(c) Fixed asset purchases.

(d) Telecommunications.

(e) Advertising.

(f) Professional fees.

(g) Travel and freight.

(h) Royalties.

(i) Warranties.

(j) Reorganisation costs.

9:27.2.1 *Other unrecorded liabilities*

In addition to other procedures, the auditor should search for material unrecorded liabilities by carrying out the following procedures:

(a) Examining the purchase, payment and payroll records after the balance sheet date and testing individual items to see whether they should have been recorded as creditors at that date. The auditor should enquire whether any significant invoices have been received after the balance sheet date but not processed at the date of the audit.

(b) Reviewing and, where appropriate, examining payments made after the balance sheet date to determine whether they satisfied liabilities that should have been recorded at that date. If they did, the auditor should check that an adequate accrual was made at the balance sheet date.

9:27.2.2 *Provisions, contingencies and commitments*

FRS 12 'Provisions, contingent liabilities and contingent assets' sets out the accounting procedure which should be followed. FRS 12 superseded SSAP 18, and introduced stricter criteria for adopting a provision in the accounts. The auditor should ensure that where the client has identified an area where a provision is required, or a contingent liability exists, it has been correctly accounted for and disclosed in the financial statements. Particular attention should be paid to matters where there is uncertainty, or where there are commitments in respect of forward purchases or sales. The client's list of provisions, contingencies and commitments might be reviewed by reference to the following:

(a) Minutes of meetings of shareholders, the board of directors and any committees thereof, at which contracts, agreements, pending or threatened litigation or other matters relating to contingencies and commitments would be discussed. The review should include minutes of meetings held after the balance sheet date but before to the date of the audit report. The auditor should review any agreements the client has entered into, noting particularly the terms of the transactions, to identify any items requiring accounting recognition or disclosure, e.g. , the nature of rights given or received; any security given; and all significant requirements, restrictions and covenants (e.g., dilapidation clauses in leases).

(b) Confirmations received from banks in connection with substantive testing of bank balances (as discussed in **Section 9:23**, 'Bank and cash balances'). These frequently identify contingencies and commitments (e.g., guarantees and forward foreign exchange contracts).

(c) Records of open purchase commitments (for items incurred not in the ordinary course of business).

(d) Records of authorisation for expenditure on and disposals of property, plant and equipment.

(e) Records of leased assets and lease agreements.

(f) Records of authorisation for the purchase and sale of investments held as fixed assets.

(g) A review of the tax and VAT position and correspondence.

(h) Reports from auditors of branches or subsidiaries.

(i) Actuarial valuations (to identify pension commitments).

(j) Correspondence with the Inland Revenue (to identify unresolved PAYE disputes).

To ensure that all potential liabilities arising from pending or threatened litigation have been properly taken into account, it is necessary to consider whether the procedures adopted for bringing these matters to the attention of the board are adequate. The auditor should also discuss the arrangements for instructing solicitors with the members of management responsible for legal matters and should ask for a list of matters referred to solicitors, with estimates of the possible ultimate liabilities. This list should be reviewed with the available information, e.g. bills from solicitors and correspondence with them. The auditor should request that the client ask the solicitors to provide bills or estimates of charges to date, or to confirm that there are no unbilled charges. The auditor should obtain letters from the client's solicitors regarding legal matters. The factors that should be considered, and the procedures to be followed, are discussed in **Section 9:10**, 'Enquiry of a client's solicitors concerning lawsuits, claims and other actions'.

Frequently, the liabilities or contingencies that are disclosed through these procedures will be difficult to quantify and affected by some degree of uncertainty. Their measurement will therefore require judgement and the auditor should discuss them with senior client management. Accordingly, the auditor should draw the existence of these items to the attention of the engagement manager as early as possible, and they should be recorded in the issues documentation.

9:27.2.3 Representations from management

The auditor should enquire of management whether there are any significant liabilities, contingencies or commitments not recorded in the financial statements and whether adequate provision has been made in respect of any contingent losses. The auditor should record in the working papers significant matters arising from this discussion, including the names of the members of management with whom the matters were discussed.

The auditor should obtain written representations from the client, as to the completeness of other creditors, provisions, contingencies and commitments, in the form of a letter of representation. Further guidance in connection with letters of representation is given in **Section 10:4**, 'Representations from management'.

9:27.3 Accuracy; Existence; Cut-off; Valuation; Rights and obligations

9:27.3.1 Sources of assurance

The work described in **Sections 9:27.3.2** to **9:27.3.8** should normally enable the auditor to conclude on all these objectives, without the need to carry out additional procedures. Some of the procedures will also provide secondary assurance with respect to the completeness objectives. The work is discussed under the following main headings:

(a)   Salaries and wages.

(b)   Pension scheme costs.

(c)   Leasing liabilities.

(d)   Loans.

(e)   Bills payable.

(f)   Other liabilities and provisions.

(g)   Deferred income.

If any creditors or contingencies are denominated in foreign currencies, the auditor should check they have been translated into sterling at the appropriate exchange rate.

9:27.3.2 Salaries and wages

Salaries are usually paid on the last working day of the month and therefore an accrual will often not be necessary. However, it is more common for wages to be paid in arrears. Any accruals should be checked with the payroll records and the correct apportionment of the accrual checked.

9:27.3.2.1 Bonuses and commissions

Frequently, it is possible to re-compute accruals for bonuses and commissions by reference to the original agreement or other documentation. If this is not possible, the auditor may be able to develop an estimate of the accrual by reference to the prior year's amount adjusted by, e.g., the number of eligible employees and changes in the bonus or commission percentage. If neither of these procedures is possible, the auditor should test a sample of items comprising the total.

9:27.3.2.2 Holiday pay

The auditor should examine the basis of any holiday pay entitlement, review such basis for reasonableness and check the client's calculations.

9:27.3.2.3 PAYE and NI

Credits to the PAYE and NI accounts should normally be tested as part of the work on payrolls (as discussed in **Section 9:32**, 'Payrolls'). The auditor should therefore test the debits by, e.g., checking payments to the Inland Revenue with supporting documentation. If a specific risk of fraud has been identified, it is necessary to inspect the paid cheque or bank transfer.

The Inland Revenue is empowered to examine employers' records to ensure that the PAYE and NI regulations are being followed. It is normal practice for the Inland Revenue to examine the records of companies on a rotation basis, in addition to carrying out examinations where it has reason to believe there may have been contravention of the regulations. During such examinations, the PAYE investigators direct particular attention to determining whether payments have been made to, or on behalf of, employees without deduction of income tax, and they are empowered to examine records going back over a six-year period. Thus, if there are irregularities, the additional tax to be paid over (together with penalties, which themselves can be substantial) could be material to the financial statements.

Accordingly, in addition to reviewing procedures for deducting PAYE and NI and paying it over to the Inland Revenue, the auditor should ascertain whether the client makes cash payments to, or enters into other arrangements with, employees and others, or provides them with benefits in kind. If so, the auditor should ascertain whether PAYE and NI are accounted for properly, and whether the payments or benefits are reported to the Inland Revenue or their tax treatment has been agreed with the Inland Revenue.

Audit enquiries, together with a brief review of petty cash files and employee expense claims, may identify such items as the following:

(a)   Payments out of petty cash to casual or part-time labour or outworkers, without setting up the necessary PAYE records or deducting income tax and NI.

(b)   Payments to 'contractors' or to 'consultants' claiming to be self-employed but who are, in reality, employees.

(c)   Payments to directors, particularly bonuses, or payments made on behalf of directors for purchases or other items (e.g., credit card accounts), without either (in the case of payments to third parties) including them as emoluments for PAYE and NI purposes, or reporting them on P11D forms.

(d)   Excessive or unsupportable (e.g., round-sum) subsistence 'allowances' paid without tax deductions for mileage, subsistence, car cleaning, garaging or other expenses.

(e)   Home telephone rentals paid by the employer.

(f)   'Call-out' allowances (e.g., for maintenance staff).

(g)   Home to work travel, or inadequate identification of business petrol.

(h)   Gifts to customers or employees.

(i)   Sales incentives, excessive or frequent staff parties, or conferences with an insubstantial element of training.

It may be entirely reasonable for clients to make some of the types of payment listed above without accounting for PAYE. Other payments might, while not attracting PAYE, represent benefits on which the employer is liable to penalties if they are not declared.

If it appears that PAYE or NI may not have been accounted for properly, or if benefits have not been reported properly, the auditor should first consult a tax specialist. Because of the potential sensitivity of these matters, the auditor should consult the engagement partner before discussing the matter with the client.

9:27.3.2.4 Other payroll deductions

By the nature of payroll deductions, there will not normally be any independent evidence to support the year-end accruals. The auditor should, therefore, test the accruals by reference to the individual debits and credits which underlie them. In the audit work on payroll deductions (as discussed in **Section 9:32**, 'Payrolls'), the credits should be tested. The debits should be tested to the deductions accounts by inspecting supporting documentary evidence (e.g., journal transfers).

The auditor should request the client to analyse the accrual for payroll deductions over the various deduction accounts and to reconcile the balances to the relevant payrolls.

9:27.3.3 Pension scheme costs

If the client has a pension scheme, it is important for the auditor to understand the nature and type of the scheme.

The auditor should consider matters such as:

(a)   The date and results of the latest actuarial valuation and the results of any subsequent discussions with the actuary.

(b)   The competence and objectivity of the actuary.

(c)   The treatment of any surplus or deficiency arising from the actuarial valuation.

(d)   The effect on the scheme of any changes of accounting policy, including, where appropriate, any changes in the basis of the actuarial valuation.

(e)   The effect on the scheme of events such as major plant closures or mergers.

If the auditor plans to consult the pension scheme actuary, it may be useful to take into account the matters discussed in the APC's Audit Brief: 'The work of a pension scheme actuary'.

9:27.3.4 Leasing liabilities

If finance leases are capitalised, the auditor should obtain a schedule of liabilities showing the following information:

(a)   Liabilities arising from leasing agreements entered into during the period.

(b)   Liabilities arising from leasing arrangements existing at the beginning of the period, which should agree with prior year working papers.

For new leases entered into during the period, the auditor should test the client's calculations of the net present value of future payments, either in total or for individual items, and agree the result of the calculation with the value capitalised within fixed assets. Usually this should be done in conjunction with the substantive testing of tangible fixed assets (described in **Section 9:16**, 'Tangible fixed assets').

For payments made under leasing arrangements, the auditor should obtain the client's calculations of the finance charge element of the payments and check that these amounts are included in the charge in the profit and loss account and that the obligation for future rentals is appropriately reduced. The client's calculations should be re-performed for a selection of leases.

The auditor should also obtain the client's analysis of the total liability for finance lease payments for future periods and test the allocation of payments as between those payable:

(a)   in the next year;

(b)   between one and five years from the balance sheet date;

(c)   in more than five years from the balance sheet date.

It may be possible to use software to assist in the audit of leases. Packages can help to categorise leases as finance leases or operating leases, and to provide the accounting information needed for the disclosures required by SSAP 21.

9:27.3.5 Bills payable

For any bills of exchange payable that are included in other creditors, it is necessary to obtain a listing of the individual bills and check or test the additions of the list. The auditor should also carry out the following procedures:

(a)   Trace bills to the records of bills payable and vice versa.

(b)   Confirm, if bills have been paid since the balance sheet date, that they were met on their due dates, and inspect some of the cancelled bills.

(c)   If bills have been renewed or renegotiated since the balance sheet date, ascertain the reasons and, if there is any indication that they were renewed or renegotiated because the client is in financial difficulties, draw the matter to the attention of the engagement manager.

9:27.3.6 Other liabilities and provisions

The auditor should test other liabilities, such as rents or professional fees, to supporting documentation, checking the calculation of the accrual. It may be necessary to confirm the amounts outstanding with the third parties involved.

The auditor should examine the movements on any significant provisions and check, by reference to relevant supporting documentation, that the balances at the substantive testing date are reasonable in relation to the liabilities or expected losses for which they have been established.

If the client has warranty provisions, the auditor should examine the client's procedures for accruing the provisions, and consider whether the accounting policies used are appropriate and applied consistently. A substantive analytical review may be useful, and an expectation of the provision may be developed from, e.g., the prior years' provisions and the level of sales in the current year. However, the auditor should remain alert for other evidence which might indicate that the provision is inappropriate. Such evidence may include correspondence with customers, quality control reports, significant changes in rectification costs, and an apparent increase in the credit period being taken by customers (which could indicate dissatisfaction with the products).

9:27.3.7 Deferred income

A common source of deferred income is government grants. As discussed in **Section 9:16**, 'Tangible fixed assets', the auditor should consider whether any additions to fixed assets are eligible for grants. It is important to check that any grants are released over the life of the related asset and that the calculations of the amounts released are correct. It is also important to check that the assets are still used for the purpose for which the grants were given; a change in the use of an asset, on its disposal, may render a grant repayable.

The procedures to be applied to other deferred income will vary according to the nature of the particular item. However, the auditor should check that the amount is being released over an appropriate period and that the calculation of the amount released is correct.

9:27.3.8 Agreement with accounting records

The auditor should obtain assurance that the other creditors in the general ledger agree with the financial statements, by tracing the general ledger account balances via the trial balance to the financial statements.

9:27.4 Presentation and disclosure

To help achieve the presentation and disclosure objective the auditor should, at the end of the audit, review the financial statements and consider the matters set out in a UK GAAP checklist. Also, it is important to be alert for any matters that require disclosure and which can more efficiently be identified during fieldwork, including, e.g., any part of a creditor balance which is not payable within 12 months of the balance sheet date.

9:28 Long-term borrowings (including related interest)

9:28.1 Introduction

This section is designed to help to develop a programme of substantive tests in accordance with the approved strategy or, if prepared, the substantive testing plan (STP) for long-term borrowings, including debentures and loans and the related interest charged and accrued. Other long-term liabilities, including, e.g., leasing liabilities are discussed in **Section 9:27**, 'Other creditors and contingencies'. The strategy should specify the planned response to the assessment of the risk of material misstatement, including the nature, extent and timing of substantive tests.

This section should be read in conjunction with the general guidance on substantive testing in the following sections:

- **Section 9:3**, 'Analytical procedures'

- **Section 9:4**, 'Tests of details'

- **Section 9:5**, 'Evaluating the results of substantive testing'

9:28.1.1 Essential audit objectives

The specific audit objectives for long-term borrowings are set out below for each of the seven general audit objectives. The auditor should obtain sufficient evidence to achieve these specific objectives:

• **Completeness; Accuracy; Cut-off; Rights and obligations**	All long-term borrowings have been recorded in the financial statements.
	The amounts of long-term borrowings have been accurately determined, summarised and recorded.
	All changes in long-term borrowings have been recorded in the correct accounting period.
	Interest charges and accruals have been recorded in the correct accounting period.
	The amounts reported in the financial statements are in agreement with the accounting records.
	Long-term borrowings are obligations of the client.
	All terms, requirements and restrictions with respect to any loan agreements have been complied with.
• **Existence**	Only valid long-term borrowings have been included in the financial statements.

- **Valuation**   The amounts at which long-term borrowings have been stated make appropriate recognition of any premium or discount on issue or redemption.

- **Presentation and disclosure**   Long-term borrowings and the related interest have been properly classified, described and disclosed in the financial statements.

Sometimes, the auditor may conclude that there is a negligible risk of material misstatement in relation to a particular audit objective and that consequently no specific substantive procedures are necessary.

9:28.1.2 Early substantive testing

The auditor should consider carrying out some of the procedures discussed in this section at an interim date, as part of early substantive testing (discussed in **Section 4:7**, 'The audit programme). The strategy or STP, if prepared, for long-term borrowings should specify which procedures will be carried out at an interim date and whether it is expected that it will be necessary to repeat or extend them at the balance sheet date. The audit programme for long-term liabilities should set out the procedures to be performed in respect of the intervening period.

9:28.2 Completeness; Accuracy; Cut-off; Rights and obligations

The audit objectives for completeness, accuracy, cut-off and rights and obligations are discussed together because usually they will be achieved most efficiently by means of direct confirmation either from lenders or, in the case of debentures or loan stocks, from the registrars. The auditor should ensure that confirmation procedures are applied to a complete population of liabilities. To do this, the auditor should normally select items from the population of liabilities at the beginning of the accounting period and the new liabilities assumed during the period.

The auditor may identify new liabilities from the business review, a review of the minutes and statutory books, and by means of the following:

(a) Identifying costs, such as issue costs, associated with new borrowings or interest payments.

(b) Examining loan agreements entered into during the period.

(c) Scrutinising press reports, offer documents, EXTEL cards and other evidence of potential liabilities.

9:28.2.1 Direct confirmation

The auditor should request confirmation of the following:

(a) The balance at the substantive testing date.

(b)   Repayments of principal during the period.

(c)   Interest paid during the period.

(d)   Accrued interest at the substantive testing date.

(e)   Particulars of any security for the loan.

(f)   The terms of repayment.

If the lender is a bank, the auditor should use the standard bank letter. In other cases, the guidance on confirmation procedures set out in **Section 9:21**, 'Trade debtors', should be followed. For debentures or loan stocks, confirmation of the outstanding balance may be obtained from the registrars.

If the debentures or loan stocks are administered by the client and not by independent registrars the auditor should carry out the following tests:

(a)   Check that the total amount outstanding agrees with the schedule of detailed balances on the client's registers.

(b)   Test the additions of the schedule.

(c)   Confirm directly the balances due to lenders.

9:28.2.2 Alternative procedures

If unable to obtain confirmation of balances, the auditor should carry out alternative procedures. These will normally comprise checking the amounts of loans against the relevant signed documentation, testing that repayments made during the year are in accordance with the terms of the loan agreement and, if a specific risk of fraud has been identified in respect of payments, inspecting the returned cheques. The auditor should also check that interest payments have been correctly made during the period.

9:28.2.3 Foreign exchange

Where long-term borrowings are denominated in foreign currencies, the auditor should check that they have been translated into sterling at the correct rate.

9:28.2.4 Interest amounts

The auditor should normally carry out work on interest charged and accrued on long-term borrowings in conjunction with work on the liabilities themselves. The evidence required may be obtained from the information included in the replies to confirmation requests (*see* **Section 9:28.2.1**), or by means of the following procedures:

(a)   Re-computation of the total interest on individual loans by reference to the rates set out in the loan agreement.

(b)   Substantive analytical review (e.g., by developing an expectation of the total interest expense based on known interest rates and outstanding debt).

(c)   Tests of details.

9:28.2.5 *Agreement with accounting records*

The auditor should obtain evidence that the long-term borrowings balances and interest balances in the general ledger agree with the financial statements, by tracing the general ledger account balances via the trial balance to the financial statements.

9:28.2.6 *Compliance with terms of borrowing and borrowing powers*

The client's borrowing powers may be restricted under the terms of loan agreements, debenture trust deeds or the Memorandum and Articles of Association. Such restrictions will normally be expressed in terms of an overall limit on borrowing or interest payments together with, e.g., ratios of secured to unsecured borrowings. The auditor should check that these have been complied with. The auditor may be required to issue a separate report on compliance with loan covenants, in which case the work on that report should, where possible, be co-ordinated with audit work on the financial statements.

The auditor should check that loan repayments and interest payments are being made in accordance with the terms of the agreement. It is also important to check that, if any liabilities are secured, details of the security have been properly recorded in the Register of Charges. If the Register of Charges has not been written up it may be necessary for the auditors to check whether any liabilities are secured by requesting a search of the company's file at Companies House.

If the auditor encounters an 'off-balance-sheet' scheme which has as its aim the removal of a long-term borrowing from the balance sheet, it is important to consider whether this might result in the client's borrowing powers being exceeded.

9:28.3 Existence

A satisfactory confirmation of a long-term borrowings balance will provide adequate evidence that the liability existed at the balance sheet date and was not overstated. Accordingly, the auditor will normally obtain sufficient assurance from the confirmation of balances selected as discussed in **Section 9:28.2.1** (first paragraph). However, if the balance of recorded liabilities not selected is material, further balances may be selected for confirmation.

9:28.4 Valuation

For long-term borrowings issued, or to be redeemed, at a premium or discount, the auditor should check that the premium or discount has been correctly calculated and properly accounted for. The auditor should do this by verifying the terms of issue or redemption to supporting documentation, or to the reply to the confirmation request. In the case of complex capital issues (such as deep-discounted, convertible, zero-coupon or index-linked bonds) it is important to refer to current technical accounting guidance.

9:28.5 Presentation and disclosure

The auditor will normally achieve the presentation and disclosure objective at the end of the audit by reviewing the financial statements and considering the matters set out in a UK GAAP checklist. Also, it is important to be alert for any matters that require disclosure and which can be more efficiently identified during fieldwork. These include:

(a) secured borrowings and the nature of the security given;

(b) the current portion of debt which should be classified as a creditor payable in less than 12 months;

(c) redeemed debentures that the client can reissue.

(d) 'Off-balance-sheet' arrangements that the client may have entered into for the purpose of reducing the disclosed long-term liabilities in the balance sheet. When the auditor encounters such arrangements, it is necessary to decide whether they should be accounted for as part of long-term borrowings. The auditor should consult the engagement manager when dealing with them. These arrangements are also discussed in **Section 9:13**, 'Window dressing and off-balance-sheet finance'.

9:29 Capital and statutory records

9:29.1 Introduction

This section is designed to help to develop a programme of substantive tests in accordance with the strategy or, if prepared, the approved substantive testing plan (STP) for share capital, reserves and dividends, as defined below. It is also designed to assist with carrying out work on the client's statutory records.

The strategy or STP, if prepared, for share capital, reserves and dividends should specify the planned response to the assessment of the risk of material misstatement, including the nature, extent and timing of substantive tests.

This section should be read in conjunction with the general guidance on substantive testing in the following sections:

● **Section 9:3**, 'Analytical procedures'

● **Section 9:4**, 'Tests of details'

● **Section 9:5**, 'Evaluating the results of substantive testing'

For the purposes of this section, the following definitions apply:

(a) **Share capital** is the authorised and issued capital of incorporated entities.

(b)   **Reserves** comprise the share premium account, revaluation reserve, profit and loss account, and all other reserves (e.g., capital redemption reserve, reserve for own shares and reserves provided for by the Articles).

(c)   **Dividends** are all distributions, either made or proposed.

9:29.1.1 *Essential audit objectives*

The specific audit objectives for share capital, reserves and dividends are set out below for each of the seven general audit objectives. The auditor should obtain sufficient evidence to achieve these specific objectives:

● **Completeness; Accuracy; Existence; Valuation**	All changes in the authorised or allotted share capital have been properly accounted for.
	All movements on reserves have been properly accounted for and items which should be reserve movements have been included as such.
	All dividends have been approved and properly accounted for.
	The authorised share capital is in agreement with the Memorandum of Association, and the allotted share capital is in agreement with the share register.
	All dividends have been correctly calculated.
	Transfers to, and movements between, reserves have been correctly made in accordance with appropriate resolutions, minutes, or other authorisations.
	The amounts reported in the financial statements are in agreement with the accounting records.
	All amounts shown in respect of share capital and reserves have been correctly valued.
	Appropriate policies have been applied to account for the issue of shares at nominal or fair value.
● **Cut-off**	Movements in share capital and reserves have been accounted for in the correct accounting period.
● **Rights and obligations**	Rights and obligations relating to share capital, reserves and dividends have been correctly identified.
● **Presentation and disclosure**	Share capital, reserves and dividends have been properly classified, described and disclosed in the financial statements.

In some cases the auditor may conclude that there is a negligible risk of material misstatement in relation to one or more of these audit objectives, and that consequently no specific substantive procedures are necessary.

As discussed in **Sections 9:29.2.1** to **9:29.2.2.7**, it is also necessary to ensure that the client's statutory records have been accurately maintained and are up to date.

9:29.1.2 Early substantive testing

The auditor should consider carrying out some of the procedures discussed in this section at an interim date, as **part** of early substantive testing (discussed in **Section 4:7**, 'The audit programme'). Sometimes, depending principally on the assessment of control effectiveness, it may be necessary to repeat or extend the procedures as at the balance sheet date. The strategy or STP, if prepared, for share capital, reserves and dividends should specify which procedures will be carried out at an interim date and whether it is expected that it will be necessary to repeat or extend them as at the balance sheet date. The audit programme for share capital, reserves and dividends should set out the procedures to be performed in respect of the intervening period.

9:29.2 Minutes and statutory records

9:29.2.1 Minutes

As part of the business review the auditor should read the minutes of meetings of the board and of management because they will normally be a valuable source of information regarding the client's business activities. The minutes will also provide audit evidence in relation to authorisations by the client. For example, the following matters should normally be authorised by the board of directors, and be properly minuted:

(a) Directors' remuneration.

(b) Contracts or trading arrangements in which directors or officers have an interest.

(c) Individual transactions large enough to have a significant effect on the business (e.g., major capital projects).

(d) Matters of opinion affecting the financial statements (e.g., directors' valuations of properties).

(e) Delegation to committees of authorities normally retained by the directors.

(f) Unusual transactions or events, especially when it is difficult to determine an arm's length value.

(g) Continued support to group companies (discussed in **Section 9:8**, 'Considerations in respect of going concern').

(h) Interim and proposed final dividends.

(i) Interim statements and preliminary announcements.

The review of the minutes should be updated as part of the post-balance-sheet events procedures.

9:29.2.2 *Statutory records*

9:29.2.2.1 *Inspection of company file*

For a new client, the auditor should read the company's file kept by the Registrar of Companies ensuring, where relevant, that the previous auditor's notice of resignation has been filed.

   In subsequent years, the auditor should consider whether to carry out a further review of the company's file. This might be appropriate where, e.g.:

(a)   there is an uncertainty regarding the existence of a charge over the company's assets; or

(b)   there is a suspicion that documents have, either carelessly or deliberately, not been filed, or that incorrect documents have been filed.

9:29.2.2.2 *Accounting reference date*

The auditor should ensure that the financial statements being audited are for a period ending within seven days of the accounting reference date. (Section 223(3) of the Companies Act 1985 allows those companies that find it convenient to prepare their financial statements as at a particular day of the week to do so; this applies in particular to those in the retail trade.) Also, it is important to ensure that any change in accounting reference date is in accordance with the Act and has been notified to the Registrar of Companies.

9:29.2.2.3 *Filing of previous financial statements*

The auditor should enquire whether a copy of the previous period's financial statements has been filed with the Registrar of Companies within the required time period. This period is seven months from the accounting reference date for a public company and ten months for a private company. Directors of the company are liable to be fined for late submission of financial statements to the Registrar.

9:29.2.2.4 *Register of mortgages and charges*

The auditor should examine the register to ascertain whether any mortgages or charges were created or repaid during the year. This will be necessary to achieve the completeness objective for long-term borrowings (*see* **Section 9:28**, 'Long-term borrowings (including related interest)'). The creation of mortgages or charges should be also recorded in the client's minutes.

9:29.2.2.5 Register of directors and secretaries

The auditor should inspect the register, noting any changes and enquiring whether returns of all changes have been filed with the Registrar of Companies.

The auditor should check, by reference to the appropriate minutes of meetings, that all appointments, resignations or removals of directors or of the secretary have been properly made.

The auditor should check that the client complied with the Companies Act requirements for the minimum number of directors, and that the requirements regarding age limits were also complied with, if appropriate.

9:29.2.2.6 Other registers

The auditor should inspect the register of directors' interests in company or group shares and debentures and the register of substantial individual interests in the company's share capital to establish that:

(a)   they contain the necessary information; and

(b)   the information appears to be up to date.

9:29.2.2.7 Directors' service contracts

The auditor should check that the client is complying with the requirement to make directors' service contracts available for inspection by members.

9:29.3 Share capital, reserves and dividends

9:29.3.1 Completeness; Accuracy; Existence; Valuation

9:29.3.1.1 Reconciliation and review of share capital movements

The auditor should obtain an analysis which reconciles the figures at the balance sheet date with those at the previous year-end for each class of share capital, by both number and value.

The auditor should review this analysis in the light of the business review and examination of the minutes, both of which might indicate events requiring, or resulting in, a change in share capital (e.g., the issue of shares to fund an acquisition, bonus issues, a call on partly paid shares, conversion or redemption of certain classes of share and the issue of shares as part of a profit-sharing or share-option scheme).

9:29.3.1.2 *Independent confirmation*

When the share registers are kept by independent registrars, it is normally possible to obtain confirmation of all changes from the registrars (together with particulars of directors' shareholdings and unclaimed dividends). However, the auditor should first consider whether it is necessary to make enquiries about the registrar's system of internal control. Some independent registrars are affiliated to major banks and, in these cases, it can normally be assumed that controls are satisfactory. However, it might be necessary to make enquiries of such registrars if, e.g.:

(a) the confirmation differs significantly from the client's records and follow-up indicates that the difference was due to errors on the part of the registrars; or

(b) the auditor has knowledge of a history of error involving a particular registrar.

9:29.3.1.3 *Direct testing*

If the auditor does not rely on confirmation from independent registrars, share capital movements should be checked directly. Because the number of changes is normally small, and each one significant, it is normally appropriate to check them all. However, if there are many small changes, such as may occur (e.g.) when shares are regularly issued under the terms of a share-option scheme, a check based on a sample of items may be sufficient.

9:29.3.1.4 *Share issues*

For share issues, the auditor should carry out the following procedures:

(a) Check the issue against supporting documentation, such as minutes and prospectuses, and note the reason for making the issue.

(b) Ensure that the cash or other consideration has been received or is included in called-up share capital not paid.

(c) Check any changes in the authorised share capital against the Articles of Association.

(d) For redeemable shares issued during the year, check that the terms of redemption provide for payment on redemption and that the Memorandum or Articles specify the method and terms by which the redemption may be effected.

The auditor should consider the following matters:

(a) When shares have been issued by a public company for a non-cash consideration, the auditor should verify that a fair value has been ascribed to the shares. The auditor should review the valuation certificate which is required under s. 103 of the Companies Act 1985.

(b) When shares have been issued at a premium, the auditor should check that a sum equal to the aggregate amount or value of the premium has been transferred to the share premium account, unless merger relief under s. 131 of the Companies Act 1985 is available.

9:29.3.1.5 Share purchases or redemptions

For any purchase or redemption of shares during the period the auditor should carry out the following procedures:

(a) Ensure that the company is authorised against do so by its Articles of Association.

(b) Check the purchase/redemption against supporting documentation such as minutes.

(c) Check that, after the purchase, the company has other shares in issue which are not redeemable and that the company has at least two members.

(d) Verify that only fully paid shares have been purchased or redeemed.

(e) Agree the total value of shares purchased or redeemed against the list of cheques issued to registered holders.

(f) Where shares are redeemed out of profits, ensure that an amount equal to the reduction of the issued share capital has been transferred to the capital redemption reserve.

9:29.3.1.6 Agreement with underlying records

The auditor should check the reported authorised share capital with the Memorandum of Association or, for a company not incorporated under the Companies Act, with the Royal Charter, Act of Parliament, or other appropriate documentation.

The auditor should reconcile the allotted capital with the share register (or check the client's reconciliation), ensure that the share register is balanced and test the additions. The total amount of issued share capital at the balance sheet date should be agreed to the general ledger. For a public company, it is necessary to ensure that the allotted share capital is in excess of £50,000.

9:29.3.1.7 Movements on reserves

In relation to overall reconciliation, the auditor should obtain a reconciliation of reserves between the opening and closing balance sheets for:

(a) share premium account;

(b) revaluation reserve;

(c) profit and loss account;

(d) other reserves (e.g., capital redemption reserve, reserve for own shares, and reserves provided for by the Articles of Association).

Only certain types of transaction may be treated as movements on reserves. The auditor should, therefore, check that the items shown in the reconciliation fall into those categories, and should also consider whether items in the profit and loss account should be properly treated as movements on reserves.

In relation to the share premium account, the auditor should confirm movements in the share premium account during the period by re-computation. If there is a reduction in the share premium account the auditor should check the uses of the account, in addition to the amount, to ensure that it has only been used for the following purposes:

(a)   To pay up fully paid bonus shares.

(b)   To write off preliminary expenses.

(c)   To write off expenses of any issue of shares or debentures.

(d)   To write off commission paid, or discount allowed, on any issue of shares or debentures.

(e)   To provide for the premium payable on any redemption of debentures.

In the relation to the revaluation reserve, the auditor must, under the 'alternative' accounting rules (para. 34 of Sch. 4 to the Companies Act 1985) account for any surplus or deficit arising on the revaluation of any asset in a revaluation reserve. The auditor should check the movements against the relevant section of the working papers where the work on the revaluation has been carried out.

In relation to the profit and loss account, the auditor should carry out the following procedures for movements during the period:

(a)   Check total dividends paid and payable with the minutes, the number of shares in issue and ranking for dividends at the relevant time, and the cash payments records.

(b)   Ensure that, for each dividend paid or payable, an appropriate ACT liability is recorded (unless the dividend is paid to the parent company and there is a group election in force), and that there are sufficient distributable profits to cover the dividend.

(c)   Check any prior year adjustment and review the accounting treatment.

In relation to other reserves, the auditor should check movements during the period with the minutes and other supporting documentation, ensuring that the entries are justified by the circumstances.

9:29.3.1.8 Low or negative reserves

If the reserves are low or negative the auditor should consider whether any of the following situations exists:

(a)   The requirements of any loan stock or similar deeds may have been breached.

(b)   For a public company, an extraordinary general meeting has been called if the company's net assets are less than half its called-up share capital.

(c)   The company is trading while insolvent. (Under the Insolvency Act 1986 directors can become personally liable for the company's debt if they continue to trade while knowingly insolvent.)

(d)   Any proposed distributions may be illegal.

9:29.3.1.9 Dividends

In relation to dividends paid, Audit work should cover dividends both paid and declared during the period. The auditor should prove the amount of dividends by re-computation, and should also check that interim dividends have been approved by the directors and that final dividends have been approved by the company either in general meeting or, in the case of private companies, by written resolution.

If a dividend is distributed by independent registrars the auditor may, if satisfied with the independence and solvency of the registrars, place reliance on an examination of the total payment made by the client to the registrars, and it will not normally be necessary to test the individual payments made to shareholders.

If dividends are distributed to shareholders by the client itself, the auditor should test a sample of payments by checking the shareholding against the share register, checking the calculation of the dividend, and examining the returned warrant or cheque for evidence of payment.

In relation to dividends accrued, if a dividend has been declared but not distributed at the balance sheet date, the auditor should check the accrual by re-computation. Also, to ensure the completeness of the total liability for dividends, the auditor must check the validity of the payment of any accrued dividends brought forward from the previous period.

Accrued dividends may be represented by the balance on a special bank account set up to pay dividends. The auditor should check that the unpaid liability equals the balance on the bank account.

If the audit report has been qualified, the auditor will need to make an additional statement to the members of the company regarding the legality of the proposed distribution. This is discussed in **Section 13:18**, 'Additional reports under s. 271 of the Companies Act 1985 (distributions)'.

9:29.3.1.10 Agreement with accounting records

The auditor should check that the amounts of share capital, reserves and dividends in the general ledger agree with the financial statements, by tracing the general ledger account balances to the financial statements via the trial balance.

9:29.4 Cut-off

The auditor should obtain sufficient evidence that changes in authorised or allotted share capital have been recorded in the correct accounting period. This objective will only be relevant when issues or redemptions are made close to the balance sheet date, and will normally be achieved from work on share issues and redemptions set out in **Sections 9:29.3.1.4** and **9:29.3.1.5**.

Assurance concerning the cut-off objective for reserves and dividends will be obtained from the work carried out in relation to the completeness, accuracy and existence objectives described in **Sections 9:29.3.1.7** to **9:29.3.1.10**.

9:29.5 Rights and obligations

The auditor should obtain sufficient evidence from a review of minutes, resolutions of members and other documentation that all the rights and obligations relating to share capital, reserves and dividends have been identified. The team leader should discuss the consequences of complex capital issues with the engagement manager and the engagement partner.

9:29.6 Presentation and disclosure

The auditor will normally achieve the presentation and disclosure objective at the end of the audit by reviewing the financial statements and considering the matters set out in a UK GAAP checklist. Also, it is important to be alert for any matters that require disclosure and which can be more efficiently identified during fieldwork. These include:

(a)   details of interests of any person (other than a director) in 3 per cent or more of the nominal value of any class of voting capital of a listed company;

(b)   particulars of called-up share capital not paid;

(c)   the amounts of distributable reserves, if they are materially different from the balance on the profit and loss account;

(d)   details of any arrears of fixed cumulative dividends.

9:30 Turnover and other income

9:30.1 Introduction

This section is designed to help to develop a programme of substantive tests in accordance with the strategy or the approved substantive testing plan (STP) for turnover and other income. The strategy or STP, if prepared, for turnover and other income should specify the planned response to the assessment of the risk of material misstatement, including the nature, extent and timing of substantive tests.

This section should be read in conjunction with the general guidance on substantive testing in the following sections:

- **Section 9:3**, 'Analytical procedures'
- **Section 9:4**, 'Tests of details'
- **Section 9:5**, 'Evaluating the results of substantive testing'

This section does not cover investment income, which is discussed in **Section 9:18**, 'Investments (including investment income)', or income arising from long-term contracts, which is discussed in **Section 9:20**, 'Long-term contracts'.

9:30.1.1 *Essential audit objectives*

The specific audit objectives for turnover and other income are set out below for each of the general audit objectives. The auditor should obtain sufficient evidence to achieve these specific objectives:

Completeness	All amounts chargeable to customers for goods and/or services supplied, less any trade discounts, returns or allowances, have been recorded in the financial statements.
Accuracy	Transactions have been accurately determined, summarised and recorded.
	The amounts reported in the financial statements are in agreement with the accounting records.
Existence; Valuation; Rights and obligations	Recorded turnover and other income represent either valid sales of goods and services of the client, or valid rights accruing to the client.
Cut-off	Turnover and other income have been recorded in the correct accounting period.
Presentation and disclosure	Turnover and other income have been properly classified, described and disclosed in the financial statements.

Sometimes the auditor may conclude that there is a negligible risk of material misstatement in relation to one or more of these audit objectives, and that consequently no specific substantive procedures are necessary.

9:30.1.2 Early substantive testing

The auditor should normally carry out some of the procedures discussed in this section at an interim date as part of early substantive testing (discussed in **Section 4:7**, 'The audit programme'). The strategy or the substantive testing plan (STP), if prepared, for turnover and other income should specify which procedures will be carried out at an interim date, and how these procedures will be updated to the balance sheet date.

9:30.2 Completeness

9:30.2.1 Accounting policies

The client's accounting policies governing the recognition of a sale should ensure that turnover includes all amounts to which the client is entitled. The auditor should review such policies for acceptability and consistency of application. The problems which might be encountered in certain industries are referred to in **Section 9:30.4.2**.

   The auditor should also consider whether the client takes in a full calendar year's turnover, or whether the turnover includes transactions up to some convenient date (e.g., the last Friday before the year-end). If so, it is necessary to consider whether the effect is material in relation both to the current year and to the preceding year.

9:30.2.2 Re-computation in total

It may be possible to re-compute the total turnover on the basis of known prices and independent despatch or production records. This approach is often effective for clients whose sales consist of a small number of high-value items, or whose sales are of one, or few, products or services the prices of which are not subject to frequent variation. It has been successfully used in the audit of mines, oil and chemical companies, and employment agencies operating on a commission basis.

9:30.2.3 Substantive analytical review

Often it will be efficient to develop an expectation of sales or other income on the basis of the prior year's results, adjusted for known changes and for other variables such as the following:

(a) price increases (dates and percentages);

(b) major customers gained and lost;

(c) changes in credit policies;

(d) new products, discontinued products or changes in the product mix;

(e) seasonal variations.

For example, an estimate of sales for the current period might be developed by adjusting the prior period (audited) sales figure for the following variables:

(a)   Changes in units sold, using details of units manufactured and despatched obtained from the client's management information system.

(b)   Changes in selling prices, obtained from authorised price lists.

Alternatively, an expectation might be developed by reference to known plausible relationships between current year data, e.g. as in the following tabulation.

Class of transactions of audit interest	Related data
● Sales of goods	Purchases, cost of sales, gross margin, product mix, sales area, units despatched.
● Interest receivable	Balances on deposit, interest rates.
● Commission receivable	Number of units sold, commission rates.
● Apartment income	Number of rooms, room tariff index.
● Newspaper advertising	Space taken, price index, revenue.
● Freight income	Number of containers lifted, freight index.

It may be possible to use the client's own budgets as a reasonable expectation. If this is done, however, the auditor should obtain sufficient assurance that the budgets are reasonable and that they are affected neither by undue optimism nor by excessive caution. Their compilation should be reviewed with care.

The nature of audit procedures should vary according to the characteristics of the business and the level of assurance required. For example, to achieve low assurance in a company with few products and stable prices, a single expectation might be developed for the entire period, whereas in a company with several product lines and different pricing policies for each product group, the expectation would be developed at a disaggregated level (e.g., by product or monthly periods) to achieve a similar level of assurance.

9:30.2.4 Tests of details

9:30.2.4.1 Source populations for samples

To test that all sales are recorded, the auditor must select from records that enable potential sales to be identified at the earliest stage in the recording process. Such records should be both complete and independent of the sales recording system. Examples of suitable populations (which are termed 'reciprocal' populations) from which samples might be selected are discussed below:

(a)   **Manufacturing or finished goods**: Goods despatched notes or customers' orders that are subject to controls for completeness are a suitable population. Alternatively, if the client records cost of sales by transfers from stock, the cost of sales account may be used. However, this latter method should not be used if there is evidence that the stock records might not be reliable (e.g., if there is a history of material stock adjustments).

(b) **Service industries**: When turnover is generated by charges for labour supplied plus overheads (e.g., in the case of employment agencies, cleaning contractors, contract labour and professional practitioners) the cost of labour may be used as a reciprocal population. Alternatively, a complete population of contracts might be used. In service industries that receive a commission (e.g., travel agents and insurance brokers) items such as the cost of airline tickets may be used as a suitable reciprocal population.

(c) **Rental income** (other than that covered by leasing agreements) is often best tested by sampling from the income generating assets.

9:30.2.4.2 *Testing the sample*

The auditor should examine the available evidence to obtain assurance that:

(a) the selected item has resulted in a sales invoice showing correct details of all the goods or services supplied.

(b) the selling prices are properly authorised and are based on authorised price lists, catalogues, contracts, agreements or other evidence;

(c) the extensions and additions on the invoice are correct (and, if the sale is in a foreign currency, the translation into sterling is correct);

(d) the sale has been included in the general ledger (the auditor should trace the item through initial and intermediate records);

(e) the additions of the income accounts are correct. It should not normally be necessary to check the additions of all records provided the auditor can be satisfied that the selection is included in the total.

9:30.2.5 *Cash sales*

When considering the effectiveness of controls over cash, the auditor must remember that cash is susceptible to employee theft, and that this can be concealed if there is inadequate accountability over the cash receipts. For example, this risk exists where employees with access to cash receipts also have uncontrolled access to the related accounting records, or if security arrangements and controls are inadequate.

If cash sales are an immaterial portion of the client's total sales and the auditor plans to do limited work, or none at all, in this area, this strategy should be explained to the client.

9:30.2.5.1 *Substantive analytical review*

Substantive analytical review may be used to obtain assurance concerning the completeness of recorded cash sales by developing an expectation as discussed in **Section 9:30.2.3**.

9:30.2.5.2 *Tests of details*

Tests of details of cash sales should normally involve the following processes:

(a)   Testing the completeness of till rolls or cash sales vouchers, and obtaining (and adequately verifying) explanations for any missing documents.

(b)   For selected items, tracing amounts to sales summaries and banking documents.

(c)   Testing the additions of the cash sales summaries.

(d)   Checking that sales summaries have been posted to the sales account.

9:30.2.6 Other income

The choice of tests on other income will largely be determined by the type of income involved. For example:

(a)   **Sales of scrap materials**: Often, these can be tested most effectively by estimating the income on the basis of production reports detailing scrap levels and current scrap prices.

(b)   **By-products**: The auditor might ascertain the nature and volume of by-products by reference to production records and from discussions with production personnel. An estimated income figure can then be developed using independent pricing information.

(c)   **Rental income**: The terms of any leases or sub-leases should be examined. It is important to consider whether all appropriate recharges have been made. The auditor should recompute the total amounts of such income. It is also important to review the board minutes to ensure that all significant leases have been identified.

(d)   **Charges levied on overdue accounts**: If sale agreements include terms for interest on overdue accounts, the auditor should estimate the expected monetary effect by reference to the average overdue debts during the year, the client's aged analysis, and the interest rate applicable.

(e)   **Income from consequential loss insurance claims**: The auditor should consider, based on knowledge of the client gained from the business review or other audit work, whether there have been any events which are likely to give rise to a claim under the client's insurance. The potential amount of any claim should be discussed with management and, if appropriate, with the loss adjusters.

(f)   **Royalties and other contractual rights**: When other income is based on legal agreements such as royalty agreements, the auditor should check that the income has been correctly accounted for in accordance with the terms of the relevant agreement.

9:30.2.7 Sales returns and allowances

It may be possible to obtain assurance on sales returns and allowances by using recomputation in total or substantive analytical review. If tests of details are carried out, the auditor should test a sample by tracing the selected items to the relevant supporting documentation such as goods returned notes, invoices, correspondence or internal authorisations for write-offs, to ensure that the amounts are valid and fairly stated, and were incurred during the current period.

9:30.3 Accuracy

9:30.3.1 Sources of assurance

The auditor will normally obtain the required assurance in respect of this objective from work in relation to the other objectives for turnover and from the corollary effect of work on trade debtors. In particular:

(a) The procedures discussed in **Sections 9:30.2.2** to **9:30.2.6** will provide assurance that sales transactions were accurately recorded, summarised, and posted.

(b) The risk of underpricing will be covered by the checking of sales invoice prices to authorised price lists, catalogues, contracts or agreements, as discussed in **Section 9:30.2.4.2**.

(c) The risk of overpricing of sales transactions will be covered by the trade debtors circularisation procedures (discussed in **Section 9:21**, 'Trade debtors').

9:30.3.2 Agreement with accounting records

The auditor should check that the sales and other income accounts in the general ledger agree with the financial statements, normally by tracing the general ledger accounts to the financial statements via the trial balance.

9:30.4 Existence; Valuation; Rights and obligations

9:30.4.1 Sources of assurance

Because the majority of clients' recorded sales will comprise settled transactions, the auditor will normally (in the absence of identified risks of misstatement) obtain sufficient assurance that they are valid from the corollary effect of testing of balance sheet accounts, particularly bank and cash balances. Similarly, assurance on unsettled transactions will be obtained from the circularisation of debtor balances and direct tests of cut-off, as discussed in **Section 9:21**, 'Trade debtors'. A re-computation in total or a substantive analytical review (**Sections 9:30.2.2** and **9:30.2.3**) will also frequently provide sufficient evidence that recorded sales are valid.

9:30.4.2 Client's policies

In certain industries, however, the risk of incorrect recognition of sales revenue is often high (e.g., leasing and software development). This may be because:

(a) the determination of income is complex, and thus prone to error; and/or

(b) the choice and application of accounting policies for recognising income may be inappropriate or incorrect.

The auditor should identify any risks of material misstatement caused by these factors during the business review.

If the auditor considers the accounting policies adopted by the client are inappropriate and likely to result in material misstatement, after appropriate consultation with other partners (discussed in **Section 5:5**, 'Consultation and concurring reviews'), the auditor should discuss the problem with senior client management with a view to having the accounting policies revised.

9:30.4.3 Tests of details

If a risk of material misstatement relating to the inclusion of invalid sales has been identified, the auditor should consider carrying out appropriate tests of details by, for example, carrying out the following procedure:

(a) Selecting a sample of recorded sales, and examining supporting documentation such as customers' orders, despatch documents and contracts.

(b) Considering the terms of sales to ensure that no 'sale or return' clause or equivalent undertaking leads to doubts about the validity of including the sale in the current period.

(c) Direct confirmation with customers of the terms of sale.

(d) Analysis of contracts, especially with government departments, to ensure that the billing is based on the relevant criteria and that, e.g., only eligible costs have been included.

9:30.5 Cut-off

Audit work on cut-off should be designed to ensure that the following have **not** occurred:

(a) Inclusion of 'old year' sales in the 'new year' (with or without the items sold being removed from stock).

(b) 'New year' sales recorded incorrectly in the 'old year' (with or without the items sold being removed from stock).

The auditor should carefully consider the following:

(a) When the title to goods passes.

(b) The date that goods leave the client's premises.

(c) Terms laid down in contracts.

(d) Special arrangements made with customers regarding delivery or payment.

9:30.5.1 Tests of details

The tests to perform in relation to sales cut-off are discussed in **Section 9:21**, 'Trade debtors'.

9:30.6 Presentation and disclosure

To help achieve the objective of presentation and disclosure the auditor should, at the end of the audit, review the financial statements and consider the matters set out in a UK GAAP checklist. Also, it is important to be alert for any matters that require disclosure and which can more efficiently be identified during fieldwork. These include:

(a)　sales to group companies and other related parties;

(b)　sales to locations not previously supplied by the client (this may affect the geographical analysis);

(c)　sales of new products (this may affect the segmental analysis);

(d)　deduction of all applicable amounts from the disclosed turnover (e.g., VAT, returns of goods, credit notes and commissions deducted at source);

(e)　income requiring separate classification (e.g., deposit interest, investment income, sales of fixed assets).

9:31　Purchases and expenses

9:31.1　Introduction

This section is designed to help to develop a programme of substantive tests in accordance with the strategy or the approved substantive testing plan (STP), if prepared, for purchases and expenses. The strategy or STP, if prepared, for purchases and expenses should specify the planned response to the assessment of the risk of material misstatement, including the nature, extent and timing of substantive tests.

This section should be read in conjunction with the general guidance on substantive testing in the following sections:

- **Section 9:3**, 'Analytical procedures'
- **Section 9:4**, 'Tests of details'
- **Section 9:5**, 'Evaluating the results of substantive testing'

The following expenses are discussed in other sections:

- **Depreciation: Section 9:16**, 'Tangible fixed assets'.

- **Payroll costs: Section 9:32**, 'Payrolls'.
- **Directors' emoluments: Section 9:9**, 'Directors' emoluments, transactions and loans'.

9:31.1.1 Essential audit objectives

The specific audit objectives for purchases and expenses are set out below for each of the seven general audit objectives. The auditor should obtain sufficient evidence to achieve these specific objectives:

• **Completeness**	All purchases and expenses have been recorded in the financial statements.
• **Accuracy; Existence; Rights and obligations**	Transactions have been accurately determined, summarised and recorded.
	Recorded purchases and expenses represent valid expenditure for the purposes of the business.
	The amounts reported in the financial statements are in agreement with the accounting records.
• **Cut-off**	Purchases and expenses have been recorded in the correct accounting period.
• **Valuation**	This is not a relevant objective for purchases and expenses.
• **Presentation and disclosure**	Purchases and expenses have been properly classified, described and disclosed in the financial statements.

Sometimes the auditor may conclude that there is a negligible risk of material misstatement in relation to one or more of these audit objectives, and that consequently no specific substantive procedures are necessary.

9:31.1.2 Early substantive testing

The auditor should normally be able to carry out some of the procedures discussed in this section at an interim date, as part of early substantive testing (discussed in **Section 4:7**, 'The audit programme'). The strategy or STP, if prepared, for purchases and expenses should specify which procedures will be carried out at an interim date and how they will be updated to the balance sheet date.

9:31.2 Completeness

The auditor will normally obtain sufficient assurance in relation to the completeness objective from the corollary effect of direct testing of creditors for completeness. However, if additional assurance is required, it may be possible to:

(a) rely on a substantive analytical review carried out to achieve the existence, accuracy, and rights and obligations objectives, as discussed in **Section 9:31.3.2** (provided the auditor is satisfied that this provides the additional required assurance in respect of completeness); or

(b) carry out tests of details aimed at the specific risks identified (e.g., the auditor may request direct confirmation from suppliers of goods purchased during the period of audit interest, or may extend cut-off tests); or

(c) rely on a combination of these procedures.

9:31.3 Accuracy; Existence; Rights and obligations

The procedures of re-computation, substantive analytical review, and tests of details discussed in **Sections 9:31.3.1** to **9:31.3.5.2** will provide assurance in respect of all the specific objectives under accuracy, existence, and rights and obligations.

9:31.3.1 Re-computation in total

Sometimes (e.g., in process industries) it may be possible to re-compute the cost of purchases by reference to an independent record of quantities delivered, applying unit cost information obtained from, e.g., suppliers' price lists. If the client deals with one supplier for a substantial proportion of its purchases it may be possible to obtain direct confirmation of the purchases for the period. Alternatively, it may be possible to calculate the total purchases in the period by reference to the supplier's statements.

This technique is effective when the client makes most or all of its purchases from a company in the same group, or where the client is a distributor. Re-computation is also effective as a test of expenses such as rates and rent.

9:31.3.2 Substantive analytical review

To develop an expectation for substantive analytical review purposes, the auditor should use an understanding of the business to identify those variables upon which the purchase or expense items are dependent. Examples are:

Type of purchase/expense	Related data
● Cost of sales	Sales; gross margin; product mix; over head absorption rate.
● Total purchases	Volume; weight or units purchased; price index.
● Raw materials	Volume/weight processed; price index.
● Overheads	Prices; size of business; inflation rate; staffing levels; floor area occupied.

Thus, e.g., the auditor might develop an expectation of raw material costs by applying average purchase prices, obtained from a review of suppliers' invoices at various points during the period of audit interest, to the quantities of raw materials used in production.

To obtain higher levels of assurance, the auditor may need to do one or more of the following:

(a) Increase the extent of disaggregation of the data by, e.g., developing a separate expectation for each major type of raw material.

(b) Consider additional data which might affect the expectation (e.g., by taking into account any wastage of materials during the production process).

(c) Examine relevant data in greater detail by, e.g., developing a weighted average for the price of materials by reference to the timing of major purchases.

9:31.3.3 *Tests of details*

9:31.3.3.1 *Sampling*

If the auditor decides to carry out tests of details based on a sample, the selection may be made from either:

(a) the purchase and expense accounts in the general ledger; or

(b) the cash payment records. In this case the auditor should trace the total to the general ledger, and review the general ledger accounts for any unusual items not derived from the cash payment records.

If the client has a standard costing system and the auditor decides to select debits from the stock account, the debits selected will be at standard cost. In such cases a sample should also be selected from debits to the variance account.

9:31.3.3.2 *Testing the sample*

The auditor should substantiate the validity of each selected transaction by examining the supplier's invoice to check that:

(a) it is addressed to the client;

(b) the goods or services were ordered by the client; and

(c) the delivery address is one of the client's locations.

If there is no written order (e.g., for transactions relating to the supply of electricity or water), it is necessary to establish that the invoice or other supporting documentation appears reasonable. If the goods or services were supplied by a company in the same group, the auditor should check that the price is a reasonable 'arm's length' price. If the transaction does not appear to be priced on normal commercial terms, the auditor should bring the matter to the attention of the engagement manager.

The auditor should also check that the recorded goods or services were actually received. For goods, this can normally be done by inspection of receiving records; but finding evidence of the receipt of services may be more difficult. In some cases, such as office cleaning and telephone and telex charges, there may be specific evidence. However, it should often be possible to reach a conclusion that the service was received by reference to the scale of operations of the client, or by observation or, in the case of freight charges on stock, by checking the delivery of the related goods.

The auditor should also confirm the following:

(a) **The transaction is correct**: This is done by testing invoice prices to purchase orders, price lists or other available evidence, and by testing the arithmetical accuracy of the invoice.

(b) **The transaction is properly authorised**: The auditor should ensure that the invoice has been passed for payment by a responsible official.

(c) **The transaction is allocated to the correct account in the general ledger, and to the correct supplier's account in the purchase ledger.**

In the absence of an identified risk of fraud, the auditor will normally obtain sufficient assurance regarding payment for the transaction from inspection and reconciliation of suppliers' statements (*see* **Section 9:24**, 'Trade creditors').

9:31.3.4 *Cost of sales*

Cost of sales is usually determined by one of the following methods:

(a) Each time an item is sold there is a corresponding transfer from finished goods to the cost of sales account.

(b) Cost of sales is calculated periodically from purchases and expenses during the period (adjusted for stock movements based on stock counts).

In the circumstances described in point (a) above, the auditor should test the cost of sales account by selecting debits to that account and ensuring that they represent transfers from the finished goods account only. Sometimes, it may be possible to prove the transfers in total. Because the debits to the finished goods account will have been audited during the testing of purchases discussed in **Section 9:31.3.3.2**, no further testing of the cost of sales account is necessary.

In the circumstances described in point (b) above, the cost of sales account will comprise purchases, plus or minus the movement in stock, plus labour and overheads allocated by journal transfer. The auditor will normally test the underlying materials, payrolls and expense accounts separately as discussed in **Sections 9:31.3.1 to 9:31.3.3.2** and in **Section 9:32**, 'Payrolls'. Work on the cost of sales account will, therefore, concentrate on ensuring that the basis of allocating labour and overheads is appropriate.

9:31.3.5 Purchase returns

The level of purchase returns will depend on the nature of the client's business. The auditor should test purchase returns only when they are expected to be material or if a risk of material misstatement has been identified. This may be ascertained either from knowledge of the business or from a review of the receiving records for evidence of goods received in an unsatisfactory condition.

9:31.3.5.1 Substantive analytical review

The auditor may re-estimate current year amounts for substantive analytical review purposes. The estimate should normally be based on the relationships of the previous year's returns and purchases adjusted for any known changes in the pattern of the business.

9:31.3.5.2 Tests of details

For tests of details, a sample should be selected from a suitable reciprocal population such as goods returned notes, inspection records or correspondence with suppliers. The auditor should test that the amounts are the same as for the original purchase and trace them (and any VAT) to the relevant ledger accounts, and should test the additions of those accounts.

9:31.3.6 Value added tax

It is often convenient and efficient to test the debit entries in the VAT control account at the same time as work on purchases and expenses. There are two types of entry:

(a)   **Payments of VAT to Customs & Excise**: The auditor should test these by examining a copy of the appropriate VAT return and, if a specific risk of fraud has been identified in relation to payments, inspecting the paid cheque or credit transfer authorisation. To ensure that the correct amount was paid it is necessary to check that the return agrees with the records.

(b)   **VAT on purchases and expenses**: The auditor should test this by checking the calculation of VAT on the relevant invoice.

Detailed guidance on the audit of VAT is set out in **Section 9:26**, 'Value added tax'.

9:31.3.7 Agreement with accounting records

The auditor should obtain sufficient evidence that the purchase and expense accounts in the general ledger agree with the financial statements. This should be done by tracing the general ledger accounts to the financial statements via the trial balance.

9:31.4 Cut-off

The auditor will normally obtain the required assurance in relation to purchases cut-off from work on creditors, as discussed in **Sections 9:21** and **9:27**, 'Trade creditors', and 'Other creditors and contingencies'.

9:31.5 Presentation and disclosure

The auditor will normally achieve the objective of presentation and disclosure at the end of the audit by reviewing the financial statements and considering the matters set out in a UK GAAP checklist. Also, it is important to be alert for any matters that require disclosure and that should more efficiently be identified during fieldwork. These include:

(a)   items which should be capitalised;

(b)   transactions involving directors or related parties;

(c)   purchases from suppliers who have included reservation of title in their terms of trade;

(d)   correct classification of purchases and expenses to comply with the prescribed formats of the Companies Act;

(e)   items which should be disclosed as extraordinary or exceptional.

9:32 Payrolls

9:32.1 Introduction

This section is designed to help to develop a programme of substantive tests for payrolls in accordance with the testing plan for payrolls. The strategy for payrolls should specify the planned response to the assessment of the risk of material misstatement, including the nature, extent and timing of substantive tests.

   This section should be read in conjunction with the general guidance on substantive testing in the following sections:

- **Section 9:3**, 'Analytical procedures'
- **Section 9:4**, 'Tests of details'
- **Section 9:5**, 'Evaluating the results of substantive testing'

Directors' emoluments are discussed in **Section 9:9**, 'Directors' emoluments, transactions and loans'.

9:32.1.1 *Essential audit objectives*

The specific audit objectives for payrolls are set out below for each of the seven general audit objectives. The auditor should obtain sufficient evidence to achieve these specific objectives:

- **Completeness**   All payroll costs have been recorded in the financial statements.

- **Accuracy; Existence;**   Gross payroll costs represent amounts to which the
  Rights and obligations   client's employees are properly entitled.

                                     Employers' additional payroll costs represent payments for which the client is liable.

                                     Deductions from gross payroll are complete, authorised, correctly calculated and properly accounted for.

                                     The amounts recorded in the financial statements are in agreement with the accounting records.

- **Cut-off**   Payroll costs have been recorded in the correct accounting period.

- **Valuation**   This is not a relevant audit objective for payrolls.

- **Presentation and disclosure**   Payroll costs have been properly classified, described and disclosed in the financial statements.

In some cases the auditor may conclude that there is a negligible risk of material misstatement in relation to one or more of these audit objectives, and that consequently no specific substantive procedures are necessary.

  This area of the client's records is usually computerised. This means that payroll calculations are automatic, and often outside the client's control. Payments may be made by BACS, and many clients use a bureau for payroll work.

9:32.1.2 *Early substantive testing*

The auditor should normally be able to carry out some of the procedures discussed in this section at an interim date as part of early substantive testing (discussed in **Section 4:7**, 'The audit programme'). The strategy or substantive testing plan (STP), if prepared, for payrolls should specify which procedures will be carried out at an interim date and how they will be updated to the balance sheet date.

9:32.2 Completeness

The risk of material misstatement relating to the completeness of payroll costs is normally low, principally because most employees have a strong interest in ensuring that they are paid promptly and fully. Accordingly, it is normally possible to conclude on this objective on the basis of the corollary effect of work on payroll accruals (as discussed in **Section 9:27**, 'Other creditors and contingencies').

However, if a risk of material misstatement relating to the completeness of payrolls has been identified (e.g., in a company with many casual employees who might wish to avoid incurring income tax), it is necessary to consider carrying out appropriate direct tests. Such tests might include calculating the necessary workforce to maintain production or services and comparing that calculation with the recorded number. Alternatively, the auditor might identify individual employees during audit visits to the client's locations and ensure that such employees appeared on the payroll and were recorded as having been paid the full wage.

9:32.3 Accuracy; Existence; Rights and obligations

9:32.3.1 Gross payroll

9:32.3.1.1 Re-computation in total

If the number of employees is small, and variables such as overtime are not material, it may be possible to re-compute part or all of the gross payroll costs. To do this the auditor should carry out the following procedures:

(a)   Obtain a list of the employees (including leavers and joiners), together with their salaries at the beginning of the year and the dates and amounts of salary changes.

(b)   Test the accuracy of this information and confirm that the employees exist (referred to in **Section 9:32.3.1.3** (fourth paragraph, point (a))).

(c)   Investigate any significant discrepancies between the recomputed amounts and the recorded amounts by obtaining and corroborating explanations from the client.

In manufacturing businesses, production departments often maintain records that account for all the direct labour payroll costs, and it may be possible to use such information to prove the payroll costs in total. The auditor should, however, be satisfied that the records are independent of those kept in the payroll department.

9:32.3.1.2 Substantive analytical review

Substantive analytical reviews of payroll costs will normally involve developing an estimate of the current year charge based on the prior year amounts, adjusted for known changes in average employee numbers and pay rates.

The way the estimate is developed, and the information which should be taken into account, will vary according to:

(a)   the size and complexity of the client; and

(b)   the level of assurance the auditor is seeking from the procedure.

Thus, for a small client with few employees, it might be possible to base the estimate on the prior year's total payroll charge adjusted for an average pay increase, whereas for a client with numerous employees and a complex pay and benefit structure it would be necessary to take into account the number of employees and their rates of pay analysed by category, and/or location and/or cost centre.

Similarly, for a low level of assurance, the auditor might develop a single expectation covering the entire period, whereas for higher levels of assurance it would be necessary to take account of one or more of the following:

(a)   Further disaggregation of the data into, e.g., months or weeks, type of work and location, division or cost centre.

(b)   Additional key factors such as changes of employee 'mix', and pay increases that differ according to the nature of the work.

(c)   The examination of additional corroborative evidence (e.g., the records of the number of employees or payment records) to verify that pay rises were effected at the relevant date.

9:32.3.1.3 Tests of details

Sampling: If tests of details are to be carried out, the auditor should normally use a suitable form of representative sampling. Guidance on selecting samples is given in **Section 9:4**, 'Tests of details'.

The sample should normally be selected from the gross payroll costs in the general ledger. However, if the client maintains a costing system, it may be necessary to select directly from the payroll records. In the latter case, it is important to ensure that the sample is taken from a complete population by checking that the totals of the payroll records agree with those in the general ledger.

When companies pay the employees of other group companies through a centralised payroll department, the auditor should be careful to select samples to reflect the materiality and risk associated with each company. It is also necessary to ensure that the payroll costs reconcile with the amounts debited in the accounting records of the companies concerned.

Testing the sample: The auditor should examine the available evidence to obtain assurance on the following matters:

(a)   **Is the employee genuine?** This can be tested by reference to personnel records that are independent of the payroll department's records. Alternatively, the auditor might make enquiries of independent members of management (who should not be in a position to initiate employee records), or observe a cash wages pay-out (referred to in (c) below). An independently maintained internal telephone directory may provide evidence of existence. It is also important to scrutinise the payroll to ensure that the selected employees do not appear more than once.

(b) **Is the amount of gross pay correct?** Details of pay rates should be checked to authorised salary revision lists, agreed pay scales, and status change documents. Where appropriate, evidence of hours worked or production achieved should be examined (e.g., clock cards, piece-work tickets or bonus records). The auditor should check the accuracy of the calculation of the gross pay, or overtime, and confirm that the gross pay, less the deductions, equals the net pay.

(c) **Has the amount due to the employee been paid?** The paid cheque, or the signed receipt for cash wages, should be examined. If the amount is paid by bank transfer, it is important to check that it is included in the list of payments sent to the bank. The auditor should check that the payroll sheets are approved by a responsible member of management at the time the cheque is drawn or the direct credit transfer advice is approved. The total of net wages should be agreed to the cash book payment in respect of at least one payment. If significant amounts of wages are paid in cash, the auditor should observe the making up of pay packets and the distribution of pay (discussed in **Section 9:32.3.1.4**).

In addition the auditor should agree the general ledger amount to the payroll in respect of at least one recorded monthly or weekly payroll.

9:32.3.1.4 *Attendance at cash wages pay-out*

Attendance at the cash wages pay-out will enable the auditor to:

(a) gain evidence of the efficiency of internal control procedures over cash wages by observing the pay-out;

(b) check the existence of employees;

(c) observe the controls over unclaimed wages and the follow-up procedures.

When attending a wages pay-out, the auditor should seek to ensure that those responsible for the pay-out do not have prior knowledge of this attendance (although management should be informed of the intention to attend). If more than one pay-out takes place simultaneously, enough members of the audit team should be allocated to cover all selected paypoints.

9:32.3.1.5 *Payroll department personnel*

Employees who prepare, handle, or approve status change documents, payroll master files or payrolls are normally in a position to adjust their own pay. Consequently, it is necessary to consider carrying out additional tests on such employees' pay, irrespective of how the audit assurance is obtained for payrolls as a whole. The tests which should be carried out are the same as those described in **Section 9:32.3.1.3** (fourth paragraph).

9:32.3.1.6 *Redundancy payments*

Redundancy payments should normally be tested because, as unusual transactions, they present a risk of misstatement. The auditor should check the terms as agreed by management and the calculation of the amount, and confirm that the amounts are at least equal to the statutory minimum levels. It is also important to check that any government rebates to which the client is entitled have been claimed and accounted for.

9:32.3.2 *Additional payroll costs*

Employer's additional payroll costs generally comprise national insurance, pension contributions and benefits in kind. Certain transactions (e.g., benefits in kind for senior employees) may be complex or unusual and therefore present a greater risk of misstatement.

9:32.3.2.1 *Re-computation in total*

Because national insurance and pension contributions are directly related to gross pay, it may be possible to re-compute them by applying the appropriate percentages to gross pay.

9:32.3.2.2 *Substantive analytical review*

It is possible to carry out a substantive analytical review of the employer's additional payroll costs by estimating the current year's figures by reference to actual costs for the previous year and known changes since then. Alternatively, for pension contributions, if employees' pension deductions have been audited to provide adequate assurance of their accuracy, it may be possible to estimate the employer's costs because there is often a direct relationship between the two figures.

9:32.3.2.3 *Tests of details*

Sampling: To carry out tests of details, a sample should be selected from the employer's additional payroll costs in the general ledger. The auditor should ensure that all the accounts that include employer's additional costs are covered by the sample.

   Testing the sample*:* Tests should comprise:

(a) **National insurance**: This involves checking the calculation of the employer's contribution. The auditor should have regard to the employee's pay in the period, whether he or she is contracted in or out of the government pension scheme, and other appropriate details. (For example, children under 16, married women, widows and people over pensionable age may attract different employer's contributions.)

(b) **Pensions**: This involved checking the calculation of the charge for pensions by reference to the terms of employment and the conditions of the pension fund. Generally, the employer's contribution will be a fixed percentage of the employee's basic salary. The auditor should check that the appropriate rate has been applied and that the employee is eligible to join the scheme. If there has been a recent actuarial valuation of the pension fund, it is important to consider whether it has caused any change in the contribution rate.

(c) **Other costs**: These include health insurance, car schemes, luncheon vouchers and canteen subsidies. The auditor should agree selected items against appropriate supporting documents.

(d) **Postings**: The auditor should check that all items tested in (a), (b) and (c) have been posted to an appropriate liability account.

9:32.3.3 Deductions from gross payroll

Employees' tax, national insurance and pension contributions are normally the most material deductions from payroll. However, deductions may also include season tickets, loan repayments, savings schemes and club and union subscriptions. When auditing deductions, it is important to remember that, in general, no deduction can be made from an employee's pay unless it is:

(a) required or authorised by statute (e.g., income tax and national insurance);

(b) authorised by a 'relevant provision' of the employee's contract of employment. A 'relevant provision' is either a written term of the contract, or an express or implied term where the employee has been notified of its existence and effect before any deduction is made;

(c) agreed to in writing by the employee before the deduction is made;

(d) in respect of overpayment of wages, as a result of any statutory disciplinary procedure or in respect of strikes or other industrial action.

9:32.3.3.1 Re-computation in total

In the same way that it is sometimes possible to re-compute the cost of the employer's national insurance and pension contributions, it is also possible to re-compute the employees' contributions. In particular, pension deductions normally bear a fixed relationship to gross pay and, consequently, to the employer's contributions. Therefore, if the auditor re-computes the employer's contribution, it may be possible to apply a simple ratio to that amount to re-compute the deductions.

9:32.3.3.2 Substantive analytical review

It may be possible to carry out an effective substantive analytical review on deductions by reference to the amounts deducted in previous years and by comparing the deductions with the budgets. However, because pension and national insurance contributions can vary, the auditor should normally check whether there are unusual features in the composition of the payroll, such as a significant number of low-paid or part-time employees who pay no national insurance contributions. Provided that no significant unusual features exist (or, if they do, that they can be adjusted for), substantive analytical review will normally be effective.

9:32.3.3.3 Tests of details

(a) **Sampling**: Usually, the most suitable population for testing deductions for completeness is the sample selected for testing gross pay discussed in **Section 9:32.3.1.3** (first three paragraphs). However, if the gross payroll costs are being tested by substantive analytical review or re-computation, but the auditor wishes to carry out tests of details on deductions, the sample should normally be selected from the gross amounts in the detailed payroll itself.

(b) **Testing the sample**: For every deduction selected, the auditor should either check the calculation (e.g., by reference to tax tables or the pension scheme conditions) or confirm that the amount of the deduction is reasonable and credible. It is then necessary to test the casts of the deductions and the postings to, and casts of, the deductions account.

9:32.3.3.4 *Temporary and contract labour*

Where the client employs temporary labour, labour-only subcontractors in the construction industry or agency staff, it is important to check to ensure that appropriate deductions are made and accounted for. In addition, the auditor should check that the PAYE regulations are followed for all temporary employees. Frequently, such employees' pay is processed through the cash records or petty cash. If so, it is necessary to enquire whether PAYE has been deducted and accounted for.

Where construction industry subcontractors are employed, they should normally have tax deducted by the employer. If tax has not been deducted, the auditor should check that the employer has confirmed that the subcontractor has the appropriate exemption certificate.

Agency staff should be paid by the agency, which will invoice the client. If, for any reason, the client does not pay the agency direct, the client should operate PAYE.

9:32.3.3.5 *PAYE*

PAYE liabilities may fall on the client if the transactions described in **Section 9:32.3.3.4** are not accounted for correctly. In such cases, the Inland Revenue will often make assessments for errors which occurred over a number of years. Consequently, in determining whether there is a material risk of misstatement, it may be necessary to have regard to the likelihood of a relatively small misstatement accumulating to a material amount over several years.

The auditor should also enquire whether expense payments and benefits in kind for all employees have been returned to the Inland Revenue on form P11D or P9D. The main disclosures are the following:

(a) Round-sum payments, unless they are included in a dispensation by the Inspector of Taxes.

(b) Entertainment expenses.

(c) Subscriptions.

(d) Cars.

(e) Accommodation.

(f) Educational assistance.

(g)   Luncheon or travel vouchers.

(h)   Home telephone bills.

(i)   Medical expenses or insurance.

(j)   Prizes or other rewards (e.g., holidays) awarded for performance.

(k)   Beneficial loans.

Because the Inland Revenue has extensive powers to investigate and levy penalties on businesses that have not complied with PAYE and related regulations, the auditor should draw any areas of non-compliance to the attention of the engagement manager.

9:32.3.3.6 Pension scheme

If also responsible for the audit of the client's pension scheme, the auditor should liaise with the audit team responsible for that audit, to ensure that testing includes all the matters that are relevant to the audit of the scheme.

9:32.3.4 Agreement with accounting records

The auditor should check that the payroll amount in the general ledger agrees with the financial statements. This should be done by tracing the general ledger accounts to the financial statements via the trial balance.

9:32.4 Cut-off

Payroll costs are normally paid in arrears. Accordingly, the assurance required in relation to the cut-off objective will normally be obtained from work on payroll accruals discussed in **Section 9:27**, 'Other creditors and contingencies'.

9:32.5 Presentation and disclosure

To help achieve the objective of presentation and disclosure the auditor should, at the end of the audit, review the financial statements and consider the matters set out in a UK GAAP checklist. Also, it is important to be alert for any matters that require disclosure and which can more efficiently be identified during fieldwork including, e.g., the analysis of staff costs.

9:33 Trial balance and general ledger

9:33.1 Essential audit objectives

The auditor should obtain assurance that:

(a)   the balances at the end of the preceding accounting period have been correctly brought forward;

(b)   the trial balance has been properly balanced;

(c)   all items in the financial statements are in agreement with the trial balance and accounting records, and have been subject to audit.

9:33.2 Brought forward balances

At an early stage of the audit the auditor should trace the balances from the previous year's trial balance to the current year's accounting records and investigate any discrepancies. The auditor should also investigate any amounts in the current year's records that are described as opening balances but which do not appear on the previous year's closing trial balance.

9:33.3 Trial balance

The auditor should obtain evidence as to the arithmetical accuracy of the trial balance by checking the additions. However, this is not necessary if all amounts in the trial balance have been referenced to working papers and then to the financial statements. This is because any imbalance in the trial balance would automatically be reflected in the financial statements.

If the trial balance is not properly balanced the auditor should ascertain the reasons and ensure that the matter is properly investigated and resolved. If the client is still unable to balance the trial balance properly, the audit staff should report the matter in issues documentation, and the engagement partner should consider whether proper accounting records have been kept in accordance with s. 221 of the Companies Act 1985.

9:33.4 Agreement with accounting records

Each section of this Manual dealing with an area of the financial statements includes a specific audit objective to ensure that the accounting records agree with the financial statements. The auditor should normally achieve this by tracing items from the general ledger to the trial balance and then to the financial statements via the audit working papers.

The auditor should normally agree the trial balance to the general ledger at an early stage of the final audit, and then control and check subsequent adjustments to the trial balance. The members of the audit team responsible for each area should check that the amounts subject to audit agree with the adjusted trial balance. They should also trace the amounts into the financial statements. The auditor should reference both the adjusted trial balance and the financial statements to the relevant working papers.

As part of the final review, the team leader should ensure that the amounts and descriptions in the financial statements agree with the working papers and that they, in turn, agree with the trial balance. The team leader should take particular care to ensure that all late adjustments to the trial balance have been reflected in the working papers and in the financial statements and that, where appropriate, they have been subject to audit.

9:33.5　Scrutiny of the general ledger

Based on the results of the substantive testing procedures in respect of the profit and loss account, and also in respect of assets and liabilities, the auditor should consider whether, and to what extent, the general ledger should be scrutinised.

The objectives of carrying out a scrutiny are:

(a)　to see what is in the accounting records and from where the entries originate; and

(b)　to identify any items, not otherwise examined, that require specific verification.

The extent of scrutiny of the general ledger will depend on whether it is well controlled. It is preferable for the general ledger to be kept, under the direct control of the chief accountant, by an employee or employees who are not concerned with other aspects of the accounting procedures (e.g., cash, wages and salaries, purchases, sales, stock and work-in-progress or fixed assets). Transfers between accounts should be supported by journal vouchers which should be authorised by a responsible official.

Charges and credits to profit and loss account items which originate from records subject to adequate internal control procedures will normally have been adequately covered by tests of application controls. The entries to which attention should be directed are those which do not originate from a subsidiary accounting record which has already been examined (e.g., transfers from one account to another). Any transfer between ledger accounts should be supported by a journal entry. A review of the general ledger may indicate that such a procedure is not being followed. In that event, the auditor should investigate the transactions concerned.

In the event either that the company's procedures are inadequate or where the auditor's attention is drawn to account balances or specific items that merit further examination, the auditor should consider what further steps are necessary. For example, in respect of an account balance the auditor may obtain an analysis of its make-up, and perform a further scrutiny to identify large and/or unusual transactions for substantive testing.

Where it is decided that scrutinies should be performed it will often be appropriate to carry them out before the year-end for the completed part of the year. Such scrutinies will later require updating to the year-end.

Chapter 10

Audit completion

10:1　Audit completion

10:1.1　Introduction

This section discusses the procedures the auditor should carry out to complete the audit in an orderly and proper manner under the following main headings:

(a)　Final review of draft financial statements.

(b)　Completion of fieldwork.

(c)　Drafting the audit report.

(d)　Issues documentation.

(e)　Audit completion checklist.

(f)　Signature.

(g)　Reporting to the board and to management.

(h)　Debriefing.

(i)　Consideration of desirability of reappointment.

These procedures will normally be performed from receipt of the client's draft financial statements to final completion of the audit, although not necessarily in the order above. As discussed below further guidance on certain of these procedures is contained in the other sections in this chapter.

10:1.2　Final review of draft financial statements

The auditor should carry out a final review of the draft financial statements sufficient, in conjunction with the conclusions drawn from other evidence obtained, to provide a reasonable basis for the audit opinion. As a preliminary to this, the financial statements (including the notes to the financial statements and the directors' report) should be cross-referenced to the working papers. If the auditor has assisted the client in preparing any of the amounts included in the financial statements, they should be agreed with the client and this fact noted in the relevant working paper. The audit evidence supporting the figures and disclosure should be recorded.

Guidance on the final review of the draft financial statements is contained in **Section 10:3**, 'Reviewing the financial statements'.

10:1.3　Completion of fieldwork

The engagement manager should ensure that all fieldwork has been completed and reviewed, except as indicated in issues documentation, before the files are presented for final review by the engagement partner. The engagement manager should be satisfied that:

(a)   adequate working paper review is evidenced in the file;

(b)   all review notes have been satisfactorily cleared and have been removed from the files, any comments relating to matters of substance affecting the opinion having been transferred to the issues documentation.

This is described in more detail in **Section 5:3**, 'Supervision and reviews'.

10:1.3.1 Letter of representation

In addition to any written representations which may have been requested from the client during the audit (e.g., in relation to directors' emoluments), the auditor should consider obtaining a letter of representation from the directors. This procedure is described in detail in **Section 10:4**, 'Representations from management'.

10:1.3.2 Subsequent events review

The auditor should carry out procedures designed to identify all material subsequent events. These procedures should cover the period from the balance sheet date to the date the audit report is signed, and the work done and conclusions drawn should be evidenced on file. This review of subsequent events will normally consist of a combination of discussions with management and inspection of relevant documentation. This is described in more detail in **Section 10:5**, 'Subsequent events'.

10:1.4 Drafting the audit report

The draft financial statements presented to the engagement partner for review should include the draft audit report. The audit report should use the standard wording for an unqualified opinion. If the engagement partner intends to use a special form of wording, or proposes to qualify the opinion, the guidance in **Chapter 13** should be followed. It is also important to consider the consultation procedures set out in **Section 5:5**, 'Consultation and concurring reviews'.

10:1.5 Issues documentation

To assist the partner in the efficient review of the financial statements and clearance of the audit, it is helpful for the audit team to prepare issues documentation. The contents and compilation of issues documentation are discussed in detail in **Section 10:2**, 'Issues documentation'. The engagement partner may evidence clearance of the opinion on the financial statements by signing-off the issues documentation. If a concurring review is required the review partner may also evidence approval of the audit conclusions by signing-off the issues documentation or an equivalent record (*see* **Section 5:5**, 'Consultation and concurring reviews').

10:1.6 Audit completion checklist

To help ensure that all relevant matters are attended to before the audit report is signed, it is often useful to provide an 'Audit completion checklist'. This could be a manual record or use technology. When final issues documentation is first 'presented' to partners for initial clearance it is likely that some of the matters (e.g., the subsequent events review) will not have been completed. However, the auditor should deal with all matters on the checklist before 'presenting' the issues documentation (with the checklist) for final clearance.

10:1.7 Signature

It may be useful to record information relating to signature of the master copy of the financial statements. The audit file could also contain a record of the location and movement of draft and signed copies, the numbers required for printing and the persons to whom copies have been sent. This record will normally be signed by the engagement manager and the engagement partner to evidence completion of the audit and dating of the opinion in accordance with SAS 600.

10:1.8 Reporting to the board and to management

As well as considering the audit report on the financial statements, the auditor should draw together conclusions and other matters appropriate for inclusion in the report to the board and in other reports to management. Detailed guidance is contained in **Chapter 12**.

10:1.9 Debriefing

10:1.9.1 Objectives

The objectives of debriefing at the end of the audit are:

(a)   To ensure that all matters that may need to be reported to the board and to management are identified.

(b)   To assist in the on-assignment training and development of the audit team.

(c)   To improve the efficiency and effectiveness of future audits.

Debriefing is important to future audit planning irrespective of the size of the audit. Members of the audit team often raise matters during an audit which the engagement manager and the engagement partner need to consider, and which may also require discussion with the client's senior management. When the matter is resolved the member of the audit team who first raised it may be unaware of the way in which it was cleared and of all the factors that were considered. Debriefing at the end of an audit allows each person concerned to be told not only that the matter they raised was followed up but also how it was resolved.

Additionally, during an audit, individual members of the audit team will accumulate ideas for improving the audit strategy and its implementation. It is important that these ideas are passed on to the engagement manager so that, where appropriate, those ideas can be carried forward and used in future. A debriefing meeting involving all members of staff on an audit team will ensure that all planning points for future audits are collected.

10:1.9.2 Practical aspects of debriefing

Debriefing meetings should be held shortly after the end of the audit. Holding the meeting at this time will ensure that matters are still fresh in the minds of everybody concerned. All members of the audit team should attend if possible.

A record of the matters covered in the debriefing should be retained in the working papers for carry-forward to the next period, preferably in the form of planning suggestions for next year.

10:1.10 Consideration of desirability of reappointment

The auditor should consider whether the circumstances of the client have changed in such a way as to make it undesirable to continue as the client's auditor. A decision is needed before the auditor signifies willingness to be reappointed at the company's AGM. It is necessary to be alert for conditions that might have caused a rejection of the client had they existed when the appointment was initially accepted. In case of doubt, the engagement partner should consult other partners. This is considered in more detail in **Section 3:2**, 'Appointment and continuation as auditor'. The steps to be taken when a firm ceases to act as auditor are set out in **Section 14:1**, 'Cessation as auditor'.

10:1.11 File completion procedures prior to archiving

The audit files may be scrutinised by others at a later stage. It is therefore important that the final state of the audit files is considered prior to archiving. For example, careless or superficial comments should be avoided, lists of outstanding work should be cleared, open items or unfinished business should be dealt with. Any papers not required for audit purposes, or which have been superseded and have no value, should be destroyed.

10:2 Issues documentation

10:2.1 Introduction

The auditor should prepare issues documentation to provide an appropriate record of matters of significance that arise from audit work. This might record:

(a)   All significant matters affecting the audit opinion on which an initial decision has been made by the engagement manager, and which are subject to review and approval by the engagement partner. (Further guidance on the matters to be included is given in **Section 10:2.3** (first paragraph).)

(b) Decisions that the engagement partner makes on issues, including those in (a) above.

(c) Particulars of the eventual resolution of matters that the engagement partner decides should be discussed with the client, including the reasoning involved in their resolution.

10:2.2 Requirements for issues documentation

10:2.2.1 Timing of issues documentation

Matters which require consideration by the engagement partner may arise at any time after the strategy has been determined. It is important to both the efficiency of the conduct of an audit and the maintenance of good relations with the client that matters of principle which are expected to be significant should be identified promptly. This not only gives the engagement partner more time to consider them, but also usually results in the client's being more receptive than if a matter is raised only in the final stages of the audit. Matters that should be submitted to the engagement partner well before the end of the audit are referred to here as 'interim issues documentation' and those that are submitted towards the end of the audit are referred to as 'final issues documentation'. This is not intended to signify that two separate stages are always appropriate.

10:2.2.2 Evidence of review and quality control procedures

Final issues documentation should be designed to ensure that the audit has been performed in accordance with the approved audit strategy, that review and quality control procedures have been carried out before the audit report is signed and that reporting to the board and to management has been properly considered. To achieve these purposes, it may be useful for final issues documentation to be accompanied by a sign-off by the engagement manager and the engagement partner. The manager might confirm such matters as the following:

(a) The manager has reviewed the working papers and is satisfied that the audit programmes are in accordance with the agreed strategy, and the work is complete.

(b) Questions and exceptions arising from the audit have been satisfactorily resolved.

(c) There has been no limitation in the scope of the audit.

(d) The manager has reviewed the financial statements and is satisfied that they show a true and fair view.

(e) The proposed audit report is consistent with the results of the audit.

(f) The audit completion checklist has been completed.

(g) Significant matters for reporting to management are recorded in issues documentation.

If the manager is unable to confirm any of the above points, one might expect details to be set out in the issues documentation. If a large number of points remain outstanding, they should be resolved as far as possible before the partner reviews the working papers.

The issues clearance process can also provide for the engagement partner to record clearance of issues documentation at the following times:

(a)   When issues documentation is first submitted, subject to any matters which cannot be cleared at that time. The engagement partner should review the draft financial statements and proposed audit report at this time and may clear some of the issues documentation on a provisional basis.

(b)   When all outstanding matters have been cleared.

The engagement manager should normally be responsible for ensuring that all matters outstanding from the first clearance of issues documentation by the engagement partner are settled, and that all other completion procedures have been carried out (these are discussed in **Section 10:1**, 'Audit completion'), before the final clearance of issues documentation by the engagement partner. However, the team leader and relevant members of the audit team should be involved in this process, so that they are aware of the work required to complete the audit. If the issues documentation contains a list of outstanding matters at the time of the first clearance, these should be marked off by the engagement manager indicating the date on which the matter was cleared.

The engagement manager should present final issues documentation to the partner for final clearance on the date appearing on the audit report. This should be the same date as that on which the audit report is actually signed, and after the date that the directors have approved the financial statements. If, however, there is delay over printing the financial statements, issues documentation should nevertheless be presented to the partner on the date appearing on the audit report. This is because it is the date the auditor has declared a willingness to sign the audit report; even if the audit report on the printed version is actually signed later.

10:2.3 Items for inclusion in issues documentation

The engagement manager, in consultation with the engagement partner if necessary, should decide the matters that are included in issues documentation. However, the following should normally be considered for inclusion:

(a)   **The business**: Comments on significant changes in the client's operations, including significant matters arising from analytical reviews, such as unusual variations in important operating ratios or performance indicators. Subject to the engagement partner's requirements this commentary can be kept brief; duplication of material on the audit file is normally best avoided (*see* the next but one paragraph).

(b)   **The financial statements**

    (i)   Particulars of any material respect in which the financial statements fail to comply with the requirements of statute or other relevant regulations (e.g., the

Companies Act, SSAPs, FRSs, the Stock Exchange 'Admission of securities to listing', or, where relevant, SEC requirements).

(ii) Particulars of any failure of the financial statements to comply with acceptable accounting policies. If difficult questions of principle or judgement arise, the auditor should summarise the relevant information and bases for conclusions, including the results of any consultations with others in the firm.

(iii) Information on significant changes in the client's accounting policies or new accounting policies.

(c) The audit

(i) Particulars of any significant changes to the audit strategy or the substantive testing plan affecting the scope of the work.

(ii) Information concerning significant audit queries or matters to be followed up that have still to be resolved (e.g., missing information bearing on the existence or amount of an asset or liability).

(iii) A summary of the aggregate effect of the auditor's estimates of likely misstatement and an overall conclusion on the implications for the audit opinion.

(iv) Conclusions on, and explanation of, any pending litigation and other fundamental uncertainties.

(v) Information on any failure to comply with the requirements of the company's Memorandum and Articles or with trust deeds governing loans or debentures.

(d) **Reporting to the board and to management**: Information on the key matters for reporting to the client.

(e) **Other**

(i) The disposal of any matters marked on the previous year's issues documentation to be carried forward to the current audit.

(ii) Information on any special matters affecting the client's taxation position.

The auditor may also record in issues documentation any other important information that is not otherwise obvious from the financial statements in issues documentation so that the engagement partner is fully aware of any important developments and is able to discuss the client's business effectively with the directors.

Issues documentation need not repeat details of a particular matter that are already included elsewhere on the audit files. A brief summary and a reference to where the full particulars can be found in the working papers are sufficient. Similarly, it is not normally necessary to include in issues documentation comments on every material item in the balance sheet and profit and loss account, or comment on insignificant variations.

10:2.4 Completion of issues documentation

Issues documentation should generally be prepared by the team leader, although other members of the audit team should be encouraged to contribute issues documentation for sections of the work they have completed. The engagement manager, who is normally responsible for ensuring that the audit work is of adequate quality and complete, may then confirm the various matters in **Section 10:2.2.2** (first paragraph) by signing off the issues as complete.

10:2.4.1 Disposal of issues raised

The engagement partner should record the disposal of each issue, or at least those that are critical to the audit opinion, and the supporting rationale. Matters listed on interim issues documentation should be cleared promptly. The engagement partner should sign-off to indicate that the items are cleared.

The engagement partner may decide that some of the matters can properly be resolved only by discussion with the client. After such discussion, a record should be made of what took place and of the reasons that affected the final decision, both those advanced by the client and those advanced by the auditor. The disposal note on issues documentation should record briefly the decision reached. If sufficient space is not available on the form for that purpose, a full account of the discussion should be recorded elsewhere in the working papers. This should be cross-referenced to the disposal note on issues documentation.

10:2.5 Group issues documentation

10:2.5.1 Clearance on consolidation packages

For subsidiary companies, if the auditor has to report first on a consolidation package and later on statutory financial statements, the matters that are brought to the attention of the engagement partner in connection with the opinion on the consolidation package should be recorded on final issues documentation. If possible, the issues documentation should also include matters arising that are relevant to the statutory financial statements so that they are drawn to the engagement partner's attention at the earliest opportunity.

If, however, it is not possible to dispose of all matters that are relevant to the statutory financial statements at the time clearance of the consolidation package is given, the auditor should consider the need to prepare further financial statement issues documentation.

10:2.6 Confidentiality

Because issues documentation will often contain discussion of sensitive issues, the auditor should consider carefully the circumstances before allowing third parties access to them. General guidance on making working papers available to third parties is included in **Section 6:4**, 'Access to audit working papers'.

10:3 Reviewing the financial statements

10:3.1 Scope

This section discusses the following matters:

(a) Disclosures and forms of presentation required by the Companies Act 1985, Statements of Standard Accounting Practice (SSAPs), Financial Reporting Standards (FRSs), and the Stock Exchange Continuing Obligations for listed companies.

(b) Reviewing the financial statements for clerical accuracy, consistency and credibility.

Procedures to be followed for calling over, processing and printing of draft financial statements that are prepared on behalf of clients are set out in the appendix to this section (*see* **Section 10:3.5**). Most of these procedures also apply when clients produce their own annual report and where the auditor is required to check a series of printer's proofs.

10:3.2 Essential audit objectives

SAS 470, 'Overall review of financial statements', requires the auditor to:

> *carry out a review of the financial statements that is sufficient, in conjunction with the conclusions drawn from the other audit evidence obtained, to give a reasonable basis for the opinion on the financial statements.*

This section identifies and discusses the following two essential audit objectives which are common to most sets of financial statements and which the auditor should satisfy:

(a) In respect of disclosure items included in the financial statements, the amounts are not materially misstated and wording is appropriate, consistent, clear and unambiguous.

(b) The interrelationships between the amounts disclosed in the financial statements are credible and the financial statements are free from inconsistencies and from arithmetical or other clerical errors.

10:3.3 Disclosure items

10:3.3.1 Introduction

Information in the financial statements is of the following types:

(a) Information that should be included in the financial statements on which the auditor reports to give a true and fair view.

(b) Other information (e.g., the Directors' Report or Chairman's Statement) issued with the financial statements to comply with legal requirements or specific regulations such as the Listings Rules of the London Stock Exchange.

The essential difference between the two types of information lies in the duty of care imposed on the auditor as auditor. Disclosure information included in the basic financial statements (e.g. balance sheet, profit and loss account, cash flow statement and notes to the financial statements, including statements of accounting policies) is covered by the audit report and it is necessary to form an opinion on each item irrespective of its size. A separate materiality level should therefore be considered in respect of each item. Because such materiality levels will often be lower than the overall materiality level established for the audit as a whole, it may not be sufficient merely to trace the disclosure amounts to the client's audited trial balance. Specific procedures may be necessary to obtain the additional assurance required.

On the other hand, in accordance with SAS 160, 'Other Information in Documents Containing Audited Financial Statements', the auditor should examine information contained in those parts of the annual report that are not covered by the audit report only (subject to client expectations) to the extent necessary to provide sufficient assurance that the information is arithmetically accurate, and appears reasonable and consistent with the basic financial statements. If the auditor identifies any inconsistency between the financial statements and the other information, the auditor should seek to resolve the matter through discussion with the directors. If the matter remains unresolved, the auditor may consider including in the audit report an explanatory paragraph describing the apparent misstatement or inconsistency,

It is important to remember that the auditor has a statutory duty to disclose in the audit report any inconsistency between the Directors' Report and the financial statements. **Section 10:3.3.4.2** provides guidance on the auditor's work in respect of directors' reports.

10:3.3.2 Identifying 'true and fair' disclosure items

The audit work should be planned to enable all necessary information to be obtained and supplied to the auditor in a timely fashion. Wherever possible, the information should be provided by the client in sufficient time for it to be examined adequately within the reporting deadlines. Therefore the auditor should, at the planning stage, identify the information required, and agree with the client:

(a)   the specific information needed; and

(b)   a timetable for its delivery to the auditor.

During later phases of the audit it is important to be alert for any further disclosure matters that arise from circumstances, conditions or events which were not contemplated at the planning stage. The auditor should also have regard to those particular disclosure matters discussed in each of the sections dealing with specific areas of the financial statements.

The auditor may use a manual UK GAAP checklist or suitable software to help ensure that all relevant matters have been properly identified and disclosed. The member of the audit team who completes the checklist should tick or sign off each step and the engagement manager should review the work. If software is used, the engagement manager should review the reports showing the assumptions made, and those questions which were either answered as 'unsatisfactory', or not answered at all.

10:3.3.3 *Auditing 'true and fair' disclosure items*

The auditor should examine disclosure information to ensure that:

(a)   financial amounts are not materially misstated; and

(b)   narratives, descriptions, and wording generally, are appropriate and consistent, and convey clearly and unambiguously the information they are required to convey.

Each disclosure item should be cross-referenced in the working papers to the trial balance or, in the case of consolidated financial statements, to the consolidation schedules. The auditor should support any item which cannot be referenced in one of these ways with a working paper that links the item with its source.

The auditor should review each disclosure item, including numbers and captions in the financial statements, for sense, by comparing it both with the preceding year's amounts and wording and with other related amounts in the current financial statements. It is necessary to establish that the amounts have been compiled on a reasonable and consistent basis, and to obtain and corroborate explanations for any significant fluctuations and discrepancies. These explanations should be recorded in the working papers, together with the conclusions.

For disclosures not derived directly from figures in the trial balance, the auditor should ascertain how the figures have been compiled and determine whether the method of compilation is reasonable and has been properly applied.

10:3.3.3.1 *Earnings per share (EPS)*

The auditor should review the calculation of earnings per share for compliance with FRS 14 and ensure that it has been properly based on profit after tax, as disclosed in the financial statements, and on the number of shares in issue. If there has been a share issue in the year the calculation of the average number of shares in issue should be checked. The auditor should also check whether a 'fully diluted' EPS should be disclosed.

10:3.3.3.2 *Statement of cash flows*

The client should be requested to prepare a working paper showing how the cash flow statement has been compiled. The auditor should carry out the following procedures:

(a)   Trace and reconcile the details to the working papers.

(b)   Obtain or prepare a supporting analysis of items, such as tax payments and proceeds of disposals of fixed assets, that do not already appear on the working papers.

(c)   Cross-check the amounts of any items (e.g., depreciation) that appear elsewhere in the financial statements.

(d)   Review the statement for reasonableness.

10:3.3.3.3 Capital commitments

The auditor should obtain particulars of capital expenditure contracted but not provided for.

If the client has a formal procedure for authorising capital expenditure, the auditor should check that all authorised expenditure has been included in capital commitments (or, alternatively, has actually been expended and capitalised). If there is no formal system in existence it is necessary to review the board/management minutes for evidence of capital commitments.

The auditor should consider the capital projects in progress and ascertain any further commitments in respect thereof. Further evidence may be obtained by reviewing invoices for capital purchases received after the balance sheet date and by reviewing unfulfilled purchase orders at that date.

10:3.3.4 Information issued with audited financial statements

10:3.3.4.1 Introduction

The financial information issued with audited financial statements to comply with legal requirements or with specific regulations normally comprises the Directors' Report and the Chairman's Statement. However, other reports might also be included such as an operating and financial review, a value added statement, a summary of past results or any report on operations. **Sections 10:3.3.4.2** and **10:3.3.4.3**, therefore, are relevant to any such financial information issued with audited financial statements even though only the Directors' Report and Chairman's Statement are referred to specifically.

10:3.3.4.2 Directors' Report

Much of a Directors' Report comprises narrative comment on matters required by the Companies Act, and the Listings Rules of the London Stock Exchange. Before signing the audit report, the auditor should review the directors' comments on these matters for completeness, and should be satisfied that their comments are neither misleading nor inconsistent with the financial statements.

The auditor should reference all monetary amounts disclosed in the Directors' Report to the financial statements, the trial balance and the extracts of the statutory registers in the working papers. The procedures that the client has used to obtain any amounts which cannot be referenced should be reviewed, and the amounts considered for sense and reasonableness. Details of this work should be recorded in the working papers, together with the conclusions.

A specimen audit programme may be drafted that indicates the nature and extent of the audit procedures that the auditor should carry out in relation to the items required to be disclosed in the Directors' Report.

The auditor should take steps during the audit to ensure that the Directors' Report is available in good time to permit an effective review by the engagement manager and the engagement partner. The Directors' Report and the Chairman's Statement should be reviewed for any tax implications. Accordingly, the engagement manager may wish to send copies of these documents to a specialist tax partner or tax manager as soon as they are available.

Errors of fact should be corrected; normally there should be no difficulty in getting the client to do this. If it appears that the Directors' Report contains a significantly misleading statement, or if information contained therein is materially inconsistent with the audited financial statements, matters arising should be included in issues documentation and the auditor should consider the effect on the audit report. In the case of inconsistent information, the Companies Act requires the auditor to state that fact in the audit report. Any audit report which includes references to the Directors' Report will constitute a non-standard report and it should be dealt with in accordance with the procedures for consultation as discussed in **Section 5:5**, 'Consultation and concurring reviews'.

10:3.3.4.3 Chairman's Statement

Before signing the audit report, the auditor should review the Chairman's Statement and any other supplementary financial information included with an Annual Report, in case the views expressed and any financial information given therein are materially misleading or incompatible with the financial statements. The procedures that should be applied should be similar to those used on the Directors' Report. The evidence that should be included in the working papers should comprise adequate cross-referencing to the financial statements, trial balance or working papers (where applicable), together with the conclusions.

If any difficulties arise, the engagement partner should discuss the matter with the chairman, managing director or other senior members of management. If they are unable to provide a satisfactory explanation the auditor should consider whether the financial statements, the Directors' Report or the other financial information should be amended.

If the auditor considers that the financial statements should be amended, but the directors are unwilling to do this, there is no statutory requirement to comment in the report. However, there may be occasions when a matter is potentially so misleading to a reader of the financial statements that it would be inappropriate to remain silent. In these circumstances, the engagement partner should follow the consultation procedures set out in **Section 5:5**, 'Consultation and concurring reviews', and it may be necessary to obtain legal advice.

10:3.4 Final review

SAS 470 states that:

> *auditors should consider whether the financial statements as a whole and the*
> *assertions contained therein are consistent with their knowledge of the entity's*

business and with the results of other audit procedures, and the manner of disclosure is fair.

The final review of the financial statements, apart from providing confirmation that they indeed give a true and fair view, should normally comprise:

(a)   A review of the credibility of the relationships between amounts disclosed in the financial statements.

(b)   A review for clerical accuracy and for consistency within the financial statements.

10:3.4.1 *Review for credibility*

The purpose of the review is to:

(a)   identify unusual fluctuations by reference to the interrelationships between amounts included in the financial statements;

(b)   compare the findings with those arising from substantive auditing procedures, and ensure that satisfactory corroborated explanations have been obtained for them;

(c)   where necessary, make further enquiries and carry out further testing to explain the fluctuations;

(d)   decide in the light of (a) to (c) whether the financial statements as a whole reflect the underlying events and transactions.

The auditor should compare the ratios developed at the preliminary and final phases of the audit to identify any large or unusual fluctuations and ensure that sufficient understanding of their causes has been obtained.

The auditor may also prepare a summary of the major components of the amounts reported in the financial statements. For example, although it is helpful to calculate the client's overall gross profit margin and compare it with prior periods and the budget, it is often more useful to prepare such comparisons for major product lines and, wherever possible, to incorporate volumes as well as values sold.

Firms may develop software packages to assist in this review. Where such a package is used, the reports produced should be filed with the working papers, and all review comments generated by the program should be cleared.

10:3.4.2 *Review for clerical accuracy and consistency*

Although the audit opinion will rarely be invalidated by minor inconsistencies in the financial statements, such inconsistencies (and other minor errors) will lead the users of the financial statements to question the quality of the audit work. Consequently, before the financial statements are issued, the engagement manager should read the financial statements (including the Directors' Report, the Chairman's Statement and other financial disclosures not covered by the report) carefully for sense and consistency.

The engagement manager should also ensure that:

(a)   all the additions are correct;

(b)   amounts disclosed in the Notes and in the Directors' Report agree with the corresponding amounts in the balance sheet, profit and loss account and cash flow statement (e.g., the amount disclosed as the depreciation charge should be the same in the fixed assets note and in the cash flow statement);

(c)   cross-references within the financial statements are complete and correct (e.g., the note references on the balance sheet should agree with the note numbers);

(d)   all significant disclosures are supported by working papers;

(e)   the audit report is appropriately worded and properly dated (audit reports are discussed in **Chapter 13**);

(f)   comparative figures agree with the published prior year financial statements (or the differences have been reconciled and adequately explained);

(g)   no spelling or typographical errors have been overlooked;

(h)   all the matters discussed in **Sections 10:3.4** and **10:3.4.1** have been satisfactorily dealt with.

The engagement manager should evidence completion of the review.

10:3.5 Appendix A Calling over and processing financial statements

10:3.5.1 Financial statements printed by the audit firm

The draft financial statements approved by the engagement partner should be used as the basis for processing the master copy and should be clearly identified for this purpose (normally by the engagement partner initialling the draft). The approved draft should be retained on the audit file. After any final matters arising on the financial statements have been cleared by the engagement partner, the financial statements should be processed.

10:3.5.1.1 Calling over and printing

The detailed arrangements recommended for processing financial statements are set out in the following paragraphs of **Section 10:3.5.1.1**. However, each firm should determine its own administrative procedures for controlling and processing financial statements, and also any circumstances in which it is permitted to depart from the standard procedure.

Audit staff should call over the master copy with the approved draft, and check calculations and additions (including the cross-casts) before the master copy is printed or presented to the engagement partner for signature. The members of the audit team who carry out these procedures should sign the master copy.

Errors found on calling over should be marked on a copy (or listed on a separate sheet), and the work returned for correction. If practicable, those who carried out the original calling over should check that the corrections are properly made. If the master copy is corrected a number of times, each processed version should be dated and consecutively numbered for identification purposes to avoid possible confusion.

Audit staff should call over financial statements in a common-sense way and ensure that numbers, references and statements are consistent throughout the document. In particular, they should check that:

(a)   all pages and paragraphs are numbered and follow in sequence;

(b)   dates have been changed from the previous period's financial statements;

(c)   if the reporting date has changed, the term 'period' or 'year' is used, as appropriate;

(d)   all page and column headings are correct;

(e)   references to pages, paragraphs and notes (numbers and amounts) are correct. These should be checked both ways and page numbers in the audit report should be checked to the actual pages in the financial statements; and

(f)   directors' names and initials are accurately and consistently disclosed.

Audit staff should be alert for inconsistencies in statements or figures which are identifiable in, or can be derived from, other figures in the financial statements. For example, they should check:

(a)   that the balance on the reconciliation of movements in shareholders' funds agrees with the corresponding figure in the balance sheet;

(b)   that the depreciation charge disclosed in the profit and loss account note agrees with the tangible fixed asset note to the balance sheet;

(c)   all the figures in the cash flow statement.

After the calling over, and before sending (or releasing) the financial statements for printing, the engagement manager should arrange for the master copy to be fully cross-referenced to the working papers and should read through the document.

The engagement manager should check the printed copies to ensure that all pages have been properly printed.

10:3.5.2 *Financial statements prepared by the client*

The auditor should follow the procedures described above (amended as appropriate in the circumstances) when the financial statements are produced by the client or by an outside printer. For example, a referenced draft should still be prepared for presentation to the engagement partner and for checking against the final document, and calculations and additions should be checked.

The auditor should ensure that all amendments to the financial statements have been authorised by the client. It may be necessary, particularly in the case of a public company, to call over each major proof in full until all corrections are made.

10:3.5.3 Other documents

The auditor should follow the calling over procedures described above (as appropriate in the circumstances) for other documents sent to clients, such as the audit report to the board.

10:4 Representations from management

10:4.1 Representations as audit evidence

To form an opinion on a client's financial statements the auditor needs to obtain relevant and reliable evidence sufficient to draw reasonable conclusions in respect of all material items in the financial statements. One source of relevant audit evidence is the information the auditor obtains from the client's directors and management, referred to as 'representations from management'. The following sections should be read in conjunction with SAS 440, 'Management representations'.

SAS 440 states that 'auditors should obtain written confirmation of appropriate representations from management before their report is issued'.

During the audit the auditor will receive oral representations from management in answer to specific enquiries. The auditor can nearly always corroborate such representations with other evidence obtained from the audit fieldwork. For example, management might have advised the auditor that it was not in a position to exercise significant influence over an associated company, and the auditor may have been able to corroborate this by reviewing minutes of that company's board and executive committee meetings, and by inspecting correspondence. Where this applies, the auditor does not need to ask the client's management to confirm in writing its oral representations.

Sometimes, however, the auditor may not be able to obtain adequate corroborative evidence, and it will not be reasonable to expect such evidence to be available. This might apply, e.g., where the facts concerned were known only to management, or where the matter principally involved judgement and opinion. In such cases the auditor should:

(a)   compile a summary of the uncorroborated oral representations received from management during the audit;

(b)   ensure that there is no other evidence which conflicts with management's oral representations;

(c)   obtain senior management's written confirmation of the oral representations; and

(d)   consider whether, in the circumstances, those representations, together with such other audit evidence obtained, are sufficient to enable the auditor to form an unqualified opinion on the financial statements.

The management's written representations are often referred to as 'the representation letter'. Some audit firms may adopt a policy of requesting the board of directors to minute the representations required rather than writing the auditor a letter. This is discussed further below.

10:4.2 Drafting the representation letter

The draft representation letter should be available for review by the engagement partner at the time of clearing the audit. Its drafting should not be left too late in the audit and if the client has difficulty in providing it there may be an impact on the audit opinion because the letter forms an essential part of the audit evidence.

The draft presented to management should concentrate on the important issues so that management focuses clearly on its responsibilities in relation to the sensitive matters in the financial statements. Accordingly, the draft should:

(a)   be tailored specifically to the client's circumstances; and

(b)   subject to the qualification is the next paragraph, include only those representations that:

> (i)   are uncorroborated by sufficient other audit evidence; and
>
> (ii)   relate to material matters for which the auditor considers that the representation is a necessary part of the audit evidence.

The auditor should remember to include any matters that arise between the date on which the fieldwork is completed and the date on which the letter of representation is presented for signature by the client. The auditor should normally obtain separate representations on directors' emoluments and transactions, as discussed in **Section 9:9**, 'Directors' emoluments, transactions and loans'.

If the engagement partner considers that there is increased risk to the firm, because of either a poor control environment or significant deficiencies in the internal accounting controls, the letter of representation may need to be more comprehensive and could include the paragraphs in the appendix to this section (*see* **Section 10:4.7**).

The representation letter should be addressed to the audit firm and, because the representations are those of management, the auditor should request the client to prepare it on headed notepaper. The auditor should ask that the draft letter be considered by the board, and for such consideration to be minuted. Alternatively, as mentioned, the detail may be minuted (*see* **Section 10:4.4** (second paragraph)).

10:4.3 Signing and dating

The letter of representation should be signed by a director on behalf of the board, and it should be dated and received before the audit report is signed. If there is a delay greater than one week between the date of the letter and the date of the audit report, the auditor should obtain an updated letter.

10:4.4 Difficulties in obtaining written representations

Directors are sometimes reluctant to sign a representation letter for one or more of the following reasons:

(a) They may consider that the board of directors accepts full responsibility for the truth and fairness of the financial statements and for their completeness when the board approves them for signature, and that specific representations are therefore unnecessary. That may be correct so far as the board is concerned but, in forming an opinion on the financial statements, the auditor has taken into account a number of management representations on specific matters (and, in the case of a comprehensive letter, a number of implied representations on other matters). The representation letter provides the evidence that management made these representations and that the auditor did not misunderstand them.

(b) The directors may consider that the letter refers either to matters on which the auditor ought to be able to form an opinion without requiring representations from them, or to matters that are irrelevant to their business. It is for these reasons that the draft letter should, except where the auditor requires a comprehensive letter, only include those matters that are both material and significant in the particular circumstances of the client.

(c) The directors themselves may be uncertain about a particular matter on which the auditor is seeking representations.

(d) The directors may consider they have no obligation to give the auditor the information requested. The auditor should explain that an auditor is entitled in law to obtain all the information and explanations the auditor considers relevant to the opinion.

SAS 440 states 'if management refuses to provide written confirmation of a representation that the auditors consider necessary, the auditors should consider the implications of this scope limitation for their next report'.

If the directors refuse either to sign a representation letter or to pass a board minute recording the representations made, the preferred procedure is that the firm should write to the client, setting out the principal representations which have been made during the audit, and requesting the client to reply in writing confirming that the auditor's understanding as regards those matters is correct.

Alternatively, or in addition to the procedures outlined above, the engagement partner may request to attend the board meeting at which the financial statements are to be approved, for the purpose of explaining the significance of the matters upon which the firm is seeking representations, and to obtain:

(a) the directors' agreement that those matters were taken into account when the financial statements were prepared; and

(b) their confirmation that the auditor's understanding is correct.

In deciding which course of action is more appropriate, the engagement partner should take into account the sensitivity and/or significance of the matters affecting the financial statements upon which written confirmation of management's representations is sought.

In the rare cases where the auditor does not consider it appropriate to record the understanding by writing to the client as discussed in the last paragraph but one above, and the request to attend the board meeting is refused, the engagement partner should follow the consultation procedures discussed in **Section 5:5**, 'Consultation and concurring reviews', regarding the circumstances leading to the refusal. If, after any necessary further discussions with the client, the partners concerned do not accept the directors' reasons for withholding their representations, the engagement partner should explain to the client that, because all the information and explanations required have not been obtained, the audit report will be qualified. The auditor should consider taking legal advice.

10:4.5 Parent companies

Where the firm is the auditor of a parent company that produces consolidated financial statements, it may need to obtain additional representations from the board of directors of the parent company. These should cover any aspects of the consolidated financial statements that cannot be adequately dealt with by representations in respect of individual companies in the group (e.g., consolidation adjustments on such matters as deferred taxation).

10:4.6 Subsidiary companies

When auditing a subsidiary company, the auditor may need to obtain additional representations from the management of the parent company on matters that affect the subsidiary's financial statements. Such matters could include, for example, confirmation of the allocation of management charges, and confirmation of the intention to pass group relief between the companies.

10:4.7 Appendix A Paragraphs for inclusion in a comprehensive representation letter

The following paragraphs should be included in a representation letter when the engagement partner considers that there is increased risk to the firm, as discussed in **Section 10:4.2** (third paragraph). They should be included in addition to any specific matters on which representations might be required as audit evidence.

10:4.7.1 Introduction

We acknowledge as directors our responsibility for ensuring:

(a) the accuracy of the accounting records and the financial statements prepared from them; and

(b) that the financial statements give a true and fair view of the state of affairs of the company as at .... and of the profit and cash flows for the year [*period*] then ended.

We confirm to the best of our knowledge and belief, and having made appropriate enquiries of other directors and officials of the company, the following representations given to you in connection with your audit of the company's financial statements for the year [*period*] ended ....

10:4.7.2 Accounting records and transactions

All the accounting records have been made available to you for the purpose of your audit, and all the transactions undertaken have been properly reflected and recorded in the accounting records. All other records and related information which might affect the truth and fairness of, or necessary disclosure in, the financial statements, including minutes of directors' and shareholders' meetings [*and of all relevant management meetings*], have been made available to you and no such information has been withheld.

10:4.7.3 Assets

Provisions for depreciation and diminution in value, including obsolescence, have been made against fixed assets on bases and at rates calculated to reduce the net book amount of each asset to its estimated residual value by the end of its probable useful life in the company's business. In this respect we are satisfied that the probable useful lives have been realistically estimated.

current assets in the balance sheet are expected to produce not less than the net book amounts at which they are stated.

All assets included in the balance sheet were at that date and remain free from any lien, encumbrance or charge [*except as disclosed in the financial statements*].

10:4.7.4 Liabilities

Full provision has been made for all liabilities at the balance sheet date, including guarantees, commitments and contingencies where the items are expected to result in significant loss [*except as follows*]. Other such items, where in our opinion provision is unnecessary, have been appropriately disclosed in the financial statements [*except as follows*].

We are not aware of any pending or threatened litigation, proceedings, hearings or claims negotiations which may result in significant loss to the company [*except as follows/other than the matters listed in the memorandum dated .... supplied to you*].

10:4.7.5 *Related parties*

We confirm that the ultimate controlling party of the company is *[insert name]*, that we have disclosed all related party transactions relevant to the company and that we are not aware of any other such matters required to be disclosed in the financial statements whether under FRS 8 or other requirements, for example, [*the Listings Rules or*] the Companies Act 1985.

10:4.7.6 *Laws and regulations*

Other than [*specify*], we are not aware of any instances of actual or potential breaches of or non-compliance with laws and regulations that are central to the company's ability to conduct its business or that could have a material effect on the financial statements.

Other than [*specify*], we are not aware of any irregularities, or allegations of irregularities including fraud, involving management or employees who have a significant role in the accounting and internal controls systems, or that could have a material effect on the financial statements.

10:4.7.7 *Other matters*

We are not aware of any irregularities, including fraud, involving management or employees of the company, nor are we aware of any breaches or possible breaches of statute, regulations, contracts, agreements or the company's Memorandum and Articles of Association which might prejudice the company's going concern status or that might result in the company's suffering significant penalties or other loss. No allegations of such irregularities, including fraud, or such breaches have come to our notice [*except as follows*].

No circumstances have arisen, or events occurred, between the balance sheet date and the date of this letter in respect of matters which would require adjustment to or disclosure in the financial statements, or which should be disclosed to shareholders through some other medium [*except as follows*]. We have no plans or intentions that may materially affect the carrying value or classification of assets and liabilities [*except as follows*].

Except as disclosed in the financial statements, no transactions involving directors, officers and others requiring disclosure in the financial statements under the Companies Act have been entered into [*except as follows*].

10:5 Subsequent events

10:5.1 Audit objective

The auditor should obtain assurance that events occurring after the subsequent sheet date have, where necessary to give a true and fair view, been appropriately dealt with in the financial statements. SAS 150, 'Subsequent Events', provides guidance on the auditor's responsibilities regarding subsequent events occurring:

(a)   between the period end and the date of the auditor's report;

(b)   between the date of the auditor's report and the issue of the financial statements; and

(c)   after the financial statements have been issued, but before they are laid before the members or equivalent.

10:5.2 Definition

SAS 150 defines subsequent events as those relevant events (favourable or unfavourable) which occur and those facts which are discovered between the period and the laying of the financial statements before the members or equivalent. Relevant events are defined as those which:

(a)   provide additional evidence relating to conditions existing at the balance sheet date; or

(b)   concern conditions which did not exist at the balance sheet date, but which may be of such materiality that their disclosure is required to ensure that the financial statements are not misleading.

SSAP 17 defines subsequent events (post-balance-sheet events) as:

> *those events, both favourable and unfavourable, which occur between the balance sheet date and the date on which the financial statements are approved by the board of directors.*

A subsequent event may require either an adjustment to the amounts disclosed in the financial statements (an 'adjusting event') or disclosure in the financial statements (a 'non-adjusting event'). The procedures discussed in this section are designed to identify events after the balance sheet date. The treatment of any such events should be decided in the light of SSAP 17 and the overriding requirement to show a true and fair view. Examples of subsequent events include:

(a) **Adjusting events**

    (i) Fixed assets. The subsequent determination of the purchase price or the proceeds of sale of assets purchased or sold before the year-end.

    (ii) Debtors. The renegotiation of amounts owing by debtors, or the insolvency of a debtor.

(b) **Non-adjusting events**

    (i) Mergers and acquisitions.

    (ii) Strikes and labour disputes.

    (iii) Losses of fixed assets or stocks as a result of catastrophe such as fire or flood.

Subsequent events do not include matters under preliminary consideration by the directors which may be the subject of a future decision by them.

The date of approval, which will normally be the date of the board meeting at which the financial statements are approved, should be disclosed in the financial statements. This is normally achieved either by including the date under the directors' signatures on the balance sheet or by referring to it in a note to the financial statements.

Although the SSAP 17 definition of post-balance-sheet events only applies up to the date on which the financial statements are approved by the board of directors, the auditor should also search for similar events up to the date on which the audit report is signed. Some responsibility may also be retained after the date on which the audit report is signed (as discussed in **Sections 10:5.6** to **10:5.6.2**).

10:5.3 Subsequent events between the balance sheet date and the date of the auditor's report

SAS 150 states that:

> *auditors should perform procedures designed to obtain sufficient appropriate audit evidence that all material subsequent events up to the date of their report which require adjustment of, or disclosure in, the financial statements have been identified and properly reflected therein.*

Subsequent events might affect the amounts at which items are stated in the financial statements or they might require disclosure. It is therefore important to be alert to the possibility of such events at all stages of the audit. In addition, specific audit procedures should be carried out to ascertain whether such events have occurred. The objective of these procedures should be to provide reasonable assurance that all material subsequent events, including 'window dressing' transactions (discussed in **Section 9:13**, 'Window dressing and off-balance-sheet financing'), have been identified and, where appropriate, either disclosed or accounted for. Audit procedures should cover the period between the balance sheet date and the date the audit report is signed. The report should not be backdated to the date the fieldwork was completed.

10:5.3.1 Specific procedures

The review of subsequent events should consist of a combination of discussions with management and inspection of relevant documentation. Such procedures should be performed as near as practicable to the date of the auditor's report and might include the following:

(a)   Ascertaining and evaluating the way management identifies subsequent events and decides whether a subsequent event requires disclosure or adjustment in the financial statements.

(b)   Reviewing the management accounts for periods after the date of the balance sheet and considering whether these identify any adverse trends or significant movements in balance sheet headings.

(c)   Reviewing other relevant accounting records and reading the latest available financial information such as interim financial statements, budgets, cash flow forecasts and other related management accounts.

(d)   Determining the outcome of known uncertainties and contingent liabilities at the balance sheet date, in particular those relating to litigation, provisions and the outcome of sale negotiations relating to significant fixed assets.

(e)   Examining the effect of inherent risks identified during the audit (e.g., the possible effects of currency fluctuations).

(f)   Reviewing the subsequent year's cash flow forecasts and budgets for evidence of subsequent events.

(g)   Reviewing the replies to letters of confirmation from solicitors and banks. Where practicable, the response from the solicitors should include events to a date as close as possible to the date of the approval of the financial statements.

(h)   Reviewing cash payments and suppliers' invoices after the balance sheet date.

(i)   Reviewing journal entries after the balance sheet date for evidence of significant adjustments or write-offs that relate to the period under audit.

(j)   Reading the minutes of meetings of members, the board of directors, and its executive committees or any other relevant committees since the balance sheet date and enquiring about matter discussed at meetings for which minutes are not yet available.

(k)   Considering carefully whether any other knowledge has come to light, from either inside or outside the client, that would indicate the occurrence of subsequent events. The auditor should consider, e.g., press comment, changes in the trading pattern of the client, changes in law or other legislation such as tax regulations, currency devaluations and major fires or catastrophes.

(l)   Making enquiries of management and where necessary obtaining representations as to the occurrence, or absence, of events subsequent to the balance sheet date that might require adjustment to, or disclosure in, the financial statements.

Examples of specific enquiries which may be made of management include:

(a)   The current status of items involving subjective judgment or which were accounted for on the basis of preliminary data, e.g. litigation in progress.

(b)   Whether new commitments, borrowing or guarantees have been entered into.

(c)   Whether sales of assets have occurred or are planned or assets have been destroyed.

(d)   Whether the issue of new shares or debentures, or an agreement to merge or to liquidate, has been made or is planned.

(e)   Whether there have been any developments regarding risk areas or contingencies.

(f)   Whether any unusual accounting adjustments have been made or are contemplated.

(g)   Whether any events have occurred or are likely to occur which might bring into question the appropriateness of the accounting policies used in financial statements, e.g. if such events called into question the validity of the going concern basis.

10:5.4 Issues documentation

The engagement manager should be prepared to confirm, for instance by signing-off the issues documentation before final clearance by the engagement partner, that appropriate subsequent events review procedures have been completed. Because the final clearance of issues documentation should take place close to the date of the audit report, the engagement manager, in providing this confirmation, should ensure that appropriate procedures have been performed not only up to the time when final issues documentation was first presented to the engagement partner (i.e., normally at the time the fieldwork is completed), but also up to the date of the audit report. Where there is a significant lapse of time between completion of the fieldwork and the date of the audit report, the auditor should update the procedures that were carried out before that date.

10:5.5 Group financial statements

If the auditor of a subsidiary company comes into possession of information which should have been reflected in the subsidiary's financial statements after those financial statements have been signed, the auditor of the parent company should be consulted. If the matter is likely to be material to the group, the subsidiary auditor should consider whether to notify the parent company auditor immediately.

When relying on other auditors, e.g. those of a division, branch or subsidiary undertaking, the parent company auditors should satisfy themselves that the other auditors have performed appropriate subsequent event procedures up to the date of the parent company's auditor's report.

10:5.6 Events discovered after the date of the audit report but before the financial statements are issued

It is the responsibility of the directors to issue financial statements which give a true and fair view and are not otherwise misleading. The directors may be expected to inform the auditor of any material and subsequent events occurring after the date of the audit report but before the financial statements are issued. The auditor does not however have any obligation to perform procedures or make enquiries regarding the financial statements after the date of the audit reports.

If the auditors become aware of material subsequent events occurring after the date of the audit report but before the financial statements are issued SAS 150 states that the auditor should:

> *establish whether the financial statements need amendment, should discuss the matter with the directors and should consider the implications for their report taking additional action as appropriate.*

> *Where the directors amend the financial statements the auditor should extend his or her audit procedures to the date that the new report on the amended financial statements is signed. Where the directors do not amend the financial statements before seeing them, if the auditor believes they should be amended the auditor should consider taking steps to prevent reliance on their report, e.g. making an appropriate statement at the AGM.*

10:5.6.1 Subsequent events discovered after the financial statements have been issued but before their laying before the members, or equivalent

After the financial statements have been issued, the auditor has no obligation to perform procedures or make any enquiries regarding such financial statements. SAS 150 requires that:

> *When, after the financial statements have been issued, but before they have been laid before the members or equivalent, auditors become aware of subsequent events which, had they occurred and been known of at the date their report, might have caused them to issue a different report, they should consider whether the financial statements need amendment, should discuss the matter with the directors, and should consider the implications for their report, taking additional action as appropriate.* (SAS 150.4)

The SAS distinguishes between two events:

(a) An event which occurred before the date of the audit report, but which the auditor became aware of thereafter; and

(b) An event which occurred after the date of the audit report.

Where an event occurred before the date of the audit report but the auditor was not aware of the event before signing the audit report the auditor should consider with the directors whether the financial statements should be revised (e.g. under the statutory provisions relating to the revision of company annual financial statements and directors' reports as set out in ss. 245 to 245C of the Companies Act 1985 and in the Arts. 253 to 253C of the Companies (Northern Ireland) Order 1986). When an event occurred after the date of the audit report there are no statutory provisions for revising financial statements in which case the auditor may wish to take advice on whether it might be possible to withdraw the report. In both examples other possible courses of action include the making of a statement by the directors or auditor at the AGM. In any event legal advice may be helpful.

When the directors revise the financial statements, the auditor should:

(a) Carry out the audit procedures necessary in the circumstances;

(b) Consider, where appropriate, whether Stock Exchange regulations require the amendment to be publicised;

(c) Considering where there is any requirement, in the case of businesses authorised under the Financial Services Act 1986 or other regulated businesses, to communicate with the appropriate regulator;

(d) Reviewing the steps taken by the directors to ensure that anyone in receipt of the previously issued financial statements together with the audit report thereon is informed of the situation; and

(e) Issuing a new audit report on the revised financial statements.

If the client issues amended financial statements, the auditor should, if practicable, ensure that all copies of those previously issued are returned and destroyed. However, if this is not possible, the amended financial statements and the audit report should indicate that they represent amendments of previously issued information. The auditor should consider whether to request written assurance from the client that copies of the amended financial statements will be sent to, or made available to, all persons who received copies of the original financial statements.

When the auditor issues a new audit report on the revised financial statements he or she should:

(a) Refer in the report to the note to the financial statements that explains in more detail the reason for the revision of the previously issued financial statements, or to set out reason in the report;

(b) Refer to the earlier audit report issued on the financial statements;

(c) Date the new audit report not earlier than the date the revised financial statements are approved; and

(d) Have regard to the guidance relating to reports on revised annual financial statements and directors' reports as set out in APB's Practice Note 8, 'Reports by Auditors Under Company Legislation in the United Kingdom'.

If the directors do not revise the financial statements which the auditor believes need to be revised and these statements are issued but have not yet been laid before the members or equivalent, or if the directors do not intend to make an appropriate statement at the AGM, then the auditor considers steps to take on a timely basis to prevent reliance on the report. For example, the auditor may consider making an appropriate statement at the AGM. The auditor may also consider taking legal advice on his or her position. An auditor does not have a statutory right to communicate directly in writing with the members although, if he or she resigns or is removed or is not reappointed, he or she has, e.g., various duties under company law.

10:5.6.2 Procedures with respect to amended financial information

The audit report on amended financial statements should not be dated before the date on which such financial statements are approved by the directors. The auditor should also ensure that subsequent events audit procedures are extended to cover the period to the date of the report on the amended financial statements or, if the information is being separately disclosed to shareholders and others, the date of approval of that information by the directors.

Clients are usually co-operative in the circumstances referred to in **Sections 10:5.6** and **10:5.6.1**. Sometimes, a client may refuse to permit the auditor to make the necessary investigation or refuse to make suitable notifications to members and others, because it does not believe the situation warrants such action or for other reasons. In such situations, the auditor should consider any professional responsibilities, including whether to make a statement at the general meeting at which the financial statements are laid before the members. It is usually advisable to seek legal advice. An auditor does not have a statutory right to communicate directly in writing with the members but, depending upon the circumstances, there may be a responsibility to notify directly members and others relying on the financial statements and, if the client is a listed company, the International Stock Exchange.

10:5.6.3 Revision of defective financial statements

Provisions in the Companies Act 1989 permit directors to revise financial statements. These provisions are explained in **Section 13:20**, 'Revision of defective accounts'.

10:5.7 Events arising after approval by the members

SAS 150 does not provide guidance on facts discovered after the approval of the financial statements by the members. However, if, after the date of the general meeting at which the financial statements are laid before the members, information comes to light concerning any events which could materially affect those financial statements, the auditor should inform the directors and establish what steps they intend to take to deal with the situation which might include issuing revised financial statements as discussed in **Section 13:20**, 'Revision of defective accounts'. It may be necessary to take legal advice on the position, especially if it appears that the directors are not taking appropriate steps.

10:5.8 Requests for additional copies of audit reports

Clients sometimes ask at a later date for the auditor to provide additional copies of the financial statements. Such requests can normally be complied with, because the services being provided are merely printing or reproduction and the request does not create any obligation to undertake additional audit procedures. However, if the auditor is aware of any significant event that has occurred since the completion of the financial statements and the release of the report and which is not reflected in the financial statements, the auditor must consider whether providing additional copies of financial statements that do not reflect this event could involve any professional responsibility or liability.

Chapter 11

Group audits

11:1 Introduction to group audits

11:1.1 Scope of the chapter

The basic procedures and policies that an auditor should follow for any audit are set out in **Section 1:3**, 'The audit approach'. These steps also apply to the audit of group financial statements; guidance on the extra procedures that apply in the case of the audit of group financial statements are set out in this chapter.

The term 'group financial statements' as used in this chapter represents the financial statements of the parent and its business units. The chapter is therefore concerned with auditing the consolidated financial statements of a parent and its subsidiaries, associates and other relevant undertakings. It also applies, however, to multi-location audits, such as a head office with a number of branches.

The chapter primarily deals with those situations where the auditor is responsible for the audit of the parent (the 'referring office') and refers work to other offices of the firm ('performing offices'), or to other auditors. However, it is also relevant where the auditor is the performing office, undertaking work which has been referred by another office or by other auditors.

11:1.2 Overview of group audits

The approach to group audits depends on whether the auditor is the referring or performing office. If the auditor is the referring office reporting on the group financial statements, the auditor carries out the audit of the parent and of the consolidation, and may audit business units directly or refer the work to business unit auditors. If the auditor is the performing office, the audit of a business unit is carried out in accordance with the group audit strategy, which takes into account specific statutory or other reporting requirements applicable to the business unit. Alternatively, the auditor may be requested to perform a review of the work of other auditors which audit local business units.

The paragraphs below outline the auditor's approach when acting as:

(a)   the referring office, **Sections 11:1.3.1 to 11:1.3.8.2**;

(b)   the performing office, **Sections 11:1.4.1 to 11:1.4.3**.

11:1.3 Referring office responsibilities

11:1.3.1 Group business review

Section 11:2, 'Group business review', sets out the elements of the business review for a group. The auditor begins a group audit by gathering or updating knowledge of the group. The auditor considers changes in the group structure, business activities and reporting requirements. Procedures may include discussions with key members of parent management, visits to major business units and liaison with other auditors.

The auditor applies preliminary analytical reviews to high-level aggregations of data, such as consolidated management accounts, in order to establish familiarity with the group's financial position and to understand which business units are important to the group's results. The auditor considers whether there are any unusual or unexpected relationships or balances applicable to individual business units or groups of business units.

The auditor reviews whether the group's significant accounting policies are appropriate in the light of legislation, accounting standards, industry norms and requirements as to good practice. The auditor considers whether these accounting policies are applied consistently throughout the group.

The auditor makes preliminary judgements concerning the materiality for the group financial statements and considers the materiality to be applied to the audits of the business units. Where appropriate the auditor applies a group materiality to the work performed on business units.

The auditor assesses the risk of material misstatement in the group financial statements. Where these risks have an impact on the audits of individual business units, the auditor notifies the auditors concerned of these risks. The auditor also considers the risk to the firm of conducting the group audit.

11:1.3.2 Assessing the control environment

Section 11:3, 'Assessing the control environment of a group', describes how the auditor may assess the control environment in the parent company, in particular the extent of control which parent management exercises over business units. Favourable features of the control environment can help the auditor reduce the extent of testing of business units, and of the consolidation.

11:1.3.3 Determining the group audit strategy

Section 11:4, 'Determining the group audit strategy', describes the matters that should be considered in determining a strategy for the audit of group financial statements. The group audit strategy describes, in broad terms, the principal features of the audit firm's proposed approach to the group audit. It is developed from the understanding of the group, from the evaluation of inherent risks, and from the review of the control environment.

The strategy records the extent of audit assurance the auditor requires in relation to individual business units and the means by which this will be obtained. The assurance will be derived from a combination of the following strategy options for the scope of work to be carried out at individual business units:

(a)   Unrestricted audits, normally undertaken only when a separate audit is required on the business unit for statutory or other reasons.

(b)   Limited scope audits, based on prescribed materiality levels or restricted to particular account balances or classes of transactions.

(c) Reviews of business units or of particular account balances and classes of transactions.

(d) Visits to business units to carry out discussions with management and other limited procedures.

In some cases, e.g. when a business unit is immaterial in relation to the group financial statements, no work will be performed on the business unit.

For geographical or other reasons, business units might be audited by other firms of auditors. The group audit strategy should indicate how the auditor plans to obtain confirmation regarding the quality of work of the other auditors.

The auditor determines the strategy for testing the aggregation of the financial information provided by each separate accounting entity taking into account the assessment of the parent company control environment. Many clients use a standard consolidation software package and the auditor might find it efficient to obtain some of the audit assurance by testing the controls over the package. The auditor checks that all business units have been included in the aggregation and that the aggregation process is arithmetically accurate, including foreign currency translation calculations. The auditor also tests the consolidation adjustments made by the parent.

11:1.3.4 Planning and control

A group audit can be complex, so proper planning and control are essential. Guidance on the procedures that the auditor should follow is set out in **Section 11:5**, 'Planning and control of group audits'. The auditor sends instructions to performing offices and to other auditors who are responsible for undertaking work on business units. These instructions set out the work required in accordance with the group audit strategy, including the nature of the report required and the reporting timetable.

The auditor also sends instructions to performing offices when requesting them to review the work of other auditors and to report on whether the work was satisfactory.

11:1.3.5 Work of other auditors

Guidance on the procedures that the auditor should follow to confirm that the work of other auditors is satisfactory is set out in **Section 11:6**, 'Work performed by other auditors'. These procedures might include:

(a) Questionnaires.

(b) Visits to business unit management and/or the other auditors.

(c) Reviews of other auditors' working papers.

The auditor should communicate regularly with other auditors and ensure that they are notified of any significant issues that arise as a result of their audit work which might affect the report on the group financial statements.

11:1.3.6 *Auditing the consolidation*

Guidance on development of a programme of tests to audit the consolidation is set out in **Section 11:7**, 'Auditing the consolidation'. The auditor receives information from business units and their auditors, including the following:

(a)   The financial information, generally included in a standard package (referred to in this Manual as a 'consolidation package').

(b)   Audit reports.

(c)   Issues documentation, or equivalent.

(d)   Questionnaires and reports.

The auditor reviews this information to identify any matters which affect the auditor as group auditor, e.g., qualifications in the audit reports of business units relating to matters which are material in relation to the group financial statements.

The auditor carries out a final analytical review. The data are analysed by business unit, or geographically, to enable the auditor to investigate and explain significant fluctuations compared to the prior year or to the client's forecasts. The auditor reviews movements on account balances such as goodwill and reserves.

11:1.3.7 *Audit completion*

Guidance on those matters particularly relevant to group audits that the auditor should consider at the completion of a group audit is set out in **Section 11:8**, 'Group audit completion procedures'. Before signing the audit report on the group financial statements the auditor completes the fieldwork and reviews it for quality. The auditor ensures that all audit work on the business units has been satisfactorily completed and, where appropriate, that the business units' statutory financial statements have been signed.

If necessary, a review partner carries out a concurring review covering, as a minimum, either the draft issues documentation or a summary of them and the draft financial statements, proposed audit report and other parts of the client's annual report.

Significant matters that could affect the audit opinion or which need to be reported to the referring partner highlighted in the issues documentation. These include significant matters arising from the audits of business units. Before the auditor finalises the audit opinion, the audit findings are discussed with parent management to ensure the auditor has obtained all the relevant information and explanations and to explain to management any concerns that the auditor might have.

11:1.3.8 Reporting

11:1.3.8.1 The audit opinion

If the auditor has achieved sufficient audit assurance, including assurance regarding work carried out by other auditors, and is satisfied that the client has met the appropriate legal and accounting requirements, the auditor gives a standard unqualified report for groups. If not satisfied with the audit outcome, including when there is a material qualification relating to a business unit, the auditor may wish to follow the firm's consultation procedures. The guidance on audit reports in **Chapter 13**, 'Audit reporting to members', also applies to group audits.

11:1.3.8.2 Reporting to the board and to management

The auditor will want to report in a positive and constructive way the main findings and recommendations arising from the group audit. Included in the report should be those significant matters arising from the audits of business units which the auditor considers are of interest to parent management.

11:1.4 Performing office responsibilities

11:1.4.1 Auditing a business unit

Guidance on the responsibility of a performing office is set out in **Section 11:9**, 'Responsibilities of a performing office'. The auditor ensures that the instructions issued by the referring office include the scope and nature of the report the auditor is being asked to give. The auditor carries out the work in accordance with these instructions, or reports significant changes to the referring office. Subject to the requirements set out by the referring office, normal audit procedures are applied to this work.

   The auditor communicates regularly with the group auditors and ensures that they are notified of any significant issues that arise as a result of this audit work which might affect their report on the group financial statements.

   The auditor reports on the work to the referring office and, if required, to the parent. The form and wording of the report are normally specified by the referring office. If the auditor plans a qualification in the report, the matter will need to be discussed with business unit management and the referring office before the report is finalised.

11:1.4.2 Letters of support

In many groups the auditor may find that a business unit being audited is dependent for its continuing existence as a going concern on support from the parent or a fellow business unit. This support is often provided by means of a letter of support or a letter of subordination. The auditor considers whether the letter needs to be legally binding and, if so, whether it properly meets this objective. The auditor may need to seek assistance from the referring office or a business unit auditor to do this. Detailed guidance is set out in **Section 11:10**, 'Letters of support'.

11:1.4.3 *Reviewing the work of another auditor*

The referring office might ask the performing office to review the work of other auditors. The nature and extent of this work will be based primarily on specific instructions received from the referring office (*see* **Section 11:1.3.4** (second paragraph)).

11:1.5 Small businesses

The procedures described in the paragraphs above apply to all audits of groups, regardless of their size. The extent to which the auditor needs to follow the detailed procedures set out in the remaining sections of this chapter will depend on the complexity of a group's structure and operation rather than its size. For example, the auditor of a small group with one significant overseas subsidiary will need to follow the guidance in **Section 11:6**, 'Work performed by other auditors'. The guidance included in **Section 11:10**, 'Letters of support', may be particularly relevant to the auditor of a small subsidiary of a larger group.

11:2 Group business review

11:2.1 Introduction

The elements of the business review for a group are the same as those for an individual business unit:

(a) Developing or updating the understanding of the client's business.

(b) Carrying out preliminary analytical reviews.

(c) Reviewing and obtaining an understanding of the client's significant accounting policies.

(d) Making a preliminary assessment of materiality.

11:2.2 Developing or updating the auditor's understanding of the client's business

In a group audit, the following issues will be of particular relevance:

(a) Group structure and business activities.

(b) Reporting requirements.

(c)   The control environment, in particular the style, philosophy and methods of the parent's management. This is discussed in **Section 11:3**, 'Assessing the control environment of a group'.

(d)   The audit environment.

(e)   The consolidation process.

11:2.2.1 Group structure and business activities

The auditor should obtain an understanding of the various elements of the organisational structure of the group, e.g. the management and operating structure, the financial reporting structure and the legal structure. The auditor should obtain, develop or update an organisation chart to record all interests of the parent in business units, including the dates of changes in the group structure. The auditor should separately identify those interests which are to be consolidated, those which are to be treated as associates or joint ventures and those which are to be excluded from consolidation.

The auditor should be alert to the need to record information on 'permanent' consolidation adjustments as supporting documentation and include it in carry-forward material. Further guidance on this is set out in **Section 11:7**, 'Auditing the consolidation'.

A group operating structure which does not fit the needs of the business can expose the group to risks, e.g.:

(a)   If a group is operationally or geographically dispersed and there is no structure to permit the adequate flow of management information, there may be an increased risk of concealed losses.

(b)   If management is able to bypass established procedures, it might be able to undermine the effectiveness of controls.

(c)   If accountability is not clearly defined, it is easier to conceal fraud or error. An inappropriate operating structure can also lead to misstatement caused by persistent conflicts and low morale among management and employees.

The auditor should update the understanding of the significant business activities of the group and the political and economic environments in which they take place. For example, if a group has some business units which operate in foreign countries it might be exposed to risks through factors such as:

(a)   Government intervention in areas such as trade and fiscal policy, and restrictions on currency and dividend movements.

(b)   Fluctuations in exchange rates.

(c)   A lack of understanding in the group of local conditions generated by cultural, political or sociological influences.

(d)   The impact of local legislation, e.g. on matters such as product liability.

The auditor should be fully aware of any changes in the group structure or business activities which might affect the assessment of risk and the scope of the audit work. **Sections 11:2.2.1.1** to **11:2.2.1.7** provide further guidance on the effect of changes.

11:2.2.1.1 Acquisitions

If the group has made, or proposes to make, an acquisition in the year the auditor should carry out the following procedures:

(a)   Agree at an early stage whether it is to be accounted for as an acquisition or as a merger and ensure that the accounting treatment adopted complies with FRS 6.

(b)   Identify and agree the date on which control passes to the parent, i.e., the effective date of acquisition for group reporting purposes and ensure it has been computed in accordance with FRS 2.

(c)   Enquire whether a special consolidation package is to be prepared for the period between acquisition and the balance sheet date or whether the annual financial statements will be prepared and prorated. In either event the auditor will need to devise appropriate procedures or modified instructions to relevant auditors.

(d)   If acquisition accounting is to be adopted, identify the steps that the group intends to take to arrive at the fair value of the acquired assets and liabilities and be satisfied that they are appropriate and acceptable. The auditor should also ensure that the fair value exercise is carried out and audited in a timely manner and complies with FRS 7; and that the letter of instruction to the relevant business unit auditors includes procedures for a review of these fair values.

(e)   Determine the client's proposed treatment of any goodwill that may arise (including that arising on the acquisition of an associate) and request that supporting evidence be prepared for the useful economic life of the goodwill.

(f)   Enquire whether the acquired business unit has any accounting policies that do not comply with those of the group and ensure that arrangements are made to amend the policies or, at least, to evaluate the effect of such non-compliance to enable any necessary consolidation adjustment to be made.

(g)   If the acquired business unit has an accounting date that differs from that of the group, ascertain whether its year-end is to be brought into line. If it is not brought into line (perhaps for tax reasons) the auditor should ascertain what steps are being taken to produce necessary figures at the balance sheet date. Alternatively, if financial statements with a differing year-end are to be incorporated into the group financial statements, the auditor should review the business unit's results between its year-end and that of the group for significant matters that need to be reflected in the group financial statements.

(h)   Where appropriate, review any work carried out by the firm in connection with the acquisition to help develop the auditor's understanding of the acquired business unit.

11:2.2.1.2 Disposals

If the group has made a disposal in the year, the auditor should consider the following matters:

(a) There might be difficulties when a group does not obtain detailed information on the relevant component's results for the period up to the date of the disposal and on its balance sheet at that date. If the amounts involved are likely to be material and the auditor is aware that such a disposal is planned, the auditor should ask the client to arrange for the information (or a reasonable estimate thereof) to be obtained to permit an accurate analysis to be made of the results as between:

    (i)   the trading profit or loss to the date of disposal; and

    (ii)   the profit or loss on disposal.

In many cases, normal management accounts may be sufficient for this purpose, provided the auditor has assessed them to be reliable.

(b) The auditor should consider the arrangement for auditing the transactions for the period prior to disposal.

(c) The auditor should carefully check the effective date of disposal to ensure that it is the date that the parent loses control in accordance with FRS 2.

(d) The auditor should ensure the profit or loss on disposal has been calculated in accordance with FRS 3 and the disclosure of the disposal also complies with this accounting standard.

11:2.2.1.3 Cessation of trading

If a business unit has ceased trading in the period the auditor will normally need to pay particular attention to ensuring that the basis and calculation of those amounts that might be treated as extraordinary are acceptable.

11:2.2.1.4 Reorganisations

The auditor should ascertain the reasons for any group reorganisation in the year. If the auditor cannot determine any obvious business reason for the reorganisation the auditor should consider whether a principal reason may have been to generate distributable profits artificially.

11:2.2.1.5 Artificial transactions

As regards any acquisitions or disposals in the year the auditor should enquire about the relationship between the group and the seller or purchaser of the relevant business unit. Where business units are under common control or there is any indication of influence being exercised, or capable of being exercised, by or on the group the auditor should investigate the matter thoroughly. This is because transactions between such parties can be used to generate an artificial profit, by entering into a transaction on terms that are not calculated on an arm's length basis.

11:2.2.1.6 *Existing subsidiaries and associates*

The auditor should consider whether it is appropriate for existing subsidiaries and associates to continue to be included on the basis used previously. There may be particular difficulties in relation to associates because of the problems in determining the extent of the group's influence. In particular, the auditor should consider whether other, more influential, shareholders exist which might indicate that they should not be treated as subsidiaries or associates. Details of undertakings which should be included in the consolidation are given in FRS 2.

In other situations, difficulties might arise where economic or political considerations cause a parent to provide support that implies a closer legal relationship than actually exists. Such support might take the form of actual or implied guarantees of bank borrowings. Other possible contingent liabilities can arise from political considerations. Where, for instance, an associate is essentially a joint venture or partnership with a foreign government or a foreign company there could be severe repercussions on the group's business in that country if the joint venture or partnership fails. In such a case there might be a real risk that the group would have to bear all the losses of that associate, rather than merely its legal share. In addition, further liabilities and commitments might flow from the assumption of such losses and liabilities and have a material effect on the parent.

The auditor should identify at an early stage any circumstances (including those described in the two preceding paragraphs) in which a group might be in danger of assuming responsibilities or obligations that are not legally reflected in the financial statements as either actual or contingent liabilities. The auditor should discuss these with parent management, and should suggest that particular attention be paid to the risk areas, both by parent management and by the auditor, by means of the following procedures:

(a)   Specific management and board level reviews of associates, joint ventures and partnerships.

(b)   Contact with local auditors and business unit management.

(c)   Regular assessment of overseas political and economic factors, and of the exposure of group business units to those factors.

(d)   Clear guidelines regarding the extent of financial support to be provided to associates, joint ventures and partnerships.

11:2.2.1.7 *Tax implications*

The auditor should consider the tax implications of any changes in group structure, e.g.:

(a)   Capital gains tax implications of business units leaving the group, including charges to tax arising on the group.

(b) The impact of anti-avoidance legislation on changes in the group structure and group reliefs previously granted or available.

In respect of all changes in the group structure in the UK, the auditor should check that the client has considered the question of VAT registration/deregistration. In cases of doubt, the auditor should consult a VAT specialist.

11:2.2.2 Reporting requirements

The auditor should ensure that the consolidation package will collect all the information necessary to produce the group financial statements and allow compliance with the disclosure requirements of the Companies Act, accounting standards and other relevant requirements. The auditor should carefully review the group's consolidation package, and ensure that if any changes in the group's activities, company law or accounting standards have taken place then the package has been amended accordingly.

Where the client operates in a specialised or regulated business the auditor should gain an understanding of any specific accounting and reporting requirements and ensure that reporting complies with the requirements of SAS 120, 'Consideration of Laws and Regulations'.

Because collection of information in a large group is often a complex administrative process the auditor should try to anticipate future changes in reporting requirements. For example, if a new accounting standard is to take effect in a year's time the auditor should ensure that the consolidation package is amended so that the information to be included as comparative figures in the next year's financial statements can be collected and reported upon in the current year.

The auditor should notify business unit auditors that the consolidation package has been reviewed. However, there might be other matters that they will need to review. In such cases, they might find it helpful to receive an up-to-date copy of a UK GAAP checklist.

11:2.2.3 The audit environment

Where the auditor does not audit all business units in a group, the auditor should update the information on business unit auditors. For example, the auditor may establish that an overseas auditor has been replaced. As discussed in **Section 11:4**, 'Determining the group audit strategy', the involvement of other auditors can result in risk to the firm, and if there are any concerns the auditor should discuss them with parent management at an early stage.

If the group made an acquisition during the year, the auditor should discuss the audit arrangements for the business unit acquired. If the firm does not already audit the business unit, the auditor may discuss with management whether a change is planned. If the firm is not appointed auditor after a significant acquisition, the auditor should consider the risk to the firm.

11:2.2.4 *The consolidation process*

The auditor should obtain an understanding of the consolidation process, including the extent of use of computers. For example, the auditor should enquire whether the client plans to use an established packaged consolidation system and whether there have been any changes in staff or procedures since the previous audit.

11:2.3 Sources of information

The sources of information will include:

(a)   discussions with group and business unit management;

(b)   visits to locations.

11:2.3.1 *Discussions with group and business unit management*

Where the auditor conducts discussions with senior management to gain an understanding of matters that might affect the strategy and key business issues, questions should not be restricted to finance and accounting officials. The auditor should address questions to executives in non-financial fields such as production, distribution, marketing and treasury and to those executives responsible for significant business segments. Such discussions are useful for assessing risk and concentrating client service efforts more effectively and for developing a closer relationship between the key decision makers and the engagement team.

11:2.3.2 *Visits to locations*

The auditor should visit important client locations. Such visits should be carried out periodically and may be co-ordinated with visits by members of parent management, where appropriate.

The auditor should inform the business unit auditor in advance of the nature and purpose of the visit and the business unit auditor might be involved in the visit. The auditor should ensure that the visit does not suggest a lack of confidence in the personnel or procedures of the business unit auditor.

Visits to locations serve the following purposes:

(a)   To increase the auditor's knowledge of local operations and conditions.

(b)   To improve the auditor's understanding of the problems faced by the business unit.

(c)   To provide opportunities to establish lines of communication and foster good client relationships.

(d)   To improve the quality of service provided to the client through the auditor's being better able to respond to client needs.

The auditor may also visit business units which appear to be immaterial to the group financial statements. The objective of such visits is to confirm that there is no significant audit risk. This is discussed further in **Section 11:4**, 'Determining the group audit strategy'.

11:2.4 Preliminary analytical reviews

The auditor should carry out preliminary analytical reviews to help determine materiality and to identify risks of misstatement that might affect the group audit strategy. In addition, it will extend or confirm the understanding of the group, enabling the auditor to direct audit attention to business units within the group that are material to the group's current financial position and results of operations.

11:2.4.1 Scope

The preliminary analytical reviews should be sufficient to help the auditor to determine the group audit strategy. Because they are not intended to provide substantive audit evidence, extensive reviews such as those required for substantive analytical reviews are not required. The auditor should direct attention to high-level aggregations such as consolidated management accounts, and supporting information which allows analysis by business unit.

11:2.4.2 Nature

Preliminary analytical reviews might include consideration of the following:

(a) **Analysis by business unit**: The auditor should identify the business units which make a significant contribution to the group's turnover and results for the period and its assets and liabilities. Where appropriate, the auditor should produce this analysis for each significant account balance and class of transactions. Similarly, the auditor should identify those business units which appear immaterial to the group financial statements.

(b) **Prior period amounts or current period budgets and forecasts**: The auditor may compare significant business units' performance against prior period results, or against budgets and forecasts. This might indicate a risk of misstatement in particular business units which can be addressed in the group audit strategy.

(c) **Financial ratios**: The auditor may analyse liquidity ratios, asset utilisation ratios, credit ratios and other operating ratios. For example, the auditor may calculate the group's gearing ratio when reviewing its level of borrowings.

(d) **Other key 'performance indicators'**: The auditor should establish the key indicators used by management to monitor the performance of business units and review them to improve the understanding of the group's activities and performance and to identify where there might be particular risks.

11:2.5 Understanding the significant accounting policies

A DTI Inspector's report criticised the principal auditor for not adequately reviewing the accounting policies of a subsidiary, after the subsidiary went into liquidation.

> **We are surprised at the degree of reliance placed by [*the principal auditors*] upon [*the business unit auditors'*] audit. [*The principal auditors'*] incomplete review of [*the business units*] accounting policies should have provided sufficient grounds for concluding that [*the business unit*] was a high risk audit area, and we are surprised that [*the principal auditors*] did not pursue their enquiries in order to provide a better knowledge and understanding as a basis for their audit.**

The auditor should review the group accounting policies each year to ensure that they remain the most appropriate for the group. The auditor should discuss with the client any policies which do not comply with generally accepted accounting principles GAAP, and any which are:

- new
- significantly affected by changes in the group business
- not the predominant industry practice
- controversial
- complex by nature
- inconsistent within the group

If the client plans to use a controversial policy, the engagement partner should discuss the matter with client management. This will include those situations where the client wishes to invoke the 'true and fair' override to justify departure from the application of an accounting standard or the Companies Act in accordance with UITF abstract 7. If there are doubts concerning the acceptability of the policy, the engagement partner should also follow the consultation procedures set out in **Section 5:5**, 'Consultation and concurring reviews'.

Inconsistent accounting policies are most likely to arise where business units have diverse activities or are based in foreign countries which apply different rules, e.g. the United States. Such inconsistencies will normally be eliminated either by parent management's requiring business units to prepare consolidation packages using group accounting policies, or by its requiring additional information on the effect of any differences. Where there are, or could be, differences, management will need to consider whether adjustments are required on consolidation. The auditor should consider significant matters arising when determining the strategy.

To assist business unit auditors in their work, the letter of instruction should make it clear whether compliance with group accounting policies will normally ensure compliance with UK GAAP.

Accounting policies which may be especially important to groups include the following:

(a)   The basis of consolidation.

(b)   Policies in respect of participating interests and associates.

(c)   The treatment of goodwill and intangible assets.

(d)   Foreign currency exchange methods of translation.

11:2.5.1 Changes in policies

The auditor should discuss changes in policies with the client to evaluate their effect. Instructions to business unit auditors will normally need to be amended to emphasise the additional work and reporting requirements arising from any changes.

The auditor should also ascertain the reason for any change. Any change that is not the result of a new or revised accounting standard should be treated with scepticism, and evidence should be obtained to show that the change is to a policy both acceptable under UK GAAP and more appropriate to the client's particular circumstances. The auditor should be especially careful when considering any change in a policy that has itself been changed in recent years.

11:2.6 Preliminary assessment of materiality

The auditor should make a preliminary assessment of group materiality in the light of the results from the preliminary analytical reviews of the group. Guidance on determining materiality is given in **Section 2:2**, 'Materiality in financial statements'. As part of the group audit strategy, the auditor may prescribe materiality levels to be used in the audit or review of individual business units. This is discussed in **Section 11:4**, 'Determining the group audit strategy'.

11:2.7 Evaluating inherent risk

11:2.7.1 Searching for inherent risks

The auditor's search for inherent risk should be made in the light of the understanding of the group's business, its control environment (including the assessment of parent management's motivation to distort the group financial statements) and its accounting systems (including the procedures adopted for the consolidation). Detailed guidance on evaluating risk is given in **Section 4:4**, 'Evaluating inherent risk'.

The auditor should consider any circumstances that might cause increased risk in a business unit, including the following:

11:2.7.1.1 Significant changes

(a) A change in key management.

(b) A business unit which is new or has been reorganised and which, as a result, has no past performance to provide a basis on which it can be judged by management.

11:2.7.1.2 Nature of operations and management

(a) Operations which differ significantly from those of other business units within the group, making it difficult for parent management to compare the performance of individual business units and generally to control the operations of the business unit.

(b) Operations which are particularly complex.

(c) Trading activities involving high risk, such as long-term contracts or trading in futures.

(d) A parent management style which emphasises local autonomy, or doubts as to the effectiveness of the controls exercised by the parent over the business unit.

11:2.7.1.3 Trading difficulties

(a) Deteriorating economic conditions, placing additional strains on the business unit.

(b) Business units which operate in a foreign country where business strategies might be affected by, or exposure to unforeseen losses created by, factors such as:

    (i) relations with minority investors, trade policies, tax agreements and foreign exchange and dividend restrictions;

    (ii) the strength and stability of the country's currency;

    (iii) government intervention;

    (iv) less frequent monitoring by parent management.

(c) A business unit which has recurring losses and where there is an increased risk that it will not be able to realise assets and meet its financial commitments.

11:2.7.1.4 Accounting and audit

(a) Accounting procedures or policies which are significantly different from group procedures and policies.

(b) Problems which have arisen in past audits or which are expected to arise this year.

(c) Significant differences between management reporting and reporting for statutory financial statements purposes.

The auditor should liaise with the business unit auditors and with parent management to ensure that all significant audit risks are identified. The auditor should use the results to help determine the group audit strategy, e.g. by planning an appropriate response to risks identified in particular business units.

The auditor should also consider the risks associated with the consolidation including, e.g.:

(a) **Complex transactions**: Transactions involving the acquisition and disposal of business units are often complex and prone to the risk of misstatement.

(b) **Risks associated with the accounting process**: These might arise if, e.g., consolidation procedures are performed infrequently and consequently client staff might be inexperienced in carrying out the work.

(c) **Account balances derived from estimates**: Estimates might be required in relation to, e.g., applying fair values in acquisition accounting or provisions for group reorganisations.

(d) **Reported results and financial position of overseas business units**: The results and financial position of overseas business units might be prone to misstatement because they will need to be restated to comply with the law and applicable Accounting Standards. Unfamiliarity with overseas or UK accounting practices can lead to possible misstatement in the consolidation packages or consolidation adjustments.

11:2.7.2 *Evaluating the significance of identified risks*

At a group level, the auditor should evaluate inherent risks by considering the likely materiality of any consequent misstatement by reference to the group financial statements. In the case of risks associated with individual business units, however, the business unit auditors will need to evaluate the significance of the risk by referring to the materiality level for the particular business unit where this is different, because, e.g., a statutory audit of the business unit is required.

11:3 Assessing the control environment of a group

11:3.1 Introduction

The auditor should assess the control environment at parent company level as part of determining the strategy for the audit of the parent and for the group audit. General guidance on making the assessment is given in **Section 8:1.3**, 'Assessing the control environment'. This section provides guidance specific to the effect on the group audit strategy of the control that the parent exercises over business units.

The specific objectives in assessing the control environment are as follows:

(a) To determine whether it is conducive to the maintenance of effective accounting and control procedures within business units.

(b)   To consider management's ability to make the informed judgements and estimates necessary in the preparation of the group financial statements.

(c)   To assess the incentives and opportunities for intentional misrepresentation or distortion of the financial statements by management at business unit or at parent level.

(d)   To identify key indicators, reports and procedures that management uses to control the group and which may be relevant for audit purposes at parent or business unit level, or for the consolidation.

(e)   To identify the impact of particular control environment factors, both favourable and unfavourable, on the risk of material misstatement at business unit or group level.

11:3.2 Features of the parent control environment

Many of the features of the parent control environment are the same as for a single entity. However, the auditor should consider in particular the group management style, and the effect of management style on the control exercised by parent management.

11:3.2.1 Group management style

The management style adopted by main board directors and senior management will affect the approach to control adopted by parent management. There are two main methods of control:

(a)   **Planning**, whereby the parent directly influences the plans of business units and the future action of managers.

(b)   **Control**, whereby the parent monitors the past and present performance of the business units against specified objectives and takes remedial action, where necessary.

Planning and control are complementary activities but the balance of emphasis and degree of involvement of the parent varies with the management style adopted. Between these two there is a variety of styles, the effectiveness of which will vary according to the degree of parent management control and the particular mix of control arrangements and monitoring procedures employed by the parent. The most popular styles are:

- strategic planning
- strategic control
- financial control

11:3.2.2 Control exercised by parent management

Depending on the style adopted by parent management, control can be exercised in one or more of the following ways:

(a)   **Establishing the organisational structure of the group**: This needs to facilitate the flow of information downwards from the board and senior management in order to communicate policies and decisions to business units. Equally, the organisational structure needs to facilitate feedback from business unit management on key business developments and performance to parent management.

(b) **Involvement in the business units' planning and budgetary processes**: This may take the form of, e.g.:

    (i)   establishing business objectives and financial, operational and service standards; and

    (ii) reviewing, discussing and contributing to business strategies and plans, and exercising control over the allocation of resources (e.g. manning levels and capital investment).

(c) **Establishing policies and procedures defining the framework, guidelines or requirements for the way particular activities are carried out**: This may be done by, e.g., formulating accounting systems and related control procedures in finance manuals or similar documentation to be used by business units.

(d) **Implementing centralised management information systems that facilitate a high degree of central control.**

(e) **Restricting the extent of authority of business unit management.**

(f) **Supervising senior business unit management appointments.**

(g) **Applying incentives and sanctions to business unit management** to encourage good performance or to take remedial action.

The parent can monitor the effectiveness of the operation of accounting systems and controls established in business units in one or more of the following ways:

(a) Establishing monthly reporting routines and monitoring business units' performance against agreed financial, operational and service standards.

(b) Analysing monthly management information produced by business units and taking corrective action.

(c) Conducting internal audits or other reviews of business units to assess compliance with established policies and procedures.

(d) Arranging regular meetings with management to obtain feedback on significant business developments and to review performance as a basis for taking corrective action.

11:3.3 Timing of the auditor's assessment

The auditor should make a preliminary assessment for group audit strategy purposes. Because the assessment might be relevant to the auditors of business units, the auditor should complete it in time to allow the findings to be communicated to them for consideration in developing their own audit strategies.

11:3.4 How to assess the parent control environment

11:3.4.1 Assessment of the parent company's control environment

The auditor's assessment of the control environment of a parent company is similar to that applying to a single entity. As described in **Section 8:1.3**, 'Assessing the control environment', to assist the auditor in making this assessment each firm may find it useful to prepare a parent company control environment checklist or diagnostic aid that sets out the factors to be considered. Appropriate headings might be:

(a)   Effectiveness of the group organisation structure.

(b)   Role of the group board of directors and key management.

(c)   Role of the audit committee and internal audit.

(d)   Reasonableness of parent company management plans and budgets.

(e)   Relevance and reliability of management information.

(f)   Reliability of management estimates.

(g)   Existence of adequate policies and procedures for controlling the group.

(h)   Risk that management might intentionally misstate the financial statements.

(i)   Effectiveness of management control over IT organisation.

(j)   Effectiveness of management control, excluding IT organisation.

11:3.4.2 Assessment of the parent company's management practices

To help support the auditor's assessment of the control environment the auditor should also assess the effectiveness of parent company management practices. In particular, the auditor should assess the main information systems operated within the parent company. To assist the auditor making this assessment any firm preparing a parent company management checklist or diagnostic aid might arrange for it to set out examples of good and bad management practices. Such a diagnostic aid could be designed to help the auditor to:

(a)   improve the understanding of the key business issues of concern to parent management and make a better risk assessment;

(b)   make a better assessment of the parent control environment and main information systems operated by and within the parent;

(c)   improve the reporting to the group board and parent management.

The diagnostic aid could provide guidance on the management styles referred to in **Section 11:3.2.1** (first paragraph), and analyse the implications of different management styles for the control environment. It could focus on the following important areas of the parent control environment:

(a)   The role of the board and senior management.

(b)   The role of the parent (the 'group headquarters').

(c)   The group organisational structure.

(d)   Group strategy and planning.

(e)   Group budgetary processes.

(f)   Group management information systems.

11:3.5 Significance of the parent control environment

The assessment of the parent control environment will normally identify favourable and unfavourable features relating to controls over business units exercised by parent management. In some cases, the effect may be pervasive and affect many, or all, business units.

The auditor should take credit for strengths of the parent control environment which reduce inherent risks. The auditor should identify specific features of control exercised by parent management which can help the auditor to reduce the scope of work needed at parent level or on individual business units. For example, reviews by the parent of financial information from business units might provide assurance that the assessment of a business unit as immaterial is satisfactory.

The auditor should bear in mind risks which might arise from unfavourable features of the parent control environment. For example, there might be pressure on business unit management to achieve targets. Where parent management adopts the financial control management style, it will be likely readily to apply incentives and sanctions to business unit managers to reward success and to penalise managers who are not delivering. This style can therefore create a greater pressure for success than any other management style, with a greater likelihood of material misstatement.

11:3.5.1 Evidence

If the auditor seeks to obtain assurance from positive features of the control environment which reduce inherent risks and, thereby, restrict the amount of work required at parent and business unit levels, the auditor should carry out the following procedures:

(a)   Identify the specific controls that give assurance.

(b)   Record the conclusions on their effectiveness, supported by the auditor's evidence.

For example, if the auditor wished to obtain assurance that comparing business unit activities against budget is an effective internal control, the auditor may identify that business unit budgets have been properly prepared by considering the following:

(a) The existence of central budget preparation guidelines and timetables.

(b) The involvement of parent and business unit management in preparation and approval.

(c) Authorisation of the budgets by the group board.

(d) Proper communication of the budgets within the group.

The amount of assurance the auditor obtains from positive features of the control environment is a matter of professional judgement and will depend partly on the quality of the evidence. For example, by evaluating the monitoring controls applied by the parent company alone, the auditor will obtain a low level of assurance in respect of the success of control effectiveness in reducing an inherent risk. If the auditor wishes to take a significant amount of assurance, e.g. to support a strategy of no work to be performed at certain business units, the auditor should assess the management practices and the effectiveness of management control in sufficient detail. The auditor should support conclusions with direct or indirect evidence.

11:3.6 Communicating information to business units

The auditor should include conclusions on the parent's control environment in the letter of instruction sent to business unit auditors if those conclusions are relevant to the audit of the business unit. Certain information, such as the role of internal audit, might be common to a number of business units, and will be relevant to the assessment of the control environment for those business units. The auditor should request business unit auditors to provide details of any favourable or unfavourable features of the business unit control environment which might lead the parent company auditor to reconsider the assessment of the control environment for the group.

The auditor's assessment of the control environment might contain sensitive matters. The auditor should request, therefore, that the business unit auditors ensure that they keep confidential any information that the auditor gives to them.

11:4 Determining the group audit strategy

11:4.1 Introduction

This section is designed to help the auditor determine the strategy for the audit of a group. Although many of the considerations applicable to the audit of a group are similar to those which apply to the audits of single entities, there are particular matters which the auditor should consider, including:

(a) The involvement of business unit auditors.

(b)   Available strategy options and factors influencing their selection for each business unit in the group.

(c)   The responsibility for determining the group audit strategy.

Guidance on the general principles and procedures that apply in determining audit strategy is given in **Section 4:6**, 'Determining the strategy'.

11:4.2 Involvement of business unit auditors

11:4.2.1 Other auditors

Statement of Auditing Standards 510, 'The Relationship Between Principal Auditors and Other Auditors', requires that 'When using the work of other auditors, principal auditors should determine how that work will affect their audit'.

If all the necessary work is carried out by offices of one firm the auditor is more easily able to ensure that the work is done to the auditor's standards by properly trained and competent staff. Moreover, it can help the client because it eliminates the time the auditor would otherwise have to spend assessing other auditors' work.

There is no statutory or professional minimum requirement for the proportion of a group which should be audited directly by the firm responsible for the group audit. However, the auditor should recognise that the involvement of other auditors might increase the risk to the firm. The auditor should discuss this with parent company management to ensure that it is aware of any concerns, and of the potential impact on audit costs of the additional audit work the auditor may need to carry out. If the proportion of the group audited by other auditors is significant, the engagement partner should follow the consultation procedures set out in **Section 5:5**, 'Consultation and concurring reviews'.

When determining the strategy, the auditor should consider the procedures for ensuring that the quality of the audit work that other auditors carry out is adequate to provide the assurance the auditor requires to express an opinion on the group financial statements. This is discussed in **Section 11:6**, 'Work performed by other auditors'.

11:4.2.2 Other offices of the firm

If the auditor refers work to other offices of the firm the auditor should send them instructions, in accordance with **Section 11:5**, 'Planning and control of group audits'. The auditor would not normally need to carry out any procedures to assess the quality of work of these offices.

11:4.3 Strategy options

The primary audit objective is to obtain sufficient relevant and reliable evidence to enable the auditor to express an opinion on the group financial statements. At business unit level, unless there are separate statutory or other obligations in respect of the business unit's financial statements, the objective is to provide assurance that misstatement which is material to the group as a whole has not occurred. In order to achieve this objective effectively and efficiently, the auditor should consider the nature, extent and timing of audit work to be performed on each business unit of the group.

11:4.3.1 Range of strategy options

There is a range of strategy options available to ensure that the auditor obtains sufficient assurance in relation to a business unit and the group as a whole, including:

(a) An unrestricted audit.

(b) Prescribing materiality levels for the work higher than that which would be established by the business unit auditor if auditing an independent entity.

(c) Instructing the business unit auditor to restrict the scope of work to be performed on the business unit to:

  (i) an audit of particular account balances and/or classes of transactions;

  (ii) performing specified procedures;

  (iii) a review of the financial statements or of particular account balances and/or classes of transactions; or

  (iv) a visit.

(d) Deciding that no work need be performed on the business unit.

Guidance on the work involved in each of these options is given in **Sections 11:4.3.2** to **11:4.3.7**. Factors affecting the selection of options are set out in **Section 11:4.3.8** to **11:4.4.4**. Where a business unit's financial statements are separately reported on because of statutory, client or other reporting requirements, the strategy should normally be an unrestricted audit.

11:4.3.2 Unrestricted audit

An unrestricted audit of a business unit will normally only be necessary in one of the following situations:

(a) To satisfy statutory, client or other reporting requirements.

(b) Where the business unit is so significant that the materiality levels established for the audit of the financial statements of the business unit are effectively the same as those for the group as a whole.

In other cases, the auditor should seek to reduce the scope of audit work to the minimum necessary to achieve group audit objectives.

11:4.3.3 Prescribing materiality levels

If a report is not required on the business unit's financial statements (e.g., in the case of an overseas business unit where local laws do not require an audit) the auditor should normally, for audit efficiency reasons, determine materiality levels for the business unit by reference to the circumstances of the group and not to those of the business unit itself. Thus the materiality would normally be higher than would be established for an unrestricted audit of the financial statements of the business unit. However, the materiality levels might need to be lower than those established for the group financial statements as a whole. This is because materiality is related in part to the aggregate amount of misstatements from all business units that can be accepted before a qualified or otherwise modified opinion on the group financial statements becomes necessary.

The auditor may wish to discuss with parent management the implications of the materiality levels, so that they are aware of the restricted extent of the examination of the business unit's financial statements. When the auditor does report on the business unit's financial statements, the auditor should normally set the materiality in relation to those financial statements.

11:4.3.4 Audit of particular account balances or performing specified procedures

When the parent exercises effective management control over the business unit and the auditor can gather or update sufficient information to determine the audit strategy and testing plans for the business unit, the auditor may instruct the business unit auditor to perform an audit of particular account balances/classes of transactions or to perform specified procedures.

11:4.3.4.1 Audit of particular account balances

When the auditor instructs the business unit auditor to conduct an audit of, and express positive assurance on, particular account balances/classes of transactions of a business unit, the auditor should normally inform the business unit auditor of the materiality to be used. The auditor should request the business unit auditor to carry out the following procedures:

(a) To consider, in determining the audit procedures to be applied, other account balances/classes of transactions which are interrelated with and which could materially affect, the account balances on which the business unit auditor is reporting.

(b) To consult the auditor when the results of procedures indicate any matters that could give rise to material misstatements in other account balances/classes of transactions and, if deemed appropriate, to extend the audit procedures to cover these account balances/classes of transactions.

11:4.3.4.2 Performing specified procedures

When the auditor instructs the business unit auditor to carry out specified procedures in relation to particular account balances/classes of transactions of the business unit, the auditor will find it most efficient to set out, in many cases, the specified procedures in a work programme. The auditor should determine the extent of testing. The auditor should request the business unit auditor to carry out the following procedures:

(a) To indicate in the report the factual findings as a result of performing the specified procedures, including sufficient details of exceptions and errors found.

(b) To complete and return the work programme.

(c) To consult the auditor where the results of the procedures indicate any matters that could give rise to material misstatement in the group financial statements and, if deemed appropriate, to extend the procedures.

(d) To report to the auditor any unusual matters noted in the extended procedures.

11:4.3.5 Review of financial statements or of particular account balances/classes of transactions

The auditor may instruct the business unit auditor to conduct a review of the financial statements of the business unit, e.g. when there are a large number of business units with similar operations subject to effective parent management control and predictable financial results. Retail stores and food and drink outlets, e.g., sometimes fall into this category. Alternatively, the auditor may instruct the business unit auditor to conduct a review of particular account balances/classes of transactions to address specific risks in a less significant business unit. In either case, the auditor may find it efficient to prescribe the materiality levels to be used for the review.

A review involves less work than an audit and results in only a limited level of assurance that the financial statements (or particular account balances/classes of transactions) are free from material misstatement, expressed in the form of a negative assurance report. The auditor should request the business unit auditor to carry out the following procedures:

(a) To consult the auditor when the results of the review indicate the existence of any matters that could give rise to material misstatement in the group financial statements, and, if deemed appropriate, to extend enquiries and other review procedures.

(b) To report to the auditor any unusual matters noted in the extended review.

11:4.3.6 Visit

When the operations of a business unit appear to be immaterial to the group financial statements and there is no audit risk associated with the business unit that is likely to be of significance to the group financial statements, the auditor may restrict the scope of the work to a visit. Visits may be made on a cyclical basis.

The objective of a visit is to confirm the judgements made that the business unit is immaterial and that there is no significant audit risk. Accordingly, the work performed will normally only involve observing the nature and extent of operations, reading recent financial information and holding discussions with the business unit's management.

It may prove efficient for the visit to the business unit to be performed by referring office personnel. The timing of visits is often flexible, and the auditor might be able to schedule visits at times which allow the auditor to avoid undue pressure on staff utilisation. Alternatively, the auditor may request a business unit auditor to carry out the visit. The auditor should ensure that the personnel visiting the business unit possess an appropriate knowledge of the relevant laws and regulations applicable to the business unit.

Where the auditor carries out the visit no report is necessary; the documentation of the visit will normally provide sufficient evidence for the conclusions reached. Where a business unit auditor carries out the visit, the auditor should request that auditor to report on the results of the visit.

The auditor also carries out visits to significant business units, as discussed in **Section 11:2**, 'Group business review', to enhance the understanding of the business.

11:4.3.7 No work to be performed on business unit

The auditor may decide that no work need be performed on a business unit in the course of the current year's audit. If this is the case, the auditor should ensure by review of the financial statements of the business unit and discussion with parent management that the risk of material misstatement is negligible and that the parent continues to exercise adequate control over the business unit.

11:4.3.8 Rotation of strategy options

Rotation of strategy options over a number of years might be efficient. The auditor should consider it when, e.g., there are no particular reporting requirements affecting business units and there are no business units which are material in their own right.

11:4.4 Factors affecting choice of option

Because factors affecting the selection of the scope of work vary among clients, the auditor should use professional judgement to determine whether the scope selected for each business unit results in sufficient work performed to form an opinion on the group financial statements. In addition to the statutory or other requirements and to the factors specific to the various strategy options set out above, the auditor should consider the following:

(a) The relative size and materiality of each business unit.

(b) The assessment of risk.

(c) The involvement of other auditors.

(d) Internal audit.

11:4.4.1 Relative size and materiality of each business unit

The auditor should consider the following matters:

(a) **The relative materiality of business units to the group financial statements**: The auditor should ascertain the contribution which each business unit makes to the major account balances and classes of transactions in the group financial statements. The auditor may do this by using the previous year's financial statements, or the latest forecast for the current year if past experience has shown that these are reliable.

(b) **The number of business units and their sizes in relation to each other**: If business units are numerous and not individually dominant in relation to group materiality, the auditor should normally perform procedures on more business units to obtain adequate coverage.

(c) **A business unit that would otherwise be regarded as immaterial might have a function that is significant to the overall operations of the group**: The auditor should take particular care to identify any business units that, although not individually material, might result in material misstatement in the group financial statements. For example, a commodity dealing company without material assets or profit might have a significant risk of material misstatement arising from unhedged forward contracts.

11:4.4.2 Assessment of risk

If the auditor has identified specific risks affecting a business unit, the auditor should ensure that the strategy option provides an adequate response to these risks. Guidance on the assessment of risk is given in **Section 11:2**, 'Group business review', and, in relation to risks arising from the auditor's assessment of the parent control environment, in **Section 11:3**, 'Assessing the control environment of a group'.

11:4.4.3 Involvement of other auditors

As discussed in **Section 11:4.2.1**, the involvement of other auditors might result in risk to the firm. The auditor may respond to this risk by amending the strategy options for the relevant business units.

11:4.4.4 Internal audit

Effective co-operation with a properly organised internal audit function can often result in significant reduction in the extent of the auditor's audit work in a group. In groups, internal audit will normally be organised as a central function and it will therefore be necessary for a preliminary assessment of internal audit for strategy purposes to be carried out wholly or primarily by the referring office. The auditor should set out arrangements for liaison with internal audit in the group audit instructions. The auditor should obtain the client's permission before making any relevant internal audit reports available to business unit auditors.

The use that the auditor may make of the work of internal auditors is discussed in **Section 7:5**, 'Using the work of internal audit'.

11:4.5 Reports by business unit auditors

The auditor will require reports from business unit auditors in accordance with the group audit strategy. Such reports will normally be reports on consolidation packages, for the following reasons:

(a) When the business unit is required to prepare audited statutory financial statements and the statutory financial statements are not available before the auditor completes the audit of the group financial statements, the auditor needs the business unit auditors to confirm that they have completed their audit (discussed in **Section 11:8**, 'Group audit completion procedures').

(b) The business unit might not be required to prepare audited statutory financial statements because there is no local requirement.

(c) Because of local requirements, the business unit's statutory financial statements might sometimes be prepared using accounting policies that are different from those used in the group financial statements. The auditor cannot rely merely on the auditor's report on the statutory financial statements, because additional information is required. The auditor should obtain a report from the business unit auditor on the consolidation package or at least on the additional information required.

The auditor should discuss the form of report required on the consolidation package when determining the group audit strategy. The form of report might vary between business units, depending on the scope of work required. The auditor should refer in the letter of instruction to the form of report required. Guidance on the nature of reports on consolidation packages is given in **Section 11:9**, 'Responsibilities of a performing office'.

11:4.6 Responsibility for determining the group audit strategy

The engagement partner is responsible for determining the group audit strategy, for the overall direction of the work at each business unit and for ensuring that the audit work is performed in accordance with acceptable auditing standards. The auditor should liaise closely on all these aspects with the auditors of the various business units.

In the case of work referred to a performing office the respective responsibilities are as follows:

(a) The engagement partner is responsible for issuing such instructions as are appropriate to meet the reporting requirements.

(b) The performing office partner is responsible for ensuring that the requirements of the engagement partner are met and for keeping the engagement partner informed of all significant matters in relation to the client.

When the auditor instructs a business unit auditor to perform work on a business unit resulting in the issuance of any form of assurance (e.g., an audit or review) that auditor is responsible for the strategy and testing plan decisions for the business unit. The auditor should advise the business unit auditor of any matters significant to the business unit's strategy and should consider whether to review the strategy prepared by the business unit auditor before commencement of the work.

When the business unit auditor is not required to issue any form of audit assurance (e.g., if the business unit auditor is performing specified procedures) the auditor will normally take responsibility for strategy and testing plan decisions for the business unit by including appropriate details in the overall audit strategy and testing plans for the group. However, in small groups or overseas groups, where the commercial environment requires local knowledge, it might be more efficient for the business unit auditor to do this.

11:4.7 Documenting the strategy

The auditor should record strategy decisions in a group audit strategy memorandum, following the guidance set out in **Section 4:6**, 'Determining the strategy', and should follow similar approval procedures.

The auditor will normally include in the memorandum the matters referred to in **Section 4:6**, and the following matters specific to the audit of groups:

(a)   The strategy option for each business unit within the group.

(b)   The procedures the auditor will adopt to obtain assurance on the work of other auditors including, if applicable, a timetable for completion and submission of questionnaires, the timetable and arrangements for any file reviews and arrangements for meeting the other auditors.

(c)   The strategy for auditing the consolidation.

The auditor should inform the business unit auditors of the scope of work to be performed at their respective business units in a letter of instruction (discussed in **Section 11:5**, 'Planning and control of group audits'). In addition, the scope of work may be discussed with partners and senior audit staff from performing offices if they attend the strategy meeting.

11:4.8 Communicating with the client

Before a final decision is made on the scope of work to be performed at each business unit, the engagement partner should consider discussing the scope proposals with parent management to ensure that the proposals are compatible with their expectation and that their specific concerns have been addressed appropriately. For example, the client might express a preference that the auditor performs more work at a particular business unit than the auditor might otherwise have done.

The auditor, however, retains full responsibility for determining the group audit strategy and should not be dissuaded from undertaking any work which the auditor judges to be appropriate in the light of the materiality, risk and controls associated with each business unit.

It may also be appropriate for performing offices and other auditors to communicate with the management of business units regarding scope proposals, particularly where the business units are statutory entities such as subsidiaries or associates.

11:5 Planning and control of group audits

11:5.1 Introduction

Good planning is fundamental to the success of a group audit, probably to an even greater extent than in the audit of a single entity. This is equally true for both the client and the auditor. Many groups are widely dispersed, responses to requests for information may be relatively slow and there is a high risk of misunderstanding and of communication failures.

11:5.2 Initial steps

Audit planning and control is a continuous process involving regular meetings with the client by members of the client handling team. Before formally starting the information gathering process, key members of the client handling team may need to meet to review matters arising from the previous year's audit and from other subsequent contacts with the client. The purpose of this initial meeting should be to plan the early stages leading up to determining the group audit strategy and agreeing it with the client.

Initial meetings should normally be attended by at least the engagement partner, the engagement manager and the in-charge, and perhaps also:

(a)   partners and senior audit staff from performing offices, especially if information specific to business units is needed and is not available at the parent;

(b)   partners and senior specialists involved with the client, e.g. computer and tax specialists.

The engagement partner and the engagement manager should discuss the proposed audit arrangements with the client.

11:5.3 Planning the implementation of the group audit strategy

The detail of planning required will necessarily be dependent on the complexity and size of the group audit. It should, however, be in sufficient detail to enable the approved group audit strategy to be properly implemented. This will involve:

(a) Setting timetables.

(b) Preparing time and fee budgets and discussing them with the client.

(c) Liaising with business unit auditors.

(d) Assigning staff to the engagement.

11:5.3.1 Setting timetables

Before setting the audit timetable the auditor should hold preliminary discussions with those members of the client's staff who are responsible for preparing the group financial statements. The auditor should take adequate account of the client's ability to produce the information required by the intended commencement date. The timing of the audit work should take account of the client's requirements, the timetable adopted by the client for the completion of the business units' and the group financial statements and the availability of suitable audit staff.

An accurate and realistic group reporting timetable is essential for the efficient completion of the group audit. The auditor should review the timetable in detail to ensure that each business unit has sufficient time to prepare its consolidation package and its financial statements and to have them audited. The auditor should also check that there is adequate time for the central consolidation, review and audit to be completed before the results are announced. The dates set out in the group timetable should normally cover at least the following steps:

(a) Reconciliation of group balances.

(b) Agreement of group tax provisions.

(c) Submission of consolidation package for each business unit.

(d) Submission of business units' signed financial statements, where applicable.

(e) Submission of business unit auditors' points for inclusion in the group audit report to the board.

(f) Various drafts of the group financial statements.

(g) The auditor's final meeting with the board.

(h) The preliminary announcement.

(i) The signing of the group financial statements.

(j) The despatch of financial statements and notice of the AGM to shareholders.

(k) The AGM.

The proposed audit timetable, together with a time and fee budget and a note of staff assigned to the engagement, should be discussed and agreed with the engagement partner during the group audit strategy meeting or shortly after the strategy has been approved.

The auditor should ensure that the group timetable is sent out well before the year-end, and that business units are required to confirm that they can meet their deadline. The parent's instructions should also include a requirement for business units to report any likely delays or problems as soon as they arise.

11:5.3.2 Preparing time and fee budgets

The auditor should prepare a budget for the audit of the parent and the consolidation. In accordance with the client's requirements, the auditor might need to prepare a budget for the group audit, and agree this budget with parent management. Fees for work referred to a performing office will normally be negotiated in one of three ways:

(a) The performing office will negotiate the fee independently with the local client and bill direct.

(b) The auditor may negotiate a fee with parent management on behalf of the performing office, normally after the performing office has consulted business unit management.

(c) The auditor may negotiate a global fee with the parent in advance of the engagement.

11:5.3.3 Liaising with business unit auditors

After agreeing the proposed audit arrangements with the client, the auditor should, as soon as possible, give all business unit auditors a broad indication of the reporting requirements and, if the engagement is a continuing one, advise them whether the requirements differ significantly from those of the previous year. Such 'early warnings' should be followed by detailed instructions as soon as practicable, and, if possible, at least two months before the estimated date for beginning the work.

The auditor should issue a letter of instruction setting out clearly the reporting requirements and the procedures requested to be performed. The letter should be comprehensive and precise as to the nature of the work to be performed and the report to be issued thereon. This is particularly important if the business unit auditors are overseas because, in the absence of explicit instructions, the auditors might apply local standards which result in the timing, nature and extent of testing differing from that required.

Although the auditor should give instructions in writing, the business unit auditors should not delay work until written instructions are received if the auditor made clear orally the scope of the work.

11:5.3.3.1 Form of letter of instruction

The auditor should normally prepare letters of instruction, in a form which communicates the essential information as clearly and concisely as possible and is cost efficient. The letters of instruction should include documentation or contain relevant enclosures of all matters that will be of significance to the business unit auditors in planning, performing and reporting on their work. Guidance on specific contents is given in **Section 11:5.3.3.3**. The following are general guidelines:

(a)   Keep instructions brief, crystallising the essential information. Keep in mind the cost of preparing instructions and the cost to the business unit auditor of reading them.

(b)   Avoid duplicating material contained in the client's manuals. Instead, make reference thereto.

(c)   Tailor the instructions to particular business units or identify the paragraphs in the instructions which apply only to particular business units.

(d)   Update the instructions each year. Highlight changes from previous instructions.

(e)   Avoid jargon. Recipients in overseas offices might need to translate the letter into their own language.

When the letter has been drafted, the auditor should read it over, reviewing it, as a recipient and focusing on clarity and completeness of instructions and the time required to read it. The better the letter the fewer the problems that are likely to arise.

    If necessary, the auditor should use supplements to the letter of instruction to:

(a)   modify the instructions; and/or

(b)   give further specific instructions to a business unit auditor that do not apply to other business unit auditors.

The auditor should consecutively number and date the supplements, so that the business unit auditor can ensure that all the necessary supplements have been received.

11:5.3.3.2 Acknowledgement of letter of instruction

The auditor should request each business unit auditor to acknowledge in writing receipt and understanding of the letter of instruction and all supplements.

11:5.3.3.3 Letters of instruction to other auditors

The auditor might include the following matters in a letter of instruction addressed to the other auditor:

(a)   The due dates for audit clearance of the business unit's consolidation package and financial statements and for the receipt of the audit report and management letter, and the arrangements for sending copies of each document to the group auditors.

(b)   Details regarding the scope and conduct of the work to be performed.

(c)   Auditing standards to be observed.

(d)   The form of report required.

(e)   Special or unusual requirements of the engagement with respect to the audit report or management letter.

(f)   Procedures for notifying the group auditor of any significant matters arising as early as possible, particularly in relation to any intention to qualify the financial statements. This should normally include arrangements for sending to the auditor the equivalent of interim and final issues documentation. However, for non-material business units it will sometimes be more appropriate to request confirmation that there are no matters which need to be brought to the auditor's attention.

(g)   Guidance as to what would be considered a significant matter, e.g. by disclosing a threshold of materiality.

(h)   Specific matters relevant to the referred engagement, such as parent company guarantees, related parties and tax.

(i)   Any specific requirements concerning post-balance-sheet event reviews.

(j)   Background information on the client that may assist in understanding the business and its associated risks, or otherwise assist the business unit auditor in completing the engagement, unless that information is confidential to the client and the firm. This should include, e.g., points relevant to the assessment of the business unit's control environment and any identified risks which have an impact on the business unit. It may be appropriate to send an abridged group audit strategy memorandum outlining the results of the preliminary business review for the group as a whole.

(k)   Matters relating to the administration of the engagement (including fee and billing arrangements).

(l)   Details of any arrangements for meetings with the client to discuss with the auditor (or the performing office to which the review is delegated) matters arising from the work, or for reviewing the working papers.

(m) A copy of the questionnaire which the other auditors are required to complete (discussed in **Section 11:6**, 'Work performed by other auditors').

11:5.3.3.4 Letters of instruction to performing offices

Letters of instruction to performing offices might contain matters similar to those referred to in **Section 11:5.3.3.3**.

11:5.3.3.5 Instructions to reviewers of other auditors

Where, for geographical or other reasons, the auditor requires another office to undertake a review of the work of other auditors, the auditor should issue instructions which include:

(a)   A copy of the letter of instruction to the other auditors.

(b)   Special reporting requirements, such as a review of the other auditors' commentary for accuracy and completeness, or work to be carried out on the other auditors' post-balance-sheet events review.

(c)   A copy of any standard checklist to be used when reviewing the work of another auditor.

(d)   A copy of the auditor's audit manual if it is not already available locally.

The auditor should normally send instructions at a stage which allows each performing office to contact the other auditor before their final audit begins.

If the review is to be performed by a non-UK office, the auditor should request the relevant office wherever possible to assign the work to staff with knowledge of UK accounting and auditing standards.

11:5.3.3.6 Monitoring costs against budget

The auditor should request business unit auditors to notify any material discrepancies which are likely to arise between the budget and the expected time costs, preferably before the time is actually incurred. Also, the in-charge should advise the engagement manager of any material discrepancies which are likely to arise in relation to the audit of the parent and the consolidation. The engagement manager should discuss all material discrepancies with the engagement partner. Where appropriate, the auditor should advise the client and negotiate a revised fee as soon as possible.

11:5.3.4 Assignment of staff

A group audit will often be complex and large, and for these and other reasons there might be a significant risk to the firm. Accordingly, the engagement manager should ensure that the parent audit team has the necessary experience. The engagement manager should discuss and agree the composition of the parent audit team with the engagement partner.

For large group audits, particularly if business units and their auditors are located overseas, the extent of liaison with business unit auditors might require a member of the audit team to be engaged specifically on this task.

11:5.4 Liaison with internal audit

Where the auditor intends to rely on the work of the client's internal audit function as part of the group audit strategy, the engagement manager should liaise with the client's internal audit department and make arrangements to review its work following the guidance set out in **Section 7:5**, 'Using the work of internal audit'.

11:6 Work performed by other auditors

11:6.1 Introduction

The group auditor has sole responsibility for the opinion expressed in the audit report on the group financial statements. The auditor therefore needs to form an opinion on whether the financial statements of all business units are acceptable for incorporation in those of the group. Sometimes, because of established custom or the geographical location of the business or the wishes of the client, the auditor has to make use of the work and the opinion of another auditor, or auditors, to form an opinion on the group financial statements. The auditor cannot discharge this responsibility by an uninformed acceptance of other auditors' work. This section is designed to provide guidance on the procedures the auditor should adopt to obtain evidence on other auditors' work.

11:6.2 Objectives

Statement of Auditing Standards 510, 'The Relationship Between Principal Auditors and Other Auditors', requires that:

> *When planning to use the work of other auditors, principal auditors should consider the professional qualifications, experience and resources of the other auditors in the context of the specific assignment.*

The auditor should be satisfied that the other auditors:

(a)   are aware that the financial statements of the business unit are to be included in the group financial statements on which the auditor is reporting and that the auditor will be relying on those other auditors' work;

(b)   are aware of UK accounting policies and auditing standards and will conduct the audit and report in accordance therewith or disclose variations therefrom;

(c)   have issued a report on the consolidation package;

(d)   have knowledge of any other financial reporting requirements relevant to the engagement; and

(e)   have determined either that the accounting policies followed conform with those prescribed by the parent or that variations are disclosed so that the auditor can be satisfied as to the consistency of application of accounting policies among the business units included in the group financial statements.

These requirements will apply to all other auditors involved.

11:6.3 Obtaining evidence on other auditors' work

SAS 510 states that 'Principal auditors should obtain sufficient appropriate audit evidence that the work of the other auditors is adequate for the principal auditors' purposes.'

11:6.3.1 Questionnaire

To provide a basis for assessing the other auditors' work the auditor may request them to complete and return a questionnaire confirming the following:

(a)   They are aware that the auditor will be relying on their work in forming the opinion on the group financial statements.

(b)   They have maintained their independence from the client.

(c)   They have carried out their audit in accordance with UK (or equivalent) auditing standards.

11:6.3.2 Additional evidence

If the auditor requires additional evidence to be satisfied that the auditor can rely on the work of another auditor the auditor should carry out one or more of the following procedures:

(a)   Request the other auditor to complete a more detailed questionnaire than that referred to in **Section 11:6.3.1**.

(b)   Meet the other auditor to discuss significant audit issues.

(c)   Review some or all of the other auditor's working papers.

In relation to (b) and (c) above, the auditor may carry out this work, or may refer the work to another office of the auditing firm.

11:6.3.2.1 More detailed questionnaire

The purpose of a more detailed questionnaire would be to obtain information about the work performed by the other auditor and to obtain direct confirmation that specified procedures, such as attendance at a stocktake, have been carried out. The auditor might use such a questionnaire if uncertain as to whether the other auditor is fully aware of, and has performed the audit in accordance with, UK auditing standards. The auditor may tailor the questionnaire to the particular circumstances of the client.

11:6.3.2.2 Meeting the other auditor

The auditor should decide whether it is appropriate to meet the other auditor to discuss matters arising from the audit and to help form a conclusion on the other auditor's standards of work. The auditor might identify these matters from the following:

(a)   A preliminary visit to the business unit to meet management of the business unit and/or the other auditor.

(b)   The work at the parent, including the preliminary analytical review.

(c)   The review of the other auditor's issues documentation, or equivalent.

If the auditor is unable to meet the other auditor, or if it is inefficient to do so, the auditor may request a partner and/or manager from another office of the auditing firm to meet the other auditor and report to the auditor.

11:6.3.2.3 Reviewing the work of other auditors

The auditor may decide that it is appropriate to review the other auditor's working papers. In doing so, the primary purpose is to seek evidence that the client's financial statements are suitable for inclusion in those of the group. The auditor may find deficiencies in the other auditor's work which leads the auditor to question the effectiveness or efficiency of the other auditor but which nevertheless are not material in the context of the group financial statements. However, some deficiencies may affect the quality of the other auditor's opinion on one or more aspects of the client's financial statements. Consequently it is helpful to divide the purpose of the work to be carried out into two categories:

(a)   Obtaining evidence to satisfy the auditor that the financial statements are suitable for inclusion in the group financial statements.

(b)   Identifying weaknesses and omissions in the other auditor's work which, regardless of whether they invalidate the conclusions under (a) above, should be brought to the other auditor's attention and followed up appropriately (*see* further guidance below).

Guidance on carrying out a review is given in **Section 11:9**, 'Responsibilities of a performing office'.

11:6.4 Determining which procedures to carry out

To determine the most appropriate procedures to carry out the auditor should assess the risks arising from relying on the work of other auditors. In making this assessment, the auditor should consider the following:

(a)   The assessment of the independence, standing and reputation of the other auditors.

(b)   The materiality of the business units audited by other auditors.

(c)   Specific risks identified.

(d)   Client relationships.

11:6.4.1 Independence, standing and reputation of the other auditors

11:6.4.1.1 General

At the earliest possible stage the auditor should consider the independence, standing and reputation of the other auditors to be satisfied that:

(a)   they are independent of their client;

(b) they are professionally qualified to carry out the work;

(c) their reputation for work standards or ethics is not in question.

The auditor may wish to consult a local office of the firm which may be able to provide additional information concerning the other auditors. The auditor may refer also to other parties, such as banks or other firms of auditors. Sometimes, the auditor will not be able to complete this assessment without meeting, or reviewing the work of, the other auditors.

If several business units are audited by members of an international firm the auditor might be able to obtain the necessary assurance by consulting with the other auditors centrally. The auditor should be satisfied about their methods of ensuring consistent quality throughout their organisation.

If there are questions concerning the other auditors' independence or standing and repute the engagement partner should discuss the matter with parent management. If the matter is not resolved, e.g. by the auditor carrying out audit work on the business unit, the engagement partner should follow the consultation procedures set out in **Section 5:5**, 'Consultation and concurring reviews'.

11:6.4.1.2 Independence

The ICAEW's 'Guide to professional ethics' states:

> *A member's objectivity must be beyond question if he or she is to report as an auditor. That objectivity can only be assured if the member is, and is seen to be, independent.*

To be satisfied that the other auditors are not inhibited in carrying out their work independently the auditor should consider the following questions:

(a) Have the other auditors refrained from holding any office with their client or from being party to any arrangement that might conflict with their duties as auditors?

(b) What, if any, clerical, accounting, taxation or other non-audit work do the other auditors perform for the client? (Although in the UK such services may be provided in addition to audit, the auditor should ensure that in doing so the other auditors have not become too closely connected with their client or over-dependent on the related fee income.)

(c) Is there anything to indicate that the client has attempted to place a restriction on the scope of the audit work and that the auditors have responded in an unsatisfactory way?

In addition to drawing on existing knowledge of the other auditors, the auditor may obtain written representations confirming their independence by use of a questionnaire, as referred to in **Section 11:6.3.1**. The auditor may, however, wish to discuss the question of independence directly with them and minute the results and conclusions of those discussions.

11:6.4.1.3 Standing and reputation

Although it is not possible to lay down specific procedures which can be followed in all cases, the auditor should have regard to whether the other auditors are members of a recognised accountancy body, and whether they have been the subject of disciplinary or other proceedings that might cast doubt on their professional standards.

11:6.4.2 Materiality of the business unit

When deciding the procedures to carry out in respect of other auditors' work the auditor should consider the following:

(a) The significance to the group financial statements as a whole of the business unit audited by the other auditors.

(b) The significance of individual account balances and classes of transactions, or items of disclosure, e.g., stock or contingent liabilities.

The auditor may need to carry out more extensive work on other auditors' work if, although business units or account balances and classes of transactions in business units are not individually material, taken together they result in a combination which is material.

11:6.4.3 Specific risks identified

The auditor should ensure that any specific risks identified and communicated to the other auditors in the letter of instruction are discussed with the other auditors or are adequately dealt with in their issues documentation or equivalent. The auditor may need to review the evidence that the other auditors have considered specific area(s) of risk.

11:6.4.4 Client relationships

The auditor should normally respond to the client's expectations of the auditor's own work on the group. For example, the client may wish the auditor to visit a business unit and to meet management of the business unit and/or the other auditors. Such visits will often be carried out with members of parent management or internal auditors.

11:6.5 Discussions with parent management

The auditor should discuss the results of the assessment of the other auditors with parent management. In particular, the auditor should draw to the attention of parent management any instances where the auditor has reason to doubt the quality of business unit auditors and where, as a consequence, the auditor plans to adopt more extensive procedures in order to be satisfied about their work.

11:6.6 Availability of information

SAS 510.6 states: 'Other auditors, knowing the context in which the principal auditors intend to use their work, should co-operate with and assist the principal auditors.'

If the business unit reported on by another auditor is a subsidiary, and both the parent company and the subsidiary are incorporated in Great Britain, s. 389A(3) of the Companies Act 1985 requires the management of the subsidiary and its auditors to give the parent company auditor such information and explanations as the auditor may reasonably require for the purposes of the auditor's duties as auditor of the parent. Equivalent legislation exists when both companies, or the parent only, are incorporated in Northern Ireland. In any other case s. 389A(4) requires the parent to take any steps reasonably open to it to obtain such information and explanations from the subsidiary.

In other cases the auditor has no statutory right to approach the other auditor, e.g. auditors of associates, but the auditor should request the client to arrange for the business unit to instruct the other auditor to co-operate. Such request should be satisfactory because the parent, if it is entitled to account for its interest as an associate, should be able to exercise significant influence over the operating and financial policy of the associate.

If the auditor is not satisfied with the co-operation received from other auditors, e.g. because they fail to respond satisfactorily to questionnaires, the auditor should discuss the matter with parent management. The auditor should request the parent management to raise the matter with business unit management.

If the auditor does not receive adequate information from other auditors, e.g. if still denied access to the other auditors' working papers or they still limit reviews to such an extent that the auditor is unable to conclude on their work, the auditor should consider:

(a)   The possible reasons for the restriction of scope and whether there are implications for other areas of the group audit.

(b)   The impact of the limitation of the scope of the work on the ability to report without qualification on the group financial statements.

11:6.7 Disclosing the involvement of other auditors

The auditor has sole responsibility for his or her audit opinion on the group financial statements. Any reference to the other auditors in the report may be misunderstood and interpreted as a qualification of the opinion or a division of responsibility, neither of which would be appropriate.

If the other auditors have qualified their opinion on the consolidation package/financial statements or included an explanatory paragraph referring to fundamental uncertainty, the auditor should consider the nature and significance of this uncertainty, in relation to the group financial statements, and consider whether it needs to be reflected in the audit report.

11:7 Auditing the consolidation

11:7.1 Introduction

This section is designed to help the auditor develop a programme of tests to audit the consolidation. It excludes guidance on accounting issues.

11:7.2 Consolidation audit programme

The auditor should consider preparing a consolidation audit programme for every group audit. The programme could be prepared either by tailoring a specimen consolidation programme, or by drawing up a programme without reference to a specimen. The programme might include the following elements:

(a)   Reviewing information relating to business units.

(b)   Auditing the aggregation.

(c)   Auditing the consolidation adjustments.

(d)   Analytical review and other procedures.

Further guidance on audit programmes is given in **Section 9:2**, 'Audit programmes'. The policies in that section regarding matters such as completion and review of programmes would apply to the consolidation audit programme.

11:7.3 Reviewing information relating to business units

The auditor should review the following in respect of significant business units:

(a)   **Consolidation packages**: In respect of each significant business unit's consolidation package the auditor should check that it is prima facie complete and that it has been properly authorised, e.g. signed by directors of the business unit.

(b)   **Audit reports**: In respect of each significant business unit's audit report the auditor should:

  (i)   check that it has been manually signed, and note the date on which such signature was given;

  (ii)   ensure that it complies with the requested wording;

  (iii)   ensure that it is free of any qualification or, if qualified, consider whether any qualification is so material as to affect the opinion on the group financial statements.

(c)   **Issues documentation (or equivalent)**: The auditor should review issues documentation (or equivalent) received from business unit auditors. For each significant business unit the auditor should:

  (i)   confirm that the information required by the instructions is given;

  (ii)   review the contents for consistency with the consolidation package;

(iii) note any material fluctuations from year to year in the balance sheet and profit and loss account;

(iv) identify any matters that need to be followed up with parent management, or which might require adjustment or disclosure in the group financial statements;

(v) note any matters, e.g. control weaknesses or client service issues, identified in a business unit that the auditor should report to parent management.

(d) **Questionnaires and reports**: The auditor should review questionnaires completed by other auditors, together with any reports on other auditors' work submitted by performing offices. If the auditor identifies particular concerns about the quality of work of other auditors, either because of unsatisfactory answers to the questionnaire, or arising from a review of their work by a performing office, the auditor should discuss the matter with parent management. If necessary, the auditor should arrange to carry out specific work on the business unit concerned.

11:7.4 Auditing the aggregation

The nature and extent of testing of the aggregation of data from business units depends on the nature of the aggregation process and on the auditor's assessment of inherent risk and the effectiveness of controls.

11:7.4.1 Inherent risk

The auditor should identify and evaluate any inherent risks relating to the consolidation process. The auditor should consider the results of previous years' audits and subsequent information which might indicate whether the client's consolidation systems are functioning properly, with a consequent effect on the auditor's assessment of control effectiveness.

11:7.4.2 Control effectiveness

The auditor should take into account the following:

(a) The evaluation of the parent control risk in so far as it might affect the aggregation process.

(b) The consolidation systems used by the client and the controls in place over those systems.

(c) The frequency with which the client's consolidation procedures are performed (e.g., monthly), to establish whether personnel involved are fully familiar with the procedures and controls.

Consolidation systems might be based on mini or microcomputers, developed and operated by a small number of personnel who are generally outside the control of the computer operations department. Accordingly, such systems might form a separate IT environment from that for the client's other accounting systems. If the audit strategy is to evaluate IT control risks the auditor might need to undertake a separate evaluation of the IT controls relating to the consolidation system.

Many clients use consolidation software packages, some of which are well proven so that the risk of random error is low. In such cases, the auditor might find it efficient to make an extended assessment of IT controls. Other systems might adopt spreadsheet packages, where there might be a greater risk of error because of the need to develop the consolidation application, and the auditor might not find it efficient to rely on IT controls.

11:7.4.3 Substantive testing

The auditor should carry out the following procedures:

(a)   Compare the client's consolidation schedules with the list of business units to ensure that all consolidation packages have been input.

(b)   Test check items in the consolidation package with the consolidation schedules (and vice versa) to ensure that amounts recorded are accurate and properly classified.

(c)   Check the currency translations. The auditor should verify the exchange rates used by the client with published rates ruling at the balance sheet date, and test the calculation of the currency translation for a sample of transactions. The auditor should also check that the accounting treatment of any profit or loss arising from the translation is in accordance with the group accounting policy.

(d)   Check the additions and cross-casts of the consolidation schedules.

The extent of work necessary will depend principally on the auditor's assessments of inherent risk and control effectiveness. Where risk is low the work may be performed mainly by more junior members of the team, under proper direction and supervision.

11:7.5 Audit software

The auditor may wish to use computer-assisted audit techniques (CAATs) because they enhance the efficiency and effectiveness of the substantive procedures. For example:

(a)   Developing an interrogation programme to produce an exception report which identifies unusually low items compared with the previous year (which might indicate that some consolidation packages have been omitted from input), and which checks additions and currency translation calculations.

(b)   Parallel input of data, e.g. by using the auditor's own financial consolidation, modelling and reporting system.

General guidance on the use of CAATs is given in **Section 9:7**, 'Computer-assisted audit techniques'.

11:7.6 Auditing the consolidation adjustments

The auditor should ensure that consolidation journal entries have been made where required and have been properly authorised by the client. The audit procedures the auditor should follow in respect of each journal adjustment will be determined by whether it is a 'permanent' or a current period adjustment. The often complex nature of the transactions giving rise to consolidation adjustments will mean that this work should normally be performed by the in-charge, the engagement manager or the partner. It should be considered in advance who is best placed to audit the consolidation adjustments in order to avoid duplication of effort.

11:7.6.1 Permanent consolidation adjustments

Many adjustments, e.g. those relating to the acquisition of subsidiaries in prior years, will not change from year to year. In the case of an existing client, the auditor will have audited these 'permanent' adjustments in prior years, and, as discussed in **Section 11:2**, 'Group business review', recorded the details in the carry-forward documentation.

Accordingly, the auditor can limit the current year's audit work to confirming the continuing relevance of the adjustments, checking them to the carry-forward schedule and ensuring that the journal entries have been correctly posted.

If there are amendments to any permanent adjustments, e.g. because of an acquisition or disposal of subsidiaries, the auditor should check the journal entry, including:

(a) Checking the calculation of pre-acquisition reserves for any subsidiaries accounted for as acquisitions.

(b) Checking that goodwill arising on consolidation has been accounted for in accordance with accounting standards.

(c) Checking that fair values of assets and liabilities have been properly evaluated.

(d) Confirming that profits or losses arising on the sale of subsidiaries have been properly calculated.

The auditor should consider referring in consolidation issues documentation to any major complex or unusual adjustments occurring for the first time in the current year.

When auditing the consolidation for the first time, the auditor should review the permanent adjustments and be satisfied that the accounting treatment adopted is appropriate.

11:7.6.2 Current period consolidation adjustments

Current period consolidation adjustments relate primarily to the elimination of intra-group transactions and account balances including:

(a) Intra-group sales and cost of sales, interest paid and received, or management fees.

(b)   Unrealised intra-group profits on stocks acquired from other business units.

(c)   Intra-group indebtedness.

The auditor should ensure that intra-group transactions and account balances cancel out, and review and corroborate any work carried out by the client to investigate and deal with any differences. The auditor should investigate any differences not resolved satisfactorily by the client.

Other adjustments might be required in the current period, e.g. to adjust account balances and classes of transactions to comply with group accounting policies. A suitably experienced auditor should review all significant journal entries. In particular, the auditor should check that all material adjustments have been authorised, that they agree with appropriate supporting evidence and that they have been correctly posted.

11:7.6.3 Impact on business units

The auditor should also consider whether any journal entries should be recorded in the financial statements of the underlying business unit(s) affected. The auditor should review the client's procedures for notifying such adjustments to business unit management and consider the need to inform the business unit auditors direct.

11:7.7 Analytical review

For each account balance and class of transactions, unless it is clear from the consolidation schedules, the auditor should obtain or prepare a schedule that shows the current and the corresponding amounts. In large and complex groups the auditor might need to analyse the amounts by significant business unit, or geographically. The auditor should obtain explanations for any significant fluctuation between periods from discussion with parent management together with analysis of comments in business unit auditors' issues documentation which explain significant fluctuations in individual business units. The auditor should pay particular attention to account balances and classes of transaction where there has been a change of accounting policy, or where there are differences in accounting policies applied by business units for local reasons.

11:7.7.1 Movements on group balance sheet accounts

In addition, the auditor should obtain working papers detailing the movements on the following group balance sheet accounts:

(a)   Goodwill.

(b)   Investments in associates.

(c)   Reserves, by major category.

(d)   Minority interests.

In respect of each of the accounts in the above list the auditor should carry out both of the following procedures:

(a) Trace the amounts to the consolidation schedules.

(b) Review all movements to ensure they are correctly classified and comply with the group's accounting policies and relevant legislation.

The auditor should have particular regard to any unusual movements on reserves in the year, such as the following:

(a) The treatment of exchange differences arising on translation of business units that report in a foreign currency and the offset of differences on foreign currency loans taken out as a hedge against such movements.

(b) Transfers between revaluation reserve and profit and loss account. (These should be supported by calculations based on the original revaluation.)

(c) Attempts to offset permanent diminutions in the value of fixed assets against a revaluation of other fixed assets.

If the reserves are low or negative, the auditor should consider whether the group is in breach of covenants or similar agreements.

11:7.7.2 Segmental reporting

The auditor should obtain or prepare working papers which support the segmental information disclosed in the financial statements, and ensure that the disclosure is in accordance with the requirements of the Companies Act 1985, the Stock Exchange and Accounting Standards.

11:7.7.3 Directors' emoluments and transactions

The auditor must be satisfied in relation to directors' emoluments, loans and other transactions. The auditor should obtain or prepare working papers detailing the emoluments paid to or receivable by directors of the parent company in respect of services to all group companies and any transactions favouring directors. The details should be agreed to supporting evidence, e.g.:

(a) Representations from directors.

(b) Articles of association.

(c) Board minutes.

(d) Remuneration committee minutes.

The auditor's letter of instruction to the auditors of the business units should request that they provide details of any emoluments paid to the parent company directors.

11:7.7.4 *Exceptional items*

The auditor should ensure that exceptional items are correctly accounted for in accordance with FRS 3. Only those amounts which properly qualify as 'super exceptional' should be classified after operating profit and before interest.

Unusual profit and loss account items should be scrutinised to ensure that all exceptional items are included as such. This includes, e.g., credits arising from the release of provisions classified as exceptional in prior periods.

11:7.7.5 *Extraordinary Items*

Because the definition of ordinary activities is now so widely drawn the incidence of extraordinary items will be extremely rare. If extraordinary items were to arise the auditor should ensure that they have been accounted for in accordance with FRS 3.

11:7.7.6 *Cash flow statement*

The auditor should obtain the client's schedules supporting the group cash flow statement, showing current period and prior period amounts, and perform the following procedures:

(a)   All items appearing elsewhere in the financial statements should be cross-checked, e.g., depreciation.

(b)   The analyses of movements or balances which do not themselves appear elsewhere should be reviewed to ensure they reconcile to the balance sheet and profit and loss account and appear reasonable, e.g., tax payments made and proceeds on the disposal of fixed assets.

(c)   Analytical review should be performed on the balances to ensure the auditor understands significant fluctuations.

(d)   The auditor should ensure that disclosure of all items required by FRS 1 has been made.

11:7.7.7 *Taxation*

The auditor should carry out the audit of the group tax position in accordance with the guidance set out in **Section 9:25**, 'Taxation'. The auditor should consider and check that evidence exists to support any arrangements related to the following:

(a)   Group relief for losses.

(b)   ACT surrenders.

(c) Group income elections.

(d) The consequences of assets transferred within the group.

(e) Payment for group relief and ACT.

The auditor should consider preparing or obtaining a proof of the consolidated tax charge for the group. In general terms this will represent an aggregation of the proofs of tax charges of the business units, but the auditor should make necessary adjustments for matters such as group relief. It will generally be appropriate to include only companies resident in the United Kingdom in this exercise.

The auditor should check the tax implications of consolidation adjustments dealing with, e.g., intra-group transactions and elimination of unrealised profits on intra-group sales.

The auditor should check that the parent informs the business unit(s) and their auditors of any tax adjustments made centrally which need to be recorded in the accounting records and financial statements of the business unit(s).

11:7.8 Group issues documentation

The auditor should record any significant matters arising from the audit of the consolidation of group issues documentation. This is discussed in **Section 11:8**, 'Group audit completion procedures'.

11:8 Group audit completion procedures

11:8.1 Introduction

Most of the matters the auditor needs to consider at the completion stage of a group audit do not differ significantly from those of any other audit (discussed in **Section 10:1**, 'Audit completion'). This section discusses those matters which are of particular relevance to group audits.

11:8.2 Final review of the draft group financial statements

Statement of Auditing Standards 470, 'Overall Review of Financial Statements', requires that:

> *Auditors should carry out such a review of the financial statements as is sufficient, in conjunction with the conclusions drawn from the other audit evidence obtained, to give them a reasonable basis for their opinion on the financial statements.*

The auditor should carry out a final review of the draft group financial statements sufficient, in conjunction with the conclusions drawn from other evidence obtained, to provide a reasonable basis for the auditor's opinion. For all entities this review should comprise the following:

(a)   Confirmation of compliance with relevant legislation and acceptable accounting policies which have been consistently applied.

(b)   Consideration of disclosures, e.g., in relation to directors' remuneration, benefits, loans and other transactions.

(c)   Confirmation of the validity of the 'going concern' basis.

(d)   Review of transactions with related parties.

(e)   A final review for credibility.

In the context of groups the auditor should consider in particular whether:

(a)   like items from business units' financial statements have been reasonably and consistently aggregated;

(b)   the basis for consolidation complies with relevant legislation and applicable accounting standards;

(c)   group accounting policies have been consistently applied, or if not, whether there is appropriate justification; and

(d)   assets and retained profits of non-UK business units operating under exchange controls or other legal restrictions have been properly treated.

The auditor should record specific matters arising from this review in the working papers.

   Where the relevant disclosure requirements are those of UK legislation and accounting standards, the auditor should use a UK GAAP checklist.

11:8.3 Concurring review

Most groups will fall within the definition, suggested in **Section 5:5**, 'Consultation and concurring reviews', of clients for which a review partner should be appointed. The role of the review partner is explained in **Section 5:5**.

11:8.4 Completion of fieldwork

The engagement manager should ensure, before the consolidation audit files are presented for final review by the referring partner, that the consolidation fieldwork has been completed and reviewed, and that any matters relating to business unit audits have been cleared, except as indicated on group issues documentation.

11 Group audits   11:8.5 – 11:8.6

11:8.5 Subsequent events review

Statement of Auditing Standards 150, 'Subsequent Events', requires that 'Auditors should consider the effect of subsequent events on the financial statements and on their report'.

Before signing the report on the group financial statements the auditor should carry out procedures designed to identify all material post-balance-sheet events at the parent and business units. For this purpose the auditor needs initially to consider all business units in the group. The auditor should decide the extent to which a subsequent events review can be carried out centrally for the group as a whole, particularly in respect of non-material business units, and the extent to which the auditor requires information from each business unit. The procedures should comprise, as a minimum, both of the following:

(a)   A request in the letter of instruction to all business unit auditors to report any material post-balance-sheet event or to report that no such event has occurred. If it is more convenient, the auditor may carry out the review after first informing the business unit auditors of this intention.

(b)   Positive enquiries directed to the board or management of the parent, who may be aware of, or have instigated, events which have not been communicated to business units' management. The auditor should ensure that, where appropriate, business unit management and its auditors are notified of any such events.

The subsequent events review should cover the period between the date of the consolidation packages and the date the auditor signs the group financial statements. The auditor should remember that, where business units produce statutory financial statements, the directors may make late amendments or additions to reflect, e.g., events occurring or information becoming available after the consolidation packages have been submitted. The auditor should inspect statutory financial statements in all cases to ensure that any such amendments or additions are reflected in the group financial statements.

The auditor should consider and summarise the results of the subsequent events review, and record any significant matters arising on group issues documentation.

11:8.6 Letters of support

The parent might be required to provide a letter of support to one or more business units which might not be a going concern without such support. In such cases, the auditor should discuss this matter with the business unit auditors involved and carry out any procedures they request, e.g. checking that the letter is properly authorised by the parent's board of directors. Guidance on letters of support is given in **Section 11:10**, 'Letters of support'.

11/52

11:8.7 Letter of representation

Statement of Auditing Standards 440, 'Management Representations', requires that 'Auditors should obtain written confirmation of appropriate representations from management before their report is issued'.

The auditor should obtain written representations for those uncorroborated oral representations received from parent management during the group audit. The way in which the auditor obtains these representations will depend upon the group management style, which can vary both between and within groups. For example, the auditor may be able to obtain written representations regarding the group financial statements from the directors of the parent where they are closely involved in the management of the business units. Alternatively, there will be circumstances where parent management is reluctant to make representations about business units' information. In this case the auditor should obtain copies of written representations made by directors of business units to their auditors, but the auditor should consider the reliability of such representations in the context of the group financial statements.

11:8.8 Drafting the group audit report

Guidance on drafting audit reports on group financial statements is given in **Sections 13:3**, 'Unqualified reports to the members of limited companies in Great Britain', and **13:16**, 'Qualified and modified reports to the members of limited companies and other organisations in Great Britain'.

If the auditor's report of a business unit is qualified the auditor should consider whether the qualification is so material as to affect the opinion on the group financial statements. If the auditor proposes to qualify the opinion the guidance in **Sections 13:16** to **13:19** should be followed, as should the consultation procedures set out in **Section 5:5**, 'Consultation and concurring reviews'.

11:8.9 Issues documentation

The auditor should prepare an appropriate record of matters of significance that arise from audit work on the group. In addition to the matters of significance that arise from audit work on the parent and on the consolidation, group issues documentation should include all matters relevant to opinion on the group financial statements highlighted by auditors of business units, in relation both to the consolidation packages and to the financial statements of business units.

Therefore, as described in **Section 11:5**, 'Planning and control of group audits', the auditor should request in the letter of instruction a copy of issues documentation on all material business units from performing offices and should request similar information from other auditors of material business units. Sometimes the management of the business unit might be reluctant to have such information released (e.g. where the business unit is an associate). In such cases, the auditor should first ask the parent to request the co-operation of business unit management.

Other auditors might be reluctant to prepare the equivalent of issues documentation on the grounds that they will incur additional cost which they will be unable to recover. However, provided that the information requested is reasonable, the auditor should point out that the request only includes details of matters that they would normally need for their audit opinion and that consequently, by careful planning, they can minimise any additional cost.

11:8.9.1 Clearance of consolidation packages

The auditor should request that issues documentation, or equivalent, are prepared to accompany the clearance of the consolidation package by the auditors of business units. Where they are unable to dispose of all matters relevant to the statutory financial statements at the time of the clearance of the consolidation package, the auditor should request a second set of final issues documentation from the business unit auditor to ensure that all matters relevant to the statutory financial statements have been addressed in group issues documentation.

11:8.9.2 Clearance of matters referred by business units' auditors

The auditor should clear any matters addressed to the referring office by business units' auditors as quickly as possible. Where copies of issues documentation are submitted, the auditor should report clearance by memorandum or letter to the business unit auditor.

11:8.9.3 Content of group issues documentation

The contents and compilation of issues documentation generally are considered in **Section 10:2**, 'Issues documentation'. In addition to the matters referred to in **Section 10:2**, to the extent that they are relevant to the audit of groups the following matters may need to be covered:

(a) **Business review and review of control environment**:

  (i)   Significant changes in the group's activities or business environment to the extent not covered in the group audit strategy.

  (ii) Significant matters arising from the assessment of the control environment, including that of the parent, affecting the auditor's view as to the reliability of the financial information produced within the group.

  (iii) Other matters identified at the strategy stage to be examined and reported upon in group issues documentation.

(b) **Accounting policies and disclosure matters**:

  (i)   The consolidation treatment for any acquisition or disposals.

  (ii) Details of any changes in the basis of consolidation.

  (iii) Details of any significant inconsistencies in accounting policies applied at business units, in particular, policies not in accordance with group policies, and how these have been dealt with in producing the group financial statements.

(iv) Particulars of financial information of any subsidiary material to the group included in the group financial statements because the subsidiary has a different year-end from that of the parent.

(v) Any significant matters relating to presentation or disclosure in the group financial statements.

(c) **Matters arising from audits of business units**:

(i) Any significant changes necessary to instructions given to business unit auditors after the release of the group instructions.

(ii) Any respects in which significant information required has not been obtained, or unsatisfactory answers have been received, from other auditors.

(iii) Any significant work required of business unit auditors, or that the auditor was required to clear by the business unit auditors, that is still outstanding.

(iv) Conclusions if the review processes indicate that the auditor is unable to place reliance on the audited financial statements of a business unit for inclusion in the group financial statements.

(v) Particulars of the nature of any qualifications in the audit reports of business units and the materiality of the amounts involved in relation to the group.

(vi) Information on any major weaknesses in the system of internal control of a business unit.

(d) **Summary information**:

(i) A summary of the aggregate effect of the auditor's estimate of the likely misstatement, including matters reported by the auditors of business units.

(ii) A summary of the percentage of group profits and net assets audited by other auditors, indicating the principal business units concerned.

(e) **Reporting to parent management and to the parent board**:

(i) Significant matters to be reported to senior parent management/to the parent board, including the proposed method and timing of the communication.

11:8.10 Confidentiality

11:8.10.1 Referring office considerations

Group issues documentation may contain discussion of sensitive client issues and they will not normally be designed to be made available to third parties. If parent management requests access to this information the auditor should find out the reason for the request and discuss the matter with the performing partners or with the other auditors of business units referred to in the group issues documentation. If it is decided to agree to the request, the auditor may wish to add the following notation to any issues documentation that were prepared by a performing office:

> **This memorandum/letter is an internal communication within [*name of the firm*] and should not be relied upon for other purposes.**

11:8.10.2 Performing office considerations

The management of a business unit might ask for a copy of issues documentation from the auditor of the business unit. In such a case the auditor should find out the reason for the request and, where appropriate, the auditor should discuss it with the referring office or other auditors before agreeing to the request. Normally there is no objection to providing a copy where the client confirms that the only reason for the request is to have a record of the matters the auditor has raised (just as the auditor would deal with any other client requests for copies of consolidation working papers or analyses of particular accounts). In the light of the particular circumstances the engagement partner should decide whether to agree to the request, and should review the issues documentation to ensure that only relevant information appropriate for disclosure to management is included.

If it is decided to agree to the request the auditor may wish to add the following notation to the copy of any report given to the client:

> **This memorandum/letter is an informal commentary to the auditor of the parent undertaking for the purpose of their audit of the consolidation and it should not be relied upon for other purposes.**

11:8.11 Signing the group financial statements

11:8.11.1 Duties of directors in relation to group financial statements

Section 227 of the Companies Act 1985 requires directors to prepare group financial statements if at the end of the year the company is a parent company. The group financial statements are required to be in consolidated form.

This means that they should incorporate in full the information contained in the individual financial statements of the business units included in the consolidation, subject to the adjustments that are authorised by the Act or by generally accepted accounting principles (consolidation adjustments). The Act states that the group financial statements shall give a true and fair view.

11:8.11.2 Signed financial statements of business units

It is therefore the parent's directors' responsibility to ensure that the financial statements of business units which are used for consolidation purposes are suitable for inclusion in the group financial statements. For business units incorporated in the UK and the Republic of Ireland, it is reasonable for directors to expect and to arrange for signed statutory financial statements of business units to be available before the group financial statements are signed in order to fulfil their obligation to ensure that the group financial statements give a true and fair view. For other business units, if necessary, consolidation packages may be prepared so as to give equivalent information to that contained in statutory financial statements. Further explanation is provided below.

11:8.11.2.1 UK and Republic of Ireland companies

In relation to business units incorporated in the UK and the Republic of Ireland:

(a) The group consolidation will be based on statutory financial statements.

(b) Alternatively, the consolidation is initially based on consolidation packages and the auditor then reviews the statutory financial statements before signing the report on the group financial statements.

The auditor should not normally report on the group financial statements before the audit reports on the statutory financial statements of all major business units have been signed.

In particular, if a group is raising finance and the group financial statements are important for that purpose, the auditor should not report on the group financial statements before the audit reports on the statutory financial statements of all major business units have been signed.

The auditor may accept consolidation packages signed by the business units' directors and auditors for minor business units, provided they are in the form of financial statements and contain information equivalent to statutory financial statements. This recognises that in practice the completion of printed signed statutory financial statements for all such business units might not be possible before the group financial statements are signed by the directors. When the statutory financial statements are printed they should be dated with the actual date on which they are signed, and not with the date on which the consolidation packages were agreed.

Except where the consolidation has been prepared directly from statutory financial statements, the auditor should ensure that the information in the statutory financial statements is in accordance with that shown in the consolidation packages. The auditor should ask the business unit auditors to report on any differences between the consolidation packages and the statutory financial statements covering the following matters:

(a) The principal items appearing in the profit and loss account, balance sheet and cash flow statements.

(b) The accounting policies adopted.

(c) Significant information contained in the notes to the financial statements.

11:8.11.2.2 Other business units

In some countries statutory financial statements are required which differ from the financial statements submitted in the form of consolidation packages for consolidation purposes, e.g. because such statutory financial statements may be produced for tax purposes only or because different accounting policies are used for other reasons. In such cases consolidation packages should be used for consolidation purposes. However, the parent should receive details of reconciling items between the consolidation packages and the statutory financial statements and the auditor should inspect these.

The consolidation packages should be formally approved by the business units' board of directors (or executive management where there is no formally constituted board), so as to minimise any risk of subsequent objection or amendment to them. The arrangements for evidencing such approval may vary, depending upon, e.g., local practice and legislation, but the consolidation packages should normally be signed by at least a director with specific authority to sign on behalf of the board as a whole. In all cases the arrangements for signature should be clearly explained in written instructions to both the business unit and its auditors.

The auditor should not report on the group financial statements before the audit reports on the consolidation packages have been signed.

The auditor need not normally request business units' auditors to confirm that the consolidation packages comply with the disclosure requirements of the Companies Act, provided that the auditor takes suitable steps to ensure that the consolidation packages cover all the matters required to be disclosed in the group financial statements.

11:8.12 Reporting to the parent board and to group management

The engagement manager should discuss with parent management its requirements, if any, for the submission of management reports for the group as a whole. The auditor can often provide the senior management of the parent with useful information regarding affairs of business units, particularly if the business units are situated in other countries. In these circumstances, the auditor may offer to extend the service provided in respect of the parent company by arranging for a composite report to be submitted to the parent incorporating significant comments regarding the group as a whole. Areas that the auditor might cover are:

(a) Impact of head office controls on the business unit.

(b) Financial accounting at the business unit.

(c) Financial stewardship at the business unit.

(d) Business controls at the business unit.

(e) Interpretation of results.

The auditor should ensure that parent management is aware of significant control weaknesses in business units. The auditor should obtain the necessary information from other offices and/or from detailed enquiries made from other auditors regarding business units audited by them. Further guidance is included in **Section 12:1**, 'Audit reporting to the board and to management'.

11:8.13 Debriefing

So far as is practicable, the auditor should arrange a meeting of representatives of offices involved in the audit to obtain adequate debriefing on the group audit, and in particular, on any problems experienced by performing offices in dealing with their instructions. The auditor should invite offices unable to attend for geographical and/or cost reasons to submit written comments on the conduct of the audit and the adequacy of their instructions. The auditor should send all offices notes of the debriefing meeting. Further guidance on the objectives and practical aspects of debriefing is set out in **Section 10:1**, 'Audit completion'.

11:9 Responsibilities of a performing office

11:9.1 Introduction

Generally, the policies and procedures that apply when carrying out work on a business unit are the same as for an individual entity. This section is generally expressed as covering matters specific to the auditor's role as performing office for an engagement referred by another office of the same firm. Where the auditor is performing work referred by another firm similar principles will apply but all the detailed procedures contained in this section will not necessarily need to be followed. The onus will be on the other auditor to issue instructions.

Referred work might comprise either of the following:

(a) Carrying out an audit or other procedures in relation to a business unit, in accordance with the group audit strategy.

(b) Reviewing the work of other auditors.

11:9.2 Strategy and planning

The auditor may attend the group audit strategy meeting with the engagement partner, the engagement manager and others from the referring office, especially if information specific to the business unit is needed and is not available at the parent.

The auditor will normally receive from the referring office a letter of instruction setting out the part of the group audit strategy relevant to the audit of the appropriate business unit. When a letter of instruction is received from the referring office, the auditor should carry out the following procedures:

(a)   Acknowledge immediately the receipt of instructions.

(b)   Advise the referring office immediately if:

  (i)   the auditor cannot comply with a specific instruction for any reason (e.g., because of local professional restrictions);

  (ii)   the auditor lacks information as to the accounting standards applicable to the country in which the referring office is situated; or

  (iii)   the auditor does not have the most recent version of the referring office's audit manual that might be needed to assist in complying with the letter of instruction.

(c)   Immediately seek clarification from the referring office if anything in the letter of instruction is unclear (e.g., if it is not clear where the responsibility lies for performing particular procedures, or where there appear to be omissions).

(d)   Ask the referring office to reconsider any requirements that the auditor believes may not be needed or justified in the circumstances.

When the auditor is instructed by the referring office to perform work on a business unit resulting in the issuance of any form of assurance (e.g., an audit or review) the auditor is responsible for the strategy and testing plan decisions. When not required to issue any form of assurance (e.g., when performing specified procedures) the referring office will normally be responsible for strategy and testing plan decisions.

The auditor should ensure that the staff assigned to the client are sufficiently experienced, and are familiar with the referring office's requirements.

11:9.3 Liaison with the referring office

The auditor should comply with the requests of the referring office on or before the time deadlines agreed upon.

The auditor should keep the referring office informed of any matters that arise that have a significant bearing on the work performed. Sometimes it is possible that the referring office might not appreciate local conditions and constraints so that the auditor might be unable to carry out the instructions of the referring office or might have to exceed those instructions, e.g. because of local statutory audit requirements. The auditor should, therefore, communicate immediately with the referring office whenever obliged to vary any part of the matters covered by the letter of instruction from the referring office.

The auditor should inform the referring office as soon as it seems likely that a reservation or qualification of the standard report will be necessary. This is particularly important because the referring office may wish to take the matter up with the parent before the wording of the reservation or qualification is finalised. Furthermore, in many cases, arrangements may be made that remove the need for a reservation or qualification. Thus the auditor should only sign a report containing a reservation or qualification in respect of an engagement referred by another office after the proposed wording of the report has been discussed with the referring office.

The auditor should also advise the referring office of any information which, while not resulting in a reservation or qualification in the standard report, would be of interest to the referring office. In the case of limited scope engagements (discussed in **Section 11:9.5.3**), such information might typically take the form of a statement along the following lines:

(a)   The amount of an account balance not covered in the limited scope procedures has increased, or the risk of its misstatement changed, to an extent which leads the auditor to recommend to the referring office that work additional to that in the original instructions should be performed.

(b)   Enquiries of management indicate that an account balance not covered in the limited procedures may be misstated.

It may be desirable for the auditor to discuss matters of contention with the client before reporting them to the referring office, to avoid errors of fact or emphasis.

11:9.4 Letters of support

The auditor may find that the business unit being audited depends for its continuing existence as a going concern on support from the parent or from a fellow business unit. This support might be provided by means of a letter of support or a letter of subordination. Guidance on the matters the auditor should consider in relation to such letters is given in **Section 11:10**, 'Letters of support'.

11:9.5 Reports on consolidation packages

Before issuing the report on the consolidation package the auditor should ensure that the package has been formally approved either by directors of the business unit or, if appropriate, by the senior management. Normally the parent will require that this formal approval is evidenced by the signing of the package by the directors or managers.

The report on the consolidation package may be an internal communication or it may be addressed to both the referring office and the parent. The engagement partner should sign the communication whatever form it takes.

Some clients require the auditor to initial one copy of the consolidation package so that the auditor can refer to that particular copy in correspondence and also in the audit report, if any. If the consolidation package is initialled, the auditor should clearly mark each page to indicate that it has been initialled for identification purposes only. The auditor may not need to initial the consolidation package sent directly to the referring office.

If the report on the client's consolidation package is intended as an internal communication only, the auditor should not normally give the client a copy of it. Sometimes, however, the client may ask for a copy of it. In that circumstance, a copy may be provided, just as the auditor might give a client a copy of consolidation working papers or analyses of particular accounts. The auditor should, however, take care to omit from those copies any references to significant auditing procedures. If the auditor gives a copy of the report to the client, it should be made clear to the client that it is an internal communication, and not a formal report. The auditor should add a notation on any copy given to the client to indicate that the inter-office memorandum was intended as an internal communication within the firm and that, accordingly, it may not be sufficient for other purposes. This notation is particularly important when the referring office has limited the scope of the audit.

11:9.5.1 Unqualified reports

Where a full audit is carried out and the financial statements contain all the information required by generally accepted accounting principles the auditor may use the wording set out in **Appendix A** (*see* **Section 11:9.8**).

11:9.5.2 Qualifications – financial statements that do not contain all the information required by generally accepted accounting principles

Sometimes the auditor will need to include a qualification solely because the financial statements do not comply with generally accepted accounting principles in that, being prepared for consolidation purposes rather than for publication outside the client group, they may not include full note disclosure of matters that are required to be disclosed under generally accepted accounting principles or to comply with local requirements. In such cases, the auditor should observe the requirements of **Section 11:9.3** (third paragraph) requiring consultation with the referring office. The audit report may use the wording set out in **Appendix B** (*see* **Section 11:9.9**).

11:9.5.3 Limited scope reports

When the referring office requires the performing office to undertake a limited scope engagement it will normally indicate the scope of the work required by either of the following methods:

(a) By specifying the report it wishes to receive as a result of the work (e.g., by requesting the performing office to report that the business unit's financial statements do not require adjustment in excess of a specified level of materiality), in which case the auditor will determine the procedures to be applied to enable the auditor to comply with the referring office's request. The referring office may, however, suggest procedures for consideration.

(b) By specifying the procedures it wishes the firm to follow, in which case the auditor should apply those procedures and advise the referring office of any exceptions found.

The form of the report will depend on which of the alternative methods of instruction described above is selected:

(a) Where the referring office indicates the nature of the report it wishes to receive (point (a) above), the report may take the form of an expression of assurance along the lines of the example in **Appendix C** (*see* **Section 11:9.10**).

(b) Where the referring office indicates the procedures to be followed (point (b) above), the report should describe the work done (preferably by reference to the letter of instruction) and the exceptions found. If the work performed differs from the procedures set out in the letter of instruction, the report should describe concisely the work performed and the reasons why the instructions were varied. An example form of report appropriate for use under this alternative is shown in **Appendix D** (*see* **Section 11:9.11**).

Both types of report referred to in the last paragraph should:

(a) be addressed to the referring office;

(b) identify the financial information that the auditor has reviewed;

(c) state that the work performed does not constitute an audit and that the auditor does not express an audit opinion on the financial statements;

(d) describe adjustments proposed, if any, to the financial information that the auditor has reviewed; and

(e) refer to any other matters that come to the auditor's attention that may affect the referring office's use of the financial statements or information.

Generally, a report as discussed in the last two paragraphs will be for the sole use of the referring office. The referring office should not distribute copies of such a report to its client or any other party without the performing office's consent. The auditor should include a paragraph in the reports setting out this restriction.

11:9.5.3.1 *Reports where scope is limited by applying a group materiality level*

When the scope of the audit of a business unit is limited by applying a group materiality level the auditor should perform sufficient work on the business unit to support the audit opinion, having regard to the increased materiality level. The auditor should still prepare audit programmes and issues documentation.

An example of a report where the referring office asks the auditor to audit based on a group materiality level is set out in **Appendix C** (*see* **Section 11:9.10**).

11:9.5.3.2 Reports where scope is limited by an instruction to carry out only specified procedures

An example of a report where the referring office sets the materiality level and further restricts the scope of the audit work by requiring the auditor to carry out only specified procedures is set out in **Appendix D** (*see* **Section 11:9.11**). In this report the auditor gives only negative assurance based on the limited procedures that have been carried out.

11:9.5.3.3 Reports on a review of the financial statements or of particular account balances

Where the auditor has carried out a review of the financial statements or of particular account balances the auditor should issue a negative assurance report. An example of such a report where the referring office has specified the materiality levels to be used for the review is set out in **Appendix E** (*see* **Section 11:9.12**).

11:9.5.3.4 Reports following a visit to a business unit

The report should identify the location visited and the nature of the procedures the auditor has carried out, e.g. observing the nature of operations, reading recent financial information and holding discussions with local management. The auditor should report any matters arising which are considered to be of interest to the referring office.

   The report should state that the auditor has not performed an audit or review and, accordingly, no form of assurance is being expressed on the financial statements. An example of such a report is set out in **Appendix F** (*see* **Section 11:9.13**).

11:9.6 Reporting to the board and to management

There is no obligation for the auditor to send copies of management reports to the parent company auditor. However, the auditor should normally send a copy of each report sent to the business unit to its parent and may, at the request of the client, send a copy to the referring office. The auditor should agree with the client in the engagement letter, or otherwise in advance in writing, the arrangements for the distribution of such reports.

11:9.7 Review of the work of another auditor

The next two paragraphs, and **Sections 11:9.7.1** to **11:9.7.5**, set out the matters to be considered when an auditor is requested by the referring office to review another auditor's working papers.

   The auditor should discuss immediately with the referring office any matters that are not dealt with by the instructions or that are unclear. The auditor should ensure that, in particular, there is a clear understanding of the following matters:

(a) The reporting requirements and deadline.

(b) Areas in which the referring office has identified significant risks of misstatement.

(c) The group materiality level, if applicable.

(d) The consolidation package and instructions. (The auditor should ensure that a copy of the client's group accounting instructions is received.)

(e) Instructions issued to the other auditor.

(f) The group accounting policies.

(g) Special reporting requirements, e.g. a review of the other auditor's issues documentation, or work to be carried out on the other auditor's post-balance-sheet events review.

The auditor will normally receive instructions from the referring office in time to contact the other auditor before the final audit begins. In this way the auditor can ensure that the instructions are clearly understood and may be able to review the other auditor's plans to ensure that areas of concern will be dealt with adequately. It is also important to establish that the other auditor intends to co-operate fully.

11:9.7.1 Assigning staff to the review

The instructions will normally indicate the desired experience and seniority of the reviewer. In the absence of such instructions from the referring office, the work should normally be carried out by a manager or partner.

11:9.7.2 Timing and location of the review

Frequently the group reporting deadline will be such that the other auditor's work will not be complete by the time the review is due to start. The other auditor may, e.g., have completed enough work to release the consolidation package but not enough to enable the signing of the report on the statutory financial statements. Accordingly, to help meet the reporting deadline, the auditor should arrange to carry out the review at the client's premises whenever possible. This will also make it easier to meet the local client management to clarify any uncertain matters if the need arises.

11:9.7.3 Carrying out the review

To obtain sufficient evidence the auditor should carry out a combination of general procedures and certain specific procedures for each significant area selected for review.

11:9.7.3.1 Selecting the areas for review

The auditor should not normally need to review all the other auditor's audit working papers. Instead the auditor should be selective in approach and concentrate on those areas in which there is the greatest risk of material misstatement. In making this decision the auditor should have regard to the following:

(a)   The auditor's assessment of the other auditor.

(b)   The relative importance of the various audit areas, taking into account the group materiality.

(c)   The nature of the company's business and the industry in which it operates.

(d)   The nature of any identified risks of misstatement in each audit area.

(e)   The auditor's knowledge of problems in previous periods.

(f)   Specific instructions received from the referring office.

The auditor should decide on these matters in the light of the latest financial information (whether it be draft financial statements, consolidation packages or management accounts), knowledge of the particular industry and, if applicable, the results of its reviews in prior years. The auditor's own assessment should be compared with that of the other auditor, both to confirm the auditor's conclusions and to assess understanding of the business.

11:9.7.3.2   General procedures

The auditor should carry out the following procedures:

(a)   Read all review comments and identify any matters that appear not to have been cleared satisfactorily.

(b)   Read the minutes, or extracts thereof held on file, of the board and other executive committees and consider whether, *prima facie*, all relevant minutes have been inspected and all significant matters have been reviewed and followed up.

(c)   Read the audit strategy memorandum and the issues documentation (or equivalents).

(d)   Check that significant risks appear to have been addressed by the other auditor.

(e)   Ascertain whether there is evidence of a review of the financial statements.

11:9.7.3.3 Procedures for specific areas

For each specific area selected for review the auditor should consider the following issues:

(a)   Has the other auditor addressed appropriate audit objectives?

(b)   Was the design of the substantive testing procedures appropriate to achieve the other auditor's objectives?

(c)   Was the testing sufficient to support the conclusions drawn?

(d)   Were any internal controls that were relied on to restrict the extent of substantive testing suitably tested and confirmed as operating satisfactorily?

(e)   Were exceptions properly evaluated and summarised so as to demonstrate that the conclusions were valid?

(f)   Were adequate review procedures applied by a manager or equivalent?

(g)   Were additional procedures appropriate to a group business unit designed and carried out satisfactorily (e.g., in relation to related party transactions).

11:9.7.3.4 Completing the review

In addition to considering the adequacy of the other auditor's work the auditor should check that the other auditor has complied with the requirements of the referring office. This may involve, e.g., reviewing the issues documentation, or equivalent, or checking that the other auditor's procedures to be applied to the post-balance-sheet events review are appropriate.

If the issues documentation or equivalent are unclear, or do not adequately describe significant matters of interest to the referring office, the auditor should ask the other auditor for further information. Failing that, the auditor should report the particulars of such matters directly to the referring office after first checking the facts with the other auditor.

11:9.7.4 Procedures if the auditor is not satisfied with the other auditor's work

If, following the review of the other auditor's working papers, the auditor is not satisfied that there is sufficient evidence to support the other auditor's conclusions the auditor should first discuss the problem with the other auditor. The auditor may establish that there is inadequate recording rather than failure to carry out sufficient work, in which case the other auditor should be asked to record the additional explanations on the relevant files. The auditor should, in any event, make careful and complete notes of the discussions and of the information and explanations received.

If, after discussing matters with the other auditor, the auditor is still not satisfied, the reasons should be explained and the auditor should request the other auditor to carry out such further work as is considered necessary. However, before doing so, the auditor may wish to request the referring partner to confirm that, in the context of the group financial statements, such additional work is necessary. If the other auditor refuses to carry out any necessary additional auditing procedures (or indicates that the client will incur significant extra costs as a result) the auditor should draw this to the attention of the referring office so that it can be raised with parent management.

11:9.7.5 Reporting the results of the review

Because the principal purpose of the review is to conclude on the suitability of the financial statements for inclusion in those of the group, the auditor should normally report by concluding on the significant matters arising from the review. These might include the following:

(a)   Comments on the performance of the other auditor (including positive assurance that this work was satisfactory).

(b)   Particulars of any areas with significant risks of misstatement that were identified and reviewed in detail.

11:9.8 Appendix A Unqualified reports

Where a full audit is carried out and the financial statements contain all the information required by generally accepted accounting principles the auditor's report should be worded as follows:

> **We have audited the standard financial statements on pages x to xx and supporting schedules xx to xx of [*the 'Company'*] for the period ended [*give date*] that have been prepared solely for the purpose of preparing the consolidated financial statements of ABC PLC.**
>
> **Respective responsibilities of directors and auditors**
>
> **The directors of the Company are responsible for the preparation of the financial statements and supporting schedules. It is our responsibility to form an independent opinion, based on our audit, on those statements and schedules and to report our opinion to you.**
>
> **Basis of opinion**
>
> **As required by United Kingdom Auditing Standards, we conducted our audit in accordance with Auditing Standards issued by the United Kingdom Auditing Practices Board. An audit includes examination, on a test basis, of evidence relevant to the amounts and disclosures in the financial statements and supporting schedules. It also includes an assessment of the significant estimates and judgements made by the directors in the preparation of the financial statements and supporting schedules, and of whether the accounting policies are in accordance with generally accepted accounting principles in the United Kingdom, consistently applied and adequately disclosed.**
>
> **We planned and performed our audit so as to obtain all the information and explanations that we considered necessary in order to provide us with sufficient evidence to give reasonable assurance that the financial statements and supporting schedules are free from material misstatement, whether caused by fraud or other irregularity or error. In forming our opinion we also evaluated the overall adequacy of the presentation of information in the financial statements and supporting schedules.**

Opinion

In our opinion the standard financial statements and supporting schedules:

(a) have been prepared to give the information required to be shown in accordance with the Group consolidation instructions dated [*date*];

(b) give a true and fair view (present fairly in all material respects) the financial position of the Company for the purpose of preparing the consolidated financial statements of ABC PLC; and

(c) are in accordance with accounting principles that are generally accepted in the United Kingdom, applied on a basis consistent with that of the previous year.

Use of this report

This report is solely for your information and is not to be used for any other purpose. It should not be included or referred to in any document or publication made available to persons outside your firm without our consent.

Note: The words 'in the United Kingdom' in the first paragraph need not be included in reports issued from offices in the United Kingdom.

Some consolidation packages may contain some schedules or information that has not been subjected to audit. The audit report should make it clear which schedules were examined, and the auditor should disclaim an opinion on those schedules not examined. In these cases, the auditor should ensure that the first paragraph refers only to the supporting schedules that have been audited and the auditor should add the following paragraph at the end of the report:

We did not examine those supporting schedules and other information set out on pages xx and xxx and, accordingly, we do not express an opinion on them.

11:9.9 Appendix B Qualified report where financial statements do not contain all the information required by generally accepted accounting principles

Sometimes the auditor should include a qualification solely because the financial statements do not comply with generally accepted accounting principles in that, being prepared for consolidation purposes rather than for publication outside the client group, they do not include full note disclosure of matters that are required to be disclosed under generally accepted accounting principles or in compliance with local requirements. The audit report should refer to the omission in the basis of opinion paragraph, in the following manner:

The financial statements have been presented on standard forms specified by ABC PLC. They do not include disclosure of all information that would be required by generally accepted accounting principles and are to be used solely for consolidation purposes.

The opinion paragraph will therefore be amended to read:

In our opinion, except for the omission of information indicated in the preceding paragraph, the financial statements and supporting schedules:

(a) have been prepared to give the information required to be shown in accordance with the Group consolidation instructions dated [*date*];

(b) give a true and fair view (present fairly in all material respects) of the financial position of the Company for the purpose of preparing the consolidated financial statements of ABC PLC; and

(c) are in accordance with accounting principles that are generally accepted in the United Kingdom, applied on a basis consistent with that of the previous year.

Some consolidation packages may contain some schedules or information that have not been subjected to audit. The audit report should make it clear which schedules were examined, and the auditor should disclaim an opinion on those schedules not examined. In these cases, the auditor should ensure that the first paragraph refers only to the supporting schedules that have been audited and the auditor should add the following paragraph at the end of the report:

We did not examine those supporting schedules and other information set out on pages xx and xxx and, accordingly, we do not express an opinion on them.

11:9.10 Appendix C Report where scope is limited by applying a group materiality level

An example of a report where the referring office asks the auditor to apply limited procedures based on a group materiality level is set out below:

> We have audited the standard financial statements on pages x to xx and supporting schedules x to xx of [*the 'Company'*] for the period ended [*date*] that have been prepared solely for the purpose of preparing the consolidated financial statements of ABC PLC.
>
> **Respective responsibilities of directors and auditors**
>
> The directors of the Company are responsible test basis, of evidence relevant to the amounts and disclosures in the financial statements and supporting schedules. It also includes an assessment of the significant estimates and judgements made by the directors in the preparation of the financial statements and supporting schedules, and of whether the accounting policies are in accordance with generally accepted accounting principles in the United Kingdom consistently applied and adequately disclosed.
>
> As required by UK Auditing Standards, we planned our audit so as to obtain all the information and explanations which we considered necessary in order to provide us with sufficient evidence to give reasonable assurance that the financial statements and supporting schedules are free from material misstatement, whether caused by fraud or other irregularity or error. However, in accordance with your letter of instructions dated [*date*], the scope of our audit was limited by the materiality levels set out in those instructions.
>
> In forming our opinion we also evaluated the overall adequacy of the presentation of information in the financial statements and supporting schedules.
>
> **Opinion**
>
> Based on our restricted audit, and within the limits of materiality referred to above, in our opinion the financial statements of the Company at [*date*] and for the period then ended:
>
> (a) have been prepared in accordance with generally accepted accounting principles in the United Kingdom, applied on a basis consistent with the previous year [*state exceptions, if any*]; and

(b) are appropriate for consolidation [*or equity accounting*] purposes [*state exceptions, if any*].

Use of this report

This report is solely for your information and is not to be used for any other purpose. It should not be included or referred to in any document or publication made available to persons outside your firm without our consent.

Some consolidation packages may contain some schedules or information that have not been subjected to audit. The audit report should make it clear which schedules were examined, and the auditor should disclaim an opinion on those schedules not examined. In these cases, the auditor should ensure that the first paragraph refers only to the supporting schedules that have been audited and the auditor should add the following paragraph at the end of the report:

We did not examine those supporting schedules and other information set out on pages xx and xxx and, accordingly, we do not express an opinion on them.

11:9.11 Appendix D Report where scope is limited by an instruction to carry out only specific procedures

An example of a report where the referring office sets the materiality and specifies the procedures to be followed by the performing office is set out below:

We have performed the procedures requested in your letter of instruction of (date) (or list specific procedures), using the materiality level of (specify amount) contained therein on the standard financial statements on pages x to x and supporting schedules x to xx of [*the 'Company'*] for the period ended [*date*].

Respective responsibilities of directors and auditors

The directors of the Company are responsible for the preparation of the standard financial statements and supporting schedules. It is our responsibility to report to you the factual findings of our work.

Basis of opinion

We planned and performed our work based on the procedures requested in your letter of instruction dated [*date*].

Opinion

During the course of applying these procedures no discrepancies were found [*state exceptions, if any*].

Because the procedures performed do not constitute either an audit or a review made in accordance with Auditing Standards in the United Kingdom, we do not imply or express any form of assurance on the financial statements and supporting schedules.

Use of this report

This report is solely for your information and is not to be used for any other purpose. It should not be included or referred to in any document or publication made available to persons outside your firm without our consent.

11:9.12 Appendix E Report on a review of the financial statements or of particular account balances

An example of a report where the auditor has carried out a review of the financial statements or of particular account balances and where the referring office has specified the materiality levels to be used for the review is set out below:

We have reviewed the financial statements on pages x to xx and supporting schedules x to xx of [*the 'Company'*] for the period ended [*date*] that have been prepared solely for the purpose of preparing the consolidated financial statements of ABC PLC. The financial statements and supporting schedules are the responsibility of the directors. Our responsibility is to report on the results of our review.

Our review consisted principally of applying analytical procedures to the underlying financial data, assessing whether accounting policies have been consistently applied, and making enquiries of management responsible for financial and accounting matters. The review excluded audit procedures such as tests of controls and verification of assets and liabilities and was therefore substantially less in scope than an audit performed in accordance with United Kingdom Auditing Standards. Accordingly we do not express an audit opinion on the financial statements and supporting schedules.

In accordance with your letter of instruction dated [*date*], the scope of our review was further restricted by the materiality levels set out in those instructions.

Based on our restricted review, and within the limits of materiality referred to above, nothing has come to our attention that causes us to believe that the financial statements of ABC PLC as at [*date*] and for the year then ended:

(a) have not been prepared in accordance with generally accepted accounting principles in the United Kingdom applied on a basis consistent with the previous year [*state exceptions, if any*]; and

(b) are not appropriate for consolidation [*or equity accounting*] purposes [*state exceptions, if any*].

Use of this report

This report is solely for your information and is not to be used for any other purpose. It should not be included or referred to in any document or publication made available to persons outside your firm without our consent.

11:9.13 Appendix F Report following a visit to a business unit

An example report that may be used following a visit to a business unit is set out below:

We enclose the [*description of financial statements*]. We have not carried out either an audit or a review and, accordingly, we do not imply or express any form of assurance on the truth and fairness of these financial statements.

In accordance with your letter of instructions dated [*date*], we visited [*location and name of business unit*] and carried out the following procedures:

[*specify procedures performed, e.g. held discussions with senior management*].

Based on these very limited procedures, no matters came to our attention [*state exceptions, if any*] that we believe should be reported to you.

This report is solely for your information and is not to be used for any other purpose. It should not be included or referred to in any document or publication made available to persons outside your firm without our consent.

11:10 Letters of support

11:10.1 Introduction

This section discusses letters of support and subordination agreements and provides guidance on the matters the auditor may need to consider if letters of support and subordination agreements are intended to be legally binding. This section does not anticipate any changes to auditing practices resulting from future pronouncements by the Auditing Practices Board (APB) on going concern matters.

There are many different ways of giving financial support between companies and the auditor should give careful consideration to the circumstances of the case, exercising a high level of professional judgement. Discussions with clients and others concerning intra-group indebtedness issues should normally be conducted by the engagement partner or manager.

11:10.2 Letters of support and subordination agreements

If a client is a subsidiary and it appears that it might not be a going concern, the auditor should immediately discuss the situation with the subsidiary's directors and, if also the group auditor, with parent management, to establish whether the parent:

(a)   will provide new permanent capital or make a non-repayable capital contribution; or, if not,

(b)   is prepared to issue a letter of support to the subsidiary (or, if appropriate, enter into a subordination agreement with it).

A *letter of support* is an agreement normally made between a company and its subsidiary or fellow subsidiary under which one company ('the donor') agrees to provide support in the form of funding to enable the other company ('the recipient') to meet its debts and liabilities, usually for a specified period of time, to the extent that the recipient cannot meet them itself.

A *subordination agreement* is an agreement, generally made between group companies, under which the donor (usually the parent) agrees not to demand repayment of specified loans already made to it by the recipient. A subordination agreement does not have the effect of placing additional funds with, or of promising additional funds to, the recipient.

As a general rule, if a subsidiary is able to pay all its creditors except the parent as and when it is required to do so, either form of support is appropriate. However, if it appears that the subsidiary will be unable to pay non-group creditors as they fall due, a subordination agreement would not be appropriate and the subsidiary's directors need to consider obtaining a letter of support.

It is desirable to identify situations in which such financial support may be required as early as possible during the audit to enable the planning to take place well before the year-end for whatever document will be required. This will save time, enable the directors of the subsidiary to consider their responsibilities under the Companies Act, encourage the client to obtain legal advice at an early stage, and generally assist with what can otherwise be a matter of aggravation at a busy time. It will also allow time for the client to make any amendments to its Memorandum or Articles if this is necessary (*see* **Section 11:10.5.4.1** (second paragraph)).

11:10.2.1 Should the letter of support be legally binding?

Parent companies might be reluctant for commercial or financial reasons to enter into legally binding commitments, or may consider the formality of obtaining the agreement to be unnecessary. They may reasonably expect that the auditor will be satisfied with their formal representations, possibly recorded in board minutes, that they 'intend to continue support for the foreseeable future' (or similar style of wording). The auditor should be aware, however, that such informal letters might not be legally binding.

For example, in *Kleinwort Benson* v *Malaysian Mining Corporation Bhd* [1989] 1 All ER 785, CA the Court of Appeal decided that the words 'it is our policy to ensure that the business of MMC is at all times in a position to meet its liabilities to Kleinwort Benson Limited' were, in the circumstances of that case, no more than a representation of present fact and did not express any contractual promise as to future policy and that the letter could not therefore be enforced by the court (*see also National Australia Bank Ltd* v *Soden & Avon* [1995] BCC 696). The court did, however, indicate that in certain circumstances a letter of support might constitute a legal commitment. Thus, the enforceability of the letter of support will depend on the particular circumstances of each case, and, where it is necessary for the letter of support to be legally binding, it should be in the form of a legal agreement and not an informal letter.

11:10.2.2 Benefits of a legally binding agreement

The use of letters of support has been common practice for many years. A letter of support that is legally binding will protect the directors of the recipient in the event that the support is not forthcoming. For example, if the recipient continued to trade in these circumstances and then went into liquidation, the directors could not be liable for wrongful trading under s. 214 of the Insolvency Act 1986. Also, if the auditor had relied on a legally binding letter in forming an opinion on whether the subsidiary was a going concern and it subsequently transpired that the support was not forthcoming, the auditor should be able more easily to demonstrate that the opinion was reasonable.

This is not to say that the auditor or the directors would not be protected if the letter of support were not legally binding, if it can be demonstrated that it was reasonable to assume that the undertaking to provide support would be honoured. However, there is clearly more room for doubt where the letter is not legally binding.

Furthermore, some insolvency specialists believe that a parent which keeps its subsidiary undercapitalised, providing support as and when it considers it necessary, may be considered to be acting recklessly and be liable as a shadow director for wrongful trading under s. 214 of the Insolvency Act 1986. The basis for this view is that the parent would have enabled its subsidiary to carry on trading and incurring debts in circumstances where the subsidiary's creditors might not be paid in full. Thus, if an undercapitalised subsidiary, which had been supported by its parent in the past, is allowed to go into insolvent liquidation, the parent, or its board, as shadow directors, might be liable to contribute to the subsidiary company's assets.

11:10.3 Requirement for a legally binding agreement

The auditor does not need to insist on the formality of a legally binding agreement **provided that** the engagement partner is satisfied that the necessary support will be available during the minimum audit period defined in **Section 9:8**, 'Considerations in respect of going concern'.

In reaching a conclusion on this matter the engagement partner should consider:

(a) The prior knowledge of the company giving the support.

(b) Its past record in providing support.

(c) The intention of the parties, based upon discussions with the directors and on management's representations.

Whenever the auditor obtains audit assurance from commitments of support which are not legally binding, the engagement partner should ensure that the considerations listed in the preceding paragraph are fully documented on the audit file and referred to in issues documentation. In addition to written representations the auditor should also obtain copies of relevant board minutes and significant correspondence.

If the engagement partner is unable to conclude that the necessary support is likely to be forthcoming, the auditor should insist that the arrangements to provide support are made legally binding or consider the implications for the audit report. The engagement partner should follow the consultation procedures set out in **Section 5:5**, 'Consultation and concurring reviews'.

When legally binding support is proposed, the client should take legal advice on the implications of a legally binding letter and on its form. The giving of a legally binding letter can have implications for the donor who should also take legal advice if it is thought necessary. The auditor should not attempt to draft any of the documentation because this might imply that legal advice is being given, which the auditor cannot and must not do.

11:10.4 Enforceability of letters of support: questions to consider

The remainder of this section discusses the matters that are relevant in assessing whether a letter of support is legally binding. The following issues are addressed:

(a) **Ability to give support**:

    (i)   What support should be promised?

    (ii)   Has the donor the necessary finances to promise support?

    (iii) Has the donor the power to promise support?

    (iv) Has the recipient the power to borrow?

(b) **Form and content of letter of support**:

    (i)   Should a letter of support be in a particular form?

    (ii)   Does a letter of support need to be in the form of a deed?

    (iii) Can a letter of support be revocable?

    (iv) For what period should the support continue?

    (v)   On what terms should the support be given?

    (vi) Should the letter contain a subordination clause?

    (vii) Should the donor have the right to stop providing support if it sells the subsidiary?

(c) **Signing formalities**:

    (i)   Letters of support made by deed and for consideration.

    (ii)   Letters of support not made by deed.

    (iii) Does a letter of support need to be minuted?

(d) **Other considerations**:

    (i)   Donor companies registered outside England and Wales.

    (ii)   Does the donor become a 'shadow director'?

    (iii) What are the risks if support is withdrawn?

11:10.5 Ability to give support

11:10.5.1 What support should be promised?

The amount or nature of the support promised should be adequate to ensure that the recipient continues as a going concern. What is adequate will depend on the precise circumstances of each case, and should be considered in conjunction with the period during which the support should continue (*see* **Section 11:10.6.4**).

The type of support that will usually be appropriate is where the donor undertakes to provide the recipient with such financial support as the recipient might require to continue trading as a going concern, and consequently to make available to the recipient such sums as the recipient might request.

11:10.5.2 *Has the donor the necessary finances to promise support?*

The donor should be financially able to give the support for the period promised. If this cannot be demonstrated, then the letter of support will be of no use. Also, under the Insolvency Act 1986 the transactions into which such a donor enters may be viewed as a 'preference or transaction at an under value' if it becomes insolvent, irrespective of their enforceability at law.

11:10.5.3 *Has the donor the power to promise support?*

11:10.5.3.1 *Identifying* ultra vires *transactions*

It is necessary to consider whether the promise of support by a donor is a transaction which is within the capacity of the donor company to enter into and within the authority of the board of directors. This can generally be established by looking at the Memorandum and Articles of the donor. The objects clause in the Memorandum defines the capacity of a company. A company has no existence, and cannot act as a legal person outside the purposes (*ultra vires*) defined in the objects clause, or beyond its powers (whether expressed in the memorandum or implied).

Theoretically, if the company concludes a contract which is *ultra vires* neither the company nor the other contracting party can sue on it. In practice, a contracting party may be able to claim the protection of s. 35 of the Companies Act 1985 provided it acted in good faith. However, the protection afforded by s. 35 was thought not to be clear and consequently a new s. 35 was substituted by the Companies Act 1989. Although this section seeks to clarify and reform the *ultra vires* rule it is not thought (*see* below) to abolish it.

In assessing whether the giving of the support is *ultra vires* the donor the auditor should take into account the following factors:

(a)   The new s. 35.

(b)   The Memorandum and Articles of Association of the donor.

(c)   Other *ultra vires* considerations.

The new s. 35: This section amends the law on *ultra vires* with a view to protecting third parties which deal with companies. It provides that the validity of an act done by a company cannot be called into question on the ground of lack of capacity by reason of anything in the company's Memorandum. Also, an act that is outside the powers of the board of directors will be deemed free of any restriction in the company's constitution if the other contracting party deals in good faith. A person is not to be regarded as acting in bad faith by reason only of knowing that an act is beyond the powers of the directors.

These provisions appear to leave it open to be argued that the *ultra vires* rule has not been abolished where the other contracting party knew of the limitations in the company's Memorandum. If this is right, *ultra vires* should still be considered in the context of letters of support.

Shareholders may ratify an *ultra vires* act by special resolution, but this will not relieve the directors or a third party of liability incurred by committing the act unless a further special resolution is passed to relieve them of this liability. The protection given by s. 35 is further limited where a company enters into a transaction to which the parties include a person 'connected' with, or a company 'associated' with, a director (*see* s. 346 of the 1985 Act). In such a case the transaction will be voidable at the instance of the company.

Memorandum and Articles of Association: The auditor should look carefully at the donor's Memorandum and Articles of Association. A company's Memorandum is sometimes complex and difficult to construe and in such circumstances the auditor should take legal advice. Under its objects clause (clause 3 of the Memorandum) the donor should be permitted:

(a)   to carry on the type of business it actually carries on and to act as a parent (unless the donor is a fellow subsidiary); and

(b)   to lend and advance money or to give credit to any company (if the support is in the form of a loan or loan account); or

(c)   if the support is in the form of a guarantee, to guarantee or to give guarantees or indemnities for the payment of money or the performance of contracts or obligations by, or become security for, any company.

In addition, the donor's Articles of Association should not place any restriction on the directors' powers to lend, to give guarantees or to enter into other contingent liabilities of the nature proposed.

If there is any doubt as to whether the giving of a letter of support is *intra vires*, the Memorandum should be altered. For example, where the donor is providing support to its parent or to a fellow subsidiary, satisfying the conditions described in the preceding two paragraphs will be more difficult and legal advice should be taken.

Other *ultra vires* considerations: A third party seeking to rely on a transaction which is within the capacity of the donor as set out in its Memorandum may still not be protected unless the giving of the support can be shown to be:

(a)   reasonably incidental to the carrying on of the donor's business;

(b)   not given gratuitously (e.g., given for some genuine commercial benefit) unless the objects clause permits the donor to part with its funds gratuitously or for a non-commercial purpose. However, the question of whether the transaction was gratuitous may be relevant in considering if the transaction is in the best interest of the company; and

(c)   a *bona fide* transaction.

In addition to their relevance in ultra vires matters, the matters in points (b) and (c) above are important in an examination of whether the transaction is in the best interests of the company and directors' fiduciary duties generally. For example, if the directors are acting in an improper manner, it may be possible for the transaction to be set aside or rescinded and for the directors to be required to give up any profits and advantages obtained.

11:10.5.3.2 Audit work

To establish whether a company has the power to provide a letter of support, the auditor should obtain one of the following:

(a)   Written confirmation from the donor's solicitors to the effect that the giving of the support is permitted under the donor's constitution and is not *ultra vires* the company, and that it is within the powers of the board of directors to give the support.

(b)   (If the transaction is not permitted by the Memorandum), a certified copy of the special resolution amending the Memorandum to give the donor the necessary capacity to give the letter of support, and (if the Articles contain a limitation on the directors' powers) a certified copy of the special resolution of the company appropriately amending the Articles or giving the directors the necessary authority.

The auditor should also consider the matters referred to in **Section 11:10.5.3.1** (last paragraph).

   The donor might be under an obligation under some other agreement to which it is a party not to enter into commitments of support, particularly if the support arrangements involve the giving of security. Accordingly, if a letter of support is intended to be legally binding, the auditor should check (and obtain confirmation in writing from the donor) that the donor is under no such restriction. The recipient's auditors may need to request the donor's auditor to carry out this work on their behalf.

11:10.5.4 Has the recipient the power to borrow?

11:10.5.4.1 Identifying ultra vires transactions

Where the letter of support will result in the recipient's borrowing money from the donor, there should be an express provision in the objects clause of the recipient's Memorandum permitting the recipient to borrow or raise or secure payment of money in such manner as it might think fit. The absence of such a provision means that the transaction is likely to be *ultra vires*.

In addition, the directors of the recipient should be empowered by the Articles to exercise the power to borrow. The Articles should be reviewed to see what borrowing powers the directors are given. For example, under Art. 70 of the current Table A, the directors may exercise all the powers of the company. However, where the company has not adopted Table A (either the current version of Table A or a previous one), directors may often be restricted from borrowing above a certain limit without the prior sanction of the company in general meeting. The London Stock Exchange does not require any similar provision to be included, but it is quite usual for borrowing restrictions to be imposed on directors by the Articles.

11:10.5.4.2 Audit work

To establish whether a company has the power to borrow the auditor should obtain one of the following:

(a)   Via the client, a written confirmation from the recipient's solicitors that the transaction is not *ultra vires*, that the recipient has the capacity under its constitution to accept the support and that it is within the directors' powers in the Articles to borrow the amount stated.

(b)   (If the transaction is not permitted by the Memorandum) a certified copy of the special resolution amending the Memorandum to give the recipient the necessary capacity, and (if the Articles contain a limitation on the directors' powers) a certified copy of the special resolution of the company appropriately amending the Articles or giving the directors the necessary authority.

Additionally, the auditor should obtain formal representations from the recipient that the terms of any existing agreements (e.g., loan agreements, debenture stock trust deeds or guarantees) do not prohibit the recipient from entering into the further borrowing commitments implied by the support agreements. If such restrictions do exist, the creation of a new loan account might trigger the default provisions of existing agreements.

11:10.6 Form and content of letters of support

11:10.6.1 Should a letter of support be in a particular form?

It is preferable for a letter of support to be in a particular form. Although it is possible for a legally binding agreement to be in the form of a simple letter, the parties are more likely to succeed in evidencing their **intention** to create legal relations between each other (a necessary condition for an agreement to be enforceable) if the letter of support is a properly drafted contract or deed. If the agreement is in the form of a letter, it should be from the donor to the recipient and should contain an acknowledgement by both parties that the letter is intended to create binding legal relations between them. The consideration for the giving of the support will also need to be clearly expressed if the letter is not in the form of a deed.

Where the recipient is a financial services company a special form of loan agreement will be necessary if the loan is to be deemed qualifying capital. For such companies, the auditor should consult a financial regulation specialist.

11:10.6.2 Does a letter of support need to be in the form of a deed?

A letter of support does not need to be under seal, provided that it is in the form of an agreement given for consideration. However, where, e.g., it is not intended that interest shall be charged on, or repayment made of, the support, then it is advisable to have the agreement under seal.

If the letter of support is neither a deed nor an agreement given for consideration it will not be legally enforceable.

11:10.6.3 Can a letter of support be revocable?

A letter of support can be revocable. An agreement can always be terminated or varied by agreement of *all* the parties to it. Consequently, where the only parties to the contract are the donor and the recipient, they can agree to terminate (or revoke) the letter. This situation should be distinguished from the situation where the donor has the *right* to terminate the support unilaterally under a provision in the letter of support.

Accordingly, if it is important for audit purposes that a letter of support is legally enforceable, the auditor should carry out the following procedures:

(a) Check that the letter of support has not been varied or terminated. (This could be done by requesting written confirmation to that effect from the client, and from any third parties involved, e.g., a bank which provides finance against the guarantee of the 'donor'.)

(b) Assess whether (to the extent that it is possible to do so) termination is likely to occur in the relevant future period (*see* **Section 11:10.6.4**).

11:10.6.4 For what period should the support continue?

Statement of Auditing Standards 130, 'The Going Concern Basis in Financial Statements', states:

> *Any consideration involving the foreseeable future involves a judgement, at a particular time, about events which are inherently uncertain.*

However, it goes on to state that:

> *If the period to which the directors have paid particular attention in assessing going concern is less than one year from the date of approval of the financial statements, and the directors have not disclosed that fact, the auditors should do so within their report setting out the basis of opinion, unless the fact is clear from any other references in their report. They should not qualify their opinion on the financial statements on these grounds alone.*

Consequently, a letter of support should **as a minimum** cover the period from the balance sheet date to the dates suggested above and should not be stated to be terminable by the donor during that period.

11:10.6.5 On what terms should the support be given?

A letter of support in the form of a loan agreement or agreement to make funds available should specify the following:

(a) The maximum amount of the facility (if any).

(b) When funds will be available.

(c) The rate of interest.

(d) The date on which the facility will cease.

(e) When repayment should be made.

11:10.6.6 Should the letter contain a 'subordination' clause?

The letter should contain a 'subordination' clause, if the donor has put a limit on the amount of support it is willing to provide to the recipient. The intention of a subordination clause is generally to create a type of debt which, in a winding up, will rank behind all or certain other debts of the company.

The main difficulty with subordination clauses (whether in a letter of support or in a subordination agreement) is that their validity could be questioned as an attempt to contract out of the statutory rules relating to the application of assets in a winding up, even though their effect would be to benefit other creditors, by permitting the subsidiary's general creditors to be paid before the donor.

Accordingly, a subordination clause in a letter of support should be of a kind in which the donor agrees not to demand repayment or enforce its claims where to do so would make the recipient insolvent, rather than one in which the donor merely agrees that the recipient may defer payment to the donor until all other debts have been paid. If the auditor has any doubt about the form of the subordination provision, the auditor should seek legal advice.

11:10.6.7 Should a donor have the right to stop providing support if it sells the subsidiary?

If there is a provision in the letter of support or loan agreement permitting the donor to stop providing support to its subsidiary when the subsidiary ceases to be a subsidiary (or indeed for any other reason) it will be harder to demonstrate that the support will be available, and consequently that the subsidiary will remain a going concern, during the minimum period referred to in **Section 11:10.6.4**.

Accordingly, to ensure enforceability, provisions to this effect should not normally be included unless the letter of support contains a further provision that the donor will arrange for a letter of support in the same terms to be provided, and that the donor will not be released from its obligation to support the recipient until such a binding letter of support has been obtained from a purchaser which is financially able to grant the necessary support for the required period. Where the auditor is aware of an impending sale, the auditor should carry out the same checks on the purchaser as on the donor.

11:10.7 Signing formalities

11:10.7.1 Letters of support made by deed

The documents comprising the deed should be sealed by both the donor and the recipient and signed on behalf of each party, in most cases either by a director and the company secretary or by two directors. However, the Articles of both the donor and the recipient should be checked to see what the formalities are for attaching the company seal. The Companies Act 1989 contains a provision which makes it no longer necessary for a company to have a common seal. A document signed by two directors or by a director and the company secretary on behalf of the company and expressed to be executed by the company will take effect as a deed if it is clear that the persons signing intend it to be a deed. The board of directors both of the donor and of the recipient should approve by resolution, in the case of the donor, the granting of the support and, in the case of the recipient, the obtaining of the support, and in both cases authorise the execution of the letter of support as a deed.

11:10.7.2 Letters of support not made by deed

It will be necessary for all directors signing the letter of support on behalf of the donor and the recipient to have the authority to bind their respective companies. To ascertain this, the auditor should check Articles for any conditions or formalities to be complied with. Additionally, the board of directors of each of the companies should authorise by resolution:

(a) (In the case of the donor) the granting of the support.

(b) (In the case of the recipient) the obtaining of the support.

(c) In both these cases the signing of the letter of support by the director(s) on behalf of their respective companies.

Any manuscript amendments to the letter of support should be initialled by all the signatories on each side.

11:10.7.3 *Does a letter of support need to be minuted?*

A letter of support must be minuted, by the board of directors both of the donor and of the recipient. Each board should agree, and formally approve by board resolution, the giving of the letter of support by the donor, the reasons for it and the benefits expected. The appropriate minutes recording the proceedings of the board meetings should be entered into each company's minute book.

In addition, each side should comply with the following procedural requirements for the board meeting:

(a) Reasonable notice of the meeting should be given to all directors. What is regarded as 'reasonable' will depend on the company's normal practice and is not laid down by law.

(b) The quorum of directors required under the company's Articles of Association should be present. If the company has adopted Table A, the quorum will be two unless the directors have fixed a different number.

(c) A director of the donor who is also a director of the recipient should disclose any interest in the letter of support at the donor company's board meeting in accordance with s. 317 of the Companies Act 1985. The company should ensure by checking the Articles that such a director is eligible to vote on a contract in which that director is interested. (It is a common provision of Articles of Association that a director is not to be counted in the quorum present at a board meeting in relation to a resolution on which the director is not entitled to vote; however, many Articles will, in fact, permit an interested director to vote where the only interest held is as a director of the other party to the contract.)

(d) Any voting requirements in the company's Articles of Association should be complied with.

The auditor of the recipient should request the donor's auditor to check that the board minutes record the approval of the letter of support, or request a certified copy of the board minutes.

11:10.8 Other considerations

11:10.8.1 Donor companies registered outside England and Wales

If the auditor is relying on the enforceability of a letter of support from a foreign-registered donor the auditor will need to obtain from lawyers in the non-UK country general legal advice on the enforceability of the letter of support. It should be noted that for this purpose Northern Ireland and Scotland are to be treated as foreign countries. Additionally, the auditor should obtain some form of assurance to the effect that:

(a) the company is empowered under its constitution to give the support; and

(b) all local formalities have been complied with.

The auditor should also specifically enquire of the auditor of the non-UK donor whether the donor is financially capable of honouring the support.

To facilitate enforceability by a UK-registered company, the letter of support should be expressed to be governed by the laws of England and should confer jurisdiction on the English courts to hear and determine any dispute arising out of the agreement. The auditor may need to give further consideration as to whether the recipient would be financially able to afford overseas legal costs, should it become necessary to enforce the agreement.

11:10.8.2 Does the donor become a 'shadow director'?

A parent will normally not itself be a director of its subsidiary (although, subject to the Articles of Association of the subsidiary, there is nothing to prevent this). However, it might be deemed to be a shadow director because of its ability to influence the management of the subsidiary's affairs. The influence might amount to complete control if the subsidiary is wholly owned and its directors are mere nominees of the holding company.

A parent will be deemed to be a 'shadow director' of its subsidiary where the board of the subsidiary is accustomed to act in accordance with the parent's directions or instructions. Many of the provisions of the Companies Act 1985, the Insolvency Act 1986 and the Company Directors Disqualification Act 1986 relating to directors will apply to shadow directors. Accordingly, if a subsidiary company were to go into an insolvent liquidation and, at some time prior to that, a company which was a shadow director knew or ought to have concluded there was no reasonable prospect of avoiding this, then the shadow director could be made liable to contribute to the subsidiary company's assets (Insolvency Act 1986, s. 214).

Clearly, the auditor cannot place any reliance on this possibility as an alternative to a letter of support. However, the auditor should consider whether a parent client is likely to be exposed as a consequence of the possibility and should inform it of the risks of permitting its subsidiary to continue trading while insolvent.

11:10.8.3 What are the risks if support is withdrawn?

There are several risks connected with the withdrawal of support:

(a)   If a loan is repaid by a recipient which is a subsidiary or associate of the donor (or otherwise 'connected' to it as defined in s. 249 of the Insolvency Act) within the two years prior to an administration order being made in respect of the recipient or the recipient going into liquidation, such payment could be regarded as a 'preference' within the meaning of s. 239 of the Insolvency Act 1986. In such cases an administrator or liquidator can apply to the court for an order to restore the position to what it would have been had the repayment not been made by ordering the donor to repay the loan.

(b)   By repaying or agreeing to a withdrawal of support with no or insufficient substitute support or funds being provided, the recipient may be entering into a transaction at an undervalue under s. 238 of the Insolvency Act or a transaction defrauding creditors under s. 423 of the Insolvency Act (e.g., if the repayment is made for the purpose of putting assets beyond reach of creditors). The court has the power to order the donor to repay, or to make such order as it thinks fit.

(c)   The withdrawal of support by the donor might result in the donor's being liable as a party to fraudulent trading (e.g., on the basis that the donor had close control of the recipient's business and the recipient's business was carried on with intent to defraud creditors). Fraudulent trading is a criminal offence under s. 458 of the Companies Act 1985, and s. 213 of the Insolvency Act 1986 provides certain civil remedies where in a winding up it is shown that business has been carried on to defraud creditors.

(d)   Upon withdrawing support the donor might be in danger of a claim from third parties which continued business with the recipient on the strength of such support. Particular care should be taken where the donor itself has dealings with creditors of the recipient, e.g. inducing suppliers to do business with it.

If the letter of support is for a specified period the directors of the recipient should continually monitor their position. If at any point they become aware of the possibility that the support will not be continued at the end of the period (or indeed earlier) they should seek legal advice. There is the risk of incurring liability for wrongful trading under s. 214 of the Insolvency Act 1986 if at some time before the commencement of the winding up of a company a director knew or ought to have concluded that there was no reasonable prospect that the company would avoid going into insolvent liquidation, and did not take every step possible with a view to minimising the potential loss to creditors.

11:10.8.4 Disclosure by the donor

To comply with Sch. 4A to the Companies Act 1985 on group accounts the **donor's** financial statements should disclose the following:

(a)   **Particulars of the letter of support,** if it is a financial commitment that has not been provided for and it is relevant to an assessment of the donor's state of affairs.

(b)   **The amount of the liability,** its legal nature and details of any security furnished, if the letter of support is a contingent liability that has not been provided for.

(c) **The nature and amount of support generally**, if this information is relevant to the truth and fairness of the financial position of the donor company.

(d)   In (a) and (b) above any commitments for the benefit of a group company must be shown separately.

If the donor has to comply with Sch. 9 to the Companies Act 1985 its financial statements need only provide the disclosures referred to in (b) and (c) of the preceding paragraph.

11:10.8.5 *Disclosure by the recipient*

To comply with Sch. 4 to the Companies Act 1985, the recipient's financial statements should disclose, in addition to the normal disclosures of its indebtedness to the donor, the nature and amount of support generally if such information is relevant to the truth and fairness of the financial position of the company.

11:10.8.6 *Related party disclosures under FRS 8*

FRS 8 requires the disclosure of certain information and balances in respect of related party transactions. Related party transactions are likely to include letters of support and subordination agreements both binding and non-binding, as examples of such transactions in the FRS include the provision of finance (including loans and equity contributions), guarantees and the provision of collateral security as well as the performance of services by, to or for a related party, regardless of whether a price is charged. Where the donor and recipient are part of the same group they are likely to be exempt under the standard from most disclosure.

For instance, FRS 8 does not require disclosure, in the financial statements of a recipient which is a 90 per cent subsidiary, of transactions with its donor or parent, provided the subsidiary is included in publicly available consolidated financial statements. Disclosure will also not be required, in the consolidated financial statements of the donor or parent, of any transactions and balances which have been eliminated on consolidation, or in the donor or parent's own financial statements when presented together with its consolidated financial statements. Recipients and donors that cannot take advantage of these exemptions will need to disclose the required information regarding the letter of support or subordination agreement. *See* Chapter 35 of the Coopers & Lybrand, *Manual of Accounting* (Croydon: Tolley Publishing Co. Ltd) for the disclosures necessary.

11:10.9 Subordination agreements

If the auditor is placing reliance on the adequacy and enforceability of a subordination agreement many of the matters discussed in relation to letters of support will also apply. Generally, a subordination agreement will need to be by deed.

In particular, the auditor should examine the original loan agreement relating to the loan or loans to be subordinated and be satisfied that:

(a)   taking into account any undrawn facilities under the loan agreement, the recipient has adequate financial resources to enable it to continue as a going concern;

(b)   the donor cannot withdraw or demand repayment of the loan(s) during the minimum post-balance-sheet period referred to in **Section 9:8**, 'Considerations in respect of going concern';

(c)   proper regard has been given to the matters discussed in the following sections:

  (i)   **11:10.6.1** (first paragraph) and **11:10.6.2** to **11:10.6.4** (form, use of seal, mutual termination);

  (ii)   **11:10.7.1** to **11:10.7.3** (signing formalities);

  (iii)   **11:10.8.1** (donor registered overseas);

  (iv)   **11:10.8.3** (withdrawal).

A subordination agreement should contain an undertaking by the donor that it will not:

(a)   demand payment from the recipient of all or any sums due; or

(b)   enforce its rights or claims against the recipient in respect of the loans being subordinated,

if and to the extent that the recipient would become insolvent as a consequence of the payment or enforcement in question. The agreement should also contain an undertaking that no payment or enforcement can be made at a time when the recipient is insolvent.

Chapter 12

Audit reporting to management

12:1 Audit reporting to the board and to management

12:1.1 Introduction

The auditor should report to the client significant matters that arise during an audit. This is one of the most important parts of a total audit service. Keeping the board and management informed of what the auditor is doing, why the auditor is doing it and what the auditor has found is also the key to a good client relationship. Without effective dialogue, misunderstanding and even mistrust can result. All the auditor's communications, whether oral or written, should be well prepared and of a high standard. SAS 610, 'Reports to Directors or Management', establishes standards and provides guidance in this area.

The work the auditor carries out, and the broad experience of the audit firm's partners, managers and staff, are potentially a source of great value to clients. It is only through effective reporting to management that this value can be realised.

The auditor should be positive and constructive in conveying views and opinions to clients. Such an approach is more likely to lead the client to address weaknesses which are identified and reported.

The auditor need not restrict the matters reported to the financial statements and accounting procedures and controls. SAS 610 states that other constructive advice, such as comments on potential economies, or improvements in efficiencies, should also be considered for inclusion in reports to directors or management. This is discussed further in **Section 1:5**, 'Adding value to the audit'.

The auditor should report either orally or in writing or both (e.g. if material weaknesses in the internal control system have been identified). Oral communication has the advantage of being less formal, allowing the listeners to raise questions on matters which need clarification to avoid misunderstanding. It is also more immediate. Written communication has the advantage of providing a formal record of matters reported, both for the client and for the auditor's records, and of being available for distribution to members of the board or client's staff not directly involved in the reporting process.

An effective combination of oral and written reporting can be achieved by, e.g., presenting a formal written report in a summarised form and using it as the basis for an oral presentation, or by holding a meeting with members of the client's management and following this up with a concise written record of the main points of the meeting. Some clients may, however, prefer a traditional 'management letter'.

Regulatory authorities may request from clients copies of these reports. Special care should therefore be exercised to ensure that all comments are factually correct and fair from the standpoint of an independent auditor. This section does not provide guidance on specific reporting requirements in relation to regulations introduced for particular industries such as financial services.

12:1.2 Audit report to the board

SAS 610 requires that auditors should consider the matters which have come to their attention during the audit, and whether they should be included in a report to directors or management. The standard goes on to require that when material weaknesses in the accounting and internal control systems are so identified, auditors should report them in writing to the directors, the audit committee or an appropriate level of management on a timely basis. Where no material weaknesses have been identified, there is no requirement for the auditor to produce such a report. However, except where a company has been dormant throughout the year, it will be rare for there to be no matters of significance which need to be drawn to the attention of management. This Manual assumes that at the end of the audit the auditor will normally provide the client with an 'Audit report to the board'. Its objectives will be:

(a)   Reporting to the most senior level of management, usually the full board.

(b)   Reporting promptly the findings from the audit.

(c)   Reporting matters of direct relevance to the business rather than just accounting issues.

(d)   Meeting client expectations of the auditor's role, e.g. as to the amount of systems work and thus the potential for commenting on strengths and weaknesses in the company's control system.

The audit report to the board will normally be arranged as follows:

(a)   An executive summary (perhaps of no more than two pages) addressing clearly and succinctly the key points of relevance to the board.

(b)   A section setting out the client's needs and expectations, and the auditor's response to them.

(c)   Attachments, typically comprising:

  (i)   A report on the client's business control systems, expanding on relevant points in the executive summary and providing recommendations for improvement.

  (ii)   Further suggestions, if any, for improvements to operational performance.

  (iii)   A review of the key audit issues. This should normally be based on the contents of issues documentation, which can contribute valuable commentary for the client.

  (iv)   A brief statement of the audit approach. This can be used to explain the scope of audit work and the auditor's responsibilities generally and in reporting to management (*see* **Sections 12:1.12** to **12:1.12.2**).

The auditor should be flexible when determining the structure and the content of the audit report to the board to ensure that it meets client circumstances and that reports do not become stereotyped. None the less, a degree of standardisation may be desirable so that the style of reporting by an audit firm is reasonably consistent. The use of technology and standard forms of reports may assist in this process.

12:1.3 Planning

12:1.3.1 Audit arrangements

In audit planning the auditor should consider the steps required to ensure effective reporting. The engagement partner and the engagement manager should agree with the client:

(a) The most appropriate method and timing of reporting audit findings.

(b) Procedures for discussing the form and content of the audit report to the board and other reports. Reports to the board may, if agreed in advance, be addressed to the audit committee.

(c) A timetable for issue and response.

(d) The addressee(s) and distribution of audit reports to the board and other reports, including the client's reply. It may be appropriate to produce different types of report for different addresses.

The budget should include sufficient time for the preparation and clearance of reports. The audit timetable should include key dates for the preparation and clearance of reports.

The need to obtain the comments and responses of line management for inclusion in reports will add to the time required to finalise them. The auditor need not, however, allow delays in responses by local management to jeopardise the timetables agreed with senior management. If a timetable for responses has been planned and agreed with the client, the auditor might decide to adhere to the timetable, explaining (if necessary) the reason for the lack of comment by local management.

The preparation of the audit report to the board should be planned so as to avoid time being wasted on needless revision. Adequate time should be allowed if the matters that are likely to be reported are not routine or if the report is likely to require substantial involvement from the engagement partner (e.g., if the audit report involves a wide range of business-related matters as well as accounting control matters). Accordingly, the engagement manager should normally discuss with the engagement partner the proposed form and content of the audit report to the board as early as possible and preferably before the initial draft is prepared.

The engagement manager will need to monitor the progress of the reporting steps and ensure that the relevant matters are brought to the attention of the engagement partner as soon as possible.

12:1.4 Timing

Many clients view the auditor's responsiveness to their priorities and deadlines as the single most important factor in evaluating service and performance. Although particular requirements and expectations vary from client to client, audit recommendations will be perceived as more valuable if they are reported without any delay. Moreover, in the case of internal control weaknesses, some clients will be reluctant to accept resulting increased audit costs if the auditor does not report the weakness immediately.

Communication with clients should be frequent and ongoing, albeit often informal. Formal meetings with clients, at which reports will be tabled, should be held on at least the following occasions:

(a) At the planning/strategy stage, presenting the findings of the auditor's risk assessment, including any recommendations, along with the auditor's proposed audit approach. The auditor should seek client input and agreement to the approach where appropriate.

(b) Upon completion of the interim audit. The auditor should present the findings of his or her work on controls and systems and agree any changes to the scope and timing of the final audit.

(c) Upon completion of the final audit work, preferably in advance of signing the audit report. The auditor should present all significant judgmental issues and their expected resolution, control weaknesses and recommendations for improvement.

The exact timing of meetings should be discussed and agreed with the client before audit work commences. The auditor may, however, find it necessary to arrange additional meetings during the audit, depending on the number and magnitude of the issues identified.

12:1.4.1 *Immediate notification*

There are a number of circumstances in which it is desirable for the auditor to report findings and recommendations to the client immediately. These include:

(a) When there are specific industry requirements, such as those for banks and building societies.

(b) If there is a risk that the client will lose assets, or incur liabilities, if the report is delayed.

(c) If the auditor identifies significant weaknesses in internal accounting controls, in particular if assets are susceptible to theft or loss.

(d) If there is a risk that information on which management is basing important decisions might require adjustments.

(e) When there is a possibility of avoiding an increase in audit time at a subsequent visit through prompt client action.

(f) When the client has requested that findings of a certain type, or all of them, should be reported immediately.

The auditor should consider the relevance and importance of all findings from the client's perspective and decide whether they should be reported immediately.

12:1.4.2 Audit approach and strategy

Once the audit strategy work is complete the auditor should consider advising the client of the broad audit approach the auditor will adopt, including the assessment of the control environment. Providing this information helps management to appreciate the extent of audit effort, and presents an opportunity for management to raise questions on audit risks and other aspects of the work. Matters that might be addressed, either in a formal presentation or in an informal discussion, include:

(a)   The auditor's understanding of any major changes or external factors affecting the business.

(b)   The key risk areas identified, to confirm that the client is not aware of other areas that should be addressed. The auditor might also explain the broad approach to risks from an audit point of view, e.g. in relation to computer security.

(c)   Informing the client of which locations and principal systems are to be examined, provided this is appropriate in the circumstances.

The auditor should ensure that the client is made aware of the intended arrangements for conducting the audit, such as the timing of visits. The auditor should discuss this with usual management contacts to ensure that the client's own arrangements and reporting timetable are not disrupted.

12:1.4.3 Interim findings

The auditor should report significant audit findings to management, and if necessary the board, following any interim audit visit. The form of an interim report will depend on the size and circumstances of the client, the relationship with client management and the nature and seriousness of matters to be reported.

Matters that might be discussed include:

(a)   The stage reached in the audit, including any difficulties encountered.

(b)   Significant weaknesses in controls, including comments on the control environment, the effectiveness of accounting systems and whether internal accounting controls are operating effectively, and matters reported in previous years that have not been addressed by the client.

(c)   Plans for completing the audit including:

   (i)   planned timing of visits;

   (ii)   changes to the audit approach;

   (iii) changes in risk assessments, including new areas that the auditor believes may become audit issues; and

   (iv)   where appropriate, findings from early substantive tests and procedures which the client could undertake to reduce final audit work.

12:1.4.4 Audit completion

At this stage the auditor normally makes the main report by means of an 'Audit report to the board', discussed in **Section 12:1.2**. The auditor should normally report more detailed matters, e.g. those relating to accounting procedures and audit adjustments, to lower levels of management responsible for ensuring that action is taken.

The audit report to the board might provide a summary of key points arising from the audit. Much of the detailed information about these contained in issues documentation may be of interest to management. Therefore, as discussed in **Section 12:1.15**, all issues should be recorded in as final a form as possible.

12:1.5 Recommendations

Clients will adopt a normal business approach in reacting to the auditor's reports. Recommendations will tend only to be implemented if the benefits clearly outweigh the time and costs involved.

Wherever practicable, the audit report to the board and other reports pointing out weaknesses should include recommendations for corrective action. Positive reports are likely to have more impact than those that do not recommend specific action. To increase the impact of the recommendations the auditor should, where practicable, point out the financial benefit of implementing the recommendation.

In many cases it is neither possible nor desirable for the auditor to carry out detailed cost-benefit analyses to support recommendations. Nevertheless, clients will generally appreciate this if the auditor shows an understanding of the relevant issues.

One of the possible approaches to cost-benefit analysis is to tabulate recommendations on the basis of an initial estimate of the potential benefits and effort required, in the following way:

Benefits	Effort
High	Low
High	Medium
High	High
Medium	Low
Medium	Medium
Medium	High
Low	Low
Low	Medium*
Low	High*

(* These recommendations should be reconsidered, before submission of a draft to the client, to determine if they are, in fact, worth while.)

If recommendations are included, the auditor should be satisfied that sufficient supporting information has been obtained, even if this cannot be derived from the normal audit examination. Sometimes, before making specific recommendations, it may be necessary for the auditor to review them with in-house specialists who advise on systems. If the auditor decides that it is not appropriate to make specific recommendations, it may be appropriate to suggest that the client should carry out a detailed study and evaluation of the problem. As an alternative, the auditor may offer assistance from in-house specialist departments.

12:1.6 Addressee

Each comment and recommendation should be addressed to the appropriate level of client management. Reporting too much detail to senior levels of management may make it difficult for them to identify the points of significance. However, failing to make management, in particular senior management, aware of problems may result in loss to the client and increased risk to the auditor should weaknesses not be corrected.

The auditor should adopt the following principles in determining whether points arising should be included in the audit report to the board or communicated to lower levels of management:

(a)   Matters should be included in the audit report to the board or audit committee if they are matters that the auditor would expect normally to be discussed by the board. These may be different for larger clients than for smaller clients, and for clients which are centralised rather than decentralised.

(b)   Detailed accounting matters which do not present serious risks should not normally be included in the audit report to the board.

(c)   Points should be addressed to those individuals who are in a position to take action to ensure that matters are corrected.

(d)   Points should be addressed to a level of management more senior than the employees responsible for a particular weakness, breakdown or error noted. As a matter of courtesy, and to confirm the facts, such matters would usually be discussed first with the employees concerned.

(e)   Where, in addition to the report to the board, a report is submitted to other levels of management, the auditor should normally include a brief reference in the report to the board stating that fact and the members of management to whom they have been reported. It may be appropriate to note briefly the points so discussed.

If a report is addressed to a member of the client's staff who fails to act on important matters within a reasonable time, the auditor should consider whether to report the matters to a higher level of management. It may be necessary to do this, in particular, in groups of companies. It may also be necessary to do this where the board of a company comprises non-executive directors and a limited number of executive directors, in which case the auditor may need to report matters to the non-executive directors.

If a client has an audit committee, usually it will rely on the auditor to keep it informed of audit findings and will expect to receive a report, either written or oral, or both. In most cases the report to the board should be presented to the audit committee, either in addition to the presentation to the full board or in place of it. The auditor should normally make an oral presentation so that members of the audit committee, who will usually be non-executive directors, can raise questions for more information and explanation.

The auditor should ensure that copies of the audit report to the board are given to all members of the board. If the audit report to the board is presented only to an audit committee, copies should normally also be given to members of the board not represented on the audit committee. There may on occasion be matters which are so significant that the auditor requests that they be actively considered by the whole board.

12:1.7 Groups of companies

For group audits the engagement manager should discuss with the parent company's management its requirements, if any, for the submission of management reports for the group as a whole. If the client has divisions, branches or subsidiaries (for this purpose collectively referred to as 'subsidiaries'), particularly if the subsidiaries are situated in other countries, the auditor can often provide the senior management of the parent company with useful information regarding affairs of such subsidiaries. In these circumstances the auditor may offer to extend the service provided by arranging for a composite report to be submitted to the parent company incorporating significant comments regarding the group as a whole. Areas that might be covered, in writing or only orally, are:

(a) Impact of head office controls on the subsidiary.

(b) Financial accounting at the subsidiary.

(c) Financial stewardship at the subsidiary.

(d) Business controls at the subsidiary.

(e) Interpretation of results.

(f) Effectiveness of key people at the subsidiary.

The auditor should ensure that parent company management is aware of significant control weaknesses in subsidiaries. Weaknesses reported in this way should be put in the right context.

As parent company auditor, the auditor should obtain the necessary information from other offices and/or from detailed enquiries made of other auditors regarding subsidiaries audited by them.

If the client is a subsidiary company, but the parent is also audited by the firm, the auditor should also normally send a copy of each report sent to the subsidiary to its parent company. The auditor should agree the distribution with the parent and the subsidiary company before despatching any such reports. The auditor should agree with the client in the engagement letter the arrangements in relation to the items considered above, or otherwise in advance in writing.

12:1.8 Effect of matters reported on assessment of accounting records

When reporting in accordance with the Companies Act, the auditor has a duty to consider the adequacy of a client's accounting records and state if, in his or her opinion, they are not adequate. The audit approach of this Manual, in particular the need to obtain at least overview information about internal control, is designed to provide the information that the auditor needs to do this when all the results of the audit are taken into account.

The auditor should consider the effects of any weaknesses in accounting procedures and controls which are reported to management, together with the overall impact of comments made in the audit report to the board, to determine whether they could be regarded as inconsistent with the opinion on whether proper accounting records have been kept. These matters need to be considered before the audit is finalised, because of the potential impact on the audit report on the financial statements.

12:1.9 Matters raised previously

The auditor should consider weaknesses and recommendations that were reported in previous years to determine whether the client has taken appropriate action. Where it appears that weaknesses have been rectified or recommendations implemented, the auditor may usefully mention this in the current audit report to the board or other reports.

If such weaknesses have not been corrected, or recommendations have not been implemented, the auditor should consider whether they are still valid, and should discuss them with management to determine why the points have not been addressed. It may be that the client's explanation is valid, e.g. because the cost of implementation was found not to be justified by the potential risk. Where risk still remains, but a cost-effective solution cannot be found, the auditor should refer to this in the next report. If recommendations have not been implemented and no valid reason is given by management, the point should normally be repeated in the current year, or reference should be made to the point made previously. It should be noted that over time the cumulative effect of a weakness may become material whereas it could be considered not material if only considered in the context of one accounting period.

12:1.10 Matters identified by internal auditors

If the work of internal auditors reveals weaknesses in internal controls, the external auditor should consider whether it is sufficient to draw management's attention to a report of the internal auditors or whether the same point should also be included in the report to management. The external auditor should make a separate report if management's response to internal audit reports appears to be inadequate or the weaknesses are significant.

12:1.11 Management responses

The auditor should request a reply indicating what action management intends to take in response to the points raised in the audit report to the board and other reports. If this takes the form of an oral presentation to the board, the responses of the board may be recorded in the form of minutes. Usually, however, management will wish to give careful consideration to the points raised and a formal response from management may then be appropriate.

The auditor should normally include a note of the action that local management has taken, or intends to take, in the light of audit findings and recommendations. This should add to the effectiveness of audit reports as a management aid, particularly in the case of groups of companies, and to their impact on senior management. Many clients require that the auditor should incorporate comments or responses from line management. As discussed in **Section 12:1.3.1** (third paragraph), adequate provision should be made in the timetable for incorporating management's comments. However, the auditor should not allow delay in obtaining these comments for inclusion in the report to jeopardise overall reporting deadlines.

One way to keep to the timetable is:

(a)   first, to ensure that audit findings and recommendations have been discussed with appropriate members of local management in good time and that the facts have been agreed; and

(b)   second, to ask local management to draft the responses to the recommendations, having regard to the auditor's timetable.

During discussion of the draft report, management might try to persuade the auditor to omit certain matters or to change the wording. This will normally be for one of the following reasons:

(a)   **Management disagrees with the auditor's findings and is able to produce additional information or cast further light on the problem**: If additional information is provided which justifies a change in the audit conclusions, the auditor should be prepared to modify, or even delete, comments.

(b)   **Management accepts the auditor's findings but does not consider the point to be of substance**: The auditor should review the comments and recommendations from a business perspective. If this further review confirms the initial judgement, it is necessary to state the facts as the auditor sees them. The report might also include a comment that local management does not accept the recommendations and include a note of the reasons why.

(c)   **Management does not wish the comments to be brought to the attention of more senior colleagues**: It is necessary to review the matter from an independent perspective and, if necessary, ensure that the facts are stated as the auditor sees them.

Whenever, following discussions with management, the auditor decides to make significant changes to the draft, or to omit any points, consideration should be given as to whether the reasons for the changes need to be recorded in the working papers.

It is not helpful to include management's responses if they consist of defensive and generalised self-justification. If there is no disagreement with the facts the auditor should seek to influence management into accepting the recommendations.

On rare occasions, management's response to a part of the report will be unacceptable to the auditor. Generally, it should be possible for the auditor to avoid these circumstances by producing evidence to support the findings. However, if the auditor believes that management's response is incorrect, and if it cannot be changed, it may be appropriate to comment on it in the report. Before taking this action, however, the auditor should explain the reasons for it to management.

Where the report to management takes the form of a record of discussions with management, this record should preferably include management's response and a record of the action it intends to take.

The engagement manager should ensure that all replies from the client are seen by the engagement partner and should inform the partner if the client has not replied within a reasonable time or has declined to rectify major weaknesses. If appropriate, e.g. where the matters raised are particularly important and loss to the client could arise, this should be followed up with the client. If, in the absence of a reply, the auditor holds a meeting to discuss the report, it is important for the auditor to send a copy of the notes of the meeting to the client. Unless some other notification is received, these notes would constitute the client's reply. The auditor should consider the reasons for inadequate response by the client in case they reflect on the quality of the audit report to the board, or in case they indicate that it was addressed to the wrong level of client management.

12:1.12 Limitations of the audit and the auditor's reporting

The auditor should make clear the principles underlying the 'Audit report to the board' and other reports to management. Accordingly, such reports should preferably include, either in the main body of the report or in an attachment, the following:

(a)   A statement, normally at the beginning, that the auditor is carrying out, or has carried out, an audit of the financial statements.

(b)   A statement that the report is prepared solely for the use of the addressee(s) and the client. The specimen wording in **Section 12:1.12.1** (first paragraph) may be used.

(c)   A statement, which might be included in an attachment to the report, that the principal objective of audit procedures is to enable the auditor to express an opinion on the truth and fairness of the financial statements as a whole, and that accordingly such work cannot be expected to identify all misstatements and weaknesses which a special investigation might reveal. This may be covered by the specimen wording in **Section 12:1.12.2** (second paragraph).

An acknowledgement of the assistance that the auditor has received from the client's management and staff might also be included as a matter of courtesy.

An alternative to covering the above points in each communication to the client is to set them out fully in the audit engagement letter and to refer to that when reporting to the client.

12:1.12.1 Use of reports by third parties

The audit report to the board and other management reports are prepared to assist the client beyond the legal duties of auditors. They are not prepared for use by third parties. The following wording may be used to make this clear:

> **We have prepared this report for use within [*name of client*]. It forms part of a continuing dialogue between us and is not intended to include every matter that came to our attention. If a third party were to obtain a copy without our prior written consent, we would not accept any responsibility for any reliance that they might place on it.**

The auditor should not reveal the contents of management reports to any third party, including parent company management and auditor, without the prior consent of the client.

After the auditor issues a report, the client might request consent to make the report available to a third party. In this situation the auditor should:

(a)   ask the client the identity of the third party;

(b)   establish the intended use of the report by that party.

Depending on the results of these enquiries, the engagement partner should ensure that the limitations on the audit firm's responsibility to the third party have been clearly explained and should ask the client to set out these limitations in a covering letter from the client to the third party.

12:1.12.2 Explanation of the audit approach

To explain the audit approach properly and to put reports in their context, the auditor should set out the limitations of the audit, together with certain points of which the reader should be aware, covering the following matters:

(a)   The objectives and limitations of the audit. The explanation should refer to the letter of engagement, and make it clear that the audit is risk based and is directed at material amounts.

(b)   The way in which controls are assessed, making clear that not all controls are assessed in detail.

(c) A reference to management's responsibility for maintaining adequate controls.

(d) The auditor's limited responsibility in relation to the detection of fraud and a reminder that management is responsible for the prevention of fraud.

To do this, the following wording may be used:

> **Our audit approach**
>
> **The principal objective of our audit procedures is to enable us to express our opinion on the truth and fairness of the financial statements as a whole. An audit opinion is based on the concept of reasonable assurance. It is not a guarantee that the financial statements are free of misstatement. We explained our audit responsibilities, and their limitations, in our letter of engagement of [*date*]**
>
> **Our audit procedures are tailored to our assessment of risk of material misstatement taking into account the inherent risks of error or fraud and our assessment of the effectiveness of controls in eliminating or reducing those risks.**
>
> **It is not necessary for us to examine every operating activity or accounting procedure in the company, nor can we substitute for management's responsibility to maintain adequate controls at all levels of the business. Our work cannot, therefore, be expected to identify all weaknesses in your systems and procedures which a special investigation directed at those systems and procedures might reveal.**
>
> **As to the possibility of fraud, we plan our audit to have a reasonable expectation of its disclosure if the potential effects of the fraud would be material to the financial statements. However, there are many kinds of fraudulent activity, particularly those involving forgery, collusion and management override of control systems, which it would be unreasonable to expect the normal statutory audit to uncover.**

The wording of this description of the audit approach may be varied, provided that the main points are addressed. It may, e.g., be possible to tailor the wording to make it more relevant to the client by:

(a) briefly describing the procedures for reviewing the company's internal controls or for liaising with the client's internal auditors;

(b) stating the particular locations visited;

(c) specifically describing the approach adopted in particular audit areas.

12:1.13 Absence of matters to report

Except where a company has been dormant throughout the year, it will be rare for there to be no matters of significance which need to be drawn to the attention of management. In such circumstances, for the avoidance of doubt, the auditor might write to the client, stating that there are no significant matters to report that have come to the auditor's attention.

12:1.14 Clients unreceptive to management reports

Some clients may inform the auditor that they want the minimum statutory audit opinion and that preparation of reports to management is not required or wanted. It is necessary to explain to the client that there is a professional duty to report to management any significant weaknesses coming to light during the course of the audit, and the client should benefit from the process. If the client does not accept this, the engagement partner should follow the consultation procedures set out in **Section 5:5**, 'Consultation and concurring reviews'.

If management asks the auditor not to prepare a written report, it is necessary for the auditor to consider whether to report matters orally, following this up with a note of the meeting. If the weaknesses found are expressed in the context of a generally positive report, and if the auditor points out that no additional cost has been incurred on the audit to provide the report, the client may become more receptive to written reports in future.

12:1.15 Recording audit findings

As the audit progresses, the auditor should keep a proper record of matters arising for subsequent reporting to the board and to management so that reports can be assembled quickly and efficiently at the appropriate time. These matters may arise from any of the work carried out on the audit, so there is a need for careful extraction and collation of the relevant points, and effective communication within the audit team as a whole. The auditor should adopt a 'right first time' approach, recording points in as final a form as possible, thereby eliminating the need for rewrites before communicating with the client.

12:1.16 Approval

The engagement partner should have overall responsibility for reports to the board and to management. The detailed preparation of the audit report to the board and other reports to management and their discussion with client personnel would normally be the responsibility of the engagement manager and/or the team leader. All team members should have a responsibility for identifying points for inclusion.

12:1.17 Clearance

The engagement manager should plan to submit a draft audit report to the board to the engagement partner for review no later than when the issues documentation is presented.

If a draft is not available, then the issues documentation should contain a list of matters to be discussed with the client at the audit clearance meeting. Issues documentation should include comments on the effect of significant weaknesses which may affect the audit opinion. The engagement partner should review the proposals for reporting to management when giving the preliminary clearance of issues documentation.

Chapter 13

Audit reporting to members

13:13 Reports on initial financial statements required by s. 270 of the Companies Act 1985

13:13.1 Introduction
13:13.2 Contents of a report on initial financial statements of a public company
13:13.3 Example of an unqualified report
13:13.4 Qualified report

13:14 Reports on reregistration as a public company by a private or joint stock company

13:14.1 Introduction
13:14.2 Contents of the audit report
13:14.3 Example of an audit report prepared other than in respect of the normal accounting reference period
13:14.4 Example of a written statement under s. 43(3)(b)
13:14.5 Change of auditors
13:14.6 Qualified report or statement

13:15 Unqualified reports to management on financial statements not prepared under s. 226 of the Companies Act 1985

13:15.1 Introduction
13:15.2 Contents of an audit report
13:15.3 Examples of audit reports

13:16 Qualified and modified reports to the members of limited companies and other organisations in Great Britain

13:16.1 Introduction
13:16.2 Principles
13:16.3 Qualified reports
13:16.4 Forms of qualification
13:16.5   Inherent uncertainties
13:16.6 Fundamental uncertainties
13:16.7 Going concern
13:16.8 Reporting fraud and error and non-compliance with law or regulations
13:16.9 Departures from standard accounting practice
13:16.10 Small businesses
13:16.11 Preceding period's qualifications
13:16.12 Misstated corresponding amounts
13:16.13 Decision chart – qualifications
13:16.14 Appendix A Decision chart – qualifications
13:16.15 Appendix B Examples of qualified and modified reports

13:17 Qualified reports – departures from standard accounting practice

13:17.1 Authority and scope
13:17.2 Limitations to general scope
13:17.3 Disclosure of significant departures
13:17.4 Additional primary statements required by accounting standards
13:17.5 Omission of a primary statement

13:1 Introduction

13:1.1 Structure

The Manual sections that follow describe the forms of reports which auditors are required to make when reporting to third parties in accordance with Auditing Standards issued by the Auditing Practices Board (APB) and other reports which they may issue. **Section 13:2**, 'General matters relating to reports on financial statements', describes the general principles of audit reports to members, and includes an explanation of some of the terms which are used. This chapter also includes guidance on specific types of report as follows:

- audit reports: **Sections 13:2 to 13:6;**

- unqualified reports on audit related engagements: **Sections 13:7 to 13:15;**

- qualified and modified reports: Sections **13:16 to 13:21;**

- reports on non-audit engagements: **Sections 13:22 and 13:23.**

This Manual does not include:

(a) reports that are primarily concerned with corporate finance matters, such as the reports that are issued when a company is giving financial assistance for the purchase of its own shares or long-form reports for prospectuses; and

(b) reports on specialised industry clients, such as charities, banks, building societies, insurance companies and other financial institutions. However, reports on non-incorporated clients are included here.

13:1.2 Companies Act 1985

The sections that follow have been written on the basis of the Companies Act 1985 as amended by the Companies Act 1989.

13:1.3 Auditing Standards

The sections in this chapter are principally based on SAS 600, 'Auditors' Reports on Financial Statements', issued by the APB in May 1993 and effective in respect of audits of financial statements for financial periods ending on or after 30 September 1993. They also include reference to other standards (e.g., SAS 130, 'The Going Concern Basis in Financial Statements') as appropriate.

13:2 General matters relating to reports on financial statements

13:2.1 Introduction

Audit reports are the end-products of the audit work by which the auditor will be judged. Consequently, it is essential that the reports are of the highest standard. Reports to members of limited companies are governed by the requirements of the Companies Act 1985 and by SAS 600 'Auditors' reports on financial statements'. These requirements enable the auditor to standardise the wording of unqualified reports.

The report should be drafted with care. The previous year's report should not merely be copied without considering all the facts. The engagement partner has the final responsibility for the wording of the report, but the team leader should normally prepare a draft before presenting the working papers for review.

13:2.2 Accounts or financial statements

The Companies Act refers to accounts but Statements of Auditing Standards refer to financial statements. Although 'financial statements' is more commonly used some clients may wish to refer to 'accounts'. Either description may be used, provided it is used consistently within each report. Financial statements embrace not only the accounts (balance sheets, profit and loss accounts and notes) but additional statements such as statements of cash flows and total recognised gains and losses or current cost accounts.

13:2.3 Title and addressee

All reports should state the addressee. Reports to members of limited companies should been titled 'Report of the auditors', and they should be addressed to the members, as required by s. 235 of the Companies Act 1985, which states:

> *A company's auditors shall make a report to the company's members on all annual accounts of the company of which copies are to be laid before the company in general meeting during their tenure of office.*

It is customary to combine the title and the address as follows:

Report of the auditors to the members of Blank Company Limited

13:2.4 Signature and dating

It is stated at SAS 600.9 that:

> *(a) Auditors should not express an opinion on financial statements until those statements and all other financial information contained in a report of which the audited financial statements form a part have been approved by the directors, and the auditors have considered all necessary available evidence.*

(b) The date of an auditors' report on a reporting entity's financial statements is the date on which the auditors signed their report expressing an opinion on those statements.

Audit reports must be dated. In principle, the date used must be that on which the auditor actually signs the report on the financial statements. Reports must not be dated earlier than the date on which the complete financial statements were approved by the directors, or their equivalent where the undertaking is not a limited company. The auditor must ensure that all material evidence necessary to support the audit opinion in accordance with Auditing Standards is received by the date of the report. The final clearance of the issues relevant to the audit opinion by both the engagement partner and the review partner, if any, should be given on or before the date of the audit report. The financial statements should disclose the date on which they were approved by the directors.

The audit report should not be signed or dated before the directors have approved the financial statements in their final form. Therefore, the auditor should not generally sign a draft of the report nor complete any record of signature before the date of the directors' approval. In practice, the auditor may (orally or in writing) 'signify willingness to express an opinion' based on the final draft of the financial statements, after completing the audit work but before the directors have met, on the assumption that the directors will approve the financial statements. If the directors then approve those financial statements the auditor may then date the report at the date confirmation of the directors' approval is received.

The board of directors will authorise one or more directors to sign the financial statements on its behalf. Normally, two copies of the financial statements should be signed at the board meeting when the financial statements are approved, and the auditor should sign the report shortly afterwards. In addition to the signature the report should state the name of the firm, *see* **Section 13:2.6**. One copy should be returned to the client, and one copy retained on the audit files. In addition, a third copy will need to be signed and the firm's name stated for filing with the Registrar of Companies in accordance with s. 242 of the Companies Act 1985. Other copies of the report need not be signed, but must state the firm's name.

The auditor should ask clients to ensure that in no circumstances will they distribute final copies of the financial statements either to the shareholders or to any other persons before these have been seen by the auditor, and the audit report has been signed. Section 240(1) of the Companies Act 1985 requires that if a company publishes any of its statutory accounts, they must be accompanied by the relevant auditors' report.

13:2.5 Subsequent events

The financial statements and other financial information approved by the directors, and which the auditor considers when finally expressing an opinion, may be in the form of final drafts from which printed documents will be prepared. Subsequent production of printed copies of the financial statements and of the audit report does not constitute the creation of a new document. The engagement partner should sign and date a copy of the audit opinion when the firm finally express it, to provide evidence that this is the appropriate date to be used. Copies of the audit report that are produced for circulation to shareholders or others may therefore show the date when the opinion was expressed, even though the date of signing the printed audit report is later. The auditor should only do this when there is a delay in finalising the financial statements for administrative reasons, such as the need for final processing of agreed changes and/or printing.

If in exceptional circumstances the date on which the auditor signs the report is later than that on which the directors approved the financial statements, the auditor should:

(a)   obtain assurance that the directors would have approved the financial statements on that later date (e.g., by obtaining confirmation from specified individual members of the board to whom authority has been delegated for this purpose);

(b)   ensure that audit procedures for reviewing subsequent events cover the period up to that date; and

(c)   ensure that the representation letter from the directors is dated not more than one week before the date of the audit report.

When auditing group financial statements, the auditor should refer to the guidance in **Section 11:8**, 'Group audit completion procedures'.

The longer the gap between the date of the directors' approval and the auditor's signing of the audit report, the more important it is to perform subsequent events procedures. In order, therefore, to ensure there is no significant gap, the auditor should ask the finance director or another senior officer to telephone or fax as soon as possible with confirmation of the directors' approval of the draft accounts without change. The auditor should ensure that a record of this is kept on file. The auditor may then sign a copy of the audit report in, e.g., the final draft annual report, and a copy of the version that is sent to the typesetters or printers. This date will be the date of the audit report. If this is on the same day as the directors' approval the auditor will not need to consider further subsequent events procedures.

Sometimes clients delay informing the auditor that the financial statements were approved. In this case the auditor must not sign the audit report until he or she knows that the financial statements are approved. The auditor (and the client) should accept that it may be necessary to reconfirm that there have been no subsequent events up to the date the auditor actually signs the opinion. In practice this need not be too onerous. Three situations may apply:

(a)   If there is only an insignificant delay, provided the auditor is satisfied there is negligible risk of a material subsequent event, there is no need to perform further procedures.

(b)   If the entity's history is stable and there is no reason to believe there could be a material subsequent event, and the auditor signs within, say, seven days of the directors' approval, a note of a telephone conversation with, or a fax from, the financial director or other senior officer, included on the audit file, may be sufficient to confirm that nothing has happened and no further procedures are necessary.

(c)   If the entity's history is more volatile, or a material event may have taken place in relation to uncertainties surrounding the financial statements, or the delay is longer, additional procedures to update the auditor's earlier subsequent events review will be necessary.

Where the auditor's first signature of the audit report was based on oral, fax or other written confirmation from the client that the financial statements were approved, the auditor should subsequently see a final version of the financial statements that the directors have signed and sign the audit report based on this set.

13:2.6 Use of the term 'Registered auditors'

The audit report should state at the foot the name of the firm. The description 'Registered auditors' or, if appropriate, 'Chartered accountants and Registered auditors', should appear after the name of the firm. The address of the office (limited to the city or town) of the firm's practice partnership that was appointed as auditors should also appear after the firm's name. The address to be used should normally be that of the office issuing the engagement letter.

The requirement to state the term 'Registered auditors' is from the *'Audit regulations and guidance'* issued by ICAEW, ICAS and ICAI. These regulations require that any audit reports have to be signed by the firm with the added description 'Registered auditors'.

An audit report is defined in the *'Audit regulations and guidance'* as 'a report by a company's auditor which relates to an audit'. The *'Audit regulations and guidance'* provides a list of the various sources of legislation which require that an audit opinion be given.

13:3 Unqualified reports to the members of limited companies in Great Britain

13:3.1 Contents of reports under the Companies Act 1985

SAS 600 states:

> *An auditors' report should contain a clear expression of opinion on the financial statements and on any further matters required by statute or other requirements applicable to the particular engagement.*

Any reports given by the auditor under s. 235 of the Companies Act 1985 are required to state whether, in the auditor's opinion, the financial statements give a true and fair view of the state of the company's affairs at the balance sheet date and of the profit or loss for the financial period then ended. The auditor is also required to state whether the financial statements have been properly prepared in accordance with the provisions of the Companies Act 1985. The auditor must also consider whether, in his or her opinion:

(a)   proper accounting records have been kept;

(b)   the auditor has received all the information and explanations considered necessary for the purposes of the audit;

(c)   proper returns, adequate for audit purposes, have been received from branches not visited by the auditor;

(d)   the financial statements are in agreement with the accounting records and returns;

(e)   the information given in the directors' report is consistent with the financial statements;

(f)   any qualification is material in determining the legality of a distribution.

If the auditor is satisfied about the matters in (a) to (e), there is no need to refer to them in the audit report. The auditor should consider (f) whenever there is a qualification (*see* **Section 13:18**, 'Additional reports under s. 271 of the Companies Act 1985 (distributions)').

If the financial statements do not give all the information required by the Act or the London Stock Exchange (*see* **Section 13:21**, 'Qualified or modified reports on directors' emoluments and other benefits') in respect of directors' emoluments, directors' emoluments waived and loans to, and other dealings in favour of, directors and officers, then the auditor must give the necessary information in the audit report.

13:3.2 Identification of financial statements

The auditor must identify in the first sentence of the report the financial statements covered by the report, by referring to the page numbers on which the financial statements are set out.

Sometimes a company includes information, which is required by law or Accounting Standards to be contained in the financial statements, in the directors' report or other document which is attached to the financial statements. For example, certain information on directors' emoluments may be included in a separate 'Report of the Remuneration Committee', with a cross-reference from the financial statements.

Where the information that is subject to audit is included in the Remuneration Committee report and is clearly cross-referenced from the financial statements, there is no need to make specific reference to the pages on which the information is included. However, where it is not clearly cross-referenced the auditor should clearly identify the information included in the report of the Remuneration Committee which is covered by the audit report, while making sure that other information in that document is not covered by the report. If, for example the information that is required to be audited is not clearly cross-referenced and is contained in paragraphs numbered 3 and 4 of the report of the Remuneration Committee, the report might begin:

We have audited the financial statements on pages x to y including paragraphs 3 and 4 on page 3, which have been prepared under the historical cost convention and the accounting policies set out on page x.

If the information to be audited in the report of the Remuneration Committee is not numbered but appears under a specific heading, 'Directors' Detailed Remuneration', the report would begin:

> **We have audited the financial statements on pages x to y, which have been prepared under the historical cost convention [*as modified by the revaluation of certain fixed assets*] and the accounting policies set out on page x including the information appearing under the heading 'Directors' Detailed Remuneration' on page 3.**

13:3.3 Accounting convention – historical cost or current cost

SAS 600 states that the auditors' report may refer to the accounting convention and accounting policies which have been followed in preparing the financial statements. It refers to the accounting convention in the example audit reports. Some audit firms may prefer not to follow this style. However, where the notes to the financial statements do not adequately describe the convention used, specific reference should be made to the accounting convention in the audit report. This should be done by amending the first sentence of the audit report, as in the following example:

> **We have audited the financial statements on pages x to x which have been prepared under the historical cost convention as modified by the revaluation of certain fixed assets, and the accounting policies set out on page xx.**

Other conventions that may be used are 'historical cost' or 'current cost'.

Where the company on which the auditor is reporting is dormant the above will only apply if the balance sheet includes any non-monetary assets (e.g., an investment in a subsidiary).

13:3.4 Statements of responsibilities

SAS 600 states:

> (a) *Auditors should distinguish between their responsibilities and those of the directors by including in their report*
>
> > (i) *a statement that the financial statements are the responsibility of the reporting entity's directors;*
> >
> > (ii) *a reference to a description of those responsibilities when set out elsewhere in the financial statements or accompanying information; and*
> >
> > (iii) *a statement that the auditors' responsibility is to express an opinion on the financial statements.*
>
> (b) *Where the financial statements or accompanying information (for example, the directors' report) do not include an adequate description of directors' relevant responsibilities, the auditors' report should include a description of those responsibilities.*

13:3.4.1 Directors' responsibilities

The audit report must include a statement that the financial statements are the responsibility of the directors. The auditor must also cross-refer in the audit report to where in the financial statements or accompanying information a description of the directors' responsibilities is contained.

A description of the directors' responsibilities should include, as a minimum, the following points:

(a) Company law requires directors to prepare financial statements for each financial year that give a true and fair view of the company's (and group's, where relevant) state of affairs at the end of the year and of its (or the group's, where relevant) profit or loss for the year then ended.

(b) In preparing those financial statements, the directors are required to carry out the following procedures:

(i) Select suitable accounting policies and then apply them on a consistent basis, making judgements and estimates that are prudent and reasonable.

(ii) Confirm that applicable accounting standards have been followed, subject to any material departures disclosed and explained in the financial statements. (This requirement does not, however, apply to small and medium-sized companies.)

(iii) Where no separate statement on going concern is made by the directors, prepare the financial statements on a going concern basis unless it is not appropriate to presume that the company will continue in business.

(c) The directors are responsible for keeping proper accounting records, for safeguarding the assets of the company (or group) and for taking reasonable steps for the prevention and detection of fraud and other irregularities.

Where the statement is included in the financial statements or accompanying information, the auditor must cross-refer to the page on which it appears. A suitable wording in the audit report would be as follows:

As described on page x the company's directors are responsible for the preparation of financial statements.

The provision in the annual report of a statement of directors' responsibilities does not absolve the directors from providing a letter of representation for audit purposes. However, the contents of the statement need not be repeated in the letter of representation.

Where there is no description of the directors' responsibilities in the financial statements or accompanying information or where there is an inadequate description, the auditor must include a description in the audit report. In such circumstances the following wording should be used instead of the wording suggested (suitably amended where group financial statements are presented):

Company law requires the directors to prepare financial statements for each financial year which give a true and fair view of the state of affairs of the company and of the profit or loss of the company for that period. In preparing those financial statements, the directors are required to:

- select suitable accounting policies and then apply them consistently;

- make judgements and estimates that are reasonable and prudent;

- state whether applicable accounting standards have been followed, subject to any material departures disclosed and explained in the financial statements [*not applicable for small and medium-sized companies*];

- prepare the financial statements on the going concern basis unless it is inappropriate to presume that the company will continue in business [*only if no separate statement on going concern is made by the directors*].

The directors are responsible for keeping proper accounting records which disclose with reasonable accuracy at any time the financial position of the company and to enable them to ensure that the financial statements comply with the Companies Act 1985. They are also responsible for safeguarding the assets of the company and hence for taking reasonable steps for the prevention and detection of fraud and other irregularities.

Where the auditor reports on financial statements of an entity which does not have directors, such as a pension scheme or a trust, the statement of responsibilities will need to be given by the trustees or other governing body. The statement itself should be tailored to cover the specific legal responsibilities of such trustees or other governing body, as should the reference made in the audit report to the statement.

13:3.4.2 Auditors' responsibilities

The audit report must include a statement of the auditor's responsibility for expressing an opinion on the financial statements. This should be as follows:

It is our responsibility to form an independent opinion, based on our audit, on the financial statements and to report our opinion to you.

The APB may issue further guidance on the contents and location of the auditor's responsibilities statement.

13:3.5 Basis of opinion

SAS 600 states:

Auditors should explain the basis of their opinion by including in their report:

(a) a statement as to their compliance or otherwise with Auditing Standards, together with the reasons for any departure therefrom;

(b) *a statement that the audit process includes*

> (i) *examining, on a test basis, evidence relevant to the amounts and disclosures in the financial statements,*

> (ii) *assessing the significant estimates and judgements made by the reporting entity's directors in preparing the financial statements,*

> (iii) *considering whether the accounting policies are appropriate to the reporting entity's circumstances, consistently applied and adequately disclosed;*

(c) *a statement that they planned and performed the audit so as to obtain reasonable assurance that the financial statements are free from material misstatement, whether caused by fraud or other irregularity or error, and that they have evaluated the overall presentation of the financial statements.*

13:3.6 Explanatory paragraph – fundamental uncertainty

Where an uncertainty exists which in the auditor's opinion is fundamental but it is adequately disclosed in the financial statements, the auditor must include an explanatory paragraph in the 'Basis of opinion' section of the audit report referring to the fundamental uncertainty. There must be a clear indication that the auditor's opinion on the financial statements is not qualified.

A fundamental uncertainty is an uncertainty, the potential impact of which is so great that, without clear disclosure of its nature and implications, the view given by the financial statements as a whole would be seriously misleading. Where a fundamental uncertainty is not adequately disclosed in the financial statements the auditor must qualify the audit opinion. Further guidance is contained in **Section 13:16**, 'Qualified and modified reports to the members of limited companies and other organisations in Great Britain'.

13:3.7 Opinion

SAS 600 states:

> *Auditors' reports on financial statements should contain a clear expression of opinion, based on review and assessment of the conclusions drawn from evidence obtained in the course of the audit.*

The opinion section of the audit report contains the auditor's opinion on the financial statements. The minimum legal requirement is for the report to state whether in the opinion of the auditor the financial statements give a true and fair view of the company's (and group's, where applicable) state of affairs at the end of the financial year and of the profit or loss for that year and whether the financial statements have been properly prepared in accordance with the Companies Act 1985. The auditor may also wish to express an opinion as to whether the financial statements give a true and fair view of the cash flows. This is because the cash flow statement, although necessary in order to give a true and fair view of the state of affairs and profit or loss, is a primary statement in its own right and is also intended to give a true and fair view of cash flows. While the statement of total recognised gains and losses is also a primary statement, the auditor does not refer to total recognised gains in his or her audit report as it is considered to be less important than cash flows. If, however, a company wishes it, the auditor may refer to total recognised gains in his or her audit report. It is not acceptable to refer to total recognised gains but not to cash flows.

13:3.8 Standard forms of report

SAS 600 states:

> Auditors' reports on financial statements should include the following matters:
>
> (a) a title identifying the person or persons to whom the report is addressed;
>
> (b) an introductory paragraph identifying the financial statements audited;
>
> (c) separate sections, appropriately headed, dealing with
>
>> (i) respective responsibilities of directors (or equivalent persons) and auditors,
>>
>> (ii) the basis of the auditors' opinion,
>>
>> (iii) the auditors' opinion on the financial statements;
>
> (d) the manuscript or printed signature of the auditors; and
>
> (e) the date of the auditors' report.

The standard forms of report the auditor is expected to use are given in the following paragraphs. The reports include the following matters as required by SAS 600:

(a) a title identifying the person or persons to whom the report is addressed;

(b) an introductory paragraph identifying the financial statements audited;

(c) a section entitled 'Respective responsibilities of directors and auditors';

(d) a section entitled 'Basis of opinion';

(e) a section entitled 'Opinion';

(f) the manual or printed signature of the audit firm; and

(g) the date of the report.

The standard report for a single company is as follows:

Report of the auditors to the members of Blank PLC

We have audited the financial statements on pages x to x, which have been prepared under the historical cost convention [*as modified by the revaluation of certain fixed assets*] and the accounting policies set out on page x.

Respective responsibilities of directors and auditors

As described on page x the company's directors are responsible for the preparation of financial statements. It is our responsibility to form an independent opinion, based on our audit, on those statements and to report our opinion to you.

Basis of opinion

We conducted our audit in accordance with Auditing Standards issued by the Auditing Practices Board. An audit includes examination, on a test basis, of evidence relevant to the amounts and disclosures in the financial statements. It also includes an assessment of the significant estimates and judgements made by the directors in the preparation of the financial statements, and of whether the accounting policies are appropriate to the company's circumstances, consistently applied and adequately disclosed.

We planned and performed our audit so as to obtain all the information and explanations that we considered necessary in order to provide us with sufficient evidence to give reasonable assurance that the financial statements are free from material misstatement whether caused by fraud or by other irregularity or error. In forming our opinion we also evaluated the overall adequacy of the presentation of information in the financial statements.

Opinion

In our opinion the financial statements give a true and fair view of the state of the company's affairs at 31 December 20XX and of its profit/[*loss*], and cash flows for the year then ended and have been properly prepared in accordance with the Companies Act 1985.

XYZ & Co

Chartered Accountants and Registered Auditors

City or Town

Date

The standard report for group financial statements is as follows:

Report of the auditors to the members of Blank Holdings PLC

We have audited the financial statements on pages x to x, which have been prepared under the historical cost convention [*as modified by the revaluation of certain fixed assets*] and the accounting policies set out on page x.

Respective responsibilities of directors and auditors

As described on page x the company's directors are responsible for the preparation of financial statements. It is our responsibility to form an independent opinion, based on our audit, on those statements and to report our opinion to you.

Basis of opinion

We conducted our audit in accordance with Auditing Standards issued by the Auditing Practices Board. An audit includes examination, on a test basis, of evidence relevant to the amounts and disclosures in the financial statements. It also includes an assessment of the significant estimates and judgements made by the directors in the preparation of the financial statements, and of whether the accounting policies are appropriate to the company's circumstances, consistently applied and adequately disclosed.

We planned and performed our audit so as to obtain all the information and explanations that we considered necessary in order to provide us with sufficient evidence to give reasonable assurance that the financial statements are free from material misstatement, whether caused by fraud or by other irregularity or error. In forming our opinion we also evaluated the overall adequacy of the presentation of information in the financial statements.

Opinion

In our opinion the financial statements give a true and fair view of the state of affairs of the company and the group at 31 December 20XX and of the profit/[loss] and cash flows of the group for the year then ended and have been properly prepared in accordance with the Companies Act 1985.

XYZ & Co

Chartered Accountants and Registered Auditors

City or Town

Date

The standard report for a dormant company is as follows:

Report of the auditors to the members of Dormant Company Limited

We have audited the financial statements on pages x to x, which have been prepared under the historical cost convention [*as modified by the revaluation of certain fixed assets*] and the accounting policies set out on page x.

Respective responsibilities of directors and auditors

As described on page x the company's directors are responsible for the preparation of financial statements. It is our responsibility to form an independent opinion, based on our audit, on those statements and to report our opinion to you.

Basis of opinion

We conducted our audit in accordance with Auditing Standards issued by the Auditing Practices Board. An audit includes examination, on a test basis, of evidence relevant to the amounts and disclosures in the financial statements. It also includes an assessment of the significant estimates and judgements made by the directors in the preparation of the financial statements, and of whether the accounting policies are appropriate to the company's circumstances, consistently applied and adequately disclosed.

We planned and performed our audit so as to obtain all the information and explanations that we considered necessary in order to provide us with sufficient evidence to give reasonable assurance that the financial statements are free from material misstatement, whether caused by fraud or by other irregularity or error. In forming our opinion we also evaluated the overall adequacy of the presentation of information in the financial statements.

Opinion

In our opinion the financial statements give a true and fair view of the state of the company's affairs at 31 December 20XX and have been properly prepared in accordance with the Companies Act 1985.

XYZ & Co

Chartered Accountants and Registered Auditors

City or Town

Date

Where both the balance sheet and the notes to the balance sheet are set out on one page, the auditor may use the words 'balance sheet' instead of 'financial statements'.

If a dormant company has availed itself of the exemption under s. 250 of the Companies Act 1985 and resolved not to appoint auditors, it will of course not require any audit report on its financial statements.

13:3.9 Modifications which are not qualifications

Sometimes, the auditor may need to modify the above standard forms of report. The modifications discussed following this example do not constitute qualifications or modifications involving an explanatory paragraph, which are dealt with separately in other sections. The notes indicated by the letters in brackets in this example are explained in the paragraph that follows the example.

Report of the auditors to the members of Blank PLC

We have audited the accompanying [a] financial statements which comprise the balance sheet, the profit and loss account, and the cash flow statement which have been prepared under the historical cost convention as modified by the revaluation of certain fixed assets [b], and in accordance with the accounting policies set out on page x.

Respective responsibilities of directors and auditors

As described on page x the company's directors are responsible for the preparation of financial statements. It is our responsibility to form an independent opinion, based on our audit, on those statements and to report our opinion to you.

Basis of opinion

We conducted our audit in accordance with Auditing Standards issued by the Auditing Practices Board. An audit includes examination, on a test basis, of evidence relevant to the amounts and disclosures in the financial statements. It also includes an assessment of the significant estimates and judgements made by the directors in the preparation of the financial statements, and of whether the accounting policies are appropriate to the company's circumstances, consistently applied and adequately disclosed.

We planned and performed our audit so as to obtain all the information and explanations that we considered necessary in order to provide us with sufficient evidence to give reasonable assurance that the financial statements are free from material misstatement, whether caused by fraud or by other irregularity or error. In forming our opinion we also evaluated the overall adequacy of the presentation of information in the financial statements.

Opinion

In our opinion the financial statements give a true and fair view of the state of the company's affairs at 31 December 20XX and of its result [c], and cash flows for the period [d] from 1 April 20XX to 31 December 20XX and have been properly prepared in accordance with the Companies Act 1985.

The following notes are relevant to the above:

(a)   When the pages on which the financial statements appear are not numbered, the auditor should identify the financial statements on which he or she is reporting by using the titles used in the financial statements. The word 'accompanying' is preferable to the words 'attached', 'annexed' or 'above'.

(b)   When the financial statements do not adequately describe the basis of accounting (e.g., historical cost) the auditor should make specific reference to this basis (*see* **Section 13:3.3** (first paragraph)).

(c)   Where the profit and loss account shows neither a profit nor a loss for the financial year, the audit report may use the word 'result'.

(d)   Where the period covered by the profit and loss account is not a year, the audit report should state the period.

13:3.10 Standard forms of report – specialised entities

Certain types of company and other entities are required by law or regulations to include auditors' reports with their financial statements, the wording of which differs from the standard formats illustrated in the preceding paragraphs.

Where such a specialised entity is being audited, advice on the wording of the audit report should be obtained from an appropriate industry specialist.

The following represent the principal types of specialised entity where consultation may be required over the form of wording of reports and review procedures:

- Banking companies
- Building societies
- Charities
- Financial services
- Friendly societies
- Housing associations
- Insurance companies
- Investment and unit trusts
- Leasing companies
- Pension schemes

13:3.11 Standard forms of report – current cost financial statements

Current cost financial statements may take the form of either unabridged or abridged financial statements. An unabridged set of financial statements is one that, together with notes, gives all the information required for financial statements intended to give a true and fair view, under current cost principles, of the state of affairs and the results for the year. Where these are the main or only financial statements, the auditor will usually have a statutory obligation to report in true and fair terms. An abridged set of financial statements cannot give a true and fair view and must either be supplementary to the historical cost financial statements or be included in the notes to the historical cost financial statements. However, the auditor can express an opinion on whether abridged financial statements have been properly prepared.

A standard form of report on current cost main financial statements giving a true and fair view is as follows:

Report of the auditors to the members of Blank PLC

We have audited the financial statements on pages x to x which have been prepared using the current cost principles, accounting policies and methods described on page x.

Respective responsibilities of directors and auditors

As described on page x the company's directors are responsible for the preparation of financial statements. It is our responsibility to form an independent opinion, based on our audit, on those statements and to report our opinion to you.

Basis of opinion

We conducted our audit in accordance with Auditing Standards issued by the Auditing Practices Board. An audit includes examination, on a test basis, of evidence relevant to the amounts and disclosures in the financial statements. It also includes an assessment of the significant estimates and judgements made by the directors in the preparation of the financial statements, and of whether the accounting policies are appropriate to the company's circumstances, consistently applied and adequately disclosed.

We planned and performed our audit so as to obtain all the information and explanations that we considered necessary in order to provide us with sufficient evidence to give reasonable assurance that the financial statements are free from material misstatement, whether caused by fraud or by other irregularity or error. In forming our opinion we also evaluated the overall adequacy of the presentation of information in the financial statements.

Opinion

In our opinion the financial statements give, on a current cost basis, a true and fair view of the state of the company's affairs at 31 December 20XX and of its profit and cash flows for the year then ended and have been properly prepared in accordance with the Companies Act 1985.

A standard form of report for current cost supplementary financial statements also giving a true and fair view is as follows:

Report of the auditors to the members of Blank PLC

We have audited the historical cost financial statements, which have been prepared under the historical cost convention [*as modified by the revaluation of certain fixed assets*] and the accounting policies set out on page x and the supplementary current cost financial statements on pages x to x.

Respective responsibilities of directors and auditors

As described on page x the company's directors are responsible for the preparation of financial statements. It is our responsibility to form an independent opinion, based on our audit, on those statements and to report our opinion to you.

Basis of opinion

We conducted our audit in accordance with Auditing Standards issued by the Auditing Practices Board. An audit includes examination, on a test basis, of evidence relevant to the amounts and disclosures in the financial statements. It also includes an assessment of the significant estimates and judgements made by the directors in the preparation of the financial statements, and of whether the accounting policies are appropriate to the company's circumstances, consistently applied and adequately disclosed.

We planned and performed our audit so as to obtain all the information and explanations that we considered necessary in order to provide us with sufficient evidence to give reasonable assurance that the financial statements are free from material misstatement, whether caused by fraud or by other irregularity or error. In forming our opinion we also evaluated the overall adequacy of the presentation of information in the financial statements.

Opinion

In our opinion the historical cost financial statements give, on that basis, a true and fair view of the state of the company's affairs at 31 December 20XX and of its profit and cash flows for the year then ended and have been properly prepared in accordance with the Companies Act 1985.

In our opinion the supplementary current cost financial statements have been properly prepared in accordance with the current cost principles, accounting policies and methods described in notes x to x and give, under that current cost convention, a true and fair view of the state of the company's affairs at 31 December 20XX and of its profit and cash flows for the year then ended.

A standard form of report for current cost supplementary financial statements not intended to give a true and fair view because they are abridged is as follows:

Report of the auditors to the members of Blank PLC

We have audited the financial statements on pages x to x, which have been prepared under the historical cost convention [*as modified by the revaluation of certain fixed assets*] and the accounting policies set out on page x.

Respective responsibilities of directors and auditors

As described on page x the company's directors are responsible for the preparation of financial statements. It is our responsibility to form an independent opinion, based on our audit, on those statements and to report our opinion to you.

Basis of opinion

We conducted our audit in accordance with Auditing Standards issued by the Auditing Practices Board. An audit includes examination, on a test basis, of evidence relevant to the amounts and disclosures in the financial statements. It also includes an assessment of the significant estimates and judgements made by the directors in the preparation of the financial statements, and of whether the accounting policies are appropriate to the company's circumstances, consistently applied and adequately disclosed.

We planned and performed our audit so as to obtain all the information and explanations that we considered necessary in order to provide us with sufficient evidence to give reasonable assurance that the financial statements are free from material misstatement, whether caused by fraud or by other irregularity or error. In forming our opinion we also evaluated the overall adequacy of the presentation of information in the financial statements.

Opinion

In our opinion the financial statements on pages x to x give a true and fair view of the state of the company's affairs at 31 December 20XX and of its profit and cash flows for the year then ended and have been properly prepared in accordance with the Companies Act 1985.

In our opinion the abridged supplementary current cost financial statements on pages x to x have been properly prepared in accordance with the current cost principles, accounting policies and methods described in notes x to x.

The page numbers referred to in the scope paragraph of this report should include the pages on which the abridged supplementary current cost financial statements are set out because the audit work in accordance with Auditing Standards extends to audit work on current cost financial statements. This applies even though the auditor is reporting only that they have been properly prepared.

Where companies include current cost information by way of a note to main historical cost financial statements, the auditor may be requested either to report specifically on the information or to include it in the scope of the statutory audit report on the main historical cost financial statements.

Where the auditor is requested to report specifically on the current cost information, a suitable form of wording, to be added as a separate paragraph following the audit opinion on the main historical cost financial statements, is as follows:

> **In our opinion the information in note x on pages x to x on the effects of changing prices has been properly prepared in accordance with the current cost principles, accounting policies and methods described in that note.**

Where the current cost information is included within the scope of the audit report on the main historical cost financial statements, the auditor should make this clear by identifying the information in the first paragraph of the report. In this case the auditor should only specifically refer to the current cost information in the opinion paragraph of the report where it affects the truth and fairness of the financial statements. Such reference would be required, e.g., if the current cost information were misleading or inconsistent with the historical cost information. An example of a first paragraph identifying the current cost information is as follows:

> **We have audited the financial statements on pages x to x which have been prepared under the historical cost convention [*as modified by the revaluation of certain fixed assets*] including the supplementary current cost information in note x and the accounting policies set out on page x.**

13:4 Reports on summary financial statements

13:4.1 Introduction

Listed public companies may in certain circumstances send to members a summary financial statement instead of full statutory financial statements. 'Listed' means admitted to the Official List of The International Stock Exchange of the United Kingdom and the Republic of Ireland Limited (which trades as the 'London Stock Exchange'). The summary financial statement must be derived from the company's annual financial statements and directors' report, and the form and contents of the statement are laid down in The Companies (Summary Financial Statement) Regulations 1995 (SI No. 2092). This replaces SI 1992 No. 3075 ('the 1992 regulations') and re-enacts the provisions of the 1992 regulations, but with changes that principally affect the way in which a listed company ascertains whether shareholders and others entitled to receive the full financial statements instead wish to receive summary financial statements. It also modifies the contents of the summary financial statement for insurance companies and groups to reflect changes in the law relating to the full financial statements of such entities.

In particular, the summary financial statement must state the following:

(a)   That it is only a summary of information in the company's annual financial statements and directors' report.

(b)   Whether it is the opinion of the auditors that the summary financial statement is consistent with the annual financial statements and directors' report and complies with the requirements of the relevant Companies Act section (s. 251) and regulations made under that section.

(c)   Whether the auditors' report on the annual financial statements was unqualified or qualified, and, if it was qualified, it must set out the report in full, together with any further material needed to understand the qualification.

(d)   Whether the auditors' report on the annual financial statements contained a statement under:

   (i)   s. 237(2) (accounting records or returns inadequate or accounts not agreeing with records and returns); and/or

   (ii)   s. 237(3) (failure to obtain necessary information and explanations);

and if so, it must set out the statement in full.

13:4.2 Audit implications

13:4.2.1 APB Bulletin 1999/6

The APB issued Bulletin 1999/6 'The auditors' statement on the summary financial statement' (which supersedes Auditing Guideline 506). The guidance given in the following paragraphs is consistent with the Bulletin.

13:4.2.2 'Health warning'

The auditor is required to state whether in his or her opinion the summary financial statement is consistent with the annual financial statements and the directors' report. The auditor is not, however, required to form an opinion on whether the summary financial statement gives a true and fair view. The summary financial statement must contain a statement that it does not contain sufficient information to allow as full an understanding of the results of the company (or group, as applicable) and state of affairs of the company (or group, as applicable) as would be provided by the full annual financial statements and reports, and that members and debenture holders requiring more detailed information have the right to obtain, free of charge, a copy of the company's last full annual financial statements and reports.

13:4.2.3 *Scope and timing of the work*

Usually, the work performed by the auditor on the company's full financial statements, coupled with a review of the summary financial statement, will be sufficient to enable the auditor to make the required statement.

The auditor should normally carry out the work on the summary financial statement at the same time as completing the audit of the annual financial statements and directors' report, so that the auditor's statement on the summary financial statement may be issued at the same time as the audit report.

The auditor should design the review of the summary financial statement in such a way as to ensure that the statement includes, as appropriate, at least the information required by s. 251 of the Companies Act 1985 and the regulations (*see* **Section 13:4.1** (second paragraph)) and to ensure also that the amounts and the other information are consistent with the company's annual financial statements and the directors' report. The auditor should also consider whether, within the inherent limitations of a summary financial statement, the overall impression given is compatible with that given by the annual financial statements and the directors' report.

Where summary financial statements include information beyond that required by statute, the auditor should ascertain whether the other information contains apparent misstatements or material inconsistencies with the summary financial statement (*see* **Section 13:4.4**).

13:4.2.4 *Inconsistency*

Inconsistency may result in the following circumstances:

(a) If the information in the summary financial statement has been incorrectly extracted from the annual financial statements and the directors' report (e.g., incorrect classification of balance sheet items).

(b) Use of headings in the summary financial statements that are incompatible with the full annual accounts

(c) If information has been omitted which should be included in the summary financial statement in order that the overall impression is compatible with that given by the annual financial statements and the directors' report. This applies even where such information is not specifically required by the regulations (e.g., omission of information relating to an exceptional item or a non-adjusting post-balance-sheet event which the auditor considers fundamental to a shareholder's understanding of the company's results or financial position).

(d)   If information is included which in the opinion of the auditor has been summarised in a manner that is not compatible with the annual financial statements and the directors' report (e.g., unduly selective summarisation of the directors' report).

If the auditor identifies an inconsistency, it should be discussed with management. The auditor should ask management to remove the inconsistency by amending the summary financial statement – e.g., by providing additional information. If discussion with management does not result in elimination of the inconsistency, the auditor should qualify the opinion.

13:4.2.5 Unqualified statements

In addition to complying with the legal requirement to express an opinion on the consistency of the summary financial statement with the annual financial statements and directors' report (*see* **Section 13:4.1** (second paragraph (point (b)))) the auditor should extend the information given in the statement to include information on the responsibilities of directors and auditors and on the basis of the opinion on the summary financial statement. The auditor should also draw attention to any mention that has been made in the audit report on the annual financial statements of the auditor's consideration of the disclosure of fundamental uncertainties (*see* **Section 13:4.2.7** (first paragraph)).

The auditor's statement therefore should include the following:

(a)   Addressee – the Act does not specify to whom the auditor should address the statement; in the absence of any other requirement it should be addressed to the members.

(b)   Introductory paragraph – identifying the summary financial statement.

(c)   Respective responsibilities, distinguishing between the auditor's responsibilities and those of the directors, and stating that the auditor's responsibility is limited to determining whether the requirements concerning consistency and compliance have been met.

(d)   Basis of opinion, indicating that the audit work was conducted in accordance with the APB Bulletin 1999/6, 'The auditors' statement on the summary financial statement' (*see* **Section 13:4.2.1**).

(e)   Opinion, stating that in the opinion of the auditor:

    a.   the summary financial statement is consistent with the full annual accounts and directors' report of the company for the year concerned; and

    b.   the statement complies with the requirements of s. 251 of the Companies Act 1985 and regulations made under it.

(f)   Other information required – if the auditors' report on the full annual accounts is qualified, the auditors state that fact and reproduce the qualified audit report in full. If the auditors' report on the full accounts includes an explanatory paragraph dealing with a fundamental uncertainty, auditors refer to the uncertainty in their statement on the summary financial statement in sufficient detail for the reader to obtain a proper understanding of the issue or issues involved.

The date of the audit report should be the date on which the auditor signs (in manuscript) the report. The auditor will not be in a position to do this until after the directors have approved and signed the summary statement. The auditor should complete and sign the statement as soon as possible after the date of the report on the annual financial statements, thereby avoiding the impression that the statement on the summary financial statement in any way 'updates' the audit report on the annual financial statements.

An example of an unqualified statement on the summary financial statement is as follows:

Auditors' statement to the members of Blank PLC

We have examined the summary financial statement set out above/on page x.

Respective responsibilities of directors and auditors

The directors are responsible for preparing the summarised annual report. Our responsibility is to report to you our opinion on the consistency of the summary financial statement within the summarised annual report with the full annual accounts and directors' report, and its compliance with the relevant requirements of section 251 of the Companies Act 1985 and the regulations made thereunder. We also read the other information contained in the summarised annual report, and consider the implications for our report if we become aware of any apparent misstatements or material inconsistencies with the summary financial statement.

Basis of opinion

We conducted our work in accordance with Bulletin 1999/6 'The auditors' statement on the summary financial statement' issued by the Auditing Practices Board.

Opinion

In our opinion the summary financial statement is consistent with the full annual accounts and the directors' report of Blank PLC for the year ended 31 December 20xx and complies with the requirements of s. 251 of the Companies Act 1985, and the regulations made thereunder.

XYX & Co

Registered Auditors

City or Town

Date

13:4.2.6 *Qualifications or modifications in the report on the annual financial statements*

The effect on the summary financial statement where the auditor has issued a qualified or modified report on the annual financial statements is dealt with in the remaining paragraphs of **Section 13:4.2.6** and in **Section 13:4.2.7**. Qualified statements on the summary financial statement are dealt with in **Sections 13:4.3.1** and **13:4.3.2**.

If the report on the annual financial statements was qualified, or if it included a statement under s. 237(2) or (3) of the Companies Act 1985, the auditor must ensure that the summary financial statement reproduces the qualified report or statement accurately. Where the qualification includes a reference to a note to the annual financial statements, without stating all the relevant information contained in the note, the auditor should ensure that the full text of the note is reproduced in the summary financial statement. This is because the Act requires that any further material needed to understand the qualified report be set out (*see* **Section 13:4.1** (second paragraph point (c))).

The auditor should refer to the qualification on the annual financial statements in the unqualified statement by including in the 'Basis of opinion' section a reference to the relevant note to the summary financial statement – e.g.:

Auditors' statement to the members of Blank PLC

We have examined the summary financial statement above/on page x.

Respective responsibilities of directors and auditors

The directors are responsible for preparing the summarised annual report. Our responsibility is to report to you our opinion on the consistency of the summary financial statement within the summarised annual report with the full annual accounts and directors' report, and its compliance with the relevant requirements of section 251 of the Companies Act 1985 and the regulations made thereunder. We also read the other information contained in the summarised annual report, and consider the implications for our report if we become aware of any apparent misstatements or material inconsistencies with the summary financial statement

Basis of opinion

We conducted our work in accordance with Bulletin 1999/6 'The auditors' statement on the summary financial statement' issued by the Auditing Practices Board.

Our opinion on the company's annual financial statements was qualified as a result of a disagreement with the accounting treatment of the company's investment properties. That opinion and details of the circumstances giving rise to that opinion are set out in note x of the summary financial statement.

Opinion

In our opinion the summary financial statement is consistent with the annual financial statements and the directors' report of Blank PLC for the year ended 31 December 20xx and complies with the requirements of s. 251 of the Companies Act 1985 and the regulations made thereunder.

If the qualification referred to in the second paragraph of **Section 13:4.2.6** above relates to information not included in the summary financial statement and which is not essential to an understanding of the qualification, it will usually be helpful to a reader if this fact is explained. Management may, for example, include an explanatory note close to the text of the qualified report. If management does not wish to do this, the auditor should still include an appropriate reference in the 'Basis of opinion' section of the statement. For example, this could be reported as follows:

Our opinion on the company's annual financial statements was qualified as a result of a disagreement regarding the omission of a cash flow statement and the opinion is reproduced in note x to the summary financial statement. Details of cash flows are not included and are not required to be included in the summary financial statement.

13:4.2.7 *Fundamental uncertainties*

If the audit report on the annual financial statements contained a reference to a fundamental uncertainty, this should also be referred to in the 'Basis of opinion' section in the statement on the summary financial statement. This might be done as follows:

Our report on the company's annual financial statements contained an explanatory paragraph concerning a fundamental uncertainty, arising from the outcome of possible litigation against the company, for an alleged breach of environmental regulations. Details of the circumstances relating to this fundamental uncertainty are described in note x to the summary financial statement. Our opinion on the annual financial statements is not qualified in this respect.

This example assumes that the note relating to the contingent liability has been reproduced in the summary financial statement. Where the audit report on the annual financial statements contains reference to a fundamental uncertainty that is described in a note to the annual financial statements, the auditor should ensure that the full text of the note is reproduced in the summary financial statement.

Where the auditor has included an explanatory paragraph in the audit report on the annual financial statements, the full audit report need not be reproduced in the summary financial statement. This contrasts with the requirement to reproduce the audit report on the annual financial statements where it has been qualified (*see* **Section 13:4.1** (second paragraph, point (c))). None the less the auditor should still draw attention to the fundamental uncertainty and to the fact that it has been referred to in the report on the annual financial statements, as described in the two preceding paragraphs.

13:4.3 Qualified statement

There may be cases where the summary financial statement does not contain information required by the Act, or where the auditor considers that the information given is not consistent with the annual financial statements and the directors' report. Examples of reports in such circumstances are given below:

13:4.3.1 Information not disclosed

Auditors' statement to the members of Blank PLC

We have examined the summary financial statement set out above/on page x.

Respective responsibilities of directors and auditors

The directors are responsible for preparing the summarised annual report. Our responsibility is to report to you our opinion on the consistency of the summary financial statement within the summarised annual report with the full annual accounts and directors' report, and its compliance with the relevant requirements of section 251 of the Companies Act 1985 and the regulations made thereunder. We also read the other information contained in the summarised annual report, and consider the implications for our report if we become aware of any apparent misstatements or material inconsistencies with the summary financial statement

Basis of opinion

We conducted our work in accordance with Bulletin 1999/6 'The auditors' statement on the summary financial statement' issued by the Auditing Practices Board.

Qualified opinion resulting from disagreement about disclosure

The summary financial statement does not disclose net interest payable of £5 million as required by the Companies (Summary Financial Statement) Regulations 1995.

Except for the non-disclosure of net interest payable, in our opinion the summary financial statement is consistent with the annual financial statements and the directors' report of Blank PLC for the year ended 31 December 20xx and complies with the requirements of s. 251 of the Companies Act 1985 and the regulations made thereunder.

13:4.3.2 Inconsistency with annual financial statements and the directors' report

Auditors' statement to the members of Blank PLC

We have examined the summary financial statement set out above/on page x.

Respective responsibilities of directors and auditors

The directors are responsible for preparing the summarised annual report. Our responsibility is to report to you our opinion on the consistency of the summary financial statement within the summarised annual report with the full annual accounts and directors' report, and its compliance with the relevant requirements of section 251 of the Companies Act 1985 and the regulations made thereunder. We also read the other information contained in the summarised annual report, and consider the implications for our report if we become aware of any apparent misstatements or material inconsistencies with the summary financial statement

Basis of opinion

We conducted our work in accordance with Bulletin 1999/6 'The auditors' statement on the summary financial statement' issued by the Auditing Practices Board.

Qualified opinion resulting from inconsistency with annual financial statements

The summary financial statement includes in the figure of turnover the share of turnover of associated companies attributable to the company's interests which amounts to £50 million. In the annual financial statements this amount is not included in the total turnover shown in the profit and loss account.

Except for the matter referred to above, in our opinion the summary financial statement is consistent with the annual consolidated financial statements and the directors' report of Blank PLC for the year ended 31 December 20xx and complies with the requirements of s. 251 of the Companies Act 1985 and the regulations made thereunder.

13:4.4 Summary financial statement issued as part of a larger document

A summary financial statement may be issued as part of a larger document, such as a newsletter containing information on the company's products. In such circumstances, the summary financial statement should form a separate and clearly identified part of the larger document. Where summary financial statements include information beyond that required by statute, the auditor should ascertain whether the other information contains apparent misstatements or material inconsistencies with the summary financial statement. The auditor should therefore arrange to see, prior to publication, any document in which the summary financial statement is to be included. If the auditor disagrees with any of the material in that document, it should be discussed with management. If the amendments that the auditor considers necessary are not made, the auditor should consider the implications for the audit report. In these circumstances, the engagement partner should follow the consultation procedures set out in **Section 5:5**, 'Consultation and concurring reviews'.

13:4.5 Approval of statement

The engagement partner should decide on the form of the statement which should be used. If a qualified statement is being considered, the engagement partner must follow the consultation procedures set out in **Section 5:5**, 'Consultation and concurring reviews'.

13:5 Preliminary statements of annual results

13:5.1 Introduction

The Listing Rules ('Yellow Book') of the London Stock Exchange require that a preliminary statement of annual results issued by a company is agreed for release with the company's auditors. If the auditors' report is likely to be qualified, the preliminary announcement should give details of the nature of the qualification.

13:5.2 APB Bulletin 1998/7

The Auditing Practices Board published guidance for auditors in Bulletin 1998/7 'The Auditors' Association with preliminary announcements'. The following paragraphs are consistent with this guidance.

Where the preliminary announcement is to be based on the audited financial statements the auditor should have signed the audit report before agreeing to the release of a preliminary announcement which claims that the information is audited. Thus the auditor will need to plan the completion of his or her audit work to meet the company's timetable.

Where the preliminary announcement is to be based on draft financial statements (and therefore will not claim to be audited) the auditor should ensure that he or she is informed of the company's timetable so that he or she can plan to have completed the audit other than for the matters set out in **Section 13:5.3** below.

The auditor must ensure that before release of the preliminary announcement the audit work is sufficiently advanced on the financial statements to enable him or her to be satisfied that any matters outstanding will be unlikely to result in changes to the information contained in the preliminary announcement.

13:5.3 Audit implications

The auditor must not agree to the release of a company's preliminary announcement unless he or she has:

(a)   completed the audit and signed the audit report (if the information in the announcement claims to be 'audited'; or

(b)   substantially completed the audit of the financial statements (if the information in the announcement does not claim to be 'audited').

Completion should be subject only to:

(a)   clearing outstanding audit matters that the auditor considers will not materially affect the figures or disclosures in the preliminary announcement;

(b)   completing the audit procedures on the note disclosures that will not affect materially the financial statements (any note disclosures that do materially affect the financial statements must be audited before the auditor agrees to the release of the preliminary announcement) and completing the reading of the other information in the annual report in accordance with SAS 160, 'Other Information in Documents Containing Audited Financial Statements';

(c)   updating the subsequent events review to cover the period between the issue of the preliminary announcement and the date of signing the report on the audited financial statements; and

(d)   obtaining final written representations from management and establishing that the financial statements have been reviewed and approved by the directors.

This will entail, as a minimum, evidence of preliminary clearance in issues documentation, without any major matters in the issues documentation affecting the results and financial position remaining outstanding.

13:5.4 Audit procedures

Although the financial statements may not be complete or in final form, the auditor should be satisfied that all the figures appearing in the preliminary announcement agree with the figures in the draft financial statements on which the audit has been substantially completed, and that they are not inconsistent or misleading. The auditor should aim to ensure that there will be no material differences between the results shown in the preliminary announcement and the results expected to be shown by the equivalent information in the statutory financial statements. The auditor should also consider other non-financial information or commentary in the preliminary announcement to ensure that it is consistent with the preliminary announcement and draft financial statements.

To achieve the above objectives the auditor should carry out the following procedures:

(a)   Check that the figures in the preliminary announcement have been accurately extracted from the audited or latest draft of the financial statements on which the auditor has performed his or her audit work to reflect the presentation to be adopted in the annual financial statements, e.g. any summarisation should not change the order in which items are presented where this is specified by law or accounting standards.

(b)   Check that the preliminary announcement is not inconsistent with other expected contents of the annual report of which the auditor is aware.

(c)   Check, based on the audit work to date, that the preliminary announcement is not misleading – e.g., because of the omission of significant information, such as changes in accounting policies, of which the auditor has been made aware.

(d)   Check that the preliminary announcement complies with the relevant Stock Exchange and statutory requirements as to its form and content – i.e., the Listing Rules and the non-statutory financial statements requirements of s. 240 of the Companies Act 1985.

(e)   If the auditor considers it necessary, written representations should be obtained from directors and management on the contents of the announcement, to the extent not already obtained for audit purposes.

(f)   Ensure that the preliminary announcement has been formally approved by the board of directors. Approval by the audit committee will be sufficient if it has the board's authority. The auditor should not agree to the release of a preliminary announcement until it has been so approved.

The above list of procedures is not exhaustive and the auditor may need to carry out additional procedures where there are special circumstances – e.g., where a qualification or modification of the audit report on the statutory financial statements is being considered.

13:5.4.1   *Management commentary and final interim period*

The ASB's statement 'Preliminary Announcements' issued in July 1998 recommends that a company should provide a balanced management commentary on the company's performance during the year and its position at the year end. The ASB statement encourages preparers to comment specifically on the final interim period in the preliminary announcement and to present figures for that final interim period separately to the extent necessary to support the management commentary.

The auditor should read the management commentary and other narrative disclosures and any final interim period figures and consider whether they are in conflict with the information that the auditor has obtained in the course of the audit. If the auditor becomes aware of inconsistencies with information obtained during the audit or with the draft financial statements (including the chairman's statement, Operating and Financial Review (OFR) or similar document) the auditor should seek to resolve them with the directors. If they cannot be resolved the auditor should not agree to the issue of the preliminary announcement and the consultation procedures should be followed.

13:5.4.2 *Qualified or modified audit report*

Where the auditor has completed his or her audit and has issued a qualified or modified report (having followed the consultation procedures) the auditor must ensure that the preliminary announcement discloses that fact and the nature of the qualification or modification. The auditor should take care to ensure that the requirements of s.240 of the Companies Act are complied with in the preliminary announcement.

Where the auditor has not yet signed the audit report and is considering whether he or she may need to qualify or modify (e.g. by adding an explanatory paragraph) the opinion on the financial statements, engagement teams should consult in accordance with the procedures set out in **Section 5:5**, 'Consultation and concurring reviews'.

If the auditor decides, after consultation, to issue a qualified audit report, he or she must ensure that the fact that the audit report will be qualified or modified, and the nature of the proposed qualification or modification, are disclosed in the preliminary statement.

If it is possible, but not certain, that the report will be qualified, the auditor must also ensure that the preliminary announcement gives a full explanation of the circumstances and of the possibility that the report will be qualified.

Whereas disclosure of the fact that the report is likely to be qualified and the nature of the qualification in the preliminary announcement is a specific requirement of the Stock Exchange, there is not a specific requirement to disclose if the auditor is going to modify the report by way of an explanatory paragraph. However, the Stock Exchange rules require that the preliminary statement should include sufficient information to enable assessment of the results being announced. If, therefore, there is a fundamental uncertainty (e.g., concerning the validity of the going concern basis in the preparation of the financial statements), it should be fully disclosed in the preliminary statement in order to meet this requirement. In practice the disclosure often takes the form of reproducing the full note that will appear in the statutory financial statements. The auditor must not agree to release of the preliminary announcements unless disclosure of the fundamental uncertainties has been made.

Where the auditor is likely or certain to include an explanatory paragraph in the unqualified audit report, both that fact and the circumstances should also be disclosed in the preliminary statement.

While the APB guidance states that there is no need for the preliminary announcement to refer to the auditor in this context, consider that where the auditor is likely or certain to include an explanatory paragraph in the unqualified audit report, the auditor should ensure that both that fact and the circumstances are also disclosed in the preliminary announcement.

In practice the reference to the modification of the report may be made as part of the s. 240 statement, using wording such as:

> **The figures and financial information for the year ended [*20X1*] do not constitute the statutory financial statements for that year. Those financial statements have not yet been delivered to the Registrar, nor have the**

auditors yet reported on them. The auditors have indicated that their report, will contain reference to the fundamental uncertainty disclosed in note x above. The figures and financial information for the year ended 20X0 do not constitute the statutory financial statements for that year. Those financial statements have been delivered to the Registrar and included the auditors' report which was unqualified and did not contain a statement under either section 237(2) or section 237(3) of the Companies Act 1985.

Where the auditor has already signed a modified report, the wording of the first sentence of the above note would be changed to:

The figures and financial information for the year ended 20X1 do not constitute the statutory financial statements for that year. Those financial statements have [*have not yet*] been delivered to the Registrar and include the auditors' report which, whilst unqualified, contains reference to the fundamental uncertainty disclosed in note x above. The auditors' report does not contain a statement under either section 237(2) or section 237(3) of the Companies Act 1985.

13:5.4.3 Adjusting post-balance-sheet events

On rare occasions, an adjusting post-balance-sheet event (e.g., the insolvency of a major debtor) may occur between the issue of the preliminary announcement and the date on which the full financial statements are formally approved by the board and the audit report is signed. In such circumstances the necessary adjustments should be made in the financial statements, and the company may need to make a further announcement to the Stock Exchange.

13:5.4.4 Reporting on the preliminary announcement

There is no requirement placed on the auditor by the Stock Exchange to issue a report on the preliminary announcement. However, if requested, the auditor should issue an opinion in writing to the directors. A written report allows the audit firm to clarify the extent of its responsibility, the basis of the opinion it is providing and the nature of the opinion itself. Some companies may suggest that the report is published. This is not recommended, and the auditor should not agree to it without consultation in accordance with the procedures referred to in the first paragraph of **Section 13:5.4.1**.

Even though the directors may not request a written report, the auditor should perform procedures on the preliminary statement along the lines referred to in **Section 13:5.4** (second paragraph) and record the work done. Any concerns that the auditor has about the statement should be communicated to the directors, preferably in writing.

The form of the review report to the directors that might be made on a preliminary announcement is illustrated below, along with an explanation of the circumstances in which it might be made, namely that the audit is substantially complete and that some audit evidence is outstanding, but that no qualification or modification of the audit opinion is contemplated. The timing of the issue of the preliminary announcement is in the company's control but it has to be communicated in advance to the Stock Exchange. The auditor should ask to be informed of the date so that the work necessary can be properly planned. In some cases there may be more audit work outstanding than is indicated in the report below. If it is not possible for the auditor to issue an opinion on the basis described in the illustrative report, an alternative wording should be used explaining the actual basis. It is, however, in the auditor's interests to manage the audit so that substantially all work that might affect the audit opinion on the statutory financial statements has been completed by the time that agreement to the preliminary statement is requested.

Review report by the auditors to the directors of XYZ plc

In accordance with the terms of our engagement letter dated *[date]* we have reviewed the attached proposed preliminary announcement of XYZ plc for the year ended [date]. Our work was conducted having regard to Bulletin 1998/7 issued by the Auditing Practices Board. As directors you are responsible for preparing and issuing the preliminary announcement.

Our responsibility is solely to give our agreement to the preliminary announcement having carried out the procedures specified in the Bulletin as providing a basis for such agreement. In this regard we agree to the preliminary announcement being notified to the [*London*] [*Irish*] Stock Exchange.

[*As you are aware we are not in a position to sign our report on the annual financial statements as they have not yet been approved by the directors and we have not yet [insert significant procedures that are to be completed, e.g. completing the subsequent events review and obtaining final representations from directors]. Consequently there can be no certainty that we will be in a position to issue an unmodified audit opinion on financial statements consistent with the results and financial position reported in the preliminary announcement. However, at the present time, we are not aware of any matters that may give rise to a modification to our report. In the event that such matters do come to our attention we will inform you immediately.*]

XYZ & Co

Chartered Accountants

City or Town

Date

13:5.4.5 Agreement to release preliminary announcement

Even though the auditor may have issued a report on the preliminary announcement, it will be inappropriate for the preliminary announcement to be described by the company as 'audited' unless the audit has been completed, and the report on the financial statements signed. If this is the case, the wording of the above report will not be appropriate and the auditor should use a form of words for the report on the preliminary announcement reflecting the fact that the audit work has been completed.

It is unnecessary for a company to refer in its preliminary statement to the fact that it has been agreed with the auditor. Nevertheless, some companies may suggest that a statement to this effect is included. As a minimum, the engagement letter should stipulate that the directors do not make any statement about the auditor's involvement without this being agreed by the auditor. However, as discussed in **Section 13:5.4.3** (first paragraph), public reports on preliminary statements are not recommended.

If the auditor is unable to agree to the release of the preliminary announcement by the date that it is due to be announced, this fact should be discussed with the directors. The directors may then wish to discuss with the Stock Exchange a delay in the announcement. If the directors do not wish to delay the announcement the auditor must ensure that the preliminary statement clearly states that it has not been agreed by the auditor.

13:5.5 Engagement letters

The auditor should include in the audit engagement letter his or her responsibilities in relation to the preliminary announcement. Alternatively the auditor may include a separate engagement letter. Matters that should be dealt with in the engagement letter include:

(a)   The responsibilities of the directors to prepare the preliminary announcement.

(b)   The fact that the auditor will conduct the work in accordance with the APB Bulletin 1998/7.

(c)   A statement as to whether the auditor believes it is management's intention to base the preliminary announcement on audited financial statements or on draft financial statements which the auditor has not yet reported on.

(d)   A statement that the auditor will issue a letter confirming, or otherwise, the agreement of the preliminary announcement.

(e)   A statement explaining the inherent limitations on the work.

(f)   A statement confirming that the directors will not refer publicly to the auditor's association, or make any private report from the auditor available to members or to a third party without the auditor's prior written consent.

Examples of specimen paragraphs for engagement letters in the two situations where either the audit has been completed or the audit has not yet been completed, are given below:

Example paragraphs for engagement letter – audit completed

Extract from Letter of Engagement

The Listing Rules state that 'a preliminary statement of the annual results ... must have been agreed with the company's auditors'. As directors of the company, you are responsible for preparing and issuing the preliminary statement of annual results and ensuring that we agree with its release.

We understand that the preliminary statement of annual results will be prepared in accordance with the recommendations of the Accounting Standards Board in their statement 'Preliminary Announcements'.

We undertake to review the preliminary announcement having regard to Bulletin 1998/7 'The Auditors' Association with Preliminary Announcements' issued by the Auditing Practices Board. Accordingly, our review will be limited to checking the accuracy of extraction of the financial information in the preliminary announcement from the audited financial statements of the company for that year and reading the management commentary, including any comments on or separate presentation of the final interim period figures, and considering whether it is in conflict with the information that we obtained in the course of our audit.

You will provide us with such information and explanations as we consider necessary for the purposes of our work. We shall request sight of the preliminary announcement in sufficient time to enable us to complete our work. The Board/committee of the Board will formally approve the preliminary announcement before we agree to it.

You agree not to refer to us in the preliminary announcement or make available copies of our letter indicating our agreement to any other party without our prior written consent.

Example paragraphs for engagement letter – audit not completed

Extract from Letter of Engagement

The Listing Rules state that 'a preliminary statement of the annual results ... must have been agreed with the company's auditors'. As directors of the company, you are responsible for preparing and issuing the preliminary statement of annual results and ensuring that we agree with its release.

We understand that the preliminary statement of annual results will be prepared in accordance with the recommendations of the Accounting Standards Board in their statement 'Preliminary Announcements'.

We undertake to review the preliminary announcement having regard to Bulletin 1998/7 'The Auditors' Association with Preliminary Announcements' issued by the Auditing Practices Board. Accordingly, our review will be limited to checking the accuracy of extraction of the financial information in the preliminary announcement from the latest available draft financial statements of the company for that year and reading the management commentary, including any comments on or separate presentation of the final interim period figures, and considering whether it is in conflict with the information that we have obtained in the course of our audit.

You will provide us with such information and explanations as we consider necessary for the purposes of our work. We shall request sight of the preliminary announcement in sufficient time to enable us to complete our work. The Board/committee of the Board will formally approve the preliminary announcement before we agree to it. You will also make available to us the proposed text of the company's annual report.

We will not agree to the release of the preliminary announcement until the audit is complete subject only to the following:

(a)   clearing outstanding audit matters that we consider will not materially affect the figures or disclosures in the preliminary announcement;

(b)   completing our audit procedures on the note disclosures to the financial statements and completing our reading of the other information in the annual report;

(c)   updating our subsequent events review to cover the period between the date of the preliminary announcement and the date of signing our report on the financial statements;

(d)   obtaining final written representations from management and establishing that the financial statements have been reviewed and approved by the directors.

The scope of our work will be necessarily limited in that, we will only be able to check the consistency of the preliminary announcement with draft financial statements on which our audit is incomplete. Accordingly, we shall not, at that stage, know whether further adjustments may be required to those draft financial statements. Consequently, there is an unavoidable risk that the company may wish to revise its preliminary announcement in the light of audit findings or other developments arising between the preliminary announcement being notified to the Stock Exchange and the completion of the audit.

You agree not to refer to us in the preliminary announcement or make available copies of our letter indicating our agreement to any other party without our prior written consent.

In the event that we disagree with the release of the preliminary announcement we will send you a letter setting out the reasons why.

13:6 Reading the audit report at annual general meetings

13:6.1 Introduction

The Companies Act 1985 does not require the auditor to read the audit report at the client's annual general meeting. It is enough, and indeed it is required, that the annual financial statements and the auditor's report thereon are laid before the members.

However, in many companies it has been the practice for the engagement partner to attend the annual general meeting and read the audit report aloud to the members.

Because of the length of the standard audit report in accordance with SAS 600 the auditor may, if asked to read the report at the annual general meeting, prefer to read only highlights of the report.

If the auditor reads only the highlights of the report, he or she should make sure that:

(a) what is read out cannot be construed as the full report; and

(b) where there is a need to modify the normal wording of the audit report, the modifications are made clear.

13:6.2 Suitable highlights wording

A suitable highlights wording for a group is as follows:

The firm's report on the annual financial statements is set out on page x of the annual report and financial statements. This includes confirmation that we have performed our audit in accordance with Auditing Standards and that in our opinion the financial statements give a true and fair view of the state of affairs of the company and group at [*date*] and of the profit and cash flows of the group for the year then ended and have been properly prepared in accordance with the Companies Act 1985.

13:7 Reports on small companies and groups – preparation exemptions

13:7.1 Introduction

The Companies Act 1985, Part VII, ss. 246, 247A and 248A permits small companies and groups to take advantage of certain exemptions in the preparation of their financial statements and their directors' report. These exemptions are incorporated in a new Sch. 8 to the Companies Act 1985 which was introduced by the Companies Act 1985 (Accounts of Small and Medium-sized Companies and Minor Accounting Amendments Regulations

1997 (SI No. 220). The exemptions do not apply to public companies, banking or insurance companies or authorised persons under the Financial Services Act 1986 or members of an ineligible group.

13:7.2 Small companies

13:7.2.1 Preparation of financial statements

The exemptions which may be taken by small companies and groups in the preparation of their financial statements and directors' report and the detailed requirements that **do** apply to small companies are set out in ss. 246 and 248A of and Sch. 8 to the Companies Act 1985. Where advantage is taken of the exemptions, the requirements set out in **Section 13:7.2.2** apply.

Small companies may prepare their accounts using the Financial Reporting Standard for Smaller Enterprises (FRSSE) rather than FRSs and other accounting standards. Auditing Guidance on the FRSSE is given by the Auditing Practices Board in Practice Note 13 and Bulletin 1997/3.

13:7.2.2 Statements to be made where advantage is taken of the exemptions

Section 246(8) of the Companies Act 1985 (as inserted by SI 1997 No. 220) requires that where advantage has been taken of the exemptions in preparation of small company accounts and directors' report a statement must be made in a prominent position on the balance sheet, in the case of accounts, and on the report, in the case of the directors' report, that they are prepared in accordance with the special provisions of Part VII of the Companies Act 1985 relating to small companies. The statement must be positioned above the director's signature, in the case of the balance sheet, and above the director's or secretary's signature, in the case of the directors' report.

Suitable wording for the statement on the balance sheet would be:

> **These financial statements have been prepared in accordance with the special provisions of Part VII of the Companies Act 1985 relating to small companies.**

Suitable wording for the statement in the directors' report would be:

> **This report has been prepared in accordance with the special provisions of Part VII of the Companies Act 1985 relating to small companies.**

13:7.2.3 Audit report

It is generally accepted that, normally, financial statements that are prepared using the exemptions will still give a true and fair view. Accordingly, the auditor should continue to refer to 'true and fair' in the report. However, the auditor should explain in the introductory paragraph that the financial statements have been prepared in accordance with the provisions of the Companies Act 1985 relating to small companies. The auditor should use the following wording for an unqualified report on a small company that takes advantage of the exemptions:

Report of the auditors to the members of Blank Limited

We have audited the financial statements on pages x to x, which have been prepared under the historical cost convention [*as modified by the revaluation of certain fixed assets*] and the accounting policies set out on page x and which have been prepared in accordance with the special provisions of Part VII of the Companies Act 1985 relating to small companies.

Respective responsibilities of directors and auditors

As described on page x the company's directors are responsible for the preparation of financial statements. It is our responsibility to form an independent opinion, based on our audit, on those statements and to report our opinion to you.

Basis of opinion

We conducted our audit in accordance with Auditing Standards issued by the Auditing Practices Board. An audit includes examination, on a test basis, of evidence relevant to the amounts and disclosures in the financial statements. It also includes an assessment of the significant estimates and judgements made by the directors in the preparation of the financial statements, and of whether the accounting policies are appropriate to the company's circumstances, consistently applied and adequately disclosed.

We planned and performed our audit so as to obtain all the information and explanations that we considered necessary in order to provide us with sufficient evidence to give reasonable assurance that the financial statements are free from material misstatement, whether caused by fraud or by other irregularity or error. In forming our opinion we also evaluated the overall adequacy of the presentation of information in the financial statements.

Opinion

In our opinion the financial statements give a true and fair view of the state of the company's affairs at 31 December 20XX and of its profit/[*loss*] and cash flows (where applicable) for the year then ended, and have been properly prepared in accordance with the Companies Act 1985.

There may be instances where the use of the exemptions means that the financial statements do not give a true and fair view. The exemptions available fall into two types:

(a)   The company may combine certain format headings and show one figure rather than figures for each of the relevant format headings.

(b)   The exemptions provide that certain disclosures need not be made.

The financial statements may fail to give a true and fair view if the auditor considers that a particular item is of such significance that it should be separately disclosed, but instead it has been combined with other format headings using the exemptions in the Act. They may also fail to give a true and fair view if the auditor considers that an item is of such significance that it should be disclosed, but the exemptions permit that it is not disclosed. The financial statements may also fail to give a true view for some reason other than that the exemptions have been used.

Where the financial statements of a small company fail to give a true and fair view for any of the reasons described in the preceding paragraph, the auditor should qualify the audit report. Guidance on qualified reports is contained in **Section 13:16**, 'Qualified and modified reports to members of listed companies and other organisations in Great Britain'.

13:7.3 Small groups

13:7.3.1 Preparation of financial statements

Small and medium-sized companies which are parent companies are exempt from preparing group financial statements, subject to certain conditions. Details are given in **Section 13:8**, 'Reports on small and medium-sized companies and groups – filing exemptions', and **Section 13:8.2.5**. Where, however, a small company is exempt from preparing group financial statements, but none the less chooses to do so, it may prepare the group financial statements taking the same exemptions as are available in the preparation of small company financial statements, suitably modified for group financial statements. In such a case the following paragraphs would apply.

13:7.3.2 Statements to be made where advantage is taken of the exemptions

The statements would be as for small companies preparing financial statements and taking the exemptions except that they would refer to exemptions applicable to small companies and groups (*see* **Section 13:7.2.2**).

13:7.3.3 Audit report

The introductory paragraph of the audit report set out in **Section 13:7.2.3** would refer to 'Small companies and groups' and the opinion paragraph would be modified to apply to the group financial statements as follows:

Opinion

In our opinion the financial statements give a true and fair view of the state of affairs of the company and the group at 31 December 20XX and of the profit/[*loss*] and cash flows (where applicable) of the group for the year then ended and have been properly prepared in accordance with the Companies Act 1985.

If the auditor considers that the group financial statements do not give a true and fair view either because the group has taken advantage of the exemptions, or for any other reason, he or she should qualify the audit report. (*See* **Section 13:7.2.3** (final paragraph).)

13:7.4 Audit implications

The auditor must be satisfied that a company or group, which proposes to take advantage of the exemptions, qualifies as a small company or group under s. 247 or s. 249 respectively. The auditor must therefore ensure that the relevant criteria set out in those sections are satisfied and that there is no uncertainty or disagreement which might affect the amounts of turnover or total assets or the number of employees.

The auditor must also examine the financial statements to ensure that the exemptions have been properly applied, and that use of the exemptions has not resulted in the financial statements' failing to give a true and fair view and that the financial statements do not fail to give a true and fair view for any other reason. (*See* **Section 13:7.2.3** (second and third paragraphs).)

13:7.5 Filing of financial statements

Section 246(5) of the Companies Act 1985 allows small companies to deliver financial statements (prepared in accordance with the exemptions described above) to the registrar which exclude:

(a)   the profit and loss account for the year; and

(b)   the directors' report for the year.

Small companies may also file, instead of the balance sheet prepared using the exemptions described above, a balance sheet which takes advantage of the exemptions in filing accounts which are contained in Sch. 8A to the Companies Act 1985.

For details of reports and statements that are required where Sch. 8A exemptions are taken in respect of filing accounts *see* **Section 13:9**.

13:8 Reports on small and medium-sized companies and groups – filing exemptions

13:8.1 Introduction

The Companies Act 1985, Part VII, ss. 246, 246A, 247A and 247B permits small and medium-sized companies to take advantage of certain exemptions in the financial statements which they file with the Registrar. For small companies the exemptions are set out in s. 246 of and Sch. 8A to the Companies Act 1985. For medium-sized companies the exemptions are set out in s. 246A of the Companies Act 1985. In both cases the auditors must make a special report and the requirements relating to this report are set out in s. 247B of the Companies Act 1985. The exemptions do not apply to public companies, banking or insurance companies or authorised persons under the Financial Services Act 1986. There is no provision in the Companies Act 1985 for delivery of abbreviated group accounts as both small and medium-sized groups may take advantage of exemptions from preparing group accounts (*see* **Section 13:8.3.1** (first paragraph)).

This section provides guidance on the reporting requirements in situations where a client takes advantage of provisions in the Companies Act which enable:

(a)   filing of abbreviated financial statements; or

(b)   exemptions from preparing group financial statements.

13:8.2 Small and medium-sized companies

13:8.2.1 Audit reports

Small or medium-sized companies are permitted to file 'abbreviated' financial statements with the Registrar of Companies. Before the directors deliver abbreviated financial statements to the Registrar, the company's auditors must consider whether, in their opinion, the company is entitled, under s. 247 of the Companies Act 1985, to the exemptions conferred by s. 246(5) or (6) ('the relevant provision') of and Sch. 8A to (small companies) or s. 246A(3) ('the relevant provision') (medium-sized companies) of the Companies Act 1985. If it is, the auditor must prepare a special report under s. 247B of the Companies Act 1985 which is addressed to the directors. This report must accompany the abbreviated financial statements that are filed with the Registrar. Within the special report, the auditor must state whether in his or her opinion the company is entitled to deliver abbreviated accounts prepared in accordance with the relevant provision and whether the abbreviated accounts to be delivered are properly prepared in accordance with that provision. Examples of such reports are set out below.

13:8.2.1.1 Small company filing abbreviated financial statements which has also taken advantage of exemptions in the preparation of its financial statements

For details of the exemptions in the preparation of its financial statements of which a small company may take advantage, *see* **Section 13:7**, 'Reports onsmall companies and groups – preparation exemptions'.

Report of the auditors to the directors of Blank Limited under s. 247B of the Companies Act 1985

We have examined the abbreviated financial statements on pages x to x together with the annual financial statements of Blank Limited for the year ended 31 December 20XX, which have been prepared under the historical cost convention [*as modified by the revaluation of certain fixed assets*] and the accounting policies set out on page x.

Respective responsibilities of directors and auditors

The directors are responsible for preparing the abbreviated financial statements in accordance with s. 246 of and Sch. 8A to the Companies Act 1985. It is our responsibility to form an independent opinion as to the company's entitlement to deliver abbreviated financial statements prepared in accordance with s. 246(5) and (6) of the Companies Act 1985 and whether the abbreviated financial statements are properly prepared in accordance with those provisions and to report our opinion to you.

Basis of opinion

We have carried out the procedures we considered necessary to confirm, by reference to the annual financial statements, that the company is entitled to deliver abbreviated financial statements and that the abbreviated financial statements are properly prepared from those financial statements. The scope of our work for the purpose of this report does not include examining or dealing with events after the date of our report on the annual financial statements.

Opinion

In our opinion the company is entitled to deliver abbreviated financial statements prepared in accordance with s. 246(5) and (6) of the Companies Act 1985 and the abbreviated financial statements to be delivered are properly prepared in accordance with those provisions.

(*Note:* The above report assumes that the exemptions in both s. 246(5) and 246(6) are taken. If the exemptions in only one of the subsections are taken the references in the report would be amended accordingly.)

13:8.2.1.2 Medium-sized company filing abbreviated financial statements

Report of the auditors to the directors of Blank Limited under s. 247B of the Companies Act 1985

We have examined the abbreviated financial statements on pages x to x together with the annual financial statements of Blank Limited for the year ended 31 December 20XX, which have been prepared under the historical cost convention [*as modified by the revaluation of certain fixed assets*] and the accounting policies set out on page x.

Respective responsibilities of directors and auditors

The directors are responsible for preparing the abbreviated financial statements in accordance with s. 246A of the Companies Act 1985. It is our responsibility to form an independent opinion as to the company's entitlement to deliver abbreviated financial statements prepared in accordance with s. 246A(3) of the Companies Act 1985 and whether the abbreviated financial statements are properly prepared in accordance with that provision and to report our opinion to you.

Basis of opinion

We have carried out the procedures we considered necessary to confirm, by reference to the annual financial statements, that the company is entitled to deliver abbreviated financial statements and that the abbreviated financial statements are properly prepared from those financial statements. The scope of our work for the purpose of this report does not include examining or dealing with events after the date of our report on the annual financial statements.

Opinion

In our opinion the company is entitled to deliver abbreviated financial statements prepared in accordance with s. 246A(3) of the Companies Act 1985 and the abbreviated financial statements to be delivered are properly prepared in accordance with that provision.

As mentioned in **Section 13:8.2.1** (first paragraph), the auditor's special report must accompany the abbreviated financial statements that are delivered to the Registrar.

13:8.2.2 Qualified or modified audit reports

The special report that is filed with the Registrar (*see* **Section 13:8.2.1**) need not contain the auditor's report under s. 235 on the statutory financial statements unless that report was qualified or contained a statement under s. 237(2) (proper accounting records) or s. 237(3) (failure to obtain necessary information and explanations). If the audit report on the statutory financial statements was qualified then the special report on the abbreviated financial statements must set out the s. 235 report in full, together with any further material necessary to understand the qualification. If the audit report on the statutory financial statements contained a statement under s. 237(2) or (3)) that statement must be set out in full in the special report.

The disclosures described in the preceding paragraph are the minimum requirements of the Companies Act. They do not preclude the inclusion in the auditor's special report of other information that the auditor considers important for a proper understanding of that report. The special report should also set out the auditor's s. 235 report in full, when that report was unqualified but contained an explanatory paragraph regarding a fundamental uncertainty (together with any further material necessary for an understanding of the explanatory paragraph).

The auditor must also consider whether he or she can issue a s. 247B special report if the audit report on the annual financial statements has been qualified or contains reference to a fundamental uncertainty in either the current or the previous period in relation to one of the criteria for exemption. The auditor must be satisfied that the maximum effect of the qualification or uncertainty cannot take the turnover, total assets or total number of employees over the exemption limits. Abbreviated financial statements are permitted only where a company satisfies two or more of the criteria for exemption.

Qualifications to the audit report on the annual financial statements that do not affect either the turnover or the items included in the balance sheet total will not normally affect the audit opinion in the s. 247B special report. If the auditor has issued a qualified or modified report on the annual financial statements, that report should be repeated in the s. 247B report without amplification. However, where the qualification or modification includes a reference to a note to the annual financial statements, without stating explicitly all the relevant information contained in that note, the full text of the note should be reproduced in the report on the abbreviated financial statements immediately following the text of the qualified or modified report on the annual financial statements. This is because, as noted in the first two paragraphs of **Section 13:8.2.2**, s. 247B requires that, if the report was qualified or modified, both the s. 235 report and any further material necessary to understand the qualification or modification should be included.

The 1985 Act makes no provision for the delivery of a qualified s. 247B special report to the Registrar of Companies. It would appear, therefore, that the directors would be in breach of s. 247B if abbreviated financial statements were delivered to the Registrar with other than an unqualified special report (regardless of whether that report contained a qualified report on the annual financial statements).

13:8.2.3 Statements to be made where advantage is taken of the exemptions

Sections 246(8) (small companies) and 246A(4) (medium-sized companies) of the Companies Act 1985 require that, where abbreviated financial statements are delivered, the company's abbreviated balance sheet shall contain a statement that the abbreviated financial statements are prepared in accordance with the special provisions of Part VII of the Companies Act 1985 relating to small companies/medium-sized companies (as applicable). The statement should appear in a prominent position on the abbreviated balance sheet above the director's/directors' signatures.

For small companies filing abbreviated financial statements the statement would be as follows:

> **The abbreviated financial statements have been prepared in accordance with the special provisions of Part VII of the Companies Act 1985 relating to small companies.**

For medium-sized companies filing abbreviated financial statements, the statement would be as follows:

> **The abbreviated financial statements have been prepared in accordance with the special provisions of Part VII of the Companies Act relating to medium-sized companies.**

13:8.2.4 Audit implications

Usually, the work the auditor performs on the company's annual financial statements, coupled with a review of the abbreviated financial statements, will be sufficient to enable the auditor to make the required report.

The auditor should design the review of the abbreviated financial statements in such a way as to ensure that it includes at least the information required by s. 246 of and Sch. 8A to (small companies) or s. 246A of (medium-sized companies) the Act and to ensure also that the amounts correspond correctly with the company's annual financial statements.

Where there is to be a change of auditors, it should be arranged for the auditors of the annual financial statements to report on the abbreviated financial statements. If this is not possible and the new auditors have to report on the abbreviated financial statements, the new auditors can accept the audited annual financial statements as a basis for their work unless they have grounds to doubt the accuracy of the criteria for exemption, e.g. because of a qualified opinion. The new auditors should indicate in their report who carried out the audit of the annual financial statements.

13:8.2.5 Groups

There is no provision in the Companies Act 1985 for abbreviated group financial statements. Hence, if an eligible small or medium-sized group does not take advantage of the exemption from the requirement to prepare group financial statements available under s. 248 (*see* **Section 13:8.3.1**), they must file the group financial statements which they prepare for their members. In the case of small companies, however, those group financial statements may take advantage of exemptions in the preparation of such statements (*see* **Section 13:7**, 'Reports on financial statements of small companies and groups taking advantage of exemptions in preparation of financial statements'). (Medium-sized companies may also file financial statements taking advantage of a minor exemption in preparation relating to para. 36A of Sch. 4. *See* s. 246A(2) of the Companies Act 1985.)

13:8.3 Small/medium-sized groups

13:8.3.1 Audit report

A parent company is not required to prepare group financial statements for a financial year in relation to which the group headed by that company qualifies as a small or medium-sized group and is not an ineligible group. An ineligible group is one which has as a member:

(a)   a public company or other body corporate that has power to offer shares or debentures to the public; or

(b)   an authorised institution under the Banking Act 1987; or

(c)   an insurance company to which Part II of the Insurance Companies Act 1982 applies; or

(d)   an authorised person under the Financial Services Act 1986.

The detailed criteria that must be satisfied before a group may qualify as small or medium-sized are set out in s. 249 of the Companies Act 1985 as amended by SI 1992 No. 2452.

SI 1996 No. 189 introduced a requirement into s. 237 effective for any annual financial statements approved by the directors on or after 2 February 1996 that if the directors of a company have taken advantage of the exemptions from preparing group accounts described in **Section 13:8.2.4** (first paragraph), and in the auditors' opinion they were not entitled to do so, the auditors must state that fact in their report on the company's individual financial statements.

13:8.3.2 Modified audit reports on the individual financial statements

In determining whether it is necessary to make a statement in the audit report on the individual financial statements, the auditor must consider whether the audit report on the financial statements of the company or any of its subsidiaries has been qualified in either the current or the previous year in relation to one of the criteria for exemption set out in s. 249. The auditor must be satisfied that the maximum effect of the qualification or qualifications cannot take the turnover, total assets or number of employees over the exemption limits. Where a subsidiary undertaking's financial statements are not audited, the auditor must carry out sufficient audit work to be satisfied that the turnover, total assets or number of employees of the group would not exceed the exemption limits. A group qualifies as small or medium-sized only where it satisfies two or more of the criteria for exemption.

Qualifications to the audit reports on the financial statements of the company and/or its subsidiaries that do not affect the turnover, the total assets or the number of employees will not normally require the auditor to make the statement referred to in **Section 13:8.3.1** (second paragraph) in the audit report on the company's individual financial statements.

13:8.4   Consultation

Whenever the auditor is considering issuing a modified report, the consultation procedures set out in **Section 5:5**, 'Consultation and concurring reviews', must be followed.

13:9   Audit exemption for small companies and groups

13:9.1   Introduction and applicability of Companies Act regulations

The Companies Act 1985 (Audit Exemption) Regulations 1994 (SI 1994 No. 1935) introduced amendments to the 1985 Act which permitted companies meeting the qualifying conditions to exempt themselves from audit. Where the conditions for total exemption were not met but a company still met certain other conditions an accountants' report but not a full audit was required. In April 1997 the Companies Act 1985 (Audit Exemption) (Amendment) Regulations 1997 (SI 1997 No. 936) were introduced which amended the 1985 Act to abolish accountants' reports for all companies except charitable companies. It also raised the total exemption from audit limits.

    The following guidance is therefore applicable to small companies other than charitable companies (which are outwith the scope of this manual).

References are to the Companies Act 1985 sections as amended by SI 1997 No. 936.

13:9.2   Exemption conditions

SI 1997 No. 936 raised the audit exemption limit to £350,000 in relation to turnover. The conditions for total exemption from audit with effect for accounting periods ending on or after 15 June 1997 are set out in s. 249A(3) and are as follows:

(a)   The company must qualify as a small company in relation to the financial year for the purposes of s. 246.

(b)   Its turnover in that year must be not more than £350,000.

(c)   Its balance sheet total for the year must be not more than £1.4 million.

13:9.3   Companies not entitled to the exemption

Section 249(B)(1) and subs. 1A to 1C stipulate that the following types of company are not entitled to exemption from audit, even if they qualify as small companies and meet the total exemption conditions set out above, if at any time in the financial year they were any of the following:

(a)   A public company.

(b)   A banking or insurance company.

(c)   A company enrolled on a list maintained by the Insurance Brokers Registration Council under s. 4 of the Insurance Brokers (Registration) Act 1977.

(d)   An authorised person or appointed representative under the Financial Services Act 1986.

(e)   A special register body as defined in s. 117(1) of the Trade Union and Labour Relations (Consolidation) Act 1992 or an employers' association as defined by s. 122 of that Act.

(f)   A parent company or subsidiary undertaking unless it is:

   (i)   a subsidiary undertaking that qualifies as dormant under s. 250 of the Companies Act (no special resolution under s. 250 is, however, required for it to qualify under this exemption); or

   (ii)   a parent or a subsidiary undertaking in a small group (that qualifies as such under s. 249), provided that the turnover of the group is not more than £350,000 net or £420,000 gross (both as calculated in accordance with s. 249) and the group's balance sheet total is not more than £1.4 million net or £1.68 million gross (again as calculated in accordance with s. 249) and the group is not an ineligible group within the meaning of s. 248(2).

A company is also not exempt if members holding 10% or more of the share capital serve notice that they require an audit.

13:9.4 Reporting

There are no specific reports required from the auditor in relation to the rules set out above as a company is either exempt from audit or it is not. The directors of a company taking advantage of an exemption must make a statement on the balance sheet, acknowledging their responsibility for ensuring that proper accounting records are kept, and for preparing accounts that give a true and fair view and comply with the Companies Act.

13:10 Reports on international financial statements

13:10.1 Introduction

For the purpose of this section, international financial statements are defined as those financial statements that a client prepares primarily for the benefit of users domiciled in a foreign country.

   In deciding whether financial statements constitute international financial statements, the auditor should consider the views expressed by the client's management and any other indications there may be of the intended use of the statements. The auditor should presume that those financial statements that meet any of the following conditions are prepared primarily for the benefit of users in a foreign country:

(a)   The statements are presented in a language other than an official language of the country in which the client is domiciled.

(b)   The statements are presented in a currency or a composite of currencies (such as the Special Drawing Rights of the International Monetary Fund) other than that of the country in which the client is domiciled.

(c)   The statements disclose that they conform to International Accounting Standards or to accounting standards used in a country or countries other than the one in which the client is domiciled.

(d)   The related auditors' report indicates that the audit conforms to International Standards on Auditing or to auditing standards of a country or countries other than the one in which the client is domiciled.

(e)   The client has its principal place of business in a country other than the one in which it is domiciled.

Although a client's financial statements may meet one or more of the preceding criteria, if the auditor decides, after following the consultation procedures set out in **Section 5:5**, 'Consultation and concurring reviews', that the presumption in the preceding paragraph is invalid for other reasons, those reasons should be indicated in the audit working papers.

13:10.2 Disclosures in international financial statements

In addition to the other disclosures that are required by the accounting policies used, the international financial statements should disclose the following:

(a)   The country whose accounting principles have been followed in the presentation of the financial statements, or that they have been prepared in accordance with International Accounting Standards, as applicable. If the principles of two or more countries are compatible in so far as they apply to the financial statements of the entity, the financial statements may refer to more than one set of accounting principles.

(b)   The currency in which the financial statements are presented.

(c)   The purpose of translating the local currency amounts into foreign currency amounts, if applicable, and (when the standards followed allow alternative translation methods) the method used.

The financial statements of a company incorporated abroad that have been prepared in accordance with United Kingdom standard accounting practice may not agree with the company's records maintained in accordance with accounting principles accepted in the country of incorporation. In such a case, the differences and their effect on the company's results and state of affairs should be summarised in the notes to the financial statements.

13:10.3 Disclosures in auditors' report

In the audit report on international financial statements, disclosure should be made of the country whose auditing standards the auditor has followed, or a statement that International Standards on Auditing were followed (*see also* **Section 13:10.8**), as applicable. If there are no significant inconsistencies among the auditing standards of two or more countries in so far as they relate to the audit, the auditor may disclose that the audit of those financial statements has been carried out in accordance with the standards of such countries.

If the client's management refuses to disclose in its financial statements the country or countries whose accounting principles it has followed, and the currency in which it has presented the financial statements, the auditor should make such disclosures in the audit report.

13:10.4 Applicability of 'true and fair' opinions

If the financial statements have been prepared in accordance with the accounting principles of a country outside the United Kingdom and the Republic of Ireland, and these accounting principles do not accord in all material respects with United Kingdom standard accounting practice, then the words 'true and fair' should not be used in the audit report. Similarly, the words 'true and fair' should not normally be used if the financial statements are not expressed in sterling. In both these circumstances the auditor should use the words 'present fairly'. An exception to this applies for companies which report under the Companies Act 1985. In this case the auditor is bound to report on the statutory accounts in true and fair terms regardless of whether the financial statements are prepared in a foreign currency. In this respect it should be noted that the Registrar of Companies will not accept financial statements prepared in accordance with the Companies Act 1985, but which are in a foreign currency, unless the rate of exchange from that currency to the pound sterling at the balance sheet date is disclosed.

13:10.5 Auditing standards

In all cases where the auditor proposes to issue an audit report, the auditor is recommended to carry out the examination of the financial statements in accordance with the auditing standards laid down in this manual.

13:10.6 Illustrative forms of report

In the two different circumstances described below, the forms of report given are appropriate.

13:10.6.1 Financial statements prepared in local currency in accordance with accounting principles generally accepted in the country of incorporation with adequate disclosure of the basis of accounting (e.g., historical cost), but not in accord with United Kingdom accounting practice

In this case, the audit was conducted in accordance with Auditing Standards in the United Kingdom.

Report of the auditors to the members of Blank SA

We have audited the financial statements on pages x to x, which have been prepared in French francs under the historical cost convention [*as modified by the revaluation of certain fixed assets*], in accordance with accounting principles generally accepted in France on the basis of the accounting policies set out on pages x to x.

Respective responsibilities of directors and auditors

As described on page x the company's directors are responsible for the preparation of financial statements. It is our responsibility to form an independent opinion, based on our audit, on those statements and to report our opinion to you.

Basis of opinion

We conducted our audit in accordance with Auditing Standards issued by the Auditing Practices Board in the United Kingdom. An audit includes examination, on a test basis, of evidence relevant to the amounts and disclosures in the financial statements. It also includes an assessment of the significant estimates and judgements made by the directors in the preparation of the financial statements, and of whether the accounting policies are appropriate to the company's circumstances, consistently applied and adequately disclosed.

We planned and performed our audit so as to obtain all the information and explanations that we considered necessary in order to provide us with sufficient evidence to give reasonable assurance that the financial statements are free from material misstatement, whether caused by fraud or by other irregularity or error. In forming our opinion we also evaluated the overall adequacy of the presentation of information in the financial statements.

Opinion

In our opinion the financial statements present fairly the state of the company's affairs at 31 December 20XX and its profit and cash flows for the year then ended.

If, however, the financial statements are expressed in sterling, the auditor must be satisfied that the basis of translation from local currency is appropriate, and that there is adequate disclosure of the basis in the notes. If so satisfied, the auditor need not refer to the currency translation in the report.

13:10.6.2 *Company incorporated overseas and a subsidiary or an associate of a company incorporated in the United Kingdom*

In this case, the notes to the financial statements should specifically indicate (a) that the statements have been prepared in accordance with United Kingdom standard accounting practice, and (b) the currency of the financial statements.

Report of the auditors to the members of Blank SA

We have audited the financial statements on pages x to x which have been prepared under the historical cost convention [*as modified by the revaluation of certain fixed assets*] and the accounting policies set out on page x.

Respective responsibilities of directors and auditors

As described on page x the company's directors are responsible for the preparation of financial statements. It is our responsibility to form an independent opinion, based on our audit, on those statements and to report our opinion to you.

Basis of opinion

We conducted our audit in accordance with Auditing Standards issued by the Auditing Practices Board in the United Kingdom. An audit includes examination, on a test basis, of evidence relevant to the amounts and disclosures in the financial statements. It also includes an assessment of the significant estimates and judgements made by the directors in the preparation of the financial statements, and of whether the accounting policies are appropriate to the company's circumstances, consistently applied and adequately disclosed.

We planned and performed our audit so as to obtain all the information and explanations that we considered necessary in order to provide us with sufficient evidence to give reasonable assurance that the financial statements are free from material misstatement, whether caused by fraud or by other irregularity or error. In forming our opinion we also evaluated the overall adequacy of the presentation of information in the financial statements.

Opinion

In our opinion the financial statements give a true and fair view of the state of the company's affairs at 31 December 20XX and of its profit and cash flows for the year then ended.

13:10.7 Overseas companies

All overseas companies (i.e., all companies that are incorporated outside Great Britain and which have an established place of business in Great Britain) must file their financial statements with the Registrar of Companies. These financial statements must contain the same information (subject to specified modifications and exemptions) as would have been required under the Companies Act 1985 if such an overseas company was in fact a company within the meaning of that Act. The modifications and exemptions for overseas companies are listed in 'The Overseas Companies (Accounts) (Modifications and Exemptions) Order 1990 (SI No. 440)'.

Where an overseas company avails itself of the exemptions, the content of the financial statements will be substantially different from the content of the financial statements of a company incorporated in Great Britain. Consequently, it is recommended that any overseas company that takes advantage of the provisions of the regulation should disclose this fact in the notes to the financial statements, regardless of whether those financial statements are audited.

Where the financial statements of an overseas company are audited, the report should state that they have been properly prepared in accordance with:

the Companies Act 1985 applicable to overseas companies.

The auditor may be unable to give a 'true and fair' report where an overseas company takes advantage of the exemptions from disclosure.

If the financial statements do not make it clear why certain information has been omitted, the report should provide an explanation in the following terms:

The company has taken advantage of the modifications and exemptions from disclosure that are set out in the Overseas Companies (Accounts) (Modifications and Exemptions) Order 1990 (SI No. 440).

This paragraph should appear before the opinion paragraph of the audit report.

13:10.8 Reporting in accordance with International Standards on Auditing

The auditor may be asked to carry out an audit of international financial statements in accordance with International Standards on Auditing issued by the International Auditing Practices Committee of the International Federation of Accountants (IFAC). Where this is the case, the auditor should ensure that the work is carried out in accordance with those standards. The form of report set out in the International Standard on Auditing, 'The auditor's report on financial statements', should be used.

If the auditor is qualifying or modifying the audit report in accordance with International Standards on Auditing, he or she should refer to the above standard or to other relevant standards – e.g., the International Standard on Auditing, 'Going concern'.

Where the auditor intends to qualify or modify the audit report in accordance with International Standards on Auditing, the consultation procedures set out in **Section 5:5**, 'Consultation and concurring reviews', should be followed.

13:11 Reports on unincorporated organisations

13:11.1 Content of reports

Audit reports on businesses and other organisations that are not companies should, unless specifically required otherwise by the terms of the appointment or by specific legislation covering the organisation concerned, such as legislation applicable to charities, generally follow the wording of reports given under the Companies Act 1985. However, the following three exceptions apply:

(a)   Reference to the Companies Act 1985 is not relevant and should therefore be omitted.

(b)   Where the client does not carry on a business for the purpose of making a profit, the reference to profit (or loss) is not appropriate. Reference might instead be made to excess of income (expenditure) over expenditure (income).

(c)   The statement of responsibilities should refer to the specific responsibilities of the body (e.g., trustees) responsible for the financial statements.

13:11.2 Forms of reports

Financial statements of unincorporated organisations that are intended to give a true and fair view must disclose all the information necessary, including a statement of accounting policies. Likewise, the accounting policies adopted will need to comply with accounting standards. In such cases, the following are examples of reports on unincorporated organisations:

13:11.2.1 Partnerships

Report of the auditors to the partners of Blank and Partners

We have audited the financial statements on pages x to x which have been prepared under the historical cost convention [*as modified by the*

revaluation of certain fixed assets] and the accounting policies set out on page x.

Respective responsibilities of partners and auditors

As described on page x the partners are responsible for the preparation of the financial statements. It is our responsibility to form an independent opinion, based on our audit, on those statements and to report our opinion to you.

Basis of opinion

We conducted our audit in accordance with Auditing Standards issued by the Auditing Practices Board. An audit includes examination, on a test basis, of evidence relevant to the amounts and disclosures in the financial statements. It also includes an assessment of the significant estimates and judgements made by the partners in the preparation of the financial statements, and of whether the accounting policies are appropriate to the partnership's circumstances, consistently applied and adequately disclosed.

We planned and performed our audit so as to obtain all the information and explanations that we considered necessary in order to provide us with sufficient evidence to give reasonable assurance that the financial statements are free from material misstatement, whether caused by fraud or by other irregularity or error. In forming our opinion we also evaluated the overall adequacy of the presentation of information in the financial statements.

Opinion

In our opinion the financial statements give a true and fair view of the state of the partnership's affairs at 31 December 20XX and of its profit and cash flows for the year then ended.

13:11.2.2 *Non-profit-making organisations*

Report of the auditors to the members of the Blank Society

We have audited the financial statements on pages x to x which have been prepared under the historical cost convention [*as modified by the revaluation of certain fixed assets*] and the accounting policies set out on page x.

Respective responsibilities of directors/members/trustees and auditors

As described on page x the Society's directors/members/trustees are responsible for the preparation of the financial statements. It is our responsibility to form an independent opinion, based on our audit, on those statements and to report our opinion to you.

Basis of opinion

We conducted our audit in accordance with Auditing Standards issued by the Auditing Practices Board. An audit includes examination, on a test basis, of evidence relevant to the amounts and disclosures in the financial statements. It also includes an assessment of the significant estimates and judgements made by the directors/members/trustees in the preparation of the financial statements, and of whether the accounting policies are appropriate to the Society's circumstances, consistently applied and adequately disclosed.

We planned and performed our audit so as to obtain all the information and explanations that we considered necessary in order to provide us with sufficient evidence to give reasonable assurance that the financial statements are free from material misstatement, whether caused by fraud or by other irregularity or error. In forming our opinion we also evaluated the overall adequacy of the presentation of information in the financial statements.

Opinion

In our opinion the financial statements give a true and fair view of the state of the Society's affairs at 31 December 20XX and of its excess of income over expenditure (expenditure over income) and cash flows for the year then ended.

13:11.3 Statement of responsibilities

Each of the example reports given above assumes that there is a statement of the responsibilities of the partners/members/trustees or other governing body in the financial statements. In some cases the auditor may need to refer to partnership agreements, trust deeds or specific legislation that applies to the organisation, in order to determine these responsibilities. Where there is an appropriate industry group within the auditor's firm, reference should also be made to guidance issued by that group.

If there is no statement of responsibilities the auditor should set out in the report a summary of the responsibilities.

13:11.4 Reports on unaudited financial statements

Auditors may be asked to prepare or to assist in preparing financial statements. Such engagements are covered by **Section 13:23**, 'Reports on reviews (other than on interim financial information), agreed-upon procedures and compilation engagements'.

The auditor may also undertake engagements to perform specific procedures which the firm has agreed with the client and to present his or her factual findings in a report. Such engagements are also discussed in **Section 13:23**.

The auditor may be asked to review financial information. Such engagements are covered either by **Section 13:22**, 'Review engagements on interim financial information', where the review is of interim financial information, or by **Section 13:23**.

13:12 Reports under s. 343(6) of the Companies Act 1985

13:12.1 Introduction

This section deals with the reports that auditors are required to make under s. 343(6) of the Companies Act 1985 in respect of the statement of transactions entered into by banking companies and parent companies of credit institutions for a director or a person connected with a director.

Banking companies and the parent companies of credit institutions are entitled under para. 2 of Part IV of Sch. 9 to the Companies Act 1985 to disclose in their financial statements aggregate amounts rather than the detailed information otherwise required by Part II of Sch. 6 (loans, quasi-loans and other dealings) in relation to a transaction or arrangement of a kind included in s. 330, or an agreement to enter into such a transaction or arrangement, to which that banking company or credit institution is a party. However, such a company is required by s. 343(4) to make a statement available at the registered office of the company (unless it is a banking company which is a wholly owned subsidiary of a company incorporated in the UK). The statement must be available for inspection by the members for not less than 15 days before the annual general meeting, and must contain the particulars of transactions, arrangements and agreements which the company would, but for para. 2 of Part IV of Sch. 9, be required to disclose in its individual or group financial statements for the financial year preceding the annual general meeting – i.e., the disclosures required by Part II of Sch. 6. There is a *de minimis* exemption if the total value of all transactions for each director does not exceed £2,000 (s. 344(1) of the Companies Act 1985).

The Act requires the auditors to examine the statement before it is made available to the members of the company. On the basis of this inspection the auditors are required to make a report to the members on that statement. This report must be annexed to the statement before the statement is made available (s. 343(6) of the Companies Act 1985).

13:12.2 Auditors' report

The auditor should state in the report whether, in his or her opinion, the statement contains the required particulars. If not, the report should include a statement that gives those particulars as far as the auditor is reasonably able to do this. The report may take the following form:

We have examined the attached statement of transactions with directors for the year ended 31 December 20XX. In our opinion the statement contains the particulars required by s. 343(4) of the Companies Act 1985.

13:13 Reports on initial financial statements required by s. 270 of the Companies Act 1985

13:13.1 Introduction

Section 270(4) of the Companies Act 1985 requires a company to prepare initial financial statements when it proposes to declare a distribution during its first accounting reference period or before it lays or files any financial statements in respect of that period. Initial financial statements of a public company (but not a private company) must be audited and filed with the Registrar.

13:13.2 Contents of a report on initial financial statements of a public company

Section 273(4) of the Companies Act 1985 requires the auditors to state in their report whether, in their opinion, the financial statements have been properly prepared. Sections 273(3) and 272(3) define 'properly prepared' to mean that the financial statements comply with s. 226 of the Companies Act 1985 (applying that section and Sch. 4 with such modifications as are necessary because the financial statements are prepared otherwise than in respect of an accounting reference period), that they have been signed, and that they give a true and fair view. In these circumstances, group financial statements need not be prepared.

The audit report must be unqualified if it is to support a distribution. Alternatively, the auditor must state in writing whether, in his or her opinion, the matter giving rise to the qualification is material for the purpose of determining whether the proposed distribution is lawful.

13:13.3 Example of an unqualified report

An example of the wording of an unqualified report is as follows:

Report of the auditors to the directors of Blank PLC under s. 273(4) of the Companies Act 1985

We have audited the financial statements of Blank PLC on pages x to x which have been prepared under the historical cost convention [*as modified by the revaluation of certain fixed assets*] and the accounting policies set out on page x.

Respective responsibilities of directors and auditors

As described on page x the company's directors are responsible for the preparation of financial statements. It is our responsibility to form an independent opinion, based on our audit, on those statements and to report our opinion to you.

Basis of opinion

We conducted our audit in accordance with Auditing Standards issued by the Auditing Practices Board. An audit includes examination, on a test basis, of evidence relevant to the amounts and disclosures in the financial statements. It also includes an assessment of the significant estimates and judgements made by the directors in the preparation of the financial statements, and of whether the accounting policies are appropriate to the company's circumstances, consistently applied and adequately disclosed.

We planned and performed our audit so as to obtain all the information and explanations that we considered necessary in order to provide us with sufficient evidence to give reasonable assurance that the financial statements are free from material misstatement, whether caused by fraud or by other irregularity or error. In forming our opinion we also evaluated the overall adequacy of the presentation of information in the financial statements.

Opinion

In our opinion, the financial statements for the period from . . . to . . . have been properly prepared in accordance with s. 273 of the Companies Act 1985.

13:13.4 Qualified report

If the audit report is qualified, the auditor should consider the matters discussed in **Section 13:18**, 'Additional reports under s. 271 of the Companies Act 1985 (distributions)'. The consultation procedures set out in **Section 5:5**, 'Consultation and concurring reviews', must be followed.

13:14 Reports on reregistration as a public company by a private or joint stock company

13:14.1 Introduction

If a private company or a joint stock company seeks to become a public company, it must make an application in the format laid down by s. 43 (private companies) or s. 685 (joint stock companies) of the Companies Act 1985.

The Companies Act 1985 requires that the application should be accompanied by a balance sheet prepared not more than seven months before the date of the application (a 'relevant balance sheet'), together with an unqualified audit report. With a private company the audit report must be made by the company's auditors. With a joint stock company, the report must be made by a person who would be qualified for appointment as auditor of a company if it were a company registered under the Companies Act.

Section 43(3)(b) of the Act requires in addition that the application should be accompanied by a written statement by the auditors of the company (or, with a joint stock company, by a person who would be qualified for appointment as auditor), stating that, in their opinion, the relevant balance sheet shows that, at the balance sheet date, the amount of the company's net assets was not less than the aggregate of its called-up share capital and undistributable reserves.

13:14.2 Contents of the audit report

An unqualified audit report on a relevant balance sheet is defined as one that states, without material qualification, the auditors' opinion that the balance sheet has been properly prepared in accordance with the Companies Act 1985. If the balance sheet was not prepared as at the end of the company's accounting reference period, an unqualified report is defined as one that states, without material qualification, the auditors' opinion that the balance sheet has been properly prepared in accordance with the provisions of the Act that would have applied if it had been so prepared. A qualification is treated as being not material if the person making the report states in the report that the matter that has given rise to the qualification is not material for the purpose of determining by reference to the company's balance sheet whether, at the balance sheet date, the amount of the company's net assets was not less than the aggregate of its called-up share capital and undistributable reserves.

13:14.3 Example of an audit report prepared other than in respect of the normal accounting reference period

Where a balance sheet is prepared as part of the financial statements for an accounting reference period, then the audit report on those financial statements will normally be sufficient. However, where a balance sheet is prepared other than in respect of the accounting reference period (e.g., because the accounting reference period ends more than seven months before the date of the application), then the form of the report on the balance sheet should be as follows:

Report of the auditors to the directors of Blank Limited

We have audited the balance sheet and related notes on pages x to x which have been prepared under the historical cost convention [*as modified by the revaluation of certain fixed assets*] and the accounting policies set out on page x.

Respective responsibilities of directors and auditors

As described on page x the company's directors are responsible for the preparation of the balance sheet. It is our responsibility to form an independent opinion, based on our audit, on the balance sheet and to report our opinion to you.

Basis of opinion

We conducted our audit in accordance with Auditing Standards issued by the Auditing Practices Board. An audit includes examination, on a test basis, of evidence relevant to the amounts and disclosures in the balance sheet. It also includes an assessment of the significant estimates and judgements made by the directors in the preparation of the balance sheet, and of whether the accounting policies are appropriate to the company's circumstances, consistently applied and adequately disclosed.

We planned and performed our audit so as to obtain all the information and explanations that we considered necessary in order to provide us with sufficient evidence to give reasonable assurance that the balance sheet is free from material misstatement, whether caused by fraud or by other irregularity or error. In forming our opinion we also evaluated the overall adequacy of the presentation of information in the balance sheet.

Opinion

In our opinion the balance sheet and related notes give a true and fair view of the state of the company's affairs at 31 December 20XX and have been properly prepared in accordance with the provisions of the Companies Act 1985 which would have applied had the balance sheet been prepared for a financial year of the company.

13:14.4 Example of a written statement under s. 43(3)(b)

The wording of a written statement should read as set out below. The example assumes that the balance sheet referred to was included in the last annual financial statements, but if the auditor is referring to a balance sheet other than in respect of an accounting reference period the wording of the first paragraph should be amended to delete reference to the financial statements for the year.

Auditors' statement to the directors of Blank Limited under s. 43(3)(b) (or under s. 685(4)(b)) of the Companies Act 1985

We have examined the balance sheet of Blank Limited at 31 December 20XX which has been prepared under the historical cost convention [*as modified by the revaluation of certain fixed assets*] and the accounting policies set out on page x, and which formed part of the financial statements for the year then ended audited by us/ABC and Co.

Basis of opinion

The scope of our work for the purpose of this statement was limited to an examination of the relationship between the company's net assets and its called-up share capital and undistributable reserves as stated in the audited balance sheet in connection with the company's proposed re-registration as a public company.

Opinion

In our opinion the balance sheet shows that at 31 December 20XX the amount of the company's net assets was not less than the aggregate of its called-up share capital and undistributable reserves.

If the audit report on the relevant balance sheet was qualified and the auditor considers that the qualification was not material for the purposes of the statement, the following paragraph should be included:

We audited the financial statements of Blank Limited for the year ended 31 December 20XX in accordance with Auditing Standards issued by the Auditing Practices Board and expressed a qualified opinion thereon. The matter giving rise to our qualification is not material for determining by reference to the balance sheet at 31 December 20XX whether at that date the net assets of the company were not less than the aggregate of its called-up share capital and undistributable reserves.

13:14.5 Change of auditors

If the auditors have recently been appointed, they can rely on the balance sheet audited by their predecessor as a basis for the statement, unless the audit report on the balance sheet was qualified. The new auditors should state in their report the name of the auditors of the relevant balance sheet. If the audit report signed by the predecessor auditors was qualified, the new auditors will have to ascertain the reasons for the qualification and discuss the reasons with the previous auditors. If, having discussed the reasons, and carried out any additional work considered necessary, the new auditors are satisfied that the matter giving rise to the qualification is not material for the purpose of their report, they may adopt wording similar to that set out in **Section 13:14.4**, last paragraph. In this report the auditor should explain that the audit of the balance sheet was carried out by another firm, but that the subject of the qualification is not material for the purpose of determining whether net assets are not less than the aggregate of called-up share capital and undistributable reserves.

13:14.6 Qualified report or statement

If the auditor qualifies the report or statement, the matters discussed in **Section 13:18**, 'Additional reports under s. 271 of the Companies Act 1985 (distributions)', are relevant. Where the report or statement is qualified, or includes reference to fundamental uncertainties, the consultation procedures set out in **Section 5:5**, 'Consultation and concurring reviews', must be followed.

13:15 Unqualified reports to management on financial statements not prepared under s. 226 of the Companies Act 1985

13:15.1 Introduction

Section 226 of the Companies Act 1985 requires the directors of every company to prepare financial statements for each financial year. Section 242 requires the directors to deliver these financial statements to the Registrar of Companies.

Management will sometimes request the auditor to carry out an audit for a period other than an accounting reference period or to adjust the company's financial statements in accordance with a formula. Such requests will normally be connected with:

(a)   changes in management;

(b)   changes in ownership;

(c)   profit or net asset warranties;

(d)   accounting problems;

(e)   fraud;

(f)   financial statements prepared in anticipation of a flotation.

In some cases the work requested by management will not constitute a full audit of financial statements but will be an engagement to perform specific procedures. In such cases reference should be made to **Section 13:23**, 'Reports on reviews (other than on interim financial information), agreed-upon procedures and compilation engagements'.

13:15.2 Contents of an audit report

Any report that the auditor makes to management will normally be either a report on the truth and fairness of the financial statements or a report for the purposes of an agreement.

If the auditor is to report on truth and fairness, the financial statements must include a profit and loss account, a balance sheet and notes of accounting policies. All financial statements intended to give a true and fair view must comply with accounting standards and must therefore contain a cash flow statement (unless exempt under FRS 1) and a statement of total recognised gains and losses (or a note that there are no such gains and losses other than profit or loss for the year). However, the financial statements do not necessarily have to comply with all of the disclosure requirements of the Companies Act. It is not possible to be more specific as to the precise disclosures required in order that the financial statements give a true and fair view. This will depend upon the circumstances of each individual situation.

If the auditor is to report for the purposes of an agreement, he or she should report that the documents present information fairly, and are appropriate for the purposes of the agreement. The contents of the statements on which the auditor reports will depend on the wording of the agreement, and they may involve only very limited disclosure of information.

13:15.3 Examples of audit reports

13:15.3.1 True and fair view report

An example of a report expressed in true and fair view terms is set out below:

Report of the auditors to the directors of Blank PLC

We have audited the financial statements on pages x to x which have been prepared under the historical cost convention [*as modified by the revaluation of certain fixed assets*] and the accounting policies set out on page x.

These financial statements have not been prepared under s. 226 of the Companies Act 1985 and were prepared solely for the purposes of management.

Respective responsibilities of directors and auditors

As described on page x the company's directors are responsible for the preparation of financial statements. It is our responsibility to form an independent opinion, based on our audit, on those statements and to report our opinion to you.

Basis of opinion

We conducted our audit in accordance with Auditing Standards issued by the Auditing Practices Board. An audit includes examination, on a test basis, of evidence relevant to the amounts and disclosures in the financial statements. It also includes an assessment of the significant estimates and judgements made by the directors in the preparation of the financial statements, and of whether the accounting policies are appropriate to the company's circumstances, consistently applied and adequately disclosed.

We planned and performed our audit so as to obtain all the information and explanations that we considered necessary in order to provide us with sufficient evidence to give reasonable assurance that the financial statements are free from material misstatement, whether caused by fraud or by other irregularity or error. In forming our opinion we also evaluated the overall adequacy of the presentation of information in the financial statements.

Opinion

In our opinion, the financial statements give a true and fair view of the state

of the company's affairs at 30 September 20XX and of its profit and cash flows for the period from 21 June 20XX to 30 September 20XX.

The first note to the financial statements should state:

These financial statements are not prepared under s. 226 of the Companies Act 1985. The financial statements have been prepared on the historical cost basis, solely for the purposes of management.

13:15.3.2 Report for the purposes of an agreement

An example of a report for the purposes of an agreement between A Plc and B is set out below:

Report of the auditors of Blank PLC to A PLC and B

We have audited Blank PLC's statements of operating profit and adjusted operating profit on pages x and x which have been prepared under the historical cost convention [*as modified by the revaluation of certain fixed assets*] and the accounting policies set out on page x.

These statements have been prepared solely for the purposes of the agreement dated 21 July 20XX between A PLC and B. They have not been prepared under s. 226 of the Companies Act 1985 and accordingly they do not disclose all the information that would be necessary for them to show a true and fair view.

Respective responsibilities of directors and auditors

As described on page x the company's directors are responsible for the preparation of the statements. It is our responsibility to form an independent opinion, based on our audit, on the statements and to report our opinion to you.

Basis of opinion

We conducted our audit in accordance with Auditing Standards issued by the Auditing Practices Board. An audit includes examination, on a test basis, of evidence relevant to the amounts and disclosures in the statements. It also includes an assessment of the significant estimates and judgements made by the directors in the preparation of the statements, and of whether the accounting policies are appropriate to the company's circumstances, consistently applied and adequately disclosed.

We planned and performed our audit so as to obtain all the information and explanations that we considered necessary in order to provide us with sufficient evidence to give reasonable assurance that the statements are free from material misstatement, whether caused by fraud or by other irregularity or error. In forming our opinion we also evaluated the overall adequacy of the presentation of information in the statements.

Opinion

In our opinion:

(a) **The statement of operating profit fairly presents, for the purpose of the aforementioned agreement, the operating profit for the year ended 1 August 20XX.**

(b) **The adjusted operating profit of £xxx, being less than the warranted profit, is appropriate for establishing the deficit for the purpose of paragraph x of the aforementioned agreement.**

13:16 Qualified and modified reports to the members of limited companies and other organisations in Great Britain

13:16.1 Introduction

This Manual section outlines some of the circumstances in which the auditor may have either to modify or to qualify the normal audit report on companies' financial statements under the Companies Act 1985 or on unincorporated organisations. It also gives guidance on drafting such reports. In this context a modified report is one where the opinion is unqualified but the 'Basis of opinion' section is expanded to include reference to the auditor's review of disclosures relating to a fundamental uncertainty or to include reference to other disclosures – e.g., loans to directors, to which the auditor wishes to draw the readers' attention.

It is not possible to foresee, and thereby discuss in this section, all of the circumstances in which the auditor may need either to modify or to qualify the report. The engagement partner must consider the facts of each case, and decide on the form of report and follow the procedures set out in **Section 5:5**, 'Consultation and concurring reviews'. The auditor must consider proposals to repeat a qualification used in the previous year in the light of any changes in the circumstances, and must again follow the consultation procedures.

In any case where a situation may arise that could require the auditor to qualify the report, the matter must be discussed with the client so that the client has the opportunity either to rectify the matter or to satisfy the auditor in some other way. Likewise, the client must be given the opportunity to review the wording of the audit report. Where the subject matter of the report is particularly contentious or includes references to illegal or potentially illegal acts, the auditor should also consider whether the wording should be reviewed by the firm's legal advisers. It must be remembered that the auditor is solely responsible for the content of the report.

The financial statements and the auditors' report may be examined not only by the shareholders but also by professional advisers, prospective shareholders and their advisers, bankers, creditors and inspectors of taxes. Some of these readers may be skilled in interpreting financial statements, but whoever they may be, or whatever skills they may have, they are entitled to an auditors' report written in clear and unequivocal terms. Accordingly, the auditor should ensure that the qualifications or modifications in reports are clear and concise so that any person reading them will be in no doubt as to their meaning. They must be free of technical jargon.

13:16.2 Principles

The following principles should be observed:

(a)   The auditor must clearly identify, in the report, the financial statements on which he or she is reporting. Financial statements comprise the balance sheet, profit and loss account, statements of cash flows and total recognised gains and losses, notes and other statements and explanatory material.

(b)   The report should, wherever practicable, be complete in itself. It is normally unsatisfactory to include, in the report, references to either notes to the financial statements or paragraphs in the directors' report (with the exception of reference to the directors' responsibility statement) without also describing the basic circumstances and their effect on the financial statements. Where it would be inappropriate to repeat a lengthy note, the auditor should summarise it and give sufficient information to ensure that the meaning of the report is clear.

(c)   The wording must be specific as to the matters concerned. The auditor should describe the matters, quantify them if practicable and, if relevant, relate them to recognisable items in the financial statements.

(d)   The auditor must follow any matters to which he or she refers with a clear indication of how they affect the audit opinion. It is unsatisfactory to include, in the report, references to such matters as the basis of preparation of the financial statements, unsatisfactory items in the financial statements and inadequate records or inadequate explanations, without also giving an indication of the extent to which the matters referred to affect the opinion on the financial statements.

(e)   The auditor must, as far as possible, make clear the monetary effect of the matters on which the report has been qualified.

(f)   The auditor must comply with the specific requirements of the Companies Act 1985 and the London Stock Exchange as to statements to be included in the audit report.

13:16.3 Qualified reports

The auditor should qualify the audit report where the matters at issue are material, but should not qualify his or her opinion if matters are not material.

Materiality is defined in SAS 600 as follows:

> *A matter is material if its omission or misstatement would reasonably influence the decisions of a user of the financial statements. Materiality may be considered*

*in the context of the financial statements as a whole, any individual primary
statement within the financial statements or individual items included in them.*

Materiality is recognised in law in that para. 86 of Sch. 4 and para. 5 of Sch. 4A to the
Companies Act 1985 state:

*Amounts which in the particular context of any provision of this Schedule are not
material may be disregarded for the purposes of that provision.*

Materiality is not capable of general mathematical definition as it has both qualitative and
quantitative aspects.

The basic reasons for qualifying audit reports are dealt with in SAS 600. In summary,
they are as follows:

(a)　Where the auditor is not able either to carry out or to complete those audit
procedures that he or she regards as essential, or where the scope of the examination is
limited so that the auditor is prevented from obtaining sufficient evidence to express an
unqualified opinion. In other words, the auditor has not received all of the information and
explanations that were considered necessary for the purpose of the audit.

(b)　When, in the opinion of the auditor, the financial statements are not prepared in
accordance with recognised accounting principles and as a result do not give a true and
fair view. This may be because:

(i)　the method of computing balance sheet or profit and loss items is, in the
opinion of the auditor, either inappropriate or incorrect;

(ii)　the accounting principles applied are inconsistent with those of the previous
year, and no explanation is given. Also, the effect is not quantified either in a
note or on the face of the financial statements;

(iii)　the financial statements do not disclose information which in the opinion of the
auditor is necessary in order to give a true and fair view;

(iv)　information is given either in a note to the financial statements or in the
directors' report or other information issued with the financial statements that
materially alters the view the financial statements otherwise give (*see* **Section
13:19,** 'Qualified reports on information contained in the directors' report and
on other information in documents containing audited financial statements').

(c)　When in the opinion of the auditor:

(i)　proper accounting records have not been kept in accordance with s. 221 of the
Companies Act 1985;

(ii)　proper returns, adequate for the purposes of the audit, have not been received
from branches not visited by the auditor;

(iii)　the balance sheet and (unless it is framed as a consolidated profit and loss
account) the profit and loss account are not in agreement with the accounting
records and the returns.

(d)   When the financial statements have not been properly prepared in accordance with the disclosure and other requirements of the Companies Act 1985 or other relevant legislation.

The nature of the circumstances that give rise to the auditor qualifying his or her opinion will generally fall into one of the following categories:

(a)   Where there is a limitation on the scope of the examination that prevents the auditor from forming an opinion on a matter, or on the financial statements as a whole.

(b)   Where the auditor disagrees with the treatment or disclosure of a matter in the financial statements.

Each of these categories gives rise to alternative forms of qualification depending upon whether the auditor considers that the subject matter of the limitation on scope or the disagreement is so material or pervasive that the auditor:

(a)   has not been able to obtain sufficient evidence to support and accordingly to express an opinion on the financial statements (in the case of a limitation on scope); or

(b)   concludes that the financial statements are seriously misleading (in the case of a disagreement).

13:16.3.1 Limitations on scope

SAS 600 states:

> *When there has been a limitation on the scope of the auditors' work that prevents them from obtaining sufficient evidence to express an unqualified opinion*
>
> *(a)   the auditors' report should include a description of the factors leading to the limitation in the opinion section of their report;*
>
> *(b)   the auditors should issue a disclaimer of opinion when the possible effect of a limitation on scope is so material or pervasive that they are unable to express an opinion on the financial statements;*
>
> *(c)   a qualified opinion should be issued when the effect of the limitation is not so material or pervasive as to require a disclaimer, and the wording of the opinion should indicate that it is qualified as to the possible adjustments to the financial statements that might have been determined to be necessary had the limitation not existed. (SAS 600.7)*

Where there has been a limitation on scope the auditor must include in the audit report a description of the factors leading to the limitation. Although SAS 600 states that this should be in the 'Opinion' section of the report, in practice this description should be given in the 'Basis of opinion' section of the report and reference made to it in the

'Opinion' section. This is the practice adopted in the examples given in SAS 600. Where this is done, the auditor should also amend the standard wording of the 'Basis of opinion' section by changing the words 'We planned and performed our audit . . . ' to 'We planned our audit . . . ' (*see* example reports in **Appendix B – Section 13:16.15**).

In considering whether a limitation on scope results in a lack of evidence necessary to form an opinion the auditor should assess:

(a) The quantity and type of evidence that may reasonably be expected to be available to support a particular figure or disclosure in the financial statements.

(b) The possible effect on the financial statements of the matter for which insufficient evidence is available. Where the auditor considers that the possible effect is material to the financial statements, he or she should issue a qualified opinion.

The auditor must describe the factors that have led to a limitation on the scope of work in the report. The description should be in the 'Basis of opinion' section of the report (*see* above) and should be sufficient to enable the reader to understand the factors and to distinguish between the following limitations:

(a) Those that are imposed upon the auditor – e.g., where certain of the accounting records are not made available or where the directors prevent the auditor from carrying out audit procedures that are considered necessary to enable him or her to form an opinion.

(b) Those that are outside the control of the directors or the auditor – e.g., where the auditors are appointed after the year-end and are thus unable to attend the company's stocktake and there are no alternative audit procedures that can be adopted to verify the existence of stocks.

13:16.3.2 Disclaimer of opinion

Where a limitation on scope is so material or pervasive that the auditor is unable to obtain sufficient evidence to support, and accordingly to express an opinion on the financial statements, the auditor must disclaim an opinion on the financial statements.

SAS 601 'Imposed limitation of audit scope' outlines the additional steps an auditor should take in circumstances where the directors impose a limitation on the scope of the audit work such that the auditor is likely to issue a disclaimer of opinion in the financial statements. In this situation, the auditor should first request the removal of the limitation. If the limitation is not removed, the auditor should consider resigning from the audit engagement.

13:16.3.3 'Except for' opinion

Where a limitation on scope is not so significant as to require a disclaimer the auditor must issue an opinion that is qualified by stating that the financial statements give a true and fair view except for the effects of any adjustments that might have been found necessary had the limitation not affected the evidence available.

13:16.3.4 Disagreements

SAS 600 states:

> *Where the auditors disagree with the accounting treatment or disclosure of a matter in the financial statements, and in the auditors' opinion the effect of that disagreement is material to the financial statements*
>
> *(a) the auditors should include in the opinion section of their report*
>
>> *(i) a description of all substantive factors giving rise to the disagreement;*
>>
>> *(ii) their implications for the financial statements;*
>>
>> *(iii) whenever practicable, a quantification of the effect on the financial statements;*
>
> *(b) when the auditors conclude that the effect of the matter giving rise to disagreement is so material or pervasive that the financial statements are seriously misleading, they should issue an adverse opinion;*
>
> *(c) in the case of other material disagreements, the auditors should issue a qualified opinion indicating that it is expressed except for the effects of the matter giving rise to the disagreement.* (SAS 600.8)

Where the auditor disagrees with an accounting treatment or disclosure in the financial statements, and considers that the effect of the disagreement is material to the financial statements the auditor must issue a qualified opinion.

The auditor's opinion must clearly describe all of the substantive factors giving rise to the disagreement and should explain the implications for the financial statements. Wherever practicable the auditor must quantify the effect of the disagreement on the financial statements.

13:16.3.5 Adverse opinion

Where a disagreement is so material or pervasive that the auditor concludes that the financial statements are seriously misleading the auditor must express an adverse opinion by stating that the financial statements do not give a true and fair view.

13:16.3.6 'Except for' opinion

Where a disagreement is not so significant as to require an adverse opinion, the auditor must issue an opinion that is qualified by stating that the financial statements give a true and fair view except for the effects of the matter giving rise to the disagreement.

13:16.4 Forms of qualification

The forms of qualification that auditors should use in different circumstances are shown in **Table 13.1**.

Table 13.1 *Forms of qualification*

Nature of circumstances	Qualification	Reason
Limitation on scope	Disclaimer of opinion	Possible effect of the limitation is so material or pervasive that the auditor cannot express an opinion.
Limitation on scope	'Except for' opinion	Possible effect of the limitation is material but not so material or pervasive that the auditor cannot express an opinion.
Disagreement	Adverse opinion	The effect of the matter giving rise to the disagreement is so material or pervasive that the financial statements are seriously misleading.
Disagreement	'Except for' opinion	The effect of the matter giving rise to the disagreement is material but not so material or pervasive that the financial statements are seriously misleading.

In a limitation on scope disclaimer of opinion the auditor states that he or she is unable to form an opinion as to whether the financial statements give a true and fair view. The auditor must also state that he or she has not obtained all the information and explanations that were considered necessary for the purpose of the audit.

In a limitation on scope 'except for' opinion the auditor states that, except for any adjustments that might have been found to be necessary had the auditor been able to obtain sufficient evidence, the financial statements give a true and fair view. The auditor must also state that he or she has not obtained all the information and explanations that were considered necessary for the purpose of the audit.

In an adverse opinion the auditor states that in his or her opinion the financial statements do not give a true and fair view.

In a disagreement 'except for' opinion the auditor expresses an adverse opinion on a particular matter within the financial statements, but not on the financial statements as a whole.

The disclaimer of opinion and the adverse opinion are the extreme forms of the two main categories of qualification and should be used as measures of last resort.

13:16.5 Inherent uncertainties

SAS 600 states:

(a) In forming their opinion on financial statements, auditors should consider whether the view given by the financial statements could be affected by inherent uncertainties which, in their opinion, are fundamental.

(b) When an inherent uncertainty exists which

(i) in the auditors' opinion is fundamental, and

(ii) is adequately accounted for and disclosed in the financial statements,

the auditors should include an explanatory paragraph referring to the fundamental uncertainty in the section of their report setting out the basis of their opinion.

(c) When adding an explanatory paragraph, auditors should use words which clearly indicate that their opinion on the financial statements is not qualified in respect of its contents. (SAS 600.6)

The auditor must consider the nature and disclosure in the financial statements of inherent uncertainties that may affect the financial statements. An inherent uncertainty is defined in SAS 600 as:

an uncertainty whose resolution is dependent upon uncertain future events outside the control of the reporting entity's directors at the date the financial statements are approved.

Inherent uncertainties about the outcome of future events frequently affect a wide range of components of financial statements. An example is where development expenditure on a new product is capitalised in accordance with SSAP 13. In such a case capitalisation is permitted provided that certain conditions that reduce the inherent uncertainty are satisfied. Similarly, there is always inherent uncertainty in the amounts provided for deferred taxation under the partial provision basis set out in SSAP 15.

As part of the audit, the auditor should assess whether there is sufficient evidence to support the directors' analysis of relevant existing conditions, including uncertainties about future events and their effect on financial statements.

Provided that the auditor can obtain sufficient evidence to support the directors' analysis and he or she agrees that the analysis is reasonable, the inherent uncertainty does not give rise to a limitation on the scope of the audit work.

Where, however, evidence exists or could reasonably be expected to exist concerning an inherent uncertainty, and that evidence is not available to the auditor, the scope of the work will be limited and the auditor must issue a qualified opinion (*see* **Sections 13:16.3.1** to **13:16.3.6**).

In addition, the auditor should consider the adequacy of the accounting treatment of inherent uncertainties. This involves consideration of:

(a)   The appropriateness of accounting policies dealing with uncertain matters.

(b)   The reasonableness of the estimates included in the financial statements in respect of inherent uncertainties.

(c)   The adequacy of disclosure.

If the auditor disagrees with any of these matters in respect of an inherent uncertainty and the effect of the disagreement is material, the auditor must issue a qualified opinion.

If the auditor is satisfied as to the adequacy of the accounting treatment, estimate and disclosure of an inherent uncertainty, the auditor should make no reference in the audit report unless the inherent uncertainty is fundamental.

13:16.6 Fundamental uncertainties

A fundamental uncertainty is defined in SAS 600 as an inherent uncertainty the magnitude of whose potential impact is so great that, without clear disclosure of the nature and implications of the uncertainty, the view given by the financial statements would be seriously misleading.

In assessing whether an inherent uncertainty is fundamental the auditor should consider:

(a)   The risk that the estimate included in the financial statements may be subject to change.

(b)   The range of possible outcomes.

(c)   The consequences of those outcomes on the view shown in the financial statements.

The auditor should regard inherent uncertainties as fundamental when they involve a significant level of concern about the validity of the going concern basis or other matters whose potential effect on the financial statements is unusually great. A common example of a fundamental uncertainty is the outcome of major litigation. Other examples might include significant uncertainty about the recoverability of capitalised development expenditure, about whether provisions made in the financial statements are adequate or excessive or about the values of stock or fixed assets.

Although the question of whether an inherent uncertainty is fundamental must be a matter of judgement, the auditor should usually consider the following criteria in making the judgement:

(a)   The amounts should be material.

(b)   The uncertainty should be so great that the auditor is not able to form an opinion on the matter.

(c)   The uncertainty need not be pervasive – i.e., it need not be such that the auditor cannot form an opinion on the financial statements as a whole. It is sufficient that the auditor is unable to form an opinion on a particular matter, provided that the matter is material.

13:16.6.1 Disclosure in financial statements

Where the auditor concludes that an inherent uncertainty is fundamental the auditor must consider the disclosure of that uncertainty in the financial statements. Where the fundamental uncertainty relates to going concern, reference should be made to **Sections 13:16.7** to **13:16.7.7**. The next paragraph and **Sections 13:16.6.2** and **13:16.6.3** deal with fundamental uncertainties other than those relating to going concern.

The auditor must ensure that the disclosure gives full particulars of the matter giving rise to the uncertainty, with quantification where practicable of the possible effects on the financial statements. An example of disclosure of a fundamental uncertainty relating to litigation is given in **Appendix B, Example 2** – *see* **Section 13:16.15.2**.

13:16.6.2 Audit report – explanatory paragraph

If the auditor considers that the disclosure is adequate, he or she should issue an unqualified opinion. However, the auditor must include in the 'Basis of opinion' section of the audit report an explanatory paragraph. In this paragraph the auditor should explain that in forming an audit opinion the adequacy of the disclosures concerning the possible outcome of the uncertainty were considered, and the auditor should describe the uncertainty, the possible outcome and its effect and finally make clear that the audit opinion is unqualified.

13:16.6.3 Audit report – qualifications

If the auditor considers that the disclosure in the financial statements relating to the fundamental uncertainty is inadequate or misleading, he or she must qualify the audit opinion. The qualification is 'except for' the effect of the matter giving rise to the disagreement or 'not true and fair' if the auditor considers that the effect of the matter is so material or pervasive that the financial statements are seriously misleading (*see* **Section 13:16.4**).

If the scope of the auditor's work has been limited such that he or she is unable to assess the adequacy of the accounting treatment and disclosure of a fundamental uncertainty, the auditor must qualify the report. The qualification is 'except for' any adjustments that might have been found to be necessary had the auditor been able to obtain sufficient evidence, or a 'disclaimer of opinion' if the auditor considers that the possible effect of the limitation is so material or pervasive that he or she cannot express an opinion (*see* **Section 13:16.4**).

13:16.7 Going concern

Where a fundamental uncertainty relates to going concern the auditor should have regard to SAS 130, 'The going concern basis in financial statements'. This standard is broadly consistent with the guidance contained in SAS 600. In some areas, however, there are minor differences which are explained below.

13:16.7.1 Disclosure

SAS 130 includes the following auditing standard:

> *Where the auditors consider that there is a significant level of concern about the entity's ability to continue as a going concern, but do not disagree with the preparation of the financial statements on the going concern basis, they should include an explanatory paragraph when setting out the basis of their opinion. They should not qualify their opinion on these grounds alone, provided the disclosures in the financial statements of the matters giving rise to the concern are adequate for the financial statements to give a true and fair view. (SAS 130.6)*

While making it plain that its guidance does not constitute an accounting standard, SAS 130 indicates that the matters that should be disclosed in the financial statements where there is significant concern include:

(a)   A statement that the financial statements have been prepared on the going concern basis.

(b)   A statement of the pertinent facts.

(c)   The nature of the concern.

(d)   A statement of the assumptions adopted by the directors, which should be clearly distinguishable from the pertinent facts.

(e)   Where appropriate and practicable, a statement regarding the directors' plans for resolving the matters giving rise to the concern.

(f)   Details of any relevant actions by the directors.

If the going concern basis is not appropriate a statement of the effects should also normally be given (*see* **Section 13:16.7.2.2**).

SAS 130 provides the following list of indications that may suggest that there is significant uncertainty about the appropriateness of the going concern basis. Where any of these indications are present, they would be pertinent facts that should be considered for disclosure where there is a significant level of concern about the client's ability to continue as a going concern:

Financial

- an excess of liabilities over assets;
- net current liabilities;
- necessary borrowing facilities have not been agreed;.
- default on terms of loan agreements, and potential breaches of covenant (or of the client's borrowing powers in its Articles);
- significant liquidity or cash flow problems;

- major losses or cash flow problems which have arisen since the balance sheet date and which threaten the client's continued existence;
- substantial sales of fixed assets not intended to be replaced;
- major restructuring of debt;
- denial of (or reduction in) normal terms of trade credit by suppliers;
- major debt repayment falling due when refinancing is necessary to the client's continued existence;
- inability to pay debts as they fall due;

Operational

- fundamental changes in the market or technology to which the client is unable to adapt adequately;
- externally forced reductions in operations (e.g., as a result of legislation or regulatory action);
- loss of key management or staff, labour difficulties or excessive dependence on a few product lines where the market is depressed;
- loss of key suppliers or customers or technical developments which render a key product obsolete;

Other

- major litigation in which an adverse judgement would imperil the client's continued existence;
- issues which involve a range of possible outcomes so wide that an unfavourable result could affect the appropriateness of the going concern basis.

Clearly, not all of the above factors will be present in each situation. Equally, in other situations there may be other facts which need disclosure and which are not included in the list above. Where there is any doubt about the matters that need to be disclosed in individual cases, consultation procedures set out in **Section 5:5**, 'Consultation and concurring reviews', should be followed.

13:16.7.2 *Reporting – explanatory paragraphs*

The standard reproduced in **Section 13:16.7.1** (first paragraph) requires the auditor to include an explanatory paragraph in the 'Basis of opinion' section of the report, where the auditor considers that there is a significant uncertainty about the entity's ability to continue as a going concern, but the auditor does not disagree with that basis and is satisfied that the disclosure in the financial statements is adequate. In this regard SAS 130 uses the term 'significant level of concern', whereas SAS 600 uses the term 'fundamental uncertainty'. As 'significant level of concern' is not defined in SAS 130, reference should be made to the definition of 'fundamental uncertainty' in SAS 600 when determining the meaning of 'significant level of concern'. As mentioned in **Section 13:16.6** (first paragraph), SAS 600 defines 'fundamental uncertainty' as an inherent uncertainty that becomes fundamental when the magnitude of its potential impact is so great that, without clear disclosure of the nature and implications of the uncertainty, the view given by the financial statements would be seriously misleading.

SAS 600 includes an example of a report with an explanatory paragraph given in the above circumstances. Although the examples in SAS 130 differ in minor respects, the example in SAS 600 and the examples in **Appendix B** (*see* **Section 13:16.15**) are consistent with the standard reproduced in **Section 13:16.7.1** (first paragraph). *See* **Appendix B, Examples 5 and 7 (Sections 13:16.15.6 and 13:16.15.8).**

The minor differences between the examples in SAS 130 and the examples in SAS 600 and this section concern:

(a)   The heading of the explanatory paragraph.

(b)   Disclosure of the effects if the going concern basis is not valid.

(c)   References to the note describing the uncertainty.

(d)   The absence of reference to 'fundamental uncertainty' in the SAS 130 examples.

13:16.7.2.1 The heading of the explanatory paragraph

In the SAS 600 example the heading of the explanatory paragraph is 'Fundamental uncertainty'. In the SAS 130 examples it is 'Going concern'. Although either may be used, a heading referring to 'Going concern' should also preferably refer to the uncertainty by using words such as 'Uncertainty – going concern'. The heading used should not give a misleading impression of the importance of the paragraph.

13:16.7.2.2 Disclosure of the effects if the going concern basis were not valid

The guidance notes to SAS 130 indicate that neither the explanatory paragraph nor the disclosure in the financial statements need refer to the possible effects if the going concern basis were not valid. This may be unhelpful to a reader and inconsistent with the treatment of other fundamental uncertainties under SAS 600 and so reference should preferably be made to the potential effects. The examples in **Appendix B** – *see* **Section 13:16.15** do this by including, in the specimen note disclosure, wording such as:

> **If the company were unable to continue in operational existence for the foreseeable future, adjustments would have to be made to reduce the balance sheet values of assets to their recoverable amounts, to provide for further liabilities that might arise, and to reclassify fixed assets and long-term liabilities as current assets and liabilities.**

In the explanatory paragraph there is wording as follows:

> **The financial statements do not include any adjustments that would result from a failure to obtain funding.**

The above wording should be used, suitably adapted to the particular circumstances of the client.

13:16.7.2.3 Reference to the financial statements note

In the SAS 130 examples references to the financial statements note that describes the uncertainty relating to going concern are accompanied by the words, 'In view of the significance of this uncertainty we consider that it should be drawn to your attention but our opinion is not qualified in this respect.' In contrast, the examples in SAS 600 and **Examples 5** and **7** in **Appendix B** – *see* **Sections 13:16.15.6** and **13.16.15.8** – specifically refer to the 'fundamental' uncertainty by saying, 'Details of the circumstances relating to this fundamental uncertainty are described in note x. Our opinion is not qualified in this respect.'

13:16.7.2.4 Reference to 'fundamental uncertainty'

Either style may be adopted, but if the SAS 130 approach is used the wording should be adapted to refer to the uncertainty as a 'fundamental' uncertainty. This ensures that the reader is in no doubt as to the seriousness of the situation. The approach is also consistent with the view that the potential effects of the uncertainty should also be described.

An example of an SAS 130 style explanatory paragraph, modified to include the recommendations in **Sections 13:16.7.2.1** to **13:16.7.2.4** (first paragraph), is included as **Example 6** in **Appendix B** (*see* **Section 13:16.15.7**).

13:16.7.3 Reporting – period covered by directors' assessment

SAS 130 contains a standard which relates to the period to which the directors have paid particular attention in assessing going concern. The standard states:

> *If the period to which the directors have paid particular attention in assessing going concern is less than one year from the date of approval of the financial statements, and the directors have not disclosed that fact, the auditors should do so within the section of their report setting out the basis of their opinion, unless the fact is clear from any other references in their report. They should not qualify their opinion on the financial statements on these grounds alone.* (SAS 130.7)

Although SAS 130 recognises that the directors pay 'particular attention' to a future period, it does not provide guidance on what this means. Some major areas in which the auditor might expect the directors to have carried out procedures in paying 'particular attention' to the future period are as follows:

(a) **Forecasts and budgets**: As a minimum these are likely to be prepared to cover the period to the next balance sheet date, but they may be prepared on a rolling basis for at least 12 months ahead. Where they do not cover one year from the date of approval of the financial statements the auditor should consider whether other medium or long-term plans provide sufficient detail.

(b) **Borrowing requirements**: Facilities should be reviewed and compared with cash flow forecasts.

(c) **Liability management**: Financial plans should indicate adequate matching of projected cash inflows with known cash outflows including, e.g., loan repayments, tax payments and other commitments which may be recorded off-balance sheet.

(d) **Contingent liabilities**: The directors should consider the company's exposure to liabilities arising from, e.g., legal proceedings, guarantees and product liability.

(e) **Products and markets**: Directors should consider the size and strength of their main product markets, the market share and whether economic, political or other factors might result in change.

(f) **Financial risk management**: Risks arising from, e.g., exposure to movements in foreign currency rates should be considered.

(g) **Other factors** specific to the client's circumstances.

Appendix 3 to SAS 130 envisages four situations arising and sets out the appropriate action to be taken by the auditors, as follows:

(a) The auditor concludes that there is a significant level of concern regarding going concern, but there is adequate disclosure. In this case the auditor should include an explanatory paragraph in the report (*see* **Section 13:16.7.2** and **Examples 5, 6** and **7** in **Appendix B** – *see* **Sections 13:16.15.6** to **13:16.15.8**).

(b) The auditor concludes that there is no significant level of concern about going concern, but the directors do not disclose, either in the financial statements or in accompanying information (e.g., the operating and financial review), that they have not paid particular attention to a period ending one year from the date of approval of the financial statements. In such a case the auditor should include a paragraph in the 'Basis of opinion' section of the report pointing this out, but the report should be unqualified. This situation should not arise commonly in practice and the auditor should always seek to persuade the directors to include appropriate disclosure, using the example below only as a last resort:

Assessment of going concern by the directors

In assessing whether it is appropriate to prepare the financial statements on a going concern basis the directors have paid particular attention to a period of [*only state period*]/[*less than 12 months from the date of approval of the financial statements*]. In accordance with Auditing Standards we are required to draw your attention to this fact, but our opinion is not qualified in this respect.

(c) The situation is as (b) but the directors make the necessary disclosure. In this case the auditor need make no reference to the matter in the report.

(d)   The auditor concludes that the directors have not taken adequate steps to satisfy themselves that it is appropriate to adopt the going concern basis. Accordingly, there is a limitation on the scope of the audit work and the auditor should qualify the report. (*See* **Section 13:16.3.1** and **Example 8** in **Appendix B** – *see* **Section 13:16.15.9**.)

13:16.7.4 Reporting – consideration of level of uncertainty

The guidance notes to SAS 130, but **not** the standards themselves, indicate that there may be circumstances where, although there is no **significant** concern about the ability of the client to continue as a going concern, there is some concern. In such cases the guidance states that without disclosure of the reasons for the concern the auditors might decide to qualify the audit opinion on the grounds that disclosure should be made. The auditor should not normally qualify the audit opinion regarding the absence of disclosure unless he or she considers that there is a significant level of concern (fundamental uncertainty).

An unwillingness to disclose material facts might indicate in some circumstances that disclosure could affect whether an uncertainty is fundamental. The auditor should reassess whether his or her assessment shows that the uncertainty is fundamental and, if so, the auditor should qualify the opinion if he or she believes the disclosure is inadequate.

Where a client is willing to disclose circumstances relating to the going concern position, this does not relieve the auditor of the responsibility to assess whether there is a significant level of concern that should be referred to in the audit opinion by means of an explanatory paragraph.

13:16.7.5 Reporting – disagreement

Where there is a significant level of concern about going concern, but the disclosure in the financial statements is inadequate, the auditor must qualify the report. An example of such a qualified report is given in **Example 9** of **Appendix B** – *see* **Section 13:16.15.11**. The form of this example is broadly similar to the example in SAS 130.

There may be rare circumstances where the auditor disagrees with the preparation of financial statements on the going concern basis. In such a case SAS 130 states as a standard:

> *Where the auditors disagree with the preparation of the financial statements on the going concern basis, they should issue an adverse audit opinion.* (SAS 130.8)

As this situation is likely to be very rare it is inappropriate to give examples in this section and the consultation procedures referred to in **Section 13:16.7.1** (last paragraph) should be followed if this situation arises.

13:16.7.6 Reporting – financial statements not prepared on a going concern basis

SAS 130 includes the following standard:

> *In rare circumstances, in order to give a true and fair view, the directors may have prepared financial statements on a basis other than that of a going concern. If the auditors consider this other basis to be appropriate in the specific circumstances, and if the financial statements contain the necessary disclosures, the auditors should not qualify their audit opinion in this respect.* (SAS 130.9)

Although **Appendix B (Section 13:16.15)** does not contain an example of a report given in these circumstances, the situation is frequently met in practice where a subsidiary company has, for example, been put into voluntary liquidation after the year-end, or has transferred its trade to another group company.

In such circumstances the auditor should normally add an explanatory paragraph headed 'Basis of preparation' at the end of the 'Basis of opinion' section of the report. The paragraph should refer to disclosures in the financial statements and one particular circumstance might be summarised as follows:

Basis of preparation

We draw your attention to note 1 which explains that following the year-end the directors have decided that the company will cease trading. Accordingly the going concern basis of accounting is no longer appropriate. Adjustments have been made in these financial statements to reduce assets to their realisable values, to provide for liabilities arising from the decision, and to reclassify fixed assets and long-term liabilities as current assets and liabilities. Our opinion is not qualified in this respect.

13:16.7.7 Further guidance – decision chart on going concern

SAS 130 contains a useful decision chart on going concern and reporting on the financial statements.

13:16.8 Reporting fraud and error and non-compliance with law or regulations

The auditor's responsibilities in relation to reporting to shareholders on suspected fraud and error or on non-compliance with law or regulations are set out in SAS 110, 'Fraud and error', and SAS 120, 'Consideration of law and regulations', respectively. Guidance is given in **Section 2:7**, 'Fraud and error', and **Section 2:8**, 'Law and regulations'.

SAS 110 states:

Where the auditors conclude that the view given by the financial statements could be affected by a level of uncertainty concerning the consequences of a suspected or actual error or fraud which, in their opinion, is fundamental, they should include an explanatory paragraph referring to the matter in their report.

Where the auditors conclude that a suspected or actual instance of fraud or error has a material effect on the financial statements and they disagree with the accounting treatment or with the extent, or the lack, of disclosure in the financial statements of the instance or of its consequences they should issue an adverse or qualified opinion. If the auditors are unable to determine whether fraud or error has occurred because of limitation in the scope of their work, they should issue a disclaimer or a qualified opinion.

SAS 120 states:

Where the auditors conclude that the view given by the financial statements could be affected by a level of uncertainty concerning the consequences of a suspected or actual non-compliance which, in their opinion, is fundamental, they should include an explanatory paragraph referring to the matter in their report.

Where the auditors conclude that a suspected or actual instance of non-compliance with law or regulation has a material effect on the financial statements and they disagree with the accounting treatment or with the extent, or the lack, of any disclosure in the financial statements of the instance or of its consequences they should issue an adverse or qualified opinion. If the auditors are unable to determine whether non-compliance with law or regulations has occurred because of limitation in the scope of their work, they should issue a disclaimer or a qualified opinion.

The guidance on reporting in SAS 110 and SAS 120 is almost identical and is summarised in the following paragraphs.

When the auditor is deciding whether the disclosures concerning the suspected or actual instance of fraud or error or non-compliance with law and regulations are adequate, or whether an explanatory paragraph should be included in the report, the auditor should base the decision primarily on the adequacy of the overall view given by the financial statements. Where management has taken steps to regularise or correct the position, or where the effect of a qualification might be to precipitate adverse legal or other consequences for the company, these are not, on their own, grounds on which the auditor can avoid qualifying the opinion or including an explanatory paragraph to reflect a fundamental uncertainty.

When deciding whether the directors have properly treated a possible or actual instance of dishonesty or fraud or non-compliance with law or regulations that may require disclosure in the financial statements, the auditor must consider whether the financial statements are free from material misstatements, whether shareholders require information about the matter to enable them to assess the performance of the company and any potential implications for the future operations or reputation of the company. Corrections to the financial statements need to be made where errors have been identified. Where a suspected or actual instance of dishonest or fraudulent conduct or non-compliance with law and regulations needs to be reflected in the financial statements, a true and fair view will require that sufficient particulars are given to enable the users of the financial statements to appreciate the full significance of the information disclosed. This will usually require the full potential consequences to be disclosed and, in some cases, it may be necessary for this purpose that the financial statements indicate that fraudulent or dishonest conduct or non-compliance with law or regulations is or may be involved.

When considering whether the possible consequences of any suspected or actual dishonest or fraudulent conduct or non-compliance with law or regulations need to be reflected in financial statements, the auditor should have regard to the requirements of SSAP 18, 'Accounting for contingencies'. Suspected or actual dishonest or fraudulent conduct or non-compliance with law or regulations may require disclosure in the financial statements because, although the immediate financial effect on the entity may not be material, there could be future material consequences such as fines or litigation.

Where suspected or actual dishonest or fraudulent conduct or non-compliance with laws or regulations is encountered, the auditor should follow the procedures in **Section 2:7**, 'Fraud and error', and **Section 2:8**, 'Laws and regulations'. Where the audit report is to include reference to such conduct the auditor should consider obtaining a review of the wording from the firm's legal advisers, as mentioned in **Section 13:16.1**.

The preceding paragraphs **Section 13:16.8** deal with reporting where there are fundamental uncertainties, disagreement about accounting treatment or disclosure or limitation on audit scope. However, there are other circumstances, when none of the above is involved, where the auditor should still add an explanatory paragraph drawing attention to the disclosures made in the financial statements. These circumstances are where there have been illegal transactions with directors or illegal dividends. Separate guidance on each of these circumstances is considered below.

13:16.8.1 Explanatory paragraph – illegal transactions with directors

In exceptional circumstances, where there have been illegal loans or other transactions in favour of directors, the auditor may consider that the attention of members should be drawn to these matters and to the fact that they may be illegal. The auditor should do this by adding an explanatory paragraph in the 'Basis of opinion' section of the report, in which the auditor should explain that in forming an audit opinion, the auditor has considered the adequacy of the disclosures made in the financial statements concerning the loans or other transactions. The auditor should also give brief details of the circumstances and cross-refer to the note in which full details are given. Finally, the auditor should clearly state that the audit opinion is unqualified in this respect.

The exceptional circumstances referred to above may include wilful disregard of the legal requirements by directors, situations where matters of public interest are involved or amounts which are material in the context of the financial statements. Normally, however, where such matters do not fall into these categories and the transactions are properly disclosed in the financial statements, no explanatory paragraph will be required. Where they are not properly disclosed the auditor must give the information in the audit report and qualify the report (*see* **Section 13:16.8** (third paragraph)). Where the auditor is unable to determine whether certain transactions have been properly disclosed or whether they affect the truth and fairness of the financial statements (e.g., because recovery of the amounts advanced may be doubtful), the auditor must consider whether there is a limitation on scope or fundamental uncertainty respectively which would lead him or her to qualify or modify the audit report (*see* **Section 13:16.8** (third paragraph)). If the legal requirements are persistently flouted by a client to a material degree the auditor should consider whether he or she should resign.

13:16.8.2 *Explanatory paragraph – illegal dividends*

There may be occasions where a company has paid a dividend illegally during the year. This could happen, for example, where the relevant financial statements did not show sufficient distributable profits to justify the dividend.

Where this happens there should be full disclosure of the facts in the financial statements. Such disclosure should include a statement of the fact that the dividend has been illegally paid, the consequences, if any, for the financial statements and the action that the directors have taken or are going to take.

In all cases, where a dividend paid was illegal or where there is doubt about whether a dividend paid was lawful the auditor should advise the company to take legal advice, and if the company does not do so, the auditor should also take legal advice.

Where the auditor concludes that the view given by the financial statements could be affected by a level of uncertainty concerning the consequences of an illegal dividend which, in the opinion of the auditor, is fundamental, the auditor should include an explanatory paragraph in the 'Basis of opinion' section of the audit report referring to the matter and to the uncertainty (*see* **Section 13:16.8** (third paragraph)). An example of such a fundamental uncertainty might be where a dividend had been paid which was potentially recoverable by the company, but recovery was uncertain.

Where the auditor concludes that the consequences of payment of an illegal dividend may have a material effect on the financial statements and the auditor disagrees either with the accounting treatment or with the extent, or the lack, of any disclosure in the financial statements of the payment or its consequences, the auditor should issue an adverse or 'except for' opinion (*see* **Section 13:16.8** (third paragraph)).

If the auditor is unable to determine whether non-compliance with the law relating to dividends has occurred because of a limitation on the scope of the audit work, the auditor should issue a disclaimer of opinion or an 'except for' opinion (*see* **Section 13:16.8** (third paragraph)). An example of a limitation on scope might be where a private company should have prepared interim financial statements to justify a dividend, but there is no evidence that such financial statements were prepared or considered by the board.

Even where full disclosure of an illegal dividend is made and there is no fundamental uncertainty, disagreement or limitation on scope, there may be exceptional circumstances where the auditor would still add an explanatory paragraph to the 'Basis of opinion' section of the audit report drawing attention to the disclosures.

'Exceptional circumstances' may include wilful disregard of legal requirements, or where the practical effect of the consequences of the illegal payment is that there has been, or is likely to be, a material impact on the financial statements. An example of wilful disregard of the legal requirements is where the board was clearly aware of the legal requirements but deliberately chose to ignore them. An example of where the payment of an illegal dividend has a material impact on the financial statements is where the payment has depleted the company's cash resources such that it has necessitated substantial additional borrowings to be taken out to enable the company to continue its operations. Where such matters do not fall into these categories and the details are properly disclosed in the financial statements no explanatory paragraph will be required.

A form of wording where the auditor considers that an explanatory paragraph should be added to the audit report might be as follows. The paragraph would appear after the 'Basis of opinion' paragraph and before the 'Opinion' paragraph.

Unlawful distributions

In forming our opinion we have considered the adequacy of the disclosures made in the financial statements concerning certain dividend payments made by the company during the year and prior years which were in breach of the Companies Act 1985 as the company did not have sufficient distributable reserves at the time of payment. Details of the circumstances relating to these unlawful distributions are described in note 9. Our opinion is not qualified in this respect.

In all cases where a company has paid an illegal dividend the auditor must follow the consultation procedures set out in **Section 5:5**, 'Consultation and concurring reviews', as if the matter were a proposed qualified or modified report.

13:16.9 Departures from standard accounting practice

Departures from standard accounting practice are dealt with in **Section 13:17**, 'Qualified reports – departures from standard accounting practice'. That section includes an example of the form of qualification required if a primary statement that is required by accounting standards is omitted from the financial statements. The two primary statements that are specifically required by accounting standards are the cash flow statement and the statement of total recognised gains and losses.

13:16.10 Small businesses

There can be particular problems associated with the audit of small companies. The auditor needs to obtain the same degree of assurance in order to give an unqualified opinion on the financial statements of small enterprises as on large enterprises. The most effective practicable form of internal control for small companies is generally the close involvement of the directors. This involvement will, however, enable them to override controls and purposely to exclude transactions from the records. This possibility can give rise to difficulties for the auditor, not only because there may be a lack of controls, but also, or instead, because of insufficient evidence as to their operation and the completeness of the records.

Often the auditor will be able to reach a conclusion that will support an unqualified opinion on the financial statements by combining the evidence obtained from substantive testing with a careful review of costs and margins. However, in some businesses, such as those where most transactions are for cash and there is no regular pattern of costs and margins, the documentary or other evidence available may be inadequate to support an opinion on the financial statements and may thus constitute a limitation on the scope of the audit work.

Where the auditor is satisfied that evidence from substantive testing and from knowledge of the client is sufficient to support an unqualified opinion the auditor should make no reference in the audit report to the less formal nature of internal control. Nor should the auditor refer to any representations that have been received from the directors as to the completeness and correctness of recording of transactions, in case such reference should be misconstrued as a form of qualification.

Where the auditor is not satisfied that the evidence and any representations received are sufficient to support an unqualified opinion, and provided that there is no matter that would give rise to an adverse opinion, the auditor should express an 'except for' opinion, or, in extreme cases, a disclaimer. This is because there has been a limitation on the scope of the audit work.

The particular circumstances in which a qualification will be necessary must always remain the responsibility of each engagement partner who should review and evaluate all of the available evidence.

If the auditor needs to qualify the audit report, he or she should always specify the particular areas of the financial statements where he or she has been unable to obtain the evidence considered necessary. If the auditor is unable to identify any particular area or amounts because the uncertainties are pervasive to the financial statements, the auditor should consider whether a disclaimer of opinion is required. Having regard to the other evidence available, however, the auditor may decide that a disclaimer is not justified. In such cases the auditor should use an 'except for' qualification, e.g., except for any adjustments that might have been found to be necessary had the auditor been able to obtain sufficient evidence concerning the completeness and accuracy of the accounting records.

All such qualifications must be reviewed in accordance with the procedures set out in **Section 5:5**, 'Consultation and concurring reviews'.

An example of a qualification caused by lack of evidence of satisfactory controls is set out in **Appendix B, Example 4** – *see* **Section 13:16.15.4**.

13:16.11 Preceding period's qualifications

If the audit report on the preceding period's financial statements was qualified or otherwise modified, but the matter that gave rise to the qualification or modification has been resolved and properly dealt with in the financial statements, then normally the auditor need make no reference to the previous qualification or modification in the current period's audit report. If, however, the matter remains unresolved and is material in relation to the current period's financial statements, the auditor must qualify or modify the report. In such a case the auditor should ensure that the notes to the financial statements adequately disclose the circumstances giving rise to the qualification or modification. The auditor should normally refer to the previous qualification or modification so as to make clear that the matter giving rise to the qualification or modification of the report on the financial statements of the current period arose in a previous period. An example of such a report is set out in **Appendix B, Example 20** – *see* **Section 13:16.15.21**.

13:16.12 Misstated corresponding amounts

The auditor should refer in the audit report to an actual or possible material misstatement in the corresponding amounts even though the misstatement does not directly affect the current period's figures. Such a misstatement may result from:

(a) a limitation on scope affecting the preceding period's profit and loss account, but not the balance sheet;

(b) misclassification of amounts in the preceding period's financial statements; or

(c) restatement of the preceding period's figures where the auditor does not concur with the restatement, or if in the auditor's opinion a restatement is necessary but has not been made.

An example of a report qualified because of a limitation on scope relating to comparative figures is set out in **Appendix B, Example 21** – *see* **Section 13:16.15.22**.

13:16.13 Decision chart – qualifications

A decision chart which the auditor may use as a guide to when qualifications are required, and as a means of determining the appropriate form of qualification, is set out in **Appendix A** – *see* **Section 13:16.14**. It is based on an example in SAS 600.

13:16.14 Appendix A   Decision chart – qualifications

To be included in Supplement 1.

13:16.15 Appendix B   Examples of qualified and modified reports

13:16.15.1   Example 1   Fundamental uncertainty

This example is an unqualified but modified report based on a fundamental uncertainty regarding future events that cannot be determined, and this leads to the inclusion of an explanatory paragraph describing the uncertainty in the 'Basis of opinion' section of the report.

[Text continues on page 13/92.]

Report of the auditors to the members of Blank PLC

We have audited the financial statements on pages x to x which have been prepared under the historical cost convention [*as modified by the revaluation of certain fixed assets*] and the accounting policies set out on page x.

Respective responsibilities of directors and auditors

As described on page x the company's directors are responsible for the preparation of financial statements. It is our responsibility to form an independent opinion, based on our audit, on those statements and to report our opinion to you.

Basis of opinion

We conducted our audit in accordance with Auditing Standards issued by the Auditing Practices Board. An audit includes examination, on a test basis, of evidence relevant to the amounts and disclosures in the financial statements. It also includes an assessment of the significant estimates and judgements made by the directors in the preparation of the financial statements, and of whether the accounting policies are appropriate to the company's circumstances, consistently applied and adequately disclosed.

We planned and performed our audit so as to obtain all the information and explanations that we considered necessary in order to provide us with sufficient evidence to give reasonable assurance that the financial statements are free from material misstatement, whether caused by fraud or by other irregularity or error. In forming our opinion we also evaluated the overall adequacy of the presentation of information in the financial statements.

Fundamental uncertainty

In forming our opinion we have considered the adequacy of the disclosures in the financial statements concerning the provision of £X million made in respect of the costs expected to be incurred as a result of the decision to discontinue the design, manufacture and marketing of radar-based products. By its nature the provision is based on directors' estimates of the realisable value of assets and of costs to be incurred and may be subject to material change as the discontinuance progresses. Details of the circumstances relating to this fundamental uncertainty are described in note x. Our opinion is not qualified in this respect.

Opinion

In our opinion the financial statements give a true and fair view of the state of the company's affairs at 31 December 20XX and of its loss and cash flows for the year then ended and have been properly prepared in accordance with the Companies Act 1985.

Set out below is the note to the financial statements referred to in the report:

During the year the Board made a decision, after extensive review, that the company's major operating division, responsible for the design, manufacture and marketing of radar-based products, should be discontinued. A provision of £X million has been established and is disclosed after operating profit in the profit and loss account. The provision comprises £Y million in respect of reductions to the carrying value of fixed assets and £Z million in respect of redundancies. Both of these amounts are based on the directors' best estimates of the amounts required. However, the amounts may be subject to material change as the discontinuance progresses, due to the fact that there exists only a limited market for the specialised plant, making realisable values difficult to forecast, and because it is the directors' intention to seek to reduce the level of redundancies by placing employees with other group companies.

13:16.15.2 Example 2 Fundamental uncertainty

This example is an unqualified but modified report based on fundamental uncertainty regarding future events that cannot be determined by the directors that leads to the inclusion of an explanatory paragraph describing the uncertainty in the 'Basis of opinion' section of the report.

Report of the auditors to the members of Blank PLC

We have audited the financial statements on pages x to x which have been prepared under the historical cost convention [*as modified by the revaluation of certain fixed assets*] and the accounting policies set out on page x.

Respective responsibilities of directors and auditors

As described on page x the company's directors are responsible for the preparation of financial statements. It is our responsibility to form an independent opinion, based on our audit, on those statements and to report our opinion to you.

Basis of opinion

We conducted our audit in accordance with Auditing Standards issued by the Auditing Practices Board. An audit includes examination, on a test basis, of evidence relevant to the amounts and disclosures in the financial statements. It also includes an assessment of the significant estimates and judgements made by the directors in the preparation of the financial statements, and of whether the accounting policies are appropriate to the company's circumstances, consistently applied and adequately disclosed.

We planned and performed our audit so as to obtain all the information and explanations that we considered necessary in order to provide us with sufficient evidence to give reasonable assurance that the financial statements are free from material misstatement, whether caused by fraud or by other irregularity or error. In forming our opinion we also evaluated the overall adequacy of the presentation of information in the financial statements.

Fundamental uncertainty

In forming our opinion we have considered the adequacy of the disclosures made in the financial statements concerning the possible outcome to litigation against the company for alleged delays in the construction of a refinery, breaches of the construction contract, loss of profits and misrepresentation. On the basis of information presently available the directors and their legal advisers are of the opinion that the legal action will be successfully defended. However if the action were to be decided against the company, there could be a materially adverse effect on the financial position disclosed in these financial statements. Details of the circumstances relating to this fundamental uncertainty are described in note x. Our opinion is not qualified in this respect.

Opinion

In our opinion the financial statements give a true and fair view of the state of the company's affairs at 31 December 20XX and of its profit and cash flows for the year then ended and have been properly prepared in accordance with the Companies Act 1985.

Set out below is the note to the financial statements referred to in the report:

Refinery litigation

In January 20XX the company wrote off debtors of £1,400,000 and Canadian $9,200,000 due from XYZ Company Limited in connection with the construction of a refinery in Newfoundland, operated by XYZ Company Limited. In February 20XX XYZ Company Limited instituted a lawsuit against the company in the Supreme Court of New York in the amount of US $189,000,000 relating to alleged delays in constructing the refinery, breaches of the construction contract and misrepresentation.

In September 20XX, the company instituted a lawsuit against XYZ Company Limited to claim the amounts due in connection with the construction of the refinery. In October 20XX, the defendant filed a counterclaim in the London High Court for Canadian $18,000,000 for alleged equipment failure and Canadian $104,000,000 for loss of profits and other damages. The counterclaim alleged delay, negligence and fundamental breach of contract.

If the above claims and counterclaims were decided against the company there could be a materially adverse effect on the financial position disclosed in these financial statements. However, in the opinion of the company's legal advisers, the contingent liability under all these claims is limited to US $500,000 in respect of any damages recoverable under the contract for defective work and this amount was paid into the London High Court during 20XX. The company has issued proceedings against its subcontractors for recovery of monies which may be payable under the above claims.

On the basis of information available to them, the directors and their legal advisers are of the opinion that all of the abovementioned suits and counterclaims against the company can be successfully defended. Costs of the defence are being met by the company.

13:16.15.3 *Example 3 Limitation on scope and disagreement*

This example is based on a limitation on the scope of audit work caused by the absence of audited financial statements of certain subsidiaries and an associate. There is also a qualification arising from disagreement on the failure to depreciate buildings and this gives rise to a multiple qualification.

Report of the auditors to the members of Blank Holdings PLC

We have audited the financial statements on pages x to x which have been prepared under the historical cost convention [*as modified by the revaluation of certain fixed assets*] and the accounting policies set out on page x.

Respective responsibilities of directors and auditors

As described on page x the company's directors are responsible for the preparation of financial statements. It is our responsibility to form an independent opinion, based on our audit, on those statements and to report our opinion to you.

Basis of opinion

We conducted our audit in accordance with Auditing Standards issued by the Auditing Practices Board, except that the scope of our work was limited as explained below.

An audit includes examination, on a test basis, of evidence relevant to the amounts and disclosures in the financial statements. It also includes an assessment of the significant estimates and judgements made by the directors in the preparation of the financial statements, and of whether the accounting policies are appropriate to the company's circumstances, consistently applied and adequately disclosed.

We planned our audit so as to obtain all the information and explanations that we considered necessary in order to provide us with sufficient evidence to give reasonable assurance that the financial statements are free from material misstatement, whether caused by fraud or other irregularity or error. However, the evidence available to us was limited because the financial statements of certain subsidiaries registered abroad and of an associated company have not been audited and it was not therefore possible for us to form an opinion on the amounts of the attributable net assets of £X million and profits of £Y million which are shown in note x.

In forming our opinion we also evaluated the overall adequacy of the presentation of information in the financial statements.

As stated in note x to the financial statements depreciation is not provided on freehold buildings. Had depreciation been provided in accordance with standard accounting practice in our opinion, based on a rate of 2 per cent per annum, the profit for the year would have been reduced by £240,000 and the profit and loss account reserve and net book value of freehold properties would have been reduced by £720,000.

Except for any adjustments that might have been found to be necessary had we been able to obtain sufficient evidence concerning the net assets and profits of unaudited subsidiaries and the associated company and except for the adjustments that would have been necessary had depreciation been provided on freehold buildings, in our opinion the financial statements give a true and fair view of the state of affairs of the company and the group at 31 December 20XX and of the profit and cash flows of the group for the year then ended and have been properly prepared in accordance with the Companies Act 1985.

In respect alone of the limitation on our work relating to the subsidiaries and associated company referred to above:

(a) we have not obtained all the information and explanations that we considered necessary for the purpose of our audit; and

(b) we were unable to determine whether proper accounting records had been kept.

13:16.15.4   *Example 4 Limitation scope – 'except for' opinion*

This example is based on a limitation on the scope of the work caused by the lack of evidence of the operation of internal controls coupled with our inability to adopt alternative auditing procedures to compensate. This results in an 'except for' opinion.

Report of the auditors to the members of Blank Limited

We have audited the financial statements on pages x to x which have been prepared under the historical cost convention and the accounting policies set out on page x.

Respective responsibilities of directors and auditors

As described on page x the company's directors are responsible for the preparation of financial statements. It is our responsibility to form an independent opinion, based on our audit, on those statements and to report our opinion to you.

Basis of opinion

We conducted our audit in accordance with Auditing Standards issued by the Auditing Practices Board, except that the scope of our work was limited as explained below.

An audit includes examination, on a test basis, of evidence relevant to the amounts and disclosures in the financial statements. It also includes an assessment of the significant estimates and judgements made by the directors in the preparation of the financial statements, and of whether the accounting policies are appropriate to the company's circumstances, consistently applied and adequately disclosed.

We planned our audit so as to obtain all the information and explanations that we considered necessary in order to provide us with sufficient evidence to give reasonable assurance that the financial statements are free from material misstatement, whether caused by fraud or other irregularity or error. However, the evidence available to us was limited because £X of the company's recorded turnover of £Y comprises cash sales, over which there was no system of control on which we could rely for the purpose of our audit. There were no other satisfactory audit procedures that we could adopt to confirm independently that all cash sales were properly recorded.

In forming our opinion we also evaluated the overall adequacy of the presentation of information in the financial statements.

Qualified opinion arising from limitation on audit scope

Except for any adjustments that might have been found to be necessary had we been able to obtain sufficient evidence concerning cash sales, in our opinion the financial statements give a true and fair view of the state of the company's affairs at 31 December 20XX and of its profit and cash flows for the year then ended and have been properly prepared in accordance with the Companies Act 1985.

In respect alone of the limitation on our work relating to cash sales:

(a) we have not obtained all the information and explanations that we considered necessary for the purpose of our audit; and

(b) we were unable to determine whether proper accounting records had been kept.

13:16.15.5 Uncertainty of going concern – Examples 5 and 6

Situations can arise where the auditor will need to include an explanatory paragraph in the 'Basis of opinion' section of the audit report to explain that in forming an unqualified opinion the auditor has considered the disclosures in the financial statements relating to fundamental uncertainty about the validity of going concern basis. Example 5 includes such an explanatory paragraph but is unqualified. Example 5 is distinguished from Example 6 because it is based on the Example in SAS 600 whereas Example 6 is based on SAS 130, 'The going concern basis in financial statements', with appropriate amendments (*see* **Section 13:16.7.2**). Either example may be used when including an explanatory paragraph on going concern.

13:16.15.6 Example 5 Fundamental uncertainty of going concern

This example applies when the auditor is reasonably certain that support will be given.

Report of the auditors to the members of Blank PLC

We have audited the financial statements on pages x to x which have been prepared under the historical cost convention [*as modified by the revaluation of certain fixed assets*] and the accounting policies set out on page x.

Respective responsibilities of directors and auditors

As described on page x the company's directors are responsible for the preparation of financial statements. It is our responsibility to form an independent opinion, based on our audit, on those statements and to report our opinion to you.

Basis of opinion

We conducted our audit in accordance with Auditing Standards issued by the Auditing Practices Board. An audit includes examination, on a test basis, of evidence relevant to the amounts and disclosures in the financial statements. It also includes an assessment of the significant estimates and judgements made by the directors in the preparation of the financial statements, and of whether the accounting policies are appropriate to the company's circumstances, consistently applied and adequately disclosed.

We planned and performed our audit so as to obtain all the information and explanations that we considered necessary in order to provide us with sufficient evidence to give reasonable assurance that the financial

statements are free from material misstatement, whether caused by fraud or by other irregularity or error. In forming our opinion we also evaluated the overall adequacy of the presentation of information in the financial statements.

Fundamental uncertainty

In forming our opinion, we have considered the adequacy of the disclosures made in the financial statements concerning the directors' negotiations with lenders to the group for new terms for amounts borrowed totalling £A million, and their plans for raising funds for approximately £B million from a share issue by the company. The financial statements have been prepared on a going concern basis, the validity of which depends on the successful conclusion of the negotiations with the group's lenders and the raising of additional funds by the share issue. The financial statements do not include any adjustments that would result from a failure to obtain this funding. Details of the circumstances relating to this fundamental uncertainty are described in note 1. Our opinion is not qualified in this respect.

Opinion

In our opinion the financial statements give a true and fair view of the state of affairs of the company and the group at 31 December 20XX and of the profit and cash flows of the group for the year then ended and have been properly prepared in accordance with the Companies Act 1985.

Set out below is the note to the financial statements referred to in the audit report:

Basis of preparing the financial statements – going concern assumption

The company and certain of its subsidiaries have not complied with the covenants relating to certain of their borrowings included in the financial statements. Under the terms of these covenants, the publication of these financial statements therefore gives rise to defaults on covenants relating to certain of the group's borrowings. These defaults result in the related borrowings becoming repayable on demand.

The directors are currently negotiating with lenders to the group for new terms for amounts borrowed totalling £A million. In addition, the directors' plans for raising funds of approximately £B million from a share issue by the company are at an advanced stage.

The financial statements have been prepared on the going concern basis which assumes that the company and its subsidiaries will continue in operational existence for the foreseeable future.

The validity of this assumption depends on the successful conclusion of the negotiations with the group's lenders and the raising of additional funds by a share issue. Certain of these arrangements will require approval of shareholders in a general meeting.

If the company or its subsidiaries were unable to continue in operational existence for the foreseeable future, adjustments would have to be made to reduce the balance sheet values of assets to their recoverable amounts, and to provide for further liabilities that might arise, and to reclassify fixed assets and long term liabilities as current assets and liabilities.

Although the directors are at present uncertain as to the outcome of the matters mentioned above, they believe that it is appropriate for the financial statements to be prepared on the going concern basis.

13:16.15.7 Example 6 Fundamental uncertainty of going concern

This example applies when the auditor is reasonably certain that support will be given.

Report of the auditors to the members of Blank PLC

We have audited the financial statements on pages x to x which have been prepared under the historical cost convention [*as modified by the revaluation of certain fixed assets*] and the accounting policies set out on page x.

Respective responsibilities of directors and auditors

As described on page x the company's directors are responsible for the preparation of financial statements. It is our responsibility to form an independent opinion, based on our audit, on those statements and to report our opinion to you.

Basis of opinion

We conducted our audit in accordance with Auditing Standards issued by the Auditing Practices Board. An audit includes examination, on a test basis, of evidence relevant to the amounts and disclosures in the financial statements. It also includes an assessment of the significant estimates and judgements made by the directors in the preparation of the financial statements, and of whether the accounting policies are appropriate to the company's circumstances, consistently applied and adequately disclosed.

We planned and performed our audit so as to obtain all the information and explanations that we considered necessary in order to provide us with sufficient evidence to give reasonable assurance that the financial statements are free from material misstatement, whether caused by fraud or by other irregularity or error. In forming our opinion we also evaluated the overall adequacy of the presentation of information in the financial statements.

Uncertainty – going concern

In forming our opinion, we have considered the adequacy of the disclosures made in note 1 of the financial statements concerning the uncertainty as to the outcome of negotiations with the group's lenders for new terms for amounts borrowed totalling £A million, and the proposed raising of additional funds of approximately £B million by a share issue. The financial statements do not include any adjustments that would result from a failure to obtain this funding. In view of the significance of this fundamental uncertainty we consider that it should be drawn to your attention but our opinion is not qualified in this respect.

Opinion

In our opinion the financial statements give a true and fair view of the state of affairs of the company and the group at 31 December 20XX and of the profit and cash flows of the group for the year then ended and have been properly prepared in accordance with the Companies Act 1985.

Note 1 to the financial statements is the same as in Example 5.

13:16.15.8 Example 7 Fundamental uncertainty of going concern

This example covers the common situation where the validity of the going concern basis depends on the continued support of the company's bankers (or parent company). There is a fundamental uncertainty which is referred to in an explanatory paragraph of the 'Basis of opinion' section of the report, which is unqualified because the auditor is satisfied with the disclosure.

This example is based on the SAS 600 example (*see* **Example 5** above) but may be suitably amended to conform to the SAS 130 example (*see* **Example 6** above).

Report of the auditors to the members of Blank Limited

We have audited the financial statements on pages x to x which have been prepared under the historical cost convention [*as modified by the revaluation of certain fixed assets*] and the accounting policies set out on page x.

Respective responsibilities of directors and auditors

As described on page x the company's directors are responsible for the preparation of financial statements. It is our responsibility to form an independent opinion, based on our audit, on those statements and to report our opinion to you.

Basis of opinion

We conducted our audit in accordance with Auditing Standards issued by the Auditing Practices Board. An audit includes examination, on a test basis, of evidence relevant to the amounts and disclosures in the financial statements. It also includes an assessment of the significant estimates and judgements made by the directors in the preparation of the financial statements, and of whether the accounting policies are appropriate to the company's circumstances, consistently applied and adequately disclosed.

We planned and performed our audit so as to obtain all the information and explanations that we considered necessary in order to provide us with sufficient evidence to give reasonable assurance that the financial statements are free from material misstatement, whether caused by fraud or by other irregularity or error. In forming our opinion we also evaluated the overall adequacy of the presentation of information in the financial statements.

Fundamental uncertainty

In forming our opinion we have considered the adequacy of the disclosures made in the financial statements concerning the basis of preparation. The financial statements have been prepared on a going concern basis and the validity of this depends on the continued support of the company's [*bankers*] parent company by providing adequate [*overdraft*] loan facilities. The financial statements do not include any adjustments that would result from a failure to obtain such continued support. Details of the circumstances relating to this fundamental uncertainty are described in note 1. Our opinion is not qualified in this respect.

Opinion

In our opinion the financial statements give a true and fair view of the state of the company's affairs at 31 December 20XX and of its loss and cash flows for the year then ended and have been properly prepared in accordance with the Companies Act 1985.

Note: In this example, which differs from Examples 5 and 6, no new finance is needed, only continuation of existing facilities. The notes to the financial statements must include an adequate description of the circumstances of the fundamental uncertainty and its effects. There will be a wide variety of situations and it is not possible to give examples of them all. Examples of extracts from notes to the financial statements for two situations are given below:

Validity of going concern basis dependent on bank support

Basis of preparing the financial statements – going concern

During the year the company incurred a loss of £xx and at the balance sheet date its current liabilities exceeded its current assets by £xx. The company meets its day-to-day working capital requirements through a bank overdraft facility which, in common with all such facilities, is repayable on demand. At the balance sheet date the overdraft was £xx which was within its agreed facility of £xx.

The company's bankers have agreed to continue the facility on a day-to-day basis, conditional on the company's meeting its projected cash flow forecasts for the year to [*date*]. These cash flow forecasts indicate that the company will be able to remain within its agreed facility. However the nature of the company's business is such that there can be considerable variation in the timing of cash inflows and there is therefore uncertainty about whether the cash flow forecasts will be met.

The financial statements have been prepared on a going concern basis which assumes that the company will continue in operational existence for the foreseeable future.

The validity of this assumption depends on the company's being able to meet its projected cash flow forecasts and on the company's bankers continuing their support by providing adequate overdraft facilities.

If the company were unable to continue in operational existence for the foreseeable future, adjustments would have to be made to reduce the balance sheet values of assets to their recoverable amounts, to provide for further liabilities that might arise and to reclassify fixed assets and long-term liabilities as current assets and liabilities.

Although the directors are at present uncertain as to the outcome of the matters mentioned above, they believe that it is appropriate for the financial statements to be prepared on a going concern basis.

Validity of going concern basis dependent on support from parent company

Basis of preparing the financial statements – going concern

During the year the company incurred a loss of £xx and at the balance sheet date its current liabilities exceeded its current assets by £xx.

The company is in a start-up situation and relies on its parent company for financial support which has been provided by a loan amounting to £xx at the balance sheet date. The loan is repayable on demand. The parent company has considered forecasts prepared by the company of the future sales revenue and cash flows that the company's new product is expected to generate. These forecasts indicate that the current level of parent company support will be adequate for the company's needs in the future and the parent company has indicated that it will continue its support at the current level on condition that these forecasts prove to be reliable and are substantially met in the coming year. The forecasts have been prepared on the basis of extensive market research but because the product is new they involve assumptions which are subject to a considerable degree of uncertainty.

The financial statements have been prepared on a going concern basis which assumes that the company will continue in operational existence for the foreseeable future.

The validity of this assumption depends on the company's being able to meet its forecasts of sales revenue and cash flows and on the parent company's continuing its support by providing adequate loan facilities.

If the company were unable to continue in operational existence for the foreseeable future, adjustments would have to be made to reduce the balance sheet values of assets to their recoverable amounts, to provide for further liabilities that might arise and to reclassify fixed assets and long-term liabilities as current assets and liabilities.

Although the directors are at present uncertain as to the outcome of the matters mentioned above they believe that it is appropriate for the financial statements to be prepared on a going concern basis.

13:16.15.9 *Example 8 Limitation on scope – going concern*

This example is based on a limitation on the scope of audit work that results from the evidence available to the auditor being limited because, when considering the appropriateness of the going concern basis, the directors have not paid particular attention to a period of at least one year from the date of approval of the financial statements. It leads to a disclaimer of opinion.

Report of the auditors to the members of Blank Limited

We have audited the financial statements on pages x to x which have been prepared under the historical cost convention [*as modified by the revaluation of certain fixed assets*] and the accounting policies set out on page x.

Respective responsibilities of directors and auditors

As described on page x the company's directors are responsible for the preparation of financial statements. It is our responsibility to form an independent opinion, based on our audit, on those statements and to report our opinion to you.

Basis of opinion

We conducted our audit in accordance with Auditing Standards issued by the Auditing Practices Board, except that the scope of our work was limited as explained below.

An audit includes examination, on a test basis, of evidence relevant to the amounts and disclosures in the financial statements. It also includes an assessment of the significant estimates and judgements made by the directors in the preparation of the financial statements, and of whether the accounting policies are appropriate to the company's circumstances, consistently applied and adequately disclosed.

We planned our audit so as to obtain all the information and explanations that we considered necessary in order to provide us with sufficient evidence to give reasonable assurance that the financial statements are free from material misstatement, whether caused by fraud or by other irregularity or error. However, the evidence available to us was limited because the company has prepared cash flow forecasts and other information needed for the assessment of the appropriateness of the going concern basis of preparation of the financial statements only for a period of [*state period*] from the date of approval of these financial statements. We consider that the circumstances of the company [*the nature of the company's business*] require that such information be prepared, and reviewed by the directors and ourselves, for a period of at least 12 months from the date of approval of the financial statements. In the absence of such information we have been unable to form an opinion on whether it is appropriate to prepare the financial statements on a going concern basis.

In forming our opinion we also evaluated the overall adequacy of the presentation of information in the financial statements.

Opinion: disclaimer on view given by financial statements

Because of the possible effect of the limitation in evidence available to us, we are unable to form an opinion as to whether the financial statements give a true and fair view of the state of the company's affairs at 31 December 20XX and of its profit for the year then ended.

In our opinion the cash flow statement gives a true and fair view of the company's cash flows for the year ended 31 December 20XX and in all other respects the financial statements have been properly prepared in accordance with the Companies Act 1985.

In respect alone of the limitation on our work relating to going concern we have not obtained all the information and explanations that we considered necessary for the purpose of our audit.

Notes:

(a)   Because the going concern basis is fundamental to the preparation of financial statements a disclaimer of opinion is most likely where the effects could be significant were the going concern basis not appropriate. If the potential adjustments are minor, however, an 'except for' opinion might be more appropriate.

(b)   The opinion does not contain any statement about accounting records, as it is assumed that 'accounting records' applies to records of transactions that have occurred rather than forecasts of future transactions.

13:16.15.10 Example 9 Disagreement – going concern

This example covers the situation where there is a fundamental uncertainty about a group's ability to continue as a going concern. Instead of including an explanatory paragraph in the 'Basis of opinion' paragraph and issuing an unqualified report the auditor must issue an 'except for' opinion because in this case there is disagreement with the disclosures given in the financial statements because they omit material facts.

Report of the auditors to the members of Blank PLC

We have audited the financial statements on pages x to x which have been prepared under the historical cost convention [*as modified by the revaluation of certain fixed assets*] and the accounting policies set out on page x.

Respective responsibilities of directors and auditors

As described on page x the company's directors are responsible for the preparation of financial statements. It is our responsibility to form an independent opinion, based on our audit, on those statements and to report our opinion to you.

Basis of opinion

We conducted our audit in accordance with Auditing Standards issued by the Auditing Practices Board. An audit includes examination, on a test basis, of evidence relevant to the amounts and disclosures in the financial statements. It also includes an assessment of the significant estimates and judgements made by the directors in the preparation of the financial statements, and of whether the accounting policies are appropriate to the company's circumstances, consistently applied and adequately disclosed.

We planned and performed our audit so as to obtain all the information and explanations that we considered necessary in order to provide us with sufficient evidence to give reasonable assurance that the financial statements are free from material misstatement, whether caused by fraud or by other irregularity or error. In forming our opinion we also evaluated

the overall adequacy of the presentation of information in the financial statements.

Qualified opinion arising from disagreement about disclosure of fundamental uncertainty

Note 1 contains disclosures regarding the directors' negotiations with lenders to the group for new terms for amounts borrowed totalling £A million, and their plans for raising funds of approximately £B million from a share issue by the company. The financial statements have been prepared on a going concern basis, the validity of which depends on the successful conclusion of the negotiations with the group's lenders and the raising of additional funds by the share issue. The financial statements do not include any adjustments that would result from a failure to obtain this funding. Details of the circumstances relating to this fundamental uncertainty are described in note 1.

In our opinion the financial statements should also disclose that the company and certain of its subsidiaries have not complied with covenants relating to certain of their borrowings included in the financial statements. Under the terms of these covenants, the publication of the financial statements gives rise to defaults on covenants relating to certain of the group's borrowings. These defaults result in the related borrowings becoming repayable on demand.

In our opinion the financial statements give a true and fair view of the profit and cash flows of the group for the year ended 31 December 20XX and, except for the absence of the disclosure referred to in the paragraph above, of the state of affairs of the company and the group at that date and have been properly prepared in accordance with the Companies Act 1985.

Set out below is the note to the financial statements referred to in the audit report:

Basis of preparing the financial statements – going concern assumption

The directors are currently negotiating with lenders to the group for new terms for amounts borrowed totalling £A million. In addition, the directors' plans for raising funds of approximately £B million from a share issue by the company are at an advanced stage.

The financial statements have been prepared on the going concern basis which assumes that the company and its subsidiaries will continue in operational existence for the foreseeable future.

The validity of this assumption depends on the successful conclusion of the negotiations with the group's lenders and the raising of additional funds by a share issue. Certain of these arrangements will require the approval of shareholders in a general meeting.

If the company or its subsidiaries were unable to continue in operational existence for the foreseeable future, adjustments would have to be made to reduce the balance sheet values of assets to their recoverable amounts, and to provide for further liabilities that might arise, and to reclassify fixed assets and long-term liabilities as current assets and liabilities.

Although the directors are at present uncertain as to the outcome of the matters mentioned above, they believe that it is appropriate for the financial statements to be prepared on the going concern basis.

13:16.15.11 Example 10 Limitation on scope – disclaimer of opinion

This example is based on a limitation on the scope of audit work caused by the date of the auditor's appointment. This leads to a disclaimer of opinion on the profit and loss account and statement of total recognised gains and losses.

Report of the auditors to the members of Blank PLC

We have audited the financial statements on pages x to x which have been prepared under the historical cost convention [*as modified by the revaluation of certain fixed assets*] and the accounting policies set out on page x.

Respective responsibilities of directors and auditors

As described on page x the company's directors are responsible for the preparation of financial statements. It is our responsibility to form an independent opinion, based on our audit, on those statements and to report our opinion to you.

Basis of opinion

We conducted our audit in accordance with Auditing Standards issued by the Auditing Practices Board, except that the scope of our work was limited as explained below.

An audit includes examination, on a test basis, of evidence relevant to the amounts and disclosures in the financial statements. It also includes an assessment of the significant estimates and judgements made by the directors in the preparation of the financial statements, and of whether the accounting policies are appropriate to the company's circumstances, consistently applied and adequately disclosed.

We planned our audit so as to obtain all the information and explanations that we considered necessary in order to provide us with sufficient evidence to give reasonable assurance that the financial statements are free from material misstatement, whether caused by fraud or by other irregularity or error. However, the evidence available to us was limited because we were not appointed auditors until [*date*] and in consequence did not report on the financial statements for the year ended [*preceding year*]. It was not possible for us to carry out the auditing procedures necessary to obtain our own assurance as regards certain stock and work-in-progress appearing in the preceding period's financial statements at £X. Any adjustment to this figure would have a consequential effect on the profit and total recognised gains for the year ended 31 December 20XX.

In forming our opinion we also evaluated the overall adequacy of the presentation of information in the financial statements.

Opinion: disclaimer on view given by the profit and loss account

Because of the possible effect of the limitation in evidence available to us, we are unable to form an opinion as to whether the profit and loss account and cash flow statements give a true and fair view of the company's profit and cash flows for the year ended 31 December 20XX.

In our opinion the balance sheet gives a true and fair view of the company's state of affairs at 31 December 20XX and in all other respects the financial statements have been properly prepared in accordance with the Companies Act 1985.

In respect alone of the limitation on our work relating to opening stock and work-in-progress:

(a) we have not obtained all the information and explanations that we considered necessary for the purpose of our audit; and

(b) we were unable to determine whether proper accounting records had been kept.

13:16.15.12   Example 11   Limitation on scope – disclaimer of opinion

This example is based on a limitation on the scope of audit work caused by inadequate internal control that leads to a disclaimer of opinion on the financial statements as a whole.

Report of the auditors to the members of Blank PLC

We have audited the financial statements on pages x to x which have been prepared under the historical cost convention [*as modified by the revaluation of certain fixed assets*] and the accounting policies set out on page x.

Respective responsibilities of directors and auditors

As described on page x the company's directors are responsible for the preparation of financial statements. It is our responsibility to form an independent opinion, based on our audit, on those statements and to report our opinion to you.

Basis of opinion

We conducted our audit in accordance with Auditing Standards issued by the Auditing Practices Board, except that the scope of our work was limited as explained below.

An audit includes examination, on a test basis, of evidence relevant to the amounts and disclosures in the financial statements. It also includes an assessment of the significant estimates and judgements made by the directors in the preparation of the financial statements, and of whether the accounting policies are appropriate to the company's circumstances, consistently applied and adequately disclosed.

We planned our audit so as to obtain all the information and explanations that we considered necessary in order to provide us with sufficient evidence to give reasonable assurance that the financial statements are free from material misstatement, whether caused by fraud or by other irregularity or error. However, the evidence available to us was limited because during the year the company transferred all its accounting records to a computer bureau and in our opinion the control over the records submitted to the bureau and over the examination of data produced by the bureau was inadequate. As a result we could not rely on those data and there were no other satisfactory audit procedures that we could adopt to confirm the completeness and accuracy of the accounting records.

In forming our opinion we also evaluated the overall adequacy of the presentation of the information in the financial statements.

Opinion: disclaimer on view given by financial statements

Because of the possible effect of the limitation in evidence available to us, we are unable to form an opinion as to whether:

(a) the financial statements give a true and fair view of the state of the company's affairs at 31 December 20XX and of its profit and cash flows for the year then ended.

(b) the financial statements have been properly prepared in accordance with the Companies Act 1985.

In respect of the limitation on our work referred to above:

(a) we have not obtained all the information and explanations that we considered necessary for the purpose of our audit; and

(b) in our opinion proper accounting records have not been kept.

13:16.15.13 Example 12 Limitation on scope – disclaimer of opinion

This example is based on a limitation on the scope of audit work caused by unsatisfactory accounting records that leads to a disclaimer of opinion on the financial statements as a whole.

Report of the auditors to the members of Blank Limited

We have audited the financial statements on pages x to x which have been prepared under the historical cost convention [*as modified by the revaluation of certain fixed assets*] and the accounting policies set out on page x.

Respective responsibilities of directors and auditors

As described on page x the company's directors are responsible for the preparation of financial statements. It is our responsibility to form an independent opinion, based on our audit, on those statements and to report our opinion to you.

Basis of opinion

We conducted our audit in accordance with Auditing Standards issued by the Auditing Practices Board, except that the scope of our work was limited as explained below.

An audit includes examination, on a test basis, of evidence relevant to the amounts and disclosures in the financial statements. It also includes an assessment of the significant estimates and judgements made by the directors in the preparation of the financial statements, and of whether the accounting policies are appropriate to the company's circumstances, consistently applied and adequately disclosed.

We planned our audit so as to obtain all the information and explanations that we considered necessary in order to provide us with sufficient evidence to give reasonable assurance that the financial statements are free from material misstatement, whether caused by fraud or by other irregularity or error. However, the evidence available to us was limited because in our opinion the system of accounting was unsatisfactory during the year and certain records of income and expenditure necessary for the purpose of our audit were not maintained by the company. In addition we have not been able to satisfy ourselves that all assets and liabilities of the company have been included in the financial statements or that the assets and liabilities included in the financial statements are stated at their proper amounts.

In forming our opinion we also evaluated the overall adequacy of the presentation of information in the financial statements.

Opinion: disclaimer on view given by financial statements

Because of the possible effect of the limitation in evidence available to us, we are unable to form an opinion as to whether:

(a) the financial statements give a true and fair view of the state of the company's affairs at 31 December 20XX and of its profit and cash flows for the year then ended.

(b) the financial statements have been properly prepared in accordance with the Companies Act 1985.

In respect of the limitation on our work referred to above:

(a) we have not obtained all the information and explanations that we considered necessary for the purpose of our audit; and

(b) in our opinion proper accounting records have not been kept.

13:16.15.14 Example 13 Limitation on scope – 'except for' opinion

This example is based on a limitation on the scope of audit work caused by a lack of information that is not so material or pervasive in relation to the financial statements as a whole that the auditor considers it is necessary to disclaim an opinion, but which is material enough that the auditor needs to issue an 'except for' opinion.

Report of the auditors to the members of Blank PLC

We have audited the financial statements on pages x to x which have been prepared under the historical cost convention [*as modified by the revaluation of certain fixed assets*] and the accounting policies set out on page x.

Respective responsibilities of directors and auditors

As described on page x the company's directors are responsible for the preparation of financial statements. It is our responsibility to form an independent opinion, based on our audit, on those statements and to report our opinion to you.

Basis of opinion

We conducted our audit in accordance with Auditing Standards issued by the Auditing Practices Board, except that the scope of our work was limited as explained below.

An audit includes examination, on a test basis, of evidence relevant to the amounts and disclosures in the financial statements. It also includes an assessment of the significant estimates and judgements made by the directors in the preparation of the financial statements, and of whether the accounting policies are appropriate to the company's circumstances, consistently applied and adequately disclosed.

We planned our audit so as to obtain all the information and explanations that we considered necessary in order to provide us with sufficient evidence to give reasonable assurance that the financial statements are free from material misstatement, whether caused by fraud or by other irregularity or error. However, the evidence available to us was limited in respect of the investment in ABC Limited, a company under the common control of the directors, which is shown in the balance sheet at a cost of £XX comprising an investment in share capital of £XX and unsecured loans of £XX. The latest available financial statements of ABC Limited were made up to 31 December 20XX and showed net assets at that date amounting to £YY. No further financial statements or other financial information concerning this investment have been made available to us. Consequently we are unable to determine whether any provisions need to be made against the carrying value of the investment or the unsecured loans due.

In forming our opinion we also evaluated the overall adequacy of the presentation of information in the financial statements.

Qualified opinion arising from limitation on audit scope

Except for any adjustments that might have been found to be necessary had we been able to obtain sufficient evidence concerning the investment in ABC Limited, in our opinion the financial statements give a true and fair view of the state of the company's affairs at 31 December 20XX and of its profit for the year then ended and have been properly prepared in accordance with the Companies Act 1985.

In our opinion the cash flow statement gives a true and fair view of the company's cash flows for the year ended 31 December 20XX.

In respect alone of the limitation on our work relating to the investment in ABC Limited we have not obtained all the information and explanations that we considered necessary for the purpose of our audit.

13:16.15.15 Example 14 Limitation on scope – disclaimer of opinion

This example is based on a limitation on the scope of audit work placed by the company's management that leads to a disclaimer of opinion on the financial statements as a whole.

Report of the auditors to the members of Blank Limited

We have audited the financial statements on pages x to x which have been prepared under the historical cost convention [*as modified by the revaluation of certain fixed assets*] and the accounting policies set out on page x.

Respective responsibilities of directors and auditors

As described on page x the company's directors are responsible for the preparation of financial statements. It is our responsibility to form an independent opinion, based on our audit, on those statements and to report our opinion to you.

Basis of opinion

We conducted our audit in accordance with Auditing Standards issued by the Auditing Practices Board, except that the scope of our work was limited as explained below.

An audit includes examination, on a test basis, of evidence relevant to the amounts and disclosures in the financial statements. It also includes an assessment of the significant estimates and judgements made by the directors in the preparation of the financial statements, and of whether the accounting policies are appropriate to the company's circumstances, consistently applied and adequately disclosed.

We planned our audit so as to obtain all the information and explanations that we considered necessary in order to provide us with sufficient evidence to give reasonable assurance that the financial statements are free from material misstatement, whether caused by fraud or by other irregularity or error. However, the evidence available to us was limited because when the company ceased trading on 9 November 20XX the documents substantiating the trading transactions of the company for the period to that date were placed into storage and have not been made available to us.

In these circumstances we were unable to carry out all the auditing procedures or to obtain all the information and explanations we considered necessary. Furthermore we have not been able to confirm or assess the collectability of the amounts due from the parent company and fellow subsidiary companies totalling £xx.

In forming our opinion we also evaluated the overall adequacy of the presentation of information in the financial statements.

Opinion: disclaimer on view given by financial statements

Because of the possible effect of the limitation in evidence available to us we are unable to form an opinion as to whether:

(a) the financial statements give a true and fair view of the state of the company's affairs at 31 December 20XX and of its profit and cash flows for the year then ended.

(b) the financial statements have been properly prepared in accordance with the Companies Act 1985.

In respect of the limitation on our work referred to above:

(a) we have not obtained all the information and explanations that we considered necessary for the purpose of our audit; and

(b) we were unable to determine whether proper accounting records had been kept.

13:16.15.16 Example 15 Adverse opinion

This example covers the situation where there is a fundamental uncertainty regarding future events. Instead of including an explanatory paragraph in the 'Basis of opinion' section and issuing an unqualified report, the auditor must issue an adverse opinion because in this case the auditor disagrees with the disclosures given in the financial statements because they omit material facts. The omission is so material that the auditor considers that the financial statements are seriously misleading.

Report of the auditors to the members of Blank PLC

We have audited the financial statements on pages x to x which have been prepared under the historical cost convention [*as modified by the revaluation of certain fixed assets*] and the accounting policies set out on page x.

Respective responsibilities of directors and auditors

As described on page x the company's directors are responsible for the preparation of financial statements. It is our responsibility to form an independent opinion, based on our audit, on those statements and to report our opinion to you.

Basis of opinion

We conducted our audit in accordance with Auditing Standards issued by the Auditing Practices Board. An audit includes examination, on a test basis, of evidence relevant to the amounts and disclosures in the financial statements. It also includes an assessment of the significant estimates and judgements made by the directors in the preparation of the financial statements, and of whether the accounting policies are appropriate to the company's circumstances, consistently applied and adequately disclosed.

We planned and performed our audit so as to obtain all the information and explanations that we considered necessary in order to provide us with sufficient evidence to give reasonable assurance that the financial statements are free from material misstatement, whether caused by fraud or by other irregularity or error. In forming our opinion we also evaluated the overall adequacy of the presentation of information in the financial statements.

Qualified opinion arising from disagreement about disclosure of fundamental uncertainty

The estimates of losses to completion amounting to £x on long-term construction contracts depend on assumptions including those relating to substantially increased productivity that have yet to be achieved. Further details of the circumstances relating to this fundamental uncertainty are described in note 1.

In our opinion the financial statements should also disclose that the increased productivity will only be possible if agreements are reached with unions to enable double-shift working to take place. Negotiations regarding such agreements have at present broken down but the directors expect them to resume shortly and that agreement will be reached so as to enable the increased productivity to be achieved.

In view of the effect of the absence of the disclosure referred to in the paragraph above in our opinion the financial statements do not give a true and fair view of the state of the company's affairs at 31 December 20XX and of its profit for the year then ended.

In our opinion the cash flow statement gives a true and fair view of the company's cash flows for the year ended 31 December 20XX and in all other respects the financial statements have been properly prepared in accordance with the Companies Act 1985.

13:16.15.17 Example 16 Disagreement – 'except for' opinion

This example covers the situation where there is a disagreement that is not sufficiently material or pervasive to require an adverse report on the financial statements as a whole, and this results in an 'except for' opinion.

Report of the auditors to the members of Blank PLC

We have audited the financial statements on pages x to x which have been prepared under the historical cost convention [*as modified by the revaluation of certain fixed assets*] and the accounting policies set out on page x.

Respective responsibilities of directors and auditors

As described on page x the company's directors are responsible for the preparation of financial statements. It is our responsibility to form an independent opinion, based on our audit, on those statements and to report our opinion to you.

Basis of opinion

We conducted our audit in accordance with Auditing Standards issued by the Auditing Practices Board. An audit includes examination, on a test basis, of evidence relevant to the amounts and disclosures in the financial statements. It also includes an assessment of the significant estimates and judgements made by the directors in the preparation of the financial statements, and of whether the accounting policies are appropriate to the company's circumstances, consistently applied and adequately disclosed.

We planned and performed our audit so as to obtain all the information and explanations that we considered necessary in order to provide us with sufficient evidence to give reasonable assurance that the financial statements are free from material misstatement, whether caused by fraud or by other irregularity or error. In forming our opinion we also evaluated the overall adequacy of the presentation of information in the financial statements.

Qualified opinion arising from disagreement about accounting treatment

As stated in note x on page x the financial statements have been prepared on a realisable value basis that has regard to the ultimate parent company's corporate strategy to withdraw from European nylon operations and to close down production facilities in July 20XX. Accordingly, plant and equipment was written down by £xx to its estimated net realisable value of £xx and provisions of £xx were made to reduce other assets to their net realisable value and to provide for the anticipated closure costs.

The realisation of all plant and equipment and other assets and the utilisation of the closure provision subsequent to 31 December 20XX show that total net provisions have been understated by £xx. In our opinion this amount should have been provided for in the financial statements.

Except for the absence of a provision for the amount referred to in the preceding paragraph, in our opinion the financial statements give a true and fair view of the state of the company's affairs at 31 December 20XX and of its loss for the year then ended and have been properly prepared in accordance with the Companies Act 1985.

In our opinion the cash flow statement gives a true and fair view of the company's cash flows for the year ended 31 December 20XX.

13:16.15.18   Example 17   Disagreement – 'except for' qualification

This is an example of a qualification on supplementary current cost financial statements (where such financial statements have been prepared and the auditor is reporting on them).

Report of the auditors to the members of Blank PLC

We have audited the financial statements on pages x to x which have been prepared under the historical cost convention [*as modified by the revaluation of certain fixed assets*] and the accounting policies set out on page x.

Respective responsibilities of directors and auditors

As described on page x the company's directors are responsible for the preparation of financial statements. It is our responsibility to form an independent opinion, based on our audit, on those statements and to report our opinion to you.

Basis of opinion

We conducted our audit in accordance with Auditing Standards issued by the Auditing Practices Board. An audit includes examination, on a test basis, of evidence relevant to the amounts and disclosures in the financial statements. It also includes an assessment of the significant estimates and judgements made by the directors in the preparation of the financial statements, and of whether the accounting policies are appropriate to the company's circumstances, consistently applied and adequately disclosed.

We planned and performed our audit so as to obtain all the information and explanations that we considered necessary in order to provide us with sufficient evidence to give reasonable assurance that the financial statements are free from material misstatement, whether caused by fraud or by other irregularity or error. In forming our opinion we also evaluated the overall adequacy of the presentation of information in the financial statements.

Opinion on historical financial statements

In our opinion the financial statements give a true and fair view of the state of the company's affairs at 31 December 20XX and of its profit and cash flows for the year then ended and have been properly prepared in accordance with the Companies Act 1985.

Qualified opinion on supplementary current cost financial statements arising from disagreement about accounting treatment

As stated in note x on page x, no current cost adjustments have been made in respect of associated companies. Except for the effects of this treatment, in our opinion the abridged supplementary current cost financial statements on page x to x have been properly prepared in accordance with the current cost principles, accounting policies and methods described in notes x to x.

13:16.15.19 Example 18 Disagreement – adverse opinion

This example covers the situation where there is a disagreement so material or pervasive as to require an adverse report on the financial statements as a whole.

Report of the auditors to the members of Blank PLC

We have audited the financial statements on pages x to x which have been prepared under the historical cost convention [*as modified by the revaluation of certain fixed assets*] and the accounting policies set out on page x.

Respective responsibilities of directors and auditors

As described on page x the company's directors are responsible for the preparation of financial statements. It is our responsibility to form an independent opinion, based on our audit, on those statements and to report our opinion to you.

Basis of opinion

We conducted our audit in accordance with Auditing Standards issued by the Auditing Practices Board. An audit includes examination, on a test basis, of evidence relevant to the amounts and disclosures in the financial statements. It also includes an assessment of the significant estimates and judgements made by the directors in the preparation of the financial statements, and of whether the accounting policies are appropriate to the company's circumstances, consistently applied and adequately disclosed.

We planned and performed our audit so as to obtain all the information and explanations that we considered necessary in order to provide us with sufficient evidence to give reasonable assurance that the financial statements are free from material misstatement, whether caused by fraud or by other irregularity or error. In forming our opinion we also evaluated the overall adequacy of the presentation of information in the financial statements.

Adverse opinion

The company's principal asset comprises work-in-progress stated at £xx. In our opinion a provision of approximately £x is required to reduce work-in-progress to its net realisable value.

In view of the effect of the failure to make the provision referred to above, in our opinion the financial statements do not give a true and fair view of the state of the company's affairs at 31 December 20XX and of its profit for the year then ended.

In our opinion the cash flow statement gives a true and fair view of the company's cash flows for the year ended 31 December 20XX and in all other respects the financial statements have been properly prepared in accordance with the Companies Act 1985.

13:16.15.20 Example 19 Disagreement – adverse opinion

This example covers the situation where there is a disagreement so material or pervasive as to require an adverse report on the balance sheet and profit and loss account.

Report of the auditors to the members of Blank Limited

We have audited the financial statements on pages x to x which have been prepared under the historical cost convention [*as modified by the revaluation of certain fixed assets*] and the accounting policies set out on page x.

Respective responsibilities of directors and auditors

As described on page x the company's directors are responsible for the preparation of financial statements. It is our responsibility to form an independent opinion, based on our audit, on those statements and to report our opinion to you.

Basis of opinion

We conducted our audit in accordance with Auditing Standards issued by the Auditing Practices Board. An audit includes examination, on a test basis, of evidence relevant to the amounts and disclosures in the financial statements. It also includes an assessment of the significant estimates and judgements made by the directors in the preparation of the financial statements, and of whether the accounting policies are appropriate to the company's circumstances, consistently applied and adequately disclosed.

We planned and performed our audit so as to obtain all the information and explanations that we considered necessary in order to provide us with sufficient evidence to give reasonable assurance that the financial statements are free from material misstatement, whether caused by fraud or by other irregularity or error. In forming our opinion we also evaluated the overall adequacy of the presentation of information in the financial statements.

Adverse opinion

As explained in note x the major source of income of the subsidiary company was terminated following discussions initiated by the government of xxx. In our opinion provision should have been made in the financial statements for the year ended 31 December 20XX for the probable long-term diminution in the value of the investment in the subsidiary which is included in the balance sheet at 31 December 20XX at a book value of £xx compared with net assets having a book value of £x.

In our opinion, in view of the effect of the probable reduction in the long-term value of the investment in the subsidiary for which no provision has been made, the financial statements do not give a true and fair view of the state of the company's affairs at 31 December 20XX and of its profit for the year then ended.

In our opinion the cash flow statement gives a true and fair view of the company's cash flows for the year ended 31 December 20XX and in all other respects the financial statements have been properly prepared in accordance with the Companies Act 1985.

13:16.15.21   Example 20   Fundamental uncertainty – current and prior periods

This example is based on a fundamental uncertainty that first arose in a prior period and resulted in an explanatory paragraph in the 'Basis of opinion' section of the audit report. As the uncertainty has not yet been resolved the matter gives rise to a further explanatory paragraph in the opinion on the current period's financial statements.

Report of the auditors to the members of Blank PLC

We have audited the financial statements on pages x to x which have been prepared under the historical cost convention [*as modified by the revaluation of certain fixed assets*] and the accounting policies set out on page x.

Respective responsibilities of directors and auditors

As described on page x the company's directors are responsible for the preparation of financial statements. It is our responsibility to form an independent opinion, based on our audit, on those statements and to report our opinion to you.

Basis of opinion

We conducted our audit in accordance with Auditing Standards issued by the Auditing Practices Board. An audit includes examination, on a test basis, of evidence relevant to the amounts and disclosures in the financial statements. It also includes an assessment of the significant estimates and judgements made by the directors in the preparation of the financial statements, and of whether the accounting policies are appropriate to the company's circumstances, consistently applied and adequately disclosed.

We planned and performed our audit so as to obtain all the information and explanations that we considered necessary in order to provide us with sufficient evidence to give reasonable assurance that the financial statements are free from material misstatement, whether caused by fraud or by other irregularity or error. In forming our opinion we also evaluated the overall adequacy of the presentation of information in the financial statements.

Fundamental uncertainty

In forming our opinion, we have considered the adequacy of the disclosures made in the financial statements concerning the possible outcome of litigation relating to an amount of £x included in debtors. The future settlement of this litigation could result in this amount not being recoverable in part or in full. However as the litigation is at an early stage no provision has been made in these financial statements. We referred to this same uncertainty in our audit report on the financial statements at [*date of preceding financial statements*]. Details of the circumstances relating to this fundamental uncertainty are described in note x. Our opinion is not qualified in this respect.

Opinion

In our opinion the financial statements give a true and fair view of the state of the company's affairs at 31 December 20XX and of its profit and cash flows for the year then ended and have been properly prepared in accordance with the Companies Act 1985.

13:16.15.22 *Example 21 Limitation on scope – prior periods*

This example covers the situation where there is a limitation on the scope of audit work relating to corresponding amounts, and this leads to an 'except for' opinion on compliance with the Companies Act.

Report of the auditors to the members of Blank PLC

We have audited the financial statements on pages x to x which have been prepared under the historical cost convention [*as modified by the revaluation of certain fixed assets*] and the accounting policies set out on page x.

Respective responsibilities of directors and auditors

As described on page x the company's directors are responsible for the preparation of financial statements. It is our responsibility to form an independent opinion, based on our audit, on those statements and to report our opinion to you.

Basis of opinion

We conducted our audit in accordance with Auditing Standards issued by the Auditing Practices Board except that the scope of our work was limited as explained below.

An audit includes examination, on a test basis, of evidence relevant to the amounts and disclosures in the financial statements. It also includes an assessment of the significant estimates and judgements made by the directors in the preparation of the financial statements, and of whether the accounting policies are appropriate to the company's circumstances, consistently applied and adequately disclosed.

We planned our audit so as to obtain all the information and explanations that we considered necessary in order to provide us with sufficient evidence to give reasonable assurance that the financial statements are free from material misstatement, whether caused by fraud or by other irregularity or error. However, the evidence available to us was limited in respect of the corresponding amounts in the current period's financial statements which are derived from the financial statements for the year ended [*date of preceding financial statements*]. In our report on those financial statements we stated that we were unable to express an opinion on the profit for the year ended on that date because we were unable to substantiate the amount of stocks at 1 January 20XX/[*preceding year*]. Accordingly the corresponding amounts shown for the profit and loss account may not be comparable with the figures for the current year.

In forming our opinion we also evaluated the overall adequacy of the presentation of information in the financial statements.

Qualified opinion arising from limitation on audit scope

In our opinion the financial statements give a true and fair view of the state of the company's affairs at 31 December 20XX and of its profit and cash flows for the year then ended and, except for any adjustments that might have been found to be necessary had we been able to obtain sufficient evidence concerning the amount of stocks at 1 January 20XX/[*preceding year*] have been properly prepared in accordance with the Companies Act 1985.

13:17 Qualified reports – departures from standard accounting practice

13:17.1 Authority and scope

Financial Reporting Standards and Statements of Standard Accounting Practice issued or adopted by the ASB contain accounting standards that apply to all financial statements intended to give a true and fair view of the financial position and the profit or loss.

Accounting standards are persuasive in determining what gives a true and fair view. It is a requirement of Schs 4, 9 and 9A to the Companies Act 1985 that the financial statements should contain a statement as to whether they have been prepared in accordance with applicable accounting standards. (However, the requirement does not apply to small and medium-sized companies.)

13:17.2 Limitations to general scope

Any limitation of the above general scope is made clear in the text of the statements. For example, FRS 14 (which requires the disclosure of earnings per share) does not apply either to the financial statements of unlisted companies (other than companies dealt in on the AIM) or to the financial statements of those listed companies that enjoy the exemptions of Schs. 9 or 9A to the Companies Act 1985. Hence, the omission of information regarding earnings per share in such cases is not a departure.

13:17.3 Disclosure of significant departures

Material departures from applicable accounting standards in financial statements should be disclosed and explained in the financial statements. This is a requirement of para. 36A of Sch. 4, para. 49 of Sch. 9 and para. 56 of Sch. 9A to the Companies Act 1985. (This requirement does not apply to small and medium-sized companies. However, there is a similar requirement in the Foreword to Accounting Standards which applies to all companies, irrespective of size.) Unless the auditor concurs with the departure, the audit report should refer to any material departure from an accounting standard. This applies regardless of whether the departure is disclosed in the financial statements.

If the departure is material, the engagement partner must document the basis on which the audit firm concurs with the departure, and follow the procedures set out **Section 5:5**, 'Consultation and concurring reviews'.

The directors should estimate and disclose the financial effect of material departures unless this would be impracticable or misleading in the context of giving a true and fair view (discussed further in **Section 13:17.3.2** (fourth paragraph)). If the financial effects of a departure from a standard are not disclosed, the directors should state the reasons for non-disclosure.

The extent of the detailed description in the audit report of the departure and of its financial effect will depend upon whether the departure is fully explained in the financial statements. If it is, the auditor may need to make only a brief reference to the circumstances in the report. But if it is not, the auditor must make a more detailed reference. Two examples are given below:

13:17.3.1 Full disclosure is made in the financial statements and the auditor does not concur with the departure

Report of the auditors to the members of Blank Limited

We have audited the financial statements on pages x to x which have been prepared under the historical cost convention [*as modified by the revaluation of certain fixed assets*] and the accounting policies set out on page x.

Respective responsibilities of directors and auditors

As described on page x the company's directors are responsible for the preparation of financial statements. It is our responsibility to form an independent opinion, based on our audit, on those statements and to report our opinion to you.

Basis of opinion

We conducted our audit in accordance with Auditing Standards issued by the Auditing Practices Board. An audit includes examination, on a test basis, of evidence relevant to the amounts and disclosures in the financial statements. It also includes an assessment of the significant estimates and judgements made by the directors in the preparation of the financial statements, and of whether the accounting policies are appropriate to the company's circumstances, consistently applied and adequately disclosed.

We planned and performed our audit so as to obtain all the information and explanations that we considered necessary in order to provide us with sufficient evidence to give reasonable assurance that the financial statements are free from material misstatement, whether caused by fraud or by other irregularity or error. In forming our opinion we also evaluated the overall adequacy of the presentation of information in the financial statements.

Qualified opinion arising from disagreement about accounting treatment

As explained in note x, regional development grants have been credited in full to profits instead of being spread over the lives of the relevant assets as required by standard accounting practice; the effect of so doing has been to increase profits before and after tax for the year by £xx (20XX £xx) and to overstate reserves by £yy (20XX £yy).

Except for the effects of accounting for regional development grants in the manner described in the preceding paragraph, in our opinion the financial statements give a true and fair view of the state of the company's affairs at 31 December 20XX and of its profit for the year then ended.

In our opinion the cash flow statement gives a true and fair view of the company's cash flows for the year ended 31 December 20XX and in all other respects the financial statements have been properly prepared in accordance with the Companies Act 1985.

13:17.3.2 Either no disclosure or inadequate disclosure in the financial statements and the auditor does not concur with the departure

In this example there is no dispute between the auditor and the company that X Limited is an associated company.

Report of the auditors to the members of Blank Holdings PLC

We have audited the financial statements on pages x to x which have been prepared under the historical cost convention [*as modified by the revaluation of certain fixed assets*] and the accounting policies set out on page x.

Respective responsibilities of directors and auditors

As described on page x the company's directors are responsible for the preparation of financial statements. It is our responsibility to form an independent opinion, based on our audit, on those statements and to report our opinion to you.

Basis of opinion

We conducted our audit in accordance with Auditing Standards issued by the Auditing Practices Board. An audit includes examination, on a test basis, of evidence relevant to the amounts and disclosures in the financial statements. It also includes an assessment of the significant estimates and judgements made by the directors in the preparation of the financial statements, and of whether the accounting policies are appropriate to the company's circumstances, consistently applied and adequately disclosed.

We planned and performed our audit so as to obtain all the information and explanations that we considered necessary in order to provide us with sufficient evidence to give reasonable assurance that the financial statements are free from material misstatement, whether caused by fraud or by other irregularity or error. In forming our opinion we also evaluated the overall adequacy of the presentation of information in the financial statements.

Qualified opinion arising from disagreement about accounting treatment

The company follows the policy of including in the consolidated financial statements only dividends received from X Limited, its associated company.

This is not in accordance with standard accounting practice. If the company had recorded its share of profits of X Limited in accordance with standard accounting practice, the profit before taxation shown in the consolidated profit and loss account would have been increased by £xx (20XX £xx) and the taxation charge would have been increased by £xx (20XX £xx). Also, the company's interest in X Limited, as shown in the consolidated balance sheet, would have been increased by £xx (20XX £xx) being the company's share of post-acquisition profits retained by X Limited.

In our opinion the balance sheet of the company gives a true and fair view of the state of the company's affairs at 31 December 20XX.

Except for the effects of accounting for its interest in its associated company in the manner described above, in our opinion the consolidated financial statements give a true and fair view of the state of the group's affairs at 31 December 20XX and of its profit and cash flows for the year then ended and in all other respects the financial statements have been properly prepared in accordance with the Companies Act 1985.

In applying accounting standards it is important to have regard to the spirit of the standards and the reasoning behind them. They are not intended to be a comprehensive code of rigid rules. They do not overrule the exercise of an informed judgement in determining what constitutes a true and fair view in each circumstance.

Financial Reporting Standards and Statements of Standard Accounting Practice recognise that there may be situations in which, for justifiable reasons, accounting standards are not strictly applicable. In particular, this may be where application would conflict with giving a true and fair view.

In all such cases, the directors must adopt either modified or alternative treatments. However, such departures must still be disclosed and explained in the financial statements. In judging exceptional or borderline cases it is important for the directors to have regard to the spirit of the accounting standards as well as to their precise terms. It is also important that they bear in mind the overriding requirement to give a true and fair view. Section 226 of the Companies Act 1985 provides that where information additional to that which the Act requires is needed for the financial statements to give a true and fair view, those statements shall include that additional information. Similarly, s. 226 provides that where, in special circumstances, compliance with a requirement of the Act is inconsistent with the requirement to give a true and fair view, the directors shall depart from that requirement to the extent necessary to give a true and fair view. It should be stressed, however, that such a departure will be necessary only in special circumstances.

When there is a departure, the notes to the financial statements must disclose particulars of the reasons for and the effect of, the departure. The Urgent Issues Task Force has issued Abstract 7, 'True and fair override disclosures', which sets out standards of disclosure that must be observed.

There may be exceptional circumstances where the auditor considers that, in preparing the financial statements, the directors have departed from an accounting standard because it was necessary in order to show a true and fair view. Provided the departure has been disclosed in the financial statements, the auditor need not refer to the departure in the audit report. The auditor must follow the consultation procedures referred to in **Section 13:17.3** (third paragraph) before he or she can concur with such a departure.

The auditor may consider that a departure is not justified and that this impairs the true and fair view shown by the financial statements. If so, the auditor should, in addition to referring to the notes and disclosing the necessary information in the audit report, express a qualified opinion. The auditor should also quantify the financial effect of the departure unless this is impracticable. If the auditor considers it is impracticable to give this quantification he or she should state the reasons.

13:17.3.3 Adverse opinion

Occasionally, a departure from an accounting standard may be so fundamental that it leads to an adverse opinion on the financial statements as a whole. If so, the auditor should report on the lines shown in the example below:

Report of the auditors to the members of Blank Limited

We have audited the financial statements on pages x to x which have been prepared under the historical cost convention [*as modified by the revaluation of certain fixed assets*] and the accounting policies set out on page x.

Respective responsibilities of directors and auditors

As described on page x the company's directors are responsible for the preparation of financial statements. It is our responsibility to form an independent opinion, based on our audit, on those statements and to report our opinion to you.

Basis of opinion

We conducted our audit in accordance with Auditing Standards issued by the Auditing Practices Board. An audit includes examination, on a test basis, of evidence relevant to the amounts and disclosures in the financial statements. It also includes an assessment of the significant estimates and judgements made by the directors in the preparation of the financial statements, and of whether the accounting policies are appropriate to the company's circumstances, consistently applied and adequately disclosed.

We planned and performed our audit so as to obtain all the information and explanations that we considered necessary in order to provide us with sufficient evidence to give reasonable assurance that the financial statements are free from material misstatement, whether caused by fraud or by other irregularity or error. In forming our opinion we also evaluated the overall adequacy of the presentation of information in the financial statements.

Adverse opinion

Development expenditure included in the balance sheet at £xx relates to a project which is unlikely to prove commercially viable in the light of the existing consumer and environmental legislation. In our opinion standard accounting practice would require that this expenditure should be written off in the profit and loss account.

Because of the significance of the foregoing matter, in our opinion the financial statements do not give a true and fair view of the state of the company's affairs at 31 December 20XX or of its profit for the year then ended.

In our opinion the cash flow statement gives a true and fair view of the company's cash flows for the year ended 31 December 20XX and in all other respects the financial statements have been properly prepared in accordance with the Companies Act 1985.

13:17.4 Additional primary statements required by accounting standards

Accounting standards contained in Financial Reporting Standards (FRS) require, in certain circumstances, further primary statements in addition to the balance sheet and profit and loss account that are required by the Companies Act 1985. The statement of total recognised gains and losses required by FRS 3, 'Reporting Financial Performance', and the cash flow statement required by FRS 1, 'Cash Flow Statements' are both primary statements.

There are two views on whether the audit report should make reference to additional primary statements that are required by accounting standards.

One view is that compliance with accounting standards is necessary to meet the requirement of company law that the directors prepare annual financial statements that give a true and fair view of a company's state of affairs and profit or loss. This view sees the additional primary statements only as necessary additional information if the financial statements are to give a true and fair view of the state of affairs and profit or loss. To mention these statements separately in the report would detract from their role of supporting the information contained in the company's balance sheet and profit and loss account. This is the view expressed in SAS 600. Accordingly, the example reports in SAS 600 do not specifically refer to cash flows or total recognised gains/losses.

An alternative view is that reference to cash flows, at least, is desirable in view of the importance of this primary statement. This does not detract from the auditor's opinion on the truth and fairness of the profit for the year or the state of affairs at the balance sheet date. The standard audit report in this Manual, therefore, differs in this respect from the example reports in SAS 600. If a client objects and wishes the auditor to limit the report to profit and state of affairs, the auditor may do so by using the wording in SAS 600.

13:17.5 Omission of a primary statement

Because the primary statements required by FRS 1 and FRS 3 support the information contained in the company's balance sheet and profit and loss account, omission of either statement will usually affect the truth and fairness of the state of affairs and profit or loss for the financial year.

Where such a primary statement is omitted, the auditor must assess whether the effect of the omission is so material or pervasive that the financial statements do not give a true and fair view. If the effect is to prevent the financial statements from giving a true and fair view the auditor must issue an adverse opinion. Where the effect is material, but not so material or pervasive that the financial statements do not give a true and fair view, the auditor must issue an 'except for' opinion.

An example of an 'except for' qualified opinion because of omission of a cash flow statement is as follows:

Report of the auditors to the members of Blank PLC

We have audited the financial statements on pages x to x which have been prepared under the historical cost convention [*as modified by the revaluation of certain fixed assets*] and the accounting policies set out on page x.

Respective responsibilities of the directors and auditors

As described on page x the company's directors are responsible for the preparation of financial statements. It is our responsibility to form an independent opinion, based on our audit, on those statements and to report our opinion to you.

Basis of opinion

We conducted our audit in accordance with Auditing Standards issued by the Auditing Practices Board. An audit includes examination, on a test basis, of evidence relevant to the amounts and disclosures in the financial statements. It also includes an assessment of the significant estimates and judgements made by the directors in the preparation of the financial statements, and of whether the accounting policies are appropriate to the company's circumstances, consistently applied and adequately disclosed.

We planned and performed our audit so as to obtain all the information and explanations that we considered necessary in order to provide us with sufficient evidence to give reasonable assurance that the financial statements are free from material misstatement, whether caused by fraud or by other irregularity or error. In forming our opinion we also evaluated the overall adequacy of the presentation of information in the financial statements.

Qualified opinion arising from omission of cash flow statement

As explained in note x the financial statements do not contain a statement of cash flows as required by Financial Reporting Standard 1. The net decrease in cash and cash equivalents for the year ended 31 December 20XX amounted to £x and in our opinion information about the company's cash flows is necessary for proper understanding of the company's state of affairs and profit/[*loss*].

Except for the failure to provide information about the company's cash flows, in our opinion the financial statements give a true and fair view of the state of the company's affairs at 31 December 20XX and of its profit/[*loss*] for the year then ended and have been properly prepared in accordance with the Companies Act 1985.

In the above example there is no reference specifically on cash flows, other than to qualify on the omission of the cash flow statement, because in this instance the auditor cannot form an opinion on a statement that is not given.

Where there are no recognised gains or losses other than the profit or loss for the period, FRS 3 allows a company to omit the statement provided that an explanation of this fact is given immediately below the profit and loss account.

13:18 Additional reports under s. 271 of the Companies Act 1985 (distributions)

13:18.1 Introduction

The distribution rules that apply to public and private companies are set out in the Companies Act 1985. Sections 271(4) and 273(5) require the auditors, if they have qualified their opinion on the financial statements, to state in writing whether the subject matter of their qualification is material in determining the legality of any distribution. Consequently, where the auditor qualifies the report on the financial statements of a company that is proposing to pay a dividend, the auditor will need to make an additional statement to the members of the company. That statement must be laid before the company in general meeting before the dividend is paid.

13:18.2 Companies Act requirements

Section 263 of the Companies Act 1985 states that a company shall not make a distribution except out of profits available for the purpose. It is important that clients should keep sufficient records to enable them to distinguish between reserves that are distributable and those which are not. The auditor should ensure that the dividend is permitted by the legislation.

Where the audit report is qualified, special considerations arise. Section 271(4) of the Companies Act 1985 states that:

> **The auditors must in that case [*i.e. if the report is a qualified report*] also have stated in writing (either at the time of their report or subsequently) whether, in their opinion, the matter in respect of which their report is qualified is material for determining, by reference to items mentioned in section 270(2), whether the distribution would contravene the relevant section; and a copy of the statement must have been laid before the company in general meeting.**

13:18.3 Relevant qualifications

A qualified report for the purposes of s. 271(4) of the Companies Act 1985 is one in which the auditor is unable to report without qualification that the financial statements have been properly prepared in accordance with the Act. This would include all qualifications relating to the true and fair view, but would not include explanatory paragraphs in the 'Basis of opinion' section of the audit report, referring to fundamental uncertainties which are adequately disclosed in the financial statements.

13:18.4 The meaning of 'material'

A qualification is material in the context of a particular dividend if, were the financial statements to be adjusted so that the qualification could be removed, the amount of profits distributable in terms of ss. 263 to 267 and 275 of the Companies Act 1985 would, or might, be reduced to such an extent that the intended distribution was illegal.

Certain types of qualification cannot be material in this context, because they do not affect the determination of accumulated profits. Examples are:

(a) Qualifications relating to the classification of profits and losses (e.g., between ordinary activities and extraordinary items, or between the current year and prior years).

(b) Qualifications that only affect the consolidated financial statements.

(c) Qualifications related to disclosure.

(d) Qualifications on illegal loans to directors (unless the value of the loan is in question).

13:18.5 Effect of qualified audit reports

Set out below are some of the matters that the auditor should consider when determining the format of the additional statement to the members and the wording that should be used.

13:18.5.1 An 'except for' opinion relating to disagreement about amounts

Where an audit report qualification arises from a disagreement between the auditor and the directors as to the amount at which an item should appear in the financial statements, generally the auditor will have no difficulty in deciding whether the qualification is material in determining the legality of the proposed distribution. The report set out below illustrates this point:

Report of the auditors to the members of Blank PLC

We have audited the financial statements on pages x to x which have been prepared under the historical cost convention [*as modified by the revaluation of certain fixed assets*] and the accounting policies set out on page x.

Respective responsibilities of directors and auditors

As described on page x the company's directors are responsible for the preparation of financial statements. It is our responsibility to form an independent opinion, based on our audit, on those statements and to report our opinion to you.

Basis of opinion

We conducted our audit in accordance with Auditing Standards issued by the Auditing Practices Board. An audit includes examination, on a test basis, of evidence relevant to the amounts and disclosures in the financial statements. It also includes an assessment of the significant estimates and judgements made by the directors in the preparation of the financial statements, and of whether the accounting policies are appropriate to the company's circumstances, consistently applied and adequately disclosed.

We planned and performed our audit so as to obtain all the information and explanations that we considered necessary in order to provide us with sufficient evidence to give reasonable assurance that the financial statements are free from material misstatement, whether caused by fraud or by other irregularity or error. In forming our opinion we also evaluated the overall adequacy of the presentation of information in the financial statements.

Qualified opinion arising from disagreement about accounting treatment

No provision has been made against an amount of £xx owing by a company which has been placed in liquidation since the year-end. The liquidator has indicated that unsecured creditors are unlikely to receive any payment and in our opinion full provision should be made.

Except for the failure to provide the amount described above, in our opinion the financial statements give a true and fair view of the state of the company's affairs at 31 December 20XX and of its profit for the year then ended.

In our opinion the cash flow statement gives a true and fair view of the company's cash flows for the year ended 31 December 20XX and in all other respects the financial statements have been properly prepared in accordance with the Companies Act 1985.

In these circumstances, the proposed distribution would be legal, if, by deducting from distributable reserves the amount of the required provision against the debt, the net figure is adequate for the purposes of the distribution.

13:18.5.2 An 'except for' opinion relating to a limitation on the scope of our work

Where an audit report qualification arises from a limitation on the scope of the audit work, the auditor will be able to decide whether the qualification is material in determining the legality of the proposed distribution only if he or she can place an upper limit on the liabilities affected and a lower limit on the assets affected. The report set out below illustrates this point:

Report of the auditors to the members of Blank PLC

We have audited the financial statements on pages x to x which have been prepared under the historical cost convention [*as modified by the revaluation of certain fixed assets*] and the accounting policies set out on page x.

Respective responsibilities of directors and auditors

As described on page x the company's directors are responsible for the preparation of financial statements. It is our responsibility to form an independent opinion, based on our audit, on those statements and to report our opinion to you.

Basis of opinion

We conducted our audit in accordance with Auditing Standards issued by the Auditing Practices Board, except that the scope of our work was limited as explained below.

An audit includes examination, on a test basis, of evidence relevant to the amounts and disclosures in the financial statements. It also includes an assessment of the significant estimates and judgements made by the directors in the preparation of the financial statements, and of whether the accounting policies are appropriate to the company's circumstances, consistently applied and adequately disclosed.

We planned our audit so as to obtain all the information and explanations that we considered necessary in order to provide us with sufficient evidence to give reasonable assurance that the financial statements are free from material misstatement, whether caused by fraud or by other irregularity or error. However the evidence available to us was limited because one branch of the company did not carry out a physical count of stock at 31 December 20XX and there were no practicable alternative auditing procedures that we could apply to obtain all the information and explanations that we considered necessary to satisfy ourselves as to the existence of stock valued at £xx at 31 December 20XX which is included as part of the total stocks of £xx in the balance sheet.

In forming our opinion we also evaluated the overall adequacy of the presentation of information in the financial statements.

Qualified opinion arising from limitation on audit scope

Except for any adjustments that might have been found to be necessary had we been able to obtain sufficient evidence concerning the branch stocks referred to above, in our opinion the financial statements give a true and fair view of the state of the company's affairs at 31 December 20XX and of its profit and cash flows for the year then ended and have been properly prepared in accordance with the Companies Act 1985.

In respect alone of the limitation on our work relating to branch stocks:

(a) we have not obtained all the information and explanations that we considered necessary for the purpose of our audit; and

(b) in our opinion proper accounting records have not been kept.

In these circumstances, the proposed distribution would be legal, if, after deducting from distributable reserves the amount of the stock affected (e.g., by valuing that stock either at nil or at a reduced amount that depends on the nature of the qualification), the net figure is adequate for the purpose of the distribution.

If the auditor cannot quantify the financial effect of a matter for which, as a result of a limitation on scope, the auditor has been unable to obtain sufficient evidence, the auditor should regard the effect as infinite in respect of a possible understatement of liabilities. In respect of a possible overstatement of assets, the auditor should regard the effect as being limited to the amount at which the asset is stated.

13:18.5.3 A disclaimer of opinion

In circumstances where the auditor disclaims an opinion because the possible effect of a limitation on scope is so material or pervasive that the auditor cannot form an opinion on the financial statements as a whole, the auditor will not be in a position to confirm the amount at which the company's net assets are stated. Accordingly, the auditor will not be able to state that the qualification is not material in determining the legality of the proposed distribution.

13:18.5.4 An 'except for' opinion relating to disclosure only

Where there is an inherent uncertainty that the auditor considers to be fundamental, the auditor should normally refer to this by way of an explanatory paragraph in the 'Basis of opinion' section of the report, if the disclosure relating to the uncertainty in the financial statements is adequate. Where it is inadequate the auditor must qualify the report. Such a qualification will, however, not be material for the purpose of determining the legality of any proposed dividend. Although this may seem strange, because a fundamental uncertainty could, e.g., include uncertainty about the validity of the going concern basis of accounting, the qualification is not material because it relates solely to the disclosure in the financial statements and not to amounts.

13:18.5.5 An adverse opinion

Where an adverse opinion is given, the financial statements as a whole do not give a true and fair view. If the auditor is able to quantify the maximum effect of the disagreement and adjust distributable reserves to determine whether the balance would or would not render the proposed dividend illegal, the auditor will be able to report on whether the qualification is material. If the effect of the disagreement is not capable of quantification, however, the auditor will not be able to state that the qualification is not material in determining the legality of the proposed distribution.

13:18.5.6 The audit report qualification is material, but 'favourable'

In circumstances where the audit report qualification is material in determining the legality of the proposed distribution, but is a 'favourable' qualification, the auditor does not need to regard it as material for the purposes of the distribution. For example, where the auditor considers that a provision for a possible loss is excessive, an adjustment of the financial statements would increase either net assets or realised profits.

13:18.6 The wording of the additional statement

Section 271 of the Companies Act 1985 envisages that the additional statement will be made separately to the members of the company and the auditor must so make it if the directors request this. However, as an alternative, the statement may be incorporated as a separate paragraph in the report. In any situation where it appears that the effect of the qualification would, or might, make the distribution illegal, then the auditor should endeavour to include the statement in the report. Section 271(4) requires that a copy of this statement must have been laid before the company in general meeting.

Where the audit qualification is 'unfavourable', but is not material in determining the legality of the proposed distribution, the auditor should add the following paragraph as the final paragraph to the audit report:

In our opinion the qualification is not material for the purpose of determining, by reference to these financial statements, whether the final dividend for the year ended 31 December 20XX proposed by the company is permitted under ss. 263 (and 264)* of the Companies Act 1985.

* public companies only

Where the auditor reports separately to the members of the company the statement should be as follows:

Statement of the auditors to the members of Blank PLC under s. 271(4) of the Companies Act 1985

We have audited the financial statements of Blank PLC for the year ended 31 December 20XX in accordance with Auditing Standards issued by the Auditing Practices Board and have expressed a qualified opinion on them.

In our opinion that qualification is not material for the purpose of determining, by reference to those financial statements, whether the distribution proposed by the company is permitted under ss. 263 (and 264)* of the Companies Act 1985.

* public companies only

Where the audit qualification is material in determining the legality of the proposed distribution, the auditor should delete the word 'not' before the word 'material'. In addition, the auditor should, if practicable, add a brief explanation of the effect the qualification has on the company's ability to make the distribution.

Where the effect of the audit qualification is favourable, the auditor can word the additional statement as follows to cover any future distributions:

In our opinion the qualification is not material for the purpose of determining whether any distribution payable by reference to these financial statements is permitted under ss. 263 (and 264)* of the Companies Act 1985.

* public companies only

Where the auditor can quantify the effect of an audit qualification that is unfavourable but is not material for this purpose, he or she can word the statement as follows to cover any future distributions:

In our opinion the qualification is not material for the purpose of determining whether distributions not exceeding £xx in total payable by

reference to these financial statements are permitted under ss. 263 (and 264)* the Companies Act 1985.

* public companies only

Because most companies will want to pay an interim dividend in the following year, and the financial statements on which the auditor is reporting will constitute the relevant financial statements for the purposes of that interim dividend, the auditor should, where appropriate, word the statement in the manner of the preceding two examples. If the auditor does not do so, but instead limits the statement solely to the final dividend proposed, the auditor will have to make a further statement in respect of the interim dividend. The company would then have to hold a general meeting in order to lay this statement before the members.

Where a company has preference shares, the statement will need to cover distributions by way of dividends on those shares.

13:18.7 Audit implications

Where the auditor intends to qualify the audit opinion on the financial statements of a company that is bound by the distribution rules set out in the Companies Act 1985, the auditor should carry out the following procedures:

(a)   Ascertain whether the qualification is material in determining the legality of the proposed distribution.

(b)   Draft an appropriate additional paragraph to the qualified audit report, or a separate statement to the members.

(c)   Follow the consultation procedures set out in **Section 5:5**, 'Consultation and concurring reviews'.

13:18.8 Fundamental uncertainties

Where the audit report contains an explanatory paragraph referring to a fundamental uncertainty, but is unqualified, there is no legal requirement to make any statement under s. 271(4) of the Companies Act 1985 (*see* **Section 13:18.3**). However, where there is a fundamental uncertainty, the effect of which could be material to a dividend proposed in the financial statements, the auditor should consider whether the disclosure of the effects of the fundamental uncertainty in the financial statements adequately reflects this fact.

Where the auditor adds an explanatory paragraph relating to a fundamental uncertainty to the audit report, he or she must also follow the consultation procedures referred to in **Section 13:18.7** (point (c)). Such consultation should include consideration of the matters referred to in the preceding paragraph.

13:19 Qualified reports on information contained in the directors' report and on other information in documents containing audited financial statements

13:19.1 Introduction

Section 235 of the Companies Act 1985 extends the responsibilities of the auditor to the directors' report as follows:

> *The auditors shall consider whether the information given in the directors' report for the financial year for which the annual accounts are prepared is consistent with those accounts; and if they are of the opinion that it is not they shall state that fact in their report.*

Guidance on the auditors' responsibilities is given in SAS 160, 'Other Information in Documents Containing Audited Financial Statements', revised by the APB in October 1999.

The types of other information, apart from the directors' report, which may be included with the audited financial statements are:

(a)   The chairman's statement.

(b)   An operating and financial review.

(c)   Financial summaries.

(d)   Employment data.

(e)   Planned capital expenditures.

(f)   Financial ratios.

(g)   Selected quarterly data.

To this can be added information on individual directors' emoluments and other information that should be included in a remuneration committee report to be presented by listed companies as part of, or annexed, to their annual report and financial statements (*see also* **Section 13:21**, 'Qualified or modified reports on directors' emoluments and other benefits').

13:19.2 Audit implications

13:19.2.1 Procedures

SAS 160 states:

> *Auditors should read the other information. If as a result they become aware of any apparent misstatements therein, or identify any material inconsistencies with the audited financial statements, they should seek to resolve them.*

The auditor should examine the directors' report and any other information issued with the audited financial statements, or in which audited financial statements are included, as discussed in **Section 10:3**, 'Reviewing the financial statements'. The auditor should consider whether the directors' report and other information are consistent with the financial statements and with other information known to the auditor. This should be done by a senior member of the audit team who can be expected to detect inconsistencies.

SAS 160 states, in relation to inconsistencies or misstatements:

> *If auditors identify an inconsistency between the financial statements and the other information, or a misstatement within the other information, they should consider whether an amendment is required to the financial statements or to the other information and should seek to resolve the matter through discussion with the directors.*

A misstatement within the other information exists when the other information is stated incorrectly or presented in a misleading manner.

An inconsistency exists when the other information contradicts, or appears to contradict, information contained in the financial statements. An inconsistency may raise doubt about the audit conclusions drawn from audit evidence previously obtained and possibly about the basis for the audit opinion on the financial statements. An example is a situation where the going concern basis was in doubt because of the loss of a major customer and the financial statements contained disclosures relating to this uncertainty, but the chairman's statement referred to expectations of a major new contract from that customer.

If the auditor identifies an inconsistency or a misstatement he or she should consider whether an amendment is required to the financial statements. The auditor should hold discussions with management in order to achieve the elimination of material inconsistencies or misstatements. The auditor should keep a written record of the matters discussed.

SAS 160 states, in relation to discussions:

> *If, after discussion with the directors, the auditors conclude:*
>
> *that the financial statements require amendment and no such amendment is made, they should consider the implications for their report; or*
>
> *that the other information requires amendment and no such amendment is made, they should consider appropriate action including the implications for their report.*

13:19.2.2 *Effect of inconsistencies and misstatements on the audit report*

If the auditor is unable to eliminate inconsistencies or misstatements, he or she should consider the implications for the audit report. Where the inconsistency is between the directors' report and the financial statements, the auditor must draw attention to the inconsistency in the audit report, because this is required by the Companies Act 1985 (*see* **Section 13:19.1**).

Matters which may require resolution or to which the auditor may need to refer in an explanatory paragraph within the audit report include:

(a)   An inconsistency between amounts or narrative appearing in the financial statements and the directors' report.

(b)   An inconsistency between the bases of preparation of related items appearing in the financial statements and the directors' report, where the figures themselves are not directly comparable and the different bases are not disclosed.

(c)   An inconsistency between figures contained in the financial statements and a narrative interpretation of the effect of those figures in the directors' report.

Set out below is an example of an audit report on an inconsistency between the directors' report and the financial statements in circumstances where it is the directors' report that requires amendment:

> **Report of the auditors to the members of Blank PLC**
>
> **We have audited the financial statements on pages x to x which have been prepared under the historical cost convention [*as modified by the revaluation of certain fixed assets*] and the accounting policies set out on page x.**
>
> **Respective responsibilities of directors and auditors**
>
> **As described on page x the company's directors are responsible for the preparation of financial statements. It is our responsibility to form an independent opinion, based on our audit, on those statements and to report our opinion to you.**
>
> **Basis of opinion**
>
> **We conducted our audit in accordance with Auditing Standards issued by the Auditing Practices Board. An audit includes examination, on a test basis, of evidence relevant to the amounts and disclosures in the financial statements. It also includes an assessment of the significant estimates and judgements made by the directors in the preparation of the financial statements, and of whether the accounting policies are appropriate to the company's circumstances, consistently applied and adequately disclosed.**

We planned and performed our audit so as to obtain all the information and explanations that we considered necessary in order to provide us with sufficient evidence to give reasonable assurance that the financial statements are free from material misstatement whether caused by fraud or by other irregularity or error. In forming our opinion we also evaluated the overall adequacy of the presentation of information in the financial statements.

Opinion

In our opinion the financial statements give a true and fair view of the state of the company's affairs at 31 December 20XX and of its profit/[*loss*] and cash flows for the year then ended and have been properly prepared in accordance with the Companies Act 1985.

Inconsistency between the financial statements and the directors' report

As stated in note x to the profit and loss account, the turnover for the company's Australian division amounted to £xx. The directors' report states, however, that the company, which has a total turnover of £xx, has made very substantial sales during the year to Australia, representing a large proportion of the company's total turnover. In our opinion this statement in the directors' report is not consistent with the company's financial statements for the year.

Note: The above form of report is not a qualified report for the purposes of ss. 240(3)(d) (publication of non-statutory financial statements) or 271(4) (auditors' statement if financial statements are qualified and dividend proposed to be paid – *see* **Section 13:18**, 'Additional reports under s. 271 of the Companies Act 1985 (distributions)') of the Companies Act 1985, as the opinion on the financial statements is unaffected.

13:19.2.3 Further action

If the auditor concludes that the other information contains any misstatements or inconsistencies with the financial statements, in circumstances other than those in which **Section 13:19.2.2** (first paragraph) applies, and the auditor is unable to resolve them through discussion with the directors, the auditor should consider including in the audit report an explanatory paragraph describing the apparent misstatement or material inconsistency. The auditor may need to seek legal advice when considering such action. In particular, the auditor may need legal advice on whether he or she would be protected by qualified privilege from a defamation claim if the auditor were to refer to the matters in the audit report or subsequently.

Set out below is an example of an explanatory paragraph where the auditor considers that other information is inconsistent with the financial statements. The paragraph would appear below the opinion paragraph of the audit report.

Inconsistency between the financial statements and the chairman's statement

We do not express any opinion on the financial information contained in the other statements issued with the financial statements identified above. We do, however, draw attention to the inconsistency between the chairman's statement and the profit and loss account. The operating result as shown in the profit and loss account is a loss of £xx. The third sentence of the chairman's report, however, indicates that the operating result is £xx by taking account of a profit from the sale of land £xx.

Auditors of a limited company may use the right under s. 390 of the Companies Act 1985 to be heard at any general meeting of the members on any part of the business of the meeting which concerns them as auditors.

The auditor may also consider resigning from the audit engagement. For auditors of limited companies, the requirements of s. 394 of the Companies Act 1985 for auditors to make a statement on their ceasing to hold office as auditors apply.

13:19.3 Timing considerations

In order that the auditor can consider the other information included in the annual report, appropriate arrangements should be made with the client to obtain timely access to such information before the date of the audit report. SAS 600, 'Auditors' reports on financial statements', requires all other information to be approved by the entity, and auditors to consider all necessary evidence, before the audit opinion is expressed.

13:19.4 Consultation

In all cases where the auditor is considering adding an explanatory paragraph to the audit report to draw attention to an inconsistency between the directors' report or other information and the financial statements, or where the auditor intends to seek legal advice, the procedures set out in **Section 5:5**, 'Consultation and concurring reviews', must be followed.

13:19.5 Appendix A Determining a course of action regarding material misstatements and inconsistencies

The process described below is to be followed in respect of each individual material inconsistency between the financial statements and the other information, and each material misstatement within the other information.

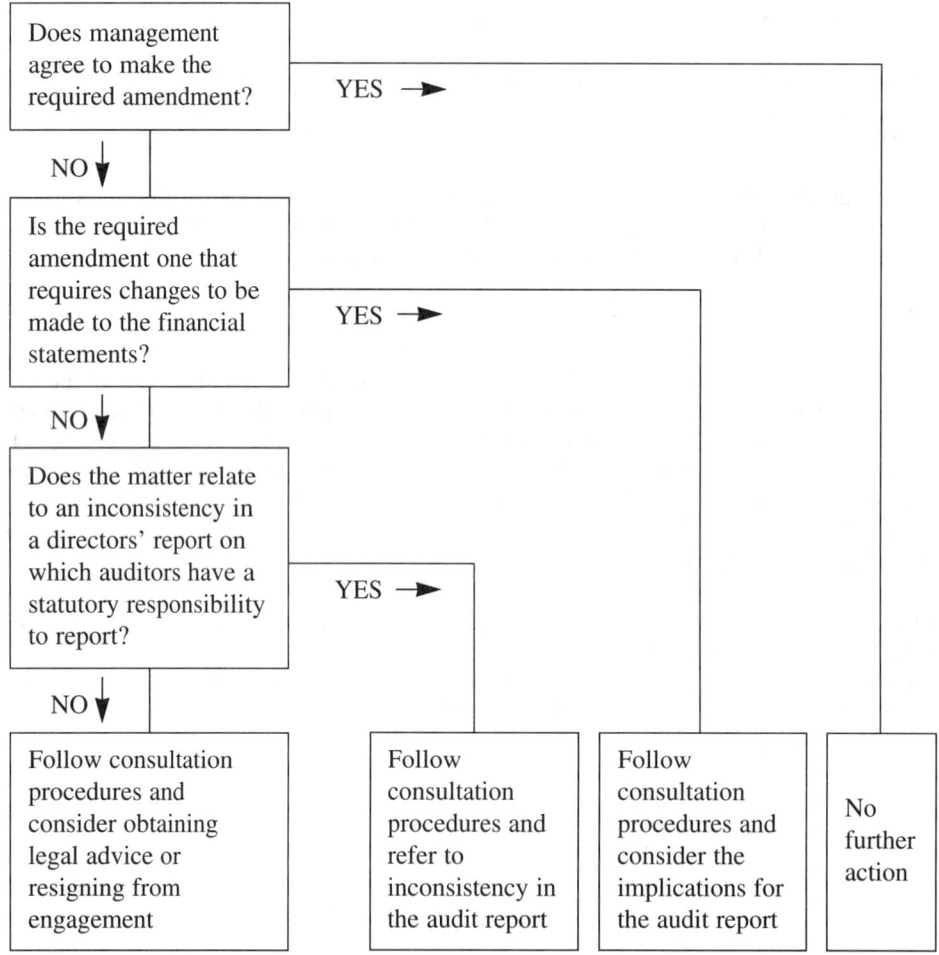

13:20 Revision of defective accounts

13:20.1 Introduction

Before the Companies Act 1989 there was no legal provision for the revision of financial statements or directors' reports. In practice, when revisions took place the Registrar of Companies would accept the revised financial statements and directors' report and put them on the company's file. However, there was no legal requirement for him to do so and the original financial statements and directors' report were not removed from the file.

13:20.2 The Companies Act 1989

The Companies Act 1989 amended the 1985 Act by introducing provisions which:

(a)   permit directors to prepare revised financial statements or a revised directors' report where it appears to them that the annual financial statements or directors' report did not comply with the Companies Act 1985 ('voluntary revision'); and

(b)   permit the Secretary of State (in the absence of a satisfactory explanation from the directors of a company to the question of whether the financial statements or directors' report comply with the Companies Act 1985), to apply to the court for an order that revised financial statements should be prepared. Application may also be made by a person authorised by the Secretary of State (the Review Panel of the Financial Reporting Council is such a person); this is known as 'compulsory revision'.

The provisions referred to above are contained in ss. 245, 245A, 245B and 245C of the Companies Act 1985.

   The detailed regulations governing the preparation, audit and issuance of revised financial statements and directors' reports, where the revision is voluntary, are contained in The Companies (Revision of Defective Accounts and Report) Regulations 1990 (SI No. 2570) ('the regulations') as amended by The Companies (Summary Financial Statement) Regulations 1992 (SI No. 3075), The Companies Act 1985 (Audit Exemption) Regulations 1994 (SI No. 1935) and The Companies (Revision of Defective Accounts and Report)(Amendment) Regulations 1996 (SI No. 315).

   There are no regulations governing the preparation, audit and issuance of financial statements and directors' reports that are compulsorily revised, as the court is empowered to give directions as to these and other matters as it thinks fit. The remainder of this section therefore deals only with voluntary revisions, the requirements of the regulations and audit issues that may arise.

13:20.3 Circumstances in which a voluntary revision may be made

The directors may revise the financial statements or the directors' report if it appears to them that the original financial statements or the directors' report did not comply with the requirements of the Companies Act 1985 ('the Act'). The revisions must be confined to the correction of those respects in which the previous financial statements or directors' report did not comply with the Act and any consequential amendments.

13:20.4 Type of revision

Revision of the financial statements or directors' report may be made either by preparing replacement financial statements or directors' reports or by preparing a supplementary note indicating corrections to be made to the original financial statements or directors' report.

13:20.5 Revision of financial statements or directors' report

Where a decision has been made to replace the original financial statements or directors' report, they should be prepared in the normal way in accordance with the provisions of the Act which were in force at the date on which the original financial statements and directors' report were approved. (Thus, contrary to what might have been expected, the relevant provisions are **not** those in force at the date of the company's year-end.) There could therefore be additional consequential amendments to be made as a result of changes in the Act between the company's year-end and the date of approval of the original financial statements. In the case of revisions to abbreviated financial statements, references to provisions of the Act are to provisions in force at the date of delivery of the original abbreviated financial statements. In the case of revisions to summary financial statements, references to s. 251 or to the regulations regarding summary financial statements are to that section or those regulations in force at the date of sending out the original summary financial statement.

13:20.6 Subsequent events

The regulations state that the provisions of the Act as to the matters to be included in the annual financial statements of a company shall apply to the revised financial statements **as if the revised financial statements were prepared and approved by the directors as at the date of approval of the original financial statements.**

The purpose of this is to exclude from consideration events that occur between the date of approval of the original financial statements and the date of approval of the revised financial statements.

13:20.7 Approval and signature of revised financial statements or directors' report

13:20.7.1 Revised financial statements

The regulations provide that revised financial statements must be approved by the board and signed by a director on the board's behalf. In the case of revision by supplementary note the signature should be on the supplementary note. The following must be stated in financial statements that are revised by replacement, if the original financial statements have been sent to members, laid before the company in general meeting or delivered to the Registrar:

(a)   That the revised financial statements replace the original financial statements for the financial year (specifying it).

(b)   That they are now the statutory financial statements of the company for that financial year.

(c)   That they have been prepared as at the date of the original annual financial statements (i.e., the date on which the original financial statements were approved) and not as at the date of revision (i.e., the date of approval of the revised financial statements) and accordingly do not deal with events between those dates.

(d)   The respects in which the original financial statements did not comply with the requirements of the Act.

(e)   Any significant amendments made consequential upon the remedying of those defects.

Where the financial statements are revised by supplementary note, the following statements must be made in the note:

(a)   That the note revises in certain respects the original annual financial statements of the company and is to be treated as forming part of those financial statements.

(b)   That the annual financial statements have been revised as at the date of the original financial statements and not as at the date of revision (*see* **Section 13:20.7.1** (c) above) and accordingly do not deal with events between those dates.

The date of the approval of the revised financial statements must be given in those financial statements (in the case of revision by supplementary note, the date should be given in the note).

13:20.7.2 *Revised directors' report*

Similar considerations apply to a revised directors' report. The revised report must be approved by the board and signed on its behalf by a director or the secretary. In the case of revision by supplementary note the signature must be on the supplementary note. Where the original directors' report has been sent to members, laid before the company in general meeting or delivered to the Registrar, the revised report must state, where it is revised by replacement the following:

(a)   That the revised report replaces the original report for the financial year (specifying it).

(b)   That it has been prepared as at the date of (approval of) the original directors' report and not as at the date of (approval of) the revision and accordingly does not deal with any events between those dates.

(c)   The respects in which the original directors' report did not comply with the requirements of the Act.

(d)   Any significant amendments made consequential upon the remedying of those defects.

Where it is revised by supplementary note the note must state the following:

(a)   That the note revises in certain respects the original directors' report of the company and is to be treated as forming part of that report.

(b)   That the directors' report has been revised as at the date of (approval of) the original directors' report and not as at the date of (approval of) the revision and accordingly does not deal with events between those dates.

The date of approval of the revised report must be given in the revised report (or in the supplementary note, if revised by supplementary note).

13:20.8 Auditors' report on revised financial statements and directors' report

If there has been a change of auditors between the date of the original financial statements and the date of the revised financial statements, the report on the revised financial statements must be made by the new auditors unless the directors resolve that it be made by the former auditors (provided that the former auditors agree to do so and that they would be qualified for appointment as auditors of the company). Where new auditors or former auditors are requested by the directors to report on revised financial statements the firm should consider all the implications and follow the firm's consultation procedures (*see* **Section 13:20.16** below).

Whether the auditors are reporting as present or former auditors, the contents of the audit report must be the same. It must state whether in the opinion of the auditor:

(a)   the revised financial statements have been properly prepared in accordance with the provisions of the Act as they have effect under the regulations;

(b)   a true and fair view, **seen as at the date when the original financial statements were approved**, is given by the revised financial statements of the state of the company's affairs at the end of the financial year, and of the profit or loss of the company for the financial year (or, in the case of consolidated financial statements, of the state of affairs of the company and the group at the end of the financial year and of the profit or loss of the group for the financial year); and

(c)   the original annual financial statements failed to comply with the requirements of the Act in the respects identified by the directors:

    (i)   (in the case of revision by replacement) in the statement the directors are required to make in the revised financial statements; or

    (ii)   (in the case of revision by supplementary note) in the supplementary note.

The auditor must also consider whether the information in the original or, if it has been revised, the revised directors' report is consistent with the revised financial statements and, if it is not, that fact must be stated in the audit report. The auditor must sign the report which, after being signed, replaces the original audit report as the audit report on the company's financial statements.

13:20.9 Auditors' report on revised directors' report alone

Where the financial statements are not being revised, but the directors' report is and there has been a change of auditors, the company's current auditors must report on the revised directors' report unless the directors resolve that the auditors' report be made by the former auditors (provided that the former auditors agree to do so and that they would be qualified for appointment as auditors of the company). The firm (who may be the present or former auditors, as the directors decide) is not required to report on the revised financial statements. The firm must, however, report on the revised directors' report. The report must state that the auditor has considered whether the information in the revised report is consistent with the annual financial statements for the financial year and:

(a)   if the auditor is of the opinion that it is; or

(b)   if the auditor is of the opinion that it is not, the auditor must state that fact in the report. The report must be signed and dated.

13:20.10 Publication of revised financial statements and directors' report

If the original financial statements and directors' report have already been sent to members and others entitled to receive copies, the directors must send copies of the revised financial statements and directors' report, together with the auditors' report, to those persons not more than 28 days from the date of approval of the revised financial statements and report. Where, however, the revision has been by supplementary note the directors need only send the supplementary note, and the auditors' report on the revised financial statements (or as the case may be, on the revised report). The directors must also (again within 28 days of the date of approval of the revised financial statements and report) send copies of the revised financial statements or report, together with the audit report, to persons who are at the date on which the revised financial statements or report are approved:

(a)   a member of the company;

(b)   a holder of the company's debentures; or

(c)   a person who is entitled to receive notice of general meetings.

13:20.11 Laying of revised financial statements and directors' report

Where the original financial statements and directors' report have already been laid before members, the company will have to lay the revised financial statements and report, together with the auditors' report, before the next general meeting at which annual financial statements are laid, unless they choose to lay them before an earlier general meeting.

13:20.12 Delivery of revised financial statements and directors' report

Where the original financial statements and directors' report have already been delivered to the Registrar, the directors must deliver the revised financial statements and report together with the auditors' report, to the Registrar within 28 days of the date of approval of the revised financial statements and report. Where the revision has been by supplementary note, only that note and the auditors' report on the revised financial statements (or on the revised report as the case may be) need be delivered.

13:20.13 Small and medium-sized companies and dormant companies

The regulations provide for the revision of abbreviated financial statements where these are affected by the revision of a company's full financial statements. In this case **either** the revised abbreviated financial statements should be delivered to the Registrar with a statement as to the effect of the revisions made, **or** the company must deliver a copy of the revised financial statements and directors' report together with the auditors' report thereon. The latter alternative must be adopted, if, as a result of the revision, the company is no longer entitled to file abbreviated financial statements. Where abbreviated financial statements are not affected by the revision to the full financial statements, a note stating that the full financial statements have been revised in a respect that has no bearing on the abbreviated financial statements, together with a copy of the auditors' report on the revised financial statements, must be delivered to the Registrar.

Where the abbreviated financial statements are not affected by a revision to the full financial statements but they fail to comply with the Act in some other respect the abbreviated financial statements alone must be revised. The directors must prepare revised abbreviated financial statements and deliver them to the Registrar within 28 days of the date of approval of the revised abbreviated financial statements. The revised abbreviated financial statements must contain a statement as to the effect of the revisions made.

13:20.14 Summary financial statements

Where the summary financial statement has been sent to members and others entitled to receive it, and its contents are affected by the revision of the annual financial statements such that the original summary financial statement no longer complies with the Act, the company must prepare a revised statement. The revised summary financial statement must contain a short statement of the revisions and their effect. The company must send the revised statement to all those who received the original summary statement and to any person to whom the company would be entitled to send such a statement as at the date of preparation of the revised statement.

If, however, the original summary financial statement is not affected by the revision of the annual financial statements, the company must send a note stating that the annual financial statements or directors' report for the year have been revised in a respect that has no bearing on the summary financial statement for that year. This note should be sent to the same persons as mentioned in the preceding paragraph. If the auditors' report on the revised financial statements or directors' report has been qualified, a copy of that report must also be sent out attached to the note.

The revised statement or note must be sent within 28 days of the date of approval of the revised financial statements or directors' report.

13:20.15 Companies exempt from audit

Under certain circumstances small companies may be exempt from audit by virtue of s. 249A of the Companies Act 1985. Details are given in Section 13:9, 'Audit exemption for small companies and groups'.

Where a small company is exempt from audit, the regulations regarding revisions of defective accounts apply as if any reference to an auditors' report, or to the making of such a report, were omitted. In practice, this means that as there was no auditors' report on the original financial statements, there is no auditors' report on the revised financial statements.

Where a company that met the exemption conditions in its original financial statements does not meet the conditions in its revised financial statements, the company must obtain a full audit opinion on the revised financial statements.

The auditors' report must be delivered to the Registrar of Companies within 28 days after the date of the revision of the financial statements.

13:20.16 Audit implications

In all cases where the auditor is reporting on revised financial statements and directors' reports, the auditor should carry out the following procedures:

(a)   Determine the reasons for revision and form a view from available evidence as to whether those reasons are valid. If they are not valid the auditor should not report on the revised financial statements. If there is uncertainty, the auditor should discuss the reasons with the directors before commencing work. In all cases where a report on revised financial statements is being considered the auditor must follow the procedures in **Section 5:5**, 'Consultation and concurring reviews'.

(b)   Review the audit planning and testing carried out on the audit of the original financial statements and in particular review all matters of judgement involved in the preparation of those financial statements.

(c)   Reconsider the integrity of management and the nature of management's earlier representations.

(d)   Obtain evidence to substantiate the changes being made to the original financial statements.

(e)   Update the existing subsequent events review work, to the date of the original audit report.

(f)   Review the revised financial statements and directors' report.

Where the auditor did not audit the original financial statements, the extent of the audit work on the revised financial statements will normally be increased considerably.

13:20.17 Subsequent events and dual dating

The auditor must state his or her opinion as at the date the original financial statements were approved, despite the fact that the report will be dated as at the date the auditor actually signs the report on the revised financial statements. The report should therefore make clear the basis on which the financial statements have been prepared and that the auditor's opinion is 'as of' a date that differs from the date on which he or she signs the report. The auditor may also need to include in the report a reference to the fact that the revised financial statements do not take account of events subsequent to the date of approval of the original financial statements.

   Although the auditor has no duty to search for events that take place after the date of approval of the original financial statements, in some circumstances the auditor might become aware of events that have occurred subsequent to that date which are of such significance that the auditor might be unwilling to sign the audit report on the revised financial statements. In such circumstances the auditor must follow the consultation procedures referred to in **Section 13:20.16** (a) above.

13:20.18 Example reports

Examples of reports that should be used in the various situations covered in this section are as follows:

13:20.18.1 *Example of a report where the financial statements and directors' report have been revised by replacement*

Report of the auditors to the members of Blank PLC

We have audited the revised financial statements on pages x to x which have been prepared under the historical cost convention [*as modified by the revaluation of certain fixed assets*] and the accounting policies set out on page x. The revised financial statements replace the original financial statements approved by the directors on 2 March 20X2.

Respective responsibilities of directors and auditors

As described on page x the company's directors are responsible for the preparation of financial statements. It is our responsibility to form an independent opinion, based on our audit, on those statements and to report our opinion to you. We are also required to report whether in our opinion the original financial statements failed to comply with the requirements of the Companies Act 1985 in the respects identified by the directors.

Basis of opinion

We conducted our audit in accordance with Auditing Standards issued by the Auditing Practices Board. An audit includes examination, on a test basis, of evidence relevant to the amounts and disclosures in the financial statements. It also includes an assessment of the significant estimates and judgements made by the directors in the preparation of the financial statements, and of whether the accounting policies are appropriate to the company's circumstances, consistently applied and adequately disclosed. The audit of revised financial statements includes the performance of additional procedures to assess whether the revisions made by the directors are appropriate and have been properly made.

We planned and performed our audit so as to obtain all the information and explanations that we considered necessary in order to provide us with sufficient evidence to give reasonable assurance that the financial statements are free from material misstatement, whether caused by fraud or by other irregularity or error. In forming our opinion we also evaluated the overall adequacy of the presentation of information in the financial statements.

Opinion

In our opinion the revised financial statements give a true and fair view, seen as at 3 March 20x2, the date the original financial statements were approved, of the state of the company's affairs at 31 December 20x1 and of its profit and cash flows for the year then ended and have been properly prepared in accordance with the provisions of the Companies Act 1985 as they have effect under The Companies (Revision of Defective Accounts and Report) Regulations 1990.

[*In our opinion the revised financial statements give a true and fair view, seen as at 3 March 20x2, the date the original financial statements were approved, of the state of affairs of the company and the group at 31 December 20x1 and of the profit and cash flows of the group for the year then ended and have been properly prepared in accordance with the provisions of the Companies Act 1985 as they have effect under The Companies (Revision of Defective Accounts and Report) Regulations 1990.*]

In our opinion the original financial statements for the year ended 31 December 20x1 failed to comply with the requirements of the Companies Act 1985 in the respects identified by the directors in note x to these financial statements.

Notes:

(a)   The auditor must consider whether the information contained in the directors' report, whether revised or not, is consistent with the revised financial statements. If the auditor is of the opinion that it is not, that fact must be stated in the report.

(b)   The paragraph in brackets should be substituted for the preceding paragraph where the auditor reports on group financial statements.

13:20.18.2 Example of a report where the financial statements only have been revised by supplementary note

Report of the auditors to the members of Blank PLC

We have audited the revised financial statements of Blank PLC for the year ended 31 December 20x1. The revised financial statements replace the original financial statements approved by the directors on 3 March 20x2 and consist of the attached supplementary note together with the original financial statements which were circulated to members on [*date*].

Respective responsibilities of directors and auditors

As described on page x of the original financial statements the company's directors are responsible for the preparation of financial statements. It is our responsibility to form an independent opinion, based on our audit, on those statements and to report our opinion to you. We are also required to report whether in our opinion the original financial statements failed to comply with the requirements of the Companies Act 1985 in the respects identified by the directors.

Basis of opinion

We conducted our audit in accordance with Auditing Standards issued by the Auditing Practices Board. An audit includes examination, on a test basis, of evidence relevant to the amounts and disclosures in the financial statements. It also includes an assessment of the significant estimates and judgements made by the directors in the preparation of the financial statements, and of whether the accounting policies are appropriate to the company's circumstances, consistently applied and adequately disclosed. The audit of revised financial statements includes the performance of additional procedures to assess whether the revisions made by the directors are appropriate and have been properly made.

We planned and performed our audit so as to obtain all the information and explanations that we considered necessary in order to provide us with sufficient evidence to give reasonable assurance that the revised financial statements are free from material misstatement, whether caused by fraud or by other irregularity or error. In forming our opinion we also evaluated the overall adequacy of the presentation of information in the revised financial statements.

Opinion

In our opinion the revised financial statements give a true and fair view, seen as at 3 March 20x2, the date the original financial statements were approved, of the state of the company's affairs at 31 December 20x1 and of its profit and cash flows for the year then ended and have been properly prepared in accordance with the provisions of the Companies Act 1985 as they have effect under The Companies (Revision of Defective Accounts and Report) Regulations 1990.

[*In our opinion the revised financial statements give a true and fair view, seen as at 3 March 20x2, the date the original financial statements were approved, of the state of affairs of the company and the group at 31 December 20x1 and of the profit and cash flows of the group for the year then ended and have been properly prepared in accordance with the provisions of the Companies Act 1985 as they have effect under The Companies (Revision of Defective Accounts and Report) Regulations 1990.*]

In our opinion the original financial statements for the year ended 31 December 20x1 failed to comply with the requirements of the Companies Act 1985 in the respects identified by the directors in the supplementary note.

Notes:

(a)   The auditor must also consider whether the information contained in the directors' report is consistent with the revised financial statements. If the auditor is of the opinion that it is not, that fact must be stated in the report.

(b)   Although there may be rare occasions where the financial statements and the directors' report are *both* revised by supplementary note, and the wording of the audit report might alter in such a case, it is not considered worth while to include an example of such a report here.

(c)   The paragraph in brackets should be substituted for the preceding paragraph where the auditor reports on group financial statements.

13:20.18.3 Example of a report where the directors' report only has been revised by replacement

Report of the auditors to the members of Blank PLC

We have considered whether the information given in the revised directors' report is consistent with the financial statements for the year ended 31 December 20X1.

As explained on page x of the directors' report the report has been prepared as at 3 March 20X2, the date on which the directors approved the original directors' report, and not as at 7 September 20X2, the date on which the revised directors' report was approved. Accordingly the revised directors' report does not deal with events between those dates.

As at 3 March 20X2 in our opinion the information given in the revised report is consistent with the annual financial statements for the year ended 31 December 20X1.

Notes:

(a)   If the auditor does **not** consider that the information is consistent, he or she must say so in the audit report.

(b)   The words, 'As at 3 March 20X2', are considered necessary although the regulations do not in this case provide for dual dating.

13:20.18.4 *Example of a report where the directors' report only has been revised by supplementary note*

Report of the auditors to the members of Blank PLC

We have considered whether the information given in the revised directors' report is consistent with the financial statements for the year ended 31 December 20X1. The revised directors' report comprises the attached supplementary note and the original directors' report which was approved by the directors on 3 March 20X2. The revised directors' report replaces the original directors' report as from 7 September 20X2 (the date on which the supplementary note is approved and signed).

As explained in the attached supplementary note the directors' report has been revised as at 3 March 20X2, the date on which the directors approved the original financial statements and not as at 7 September 20X2, the date on which the revised directors' report was approved. Accordingly the revised directors' report does not deal with events between those dates.

As at 3 March 20X2 in our opinion the information given in the revised report is consistent with the annual financial statements for the year ended 31 December, 20X1.

Notes:

(a)   If the auditor does **not** consider that the information is consistent, he or she must say so in the audit report.

(b)   The words, 'As at 3 March 20X2', are considered necessary although the regulations do not in this case provide for dual dating.

13:21 Qualified or modified reports on directors' emoluments and other benefits

13:21.1 Introduction

Section 237 of the Companies Act 1985 requires the auditors to include details of directors' emoluments and directors' and officers' other benefits such as loans in their report if such details are required by law to be given in the financial statements, but have not been given. The section states:

> *If the requirements of Schedule 6 (disclosure of information: emoluments and other benefits of directors and others) are not complied with in the annual accounts, the auditors shall include in their report, so far as they are reasonably able to do so, a statement giving the required particulars.*

(Section 232 of the Act requires the disclosure set out in Sch. 6 to be included in the financial statements.)

13:21.2 Greenbury Report

The Stock Exchange has adopted certain aspects of the Greenbury Report (1995) ('Greenbury'). Following the implementation of its listing requirement for UK-listed companies to include additional details concerning directors' emoluments in accordance with Greenbury, it also requires the auditors to make a statement giving the required particulars in their audit report if those details are not included in the financial statements. The additional matters that are subject to audit under the Stock Exchange rules are the disclosures of the following:

(a)   The amount of each element in the remuneration package for the period under review of each director by name, including, but not restricted to, basic salary and fees, the estimated money value of benefits in kind, annual bonuses, compensation for loss of office and payments for breach of contract or other termination payments, together with the total for each director for the period under review and for the corresponding prior period, and any significant payments made to former directors during the period under review; such details should be presented in tabular form, unless inappropriate, together with explanatory notes as necessary.

(b)   Information on share options, including SAYE options, for each director by name in accordance with the recommendations of the Accounting Standards Board's Urgent Issues Task Force, Abstract 10; such information should be presented in tabular form, together with explanatory notes as necessary.

(c)   Details of any long-term incentive schemes, other than share options, where the details have been disclosed under (b) above, including the interests of each director by name in the long-term incentive schemes at the start of the period under review; entitlements or awards granted and commitments made to each director under such schemes during the period, showing which crystallise either in the same year or in subsequent years; the money value and number of shares, cash payments or other benefits received by each director under such schemes during the period; and the interests of each director in the long-term incentive schemes at the end of the period.

(d)   For defined benefit schemes (as in Part 1 of Sch. 6 to the Companies Act 1985);

    (i)   details of the amount of the increase during the period under review (excluding inflation) and of the accumulated total amount at the end of the period in respect of the accrued benefit to which each director would be entitled on leaving service or is entitled having left service during the period under review;

    (ii) and either:

        — the transfer value (less director's contributions) of the relevant increase in accrued benefit (to be calculated in accordance with Actuarial Guidance Note GN11 but making no deduction for any under-funding) as at the end of the period; or

        — so much of the following information as is necessary to make a reasonable assessment of the transfer value in respect of each director:

- current age;
- normal retirement age;
- the amount of any contributions paid or payable by the director under the terms of the scheme during the period under review;
- details of spouse's and dependants' benefits;
- early retirement rights and options, expectations of pension increases after retirement (whether guaranteed or discretionary); and
- discretionary benefits for which allowance is made in transfer values on leaving and any other relevant information which will significantly affect the value of the benefits.

Voluntary contributions and benefits should not be disclosed.

(e)   For money purchase schemes (as in Part 1 of Sch. 6 to the Companies Act 1985) details of the contribution or allowance payable or made by the company in respect of each director during the period under review.

The other Stock Exchange requirements relating to its implementation of the Greenbury Report, although not specifically subject to audit, should be considered in the context of 'Information contained in the directors' report and other information in documents containing audited financial information.'

13:21.3 Information clearly cross-referenced

Where the Stock Exchange information that is subject to audit is included in the board's report on directors' remuneration and is clearly cross-referenced from the financial statements the auditor need make no specific reference in the audit report to the pages on which the information is included. Where statutory directors' remuneration disclosures are also included in the report on directors' remuneration they must be cross-referenced from the financial statements and the cross-reference must make clear that the statutory disclosures form part of the financial statements.

13:21.4 Information not clearly cross-referenced

Where the Stock Exchange information that is required to be audited is not clearly cross-referenced from the financial statements to the board's report on directors' remuneration, the auditor should clearly identify in the audit report the information the auditor is reporting on. The auditor should do this by beginning the report as follows (note that the reference to page 3 below does not encompass other information in the report on the directors' remuneration that is not subject to audit):

> **We have audited the financial statements on pages 5 to 14. We have also examined the amounts disclosed relating to the emoluments, share options, long term incentive scheme interests and pension benefits of the directors which form part of the report by the Board to the shareholders on directors remuneration on page 3.**

If, in exceptional circumstances, it is not possible to describe clearly in the report the information that has been audited, the auditor should consider whether it is then necessary to reproduce the detailed disclosures in the report.

13:21.5 Non-disclosure of information required by Sch. 6 to the Companies Act 1985

Where the financial statements (including, where relevant, statutory disclosures contained in the remuneration committee report) do not include all of the information that is required to be disclosed by Sch. 6 to the Companies Act, the auditor must include that information in the audit report on the financial statements so far as the auditor is able. This will mean that the auditor is also unable to state without qualification that the financial statements have been prepared in accordance with the Companies Act, although generally the auditor should still be able to report that the financial statements give a true and fair view of the state of affairs and profit.

   An example report in these circumstances is as follows. (The report assumes that there is no clear reference from the financial statements to the statutory information contained in the remuneration committee report – *see* **Section 13:21.4** (first paragraph).)

> **Report of the auditors to the members of Blank plc**
>
> **We have audited the financial statements on pages x to x including the information in paragraphs x to x on page x, which have been prepared under the historical cost convention [*as modified by the revaluation of certain fixed assets*] and the accounting policies set out on page x.**

Respective responsibilities of directors and auditors

As described on page x the company's directors are responsible for the preparation of financial statements. It is our responsibility to form an independent opinion, based on our audit, on those statements and to report our opinion to you.

Basis of opinion

We conducted our audit in accordance with Auditing Standards issued by the Auditing Practices Board. An audit includes examination, on a test basis, of evidence relevant to the amounts and disclosures in the financial statements. It also includes an assessment of the significant estimates and judgements made by the directors in the preparation of the financial statements, and of whether the accounting policies are appropriate to the company's circumstances, consistently applied and adequately disclosed.

We planned and performed our audit so as to obtain all the information and explanations that we considered necessary in order to provide us with sufficient evidence to give reasonable assurance that the financial statements are free from material misstatement whether caused by fraud or by other irregularity or error. In forming our opinion we also evaluated the overall adequacy of the presentation of information in the financial statements.

Qualified opinion arising from non-disclosure of information relating to director's remuneration

The following information has been omitted from the financial statements contrary to s. 232 of the Companies Act 1985.

The financial statements do not disclose the aggregate of the amount of gains made by directors on the exercise of share options during the year. The amount that should be disclosed is £2,560,000.

In our opinion the financial statements give a true and fair view of the state of the company's affairs at 31 December 20XX and of its profit and cash flows for the year then ended and, except for the omission of the information referred to above concerning the loan to a director, have been properly prepared in accordance with the Companies Act 1985.

(Note: The qualification would apply to listed or AIM companies only, as unlisted companies do not have to disclose this information.)

13:21.6 Non-disclosure of information required by Stock Exchange Listing Rules

Where the financial statements include all the information required by law, but do not include the information in **Section 13:21.2** (first paragraph), disclosure of which is required by the Listing Rules of the Stock Exchange, the auditor must include a statement, so far as he or she is able, of the required particulars. Because these particulars are not required by law the report should not refer to a departure from the Companies Act, nor will omission of the particulars normally affect the true and fair view of the state of affairs or profit.

An example of the opinion paragraph of a report in these circumstances is as follows:

Opinion

The following information relating to directors' share options, which is required to be given in the report by the board to shareholders or directors remuneration by the Listing Rules of the London Stock Exchange, has been omitted from that report.

Name	At 1.1.9x	At 31.12.9x	Exercise price	Date from which exercisable	Expiry date
Mr A	5,000	5,000	258p	1997	2000
Ms B	10,000	10,000	260p	1998	2001
Mr C	3,000	3,000	258p	1997	2000

No options were granted or exercised in the year. The price of the company's shares at 1.1.9x was 258p and at 31.12.9x it was 298p. The high for the year was 298p. There are no performance criteria attached to the options.

In our opinion the financial statements give a true and fair view of the state of the company's affairs at 31 December 199x and of its profit and cash flows for the year then ended and have been properly prepared in accordance with the Companies Act 1985.

13:21.7 Non-disclosure of information required by Sch. 7 to the Companies Act 1985 to be given in the directors' report

In the above example, the information omitted includes reference to options granted and exercised during the year. If options had been granted or exercised but disclosure had not been made, this would have been a departure from the requirements of Sch. 7 to the Companies Act, which requires such disclosure to be made in the directors' report. However, omission of such information from the directors' report would not necessarily result in a qualification of the audit opinion, because the auditor is required by law to report on the financial statements, not on the directors' report.

Where, however, information required by Sch. 7 to be given in the directors' report is duplicated by the Stock Exchange requirements, e.g. options granted and exercised, the auditor must include that information in the audit report if it is not included in the report of the remuneration committee. Where the Sch. 7 information that is not included in the Stock Exchange requirements (e.g., details of the company's policy towards disabled employees) is excluded, the auditor should neither include a statement of the information in the audit report nor qualify that report. However, the auditor should point out the omission to the company and check that it is rectified. If the inclusion or exclusion of information required by Sch. 7 creates an inconsistency with the financial statements the auditor should draw attention to this in the audit report because this is a legal requirement.

13:21.8 Information required by the Listing Rules or Sch. 6 incorrectly stated

Where the company has included information required by the Listing Rules or Sch. 6, but that information is incorrect, the auditor should follow the above rules as if the information required had not been given because it is implicit in the Listing Rules and Sch. 6 that the information given must be the correct information. Accordingly in such a case the auditor should include in the audit report a statement that whereas the information has been given it is not the correct information, and the auditor should then include the correct information, so far as he or she is able.

13:21.9 Pension entitlements disclosure – audit considerations

The audit of pension entitlement disclosures may require specialist advice and in cases where this is so actuarial experts should be consulted.

In particular the APB discussed the difficulties faced by auditors in auditing the Stock Exchange requirement which requires disclosure of 'any other relevant information which will significantly affect the value of the benefits'. The difficulties occur because of the open ended nature of the requirement. Consequently the APB recommends, in respect of this requirement, that auditors should only take account of information of which they are aware from:

(a)   their normal audit work on the financial statements; and

(b)   reasonable enquiry of the directors and the company's pension advisers.

13:21.10 Engagement letters

The Listing Rules are an agreement between the Stock Exchange and listed companies. Therefore the auditor needs to agree with the directors of the client that the scope of the audit includes the requirement to audit the information described in **Section 13:21.9** above. The engagement letter should therefore expressly encompass the audit of this information.

13:21.11 Consultation

Where the auditor is considering modifying the audit report in any of the circumstances described above the consultation procedures set out in **Section 5:5**, 'Consultation and concurring reviews', must be followed.

13:22 Review engagements on interim financial information

13:22.1 Introduction

The Listing Rules require that listed companies produce a half-yearly report containing figures in table form, amounting to a summarised profit and loss account and an explanatory statement relating to the company's activities for the first six months of each financial year. Companies may choose to have this information reviewed by auditors.

Where the figures in the interim report have been reviewed by auditors, the Listing Rules require that the review report be published with the interim report.

In July 1999 the APB issued Bulletin 1999/4 'Review of interim financial information'. This provides guidance to auditors in reviewing and reporting on financial information in interim reports produced by listed companies.

13:22.2 Nature of a review engagement

A review of interim financial information is substantially less in scope than an audit, because, *inter alia*, a review does not include the following:

(a) Tests of accounting records through inspection, observation, or confirmation.

(b) Obtaining corroborating evidence in response to enquiries.

(c) The application of certain other procedures normally performed during an audit, e.g. tests of controls and verification of assets and liabilities.

A review may bring to the auditor's attention significant matters affecting the interim financial information, but does not ensure that the auditor will become aware of all significant matters that would be disclosed in an audit.

Because a review is limited in its scope, the auditors' review report conveys a level of assurance significantly below that of an audit opinion and therefore the auditor should state in the review report that an audit opinion is not expressed on the interim financial information.

13:22.3 Agreeing the terms of the engagement

The auditor must assess the risk relating to a client's interim financial information before agreeing to a review engagement. This should normally include the following:

(a)   Updating the assessment of the risk to the audit firm by considering any significant changes since the last audit; and

(b)   Considering risks specific to the interim financial information, e.g. whether the client appears to have procedures in place to ensure that the interim financial information is properly prepared.

   The auditor must also send an engagement letter to the client. This should normally include the following matters:

(a)   An explanation that the review report is prepared to assist the company in meeting Stock Exchange requirements, and in the proper control of its affairs and that the review is performed, and the review report is issued, for these purposes only.

(b)   An explanation that the interim financial information is the responsibility of the client's directors.

(c)   Confirmation that the review will be conducted in accordance with Bulletin 1999/4.

(d)   Identification of the financial information to be reviewed.

(e)   The scope of the review, including sufficient description of the procedures to explain the extent of the auditor's involvement and the consequences of any limitations in scope.

(f)   An explanation that such procedures are substantially less in scope than an audit performed in accordance with Auditing Standards, and that the review therefore provides a lower level of assurance than an audit.

(g)   A description of the form of the proposed review report.

A specimen engagement letter is given in **Appendix A** – *see* **Section 13:22.17**. It should be tailored to the client's circumstances.

13:22.4 Planning

The auditor should update his or her knowledge of the business and consider the client's organisation, accounting and control systems, operating characteristics and the nature of its assets, liabilities, revenues and expenses. The auditor should focus the audit work on areas of potential risk of material misstatement based on knowledge from previous audits.

   The auditor should use professional judgement to determine the nature, timing and extent of review procedures, based on an assessment of the risk of material misstatement. In determining the procedures the auditor should take into account such matters as the following:

(a)   Knowledge acquired in carrying out audits of the annual financial statements and reviews of interim financial information for prior periods.

(b)   Knowledge of the business, including accounting principles and practices of the industry in which the client operates.

(c)   Knowledge of the client's accounting systems.

(d)   The extent to which a particular item is affected by management judgement.

(e)   The materiality of transactions and account balances.

(f)   Management's own assessment of the risks underlying the interim financial information and the monitoring and other controls established to mitigate those risks.

13:22.4.1 *Groups and multi-location engagements*

Where the auditor is reporting on the interim financial information for a group, the auditor should establish the scope of review work required, if any, for each division and subsidiary and associated undertaking, taking into account the assessment of the risk of material misstatement. If the auditor needs to involve other firms of auditors they should be sent letters of instruction which include the nature and extent of work required, the report required and the reporting timetable. Additionally, the auditor should plan to carry out appropriate procedures to be satisfied that the work of other auditors is adequate for the purposes of the review.

For multi-location engagements the auditor should consider the need to visit operating locations. There may be benefit in visiting significant operating locations to facilitate the review of divisional interim financial data, but generally it is not necessary to visit all locations. The decision whether to visit operating locations will be based on the assessment of risk associated with each location, taking into account its effect on the consolidated interim financial information.

13:22.4.2 *Involvement of review partner*

Reviews of interim financial information undertaken for most clients will fall within the definition in **Section 5:5**, 'Consultation and concurring reviews', of clients for which, for audit purposes, a review partner may be appointed. Where a review partner has been so appointed, the engagement partner should determine the extent of the review partner's involvement on the interim review engagement, but as a minimum the review partner should be consulted on:

(a)   the overall scope of the review;

(b)   any significant issues arising, e.g. inconsistencies in accounting policies compared with them of the previous annual financial statements; and

(c)   any proposed qualification or modification of the review report.

13:22.5 Review procedures

The auditor should obtain evidence primarily through enquiry and analytical procedures and document that evidence. The auditor should normally carry out the following procedures:

(a) Review prior-year matters, including any points raised in reports to the board submitted after the preceding statutory audit, paying particular attention to matters which may have a material effect on the interim financial information. For example:

> (i)   matters relating to the adequacy of systems and controls over accounting and financial reporting;
>
> (ii) any findings relating to the quality and reliability of management accounts;
>
> (iii) the nature and extent of adjustments and errors; and
>
> (iv) the appropriateness of accounting policies.

(b) Update the auditor's understanding of the client's business and the industry in which it operates, by discussion with management and from other relevant sources of information.

(c) Enquire whether there have been any significant changes during the interim period (e.g., changes in ownership or capital structure, changes in accounting policies and, in groups, significant acquisitions or disposals).

(d) Consider the results of the subsequent events review carried out for the preceding annual audit where these are relevant to the interim financial information.

(e) Enquire whether significant changes are planned – e.g., disposals of major assets or divisions and subsidiary and associated undertakings.

(f) Update the assessment of the control environment, responding to any significant changes.

(g) Enquire of management, including internal audit, whether there have been any changes in the financial reporting systems (including computer systems) or internal controls, or any breakdowns in systems and controls, which might affect the reliability of the interim financial information.

(h) Enquire about changes in the client's procedures for recording, classifying and summarising transactions, accumulating information for disclosure and preparing the interim financial information.

(i) Check significant balances in the interim financial information to the trial balance or the accounting records from which the interim financial information is derived.

(j) Review minutes of, and enquire about actions taken at meetings of, shareholders, the board of directors, audit committee and other committees of the board of directors and other relevant meetings.

(k) Perform analytical procedures designed to identify relationships and individual items that appear unusual, including comparison of the interim financial information with profit and loss account and balance sheet information for prior periods and with anticipated results and financial position. In applying these procedures, the auditor should consider the types of matters that required accounting adjustments in prior periods. (Further guidance on analytical procedures is given in **Section 13:22.5.1.**)

(l)   Consider whether the interim financial information is prepared on a basis consistent with generally accepted accounting principles appropriate to the preparation of interim financial information, and on the basis of accounting policies consistent with those used in the preparation of the annual financial statements.

(m)   Read the interim financial information to consider, in the light of the matters coming to the auditor's attention during the review engagement, whether the interim financial information appears to conform with the basis of accounting described in the notes thereto and is consistent with the auditor's knowledge of the client and the findings of the review engagement.

(n)   Obtain reports from other auditors, if any, whom the auditor has engaged to review the interim financial information of divisions and subsidiary and associated undertakings.

(o)   Reassess the results of the going concern procedures which the auditor carried out as part of the audit of the preceding annual financial statements. The auditor should consider the remaining period of time which was relevant for that audit. The auditor should limit the review to enquiries of management regarding any significant changes in cash flow forecasts and banking arrangements.

(p)   Follow up questions which have arisen in the course of applying the foregoing procedures.

(q)   Check the clerical accuracy and consistency of the interim financial information, and that it has been approved by the directors.

APB Bulletin 1999/4 contains a specimen programme for interim review engagements which may be used to help develop a review programme. The specimen programme should be tailored to the client's circumstances.

The review procedures above assume the following:

(a)   That profit and loss, balance sheet and cash flow information is produced, even though only profit and loss information is currently required to be published. Where such other information, in particular balance sheet information, is not available for analytical procedures, the auditor may not necessarily obtain sufficient evidence from reviewing the profit and loss information in isolation to enable him or her to issue an unqualified review report.

(b)   The auditor has audited the annual financial statements for the previous financial year and has reviewed the corresponding interim financial information in the previous year. Where this is not the case, e.g. if it is a new engagement or where the auditor is newly appointed, the auditor is likely to have significantly less knowledge of the client's business organisation and accounting and control systems. Accordingly, in such circumstances, the auditor should normally perform significantly more review procedures.

13:22.5.1 Analytical procedures

The auditor should normally consider carrying out the following analytical procedures:

(a) Comparison of the interim financial information with comparable information for the immediately preceding interim period and for corresponding previous period(s).

(b) Evaluations of the interim financial information made by consideration of plausible relationships among both financial and, where relevant, non-financial data.

(c) Comparisons of amounts, or ratios developed from these amounts, with expectations.

The auditor's expectations should be based on an understanding of the client and of the industry in which the client operates. Relevant sources of information might include:

(a) Financial information for comparable prior period(s), giving consideration to known changes.

(b) Anticipated results – e.g., budgets or forecasts, including extrapolations from interim or annual data.

(c) Relationships among elements of financial information within the period.

(d) Information regarding the industry in which the client operates – e.g., gross margin information.

(e) Relationships of financial information with relevant non-financial information.

13:22.6 Issues management

The content of issues documentation should reflect the nature of the engagement, covering as a minimum:

(a) Matters arising in response to significant risks identified at the planning stage.

(b) Any exceptions identified, e.g. inconsistent accounting policies.

(c) Uncertainties in significant estimates made by management.

(d) For groups, significant issues reported by other auditors.

13:22.7 Evaluating the results of the review

If the auditor has reason to believe that the interim financial information may contain material misstatements, the auditor should discuss the matter with the directors and the audit committee.

The auditor should explain the nature of any additional or more extensive procedures that are required to enable the auditor to issue an unqualified review report or to confirm that a qualified review report is required, and the reasons why the auditor considers such procedures necessary. The auditor should agree an appropriate variation order for any further procedures before performing them.

13:22.8 Subsequent events

The auditor should enquire about events up to the date of approval of the interim financial information, such as significant changes to the business, that may require adjustment of, or disclosure in, the interim financial information.

13:22.9 Management representations

The auditor should obtain written representations from the directors tailored to the client's circumstances. Such representations should normally include:

(a) Acknowledgement by the directors that the auditors' review is substantially less in scope than an audit, and that the auditors do not express an audit opinion.

(b) Acknowledgement of the directors' responsibility for the interim financial information and the completeness of the financial records and of the minutes (and summaries of meetings for which minutes have not been prepared) that were made available for the purposes of the audit review.

(c) Confirmation that the directors have made and effected all judgements necessary in the preparation of the interim financial information.

(d) Confirmation that the directors have assessed the appropriateness of the going concern basis of accounting.

(e) Notification of any subsequent events that would require adjustment to, or disclosure in, the interim financial information.

(f) Other matters, if any, for which the auditor considers written representations are appropriate in the circumstances. Such matters might include, e.g., the substance of significant assertions, estimates, judgements or interpretations of facts by the directors that have a significant effect on the interim financial information.

13:22.10 Other information in documents containing interim financial information

A client may publish other information with the interim financial information including, possibly, prospective financial information. Although the auditor does not report thereon, the other information should be read in order to establish whether or not it contains any matters which are inconsistent with the interim financial information.

13:22.11 Discussion of findings with the audit committee and board of directors

In addition to the review report, the auditor should communicate the results of the findings from the interim review to the client's audit committee and, where appropriate, the board of directors. Matters which the auditor may need to report and discuss include the following:

(a) The scope and the results of the review procedures, including the extent of visits undertaken, if any, to operating locations.

(b) The general process by which the interim financial information has been prepared, and in particular the process used by management in formulating particularly sensitive accounting estimates and the basis for the auditor's conclusions regarding the reasonableness of those estimates.

(c) Whether significant accounting policies, including any changes, affecting the interim financial information are appropriate.

(d) Issues which have been discussed with management, such as:

  (i) any matters that cause the auditor to believe that the interim financial information is probably materially misstated as a result of a departure from generally accepted accounting principles applicable to interim financial information;

  (ii) an update on any material weaknesses in internal control reported to the audit committee or the board during the most recent statutory audit;

  (iii) any significant adjustments resulting from the review; and

  (iv) any inconsistencies in other information presented with the interim financial information.

13:22.12 Completion

The completion of the review engagement must be supported by the audit firm's relevant documentation, with the wording tailored to the review engagement, and must be signed off before the date of the review report on the interim financial information.

13:22.13 Reporting

The auditor's review report should state that the auditor is not aware of any material modifications that should be made to the interim financial information as presented, unless the review has revealed matters that the auditor considers require him or her to modify this opinion (*see* **Sections 13:22.13.2** to **13:22.13.2.5**).

The auditor should include in the review report the following matters:

(a) A title identifying the person(s) to whom the report is addressed, clearly indicating that this is a review report.

(b) An introductory paragraph identifying the interim financial information reviewed.

(c) A statement that the interim financial information is the responsibility of, and has been approved by, the directors.

(d) A statement that the review was carried out in accordance with Bulletin 1999/4

(e) A description of the work performed in undertaking the review.

(f) A review conclusion.

(g) The auditor's name and signature and designation.

(h) The date of the review report.

The date of the review report on a client's interim financial information should be the date on which the auditor signs the review report. The auditor should not date the review report earlier than the date on which the interim financial information was approved by the directors.

   Example 1 in **Appendix B** – *see* **Section 13:22.18** – illustrates an unqualified review report.

13:22.13.1 Basis of the review

The auditor's report should describe the scope of the engagement, to enable the reader to understand the nature of the work performed and to make it clear that the work was substantially less in scope than an audit and, therefore, that an audit opinion is not expressed.

   The audit firm should state that its responsibility is to report on the results of its review. The explanation of the basis of the firm's review should include a statement that the review:

(a)   consisted principally of making enquiries of management and applying analytical procedures;

(b)   included an assessment of whether accounting policies have been consistently applied;

(c)   excluded audit procedures such as tests of controls and the verification of assets and liabilities; and

(d)   was substantially less in scope than an audit performed in accordance with Auditing Standards, and therefore provides a lower level of assurance than an audit.

13:22.13.2 Modification of the review report

The auditor should modify the review report if, based on the review, the auditor considers that a material modification is required to the interim financial information as presented.

   Guidance on the form of qualification or modification is given in **Sections 13:22.13.2.1** to **13:22.13.2.5**. Further guidance may be obtained from **Section 13:16**, 'Qualified and modified reports to the members of limited companies and other organisations in Great Britain'.

13:22.13.2.1 Inconsistencies in accounting policies

The auditor may require to modify the review report where:

(a)   an accounting policy or the presentation applied is materially inconsistent with that used in the preceding annual financial statements and the changes, and reasons for them, are not adequately disclosed;

(b)   the financial information has not been adjusted for a known accounting policy change to be made in the subsequent annual financial statements, no estimate of the change has been made, and no statement of explanation has been made;

(c)   a new accounting policy has not been adopted where required by accounting standards or otherwise;

(d)   a change in accounting policy has not been disclosed;

(e)   an inappropriate accounting policy has been applied;

(f)   there is inadequate disclosure of a fundamental uncertainty.

Inconsistencies between the accounting policies used in the interim financial information and those used in the preceding annual financial statements may be justified, if the changes of policy have been made to conform to changes in the client's next annual financial statements. The London Stock Exchange Listing Rules state:

> The accounting policies and presentation applied to interim figures must be consistent with those applied in the latest published annual accounts save where:
>
> (a) such policies and presentation are to be changed in the subsequent annual financial statements to ensure consistency with company law and accounting standards and the changes and reasons therefor are disclosed in the half yearly report; or
>
> (b) the Exchange otherwise agrees.

Following a change in accounting policy, the amounts of the current and prior periods should be stated on the basis of the new policies and the cumulative effect of the policy change on the opening reserves should be disclosed. A description should be given to help users understand the nature of the change. The auditor should review the adjustments and disclosures made. If the auditor does not consider that accounting policy changes have been properly reflected in the financial information, he or she should consider the implications for the review report.

Other inconsistencies in accounting polices that do not fall within the allowed changes referred to above, and other matters that the auditor considers should be reflected by making material modifications to the interim financial information, will, if they are not amended, result in modification of the review report.

13:22.13.2.2 Disagreement

Where there is disagreement about accounting treatment or disclosure in the circumstances described above, the auditor should modify the review report to describe the nature of the matter identified and, if practicable, state the effects on the interim financial information. **Example 2** in **Appendix B** – *see* **Section 13:22.18** – illustrates such a report.

   The auditor should also modify the review report where any other information published along with the interim financial statements contains an apparent misstatement or material inconsistency with the financial information.

13:22.13.2.3 Limitation on scope

If there has been a limitation on the scope of the auditor's work that prevents him or her from obtaining sufficient evidence to provide an unqualified review report, the auditor should describe the limitation and indicate that the review report is qualified as to the possible adjustments to the interim financial information that might have been determined to be necessary had the limitation not existed.

   In rare cases when there has been a limitation on the scope of the auditor's work which the auditor believes to be so significant that he or she concludes that no assurance can be given, the auditor should issue a denial of review conclusion, and consider the implications for their appointment.

13:22.13.2.4 Fundamental uncertainty

If there is a fundamental uncertainty, e.g. substantial doubt about the company's ability to continue as a going concern, the auditor should include an additional paragraph in the report, provided that the interim financial information appropriately discloses such matters.

13:22.13.2.5 Prior period qualifications

If the prior period review report on the interim financial information, or the review report on the preceding annual financial statements, was qualified, and the matter that gave rise to the qualification has not been resolved, the auditor should refer in the review report to the qualification and discuss the current status of the matter giving rise to the qualification.

13:22.14 Requests to discontinue an interim review engagement

There may be rare circumstances in which the auditor indicates in advance to the directors that the review report may be qualified for one or more of the factors described in **Section 13:22.13.2.1** and **Sections 13:22.13.2.2** to **13:22.13.2.5**. In these cases the directors may request that the auditor discontinue the review engagement rather than include a qualified review report in the interim financial information, or may indicate that they will not publish the review report.

The auditor should inform the audit committee of this situation as soon as practicable. This communication may be oral or written, but if information is communicated orally, the auditor should subsequently document the communication as appropriate. If, in the auditor's judgement, the client does not take appropriate action to address the concerns regarding the interim financial information to be published, the auditor should consider requesting the directors to discuss the matter with the company's brokers, including whether the matter should be reported to the London Stock Exchange. The auditor should also evaluate whether:

(a) to discontinue the review engagement; and

(b) to resign as the company's auditors and include the reasons for resigning in a statement of circumstances in accordance with s. 394 of the Companies Act 1985.

The auditor may need to take legal advice when considering the above matters.

13:22.15 Consultation

In all cases where the auditor is considering modifying the review report on interim financial information, the procedures set out in **Section 5:5**, 'Consultation and concurring reviews', should be followed.

13:22.16 Working papers

The guidance regarding working papers set out in **Section 6:2**, 'Audit working papers', including policies for review of working papers, applies to an engagement to review interim financial information. Much of the auditor's work will comprise discussions with client management, and therefore the auditor should include in the working papers:

(a) The name and position of the person(s) concerned.

(b) The date on which enquiries were made.

(c) The nature of the enquiries and the responses obtained.

(d) Further corroborative work performed, where necessary.

13:22.17   Appendix A   Illustrative engagement letter

[*To be tailored to the company's circumstances*]

Board of Directors

XYZ PLC   Date

XYZ PLC interim financial information for the six months ended 30 June 20XX

Dear Sirs

As discussed with . . . at our meeting on . . . this letter sets out our understanding of the terms of our engagement to review the interim financial information of XYZ PLC for the six months ended 30 June 20XX. This letter explains the scope of the work which we will undertake and the form of our proposed review report and draws attention to the inherent limitations of a review.

Directors' responsibilities

As directors of XYZ PLC you are responsible under the Companies Act 1985 for keeping proper accounting records. You are also responsible for presenting interim financial information complying, as a minimum, with the requirements of the Continuing Obligations for companies listed on the London Stock Exchange.

For the purpose of our review you will make available to us all of the company's accounting records and all other related information, including minutes of directors' and shareholders' meetings and of all relevant management meetings, that we consider necessary.

Scope and limitations of our review

We will review the interim financial information of XYZ PLC for the six months ended 30 June 20XX. This financial information will comprise [*specify the content, e.g. balance sheet information as at 30 June 20XX, and profit and loss and cash flow information for the six months then ended*].

Our review will be substantially less in scope than an audit in accordance with Auditing Standards and therefore provides a lower level of assurance than an audit. It will consist principally of applying analytical procedures to financial data, assessing whether accounting policies have been consistently applied, and making enquiries of [*Group*] management responsible for financial and accounting matters. It will not include audit procedures such as tests of controls and verification of assets and liabilities. Our review will have regard to the guidance contained in the Bulletin 1999/4, 'Review of interim financial information', issued by the Auditing Practices Board.

[*If appropriate, e.g. to avoid any subsequent misunderstanding, provide a more detailed explanation of the procedures including the consequences of any proposed limitation in scope.*]

If in the course of our review we find increased risk of potential misstatements in the interim financial information we may decide that further more detailed enquiries or examinations are necessary for us to reach conclusions. We will discuss the nature and extent of these procedures with you and with the audit committee.

Our review is not designed to, and therefore cannot be relied upon to, disclose any irregularities, including fraud, which may exist.

Our review is not designed to, and therefore will not necessarily, reveal weaknesses in internal controls, errors in the accounting records, misstatements of management estimates or other matters which might be revealed if we were to conduct an audit in accordance with Auditing Standards.

There is no assurance that our review will reveal all matters of significance related to the interim report. However, we shall report to you and to the audit committee, any significant findings from our work which we consider should be brought to your attention.

Reporting

As we will not carry out an audit of the interim financial information in accordance with Auditing Standards we will not express an audit opinion thereon but we will issue a review report in accordance with Bulletin 1999/4, addressed to the Company, for publication with the interim financial information. Our report will be prepared to assist the company in meeting Stock Exchange requirements, and in the proper control of its affairs; our review will be performed and our report will be issued for these purposes only. Our report will not be prepared for any purpose connected with any specific transaction, and should not be relied upon for any such purpose.

We expect to report on the interim financial information as follows:

[*Insert proposed text of report – see Appendix B – Section 13:22.18 – Example 1.*]

Representations by management

As part of our procedures, we shall request you to provide written confirmation of oral representations which we have received from you during the course of the review engagement.

Documents issued with the interim financial information

To assist us with our work, we shall request sight of all documents or statements which are due to be issued with the interim financial information.

Other auditors

[*A paragraph along the following lines should be included where the auditor is reporting on a group and divisions and subsidiary and associated undertakings are audited by other auditors.*] In carrying out the engagement we shall instruct the auditors of divisions and subsidiary and associated undertakings to make such enquiries, and to report to us the results of their work, to the extent which we consider necessary for the purposes of making our report.

Quality of service

It is our desire to provide you at all times with a high-quality service to meet your needs. If, at any time, you believe that our service to you could be improved, or if you are dissatisfied with any aspect of our services, please raise the matter immediately with the partner responsible for that aspect of our services to you. If, for any reason, you would prefer to discuss these matters with someone other than that partner, please contact . . . in our office at . . . . In this way we are able to ensure that your concerns are dealt with carefully and promptly. In the unlikely event that we are unable thus to satisfy your concerns, you may then choose to take the matter up with the Institute of Chartered Accountants in England and Wales [*or other relevant professional body*].

Fees and terms

Our fees are computed on the basis of the time spent on the review of the interim financial information by the partners and our staff, and on the levels of skill and responsibility involved. Our fees will be billed [*on completion of/at intervals during*] the engagement.

Agreement of terms

We shall be grateful if you could confirm in writing your agreement to the terms of this letter by signing and returning the enclosed copy. If you wish to discuss the terms of this engagement letter further before replying, please let us know.

Yours faithfully,

XYZ & Co

Chartered Accountants

Office

13:22.18 Appendix B Example review reports

13:22.18.1 Example 1 Unqualified and unmodified review report on interim financial information

Independent review report XYZ plc

Introduction

We have been instructed by the company to review the interim financial information set out on pages x to x, and we have read the other information contained in the interim report and considered whether it contains any apparent misstatements of material inconsistencies with the financial information.

Directors' responsibilities

The interim report, including the financial information contained therein, is the responsibility of, and has been approved by, the directors. The Listing Rules of the London Stock Exchange require that the accounting policies and presentation applied to the interim figures should be consistent with those applied in preparing the preceding annual accounts except where any changes, and the reasons for them, are disclosed.

Review work performed

Our review was carried out in accordance with guidance contained in Bulletin 1999/4, 'Review of Interim Financial Information', issued by the Auditing Practices Board. This review consisted principally of making enquiries of [*group*] management and applying analytical procedures to the financial information and underlying financial data and based thereon, assessing whether accounting policies and presentation have been consistently applied unless otherwise disclosed. The review excluded audit procedures such as tests of controls and verification of assets, liabilities and transactions and was therefore substantially less in scope than an audit performed in accordance with Auditing Standards, and therefore provides a lower level of assurance than an audit. Accordingly we do not express an audit opinion on the interim financial information.

Review conclusion

On the basis of our review, we are not aware of any material modifications that should be made to the financial information as presented for the six months ended 30 June 20XX.

XYZ & Co

Chartered Accountants

Town or City

Date

13:22.18.2 Example 2 Modified review report

This example is based on the example in the APB Bulletin. The circumstances are that in the auditor's opinion provision should be made for a doubtful debt, and accordingly the report is qualified because of disagreement about accounting treatment.

Review report by the auditors to XYZ PLC

Independent review report XYZ plc

Introduction

We have been instructed by the company to review the interim financial information set out on pages x to x, and we have read the other information contained in the interim report and considered whether it contains any apparent misstatements of material inconsistencies with the financial information.

Directors' responsibilities

The interim report, including the financial information contained therein, is the responsibility of, and has been approved by, the directors. The Listing Rules of the London Stock Exchange require that the accounting policies and presentation applied to the interim figures should be consistent with those applied in preparing the preceding annual accounts except where any changes, and the reasons for them, are disclosed.

Review work performed

Our review was carried out in accordance with guidance contained in Bulletin 1999/4, 'Review of Interim Financial Information', issued by the Auditing Practices Board. This review consisted principally of making enquiries of [*group*] management and applying analytical procedures to the financial information and underlying financial data and based thereon, assessing whether accounting policies and presentation have been consistently applied unless otherwise disclosed. The review excluded audit procedures such as tests of controls and verification of assets, liabilities and transactions and was therefore substantially less in scope than an audit performed in accordance with Auditing Standards, and therefore provides a lower level of assurance than an audit. Accordingly we do not express an audit opinion on the interim financial information.

Review conclusion

Included in debtors shown on the balance sheet is an amount of £Y due from a company which has ceased trading. XYZ PLC has no security for this debt. In our opinion the company is unlikely to receive any payment and full provision of £Y should have been made, reducing profit before tax and net assets by that amount.

On the basis of our review, with the exception of the matter described in the preceding paragraph, we are not aware of any material modifications that should be made to the financial information as presented for the six months ended 30 June 20XX.

XYZ & Co

Chartered Accountants

Town or City

Date

13:23 Reports on reviews (other than on interim financial information), agreed-upon procedures and compilation engagements

13:23.1 Introduction

From time to time audit firms are asked to carry out reviews of, or to perform agreed-upon procedures on, financial information. Firms may also be asked to compile financial information or financial statements. Such engagements are not audits, and the level of assurance that the auditor can provide as a result of this work is significantly less than the auditor can provide if a full audit is carried out. It ranges from 'negative assurance' to no assurance.

This section provides a general description of each type of engagement. It does not deal with reviews of interim financial information, which are dealt with in **Section 13:22**, 'Review engagements on interim financial information'. The guidance in this section is consistent with the following International Standards on Auditing, issued by the International Federation of Accountants (IFAC); 'Engagements to Review Financial Statements', 'Engagements to Perform Agreed-Upon Procedures Regarding Financial Information' and 'Engagements to Compile Financial Information'.

13:23.2 Definitions

The three types of engagement are defined as follows:

(a) **Review engagements**, in which the audit firm provides a limited level of assurance that the information subject to review is free from material error, reported in the form of negative assurance on an assertion, e.g.:

> **Based on our review, nothing has come to our attention that causes us to believe that material modifications should be made to the financial statements in order for them to be in conformity with generally accepted accounting principles.**

(b) **Agreed-upon procedures**, in which the audit firm is engaged to carry out specific procedures to which the auditor and the client have agreed and to present factual findings in the report.

(c) **Compilations**, in which the audit firm gathers, classifies and summarises information provided by management without undertaking to test the underlying assertions or express any assurance on that information.

13:23.3 Acceptance of clients, engagement letters and limitation of liability

On each type of engagement the firm must follow its standard procedures for acceptance and continuance of engagements and must obtain an engagement letter.

13:23.4 Forms of report

Where the audit firm is engaged to perform several services for a client, e.g., if the firm is asked to compile financial statements and to carry out agreed-upon procedures on those statements the form of report the firm should use will be that which gives the greatest level of assurance. If the firm is compiling financial statements and is asked to audit them, the firm should carry out a full audit and the report given should be the firm's standard audit report, modified as necessary if the entity the firm is auditing is unincorporated. Normally, where the audit firm issues a report of the type under discussion in this section the report will be addressed to the directors.

13:23.4.1 Reviews

A standard form of report where the audit firm carries out a review, other than a review of interim financial information, is as follows:

> **Accountants' report to the directors of XYZ Ltd.**
>
> **We have reviewed the financial statements on pages x to x in accordance with [*International Standards on Auditing*] [*your letter of instruction dated***

x].* All information in these financial statements is the representation of management of XYZ limited.

A review is limited primarily to enquiries of company personnel and analytical procedures applied to financial data and thus it provides less assurance than an audit. We have not performed an audit and, accordingly we do not express an audit opinion.

Based on our review, nothing has come to our attention that causes us to believe that the financial statements are not in all material respects in accordance with [*International Accounting Standards*][*Applicable accounting standards*][*other relevant requirements*].**

The use of this report is limited to the parties to whom it is addressed or to [*state other parties*].

XYZ & Co

Chartered Accountants

Town or city

Date

Notes:
*   The report should state whether the firm has used the International Standard on Auditing relating to reviews (*see* **Section 13:23.1** (second paragraph)) or whether the firm has carried out the review in accordance with specific instructions from the client.

**   The report should also refer to the appropriate accounting, legislative or other requirements with which the financial statements comply.

13:23.4.2 *Agreed-upon procedures*

An example form of report for agreed-upon procedures is as follows:

Accountants' report to the directors of XYZ Ltd of factual findings in connection with the recorded claims of creditors

We have performed the procedures agreed with you and enumerated below with respect to the recorded claims of creditors of XYZ Ltd at 31 May 20XX, set out in the accompanying schedules. The procedures we performed are summarised as follows:

(a) We checked the addition of the trial balance of accounts payable at 31 May 20XX, prepared by the company, and compared the total to the balance in the company's related general ledger account.

(b) We compared the claims received from creditors to the trial balance of accounts payable.

(c) We examined documentation submitted by the creditors in support of their claims and compared it to documentation in the company's files including invoices, receiving records and other evidence of receipt of goods or services.

With respect to procedure (a) no discrepancies were found. Our findings relating to procedures (b) and (c) are presented in the accompanying schedules set out on pages x to x. Schedule A lists claims that are in agreement with the company's records. Schedule B lists claims that are not in agreement with the company's records and sets out the differences in amount.

Because the above procedures do not constitute either an audit or a review we do not imply or express any assurance on the accounts payable at 31 May 20XX. This report relates only to the accounts and items specified above.

We make no representation regarding the sufficiency of the above procedures for your purposes.

Our report is solely for your information and is not to be used or referred to for any other purpose.

XYZ & Co

Chartered Accountants

Town or city

Date

13:23.4.3 Compilations

An example of a compilation report is as follows:

Accountants' report to the directors of XYZ Ltd*

On the basis of information supplied by you we have compiled the accompanying financial statements for the year ended 31 December 20XX. You are solely responsible for this information. We have not audited or reviewed the financial statements and, accordingly, do not imply or express an opinion or any other form of assurance on them. Readers are cautioned that the financial statements may not be appropriate for their purposes.

XYZ & Co

Chartered Accountants

Town or city

Date

Note:
*   Although the heading in the example indicates that such a report may be given to the directors of a company, this would normally only be done if the firm were not the auditors, or if the company was exempt, because of its size, from having both an audit and a report by reporting accountants under the Companies Act. It is likely that more often the report will be requested by smaller entities such as sole traders.

13:23.5 Misleading information

Where an audit firm is carrying out a compilation engagement and comes across financial statements or other information that is misleading, the audit firm should first seek to have the information corrected. If this fails, either the firm should refer to the matter in the compilation report, or, if the matter is such that the firm does not consider that it should be associated with the financial statements, the firm should resign. In circumstances where the firm believes that the financial statements may be misleading and is considering what action to take, the consultation procedures, set out in **Section 5:5**, 'Consultation and concurring reviews', should be followed.

An example of the inclusion of an explanatory paragraph drawing attention to misleading information in financial information is as follows. The paragraph would be added to the compilation report set out in **Section 13:23.4.3**.

> **In preparing the financial statements it has come to our attention that the balance sheet total of fixed assets includes £x in respect of a motor vehicle that was severely damaged in a crash shortly before the year-end. No provision has been made against this amount as you have informed us that you expect to succeed in recovering the value from your insurers.**

Chapter 14

Cessation as auditor

14:1 Cessation as auditor

14:1.1 Introduction

When a firm is notified that a client intends to nominate another firm to be appointed in its place, or when the firm wishes to cease to act as auditor to a client, the correct legal and professional procedures must be followed. The legal procedures are contained in ss. 391 to 394 of the Companies Act 1985, which were amended by the Companies Act 1989. The professional procedures are set out in the ethical guidance published by each of the professional bodies (referred to, in particular, in **Section 14:1.6.2** (first paragraph)). The action that the auditor has to take will vary depending upon whether the reason for the change is removal, resignation or non-reappointment.

14:1.2 General

The engagement partner should ensure that all correspondence relating to the removal, resignation or non-reappointment as auditor is dealt with in the appropriate manner.

If a client notifies the firm of its intention to nominate another firm of auditors in its place, the auditor should acknowledge receipt of the notification in writing, irrespective of the reason for the change. At that stage, however, the auditor should not commit the firm further. A specimen letter of acknowledgement is set out in **AppendixA** (*see* **Section 14:1.7**). The engagement partner should follow the consultation procedures set out in **Section 5:5**, 'Consultation and concurring reviews', before any further action is taken.

When the auditor proposes either to make representations to the members in respect of the proposed removal or non-reappointment or to give details of the circumstances of the auditor's resignation to the members or the creditors, the engagement partner should follow the consultation procedures set out in **Section 5:5**, 'Consultation and concurring reviews'.

14:1.3 Removal during term of office

Section 391 of the Companies Act 1985 refers to the removal of auditors, i.e., auditors being asked to cease to act before the term of their appointment expires. Under s. 391A, the client is obliged to send the auditor a copy of the resolution that will be put to a general meeting proposing that the firm be removed as auditor before its term of office expires. The auditor may then make representations in writing to the client as to why the auditor believes that the auditor should not be removed. The company is obliged to send a copy of these representations to every member of the company unless they are received too late. If these representations are not sent to members, the auditor has the right to require that the representations are read out at the general meeting. After the general meeting of the company, the auditor should ascertain from the client whether the resolution was passed.

The auditor must deposit at the company's registered office a statement (not later than 14 days after the date on which the auditor ceases to hold office) that there are no circumstances connected with the auditor's ceasing to hold office which the auditor considers should be brought to the attention of the members or the creditors, or else give details of any such circumstances as do exist. A specimen statement is set out in the **Appendix A** (*see* **Section 14:1.7**).

14:1.4 Resignation during term of office

If a firm is resigning as auditor (i.e., asking to cease to act before the term of office expires), s. 392 of the Companies Act 1985 requires the auditor to deposit a notice of resignation at the company's registered office. The auditor should either send the notice by recorded delivery or deliver it directly. The notice must be accompanied by a statement that there are no circumstances connected with the auditor's ceasing to hold office which the auditor considers should be brought to the attention of the members or the creditors, or else give details of any such circumstances as do exist. A specimen notice and statement are given in the **Appendix A** (*see* **Section 14:1.7**). The auditor should normally fulfil the responsibility to complete the current engagement when making the decision to resign during the period of appointment.

14:1.5 Non-reappointment at end of term

When a firm is not being reappointed (i.e., the term of office has expired and the company proposes to appoint another firm), the client is obliged under s. 391A of the Companies Act 1985 to send the auditor a copy of the resolution proposing the appointment of another firm as auditor. If the change is made at the client's request and the auditor does not agree with it, the auditor may make representations, as described in **Section 14:1.3** (first paragraph). The auditor must deposit, not less than 14 days before the end of the time allowed for next appointing auditors, a statement that there are no circumstances connected with the auditor's ceasing to hold office which the auditor considers should be brought to the attention of the members or the creditors, or else give details of any such circumstances as do exist. A specimen statement is set out in the **Appendix A** (*see* **Section 14:1.7**). Such a statement is required for each company if, e.g., the auditor is not reappointed to a group of companies following a takeover.

14:1.6 Procedure to be followed when a firm ceases to act as auditor

14:1.6.1 Statements under s. 394 of the Companies Act 1985

In all cases where the auditor has issued a statement of 'circumstances' which refers to matters that the auditor considers should be brought to the attention of members or creditors, the auditor must, in addition, send a copy of the statement to the Registrar of Companies within 28 days of the date of deposit of the statement at the company's registered office. Section 394 allows a company to apply to the court to prevent the statement from being issued, in which case the time limit may vary. There is no requirement for the auditor to send the statement to the Registrar of Companies if it does not contain 'circumstances' that the auditor considers should be brought to the attention of members or creditors.

14:1.6.2 Communications with new auditor

The ethical guidance published by each of the professional bodies imposes on the auditor a duty to give information to the new auditor which will be relevant to whether that firm should accept the nomination. The purpose is to avoid an incoming auditor from unwittingly becoming the means by which any unsatisfactory practices of an entity, or any impropriety in the conduct of its affairs, may be enabled to continue or be concealed from shareholders or other legitimately interested persons. Communication between auditors is intended to ensure that all relevant facts are known to the prospective new auditor, who can then accept or reject the nomination. Relevant matters to be communicated would include, e.g., serious doubts regarding the integrity of the directors of the client company or the deliberate withholding of information from the existing auditor.

If the proposed new auditor is following the correct professional procedures, that firm will request that the existing auditor write to it. Before doing so, the auditor should obtain the client's written authority to discuss its affairs with the proposed new auditor. A specimen letter for this purpose is set out in the **Appendix A** (*see* **Section 14:1.7**). If the existing auditor does not receive any communication from the proposed new auditor, the auditor should not volunteer information to that firm.

If there is no information of which the proposed new auditor needs to be aware before deciding whether to accept nomination, the existing auditor should write to that firm in accordance with the specimen letter in the **Appendix A** (*see* **Section 14:1.7**).

If, however, there are reasons for the proposed change of which the proposed new auditor needs to be aware before deciding whether to accept the nomination, the existing auditor should write to that firm as indicated in the specimen letter in **Appendix A** (*see* **Section 14:1.7**), setting out all the matters which the auditor brought to the attention of the members or the creditors. The engagement partner should follow the consultation procedures set out in **Section 5:5**, 'Consultation and concurring reviews', before sending such a letter to the proposed new auditor.

Further guidance on the legal position of an outgoing auditor who communicates to a proposed new auditor matters damaging to the client or other individuals concerned with the client's business is given in the published ethical guidance.

It is important that the existing auditor should answer all communications without delay. The new auditor should request the existing auditor or the client to deal with the relevant matter in writing, rather than orally.

14:1.7 Appendix A Specimen letters

14:1.7.1 Specimen letter to client in reply to notification of intent to nominate another firm

A specimen letter addressed to the company secretary or the directors in reply to the client's notification of its intention to nominate another firm of auditors in place of the existing auditor is set out below:

> **Dear Sir(s),**
>
> **We acknowledge receipt of your letter dated informing us of your intention to nominate another firm of auditors to XYZ Company Limited in our place.**
>
> **Yours faithfully,**

14:1.7.2 Specimen statement where the firm ceases to act as auditor

A specimen statement, to be deposited at the company's registered office, addressed to the company secretary or the directors of the client where the auditor ceases to act as auditor for any reason is set out below. If the statement contains 'circumstances' it must also be sent by the auditor to the Registrar of Companies within 28 days of the date of deposit unless the company applies to the court to direct that the statement should not be sent out. If it does not contain 'circumstances' it need not be sent to the Registrar.

> **Dear Sir(s),**
>
> **In accordance with s. 394 of the Companies Act 1985, we confirm that there are no circumstances connected with our ceasing to hold office that we consider should be brought to the attention of the company's members or creditors.**
>
> **Yours faithfully,**

14:1.7.3 Specimen letter where the auditor resigns

If the auditor is resigning, the auditor should send the statement set out in **Section 14:1.7.2** with the letter of resignation, which may be worded as follows:

> **Dear Sirs,**
>
> **Notice of resignation as auditors**
>
> **In accordance with section 392 of the Companies Act 1985, we give notice that we are resigning as auditors of [*name of client*] with effect from [*date*].**

Statutory notice under section 394

In accordance with section 394 of the Companies Act 1985, we confirm that there are no circumstances connected with our resignation which we consider should be brought to the notice of the shareholders or creditors of [*name of client*].

Yours faithfully,

For UK purposes this letter may be split into two (the notification and the statutory notice) as the Companies Act 1985 (as amended by the Companies Act 1989) requires the auditors' notification of resignation (s. 392) to be filed with the Registrar of Companies in all cases but only requires the statutory notice to be filed with the Registrar if the statement of circumstances is positive.

14:1.7.4 Specimen letter to client requesting written authority to discuss client's affairs

A specimen letter to the company secretary or the directors requesting the client to give the existing auditor written authority to discuss its affairs with the auditor who has been nominated in place of the existing auditor is set out below:

Dear Sirs,

We have received a letter from [*name of proposed auditors*], who have been asked to accept nomination/appointment* as auditors to the company, seeking information which could influence their decision as to whether they may properly accept nomination/appointment*.

We shall be obliged if you will sign and return the enclosed copy of this letter, providing us with written authority to discuss the affairs of the company with the proposed new auditors.

Yours faithfully,

We authorise you to discuss the affairs of the company with [*name of proposed auditors*].

Signed   ....

Name and position   ....

for and on behalf of ....

Date   ....

* delete as appropriate

It may be considered appropriate to include a sentence in this letter indicating that discussion will take place after a certain time if no written authority is received. The letter should be sent by recorded delivery.

14:1.7.5 Specimen letter to successor auditor — no matters to report

A specimen letter in reply to the new auditor when there are no reasons for the proposed change of which that firm need be aware is set out below:

Dear Sirs,

[*Name of Client*]

Thank you for your letter dated *[date]* **relating to your proposed nomination/appointment* as auditor to the above-named company.**

In our opinion there are no matters of which you should be aware that could influence your decision as to whether or not you may properly accept nomination/appointment*.

[*Note: If the auditor is being removed or resigning as opposed to not seeking re-appointment: We enclose a copy of the letter we have written to the company.*]*

We enclose a copy of the statement made under section 394 of the Companies Act 1985 which we have deposited at the company's registered office [*and which has been sent to the Registrar of Companies*].

Yours faithfully,

* delete as appropriate

14:1.7.6 Specimen letter to successor auditor – matters to report

A specimen letter in reply to the new auditor setting out the reasons for the proposed change of which that firm need be aware is set out below:

Dear Sirs,

[*Name of client*]

Thank you for your letter dated *[date]* **relating to your proposed nomination/appointment* as auditor to the above company.**

In this regard we consider that there are matters of which, in our opinion, you should be aware and we set these out below for your consideration. We have/have not* communicated these points in a written representation to the company for the information of its members. We enclose a copy of the

letter we have written to the company. [*Note: If all the reasons are fully detailed in the representation it is sufficient to refer to the representation rather than give the full details in the main body of the letter.*]

We also enclose a copy of the statement* under Section 394 of the Companies Act 1985 which we have deposited at the company's registered office.

If you wish to discuss furt*her* any of the matters raised in this letter please contact [*name of partner*].

Yours faithfully,

Note: *The auditor should ensure, before sending a copy of the statement, that the company has not applied to the court under s. 394(3), (4) and (5) of the Companies Act 1985, to direct that the statement need not be sent out.

Index

Index

C

G

Index

M

Index

O

Index

W